Published by Collins
An imprint of HarperCollins Publishers
77-85 Fulham Palace Road,
Hammersmith,
London W6 8JB

www.harpercollins.co.uk

First published by Geographia Ltd 1977

21st edition 2013

Mapping generated from Collins Bartholomew digital databases

London Underground Map by permission of Transport Trading Limited
Registered User No. 13/2428/P

Information on fixed speed camera locations provided by PocketGPSWorld.Com Ltd.

The grid on this map is the National Grid taken from the Ordnance Survey map with the permission of the Controller of Her Majesty's Stationery Office.

Printed in China by South China Printing Co. Ltd

Paperback ISBN 978 0 00 749446 0
Imp 001

Queries concerning this product to be addressed to:
Collins RoadCheck,
Collins Geo,
HarperCollins Publishers,
Westerhill Road,
Bishopbriggs,
Glasgow,
G64 2QT

e-mail: roadcheck@harpercollins.co.uk

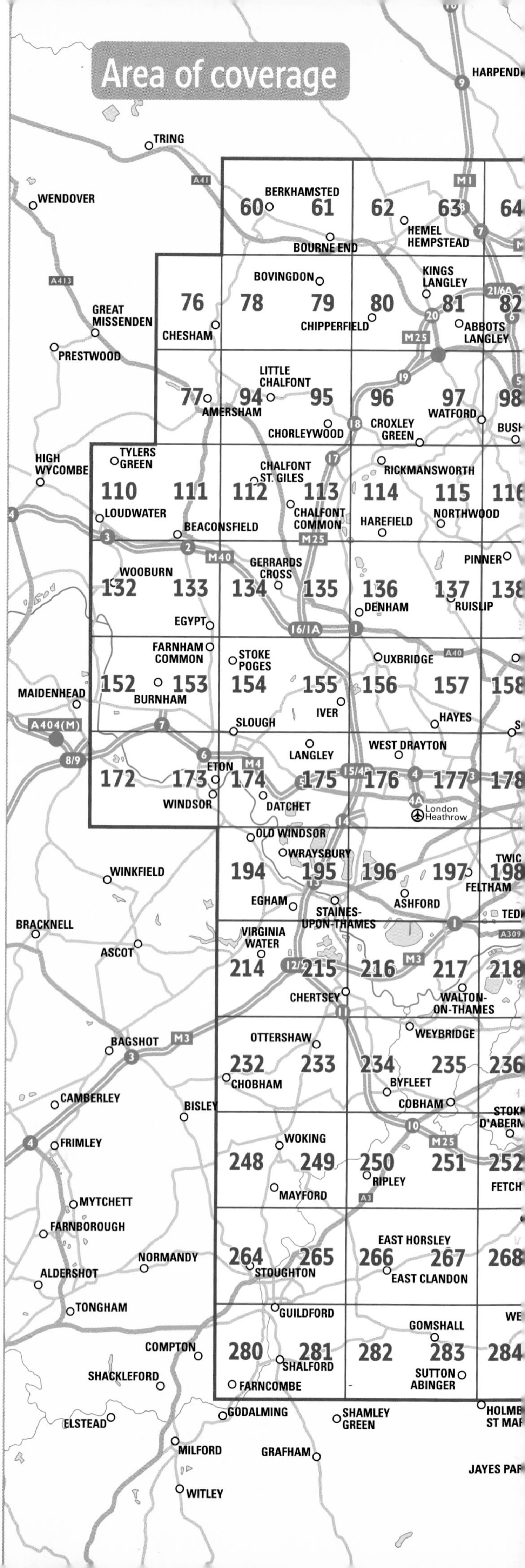

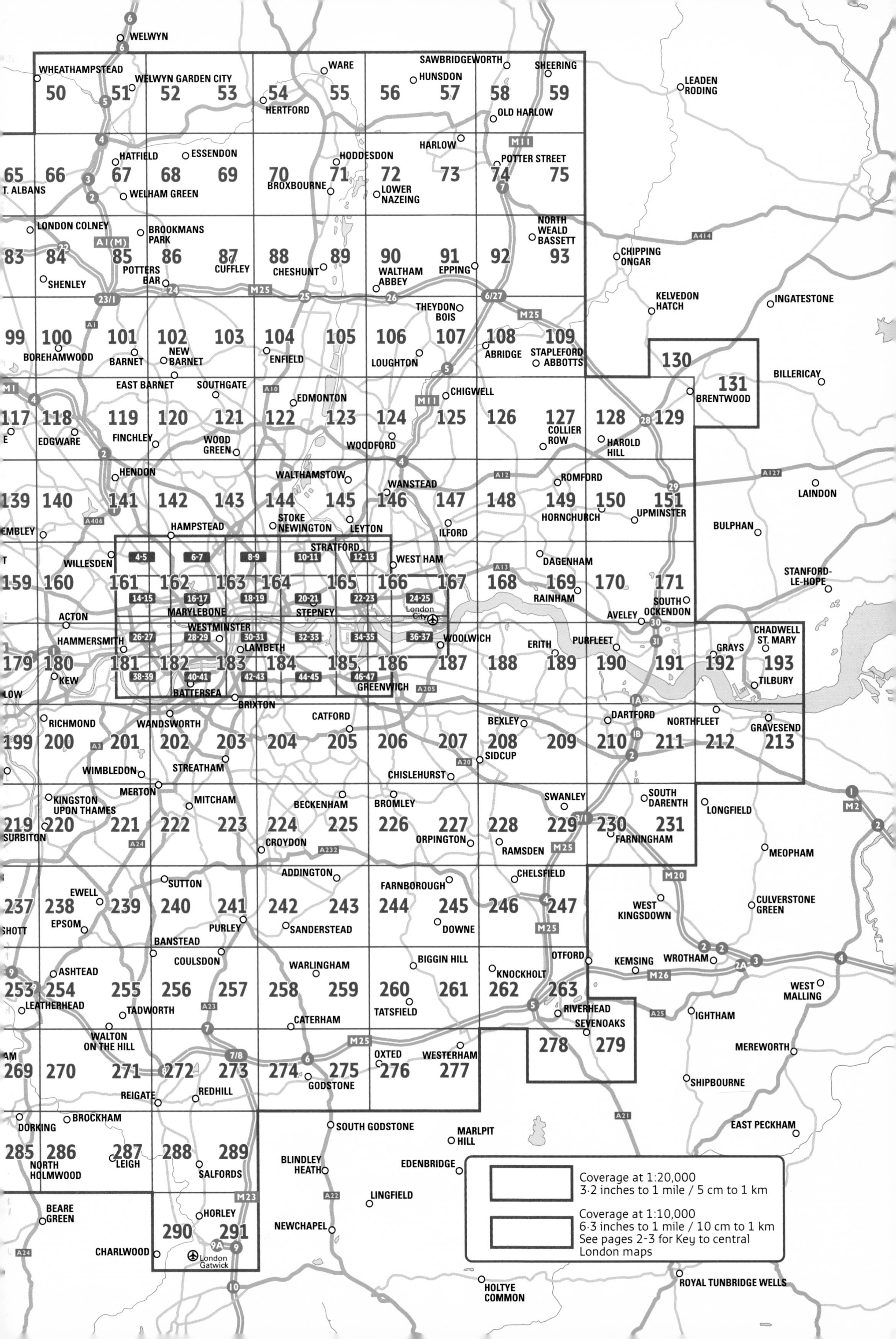

WELWYN
WHEATHAMPSTEAD
WELWYN GARDEN CITY
WARE
SAWBRIDGEWORTH
HUNSDON
SHEERING
LEADEN RODING
50
51
52
53
54
55
56
57
58
59
HERTFORD
OLD HARLOW
HARLOW
M11
HATFIELD
ESSENDON
HODDESDON
POTTER STREET
65
66
67
68
69
70
71
72
73
74
75
T. ALBANS
BROXBOURNE
LOWER NAZEING
WELHAM GREEN
LONDON COLNEY
BROOKMANS PARK
NORTH WEALD BASSETT
A1(M)
A414
83
84
85
86
87
88
89
90
91
92
93
CHIPPING ONGAR
POTTERS BAR
CUFFLEY
CHESHUNT
WALTHAM ABBEY
EPPING
SHENLEY
M25
KELVEDON HATCH
INGATESTONE
THEYDON BOIS
99
100
101
102
103
104
105
106
107
108
109
BOREHAMWOOD
BARNET
NEW BARNET
ENFIELD
LOUGHTON
ABRIDGE
STAPLEFORD ABBOTTS
130
131
BRENTWOOD
BILLERICAY
EAST BARNET
SOUTHGATE
EDMONTON
CHIGWELL
117
118
119
120
121
122
123
124
125
126
127
128
129
EDGWARE
FINCHLEY
WOOD GREEN
WOODFORD
COLLIER ROW
HAROLD HILL
HENDON
WALTHAMSTOW
WANSTEAD
ROMFORD
A12
A127
139
140
141
142
143
144
145
146
147
148
149
150
151
LAINDON
EMBLEY
A406
HAMPSTEAD
STOKE NEWINGTON
LEYTON
ILFORD
HORNCHURCH
UPMINSTER
BULPHAN
STRATFORD
WEST HAM
DAGENHAM
WILLESDEN
4-5
6-7
8-9
10-11
12-13
A13
159
160
161
162
163
164
165
166
167
168
169
170
171
STANFORD-LE-HOPE
14-15
16-17
18-19
20-21
22-23
24-25
London City
RAINHAM
SOUTH OCKENDON
ACTON
MARYLEBONE
STEPNEY
AVELEY
WESTMINSTER
HAMMERSMITH
26-27
28-29
30-31
32-33
34-35
36-37
WOOLWICH
ERITH
PURFLEET
GRAYS
CHADWELL ST. MARY
LAMBETH
179
180
181
182
183
184
185
186
187
188
189
190
191
192
193
KEW
38-39
40-41
42-43
44-45
46-47
GREENWICH
A205
TILBURY
LOW
BATTERSEA
BRIXTON
RICHMOND
WANDSWORTH
CATFORD
BEXLEY
DARTFORD
NORTHFLEET
GRAVESEND
199
200
201
202
203
204
205
206
207
208
209
210
211
212
213
A3
A20
SIDCUP
WIMBLEDON
STREATHAM
CHISLEHURST
MERTON
KINGSTON UPON THAMES
MITCHAM
BECKENHAM
BROMLEY
SWANLEY
SOUTH DARENTH
LONGFIELD
M2
219
220
221
222
223
224
225
226
227
228
229
230
231
SURBITON
A24
CROYDON
A232
ORPINGTON
RAMSDEN
FARNINGHAM
M25
MEOPHAM
ADDINGTON
CHELSFIELD
M20
SUTTON
FARNBOROUGH
EWELL
237
238
239
240
241
242
243
244
245
246
247
WEST KINGSDOWN
CULVERSTONE GREEN
EPSOM
PURLEY
SANDERSTEAD
DOWNE
SHOTT
BANSTEAD
COULSDON
WARLINGHAM
BIGGIN HILL
OTFORD
KEMSING
WROTHAM
ASHTEAD
KNOCKHOLT
M26
WEST MALLING
253
254
255
256
257
258
259
260
261
262
263
LEATHERHEAD
TADWORTH
A23
TATSFIELD
RIVERHEAD
A25
IGHTHAM
CATERHAM
SEVENOAKS
WALTON ON THE HILL
278
279
MEREWORTH
OXTED
WESTERHAM
AM
269
270
271
272
273
274
275
276
277
GODSTONE
REIGATE
REDHILL
SHIPBOURNE
DORKING
BROCKHAM
A21
SOUTH GODSTONE
MARLPIT HILL
EAST PECKHAM
285
286
287
288
289
NORTH HOLMWOOD
LEIGH
SALFORDS
BLINDLEY HEATH
EDENBRIDGE
M23
A22
LINGFIELD
BEARE GREEN
HORLEY
290
291
NEWCHAPEL
CHARLWOOD
London Gatwick
A24
HOLTYE COMMON
ROYAL TUNBRIDGE WELLS
Coverage at 1:20,000
3·2 inches to 1 mile / 5 cm to 1 km
Coverage at 1:10,000
6·3 inches to 1 mile / 10 cm to 1 km
See pages 2-3 for Key to central London maps

London Underground map

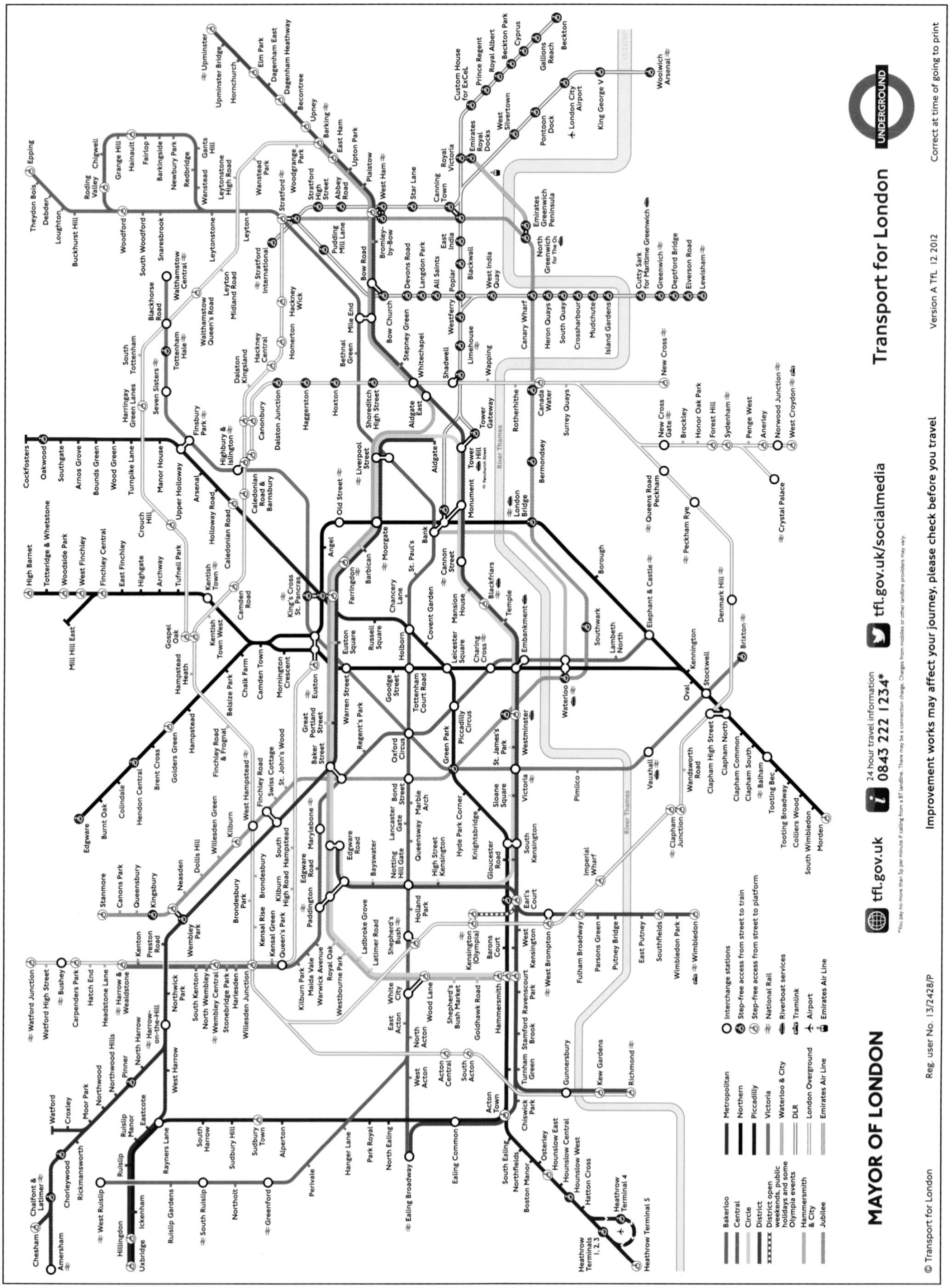

Collins
GREATER LONDON
STREET ATLAS

CONTENTS

CENTRAL AREA MAPS

Key to central London maps 2-3
Key to map symbols 3
Central area maps 4-47

LONDON STREET MAPS

Key to London street maps 48-49
Key to map symbols 49
London street maps 50-291

URBAN AREA MAPS

Key to London urban area maps 292-293
Key to map symbols 293
London urban area maps 294-311

INFORMATION PAGES

M25 London orbital motorway 312-313
Airport plans 314
London Congestion Charging and Low Emission zones 315
Index to street names, places of interest, place names, stations, hospitals, schools, colleges and universities 316-481
Administrative areas 482-483

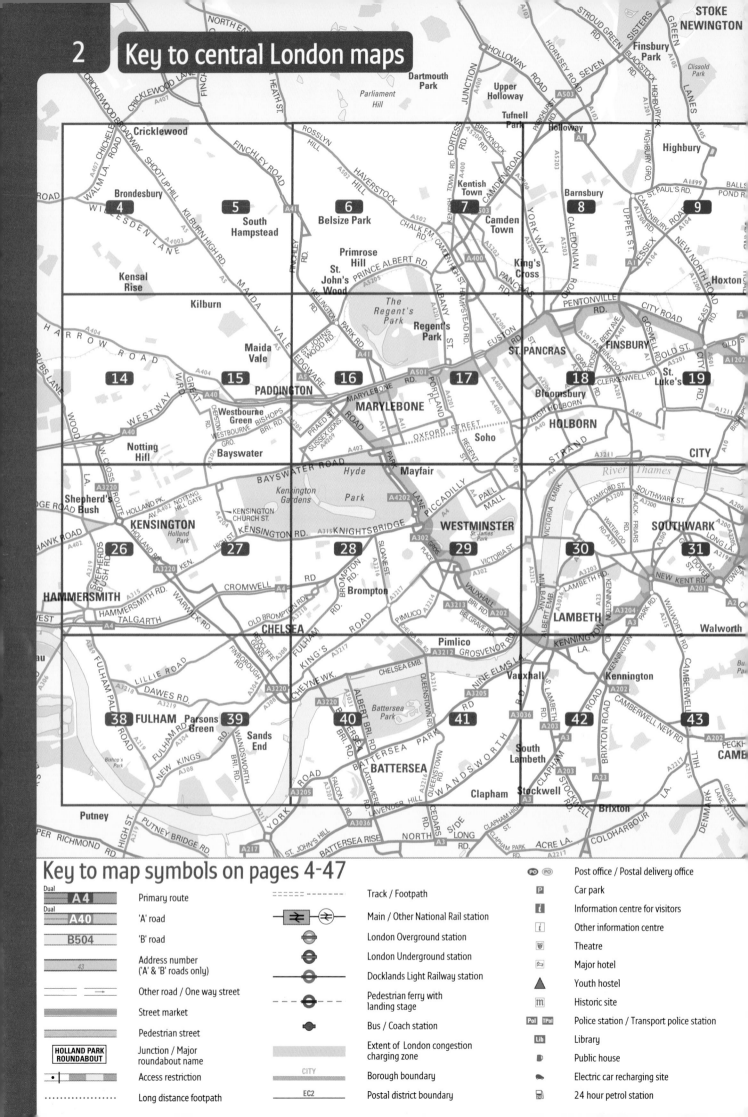

Key to central London maps

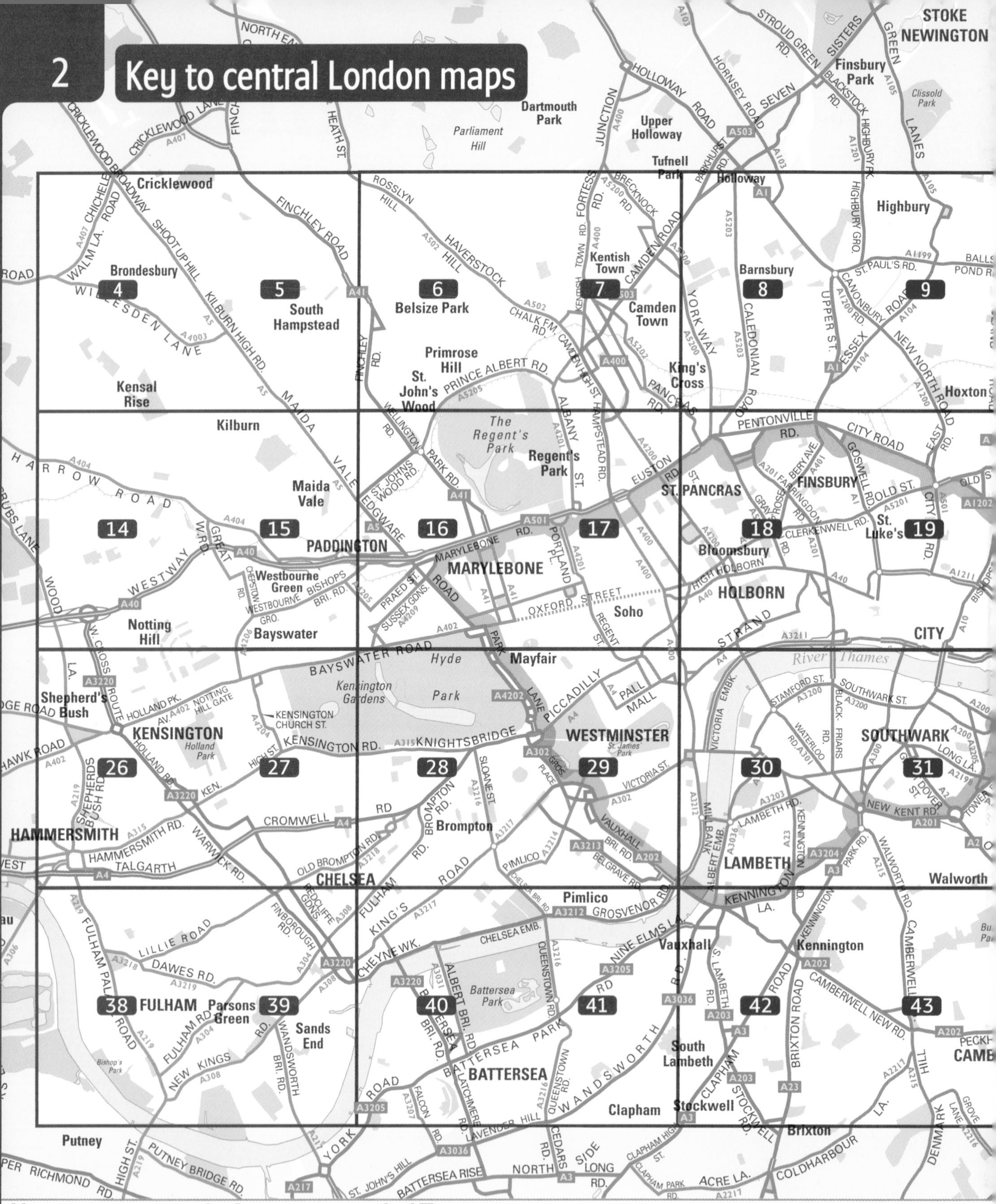

Key to map symbols on pages 4-47

Dual A4	Primary route
Dual A40	'A' road
B504	'B' road
43	Address number ('A' & 'B' roads only)
	Other road / One way street
	Street market
	Pedestrian street
HOLLAND PARK ROUNDABOUT	Junction / Major roundabout name
	Access restriction
	Long distance footpath
	Track / Footpath
	Main / Other National Rail station
	London Overground station
	London Underground station
	Docklands Light Railway station
	Pedestrian ferry with landing stage
	Bus / Coach station
	Extent of London congestion charging zone
CITY	Borough boundary
EC2	Postal district boundary
PO PO	Post office / Postal delivery office
P	Car park
i	Information centre for visitors
i	Other information centre
	Theatre
	Major hotel
	Youth hostel
m	Historic site
Pol TPol	Police station / Transport police station
Lib	Library
	Public house
	Electric car recharging site
24	24 hour petrol station

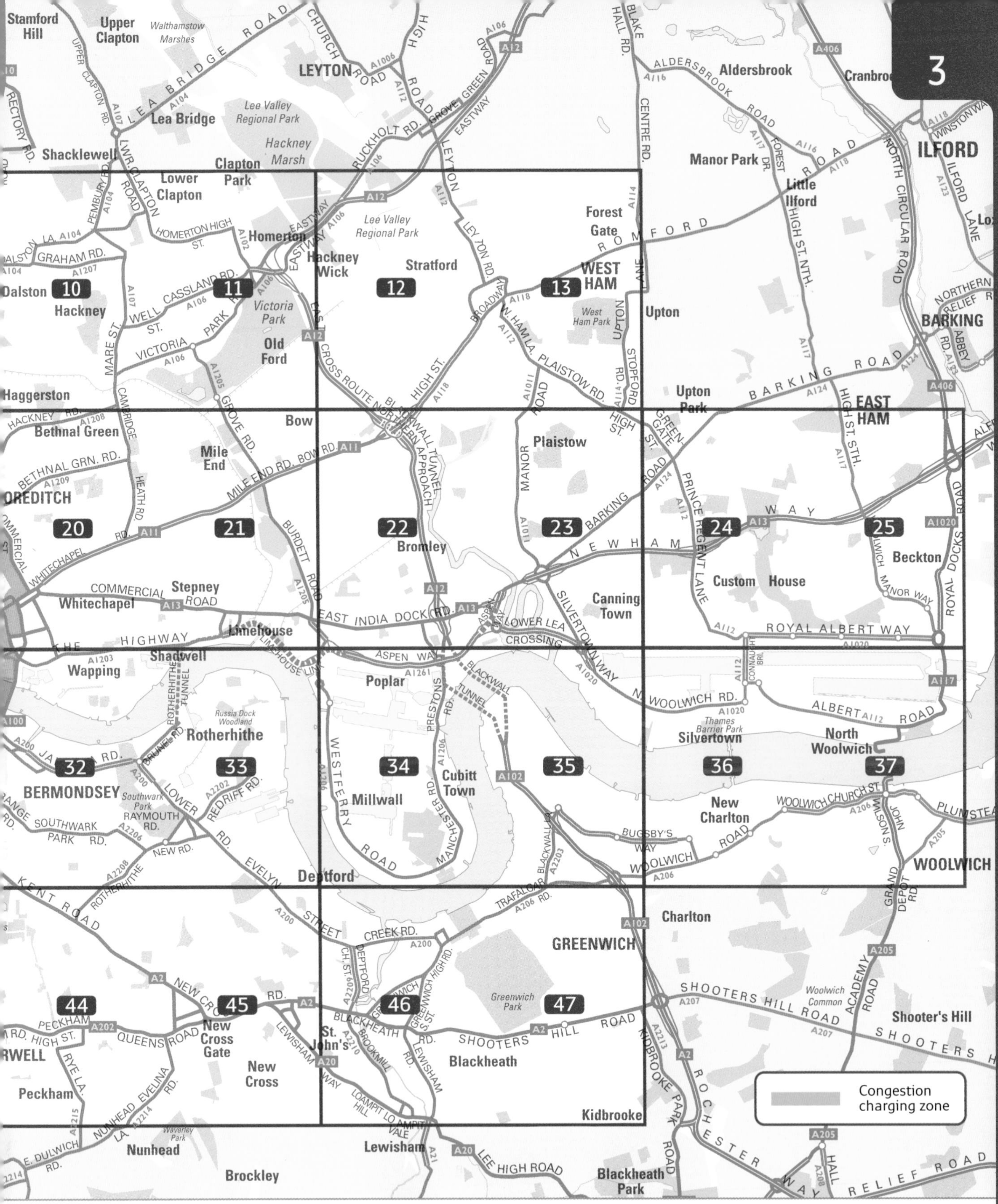

USA	Embassy
Fire Sta / Amb Sta	Fire station / Ambulance station
	Monument / Statue
Comm Cen	Community centre / Hall
	Public toilet
	Residential tower block
	Cinema
	Church
	Mosque
	Synagogue
Mormon	Other place of worship
BARCLAYS	Cycle hire docking station

Leisure & tourism	Education	Golf course
Shopping	Major office	Woodland
Market	Industry & commerce	Public open space
Administration & law	Other landmark building / Tower block	Park / Garden / Sports ground
Health & welfare	Built-up area	Cemetery

161 5 Page continuation number

26 National Grid kilometre square

SCALE

0 — 1/4 — 1/2 mile

0 — 0.25 — 0.5 — 0.75 kilometre

1: 10,000 6.3 inches (16cm) to 1 mile / 10cm to 1 km

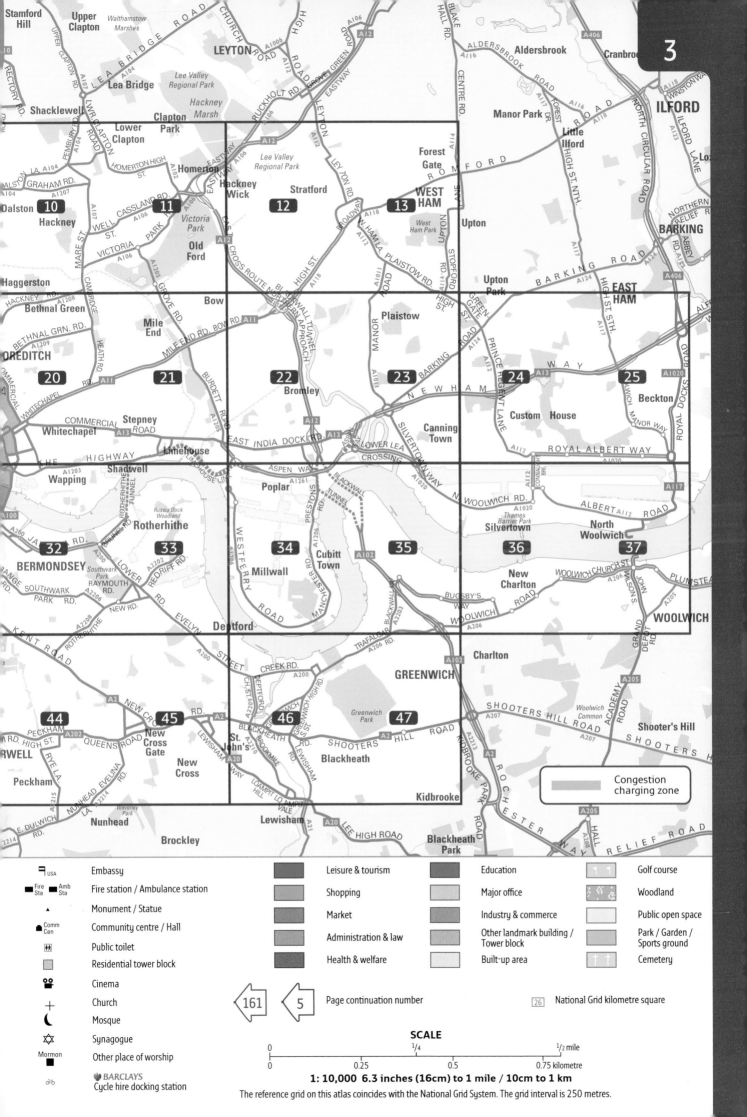

The reference grid on this atlas coincides with the National Grid System. The grid interval is 250 metres.

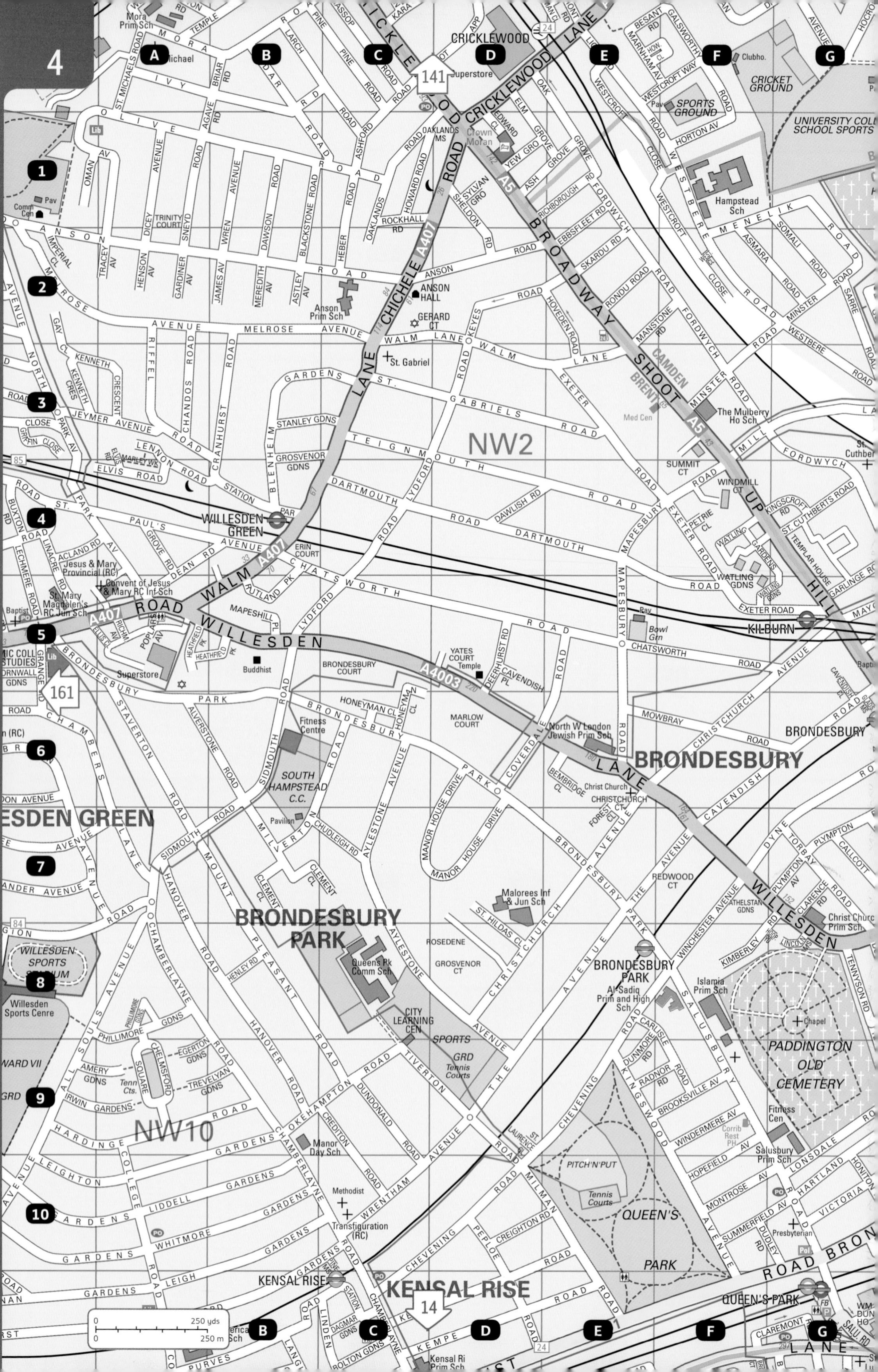
A
B
C
D
E
F
G
1
2
3
4
5
6
7
8
9
10
141
161
14
CRICKLEWOOD
NW2
NW10
BRONDESBURY
BRONDESBURY PARK
KENSAL RISE
ESDEN GREEN
Mora Prim Sch
TEMPLE RD
MORA RD
Michael
IVY RD
OLIVE RD
ST. MICHAEL'S ROAD
BRIAR RD
AGAVE RD
LARCH RD
PINE RD
CEDAR RD
ASSOP
ASHFORD RD
CRICKLEWOOD LANE
CRICKLEWOOD BROADWAY
Superstore
OAKLANDS MS
Crown Moran
EDWARD CL
ELM GROVE
OAK GROVE
YEW GRO
ASH GROVE
Lib
OMAN AV
AVENUE
ROAD
Pav
Comm Cen
ANSON ROAD
IMPERIAL
TRACEY AV
HENSON AV
DICEY AV
TRINITY COURT
SNEYD ROAD
GARDINER AV
JAMES AV
WREN AVENUE
MEREDITH AV
DAWSON RD
ASTLEY AV
BLACKSTONE ROAD
HEBER ROAD
OAKLANDS
HOWARD ROAD
ROCKHALL RD
SYLVAN GRO
SHELDON RD
RICHBOROUGH RD
EBBSFLEET RD
SKARDU RD
FORDWYCH RD
BROADWAY
SHOOT UP HILL
A5
A407
A4003
ANSON HALL
Anson Prim Sch
GERARD CT
MELROSE AVENUE
WALM LANE
St. Gabriel
ST. GABRIELS ROAD
GAY CL
KENNETH CRES
KENNETH CRESCENT
RIFFEL RD
CHANDOS ROAD
CRANHURST ROAD
NORTH PARK AV
CLOSE
GRIFFIN CLOSE
JEYMER AVENUE
ELVIS RD
MARLEY WK
LENNON ROAD
STATION PAR
STANLEY GDNS
GROSVENOR GDNS
BLENHEIM
TEIGNMOUTH ROAD
DARTMOUTH ROAD
LYDFORD ROAD
KEYES ROAD
HOVEDEN ROAD
EXETER ROAD
DAWLISH RD
RONDU ROAD
MANSTONE RD
CAMDEN
BRENT
Med Cen
The Mulberry Ho Sch
MINSTER ROAD
SUMMIT CT
WINDMILL CT
MILL LANE
St. Cuthbert
KINGSCROFT RD
ST. CUTHBERTS ROAD
TEMPLAR HOUSE
PETRIE CL
WATLING GARDENS
WATLING GDNS
MAPESBURY ROAD
GARLINGE RD
WILLESDEN GREEN
ST. PAUL'S AVENUE
BUXTON RD
LECHMERE ROAD
LINACRE RD
ACLAND RD
Jesus & Mary Provincial (RC)
Convent of Jesus & Mary RC Inf Sch
St. Mary Magdalen's RC Jun Sch
Baptist
DEAN RD
GROVE RD
ERIN COURT
CHATSWORTH ROAD
RUTLAND PK
MAPESHILL PL
WALM ROAD
WILLESDEN LANE
POPLARS AV
HEATHFIELD PK
Superstore
Buddhist
BRONDESBURY COURT
YATES COURT
Temple
DEERHURST RD
CAVENDISH RD
Bowl Grn
KILBURN
EXETER ROAD
MIC COLL STUDIES
CORNWALL GDNS
GRANGE RD
BRONDESBURY PARK
HONEYMAN CL
MARLOW COURT
MOWBRAY ROAD
CHRISTCHURCH AVENUE
BRONDESBURY
North W London Jewish Prim Sch
STAVERTON ROAD
CHAMBERS LANE
ALVERSTONE ROAD
SIDMOUTH ROAD
Fitness Centre
SOUTH HAMPSTEAD C.C.
Pavilion
AYLESTONE AVENUE
MANOR HOUSE DRIVE
COVERDALE RD
BEMBRIDGE CL
Christ Church
CHRISTCHURCH CT
FOREST CL
CAVENDISH ROAD
DYNE RD
TORBAY RD
PLYMPTON RD
CALLCOTT RD
MILVERTON RD
CHUDLEIGH RD
CLEMENT CL
MOUNT PLEASANT
HANOVER ROAD
REDWOOD CT
Malorees Inf & Jun Sch
ST. HILDAS CL
ATHELSTAN GDNS
CLARENCE RD
Christ Church Prim Sch
KIMBERLEY RD
LINCOLN RD
WILLESDEN SPORTS STADIUM
Willesden Sports Centre
ALL SOULS AVENUE
CHAMBERLAYNE ROAD
HENLEY RD
Queens Pk Comm Sch
ROSEDENE
GROSVENOR CT
BRONDESBURY PARK
Al-Sadiq Prim and High Sch
Islamia Prim Sch
Chapel
PADDINGTON OLD CEMETERY
TENNYSON RD
WINCHESTER AVENUE
CITY LEARNING CEN
SPORTS GRD
Tennis Courts
PHILLIMORE GDNS
CHELMSFORD SQUARE
EGERTON GDNS
AMERY GDNS
TREVELYAN GDNS
Tenn Cts.
IRWIN GARDENS
HARDINGE ROAD
LEIGHTON GARDENS
COLLEGE ROAD
LIDDELL GARDENS
WHITMORE GARDENS
OKEHAMPTON ROAD
DUNDONALD ROAD
CREDITON ROAD
TIVERTON ROAD
WRENTHAM AVENUE
Manor Day Sch
Methodist
Transfiguration (RC)
CARLISLE RD
DUNMORE RD
RADNOR RD
KINGSWOOD AVENUE
BROOKSVILLE AV
WINDERMERE AV
HOPEFIELD AV
MONTROSE AV
SUMMERFIELD AV
SALUSBURY ROAD
Corrib Rest
Fitness Cen
Salusbury Prim Sch
LONSDALE RD
HARTLAND RD
VICTORIA RD
DUDLEY RD
Presbyterian
ST LAURENCE CL
PITCH'N'PUT
QUEEN'S PARK
CHEVENING ROAD
MILMAN RD
PEPLOE RD
CREIGHTON RD
KENSAL RISE
LEIGH GARDENS
STATION TER
DAGMAR GDNS
LINDEN AV
BOLTON GDNS
KEMPE ROAD
Kensal Ri Prim Sch
PURVES RD
QUEEN'S PARK
ROAD BRONDESBURY
CLAREMONT RD
LANE
0
250 yds
250 m
24
WARD VII
GRD
ANDER AVENUE
DON AVENUE
Clubho.
CRICKET GROUND
SPORTS GROUND
UNIVERSITY COLL SCHOOL SPORTS
BESANT RD
GALSWORTHY
MARNHAM AV
WESTCROFT WAY
WESTCROFT CLOSE
HORTON AV
WESTBERE ROAD
Hampstead Sch
MENELIK ROAD
SOMALI ROAD
ASMARA ROAD
SARRE RD
MINSTER ROAD

WEST HAMPSTEAD
SOUTH HAMPSTEAD
KILBURN
NW3
NW6
NW8
HAMPSTEAD
FINCHLEY ROAD
WEST END LANE
KILBURN HIGH ROAD
BELSIZE ROAD
ABBEY ROAD
MAIDA VALE
FITZJOHN'S AV
COLLEGE CRES
BOUNDARY ROAD
FINCHLEY ROAD & FROGNAL
WEST HAMPSTEAD (THAMESLINK)
KILBURN PARK
HAMPSTEAD C.C.
KILBURN GRANGE PARK
FORTUNE GREEN
CAMDEN ARTS CEN
FREUD MUSEUM
The Jack Taylor Sch
George Eliot Inf & Jun Schs
Quintin Kynaston Sch
The American Sch in London
University Coll Sch
ABBEY ROAD ESTATE
MORTIMER ESTATE
WEBHEATH ESTATE
CAMDEN
WESTMINSTER
142
15
H
J
K
L
M
N
P
1
2
3
4
5
6
7
8
9
10

A
B
C
D
E
F
G
1
2
3
4
5
6
7
8
9
10
HAMPSTEAD
NW3
BELSIZE PARK
NW8
PRIMROSE HILL
THE REGENT'S
PARLIAMENT HILL
ATHLETICS TRACK
CRICKET GROUND
PREACHER'S
27
28
142
5
16
HAMPSTEAD HIGH ST
A502
ROSSLYN HILL
HAVERSTOCK HILL
HAVERSTOCK
FITZJOHN'S AV
B511
FINCHLEY ROAD
A41
ADELAIDE ROAD
B509
WELLINGTON RD
PRINCE ALBERT ROAD
AGINCOURT RD
FLEET ROAD
B518
MANSFIELD ROAD
SOUTHAMPTON RD
MALDEN
ROYAL FREE HOSP
HAMPSTEAD HEATH
BELSIZE PK
CHALK FARM
SWISS COTTAGE
SOUTH HAMPSTEAD
ST. JOHN'S WOOD
FINCHLEY ROAD
FREUD MUSEUM
KEATS HOUSE
TAVISTOCK CEN
CENTRAL SCH OF SPEECH & DRAMA
ODEON
EVERYMAN
TOWN HALL CEN
Premier Inn
Marriott Regents Park
Britannia Hampstead
REGENT'S CANAL
RUNNING TRACK
ZSL LONDON ZOO
Main Gate
Cov Res
CAMDEN
MAITLAND PARK ESTATE
ST. SILAS STREET ESTATE
TOWNSHEND ESTATE
Quintin Kynaston Sch
George Eliot Inf & Jun Schs
The American Sch in London
ROUNDHOUSE
250 yds
250 m

TUFNELL PARK
GOSPEL OAK
NW5
N7
KENTISH TOWN
KENTISH TOWN WEST
KENTISH TOWN
CAMDEN ROAD
CAMDEN TOWN
NW1
N1
KING'S CROSS
REGENT'S PARK
MORNINGTON CRESCENT
ST. PANCRAS
H.M.P. HOLLOWAY
HILLDROP ESTATE
BRECKNOCK ROAD ESTATE
AGAR GROVE ESTATE
ST. PANCRAS HOSPITAL
ST. PANCRAS GARDENS
Holloway School
Camden Sch for Girls
Camden Lock Mkt
Stables Mkt
JEWISH MUS
CENTRAL SAINT MARTINS COLLEGE OF ART AND DESIGN KING'S CROSS
Camley Street Natural Park
ROYAL VETERINARY COLL
THE FORUM
CANTELOWES GDNS
CAMDEN SQ GDNS
ST. MARTIN'S GARDENS
Gloucester Gate
FORTESS ROAD
KENTISH TOWN ROAD
CAMDEN ROAD
CAMDEN HIGH ST
BRECKNOCK ROAD
YORK WAY
ST. PANCRAS WAY
CAMDEN PARK RD
AGAR GROVE
PARKWAY
DELANCEY STREET
ALBANY ST
CHALK FARM RD
PRATT ST
CROWNDALE RD
EVERSHOLT ST
HAMPSTEAD RD
OAKLEY SQ
PANCRAS ROAD
MIDLAND RD
PRINCE OF WALES ROAD
HIGHGATE ROAD
LEIGHTON RD
ROYAL COLLEGE ST
A400
A503
A5200
A5202
A5205
B518
B512
143
8
17
H
J
K
L
M
N
P
1
2
3
4
5
6
7
8
9
10

HOLLOWAY
LOWER HOLLOWAY
BARNSBURY
ISLINGTON
KING'S CROSS
PENTONVILLE
N7
NW1
HIGHBURY FIELDS
EMIRATES STADIUM ARSENAL FC
H.M.P. HOLLOWAY
H.M.P. PENTONVILLE
HOLLOWAY ROAD
CALEDONIAN ROAD
CAMDEN ROAD
YORK WAY
LIVERPOOL ROAD
UPPER STREET
PENTONVILLE ROAD
COPENHAGEN STREET
MARKET ROAD
CALEDONIAN PARK
SPORTS GROUND
PARADISE PARK
BARNSBURY WOOD
THORNHILL SQ
REGENT'S CANAL
DRAYTON PARK
HOLLOWAY ROAD
CALEDONIAN ROAD & BARNSBURY
HIGHBURY & ISLINGTON
ANGEL
KING'S CROSS ST. PANCRAS
BUSINESS DESIGN CEN
CENTRAL ST MARTINS COLLEGE OF ART AND DESIGN (KING'S CROSS)
LONDON MET UNI
NAGS HEAD
A B C D E F G
1 2 3 4 5 6 7 8 9 10
143
18
7
250 yds
250 m

HIGHBURY
N5
CANONBURY
N1
N16
E8
KINGSLAND
DE BEAUVOIR TOWN
SHOREDITCH
HOXTON
DALSTON KINGSLAND
DALSTON JUNCTION
HAGGERSTON
ESSEX ROAD
CANONBURY
HIGHBURY ESTATE
SHOREDITCH PARK
KINGSGATE ESTATE
COLVILLE ESTATE
HOBBS PLACE ESTATE
WHITMORE ESTATE
ROSEMARY GDNS
DE BEAUVOIR ESTATE
CRANSTON ESTATE
GEFFRYE MUSEUM
REGENT'S CANAL
KINGSLAND BASIN
WENLOCK BASIN
CITY ROAD BASIN
HIGHBURY GROVE
HIGHBURY PARK
PAUL'S ROAD
BALLS POND ROAD
ESSEX ROAD
NEW NORTH ROAD
SOUTHGATE ROAD
KINGSLAND ROAD
KINGSLAND HIGH ST
STOKE NEWINGTON ROAD
NEWINGTON GRN
ALBION ROAD
MILDMAY PARK
MILDMAY GROVE NORTH
MILDMAY GROVE SOUTH
ST. PAUL'S ROAD
CANONBURY ROAD
DOWNHAM ROAD
EAGLE WHARF ROAD
SHEPHERDESS WALK
NORTHCHURCH ROAD
ENGLEFIELD ROAD
GREEN LANES
A1201
A1199
A1200
A104
A105
A10
B102
B104
144
10
19
H
J
K
L
M
N
P
1
2
3
4
5
6
7
8
9
10

N16
SHACKLEWELL
HACKNEY DOWNS
DALSTON KINGSLAND
DALSTON JUNCTION
HACKNEY DOWNS
HACKNEY CENTRAL
HACKNEY
E8
DALSTON
LONDON FIELDS
SOUTH HACKNEY
HAGGERSTON
HAGGERSTON PARK
E2
N1
CAMBRIDGE HEATH
STOKE NEWINGTON ROAD
KINGSLAND HIGH ST
KINGSLAND ROAD
A10
DALSTON LANE
GRAHAM ROAD
A1207
A104
PEMBURY ROAD
CRICKETFIELD ROAD
AMHURST ROAD
A107
MARE STREET
CAMBRIDGE HEATH ROAD
LWR CLAPTON RD
QUEENSBRIDGE ROAD
B108
RICHMOND ROAD
MIDDLETON ROAD
WELL STREET
A106
VICTORIA
REGENTS ROW
HACKNEY ROAD
A1208
DOWNS PARK ROAD
SANDRINGHAM ROAD
Kingsland Shopping Cen
Petchey Academy
Mossbourne Comm. Academy
Hackney City Farm
Geffrye Museum
Gas Works
BUS DEPOT
St. Joseph's Hospice
144
9
20
0
250 yds
250 m

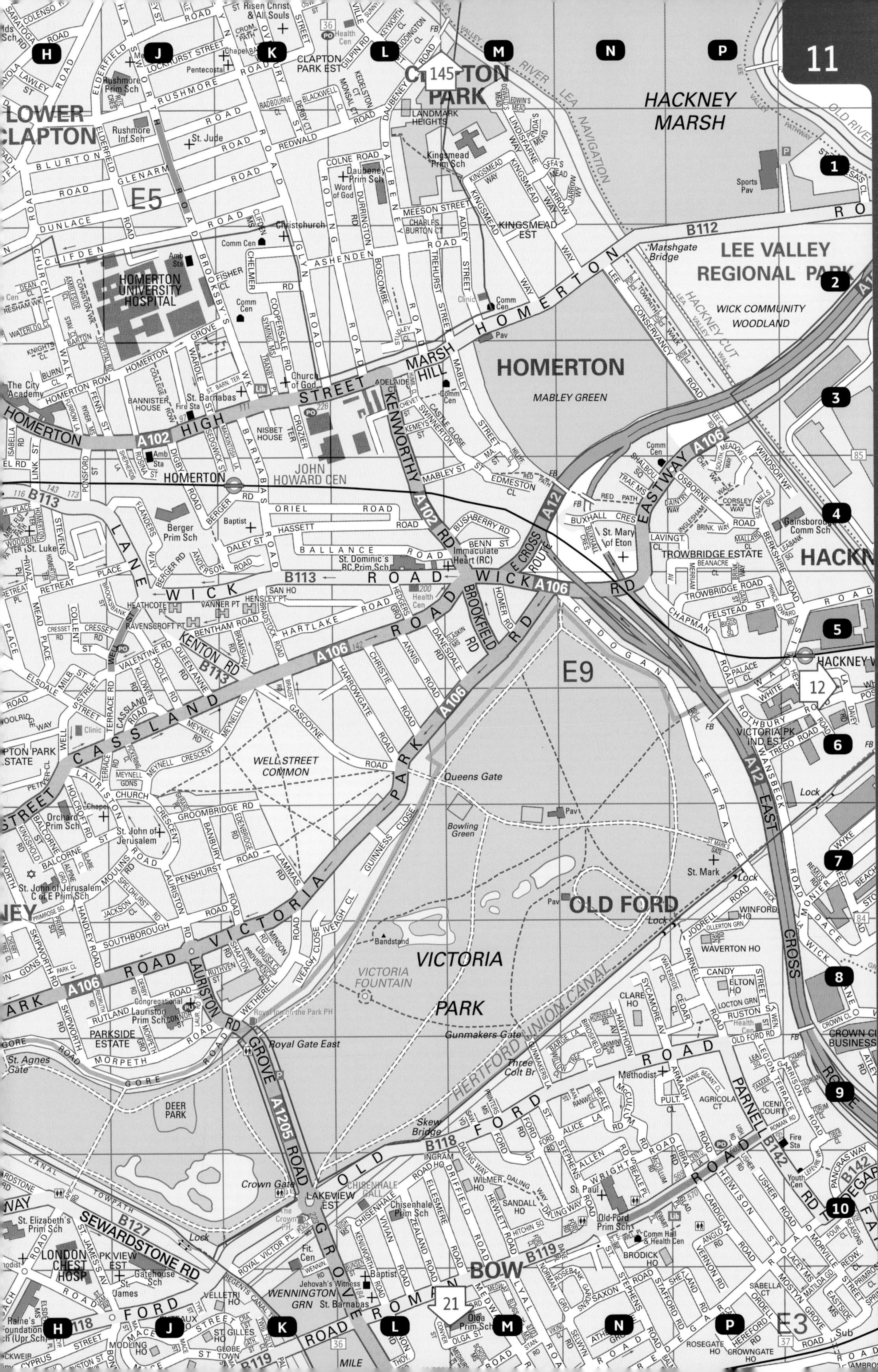
LOWER CLAPTON
CLAPTON PARK
HACKNEY MARSH
LEE VALLEY REGIONAL PARK
WICK COMMUNITY WOODLAND
HOMERTON
MABLEY GREEN
HOMERTON UNIVERSITY HOSPITAL
JOHN HOWARD CEN
KINGSMEAD EST
TROWBRIDGE ESTATE
WELL STREET COMMON
VICTORIA PARK
VICTORIA FOUNTAIN
OLD FORD
BOW
DEER PARK
LONDON CHEST HOSP
PARKSIDE ESTATE
LAKEVIEW EST
VICTORIA PK IND EST
HERTFORD UNION CANAL
RIVER LEA NAVIGATION
HACKNEY CUT
Queens Gate
Gunmakers Gate
Royal Gate East
Crown Gate
St. Agnes Gate
Bowling Green
Bandstand
Skew Bridge
Three Colt Br
Marshgate Bridge
E5
E9
E3
A102
A106
A12
A1205
B112
B113
B118
B119
B127
B142
HOMERTON HIGH STREET
WICK ROAD
CASSLAND ROAD
VICTORIA PARK ROAD
GROVE ROAD
OLD FORD ROAD
ROMAN ROAD
PARNELL ROAD
EAST CROSS ROUTE
SEWARDSTONE RD
MARSH HILL
KENWORTHY RD
BROOKFIELD RD
CADOGAN TERRACE
WELL STREET
LAURISTON RD
GORE ROAD
145
12
21
H J K L M N P
1 2 3 4 5 6 7 8 9 10

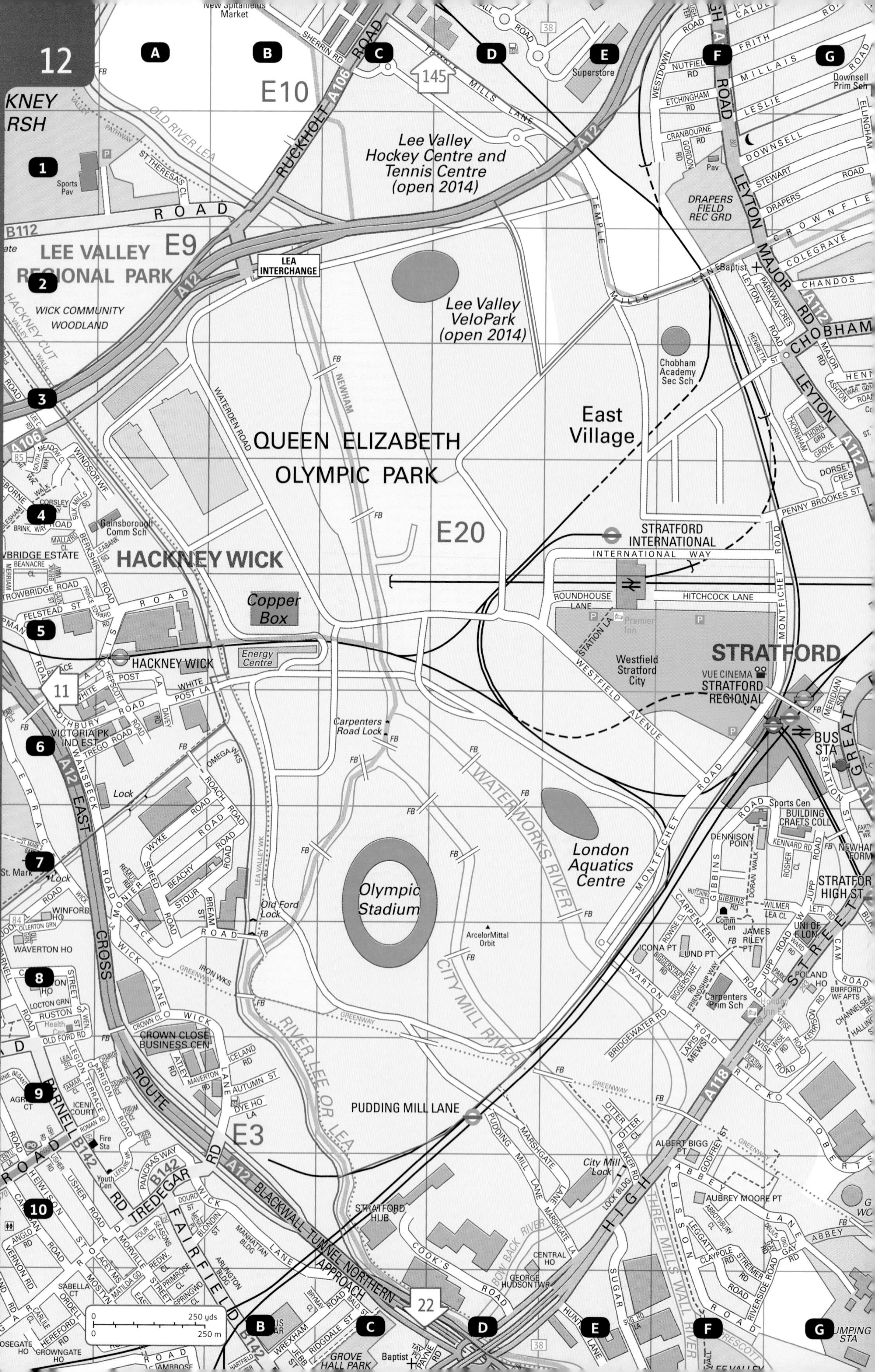
A
B
C
D
E
F
G
1
2
3
4
5
6
7
8
9
10
E10
E9
E20
E3
KNEY
RSH
New Spitalfields Market
Superstore
145
11
22
38
Lee Valley
Hockey Centre and
Tennis Centre
(open 2014)
LEE VALLEY
REGIONAL PARK
WICK COMMUNITY
WOODLAND
LEA
INTERCHANGE
Lee Valley
VeloPark
(open 2014)
Chobham
Academy
Sec Sch
East
Village
QUEEN ELIZABETH
OLYMPIC PARK
STRATFORD
INTERNATIONAL
INTERNATIONAL WAY
ROUNDHOUSE LANE
HITCHCOCK LANE
Premier Inn
Westfield
Stratford
City
STRATFORD
VUE CINEMA
STRATFORD
REGIONAL
BUS STA
HACKNEY WICK
Gainsborough
Comm Sch
Copper
Box
Energy
Centre
Carpenters
Road Lock
London
Aquatics
Centre
Olympic
Stadium
ArcelorMittal
Orbit
Old Ford
Lock
VICTORIA PK
IND EST
Lock
St. Mark
WINFORD HO
WAVERTON HO
CROWN CLOSE
BUSINESS CEN
PUDDING MILL LANE
City Mill
Lock
STRATFORD
HUB
CENTRAL HO
GEORGE
HUDSON TWR
DRAPERS
FIELD
REC GRD
Downsell
Prim Sch
Sports
Pav
Pav
Baptist
Sports Cen
BUILDING
CRAFTS COLL
DENNISON
POINT
STRATFORD
HIGH ST
UNI OF
E LON
JAMES
RILEY
PT
ICONA PT
LUND PT
Carpenters
Prim Sch
Holiday
Inn Ex
POLAND HO
BURFORD
WF APTS
ALBERT BIGG PT
AUBREY MOORE PT
GROVE
HALL PARK
CROWNGATE HO
Youth Cen
Fire Sta
Health Cen
RUCKHOLT ROAD
A106
A12
A112
A118
B112
B142
OLD RIVER LEA
ST THERESA'S CL
TEMPLE MILLS LANE
LEYTON ROAD
LEYTON MAJOR RD
CHOBHAM
WESTDOWN RD
FRITH RD
MILLAIS RD
LESLIE RD
NUTFIELD RD
ETCHINGHAM RD
CRANBOURNE RD
DOWNSELL RD
STEWART RD
DRAPERS RD
CROWNFIELD RD
COLEGRAVE RD
CHANDOS RD
HENRIETTA ST
PARKWAY CRES
THORNHAM GRO
DORSET CRES
PENNY BROOKES ST
MONTFICHET ROAD
WESTFIELD AVENUE
STATION LA
NEWHAM GREENWAY
WATERDEN ROAD
WATERWORKS RIVER
CITY MILL RIVER
RIVER LEE OR LEA
BOW BACK RIVER
THREE MILLS WALL RIVER
HACKNEY CUT
LEA VALLEY WK
WHITE POST LA
HEPSCOTT RD
WANSBECK RD
TREGO ROAD
OMEGA WKS
ROACH ROAD
WYKE ROAD
SMEED ROAD
BEACHY ROAD
STOUR ROAD
BREAM ST
MONIER ROAD
DACE ROAD
WICK LANE
IRON WKS
EAST CROSS ROUTE
HACKNEY WICK
BERKSHIRE ROAD
FELSTEAD ST
TROWBRIDGE ROAD
WINDSOR WF
BEANACRE CL
CORSLEY WAY
WARTON ROAD
CARPENTERS ROAD
BRIDGEWATER RD
GIBBINS RD
ROWSE CL
BIGGERSTAFF RD
FRIENDSHIP WAY
LAPIS MEWS
RICKS ROAD
ROBERTS ROAD
JUPP ROAD
WARD RD
KENNARD RD
ROSHER CL
WILMER LEA CL
LETT RD
KERRISON RD
WISE ROAD
DEASON ST
PUDDING MILL LANE
MARSHGATE LANE
OTTER CL
BLAKER RD
LOCK BLDG
HIGH ST
ABBEY LANE
GODFREY ST
BISSON RD
LEGGATT RD
CLAYPOLE RD
STREIMER ROAD
RIVERSIDE ROAD
SUGAR HOUSE LANE
ABBOTSBURY
BLACKWALL TUNNEL NORTHERN APPROACH
COOK'S ROAD
TREDEGAR RD
FAIRFIELD RD
WICK LANE
PARNELL RD
OLD FORD RD
ROMAN ROAD
MANHATTAN BLDG
ARLINGTON BLDG
AUTUMN ST
ICELAND RD
DYE HO LA
MAVERTON RD
ATLEY RD
WREXHAM RD
RIDGDALE ST
MORVILLE ST
STOCKTON ROAD
HEWISON ST
USHER ROAD
VERNON RD
MOSTYN GRO
ORDELL RD
HEREFORD RD
CARLILE CL
0 250 yds
0 250 m

FOREST GATE
WEST HAM
E7
E13
E15
MARYLAND
PLAISTOW
ABBEY ROAD
JEWISH CEMETERY
WEST HAM CEMETERY
WEST HAM PARK
SPORTS GROUND
STRATFORD PARK
STRATFORD MARKET DEPOT
The Stratford Centre
THEATRE ROYAL
PICTURE HOUSE ARTS CEN
UNI OF EAST LONDON (Stratford Campus)
NEWHAM COLL OF FURTHER ED (Stratford Campus)
FOREST LANE PK
CLAPTON FC
ROMFORD ROAD
A118
A112
A114
A1011
B164
B165
B161
LEYTONSTONE ROAD
WATER LANE
UPTON LANE
WOODGRANGE ROAD
PORTWAY
PLASHET
STOPFORD ROAD
PLAISTOW ROAD
NEW PLAISTOW RD
MANOR ROAD
BROADWAY
WEST HAM LA
VICARAGE LANE
FOREST LANE
CORPORATION
GREENWAY
146
166
23
H
J
K
L
M
N
P
1
2
3
4
5
6
7
8
9
10

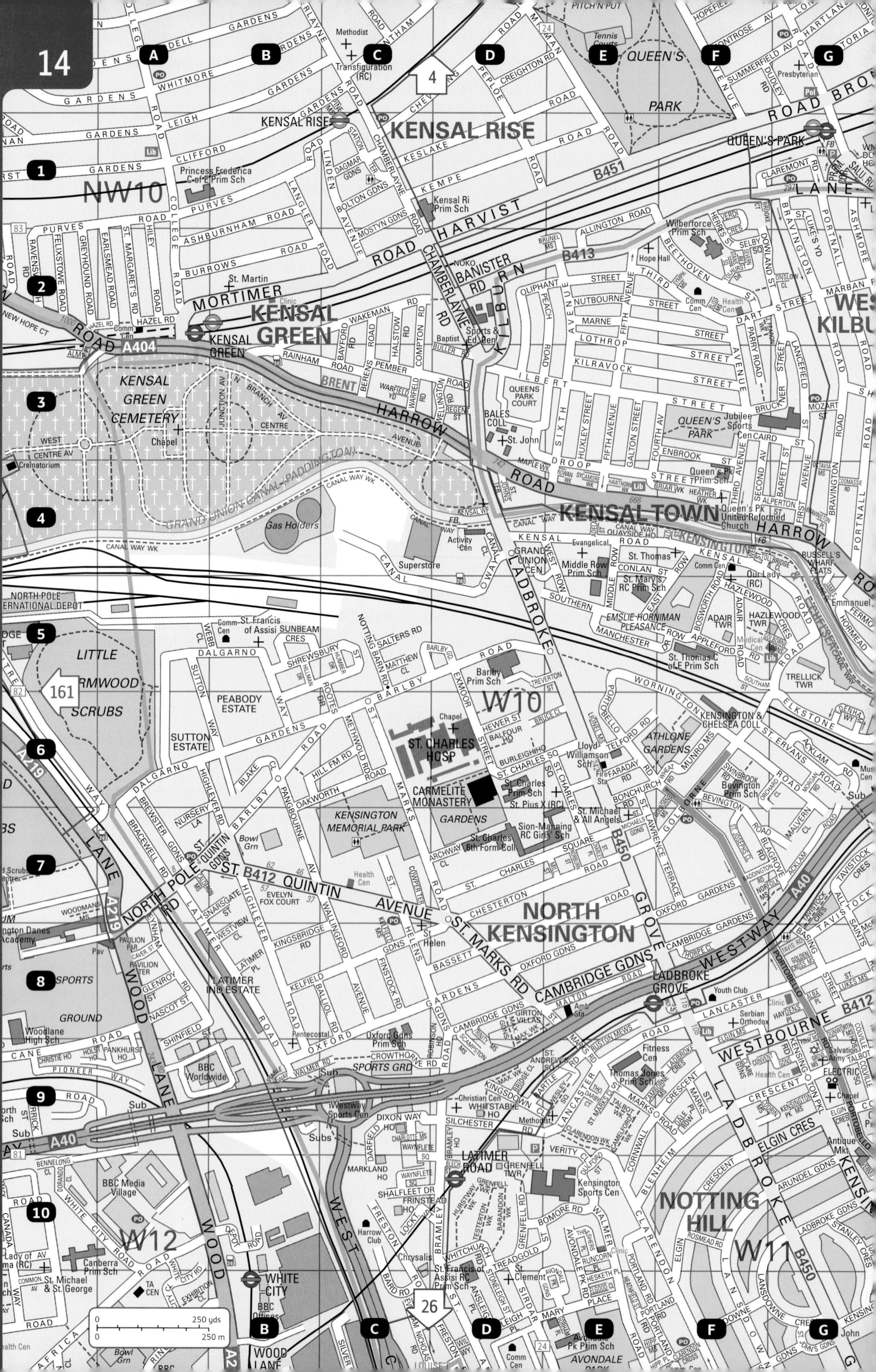
KENSAL RISE
KENSAL GREEN
KENSAL GREEN CEMETERY
KENSAL TOWN
NW10
W10
W11
W12
NORTH KENSINGTON
NOTTING HILL
QUEEN'S PARK
LITTLE WORMWOOD SCRUBS
KENSINGTON MEMORIAL PARK
ST. CHARLES HOSP
CARMELITE MONASTERY GARDENS
PEABODY ESTATE
SUTTON ESTATE
LATIMER IND ESTATE
ATHLONE GARDENS
EMSLIE HORNIMAN PLEASANCE
GRAND UNION CANAL (PADDINGTON)
Gas Holders
Superstore
NORTH POLE INTERNATIONAL DEPOT
HARROW ROAD
A404
B451
B413
B412
B450
A40
A219
WESTWAY
LADBROKE GROVE
LATIMER ROAD
WHITE CITY
BBC Media Village
BBC Worldwide
WOOD LANE
ST. QUINTIN AVENUE
NORTH POLE RD
WESTBOURNE PARK
QUEEN'S PARK
KENSAL RISE
KENSAL GREEN
CHAMBERLAYNE RD
KILBURN LANE
LADBROKE GROVE
PORTOBELLO RD
ST. MARKS RD
CAMBRIDGE GDNS
Kensington Sports Cen
Westway Sports Cen
4
26
161
0 250 yds
0 250 m

KILBURN
KILBURN PARK
MAIDA VALE
MAIDA HILL
WESTBOURNE GREEN
PADDINGTON
BAYSWATER
ROYAL OAK
WARWICK AVENUE
ST. JOHN'S WOOD
NW6
NW8
W9
W2
MAIDA VALE
ABBEY ROAD
GROVE END ROAD
CARLTON VALE
KILBURN PARK ROAD
SHIRLAND ROAD
ELGIN AVENUE
HARROW ROAD
WESTWAY
WESTBOURNE PARK ROAD
WESTBOURNE GROVE
CHEPSTOW ROAD
PEMBRIDGE VILLAS
BISHOPS BRIDGE RD
EASTBOURNE TER
CRAVEN ROAD
QUEENSWAY
PORCHESTER RD
LEINSTER TER
BAYSWATER ROAD
EDGWARE RD
PADDINGTON RECREATION GROUND
ATHLETICS TRACK
CRICKET GROUND
Little Venice
PADDINGTON GREEN
ST. MARY'S HOSP
Lancaster Gate
WARWICK AVENUE
BLOMFIELD RD
SUTHERLAND AVENUE
RANDOLPH AVENUE
HAMILTON TERRACE
CLIFTON GDNS
WARRINGTON CRESCENT
A5
A40
A404
A402
A4206
A4207
B413
B414
B411
B415
B507
5
16
27
25
26

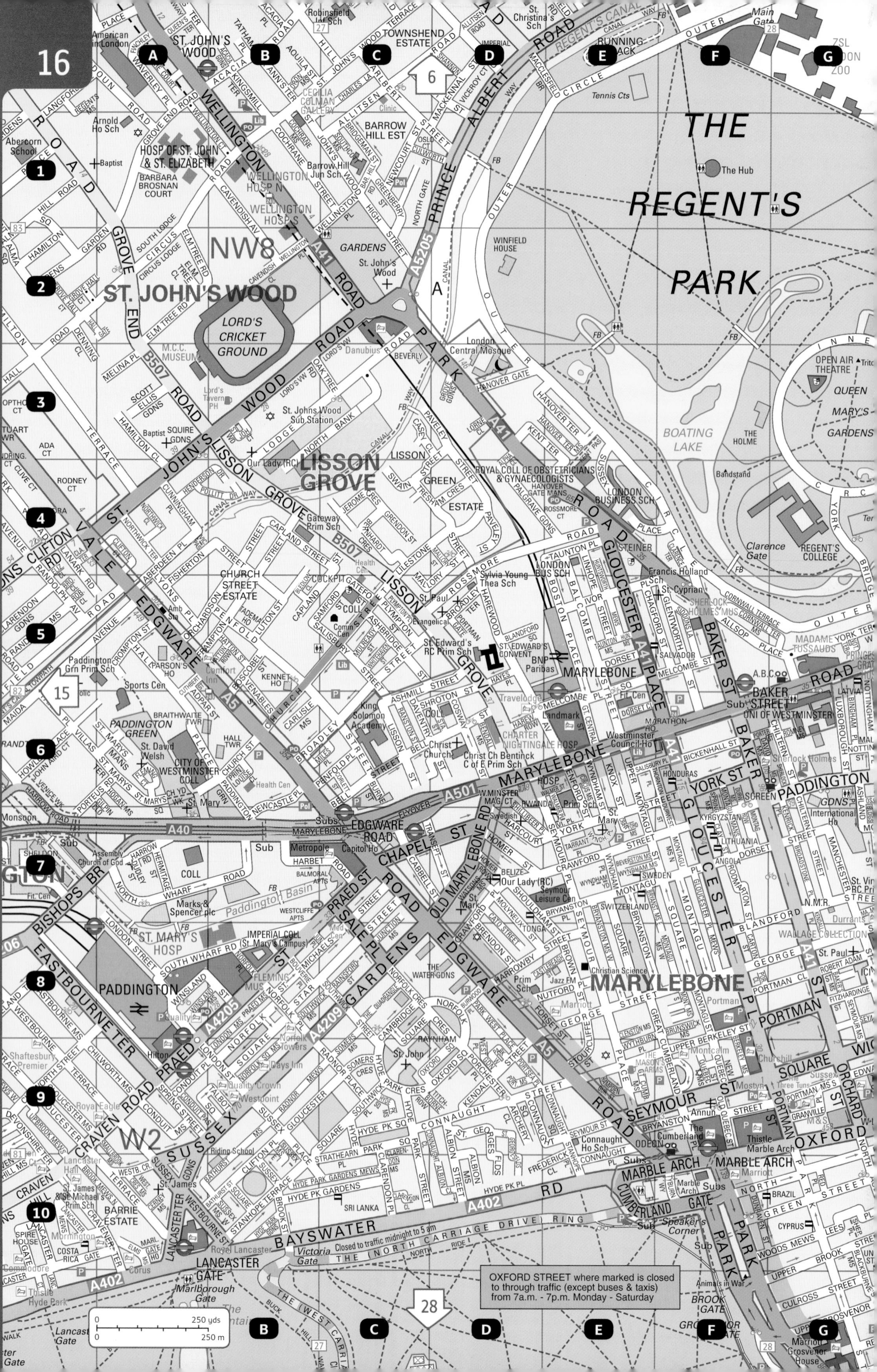
A
B
C
D
E
F
G
1
2
3
4
5
6
7
8
9
10
6
15
28
THE REGENT'S PARK
ST. JOHN'S WOOD
NW8
LORD'S CRICKET GROUND
M.C.C. MUSEUM
LISSON GROVE
MARYLEBONE
PADDINGTON
W2
ST. JOHN'S WOOD
WELLINGTON ROAD
PRINCE ALBERT ROAD
OUTER CIRCLE
REGENT'S CANAL
RUNNING TRACK
Tennis Cts
The Hub
WINFIELD HOUSE
London Central Mosque
HANOVER GATE
BOATING LAKE
THE HOLME
Bandstand
OPEN AIR THEATRE
QUEEN MARY'S GARDENS
Clarence Gate
REGENT'S COLLEGE
LONDON BUSINESS SCH
ROYAL COLL OF OBSTETRICIANS & GYNAECOLOGISTS
HOSP OF ST. JOHN & ST. ELIZABETH
WELLINGTON HOSP N
WELLINGTON HOSP S
BARROW HILL EST
TOWNSHEND ESTATE
CHURCH STREET ESTATE
LISSON GREEN ESTATE
ST. JOHN'S WOOD ROAD
GROVE END ROAD
EDGWARE ROAD
MARYLEBONE ROAD
BAKER STREET
GLOUCESTER PLACE
PARK ROAD
MADAME TUSSAUDS
Sherlock Holmes
SHERLOCK HOLMES MUS
CITY OF WESTMINSTER COLL
PADDINGTON GREEN
Paddington Basin
ST. MARY'S HOSP
IMPERIAL COLL (St. Mary's Campus)
EASTBOURNE TER
PRAED ST
SUSSEX GARDENS
CRAVEN ROAD
BISHOPS BR
BAYSWATER RD
A402
A40
A41
A5
A501
A4205
A4209
A5205
B507
MARBLE ARCH
CUMBERLAND GATE
Speaker's Corner
PARK LANE
OXFORD STREET
PORTMAN SQUARE
SEYMOUR ST
HYDE PARK GARDENS
HYDE PARK CRES
CONNAUGHT ST
LANCASTER GATE
Victoria Gate
Marlborough Gate
THE (NORTH CARRIAGE DRIVE) RING
Closed to traffic midnight to 5 am
Animals in War
BROOK GATE
GROSVENOR GATE
OXFORD STREET where marked is closed to through traffic (except buses & taxis) from 7a.m. - 7p.m. Monday - Saturday
0 250 yds
0 250 m

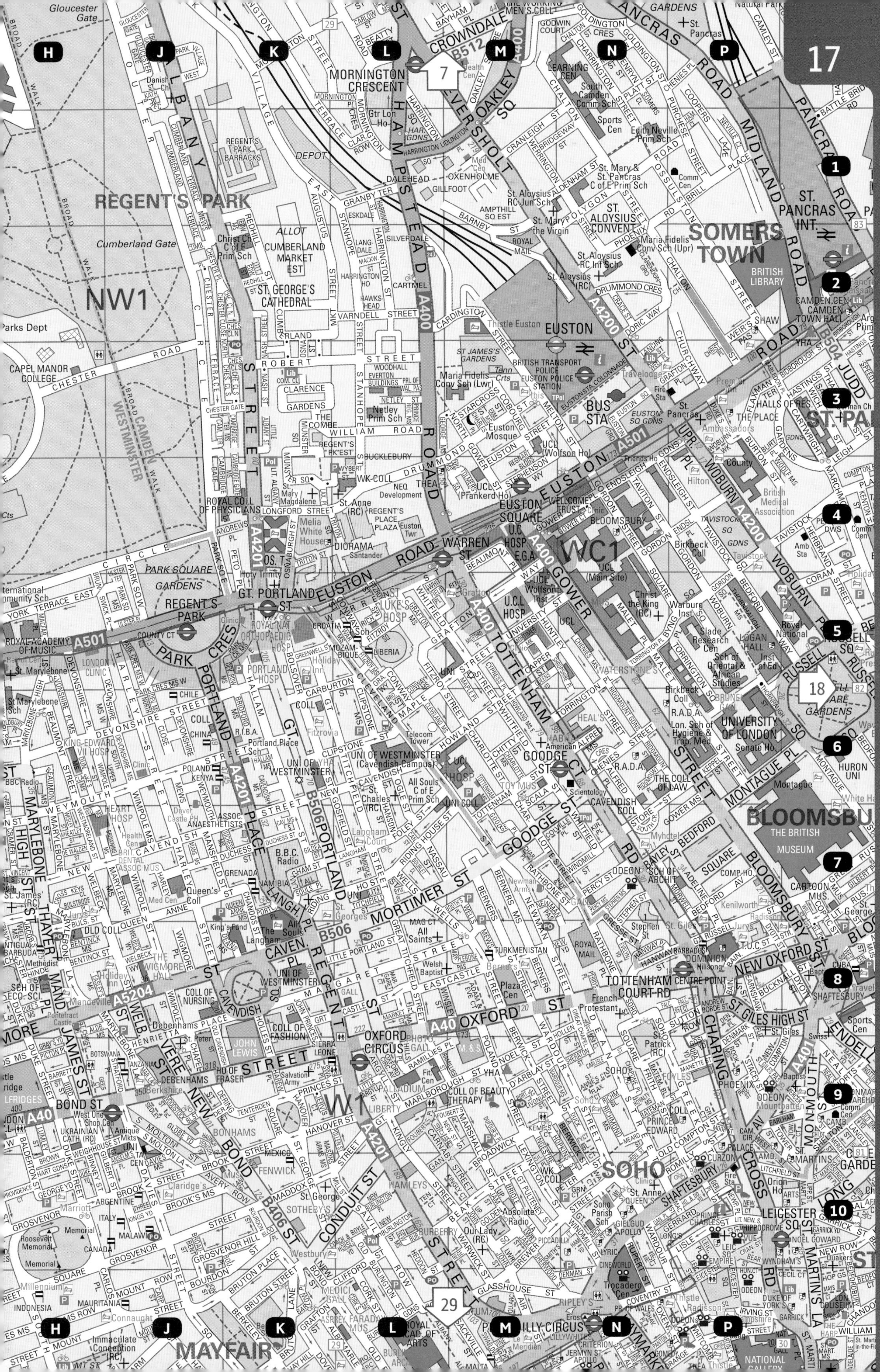
H
J
K
L
M
N
P
1
2
3
4
5
6
7
8
9
10
7
18
29
REGENT'S PARK
NW1
WC1
W1
SOMERS TOWN
BLOOMSBU
SOHO
MAYFAIR
ST. PANCRAS INT.
BRITISH LIBRARY
EUSTON
EUSTON SQUARE
WARREN ST
GT. PORTLAND ST
REGENT'S PARK
MORNINGTON CRESCENT
GOODGE ST
TOTTENHAM COURT RD
OXFORD CIRCUS
BOND ST
PICCADILLY CIRCUS
LEICESTER SQ
EUSTON ROAD
OXFORD ST
REGENT ST
TOTTENHAM COURT RD
GOWER ST
HAMPSTEAD ROAD
CHARING CROSS RD
SHAFTESBURY
NEW OXFORD ST
WOBURN PL
RUSSELL SQ
BLOOMSBURY ST
MIDLAND ROAD
PANCRAS ROAD
PORTLAND PLACE
MARYLEBONE HIGH ST
NEW BOND ST
CONDUIT ST
THE BRITISH MUSEUM
UNIVERSITY OF LONDON
UCL (Main Site)
A501
A400
A4200
A4201
A40
A5204
B506
B406
A401
B504
B512
A4200

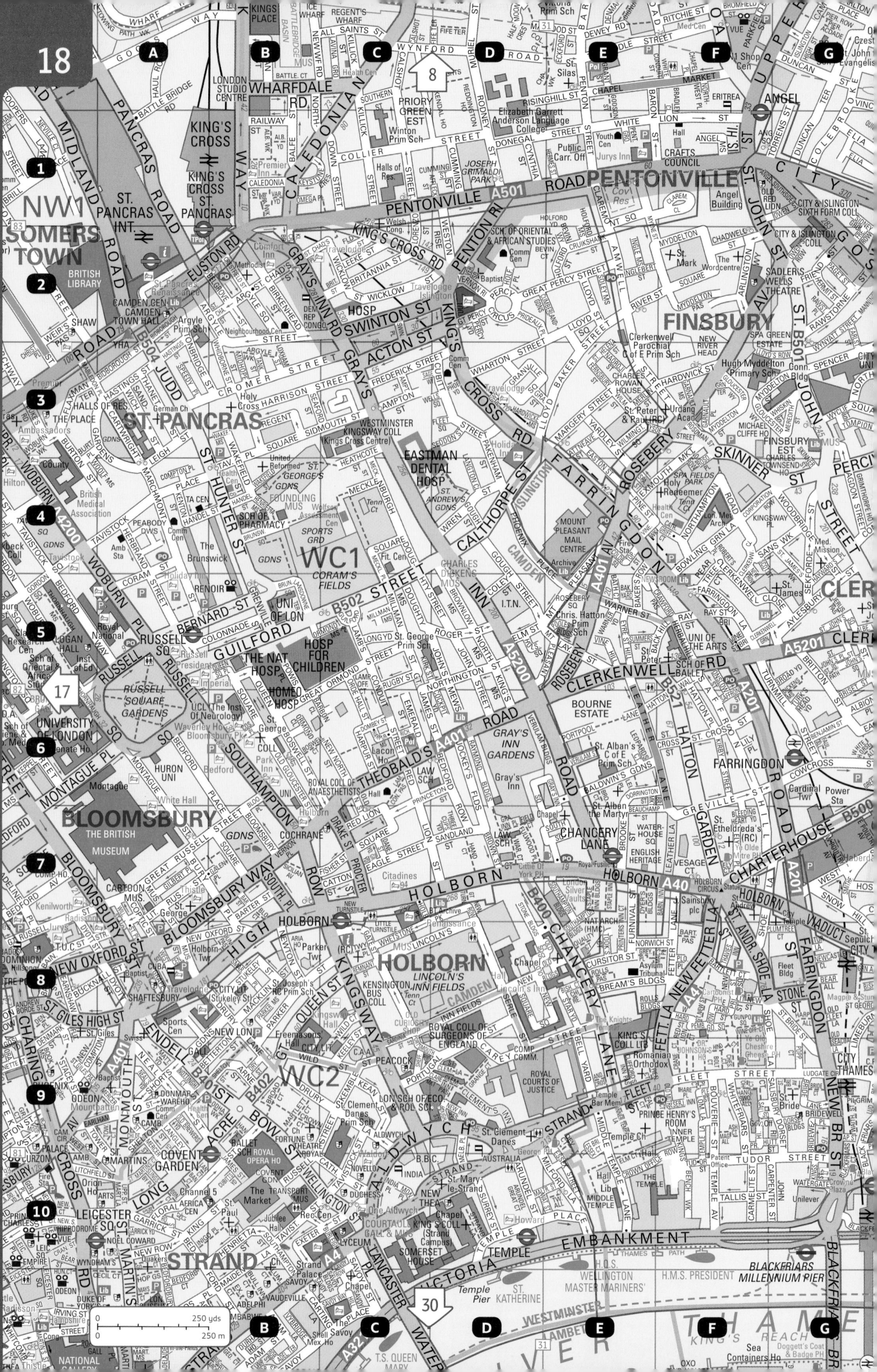
A
B
C
D
E
F
G
1
2
3
4
5
6
7
8
9
10
8
17
30
NW1
SOMERS TOWN
KING'S CROSS
ST. PANCRAS INT.
KING'S CROSS ST. PANCRAS
BRITISH LIBRARY
PENTONVILLE
ANGEL
FINSBURY
ST PANCRAS
WC1
CORAM'S FIELDS
BLOOMSBURY
THE BRITISH MUSEUM
HOLBORN
LINCOLN'S INN FIELDS
WC2
COVENT GARDEN
STRAND
CHANCERY LANE
FARRINGDON
TEMPLE
RUSSELL SQUARE GARDENS
GRAY'S INN GARDENS
EASTMAN DENTAL HOSP
HOSP FOR CHILDREN
MOUNT PLEASANT MAIL CENTRE
ROYAL COURTS OF JUSTICE
SOMERSET HOUSE
VICTORIA EMBANKMENT
BLACKFRIARS MILLENNIUM PIER
THAMES
PENTONVILLE ROAD
EUSTON RD
GRAY'S INN RD
KING'S CROSS RD
FARRINGDON RD
ROSEBERY AV
CLERKENWELL RD
THEOBALD'S ROAD
HOLBORN
HIGH HOLBORN
KINGSWAY
ALDWYCH
FLEET ST
CHARTERHOUSE
SOUTHAMPTON ROW
WOBURN PL
GUILFORD ST
CHARING CROSS
SHAFTESBURY
LEICESTER SQ
250 yds
250 m

H
J
K
L
M
N
P
1
2
3
4
5
6
7
8
9
10
9
20
31
SHOREDITCH
SPORTS GRD PARK
SHOREDITCH PARK GARDEN
N1
HOXTON
ARDEN ESTATE
CRANSTON ESTATE
PITFIELD ESTATE
GEFFRYE MUSEUM
CITY ROAD BASIN
WENLOCK BASIN
REGENT'S CANAL
EAGLE WHARF
SHEPHERDESS WALK
NEW NORTH RD
CITY ROAD
PITFIELD ST
KINGSLAND ROAD
HACKNEY ROAD
OLD STREET
MOORFIELDS EYE HOSP
EC1
ST. LUKE'S
KING SQUARE GDN
BUNHILL FIELDS BURIAL GRD
BUNHILL FIELDS
GREAT EASTERN STREET
SHOREDITCH HIGH STREET
CALVERT AV
ARNOLD CIRCUS
CLERKENWELL RD
GOSWELL RD
ALDERSGATE ST
BARBICAN
CHISWELL ST
FINSBURY SQ
BROADGATE
LIVERPOOL STREET
EC2
BISHOPSGATE
COMMERCIAL ST
E1
OLD SPITALFIELDS MARKET
MOORGATE
LONDON WALL
BARTHOLOMEW'S HOSPITAL
NEWGATE ST
ST. PAUL'S
ST. PAUL'S CATHEDRAL
CHEAPSIDE
BANK
Bank of England
MANSION HOUSE
CANNON ST
MONUMENT
FENCHURCH ST
HOUNDSDITCH
ALDGATE
MINORIES
TOWER HILL
EC3
EC4
BLACKFRIARS
MILLENNIUM BRIDGE
SOUTHWARK BRIDGE
LONDON BRIDGE
Southwark Bridge Steps
Swan Lane Pier
TOWER OF LONDON
BLACKFRIARS FOR BANKSIDE AND SOUTH BANK
SHAKESPEARE'S GLOBE THEATRE

HAGGERSTON
HOXTON
SHOREDITCH
BETHNAL GREEN
WHITECHAPEL
E2
E1
EC3
HACKNEY ROAD
KINGSLAND
SHOREDITCH HIGH STREET
COMMERCIAL STREET
COMMERCIAL ROAD
WHITECHAPEL HIGH ST
WHITECHAPEL RD
MILE END RD
CAMBRIDGE HEATH RD
OLD BETHNAL GREEN ROAD
BETHNAL GREEN ROAD
ROMAN ROAD
COLUMBIA RD
GOSSET ST
VALLANCE RD
CANNON STREET RD
CABLE STREET
ROYAL MINT ST
MINORIES
HOUNDSDITCH
LEMAN STREET
BRICK LANE
MANSELL ST
DOCK ST
ALDGATE
ALDGATE EAST
TOWER HILL
TOWER GATEWAY
SHADWELL
WHITECHAPEL
BETHNAL GREEN
SHOREDITCH HIGH STREET
FENCHURCH ST
WEAVERS FIELDS
ALLEN GDNS
JEWISH BURIAL GROUND
ROYAL LONDON HOSP
OLD SPITALFIELDS MARKET
Spitalfields City Farm
Hackney City Farm
GEFFRYE MUSEUM
MUSEUM OF CHILDHOOD
IONA SQUARE GARDENS
SPORTS GROUND
HAGGERSTON PARK
BETHNAL GREEN GDNS
250 yds
250 m
A B C D E F G
1 2 3 4 5 6 7 8 9 10
10
19
32

H
J
K
L
M
N
P
1
2
3
4
5
6
7
8
9
10
11
22
33
BOW
MILE END
STEPNEY
LIMEHOUSE
E3
E14
SEWARDSTONE RD
ROMAN ROAD
GROVE ROAD
BOW ROAD
MILE END ROAD
BURDETT ROAD
COMMERCIAL ROAD
CABLE STREET
STEPNEY GREEN
BEN JONSON ROAD
COBORN ROAD
ST. PAULS WAY
EAST INDIA DOCK ROAD
ROTHERHITHE TUNNEL
NARROW STREET
BOW COMMON LANE
MILE END PARK
TOWER HAMLETS CEMETERY PARK
MILE END HOSPITAL
QUEEN MARY UNI OF LONDON
LONDON CHEST HOSP
LONDON INDEP. HOSP
MEATH GARDENS
SHANDY PARK
STEPNEY GREEN PARK
MILE END STADIUM
RAGGED SCHOOL MUSEUM
LIMEHOUSE BASIN
ROPEMAKERS FIELD
OCEAN ESTATE
LOCKSLEY ESTATE
LIMEHOUSE CUT
KING EDWARD VII MEMORIAL PK
Crown Gate
Stone Stairs
Ratcliffe Cross Stairs
Limehouse Hole Stairs
THAMES
WESTFERRY
STEPNEY GREEN
MILE END
BOW ROAD
LIMEHOUSE

A
B
C
D
E
F
G
1
2
3
4
5
6
7
8
9
10
12
21
34
E15
E3
E14
BLACKWALL TUNNEL NORTHERN APPROACH
FAIRFIELD ROAD
B142
A12
A11
A13
B140
A1206
A1261
B125
BOW ROAD
BOW CHURCH
DEVONS ROAD
BROMLEY BY BOW
LANGDON PARK
ALL SAINTS
WESTFERRY
POPLAR
BLACKWALL
WEST INDIA QUAY
BROMLEY
TOWER HAMLETS CEMETERY PARK
GROVE HALL PARK
LEE VALLEY PARK-THREE MILLS GREEN
LEE VALLEY PARK
Three Mills Studios
GAS WORKS
Gas Works
MEMORIAL GARDENS
Dudley Stationers
Mail Centre
BUS GAR
BOW TRIANGLE BUS. CEN
DEVONS ESTATE
BOW BRIDGE ESTATE
LANSBURY EST
FURZE GREEN
BARTLETT PARK
LANGDON PARK
JOLLY'S GREEN
LIMEHOUSE CUT
THOMAS ROAD IND EST
BARRATT IND PK
POPLAR BUSINESS PARK
TOWER HAMLETS COLL
EAST INDIA DOCK ROAD
DEVAS STREET
DEVONS ROAD
ST PAULS WAY
BOW COMMON LANE
POPLAR HIGH STREET
ASPEN WAY
A1261 WAY
LIMEHOUSE CAUSEWAY
COTTON STREET
ABBOTT ROAD
THREE MILL LANE
ABBEY LANE
SUGAR HOUSE LANE
BOW BACK RIVER
THREE MILLS WALL RIVER
PRESCOTT CHANNEL
RIVER LEA
Superstore
Global Switch
COUNCIL OFFICES
East India Dock Ho
0
250 yds
250 m

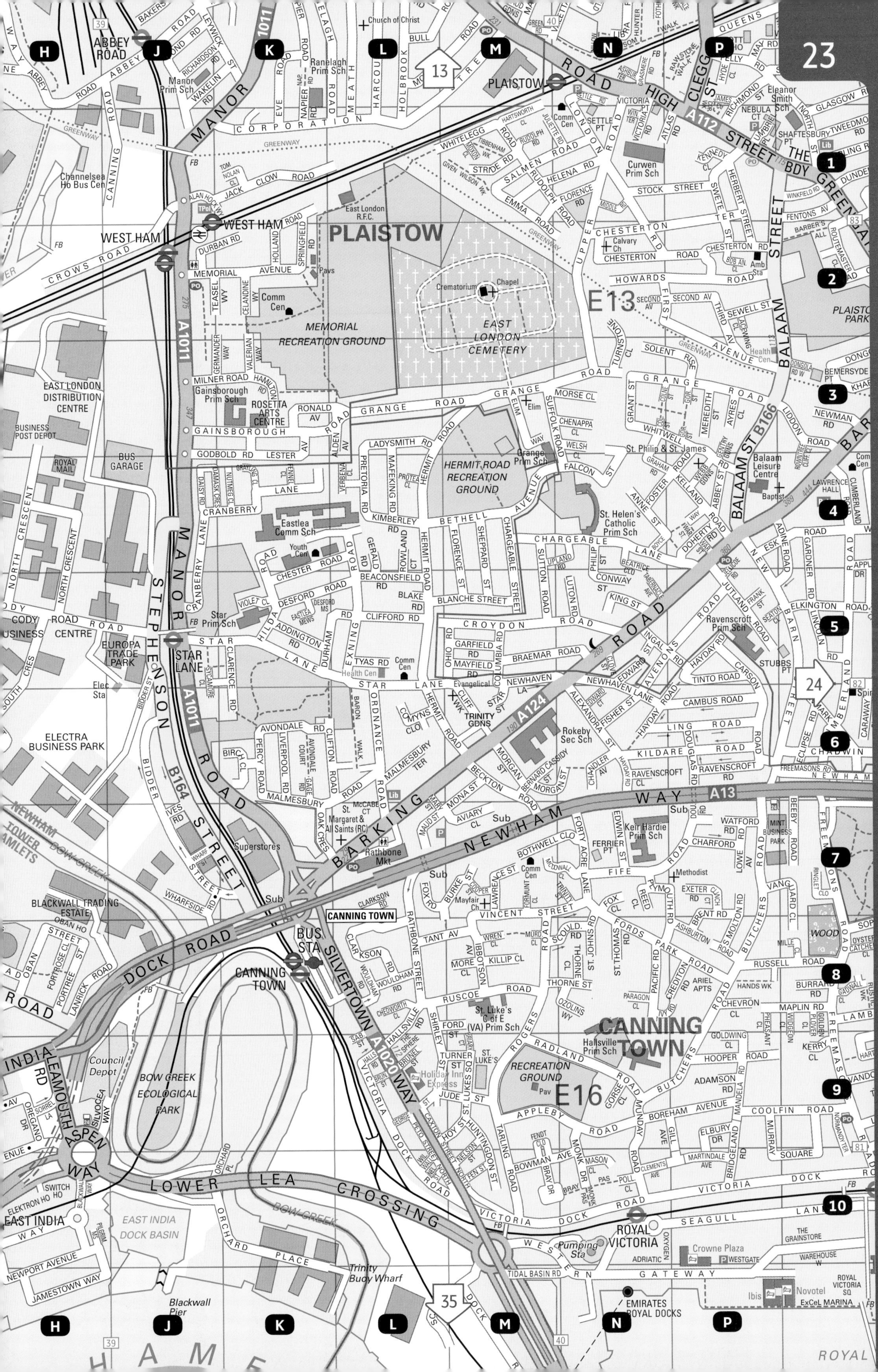
H
J
K
L
M
N
P
1
2
3
4
5
6
7
8
9
10
13
24
35
ABBEY ROAD
Manor Prim Sch
Ranelagh Prim Sch
Church of Christ
PLAISTOW
HIGH STREET
A112
CLEGG ST
QUEENS
Eleanor Smith Sch
GLASGOW RD
CORPORATION ROAD
GREENWAY
MANOR ROAD
A1011
Channelsea Ho Bus Cen
JACK CLOW ROAD
WEST HAM
CROWS ROAD
MEMORIAL AVENUE
DURBAN RD
HOLLAND RD
SPRINGFIELD RD
Pavs
East London R.F.C.
PLAISTOW
Comm Cen
MEMORIAL RECREATION GROUND
Crematorium
Chapel
EAST LONDON CEMETERY
E13
WHITELEGG ROAD
SALMEN ROAD
HELENA RD
RUDOLPH RD
FLORENCE RD
EMMA ROAD
Curwen Prim Sch
STOCK STREET
CHESTERTON ROAD
Calvary Ch
HOWARDS ROAD
SECOND AV
SEWELL ST
BALAAM STREET
PLAISTOW PARK
SOLENT RISE
GRANGE ROAD
EAST LONDON DISTRIBUTION CENTRE
BUSINESS POST DEPOT
ROYAL MAIL
BUS GARAGE
MILNER ROAD
Gainsborough Prim Sch
ROSETTA ARTS CENTRE
RONALD AV
GAINSBOROUGH
GODBOLD RD
LESTER AV
LADYSMITH AV
HERMIT ROAD RECREATION GROUND
Grange Prim Sch
MORSE CL
CHENAPPA CL
WELSH CL
FALCON ST
St. Philip & St. James
Balaam Leisure Centre
Baptist
B166
BALAAM ST
NEWMAN RD
CUMBERLAND RD
St. Helen's Catholic Prim Sch
CRANBERRY LANE
Eastlea Comm Sch
Youth Cen
CHESTER ROAD
BEACONSFIELD RD
KIMBERLEY RD
BETHELL AV
CHARGEABLE LANE
CONWAY ST
KING ST
ESK RD
ELKINGTON ROAD
Ravenscroft Prim Sch
STUBBS PT
CODY ROAD
BUSINESS CENTRE
NORTH CRESCENT
Star Prim Sch
DESFORD ROAD
ADDINGTON RD
CLIFFORD RD
BLANCHE STREET
CROYDON ROAD
GARFIELD RD
MAYFIELD RD
BRAEMAR ROAD
BARKING ROAD
A124
STAR LANE
STEPHENSON STREET
EUROPA TRADE PARK
Elec Sta
TYAS RD
Comm Cen
Health Cen
Evangelical
NEWHAVEN LANE
TINTO ROAD
CAMBUS ROAD
ELECTRA BUSINESS PARK
AVONDALE RD
PERCY ROAD
LIVERPOOL RD
CLIFTON ROAD
MALMESBURY RD
TRINITY GDNS
Rokeby Sec Sch
LING ROAD
KILDARE ROAD
RAVENSCROFT RD
CHADWIN
NEWHAM WAY
A13
B164
BIDDER STREET
Superstores
St. Margaret & All Saints (RC)
Rathbone Mkt
Lib
Keir Hardie Prim Sch
FERRIER PT
FIFE
Methodist
WATFORD RD
CHARFORD RD
MINT BUSINESS PARK
WOOD
NEWHAM TOWER HAMLETS
BOW CREEK
BLACKWALL TRADING ESTATE
OBAN HO
WHARFSIDE RD
CANNING TOWN
BUS STA
DOCK ROAD
SILVERTOWN WAY
A1020
VINCENT STREET
Mayfair Ch
TANT AV
KILLIP CL
RUSCOE ROAD
St. Luke's C of E (VA) Prim Sch
CANNING TOWN
Hallsville Prim Sch
RUSSELL ROAD
MAPLIN RD
HOOPER ROAD
ADAMSON RD
RECREATION GROUND
Pav
E16
Holiday Inn Express
APPLEBY ROAD
BOREHAM AVENUE
COOLFIN ROAD
MURRAY SQUARE
Council Depot
BOW CREEK ECOLOGICAL PARK
EAST INDIA
LEAMOUTH RD
ASPEN WAY
LOWER LEA CROSSING
VICTORIA DOCK ROAD
ROYAL VICTORIA
Pumping Sta
Crowne Plaza
WESTGATE
THE GRAINSTORE
WAREHOUSE W
GATEWAY
TIDAL BASIN RD
EMIRATES ROYAL DOCKS
Novotel
Ibis
ExCeL MARINA
ROYAL VICTORIA SQ
EAST INDIA DOCK BASIN
NEWPORT AVENUE
JAMESTOWN WAY
ORCHARD PLACE
Trinity Buoy Wharf
Blackwall Pier
THAMES
ROYAL

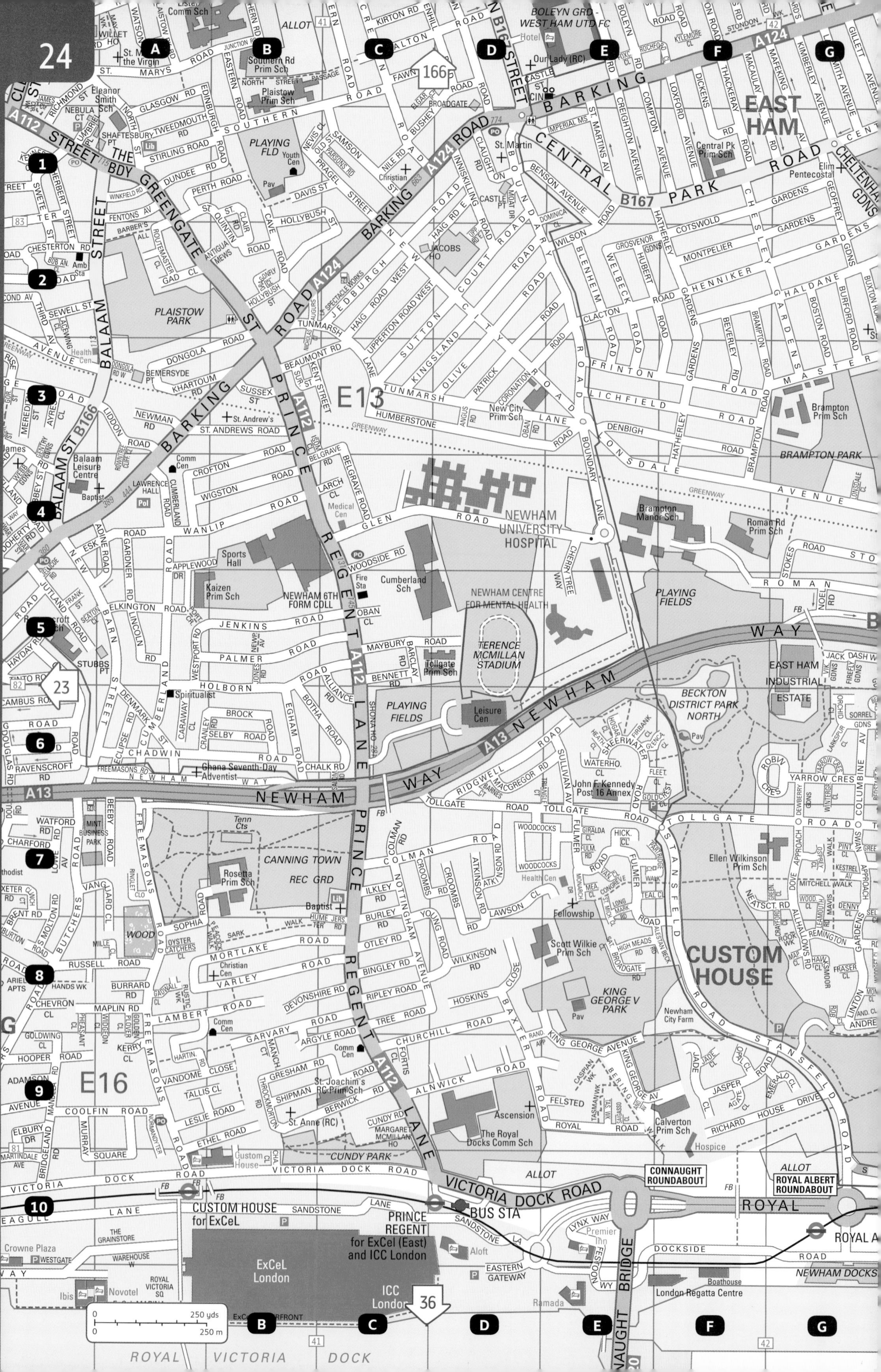

A
B
C
D
E
F
G
1
2
3
4
5
6
7
8
9
10
BOLEYN GRD - WEST HAM UTD FC
EAST HAM
E13
E16
BARKING ROAD
A124
A112
A13
NEWHAM WAY
PRINCE REGENT LANE
GREENGATE STREET
BALAAM STREET
CENTRAL PARK ROAD
B167
TOLLGATE ROAD
VICTORIA DOCK ROAD
PLAISTOW PARK
PLAYING FLD
NEWHAM UNIVERSITY HOSPITAL
NEWHAM CENTRE FOR MENTAL HEALTH
TERENCE MCMILLAN STADIUM
PLAYING FIELDS
BECKTON DISTRICT PARK NORTH
EAST HAM INDUSTRIAL ESTATE
BRAMPTON PARK
CANNING TOWN REC GRD
KING GEORGE V PARK
CUSTOM HOUSE
CUNDY PARK
CONNAUGHT ROUNDABOUT
ROYAL ALBERT ROUNDABOUT
CUSTOM HOUSE for ExCeL
PRINCE REGENT for ExCel (East) and ICC London
ExCeL London
ICC London
BUS STA
NEWHAM DOCKS
London Regatta Centre
ROYAL VICTORIA DOCK
23
36
166
250 yds
250 m

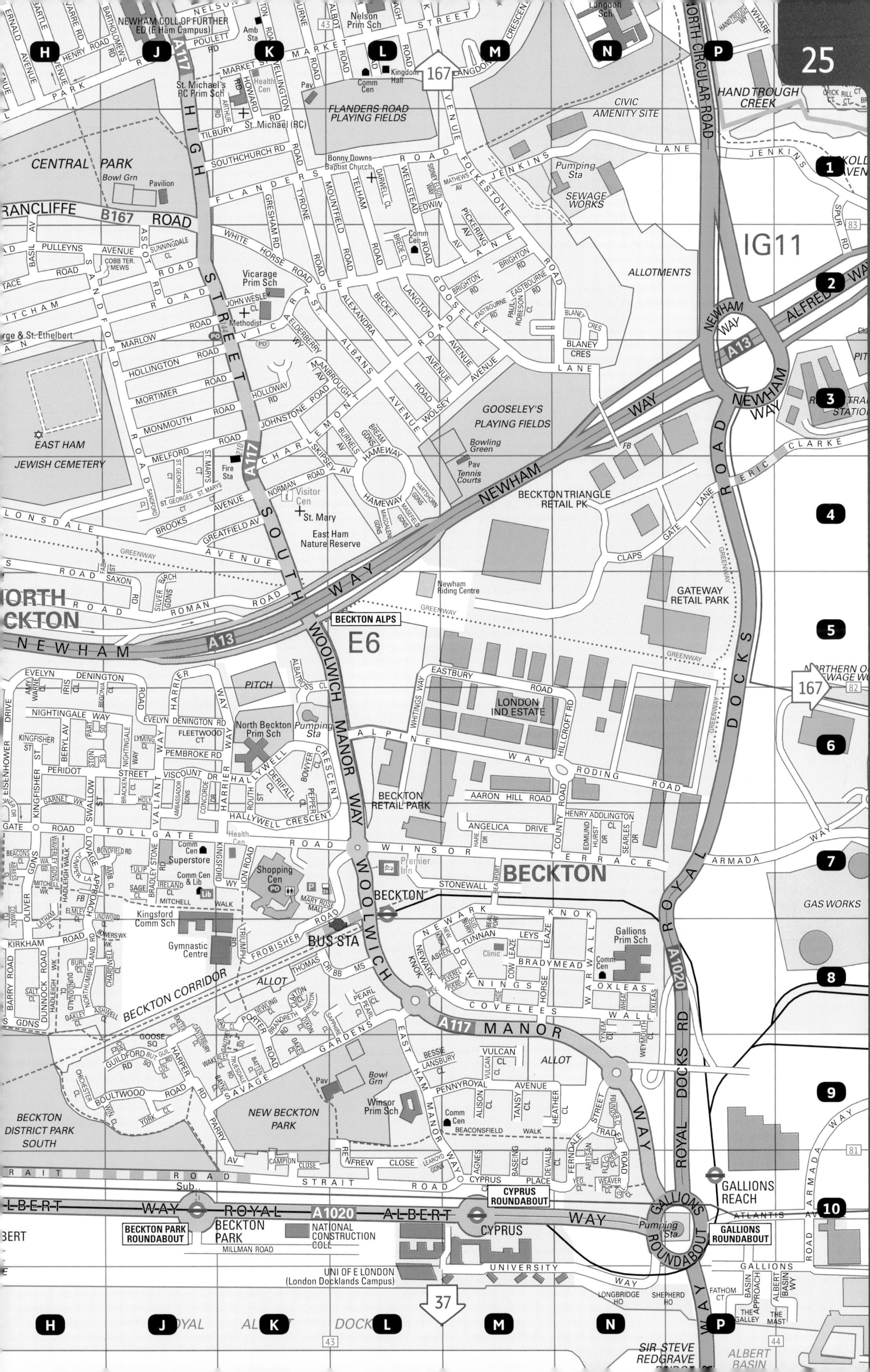
H
J
K
L
M
N
P
1
2
3
4
5
6
7
8
9
10
NEWHAM COLL OF FURTHER ED (E Ham Campus)
Amb Sta
Nelson Prim Sch
Langdon Sch
167
St. Michael's RC Prim Sch
Health Cen
Comm Cen
Kingdom Hall
St. Michael (RC)
FLANDERS ROAD PLAYING FIELDS
HAND TROUGH CREEK
CIVIC AMENITY SITE
NORTH CIRCULAR ROAD
CENTRAL PARK
Bowl Grn
Pavilion
Bonny Downs Baptist Church
Pumping Sta
SEWAGE WORKS
IG11
ALLOTMENTS
RANCLIFFE B167 ROAD
HIGH STREET
A117
SOUTHCHURCH RD
FLANDERS ROAD
WHITE HORSE ROAD
Vicarage Prim Sch
JOHN WESLEY CL
Methodist
NEWHAM WAY
A13
ALFRED WAY
BLANEY CRES
GOOSELEY'S PLAYING FIELDS
Bowling Green
Pav
Tennis Courts
EAST HAM JEWISH CEMETERY
Fire Sta
Visitor Cen
St. Mary
East Ham Nature Reserve
BECKTON TRIANGLE RETAIL PK
ERIC CLARKE LANE
RETAIL STATION
CLAPS GATE LANE
GREENWAY
Newham Riding Centre
GATEWAY RETAIL PARK
NORTH BECKTON
BECKTON ALPS
E6
NEWHAM WAY
NORTHERN OUTFALL SEWAGE WORKS
PITCH
LONDON IND ESTATE
North Beckton Prim Sch
Pumping Sta
BECKTON RETAIL PARK
ALPINE WAY
RODING ROAD
WOOLWICH MANOR WAY
ROYAL DOCKS ROAD
TOLLGATE ROAD
WINSOR TERRACE
Superstore
Comm Cen & Lib
Shopping Cen
Premier Inn
BECKTON
GAS WORKS
Kingsford Comm Sch
Gymnastic Centre
BUS STA
Gallions Prim Sch
Clinic
BECKTON CORRIDOR
ALLOT
A117 MANOR WAY
A1020
Bowl Grn
Winsor Prim Sch
NEW BECKTON PARK
BECKTON DISTRICT PARK SOUTH
STRAIT ROAD
CYPRUS ROUNDABOUT
BECKTON PARK ROUNDABOUT
ROYAL ALBERT WAY
BECKTON PARK
NATIONAL CONSTRUCTION COLL
CYPRUS
GALLIONS REACH
GALLIONS ROUNDABOUT
UNI OF E LONDON (London Docklands Campus)
UNIVERSITY WAY
37
LONGBRIDGE HO
SHEPHERD HO
FATHOM CT
THE GALLEY
THE MAST
ROYAL ALBERT DOCK
SIR STEVE REDGRAVE
ALBERT BASIN

A
B
C
D
E
F
G
1
2
3
4
5
6
7
8
9
10
14
38
181
NOTTING HILL
W12
W11
W14
W6
SHEPHERD'S BUSH
Westfield
VUE CINEMA
HAMMERSMITH
HOLLAND PARK ROUNDABOUT
HAMMERSMITH BROADWAY
KENSINGTON (OLYMPIA)
OLYMPIA
BBC Media Village
BBC Television Centre
HAMMERSMITH PARK
WHITE CITY
WOOD LANE
SHEPHERD'S BUSH MARKET
SHEPHERD'S BUSH
GOLDHAWK ROAD
HAMMERSMITH
BARONS COURT
HOLLAND PARK
WEST CROSS ROUTE
A3220
A219
A4020
A402
A315
A4
B450
UXBRIDGE ROAD
SHEPHERDS BUSH GREEN
SHEPHERDS BUSH COMMON
HOLLAND PARK
HOLLAND ROAD
ADDISON ROAD
KING STREET
HAMMERSMITH ROAD
TALGARTH ROAD
HAMMERSMITH FLYOVER
FULHAM PALACE ROAD
SHEPHERDS BUSH ROAD
BROOK GREEN
NORTH END ROAD
WEST CROMWELL ROAD
HAMMERSMITH & FULHAM
KENSINGTON & CHELSEA
AVONDALE PARK
SPORTS GROUND
HAMMERSMITH CEMETERY
HAMMERSMITH & W LONDON COLL
ACADEMY OF MUSIC & DRAMATIC ART
St. Paul's Girls Sch
BLYTHE HOUSE
SPRINGVALE ESTATE
QUEEN CAROLINE ESTATE
HarperCollins Publishers
Novotel London West
NAZARETH HOUSE CONVENT
Hilton Olympia
CHARLES HO GOVT OFFICES
0
250 yds
250 m

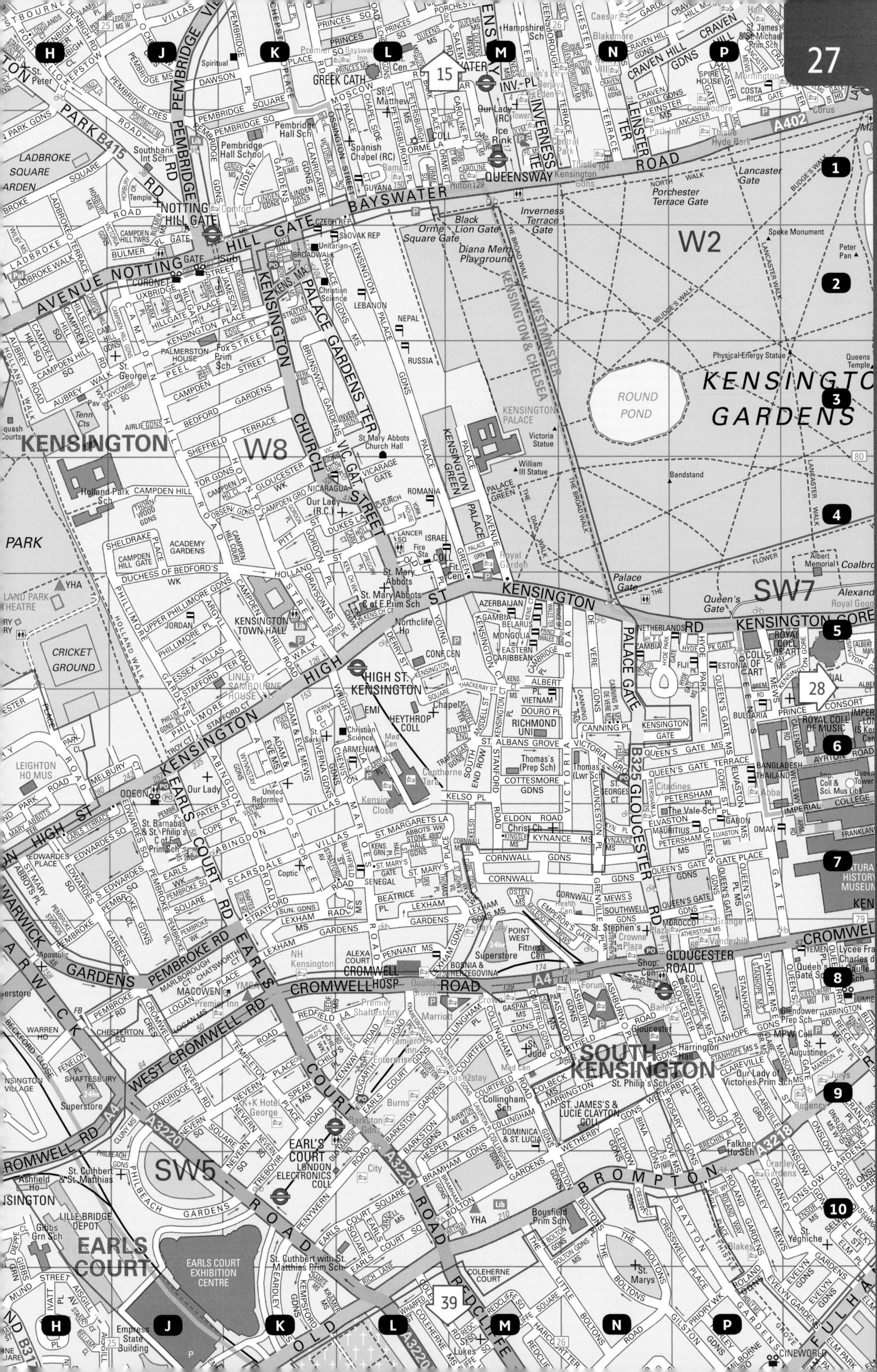
KENSINGTON
KENSINGTON GARDENS
SOUTH KENSINGTON
EARLS COURT
W2
W8
SW7
SW5
NOTTING HILL GATE
QUEENSWAY
HIGH ST. KENSINGTON
EARL'S COURT
BAYSWATER ROAD
KENSINGTON HIGH ST
CROMWELL ROAD
WEST CROMWELL RD
BROMPTON ROAD
KENSINGTON CHURCH STREET
ROUND POND
KENSINGTON PALACE
KENSINGTON TOWN HALL
HOLLAND PARK
CRICKET GROUND
EARLS COURT EXHIBITION CENTRE
NATURAL HISTORY MUSEUM
ROYAL COLL OF MUSIC
IMPERIAL COLLEGE
ROYAL COLL OF ART
Albert Memorial
Physical Energy Statue
Speke Monument
Peter Pan
Lancaster Gate
Palace Gate
Queen's Gate
Diana Mem Playground
15
28
39
H J K L M N P
1 2 3 4 5 6 7 8 9 10

HYDE PARK
KENSINGTON GARDENS
W2
SW7
SW3
BROMPTON
THE SERPENTINE
THE LONG WATER
The Fountains
Bird Sanctuary
Lido
Diana Princess of Wales Memorial
SERPENTINE GALLERY
Albert Memorial
Physical Energy Statue
Speke Monument
Peter Pan
Queens Temple
Holocaust Memorial
Bandstand
Joy of Life Fountain
Animals in War
Speakers' Corner
MARBLE ARCH
LANCASTER GATE
Victoria Gate
Brook Gate
Grosvenor Gate
Albert Gate
Edinburgh Gate
Rutland Gate
Prince of Wales Gate
Alexandra Gate
Queen's Gate
Coalbrookdale Gate
BAYSWATER RD
KENSINGTON RD
KENSINGTON GORE
KNIGHTSBRIDGE
BROMPTON ROAD
CROMWELL RD
KING'S ROAD
FULHAM ROAD
SLOANE STREET
PONT STREET
EXHIBITION ROAD
ROTTEN ROW
SERPENTINE ROAD
SOUTH CARRIAGE DRIVE
PARK LANE
A402
A4
A315
A3216
A3218
A308
B304
B319
B302
A4202
HARRODS
HARVEY NICHOLS
ROYAL COLL OF ART
IMPERIAL COLL
ROYAL COLL OF MUSIC
SCIENCE MUSEUM
NATURAL HISTORY MUSEUM
VICTORIA & ALBERT MUSEUM
Brompton Oratory
THE ROYAL MARSDEN
ROYAL BROMPTON HOSP
SOUTH KENSINGTON
KNIGHTSBRIDGE
SLOANE SQ
Saatchi Gallery
BURTON'S CT
ROYAL HOSPITAL
HYDE PARK BARRACKS
16
27
40
A
B
C
D
E
F
G
1
2
3
4
5
6
7
8
9
10
250 yds
250 m

H
J
K
L
M
N
P
17
SOHO
W1
MAYFAIR
PICCADILLY CIRCUS
PICCADILLY
NATIONAL GALLERY
TRAFALGAR SQ.
HAYMARKET
PALL MALL
ST. JAMES'S
THE GREEN PARK
ST. JAMES'S PARK
BUCKINGHAM PALACE GARDENS
BUCKINGHAM PALACE
SW1
WESTMINSTER
30
VICTORIA
PIMLICO
TATE BRITAIN
GRAVIA
1
2
3
4
5
6
7
8
9
10
41
HORSE GUARDS ROAD
BIRDCAGE WALK
CONSTITUTION HILL
VICTORIA ST
VAUXHALL BRIDGE ROAD
BELGRAVE RD
HORSEFERRY ROAD
MILLBANK
MARSHAM STREET
GROSVENOR PLACE
PARK LANE
HYDE PARK CORNER
GREEN PARK
WHITEHALL
PARLIAMENT ST
H.M. TREASURY
FOREIGN & COMMONWEALTH OFFICE
PLAYING FIELDS
GROSVENOR ESTATE
CHELSEA COLL OF ARTS & DESIGN
RIVERSIDE WK GARDENS
COACH STA
DEPOT

A
B
C
D
E
F
G
1
2
3
4
5
6
7
8
9
10
18
29
42
STRAND
WC2
SE11
SW1
LAMBETH
VAUXHALL
RIVER THAMES
KING'S REACH
VICTORIA EMBANKMENT
EMBANKMENT
TEMPLE
NATIONAL GALLERY
TRAFALGAR SQ
CHARING CROSS
WHITEHALL
HORSE GUARDS AV
MINISTRY OF DEFENCE
DOWNING ST
H.M. TREASURY
WESTMINSTER
HOUSES OF PARLIAMENT
The Clock Tower (Big Ben)
WESTMINSTER ABBEY
BRIDGE ST
WESTMINSTER BRI
LAMBETH BRI
MILLBANK
TATE BRITAIN
VICTORIA TOWER GARDENS
LONDON EYE MILLENNIUM PIER
LONDON FILM MUSEUM
JUBILEE GDNS
ROYAL FESTIVAL HALL
NATIONAL THEATRE
BFI SOUTHBANK
BFI IMAX
WATERLOO
WATERLOO BRI
WATERLOO EAST
ST. THOMAS' HOSP
LAMBETH PALACE GDNS
ARCHBISHOP'S PARK
LAMBETH NORTH
GERALDINE MARY HARMSWORTH PARK
IMPERIAL WAR MUS
KENNINGTON ROAD
KENNINGTON
KENNINGTON LANE
ALBERT EMBANKMENT
BLACKFRIARS ROAD
BLACKFRIARS MILLENNIUM PIER
STAMFORD STREET
UPPER GROUND
THE CUT
ST. GEORGE'S ROAD
LAMBETH ROAD
0 250 yds
0 250 m

H
J
K
L
M
N
P
19
EC4
SOUTHWARK
CANNON ST
BANKSIDE PIER
SHAKESPEARE'S GLOBE THEATRE
TATE MODERN
Swan Lane Pier
Fishmongers' Hall
MONUMENT
EASTCHEAP
FENCHURCH ST
TOWER HILL
Old Billingsgate
H. M. Revenue & Customs
Tate & Lyle plc
TOWER OF LONDON
Tower Millennium Pier
EC3
LONDON BRIDGE CITY PIER
LONDON BRIDGE HOSP.
SOUTHWARK CATHEDRAL
GOLDEN HINDE
CLINK PRISON
VINOPOLIS
Borough Mkt.
H.M.S. BELFAST
TOWER HAMLETS
TOWER BRIDGE
POTTERS FIELDS PARK
Hay's Galleria
The Shard
LONDON BRIDGE
GUY'S HOSP
TOOLEY ST
ST. THOMAS ST
BERMONDSEY STREET
CRUCIFIX LA
DRUID ST
SE1
SOUTHWARK
SOUTHWARK STREET A3200
UNION STREET B300
BLACKFRIARS RD
Blue Fin Building
PEABODY TRUST
BOROUGH HIGH ST
MARSHALSEA RD
LONG LANE
THE BOROUGH
BOROUGH ROAD
GREAT DOVER STREET
TABARD GARDENS ESTATE
ELIM ESTATE
LEATHERMARKET GARDENS
THE LEATHER MKT
KIPLING EST
A2198
ABBEY
32
ST. JOHN'S ESTATE
LONDON SOUTH BANK UNI
NEWINGTON CAUSEWAY
NEW KENT ROAD A201
BRICKLAYER'S ARMS ROUNDABOUT
OLD KENT RD
TOWER BRIDGE RD
GRANGE ROAD
BERMONDSEY
ELEPHANT & CASTLE
NEWINGTON BUTTS
NEWINGTON
WALWORTH
SE17
WALWORTH ROAD
EAST STREET
SURREY SQUARE PARK
FARADAY GARDENS
AYLESBURY EST
43
Bricklayer's Arms Distribution Centre
Royal Mail
Walworth Academy
SURREY GDNS
33
1
2
3
4
5
6
7
8
9
10

A
B
C
D
E
F
G
1
2
3
4
5
6
7
8
9
10
20
31
44
TOWER HILL
TOWER GATEWAY
ROYAL MINT ST
PRESCOT ST
CABLE ST
DOCK ST
THE HIGHWAY
A1203
B126
SHADWELL
TOWER OF LONDON
Chapel
All Hallows
Tower Pl W
Tate & Lyle plc
Tower Millennium Pier
EC3
E1
TOWER HAMLETS
SOUTHWARK
H.M.S. BELFAST
TOWER BRIDGE
TOWER BRIDGE APP
TOWER BRIDGE EXHIBITION
EAST SMITHFIELD
ST. KATHARINE DOCKS
St. Katharine's Pier
Ivory Ho
Devon Ho
Alderman Stairs
THOMAS MORE ST
THOMAS MORE SQ
Trinity Tower
Superstore
WAPPING
Hermitage Prim Sch
John Orwell (Wapping) Sports Cen
Tobacco Dock
PENNINGTON STREET
WAPPING LANE
WAPPING HIGH ST
WAPPING
Wapping Dock Stairs
Wapping Old Stairs
Wapping New Stairs
Waterside Gardens
TOWN OF RAMSGATE PH
St. Patrick (RC)
St. Peter
Oswell Ho
St. Peter's Prim Sch
Superstore
THE SCOOP
MORE LONDON RIVERSIDE
CITY HALL (Greater London Authority)
POTTERS FIELDS PARK
BUTLERS WHARF
ENGINE HOUSE
George's Stairs
DESIGN MUSEUM
SHAD THAMES
UPPER POOL
THE POOL
LOWER POOL
Mill Stairs
East Lane Stairs
Cherry Garden Pier
King's Stairs
Princes Stairs
The Angel PH
KING'S STAIRS GARDENS
BRUNEL MUSEUM & ENGINE HOUSE
Mayflower PH
St. Mary with All Saints
ST. OLAVE'S EST
DRUID ST
TOWER BRIDGE RD
Tower Br. Prim Sch
ST. JOHN'S ESTATE
TANNER ST
SE1
BUTLERS & COLONIAL WF
NEW CONCORDIA WHARF
LUNA HOUSE
St. Michael's RC Sch
Most Holy Trinity (RC)
DICKENS ESTATE
St. Joseph's RC Prim Sch
ARNOLD EST
JAMAICA ROAD
A200
Riverside Prim Sch
BERMONDSEY
KIRBY ESTATE
MILLPOND EST
St. Peter (RC)
ROTHERHITHE
St. Saviour's Est
Mission
St. James' C of E Prim Sch
St. James
St. Crispin
NEW PLACE SQUARE
MORETON HO
ARICA HOUSE
SE16
SOUTHWARK
SOUTHWARK PARK
Evangelical London Christian Sch
Seven Islands Leisure C
B202
NECKINGER EST
AYLWYN EST
BERMONDSEY
COUNCIL OFF
SPA ROAD
A2206
RICH IND EST
BERMONDSEY SPA GDNS
VAUBAN ESTATE
EVELINE LOWE EST
SOUTHWARK COLL
LOCKWOOD SQUARE
MARDEN SQUARE
Baptist
Southwark Pk Prim Sch
MAYDEW HOUSE
Boutcher C of E Prim Sch
Harris Academy Bermondsey
Cherry Gdn Sch
Alma Prim Sch
SOUTHWARK PARK ROAD
RAYMOUTH RD
Royal Mail
LONGFIELD ESTATE
St. Anne & St. Augustine
Christian Cen
MANOR ESTATE
Methodist
TREVITHICK HO
RENNIE ESTATE
St. Gertrude (RC)
B203
DUNTON RD
LYNTON RD
LYNTON EST
City of London Academy
PATERSON PARK
ADMIRAL HYSON TRADING EST
A2208
ROTHERHITHE NEW ROAD
Superstores
ROLLS ROAD
B204
A2
OLD KENT ROAD
Fire Sta
Walworth Academy
St. Philip & St. Mark
Eveline Lowe Prim Sch
MAWBEY ESTATE
SIX BRIDGES TRADING EST
CATLIN STREET
Comm Cen
ILDERTON RD
Ilderton Prim Sch
VERNEY ROAD
0 250 yds
0 250 m

LIMEHOUSE
RIVER THAMES
ROTHERHITHE
E14
SE8
DEPTFORD
CANARY WHARF PIER
HILTON DOCKLANDS NELSON DOCK PIER
GREENLAND PIER
CANADA WATER
SURREY QUAYS
ROTHERHITHE TUNNEL
SALTER ROAD
B205
A2202
REDRIFF ROAD
LOWER ROAD
A200
EVELYN STREET
PLOUGH WAY
B206
GROVE STREET
WESTFERRY ROAD
WESTFERRY CIRCUS
LIMEHOUSE REACH
TOWER HAMLETS
SOUTHWARK
LEWISHAM
GREENLAND DOCK
SOUTH DOCK
CANADA WATER
SURREY WATER
ECOLOGICAL PARK
RUSSIA DOCK WOODLAND
MELLISH SPORTS GROUND
SPORTS GROUND
Stave Hill
Surrey Quays Shopping Centre
Associated Newspapers Print Works
MULBERRY BUSINESS CENTRE
CANNON WHARF BUSINESS CENTRE
DEPTFORD PARK
PEPYS PARK
REDRIFF ESTATE
ALBION ESTATE
AYLTON ESTATE
ROTHERHITHE NEW ROAD
EVELYN
TRUNDLEYS
BESTWOOD ST
ROTHERHITHE OLD RD
HAWKSTONE RD
NARROW STREET
THE DEN MILLWALL FC
Power Station
GEMINI PROJECT
Duke Shore Wharf
Limehouse Hole Stairs
Lavender Wharf
Sunderland Wharf
Ordnance Wharf
Lawrence Wharf
Columbia Wharf
New Atlas Wharf
West India Dock Pier
Surrey Docks Water Sports Cen
St. George's Stairs
South Lock
H J K L M N P
1 2 3 4 5 6 7 8 9 10
21
34
45
36
37

A
B
C
D
E
F
G
1
2
3
4
5
6
7
8
9
10
22
33
46
E14
SE8
POPLAR
ISLE OF DOGS
MILLWALL
CUBITT TOWN
DEPTFORD
LIMEHOUSE
WESTFERRY
WEST INDIA QUAY
CANARY WHARF
HERON QUAYS
SOUTH QUAY
CROSSHARBOUR
MUDCHUTE
ISLAND GARDENS
BLACKWALL
ALL SAINTS
WESTFERRY ROAD
MANCHESTER ROAD
MARSH WALL
EAST FERRY ROAD
PRESTONS ROAD
ASPEN WAY
A1261
A1206
A13
POPLAR HIGH STREET
LIMEHOUSE CAUSEWAY
WEST INDIA DOCKS
MILLWALL INNER DOCK
MILLWALL OUTER DOCK
BLACKWALL BASIN
POPLAR DOCK
MILLWALL PARK
MUDCHUTE FARM
Billingsgate Mkt
Museum of London Docklands
Cabot Place
Jubilee Pk
1 Canada Sq
Telegraph & Express Print Works
Docklands Sailing & Watersport Cen
Masthouse Terrace Pier
Canary Wharf Pier
West India Dock Pier
George Green's Sch
Greenwich Foot Tunnel
RIVER THAMES
GREENWICH REACH
LIMEHOUSE REACH
TOWER HAMLETS
SOUTHWARK
LEWISHAM
GREENWICH
0 250 yds
0 250 m

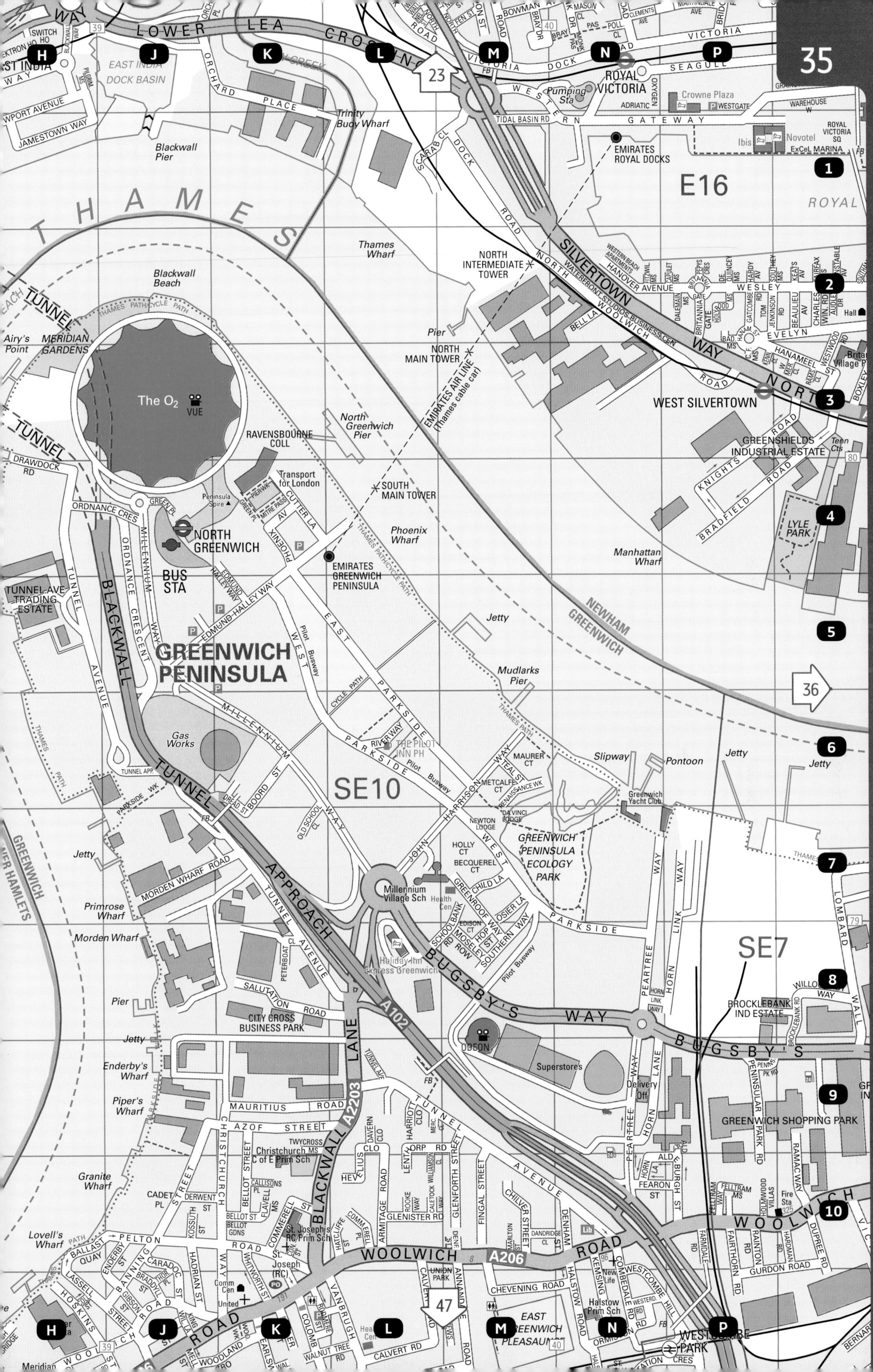

H
J
K
L
M
N
P
LOWER LEA CROSSING
EAST INDIA DOCK BASIN
ORCHARD PLACE
Trinity Buoy Wharf
Blackwall Pier
JAMESTOWN WAY
NEWPORT AVENUE
VICTORIA DOCK ROAD
ROYAL VICTORIA
SEAGULL
Pumping Sta
Crowne Plaza
WESTGATE
ADRIATIC
OXYGEN
WESTERN GATEWAY
TIDAL BASIN RD
WAREHOUSE W
ROYAL VICTORIA SQ
Ibis
Novotel
ExCeL MARINA
EMIRATES ROYAL DOCKS
E16
ROYAL
THAMES
SCARAB CL
DOCK ROAD
SILVERTOWN WAY
NORTH WOOLWICH ROAD
Thames Wharf
NORTH INTERMEDIATE TOWER
WATERFRONT STUDIOS BUSINESS CEN
HANOVER AVENUE
WESLEY
EVELYN
HANAMEEL ST
BELL LA
WEST SILVERTOWN
Blackwall Beach
BLACKWALL TUNNEL
THAMES PATH/CYCLE PATH
Airy's Point
MERIDIAN GARDENS
The O2
VUE
Pier
NORTH MAIN TOWER
EMIRATES AIR LINE (Thames cable car)
North Greenwich Pier
RAVENSBOURNE COLL
Transport for London
GREENSHIELDS INDUSTRIAL ESTATE
KNIGHTS ROAD
BRADFIELD ROAD
LYLE PARK
Tenn Cts
80
DRAWDOCK RD
ORDNANCE CRES
Peninsula Spire
NORTH GREENWICH
CUTTER LA
SOUTH MAIN TOWER
Phoenix Wharf
PHOENIX AV
EMIRATES GREENWICH PENINSULA
BUS STA
MILLENNIUM WAY
ORDNANCE CRESCENT
EDMUND HALLEY WAY
TUNNEL AVE TRADING ESTATE
TUNNEL AVENUE
BLACKWALL TUNNEL APPROACH
Manhattan Wharf
NEWHAM
GREENWICH
Jetty
GREENWICH PENINSULA
WEST PARKSIDE
EAST PARKSIDE
Pilot Busway
Mudlarks Pier
36
Gas Works
CYCLE PATH
RIVER WAY
THE PILOT INN PH
Slipway
Pontoon
Jetty
SE10
BOORD ST
MAURER CT
TEAL ST
METCALFE CT
RENAISSANCE WK
Greenwich Yacht Club
DA VINCI LODGE
NEWTON LODGE
JOHN HARRISON WAY
HOLLY CT
BECQUEREL CT
GREENWICH PENINSULA ECOLOGY PARK
TUNNEL APP
PARKSIDE WK
DREADNOUGHT ST
OLD SCHOOL CL
MORDEN WHARF ROAD
Primrose Wharf
Morden Wharf
Millennium Village Sch
Health Cen
CHILD LA
GREENROOF WAY
OSIER LA
SCHOOLBANK RD
EDISON CT
HOP ST
MOSELEY ROW
SOUTHERN WAY
PARKSIDE
PEARTREE WAY
HORN LINK WAY
SE7
LOMBARD WALL
79
WILLOUGHBY WAY
BROCKLEBANK IND ESTATE
BROCKLEBANK RD
PETERBOAT CL
TUNNEL AVENUE
Holiday Inn Express Greenwich
BUGSBY'S WAY
SALUTATION ROAD
A102
Pier
CITY CROSS BUSINESS PARK
Jetty
ODEON
Superstores
Delivery Off
PENINSULAR PARK RD
GREENWICH SHOPPING PARK
RAMAC WAY
Enderby's Wharf
BLACKWALL LANE
A2203
TUNNEL AVE
Piper's Wharf
MAURITIUS ROAD
AZOF STREET
TWYCROSS MS
Christchurch C of E Prim Sch
CHRISTCHURCH WAY
BELLOT STREET
CALLISONS PL
FLAVELL MS
DAVERN CL
HARRIOTT CL
MERCURY CL
ORPWOOD RD
HELVETIUS CL
ARMITAGE ROAD
LENTHORP RD
ROOKE WAY
WILLIAMSON CL
GLENFORTH STREET
FINGAL STREET
CHILVER STREET
TUNNEL AVENUE
HORN LANE
FEARON ST
PEARTREE WAY
FELLTRAM WAY
FELLTRAM MS
HOLLYWOOD VILLAS
Fire Sta
WOOLWICH ROAD
Granite Wharf
CADET PL
DERWENT ST
KOSSUTH ST
BELLOT ST
BELLOT GDNS
COMMERELL ST
St. Joseph's RC Prim Sch
St. Joseph (RC)
GLENISTER RD
DANDRIDGE CL
DENHAM ST
Lib
Lovell's Wharf
BALLAST QUAY
PELTON ROAD
ENDERBY ST
BANNING ST
CARADOC ST
HADRIAN ST
WHITWORTH ST
A206
WOOLWICH ROAD
UNION PARK
CHEVENING ROAD
HALSTOW ROAD
KEMSING RD
COMBEDALE RD
WESTCOMBE HILL
FARMDALE RD
FAIRTHORN RD
RAINTON RD
HARDMAN RD
GURDON ROAD
DUPREE RD
LASSELL ST
HOSKINS ST
Comm Cen
United
VANBRUGH HILL
COLOMB ST
Health Cen
47
EAST GREENWICH PLEASAUNCE
Halstow Prim Sch
WESTERDALE RD
WESTCOMBE PARK
CALVERT RD
WALNUT TREE RD
WOODLAND GRO
Meridian
39
40

A
B
C
D
E
F
G
1
2
3
4
5
6
7
8
9
10
VICTORIA DOCK ROAD
CONNAUGHT ROUNDABOUT
ROYAL ALBERT ROUNDABOUT
ROYAL
ALLOT
CUSTOM H
for ExCeL
SANDSTONE
24
Crowne Plaza
WESTGATE
THE GRAINSTORE
WAREHOUSE W
ExCeL London
ICC London
for ExCel (Ea
and ICC London
Aloft
EASTERN GATEWAY
Premier Inn
DOCKSIDE
ROAD
NEWHAM DOC
Boathouse
London Regatta Centre
Ibis
Novotel
ROYAL VICTORIA SQ
ExCeL MARINA
ExCeL WATERFRONT
Ramada
E16
ROYAL VICTORIA DOCK
CONNAUGHT BRIDGE
A1020
JET CENTRE
London C
MILLENNIUM MILLS
PONTOON DOCK
AIRPORT ROUNDABOUT
Travelodge
CONNAUGHT ROAD
HARTMANN ROAD
LONDON CITY AIRPORT
CAMEL RD
DREW ROAD
WESLEY AVENUE
EVELYN ROAD
HANAMEEL ST
Britannia Village Prim Sch
Hall
PIRIE ST
FORT STREET
MILL ROAD
Fire Sta
N WOOLWICH ROUNDABOUT
CONN. BR
NORTH WOOLWICH ROAD
MUSIC HALL
Etap
ORIENTAL RD
NORTH WOOLWICH ROAD
A1020
BRAMWELL WAY
AGNES GEORGE WK
BOOTH RD
THAMES ROAD
PONTOON DOCK
BARRIER POINT ROAD
GREENSHIELDS INDUSTRIAL ESTATE
KNIGHTS ROAD
Tenn Cts
LYLE PARK
Pav
THAMES BARRIER PARK
SILVERTOWN
WARDS WHARF APPROACH
FACTORY
THAMESIDE INDUSTRIA
A112
Tate & Lyle Jetty
WOOLWICH REACH
RIVER
THAMES FLOOD BARRIER
35
Barrier Gardens Pier
Jetty
THAMES BARRIER LEARNING CEN
MELLISH IND ESTATE
HARRINGTON WAY
VISITORS CEN
BOWATER ROAD
UNITY WAY
BARRIER CONTROL BUILDING
HARLINGER ST
THAMES PATH
RIVERSIDE
ANCHORAGE PT INDUSTRIAL EST
HERRINGHAM ROAD
NEW LYDENBURG ST
WESTMOOR
EASTMOOR
FARADAY WAY
WESTFIELD STREET
RUSTON
LOMBARD WALL
ANCHOR & HOPE LANE
MERIDIAN TRADING ESTATE
WILLOUGHBY WAY
BROCKLEBANK IND ESTATE
PARCELFORCE
ROPERY BUSINESS PARK
NEW CHARLTON
HOLBORN COLL
St. Catherine (RC)
A206
MARYON
WOOLWICH ROAD
PENHALL ROAD
BUGSBY'S WAY
Superstores
SE7
GREENWICH IND ESTATE
CHARLTON GATE
STONE LAKE ROUNDABOUT
STONE LAKE RETAIL PARK
CABLE TRADE PK
HICKIN CLOSE
GREENWICH SHOPPING PARK
GALLIONS ROAD
HORIZON WAY
PENINSULAR PARK RD
RAMAC WAY
MARYON PARK
PRENTISS CT
Clinic
HARVEY GDNS
HARVEY GARDENS
GALLON CLO
BARNEY CLOSE
TROUGHTON ROAD
COXMOUNT RD
Thorntree Inf Sch
St. Thomas
PARK FARM
WOODLAND
KINVEACHY
Fire Sta
WOOLWICH
TROUGHTON
CHARLTON
THE VALLEY CHARLTON ATHLETIC FC
FLOYD ROAD
VALLEY GRO
VALIANT HO
RATHMORE RD
DELAFIELD ROAD
SUNDORNE ROAD
GURDON ROAD
WELLESLEY CL
186
LANSDOWNE MS
WOLFE CRES
THORNTREE ROAD
CHARLTON LANE
MARYON WILSON PARK
FLAMSTEED RD
250 yds
250 m
WESTCOMBE PARK
CALYDON RD
Health Cen
CHARLTON

GALLIONS REACH
BECKTON PARK ROUNDABOUT
BECKTON PARK
NATIONAL CONSTRUCTION COLL
CYPRUS ROUNDABOUT
CYPRUS
GALLIONS ROUNDABOUT
A1020
ROYAL ALBERT WAY
25
UNI OF E LONDON (London Docklands Campus)
UNIVERSITY WAY
ROYAL ALBERT DOCK
SIR STEVE REDGRAVE BRIDGE
ALBERT BASIN
Airport
KING GEORGE V DOCK
KING GEORGE V
HARTMANN ROAD
NEWLAND STREET
ALBERT ROAD
FACTORY ROAD
A112
A117
WOOLWICH MANOR WAY
NORTH WOOLWICH
STANDARD INDUSTRIAL ESTATE
BT London Teleport
Pumping Sta
THE SIDINGS APARTMENTS
ROYAL VICTORIA GDNS
Waldair Wharf
PIER ROAD
North Woolwich Pier
Woolwich Ferry Pier
WOOLWICH FREE FERRY
WOOLWICH FOOT TUNNEL
THAMES
NEWHAM
GREENWICH
187
WOOLWICH ARSENAL PIER
WOOLWICH
GREENWICH HERITAGE CEN
FIREPOWER
THAMES PATH
South Pontoon
S.E. London Aquatic Cen
WOOLWICH HIGH ST
WOOLWICH MKT HILL
BERESFORD ST
WOOLWICH CHURCH STREET
A206
WOOLWICH DOCKYARD IND EST
WOOLWICH DOCKYARD
St. Mary Magdalene
JOHN WILSON ST
A205
SE18
PLUMSTEAD RD
WOOLWICH ARSENAL
ROYAL CARRIAGE MEWS
GREENWICH COMMUNITY COLL (Burrage Cen)
WOOLWICH CENTRE
TOWN HALL
B210
WELLINGTON STREET
ARTILLERY PLACE
ROYAL ARTILLERY BARRACKS
HILLREACH
HEATH
GRAND DEPOT ROAD
BARRACK FIELD
The Royal Garrison Church of St. George
St. Peter's RC Prim Sch
Foxfield Prim Sch
Nightingale Prim Sch
St. Margaret's C of E Prim Sch
H J K L M N P
1 2 3 4 5 6 7 8 9 10

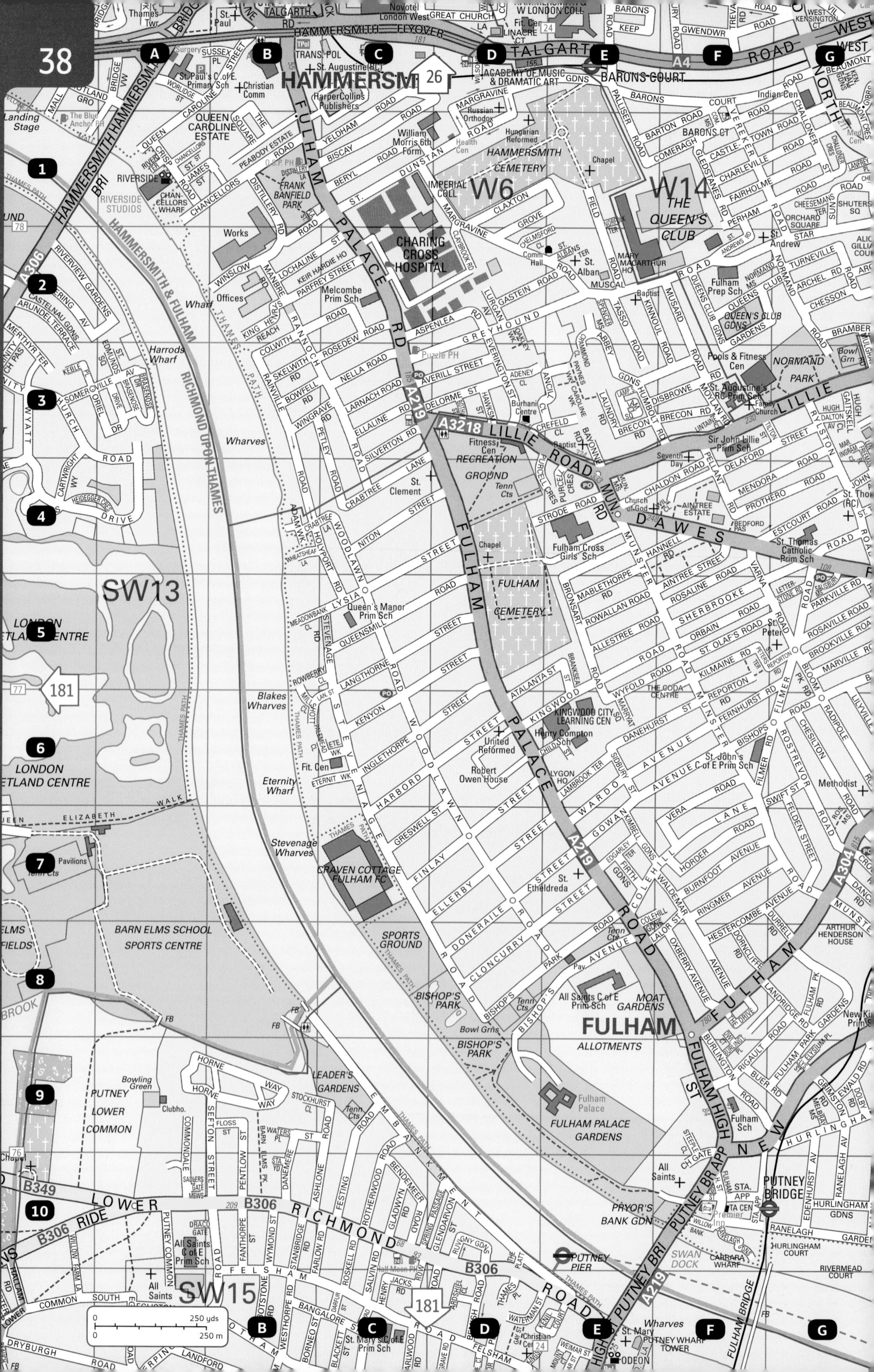
A
B
C
D
E
F
G
1
2
3
4
5
6
7
8
9
10
HAMMERSMITH
HAMMERSMITH FLYOVER
TALGARTH RD
Novotel London West
GREAT CHURCH LA
W LONDON COLL
BARONS KEEP
GWENDWR RD
WEST KENSINGTON CT
A4
WEST CROMWELL ROAD
BARONS COURT
26
ACADEMY OF MUSIC & DRAMATIC ART
St. Paul's C of E Primary Sch
Christian Comm
St. Augustine (RC)
HarperCollins Publishers
QUEEN CAROLINE ESTATE
The Blue Anchor PH
Landing Stage
RIVERSIDE STUDIOS
HAMMERSMITH BRIDGE
A306
HAMMERSMITH & FULHAM
RICHMOND UPON THAMES
THAMES PATH
FULHAM PALACE RD
A219
FRANK BANFIELD PARK
William Morris 6th Form
IMPERIAL COLL
CHARING CROSS HOSPITAL
HAMMERSMITH CEMETERY
Hungarian Reformed
Russian Orthodox
MARGRAVINE GDNS
W6
W14
THE QUEEN'S CLUB
MARY MACARTHUR HO
St. Alban
Melcombe Prim Sch
Works
Offices
Wharf
Harrods Wharf
Wharves
Puzzle PH
A3218 LILLIE ROAD
Fitness Cen
RECREATION GROUND
Burhani Centre
St. Clement
Fulham Prep Sch
QUEEN'S CLUB GDNS
Pools & Fitness Cen
NORMAND PARK
St. Augustine's RC Prim Sch
Sir John Lillie Prim Sch
MUNSTER RD
DAWES ROAD
AINTREE ESTATE
Fulham Cross Girls' Sch
St. Thomas Catholic Prim Sch
FULHAM CEMETERY
Chapel
Queen's Manor Prim Sch
SW13
LONDON WETLAND CENTRE
181
Blakes Wharves
Eternity Wharf
Stevenage Wharves
CRAVEN COTTAGE FULHAM FC
KINGWOOD CITY LEARNING CEN
Henry Compton Sch
United Reformed
Robert Owen House
THE CODA CENTRE
St. John's C of E Prim Sch
St. Etheldreda
Methodist
Pavilions
Tenn Cts
BARN ELMS SCHOOL SPORTS CENTRE
SPORTS GROUND
BISHOP'S PARK
Bowl Grns
All Saints C of E Prim Sch
MOAT GARDENS
FULHAM
ALLOTMENTS
A304
ARTHUR HENDERSON HOUSE
PUTNEY LOWER COMMON
Bowling Green
LEADER'S GARDENS
EMBANKMENT
FULHAM PALACE GARDENS
Fulham Palace
Fulham Sch
FULHAM HIGH ST
NEW KINGS ROAD
All Saints
PUTNEY BRIDGE
PRYOR'S BANK GDN
Premier Inn
HURLINGHAM GDNS
HURLINGHAM COURT
RIVERMEAD COURT
PUTNEY PIER
SWAN DOCK
CARRARA WHARF
B349
LOWER RICHMOND ROAD
B306
All Saints C of E Prim Sch
All Saints
SW15
St. Mary's C of E Prim Sch
Half Moon PH
St. Mary
PUTNEY WHARF TOWER
ODEON
FULHAM BRIDGE
PUTNEY BRIDGE
250 yds
250 m

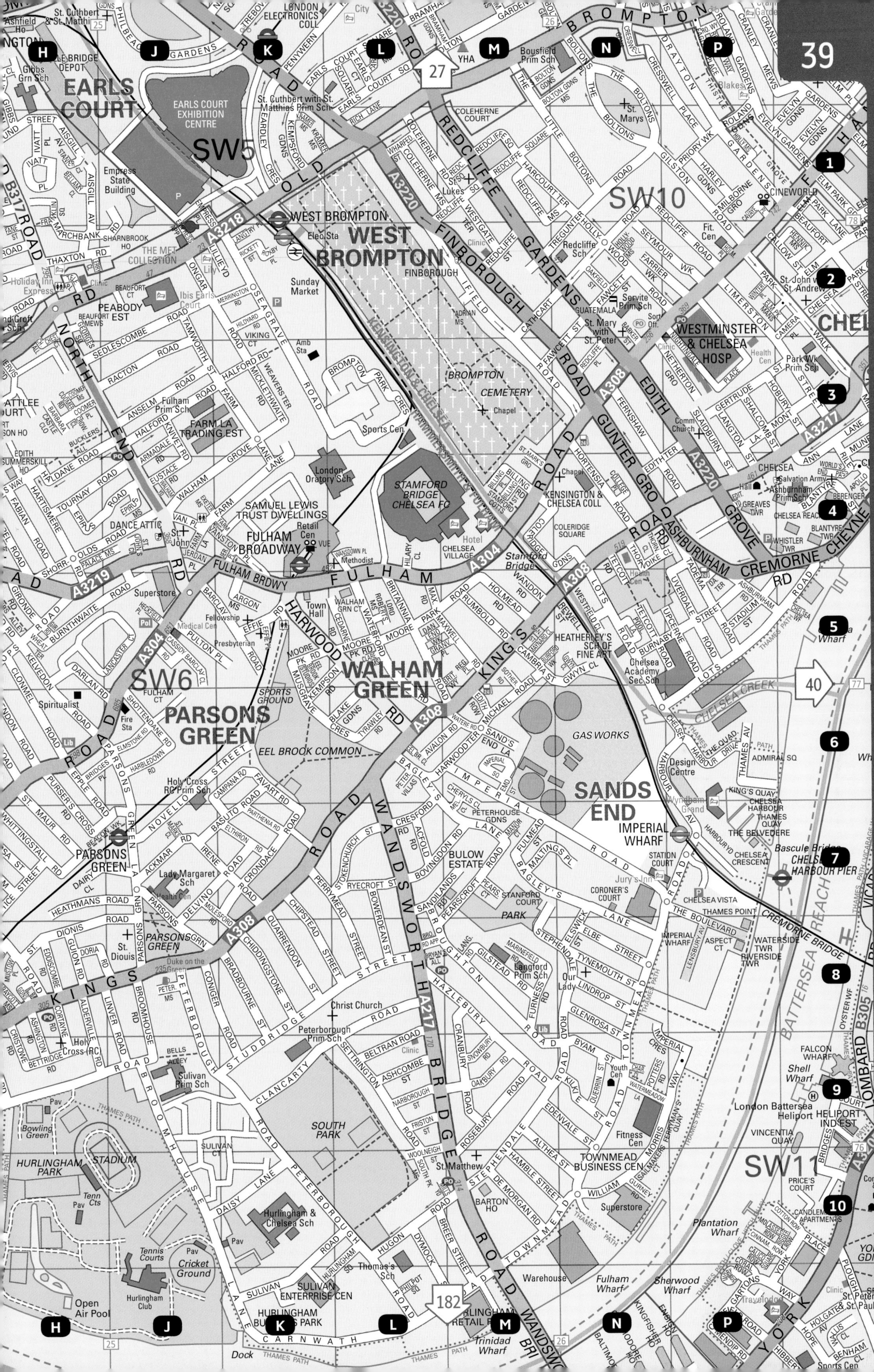
EARLS COURT
EARLS COURT EXHIBITION CENTRE
SW5
Empress State Building
LONDON ELECTRONICS COLL
BROMPTON
OLD BROMPTON ROAD
REDCLIFFE GARDENS
THE BOLTONS
St. Marys
SW10
CINEWORLD
WEST BROMPTON
WEST BROMPTON
BROMPTON CEMETERY
Chapel
KENSINGTON & CHELSEA
FINBOROUGH ROAD
Sunday Market
Sports Cen
London Oratory Sch
STAMFORD BRIDGE CHELSEA FC
CHELSEA VILLAGE
Hotel
WESTMINSTER & CHELSEA HOSP
FULHAM BROADWAY
FULHAM BRDWY
FULHAM
Town Hall
WALHAM GREEN
PEABODY EST
THE MET COLLECTION
Ibis Earls Court
NORTH END RD
FARM LA TRADING EST
SAMUEL LEWIS TRUST DWELLINGS
DANCE ATTIC
Superstore
KENSINGTON & CHELSEA COLL
COLERIDGE SQUARE
HEATHERLEY'S SCH OF FINE ART
Chelsea Academy Sec Sch
KING'S ROAD
CREMORNE RD
GUNTER GRO
EDITH GROVE
ASHBURNHAM RD
SW6
PARSONS GREEN
SPORTS GROUND
EEL BROOK COMMON
GAS WORKS
SANDS END
IMPERIAL WHARF
CHELSEA CREEK
Chelsea Wharf
Design Centre
KING'S QUAY
CHELSEA HARBOUR
THE BELVEDERE
CHELSEA HARBOUR PIER
Bascule Bridge
CREMORNE BRIDGE
IMPERIAL ROAD
WANDSWORTH BRIDGE RD
BULOW ESTATE
STANFORD COURT
PARK
Lady Margaret Sch
Holy Cross RC Prim Sch
KINGS ROAD
Christ Church
Peterborough Prim Sch
SOUTH PARK
Langford Prim Sch
TOWNMEAD BUSINESS CEN
Superstore
Fitness Cen
Falcon Wharf
Shell Wharf
London Battersea Heliport
HELIPORT IND EST
VINCENTIA QUAY
SW11
PRICE'S COURT
Plantation Wharf
Sherwood Wharf
Fulham Wharf
Warehouse
Travelodge
HURLINGHAM PARK
STADIUM
Tennis Courts
Cricket Ground
Open Air Pool
Hurlingham Club
Hurlingham & Chelsea Sch
SULIVAN ENTERPRISE CEN
HURLINGHAM BUSINESS PARK
Trinidad Wharf
Dock
THAMES PATH
St. Matthew
BATTERSEA REACH
LOMBARD
YORK
27
40
182
H
J
K
L
M
N
P
1
2
3
4
5
6
7
8
9
10

A
B
C
D
E
F
G
1
2
3
4
5
6
7
8
9
10
THE ROYAL MARSDEN
ROYAL BROMPTON HOSP
St. Luke
28
SW3
BURTON'S COURT
MUSEUM
ROYAL HOSP CHELSEA
NATIONAL ARMY MUSEUM
CHELSEA PHYSIC GARDEN
CHELSEA
WESTMINSTER & CHELSEA HOSP
FULHAM ROAD
KING'S ROAD
CINEWORLD
Chelsea Old Town Hall
Antique Mkt
SIR THOMAS MORE EST
CARLYLE'S HO (NT)
Chelsea Old Ch
Holy Redeemer (RC)
Moravian
CHEYNE WALK
CHELSEA EMBANKMENT
CADOGAN PIER
KENSINGTON & CHELSEA
WANDSWORTH
ALBERT BRI
BATTERSEA BRI
CREMORNE EST
WORLD'S END
Ashburnham Prim Sch
CHELSEA REACH TWR
Waterside Point
ALBION RIVERSIDE BUILDING
Dock
Peace Pagoda
CHILDREN'S ZOO
BATTERSEA PARK
REC GRDS
Fountain Lake
Bandstand
ROYAL COLL OF ART
RANSOME'S DOCK BUS CEN
St. Mary-le-Park
Chelsea Wharf
SW10
39
MONTEVETRO
Westbridge Prim Sch
SOMERSET EST
SURREY LANE EST
St. Mary
Wharves
KING'S QUAY
CHELSEA HARBOUR
THE BELVEDERE
Bascule Bridge
CHELSEA HARBOUR PIER
CHELSEA VISTA
THAMES POINT
CREMORNE BRIDGE
BATTERSEA REACH
ROYAL ACAD OF DANCE
Thomas's Sch
St John Bosco Sch
Sacred Heart (RC)
PRINCE OF WALES DR
SW11
United Reformed
Assemblies of the First Born
Theatre503
Battersea Park Sch
Chesterton Prim Sch
SW6
FALCON WHARF
Shell Wharf
London Battersea Heliport
HELIPORT IND EST
VINCENTIA QUAY
PRICE'S COURT
CANDLEMAKERS APARTMENTS
Plantation Wharf
YORK GDNS
WINSTANLEY EST
Thames Christian Coll
Falconbrook Prim Sch
Christchurch
Sacred Heart Prim Sch
Muslim Comm Cen
Christchurch Prim Sch
FALCON PARK
Leisure Cen
Shaftesbury Pk Prim Sch
Church of the Nazarene
182
Superstores
Church of the Ascension
ARTS CEN
United Reformed
Travelodge
250 yds
250 m
BATTERSEA PARK ROAD
LATCHMERE ROAD
BATTERSEA BRIDGE ROAD
FALCON ROAD
LOMBARD ROAD
WESTBRIDGE ROAD
VICARAGE CRES
CREMORNE RD
ALBERT BRIDGE ROAD
CARRIAGE DRIVE NORTH
PARKGATE
SHUTTLEWORTH
SIMPSON
GWYNNE ROAD
KNOWSLEY ROAD
SHEEPCOTE LANE
EVERSLEIGH
HEATHWALL ST

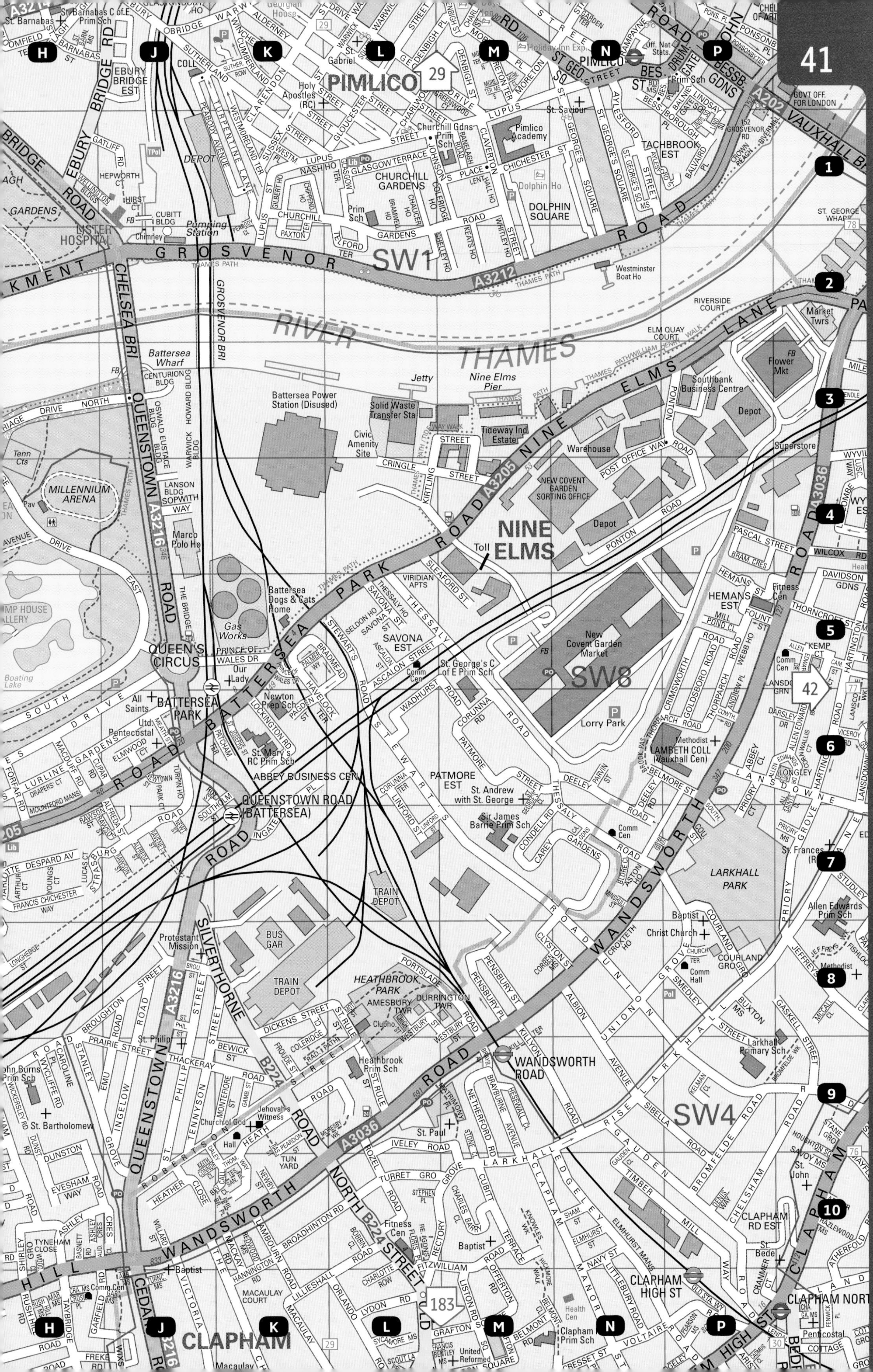
PIMLICO
29
SW1
GROSVENOR ROAD
A3212
RIVER THAMES
CHURCHILL GARDENS
DOLPHIN SQUARE
TACHBROOK EST
EBURY BRIDGE EST
Pimlico Academy
Dolphin Ho
Westminster Boat Ho
VAUXHALL BR
A202
GOVT OFF. FOR LONDON
ST. GEORGE WHARF
Battersea Power Station (Disused)
Nine Elms Pier
Jetty
Battersea Wharf
NINE ELMS LANE
A3205
Tideway Ind Estate
NEW COVENT GARDEN SORTING OFFICE
Flower Mkt
Market Twrs
Southbank Business Centre
Superstore
NINE ELMS
Toll
MILLENNIUM ARENA
QUEENSTOWN ROAD
A3216
Marco Polo Ho
Gas Works
Battersea Dogs & Cats Home
BATTERSEA PARK ROAD
QUEEN'S CIRCUS
BATTERSEA PARK
SAVONA EST
New Covent Garden Market
SW8
Lorry Park
HEMANS EST
LAMBETH COLL (Vauxhall Cen)
PATMORE EST
ABBEY BUSINESS CEN
QUEENSTOWN ROAD (BATTERSEA)
42
LARKHALL PARK
TRAIN DEPOT
BUS GAR
HEATHBROOK PARK
WANDSWORTH ROAD
A3036
SW4
SILVERTHORNE ROAD
B224
LARKHALL RISE
CLAPHAM ROAD
CLAPHAM RD EST
CLAPHAM HIGH ST
CLAPHAM NORTH
183
CLAPHAM
WANDSWORTH ROAD
H
J
K
L
M
N
P
1
2
3
4
5
6
7
8
9
10

A
B
C
D
E
F
G
1
2
3
4
5
6
7
8
9
10
30
41
183
SW1
SW8
SW9
SW4
SE11
VAUXHALL
KENNINGTON
SOUTH LAMBETH
STOCKWELL
RIVERSIDE WK GARDENS
GOVT OFF. FOR LONDON
Eighty9 Albert Embankment
DRAW DOCK
SIS/ MI6
VAUXHALL BRI
BRIDGEFOOT
WANDSWORTH RD
BUS STATION
PARRY ST
Market Twrs
Flower Mkt
Southbank Business Centre
Depot
Superstore
VAUXHALL PARK
SPRING GDNS
KENNINGTON LANE
HARLEYFORD ROAD
KENNINGTON OVAL
THE KIA OVAL (SURREY C.C.C.)
GAS WORKS
KENNINGTON PARK
SPORTS GRD
CITY & GUILDS OF LONDON ART SCH
CAMBERWELL
CLAPHAM ROAD
BRIXTON ROAD
SOUTH LAMBETH ROAD
STOCKWELL ROAD
LAMBETH HOSPITAL
CLAPHAM NORTH
LARKHALL PARK
SLADE GDNS
MAX ROACH PARK
LOUGHBOROUGH ESTATE
ANGELL TOWN ESTATE
STOCKWELL PARK ESTATE
STOCKWELL GARDENS EST
STUDLEY ESTATE
CLAPHAM RD EST
WYCK GARDENS
O2 ACADEMY BRIXTON
250 yds
250 m

WALWORTH
SE17
CAMBERWELL
SE5
SE15
BURGESS PARK
SURREY SQUARE PARK
SURREY GDNS
FARADAY GARDENS
RUSKIN PARK
LUCAS GDNS
KING'S COLLEGE HOSPITAL
MAUDSLEY HOSPITAL
DENMARK HILL
CAMBERWELL GREEN
LOUGHBOROUGH JUNCTION
GREEK CATHEDRAL
BURGESS BUSINESS PARK
CAMBERWELL COLL OF ARTS
S LONDON GALL
TOWN HALL
WILLIAM BOOTH COLL
CHAMPION PARK EST
DOG KENNEL HILL EST
CHAMPION HILL ESTATE
KING'S COLL (Denmark Hill Campus)
AYLESBURY EST
ELIZABETH EST
WYNDHAM ESTATE
ELMINGTON ESTATE
DOWLAS ESTATE
CRAWFORD ESTATE
VALMAR TRADING ESTATE
PELICAN ESTATE
PEABODY ESTATE
KENBURY GARDENS
SCEAUX GDNS
SPORTS GRD
Kart Track
Tennis Cen
Football Pitch
Bandstand
Bowling Green
PITCHES
ALLOT
BUS GAR
CAMBERWELL CHURCH ST
PECKHAM
CAMBERWELL ROAD
DENMARK HILL
CAMBERWELL NEW ROAD
ALBANY ROAD
WELLS WAY
ST GEORGES WAY
SOUTHAMPTON WAY
CHURCH STREET
COLDHARBOUR LANE
CHAMPION PK
GROVE LANE
DOG KENNEL
CAMBERWELL GROVE
EAST STREET
WESTMORELAND ROAD
NEATE STREET
SURREY LINEAR
A215
A202
A2217
A2216
B214
31
44
184
H
J
K
L
M
N
P
1
2
3
4
5
6
7
8
9
10

A
B
C
D
E
F
G
1
2
3
4
5
6
7
8
9
10
32
43
184
SE1
SE5
SE15
PECKHAM
PATERSON PARK
ROLLS ROAD
ABERCORN WAY
CATLIN STREET
ROTHERHITHE NEW ROAD
ILDERTON ROAD
VERNEY ROAD
OLD KENT ROAD
BURGESS PARK
SURREY LINEAR CANAL PARK
TRAFALGAR AV
SUMNER RD
WILLOWBROOK RD
PECKHAM HILL STREET
PECKHAM PARK ROAD
COMMERCIAL WAY
PECKHAM HIGH STREET
QUEENS ROAD
PECKHAM ROAD
HANOVER PK
RYE LANE
PECKHAM RYE
LYNDHURST GROVE
CHOUMERT ROAD
NUNHEAD LANE
EVELINA ROAD
ASYLUM ROAD
FRIARY ESTATE
FRANCISCAN FRIARY
LEDBURY EST
LINDLEY ESTATE
BELLS GARDEN EST
OLIVER-GOLDSMITH ESTATE
PELICAN ESTATE
MAWBEY ESTATE
SIX BRIDGES TRADING EST
KENT PARK IND EST
Gas Works
TUSTIN ESTATE
CAROLINE GARDENS
BRIMMINGTON PARK
QUEENS ROAD PECKHAM
PECKHAM RYE
BUS STA
Aylesham Centre
Harris Academy Peckham
Highshore Sch
Peckham Pk Sch
John Donne Prim Sch
COSSALL PARK
St. Thomas the Apostle Coll
St. Mary Magdalene Prim Sch
SOUTHWARK ADULT ED (Thomas Calton Cen)
Bellenden Prim Sch
SPORTS GROUND
WARWICK GDNS
DOG KENNEL HILL EST
Rye Oak Sch
Walworth Academy
Cobourg Prim Sch
SPORTS GRD
Cantium Retail Park
Superstore
Pulse Fitness Cen
CAMBERWELL COLL OF ARTS
S LONDON GALL
Oliver Goldsmith Prim Sch
250 yds
250 m

H
J
K
L
M
N
P
1
2
3
4
5
6
7
8
9
10
33
46
185
DEPTFORD
SE8
SE14
SE4
NEW CROSS GATE
NEW CROSS
NUNHEAD
DEPTFORD PARK
SAYES COURT PARK
FOLKESTONE GARDENS
BRIDGE HOUSE MEADOWS
ECKINGTON GDNS
FORDHAM PARK
THE DEN MILLWALL FC
GEMINI PROJECT
Power Station
DEPTFORD TRADING EST
PARKSIDE BUSINESS ESTATE
ORION BUS. CEN
HATCHAM MS BUSINESS CEN
Superstore
NEW CROSS GATE
NEW CROSS
DEPTFORD
BROCKLEY
BUS GARAGE
UNI OF LONDON GOLDSMITHS COLL
NEW CROSS GATE CUTTING NATURE RESERVE
TELEGRAPH HILL PARK
NUNHEAD CEMETERY
HABERDASHERS ASKE'S PLAYING FIELD
Haberdashers Aske's Hatcham Coll
CROSSWAYS SIXTH FORM
Sir Francis Drake Prim Sch
Deptford Grn Sch
Childeric Prim Sch
Edmund Waller Prim Sch
Myatt Gdn Prim Sch
John Stainer Prim Sch
Hollydale Prim Sch
Kender Prim Sch
Hatcham Temple Grove Primary Sch.
St.James Hatcham C of E Prim Sch
Grinling Gibbons Prim Sch
Lucas Vale Prim Sch
Addey & Stanhope Sch.
NEW CROSS ROAD
LEWISHAM WAY
EVELYN STREET
DEPTFORD HIGH STREET
DRAKEFELL ROAD
B2142 ROAD
BROCKLEY CROSS
ENDWELL RD
SURREY CANAL ROAD
COLD BLOW LA
SANFORD STREET
PAGNELL ST
AMERSHAM RD
FLORENCE RD
LAUSANNE ROAD
KENDER STREET
POMEROY STREET
GELLATLY RD
MALPAS
UPPER BROCKLEY ROAD
VESTA ROAD
ARBUTHNOT ROAD
MUSGROVE ROAD
SHERWIN ROAD
OMMANEY ROAD
PEPYS ROAD
ERLANGER ROAD
WALLER ROAD
JERNINGHAM
ST. DONATTS RD
SHARDELOES ROAD
MILLMARK GROVE
ASHBY ROAD
WICKHAM

DEPTFORD
SE8
E14
GREENWICH REACH
TOWER HAMLETS
GREENWICH
GREENWICH PIER
Greenwich Pier
Masthouse Terrace Pier
Palmer's Wharf
Payne's Wharf
Borthwick Wharf
Landing Stage
Wood Wharf
Sailing Centre
ISLAND GARDENS
MANCHESTER ROAD
CREEK ROAD
DEPTFORD CHURCH STREET
DEPTFORD HIGH STREET
ROMNEY ROAD A206
GREENWICH HIGH ROAD
GREENWICH SOUTH STREET
BLACKHEATH ROAD
BLACKHEATH HILL A2
SHOOTERS HILL
ROYAL HILL
CROOMS HILL
NATIONAL MARITIME MUSEUM
QUEEN'S HOUSE
CUTTY SARK
GREENWICH FOOT TUNNEL
UNI OF GREENWICH (Maritime Greenwich Campus)
TRINITY COLL OF MUSIC
Old Royal Navy Coll.
DEPTFORD BRIDGE
BROOKMILL ROAD
A2210
RIVER RAVENSBOURNE
ST. JOHN'S
LEWISHAM WAY
LEWISHAM COLL (Lewisham Way Campus)
SE14
SE13
SE10
LOAMPIT HILL A20
LOAMPIT VALE
THURSTON ROAD
LEWISHAM
LEWISHAM HIGH ST
LEWISHAM ROAD A2211
ELVERSON ROAD
BLACKHEATH BUS. EST
GRANVILLE PK
BELMONT
LOAMPIT VALE
BUS STA
DEPTFORD
GREENWICH
34
45
185
250 yds
250 m

H
J
K
L
M
N
P
35
186
Lovell's Wharf
Granite Wh
Power Sta
Meridian Prim Sch
Arches Leisure Cen
WOOLWICH ROAD
A206
TRAFALGAR ROAD
ROMNEY
MAZE HILL
WESTCOMBE PARK
WESTCOMBE PARK ROAD
EAST GREENWICH PLEASAUNCE
CHEVENING ROAD
HALSTOW ROAD
Halstow Prim Sch
ANNANDALE ROAD
VANBRUGH HILL
CALVERT RD
HUMBER ROAD
DINSDALE RD
LEMMON RD
SEREN PARK GDNS
LEAMINGTON CT
ULUNDI ROAD
COLERAINE ROAD
FOYLE ROAD
BEACONSFIELD ROAD
MYCENAE ROAD
KIRKSIDE ROAD
St. George
SIEBERT ROAD
Invicta Inf Sch
INVICTA ROAD
Kingdom Hall
Comm Cen
John Roan Sec Sch
HIGHMORE RD
WESTCOMBE CT
FERNDALE CT
Blackheath High Sch
ST. ANDREWS MS
SE7
A102
BRAMSHOT AVENUE
EASTCOMBE AVE
CHARLTON
ONE TREE HILL
Maze Hill House Gate
Maze Hill Gate
GREENWICH PARK
ROYAL OBSERVATORY GREENWICH (FLAMSTEED HOUSE)
Gen. James Wolfe
Peter Harrison Planetarium
BLACKHEATH AVENUE
GREAT CROSS AVENUE
Bandstand
THE GARDENS
THE WILDERNESS (DEER PARK)
Vanbrugh Park Gate
Cov Res
Tenn Cts
RANGER'S HOUSE
Blackheath Gate
Creed Place Gate
Park Row Gate
VANBRUGH PARK
VANBRUGH WAY
B210
OLD DOVER
Royal Standard PH
St. John
HEATHWAY
JOHN'S PARK
Bardon Lodge
The Pointer Sch
LANGTON WAY
STRATHEDEN ROAD
SHOOTERS HILL ROAD
A2
CHARLTON ROAD
KIDBROOKE PARK ROAD
ROSSE MS
ANNESLEY RD
PILGRIMS CT
Blackheath Nursery & Prep Sch
PRINCE OF WALES ROAD
B212
ST. GERMAN'S PLACE
BLACKHEATH
SE3
LONG POND ROAD
DUKE HUMPHREY ROAD
PRINCE CHARLES ROAD
Andrew Gibb Mem
GOFFERS ROAD
WHITFIELD ROAD
TALBOT PLACE
MOUNTS POND RD
All Saints Cof E Prim Sch
HARE & BILLET ROAD
ELIOT PLACE
ELIOT VALE
HEATHFIELD GDNS
John Ball Sch
BAIZDON ROAD
TRANQUIL VALE
ROYAL PAR
MONTPELIER ROW
MONT. VALE
All Saints
Clarendon Hotel
Blackheath High Sch (Jun Dept)
PARAGON PLACE
RYCULFF SQUARE
SOUTH ROW
THE PARAGON
Morden College
Chapel
FULTHORP ROAD
MORDEN ROAD
HUNT'S CL
THE PLANTATION
SWEYN PL
SPORTS GROUNDS
Tenn Cts
Pav
St. James
KIDBROOKE GARDENS
KIDBROOKE GROVE
WESTBROOK RD
LISKEARD GARDENS
A2213
BLACKHEATH PARK
CORNER GREEN
BERNERSMEDE
St. Michael & All Angels
Our Lady (RC)
BLACKHEATH HALLS
BLACKHEATH VILLAGE
BENNETT PARK
CRESSWELL PARK
Quakers
BLACKHEATH
LEE TERRACE
B220
LEE ROAD
B21
BLACKHEATH HOSP
LDS Church
St. Matthew Academy
CEMETERY
ST. JOSEPH'S VALE
BELMONT HALL CT
Brooklands JMI Sch
BROOKLANDS PARK
CASTERBRIDGE ROAD
MOOREHEAD
Wingfield Prim Sch
GOLDMARK HO
Bowl Grn
MEADOWBANK
KIDB

Key to London street maps

London Luton

WELWYN

HARPENDEN

WHEATHAMPSTEAD 50 51 WELWYN GARDEN CITY 52 53 54 HERTFORD WARE 55 56

TRING

BERKHAMSTED 60 61 62 63 HEMEL HEMPSTEAD 64 ST. ALBANS 65 66 HATFIELD 67 ESSENDON 68 69 70 BROXBOURNE HODDESDON 71 72 LOWER NAZEING

BOURNE END WELHAM GREEN

GREAT MISSENDEN

76 CHESHAM BOVINGDON 78 79 CHIPPERFIELD 80 KINGS LANGLEY 81 ABBOTS LANGLEY 82 BRICKET WOOD 83 LONDON COLNEY 84 SHENLEY 85 POTTERS BAR BROOKMANS PARK 86 87 CUFFLEY 88 CHESHUNT 89 90 WALTHAM ABBEY

77 AMERSHAM LITTLE CHALFONT 94 95 CHORLEYWOOD 96 CROXLEY GREEN 97 WATFORD 98 BUSHEY 99 100 BOREHAMWOOD 101 BARNET 102 NEW BARNET 103 104 ENFIELD 105 106 LOUGHTON

TYLERS GREEN 110 LOUDWATER 111 CHALFONT ST. GILES 112 113 CHALFONT COMMON BEACONSFIELD RICKMANSWORTH 114 HAREFIELD 115 NORTHWOOD 116 STANMORE 117 118 EDGWARE EAST BARNET 119 FINCHLEY SOUTHGATE 120 121 WOOD GREEN 122 EDMONTON 123 124 WOODFORD

WOOBURN 132 133 EGYPT GERRARDS CROSS 134 135 136 DENHAM PINNER 137 RUISLIP 138 HARROW 139 WEMBLEY 140 HENDON 141 142 HAMPSTEAD 143 WALTHAMSTOW 144 STOKE NEWINGTON 145 LEYTON 146 WANSTEAD

FARNHAM COMMON 152 153 BURNHAM MAIDENHEAD STOKE POGES 154 SLOUGH 155 IVER UXBRIDGE 156 157 HAYES NORTHOLT 158 SOUTHALL 159 160 ACTON WILLESDEN 161 PADDINGTON 162 MARYLEBONE 163 164 STRATFORD 165 STEPNEY 166 WEST HAM

172 173 WINDSOR ETON 174 DATCHET LANGLEY 175 WEST DRAYTON 176 177 London Heathrow 178 HOUNSLOW 179 180 KEW HAMMERSMITH 181 BATTERSEA 182 WESTMINSTER 183 BRIXTON LAMBETH 184 PECKHAM 185 186 GREENWICH

WINKFIELD OLD WINDSOR WRAYSBURY 194 EGHAM 195 196 ASHFORD 197 FELTHAM TWICKENHAM 198 199 TEDDINGTON RICHMOND 200 WIMBLEDON 201 WANDSWORTH 202 STREATHAM 203 204 CATFORD 205 206 CHISLEHURST

ASCOT VIRGINIA WATER 214 215 STAINES-UPON-THAMES CHERTSEY 216 217 WALTON-ON-THAMES 218 219 SURBITON KINGSTON UPON THAMES 220 221 MERTON 222 MITCHAM 223 224 CROYDON BECKENHAM 225 BROMLEY 226

BAGSHOT CAMBERLEY OTTERSHAW 232 CHOBHAM 233 234 BYFLEET WEYBRIDGE 235 COBHAM 236 ESHER 237 OXSHOTT 238 EWELL EPSOM 239 SUTTON 240 BANSTEAD 241 PURLEY 242 ADDINGTON SANDERSTEAD 243 244 FARNBOROUGH

BISLEY FRIMLEY WOKING 248 249 MAYFORD 250 RIPLEY 251 STOKE D'ABERNON 252 FETCHAM 253 LEATHERHEAD ASHTEAD 254 255 TADWORTH 256 COULSDON 257 258 WARLINGHAM CATERHAM 259 260 TATSFIELD

MYTCHETT NORMANDY 264 STOUGHTON 265 EAST HORSLEY 266 EAST CLANDON 267 268 GREAT BOOKHAM 269 270 WALTON ON THE HILL 271 REIGATE 272 REDHILL 273 274 GODSTONE 275 OXTED 276

TONGHAM GUILDFORD 280 SHALFORD FARNCOMBE 281 282 GOMSHALL 283 SUTTON ABINGER 284 WESTCOTT 285 DORKING 286 BROCKHAM NORTH HOLMWOOD 287 LEIGH 288 SALFORDS 289 SOUTH GODSTONE BLINDLEY HEATH

COMPTON SHACKLEFORD ELSTEAD GODALMING MILFORD WITLEY GRAFHAM SHAMLEY GREEN HOLMBURY ST MARY JAYES PARK BEARE GREEN CHARLWOOD 290 HORLEY 291 London Gatwick NEWCHAPEL LINGFIELD EDENBRIDGE

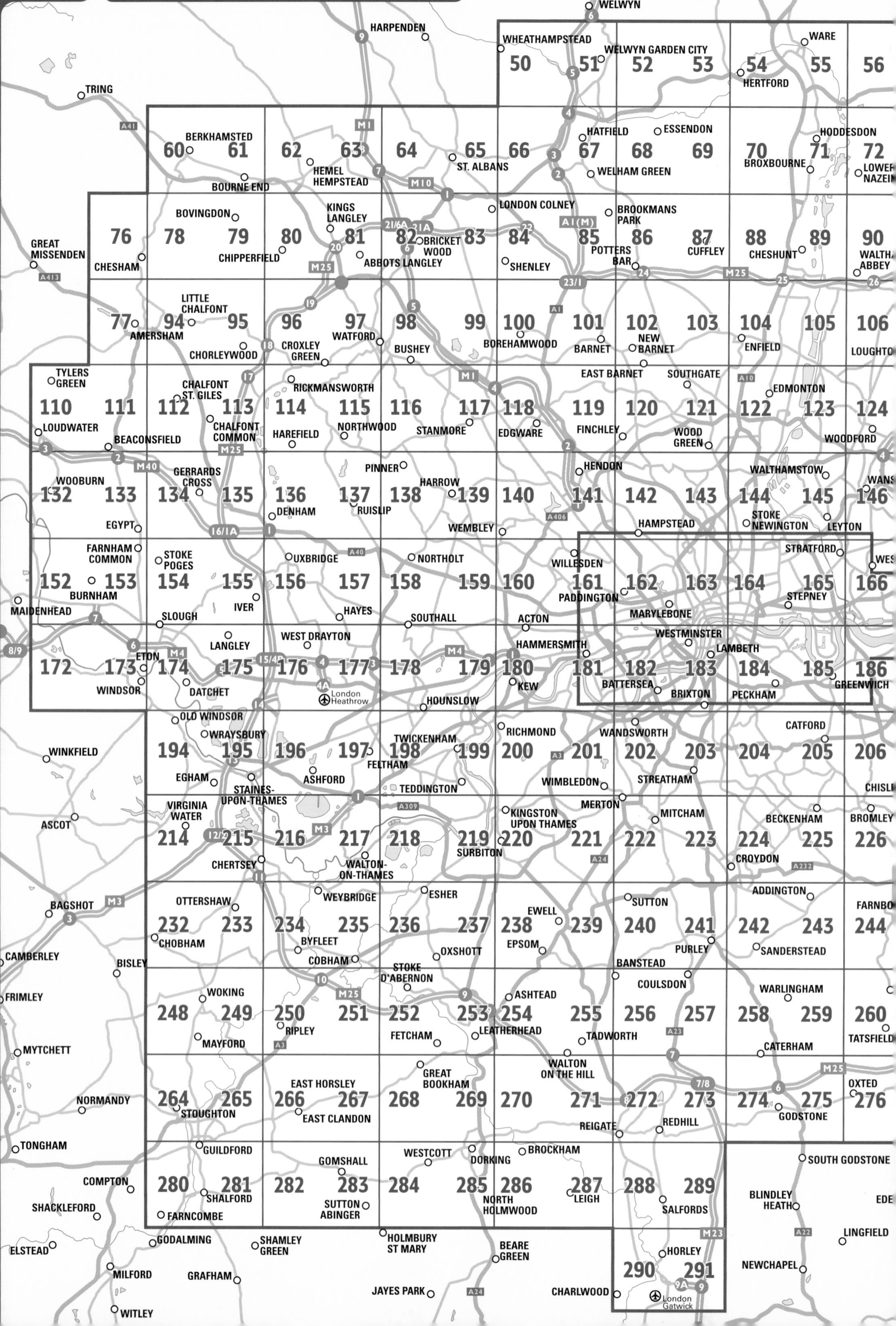

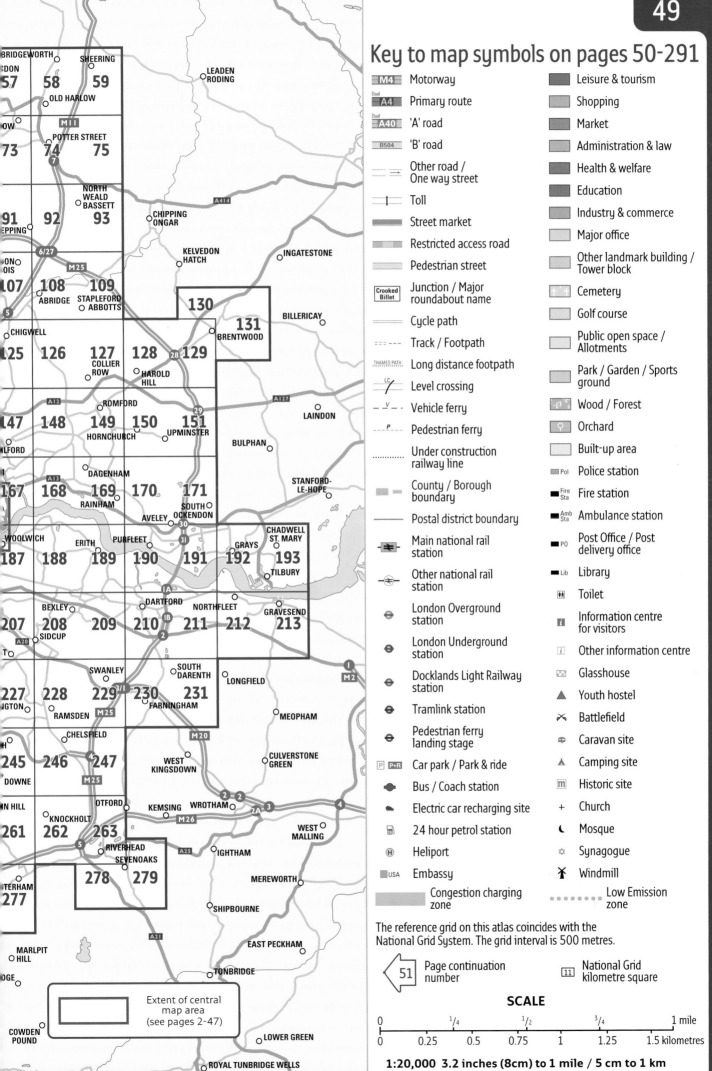

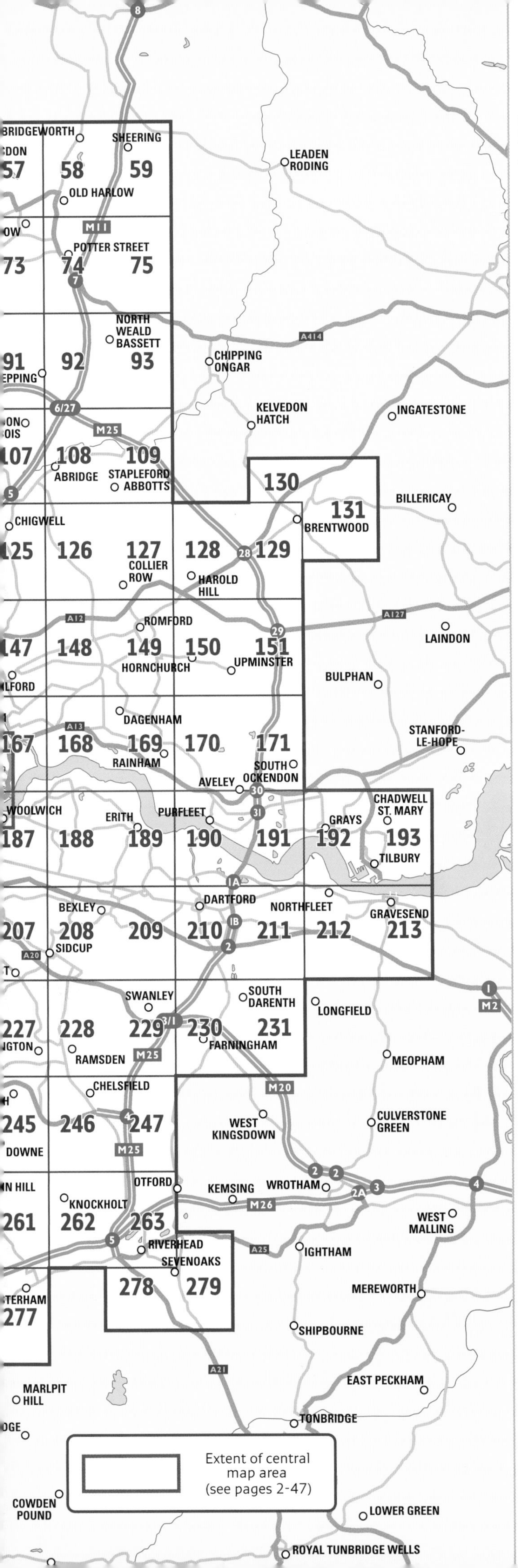

Key to map symbols on pages 50-291

- M4 Motorway
- Dual A4 Primary route
- Dual A40 'A' road
- B504 'B' road
- Other road / One way street
- Toll
- Street market
- Restricted access road
- Pedestrian street
- Crooked Billet Junction / Major roundabout name
- Cycle path
- Track / Footpath
- THAMES PATH Long distance footpath
- LC Level crossing
- V Vehicle ferry
- P Pedestrian ferry
- Under construction railway line
- County / Borough boundary
- Postal district boundary
- Main national rail station
- Other national rail station
- London Overground station
- London Underground station
- Docklands Light Railway station
- Tramlink station
- Pedestrian ferry landing stage
- P P+R Car park / Park & ride
- Bus / Coach station
- Electric car recharging site
- 24 hour petrol station
- H Heliport
- USA Embassy
- Congestion charging zone
- Leisure & tourism
- Shopping
- Market
- Administration & law
- Health & welfare
- Education
- Industry & commerce
- Major office
- Other landmark building / Tower block
- Cemetery
- Golf course
- Public open space / Allotments
- Park / Garden / Sports ground
- Wood / Forest
- Orchard
- Built-up area
- Pol Police station
- Fire Sta Fire station
- Amb Sta Ambulance station
- PO Post Office / Post delivery office
- Lib Library
- Toilet
- Information centre for visitors
- Other information centre
- Glasshouse
- Youth hostel
- Battlefield
- Caravan site
- Camping site
- Historic site
- Church
- Mosque
- Synagogue
- Windmill
- Low Emission zone

The reference grid on this atlas coincides with the National Grid System. The grid interval is 500 metres.

- 51 Page continuation number
- 11 National Grid kilometre square

SCALE

0	$^1/_4$	$^1/_2$	$^3/_4$	1 mile		
0	0.25	0.5	0.75	1	1.25	1.5 kilometres

1:20,000 3.2 inches (8cm) to 1 mile / 5 cm to 1 km

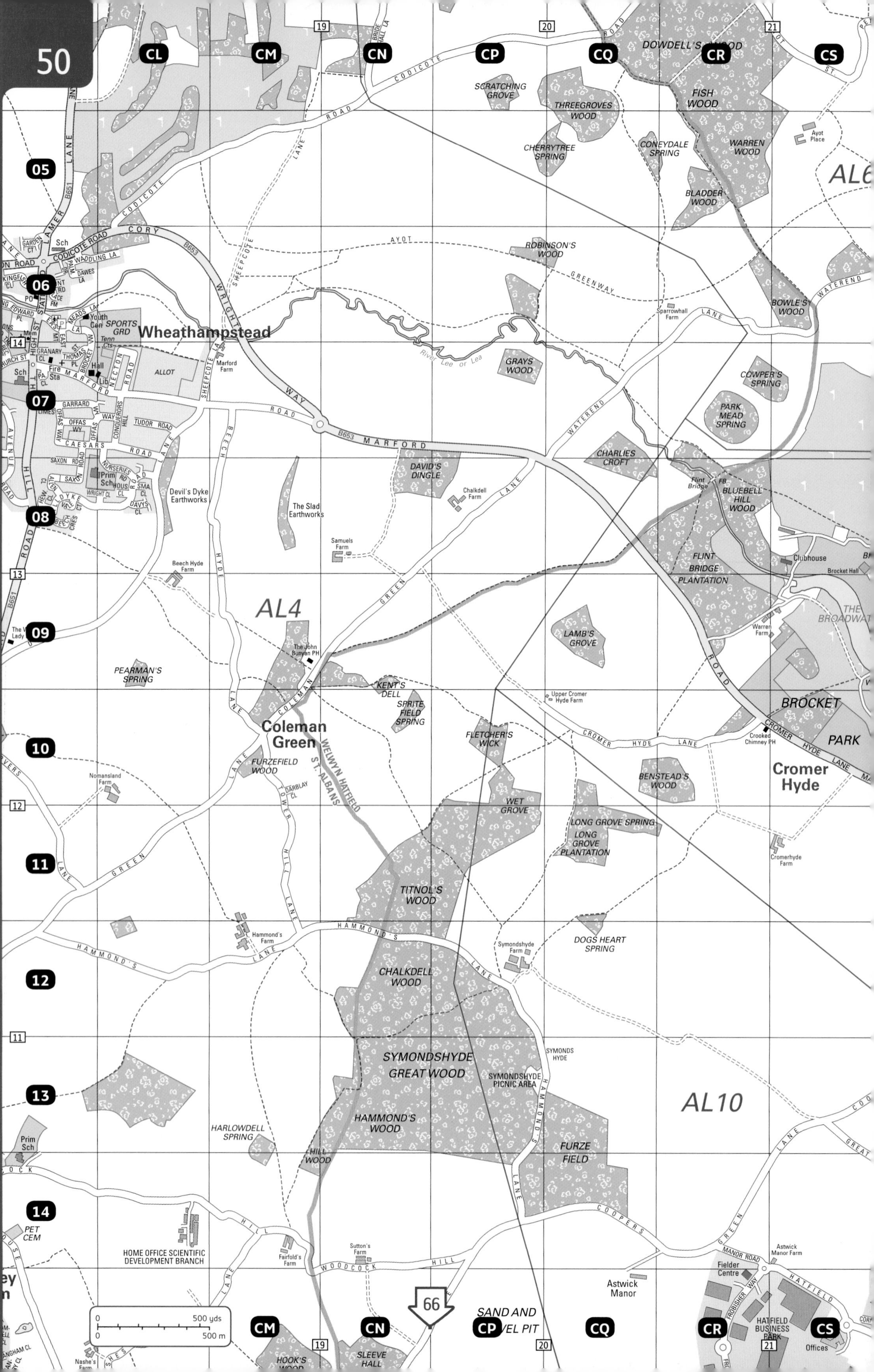

CL
CM
CN
CP
CQ
CR
CS
19
20
21
05
06
07
08
09
10
11
12
13
14
14
13
12
11
DOWDELL'S WOOD
SCRATCHING GROVE
THREEGROVES WOOD
CHERRYTREE SPRING
CONEYDALE SPRING
FISH WOOD
WARREN WOOD
BLADDER WOOD
Ayot Place
AL6
CODICOTE ROAD
CODICOTE
LAMER LANE
B651
Sch
CORY
B653
WRIGHT WAY
SHEEPCOTE
AYOT GREENWAY
ROBINSON'S WOOD
Sparrowhall Farm
LANE
WATEREND
BOWLE'S WOOD
GARDEN CT
CODICOTE ROAD
WADDLING LA
DAWES LA
PO
Youth Cen
SPORTS GRD
Tenn Cts
Wheathampstead
ALLOT
Marford Farm
River Lee or Lea
GRAYS WOOD
COWPER'S SPRING
PARK MEAD SPRING
Mem
GRANARY CL
THOMAS PL
Hall
Lib
Fire Sta
Sch
MARFORD
NECTON ROAD
GARRARD
OFFAS WY
TUDOR ROAD
CONQUERORS HILL
CAESARS
ROAD
SAXON RD
NURSERIES ROAD
Prim Sch
WRIGHT CL
DAVYS CL
Devil's Dyke Earthworks
HILL
ROAD
BEECH HYDE
MARFORD ROAD
B653
DAVID'S DINGLE
Chalkdell Farm
CHARLIES CROFT
Flint Bridge
FB
BLUEBELL HILL WOOD
Clubhouse
Brocket Hall
The Slad Earthworks
Samuels Farm
FLINT BRIDGE PLANTATION
THE BROADWATER
Beech Hyde Farm
AL4
GREEN
LAMB'S GROVE
Warren Farm
The Lady
The John Bunyan PH
PEARMAN'S SPRING
COLEMAN
KENT'S DELL
SPRITE FIELD SPRING
Upper Cromer Hyde Farm
ROAD
BROCKET PARK
Coleman Green
FLETCHER'S WICK
CROMER HYDE LANE
Crooked Chimney PH
Cromer Hyde
WELWYN HATFIELD
ST. ALBANS
Nomansland Farm
FURZEFIELD WOOD
DARBLAY CL
LOWER HILL LANE
BENSTEAD'S WOOD
WET GROVE
LONG GROVE SPRING
LONG GROVE PLANTATION
Cromerhyde Farm
GREEN LANE
TITNOL'S WOOD
Hammond's Farm
HAMMOND'S LANE
DOGS HEART SPRING
Symondshyde Farm
CHALKDELL WOOD
SYMONDSHYDE GREAT WOOD
SYMONDS HYDE
SYMONDSHYDE PICNIC AREA
HAMMOND'S WOOD
AL10
HARLOWDELL SPRING
HILL WOOD
FURZE FIELD
Prim Sch
PET CEM
HOME OFFICE SCIENTIFIC DEVELOPMENT BRANCH
HILL
COOPERS
LANE
GREEN LANE
Fairfold's Farm
Sutton's Farm
WOODCOCK HILL
Astwick Manor
Astwick Manor Farm
MANOR ROAD
Fielder Centre
FROBISHER WAY
HATFIELD
HATFIELD BUSINESS PARK
Offices
66
SAND AND GRAVEL PIT
0
500 yds
0
500 m
HOOK'S WOOD
SLEEVE HALL
Nashe's Farm

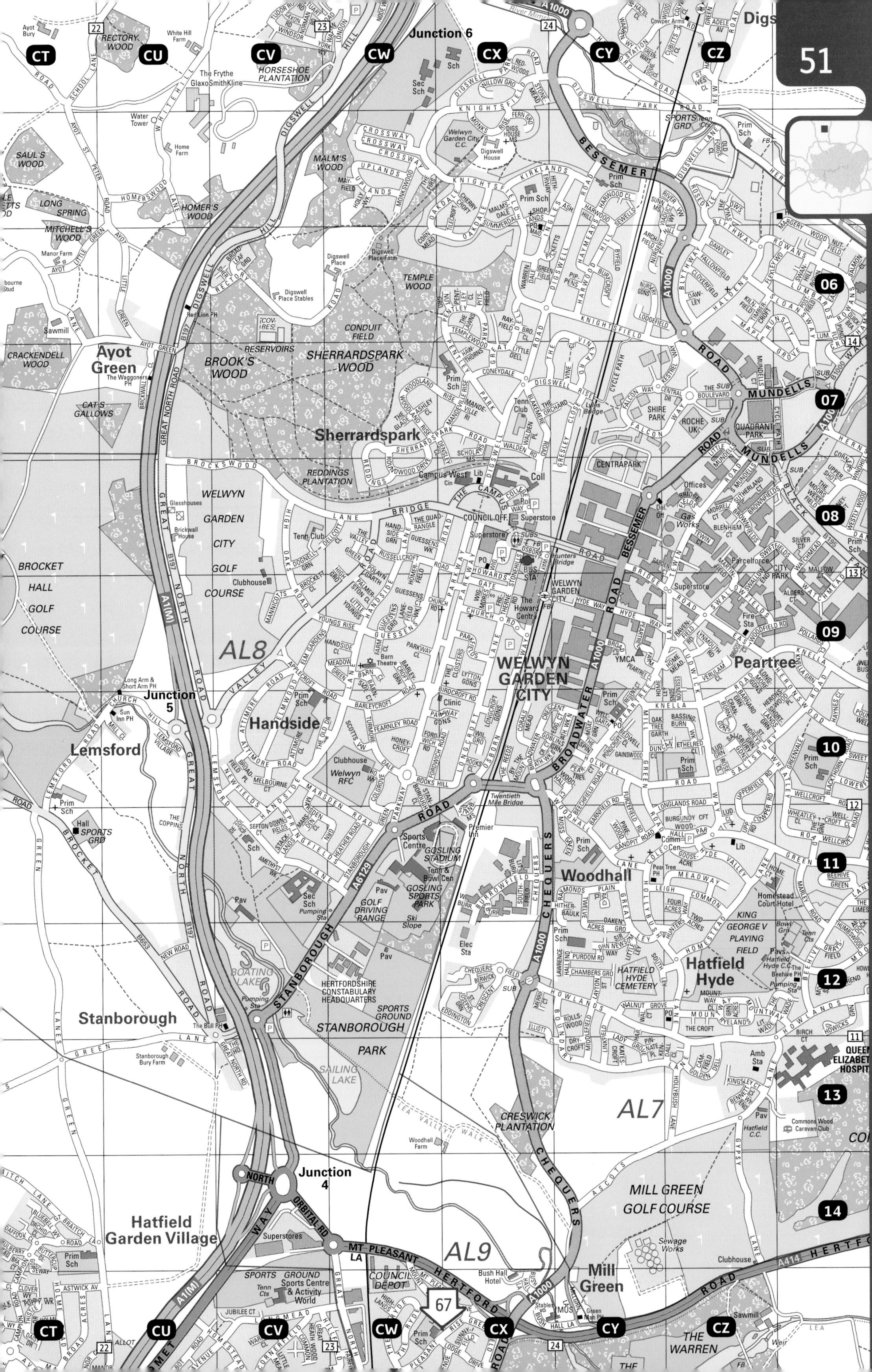

CT
CU
CV
CW
CX
CY
CZ
22
23
24
Junction 6
Ayot Bury
RECTORY WOOD
White Hill Farm
The Frythe GlaxoSmithKline
HORSESHOE PLANTATION
Digswell
Water Tower
SAUL'S WOOD
Home Farm
LONG SPRING
MITCHELL'S WOOD
HOMER'S WOOD
MALM'S WOOD
Manor Farm
Digswell Place
Digswell Place Farm
TEMPLE WOOD
Digswell Place Stables
Red Lion PH
CONDUIT FIELD
RESERVOIRS
SHERRARDSPARK WOOD
BROOK'S WOOD
Ayot Green
The Waggoners PH
CRACKENDELL WOOD
CAT'S GALLOWS
Sawmill
Sherrardspark
REDDINGS PLANTATION
Welwyn Garden City C.C.
Digswell House
DIGSWELL LAKE
BESSEMER
Prim Sch
SPORTS GRD
06
07
08
09
10
11
12
13
14
MUNDELLS
QUADRANT PARK
CENTRAPARK
SHIRE PARK
ROCHE UK
Campus West
Coll
COUNCIL OFF.
Superstore
BUS STA
Hunters Bridge
WELWYN GARDEN CITY
The Howard Centre
Parcelforce
Gas Works
WELWYN GARDEN CITY GOLF COURSE
BROCKET HALL GOLF COURSE
Glasshouses
Brickwall House
Clubhouse
Tenn Club
AL8
Handside
Barn Theatre
Peartree
Fire Sta
Junction 5
Long Arm & Short Arm PH
Sun Inn PH
Lemsford
Hall
SPORTS GRD
THE COPPINS
Welwyn RFC
Twentieth Mile Bridge
Premier Inn
Sports Centre
GOSLING STADIUM
Tenn & Bowl Cen
GOSLING SPORTS PARK
GOLF DRIVING RANGE
Ski Slope
Sec Sch
Pumping Sta
Woodhall
Elec Sta
HATFIELD HYDE CEMETERY
Hatfield Hyde
KING GEORGE V PLAYING FIELD
Homestead Court Hotel
QUEEN ELIZABETH HOSPITAL
Amb Sta
BOATING LAKE
HERTFORDSHIRE CONSTABULARY HEADQUARTERS
SPORTS GROUND
STANBOROUGH PARK
SAILING LAKE
Stanborough
The Bull PH
Stanborough Bury Farm
CRESWICK PLANTATION
AL7
Hatfield C.C.
Commons Wood Caravan Club
Woodhall Farm
Junction 4
NORTH ORBITAL RD
MILL GREEN GOLF COURSE
Sewage Works
Hatfield Garden Village
Superstores
AL9
MT PLEASANT
COUNCIL DEPOT
SPORTS GROUND
Sports Centre & Activity World
Bush Hall Hotel
Mill Green
Green Man PH
Clubhouse
Sawmill
THE WARREN
67
A1(M)
A1000
A6129
A414
B197
B653
B195
B1000

DA
DB
DC
DD
DE
DF
DG
26
27
28
05
06
07
08
09
10
11
12
13
14
DAWLEY WOOD
DAWLEY PLANTATION
BRAMFIELD PARK WOOD
Tewin
GODFRIES CL
BACK LANE
LOWER GRN
Prim Sch
PO
HERTFORD ROAD
Muspatts Farm
AL6
HOME WOOD
Holdens
Weirs
WESTLEY WOOD
War Memorial
RECTORY WOOD
Tewin Bury Farm Hotel
Tewin Lodge
FLEXLEYS WOOD
LAMB DELL WOOD
HOME WOOD
RED WOOD
Marden Hill
PANSHANGER GOLF COURSE
Fairway Tavern PH
Clubhouse
Tewin Mill Farm
Tewin Mill House
MUNDELLS
QUADRANT PARK
ROCHE UK
Pitch 'n' Putt
Welwyn Garden City FC Clubho
River Mimram
Warrengate Farm
Archers Green
BERRICOT GREEN
PANSHANGER AERODROME
POPLARS GREEN
BROCKET HILL
Comm Cen
Prim Sch
Swim Pool
Sec Sch
Panshanger
Surgery
Gas Works
Parcelforce
CITY PARK
Superstore
Fire Sta
Attimore Hall PH
Superstore
WELTECH BUSINESS CEN
Hangar
Flying Sch
HENRY WOOD
MONEYHOLE LANE PARK
Tenn Cts
Pav
Peartree
51
ALLOT
Pumping Stal
BIRCHALL WOOD
HIGH GROVE
AL7
Prim Sch
ROLLS WOOD
Lib
Birchall
GREAT CAPTAIN'S WOOD
BIRCHALL LANE
Cole Green
Munn's Farm
Cowper Arms PH
Homestead Court Hotel
KING GEORGE V PLAYING FIELD
Hall Grove
Hatfield
Hatfield Hyde C.C.
The Beehive PH
Holwell Hyde Farm
EAST HERTS
WELWYN HATFIELD
COLE GREEN WAY
LEA VALLEY WALK
Prim Sch
QUEEN ELIZABETH II HOSPITAL
Amb Sta
Pumping Sta
AL9
DEADFIELD
LETTY GRN
Holwell Court Farm
Pav
Hatfield C.C.
Commons Wood Caravan Club
THE COMMONS
Burnside Farm
Holwell Court
MILL GREEN GOLF COURSE
HATFIELD ROAD
HOLWELL CARAVAN SITE
A414 HERTFORD ROAD
Clubhouse
Sawmill
THE WARREN
68
River Lee or Lea
Holwell Manor
Holwell Bridge
Essendon Mill
B158 ROAD
500 yds
500 m

Bramfield
Bramfield Place Farm
PRIEST WOOD
Waterford Hall
BARLEYCROFT GROVE
DH
DJ
DK
DL
DM
DN
DP
29
30
31
HIGH ROAD
BRAMFIELD LANE
VICARAGE LANE
SACOMBE LANE
Waterford
WATERFORD PLANTATION
WATERFORD COMMON
WATERFORD HEATH COMMUNITY NATURE PARK
WATERFORD MARSH
TIMBER ORCHARD
A119
NORTH ROAD
HOLLY GROVE ROAD
TATTLE HILL
GOLDINGS LANE
GOLDINGS
Goldings Hall
GREAT MOLE WOOD
THE ORCHARD
THE WICK
06
07
08
09
10
11
12
13
14
OAKFIELD PLANTATION
GREAT MOLEWOOD
HIGH MOLEWOOD
Prim Sch
Broadoak End
ICEHOUSE WOOD
HOOK'S BUSHES
BARNSLEYS WOOD
CHATTERSFIELD PLANTATION
HANGING GROVE
Windyridge Farm
ELEVEN ACRE WOOD
River Beane
Goldings Canal
Water Tower
Bengeo
WESTFIELD ROAD
LITTLE MOLE WOOD
SELEBROOM WOOD
ARCHER'S SPRING
LONG WOOD
Lafarge Redlands Aggregates
Comm Cen
RIDGEWAY
CHERRY TREE GRN
BURNETT SQUARE
HERTFORD CEMETERY
ALLOT
WELWYN ROAD
BENTLEY ROAD
LAWRENCE CL
CALTON AVENUE
CARDE CL
EVERGREEN WOOD
GARDEN WOOD
BROADWATER
Weir
BLAKEMORE WOOD
Golden Griffin PH
B1000
SAND PIT
Sec Sch
Prim Sch
FORDWICH RD
HERTFORD NORTH
PORT VALE
SPORTS GRD
ST. ANDREW
SG14
LADY HUGHES'S WOOD
CHESHER'S PLANTATION
THIEVES LANE
LADYWOOD ROAD
HALLEYS RIDGE
CHELMSFORD WOOD
HERTFORD COUNTY HOSP
54
GASCOYNE
HERTFORD
OSIER BEDS
River Mimram
BYPASS
HERTINGFORDBURY
A414
Mill Farm
Epcombs
THE COURTYARD
THE MILL
CHISEL SHELF
GREEN
FB
Hertingfordbury
White Horse Hotel
Hall
Prince of Wales PH
MAYFLOWER CL
Hertford Town FC
Pav
WALK
Tenn Cts
Cricket Ground
THE OLD COACH ROAD
COACH ROAD
War Memorial
Prim Sch
STAINES GREEN
The Bury Farm
Hertingfordbury C.C.
Tenn Cts
Sch
COLE GREEN WAY
LEA VALLEY WALK
TERRACE WOOD
Terrace Wood Nursery
Birch Green
BIRCH GREEN
Birch Grove Nursery
KIT'S DOCKINGS
FOXDELLS
COLE GREEN WAY · LEA VALLEY WALK
River Lee or Lea
HORNS MILL ROAD
Riverside Garden Centre
SPORTS GRD
CECIL ROAD
CHAPEL LANE
Letty Green Fruit Farm
PONTERS GROVE
Eastendgreen Farm
SOUTHFIELD WOOD
Bayfordbury Park Farm
THE PINETUM
Letty Green
Rochfords Nursery
Pipers End
East End Green
CHALK DELL
SG13
B158
WOOLMERS LA
GROTTO WOOD
Bayfordbury
Roxford
Bayfordbury Mansion
Uni of Herts-Field Station & Observatory
Glasshouse
Woolmers Park
GRAVEL PIT
HATFIELD ROAD
GRAVEFIELD GROVE
Home Farm
SPRING WOOD
THE PIGHTLE
LARCH PLANTATION
BAYFORD LANE
HOOK'S GROVE
SAILOR'S GROVE
GRAVEL PIT
69
Water Hall Farm
BROADGREEN WOOD

DQ
DR
DS
DT
DU
DV
DW
33
34
35
05
06
07
08
09
10
11
12
13
14
53
70
SG14
SG13
ST. JOHNS WOOD
OAK WOOD
WATERFORD HEATH COMMUNITY NATURE PARK
EIGHT ACRE PLANTATION
COWSHED CORNER
Ware Park
Ware Park Farm
Ware Park Manor
Bardon Farm
Nursery
MONASTERY
GREAT MOLE WOOD
BENGEO MEADOWS
Kennel Corner
Bengeo
LITTLE MOLE WOOD
KING'S MEADS
Chadwell Spring
CHADWELL SPRINGS GOLF COURSE
Clubhouse
LOCK HOUSE IND EST
MEAD LANE IND EST
MEAD BUSINESS CENTRE
DICKER MILL EST
HARTHAM COMMON
THE WARREN
Madford Retail Pk
FOXHOLES BUSINESS PARK
HERTFORD
COUNTY HALL
BURIAL GRD
BALLS PARK
THE CANAL
Hertford Cricket Club
Foxholes Farm
Jenningsbury Court
Rush Green Farm
Amwell Place Farm
Dunkirks Farm
Caravan Club Site
GREAT STOCK WOOD
LITTLE STOCK WOOD
Hertford Heath
HERTFORD HEATH NATURE RESERVE
Swallow Grove Farm
BALLS WOOD
HIGH WOOD
HOBBYHORSE WOOD
Research Centre
Brickendonbury
Bayfordbury Mansion
THE ARBORETUM
SAILOR'S GROVE
THE GROVE
Clements Farm
Blackfields Farm
East Herts Equestrian Centre
BOX
WARE CEM
SPORTS GRD
WARE ROAD
LONDON ROAD
HERTFORD ROAD
STANSTEAD ROAD
GASCOYNE WAY
A10
A414
A119
B158
B1197
B1502
River Lee or Lea
River Beane
River Rib
New River
0
500 yds
500 m

DX
DY
DZ
EA
EB
EC
ED
06
07
08
09
10
11
12
13
14
56
71
36
37
38
Great Cozens
Morley Hall
Moat
JACKSON'S GROVE
Swades Farm
Ford
Newhole Farm
HARCAMLOW WAY
B1004
WARE
PRIOR'S WOOD
DOGHOUSE WOOD
LADY GROVE
YOUNG WOOD
SG12
Easneye
Waters Place Farm
Weir
Brokengall Hill
Widburyhill Farm
WIDBURY WOOD
MEAD WOOD
The Dairy Farm
River Ash
EASNEYE WOOD
All Nations Christian Coll
SPORTS GRD
HOLLYCROSS ROAD
WIDBURY HILL
KING GEORGE'S FLD
THE VINEYARD
WARE
HIGH ST
A1170
BALDOCK ST
VIADUCT
AMWELL END
LONDON RD
PEERGLOW CEN
CRANE MEAD BUS PK
Coll
PETER'S WOOD
Sec Sch
POST WOOD
Nurseries
Sch
PRESDALES RECREATION GROUND
Amwellbury Farm
WALNUT TREE WALK
Hardmead Lock
LEE VALLEY REGIONAL PARK
RIVER LEE NAVIGATION
AMWELL QUARRY NATURE RESERVE
LEE VALLEY CYCLE ROUTE
Weirs
New River
CHURCH PATH
War Memorial
Van Hage Garden Centre
Great Amwell
Prim Sch
St. Margarets
Glasshouses
Stanstead Lock
Stanstead Mill Stream
CAPPELL ROAD
Stanstead Abbotts
The Maltings
HUNSDON ROAD
B181
ROYDON ROAD
LEE VALLEY REGIONAL PARK
Nursery
Ryegate Farm
B1502
LEAFYOAK WOOD
MUCH WOOD
GYPSY LANE
HERTFORD ROAD
Amwell Roundabout
STATION ROAD
St. Margaretsbury Rec Grd
Cricket Club
Tenn Cts
GOLDING'S WOOD
A414
A10
HODDESDON BYPASS
SPORTS GROUND
HAILEY WOOD
Hailey
Haileybury
Coll
Tenn Cts
The Galley Hall PH
HAILEY LANE
EN11
DELLS WOOD
Woollensbrook
BROXBOURNE
Surgery
Sports Cen
Sec Sch
SPORTS GRD
CEM
RYE MEADS NATURE RESERVE
RSPB RYE MEADS
Visitor Centre
Toll House Stream
Filter Beds
Sewage Works
Sludge Lagoons
Showman's Caravan Site
RYE HOUSE SPEEDWAY
Rye House Gatehouse
RYE HOUSE
KARTING

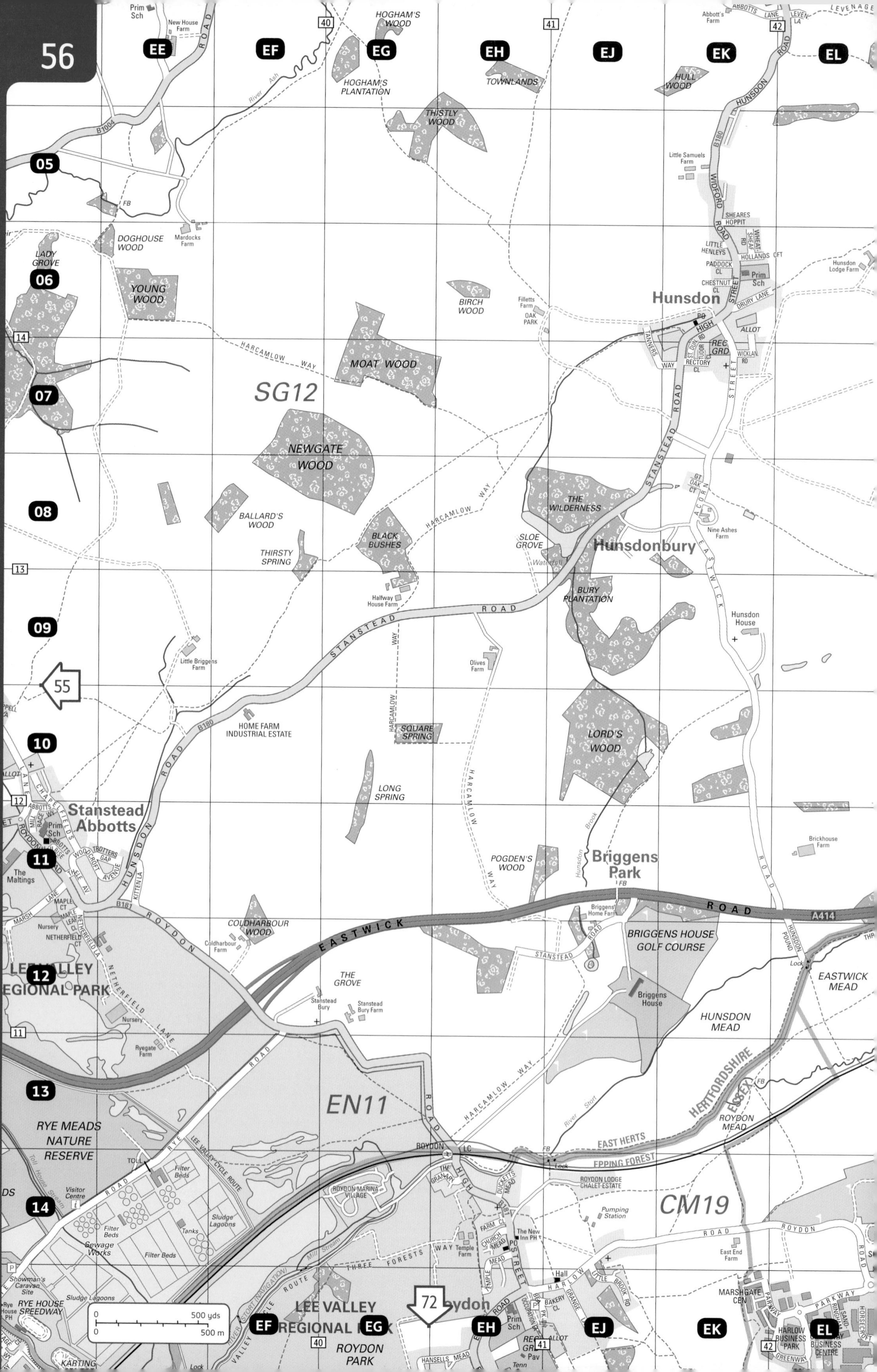

EE
EF
EG
EH
EJ
EK
EL
40
41
42
05
06
07
08
09
10
11
12
13
14
Prim Sch
New House Farm
ROAD
B1004
River Ash
FB
HOGHAM'S WOOD
HOGHAM'S PLANTATION
THISTLY WOOD
TOWNLANDS
HULL WOOD
Abbott's Farm
ABBOTTS LANE
LEVEN LA
LEVENAGE
HUNSDON ROAD
B180
Little Samuels Farm
WIDFORD ROAD
SHEARES HOPPIT
WHEAT SHEAF RD
LITTLE HENLEYS
HOLLANDS CFT
PADDOCK CL
CHESTNUT CL
Prim Sch
Hunsdon Lodge Farm
DRURY LANE
Hunsdon
PO
HIGH
TANNERS WAY
REC GRD
ST DUNSTAN
TUDOR
RECTORY CL
WICKLAND RD
ALLOT
STREET
Mardocks Farm
DOGHOUSE WOOD
LADY GROVE
YOUNG WOOD
BIRCH WOOD
Filletts Farm
OAK PARK
HARCAMLOW WAY
MOAT WOOD
SG12
NEWGATE WOOD
BALLARD'S WOOD
THIRSTY SPRING
BLACK BUSHES
STANSTEAD ROAD
GT OAK CT
ACORN
THE WILDERNESS
Nine Ashes Farm
SLOE GROVE
Waterfall
Hunsdonbury
BURY PLANTATION
Halfway House Farm
EASTWICK
Hunsdon House
Olives Farm
Little Briggens Farm
55
HOME FARM INDUSTRIAL ESTATE
SQUARE SPRING
LORD'S WOOD
LONG SPRING
HARCAMLOW WAY
Brickhouse Farm
Stanstead Abbotts
CHAPELFIELDS
ABBOTTS
MILL RACE
ROYDON
TROTTERS GAP
WOODCROFT AVENUE
THE AV
KITTEN LA
HUNSDON ROAD
POGDEN'S WOOD
Hunsdon Brook
Briggens Park
FB
The Maltings
MAPLE CT
MARSH LANE
Nursery
NETHERFIELD CT
B181
ROYDON
COLDHARBOUR WOOD
Coldharbour Farm
EASTWICK ROAD
A414
Briggens Home Farm
STANSTEAD
BRIGGENS HOUSE GOLF COURSE
HUNSDON POUND
Lock
EASTWICK MEAD
LEE VALLEY REGIONAL PARK
NETHERFIELD LANE
THE GROVE
Stanstead Bury
Stanstead Bury Farm
Briggens House
HUNSDON MEAD
Nursery
Ryegate Farm
HERTFORDSHIRE
ESSEX
FB
ROYDON MEAD
EN11
RYE MEADS NATURE RESERVE
RYE ROAD
LEE VALLEY CYCLE ROUTE
ROAD
River Stort
EAST HERTS
EPPING FOREST
ROYDON
LC
THE GRANARY
HIGH
DUCKETTS MEAD
FB
Lock
ROYDON LODGE CHALET ESTATE
TOLL
Filter Beds
Visitor Centre
ROYDON MARINA VILLAGE
Pumping Station
CM19
Sludge Lagoons
Tanks
Filter Beds
Sewage Works
Filter Beds
Mill Stream
FARM CL
CHURCH MEAD
PO
The New Inn PH
ROYDON ROAD
MEAD
WAY
Temple Farm
THREE FORESTS WAY
East End Farm
Showman's Caravan Site
Sludge Lagoons
Rye House PH
RYE HOUSE SPEEDWAY
KARTING
RIVER STORT (NAVIGATION)
ROUTE
Hall
HARLOW
LITTLE BROOK RD
GRANGE
BAKERY CL
MARSHGATE CEN
PARKWAY
72
Roydon
LEE VALLEY REGIONAL PARK
ROYDON PARK
Prim Sch
REC GRD
ALLOT
Pav
Tenn
HANSELLS MEAD
HARLOW BUSINESS PARK
BUSINESS CENTRE
RINGWAY
SAND
HORSECROFT
GREENWAY
0
500 yds
500 m

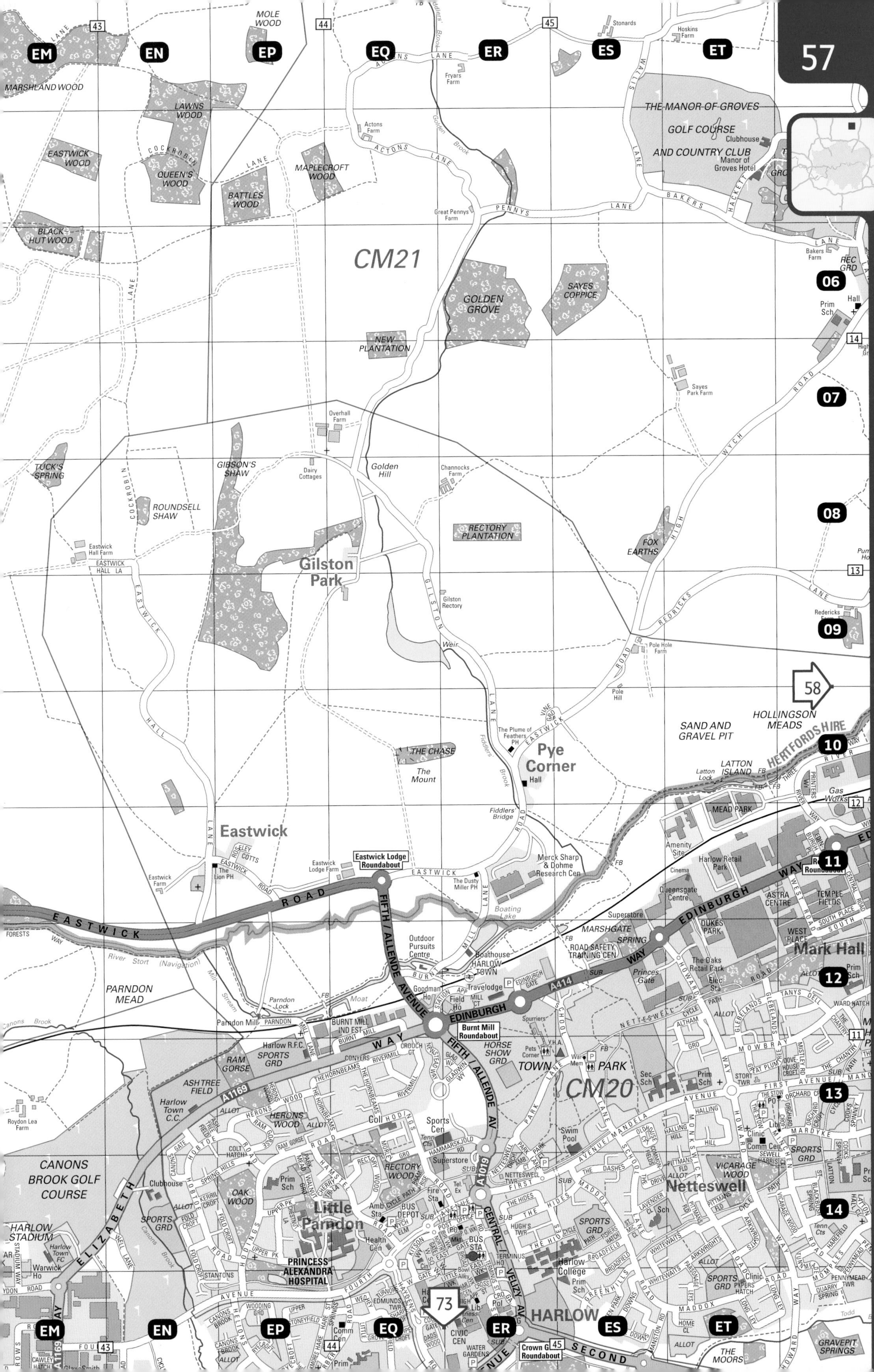
EM
EN
EP
EQ
ER
ES
ET
43
44
45
MOLE WOOD
Stonards
Hoskins Farm
MARSHLAND WOOD
ACTONS LANE
Fryars Farm
THE MANOR OF GROVES GOLF COURSE AND COUNTRY CLUB
Clubhouse
Manor of Groves Hotel
LAWNS WOOD
Actons Farm
EASTWICK WOOD
COCKROBIN LANE
QUEEN'S WOOD
BATTLES WOOD
MAPLECROFT WOOD
Golden Brook
WALLIS LANE
BAKERS LANE
HACKETT
Great Pennys Farm
PENNYS LANE
BLACK HUT WOOD
Bakers Farm
REC GRD
CM21
06
GOLDEN GROVE
SAYES COPPICE
Hall
Prim Sch
14
NEW PLANTATION
Sayes Park Farm
07
WYCH ROAD
HIGH
Overhall Farm
TUCK'S SPRING
GIBSON'S SHAW
Dairy Cottages
Golden Hill
Channocks Farm
ROUNDSELL SHAW
08
RECTORY PLANTATION
FOX EARTHS
Eastwick Hall Farm
EASTWICK HALL LA
Gilston Park
GILSTON LANE
Gilston Rectory
13
REDRICKS LANE
Redericks
09
EASTWICK HALL LANE
Weir
Pole Hole Farm
ROAD
Pole Hill
58
HOLLINGSON MEADS
SAND AND GRAVEL PIT
HERTFORDSHIRE
The Plume of Feathers PH
VINE GRO
EASTWICK
THE CHASE
Pye Corner
Hall
10
The Mount
Fiddlers' Brook
Latton Lock
LATTON ISLAND
FB
Gas Works
12
MEAD PARK
Fiddlers' Bridge
Eastwick
Eastwick Lodge Farm
Eastwick Lodge Roundabout
Merck Sharp & Dohme Research Cen
Amenity Site
Harlow Retail Park
11
Eastwick Farm
The Lion PH
EASTWICK ROAD
The Dusty Miller PH
Cinema
Queensgate Centre
EDINBURGH WAY
ASTRA CENTRE
TEMPLE FIELDS
Boating Lake
FORESTS WAY
Superstore
DUKES PARK
MARSHGATE SPRING
WEST PLACE
Mark Hall
Outdoor Pursuits Centre
River Stort (Navigation)
FIFTH / ALLENDE AVENUE
Boathouse
HARLOW TOWN
ROAD SAFETY TRAINING CEN
The Oaks Retail Park
Princes Gate
PARNDON MEAD
Travelodge
A414
Goodman Ho
Field Ho
Moat
Parndon Lock
Burnt Mill Roundabout
Spurriers
Parndon Mill
BURNT MILL IND EST
NETTESWELL
ALTHAM
Harlow R.F.C. SPORTS GRD
RAM GORSE
HORSE SHOW GRD
Pets Corner
Y.H.A.
War Mem
TOWN PARK
Sec Sch
Prim Sch
ASH TREE FIELD
A1169
Harlow Town C.C.
HERONS WOOD
CM20
13
Roydon Lea Farm
Coll
Sports Cen
Superstore
A1019
Swim Pool
CANONS BROOK GOLF COURSE
Clubhouse
Prim Sch
OAK WOOD
RECTORY WOOD
VICARAGE WOOD
SPORTS GRD
Netteswell
HARLOW STADIUM
Harlow Town FC
SPORTS GRD
Little Parndon
Fire Sta
Amb Sta
BUS DEPOT
Health Cen
BUS STA
Harlow College
14
Warwick Ho
PRINCESS ALEXANDRA HOSPITAL
ELIZABETH WAY
SPORTS GRD
Clinic
73
HARLOW
CIVIC CEN
WATER GARDENS
Crown Gate Roundabout
SECOND AVENUE
THE MOORS
GRAVEPIT SPRINGS

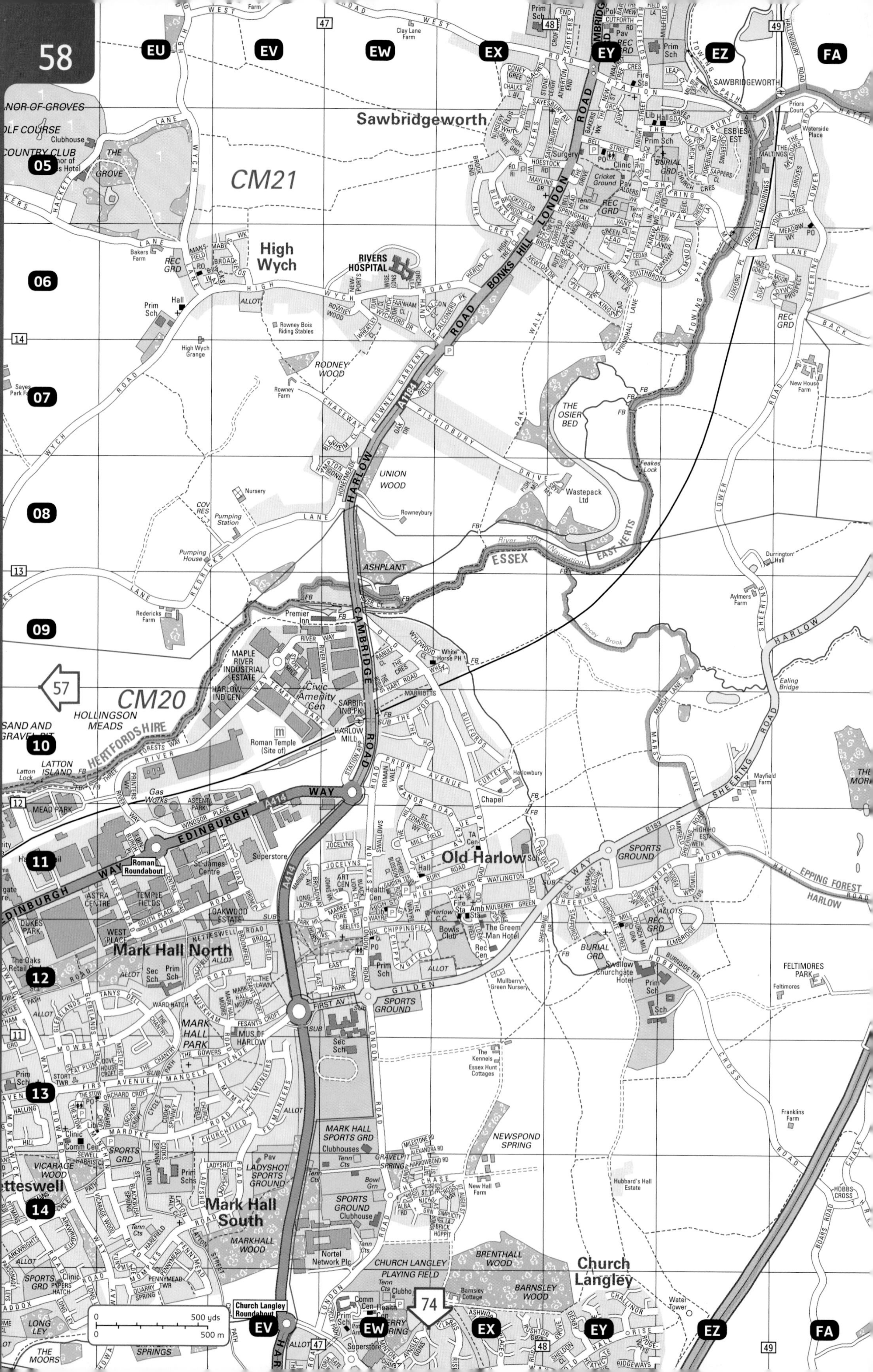
EU
EV
EW
EX
EY
EZ
FA
05
06
07
08
09
10
11
12
13
14
57
74
Sawbridgeworth
CM21
CM20
High Wych
RIVERS HOSPITAL
Old Harlow
Mark Hall North
Mark Hall South
Church Langley
Netteswell
HARLOW ROAD
LONDON ROAD
CAMBRIDGE ROAD
BONKS HILL
EDINBURGH WAY
A414
A1184
B183
ESSEX
EAST HERTS
HERTFORDSHIRE
River Stort (Navigation)
Pincey Brook
THE OSIER BED
UNION WOOD
RODNEY WOOD
ASHPLANT
HOLLINGSON MEADS
LATTON ISLAND
MAPLE RIVER INDUSTRIAL ESTATE
HARLOW IND CEN
Civic Amenity Cen
Roman Temple (Site of)
HARLOW MILL
Roman Roundabout
Church Langley Roundabout
MARK HALL SPORTS GRD
SPORTS GROUND
NEWSPOND SPRING
BRENTHALL WOOD
BARNSLEY WOOD
MARKHALL WOOD
LADYSHOT SPORTS GROUND
VICARAGE WOOD
Nortel Network Plc
Swallow Churchgate Hotel
The Green Man Hotel
FELTIMORES PARK
Franklins Farm
Hubbard's Hall Estate
Mayfield Farm
Aylmers Farm
Durrington Hall
New House Farm
Wastepack Ltd
Feakes Lock
Ealing Bridge
Rowney Farm
Rowney Bois Riding Stables
High Wych Grange
Redericks Farm
Bakers Farm
Pumping Station
Pumping House
Nursery
Rowneybury
Premier Inn
White Horse PH
Superstore
St James Centre
ASTRA CENTRE
TEMPLE FIELDS
OAKWOOD ESTATE
DUKES PARK
WEST PLACE
MEAD PARK
Gas Works
MUS OF HARLOW
Mullberry Green Nursery
The Kennels
Essex Hunt Cottages
New Hall Farm
Water Tower
ESSEX
EPPING FOREST
HARLOW
SHEERING ROAD
0 500 yds
0 500 m

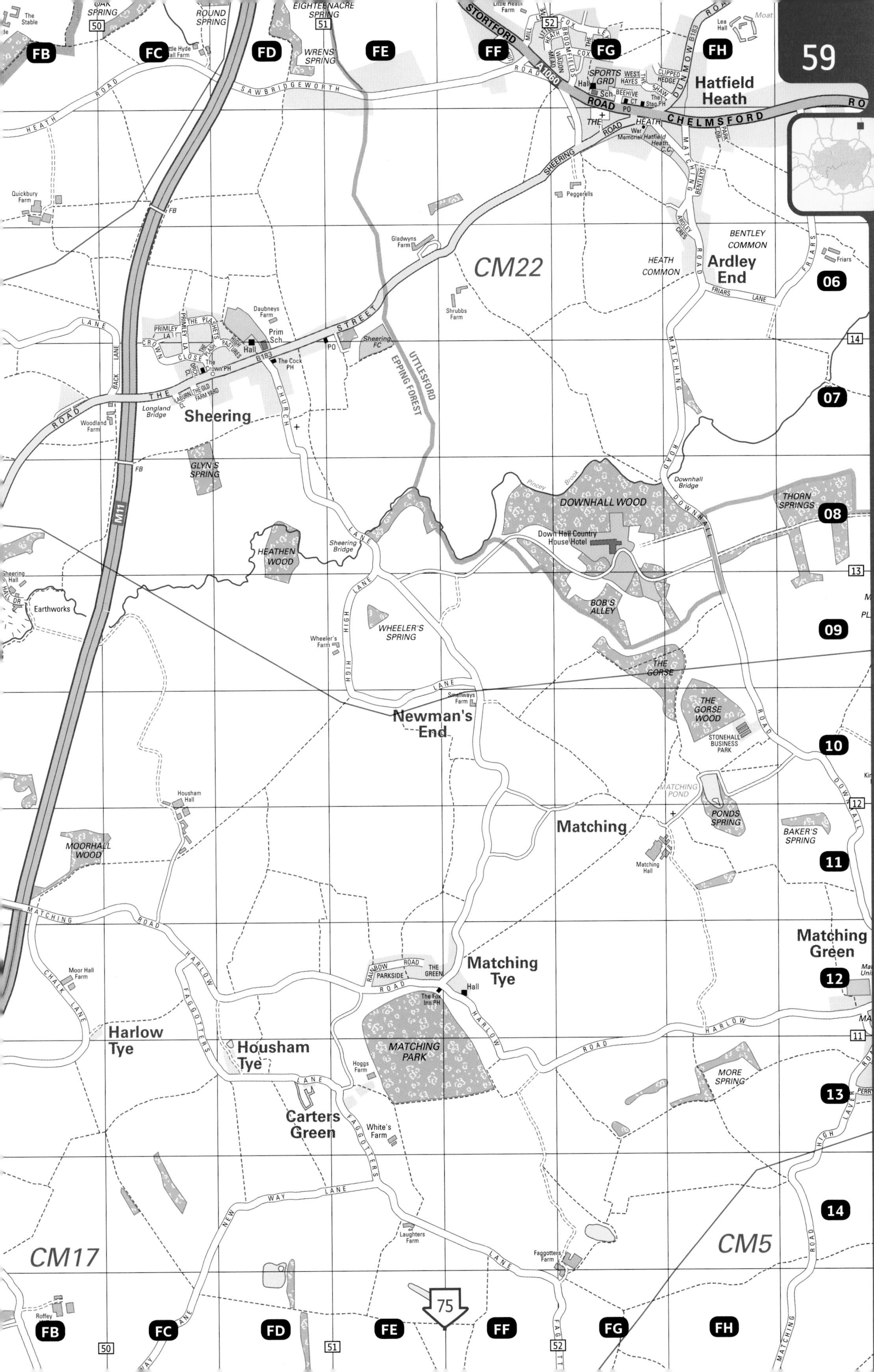

FB
FC
FD
FE
FF
FG
FH
The Stable
OAK SPRING
ROUND SPRING
EIGHTEENACRE SPRING
Little Hyde Hall Farm
WRENS SPRING
Little Heath Farm
STORTFORD ROAD
A1060
Lea Hall
Moat
Hatfield Heath
SPORTS GRD
Hall
Sch
PO
Stag PH
THE HEATH
War Memorial
Hatfield Heath C.C.
CHELMSFORD ROAD
DUNMOW B183
SAWBRIDGEWORTH ROAD
HEATH ROAD
SHEERING ROAD
MATCHING ROAD
BENTLEYS
ARDLEY CRES
Peggerells
Quickbury Farm
FB
Gladwyns Farm
CM22
BENTLEY COMMON
HEATH COMMON
Ardley End
FRIARS LANE
Friars
06
07
08
09
10
11
12
13
14
Shrubbs Farm
Daubneys Farm
Prim Sch
Hall
PO
Sheering FC
The Cock PH
The Crown PH
THE STREET
B183
BACK LANE
THE ROAD
Longland Bridge
Woodland Farm
Sheering
CHURCH
UTTLESFORD
EPPING FOREST
GLYN'S SPRING
M11
FB
Downhall Bridge
DOWNHALL WOOD
Pincey Brook
Down Hall Country House Hotel
THORN SPRINGS
HEATHEN WOOD
Sheering Bridge
Sheering Hall
Earthworks
BOB'S ALLEY
WHEELER'S SPRING
Wheeler's Farm
HIGH LANE
THE GORSE
Smallways Farm
Newman's End
THE GORSE WOOD
STONEHALL BUSINESS PARK
MATCHING POND
PONDS SPRING
Housham Hall
Matching
Matching Hall
BAKER'S SPRING
DOWNHALL ROAD
MOORHALL WOOD
MATCHING ROAD
Matching Green
Moor Hall Farm
CHALK LANE
RAINBOW ROAD
PARKSIDE
THE GREEN
Matching Tye
Hall
The Fox Inn PH
HARLOW ROAD
FAGGOTTERS
Harlow Tye
Housham Tye
MATCHING PARK
Hoggs Farm
MORE SPRING
Carters Green
White's Farm
NEW WAY LANE
Laughters Farm
CM17
CM5
Faggotters Farm
HIGH LAVER ROAD
Roffey
75
50
51
52

NORTHCHURCH COMMON NT
AS
AT
AU
AV
AW
AX
AY
FIRTHSDEN BEECHES
NATIONAL TRUST
98
99
00
Hill Farm
NEW ROAD
Pumping Station
15
16
17
18
19
20
21
22
23
24
09
08
07
06
Gorseside Farm
Northchurch Farm
GRAND UNION CANAL
Dudswell
DUDSWELL LANE
BERKHAMSTED GOLF COURSE
ALLOT
Tenn Cts
Pav
REC GRD
HIGH STREET
A4251
ROAD
HP4
Well Farm
Sec Sch
New Farm
CEM
Northchurch
RECYCLING CEN
CANAL-SIDE
BERKHAMSTED
SPORTS GRD
Clubhouse
BERKHAMSTED PLACE
SPORTS GRD
Social Cen
Hospice
THE ROOKERY
Woodcock Hill
COX DELL
Sch
THE PLANTATION
SHOOTERSWAY
BERKHAMSTED A41 BYPASS
Youth Club
Sports Cen
Health Cen
GOSSOMS END
BERKHAMSTED CASTLE (ruins)
BERKHAMSTED
Berkhamsted Town FC
Superstore
THE MOOR
Amb Sta
Fire Sta
CIVIC CEN
Lib
Hall
Prim Sch
Clinic
REC GRD
Prep Sch
LONDON ROAD
KINGS ROAD
A416
Tower
PLAYING FIELD
PLAYING FIELD
Sec Sch
REC GRD
Prim Sch
National Film & Television Archive
KINGSHILL WAY
CEM
Ashlyns Farm
Ashlyns Hall
PANCAKE WOOD
HOCKERIDGE WOOD
WILLOW WOOD
BERKHAMSTED A41 BYPASS
CHESHAM ROAD
SANDPIT GREEN
DROPPING'S WOOD
COKER'S SPRING
Johns Lane Farm
Sch
Haresfoot Farm
William Hill Farm
Hockeridge Farm
HP5
Brickies Farm
Harriotts End Farm
THE LARCHES
HEATHEN GROVE
Snowhill Farm
Old Oak Farm
Brickies Farm
PO
Hall
Sewage Works
Ashley Green
Hall
Flamstead Farm
SHORT WOOD
BACORUM HERTFORDSHIRE
CHILTERN BUCKINGHAMSHIRE
Whelpley Hill Farm
Kenmore Farm
GREAT WOOD
78
0 500 yds
0 500 m
Sale's Farm
Spencer's Farm
Hemming's Farm
GRD
STRAWE

AZ
BA
BB
BC
BD
BE
BF
01
02
03
NATIONAL TRUST
LITTLE FRITHSDEN COPSE
FRITHSDEN VINES
Hollybush Farm
Alford Arms PH
Crossways Farm
HERDIN'S WOOD
Strathgade Farm
Bingham's Park Farm
Poultry Farm
Rumblers Farm
BROWN'S SPRING WOOD
HOLLYBUSH WOOD
Woodcroft Farm
CATSTAIL WOOD
16
Potten End
DELL WOOD
09
Boxted Farm
17
COV RES
Gutteridge Farm
GUTTERIDGE WOOD
LITTLE HEATH NT
Little Heath Farm
Bowling Green
Boxted Pig Farm
Gadebridge
SPORTS GROUND
18
Little Heath Great Farm
Lower Little Heath Farm
Fields End Farm
WARNERS END
Warners End
19
62
BULLBEGGAR'S WOOD
HP1
SHRUB HILL COMMON
NORTHRIDGE PARK
20
Berkhamsted Sewage Works
Chaulden
21
Pouchen End Farm
Broadway Farm
Pix Farm
The Three Horseshoes PH
Watermill Hotel
CHAULDEN LANE PLAYING FIELD
Rugby Ground
22
Bourne End
BOURNE END MILLS
Moorend Farm
HEMEL HEMPSTEAD
06
23
UPPER ROUGHDOWN
Premier Inn
Vale Farm
GREEN CROFT
HAY WOOD
Prep Sch
HANGING WOOD
Clubhouse
LITTLE HAY GOLF COMPLEX
BOXMOOR GOLF COURSE
24
COLESHILL WOOD
HP3
SHEETHANGER COMMON
Felden Lodge
Howe's Retreat
GORSEFIELD WOOD
79
BURY WOOD
Tower Farm
Felden Grange
Felden Manor
Longcroft Farm
COVERED RESERVOIR
A41
A4251
A4146
KINGS LANGLEY BYPASS
BERKHAMSTED BYPASS
LONDON ROAD

BG
BH
BJ
BK
BL
BM
BN
05
06
07
08
09
15
16
17
18
19
20
21
22
23
24
61
80
VARNEY'S WOOD
Wood Farm
Lovetts End Farm
The Red Lion PH
A4146
THRIFT WOOD
Grist House Farm
Watercress Beds
Strathgade Farm
Noake Mill
Gaddesden Hall
Fish Farm
Piccotts End Garden Centre
Fish Ponds
Electricity Station
BUZZARD
Piccotts End
New Farm House
DELL WOOD
Piccotts End Farm
Boars Head PH
Marchmont Farm
WARNERS END WOOD
HOME WOOD
GADEBRIDGE
LINK
ROAD
A4147
HOWE GROVE
GROVEHILL PLAYING FIELDS
Grovehill
MARGARET LLOYD PARK
Cupid Green
Amenity Site
Superstore
PENNINE WAY SPORTS GROUND
YEWTREE WOOD
REDBOURN ROAD
SWALLOWDALE LA
PLAYING FLD
Highfield
RANDALL PARK
SPORTS GROUND
LEIGHTON BUZZARD ROAD
GADEBRIDGE PARK
HP1
VALLEY
WARNERS END
KEEN FIELDS
QUEENSWAY
Hammerfield
West Herts Coll
DACORUM CIVIC CENTRE
BUS STA
NORTHRIDGE PARK
Adeyfield
REITH FIELDS
HEATH LANE CEMETERY
HEMEL HEMPSTEAD GENERAL HOSP
HEMEL HEMPSTEAD
The Marlowes Centre
Plough Roundabout
ST. ALBANS ROAD
A414
JARMAN PARK
Leisure World
Cinema
Ice Arena
DACORUM ATHLETICS TRACK
The Snow Centre
Boxmoor
Rugby Ground
Cricket Ground
Cricket Club
LONDON ROAD
A41
STATION ROAD
TWO WATERS RD
HP3
LIME WALK
Bennetts End
BELSWAINS PLAYING FIELDS
Gas Holder
Gas Holders
UPPER ROUGHDOWN
LOWER ROUGHDOWN
A4251
KINGS LANGLEY BYPASS
Three Fields Farm
Felden
HOME WOOD
Superstores
APSLEY MILLS RETAIL PARK
Holiday Inn Express
Apsley
SHENDISH MANOR GOLF COURSE
HEN'S HEAD WOOD
Tower Farm
Felden Lodge
Howe's Retreat
GRAND UNION CANAL
500 yds
500 m

BP
BQ
BR
BS
BT
BU
BV
08
09
10
Dane End Farm
Superstore
Med Cen
Prim Sch
HEMEL HEMPSTEAD ROAD
CYCLE PATH
Bohemia House
Hill Farm
Prim Schs
Comm Cen
B487
HUNTERS
CHERRY TREE LANE
DACORUM
ST. ALBANS
Wood End Farm
Cherry Tree Farm
LILLY LANE
PUNCH BOWL LANE
HP2
PRATTS DELL
Southend Farm
HEMEL HEMPSTEAD INDUSTRIAL ESTATE
MAXTED ROAD
BOUNDARY ROAD
BUNCEFIELD LANE
HOGG END LANE
Oil Tanks
AL3
Old Jeromes
Butler's Farm
Buncefield Terminal
Oil Tanks
Kettlewell's Farm
GROVELANDS BUS. CEN.
SARACEN INDUSTRIAL AREA
Dixons Group Plc
BOUNDARY WAY
KENTISH WOOD
WINDMILLHILL WOOD
THE VISTAS
THE WILDERNESS
CHALK DELL
GORHAMBURY
WOODWELLS FARM CEMETERY
Peoplebuilding
Fitness Cen
Depot
Caravan Club
Elec Sta
BREAKSPEAR WAY
Holiday Inn
B.P. Plc
MARCHMONT HOUSE POND
BRUCE'S PLANTATION
Gorhambury (Ruins)
64
Juntions 7 & 8
BRICKKILN WOOD
A4147
AVENUE
A414
LEVERSTOCK GRN WAY
GREEN LANE
M1
Mayers Farm Stud Cottages
Prim Sch
Westwick Farm
Leverstock Green FC
Leverstock Green
Comm Cen
Lib
Westwick Hall
Westwick Row Farm
WESTWICK ROW
Cricket Ground
Pav
Hill End Farm
BEECHTREE LANE
Tenn Club
Sch
Corner Farm
Westwick House
HEMEL HEMPSTEAD ROAD
06
07
LONGFIELD SPRING
Maiden Crouch Farm
APPSPOND LANE
Prim Sch
Sports Cen
Sec Sch
CATSDELL BOTTOM
CHAMBERSBURY LANE
BLACKWATER LANE
BLACKWATER WOOD
Bunkers Farm
Well Farm
THREE RIVERS
BEDMOND ROAD
Highwood Hall Farm
High Herts Farm
The Swan PH
APPSPOND WOOD
POTTERS CROUCH PLANTATION
WOODHALL LANE
BUNKERS LANE
SILVERTHORN DRIVE
LONG DEANS
81
Bedmond House
Rose Acre
WD5
BEDMOND LANE
16
17
18
19
20
21
22
23
24

BW
BX
BY
BZ
CA
CB
CC
12
13
14
15
16
17
18
19
20
21
22
23
24
09
08
07
06
Punch Bowl PH
Pumping Sta
Mill Stream
BUSH WOOD
Childwick Bury
KIDMAN'S SPRING WOOD
HILL
FARM
LANE
BOWL
Hill Farm
New Jerome Cottage
PUNCH
A5183
REDBOURN
WATLING STREET (ROMAN ROAD)
River Ver
Mill Race
THE PLANTATION
Woodlands Farm
TOULMIN DRIVE SPORTS GROUND
Sec Sch
Pav
Stafford Farm
Stafford Stud
LADIES GROVE WOOD
BATCH WOOD
END
HOGG
ROAD
WHITEHEDGE SPRING
Golf & Tennis Cen
Tenn Cts
Bowling Green
Batchwood Hall
BATCHWOOD HALL GOLF COURSE
Bow Bridge
Butler's Farm
AL3
Maynes Farm
DRIVE
Hospice
REC GRD
ST. ALBANS CITY HOSP
WINDMILLHILL WOOD
THE WILDERNESS
CHALK DELL
GORHAMBURY
ONE ACRE
Gorhambury
CHURCHYARD MEADOW
REDBOURN
A5183
ROAD
Shepherds Cottage
GILPINS
HUGO'S SPINNEY
Course of Roman Wall
VERULAM
FOLLY
ALBANY LODGE
Gorhambury (Ruins)
63
CYPRESS WOOD
The Fosse
KINGSBURY WATERMILL
Roman Open Air Theatre
VERULAMIUM MUSEUM
BELL MEADOW
LORD BACON'S MOUNT
TEMPLE WOOD
Site of Roman Verulamium
HEMEL HEMPSTEAD
Mayers Farm Stud Cottages
Prae Wood House
PRAE WOOD
Prae Wood Farm
VERULAMIUM PARK
Hypocaust
Tennis Courts
THE LAKE
Ye Olde Fighting Cocks PH
SQUARE WOOD
ROAD
A4147
Verulam Hills
ATHLETICS TRACK
Leisure Centre
Hill End Farm
Superstore
Prim Sch
ABBEY VIEW GOLF COURSE
HEMPSTEAD
HEMEL
Sch
ST STEPHENS HILL
St. Stephens
A414
LONGFIELD SPRING
Maiden Crouch Farm
MADAM'S WOOD
Windridge Farm
BEDMOND
BIRCH WOOD
NETHERWAY OPEN SPACE
WATLING STREET
A5183
Sec Sch
PO
BIRCH WOOD
BEDMOND LANE
PARK WOOD
Westfields Farm
APPSPOND WOOD
Holly Bush PH
Potters Crouch East Farm
Potters Crouch Farm
RAGGED HALL LANE
SQUARE WOOD
SCRUBBS WOOD
Cuckman's Farm
AL2
Surgery
ALLOT
REC GRD
Prim Sch
ST. JULIAN'S WOOD
Park Street Roundabout
M1
WD5
Potters Crouch
500 yds
500 m
82
FURZE
Plaistowes
A405
WATLING STREET CARAVAN TRAVELLERS

CD
CE
CF
CG
CH
CJ
CK
15
16
17
HOME OFFICE SCIEN
DEVELOPMENT BRA
16
09
17
18
08
19
20
07
21
22
06
23
24
66
83
Harpenden Road
Woollams Playing Field
Jersey Farm
Jersey Farm Woodland Park
New Greens
Marshalswick
Townsend
Bernards Heath
AL4
AL1
St. Albans
Fleetville
The Camp
Highfield Park
Tyttenhanger
Verulam Golf Course
St. Julians
Hatfield Road
London Road
St. Albans Cemetery
Longacres Playing Field
Home Wood
Skys Wood
The Wick
Sandpit Lane
North Orbital Road
London Colney Rbt
Verulamian RFC
Chalkdell Wood
Sopwell House Hotel
Oaklands College
Clarence Park
Junction 1
A1081
A1057
A414
A5183
B651
B691

CL
CM
CN
CP
CQ
CR
CS
50
84
65
15
16
17
18
19
20
21
22
23
24
08
07
06
09
19
20
21
HOME OFFICE SCIENTIFIC DEVELOPMENT BRANCH
Fairfold's Farm
Sutton's Farm
WOODCOCK HILL
Nashe's Farm
NASHES FARM LANE
HILL
SAND AND GRAVEL PIT
SAND & GRAVEL PIT
Astwick Manor
Astwick Manor Farm
MANOR ROAD
Fielder Centre
HATFIELD BUSINESS PARK
Offices
FROBISHER WAY
HOOK'S WOOD
SLEEVE HALL WOOD
BALL'S COVERT
OAK WOOD
Beech Farm
ROUND WOOD
HOME COVERT
ASH GREEN
Oak Farm
COOPERS GREEN LANE
WELWYN HATFIELD
ST. ALBANS
AL10
Prim Sch
Fitness Cen
University of Hertfordshire de Havilland Campus
Sports Cen
BISHOP SQUARE
Ramada
OAKLANDS LANE
NORTH
RICHMOND WALK
CRESCENT
RIPON WAY
NEWGATE CL
HOUSE LANE
Radio Nursery
PASTURE VIEW
Popefield Farm
ST. ALBANS ROAD WEST
Wilkin's Green
Ellenbrook
Glasshouses
College Farm Buildings
EAST DRIVE
Oaklands Coll
Tenn Cts
BAGGYMEAD SPRING
Notcutts Garden Cen.
A1057
HATFIELD ROAD
Wilkin's Green Farm
Nast Hyde Farm
ALBAN WAY CYCLE ROUTE
Smallford
Smallford Nursery
STATION ROAD
WILKINS GREEN LANE
Junction 3
COMET WAY
ROEHYDE
HOME WOOD
Coll
Superstores
HATHAWAY CT
FIRWOOD AVENUE
STATION YD
SUB
AL4
Sleapshyde
Sleapshyde Farm
SLEAPSHYDE LANE
SMITHS CRES
SLEAPCROSS GARDENS
A414
HOBBS CL
Sec Sch
HIXBERRY LANE
Pav
SPORTS GRD
ALLOT
HEATH
Smallford Farm
BUTTERWICK LANE
JOHNSON'S SPRING
Bullen's Green
HIGHFIELD PARK
Cricket Ground
BARLEY MOW CARAVAN PARK
ORBITAL
FB
SPORTS GRD
Prim Sch
Clubhouse
Tenn Cts
BURIAL GRD
Barley Mow Stables
Roundhouse Farm
Colney Heath
Pumping Sta
ROESTOCK PARK
SPORTS GRD
Hall
The Plough PH
GREEN BARLEY
Tyttenhanger
SAND AND GRAVEL PIT
River Colne
PARK CORNER
Hall
STREET
PO
Queens Head PH
Colney Heath Farm
TOLLGATE ROAD
FELLOWES LANE
DELLSOME
Roestock
Highfield Farm
HIGHFIELD LANE
KNIGHT'S WOOD
ST. ALBANS HERTSMERE
SAND AND GRAVEL PIT
Warren Farm
THE WARREN
COURSERS ROAD
Highfield Hall
HIGHFIELD MANOR
BLOUNT SPRING
FREDERICK'S WOOD
WELWYN HATFIELD
Tyttenhanger Farm
NORTH ORBITAL A414
LONDON
FIVE ACRES
COPPICE
500 yds
500 m
Tyttenhanger House
GARDEN WOOD
THE NEW PLANTATION
Coursers Farm
HERTS

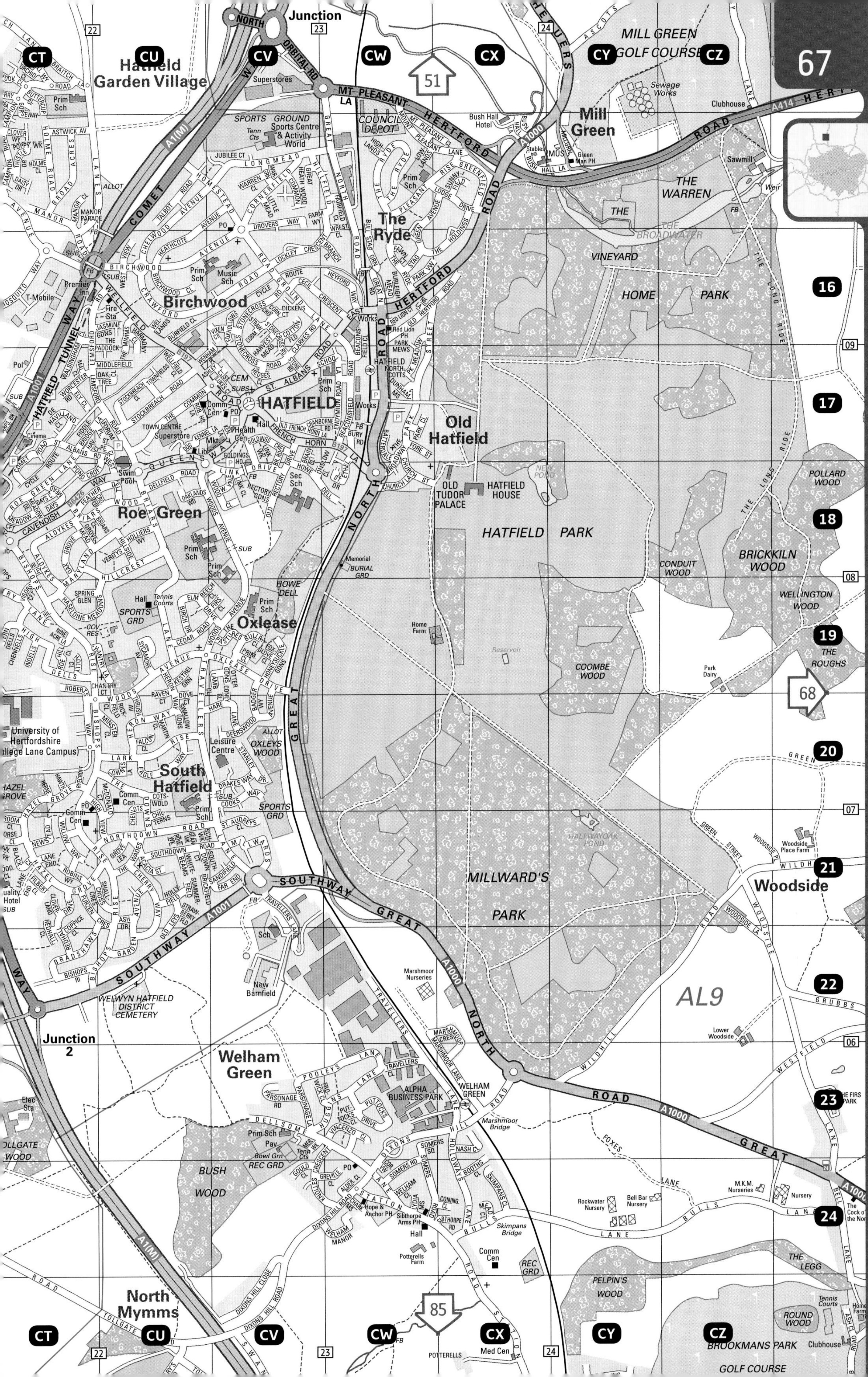
Junction 23
CT
CU
CV
CW
CX
CY
CZ
51
Hatfield Garden Village
MILL GREEN GOLF COURSE
Sewage Works
Clubhouse
Mill Green
Bush Hall Hotel
MUS
Green Man PH
Superstores
NORTH ORBITAL RD
MT PLEASANT LA
HERTFORD ROAD
A414
COUNCIL DEPOT
SPORTS GROUND
Sports Centre & Activity World
Tenn Cts
A1(M)
COMET WAY
A1000
Sawmill
Weir
THE WARREN
THE BROADWATER
THE VINEYARD
HOME PARK
THE LONG RIDE
16
09
17
18
08
19
68
20
07
21
22
06
23
24
Prim Sch
The Ryde
Birchwood
Music Sch
Premier Inn
T-Mobile
Fire Sta
HATFIELD
Old Hatfield
OLD TUDOR PALACE
HATFIELD HOUSE
NEW POND
HATFIELD PARK
POLLARD WOOD
BRICKKILN WOOD
CONDUIT WOOD
WELLINGTON WOOD
THE ROUGHS
Memorial
BURIAL GRD
HOWE DELL
Home Farm
Reservoir
COOMBE WOOD
Park Dairy
Roe Green
Oxlease
Swim Pool
Cinema
TOWN CENTRE
Superstore
Health Cen
Lib
Mkt
Sec Sch
SPORTS GRD
Tennis Courts
University of Hertfordshire (College Lane Campus)
South Hatfield
Leisure Centre
OXLEYS WOOD
HALFWAYOAK POND
MILLWARD'S PARK
Woodside
Woodside Place Farm
AL9
Lower Woodside
SOUTHWAY
GREAT NORTH ROAD
Junction 2
WELWYN HATFIELD DISTRICT CEMETERY
New Barnfield
Sch
Marshmoor Nurseries
Welham Green
ALPHA BUSINESS PARK
WELHAM GREEN
Marshmoor Bridge
Elec Sta
TOLLGATE WOOD
BUSH WOOD
Prim Sch
Pav
Bowl Grn
Tenn Cts
REC GRD
Hope & Anchor PH
Sibthorpe Arms PH
Hall
Potterells Farm
Skimpans Bridge
Comm Cen
REC GRD
Rockwater Nursery
Bell Bar Nursery
M.K.M. Nurseries
Nursery
The Cock o' the North
THE LEGG
PELPIN'S WOOD
North Mymms
85
Med Cen
POTTERELLS
Tennis Courts
ROUND WOOD
Home Farm
BROOKMANS PARK GOLF COURSE
Clubhouse
22
23
24

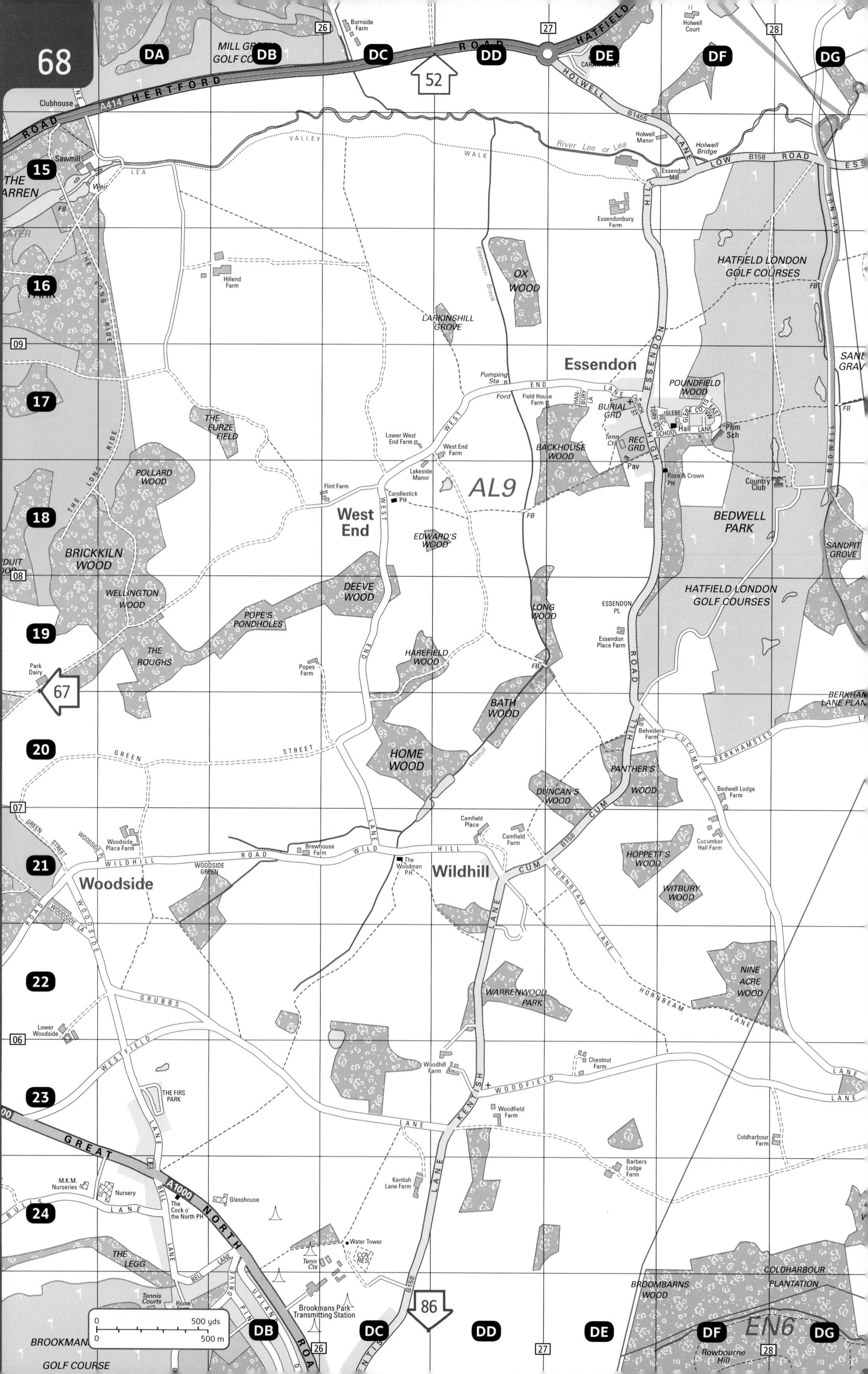
DA
DB
DC
DD
DE
DF
DG
26
27
28
52
MILL GREEN GOLF COURSE
Burnside Farm
Holwell Court
HATFIELD
ROAD
HOLWELL
CARAVAN SITE
HERTFORD
A414
Clubhouse
ROAD
B1455
Holwell Manor
Holwell Bridge
LANE
River Lee or Lea
VALLEY
WALK
LEA
Sawmill
Weir
THE WARREN
15
FB
Essendon Mill
LOW
B158
ROAD
Essendonbury Farm
HILL
16
THE LONG RIDE
Hillend Farm
OX WOOD
Essendon Brook
HATFIELD LONDON GOLF COURSES
AVENUE
LARKINSHILL GROVE
09
Essendon
Pumping Sta
END
LANE
ESSENDON
POUNDFIELD WOOD
CHURCH ST
HAN-BURY LA
TORY CT
REC
GLEBE CL
GLEBE COTTS
EAST VW
SCHOOL
Hall
LANE
Prim Sch
BURIAL GRD
Ford
Field House Farm
Tenn Cts
REC GRD
Pav
Rose & Crown PH
HIGH
17
THE FURZE FIELD
WEST
Lower West End Farm
West End Farm
Lakeside Manor
BACKHOUSE WOOD
BEDWELL
Country Club
POLLARD WOOD
Flint Farm
Candlestick PH
AL9
FB
18
West End
WEST
EDWARD'S WOOD
BEDWELL PARK
SANDPIT GROVE
SAND GRAV
BRICKKILN WOOD
08
WELLINGTON WOOD
DEEVE WOOD
LONG WOOD
ESSENDON PL
HATFIELD LONDON GOLF COURSES
POPE'S PONDHOLES
Essendon Place Farm
19
THE ROUGHS
END
HAREFIELD WOOD
Popes Farm
Park Dairy
67
FB
BATH WOOD
Brook
ROAD
BERKHAMSTED LANE PLAN
20
GREEN
STREET
HOME WOOD
Wildhill
HILL
Belvedere Farm
CUCUMBER
BERKHAMSTED
PANTHER'S WOOD
DUNCAN'S WOOD
Bedwell Lodge Farm
07
GREEN
STREET
WOODSIDE PL
Woodside Place Farm
LANE
Camfield Place
Camfield Farm
CUM
CUM
Cucumber Hall Farm
WILDHILL
ROAD
Brewhouse Farm
WILD
HILL
The Woodman P.H.
B158
HOPPETT'S WOOD
21
Woodside
WOODSIDE GREEN
Wildhill
HORNBEAM
WITBURY WOOD
ROAD
WOODSIDE LA
WOODSIDE
LANE
LANE
22
GRUBBS
WARRENWOOD PARK
NINE ACRE WOOD
HORNBEAM
LANE
Lower Woodside
06
WESTFIELD
Woodhill Farm
Chestnut Farm
LANE
KENTISH
WOODFIELD
LANE
23
THE FIRS PARK
Woodfield Farm
LANE
GREAT
LANE
Coldharbour Farm
M.K.M. Nurseries
Nursery
BELL
A1000
NORTH
Glasshouse
Barbers Lodge Farm
Kentish Lane Farm
24
BULLS
LANE
The Cock o' the North PH
THE LEGG
BELL
LANE
Water Tower
COV RES
Tenn Cts
COLDHARBOUR PLANTATION
BROOMBARNS WOOD
Tennis Courts
Home Farm
DRIVE
PINE
UPLANDS
B158
Brookmans Park Transmitting Station
86
0 500 yds
0 500 m
BROOKMANS
GOLF COURSE
ROAD
EN6
Rowbourne Hill

GRAVEL PIT
Roxford
HATFIELD
Uni of Herts-Field Station & Observatory
Bayfordbury Mansion
Glasshouse
Home Farm
53
FIELD GROVE
LARCH PLANTATION
SPRING WOOD
THE PIGHTLE
HOOK'S GROVE
SAILOR'S GROVE
GRAVEL PIT
Water Hall Farm
LOWER ROAD
BAYFORD
BROAD GRN WD
BROADGREEN WOOD
The Home Field
HILL
POLLARD WOOD
STOCKINGS
MARLEYS BROW
WEEPINGS WOOD
GRAVEL PIT
Bayford Hall Farm
Bayford Hall
Bayford & Hertford C.C.
Cricket Club
LANE
CULVER WOOD
FB
CHURCH LA
HARMOND'S WOOD
Ashfield Farm
Warren House
Place Farm
STOCKINGS LANE
NEST
Culverwood Farm
GREAT GROVES
STOCKINGS
WELL ROW
BROAD GREEN
FURZE FIELD
WILLOW CORNER
FOURWAYS
Bayford
Baker Arms PH
Moat
BAYFORD
BAYFORD WOOD
Prim Sch
Hall
ROAD
BRICKENDON
STOCKING
BACK LANE
Fanshaws
SWEET
Little Berkhamsted
BREACH LANE
The Farmer Boy PH
FANSHAWS
ROBINS
Fanshaws Farm
Tenn Cts
Danes Farm
BUCKS
GIDNER'S WOOD
HARRY'S GROVE
BRICKENDON
BRICKENDON GREEN
LANE
ORCHARD CL
PO
THE BOUND
CHURCH
Five Horseshoes PH
SPORTS GRD
Hall
GODDARDS CL
MORLEY GROVE
Clubhouse
LITTLE BERKHAMSTED
ALLEY
EVES LOT
BUCK'S ALLEY WOOD
Poultry Houses
BELL'S WOOD
GRANGE
70
CLAY WOOD
Buck's Farm
SG13
Bush Farm
ASHENDENE
Airshaft
GOLF COURSE
STARCH GROVE
Poultry Houses
LANE
STUBBS
LANE
Kingfisher Garden Centre
Old Claypits Farm
The Beehive PH
ASHEN GROVE
Airshaft
CALAIS WOOD
HENDERSON
PLACE
Epping Green
DEVIL'S
Mast
ROAD
Homewood Farm
WHITE
Epping Green Farm
Ponsbourne Lodge Farm
CALVES GROVE
Bayford Kennels & Cattery
WHITE STUBBS
EAST HERTS
WELWYN HATFIELD
NEWGATE
Airshaft
OLD GROVE
GRANDSIDE GROVE
Woodcock Lodge Farm
Beavers Lodge Farm
STREET
Ponsbourne Tunnel
FB
CAUSEWAY
Tylers Causeway
Airshaft
WORMLEY WOOD NATURE RESERVE
Wormleybury Brook
BIRCH WOOD
NEWGATE
TYLERS
THE WARREN
THE ROUGHS
EAST HERTS
BROXBOURNE
Ponsfall Farm
Tenn Cts
Pav
Home Farm
Ponsbourne Park Hotel
Airshaft
HOTEL GOLF COURSE
DRIVE
WELLFIELD GROVE
WESTFIELD GROVE
FOREST HILLS
GOLF
Clubhouse
COURSE
DERRYS WOOD
LONG GROVE
Turnford Brook
Newpark Farm
THE
Boswell's Livery Stables
FB
HAZEL GROVE
Newgate Street
NEW PARK ROAD
Ponsbourne Riding Centre
CALVES CROFT
Turnford
Prim Sch
Home Farm
PO
Hall
REC GRD
Tenn Cts
NEWGATE
Tanfield Stud Farm
MILBROOK
GOLF
COURSE
Tolmers Park Farm
87
St. Lawrence Farm
EN7
TOLMERS
TOLMERS PK
VILLAGE
DARNICLE
HILL
Nursery
Newgate Street Bridge
SHAMBROOK
HAMMOND STREET
WALTERS
NIGHT
DAHLIA CL
BRACE CL
DH
DJ
DK
DL
DM
DN
DP
29
30
31
09
08
07
06
16
17
18
19
20
21
22
23
24

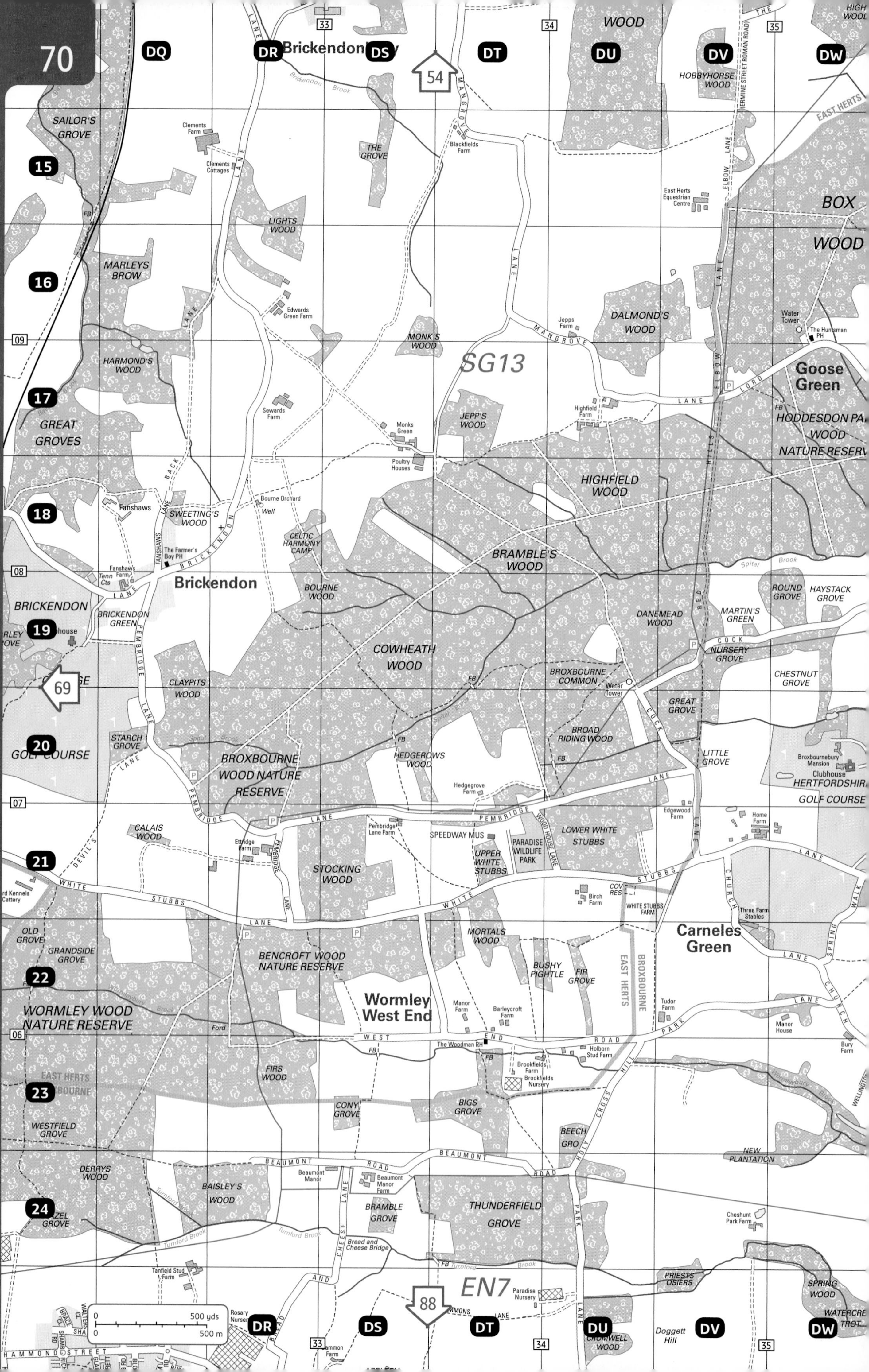
DQ
DR
Brickendonbury
DS
54
DT
DU
DV
DW
33
34
35
WOOD
HOBBYHORSE WOOD
ERMINE STREET ROMAN ROAD
EAST HERTS
Brickendon Brook
SAILOR'S GROVE
15
Clements Farm
Clements Cottages
LANE
MANGROVE
Blackfields Farm
THE GROVE
ELBOW LANE
East Herts Equestrian Centre
BOX WOOD
LIGHTS WOOD
MARLEYS BROW
16
LANE
Edwards Green Farm
DALMOND'S WOOD
Water Tower
The Huntsman PH
09
HARMOND'S WOOD
MONK'S WOOD
MANGROVE
Jepps Farm
SG13
Goose Green
17
Sewards Farm
Highfield Farm
LANE
LORD
JEPP'S WOOD
FB
HODDESDON PARK WOOD NATURE RESERVE
GREAT GROVES
Monks Green
Poultry Houses
BACK
HIGHFIELD WOOD
MILLS
Fanshaws
18
SWEETING'S WOOD
Bourne Orchard
Well
CELTIC HARMONY CAMP
FANSHAWS LANE
The Farmer's Boy PH
BRICKENDON
BRAMBLE'S WOOD
Spital Brook
08
Fanshaws Farm
Tenn Cts
LANE
Brickendon
BOURNE WOOD
ROUND GROVE
HAYSTACK GROVE
BRICKENDON
BRICKENDON GREEN
DANEMEAD WOOD
MARTIN'S GREEN
RED
19
COCK
NURSERY GROVE
PEMBRIDGE
COWHEATH WOOD
CHESTNUT GROVE
69
CLAYPITS WOOD
FB
BROXBOURNE COMMON
Water Tower
GREAT GROVE
COCK
STARCH GROVE
BROAD RIDING WOOD
20
GOLF COURSE
Spital Brook
FB
HEDGEROWS WOOD
LITTLE GROVE
BROXBOURNE WOOD NATURE RESERVE
FB
Broxbournebury Mansion
Clubhouse
HERTFORDSHIRE GOLF COURSE
LANE
Hedgegrove Farm
07
PEMBRIDGE
LANE
PEMBRIDGE
Edgewood Farm
CALAIS WOOD
Pembridge Lane Farm
SPEEDWAY MUS
WOOD HOUSE LANE
LOWER WHITE STUBBS
Home Farm
Ettridge Farm
PEMBRIDGE
PARADISE WILDLIFE PARK
UPPER WHITE STUBBS
LANE
DEVIL'S
STOCKING WOOD
21
Kennels Cattery
WHITE
STUBBS
LANE
STUBBS
CHURCH
WALK
COV RES
Birch Farm
WHITE STUBBS FARM
WHITE
Three Farm Stables
OLD GROVE
LANE
MORTALS WOOD
Carneles Green
SPRING
GRANDSIDE GROVE
BENCROFT WOOD NATURE RESERVE
BUSHY PIGHTLE
FIR GROVE
EAST HERTS
BROXBOURNE
LANE
22
Wormleybury Brook
Wormley West End
Tudor Farm
WORMLEY WOOD NATURE RESERVE
Manor Farm
Barleycroft Farm
CHURCH
Ford
PARK
Manor House
06
WEST
END
ROAD
The Woodman PH
FB
FB
Holborn Stud Farm
Bury Farm
EAST HERTS
BROXBOURNE
FIRS WOOD
Brookfields Farm
Brookfields Nursery
HILL
Wormleybury Brook
23
CONY GROVE
BIGS GROVE
CROSS
WESTFIELD GROVE
BEECH GROVE
HOLY
NEW PLANTATION
BEAUMONT
ROAD
BEAUMONT
ROAD
DERRYS WOOD
Beaumont Manor
Beaumont Manor Farm
BAISLEY'S WOOD
Turnford Brook
BRAMBLE GROVE
THUNDERFIELD GROVE
24
HAZEL GROVE
LANE
PARK
Cheshunt Park Farm
Turnford Brook
CHEESE
Bread and Cheese Bridge
FB
Turnford Brook
Tanfield Stud Farm
AND
PRIESTS OSIERS
SPRING WOOD
EN7
Paradise Nursery
88
Rosary Nursery
0
500 yds
0
500 m
DR
DS
DT
DU
DV
DW
LANE
Doggett Hill
CROMWELL WOOD
33
34
35
HAMMOND STREET

DX
DY
DZ
EA
EB
EC
ED
55
72
89
RSPB RYE MEADS
Visitor Centre
Sewage Works
Filter Beds
DELLS WOOD
Woollensbrook
HODDESDON
EN11
Rye Park
RYE HOUSE SPEEDWAY
KARTING CENTRE
Rye House Gatehouse
HODDESDON IND CEN
IMPRESA PARK
OPTIMA BUS PK
TRIDENT IND EST
Power Station
Gerald Game Bridge
MAPLE PARK
NICHOLSON CT
BELCON IND EST
Electricity Stations
Electricity Station
Dobb's Weir
HIGH LEIGH BARNS
HIGH LEIGH CONFERENCE CENTRE
BARCLAY PARK
Hoddesdon Town FC
SPORTS GROUND
ADMIRALS WALK LAKE
Spitalbrook
LUCERN WARREN
CRABTREE PLANTATION
ICEHOUSE GROVE
THE FERNERY
NAZEING MEAD
Dobb's Weir Lock
CM19
SLURRY PIT
Gasholder
BROXBOURNE
Sailing Club
CARTHAGENA ESTATE
BOATING LAKE
PLAIN LARCH
BROXBOURNE
COZENS GROVE
Baas Hill
Tudor House
KEYSERS ESTATE
GLASS MUS
HILLGROVE BUSINESS PARK
BROXBOURNE PAR 3 GOLF COURSE
EN10
Clubhouse
Chime Garden Centre
WORMLEY PLAYING FIELDS
Sports Club Pavs.
LEE VALLEY REGIONAL PARK
FLOOD RELIEF CHANNEL
Wormley
NURSERY WOOD
NAZEING MARSH
HERTFORDSHIRE
ESSEX
King's Weir
EN9
Sluice
Turnford
New River Arms
College
Turnford Marsh
HELL WOOD
Lower Nazeing
Clayton Hill
Oakleys Nursery
Hallmead Nursery
Lakeside Nursery
Paynes Farm
Paynes Farm Nursery
Larksmead Nursery
Leafield Nursery
Langridge Nursery
St. Leonards Farm
Mushroom Farm
HODDESDON BY PASS
A10
A1170
B194
16
17
18
19
20
21
22
23
24
36
37
38

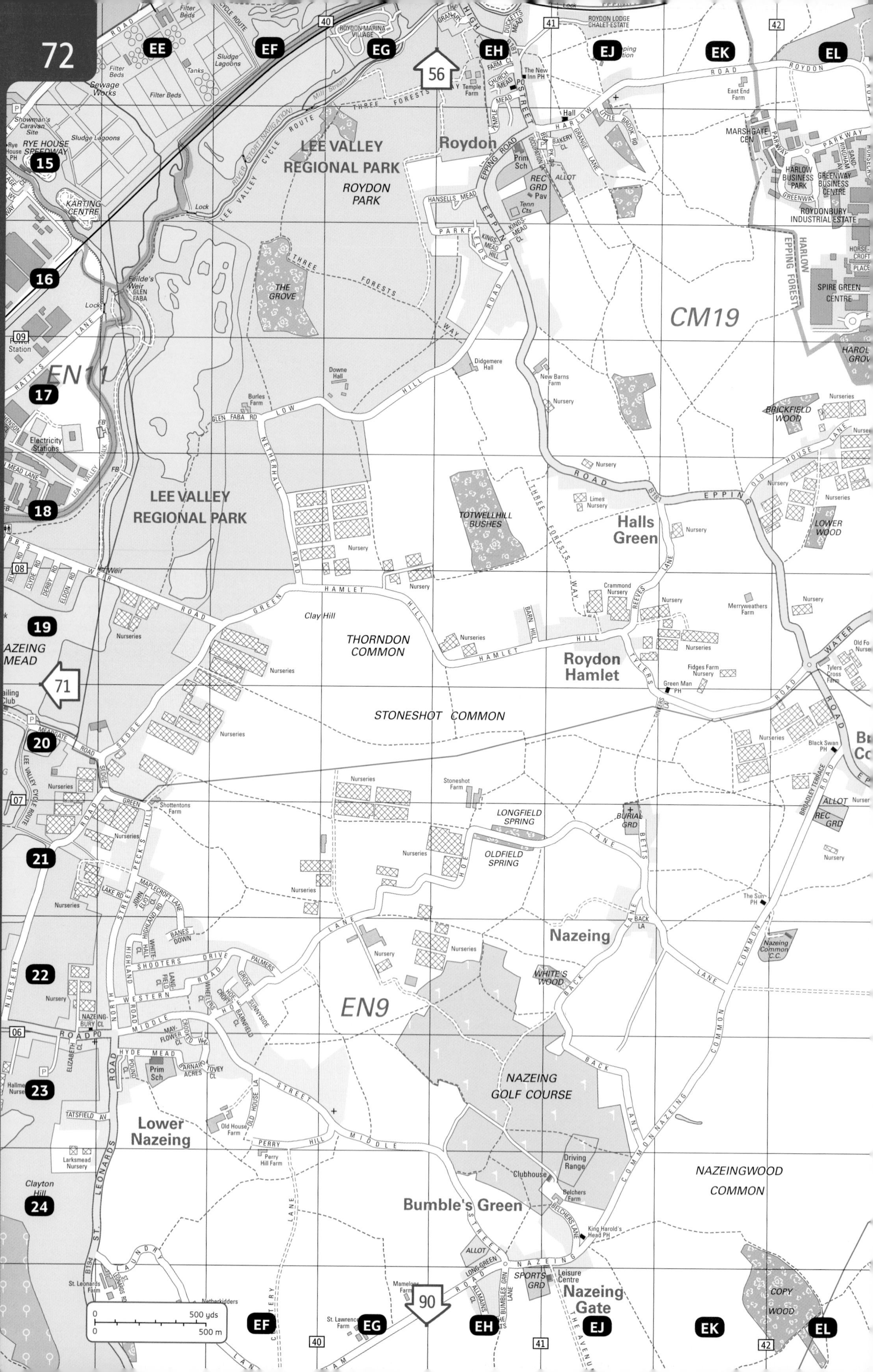
EE
EF
EG
EH
EJ
EK
EL
40
41
42
56
71
90
09
08
07
06
15
16
17
18
19
20
21
22
23
24
Filter Beds
Sewage Works
Sludge Lagoons
Tanks
Showman's Caravan Site
RYE HOUSE SPEEDWAY
Rye House PH
KARTING CENTRE
Lock
Feilde's Weir
GLEN FABA
Power Station
EN11
RATTY'S LANE
Electricity Stations
MEAD LANE
LEA VALLEY WALK
FB
ROYDON MARINA VILLAGE
ROYDON LODGE CHALET ESTATE
RIVER STORT (NAVIGATION)
Mill Stream
THREE FORESTS WAY
LEE VALLEY CYCLE ROUTE
LEE VALLEY REGIONAL PARK
ROYDON PARK
THE GROVE
Roydon
HIGH STREET
Temple Farm
FARM CL
CHURCH MEAD
The New Inn PH
Hall
HARLOW ROAD
LITTLE BROOK RD
GRANGE LANE
BAKERY CL
Prim Sch
REC GRD
Pav
Tenn Cts
ALLOT
EPPING ROAD
HANSELLS MEAD
PARKFIELDS
KINGSMEAD HILL
KINGSMEAD CL
ROYDON ROAD
East End Farm
MARSHGATE CEN
HARLOW BUSINESS PARK
GREENWAY BUSINESS CENTRE
ROYDONBURY INDUSTRIAL ESTATE
PARKWAY
HARLOW EPPING FOREST
HORSECROFT PLACE
SPIRE GREEN CENTRE
CM19
HAROLD GROVE
Didgemere Hall
New Barns Farm
Nursery
Downe Hall
Burles Farm
GLEN FABA RD
LOW HILL
NETHERHALL ROAD
BRICKFIELD WOOD
Nurseries
OLD HOUSE LANE
Limes Nursery
TOTWELLHILL BUSHES
Halls Green
EPPING ROAD
LOWER WOOD
LEE VALLEY REGIONAL PARK
WEIR ROAD
Weir
CLYDE RD
DERBY RD
ELDON RD
HAMLET HILL
Clay Hill
GREEN
THORNDON COMMON
Cranmond Nursery
REEVES LANE
BARN HILL
Merryweathers Farm
Roydon Hamlet
TYLERS ROAD
Fidges Farm Nursery
Green Man PH
WATER LANE
Old Fo Nurse
Tylers Cross Farm
NAZEING MEAD
Sailing Club
STONESHOT COMMON
TINKERS LA
Black Swan PH
MEADGATE ROAD
SEDGE GREEN
LEE VALLEY CYCLE ROUTE
Shottentons Farm
Stoneshot Farm
LONGFIELD SPRING
BURIAL GRD
BETTS LANE
BROADLEY TERRACE
ALLOT
REC GRD
PECKS HILL
HOE LANE
OLDFIELD SPRING
LAKE RD
MAPLECROFT LANE
JOHN EILOT CL
HIGHLAND RD
BANES DOWN
WHITE HALL CL
The Sun PH
BACK LA
Nazeing
Nazeing Common C.C.
SHOOTERS DRIVE
LANGFIELD CL
HOECROFT
PALMERS GROVE
WESTERN ROAD
WHEELERS CL
BARNFIELD
SUNNYSIDE
WHITE'S WOOD
BACK LANE
COMMON LANE
EN9
NURSERY ROAD
NAZEINGBURY CL
NORTH STREET
MIDDLE STREET
MAYFLOWER CL
CROOKED WAY
ROAD PO
ELIZABETH CL
HYDE MEAD
POUND CL
BARNARD ACRES
TOVEY CL
Prim Sch
Hallmead Nursery
NAZEING GOLF COURSE
OLD HOUSE LA
Lower Nazeing
TATSFIELD AV
Old House Farm
PERRY HILL
Perry Hill Farm
Larksmead Nursery
Clayton Hill
COMMON NAZEING
NAZEINGWOOD COMMON
Driving Range
Clubhouse
Belchers Farm
Bumble's Green
BELCHERS LANE
King Harold's Head PH
ST LEONARDS ROAD
B194
LAUNDRY LANE
CEMETERY LANE
ALLOT
LONG GREEN
NAZEING ROAD
SPORTS GRD
Leisure Centre
Nazeing Gate
THE AVENUE
ALLMAINS CL
BUMBLES GRN LANE
COPY WOOD
St. Leonards Farm
Netherkidders
Mamelons Farm
St. Lawrence Farm
0
500 yds
500 m

CANONS BROOK GOLF COURSE
HARLOW STADIUM
Little Parndon
PRINCESS ALEXANDRA HOSPITAL
Netteswell
CM20
HARLOW
Harlow College
Crown Gate Roundabout
SECOND AVENUE
A1025
NETTLESWELL PLANTATION
Pinnacles
COLDHARBOUR PINNACLES ESTATE
HARLOW BUSINESS CENTRE
Whitehall Roundabout
THIRD AVENUE
NEW FRONTIERS SCIENCE PARK
Hare Street
Great Parndon
CM18
Passmores House
Brays Grove
Tye Green
Passmores
Katherines
KATHERINES WAY
A1169
SOUTHERN WAY
THE LATTON BUSH CENTRE
Latton Bush
Stewards
Staple Tye Shop Cen
Sumners
Leisure Centre
BURNETT'S WOOD
MAUND'S WOOD
Kingsmoor
PARNDON WOOD NATURE RESERVE
PARNDON WOOD CEM
RISDEN'S WOOD
HOSPITAL WOOD
Jacks Hatch
Rye Hill
Dorrington Farm
Rivetts Farm
HARLOW EPPING FOREST
CM16
Marles Farm
Sumners Farm
Travellers Friend PH
Epping Green
EPPING LONG GRN
Epping Upland
Hayleys Manor Farm
BARN MEADOW
Rose Farm
Pinch Timber Farm
Cobbin's Brook
B181
EPPING GREEN ROAD
57
74
91
EM EN EP EQ ER ES ET
43 44 45
16 17 18 19 20 21 22 23 24
09 08 07 06

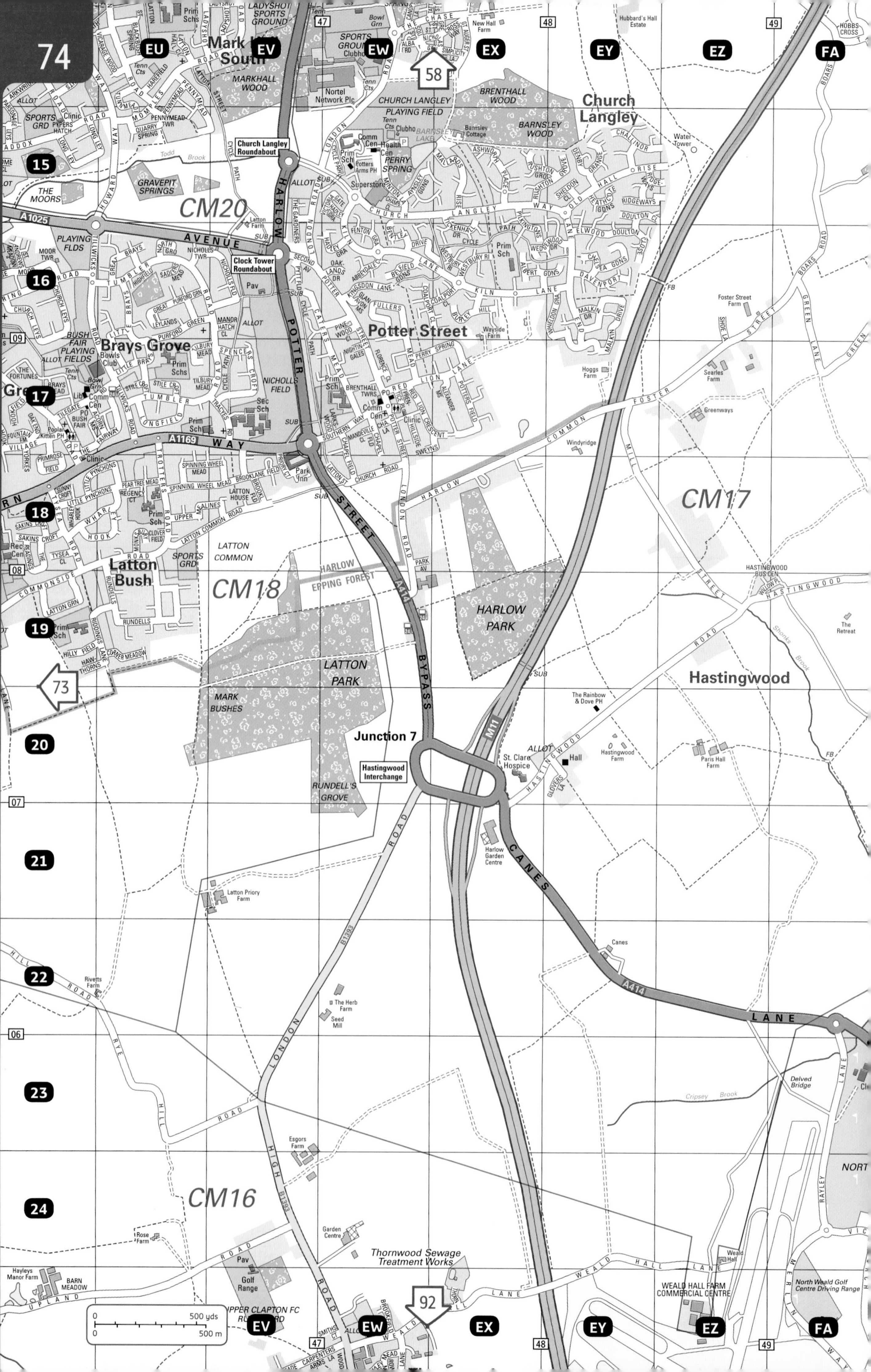
EU
EV
EW
EX
EY
EZ
FA
47
48
49
58
73
92
15
16
17
18
19
20
21
22
23
24
09
08
07
06
Mark Hall South
MARKHALL WOOD
SPORTS GROUND
Nortel Network Plc
CHURCH LANGLEY PLAYING FIELD
BRENTHALL WOOD
BARNSLEY WOOD
Church Langley
Hubbard's Hall Estate
HOBBS CROSS
New Hall Farm
THE CHASE
Church Langley Roundabout
Clock Tower Roundabout
GRAVEPIT SPRINGS
THE MOORS
CM20
A1025
AVENUE
HARLOW
POTTER
STREET
Potters Arms PH
Superstore
PERRY SPRING
CHURCH LANGLEY WAY
KILN LANE
Barnsley Cottage
Water Tower
Potter Street
Brays Grove
Bowls Club
BUSH FAIR PLAYING FIELDS
NICHOLLS FIELD
Sec Sch
Prim Schs
Foster Street Farm
Hoggs Farm
Searles Farm
Greenways
Windyridge
Wayside Farm
FOSTER STREET
A1169
WAY
Park Inn
CHURCH ROAD
LATTON COMMON
Latton Bush
CM18
HARLOW EPPING FOREST
A414
BYPASS
HARLOW PARK
CM17
HASTINGWOOD BUS CEN
HASTINGWOOD ROAD
The Retreat
Shonks Brook
Hastingwood
The Rainbow & Dove PH
M11
LATTON PARK
MARK BUSHES
Junction 7
Hastingwood Interchange
RUNDELL'S GROVE
St. Clare Hospice
Hall
Hastingwood Farm
Paris Hall Farm
Harlow Garden Centre
CANES
Canes
A414
LANE
Latton Priory Farm
Rivetts Farm
HILL ROAD
RYE HILL ROAD
LONDON ROAD
B1393
The Herb Farm
Seed Mill
Delved Bridge
Cripsey Brook
Esgors Farm
HIGH ROAD
CM16
Rose Farm
Garden Centre
Thornwood Sewage Treatment Works
Weald Hall
WEALD HALL LANE
WEALD HALL FARM COMMERCIAL CENTRE
North Weald Golf Centre Driving Range
Hayleys Manor Farm
BARN MEADOW
UPLAND ROAD
Pav
Golf Range
UPPER CLAPTON FC
0
500 yds
0
500 m
NORT

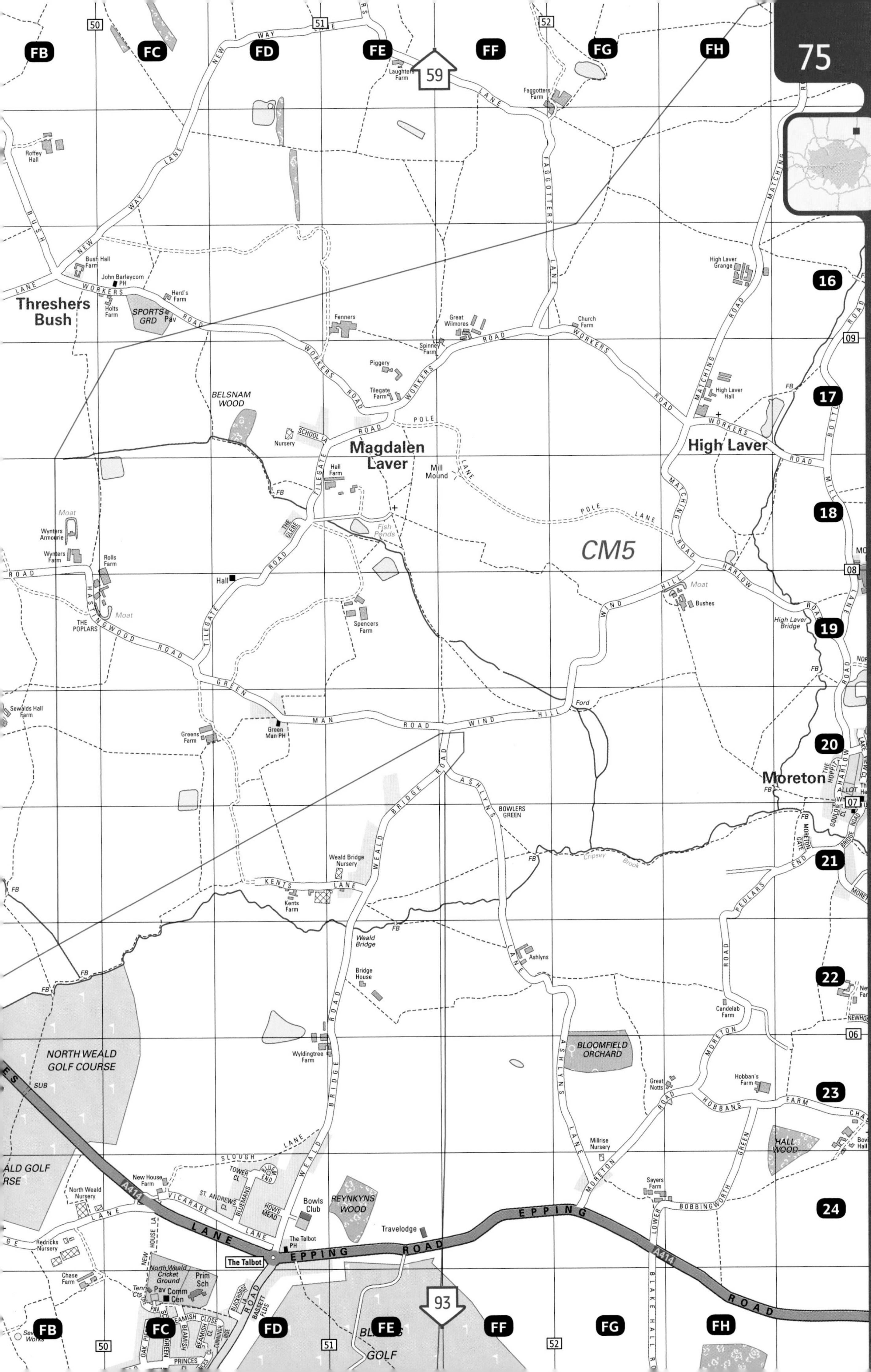
FB
FC
FD
FE
FF
FG
FH
50
51
52
59
Laughters Farm
Faggotters Farm
Roffey Hall
NEW WAY LANE
BUSH LANE
FAGGOTTERS LANE
MATCHING ROAD
Bush Hall Farm
John Barleycorn PH
Herd's Farm
Holts Farm
Threshers Bush
SPORTS GRD
Pav
WORKERS ROAD
Fenners
Great Wilmores
Spinney Farm
Church Farm
High Laver Grange
16
09
Piggery
Tilegate Farm
High Laver Hall
17
BELSNAM WOOD
SCHOOL LA
POLE LANE
Nursery
Magdalen Laver
High Laver
Mill Mound
Hall Farm
TILEGATE ROAD
FB
Moat
Wynters Armourie
Wynters Farm
Rolls Farm
THE GLEBE
Fish Ponds
CM5
18
Hall
HARLOW ROAD
Moat
Bushes
08
Moat
THE POPLARS
HASTINGWOOD ROAD
Spencers Farm
WIND HILL
High Laver Bridge
19
GREEN MAN ROAD
Ford
Sewalds Hall Farm
Greens Farm
Green Man PH
20
Moreton
ASHLYNS
BOWLERS GREEN
BRIDGE ROAD
07
Weald Bridge Nursery
FB
Cripsey Brook
MORETON GATE
21
KENTS LANE
Kents Farm
PEDLARS END
FB
Weald Bridge
Ashlyns
Bridge House
22
FB
Candelab Farm
NORTH WEALD GOLF COURSE
WEALD BRIDGE ROAD
BLOOMFIELD ORCHARD
06
Wyldingtree Farm
MORETON ROAD
Hobban's Farm
Great Notts
HOBBANS FARM
23
SUB
HALL WOOD
SLOUGH LANE
Millrise Nursery
ALD GOLF RSE
New House Farm
TOWER CL
North Weald Nursery
ST. ANDREWS CL
BLUEMANS
VICARAGE LANE
HOWS MEAD
Bowls Club
REYNKYNS WOOD
Sayers Farm
BOBBINGWORTH GREEN
24
EPPING ROAD
A414
Redricks Nursery
Travelodge
The Talbot PH
The Talbot
LOWER BOBBINGWORTH GREEN
BLAKE HALL ROAD
North Weald Cricket Ground
Prim Sch
Chase Farm
Pav
Comm Cen
Tenn Cts
BEAMISH CLOSE
BASSETT FLDS
BLACKHORSE ROAD
PRINCES CL
93
GOLF

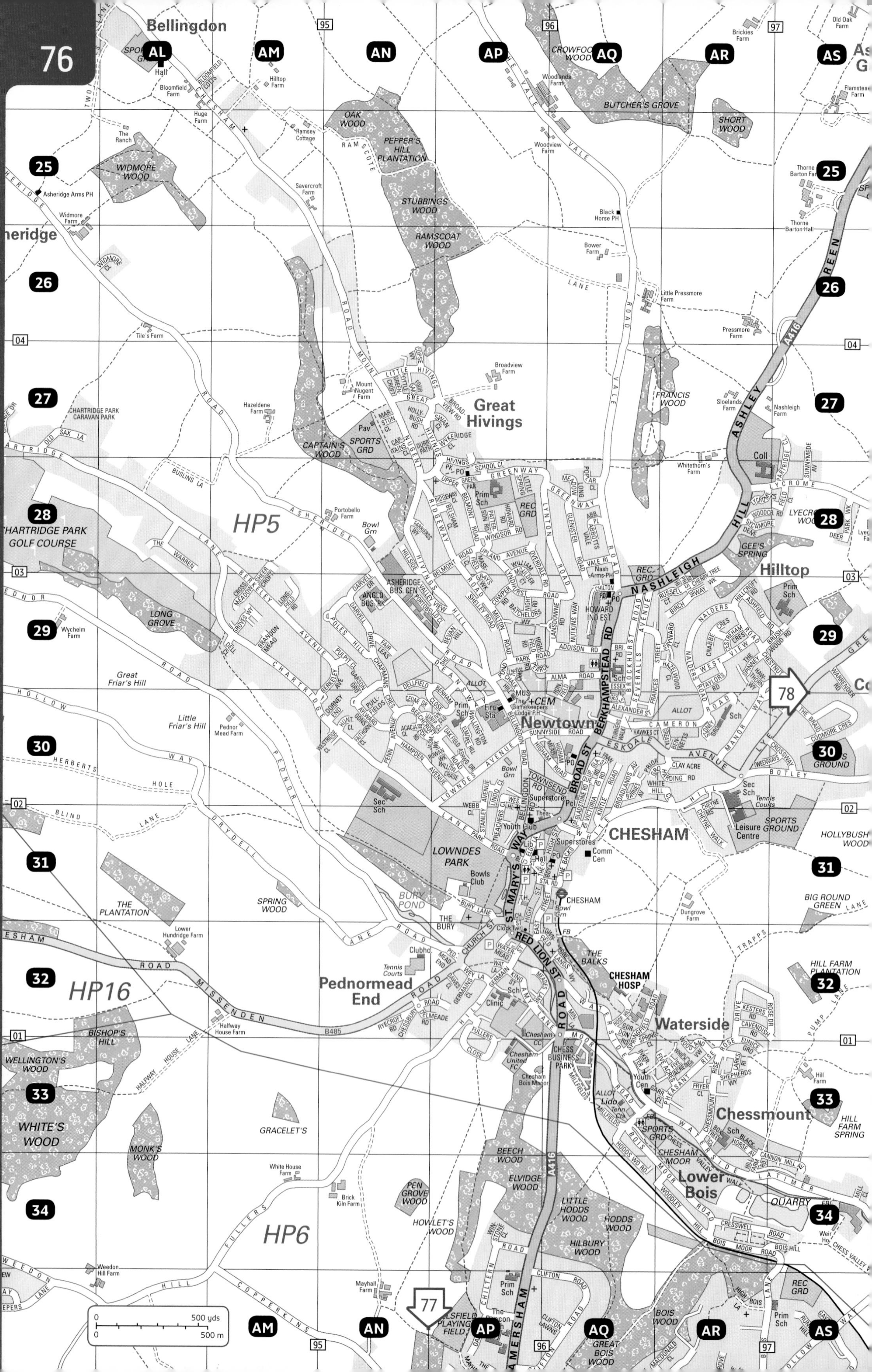

Bellingdon
AL
AM
AN
AP
AQ
AR
AS
95
96
97
Hall
Bloomfield Farm
Huge Farm
CHESHAM
The Ranch
Hilltop Farm
Ramsey Cottage
OAK WOOD
PEPPER'S HILL PLANTATION
RAMSCOTE
CROWFOOT WOOD
Woodlands Farm
BUTCHER'S GROVE
SHORT WOOD
Woodview Farm
VALE
Brickies Farm
Old Oak Farm
Flamstead Farm
25
WIDMORE WOOD
Asheridge Arms PH
Savercroft Farm
STUBBINGS WOOD
Black Horse PH
Thorne Barton Farm
Thorne Barton Hall
Widmore Farm
heridge
RAMSCOAT WOOD
Bower Farm
LANE
26
WIDMORE CL
Little Pressmore Farm
Pressmore Farm
04
Tile's Farm
MOUNT
ROAD
Broadview Farm
A416
27
CHARTRIDGE PARK CARAVAN PARK
Hazeldene Farm
Mount Nugent Farm
Great Hivings
FRANCIS WOOD
Sloelands Farm
Nashleigh Farm
ASHLEY
OLD SAX LA
CAPTAIN'S WOOD
SPORTS GRD
Pav
Coll
Whitethorn's Farm
BUSLINS LA
28
CHARTRIDGE PARK GOLF COURSE
HP5
Portobello Farm
Bowl Grn
REC GRD
LYECROFT WOOD
GEE'S SPRING
THE WARREN
ASHERIDGE BUS. CEN
Hilltop
03
NASHLEIGH
HILL
HOWARD IND EST
Nash Arms PH
LONG GROVE
29
Wychelm Farm
ANGLO BUS. PK
BERKHAMSTEAD RD
Great Friar's Hill
ALLOT
MUS
The Gamekeepers Lodge PH
CEM
Newtown
78
30
Little Friar's Hill
Pednor Mead Farm
HERBERTS
HOLE
WAY
BROAD ST
SUNNYSIDE ROAD
ESKDALE
AVENUE
CAMERON
GROUND
02
BLIND
LANE
Sec Sch
Superstore
Superstores
CHESHAM
Leisure Centre
SPORTS GROUND
Tennis Courts
HOLLYBUSH WOOD
31
LOWNDES PARK
Bowls Club
Comm Cen
Lib
SPRING WOOD
BURY POND
THE BURY
CHESHAM
Dungrove Farm
BIG ROUND GREEN
TRAPPS
THE PLANTATION
Lower Hundridge Farm
ESHAM
ROAD
Clubhouse
Tennis Courts
Pednormead End
THE BALKS
CHESHAM HOSP
HILL FARM PLANTATION
32
HP16
MISSENDEN
B485
Waterside
PUMP LANE
01
BISHOP'S HILL
Halfway House Farm
Clinic
Chesham CC
CHESS BUSINESS PARK
Chesham United FC
Chesham Bois Manor
Hill Farm
WELLINGTON'S WOOD
33
WHITE'S WOOD
MONK'S WOOD
GRACELET'S
Youth Cen
Lido
Chessmount
HILL FARM SPRING
BEECH WOOD
ELVIDGE WOOD
SPORTS GRD
CHESHAM MOOR
Lower Bois
White House Farm
Brick Kiln Farm
PEN GROVE WOOD
LITTLE HODDS WOOD
HODDS WOOD
HILBURY WOOD
QUARRY
34
HP6
HOWLET'S WOOD
Weir Ho
CHESS VALLEY
Weedon Hill Farm
COPPERKINS
Mayhall Farm
77
CLIFTON ROAD
REC GRD
Prim Sch
BOIS WOOD
GREAT BOIS WOOD
AMERSHAM
0
500 yds
500 m

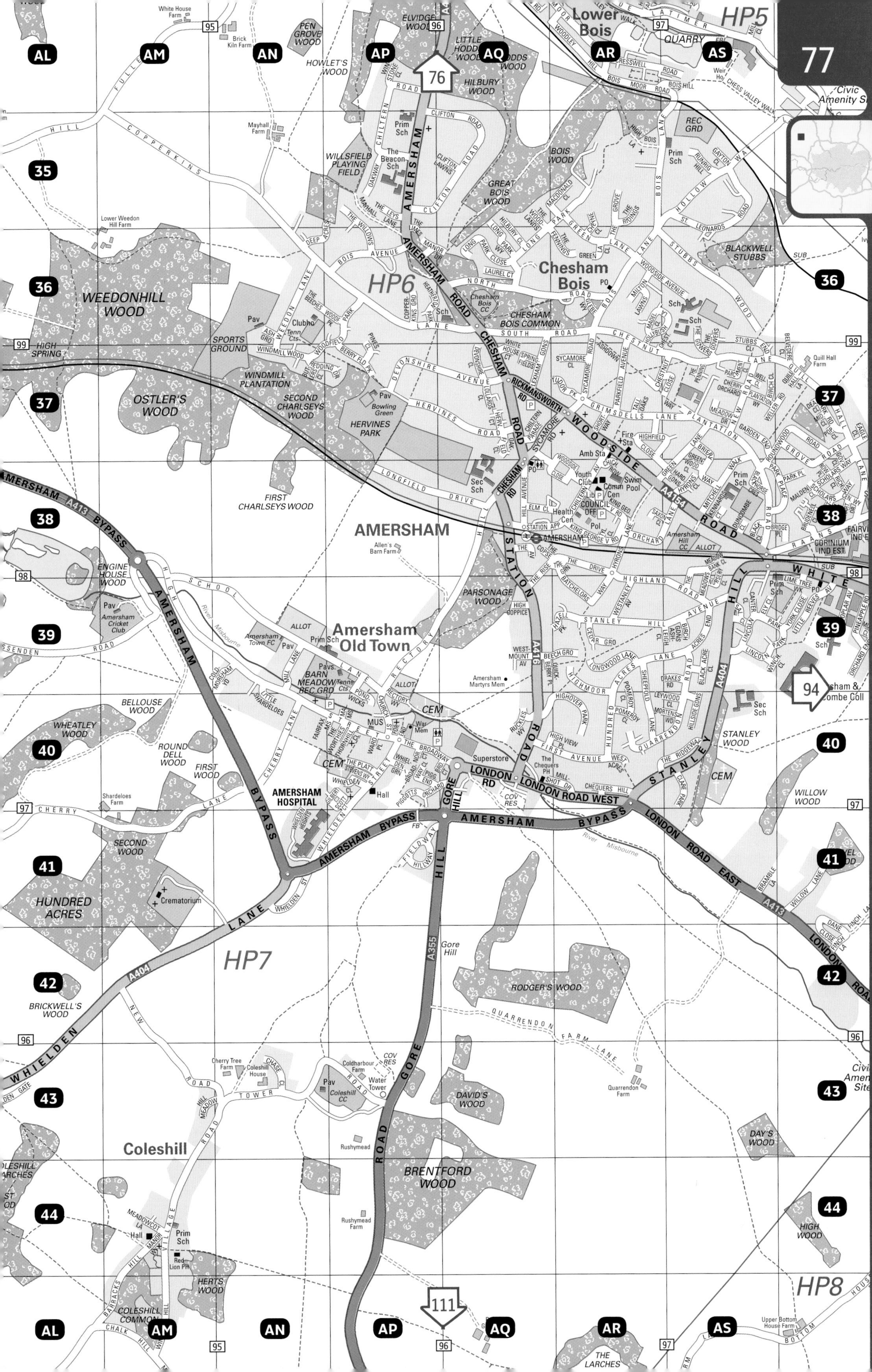

AL
AM
AN
AP
AQ
AR
AS
35
36
37
38
39
40
41
42
43
44
76
94
111
HP5
HP6
HP7
HP8
Lower Bois
Chesham Bois
AMERSHAM
Amersham Old Town
Coleshill
WEEDONHILL WOOD
OSTLER'S WOOD
WINDMILL PLANTATION
SECOND CHARLSEYS WOOD
FIRST CHARLSEYS WOOD
HERVINES PARK
SPORTS GROUND
HIGH SPRING
ENGINE HOUSE WOOD
Amersham Cricket Club
BELLOUSE WOOD
WHEATLEY WOOD
ROUND DELL WOOD
FIRST WOOD
SECOND WOOD
Shardeloes Farm
HUNDRED ACRES
Crematorium
BRICKWELL'S WOOD
AMERSHAM HOSPITAL
PARSONAGE WOOD
Allen's Barn Farm
Amersham Martyrs Mem
STANLEY WOOD
WILLOW WOOD
Gore Hill
RODGER'S WOOD
DAVID'S WOOD
BRENTFORD WOOD
Rushymead
Rushymead Farm
Coldharbour Farm
Water Tower
Coleshill CC
Cherry Tree Farm
Coleshill House
Quarrendon Farm
DAY'S WOOD
HIGH WOOD
HERTS WOOD
COLESHILL COMMON
Upper Bottom House Farm
THE LARCHES
Lower Weedon Hill Farm
Mayhall Farm
White House Farm
Brick Kiln Farm
PEN GROVE WOOD
HOWLET'S WOOD
ELVIDGE WOOD
LITTLE HODDS WOOD
HODDS WOOD
HILBURY WOOD
WILLSFIELD PLAYING FIELD
GREAT BOIS WOOD
BOIS WOOD
BLACKWELL STUBBS
CHESHAM BOIS COMMON
REC GRD
Quill Hall Farm
Civic Amenity Site
CORINIUM IND EST
FAIRVIEW IND EST
AMERSHAM BYPASS
AMERSHAM ROAD
CHESHAM ROAD
RICKMANSWORTH RD
WOODSIDE ROAD
STATION ROAD
LONDON ROAD WEST
LONDON ROAD EAST
WHIELDEN LANE
GORE HILL
GORE ROAD
STANLEY HILL
WHITE LION ROAD
QUARRENDON FARM LANE
CHERRY LANE
COPPERKINS LANE
SOUTH ROAD
LONGFIELD DRIVE
HIGHLAND ROAD
BOIS AVENUE
THE BROADWAY
A413
A416
A4154
A355
A404

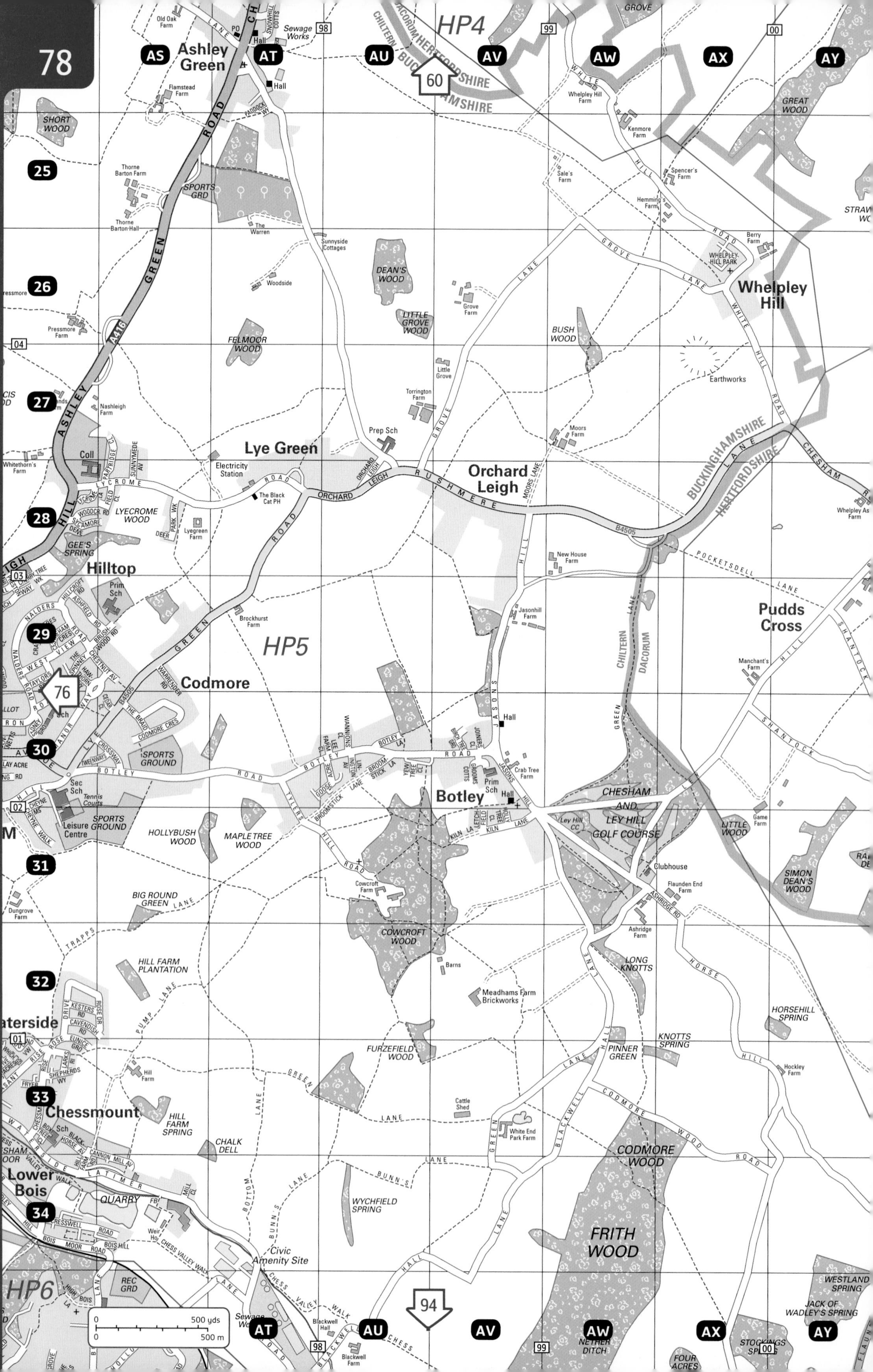
HP4
HP5
HP6
60
76
94
AS
AT
AU
AV
AW
AX
AY
25
26
27
28
29
30
31
32
33
34
98
99
00
04
03
02
01
Ashley Green
Old Oak Farm
PO
Hall
SNOWHILL COTTS
Sewage Works
CHILTERN
DACORUM
HERTFORDSHIRE
BUCKINGHAMSHIRE
GROVE
Flamstead Farm
PADDOCK WY
SHORT WOOD
GREAT WOOD
Whelpley Hill Farm
Kenmore Farm
Thorne Barton Farm
SPORTS GRD
Sale's Farm
Spencer's Farm
Hemming's Farm
Thorne Barton Hall
The Warren
Sunnyside Cottages
Berry Farm
WHELPLEY HILL PARK
Whelpley Hill
DEAN'S WOOD
Woodside
Grove Farm
LITTLE GROVE WOOD
Pressmore
Pressmore Farm
A416
FELMOOR WOOD
BUSH WOOD
Little Grove
Earthworks
Torrington Farm
Nashleigh Farm
ASHLEY GREEN ROAD
Prep Sch
Moors Farm
Lye Green
Coll
Whitethorn's Farm
PARTRIDGE CL
SUNNYMEDE AV
Electricity Station
Orchard Leigh
MOORS LANE
LYCROME ROAD
The Black Cat PH
ORCHARD LEIGH
RUSHMERE LANE
CHESHAM ROAD
Whelpley Ash Farm
LYECROME WOOD
WOODCR RD
SYCAMORE DENE
PARK WK
DEER
Lyegreen Farm
B4505
GEE'S SPRING
POCKETSDELL LANE
New House Farm
Hilltop
HILLCROFT RD
Prim Sch
NALDERS
ASHFIELD RD
Brockhurst Farm
Jasonhill Farm
Pudds Cross
WEST
Manchant's Farm
SHANTOCK HALL LANE
Codmore
WARRENDER RD
CHESTNUT AV
JASONS HILL
Hall
CODMORE CRES
THE BRAID
CEDAR
CROSSWAY
TWEENWAYS
SPORTS GROUND
Sec Sch
Tennis Courts
BOTLEY ROAD
BOTLEY LA
WANNIONS CL
Crab Tree Farm
Botley
Sch
Leisure Centre
CHESHAM AND LEY HILL GOLF COURSE
Ley Hill CC
LITTLE WOOD
Game Farm
HOLLYBUSH WOOD
MAPLE TREE WOOD
TYLERS HILL ROAD
BROOMSTICK LANE
KILN LANE
KILN LA
Clubhouse
Flaunden End Farm
ASHRIDGE RD
SIMON DEAN'S WOOD
BIG ROUND GREEN LANE
Cowcroft Farm
Dungrove Farm
COWCROFT WOOD
Ashridge Farm
HORSE HILL
TRAPPS
HILL FARM PLANTATION
Barns
LONG KNOTTS
PUMP LANE
Meadhams Farm Brickworks
HORSEHILL SPRING
aterside
KESTERS RD
CAVENDISH RD
ROSE DR
EUNICE GR
SHEPHERDS WY
Hill Farm
FURZEFIELD WOOD
KNOTTS SPRING
PINNER GREEN
HALL LANE
Hockley Farm
GREEN LANE
Cattle Shed
Chessmount
Sch
HILL FARM SPRING
CODMORE WOOD ROAD
White End Park Farm
BLACKWELL HALL LANE
CHALK DELL
CODMORE WOOD
Lower Bois
LATIMER RD
CANNON MILL AV
QUARRY
MILL CL
BUNN'S LANE
BOTTOM LANE
WYCHFIELD SPRING
FRITH WOOD
RESSWELL ROAD
BOIS MOOR ROAD
BOIS HILL
Weir Ho
CHESS VALLEY WALK
Civic Amenity Site
REC GRD
WESTLAND SPRING
JACK OF WADLEY'S SPRING
HIGH BOIS LA
Sewage Works
Blackwell Hall
Blackwell Farm
500 yds
500 m
NETHER DITCH
STOCKINGS SPRING
FOUR ACRES
FLAUNDEN

HP1
HP3
WD3
WD4
Bovingdon
Hogpits Bottom
Flaunden
Belsize
COLESHILL WOOD
HANGING WOOD
GOLF COMPLEX
Clubhouse
Prep Sch
HAY WOOD
BOXMOOR GOLF COURSE
SHEETHANGER COMMON
Felden Lodge
Howe's Retreat
RAMACRE WOOD
GORSEFIELD WOOD
BURY WOOD
BOX LANE
BURY RISE
UPPER BOURNE END LANE
COVERED RESERVOIR
ROAD
B4505
BUSHFIELD ROAD
SHOTHANGER WAY
Longcroft Farm
LONGCROFT
RAINHILL SPRING
RAINHILL DELL
KINGSHILL DELL
Macdonald Bobsleigh Hotel
Disused Airfield
H.M. THE MOUNT PRISON
Duckhall Farm
Honours Farm
Random Farm
HOMEFIELD SPRING
STONEY LANE
Bury Farm
SHORTRIDGE WOOD
OLD DEAN
FLAUNDEN LANE
BULSTRODE LANE
HEMPSTEAD ROAD
CHESHAM ROAD
Lib
Sch
Hall
PO
CHURCH ST
VICARAGE LANE
BALFOUR MEWS
MOLYNEAUX AVENUE
HYDE LANE
HYDE MEADOWS
RYDER CLOSE
CHIPPERFIELD ROAD
Lane Farm
Dormers
Nuffield Farm
RUCKLERS LANE
LONGCROFT LANE
Street Farm
Rent Street Farm
Darley Ash
Greinan Farm
Bulstrode Farm
Cross Farm
Bovingdon Grange
Grange Farm
Pav
Bovingdon FC
BOVINGDON GREEN
Green Farm
GREEN LANE
kworks
TOWER HILL
Bryants Nurseries
Wyevale Garden Centre
Tenements Farm
NEW RD
The Boot PH
Stoney Lane Nursery
STONEY LA
Tuffs Farm
Frenches Farm
Chipperfield House
SCATTERDELLS
BAKER'S WOOD
Bell Farm
HUNTERS CL
THE HOLLIES
Long Lane Farm
MIDDLE LANE
WATER LANE
Riding School
Cottingham Farm
Mast
Meadow Way Farm
Shantock Nursery
Shantock Farm
Chiltern Farm
LONG LANE
VENUS HILL
Venus Hill Dairy Farm
HOLLY HEDGES LANE
Crumlin Farm
New Maulden Farm
Garden Centre
CHAPEL CROFT
Royal Oak PH
Prim Sch
Hall
Pav
Tenn Cts
ALLOT
THE COMMON
Rose Farm
WOODMAN'S WOOD
Woodman's Farm
FLAUNDEN PARK
HOGPITS BOTTOM
Bricklayer's Arms PH
LOWER PLANTATION
OLLEBERRIE LANE
WINDMILL HILL
LITTLE WINDMILL HILL
DUNNY LANE
Cherry Tree Farm
Olleberrie Farm
The Plough PH
PENMAN'S GREEN
PENMANS HILL
Stables
Sharlowe's Farm
BIRCH LANE
HOG PITS
Dale Farm
FLAUNDEN LANE
Hall
FLAUNDEN SPRING
FLAUNDEN HILL
Springview Farm
LIMEDELL SPRING
Whitedell Farm
BRAGMANS LANE
POLES HILL
PLOUGH LANE
Hillmeads Farm
Newhouse Farm
Rose Hall Farm
DEBARDINE WOOD
ROSEHALL WOOD
PLOUGH WOOD
HILLMEADS SPRING
BOTTOM
HANGING CROFT
Moonshine Farm
Great Sarratt Hall Farm
Great Sarratt Hall
DACORUM
THREE RIVERS
CHENIES HILL
Mast
R.A.F. Chenies
TOP SPRING
OLDCROFT WOOD
LONG WOOD
Martin Top Farm
BRAMBLE
HANGINGLANE WOOD
DAFFODIL SPRING
THE RED LION
The Boot PH
AZ
BA
BB
BC
BD
BE
BF
01
02
03
04
61
80
95
26
27
28
29
30
31
32
33
34

BG
BH
BJ
BK
BL
BM
BN
62
79
96
Felden
Three Fields Farm
Felden Lodge
Howe's Retreat
Tower Farm
Felden Grange
Felden Manor
HP3
Apsley
APSLEY MILLS RETAIL PARK
Superstore
Holiday Inn Express
SHENDISH MANOR GOLF COURSE
COCK'S HEAD WOOD
HEN'S HEAD WOOD
THE COURTYARD
SHENDISH MANOR
GRAND UNION CANAL
A4251
LONDON ROAD
TWO WATERS
A41
LANGLEY BYPASS
KINGS LANGLEY BYPASS
GREAT WOOD
PHASELS WOOD
Phasels Wood Activity Centre
OLD DEAN
RUCKLERS LANE
RUCKLERS WOOD
DARK WOOD
THE HANGINGS
THE NUCKET
MERCEYS WOOD
BARNES LANE
Barnes Farm
Barnes Lodge
HEMPSTEAD ROAD
Hall
Rec Cen
Shafford's Knoll Farm
SCATTERDELLS WOOD
THE GROVE
THE WINGS
Sec Sch
Prim Sch
Hill Farm
KING LANGLEY COMMON
Kings Langley C.C.
Priory (Remains of)
Premier Travel Inn
Rectory Farm
Kings Langley
CEM
Wayside Farm
Meggacres Farm
Whippendell Farm
Whippendell Bottom
Whippendell Hill
CHIPPERFIELD ROAD
Ballspond Farm
Kings Langley Riding School
The Boot PH
Chipperfield House
Garden Centre
Chipperfield
Royal Oak PH
Two Brewers PH
Rose Farm
Chipperfield CC
WD4
ROOKERY WOOD
Manor House
Berrybush Farm
Sunbury Hill Farm
Langley Lodge
Langley Lodge Farm
Burlew Farm
Middle Farm
LANGLEY LODGE LANE
CHIPPERFIELD COMMON
PENMAN'S GREEN
Belsize
DACORUM
THREE RIVERS
Hillmeads Farm
Callipers Hall
Callipers Hall Farm
BERRYBUSHES WOOD
DELLSHOT SPRING
DEBARDINE WOOD
PLOUGH WOOD
HILLMEADS SPRING
Cart & Horses PH
QUICKMOOR LANE
Baytree Farm
Model Farm
SHEEPCOTE SPRING
LANGLEYBURY FIELDS
Commonwood
COMMONWOOD COMMON
HAWK SPRING
Bucks Hill
Bucks Hill Farm
Great Sarratt Hall
BEECHEN BOTTOM
Little Westwood Farm
Sarratt
The Boot PH
HIGH SPRING
JUNIPER
500 yds
500 m
25
26
27
28
29
30
31
32
33
34
01
02
03
04
05
06
07

BP
BQ
BR
BS
BT
BU
BV
08
09
10
63
82
97
POTTERS CROUCH PLANTATION
LONG DEANS
HP3
Sports Hall
Highwood Hall Farm
High Herts Farm
Bedmond House
Rose Acre
Radio Station
Hyde Meadow Farm
HYDE LANE SPRING
Hyde Springs
Hyde Farm
Hyde Lane Farm
Hart Hall Farm
NEW PLANTATION
Hart Hall
Green End Farm
White House Farm
Woodlands Poultry Farm
Verulam Farm
NEWLANDS PARK
ST. ALBANS
THREE RIVERS
WELLFIELD SPRING
DEADMAN WOOD
BEDMOND WOOD
PIECORNER WOOD
HANGING WOOD
FURZEFIELD WOOD
JOB'S WOOD
Whitehouse Farm
Searches Farm
Millhouse Farm
Ninnings Farm
Poultry Farm
Tenements Farm
WD5
Bedmond
Bell Inn PH
BEDMOND PLAYING FIELDS
Prim Sch
MOOR WOOD
LONG SPRING
Hilltop Farm
HIGH VIEW CARAVAN PARK
Benmore Farm
Glasshouse
GREAT NOTLEY
M25
M1
Junction
Junction
STOWES WOOD
LITTLE NOTLEY
Mansion House Farm
COV RES
Numbers Farm
LONG WOOD
ROUND WOOD
Wind Turbine & Renewable Energy Systems
KINGLEY PK
Fishing Club
MONACO WORKS
HOME PK IND. EST.
KINGS LANGLEY
CEM
Fortunes Farm
BLOOM WOOD
LEAVESDEN COUNTRY PARK
ABBOTS LANGLEY
MANOR HOUSE GROUNDS
The Compasses PH
TANNERS WOOD
LEAVESDEN COUNTRY PARK
Junction 20
WATFORD ROAD
GRAND UNION CANAL
WOODSIDE STADIUM
Leisure Cen
WD25
ALBAN WOOD
WOODSIDE PLAYING FIELDS
Watford Town C.C.
Leisure Park
Hunton Bridge
The Kings Head
Langleybury
THE ROOKERY
SPORTS GROUND
Langleybury Children's Farm
Home Farm
SOUTH WAY PLAYING FLD
Leavesden Studios
Hunton Park
HILL FARM IND EST
Woodside
Leavesden Green
NORTH ORBITAL ROAD
A405
A41
KINGSWAY
Kingswood
Garston
Airshafts
NORTH WATFORD CEMETERY
STANBOROUGH PARK
WESTERN AVENUE
Hunton Bridge
Leavesden Green
26
27
28
29
30
31
32
33
34
04
03
02
01

BW
BX
BY
BZ
CA
CB
CC
64
81
98
25
26
27
28
29
30
31
32
33
34
12
13
14
04
03
02
01
APPSPOND WOOD
PARK WOOD
Westfields Farm
Holly Bush PH
Potters Crouch East Farm
Potters Crouch Farm
SQUARE WOOD
SCRUBBS WOOD
Cuckman's Farm
Park Street Roundabout
ST. JULIAN'S WOOD
Prim Sch
WATLING STREET CARAVAN SITE (TRAVELL
Potters Crouch
WELLFIELD SPRING
Plaistowes Farm
Royal Entemological Society
Bone Hill
RNRS GDNS OF THE ROSE
Chiswellgreen Farm
Three Hammers PH
GREENWOOD PARK
Pavs
Tennis Courts
AL2
Chiswell Green
Whitehouse Farm
Noke Farm
Noke Lane Business Centre
Thistle
Burston Manor Farm
Moat
Birchwood Farm
Burston Garden Centre
HOLT WOOD
Holt Farm
Searches Farm
Millhouse Farm
BIRCH WOOD
SPIELPLATZ
SUNFOLKS
Sch
WD5
Junction 21A
Junction 21 M25
Junction 6A M1
WINCH HILL WOOD
Bricket Wood
BLACKGREEN WOOD
BLACKGREEN WOOD
BLACK GREEN
SMUG OAK GREEN BUSINESS CENTRE
HORSESHOE BUSINESS PARK
Social Club
SMUG OAK GREEN
The Gate PH
Hall
SPORTS GROUND
THE LAKES
Sports Centre
Fortunes Farm
Junction 6
Waterdale
BLOOM WOOD
Prim Sch
BRICKET WOOD
NOTTLERS WOOD
Nottlers House
Household Waste Centre
Depot
Sec Sch
Sports Centre
BENSKINS SPORTS GRD
Crem
Brookdell Farm
PENFOLD PARK GOLF COURSE
BRICKET
BUILDING RESEARCH ESTABLISHMENT
JACK WILLIAM'S WOOD
WOOD
NEW PLANTATION
Site of Roman Villa
WD25
SPORTS GRD
Garston Manor Sch
Prim Sch
WOODSIDE STADIUM
Leisure Cen
PITCH
Prim Sch
COMMON
MUTCHETTS WOOD
Little Munden Farm
WD25
WOODSIDE PLAYING FIELDS
Watford Town C.C.
Cinema
Leisure Park
Premier Inn
COLDHARBOUR PLANTATION
FOUR ACRE PLANTATION
GARSTON PARK
PEARTREE WOOD
CRAB WOOD
Munden
River Colne
Medical Cen
Kingswood
BUS GAR
MUNDEN SPRING
ST. ALBANS
HERTSMERE
WATFORD
Munden House
GARSTON
Sch
500 yds
500 m
Meriden
STANBOROUGH PARK
M1
M25
A405
A412
NORTH ORBITAL ROAD
ST ALBANS ROAD
KINGSWAY

AL1
AL2
AL4
WD7
65
84
99
Park Street
Frogmore
Colney Street
LONDON COLNEY
KINGSLEY GREEN
RADLETT
SHENLEY PARK
NORTH ORBITAL ROAD
A414
A1081
LONDON ROAD
London Colney Rbt
NORTH ORBITAL COMMERCIAL PARK
CHALKDELL WOOD
Hedges Farm
Sopwell House
Aylett Nurseries
VERULAMIANS RFC
COLUMBANS SPORTS GRD
SPORTS GROUND
GRAVEL PIT
PARK STREET
A5183
FROGMORE
RADLETT ROAD
WATLING STREET
M25
BELL LANE
SHENLEY LANE
B5378
B556
HARPER LANE
Harper Lane Rail Depot
RADLETT GOLF CENTRE
HOUND'S WOOD
NINE ACRES
ALL SAINTS PASTORAL CENTRE
BROAD COLNEY LAKES NATURE RESERVE
Fir Tree Farm
Broad Colney Bridge
River Colne
River Ver
COLNEY PARK
SPORTS GRDS
HERTSMERE
ST. ALBANS
VENTURA PARK
Old Parkbury
Premier Inn
Colney Street Farm
Colney Street Bridge
Pumping Sta
Netherwylde Farm
Hill Farm
Oakridge Lane Sewage Treatment Works
Starveacres
PORTERS PARK GOLF COURSE
SAND PLANTATION
The Shenley Cricket Centre
Clubhouse
Wild Farm
Moat
COW BANKS
RIVERSIDE ESTATE
MORRIS PLAYING FLD
SPORTS GROUND
PARK IND EST
CURO PARK
FROGMORE HOME PARK
CD
CE
CF
CG
CH
CJ
CK
15
16
17
26
27
28
29
30
31
32
33
34
04
03
02
01

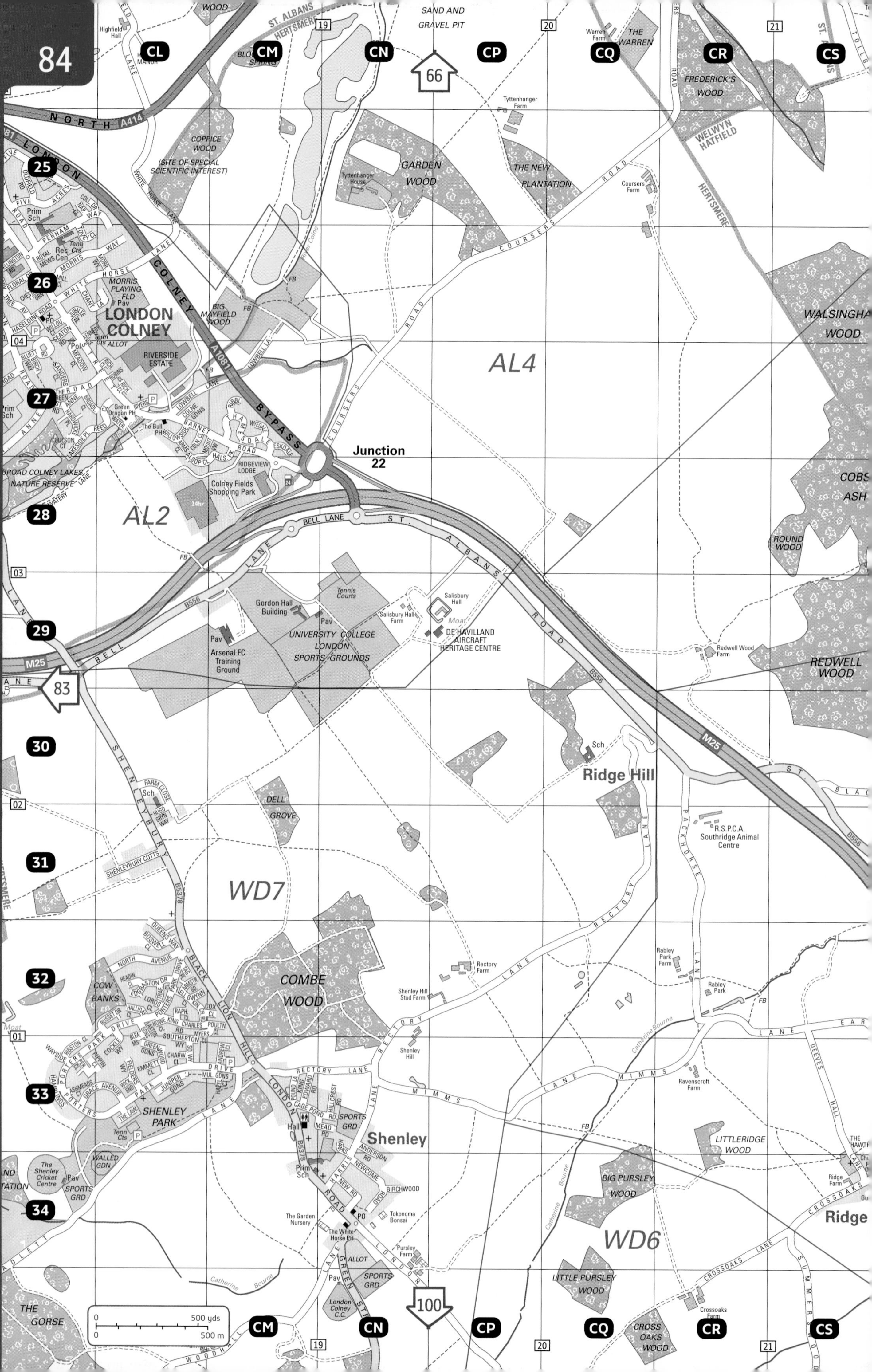

CL
CM
CN
CP
CQ
CR
CS
66
83
100
19
20
21
03
02
01
04
25
26
27
28
29
30
31
32
33
34
SAND AND GRAVEL PIT
ST. ALBANS HERTSMERE
WELWYN HATFIELD
HERTSMERE
Highfield Hall
WOOD
Warren Farm
THE WARREN
FREDERICK'S WOOD
NORTH A414
A1081 LONDON COLNEY BYPASS
COPPICE WOOD
(SITE OF SPECIAL SCIENTIFIC INTEREST)
WHITE HORSE LANE
Tyttenhanger Farm
Tyttenhanger House
GARDEN WOOD
THE NEW PLANTATION
COURSERS ROAD
Coursers Farm
River Colne
BIG MAYFIELD WOOD
LONDON COLNEY
MORRIS PLAYING FLD
RIVERSIDE ESTATE
Prim Sch
Rec Cen
Tenn Cts
Green Dragon PH
The Bull PH
ALLOT
RIDGEVIEW LODGE
Colney Fields Shopping Park
24hr
BROAD COLNEY LAKES NATURE RESERVE
WALSINGHAM WOOD
AL4
AL2
Junction 22
BELL LANE
ST. ALBANS ROAD
B556
M25
COBS ASH
ROUND WOOD
Tennis Courts
Gordon Hall Building
Salisbury Hall
Salisbury Hall Farm
Moat
DE HAVILLAND AIRCRAFT HERITAGE CENTRE
UNIVERSITY COLLEGE LONDON SPORTS GROUNDS
Pav
Arsenal FC Training Ground
Redwell Wood Farm
REDWELL WOOD
Sch
Ridge Hill
SHENLEYBURY
FARM CLOSE
HUGO GRYN WAY
SHENLEYBURY COTTS
DELL GROVE
WD7
R.S.P.C.A. Southridge Animal Centre
PACKHORSE LANE
B5378
BLACK LION HILL
COMBE WOOD
COW BANKS
RECTORY LANE
Rectory Farm
Shenley Hill Stud Farm
Shenley Hill
Rabley Park Farm
Rabley Park
Catherine Bourne
MIMMS LANE
DEEVES HALL
Ravenscroft Farm
SHENLEY PARK
PORTERS PARK DRIVE
Tenn Cts
WALLED GDN
The Shenley Cricket Centre
SPORTS GRD
Hall
LONDON ROAD
Shenley
Prim Sch
NEWCOME
HARRIS LANE
BIRCHWOOD
The Garden Nursery
PO
Tokonoma Bonsai
The White Horse PH
Pursley Farm
GREEN STREET
London Colney C.C.
LITTLERIDGE WOOD
BIG PURSLEY WOOD
WD6
LITTLE PURSLEY WOOD
CROSS OAKS WOOD
Crossoaks Farm
CROSSOAKS LANE
SUMMERSWOOD
Ridge Farm
Ridge
THE GORSE
RADLETT
WOODHALL
0 500 yds
0 500 m

CT
CU
CV
CW
CX
CY
CZ
67
North Mymms
NORTH MYMMS PARK
Mansion House
Water End
The Woodman Inn PH
The Old Maypole PH
BRICK KILN WOOD
Royal Veterinary College (Hawkshead)
BROOKMANS PARK
BROOKMANS PARK GOLF COURSE
PELPIN'S WOOD
GOBIONS OPEN SPACE
GOBIONS GARDEN
GOBIONS POND
AL9
Deep Bottom
SWALLOW HOLES
CANGSLEY WOOD
HAWKSHEAD WOOD
MYMMSHALL WOOD
WELWYN HATFIELD
HERTSMERE
SPORTS GROUND
PILVAGE WOOD
Site of Motte & Baileys
Royal Veterinary College (Boltons Park Farm)
POTTERS BAR GOLF COURSE
86
FURZEFIELD WOOD
CRANBORNE INDUSTRIAL ESTATE
KING GEORGE V PLAYING FLDS
Warrengate Farm
Mimms Hall Farm
Windmore Hall
EN6
South Mimms
Town Farm
Black Horse PH
The White Hart PH
Bridgefoot
Bridgefoot House
Premier Inn South Mimms
South Mimms Services
Days Inn
Bignell's Corner
Cancer Research UK
Blanche Farm
Dugdale Hill
Rydal Mount
Rydal Mount Stables
Elm Farm
Bentley Heath Farm
Bentley Heath
101
Junction 23 (M25) Junction 1 A1(M)
A1(M)
M25
26
27
28
29
30
31
32
33
34

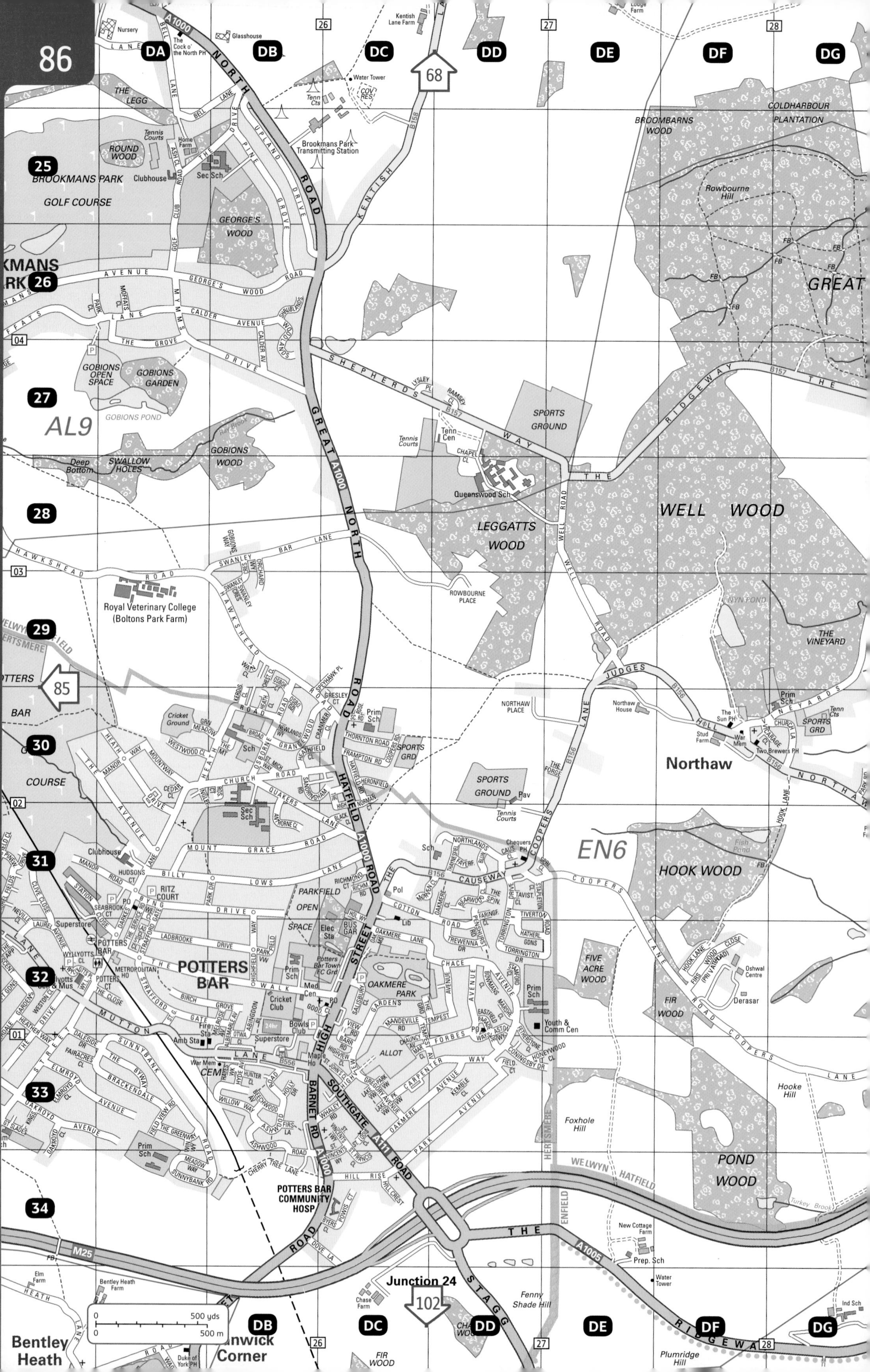
DA
DB
DC
DD
DE
DF
DG
26
27
28
68
85
102
25
26
27
28
29
30
31
32
33
34
04
03
02
01
Nursery
Glasshouse
The Cock o' the North PH
Kentish Lane Farm
Water Tower
COV RES
Tenn Cts
Brookmans Park Transmitting Station
THE LEGG
ROUND WOOD
BROOKMANS PARK GOLF COURSE
Clubhouse
Sec Sch
Home Farm
Tennis Courts
GEORGE'S WOOD
BROOMBARNS WOOD
COLDHARBOUR PLANTATION
Rowbourne Hill
FB
GREAT
GEORGE'S WOOD ROAD
CALDER AVENUE
SHEPHERDS WAY
THE RIDGEWAY
B157
B158
A1000
GOBIONS OPEN SPACE
GOBIONS GARDEN
GOBIONS POND
AL9
GOBIONS WOOD
Deep Bottom
SWALLOW HOLES
SPORTS GROUND
Tennis Courts
Tenn Cen
Queenswood Sch
LEGGATTS WOOD
WELL WOOD
WELL ROAD
HAWKSHEAD ROAD
SWANLEY BAR LANE
Royal Veterinary College (Boltons Park Farm)
ROWBOURNE PLACE
NYN POND
THE VINEYARD
GREAT NORTH ROAD
JUDGES HILL
NORTHAW PLACE
Northaw House
The Sun PH
War Mem
Stud Farm
Two Brewers PH
Prim Sch
SPORTS GRD
Northaw
B156
THE FORGE
SPORTS GROUND
Pav
Tennis Courts
EN6
Chequers PH
COOPERS LANE
HOOK WOOD
Fish Pond
HOOK LANE
Cricket Ground
SPORTS GRD
HATFIELD ROAD
A1000
Sec Sch
Sch
COURSE
MOUNT GRACE ROAD
Clubhouse
BILLY LOWS LANE
RITZ COURT
PARKFIELD OPEN SPACE
Elec Sta
BUS GAR
Superstore
POTTERS BAR
DARKES LANE
Lib
Pol
THE CAUSEWAY
HIGH STREET
OAKMERE PARK
FIVE ACRE WOOD
FIR WOOD
Oshwal Centre
Derasar
Youth & Comm Cen
Prim Sch
Cricket Club
Bowls Club
Superstore
Amb Sta
Fire Sta
War Mem
CEM
Med Cen
MUTTON LANE
B556
ALLOT
Maple Ho
SOUTHGATE ROAD
A111
BARNET RD
Foxhole Hill
Hooke Hill
POND WOOD
Turkey Brook
HERTSMERE
ENFIELD
WELWYN HATFIELD
POTTERS BAR COMMUNITY HOSP
M25
THE RIDGEWAY
A1005
New Cottage Farm
Prep. Sch
Water Tower
Junction 24
STAGG HILL
Fenny Shade Hill
Chase Farm
Elm Farm
Bentley Heath Farm
Bentley Heath
Duke of York PH
Ganwick Corner
FIR WOOD
Plumridge Hill
Ind Sch
0
500 yds
500 m

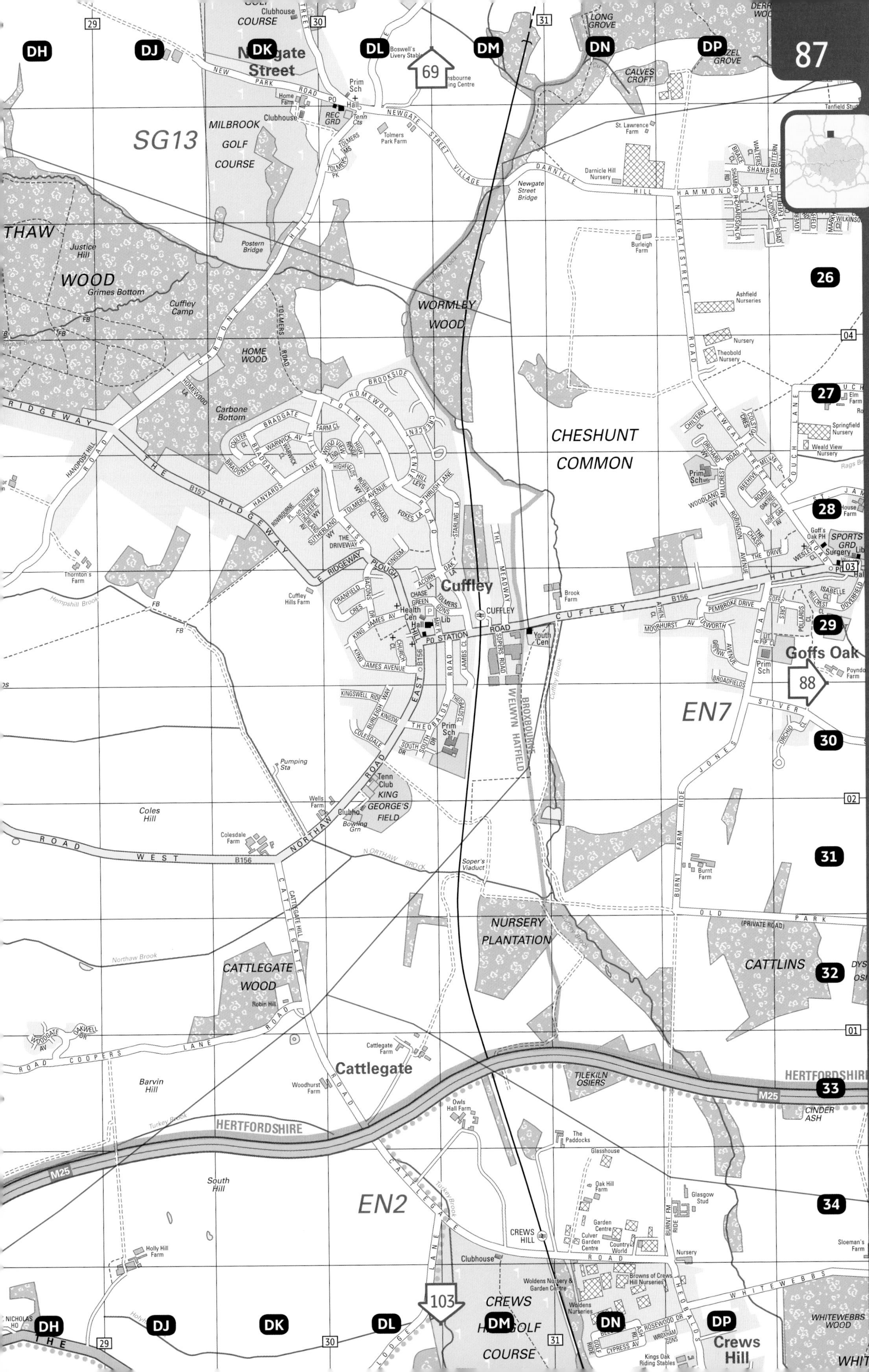
DH
DJ
DK
DL
DM
DN
DP
69
Newgate Street
NEW PARK ROAD
Clubhouse
COURSE
Boswell's Livery Stables
LONG GROVE
HAZEL GROVE
CALVES CROFT
Prim Sch
Hall
Home Farm
PO
REC GRD
Tenn Cts
NEWGATE STREET VILLAGE
Tolmers Park Farm
TOLMERS MS
TOLMERS PK
SG13
MILBROOK GOLF COURSE
Newgate Street Bridge
DARNICLE HILL
Darnicle Hill Nursery
St. Lawrence Farm
HAMMOND STREET
Tanfield Stud
WALTERS CL
BRICE RD
SHAMBROOK RD
BITTERN
RICHARDSON CR
GLADDING RD
WILKINSON CL
THAW WOOD
Justice Hill
Postern Bridge
Burleigh Farm
NEWGATE STREET ROAD
26
Grimes Bottom
Cuffley Camp
WORMLEY WOOD
Cuffley Brook
Ashfield Nurseries
HOME WOOD
TOLMERS ROAD
CARBONE HILL
Nursery
Theobold Nursery
04
27
Elm Farm
Springfield Nursery
Weald View Nursery
CROUCH LANE
Rags Brook
HOMEWOOD LA
Carbone Bottom
RIDGEWAY
HANDPOST HILL ROAD
BROOKSIDE
HOMEWOOD
TOLMERS AVENUE
CRESCENT
BRADGATE
BRADGATE CL
COULTER CL
WARWICK AV
WARWICK CL
FARM CL
WOOD VIEW
HIGH RIDGE
HIGHFIELDS
HILL LEYS
THRUSH LANE
CHESHUNT COMMON
CHILTERN CL
NEWGATE STREET ROAD
ORCHARD WY
COLSTON CRES
MELVIN CL
Prim Sch
MILLCREST RD
BEEHIVE LA
WOODLAND WY
ROBINSON AVENUE
THE CHASE
OAKTREE CL
GOFF OAK AV
THE DRIVE
Goff's Oak PH
SPORTS GRD
Surgery
Lib
Hall
House Farm
28
ST JAMES
HANYARDS LANE
ROWBOURNE PL
SUTHERLAND AV
ROBIN WY
ORCHARD CL
FOXES LA
STARLING LA
THE DRIVEWAY
THE RIDGEWAY
B157
Thornton's Farm
Cuffley Hills Farm
KINGSMEAD
PLOUGH HILL
ACORN LA
OAK LA
THE MEADWAY
Brook Farm
Cuffley
CHASE GREEN
CRANFIELD CRES
BACONS DR
KING JAMES AV
Health Cen
Lib
Hall
PO
STATION ROAD
CUFFLEY
CUFFLEY HILL
B156
SOPERS ROAD
Youth Cen
ATHEN PL
MOORHURST AV
PEMBROKE DRIVE
LULWORTH AV
GREENWAY
ISABELLE CL
HILLCREST CL
DOVERFIELD
POLLARDS CL
GOFFS CRES
29
Goffs Oak
Prim Sch
Poynders Farm
88
Hempshill Brook
FB
CHURCH CL
KING JAMES AVENUE
EAST RIDGEWAY
B156
LAMBS CL
WELWYN HATFIELD
BROXBOURNE
BROADFIELDS
SILVER ST
EN7
ORCHID CL
30
KINGSWELL RIDE
BURLEIGH WAY
KINGSWELL
COLESDALE
THEOBALDS ROAD
SOUTH DR
Prim Sch
Pumping Sta
JONES ROAD
Tenn Club
KING GEORGE'S FIELD
Bowling Grn
Clubho
Wells Farm
Coles Hill
Colesdale Farm
02
NORTHAW ROAD
ROAD WEST
B156
NORTHAW BROOK
Soper's Viaduct
BURNT FARM RIDE
Burnt Farm
31
CATTLEGATE HILL
NURSERY PLANTATION
OLD PARK
(PRIVATE ROAD)
Northaw Brook
CATTLEGATE WOOD
Robin Hill
CATTLINS
32
01
WOODGATE AV
OAKWELL DR
COOPERS LANE ROAD
Cattlegate Farm
Cattlegate
TILEKILN OSIERS
HERTFORDSHIRE
33
M25
Barvin Hill
Woodhurst Farm
CINDER ASH
Owls Hall Farm
Turkey Brook
HERTFORDSHIRE
The Paddocks
Glasshouse
M25
South Hill
Oak Hill Farm
Glasgow Stud
34
EN2
CATTLEGATE ROAD
Garden Centre
Culver Garden Centre
Country World
CREWS HILL
BURNT FM RIDE
Nursery
Sloeman's Farm
Holly Hill Farm
Clubhouse
ROAD
Woldens Nursery & Garden Centre
Browns of Crews Hill Nurseries
WHITEWEBBS
LANE
103
CREWS HILL GOLF COURSE
Woldens Nurseries
WHITEWEBBS WOOD
ST. NICHOLAS HO
ROSEWOOD DR
WROXHAM GDNS
CYPRESS AV
GOLF RIDE
THEOBALDS
Crews Hill
Kings Oak Riding Stables
LODGE
29
30
31

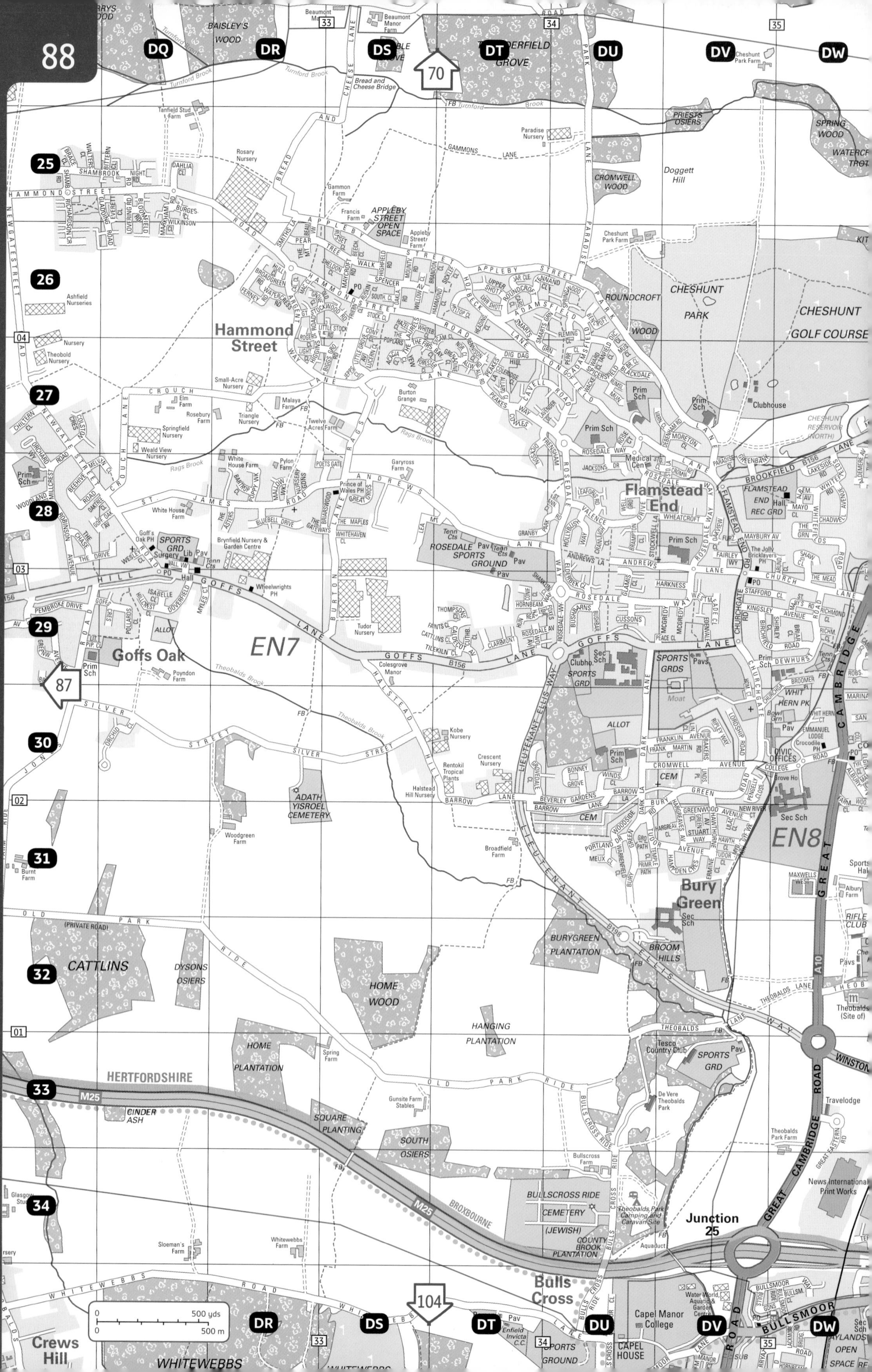
DQ
DR
DS
DT
DU
DV
DW
70
87
104
25
26
27
28
29
30
31
32
33
34
35
BAISLEY'S WOOD
Turnford Brook
Beaumont Manor Farm
Bread and Cheese Bridge
Tanfield Stud Farm
Paradise Nursery
GAMMONS LANE
PRIESTS OSIERS
SPRING WOOD
Cheshunt Park Farm
Doggett Hill
CROMWELL WOOD
Cheshunt Park Farm
CHESHUNT PARK
CHESHUNT GOLF COURSE
ROUNDCROFT WOOD
Clubhouse
CHESHUNT RESERVOIR (NORTH)
HAMMOND STREET
NEWGATESTREET ROAD
SHAMBROOK
Rosary Nursery
Gammon Farm
Francis Farm
APPLEBY STREET OPEN SPACE
Appleby Street Farm
APPLEBY STREET
HAMMOND STREET ROAD
Ashfield Nurseries
Nursery
Theobald Nursery
Hammond Street
Small-Acre Nursery
CROUCH LANE
Elm Farm
Rosebury Farm
Springfield Nursery
Weald View Nursery
Malaya Farm
Triangle Nursery
Twelve Acres Farm
Burton Grange
Rags Brook
White House Farm
Pylon Farm
Garyross Farm
Prince of Wales PH
ST JAMES ROAD
ANDREWS LANE
White House Farm
Goff's Oak PH
SPORTS GRD
Surgery
Pav
Tenn Cts
Brynfield Nursery & Garden Centre
Wheelwrights PH
ROSEDALE SPORTS GROUND
GOFFS LANE
EN7
Tudor Nursery
Colesgrove Manor
Goffs Oak
Prim Sch
Poyndon Farm
Theobalds Brook
SILVER STREET
Kobe Nursery
Rentokil Tropical Plants
Crescent Nursery
Halstead Hill Nursery
ADATH YISROEL CEMETERY
Woodgreen Farm
Broadfield Farm
Burnt Farm
Flamstead End
FLAMSTEAD END REC GRD
The Jolly Bricklayers PH
SPORTS GRDS
Moat
ALLOT
CEM
CIVIC OFFICES
Grove Ho
Sec Sch
EN8
LIEUTENANT ELLIS WAY
GREAT CAMBRIDGE ROAD
A10
Bury Green
BROOM HILLS
BURYGREEN PLANTATION
RIFLE CLUB
Theobalds (Site of)
Albury Farm
OLD PARK RIDE
(PRIVATE ROAD)
CATTLINS
DYSONS OSIERS
HOME WOOD
HANGING PLANTATION
HOME PLANTATION
Spring Farm
Tesco Country Club
SPORTS GRD
De Vere Theobalds Park
Travelodge
Theobalds Park Farm
News International Print Works
HERTFORDSHIRE
M25
CINDER ASH
Gunsite Farm Stables
SQUARE PLANTING
SOUTH OSIERS
Bullscross Farm
BULLSCROSS RIDE CEMETERY (JEWISH)
COUNTY BROOK PLANTATION
Theobalds Park Camping and Caravan Site
Junction 25
BROXBOURNE
Glasgow Stud
Whitewebbs Farm
Sloeman's Farm
WHITEWEBBS ROAD
Bulls Cross
Water World Aquatic & Garden Centre
Capel Manor College
CAPEL HOUSE
Enfield Invicta C.C.
SPORTS GROUND
BULLSMOOR
Crews Hill
WHITEWEBBS
0 500 yds
0 500 m

DX
DY
DZ
EA
EB
EC
ED
36
37
38
71
90
105
26
27
28
29
30
31
32
33
34
04
03
02
01
Wormley
Turnford
NAZEING MARSH
HERTFORDSHIRE
ESSEX
King's Weir
Paynes Farm Nursery
Clayton Hill
Langridge Nursery
Larksmead Nursery
EN10
A10
Turnford
New River Arms
HIGH ROAD TURNFORD
Comm Cen
College
Turnford Marsh
HOLYFIELD LAKE
Aqueduct Lock
Sailing Club
St. Leonards Farm
COLEMAN'S LANE
COLEMAN'S SHAW
LEE VALLEY REGIONAL PARK
ASHLEY
Weir
Marriott Cheshunt
Bull's Head
NEW RIVER TRADING EST
HALFHIDE LANE
BROOKFIELD CENTRE
HODDESDON ROAD
GREAT CAMBRIDGE RD
Holyfield Marsh
Holyfield Hall Farm
Marsh Hill
Elec Station
Peartree Farm
THE NIGHTLEYS
CHESHUNT
Lee Valley Park Farm & Information Service
Holyfield
Hayes Hill
NORTH METROPOLITAN PIT
Cheshunt Lock
SEVENTY ACRES LAKE
STUBBINS HALL LANE
North Lodge Farm
Nursery
Grubbs Hill
PUCK LANE
HOMEFIELD WOOD
CHESHUNT LAKE
RIVER LEE NAVIGATION
Turnershill Marsh
Holyfield Fishery
FISHERS GREEN LANE
EN9
Holyfield Farm
MONKHAMS
YHA
Young Mariners Base
Police Pit
Hooks Marsh Lake
KENNEL WOOD
CHESHUNT
Thistly Marsh
CLAYGATE LANE
SPORTS GRD
Tesco HQ
SPORTS GROUND
GRUNDY PARK
Leisure Cen
HOSP
Cheshunt Junction
Friday Lake
Waltham Common Lock
Sluice
WALTHAM ABBEY WOODS
Cornmill Stream
CROOKED MILE
ALLOT
Hall Marsh Scrape
Mile Nursery
Waltham Abbey Plant Centre
Lee Valley Nursery
Abbey View Nursery
BOWYER'S WATER
BROXBOURNE
EPPING FOREST
Cornmill Meadows
Old River Lea or Lee
LEA VALLEY WALK
LEE VALLEY PATHWAY
THEOBALDS GROVE
Marsh Bridge
PARKLANDS
ROYAL GUNPOWDER MILLS
Crooked Mile Roundabout
Cheshunt Marsh
Waltham Marsh
WALTHAM ABBEY (Ruins)
ABBEY GARDENS
ABBEY CHURCHYARD
Prim Schs
WALTHAM CROSS
Lee Valley White Water Centre
Britannia Nursery
Waltham Town Lock
HIGHBRIDGE ST
Abbey Vw Roundabout
STATION ROAD
ELEANOR CROSS RD
MONARCHS WAY
MERIDIAN WAY
A121
TOWN MEAD
LWR ISLAND
Holdbrook
BRITANNIA BUSINESS PK
NEW FORD BUSINESS CEN
LEA RD TRADING EST
IO CENTRE
CEM
WALTHAM ABBEY FC
LARSENS REC GRD
SPORTS GROUND
Swim Pool
Pitches
M25
Freezywater
MOLLISON AVENUE
A1055
RAMMEY MARSH
MERIDIAN WAY A121
Cobbin's Brook
LODGE LANE
Quinton Hill Farm
Sewardstone Roundabout
SEWARDSTONE ROAD

EE
EF
EG
EH
EJ
EK
EL
25
26
27
28
29
30
31
32
33
34
40
41
42
04
03
02
01
72
89
106
Hill Farm
Range
Clubhouse
NAZEINGWOOD
COMMON
Bumble's Green
Belchers Farm
BELCHERS LANE
King Harold's Head PH
ALLOT
LONG GREEN
NAZEING
SPORTS GRD
Leisure Centre
Nazeing Gate
THE AVENUE
BUMBLES GRN LANE
ALLMAINS CL
THE HTS
COPY WOOD
LAUNDRY LANE
ST. LEONARDS ROAD
B194
St. Leonards Farm
Netherkidders Farm
Mushroom Farm
CEMETERY LANE
Mamelons Farm
St. Lawrence Farm
WALTHAM ROAD
Harold's Park Farm
LONGFIELD SHAW
COLEMAN'S LANE
COLEMAN'S SHAW
Coach & Horses PH
Denver Lodge Farm
GALLEYHILL GREEN
THE SPRINGS
DEERPARK WOOD
Parvills Farm
Marsh Hill
Galley Hill
Kennels
Peartree Farm
Claverhambury Manor
Claverhambury Farm
Claverhambury Carp Farm
CLAVERHAMBURY ROAD
Holyfield
HOLYFIELD
GALLEYHILL WOOD
BROADGATE SPRINGS
BRAYSHILL SPRING
Reevesgate Farm
LONGCROFT GROVE
Three Gates
STOCKING GROVE
COBBINSEND
Aimes Green
PUCK LANE
Aimesgreen Farm
Nightingales
Cobbinsend Farm
Maynards Farm
EN9
MAPLE SPRINGS
BREACH BARN MOBILE HOME PARK
Cobbin's Brook
KENNEL WOOD
Breach Barns Farm
Fernhall Farm
FERNHALL WOOD
CLAYGATE
BREACH BARNS LANE
Oakwood Nursery
Fourways Nursery
Dallance Farm
Obelisk
GALLEY HILL
BROOKMEADOW WOOD
FERNHALL LANE
LONG STREET
Newhouse Farm
Nicholls Farm
Home Farm
Monkswood Nursery
Mushroom Farm
COBBIN POND
COPPED HALL GREEN
Springfield Nursery
Upshire Nursery
Obelisk Farm
Glyn Gates
Abbey View Nursery
Knollys Nursery
GDNS
The Temple
Lea Valley Nursery
Paternoster Hill Nursery
Paternoster Nursery
Paternoster House
PICK HILL
Warlies Park House
WARLIES PARK
Burgess Farm
PARKLANDS
Upshire
Hall
Warlies Lodge
The Horseshoes PH
HORSESHOE HILL
CROWN HILL
Prim Schs
Sports Cen
Prim Sch
SPORTS GROUND
UPSHIRE ROAD
NINEFIELDS
SERGEANTS GREEN LA
RUGGED LANE
OXLEYS WOOD
WOODREDON FARM LANE
Copthall Green
Crown Hill Nursery
WOODGREEN ROAD
Clubho
LARSENS REC GRD
ALLOT
BLIND LA
GREEN LANE
POTKILN WOOD
BRAMBLY SHAW
Woodgreen Farm
Green Lane Bungalows
ROUNDHILLS
Southend Farm
SOUTHEND LA
Woodredon House
WALTHAM ABBEY FC
Marriott Waltham Abbey
Upshire Hall
CLAY PIGEON RANGE
WOODBINE CLOSE
CONYBURY WOOD
ALLOT
Swim Pool
SPORTS GROUND
WALTHAM ABBEY
Sudbury Farm
Woodbine Inn PH
Woodredon Farm
The Lodge
Skillet Hill Farm
STABLES SHAW
Junction 26
SKILLET HILL
HONEY LANE
A121
WOODRIDGE
Volunteer PH
Woodredon Riding School
M25
Quinton Hill Farm
Sewardstone Roundabout
BEECHFIELD WALK
LODGE LANE
500 yds
500 m

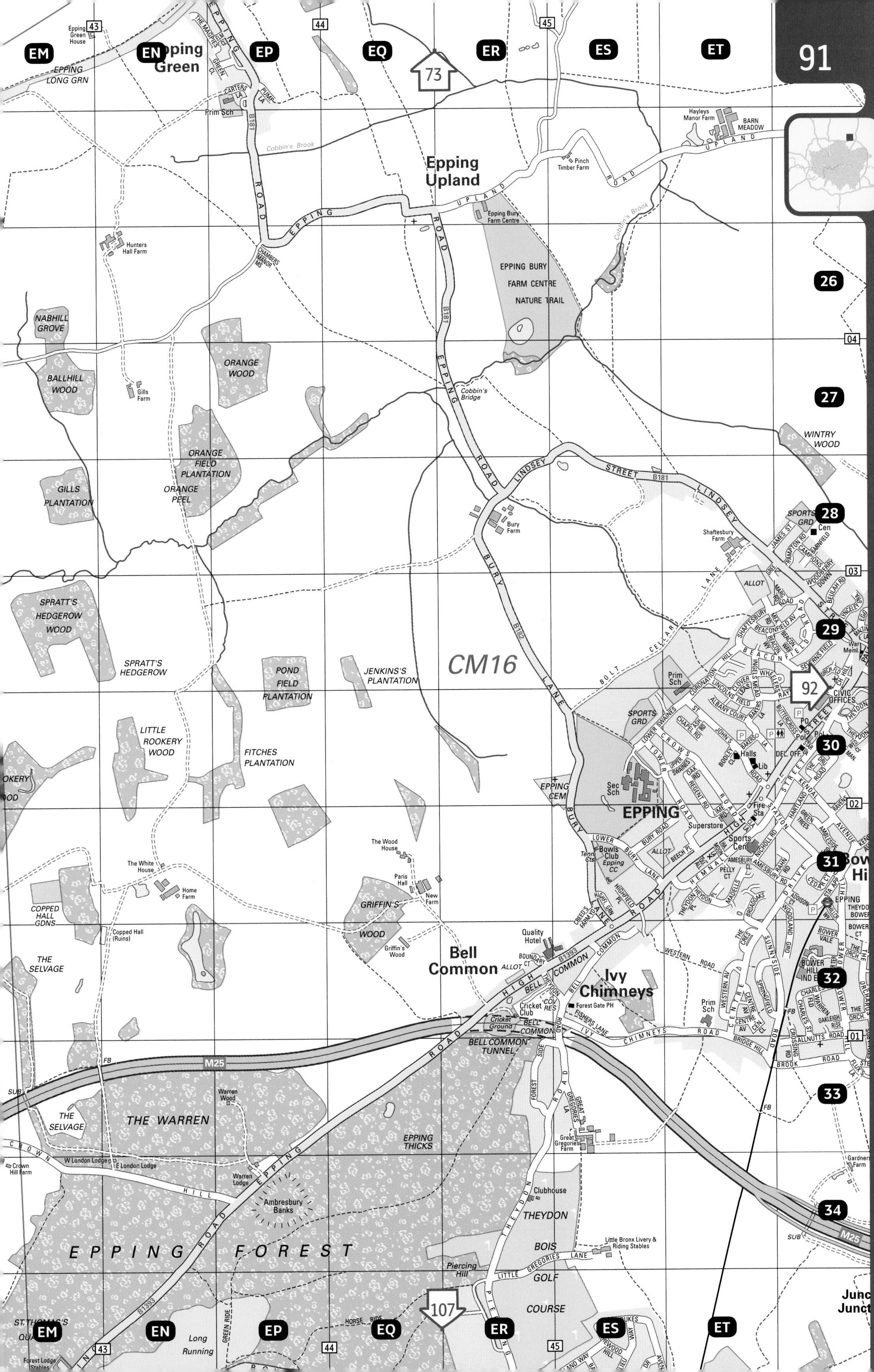
EM
EN
EP
EQ
ER
ES
ET
73
Epping Green House
Epping Green
EPPING LONG GRN
THE MAGPIES
CARTERS LA
PUMP LA
GREEN CL
Prim Sch
B181
Cobbin's Brook
Hayleys Manor Farm
BARN MEADOW
UPLAND ROAD
Pinch Timber Farm
Epping Upland
EPPING UPLAND
Epping Bury Farm Centre
Hunters Hall Farm
CHAMBERS MANOR MS
EPPING ROAD
EPPING BURY FARM CENTRE NATURE TRAIL
26
04
NABHILL GROVE
BALLHILL WOOD
ORANGE WOOD
Gills Farm
Cobbin's Bridge
27
WINTRY WOOD
ORANGE FIELD PLANTATION
ORANGE PEEL
GILLS PLANTATION
LINDSEY STREET
B181
Bury Farm
28
SPORTS GRD
Cen
Shaftesbury Farm
03
ALLOT
SPRATT'S HEDGEROW WOOD
SPRATT'S HEDGEROW
POND FIELD PLANTATION
JENKINS'S PLANTATION
CM16
BURY LANE
B182
CELLAR LANE
BOLT
29
War Meml
92
CIVIC OFFICES
Prim Sch
SPORTS GRD
LITTLE ROOKERY WOOD
FITCHES PLANTATION
30
Halls
Lib
DEL OFF
Po
Pol
EPPING CEM
Sec Sch
EPPING
02
Superstore
Fire Sta
Sports Cen
HIGH STREET
STATION ROAD
LOWER BURY LANE
Bowls Club
Epping CC
ALLOT
31
The Wood House
The White House
Home Farm
Paris Hall
New Farm
COPPED HALL GDNS
Copped Hall (Ruins)
GRIFFIN'S WOOD
Griffin's Wood
EPPING
THEYDON BOWER
Quality Hotel
Bell Common
ALLOT
THE SELVAGE
Ivy Chimneys
WESTERN ROAD
32
Cricket Club
Forest Gate PH
Prim Sch
Cricket Ground
BELL COMMON
BELL COMMON TUNNEL
IVY CHIMNEYS ROAD
01
M25
FB
BROOK ROAD
SUB
THE SELVAGE
Warren Wood
THE WARREN
EPPING THICKS
FOREST SIDE
GREAT GREGORIES LA
Great Gregories Farm
33
CROWN HILL
Crown Hill Farm
W London Lodge
E London Lodge
Warren Lodge
Ambresbury Banks
Clubhouse
THEYDON BOIS GOLF COURSE
Gardners Farm
34
M25
EPPING FOREST
EPPING ROAD
Little Bronx Livery & Riding Stables
LITTLE GREGORIES LANE
Piercing Hill
B1393
107
HORSE RIDE
GREEN RIDE
Long Running
ST THOMAS'S QUARTERS
Forest Lodge Stables
43
44
45
Junc

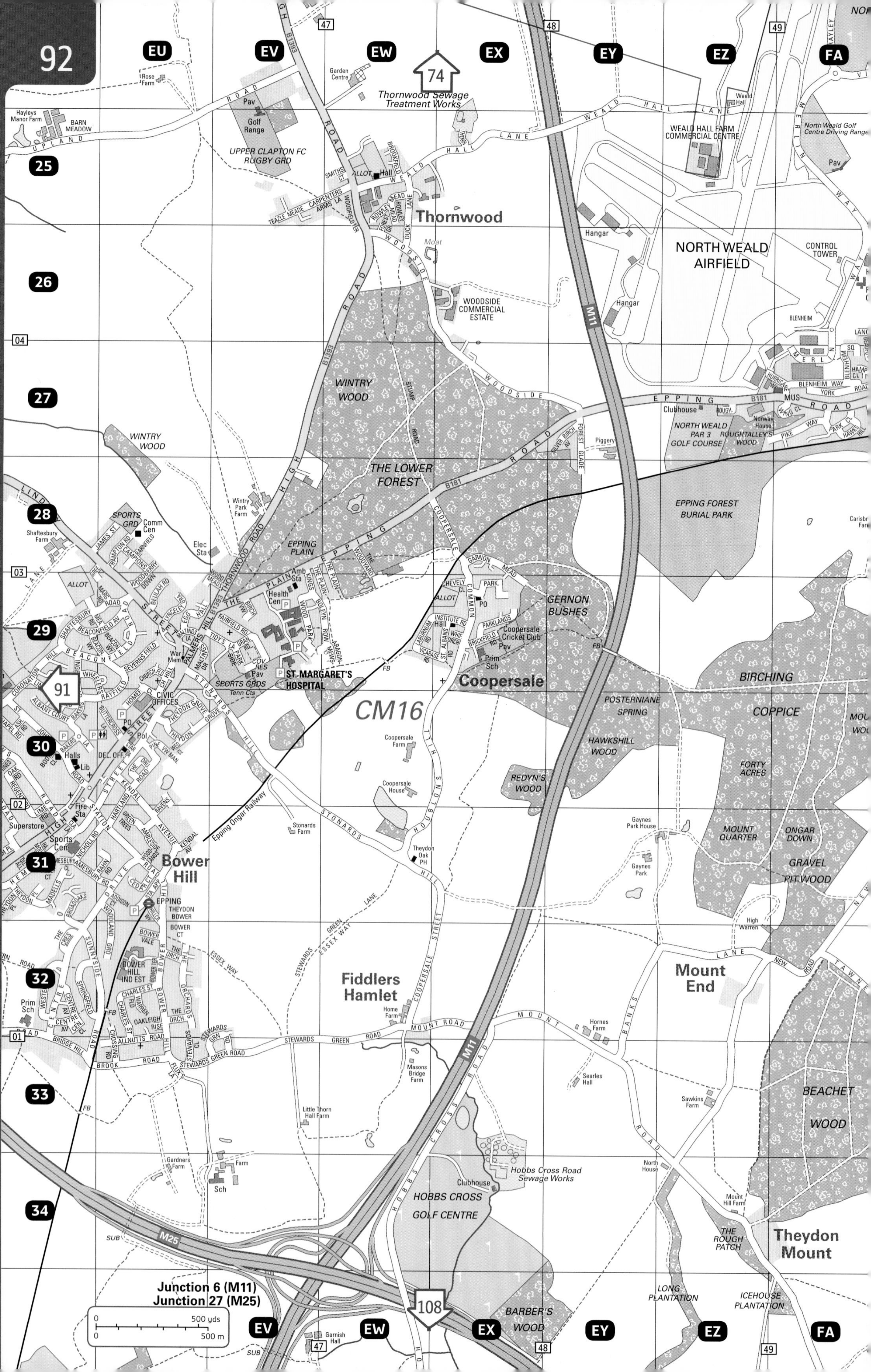

EU
EV
EW
EX
EY
EZ
FA
74
108
91
25
26
27
28
29
30
31
32
33
34
04
03
02
01
47
48
49
Thornwood Sewage Treatment Works
Garden Centre
Rose Farm
Hayleys Manor Farm
BARN MEADOW
UPLAND ROAD
Pav
Golf Range
UPPER CLAPTON FC RUGBY GRD
Thornwood
Hall
ALLOT
Moat
WOODSIDE COMMERCIAL ESTATE
WEALD HALL LANE
Weald Hall
WEALD HALL FARM COMMERCIAL CENTRE
North Weald Golf Centre Driving Range
Hangar
NORTH WEALD AIRFIELD
CONTROL TOWER
BLENHEIM
MUS
EPPING ROAD
B181
B1393
M11
Clubhouse
NORTH WEALD PAR 3 GOLF COURSE
ROUGHTALLEY'S WOOD
Piggery
EPPING FOREST BURIAL PARK
WINTRY WOOD
THE LOWER FOREST
Wintry Park Farm
EPPING PLAIN
Elec Sta
SPORTS GRD
Comm Cen
Shaftesbury Farm
ALLOT
Amb Sta
Health Cen
COV RES
Pav
SPORTS GRDS
Tenn Cts
ST. MARGARET'S HOSPITAL
War Mem
CIVIC OFFICES
Halls
Lib
Fire Sta
Superstore
Sports Cen
PO
Pol
GERNON BUSHES
Coopersale Cricket Club
Prim Sch
Coopersale
CM16
BIRCHING COPPICE
POSTERNIANE SPRING
HAWKSHILL WOOD
REDYN'S WOOD
FORTY ACRES
MOUNT QUARTER
ONGAR DOWN
GRAVEL PIT WOOD
Coopersale Farm
Coopersale House
Stonards Farm
Theydon Oak PH
Gaynes Park House
Gaynes Park
High Warren
Epping Ongar Railway
Bower Hill
EPPING
THEYDON BOWER
BOWER CT
BOWER HILL IND EST
Prim Sch
Fiddlers Hamlet
Home Farm
Mount End
Hornes Farm
Searles Hall
Masons Bridge Farm
MOUNT ROAD
STEWARDS GREEN ROAD
ESSEX WAY
Little Thorn Hall Farm
Sawkins Farm
BEACHET WOOD
North House
Mount Hill Farm
THE ROUGH PATCH
Theydon Mount
Gardners Farm
Farm
Sch
Hobbs Cross Road Sewage Works
Clubhouse
HOBBS CROSS GOLF CENTRE
M25
LONG PLANTATION
ICEHOUSE PLANTATION
BARBER'S WOOD
Garnish Hall
Junction 6 (M11)
Junction 27 (M25)
0 500 yds
0 500 m

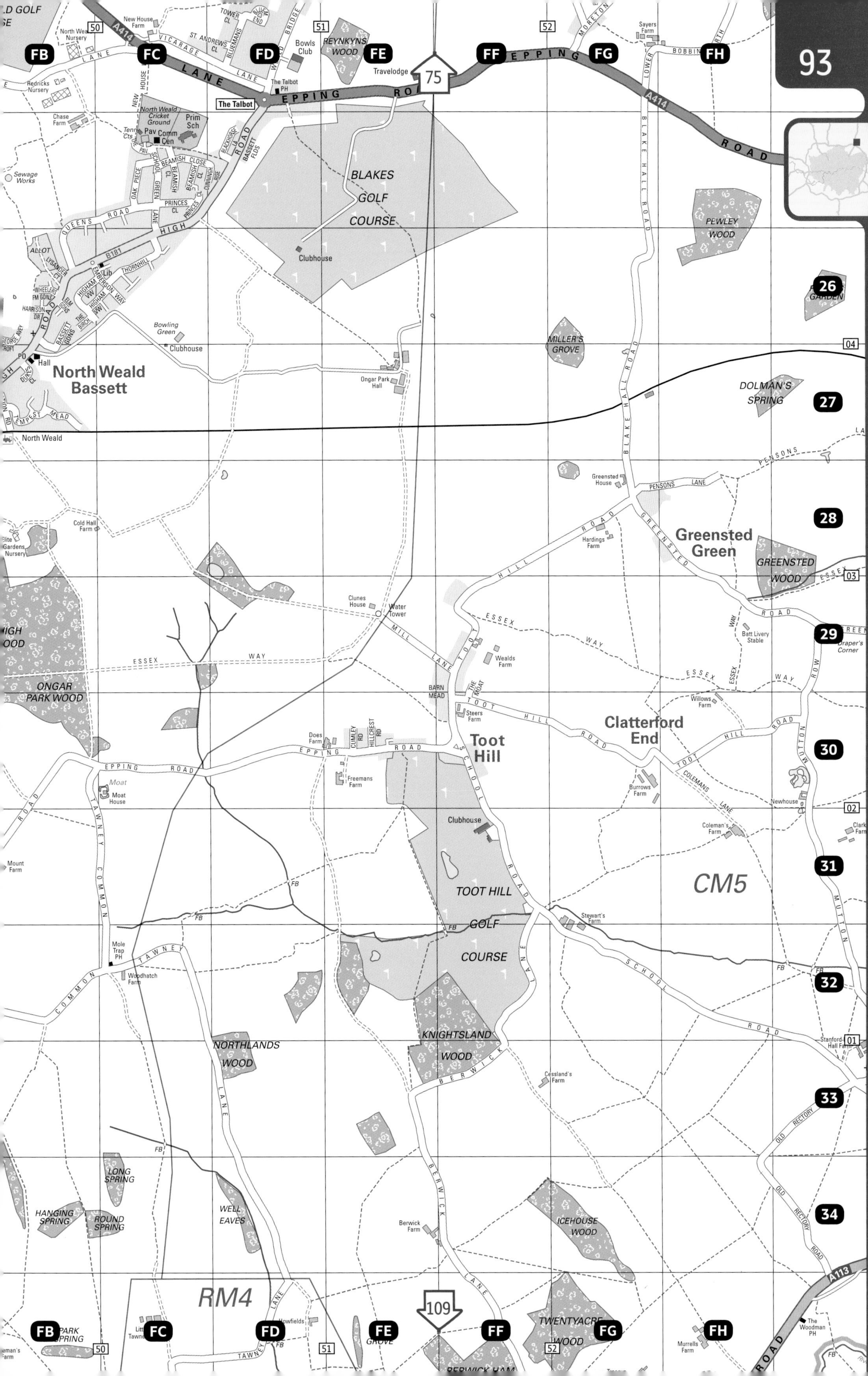
North Weald Bassett
Blakes Golf Course
Clubhouse
The Talbot
Travelodge
Epping Road
Reynkyns Wood
Bowls Club
The Talbot PH
Vicarage Lane
New House Farm
North Weald Nursery
Redricks Nursery
Chase Farm
North Weald Cricket Ground
Prim Sch
Pav
Comm Cen
Sewage Works
Queens Road
High Road
Bowling Green
Clubhouse
Ongar Park Hall
North Weald
Pewley Wood
Miller's Grove
Dolman's Spring
Blake Hall Road
Sayers Farm
Pensons Lane
Greensted House
Greensted Green
Greensted Wood
Hardings Farm
Toot Hill Road
Cold Hall Farm
Ongar Park Wood
Essex Way
Clunes House
Water Tower
Mill Lane
Wealds Farm
Batt Livery Stable
Draper's Corner
Barn Mead
The Moat
Steers Farm
Toot Hill
Willows Farm
Clatterford End
Does Farm
Cumley Rd
Hillcrest Rd
Freemans Farm
Moat House
Burrows Farm
Colemans Lane
Coleman's Farm
Newhouse
Clubhouse
School Road
Toot Hill Golf Course
Stewart's Farm
CM5
Mutton Row
Tawney Common
Mount Farm
Mole Trap PH
Woodhatch Farm
Knightsland Wood
Northlands Wood
Berwick Lane
Cessland's Farm
Stanford Hall Farm
Old Rectory Road
Long Spring
Hanging Spring
Round Spring
Well Eaves
Icehouse Wood
Berwick Farm
RM4
Twentyacre Wood
Murrells Farm
The Woodman PH
A113
A414
B181
Park Spring
Howfields
75
109
FB FC FD FE FF FG FH
26 27 28 29 30 31 32 33 34
50 51 52
04 03 02 01

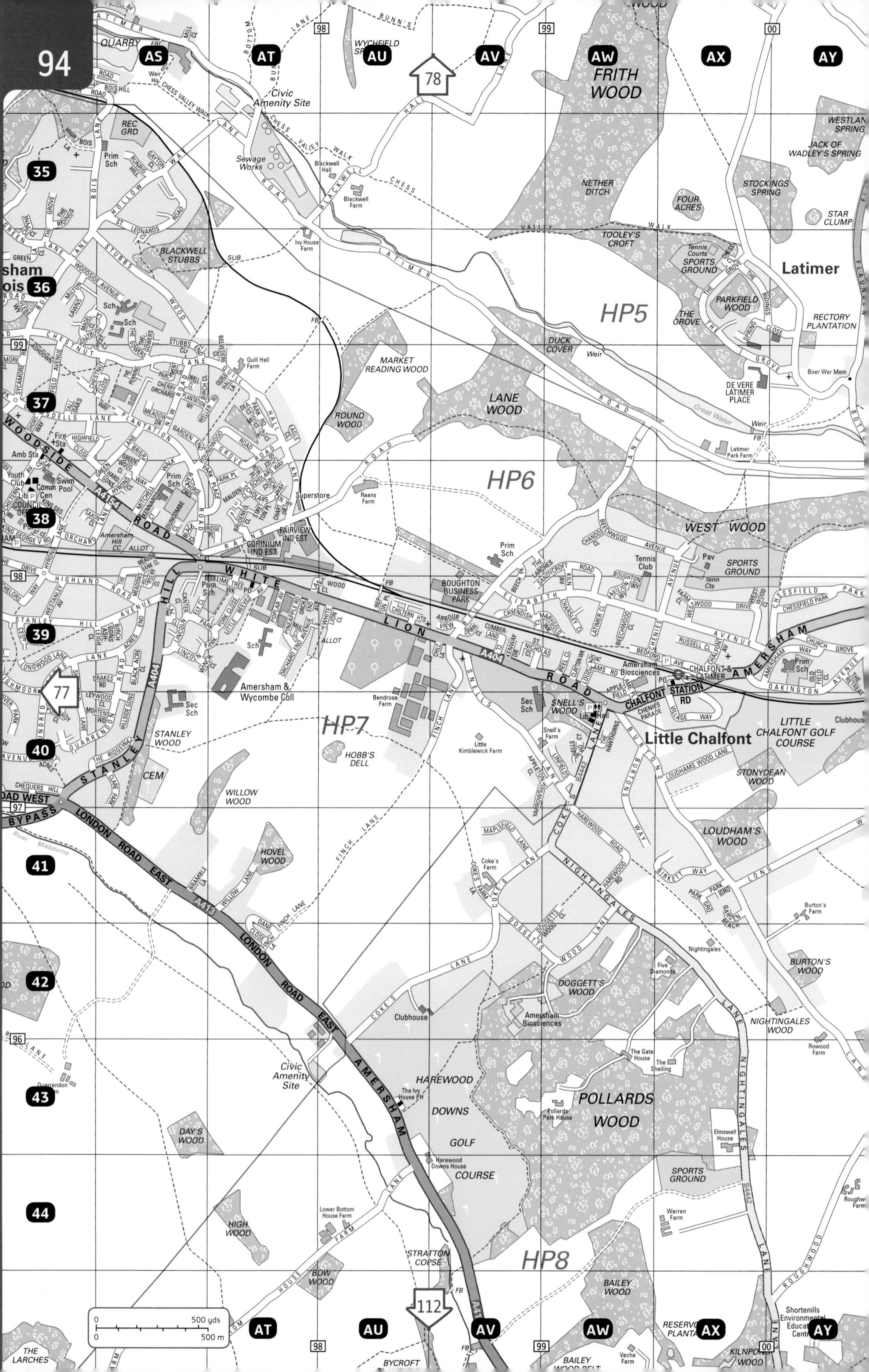
AS
AT
AU
AV
AW
AX
AY
78
98
99
00
QUARRY
FRITH WOOD
WYCHFIELD
Civic Amenity Site
Sewage Works
Blackwell Hall
Blackwell Farm
CHESS VALLEY WALK
BLACKWELL ROAD
BUNN'S LANE
HALL LANE
REC GRD
Prim Sch
BOIS HILL
BOIS LANE
HIGH BOIS LA
GAYTON WAY
RUNRIG HILL
HOLLOW WAY
ST. LEONARDS ROAD
BLACKWELL STUBBS
STUBBS WOOD
NETHER DITCH
FOUR ACRES
STOCKINGS SPRING
WESTLAN SPRING
JACK OF WADLEY'S SPRING
STAR CLUMP
TOOLEY'S CROFT
VALLEY WALK
Tennis Courts
SPORTS GROUND
PARKFIELD WOOD
Latimer
THE GROVE
RECTORY PLANTATION
HP5
River Chess
Ivy House Farm
LATIMER ROAD
DUCK COVER
Weir
Boer War Mem
DE VERE LATIMER PLACE
Great Water
Latimer Park Farm
MARKET READING WOOD
LANE WOOD
ROUND WOOD
Quill Hall Farm
35
36
37
38
39
40
41
42
43
44
sham
ois
GREEN
WOODSIDE AVENUE
CHESTNUT LANE
STUBBS END CL
QUILL HALL LANE
PLANTATION ROAD
GARDEN END
HIGHFIELD CLOSE
Fire Sta
Amb Sta
Youth Club
Comm Cen
Swim Pool
Lib
COUNCIL OFF
WOODSIDE ROAD
A4154
Prim Sch
Superstore
Raans Farm
HP6
RAANS ROAD
FAIRVIEW IND EST
CORINIUM IND EST
Amersham Hill CC
ALLOT
SUB
HIGHLAND ROAD
WHITE LION ROAD
A404
HILL AVENUE
STANLEY HILL
BOUGHTON BUSINESS PARK
CHILTERN HTS
Prim Sch
WEST WOOD
Tennis Club
Pav
SPORTS GROUND
Tenn Cts
CHESSFIELD PARK
ELIZABETH AVENUE
CHENIES AVENUE
Amersham Biosciences
CHALFONT & LATIMER
CHALFONT STATION RD
AMERSHAM ROAD
Prim Sch
OAKINGTON AVENUE
Sch
ALLOT
Amersham & Wycombe Coll
Bendrose Farm
HP7
HOBB'S DELL
Little Kimblewick Farm
Sec Sch
SNELL'S WOOD
Snell's Farm
Lib
Hall
Little Chalfont
LITTLE CHALFONT GOLF COURSE
Clubhouse
LOUDHAMS WOOD LANE
STONYDEAN WOOD
77
Sec Sch
STANLEY WOOD
CEM
WILLOW WOOD
QUARRENDON
THE RIDGEWAY
97
BYPASS
ROAD WEST
CHEQUERS HILL
LONDON ROAD EAST
A413
River Misbourne
HOVEL WOOD
FINCH LANE
MAPLEFIELD LANE
HAREWOOD ROAD
LOUDHAM'S WOOD
BIRKETT WAY
Coke's Farm
COKE'S LANE
NIGHTINGALES LANE
Burton's Farm
Nightingales
DOGGETTS WOOD LANE
Five Diamonds
BURTON'S WOOD
DOGGETT'S WOOD
Clubhouse
Amersham Biosciences
NIGHTINGALES WOOD
Rowood Farm
96
Quarrendon
Civic Amenity Site
HAREWOOD DOWNS GOLF COURSE
The Ivy House PH
The Gate House
The Sheiling
POLLARDS WOOD
Pollards Park House
Elmswell House
DAY'S WOOD
Harewood Downs House
SPORTS GROUND
B4442
Warren Farm
Lower Bottom House Farm
HIGH WOOD
STRATTON COPSE
BOW WOOD
HP8
BAILEY WOOD
ROUGHWOOD LANE
112
FB
500 yds
500 m
0
THE LARCHES
BYCROFT
BAILEY WOOD BELT
Vache Farm
RESERVOIR PLANTA
KILNPOND WOOD
Shortenills Environmental Educat Centr
Roughw Farm

AZ
BA
BB
BC
BD
BE
BF
01
02
03
79
96
113
HANGING CROFT
HP3
WD3
Mast
R.A.F. Chenies
Moonshine Farm
DACORUM
THREE RIVERS
TOP SPRING
OLDCROFT WOOD
WOOD
PLOUGH WOOD
Great Sarratt Hall Farm
Great Sarratt Hall
LONG WOOD
Martin Top Farm
HANGINGLANE WOOD
BRAMBLE CROFT
DAFFODIL SPRING
OLDFIELD SPRING
LIMESHILL WOOD
FLAUNDEN GROVE
BALDWIN'S WOOD
WALLACE'S WOOD
Valley Farm
DAWES COMMON
SANDFIELD WOOD
Moor Cottage
Watercress Beds
Mill Farm
MOUNT WOOD
ALLOT
Green End Business Cen
River Chess
CHENIES BOTTOM
Chenies Place
PLACEHOUSE COPSE
CONEY WOOD
Greathouse Farm
Prim Sch
Chenies Manor
Mountwood Farm
NICHOLAS SPRING
WALK WOOD
Bedford Arms PH
Chenies
TURVEYLANE WOOD
Football Ground
Chenies Garden Centre
Chenies & Latimer CC
Pav
WYBURN WOOD
SCRUBBS WOOD
BLUNTS WOOD
Sarrattmill Bridge
Water Works
MEAD SPRING
Weir
Weirs
FB
A404
AMERSHAM ROAD
CHENIES ROAD
RICKMANSWORTH ROAD
OLD HANGING WOOD
CHILTON'S WOOD
CHILTERN
Great Greenstreet Farm
Little Greenstreet Farm
Stubbs Farm
NEW HANGING WOOD
HALSEY'S WOOD
LODGE COPSE
Sec Sch
Field Study Centre
Tennis Club
Chorleywood House
DELL WOOD
Lodge Farm
BUCKINGHAMSHIRE
HERTFORDSHIRE
WHITELANDS WOOD
HILLAS WOOD
CARPENTER'S WOOD
CEM
Chorleywood Cricket Club
Prim Sch
White Horse PH
Arts Centre
Clubhouse
Hall
CHORLEYWOOD COMMON
CHORLEYWOOD GOLF COURSE
Newhouse Farm
Prim Sch
PO
CHORLEYWOOD
Lib
Black Horse PH
HOME WOOD
The Cedars
Chorleywood
CROSSLANE WOOD
Roughwood Park
Fairfield Farm & Livery Stables
Berry Farm
THE SCREEN
SOLOMON'S WOOD
The Hall Farm
Penn Farm
West Herts Riding School
PHEASANTS WOOD
COV RES
Prim Sch
Hill Farm
Chorleywood Bottom
The Swillet
ALLOT
Bullsland Farm
GROVE WOOD
Heronsgate
M25

Commonwood
BG
BH
BJ
BK
BL
BM
BN
80
Bucks Hill
Baytree Farm
Model Farm
HILLMEADS SPRING
COMMONWOOD COMMON
Bucks Hill Farm
Great Sarratt Hall
HAW SPRING
BEECHEN BOTTOM
Little Westwood Farm
Great Westwood Equestrian Park
WD4
35
Sarratt
RED LION LANE
BOTTOM LANE
HOUSE LANE
OLD HOUSE LANE
HIGH SPRING
JUNIPER HILL
The Boot PH
Tennis Courts
SPORTS GROUND
Pav
Poultry Houses
Buckshill Bottom
Newhall Farm
36
DAWS COMMON
Cricketers PH
PO
Prim Sch
Hall
DIMMOCKS LANE
DEADMAN'S ASH LANE
Junction 19
TEMPLEPAN WOOD
SANDFIELD WOOD
Adams Nurseries
TEMPLEPAN LANE
Yew Court Farm
ALLOT
37
Green End Business Cen
BIRCH SPRING
DARTPATH WOOD
Potten's Farm
Mickleford Green Farm
GREAT WOOD
WHITE SHACK LANE
SHEEPYARD SPRING
M25
Chandler's Cross
38
New Model Farm
SAWPIT SPRING
Coltspring Riding Stables
Coltyard Farm
Cottage Farm
Blacketts Nurseries
SCRUBBS WOOD
98
WILLOW WOOD
HARROCKS WOOD
BLUNTS WOOD
Sarrattmill Bridge
39
MEAD SPRING
Redhall Farm
WELLING GROVE
MERLIN'S WOOD
95
Weir
Micklefield Hall Farm
Micklefield Hall
MERLIN'S SPRING
40
Beechen Hill
WD3
BEECHENGROVE WOOD
ROUND SPRING
Model Farm
York Ho Sch
MILLFIELD PLANTATION
LONG SPRING
UPPER PLANTATION
WATERDELL SPRING
97
41
Highlands Water Gardens
Solesbridge Mill Water Gardens
Waterdell House
Loudwater
Croxley House
Killingdown Farm
LITTLE LADY'S WOOD
Junction 18
Loudwater House
Whitestocks Farm
PARROT'S DELL
CROXLEY GREEN
42
Weirs
Mont Au Source
The Cedars
HOME WOOD
CHORLEYWOOD ROAD
Loudwater Farm
BALDWINS LANE RECREATION GROUND
96
COPTHORNE WOOD
SPORTS GROUND
Pav
43
ROUND SPRING
Coach & Horses PH
Prim Sch
SPORTS GROUND
Croxley Green
THE SCREEN
SOLOMON'S WOOD
Sch
West Herts Riding School
44
PHEASANTS WOOD
Prim Sch
Rickmansworth Masonic Sch
HOCKEY GRD
PLAYING FIELD
CRICKET GRD
Clubhouse
Sec Sch
Prim Sch
SPORTS GROUND
A404
CEM
114
FORTUNE COMMON
CROXLEY HALL WOODS
LONG VALLEY WOOD
RICKMANSWORTH PARK
RICKMANSWORTH
SCOTS HILL
WATFORD ROAD
0 500 yds
0 500 m
05
06
07

Langleybury
Leavesden Green
Kingswood
81
NORTH WESTERN AVENUE
Hunton Bridge Interchange
Leavesden Green
The Dome
NORTH WATFORD CEMETERY
STANBOROUGH PARK
HEATH WOOD
The Grove Hotel
THE GROVE
GOLF COURSE
WD24
NORTH WATFORD
CALLOWLAND REC GRD
CHARLOTTE'S VALE
ROUGH WOOD
SPORTS GROUND
WHIPPENDELL WOOD
WEST HERTS GOLF COURSE
HEMPSTEAD ROAD
CASSIOBURY PARK
NATURE RESERVE
Paddling Pools
WATFORD
WD17
Watford Junction
West Herts College
THE COLOSSEUM
TOWN HALL
98
RICKMANSWORTH ROAD
WEST WATFORD
VICARAGE RD CEMETERY
VICARAGE RD STADIUM WATFORD FC & SARACENS RFC
WATFORD GENERAL HOSP
WD18
Holywell
WATFORD BUSINESS PARK
CROXLEY GREEN BUSINESS PARK
HOLYWELL IND EST
KING GEORGE V PLAYING FIELDS
RIVERSIDE PARK
Electricity Transmission Station
LONG VALLEY WOOD
COMMON MOOR
115
WATFORD HIGH STREET
BP
BQ
BR
BS
BT
BU
BV
36
37
38
39
40
41
42
43
44

BW
BX
BY
BZ
CA
CB
CC
82
97
116
12
13
14
35
36
37
38
39
40
41
42
43
44
Garston
Meriden
NORTH WATFORD
WD24
WD17
WD19
WD25
WD23
Munden
MUNDEN SPRING
PEARTREE WOOD
ST. ALBANS
HERTSMERE
WATFORD
STANBOROUGH PARK
The Dome
Superstore
Superstores
ODHAMS TRADING EST
THE WENTA BUSINESS CEN
PARAMOUNT IND EST
MOWAT IND EST
SANDOWN RD IND EST
THE EMPIRE CENTRE
TRIDENT CENTRE
HOLLY IND PARK
PENFOLD TRADING EST
IMPERIAL PARK
WATFORD JUNCTION
TOP GOLF GAME CENTRE
Junction 5
Berrygrove Interchange
ALDENHAM GOLF COURSE & COUNTRY CLUB
Aldenham
Hartswood
Hilton Watford
Bushey Hall Farm
SCOTTS WOOD
BUSHEY HALL GOLF COURSE
ICEDALE WOODS
RADLETT ROAD PLAYING FIELDS
The Purcell School
METROPOLITAN POLICE BUSHEY SPORTS GROUND
BUSHEY JEWISH CEMETERY
The Lincolnsfields Centre
Leisure Cen
GREATHAM RD IND EST
Premier Inn
Waterfields
Waterfields Retail Park
Colne Valley Retail Park
Veolia Water
Gas Works
Watford Arches Retail Park
WATFORD HIGH STREET
The Harlequin
Charter Place
STADIUM WATFORD FC & SARACENS RFC
FISHER'S IND EST
WIGGENHALL RD GOODS YD
OXHEY PARK
OXHEY
BUSHEY
BUSHEY GOLF COURSE & COUNTRY CLUB
KING GEORGE REC GROUND
MOAT-FIELD REC GRD
BURIAL GRD
ST ALBANS ROAD
COLNE WAY (NORTH WESTERN AVENUE)
OTTERSPOOL WAY
ELTON WAY (NORTH WESTERN AVENUE)
BERRY GROVE LANE
HARTSPRING LANE
ALDENHAM ROAD
STEPHENSON WAY
WATERFIELDS WAY
BEECHEN GROVE
EXCHANGE ROAD
VICARAGE ROAD
WIGGENHALL ROAD
DEACONS HILL
EASTBURY ROAD
PINNER ROAD
CHALK HILL
LONDON ROAD
HIGH ROAD
HIGH STREET
SPARROWS HERNE
A41
A412
A411
A4008
A4125
A4178
B462
M1
0 500 yds
0 500 m

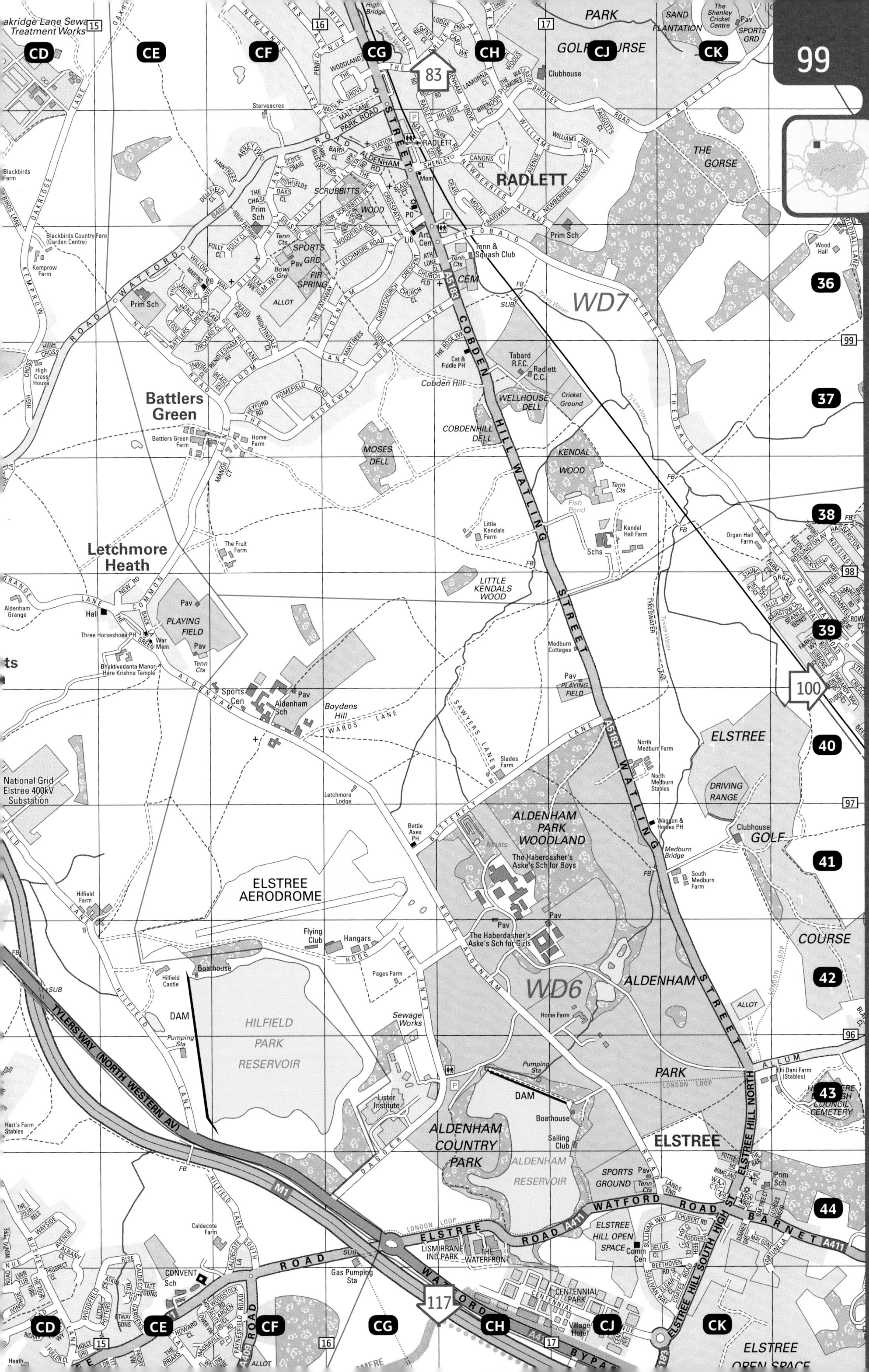
CD
CE
CF
CG
CH
CJ
CK
83
100
117
36
37
38
39
40
41
42
43
44
15
16
17
99
98
97
96
Oakridge Lane Sewage Treatment Works
High Bridge
PARK
SAND PLANTATION
The Shenley Cricket Centre
Pav
SPORTS GRD
GOLF COURSE
Clubhouse
RADLETT
THE GORSE
Wood Hall
WD7
Starveacres
Blackbirds Farm
Blackbirds Country Fare (Garden Centre)
Kemprow Farm
High Cross House
Prim Sch
SCRUBBITTS WOOD
SPORTS GRD
FIR SPRING
ALLOT
Bowl Grn
Tenn Cts
Lib
Arts Cen
CEM
Tenn & Squash Club
Tabard R.F.C.
Radlett C.C.
Cricket Ground
Cat & Fiddle PH
Cobden Hill
WELLHOUSE DELL
COBDENHILL DELL
MOSES DELL
KENDAL WOOD
Fish Pond
Little Kendals Farm
Kendal Hall Farm
Schs
LITTLE KENDALS WOOD
Organ Hall Farm
Battlers Green
Battlers Green Farm
Home Farm
Letchmore Heath
The Fruit Farm
Aldenham Grange
Hall
PLAYING FIELD
Three Horseshoes PH
War Mem
Bhaktivedanta Manor-Hare Krishna Temple
Sports Cen
Aldenham Sch
Boydens Hill
Medburn Cottages
PLAYING FIELD
North Medburn Farm
North Medburn Stables
Slades Farm
ELSTREE
DRIVING RANGE
Clubhouse
GOLF COURSE
National Grid Elstree 400kV Substation
Letchmore Lodge
Battle Axes PH
ALDENHAM PARK WOODLAND
Moats
The Haberdasher's Aske's Sch for Boys
Waggon & Horses PH
Medburn Bridge
South Medburn Farm
ELSTREE AERODROME
Hilfield Farm
Flying Club
Hangars
The Haberdasher's Aske's Sch for Girls
WD6
ALDENHAM
ALLOT
Boathouse
Hilfield Castle
Pages Farm
DAM
Pumping Sta
HILFIELD PARK RESERVOIR
Sewage Works
Home Farm
Pumping Sta
PARK
LONDON LOOP
Elli Dani Farm (Stables)
HERTSMERE COUNCIL CEMETERY
Hart's Farm Stables
Lister Institute
DAM
Boathouse
Sailing Club
ALDENHAM COUNTRY PARK
ALDENHAM RESERVOIR
ELSTREE
SPORTS GROUND
Tenn Cts
Prim Sch
TYLERS WAY (NORTH WESTERN AV)
M1
Caldecote Farm
LISMIRRANE IND PARK
THE WATERFRONT
ELSTREE HILL OPEN SPACE
Comm Cen
CONVENT Sch
Gas Pumping Sta
CENTENNIAL PARK
Village Hotel
ELSTREE OPEN SPACE
WATLING STREET
COBDEN HILL
A5183
WATFORD ROAD
ELSTREE ROAD
BARNET LANE
ALDENHAM ROAD
ELSTREE HILL NORTH
ELSTREE HILL SOUTH
A411
A409
ELSTREE BYPASS

CL
CM
CN
CP
CQ
CR
CS
84
99
118
35
36
37
38
39
40
41
42
43
44
WD7
WD6
Green Street
THE MEADOWS
Well End
BOREHAMWOOD
ELSTREE
BIG PURSLEY WOOD
LITTLE PURSLEY WOOD
CROSS OAKS WOOD
BIRCH WOOD
Crossoaks Farm
The Garden Nursery
Tokonoma Bonsai
The White Horse PH
Pursley Farm
SPORTS GRD
ALLOT
London Colney C.C.
Auriol Farm
Wood Hall Farm
Wood Hall
Kitwells Farm
Villa Scalabrini
Lyndhurst
SILVER HILL
High Canons
High Canons Farm
Holmshill House
Buckettsland Farm
Wheatsheaf Farm
Maxwelton Nurseries
Well End Farm
Cowley Hill Farm
Organ Hall Farm
Strangeways Farm
Rowley Farm
Mops & Brooms PH
AYCLIFFE ROAD PITCHES
SPORTS GROUND
ABERFORD PARK
MEADOW PARK
Hertswood School (Upper School)
Oaklands College
BOREHAMWOOD IND PARK
NEW HORIZONS
Millennium Studios
DEVONSHIRE BUSINESS PARK
B.B.C. Elstree Studios
Elstree Film Studios
ELSTREE BUSINESS CENTRE
Hertsmere Ind Pk
KENILWORTH PARK
Borehamwood Shopping Park
Kinetic Bus Cen
The Point
MAXWELL PK
Travelodge
Holiday Inn
A1 DRIVING RANGE
ROWLEY LANE SPORTS GRD
ROWLEY LANE GOLF COURSE
RIPON PARK
ELSTREE & BOREHAMWOOD
Gas Works
Furze Hill
STIRLING IND CEN
Stirling Retail Pk
Stirling Corner
DRIVING RANGE
GOLF COURSE
Clubhouse
South Medburn Farm
Elli Dani Farm (Stables)
HERTSMERE BOROUGH COUNCIL CEMETERY
Woodcock Hill Farm
BUPA Nursing Home
Deacons Hill
DEACONS HILL OPEN SPACE
Elstree Manor
Penniwells Farm
SCRATCH WOOD
FROGHALL WOOD
BOYS HILL WOOD
THISTLE WOOD
ARKLEY PARK
Hyver Hall
GRAVEL PITWOOD
ELSTREE OPEN SPACE
TUNNEL
Airshafts
A411
A5135
B5378
BARNET BYPASS
ELSTREE WAY
BARNET LANE
SHENLEY ROAD
ALLUM LANE
ELSTREE HILL NORTH
ELSTREE HILL SOUTH
LONDON LOOP
500 yds
500 m

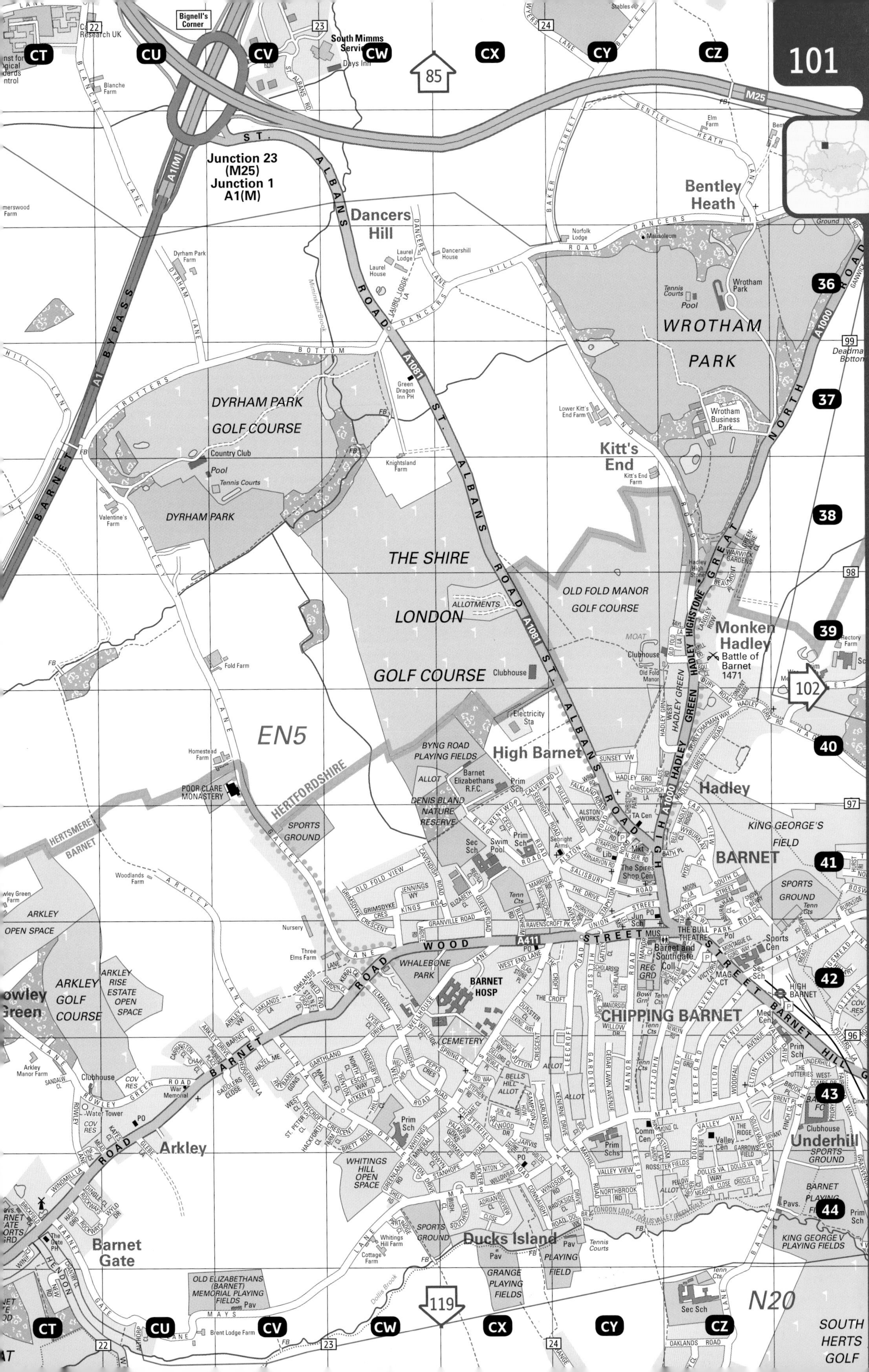

CT
CU
CV
CW
CX
CY
CZ
85
Bignell's Corner
Research UK
South Mimms Services
Days Inn
Blanche Farm
BLANCHE LANE
M25
BENTLEY HEATH
Elm Farm
Junction 23 (M25) Junction 1 A1(M)
A1(M)
ST. ALBANS ROAD
BAKER STREET
WYERS LANE
Stables
Bentley Heath
Dancers Hill
Norfolk Lodge
DANCERS HILL ROAD
Mausoleum
Laurel Lodge
Dancershill House
Laurel House
LAUREL LODGE LA
Dyrham Park Farm
DYRHAM LANE
Mimmshall Brook
Tennis Courts
Pool
Wrotham Park
WROTHAM PARK
A1000
NORTH ROAD
GANWICK
99
Deadman Bottom
36
37
38
39
40
41
42
43
44
A1 BYPASS
BOTTOM LANE
TROTTERS
A1081
Green Dragon Inn PH
DYRHAM PARK GOLF COURSE
Country Club
Pool
Tennis Courts
FB
Lower Kitt's End Farm
KITT'S END ROAD
Wrotham Business Park
Knightsland Farm
Kitt's End
Kitt's End Farm
BARNET LANE
Valentine's Farm
DYRHAM PARK
GALLEY LANE
THE SHIRE LONDON GOLF COURSE
ALLOTMENTS
Clubhouse
OLD FOLD MANOR GOLF COURSE
MOAT
Clubhouse
Old Fold Manor
Hadley High Stone
GREAT NORTH ROAD
GREEN-ACRE CL
WARWICK GARDENS
BEAUMONT PL
98
Monken Hadley
Battle of Barnet 1471
Rectory Farm
102
HADLEY GREEN
HADLEY HIGHSTONE
LANGLEY ROW
Fold Farm
Electricity Sta
EN5
HERTFORDSHIRE
Homestead Farm
BYNG ROAD PLAYING FIELDS
High Barnet
POOR CLARE MONASTERY
ALLOT
Barnet Elizabethans R.F.C.
Prim Sch
DENIS BLAND NATURE RESERVE
SPORTS GROUND
HERTSMERE
BARNET
Hadley
97
KING GEORGE'S FIELD
BARNET
Woodlands Farm
ARKLEY LANE
ARKLEY OPEN SPACE
Sec Sch
Swim Pool
Prim Sch
Sebright Arms
TA Cen
Mkt
Lib
The Spires Shop Cen
SPORTS GROUND
Tenn Cts
Rowley Green Farm
OLD FOLD VIEW
JENNINGS WY
GRIMSDYKE CRES
KINGS RD
Tenn Cts
SALISBURY
THE DRIVE
UNION STREET
Jun Sch
PO
MUS
THE BULL THEATRE
PARK RD
Pol
Sports Cen
Nursery
GRANVILLE ROAD
RAVENSCROFT PK
A411
WOOD STREET
Barnet and Southgate Coll
REC GRD
MAG CT
HIGH STREET
HIGH BARNET
Sec Sch
Three Elms Farm
WHALEBONE PARK
BARNET HOSP
WEST END LANE
THE CROFT
ARKLEY RISE ESTATE OPEN SPACE
ARKLEY GOLF COURSE
Rowley Green
CHIPPING BARNET
Med Cen
BARNET HILL
96
CEMETERY
Tenn Cts
Bowl Grn
Tenn Cts
Prim Sch
THE POTTERIES
Arkley Manor Farm
Clubhouse
COV RES
ROWLEY GREEN ROAD
War Memorial
BARNET ROAD
BELLS HILL ALLOT
ALLOT
ALLOT
Clubhouse
Water Tower
PO
Prim Sch
Comm Cen
Prim Schs
Valley Cen
Underhill
SPORTS GROUND
Arkley
MAYS LANE
VALLEY VIEW
WHITINGS HILL OPEN SPACE
ROSSITER FIELDS
ALLOT
BARNET PLAYING FIELDS
Pavs.
Prim Sch
LONDON LOOP / DOLLIS VALLEY GREENWALK
SPORTS GROUND
Ducks Island
Pav
Tennis Courts
Whitings Hill Farm
Cottage Farm
Pav
PLAYING FIELD
KING GEORGE V PLAYING FIELDS
Barnet Gate
The Gate PH
HENDON WOOD LANE
Dollis Brook
GRANGE PLAYING FIELDS
119
OLD ELIZABETHANS (BARNET) MEMORIAL PLAYING FIELDS
Pav
Tenn Cts
Sec Sch
N20
Brent Lodge Farm
22
23
24
OAKLANDS ROAD
SOUTH HERTS GOLF

DA
DB
DC
DD
DE
DF
DG
POTTERS BAR COMMUNITY HOSP
M25
86
Junction 24
WELWYN HATFIELD
THE RIDGEWAY
A1005
New Cottage Farm
Prep. Sch
Water Tower
WOOD
Elm Farm
Bentley Heath Farm
Bentley Heath
Garden Centre
Ganwick Corner
Duke of York PH
Cricket Ground
Pav
Fenny Shade Hill
CHASE WOOD
Chase Farm
FIR WOOD
Plumridge Hill
PLUMRIDGE WOOD
South Ba Farm
VAULT HILL WOOD
Wrotham Park
Pool
WROTHAM PARK
Three Oak Hill
Hornbeam Hills
HERTFORDSHIRE
Cockshot Hill
Plumridge Farm
Deadman's Bottom
Ganwick Farm
SPOILBANK WOOD
HERTSMERE
ENFIELD
Salmon's Brook
Slopers Pond Farm
Roundhe Hill
Wrotham Business Park
WAGGON ROAD
ENFIEL
BARTRAMS QUASH
Tenn Club
Prim Sch
HADLEY WOOD
CLAREMONT ROAD
COURTLEIGH AV
KINGWELL ROAD
Monken Mead Brook
West Lodge Park Hotel
ASH WOOD
COCKFOSTERS ROAD
LANCASTER AVENUE
DOUGLAS CLOSE
HADLEY WOOD
FERNY HILL
Ferny Hill Farm
Great Broadgates Hill
BEECH HILL
CAMLET WAY
WALMAR CLOSE
Clubhouse
FERNYHILL WOOD
ROUG LOT
Monken Hadley
Battle of Barnet
Rectory Farm
Sch
War Memorial
BEECH HILL PARK
HADLEY WOOD GOLF COURSE
Green Brook
COVERT WAY OPEN SPACE
Sewit's Hill
Fish Ponds
SEEDFIELD SPINNEY
Bournwell Hill
MONKEN HADLEY COMMON
Priddeon's Hill
Newman's Hill
EN4
BEECH HILL LAKE
Water Tower
OAK WOOD
Hadley
TUDOR GOLF COURSE
TUDOR SPORTS GRD
KING GEORGE'S FIELD
EN5
BARNET
Jewish Comm. Sec Sch
SPORTS GROUND
Gas Works
VICTORIA REC GRD
SPORTS GROUND
TRENT PARK CEM
COCKFOSTERS
Monument
CHURCH
NEW BARNET
HIGH BARNET
COCKFOSTERS
BARNET
EAST BARNET ROAD
NEW BARNET
A110
A1000
A111
GREAT NORTH ROAD
STATION ROAD
Underhill
SPORTS GROUND
BARNET FC
BARNET PLAYING FIELDS
KING GEORGE V PLAYING FIELDS
BROOKHILL ROAD
CAT HILL
Middlesex Uni
EAST BARNET
Oak Hill College
OAK HILL PARK
Bandstand
Miniature Golf Course
N20
WYATTS FARM OPEN SPACE
120
101
500 yds
500 m
GOLF

M25
South Hill
87
Crews Hill
Clubhouse
CREWS HILL GOLF COURSE
Crews Hill
Kings Oak Plain
WILDWOOD
THE RIDGEWAY
Botany Bay
Botany Bay C.C.
Botany Bay Farm
LITTLE BEECHILL WOOD
A1005
Prim Sch
STRAYFIELD ROAD CEMETERY
Rendlesham Viaduct
Kingswood
Clay Hill
CHASE
HILLY FIELDS PARK
EN2
LAVENDER HILL CEMETERY
THE KING'S OAK HOSPITAL
CHASE FARM HOSPITAL
Cuckolds Hill
Park Farms
HADLEY ROAD
MOAT WOOD
Camlet Hill
RIDE WOOD
Parkside Farm
Pumping Station
Royal Chace Hotel
Vicarage Farm
Leeging Beech Gutter
Salmon's Brook
Hog Hill
WILLIAMS WOOD
Fish Pond
ICEHOUSE WOOD
Middlesex University
SHAWS WOOD
NUFFIELD HOSP
104
Tennis Courts
SPORTS GROUND
TRENT PARK GOLF COURSE
Merryhills Brook
SLADES HILL
WINDMILL HILL
A110
World's End
ENFIELD GOLF COURSE
TRIANGULAR WOOD
South Lodge Farm
ENFIELD ROAD
Trent Park Equestrian Centre
Driving Range
Clubhouse
Sec Sch
Prim Sch
CHEYNE WALK
GRANGE PARK
OAKWOOD
BRAMLEY ROAD
PRIORY
N21
SPORTS GROUND
Pitch 'n' Putt
OAKWOOD PARK
YACHTING POND
121
WINCHMORE HILL
N14
Bush Hill Park Golf Course
DH
DJ
DK
DL
DM
DN
DP
29
30
31
36
37
38
39
40
41
42
43
44
96
97
98
99

DQ
DR
DS
DT
DU
DV
DW
33
34
35
88
103
122
Junction 25
News International Print Works
BULLSCROSS RIDE
CEMETERY (JEWISH)
COUNTY BROOK PLANTATION
Theobalds Park Camping and Caravan Site
Aquaduct
Sloeman's Farm
Whitewebbs Farm
WHITEWEBBS ROAD
Bulls Cross
Capel Manor College
CAPEL HOUSE
BULLSMOOR LANE
Water World, Aquatic & Garden Centre
AYLANDS OPEN SPACE
Crews Hill
WHITEWEBBS WOOD
WHITEWEBBS PARK
WHITEWEBBS GOLF COURSE
White Webbs House
Roman Villa
Enfield Invicta C.C.
SPORTS GROUND
Myddelton Farm
BULLS CROSS FIELD
Orchardside Nurseries
Wilfwoods Water Garden Centre
WILDWOOD
Hill Side Nursery
Myddelton House
Gardens
Turkey Brook
LONDON LOOP
New River (Old Course)
Cuffley Brook
EN2
Brayside Farm
Clubhouse
The Fallow Buck PH
North Enfield
Queenswood Farm
Kingswood
Clay Hill
Clay Hill House
Rose & Crown PH
FORTY HALL COUNTRY PARK
Forty Hill
Forty Hall Farm
FORTY HALL & MUSEUM
Maiden's Bridge
Bullsmoor
TURKEY STREET
THE DELL
War Memorial
CEMETERY
Crematorium
HILLY FIELDS PARK
ALLOTMENTS
Clockhouse Nursery
Clock House
CEDAR HILL CEMETERY
FOUR HILLS EST
HOLTWHITES SPORTS & SOCIAL CLUB
Holtwhites Hotel
ENFIELD CEMETERY (JEWISH)
REC GRD
Fitness Centre
QUEEN ELIZABETH STADIUM
EN1
ENFIELD PLAYING FIELDS
ENFIELD
SPORTS GROUND
BASEBALL GROUND
Pavilion
Leisure Cen
ST. GEORGE'S FIELD
Boys Club
Health Cen
ENFIELD TOWN
CIVIC CENTRE
Palace Gardens
Palace Exchange
CHURCH ST
SOUTHBURY ROAD
WINDMILL HILL
ENFIELD CHASE
TOWN PARK
CONVENT
Superstore
Superstores
ENFIELD RETAIL PK
Enfield Coll
GREAT CAMBRIDGE ROAD
HERTFORD ROAD
Cinema
SOUTHBURY
BUSH HILL PARK
Croquet Lawn
Enfield C.C.
BUSH HILL PARK GOLF COURSE
GRANGE PARK
CHEYNE WALK
MARTINBRIDGE TRADING ESTATE
HASLEMERE BUSINESS CENTRE
GREAT CAMBRIDGE IND EST
Bowls & Tenn Club
Tenn Club
N21
Salmon's Brook
Tenn & Squash Club
JUBILEE PARK
ALLOTMENTS
Sadlers Mill
0 500 yds
0 500 m

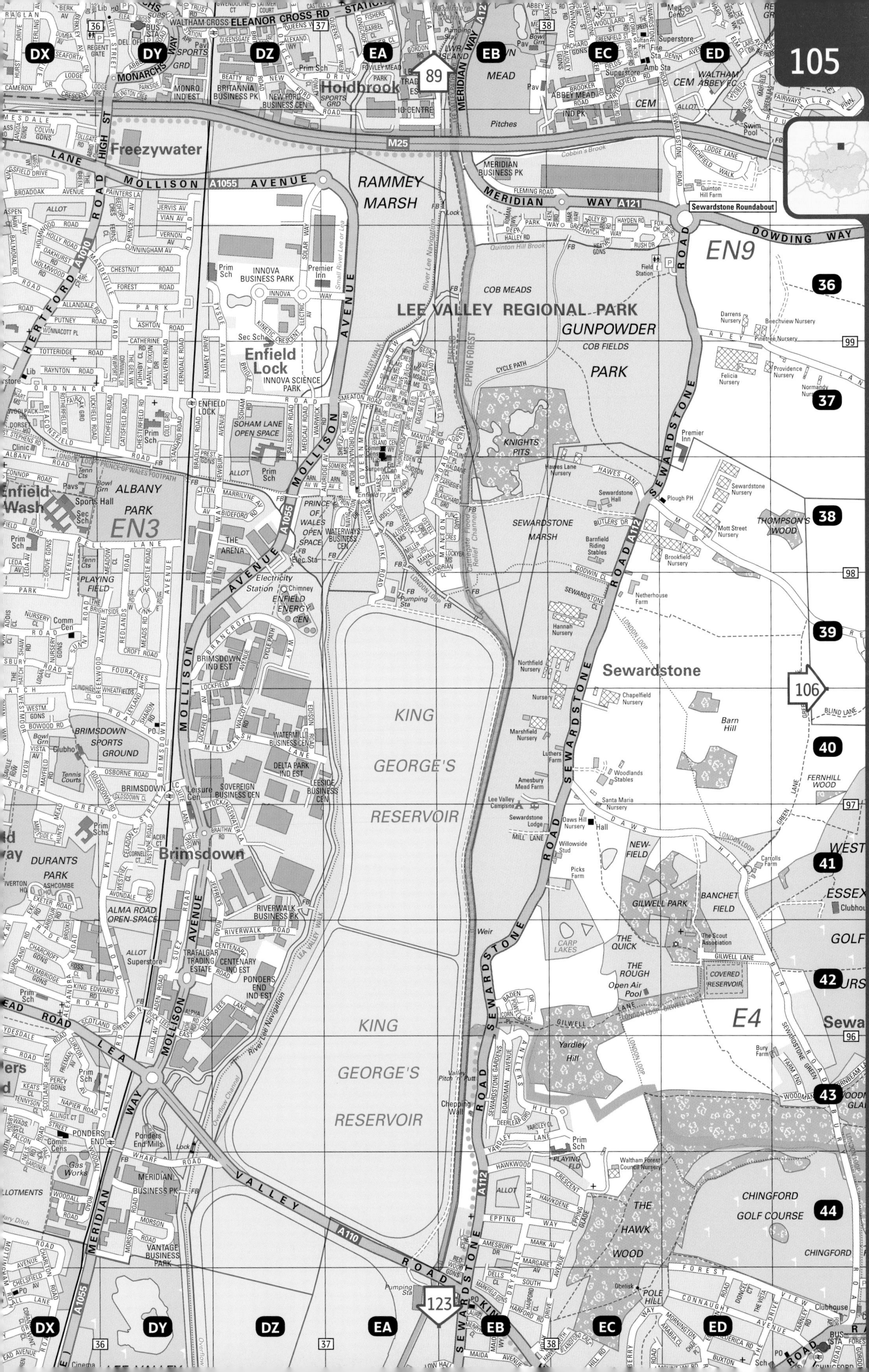
DX
DY
DZ
EA
EB
EC
ED
89
Holdbrook
WALTHAM CROSS
ELEANOR CROSS RD
MONARCHS WAY
MERIDIAN WAY
WALTHAM ABBEY F.C.
M25
Freezywater
MOLLISON AVENUE
A1055
RAMMEY MARSH
MERIDIAN BUSINESS PK
Sewardstone Roundabout
DOWDING WAY
A121
EN9
36
37
38
39
40
41
42
43
44
INNOVA BUSINESS PARK
Enfield Lock
INNOVA SCIENCE PARK
LEE VALLEY REGIONAL PARK
GUNPOWDER PARK
COB MEADS
COB FIELDS
HERTFORD ROAD
A1010
ENFIELD LOCK
SOHAM LANE OPEN SPACE
KNIGHTS PITS
Premier Inn
Plough PH
SEWARDSTONE ROAD
A112
ALBANY PARK
Enfield Wash
EN3
THE ARENA
PRINCE OF WALES OPEN SPACE
WATERWAYS BUSINESS CEN
SEWARDSTONE MARSH
THOMPSON'S WOOD
Electricity Station
ENFIELD ENERGY CEN
BRIMSDOWN IND EST
Sewardstone
106
KING GEORGE'S RESERVOIR
BRIMSDOWN SPORTS GROUND
DELTA PARK IND EST
LEESIDE BUSINESS CEN
SOVEREIGN BUSINESS CEN
Barn Hill
FERNHILL WOOD
Brimsdown
DURANTS PARK
NEW-FIELD
RIVERWALK BUSINESS PK
ALMA ROAD OPEN SPACE
GILWELL PARK
BANCHET FIELD
TRAFALGAR TRADING ESTATE
CENTENARY IND EST
PONDERS END IND EST
THE QUICK
THE ROUGH
CARP LAKES
E4
Yardley Hill
PONDERS END
MERIDIAN BUSINESS PK
VANTAGE BUSINESS PARK
CHINGFORD GOLF COURSE
THE HAWK WOOD
POLE HILL
CHINGFORD
LEA VALLEY ROAD
A110
123

EE
EF
EG
EH
EJ
EK
EL
90
WALTHAM ABBEY
SPORTS GROUND
Prim Schs
Swim Pool
Marriott Waltham Abbey
Junction 26
HONEY LANE
Skillet Hill Farm
M25
Sewardstone Roundabout
Quinton Hill Farm
DOWDING WAY
A121
EN9
Inner Lodge
LORD PADGETS WOOD
POPLARS SHAW
WALTHAM ABBEY CEMETERY (JEWISH)
Volunteer PH
HONEY LANE PLAIN
WOODRIDDEN
Southend Farm
Upshire Hall
SOUTHEND LA
CLAY PIGEON RANGE
The Lodge
Sudbury Farm
WOODBINE CLOSE
Woodbine Inn PH
Woodgreen Farm
POTKILN WOOD
CONYBURY WOOD
Woodredon House
Woodredon Farm
Woodredon Riding School
STABLES SHAW
BRAMBLY SHAW
HONEY LANE QUARTERS
SUNSHINE PLAIN
THREE FORESTS WAY
Round Hills
Darrens Nursery
Beechview Nursery
Pinetree Nursery
Felicia Nursery
Providence Nursery
Normandy Nursery
AVEY LANE
Avey Lane Farm
Beech Hill Park
BEECH HILL PARK
Hanbury Riding School
HIGH BEECH GOLF COURSE
Tile Hill Farm
Clubho
Duke of Wellington PH
PYNEST GRN
Pynest Green
High Beech Riding School
High Beech Nursery
Avey Cottages
Bowl Club
Earthworks
King's Oak PH
Epping Forest Field Cen
Premier Inn
Sewardstone Nursery
Mott Street Nursery
THOMPSON'S WOOD
Manor Farm
Prim Sch
Manor House
MANOR ROAD
Paul's Nursery
Oak Farm
MOTT STREET
Wallsgrove House
ALDERGROVE WOOD
High Beach C.C.
High Beach
CHURCH ROAD
LIPPITTS HILL
BLIND LANE
Barn Hill
105
Day's Farm
FERNHILL WOOD
Police Training Centre
THE ELMS
Elms Caravan & Camping Park
Suntrap Field Study Centre
Pipers Farm
THE OWL
Owl PH
HILL WOOD
CENTENARY WALK
EPPING FOREST
IG10
A104
EPPING NEW ROAD
LITTLE MONK WOOD
Mount Pleasant
Broom Hill
Kate's Cellar
Shelley's Hill
Robin Hood PH
Loughton Camp
Wake Valley
Staples Hill
Strawberry Hill
WEST ESSEX GOLF COURSE
Clubhouse
Carrolls Farm
BANCHET FIELD
The Scout Association
GILWELL LANE
Springfield Farm
Piggeries
WHITEHOUSE PLAIN
ROUND THICKET
ALMSHOUSE PLAIN
North Long Hills
Fairmead Bottom
FAIRMEAD POND
STRAWBERRY HILL PONDS
E4
Sewardstonebury
Bury Farm
WOODMAN LA
WOODMAN'S GLADE
BURY WOOD
Cuckoo Pits
Grimston's Oak
Long Hills
HORSE RIDE
GREEN RIDE
Obelisk
Glasshouses
Tenn Cts
Oaklands Sch
Health Cen
Hall
Clubho
Fire Sta
Superstore
Sec Sch
Tenn Club
LOUGHTON
Magpie Hill
CONNAUGHT WATER
CHINGFORD GOLF COURSE
CHINGFORD PLAIN
A1069
QUEEN ELIZABETH'S HUNTING LODGE
Warren Hill House
Warren Hill
MANOR ROAD
Holmhurst
North Farm House
124
Warren Wood PH
Buckhurst Hill
Oak Hall
Tenn & Bowl
Cricket Ground
ROEBUCK LA
500 yds
500 m
35
36
37
38
39
40
41
42
43
44
99
98
97
96

EM
EN
EP
EQ
ER
ES
ET
43
44
45
91
EPPING FOREST
Ambresbury Banks
Warren Lodge
THEYDON BOIS GOLF COURSE
Clubhouse
Little Bronx Livery & Riding Stables
LITTLE GREGORIES LANE
Piercing Hill
PIERCING HILL
ST. THOMAS'S QUARTERS
Forest Lodge Stables
Long Running
GREEN RIDE
HORSE RIDE
Jacks Hill
COPPICE ROW
B172
B1393
EPPING ROAD
Wake Arms
Oak Hill
Oak Hill Farm
Sixteen String Jack PH
Birch Hall
Birch Hall Farm
THEYDON PLAIN
THE COPPICE
Hall
Prim Sch
DUKES AVENUE
WOODLAND WAY
MORGAN CRESCENT
ELIZABETH DR
BUXTON RD
Theydon Bois
THEYDON BOIS
STATION APP
ABRIDGE ROAD
THEYDON GREEN
SPORTS GRD
Tenn Club
Cricket Club
ALLOTS
Youth Cen
ROBERT DANIELS CT
COOPERSALE ROAD
Thrifts Hall Farm
CM16
36
37
38
39
40
41
42
43
44
99
98
97
96
Dulsmead Hollow
HELTER PLAIN
COPLEY PLAIN
FURZE GROUND
BIRCH WOOD
RED OAK WOOD
GAUNT'S WOOD
GOLDINGS HILL
A121
GREAT MONK WOOD
BROADSTROOD PLAIN
GREGSON'S RIDE
THE DITCHES RIDE
Ripley Grange
Debden Green
Debden Ho Cen
DEBDEN LANE
LOUGHTON GOLF COURSE
Clubhouse
CLAY'S LANE
Sec Sch
THEYDON PARK ROAD
THEYDON BOIS CEMETERY
Theydon Hall Farm
Theydon Hall
M11
108
LONG SHAW
BROADFIELD SHAW
RM4
THEYDON MEAD
WILLINGALE ROAD
Prim Sch
HILLYFIELDS OPEN SPACE
RECTORY LANE
A1168
Debden
SPORTS GROUND
Sec Sch
ALLOTMENTS
CEM
Sch
Plume of Feathers PH
ST. NICHOLAS
BORDERS LANE
Old Golden Lion PH
Comm. & Sports Cens
Coll
Epping Forest Coll
Sir Winston Churchill PH
Drama Sch
Health Cen
Amb Sta
Thea
Comm Cen
Lib
PO
SPORTS GROUND
Printing Works
IMPRIMO PARK
PROSPECT BUSINESS PARK
Tenn Cts
Pav
Bowl Grn
DEBDEN
LOUGHTON BUSINESS CEN
Higgins Homes
OAKWOOD HILL INDUSTRIAL ESTATE
CHIGWELL LANE
LANGSTON ROAD
LOUGHTON
Prim Schs
Clubhouse
SPORTS GROUND
Loughton Bridge
Junction 5
WOOLSTON MANOR GOLF & COUNTRY CLUB
Fitness Centre
Driving Range
Woolston Hall
Pool
Clubhouse
River Roding
IG7
A113
Little London
LONDON ROAD
GRAVEL LANE
ABRIDGE PARK
Great Downs Farm
Turnours Hall
Marchings
Marchings Farm
A1112
ABRIDGE ROAD
PUDDING LANE
Home Farm
Rolls Park Roundabout
125
Rolls Park Farm
Pettits Hall
Taylor May's Farm
SPORTS GROUND
LOUGHTON
OAKWOOD HILL
RIVER WAY
SOUTH VIEW RD
LONDON ROAD

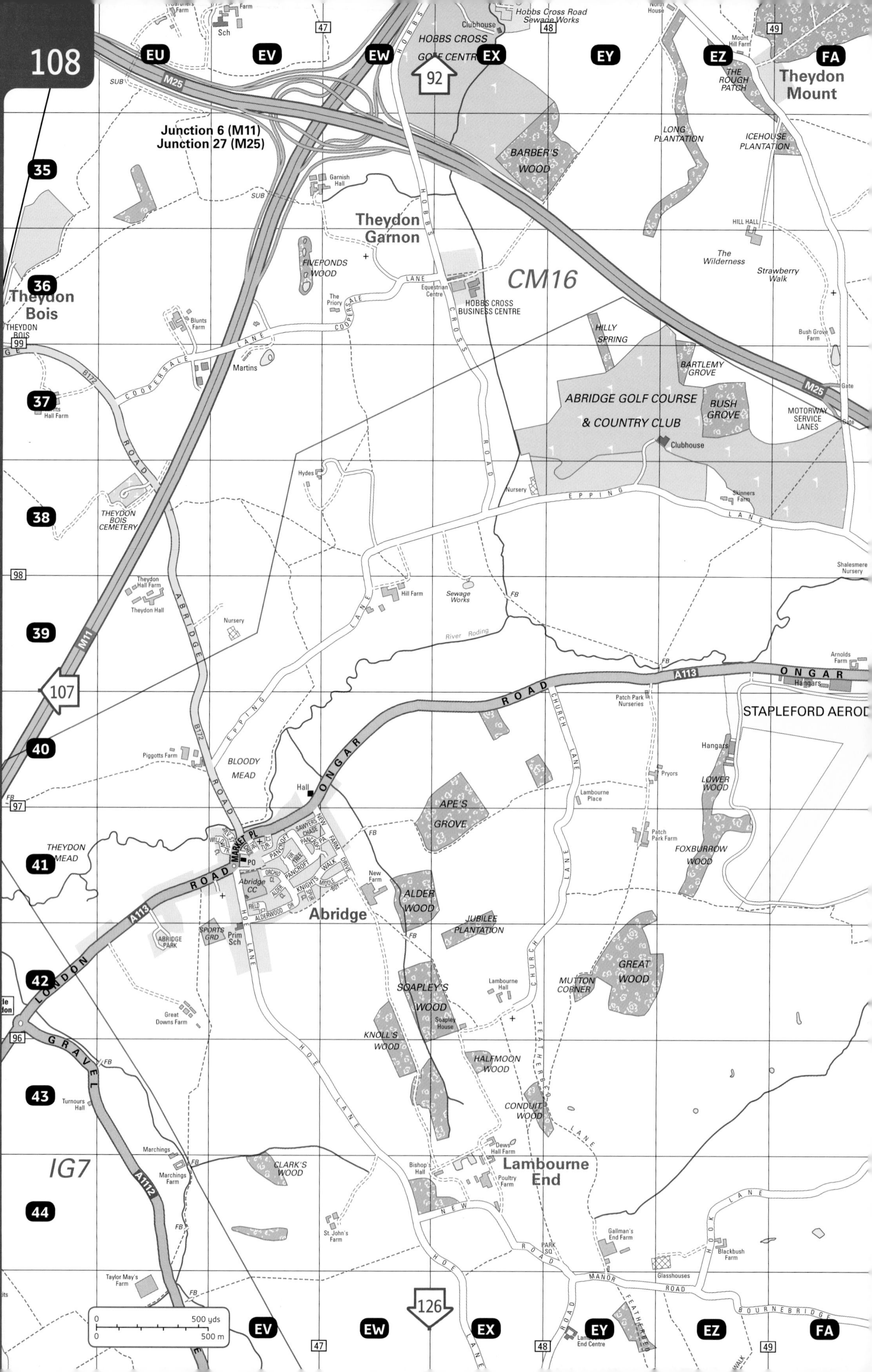
EU
EV
EW
EX
EY
EZ
FA
47
48
49
92
107
126
35
36
37
38
39
40
41
42
43
44
99
98
97
96
Sch
Farm
Hobbs Cross Road Sewage Works
Clubhouse
HOBBS CROSS GOLF CENTRE
North House
Mount Hill Farm
THE ROUGH PATCH
Theydon Mount
SUB
M25
Junction 6 (M11)
Junction 27 (M25)
BARBER'S WOOD
LONG PLANTATION
ICEHOUSE PLANTATION
Garnish Hall
Theydon Garnon
HILL HALL
The Wilderness
Strawberry Walk
FIVEPONDS WOOD
CM16
Equestrian Centre
HOBBS CROSS BUSINESS CENTRE
The Priory
Theydon Bois
THEYDON BOIS
Blunts Farm
COOPERSALE LANE
Martins
HILLY SPRING
Bush Grove Farm
BARTLEMY GROVE
ABRIDGE GOLF COURSE & COUNTRY CLUB
BUSH GROVE
MOTORWAY SERVICE LANES
Gate
Clubhouse
B172
Hall Farm
ROAD
Hydes
Nursery
EPPING LANE
Skinners Farm
THEYDON BOIS CEMETERY
Shalesmere Nursery
Theydon Hall Farm
Theydon Hall
Hill Farm
Sewage Works
FB
ABRIDGE
River Roding
M11
Arnolds Farm
A113
ONGAR ROAD
Hangars
Patch Park Nurseries
CHURCH LANE
STAPLEFORD AEROD
Piggotts Farm
BLOODY MEAD
Hangars
Pryors
LOWER WOOD
Hall
APE'S GROVE
Lambourne Place
Patch Park Farm
THEYDON MEAD
MARKET PL
SAWYERS CHASE
PANCROFT
NEW FARM DRIVE
FOXBURROW WOOD
PO
Abridge CC
ORCHID CL
ALDER CL
FIR TREE
KNIGHTS WALK
MIDDLE BOY
FIELD
ALDERWOOD DR
New Farm
ALDER WOOD
Abridge
LONDON ROAD
SPORTS GRD
Prim Sch
ABRIDGE PARK
HOE LANE
JUBILEE PLANTATION
GREAT WOOD
SOAPLEY'S WOOD
Lambourne Hall
MUTTON CORNER
Great Downs Farm
Soapley House
KNOLL'S WOOD
GRAVEL
HALFMOON WOOD
Turnours Hall
CONDUIT WOOD
FEATHERBED LANE
Marchings
Dews Hall Farm
IG7
Marchings Farm
CLARK'S WOOD
Bishop's Hall
Lambourne End
Poultry Farm
A1112
NEW ROAD
HOOK LANE
St. John's Farm
Gallman's End Farm
PARK SQ
Blackbush Farm
Taylor May's Farm
MANOR ROAD
Glasshouses
BOURNEBRIDGE
Lambourne End Centre
500 yds
500 m
0

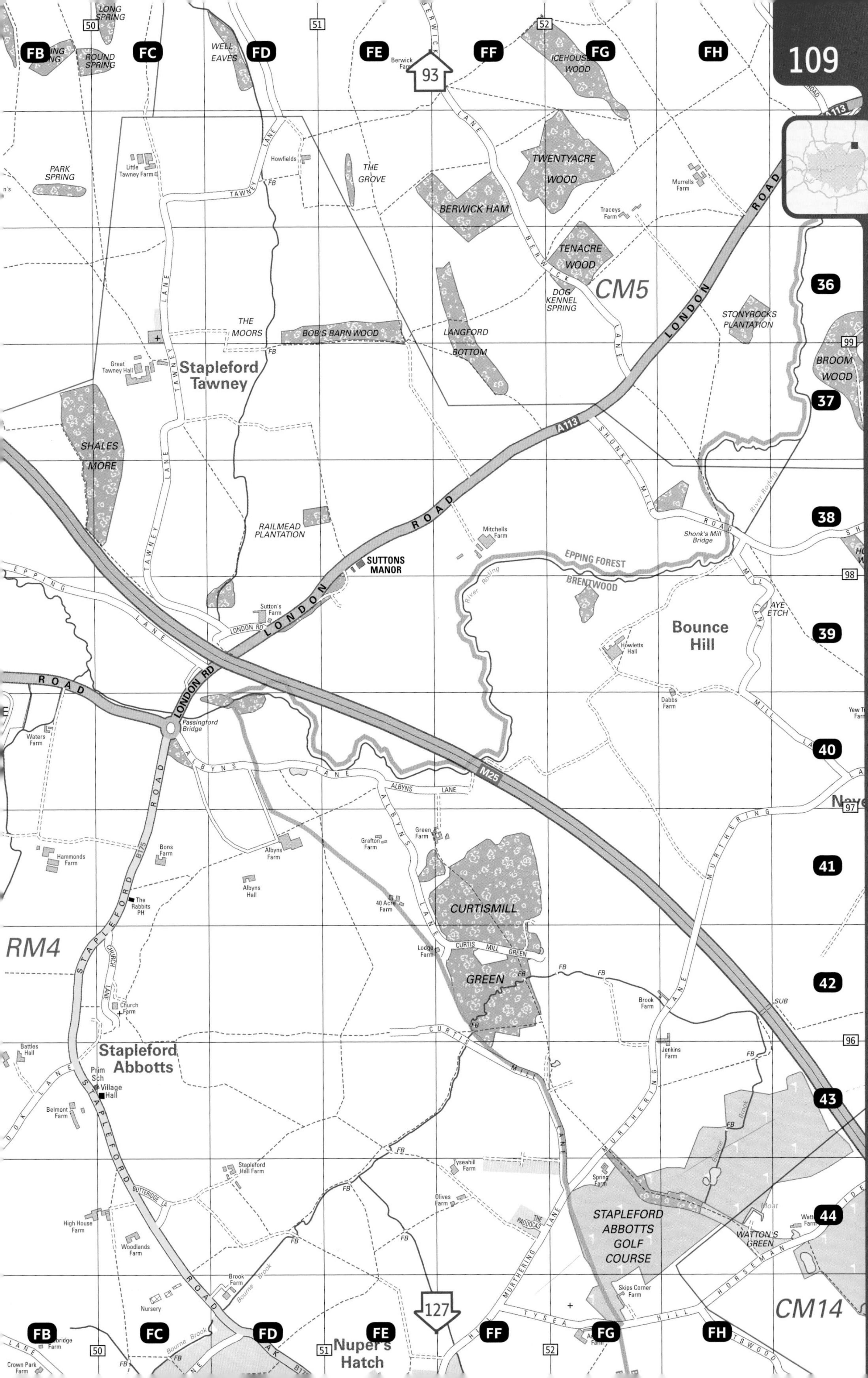
LONG SPRING
ROUND SPRING
WELL EAVES
ICEHOUSE WOOD
Berwick Farm
93
FB
FC
FD
FE
FF
FG
FH
50
51
52
PARK SPRING
Little Tawney Farm
Howfields
THE GROVE
TWENTYACRE WOOD
BERWICK HAM
Murrells Farm
Traceys Farm
TENACRE WOOD
DOG KENNEL SPRING
CM5
BERWICK LANE
TAWNEY LANE
LONDON ROAD
A113
THE MOORS
BOB'S BARN WOOD
LANGFORD BOTTOM
STONYROCKS PLANTATION
BROOM WOOD
Great Tawney Hall
Stapleford Tawney
SHALES MORE
SHONKS MILL ROAD
RAILMEAD PLANTATION
Mitchells Farm
Shonk's Mill Bridge
River Roding
SUTTONS MANOR
EPPING FOREST
BRENTWOOD
EPPING LANE
Sutton's Farm
LONDON RD
AYE ETCH
Bounce Hill
Howletts Hall
MILL LANE
ROAD
Passingford Bridge
Dabbs Farm
Waters Farm
M25
ALBYNS LANE
Yew Tree Farm
Hammonds Farm
Bons Farm
Albyns Farm
Grafton Farm
Green Farm
MURTHERING LANE
Albyns Hall
The Rabbits PH
40 Acre Farm
CURTISMILL GREEN
RM4
STAPLEFORD ROAD
CHURCH LANE
Lodge Farm
CURTIS MILL GREEN
B175
Brook Farm
SUB
Church Farm
Battles Hall
Stapleford Abbotts
Jenkins Farm
Prim Sch
Village Hall
Belmont Farm
CURTIS MILL LANE
Brook
Stapleford Hall Farm
Tyseahill Farm
GUTTERIDGE LA
Spring Farm
Olives Farm
Moat
High House Farm
THE PADDOCKS
STAPLEFORD ABBOTTS GOLF COURSE
WATTON'S GREEN
Woodlands Farm
Brook Farm
Bourne Brook
Skips Corner Farm
HORSEMAN SIDE
Nursery
127
TYSEA HILL
CM14
Nuper's Hatch
Crown Park Farm
36
37
38
39
40
41
42
43
44
99
98
97
96
FB

HP15
AC
AD
AE
AF
AG
AH
AJ
91
92
93
TYLERS GREEN
COMMON WOOD
THE LARCHES
CHARCOLE GROVE
THE COPSE
Penn Street Farm
Winchmore Hill CC
Penn House
PENNHOUSE GROVE
Winchmore Hill Farm
Goodwins Nursery
GLORY BELT
PUGH'S WOOD
BROOK WOOD
Pennhouse Farm
ROUND WOOD
BRANCHES WOOD
Cricket Ground
Tennis Courts
Clubhouse
SPORTS GRD
Puttenham Place Farm
The Red Lion PH
The Old Queen's Head PH
Prim Sch
SPORTS GROUND
KING'S WOOD
VICARAGE WOOD
DOWNHAM GROVE
WESTFIELD PIECES
WITHERIDGE WOOD
Penn
The Crown PH
PENBURY GROVE
CHURCH PATH WOOD
Saucy Corner
Knotty Green
Stumpwell
POND WOOD
LITTLE GOMMS WOOD
Fieldgrove Nurseries
HP10
Town House Farm
Bottom Farm
GATEMOOR WOOD
CORKERS WOOD
STANDERS WOOD
Parsonage Farm
WYCOMBE HEIGHTS GOLF CENTRE
MAGPIE WOOD
DRIVING RANGE
VINEYARD
COPPICE WOOD
Lude Farm
LONGFIELD WOOD
The Royal Standard of England PH
Forty Green
THROSHERS WOOD
ROUNDHEADS WOOD
SNIGGS WOOD
CHILTERN WYCOMBE
MOBILE HOME PARK
Electricity Station
Upper Derehams Farm
HOGBACK WOOD
KINGSMEAD BUSINESS PARK
CEM
ALLOT
Holtspur Bottom Farm
Whitehouse Farm
Loudwater
KNAVES BEECH IND EST
TREADAWAY TECH CEN
Superstore
Superstores
Junction 3
GREEN VALLEY
CUT-THROAT WOOD
Holtspur
Beacon Centre
Thea Youth Club
Bandstand
Highwayman's Farm
FENNELL'S WOOD
Clubhouse
The Three Horseshoes PH
FLACKWELL HEATH
SPORTS GRD
The Falcon PH
132
A40
B474
HAZLEMERE ROAD
ELM ROAD
CHURCH ROAD
BEACON HILL
WITHERIDGE LANE
PENN BOTTOM
HAMMERSLEY LANE
LONDON ROAD
OXFORD ROAD
BOUNDARY ROAD
WYCOMBE ROAD
WHITE HILL
0 500 yds
0 500 m
45
46
47
48
49
50
51
52
53
54

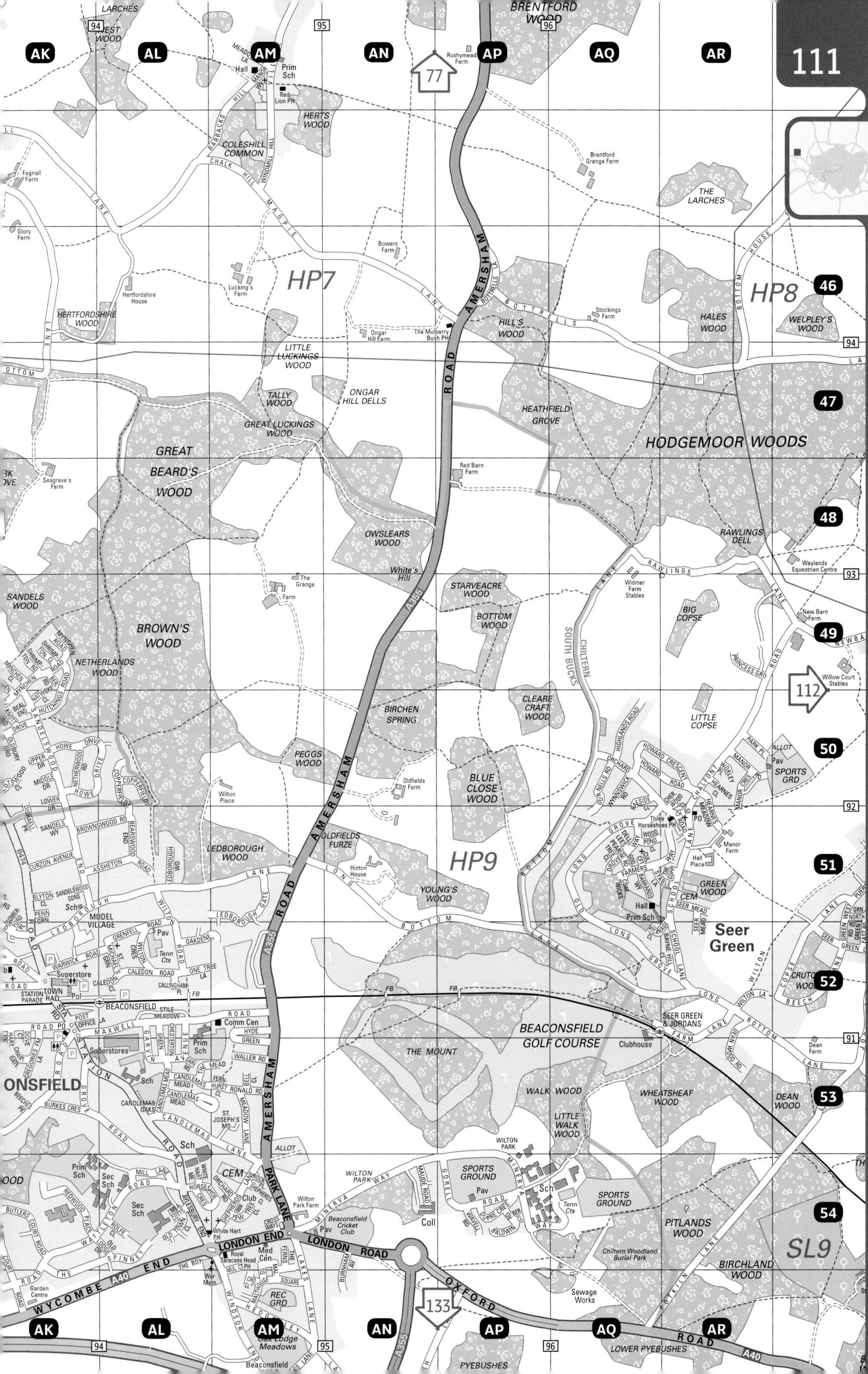
AK
AL
AM
AN
AP
AQ
AR
46
47
48
49
50
51
52
53
54
94
95
96
93
92
91
77
112
133
LARCHES
WEST WOOD
BRENTFORD WOOD
Rushymead Farm
Hall
Prim Sch
Red Lion PH
HERTS WOOD
COLESHILL COMMON
BARRACKS HILL
CHALK HILL
WINDMILL HILL
MAGPIE LANE
Fagnall Farm
Glory Farm
Brentford Grange Farm
THE LARCHES
HOUSE
BOTTOM
Bowers Farm
HP7
HP8
Lucking's Farm
Hertfordshire House
HERTFORDSHIRE WOOD
AMERSHAM ROAD
BOTTRELLS LA
BOTTRELLS LANE
Stockings Farm
HALES WOOD
WELPLEY'S WOOD
HILL'S WOOD
The Mulberry Bush PH
Ongar Hill Farm
LITTLE LUCKINGS WOOD
ONGAR HILL DELLS
TALLY WOOD
GREAT LUCKINGS WOOD
HEATHFIELD GROVE
HODGEMOOR WOODS
GREAT BEARD'S WOOD
Red Barn Farm
Seagrave's Farm
OWSLEARS WOOD
RAWLINGS DELL
Waylands Equestrian Centre
RAWLINGS LANE
White's Hill
STARVEACRE WOOD
BOTTOM WOOD
Widmer Farm Stables
BIG COPSE
New Barn Farm
SANDELS WOOD
The Grange
Farm
A355
BROWN'S WOOD
NETHERLANDS WOOD
SOUTH BUCKS
CHILTERN
PRINCESS GRO
Willow Court Stables
CLEARE CRAFT WOOD
BIRCHEN SPRING
HIGHLANDS ROAD
LITTLE COPSE
PEGGS WOOD
BLUE CLOSE WOOD
Oldfields Farm
Wilton Place
HOWARD CRESCENT
HOWARD ROAD
ORCHARD
PARK PL
ALLOT
Pav
SPORTS GRD
MANOR RD
WORLEY PL
HEARNES CL
MANOR CRES
CHALFONT ROAD
Three Horseshoes PH
Po
Manor Farm
OLDFIELDS FURZE
LEDBOROUGH WOOD
HP9
Hinton House
YOUNG'S WOOD
LONG BOTTOM
GREEN WOOD
CEM
Hall
Prim Sch
SEER MEAD
SCHOOL LANE
Seer Green
WILTON LA
CRUTCHES WOOD
BEECH
MODEL VILLAGE
LEDBOROUGH LANE
LEDBOROUGH GATE
WILTON ROAD
OAKDENE
Tenn Cts
CALEDON ROAD
ONE TREE LA
CALLINGHAM PL
FB
BEACONSFIELD
STATION PARADE
TOWN HALL
Pol
Superstore
WARWICK ROAD
Comm Cen
MAXWELL ROAD
Superstores
Prim Sch
WALLER RD
HYDE GREEN
THE MEAD
SEER GREEN & JORDANS
FARM LANE
BEACONSFIELD GOLF COURSE
Clubhouse
THE MOUNT
DEAN WOOD RD
Dean Farm
ONSFIELD
Sch
CANDLEMAS MEAD
CANDLEMAS LANE
CANDLEMAS OAKS
ST. JOSEPH'S MS
MEADOW LANE
BURKES CRES
WALK WOOD
LITTLE WALK WOOD
WHEATSHEAF WOOD
DEAN WOOD
ALLOT
Sch
CEM
Prim Sch
Sec Sch
WILTON PARK WAY
WILTON PARK
MINERVA WAY
SPORTS GROUND
SPORTS GROUND
Pav
Tenn Cts
Wilton Park Farm
MILL LANE
REDWOOD PLACE
Club
White Hart PH
OLD TOWN
PARK LANE
AMERSHAM ROAD
LONDON END
LONDON ROAD
Beaconsfield Cricket Club
Coll
GORELL ROAD
MAUDE ROAD
PITLANDS WOOD
Chiltern Woodland Burial Park
SL9
BIRCHLAND WOOD
POTKILN LANE
Royal Saracens Head
Med Cen
War Mem
THE SPINNEY
WYCOMBE END
A40
BUTLERS COURT ROAD
Garden Centre
REC GRD
OXFORD ROAD
Sewage Works
LOWER PYEBUSHES
PYEBUSHES
Oak Lodge Meadows
Beaconsfield
HEDGERLEY LANE
WINDSOR ROAD
THE LAKES LANE

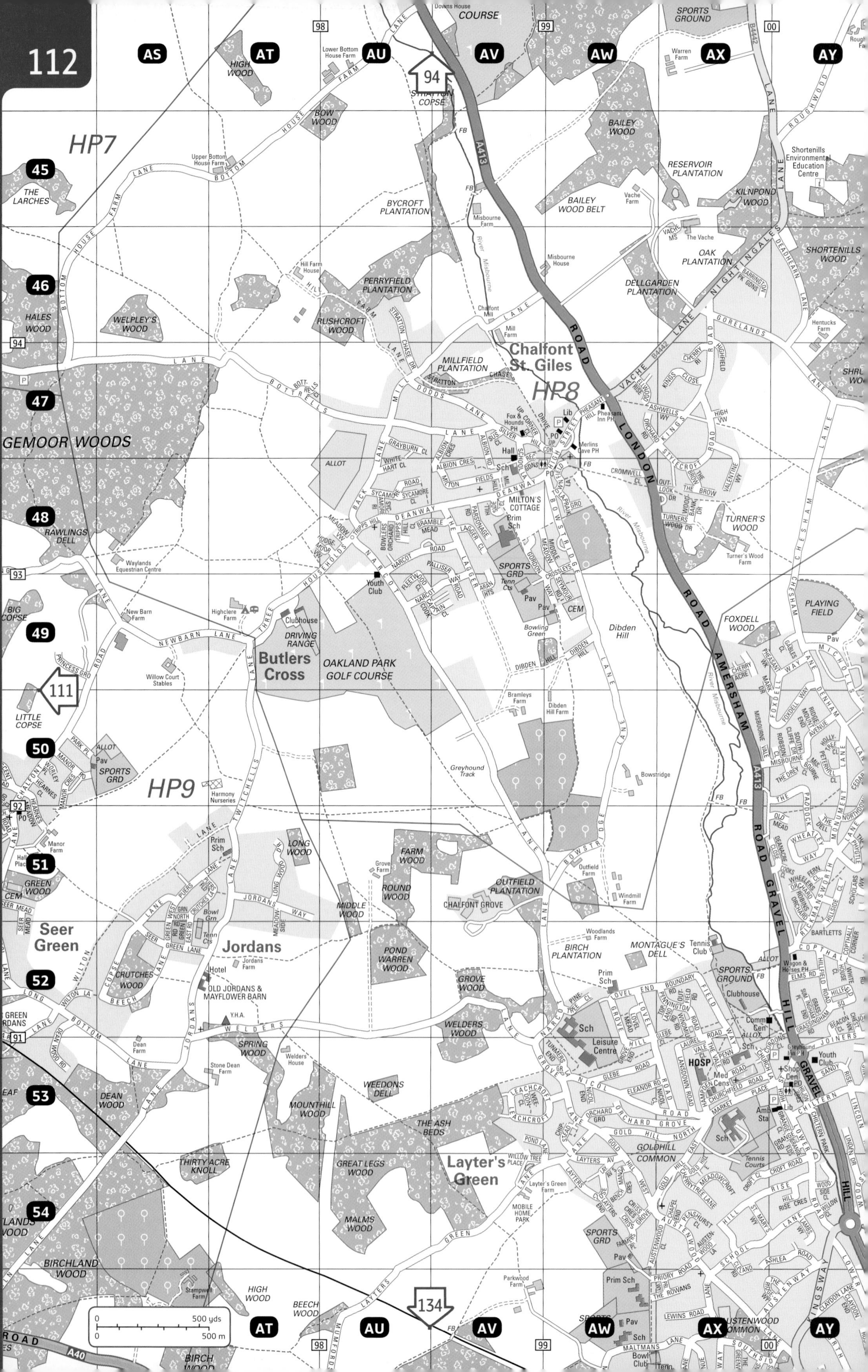
AS
AT
AU
AV
AW
AX
AY
94
111
134
HP7
HP8
HP9
45
46
47
48
49
50
51
52
53
54
HIGH WOOD
BOW WOOD
Lower Bottom House Farm
STRATTON COPSE
Downs House
COURSE
SPORTS GROUND
Warren Farm
BAILEY WOOD
RESERVOIR PLANTATION
Shortenills Environmental Education Centre
KILNPOND WOOD
BAILEY WOOD BELT
Vache Farm
The Vache
OAK PLANTATION
SHORTENILLS WOOD
DELLGARDEN PLANTATION
Hentucks Farm
Upper Bottom House Farm
THE LARCHES
BYCROFT PLANTATION
Misbourne Farm
Misbourne House
River Misbourne
Hill Farm House
PERRYFIELD PLANTATION
RUSHCROFT WOOD
WELPLEY'S WOOD
HALES WOOD
Chalfont Mill
Mill Farm
MILLFIELD PLANTATION
Chalfont St. Giles
GEMOOR WOODS
Fox & Hounds PH
Pheasant Inn PH
Merlins Cave PH
ALLOT
Hall
Sch
Lib
PO
MILTON'S COTTAGE
Prim Sch
SPORTS GRD
Tenn Cts
Pav
CEM
Bowling Green
TURNER'S WOOD
Turner's Wood Farm
RAWLINGS DELL
Waylands Equestrian Centre
Youth Club
PLAYING FIELD
FOXDELL WOOD
Dibden Hill
BIG COPSE
New Barn Farm
Highclere Farm
Clubhouse
DRIVING RANGE
Butlers Cross
OAKLAND PARK GOLF COURSE
Willow Court Stables
Bramleys Farm
Dibden Hill Farm
LITTLE COPSE
Greyhound Track
Bowstridge
Harmony Nurseries
LONG WOOD
FARM WOOD
Grove Farm
ROUND WOOD
OUTFIELD PLANTATION
Outfield Farm
Windmill Farm
Manor Farm
Hall Place
GREEN WOOD
CEM
MIDDLE WOOD
CHALFONT GROVE
Seer Green
Jordans
Jordans Farm
Hotel
OLD JORDANS & MAYFLOWER BARN
CRUTCHES WOOD
POND WARREN WOOD
Woodlands Farm
BIRCH PLANTATION
MONTAGUE'S DELL
Tennis Club
SPORTS GROUND
Clubhouse
GROVE WOOD
Prim Sch
Wagon & Horses PH
BARTLETTS
Y.H.A.
WELDERS WOOD
Leisure Centre
Comm Cen
Greyhound Inn PH
Youth Club
Dean Farm
SPRING WOOD
Welders House
Stone Dean Farm
HOSP
Med Cens
Shop Cen
Amb Sta
DEAN WOOD
WEEDONS DELL
MOUNTHILL WOOD
THE ASH BEDS
GOLDHILL COMMON
Tennis Courts
THIRTY ACRE KNOLL
GREAT LEGS WOOD
Layter's Green
Layter's Green Farm
MOBILE HOME PARK
MALMS WOOD
SPORTS GRD
Pav
Prim Sch
BIRCHLAND WOOD
Stampwell Farm
HIGH WOOD
BEECH WOOD
Parkwood Farm
AUSTENWOOD COMMON
BIRCH WOOD
A413
A40
B4442
LONDON ROAD
AMERSHAM ROAD
GRAVEL HILL
0 500 yds
0 500 m

AZ
BA
BB
BC
BD
BE
BF
01
02
03
95
135
114
Chorleywood Bottom
The Swillet
Heronsgate
Mill End
Junction 17
Maple Cross Roundabout
WD3
Maple Cross
Chalfont Common
SL9
West Hyde
UB9
CHALFONT ST. PETER
GROVESPRING WOOD
PHILIPSHILL WOOD
NEWLAND GORSE
NEWLAND PARK
CHILTERN OPEN AIR MUSEUM
Buckinghamshire Chilterns University College
SPORTS GROUND
FIVE PLANTATIONS
BOTTOM WOOD
LADYWALK WOOD
POLLARDSHILL WOOD
BEECHEN WOOD
FRANKLINS SPRING
KILN WOOD
ROBERT'S WOOD
ROUND ROCKET PLANTATION
QUARRY & LANDFILL SITE
MIDDLE WOOD
BLOOM WOOD
GRAVEL PIT
HOGTROUGH WOOD
GERRARDS CROSS GOLF COURSE
LITTLE HANGING WOOD
NOCKHILL WOOD
JUNIPER WOOD
Denham Grove
Maple Lodge Sewage Treatment Works
LYNSTERS LAKE
PYNESFIELD LAKE
SPRINGWELL LAKE
Horseshoe Bay
Sailing Club
WILLIAM PENN MULTISPORTS ARENA
Leisure Centre
HERTFORDSHIRE
BUCKINGHAMSHIRE
THREE RIVERS
CHILTERN
SOUTH BUCKS
M25
A412
A405
DENHAM WAY
NORTH ORBITAL
UXBRIDGE ROAD
CHALFONT ROAD
CHALFONT LANE
HORNHILL ROAD
RICKMANSWORTH LANE
SHIRE LANE
OLD SHIRE LANE
TILEHOUSE LANE
LONG LANE
River Colne
46
47
48
49
50
51
52
53
54

BG
BH
BJ
BK
BL
BM
BN
96
05
06
07
45
46
47
48
49
50
51
52
53
54
94
93
92
91
113
136
M25
SOLOMON'S WOOD
PHEASANTS WOOD
Prim Sch
UPPER HILL RISE
BEACON WAY
SHEPHERDS WAY
PHEASANTS WAY
THE MOUNT
WINCHFIELD WAY
NIGHTINGALE ROAD
Masonic Sch
HOCKEY GRD
PLAYING FIELD
CRICKET GRD
Pav
Clubhouse
SCOTS HILL
Sec Sch
SPORTS GROUND
CHALMERS COURT
CROXLEY HALL WOODS
LONG VALLEY WOOD
LAVROCK LANE
CEM
A404
CHESS VALLEY WALK
FORTUNE COMMON
RICKMANSWORTH PARK
Superstore
THE CLOISTERS
COUN. OFF
MUS
Comet House
Lib
PO
Watersmeet Cen
RICKMANSWORTH
Croxley Great Barn
Lot Mead Lock
RECTORY RD
Mill End
Leisure Centre
Swim Pool
WILLIAM PENN MULTISPORTS ARENA
Moneyhill
Prim Sch
Comm Cens
Tenn Club
Amb Sta
Fire Sta
Pol
Clinics
Halfway House PH
Boathouse
RIVERSIDE DRIVE
Batchworth Roundabout
Hampton Hall Farm
The Alders
ROAD
A412
UXBRIDGE
BATCHWORTH LAKE
THE AQUADROME
BURY LAKE
WD3
Recycling Cen
Trinity Ct
The White Bear PH
LONDON RD
Three Valleys Water
MOOR LANE
Green Knoll
Batchworth
Clubhouse
RICKMANSWORTH
MOOR PARK GOLF COURSE
GRAND UNION CANAL
STOCKER'S LAKE
STOCKER'S LAKE NATURE RESERVE
Stocker's Lock
Stocker's Farm
Pumping Sta
Prim Sch
THE GROVE
BATCHWORTH PARK GOLF COURSE
Moor Park Farm
BATCHWORTH HILL
MOOR PARK
Whip & Collar PH
River Colne
Mill End Pumping Sta
Froghall Farm
GARRETT WOOD
HIGH WOOD
CHALK PIT
Andrews Ley Farm
Juniper Dell
Greenbroom Spring
Sandfield Spring
WOODCOCK HILL CEMETERY
Springwell Lock
SPRINGWELL CHALK PIT
SPRINGWELL LAKE
HERTFORDSHIRE
WOODCOCK HILL INDUSTRIAL ESTATE
Pipers Farm
HOME FARM RD
Home Farm House
Bush Spring
Batchworth Heath
BATCHWORTH HEATH HILL
Batchworth Heath Farm
COCKS WOOD
Clubhouse
Maple Lodge Sewage Treatment Works
Filter Beds
Sludge Beds
THREE RIVERS
HILLINGDON
LONDON LOOP
Rose & Crown PH
HAREFIELD ROAD
WOODCOCK HILL
LONG SPRING
PARK WOOD
Cripps House Farm
BISHOP'S WOOD
POORFIELD
LOCKWELL WOOD
HILLINGDON
LYNSTERS LAKE
Waybeards Farm
Hill End
White Heath Farm
PEARSON'S WOOD
Harefield Grove
SHRUBS RD
COVERED RESERVOIR
FRENCH GROVE
Battlers Wells Farm
BATTLERS WELLS WOOD
JACKETS LANE
ALLOT
WATTS COMMON
TAYLORS MEADOW
Harefield Grove Farm
Little Bourne Farm (Equestrian Stables)
PARK WOOD
Nature Reserve
MOUNT PLEASANT SPORTS GRD
UB9
Shepherds Hill Farm
Shepherds Hill House
HAREFIELD HOSPITAL
Sec Sch
NORTHWOOD ROAD
SPORTS GRD
Health Cen
THE GREEN
HAREFIELD
FURZEFIELD
DEADMAN'S GROVE
Horseshoe Bay
Weir
Sailing Club
Black Jack's Lock
Prim Schs
Lib
Comm Cen
Harefield CC
Harefield United FC
ASHAIN SPRING
SCARLET SPRING
KILN POND
CLAYPITS
RAVENERS SPRING
DELL
Shooting School
HIGHBONES
Knightscote Farm
Langley Farm
Bourne Farm
BREAKSPEAR ROAD
NORTH ORBITAL ROAD
LONDON LOOP/TOWING PATH
0
500 yds
500 m

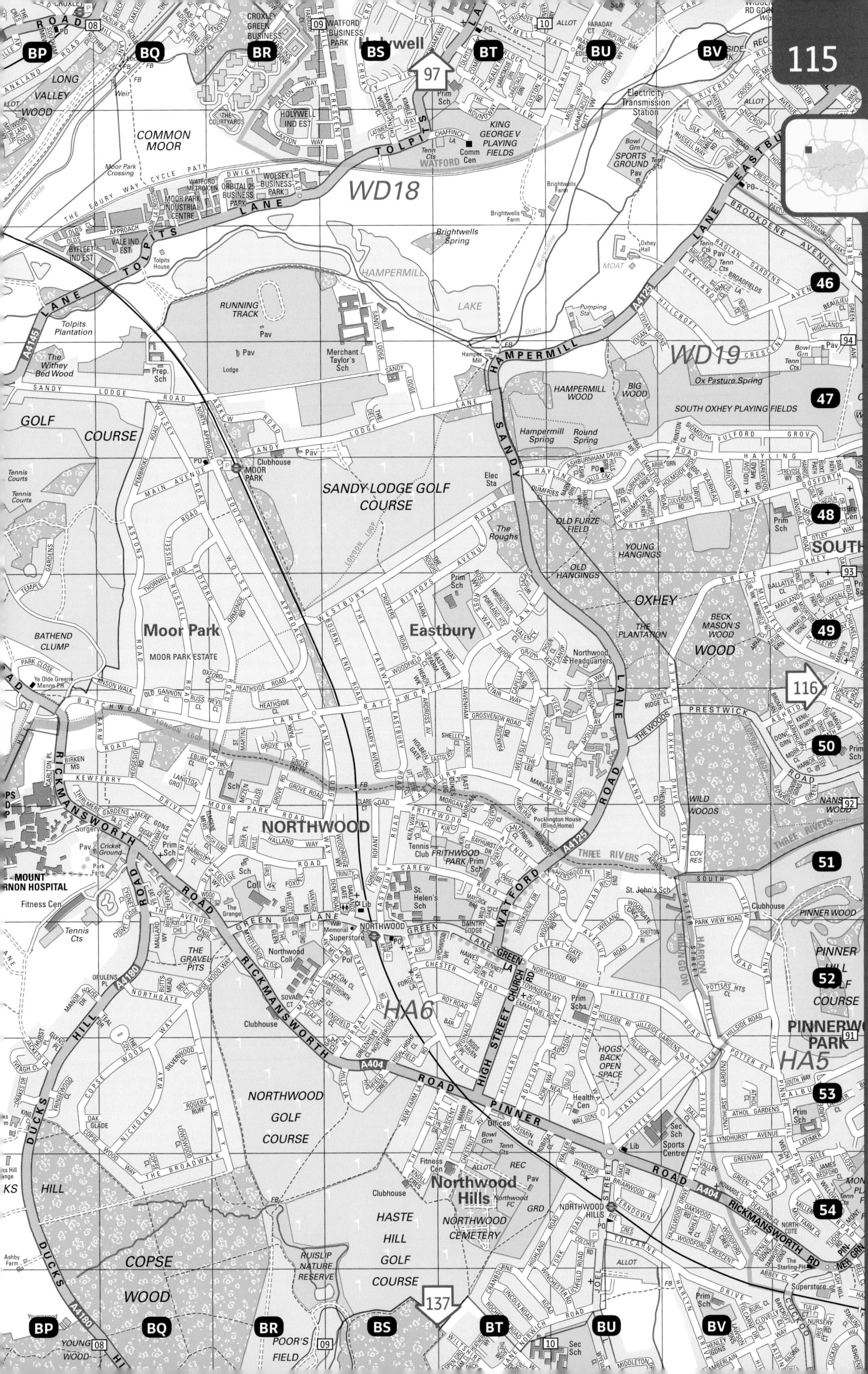
BP
BQ
BR
BS
BT
BU
BV
97
116
137
46
47
48
49
50
51
52
53
54
Holywell
WATFORD BUSINESS PARK
CROXLEY GREEN BUSINESS
HOLYWELL IND EST
LONG VALLEY WOOD
COMMON MOOR
KING GEORGE V PLAYING FIELDS
Electricity Transmission Station
SPORTS GROUND
WD18
WD19
WATFORD METROCEN
ORBITAL 25 BUSINESS PARK
WOLSEY BUSINESS PARK
MOOR PARK INDUSTRIAL CENTRE
VALE IND EST
BYFLEET IND EST
TOLPITS LANE
Brightwells Spring
HAMPERMILL LAKE
RUNNING TRACK
Tolpits Plantation
The Withey Bed Wood
Merchant Taylor's Sch
HAMPERMILL WOOD
BIG WOOD
Ox Pasture Spring
SOUTH OXHEY PLAYING FIELDS
Hampermill Spring
Round Spring
GOLF COURSE
SANDY LODGE GOLF COURSE
MOOR PARK
OLD FURZE FIELD
YOUNG HANGINGS
OLD HANGINGS
OXHEY
THE PLANTATION
BECK MASON'S WOOD
WOOD
SOUTH
Moor Park
MOOR PARK ESTATE
Eastbury
BATHEND CLUMP
Northwood Headquarters
NORTHWOOD
WILD WOODS
THREE RIVERS
MOUNT VERNON HOSPITAL
FRITHWOOD PARK
St. Helen's Sch
St. John's Sch
PINNER WOOD
PINNER HILL GOLF COURSE
PINNERWOOD PARK
HA5
HA6
THE GRAVEL PITS
HOGS BACK OPEN SPACE
NORTHWOOD GOLF COURSE
DUCKS HILL
Northwood Hills
NORTHWOOD CEMETERY
HASTE HILL GOLF COURSE
RUISLIP NATURE RESERVE
COPSE WOOD
POOR'S FIELD
YOUNG WOOD
RICKMANSWORTH ROAD
PINNER ROAD
HIGH STREET
WATFORD ROAD
SANDY LANE
HAMPERMILL LANE
A4125
A4145
A4180
A404
Superstore
Pocklington House (Blind Home)

BUSHEY
BUSHEY GOLF COURSE & COUNTRY CLUB
WATFORD HEATH
OXHEY PARK
OXHEY PARK GOLF COURSE
WD19
SOUTH OXHEY PLAYING FIELDS
CARPENDERS PARK
MERRY HILL
WD23
HARTSBOURNE GOLF COURSE & COUNTRY CLUB
SOUTH OXHEY
CARPENDERS PARK CEMETERY
GRIM'S DYKE GOLF COURSE
HATCH END
SHAFTESBURY PLAYING FIELDS
PINNER HILL GOLF COURSE
HA5
PINNERWOOD PARK
PINNER GREEN
PINNER PARK
LITTLE COMMON
HATCH END PLAYING FIELD
HEADSTONE MANOR
HA2
KING GEORGE REC GROUND
BANNISTER STADIUM
RAGHUVANSHI CHARITABLE TRUST SPORTS GROUND
SADDLERS MEAD REC GROUND
EASTBURY LANE
PRESTWICK ROAD
OXHEY LANE
UXBRIDGE ROAD
HIGH STREET
LONDON ROAD
ST. THOMAS' DRIVE
HERTFORDSHIRE
THREE RIVERS
HERTSMERE
HARROW
98
115
138
BW
BX
BY
BZ
CA
CB
CC
45
46
47
48
49
50
51
52
53
54
500 yds
500 m

CD
CE
CF
CG
CH
CJ
CK
99
118
139
HA7
HA3
HA8
WD6
BUSHEY HEATH
STANMORE COMMON
BENTLEY PRIORY OPEN SPACE
STANMORE
STANMORE GOLF COURSE
HARROW WEALD
BELMONT
QUEENSBURY
WEALDSTONE
ROYAL NATIONAL ORTHOPAEDIC HOSP
STANMORE COUNTRY PARK (NATURE RESERVE)
PEAR WOOD
CLOISTERS WOOD
ELSTREE HILL OPEN SPACE
ELSTREE OPEN SPACE
Junction 4
SPIRE HOSPITAL
Stanmore College
Harrow College
HARROW WEALD CEMETERY
GROVE FIELDS
LITTLE COMMON
DEER PARK
BROCKLEY HILL DRIVING RANGE
GOLF PARK
CANONS PARK
KING GEORGE V MEML GDNS
SPORTS GROUND
PLAYING FIELD
WATFORD BY-PASS
UXBRIDGE ROAD
LONDON ROAD
STANMORE HILL
HONEYPOT LANE
BROCKLEY HILL
EDGWARE WAY
HEATHBOURNE ROAD
BROOKSHILL
COMMON ROAD
ELSTREE ROAD
HIGH ROAD
STANMORE MARSH
CENTENNIAL PARK
46
47
48
49
50
51
52
53
54

CL
CM
CN
CP
CQ
CR
CS
100
140
117
A411
BARNET LA
Stirling Corner
Stirling Retail Pk
Woodcock Hill Farm
Deacons Hill
DEACONS HILL OPEN SPACE
SCRATCH WOOD
FROGHALL WOOD
BOYS HILL WOOD
Elstree Manor
Penniwells Farm
Corus Hotel
BUPA Nursing Home
ELSTREE OPEN SPACE
WD6
HERTSMERE
BARNET
M1
Junction 4
THISTLE WOOD
GRAVEL PIT WOOD
CLUMP OF TREES WOOD
TARGET WOOD
MILL HILL GOLF COURSE
NUT WOOD
London Gateway Services
HEMMINGS WOOD
STONEY WOOD
Bury Farm
EDGWAREBURY CEMETERY
SPORTS GRD
REC GRD
EDGWAREBURY PARK
Days Hotel
BROCKLEY HILL DRIVING RANGE
EDGWAREBURY GOLF COURSE
BROCKLEY PARK
A41 (WATFORD BY-PASS)
EDGWARE WAY
Canons Corner
SPUR ROAD
A410
STONEGROVE
CONVENT
Apex Corner
A5100
EDGWARE
STONEGROVE PARK
N London Collegiate Sch
KING GEORGE V MEML GDNS
CANONS PARK
BUS STA
Broadwalk Shopping Centre
BUS DEPOT
HA8
LYNDHURST PARK
HIGH STREET
A5
BURNT OAK
DEANSBROOK ROAD
EDGWARE COMMUNITY HOSPITAL
CHANDOS RECREATION GROUND
HA7
PRINCE EDWARD PLAYING FIELD
HONEYPOT BUSINESS CEN
BARNET F.C. TRAINING GROUND
WILLIAM ELLIS SPORTS GROUND
WATLING PARK
SPORTS GROUND
ADASTRAL ESTATE
MONTROSE PLAYING FIELDS
NW LONDON HEALTH PROTECTION UNIT
NHS BLOOD AND TRANSPLANT
COLINDALE BUSINESS PK
COLINDALE
BRITISH LIBRARY NEWSPAPERS
QUEENSBURY
A4140
HONEYPOT LANE
BROADWAY
0 500 yds
0 500 m

CT
CU
CV
CW
CX
CY
CZ
22
23
24
101
120
141
Barnet Gate
Ducks Island
OLD ELIZABETHANS (BARNET) MEMORIAL PLAYING FIELDS
GRANGE PLAYING FIELDS
Brent Lodge Farm
Dollis Brook
N20
OLD CHOLMELEIAN SPORTS GROUND
TOTTERIDGE FIELDS NATURE RESERVE
TOTTERIDGE PARK
TOTTERIDGE COMMON
A5109
TOTTERIDGE
TOTTERIDGE VILLAGE
TOTTERIDGE GREEN
Mote End Farm
Ellern Mede Farm
Fairlawn
The Lynch House
HENDON PARK WOOD
HIGHWOOD HILL
Highwood Hill
Holcombe Dales
Folly Brook
DARLANDS LAKE NATURE RESERVE
Folly Farm
Consolata Missionary Coll
SPORTS GROUND
Clubhouses
Burtonhole Farm
N12
NW7
THE MILL FIELD
Three Hammers PH
Belmont Farm
CHALET ESTATE
MARSHALL ESTATE
Mill Hill Circus
Nat Inst for Medical Research
THE RIDGEWAY
The Mount Sch
Drivers Hill
Watch Tower House
MILL HILL
ARRANDENE OPEN SPACE
Milespit Hill
Featherstone Hill
Uni of London Observatory
MILL HILL PARK
INGLIS BARRACKS
MILL HILL CEM
BITTACY HILL PARK
FINCHLEY GOLF COURSE
Nether Court (Clubhouse)
Council Depot
MILL HILL EAST
BITTACY BUS. CEN
WATFORD WAY
Mill Hill Ind Est
Pentavia Retail Park
CHASE LODGE PLAYING FIELD
METRO GOLF RANGE
Leisure Cen
HENDON
BARNET COPTHALL STADIUM
Crematorium
HENDON CEMETERY
HENDON GOLF COURSE
HOLDERS HILL
COPTHALL PLAYING FIELDS
COPTHALL SPORTS GROUND
Junction 2
Five Ways Corner
Barnet and Southgate College
RAF MUSEUM
Hendon RFC
NW4
SUNNY HILL PARK
GREAT NORTH WAY
A1
M1
A41
Hendon Hall Hot
GARDEN HOSP
WINDSOR OPEN SPACE
N3
CHURCH END
FINCHLEY CENTRAL
REGENTS PARK ROAD
GRAVEL HILL
EAST END ROAD
A504
Metropolitan Pol Training & Driving Sch
NW9
46
47
48
49
50
51
52
53
54
91
92
93
94

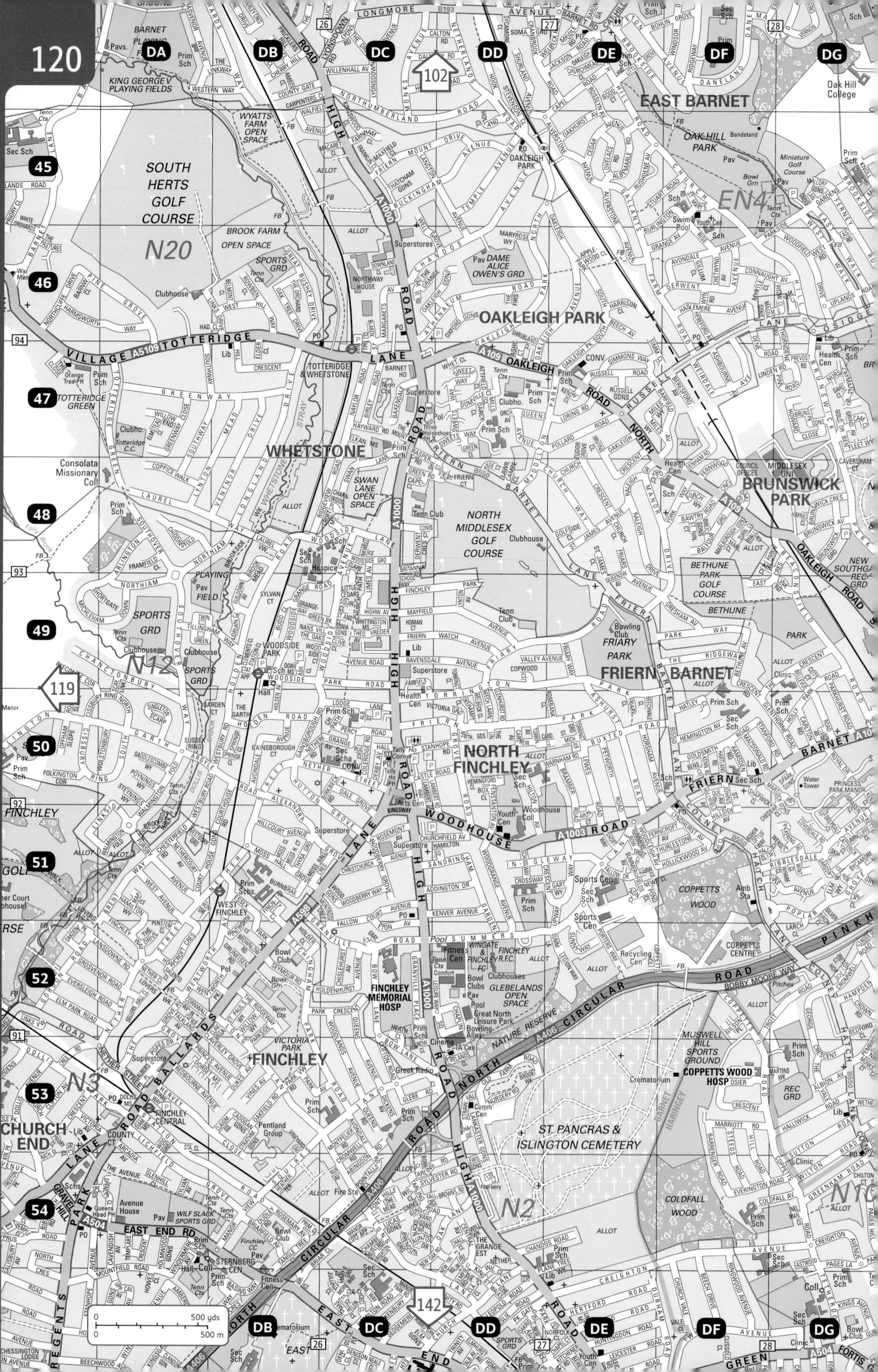
DA
DB
DC
DD
DE
DF
DG
102
119
142
45
46
47
48
49
50
51
52
53
54
EAST BARNET
OAK HILL PARK
Oak Hill College
EN4
SOUTH HERTS GOLF COURSE
N20
WYATTS FARM OPEN SPACE
BROOK FARM OPEN SPACE
SPORTS GRD
DAME ALICE OWEN'S GRD
OAKLEIGH PARK
TOTTERIDGE GREEN
VILLAGE
TOTTERIDGE LANE
TOTTERIDGE & WHETSTONE
WHETSTONE
SWAN LANE OPEN SPACE
NORTH MIDDLESEX GOLF COURSE
MIDDLESEX UNI
BRUNSWICK PARK
BETHUNE PARK GOLF COURSE
NEW SOUTHGATE REC GRD
FRIARY PARK
FRIERN BARNET
OAKLEIGH ROAD NORTH
N12
WOODSIDE PARK
NORTH FINCHLEY
WOODHOUSE ROAD
COPPETTS WOOD
COPPETTS CENTRE
FINCHLEY MEMORIAL HOSP
GLEBELANDS OPEN SPACE
NORTH CIRCULAR ROAD
MUSWELL HILL SPORTS GROUND
COPPETTS WOOD HOSP
ST. PANCRAS & ISLINGTON CEMETERY
COLDFALL WOOD
N2
N10
N3
FINCHLEY
CHURCH END
VICTORIA PARK
FINCHLEY CENTRAL
WEST FINCHLEY
REGENTS PARK
EAST END RD
HIGH ROAD
BALLARDS LANE
0
500 yds
0
500 m

DH
DJ
DK
DL
DM
DN
DP
103
OAKWOOD
OAKWOOD PARK
WINCHMORE HILL
GROVELANDS PARK
PRIORY HOSPITAL
N14
N21
OSIDGE
SOUTHGATE
Barnet and Southgate College
SOUTHGATE CEMETERY
PALMERS GREEN
ARNOS PARK
NEW SOUTHGATE
BROOMFIELD PARK
N13
122
Clockhouse Junction
THE PAULIN GROUND
CLOWES SPORTS GROUND
HAZELWOOD SPORTS GRD
TOTTENHALL SPORTS GROUND
BOUNDARY PLAYING FIELDS
BOWES PARK
N11
FRIERN BRIDGE RETAIL PARK
MUSWELL HILL GOLF COURSE
SCOUT PARK
RECREATION GROUND
NEW RIVER SPORTS CENTRE
N22
WOOD GREEN
NOEL PARK
ALEXANDRA PALACE
ALEXANDRA PARK
MUSWELL HILL
HORNSEY
143
46
47
48
49
50
51
52
53
54

DQ
DR
DS
DT
DU
DV
DW
104
121
144
45
46
47
48
49
50
51
52
53
54
33
34
35
91
92
93
94
N21
N13
N18
N9
N17
N22
LOWER EDMONTON
EDMONTON
UPPER EDMONTON
TOTTENHAM
TOTTENHAM HALE
TOTTENHAM MARSHES
EDMONTON CEMETERY
TOTTENHAM CEMETERY
PYMMES PARK
JUBILEE PARK
CHURCHFIELD REC GRD
CHURCH STREET REC GRD
FIRS FARM PLAYING FIELDS
CLOWES SPORTS GROUND
THE PAULIN GROUND
TATEM PARK REC GRD
HOLLYWOOD GDNS
HAZELWOOD SPORTS
TOTTENHALL SPORTS GROUND
BOUNDARY PLAYING FIELDS
LORDSHIP RECREATION GROUND
BRUCE CASTLE PARK
DOWN LANE REC GRD
EDMONTON FEDERATION CEMETERY (JEWISH)
TOTTENHAM PARK CEMETERY
MONTAGU RECREATION GROUND
WESTERN SYNAGOGUE CEMETERY
NORTH MIDDLESEX UNIVERSITY HOSPITAL
Great Cambridge Junction
Kenninghall
TOTTENHAM HOTSPUR FC
NORTHUMBERLAND PARK
LOCKWOOD RESERVOIR
GREAT CAMBRIDGE ROAD
HERTFORD ROAD
FORE STREET
HIGH ROAD
NORTH CIRCULAR ROAD
STERLING WAY
ANGEL ROAD
MERIDIAN WAY
WATERMEAD WAY (NORTH-SOUTH ROUTE)
LORDSHIP LANE
THE ROUNDWAY
BRUCE GROVE
RIDGE AVENUE
GREEN LANES
SILVER STREET
WHITE HART LANE
0 500 yds
0 500 m

DX
DY
DZ
EA
EB
EC
ED
105
124
145
36
37
38
LEE VALLEY
WILLIAM
GIRLING
RESERVOIR
GOLF
COURSE
LEE VALLEY
REGIONAL
PARK
MERIDIAN BUSINESS PK
VANTAGE BUSINESS PARK
Lee Valley Athletics Centre
Lee Valley Leisure Complex Camping & Caravan Park
DEEPHAMS SEWAGE TREATMENT WORKS
Lidl UK GmbH Distribution Centre
CLAVERINGS IND EST
Pickett's Lock
THE HAWK WOOD
POLE HILL
CHINGFORD GOLF CO
CHINGFORD
E4
FRIDAY HILL
PIMP HALL PARK
CHINGFORD
MANSFIELD PARK
LEA VALLEY PLAYING FIELDS
Chingford Golf Range
RIDGEWAY PARK
CHINGFORD MOUNT CEMETERY
CHINGFORD HALL PARK
SOUTH CHINGFORD
CHINGFORD HATCH
LARKSWOOD PLAYING FIELDS
LARKS WOOD
WAR MEMORIAL REC GRD
JUBILEE SPORTS GRD
HIGHAMS PARK
HALE END
AINSLIE WOOD (Nat Res)
ROLLS SPORTS GRD
HIGHAMS IND EST
GOALS CHINGFORD
SPORTS GRD
BANBURY RESERVOIR
MUSLIM BURIAL GROUND
FAIRWAY GOLF RANGE
BRITANNIA SPORTS GROUND
THE LONDON HOSPITAL SPORTS GRD
Sports Centre
Crooked Billet
Cooks Ferry
Hall La
CHINGFORD IND CEN
CORK TREE RETAIL PK
RAVENSIDE RETAIL PK
LEE VALLEY TRAD EST
HASTINGWOOD TRADING ESTATE
Lee Valley Watersports
BUS DEPOT
SOUTHEND RD
NORTH CIRCULAR RD
A406
A110
A112
A1009
A1037
A1055
A503
B160
B179
IG8
EPPING
WALTHAM FOREST
HIGHAM HILL REC GRD
HIGHAM HILL
UPLANDS BUSINESS PARK
HIGHAMS LODGE BUSINESS CEN
E17
LLOYD PARK
WALTHAMSTOW
Sir George Monoux Coll
WALTHAM FOREST TRACK
CHESTNUTS SHOWGROUND
WADHAM LODGE SPORTS GRD
LRT FB SPORTS GRD
WALTHAMSTOW BUSINESS CEN
Wood Street
TOWN HALL
Waltham Forest Coll
ASSEMBLY HALL
THORPE COOMBE HOSP
The Bell
46
47
48
49
50
51
52
53
54
91
92
93
94

EE
EF
EG
EH
EJ
EK
EL
106
123
146
IG10
IG9
IG8
E4
E17
E18
Buckhurst Hill
CHINGFORD GREEN
FRIDAY HILL
HIGHAMS PARK
HALE END
WOODFORD GREEN
Woodford Wells
WOODFORD
SOUTH WOODFORD
CHINGFORD
CHINGFORD PLAIN
QUEEN ELIZABETH'S HUNTING LODGE
THE WARREN
HATCH FOREST
WHITEHALL PLAIN
LORD'S BUSHES
Knighton Wood
WOODFORD GOLF COURSE
THE HIGHAMS PARK
EPPING FOREST
WALTHAMSTOW FOREST
BLUEHOUSE GROVE
HATCH GROVE
REED'S FOREST
RAY PARK
ASHTON PLAYING FIELD
LUXBOROUGH LANE TREATMENT WORKS
Waterworks Corner
George Lane Roundabout
Charlie Brown's Roundabout
HOLLY HOUSE HOSP
RANGERS ROAD
EPPING NEW ROAD
HIGH ROAD
NORTH CIRCULAR RD
SOUTHEND ROAD
CHIGWELL ROAD
WOODFORD NEW ROAD
BROADMEAD ROAD
A1069
A104
A121
A110
A1009
A1199
A113
A406
A503
500 yds
500 m

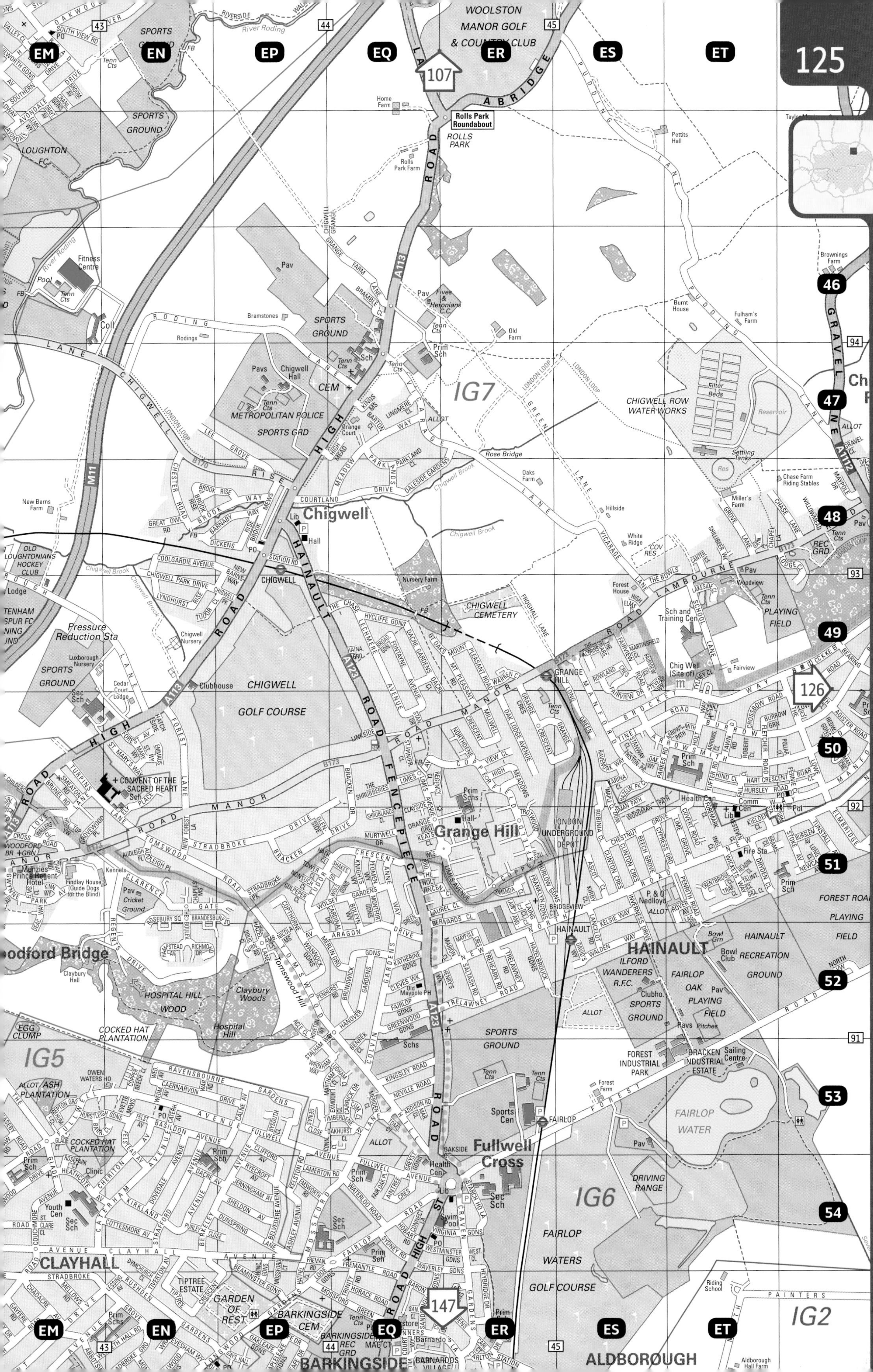
WOOLSTON MANOR GOLF & COUNTRY CLUB
107
ABRIDGE ROAD
Rolls Park Roundabout
ROLLS PARK
LOUGHTON FC
SPORTS GROUND
River Roding
Fitness Centre
CHIGWELL GRANGE
GRANGE FARM LANE
SPORTS GROUND
Fives & Heronians C.C.
Old Farm
Pettits Hall
PUDDING LANE
Burnt House
Fulham's Farm
Brownings Farm
GRAVEL LANE
RODING LANE
Bramstones
Rodings
Chigwell Hall
CEM
METROPOLITAN POLICE SPORTS GRD
IG7
CHIGWELL ROW WATER WORKS
Filter Beds
Reservoir
Settling Tanks
Chase Farm Riding Stables
Miller's Farm
CHIGWELL LANE
LONDON LOOP
GREEN LANE
Rose Bridge
Oaks Farm
Hillside
VICARAGE LANE
White Ridge
COV RES
LAMBOURNE ROAD
Forest House
Sch and Training Cen
PLAYING FIELD
REC GRD
Chigwell
New Barns Farm
OLD LOUGHTONIANS HOCKEY CLUB
Chigwell Brook
COOLGARDIE AVENUE
CHIGWELL PARK DRIVE
STATION RD
CHIGWELL
Nursery Farm
CHIGWELL CEMETERY
FROGHALL LANE
Pressure Reduction Sta
Luxborough Nursery
SPORTS GROUND
Chigwell Nursery
CHIGWELL GOLF COURSE
HAINAULT ROAD
Clubhouse
GRANGE HILL
Chig Well (Site of)
BROCKET WAY
126
MANFORD WAY
CONVENT OF THE SACRED HEART
MANOR ROAD
FENCEPIECE ROAD
Grange Hill
LONDON UNDERGROUND DEPOT
Health Cen
Lib
Fire Sta
Prim Sch
FOREST ROAD
PLAYING FIELD
HAINAULT RECREATION GROUND
Woodford Bridge
Menzies Prince Regent Hotel
Findlay House (Guide Dogs for the Blind)
Pav Cricket Ground
TOMSWOOD ROAD
STRADBROKE DRIVE
Claybury Hall
HOSPITAL HILL WOOD
Claybury Woods
Hospital Hill
Tomswood Hill
HAINAULT
P & O Nedlloyd
ILFORD WANDERERS R.F.C.
FAIRLOP OAK PLAYING FIELD
SPORTS GROUND
Bowl Club
EGG CLUMP
COCKED HAT PLANTATION
IG5
ASH PLANTATION
OWEN WATERS HO
RAVENSBOURNE GARDENS
FULLWELL AVENUE
SPORTS GROUND
FOREST INDUSTRIAL PARK
BRACKEN INDUSTRIAL ESTATE
Sailing Centre
Forest Farm
Sports Cen
FAIRLOP
FAIRLOP WATER
DRIVING RANGE
Fullwell Cross
CLAYHALL
IG6
FAIRLOP WATERS GOLF COURSE
Sec Sch
Swim Pool
TIPTREE ESTATE
GARDEN OF REST
BARKINGSIDE CEM
BARKINGSIDE REC GRD
147
Riding School
PAINTERS
IG2
BARKINGSIDE
Barnardo's
BARNARDOS VILLAGE
ALDBOROUGH
Aldborough Hall Farm
EM EN EP EQ ER ES ET
43 44 45
46 47 48 49 50 51 52 53 54
91 92 93 94

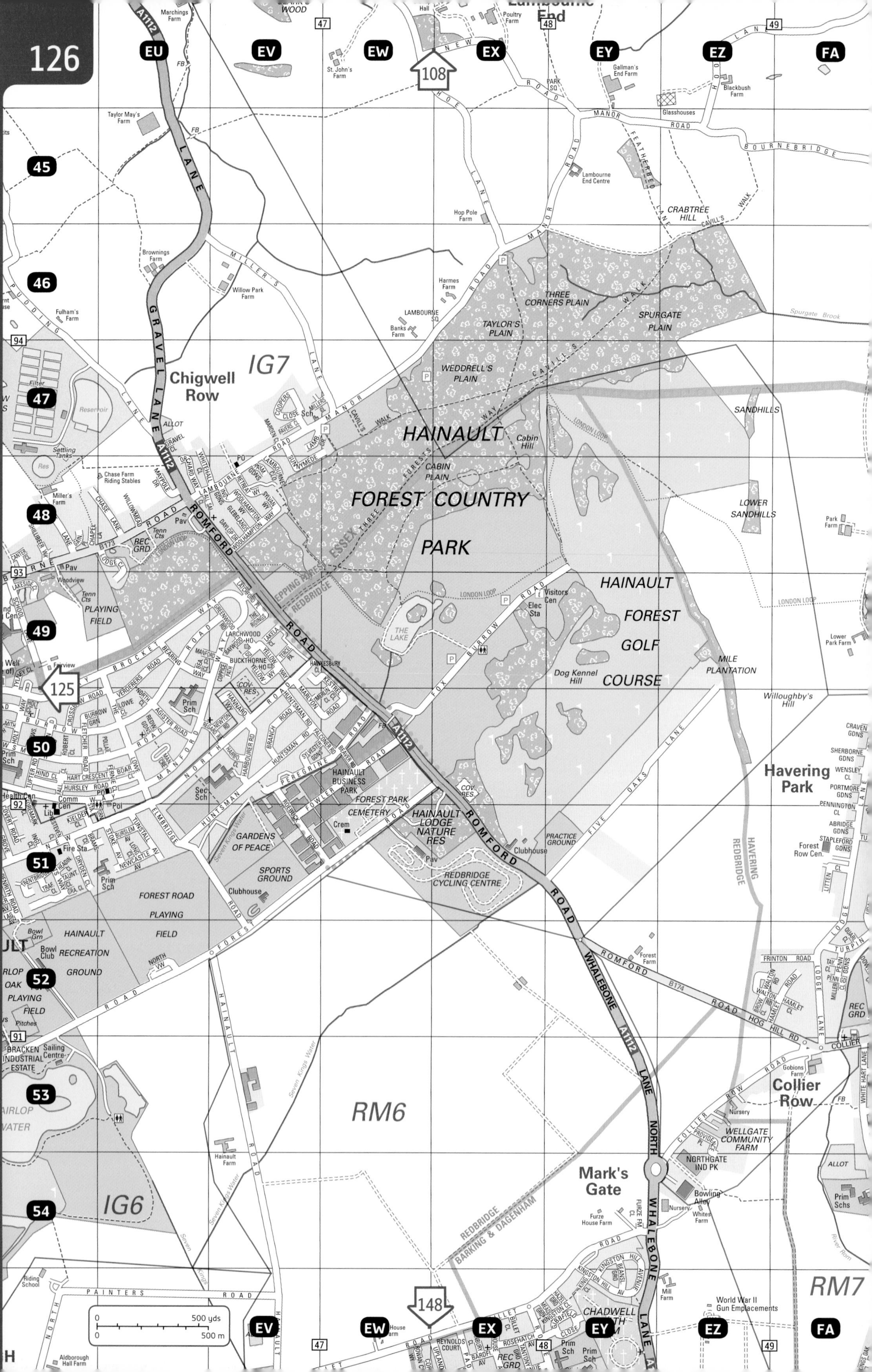
EU
EV
EW
EX
EY
EZ
FA
108
125
148
45
46
47
48
49
50
51
52
53
54
Marchings Farm
Poultry Farm
Gallman's End Farm
St. John's Farm
Blackbush Farm
Glasshouses
Taylor May's Farm
Lambourne End Centre
MANOR ROAD
BOURNEBRIDGE
CRABTREE HILL
Hop Pole Farm
Brownings Farm
Willow Park Farm
Harmes Farm
Fulham's Farm
LAMBOURNE SQ
Banks Farm
THREE CORNERS PLAIN
TAYLOR'S PLAIN
SPURGATE PLAIN
Spurgate Brook
WEDDRELL'S PLAIN
Chigwell Row
IG7
GRAVEL LANE
A1112
SANDHILLS
HAINAULT
FOREST COUNTRY
PARK
Cabin Hill
CABIN PLAIN
LONDON LOOP
Reservoir
Settling Tanks
Chase Farm Riding Stables
Miller's Farm
LOWER SANDHILLS
Park Farm
ROMFORD ROAD
ESSEX
EPPING FOREST
REDBRIDGE
THE LAKE
Visitors Cen
Elec Sta
HAINAULT FOREST GOLF COURSE
Dog Kennel Hill
MILE PLANTATION
Lower Park Farm
Willoughby's Hill
PLAYING FIELD
Woodview
Fairview
Tenn Cts
REC GRD
Prim Sch
Sec Sch
HAINAULT BUSINESS PARK
FOREST PARK CEMETERY
Crem
HAINAULT LODGE NATURE RES
Clubhouse
PRACTICE GROUND
REDBRIDGE CYCLING CENTRE
GARDENS OF PEACE
SPORTS GROUND
FOREST ROAD PLAYING FIELD
HAINAULT RECREATION GROUND
Fire Sta
Health Cen
Comm Cen
Lib
Pol
FIVE OAKS LANE
FOX BURROW ROAD
Havering Park
HAVERING
REDBRIDGE
Forest Farm
ROMFORD ROAD
B174
HOG HILL RD
WHALEBONE LANE
Bowl Club
BRACKEN INDUSTRIAL ESTATE
Sailing Centre
RM6
HAINAULT ROAD
Seven Kings Water
Hainault Farm
Collier Row
Gobions Farm
Nursery
WELLGATE COMMUNITY FARM
NORTHGATE IND PK
Mark's Gate
Furze House Farm
Bowling Alley
Whites Farm
Prim Schs
ALLOT
REDBRIDGE
BARKING & DAGENHAM
IG6
Riding School
PAINTERS ROAD
Mill Farm
World War II Gun Emplacements
RM7
CHADWELL HEATH
Aldborough Hall Farm
0 500 yds
0 500 m
47
48
49

FB
FC
FD
FE
FF
FG
FH
109
128
149
CM14
RM4
RM5
RM1
RM2
RM3
Nuper's Hatch
Havering-atte-Bower
Chase Cross
Gidea Park
NOAK HILL ROAD
BOURNEBRIDGE LANE
TYSEA HILL
MURTHERING LANE
NORTH ROAD
BROXHILL ROAD
CLOCKHOUSE LANE
ORANGE TREE HILL
HAVERING ROAD
LOWER BEDFORDS ROAD
EASTERN AVENUE
MAIN ROAD
COLLIER ROW
HORSEMAN SIDE
GOATSWOOD LANE
Hall Farm
High House Farm
Woodlands Farm
Brook Farm
Nursery
Bournebridge Farm
Crown Park Farm
Olives Farm
Spring Farm
Skips Corner Farm
Asheton Farm
Home Farm
Widdrington Farm
Bower Farm
Round House Farm
Upper Bedfords Farm
Chase End
STAPLEFORD ABBOTTS GOLF COURSE
WATTON'S GREEN
BRENTWOOD
EPPING FOREST
ESSEX
HAVERING
STRAIGHTS PLANTATION
PALACE PLANTATION
SANDPITS PLANTATION
WITCH HILL PLANTATION
HILLY PARK
OSIER BED
TRENCH POND PLANTATION
SOUTH PARK PLANTATION
PYRGO PARK
FOXBURROW WOOD
PHEASANT WOOD
AVENUE WOOD
DELL POND
HAVERING COUNTRY PARK
FURRY FIELD
PINE WOOD
KILN WOOD
ROUND WOOD
BIG FIELD
BEAN FIELD
ST. FRANCIS HOSPICE
BEDFORD'S PARK
SPORTS GROUND
BOWER WOOD
SPRING WOODS
LARCH WOOD
NURSERY WOOD
Foxes Hill
BEDFORDS LAKE
Water Works
RISEBRIDGE GOLF COURSE
RISE PARK
LAWNS REC GRD
RAPHAEL PARK
ROMFORD GOLF COURSE
GIDEA PARK SPORTS GRD
KING GEORGE'S PLAYING
HUBBINET IND EST
LONDON LOOP
Prim Sch
Sec Sch
Youth Cen
Fire Sta
Tennis Club
Clubhouse
Driving Range
Med Cen
Comm Cen
Clinic
Lib
PO
A12
B175
B174
B1459
46
47
48
49
50
51
52
53
54
91
92
93
94

FJ
FK
FL
FM
FN
FP
FQ
54
55
56
45
46
47
48
49
50
51
52
53
54
94
93
92
91
PRIORS GOLF COURSE
CURTIS PLANTATION
WABBING'S PLANTATION
LOCKSMITH WOOD
GOLDSMITH WOOD
Frieze Hall
The Chequers PH
Weald Bridge
ESSEX
BRENTWOOD
HAVERING
SEVENACRE PLANTATION
Old Macdonalds Farm
Wright's Bridge
Wrightsbridge Farm
Wealdside
Rochetts Farm
Hou Hatch
St. Vincent's Hamlet
M25
Pentowan Farm
SPICE PITS WOOD
Spice Pits Farm
Hill Farm
NOAK HILL SPORTS GRD
Hall
Noak Hill
RM4
Widdrington Farm
TRENCH POND PLANTATION
LONDON LOOP
FOXBURROW
THE OSIERS
BURNT WOOD
Manor Farm
DAGNAM PARK
FIR WOOD
COCK WOOD
ALDER WOOD
MAYLANDS GOLF COURSE
Havering Coll
HATTER'S WOOD
Dycorts Sch
Sec Sch
Prim Sch
DUCK WOOD NATURE RESERVE
127
COUNCIL OFFICES
CENTRAL PARK
Harold Hill
LONG WOOD
SALE WOOD
Leisure Cen
Health Cen
Comm Cen
Youth Club
Youth Centre
Ardleigh Green Cricket Club
Clubhouse
Maylands
SPORTS GRD
SHOULDER OF MUTTON WOOD
The Saxon King PH
RM3
COLCHESTER ROAD
A12
PLAYING FIELD
Harold Park
BATES INDUSTRIAL EST
Sludge Beds
Harold Court
HAROLD COURT WOODS
Roots & Shoots Garden Cen
Ivy Lodge Farm
HAROLD HILL INDUSTRIAL ESTATE
FALCON BUS. CEN
Fire Sta
Superstore
Gallows Corner
AVENUE INDUSTRIAL ESTATE
GIDEA PARK SPORTS GRD
HAROLD WOOD
King Harold PH
Clinic
Comm Cen
Cockabourne Bridge
Pages Farm
Riding Stables
RM1
RM2
STAFFORD INDUSTRIAL ESTATE
SOUTHEND
A127
Harold Wood Cricket Club
HAROLD WOOD PARK
Sec Sch
PAGES WOOD
150
Health Club
Prospect Farm
500 yds
500 m

FR
FS
FT
FU
FV
FW
FX
57
58
59
130
131
151
46
47
48
49
50
51
52
53
54
94
93
92
91
CM15
CM14
CM13
WEALD COUNTRY PARK
BRENTWOOD
South Weald
Brook Street
Warley
Great Warley
Junction 28
WARLEY COUNTRY PARK
BRENTWOOD BYPASS
A12
A1023
A128
B186
M25
ONGAR ROAD
BRENTWOOD
HIGH STREET
LONDON ROAD
BROOK STREET
WEALD ROAD
SHENFIELD ROAD
INGRAVE ROAD
QUEENS ROAD
KINGS ROAD
WARLEY HILL
WARLEY ROAD
EAGLE WAY
THE AVENUE
HARTSWOOD ROAD
MIDDLETON HALL LANE
MAGPIE LANE
BIRD LANE
DARK LANE
NAGS HEAD LANE
MASCALLS LANE
GREAT ROPERS LANE
HONEYPOT LANE
SANDPIT LANE
LODGE FIELD
MARSH FIELD
LAKE FIELD
SOUTH WEALD LAKE
BELVEDERE FIELD
THE FOREST
LANGTONS WOOD
FOXDOWN WOOD
THE PARK
HIGH WOOD
LARKINS PLAYING FIELDS
THE SPINNEY
Calcott Hall Farm
Langtons Farm
Halfway House Farm
Tower Arms PH
Holiday Inn Brentwood
Nags Head PH
VICARAGE WOOD
LOWER VICARAGE WOOD
Old Vicarage
Bennett's Farm
Tomlins Nursery
Mascalls
LOWER BELT
BACHELOR'S WALK
Leverton House
Leverton Hall
Boyles Court Farm
TOP PLANTATION
TYLERS SHAW
JACKSONS WOOD
WORMWALK SHAW
JERMAINS WOOD
BRIDGE WOOD
Tylers Hall
TYLERS WOOD
FOXBURROW WOOD
COOMBE WOOD
Stonyhills Farm
Stonyhills House
Coombe Lodge
Thatchers Arms PH
WARLEY PLACE NATURE RESERVE
Warley Lea Farm
Tooks Farm
Hole Farm
Suttons Farm
BRENTWOOD
HAVERING
ESSEX
CLEMENT'S WOOD
MASCALLS PARK
WARLEY HILL BUSINESS PK
WARLEY PLAYING FIELDS
MARILLAC HOSPITAL
SPIRE HARTSWOOD HOSP
BRENTWOOD LEISURE PARK
HOLDEN'S WOOD
WARLEY GAP
ELLEN'S WOOD
RUSHY PIECE
WARLEY PARK GOLF COURSE
Driving Range
Clubhouse
Little Warley Lodge
Home Farm
Pump Farm
Clap Gate Farm
DONKEY LANE PLANTATION
BARRACK WOOD
CEMETERY
DEVIL'S HEAD PLANTATION
ESSEX NUFFIELD HOSP
SPORTS GROUND
BRENTWOOD C.C.
WILSONS CORNER
TOWN HALL
B.T. Offices
LONDON ROAD CEM
LA PLATA WOOD
BRENTWOOD
Sawyer's Hall Farm
Great & Little Warley CC
Horse & Groom PH
Great Ropers

Kelvedon Hatch Camping & Caravanning Site
BENTLEY GOLF COURSE
FS
FT
FU
FV
FW
FX
FY
58
59
60
Bentley
SPORTS GROUND
Country Club
Crow Green
Ashwells Farm
Wishfields Farm
Sumner's Farm
Howe's Farm
Martin McColl Ho
Beads Hall Nursery
Days Farm
Crow Green Farm
Brick House Farm
Graytoni Stud Farm
Straight Mile Nursery
BEADS HALL LAKE
BRICK HOUSE WOOD
Pilgrims Hall
Bleak House Farm
Moat House
Canterbury Tye Farm
CANTERBURY TYE SPRING
Pilgrim's Hatch
CM15
41
42
43
44
45
46
47
48
49
50
96
95
94
93
Coxtie Green Farm
Orchard Nursery
Bentley Cricket Club
RECYCLING CENTRE
Black Horse PH
SPORTS GRD
BISHOP'S HALL PARK
Brentwood Centre
LARCH WOOD
FOX WOOD
TOWER PLANTATION
LANGTONS WOOD
FOXDOWN WOOD
LODGE FIELD
THE FOREST
HIGH WOOD
LARKINS PLAYING FIELDS
Langtons Farm
Sawyer's Hall Farm
HALL WOOD
WEALD COUNTRY PARK
128
SOUTH WEALD LAKE
BELVEDERE FIELD
THE PARK
Calcott Hall Farm
Cricket Ground
THE SPINNEY
Brookweald Cricket Club
Halfway House Farm
Visitor Cen
Tower Arms PH
CM14
BRENTWOOD
SPORTS GRD
ESSEX NUFFIELD HOSP
SPORTS GROUND
Brentwood Sch
South Weald
Bennett's Farm
VICARAGE WOOD
Old Vicarage
LONDON ROAD CEM
B.T. Offices
TOWN HALL
High Sch
Sec Sch
SHENFIELD COMMON
LOWER VICARAGE WOOD
Holiday Inn Brentwood
Junction 28
Nags Head PH
Brook Street
WARLEY COUNTRY PARK
Tomlins Nursery
Warley
CEMETERY
DONKEY LANE PLANTATION
HARTSWOOD
Mascalls
CLEMENT'S WOOD
WARLEY HILL BUSINESS PK
Fitness Centre
WARLEY PLAYING FIELDS
LOWER BELT
129
MASCALLS PARK
BARRACK WOOD
Leverton House
Great Ropers
Horse & Groom PH
MARILLAC HOSPITAL
BRENTWOOD BYPASS
ONGAR ROAD
LONDON ROAD
BROOK STREET
HIGH STREET
SHENFIELD ROAD
INGRAVE ROAD
WEALD ROAD
A128
A12
A1023
0
500 yds
500 m

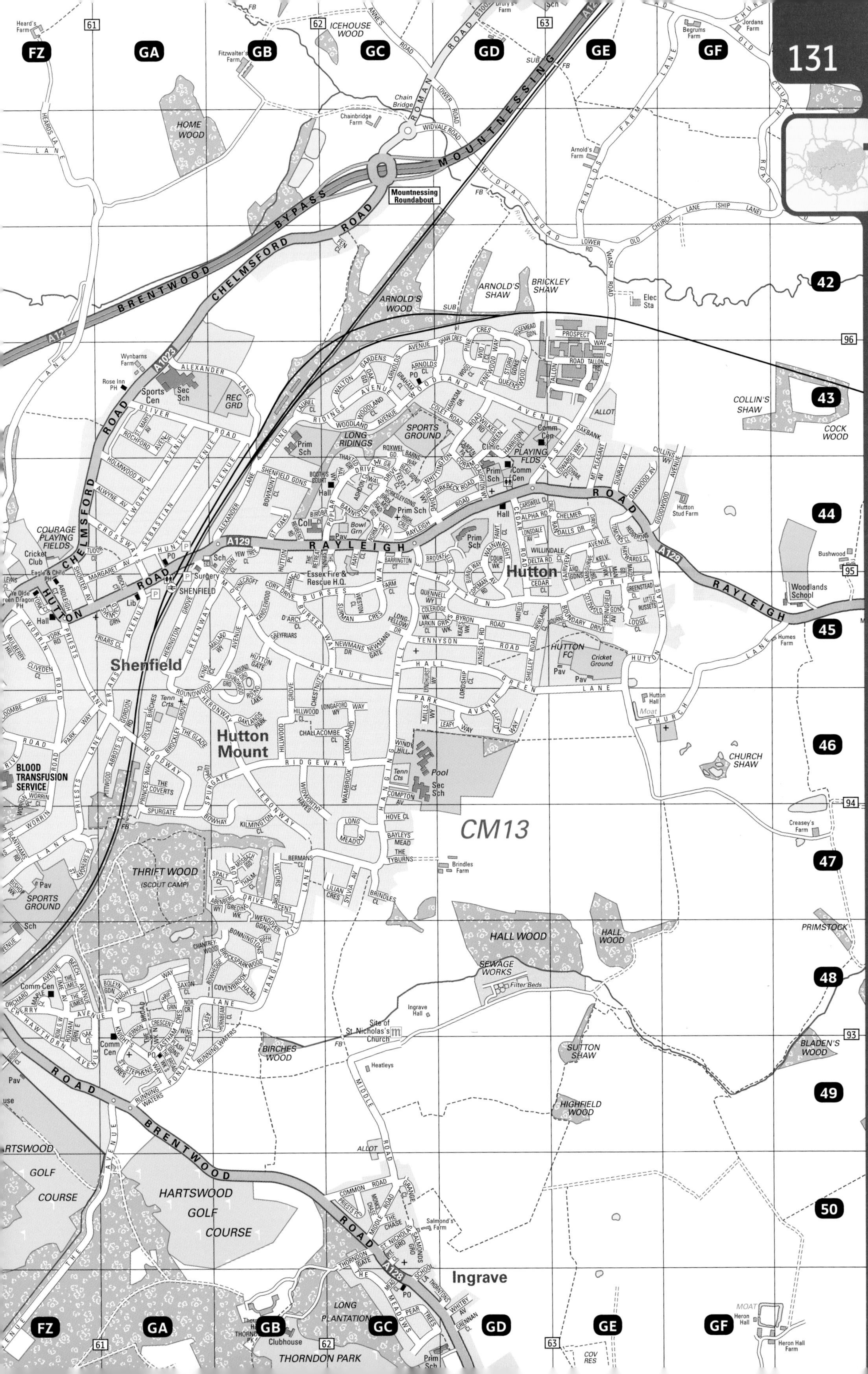
FZ
GA
GB
GC
GD
GE
GF
61
62
63
ICEHOUSE WOOD
Heard's Farm
Fitzwalter's Farm
Begrums Farm
Jordans Farm
HOME WOOD
Chain Bridge
Chainbridge Farm
WIDVALE ROAD
MOUNTNESSING
BRENTWOOD BYPASS
CHELMSFORD ROAD
Mountnessing Roundabout
Arnold's Farm
ARNOLD'S WOOD
ARNOLD'S SHAW
BRICKLEY SHAW
Elec Sta
42
43
44
45
46
47
48
49
50
96
95
94
93
COLLIN'S SHAW
COCK WOOD
Wynbarns Farm
Rose Inn PH
Sports Cen
Sec Sch
REC GRD
LONG RIDINGS
SPORTS GROUND
PLAYING FLDS
Prim Sch
Comm Cen
Clinic
Hall
Coll
Hutton Stud Farm
COURAGE PLAYING FIELDS
Cricket Club
A129
RAYLEIGH ROAD
Essex Fire & Rescue H.Q.
Surgery
SHENFIELD
Lib
Hutton
Bushwood
Woodlands School
Humes Farm
Shenfield
HUTTON FC
Cricket Ground
Pav
Hutton Hall
Moat
Hutton Mount
BLOOD TRANSFUSION SERVICE
Pool
Sec Sch
CHURCH SHAW
CM13
Creasey's Farm
Brindles Farm
THRIFT WOOD (SCOUT CAMP)
SPORTS GROUND
HALL WOOD
PRIMSTOCK
SEWAGE WORKS
Filter Beds
Ingrave Hall
Site of St Nicholas's Church
BIRCHES WOOD
SUTTON SHAW
BLADEN'S WOOD
Heatleys
HIGHFIELD WOOD
BRENTWOOD ROAD
HARTSWOOD GOLF COURSE
Salmond's Farm
A128
Ingrave
LONG PLANTATION
Clubhouse
THORNDON PARK
Heron Hall
Heron Hall Farm
COV RES

AC
AD
AE
AF
AG
AH
AJ
110
152
91
92
93
89
88
87
86
55
56
57
58
59
60
61
62
63
64
Holtspur
Beacon Centre
Junction 3
Superstore
Superstores
LONDON ROAD
OXFORD ROAD
M40
WYCOMBE END
WHITE HILL
BOUNDARY ROAD
A4094
FLACKWELL HEATH GOLF COURSE
FLACKWELL HEATH
Juniper Hill
NORTHERN WOODS
OLD MEADOWS
RONALD WOODS
Wooburn Green
SPORTS FIELD
CEM
QUARRY
MERCURY PARK
Clubhouse
SPORTS FLD
The Eagle PH
The Falcon PH
Glory Hill Farm
Over's Farm
MILL WOOD
Glass Craft
Lillyfee Farm
HP10
Wooburn
Cricket Club
WOOBURN PARK
WYCOMBE
SOUTH BUCKS
Castleman's Farm
ODDS FARM PARK
ODDS FARM ESTATE
The Royal Standard PH
SHEEPCOTE WOODS
SOHO MILLS IND EST
WOOBURN IND PARK
Sports Club
Sec Sch
SPORTS GRD
CEM
WASH HILL WOOD
FARM WOOD
THE SWILLEY
Clubhouse
COVERED RESERVOIR
HEDSOR GOLF COURSE
Sheepcote Farm
Meca Riding Centre
ASHEN COPPICE
Hawk's Hill
SAPPERS FIELD
The Chequers Inn PH
Hedsor Farmhouse
BOURNE END
SL8
Hollands Farm
Tower Hill
WOOLMAN'S WOOD
BRISTLES WOOD
HOLLYBUSH WOOD
White Hill
Bourne End Garden Centre
Priory Nursery
THE DENE
Hedsor Court
JOHNSON'S COPPICE
Hedsor Wharf
Hedsor Priory
Hedsor House
PARK TOP
DROPMORE PARK
THE ROOKERY
HEDSOR PARK
OAKEN GROVE
WINDSOR & MAIDENHEAD
SL6
BURWOOD
ESTATE
ROOT MOUND
ABBEY WOOD
Brook End Farm
SL1
LOCK CUT
Cookham Lock
Cookham Bridge
ODNEY COMMON
ODNEY CLUB SPORTS GRD
Tennis Courts
Cricket Ground
Mill House
Formosa Court
Cliveden House & Hotel
CLIVEDEN NT
GULLEY WOOD
CADBROOK WOOD
LITTLE BARNS WOOD
LAMBOURNE GOLF COURSE
Clubhouse
LAMBOURNES WOOD
The Feathers Inn PH
Cookham
Formosa Place
Seven Gables Cottage
Boathouse
Burwood House
WYMERS WOOD
BUCKINGHAMSHIRE
0 500 yds
0 500 m

HP9
SL9
SL2
Junction 2
WYCOMBE END
LONDON END
LONDON ROAD
OXFORD ROAD
PARK LANE
WINDSOR ROAD
COLLINSWOOD ROAD
BEACONSFIELD ROAD
HEDGERLEY LANE
M40
A40
A355
Beaconsfield Cricket Club
SPORTS GROUND
PITLANDS WOOD
BIRCHLAND WOOD
Chiltern Woodland Burial Park
Sewage Works
LOWER PYEBUSHES
PYEBUSHES
Oak Lodge Meadows
Beaconsfield RFC
Hall Barn Gardens
Beaconsfield SYCOB FC & Slough Town FC
Hyde Farm
Bellhouse Hotel
GREEN BROOM
SAND AND GRAVEL PIT
THE GROVE
DUKE'S UNDERWOOD
Beaconsfield Service Area
CAVE WOOD
BIRCHEN SPRING COPPICE
HILL WOOD
BURTLEY WOOD
HILLMOTTS WOOD
Hillmotts Farm
Slade Farm
HOLLYBUSH WOOD
Woodlands Farm
BOWER WOOD
HILLMOTTS FURZE
HANGINGS WOOD
Downey Bottom
BROOMHILL COPPICE
JENNINGS WOOD
SUTTON'S WOOD
Jennings Farm
Dorney Bottom
Mount Pleasant Farm
PENNLANDS WOOD
MOLL HAYES WOOD
Hedgerley
Gas Works
Pennlands Farm
LITTLE WOOD
KILN WOOD
BOVENEY WOOD
HEALY'S GORSE
HANGING WOOD
Water Tower
The Yew Tree PH
TREETOPS CAMPSITE
Abbey Park Farm
SUMMERLINS WOOD
FOOTPATH WOOD
LITTLE BURNT COPPICE
Hollybush Corner
BLACK GROVE
Boveney Wood Farm
HEATHFIELD WOOD
PONDS WOOD
STAPLEFURZE WOOD
The Blackwood Arms PH
SCHOOL WOOD
TWELVE ACRE WOOD
EGYPT WOODS
TIMBER WOOD
Littleworth Corner
WHITESPARK WOOD
GREAT BURNT COPPICE
NINE ACRE WOOD
Clubhouse
SPORTS GRD
DORNEY WOOD
HARTLEY COURT MOAT
EGYPT
FLEET WOOD
TOWER WOOD
BURNHAM BEECHES
BROCKHURST WOOD
INGRAM'S COPSE
Pumpkin Hill
JUNIPER GROVE
EAST BURNHAM COMMON
Farnham Common
111
134
153
AK
AL
AM
AN
AP
AQ
AR
56
57
58
59
60
61
62
63
64
94
95
96
89
88
87
86

AS
AT
AU
AV
AW
AX
AY
112
133
154
Layter's Green
THIRTY ACRE KNOLL
GREAT LEGS WOOD
MALMS WOOD
MOBILE HOME PARK
BIRCHLAND WOOD
Stampwell Farm
HIGH WOOD
BEECH WOOD
BIRCH WOOD
Bellhouse Hotel
OXFORD ROAD
A40
Wapsey's Wood Landfill Site
SAND AND GRAVEL PIT
FURTHER WARREN WOOD
Mumfords Farm
MUMFORDS LANE
LAYTERS GREEN
Parkwood Farm
SIBLET'S WOOD
SPORTS GRD
Prim Sch
Pav
Sch
CHANTRY WOOD
AUSTENWOOD COMMON
Bowls Club
Tenn Club
MALTMANS LANE
Raylands Farm
CHILTERN
SOUTH BUCKS
WEST PLANTATION
SL9
Jarretts Hill
BULSTRODE PARK
Bulstrode
MENAGERIE WOOD
GROVE PLANTATION
The Bull Hotel
GERRARDS CROSS
GERRARDS CROSS COMMON
Bulstrode Camp
Crab Hill
Ponders
Slade Farm
HEDGERLEY LANE
WAPSEYS LANE
HEDGERLEY GREEN
SUTTON'S WOOD
LEITH GROVE
RSPB NATURE RESERVE
CHURCH WOOD
Hedgerley
The White Horse PH
UPPER MEADOW
High Meadows
WINDSOR ROAD
B416
M40
SUB
HANGING WOOD
MOUNTHILL WOOD
Mount Hill Farm
HEDGERLEY PARK
BLACK GROVE
Park House
DUKE'S ORCHARD
Riding Stables
French Horn PH
Cricket Ground
Clubhouse
PARKSIDE CEMETERY
PICKERIDGE WOOD
Tara
Hedgerley Park Farm
Low Farm
HAY WOOD
TIMBER WOOD
STOKE WOOD
COLLUM GREEN ROAD
Pickeridge Farm
Kestrel Farm
SL3
Fulmer
Fulmer Hall
Prim Sch
Church Farm
Fulmer House Farm
SL2
TEMPLEWOOD LANE
STOKE COMMON ROAD
STOKE COMMON
BROCKHURST WOOD
FRAME WOOD
Fernacres Farm
PENN WOOD
Fulmer C.C.
Black Firs
Fernacres House
Framewood Manor
WEXHAM
Alder Bourne
Fish Pond
0 500 yds
0 500 m

HOGTROUGH WOOD
AZ
BA
BB
BC
BD
BE
BF
01
02
03
113
GERRARDS CROSS GOLF COURSE
Pav
Clubhouse
CHALFONT PARK
River Misbourne
A413
SLADE LANE
SOUTH BUCKS
CHILTERN
SQUARE COPSE
Coldharbour Farm
ROUND COPSE
NOCKHILL WOOD
JUNIPER WOOD
QUARTERS WOOD
OAK LANE
THREE RIVERS
SOUTH BUCKS
SHIRE LANE
LITTLE HANGING WOOD
Little Halings
Denham Grove
TILEHOUSE LANE
GREAT HALINGS WOOD
HALINGS LANE
Caravan Club
WYATTS COVERT
NORTHMOOR HILL (NATURE RESERVE)
UXBRIDGE ROAD
NORTH ORBITAL ROAD
A412
Weir
56
BATTLESFORD WOOD
89
RANSTON COVERT
57
Meadow Grange
OAKEND WOOD
MARISH LANE
Denham Park Farm
Pilot Centre
Hangars
DENHAM MARSH WOOD
Owls Oak
MIRRIE LANE
DENHAM AERODROME
OAKEND WOOD
WADLEY COVERT
NIGHTINGALE WOOD
HOLLY HILL WOOD
DENHAM MEDIA PARK
Flying Schools
WOODHURST DR
Comm Cen
FB
M25
Isle of Wight Farm
OVER THE MISBOURNE
SLADE OAK LANE
DENHAM GOLF COURSE
Sherwood House
Denham Green
NEWSTEAD WOOD
Prim Sch
58
COLLSELS WOOD
Clubhouse
LOWER ROAD
AMERSHAM ROAD
WOODLANDS ROAD
VICARAGE WAY
WOODHILL AV
HILLCREST WAYE
BEECH WAYE
MORELAND DR
MILL WOOD
DENHAM GOLF CLUB
Higher Denham
DOGGETTS FARM RD
UPPER ROAD
MIDDLE ROAD
ASHCROFT DRIVE
TILEHOUSE WAY
88
Medical Cen
PO
STATION YARD
DENHAM
59
UB9
GALLOWS WOOD
Elec Sta
Sewage Works
Gas Works
TOM WILLIAM'S WOOD
Moor House Farm
Comm Cen
BRADBURY'S ISLAND
OLD RECTORY LANE
MARTINSFIELD SPORTS GRD
Clubhouse
136
HEUSDEN WAY
LITTLE GALLOWS WOOD
THE RANCHO
OXFORD ROAD
Mushroom Farm
CAPS WOOD
MISBOURNE MEADOWS
The Prescotts
River Misbourne
60
Pol
Fire Sta
Gas Pipeline Sta
A40
CAPSWOOD BUS.CEN
S.BUCKS DISTRICT COUNCIL
BROKENGATE LANE
BAKER'S WOOD
Denham Place
THE PYGHTLE
87
St. Hubert's
St. Hubert's Home Farm
PINSTONE WAY
Ugly Duckling PH
SKYLARK RD
Tatling End
RED HILL
DENHAM AVENUE
VILLAGE ROAD
Hall
FULMER LANE
Little Prestwick
Old Prestwick
Prestwick Cottage
Hollybush Farm
HOLLYBUSH LANE
BLACKSMITHS LANE
MOUNT LANE
61
Wellers Mead
NABOTH
Grayleigh
Alderbourne Manor
Glasshouse
Denham Mount
FIELD ROAD
ASHMEAD
Prim Sch
Bowl
REC Club GRD
Little Acres Farm
Oldhouse Farm
GALDWINS WOOD
BROADSPRING WOOD
FROGGY LANE
62
PRIORY
HAWKS
Hawkswood
WOOD
Holly Bush
Glasshouses
Farm
Furzeney
FURZENEY WOOD
Junction 16 (M25)
86
Denham Roundabout
M40
FIELD ROAD
63
FURZENEY WOOD
HAWKS WOOD
Alderbourne Arches
BROADSPRING WOOD
Junction 1a (M40)
Rush Green Farm
New House Farm
WILLETTS LANE
GOSSAMS WOOD
Durham House
Cornerfields
HAWKSWOOD LANE
Watersplash Farm
FB
Alder Bourne
Fulmer Rise Manor
BROWN'S WOOD
Field End Farm
Ways Farm
OLDHOUSE WOOD
SOUTHLANDS ROAD
64
Alderbourne Farm
PARKSPRING WOOD
Cherry Orchard Farm
Blanchard's Farm
Kingcup Farm
MOUNT FIDGET WOOD
Saul's Farm
SEVEN HILLS ROAD
SL0
FULMER RISE
Fulmer Plant Park
BRIDGETTINE CONVENT
LANGLEY COMMON
PINEWOOD ROAD
155
LONG COPPICE
Sevenhills
PLAYING FIELD
Copse Hill Farm
DENHAM ROAD
Southlands Manor
Langley Corner
Dromenagh

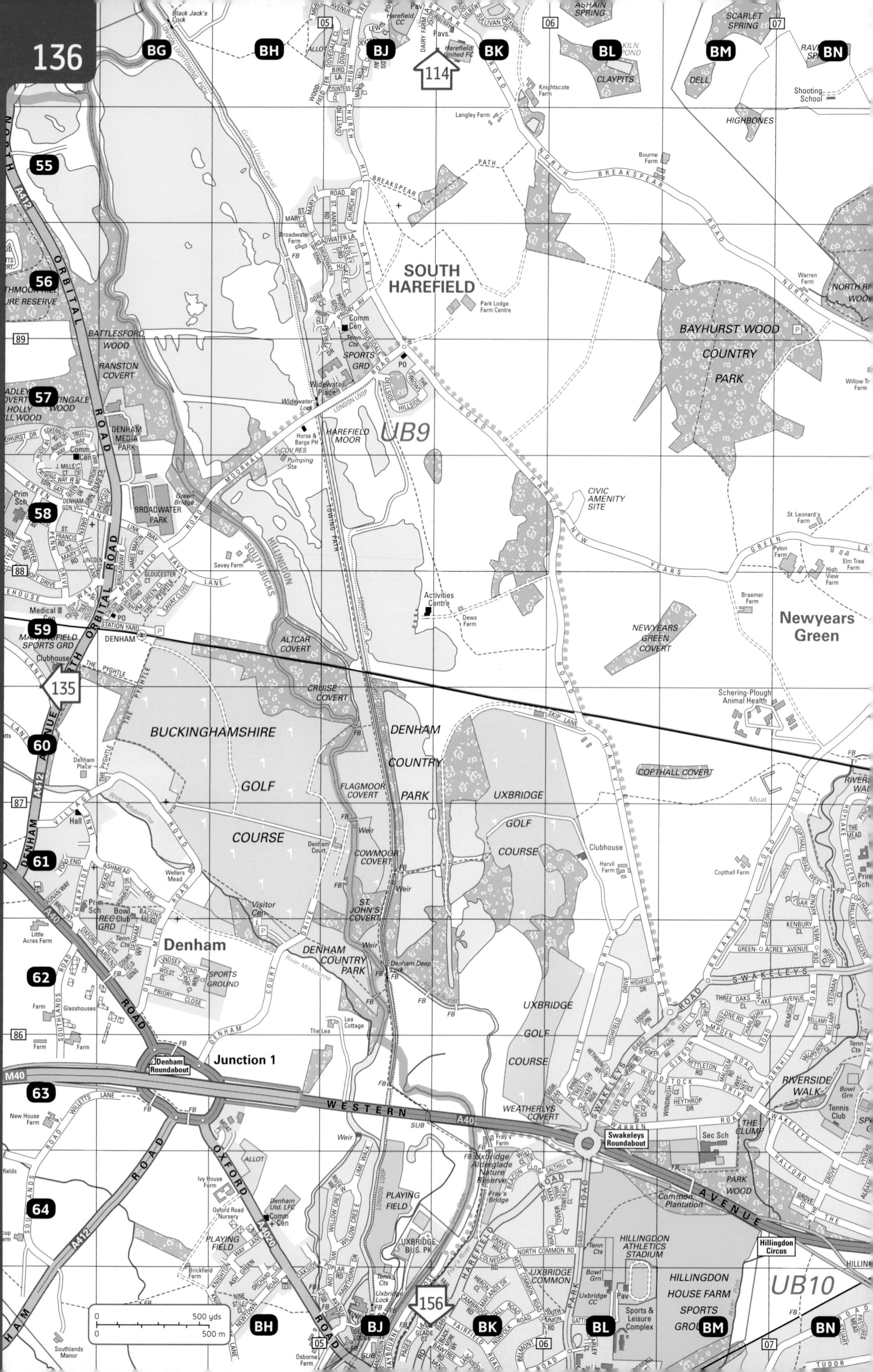
BG
BH
BJ
BK
BL
BM
BN
114
135
156
55
56
57
58
59
60
61
62
63
64
89
88
87
86
05
06
07
SOUTH HAREFIELD
UB9
UB10
Newyears Green
Denham
Junction 1
Denham Roundabout
Swakeleys Roundabout
Hillingdon Circus
BUCKINGHAMSHIRE GOLF COURSE
DENHAM COUNTRY PARK
UXBRIDGE GOLF COURSE
BAYHURST WOOD COUNTRY PARK
HARVIL ROAD
NORTH ORBITAL ROAD
DENHAM AVENUE
NORTH BREAKSPEAR ROAD
BREAKSPEAR PATH
MOORHALL ROAD
SAVAY LANE
NEW YEARS GREEN LANE
SKIP LANE
SWAKELEYS ROAD
WESTERN AVENUE
OXFORD ROAD
DENHAM ROAD
PARK ROAD
HAREFIELD ROAD
THE DRIVE
SOUTH BREAKSPEAR ROAD
WILLETTS LANE
VILLAGE ROAD
Grand Union Canal
River Misbourne
Frays River
HAREFIELD MOOR
DENHAM MEDIA PARK
BROADWATER PARK
BATTLESFORD WOOD
RANSTON COVERT
ALTCAR COVERT
CRUISE COVERT
FLAGMOOR COVERT
COWMOOR COVERT
ST. JOHN'S COVERT
COPTHALL COVERT
NEWYEARS GREEN COVERT
WEATHERLYS COVERT
CIVIC AMENITY SITE
Activities Centre
Dews Farm
Savay Farm
Schering-Plough Animal Health
Braemer Farm
Pylon Farm
Elm Tree Farm
St. Leonard's Farm
Copthall Farm
Harvil Farm
Langley Farm
Knightscote Farm
Bourne Farm
Warren Farm
Park Lodge Farm Centre
Broadwater Farm
Widewater Place
Widewater Lock
Horse & Barge PH
Pumping Sta
CLAYPITS
DELL
HIGHBONES
SCARLET SPRING
Shooting School
Harefield United FC
Harefield CC
Visitor Cen
Denham Court
Wellers Mead
Denham Place
Denham Deep Lock
The Lea
Lea Cottage
Frays Farm
Uxbridge Alderglade Nature Reserve
Frays Bridge
UXBRIDGE COMMON
UXBRIDGE BUS. PK
PLAYING FIELD
HILLINGDON ATHLETICS STADIUM
HILLINGDON HOUSE FARM SPORTS GROUND
Sports & Leisure Complex
Uxbridge CC
RIVERSIDE WALK
PARK WOOD
Common Plantation
THE CLUMP
Sec Sch
Tennis Club
Ivy House Farm
Oxford Road Nursery
Denham Utd. LFC
Brickfield Farm
New House Farm
Little Acres Farm
Southlands Manor
Osborne Farm
MARKSFIELD SPORTS GRD
SPORTS GROUND
Bowl REC Club GRD
DENHAM

Northwood Hills
HILL GOLF COURSE
RUISLIP NATURE RESERVE
COPSE WOOD
HA6
YOUNG WOOD
MAD BESS WOOD
POOR'S FIELD
RUISLIP LIDO
PARK WOOD
RUISLIP COMMON
Breakspear Crematorium
Hillingdon Borough FC
HA5
EASTCOTE VILLAGE
Haydon Hall
EASTCOTE HO GRD
CUCKOO HILL
Eastcote Hockey & Badminton Club
KINGS COLLEGE PLAYING FIELDS
HA4
RUISLIP
Ruislip CC
Swim Pool & Fitness Cen
WARRENDER PARK
EASTCOTE
RUISLIP GOLF COURSE
DRIVING RANGE
RUISLIP MANOR
Windmill Hall
CAVENDISH REC GRD
PINE GDNS
WEST RUISLIP
MAD FIELD COVERT
Ickenham C.C.
SPORTS GROUND
Wealdstone F.C.
Ruislip R.F.C.
BESSINGBY FIELD
NEW POND FARM FIELDS
Ruislip High Sch
RUISLIP GARDENS
ICKENHAM
Compass Theatre
BRAINTREE INDUSTRIAL ESTATE
SOUTH RUISLIP
Days Hotel
ODYSSEY BUSINESS PARK
Ickenham Marsh
Warehouse Hangar
Hangars
RAF NORTHOLT
FREEZELAND COVERT
WESTERN AVENUE
WEST END ROAD
HIGH STREET
BURY STREET
DUCKS HILL ROAD
A4180
A404
B466
115
138
157
BP
BQ
BR
BS
BT
BU
BV
56
57
58
59
60
61
62
63
64
08
09
10
86
87
88
89

BW
BX
BY
BZ
CA
CB
CC
116
137
158
55
56
57
58
59
60
61
62
63
64
PINNER GREEN
MONTESOLE PLAYING FIELDS
LITTLE COMMON
PINNER
PINNER MEMORIAL PARK
PINNER NEW CEMETERY
HEADSTONE MANOR RECREATION GROUND
HEADSTONE
CUCKOO HILL
HA5
EASTCOTE VILLAGE
PINNER VILLAGE GARDENS
NORTH HARROW
EASTCOTE
THE CROFT PLAYING FIELD
WEST HARROW
WEST HARROW REC GRD
RAYNERS LANE
HA2
ROXBOURNE PARK
CAVENDISH REC GRD
PINE GDNS
BESSINGBY FIELD
RECREATION GROUND
NEWTON PARK WEST
NEWTON FM ECOLOGY PK
SOUTH HARROW
ALEXANDRA PARK
SOUTH RUISLIP
SOUTH RUISLIP PLAYING FIELD
DEANE PARK
BRAINTREE INDUSTRIAL ESTATE
ODYSSEY BUSINESS PARK
HA4
Ruislip Retail Park
Victoria Retail Park
Brook Retail Park
Civic Amenity Site
NORTHOLT RECREATION GRD
EARLSMEAD STADIUM
UB5
LORD HALSBURY MEMORIAL GRD
ALEXANDRA AVENUE
A4090
A404
A312
PINNER ROAD
GEORGE V AVENUE
NORTHOLT ROAD
WEST END ROAD
0
500 yds
500 m

WEALDSTONE
KENTON
QUEENSBURY
HARROW ON THE HILL
NORTH WEMBLEY
SUDBURY
PRESTON
HA1
HA3
HA7
HA9
HA0
UB6
HARROW & WEALDSTONE
NORTHWICK PARK
NORTHWICK PARK HOSP
ST. MARK'S HOSP
OLYMPIC MEDICAL INSTITUTE
University of Westminster
HARROW SCHOOL PLAYING FIELDS
HARROW SCHOOL GOLF COURSE
CLEMENTINE CHURCHILL HOSPITAL
BOWDEN HOUSE
VALE FARM SPORTS GROUND
BARHAM PARK
PRESTON PARK
WOODCOCK PARK
KENTON RECREATION GROUND
ST. LUKE'S HOSPICE
WEMBLEY COMMERCIAL CENTRE
KING EDWARD VII PARK
JOHN BILLAM SPORTS GRD
JOHN LYON RBT
WEMBLEY CENTRAL
SOUTH KENTON
SUDBURY HILL
SUDBURY TOWN
WAVERLEY IND PARK
WHITEFRIARS IND EST
PHOENIX IND EST
ROXETH
117
140
159
CD
CE
CF
CG
CH
CJ
CK
56
57
58
59
60
61
62
63
64

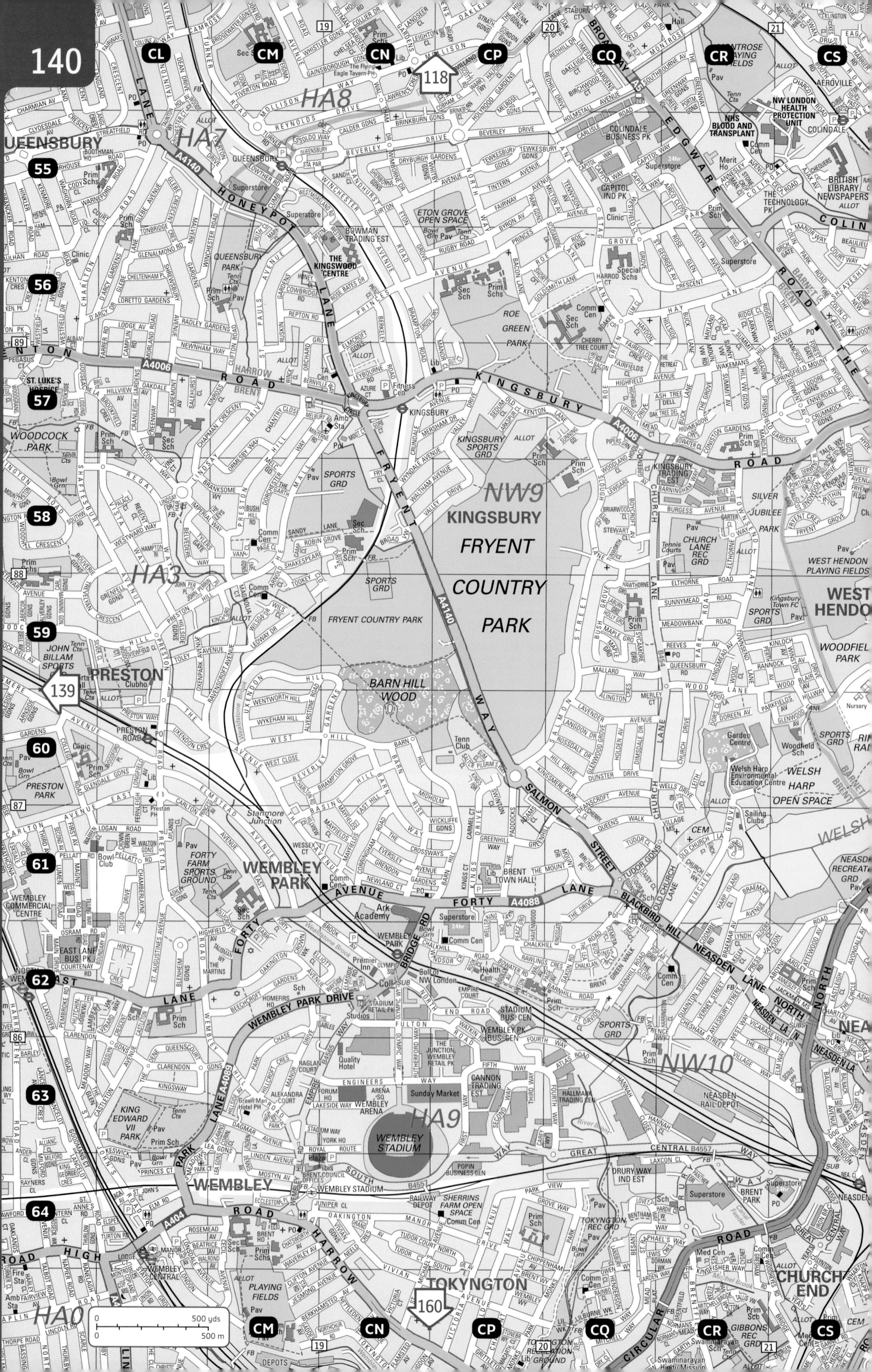
CL
CM
CN
CP
CQ
CR
CS
118
HA8
HA7
QUEENSBURY
55
56
57
58
59
60
61
62
63
64
A4140
HONEYPOT LANE
A5 EDGWARE ROAD
COLINDALE BUSINESS PK
COLINDALE
NW LONDON HEALTH PROTECTION UNIT
NHS BLOOD AND TRANSPLANT
BRITISH LIBRARY NEWSPAPERS
THE TECHNOLOGY PK
CAPITOL IND PK
MONTROSE PLAYING FIELDS
ETON GROVE OPEN SPACE
BOWMAN TRADING EST
THE KINGSWOOD CENTRE
QUEENSBURY PARK
ROE GREEN PARK
CHERRY TREE COURT
A4006 KENTON ROAD
KINGSBURY ROAD
KINGSBURY
ST. LUKE'S HOSPICE
WOODCOCK PARK
KINGSBURY SPORTS GRD
KINGSBURY TRADING EST
SILVER JUBILEE PARK
NW9
KINGSBURY FRYENT COUNTRY PARK
FRYENT COUNTRY PARK
FRYENT WAY
CHURCH LANE REC GRD
WEST HENDON PLAYING FIELDS
WEST HENDON
HA3
JOHN BILLAM SPORTS GRD
PRESTON
139
BARN HILL WOOD
WOODFIELD PARK
WELSH HARP OPEN SPACE
Welsh Harp Environmental Education Centre
PRESTON PARK
Stanmore Junction
SALMON STREET
FORTY FARM SPORTS GROUND
WEMBLEY PARK
BRENT TOWN HALL
FORTY AVENUE
FORTY LANE A4088
BLACKBIRD HILL
NEASDEN LANE
WEMBLEY COMMERCIAL CENTRE
EAST LANE BUS PK
Ark Academy
Superstore
WEMBLEY PARK
BRIDGE RD
Premier Inn
Coll of NW London
EMPIRE COURT
STADIUM BUS CEN
WEMBLEY PARK DRIVE
STADIUM RETAIL PK
WEMBLEY PK BUS CEN
THE JUNCTION WEMBLEY RETAIL PK
NW10
Quality Hotel
CANNON TRADING EST
HALLMARK TRADING CEN
NEASDEN RAIL DEPOT
Sunday Market
WEMBLEY ARENA
HA9
WEMBLEY STADIUM
KING EDWARD VII PARK
GREAT CENTRAL WAY B4557
POPIN BUSINESS CEN
DRURY WAY IND EST
BRENT PARK
WEMBLEY
WEMBLEY STADIUM
SHERRINS FARM OPEN SPACE
TOKYNGTON REC GRD
A404 HARROW ROAD
HIGH ROAD
WEMBLEY CENTRAL
PLAYING FIELDS
TOKYNGTON
160
NORTH CIRCULAR ROAD
CHURCH END
GIBBONS REC GRD
HA0
500 yds
500 m
19
20
21
DEPOTS
NEASDEN

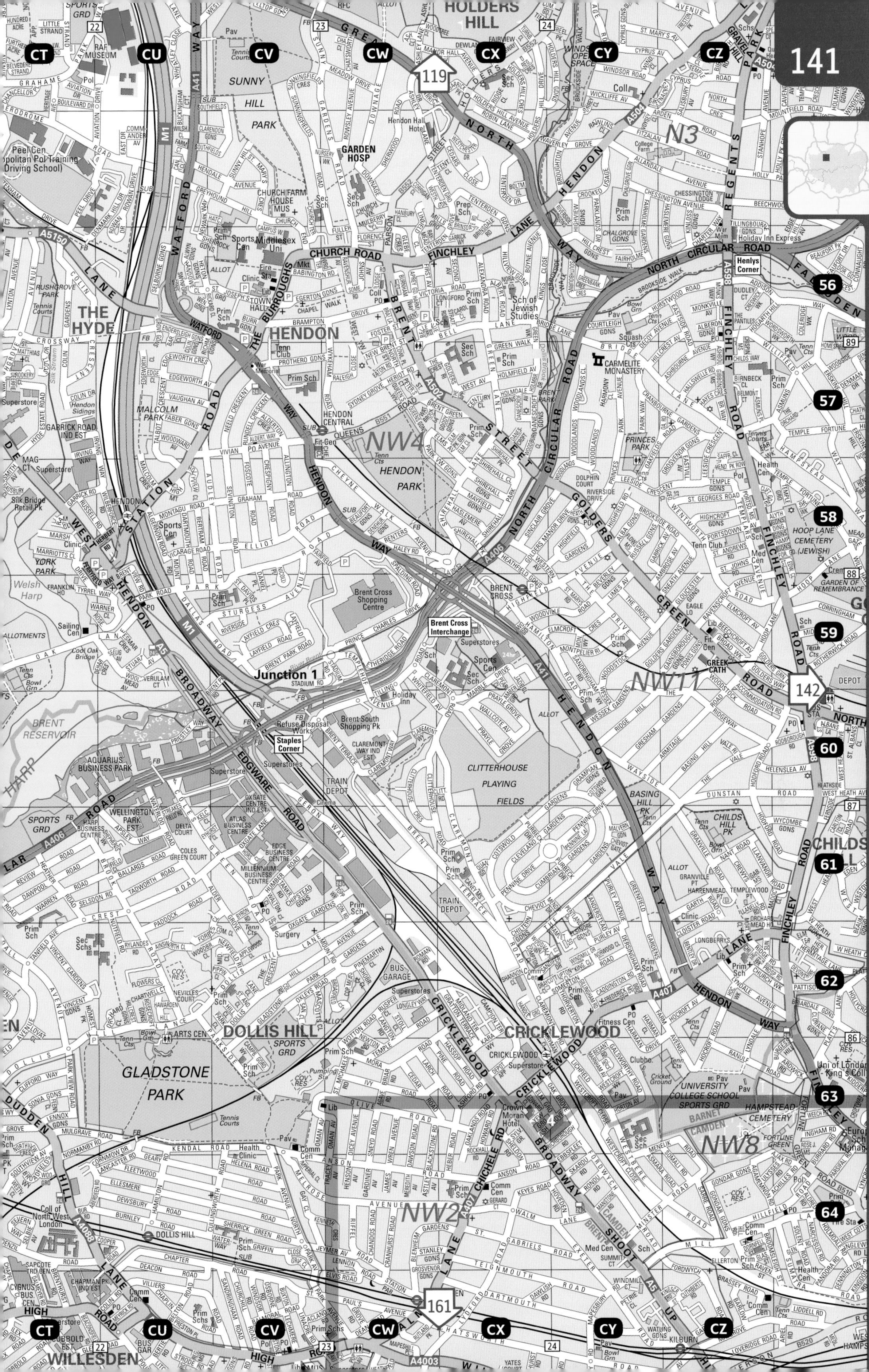

CT
CU
CV
CW
CX
CY
CZ
119
HOLDERS HILL
SUNNY HILL PARK
N3
GARDEN HOSP
Hendon Hall Hotel
Peel Cen
(Metropolitan Pol Training & Driving School)
RAF MUSEUM
CHURCH FARM HOUSE MUS
Middlesex Uni
TOWN HALL
Sch of Jewish Studies
CARMELITE MONASTERY
Henlys Corner
Holiday Inn Express
NORTH CIRCULAR ROAD
REGENTS PARK ROAD
FINCHLEY ROAD
THE HYDE
HENDON
HENDON CENTRAL
NW4
HENDON PARK
PRINCES PARK
WATFORD WAY
THE BURROUGHS
CHURCH ROAD
FINCHLEY LANE
BRENT STREET
QUEENS ROAD
MALCOLM PARK
GARRICK ROAD IND EST
Silk Bridge Retail Pk
YORK PARK
Welsh Harp
Sailing Cen
Cool Oak Bridge
HENDON WAY
Brent Cross Shopping Centre
BRENT CROSS
Brent Cross Interchange
Junction 1
HOOP LANE CEMETERY (JEWISH)
GARDEN OF REMEMBRANCE
GOLDERS GREEN ROAD
NW11
GREEK CATH
142
BRENT RESERVOIR
AQUARIUS BUSINESS PARK
Staples Corner
Refuse Disposal Works
Brent South Shopping Pk
CLAREMONT WAY IND EST
CLITTERHOUSE PLAYING FIELDS
BASING HILL PK
CHILDS HILL PK
CHILDS HILL
WELLINGTON PARK EST
OXGATE CENTRE IND EST
ATLAS BUSINESS CENTRE
EDGE BUSINESS CENTRE
MILLENNIUM BUSINESS CENTRE
EDGWARE ROAD
NORTH CIRCULAR ROAD
TRAIN DEPOT
BUS GARAGE
DOLLIS HILL
GLADSTONE PARK
CRICKLEWOOD
CRICKLEWOOD BROADWAY
Crown Moran Hotel
UNIVERSITY COLLEGE SCHOOL SPORTS GRD
HAMPSTEAD CEMETERY
BARNET
CAMDEN
NW8
NW2
Coll of North West London
DOLLIS HILL
SHOOT UP HILL
KILBURN
WILLESDEN
161
56
57
58
59
60
61
62
63
64
22
23
24

N3
EAST FINCHLEY CEMETERY
Crematorium
EAST FINCHLEY
N2
FORTIS GREEN
HIGHGATE WOOD
HAMPSTEAD GARDEN SUBURB
BIG WOOD
LITTLE WOOD
N6
HIGHGATE GOLF COURSE
HOOP LANE CEMETERY (JEWISH)
HAMPSTEAD HEATH EXTENSION
HAMPSTEAD GOLF COURSE
GOLDERS GREEN
NW11
Bunkers Hill
TURNERS WOOD
NORTH WOOD
Kenwood House
SANDY HEATH
GOLDERS HILL PARK
CHILDS HILL
KENWOOD
HAMPSTEAD HEATH
WEST HEATH
HEATHLANDS
PARLIAMENT HILL
NW3
HIGHGATE PONDS
QUEEN MARY'S HOSP
FENTON HO
HAMPSTEAD
KEATS HOUSE
ROYAL FREE HOSP
HAMPSTEAD CEMETERY
WEST HAMPSTEAD
FINCHLEY ROAD
HAVERSTOCK HILL
NORTH CIRCULAR ROAD
FALLODEN WAY
LYTTELTON ROAD
AYLMER ROAD
ARCHWAY ROAD
GREAT NORTH ROAD
EAST END ROAD
HAMPSTEAD LANE
NORTH END ROAD
SPANIARDS ROAD
HENDON WAY
ST. DOMINIC'S PRIORY
MAITLAND PARK ESTATE
HARINGEY
BARNET
CAMDEN
120
141
162
DA
DB
DC
DD
DE
DF
DG
55
56
57
58
59
60
61
62
63
64
500 yds
500 m

NOEL PARK
ALEXANDRA PALACE
ALEXANDRA PARK
N22
MUSWELL HILL
HORNSEY
N8
CROUCH END
QUEEN'S WOOD
HARRINGAY
STROUD GREEN
FINSBURY PARK
N4
N19
UPPER HOLLOWAY
TUFNELL PARK
HOLLOWAY
N7
LOWER HOLLOWAY
KENTISH TOWN
DARTMOUTH PARK
HIGHBURY
N5
CANONBURY
EMIRATES STADIUM
ARSENAL FC
WHITTINGTON HOSPITAL
HIGHGATE CEMETERY
WATERLOW PARK
H.M. PRISON HOLLOWAY
Nags Head
121
144
163
DH
DJ
DK
DL
DM
DN
DP
56
57
58
59
60
61
62
63
64

DQ
DR
DS
DT
DU
DV
DW
122
34
35
33
55
56
57
58
59
60
61
62
63
64
89
88
87
86
143
164
9
10
LORDSHIP RECREATION GROUND
BROADWATER FARM EST
TOTTENHAM MARSHES
WOODBERRY RESERVOIR
N17
N22
BELMONT REC GRD
DOWNHILLS PARK
WEST GREEN
TOTTENHAM HALE
LOCKWOOD INDUSTRIAL PARK
LEE VALLEY TECHNOPARK
DOWN LANE REC GRD
MILMEAD INDUSTRIAL CENTRE
LOW MAYNARD RESERVOIR
MONUMENT WAY
FERRY LANE
Tottenham Hale
Tottenham Hale Retail Park
THE HIGH CROSS CENTRE
N15
Coll of N E London
TOWN HALL
BROAD LANE
CHESTNUTS PARK
ST. ANN'S HOSPITAL
SEVEN SISTERS
Seven Sisters
SOUTH TOTTENHAM
MARKFIELD REC GRD
RESERVOIR NUMBER TWO
RESERVOIR NUMBER FOUR
RESERVOIR NUMBER THREE
WARWICK RESERVOIR EAST
WARWICK RESERVOIR WEST
COPPERMILL PLAYING FIELD
LEE VALLEY REGIONAL
HARRINGAY GREEN LANES
Arena Shopping Park
FINSBURY PARK
N4
AMHURST PARK
STAMFORD HILL
WOODBERRY DOWN ESTATE
EAST RESERVOIR
WEST RESERVOIR
MANOR HOUSE
SPRINGHILL SPORTS GRD
SPRINGFIELD PARK
Walthamstow Marsh Nature Reserve
CLAPTON COMMON
UPPER CLAPTON
STAMFORD HILL ESTATE
ABNEY PARK CEMETERY
STOKE NEWINGTON
N16
CLISSOLD PARK
SPORTS GROUND
NORTH MILLFIELDS RECREATION GROUND
E5
SHACKLEWELL
HACKNEY DOWNS
N5
HIGHBURY
E8
DALSTON JUNCTION
HACKNEY CENTRAL
HACKNEY DOWNS
HIGHBURY & ISLINGTON
CANONBURY
BALLS POND ROAD
DALSTON LANE
GRAHAM ROAD
STOKE NEWINGTON HIGH ST
STAMFORD HILL
HIGH ROAD
SEVEN SISTERS ROAD
GREEN LANES
AMHURST ROAD
LOWER CLAPTON RD
REGTORY ROAD
KINGSLAND
A10
A503
A504
A107
A105
A1201
A1199
A104
A1207
B104
B105
0
500 yds
0
500 m

DX
DY
DZ
EA
EB
EC
ED
HIGHAM HILL
LLOYD PARK
123
WALTHAMSTOW
CHESTNUTS SHOWGROUND
WALTHAM FOREST TRACK
UPLANDS BUSINESS PARK
HIGHAMS LODGE BUSINESS CEN
FOREST TRADING EST
Blackhorse Road
Wood Street
THORPE COOMBE HOSP
The Bell
A503
FOREST ROAD
UPPER WALTHAMSTOW
E17
DOUGLAS EYRE PLAYING FIELDS
WALTHAMSTOW CENTRAL
WALTHAMSTOW QUEENS ROAD
The Mall
WALTHAMSTOW CEM
ST. JAMES'S PARK
LOW HALL SPORTS GROUND
FOREST BUSINESS PK
ROXWELL TRADING PK
CROMWELL IND EST
DORMA TRADING PK
EASTGATE BUS. PK
LEYTON IND VILLAGE
WHIPPS CROSS UNIVERSITY HOSPITAL
Whipps Cross
LEYTONSTONE
146
56
57
58
59
60
61
62
63
64
89
88
87
86
LEA BRIDGE ROAD
A104
A1006
A112
A106
A12
A11
A102
LEYTON
E10
LEYTON MIDLAND ROAD
LEYTON FC
LEYTON ORIENT FC
SEYMOUR ROAD PLAYING FIELD
MARSH LANE PLAYING FIELD
IVE FM SPORTS GRD
LEYTON MARSHES
The Waterworks Visitor Centre
THE WATERWORKS NATURE RESERVE
LEE VALLEY PITCH & PUTT GOLF COURSE
Lee Valley Riding Cen
TEMPLE MILLS DEPOT
New Spitalfields Market
HACKNEY MARSH
LEE VALLEY REGIONAL PARK
LEA BRIDGE
LOWER CLAPTON
CLAPTON PARK
Lee Valley Hockey Centre and Tennis Centre (open 2014)
Lea Interchange
WICK COMMUNITY WOODLAND
Lee Valley VeloPark (open 2014)
HOMERTON
HACKNEY WICK
E9
E15
E20
EAST VILLAGE
QUEEN ELIZABETH OLYMPIC PARK
165
STRATFORD INTERNATIONAL
STRATFORD
Copper Box
ST. PATRICK'S RC CEMETERY
SIDMOUTH PARK
DRAPERS FIELD REC. GRD
JOHN HOWARD CENTRE
MABLEY GREEN
EAST CROSS ROUTE
CHOBHAM ROAD
LEYTONSTONE ROAD
36
37
38

EE
EF
EG
EH
EJ
EK
EL
SOUTH WOODFORD
124
Waterworks Corner
Charlie Brown's Roundabout
NORTH CIRCULAR
SOUTHEND ROAD
WOODFORD
EPPING FOREST
E18
Junction 4
SPORTS GROUND
RODING VALLEY PARK
SPIRE RODING HOSP
RECREATION GROUND
IG4
SNARESBROOK
SNARESBROOK CROWN COURT
Whipps Cross
WHIPPS CROSS UNIVERSITY HOSPITAL
EPPING FOREST
ETON MANOR RFC
Redbridge Roundabout
EASTERN AVENUE
WANSTEAD
WANSTEAD GOLF COURSE
LEYTONSTONE
E11
145
WANSTEAD FLATS
BUSH WOOD
THE BASIN
WANSTEAD PARK
WANSTEAD GOLF COURSE
ALDERSBROOK
CITY OF LONDON CEMETERY
WANSTEAD FLATS
JEWISH CEMETERY
WEST HAM CEMETERY
MANOR PARK
MANOR PARK CEMETERY
E15
FOREST GATE
E7
WOODGRANGE PARK CEMETERY
PLASHET JEWISH CEMETERY
13
166
55
56
57
58
59
60
61
62
63
64
500 yds
500 m

EM
EN
EP
EQ
ER
ES
ET
43
44
45
125
CLAYHALL
TIPTREE ESTATE
GARDEN OF REST
BARKINGSIDE CEM
IG5
IG6
FAIRLOP WATERS GOLF COURSE
DRIVING RANGE
ALDBOROUGH HATCH
BARKINGSIDE
BARNARDOS VILLAGE
CLAYHALL PARK
REC GRD
Aldborough Hall Farm
Aldborough Hatch Farm
56
57
58
59
60
61
62
63
64
89
88
87
86
NE LONDON TREATMENT CENTRE
FORD'S SPORTS GROUND
SPORTS GROUND
SEVEN KINGS PARK
GANTS HILL
NEWBURY PARK
WOODFORD AVENUE
EASTERN AVENUE
CRANBROOK ROAD
IG2
VALENTINES PARK
VALENTINES SPORTS GROUND
MELBOURNE FIELD
Valentines Mansion
CRANBROOK
SEVEN KINGS
148
REDBRIDGE
IG1
IG3
HIGH ROAD
GREEN LANE
Eastern Roundabout
The Mall Exchange
TOWN HALL
ILFORD
CRICKLEFIELD STADIUM
ILFORD CEM
SOUTH PARK
KNOX SPORTS FIELD
LOXFORD
LOXFORD PARK
LITTLE ILFORD PARK
BARKING PARK
Indoor Bowl Club
BARRINGTON PLAYING FLDS
LONGBRIDGE ROAD
NORTH CIRCULAR ROAD
A406
A12
A118
A123
A124
A1083
A1400
167
SPORTS GROUND
E12

EU
EV
EW
EX
EY
EZ
FA
55
56
57
58
59
60
61
62
63
64
47
48
49
126
147
168
Mark's Gate
NORTHGATE IND PK
IG2
RM6
RM8
RM9
IG3
IG11
KING GEORGE HOSPITAL
GOODMAYES HOSPITAL
NE LONDON TREATMENT CENTRE
Redbridge College
CHADWELL HEATH CEM
CHADWELL HEATH
ST. CHADS PARK
CRANFIELD GOLF CENTRE
WESTLANDS PLAYING FIELDS
WEST HAM UNITED FC TRAINING GROUND
MIRRAVALE TRADING ESTATE
ELDENWALL ESTATE
CHADWELL HEATH IND PARK
GOODMAYES
GOODMAYES PARK
VALENCE PARK
BECONTREE
Becontree Heath
PARSLOES PARK
MAYESBROOK PARK
BARKING FC & ETON MANOR FC
ARENA
SPORTS GROUND
FORD'S SPORTS GROUND
SEVEN KINGS PARK
KINGS
EASTERN AVENUE
A12
HIGH ROAD
A118
GREEN LANE
A1083
LONGBRIDGE ROAD
WOOD LANE
A124
WHALEBONE LANE NORTH
WHALEBONE LANE SOUTH
A112
HEATHWAY
A1240
PORTERS AVENUE
A1153
BILLET ROAD
PAINTERS ROAD
HAINAULT ROAD
GOODMAYES LANE
BARLEY LANE
B177
REDBRIDGE BARKING & DAGENHAM
World War II Gun Emplacements
Little Heath
Moby Dick
NEWTON IND EST
Grove Farm Retail Park
GOODMAYES RETAIL PARK
VALENCE HO MUS
DAGENHAM HEATHWAY
500 yds
500 m

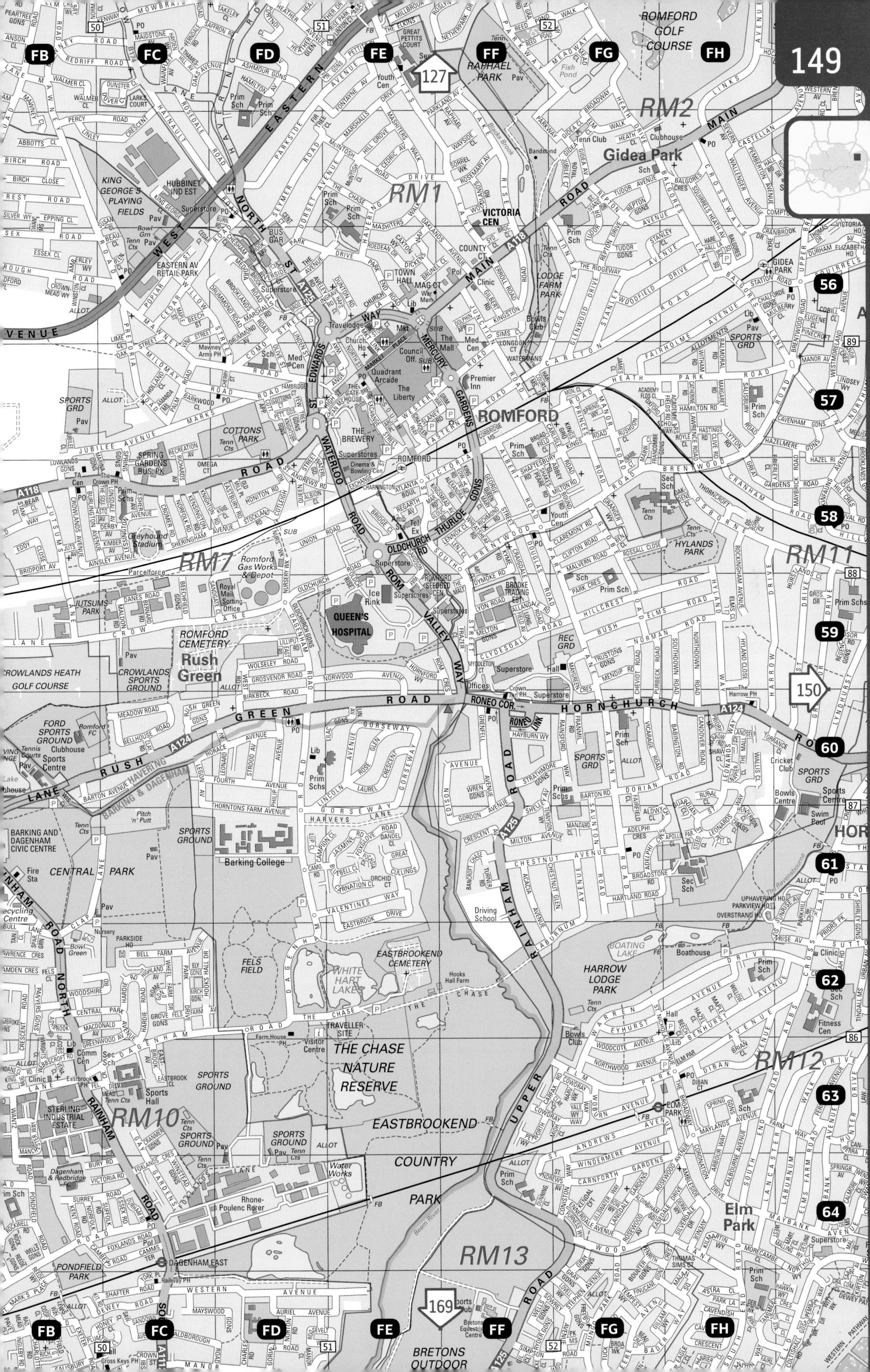
ROMFORD GOLF COURSE
RAPHAEL PARK
RM2
Gidea Park
RM1
VICTORIA CEN
KING GEORGE'S PLAYING FIELDS
HUBBINET IND EST
EASTERN AV RETAIL PARK
LODGE FARM PARK
ROMFORD
THE BREWERY
Quadrant Arcade
The Liberty
The Mall
COTTONS PARK
SPRING GARDENS BUS. PK
Greyhound Stadium
RM7
Romford Gas Works & Depot
JUTSUMS PARK
QUEEN'S HOSPITAL
BROOKE TRADING EST
HYLANDS PARK
RM11
ROMFORD CEMETERY
Rush Green
CROWLANDS HEATH GOLF COURSE
CROWLANDS SPORTS GROUND
FORD SPORTS GROUND
BARKING AND DAGENHAM CIVIC CENTRE
CENTRAL PARK
Barking College
FELS FIELD
WHITE HART LAKE
EASTBROOKEND CEMETERY
HARROW LODGE PARK
BOATING LAKE
THE CHASE NATURE RESERVE
EASTBROOKEND COUNTRY PARK
STERLING INDUSTRIAL ESTATE
RM10
RM12
Elm Park
RM13
Rhone-Poulenc Rorer
DAGENHAM EAST
PONDFIELD PARK
BRETONS OUTDOOR
127
150
169
FB
FC
FD
FE
FF
FG
FH
56
57
58
59
60
61
62
63
64

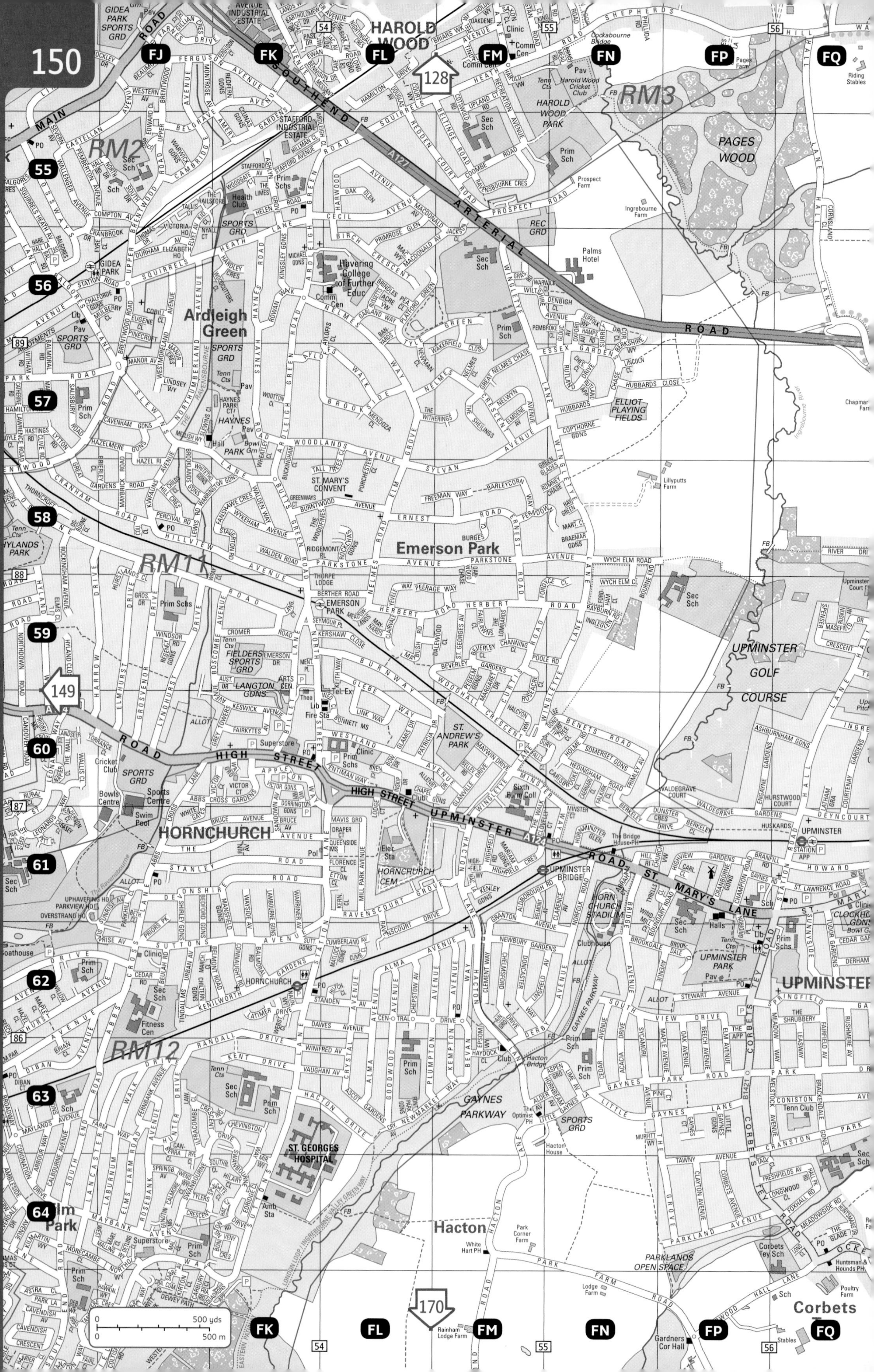
FJ
FK
FL
FM
FN
FP
FQ
128
170
149
54
55
56
55
56
57
58
59
60
61
62
63
64
89
88
87
86
HAROLD WOOD
GIDEA PARK SPORTS GRD
AVENUE INDUSTRIAL ESTATE
RM2
RM3
RM11
RM12
PAGES WOOD
HAROLD WOOD PARK
Harold Wood Cricket Club
Cockabourne Bridge
Pages Farm
Riding Stables
Prospect Farm
Ingrebourne Farm
Palms Hotel
STAFFORD INDUSTRIAL ESTATE
SOUTHEND
ARTERIAL
ROAD
A127
A124
A12
GIDEA PARK
Ardleigh Green
Havering College of Further Educ
ELLIOT PLAYING FIELDS
HAYNES PARK
Emerson Park
EMERSON PARK
ST. MARY'S CONVENT
Lillyputts Farm
HYLANDS PARK
UPMINSTER GOLF COURSE
Upminster Court
ST. ANDREW'S PARK
FIELDERS SPORTS GRD
LANGTON GDNS
HIGH STREET
UPMINSTER ROAD
HORNCHURCH
Sixth Form Coll
HORNCHURCH CEM
HORNCHURCH STADIUM
UPMINSTER BRIDGE
UPMINSTER
ST. MARY'S LANE
UPMINSTER PARK
Chapman Farm
Cricket Club
Bowls Centre
Sports Centre
Swim Pool
ST. GEORGES HOSPITAL
GAYNES PARKWAY
Hacton
Hacton Bridge
Hacton House
PARKLANDS OPEN SPACE
Park Corner Farm
White Hart PH
Lodge Farm
Rainham Lodge Farm
Gardners Cor Hall
Corbets Tey Sch
Corbets
Huntsman & Hounds PH
Poultry Farm
Stables
Elm Park
Boathouse
Fitness Cen
The Optimist PH
The Bridge House PH
Clubhouse
500 yds
500 m

129
171
CM13
RM14
Cranham
North Ockendon
Junction 29
M25
A127
B186
B187
B1421
ESSEX
BRENTWOOD
HAVERING
SOUTHEND ARTERIAL ROAD
WARLEY STREET
FOXBURROW WOOD
COOMBE WOOD
FOLKES LANE WOODLAND
PARKER'S SHAW
LATCHET'S SHAW
CODHAM HALL WOOD
POT KILN WOOD
WARLEY HALL WOOD
WARLEY PARK GOLF COURSE
UPMINSTER TRADING PARK
UPMINSTER HALL PLAYING FIELDS
CRANHAM BRICKFIELDS
CRANHAM PLAYING FIELDS
FRANKS WOOD
CLAY TYE WOOD
CRANHAM GOLF COURSE
Thames Chase Forest Centre
THAMES CHASE
Electricity Station
SPRING WOOD
CRANHAM MARSH NATURE RESERVE
MIDDLE WOOD
BONUS WOOD
UPMINSTER CEMETERY
TOP MEADOW GOLF COURSE
Driving Range
RUSSELLS LAKE
SPORTS GRD
TRAIN DEPOT
Warley Street Flyover
Suttons Farm
Howard's Farm
Emery Farm
Upminster Lodge Farm
Hole Farm
Tooks Farm
Clap Gate Farm
Warley Garden Centre
Woodlands Mushroom Farm
Folkes Farm
Codham Hall Farm
Codham Hall
Little Warley Hall Farm
Great Warley Hall
Franks Farm
Wyncray Farm
Westbury Farm
Cranham Court
Monks Farm
Elizabeth Lodge Farm
Forest View Nurseries
Bury Farm
Clay Tye Farm
Fairplay Farm
Groveland Nurseries
Whitepost Farm
Manor Farm
Hall Farm
Cranham Hall
Top Meadow Hotel
The Old White Horse PH
Jobbers Rest PH
Thatched House PH
The Plough PH
Golden Crane PH
BRIDGE COTTAGES
FR FS FT FU FV FW FX
56 57 58 59 60 61 62 63 64
57 58 59 86 87 88 89

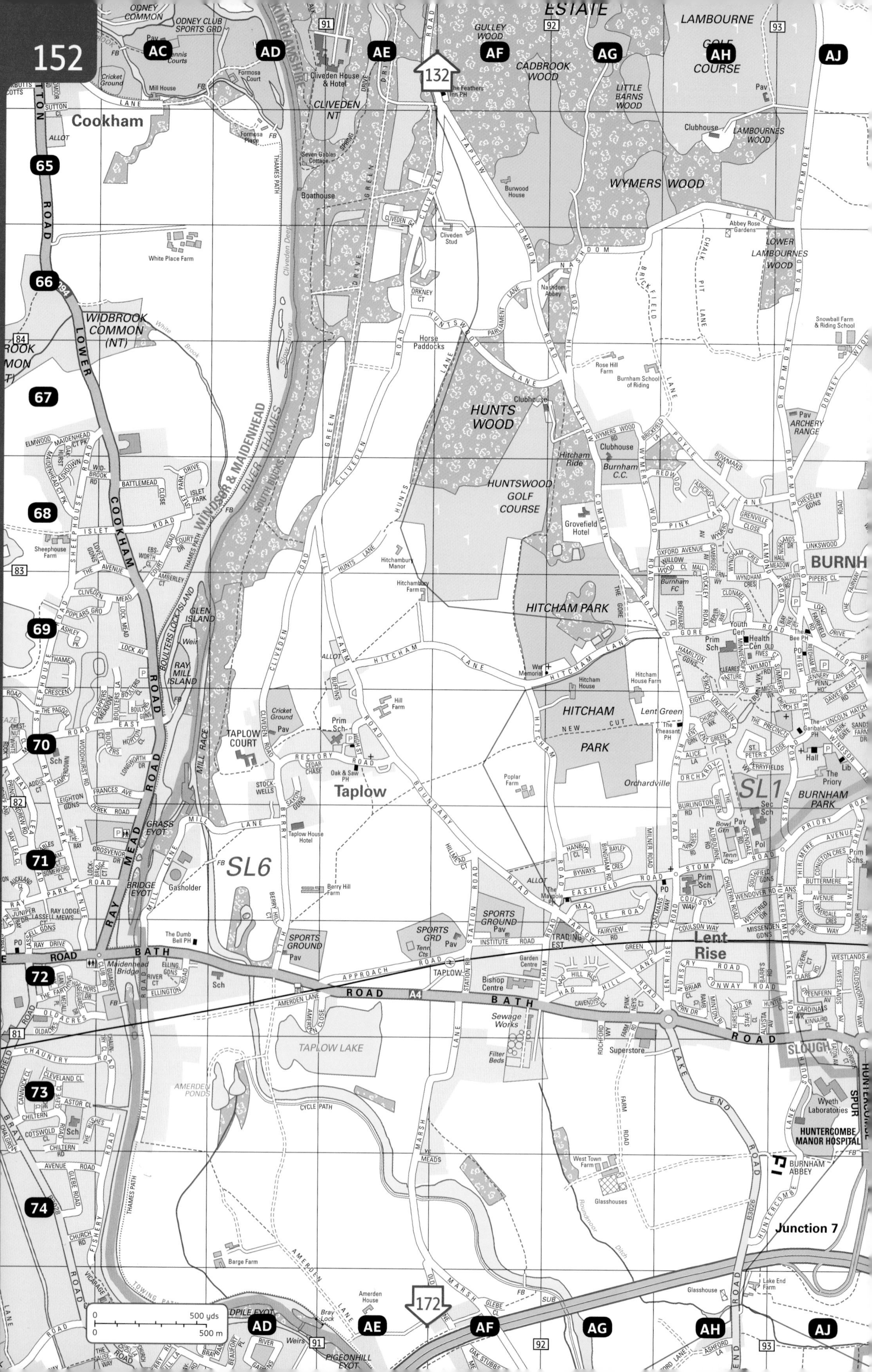

AC
AD
AE
AF
AG
AH
AJ
132
172
91
92
93
84
83
82
81
65
66
67
68
69
70
71
72
73
74
ODNEY COMMON
ODNEY CLUB SPORTS GRD
Cookham
LAMBOURNE GOLF COURSE
GULLEY WOOD
CADBROOK WOOD
LITTLE BARNS WOOD
LAMBOURNES WOOD
WYMERS WOOD
LOWER LAMBOURNES WOOD
Cliveden House & Hotel
CLIVEDEN NT
The Feathers Inn PH
Formosa Court
Formosa Place
Seven Gables Cottage
Boathouse
Burwood House
White Place Farm
Cliveden Stud
Abbey Rose Gardens
Nashdom Abbey
Snowball Farm & Riding School
WIDBROOK COMMON (NT)
Horse Paddocks
Rose Hill Farm
Burnham School of Riding
HUNTS WOOD
Clubhouse
ARCHERY RANGE
WINDSOR & MAIDENHEAD
SOUTH BUCKS
RIVER THAMES
Hitcham Ride
Burnham C.C.
HUNTSWOOD GOLF COURSE
Grovefield Hotel
BURNH
Hitchambury Manor
Hitchambury Farm
Burnham FC
HITCHAM PARK
GLEN ISLAND
RAY MILL ISLAND
Weir
Youth Cen
Prim Sch
Health Cen
Hill Farm
War Memorial
Hitcham House
Hitcham House Farm
Lent Green
HITCHAM PARK
Cricket Ground
TAPLOW COURT
Taplow
Oak & Saw PH
Poplar Farm
Orchardville
SL1
BURNHAM PARK
The Priory
SL6
Taplow House Hotel
Berry Hill Farm
Gasholder
GRASS EYOT
BRIDGE EYOT
SPORTS GROUND
TRADING EST
Lent Rise
The Dumb Bell PH
Maidenhead Bridge
TAPLOW
Bishop Centre
Garden Centre
Sewage Works
Filter Beds
Superstore
TAPLOW LAKE
AMERDEN PONDS
CYCLE PATH
SLOUGH
Wyeth Laboratories
HUNTERCOMBE MANOR HOSPITAL
BURNHAM ABBEY
West Town Farm
Glasshouses
Junction 7
Barge Farm
Amerden House
Bray Lock
Weirs
PIGEONHILL EYOT
Lake End Farm
Glasshouse
0
500 yds
500 m

AK
AL
AM
AN
AP
AQ
AR
133
154
173
66
67
68
69
70
71
72
73
74
84
83
82
81
94
95
96
BURNHAM BEECHES
EAST BURNHAM COMMON
BURNHAM BEECHES GOLF COURSE
Dorneywood House
Pumpkin Hill
Seven Ways Plain
Juniper Grove
Hawthorn Dell
Fleet Wood
Tower
Upper Pond
Middle Pond
Swilly Pond
Thompkins Wood
Farnham Common
Ingram's Copse
Parson's Wood
Old Orchard Wood
Farnham Park Golf Course
SL2
East Burnham
East Burnham Park
Kennedy's Garden Centre
Civic Amenity Site
Lock's Bottom
Bottom Waltons
Deepwood
South Bucks
Burnham Beeches Hotel
Grove Wood
Cherry Orchard Nature Park
George Pitcher Memorial Rec Grd
Cocksherd Wood
Farnham
Farnham Royal
Stoke Park Golf Course
Manor Park
Britwell Estate
Kennedy Park
Haymill Valley
Mars Ltd
Slough Trading Estate
Slough Heat & Power
Granville Playing Field
Godolphin Playing Fields
Westgate Retail Park
Slough Retail Park
Village Green
Mercian Recreation Ground
Salt Hill Park
Town Hall
Ice Arena
Slough
Cippenham
Burnham
Beaconsfield Road
Farnham Road
A355
A4
Bath Road
Buckingham Avenue
Farnham Lane
Britwell Road
Whittaker Road
Northborough Road
Stoke Poges Lane
Lord Mayors Drive
Hawthorn Lane
Allerds Road
Crown Lane
Park Lane
Church Road
Liverpool Road
Ipswich Road
Cippenham Lane
Dover Road
Bedford Avenue
Cockfield Bridge
Whitby Road
Ajax Avenue
Stirling Road
Edinburgh Avenue
Montem Lane
Windsor Road

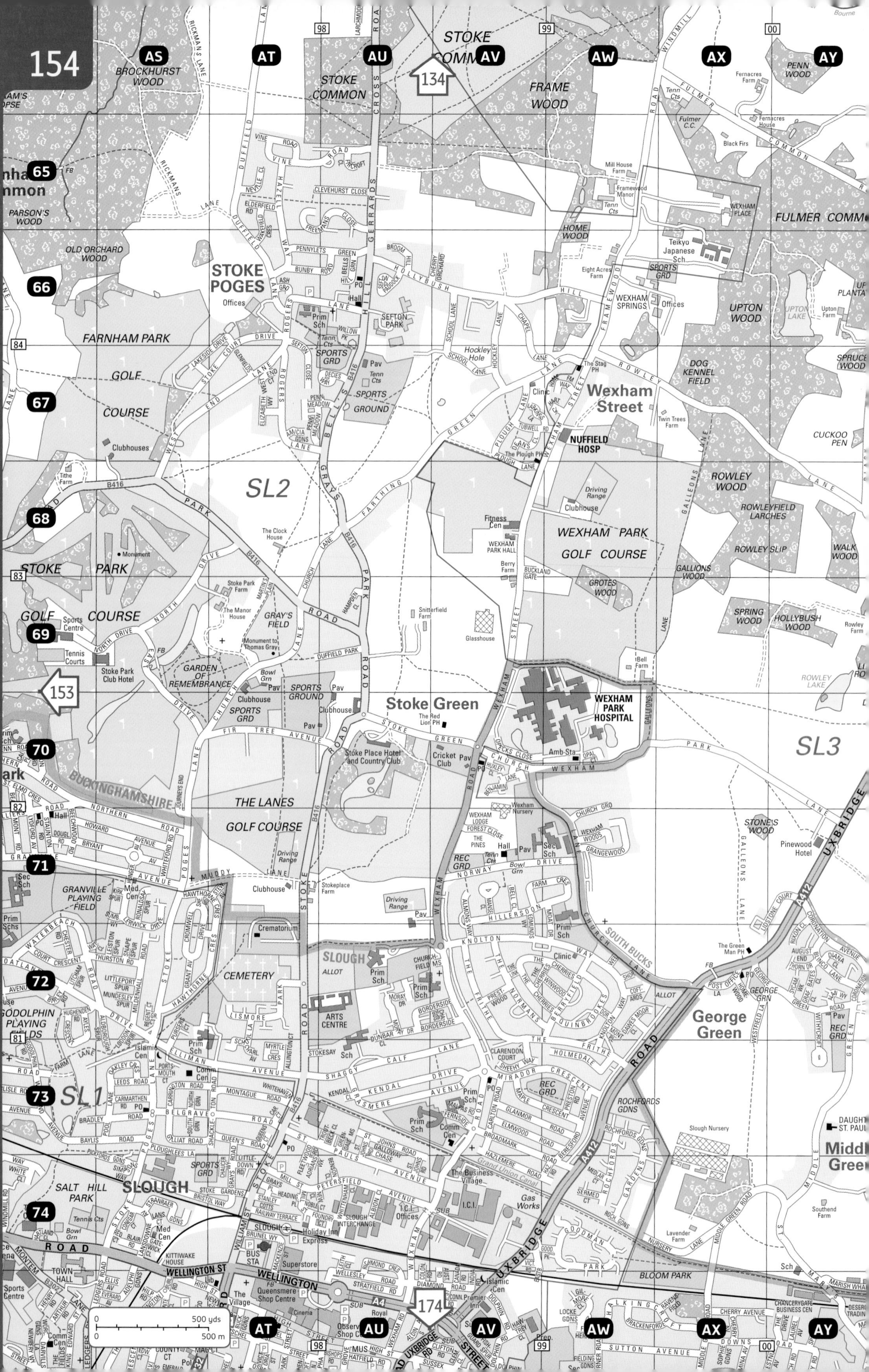

AS
AT
AU
AV
AW
AX
AY
65
66
67
68
69
70
71
72
73
74
134
153
174
BROCKHURST WOOD
STOKE COMMON
FRAME WOOD
PENN WOOD
FULMER COMMON ROAD
FULMER COMMON
PARSON'S WOOD
OLD ORCHARD WOOD
STOKE POGES
FARNHAM PARK GOLF COURSE
Clubhouses
STOKE PARK GOLF COURSE
Monument
Sports Centre
Tennis Courts
Stoke Park Club Hotel
GARDEN OF REMEMBRANCE
GRAY'S FIELD
The Manor House
Stoke Park Farm
The Clock House
Monument to Thomas Gray
SL2
SL3
SL1
Wexham Street
NUFFIELD HOSP
WEXHAM PARK GOLF COURSE
Driving Range
Clubhouse
WEXHAM PARK HALL
Fitness Cen
Berry Farm
GROTES WOOD
Snitterfield Farm
Glasshouse
WEXHAM PARK HOSPITAL
Stoke Green
The Red Lion PH
Stoke Place Hotel and Country Club
Cricket Club
HOME WOOD
Eight Acres Farm
WEXHAM SPRINGS
Teikyo Japanese Sch
WEXHAM PLACE
Mill House Farm
Framewood Manor
UPTON WOOD
UPTON LAKE
Upton Farm
DOG KENNEL FIELD
SPRUCE WOOD
CUCKOO PEN
ROWLEY WOOD
ROWLEYFIELD LARCHES
ROWLEY SLIP
WALK WOOD
GALLIONS WOOD
SPRING WOOD
HOLLYBUSH WOOD
Rowley Farm
ROWLEY LAKE
Twin Trees Farm
Hockley Hole
SEFTON PARK
The Stag PH
The Plough PH
Bell Farm
THE LANES GOLF COURSE
Stokeplace Farm
BUCKINGHAMSHIRE
GRANVILLE PLAYING FIELD
SLOUGH CEMETERY
Crematorium
ARTS CENTRE
Wexham Nursery
STONE'S WOOD
Pinewood Hotel
The Green Man PH
George Green
SOUTH BUCKS
GODOLPHIN PLAYING FIELDS
SALT HILL PARK
SLOUGH
The Business Village
I.C.I.
Gas Works
Grand Union Canal
Slough Nursery
Lavender Farm
Southend Farm
BLOOM PARK
Middle Green
Queensmere Shop Centre
Holiday Inn Express
Superstore
BUS STA
TOWN HALL
SLOUGH INTERCHANGE
The Village
Sports Centre
CHANCERYGATE BUSINESS CEN
STOKE POGES LANE
WEXHAM ROAD
UXBRIDGE ROAD
A412
A4
B416
WELLINGTON ST
WELLINGTON
STOKE ROAD
PARK ROAD
GERRARDS CROSS ROAD
WINDMILL ROAD
FRAMEWOOD ROAD
GALLEONS LANE
ROWLEY LANE
CHURCH LANE
STOKE GREEN
FARTHING GREEN
NORTHERN ROAD
BATH ROAD
0
500 yds
500 m

AZ
BA
BB
BC
BD
BE
BF
01
02
03
135
BROWN'S WOOD
Ways Farm
OLDHOUSE WOOD
Durham House
Cornerfields
Kingcup Farm
PARKSPRING WOOD
Alderbourne Farm
Saul's Farm
SEVEN HILLS ROAD
Cherry Orchard Farm
Blanchard's Farm
Belle Farm
LONG COPPICE
Sevenhills Farm
Taidswood
Copse Hill Farm
UB9
Southlands Manor
MOUNT FIDGET WOOD
Fulmer Plant Park
BRIDGETTINE CONVENT
Downings
LANGLEY COMMON
Langley Corner
FULMER COMMON ROAD
STRAWBERRY WOOD
HEATHFIELD PLANTATION
PLAYING FIELD
Dromenagh Farm
THE CLUMP
Pinewood Film Studios
NATURE RESERVE
M25
DENHAM ROAD
Round Coppice Farm
66
Heatherden Hall
PINEWOOD GREEN
BROOM WARREN
84
Park Lodge Farm
Brackenwood
Mansfield Farm
Iver Nature Study Cen
67
BLACK PARK
COUNTRY PARK
Stag & Hounds PH
Medical Cen
SPORTS GRD
Park Lodge
DIAMOND WOOD
A4007
68
CHANDLERS HILL
BLACKPARK LAKE
Warren Lodge
Warren House
Health Cen
Hall
Lib
Prim Sch
PO
The Black Horse PH
Centenary Lodge Visitors Centre
CHESTNUT WOOD
Warren House Farm
CHURCH ROAD
SLOUGH ROAD
83
Woodlands Park
Perivale Livery Stables
Five Points
ALLOT
Sch
FOXES GUTTER
COLUMN LARCHES
Crooked Billet PH
Fernleigh
Pav
Tennis Cts
SPORTS GROUND
IVER HEATH
Home Cottage Farm
SL0
Moorwards
69
156
LANGLEY PARK WOOD
RHODODENDRON GARDENS
Bangors Park Farm
Norwood Grange
LANGLEY PARK COUNTRY PARK
SPORTS GROUND
NORWOOD LANE
Nursery
70
Delaford Manor
Evreham Centre
Sports Centre
Whip & Collar PH
82
ROUGHGROUND WOOD
Coppins Farm
Lower Delaford
ARBORETUM
Five Points
Ashen Cross
BELLSWOOD LANE
71
Treal Farm
Langley Park House
Prim Sch
Shreding Green
Red Lion PH
HIGH STREET
Hall
Prim Sch
Pol
IVER
72
Burial Grd
SPORTS GROUND
ALLOT
LANGLEY PARK ROAD
Love Hill House Farm
Shredding Green Farm
81
B470
Filter Beds
73
Sewage Works
RIDGEWAY
Glasshouse
Clubhouse
Driving Range
IVER GOLF COURSE
THE ORCHARDS RESIDENTIAL PARK
Recycling Centre
Grand Union Canal (Slough Arm)
TOWING PATH
74
Water Treatment Works
BUCKINGHAMSHIRE
SOUTH BUCKS
SLOUGH
CARAVAN SITE
CANAL ESTATE
175
Chequer Bridge
LANGLEY
IVER
PO
LANGLEY BUSINESS CENTRE
Tenn Cts

BG
BH
BJ
BK
BL
BM
BN
136
155
176
65
66
67
68
69
70
71
72
73
74
UB9
UB10
UB8
UB7
SL0
UXBRIDGE
UXBRIDGE MOOR
COWLEY
YIEWSLEY
IVER
HILLINGDON
HILLINGDON ATHLETICS STADIUM
UXBRIDGE COMMON
HILLINGDON HOUSE FARM SPORTS GROUNDS
HILLINGDON COURT PARK
Hillingdon Circus
Uxbridge College (Uxbridge Campus)
HILLINGDON GOLF COURSE
HILLINGDON & UXBRIDGE CEMETERY
Brunel University
BRUNEL UNIVERSITY SPORTS PARK
HILLINGDON HOSPITAL
HUNTSMOOR PARK
FARLOWS LAKE
LITTLE BRITAIN LAKE
COWLEY LAKE
Sewage Works
Water Treatment Works
Electricity Sub Station
MIDAS INDUSTRIAL ESTATE
CHILTERN BUSINESS VILLAGE
TRADE CITY BUSINESS PARK
COWLEY BUSINESS PARK
ROCKINGHAM REC GRD
TOMO INDUSTRIAL EST
ZODIAC BUSINESS PARK
RAINBOW INDUSTRIAL ESTATE
HORTON IND PARK
Apple Tree Rbt
Colham Roundabout
Grand Union Canal (Slough Arm)
COWLEY HIGH ROAD
HIGH STREET
FALLING LANE
PARK VIEW RD
STOCKLEY RD
M25
A4020
A4007
A408
A437
B470
B483
0 500 yds
0 500 m
GOLF COURSE

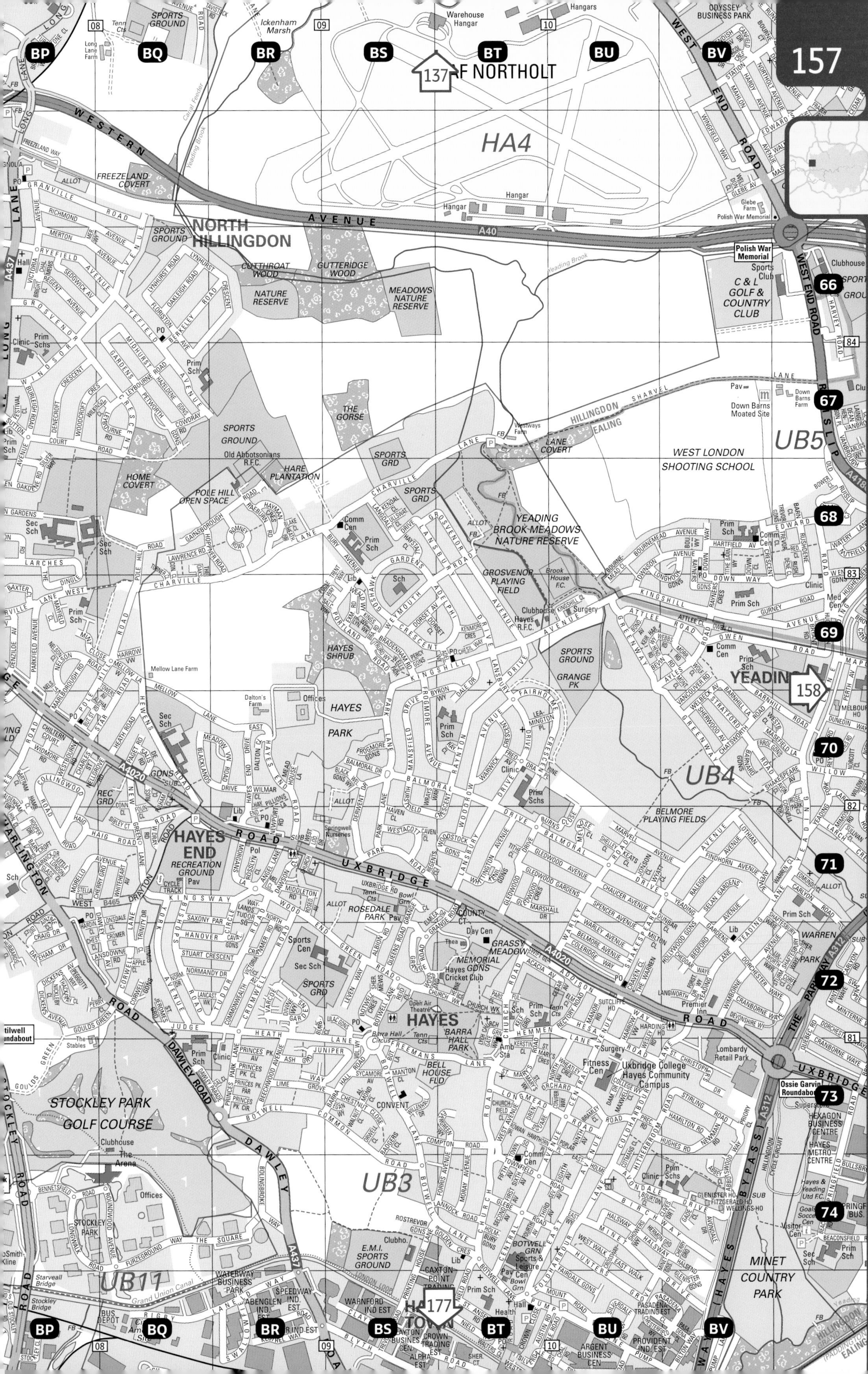
BP
BQ
BR
BS
BT
BU
BV
08
09
10
137
RAF NORTHOLT
HA4
Warehouse Hangar
Hangars
Hangar
ODYSSEY BUSINESS PARK
WEST END ROAD
WESTERN AVENUE
A40
NORTH HILLINGDON
FREEZELAND COVERT
CUTTHROAT WOOD NATURE RESERVE
GUTTERIDGE WOOD
MEADOWS NATURE RESERVE
Icknham Marsh
Yeading Brook
Polish War Memorial
C & L GOLF & COUNTRY CLUB
66
67
68
69
70
71
72
73
74
84
83
82
81
Down Barns Moated Site
UB5
WEST LONDON SHOOTING SCHOOL
HILLINGDON
EALING
LANE COVERT
THE GORSE
SPORTS GROUND
Old Abbotsonians R.F.C.
HARE PLANTATION
HOME COVERT
POLE HILL OPEN SPACE
CHARVILLE LANE
YEADING BROOK MEADOWS NATURE RESERVE
GROSVENOR PLAYING FIELD
Hayes R.F.C.
SPORTS GROUND
GRANGE PK
YEADING
158
HAYES SHRUB
HAYES PARK
Mellow Lane Farm
Dalton's Farm
UB4
BELMORE PLAYING FIELDS
A4020
HAYES END
RECREATION GROUND
UXBRIDGE ROAD
ROSEDALE PARK
GRASSY MEADOW
MEMORIAL GDNS
Hayes Cricket Club
HAYES
BARRA HALL PARK
BELL HOUSE FLD
Uxbridge College Hayes Community Campus
Lombardy Retail Park
Ossie Garvin Roundabout
HEXAGON BUSINESS CENTRE
HAYES METRO CENTRE
THE PARKWAY
A312
HAYES BYPASS
Stilwell Roundabout
STOCKLEY PARK GOLF COURSE
The Arena
STOCKLEY PARK
DAWLEY ROAD
A437
UB3
UB11
E.M.I. SPORTS GROUND
WATERWAY BUSINESS PARK
Grand Union Canal
SPEEDWAY IND. EST
ABENGLEN IND. EST
WARNFORD IND EST
CAXTON POINT TRADING EST
HAYES TOWN
177
CROWN TRADING EST
ARGENT BUSINESS CEN
PROVIDENT IND. EST
PASADENA TRADING EST
MINET COUNTRY PARK
Starveall Bridge
Stockley Bridge
BUS DEPOT

BW
BX
BY
BZ
CA
CB
CC
HA4
138
157
178
65
66
67
68
69
70
71
72
73
74
NORTHOLT
GREENFORD
SOUTHALL
DORMER'S WELLS
UB5
UB4
UB1
NORTHOLT RECREATION GRD
LORD HALSBURY MEMORIAL REC GRD
SPORTS GROUND
C & L GOLF & COUNTRY CLUB
Polish War Memorial
LIME TREE PARK GOLF COURSE
LIME TREE PARK
Down Barns Moated Site
WEST LONDON SHOOTING SCHOOL
ISLIP MANOR PARK
BELVUE PARK
BELVUE BUSINESS CENTRE
NORTHOLT TRADING ESTATE
KELVIN INDUSTRIAL ESTATE
EALING GOLF RANGE
THE METROPOLITAN CENTRE
NORTHALA FIELDS
Target Roundabout
MARNHAM FIELDS
NORTHOLT GOLF COURSE
White Hart Roundabout
RECTORY PARK
SMITHS FARM EST
RAVENOR PARK
KING GEORGE'S FIELD
GREENFORD PARK REC GRD
Willow Tree Roundabout
BROOKSIDE
JUBILEE PARK
GREENFORD PARK CEMETERY
WEST MIDDLESEX GOLF COURSE
Ossie Garvin Roundabout
Lombardy Retail Park
HEXAGON BUSINESS CENTRE
HAYES BRIDGE RETAIL PARK
HAYES METRO CENTRE
SPRINGFIELD RD BUS. CEN
BROOK INDUSTRIAL ESTATE
MINET COUNTRY PARK
HEATHROW PURPLE PARKING
SOUTHALL PARK
BARRATT IND EST
SOUTHALL RAILWAY CENTRE
WESTERN AVENUE
CHURCH ROAD
MANDEVILLE ROAD
RUISLIP ROAD
WEST END ROAD
THE PARKWAY (HAYES BYPASS)
UXBRIDGE ROAD
THE BROADWAY
HIGH STREET
GREENFORD ROAD
A40
A312
A4180
A4020
A3005
B455
0 500 yds
0 500 m

CD
CE
CF
CG
CH
CJ
CK
15
16
17
SUDBURY
139
HA0
BARHAM PARK
WHITTON AVENUE WEST
A4090
HARROW ROAD
HIGH ROAD
WEMBLEY
BRIDGEWATER ROAD
EAST
SUDBURY TOWN
HORSENDEN WOOD
HORSENDEN HILL GOLF COURSE
SUDBURY GOLF COURSE
HORSENDEN HILL
GREAT BRAMSTONES
BERKELEY FIELDS
SPORTS GROUND
HOME MEAD
UB6
A4127
GRAND UNION CANAL (PADDINGTON BRANCH)
ALPERTON CEMETERY
ONE TREE HILL OPEN SPACE
A4005
66
67
68
69
70
71
72
73
74
84
83
82
81
GREENFORD
Westway Shopping Pk
GREENFORD GRN BUS. PK
Royal Mail Centre
PERIVALE WOOD (Nature Reserve)
PERIVALE
PERIVALE PARK
PERIVALE NEW BUSINESS CENTRE
WADSWORTH BUSINESS CENTRE
FLEETWAY BUSINESS PARK
SHERATON BUSINESS CEN
ABERCORN COMMERCIAL CENTRE
PHOENIX TRADING ESTATE
CAPITAL BUSINESS CEN
ALPERTON
ALPERTON SPORTS GROUND
EALING ROAD
HANGER LANE
Greenford Roundabout
OLDFIELD REC GRD
SOUTH GREENFORD
Perivale
WESTERN AVENUE
A40
EALING CENTRAL SPORTS GRD
EALING GOLF COURSE
ATHLETICS TRACK
PERIVALE PARK SPORTS GROUND
PERIVALE PARK GOLF COURSE
PITSHANGER PARK
160
River Brent
B455
RUISLIP ROAD EAST
Greenford Bridge
SPORTS GROUND
BRENT VALLEY PARK
CLEVELAND PARK
CASTLE BAR PARK
CUCKOO PARK
W7
BRENT VALLEY GOLF COURSE
CHURCHFIELDS RECREATION GROUND
W13
W5
EALING
DRAYTON GREEN
WEST EALING
HANWELL
KENSINGTON & CHELSEA CEMETERY
HANWELL CEMETERY
PITSHANGER MANOR HOUSE & GALL
WALPOLE PARK
UXBRIDGE RD
A4020
NEW BROADWAY
BROADWAY
THE BROADWAY
Ealing Broadway Shop Cen
TOWN HALL
EALING HOSPITAL N.H.S. TRUST
ST BERNARD'S HOSPITAL
Wharncliffe Viaduct
University of West London
LAMMAS PARK
179

CL
CM
CN
CP
CQ
CR
CS
WEMBLEY
TOKYNGTON
CHURCH END
HA9
HA0
ALPERTON
STONEBRIDGE
PARK ROYAL
NORTH ACTON
WEST ACTON
ACTON
EAST ACTON
W3
W5
EALING COMMON
EALING BROADWAY
HARLESDEN
140
159
180
65
66
67
68
69
70
71
72
73
74
WEMBLEY STADIUM
WEMBLEY CENTRAL
STONEBRIDGE PARK
HANGER LANE
PARK ROYAL
NORTH EALING
ACTON TOWN
ACTON CENTRAL
ACTON MAIN LINE
CENTRAL MIDDLESEX HOSPITAL
PARK ROYAL CEN
Twyford Abbey
Diageo
Hanger Lane
Gypsy Corner
Ealing Common
NORTH CIRCULAR ROAD
WESTERN AVENUE
HANGER LANE
EALING ROAD
HARROW ROAD
HIGH ROAD
UXBRIDGE ROAD
GUNNERSBURY AVENUE
HORN LANE
VICTORIA ROAD
BRENTFIELD
HILLSIDE
CRAVEN PARK
THE MALL
THE BROADWAY
HIGH STREET
A404
A4089
A406
A40
A4020
A4000
A407
PLAYING FIELDS
ONE TREE HILL OPEN SPACE
HANGER HILL PARK
BARCLAYS BANK SPORTS GROUND
TWYFORD AVENUE SPORTS GRD
London Wasps RFC Training Grd
NORTH ACTON PLAYING FIELDS
ACTON PARK
TOKYNGTON RECREATION GROUND
GIBBONS REC GRD
STONEBRIDGE REC GRD
ACTON CEMETERY
PREMIER PARK
TOWNSEND INDUSTRIAL ESTATE
UNITED BISCUITS-McVITIE
NORTHFIELDS INDUSTRIAL ESTATE
ABBEY IND EST
GRAND UNION IND EST
GENESIS BUSINESS PARK
CUMBERLAND BUSINESS PARK
AMC BUSINESS CENTRE
PARK ROYAL METRO CEN
WESTERN TRADING EST
BUSH INDUSTRIAL EST
FROGMORE INDUSTRIAL ESTATE
VICTORIA IND EST
ROYALE LEISURE PARK
WESTPOINT TRADING EST
WESTWOOD PARK TRADING EST
Princess Royal Distribution Centre
Swaminarayan Hindu Mission
Barbara Speake Stage Sch
University of West London
500 yds
500 m

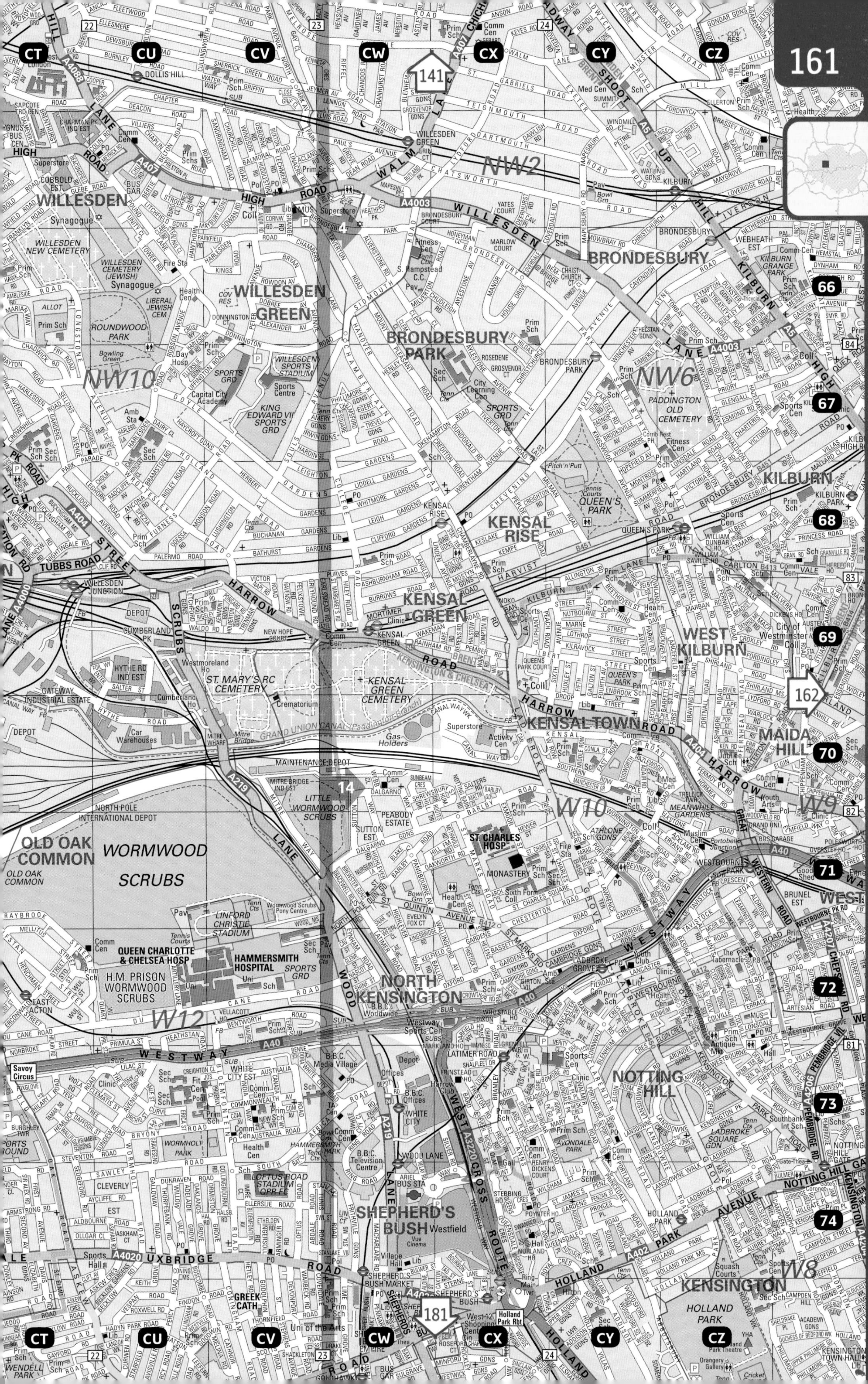
CT
CU
CV
CW
CX
CY
CZ
141
WILLESDEN
WILLESDEN NEW CEMETERY
WILLESDEN CEMETERY (JEWISH)
WILLESDEN GREEN
NW2
NW10
NW6
BRONDESBURY
BRONDESBURY PARK
KILBURN
KENSAL RISE
QUEEN'S PARK
PADDINGTON OLD CEMETERY
KENSAL GREEN
WEST KILBURN
ST. MARY'S RC CEMETERY
KENSAL GREEN CEMETERY
GRAND UNION CANAL (Paddington Branch)
KENSAL TOWN
MAIDA HILL
162
OLD OAK COMMON
WORMWOOD SCRUBS
LITTLE WORMWOOD SCRUBS
W10
W9
ST. CHARLES HOSP
LINFORD CHRISTIE STADIUM
QUEEN CHARLOTTE & CHELSEA HOSP
HAMMERSMITH HOSPITAL
H.M. PRISON WORMWOOD SCRUBS
NORTH KENSINGTON
W12
WESTWAY
NOTTING HILL
WORMHOLT PARK
LOFTUS ROAD STADIUM QPR FC
SHEPHERD'S BUSH
Westfield
HOLLAND PARK
KENSINGTON
W8
Holland Park Rbt
181
22
23
24
66
67
68
69
70
71
72
73
74
81
82
83
84

DA
DB
DC
DD
DE
DF
DG
142
WEST HAMPSTEAD
NW6
SOUTH HAMPSTEAD
KILBURN
NW8
ST. JOHN'S WOOD
BELSIZE PARK
NW3
PRIMROSE HILL
THE REGENT'S PARK
NW1
ZSL LONDON ZOO
LORD'S CRICKET GROUND
LISSON GROVE
MAIDA VALE
MAIDA HILL
W9
WESTBOURNE GREEN
PADDINGTON
MARYLEBONE
BAYSWATER
W2
KENSINGTON GARDENS
HYDE PARK
THE SERPENTINE
THE LONG WATER
ROUND POND
W8
SW7
KENSINGTON
HOLLAND PARK
161
182
65
66
67
68
69
70
71
72
73
74
FINCHLEY ROAD
MAIDA VALE
EDGWARE ROAD
WESTWAY
BAYSWATER ROAD
KENSINGTON GORE
KNIGHTSBRIDGE
MARYLEBONE
WELLINGTON RD
PARK LANE
OXFORD STREET where marked is closed to through traffic (except buses & taxis) from 7a.m.-7p.m. Monday - Saturday
500 yds
500 m

DH
DJ
DK
DL
DM
DN
DP
143
164
183
66
67
68
69
70
71
72
73
74
HOLLOWAY
LOWER HOLLOWAY
KENTISH TOWN
CAMDEN TOWN
KING'S CROSS
BARNSBURY
ISLINGTON
N7
N1
SOMERS TOWN
ST. PANCRAS
FINSBURY
CLERKENWELL
WC1
BLOOMSBURY
HOLBORN
W1
WC2
SOHO
STRAND
EC4
ST. JAMES'S
THE GREEN PARK
ST. JAMES'S PARK
SW1
SOUTHWARK
THE BOROUGH
SE1
REGENT'S PARK
MAYFAIR
RIVER THAMES

DQ
DR
DS
DT
DU
DV
DW
144
184
163
65
66
67
68
69
70
71
72
73
74
HIGHBURY
CANONBURY
KINGSLAND
DALSTON
HACKNEY
DE BEAUVOIR TOWN
SOUTH HACKNEY
HOXTON
HAGGERSTON
BETHNAL GREEN
SHOREDITCH
CLERKENWELL
BARBICAN
BROADGATE
WHITECHAPEL
STEPNEY
SHADWELL
WAPPING
SOUTHWARK
BOROUGH
N1
E8
E2
EC1
EC2
EC3
EC4
E1
SE1
RIVER THAMES
TOWER OF LONDON
TATE MODERN
GUY'S HOSPITAL
ROYAL LONDON HOSP
MOORFIELDS EYE HOSP
ST. BART'S HOSP
ST. JOSEPH'S HOSPICE
MILDMAY MISS. HOSP
LONDON BRIDGE HOSP
REGENT'S CANAL
LONDON FIELDS
0
500 yds
500 m

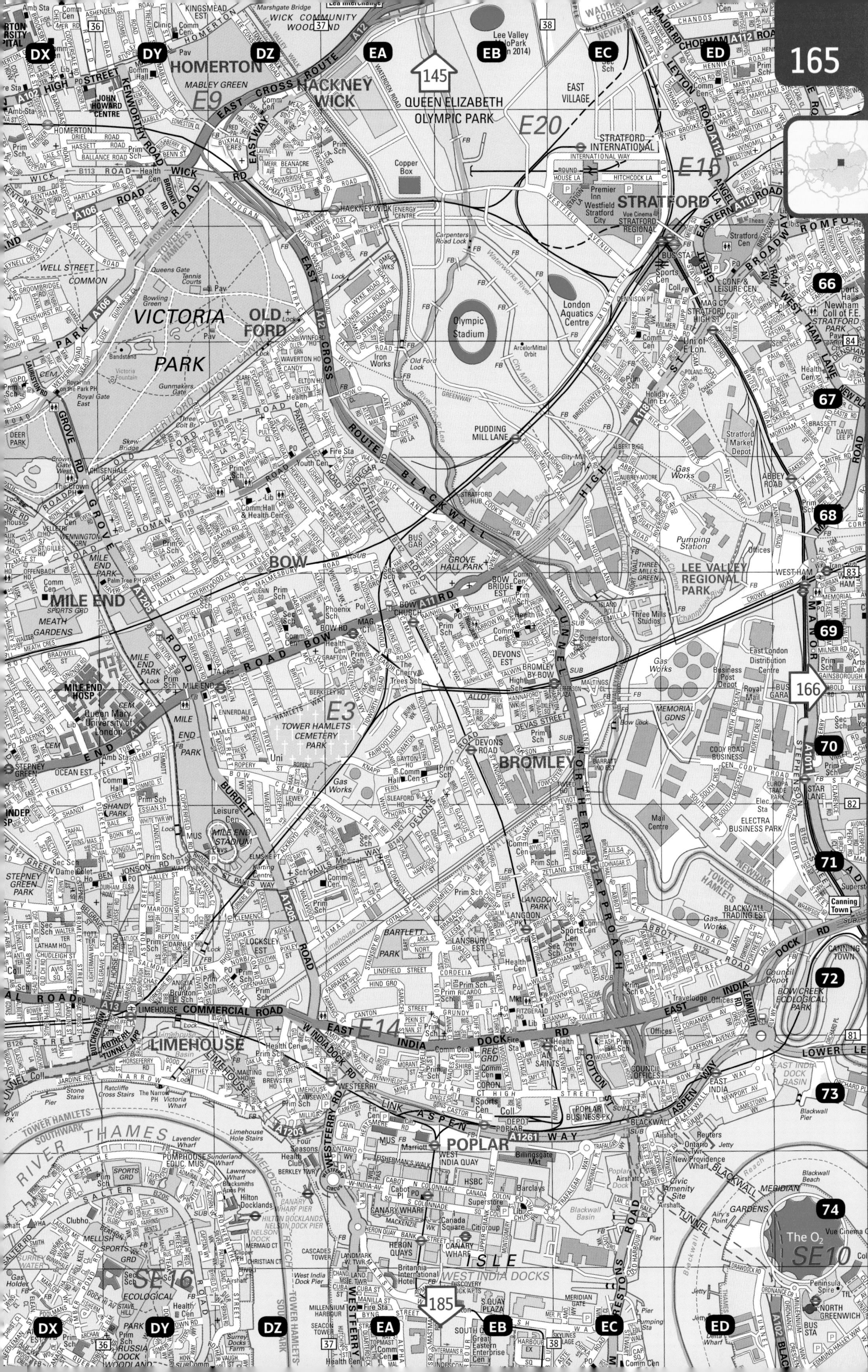

DX
DY
DZ
EA
EB
EC
ED
145
166
185
HOMERTON
HACKNEY WICK
QUEEN ELIZABETH OLYMPIC PARK
E9
E20
E15
EAST VILLAGE
STRATFORD INTERNATIONAL
STRATFORD
Westfield Stratford City
Vue Cinema STRATFORD REGIONAL
Copper Box
Olympic Stadium
ArcelorMittal Orbit
London Aquatics Centre
Lee Valley VeloPark
MABLEY GREEN
WICK COMMUNITY WOODLAND
EAST CROSS ROUTE
VICTORIA PARK
OLD FORD
WELL STREET COMMON
HERTFORD UNION CANAL
JOHN HOWARD CENTRE
PUDDING MILL LANE
BOW
MILE END
MILE END PARK
MILE END HOSP
Queen Mary University of London
E3
TOWER HAMLETS CEMETERY PARK
BROMLEY
DEVONS ROAD
BROMLEY-BY-BOW
LEE VALLEY REGIONAL PARK
Three Mills Studios
WEST HAM
East London Distribution Centre
MEMORIAL GDNS
CODY ROAD BUSINESS CEN
ELECTRA BUSINESS PARK
STAR LANE
Canning Town
CANNING TOWN
BOW CREEK ECOLOGICAL PARK
BLACKWALL TRADING EST
NORTHERN APPROACH
BLACKWALL TUNNEL
LANGDON PARK
LANSBURY EST
BARTLETT PARK
STEPNEY GREEN
STEPNEY GREEN PARK
SHANDY PARK
LIMEHOUSE
COMMERCIAL ROAD
EAST INDIA DOCK RD
E14
LIMEHOUSE
WESTFERRY
POPLAR
ALL SAINTS
BLACKWALL
EAST INDIA
EAST INDIA DOCK BASIN
WEST INDIA QUAY
CANARY WHARF
HERON QUAYS
ISLE
WEST INDIA DOCKS
Billingsgate Mkt
Poplar Dock
Blackwall Basin
RIVER THAMES
TOWER HAMLETS
SOUTHWARK
SE16
SURREY WATER
RUSSIA DOCK WOODLAND
Hilton Docklands
CANARY WHARF PIER
HILTON DOCKLANDS NELSON DOCK PIER
Limehouse Reach
Blackwall Reach
The O2
SE10
NORTH GREENWICH
Peninsula Spire
MERIDIAN GARDENS
Blackwall Pier
ISLAND GARDENS

EE
EF
EG
EH
EJ
EK
EL
146
FOREST GATE
E7
WOODGRANGE PARK CEMETERY
ROMFORD ROAD
13
PLASHET JEWISH CEMETERY
PLASHET PARK
WEST HAM PARK
Clapton FC
UPTON
WEST HAM
Stratford Cen
65
66
67
68
69
70
71
72
73
74
E15
STRATFORD
Newham Coll of F.E. STRATFORD PARK
Stratford Market Depot
UPTON PARK
PRIORY PARK
BOLEYN GRD WEST HAM UTD FC
EAST HAM JEWISH CEMETERY
24
PLAISTOW
LEE VALLEY REGIONAL PARK
MEMORIAL RECREATION GROUND
EAST LONDON CEMETERY
PLAISTOW PARK
HERMIT RD REC GRD
E13
NEWHAM UNIVERSITY HOSPITAL
TERENCE McMILLAN STADIUM
BRAMPTON PARK
E6
165
East London Distribution Centre
ELECTRA BUSINESS PARK
BLACKWALL TRADING EST
CANNING TOWN REC GRD
CANNING TOWN
CUSTOM HOUSE
KING GEORGE V PARK
BECKTON DISTRICT PARK NORTH
BECKTON DISTRICT PARK SOUTH
BOW CREEK ECOLOGICAL PARK
LOWER LEA CROSSING
EAST INDIA DOCK BASIN
Connaught Roundabout
Royal Albert Roundabout
ExCeL London
ICC London
ROYAL VICTORIA DOCK
E16
Millennium Mills
Airport Roundabout
N Woolwich Roundabout
SILVERTOWN WAY
NORTH WOOLWICH ROAD
The O2
SE10
THAMES BARRIER PARK
SILVERTOWN
THAMESIDE INDUSTRIAL EST
RIVER
WOOLWICH REACH
THAMES FLOOD
186
40
41
42
500 yds
500 m

LOXFORD
BARKING PARK
BARKING
BARKING HOSPITAL
UPNEY
IG11
RIPPLESIDE BURIAL GROUND
ALFREDS WAY IND ESTATE
WAYSIDE COMMERCIAL EST
LYON BUSINESS PARK
KATELLA TRADING EST
ABBEY WHARF INDUSTRIAL ESTATE
BECKTON SEWAGE TREATMENT WORKS
RIVER ROAD BUSINESS PARK
IO CENTRE
TRAFALGAR BUSINESS CENTRE
BUZZARD CREEK INDUSTRIAL ESTATE
CREEKMOUTH
BARKING FLOOD BARRIER
BECKTON TRIANGLE RETAIL PARK
GATEWAY RETAIL PARK
LONDON IND EST
BECKTON RETAIL PARK
BECKTON
GEMINI BUSINESS PARK
Gas Works
DLR DEPOT
NEW BECKTON PARK
GALLIONS REACH
MARGARET NESS OR TRIPCOCK POINT
THAMESMEAD
SE28
GALLIONS HILL
ALBERT DOCK
KING GEORGE V DOCK
Uni of East London
ROYAL VICTORIA GDNS
STANDARD INDUSTRIAL ESTATE
Woolwich Ferry Pier
H.M. PRISON
ALFREDS WAY
NORTH CIRCULAR ROAD
NEWHAM WAY
ROYAL DOCKS ROAD
WOOLWICH MANOR WAY
LONGBRIDGE ROAD
RIPPLE ROAD
BARKING ROAD
EM EN EP EQ ER ES ET
147
168
187
66 67 68 69 70 71 72 73 74

EU
EV
EW
EX
EY
EZ
FA
148
PARSLOES PARK
RM9
DAGENHAM HEATHWAY
BECONTREE
Boating Lake
RIPPLESIDE BURIAL GROUND
Lodge Avenue Junction
MAYBROOK MEADOW EST
CASTLE GREEN
GORESBROOK SPORTS GROUND
GORESBROOK PARK
BARKING R.F.C.
DAGENHAM LEISURE PK
BARKING INDUSTRIAL PARK
ALFREDS WAY IND ESTATE
WAYSIDE COMMERCIAL EST
RENWICK IND ESTATE
RIPPLESIDE COMMERCIAL ESTATE
PORTLAND COMM CEN
MAYBELLS COMM EST
TRAIN DEPOT
SCRATTONS FARM ECO-PARK
Freight Depot
FORD MOTOR WORKS
DAGENHAM DOCK
BARKING BUSINESS CENTRE
RIVERSIDE INDUSTRIAL ESTATE
The Ripple Nature Reserve
IG11
THAMES GATEWAY PARK
POWER STATION
Power Station
Horse Shoe Corner
Oil Storage Depot
CREEKMOUTH
TRAFALGAR BUSINESS CENTRE
BUZZARD CREEK INDUSTRIAL ESTATE
Gravel Works
BARKING FLOOD BARRIER
167
Barking or False Point
BARKING & DAGENHAM
CROSSNESS LIGHTHOUSE
THAMESMEAD NORTH
Ecology Study Area
Driving Range
Crossness Pumping Station
SE2
THAMESVIEW GOLF COURSE
COVERED RESERVOIRS
Crossness Sewage Treatment Works
Sludge Incinerator
SPORTS GROUND
Thamesmead Town FC
CROSSWAY PARK
THAMESMEAD
Thamesmere Lake
SPORTS GRD
MOORINGS
PHOENIX POINT
SPORTS GROUND
RINGSIDE
LAKESIDE CENTRE
SOUTHMERE
SOUTHMERE PARK
ERITH MARSHES
CROSSNESS NATURE RESERVE
BIRCHMERE PARK
SE28
DA18
WOODLAND WAY
ABBEY WOOD PARK
188
KENCOT CL BUS PARK
The Business Academy Bexley
EASTERN WAY
A13
A2016
A1153
A1240
500 yds
500 m

FB
FC
FD
FE
FF
FG
FH
149
189
170
RM10
RM12
RM13
DA17
South Hornchurch
RAINHAM
BRETONS OUTDOOR CENTRE
BRITTONS PLAYING FIELD
BEAM VALLEY COUNTRY PARK
HORNCHURCH MARSHES
RAINHAM MARSHES
Riverside Sewage Works
Old Man's Head
Hornchurch Shoot
DAGENHAM EAST
PONDFIELD PARK
MANOR ROAD SPORTS GRD
BMX TRACK
SPORTS GRD
THE LEYS
Clubhouse
Newtons Corner
Dovers Corner
SUTTONS BUSINESS PARK
Mudlands Industrial Est
DOVERS CORNER INDUSTRIAL ESTATE
ALBRIGHT INDUSTRIAL ESTATE
DENVER INDUSTRIAL ESTATE
CONTAINER DEPOT
FAIRVIEW INDUSTRIAL PARK
Thames Gateway Coll (CEME Campus)
CAR COMPOUND
EASTER PARK
BELVEDERE INDUSTRIAL ESTATE
ISIS REACH
Jenningtree Point
Wharf
Jetty
Pier
FLIGHTWAY WOOD
FARMFIELD WOOD
LOWFIELD WOOD
Albyns Farm
The Albion PH
The Bell Inn PH
Rainham Hall
SPORTS GROUND
Superstore
Swim Pool
South Hall Farm
Southall Bridge
WENNINGTON MARSHES
RAINHAM ROAD
RAINHAM ROAD SOUTH
DAGENHAM ROAD
NEW ROAD
A1306
A125
A13
A1112
A1311
B1335
THAMES GATEWAY
MARSH WAY
FERRY LANE
COLDHARBOUR LANE
UPMINSTER ROAD SOUTH
WENNINGTON ROAD
SOUTH END ROAD
BARKING & DAGENHAM
HAVERING
Beam River
Ingrebourne River
66
67
68
69
70
71
72
73
74
50
51
52
81
82
83
84

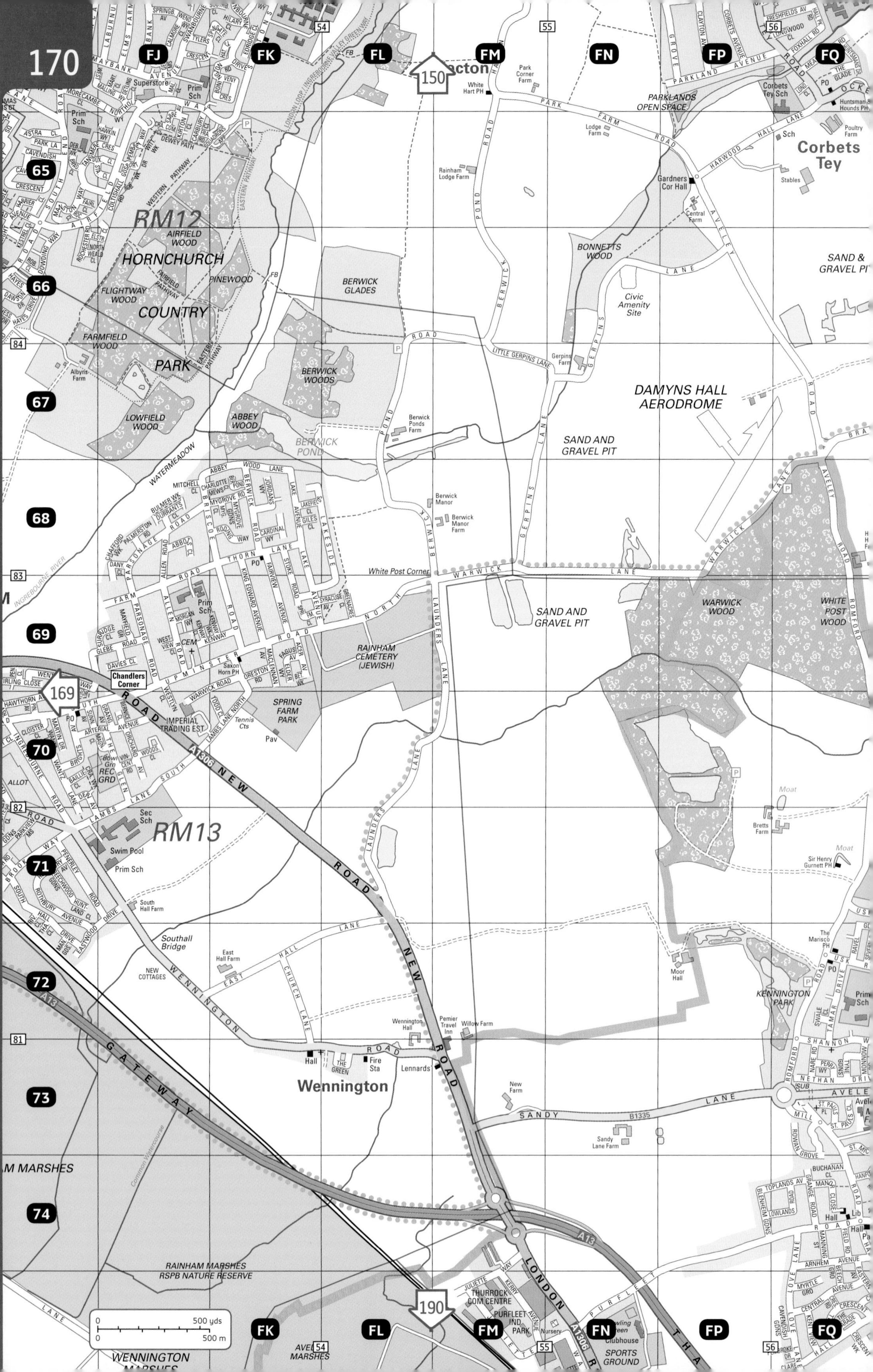
FJ
FK
FL
FM
FN
FP
FQ
150
169
190
54
55
56
84
83
82
81
65
66
67
68
69
70
71
72
73
74
RM12
RM13
HORNCHURCH
COUNTRY
PARK
AIRFIELD WOOD
FLIGHTWAY WOOD
FARMFIELD WOOD
PINEWOOD
LOWFIELD WOOD
ABBEY WOOD
BERWICK GLADES
BERWICK WOODS
BERWICK POND
Corbets Tey
PARKLANDS OPEN SPACE
BONNETTS WOOD
SAND & GRAVEL PIT
Civic Amenity Site
DAMYNS HALL AERODROME
SAND AND GRAVEL PIT
WARWICK WOOD
WHITE POST WOOD
White Post Corner
RAINHAM CEMETERY (JEWISH)
SPRING FARM PARK
Chandlers Corner
IMPERIAL TRADING EST
Southall Bridge
NEW COTTAGES
East Hall Farm
Wennington
Wennington Hall
Premier Travel Inn
Willow Farm
Lennards
New Farm
Sandy Lane Farm
Moor Hall
KENNINGTON PARK
Bretts Farm
Sir Henry Gurnett PH
The Marisco PH
Moat
Park Corner Farm
White Hart PH
Lodge Farm
Rainham Lodge Farm
Gardners Cor Hall
Central Farm
Stables
Poultry Farm
Huntsman & Hounds PH
Corbets Tey Sch
Gerpins Farm
Berwick Ponds Farm
Berwick Manor
Berwick Manor Farm
Albyns Farm
South Hall Farm
Swim Pool
Sec Sch
Prim Sch
Superstore
REC GRD
Saxon Horn PH
Tennis Cts
Pav
RAINHAM MARSHES RSPB NATURE RESERVE
THURROCK COM CENTRE
PURFLEET IND PARK
Nursery
SPORTS GROUND
WENNINGTON MARSHES
AVELEY MARSHES
Common Watercourse
INGREBOURNE RIVER
LONDON LOOP / INGREBOURNE VALLEY GREENWAY
WATERMEADOW
EASTERN PATHWAY
WESTERN PATHWAY
FAIRFIELD PATHWAY
PARK FARM ROAD
HARWOOD HALL LANE
AVELEY ROAD
BERWICK POND ROAD
GERPINS LANE
LITTLE GERPINS LANE
WARWICK LANE
LAUNDERS LANE
NORTH ROAD
UPMINSTER ROAD
NEW ROAD
SOUTH ROAD
LAMBS LANE
WENNINGTON ROAD
EAST HALL LANE
CHURCH LANE
SANDY LANE
B1335
A1306
A13
GATEWAY
LONDON ROAD
PURFLEET
ROMFORD ROAD
THORN LANE
ABBEY WOOD LANE
PARSONAGE ROAD
FARM ROAD
KING EDWARD AVENUE
FAIRVIEW AVENUE
LAKE AVENUE
LAKESIDE
ALLEN ROAD
MAYFIELD
BRISCOE ROAD
AIRFIELD WAY
MAYBANK AVENUE
PARKLAND AVENUE
0 500 yds
0 500 m

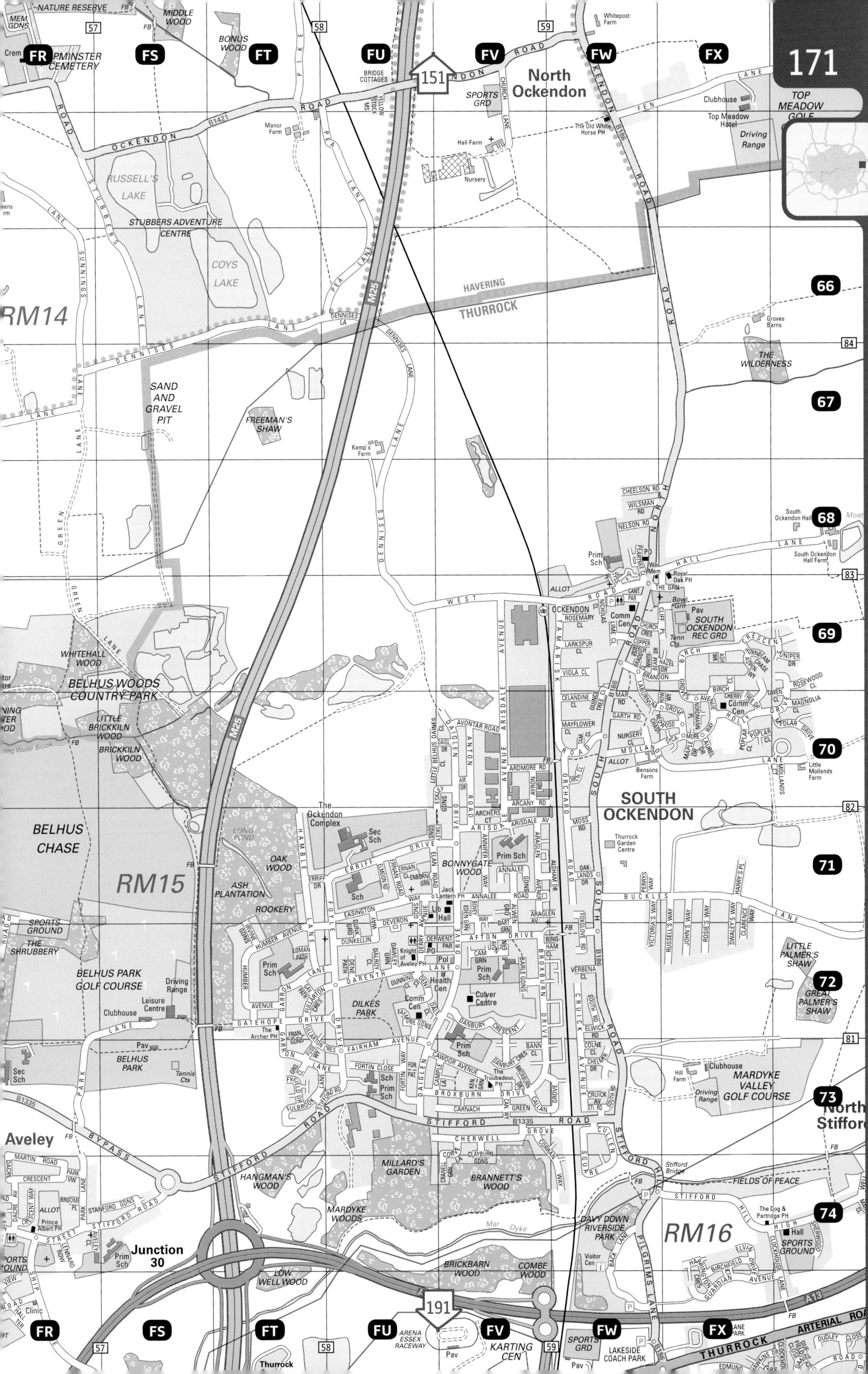
NATURE RESERVE
MEM GDNS
MIDDLE WOOD
BONUS WOOD
UPMINSTER CEMETERY
FR
FS
FT
FU
FV
FW
FX
57
58
59
151
BRIDGE COTTAGES
North Ockendon
SPORTS GRD
TOP MEADOW GOLF
Clubhouse
Top Meadow Hotel
Driving Range
The Old White Horse PH
Manor Farm
Hall Farm
Nursery
OCKENDON ROAD
B1421
RUSSELL'S LAKE
STUBBERS ADVENTURE CENTRE
COYS LAKE
HAVERING
THURROCK
M25
RM14
DENNISES LANE
SAND AND GRAVEL PIT
FREEMAN'S SHAW
Kemp's Farm
Groves Barns
THE WILDERNESS
66
67
68
69
70
71
72
73
74
84
83
82
81
South Ockendon Hall
South Ockendon Hall Farm
Moat
CHEELSON RD
WILSMAN RD
NELSON RD
Prim Sch
PO
War Mem
Royal Oak PH
THE GRN
ALLOT
WEST ROAD
OCKENDON
SOUTH OCKENDON REC GRD
Pav
Comm Cen
WHITEHALL WOOD
BELHUS WOODS COUNTRY PARK
LITTLE BRICKKILN WOOD
BRICKKILN WOOD
BELHUS CHASE
RM15
LONG POND
OAK WOOD
ASH PLANTATION
ROOKERY
The Ockendon Complex
Sec Sch
BONNYGATE WOOD
Prim Sch
Jack Lantern PH
Lib
Hall
Pol
Health Cen
Culver Centre
DILKES PARK
Knight of Aveley PH
SOUTH OCKENDON
Thurrock Garden Centre
Bensons Farm
Little Mollands Farm
BUCKLES LANE
LITTLE PALMER'S SHAW
GREAT PALMER'S SHAW
SPORTS GROUND
THE SHRUBBERY
BELHUS PARK GOLF COURSE
Driving Range
Leisure Centre
Clubhouse
BELHUS PARK
Tennis Cts
The Archer PH
The Troubadour PH
STIFFORD ROAD
B1335
Hill Farm
Clubhouse
MARDYKE VALLEY GOLF COURSE
North Stifford
Aveley
HANGMAN'S WOOD
MILLARD'S GARDEN
BRANNETT'S WOOD
MARDYKE WOODS
Stifford Bridge
FIELDS OF PEACE
DAVY DOWN RIVERSIDE PARK
Visitor Cen
The Dog & Partridge PH
RM16
Hall
SPORTS GROUND
Prince Albert PH
Junction 30
LOW WELL WOOD
BRICKBARN WOOD
COMBE WOOD
191
ARENA ESSEX RACEWAY
KARTING CEN
SPORTS GRD
LAKESIDE COACH PARK
Thurrock
THURROCK ARTERIAL ROAD
A13
Clinic

AC
AD
AE
AF
AG
AH
AJ
75
76
77
78
79
80
81
82
83
84
91
92
93
152
Junction 7
BURNHAM ABBEY
Glasshouses
Farm
HUNTERCOMBE
B3026
Lake End Farm
Glasshouse
THAMES PATH
FISHERY
ROAD
VICARAGE WK
Clubho
Cricket Grd
TOWING PATH
Barge Farm
AMERDEN LANE
Amerden House
HEADPILE EYOT
Bray Lock
Weirs
MARSH
GLEBE CL
FB
SUB
OLD MARSH LANE
CHURCH PATH
Waterside PH
BRAY ROAD
THE CAUSEWAY
Cricket Grd
Sch
Mem
BEAUFORT PL
RIVER GARDENS
PIGEONHILL EYOT
M4
Hall
OAK STUBBS LANE
MEADOW WAY
ASHFORD LANE
ASHFORD LA
Bray
OLD MILL LANE
New Thames Bridge
Prim Sch
HARCOURT ROAD
Crown Inn P.H.
HIGH ST
Hall
Jesus Hospital
ALLOT
Bray Bridge
The Cut
BINGHAMS
Weir Bank
Dorney Reach
DORNEY REACH ROAD
CYCLE PATH
LAKE END ROAD
Dorney
COURT LANE
VILLAGE B3026 ROAD
SOUTH FIELD CL
Court Farm
Hotel
MONKEY ISLAND
Dorney Court
CANON HILL DR
CANON HILL
WINDSOR
BRAY B3028 ROAD
UPPER
HASTINGS CL
CHESTNUT PK
MONKEY ISLAND LANE
Pigeonhouse Farm
COMMON
WINDSOR ROAD
AYSGARTH PARK
ESKDALE GDNS
WHITE ACRES DR
BYLAND DR
COURT CL
BRAY CT
BRAY MARINA
Riding School
CEM
GRAVEL PIT
Clubhouse
QUEEN'S EYOT
Works
SPRINGFIELD
Holyport
PO
BROADWATER PK
TITHE BARN DR
A308
BUCKINGHAMSHIRE
WINDSOR & MAIDENHEAD
DORNEY LAKE
Cress
HUXTABLE GDNS
LYNGFIELD PARK
STOMPITS RD
STROUD FARM ROAD
NEW RD
SL6
DOWN PL
DOWN PLACE
Bray Studios
RIVER THAMES
FERNDALE PARK
The Guild House
Queen's Head PH
Wayside Stables Equestrian Centre
Oakley Court Hotel
TOWING PATH
Stroud Farm
REEVE RD
GAYS
Pitch 'n' Putt
SOUTH BUCKS
Windsor Marina
RIVER ROAD
WILLOWS RIVERSIDE PARK
MAIDENHEAD
MAIN ROAD
THE HATCH
WINDSOR ROAD
CEM
FIFIELD ROAD
THE RETREAT
The Retreat Farm
MANOR GROVE
Bullock's Hatch Bridge
CONINGSBY LANE
GREEN LANE
Fifield
FIFIELD
MEADOW WY
SEWART CL
Coningsby Farm
B3024
The Rising Sun PH
GREEN ROAD
Ledger Farm
The Fifield Inn PH
Fifield House
Braywood C.C.
Pav
LEDGER LA
Prim Sch
OAKLEY GREEN ROAD
Oakley Place Farm
Kimbers Farm
Banham Farm
Bishops Farmhouse
BISHOPS FARM CL
Oakley Green
Ye Olde Red Lion PH
B3383 ROAD
Windsor Garden Centre
The Greene Oak PH
DEDWORTH
Broom Farm
CHARLTON WAY
FURNESS
Prim Sch
FARM
TARBAY LANE
Gale House Farm
SIDNEY RD
Tarbay Farm
Braywood House
BRAY WOOD
Lakeside Racing Stables
DARKHOLE RIDE
FORBE'S RIDE
Darkhole Bridge
Nightingale Corner
HOLLIDAY'S PLAIN
NOBBSCROOK
WINDSOR FOREST
Wakers Farm
Hawe Farm
DRIFT ROAD
New Lodge Farm
WINDSOR & MAIDENHEAD
BRACKNELL FOREST
The Bourne
New Lodge
Foliejon Park Farm
St. Leonard Farm
0
500 yds
0
500 m
NOBBSCROOK COPSE
FISH POND
Windsor

AK
AL
AM
AN
AP
AQ
AR
153
174
Cippenham
SL1
SL4
Chalvey
Junction 6
M4
A355
A332
A308
B3026
B3024
B3022
B3025
B3173
SLOUGH
WINDSOR & MAIDENHEAD
SOUTH BUCKS
MERCIAN RECREATION GROUND
WASTE WATER TREATMENT WORKS
JUBILEE RIVER
ETON WICK COMMON
Eton Wick
ETON GREAT COMMON
DORNEY COMMON
Boveney
RIVER THAMES
ROYAL WINDSOR RACECOURSE
Windsor Racecourse Yacht Basin
Clewer Village
SUTHERLAND GRANGE
WINDSOR RACECOURSE PARK HOMES
MAIDENHEAD ROAD
DEDWORTH MANOR OPEN SPACE
CLEWER MEMORIAL REC GRD
Dedworth
Clewer Green
Clewer New Town
ETON COLLEGE GOLF COURSE
THE PLAYING FIELDS
Eton College
ETON
THE BROCAS
SPORTS GROUND
ALEXANDRA GDNS
WINDSOR & ETON CENTRAL
WINDSOR & ETON RIVERSIDE
Royal Mews Riding Sch
South Slopes
Victoria Barracks
WINDSOR
INTERCONTINENTAL Hotels
PRINCESS MARGARET HOSP
KING EDWARD VII HOSP
Combermere Barracks
WINDSOR CEMETERY
Windsor & Eton FC
HOG COMMON
GARRISON SPORTS GROUND
QUEEN MARY'S PLANTATION
MINIATURE RIFLE RANGE
CAVALRY EXERCISE GROUNDS
ASH PLANTATION
WITHY COVER
DININGROOM CLOSE
SPITAL MEADOW
WINDSOR GREAT PARK
LEGOLAND
NEW COVER
FROGMORE
76
77
78
79
80
81
82
83
84

SLOUGH
AS
AT
AU
AV
AW
AX
AY
154
173
194
75
76
77
78
79
80
81
82
83
84
The Business Village
Gas Works
Lavender Farm
BLOOM PARK
Holiday Inn Express
BUS STA
Superstore
WELLINGTON ST
WELLINGTON
TOWN HALL
Sports Centre
Queensmere Shop Centre
Observatory Shop Centre
Royal Mail
Cinema
Travelodge
Islamic Cen
Premier Inn
Superstore
Prep. Sch
Sec Sch
CHANCERYGATE BUSINESS CEN
CHERRY AVENUE
SUTTON AVENUE
LANGLEY
SPORTS GROUND
Prim Sch
KEDERMISTER PARK
UPTON HOSP
ALBERT ST
MERE RD
YEW TREE
Upton Park
Red Cow
HERSCHEL PARK
Upton
LASCELLES PARK
Tennis Courts
SUSSEX PLACE
LONDON
UPTON COURT
SL1
UPTON COURT PARK
MOTOCROSS TRACK
SLOUGH
WINDSOR & MAIDENHEAD
Pumping Station
Clubhouse
Slough C.C.
SLOUGH R.F.C.
B.M.X. TRACK
AGARS PLOUGH PLAYING FIELDS
THAMES VALLEY ATHLETICS CENTRE
Datchet Mead Hotel
DITTON PARK
The Manor House
KINGS OAK
Computer Associates
Riding Court Farm
Eton College
THE HOME PARK RECREATION GROUND
DATCHET GOLF COURSE
Victoria Bri
EDWARD VII AVENUE
WINDSOR & ETON RIVERSIDE
WINDSOR CASTLE
EAST LAWN
Royal Mews
South Slopes
GOLF COURSE
Adelaide Lodge
The Royal Stag PH
THE GREEN
DATCHET
DATCHET CEMETERY
DATCHET SPORTS GROUND
MILL PLACE CARAVAN PARK
WINDSOR
Victoria Barracks
Long Walk Gate
THE HOME PARK
SL4
FROGMORE GARDENS
Frogmore House
Royal Mausoleum
Prince Consort's Home Farm
THAMES PATH
Southlea
Southlea Farm
Pumping Station
Albert Bridge
Windsor Hall
ROYAL GARDENS
Shaw Farm
NICKCROFT AIT
Sludge Lagoon
Sludge Lagoons
HAM ISLAND
Filter Beds
Sludge Beds
NEW CUT
Ham Bridge
Manor Farm
Clayhall Farm
PRINCESS MARGARET HOSP
GARRISON SPORTS GROUND
Sunnymeads
SUNNYMEADS
Sailing Club
St. George's Farm
Old Windsor Lock
The Manor
REMENHAM PARK
Anglo Saxon Palace (site of)
CROFT CORNER
ALLOT
M4
A4
A308
A332
B470
B376
B3021
B3022
0
500 yds
500 m

IVER GOLF COURSE
Clubhouse
Glasshouse
Recycling Centre
THE ORCHARDS RESIDENTIAL PARK
BUCKINGHAMSHIRE
SLOUGH
SOUTH BUCKS
155
Grand Union Canal (Slough Arm)
TOWING PATH
CARAVAN SITE
CANAL ESTATE
WATERSIDE DRIVE
LANGLEY
Chequer Bridge
Withy Bridge
LANGLEY BUSINESS CENTRE
E. Berkshire Coll
Market
LANGLEY
Comm Cen
MEMORIAL GROUND
Prim Sch
Swimming Pool
HARVEY PARK
Royal Mail Distribution Centre
AXIS PARK
Health Centre
Prim Sch
Sutton Court Farm
Garden Centre
Richings Park
Glasshouses
SPORTS GRD Clubhouse
Bowl Grn
IVER
SL0
RICHINGS PARK GOLF COURSE AND COUNTRY CLUB
Clubhouse
HOME WOOD
Old Slade Farm
Junction 15 (M25)
Junction 4B (M4)
M4
OAK PLANTATION
SLOUGH OLD WOOD
Sewage Works
Filter Beds
LAKESIDE IND EST
176
Incinerator
Chimney
Marriott Hotel
Junction 5
LONDON ROAD
Honda
Brands Hill
Quality Hotel Heathrow
COLNBROOK BYPASS
A4
Sailing Club
REC GRD
Brook Farm
Colnbrook
Comm Cen
Tanhouse Farm
Colnbrook Bridge
Prim Sch
PIPPINS PARK
Arora Park Hotel
COLNBROOK GOLF RANGE
Poyle
Hilton London Heathrow Airport Terminal 5
Pond
THE QUEEN MOTHER RESERVOIR
SL3
BRITANNIA INDUSTRIAL EST
MCKAY TRADING ESTATE
POYLE TECH CEN
POLYGON BUSINESS CEN.
TRIDENT INDUSTRIAL ESTATE
Poyle Farm
POYLE PARK
Travelodge
Junction 14
Lintells Bridge
HILLINGDON
AIRPORT
Ashgood Farm
Berkyn Manor Farm
Arthur Jacob Nature Reserve
Horton
Crown PH
Five Bells PH
Sailing Club
DATCHET ROAD
STANWELL ROAD
POYLE POPLARS ROAD
Golden Cross PH
WINDSOR & MAIDENHEAD
SURREY
COPPERMILL ROAD
Inlet Pier
195
WRAYSBURY
TW19
M25
BEDFONT COURT ESTATE
Mad Bridge
The Anchor PH
Hall
AZ BA BB BC BD BE BF
01 02 03
76 77 78 79 80 81 82 83 84

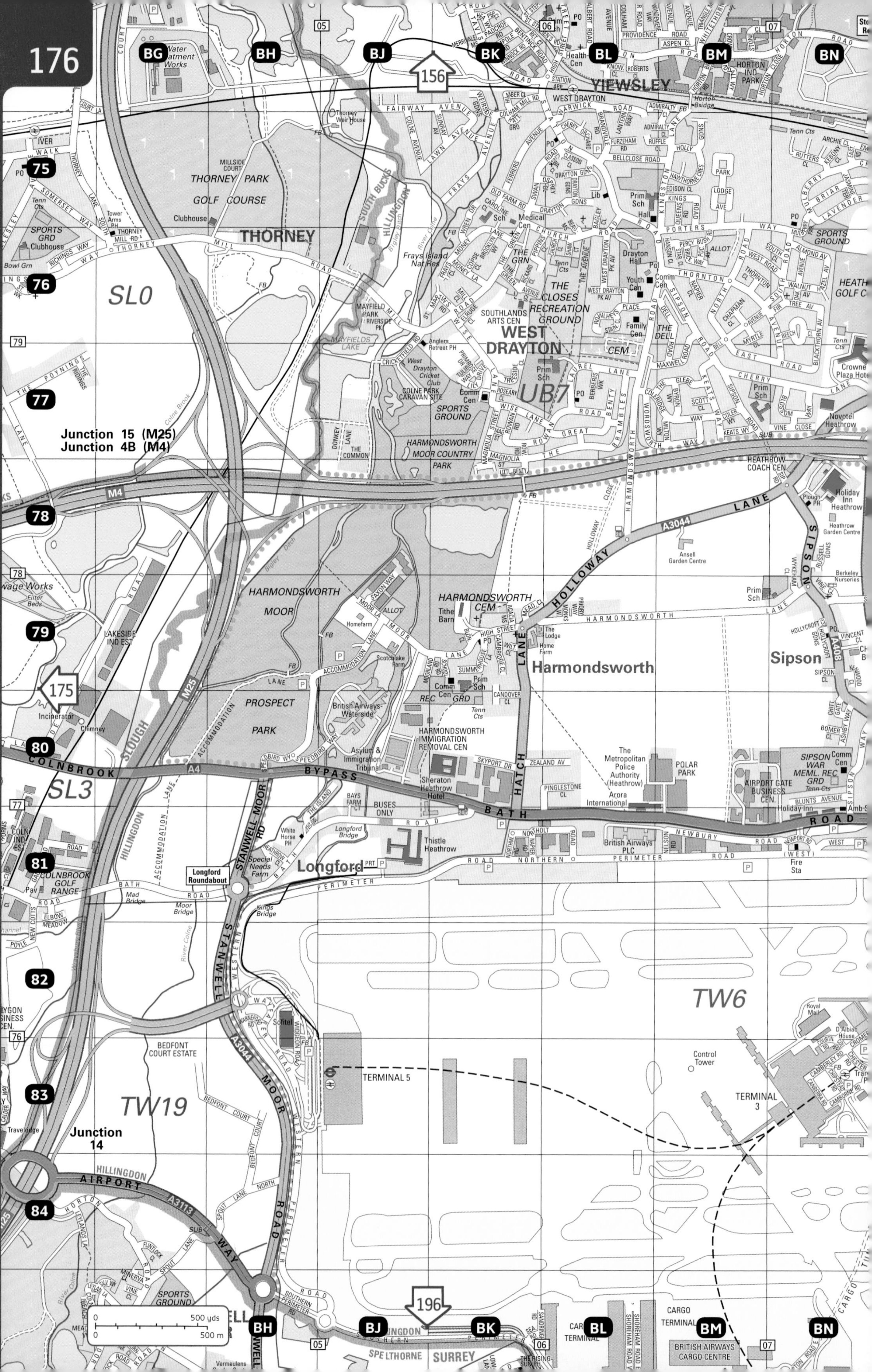

BG
BH
BJ
BK
BL
BM
BN
156
175
196
YIEWSLEY
WEST DRAYTON
Water Treatment Works
IVER
THORNEY PARK GOLF COURSE
Clubhouse
THORNEY
SL0
SPORTS GRD
Frays Island Nat Res
MAYFIELD PARK
MAYFIELDS LAKE
West Drayton Cricket Club
COLNE PARK CARAVAN SITE
SPORTS GROUND
HARMONDSWORTH MOOR COUNTRY PARK
WEST DRAYTON
UB7
SOUTHLANDS ARTS CEN
THE CLOSES RECREATION GROUND
Drayton Hall
THE DELL
SPORTS GROUND
HEATH GOLF C
Crowne Plaza Hotel
Novotel Heathrow
HEATHROW COACH CEN
Holiday Inn Heathrow
Heathrow Garden Centre
Ansell Garden Centre
Berkeley Nurseries
Junction 15 (M25)
Junction 4B (M4)
M4
M25
A3044
A4
A408
A3113
HOLLOWAY LANE
HARMONDSWORTH LANE
HARMONDSWORTH MOOR
HARMONDSWORTH CEM
Tithe Barn
Harmondsworth
Sipson
LAKESIDE IND EST
Incinerator
Chimney
PROSPECT PARK
British Airways Waterside
Asylum & Immigration Tribunal
HARMONDSWORTH IMMIGRATION REMOVAL CEN
Sheraton Heathrow Hotel
The Metropolitan Police Authority (Heathrow)
POLAR PARK
Arora International
SIPSON WAR MEML. REC GRD
AIRPORT GATE BUSINESS CEN.
Holiday Inn
COLNBROOK BYPASS
BATH ROAD
SL3
HILLINGDON
SLOUGH
Longford Roundabout
Longford
Thistle Heathrow
British Airways PLC
NORTHERN PERIMETER ROAD
COLNBROOK GOLF RANGE
Mad Bridge
Moor Bridge
Kings Bridge
STANWELL MOOR ROAD
TW6
Sofitel
TERMINAL 5
Control Tower
TERMINAL 3
Royal Mail
BEDFONT COURT ESTATE
TW19
Junction 14
Travelodge
HILLINGDON AIRPORT WAY
SPORTS GROUND
SOUTHERN PERIMETER ROAD
CARGO TERMINAL
BRITISH AIRWAYS CARGO CENTRE
SPELTHORNE
SURREY
75
76
77
78
79
80
81
82
83
84
500 yds
500 m

BP
BQ
BR
BS
BT
BU
BV
157
MINET COUNTRY PARK
STOCKLEY PARK
UB11
Grand Union Canal
E.M.I. SPORTS GROUND
HAYES TOWN
CAXTON POINT TRADING EST
WARNFORD IND EST
CLAYTON BUSINESS CEN
CROWN TRADING EST
BOTWELL GRN Sports & Leisure Cen
ARGENT BUSINESS CEN
PETER JAMES BUSINESS CENTRE
PROVIDENT IND EST
PASADENA TRADING EST
WATERWAY BUSINESS PARK
SPEEDWAY IND. EST
ABENGLEN IND. EST
ADLER IND EST
Civic Amenity Site
BUS DEPOT
Starveall Bridge
Stockley Bridge
PROLOGIS PARK HEATHROW
BOURNE FARM FIELD
ALLOTMENTS
HAYES & HARLINGTON
British Airways Engineering
SQUIRRELS TRADING ESTATE
Sports & Social Club
BEAVER INDUSTRIAL PARK
76
INTERNATIONAL TRADING EST
BULLS BRIDGE
BULLSBRIDGE IND EST
MARKET TRAD EST
Western International Market
SQUARE ONE
77
UB3
PINKWELL PARK
CHERRY LANE CEMETERY
Frog's Ditch Farm
Sports Hall
SAM PHILIP REC GRD
NORTH HYDE RD
A437
M4
Junction 4
Junction 3
THE PARKWAY
A312
Fitness Centre
Driving Range
78
SPITFIRE ESTATE
IMPERIAL COLLEGE SPORTS GROUND
LITTLE HARLINGTON FIELD
SIPSON MEADOW
SPORTS GROUND
CRANE MEADOW
CRANFORD COUNTRYSIDE PARK
TRAVELLERS SITE
BRITISH AIRWAYS SPORTS GROUND
79
Concorde Centre
PARKWAY TRADING ESTATE
REDWOOD ESTATE
178
HARLINGTON
Elder Farm
HIGH STREET
Poultry Farm
The White House
AVENUE PARK
CRANFORD
TW5
80
Junction 4A
Radisson Edwardian Hotel
Marriott Hotel
Sheraton Skyline
Holiday Inn
Ariel
Bowling Alley
Ibis
Premier Inn
Park Inn
B.A.A.
HEATHROW ACADEMY
Cardinal Pt
Renaissance Hotel
CUSTOM HOUSE
BATH ROAD
A4
Europa House
Heathrow Ho
Ramada
Travelodge
81
Waggoners Roundabout
NORTHERN PERIMETER
Parking Express
HEATHROW AIRPORT (LONDON)
Enfield Road Roundabout
EASTERN PERIMETER
Maintenance Area
Hangar
TW4
ALLOT
Prim Schs
HASLEMERE HEATHROW ESTATE
British Airways PLC
82
TERMINAL 1
Terminal 2 under construction
British Airways (Vanguard Ho)
BA Maintenance Base
Envoy Avenue Roundabout
Jurys Inn
Perishable Handling Facility
Hatton Cross Roundabout
HATTON CROSS
Hatton Cross
HEATHROW CAUSEWAY CEN
HEATHROW INT TRADING ESTATE
RIFLE RANGE
GREEN LANE OPEN SPACE
83
HATTON
BALANCING RESERVOIR
DONKEY WOOD
RADIUS PARK
GREAT SOUTH-WEST ROAD
A30
THE CAUSEWAY
Civic Amenity Site
84
TW14
197
HOUNSLOW URBAN FARM
HATTON CEM
NORTH FELTHAM TRADING EST
MERCURY CENTRE
FALCON EST
HOUNSLOW HEATH GOLF COURSE
Baber Bridge
TERMINAL
Mast

BW
BX
BY
BZ
CA
CB
CC
158
177
198
75
76
77
78
79
80
81
82
83
84
SOUTHALL
UB1
UB2
UB3
TW3
TW4
TW5
MINET COUNTRY PARK
HEATHROW PURPLE PARKING
SOUTHALL RAILWAY CENTRE
MIDDLESEX BUSINESS CENTRE
THE BRIDGE BUSINESS CENTRE
GLADE LANE CANALSIDE PARK
TENTELOW LANE SPORTS GROUND
BEAVER INDUSTRIAL PARK
Balfour Business Centre
FEATHERSTONE IND EST
INTERNATIONAL TRADING EST
BULLSBRIDGE IND EST
Western International Market
SQUARE ONE
NORWOOD GREEN
NORTH HYDE
ENDSLEIGH IND EST
AIRLINKS GOLF COURSE
Heston Services
BRITISH AIRWAYS SPORTS GROUND
PARKWAY TRADING ESTATE
AIR LINKS INDUSTRIAL ESTATE
Junction 3
M4
HESTON
HESTON INDUSTRIAL MALL
SUTTON PLAYING FIELD
Brentford FC Training Ground
OSTERL
Osterley Park Farm
LAMPTON
LAMPTON PARK
HOUNSLOW CIVIC CENTRE
Waggoners Roundabout
Henlys Roundabout
HOUNSLOW WEST
BEAVERSFORD PARK
Cavalry Barracks
HEATHROW INT TRADING ESTATE
RIFLE RANGE
GREEN LANE OPEN SPACE
HOUNSLOW
HOUNSLOW CENTRAL
HOUNSLOW EAST
The Blenheim Centre
Treaty Centre
INWOOD PARK
CENTRAL PARK EST
NORTH FELTHAM TRADING EST
FALCON EST
DONKEY WOOD
HOUNSLOW HEATH
A4
A30
A315
A3005
A3006
A3063
A4127
0 500 yds
0 500 m

CD
CE
CF
CG
CH
CJ
CK
159
180
199
76
77
78
79
80
81
82
83
84
HANWELL
HANWELL CEMETERY
EALING HOSPITAL N.H.S. TRUST
W7
W13
W5
TW7
TW8
TW9
TW1
BRENT RIVER PARK
ELTHORNE PARK
ELTHORNE PARK EXTENSION
LONG WOOD (Nature Reserve)
WATERSIDE TRADING CENTRE
RIVER BRENT BUS PARK
SPORTS GROUND
OSTERLEY PARK NT
WYKE GREEN GOLF COURSE
MACFARLANE SPORT FIELD
BOSTON MANOR
LONDON PLAYING FIELDS
BOSTON MANOR HOUSE
BOSTON MANOR PARK
GlaxoSmithKline
WEST CROSS CENTRE
CENTAURS BUSINESS CEN
BRENTSIDE EXECUTIVE CENTRE
BRENTFORD BUSINESS CENTRE
Gillette Corner
GREAT WEST ROAD
LITTLE EALING
SOUTH EALING
SOUTH EALING CEMETERY
LAMMAS PARK
WALPOLE PARK
University of West London
BRENTFORD
BRENTFORD FC
Junction 2
Watermans Arts Cen
SPRING GROVE
SPORTS GRD
ISLEWORTH CROWN CRT
West Thames Coll
SYON LANE
SYON PARK
SYON HOUSE
Syon Park Conservatory
London Syon Park
Aquatic Experience
Battles of Brentford 1016 & 1642
Duke of Northumberland Estate
RIVER THAMES
BOTANIC GARDENS
QUEEN'S COTTAGE GARDENS
Queen Charlotte's Cottage
KEW
WEST MIDDLESEX UNIVERSITY HOSP
WOODLANDS
ISLEWORTH
ISLEWORTH AIT
THORNBURY PLAYING FIELDS
VICTORY BUSINESS CENTRE
REDLEES PARK
MOGDEN SEWAGE TREATMENT WORKS
WORTON HALL ESTATE
ROYAL MID-SURREY GOLF COURSE (OLD DEER PARK)
Kew Observatory
OBSERVATORY GARDENS
OLD DEER PARK RECREATION GROUND
RICHMOND ATHLETIC GROUND
ROYAL HOSP
Richmond Circus
RICHMOND GREEN
THE SQUARE
ST. MARGARETS
St. Margarets Roundabout
IVYBRIDGE ESTATE
M4
A4
A315
A3002
A310
A316
A3004
A4020

CL
CM
CN
CP
CQ
CR
CS
160
179
200
75
76
77
78
79
80
81
82
83
84
EALING COMMON
ACTON
EAST ACTON
W5
ACTON PARK
ACTON PARK ESTATE
SOUTHFIELDS PLAYING FIELDS
POPEFIELD PLAYING FIELDS
ACTON TOWN
SOUTH ACTON
BEDFORD PARK
GUNNERSBURY PARK
W3
GUNNERSBURY
SOUTH EALING CEMETERY
CLAYPONDS HOSP
KENSINGTON CEMETERY
CHISWICK PARK
Junction 1
Chiswick Rbt
Junction 2
PHOENIX PARK
TW8
KEW BRIDGE
WELLESLEY
Kew Bridge
W4
CHISWICK
BRENTFORD
KEW GREEN
KEW
Kew Green
KEW PALACE
ROYAL
TW9
BOTANIC GARDENS
GROVE PARK
THE NATIONAL ARCHIVES
OLIVER'S ISLAND
CHISWICK HOUSE
CHISWICK HOUSE GROUNDS
UNIVERSITY OF WESTMINSTER SPORTS GROUND
CIVIL SERVICE SPORTS GROUND
DUKE'S MEADOW
DUKE'S MEADOWS GOLF CHISWICK BRIDGE
RIVER THAMES
QUEEN'S COTTAGE GARDENS
NORTH SHEEN
NORTH SHEEN CEMETERY
HAMMERSMITH CEMETERY
Chalkers Corner
Manor Circus
Richmond Circus
MORTLAKE
MORTLAKE HIGH ST
BARNES HOSP
RICHMOND
RICHMOND ATHLETIC GROUND
ROYAL HOSP
EAST SHEEN
SW14
Milestone Green
NATIONAL TENNIS CENTRE
EAST SHEEN COMMON (NT)
PALEWELL COMMON
RICHMOND GREEN
HOUNSLOW
RICHMOND UPON THAMES
0
500 yds
500 m

CT
CU
CV
CW
CX
CY
CZ
161
SHEPHERD'S BUSH
LOFTUS ROAD STADIUM QPR FC
UXBRIDGE ROAD
HOLLAND PARK
KENSINGTON
HOLLAND PARK
W14
W8
W12
W6
GOLDHAWK ROAD
RAVENSCOURT PARK
STAMFORD BROOK
KING STREET
HAMMERSMITH
HAMMERSMITH FLYOVER
GREAT WEST ROAD
TALGARTH ROAD
KENSINGTON (OLYMPIA)
OLYMPIA
EARLS COURT
SW5
EARLS COURT EXHIBITION CENTRE
CASTELNAU
CHARING CROSS HOSP
HAMMERSMITH CEMETERY
THE QUEEN'S CLUB
LILLIE ROAD
DAWES ROAD
182
SW13
LONDON WETLANDS CENTRE
38
SW6
FULHAM PALACE ROAD
PARSONS GREEN
BARN ELMS PLAYING FIELDS
BARN ELMS SCHOOL SPORTS CENTRE
RIVER THAMES
CRAVEN COTTAGE FULHAM FC
BISHOP'S PARK
FULHAM
FULHAM PALACE GARDENS
HURLINGHAM PARK
BARNES
BARNES COMMON
LOWER RICHMOND ROAD
UPPER RICHMOND ROAD
PUTNEY
PUTNEY BRIDGE
SW15
WANDSWORTH PARK
WANDSWORTH
ROEHAMPTON
ROEHAMPTON LANE
SOUTH CIRCULAR ROAD
201
22
23
24
26
76
77
78
79
80
81
82
83
84

KENSINGTON GARDENS
HYDE PARK
W8
SW7
KENSINGTON
HOLLAND PARK
SOUTH KENSINGTON
BELGRAVIA
BROMPTON
EARLS COURT
SW5
SW10
SW3
WEST BROMPTON
CHELSEA
BATTERSEA PARK
PARSONS GREEN
WALHAM GREEN
SANDS END
SW6
SW11
SW15
SW18
WANDSWORTH
CLAPHAM JUNCTION
KENSINGTON ROAD
KNIGHTSBRIDGE
CROMWELL ROAD
BROMPTON ROAD
FULHAM ROAD
KING'S ROAD
CHEYNE WALK
CHELSEA EMBANKMENT
BATTERSEA BRIDGE
ALBERT BRIDGE
CHELSEA BRIDGE
WANDSWORTH BRIDGE
LAVENDER HILL
CLAPHAM COMMON
DA
DB
DC
DD
DE
DF
DG
75
76
77
78
79
80
81
82
83
84
162
181
202
0
500 yds
500 m

DH
DJ
DK
DL
DM
DN
DP
163
THE GREEN PARK
ST. JAMES'S
ST. JAMES'S PARK
SW1
BUCKINGHAM PALACE
WESTMINSTER
VICTORIA
HOUSES OF PARLIAMENT
WATERLOO
SOUTHWARK
SE1
ST. THOMAS' HOSP
LAMBETH PALACE
LAMBETH
BOROUGH
ELEPHANT & CASTLE
WALWORTH
SE11
PIMLICO
VAUXHALL
KENNINGTON
THE KIA OVAL (SURREY C.C.C.)
RIVER THAMES
NINE ELMS
SW8
BATTERSEA
SOUTH LAMBETH
STOCKWELL
CAMBERWELL
SE5
SW9
MYATT'S FIELDS PARK
LOUGHBOROUGH JUNCTION
COLDHARBOUR
BRIXTON
CLAPHAM
SW4
SE24
TRINITY HOSPICE
LAMBETH HOSPITAL
184
203
76
77
78
79
80
81
82
83
84
41
42
29
30
31

DQ
DR
DS
DT
DU
DV
DW
164
183
204
33
34
35
75
76
77
78
79
80
81
82
83
84
43
44
WAPPING
SOUTHWARK
THE BOROUGH
NEWINGTON
BERMONDSEY
SE1
SE17
WALWORTH
CAMBERWELL
SE5
PECKHAM
SE15
SE22
SE24
BURGESS PARK
LONDON BRIDGE HOSP
GUY'S HOSPITAL
MAUDSLEY HOSPITAL
KING'S COLLEGE HOSPITAL
DULWICH COMMUNITY HOSP
TOWER BRIDGE EXHIBITION
BRUNEL MUSEUM & ENGINE HOUSE
GREEK CATHEDRAL
PECKHAM RYE COMMON
PECKHAM RYE PARK
RUSKIN PARK
MYATT'S FIELDS PARK
SOUTHWARK PARK
SOUTHWARK PARK EST
LUCAS GDNS
SURREY GDNS
NEW KENT ROAD
OLD KENT ROAD
CAMBERWELL ROAD
WALWORTH ROAD
DENMARK HILL
PECKHAM ROAD
PECKHAM HIGH ST
QUEENS ROAD
EAST DULWICH ROAD
GROVE VALE
JAMAICA ROAD
SOUTHWARK PARK ROAD
TOWER BRIDGE ROAD
BOROUGH HIGH ST
GREAT DOVER STREET
ALBANY ROAD
CAMBERWELL CH ST
LORDSHIP LANE
DOG KENNEL HILL
0 500 yds
0 500 m

DX
DY
DZ
EA
EB
EC
ED
165
186
205
76
77
78
79
80
81
82
83
84
36
37
38
45
46
SE16
SE10
SE8
SE14
SE3
SE4
SE13
E14
ROTHERHITHE
ISLE OF DOGS
MILLWALL
CUBITT TOWN
DEPTFORD
GREENWICH
GREENWICH PARK
NEW CROSS GATE
NEW CROSS
ST JOHN'S
LEWISHAM
BROCKLEY
LADYWELL
HILLY FIELDS
BLACKHEATH
MUDCHUTE FARM
WEST INDIA DOCKS
MILLWALL OUTER DOCK
DEPTFORD PARK
PEPYS PARK
ISLAND GARDENS
MILLWALL PARK
RUSSIA DOCK WOODLAND
GREENLAND DOCK
SOUTH DOCK
TOWER HAMLETS
SOUTHWARK
LEWISHAM
GREENWICH REACH
BROCKLEY CEMETERY
LADYWELL CEMETERY
TELEGRAPH HILL PARK
NEW CROSS NATURE RESERVE
NATIONAL MARITIME MUSEUM
ROYAL OBSERVATORY GREENWICH (Flamsteed House)
CUTTY SARK
MANOR PARK

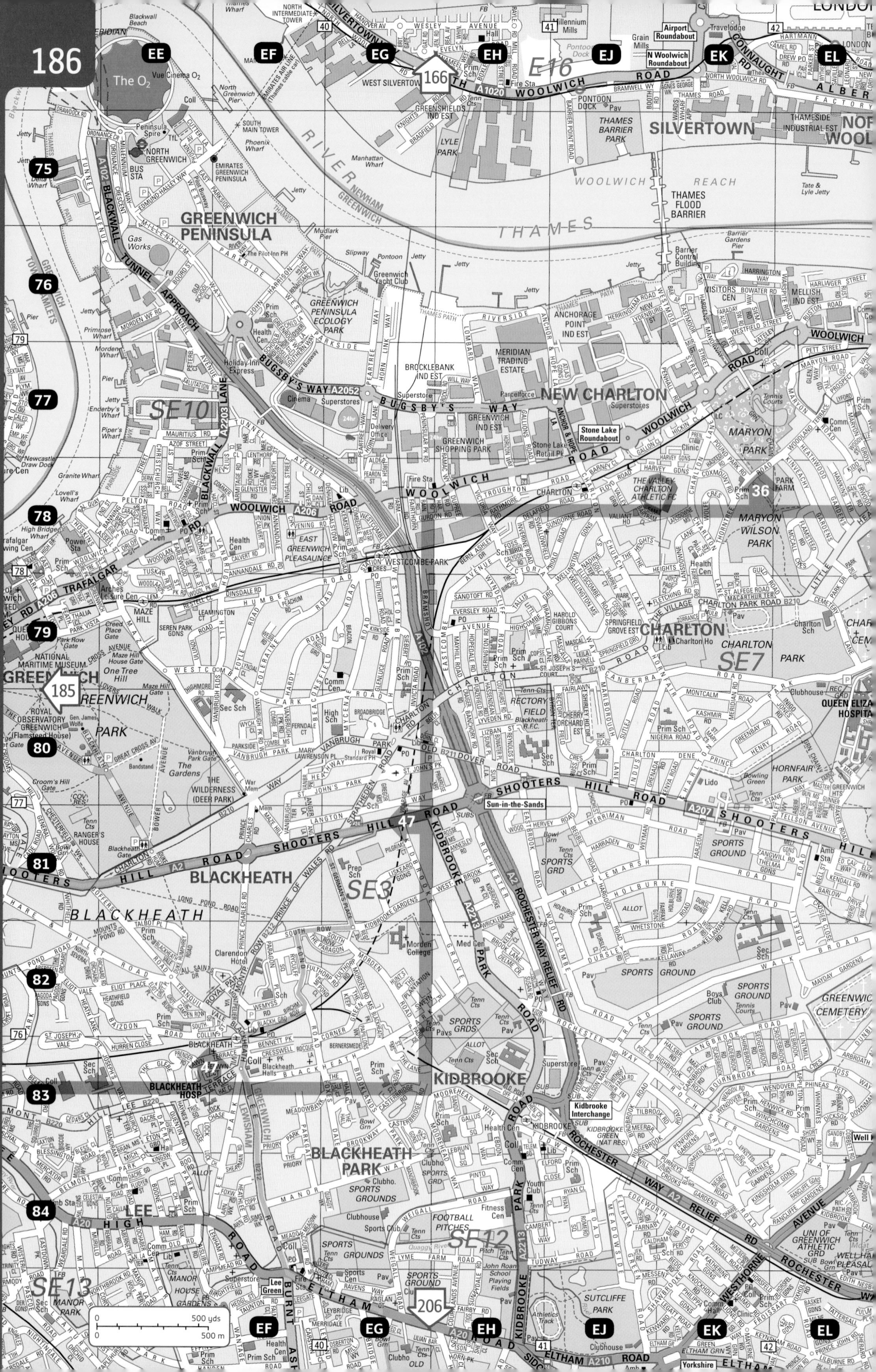
The O2
GREENWICH PENINSULA
NORTH GREENWICH
SILVERTOWN
WEST SILVERTOWN
E16
RIVER THAMES
WOOLWICH REACH
THAMES FLOOD BARRIER
THAMES BARRIER PARK
NEW CHARLTON
SE10
SE7
SE3
SE12
SE13
CHARLTON
MARYON PARK
MARYON WILSON PARK
CHARLTON PARK
GREENWICH PARK
BLACKHEATH
KIDBROOKE
BLACKHEATH PARK
LEE
HORNFAIR PARK
SUTCLIFFE PARK
GREENWICH CEMETERY
EAST GREENWICH PLEASAUNCE
GREENWICH PENINSULA ECOLOGY PARK
LYLE PARK
THE VALLEY CHARLTON ATHLETIC FC
WOOLWICH ROAD
BLACKWALL TUNNEL APPROACH
SHOOTERS HILL ROAD
ROCHESTER WAY RELIEF RD
Stone Lake Roundabout
Sun-in-the-Sands
Kidbrooke Interchange
Airport Roundabout
N Woolwich Roundabout
Lee Green
166
185
206
500 yds
500 m

KING GEORGE V DOCK
NEWHAM
GREENWICH
WOOLWICH FREE FERRY
THAMESMEAD WEST
SE28
H.M. PRISON BELMARSH
WEST THAMESMEAD BUSINESS PARK
BROADWATER GRN
SE2
PLUMSTEAD
WOOLWICH ARSENAL
WOOLWICH
BARRACK FIELD
Royal Artillery Barracks
PLUMSTEAD COMMON
WINN'S COMMON
SE18
WOOLWICH CEMETERY
WOOLWICH COMMON
SHREWSBURY PARK
SHOOTERS HILL GOLF COURSE
SHOOTER'S HILL
EAST WICKHAM OPEN SPACE
HILLVIEW CEMETERY
ELTHAM COMMON
MEMORIAL HOSPITAL
JACK WOOD
CASTLE WOOD
OXLEAS WOOD
OXLEAS MEADOW
SHEPHERDLEAS' WOOD
FALCONWOOD
DA16
DA15
SE9
ELTHAM PARK SOUTH
ELTHAM CEMETERY
ELTHAM WARREN GOLF COURSE
WELLING
EM EN EP EQ ER ES ET
167
188
207
37

EU
EV
EW
EX
EY
EZ
FA
168
SOUTHMERE PARK
ERITH MARSHES
LAKESIDE CENTRE
SOUTHMERE
BIRCHMERE PARK
SE28
DA18
WOODLAND WAY
The Business Academy Bexley
EASTERN WAY
75
76
77
78
79
80
81
82
83
84
ABBEY WOOD PARK
THISTLEBROOK INDUSTRIAL EST
SE18
ABBEY WOOD
Lesnes Abbey (ruins)
HARROW MANORWAY
KNEE HILL
SE2
BOSTALL HEATH
ABBEY WOOD CARAVAN CLUBS SITE
HIGH STREET
BOSTALL HILL
WOOLWICH ROAD
WEST HEATH
BOSTALL WOODS
GOLDIE LEIGH HOSPITAL
CLAM FIELD RECREATION GROUND
187
WOOLWICH CEMETERY
PLUMSTEAD CEMETERY
EAST WICKHAM
EAST WICKHAM OPEN SPACE
DA16
STEVENS PARK
DA7
WELLING
WELLING HIGH STREET
PARK VIEW ROAD
CROOK LOG
BROADWAY
BEXLEYHEATH CEMETERY
The Mall Bexleyheath
DANSON
PARK
DANSON ROAD
DA6
BEXLEYHEATH
208
0 500 yds
0 500 m
47
48
49

RAINHAM MARSHES
FB
FC
FD
FE
FF
FG
FH
169
190
209
ISIS REACH
BELVEDERE INDUSTRIAL ESTATE
EASTERN WAY
BELVEDERE BUS. PARK
CRABTREE MANORWAY IND EST
CHURCH MANORWAY INDUSTRIAL ESTATE
Erith Oil Works
THAMESMEAD SPINE RD
BRONZE AGE WAY
ERITH REACH
RIVER THAMES
RM13
COLDHARBOUR LANE
Sludge Pipeline
FREIGHTMASTER ESTATE
Coldharbour Point
HAVERING
BEXLEY
ERITH RANDS
Landing Stage
Chalk Fm Wharf
Erith Deep Wharf Jetty
DA17
BELVEDERE
FRANK'S PARK
Bexley Coll
LESSNESS HEATH
ERITH CEMETERY
HAMLET ESTATE
EUROPA TRADING ESTATE
Atlas Trade Park
FRASER ROAD
ERITH
QUEEN'S ROAD
Superstore
Concrete Works
MANFORD IND EST
ANCHOR BAY IND EST
Sailing Club
The Saltings
MANOR ROAD
ERITH & DISTRICT HOSP
MONASTERY
ERITH REC GRD
Sports Centre
ERITH STADIUM
DA8
CHURCH TRADING EST
NORTHUMBERLAND HEATH
NORTHEND TRD EST
SLADE GREEN
SPORTS GROUND
CRAYFORD MARSHES
HOWBURY LANE REC GRDS
RAIL DEPOT
The Grange
BURSTED WOOD
BARNEHURST
BARNEHURST GOLF COURSE
SPORTS GROUND
OPTIMA PARK
Chemical Works
Waste Reception Centre
MARTENS GROVE PARK
BAKERS FIELD
DA1
Perry Street Farm
Crayside Industrial Est
BARNES CRAY
CRAYFORD MARSHES
SHENSTONE PARK
CRAYFORD INDUSTRIAL ESTATE
ACORN INDUSTRIAL PARK
WATLING STREET
LONDON ROAD
A206
A207
A220
A2000
A2016
76
77
78
79
80
81
82
83
84
50
51
52

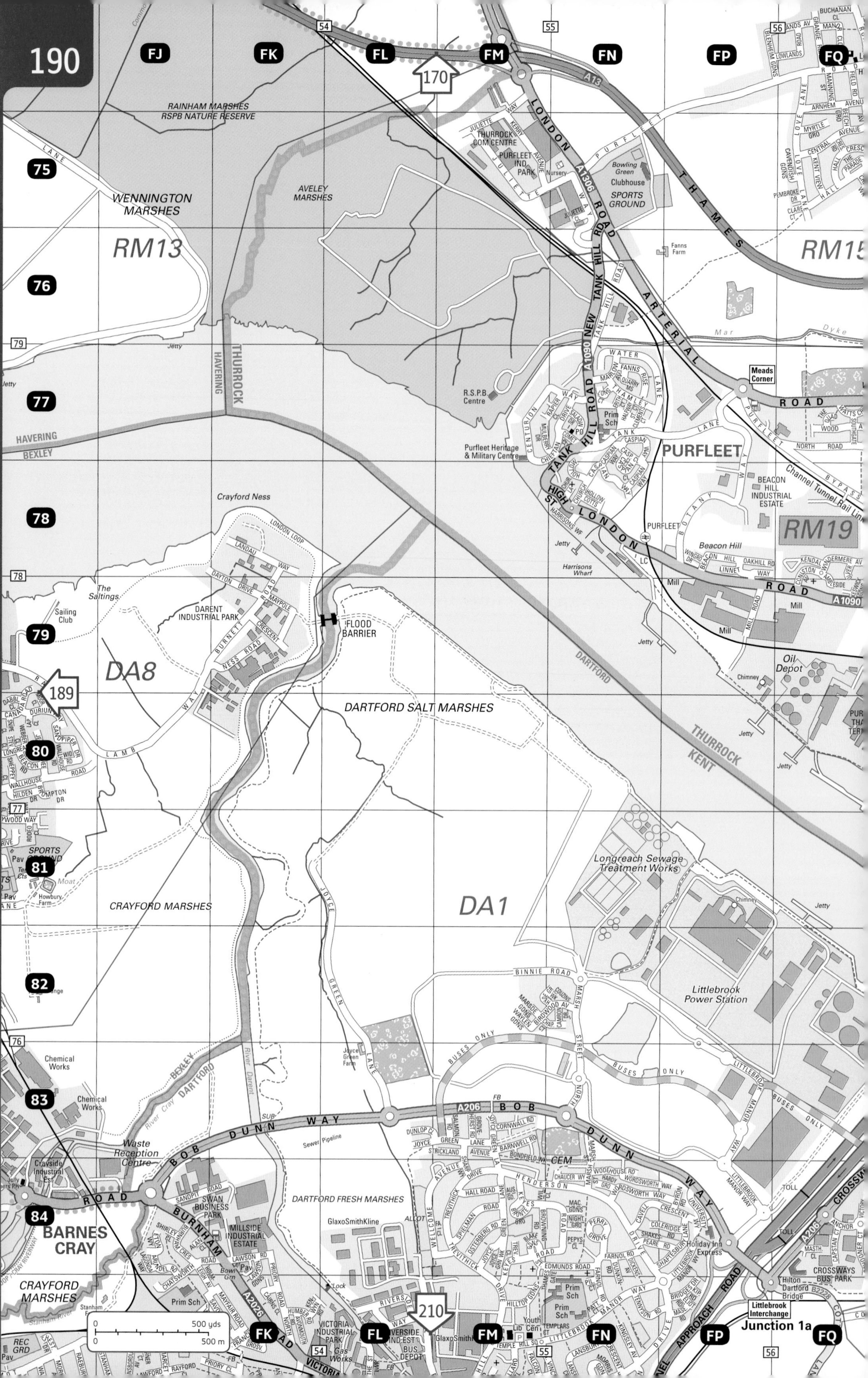
FJ
FK
FL
FM
FN
FP
FQ
170
189
210
RAINHAM MARSHES
RSPB NATURE RESERVE
WENNINGTON MARSHES
RM13
AVELEY MARSHES
HAVERING
THURROCK
BEXLEY
THURROCK
KENT
R.S.P.B. Centre
Purfleet Heritage & Military Centre
THURROCK COM CENTRE
PURFLEET IND PARK
Nursery
Bowling Green
Clubhouse
SPORTS GROUND
Fanns Farm
RM15
LONDON ROAD
A1306
NEW TANK HILL ROAD
A1090
TANK HILL ROAD
ARTERIAL
THAMES
A13
Meads Corner
PURFLEET
BEACON HILL INDUSTRIAL ESTATE
Channel Tunnel Rail Link
RM19
Beacon Hill
Harrisons Wharf
Jetty
Mill
Oil Depot
Chimney
Crayford Ness
The Saltings
Sailing Club
DARENT INDUSTRIAL PARK
FLOOD BARRIER
DA8
DARTFORD SALT MARSHES
DARTFORD
CRAYFORD MARSHES
DA1
Longreach Sewage Treatment Works
Littlebrook Power Station
BINNIE ROAD
MARSH STREET
BUSES ONLY
Joyce Green Farm
JOYCE GREEN LANE
River Darent
River Cray
Chemical Works
Waste Reception Centre
Crayside Industrial Est
BARNES CRAY
CRAYFORD MARSHES
SWAN BUSINESS PARK
MILLSIDE INDUSTRIAL ESTATE
DARTFORD FRESH MARSHES
GlaxoSmithKline
BOB DUNN WAY
A206
BURNHAM ROAD
A2026
VICTORIA INDUSTRIAL PARK
RIVERSIDE IND EST
BUS DEPOT
Gas Works
Prim Sch
CEM
Holiday Inn Express
LITTLEBROOK MANOR WAY
Littlebrook Interchange
Junction 1a
CROSSWAYS BUS PARK
Hilton Dartford Bridge
TOLL
0
500 yds
500 m
75
76
77
78
79
80
81
82
83
84
54
55
56

FR
FS
FT
FU
FV
FW
FX
57
58
59
171
192
211
76
77
78
79
80
81
82
83
84
Junction 30
Junction 31
HANGMAN'S WOOD
MARDYKE WOODS
BRANNETT'S WOOD
BRICKBARN WOOD
COMBE WOOD
LOW WELL WOOD
DAVY DOWN RIVERSIDE PARK
Visitor Cen
STIFFORD
FIELDS OF
PILGRIMS LANE
CLOCKHOUSE LANE
A13
ARENA ESSEX RACEWAY
KARTING CEN
SPORTS GRD
LAKESIDE COACH PARK
PILGRIMS LANE CARAVAN PARK
THURROCK
WEST
ARTERIAL ROAD
A1306
Thurrock Services
Travelodge
BUS & COACH STA
Superstore
Premier Inn
Fitness Cen
CHAFFORD HUNDRED
RM16
WARREN GORGE
LION GORGE
Oil Depot
DEVONSHIRE ROAD
A126
SHIP LANE CARAVAN SITE
Causeway Bri
Thurrock FC
Mar Dyke Farm
Thurrock Hotel
PURFLEET
Cinema
THE JUNCTION
LAKESIDE RETAIL PK
Lakeside
ALEXANDRA LAKE
Watersport Centre
Clocktower
WESTON AV
THURROCK WAY
B186
West Thurrock
FROGMORE ESTATE
J31 PARK
WATERGLADE INDUSTRIAL PK
QED DISTRIBUTION PARK
Distribution Centre
M25
MOTHERWELL WAY
GLADE BUSINESS CENTRE
EASTERN AVENUE
SPORTS GRD
CEM
LYNDALE ESTATE
South Stifford
MAGNET ESTATE
LONDON ROAD
WEST THURROCK WAY
STONENESS RD
ACORN TRADING ESTATE
REC GRD
Stonehouse Corner
ELECTRICITY STA
Formule 1 Hotel
Ibis Hotel
LONDON RD W THURROCK
A1090
PURFLEET BYPASS
DOVECOTE BARNS
JARRAH COTTS
High House
CANTERBURY WAY
A282
ST. CLEMENTS WAY
THURROCK TRADE PARK
OLIVER ROAD
OLIVER CLOSE
HEDLEY AVENUE
Elec Sta
ST CLEMENT
WILDLIFE SANCTUARY
Electricity Sub Station
WEST THURROCK MARSHES
RM20
Chemical Works
Oil Depot
Oil Storage Depot
Jetty
Jetties
Airshafts
QUEEN ELIZABETH II BRIDGE
TUNNEL
STONENESS LIGHTHOUSE
ST. CLEMENT'S OR FIDDLER'S REACH
RIVER THAMES
THURROCK
DARTFORD
Bell Wharf
Pier
SWANSCOMBE MARSHES
DA2
DA9
DA10
THAMES EUROPORT
Johnson's Wharf
Campanile Hotel
Crossways
CROSSWAYS BOULEVARD
NEWTONS COURT
QUADRANT COURT
Superstore
HIGH STREET
B255
THE AVENUE
CLARINDA HO
STONE CROSSING
Travelodge
LONDON ROAD
A226
GALLEY HILL TRADE PARK
NELSON HOUSE
Comm Cen
Lib
Stone
Greenhithe
GREENHITHE FOR BLUEWATER
Clinic
SPORTS GRD
Prim Sch

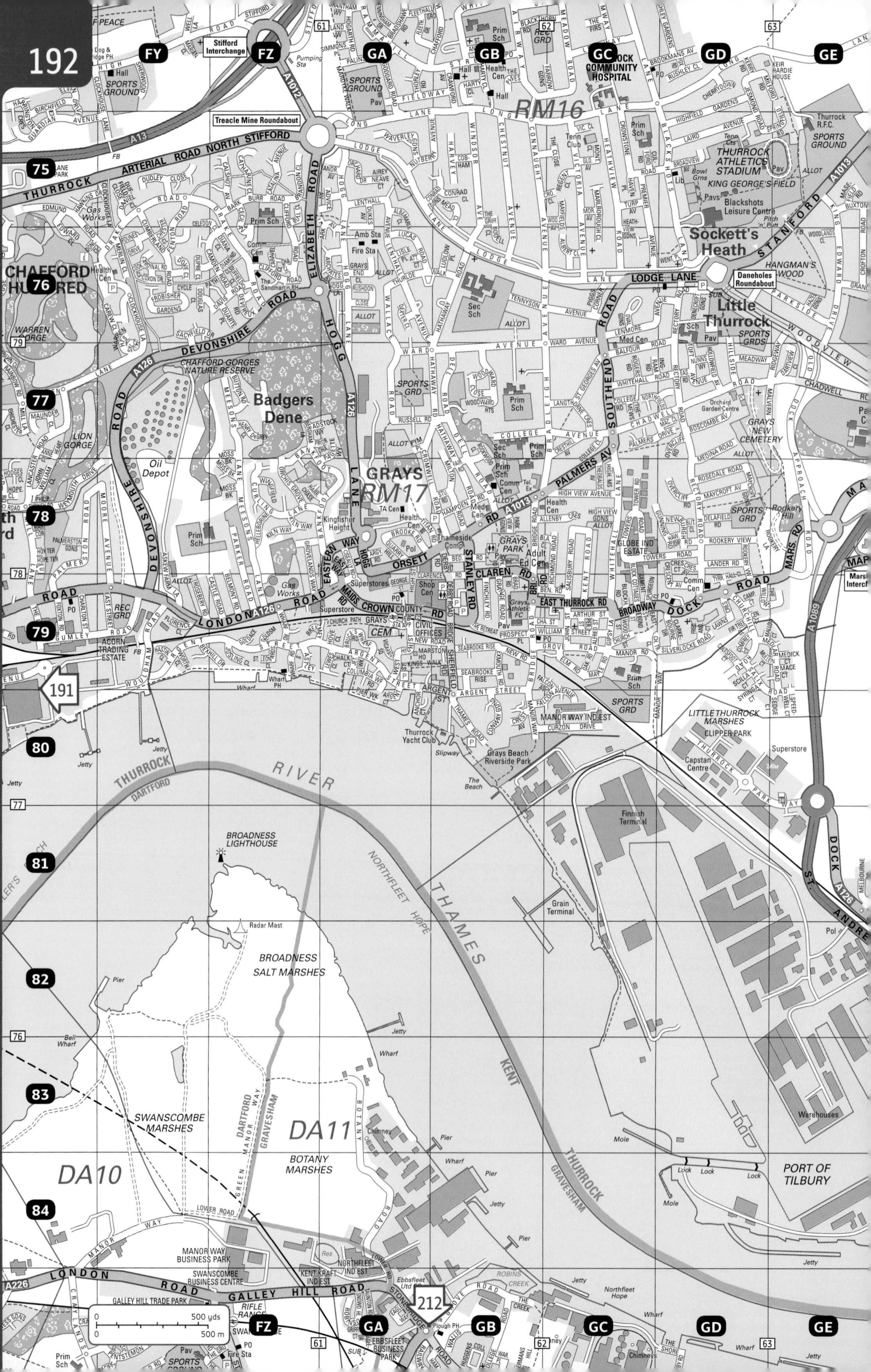
Stifford Interchange
Treacle Mine Roundabout
THURROCK ARTERIAL ROAD NORTH STIFFORD
A13
A1012
RM16
THURROCK COMMUNITY HOSPITAL
THURROCK ATHLETICS STADIUM
KING GEORGE'S FIELD
Blackshots Leisure Centre
Sockett's Heath
Daneholes Roundabout
Little Thurrock
HANGMAN'S WOOD
Thurrock R.F.C.
SPORTS GROUND
CHAFFORD HUNDRED
WARREN GORGE
CHAFFORD GORGES NATURE RESERVE
Badgers Dene
LION GORGE
Oil Depot
DEVONSHIRE ROAD
A126
ELIZABETH ROAD
HOGG LANE
GRAYS
RM17
Kingfisher Height
ORSETT RD
STANLEY RD
CLAREN. RD
EAST THURROCK RD
BROADWAY
DOCK ROAD
PALMERS AV
A1013
SOUTHEND ROAD
LODGE LANE
GRAYS NEW CEMETERY
GLOBE IND ESTATE
Rookery Hill
LONDON ROAD
ACORN TRADING ESTATE
Thurrock Yacht Club
Grays Beach Riverside Park
MANOR WAY IND EST
LITTLE THURROCK MARSHES
CLIPPER PARK
Capstan Centre
Superstore
Finnish Terminal
Grain Terminal
RIVER THAMES
THURROCK
DARTFORD
NORTHFLEET HOPE
BROADNESS LIGHTHOUSE
Radar Mast
BROADNESS SALT MARSHES
SWANSCOMBE MARSHES
DA10
DA11
BOTANY MARSHES
DARTFORD GRAVESHAM
KENT
GRAVESHAM
Warehouses
PORT OF TILBURY
Lock
Mole
MANOR WAY BUSINESS PARK
SWANSCOMBE BUSINESS CENTRE
KENT KRAFT IND EST
NORTHFLEET IND EST
GALLEY HILL TRADE PARK
GALLEY HILL ROAD
EBBSFLEET BUSINESS PARK
Northfleet Hope
DOCK APPROACH ROAD
ST. ANDREWS
A1089
FY
FZ
GA
GB
GC
GD
GE
75
76
77
78
79
80
81
82
83
84
191
212
61
62
63
0 500 yds
0 500 m

Orsett Heath
ORSETT GOLF COURSE
CHADWELL ST. MARY
Linford
SS17
Muckingford
West Tilbury
Low Street
TILBURY MARSHES
RM18
WEST TILBURY MARSHES
WALTHAM COMMON
PARSONAGE COMMON
HALLHILL COMMON
SHROVE HILL WOOD
OLD HOUSE WOOD
RAINBOW WOOD
ASHEN SHAW
GRAVEL PIT
TILBURY
KING GEORGE'S FIELD
ANCHOR FLDS PK
CUSTOM HOUSE
Tilbury Fort
Tilbury Energy & Environmental Centre
Tilbury B Power Station
Sewage Works
Electricity Station
Thurrock & Basildon College
TERRELS HEATH
Hob Hill
Broom Hill
Hutts Hill
STAR ESTATE
Tilbury FC
TILBURY STADIUM (KARTING)
FORTRESS DISTRIBUTION PARK
RIVERSIDE BUSINESS CENTRE
ENTERPRISE DISTRIBUTION CENTRE
Cold Storage
London International Cruise Terminal
Riverside Rail Terminal
DRY DOCK
RIVER THAMES
THURROCK
GRAVESHAM
GRAVESEND REACH
213
A126
A1089
B149
ST. CHAD'S ROAD
FERRY ROAD
DOCK ROAD
FORT ROAD
MUCKINGFORD ROAD
LINFORD ROAD
BRENTWOOD ROAD
RIVER VIEW
CHADWELL BYPASS
HIGH HOUSE LANE
TURNPIKE LANE
GUN HILL
BLUE ANCHOR LANE
LOW STREET LANE
CHURCH ROAD
COOPERS SHAW ROAD
RECTORY ROAD
BIGGIN LANE
SANDY LANE
HORNSBY LANE
GF GG GH GJ GK GL GM
64 65 66
76 77 78 79 80 81 82 83 84

AS
AT
AU
AV
AW
AX
AY
174
85
86
87
88
89
90
91
92
93
94
74
73
72
71
98
99
00
ALBERT ROAD
A308
ROYAL GARDENS
Glasshouses
DATCHET RD
DUNBOYNE PL
Manor Farm
Ham Bridge
NEW CUT
Filter Beds
Weir
ISLAND
HAM LANE
Sludge Beds
Sunnymeads
Sailing Club
Clayhall Farm
HOLLY DRIVE
Battle Bourne
St. George's Farm
Old Windsor Lock
The Manor
REMENHAM PARK
PARK AVENUE
ENGLISH GDNS
THE DRIVE
WELLEY ROAD
B376
CLAYHALL LANE
Moat
Tileplace Farm
STRAIGHT ROAD
Hall
Lib
ALLOT
CROFT CORNER
CHURCH ROAD
Anglo Saxon Palace (site of)
The Priory
Priory Stables
OLD FERRY DRIVE
KINGSWOOD CREEK
PETERSHILL COPSE
MILLERS LANE
Peter's Hill
OLD WINDSOR
Tenn Cts
Pav
NEWMEADOWS PLANTATION
Prim Sch
The Oxford Blue PH
CRIMP HILL
Mount Place
SAXON WAY
THE FRIARY
FRIARY ISLAND
COLNE VALLEY REGIONAL PARK
FAIRFIELD APPROACH
NURSERY WY
Prim Sch
The George Inn PH
WINDSOR ROAD
ST. ANDREW'S CL
WHARF ROAD
RIVERSIDE
OUSELEY ROAD
COPPICE DR
GARSON LANE
Moat
BEAR'S RAILS
CEM
RUSH POND
BURFIELD ROAD
Med Cen
KINGSBURY DR
Prim Sch
Burfield Lodge
Woodside Farm
RIVER THAMES
Bells of Ouzeley PH
THE EMBANKMENT
PRINCE OF WALES POND
THE LONG WALK
OLD WINDSOR WOOD
SL4
B3021
PELLING HILL
BEAUMONT HOUSE CONFERENCE CENTRE
War Memorial
WINDSOR ROAD
PATS CROFT EYOT
MAGNA CARTA LANE
MEDE CLOSE
WITHY BED
DUKE OF YORK PLANTATION
LIDDELL PLANTATION
Battersea Dogs & Cats Home
COOPER'S HILL SLOPES NT
MAGNA CARTA ISLAND
OLD COVERT
SPORTS GROUND
Tennis Courts
South Lodge Farm
RUNNYMEDE
WILD BOAR ENCLOSURE
PRINCE CONSORTS PLANTATION
SULTAN PLANTATION
Snow Hill
Home Farm
Sch
WINDSOR & MAIDENHEAD
SURREY
A328
John F Kennedy Memorial
Magna Carta Monument
Benedictine Nunnery (remains)
PRINCE OF WALES PLANTATION
QUEEN VICTORIA'S PLANTATION
Spring Hill
GORE PLANTATION
Beech Hill
Ridgemead House
PRIEST HILL
OAK LANE
Priest Hill Farm
Tennis Courts
Cookes Hill
Park Place
RIDGEMEAD ROAD
Brunel University, Runnymede Campus
Cooper's Hill Slopes
Main Gate Lodges
Bishops Gate
The Dell
Sch
Pumping Sta
COV RES
Royal Lodge
Chapel Lodge
BISHOPSGATE ROAD
Fox & Hounds PH
Bishopsgate House
Dell Park Farm
COOPER'S HILL COPPICE
Air Forces Memorial
COOPERS HILL LANE
CONSERVATORY COVERT
GREENBROOM COVERT
Round Oak
Castle Hill
HAM LANE
HOLLYCOMBE
SPORTS GROUND
Royal Holloway Coll (Hall of Residence)
KING GEORGE VI CORONATION GROVE
Tennis Courts
Savill Court Hotel
ENGLEFIELD GREEN
Castle Hill Farm
KINGSWOOD CL
RUNNYMEDE PARK
CUMBERLAND LODGE
Park Close
Englefield Green
The Barley Mow PH
TW20
Runnymede Park
PROSPECT LANE
BARLEY MOW ROAD
ST. JUDE'S ROAD
CHAPEL WOOD
Cumberland Gate
WILDERNESS
The Sun PH
KINGS LANE
WILLSON ROAD
BARNWAY
ALDERSIDE WALK
Health Cen
BOND STREET
WILLOW WK
VICTORIA STREET
ALBERT ROAD
Hall
Glasshouses
A30
Ripley Springs
Parkside House
Meadow Cottage Farm
MAGNA
OBELISK RIDE
MAIN RIDE
THE SAVILL GARDENS
LARCHWOOD
ST. JUDE'S CEMETERY
WINDSOR
SL5
SMITH'S LAWN
Visitor Centre
Parkwood
SPORTS GROUND
Prim Sch
Prim Sch
CORBY DRIVE
EGHAM HILL
University of London Royal Holloway College
CORK CLUMP
GREAT
ALDER COVERT
FUZZY CLUMP
Cumberland Obelisk
Prince Consort's Statue
OBELISK POND
PARK
SCARLETOAK PLANTATION
RHODODENDRON RIDE
FB
Blays House
Viatel
PRUNE HILL
Egham Wick
WICK LANE
WICK ROAD
ST DAVID'S DR
ROBERTS WY
SIMONS WALK
BAKEHAM LANE
LONDON ROAD
POLO GROUND
Flying Barn
EGHAM WICK PLANTATION
214
Breakheart Hill
Pav
Eton Bridge
Kurch Bri
0
500 yds
0
500 m
HEATHER GARDEN
DARKHOLE CLUMP
OUT HILLS

AZ
BA
BB
BC
BD
BE
BF
175
215
196
86
87
88
89
90
91
92
93
94
01
02
03
74
73
72
71
SL3
WRAYSBURY
RESERVOIR
TW19
TW18
Wraysbury
WRAYSBURY
COLNE VALLEY
REGIONAL PARK
KING
GEORGE VI
RESERVOIR
STAINES
MOOR
HERON
LAKE
Clubhouse
Junction
13
Hythe
End
RUNNYMEDE
PLEASURE
GROUND
RUNNYMEDE
NT
THE
ISLAND
WINDSOR ROAD
STAINES BYPASS
LONDON ROAD
THE CAUSEWAY
THE GLANTY
QUEENSMEAD
LAKE
ASHBY
REC GRD
Runnymede
Hotel
Bellweir
Lock
Pooley
Green
EGHAM
Egham Hythe
Thorpe
Lea
THORPE
LEA
REC GRD
BISHOPS WAY
REC
GRD
SPORTS
GROUND
EGHAM
PLAYING
FLD
Sports
Centre
Sailing
Club
Lower
Mill Farm
Hithermoor
Farm
Inlet
Pier
Moor
Farm
Two Rivers
Retail Park
The
Elmsleigh
Centre
Staines
Town FC
Mayflower
Nurseries
Mushroom
Farm
Glenville
Farm
Bowls
Club
Boathouse
Superstore
Travelodge
Gas Works
London
Stone
Monument
TRUSS'S
ISLAND
M25
A30
A308
A320
B376
B388
B3376
CHERTSEY
Crabtree

BG
BH
BJ
BK
BL
BM
BN
05
06
07
176
195
216
85
86
87
88
89
90
91
92
93
94
74
73
72
71
STANWELL MOOR
STANWELL
STAINES-UPON-THAMES
ASHFORD
TW19
TW17
TW18
KING GEORGE VI RESERVOIR
STAINES RESERVOIRS
QUEEN MARY
SPELTHORNE
SURREY
HILLINGDON
CARGO TERMINAL
BRITISH AIRWAYS CARGO CENTRE
Virgin Atlantic Cargo
BLACKBURN TRADING ESTATE
CAMGATE CENTRE
RECREATION GROUND
ASHFORD HOSPITAL
The Bull Dog
BURIAL GROUND
SPORTS GROUND
REC GROUND
H.M. Prison Bronzefield
SHORTWOOD COMMON
STAINES CEM
Crooked Billet Roundabout
Fordbridge Roundabout
FORDBRIDGE PARK
ASHFORD MANOR GOLF COURSE
Electricity Station
GRAVEL PIT
STAINES PARK MINI RAILWAY
Staines Town FC
Sweep's Bridge
Penton Hook Farm
Hengrove Farm
New Inn Farm
Shortwood Farm
Hithermoor Farm
Vermeulens Garden Centre
The Anchor PH
Superstore
STANWELL MOOR ROAD
LONDON ROAD
STAINES BYPASS
KINGSTON ROAD
CHURCH ROAD
SOUTHERN PERIMETER ROAD
BEDFONT ROAD
A3044
A30
A308
B378
B377
A3113
0 500 yds
0 500 m

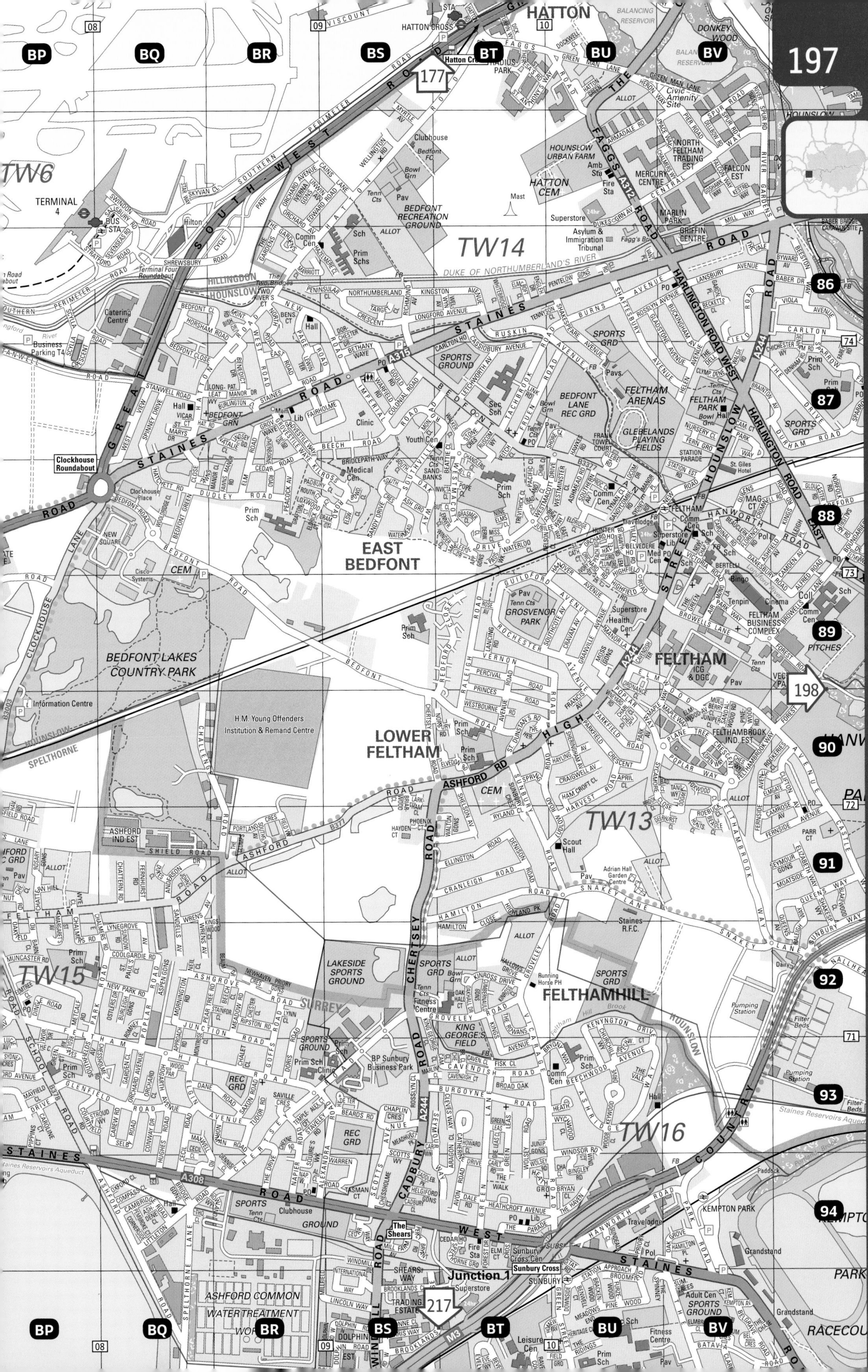
HATTON
HATTON CROSS
177
TW6
TERMINAL 4
TW14
HOUNSLOW URBAN FARM
HATTON CEM
BEDFONT RECREATION GROUND
NORTH FELTHAM TRADING EST
MERCURY CENTRE
MARLIN PARK
GRIFFIN CENTRE
Asylum & Immigration Tribunal
DUKE OF NORTHUMBERLAND'S RIVER
Clockhouse Roundabout
STAINES ROAD
GREAT SOUTH WEST ROAD
HARLINGTON ROAD WEST
HARLINGTON ROAD EAST
HOUNSLOW ROAD
BEDFONT LANE REC GRD
FELTHAM ARENAS
GLEBELANDS PLAYING FIELDS
EAST BEDFONT
BEDFONT LAKES COUNTRY PARK
Information Centre
H.M. Young Offenders Institution & Remand Centre
GROSVENOR PARK
FELTHAM
FELTHAMBROOK IND. EST
LOWER FELTHAM
198
TW13
ASHFORD IND EST
TW15
LAKESIDE SPORTS GROUND
FELTHAMHILL
KING GEORGE'S FIELD
BP Sunbury Business Park
TW16
KEMPTON PARK
Sunbury Cross
Junction 1
217
ASHFORD COMMON WATER TREATMENT WORKS
BP BQ BR BS BT BU BV
86 87 88 89 90 91 92 93 94

BW
BX
BY
BZ
CA
CB
CC
178
197
218
TW3
TW4
TW12
TW13
TW14
TW16
HOUNSLOW HEATH
HOUNSLOW HEATH GOLF COURSE
WHITTON
BOROUGH CEMETERY
TWICKENHAM CEMETERY
CRANE PARK
HANWORTH PARK
HANWORTH
FULWELL PARK
FULWELL GOLF COURSE
TWICKENHAM PARK GOLF CENTRE
KEMPTON PARK
KEMPTON PARK RESERVOIRS
HALF MOON COVERT
HAMPTON
HAMPTON TRADING ESTATE
HAMPTON BUSINESS PARK
MILL FARM BUSINESS PARK
FELTHAM BUSINESS COMPLEX
CENTRAL PARK EST
NORTH FELTHAM TRADING EST
KINGSWAY BUSINESS PARK
APEX RETAIL PARK
West Thames Coll
Crematorium
Recreation Centre
Sorting Office
STAINES ROAD
UXBRIDGE ROAD
HANWORTH ROAD
HOUNSLOW ROAD
HARLINGTON ROAD EAST
HARLINGTON ROAD WEST
GREAT CHERTSEY ROAD
HAMPTON ROAD WEST
TWICKENHAM RD
SUNBURY WAY
COUNTRY WAY
HIGH STREET
HOSPITAL BRIDGE ROAD
A312
A314
A315
A316
A244
A313
A311
85
86
87
88
89
90
91
92
93
94
0
500 yds
500 m

TW9
TW6
TW2
TW1
TW10
TW11
KT2
OLD DEER PARK RECREATION GROUND
MOGDEN SEWAGE TREATMENT WORKS
ST. MARGARETS
St. Margarets Roundabout
Whitton Rd Roundabout
London Road Roundabout
THE RUGBY FOOTBALL UNION TWICKENHAM
Royal Military Sch of Music
RICHMOND UPON THAMES COLLEGE
Twickenham Stoop Stadium
RICHMOND GREEN
RICHMOND
MARBLE HILL
MARBLE HILL HOUSE PARK
PETERSHAM MEADOWS
GLOVER'S ISLAND
MEADOWBANK
RIVER THAMES
EEL PIE ISLAND
TWICKENHAM
HAM HOUSE (NT)
HAM HOUSE GARDENS
KING GEORGE'S FIELD
TWICKENHAM RIFLE CLUB
HAM
HAM COMMON
ST. MICHAEL'S CONVENT
THE COPSE
STRAWBERRY HILL
STRAWBERRY HILL GOLF COURSE
TEDDINGTON CEM
St. Mary's Coll
Thames Young Mariners Base
Teddington Lock
Teddington Weir
Teddington Studios
TROWLOCK ISLAND
TEDDINGTON
HAMPTON HILL
CANAL PLANTATION
NATIONAL PHYSICAL LABORATORY
BUSHY HOUSE
ROUND PLANTATION
BUSHY PARK
BROOM CLUMPS
WATERHOUSE WOODLAND GARDEN
OVAL PLANTATION
HAMPTON
LEG OF MUTTON POND
STEVEN'S EYOT
BROOM ROAD REC GRD
THE CASSEL
RICHMOND GOLF C
Open during daylight hours only
179
200
219
86
87
88
89
90
91
92
93
94
CD
CE
CF
CG
CH
CJ
CK

RICHMOND PARK
TW10
SW14
KT2
RICHMOND
PETERSHAM
HAM COMMON
COOMBE
EAST SHEEN
NORTH SHEEN
Richmond Circus
UPPER RICHMOND ROAD WEST
SHEEN ROAD
PESTHOUSE COMMON
EAST SHEEN COMMON (NT)
EAST SHEEN CEMETERY
RICHMOND CEMETERY
PALEWELL COMMON
PALEWELL PLAYING FIELDS
TECK PLANTATION
SHEEN WOOD
ADAM'S POND
The Bog
SHEEN CROSS WOOD
SAWYER'S HILL
POLO FIELD
CONDUIT WOOD
BISHOP'S PONDS
Richmond Gate
BARN WOOD POND
SAW PIT PLANTATION
Open during daylight hours only
KIDNEY WOOD
JUBILEE PLANTATION
QUEEN'S RIDE
WHITE LODGE PLANTATIONS
DUCHESS WOOD
The Royal Ballet Sch
SIDMOUTH WOOD
KING HENRY VIII MOUND
QUEEN ELIZABETH'S PLANTATION
LEG OF MUTTON POND
PEN PONDS
DEER PARK
TREEBOX WOOD
KING GEORGE V JUBILEE PLANTATION
SPANKER'S HILL WOOD
Pembroke Lodge
PETERSHAM PARK
LAWN PLANTATION
POND PLANTATION
White Ash Lodge
CYCLE PATH
HORSE RIDE
Tercentenary Plantation
RICHMOND GOLF COURSE
The Wilderness
Pond Slade
MARTIN'S POND
PRINCE CHARLES'S SPINNEY
Robin Hood Gate
HAM CROSS PLANTATION
GIBBET WOOD
Ham Bottom
ISABELLA PLANTATION
Broomfield Hill
Kingston Uni (Dorich House)
BROOMFIELD HILL PLANTATION
PEG'S POND
THOMSON'S POND
STILL POND
Ham Gate
Ham Cross
Ham Dip
HIGH WOOD
Deer Fold
HORNBEAM WALK
CORONATION PLANTATION
DANN'S POND
The Flat
Thatchedhouse Lodge
Ladderstile Gate
GALLOW'S POND
Kings Clump
Dark Hill
Kingston Gate
Kingston University (Kingston Hill)
COOMBE HILL GOLF COURSE
COOMBE WOOD GOLF COURSE
KINGSTON HILL
ROBIN HOOD WAY
ROBIN HOOD LANE
RICHMOND ROAD
PETERSHAM ROAD
UPPER HAM RD
HAM GATE AVENUE
KINGSTON UPON THAMES
Ormeley Lodge
PETERSHAM MEADOWS
GLOVER'S ISLAND
MEADOWBANK
Royal Star & Garter Home
American Uni in London
Richmond Hill Hotel
TERRACE FIELD
TERRACE GDNS
POPPY FACTORY MUS
KINGSTON HOSPITAL
Kingston Lodge Hotel
BROOM ROAD REC GRD
STEVEN'S EYOT
CANBURY GDNS
COOMBE LANE WEST
NORBITON
CL
CM
CN
CP
CQ
CR
CS
85
86
87
88
89
90
91
92
93
94
180
199
220
0
500 yds
500 m

CT
CU
CV
CW
CX
CY
CZ
181
202
221
86
87
88
89
90
91
92
93
94
ROEHAMPTON
PUTNEY
WANDSWORTH
SW15
SW18
SW19
SW20
PUTNEY HEATH
WIMBLEDON
COMMON
WIMBLEDON PARK
PUTNEY VALE
COPSE HILL
COTTENHAM PARK
ROEHAMPTON GOLF COURSE
Southlands College
Digby Stuart College
Roehampton University
Froebel College
QUEEN MARY'S UNI HOSP
ROEHAMPTON PLAYING FIELDS
Roehampton Uni-Whitelands College
S. Thames Coll Downshire Ho
Kingsfarm Plantation
RICHMOND PARK GOLF COURSE
Jerry's Hill
Crematorium
PUTNEY VALE CEMETERY
WINDMILL MUSEUM
LONDON SCOTTISH GOLF COURSE
Queen's Butt (Site of)
Gravelly Hill
Farm Bog
Farm Ravine
Caesar's Camp
Fishponds Wood Nature Reserve
ROYAL WIMBLEDON GOLF COURSE
Shadwell Wood
CANNIZARO PARK
Cannizaro House Hotel
LADY JANE'S WOOD
WOLFSON NEUROREHAB CENTRE
OBERON PLAYING FIELD
SPORTS GROUND
ROYAL HOSPITAL
Tibbet's Corner
Roehampton Lane
Stag Lane
Coombe Lane
PARKSIDE HOSPITAL
Parkside Oncology Clinic
BLUEGATE GRAVEL PIT (DISUSED)
HOOKHAMSLADE POND
RUSHMERE POND
KING'S MERE
QUEEN'S MERE
ALL ENGLAND LAWN TENNIS & CROQUET CLUB
WIMBLEDON PARK GOLF COURSE
WIMBLEDON PARK Stadium
SOUTHFIELDS
WIMBLEDON PARK EST
St. Cecilia's Wandsworth Sch
DUNDONALD REC GRD
King's Coll Sch
KINGSTON ROAD
UPPER RICHMOND ROAD
WIMBLEDON PARK SIDE
PARKSIDE
HIGH ST WIMBLEDON
WIMBLEDON HILL RD
ROEHAMPTON LANE
PUTNEY HILL
KINGSTON VALE
WEST HILL
A3
A205
A219
A218
A238
A306
A3209

DA
DB
DC
DD
DE
DF
DG
182
201
222
85
86
87
88
89
90
91
92
93
94
WANDSWORTH
SW11
SW18
SW19
SW17
SOUTHFIELDS
EARLSFIELD
SUMMERSTOWN
WIMBLEDON PARK
UPPER TOOTING
BALHAM
TOOTING GRAVENEY
COLLIER'S WOOD
SOUTH WIMBLEDON
FURZE
CLAPHAM JUNCTION
Wandsworth Town
Wandsworth Common
WANDSWORTH COMMON
H.M. PRISON WANDSWORTH
WANDSWORTH CEMETERY
SPENCER PARK
KING GEORGE'S PARK
SPRINGFIELD HOSPITAL
CENTRAL LONDON GOLF CENTRE
GARRATT GREEN
STREATHAM CEMETERY
WIMBLEDON STADIUM
WIMBLEDON CEMETERY
LAMBETH CEMETERY
ST. GEORGE'S HOSPITAL
Uni of London Med Sch
WANDLE MEADOW NAT. PK
LONDON ROAD CEMETERY
FIGGE'S MARSH
Tooting Bec
Tooting Bdy
TOOTING BROADWAY
WIMBLEDON
WIMB. BR
MERTON INDUSTRIAL PARK
TRINITY ROAD
GARRATT LANE
MERTON ROAD
DURNSFORD ROAD
HAYDONS ROAD
BROADWAY
MERANTUN WAY
MITCHAM ROAD
BALHAM HIGH ROAD
UPPER TOOTING ROAD
WEST HILL
WANDSWORTH HIGH ST
ARMOURY WAY
BATTERSEA RISE
CLAPHAM COMMON W SIDE
500 yds
500 m

DH
DJ
DK
DL
DM
DN
DP
183
CLAPHAM COMMON
SW4
CLAPHAM PARK
BRIXTON
SW2
SE24
BROCKWELL PARK
STREATHAM HILL
SE21
TULSE HILL
Tulse Hill
TOOTING BEC COMMON
TOOTING GRAVENEY COMMON
STREATHAM PARK
STREATHAM
SE27
WEST NORWOOD
WEST NORWOOD CEMETERY
204
SW16
STREATHAM COMMON
NORWOOD GROVE RECREATION GROUND
SE19
STREATHAM VALE
NORBURY PARK
NORBURY
223
86
87
88
89
90
91
92
93
94
29
30
31
71
72
73
74

DQ
DR
DS
DT
DU
DV
DW
184
203
224
SE24
SE22
SE21
SE27
SE26
SE19
SE20
HERNE HILL
EAST DULWICH
DULWICH
TULSE HILL
WEST DULWICH
WEST NORWOOD
UPPER SYDENHAM
SYDENHAM
NORWOOD
NORWOOD NEWTOWN
UPPER NORWOOD
PENGE
BROCKWELL PARK
PECKHAM RYE COMMON
PECKHAM RYE PARK
CAMBERWELL OLD CEMETERY
DULWICH PARK
DULWICH & SYDENHAM HILL GOLF COURSE
SYDENHAM HILL WOOD (NATURE RESERVE)
DULWICH WOOD
WEST NORWOOD CEMETERY
NORWOOD PARK
CRYSTAL PALACE PARK
CRYSTAL PALACE NATIONAL SPORTS CENTRE
HERNE HILL VELODROME
DULWICH COMMUNITY HOSP
DULWICH PICTURE GALL
HORNIMAN MUS
HORNIMAN GDNS
WESTOW PARK
UPPER NORWOOD REC GRD
SOUTH BANK UNIVERSITY SPORTS GROUND
PECKHAM
RYE
SOUTHWARK
LAMBETH
LEWISHAM
CROYDON
Tulse Hill
Forest Hill
The Grove
85
86
87
88
89
90
91
92
93
94
33
34
35
71
72
73
74
0
500 yds
500 m

DX
DY
DZ
EA
EB
EC
ED
185
LEWISHAM
HILLY FIELDS
BROCKLEY
BROCKLEY CEMETERY
LADYWELL CEMETERY
SE4
LADYWELL
UNIVERSITY HOSPITAL LEWISHAM
LEWISHAM PARK
SE13
MANOR PARK
HITHER GREEN
CAMBERWELL NEW CEMETERY
Honor Oak Crematorium
HONOR OAK SPORTS GRD
KING'S COLLEGE SPORTS GRD
HONOR OAK PARK
BLYTHE HILL FIELDS
LADYWELL FIELDS
MOUNTFIELD PARK PLAYING FIELDS
SE23
BROCKLEY HILL PARK
Catford Gyratory
CATFORD
BROWNHILL ROAD
S CIRCULAR ROAD
STANSTEAD ROAD
A205 (SOUTH CIRCULAR ROAD)
FOREST HILL
SE6
CATFORD HILL
BROMLEY ROAD
PERRY HILL
BELL GREEN
BELLINGHAM
FORSTER MEMORIAL PARK
SPORTS GROUND
206
LOWER SYDENHAM
SOUTHEND
SOUTHEND LANE
HOME PARK
BECKENHAM HILL
BECKENHAM PLACE PARK
GOLF COURSE
SUMMERHOUSE HILL WOOD
ASH PLANTATION
LEWISHAM BOROUGH SPORTS GROUND
MIDLAND BANK SPORTS GROUND
WARREN AVE PLAYING FIELDS
NEW BECKENHAM
KENT C.C.C.
CRYSTAL PALACE FC TRAINING GROUND
ROYAL BANK OF SCOTLAND SPORTS GOUND
BR3
BR2
CATOR PARK
BECKENHAM
LEWISHAM
BROMLEY
SHORTLANDS GOLF COURSE
BROMLEY PARK
THE SLOANE HOSPITAL
225
86
87
88
89
90
91
92
93
94

EE
EF
EG
EH
EJ
EK
EL
186
85
86
87
88
89
90
91
92
93
94
205
226
SE13
SE12
SE6
BR1
BR2
HITHER GREEN
GROVE PARK
MOTTINGHAM
ELTHAM
DOWNHAM
PLAISTOW
SUNDRIDGE
ELMSTEAD
Widmore Green
BROMLEY PARK
Lee Green
Clifton's Roundabout
Yorkshire Grey
MANOR PARK
MANOR HOUSE GARDENS
HITHER GREEN CEMETERY
Crematorium
NORTHBROOK PARK
SUTCLIFFE PARK
OLD COLFEIANS SPORTS GROUND
MIDDLE PARK FIELD
QUEENSCROFT REC GRD
KING JOHN PLAYING FIELDS
MOTTINGHAM SPORTS GROUND
CHINBROOK ESTATE
CHINBROOK MEADOWS
LOWER MARVELS WOOD
GROVE PARK CEMETERY
ELMSTEAD WOOD
SUNDRIDGE PARK GOLF COURSE
Sundridge Park Manor
ROCKPIT WOOD
LOGSHILL WOOD
DOWNHAM FIELDS
DOWNHAM PLAYING FIELDS
SHAFTESBURY PARK REC GRD
KING'S MEADOW PLAYING FIELDS
LEWISHAM BOROUGH SPORTS GROUND
MIDLAND BANK SPORTS GROUND
WARREN AVE PLAYING FIELDS
SHORTLANDS GOLF
THE SLOANE HOSPITAL
FORSTER MEMORIAL PARK
UNI OF GREENWICH ATHLETIC GRD
ELTHAM PALACE
BURNT ASH HILL
BARING ROAD
WESTHORNE AVENUE
S CIRCULAR ROAD
ST MILDREDS ROAD
SIDCUP ROAD
ELTHAM ROAD
ROCHESTER WAY
KIDBROOKE PARK
BROMLEY ROAD
LONDON ROAD
BURNT ASH LANE
COLLEGE RD
BROMLEY NORTH
SUNDRIDGE PARK
GROVE PARK
Quaggy River
500 yds
500 m

EM
EN
EP
EQ
ER
ES
ET
187
208
227
DA16
DA15
DA14
SE9
BR7
ELTHAM
ELTHAM PARK SOUTH
ELTHAM WARREN GOLF COURSE
ROCHESTER WAY RELIEF ROAD
EAST ROCHESTER WAY
BEXLEY ROAD
BLACKFEN ROAD
AVERY HILL
AVERY HILL PARK
University of Greenwich Avery Hill Campus
CAMBRIDGE MISSION SPORTS GROUND
CHARLTON ATHLETIC FC TRAINING GRD
MILLWALL FC TRAINING GRD
FOOTSCRAY PLAYING FIELDS
FOOTSCRAY ROAD
ROYAL BLACKHEATH GOLF COURSE
TARN BIRD SANCTUARY
BLACKFEN
HOLLY OAK WOOD PK
LAMORBEY
OLD FARM PARK
KING GEORGE'S REC GRD
NEW ELTHAM
SIDCUP ROAD
LONGLANDS
JACK NICKLAUS GOLF CENTRE
FLAMINGO PK SPORTS GRD
LONGLANDS REC GRD
MAIN ROAD
SIDCUP
SIDCUP BYPASS
STATION ROAD
BELMONT LANE OPEN SPACE
Kemnal Manor Stables
Beaver's Wood
CHISLEHURST CEMETERY
Hoblands Wood
OLD ELTHAMIANS SPORTS GRD
UNIVERSITY COLLEGE LONDON SPORTS GRD
Frognal Corner
QUEEN MARY'S HOSP
SCADBURY PARK NATURE RESERVE
LITTLE WOOD
Perry Street Shaw
Bushy Clump
Icehouse Wood
PARK WOOD
Scadbury Moated Manor House Site
Holbrook Wood
CHISLEHURST WEST
WHYTES WOODLAND
Bird Sanctuary
CHISLEHURST
CAMDEN PARK
CHISLEHURST GOLF COURSE
CHISLEHURST COMMON
WHITE HORSE HILL
RED HILL
HIGH STREET
PERRY STREET
BROMLEY LANE
ROYAL PAR
ST. PAULS
WATTS LANE
BROMLEY HILL
86
87
88
89
90
91
92
93
94

EU
EV
EW
EX
EY
EZ
FA
188
207
228
85
86
87
88
89
90
91
92
93
94
47
48
49
74
73
72
71
DA16
DANSON
PARK
THE LAKE
The Boathouse
Danson Mansion
Bexley Grammar Sch
DA6
BEXLEYHEATH
Bowling Alley
The Mall Bexleyheath
BROADWAY
PLAYING FIELD
BEXLEYHEATH GOLF COURSE
ROCHESTER WAY
Danson Interchange
BLACKFEN
HOLLY OAK WOOD PK
PENHILL PARK
BEXLEY PARK WOOD
RIVERSIDE WALK
SIDCUP GOLF COURSE
DA15
LAMORBEY
Rose Bruford College
LAMORBEY PARK
RUTLAND SHAW
ALBANY PARK
ABBEYHILL PARK
DA5
Bexley Cricket Club
KING GEORGE'S REC GRD
SIDCUP
Sidcup Arts Cen
WARING PARK
GOLDSMITH COLLEGE SPORTS GRD
THE ALDERS
NORTH CRAY
NORTH CRAY WOOD
STABLE MEADOW
DA14
FOOTS CRAY MEADOWS
Foots Cray Place
Five Arch Bridge
GATTONS WOOD
SIDCUP PLACE
Sixth Form College
QUEEN MARY'S HOSP
Frognal Corner
SIDCUP TECHNOLOGY CENTRE
SPORTS GRD
RUXLEY CORNER INDUSTRIAL ESTATE
Ruxley Corner
GARDEN SHAW
FOOTS CRAY
SCADBURY PARK
NATURE RESERVE
LITTLE WOOD
Spring Shaw
Bank's Shaw
BLACK CLUMP
Crittall's Corner
RUXLEY WOOD
Ruxley Manor Garden Centre
BR5
SIDCUP BYPASS
A20
A2
A210
A221
A222
A223
A224
A211
A207
Scadbury Moated Manor House Site
Field Study Centre
RUXLEY PARK GOLF COURSE
CRAYFIELDS BUSINESS PARK
0 500 yds
0 500 m

FB
FC
FD
FE
FF
FG
FH
189
BARNES CRAY
Woolwich
WATLING STREET
A207
LONDON ROAD (WATLING STREET)
MARTENS GROVE PARK
SPORTS GRD
BURIAL GRD
BAKERS FIELD
Clubhouse
Gas Works
SHENSTONE PARK
BIGS HILL WOOD
CRAYFORD HIGH ST
CRAYFORD INDUSTRIAL ESTATE
ACORN INDUSTRIAL PARK
Tower Retail Park
CRAYFORD MARSHES
DA1
Stanham River
River Cray
LONDON LOOP / CRAY RIVERWAY
CRAYFORD ROAD
A207
DARTFORD ROAD (WATLING STREET)
CRAYFORD
BOURNE ROAD
A223
GRAVEL HILL
A220
Crayford Commercial Centre
CRAYFORD GREYHOUND STADIUM
Leisure Centre
Superstores
STATION APP
CRAYFORD
SPORTS GROUND
HALL PLACE
Hall Place Nursery
HALL PLACE GARDENS
Black Prince Interchange
Holiday Inn
Clubhouse
RUGBY GRD
ST. MARY'S REC GRD
OLD BEXLEY BUSINESS PARK
EAST ROCHESTER WAY
A2
QUARRY
OLD BEXLEY
THE OLD ORCHARD
Recycling Cen
CHURCHFIELD WOOD
Nature Reserve
SPORTS GROUND
SPORTS GRD
PRINCES ROAD
B2174
86
87
88
89
90
91
92
93
94
SHEPHERDS LANE
A2018
DARTFORD HEATH
DARTFORD BYPASS
OLD BEXLEY LANE
Dartford Heath
Dartford Heath Retail Park
DARTFORD GOLF COURSE
BRICKHILL WOOD
Clubhouse
North West Kent College
210
VICARAGE ROAD
DARTFORD ROAD
A2018
Coldblow
OLD BEXLEY LANE
Equestrian Centre
Littleworth Nursery
CAVEY'S SPRING
Electricity Station
Bracton Centre
DARTFORD HEATH
Horse & Groom PH
Clubhouse
SPORTS GROUND
TILE KILN LANE
SPORTS GROUND
Nursery
Turnagain Farm
HOOK GREEN LANE
Hook Green Farm
Hook Green
Hook Green Dairy
JOYDEN'S WOOD
JOYDENS WOOD
Ashlea Nurseries
DA2
Rowan Stables
ROWHILL WOOD
Piggery
Rowhill Grange Hotel
Oakleigh Farm
Wood End Farm
Joydens Wood
BIRCHWOOD PARK GOLF CENTRE
DRIVING RANGE
Clubhouse
Stonehill Woods Park
CIRCULAR PERMITTED HORSE RIDE
Stanhill Farm
ROWHILL WOOD
Furness Sch
DARTFORD
SEVENOAKS
Hextable
SPORTS GROUND
BR8
Malt House Farm
Recreation Ground
Barn End Farm
Youth Cen
Stonehill Farm
Lumbersland
Upper Ruxley Farm
Timbertops Farm
KENT
HEXTABLE GDNS
College Road Nursery
229
Glasshouse
Pembroke House
Swanley New Barn Railway
SWANLEY
Highlands Farm
Swanley Village
B2173
B258
50
51
52
71
72
73
74

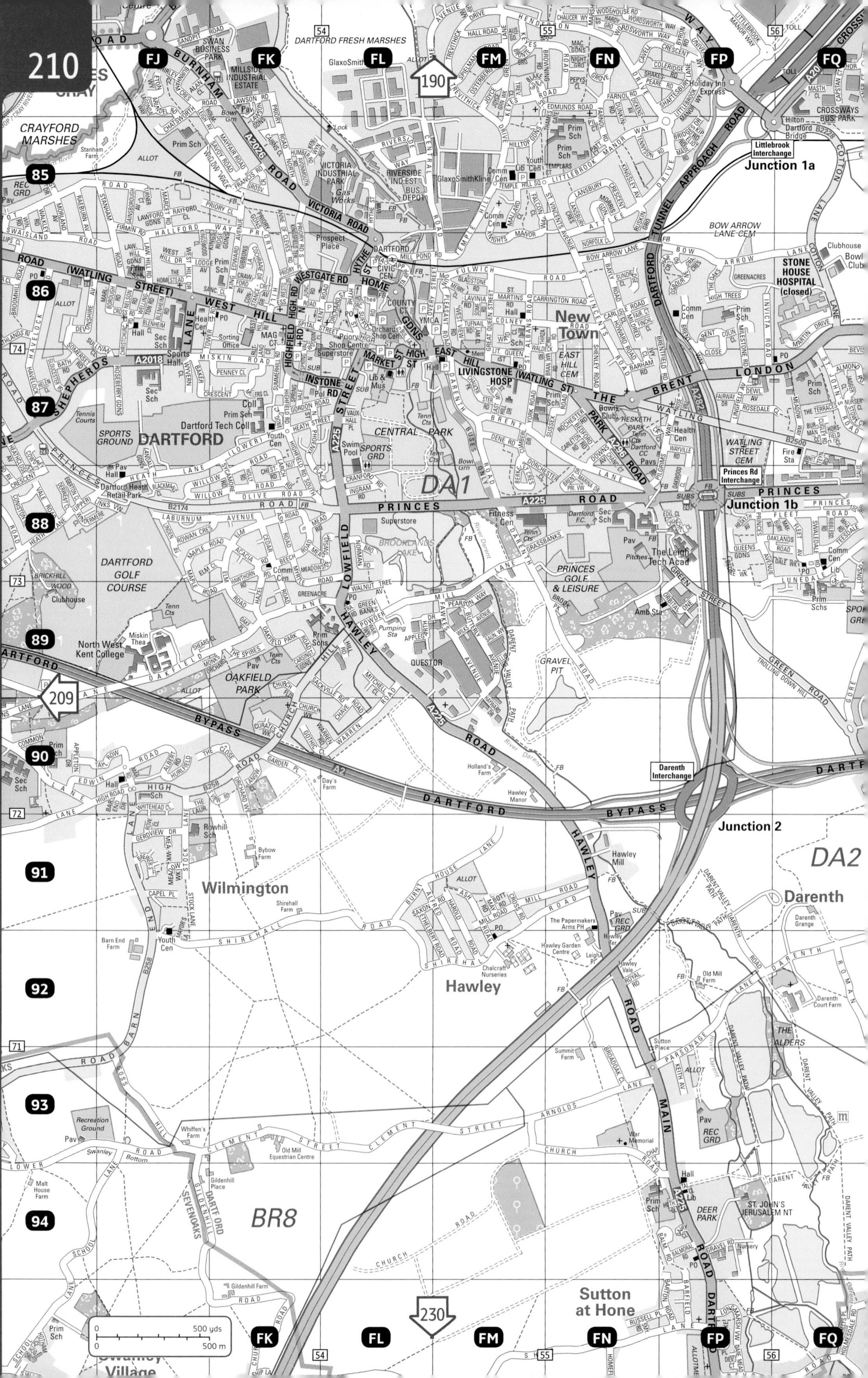
DARTFORD FRESH MARSHES
CRAYFORD MARSHES
190
209
230
FJ
FK
FL
FM
FN
FP
FQ
54
55
56
71
72
73
74
85
86
87
88
89
90
91
92
93
94
BURNHAM ROAD
A2026
SWAN BUSINESS PARK
MILLSIDE INDUSTRIAL ESTATE
GlaxoSmithKline
VICTORIA INDUSTRIAL PARK
RIVERSIDE IND EST
Gas Works
VICTORIA ROAD
Prospect Place
DARTFORD
CIVIC CEN
HOME GDNS
COUNTY CT
YMCA
Orchards Shop Cen
Priory Shop Centre
Superstore
MARKET ST
HIGH ST
EAST HILL
WEST HILL
WATLING STREET
SHEPHERDS LANE
A2018
HIGHFIELD RD
Sorting Office
MAG CT
Lib & Mus
INSTONE RD
LOWFIELD STREET
A225
CENTRAL PARK
Dartford Tech Coll
SPORTS GROUND
DARTFORD
Dartford Heath Retail Park
B2174
PRINCES ROAD
DA1
Fitness Cen
Dartford F.C.
BROOKLANDS LAKE
DARTFORD GOLF COURSE
BRICKHILL WOOD
Clubhouse
North West Kent College
Miskin Thea
OAKFIELD PARK
HAWLEY ROAD
A225
QUESTOR
Pumping Sta
PRINCES GOLF & LEISURE
GRAVEL PIT
River Darent
The Leigh Tech Acad
New Town
EAST HILL CEM
LIVINGSTONE HOSP
THE BRENT
Bowls Club
Dartford CC
Health Cen
A282
DARTFORD TUNNEL APPROACH ROAD
BOW ARROW LANE CEM
STONE HOUSE HOSPITAL (closed)
Littlebrook Interchange
Junction 1a
Holiday Inn Express
Hilton Dartford Bridge
CROSSWAYS BUS PARK
B2228
LONDON ROAD
WATLING STREET CEM
Princes Rd Interchange
Junction 1b
B2500
Amb Sta
Prim Schs
GREEN STREET
TROLLING DOWN HILL
Darenth Interchange
Junction 2
DARTFORD BYPASS
A2
Holland's Farm
Hawley Manor
Hawley Mill
DA2
Darenth
Darenth Grange
Darenth Court Farm
THE ALDERS
Wilmington
Shirehall Farm
Bybow Farm
Rowhill Sch
Day's Farm
Barn End Farm
Youth Cen
B258
B2
Hawley
Chalcraft Nurseries
The Papermakers Arms PH
Hawley Garden Centre
Old Mill Farm
Sutton Place
Summit Farm
Whiffen's Farm
Old Mill Equestrian Centre
Recreation Ground
Malt House Farm
Gildenhill Place
Gildenhill Farm
BR8
DEER PARK
ST. JOHN'S JERUSALEM NT
REC GRD
War Memorial
Sutton at Hone
Swanley Village
0 500 yds
0 500 m

Crossways
THAMES EUROPORT
Johnson's Wharf
NEWTONS COURT
QUADRANT COURT
Superstore
191
CROSSWAYS BOULEVARD
ST. MARY'S ROAD
Travelodge
CHARLES STREET
STONE CROSSING
ELIZABETH STREET
Stone
ST. CLEMENTS WAY
GREENHITHE FOR BLUEWATER
LONDON ROAD
A226
NELSON HOUSE
Greenhithe
Knockhall
Clinic
Prim Sch
Comm Cen
Lib
SPORTS GRD
Gas Works
DA9
The Bull PH
PO
STONE REC GRD
Tenn Cts
Pav
Hall
Prim Sch
Stone Castle
SWANSCOMBE HERITAGE PARK
NAT RES
ALLOT
Leisure Centre
Bowl Grn
ALKERDEN LANE
Alkerden Farm
Western Cross Farm
MOUNTS ROAD
BLUEWATER PARKWAY
Bluewater Shopping Centre
THE VILLAGE
Cinema
Plaza
BUS STA
STONE CEM
DA10
WATLING STREET
A296
BUSES ONLY
DARENT VALLEY HOSPITAL
CHALK PIT
Bean Interchange
A2
DARTFORD BYPASS
DARENTH WOOD
DARENTH COUNTRY PARK
BURIAL GRD
Knoxfield Caravan Park
Arrow Riding & Carriage Driving Centre for the Disabled
THE THRIFT
The Royal Oak PH
Caravan Site
212
COV RES
Bean
Bean Farm
Badger's Mount
BEACON DRIVE
HIGH STREET
B255
Youth Club
Prim Sch
BEACON WOOD COUNTRY PARK
Cherwell Farm
LADIES WOOD
LORDS WOOD
WALLER PARK
Lane End
SANDY LANE
SOUTHFLEET ROAD
BETSHAM HILL
B262
HIGHCROSS
Betsham C.C.
DA13
Manor Farm Garden Centre
GREEN STREET GREEN ROAD
SANDBANKS
Green Street Green
SHELLBANK LANE
ST. MARGARET'S ROAD
St. Margaret's Farm
DA4
Westwood Farm
Wheatsheaf PH
HOOK GREEN ROAD
GILL'S ROAD
Gill's Farm
Walnut Tree Farm
Chalkcroft
Ryecroft Farm
231
DARTFORD SEVENOAKS
South Darenth
QUARRY
FR FS FT FU FV FW FX
57 58 59
86 87 88 89 90 91 92 93 94
73 72 71 74

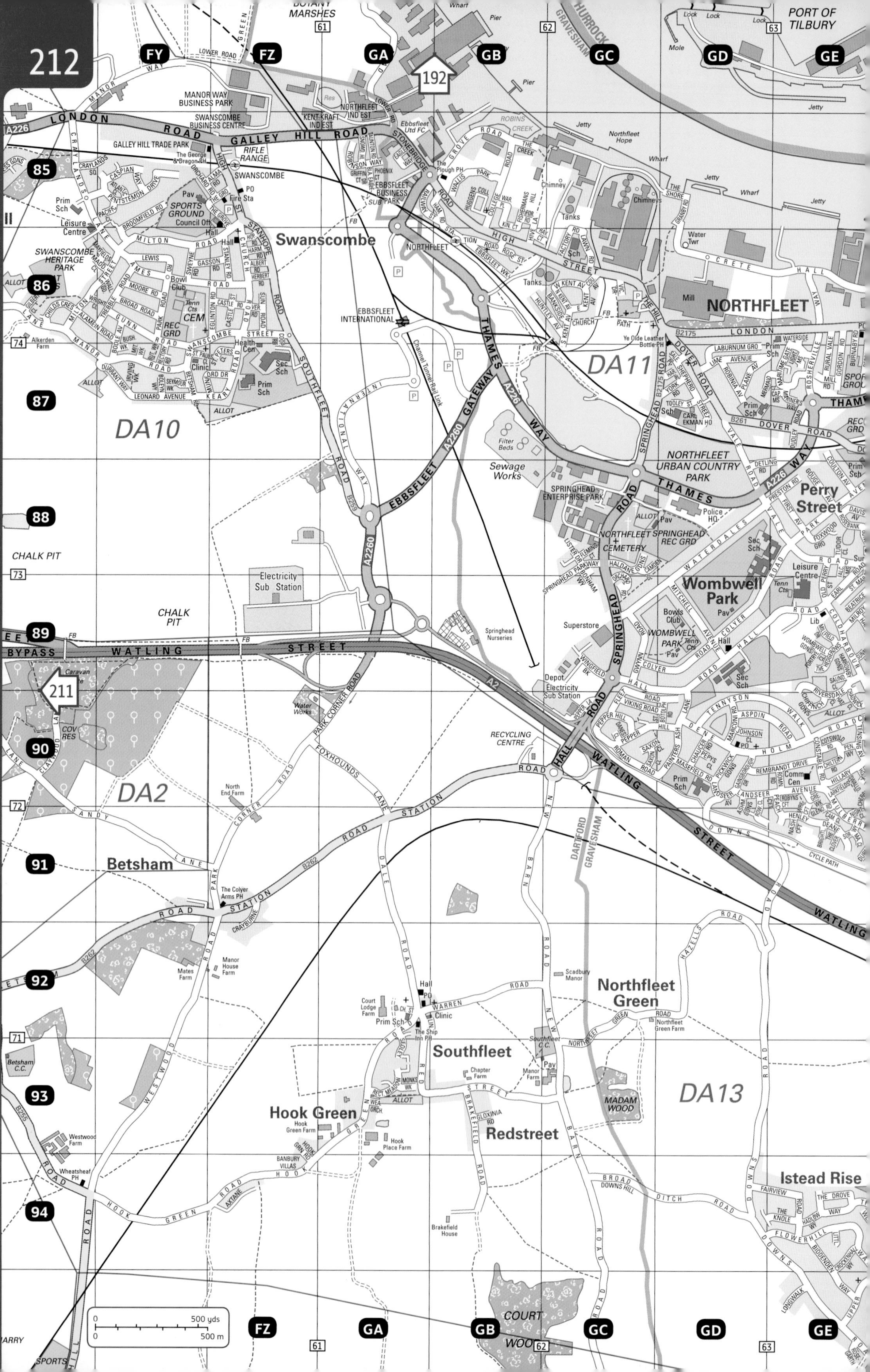
FY
FZ
GA
GB
GC
GD
GE
192
211
85
86
87
88
89
90
91
92
93
94
61
62
63
74
73
72
71
BOTANY MARSHES
PORT OF TILBURY
GRAVESHAM
MANOR WAY BUSINESS PARK
SWANSCOMBE BUSINESS CENTRE
GALLEY HILL TRADE PARK
NORTHFLEET IND EST
KENT KRAFT IND EST
Ebbsfleet Utd FC
LONDON ROAD
GALLEY HILL ROAD
RIFLE RANGE
SWANSCOMBE
EBBSFLEET BUSINESS PARK
Swanscombe
SPORTS GROUND
Leisure Centre
SWANSCOMBE HERITAGE PARK
Northfleet Hope
NORTHFLEET
EBBSFLEET INTERNATIONAL
Channel Tunnel Rail Link
DA10
DA11
DA2
DA13
THAMES WAY
EBBSFLEET GATEWAY
NORTHFLEET URBAN COUNTRY PARK
SPRINGHEAD ENTERPRISE PARK
Sewage Works
Filter Beds
NORTHFLEET CEMETERY
SPRINGHEAD REC GRD
Perry Street
Wombwell Park
CHALK PIT
Electricity Sub Station
Springhead Nurseries
Superstore
WATLING STREET
BYPASS
RECYCLING CENTRE
Water Works
North End Farm
STATION ROAD
Betsham
The Colyer Arms PH
Manor House Farm
Mates Farm
Scadbury Manor
Northfleet Green
Northfleet Green Farm
Court Lodge Farm
The Ship Inn PH
Southfleet
Chapter Farm
Manor Farm
MADAM WOOD
Hook Green
Hook Green Farm
Hook Place Farm
BANBURY VILLAS
Redstreet
Westwood Farm
Wheatsheaf PH
Brakefield House
Istead Rise
COURT WOOD
Betsham C.C.
Southfleet C.C.
DARTFORD
GRAVESHAM
CYCLE PATH
0
500 yds
0
500 m

RM18
RIVER THAMES
THURROCK
GRAVESHAM
GRAVESEND
Tilbury Fort
Riverside Rail Terminal
London International Cruise Terminal
ENTERPRISE DISTRIBUTION CENTRE
FORTRESS DISTRIBUTION PARK
RIVERSIDE BUSINESS CENTRE
193
Milton
Denton
Westcourt
Windmill Hill
Kings Farm
Parrock Farm
Riverview Park
Singlewell
Ifield
Thong
DA12
MID KENT GOLF COURSE
CLAYLANE WOOD
HUNTONDOWN WOOD
GRAVEHILL WOOD
TWENTY ACRE WOOD
WATLING STREET
WROTHAM ROAD
ROCHESTER ROAD
OVERCLIFFE
MILTON RD
OLD RD EAST
OLD RD WEST
SINGLEWELL ROAD
DENTON MARSHES
WESTCOURT MARSHES
The National Sea Training Centre
Metropolitan Police Specialist Training Centre
SINGLEWELL INFRASTRUCTURE MAINTENANCE DEPOT
GF
GG
GH
GJ
GK
GL
GM
86
87
88
89
90
91
92
93
94
64
65
66
A2
A226
A227

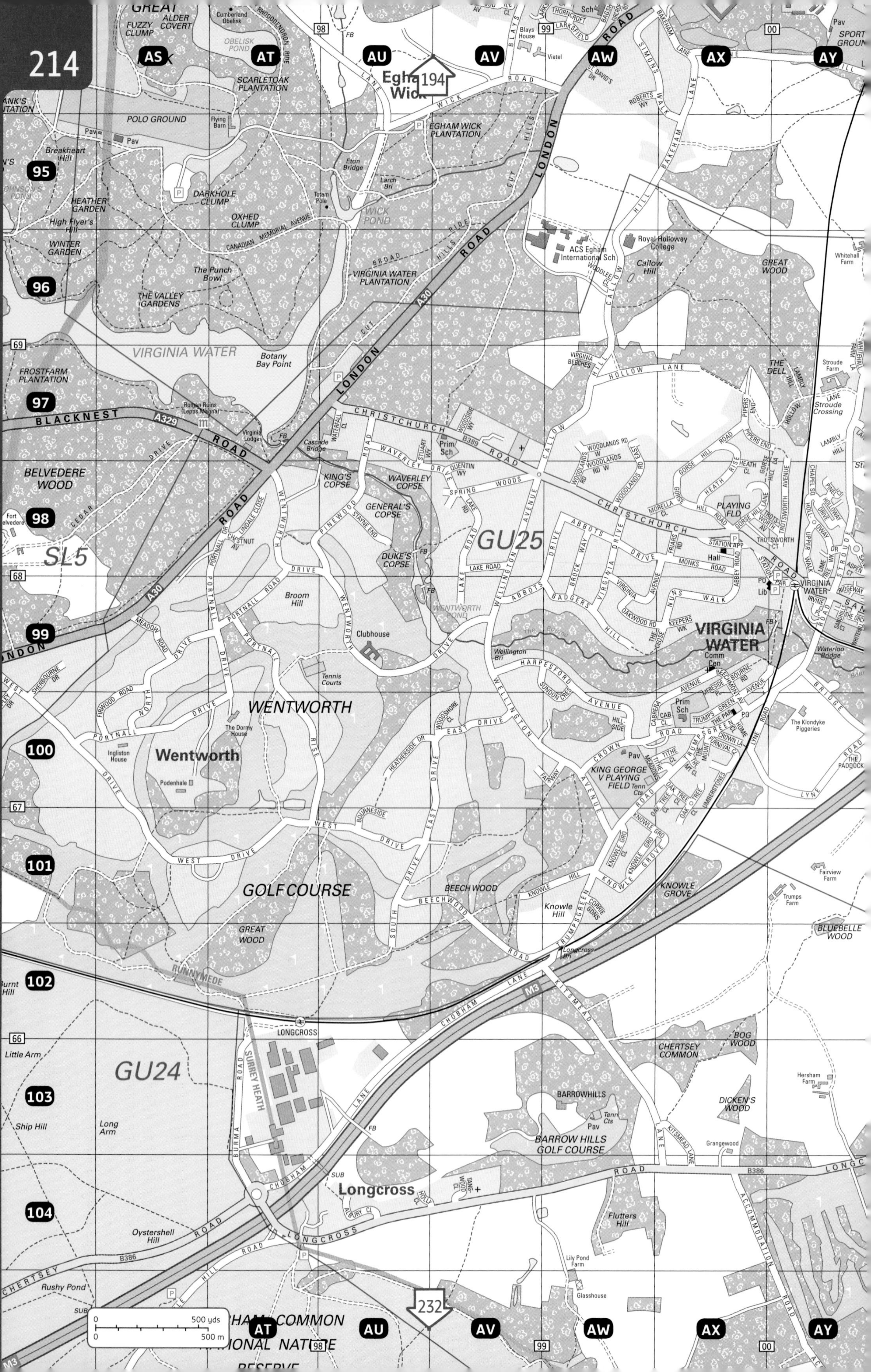
194
232
AS
AT
AU
AV
AW
AX
AY
95
96
97
98
99
100
101
102
103
104
SL5
GU25
GU24
GREAT ALDER COVERT
FUZZY CLUMP
Cumberland Obelisk
OBELISK POND
SCARLETOAK PLANTATION
POLO GROUND
Flying Barn
Pav
Breakheart Hill
HEATHER GARDEN
High Flyer's Hill
WINTER GARDEN
DARKHOLE CLUMP
OXHED CLUMP
CANADIAN MEMORIAL AVENUE
The Punch Bowl
THE VALLEY GARDENS
VIRGINIA WATER
Botany Bay Point
FROSTFARM PLANTATION
Totem Pole
WICK POND
Eton Bridge
Larch Bri
Egham Wick
EGHAM WICK PLANTATION
VIRGINIA WATER PLANTATION
BROAD HILLS RIDE
CUT HILLS
Blays House
Viatel
LONDON ROAD
A30
ROBERTS WY
BAKEHAM LANE
SIMONS WALK
ST DAVID'S DR
ACS Egham International Sch
Royal Holloway College
Callow Hill
GREAT WOOD
Whitehall Farm
SPORT GROUND
VIRGINIA BEECHES
HOLLOW LANE
THE DELL
Stroude Farm
Stroude Crossing
BLACKNEST ROAD
A329
Roman Ruins (Leptis Magna)
Virginia Lodge
Cascade Bridge
BELVEDERE WOOD
Fort Belvedere
CEDAR DRIVE
CHRISTCHURCH ROAD
B389
Prim Sch
KING'S COPSE
WAVERLEY COPSE
GENERAL'S COPSE
DUKE'S COPSE
SPRING WOODS
QUENTIN WY
LAKE ROAD
WELLINGTON AVENUE
ABBOTS DRIVE
BROCK WAY
VIRGINIA DRIVE
WOODLANDS RD
PIPERS END
GORSE HILL ROAD
HEATH RISE
PLAYING FLD
TROTSWORTH AVENUE
TROTSWORTH CT
STATION APP
Hall
MONKS ROAD
NUNS WALK
KEEPERS WK
OAKWOOD RD
BADGERS HILL
VIRGINIA WATER
PO
Lib
Comm Cen
Broom Hill
WENTWORTH DRIVE
PORTNALL DRIVE
PORTNALL ROAD
LINDALE CLOSE
CHESTNUT AV
MEADOW ROAD
Clubhouse
WENTWORTH POND
Wellington Bri
HARPESFORD AVENUE
Tennis Courts
WENTWORTH
The Dormy House
Wentworth
Ingliston House
Podenhale
FIRWOOD ROAD
NORTH DRIVE
SHERBOURNE DR
WEST DRIVE
EAST DRIVE
WOODSHORE CL
HEATHERSIDE DR
RISE
BOURNESIDE
SOUTH DRIVE
BEECHWOOD ROAD
BEECH WOOD
GOLF COURSE
GREAT WOOD
CROWN ROAD
Prim Sch
TRUMPS GREEN
KING GEORGE V PLAYING FIELD
Tenn Cts
Pav
FAIRWAY
KNOWLE HILL
KNOWLE GROVE
Knowle Hill
CORRIE GDNS
RUMPSGREEN
Longcross Bri
The Klondyke Piggeries
LYNE ROAD
LYNE LANE
Waterloo Bridge
Fairview Farm
Trumps Farm
BLUEBELLE WOOD
RUNNYMEDE
LONGCROSS
M3
CHOBHAM LANE
KITSMEAD LANE
CHERTSEY COMMON
BOG WOOD
Hersham Farm
DICKEN'S WOOD
BARROWHILLS
BARROW HILLS GOLF COURSE
Grangewood
SURREY HEATH
BURMA ROAD
Little Arm
Ship Hill
Long Arm
Longcross
CHOBHAM ROAD
B386
ROAD
ACCOMMODATION LANE
Flutters Hill
Lily Pond Farm
Glasshouse
Oystershell Hill
CHERTSEY ROAD
Rushy Pond
LONGCROSS ROAD
HILL ROAD
HAM COMMON NATIONAL NATURE RESERVE
0 500 yds
0 500 m
69
68
67
66
98
99
00

AZ
BA
BB
BC
BD
BE
BF
01
02
03
195
216
233
TW20
TW18
KT16
KT15
Stroude
Thorpe
Thorpe Green
THORPE GREEN
Lyne
CHERTSEY
ADDLESTONE CEMETERY
Great Fosters Hotel
Luddington House
Oaktree Nursery
Nursery
Crabtree Corner
THORPE INDUSTRIAL EST
EGHAM BUSINESS VILLAGE
TASIS England
Spring Farm
Manor Farm
Woodcock Farm
LONGSIDE LAKE
SPORTS GROUND
THE MOAT
WATER GARDENS
MANOR LAKE
THORPE PARK
Mountbatten Pavilion
ST. ANN'S LAKE
Abbey Lake
Britannia Arena
Fleet Lake
CEMEX UK
PENTON HOOK MARINA
PENTON HOOK ISLAND
Yacht Basin
PENTON PARK (Caravan Park)
TRUSS'S ISLAND
FISHING TEMPLE
Hurst Stud Farm
Home Farm
Rose & Crown PH
ANCHOR COPSE
St. Anne's Chapel (remains of)
Junction 2 (M3), Junction 12 (M25)
ST. ANN'S HILL PARK
Sludge Lagoons
Lyne Sewage Works
Filter Beds
Recycling Centre
Redlands Farm
Lyne Hill Farm
Ruxbury Farm
ELM FARM CARAVAN PARK
The Brooks Riding Centre
THE ROUGH
Almner Priory
Merrywood Farm
Lynefield Farm
Hillside Farm
Twynersh House PH
ABBEYFIELDS REC GRD
Chertsey Cricket Club
Chertsey Town FC
GOGMORE FM PK
Health Club
Lyne Court
Lyne Place Manor
Piggery
LYNE COPSE
RECREATION GROUND
Pantiles Nurseries
HERSHAM COPSE
FAN GROVE
FANGROVE PARK
Great Cockcrow Railway
Cockcrow Hill
Hardwick Court Farm
Lynwood Farm
Lyne Acres Farm
Trys Hill Farm
Fan Court
Squires Nursery
Westbrook Farm
Fox Hills Farm
White Lodge Centre
RUNNYMEDE HOSP
ST. PETER'S HOSP
Silverlands Farm
FOXHILLS GOLF COURSE
Clubhouse
Foxhills Country Club
Foxhills
Botleys Mansion
HOME WOOD
HOMEWOOD PARK
Hillswood Business
Kitchenride Corner
Pannells Farm
Woodside Farm
Junction 11
ALLOTMENTS
SPORTS GROUND
REC GRD
Sec Sch
M25
M3
A320
B388
B389
B386
A317
B375
STAINES ROAD
CHERTSEY LANE
GUILDFORD ROAD
MILL HOUSE LANE
THORPE BYPASS
GREEN ROAD
LYNE LANE
LYNE CROSSING ROAD
RUXBURY ROAD
WATERY LANE
ALMNERS ROAD
HARDWICK LANE
TRYS HILL
HOLLOWAY HILL
ST. PETER'S WAY
BITTAMS LANE
GUILDFORD STREET
PYRCROFT ROAD
CHILSEY GREEN RD
ST. ANNS ROAD
EASTWORTH ROAD
HANWORTH LANE
96
97
98
99
100
101
102
103
104

BG
BH
BJ
BK
BL
BM
BN
05
06
07
196
GRAVEL
QUEEN
MARY
RESERVOIR
TW18
STAINES ROAD
Sweep's Bridge
Staines Town FC
Clubhouse
SPORTS GROUND
Penton Hook Farm
Garden Centre
Penton Hook Lock
ARCADIA CARAVANS
Glasshouse
THAMESIDE
Pumping Sta
Intake Channel
Gas Pipeline Sta
ROUND COPSE
PENTON HOOK ISLAND
PENTON HOOK
PENTON HOOK MARINA
Yacht Basin
Manor Farm
Prim Sch
Hall
Youth Club
Three Horseshoes PH
War Mem
SPORTS GRD
Pav
LALEHAM
SHEPPERTON ROAD
Shepperton Studios
THE GREEN
Squires Bridge
REC GRD
LALEHAM ROAD
Laleham Nurseries
PENTON PARK (Caravan Park)
Mountbatten Pavilion
Abbey Lake
Clubhouse
LALEHAM GOLF COURSE
LALEHAM BURWAY
RESERVOIR
Filter Beds
Water Works
Rowing Club
LALEHAM PARK
Laleham Abbey
LALEHAM PARK SPORTS GROUND
Camp Site
Staines Farm
Prim Sch
Sailing Club
95
96
97
98
99
100
101
102
103
104
69
68
67
66
215
KT16
M3
Earthworks
Abbey Bridge
ABBEYFIELDS REC GRD
Abbey River
Abbey Chase House
Weir
Chertsey Lock
ABBEYFIELDS MOBILE HOME PARK
KINGFISHER PH
CHERTSEY BRIDGE ROAD
Dumsey Eyot
RYEPECK MEADOW MOORINGS
Riversleigh Farm
CHERTSEY ROAD
RENFREE
Chertsey Cricket Club
Chertsey Town FC
MUS
Old TH
LONDON STREET
GOGMORE FM PK
Comm Hall
Health Club
CHERTSEY
Prim Sch
SPORTS GROUND
Health Cen
RECREATION GROUND
CHERTSEY MEADS
SPELTHORNE
RUNNYMEDE
DOCKETT EDDY
Dockett Point
PHARAOH'S ISLAND
Shepperton Lock
LOCK ISLAND
HAMHAUGH ISLAND
Hamhaugh Point
FORDWATER TRADING EST
Fordwater Bridge
Marina
CHERTSEY MEADS
EASTWORTH ROAD
CEM
SPORTS GROUND
Pannells
SPORTS GROUND
ADDLESTONE MOOR
ADDLESTONE CEMETERY
ABBEY MOOR GOLF COURSE
Coll
Fire Sta
Woburn Park Farm
Hatch Farm
WOBURN HILL
WOBURN PARK
Tennis Cen
St. George's College
WOODLANDS
MEADOWLANDS PARK
Hamm Court Farm
HAMM COURT
The Bull Dogs
KT15
The Plantation Nursery
ST. PETER'S WAY
A317
A318
A320
The George
VICTORY PARK
Bowl Grn
SPORTS GRD
Superstore
Woodside Farm
Junction 11
234
BOURNE BUS PK
Thales
WEYBRIDGE ROAD
WEYBRIDGE BUSINESS PARK
Black Boy Bridge
Weybridge Lock
HOSP
WEYBRIDGE
0
500 yds
500 m

BP
BQ
BR
BS
BT
BU
BV
197
Junction 1
Sunbury Cross
ASHFORD COMMON WATER TREATMENT WORKS
STAINES ROAD WEST
WINDMILL ROAD
UPPER HALLIFORD ROAD
LITTLETON
UPPER HALLIFORD
SUNBURY GOLF COURSE
HAZELWOOD GOLF COURSE
DRIVING RANGE
SHEPPERTON BUSINESS PARK
TW16
SUNBURY
SUNBURY PARK
LONDON IRISH RUGBY GROUND
GAFLAC SPORTS GROUND
CEDARS REC GRD
Sivyers Lake
Sunbury Locks
SUNBURY LOCK AIT
Gas Works
WHEATLEYS EYOT
LONGWOOD BUSINESS PARK
Oil Terminal
KT12
218
96
97
98
99
100
101
102
103
104
The Swan Sanctuary
Shepperton Marina
GASTON BRIDGE ROAD
WALTON BRIDGE RD
PERTON
LAS PALMAS ESTATE
DESBOROUGH ISLAND
D'OYLY CARTE ISLAND
THAMES MEADOW
COWEY SALE
KT13
BROAD WATER
Oatlands Park Hotel
ST. MAUR'S CONV
WALTON-ON THAMES
ASHLEY PARK
ELM GROVE REC GRD
WALTON & HERSHAM FC
Unilever UK Ltd.
WALTON-ON-THAMES
OATLANDS DRIVE
OATLANDS
HERSHAM ROAD
NEW ZEALAND AVENUE
QUEENS
235
08
09
10

BW
BX
BY
BZ
CA
CB
CC
198
KEMPTON
PARK
RACECOURSE
TW16
HALF MOON COVERT
PLAYING FIELD
HAMPTON
CARLISLE PARK
Open Air Pool
KINGSWAY BUSINESS PARK
KEMPTON GATE
HYDES FIELD
Portlane Bridge
Clubhouse Football Grd
EAST
UPPER SUNBURY ROAD
A308
THAMES ST
HAMPTON
Hampton FC
STAIN HILL RESERVOIRS
KENTON COURT MEADOW
UPON THAMES
RICHMOND
GRAND JUNCTION RESERVOIR
Filter Beds
Water Works
TW12
PLATT'S EYOT
HURST PARK
GARRICK'S AIT
Garrick Temple
CONFERENCE CENTRE
SUNBURY COURT
GRAND JUNCTION ISLE
SUNBURY COURT ISLAND
RIVER THAMES
SUNNYSIDE RESERVOIR
SWAN'S REST ISLAND
RIVERMEAD ISLAND
BARGE WALK
ELMBRIDGE
MOLESEY RESERVOIRS NATURE RESERVE
HURST ROAD
A3050
SPORTS GROUND
REC GROUND
Swim Pool
95
96
97
98
99
100
101
102
103
104
69
68
67
66
SUNBURY
RIVERSIDE ARTS CEN
GALLERY
Sunbury Locks
SPELTHORNE
SUNBURY LOCK AIT
WALTON ADVANCED WATER TREATMENT WORKS
Gas Works
The Weir PH
Apps Court Farm
BESSBOROUGH RESERVOIR
KNIGHTS RESERVOIR
CEM
REC GRD
Comm Cen
WEST MOLESEY
KT8
KT12
Rivernook Farm
Bramble Hill Farm
APPLE COURT GREEN
WALTON ROAD
B369
SPORTS GROUND
HOSP
Adult Learning Cen
NEILSON PLAYING FIELD
SPORTS GROUND
Medical Cen
217
Thamesfield Farm
QUEEN ELIZABETH II RESERVOIR
Dead River
Pumping Station
Sailing Club
SAND & GRAVEL PIT
ISLAND BARN RESERVOIR
River Mole
River Ember
Walton-on-Thames
Hall
Fieldcommon Farm
FIELDCOMMON LANE
Sewage Works
Filter Beds
KT10
Bowl Grn
Sports Club
Prim Sch
GEORGE FROUDE PK
RYDENS
RYDENS ROAD REC GRD
Esher R.F.C.
Health Cen
HOSP
NORTH WEYLANDS INDUSTRIAL ESTATE
RIVER MOLE BUSINESS PARK
SANDOWN IND PK
REC GRD
Weir
Lower Green
SANDOWN GOLF COURSE
EMBER CENTRE
DRIVING RANGE
HERSHAM
Clubhouse
DRIVING RANGE
SANDOWN PARK RACECOURSE
Karting Centre
Grandstand & Exhibition Centre
Surgery
Wayneflete's or Wolsey's Tower
Sec Sch
Ski Slope
Ski Sch
Squash Club
THE WARREN
Fire Sta
Amb Sta
Unilever UK Ltd.
Prim Sch
Young Peoples Cen
CORONATION RECREATION GROUND
HERSHAM VILLAGE GOLF COURSE
Sec Sch
Prim Sch
Clinic
236
A244
PORTSMOUTH
ESHER
0 500 yds
0 500 m
12
13
14

CD
CE
CF
CG
CH
CJ
CK
199
BUSHY
PARK
TW11
BROOM CLUMPS
WATERHOUSE WOODLAND GARDEN
WARREN PLANTATION
HALF MOON PLANTATION
OVAL PLANTATION
HAMPTON WICK
Red Brick Bridge
Diana Fountain
THE ROYAL PADDOCKS
THE KINGSFIELD
HAMPTON COURT ROAD
A308
TAGG'S ISLAND
ASH ISLAND
HAMPTON COURT GREEN
HAMPTON COURT PALACE
MAZE
HAMPTON COURT GDNS
PRIVY GDN
EAST MOLESEY
CIGARETTE ISLAND PARK
KT8
HAMPTON COURT PARK
(HOME PARK)
HAMPTON COURT PALACE GOLF COURSE
The Long Water
RAVENS AIT
DITTON FIELD
THAMES DITTON ISLAND
THAMES DITTON
BOYLE FM ISLAND
KINGSTON BRIDGE
Kingston University
VICTORIA REC GRD
LONG DITTON REC GRD
KT7
WESTON GREEN
KT6
LONG DITTON
Cockcrow Hill
PORTSMOUTH ROAD
A307
HAMPTON COURT WAY
A309
THAMES DITTON & ESHER GOLF COURSE
DITTON COMMON
ESHER
Scilly Isles
HINCHLEY WOOD
LITTLEWORTH COMMON
KINGSTON BYPASS
KT9
Hook Junction
KING EDWARD REC GRD
SURBITON
Telegraph Hill
237
220
96
97
98
99
100
101
102
103
104
SURBITON HOSP
UPPER BRIGHTON ROAD
HOOK ROAD
A243
A240
PENRHYN ROAD
SURREY
RICHMOND UPON THAMES

CL
CM
CN
CP
CQ
CR
CS
200
COOMBE
COOMBE WOOD GOLF COURSE
KT2
KINGSTON HOSPITAL
NORBITON
KINGSTON UPON THAMES
KINGSTON CEMETERY
KT1
NEW MALDEN
SURBITON CEMETERY
BERRYLANDS
KT3
219
SURBITON HOSP
HOGSMILL PUBLIC OPEN SPACE
KT5
SURBITON
KT6
HOGSMILL OPEN SPACE
ALEXANDRA REC GRD
OLD MALDEN
TOLWORTH HOSPITAL
TOLWORTH
KINGSTON UNIVERSITY SPORTS GRD
KING GEORGES FIELD
KT9
238
KINGSTON BYPASS
95
96
97
98
99
100
101
102
103
104
500 yds
500 m

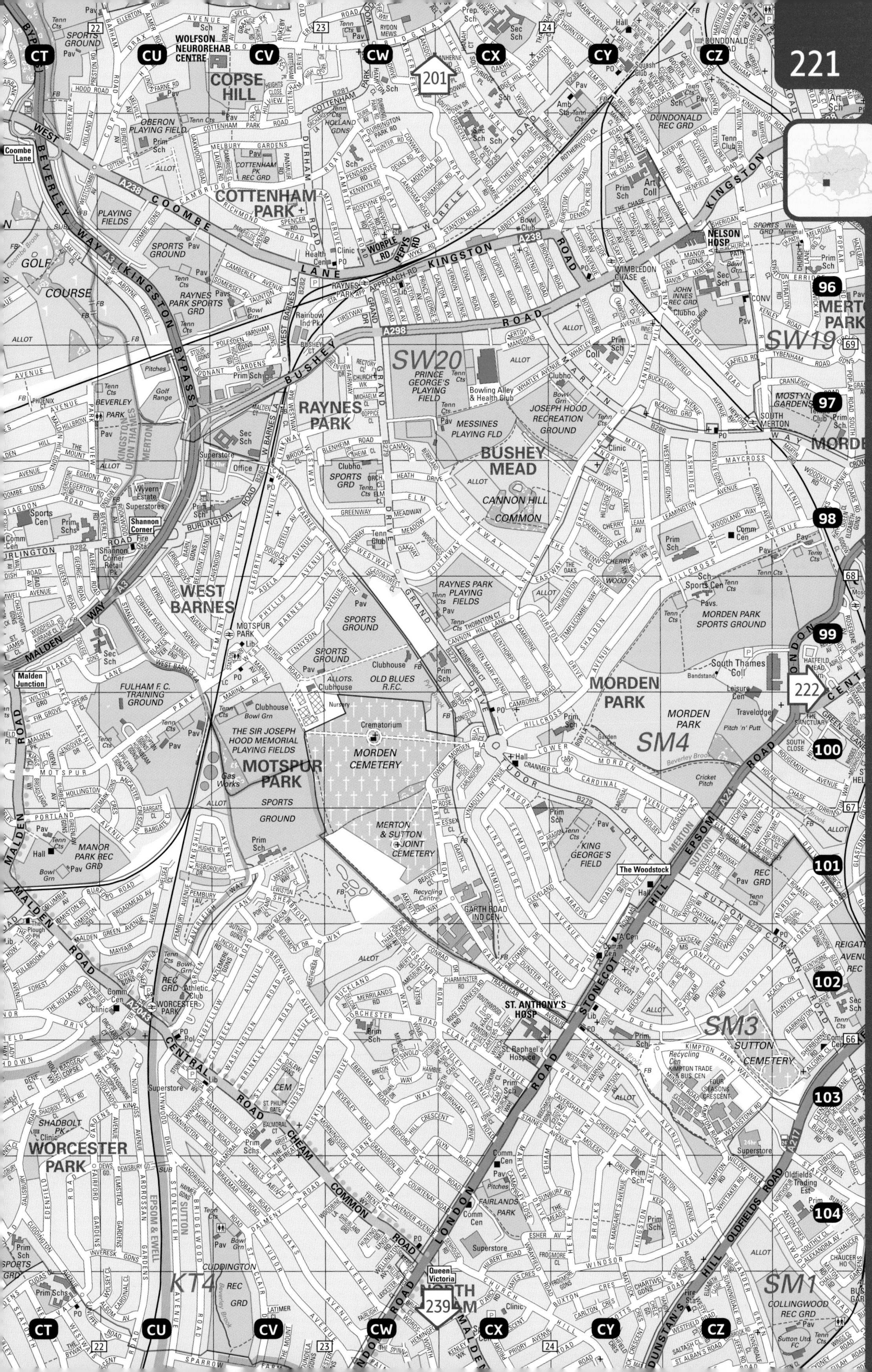
CT
CU
CV
CW
CX
CY
CZ
201
222
239
22
23
24
WOLFSON NEUROREHAB CENTRE
COPSE HILL
OBERON PLAYING FIELD
COTTENHAM PARK
COTTENHAM PK REC GRD
PLAYING FIELDS
SPORTS GROUND
GOLF COURSE
RAYNES PARK SPORTS GRD
DUNDONALD REC GRD
NELSON HOSP
JOHN INNES REC GRD
WIMBLEDON CHASE
MERTON PARK
SW19
SW20
PRINCE GEORGE'S PLAYING FIELD
Bowling Alley & Health Club
RAYNES PARK
MESSINES PLAYING FLD
JOSEPH HOOD RECREATION GROUND
BUSHEY MEAD
CANNON HILL COMMON
SOUTH MERTON
MOSTYN GARDENS
MORDEN
BEVERLEY PARK
Coombe Lane
Shannon Corner
Shannon Corner Retail Pk
WEST BARNES
RAYNES PARK PLAYING FIELDS
SPORTS GROUND
OLD BLUES R.F.C.
MORDEN PARK SPORTS GROUND
MORDEN PARK
South Thames Coll
Malden Junction
FULHAM F.C. TRAINING GROUND
THE SIR JOSEPH HOOD MEMORIAL PLAYING FIELDS
MOTSPUR PARK
MORDEN CEMETERY
Crematorium
MERTON & SUTTON JOINT CEMETERY
SM4
KING GEORGE'S FIELD
The Woodstock
MANOR PARK REC GRD
GARTH ROAD IND CEN
ST. ANTHONY'S HOSP
St. Raphael's Hospice
SM3
SUTTON CEMETERY
KIMPTON TRADE & BUS CEN
FOUR SEASONS CRESCENT
WORCESTER PARK
REC GRD
FAIRLANDS PARK
KT4
CUDDINGTON REC GRD
Queen Victoria
NORTH CHEAM
SM1
COLLINGWOOD REC GRD
Oldfields Trading Est
Sutton Utd FC
KINGSTON BYPASS
A3
A238
A298
A24
A217
A2043
B279
B282
B286
KINGSTON ROAD
BUSHEY ROAD
CENTRAL ROAD
CHEAM COMMON ROAD
LONDON ROAD
STONECOT HILL
EPSOM ROAD
MALDEN ROAD
BEVERLEY WAY
COOMBE LANE
MORDEN ROAD
96
97
98
99
100
101
102
103
104
66
67
68
69

DA
DB
DC
DD
DE
DF
DG
202
SOUTH WIMBLEDON
COLLIER'S WOOD
LONDON ROAD CEMETERY
FIGGE'S MARSH
MERTON
MERTON PARK
SW19
MORDEN
MORDEN HALL PARK
MITCHAM
SM4
MORDEN PARK SPORTS GROUND
221
ST. HELIER
ROSEHILL
SM3
SUTTON CEMETERY
SM5
BENHILTON
THE WRYTHE
SM1
240
95
96
97
98
99
100
101
102
103
104
26
27
28
69
68
67
66
500 yds
500 m

STREATHAM VALE
SW16
NORBURY
NORBURY PARK
STREATHAM PARK
CEMETERY
POLLARDS HILL
CR7
THORNTON HEATH
CR4
MITCHAM
COMMON
CROYDON CEMETERY
MAYDAY UNIVERSITY HOSPITAL
BROAD GREEN
QUEEN'S ROAD CEMETERY
CR0
WADDON
WANDLE PARK
HACKBRIDGE
SM6
BEDDINGTON
BEDDINGTON PARK
CROYDON SUB STATION
DUPPAS HILL
LONDON ROAD
PURLEY WAY
MITCHAM ROAD
CROYDON ROAD
DUPPAS HILL RD
DH
DJ
DK
DL
DM
DN
DP
29
30
31
203
224
241
96
97
98
99
100
101
102
103
104
69
68
67
66

DQ
DR
DS
DT
DU
DV
DW
UPPER NORWOOD
204
SE19
SE20
ANERLEY
BEAULIEU HEIGHTS
SOUTH NORWOOD
SE25
CR7
THORNTON HEATH
SELHURST
WOODSIDE
CROYDON
ADDISCOMBE
CR0
223
242
95
96
97
98
99
100
101
102
103
104
SOUTH NORWOOD COUNTRY PARK
BECKENHAM CEMETERY
ORCHARD SCHOOL SPORTS CENTRE
SELHURST PARK CRYSTAL PALACE FC
QUEEN'S ROAD CEMETERY
MAYDAY UNIVERSITY HOSPITAL
WHITGIFT PLAYING FIELDS
SHIRLEY PARK GOLF COURSE
LLOYD PARK
CROYDON SPORTS ARENA
ASHBURTON PARK
SHIRLEY OAKS HOSPITAL
GRANGEWOOD PARK
SOUTH NORWOOD REC GRD
CROYDON AND RYLANDS FIELDS
CROYDON DRIVING RANGE
HOCKEY PITCH
SPORTS GROUND
PARK HILL
0 500 yds
0 500 m

DX
DY
DZ
EA
EB
EC
ED
205
BECKENHAM
BECKENHAM JUNCTION
NEW BECKENHAM
CATOR PARK
KENT HOUSE
BECKENHAM ROAD
LEWISHAM
BROMLEY
RAVENSBOURNE
THE SLOANE HOSPITAL
SHORTLANDS
BECKENHAM HOSPITAL
CROYDON RD REC GROUND
BR3
BR2
KELSEY PARK
ELMERS END
CREASE PARK
HARVINGTON PLAYING FIELD
EDEN PARK
PARK LANGLEY
UPPER ELMERS END
CROUCH OAK WOOD
MONKS ORCHARD
BETHLEM ROYAL HOSPITAL
HIGH BROOM WOOD
LANGLEY PARK GOLF COURSE
THE ROOKERY
WEST WICKHAM
BR4
SHIRLEY
SPRING PARK WOOD
FOXES WOOD
KENNEL WOOD
PINEWOODS
SPARROWS DEN PLAYING FIELDS
SPRING PARK
CONEY HALL REC GRD
BLAKE REC GRD
PARKFIELDS REC GRD
GLADE WOOD
226
243
96
97
98
99
100
101
102
103
104
36
37
38
66
67
68
69
A234
A214
A222
A232
A2015
A2022
B230

EE
EF
EG
EH
EJ
EK
EL
206
225
244
95
96
97
98
99
100
101
102
103
104
40
41
42
66
67
68
69
SHORTLANDS GOLF COURSE
THE SLOANE HOSPITAL
BROMLEY PARK
BECKENHAM ROAD
SHORTLANDS
BROMLEY
QUEEN'S MEAD REC GRD
CHURCH HOUSE GDNS
MARTIN'S HILL
SPORTS GROUND
The Glades Shop Cen
BROMLEY CIVIC CENTRE
Leisure Cen
BROMLEY NORTH
BROMLEY SOUTH
Westmoreland Place
LONDON ROAD
HIGH ST
TWEEDY RD
COLLEGE RD
WIDMORE ROAD
KENTISH WAY
A21
A222
A232
A233
B228
B2212
B265
B251
Widmore Green
WIDMORE
BR1
BR2
BR4
Recycling Cen
HAVELOCK REC GRD
WHITEHALL REC GRD
BICKLEY ROAD
LOGSHILL WOOD
PLAYING FIELD
PRIORY
MASONS HILL
BROMLEY COMMON
SOUTH HILL WOOD
WESTMORELAND ROAD
HAYES ROAD
HAYES LANE
PICKHURST LANE
LANGLEY
PARK COURSE
CUPOLA WOOD
REC GRD
Fitness Cen
Bromley Town & Old Bromleians C.C.
Bromley FC
FISHER'S WOOD
NORMAN PARK RECREATION GROUND
ATHLETICS TRACK
SCROGGINHALL WOOD
Bromley College of Further & Higher Education
LORDS WOOD
BROOK WOOD
MAZZARDS WOOD
WOODCOCK GROVE
BOLDS WOOD
THE GROVE SPORTS GRD
Oakley House
HASTINGS ROAD
OAKLEY ROAD
Hayes Street Farm
Isard House
HAYES
THE KNOLL
PRIORY HOSP HAYES GROVE
Country Club
SPORTS GROUND
BARNET WOOD
PARKHOUSE F.C. RUGBY GROUND
HAYES COMMON
COLYERS WOOD
WEST WICKHAM COMMON
Coney Hall
CONEY HALL REC GRD
CROYDON ROAD
GLEBE WAY
Keston Mark
PADMALL WOOD
Baston Manor
The Oasthouse
The Lodge
Wyevale Garden Centre
Old Beccehamian R.F.C.
BURIAL GRD
RAVENSBOURNE BUSINESS CEN
J.B. Stables
500 yds
500 m

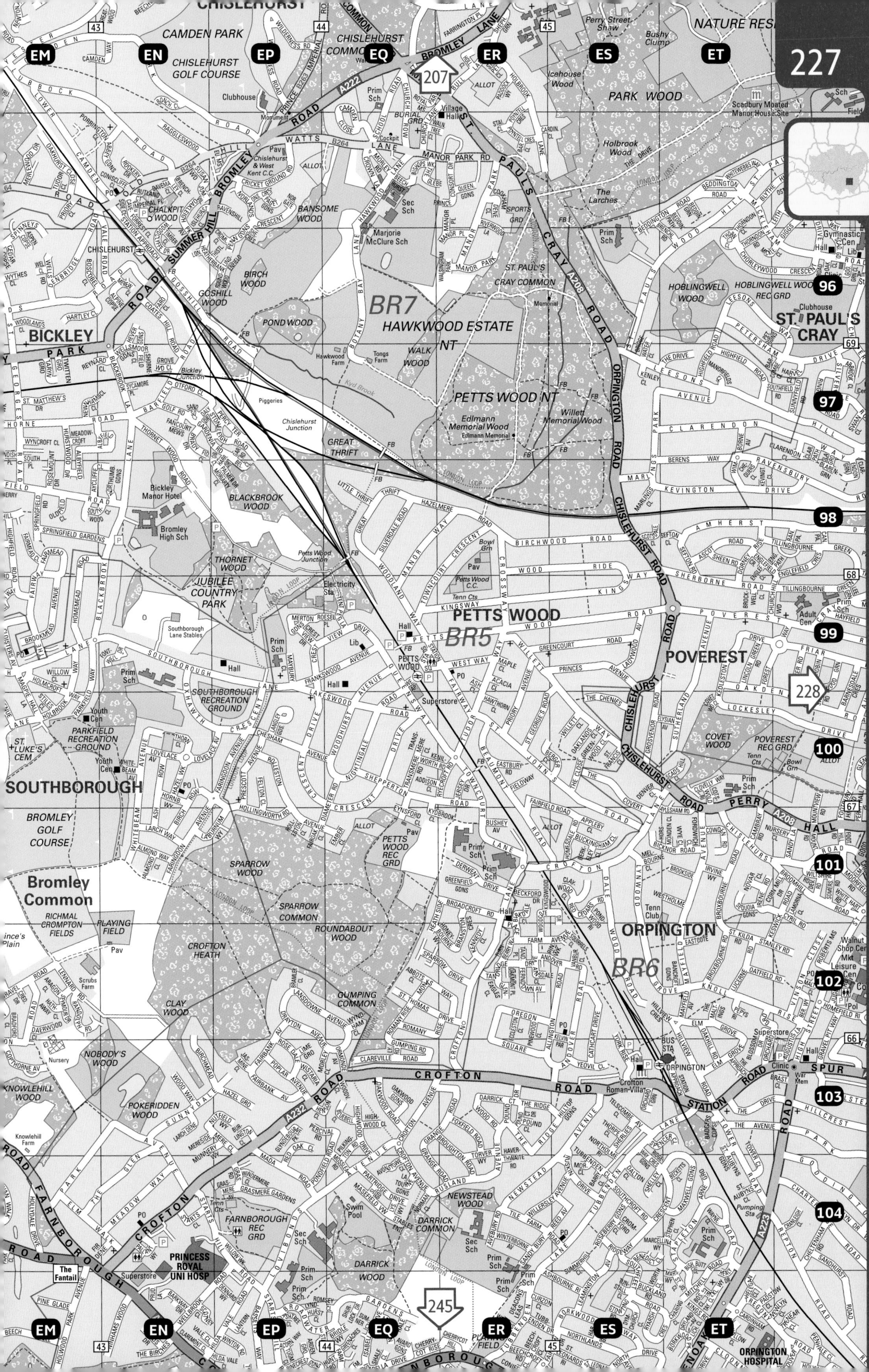
CHISLEHURST
CAMDEN PARK
CHISLEHURST COMMON
CHISLEHURST GOLF COURSE
NATURE RESERVE
Perry Street Shaw
Bushy Clump
EM
EN
EP
EQ
ER
ES
ET
207
Icehouse Wood
PARK WOOD
Scadbury Moated Manor House Site
Clubhouse
Village Hall
Holbrook Wood
The Larches
BANSOME WOOD
CHALKPIT WOOD
Marjorie McClure Sch
CHISLEHURST
BIRCH WOOD
GOSHILL WOOD
POND WOOD
BR7
HAWKWOOD ESTATE NT
ST. PAUL'S CRAY COMMON
HOBLINGWELL WOOD
HOBLINGWELL WOOD REC GRD
ST. PAUL'S CRAY
96
BICKLEY
Hawkwood Farm
Tongs Farm
WALK WOOD
Piggeries
Chislehurst Junction
PETTS WOOD NT
Edlmann Memorial Wood
Willett Memorial Wood
97
GREAT THRIFT
Bickley Manor Hotel
BLACKBROOK WOOD
Bromley High Sch
98
THORNET WOOD
Petts Wood Junction
JUBILEE COUNTRY PARK
Southborough Lane Stables
PETTS WOOD
BR5
POVEREST
99
SOUTHBOROUGH RECREATION GROUND
PARKFIELD RECREATION GROUND
ST. LUKE'S CEM
228
COVET WOOD
POVEREST REC GRD
100
SOUTHBOROUGH
BROMLEY GOLF COURSE
Bromley Common
PETTS WOOD REC GRD
SPARROW WOOD
101
RICHMAL CROMPTON FIELDS
PLAYING FIELD
SPARROW COMMON
ROUNDABOUT WOOD
CROFTON HEATH
ORPINGTON
BR6
Scrubs Farm
GUMPING COMMON
102
CLAY WOOD
NOBODY'S WOOD
ORPINGTON
Crofton Roman Villa
103
KNOWLEHILL WOOD
POKERIDDEN WOOD
Knowlehill Farm
NEWSTEAD WOOD
FARNBOROUGH REC GRD
DARRICK COMMON
104
PRINCESS ROYAL UNI HOSP
DARRICK WOOD
The Fantail
245
ORPINGTON HOSPITAL
CROFTON ROAD
FARNBOROUGH ROAD
CHISLEHURST ROAD
ORPINGTON ROAD
SPUR ROAD
A208
A222
A232
A223

EU
EV
EW
EX
EY
EZ
FA
208
227
246
95
96
97
98
99
100
101
102
103
104
47
48
49
DA14
BR7
BR5
BR6
SIDCUP BYPASS
A20
A224
A223
A208
A232
B258
SEVENOAKS WAY
CRAY AVENUE
COURT ROAD (ORPINGTON BYPASS)
PERRY HALL ROAD
SPUR ROAD
HIGH ST
Crittall's Corner
EDGINGTON
RUXLEY WOOD
Ruxley Manor Garden Centre
Scadbury Moated Manor House Site
Field-Study Centre
ST. PAUL'S CRAY
HOBLINGWELL WOOD REC GRD
CRAYFIELDS BUSINESS PARK
CRAYFIELDS IND PARK
RUXLEY PARK GOLF COURSE
CRAY VALLEY GOLF COURSE
Pilgrim Hill
Barnfield Bank
Lower Hockenden Farm
Simon's Field Shaw
The Small House
PAULS CRAY HILL PARK
HIGHLANDS WOOD
HOCKENDEN WOOD
Hogspring Cottages
MURRAY BUSINESS CEN
SPRINGVALE RETAIL PARK
BROOK IND PK
ST MARY CRAY
NUGENT SHOPPING PARK
NUGENT IND PARK
THE WARREN
Sheepcote Farm
Ringland Farm
CHILD'S WOOD
ST. MARY CRAY REC GRD
Blueberry Farm
Kevington Farm
Derry Downs
GRIGG'S CROSS
KYNASTON WOOD
Waldens Farm
Crouch Farm
Walden Manor
Heather's Holdings
Bleak House Farm
POVEREST
POVEREST REC GRD
PRIORY GARDENS
BROMLEY MUS
GRASSMEADE RECREATION GROUND
RAMSDEN
Eastwood Farm
GRIFF'S WOOD
Piggery
Byways Nurseries
SAGE WENTS
Cookham Hill Farm
Cookham Farm
Crownwood Farm
Goddington
GODDINGTON PARK
ROUNDS SMALLAMS
LILLY'S WOOD
BLACK BUSH WOOD
ORPINGTON HOSPITAL
0 500 yds
0 500 m

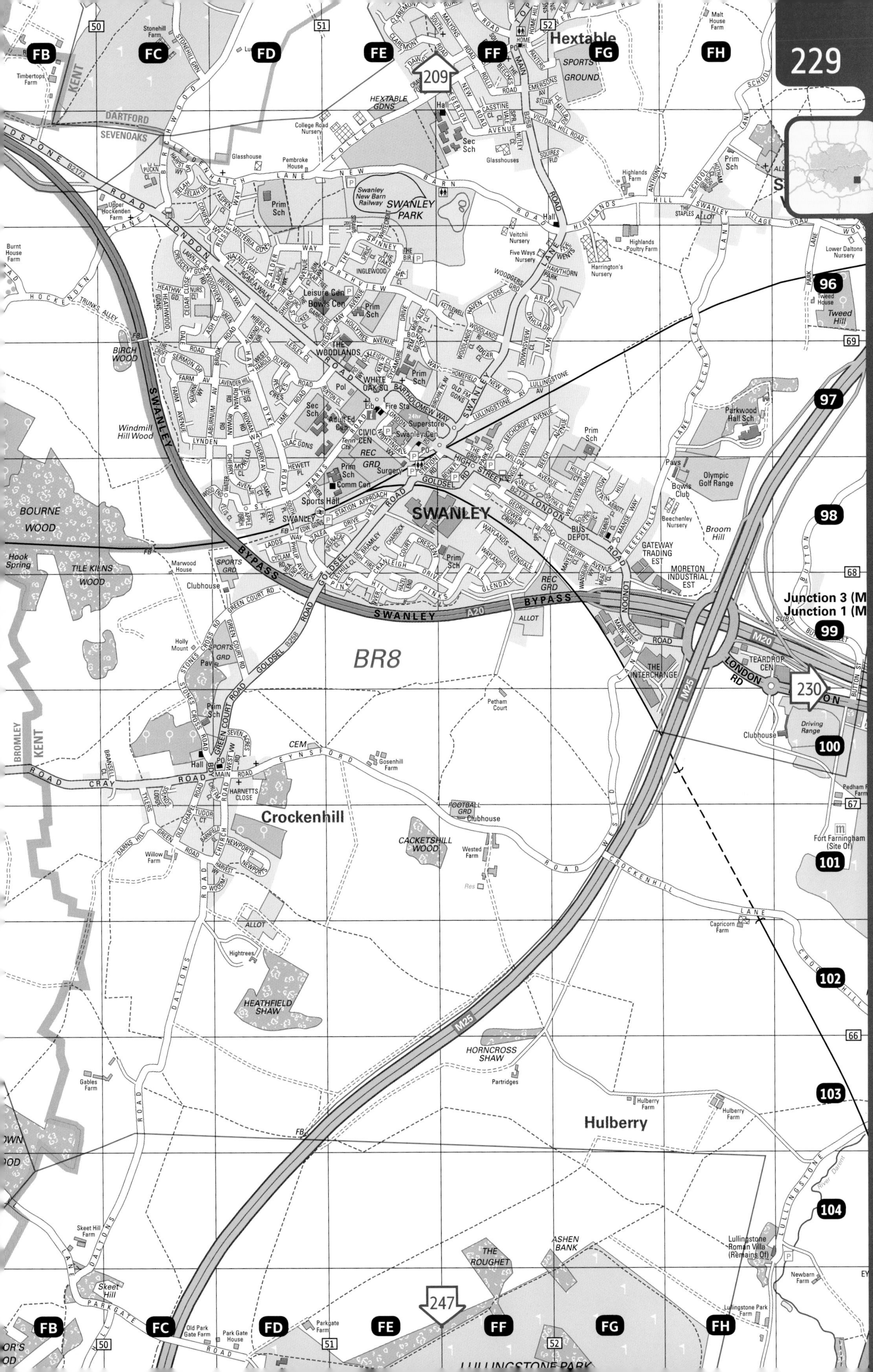

Hextable
SPORTS GROUND
HEXTABLE GDNS
College Road Nursery
Glasshouse
Pembroke House
Swanley New Barn Railway
SWANLEY PARK
Veitchii Nursery
Five Ways Nursery
Harrington's Nursery
Highlands Farm
Highlands Poultry Farm
Malt House Farm
Lower Daltons Nursery
Tweed House
Tweed Hill
Stonehill Farm
Timbertops Farm
KENT
DARTFORD
SEVENOAKS
Upper Hockenden Farm
Burnt House Farm
BIRCH WOOD
Windmill Hill Wood
BOURNE WOOD
Hook Spring
TILE KILNS WOOD
Marwood House
Clubhouse
Holly Mount
SWANLEY
THE WOODLANDS
WHITE OAK SQ
Leisure Cen
Bowls Cen
Superstore
Swanley Cen
CIVIC CEN
REC GRD
Sports Hall
BUS DEPOT
Olympic Golf Range
Bowls Club
Beechenley Nursery
Broom Hill
GATEWAY TRADING EST
MORETON INDUSTRIAL EST
Junction 3 (M
Junction 1 (M
Parkwood Hall Sch
TEARDROP CEN
THE INTERCHANGE
Driving Range
Clubhouse
Pedham Farm
Fort Farningham (Site Of)
BR8
Petham Court
Gosenhill Farm
CEM
Crockenhill
HARNETTS CLOSE
FOOTBALL GRD
CACKETSHILL WOOD
Westend Farm
Willow Farm
Hightrees
HEATHFIELD SHAW
Capricorn Farm
HORNCROSS SHAW
Partridges
Gables Farm
Hulberry
Hulberry Farm
Skeet Hill Farm
Skeet Hill
Old Park Gate Farm
Park Gate House
Parkgate Farm
THE ROUGHET
ASHEN BANK
Lullingstone Roman Villa (Remains Of)
Newbarn Farm
Lullingstone Park Farm
River Darent
BROMLEY
KENT
SWANLEY BYPASS
M25
M20
A20
B2173
B258
FB FC FD FE FF FG FH
209
230
247

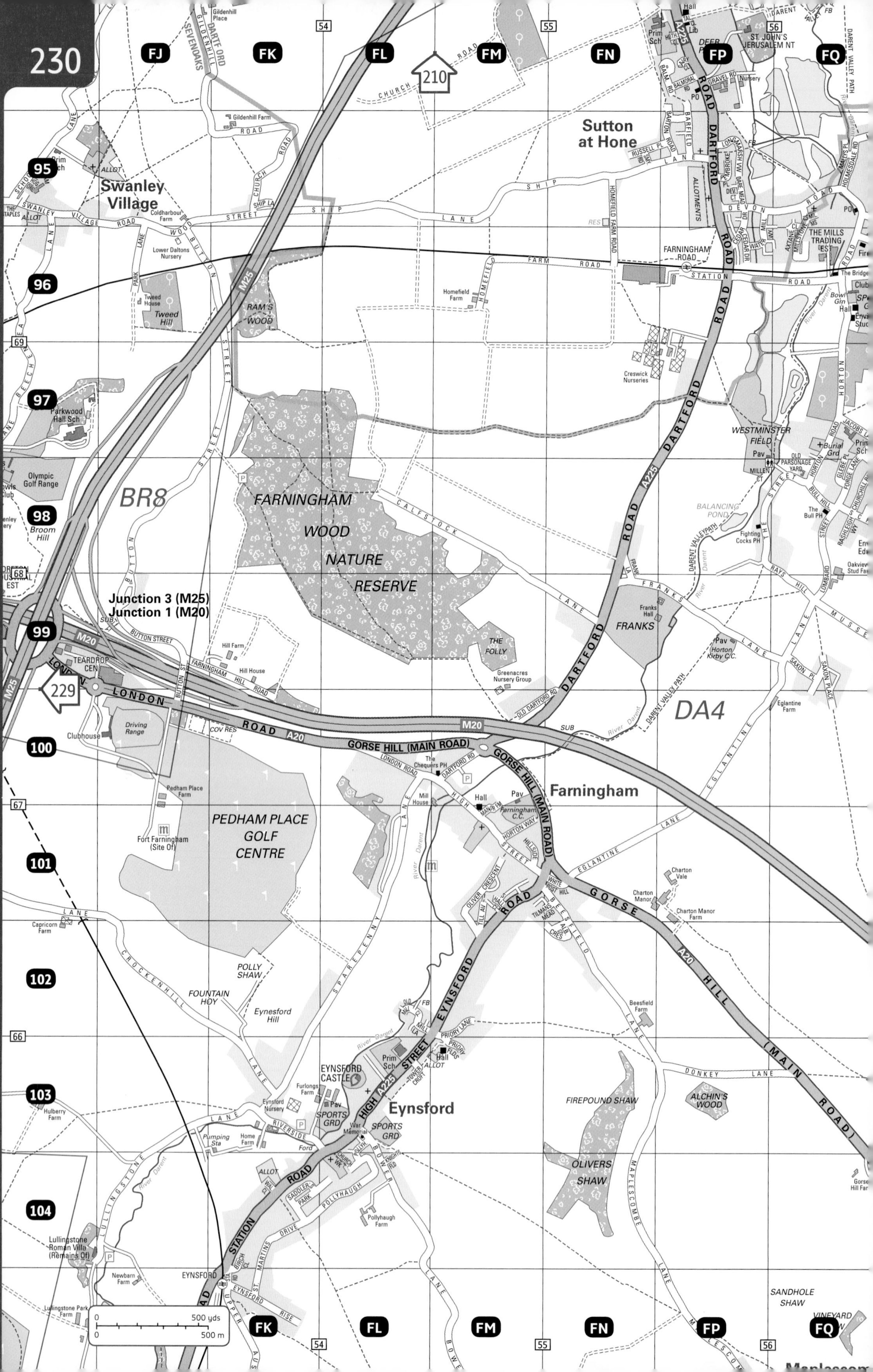

FJ
FK
FL
FM
FN
FP
FQ
54
55
56
210
229
95
96
97
98
99
100
101
102
103
104
69
68
67
66
Gildenhill Place
DARTFORD
SEVENOAKS
GILDENHILL
Gildenhill Farm
CHURCH ROAD
Sutton at Hone
Swanley Village
SWANLEY VILLAGE ROAD
SHIP LANE
SHIP STREET
SHIP LA
Coldharbour Farm
Lower Daltons Nursery
WOOD
BUTTON STREET
PARK LANE
Tweed House
Tweed Hill
RAM'S WOOD
M25
HOMEFIELD FARM ROAD
Homefield Farm
FARM ROAD
STATION ROAD
FARNINGHAM ROAD
Creswick Nurseries
DARTFORD ROAD
A225
ST. JOHN'S JERUSALEM NT
DEER
Prim Sch
Lib
Hall
PO
BALM RD
BALMORAL RD
BARTON ROAD
BARFIELD
GRAVEL RD
Nursery
RUSSELL PL
LONGMARSH VW
LANE
DEVON ROAD
ALLOTMENTS
THE MILLS TRADING EST
The Bridge
Club
Bowl Grn
Hall
WESTMINSTER FIELD
Pav
BALANCING POND
Fighting Cocks PH
The Bull PH
OLD PARSONAGE YARD
HORTON ROAD
JACOBS
Burial Grd
GLEBE PL
FORGE LANE
BULL HILL
THE STREET
RASHLEIGH
RAYS HILL
LOMBARD
Oakview Stud Fa
MUSSE
Parkwood Hall Sch
Olympic Golf Range
Broom Hill
BEECHENLEA LANE
BR8
FARNINGHAM WOOD NATURE RESERVE
CALFSTOCK LANE
THE FOLLY
Greenacres Nursery Group
Junction 3 (M25)
Junction 1 (M20)
BUTTON STREET
Hill Farm
Hill House
FARNINGHAM HILL ROAD
TEARDROP CEN
LONDON ROAD
A20
M20
COV RES
Driving Range
Clubhouse
GORSE HILL (MAIN ROAD)
The Chequers PH
DARTFORD RD
Mill House
HIGH STREET
Farningham
Farningham C.C.
HORTON WAY
HILLSIDE
OLD DARTFORD RD
FRANKS
Franks Hall
FRANKS LANE
Horton Kirby C.C.
SAXON PL
SAXON PLACE
DA4
DARENT VALLEY PATH
River Darent
Eglantine Farm
EGLANTINE LANE
Charton Vale
Charton Manor
Charton Manor Farm
GORSE HILL
WHITE POST HILL
BEESFIELD
TILMANS MEAD
OLIVER CRESCENT
Pedham Place Farm
Fort Farningham (Site Of)
PEDHAM PLACE GOLF CENTRE
Capricorn Farm
CROCKENHILL LANE
POLLY SHAW
FOUNTAIN HOY
Eynesford Hill
SPAREPENNY LANE
EYNSFORD ROAD
Beesfield Farm
DONKEY LANE
ALCHIN'S WOOD
FIREPOUND SHAW
OLIVERS SHAW
MAPLESCOMBE LANE
(MAIN ROAD)
Gorse Hill Far
PRIORY LANE
Prim Sch
Hall
ALLOT
EYNSFORD CASTLE
Furlongs Farm
Pav
SPORTS GRD
Eynsford
Eynsford Nursery
RIVERSIDE
Pumping Sta
Home Farm
Ford
War Memorial
HIGH STREET
A225
STATION ROAD
SADDLERS PARK
POLLYHAUGH
Pollyhaugh Farm
ST. MARTINS DRIVE
LULLINGSTONE LANE
Hulberry Farm
Lullingstone Roman Villa (Remains Of)
Newbarn Farm
EYNSFORD
Lullingstone Park Farm
EYNSFORD RISE
UPPER
BOWEN LANE
SANDHOLE SHAW
VINEYARD
500 yds
500 m

FR
FS
FT
FU
FV
FW
FX
57
58
59
211
St. Margaret's Farm
ST. MARGARET'S ROAD
Wheatsheaf PH
WHITEHILL ROAD
B260
GREEN STREET GREEN ROAD
Walnut Tree Farm
Chalkcroft
Ryecroft Farm
DA2
QUARRY
South Darenth
SHRUBBERY
MONTGOMERY RD
HILL
GILL'S ROAD
Gill's Farm
Orchard View
RYECROFTS WOOD
DARTFORD
SEVENOAKS
LANE
SPORTS GRD
ALLOT
Pinden
Mile End Green
Pinden End Farm
Pav
FOOTBALL PITCH
Hall
MAIN ROAD
NORTHDOWN ROAD
Lib
96
ESSEX ROAD
WEST SHAW
ROWANS CL
KENT ROAD
PO
STATION ROAD
HARTLEY RD
69
LONGFIELD
CAVENDISH SQ
BRAMBLEFIELD
OAKWOOD RISE
DENE WK
PARK DRIVE CLOSE
97
Dean Bottom Farm
RABBITS ROAD
GORRINGE AV
VICTORIA DR
PRINCE CHARLES AV
ALLOT
Tuppence Farm
SOUTHDOWNS
WILSON LANE
Rabbits Farm
CANADA FARM ROAD
Dean Bottom
CHURCHDOWN WOOD
FAWKHAM ROAD
Horton Kirby
STACK ROAD
Northdown Country Riding Club
98
BANCKSIDE
PARKFIELD
VALLEY
DOWNS
68
Churchdown Farm
CASTLE HILL
OLD DOWNS
Beeches Farm
Canada Farm
Hill Barn Farm
Hartley Green
99
FAWKHAM VALLEY GOLF COURSE
Country Club
Bowl Grn
SPORTS GRD
Tenn Cts
Pav
PENNIS LANE
Corinthian FC
Sports Cen
Clubho
SPORTS GRD
Gay Dawn Farm
Pennis Farm
Prim Sch
FAIRBY
100
SCHOOL LANE
SCUDDERS HILL
VALLEY ROAD
Lone Oak Farm
Kentdown Mushroom Farm
Nursery
THREE GATES ROAD
Elec Sta
Nursery
67
DA3
MUSSENDEN LANE
HORTON WOOD
GROVE WOOD
Grove Farm
YEWFIELD SHAW
PENNIS WOOD
101
MANOR ROAD
Hall
Prim Sch
REDLIBBETS GOLF COURSE
Clubhouse
102
HOPKINS SPRING WOOD
FAWKHAM MANOR HOSPITAL
Radio Mast
HATCHFIELD WOOD
Fawkham Manor Farm
FB
The Rookery Pig Farm
M20
66
CHAPEL WOOD
AYELANDS
MILLFIELD
Speedgate Farm
White House Farm
SPEEDGATE HILL
MANOR LANE
BUTCHERS LANE
103
New Ash Green
GABRIEL SPRING ROAD
GABRIEL SPRING WOOD
GABRIEL SPRING ROAD (EAST)
CHOAKS WOOD
SUN HILL
MICHAELS LANE
WEST YOKE
Westyoke Farm
SCRATCHERS LANE
The Rising Sun PH
War Memorial
PO
Fawkham Green
SMALL GRAINS
Oak Racing Kennels
Eaglesfield Equestrian Centre
104
Beechcroft Farm Industries
FOXBURY
PUNCH CROFT
Tenn Cts
Sports Cen
SPORTS GROUND
HATCH ROAD
FAWKHAM GREEN ROAD
TN15
Woodhall Farm
CORSE HILL (MAIN ROAD)
BRANDS HATCH KARTING
Leisure Cen
Brands Hatch Place Hotel
SAXTEN'S WOOD
Landway Farm
REDHILL
EXPO
CHAPMAN
Stewart Cen
SHETLEY SHAWS
Thistle Brands Hatch
BRANDS HATCH MOTOR RACING
GALLOWS WD
ROGERS WOOD LANE
Ash
Ash Place Farm
The White

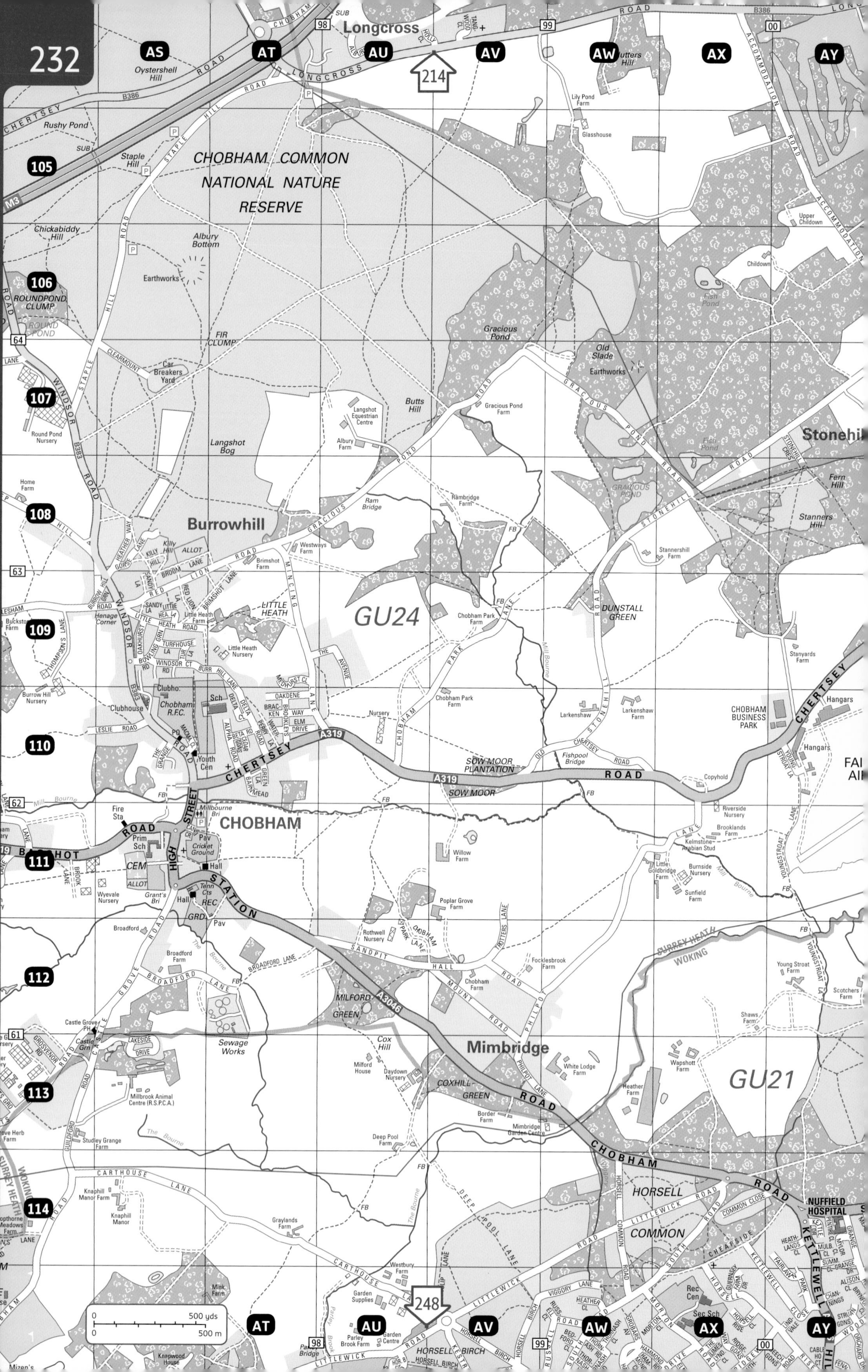
AS
AT
AU
AV
AW
AX
AY
214
Longcross
ROAD
B386
CHOBHAM
SUB
LONGCROSS
Oystershell Hill
Hutters Hill
Lily Pond Farm
Glasshouse
ACCOMMODATION ROAD
CHERTSEY
Rushy Pond
M3
Staple Hill
STAPLE HILL ROAD
CHOBHAM COMMON
NATIONAL NATURE
RESERVE
Chickabiddy Hill
Albury Bottom
Upper Childown
Childown
Fish Pond
Earthworks
ROUNDPOND CLUMP
ROUND POND
FIR CLUMP
Gracious Pond
Old Slade
Earthworks
CLEARMOUNT
Car Breakers Yard
WINDSOR ROAD
B383
Round Pond Nursery
Langshot Equestrian Centre
Butts Hill
Gracious Pond Farm
GRACIOUS POND ROAD
Stonehill
Langshot Bog
Albury Farm
Fish Pond
STONEHILL CRES
Fern Hill
Home Farm
Ram Bridge
Rambridge Farm
GRACIOUS POND
Stanners Hill
Burrowhill
Westways Farm
Stannershill Farm
STONEHILL ROAD
HEATHER WAY
KILLY HILL
ALLOT
BROOM LANE
Brimshot Farm
MINCING LANE
RED LION ROAD
BRIMSHOT LANE
LITTLE HEATH
GU24
Chobham Park Farm
DUNSTALL GREEN
Henage Corner
Little Heath Farm
LITTLE HEATH ROAD
Buckstone Farm
THOMPSON'S LANE
OAKHURST
TURFHOUSE LA
Little Heath Nursery
THE AVENUE
Stanyards Farm
WINDSOR CT
BURR HILL LANE
MEDHURST CL
Burrow Hill Nursery
Clubho.
Chobham R.F.C.
Sch
OAKDENE
Chobham Park Farm
CHOBHAM PARK LANE
Larkenshaw
Larkenshaw Farm
CHOBHAM BUSINESS PARK
Hangars
Clubhouse
LESLIE ROAD
PO
THE GRANGE
Youth Cen
CHERTSEY ROAD
A319
Nursery
SOW MOOR PLANTATION
OLD CHERTSEY ROAD
Fishpool Bridge
Copyhold
YOUNGSTROAT LANE
FB
SOW MOOR
Mill Bourne
Fire Sta
Millbourne Bri
CHOBHAM
HIGH STREET
Riverside Nursery
Brooklands Farm
Kelmstone Arabian Stud
BAGSHOT ROAD
Prim Sch
Pav
Cricket Ground
Hall
CEM
ALLOT
Willow Farm
Little Goldbridge Farm
Burnside Nursery
Sunfield Farm
Wyevale Nursery
Grant's Bri
Tenn Cts
REC
STATION ROAD
Poplar Grove Farm
Broadford
GRD
Pav
Rothwell Nursery
CHOBHAM PARK LANE
POTTERS LANE
SANDPIT HALL ROAD
SURREY HEATH
WOKING
Young Stroat Farm
Broadford Farm
BROADFORD LANE
The Bourne
Focklesbrook Farm
Chobham Farm
MOUNT ROAD
PHILPOT LANE
Scotchers Farm
GROVE
MILFORD GREEN
A3046
Shaws Farm
Castle Grove PH
Castle Grn
LAKESIDE DRIVE
Sewage Works
Cox Hill
Mimbridge
Wapshott Farm
GROSVENOR RD
Milford House
Daydown Nursery
White Lodge Farm
GU21
COXHILL GREEN
Heather Farm
Millbrook Animal Centre (R.S.P.C.A.)
Border Farm
Mimbridge Garden Centre
CHOBHAM ROAD
GUILDFORD ROAD
Deep Pool Farm
Studley Grange Farm
CARTHOUSE LANE
HORSELL COMMON
NUFFIELD HOSPITAL
Knaphill Manor Farm
Knaphill Manor
Graylands Farm
The Bourne
DEEP POOL LANE
LITTLEWICK ROAD
HORSELL COMMON ROAD
COMMON CLOSE
KETTLEWELL HILL
Westbury Farm
Mink Farm
CHEAPSIDE
Garden Supplies
248
VIGGORY LANE
HEATHER CL
Rec Cen
Sec Sch
Parley Brook Farm
Garden Centre
Parley Bridge
HORSELL BIRCH
500 yds
500 m
0
105
106
107
108
109
110
111
112
113
114
98
99
00
64
63
62
61

AZ
BA
BB
BC
BD
BE
BF
01
02
03
RUNNYMEDE HOSP
ST. PETER'S HOSP
215
GOLF COURSE
Clubhouse
Foxhills Country Club
Foxhills
Tennis Courts
Dower House
HOME WOOD
Botleys Mansion
HOMEWOOD PARK
Hillswood Business Park
FISH POND
Church Farm
Kitchenride Corner
Ten Acre Farm
Woodside Farm
Junction 11
ST. PETER'S WAY
A320
GUILDFORD ROAD
Ether Hill
QUEENWOOD GOLF COURSE
KT16
OTTERSHAW MEMORIAL FIELDS
Youth Club
Amb Sta
OTTERSHAW
The Otter Nursery
Great Grove Farm
MURRAY ROAD
B3121
SPINNEY HILL
106
107
108
109
110
111
112
113
114
64
63
62
61
Coach House
Clubhouse
A319
CHOBHAM ROAD
Timber Hill
THE COMMON
Prim Sch
Bousley Farm
Bousley End Stables
Brox Road Nursery
Southern Wood Farm
ROW TOWN
KT15
Tulk House
The Mansion
BROX COPSE
Rodwell Farm
Hall's Farm
LONG COPSE
OTTERSHAW PARK
ROSE PARK
SAMSON'S WOOD
LITTLE BLACKMOLE POND
GREAT WOOD
SANDPIT PLANTATION
GREAT BLACKMOLE POND
Holme Farm
Fallow Farm
234
THE WARREN
Anningsley Park Farm
BIRCH WOOD
WARE COPSE
Anningsley Park
DECOY PLANTATION
Dunford Bridge
Bonsey's Bridge
McLaren Technology Centre
The Bourne
HOYT WOOD
WOODHAM
RUNNYMEDE
WOKING
Sports Club
Recycling Centre
NEW ZEALAND GOLF COURSE
Clubhouse
BASINGSTOKE CANAL
Electricity Station
WEST BYFLEET
Sheerwater Bridge
ANTHONYS
Danewell Hill
Sands PH
HORSELL COMMON
SHEERWATER
SHEERWATER REC GRD
Athletic Club
Sec Sch
Comm Cen
Youth Club
KT14
Clubhouse
A245
WOODHAM ROAD
CHERTSEY ROAD
Six Cross Roads
KINGSWEY BUSINESS PARK
RIVER COURT
GENESIS BUSINESS PARK
WOKING BUSINESS PARK
WEST BYFLEET GOLF COURSE
249
Pyrford
GU22
Monument Bridge
IND EST
SPORTS GROUND

MOOR GOLF COURSE
BG
BH
BJ
BK
BL
BM
BN
216
233
250
Junction 11
105
106
107
108
109
110
111
112
113
114
63
62
61
64
05
06
07
A317 ST. PETER'S WAY
WEYBRIDGE ROAD
A317
BALFOUR RD
CHURCH ST
HOSP
WEYBRIDGE
The Plantation Nursery
Tennis Cen
St. George's College
WOODLANDS
MEADOWLANDS PARK
Hamhaugh Point
SPORTS GRD
AVIATOR PK
VICTORY PARK
Bowl Grn PARK
HOSPITALLER CONVENT
Superstore
ADDLESTONE
Comm Cen
Pol Lib
CIVIC CEN
Health Cen
Prim Sch
Sports Cen
Sec Sch
HIGH STREET
BRIGHTON ROAD
STATION ROAD
CHURCH ROAD
B3121
B312
BOURNE BUS PK
RHM Culinary Brands
Thales
WEYBRIDGE BUSINESS PARK
Black Boy Bridge
Weybridge Lock
RUNNYMEDE
ELMBRIDGE
MEADOWS
Crockford Park Nurseries
ADDLESTONE
MILL POND
Coxes Lock
WEY MEADOWS
RIVERSIDE PARK
Crockford Bridge Farm
Crockford Bridge
NEW HAW ROAD
A318
SAYES COURT PUBLIC OPEN SPACE
ALLOT
KT15
PLAYING FIELDS
CEM
Brooklands College
Crickets Hill
Conduit Hill
Weybridge Junction
Addlestone Junction
Coomelands Farm
ROW TOWN
Clubhouse
DRIVING RANGE
TOP GOLF ADDLESTONE GOLF COURSE
NEW HAW
Nine Arches Bridge
Water Works
SEVEN ARCHES APPROACH
Seven Arches Bridge
Wey Manor Farm
Hall's Farm
The Bourne
CENTRAL VETERINARY LABORATORY
MERCEDES-BENZ WORLD
BROOKLANDS MUSEUM
ST GEORGES BUSINESS PK
Memorial
BROOKLANDS
Electricity Station
BYFLEET ROAD
Grange Farm
Charwood Farm
Fallow Farm
Comm Cen
Procter & Gamble
THE HEIGHTS
Sony UK
M25
BYFLEET & NEW HAW
Byfleet Junction
BROOKLANDS INDUSTRIAL PARK
TRADE CITY
SUB
River Ditch
ALLOT
Electricity Station
Fitness Club
HEATHERVALE CARAVAN PARK
HEATHERVALE REC GRD
Botton Lock
WOODHAM
OYSTER LANE A318
BYFLEET TECHNICAL CENTRE
BROOKLANDS COMMUNITY PARK
Paddocks Retail Pk
BARNES WALLIS DR
SOPWITH DR
CAMPHILL INDUSTRIAL ESTATE
Scotland Bridge
Scotland Lock
PLAYING FIELD
Sec Sch
BASINGSTOKE CANAL
Horizon Business Village
Cricket Grd Pav
PARVIS ROAD
Wey Retail Pk
Plough Bridge
Plough Bridge Farm
WEST BYFLEET
Electricity Station
Prim Schs
A245
DARTNELL PARK
OLD WOOD
TINS WOOD
KT14
OLDWOOD POND
Bluegates Hole
OLD WOKING ROAD
THE CORNER PARVIS
Health Cen
Superstore
PLAYING FIELD
Manor Farm
BYFLEET
WEST BYFLEET
Clubhouse
Mouchel Parkman
Byfleet Mill
DODD'S WOOD
Tennis Courts
Murray's Bridge
CEM
Health Club
Dodd's Bridge
WOKING
GUILDFORD
GU22
TRADITIONS GOLF COURSE
GU23
Manor House
THE ISLAND
Park Barn Farm
COMMON MEADOWS
River Wey
Sewage Works
Filter Beds
BUXTON WOOD
0 500 yds
0 500 m

ASHLEY PARK
OATLANDS PARK
BURWOOD PARK
WALTON COMMON
ST. GEORGE'S HILL
WHITELEY VILLAGE
BURHILL GOLF COURSE (OLD COURSE)
BURHILL GOLF COURSE (NEW COURSE)
ST. GEORGE'S HILL GOLF COURSE
SILVERMERE GOLF COURSE
PAINSHILL PARK
COBHAM
KT11
KT12
KT13
QUEENS ROAD
OATLANDS DRIVE
SEVEN HILLS ROAD
BYFLEET ROAD
PORTSMOUTH ROAD
ESHER ROAD
BURWOOD ROAD
HERSHAM ROAD
A3050
A317
A245
A3
B365
217
236
251
BP
BQ
BR
BS
BT
BU
BV
106
107
108
109
110
111
112
113
114
08
09
10
61
62
63
64

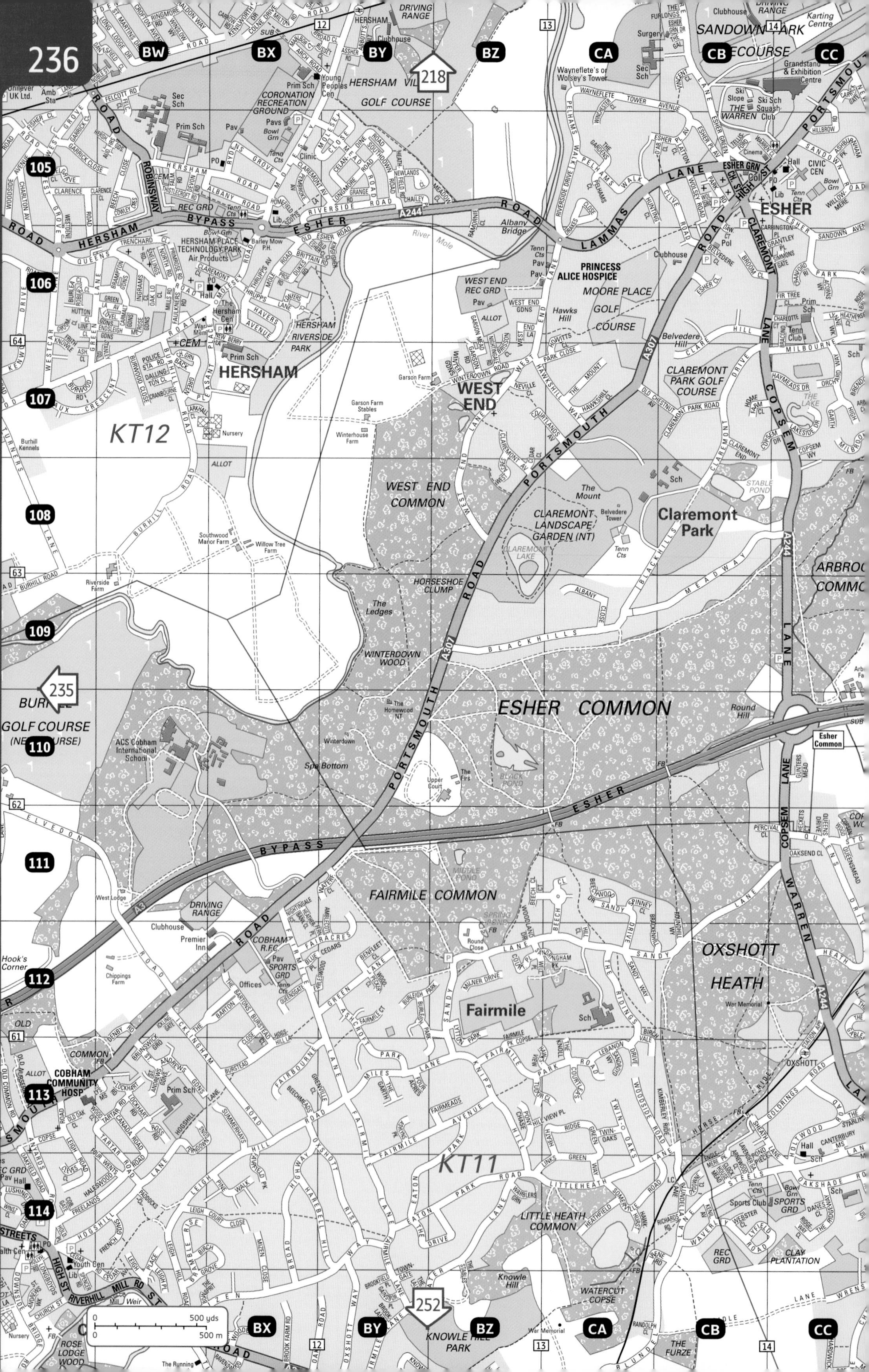
BW
BX
BY
BZ
CA
CB
CC
218
235
252
105
106
107
108
109
110
111
112
113
114
12
13
14
64
63
62
61
HERSHAM
KT12
HERSHAM VILLAGE GOLF COURSE
CORONATION RECREATION GROUND
SANDOWN PARK RACECOURSE
Grandstand & Exhibition Centre
Karting Centre
DRIVING RANGE
Wayneflete's or Wolsey's Tower
ESHER
WEST END
PRINCESS ALICE HOSPICE
MOORE PLACE GOLF COURSE
CLAREMONT PARK GOLF COURSE
Claremont Park
CLAREMONT LANDSCAPE GARDEN (NT)
HERSHAM RIVERSIDE PARK
HERSHAM PLACE TECHNOLOGY PARK
WEST END COMMON
HORSESHOE CLUMP
WINTERDOWN WOOD
ESHER COMMON
BURHILL GOLF COURSE (NEW COURSE)
ACS Cobham International School
FAIRMILE COMMON
OXSHOTT HEATH
Fairmile
KT11
COBHAM COMMUNITY HOSP
LITTLE HEATH COMMON
KNOWLE HILL PARK
CLAY PLANTATION
ROSE LODGE WOOD
THE FURZE
HERSHAM BYPASS
ESHER ROAD
PORTSMOUTH ROAD
LAMMAS LANE
COPSEM LANE
WARREN LANE
ESHER BYPASS
Esher Common
OXSHOTT
A3
A244
A307
500 yds
500 m

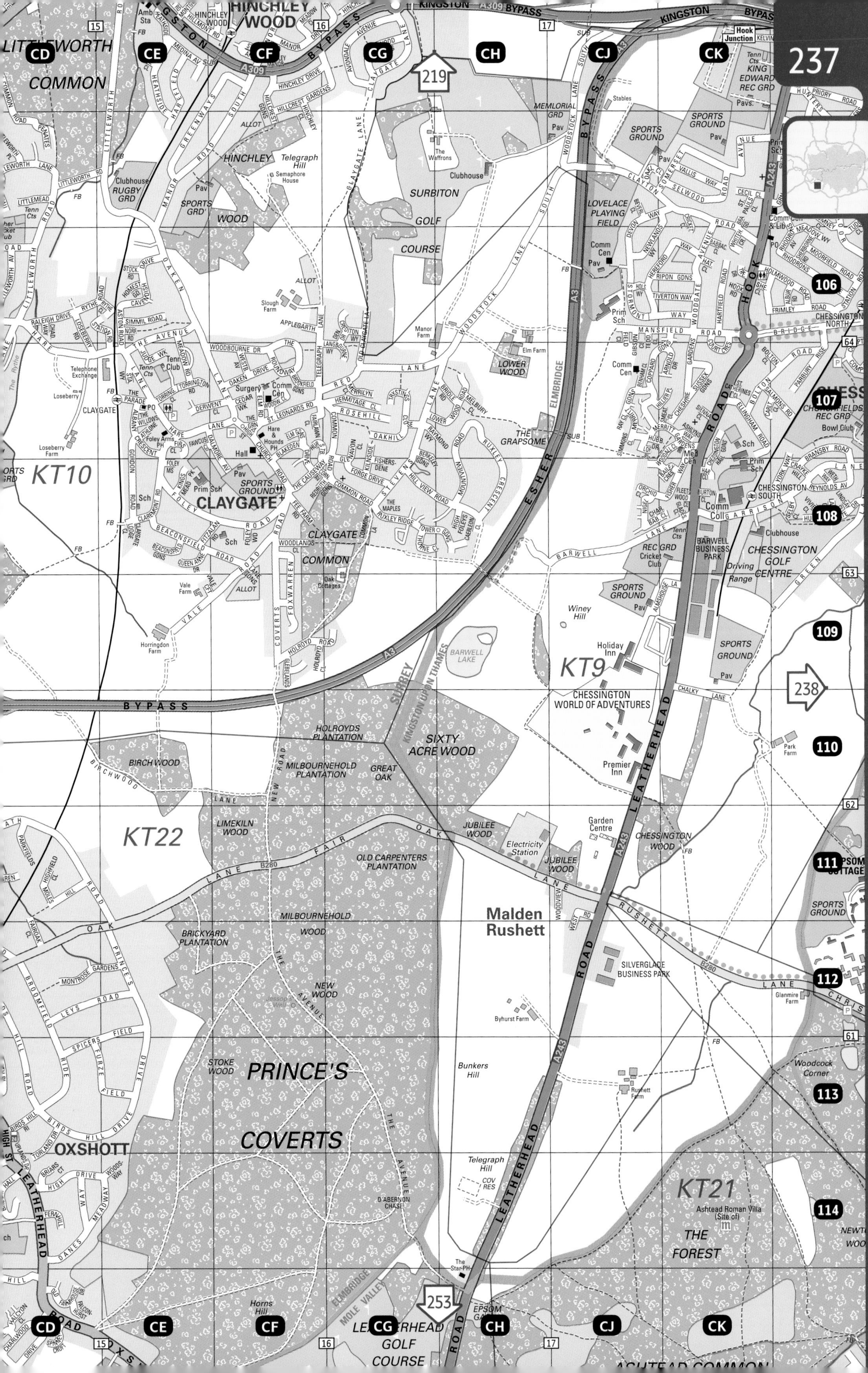

CD
CE
CF
CG
CH
CJ
CK
219
253
238
15
16
17
64
63
62
61
106
107
108
109
110
111
112
113
114
KINGSTON BYPASS
A309
HINCHLEY WOOD
Hook Junction
LITTLEWORTH COMMON
KING EDWARD REC GRD
HINCHLEY WOOD
Telegraph Hill
Semaphore House
Clubhouse
RUGBY GRD
SPORTS GRD
SURBITON GOLF COURSE
The Waffrons
MEMLORIAL GRD
SPORTS GROUND
LOVELACE PLAYING FIELD
Comm Cen
ALLOT
Slough Farm
Manor Farm
Elm Farm
LOWER WOOD
ELMBRIDGE
CHESSINGTON NORTH
Telephone Exchange
Loseberry
CLAYGATE
Loseberry Farm
KT10
CLAYGATE
SPORTS GROUND
Prim Sch
THE GRAPSOME
CHURCHFIELDS REC GRD
Bowl Club
CHESSINGTON SOUTH
CLAYGATE COMMON
Oak Cottages
Vale Farm
Horringdon Farm
REC GRD
Cricket Club
BARWELL BUSINESS PARK
CHESSINGTON GOLF CENTRE
Driving Range
Winey Hill
BARWELL LAKE
Holiday Inn
KT9
CHESSINGTON WORLD OF ADVENTURES
SPORTS GROUND
SURREY
KINGSTON UPON THAMES
BYPASS
A3
HOLROYDS PLANTATION
SIXTY ACRE WOOD
BIRCH WOOD
MILBOURNEHOLD PLANTATION
GREAT OAK
Premier Inn
Park Farm
KT22
LIMEKILN WOOD
JUBILEE WOOD
Electricity Station
Garden Centre
JUBILEE WOOD
CHESSINGTON WOOD
OLD CARPENTERS PLANTATION
OAK LANE
FAIR LANE
B280
Malden Rushett
BRICKYARD PLANTATION
MILBOURNEHOLD WOOD
SILVERGLADE BUSINESS PARK
RUSHETT LANE
Glanmire Farm
SPORTS GROUND
NEW WOOD
Byhurst Farm
STOKE WOOD
PRINCE'S COVERTS
Bunkers Hill
Woodcock Corner
Rushett Farm
OXSHOTT
Telegraph Hill
COV RES
KT21
Ashtead Roman Villa (Site of)
THE FOREST
D'ABERNON CHASE
The Star PH
LEATHERHEAD ROAD
A243
ESHER BYPASS
Horns Hill
MOLE VALLEY
LEATHERHEAD GOLF COURSE
EPSOM

CL
CM
CN
CP
CQ
CR
CS
220
254
237
19
20
21
105
106
107
108
109
110
111
112
113
114
64
63
62
61
KT9
KT19
KT18
KT21
HOOK
CHESSINGTON
HORTON
EPSOM
WEST EWELL
HORTON COUNTRY PARK
EPSOM COMMON
HORTON PARK COUNTRY CLUB GOLF COURSE
LONG GROVE PARK
HOGSMILL RIVERSIDE OPEN SPACE
KING GEORGE V REC GRD
KING GEORGES FIELD
CHESSINGTON GOLF CENTRE
CHESSINGTON TRADE PARK
KING GEORGE'S TRADING EST
DAVIS ROAD IND PK
HOOK RISE SOUTH IND PK
HOOK ROAD ARENA
ST. EBBA'S HOSPITAL
NEW EPSOM & EWELL COTTAGE HOSP
WEST PARK HOSPITAL
EPSOM GENERAL HOSP
BARWELL BUSINESS PARK
LONGMEAD BUSINESS CEN
NONSUCH INDUSTRIAL ESTATE
EPSOM TRADE PK
OLD HALEYBURIANS R.F.C.
BUTCHERS GROVE
GREAT WOOD
FOUR ACRE WOOD
POND WOOD
NEWTON WOOD
THE FOREST
Castle Hill
Earthworks
Bonesgate Open Space (Nat Res)
HORTON PARK CHILDREN'S FARM
CHESSINGTON NORTH
CHESSINGTON SOUTH
Tolworth Court Bridge
Pack Horse Bridge
SURREY
KINGSTON UPON THAMES
EPSOM
The Quadrant
TOWN HALL
UPPER HIGH STREET
HIGH ST
SOUTH STREET
ASHLEY AV
WEST HILL
CHURCH ROAD
CHRIST CHURCH ROAD
CHESSINGTON ROAD
HOOK ROAD
RUXLEY LANE
KINGSTON ROAD
WORCESTER PARK ROAD
KINGSTON BYPASS
COX LANE
HORTON LANE
CHANTILLY WAY
STEW POND
GREAT POND
Woodcock Corner
Glanmire Farm
Park Farm
Hollywood Lodge
Horton Farm
0 500 yds
0 500 m

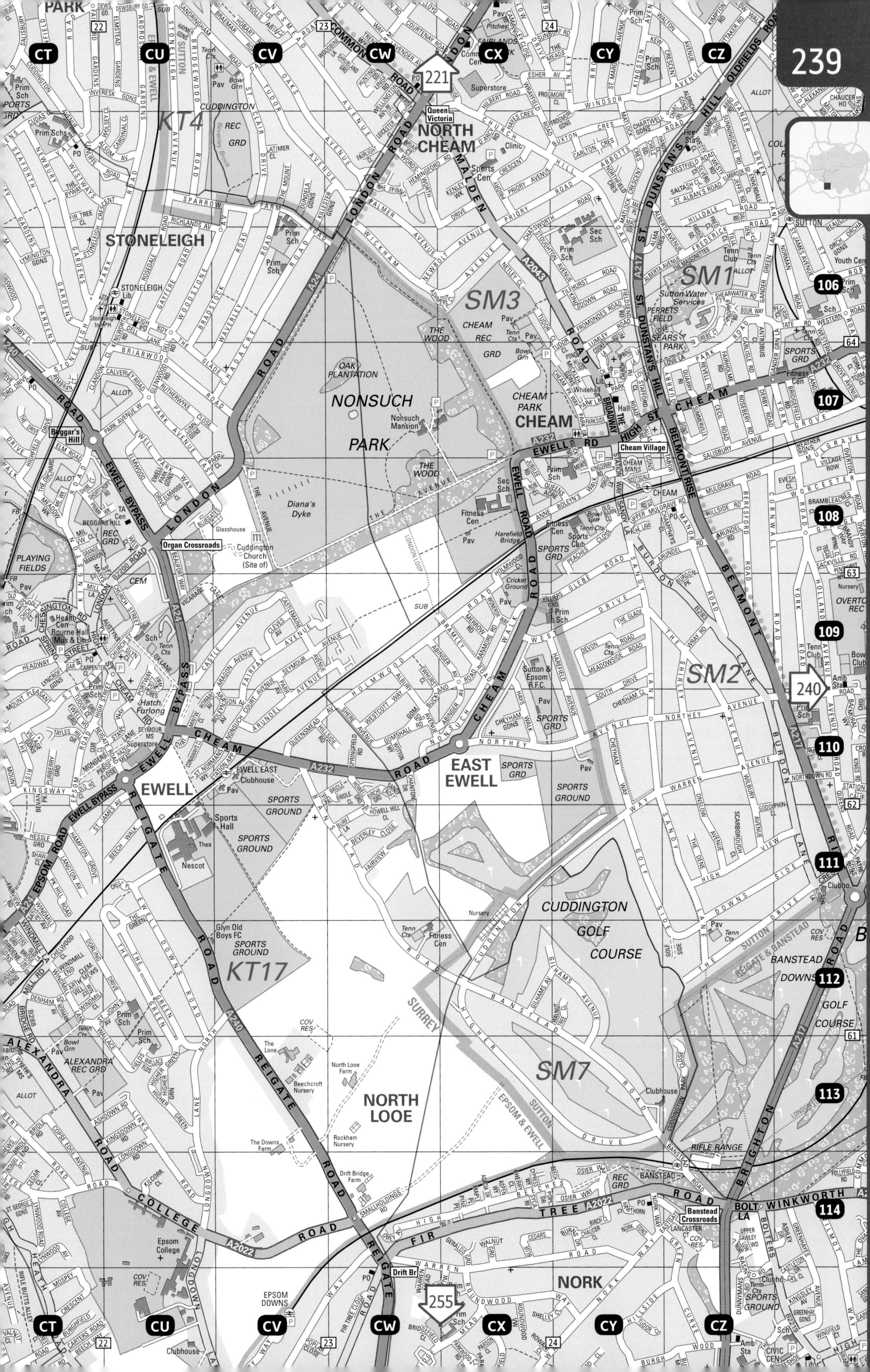
CT
CU
CV
CW
CX
CY
CZ
221
KT4
CUDDINGTON
REC GRD
NORTH CHEAM
Queen Victoria
Superstore
Sports Cen
Clinic
STONELEIGH
Stoneleigh
SM3
SM1
Sutton Water Services
PERRETS FIELD
SEARS PARK
106
107
108
109
110
111
112
113
114
OAK PLANTATION
NONSUCH PARK
Nonsuch Mansion
THE WOOD
CHEAM REC GRD
CHEAM PARK
CHEAM
Cheam Village
Beggar's Hill
Diana's Dyke
Organ Crossroads
Cuddington Church (Site of)
PLAYING FIELDS
CEM
Bourne Hall Mus & Lib
Hatch Furlong
EWELL
EWELL EAST
EAST EWELL
SPORTS GRD
SPORTS GROUND
SM2
240
Sutton & Epsom R.F.C.
Nescot
CUDDINGTON GOLF COURSE
BANSTEAD DOWNS GOLF COURSE
KT17
SM7
SURREY
EPSOM & EWELL
SUTTON
REIGATE & BANSTEAD
ALEXANDRA REC GRD
NORTH LOOE
The Looe
North Looe Farm
Beechcroft Nursery
Rockham Nursery
The Downs Farm
Drift Bridge Farm
RIFLE RANGE
Banstead Crossroads
Epsom College
EPSOM DOWNS
Drift Br
NORK
255
A24
A232
A240
A217
A2022
A2043
LONDON ROAD
EWELL BYPASS
REIGATE ROAD
BRIGHTON ROAD
COLLEGE ROAD
FIR TREE ROAD
BANSTEAD ROAD
EPSOM ROAD
ALEXANDRA ROAD
BELMONT RISE
ST DUNSTAN'S HILL
CHEAM ROAD
EWELL ROAD
22
23
24
61
62
63
64

DA
DB
DC
DD
DE
DF
DG
222
SM1
COLLINGWOOD REC GRD
Gas Works
ROYSTON PARK
THE WRYTHE REC GRD
Carshalton Coll
WILDERNESS ISLAND
THE GROVE
CARSHALTON
WEST SUTTON
SUTTON
CARSHALTON ROAD
HIGH ST
POUND ST
RUSKIN
CARSHALTON PARK
CARSHALTON BEECHES
105
106
107
108
109
110
111
112
113
114
SM2
OVERTON PARK REC GRD
BELMONT RISE
239
SM5
WELLFIELD PLANTATION
CARSHALTON BEECHES
SUTTON HOSPITAL
Uni of Lon Institute of Cancer Research
ROYAL MARSDEN HOSP
PLAYING FIELD
Diamond Riding Cen
LITTLE WOODCOTE ESTATE
BELMONT
BANSTEAD DOWNS
BANSTEAD DOWNS GOLF COURSE
BANSTEAD COMMON
H.M. PRISON DOWNVIEW
H.M. PRISON HIGH DOWN
OAKS SPORTS CENTRE GOLF COURSE
Oaks Sports Cen
THE OAKS PARK
LITTLE WOODCOTE
WOODMANSTERNE LANE
Huntersfield Riding Cen
Oaks Farm
Market Gardens
Market Garden
Evergreens Nursery
Holmdene Farm
Holmefarm Livery Stables
RIFLE RANGE
WINKWORTH ROAD
CROYDON ROAD
A2022
A217
RIFFET WOOD
SPORTS GROUND
BIG WOOD
WOODMANSTERNE PARK RECREATION GROUND
CLOCKHOUSE REC GRD
Weston Acres
Hengest Farm
Nicola Farm
SM7
256
WOODMANSTERNE
PROSPECT PLANTATION
Banstead Crossroads
500 yds
500 m
61
62
63
64
26
27
28

BEDDINGTON
WALLINGTON
SOUTH BEDDINGTON
SM6
BANDON HILL CEMETERY
DUPPAS HILL
CR0
PURLEY WAY PLAYING FIELDS
ROUNDSHAW PLAYING FIELD
ROUNDSHAW OPEN SPACE
SOUTH CROYDON
HALING PARK
CR2
WOODCOTE
PURLEY
CR8
Woodcote Park
CR5
WOODCOTE PARK GOLF COURSE
FOXLEY WOOD
HIGHER DRIVE REC GRD
RIDDLESDOWN WOOD
CROYDON ROAD
PURLEY WAY
BRIGHTON ROAD
GODSTONE ROAD
DOWNS COURT ROAD
FOXLEY LANE
WOODCOTE ROAD
SMITHAM BOTTOM LANE
WOODCOTE GROVE ROAD
Fiveways
Purley Cross
PURLEY WAR MEM. HOSP
223
242
257
DH
DJ
DK
DL
DM
DN
DP
106
107
108
109
110
111
112
113
114

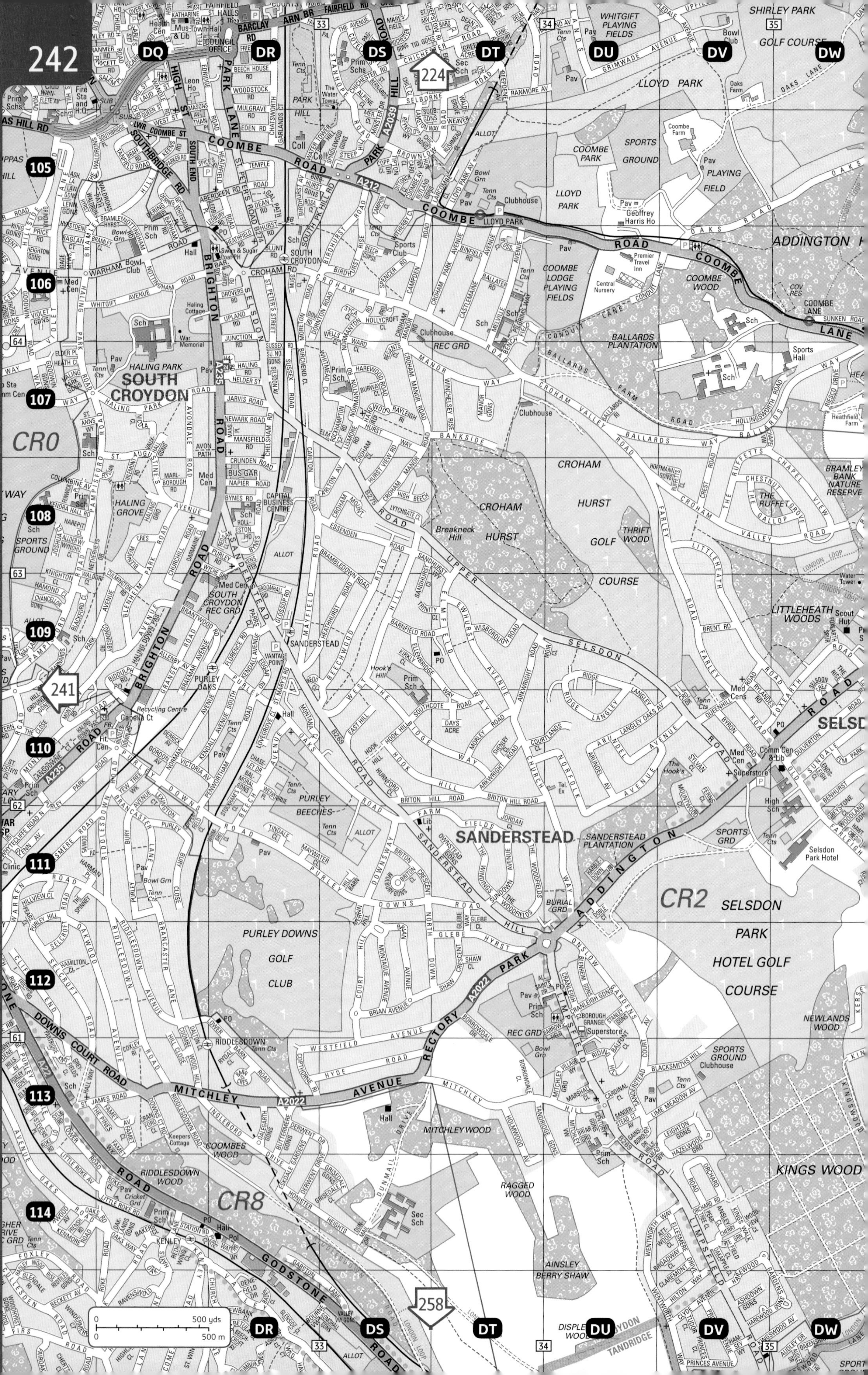
DQ
DR
DS
DT
DU
DV
DW
224
241
258
33
34
35
64
63
62
61
105
106
107
108
109
110
111
112
113
114
SHIRLEY PARK
GOLF COURSE
WHITGIFT
PLAYING
FIELDS
LLOYD PARK
GRIMWADE AVENUE
OAKS LANE
RANMORE AV
COOMBE PARK
SPORTS GROUND
PLAYING FIELD
LLOYD PARK
Clubhouse
Geoffrey Harris Ho
ADDINGTON
COOMBE ROAD
COOMBE ROAD
COOMBE WOOD
COOMBE LODGE PLAYING FIELDS
Premier Travel Inn
Central Nursery
CONDUIT LANE
BALLARDS PLANTATION
COOMBE LANE
SUNKEN ROAD
Sports Hall
HOLLINGSWORTH ROAD
Heathfield Farm
BALLARDS WAY
CROHAM VALLEY ROAD
CROHAM HURST GOLF COURSE
THRIFT WOOD
CROHAM HURST
Breakneck Hill
BRAMLEY BANK NATURE RESERVE
THE RUFFETT
LITTLEHEATH WOODS
Water Tower
Scout Hut
SELSDON ROAD
SELSDON
UPPER SELSDON ROAD
SOUTH CROYDON
HALING PARK
HALING GROVE
CR0
CR2
CR8
SPORTS GROUND
BRIGHTON ROAD
SOUTH END
HIGH ST
PARK LANE
SOUTHBRIDGE RD
COOMBE ROAD
CROHAM RD
SELSDON ROAD
SANDERSTEAD ROAD
SOUTH CROYDON REC GRD
SANDERSTEAD
VANTAGE POINT
PURLEY OAKS
Recycling Centre
PURLEY BEECHES
PURLEY DOWNS GOLF CLUB
RIDDLESDOWN
RIDDLESDOWN WOOD
COOMBES WOOD
MITCHLEY WOOD
MITCHLEY AVENUE
DOWNS COURT ROAD
GODSTONE ROAD
KENLEY
RAGGED WOOD
AINSLEY BERRY SHAW
SANDERSTEAD PLANTATION
ADDINGTON ROAD
LIMPSFIELD ROAD
REC GRD
SELSDON PARK HOTEL GOLF COURSE
Selsdon Park Hotel
NEWLANDS WOOD
SPORTS GROUND Clubhouse
KINGS WOOD
DISPLEY WOOD
TANDRIDGE
LONDON LOOP
0 500 yds
0 500 m

DX
DY
DZ
EA
EB
EC
ED
225
244
259
106
107
108
109
110
111
112
113
114
36
37
38
64
63
62
61
SHIRLEY
ADDINGTON
FORESTDALE
NEW ADDINGTON
FARLEIGH
CR0
CR6
BR4
FOXES WOOD
PINEWOODS
KENNEL WOOD
THE ADDINGTON GOLF CLUB
Clubhouse
THREEHALFPENNY WOOD
SPRING PARK
PLAYING FIELD
SPARROWS DEN PLAYING FIELDS
Old Beccehamian R.F.C.
BURIAL GRD
Pumping Station
Croydon R.F.C.
Rugby Grd
Fox Hill
FOXHILL SHAW
ROWDOWN FIELDS
BIRCH WOOD
ADDINGTON PALACE GOLF COURSE
Addington Palace
ADDINGTON PARK
Pavilion
ADDINGTON VILLAGE
SPORTS GROUND
KENT GATE WAY
GRAVEL HILL
SELSDON PARK ROAD
A212
A2022
ADDINGTON ROAD
BISHOPS WALK
LODGE LANE
FIELDWAY
KING HENRY'S DRIVE
PARKWAY
CASTLE HILL RUFFS
ROWDOWN WOOD
ADDINGTON VALE
FALCONWOOD MEADOW
Pumping Station
Water Works
REC GRD
NORTH DOWN REC GRD
Clubhouse
ADDINGTON COURT
GOLF COURSE
BEARS WOOD
(Scout Camp)
FRITH WOOD
BIRCHEN SHAW
SELSDON WOOD NT
STEVEN'S LARCH
GREENHILL SHAW
HILLOCKS WOOD
BROOM WOOD
PUPLET WOOD
Haggler's Dean
FARLEIGH COURT
GOLF COURSE
Farleigh Dean
FRYLANDS WOOD
THREECORNER GROVE
DUMPSEY DERRY
CRAB WOOD
CHAPEL HILL
LIMEKILN SHAW
COLDBLOW SHAW
BOGRAMS WOOD
HODGE GROVE
HOGCROFT SHAW
Elm Farm
Farleigh House Farm
Farleigh Court
Farleigh Cottages
Farleigh Court Manor House
Little Farleigh Green Farm
LITTLE FARLEIGH GREEN
LITTLE GREAT HILL
GT FARLEIGH GRN
MOSSYHILL SHAW
OAKEN SHAW
MOSESHILL SHAW
WELLS SHAW
BEECHES SHAW
Kingswood Lodge
Kingsmead Equestrian Centre
Scotshall Farm
FIVE ACRE SHAW
GREAT HILL SHAW
White Bear Inn PH
Fairchildes Farm
Fickleshole Farm
North Lodge
South Lodge
MILNE PARK
Health Cen
Leisure Centre
Recycling Centre
CROYDON
TANDRIDGE
SURREY
BROMLEY
LONDON LOOP
Mickleham Way Electricity Sta

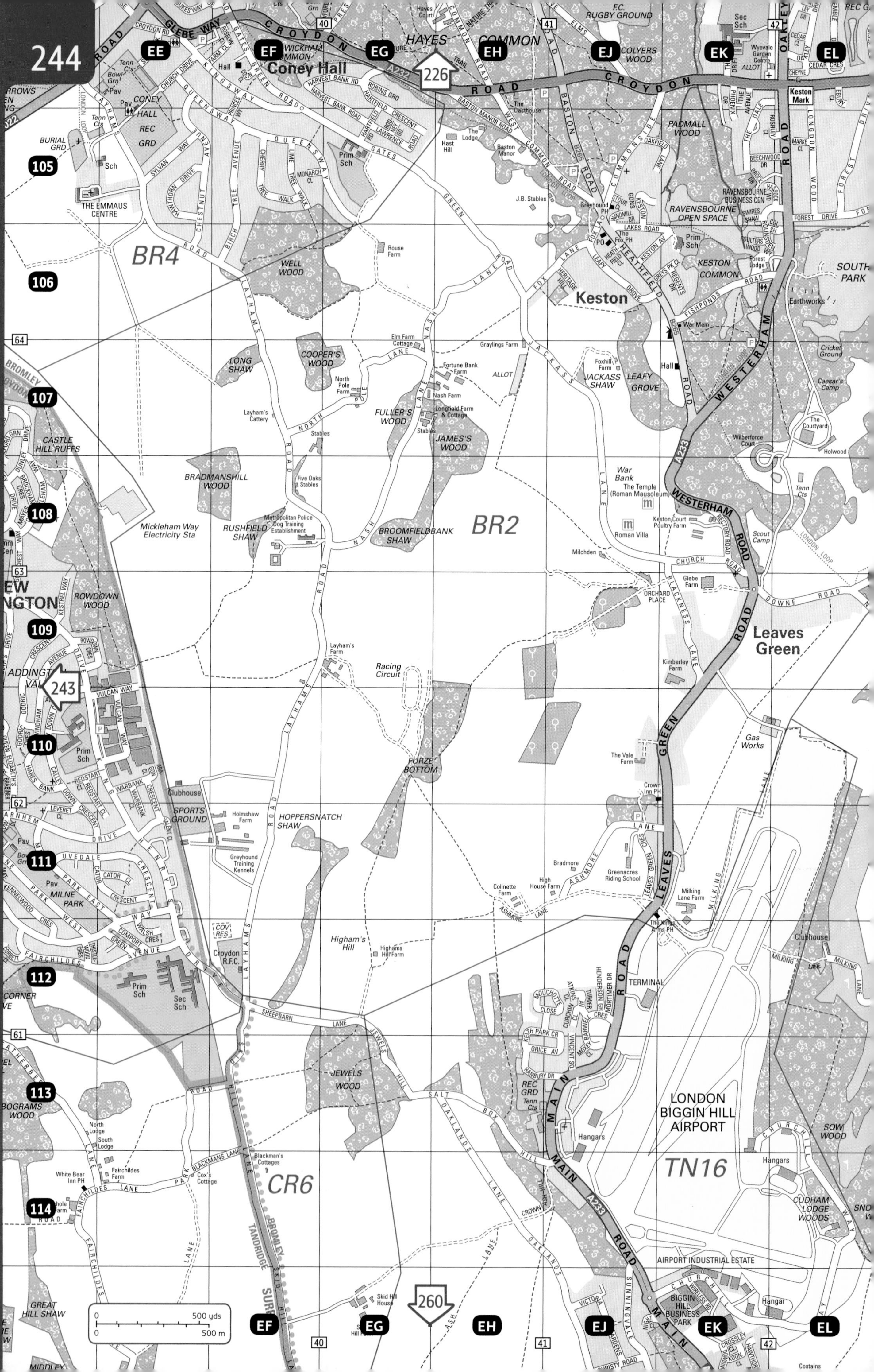
Coney Hall
HAYES COMMON
CROYDON ROAD
GLEBE WAY
WICKHAM COMMON
F.C. RUGBY GROUND
COLYERS WOOD
Keston Mark
226
EE
EF
EG
EH
EJ
EK
EL
CONEY HALL REC GRD
THE EMMAUS CENTRE
BURIAL GRD
QUEENSWAY
KINGSWAY
HARVEST BANK RD
BASTON MANOR ROAD
Baston Manor
The Oasthouse
The Lodge
Hast Hill
PADMALL WOOD
RAVENSBOURNE BUSINESS CEN
RAVENSBOURNE OPEN SPACE
FOREST DRIVE
J.B. Stables
Greyhound PH
LAKES ROAD
The Fox PH
Prim Sch
KESTON COMMON
Keston
SOUTH PARK
Earthworks
BR4
WELL WOOD
Rouse Farm
LAYHAMS ROAD
NASH LANE
FOX LANE
JACKASS LANE
HEATHFIELD
FISHPONDS
War Mem
Hall
Cricket Ground
Caesar's Camp
WESTERHAM ROAD
A233
Elm Farm Cottage
Graylings Farm
Foxhill Farm
JACKASS SHAW
LEAFY GROVE
ALLOT
LONG SHAW
COOPER'S WOOD
North Pole Farm
NORTH POLE LANE
Fortune Bank Farm
Nash Farm
Longfield Farm & Cottage
FULLER'S WOOD
JAMES'S WOOD
Layham's Cattery
Stables
The Courtyard
Wilberforce Court
Holwood
Tenn Cts
BRADMANSHILL WOOD
Five Oaks Stables
War Bank
The Temple (Roman Mausoleum)
Roman Villa
Keston Court Poultry Farm
RECTORY ROAD
Scout Camp
LONDON LOOP
Mickleham Way Electricity Sta
RUSHFIELD SHAW
Metropolitan Police Dog Training Establishment
BROOMFIELDBANK SHAW
BR2
Milchden
CHURCH ROAD
Glebe Farm
ORCHARD PLACE
BLACKNESS LANE
DOWNE ROAD
CASTLE HILL RUFFS
ROWDOWN WOOD
NEW ADDINGTON
Leaves Green
Layham's Farm
Racing Circuit
Kimberley Farm
ADDINGTON VALE
243
VULCAN WAY
Gas Works
FURZE BOTTOM
The Vale Farm
Crown Inn PH
LEAVES GREEN ROAD
Clubhouse
SPORTS GROUND
Holmshaw Farm
HOPPERSNATCH SHAW
Greyhound Training Kennels
Bradmore
Greenacres Riding School
High House Farm
Colinette Farm
ASHMORE LANE
Milking Lane Farm
MILKING LANE
The Kings Arms PH
UVEDALE
MILNE PARK
PARK EAST
PARK WEST
CRESCENT
COV RES
Croydon R.F.C.
Higham's Hill
Highams Hill Farm
FAIRCHILDES AVENUE
Prim Sch
Sec Sch
SHEEPBARN LANE
TERMINAL
JEWELS WOOD
JEWELS HILL
KEITH PARK CR
GRICE AV
HANBURY DR
REC GRD
BOGRAMS WOOD
SALT BOX HILL
OAKLANDS LANE
MAIN ROAD
Hangars
LONDON BIGGIN HILL AIRPORT
SOW WOOD
North Lodge
South Lodge
White Bear Inn PH
Fairchildes Farm
BLACKMANS LANE
Blackman's Cottages
Cox's Cottage
CR6
TN16
CUDHAM LODGE WOODS
CROWN ASH
AIRPORT INDUSTRIAL ESTATE
BIGGIN HILL BUSINESS PARK
Hangar
GREAT HILL SHAW
TANDRIDGE
SURREY
BROMLEY
SKID HILL LANE
Skid Hill House
260
0 500 yds
0 500 m
40
41
42
61
62
63
64
105
106
107
108
109
110
111
112
113
114
Costains

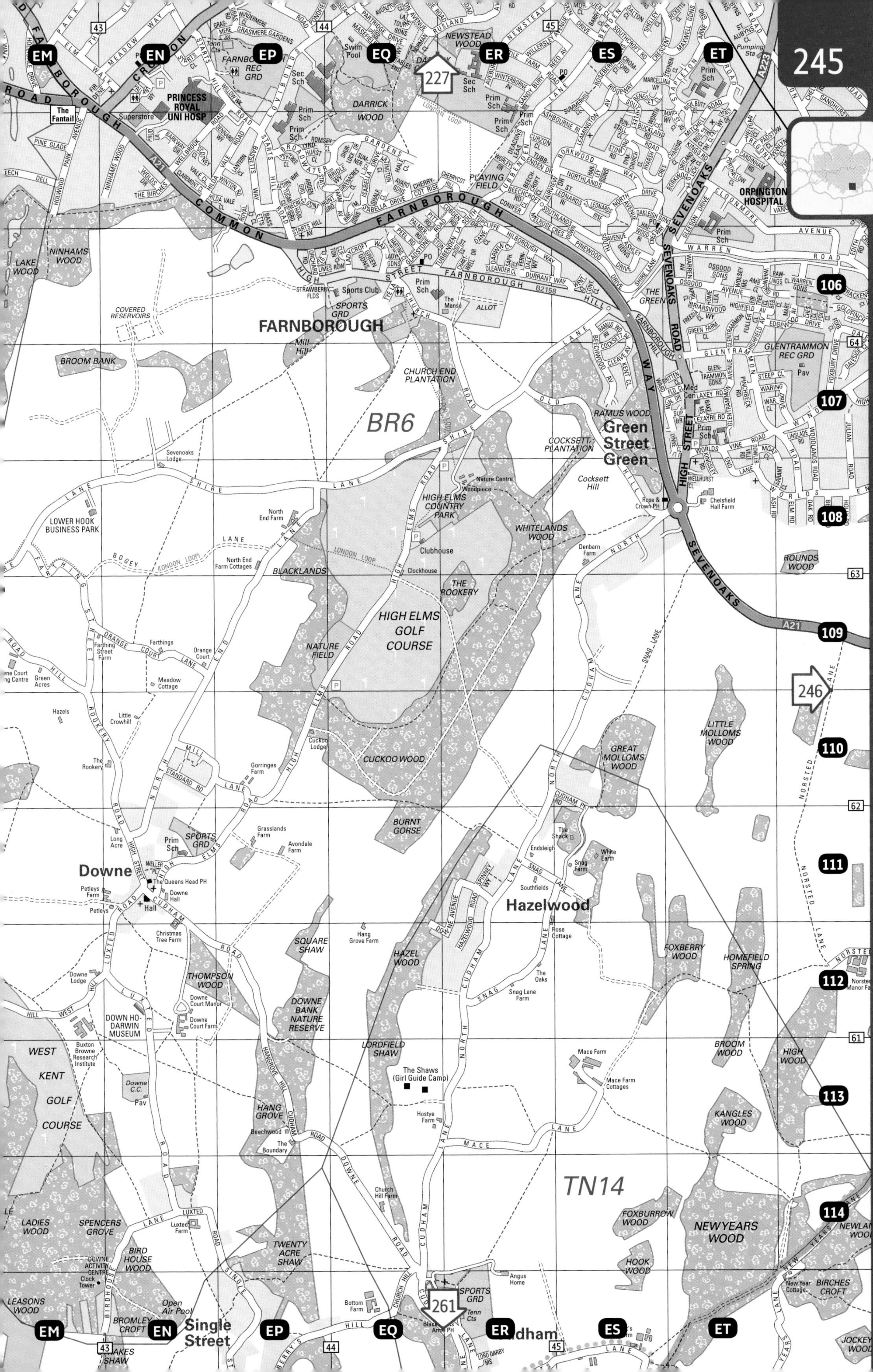
227
246
261
EM
EN
EP
EQ
ER
ES
ET
FARNBOROUGH
BR6
TN14
Green Street Green
Downe
Hazelwood
Single Street
PRINCESS ROYAL UNI HOSP
ORPINGTON HOSPITAL
FARNBOROUGH COMMON
FARNBOROUGH WAY
SEVENOAKS ROAD
SEVENOAKS WAY
A21
A223
B2158
HIGH ELMS GOLF COURSE
HIGH ELMS COUNTRY PARK
CUCKOO WOOD
BURNT GORSE
HAZEL WOOD
DOWNE BANK NATURE RESERVE
WEST KENT GOLF COURSE
DOWN HO- DARWIN MUSEUM
THOMPSON WOOD
SQUARE SHAW
LORDFIELD SHAW
HANG GROVE
TWENTY ACRE SHAW
GREAT MOLLOMS WOOD
LITTLE MOLLOMS WOOD
FOXBERRY WOOD
HOMEFIELD SPRING
BROOM WOOD
HIGH WOOD
KANGLES WOOD
NEWYEARS WOOD
FOXBURROW WOOD
HOOK WOOD
BIRCHES CROFT
LADIES WOOD
SPENCERS GROVE
BIRD HOUSE WOOD
LEASONS WOOD
BROMLEY CROFT
WHITELANDS WOOD
THE ROOKERY
NATURE FIELD
BLACKLANDS
CHURCH END PLANTATION
COCKSETT PLANTATION
RAMUS WOOD
BROOM BANK
LAKE WOOD
NINHAMS WOOD
DARRICK WOOD
NEWSTEAD WOOD
ROUNDS WOOD
GLENTRAMMON REC GRD
LOWER HOOK BUSINESS PARK
SHIRE LANE
CUDHAM LANE NORTH
SNAG LANE
NORSTED LANE
MACE LANE
LUXTED ROAD
HIGH ELMS ROAD
106
107
108
109
110
111
112
113
114
61
62
63
64
43
44
45

Goddington
GODDINGTON PARK
228
Goddington Manor
Sec Sch
Bowling Green
Clubhouse
Tennis Courts
ORPINGTON HOSPITAL
Prim Sch
CHELSFIELD
CHELSFIELD GREEN
CHELSFIELD
ASPEN SPRING
GLENTRAMMON REC GRD
HIGH BEECHES
CHELSFIELD PARK SPORTS GRD
ELEVEN OAKS
CHELSFIELD HILL WOOD
ROUNDS WOOD
LILLY'S WOOD
BLACK BUSH WOOD
BR6
CHELSFIELD PARK HOSPITAL
Lilly's Farm
Court Lodge Farm
ALLOT CHELSFIELD REC GRD
Maypole
Bucks Cross Farm
CHELSFIELD LAKES GOLF COURSE
DRIVING RANGE
Chelsfield Riding School
Hewitts Farm Market
Bo Peep PH
Bluebell Farm
KENT
CONEYEARTH WOOD
KNOCKHOLT
Elec Sta
GOSS BUSHES
Wheatsheaf Farm
BROKE HILL GOLF COURSE
Clubhouse
WATERCROFTS WOOD
SEVENOAKS ROAD A21
ORPINGTON BYPASS
COURT ROAD A224
245
LITTLE MOLLOMS
Charmwood Farm
Pratt's Bottom
Stonehouse Farm
ROCK FIELD SHAW
Bulls Head PH
Hall
Woodhill Farm
CHARM WOOD
PRATTS GROVE
Prim Sch
PRATT'S BOTTOM WOOD
RUSHMOOR HILL WOOD
HOOK WOOD
BIRTHDAY WOOD
Hill Side Farm
Stud Farm
Widmore Farm
Colgates Farm
Fairtrough Farm
HOMEFIELD SPRING
Norsted Manor Farm
LOWER BROOMS WOOD
UPPER BROOMS WOOD
LATTICE COPPICE
Coolings Nurseries
Pav SPORTS GRD
Tenn Cts
Rose & Crown P.H.
CHALKHURST WOOD
Hall
Prim Sch
PO
BROOM WOOD
HIGH WOOD
BIRCHINGBANK WOOD
Rushmore Hill Farm
KANGLES WOOD
The Washneys
PERRY WOOD
LOWER RANDLE'S WOOD
Close Heath Farm
DEERLEAP WOOD
Park Farm
Warren Court Farm
Halstead
Highlands Farm
Kangles Farm
Nursery Farm
HAYMAN'S WOOD
PIECE WOOD
New Stables Farm
NEWYEARS WOOD
NEWLANDS WOOD
Curry Farm
BROOMFIELD WOOD
New Year Cottage
BIRCHES CROFT
LONG BOTTOM SHAW
HAWFIELD WOOD
262
Singles Cross
Knockholt Pound
CHAPEL CROFT
Blueberry Farm
0 500 yds
0 500 m

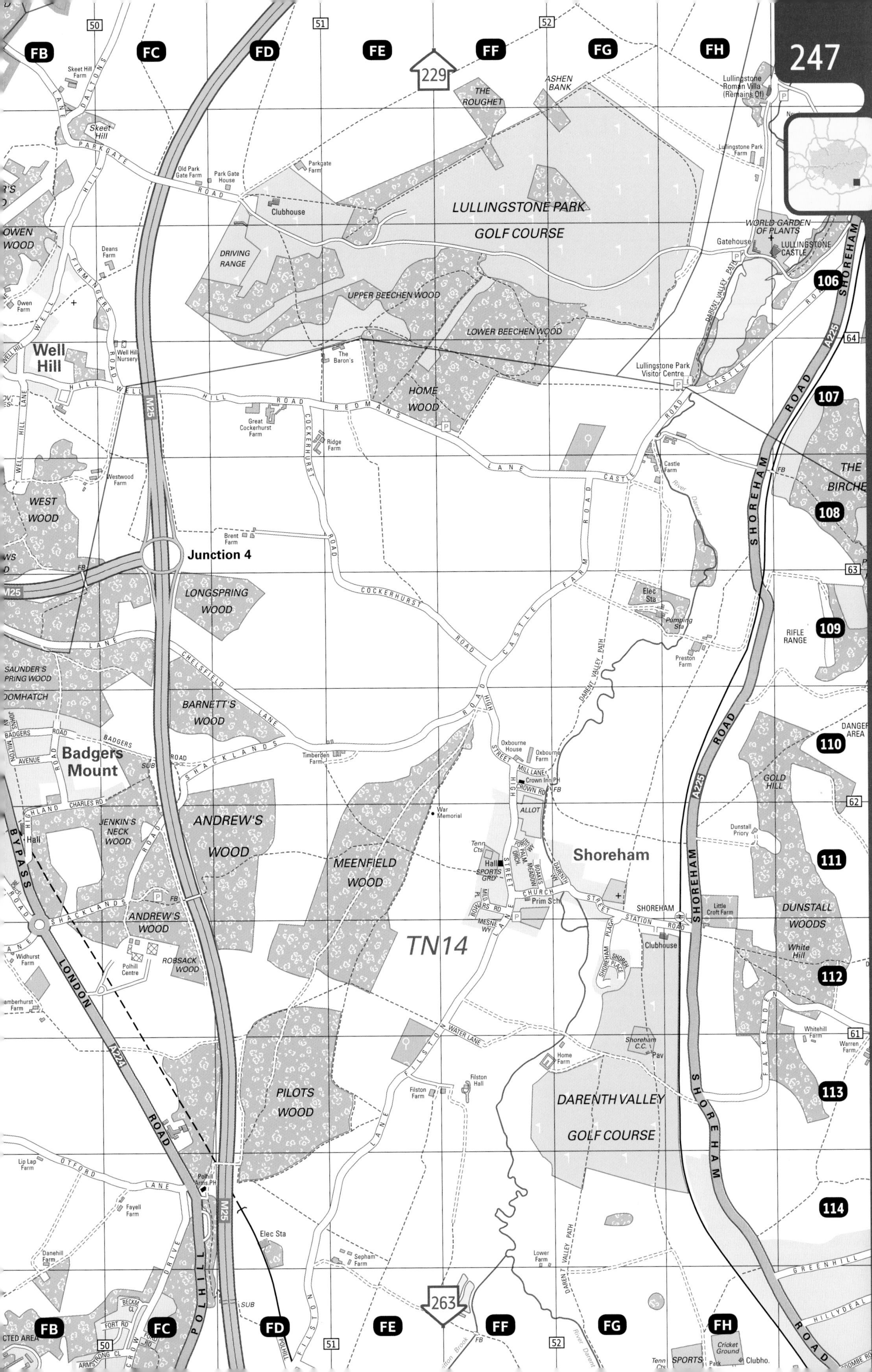
FB
FC
FD
FE
FF
FG
FH
50
51
52
229
263
Skeet Hill Farm
Skeet Hill
DALTONS
LANE
PARKGATE ROAD
Old Park Gate Farm
Park Gate House
Parkgate Farm
Clubhouse
DRIVING RANGE
THE ROUGHET
ASHEN BANK
LULLINGSTONE PARK GOLF COURSE
UPPER BEECHEN WOOD
LOWER BEECHEN WOOD
Lullingstone Roman Villa (Remains Of)
Lullingstone Park Farm
WORLD GARDEN OF PLANTS
Gatehouse
LULLINGSTONE CASTLE
DARENT VALLEY PATH
Lullingstone Park Visitor Centre
CASTLE ROAD
SHOREHAM ROAD
A225
106
107
108
109
110
111
112
113
114
64
63
62
61
OWEN WOOD
Deans Farm
FIRMINGERS ROAD
Owen Farm
Well Hill
Well Hill Nursery
WELL HILL
HILL ROAD
The Baron's
HOME WOOD
REDMANS LANE
Great Cockerhurst Farm
COCKERHURST ROAD
Ridge Farm
Castle Farm
River Darent
THE BIRCHE
Westwood Farm
WEST WOOD
M25
Brent Farm
Junction 4
FARM ROAD
LONGSPRING WOOD
Elec Sta
Pumping Sta
Preston Farm
RIFLE RANGE
SAUNDER'S SPRING WOOD
CHELSFIELD LANE
BARNETT'S WOOD
HIGH STREET
BADGERS ROAD
Badgers Mount
AVENUE
SHACKLANDS ROAD
Timberden Farm
Oxbourne House
Oxbourne Farm
MILL LANE
Crown Inn PH
CROWN RD
ALLOT
DANGER AREA
GOLD HILL
HIGHLAND
CHARLES RD
JENKIN'S NECK WOOD
ANDREW'S WOOD
War Memorial
MEENFIELD WOOD
Tenn Cts
Hall
SPORTS GRD
FORGE WY
PALM
ORCH
MEADOW
BOAKES
DARENTH
Shoreham
Dunstall Priory
BYPASS
Hall
CHURCH STREET
Prim Sch
BOWERS RD
MESNE WY
SHOREHAM
STATION ROAD
Little Croft Farm
DUNSTALL WOODS
White Hill
ANDREW'S WOOD
Widhurst Farm
Polhill Centre
ROBSACK WOOD
TN14
SHOREHAM PLACE
Clubhouse
LONDON ROAD
A224
WATER LANE
FILSTON LANE
Shoreham C.C.
Pav
Home Farm
FACKENDEN LANE
Whitehill Farm
Warren Farm
Filston Farm
Filston Hall
PILOTS WOOD
DARENTH VALLEY GOLF COURSE
Lip Lap Farm
OTFORD LANE
Polhill Arms PH
Fayell Farm
Elec Sta
Danehill Farm
POLHILL
DRIVE
Sepham Farm
Lower Farm
GREENHILL
HILLYDEAL
SUB
BECKM CL
FORT RD
CROW
ARMSTRONG CL
Cricket Ground
Park
Clubho.
SPORTS
Tenn Cts
River Darent
FB
CTED AREA

AS
AT
AU
AV
AW
AX
AY
232
264
98
99
00
GU21
GU24
GU3
115
116
117
118
119
120
121
122
123
124
59
58
57
56
CARTHOUSE LANE
Knaphill Manor
Graylands Farm
Westbury Farm
Garden Supplies
Parley Brook Farm
Garden Centre
Parley Bridge
Mink Farm
Knapwood House
LITTLEWICK COMMON
Mizen's Railway
HORSELL COMMON
LITTLEWICK ROAD
HORSELL BIRCH
TRACIOUS COPSE
Horsell
Hockey Club
GOLDSWORTH PARK REC GRD
GOLDSWORTH PARK
GOLDSWORTH PARK TRADING ESTATE
Goldsworth Park
Activity Centre
WATERERS PARK
Knaphill
LANSBURY ESTATE
Superstore
Crematorium
WOKING CEMETERY
ST. JOHN'S LYE
St. John's
Mount Hermon
LOCKFIELD DRIVE
A324
Basingstoke Canal
Premier Inn
SPORTS GRD
Hook Heath
WOKING GOLF COURSE
De Vere Gorse Hill
Fishers Hill House
Fisher's Hill
Brook Farm
Nursery
Clubhouse
WORPLESDON GOLF COURSE
Crastock Farm
Crastock Manor
SMART'S HEATH
MARTLANDS IND EST
PREY HEATH
Kemishford Bridge
WORPLESDON
Burdenshot Hill
Bonnieshott Wood Farm
Bridley Manor Farm
BRIDLEY COPSE
Havering Farm
Suttongreen Nurseries
WHITMOOR
Mayford
Jackman's Garden Centre
Mayford Centre
SPORTS GROUND
HOE VALLEY LINEAR PARK
Cricket & Bowls Club
Loampits Farm
The Mayford Arms PH
Mayford Bridge
Beech Hill
SUTTON GREEN GOLF COURSE
Pye Hill
A320
A3046
B380
Bowling Green
Tennis Club
SAUNDERS LANE
SMARTS HEATH ROAD
PREY HEATH ROAD
GUILDFORD ROAD
EGLEY ROAD
HERMITAGE ROAD
WOKING GUILDFORD
0 500 yds
0 500 m

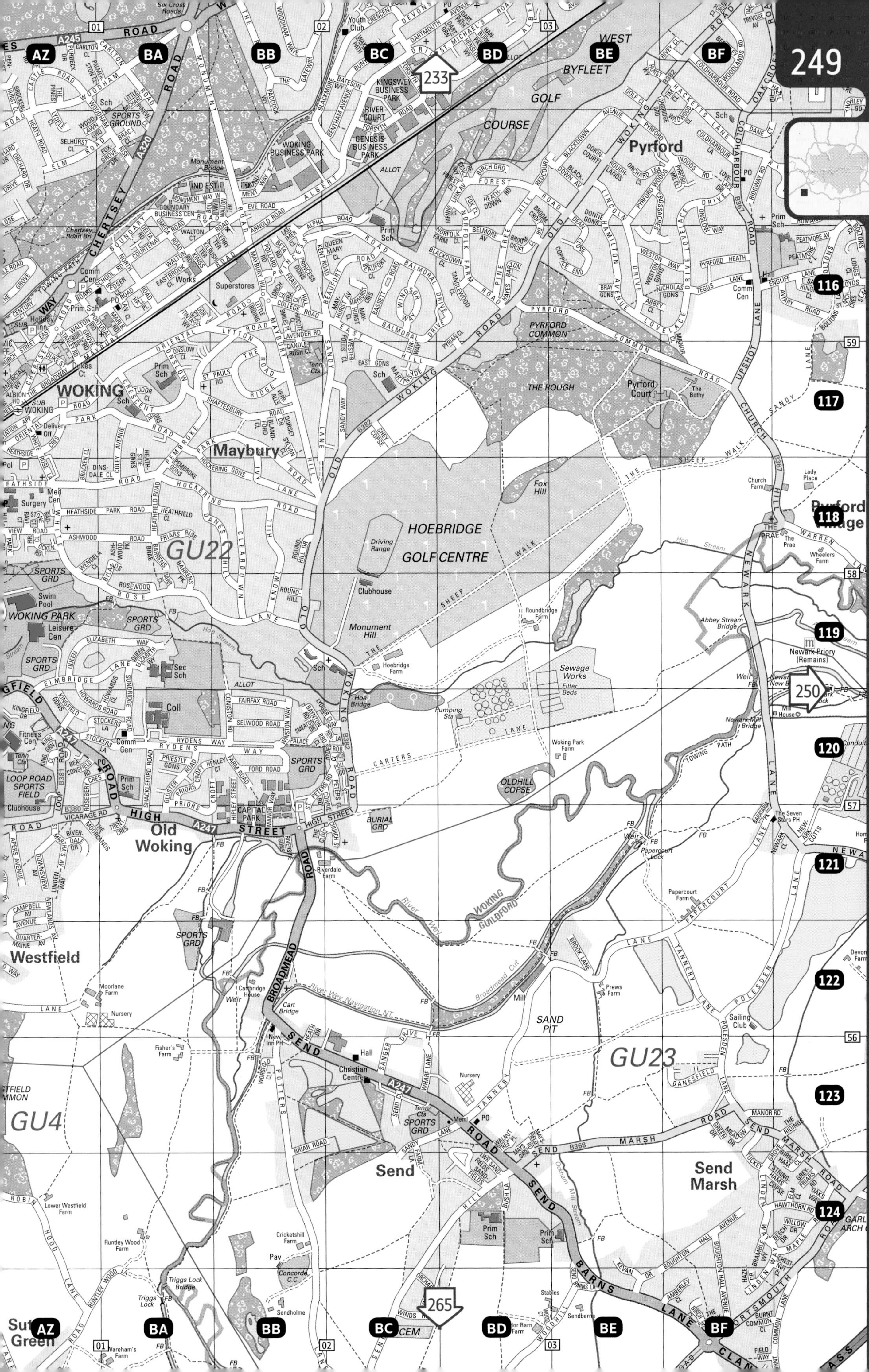
233
250
265
AZ
BA
BB
BC
BD
BE
BF
01
02
03
116
117
118
119
120
121
122
123
124
59
58
57
56
WEST BYFLEET
GOLF COURSE
Pyrford
WOKING
Maybury
GU22
HOEBRIDGE GOLF CENTRE
Driving Range
Clubhouse
Monument Hill
Fox Hill
PYRFORD COMMON
THE ROUGH
Pyrford Court
Newark Priory (Remains)
Sewage Works
Woking Park Farm
OLDHILL COPSE
Old Woking
HIGH STREET
Westfield
GU4
GU23
SAND PIT
Send
Send Marsh
WOKING BUSINESS PARK
KINGSWEY BUSINESS PARK
GENESIS BUSINESS PARK
Superstores
SPORTS GRD
WOKING PARK
Leisure Cen
LOOP ROAD SPORTS FIELD
River Wey
River Wey Navigation NT
Broadmead Cut
Hoe Stream
Papercourt Lock
Papercourt Farm
Triggs Lock
Cartbridge House
Christian Centre
BROADMEAD ROAD
SEND ROAD
SEND BARNS LANE
MARSH ROAD
PORTSMOUTH ROAD
CHERTSEY ROAD
WOKING ROAD
OLD WOKING ROAD
NEWARK LANE
CHURCH HILL
UPSHOT LANE
COLDHARBOUR ROAD
A245
A320
A247
B382
B367
B368
B380
B381

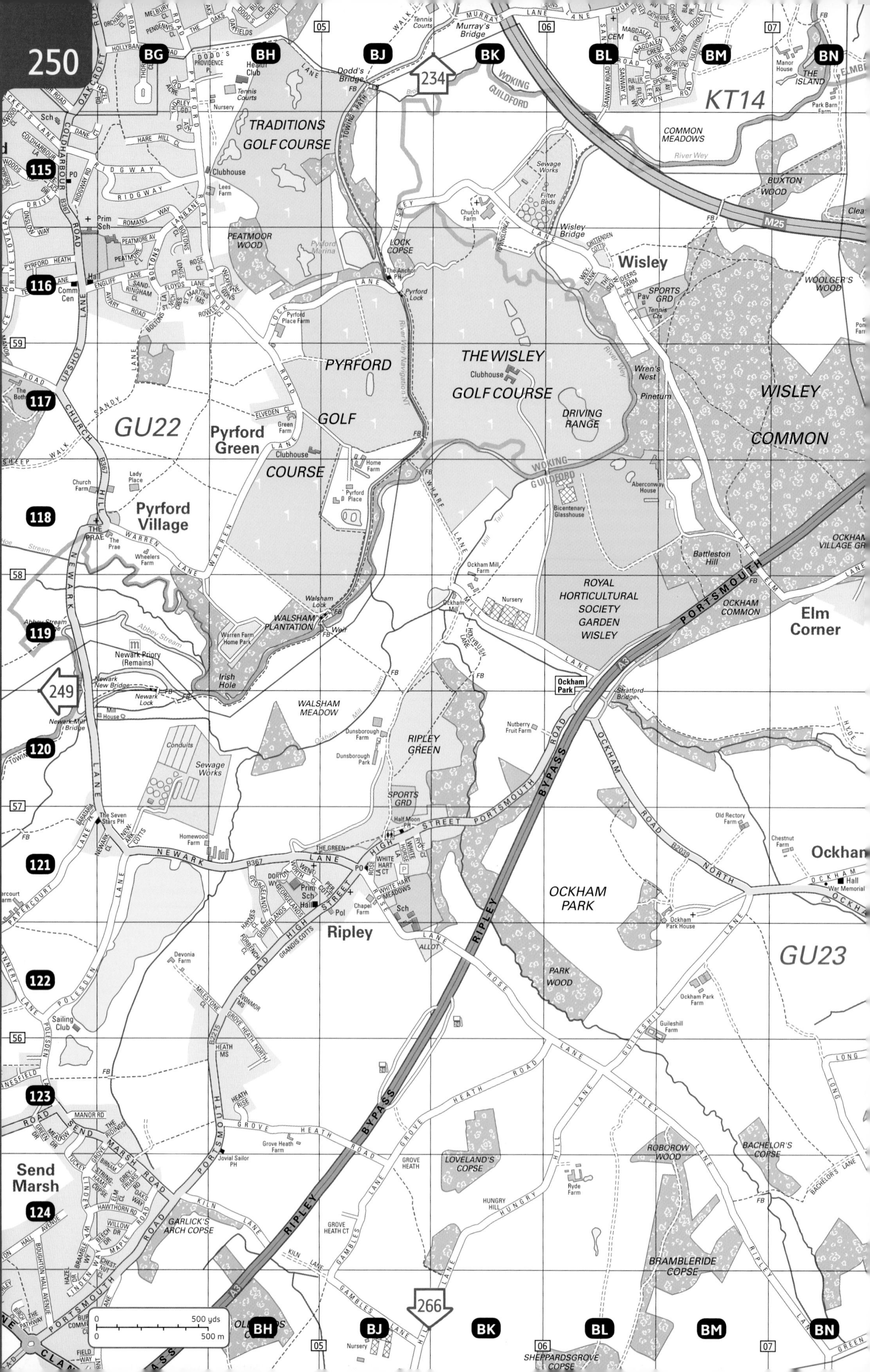

234
249
266
BG
BH
BJ
BK
BL
BM
BN
05
06
07
59
58
57
56
115
116
117
118
119
120
121
122
123
124
KT14
GU22
GU23
TRADITIONS GOLF COURSE
Clubhouse
Lees Farm
PEATMOOR WOOD
Pyrford Marina
Dodd's Bridge
Murray's Bridge
Tennis Courts
Health Club
Nursery
WOKING
GUILDFORD
Sewage Works
Filter Beds
Church Farm
Wisley Bridge
Wisley
COMMON MEADOWS
River Wey
BUXTON WOOD
M25
Manor House
THE ISLAND
Park Barn Farm
WOOLGER'S WOOD
LOCK COPSE
The Anchor PH
Pyrford Lock
Pyrford Place Farm
PYRFORD GOLF COURSE
THE WISLEY GOLF COURSE
DRIVING RANGE
River Wey Navigation
Wren's Nest
Pinetum
WISLEY COMMON
SPORTS GRD
Pav
Tennis Cts
Pyrford Green
Pyrford Village
Lady Place
Church Farm
Home Farm
Pyrford Place
Aberconway House
Bicentenary Glasshouse
Battleston Hill
OCKHAM COMMON
OCKHAM VILLAGE GREEN
Elm Corner
ROYAL HORTICULTURAL SOCIETY GARDEN WISLEY
Ockham Mill Farm
Nursery
Ockham Mill
Walsham Lock
WALSHAM PLANTATION
Weir
Warren Farm Home Park
Newark Priory (Remains)
Abbey Stream
Irish Hole
Newark New Bridge
Newark Lock
Mill House
Newark Mill Bridge
Ockham Park
Stratford Bridge
WALSHAM MEADOW
Dunsborough Farm
Dunsborough Park
RIPLEY GREEN
Nutberry Fruit Farm
Conduits
Sewage Works
SPORTS GRD
Half Moon PH
The Seven Stars PH
Homewood Farm
THE GREEN
Ripley
Prim Sch
Hall
Pol
Chapel Farm
Sch
ALLOT
OCKHAM PARK
Old Rectory Farm
Chestnut Farm
Ockham
Hall
War Memorial
Ockham Park House
PARK WOOD
Ockham Park Farm
Guileshill Farm
Devonia Farm
Sailing Club
Grove Heath Farm
Jovial Sailor PH
GROVE HEATH
LOVELAND'S COPSE
ROBOROW WOOD
BACHELOR'S COPSE
Ryde Farm
HUNGRY HILL
GROVE HEATH CT
GARLICK'S ARCH COPSE
BRAMBLERIDE COPSE
Send Marsh
SHEPPARDSGROVE COPSE
Nursery
RIPLEY BYPASS
PORTSMOUTH ROAD
NEWARK LANE
HIGH STREET
OCKHAM ROAD NORTH
ROSE LANE
RIPLEY LANE
GUILESHILL LANE
HUNGRY HILL LANE
GROVE HEATH ROAD
GROVE HEATH NORTH
KILN LANE
GAMBLES LANE
SEND MARSH ROAD
CHURCH HILL
UPSHOT LANE
COLDHARBOUR ROAD
OAKCROFT ROAD
PYRFORD ROAD
WARREN LANE
SANDY LANE
ELM LANE
WISLEY LANE
MILL LANE
WHARF LANE
HOLLYBUSH LANE
POLESDEN LANE
LONG LANE
BACHELOR'S LANE
HEATH RISE
A3
B367
B2215
B2039
0
500 yds
500 m

PAINSHILL PARK
235
BP
BQ
BR
BS
BT
BU
BV
Cobham
Visitor Centre
BELL WOOD
Long Orchard Farm
Bramble Hedge Farm
GUILDFORD ROAD
THE BROOM
Wood Hill
Gothic Temple
GROTTO
Chinese Bridge
THE LAKE
Foxwarren Park
Red Hill
PORTSMOUTH
Gothic Tower
Tower Hill
WHEEL ISLAND
Oak Pollard
Red Hill
Junction 10
CHATLEY WOOD
Redhill Bottom
POINTERS
Cockrow Hill
Wisley Interchange
Sandpit Hill
ROAD
Chatley Farm
THE BOGS
BREACH HILL WOOD
CHATLEY HEATH
CURRIE'S CLUMP
Telegraph Hill
Chatley Semaphore
OCKHAM COMMON
BOLDER MERE
HATCHFORD WOOD
HATCHFORD PARK
Wilderness Farm
HUNT'S COPSE
OLD LANE
KT11
River Mole
LODGE COPSE
POINTERS ROAD
BRAMBLE WOOD
Poynters Farm
Pointers Green
M25
LITTLE BRICKFIELD COPSE
BRICKFIELD COPSE
NORTON LANE
Cold Norton Farm
Hazeldene Farm
NORTON WOOD
Poultry Houses
The Black Swan PH
Martyr's Green
OCKHAM LANE
Pound Farm
ELMBRIDGE
GUILDFORD
TANNERS COPSE
Upton Farm
Bridge End Farm
HATCH LANE
TRULLIBER COPSE
Pav SPORTS GROUND
School Farm
CHAFFERS COPSE
May's Green
HOOK WOOD
STUMPS GROVE
Barnsthorns
Blackmoor Farm
Slade Farm
THE DRIFT GOLF COURSE
Clubhouse
BARNSTHORNS WOOD
Blue Ride
THE DRIFT
DRIFT ROAD
THE FOREST
HORSLEY CAMPING & CARAVAN SITE
Broom House
SPORTS GRD
Pav
Tenn Cts
Prim Sch
NIGHTINGALE CRESCENT
OCKHAM ROAD NORTH
B2039
267
HIGHLANDS
FOREST ROAD
HEATHWAY
FALCONWOOD
WILDWOOD CL
BRIDLEWAY
Hall
DEPOT
EFFINGHAM JUNCTION
SURREY GARDENS
OLD LANE GDNS
COPTHORNE
HOWARD ROAD
LOVELACE CL
EFFINGHAM COMMON
Effingham C.C.
Cricket Club
Slater's Oak
Hook Farm
Indian Farm
Lower Farm
LOWER FARM ROAD
Norwood Farm
KT24
GALLOWS GROVE
CLAMP ROUGH
BUSHY THICKET
THICKET COPSE
BANK'S LANE
Banks Way House
Gun Club
Newmarsh Farm
Hurst Hill
ROUNDABOUT
THE NEW PRESERVE
PEAKED ROUGH
OLD OAK COMMON
HORSLEY ROAD
Bull Riding Farm
Highway Farm
GOOSE GREEN
Halfpenny Cross
CHILBROOK ROAD
Pondtail Farm
PLOUGH LANE
Cobham Court Farm
Downside Bridge
Cobham Park Nursery
COBHAM PARK
Cobham Stud Farm
Cossins House
Cossins Farm
Downside
DOWNSIDE COMMON
Downside Sch
Hall
MIDDLETON RD
BOOKHAM
New Barn Farm
252
Cobham Services
Days Inn
ROSE LODGE WOOD
BETWEEN STREETS
A245
HIGH ST
RIVERHILL
Cobham FC
Health Cen
Youth Cen
Lib
CHURCH ST
ANVIL LA
Nursery
REC GRD
Pav
Hall
Tenn Cts
PARK WOOD
BIG ROUND
116
117
118
119
120
121
122
123
124
08
09
10
59
58
57
56

BW
BX
BY
BZ
CA
CB
CC
236
12
13
14
COBHAM
HIGH ST
RIVERHILL
MILL RD
STOKE ROAD
A245
R. Mole
ROSE LODGE WOOD
The Running Mare PH
LITTLE HEATH COMMON
Knowle Hill
WATERCUT COPSE
KNOWLE HILL PARK
War Memorial
THE FURZE
BRIDLE LANE
BLUNDEL LANE
Sports Club
SPORTS GRD
REC GRD
CLAY PLANTATION
THE COPSE
COBHAM PARK
Cobham Park Nursery
Elm Farm
COBHAM CEM
Ford
The Old Plough PH
REC GRD
Pav
Stoke D'Abernon
Mast
PARK WOOD
BIG ROUNDABOUT
LITTLE ROUNDABOUT
COBHAM & STOKE D'ABERNON
PO
Lower Farm
ALLOT
KT11
Woodlands Farm
Woodland Court Farm
Woodlands Park Hotel
WOODLANDS
Manor Farm
Garden Centre
CHELSEA F.C. TRAINING GROUND
Tennis Courts
Old Parks
Cossins House
Cossins Farm
Downside
Weir
Downside Mill
Mill Race
River Mole
SPORTS GROUND
Sch
OLD PARKS COPSE
HEATHFIELD COPSE
DOWNSIDE COMMON
Downside Farm
BEAUMONT PLANTATION
MUGGERIDGE WOOD
WRENS HILL WOOD
Stoke D'Abernon Bridge
EMBRIDGE
MOLE VALLEY
Hall
Little Slyfield House
Slyfield House
M25
New Barn Farm
THORNETS WOOD
MUGGERIDGE WOOD
Bookham Lodge Stud
LITTLE WOOD
Slyfield Farm
251
Cobham Services
Days Inn
DOWN WOOD
SPRING MEADOW WOOD
Bookham Lodge
BUSHEY COPSE
Sheepbell Farm
Riding Farm
WITHY BED
CHASEMORE WOOD
LADY CHEWTONS WOOD
PEAKED COPSE
Chasemore Farm
THE BIRCHES
Mark Oak Nursery
Barracks Farm
NEW BARN WOOD
HUNDRED POUND BRI WOOD
Hill Farm
Hundred Pound Bridge
COBHAM ROAD
Newmarsh Farm
Gun Club
GREAT BOOKHAM COMMON NT
BANK'S COMMON NT
Bank's Farm
LITTLE BOOKHAM COMMON
THICKET COPSE
BUSHY
BANKS LANE
Banks Way House
Manor Cottage
Isle of White
LITTLE MORNSHILL WOOD
GREAT MORNSHILL WOOD
THE GLADE
COMMONSIDE
KT23
ALLOT
Bookham Tunnel
BOOKHAM
Norwood Farm
Slater's Oak
Long Maddox Farm
BOOKHAM INDUSTRIAL ESTATE
PIKES POOL
HERONS REACH
LOWER FARM ROAD
Lower Farm
KT24
MALLARDS MERE
OAKEN WOOD
MOLE VALLEY
GUILDFORD
Hall
PO
Prim Sch
Youth Cen
Indian Farm
500 yds
500 m
Little Bookham
268
THORNET WOOD
GREAT BOOKHAM

CD
CE
CF
CG
CH
CJ
CK
KT9
237
THE FOREST
Ashtead Roman Villa (rem of)
LEATHERHEAD GOLF COURSE
ASHTEAD COMMON
EPSOM GAP
Horns Hill
MOLE VALLEY
ELMBRIDGE
PACHESHAM LAKE
PACHESHAM PARK
Clubhouse
Pachesham Park
KINGSTON ROAD
A243
OXSHOTT ROAD
A244
WOODLANDS PARK
Prince's Coverts
Clouds Hill Farm
Tyrwhitt House
Queen Elizabeth's Foundation Coll
M25
Junction 9
KT21
Paddock Lodge Stables
Ashley Court
WOOD FIELD
ASHTEAD
116
117
118
119
120
121
122
123
124
59
58
57
56
Rowhurst Forge
Queen Elizabeth's Foundation (Dev Cen)
TEAZLE WOOD
Clubhouse DRIVING RANGE
PACHESHAM PARK GOLF CENTRE
BALANCING PONDS
Superstores
REGENT PARK
Leatherhead Common
Brook Willow Farm
Sewage Works
Filter Beds
Pachesham Equestrian Centre
THE MOUNTS
Earthworks
Amenity Site
BUSHY PLATT
Gutter's Bridge
SPRING POND
MOLE VALLEY PREDATORS FC
RANDALLS ROAD
A245
KT22
Crematorium
RANDALLS PARK CEMETERY
ERA TECHNOLOGY LTD
PLOUGH IND EST
BYPASS ROAD
Barnettwood Farm
ALLOT
Lower Ashtead
SPORTS FLD
Junction 9
254
ASHTEAD HOSP
LEATHERHEAD BYPASS RD
Knoll Rbt
LEATHERHEAD
SPORTS GROUND
SPORTS GRD
MOLE BUSINESS PARK
LEATHERHEAD TRADE PARK
STATION RD
BULL HILL
Cannon Grove Nursery
River Mole
REC GRD
Tenn Club
HOSP
ExxonMobil House
MILL POND
Leatherhead Bridge
Leatherhead FC
Leatherhead & Cobham C.C.
Clubhouse
Leisure Centre
Thorncroft Manor
WATER PARK
Water Works
Rifle Range
Hawk's Hill
Fetcham
Downside Farm
Beaverbrook Roundabout
REIGATE ROAD
B2033
SHEPHERDS CLOSE
LEATHERHEAD BYPASS
Bocketts Farm Park
YOUNG STREET
A246
GUILDFORD ROAD
Givons Grove Roundabout
269
DORKING ROAD
B2450
B2122
15
16
17

EPSOM COMMON
CL
CM
CN
CP
CQ
CR
CS
238
NEWTON WOOD
EPSOM
EPSOM GENERAL HOSP
115
116
117
118
119
120
121
122
123
124
D COMMON
WOOD FIELD
ASHTEAD
Woodcote
HALFMOON CLUMP
WORLDS END
THE GROVE
The Durdans
RAC WOODCOTE PARK GOLF COURSE
Woodcote Park Country Club
Holiday Inn Express
ASHTEAD PARK
Ashtead Park
City of London Freemen's School
LANGLEY BOTTOM WOOD
Langley Vale
THE WARREN
KT21
KT18
KT22
253
ASHTEAD HOSP
ExxonMobil House
Chase Farm Stud
ADDLESTEAD WOOD
LITTLE HURST WOOD
M25
Tyrrell's Wood
TYRRELL'S WOOD
HAMBLETON WOOD
HEADLEY COURT
HOOK WOOD
GREAT HURST WOOD
COVERED RESERVOIR
Beaverbrook Roundabout
PIGNUT WOOD
OYSTER HILL NT
NOWER WOOD
TYRRELL'S WOOD GOLF COURSE
COSTAL WOOD
270
500 yds
500 m
Headley
EPSOM ROAD
THE STREET
DORKING ROAD
LEATHERHEAD ROAD
REIGATE ROAD
HEADLEY ROAD
EPSOM & EWELL
MOLE VALLEY

CT
CU
CV
CW
CX
CY
CZ
239
KT17
EPSOM DOWNS
Epsom College
NORK
SM7
COLLEGE ROAD
A2022
REIGATE ROAD
Drift Bridge Hotel
Drift Br
NORK WAY
Banstead Crossroads
BOLT. LA
BURGH HEATH ROAD
BUCKLE'S GAP
EPSOM GOLF COURSE
YEW TREE BOTTOM ROAD
B284
Toyota(GB)
NORK PARK
PARK WOOD
SPORTS GROUND
Nork Park Farm
PARK WOOD
TATTENHAM WAY RECREATION GROUND
TATTENHAM WAY
116
117
118
119
120
121
122
123
124
59
58
57
56
PAGES ACRE
CANONS WOOD
Superstore
Grandstands
TATTENHAM CORNER
RACE DAY PARKING
EPSOM DOWNS RACECOURSE
EPSOM DOWNS
The Hill
Tattenham Corner
Race Stables
B290
Tattenham Corner
TATTENHAM CRESCENT
GREAT TATTENHAMS
B2221
COVERED RESERVOIR
Burgh Heath
BURGH HEATH
Premier Inn
Canons Farm
256
LANGLEY VALE
WALTON DOWNS
EPSOM & EWELL
REIGATE & BANSTEAD
Banstead Athletic FC
PIT WOOD
SPORTS GROUND
Legal & General
KT20
A217
BRIGHTON ROAD
COPT HILL LANE
Garden Farm
KINGSWOOD
THE CHILDRENS TRUST
TADWORTH
B2032
BONSOR DRIVE
TADWORTH
B2220
Tumble Beacon PH
WORKHOUSE POND
Police Training School
Wingfield Stud Farm
Kingswood Warren - BBC Technical Research
KINGSWOOD
Tadworth CC
War Memorial
MERE POND
BANSTEAD HEATH
Ebbisham Farm
SANDHILL WOOD
Walton Manor
Walton Manor Farm
Walton on the Hill
The Clock Tower Riding Centre
CHIPSTEAD LANE
BEECHEN
COPSE
271
22
23
24
BANSTEAD

DA
DB
DC
DD
DE
DF
DG
240
272
255
26
27
28
59
58
57
56
115
116
117
118
119
120
121
122
123
124
WINKWORTH
A2022
CROYDON
PALMERSFIELD ROAD
BANSTEAD
SM7
WOODMANSTERNE
WOODMANSTERNE PARK RECREATION GROUND
CLOCKHOUSE REC GRD
BIG WOOD
PROSPECT PLANTATION
SPORTS GROUND
THE SHRUBBERY
Queen Elizabeth's Foundation
SCRATCH WOOD
Courtlands Farm
Place Farm
Mint Farm
The Mint PH
New Place
GREAT SOLOM'S WOOD
SOLOM'S COURT RD
PARK DOWNS
COUNCIL DEPOT
RUFFETT WOOD
PAGES ACRE
BANSTEAD WOOD
Perrotts Farm
LUNCH WOOD
FAMES ROUGH
CHIPSTEAD BOTTOM
CHIPHOUSE WOOD
WELL COPSE
Chipstead Bottom
CHIPSTEAD GOLF COURSE
Chipstead
How Hills
COVERED RESERVOIR
HOLLYMEAD
West Ridge
Tennis Club
VINCENTS CL
VINCENT GREEN
STARROCK
STARROCK SHAW
Longshaw
White Hart PH
CHIPSTEAD MEADS REC GRD
Chipstead RFC
Bowl Club
Elmore
POORFIELD WOOD
EMBERS SHAW
Court Lodge Farm
War Memorial
Hooley
Chipstead FC
Chipstead, Coulsdon & Walcountians CC
THE GROVE
Noke Farm Barns
FOURTEEN ACRE SHAW
Shabden Park
THE BELT
THE RUFFETT
ROUND WOOD
RUFFETTS WOOD
Manor Park
South Lodge
HEDGELAND SHAW
KT20
KINGSWOOD
Legal & General
SPORTS GROUND
OUTWOOD SHAW
SURREY DOWNS GOLF COURSE
OUTWOOD
THE LONG PLANTATION
Clubhouse
EYHURST PARK
KINGSWOOD GOLF COURSE AND COUNTRY CLUB
WHITE HILL
Pigeonhouse Farm
TOP SHAW
ROUND WOOD
SMUGGLERS PIT PLANTATION
Well House PH
WELLFIELD SHAW
HOMEFIELD SHAWS
Reeves Rest
Southerns Farm
BEECHEN
Mugswell
Park Farm
BOARS GREEN
HARPS OAK SHAW
Kingswood Warren
HOLLY LANE
OUTWOOD LANE
CHIPSTEAD LANE
RECTORY LANE
HIGH ROAD
HOGSCROSS LANE
COULSDON LANE
ELMORE ROAD
CASTLE ROAD
WATERHOUSE LANE
WARREN DRIVE
B2219
B2217
B2032
B2278
A217
0
500 yds
0
500 m

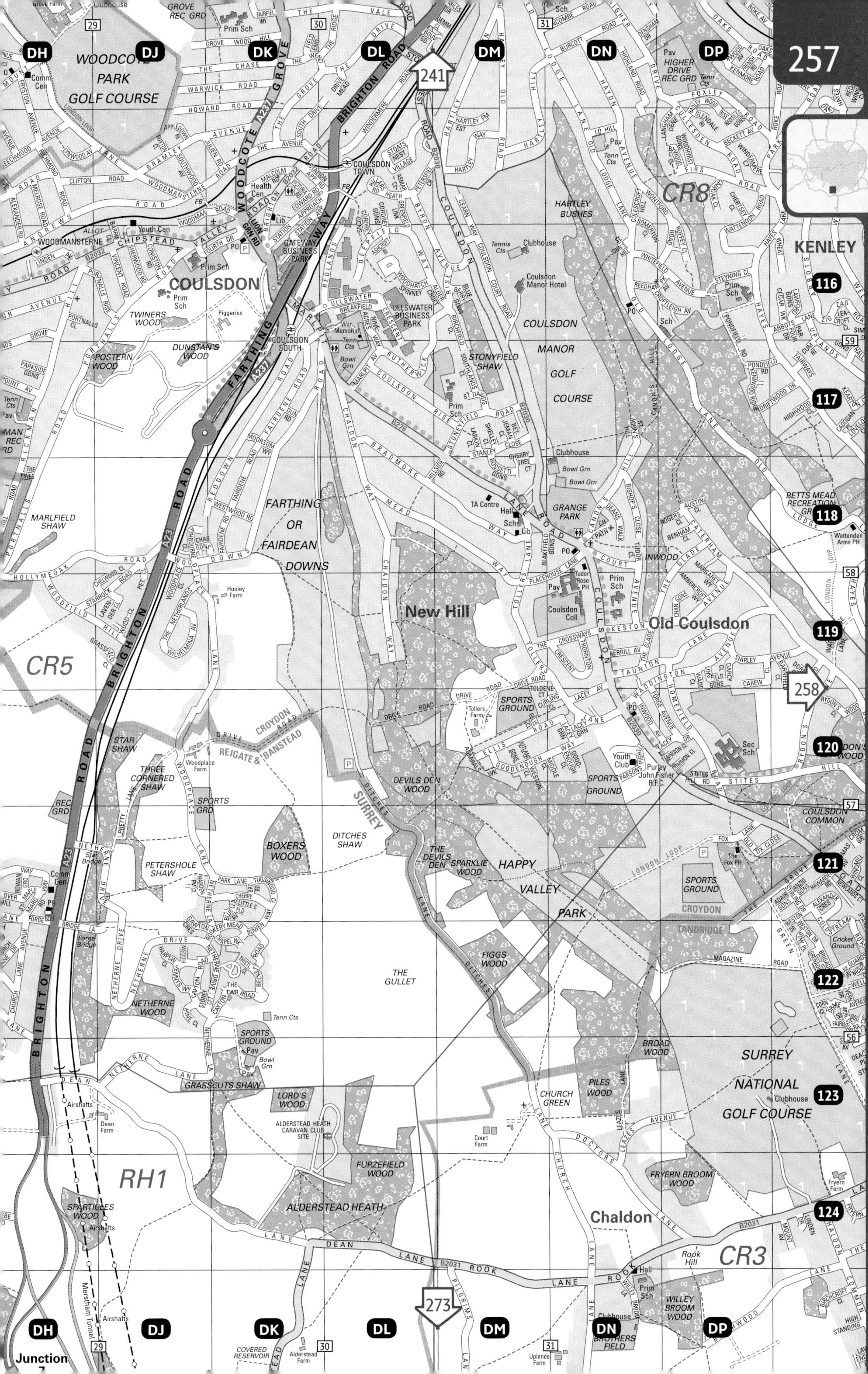
DH
DJ
DK
DL
DM
DN
DP
WOODCOTE PARK GOLF COURSE
GROVE REC GRD
Prim Sch
HIGHER DRIVE REC GRD
241
CR8
KENLEY
COULSDON TOWN
COULSDON
COULSDON SOUTH
TWINERS WOOD
DUNSTAN'S WOOD
POSTERN WOOD
GATEWAY BUSINESS PARK
ULLSWATER BUSINESS PARK
HARTLEY BUSHES
Coulsdon Manor Hotel
COULSDON MANOR GOLF COURSE
STONYFIELD SHAW
GRANGE PARK
FARTHING OR FAIRDEAN DOWNS
MARLFIELD SHAW
New Hill
Old Coulsdon
INWOOD
BETTS MEAD RECREATION GRD
CR5
258
Hooley Farm
CROYDON
REIGATE & BANSTEAD
STAR SHAW
THREE CORNERED SHAW
SPORTS GROUND
Coulsdon Coll
DEVILS DEN WOOD
DITCHES SHAW
BOXERS WOOD
PETERSHOLE SHAW
THE DEVILS DEN
SPARKLIE WOOD
HAPPY VALLEY PARK
COULSDON COMMON
The Fox PH
TANDRIDGE
FIGGS WOOD
THE GULLET
NETHERNE WOOD
SURREY
SURREY NATIONAL GOLF COURSE
BROAD WOOD
PILES WOOD
CHURCH GREEN
LORD'S WOOD
ALDERSTEAD HEATH CARAVAN CLUB SITE
Court Farm
FURZEFIELD WOOD
ALDERSTEAD HEATH
RH1
SPARTICLES WOOD
FRYERN BROOM WOOD
Chaldon
CR3
Rook Hill
WILLEY BROOM WOOD
BROTHERS FIELD
273
Mersham Tunnel
Junction 7
COVERED RESERVOIR
Alderstead Farm
Uplands Farm
116
117
118
119
120
121
122
123
124

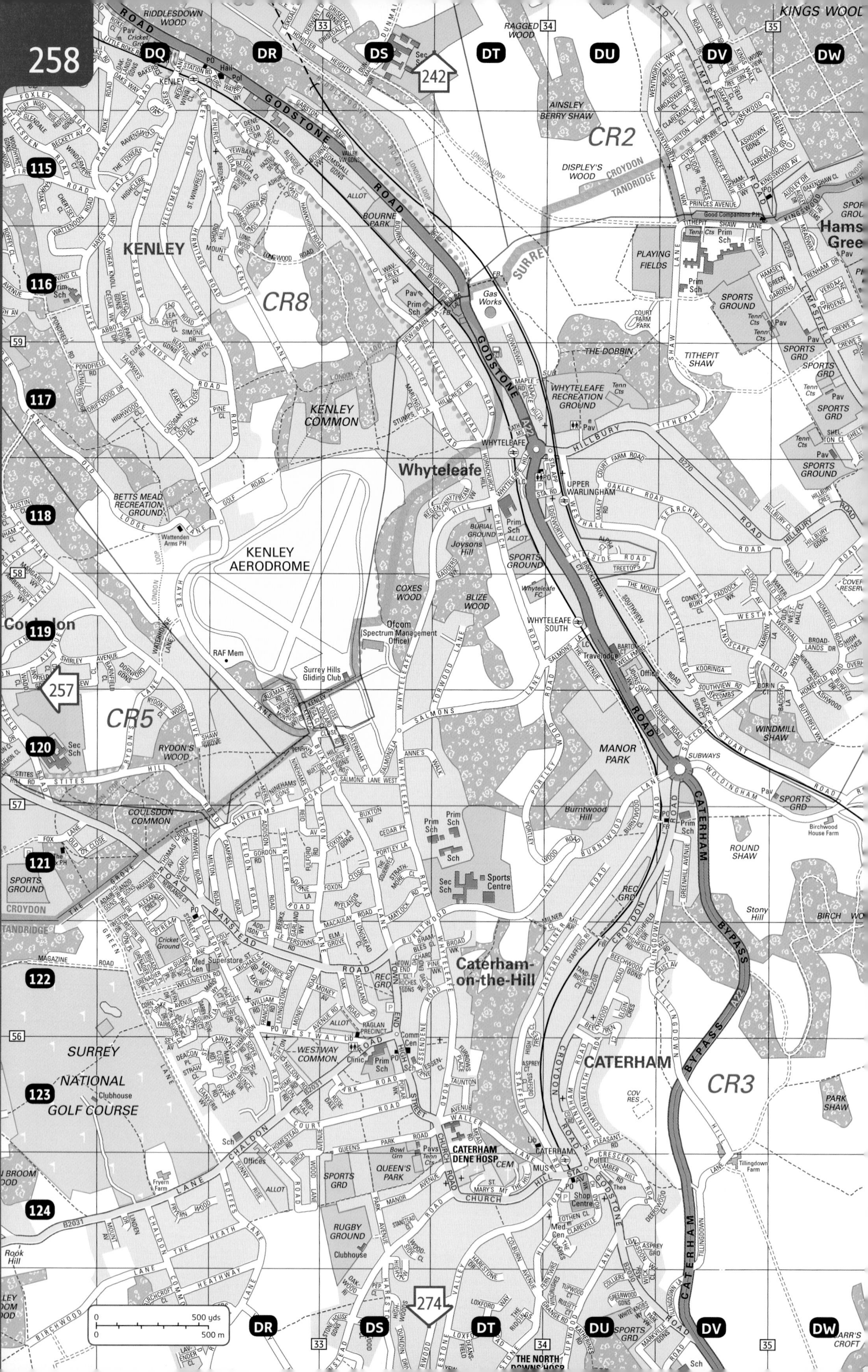

RIDDLESDOWN WOOD
RAGGED WOOD
KINGS WOOD
DQ
DR
DS
DT
DU
DV
DW
242
GODSTONE ROAD
KENLEY
AINSLEY BERRY SHAW
CR2
DISPLEY'S WOOD
CROYDON
TANDRIDGE
SURREY
BOURNE PARK
CR8
Gas Works
PLAYING FIELDS
TITHEPIT SHAW
SPORTS GROUND
THE DOBBIN
WHYTELEAFE RECREATION GROUND
KENLEY COMMON
Whyteleafe
UPPER WARLINGHAM
BETTS MEAD RECREATION GROUND
Wattenden Arms PH
KENLEY AERODROME
BURIAL GROUND
Joysons Hill
COXES WOOD
BLIZE WOOD
Whyteleafe FC
WHYTELEAFE SOUTH
Ofcom (Spectrum Management Office)
RAF Mem
Surrey Hills Gliding Club
Coulsdon
257
CR5
RYDON'S WOOD
MANOR PARK
WINDMILL SHAW
SUBWAYS
Birchwood House Farm
Burntwood Hill
ROUND SHAW
COULSDON COMMON
Sports Centre
Stony Hill
CROYDON
TANDRIDGE
Caterham-on-the-Hill
RAGLAN PRECINCT
WESTWAY COMMON
SURREY NATIONAL GOLF COURSE
Clubhouse
CATERHAM
CR3
COV RES
PARK SHAW
CATERHAM BYPASS
CATERHAM DENE HOSP
QUEEN'S PARK
SPORTS GRD
RUGBY GROUND
Fryern Farm
Tillingdown Farm
Rook Hill
274
THE NORTH DOWNS HOSP
CARR'S CROFT
0 500 yds
0 500 m
115
116
117
118
119
120
121
122
123
124
33
34
35
56
57
58
59

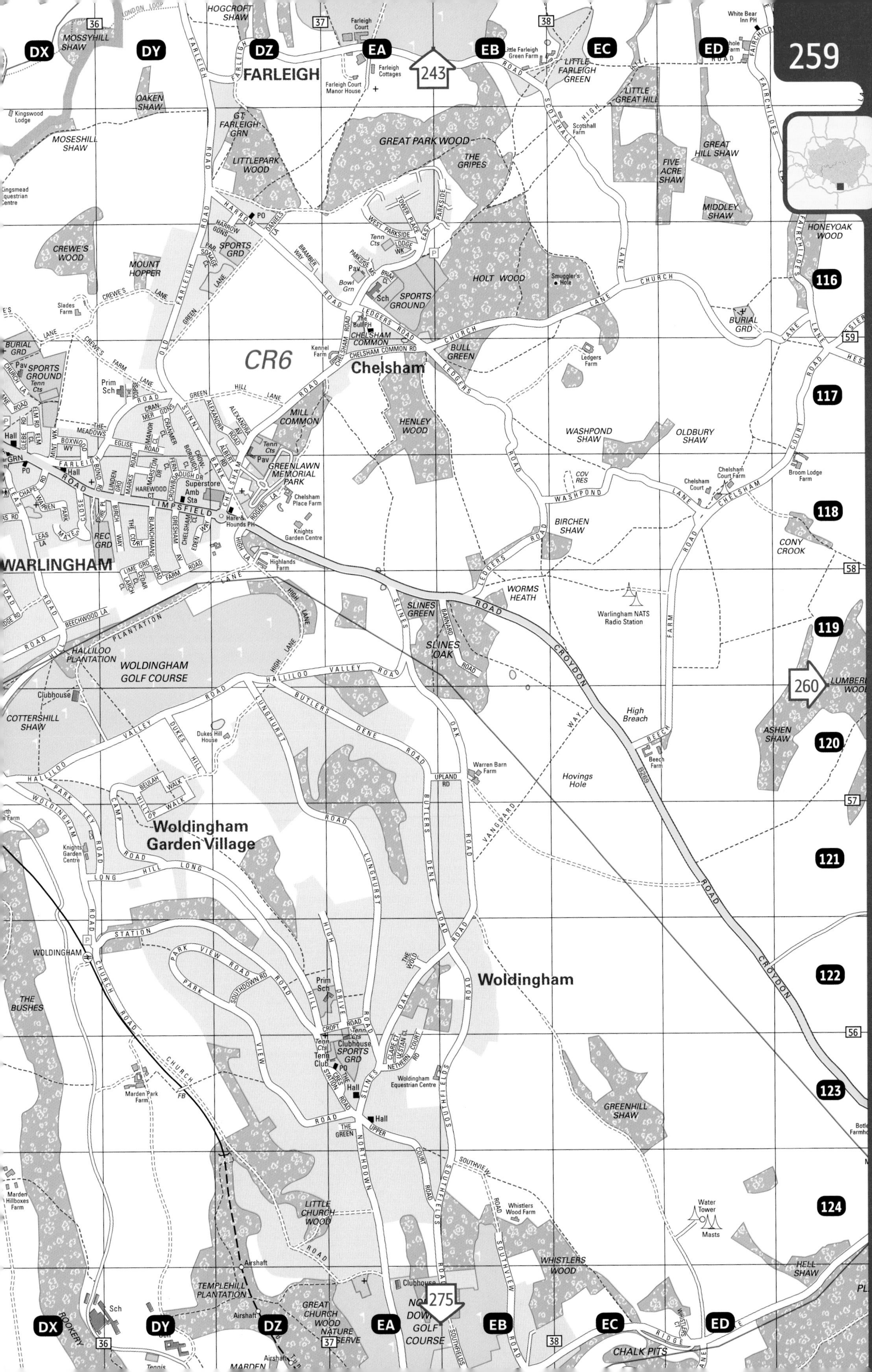
FARLEIGH
Chelsham
CR6
WARLINGHAM
Woldingham Garden Village
Woldingham
243
260
275
DX
DY
DZ
EA
EB
EC
ED
116
117
118
119
120
121
122
123
124
36
37
38
56
57
58
59
HOGCROFT SHAW
MOSSYHILL SHAW
OAKEN SHAW
MOSESHILL SHAW
GT FARLEIGH GRN
LITTLEPARK WOOD
GREAT PARK WOOD
THE GRIPES
LITTLE FARLEIGH GREEN
LITTLE GREAT HILL
GREAT HILL SHAW
FIVE ACRE SHAW
MIDDLEY SHAW
HONEYOAK WOOD
CREWE'S WOOD
MOUNT HOPPER
HOLT WOOD
BURIAL GRD
CHELSHAM COMMON
BULL GREEN
MILL COMMON
HENLEY WOOD
GREENLAWN MEMORIAL PARK
WASHPOND SHAW
OLDBURY SHAW
BIRCHEN SHAW
CONY CROOK
WORMS HEATH
SLINES GREEN
SLINES OAK
Warlingham NATS Radio Station
HALLILOO PLANTATION
WOLDINGHAM GOLF COURSE
COTTERSHILL SHAW
High Breach
Hovings Hole
ASHEN SHAW
LUMBER WOOD
THE BUSHES
GREENHILL SHAW
LITTLE CHURCH WOOD
WHISTLERS WOOD
HELL SHAW
TEMPLEHILL PLANTATION
GREAT CHURCH WOOD NATURE RESERVE
NORTH DOWNS GOLF COURSE
CHALK PITS
Farleigh Court
Farleigh Cottages
Farleigh Court Manor House
Little Farleigh Green Farm
White Bear Inn PH
Scotshall Farm
Kingswood Lodge
Kingsmead Equestrian Centre
Smuggler's Hole
Slades Farm
Kennel Farm
Ledgers Farm
Chelsham Court Farm
Chelsham Court
Broom Lodge Farm
Chelsham Place Farm
Knights Garden Centre
Hare & Hounds PH
Highlands Farm
The Bull PH
Dukes Hill House
Warren Barn Farm
Beech Farm
Knights Garden Centre
Woldingham Equestrian Centre
Marden Park Farm
Marden Hillboxes Farm
Whistlers Wood Farm
Water Tower
Masts
Airshaft
FARLEIGH ROAD
HARROW ROAD
CHURCH LANE
LEDGERS ROAD
CHELSHAM ROAD
LIMPSFIELD ROAD
CROYDON ROAD
HALLILOO VALLEY ROAD
BUTLERS DENE ROAD
LUNGHURST ROAD
STATION ROAD
CHURCH ROAD
PARK VIEW ROAD
UPPER COURT ROAD
SOUTHFIELDS
NORTHDOWN ROAD
ROOKERY
B269

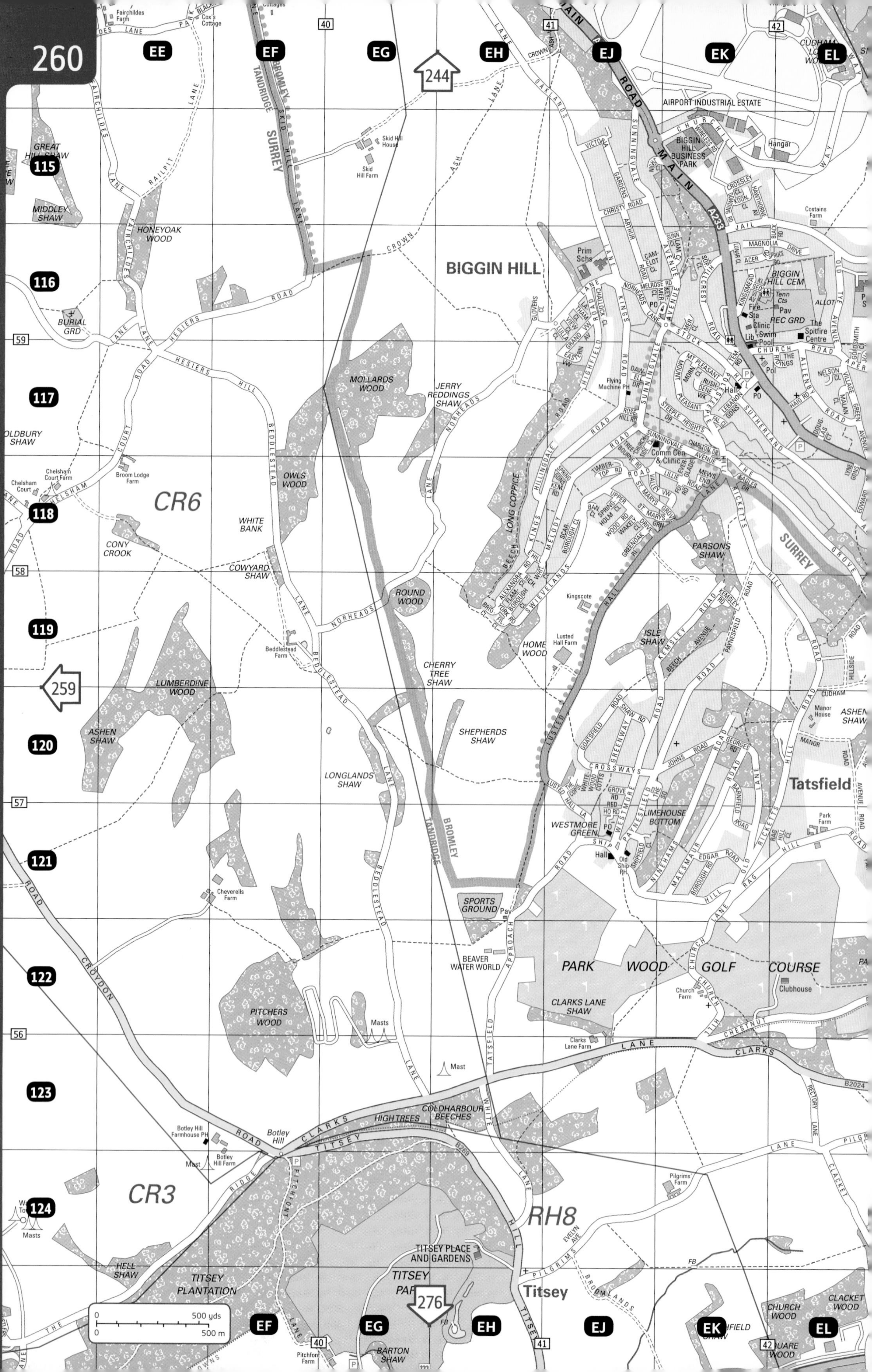
EE
EF
EG
EH
EJ
EK
EL
244
AIRPORT INDUSTRIAL ESTATE
BIGGIN HILL BUSINESS PARK
Hangar
TANDRIDGE
BROMLEY
SURREY
Skid Hill House
Skid Hill Farm
GREAT HILL SHAW
MIDDLEY SHAW
HONEYOAK WOOD
BURIAL GRD
BIGGIN HILL
Prim Schs
BIGGIN HILL CEM
REC GRD
The Spitfire Centre
MOLLARDS WOOD
JERRY REDDINGS SHAW
OLDBURY SHAW
Chelsham Court Farm
Chelsham Court
Broom Lodge Farm
CR6
OWLS WOOD
WHITE BANK
CONY CROOK
COWYARD SHAW
LONG COPPICE
Flying Machine PH
Comm Cen & Clinic
PARSONS SHAW
Kingscote
ROUND WOOD
Beddlestead Farm
Lusted Hall Farm
HOME WOOD
ISLE SHAW
CHERRY TREE SHAW
259
LUMBERDINE WOOD
ASHEN SHAW
SHEPHERDS SHAW
LONGLANDS SHAW
Tatsfield
Manor House
Park Farm
WESTMORE GREEN
LIMEHOUSE BOTTOM
Old Ship PH
Cheverells Farm
SPORTS GROUND
BEAVER WATER WORLD
PARK WOOD GOLF COURSE
Clubhouse
Church Farm
CLARKS LANE SHAW
Clarks Lane Farm
PITCHERS WOOD
Masts
Mast
HIGHTREES
COLDHARBOUR BEECHES
Botley Hill Farmhouse PH
Botley Hill
Botley Hill Farm
B269
B2024
A233
Pilgrims' Farm
CR3
RH8
TITSEY PLACE AND GARDENS
TITSEY PARK
276
Titsey
HELL SHAW
TITSEY PLANTATION
BARTON SHAW
Pitchfont Farm
CHURCH WOOD
CLACKET WOOD
SQUARE WOOD
0 500 yds
0 500 m
115
116
117
118
119
120
121
122
123
124
59
58
57
56
40
41
42

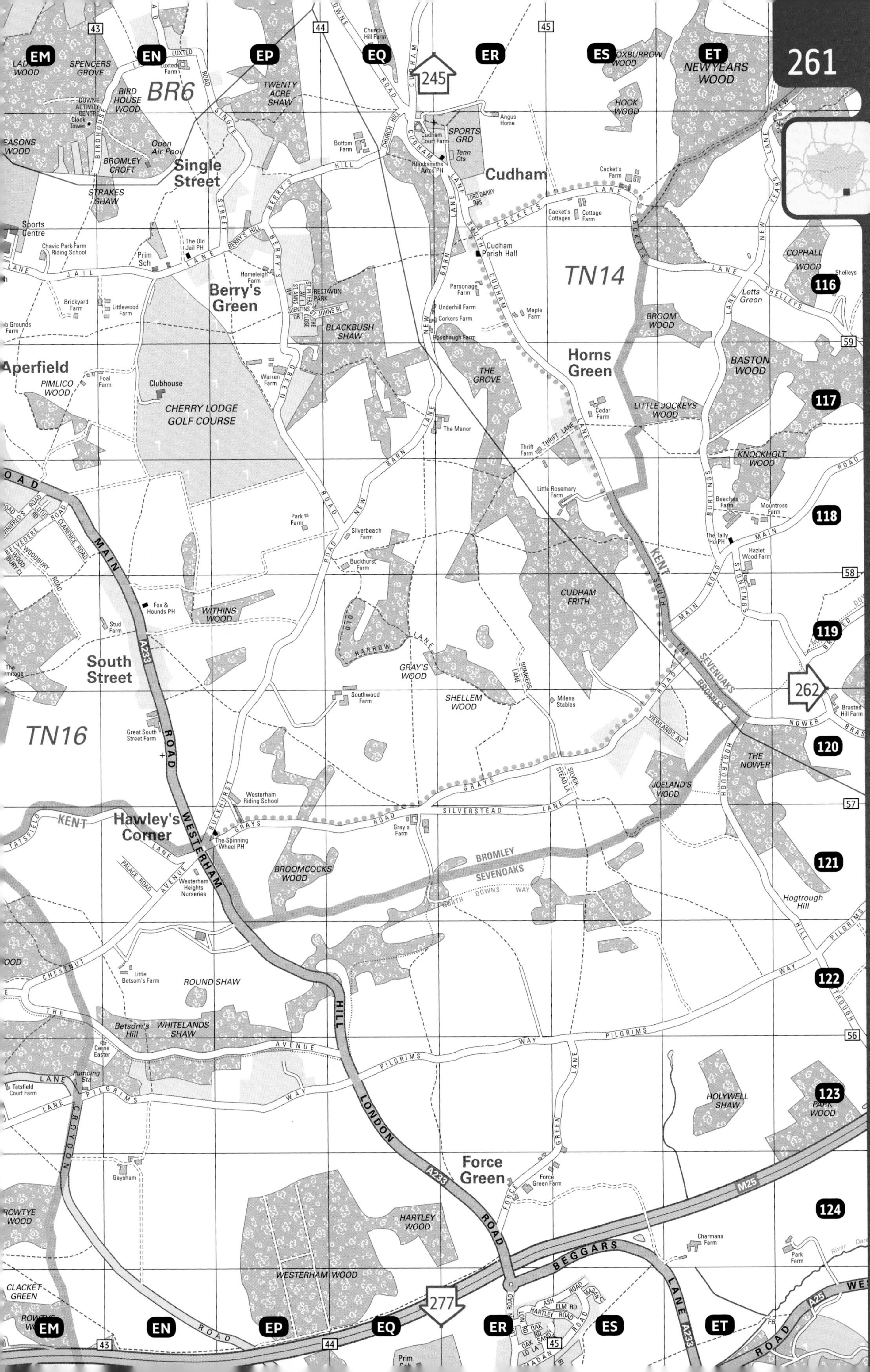
EM
EN
EP
EQ
ER
ES
ET
43
44
45
245
LADY WOOD
SPENCERS GROVE
Luxted Farm
LUXTED
BR6
BIRD HOUSE WOOD
DOWNE ACTIVITY CENTRE
Clock Tower
TWENTY ACRE SHAW
Church Hill Farm
DOWNE
CUDHAM ROAD
CHURCH HILL
Cudham Court Farm
SPORTS GRD
Tenn Cts
Angus Home
Blacksmiths Arms PH
Cudham
OXBURROW WOOD
NEW YEARS WOOD
HOOK WOOD
SEASONS WOOD
Open Air Pool
BROMLEY CROFT
Single Street
STRAKES SHAW
SINGLE STREET
Bottom Farm
HILL
BERRY'S HILL
Cacket's Farm
CACKETS LANE
Cacket's Cottages
Cottage Farm
LORD DARBY MS
SOUTH
CUDHAM LANE
Sports Centre
Chavic Park Farm Riding School
The Old Jail PH
Prim Sch
JAIL LANE
Cudham Parish Hall
TN14
COPHALL WOOD
Shelleys
116
Letts Green
SHELLEYS LANE
NEW YEARS LANE
Homeleigh Farm
Berry's Green
BERRY'S GREEN
RESTAVON PARK
ST ANNS WAY
ST PETERS AV
JOHNS RI
QUENTINS DR
THE CLOSE
Parsonage Farm
Underhill Farm
Corkers Farm
Rosehaugh Farm
Maple Farm
BROOM WOOD
Brickyard Farm
Littlewood Farm
Grounds Farm
BLACKBUSH SHAW
59
Horns Green
BASTON WOOD
Aperfield
PIMLICO WOOD
Foal Farm
Clubhouse
CHERRY LODGE GOLF COURSE
Warren Farm
THE GROVE
Cedar Farm
LITTLE JOCKEYS WOOD
117
The Manor
THRIFT LANE
Thrift Farm
KNOCKHOLT WOOD
BURLINGS LANE
ROAD
NEW BARN LANE
Little Rosemary Farm
Beeches Farm
Mountross Farm
118
MAIN ROAD
CLARENCE ROAD
WINIFRED'S RD
LOTUS RD
BELVEDERE RD
WOODBURY ROAD
Park Farm
Silverbeach Farm
The Tally Ho PH
Hazlet Wood Farm
Buckhurst Farm
KENT
SOUTH
STONINGS
58
Fox & Hounds PH
WITHINS WOOD
CUDHAM FRITH
Stud Farm
OLD HARROW LANE
GRAY'S WOOD
119
A233
South Street
The Hermitage
BOMBERS LANE
THE SEVENOAKS BROMLEY
Southwood Farm
SHELLEM WOOD
Milena Stables
262
Brasted Hill Farm
NOWER ROAD
TN16
Great South Street Farm
VIEWLANDS AV
THE NOWER
120
Westerham Riding School
GRAYS ROAD
SILVERSTEAD LA
JOELAND'S WOOD
HOGTROUGH HILL
57
TATSFIELD
KENT
Hawley's Corner
BUCKHURST
The Spinning Wheel PH
Gray's Farm
SILVERSTEAD LANE
WESTERHAM
PALACE ROAD
AVENUE
Westerham Heights Nurseries
BROOMCOCKS WOOD
BROMLEY
SEVENOAKS
NORTH DOWNS WAY
121
Hogtrough Hill
PILGRIMS WAY
CHESTNUT
Little Betsom's Farm
ROUND SHAW
HILL
122
THE AVENUE
Betsom's Hill
WHITELANDS SHAW
Cerne Easter
Pumping Sta
Tatsfield Court Farm
LANE
CROYDON
PILGRIMS WAY
56
HOLYWELL SHAW
123
PARK WOOD
LONDON ROAD
Gaysham
Force Green
FORCE GREEN LANE
Force Green Farm
M25
ROWTYE WOOD
HARTLEY WOOD
124
Charmans Farm
Park Farm
River Darent
BEGGARS LANE
WESTERHAM WOOD
CLACKET GREEN
277
ASH ROAD
ELM RD
HARTLEY ROAD
OAK RD
OAK SANDY LA
LO LA
LONDON ROAD
A25
FB
ROAD
Prim Sch

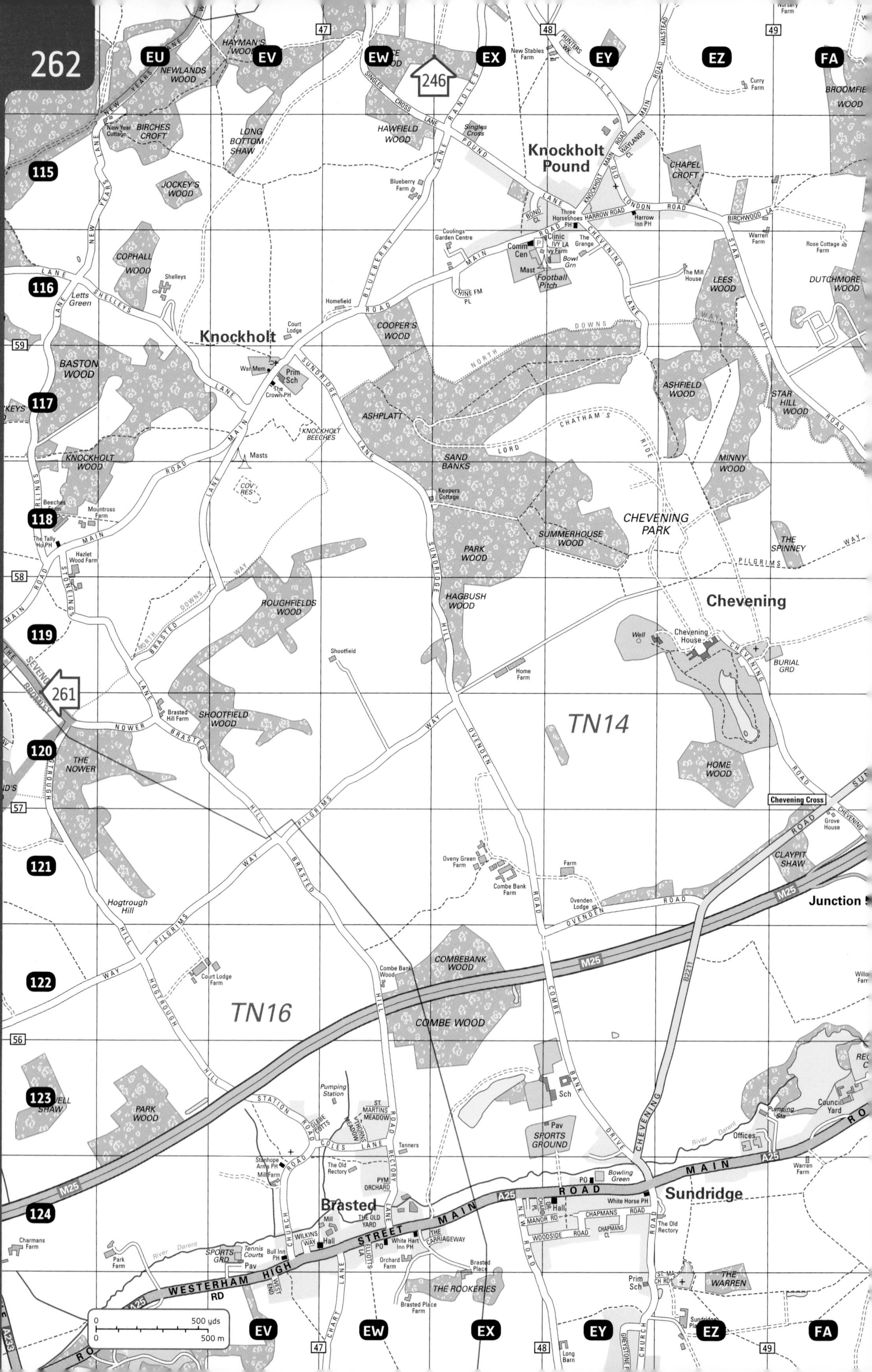
EU
EV
EW
EX
EY
EZ
FA
246
261
47
48
49
59
58
57
56
115
116
117
118
119
120
121
122
123
124
HAYMAN'S WOOD
NEWLANDS WOOD
NEW YEARS LANE
New Year Cottage
BIRCHES CROFT
LONG BOTTOM SHAW
JOCKEY'S WOOD
COPHALL WOOD
Shelleys
SHELLEYS LANE
Letts Green
Knockholt
BASTON WOOD
KNOCKHOLT WOOD
Beeches Farm
Mountross Farm
The Tally Ho PH
Hazlet Wood Farm
STONEINGS LANE
MAIN ROAD
War Mem
Prim Sch
The Crown PH
Court Lodge
Homefield
Masts
COV RES
KNOCKHOLT BEECHES
NORTH DOWNS WAY
BRASTED LANE
ROUGHFIELDS WOOD
Brasted Hill Farm
SHOOTFIELD WOOD
Shootfield
NOWER LANE
BRASTED HILL
THE NOWER
HOGTROUGH HILL
Hogtrough Hill
PILGRIMS WAY
Court Lodge Farm
TN16
SINGLES CROSS LANE
HAWFIELD WOOD
RANDLES LANE
Singles Cross
POUND LANE
Blueberry Farm
BLUEBERRY LANE
New Stables Farm
HUNTERS WK
HALSTEAD ROAD
Curry Farm
BROOMFIELD WOOD
Knockholt Pound
CHAPEL CROFT
WAYLANDS CL
OLD ROAD
KNOCKHOLT MAIN ROAD
LONDON ROAD
HARROW ROAD
Harrow Inn PH
BIRCHWOOD LA
Warren Farm
Rose Cottage Farm
STAR HILL ROAD
BOND CL
Three Horseshoes PH
Coolings Garden Centre
Comm Cen
Clinic
IVY LA
Ivy Farm
The Grange
Bowl Grn
Mast
Football Pitch
CHINE FM PL
CHEVENING LANE
The Mill House
LEES WOOD
DUTCHMORE WOOD
COOPER'S WOOD
SUNDRIDGE LANE
ASHPLATT
ASHFIELD WOOD
STAR HILL WOOD
CHATHAM'S RIDE
LORD
SAND BANKS
MINNY WOOD
Keepers Cottage
CHEVENING PARK
SUMMERHOUSE WOOD
PARK WOOD
THE SPINNEY
HAGBUSH WOOD
SUNDRIDGE HILL
Chevening
Well
Chevening House
BURIAL GRD
Home Farm
TN14
OVENDEN ROAD
HOME WOOD
Chevening Cross
CHEVENING ROAD
Grove House
CLAYPIT SHAW
Oveny Green Farm
Farm
Combe Bank Farm
Ovenden Lodge
Junction
M25
B2211
COMBEBANK WOOD
Combe Bank Wood
COMBE WOOD
COMBE BANK DRIVE
Sch
Pav
SPORTS GROUND
Pumping Station
STATION ROAD
GLEBE COTTS
ST. MARTINS MEADOW
THORNS MEADOW
COLES LANE
RECTORY LANE
Tanners
Stanhope Arms PH
Mill Farm
The Old Rectory
PYM ORCHARD
Brasted
THE OLD YARD
Mill
Hall
WILKINS WAY
CHURCH ROAD
HIGH STREET
MAIN ROAD
White Hart Inn PH
THE CARRIAGEWAY
Orchard Farm
Brasted Place
THE ROOKERIES
Brasted Place Farm
CHART LANE
ELLIOTTS LA
WEST END
Bull Inn PH
Tennis Courts
SPORTS GRD
Pav
WESTERHAM RD
A25
River Darent
Park Farm
Charmans Farm
PARK WOOD
A233
CHEVENING ROAD
Pumping Sta
Council Yard
Offices
Warren Farm
Sundridge
PO
Bowling Green
White Horse PH
CHAPMANS ROAD
CHAPMANS CL
MANOR RD
WOODSIDE ROAD
NEW ROAD
The Old Rectory
Prim Sch
ST. MARY'S CH RD
THE WARREN
Sundridge Place
GREYSTONES
CHURCH
Long Barn
500 yds
500 m
0

FB
FC
FD
FE
FF
FG
FH
247
Twitton
Otford
TN14
Dunton Green
Longford
Chipstead
Riverhead
Bessels Green
TN13
NORTH DOWNS BUSINESS PARK
QINETIQ FORT HALSTEAD
OLD GROVE
Morants Court Cross
Donnington Manor Hotel
OTFORD CEMETERY
ORCHARD HEY
BLUEBELL WOOD
GRAVEL PIT
RIVERSIDE RETAIL PARK
THE MOORS
CONNECTIONS BUSINESS PARK
EAST LAKE
SEVENOAKS WILDLIFE RESERVE
WEST LAKE
WEST KENT COLD STORAGE
CHIPSTEAD LAKE
RAKEFIELD WOOD
EDWARD SHAW
ALDER SHAW
HOME WOOD
Bat and Ball Junction
SEVENOAKS HOSP
279
RIVERHEAD PARKLAND
MONTREAL PARK
ANT WOOD
ASH PLAT WOOD
OBELISK WOOD
COLD ARBOR WOOD
LITTLE BRITAIN'S WOOD
MIDDLINGS WOOD
278
M25
M26
A25
A224
A225
A21
SEVENOAKS BYPASS
POLHILL
MORANTS COURT ROAD
LONDON ROAD
BRADBOURNE VALE ROAD
WESTERHAM ROAD
WORSHIPS HILL
AMHERST HILL
OTFORD ROAD
SEVENOAKS ROAD
STATION ROAD
HIGH STREET
DARTFORD ROAD
ST. JOHN'S HILL
SEAL ROAD
PILGRIMS WAY
116
117
118
119
120
121
122
123
124
50
51
52
56
57
58
59

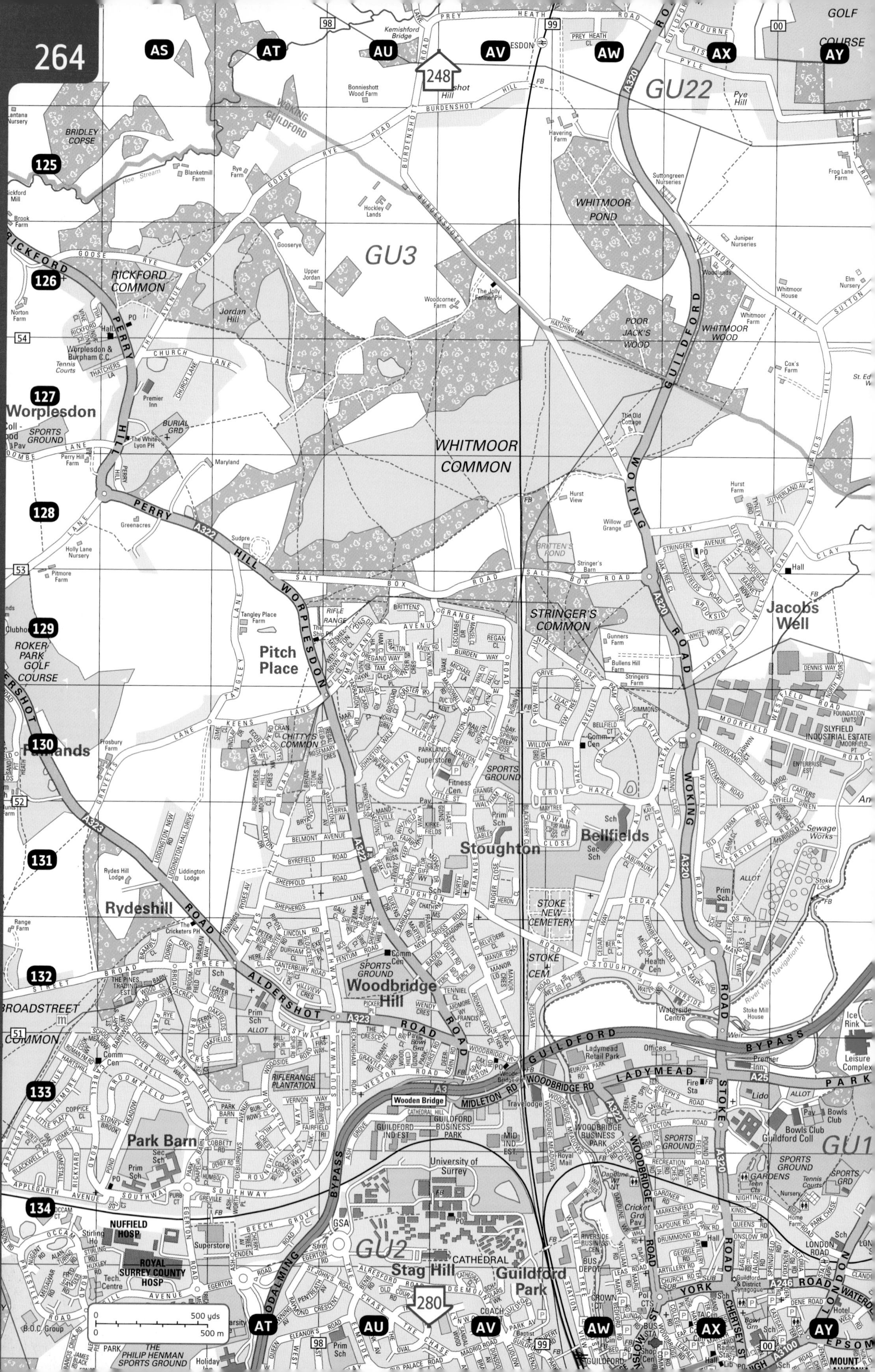

AS
AT
AU
AV
AW
AX
AY
248
280
GU22
GU3
GU2
GU1
Worplesdon
Pitch Place
Jacobs Well
Stoughton
Bellfields
Rydeshill
Woodbridge Hill
Park Barn
Stag Hill
Guildford Park
Fairlands
WHITMOOR COMMON
WHITMOOR POND
WHITMOOR WOOD
POOR JACK'S WOOD
RICKFORD COMMON
BRIDLEY COPSE
STRINGER'S COMMON
CHITTY'S COMMON
BROADSTREET COMMON
ROKER PARK GOLF COURSE
SLYFIELD INDUSTRIAL ESTATE
University of Surrey
NUFFIELD HOSP
ROYAL SURREY COUNTY HOSP
CATHEDRAL
GUILDFORD BUSINESS PARK
Ladymead Retail Park
Guildford Coll
Wooden Bridge
PERRY HILL
WORPLESDON ROAD
ALDERSHOT ROAD
WOKING ROAD
GUILDFORD BYPASS
SALT BOX ROAD
GOOSE RYE ROAD
BURDENSHOTT ROAD
STOUGHTON ROAD
WOODBRIDGE ROAD
LADYMEAD
STOKE ROAD
A3
A25
A320
A322
A323
0 500 yds
0 500 m

249
266
281
AZ
BA
BB
BC
BD
BE
BF
01
02
03
126
127
128
129
130
131
132
133
134
54
53
52
51
Send
Send Marsh
Sutton Green
Sendgrove
GU23
GU4
SUTTON PARK
Sutton Place
BURPHAM COURT FARM PARK
RIVERSIDE PARK
FRITHYS WOOD
COTTS WOOD
HIGHCOTTS WOOD
Burpham
SUTHERLAND MEMORIAL PARK
COPSE EDGE
SPORTS GROUND
MERROW COMMON
MERROW BUSINESS CEN
MERROW IND EST
DEPOT
Bushy Hill
Merrow
Abbotswood
Surrey Cricket Centre
GUILDFORD GOLF COURSE
CHALK PIT
THE WILDERNESS
CLANDON PARK
Clandon Park NT
Clandon Park Garden Centre
MERROW DOWNS
WALNUT TREE BOTTOM
RIVER WEY NAVIGATION NT
River Wey
WOKING
GUILDFORD
LONDON ROAD
A3
GUILDFORD BYPASS
RIPLEY ROAD
EPSOM ROAD
A25
A246
A247
A3100
B2215
B2234
SEND BARNS LANE
CLANDON ROAD
PORTSMOUTH ROAD
VICARAGE LANE
WOODHILL
SEND HILL
POTTERS LANE
CHURCH LANE
TOWING PATH
CLAY LANE
MERROW LANE
BOXGROVE ROAD
TRODDS LANE
NEW INN LANE
PARK LANE
KINGFISHER DRIVE
Triggs Lock
Bower's Lock
Bower's Mill
Broadoak Bridge
Weir
Westfield Farm
Runtley Wood Farm
Cricketshill Farm
Concorde C.C.
Sendholme
Wareham's Farm
Sendcourt Farm
Send Grove
Tudor Barn Farm
Sendhurst Grange
Woodhill House Farm
Old Timbers
Nutbourne Fruit Farm
Whitehouse Farm
Nuthill Farm
Gosden Hill Farm
Dedswell Manor Farm
Sutton Park House
Manor House
Stables
Sendbarns
CEM
Prim Sch
Sec Sch
Superstore
Surgery
Comm Cen
Clubhouse
Miniature Railway
Amb Sta
Bowling Green
Dance Coll
Horse & Groom PH
Tennis Courts
Fitness Cen
Merrow CC
P+R
REGT. MUS

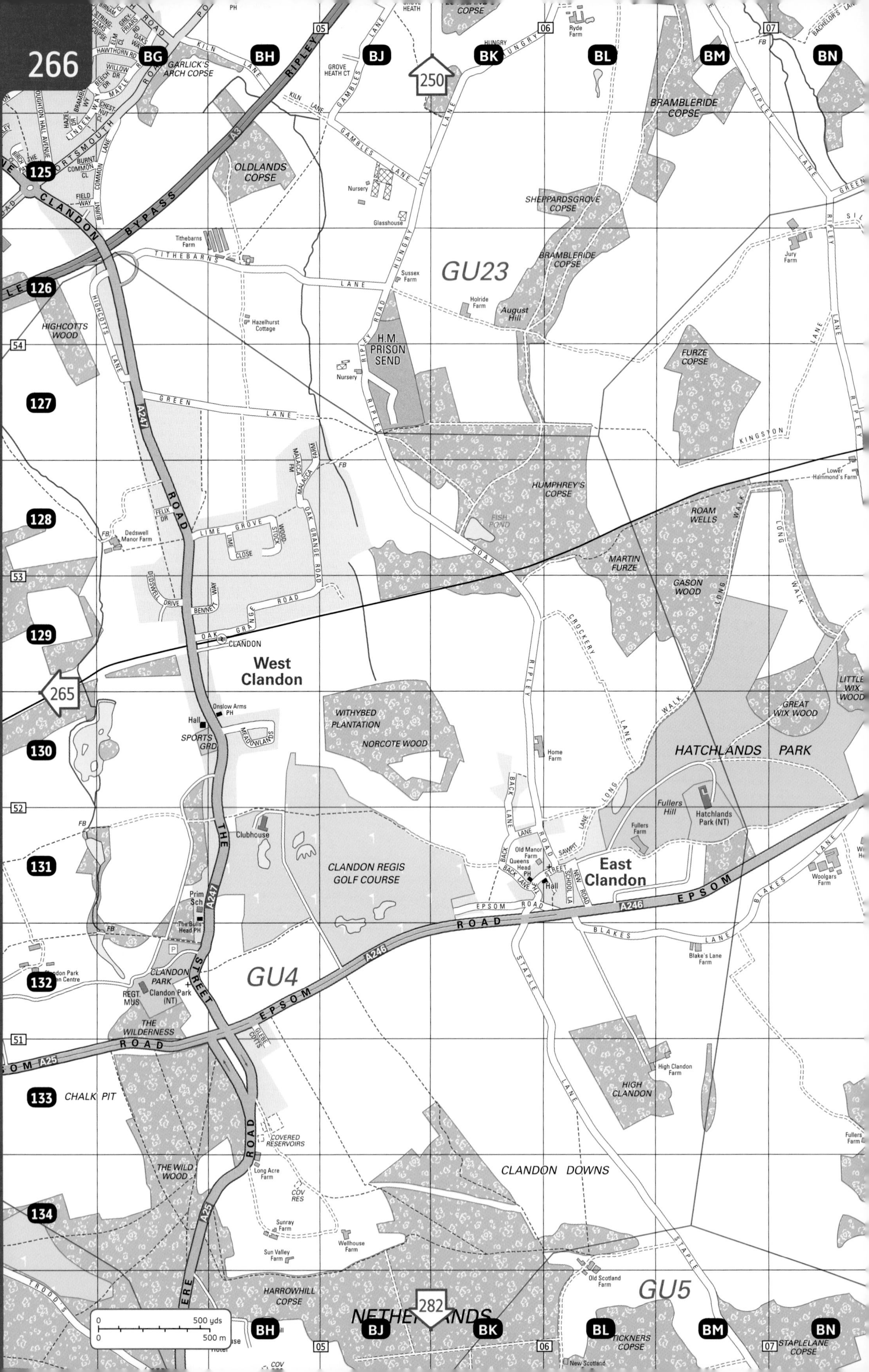
BG
BH
BJ
BK
BL
BM
BN
250
282
265
05
06
07
54
53
52
51
125
126
127
128
129
130
131
132
133
134
GARLICK'S ARCH COPSE
RIPLEY
KILN LANE
GROVE HEATH CT
GAMBLES LANE
HUNGRY HILL LANE
Ryde Farm
BRAMBLERIDE COPSE
OLDLANDS COPSE
CLANDON BYPASS
A3
Nursery
Glasshouse
SHEPPARDSGROVE COPSE
RIPLEY LANE
Tithebarns Farm
TITHEBARNS LANE
Sussex Farm
GU23
BRAMBLERIDE COPSE
Jury Farm
HIGHCOTTS WOOD
HIGHCOTTS LANE
Hazelhurst Cottage
Holride Farm
August Hill
H.M. PRISON SEND
RIPLEY ROAD
FURZE COPSE
Nursery
GREEN LANE
A247
KINGSTON
Lower Hammond's Farm
MALACCA FM
FB
HUMPHREY'S COPSE
ROAM WELLS
FELIX DR
Dedswell Manor Farm
LIME GROVE
LIME CLOSE
WOODSTOCK
OAK GRANGE ROAD
FISH POND
MARTIN FURZE
GASON WOOD
DEDSWELL DRIVE
BENNETT WAY
OAK GRANGE ROAD
CLANDON
CROCKERY LANE
LONG WALK
West Clandon
LITTLE WIX WOOD
GREAT WIX WOOD
Onslow Arms PH
Hall
SPORTS GRD
MEADOWLANDS
WITHYBED PLANTATION
NORCOTE WOOD
Home Farm
HATCHLANDS PARK
BACK LANE
Fullers Hill
Hatchlands Park (NT)
Clubhouse
Fullers Farm
THE STREET
Old Manor Farm
Queens Head PH
SAWPIT LANE
East Clandon
CLANDON REGIS GOLF COURSE
Woolgars Farm
Prim Sch
SCHOOL LA
NEW ROAD
EPSOM ROAD
A246
The Bulls Head PH
BLAKES LANE
Blake's Lane Farm
Clandon Park Garden Centre
CLANDON PARK
Clandon Park (NT)
REGT. MUS
GU4
STAPLE LANE
THE WILDERNESS
GLEBE COTTS
ROAD
A25
High Clandon Farm
HIGH CLANDON
CHALK PIT
COVERED RESERVOIRS
Fullers Farm
THE WILD WOOD
Long Acre Farm
CLANDON DOWNS
COV RES
Sunray Farm
Wellhouse Farm
Sun Valley Farm
Old Scotland Farm
GU5
HARROWHILL COPSE
TROOD'S
NETHERLANDS
TICKNERS COPSE
STAPLELANE COPSE
New Scotland
0 500 yds
0 500 m

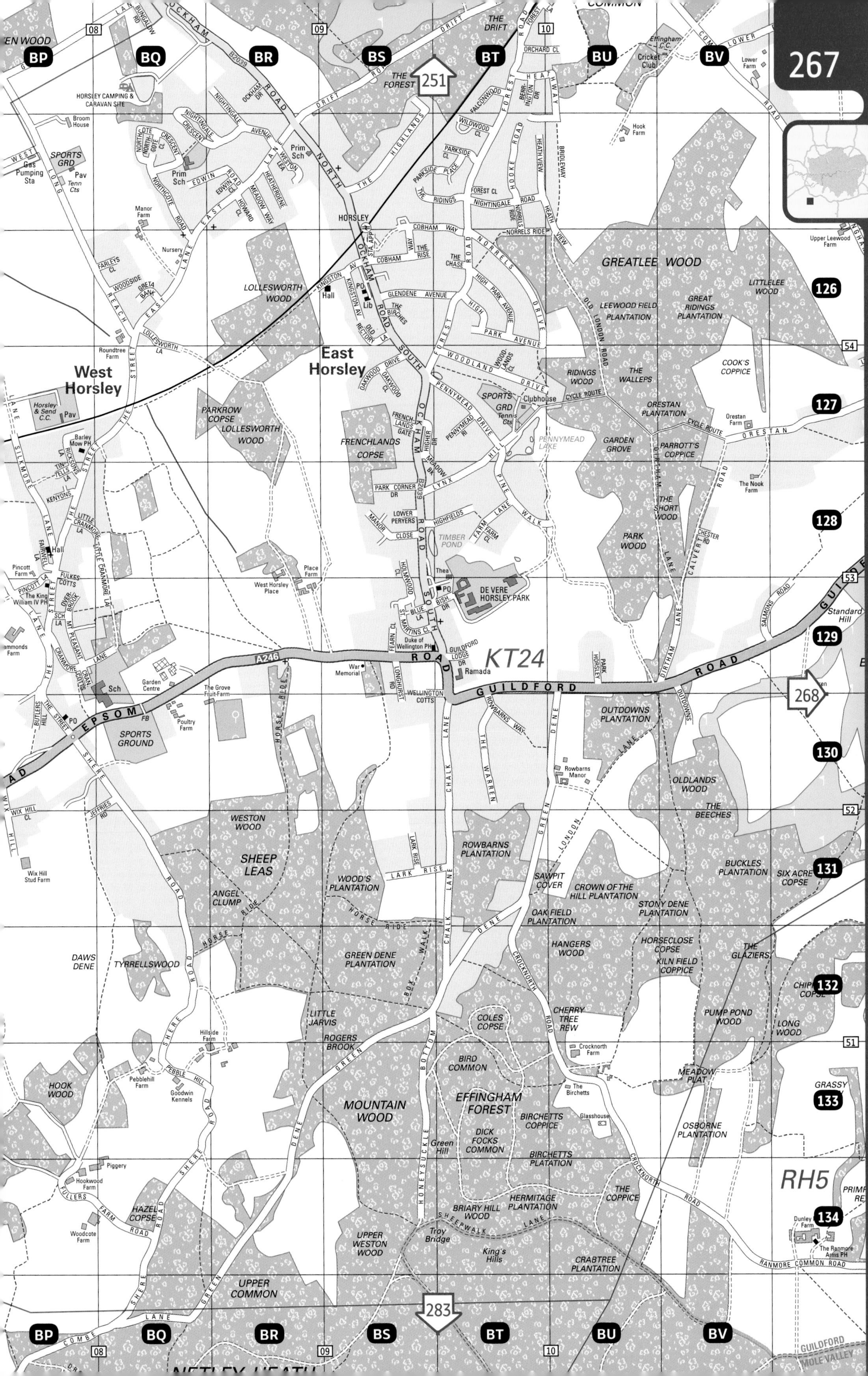

BP
BQ
BR
BS
BT
BU
BV
08
09
10
251
268
283
126
127
128
129
130
131
132
133
134
54
53
52
51
West Horsley
East Horsley
KT24
RH5
HORSLEY CAMPING & CARAVAN SITE
Broom House
SPORTS GRD
Pav
Tenn Cts
Gas Pumping Sta
Prim Sch
Manor Farm
Nursery
Roundtree Farm
Horsley & Send C.C.
Barley Mow PH
Hall
Pincott Farm
The King William IV PH
Sch
PO
SPORTS GROUND
Garden Centre
The Grove Fruit Farm
Poultry Farm
West Horsley Place
Place Farm
War Memorial
Duke of Wellington PH
Ramada
DE VERE HORSLEY PARK
Thea
Lib
PO
HORSLEY
Clubhouse
PENNYMEAD LAKE
TIMBER POND
Wix Hill Stud Farm
Hillside Farm
Pebblehill Farm
Goodwin Kennels
Piggery
Hookwood Farm
Woodcote Farm
Rowbarns Manor
Crocknorth Farm
The Birchetts
Glasshouse
Dunley Farm
The Ranmore Arms PH
Effingham C.C.
Cricket Club
Lower Farm
Hook Farm
Upper Leewood Farm
Orestan Farm
The Nook Farm
Standard Hill
THE DRIFT
THE FOREST
LOLLESWORTH WOOD
PARKROW COPSE
FRENCHLANDS COPSE
GREATLEE WOOD
LITTLELEE WOOD
LEEWOOD FIELD PLANTATION
GREAT RIDINGS PLANTATION
COOK'S COPPICE
RIDINGS WOOD
THE WALLEPS
ORESTAN PLANTATION
GARDEN GROVE
PARROTT'S COPPICE
THE SHORT WOOD
PARK WOOD
OUTDOWNS PLANTATION
OLDLANDS WOOD
THE BEECHES
BUCKLES PLANTATION
SIX ACRE COPSE
ROWBARNS PLANTATION
SAWPIT COVER
CROWN OF THE HILL PLANTATION
STONY DENE PLANTATION
OAK FIELD PLANTATION
HANGERS WOOD
HORSECLOSE COPSE
KILN FIELD COPPICE
THE GLAZIERS
CHERRY TREE REW
PUMP POND WOOD
LONG WOOD
MEADOW PLAT
GRASSY
OSBORNE PLANTATION
WESTON WOOD
SHEEP LEAS
ANGEL CLUMP
WOOD'S PLANTATION
GREEN DENE PLANTATION
DAWS DENE
TYRRELLSWOOD
LITTLE JARVIS
ROGERS BROOK
COLES COPSE
BIRD COMMON
MOUNTAIN WOOD
EFFINGHAM FOREST
BIRCHETTS COPPICE
DICK FOCKS COMMON
BIRCHETTS PLATATION
Green Hill
HOOK WOOD
HAZEL COPSE
THE COPPICE
HERMITAGE PLANTATION
BRIARY HILL WOOD
Troy Bridge
King's Hills
CRABTREE PLANTATION
UPPER WESTON WOOD
UPPER COMMON
GUILDFORD
MOLE VALLEY
OCKHAM ROAD NORTH
OCKHAM ROAD SOUTH
B2039
A246
EPSOM ROAD
GUILDFORD ROAD
DRIFT ROAD
THE HIGHLANDS
NIGHTINGALE AVENUE
NIGHTINGALE CRESCENT
EDWIN ROAD
EDWIN CL
HOWARD CL
MEADOW WAY
HEATHERDENE
WESTON LEA
NORTHCOTE ROAD
NORTHCOTE CRESCENT
EAST LANE
FARLEYS CL
WOODSIDE
LOLLESWORTH LA
LONG REACH
THE STREET
SILKMORE LANE
KENYONS
LITTLE CRANMORE LA
FULKES COTTS
PINCOTT LA
CRANMORE LANE
MT PLEASANT
BUTLERS HILL
SHERE ROAD
JEFFRIES RD
WIX HILL
WIX HILL CL
PEBBLE HILL
FULLERS FARM ROAD
COMBE LANE
SHERE LANE
COBHAM WAY
THE RISE
THE CHASE
KINGSTON AV
GLENDENE AVENUE
THE BIRCHES
OLD RECTORY LA
HIGH PARK AVENUE
PARK AVENUE
FOREST ROAD
WOODLAND DRIVE
PENNYMEAD DRIVE
PENNYMEAD RI
OAKWOOD DRIVE
FRENCH LANDS GATE
HIGHER DR
MEADOW BK
LYNX HILL
PINE WALK
PARK CORNER DR
LOWER PERYERS
MANOR CLOSE
HIGHFIELDS
FARM LANE
FARM CL
HOLMWOOD CL
BISHOPS DR
BLUE LA
ST. MARTINS CL
FEARN CL
LONGHURST RD
WELLINGTON COTTS
GUILDFORD LODGE DR
CHALK LANE
ROWBARNS WAY
THE WARREN
LARK RISE
HORSE RIDE
BOX WALK
GREEN DENE
CROCKNORTH ROAD
BOTTOM
HONEYSUCKLE
SHEEPWALK LANE
RANMORE COMMON ROAD
LONDON LANE
DIRTHAM LANE
CALVERT RD
CHESTER RD
OLD LONDON ROAD
SALMONS ROAD
ORESTAN LANE
CYCLE ROUTE
FOREST CL
HEATH VIEW
BRIDLEWAY
NORRELS DRIVE
NORRELS RIDE
HOOKE ROAD
PARKSIDE
PARKSIDE PLACE
THE RIDINGS
WILDWOOD CL
FALCONWOOD
BERRINGTON DR
HEATHWAY
ORCHARD CL
PARK HORSLEY
OUTDOWNS

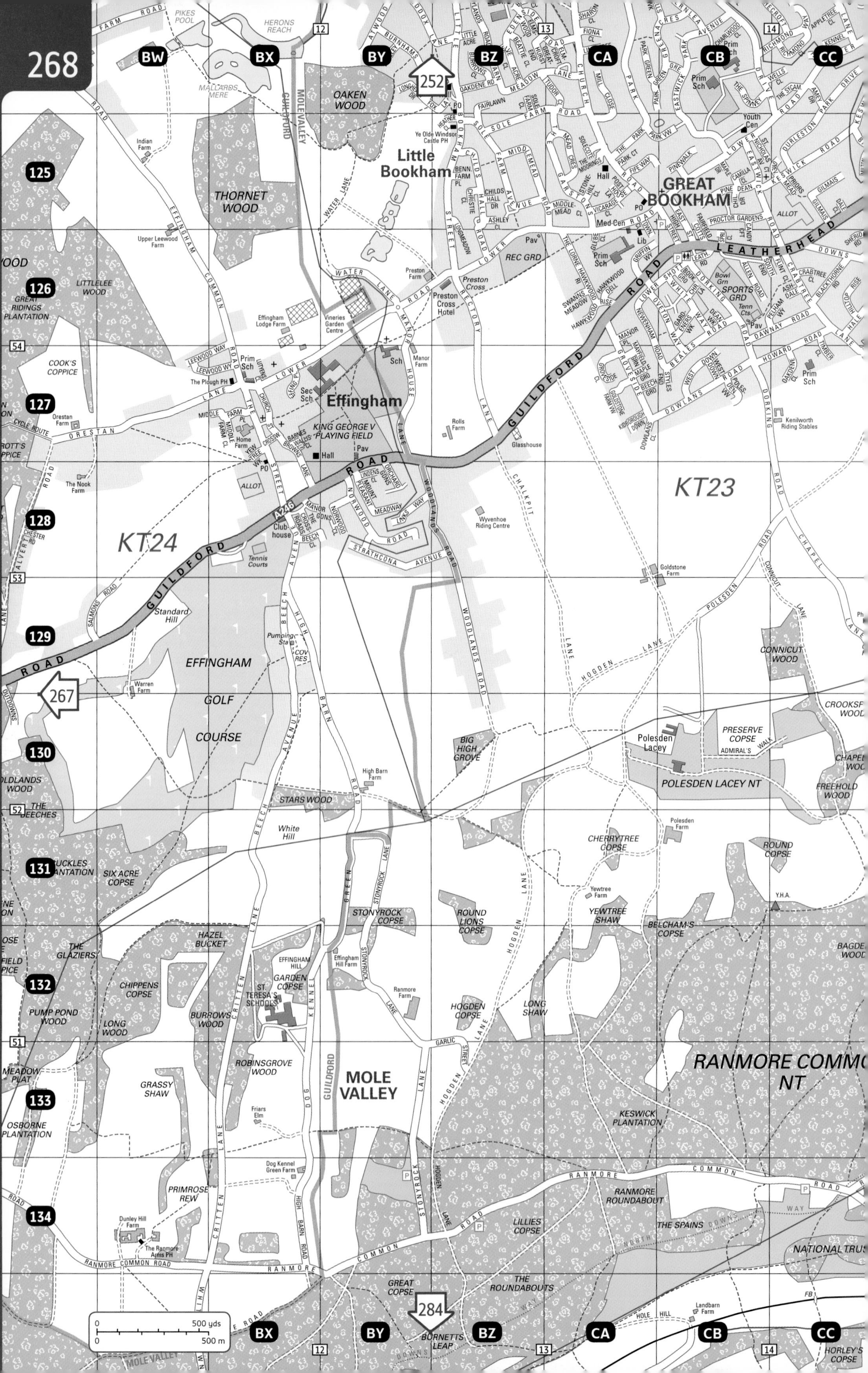
BW
BX
BY
BZ
CA
CB
CC
252
267
284
125
126
127
128
129
130
131
132
133
134
12
13
14
54
53
52
51
PIKES POOL
HERONS REACH
MALLARDS MERE
OAKEN WOOD
THORNET WOOD
LITTLELEE WOOD
GREAT RIDINGS PLANTATION
COOK'S COPPICE
Indian Farm
Upper Leewood Farm
Little Bookham
GREAT BOOKHAM
Effingham
KING GEORGE V PLAYING FIELD
KT24
KT23
EFFINGHAM
GOLF
COURSE
Standard Hill
Warren Farm
Orestan Farm
The Nook Farm
The Plough PH
Home Farm
Club-house
Tennis Courts
Effingham Lodge Farm
Vineries Garden Centre
Manor Farm
Preston Farm
Preston Cross
Preston Cross Hotel
Ye Olde Windsor Castle PH
Rolls Farm
Glasshouse
Wyvenhoe Riding Centre
Goldstone Farm
Kenilworth Riding Stables
REC GRD
SPORTS GRD
ALLOT
Youth Cen
Med Cen
Lib
Hall
Prim Sch
Sec Sch
Pav
PO
BIG HIGH GROVE
High Barn Farm
STARS WOOD
White Hill
Pumping Sta
COV RES
Polesden Lacey
PRESERVE COPSE
POLESDEN LACEY NT
Polesden Farm
CHERRYTREE COPSE
ROUND COPSE
CONNICUT WOOD
FREEHOLD WOOD
Yewtree Farm
YEWTREE SHAW
BELCHAM'S COPSE
Y.H.A.
STONYROCK COPSE
ROUND LIONS COPSE
HAZEL BUCKET
THE GLAZIERS
SIX ACRE COPSE
CHIPPENS COPSE
PUMP POND WOOD
LONG WOOD
BURROWS WOOD
ST TERESA'S SCHOOLS
EFFINGHAM HILL
GARDEN COPSE
Effingham Hill Farm
Ranmore Farm
HOGDEN COPSE
LONG SHAW
ROBINSGROVE WOOD
GRASSY SHAW
Friars Elm
MOLE VALLEY
RANMORE COMMON NT
KESWICK PLANTATION
MEADOW PLAT
OSBORNE PLANTATION
Dog Kennel Green Farm
PRIMROSE REW
Dunley Hill Farm
The Ranmore Arms PH
LILLIES COPSE
RANMORE ROUNDABOUT
THE SPAINS
NATIONAL TRUST
THE ROUNDABOUTS
GREAT COPSE
BORNETTS LEAP
Landbarn Farm
HORLEY'S COPSE
GUILDFORD ROAD
A246
LEATHERHEAD ROAD
ORESTAN LANE
EFFINGHAM COMMON ROAD
LOWER ROAD
WATER LANE
MANOR HOUSE LANE
WOODLANDS ROAD
STRATHCONA AVENUE
NORWOOD ROAD
BEECH AVENUE
HIGH BARN ROAD
CHALKPIT LANE
HOGDEN LANE
POLESDEN LANE
CHAPEL LANE
CONNICUT LANE
DORKING ROAD
RANMORE COMMON ROAD
CRITTEN LANE
STONYROCK LANE
GREEN LANE
GARLIC STREET
HOLE HILL
NORTH DOWNS WAY
0
500 yds
500 m

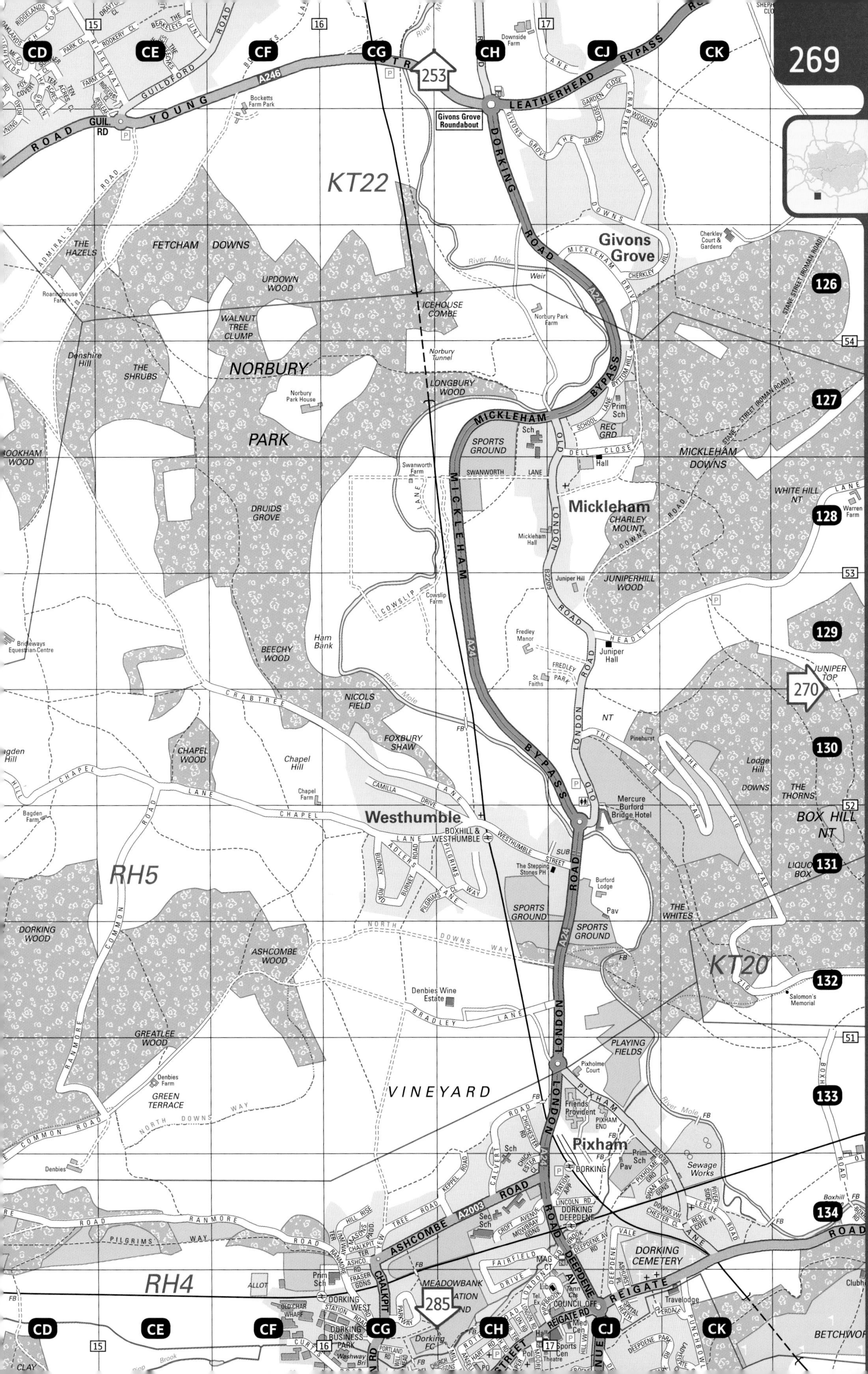
CD
CE
CF
CG
CH
CJ
CK
15
16
17
253
GUILDFORD ROAD
YOUNG STREET
A246
Bocketts Farm Park
Givons Grove Roundabout
LEATHERHEAD BYPASS
Downside Farm
KT22
DORKING ROAD
Givons Grove
Cherkley Court & Gardens
126
STANE STREET (ROMAN ROAD)
THE HAZELS
FETCHAM DOWNS
UPDOWN WOOD
Roaringhouse Farm
WALNUT TREE CLUMP
ICEHOUSE COMBE
Norbury Park Farm
Weir
River Mole
MICKLEHAM DRIVE
Norbury Tunnel
Denshire Hill
THE SHRUBS
NORBURY
Norbury Park House
LONGBURY WOOD
MICKLEHAM BYPASS
54
127
PARK
SPORTS GROUND
Sch
Prim Sch
REC GRD
DELL CLOSE
Hall
MICKLEHAM DOWNS
Swanworth Farm
SWANWORTH LANE
WHITE HILL NT
Warren Farm
128
Mickleham
CHARLEY MOUNT
Mickleham Hall
DRUIDS GROVE
53
Juniper Hill
JUNIPERHILL WOOD
LONDON ROAD
B2209
Cowslip Farm
COWSLIP LANE
Bridleways Equestrian Centre
Ham Bank
BEECHY WOOD
Fredley Manor
Juniper Hall
HEADLEY ROAD
129
FREDLEY PARK
St Faiths
JUNIPER TOP
270
CRABTREE LANE
NICOLS FIELD
A24
NT
Pinehurst
FOXBURY SHAW
Bagden Hill
CHAPEL WOOD
Chapel Hill
Lodge Hill
130
THE ZIG ZAG
DOWNS
THE THORNS
CAMILLA DRIVE
Chapel Farm
CHAPEL LANE
Bagden Farm
Westhumble
Mercure Burford Bridge Hotel
52
BOX HILL NT
BOXHILL & WESTHUMBLE
WESTHUMBLE STREET
RH5
The Stepping Stones PH
Burford Lodge
131
LIQUOR BOX
Pav
THE WHITES
SPORTS GROUND
NORTH DOWNS WAY
DORKING WOOD
ASHCOMBE WOOD
KT20
132
Salomon's Memorial
Denbies Wine Estate
BRADLEY LANE
51
GREATLEE WOOD
PLAYING FIELDS
Pixholme Court
Denbies Farm
VINEYARD
GREEN TERRACE
133
RANMORE COMMON ROAD
Friends Provident
PIXHAM END
PIXHAM LANE
Pixham
Sewage Works
Denbies
DORKING
Prim Sch
ASHCOMBE ROAD
A2003
Sec Sch
DORKING DEEPDENE
Boxhill
134
RANMORE ROAD
PILGRIMS WAY
DORKING CEMETERY
RH4
DEEPDENE AVENUE
CHALKPIT LANE
MEADOWBANK
285
REIGATE ROAD
Travelodge
DORKING WEST
DORKING BUSINESS PARK
Dorking FC
COUNCIL OFF
REIGATE RD
Med Cen
Sports Cen
Theatre
Clubhouse
BETCHWORTH
CLAY

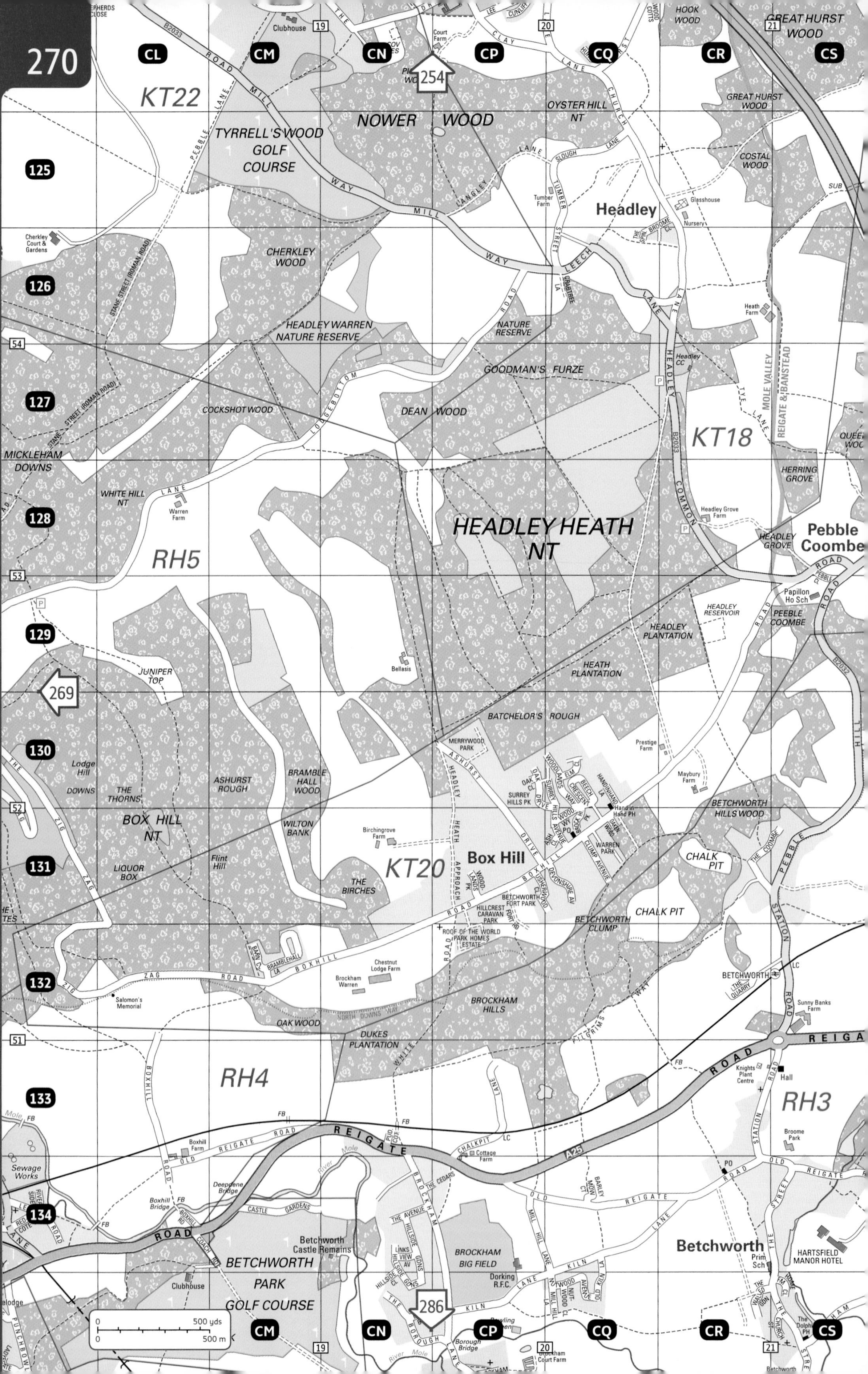
CL
CM
CN
CP
CQ
CR
CS
254
KT22
TYRRELL'S WOOD GOLF COURSE
NOWER WOOD
OYSTER HILL NT
GREAT HURST WOOD
HOOK WOOD
COSTAL WOOD
Headley
Glasshouse
Nursery
Tumber Farm
Clubhouse
Court Farm
MILL WAY
LEECH LANE
CHURCH LANE
SLOUGH LANE
TUMBER STREET
LANGLEY LANE
CLAY LANE
Cherkley Court & Gardens
CHERKLEY WOOD
HEADLEY WARREN NATURE RESERVE
NATURE RESERVE
GOODMAN'S FURZE
STANE STREET (ROMAN ROAD)
COCKSHOT WOOD
DEAN WOOD
LODGEBOTTOM ROAD
MICKLEHAM DOWNS
Headley CC
HEADLEY COMMON
KT18
MOLE VALLEY
REIGATE & BANSTEAD
TYE LANE
Heath Farm
HERRING GROVE
WHITE HILL NT
Warren Farm
RH5
HEADLEY HEATH NT
Headley Grove Farm
HEADLEY GROVE
Pebble Coombe
PEBBLE COOMBE
Papillon Ho Sch
HEADLEY RESERVOIR
HEADLEY PLANTATION
HEATH PLANTATION
JUNIPER TOP
269
Bellasis
BATCHELOR'S ROUGH
MERRYWOOD PARK
Prestige Farm
Maybury Farm
Lodge Hill
DOWNS
THE THORNS
ASHURST ROUGH
BRAMBLE HALL WOOD
BOX HILL NT
WILTON BANK
Hand-in-Hand PH
SURREY HILLS PK
WARREN PARK
BETCHWORTH HILLS WOOD
Birchingrove Farm
KT20
Box Hill
CHALK PIT
Flint Hill
LIQUOR BOX
THE BIRCHES
BETCHWORTH FORT PARK
HILLCREST CARAVAN PARK
ROOF OF THE WORLD PARK HOMES ESTATE
BETCHWORTH CLUMP
ZIG ZAG ROAD
BOXHILL ROAD
Chestnut Lodge Farm
Brockham Warren
Salomon's Memorial
BROCKHAM HILLS
NORTH DOWNS WAY
PILGRIMS WAY
OAK WOOD
DUKES PLANTATION
BETCHWORTH
Sunny Banks Farm
Knights Plant Centre
Hall
RH4
RH3
Sewage Works
Boxhill Farm
OLD REIGATE ROAD
REIGATE ROAD
Cottage Farm
A25
Broome Park
Deepdene Bridge
Boxhill Bridge
CASTLE GARDENS
Betchworth Castle Remains
BETCHWORTH PARK GOLF COURSE
Clubhouse
BROCKHAM BIG FIELD
Dorking R.F.C.
KILN LANE
MILL HILL LANE
Betchworth
Prim Sch
HARTSFIELD MANOR HOTEL
The Dolphin PH
286
Borough Bridge
Brockham Court Farm
River Mole
0 500 yds
0 500 m
125
126
127
128
129
130
131
132
133
134
51
52
53
54
19
20
21

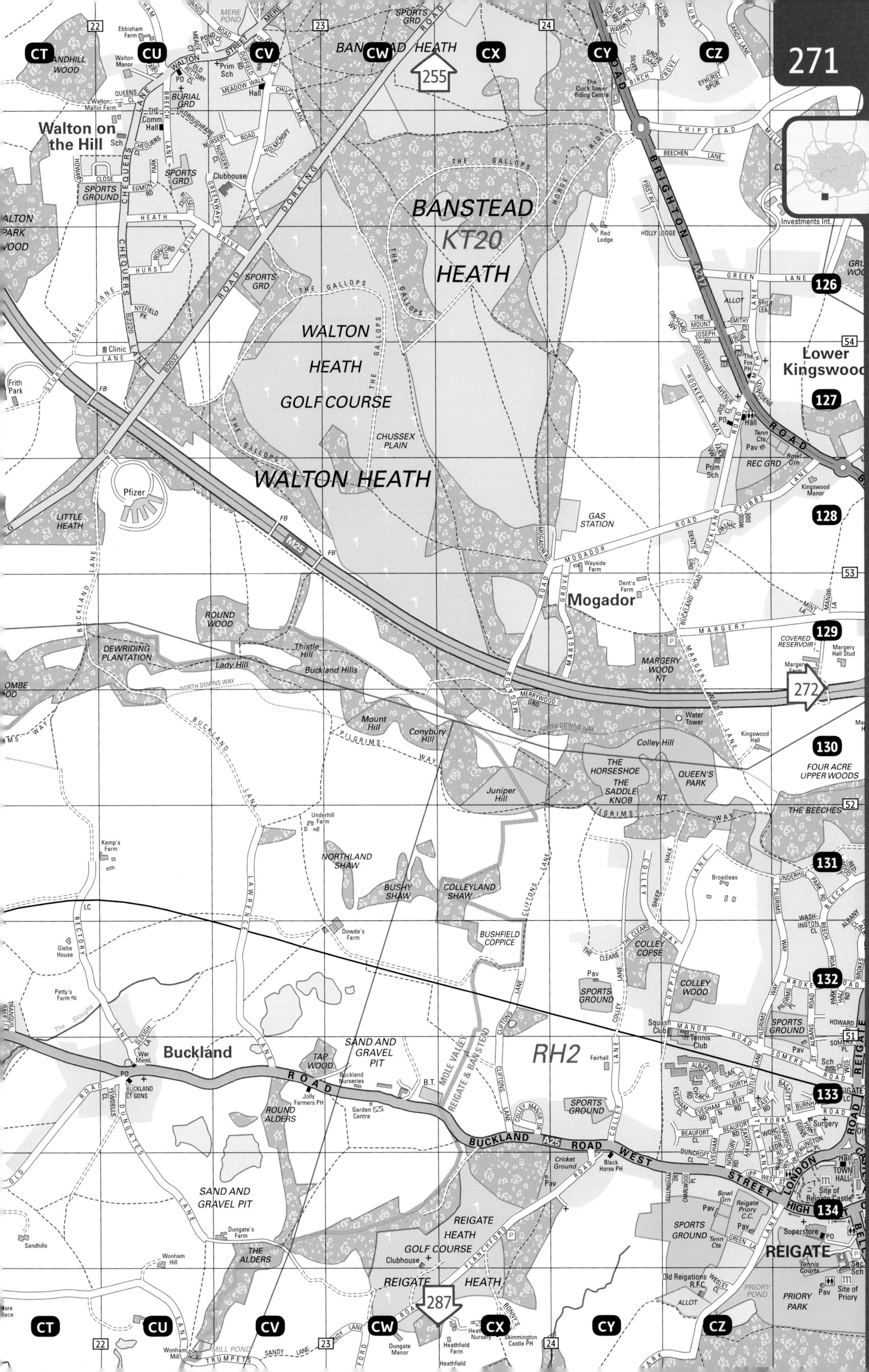

CT
CU
CV
CW
CX
CY
CZ
22
23
24
255
Walton on the Hill
SANDHILL WOOD
Ebbisham Farm
Walton Manor
Walton Manor Farm
MERE POND
BANSTEAD HEATH
SPORTS GRD
The Clock Tower Riding Centre
WALTON STREET
PO
Prim Sch
BURIAL GRD
MEADOW WALK
Hall
Comm Hall
Sch
QUEENS CL
CHEQUERS LANE
CHEQUERS CL
HOWARD CLOSE
SPORTS GROUND
EGMONT RD
PARK LANE
BREECH LANE
SPORTS GRD
Clubhouse
NURSERY CL
GREENWAYS
HOLMCROFT
CHUCKS LANE
DORKING ROAD
THE GALLOPS
BANSTEAD
KT20
HEATH
HORSE RIDE
CHIPSTEAD
BEECHEN LANE
BRIGHTON ROAD
A217
FIRST AV
Red Lodge
HOLLY LODGE
Investments Int.
HEATH DRIVE
WONFORD CL
HURST DRIVE
NYEFIELD PK
B2220
SPORTS GRD
WALTON
HEATH
GOLF COURSE
Clinic
LOVE LANE
STURTS LANE
B2032
OLD ROAD
Frith Park
FB
CHUSSEX PLAIN
WALTON HEATH
Pfizer
LITTLE HEATH
M25
GREEN LANE
126
ALLOT
BRIER LEA
ORCHARD WY
THE MOUNT
JOSEPH AV
SMITHY CL
54
Lower Kingswood
The Fox PH
JOSEPHINE AVENUE
ROOKERY WAY
127
PO
Hall
Tenn Cts
Pav
Prim Sch
REC GRD
Bowl Grn
Kingswood Manor
128
GAS STATION
STUBBS LANE
BUCKLAND ROAD
DENTS GRO
MOGADOR ROAD
Wayside Farm
Dent's Farm
53
Mogador
GROVE
MARGERY LANE
MARGERY
129
COVERED RESERVOIR
Margery Hall Stud
ROUND WOOD
DEWRIDING PLANTATION
Thistle Hill
Lady Hill
Buckland Hills
NORTH DOWNS WAY
MARGERY WOOD NT
272
MERRYWOOD GRO
Water Tower
Kingswood Hall
Mount Hill
Conybury Hill
PILGRIMS' WAY
Colley Hill
THE HORSESHOE
THE SADDLE KNOB
QUEEN'S PARK
NT
130
FOUR ACRE UPPER WOODS
Juniper Hill
THE BEECHES
52
BUCKLAND LANE
Underhill Farm
Kemp's Farm
NORTHLAND SHAW
BUSHY SHAW
COLLEYLAND SHAW
CLIFTONS LANE
Broadleas
131
UNDERHILL PARK RD
BEECH RD
PILGRIMS WAY
WASHINGTON CL
LAWRENCE LANE
Dowde's Farm
BUSHFIELD COPPICE
THE CLEARS
COLLEY COPSE
SHEEP WALK
LC
RECTORY LANE
Glebe House
Petty's Farm
The Sloughs
Pav
SPORTS GROUND
COLLEY WOOD
COPPICE LANE
132
BROKE ROAD
PILGRIMS PL
Squash Club
MANOR ROAD
Tennis Club
SPORTS GROUND
HOWARD RD
51
Buckland
SLOUGH LA
War Meml.
TAP WOOD
SAND AND GRAVEL PIT
MOLE VALLEY
REIGATE & BANSTEAD
RH2
Fairhall
COLLEY LANE
SOMERS ROAD
Sch
133
PO
BUCKLAND CT GDNS
YEWELLS CL
Buckland Nurseries
B.T.
Jolly Farmers PH
Garden Centre
ROUND ALDERS
BUCKLAND ROAD
A25
ROAD WEST
COLLEY MANOR DR
SPORTS GROUND
ALBERT RD
NORTH
EVESHAM RD
BEAUFORT CL
YORKE ROAD
Surgery
DUNCROFT CL
Black Horse PH
Cricket Ground
Pav
WEST STREET
LONDON RD
TOWN HALL
Site of Reigate Castle
HIGH ST
134
DUNGATES LANE
OLD ROAD
SAND AND GRAVEL PIT
REIGATE HEATH
GOLF COURSE
Clubhouse
FLANCHFORD ROAD
Bowl Grn
Reigate Priory C.C.
Pav
SPORTS GROUND
Tenn Cts
GREEN LA
Superstore
PO
REIGATE
Sandhills
Dungate's Farm
Wonham Hill
THE ALDERS
REIGATE HEATH
287
Old Reigations R.F.C.
WESLEY CL
PRIORY POND
ALLOT
Tennis Courts
PRIORY PARK
Pav
Site of Priory
Sec Sch
Wonham Mill
MILL POND
TRUMPETS
SANDY LANE
Dungate Manor
Heath Nursery
Heathfield Farm
Heathfield
Skimmington Castle PH
BONNY'S RD

DA
DB
DC
DD
DE
DF
DG
256
271
288
26
27
28
125
126
127
128
129
130
131
132
133
134
Mugswell
CR5
Lower Kingswood
Upper Gatton
KT20
Margery
Junction 8
Reigate Hill Interchange
RH2
Gatton
GATTON PARK
REIGATE
GOLF COU
Coles Meads
REDHILL
REIGATE
M25
A217
A242
A23
A25
B2034
UPPER GATTON WOOD
UPPER GATTON PARK
DELL WOOD
FURZEFIELD SHAW
BOARS GREEN SHAW
HARPS OAK SHAW
HEDGELAND SHAW
Ashtead Hill
JUBILEE PLANTATIONS
PARK SHAW
Kingswood Hill
MANSHIPS SHAW
GATTON FIELD SHAW
CATSBRAIN EAST
TOWER WOOD
HIGH BEECHES
GATTON BOTTOM
Driving Range
THE CROSSWAYS
MAJORITY PLANTATION
GROVE SHAW
GLEBE SHAW
GATLANDS SHAW
CATSBRAIN SHAW
JUBILEE PLANTATIONS
COLTS BUSHES
GATWICK WOOD
FURZEFIELD COPSE
LONG WOOD
LITTLE WOOD
MILLFIELD WOOD
GRUB WOOD
BEECHEN COPSE
SPORTS GRD
Fidelity Investments Int.
WELLFIELD SHAW
HOMEFIELD SHAWS
TOP SHAW
Southerns Farm
Park Farm
Manor Park
South Lodge
Reeves Rest
Home Field Farm
Highways Livery Stables
Orchard Cottage Riding Stables
Crossways Farm
Kingswood Manor
REC GRD
COVERED RESERVOIR
Margery Hall Stud
Margery Farm
TWO ACRE WOOD
BLACKHORSE WOOD
Margery Hall
Kingswood Hall
FOUR ACRE UPPER WOODS
THE BEECHES
REIGATE HILL NT
REIGATE FORT
Rock Farm
GREAT BUCK WOOD
WINGATE HILL
HALFMOON CLUMP
THE BURPIT
NUTWOOD NT
HOP GARDEN POND
ENGINE POND
SPORTS GROUND
THE LAKE
SERPENTINE WOOD
GREENCLUMP HILL
TEMPLE WOOD
QUEEN'S PARK
East Surrey Coll
WRAY COMMON
Reigate Coll
Superstore
Site of Reigate Castle
REIGATE CEMETERY
PRIORY POND
Site of Priory
Reigate Priory C.C.
Reigations R.F.C.
Bowls Club
Johnston House
Sports Cen
Surrey Fire & Rescue Service HQ
Cricket Ground
KINGSFIELD BUSINESS CEN
Gas Works
EARLSWOOD COMMON
MEML PARK
REDSTONE MANOR
GATTON ROAD
PARK ROAD
LONDON ROAD
BRIGHTON ROAD
REIGATE HILL
CROYDON ROAD
HIGH STREET
CHURCH STREET
WEST STREET
BELL STREET
STATION RD
QUEENSWAY
HATCHLANDS RD
REIGATE ROAD
0
500 yds
0
500 m

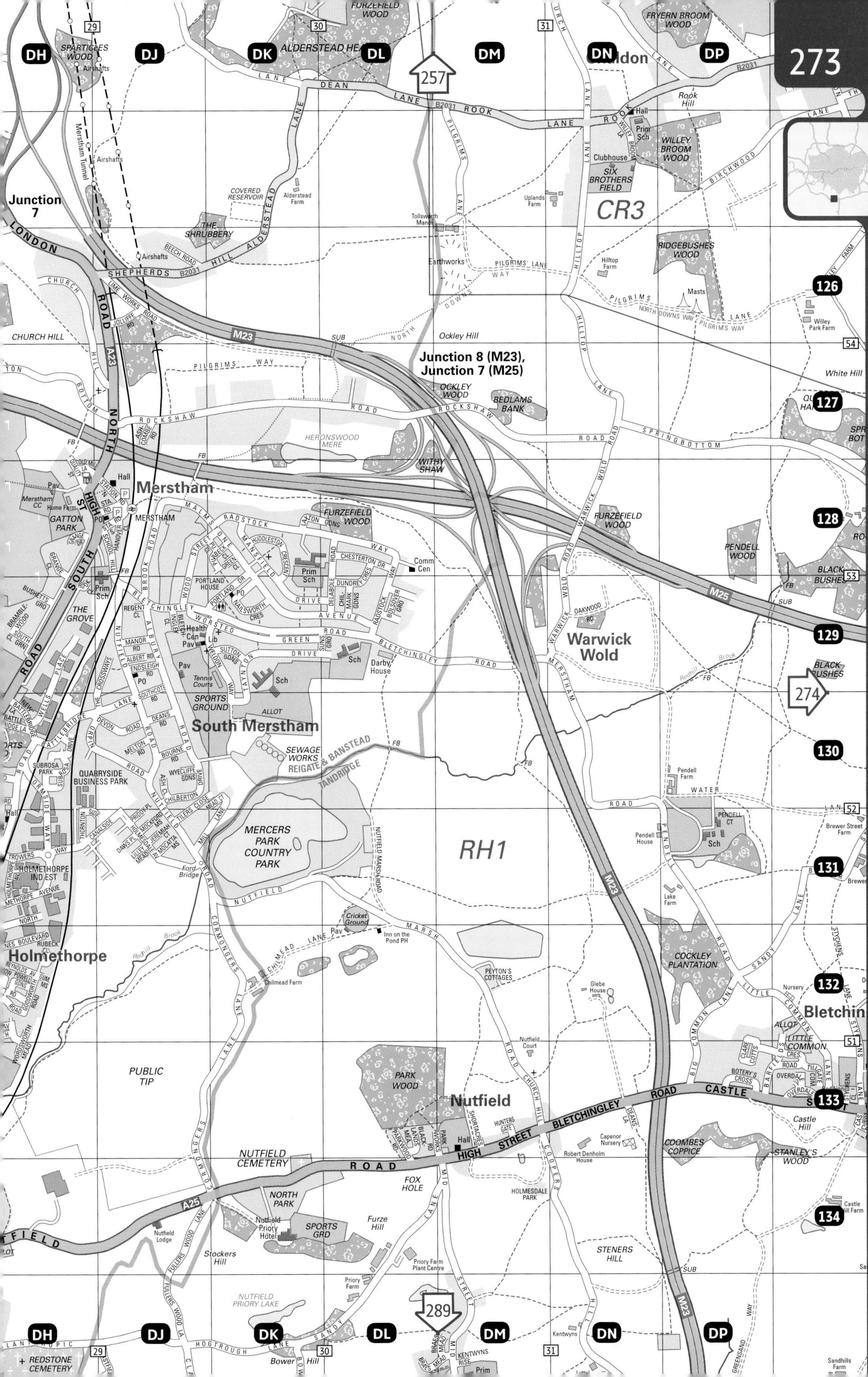
DH
DJ
DK
DL
DM
DN
DP
257
289
274
Junction 7
LONDON ROAD
SPARTICLES WOOD
Airshafts
Merstham Tunnel
ALDERSTEAD HEATH
FURZEFIELD WOOD
DEAN LANE
ROOK LANE
B2031
Chaldon
FRYERN BROOM WOOD
Rook Hill
Hall
Prim Sch
WILLEY BROOM WOOD
Clubhouse
SIX BROTHERS FIELD
BIRCHWOOD
CR3
COVERED RESERVOIR
Alderstead Farm
ALDERSTEAD HILL
THE SHRUBBERY
Tollsworth Manor
Earthworks
Uplands Farm
RIDGEBUSHES WOOD
Hilltop Farm
Masts
PILGRIMS' LANE
PILGRIMS' WAY
NORTH DOWNS WAY
SHEPHERDS HILL
CHURCH HILL
LIME WORKS ROAD
JOLLIFFE RD
M23
M25
Ockley Hill
Junction 8 (M23), Junction 7 (M25)
OCKLEY WOOD
BEDLAMS BANK
ROCKSHAW ROAD
HERONSWOOD MERE
WITHY SHAW
SPRINGBOTTOM ROAD
Willey Park Farm
White Hill
Merstham
MERSTHAM
Mersham CC
GATTON PARK
Home Farm
FURZEFIELD WOOD
RADSTOCK WAY
Comm Cen
PENDELL WOOD
BLACK BUSHES
Prim Sch
THE GROVE
PORTLAND HOUSE
OAKWOOD RD
Warwick Wold
WARWICK WOLD ROAD
BLETCHINGLEY ROAD
Darby House
Health Cen
Lib
Pav
Tennis Courts
SPORTS GROUND
ALLOT
Sch
South Merstham
SEWAGE WORKS
REIGATE & BANSTEAD
TANDRIDGE
QUARRYSIDE BUSINESS PARK
HOLMETHORPE IND EST
MERCERS PARK COUNTRY PARK
NUTFIELD MARSH ROAD
RH1
Pendell Farm
WATER LANE
Pendell House
PENDELL CT
Lake Farm
Brewer Street Farm
Redhill Brook
Ford Bridge
NUTFIELD MARSH
Cricket Ground
Inn on the Pond PH
CHILMEAD LANE
Chilmead Farm
Holmethorpe
PEYTON'S COTTAGES
Glebe House
COCKLEY PLANTATION
LITTLE COMMON LANE
SANDY LANE
Nursery
Bletchingley
CORMONGERS LANE
PUBLIC TIP
Nutfield Court
PARK WOOD
Nutfield
CHURCH HILL
HIGH STREET
BLETCHINGLEY ROAD
CASTLE STREET
Capenor Nursery
Robert Denholm House
COOMBES COPPICE
STANLEY'S WOOD
Castle Hill
Castle Hill Farm
NUTFIELD CEMETERY
A25
NUTFIELD ROAD
FOX HOLE
HOLMESDALE PARK
NORTH PARK
Nutfield Priory Hotel
SPORTS GRD
Furze Hill
Nutfield Lodge
Stockers Hill
Priory Farm Plant Centre
STENERS HILL
Priory Farm
NUTFIELD PRIORY LAKE
FULLERS WOOD LANE
HOGTROUGH LANE
Bower Hill
Kentwyns
KENTWYNS RISE
REDSTONE CEMETERY
Sandhills Farm
126
127
128
129
130
131
132
133
134
29
30
31
51
52
53
54

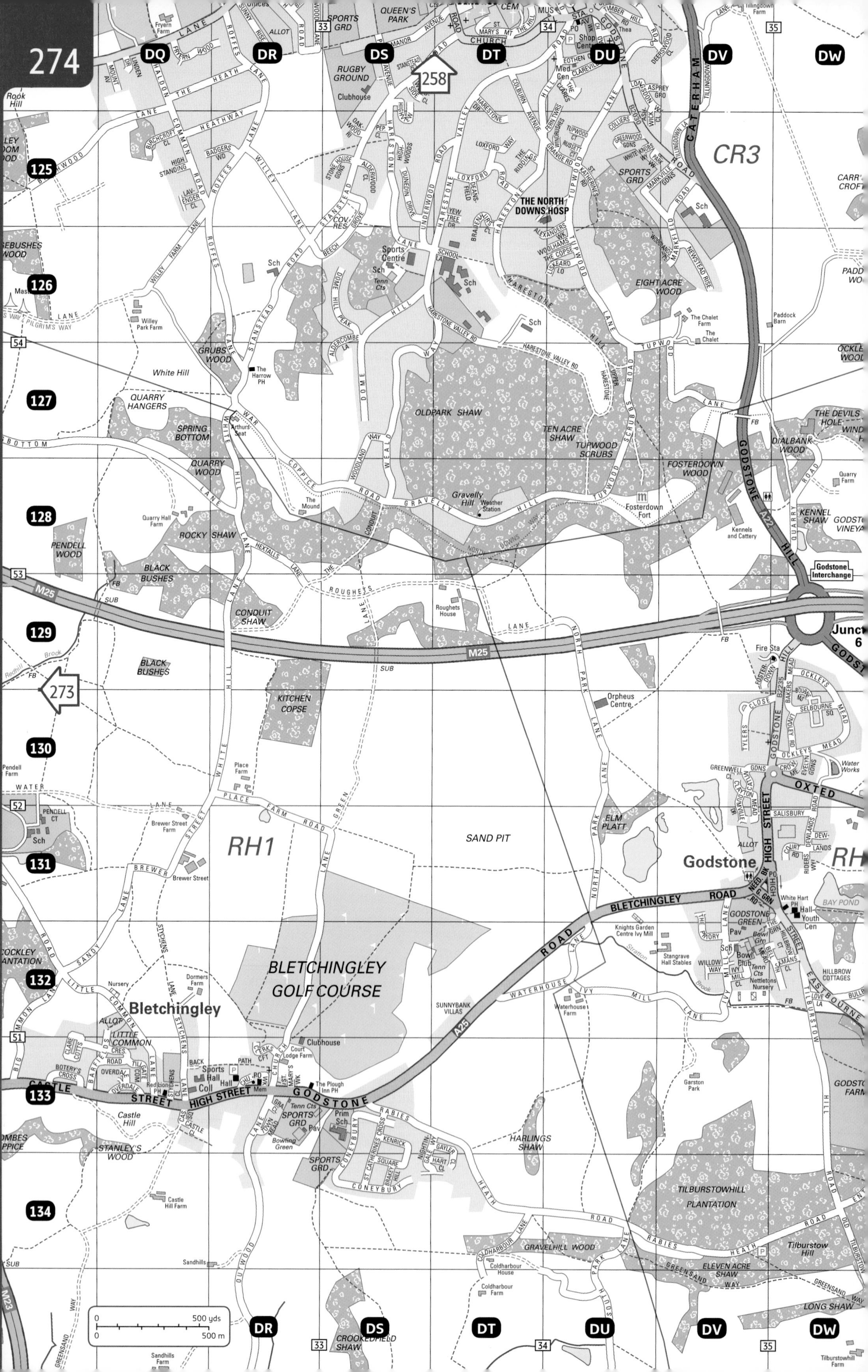
DQ
DR
DS
DT
DU
DV
DW
258
273
125
126
127
128
129
130
131
132
133
134
CR3
RH1
CATERHAM
QUEEN'S PARK
SPORTS GRD
RUGBY GROUND
Clubhouse
THE NORTH DOWNS HOSP
SPORTS GRD
EIGHT ACRE WOOD
Sports Centre
Sch
Tenn Cts
White Hill
GRUBS WOOD
The Harrow PH
QUARRY HANGERS
SPRING BOTTOM
QUARRY WOOD
OLDPARK SHAW
TEN ACRE SHAW
TUPWOOD SCRUBS
FOSTERDOWN WOOD
Gravelly Hill
Weather Station
Fosterdown Fort
The Mound
Arthur's Seat
Quarry Hall Farm
ROCKY SHAW
PENDELL WOOD
BLACK BUSHES
CONDUIT SHAW
Roughets House
M25
Godstone Interchange
Fire Sta
KITCHEN COPSE
Orpheus Centre
Place Farm
Pendell Farm
Brewer Street Farm
Brewer Street
SAND PIT
ELM PLATT
Godstone
BLETCHINGLEY ROAD
Knights Garden Centre Ivy Mill
Stangrave Hall Stables
BLETCHINGLEY GOLF COURSE
Bletchingley
Clubhouse
Court Lodge Farm
The Plough Inn PH
Red Lion PH
Castle Hill
STANLEY'S WOOD
Castle Hill Farm
SUNNYBANK VILLAS
Waterhouse Farm
HARLINGS SHAW
GRAVELHILL WOOD
Coldharbour House
Coldharbour Farm
TILBURSTOWHILL PLANTATION
Tilburstow Hill
ELEVEN ACRE SHAW
LONG SHAW
Garston Park
CROOKEDFIELD SHAW
Sandhills
Sandhills Farm
Nursery
Dormers Farm
Willey Park Farm
Kennels and Cattery
KENNEL SHAW
The Chalet Farm
The Chalet
Paddock Barn
Water Works
White Hart PH
Hall
Youth Cen
HILLBROW COTTAGES
BAY POND
A22
A25
GODSTONE HILL
HIGH STREET
OXTED ROAD
0
500 yds
0
500 m

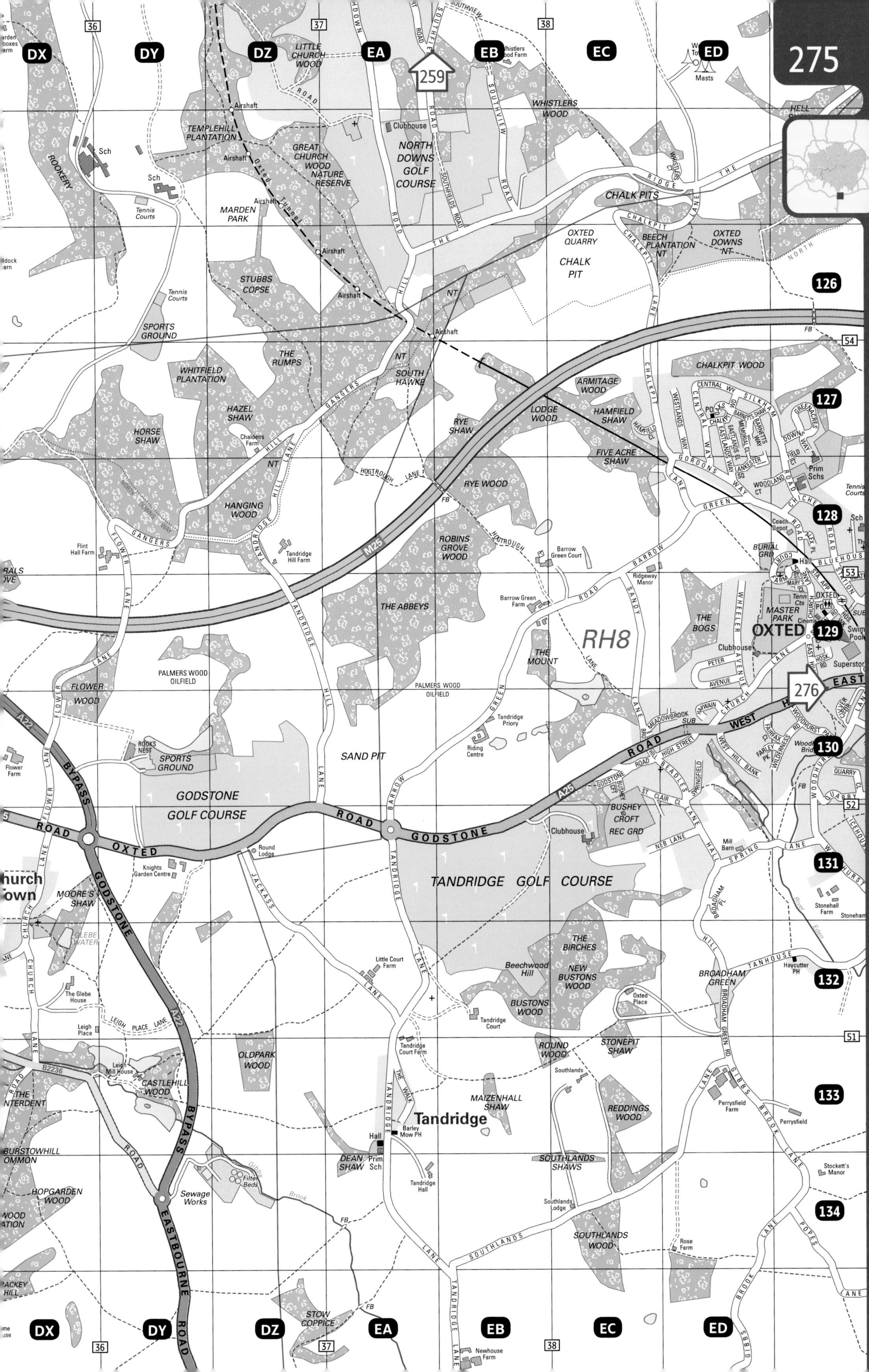
DX
DY
DZ
EA
EB
EC
ED
36
37
38
259
LITTLE CHURCH WOOD
Whistlers Wood Farm
WHISTLERS WOOD
Masts
HELL
TEMPLEHILL PLANTATION
Airshaft
Sch
ROOKERY
GREAT CHURCH WOOD NATURE RESERVE
Clubhouse
NORTH DOWNS GOLF COURSE
SOUTHFIELDS ROAD
SOUTHVIEW ROAD
RIDGE
THE RIDGE
WHISTLERS LANE
CHALK PITS
Oxted Tunnel
MARDEN PARK
Tennis Courts
STUBBS COPSE
OXTED QUARRY
CHALK PIT
CHALKPIT LANE
BEECH PLANTATION NT
OXTED DOWNS NT
NORTH
126
SPORTS GROUND
NT
FB
54
THE RUMPS
SOUTH HAWKE
WHITFIELD PLANTATION
CHALKPIT WOOD
ARMITAGE WOOD
CENTRAL WAY
SILKHAM
GREENACRES
127
HAZEL SHAW
LODGE WOOD
HAMFIELD SHAW
WESTLANDS WAY
HORSE SHAW
Chaldens Farm
GANGERS HILL
RYE SHAW
FIVE ACRE SHAW
GORDONS WAY
LANKESTER SQ
Prim Schs
HOGTROUGH LANE
RYE WOOD
WOODLAND CT
Tennis Courts
HANGING WOOD
TANDRIDGE HILL LANE
GREEN LANE
Coach Depot
128
Sch
Flint Hall Farm
FLOWER LANE
GANGERS
Tandridge Hill Farm
M25
ROBINS GROVE WOOD
HOGTROUGH
Barrow Green Court
BURIAL GRD
Hall
BLUEHOUSE
53
BARROW
Ridgeway Manor
THE ABBEYS
Barrow Green Farm
SANDY
THE BOGS
Tenn Cts
OXTED
MASTER PARK
Cinema
WHEELER AVENUE
129
Swim Pool
RH8
THE MOUNT
Clubhouse
PETER AVENUE
EAST HILL RD
Superstore
PALMERS WOOD OILFIELD
LANE
FLOWER WOOD
276
EAST
MEADOWBROOK
HAYWAIN
CHURCH LANE
WEST
Tandridge Priory
A22
ROOKS NEST
SPORTS GROUND
Riding Centre
FARRAX RD
WOODHURST PARK
130
Flower Farm
SAND PIT
HIGH STREET
WEST HILL BANK
WILDERNESS
FARLEY PK
QUARRY
BYPASS
GODSTONE GOLF COURSE
A25
ROAD
BEADLES
SPRINGFIELD
FB
52
BUSHEY CROFT REC GRD
ST. CLAIR CL
ROAD
OXTED
ROAD
GODSTONE
Round Lodge
Clubhouse
NEB LANE
Mill Barn
SPRING LANE
131
Church Town
Knights Garden Centre
JACKASS
TANDRIDGE
TANDRIDGE GOLF COURSE
MOORE'S SHAW
GODSTONE
BROADHAM PL
River Eden
Stonehall Farm
GLEBE WATER
CHURCH
THE BIRCHES
Little Court Farm
Beechwood Hill
NEW BUSTONS WOOD
TANHOUSE
Haycutter PH
BROADHAM GREEN
132
The Glebe House
BUSTONS WOOD
Oxted Place
Leigh Place
LEIGH PLACE LANE
Tandridge Court
A22
ROUND WOOD
STONEPIT SHAW
51
OLDPARK WOOD
Tandridge Court Farm
Southlands
BROADHAM GREEN RD
B2236
Leigh Mill House
CASTLEHILL WOOD
THE WALK
MAIZENHALL SHAW
REDDINGS WOOD
Perrysfield Farm
Perrysfield
GIBBS BROOK LANE
133
THE INTERDENT
Tandridge
Barley Mow PH
BURSTOWHILL COMMON
Hall
DEAN SHAW
Prim Sch
SOUTHLANDS SHAWS
Stockett's Manor
HOPGARDEN WOOD
Filter Beds
Gibbs Brook
Sewage Works
Tandridge Hall
Southlands Lodge
134
EASTBOURNE ROAD
FB
SOUTHLANDS LANE
SOUTHLANDS WOOD
Rose Farm
POPES LANE
BROOK LANE
HACKEY HILL
STOW COPPICE
FB
TANDRIDGE LANE
Newhouse Farm
B2

EE
EF
EG
EH
EJ
EK
EL
260
275
40
41
42
54
53
52
51
125
126
127
128
129
130
131
132
133
134
CR3
RH8
TITSEY PLACE AND GARDENS
TITSEY PARK
TITSEY PLANTATION
HELL SHAW
Titsey
OXTED DOWNS NT
NORTH DOWNS WAY
PILGRIMS WAY
BROOMLANDS
CHURCH WOOD
ROUGHFIELD SHAW
SQUARE WOOD
BARTON SHAW
Pitchfont Farm
Limpsfield Lodge Farm
Park Farm
PITCHFONT LANE
WATER LANE
TITSEY ROAD
River Eden
Premier Inn
TITSEY WOOD
M25
CHALKPIT WOOD
ASHEN COPPICE
Broomlands Farm
SAND PIT
GRUBSTREET SHAW
GRUBSTREET COPSE
SANDY LANE
B269
OXTED
MASTER PARK
Limpsfield
LIMPSFIELD CHART
WESTERHAM ROAD
A25
EAST HILL
WEST HILL
Superstore
Swim Pool
Gas Holder
Health Cen
COUNCIL OFF
Fire Sta
Clubhouse
GOLF COURSE
LIMPSFIELD COMMON
NT
ANDREWS WOOD
Swallowfield
Wildshaw
WEST HEATH
Limpsfield Tunnel
Woodhurst Bridge
STONESWOOD ROAD
CHAPEL ROAD
LITTLE HEATH NT
Limpsfield Chart
Chartfield House
Tenchley's Park
TENCHLEY'S WOOD
THE ALDERS
Boulthurst Farm
Stonehall Farm
Stonehamme
Mill Barn
Haycutter PH
Health Centre
Hurst Green
SPORTS GROUND
Prim Sch
LOAMPIT WOOD
Whitegates Farm
Crabbett Wood
Crabbett Wood Farm
CRABBETT WOOD
Tenchleys Manor
ITCHINGWOOD COMMON
Doghurst
REC GRD
RUNNING TRACK
Perrysfield Farm
Perrysfield
Coltsford Mill
FAIRVIEW IND EST
Holland
Red Lane Farm
PARISHCROFT WOOD
Parishcroft Wood Farm
Stockett's Manor
Depot
Sewage Works
Filter Beds
POWDERDICK SHAW
The Diamond PH
Connerton Stables
Stockenden Farm
HONESLAND WOOD
Upper Gincox Farm
COLLESTERS WOOD
MOLLSTONES WOOD
Rose Farm
0 500 yds
0 500 m

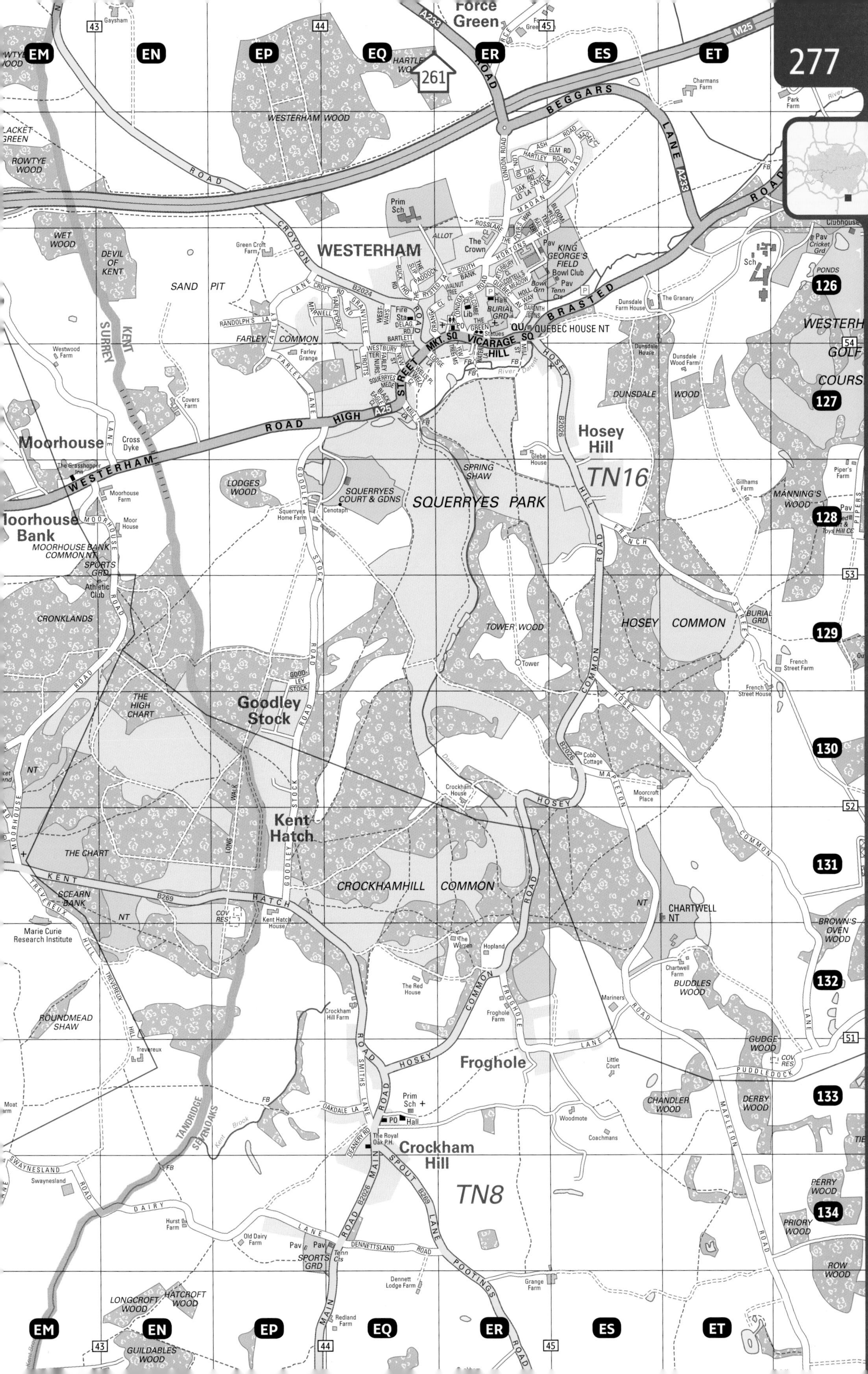
Force Green
Gaysham
EM
EN
EP
EQ
ER
ES
ET
43
44
45
261
M25
A233
BEGGARS LANE
Charmans Farm
Park Farm
WESTERHAM WOOD
ROWTYE WOOD
CROYDON ROAD
WESTERHAM
Prim Sch
The Crown
KING GEORGE'S FIELD
Bowl Club
Clubhouse
Pav
Cricket Grd
Sch
PONDS
126
127
128
129
130
131
132
133
134
WESTERHAM GOLF COURSE
WET WOOD
DEVIL OF KENT
SAND PIT
Green Croft Farm
FARLEY COMMON
Farley Grange
RANDOLPH'S LA
Westwood Farm
SURREY
KENT
B2024
MKT. SQ
VICARAGE SQ
VICARAGE HILL
QUEBEC HOUSE NT
BRASTED ROAD
Dunsdale Farm House
The Granary
Dunsdale House
Dunsdale Wood Farm
DUNSDALE WOOD
HIGH STREET
A25
WESTERHAM ROAD
Covers Farm
Moorhouse
Cross Dyke
The Grasshopper Inn
Moorhouse Farm
Moor House
Moorhouse Bank
MOORHOUSE BANK COMMON NT
SPORTS GRD
Athletic Club
LODGES WOOD
SQUERRYES COURT & GDNS
Squerryes Home Farm
Cenotaph
SQUERRYES PARK
SPRING SHAW
Glebe House
Hosey Hill
TN16
B2026
Piper's Farm
Gillhams Farm
MANNING'S WOOD
FRENCH STREET
CRONKLANDS
TOWER WOOD
Tower
HOSEY COMMON
BURIAL GRD
French Street Farm
French Street House
GOODLEY STOCK ROAD
THE HIGH CHART
Goodley Stock
Kent Hatch
Cobb Cottage
Moorcroft Place
Crockham House
River Darent
THE CHART
CROCKHAMHILL COMMON
CHARTWELL NT
KENT HATCH ROAD
B269
SCEARN BANK
NT
Marie Curie Research Institute
Kent Hatch House
The Warren
Hopland
Chartwell Farm
BUDDLES WOOD
BROWN'S OVEN WOOD
ROUNDMEAD SHAW
The Red House
Crockham Hill Farm
Froghole Farm
Mariners
MAPLETON ROAD
GUDGE WOOD
PUDDLEDOCK
COV RES
TREVEREUX HILL
Trevereux
Froghole
Little Court
CHANDLER WOOD
DERBY WOOD
Moat Farm
TANDRIDGE
SEVENOAKS
Kent Brook
OAKDALE LA
Prim Sch
PO
Hall
Woodmote
Coachmans
The Royal Oak P.H.
Crockham Hill
TN8
SWAYNESLAND ROAD
Swaynesland
DAIRY LANE
Hurst Farm
Old Dairy Farm
DENNETTSLAND ROAD
SPORTS GRD
Tenn Cts
Dennett Lodge Farm
POOTINGS ROAD
Grange Farm
PERRY WOOD
PRIORY WOOD
ROW WOOD
LONGCROFT WOOD
HATCROFT WOOD
GUILDABLES WOOD
Redland Farm
MAIN ROAD

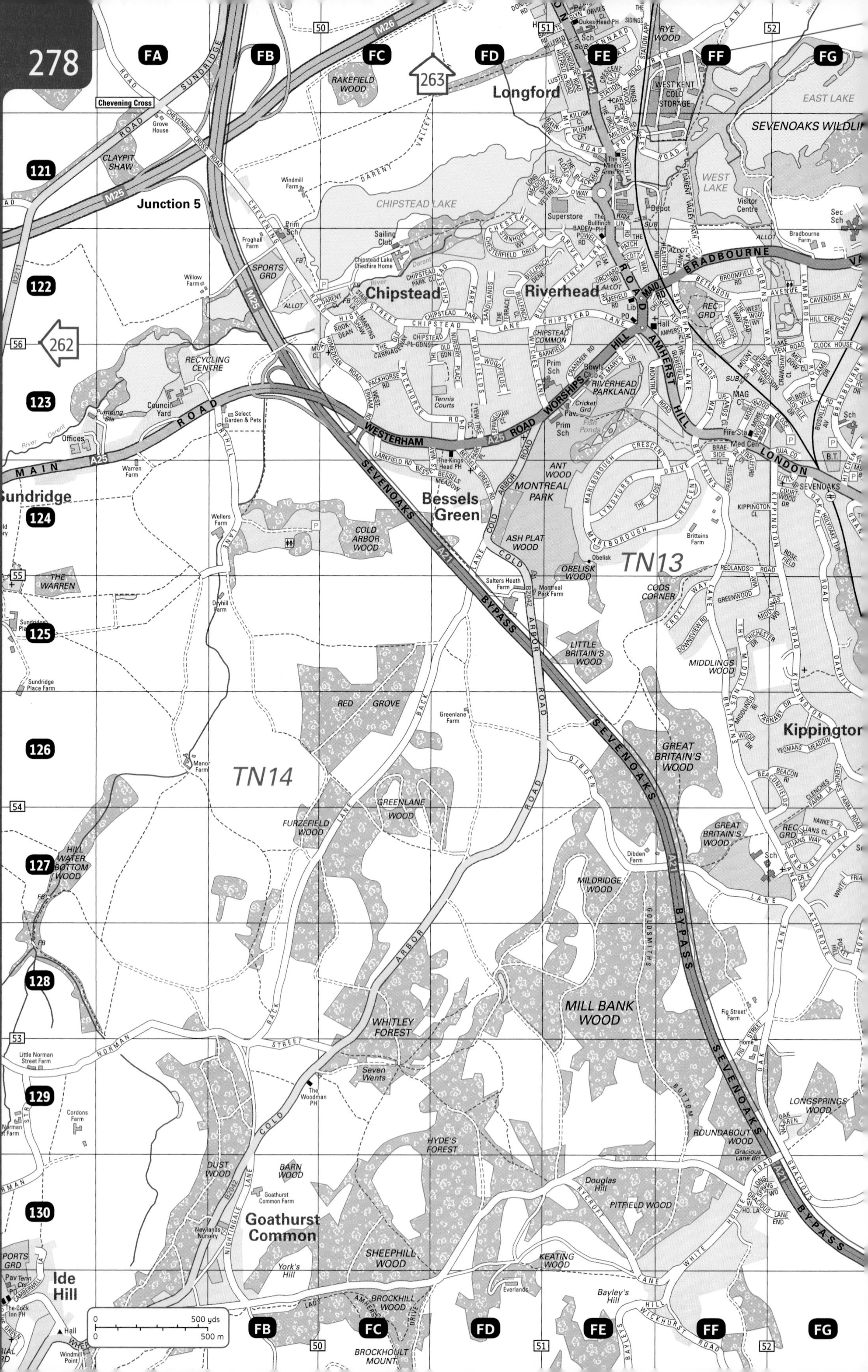
FA
FB
FC
FD
FE
FF
FG
263
262
121
122
123
124
125
126
127
128
129
130
50
51
52
53
54
55
56
Chevening Cross
Grove House
CLAYPIT SHAW
Junction 5
M25
M26
A224
A21
A25
B2042
B2211
RAKEFIELD WOOD
Longford
RYE WOOD
WEST KENT COLD STORAGE
EAST LAKE
SEVENOAKS WILDLI
WEST LAKE
Visitor Centre
Sec Sch
Bradbourne Farm
Windmill Farm
CHIPSTEAD LAKE
DARENT
Superstore
Depot
Sailing Club
Prim Sch
Froghall Farm
SPORTS GRD
Willow Farm
Chipstead Lake Cheshire Home
Chipstead
Riverhead
BRADBOURNE
Hall
Lib
PO
REC GRD
RECYCLING CENTRE
Council Yard
Pumping Sta
River Darent
Offices
Select Garden & Pets
MAIN ROAD
WESTERHAM ROAD
Tennis Courts
Bowls Club
RIVERHEAD PARKLAND
Cricket Grd
Fish Ponds
Prim Sch
The Kings Head PH
Fire Sta
Med Cen
MAG CT
LONDON ROAD
SEVENOAKS
Warren Farm
Sundridge
Bessels Green
ANT WOOD
MONTREAL PARK
ASH PLAT WOOD
COLD ARBOR WOOD
Wellers Farm
Obelisk
OBELISK WOOD
TN13
Brittains Farm
THE WARREN
Salters Heath Farm
Montreal Park Farm
CODS CORNER
Dryhill Farm
Sundridge Place
Sundridge Place Farm
SEVENOAKS BYPASS
LITTLE BRITAIN'S WOOD
MIDDLINGS WOOD
RED GROVE
Greenlane Farm
Kippington
GREAT BRITAIN'S WOOD
Manor Farm
TN14
GREENLANE WOOD
FURZEFIELD WOOD
GREAT BRITAIN'S WOOD
HILL WATER BOTTOM WOOD
REC GRD
Sch
Dibden Farm
MILDRIDGE WOOD
MILL BANK WOOD
Fig Street Farm
Little Norman Street Farm
NORMAN STREET
WHITLEY FOREST
Seven Wents
The Woodman PH
Cordons Farm
LONGSPRINGS WOOD
ROUNDABOUT WOOD
Gracious Lane Bri
HYDE'S FOREST
DUST WOOD
BARN WOOD
Goathurst Common Farm
Douglas Hill
PITFIELD WOOD
Goathurst Common
Newlands Nursery
SHEEPHILL WOOD
KEATING WOOD
York's Hill
Everlands
Bayley's Hill
SPORTS GRD
Ide Hill
The Cock Inn PH
Hall
Windmill Point
BROCKHILL WOOD
BROCKHOULT MOUNT
0 500 yds
0 500 m

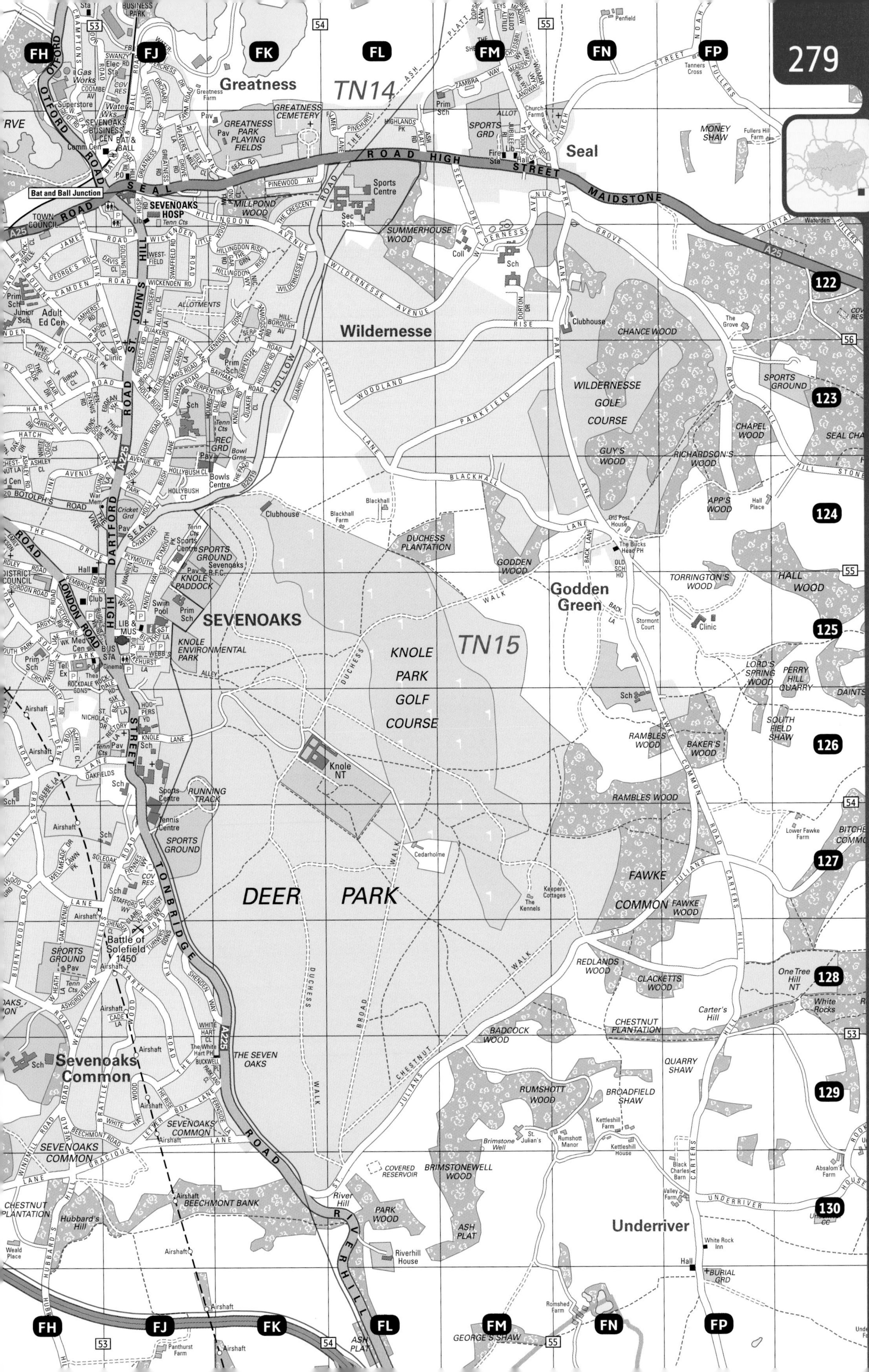
FH
FJ
FK
FL
FM
FN
FP
Greatness
TN14
Seal
Penfield
Tanners Cross
MONEY SHAW
Fullers Hill Farm
GREATNESS CEMETERY
GREATNESS PARK PLAYING FIELDS
SPORTS GRD
Bat and Ball Junction
SEAL ROAD
HIGH STREET
MAIDSTONE ROAD
A25
SEVENOAKS HOSP
MILLPOND WOOD
Sports Centre
SUMMERHOUSE WOOD
Coll
Sch
WILDERNESSE AVENUE
Wildernesse
CHANCE WOOD
WILDERNESSE GOLF COURSE
GUY'S WOOD
RICHARDSON'S WOOD
CHAPEL WOOD
SPORTS GROUND
Clubhouse
Waterden
The Grove
SEAL CHART
ALLOTMENTS
ST. JOHN'S HILL
Adult Ed Cen
Prim Sch
Clinic
BLACKHALL
Blackhall Farm
DUCHESS PLANTATION
GODDEN WOOD
Godden Green
Old Post House
The Bucks Head PH
TORRINGTON'S WOOD
HALL WOOD
Stormont Court
Clinic
APP'S WOOD
Hall Place
SEVENOAKS
SPORTS GROUND
Sevenoaks R.F.C.
KNOLE PADDOCK
KNOLE ENVIRONMENTAL PARK
DARTFORD ROAD
LONDON ROAD
DISTRICT COUNCIL
LIB & MUS
BUS STA
Cinema
KNOLE PARK GOLF COURSE
TN15
LORD'S SPRING WOOD
PERRY HILL QUARRY
SOUTH FIELD SHAW
RAMBLES WOOD
BAKER'S WOOD
Knole NT
Cedarholme
Keepers Cottages
The Kennels
DEER PARK
FAWKE COMMON
FAWKE WOOD
Lower Fawke Farm
BITCHET COMMON
HIGH STREET
Airshaft
Sports Centre
RUNNING TRACK
Tennis Centre
SPORTS GROUND
TONBRIDGE ROAD
Battle of Solefield 1450
SPORTS GROUND
REDLANDS WOOD
CLACKETTS WOOD
One Tree Hill NT
White Rocks
Carter's Hill
CHESTNUT PLANTATION
BADCOCK WOOD
QUARRY SHAW
THE SEVEN OAKS
The White Hart PH
Sevenoaks Common
SEVENOAKS COMMON
RUMSHOTT WOOD
BROADFIELD SHAW
Kettleshill Farm
Rumshott Manor
St. Julian's
Brimstone Well
Kettleshill House
COVERED RESERVOIR
BRIMSTONEWELL WOOD
Black Charles Barn
Valley Farm
Absalom's Farm
UNDERRIVER
CHESTNUT PLANTATION
Hubbard's Hill
BEECHMONT BANK
River Hill
PARK WOOD
ASH PLAT
Riverhill House
Underriver
White Rock Inn
Hall
BURIAL GRD
Weald Place
RIVERHILL
Romshed Farm
GEORGE'S SHAW
Panthurst Farm
ASH PLAT
A225
122
123
124
125
126
127
128
129
130
53
54
55
56

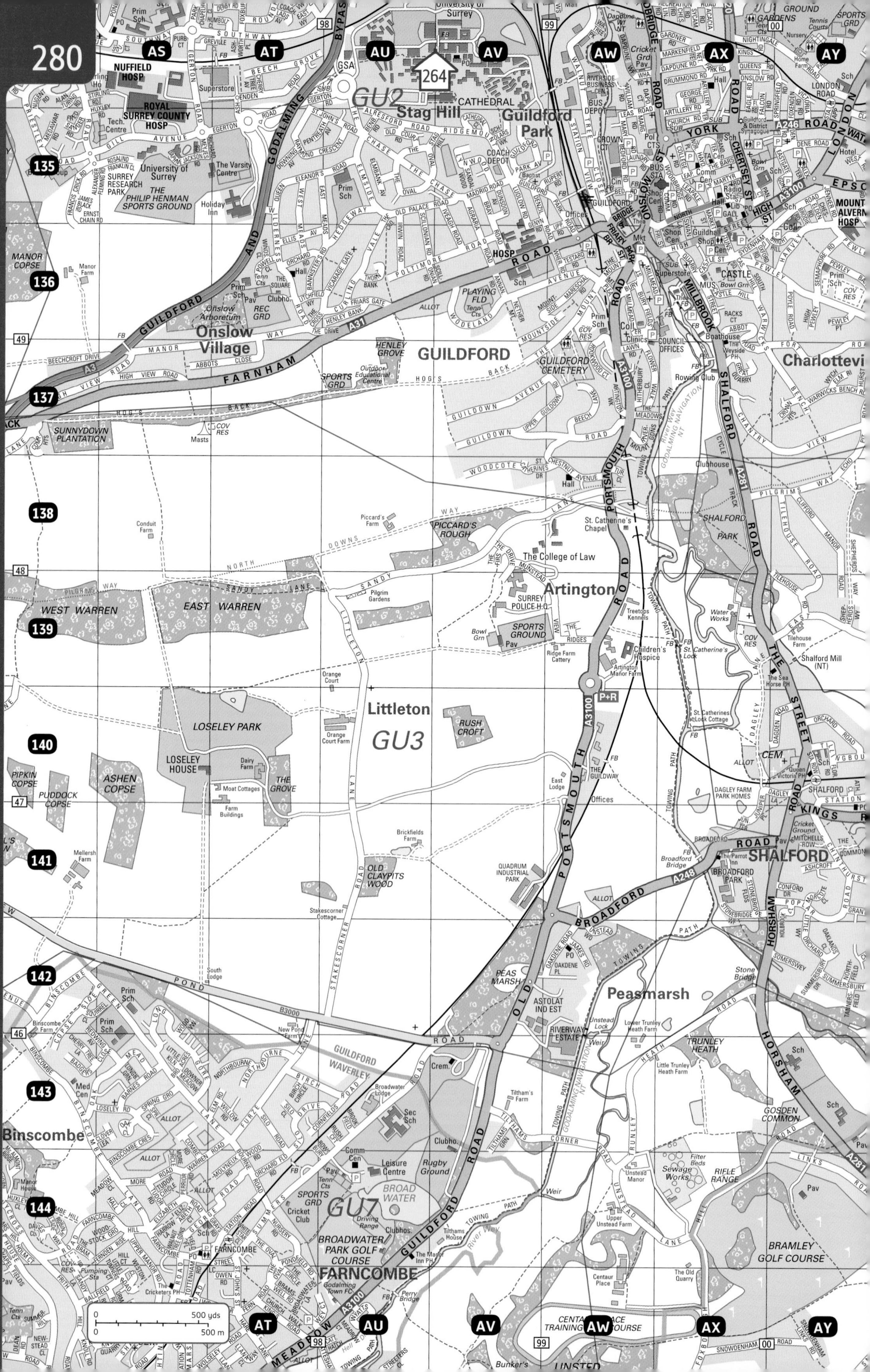

264
GU2
Stag Hill
Guildford Park
University of Surrey
NUFFIELD HOSP
ROYAL SURREY COUNTY HOSP
SURREY RESEARCH PARK
THE PHILIP HENMAN SPORTS GROUND
CATHEDRAL
Onslow Village
Onslow Arboretum
GUILDFORD
GUILDFORD CEMETERY
Charlottevi
MANOR COPSE
SUNNYDOWN PLANTATION
PICCARD'S ROUGH
The College of Law
Artington
SURREY POLICE H.Q.
WEST WARREN
EAST WARREN
SHALFORD PARK
St. Catherine's Chapel
Children's Hospice
St. Catherine's Lock
Shalford Mill (NT)
Littleton
GU3
LOSELEY PARK
LOSELEY HOUSE
RUSH CROFT
ASHEN COPSE
PIPKIN COPSE
PUDDOCK COPSE
THE GROVE
OLD CLAYPITS WOOD
QUADRUM INDUSTRIAL PARK
SHALFORD
Peasmarsh
PEAS MARSH
ASTOLAT IND EST
RIVERWAY ESTATE
TRUNLEY HEATH
GOSDEN COMMON
Binscombe
GU7
BROAD WATER
BROADWATER PARK GOLF COURSE
FARNCOMBE
BRAMLEY GOLF COURSE
PORTSMOUTH ROAD
FARNHAM ROAD
GUILDFORD AND GODALMING BYPASS
HORSHAM ROAD
SHALFORD ROAD
BROADFORD ROAD
OLD PORTSMOUTH ROAD
0 500 yds
0 500 m

AZ
BA
BB
BC
BD
BE
BF
01
02
03
265
EPSOM ROAD
A246
GUILDFORD GOLF COURSE
Clubhouse
MERROW DOWNS
WALNUT TREE BOTTOM
HAREWARREN
THE ROUGHS
SPORTS GROUND
Pav
DOWNSIDE ROAD
WARREN ROAD
ONE TREE HILL
LITTLE WARREN CL
Warren Farm
Burwood Farm
Prim Sch
GU1
ALLOT
PEWLEY DOWN
WHITE LANE
LONGDOWN
HALFPENNY LANE
COV RES
Newlands Corner
Visitor Centre
136
ALBURY DOWNS
49
137
White Lane Farm
GU5
Newbarn
Tyting Farm
Whinney Hill
South Warren Farm
PILGRIMS WAY
FARTHING COPSE
St. Martha's Hill
NORTH DOWNS WAY
St. Martha's Priory Lodge
CHANTRIES
HALFPENNY COPSE
GUILDFORD LANE
138
Great Halfpenny Farm
GU4
Old Great Halfpenny
Tilling Bourne
LIDWELL COPSE
48
MILL LA
POSTFORD POND
Chilworth Manor
Little Halfpenny Farm
DORKING ROAD
139
SHALFORD ROAD
Manor Farm
MUD WOOD
BLACKSMITH LANE
Lockner Farm
282
CUCKOO COPSE
War Memorial
Prim Sch
Chilworth
A248
CHILWORTH
140
LC
FISH POND
Tangley Mere
ALLOT
Pav
Hall
PO
BRADSTONE BROOK SPORTS GROUND
SPORTS GROUND
47
SHALFORD COMMON
CHRISTMAS HILL
NEW ROAD
Prim Sch
Chilworth Hill
Glasshouse
LOCKNER HOLT
141
Hornhatch Farm
RICES CORNER
Great Tangley Manor House
Great Tangley Manor Farm
Tangley Hill
FRANCISCAN FRIARY
NATIONAL TRUST
ROSEMARY HILL
WONERSH COMMON
War Memorial
Lower Chinthurst Farm
Tangley Way
Blackheath
The Villagers PH
142
GUILDFORD WAVERLEY
B2128
Hall
Blackheath C.C.
BLACKHEATH
46
Chinthurst Farm
Southlands Equestrian Centre
Tower
Chinthurst Hill
BLACKHEATH LANE
LITTLEFORD LANE
Derry's Hill
143
HEATHFIELDS
DERRY'S WOOD
CEM
ALLOT
GU5
BARNETT HILL CONFERENCE CENTRE
ST. MARY'S DERRYWOOD
NORTHBROOK HILL
Hallam's Farm
144
St. Catherine's Schs
The Grantley Arms PH
Wonersh
St. John's Seminary
Wonersh Court
Wonersh House
Bramley
HIGH STREET
A281
Northcote Farm
Holmcroft Nursery
GREEN LANE

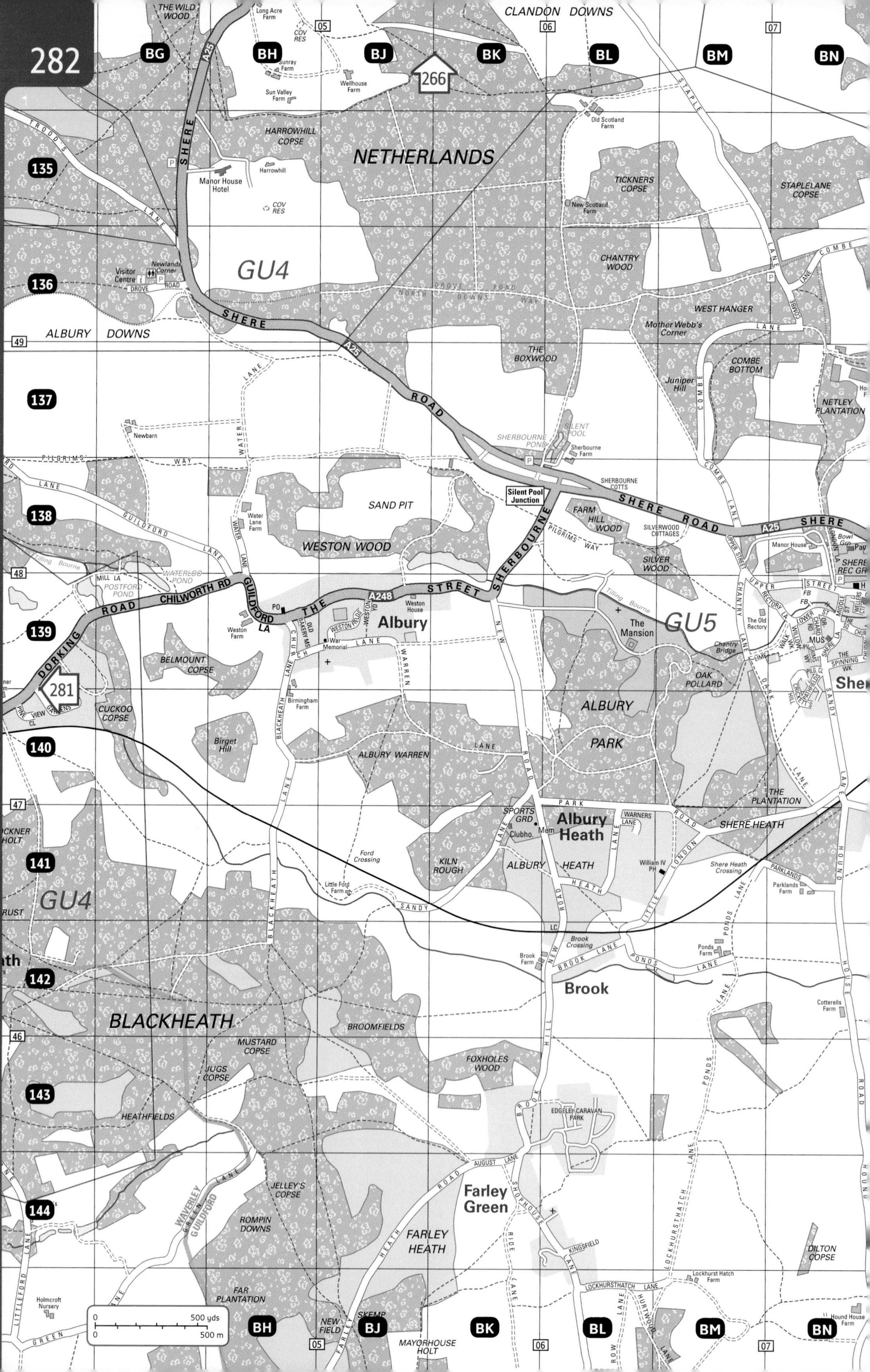

THE WILD WOOD
Long Acre Farm
COV RES
CLANDON DOWNS
BG
BH
BJ
BK
BL
BM
BN
05
06
07
266
Sunray Farm
Wellhouse Farm
Sun Valley Farm
Old Scotland Farm
STAPLE LANE
HARROWHILL COPSE
NETHERLANDS
A25
SHERE ROAD
Harrowhill
Manor House Hotel
TROOD'S LANE
TICKNERS COPSE
STAPLELANE COPSE
New Scotland Farm
CHANTRY WOOD
135
136
137
138
139
140
141
142
143
144
49
48
47
46
GU4
GU5
Visitor Centre
Newlands Corner
DROVE ROAD
NORTH DOWNS WAY
WEST HANGER
COMBE LANE
Mother Webb's Corner
ALBURY DOWNS
THE BOXWOOD
COMBE BOTTOM
Juniper Hill
NETLEY PLANTATION
WATER LANE
Newbarn
SHERBOURNE POND
SILENT POOL
Sherbourne Farm
PILGRIMS' WAY
SHERBOURNE COTTS
SAND PIT
Silent Pool Junction
FARM HILL WOOD
SILVERWOOD COTTAGES
Water Lane Farm
GUILDFORD LANE
WESTON WOOD
SHERBOURNE
Manor House
SILVER WOOD
SHERE REC GR
Tilling Bourne
WATERLOO POND
MILL LA
POSTFORD POND
CHILWORTH RD
THE STREET
A248
Weston House
UPPER STREET
Albury
The Mansion
DORKING ROAD
PO
Weston Farm
OLD BAKERY MS
WESTON YD
WESTON FIELDS
War Memorial
CHURCH LANE
WARREN LANE
NEW ROAD
The Old Rectory
Chantry Bridge
CHANTRY LANE
BELMOUNT COPSE
OAK POLLARD
281
CUCKOO COPSE
PINE VIEW CL
Birmingham Farm
ALBURY PARK
Birget Hill
BLACKHEATH LANE
ALBURY WARREN
THE PLANTATION
PARK ROAD
SPORTS GRD
Clubho.
Mem
Albury Heath
WARNERS LANE
SHERE HEATH
Ford Crossing
KILN ROUGH
ALBURY HEATH
William IV PH
LITTLE LONDON
Shere Heath Crossing
PARKLANDS
Parklands Farm
Little Ford Farm
SANDY LANE
LC
Brook Crossing
Brook Farm
BROOK LANE
PONDS LANE
Ponds Farm
Brook
HOUND HOUSE ROAD
Cotterells Farm
BLACKHEATH
BROOMFIELDS
MUSTARD COPSE
JUGS COPSE
FOXHOLES WOOD
BROOK HILL
HEATHFIELDS
EDGELEY CARAVAN PARK
AUGUST LANE
JELLEY'S COPSE
Farley Green
SHOPHOUSE LANE
LOCKHURSTHATCH LANE
ROMPIN DOWNS
FARLEY HEATH
WAVERLEY GREEN
GUILDFORD LANE
RIDE LANE
KINGSFIELD
DILTON COPSE
Lockhurst Hatch Farm
FAR PLANTATION
Holmcroft Nursery
LITTLEFORD LANE
GREEN
500 yds
500 m
NEW FIELD
SKEMP
FARLEY
MAYORHOUSE HOLT
HURTWOOD
ROW LANE
Hound House Farm

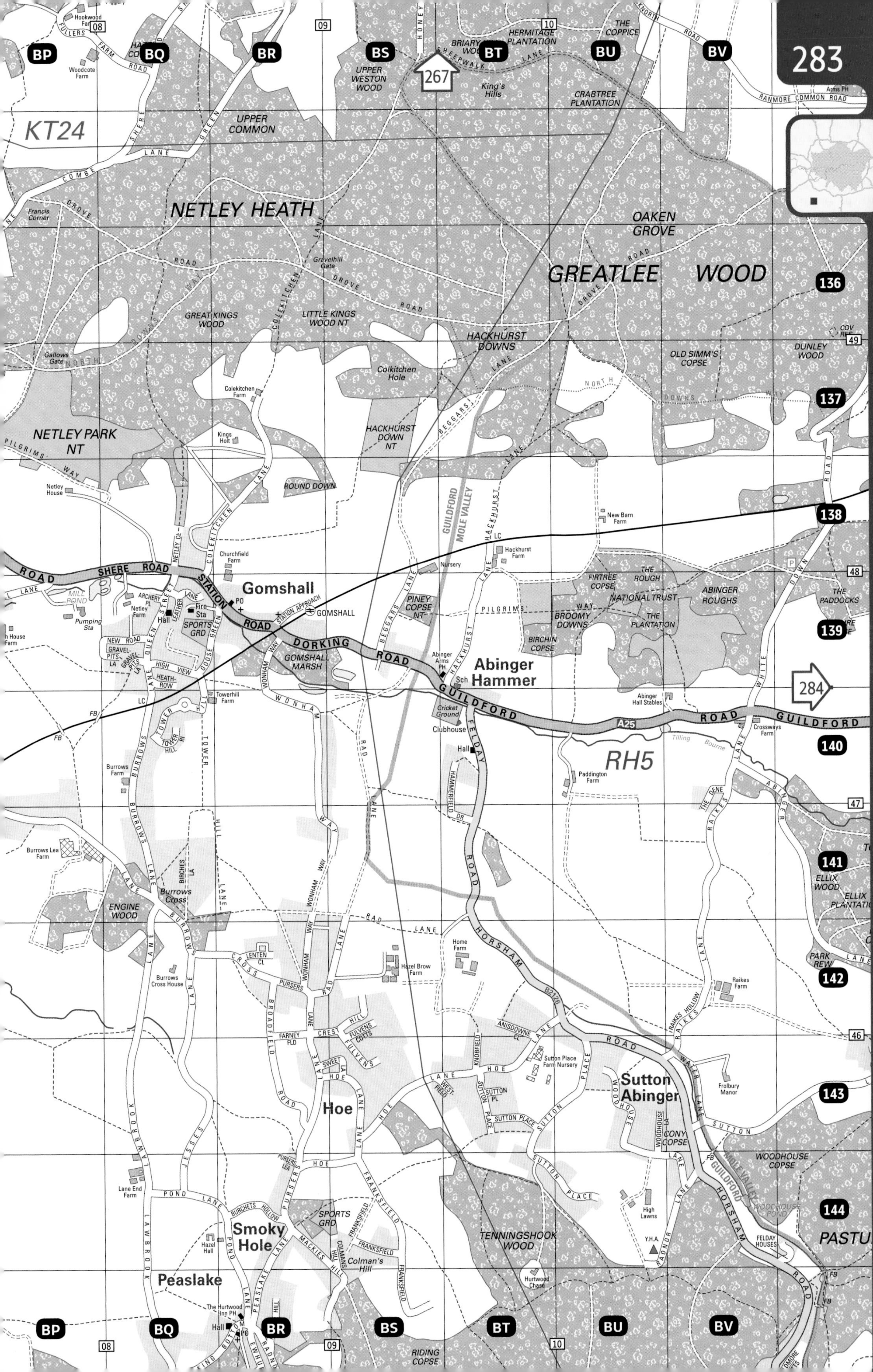

KT24
RH5
NETLEY HEATH
UPPER COMMON
UPPER WESTON WOOD
King's Hills
HERMITAGE PLANTATION
THE COPPICE
CRABTREE PLANTATION
OAKEN GROVE
GREATLEE WOOD
GREAT KINGS WOOD
LITTLE KINGS WOOD NT
Gravelhill Gate
HACKHURST DOWNS
OLD SIMM'S COPSE
DUNLEY WOOD
Gallows Gate
Colkitchen Hole
Colekitchen Farm
Kings Holt
HACKHURST DOWN NT
NETLEY PARK NT
Netley House
ROUND DOWN
Francis Corner
Hookwood Farm
Woodcote Farm
New Barn Farm
Hackhurst Farm
Churchfield Farm
Gomshall
GOMSHALL
Nursery
PINEY COPSE NT
FIRTREE COPSE
THE ROUGH
NATIONAL TRUST
ABINGER ROUGHS
THE PADDOCKS
BROOMY DOWNS
THE PLANTATION
BIRCHIN COPSE
MILL POND
Netley Farm
Pumping Sta
Fire Sta
SPORTS GRD
GOMSHALL MARSH
Abinger Arms PH
Abinger Hammer
Sch
Abinger Hall Stables
Crossways Farm
Cricket Ground
Clubhouse
Hall
Towerhill Farm
Paddington Farm
Burrows Farm
Burrows Lea Farm
Burrows Cross
ENGINE WOOD
Burrows Cross House
Home Farm
Hazel Brow Farm
Raikes Farm
ELLIX WOOD
ELLIX PLANTATION
PARK REW
Sutton Place Farm Nursery
Sutton Abinger
Frolbury Manor
CONY COPSE
WOODHOUSE COPSE
WOODHOUSE POND
Hoe
Lane End Farm
Smoky Hole
Hazel Hall
SPORTS GRD
Colman's Hill
TENNINGSHOOK WOOD
High Lawns
Y.H.A.
FELDAY HOUSES
Hurtwood Chase
Peaslake
The Hurtwood Inn PH
RIDING COPSE
PASTU
SHERE ROAD
STATION ROAD
DORKING ROAD
GUILDFORD ROAD
A25
HORSHAM ROAD
B2126
RANMORE COMMON ROAD
COMBE LANE
SHERE LANE
COLEKITCHEN LANE
BEGGARS LANE
HACKHURST LANE
WONHAM WAY
WOTTON ROAD
FELDAY ROAD
HAMMERFIELD DR
POND LANE
LAWBROOK LANE
BURROWS LANE
JESSES LANE
HOE LANE
SUTTON PLACE
WOTTON LANE
RAIKES LANE
ABINGER LANE
WHITE DOWN LANE
PILGRIMS' WAY
NORTH DOWNS WAY
GUILDFORD MOLE VALLEY
Tilling Bourne
BP BQ BR BS BT BU BV
08 09 10
136 137 138 139 140 141 142 143 144
46 47 48 49
267
284

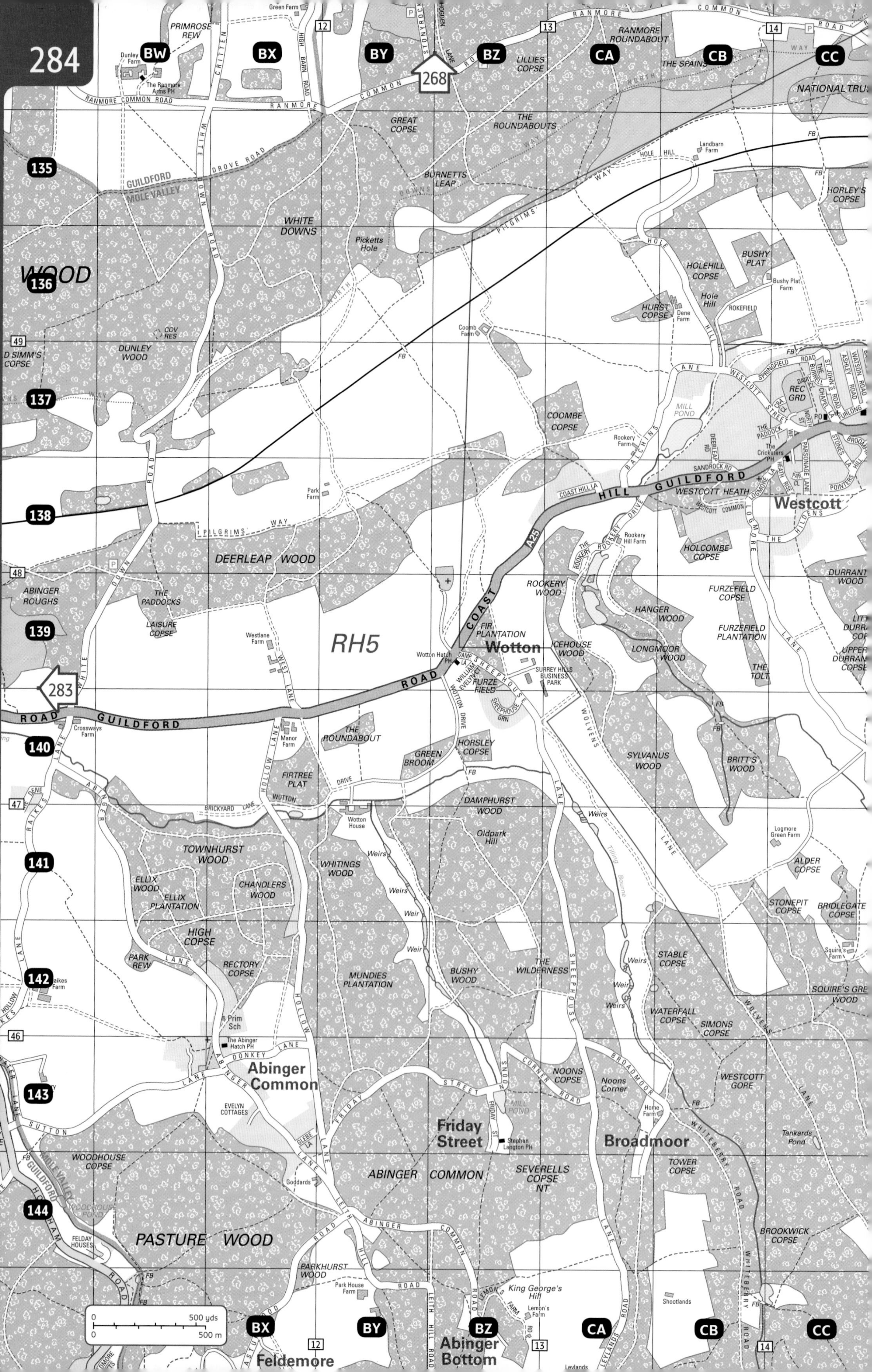
BW
BX
BY
BZ
CA
CB
CC
268
283
Green Farm
PRIMROSE REW
Dunley Farm
The Ranmore Arms PH
RANMORE COMMON ROAD
RANMORE COMMON
CRITTEN
HIGH BARN ROAD
STONYROCK
HOGDEN LANE
RANMORE ROUNDABOUT
LILLIES COPSE
THE SPAINS
NATIONAL TRUS
ROAD
GREAT COPSE
THE ROUNDABOUTS
WHITE DOWN ROAD
GUILDFORD
MOLE VALLEY
DROVE ROAD
BURNETTS LEAP
DOWNS
Landbarn Farm
HOLE HILL
HORLEY'S COPSE
WHITE DOWNS
Picketts Hole
PILGRIMS' WAY
WOOD
NORTH
BUSHY PLAT
HOLEHILL COPSE
Bushy Plat Farm
Hole Hill
ROKEFIELD
HURST COPSE
Dene Farm
COV RES
Coomb Farm
FB
D SIMM'S COPSE
DUNLEY WOOD
LANE
WESTCOTT
SPRINGFIELD ROAD
ST JOHN'S ROAD
ASHLEY
WATSON ROAD
REC GRD
MILL POND
COOMBE COPSE
BALCHINS
Rookery Farm
DEERLEAP RD
SANDROCK RD
THE PADDOCK
The Cricketers PH
PARSONAGE LANE
STONES LA
BROADMEAD
POINTERS
Park Farm
COAST HILL LA
HILL
GUILDFORD
WESTCOTT HEATH
WESTCOTT COMMON
LOGMORE LA
HEATH RISE
Westcott
ROOKERY DRIVE
Rookery Hill Farm
THE ROOKERY
HOLCOMBE COPSE
THE HILDENS
PILGRIMS' WAY
DEERLEAP WOOD
A25
COAST
ROOKERY WOOD
FURZEFIELD COPSE
DURRANT WOOD
ABINGER ROUGHS
THE PADDOCKS
HANGER WOOD
LAISURE COPSE
FIR PLANTATION
FURZEFIELD PLANTATION
Westlane Farm
RH5
Wotton
ICEHOUSE WOOD
LONGMOOR WOOD
Pipp Brook
UPPER DURRANT COPSE
Wotton Hatch PH
DAMPHURST LA
WILLIAM EVELYN CT
SHEEPHOUSE LANE
SURREY HILLS BUSINESS PARK
THE TOLT
WEST LANE
ROAD
FURZE FIELD
SHEEPHOUSE GRN
GUILDFORD
ROAD
Crossways Farm
THE ROUNDABOUT
Manor Farm
WOTTON DRIVE
HORSLEY COPSE
WOLVENS
GREEN BROOM
SYLVANUS WOOD
BRITT'S WOOD
FIRTREE PLAT
DRIVE
DENE
BRICKYARD LANE
WOTTON
RAIKES
ABINGER
DAMPHURST WOOD
Weirs
Wotton House
Oldpark Hill
Logmore Green Farm
TOWNHURST WOOD
WHITINGS WOOD
Tilling Bourne
ALDER COPSE
ELLIX WOOD
ELLIX PLANTATION
CHANDLERS WOOD
Weir
STONEPIT COPSE
BRIDLEGATE COPSE
HIGH COPSE
PARK REW
LANE
RECTORY COPSE
MUNDIES PLANTATION
BUSHY WOOD
THE WILDERNESS
STABLE COPSE
Squire's Farm
Raikes Farm
HOLLOW
SQUIRE'S GRE WOOD
Prim Sch
WATERFALL COPSE
SIMONS COPSE
The Abinger Hatch PH
DONKEY LANE
Abinger Common
NOONS CORNER ROAD
NOONS COPSE
Noons Corner
BROADMOOR
WESTCOTT GORE
STREET
Home Farm
EVELYN COTTAGES
SUTTON
FRIDAY
FRIDAY ST
MILL POND
Friday Street
Stephan Langton PH
Broadmoor
WHITEBERRY ROAD
Tankards Pond
WOODHOUSE COPSE
GLEBE LA
ABINGER COMMON
SEVERELLS COPSE NT
TOWER COPSE
HORSHAM
WOODHOUSE POND
Goddards
LEITH HILL
ABINGER COMMON
BROOKWICK COPSE
FELDAY HOUSES
PASTURE WOOD
PARKHURST WOOD
Park House Farm
ROAD
King George's Hill
LEMON'S FARM RD
Lemon's Farm
Shootlands
LEYLANDS LANE
0
500 yds
500 m
Feldemore
Abinger Bottom
Leylands
12
13
14
47
46
48
49
135
136
137
138
139
140
141
142
143
144

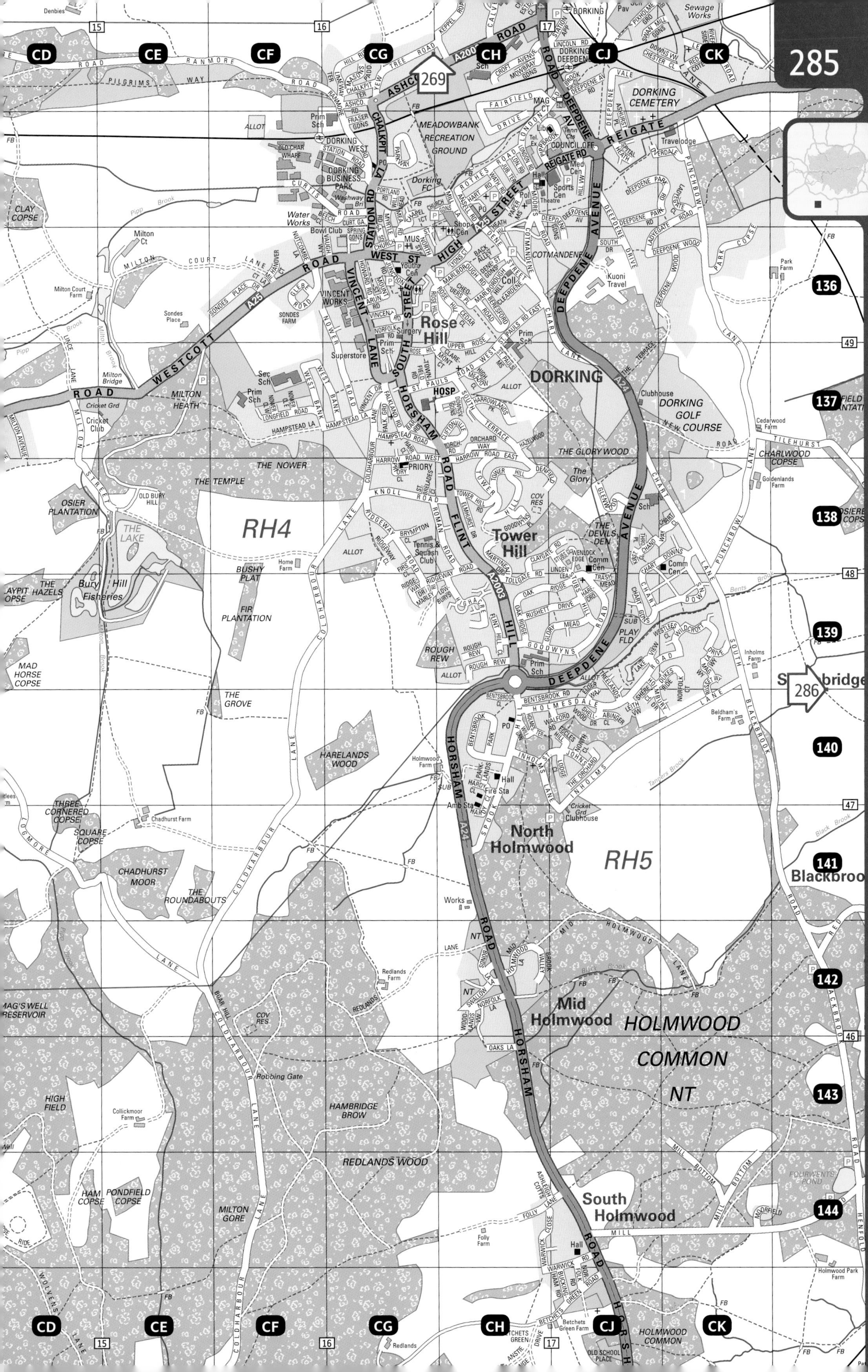
CD
CE
CF
CG
CH
CJ
CK
15
16
17
269
286
136
137
138
139
140
141
142
143
144
49
48
47
46
Denbies
RANMORE ROAD
PILGRIMS WAY
ASHCOMBE ROAD
DORKING
DORKING DEEPDENE
DORKING WEST
DORKING CEMETERY
Sewage Works
Travelodge
REIGATE ROAD
MEADOWBANK RECREATION GROUND
DORKING BUSINESS PARK
Dorking FC
Water Works
CLAY COPSE
Milton Ct
MILTON COURT LANE
Milton Court Farm
WEST ST
HIGH STREET
A25
Sports Cen
COTMANDENE
DEEPDENE AVENUE
Kuoni Travel
VINCENT WORKS
VINCENT LANE
SOUTH STREET
Rose Hill
Sondes Place
SONDES FARM
Superstore
WESTCOTT ROAD
Milton Bridge
MILTON HEATH
Cricket Club
HAMPSTEAD LA
HOSP
DORKING
A24
DORKING GOLF COURSE
Clubhouse
THE GLORY WOOD
The Glory
CHARLWOOD COPSE
Goldenlands Farm
TILEHURST
THE NOWER
THE TEMPLE
PRIORY
OSIER PLANTATION
OLD BURY HILL
THE LAKE
RH4
Home Farm
BUSHY PLAT
FIR PLANTATION
Bury Hill Fisheries
THE HAZELS
Tennis & Squash Club
FLINT HILL
A2003
Tower Hill
THE DEVILS DEN
Comm Cen
PUNCHBOWL LANE
MAD HORSE COPSE
ROUGH REW
THE GROVE
DEEPDENE
Inholms Farm
Beldham's Farm
HARELANDS WOOD
Holmwood Farm
HORSHAM ROAD
North Holmwood
RH5
Blackbrook
THREE CORNERED COPSE
SQUARE COPSE
Chadhurst Farm
CHADHURST MOOR
THE ROUNDABOUTS
COLDHARBOUR LANE
Works
Redlands Farm
MAG'S WELL RESERVOIR
Mid Holmwood
HOLMWOOD COMMON NT
Robbing Gate
HIGH FIELD
Collickmoor Farm
HAMBRIDGE BROW
REDLANDS WOOD
HAM COPSE
PONDFIELD COPSE
MILTON GORE
South Holmwood
Folly Farm
Holmwood Park Farm
Betchets Green Farm
HOLMWOOD COMMON
Redlands

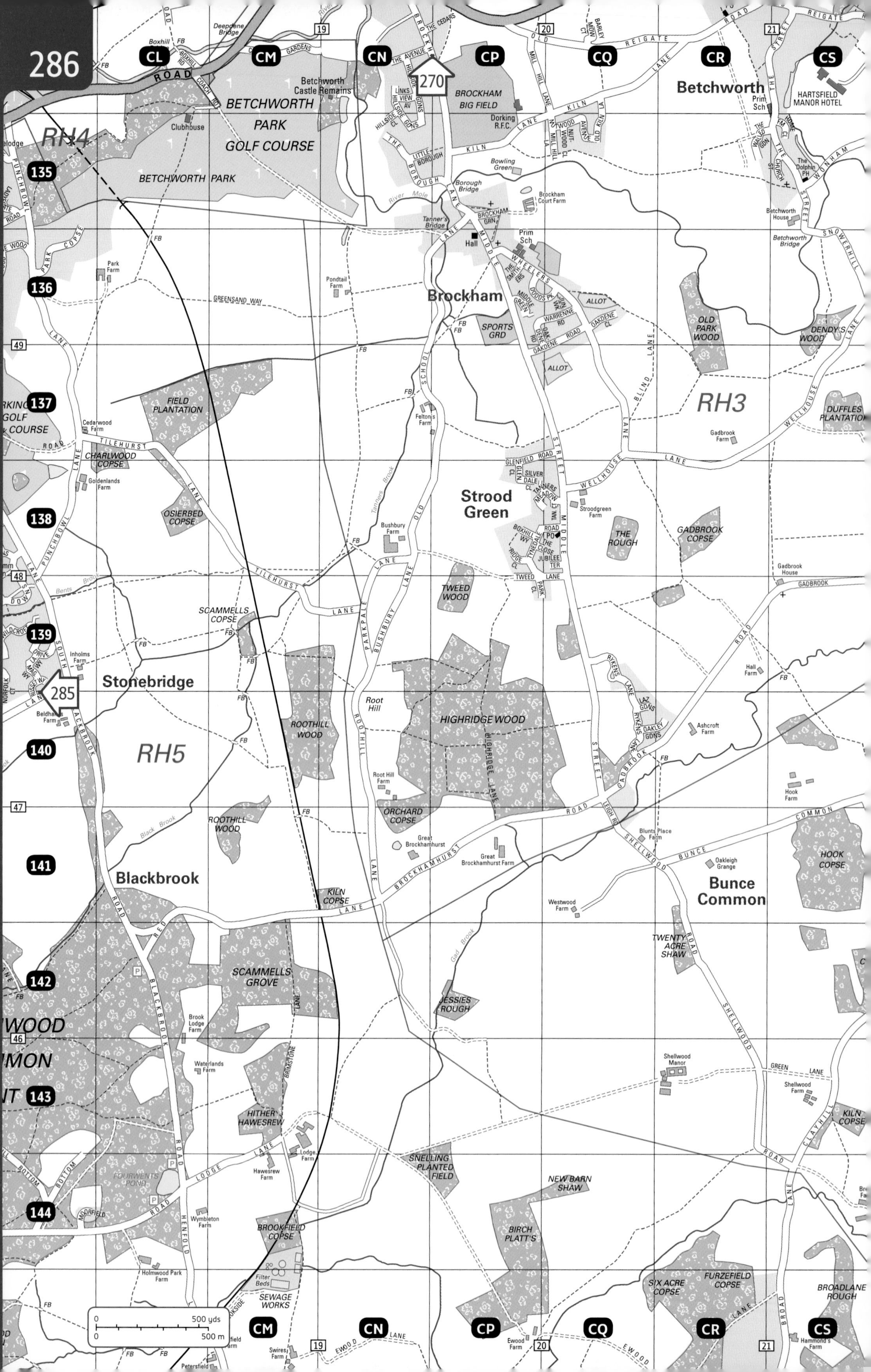
CL
CM
CN
CP
CQ
CR
CS
270
285
Betchworth
BETCHWORTH PARK GOLF COURSE
BETCHWORTH PARK
Betchworth Castle Remains
Clubhouse
RH4
RH3
RH5
BROCKHAM BIG FIELD
Dorking R.F.C.
HARTSFIELD MANOR HOTEL
Brockham
Strood Green
Stonebridge
Blackbrook
Bunce Common
Root Hill
River Mole
Borough Bridge
Tanner's Bridge
Betchworth Bridge
Brockham Court Farm
Park Farm
Pondtail Farm
GREENSAND WAY
SPORTS GRD
ALLOT
OLD PARK WOOD
DENDY'S WOOD
FIELD PLANTATION
DUFFLES PLANTATION
Cedarwood Farm
CHARLWOOD COPSE
Goldenlands Farm
OSIERBED COPSE
Feltons Farm
Gadbrook Farm
Strood Green Farm
THE ROUGH
GADBROOK COPSE
Gadbrook House
Bushbury Farm
TWEED WOOD
SCAMMELLS COPSE
Inholms Farm
Beldhams Farm
ROOTHILL WOOD
HIGHRIDGE WOOD
Root Hill Farm
ORCHARD COPSE
Great Brockhamhurst
Great Brockhamhurst Farm
Hall Farm
Ashcroft Farm
Hook Farm
Blunts Place Farm
Oakleigh Grange
HOOK COPSE
Westwood Farm
KILN COPSE
TWENTY ACRE SHAW
SCAMMELLS GROVE
JESSIES ROUGH
Brook Lodge Farm
Waterlands Farm
Shellwood Manor
Shellwood Farm
HITHER HAWESREW
Lodge Farm
Hawesrew Farm
SNELLING PLANTED FIELD
NEW BARN SHAW
FOURWENTS POND
Wymbleton Farm
BROOKFIELD COPSE
BIRCH PLATT'S
Holmwood Park Farm
Filter Beds
SEWAGE WORKS
SIX ACRE COPSE
FURZEFIELD COPSE
BROADLANE ROUGH
Ewood Farm
Swires Farm
Hammond's Farm
Petersfield
500 yds
500 m

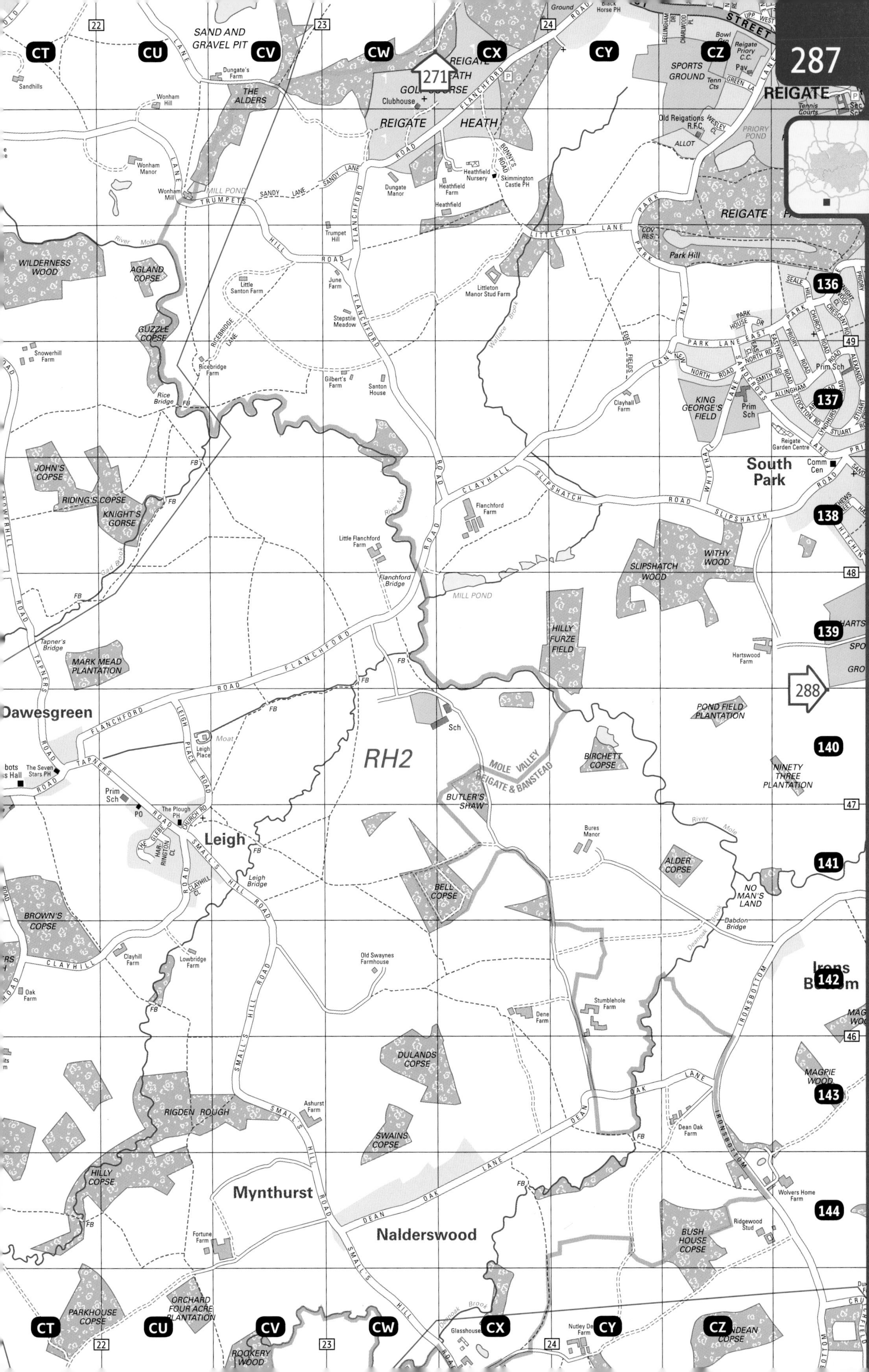

CT
CU
CV
CW
CX
CY
CZ
22
23
24
271
288
SAND AND GRAVEL PIT
Dungate's Farm
Sandhills
Wonham Hill
THE ALDERS
REIGATE HEATH GOLF COURSE
Clubhouse
REIGATE HEATH
FLANCHFORD ROAD
Black Horse PH
SPORTS GROUND
Reigate Priory C.C.
Pav
Tennis Courts
REIGATE
Old Reigatians R.F.C.
ALLOT
PRIORY POND
REIGATE
Wonham Manor
Wonham Mill
MILL POND
TRUMPETS HILL ROAD
SANDY LANE
Dungate Manor
Heathfield Farm
Heathfield Nursery
Skimmington Castle PH
Heathfield
BONNY'S ROAD
Trumpet Hill
LITTLETON LANE
COV RES
Park Hill
PARK LANE
River Mole
WILDERNESS WOOD
AGLAND COPSE
Little Santon Farm
June Farm
Littleton Manor Stud Farm
Wallace Brook
Stepstile Meadow
GUZZLE COPSE
RICEBRIDGE LANE
Snowerhill Farm
Ricebridge Farm
Gilbert's Farm
Santon House
EDES FIELDS
PARK LANE EAST
NORTH ROAD
KING GEORGE'S FIELD
Prim Sch
Clayhall Farm
Rice Bridge
FB
JOHN'S COPSE
RIDING'S COPSE
KNIGHT'S GORSE
CLAYHALL ROAD
SLIPSHATCH ROAD
WHITEHALL LANE
South Park
Comm Cen
Reigate Garden Centre
Flanchford Farm
Little Flanchford Farm
Flanchford Bridge
MILL POND
SLIPSHATCH WOOD
WITHY WOOD
Gad Brook
SNOWERHILL
Tapner's Bridge
MARK MEAD PLANTATION
HILLY FURZE FIELD
Hartswood Farm
Dawesgreen
TAPNERS ROAD
LEIGH PLACE ROAD
Moat
Leigh Place
Sch
RH2
MOLE VALLEY
REIGATE & BANSTEAD
BIRCHETT COPSE
POND FIELD PLANTATION
NINETY THREE PLANTATION
The Seven Stars PH
Prim Sch
PO
The Plough PH
CHURCH RD
Leigh
BUTLER'S SHAW
Bures Manor
ALDER COPSE
Leigh Bridge
SMALL'S HILL ROAD
BELL COPSE
NO MAN'S LAND
Dabdon Bridge
Deanoak Brook
BROWN'S COPSE
Clayhill Farm
Lowbridge Farm
CLAYHILL
Old Swaynes Farmhouse
IRONSBOTTOM
Irons Bottom
Oak Farm
Stumblehole Farm
Dene Farm
DULANDS COPSE
MAGPIE WOOD
RIGDEN ROUGH
Ashurst Farm
DEAN OAK LANE
Dean Oak Farm
SWAINS COPSE
HILLY COPSE
Mynthurst
Nalderswood
Wolvers Home Farm
Ridgewood Stud
BUSH HOUSE COPSE
Fortune Farm
ORCHARD FOUR ACRE PLANTATION
PARKHOUSE COPSE
Deanoak Brook
Glasshouse
Nutley Dean Farm
ROOKERY WOOD
136
137
138
139
140
141
142
143
144
46
47
48
49

DA
DB
DC
DD
DE
DF
DG
272
REIGATE
REDHILL
Site of Reigate Castle
TOWN HALL
Superstore
Tennis Courts
Sec Sch
Site of Priory
PRIORY PARK
PRIORY POND
Reigations R.F.C.
Bowl Grn
SPORTS GROUND
REIGATE CEMETERY
REIGATE ROAD
HIGH ST
CHURCH ST
BELL ST
LESBOURNE RD
BLACKBOROUGH
BLANFORD ROAD
WATERLOW ROAD
HIGH TREES ROAD
HATCHLANDS
WHITEPOST
RINGLEY PARK
THE CHASE
OAK WAY
REDHILL COMMON
The Garibaldi PH
Gas Works
KINGSFIELD BUSINESS CEN
Airshaft
REDSTONE MANOR
REDSTONE HILL
BRIGHTON ROAD
THE CUTTING
HOOLEY LANE
Earlswood
135
REIGATE PARK
COCKSHOT HILL
SMOKE LANE
FURZEFIELD ROAD
CRONKS HILL
CRONKS
Canon UK
Mead Vale
Clinic
Sch
Hall
WARENNE HEIGHTS
MOUNTVIEW
CARTERS COTTS
Prim Sch
ST. JOHN'S
EARLSWOOD
136
BLACKTHORN CL
COPSE ROAD
HARDWICK RD
BOX TREE WK
ARBUTUS RD
PRIORY DR
CHURCH ROAD
CRESCENT ROAD
PARK LANE EAST
NORTH ROAD
SANDCROSS LANE
49
Woodhatch
Sec Sch
Clubhouse
PENDLETON ROAD
Amb Sta
Redhill & Old Coulsdon CC
SPORTS GROUND
EARLSWOOD COMMON
HORLEY ROAD
Y.M.C.A. Comm & Sports Centre
137
K GEORGE'S FIELD
Prim Sch
ALLINGHAM
STUART ROAD
Clinic
GROSVENOR RD
Reigate Garden Centre
WOODHATCH ROAD
REDHILL AND REIGATE GOLF COURSE
EARLSWOOD LAKES
A23
ASYLUM ARCH ROAD
VICTORIA CT
South Park
Comm Cen
PRICES LANE
SANDCROSS LANE
ORCHARD WAY
KINGSLEY GROVE
MEADOW WAY
CAUSEWAY
A2044
ALLOT
Redhill FC
Clubhouse
EAST SURREY HOSPITAL
138
MATTHEWS ST
HARTSWOOD AV
The Beehive PH
BRUSHETTS
Prim Sch
New Pond Farm
Glasshouse
Filter Beds
EARLSWOOD SEWAGE WORKS
ROYAL EARLSWOOD PARK
CANADA DR
WITHY WOOD
CASTLE DR
ASHDOWN RD
ALLOT
Cricket Grd
MAPLE ROAD
THREE ARCH ROAD
48
Doversgreen
Earlswood Brook
FELLAND COPSE
HESTON RD
PETRIDGE RD
WIMBORNE AVENUE
139
HARTSWOOD SPORTS GROUND
Nursery
Pav
Dovers Farm
TURNER'S SHAW
Weir
RH2
Burnt Oak Farm
HEATHFIELD DR
HANWORTH ROAD
TOLLGATE AVENUE
PRINCE ALBERT SQUARE
Hartswood Farm
287
POND FARM PLANTATION
KILN FIELD PLANTATION
DOVERS GREEN ROAD
PETRIDGEWOOD COMMON
Maple Manor
Cricket Club
Cricket Grd
HOME GROVE
HILLFORD PL
WOODSIDE WY
Prim Sch
140
NINETY THREE PLANTATION
TWELVE ACRE PLANTATION
Sidlow Bridge
FB
LONESOME LANE
BENTING WOOD
Brookside Farm
COPSLEIGH AVENUE
47
River Mole
Riverside Meadow Farm
White Owl Farm
A217
HOLLOW SHAW
Premier Inn
141
NO MAN'S LAND
IRONSBOTTOM
Sidlow Farm
Sidlow
Lonesome Farm
Salfords Bridge
Weir
Hall
HONEYCROCK
Dabdon Bridge
Deanoak Brook
Salfords
Salfords Stream
WESTMEAD DR
SALFORDS
142
Irons Bottom
REIGATE ROAD
Kinnersley Manor
Kinnersley Manor Farm
KINNERSLEY MANOR
LODGE LANE
BONEHURST ROAD
MAGPIE WOOD
New Rivernook Farm
46
BEAUMONTS
HORLEY LODGE LA
143
MAGPIE WOOD
FONTIGARRY FARM BUSINESS PARK
MEATH GREEN LANE
SAXLEY HILL
PEAR TREE HILL
Dean Oak Farm
Ladyland Farm
Wolvers Home Farm
Lower Duxhurst Farm
144
Ridgewood Stud
DUXHURST LANE
RH6
BUSH HOUSE COPSE
Horseshoe Farm Stables
Wick Farm
Burstow Stream
Duxhurst Farm
290
COLLENDEAN COPSE
500 yds
500 m
FB
Meath Green Farm
Cheswick Farm
Moat Farm
Cambridge Hotel
Bonehurst Bridge
26
27
28

DH
DJ
DK
DL
DM
DN
DP
29
30
31
A25
NORTH PARK
FOX HOLE
HOLMESDALE PARK
Nutfield Lodge
Priory Hotel
SPORTS GRD
273
Priory Farm Plant Centre
Stockers Hill
FULLERS WOOD LANE
Priory Farm
NUTFIELD PRIORY LAKE
STENERS HILL
SUB
M23
Kentwyns
Lyttel Hall
GREENSAND WAY
REDSTONE CEMETERY
PHILANTHROPIC ROAD
HOGTROUGH LANE
SANDY
Bower Hill
Bower Hill Farm
CLAY
EASTFIELD ROAD
HAWTHORN WY
KENTWYNS RISE
Prim Sch
Hall
Bray's Farm
REC GROUND
ALLOT
South Nutfield
TRINDLES ROAD
HOLMESDALE RD
NUTFIELD
PO
FB
136
HAIGH CRES
OAKLANDS DR
CROFTERS CL
Nutfield Brook
Maple Farm
KINGS MEAD
THE COPSE
BOWER HILL
MORRIS
NETHERLEIGH PK
THE AVENUE
CRICKET HILL
Pav
South Nutfield CC
49
THEPPS SHAW
137
BOWER HILL LANE
MILL LANE
CROSS LANE
RIDGE GREEN
RIDGE GRN CL
MID STREET
THEPPS CL
KINGS CROSS
KENTWIN'S WOOD
NUTFIELD PARK
Henshaw Farm
REIGATE & BANSTEAD
TANDRIDGE
Ridge Green
Tenn Cts
THEPPSWOOD
Crab Hill House
COOPERS HILL ROAD
Hangars
Crab Hill Farm
Hale Farm
CRAB HILL
138
Hangar
THE ROOKERY
TEMPLE WOOD
RH1
KINGS LANE
White Bushes
48
Terminal
Tenn Cts
Tennis Sch
MASONS
Hazelhurst Farm
REDHILL AERODROME AND HELIPORT
139
Hangar
BRIDGE
KINGS ROAD
Salfords Stream
Sewage Works
Lawn Hill
MOATS LANE
THE PLANTATION
Burstow Park Farm
140
MASONS BRIDGE ROAD
South Hale Farm
FB
47
SPRINGFIELD WOOD
Dean Farm
RUFFET
HATCH LANE
Mason's Bridge
MOATS LANE
THE ROOKERY
141
WALES ROAD
Dairy House Farm
AXES LANE
GREEN
FURZEFIELD WOOD
JUNE LA
DUNRAVEN AV
PERRYWOOD BUSINESS PARK
Cyprus Farm
Axes Farm
NEW HOUSE LANE
FAIRACRES
Tenn Cts
SPORTS GROUND
Meesons Farm
COCKS COPSE
Shepheard's Hurst
Stone House Farm
142
NT
Christmas Farm
West View Farm
ST. GEORGES ROAD
BRICKFIELD
COBBLER'S CORNER
PERRY WOOD
Picketts
Woolborough Hatch Farm
Dog & Duck PH
CHURCH WK
War Memorial
OUTWOOD COMMON
46
TORVCROSS SHAW
ORCHARD FARM PARK
Woolborough House Farm
PRINCE OF WALES
ROAD
143
Outwood
Orchard Farm Kennels
WOOLBOROUGH
DAYSEYS HILL
BELLWETHER LA
WASP GREEN LANE
MILLERS
Hall
PICKETTS
Hunters Moon Farm
The Castle PH
MILLERS COPSE
Brightleigh Farm
CROSSOAK LANE
Rookswood Farm
LITTLE COLLINS
144
ROOKERY HILL
COLDLAND WOOD
LAKE
HATHERSHAM LANE
FB
291
ROOKERY HILL
Burstow

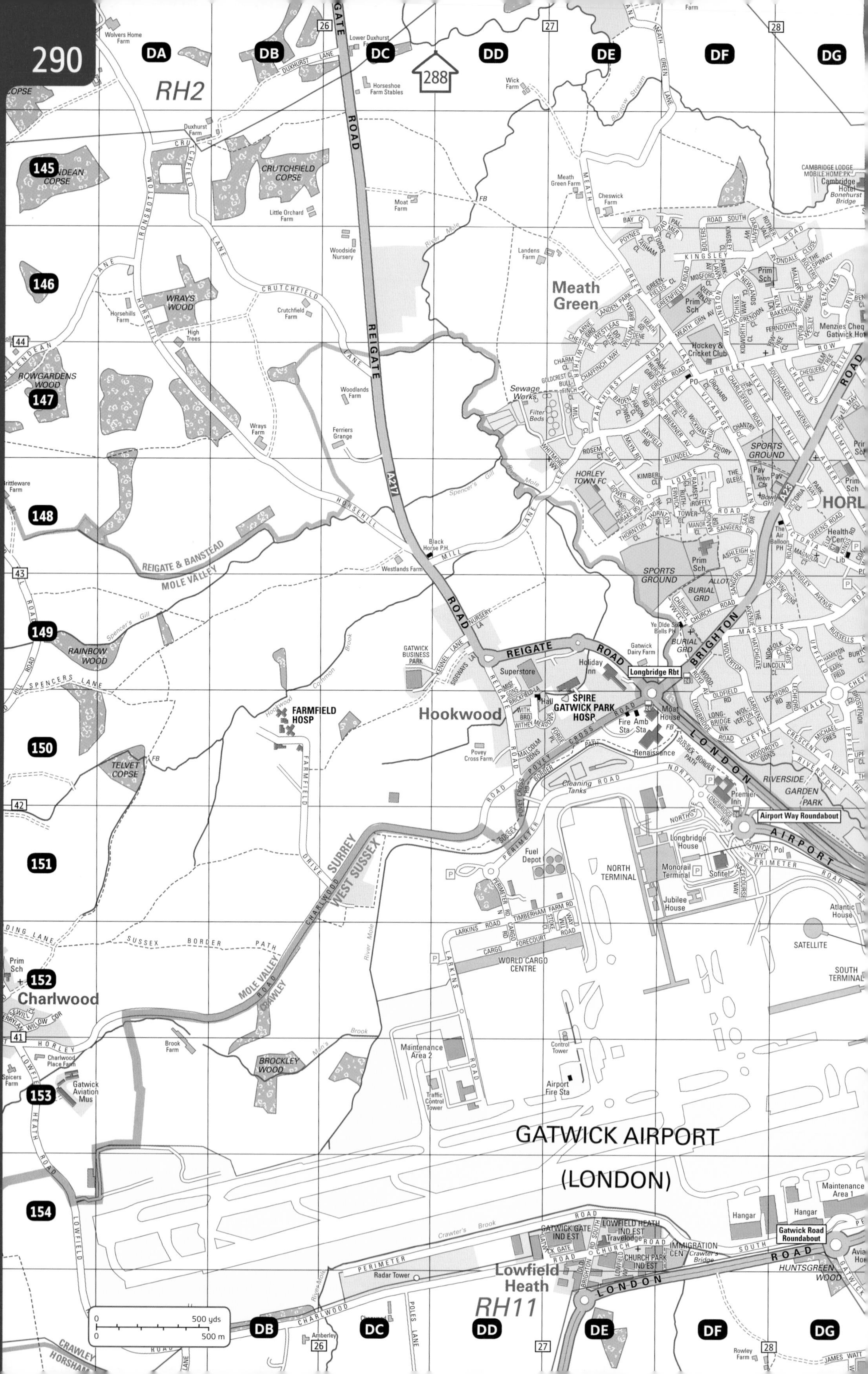
288
DA
DB
DC
DD
DE
DF
DG
26
27
28
RH2
RH11
145
146
147
148
149
150
151
152
153
154
44
43
42
41
Wolvers Home Farm
Lower Duxhurst Farm
DUXHURST LANE
Horseshoe Farm Stables
Wick Farm
Burstow Stream
MEATH GREEN LANE
CAMBRIDGE LODGE MOBILE HOME PK
Cambridge Hotel
Bonehurst Bridge
Duxhurst Farm
CRUTCHFIELD LANE
CRUTCHFIELD COPSE
DEAN COPSE
IRONSBOTTOM
Little Orchard Farm
Moat Farm
FB
Meath Green Farm
Cheswick Farm
River Mole
Woodside Nursery
Landens Farm
Meath Green
WRAYS WOOD
Horsehills Farm
HORSEHILL
High Trees
Crutchfield Farm
REIGATE ROAD
ROWGARDENS WOOD
Woodlands Farm
Ferriers Grange
Wrays Farm
Sewage Works
Filter Beds
Sports Ground
Prim Sch
Hockey & Cricket Club
HORLEY TOWN FC
Spencer's Gill
A217
Black Horse P.H.
MILL LANE
Westlands Farm
REIGATE & BANSTEAD
MOLE VALLEY
RAINBOW WOOD
SPENCERS LANE
HILL ROAD
Common Brook
GATWICK BUSINESS PARK
KENNEL LANE
NURSERY LA
Superstore
Holiday Inn
Gatwick Dairy Farm
Longbridge Rbt
SPIRE GATWICK PARK HOSP
Hookwood
FARMFIELD HOSP
Moat House
Fire Sta
Amb Sta
Renaissance
Povey Cross Farm
POVEY CROSS ROAD
TELVET COPSE
FARMFIELD DRIVE
SURREY
WEST SUSSEX
SUSSEX BORDER PATH
NORTH TERMINAL ROAD
Cleaning Tanks
Premier Inn
Airport Way Roundabout
Longbridge House
Monorail Terminal
Sofitel
Jubilee House
Fuel Depot
PERIMETER ROAD
AIRPORT WAY
Atlantic House
SATELLITE
SOUTH TERMINAL
NORTH TERMINAL
LARKINS ROAD
CARGO FORECOURT ROAD
WORLD CARGO CENTRE
TIMBERHAM FARM RD
BRIGHTON ROAD
LONDON ROAD
SPORTS GROUND
BURIAL GRD
Riverside Garden Park
Prim Sch
Charlwood
CHARLWOOD ROAD
MOLE VALLEY
CRAWLEY
HORLEY ROAD
Charlwood Place Farm
Spicers Farm
Gatwick Aviation Mus
Brook Farm
Man's Brook
BROCKLEY WOOD
Maintenance Area 2
Traffic Control Tower
Control Tower
Airport Fire Sta
GATWICK AIRPORT (LONDON)
Maintenance Area 1
Hangar
Gatwick Road Roundabout
LOWFIELD HEATH ROAD
Crawter's Brook
GATWICK GATE IND EST
LOWFIELD HEATH IND EST
Travelodge
CHURCH ROAD
CHURCH PARK IND EST
IMMIGRATION CEN
Crawter's Bridge
HUNTSGREEN WOOD
Radar Tower
PERIMETER ROAD
Lowfield Heath
POLES LANE
Amberley
Rowley Farm
JAMES WATT
CRAWLEY
HORSHAM
0 500 yds
0 500 m

DH
DJ
DK
DL
DM
DN
DP
29
30
31
289
RH1
RH6
RH10
Hunters Moon Farm
The Castle PH
MILLERS COPSE
MILLERS
Rookswood Farm
ROOKERY HILL
COLDLAND WOOD
CROSSOAK LANE
HATHERSHAM LANE
PICKETTS LAKE LANE
Hathersham Farm
Burstow Stream
Greatlake Farm
LONGYARDS SHAW
THE ROOKERY
COURTOAK GREEN
COURTOAK LANE
ROOKERY HILL
146
Burstow Manor
BURSTOW BUSINESS CENTRE
NORMANS ROAD
Hollesley Farm
44
Elec Sta
The Farmhouse PH
Tanyard Farm
LANGSHOTT
BROOK WOOD
ALDER BED
LOST SEVENS
Sewage Works
Smallfield Grid Sub Station
147
LANGSHOTT WOOD
OAK BED
WEATHERHILL COMMON
WEATHERHILL ROAD
GATWICK METRO CENTRE
Gas Holder Sta
BRIDGE IND EST
SMALLFIELD ROAD
Prim Sch
Swim Pool
Sec Sch
CAREYS WOOD
THE CRAVENS
GRANGEWAY
CRESCENT
CHAPEL ROAD
NEW ROAD
148
The Plough PH
PLOUGH LANE
Hall
Sch
PO
THE ACORNS
SPORTS GRD
PLAYING FIELD
43
WHEELERS LANE
TORONTO DR
ONTARIO CL
BRIDGEHAM WOOD
Smallfield
Green Farm
Harrowslea Green Farm
HARROWSLEY GREEN LANE
Wilgers Farm
SILVERLEA GARDENS
AVENUE GARDENS
BALCOMBE GARDENS
Haroldslea Poultry Farm
Farney Glen Farm
GREEN LANE
PERRYLANDS LANE
149
Site of Thunderfield Castle
Lower Broadbridge Farm
Broadmead Farm
CASTLE DRIVE
LIMES AVENUE
HAROLDSLEA DRIVE
B2036 BALCOMBE ROAD
Hall
LABURNUM CT
GEARY CL
150
THE ROUGHS
BROOK LANE
M23
REIGATE & BANSTEAD
TANDRIDGE
THE PLANTATION
LONE OAK
PARK ROAD
CROSS LANE
42
BAYHORNE LA
WALTERSVILLE WY
THE CLOSE
MEADOW
Flightpath Farm
Broadbridge Stables
BROADBRIDGE LANE
BELLHATCH WOOD
COLLINS WOOD
151
Junction 9a
SUSSEX BORDER PATH
Airport Way Roundabout East
AIRPORT WAY
A23
Junction 9
BRIDGES WOOD
WEST SUSSEX
SURREY
CHURCH ROAD
CHURCH LANE
Burstow
Redeham Hall
REDEHAM ROAD
152
Monorail Terminal
RING ROAD NORTH
First Point
Schlumberger House
Hilton
BUS/COACH STA
GATWICK AIRPORT
Fern Court Farm
FERNHILL ROAD
Broadfield Farm
Gatwick House
Mushroom Farm
EASTLANDS SHAW
Keepers Corner
41
EFFINGHAM LANE
CRAWLEY
TANDRIDGE
Rivington Farm
Teizers Farm
Burstow Hall
Burstow Nurseries
PEEKS BROOK LANE
CHURCH ROAD
COPTHORNE BANK
153
HORLEYLAND WOOD
Filter Beds
Sludge Lagoons
ANTLANDS LANE
The Shipley Bridge Inn PH
Shipley Bridge
B2037
KILN HEATH
New House Farm
Riding School
154
UPPER PICKETT'S
ALLEN'S WOOD
Courtlands
Burstow Park Farm
Burstow Park
SHIPLEY BRIDGE LANE
Sewage Works
Gatwick Stream
The Parsons Pig PH
BALCOMBE ROAD
Hollybush Farm
CLAY HALL LANE
KING GEORGE'S FIELD
Pav
ALLOT
ST FRANCIS
Oldlands Farm
RADFORD ROAD
STEERS LANE
GATWICK INTERNATIONAL
The Greyhound PH
BLACKCORNER WOOD

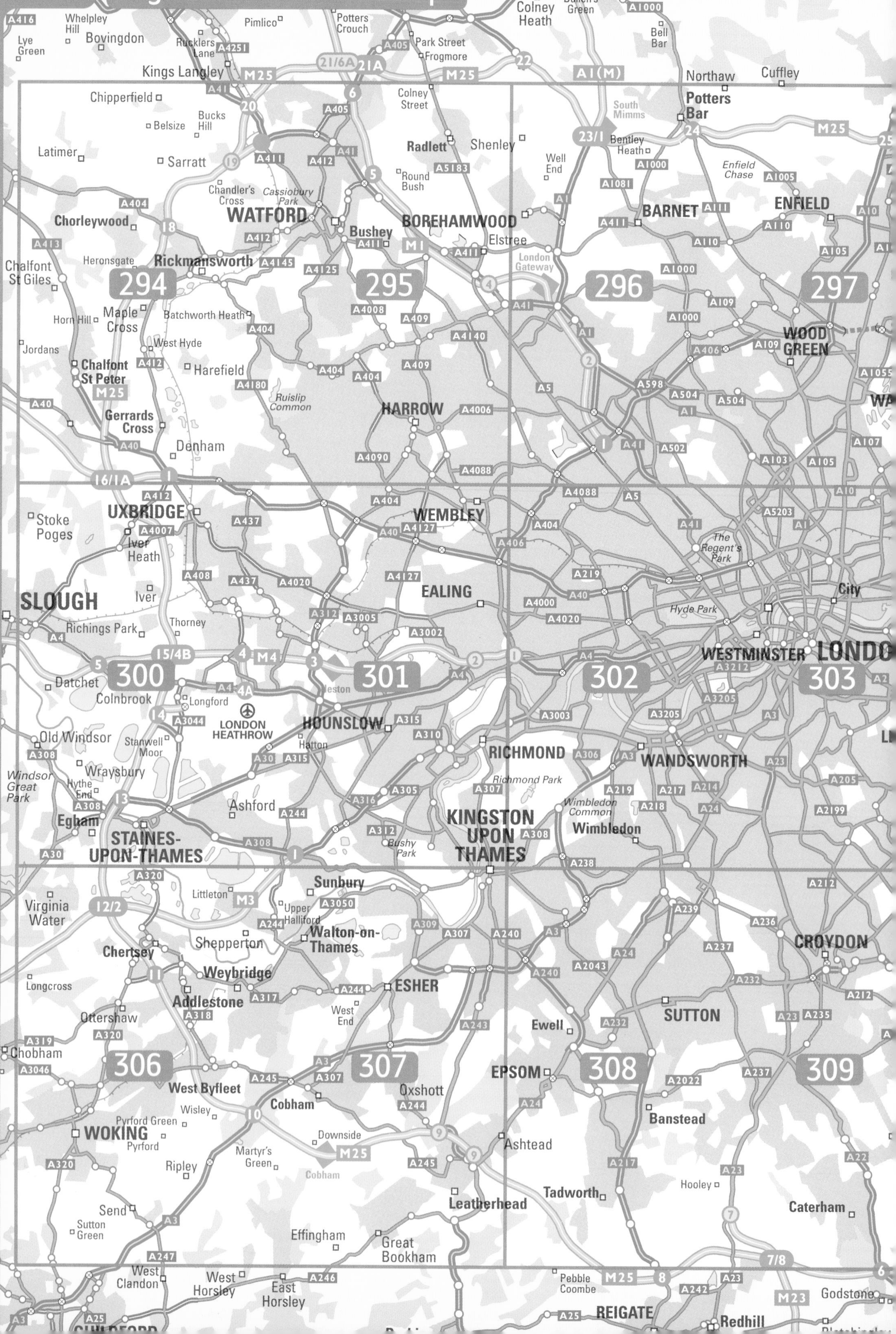
294
295
296
297
300
301
302
303
306
307
308
309
ST ALBANS
Hatfield
Wormley West End
Potten End
Whelpley Hill
Bovingdon
Lye Green
Pimlico
Potters Crouch
Rucklers Lane
Kings Langley
Park Street
Frogmore
Colney Heath
Bullen's Green
Wildhill
Epping Green
Bell Bar
Northaw
Cuffley
Chipperfield
Belsize
Bucks Hill
Latimer
Sarratt
Colney Street
Radlett
Shenley
South Mimms
Potters Bar
Bentley Heath
Well End
Round Bush
Enfield Chase
ENFIELD
Chandler's Cross
Cassiobury Park
WATFORD
Chorleywood
Bushey
BOREHAMWOOD
Elstree
BARNET
London Gateway
Heronsgate
Rickmansworth
Chalfont St Giles
Horn Hill
Maple Cross
Batchworth Heath
West Hyde
Jordans
Chalfont St Peter
Harefield
Ruislip Common
HARROW
WOOD GREEN
Gerrards Cross
Denham
UXBRIDGE
Stoke Poges
Iver Heath
WEMBLEY
The Regent's Park
SLOUGH
Iver
EALING
Thorney
Richings Park
Hyde Park
City
WESTMINSTER
LONDON
Datchet
Colnbrook
Longford
LONDON HEATHROW
HOUNSLOW
Old Windsor
Stanwell Moor
Hatton
RICHMOND
WANDSWORTH
Windsor Great Park
Wraysbury
Hythe End
Richmond Park
Wimbledon Common
Wimbledon
Ashford
Egham
KINGSTON UPON THAMES
STAINES-UPON-THAMES
Bushy Park
Sunbury
Littleton
Upper Halliford
Virginia Water
Walton-on-Thames
Shepperton
Chertsey
CROYDON
Weybridge
Longcross
ESHER
Addlestone
West End
Ottershaw
Ewell
SUTTON
Chobham
EPSOM
West Byfleet
Oxshott
Cobham
Wisley
Banstead
Pyrford Green
WOKING
Pyrford
Downside
Martyr's Green
Ashtead
Ripley
Hooley
Tadworth
Send
Leatherhead
Caterham
Sutton Green
Effingham
Great Bookham
West Clandon
West Horsley
East Horsley
Pebble Coombe
REIGATE
Redhill
Godstone
M25
M1
M3
M4
M23
A1(M)
A41
A405
A411
A412
A5183
A1000
A1081
A111
A110
A105
A404
A413
A4145
A4125
A4008
A409
A4140
A406
A109
A598
A504
A40
A4180
A4006
A502
A4090
A4088
A103
A5
A4007
A437
A4127
A5203
A408
A4020
A219
A4000
A3005
A3002
A312
A4
A3212
A3044
A3205
A3003
A315
A310
A306
A3
A30
A308
A305
A307
A219
A217
A214
A316
A244
A218
A24
A2199
A320
A238
A212
A3050
A239
A236
A309
A240
A237
A2043
A317
A232
A318
A243
A319
A3046
A245
A2022
A246
A242
A22
A247
A25

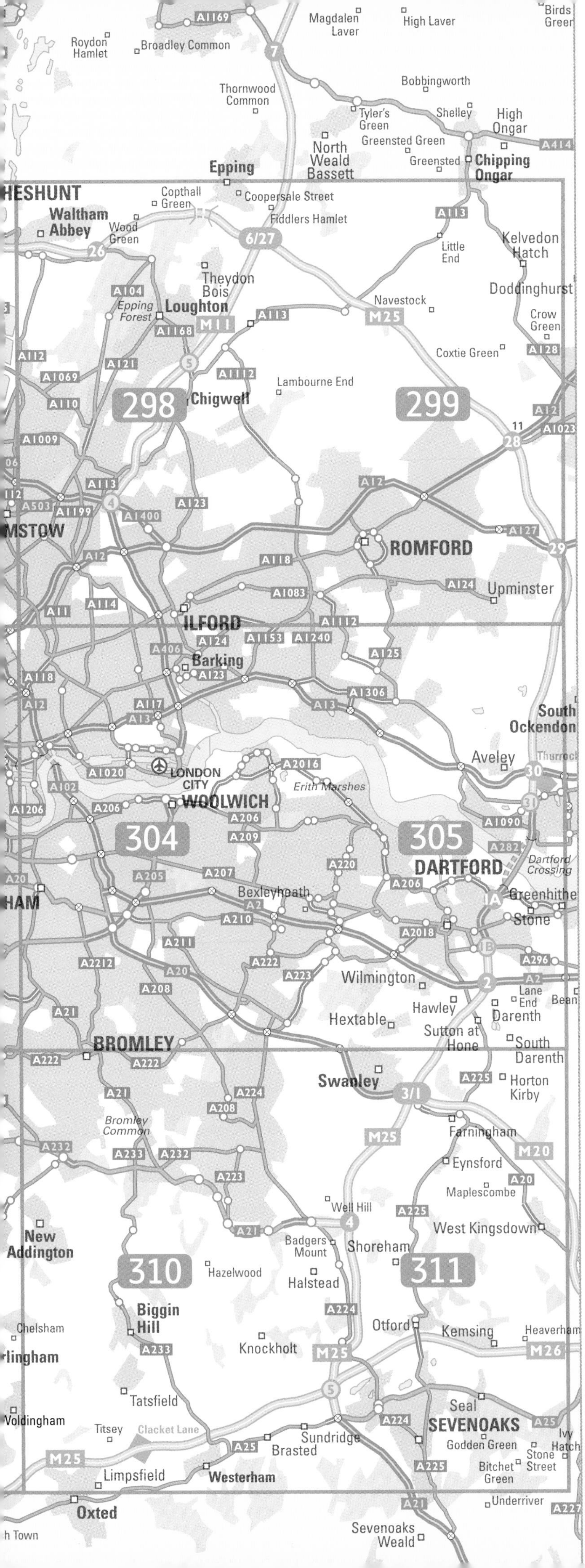

Key to map symbols on pages 294-311

M25	Motorway junctions with full access
M11	Motorway junctions with limited access
LONDON GATEWAY SERVICES	Motorway service area
A406	Primary route with dual / single carriageway
A5	'A' road with dual / single carriageway
B552	'B' road with dual / single carriageway
	Minor road with dual / single carriageway
	Road proposed or under construction
	Road tunnel
	Roundabout
Toll	Toll
	One way street / Restricted access
	Level crossing
30 V	Fixed speed camera / fixed average-speed safety camera. Speed shown by number within camera, a V indicates a variable limit.
	Long distance footpath
London City Airport	Airport with scheduled services
	Railway line / Railway tunnel
	Railway station / Light rail station
	Underground / Overground station
	Heliport
	Hospital
	Congestion charging zone
	Public building
	Built-up area
	Woodland / Park
KENT	County / Unitary Authority boundary & name
CAMDEN	Borough / District boundary & name

Aquarium	Major football club
Battle site	Major shopping centre
Camping / Caravan site	Major sports venue
Castle	Motor racing circuit
Country park	Museum
Ecclesiastical building	Nature reserve
Freight terminal	Other interesting feature
Garden	Racecourse
Golf course	Ski slope (artificial)
Historic house	Theme park
Historic site	University
Information centre	Wildlife park or zoo
Landmark public house	World Heritage Site

SCALE

0 — 1/2 — 1 — 1 1/2 — 2 miles

0 — 1 — 2 — 3 — 4 kilometres

1:63,360 1 inch (2.5cm) to 1 mile / 1.6 cm to 1 km

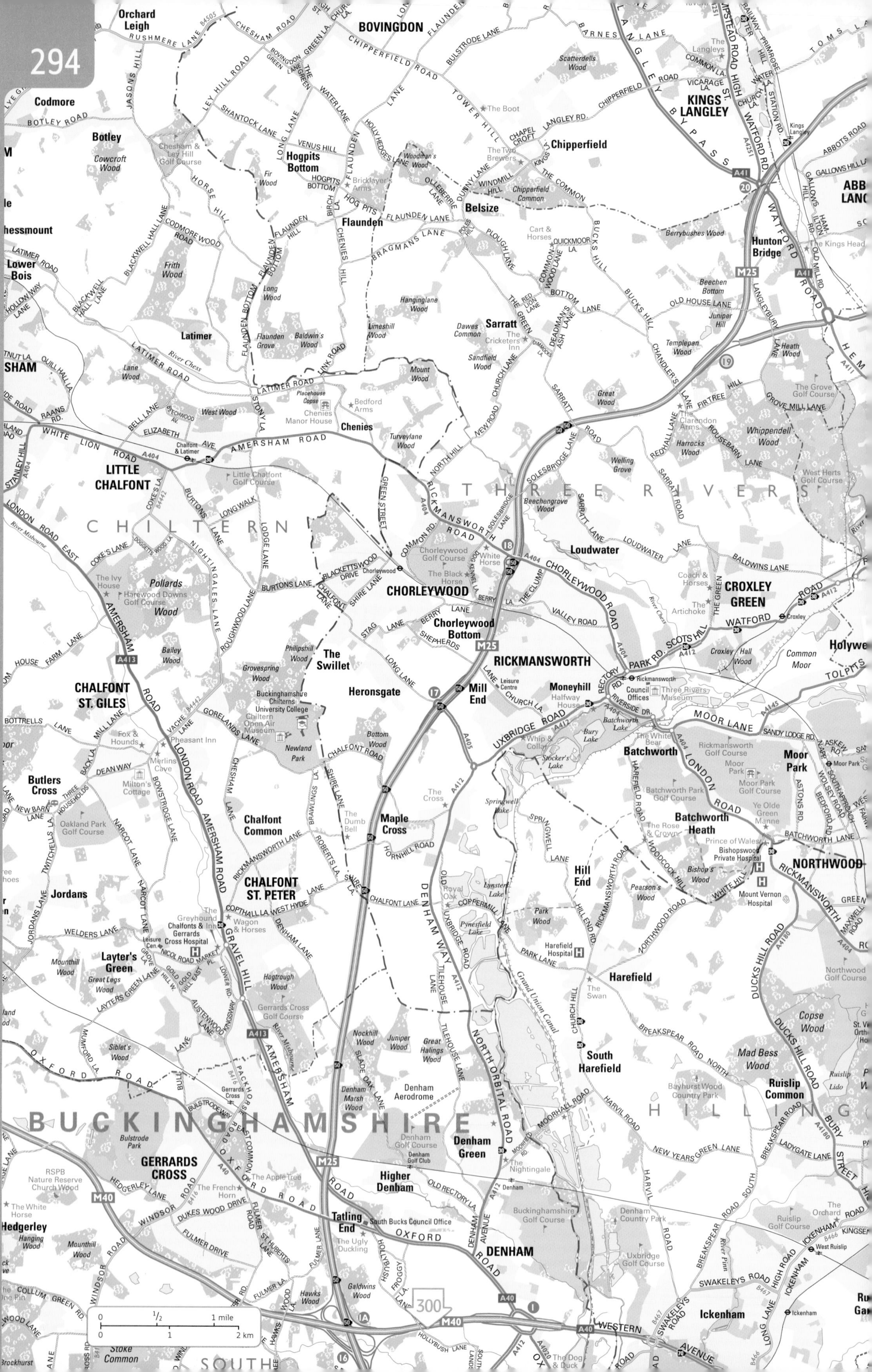
Orchard Leigh
BOVINGDON
Codmore
Botley
Cowcroft Wood
Chesham & Ley Hill Golf Course
Hogpits Bottom
Fir Wood
Flaunden
Belsize
Chipperfield
Chipperfield Common
The Two Brewers
The Boot
Scatterdells Wood
KINGS LANGLEY
The Langleys
Kings Langley
ABBOTS LANGLEY
Berrybushes Wood
Hunton Bridge
The Kings Head
Beechen Bottom
Juniper Hill
Templepan Wood
Heath Wood
The Grove Golf Course
Whippendell Wood
West Herts Golf Course
Chessmount
Lower Bois
Frith Wood
Long Wood
Latimer
River Chess
Flaunden Grove
Baldwin's Wood
Hanginglane Wood
Limeshill Wood
Dawes Common
Sarratt
The Cricketers Inn
Sandfield Wood
Great Wood
Mount Wood
Lane Wood
West Wood
Placehouse Copse
Chenies Manor House
Bedford Arms
Chenies
Turveylane Wood
The Clarendon Arms
Harrocks Wood
Welling Grove
Beechengrove Wood
LITTLE CHALFONT
Little Chalfont Golf Course
CHILTERN
THREE RIVERS
Loudwater
Chorleywood Golf Course
White Horse
The Black Horse
CHORLEYWOOD
Chorleywood Bottom
Coach & Horses
CROXLEY GREEN
The Artichoke
Croxley
The Ivy House
Pollards Wood
Harewood Downs Golf Course
Bailey Wood
Philipshill Wood
The Swillet
Grovespring Wood
Heronsgate
RICKMANSWORTH
Leisure Centre
Mill End
Moneyhill
Halfway House
Council Offices
Three Rivers Museum
Croxley Hall Wood
Common Moor
CHALFONT ST. GILES
Buckinghamshire Chilterns University College
Chiltern Open Air Museum
Newland Park
Bottom Wood
Fox & Hounds
Pheasant Inn
Merlins Cave
Milton's Cottage
Butlers Cross
Oakland Park Golf Course
Whip & Collar
Bury Lake
Batchworth Lake
Stocker's Lake
The White Bear
Batchworth
Rickmansworth Golf Course
Moor Park
Batchworth Park Golf Course
Batchworth Heath
The Rose & Crown
Ye Olde Green Manne
Prince of Wales
Bishopswood Private Hospital
Bishop's Wood
NORTHWOOD
Mount Vernon Hospital
The Cross
Springwell Lake
Chalfont Common
The Dumb Bell
Maple Cross
Jordans
CHALFONT ST. PETER
Royal Oak
Lynsters Lake
Pynesfield Lake
Hill End
Pearson's Wood
Park Wood
The Greyhound
Chalfonts & Gerrards Cross Hospital
Wagon & Horses
Layter's Green
Mounthill Wood
Great Legs Wood
Hogtrough Wood
Gerrards Cross Golf Course
Harefield Hospital
Harefield
The Swan
Grand Union Canal
Northwood Golf Course
Copse Wood
Siblet's Wood
River Misbourne
Nockhill Wood
Juniper Wood
Great Halings Wood
South Harefield
Mad Bess Wood
Ruislip Common
Ruislip Lido
Denham Marsh Wood
Denham Aerodrome
Bayhurst Wood Country Park
BUCKINGHAMSHIRE
HILLINGDON
Bulstrode Park
Gerrards Cross
Denham Golf Course
Denham Golf Club
Denham Green
GERRARDS CROSS
RSPB Nature Reserve Church Wood
The Apple Tree
The French Horn
Higher Denham
The Nightingale
Denham
The White Horse
Hedgerley
Hanging Wood
Mounthill Wood
Tatling End
South Bucks Council Office
The Ugly Duckling
Buckinghamshire Golf Course
Denham Country Park
DENHAM
Ruislip Golf Course
The Orchard
West Ruislip
Uxbridge Golf Course
River Pinn
Galdwins Wood
Hawks Wood
Ickenham
Stoke Common
Brockhurst
The Dog & Duck
M25
M40
A40
A41
A404
A412
A413
300
0 1/2 1 mile
0 1 2 km

HERTFORDSHIRE
HERTSMERE
WATFORD
HARROW
BRENT
How Wood
Frogmore
Bricket Wood
Colney Street
Ridgehill
Woodside
Kingswood
Garston
NORTH WATFORD
RADLETT
Green Street
Shenley
Ridge
Aldenham
Letchmore Heath
Patchetts Green
Elstree Aerodrome
Hilfield Park Reservoir
Aldenham Reservoir
Elstree
BOREHAMWOOD
Rowley Green
BUSHEY
Merry Hill
Oxhey
Watford Heath
Bushey Heath
Stanmore
Carpenders Park
South Oxhey
Hatch End
Pinnerwood Park
Pinner Green
Pinner
HARROW WEALD
Belmont
EDGWARE
Canons Park
Burnt Oak
Queensbury
Kenton
Headstone
Wealdstone
North Harrow
Eastcote Village
Eastcote
HARROW
West Harrow
Harrow on the Hill
Rayners Lane
Ruislip Manor
South Ruislip
South Harrow
North Wembley
WEMBLEY
Wembley Park
Kingsbury
West Hendon
Neasden
Sudbury
Wembley Complex
LONDON GATEWAY SERVICES
Elstree Studios
M25
M1
A41
A1
296
301

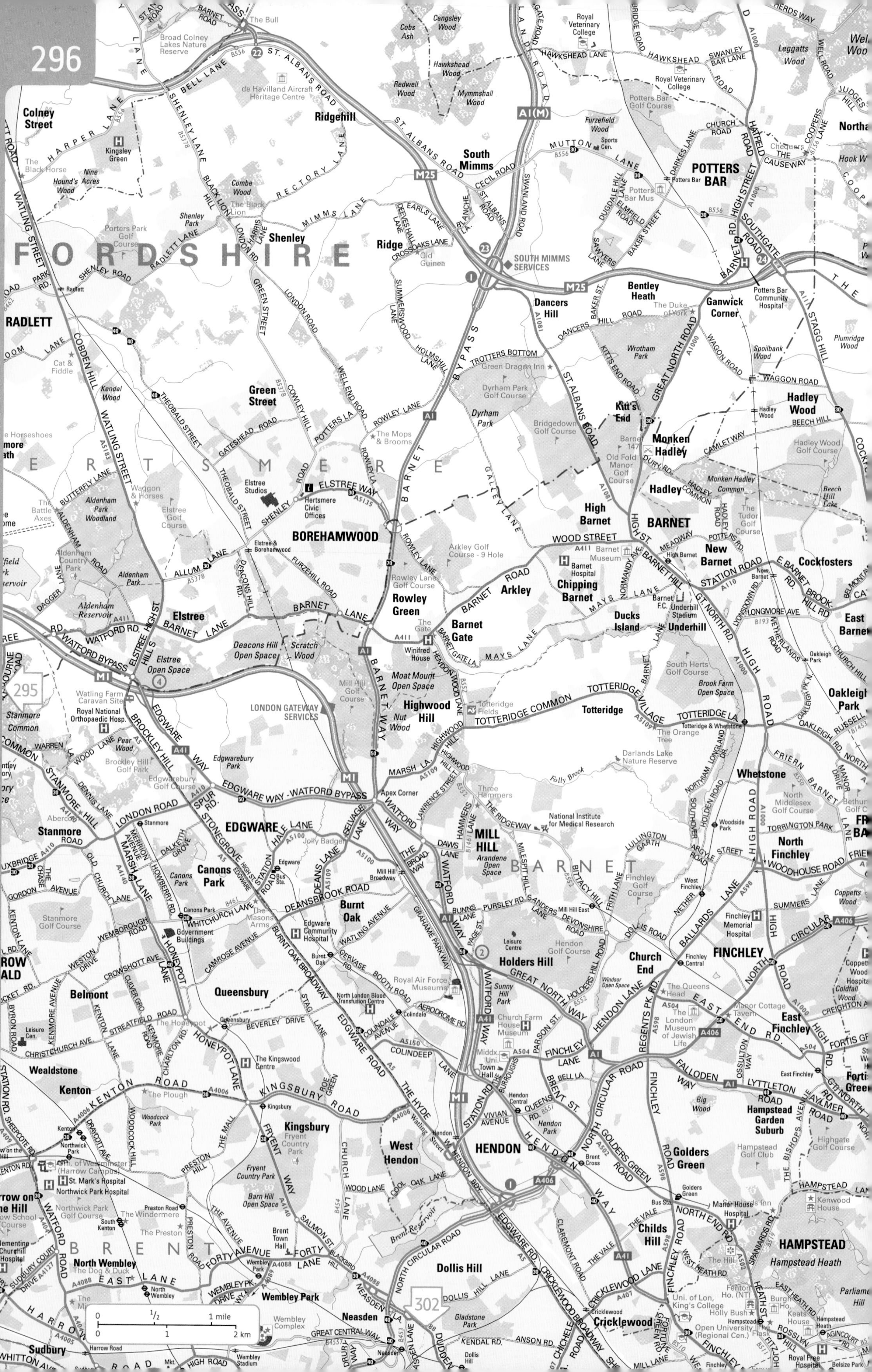

Colney Street
Broad Colney Lakes Nature Reserve
The Bull
de Havilland Aircraft Heritage Centre
Ridgehill
Cobs Ash
Cangsley Wood
Hawkshead Wood
Redwell Wood
Mymmshall Wood
Royal Veterinary College
Kingsley Green
The Black Horse
Hound's Wood
Nine Acres
Combe Wood
The Black Lion
Shenley Park
Shenley
Ridge
South Mimms
Old Guinea
SOUTH MIMMS SERVICES
POTTERS BAR
Potters Bar Golf Course
Furzefield Wood
Potters Bar Mus
Potters Park Golf Course
FORDSHIRE
RADLETT
Cat & Fiddle
Kendal Wood
Green Street
Bentley Heath
Dancers Hill
Ganwick Corner
Potters Bar Community Hospital
Wrotham Park
Green Dragon Inn
Dyrham Park Golf Course
Dyrham Park
Spoilbank Wood
Plumridge Wood
Hadley Wood
Kitt's End
Monken Hadley
Bridgedown Golf Course
The Mops & Brooms
Old Fold Manor Golf Course
Hadley Wood Golf Course
ERTSMERE
Elstree Studios
Hertsmere Civic Offices
Waggon & Horses
Aldenham Park Woodland
Elstree Golf Course
BOREHAMWOOD
High Barnet
BARNET
Hadley
Monken Hadley Common
The Tudor Golf Course
Arkley Golf Course - 9 Hole
Barnet Museum
Barnet Hospital
Chipping Barnet
Arkley
New Barnet
Cockfosters
Aldenham Country Park
Aldenham Park
Aldenham Reservoir
Rowley Lane Golf Course
Rowley Green
Elstree
Ducks Island
Underhill
Barnet Gate
East Barnet
Deacons Hill Open Space
Scratch Wood
Winifred House
Elstree Open Space
South Herts Golf Course
Brook Farm Open Space
Oakleigh Park
Watling Farm Caravan Site
Royal National Orthopaedic Hosp.
Mill Hill Golf Course
LONDON GATEWAY SERVICES
Moat Mount Open Space
Highwood Hill
Nut Wood
Totteridge Fields
Totteridge
The Orange Tree
Stanmore Common
Pear Wood
Brockley Hill Golf Park
Edgwarebury Park
Edgwarebury Golf Course
Darlands Lake Nature Reserve
Whetstone
Apex Corner
Three Hammers
National Institute for Medical Research
North Middlesex Golf Course
Stanmore
EDGWARE
Jolly Badger
MILL HILL
Arandene Open Space
North Finchley
Canons Park
Burnt Oak
BARNET
Finchley Golf Course
Coppetts Wood
The Masons Arms
Edgware Community Hospital
Government Buildings
Stanmore Golf Course
Leisure Centre
Hendon Golf Course
Holders Hill
Church End
FINCHLEY
Finchley Memorial Hospital
Queensbury
Belmont
Royal Air Force Museums
Sunny Hill Park
The Queens Head
The London Museum of Jewish Life
Manor Cottage Tavern
East Finchley
North London Blood Transfusion Centre
Church Farm House Museum
Middx. Uni.
Town Hall
Wealdstone
The Kingswood Centre
Kenton
The Plough
Kingsbury
Fryent Country Park
Woodcock Park
Big Wood
Hampstead Garden Suburb
Highgate Golf Course
West Hendon
HENDON
Hendon Park
Golders Green
Hampstead Golf Club
Univ. of Westminster (Harrow Campus)
St. Mark's Hospital
Northwick Park Hospital
Fryent Country Park
Barn Hill Open Space
Kenwood House
Northwick Park Golf Course
The Windermere
The Preston
Brent Town Hall
Brent Reservoir
Childs Hill
Manor House Hospital
HAMPSTEAD
Hampstead Heath
BRENT
North Wembley
The Dog & Duck
Wembley Park
Dollis Hill
Gladstone Park
Neasden
Wembley Complex
Cricklewood
Uni. of Lon. King's College
Open University (Regional Cen.)
Keats House
Royal Free Hospital
Sudbury
295
302
0 ½ 1 mile
0 1 2 km

Cuffley
Cheshunt Common
Goffs Oak
Flamstead End
Holyfield
Bury Green
CHESHUNT
Cattlegate
Cattlins
Waltham Cross
WALTHAM ABBEY
Holdbrook
M25
Crews Hill
Botany Bay
Whitewebbs Park
Freezy Water
Bullsmoor
Enfield Lock
Enfield Chase
Forty Hill
ENFIELD
Enfield Wash
Sewardstone
High Beach
E N F I E L D
World's End
Enfield Highway
Brimsdown
King George's Reservoir
Grange Park
Bush Hill Park
Sewardstonebury
Epping Forest
Oakwood
Winchmore Hill
Ponders End
William Girling Reservoir
Osidge
Southgate
Lower Edmonton
298
CHINGFORD
Palmers Green
New Southgate
EDMONTON
Friday Hill
Chingford Hatch
South Chingford
Bowes Park
Upper Edmonton
Highams Park
Hale End
TOTTENHAM
Banbury Reservoir
WOOD GREEN
Noel Park
Tottenham Hale
Higham Hill
WALTHAMSTOW
South Woodford
Muswell Hill
West Green
Upper Walthamstow
W A L T H A M F O R E S T
H A R I N G E Y
HORNSEY
HARRINGAY
South Tottenham
Leytonstone
Crouch End
Stroud Green
STOKE NEWINGTON
Stamford Hill
Upper Clapton
Highgate
LEYTON
Finsbury Park
Upper Holloway
Lea Bridge
Hackney Marsh
Dartmouth Park
Tufnell Park
Holloway
303
Lower Clapton
Clapton Park
Highbury
Forest Gate
H A C K N E Y
I S L I N G T O N
NORTH CIRCULAR ROAD
GREAT CAMBRIDGE ROAD
HERTFORD ROAD
LEA VALLEY ROAD
MERIDIAN WAY (NORTH - SOUTH ROUTE)
SEWARDSTONE ROAD
THE RIDGEWAY
GREEN LANES
SEVEN SISTERS RD.

EPPING FOREST
Holyfield
Galleyhill Wood
Aimes Green
Stocking Grove
Lindsey Street
Bury Lane
Civic Offices
EPPING
Fernhall Wood
Rookery Wood
Cheshunt
Old English Gentleman
Civic Off.
The Crocodile
Bury Green
CHESHUNT
River Lee Country Park
Lee Valley Regional Park
Crooked Mile
Cobbin's Brook
Bell Common
Ivy Chimneys
Upshire
Parklands
Theobalds Lane
Theobalds Grove
The Vine
Waltham Cross
Waltham Abbey
The Queens Head
WALTHAM ABBEY
Horseshoe Hill
The Horseshoes
Copthall Green
The Warren
Epping Forest
Forest Gate
Theydon Road
Theydon Bois Golf Course
Cheshunt Link Road
Eleanor Cross Road
Holdbrook
Epping Forest District Museum
The Sultan
Honey Lane
Crown Hill
Bus Sta.
Capel Manor
Bullsmoor Lane
Freezy Water
Meridian Way
M25
Woodbine Inn
The Volunteer
Woodridden Hill
The Wake Arms
Coppice Row
Sixteen Spring Jack
Piercing Hill
Theydon Bois
Dowding Way
Honey Lane Quarters
Deer shelter Plain
Avey Lane
Beech Hill Park
Birch Wood
Red Oak Wood
Turkey Street
Ordnance Road
Enfield Lock
Bullsmoor
Lee Valley Regional Park
Sewardstone Road
High Beech Golf Course
Debden House Cen. Camping Site
Broadstone Plain
Debden Green
Debden Lane
Theydon Bois
Great Monk Wood
Albany Park
The Plough
The King's Oak
Loughton Golf Course
Enfield Wash
Mollison Avenue
Hertford Road
Mott Street
Little Monk Wood
High Beach
High Wood
Sewardstone
Englands Lane
King George's Reservoir
The White Horse
Green Street
Brimsdown
Elms Caravan & Camping Park
The Robin Hood
Rectory Lane
Church Hill
The Plume of Feathers
Debden
Enfield Highway
Lee Valley Campsite
Daws Hill
West Essex Golf Course
Round Thicket
Strawberry Hill
Earl's Path
Traps Hill
Borders Lane
Leisure Centre
The Sir Winston Churchill
London Road
Gilwell Park
Nags Head Road
Southbury
Fox & Hounds
Epping Forest
Alderton Hill
Loughton
Middlesex
Lincoln Road
Yardley Hill
Sewardstonebury
King George's Reservoir
Buckhurst Hill
Ponders End
Ponders End
Lea Valley Road
Bury Wood
Connaught Water
Queen Elizabeth's Hunting Lodge
Chingford Golf Course
The Hawk Wood
Oakwood Hill
Woolston Manor Golf Course
M11
Abridge Road
Pudding Lane
Jubilee Park
Nightingale Road
William Girling Reservoir
Kings Head Hill
Rangers Road
Manor Road
Valley Hill
River Roding
Station Rd.
Chingford
Chingford Green
The Warren Wood
Loughton Way
Bounces Rd.
Monmouth Road
The Broadway
Leisure Cen.
EDMONTON
Lee Valley Leisure Golf Course
Mansfield Hill
The Ridgeway
Endlebury Rd.
Whitehall Road
Palmerston Rd.
Roding Lane
Buckhurst Hill
Holly House Hospital
Lord's Bushes
Chigwell Rise
Vicarage Lane
The Maypole
Lambourne Road
Old Church Rd.
The Green Man
CHINGFORD
Friday Hill
The Sirloin
Hatch Forest
Woodford Wells
Buckhurst Way
Forest Edge
Chigwell
CHIGWELL
Hainault Road
The Monkhams Inn
Old Hall Tavern
New Road
The Wheelwright
Woodford Golf Course
Roding Valley
Larkshall
Larks Wood
Chingford Hatch
Monkhams Lane
Chigwell Golf Course
Brocket Way
Grange Hill
Lee Valley Regional Park
South Chingford
Royston Arms
The Avenue
Highams Park
Chingford Lane
Woodford Green
Kings Avenue
Hillside Ave.
The White Hart
Manor Road
The Bald Hind
Manford
Upper Edmonton
Angel Road
A406
Highams Park
The Castle
Charter Rd.
Snakes Lane West
Snakes Lane East
Tomswood Road
Grange Hill
New North
Hart Lane
Tottenham Hotspur F.C.
Banbury Reservoir
Southend Road
Nelson Road
Selwyn Ave.
Hale End
Walthamstow Stadium (closed)
Royal Oak
Broadmead Road
Woodford
Hospital Hill Wood
Old Maypole
Hainault
HAINAULT
Northumberland Park
Lee Valley Regional Park
Epping Forest
WOODFORD
Uni. of London
Woodford Bridge
Tomswood Hill
Sports Cen.
Fairlop Plain Country Park
Fairlop Water
Billet Road
Southend Road
Roding Lane North
Fullwell Cross
Fairlop
Fairlop Water Golf Course
Lockwood Reservoir
Higham Hill
Higham Hill Road
WALTHAMSTOW
South Woodford
Southend Rd.
Clayhall Avenue
The Cocked Hat
Mossford Lane
Painters Road
Forest Road
Thorpe Coombe Hospital
Upper Walthamstow
Roding Hospital
Clayhall
Longwood Gardens
Barkingside
Aldborough Hatch
Dick Turpin
High Maynard Reservoir
Low Maynard Reservoir
Tottenham Hale
Ferry La.
Blackhorse Road
Forest Road
Wood Street
Epping Forest
Eagle Hotel
Roding Valley Park
REDBRIDGE
Cranbrook Road
Horns Road
Walthamstow Central
Bus Sta.
Vestry House Museum
Snaresbrook Road
Hermon Hill
Woodford Ave.
Gants Hill
Newbury Park
Goodmayes Hospital
Reservoir
St. James Street
Walthamstow Queens Road
Hollow Pond
Snaresbrook
Eastern Ave
Redbridge Lane East
Redbridge
Eastern Avenue
Seven Kings Park
Warwick Reservoirs
St. James's Park
Boundary Rd.
Grove Rd.
Whipps Cross Rd.
Whipps Cross University Hospital
The George
Wanstead
Wanstead Golf Course
REDBRIDGE
Perth Road
The Avenue
Seven Kings
Springfield Park
Upper Clapton
Capworth Street
Leytonstone
Wanstead
The Basin
Wanstead Park
The Drive
Valentines Park
Benton Road
Cameron Rd.
Leyton Midland Road
Leytonstone
Wanstead Golf Course
Cranbrook Road
LEYTON
Church Road
Leytonstone High Road
Aldersbrook
Cranbrook
The Kings
Clapton
Lea Bridge
Leyton Orient FC
Council Off.
Harrow Rd.
Lake House Road
Wanstead Flats
Ilford Golf Course
Ilford
Town Hall
Winston Way
Green Lane
Lee Valley Regional Park
Hackney
South Park
Sports Cen.
Lea Bridge Road
Grove Green Road
Cathall Road
Capel Road
Manor Park
ILFORD
Mortlake Road
Clacklewell
Woodgrange Rd.
Forest Gate
Wanstead Park
Station Rd.
Little Ilford
Ilford Lane
Loxford
304
297
0 1/2 1 mile
0 1 2 km
Hospital
Lee Valley Velopark
Homerton
Chobham Rd.
Forest Lane
Forest Gate
Woodgrange Park

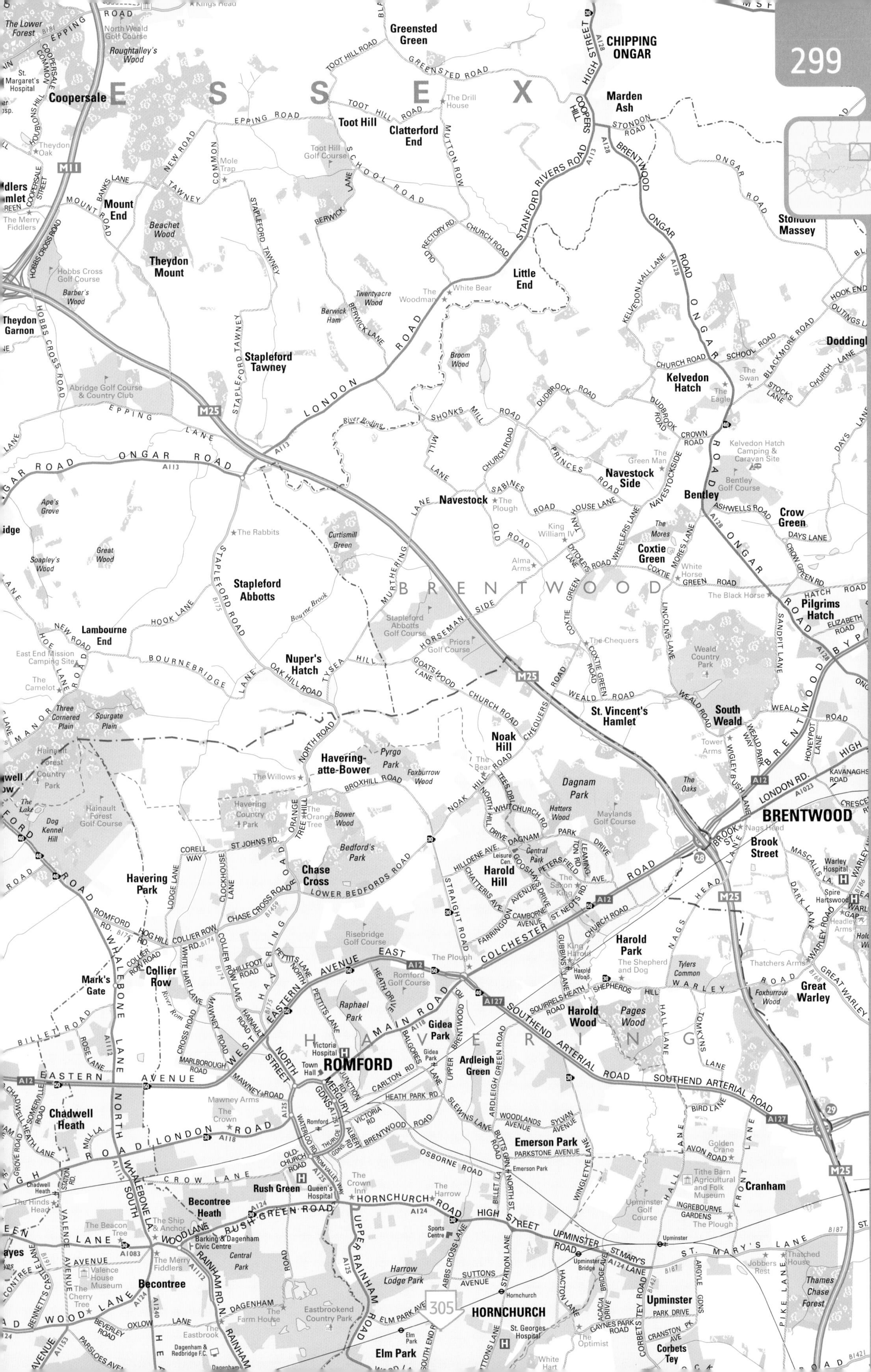
ESSEX
BRENTWOOD
HAVERING
Greensted Green
CHIPPING ONGAR
Marden Ash
Coopersale
Toot Hill
Clatterford End
Mount End
Theydon Mount
Theydon Garnon
Little End
Stondon Massey
Kelvedon Hatch
Stapleford Tawney
Navestock
Navestock Side
Bentley
Crow Green
Coxtie Green
Stapleford Abbotts
Lambourne End
Nuper's Hatch
Pilgrims Hatch
St. Vincent's Hamlet
South Weald
Noak Hill
Havering-atte-Bower
BRENTWOOD
Brook Street
Havering Park
Chase Cross
Harold Hill
Harold Park
Mark's Gate
Collier Row
Great Warley
Gidea Park
ROMFORD
Ardleigh Green
Harold Wood
Chadwell Heath
Emerson Park
Cranham
Rush Green
Becontree Heath
Becontree
HORNCHURCH
Upminster
Elm Park
Corbets Tey
Thames Chase Forest
North Weald Golf Course
Roughtalley's Wood
Hobbs Cross Golf Course
Abridge Golf Course & Country Club
Toot Hill Golf Course
Stapleford Abbotts Golf Course
Priors Golf Course
Weald Country Park
Bentley Golf Course
Kelvedon Hatch Camping & Caravan Site
Hainault Forest Country Park
Hainault Forest Golf Course
Havering Country Park
Dagnam Park
Maylands Golf Course
Risebridge Golf Course
Romford Golf Course
Upminster Golf Course
Tithe Barn Agricultural and Folk Museum
Valence House Museum
Eastbrookend Country Park
Warley Hospital
Queen's Hospital
St. Georges Hospital
M11
M25
A12
A127
A113
A128
ONGAR ROAD
LONDON ROAD
STANFORD RIVERS ROAD
SOUTHEND ARTERIAL ROAD
EASTERN AVENUE
COLCHESTER ROAD
HORNCHURCH ROAD
RUSH GREEN ROAD
UPMINSTER ROAD
ST. MARY'S LANE
WARLEY ROAD
305

294
306
DENHAM
Fulmer
SOUTH BUCKINGHAMSHIRE
Stoke Common
Stoke Poges
Wexham Street
Stoke Green
George Green
SLOUGH
Middle Green
Shreding Green
Iver Heath
Iver
Uxbridge Moor
UXBRIDGE
Ickenham
North Hillingdon
HILLINGDON
Cowley
YIEWSLEY
Hayes End
WEST DRAYTON
Thorney
Richings Park
Langley
Upton Park
Upton
Brands Hill
Colnbrook
Harmondsworth
Sipson
Harlington
Longford
Poyle
WINDSOR
Datchet
WINDSOR & MAIDENHEAD
Southlea
Horton
Sunnymeads
Old Windsor
Wraysbury
Stanwell Moor
Stanwell
London Heathrow Airport
Hythe End
Egham
Englefield Green
Pooley Green
Egham Hythe
STAINES-UPON-THAMES
Ripley Springs
Egham Wick
Thorpe Lea
Ashford
SPELTHORNE
Laleham
Thorpe
Stroude
Virginia Water
The Queen Mother Reservoir
Wraysbury Reservoir
King George VI Reservoir
Staines Reservoirs
Queen Mary Reservoir
The Home Park
Windsor Great Park
Runnymede Park (NT)
River Thames
M25
M40
M4
M3
A4
A30
A308
A40
0 ½ 1 mile
0 1 2 km

Ruislip Manor
South Ruislip
South Harrow
Northolt
North Wembley
WEMBLEY
Wembley Park
Neasden
Tokyngton
Sudbury
Perivale
Alperton
Stonebridge
Harlesden
Park Royal
North Acton
West Acton
ACTON
East Acton
South Acton
Bedford Park
Gunnersbury
Yeading
Greenford
Dormer's Wells
EALING
Hanwell
SOUTHALL
Norwood Green
North Hyde
Little Ealing
Osterley Park
Osterley
Brentford
Kew
CHISWICK
Grove Park
Cranford
HESTON
Spring Grove
Lampton
Hounslow West
Woodlands
ISLEWORTH
North Sheen
Mortlake
East Sheen
HOUNSLOW
Hatton
St. Margarets
RICHMOND
Whitton
TWICKENHAM
Petersham
FELTHAM
Lower Feltham
Strawberry Hill
Ham
Hanworth
Felthamhill
Hampton Hill
Teddington
Coombe
Hampton
Hampton Wick
KINGSTON UPON THAMES
Norbiton
Sunbury
Richmond Park
Bushy Park
HOUNSLOW
BRENT
RICHMOND UPON THAMES
KINGSTON
M4
A40
A406
A4
A316
A205
A312
295
302
307

BRENT
Wembley
WEMBLEY
Wembley Park
Wembley Complex
Sudbury
Tokyngton
Neasden
Dollis Hill
Childs Hill
HAMPSTEAD
Hampstead Heath
Cricklewood
Willesden
Brondesbury
South Hampstead
Belsize Park
Primrose Hill
St. John's Wood
Kilburn
Kensal Rise
Maida Vale
PADDINGTON
Perivale
Alperton
Stonebridge
Harlesden
Park Royal
North Acton
West Acton
Wormwood Scrubs
Westbourne Green
Bayswater
Notting Hill
Hyde Park
Kensington Gardens
EALING
ACTON
East Acton
Shepherd's Bush
KENSINGTON
Hanwell
South Acton
Bedford Park
Gunnersbury
HAMMERSMITH
Little Ealing
CHELSEA
Brentford
CHISWICK
Kew
Castelnau
FULHAM
Grove Park
Walham Green
Parsons Green
Sands End
North Sheen
BARNES
Mortlake
Putney
East Sheen
WANDSWORTH
St. Margarets
RICHMOND
Roehampton
Putney Heath
WANDSWORTH
RICHMOND
Petersham
Richmond Park
UPON THAMES
Southfields
Earlsfield
Wimbledon Park
Summerstown
Upper Tooting
Ham
Putney Vale
Kingston Vale
Wimbledon Common
Coombe
Teddington
WIMBLEDON
Tooting Graveney
Collier's Wood
Copse Hill
KINGSTON UPON THAMES
Hampton Wick
MERTON
Norbiton
KINGSTON
MERTON
MITCHAM
Raynes
Bushey Mead
HAMMERSMITH & FULHAM
0 1/2 1 mile
0 1 2 km
296
301
308

Finsbury Park
Leyton
Lea Bridge
Upper Holloway
Tufnell Park
Holloway
Highbury
Shacklewell
Lower Clapton
Clapton Park
Homerton
Hackney Wick
Stratford
Barnsbury
Dalston
Hackney
Camden Town
King's Cross
Old Ford
Hoxton
Haggerston
Bethnal Green
Bow
Regent's Park
ST. PANCRAS
FINSBURY
SHOREDITCH
St. Luke's
Mile End
Plaistow
Bloomsbury
HOLBORN
Soho
Whitechapel
Stepney
Bromley
Limehouse
Canning Town
Shadwell
Wapping
Poplar
WESTMINSTER
SOUTHWARK
Rotherhithe
BERMONDSEY
Millwall
Cubitt Town
LAMBETH
Walworth
Pimlico
Deptford
Vauxhall
Kennington
GREENWICH
CAMBERWELL
South Lambeth
New Cross Gate
St. John's
New Cross
Blackheath
Clapham
Stockwell
Peckham
Brixton
Nunhead
Lewisham
Kidbrooke
Brockley
Herne Hill
Ladywell
Clapham Park
Honor Oak
East Dulwich
Honor Oak Park
Hither Green
Lee
Streatham Hill
DULWICH
Catford
Tulse Hill
Forest Hill
Grove Park
West Dulwich
West Norwood
Upper Sydenham
Lower Sydenham
Bell Green
Bellingham
Southend
Downham
STREATHAM
Streatham Park
SYDENHAM
Furzedown
Norwood New Town
New Beckenham
Plaistow
Streatham Vale
Norwood
Penge
BECKENHAM
Norbury
Upper Norwood
South Norwood
Elmers End
Shortlands

LEYTON
Aldersbrook
Cranbrook
ILFORD
Lee Valley Regional Park
Hackney Marsh
Wanstead Flats
298
Manor Park
Little Ilford
Lower Clapton
Clapton Park
Forest Gate
Loxford
Homerton Hospital
Homerton
Hackney Wick
Stratford
WEST HAM
Upton
BARKING
Victoria Park
Old Ford
Olympic Stadium
Queen Elizabeth Olympic Park
London Aquatics Centre
Westfield Stratford City
NEWHAM
Upton Park
West Ham United F.C.
EAST HAM
TOWER HAMLETS
Bow
Mile End
Plaistow
Newham Uni. Hospital
Creekmouth
Bromley
Stepney
Beckton
Canning Town
Custom House
Whitechapel
Limehouse
Shadwell
Wapping
Poplar
ExCeL London
Royal Victoria Dock
Royal Albert Dock
London City Airport
Royal George V Dock
The O2
Rotherhithe
Silvertown
North Woolwich
Thamesmead West
Thames Barrier
Cubitt Town
Millwall
New Charlton
BERMONDSEY
Deptford
Woolwich Ferry
WOOLWICH
Plumstead
Charlton
The Valley Charlton Athletic F.C.
303
GREENWICH
National Maritime Mus
Flamsteed House (Old Royal Observatory)
Greenwich Park
Royal Artillery Barrack
Shooter's Hill
East Wickham
New Cross Gate
New Cross
St. John's
Blackheath
Kidbrooke
Eltham Common
Oxleas Wood
Welling
Nunhead
Lewisham
LEWISHAM
Brockley
Falconwood
Peckham Rye Common
Blackheath Park
Ladywell
Lee
Eltham
Avery Hill
Blackfen
Honor Oak
Honor Oak Park
Hither Green
East Dulwich
Catford
Lamorbey
Horniman Museum
Forest Hill
Grove Park
Mottingham
New Eltham
Bell Green
Bellingham
Longlands
Lower Sydenham
Southend
Downham
Elmstead
SIDCUP
SYDENHAM
Sundridge
Chislehurst West
New Beckenham
Plaistow
CHISLEHURST
Penge
BECKENHAM
Anerley
310
BROMLEY
Widmore
Bickley
Shortlands
Petts Wood
Hawkwood Estate (NT)
1/2
1 mile
0
1
2 km

Becontree
Dagenham
HORNCHURCH
Elm Park
Upminster
Corbets Tey
South Hornchurch
Rainham
South Ockendon
Belhus Park
Wennington
Aveley
Purfleet
West Thurrock
Thamesmead North
Belvedere
Lessness Heath
Erith
West Heath
Northumberland Heath
BEXLEY
Barnehurst
Bexleyheath
Crayford
Barnes Cray
Old Bexley
Coldblow
DARTFORD
New Town
Stone
North Cray
Joydens Wood
Wilmington
Hawley
Darenth
Lane End
Hextable
Swanley Village
SWANLEY
Sutton at Hone
South Darenth
Green Street Green
River Thames
Rainham Marshes
Wennington Marshes
Aveley Marshes
Erith Marshes
Dartford Salt Marshes
Crayford Marshes
West Thurrock Marshes
Ford Motor Works
Crossness Lighthouse
Jenningtree Point Lighthouse
Stoneness Lighthouse
THURROCK SERVICES
Lakeside Shopping Centre
Bluewater Shopping Centre
Dartford International Ferry Terminal
QUEEN ELIZABETH II BRIDGE
DARTFORD TUNNEL
THAMES GATEWAY
NEW ROAD
ARTERIAL ROAD PURFLEET
DARTFORD NORTHERN BYPASS
UNIVERSITY WAY
ROCHESTER WAY
WATLING STREET
DARTFORD BYPASS
A13
A282
M25
A2
A20
299
311

300
SPELTHORNE
Queen Mary Reservoir
Virginia Water
VIRGINIA WATER
Royal Holloway College
Stroude
Thorpe
Thorpe Lea
Thorpe Green
Thorpe Park
Manor Lake
St. Ann's Lake
Abbey Lake
Laleham
Laleham Golf Course
Laleham Park Camping Site
Littleton
Sunbury Golf Course
Wentworth Golf Course
Longcross
Lyne
Hersham Copse
Fan Grove
Bog Wood
Barrow Hills Golf Course
Foxhills Golf Course
St. Peter's Hospital
Runnymede Hospital
Chertsey
Chertsey Meads
Addlestone Moor
Abbey Moor Golf Course
Addlestone
Weybridge
Elmbridge Civic Cen.
Elmbridge Museum
Woburn Park
Shepperton
Desborough Island
Twynersh House
Silver Birch Caravan Site
RUNNYMEDE
SURREY HEATH
ELMBRIDGE
WOKING
GUILDFORD
Chobham Common
Queenswood Golf Course
Stonehill
Ottershaw
Ottershaw Park
Burrowhill
Row Town
New Haw
Central Veterinary Labs.
Brooklands
Brooklands Museum
St. George's Hill
St. George's Hill Golf Course
Warren Pond
Chobham
Fairoaks Airport
Great Wood
Brox Copse
Birch Wood
Hoyt Wood
Woodham
Dartnell Park
Byfleet
West Byfleet
Broadoaks Government Offices
Mimbridge
Milford Green
Castle Grove
Horsell Common
Horsell
New Zealand Golf Course
Bleak House
Basingstoke Canal
Sheerwater
Nuffield Hospital
West Byfleet Golf Course
Pyrford
Traditions Golf Course
Silvermere Golf Course
Cobham Bus Museum
Wisley
The Wisley Golf Course
Wisley Common
Wisley Gardens (RHS)
Ockham Common
Bolder Mere
Goldsworth Park
Mount Hermon
WOKING
Beechcroft Hospital
Maybury
Pyrford Green
Pyrford Golf Course
Pyrford Village
Hoebridge Golf Centre
St. John's
Knaphill
Hook Heath
Woking Golf Course
Woking Park
Old Woking
Newark Priory (rems)
River Wey
Ripley Green
Half Moon
Elm Corner
Martyr's Green
Ockham
Oakham Park
Chaffers Copse
Stumps Grove
Westfield
The Cricketers
Mayford
Mayford Arms
Fisher's Hill
Smart's Heath
Westfield Common
Sutton Green Golf Course
Sutton Green
Send
Send Marsh
Ripley
Jovial Sailor
Services
Barnsthorns Wood
Horsley Camping & Caravan Site
Worplesdon
Whitmoor Pond
Jolly Farmer
Poor Jack's Wood
The Fox & Hounds
Sendgrove
H.M. Prison Send
Lollesworth Wood
Whitmoor Common
Jacobs Well
Sutton Park
Sutton Place
Burpham Court Farm Park
Stringer's Common
Frithy's Wood
West Clandon
Clandon
King William IV
West Horsley
Cotts Wood
Onslow Arms Inn
Hatchlands Park
Burpham
Clandon Regis Golf Course
Queens Head
East Clandon
The Bulls Head
Christ College Ski Slope
Stoughton
M25
M3
A3
A320
A245
A318
A317
GUILDFORD BYPASS
PORTSMOUTH ROAD
RIPLEY BYPASS
EPSOM ROAD
0 1/2 1 mile
0 1 2 km

301
308
KINGSTON UPON THAMES
Hampton
Bushy Park
Hampton Wick
Sunbury
Kempton Park Race Course
Hampton Court Palace & Garden
East Molesey
West Molesey
Thames Ditton
Norbiton
Surbiton
SURBITON
Berrylands
Old Malden
Tolworth
Queen Elizabeth II Reservoir
Island Barn Reservoir
Rydens
Lower Green
Weston Green
Hinchley Wood
Long Ditton
Walton-on-Thames
Hersham
Ashley Park
Burwood Park
ESHER
West End
Claremont Park
Claygate
Chessington
Hook
West Ewell
Horton
EPSOM
Esher Common
Fairmile
Oxshott
Prince's Coverts
Malden Rushett
COBHAM
Stoke D'Abernon
Pachesham Park
Ashtead
Lower Ashtead
Ashtead Park
Langley Vale
Downside
Leatherhead Common
LEATHERHEAD
Fetcham
Little Bookham
Great Bookham
Effingham
Tyrrell's Wood
Headley
Givons Grove
Norbury Park
Mickleham
Westhumble
Box Hill
Pebble Coombe
Epsom Common
Ashtead Common
M25
A3
A24
A243
A307
A309
A244
A245
A246
KINGSTON
THAMES
ELMBRIDGE
EPSOM & EWELL
SURREY
MOLE VALLEY

KINGSTON UPON THAMES
Norbiton
Coombe Wood Golf Course
Kingston Hospital
New Victoria Hosp.
Wolfson Medical Rehabilitation Centre
Copse Hill
302
Merton Park
MERTON
MITCHAM
KINGSTON
UPON
THAMES
MERTON
Hampton Court Palace & Garden
Hampton Court Park
Hampton Court Palace Golf Course
Raynes Park
Bushey Mead
MORDEN
Morden Park
New Malden
West Barnes
Berrylands
Motspur Park
SURBITON
Long Ditton
Thames Ditton
Old Malden
Hinchley Wood
Tolworth
Tolworth Hospital
Government Offices
Surbiton Golf Course
Worcester Park
North Cheam
St. Helier
Rosehill
Benhilton
Carshalton
The Wrythe
SUTTON
Hook
Chessington
Stoneleigh
CHEAM
Nonsuch Park
West Ewell
Horton Country Park
Chessington World of Adventures
Claygate Common
Horton
EWELL
East Ewell
Henderson Hosp.
Sutton Hosp.
Royal Marsden Hosp.
Carshalton Beeches
Belmont
Banstead Downs
H.M. Prison Downview
H.M. Prison Highdown
EPSOM & EWELL
Malden Rushett
EPSOM
307
Epsom Common
Ashtead Common
North Looe
BANSTEAD
Woodmansterne
Pachesham Park
Ashtead
Nork
Epsom Gen. Hospital
Tattenham Corner
Epsom Downs Racecourse
Epsom Downs
Lower Ashtead
Ashtead Park
Ashtead Hospital
Langley Vale
Walton Downs
Burgh Heath
Chipstead Bottom
Tadworth
Kingswood
Tyrrell's Wood
Givons Grove
Headley
Walton on the Hill
Banstead Heath
Mugswell
Walton Heath
REIGATE & BANSTEAD
MOLE VALLEY
Mickleham
Pebble Coombe
Lower Kingswood
Mogador
Margery
Box Hill
Westhumble
M25
A24
A217
A240
A243
A3
0 ½ 1 mile
0 1 2 km

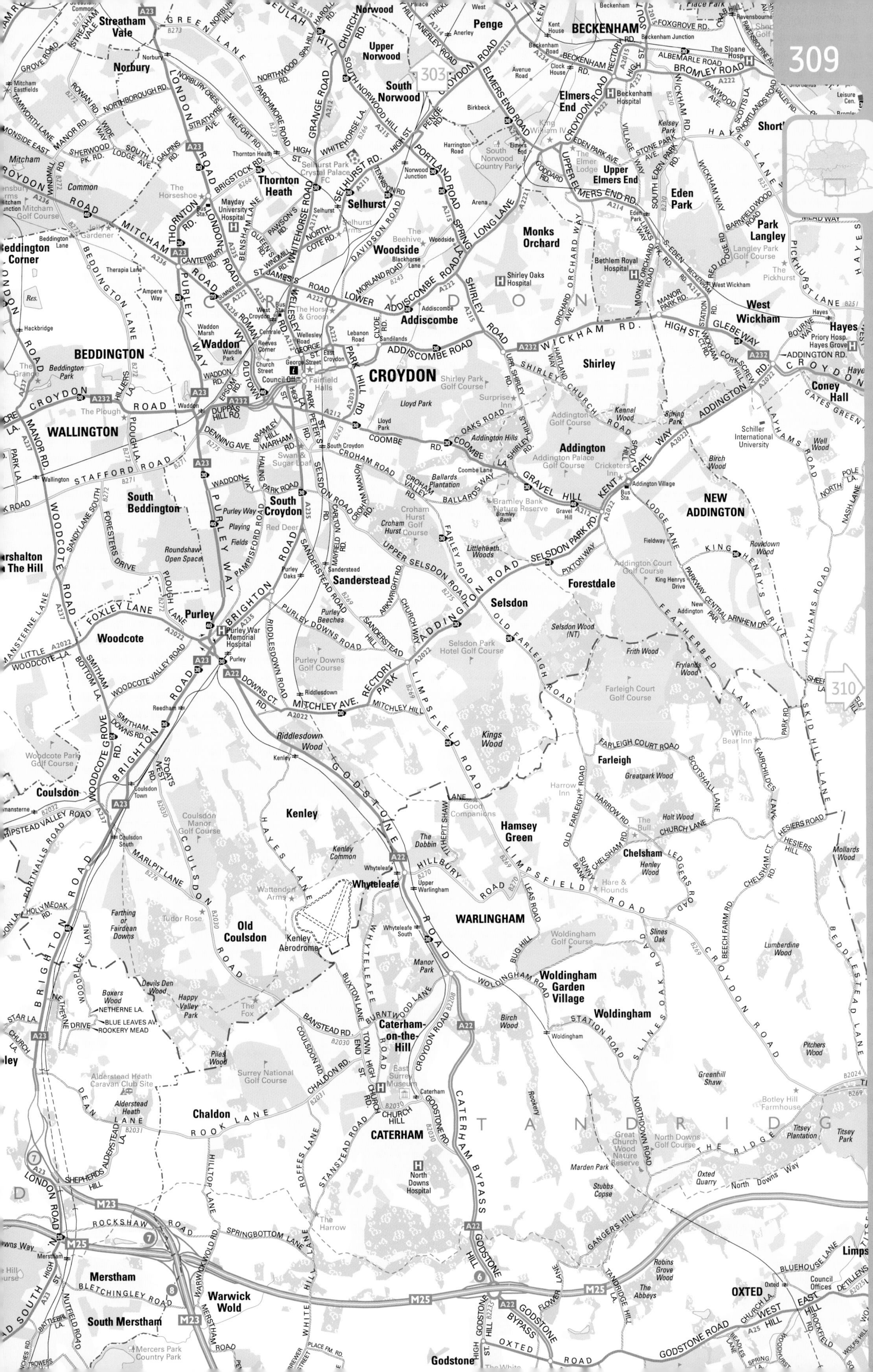
Streatham Vale
Norbury
Upper Norwood
Penge
BECKENHAM
South Norwood
303
Elmers End
Thornton Heath
Selhurst
Upper Elmers End
Eden Park
Mitcham
Common
Woodside
Monks Orchard
Park Langley
Beddington Corner
Addiscombe
West Wickham
Hayes
Waddon
CROYDON
Shirley
BEDDINGTON
Coney Hall
WALLINGTON
Addington
South Beddington
South Croydon
NEW ADDINGTON
Sanderstead
Forestdale
Selsdon
Purley
Woodcote
310
Farleigh
Coulsdon
Kenley
Hamsey Green
Chelsham
Whyteleafe
WARLINGHAM
Old Coulsdon
Woldingham Garden Village
Woldingham
Caterham-on-the-Hill
Chaldon
CATERHAM
T A N D R I D G
M23
M25
Merstham
Warwick Wold
South Merstham
OXTED
Godstone

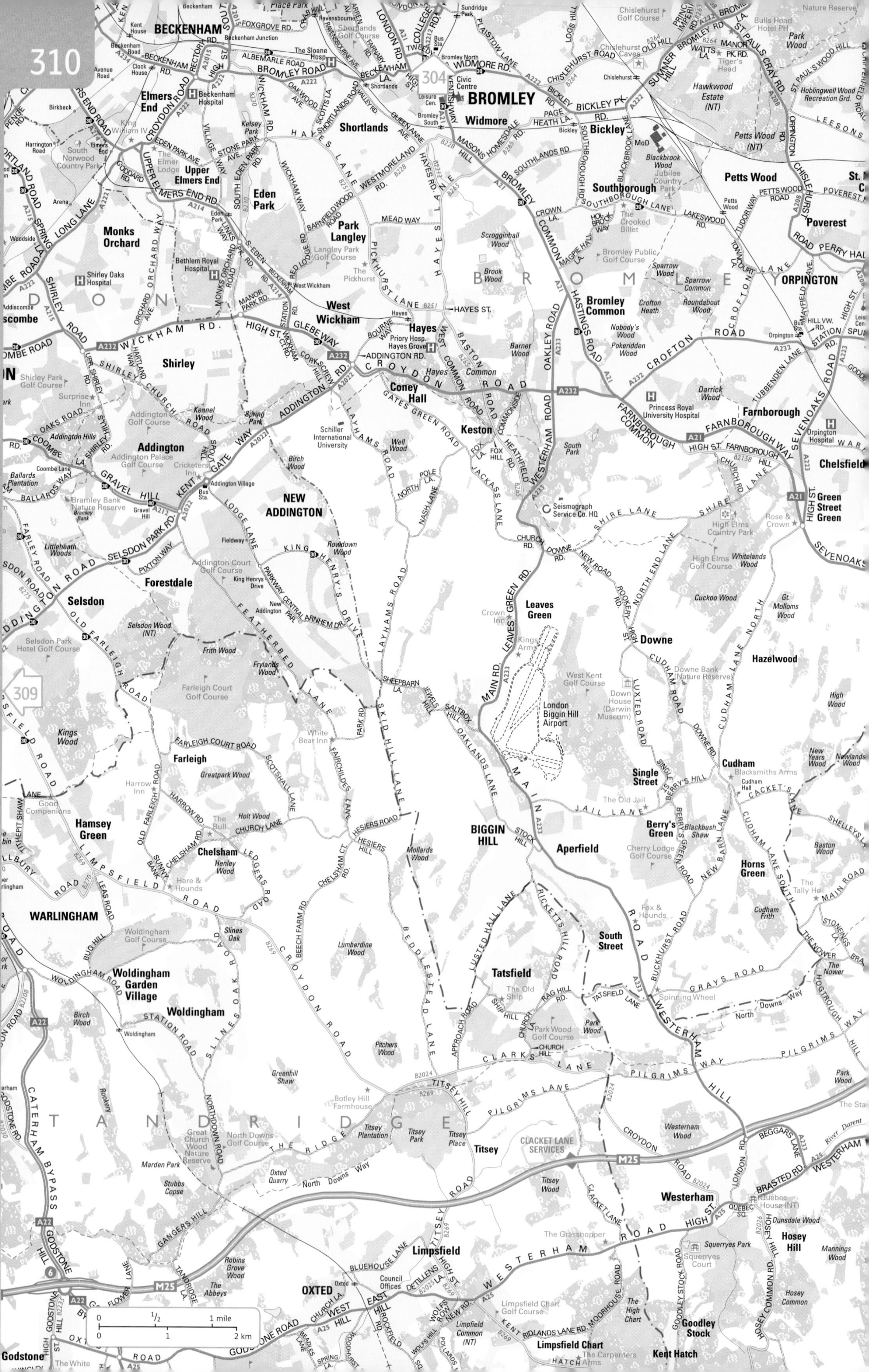
BECKENHAM
Elmers End
Shortlands
BROMLEY
Widmore
Bickley
Chislehurst Golf Course
Chislehurst Caves
Hawkwood Estate (NT)
Petts Wood (NT)
Petts Wood
Poverest
Southborough
Upper Elmers End
Eden Park
Monks Orchard
Park Langley
Langley Park Golf Course
Bromley Common
BROMLEY
ORPINGTON
West Wickham
Hayes
Shirley
Coney Hall
Keston
Farnborough
Princess Royal University Hospital
Orpington Hospital
Chelsfield
Green Street Green
Addington
Addington Palace Golf Course
NEW ADDINGTON
Selsdon
Forestdale
Farleigh Court Golf Course
Leaves Green
Downe
Down House (Darwin Museum)
London Biggin Hill Airport
West Kent Golf Course
High Elms Country Park
Hazelwood
Cudham
Single Street
Berry's Green
BIGGIN HILL
Aperfield
Farleigh
Hamsey Green
Chelsham
WARLINGHAM
Woldingham Garden Village
Woldingham
South Street
Tatsfield
Horns Green
TANDRIDGE
Titsey
CLACKET LANE SERVICES
Westerham
Hosey Hill
Limpsfield
OXTED
Limpsfield Chart
Goodley Stock
Kent Hatch
Godstone
CATERHAM BYPASS
M25
A21
A22
A25
A232
A233
304
309
0 1/2 1 mile
0 1 2 km

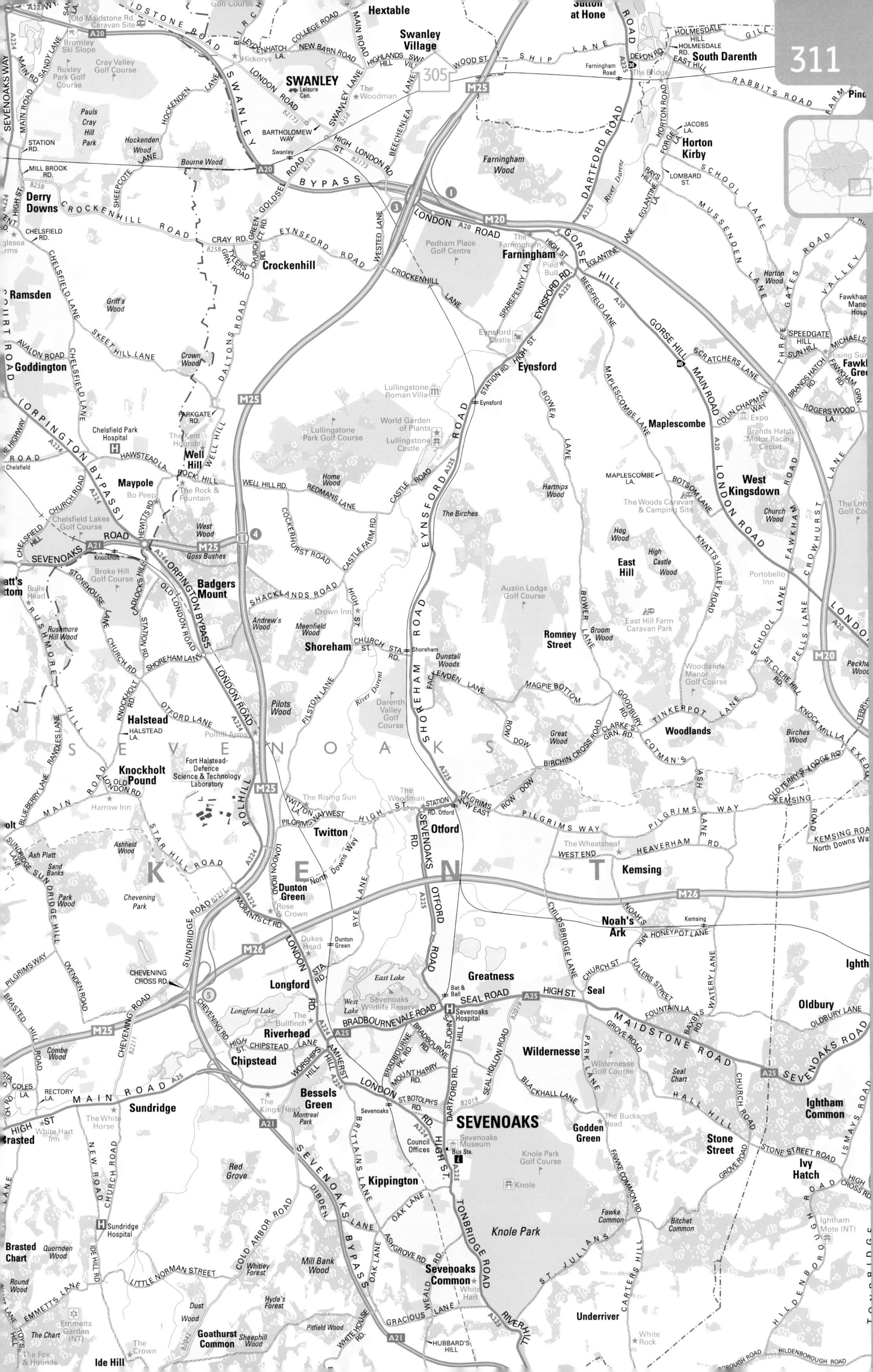
Hextable
Sutton at Hone
Swanley Village
305
SWANLEY
South Darenth
Horton Kirby
Farningham Wood
Farningham
Derry Downs
Crockenhill
Ramsden
Goddington
Eynsford
Lullingstone Roman Villa
Lullingstone Park Golf Course
Lullingstone Castle
Maplescombe
West Kingsdown
Chelsfield Park Hospital
Well Hill
Maypole
Badgers Mount
Shoreham
East Hill
Romney Street
Halstead
Knockholt Pound
Fort Halstead-Defence Science & Technology Laboratory
Woodlands
S E V E N O A K S
Otford
Twitton
Kemsing
K E N T
Dunton Green
Noah's Ark
Longford
Greatness
Seal
Oldbury
Riverhead
Chipstead
Wildernesse
Sundridge
Bessels Green
SEVENOAKS
Godden Green
Stone Street
Ightham Common
Ivy Hatch
Brasted
Kippington
Knole Park
Sevenoaks Common
Underriver
Goathurst Common
Ide Hill
Brasted Chart
Sundridge Hospital
M25
M20
M26
A20
A21
A25
A224
A225

M25 London orbital motorway

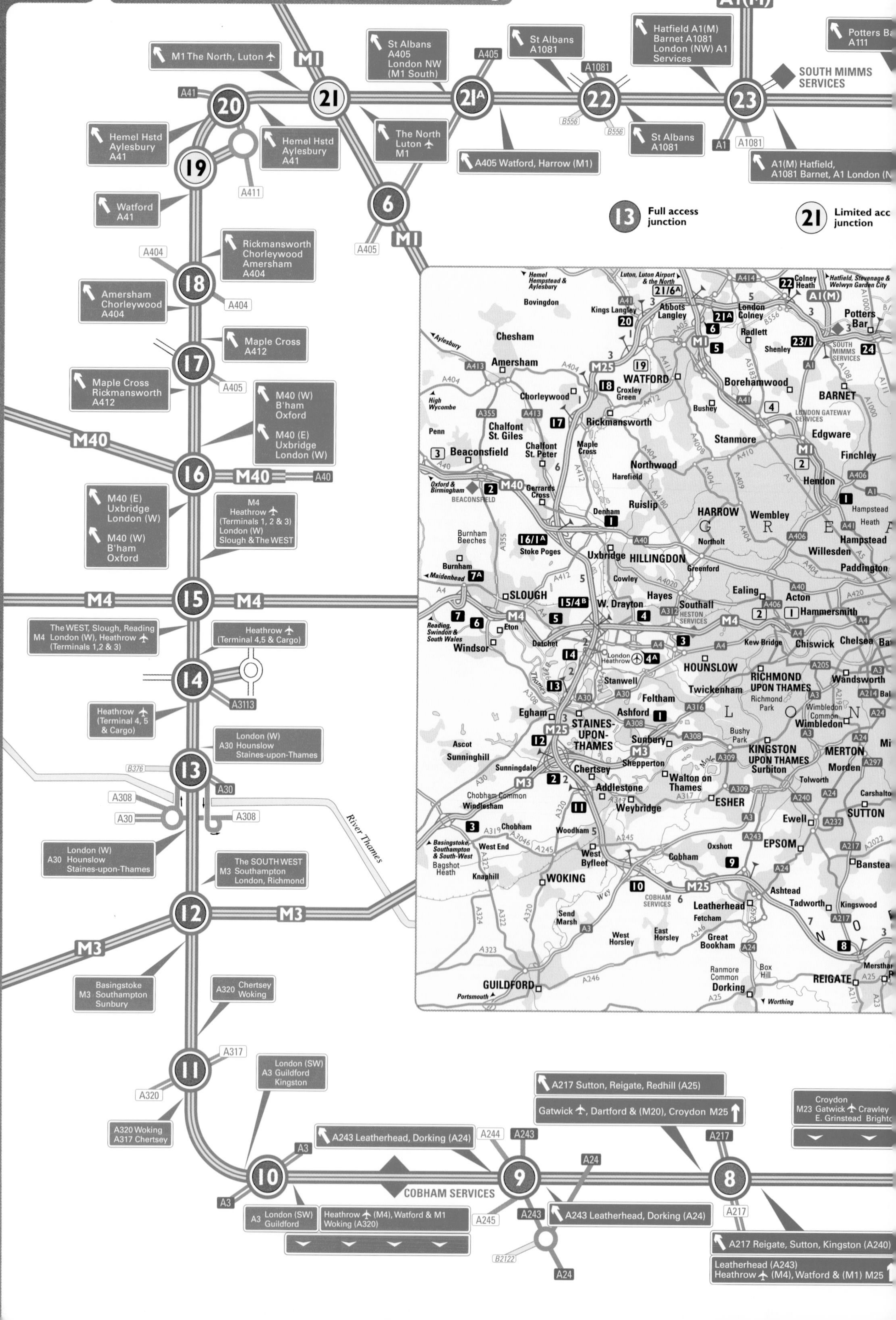

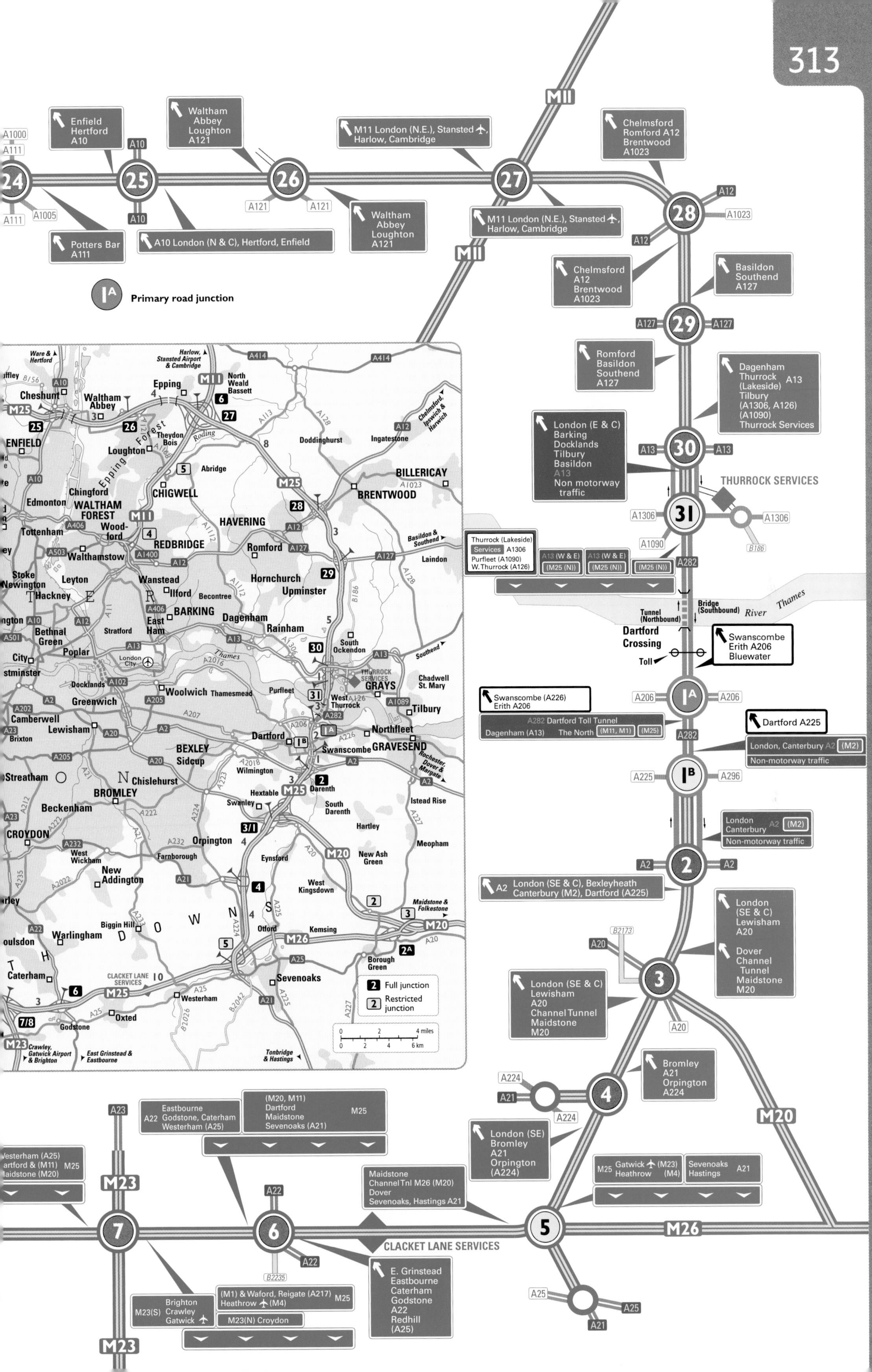
Enfield
Hertford
A10
Waltham
Abbey
Loughton
A121
M11 London (N.E.), Stansted, Harlow, Cambridge
Chelmsford
Romford A12
Brentwood
A1023
Potters Bar
A111
A10 London (N & C), Hertford, Enfield
Waltham
Abbey
Loughton
A121
M11 London (N.E.), Stansted, Harlow, Cambridge
Primary road junction
Chelmsford
A12
Brentwood
A1023
Basildon
Southend
A127
Romford
Basildon
Southend
A127
Dagenham
Thurrock (Lakeside) A13
Tilbury
(A1306, A126)
(A1090)
Thurrock Services
London (E & C)
Barking
Docklands
Tilbury
Basildon
A13
Non motorway traffic
THURROCK SERVICES
Thurrock (Lakeside)
Services A1306
Purfleet (A1090)
W. Thurrock (A126)
A13 (W & E) (M25 (N))
Bridge (Southbound)
Tunnel (Northbound)
Dartford Crossing
River Thames
Toll
Swanscombe
Erith A206
Bluewater
Swanscombe (A226)
Erith A206
A282 Dartford Toll Tunnel
Dagenham (A13) The North (M11, M1) (M25)
Dartford A225
London, Canterbury A2 (M2)
Non-motorway traffic
London
Canterbury A2 (M2)
Non-motorway traffic
A2 London (SE & C), Bexleyheath
Canterbury (M2), Dartford (A225)
London
(SE & C)
Lewisham
A20
Dover
Channel
Tunnel
Maidstone
M20
London (SE & C)
Lewisham
A20
Channel Tunnel
Maidstone
M20
Bromley
A21
Orpington
A224
London (SE)
Bromley
A21
Orpington
(A224)
M25 Gatwick (M23) Heathrow (M4)
Sevenoaks
Hastings A21
Maidstone
Channel Tnl M26 (M20)
Dover
Sevenoaks, Hastings A21
CLACKET LANE SERVICES
E. Grinstead
Eastbourne
Caterham
Godstone
A22
Redhill
(A25)
Eastbourne
A22 Godstone, Caterham
Westerham (A25)
(M20, M11)
Dartford
Maidstone
Sevenoaks (A21) M25
Westerham (A25)
Dartford & (M11) M25
Maidstone (M20)
M23(S) Brighton
Crawley
Gatwick
(M1) & Waford, Reigate (A217)
Heathrow (M4) M25
M23(N) Croydon
Full junction
Restricted junction
0 2 4 miles
0 2 4 6 km

Key to map symbols

- P Short stay car park
- P Mid stay car park
- P Long stay car park
- London underground station
- Railway station
- Monorail station
- Information centre for tourists
- Bus station
- Major hotel

Luton

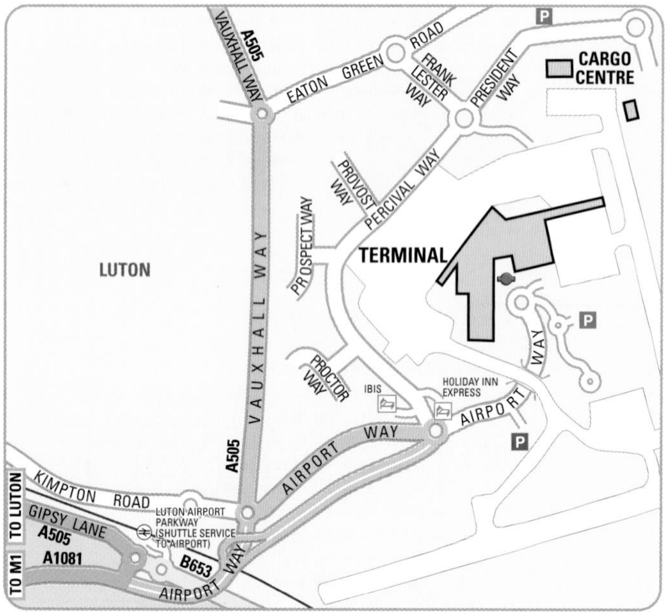

Tel. 01582 405100
www.london-luton.co.uk

Stansted

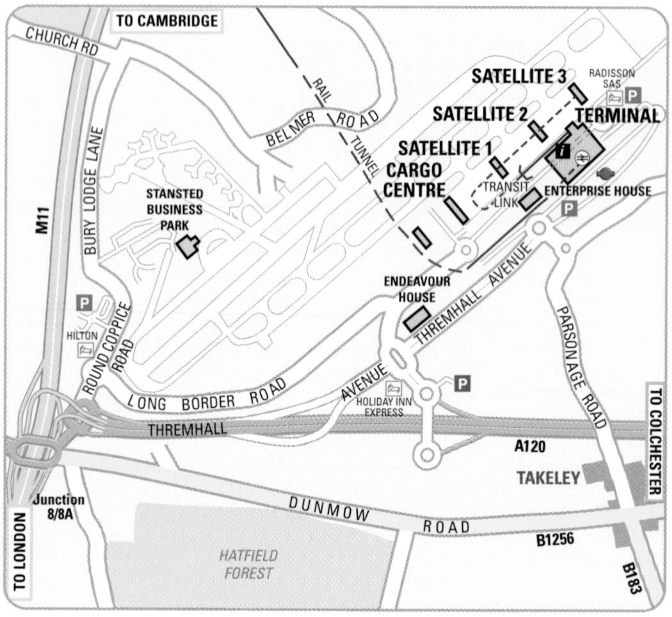

Tel. 0844 335 1803
www.stanstedairport.com

Heathrow

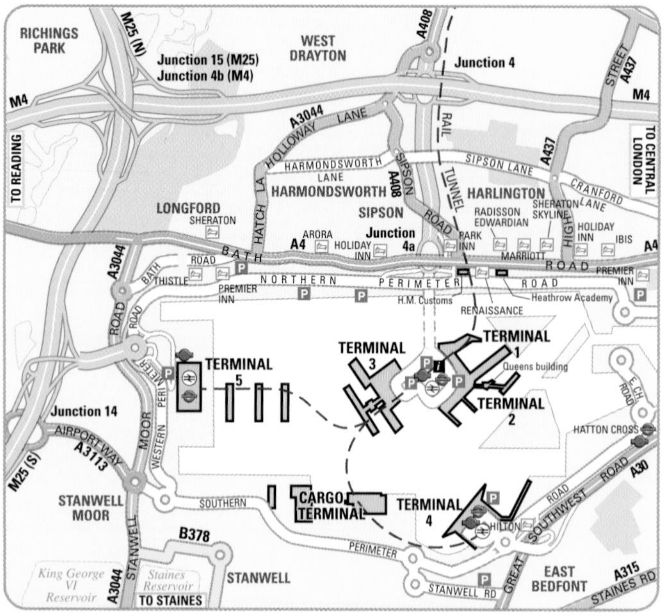

Tel. 0844 335 1801
www.heathrowairport.com

Gatwick

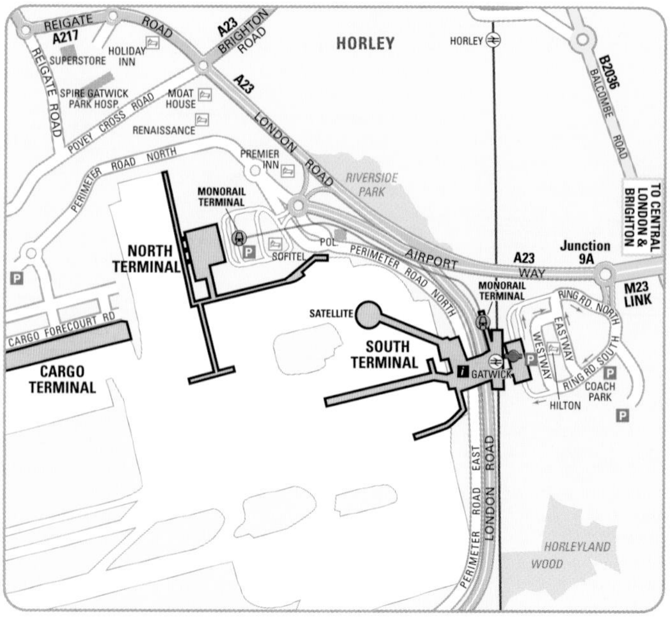

Tel. 0844 892 0322
www.gatwickairport.com

The London Congestion Charging Zone was introduced to reduce traffic congestion within Central London.

● The congestion charging zone operates inside the 'Inner Ring Road' linking Marylebone Road, Euston Road, Pentonville Road, Tower Bridge, Elephant and Castle, Vauxhall Bridge and Park Lane. The route around the zone is exempt from charge (see map below).

● The daily operating time is from 7am to 6pm, Monday to Friday, excluding public holidays and the period between Christmas Day and New Year's Day.

● Payment of the daily £10 Congestion Charge, either in advance or on the day of travel, allows the registered vehicle to enter, drive around and leave the congestion zone as many times as required on that one day.

● Payments can be made in a variety of ways but in all cases the vehicle registration number and the dates to be paid for must be given.
Charges can be paid:
- online at www.tfl.gov.uk/roadusers/congestioncharging
- by Congestion Charging Auto Pay by registering online
- by phone on 0845 900 1234
- by text message to 81099 for drivers who have pre-registered on the website or telephone.
- by post, ten days before travel, by requesting an application form from Congestion Charging, PO Box 4780, Worthing, BN11 9PQ, or downloading the form from the website and posting to the same address.
- at newsagents, convenience stores or petrol stations throughout the Greater London area where you see the Congestion Charging sign or the PayPoint logo.

● Further information, including vehicles eligible for exemption or a discount, can be found on the website **www.tfl.gov.uk/roadusers/congestioncharging** or by telephoning 0845 900 1234.

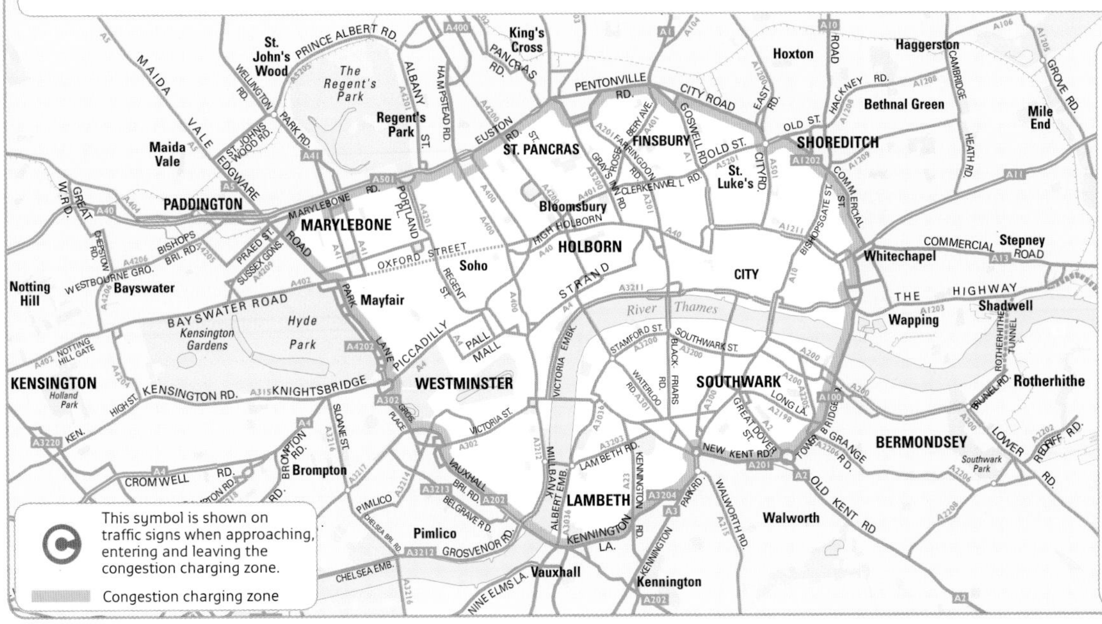

● Residents inside the congestion zone are eligible for a 90% discount upon payment of an annual £10 registration fee.

● On paying the charge the car registration number is held on a database. Cameras in and around the congestion zone record all vehicle number plates and check them against the database.
- Drivers can pay the £10 charge until midnight on the day of travel.
- Drivers who forget to pay by midnight on the day of travel can pay by midnight on the following charging day but they will then incur a £2 surcharge making the total charge £12. The £12 charge can only be paid by telephone or online.

Any driver who has not paid before midnight on the following charging day will be sent a £120 Penalty Charge Notice (PCN).
Payment within 14 days will reduce this to £60. Failure to pay within 28 days will result in the penalty being increased to £180.

Low Emission Zone

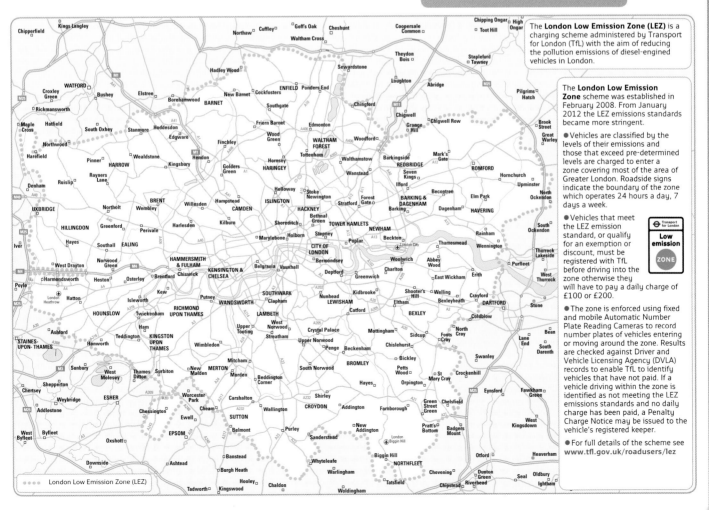

The **London Low Emission Zone (LEZ)** is a charging scheme administered by Transport for London (TfL) with the aim of reducing the pollution emissions of diesel-engined vehicles in London.

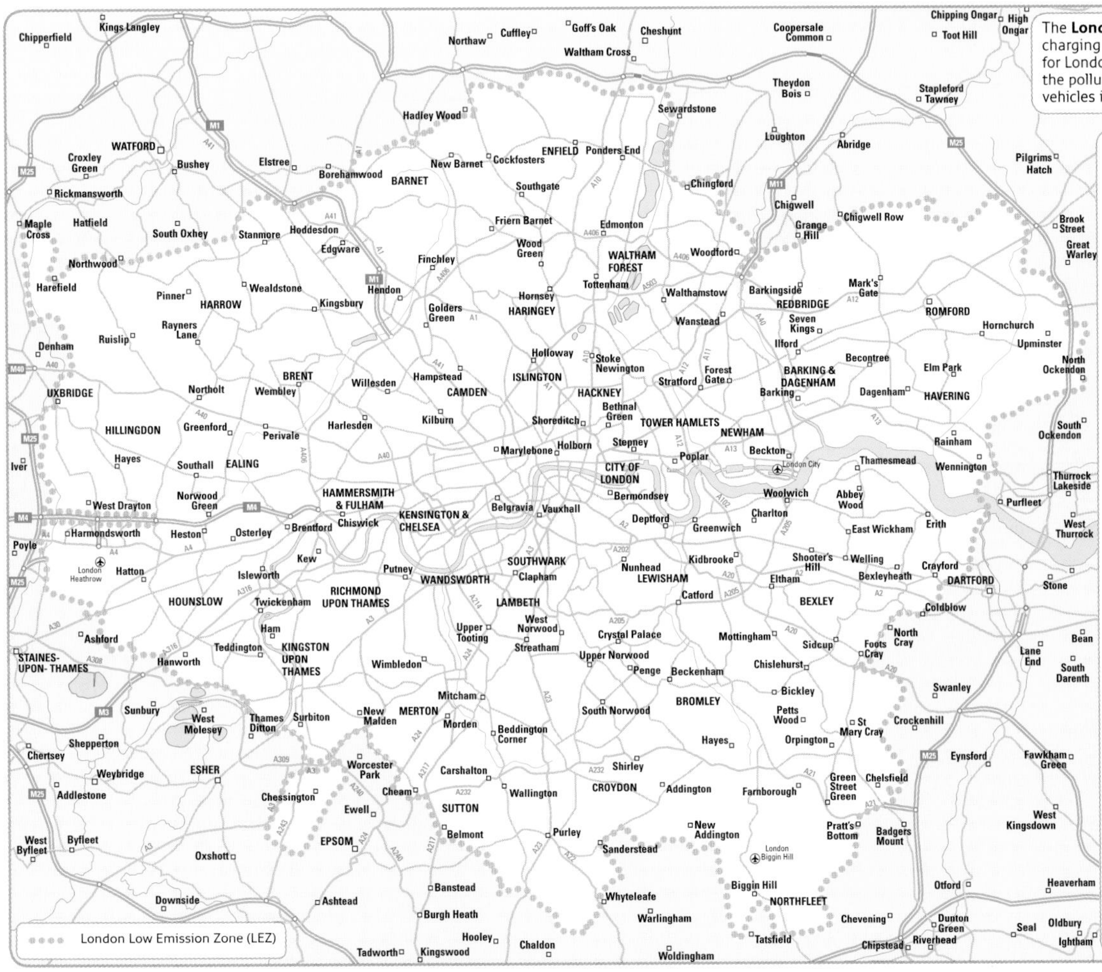

The **London Low Emission Zone** scheme was established in February 2008. From January 2012 the LEZ emissions standards became more stringent.

● Vehicles are classified by the levels of their emissions and those that exceed pre-determined levels are charged to enter a zone covering most of the area of Greater London. Roadside signs indicate the boundary of the zone which operates 24 hours a day, 7 days a week.

● Vehicles that meet the LEZ emission standard, or qualify for an exemption or discount, must be registered with TfL before driving into the zone otherwise they will have to pay a daily charge of £100 or £200.

● The zone is enforced using fixed and mobile Automatic Number Plate Reading Cameras to record number plates of vehicles entering or moving around the zone. Results are checked against Driver and Vehicle Licensing Agency (DVLA) records to enable TfL to identify vehicles that have not paid. If a vehicle driving within the zone is identified as not meeting the LEZ emissions standards and no daily charge has been paid, a Penalty Charge Notice may be issued to the vehicle's registered keeper.

● For full details of the scheme see **www.tfl.gov.uk/roadusers/lez**

Notes on how to use the index

The index starting on page 318 combines entries for street names, place names, places of interest, stations, hospitals, schools, colleges and universities.

Place names are shown in capital letters,
e.g. **ACTON**, W3 .... **160** CN74
These include towns, villages and other localities within the area covered by this atlas.

Places of interest are shown with a star symbol,
e.g. ★ **British Mus, The** WC1 ... **17** P7
These include parks, museums, galleries, other important buildings and tourist attractions.

Other features are shown by symbols as listed :-

- Railway station
- London Overground station
- London Underground station
- Docklands Light Railway station
- Tramlink station
- Pedestrian ferry landing stage
- Bus station
- Hospital
- School
- College
- University
- Road junction
- Selected industrial estate / commercial building
- Selected major shop / shopping centre / market

All other entries are for street names.

When there is more than one feature with exactly the same name then that name is shown only once in the index.
It is then followed by a list of entries for each postal district that contains a feature with that same name. London postal district references are given first in alpha-numeric order and are followed by either the post town or locality in alphabetical order. For example, there are three streets called **Ardley Close** in this atlas and the index entry shows that one of these is in London postal district NW10, one is in London postal district SE6 and one is in Ruislip HA4.
e.g. **Ardley Cl**, NW10 .... **140** CS62
SE6............................. **205** DY90
Ruislip HA4 .... **137** BQ59

In cases where there are two or more streets of the same name in the same postal area, extra information is given in brackets to aid location.
Some postal areas are abbreviated and a full list of locality and post town abbreviations used in this atlas is given on the following page.

All entries are followed by the page number and grid reference on which the name will be found. So, in the example above, **Ardley Close,** NW10 will be found on page **140** in square CS62.

All entries are indexed to the largest scale map on which they are shown.

The index also contains some features which are not actually named on the maps because there is not enough space. In these cases the adjoining or nearest named thoroughfare to such a street is shown in *italic.* The reference indicates where the unnamed street is located *off* the named thoroughfare.
e.g. **Baird Cl**, E10 *off Marconi Rd*. **145** EA60

A strict letter-by-letter alphabetical order is followed in this index. All non-alphabetic characters such as spaces, hyphens or apostrophes have not been included in the index order. For example **Belle Vue Road** and **Bellevue Road** will be found listed together.

Names beginning with a definite article (i.e. **The**) are indexed from their second word onwards with the definite article being placed at the end of the name.
e.g. **Avenue, The,** E4................. **123** ED51

Standard terms such as **Avenue, Close, Rise** and **Road** are abbreviated in the index but are ordered alphabetically as if given in full. So, for example, **Abbots Ri** comes before **Abbots Rd.** A list of these abbreviations is given below.

General abbreviations

A&E	Accident & Emergency
Acad	Academy
All	Alley
App	Approach
Apts	Apartments
Arc	Arcade
Assoc	Association
Av	Avenue
Ave	Avenue
BUPA	British United Provident Association
Bdy	Broadway
Bk	Bank
Bldg	Building
Bldgs	Buildings
Boul	Boulevard
Bowl	Bowling
Br	Bridge
C of E	Church of England
Cath	Cathedral, Catholic
CCC	County Cricket Club
Cem	Cemetery
Cen	Central, Centre
Cft	Croft
Cfts	Crofts
Ch	Church
Chyd	Churchyard
Circ	Circus
Cl	Close
Co	County
Coll	College
Comb	Combined
Comm	Community
Comp	Comprehensive
Conf	Conference
Cont	Continuing
Conv	Convent
Cor	Corner
Cors	Corners
Cotts	Cottages
Cres	Crescent
Ct	Court
Ctyd	Courtyard
Del	Delivery
Dep	Depot
Dept	Department
Dev	Development
Dr	Drive
Dws	Dwellings
E	East
Ed	Education, Educational
Embk	Embankment
Est	Estate
Ex	Exchange
Exhib	Exhibition
Ext	Extension
FC	Football Club
Fit Cen	Fitness Centre
Fld	Field
Flds	Fields
Fm	Farm
GM	Grant Maintained
Gall	Gallery
Gar	Garage
Gdn	Garden
Gdns	Gardens
Gen	General
Gra	Grange
Gram	Grammar
Grd	Ground
Grds	Grounds
Grn	Green
Grns	Greens
Gro	Grove
Gros	Groves
Gt	Great
HQ	Headquarters
Ho	House
Hos	Houses
Hosp	Hospital
HPRU	Human Psycho-pharmacology Research Unit
Hts	Heights
Ind	Industrial
Indep	Independent
Inf	Infant(s)
Inst	Institute
Int	International
JM	Junior Mixed
JMI	Junior Mixed & Infant(s)
Jun	Junior
Junct	Junction
La	Lane
Las	Lanes
Lib	Library
Lit	Literary
Lo	Lodge
Lwr	Lower
Mans	Mansions
Med	Medical
Med	Medicine
Mem	Memorial
Met	Metropolitan
Mid	Middle
Mkt	Market
Ms	Mews
Mt	Mount
Mus	Museum
N	North
NHS	National Health Service
Nat	National
Nurs	Nursery
Off	Office
PO	Post Office
PRU	Pupil Referral Unit
Par	Parade
Pas	Passage
Pk	Park
Pl	Place
Pol	Police
Poly	Polytechnic
Prec	Precinct
Prep	Preparatory
Prim	Primary
Prom	Promenade
Pt	Point
Quad	Quadrant
RC	Roman Catholic
Rbt	Roundabout
Rd	Road
Rds	Roads
Rehab	Rehabilitation
Ri	Rise
S	South
Sch	School
Schs	Schools
Sec	Secondary
Sen	Senior
Shop	Shopping
Spec	Special
Sq	Square
St	Street
St.	Saint
Sta	Station
Sts	Streets
Sub	Subway
TA	Territorial Army
Tech	Technical, Technology
Tenn	Tennis
Ter	Terrace
Thea	Theatre
Trd	Trading
Twr	Tower
Twrs	Towers
Uni	University
Upr	Upper
VA	Voluntary Aided
VC	Voluntary Controlled
Vet	Veterinary
Vil	Villas
Vil	Villa
Vw	View
W	West
Wd	Wood
Wds	Woods
Wf	Wharf
Wk	Walk
Wks	Works
Yd	Yard

Locality & post town abbreviations

Note: In the following list of abbreviations post towns are in **bold** type.

Abb.L.	**Abbots Langley**
Abin.Com.	Abinger Common
Abin.Ham.	Abinger Hammer
Add.	**Addlestone**
Alb.Hth	Albury Heath
Ald.	Aldenham
Amer.	**Amersham**
Amer.O.T.	Amersham Old Town
Art.	Artington
Ash.Grn	Ashley Green
Ashf.	**Ashford**
Ashtd.	**Ashtead**
Ayot St.P.	Ayot Saint Peter
B.End	Bourne End
B.Stort.	Bishop's Stortford
Bad.Dene	Badgers Dene
Bad.Mt	Badgers Mount
Bans.	**Banstead**
Bark.	**Barking**
Barn.	**Barnet**
Barne.	Barnehurst
Beac.	**Beaconsfield**
Beck.	**Beckenham**
Bedd.	Beddington
Bedd.Cor.	Beddington Corner
Bell.	Bellingdon
Belv.	**Belvedere**
Berk.	**Berkhamsted**
Berry's Grn	Berry's Green
Bet.	**Betchworth**
Bex.	**Bexley**
Bexh.	**Bexleyheath**
Bigg.H.	Biggin Hill
Birch Grn	Birch Green
Bkhm	Bookham
Bletch.	Bletchingley
Borwd.	**Borehamwood**
Bov.	Bovingdon
Box H.	Box Hill
Bramfld	Bramfield
Brent.	**Brentford**
Brick.Wd	Bricket Wood
Broad.Com.	Broadley Common
Brock.	Brockham
Brom.	Bromley
Brook.Pk	Brookmans Park
Brox.	**Broxbourne**
Brwd.	**Brentwood**
Buck.H.	**Buckhurst Hill**
Burgh Hth	Burgh Heath
Burn.	Burnham
Bushey Hth	Bushey Heath
Carp.Pk	Carpenders Park
Cars.	**Carshalton**
Cat.	**Caterham**
Ch.End	Church End
Ch.Lang.	Church Langley
Ch.St.G.	**Chalfont Saint Giles**
Chad.Hth	Chadwell Heath
Chad.Spr.	Chadwell Springs
Chad.St.M.	Chadwell Saint Mary
Chaff.Hun.	Chafford Hundred
Chal.St.P.	Chalfont Saint Peter
Chan.Cr.	Chandlers Cross
Chap.End	Chapmore End
Charl.	Charlwood
Chel.	Chelsham
Chels.	Chelsfield
Cher.	**Chertsey**
Chesh.	**Chesham**
Chesh.B.	Chesham Bois
Chess.	**Chessington**
Chev.	Chevening
Chig.	**Chigwell**
Chilw.	Chilworth
Chipper.	Chipperfield
Chis.	**Chislehurst**
Chob.Com.	Chobham Common
Chorl.	Chorleywood
Chsht	Cheshunt
Cipp.	Cippenham
Clay.	Claygate
Cob.	**Cobham**
Cockfos.	Cockfosters
Cole Grn	Cole Green
Colesh.	Coleshill
Coll.Row	Collier Row
Coln.Hth	Colney Heath
Coln.St	Colney Street
Colnbr.	Colnbrook
Cooper.	Coopersale
Couls.	**Coulsdon**
Cran.	Cranford
Craw.	Crawley
Cray.	Crayford
Crock.	Crockenhill
Crock.H.	Crockham Hill
Crox.Grn	Croxley Green
Croy.	**Croydon**
Dag.	**Dagenham**
Dance.H.	Dancers Hill
Dart.	**Dartford**
Denh.	Denham
Dor.	**Dorking**
Dorney R.	Dorney Reach
Down.	Downside
Dunt.Grn	Dunton Green
E.Barn.	East Barnet
E.Bed.	East Bedfont
E.Burn.	East Burnham
E.Clan.	East Clandon
E.Ewell	East Ewell
E.Hors.	East Horsley
E.Mol.	**East Molesey**
E.Til.	East Tilbury
Earls.	Earlswood
Eastcote Vill.	Eastcote Village
Eden.	Edenbridge
Edg.	**Edgware**
Eff.	Effingham
Eff.Junct.	Effingham Junction
Egh.	**Egham**
Elm Pk	Elm Park
Elm.Wds	Elmstead Woods
Els.	Elstree
Enf.	**Enfield**
Eng.Grn	Englefield Green
Epp.	**Epping**
Epp.Grn	Epping Green
Epp.Upl.	Epping Upland
Epsom Com.	Epsom Common
Essen.	Essendon
Ewell E.	Ewell East
Ewell W.	Ewell West
Eyns.	Eynsford
Far.Grn	Farley Green
Farn.Com.	Farnham Common
Farn.Royal	Farnham Royal
Farnboro.	Farnborough
Farnc.	Farncombe
Fawk.	Fawkham
Fawk.Grn	Fawkham Green
Felt.	**Feltham**
Fetch.	Fetcham
Flack.Hth	Flackwell Heath
Flam.	Flamstead
Flaun.	Flaunden
Fnghm	Farningham
Forty Grn	Forty Green
Frog.	Frogmore
Gat.	Gatwick
Gdmg.	Godalming
Gdse.	**Godstone**
Geo.Grn	George Green
Ger.Cr.	**Gerrards Cross**
Gidea Pk	Gidea Park
Gilston Pk	Gilston Park
Godden Grn	Godden Green
Goms.	Gomshall
Grav.	**Gravesend**
Green.	**Greenhithe**
Grn St Grn	Green Street Green
Grnf.	**Greenford**
Gt Amwell	Great Amwell
Gt Warley	Great Warley
Guil.	**Guildford**
H.Wyc.	High Wycombe
Hackbr.	Hackbridge
Had.Wd	Hadley Wood
Halst.	Halstead
Han.	Hanworth
Har.	**Harrow**
Har.Hill	Harrow on the Hill
Har.Wld	Harrow Weald
Hare.	Harefield
Harl.	**Harlow**
Harling.	Harlington
Harm.	Harmondsworth
Harold Wd	Harold Wood
Hast.	Hastingwood
Hat.	**Hatfield**
Hat.Hth	Hatfield Heath
Hav.at.Bow.	Havering-atte-Bower
Haz.	Hazlemere
Hedg.	Hedgerley
Hem.H.	**Hemel Hempstead**
Herons.	Heronsgate
Hert.	**Hertford**
Hert.Hth	Hertford Heath
Hext.	Hextable
High Barn.	High Barnet
Hinch.Wd	Hinchley Wood
Hkwd	Hookwood
Hlgdn	Hillingdon
Hmptn H.	Hampton Hill
Hmptn W.	Hampton Wick
Hmptn.	**Hampton**
Hodd.	**Hoddesdon**
Holm.	Holmwood
Holm.St.M.	Holmbury Saint Mary
Holt.	Holtspur
Holy.	Holyport
Horl.	**Horley**
Horn.	**Hornchurch**
Hort.Kir.	Horton Kirby
Houns.	**Hounslow**
Houns.W.	Hounslow West
Hunt.Br.	Hunton Bridge
Hutt.	Hutton
Hyde Hth	Hyde Heath
Ickhm	Ickenham
Ilf.	**Ilford**
Islw.	**Isleworth**
Ken.	**Kenley**
Kes.	**Keston**
Kgfld	Kingfield
Kgswd	Kingswood
Kings L.	**Kings Langley**
Kings.T.	**Kingston upon Thames**
Knap.	Knaphill
Knock.	Knockholt
Knock.P.	Knockholt Pound
Knot.Grn	Knotty Green
Lamb.End	Lambourne End
Let.Hth	Letchmore Heath
Letty Grn	Letty Green
Lmpfld	Limpsfield
Lmpfld Cht	Limpsfield Chart
Lmsfd	Lemsford
Lon.Col.	London Colney
Lon.Gat.Air.	London Gatwick Airport
Lon.Hthrw Air.	London Heathrow Airport
Lon.Hthrw Air.N	London Heathrow Airport N
Long Dit.	Long Ditton
Long.	**Longfield**
Longcr.	Longcross
Loud.	Loudwater
Loug.	**Loughton**
Lt.Berk.	Little Berkhamsted
Lt.Chal.	Little Chalfont
Lt.Hth	Little Heath
Lt.Warley	Little Warley
Lthd.	**Leatherhead**
Lvsdn	Leavesden
Lwfld Hth	Lowfield Heath
Lwr Kgswd	Lower Kingswood
Lwr Naze.	Lower Nazeing
Magd.Lav.	Magdalen Laver
Maid.	Maidenhead
Map.Cr.	Maple Cross
Mark Hall N.	Mark Hall North
Match.Grn	Matching Green
Match.Tye	Matching Tye
Mdgrn	Middlegreen
Merst.	Merstham
Mick.	Mickleham
Mid Holm.	Mid Holmwood
Mimbr.	Mimbridge
Mitch.	**Mitcham**
Mitch.Com.	Mitcham Common
Mord.	**Morden**
Mots.Pk	Motspur Park
Mtnsg	Mountnessing
N.Har.	North Harrow
N.Holm.	North Holmwood
N.Mal.	**New Malden**
N.Mymms	North Mymms
N.Ock.	North Ockendon
N.Stfd	North Stifford
N.Wld Bas.	North Weald Bassett
N.Wld Bas.N.	North Weald Bassett North
Nave.	Navestock
Nave.S.	Navestock Side
Naze.	Nazeing
Naze.Gate	Nazeing Gate
New Adgtn	New Addington
New Barn.	New Barnet
Newgate St	Newgate Street
Northumb.Hth	Northumberland Heath
Nthch	Northchurch
Nthflt	Northfleet
Nthlt.	**Northolt**
Nthwd.	**Northwood**
Nutfld	Nutfield
Oakl.	Oaklands
Oakley Grn	Oakley Green
Ock.	Ockham
Old Harl.	Old Harlow
Old Wind.	Old Windsor
Old Wok.	Old Woking
Ong.	Ongar
Ons.Vill.	Onslow Village
Orch.L.	Orchard Leigh
Orp.	**Orpington**
Ott.	Ottershaw
Oxt.	**Oxted**
Pans.	Panshanger
Park St	Park Street
Peasl.	Peaslake
Peasm.	Peasmarsh
Petts Wd	Petts Wood
Picc.End	Piccotts End
Pilg.Hat.	Pilgrim's Hatch
Pnr.	**Pinner**
Pond.End	Ponders End
Port.Wd	Porters Wood
Pot.B.	**Potters Bar**
Pott.Cr.	Potters Crouch
Pott.End	Potten End
Pott.St	Potter Street
Pr.Bot.	Pratt's Bottom
Pur.	**Purley**
Purf.	**Purfleet**
Putt.	Puttenham
Rad.	**Radlett**
Rain.	**Rainham**
Ran.Com.	Ranmore Common
Rayners La	Rayners Lane
Red.	**Redhill**
Redbn	Redbourn
Reig.	**Reigate**
Rich.	**Richmond**
Rick.	**Rickmansworth**
Rod.Val.	Roding Valley
Roe Grn	Roe Green
Rom.	**Romford**
Rosh.	Rosherville
Ruis.	**Ruislip**
Runny.	Runnymede
Rush Grn	Rush Green
Rvrhd	Riverhead
Rydes.	Rydeshill
S.Croy.	**South Croydon**
S.Darenth	South Darenth
S.Har.	South Harrow
S.Holm.	South Holmwood
S.Merst.	South Merstham
S.Mimms	South Mimms
S.Nutfld	South Nutfield
S.Ock.	**South Ockendon**
S.Oxhey	South Oxhey
S.Park	South Park
S.Ruis.	South Ruislip
S.Stfd	South Stifford
S.Wld	South Weald
S.le H.	Stanford-le-Hope
Salf.	Salfords
Sand.	Sandridge
Saw.	**Sawbridgeworth**
Scad.Pk	Scadbury Park
Seer Grn	Seer Green
Send M.	Send Marsh
Sev.	**Sevenoaks**
Shalf.	Shalford
Sham.Grn	Shamley Green
Sheer.	Sheerwater
Shenf.	Shenfield
Shep.	**Shepperton**
Shipley Br	Shipley Bridge
Shore.	Shoreham
Short.	Shortlands
Sid.	**Sidcup**
Slade Grn	Slade Green
Slou.	**Slough**
St.Alb.	**Saint Albans**
St.Geo.H.	Saint George's Hill
St.John's	Saint John's
St.M.Cray	Saint Mary Cray
St.P.Cray	Saint Paul's Cray
Stai.	**Staines-upon-Thames**
Stan.	**Stanmore**
Stanboro.	Stanborough
Stanfd.Riv.	Stanford Rivers
Stans.Abb.	Stanstead Abbotts
Stanw.	Stanwell
Stanw.M.	Stanwell Moor
Stap.Abb.	Stapleford Abbotts
Stap.Taw.	Stapleford Tawney
Sthflt	Southfleet
Sthl Grn	Southall Green
Sthl.	**Southall**
Stoke D'Ab.	Stoke D'Abernon
Stoke P.	Stoke Poges
Strood Grn	Strood Green
Sun.	Sunbury-on-Thames
Sund.	Sundridge
Surb.	**Surbiton**
Sutt.	**Sutton**
Sutt.Grn	Sutton Green
Sutt.H.	Sutton at Hone
Swan.	**Swanley**
Swans.	**Swanscombe**
T.Ditt.	**Thames Ditton**
Tad.	**Tadworth**
Tand.	Tandridge
Tap.	Taplow
Tats.	Tatsfield
Tedd.	**Teddington**
Th.Hth.	**Thornton Heath**
They.B.	Theydon Bois
They.Gar.	Theydon Garnon
They.Mt	Theydon Mount
Thnwd	Thornwood
Thres.B.	Threshers Bush
Til.	**Tilbury**
Tkgtn	Tokyngton
Turnf.	Turnford
Twick.	**Twickenham**
Tyr.Wd	Tyrrell's Wood
Tytten.	Tyttenhanger
Undrvr	Underriver
Upmin.	**Upminster**
Uxb.	**Uxbridge**
Vir.W.	**Virginia Water**
W.Byf.	**West Byfleet**
W.Clan.	West Clandon
W.Ewell	West Ewell
W.Hors.	West Horsley
W.Hyde	West Hyde
W.Mol.	**West Molesey**
W.Thur.	West Thurrock
W.Til.	West Tilbury
W.Wick.	**West Wickham**
Wal.Abb.	**Waltham Abbey**
Wal.Cr.	**Waltham Cross**
Wall.	**Wallington**
Walt.	**Walton-on-Thames**
Walt.Hill	Walton on the Hill
Warl.	**Warlingham**
Wat.	**Watford**
Wat.Oak.	Water Oakley
Waterf.	Waterford
Wdf.Grn.	**Woodford Green**
Wdhm	Woodham
Wealds.	Wealdstone
Well.	**Welling**
Welw.	Welwyn
Welw.G.C.	**Welwyn Garden City**
Wem.	**Wembley**
Wenn.	Wennington
West Dr.	**West Drayton**
West.	**Westerham**
Westc.	Westcott
Westh.	Westhumble
Wey.	**Weybridge**
Wheat.	Wheathampstead
Whel.Hill	Whelpley Hill
Whiteley Vill.	Whiteley Village
Whyt.	Whyteleafe
Wilm.	Wilmington
Winch.Hill	Winchmore Hill
Wind.	**Windsor**
Wink.	Winkfield
Wok.	**Woking**
Wold.	Woldingham
Won.	Wonersh
Woob.Grn	Wooburn Green
Woob.Moor	Wooburn Moor
Wor.Pk.	**Worcester Park**
Worp.	Worplesdon
Wrays.	Wraysbury
Wyc.End	Wycombe End
Yiew.	Yiewsley

1 - Add

● 1 Canada Sq, E14 34 C3
Uni 200 Pentonville Rd, Hall of Res, N1 18 C1
★ 2 Willow Rd, NW3 142 DE63
● 30 St. Mary Axe, EC3 *off St. Mary Axe* 19 P8
● 99 Bishopsgate, EC2 *off Bishopsgate* 19 N8

A

Aaron Hill Rd, E6 25 M6
Abady Ho, SW1 *off Page St* 29 P8
Abberley Ms, SW4 *off Cedars Rd* 183 DH83
Abberton Wk, Rain. RM13 *off Ongar Way* 169 FE66
Abbess Cl, E6 25 H7
SW2 203 DP88
Abbess Ter, Loug. IG10 107 EP41
Abbeville Ms, SW4 183 DK84
Abbeville Rd, N8 *off Barrington Rd* 143 DK56
SW4 203 DJ86
Abbey Av, St.Alb. AL3 64 CA23
Wembley HA0 160 CL68
● **Abbey Business Cen**, SW8 41 K6
Abbey Chyd, Wal.Abb. EN9 89 EC33
Abbey Cl, E5 144 DU63
SW8 41 P6
Hayes UB3 157 BV74
Northolt UB5 *off Invicta Gro* 158 BZ69
Pinner HA5 137 BV55
Romford RM1 149 FG58
Slough SL1 153 AL73
Woking GU22 249 BE116
Sch **Abbey C of E Prim Sch, The**, St.Alb. AL1 *off Grove Rd* 65 CD21
Abbey Ct, Wal.Abb. EN9 89 EB34
Abbey Cres, Belv. DA17 188 FA77
Abbeydale Cl, Harl. CM17 74 EW16
Abbeydale Rd, Wem. HA0 160 CN67
Abbey Dr, SW17 *off Church La* 202 DG92
Abbots Langley WD5 81 BU32
Dartford DA2 209 FE89
Staines-upon-Thames TW18 216 BJ98
Abbeyfield Cl, Mitch. CR4 222 DE96
Abbeyfield Est, SE16 *off Abbeyfield Rd* 32 G8
Abbeyfield Rd, SE16 32 G8
Abbeyfields Cl, NW10 160 CN68
Abbeyfields Mobile Home Pk, Cher. KT16 216 BK101
Abbey Gdns, NW8 15 N1
SE16 32 D8
SW1 *off Great Coll St* 30 A6
W6 38 E2
Chertsey KT16 216 BG100
Chislehurst BR7 227 EN95
Waltham Abbey EN9 89 EC33
Abbey Grn, Cher. KT16 216 BG100
Abbey Gro, SE2 188 EV77
Abbeyhill Rd, Sid. DA15 208 EW89
● **Abbey Ind Est**, Mitch. CR4 222 DF99
Wembley HA0 160 CM67
Abbey La, E15 12 F10
Beckenham BR3 205 EA94
Sch **Abbey Manor Coll**, John Evelyn Ed Cen, SE4 *off Dressington Av* 205 EA86
● **Abbey Mead Ind Pk**, Wal.Abb. EN9 89 EC34
Abbey Meadows, Cher. KT16 216 BJ101
Abbey Ms, E17 *off Leamington Av* 145 EA57
Isleworth TW7 179 CH81
Abbey Mill End, St.Alb. AL3 64 CC21
Abbey Mill La, St.Alb. AL3 64 CC21
Abbey Mills, St.Alb. AL3 64 CC21
Abbey Orchard St, SW1 29 P6
Abbey Par, SW19 *off Merton High St* 202 DC94
W5 *off Hanger La* 160 CM69
Abbey Pk, Beck. BR3 205 EA94
Abbey Pk La, Burn. SL1 133 AL61
Abbey Pl, Dart. DA1 *off Priory Rd N* 210 FK85
Sch **Abbey Prim Sch**, Mord. SM4 *off Glastonbury Rd* 222 DB101
Abbey Retail Pk, Bark. IG11 167 EP67
DLR **Abbey Road** 13 J10
Abbey Rd, E15 13 H10
NW6 5 L7
NW8 5 N9
NW10 160 CP68
SE2 188 EX77
SW19 202 DC94
Barking IG11 167 EP66
Belvedere DA17 188 EX77
Bexleyheath DA7 188 EY84
Chertsey KT16 216 BH101
Croydon CR0 223 DP104
Enfield EN1 104 DS43
Gravesend DA12 213 GL88
Greenhithe DA9 211 FW85
Ilford IG2 147 ER57
Shepperton TW17 216 BN102
South Croydon CR2 243 DX110
Virginia Water GU25 214 AX99
Waltham Cross EN8 89 DY34
Woking GU21 248 AW117
Abbey Rd Est, NW8 5 L9
Abbey St, E13 23 P4
SE1 31 P6
Abbey Ter, SE2 188 EW77
● **Abbey Trd Est**, SE26 205 DZ92
Abbey Vw, NW7 119 CT48
Radlett WD7 99 CF35
Waltham Abbey EN9 89 EB33
Watford WD25 98 BX36
Abbey Vw Rd, St.Alb. AL3 64 CC20
Rbt **Abbey Vw Rbt**, Wal.Abb. EN9 89 EB33
Abbey Wk, W.Mol. KT8 218 CB97
Abbey Way, SE2 188 EX76
● **Abbey Wf Ind Est**, Bark. IG11 167 ER68
ABBEY WOOD, SE2 188 EV76
⇌ **Abbey Wood** 188 EW76
Abbey Wd La, Rain. RM13 170 FK68
Abbey Wd Rd, SE2 188 EV77
Abbot Cl, Byfleet KT14 234 BK110
Staines-upon-Thames TW18 196 BK94
Abbot Ct, SW8 *off Hartington Rd* 42 A5
Abbot Rd, Guil. GU1 280 AX136
Abbots Av, Epsom KT19 238 CN111
St. Albans AL1 65 CE23
Abbots Av W, St.Alb. AL1 65 CD23
Abbotsbury Cl, E15 12 F10
W14 26 F5
Abbotsbury Gdns, Pnr. HA5 138 BW58
Abbotsbury Ms, SE15 184 DW83
Sch **Abbotsbury Prim Sch**, Mord. SM4 *off Abbotsbury Rd* 222 DB99
Abbotsbury Rd, W14 26 F4
Bromley BR2 226 EF103
Morden SM4 222 DB99
● **Abbots Business Pk**, Kings L. WD4 80 BN28
Abbots Cl, Guil. GU2 280 AS137
Orpington BR5 227 EQ102
Rainham RM13 170 FJ68
Ruislip HA4 138 BX62
Shenfield CM15 131 GA46
Abbots Dr, Har. HA2 138 CA61
Virginia Water GU25 214 AW98
Abbots Fld, Grav. DA12 *off Ruffets Wd* 213 GJ93
Sch **Abbotsfield Sch**, Hlgdn UB10 *off Clifton Gdns* 157 BP68
Abbotsford Av, N15 144 DQ56
Abbotsford Cl, Wok. GU22 *off Onslow Cres* 249 BA117
Abbotsford Gdns, Wdf.Grn. IG8 124 EG52
Abbotsford Lo, Nthwd. HA6 115 BS50
Abbotsford Rd, Ilf. IG3 148 EU61
Abbots Gdns, N2 142 DD56
W8 27 L7
Abbots Grn, Croy. CR0 243 DX107
Abbotshade Rd, SE16 33 K2
Abbotshall Av, N14 121 DJ48
Abbotshall Rd, SE6 205 ED88
Sch **Abbot's Hill Sch**, Hem.H. HP3 *off Bunkers La* 81 BP25
Abbots La, SE1 31 P3
Kenley CR8 258 DQ116
ABBOTS LANGLEY, WD5 81 BR31
Sch **Abbots Langley Sch**, Abb.L. WD5 *off Parsonage Cl* 81 BT30
Abbotsleigh Cl, Sutt. SM2 240 DB108
Abbotsleigh Rd, SW16 203 DJ91
Abbots Manor Est, SW1 29 J9
Abbotsmede Cl, Twick. TW1 199 CF89
Abbots Pk, SW2 203 DN88
St. Albans AL1 65 CF22
Abbot's Pl, NW6 5 L8
Abbots Pl, Borwd. WD6 100 CP37
Abbots Ri, Kings L. WD4 80 BM26
Redhill RH1 272 DG132
Abbot's Rd, E6 166 EK67
Abbots Rd, Abb.L. WD5 81 BS30
Edgware HA8 118 CQ52
Abbots Ter, N8 143 DL58
Abbotstone Rd, SW15 181 CW83
Abbot St, E8 10 A4
Abbots Vw, Kings L. WD4 80 BM27
Abbots Wk, W8 27 L7
Windsor SL4 173 AL82
Abbots Way, Beck. BR3 225 DY99
Chertsey KT16 215 BF101
Guildford GU1 265 BD133
Abbotsweld, Harl. CM18 73 ER18
Sch **Abbotsweld Prim Sch**, Harl. CM18 *off Partridge Rd* 73 ER17
Abbotswell Rd, SE4 205 DZ85
ABBOTSWOOD, Guil. GU1 265 AZ132
Abbotswood, Guil. GU1 265 AZ131
Abbotswood Cl, Belv. DA17 *off Coptefield Dr* 188 EY76
Guildford GU1 265 AZ131
Abbotswood Dr, Wey. KT13 235 BR110
Abbotswood Gdns, Ilf. IG5 147 EM55
Abbotswood Rd, SE22 184 DS84
SW16 203 DK90
Abbotswood Way, Hayes UB3 157 BV74
Abbots Yd, Guil. GU1 *off Walnut Tree Cl* 280 AW135
Abbott Av, SW20 221 CX96
Abbott Cl, Hmptn. TW12 198 BY93
Northolt UB5 158 BZ65
Abbott Rd, E14 22 E7
Abbotts Cl, N1 9 J5
SE28 168 EW73
Romford RM7 149 FB55
Swanley BR8 229 FG98
Uxbridge UB8 156 BK71
Abbotts Cres, E4 123 ED49
Enfield EN2 103 DP40
Abbotts Dr, Wal.Abb. EN9 90 EG33
Wembley HA0 139 CH61
Abbotts Pk Rd, E10 145 EC59
Abbotts Pl, Chesh. HP5 76 AQ28
Abbotts Ri, Stans.Abb. SG12 55 ED11
Abbotts Rd, Barn. EN5 102 DB42
Mitcham CR4 223 DJ98
Southall UB1 158 BY74
Sutton SM3 221 CZ104
Abbott's Tilt, Hersham KT12 218 BY104
Abbotts Vale, Chesh. HP5 76 AQ28
Abbotts Wk, Bexh. DA7 188 EX80
Caterham CR3 *off Gaist Av* 258 DV122
Abbotts Way, Slou. SL1 153 AK74
Stanstead Abbotts SG12 55 ED11
Abbotts Wf, E14 22 A8
Abbs Cross Gdns, Horn. RM12 150 FJ60
Abbs Cross La, Horn. RM12 150 FJ63
Sch **Abbs Cross Sch**, Horn. RM12 *off Abbs Cross La* 150 FJ62
Abchurch La, EC4 19 M10
Abchurch Yd, EC4 19 L10
Abdale Rd, W12 161 CV74
Abel Cl, Hem.H. HP2 62 BM20
Sch **Abel Smith Sch**, Hert. SG13 *off Churchfields* 54 DR09
Abenberg Way, Hutt. CM13 131 GB47
● **Abenglen Ind Est**, Hayes UB3 177 BR75
Aberavon Rd, E3 21 M3
Abercairn Rd, SW16 203 DJ94
Aberconway Rd, Mord. SM4 222 DB97
Abercorn Cl, NW7 119 CY52
NW8 15 N1
South Croydon CR2 243 DX112
● **Abercorn Commercial Cen**, Wem. HA0 159 CK67
Abercorn Cres, Har. HA2 138 CB60
Abercorn Dell, Bushey WD23 116 CC47
Abercorn Gdns, Har. HA3 139 CK59
Romford RM6 148 EV58
Abercorn Gro, Ruis. HA4 137 BR56
Abercorn Ms, Rich. TW10 *off Kings Rd* 180 CM84
Abercorn Pl, NW8 15 N2
Abercorn Rd, NW7 119 CY52
Stanmore HA7 117 CJ52
Sch **Abercorn Sch**, NW8 15 P1
Abercorn Wk, NW8 15 N2
Abercorn Way, SE1 32 C10
Woking GU21 248 AU118
Abercrombie Dr, Enf. EN1 *off Linwood Cres* 104 DU39
Abercrombie St, SW11 40 D8
Abercrombie Way, Harl. CM18 73 EQ16
Aberdale Ct, SE16 *off Garter Way* 33 J5
Aberdale Gdns, Pot.B. EN6 85 CZ33
Aberdare Cl, W.Wick. BR4 225 EC103
Aberdare Gdns, NW6 5 M7
NW7 119 CX52
Aberdare Rd, Enf. EN3 104 DW42
Aberdeen Av, Slou. SL1 153 AN73
Aberdeen La, N5 9 H2
Aberdeen Par, N18 *off Angel Rd* 122 DV50
Aberdeen Pk, N5 9 H2
Aberdeen Pk Ms, N5 9 K1
Aberdeen Pl, NW8 16 A5
Aberdeen Rd, N5 9 J1
N18 122 DV50
NW10 141 CT64
Croydon CR0 242 DQ105
Harrow HA3 117 CF54
Aberdeen Sq, E14 33 P2
Aberdeen Ter, SE3 46 G8
Aberdour Rd, Ilf. IG3 148 EV62
Sch **Aberdour Sch**, Burgh Hth KT20 *off Brighton Rd* 255 CZ118
Aberdour St, SE1 31 N8
Aberfeldy St, E14 22 F8
Aberford Gdns, SE18 186 EL81
Aberford Rd, Borwd. WD6 100 CN40
Aberfoyle Rd, SW16 203 DK93
Abergeldie Rd, SE12 206 EH86
Abernethy Rd, SE13 186 EE84
Abersham Rd, E8 10 B2
Abery St, SE18 187 ES77
Abigail Ms, Rom. RM3 *off King Alfred Rd* 128 FM54
Ability Twrs, EC1 19 J2
Abingdon Cl, NW1 7 N5
SE1 32 B10
SW19 202 DC93
Uxbridge UB10 156 BM67
Woking GU21 248 AV118
Wor.Pk. KT4 221 CV104
Abingdon Pl, Pot.B. EN6 86 DB32
Abingdon Rd, N3 120 DC54
SW16 223 DL96
W8 27 J6
Abingdon St, SW1 30 A6
Abingdon Vil, W8 27 J7
Abingdon Way, Orp. BR6 246 EV105
Abinger Av, Sutt. SM2 239 CW109
Abinger Cl, Bark. IG11 148 EU63
Bromley BR1 226 EL97
New Addington CR0 243 EC107
North Holmwood RH5 285 CJ140
Wallington SM6 241 DL106
ABINGER COMMON, Dor. RH5 284 BX143
Abinger Common Rd, Dor. RH5 284 BY144
Sch **Abinger Common Sch**, Abin.Com. RH5 *off Abinger La* 284 BX142
Abinger Dr, Red. RH1 288 DE136
Abinger Gdns, Islw. TW7 179 CE83
Abinger Gro, SE8 45 N3
ABINGER HAMMER, Dor. RH5 283 BT139
Sch **Abinger Hammer Village Sch**, Abin.Ham. RH5 *off Hackhurst La* 283 BT139
Abinger Keep, Horl. RH6 *off Langshott La* 291 DJ147
Abinger La, Dor. RH5 283 BV140
Abinger Ms, W9 15 J4
Abinger Rd, W4 180 CS76
Abinger Way, Guil. GU4 265 BB129
Ablett St, SE16 44 G1
Abney Gdns, N16 *off Stoke Newington High St* 144 DT61
Aboyne Dr, SW20 221 CU96
Aboyne Est, SW17 202 DD90
Sch **Aboyne Lo Sch**, St.Alb. AL3 *off Etna Rd* 65 CD19
Aboyne Rd, NW10 140 CS62
SW17 202 DD90
Abraham Cl, Wat. WD19 115 BV49
Abraham Ct, Upmin. RM14 150 FN61
ABRIDGE, Rom. RM4 108 EV41
Abridge Cl, Wal.Cr. EN8 105 DX35
Abridge Gdns, Rom. RM5 126 FA51
Abridge Pk, Abridge RM4 108 EU42
Abridge Rd, Abridge RM4 108 EU39
Chigwell IG7 107 ER44
Theydon Bois CM16 107 ES36
Abridge Way, Bark. IG11 168 EV68
Abyssinia Cl, SW11 *off Cairns Rd* 182 DE84
Abyssinia Rd, SW11 *off Auckland Rd* 182 DE84
Acacia Av, N17 122 DR52
Brentford TW8 179 CH80
Hayes UB3 157 BT72
Hornchurch RM12 149 FF61
Mitcham CR4 *off Acacia Rd* 223 DH96
Ruislip HA4 137 BU60
Shepperton TW17 216 BN99
Wembley HA9 140 CL64
West Drayton UB7 156 BM73
Woking GU22 248 AX120
Wraysbury TW19 174 AY84
● **Acacia Business Cen**, E11 *off Howard Rd* 146 EE62
Acacia Cl, SE8 33 L9
SE20 *off Selby Rd* 224 DU96
Chesham HP5 76 AN30
Cheshunt EN7 88 DS27
Petts Wood BR5 227 ER99
Stanmore HA7 117 CE51
Woodham KT15 233 BF110
Acacia Ct, Wal.Abb. EN9 *off Farthingale La* 90 EG34
Acacia Dr, Bans. SM7 239 CX114
Sutton SM3 221 CZ102
Upminster RM14 150 FN63
Woodham KT15 233 BF110
Acacia Gdns, NW8 6 B10
Upminster RM14 151 FT59
West Wickham BR4 225 EC103
Acacia Gro, SE21 204 DR89
Berkhamsted HP4 60 AV20
New Malden KT3 220 CR97
Acacia Ms, Harm. UB7 176 BK79
Acacia Pl, NW8 6 B10
Acacia Rd, E11 146 EE61
E17 145 DY58
N22 121 DN53
NW8 6 B10
SW16 223 DL95
W3 160 CQ73
Beckenham BR3 225 DZ97
Dartford DA1 210 FK88
Enfield EN2 104 DR39
Greenhithe DA9 211 FS86
Guildford GU1 264 AX134
Hampton TW12 198 CA93
Mitcham CR4 223 DH96
Staines-upon-Thames TW18 196 BH92
Acacias, The, Barn. EN4 102 DD43
Acacia St, Hat. AL10 67 CU21
Acacia Wk, Swan. BR8 229 FD96
Acacia Way, Sid. DA15 207 ET88
Academia Ave, Brox. EN10 89 DZ25
Academia Way, N17 122 DS51
Academy Ct, Borwd. WD6 100 CN42
Academy Flds Cl, Rom. RM2 149 FG57
Academy Flds Rd, Rom. RM2 149 FH57
Academy Gdns, W8 27 J4
Croydon CR0 224 DT102
Northolt UB5 158 BX68
Academy Pl, SE18 187 EM81
Islw. TW7 179 CE81
Academy Rd, SE18 187 EM81
Academy Way, Dag. RM9 148 EV63
Acanthus Dr, SE1 32 C10
Acanthus Rd, SW11 40 G10
Accommodation La, Harm. UB7 176 BJ79
Accommodation Rd, NW11 141 CZ59
Longcross KT16 214 AX104
A.C. Ct, T.Ditt. KT7 *off Harvest La* 219 CG100
Ace Par, Chess. KT9 *off Hook Rd* 220 CL104
Acer Av, Hayes UB4 158 BY71
Rainham RM13 170 FK69
Acer Ct, Enf. EN3 105 DY41
Acer Rd, Bigg.H. TN16 260 EK116
E8 10 B6
Acers, Park St AL2 82 CC28
Acfold Rd, SW6 39 L7
Achilles Cl, SE1 32 D10
Hemel Hempstead HP2 62 BM18
Achilles Pl, Wok. GU21 248 AW117
Achilles Rd, NW6 5 H2
Achilles St, SE14 45 N5
Achilles Way, W1 28 G3
Acklam Rd, W10 14 G7
Acklington Dr, NW9 118 CS53
Ackmar Rd, SW6 39 J7
Ackroyd Dr, E3 21 P6
Ackroyd Rd, SE23 205 DX87
Sch **Acland Burghley Sch**, NW5 *off Burghley Rd* 143 DJ63
Acland Cl, SE18 *off Clothworkers Rd* 187 ER80
Acland Cres, SE5 184 DR83
Acland Rd, NW2 161 CV65
Acle Cl, Ilf. IG6 125 EP52
Acme Rd, Wat. WD24 97 BU38
Acock Gro, Nthlt. UB5 138 CB63
Acol Cres, Ruis. HA4 137 BV64
Acol Rd, NW6 5 K7
Aconbury Rd, Dag. RM9 168 EV67
Acorn Cl, E4 123 EA50
Chislehurst BR7 207 EQ92
Enfield EN2 103 DP39
Hampton TW12 198 CB93
Horley RH6 291 DJ147
Romford RM1 *off Pettits La* 127 FE54
Slough SL3 *off Tamar Way* 175 BB78
Stanmore HA7 117 CH52
Acorn Ct, Ilf. IG2 147 ES58
Acorn Gdns, SE19 224 DT95
W3 160 CR71
Acorn Gro, Hayes UB3 177 BT80
Kingswood KT20 255 CY124
Ruislip HA4 137 BT63
Woking GU22 *off Old Sch Pl* 248 AY121
● **Acorn Ind Pk**, Dart. DA1 209 FF85
Acorn La, Cuffley EN6 87 DL29
Acorn Ms, Harl. CM18 73 ET17
Acorn Par, SE15 44 E5
Acorn Pl, Wat. WD24 97 BU37
Acorn Rd, Dart. DA1 209 FF85
Hemel Hempstead HP3 62 BN21
Acorns, The, Chig. IG7 125 ES49
Smallfield RH6 291 DP148
Acorn Trading Est, Grays RM20 192 FY79
Sch **Acorns Inf Sch, The**, Betchworth Site, Bet. RH3 *off The Street* 270 CR134
Leigh Site, Leigh RH2 *off Tapners Rd* 287 CU140
Acorn St, Hunsdon SG12 56 EK08
Acorns Way, Esher KT10 236 CC106
Acorn Wk, SE16 33 M2
Acorn Way, SE23 205 DX90
Beckenham BR3 225 EC99
Orpington BR6 245 EP105
Acre Dr, SE22 184 DU84
Acrefield Rd, Chal.St.P. SL9 134 AX55
Acre La, SW2 183 DL84
Carshalton SM5 240 DG105
Wallington SM6 240 DG105
Acre Pas, Wind. SL4 173 AR81
Acre Path, Nthlt. UB5 *off Arnold Rd* 158 BY65
Acre Rd, SW19 202 DD93
Dagenham RM10 169 FB66
Kingston upon Thames KT2 220 CL95
Acres End, Amer. HP7 77 AS39
Acres Gdns, Tad. KT20 255 CX119
Acre Vw, Horn. RM11 150 FL56
Acre Way, Nthwd. HA6 115 BT53
Acrewood, Hem.H. HP2 62 BL20
Acrewood Way, St.Alb. AL4 66 CM20
Acris St, SW18 202 DC85
Sch **ACS Cobham Int Sch**, Cob. KT11 *off Portsmouth Rd* 236 BW110
Sch **ACS Egham International School**, Egh. TW20 *off London Rd* 214 AW96
Sch **ACS Hillingdon Int Sch**, Hlgdn UB10 *off Vine La* 156 BM67
ACTON, W3 160 CN74
Coll **Acton & W London Coll**, W3 *off Gunnersbury La* 160 CP74
Acton Central 160 CR74
Acton Cl, N9 122 DU47
Cheshunt EN8 89 DY31
Sch **Acton High Sch**, W3 *off Gunnersbury La* 180 CN75
Acton Hill Ms, W3 *off Uxbridge Rd* 160 CP74
Acton Ho, W3 160 CQ72
Acton La, NW10 160 CS68
W3 180 CQ75
W4 180 CR76
⇌ **Acton Main Line** 160 CQ72
Acton Ms, E8 10 A8
● **Acton Pk Est**, W3 180 CR75
Actons La, High Wych CM21 57 EQ05
Acton St, WC1 18 C3
Acton Town 180 CN75
Acuba Rd, SW18 202 DB89
Acworth Cl, N9 122 DW45
Ada Cl, N11 120 DF48
Ada Ct, W9 15 P3
Ada Gdns, E14 22 G8
E15 13 L9
Adair Cl, SE25 224 DV97
Adair Gdns, Cat. CR3 258 DQ121
Adair Rd, W10 14 F5
Adair Twr, W10 14 F5
Adam & Eve Ct, W1 17 M8
Adam & Eve Ms, W8 27 K6
Adam Cl, SE6 205 DZ91
Slough SL1 153 AN74
Adam Ct, SW7 27 P8
Adam Meere Ho, E1 *off Tarling St* 20 G9
Adam Rd, E4 123 DZ51
Adams Cl, N3 120 DA52
NW9 140 CP61
Surbiton KT5 220 CM100
Adams Ct, EC2 19 M8
Adamsfield, Wal.Cr. EN7 88 DU27
Adams Gdns Est, SE16 32 G4
Adams Ho, N16 *off Stamford Hill* 144 DT60
Harlow CM20 *off Post Office Rd* 57 ER14
Adams Ms, N22 121 DM52
SW17 202 DF89
Adamson Rd, E16 23 P9
NW3 6 B6
Adamson Way, Beck. BR3 225 EC99
Adams Pl, N7 8 D3
Adams Quarter, Brent. TW8 *off Tallow Rd* 179 CJ79
Adamsrill Cl, Enf. EN1 104 DR44
Sch **Adamsrill Prim Sch**, SE26 *off Adamsrill Rd* 205 DY90
Adamsrill Rd, SE26 205 DY91
Adams Rd, N17 122 DR54
Beckenham BR3 225 DY99
Adams Row, W1 29 H1
Adams Sq, Bexh. DA6 *off Regency Way* 188 EY83
Adam St, WC2 30 B1
Adams Wk, Kings.T. KT1 220 CL96
Adams Way, Croy. CR0 224 DT100
Adam Wk, SW6 38 B4
Ada Pl, E2 10 D9
Adare Wk, SW16 203 DM90
Ada Rd, SE5 43 N5
Wembley HA0 139 CJ62
Adastral Est, NW9 118 CS53
Ada St, E8 10 E9
Adcock Wk, Orp. BR6 *off Borkwood Pk* 245 ET105
Adderley Gdns, SE9 207 EN91
Adderley Gro, SW11 *off Culmstock Rd* 202 DG85
Adderley Rd, Har. HA3 117 CF53
Adderley St, E14 22 E9
Sch **Addey & Stanhope Sch**, SE14 46 A6
ADDINGTON, Croy. CR0 243 DZ106
Addington Border, Croy. CR0 243 DY110
Addington Cl, Wind. SL4 173 AN83
Addington Ct, SW14 180 CR83
Addington Dr, N12 120 DC51
Addington Gro, SE26 205 DY91
Sch **Addington High Sch**, New Adgtn CR0 *off Fairchildes Av* 244 EE112
Addington Rd, E3 22 A2
E16 23 K5
N4 143 DN59
Croydon CR0 223 DN102
South Croydon CR2 242 DU111
West Wickham BR4 226 EE103
Addington Sq, SE5 43 K4
Addington St, SE1 30 D5
Tram **Addington Village** 243 EA107
◆ **Addington Village Interchange** 243 EA107
Addington Village Rd, Croy. CR0 243 EA106
Addis Cl, Enf. EN3 105 DX39
ADDISCOMBE, Croy. CR0 224 DT102
Tram **Addiscombe** 224 DU102
Addiscombe Av, Croy. CR0 224 DU101
Addiscombe Cl, Har. HA3 139 CJ57
Addiscombe Ct Rd, Croy. CR0 224 DS102
Addiscombe Gro, Croy. CR0 224 DR103
Addiscombe Rd, Croy. CR0 224 DS103
Watford WD18 97 BV42
Addison Av, N14 103 DH44
W11 26 E2
Hounslow TW3 178 CC81
Addison Br Pl, W14 26 G8
Addison Cl, Cat. CR3 258 DR122
Northwood HA6 115 BU53
Petts Wood BR5 227 EQ100
Addison Ct, Epp. CM16 92 EU31
Addison Cres, W14 26 F6
Addison Dr, SE12 206 EH85
Addison Gdns, W14 26 C6
Grays RM17 *off Palmers Dr* 192 GC77

Addison Gdns, Surbiton KT5 220 CM98
Addison Gro, W4 180 CS76
● Addison Ind Est, Ruis. HA4 138 BY63
Addison Pl, W11 26 E3
Southall UB1
off Atherton Pl 158 CA73
Sch Addison Prim Sch, W14 26 C6
Addison Rd, E11 146 EG58
E17 145 EB57
SE25 224 DU98
W14 26 G6
Bromley BR2 226 EJ99
Caterham CR3 258 DR121
Chesham HP5 76 AQ29
Enfield EN3 104 DW39
Guildford GU1 280 AY135
Ilford IG6 125 EQ53
Teddington TW11 199 CH93
Woking GU21
off Chertsey Rd 249 AZ117
Addison's Cl, Croy. CR0 225 DZ103
Addison Way, NW11 141 CZ56
Hayes UB3 157 BU72
Northwood HA6 115 BT53
Addle Hill, EC4 19 H10
ADDLESTONE, KT15 234 BJ106
⇌ Addlestone 234 BK105
ADDLESTONE MOOR, Add. KT15 216 BG103
Addlestone Moor, Add. KT15 216 BJ103
Addlestone Pk, Add. KT15 234 BH106
Addlestone Rd, Add. KT15 234 BL105
Addy Ho, SE16 33 H9
Adecroft Way, W.Mol. KT8 218 CC97
Adela Av, N.Mal. KT3 221 CV99
Adelaide Av, SE4 185 DZ84
Adelaide Cl, SW9
off Broughton Dr 183 DN84
Enfield EN1 104 DS38
Slough SL1
off Amerden Way 173 AN75
Stanmore HA7 117 CG49
Adelaide Cotts, W7 179 CF75
Adelaide Ct, E9 11 L3
Waltham Cross EN8
off Queens Way 89 DZ34
Adelaide Gdns, Rom. RM6 148 EY57
Adelaide Gro, W12 161 CU74
Adelaide Pl, Wey. KT13 235 BR105
Adelaide Rd, E10 145 EB62
NW3 6 B7
SW18 off Putney Br Rd 202 DA85
W13 159 CG74
Ashford TW15 196 BK92
Chislehurst BR7 207 EP92
Hounslow TW5 178 BY81
Ilford IG1 147 EP61
Richmond TW9 180 CM84
Southall UB2 178 BY77
Surbiton KT6 220 CL99
Teddington TW11 199 CF93
Tilbury RM18 193 GF81
Walton-on-Thames KT12 217 BU104
Adelaide Sq, Wind. SL4 173 AR82
Adelaide St, WC2 30 A1
St. Albans AL3 65 CD19
Adelaide Ter, Brent. TW8 179 CK78
Adelaide Wf, E2
off Queensbridge Rd 10 B9
Adela St, W10 14 E4
Adelina Gro, E1 20 G6
Adelina Ms, SW12 203 DK88
Adeline Pl, WC1 17 P7
Adeliza Cl, Bark. IG11
off North St 167 EQ66
Adelphi Ct, SE16
off Garter Way 33 J5
Adelphi Cres, Hayes UB4 157 BT69
Hornchurch RM12 149 FG61
Adelphi Gdns, Slou. SL1 174 AS75
Adelphi Rd, Epsom KT17 238 CR113
Adelphi Ter, WC2 30 B1
Adelphi Way, Hayes UB4 157 BT69
Adeney Cl, W6 38 D3
Aden Gro, N16 9 L1
Adenmore Rd, SE6 205 EA87
Aden Rd, Enf. EN3 105 DY42
Ilford IG1 147 EP59
Aden Ter, N16 144 DR63
ADEYFIELD, Hem.H. HP2 62 BN20
Adeyfield Gdns, Hem.H. HP2 62 BM19
Adeyfield Rd, Hem.H. HP2 62 BM20
Sch Adeyfield Sch, Hem.H. HP2
off Longlands 62 BN20
Adhara Rd, Nthwd. HA6
off Vega Cres 115 BU50
Adhern Ct, St.Alb. AL1 65 CJ22
Adie Rd, W6 26 A7
Adine Rd, E13 24 A4
Adisham Ho, E5
off Pembury Rd 10 E2
● Adler Ind Est, Hayes UB3 177 BR75
Adlers La, Westh. RH5 269 CG131
Adler St, E1 20 C8
Adley St, E5 11 M1
Adlington Cl, N18 122 DR50
Admaston Rd, SE18 187 EQ80
Admiral Cl, Orp. BR5 228 EX98
Admiral Ct, NW4 off Barton Cl 141 CU57
Admiral Ho, Tedd. TW11
off Twickenham Rd 199 CG91
● Admiral Hyson Trd Est, SE16 32 E9
Admiral Pl, N8 143 DP56
SE16 33 M2
Admirals Cl, E18 146 EH56
Colney Heath AL4 66 CR23
Admirals Ct, Guil. GU1 265 BB133
Admiral Seymour Rd, SE9 187 EM84
Admirals Gate, SE10 46 D6
Admiral Sq, SW10 39 P6
Admiral's Rd, Lthd. KT22, KT23 269 CD126
Admiral Stirling Ct, Wey. KT13
off Weybridge Rd 234 BM105
Admiral St, SE8 46 B7
Hertford SG13 54 DU09
Admirals Wk, NW3 142 DC62
Coulsdon CR5 257 DM120
Admiral's Wk, Dor. RH5 268 CB130
Admirals Wk, Green. DA9 211 FV85
Hoddesdon EN11 71 EA19
St. Albans AL1 65 CG23
Admirals Way, E14 34 B4
Gravesend DA12 213 GK86
★ Admiralty Arch, SW1 29 P2
Admiralty Cl, SE8 46 A6
West Drayton UB7 176 BL75
Admiralty Way, Tedd. TW11 199 CF93
Admiral Wk, W9 15 K6
Admiral Way, Berk. HP4 60 AT17
Adnams Wk, Rain. RM13
off Lovell Wk 169 FF65
Adolf St, SE6 205 EB91
Adolphus Rd, N4 143 DP61
Adolphus St, SE8 45 P4
Adomar Rd, Dag. RM8 148 EX62
Adpar St, W2 16 A5
Adrian Av, NW2
off North Circular Rd 141 CV60
Adrian Cl, Barn. EN5 101 CX44
Harefield UB9 114 BK53
Adrian Ms, SW10 39 M2
Adrian Rd, Abb.L. WD5 81 BS31
Adrians Wk, Slou. SL2 154 AT74
Adriatic, E16 23 N10
Adriatic Bldg, E14 21 L10
Adrienne Av, Sthl. UB1 158 BZ70
● Adrienne Business Cen, Sthl. UB1 off Adrienne Ave 158 BZ69
Adstock Ms, Chal.St.P. SL9
off Church La 112 AX53
Adstock Way, Bad.Dene RM17 192 FZ77
Sch ADT Coll, SW15
off West Hill 201 CZ85
Coll Adult Coll of Barking & Dagenham, The, Dag. RM9
off Fanshawe Cres 148 EZ64
Coll Adult Ed Coll Bexley, Brampton Rd Adult Ed Cen, Bexh. DA7
off Brampton Rd 188 EX83
Crayford Manor Ho Adult Ed Cen, Dart. DA1
off Mayplace Rd E 189 FE83
Southlake Cen, SE2
off Seacourt Rd 188 EX75
Advance Rd, SE27 204 DQ91
Advent Ct, Wdf.Grn. IG8
off Wood La 124 EF50
Adventurers Ct, E14
off Newport Av 35 H1
Advent Way, N18 123 DX50
Advice Av, Grays RM16 192 GA75
Adys Rd, SE15 44 B10
Aegean Apts, E16
off Western Gateway 35 P1
Sch Aerodrome Prim Sch, Croy. CR0 off Goodwin Rd 241 DP106
Aerodrome Rd, NW4 119 CT54
NW9 119 CT54
Aerodrome Way, Houns. TW5 178 BW79
Aeroville, NW9 118 CS54
Affleck St, N1 18 D1
Afghan Rd, SW11 40 C9
★ Africa Cen, WC2 18 A10
Afton Dr, S.Ock. RM15 171 FV72
Agamemnon Rd, NW6 5 H2
Agar Cl, Surb. KT6 220 CM103
Agar Gro, NW1 7 M7
Agar Gro Est, NW1 7 M7
Agar Pl, NW1 7 M7
Agars Pl, Datchet SL3 174 AU79
Agar St, WC2 30 A1
Agate Cl, E16 24 F9
NW10 160 CN69
Agate Rd, W6 26 A6
Agates La, Ashtd. KT21 253 CK118
Agatha Cl, E1 32 F2
Agaton Rd, SE9 207 EQ89
Agave Rd, NW2 4 A1
Agdon St, EC1 18 G4
Ager Ave, Dag. RM8 148 EX60
Agincourt Rd, NW3 6 E1
Agister Rd, Chig. IG7 126 EU50
Agnes Av, Ilf. IG1 147 EP63
Agnes Cl, E6 25 M10
Agnesfield Cl, N12 120 DE51
Agnes Gdns, Dag. RM8 148 EX63
Agnes George Wk, E16 36 E3
Agnes Rd, W3 161 CT74
Agnes Scott Ct, Wey. KT13
off Palace Dr 217 BP104
Agnes St, E14 21 P8
Agnew Rd, SE23 205 DX87
Agraria Rd, Guil. GU2 280 AV135
Agricola Ct, E3 11 P9
Agricola Pl, Enf. EN1 104 DT43
Aidan Cl, Dag. RM8 148 EY63
Aileen Wk, E15 13 M6
Ailsa Av, Twick. TW1 199 CG85
Ailsa Rd, Twick. TW1 199 CH85
Ailsa St, E14 22 F6
AIMES GREEN, Wal.Abb. EN9 90 EF28
Ainger Ms, NW3 6 F7
Ainger Rd, NW3 6 E7
Ainsdale Cl, Orp. BR6 227 ER102
Ainsdale Cres, Pnr. HA5 138 CA55
Ainsdale Dr, SE1 44 C1
Ainsdale Rd, W5 159 CK70
Watford WD19 116 BW48
Ainsdale Way, Wok. GU21 248 AU118
Ainsley Av, Rom. RM7 149 FB58
Ainsley Cl, N9 122 DS46
Ainsley St, E2 20 F3
Ainslie Wk, SW12 203 DH87
Ainslie Wd Cres, E4 123 EB50
Ainslie Wd Gdns, E4 123 EB49
Sch Ainslie Wd Prim Sch, E4
off Ainslie Wd Rd 123 EB50
Ainslie Wd Rd, E4 123 EA50
Ainsty Est, SE16 33 J5
Ainsworth Cl, NW2 141 CU62
SE15 43 P8
Ainsworth Rd, E9 10 G7
Croydon CR0 223 DP103
Ainsworth Way, NW8 5 N8
Aintree Av, E6 166 EL67
Aintree Cl, Colnbr. SL3 175 BE81
Gravesend DA12 213 GH90
Uxbridge UB8 157 BP72
Aintree Cres, Ilf. IG6 125 EQ54
Aintree Est, SW6 38 F4
Aintree Gro, Upmin. RM14 150 FM62
Aintree Rd, Perivale UB6 159 CH68
Aintree St, SW6 38 F5
Airco Cl, NW9 140 CR55
Aird Ct, Hmptn. TW12
off Oldfield Rd 218 BZ95
Aird Ho, SE1
off Rockingham St 31 J7
Airdrie Cl, N1 8 C7
Hayes UB4 off Glencoe Rd 158 BY71
Airedale, Hem.H. HP2
off Wharfedale 62 BL17
Airedale Av, W4 181 CT77
Airedale Av S, W4
off Netheravon Rd S 181 CT78
Airedale Cl, Dart. DA2 210 FQ88
Airedale Rd, SW12 202 DF87
W5 179 CJ76
Aire Dr, S.Ock. RM15 171 FV70
Airey Neave Ct, Grays RM17 192 GA75
Airfield Way, Horn. RM12 169 FH65
Watford WD25 81 BT34
★ Air Forces Mem, Egh. TW20 194 AX91
Airlie Gdns, W8 27 J3
Ilford IG1 147 EP60
● Air Links Ind Est, Houns. TW5 178 BW78
Air Pk Way, Felt. TW13 197 BV89
● Airport Gate Business Cen, West Dr. UB7 176 BM80
● Airport Ind Est, Bigg.H. TN16 244 EK114
Jct Airport Rbt, E16 36 E2
Airport Way, Gat. RH6 290 DG151
Staines-upon-Thames TW19 175 BF84
Jct Airport Way Rbt, Horl. RH6 290 DF151
Jct Airport Way Rbt E, Horl. RH6 291 DH151
Air St, W1 29 M1
Airthrie Rd, Ilf. IG3 148 EV61
Aisgill Av, W14 39 H1
Aisher Rd, SE28 168 EW73
Aisher Way, Rvrhd TN13 278 FE121
Aislibie Rd, SE12 186 EE84
Aiten Pl, W6 off Standish Rd 181 CU77
Aitken Cl, E8 10 C8
Mitcham CR4 222 DF101
Aitken Rd, SE6 205 EB89
Barnet EN5 101 CW43
Aitman Dr, Brent. TW8
off Chiswick High Rd 180 CN78
Ait's Vw, W.Mol. KT8
off Victoria Av 218 CB97
Ajax Av, NW9 140 CS55
Slough SL1 153 AP73
Ajax Rd, NW6 5 H2
● Ajax Wks, Bark. IG11 167 EP66
Akabusi Cl, Croy. CR0 224 DU100
Akehurst La, Sev. TN13 279 FJ125
Akehurst St, SW15 201 CU86
Akeman Cl, St.Alb. AL3
off Meautys 64 BZ22
Akenside Rd, NW3 6 A3
Akerman Rd, SW9 42 G7
Surbiton KT6 219 CJ100
Akers Ct, Wal.Cr. EN8
off High St 89 DX32
Akers Way, Chorl. WD3 95 BD44
Sch Akiva Prim Sch, N3
off East End Rd 120 DA54
Alabama St, SE18 187 ER80
Alacross Rd, W5 179 CJ75
Alamaro Lo, SE10
off Renaissance Wk 35 M6
Alamein Cl, Brox. EN10 71 DX20
Alamein Gdns, Dart. DA2 211 FR87
Alamein Rd, Swans. DA10 211 FX86
Alanbrooke, Grav. DA12 213 GJ87
Alan Cl, Dart. DA1 190 FJ84
Alandale Dr, Pnr. HA5 115 BV54
Aland Ct, SE16 33 M7
Alander Ms, E17 145 EC56
Alan Dr, Barn. EN5 101 CY44
Alan Gdns, Rom. RM7 148 FA59
Alan Hilton Ct, Ott. KT16
off Cheshire Cl 233 BD107
Alan Hocken Way, E15 23 J1
Alan Rd, SW19 201 CY92
Alanthus Cl, SE12 206 EF86
Alan Way, Geo.Grn SL3 154 AY72
Alaska, E16 off Seagull La 23 N10
Alaska Bldg, SE13
off Deals Gateway 46 C7
Alaska St, SE1 30 E3
Alba Cl, Hayes UB4
off Ramulis Dr 158 BX70
Albacore Cres, SE13 205 EB86
Alba Gdns, NW11 141 CY58
Albain Cres, Ashf. TW15 196 BL89
Alba Ms, SW18 202 DA89
Alban Av, St.Alb. AL3 65 CD18
Sch Alban City Sch, St.Alb. AL1 65 CE19
Alban Cres, Borwd. WD6 100 CP39
Farningham DA4 230 FN102
Alban Highwalk, EC2
off London Wall 19 K7
Alban Pk, St.Alb. AL4 66 CM20
Albans Vw, Wat. WD25 81 BV33
Alban Way Cycle Route, Hat. AL10 66 CQ20
St. Albans AL1, AL4 65 CK20
Sch Alban Wd Prim Sch, Wat. WD25 off The Brow 81 BV32
Albany, W1 29 L1
Albany, The, Wdf.Grn. IG8 124 EF49
Albany Cl, N15 143 DP56
SW14 180 CP84
Bexley DA5 208 EW87
Bushey WD23 99 CD44
Esher KT10 236 CA109
Reigate RH2 272 DA132
Uxbridge UB10 136 BN64
Albany Ct, E4
off Chelwood Cl 105 EB44
E10 145 EA59
Epping CM16 91 ET30
Harrow HA3 139 CK56
Albany Ctyd, W1 29 M1
Albany Cres, Clay. KT10 237 CE107
Edgware HA8 118 CN52
Albany Gate, Chesh. HP5
off Bellingdon Rd 76 AP30
Albany Hts, Grays RM17
off Hogg La 192 GA78
H Albany Lodge Comm Treatment Cen, St.Alb. AL3 64 CC19
Albany Mans, SW11 40 D5
Albany Ms, N1 8 E6
SE5 43 K3
Bromley BR1 206 EG93
Kingston upon Thames KT2 199 CK93
St. Albans AL2 82 CA27
Sutton SM1 off Camden Rd 240 DB106
Ware SG12 off Albany Quay 55 DY06
⇌ Albany Park 208 EX89
Albany Pk, Colnbr. SL3 175 BD81
Albany Pk Av, Enf. EN3 104 DW39
Albany Pk Rd, Kings.T. KT2 199 CK93
Leatherhead KT22 253 CG119
Albany Pas, Rich. TW10 200 CM85
Albany Pl, Brent. TW8
off Albany Rd 180 CL79
Egham TW20 195 BA91
Albany Quay, Ware SG12 55 DY06
Albany Rd, E10 145 EA59
E12 146 EK63
E17 145 DY58
N4 143 DM58
N18 122 DV50
SE5 43 L3
SE17 43 L3
SW19 202 DB92
W13 159 CH73
Belvedere DA17 188 EZ79
Bexley DA5 208 EW87
Brentford TW8 179 CK79
Chislehurst BR7 207 EP92
Enfield EN3 105 DX37
Hersham KT12 236 BX105
Hornchurch RM12 149 FG60
New Malden KT3 220 CR98
Old Windsor SL4 194 AU85
Pilgrim's Hatch CM15 130 FV44
Richmond TW10
off Albert Rd 200 CL85
Romford RM6 148 EZ58
Tilbury RM18 193 GG81
Windsor SL4 173 AQ82
Albanys, The, Reig. RH2 272 DA131
Sch Albany Sch, The, Horn. RM12
off Broadstone Rd 149 FH61
Albany St, NW1 7 J10
Albany Vw, Buck.H. IG9 124 EG46
Alba Pl, W11 14 G8
Alba Rd, Harl. CM17 58 EW14
Albatross Cl, E6 25 K5
Albatross Ct, Hert. SG13
off Tee Side 54 DV08
Albatross Gdns, S.Croy. CR2 243 DX111
Albatross St, SE18 187 ES80
Albatross Way, SE16 33 J5
Hatfield AL10 66 CR18
Albemarle, SW19 201 CX89
Albemarle App, Ilf. IG2 147 EP58
Albemarle Av, Chsht EN8 88 DW28
Potters Bar EN6 86 DB33
Twickenham TW2 198 BZ88
Albemarle Cl, Grays RM17 192 GA75
Albemarle Gdns, Ilf. IG2 147 EP58
New Malden KT3 220 CR98
Albemarle Pk, Stan. HA7
off Marsh La 117 CJ50
Sch Albemarle Prim Sch, SW19
off Princes Way 201 CY89
Albemarle Rd, Beck. BR3 225 EB95
East Barnet EN4 120 DE45
Albemarle St, W1 29 K1
Albemarle Way, EC1 18 G5
Albeny Gate, St.Alb. AL1 65 CD21
Albermarle Pk, Beck. BR3
off Albemarle Rd 225 EB95
Alberon Gdns, NW11 141 CZ56
Alberta Av, Sutt. SM1 239 CY105
Alberta Dr, Smallfield RH6 291 DN148
Alberta Est, SE17 31 H10
Alberta Rd, Enf. EN1 104 DT44
Erith DA8 189 FC81
Alberta St, SE17 30 G10
Albert Av, E4 123 EA49
SW8 42 C5
Chertsey KT16 216 BG97
Albert Barnes Ho, SE1 31 J7
Albert Basin, E16 37 P1
Albert Basin Way, E16 37 P1
Albert Bigg Pt, E15 12 F9
Albert Br, SW3 40 D3
SW11 40 D3
Albert Br Rd, SW11 40 D4
Albert Carr Gdns, SW16 203 DL92
Albert Cl, E9 10 F9
N22 121 DK53
Grays RM16 192 GC76
Slough SL1
off Hencroft St S 174 AT76
Albert Ct, SW7 28 A5
Waltham Cross EN8
off Queens Way 89 DZ34
Albert Cres, E4 123 EA49
Albert Dr, SW19 201 CY89
Staines-upon-Thames TW18 195 BF92
Woking GU21 233 BD114
Albert Embk, SE1 42 B1
Albert Gdns, E1 21 J9
Harlow CM17 74 EX16
Albert Gate, SW1 28 F4
Albert Gro, SW20 221 CX95
Albert Hall Mans, SW7 28 A5
Albert Ho, SE28
off Erebus Dr 187 EQ76
Albertine Cl, Epsom KT17 255 CV116
Albert Mans, SW11 40 E6
★ Albert Mem, SW7 28 A4
Albert Ms, E14 off Narrow St 21 L10
N4 143 DM60
SE4 off Arabin Rd 185 DY84
W8 27 N6
Redhill RH1 off Reed Dr 288 DG137
Albert Murray Cl, Grav. DA12
off Armoury Dr 213 GJ87
Albert Pl, N3 120 DA53
N17 off High Rd 144 DT55
W8 27 M5
Eton Wick SL4
off Common Rd 173 AN78
Albert Rd, E10 145 EC61
E16 37 H3
E17 145 EA57
E18 146 EH55
N4 143 DM60
N15 144 DS58
N22 121 DJ53
NW4 141 CX56
NW6 15 H1
NW7 119 CT50
SE9 206 EL90
SE20 205 DX94
SE25 224 DU98
W5 159 CH70
Addlestone KT15 216 BK104
Ashford TW15 196 BM92
Ashtead KT21 254 CM118
Belvedere DA17 188 EZ78
Bexley DA5 208 FA86
Bromley BR2 226 EK99
Buckhurst Hill IG9 124 EK47
Chelsfield BR6 246 EU106
Chesham HP5 76 AQ31
Dagenham RM8 148 EZ60
Dartford DA2 210 FJ90
East Barnet EN4 102 DC42
Englefield Green TW20 194 AX93
Epsom KT17 239 CT113
Hampton Hill TW12 198 CC92
Albert Rd, Harrow HA2 138 CC55
Hayes UB3 177 BS76
Horley RH6 290 DG147
Hounslow TW3 178 CA84
Ilford IG1 147 EP62
Kingston upon Thames KT1 220 CM96
Mitcham CR4 222 DF97
New Malden KT3 221 CT98
Richmond TW10 200 CL85
Romford RM1 149 FF57
St. Mary Cray BR5 228 EV100
South Merstham RH1 273 DJ129
Southall UB2 178 BX76
Sutton SM1 240 DD106
Swanscombe DA10 212 FZ86
Teddington TW11 199 CF93
Twickenham TW1 199 CF88
Warlingham CR6 259 DZ117
West Drayton UB7 156 BL74
Windsor SL4 174 AS84
Albert Rd Est, Belv. DA17 188 EZ78
Albert Rd N, Reig. RH2 271 CZ133
Watford WD17 97 BV41
Albert Rd S, Wat. WD17 97 BV41
Albert Sleet Ct, N9
off Colthurst Dr 122 DV48
Albert Sq, E15 13 K3
SW8 42 C5
Albert St, N12 120 DC50
NW1 7 K9
St. Albans AL1 65 CD21
Slough SL1 174 AT76
Warley CM14 130 FW50
Windsor SL4 173 AP81
Albert Ter, NW1 6 G8
NW10 160 CR67
W6 off Beavor La 181 CU78
Buckhurst Hill IG9 124 EK47
Albert Ter Ms, NW1 6 G9
Albert Wk, E16
off Pier Rd 37 M4
Albert Way, SE15 44 E4
Albion Av, N10 120 DG53
SW8 41 N8
Albion Cl, W2 16 D10
Hertford SG13 54 DS08
Romford RM7 149 FD58
Slough SL2 154 AU74
Albion Cres, Ch.St.G. HP8 112 AV48
Albion Dr, E8 10 A7
Albion Est, SE16 33 J5
Albion Gro, N16 144 DS63
Albion Hill, Hem.H. HP2
off Wolsey Rd 62 BK21
Loughton IG10 106 EJ43
Albion Ho, E16 off Church St 37 N3
Woking GU21 249 AZ117
Albion Ms, N1 8 E8
NW6 4 G6
W2 16 D9
W6 off Galena Rd 181 CV77
Albion Par, N16
off Albion Rd 144 DR63
Gravesend DA12 213 GK86
Albion Pk, Loug. IG10 106 EK43
Albion Pl, EC1 18 G6
W6 181 CV77
Windsor SL4 173 AN82
Sch Albion Prim Sch, SE16 33 H5
Albion Riverside Bldg, SW11 40 D4
Albion Rd, E17 145 EC55
N16 9 M2
N17 122 DT54
Bexleyheath DA6 188 EZ84
Chalfont St. Giles HP8 112 AV47
Gravesend DA12 213 GJ87
Hayes UB3 157 BS72
Hounslow TW3 178 CA84
Kingston upon Thames KT2 220 CQ95
Reigate RH2 288 DC135
St. Albans AL1 65 CF20
Sutton SM2 240 DD107
Twickenham TW2 199 CE88
Albion Sq, E8 10 A7
Albion St, SE16 33 H5
W2 16 D9
Croydon CR0 223 DP102
Albion Ter, E8 10 A7
Gravesend DA12 213 GJ86
Albion Vil Rd, SE26 204 DW90
Albion Wk, N1 18 B1
Albion Way, EC1 19 J7
SE13 185 EC84
Wembley HA9
off North End Rd 140 CP62
Albion Yd, N1 18 B1
E1 20 F6
Albon Ho, SW18
off Neville Gill Cl 202 DB86
● Albright Ind Est, Rain. RM13 169 FF71
Albrighton Rd, SE22 184 DS83
Albuhera Cl, Enf. EN2 103 DN39
ALBURY, Guil. GU5 282 BJ139
Albury Av, Bexh. DA7 188 EY82
Isleworth TW7 179 CF80
Sutton SM2 239 CW109
Albury Cl, Epsom KT19 238 CP109
Hampton TW12 198 CA93
Longcross KT16 214 AU104
Albury Ct, Sutt. SM1
off Ripley Gdns 240 DC105
Albury Dr, Pnr. HA5 116 BX52
Albury Gro Rd, Chsht EN8 89 DX30
ALBURY HEATH, Guil. GU5 282 BL141
Albury Heath, Albury GU5 282 BL141
Albury Keep, Horl. RH6
off Langshott La 291 DH147
Albury Ms, E12 146 EJ60
Albury Pk, Albury GU5 282 BL140
Albury Ride, Chsht EN8 89 DX31
Albury Rd, Chess. KT9 238 CL106
Guildford GU1 281 AZ135
Hersham KT12 235 BS107
South Merstham RH1 273 DJ129
Albury St, SE8 46 A3
Albury Wk, Chsht EN8 88 DW30
Albyfield, Brom. BR1 227 EM97
Albyn Ho, Hem.H. HP2 62 BK19
Albyn Rd, SE8 46 A7
Albyns Cl, Rain. RM13 169 FG66

Albyns La, Rom. RM4 109 FC40
Alcester Cres, E5 144 DV61
Alcester Rd, Wall. SM6 241 DH105
Alcock Cl, Wall. SM6 241 DK108
Alcock Rd, Houns. TW5 178 BX80
Alcocks Cl, Kgswd KT20 255 CY120
Alcocks La, Kgswd KT20 255 CY120
Alconbury, Welw.G.C. AL7 52 DE08
Alconbury Cl, Borwd. WD6 100 CM39
Alconbury Rd, E5 144 DU61
Alcorn Cl, Sutt. SM3 222 DA103
Alcott Cl, W7
off Westcott Cres 159 CF71
Alcuin Ct, Stan. HA7 117 CJ52
ALDBOROUGH HATCH, Ilf. IG2 147 ET55
Aldborough Rd, Dag. RM10 169 FC65
Upminster RM14 150 FM61
Aldborough Rd N, Ilf. IG2 147 ET57
Aldborough Rd S, Ilf. IG3 147 ES60
Aldborough Spur, Slou. SL1 154 AS72
Aldbourne Rd, W12 161 CT74
Burnham SL1 152 AH71
Aldbridge St, SE17 31 P10
Aldburgh Ms, W1 17 H8
Aldbury Av, Wem. HA9 160 CP66
Aldbury Cl, St.Alb. AL4
off Larkswood Ri 65 CJ15
Watford WD25 98 BX36
Aldbury Gro, Welw.G.C. AL7 52 DB09
Aldbury Ms, N9 122 DR45
Aldbury Rd, Mill End WD3 113 BF45
Aldebert Ter, SW8 42 B5
Aldeburgh Cl, E5
off Southwold Rd 144 DV61
Aldeburgh Pl, SE10 35 P9
Woodford Green IG8 124 EG49
Aldeburgh St, SE10 35 N10
Aldemere Av, Chsht EN8 88 DW28
Alden Av, E15 23 L3
ALDENHAM, Wat. WD25 98 CB38
Aldenham Av, Rad. WD7 99 CG36
Aldenham Cl, Slou. SL3 174 AX76
★ Aldenham Country Pk, Borwd. WD6 99 CG43
Aldenham Dr, Uxb. UB8 157 BP70
Aldenham Gro, Rad. WD7 83 CH34
Aldenham Rd, Bushey WD23 98 BZ42
Elstree WD6 99 CH42
Letchmore Heath WD25 99 CE39
Radlett WD7 99 CG35
Watford WD19 98 BX44
Sch Aldenham Sch, Els. WD6
off Aldenham Rd 99 CF40
Aldenham St, NW1 17 M1
Aldenholme, Wey. KT13 235 BS107
Aldensley Rd, W6 181 CV76
Alden Vw, Wind. SL4 173 AK81
Alder Av, Upmin. RM14 150 FM63
Alderbourne La, Fulmer SL3 134 AX63
Iver SL0 135 BA64
Sch Alderbrook Prim Sch, SW12
off Oldridge Rd 203 DH87
Alderbrook Rd, SW12 203 DH86
Alderbury Rd, SW13 181 CU79
Slough SL3 175 AZ75
Alderbury Rd W, Slou. SL3 175 AZ75
Alder Cl, SE15 44 B3
Englefield Green TW20 194 AY92
Erith DA18 188 EZ75
Hoddesdon EN11 71 EB15
Park Street AL2 82 CB28
Slough SL1 153 AM74
Aldercombe La, Cat. CR3 274 DS127
Alder Ct, N11 off Cline Rd 121 DJ51
Aldercroft, Couls. CR5 257 DM116
Alder Dr, S.Ock. RM15
off Laburnum Gro 171 FW70
Alder Gro, NW2 141 CV61
Aldergrove Gdns, Houns. TW3
off Bath Rd 178 BY82
Aldergrove Wk, Horn. RM12
off Pembrey Way 170 FJ65
Alder Ho, NW3 6 F4
Alderley Ct, Berk. HP4 60 AV20
Alderman Av, Bark. IG11 168 EU69
Aldermanbury, EC2 19 K8
Aldermanbury Sq, EC2 19 K7
Alderman Cl, Dart. DA1 209 FE87
North Mymms AL9 67 CW24
Alderman Judge Mall, Kings.T. KT1 off Eden St 220 CL96
Aldermans Hill, N13 121 DL49
Alderman's Wk, EC2 19 N7
Aldermary Rd, Brom. BR1 226 EG95
Alder Ms, N19 off Bredgar Rd 143 DJ61
Aldermoor Rd, SE6 205 DZ90
Alderney Av, Houns. TW5 178 CB80
Alderney Gdns, Nthlt. UB5 158 BZ66
Alderney Ho, N1 off Arran Wk 9 K5
Alderney Ms, SE1 31 L6
Alderney Rd, E1 21 J4
Erith DA8 189 FG80
Alderney St, SW1 29 K10
Alder Rd, SW14 180 CR83
Denham UB9 156 BJ65
Iver SL0 155 BC68
Sidcup DA14 207 ET90
Alders, The, N21 103 DN44
SW16 203 DJ91
Feltham TW13 198 BY91
Hounslow TW5 178 BZ79
West Byfleet KT14 234 BJ112
West Wickham BR4 225 EB102
Alders Av, Wdf.Grn. IG8 124 EE51
ALDERSBROOK, E12 146 EH61
Aldersbrook Av, Enf. EN1 104 DS40
Aldersbrook Dr, Kings.T. KT2 200 CM93
Aldersbrook La, E12 147 EM62
Sch Aldersbrook Prim Sch, E12
off Ingatestone Rd 146 EJ60
Aldersbrook Rd, E11 146 EH61
E12 146 EK62
Alders Cl, E11 146 EH61
W5 179 CK76
Edgware HA8 118 CQ50
● Alders Ct, Welw.G.C. AL7 52 DA09
Aldersey Gdns, Bark. IG11 167 ER65
Aldersey Rd, Guil. GU1 265 AZ134
Aldersford Cl, SE4 205 DX85
Aldersgate St, EC1 19 J8
Alders Gro, E.Mol. KT8 219 CD99
Aldersgrove, Wal.Abb. EN9
off Roundhills 90 EE34
Aldersgrove Av, SE9 206 EJ90
Aldershot Rd, NW6 5 H8
Guildford GU2, GU3 264 AT132
Alderside Wk, Eng.Grn TW20 194 AY92
Aldersmead Av, Croy. CR0 225 DX100
Aldersmead Rd, Beck. BR3 205 DY94
Alderson Pl, Sthl. UB2 158 CC74
Alderson St, W10 14 F4
Alders Rd, Edg. HA8 118 CQ50
Reigate RH2 272 DB132
Alderstead La, Merst. RH1 273 DK126
Alders Wk, Saw. CM21 58 EY05
Alderton Cl, NW10 140 CR62
Loughton IG10 107 EN42
Pilgrim's Hatch CM15 130 FV43
Alderton Cres, NW4 141 CV57
Alderton Hall La, Loug. IG10 107 EN42
Alderton Hill, Loug. IG10 106 EL43
Sch Alderton Inf Sch, Loug. IG10
off Alderton Hall La 107 EN43
Sch Alderton Jun Sch, Loug. IG10
off Alderton Hall La 107 EN43
Alderton Ms, Loug. IG10
off Alderton Hall La 107 EN42
Alderton Ri, Loug. IG10 107 EN42
Alderton Rd, SE24 184 DQ83
Croydon CR0 224 DT101
Alderton Way, NW4 141 CV57
Loughton IG10 107 EM43
Alderville Rd, SW6 39 H8
Alder Wk, Ilf. IG1 147 EQ64
Watford WD25
off Aspen Pk Dr 97 BV35
Alder Way, Swan. BR8 229 FD96
Alderwick Dr, Houns. TW3 179 CD83
Alderwood Cl, Abridge RM4 108 EV41
Caterham CR3 274 DS125
Alderwood Dr, Abridge RM4 108 EV41
Alderwood Ms, Barn. EN4 102 DC38
Sch Alderwood Prim Sch, SE9 off Rainham Cl 207 ES86
Alderwood Rd, SE9 207 ER86
Aldford St, W1 28 G2
⊖ Aldgate 20 A9
◆ Aldgate 20 A9
Aldgate, EC3 20 A9
Aldgate Av, E1 20 A8
⊖ Aldgate East 20 B8
Aldgate High St, EC3 20 A9
Aldham Dr, S.Ock. RM15 171 FW71
Aldin Av N, Slou. SL1 174 AU75
Aldin Av S, Slou. SL1 174 AU75
Aldine Ct, W12 26 B4
Aldine Pl, W12 26 B3
Aldine St, W12 26 B4
Aldingham Ct, Horn. RM12
off Easedale Dr 149 FG64
Aldingham Gdns, Horn. RM12 149 FG64
Aldington Cl, Dag. RM8 148 EW59
Aldington Rd, SE18 36 F7
Aldis Ms, SW17 202 DE92
Enfield EN3 105 EA37
Aldis St, SW17 202 DE92
Aldock, Welw.G.C. AL7 52 DA12
Aldred Rd, NW6 5 J2
Aldren Rd, SW17 202 DC90
Aldrich Cres, New Adgtn CR0 243 EC109
Aldriche Way, E4 123 EC51
Aldrich Gdns, Sutt. SM3 221 CZ104
Aldrich Ter, SW18
off Lidiard Rd 202 DC89
Aldridge Av, Edg. HA8 118 CP48
Enfield EN3 105 EA38
Ruislip HA4 138 BX61
Stanmore HA7 118 CL53
Aldridge Ri, N.Mal. KT3 220 CS101
Aldridge Rd, Slou. SL2 153 AN70
Aldridge Rd Vil, W11 15 H7
Aldridge Wk, N14 121 DL45
Aldrien Ct, N9
off Galahad Rd 122 DU48
Aldrington Rd, SW16 203 DJ92
Aldsworth Cl, W9 15 L5
Aldwick, St.Alb. AL1 65 CH22
Aldwick Cl, SE9 227 ER90
Aldwick Rd, Croy. CR0 223 DM104
Aldworth Gro, SE13 205 EC86
Aldworth Rd, E15 13 J7
Aldwych, WC2 18 C10
Aldwych Av, Ilf. IG6 147 EQ56
Aldwych Cl, Horn. RM12 149 FG61
Aldwych Underpass, WC2
off Kingsway 18 C9
Aldwyck Ct, Hem.H. HP1 62 BJ19
Aldykes, Hat. AL10 67 CT18
Alers Rd, Bexh. DA6 208 EX85
Alesia Cl, N22 121 DL52
Alestan Beck Rd, E16 24 F8
Alexa Ct, W8 27 L8
Sutton SM2
off Mulgrave Rd 240 DA107
Alexander Av, NW10 161 CV66
Alexander Cl, Barn. EN4 102 DD42
Bromley BR2 226 EG102
Sidcup DA15 207 ES85
Southall UB2 158 CC74
Twickenham TW2 199 CF89
Alexander Ct, Chsht EN8 89 DX30
Alexander Cres, Cat. CR3 258 DQ121
Alexander Evans Ms, SE23 205 DX88
Sch Alexander First Sch, Oakley Grn SL4 off Kenneally Row 172 AJ82
★ Alexander Fleming Laboratory Mus, W2 16 B8
Alexander Godley Cl, Ashtd. KT21 254 CM119
Alexander Ho, Kings.T. KT2
off Kingsgate Rd 220 CL95
Alexander La, Brwd. CM13, CM15 131 GB44
Sch Alexander McLeod Prim Sch, SE2 off Fuchsia St 188 EV78
Alexander Ms, SW16 203 DJ92
W2 15 L8
Harlow CM17 74 EX17
Alexander Pl, SW7 28 C8
Oxted RH8 276 EE128
Alexander Rd, N19 143 DL62
Bexleyheath DA7 188 EX82
Chislehurst BR7 207 EP92
Coulsdon CR5 257 DH115
Egham TW20 195 BB92
Greenhithe DA9 211 FW85
Hertford SG14 53 DN09
London Colney AL2 83 CJ25
Reigate RH2 288 DA137
Alexander Sq, SW3 28 C8
Alexander St, W2 15 K8
Chesham HP5 76 AQ30
Alexanders Wk, Cat. CR3 274 DT126
Alexandra Av, N22 121 DK53
SW11 40 G6
W4 180 CR80
Harrow HA2 138 BZ60
Southall UB1 158 BZ73
Sutton SM1 222 DA104
Warlingham CR6 259 DZ117
Alexandra Cl, SE8 45 N2
Ashford TW15 197 BR94
Grays RM16 193 GH75
Harrow HA2 138 CA62
Staines-upon-Thames TW18 196 BK93
Swanley BR8 229 FE96
Walton-on-Thames KT12 217 BU103
Alexandra Cotts, SE14 45 P7
Alexandra Ct, N14 103 DJ43
N16 9 P1
W9 15 P4
Ashford TW15 197 BR93
Waltham Cross EN8
off Alexandra Way 89 DZ34
Wembley HA9 140 CM63
Alexandra Cres, Brom. BR1 206 EF93
Alexandra Dr, SE19 204 DS92
Surbiton KT5 220 CN101
Alexandra Gdns, N10 143 DH56
W4 180 CS80
Carshalton SM5 240 DG109
Hounslow TW3 178 CB82
Alexandra Gro, N4 143 DP60
N12 120 DB50
Sch Alexandra Inf Sch, Beck. BR3 off Kent Ho Rd 205 DX94
Kingston upon Thames KT2
off Alexandra Rd 200 CN94
Sch Alexandra Jun Sch, SE26
off Cator Rd 205 DX93
Alexandra Ms, N2 142 DF55
SW19 off Alexandra Rd 201 CZ93
Sch Alexandra Nurs & Inf & Jun Schs, Houns. TW3
off Denbigh Rd 178 CB82
★ Alexandra Palace, N22 121 DK54
⇌ Alexandra Palace 121 DL54
Alexandra Palace Way, N22 143 DJ55
Alexandra Pk Rd, N10 121 DH54
N22 121 DK54
Sch Alexandra Pk Sch, N11
off Bidwell Gdns 121 DJ53
Alexandra Pl, NW8 5 P8
SE25 224 DR99
Croydon CR0
off Alexandra Rd 224 DS102
Guildford GU1 281 AZ136
Sch Alexandra Prim Sch, N22
off Western Rd 121 DM54
Alexandra Rd, E6 25 L2
E10 145 EC62
E17 145 DZ58
E18 146 EH55
N8 143 DN55
N9 122 DV45
N10 121 DH51
N15 144 DR57
NW4 141 CX56
NW8 5 P8
SE26 205 DX93
SW14 180 CR83
SW19 201 CZ93
W4 180 CR75
Addlestone KT15 234 BK105
Ashford TW15 197 BR94
Biggin Hill TN16 260 EH119
Borehamwood WD6 100 CR38
Brentford TW8 179 CK79
Brentwood CM14 130 FW48
Chadwell Heath RM6 148 EX58
Chipperfield WD4 80 BG30
Croydon CR0 224 DS102
Enfield EN3 105 DX42
Englefield Green TW20 194 AW93
Epsom KT17 239 CT113
Erith DA8 189 FF79
Gravesend DA12 213 GL87
Harlow CM17 58 EW13
Hemel Hempstead HP2 62 BK20
Hounslow TW3 178 CB82
Kings Langley WD4 80 BN29
Kingston upon Thames KT2 200 CN94
Mitcham CR4 202 DE94
Rainham RM13 169 FF67
Richmond TW9 180 CM82
Romford RM1 149 FF58
St. Albans AL1 65 CE20
Sarratt WD3 96 BG36
Slough SL1 173 AR76
Thames Ditton KT7 219 CF99
Tilbury RM18 193 GF82
Twickenham TW1 199 CJ86
Uxbridge UB8 156 BK68
Warlingham CR6 259 DY117
Watford WD17 97 BU40
Windsor SL4 173 AR82
Sch Alexandra Sch, S.Har. HA2
off Alexandra Av 138 CA61
Alexandra Sq, Mord. SM4 222 DA99
Alexandra St, E16 23 N6
SE14 45 M4
Alexandra Ter, Guil. GU1 280 AY135
Alexandra Wk, SE19
off Alexandra Dr 204 DS92
South Darenth DA4
off Gorringe Av 231 FS96
Alexandra Way, Epsom KT19 238 CN111
Waltham Cross EN8 89 DZ34
Alexandria Rd, W13 159 CG73
Alex Ct, Hem.H. HP2
off Alexandra Rd 62 BK19
Alexis St, SE16 32 C8
Alfan La, Dart. DA2 209 FD92
Alfearn Rd, E5 144 DW63
Alford Cl, Guil. GU4 265 AZ131
Alford Grn, New Adgtn CR0 243 ED107
Alford Ho, N6 143 DJ58
Alford Pl, N1 19 K1
Alford Rd, Erith DA8 189 FD78
Alfoxton Av, N15 143 DP56
Alfreda St, SW11 41 J6
Alfred Cl, W4 180 CR77
Alfred Ct, Whyt. CR3
off Godstone Rd 258 DU119
Alfred Gdns, Sthl. UB1 158 BY73
Alfred Ms, W1 17 N6
Alfred Pl, WC1 17 N6
Northfleet DA11 213 GF88
Alfred Prior Ho, E12 147 EN63
Alfred Rd, E15 13 L2
SE25 224 DU99
W2 15 K6
W3 160 CQ74
Aveley RM15 170 FQ74
Belvedere DA17 188 EZ78
Brentwood CM14 130 FX47
Buckhurst Hill IG9 124 EK47
Feltham TW13 198 BW89
Gravesend DA11 213 GH89
Hawley DA2 210 FL91
Kingston upon Thames KT1 220 CL97
Sutton SM1 240 DC106
Sch Alfred Salter Prim Sch, SE16 33 K5
Alfred's Gdns, Bark. IG11 167 ES68
Alfred St, E3 21 P1
Grays RM17 192 GC79
Alfreds Way, Bark. IG11 167 EQ69
● Alfreds Way Ind Est, Bark. IG11 168 EU67
Alfreton Cl, SW19 201 CX90
Alfriston, Surb. KT5 220 CM99
Alfriston Av, Croy. CR0 223 DL101
Harrow HA2 138 CA58
Alfriston Cl, Dart. DA1 209 FE86
Surbiton KT5 220 CM100
Alfriston Rd, SW11 202 DF85
Sch Alfriston Sch, Knot.Grn HP9 off Penn Rd 110 AJ49
Algar Cl, Islw. TW7
off Algar Rd 179 CG83
Stanmore HA7 117 CF50
Algar Rd, Islw. TW7 179 CG83
Algarve Rd, SW18 202 DB88
Algernon Rd, NW4 141 CU58
NW6 5 J9
SE13 46 C10
Algers Cl, Loug. IG10 106 EK43
Algers Mead, Loug. IG10 106 EK43
Algers Rd, Loug. IG10 106 EK43
Algiers Rd, SE13 185 EA84
Alibon Gdns, Dag. RM10 148 FA64
Alibon Rd, Dag. RM9, RM10 148 EZ64
Alice Cl, New Barn. EN5 102 DC42
Alice Ct, SW15 181 CZ84
Alice Gilliatt Ct, W14 38 G2
Alice La, E3 11 N9
Burnham SL1 152 AH70
Alice Ms, Tedd. TW11
off Luther Rd 199 CF92
Alice Ruston Pl, Wok. GU22 248 AW119
Alice Shepherd Ho, E14
off Stewart St 34 F5
Alice St, SE1 31 N7
Alice Thompson Cl, SE12 206 EJ89
Alice Wk, W5 159 CJ71
Alice Walker Cl, SE24
off Shakespeare Rd 183 DP84
Alice Way, Houns. TW3 178 CB84
Alicia Av, Har. HA3 139 CH56
Alicia Cl, Har. HA3 139 CJ56
Alicia Gdns, Har. HA3 139 CH56
Alie St, E1 20 B9
Alington Cres, NW9 140 CQ60
Alington Gro, Wall. SM6 241 DJ109
Alison Cl, E6 25 M9
Croydon CR0
off Shirley Oaks Rd 225 DX102
Eastcote HA5 137 BV58
Woking GU21 248 AY115
Aliwal Rd, SW11 182 DE84
Alkerden La, Green. DA9 211 FW86
Swanscombe DA10 211 FW86
Alkerden Rd, W4 180 CS78
Alkham Rd, N16 144 DT61
Alkham Twr, Orp. BR5 228 EW98
Allan Barclay Cl, N15 144 DT58
Allan Cl, N.Mal. KT3 220 CR99
Allandale, Hem.H. HP2 62 BK18
St. Albans AL3 64 CB23
Allandale Av, N3 141 CY55
Allandale Cres, Pot.B. EN6 85 CY32
Allandale Pl, Orp. BR6 228 EX104
Allandale Rd, Enf. EN3 105 DX36
Hornchurch RM11 149 FF59
Allan Way, W3 160 CQ71
Allard, NW9
off Boulevard Dr 119 CT54
Allard Cl, Chsht EN7 88 DT27
Orpington BR5 228 EW101
Allard Cres, Bushey Hth WD23 116 CC46
Allard Gdns, SW4 203 DK85
Allard Way, Brox. EN10 71 DY21
Allardyce St, SW4 183 DM84
Allbrook Cl, Tedd. TW11 199 CE92
Allcot Cl, Felt. TW14 197 BT88
Allcroft Rd, NW5 7 H3
Allder Way, S.Croy. CR2 241 DP108
Alldicks Rd, Hem.H. HP3 62 BM22
Allenby Av, S.Croy. CR2 242 DQ109
Allenby Cl, Grnf. UB6 158 CA69
Allenby Cres, Grays RM17 192 GB78
Allenby Dr, Horn. RM11 150 FL60
Sch Allenby Prim Sch, Sthl. UB1 off Allenby Rd 158 CA72
Allenby Rd, SE23 205 DY90
SE28 187 EQ76
Biggin Hill TN16 260 EL117
Southall UB1 158 CA72
Allen Cl, Mitch. CR4 223 DH95
Shenley WD7 off Russet Dr 84 CL32
Sunbury-on-Thames TW16 217 BV95
Allen Ct, Dor. RH4
off High St 285 CH136
Greenford UB6 139 CF64
Hatfield AL10
off Drakes Way 67 CV20
Allendale Av, Sthl. UB1 158 CA72
Allendale Cl, SE5 43 L8
SE26 205 DX92
Dartford DA2
off Princes Rd 211 FR88
Allendale Rd, Grnf. UB6 159 CH65
Allende Av, Harl. CM20 57 ER13
Allen Edwards Dr, SW8 42 A6
Sch Allen Edwards Prim Sch, SW4 42 A7
Allenford Ho, SW15
off Tunworth Cres 201 CT86
Allen Ho Pk, Wok. GU22 248 AW120
Allen Pl, Twick. TW1
off Church St 199 CG88
Allen Rd, E3 11 N10
N16 144 DS63
Beckenham BR3 225 DX96
Bookham KT23 268 CB126
Croydon CR0 223 DM101
Rainham RM13 170 FJ69
Allen Rd, Sunbury-on-Thames TW16 217 BV95
Allensbury Pl, NW1 7 P7
Allens Mead, Grav. DA12 213 GM88
Allens Rd, Enf. EN3 104 DW43
Allen St, W8 27 K6
Allenswood, SW19
off Albert Dr 201 CY88
Allenswood Rd, SE9 186 EL83
Allen Way, Datchet SL3 174 AW81
Allerds Rd, Farn.Royal SL2 153 AM67
Allerford Ct, Har. HA2 138 CB57
Allerford Ms, Har. HA2
off Allerford Ct 138 CB57
Allerford Rd, SE6 205 EB91
Allerton Cl, Borwd. WD6 100 CM38
Allerton Ct, NW4
off Holders Hill Rd 119 CX54
Allerton Rd, N16 144 DQ61
Borehamwood WD6 100 CL38
Allerton Wk, N7
off Durham Rd 143 DM61
Allestree Rd, SW6 38 E5
Alleyn Cres, SE21 204 DR89
Alleyndale Rd, Dag. RM8 148 EW61
Alleyn Pk, SE21 204 DR89
Southall UB2 178 BZ77
Alleyn Rd, SE21 204 DR90
Sch Alleyn's Sch, SE22
off Townley Rd 204 DS85
Allfarthing La, SW18 202 DB86
Sch Allfarthing Prim Sch, SW18
off St. Ann's Cres 202 DC86
Allgood Cl, Mord. SM4 221 CX100
Allgood St, E2 20 B1
Allhallows La, EC4 31 L1
★ All Hallows-on-the-Wall C of E Ch, EC2 19 M7
Allhallows Rd, E6 24 G7
All Hallows Rd, N17 122 DS53
Allhusen Gdns, Fulmer SL3
off Alderbourne La 134 AY63
Alliance Cl, Houns. TW4
off Vimy Cl 198 BZ85
Wembley HA0 139 CK63
● Alliance Ct, W3
off Alliance Rd 160 CP71
Alliance Rd, E13 24 C5
SE18 188 EU79
W3 160 CP70
Allied Ct, N1 9 P7
Allied Way, W3 off Larden Rd 180 CS75
Allingham Cl, W7 159 CF73
Allingham Ct, Gdmg. GU7
off Summers Rd 280 AT144
Allingham Ms, N1 9 J10
Allingham Rd, Reig. RH2 288 DA137
Allingham St, N1 9 J10
Allington Av, N17 122 DS51
Allington Cl, SW19
off High St Wimbledon 201 CX92
Gravesend DA12
off Farley Rd 213 GM88
Greenford UB6 158 CC66
Allington Ct, Enf. EN3 105 DX43
Slough SL2 154 AT73
Allington Rd, NW4 141 CV57
W10 14 E2
Harrow HA2 138 CC57
Orpington BR6 227 ER103
Allington St, SW1 29 L7
Allis Ms, Harl. CM17
off Tatton St 58 EW14
Allison Cl, SE10 46 F7
Waltham Abbey EN9 90 EG33
Allison Gro, SE21 204 DS88
Allison Rd, N8 143 DN57
W3 160 CQ72
Allitsen Rd, NW8 16 C1
Allmains Cl, Naze.Gate EN9 90 EH25
Coll All Nations Christian Coll, Easneye SG12 55 EC08
Allnutts Rd, Epp. CM16 92 EU33
Allnutt Way, SW4 203 DK85
Alloa Rd, SE8 33 K10
Ilford IG3 148 EU61
Allonby Dr, Ruis. HA4 137 BP59
Allonby Gdns, Wem. HA9 139 CJ60
Allonby Ho, E14 21 L7
Allotment La, Sev. TN13 279 FJ122
Allotment Way, NW2
off Midland Ter 141 CX62
Alloway Cl, Wok. GU21
off Inglewood 248 AV118
Alloway Rd, E3 21 M2
Allport Ms, E1 21 H5
DLR All Saints 22 E10
Sch All Saints Benhilton C of E Prim Sch, Sutt. SM1
off All Saints Rd 222 DB104
Sch All Saints Carshalton C of E Prim Sch, Cars. SM5
off Rotherfield Rd 240 DG106
Sch All Saints Cath Sch & Tech Coll, Dag. RM8 off Terling Rd 148 FA60
All Saints Cl, N9 122 DT47
SW8 42 A6
Chigwell IG7 126 EU48
Swanscombe DA10
off High St 212 FZ85
Sch All Saints C of E Jun Sch, SE19 off Upper Beulah Hill 224 DS95
Sch All Saints' C of E Prim Sch, N20 off Oakleigh Rd N 120 DD47
NW2 off Cricklewood La 141 CZ62
Sch All Saints C of E Prim Sch, SE3 47 J8
SW6 38 E8
SW15 38 A10
SW19 off East Rd 202 DC94
All Saints Cres, Wat. WD25 82 BX33
All Saints Dr, SE3 47 K8
South Croydon CR2 242 DT112
Sch All Saints Inf Sch, SE19
off Upper Beulah Hill 224 DS95
All Saints La, Crox.Grn WD3 96 BN44
All Saints Ms, Har. HA3 117 CE51
All Saints Pas, SW18
off Wandsworth High St 202 DA85
All Saints Rd, SW19 202 DC94
W3 180 CQ76
W11 14 G7
Northfleet DA11 213 GF88
Sutton SM1 222 DB104
All Saints St, N1 8 C10
Allsop Pl, NW1 16 F5
All Souls Av, NW10 161 CV68
Sch All Souls C of E Prim Sch, W1 17 L7

All Souls Pl, W1 17 K7
Allum Cl, Els. WD6 100 CL42
Allum Gro, Tad. KT20 255 CV121
Allum La, Els. WD6 100 CM42
Allum Way, N20 120 DC46
Allwood Cl, SE26 205 DX91
Allwood Rd, Chsht EN7 88 DT27
Allyn Cl, Stai. TW18
off Penton Rd 195 BF93
Alma Av, E4 123 EC52
Hornchurch RM12 150 FL63
Alma Barn Ms, Orp. BR5 228 EX103
Almack Rd, E5 10 G1
Alma Cl, Knap. GU21 248 AS118
Alma Ct, Har. HA2
off Hornbuckle Cl 139 CD61
Alma Cres, Sutt. SM1 239 CY106
Alma Cut, St.Alb. AL1 65 CE21
Alma Gro, SE1 32 B9
Alma Pl, NW10 off Harrow Rd 161 CV69
SE19 204 DT94
Thornton Heath CR7 223 DN99
Sch Alma Prim Sch, SE16 32 D8
Enfield EN3 off Alma Rd 105 DX43
Alma Rd, N10 120 DG52
SW18 202 DC85
Carshalton SM5 240 DE106
Chesham HP5 76 AQ29
Enfield EN3 105 DY43
Esher KT10 219 CE102
Eton Wick SL4 173 AM77
Northchurch HP4 60 AS17
Orpington BR5 228 EX103
Reigate RH2 272 DB133
St. Albans AL1 65 CE21
Sidcup DA14 208 EU90
Southall UB1 158 BY73
Swanscombe DA10 212 FZ85
Windsor SL4 173 AQ82
Alma Row, Har. HA3 117 CD53
Alma Sq, NW8 15 P2
Alma St, E15 12 G4
NW5 7 K4
Alma Ter, SW18 202 DD87
W8 off Allen St 27 K7
Almeida St, N1 8 G7
Almeric Rd, SW11 182 DF84
Almer Rd, SW20 201 CU94
Almington St, N4 143 DL60
Almners Rd, Lyne KT16 215 BC100
Almond Av, W5 180 CL76
Carshalton SM5 222 DF103
Uxbridge UB10 137 BP62
West Drayton UB7 176 BN76
Woking GU22 248 AX121
Almond Cl, SE15 44 D9
Bromley BR2 227 EN101
Englefield Green TW20 194 AV93
Feltham TW13
off Highfield Rd 197 BU88
Grays RM16 193 GG76
Guildford GU1 264 AX130
Hayes UB3 157 BS73
Ruislip HA4 137 BT62
Shepperton TW17 217 BQ96
Windsor SL4 173 AP82
Almond Dr, Swan. BR8 229 FD96
Almond Gro, Brent. TW8 179 CH80
Almond Rd, N17 122 DU52
SE16 32 F8
Burnham SL1 152 AH68
Dartford DA2 210 FQ87
Epsom KT19 238 CR111
Almonds, The, St.Alb. AL1 65 CH24
Almonds Av, Buck.H. IG9 124 EG47
Almond Wk, Hat. AL10
off Southdown Rd 67 CU21
Almond Way, Borwd. WD6 100 CP42
Bromley BR2 227 EN101
Harrow HA2 116 CB54
Mitcham CR4 223 DK99
Almons Way, Slou. SL2 154 AV71
Almorah Rd, N1 9 L7
Hounslow TW5 178 BX81
Alms Heath, Ock. GU23 251 BP121
Almshouse La, Chess. KT9 237 CJ109
Enfield EN1 104 DV37
Almshouses, The, Dor. RH4
off Cotmandene 285 CH135
Alnwick Gro, Mord. SM4
off Bordesley Rd 222 DB98
Alnwick Rd, E16 24 C9
SE12 206 EH87
ALPERTON, Wem. HA0 160 CM67
⊖ Alperton 160 CL67
Sch Alperton Comm Sch, Lwr Sch,
Wem. HA0 off Ealing Rd 160 CL67
Upr Sch & 6th Form Cen, Wem.
HA0 off Stanley Av 160 CL66
Alperton La, Perivale UB6 159 CK69
Wembley HA0 159 CK69
Alperton St, W10 14 F4
Alphabet Gdns, Cars. SM5 222 DD100
Alphabet Sq, E3 22 B6
● Alpha Business Pk,
N.Mymms AL9 67 CW23
Alpha Cl, NW1 16 D4
Alpha Ct, Whyt. CR3 258 DU118
Alpha Est, Hayes UB3 177 BS75
Alpha Gro, E14 34 B5
Alpha Pl, NW6 5 K10
SW3 40 D2
Sch Alpha Prep Sch, Har. HA1
off Hindes Rd 139 CE57
Alpha Rd, E4 123 EB48
N18 122 DU51
SE14 45 P6
Chobham GU24 232 AT110
Croydon CR0 224 DS102
Enfield EN3 105 DY42
Hutton CM13 131 GD44
Surbiton KT5 220 CM100
Teddington TW11 199 CD92
Uxbridge UB10 157 BP70
Woking GU22 249 BB116
Alpha St, SE15 44 C9
Alpha St N, Slou. SL1 174 AU75
Alpha St S, Slou. SL1 174 AT76
Alpha Way, Egh. TW20 215 BC95
Alphea Cl, SW19 202 DE94
Alpine Av, Surb. KT5 220 CQ103
Alpine Cl, Croy. CR0 224 DS104
Alpine Copse, Brom. BR1 227 EN96
Alpine Gro, E9 11 H7
Alpine Rd, E10 145 EB61
SE16 33 H9
Redhill RH1 272 DG131
Walton-on-Thames KT12 217 BU101
Alpine Vw, Cars. SM5 240 DE106
Alpine Wk, Stan. HA7 117 CE47
Alpine Way, E6 25 L6
Alresford Rd, Guil. GU2 280 AU135
Alric Av, NW10 160 CR66
New Malden KT3 220 CS97
Alroy Rd, N4 143 DN59
Alsace Rd, SE17 31 N10
Sch Al-Sadiq Boys & Girls Prim &
High School, NW6 5 F8
Alscot Rd, SE1 32 B8
Alscot Way, SE1 32 A8
Alsford Wf, Berk. HP4 60 AX19
Alsike Rd, SE2 188 EX76
Erith DA18 188 EY76
Alsom Av, Wor.Pk. KT4 239 CU105
Alsop Cl, Lon.Col. AL2 84 CL27
Alston Cl, Long Dit. KT6 219 CH101
Alston Rd, N18 122 DV50
SW17 202 DD91
Barnet EN5 101 CY41
Hemel Hempstead HP1 62 BG21
● Alston Wks, Barn. EN5 101 CY41
Altair Cl, N17 122 DT51
Altair Way, Nthwd. HA6 115 BT49
Altash Way, SE9 207 EM89
Altenburg Av, W13 179 CH76
Altenburg Gdns, SW11 182 DF84
Alterton Cl, Wok. GU21 248 AU117
Alt Gro, SW19
off St. George's Rd 201 CZ94
Altham Gdns, Wat. WD19 116 BX49
Altham Gro, Harl. CM20 57 ET12
Altham Rd, Pnr. HA5 116 BY52
Althea St, SW6 39 M9
Althorne Gdns, E18 146 EF56
Althorne Rd, Red. RH1 288 DG136
Althorne Way, Dag. RM10 148 FA61
Althorp Cl, Barn. EN5 119 CU45
Althorpe Gro, SW11 40 B6
Althorpe Ms, SW11 40 B7
Althorpe Rd, Har. HA1 138 CC57
Althorp Rd, SW17 202 DF88
St. Albans AL1 65 CE19
Altima Ct, SE22
off East Dulwich Rd 184 DU84
Altmore Av, E6 167 EM66
Sch Altmore Inf Sch, E6
off Altmore Av 167 EM67
Alto Ct, E15
off Plaistow Gro 13 L9
Altona Rd, Loud. HP10 110 AC52
Alton Av, Stan. HA7 117 CF52
Altona Way, Slou. SL1 153 AP72
Alton Cl, Bex. DA5 208 EY88
Isleworth TW7 179 CF82
Alton Ct, Stai. TW18 215 BE95
Alton Gdns, Beck. BR3 205 EA94
Twickenham TW2 199 CD87
Alton Ho, E3
off Bromley High St 22 D2
Alton Rd, N17 144 DR55
SW15 201 CU88
Croydon CR0 223 DN104
Richmond TW9 180 CL84
Sch Alton Sch, The, SW15
off Danebury Av 200 CS86
Alton St, E14 22 C7
Altwood Cl, Slou. SL1 153 AL71
Altyre Cl, Beck. BR3 225 DZ99
Altyre Rd, Croy. CR0 224 DR103
Altyre Way, Beck. BR3 225 DZ99
Aluric Cl, Grays RM16 193 GH77
Alvanley Gdns, NW6 5 L2
Alva Way, Wat. WD19 116 BX47
Alverstoke Rd, Rom. RM3 128 FL52
Alverstone Av, SW19 202 DA89
East Barnet EN4 120 DE45
Alverstone Gdns, SE9 207 EQ88
Alverstone Rd, E12 147 EN63
NW2 4 A6
New Malden KT3 221 CT98
Wembley HA9 140 CM60
Alverston Gdns, SE25 224 DS99
Alverton, St.Alb. AL3
off Green La 64 CC17
Alverton St, SE8 45 N1
Alveston Av, Har. HA3 139 CH55
Alveston Sq, E18 124 EG54
Alvey Est, SE17 31 N9
Alvey St, SE17 31 N10
Alvia Gdns, Sutt. SM1 240 DC105
Alvington Cres, E8 10 A2
Alvista Av, Tap. SL6 152 AH72
Alway Av, Epsom KT19 238 CQ106
Alwen Gro, S.Ock. RM15 171 FV71
Alwin Pl, Wat. WD18 97 BS42
Alwold Cres, SE12 206 EH86
Alwyn Av, W4 180 CR78
Alwyn Cl, Els. WD6 100 CM44
New Addington CR0 243 EB108
Alwyne Av, Shenf. CM15 131 GA44
Alwyne Ct, Wok. GU21 248 AY116
Alwyne La, N1 9 H6
Alwyne Pl, N1 9 J5
Alwyne Rd, N1 9 H6
SW19 201 CZ93
W7 159 CE73
Alwyne Sq, N1 9 J4
Alwyne Vil, N1 9 H6
Alwyn Gdns, NW4 141 CU56
W3 160 CP72
Alwyns Cl, Cher. KT16
off Alwyns La 216 BG100
Alwyns La, Cher. KT16 215 BF100
Alyngton, Nthch HP4 60 AS16
Alyth Gdns, NW11 142 DA58
Alzette Ho, E2 21 J2
Amalgamated Dr, Brent. TW8 179 CG79
Amanda Cl, Chig. IG7 125 ER51
Amanda Ct, Slou. SL3 174 AX76
Amanda Ms, Rom. RM7 149 FC57
Amazon Apts, N8
off New River Av 143 DM56
Amazon St, E1 20 E9
Ambassador Cl, Houns. TW3 178 BY82
Ambassador Gdns, E6 25 J7
Ambassador's Ct, SW1 29 M3
Ambassador Sq, E14 34 C9
Amber Av, E17 123 DY53
Amber Cl, New Barn. EN5 102 DB44
Amber Ct, SW17 202 DG91
Staines-upon-Thames TW18
off Laleham Rd 195 BF92
Ambercroft Way, Couls. CR5 257 DP119
Amberden Av, N3 142 DA55
Ambergate St, SE17 31 H10
Amber Gro, NW2 141 CX60
Amber La, Ilf. IG6 125 EP52
Amberley Cl, Orp. BR6 245 ET106
Amberley Cl, Pinner HA5 138 BZ55
Send GU23 265 BF125
Amberley Ct, Maid. SL6 152 AC69
Sidcup DA14 208 EW92
Amberley Dr, Wdhm KT15 233 BF110
Amberley Gdns, Enf. EN1 122 DS45
Epsom KT19 239 CT105
Amberley Gro, SE26 204 DV91
Croydon CR0 224 DT101
Amberley Pl, Wind. SL4
off Peascod St 173 AR81
Amberley Rd, E10 145 EA59
N13 121 DM47
SE2 188 EX79
W9 15 K6
Buckhurst Hill IG9 124 EJ46
Enfield EN1 122 DT45
Slough SL2 153 AL71
Amberley Way, Houns. TW4 198 BW85
Morden SM4 221 CZ101
Romford RM7 149 FB56
Uxbridge UB10 156 BL69
Amber Ms, N22
off Brampton Pk Rd 143 DN55
Amberry Ct, Harl. CM20 57 ER14
Amberside Ct, Islw. TW7 199 CD86
Amberside Ct, Hem.H. HP3
off Hardings Cl 62 BH23
Amber St, E15 13 H5
Amber Wf, E2 10 A9
Amberwood Cl, Wall. SM6 241 DL106
Amberwood Ri, N.Mal. KT3 220 CS100
Ambient Ho, Enf. EN3
off Tysoe Av 105 DZ36
Amblecote, Cob. KT11 236 BY111
Amblecote Cl, SE12 206 EH90
Amblecote Meadows, SE12 206 EH90
Amblecote Rd, SE12 206 EH90
Sch Ambler Prim Sch, N4
off Blackstock Rd 143 DP61
Ambler Rd, N4 143 DP62
Ambleside, SW19
off Albert Dr 201 CY88
Bromley BR1 205 ED93
Epping CM16 92 EU31
Purfleet RM19 190 FQ78
Ambleside Av, SW16 203 DK91
Beckenham BR3 225 DY99
Hornchurch RM12 149 FH64
Walton-on-Thames KT12 218 BW102
Ambleside Cl, E9 11 H2
E10 145 EB59
N17 off Drapers Rd 144 DT55
Redhill RH1 289 DH139
Ambleside Cres, Enf. EN3 105 DX41
Ambleside Dr, Felt. TW14 197 BT88
Ambleside Gdns, SW16 203 DK92
Ilford IG4 146 EL56
South Croydon CR2 243 DX109
Sutton SM2 240 DC107
Wembley HA9 139 CK60
Ambleside Pt, SE15 44 G4
Ambleside Rd, NW10 161 CT66
Bexleyheath DA7 188 FA82
Ambleside Wk, Uxb. UB8
off High St 156 BK67
Ambleside Way, Egh. TW20 195 BB94
Ambrey Way, Wall. SM6 241 DK109
Ambrooke Rd, Belv. DA17 188 FA76
Ambrosden Av, SW1 29 M7
Ambrose Av, NW11 141 CY59
Ambrose Cl, E6 25 J7
Crayford DA1 189 FF84
Orpington BR6
off Stapleton Rd 227 ET104
Ambrose Ms, SW11 40 E9
Ambrose St, SE16 32 E8
Ambrose Wk, E3 22 A1
● AMC Business Cen, NW10 160 CP69
Amelia, NW9
off Boulevard Dr 119 CT54
Amelia Cl, W3 160 CP74
Amelia St, SE17 31 H10
Amelle Gdns, Rom. RM3 128 FP51
Amen Cor, EC4 19 H9
SW17 202 DF93
Amen Ct, EC4 19 H8
Amenity Way, Mord. SM4 221 CW101
Amerden Cl, Tap. SL6 152 AD72
Amerden La, Tap. SL6 152 AD74
Amerden Way, Slou. SL1 173 AN75
Sch American Sch in London,
The, NW8 6 A10
America Sq, EC3 20 A10
America St, SE1 31 J3
Amerland Rd, SW18 201 CZ86
AMERSHAM, HP6 & HP7 77 AP38
⇌ Amersham 77 AQ38
⊖ Amersham 77 AQ38
Coll Amersham & Wycombe Coll,
Amersham Campus, Amer.
HP7 off Stanley Hill 94 AT39
Chesham Campus, Chesh.
HP5 off Lycrome Rd 76 AR28
Amersham Av, N18 122 DR51
Amersham Bypass, Amer. HP7 77 AN41
Amersham Cl, Rom. RM3 128 FM51
Amersham Dr, Rom. RM3 128 FL51
Amersham Gro, SE14 45 N4
H Amersham Hosp,
Amer. HP7 77 AN41
★ Amersham Mus,
Amer. HP7 77 AP40
AMERSHAM OLD TOWN,
Amer. HP7 77 AP39
Amersham Pl, Amer. HP7 94 AW39
Amersham Rd, SE14 45 N5
Beaconsfield HP9 111 AM53
Chalfont St. Giles HP8 94 AU43
Chalfont St. Peter SL9 112 AX49
Chesham HP5 77 AP35
Chesham Bois HP6 77 AP36
Coleshill HP7 111 AP46
Croydon CR0 224 DQ100
Gerrards Cross SL9 135 BB59
Little Chalfont HP6 94 AX39
Rickmansworth WD3 95 BB39
Romford RM3 128 FM51
Sch Amersham Sch, The, Amer.
HP7 off Stanley Hill 77 AS40
Amersham Vale, SE14 45 P4
Amersham Wk, Rom. RM3 128 FM51
Amersham Way, Amer. HP6 94 AX39
Amery Gdns, NW10 161 CV67
Romford RM2 150 FK55
Amery Rd, Har. HA1 139 CG61
Amesbury, Wal.Abb. EN9 90 EG32
Amesbury Av, SW2 203 DL89
Amesbury Cl, Epp. CM16 91 ET31
Amesbury Cl, Wor.Park KT4 221 CW102
Amesbury Dr, E4 105 EB44
Amesbury Rd, Brom. BR1 226 EK97
Dagenham RM9 168 EX66
Epping CM16 91 ET31
Feltham TW13 198 BX89
Slough SL1 173 AM75
Amesbury Twr, SW8 41 L8
Ames Rd, Swans. DA10 212 FY86
Amethyst Cl, N11 121 DK52
Amethyst Ct, Enf. EN3
off Enstone Rd 105 DY41
Amethyst Rd, E15 13 H1
Amethyst Wk, Welw.G.C. AL8 51 CV11
Amey Dr, Bkhm KT23 252 CC124
Amherst Av, W13 159 CJ72
Amherst Cl, Orp. BR5 228 EU98
Amherst Dr, Orp. BR5 227 ET98
Amherst Hill, Sev. TN13 278 FE122
Amherst Pl, Sev. TN13 278 FF122
Amherst Rd, W13 159 CJ72
Sevenoaks TN13 279 FH122
Sch Amherst Sch, Rvrhd
TN13 off Witches La 278 FE123
Amhurst Gdns, Islw. TW7 179 CF81
Amhurst Par, N16
off Amhurst Pk 144 DT59
Amhurst Pk, N16 144 DR59
Amhurst Pas, E8 10 C1
Amhurst Rd, E8 10 E3
N16 144 DT63
Amhurst Ter, E8 10 C1
Amhurst Wk, SE28
off Roman Sq 168 EU74
Amias Dr, Edg. HA8 118 CL49
Amicia Gdns, Stoke P. SL2 154 AT67
Amidas Gdns, Dag. RM8 148 EV63
Amiel St, E1 21 H4
Amies St, SW11 40 E10
Amina Way, SE16 32 C7
Amis Av, Epsom KT19 238 CP107
New Haw KT15 234 BG111
Amis Rd, Wok. GU21 248 AS119
Amity Gro, SW20 221 CW95
Amity Rd, E15 13 L8
Ammanford Grn, NW9
off Ruthin Cl 140 CS58
Amner Rd, SW11 202 DG86
Amor Rd, W6 26 A7
Amott Rd, SE15 184 DU83
Amoy Pl, E14 22 A9
Ampere Ho, W3
off Warple Way 180 CS75
Ampere Way, Croy. CR0 223 DL101
Tra Ampere Way 223 DM102
Ampleforth Cl, Orp. BR6 246 EW105
Ampleforth Rd, SE2 188 EV75
Amport Pl, NW7 119 CY51
Ampthill Sq Est, NW1 17 M1
Ampton Pl, WC1 18 C3
Ampton St, WC1 18 C3
Amroth Cl, SE23 204 DV88
Amroth Grn, NW9
off Fryent Gro 140 CS58
Amstel Way, Wok. GU21 248 AT118
Amsterdam Rd, E14 34 F7
Amundsen Ct, E14
off Napier Av 34 B10
Amwell Cl, Enf. EN2 104 DR43
Watford WD25
off Phillipers 98 BY35
Amwell Common, Welw.G.C.
AL7 52 DB10
Amwell Ct, Hodd. EN11 71 EA16
Waltham Abbey EN9 90 EF33
Amwell Ct Est, N4 144 DQ60
Amwell End, Ware SG12 55 DX06
Amwell Hill, Gt Amwell SG12 55 DZ08
Amwell La, Ware SG12 55 EA09
Amwell Pl, Hert.Hth SG13 54 DW11
Jct Amwell Rbt, Ware SG12 55 DZ11
Amwell St, EC1 18 E2
Hoddesdon EN11 71 EA17
Sch Amwell Vw Sch, Stans.Abb.
SG12 off Station Rd 55 EB11
Amyand Cotts, Twick. TW1
off Amyand Pk Rd 199 CH86
Amyand La, Twick. TW1
off Marble Hill Gdns 199 CH87
Amyand Pk Gdns, Twick. TW1
off Amyand Pk Rd 199 CH87
Amyand Pk Rd, Twick. TW1 199 CG87
Amy Cl, Wall. SM6 241 DL108
Sch Amy Johnson Prim Sch, Wall.
SM6 off Mollison Dr 241 DL108
Amy La, Chesh. HP5 76 AP32
Amy Rd, Oxt. RH8 276 EE129
Amyruth Rd, SE4 205 EA85
Amy Warne Cl, E6 25 H6
Anatola Rd, N19
off Dartmouth Pk Hill 143 DH61
Ancaster Cres, N.Mal. KT3 221 CU100
Ancaster Ms, Beck. BR3 225 DX97
Ancaster Rd, Beck. BR3 225 DX97
Ancaster St, SE18 187 ES80
Anchorage Cl, SW19 202 DA92
Anchorage Pt, E14 33 P4
● Anchorage Pt Ind Est, SE7 36 C7
Anchor & Hope La, SE7 36 B7
● Anchor Bay Ind Est, Erith
DA8 189 FG79
Anchor Boul, Dart. DA2 190 FQ84
Anchor Cl, Bark. IG11 168 EV69
Cheshunt EN8 89 DX28
Anchor Ct, Grays RM17 192 GA80
Anchor Dr, Rain. RM13 169 FH69
Anchor Ho, SW18
off Smugglers Way 182 DB84
Anchor La, Hem.H. HP1 62 BH21
Anchor Ms, N1 9 P5
SW11 off Westbridge Rd 40 B7
SW12 203 DH86
Anchor Retail Pk, E1 21 H5
Anchor St, SE16 32 E8
Anchor Ter, E1 21 H5
Anchor Wf, E3 off Watts Gro 22 C6
Anchor Yd, EC1 19 K4
Ancill Cl, W6 38 D3
Ancona Rd, NW10 161 CU68
SE18 187 ER78
Andace Pk Gdns, Brom. BR1 226 EJ95
Andalus Rd, SW9 183 DL83
Ander Cl, Wem. HA0 139 CK63
Andermans, Wind. SL4 173 AK81
Anderson Cl, N21 103 DM43
W3 160 CR72
Epsom KT19 238 CP112
Guildford GU2
off Tylehost 264 AV130
Anderson Cl, Harefield UB9 114 BG53
Sutton SM3 222 DA102
Anderson Ct, Red. RH1 288 DG137
Anderson Dr, Ashf. TW15 197 BQ91
Anderson Ho, Bark. IG11
off The Coverdales 167 ER68
Anderson Pl, Houns. TW3 178 CB84
Anderson Rd, E9 11 J4
Shenley WD7 84 CN33
Weybridge KT13 217 BR104
Woodford Green IG8 146 EK55
Andersons Sq, N1 8 G9
Anderson St, SW3 28 E10
Anderson Way, Belv. DA17 189 FB75
Anderton Cl, SE5 184 DR83
Andmark Ct, Sthl. UB1
off Herbert Rd 158 BZ74
Andover Av, E16 24 E9
Andover Cl, Epsom KT19 238 CR111
Feltham TW14 197 BT88
Greenford UB6 158 CB70
Uxbridge UB8 156 BH68
Andover Est, N7 143 DM61
Andover Pl, NW6 5 L10
Andover Rd, N7 143 DM61
Orpington BR6 227 ER102
Twickenham TW2 199 CD88
Andrea Av, Grays RM16 192 GA75
Andre St, E8 10 D2
Andrew Borde St, WC2 17 P8
Andrew Cl, Dart. DA1 209 FD85
Ilford IG6 125 ER51
Shenley WD7 84 CM33
Andrewes Gdns, E6 24 G8
Andrewes Ho, EC2
off The Barbican 19 K7
Sch Andrew Ewing Prim Sch,
Heston TW5
off Westbrook Rd 178 BZ80
Andrew Hill La, Hedg. SL2 133 AQ61
Andrew Pl, SW8 41 P6
Andrew Reed Ho, SW18
off Linstead Way 201 CY87
Andrews Cl, E6 24 G8
Buckhurst Hill IG9 124 EJ47
Epsom KT17 239 CT114
Harrow HA1 139 CD59
Hemel Hempstead HP2
off Church St 62 BK18
Orpington BR5 228 EX97
Worcester Park KT4 221 CX103
Andrews Crosse, WC2 18 E9
Andrewsfield, Welw.G.C. AL7 52 DC09
Andrews La, Chsht EN7 88 DU28
Sch Andrews La Prim Sch, Chsht
EN7 off Andrews La 88 DV28
Andrews Pl, SE9 207 EP86
Dartford DA2 209 FE89
Andrew's Rd, E8 10 E9
Andrew St, E14 22 E8
Andrews Wk, SE17 43 H3
Andromeda Ct, Rom. RM3
off Myrtle Rd 128 FJ51
Andwell Cl, SE2 188 EV75
Anelle Ri, Hem.H. HP3 62 BM24
Anemone Ct, Enf. EN3
off Enstone Rd 105 DY41
ANERLEY, SE20 224 DV95
⇌ Anerley 204 DV94
⊖ Anerley 204 DV94
Anerley Gro, SE19 204 DT94
Anerley Hill, SE19 204 DT93
Anerley Pk, SE20 204 DU94
Anerley Pk Rd, SE20 204 DV94
Anerley Rd, SE19 204 DU94
SE20 204 DU94
Anerley Sta Rd, SE20 224 DV95
Anerley St, SW11 40 F8
Anerley Vale, SE19 204 DT94
Anfield Cl, SW12
off Belthorn Cres 203 DJ87
Angas Ct, Wey. KT13 235 BQ106
⊖ Angel 8 F10
Angela Carter Cl, SW9
off Wiltshire Rd 42 F10
Angel All, E1 20 B8
● Angel Building, EC1 18 F1
Angel Cl, N18 122 DT49
Hampton Hill TW12
off Windmill Rd 198 CC93
Angel Cor Par, N18
off Fore St 122 DU49
Angel Ct, EC2 19 M8
Croy. CR0 224 DS103
SW1 29 M3
SW17 202 DF91
Jct Angel Edmonton, N18
off Angel Rd 122 DU50
Angelfield, Houns. TW3 178 CB84
Angel Gate, EC1 19 H2
Guildford GU1 off High St 280 AX136
Angel Hill, Sutt. SM1 222 DB104
Angel Hill Dr, Sutt. SM1 222 DB104
Angelica Cl, West Dr. UB7
off Lovibonds Av 156 BM72
Angelica Dr, E6 25 M7
Angelica Gdns, Croy. CR0 225 DX102
Angelica Rd, Guil. GU2 264 AU130
Angelis Apts, N1
off Graham St 19 H1
Angel La, E15 13 H4
EC4 off Upper Thames St 31 L1
Hayes UB3 157 BR71
Angell Pk Gdns, SW9 42 F10
Angell Rd, SW9 42 F10
Angell Town Est, SW9 42 E8
Angel Ms, E1 20 F10
N1 18 F1
SW15 201 CU87
Angelo Ms, SW16 223 DM97
Angel Pl, N18 122 DU50
SE1 31 L4
Reigate RH2
off Cockshot Hill 288 DB137
⇌ Angel Road 122 DW50
Angel Rd, N18 122 DV50
Harrow HA1 139 CE58
Thames Ditton KT7 219 CG101
● Angel Rd Wks, N18 122 DW50
Angel Southside, EC1 18 F1
Angel Sq, EC1 18 F1

Angel St, EC1 19 J8
Angel Wk, W6 26 A9
Angel Way, Rom. RM1 149 FE57
Angel Wf, N1 off Eagle Wf Rd 9 K10
Angerstein La, SE3 47 M6
Angle Cl, Uxb. UB10 156 BN67
Anglefield Rd, Berk. HP4 60 AU19
Angle Grn, Dag. RM8 148 EW60
Angle Pl, Berk. HP4 60 AU19
Angle Rd, Grays RM20 191 FX79
Anglers Cl, Rich. TW10
off Locksmeade Rd 199 CJ91
Angler's La, NW5 7 K5
Anglers Reach, Surb. KT6 219 CK99
Anglesea Av, SE18 37 N9
Anglesea Ms, SE18 37 N9
Anglesea Pl, Grav. DA11
off Clive Rd 213 GH86
Anglesea Rd, SE18 37 N9
Kingston upon Thames KT1 219 CK98
Orpington BR5 228 EW100
Anglesea Ter, W6
off Wellesley Av 181 CV76
Anglesey Cl, Ashf. TW15 196 BN90
Anglesey Ct Rd, Cars. SM5 240 DG107
Anglesey Dr, Rain. RM13 169 FG70
Anglesey Gdns, Cars. SM5 240 DG107
Anglesey Rd, Enf. EN3 104 DV42
Watford WD19 116 BW50
Anglesmede Cres, Pnr. HA5 138 CA55
Anglesmede Way, Pnr. HA5 138 BZ55
Angles Rd, SW16 203 DL91
Anglia Cl, N17 off Park La 122 DV52
Anglia Ct, Dag. RM8
off Spring Cl 148 EX60
Anglia Ho, E14 21 M9
Anglian Cl, Wat. WD24 98 BW40
Anglian Rd, E11 145 ED62
Anglia Wk, E6 167 EM67
● Anglo Business Pk,
Chesh. HP5 76 AN29
Anglo Rd, E3 11 P10
Angrave Ct, E8 10 B8
Angrave Pas, E8 10 B8
Angus Cl, Chess. KT9 238 CN106
Angus Dr, Ruis. HA4 138 BW63
Angus Gdns, NW9 118 CR53
Angus Home, Cudham TN14 261 ER115
Angus Rd, E13 24 D3
Angus St, SE14 45 M4
Anhalt Rd, SW11 40 D4
Anisdowne Cl, Abin.Ham. RH5 283 BT142
Ankerdine Cres, SE18 187 EP81
Ankerwycke Priory,
Wrays. TW19 194 AY89
Anlaby Rd, Tedd. TW11 199 CE92
Anley Rd, W14 26 C5
Anmersh Gro, Stan. HA7 117 CK53
Annabel Cl, E14 22 C9
Annabelle Ct, Rain. RM13 169 FE69
Annabels Ms, W5 159 CK70
Anna Cl, E8 10 B8
Annalee Gdns, S.Ock. RM15 171 FV71
Annalee Rd, S.Ock. RM15 171 FV71
Annandale Gro, Uxb. UB10 137 BQ62
Annandale Rd, SE10 47 L1
W4 180 CS77
Croydon CR0 224 DU103
Guildford GU2 280 AV136
Sidcup DA15 207 ES87
Anna Neagle Cl, E7
off Dames Rd 146 EG63
Annan Way, Rom. RM1 127 FD53
Anne Boleyn Ct, SE9
off Avery Hill Rd 207 ER86
Anne Boleyn's Wk, Kings.T.
KT2 200 CL92
Sutton SM3 239 CX108
Anne Case Ms, N.Mal. KT3
off Sycamore Gro 220 CR97
Anne Compton Ms, SE12 206 EF87
Anne Goodman Ho, E1
off Jubilee St 20 G8
Anne Heart Cl, Chaff.Hun.
RM16 191 FX77
Anne of Cleeves Ct, SE9
off Avery Hill Rd 207 ER86
Anne of Cleves Rd, Dart. DA1 210 FK85
Anners Cl, Egh. TW20 215 BC97
Annesley Av, NW9 140 CR55
Annesley Cl, NW10 140 CS62
Annesley Dr, Croy. CR0 225 DZ104
Annesley Rd, SE3 186 EH81
Annesley Wk, N19
off Highgate Hill 143 DJ61
Annesmere Gdns, SE3
off Highbrook Rd 186 EK83
Anne St, E13 23 N4
Anne's Wk, Cat. CR3 258 DS120
Annett Cl, Shep. TW17 217 BS98
Annette Cl, Har. HA3 117 CE54
Annette Cres, N1 9 K7
Annette Rd, N7 143 DM63
Annett Rd, Walt. KT12 217 BU101
Anne Way, Ilf. IG6 125 EQ51
West Molesey KT8 218 CB98
Annie Besant Cl, E3 11 P9
Annie Brooks Cl, Stai. TW18 195 BD90
Annie Taylor Ho, E12
off Walton Rd 147 EN63
Annifer Way, S.Ock. RM15 171 FV71
Anningsley Pk, Ott. KT16 233 BD110
Anning St, EC2 19 P4
Annington Rd, N2 142 DF55
Annis Rd, E9 11 L5
Ann La, SW10 40 A4
Ann Moss Way, SE16 32 G6
Ann's Cl, SW1 28 F5
Ann's Pl, E1 20 A7
Ann St, SE18 187 ER77
Annsworthy Av, Th.Hth. CR7
off Grange Pk Rd 224 DR97
Annsworthy Cres, SE25
off Grange Rd 224 DR96
Sch Annunciation RC Inf Sch, The,
Edg. HA8 off Thirleby Rd 118 CR53
Sch Annunciation RC Jun Sch, The,
Edg. HA8 off The Meads 118 CR51
Anscuff Rd, Slou. SL2 153 AN69
Ansdell Rd, SE15 44 G8
Ansdell St, W8 27 M6
Ansdell Ter, W8 27 M6
Ansell Gro, Cars. SM5 222 DG102
Ansell Rd, SW17 202 DE90
Dorking RH4 285 CH135
Anselm Cl, Croy. CR0 224 DT104
Anselm Rd, SW6 39 J3
Pinner HA5 116 BZ52
Ansford Rd, Brom. BR1 205 EC92
Ansleigh Pl, W11 26 D1
Ansley Cl, S.Croy. CR2 242 DV114
Anslow Gdns, Iver SL0 155 BD68
Anslow Pl, Slou. SL1 152 AJ71
Anson Cl, Bov. HP3 79 AZ27
Romford RM7 127 FB54
St. Albans AL1 65 CH22
Anson Ho, E1 21 L5
Anson Pl, SE28 187 ER75
Sch Anson Prim Sch, NW2 4 C2
Anson Rd, N7 7 M1
NW2 4 C2
Anson Ter, Nthlt. UB5 158 CB65
Anson Wk, Nthwd. HA6 115 BQ49
Anstead Dr, Rain. RM13 169 FG68
Anstey Rd, SE15 44 C10
Anstey Wk, N15 143 DP56
Anstice Cl, W4 180 CS80
Anston Ct, Guil. GU2
off Southway 264 AS134
Anstridge Path, SE9 207 ER86
Anstridge Rd, SE9 207 ER86
Antelope Av, Grays RM16
off Hogg La 192 GA76
Antelope Rd, SE18 37 J6
Antelope Wk, Surb. KT6
off Maple Rd 219 CK99
Anthony Cl, NW7 118 CS49
Dunton Green TN13 278 FE121
Watford WD19 116 BW46
Anthony La, Swan. BR8 229 FG95
Anthony Rd, SE25 224 DU100
Borehamwood WD6 100 CM40
Greenford UB6 159 CE68
Welling DA16 188 EU81
Sch Anthony Roper Prim Sch, The,
Eyns. DA4 off High St 230 FL103
Anthonys, Wok. GU21 233 BB112
Anthony St, E1 20 F8
Anthony Way, N18 123 DX51
Slough SL1 153 AK73
Anthony W Ho, Brock. RH3
off Wheelers La 286 CP136
Anthorne Cl, Pot.B. EN6 86 DB31
Anthus Ms, Nthwd. HA6 115 BS52
Antigua Cl, SE19 204 DR92
Antigua Ms, E13 24 B2
Antigua Wk, SE19 204 DR92
Antill Rd, E3 21 L2
N15 144 DU56
Antill Ter, E1 21 J8
Antlands La, Shipley Br RH6 291 DK153
Antlands La E, Horl. RH6 291 DL153
Antlands La W, Horl. RH6 291 DL153
Antlers Hill, E4 105 EB43
Antoinette Ct, Abb.L. WD5 81 BT29
Anton Cres, Sutt. SM1 222 DA104
Antoneys Cl, Pnr. HA5 116 BX54
Antonine Gate, St.Alb. AL3 64 CA21
Antonine Hts, SE1 31 N5
Anton Pl, Wem. HA9 140 CP62
Anton Rd, S.Ock. RM15 171 FV70
Anton St, E8 10 D2
Antony Ho, E5 off Pembury Pl 10 E3
Antrim Gro, NW3 6 E4
Antrim Mans, NW3 6 D4
Antrim Rd, NW3 6 E4
Antrobus Cl, Sutt. SM1 239 CZ106
Antrobus Rd, W4 180 CQ77
Anvil Cl, SW16 203 DJ94
Bovingdon HP3
off Yew Tree Dr 79 BB28
Anvil Ct, Langley SL3
off Blacksmith Row 175 BA77
Anvil La, Cob. KT11 235 BU114
Anvil Pl, St.Alb. AL2 82 CA26
Anvil Rd, Sun. TW16 217 BU97
Anvil Ter, Dart. DA2
off Pinewood Pl 209 FE89
Anworth Cl, Wdf.Grn. IG8 124 EH51
Anyards Rd, Cob. KT11 235 BV113
Anzio Gdns, Cat. CR3 258 DQ121
Apeldoorn Dr, Wall. SM6 241 DL109
Aperdele Rd, Lthd. KT22 253 CG118
APERFIELD, West. TN16 261 EM117
Aperfield Rd, Bigg.H. TN16 260 EL117
Erith DA8 189 FF79
Apers Av, Wok. GU22 249 AZ121
Apex Cl, Beck. BR3 225 EB95
Jct Apex Cor, NW7 118 CR49
● Apex Ind Est, NW10
off Hythe Rd 161 CT70
🔒 Apex Retail Pk, Felt. TW13 198 BZ90
● Apex Twr, N.Mal. KT3 220 CS97
Apley Rd, Reig. RH2 288 DA137
Aplin Way, Islw. TW7 179 CE81
Apollo, E14 34 A8
Apollo Av, Brom. BR1
off Rodway Rd 226 EH95
Northwood HA6 115 BU50
Apollo Cl, Horn. RM12 149 FH61
★ Apollo Hammersmith, W6 26 B10
Apollo Pl, E11 146 EE62
SW10 40 A4
St. John's GU21
off Church Rd 248 AU119
★ Apollo Thea, W1 17 N10
★ Apollo Victoria Thea, SW1 29 L7
Apollo Way, SE28
off Broadwater Rd 187 ER76
Hemel Hempstead HP2 62 BM18
Apostle Way, Th.Hth. CR7 223 DP96
Apothecary St, EC4 18 G9
Appach Rd, SW2 203 DN85
Apperlie Dr, Horl. RH6 291 DJ150
Apple Blossom Ct, SW8
off Pascal St 41 P4
Appleby Cl, E4 123 EC51
N15 144 DR57
Petts Wood BR5 227 ES101
Twickenham TW2 199 CD89
Uxbridge UB8 157 BQ72
Appleby Ct, W3
off Newport Rd 180 CQ75
Appleby Dr, Crox.Grn WD3 97 BP42
Romford RM3 128 FJ50
Appleby Gdns, Felt. TW14 197 BT88
Appleby Grn, Rom. RM3
off Appleby Dr 128 FJ50
Appleby Rd, E8 10 D6
E16 23 M9
Appleby St, E2 10 A10
Cheshunt EN7 88 DT26
Apple Cotts, Bov. HP3 79 BA27
Applecroft, Nthch HP4 60 AS17
Park Street AL2 82 CB28
Applecroft Rd, Welw.G.C. AL8 51 CV09
Sch Applecroft Sch, Welw.G.C.
AL8 off Applecroft Rd 51 CV10
Appledore Av, Bexh. DA7 189 FC81
Ruislip HA4 137 BV62
Appledore Cl, SW17 202 DF89
Bromley BR2 226 EF99
Edgware HA8 118 CN53
Romford RM3 128 FJ53
Appledore Cres, Sid. DA14 207 ES90
Appledore Way, NW7
off Tavistock Av 119 CX52
Appledown Ri, Couls. CR5 257 DJ115
Applefield, Amer. HP7 94 AW39
Appleford Cl, Hodd. EN11 71 DZ15
Appleford Rd, W10 14 F5
Apple Garth, Brent. TW8 179 CK77
Applegarth, Clay. KT10 237 CF106
New Addington CR0 243 EB108
Applegarth Dr, Dart. DA1 210 FL89
Ilford IG2 147 ET56
Applegarth Ho, Erith DA8 189 FF82
Sch Applegarth Nurs & Inf & Jun
Schs, New Adgtn CR0
off Bygrove 243 EB107
Applegarth Rd, SE28 168 EV74
W14 26 C7
Applegate, Brwd. CM14 130 FT43
Apple Gro, Chess. KT9 238 CL105
Enfield EN1 104 DS41
Apple Mkt, Kings.T. KT1
off Eden St 219 CK96
Apple Orchard, Swan. BR8 229 FD98
Apple Orchard, The, Hem.H.
HP2 off Highfield La 62 BM18
Apple Rd, E11 146 EE62
Appleshaw Cl, Grav. DA11 213 GG92
Appleton Cl, Amer. HP7 94 AV40
Bexleyheath DA7 189 FB82
Harlow CM19 73 EQ16
Appleton Dr, Dart. DA2 209 FH90
Appleton Gdns, N.Mal. KT3 221 CU100
Appleton Rd, SE9 186 EL83
Loughton IG10 107 EP41
Appleton Sq, Mitch. CR4
off Silbury Av 222 DE95
Appleton Way, Horn. RM12 150 FK60
Apple Tree Av, Uxb. UB8 156 BM71
West Drayton UB7 156 BM71
Appletree Cl, SE20
off Jasmine Gro 224 DV95
Leatherhead KT22 252 CC124
Appletree Ct, Guil. GU4 265 BD131
Appletree Gdns, Barn. EN4 102 DE42
Appletree La, Slou. SL3 174 AW76
Jct Apple Tree Rbt, West Dr.
UB7 156 BM73
Appletree Wk, Chesh. HP5
off Cresswell Rd 76 AR34
Watford WD25 81 BV34
Apple Tree Yd, SW1 29 M2
Applewood Cl, N20 120 DE46
NW2 141 CV62
Ickenham UB10 136 BL63
Applewood Dr, E13 24 A4
Appold St, EC2 19 N6
Erith DA8 189 FF79
Apprentice Gdns, Nthlt. UB5 158 BZ69
Apprentice Way, E5
off Clarence Rd 144 DV63
Approach, The, NW4 141 CX57
W3 160 CR72
Enfield EN1 104 DV40
Orpington BR6 227 ET103
Potters Bar EN6 85 CZ32
Upminster RM14 150 FP62
Approach Cl, N16 9 N2
Approach Rd, E2 20 G1
SW20 221 CW96
Ashford TW15 197 BQ93
Barnet EN4 102 DD42
Edgware HA8 118 CP51
Purley CR8 241 DP112
St. Albans AL1 65 CE21
Taplow SL6 152 AE72
West Molesey KT8 218 CA99
Appspond La, Pott.Cr. AL2 63 BV23
Aprey Gdns, NW4 141 CW56
April Cl, W7 159 CE73
Ashtead KT21 254 CM117
Feltham TW13 197 BU90
Orpington BR6 245 ET106
April Glen, SE23 205 DX90
April St, E8 10 B1
Aprilwood Cl, Wdhm KT15 233 BF111
Apsledene, Grav. DA12
off Miskin Way 213 GK93
APSLEY, Hem.H. HP3 80 BK25
⇌ Apsley 80 BL25
Apsley Cl, Har. HA2 138 CC57
Apsley Gra, Hem.H. HP3
off London Rd 80 BL25
🔒 Apsley Mills Retail Pk,
Hem.H. HP3 62 BL24
Apsley Rd, SE25 224 DV98
New Malden KT3 220 CQ97
Apsley Way, NW2 141 CU61
W1 29 H4
● Aquarius Business Pk,
NW2 141 CT60
Aquarius Way, Nthwd. HA6 115 BU50
★ Aquatic Experience,
Brent. TW8 179 CH81
Aquila Cl, Lthd. KT22 254 CL121
Aquila St, NW8 6 B10
Aquinas St, SE1 30 F2
Aquis Ct, St.Alb. AL3 64 CC20
Arabella Dr, SW15 180 CS84
Arabia Cl, E4 123 ED45
Arabin Rd, SE4 185 DY84
Arado, NW9
off Boulevard Dr 119 CT54
Araglen Av, S.Ock. RM15 171 FV71
Aragon Av, Epsom KT17 239 CV109
Thames Ditton KT7 219 CF99
Aragon Cl, Brom. BR2 227 EM102
Enfield EN2 103 DM38
Hemel Hempstead HP2 63 BQ15
Loughton IG10 106 EL44
New Addington CR0 244 EE110
Romford RM5 127 FB51
Sunbury-on-Thames TW16 197 BT94
Aragon Ct, SE11
off Hotspur St 30 E10
Aragon Dr, Ilf. IG6 125 EQ52
Ruislip HA4 138 BX60
Aragon Ms, Epp. CM16 92 EW29
Aragon Pl, Mord. SM4 221 CX101
Sch Aragon Prim Sch, Mord.
SM4 off Aragon Rd 221 CY101
Aragon Rd, Kings.T. KT2 200 CL92
Morden SM4 221 CX100
Aragon Twr, SE8 33 N9
Aragon Wk, Byfleet KT14 234 BM113
Aragorn Ct, Guil. GU2 264 AV132
Aran Ct, Wey. KT13
off Mallards Reach 217 BR103
Arandora Cres, Rom. RM6 148 EV59
Aran Dr, Stan. HA7 117 CJ49
Aran Hts, Ch.St.G. HP8 112 AV49
Aran Ms, N7
off Barnsbury Gro 8 E6
Arbery Rd, E3 21 L2
Arbor Cl, Beck. BR3 225 EB96
Arbor Ct, N16 144 DR61
Arboretum Pl, Bark. IG11
off Ripple Rd 167 EQ66
Arborfield Cl, SW2 203 DM88
Slough SL1 174 AS76
Arbor Ho, Orp. BR6
off Station Rd 227 ET103
Arbor Rd, E4 123 ED48
Arbour, The, Hert. SG13 54 DR11
Arbour Cl, Fetch. KT22 253 CF123
Warley CM14 130 FW50
Arbour Rd, Enf. EN3 105 DX42
Arbour Sq, E1 21 J9
Sch Arbour Vale Sch, Slou.
SL2 off Farnham Rd 153 AP69
Arbour Vw, Amer. HP7 94 AV39
Arbour Way, Horn. RM12 149 FH64
Arbroath Grn, Wat. WD19 115 BU48
Arbroath Rd, SE9 186 EL83
Arbrook Chase, Esher KT10 236 CC107
Arbrook Cl, Orp. BR5 228 EU97
Arbrook La, Esher KT10 236 CC107
Arbury Ter, SE26 204 DU90
Arbuthnot La, Bex. DA5 208 EY86
Arbuthnot Rd, SE14 45 J8
Arbutus Cl, Red. RH1 288 DC136
Arbutus Rd, Red. RH1 288 DC136
Arbutus St, E8 10 A8
Arcade, The, EC2 19 N7
Croydon CR0 off High St 224 DQ104
Hatfield AL10
off Wellfield Rd 67 CV17
Romford RM3 128 FK50
Arcade Pl, Rom. RM1 149 FE57
Arcadia Av, N3 120 DA53
Arcadia Caravans, Stai. TW18 216 BH95
🔒 Arcadia Cen, The, W5 159 CK73
Arcadia Cl, Cars. SM5 240 DG105
Arcadian Av, Bex. DA5 208 EY86
Arcadian Cl, Bex. DA5 208 EY86
Arcadian Gdns, N22 121 DM52
Arcadian Pl, SW18 201 CY87
Arcadian Rd, Bex. DA5 208 EY86
Arcadia St, E14 22 B8
Arcany Rd, S.Ock. RM15 171 FV70
Arc Ct, N11
off Friern Barnet Rd 121 DH49
★ ArcelorMittal Orbit, E20 12 D8
Archangel St, SE16 33 K5
Archates Av, Grays RM16 192 GA76
Sch Archbishop Lanfranc Sch, The,
Croy. CR0 off Mitcham Rd 223 DL100
Archbishops Pl, SW2 203 DM86
Sch Archbishop Sumner C of E
Prim Sch, SE11 30 F9
Sch Archbishop Tenison's C of E
High Sch, Croy. CR0
off Selborne Rd 224 DT104
Sch Archbishop Tenison's Sch,
SE11 42 D3
Archdale Pl, N.Mal. KT3 220 CP97
Archdale Rd, SE22 204 DT85
Sch Archdeacon Cambridge's C of E
Prim Sch, Twick. TW2
off The Green 199 CE89
Archel Rd, W14 38 G2
Archer Cl, Barn. EN5 101 CZ44
Kings L. WD4 80 BM29
Kingston upon Thames KT2 200 CL94
Archer Ho, N1
off Phillipp St 9 P9
SW11 40 A8
Archer Ms, Hmptn H. TW12
off Windmill Rd 198 CC93
SW9 42 A10
Archer Rd, SE25 224 DV98
Orpington BR5 228 EU99
Archers, Harl. CM19 73 EP20
Archers Cl, Hert. SG14 54 DQ08
Archers Ct, S.Ock. RM15 171 FV71
Archers Dr, Enf. EN3 104 DW40
Archers Fld, St.Alb. AL1 65 CF18
ARCHERS GREEN, Welw. AL6 52 DE08
Archer Sq, SE14 45 L3
Archers Ride, Welw.G.C. AL7 52 DB11
Archer St, W1 17 N10
Archer Ter, West Dr. UB7
off Yew Av 156 BL73
Archer Way, Swan. BR8 229 FF96
Archery Cl, W2 16 D9
Harrow HA3 139 CF55
Archery La, Brom. BR2 226 EK100
Archery Pl, Goms. GU5 283 BQ139
Archery Rd, SE9 207 EM85
Archery Steps, W2
off St. Georges Flds 16 D10
Arches, SW9 off Ridgeway Rd 183 DP83
Arches, The, SW6 38 G8
SW8
off New Covent Gdn Mkt 41 P4
WC2 30 B2
Harrow HA2 138 CB61
Windsor SL4 173 AQ81
Archfield, Welw.G.C. AL7 51 CY06
● Archgate Business Cen,
N12 off High Rd 120 DC50
Archibald Cl, Enf. EN3 105 DX36
Archibald Ms, W1 29 H1
Archibald Rd, N7 7 N1
Romford RM3 128 FN53
Archibald St, E3 22 A3
Archie Cl, West Dr. UB7 176 BN75
Archie St, SE1 31 P5
Coll Architectural Assoc Sch of
Architecture, WC1 17 P7
Arch Rd, Hersham KT12 218 BX104
Arch St, SE1 31 J7
⊖ Archway 143 DJ61
Archway, Rom. RM3 127 FH51
● Archway Business Cen,
N19 off Wedmore St 143 DK62
Uni Archway Campus, The,
N19 off Highgate Hill 143 DJ61
Archway Cl, N19
off Archway Rd 143 DJ61
SW19 202 DB91
W10 14 C7
Wallington SM6 223 DK104
Archway Mall, N19 143 DJ61
Archway Ms, SW15
off Putney Br Rd 181 CY84
Dorking RH4 off Chapel Ct 285 CG135
Archway Pl, Dor. RH4
off Chapel Ct 285 CG135
Archway Rd, N6 142 DG58
N19 143 DJ60
Archway St, SW13 180 CS83
Arcola St, E8 10 A2
Arcon Dr, Nthlt. UB5 158 BY70
Arctic St, NW5 7 J3
Arcus Rd, Brom. BR1 206 EE93
Ardbeg Rd, SE24 204 DR86
Arden Cl, SE28 168 EX72
Bovingdon HP3 79 BA28
Bushey Heath WD23 117 CF45
Harrow HA1 139 CD62
Reigate RH2 288 DB138
Twick. TW2 198 BZ87
Arden Ct Gdns, N2 142 DD58
Arden Cres, E14 34 B8
Dagenham RM9 168 EW66
Arden Est, N1 19 N1
Arden Gro, Orp. BR6 245 EP105
Arden Ho, SW9 42 B9
Arden Ms, E17 145 EB57
Arden Mhor, Pnr. HA5 137 BV56
Arden Rd, N3 141 CY55
W13 159 CJ73
Ardens Way, St.Alb. AL4 65 CK18
Ardent Cl, SE25 224 DS97
Ardesley Wd, Wey. KT13 235 BS105
Ardfern Av, SW16 223 DN97
Ardfillan Rd, SE6 205 ED88
Ardgowan Rd, SE6 206 EE87
Ardilaun Rd, N5 144 DQ63
Ardingly Cl, Croy. CR0 225 DX104
Ardleigh Cl, Horn. RM11 150 FK55
Ardleigh Ct, Shenf. CM15 131 FZ45
Ardleigh Gdns, Hutt. CM13
off Fairview Av 131 GE44
Sutton SM3 222 DA101
ARDLEIGH GREEN, Horn.
RM11 150 FJ56
Sch Ardleigh Grn Inf Sch, Horn.
RM11 off Ardleigh Grn Rd 150 FK55
Sch Ardleigh Grn Jun Sch, Horn.
RM11 off Ardleigh Grn Rd 150 FK55
Ardleigh Grn Rd, Horn. RM11 150 FK57
Ardleigh Ms, Ilf. IG1
off Bengal Rd 147 EP62
Ardleigh Rd, E17 123 DZ53
N1 9 M5
Ardleigh Ter, E17 123 DZ53
Ardley Cl, NW10 140 CS62
SE6 205 DY90
Ruislip HA4 137 BQ59
Ardley Cres, Hat.Hth CM22 59 FH05
ARDLEY END, B.Stort. CM22 59 FH06
Ardlui Rd, SE27 204 DQ89
Ardmay Gdns, Surb. KT6 220 CL99
Ardmere Rd, SE13 205 ED86
Ardmore Av, Guil. GU2 264 AV132
Ardmore La, Buck.H. IG9 124 EH45
Ardmore Pl, Buck.H. IG9 124 EH45
Ardmore Rd, S.Ock. RM15 171 FV70
Ardmore Way, Guil. GU2 264 AV132
Ardoch Rd, SE6 205 ED89
Ardra Rd, N9 123 DX48
Ardrossan Cl, Slou. SL2 153 AQ70
Ardrossan Gdns,
Wor.Pk. KT4 221 CU104
Ardross Av, Nthwd. HA6 115 BS50
Ardshiel Cl, SW15
off Bemish Rd 181 CX83
Ardshiel Dr, Red. RH1 288 DE136
Ardwell Av, Ilf. IG6 147 EQ57
Ardwell Rd, SW2 203 DL89
Ardwick Rd, NW2 142 DA63
🏛 Arena 224 DW99
🔒 Arena, The, Enf. EN3 105 DZ38
🔒 Arena Shop Pk, N4 143 DP58
Arena Sq, Wem. HA9 140 CN63
Arewater Grn, Loug. IG10 107 EM39
Argali Ho, Erith DA18
off Kale Rd 188 EY76
Argall Av, E10 145 DX59
Argall Way, E10 145 DX60
Argenta Way, NW10 160 CP66
● Argent Business Cen,
Hayes UB3 177 BU75
Argent Cl, Egh. TW20 195 BC93
Argent Ct, Barn. EN5 102 DC42
Grays RM17 192 GA80
Argento Twr, SW18 202 DB86
Argent St, Grays RM17 192 FY79
Argent Way, Chsht EN7 88 DR26
Argles Cl, Green. DA9
off Cowley Av 211 FU85
Argon Ms, SW6 39 K5
Argon Rd, N18 122 DW50
Argosy Gdns, Stai. TW18 195 BF93
Argosy La, Stanw. TW19 196 BK87
Argus Cl, Rom. RM7 127 FB53
Argus Way, Nthlt. UB5 158 BY69
Argyle Av, Houns. TW3 198 CA86
Argyle Cl, W13 159 CG70
Argyle Ct, Wat. WD18 97 BT42
Argyle Gdns, Upmin. RM14 151 FR61
Argyle Pas, N17 122 DT53
Argyle Pl, W6 181 CV77
Sch Argyle Prim Sch, WC1 18 A2
Argyle Rd, E1 21 J4
E15 13 J1
E16 24 B9
N12 120 DA50
N17 122 DU53
N18 122 DU49
W13 159 CG71
Barnet EN5 101 CW42
Greenford UB6 159 CF69
Harrow HA2 138 CB58
Hounslow TW3 198 CB85
Ilford IG1 147 EN61
Sevenoaks TN13 279 FH125
Teddington TW11 199 CE92
Argyle Sq, WC1 18 B2
Argyle St, WC1 18 A2
Argyle Wk, WC1 18 B3

Argyle Way, SE16 44 D1
Argyll Av, Slou. SL1 153 AN73
Southall UB1 158 CB74
Argyll Cl, SW9 42 C10
Argyll Gdns, Edg. HA8 118 CP54
Argyll Rd, SE18 187 EQ76
W8 27 J5
Grays RM17 192 GA78
Hemel Hempstead HP2 62 BL15
Argyll St, W1 17 L9
Aria Ho, WC2 18 B8
Arica Ho, SE16 32 F6
Arica Rd, SE4 185 DY84
Ariel Apts, E16
off Fords Pk Rd 23 P8
Ariel Cl, Grav. DA12 213 GM91
Ariel Rd, NW6 5 J5
Ariel Way, W12 26 B2
Hounslow TW4 177 BV83
Arisdale Av, S.Ock. RM15 171 FV71
Aristotle Rd, SW4 183 DK83
Arizona Bldg, SE13
off Deals Gateway 46 C7
Sch Ark Acad, Wem. HA9
off Forty Av 140 CN61
Ark Av, Grays RM16 192 GA76
Arkell Gro, SE19 203 DP94
Arkindale Rd, SE6 205 EC90
Arklay Cl, Uxb. UB8 156 BM70
ARKLEY, Barn. EN5 101 CU43
Arkley Ct, Hem.H. HP2
off Arkley Rd 63 BP15
Arkley Cres, E17 145 DZ57
Arkley Dr, Barn. EN5 101 CU42
Arkley La, Barn. EN5 101 CU41
Arkley Pk, Barn. EN5 100 CR44
Arkley Rd, E17 145 DZ57
Hemel Hempstead HP2 63 BP15
Arkley Vw, Barn. EN5 101 CV42
Arklow Ct, Chorl. WD3
off Station App 95 BD42
Arklow Ho, SE17 43 L2
Arklow Ms, Surb. KT6
off Vale Rd S 220 CL103
Arklow Rd, SE14 45 N3
Arkwright Rd, NW3 5 N3
Colnbrook SL3 175 BE82
South Croydon CR2 242 DT110
Tilbury RM18 193 GG82
Arkwrights, Harl. CM20 57 ET14
Arlesey Cl, SW15 201 CY85
Arlesford Rd, SW9 42 B10
Arlingford Rd, SW2 203 DN85
Arlingham Ms, Wal.Abb.
EN9 off Sun St 89 EC33
Arlington, N12 120 DA48
Arlington Av, N1 9 K9
Arlington Bldg, E3 12 B10
Arlington Cl, SE13 205 ED85
Sidcup DA15 207 ES87
Sutton SM1 222 DA103
Twickenham TW1 199 CJ86
Arlington Ct, W3
off Mill Hill Rd 160 CP74
Hayes UB3
off Shepiston La 177 BR78
Reigate RH2
off Oakfield Dr 272 DB132
Arlington Cres, Wal.Cr. EN8 89 DY34
Arlington Dr, Cars. SM5 222 DF103
Ruislip HA4 137 BR58
Arlington Gdns, W4 180 CQ78
Ilford IG1 147 EN60
Romford RM3 128 FL53
Arlington Grn, NW7 119 CX52
Arlington Ho, SE8 off Evelyn St 45 P2
SW1 off Arlington St 29 L2
West Drayton UB7
off Porters Way 176 BM75
Arlington Lo, SW2 183 DM84
Weybridge KT13 235 BP105
Arlington Ms, Twick. TW1
off Arlington Rd 199 CJ86
Arlington Pl, SE10 46 E5
Arlington Rd, N14 121 DH47
NW1 7 K9
W13 159 CH72
Ashford TW15 196 BM92
Richmond TW10 199 CK89
Surbiton KT6 219 CK100
Teddington TW11 199 CF91
Twickenham TW1 199 CJ86
Woodford Green IG8 124 EG53
Arlington Sq, N1 9 K9
Arlington St, SW1 29 L2
Arlington Way, EC1 18 F2
Arliss Way, Nthlt. UB5 158 BW67
Arlow Rd, N21 121 DN46
Armada Ct, SE8 46 A3
Grays RM16 off Hogg La 192 GA76
Armadale Cl, N17 144 DV56
Armadale Rd, SW6 39 J4
Feltham TW14 197 BU85
Woking GU21 248 AU117
Armada Way, E6 167 EQ73
Armagh Rd, E3 11 P9
Armand Cl, Wat. WD17 97 BT38
Armfield Cl, W.Mol. KT8 218 BZ99
Armfield Cres, Mitch. CR4 222 DF96
Armfield Rd, Enf. EN2 104 DR39
Arminger Rd, W12 161 CV74
Armistice Gdns, SE25 224 DU97
Armitage Cl, Loud. WD3 96 BK42
Armitage Rd, NW11 141 CZ60
SE10 35 L10
Armor Rd, Purf. RM19 191 FR77
Armour Cl, N7 8 C5
Armoury Dr, Grav. DA12 213 GJ87
Armoury Rd, SE8 46 D9
Armoury Way, SW18 202 DA85
Armstead Wk, Dag. RM10 168 FA66
Armstrong Av, Wdf.Grn. IG8 124 EE51
Armstrong Cl, E6 25 K8
Borehamwood WD6 100 CQ41
Bromley BR1 226 EL97
Dagenham RM8 148 EX59
Halstead TN14 263 FB115
London Colney AL2 84 CL27
Pinner HA5 137 BU58
Walton-on-Thames KT12 217 BU100
Armstrong Cres, Cockfos. EN4 102 DD41
Armstrong Gdns, Shenley WD7 84 CL32
Armstrong Ho, Uxb. UB8
off High St 156 BJ66
Armstrong Pl, Hem.H. HP1
off High St 62 BK19
Armstrong Rd, NW10 160 CS66
SE18 187 EQ76
SW7 28 A7
Armstrong Rd, W3 161 CT74
Englefield Green TW20 194 AW93
Feltham TW13 198 BY92
Armstrong Way, Sthl. UB2 178 CB75
Armytage Rd, Houns. TW5 178 BX80
Arnal Cres, SW18 201 CY87
Arncliffe Cl, N11 120 DG51
Arncroft Ct, Bark. IG11
off Renwick Rd 168 EV69
Arndale Wk, SW18
off Garratt La 202 DB85
Arndale Way, Egh. TW20
off Church Rd 195 BA92
Arne Gro, Horl. RH6 290 DE146
Orpington BR6 227 ET104
Arne Ho, SE11 30 C10
Arne St, WC2 18 B9
Arnett Cl, Rick. WD3 96 BG44
Sch Arnett Hills JMI Sch, Rick.
WD3 off Berry La 96 BG44
Arnett Sq, E4 123 DZ51
Arnett Way, Rick. WD3 96 BG44
Arne Wk, SE3 186 EF84
Arneways Av, Rom. RM6 148 EX55
Arneway St, SW1 29 P7
Arnewood Cl, SW15 201 CU88
Oxshott KT22 236 CB113
Arney's La, Mitch. CR4 222 DG100
Arngask Rd, SE6 205 ED87
Arnhem Av, Aveley RM15 170 FQ74
Arnhem Dr, New Adgtn CR0 243 ED111
Arnhem Pl, E14 34 A7
Arnhem Way, SE22
off East Dulwich Gro 204 DS85
Arnhem Wf, E14 off Arnhem Pl 34 A7
Sch Arnhem Wf Prim Sch, E14 34 A7
Arnison Rd, E.Mol. KT8 219 CD98
Arnold Av E, Enf. EN3 105 EA38
Arnold Av W, Enf. EN3 105 DZ38
Arnold Bennett Way, N8
off Burghley Rd 143 DN55
Arnold Circ, E2 20 A3
Arnold Cl, Har. HA3 140 CM59
Arnold Cres, Islw. TW7 199 CD85
Arnold Dr, Chess. KT9 237 CK107
Arnold Est, SE1 32 B5
Arnold Gdns, N13 121 DP50
Sch Arnold Ho Sch, NW8 16 A1
Arnold Pl, Til. RM18 193 GJ81
Arnold Rd, E3 22 A2
N15 144 DT55
SW17 202 DF94
Dagenham RM9, RM10 168 EZ66
Gravesend DA12 213 GJ89
Northolt UB5 158 BX65
Staines-upon-Thames TW18 196 BJ94
Waltham Abbey EN9 105 EC36
Woking GU21 249 BB116
Arnolds Av, Hutt. CM13 131 GC43
Arnolds Cl, Hutt. CM13 131 GC43
Arnolds Fm La, Mtnsg CM13 131 GE41
Arnolds La, Sutt.H. DA4 210 FM93
⊖ Arnos Grove 121 DJ49
Arnos Gro, N14 121 DK49
Arnos Rd, N11 121 DJ50
Arnott Cl, SE28
off Applegarth Rd 168 EW73
W4 180 CR77
Arnould Av, SE5 184 DR84
Arnsberg Way, Bexh. DA7 188 FA84
Arnside Gdns, Wem. HA9 139 CK60
Arnside Rd, Bexh. DA7 188 FA81
Arnside St, SE17 43 K2
Arnulf St, SE6 205 EB91
Arnulls Rd, SW16 203 DN93
Arodene Rd, SW2 203 DM86
Arosa Rd, Twick. TW1 199 CK86
Arpley Sq, SE20 off High St 204 DW94
Arragon Gdns, SW16 203 DL94
West Wickham BR4 225 EB104
Arragon Rd, E6 166 EK67
SW18 202 DB88
Twickenham TW1 199 CG87
Arran Cl, Erith DA8 189 FD79
Hemel Hempstead HP3 63 BQ22
Wallington SM6 241 DH105
Arran Dr, E12 146 EK60
Arran Grn, Wat. WD19
off Prestwick Rd 116 BX49
Arran Ms, W5 160 CM74
Arranmore Ct, Bushey WD23 98 BY42
Arran Rd, SE6 205 EB89
Arran Wk, N1 9 J6
Arran Way, Esher KT10 218 CB103
Arras Av, Mord. SM4 222 DC99
Arretine Cl, St.Alb. AL3 64 BZ22
Arreton Mead, Horsell GU21 232 AY114
Arrol Ho, SE1 31 K7
Arrol Rd, Beck. BR3 224 DW97
Arrow Rd, E3 22 C2
Arrowscout Wk, Nthlt. UB5
off Wayfarer Rd 158 BY69
Arrowsmith Cl, Chig. IG7 125 ET50
Arrowsmith Ho, SE11 30 C10
Arrowsmith Path, Chig. IG7 125 ET50
Arrowsmith Rd, Chig. IG7 125 ES50
Loughton IG10 106 EL41
⊖ Arsenal 143 DN62
★ Arsenal FC, N5 8 E1
Arsenal Rd, SE9 187 EM82
Arsenal Way, SE18 187 EQ76
Arta Ho, E1 21 H9
Artemis Cl, Grav. DA12 213 GL87
Arterberry Rd, SW20 201 CW94
Arterial Av, Rain. RM13 169 FH70
Arterial Rd N Stifford,
Grays RM17 192 FY75
Arterial Rd Purfleet, Purf.
RM19 190 FN76
Arterial Rd W Thurrock,
Grays RM16, RM20 191 FU76
Artesian Cl, NW10 160 CR66
Hornchurch RM11 149 FF58
Artesian Gro, Barn. EN5 102 DC41
Artesian Rd, W2 15 J9
Artesian Wk, E11 146 EE62
Arthingworth St, E15 13 J8
Arthur Ct, SW11 41 H7
W2 15 L8
Arthurdon Rd, SE4 205 EA85
Arthur Gro, SE18 187 EQ77
Arthur Henderson Ho, SW6 38 G8
Arthur Horsley Wk, E7 13 M2
★ Arthur Jacob Nature Reserve,
Slou. SL3 175 BC83
Arthur Newton Ho, SW11
off Lavender Rd 40 B10
Arthur Rd, E6 167 EM68
N7 143 DM63
Arthur Rd, N9 122 DT47
SW19 202 DA90
Biggin Hill TN16 260 EJ115
Kingston upon Thames KT2 200 CN94
New Malden KT3 221 CV99
Romford RM6 148 EW59
St. Albans AL1 65 CH20
Slough SL1 173 AR75
Windsor SL4 173 AP81
Arthur's Br Rd, Wok. GU21 248 AW117
Arthur St, EC4 31 M1
Bushey WD23 98 BX42
Erith DA8 189 FF80
Gravesend DA11 213 GG87
Grays RM17 192 GC79
Arthur St W, Grav. DA11 213 GG87
Arthur Toft Ho, Grays RM17
off New Rd 192 GB79
Arthur Vil, Epsom KT17 239 CT112
Arthur Walls Ho, E12
off Grantham Rd 147 EN62
Artichoke Dell, Chorl. WD3 95 BE43
Artichoke Hill, E1 32 E1
Artichoke Pl, SE5 43 L6
Artillery Cl, Ilf. IG2
off Horns Rd 147 EQ58
Artillery La, E1 19 P7
W12 161 CU72
Artillery Mans, SW1 29 N6
Artillery Pas, E1 19 P7
Artillery Pl, SE18 37 K9
SW1 29 N7
Harrow HA3
off Chicheley Rd 116 CC52
Artillery Rd, Guil. GU1 280 AX135
Artillery Row, SW1 29 N7
Gravesend DA12 213 GJ87
Artillery Ter, Guil. GU1 264 AX134
ARTINGTON, Guil. GU3 280 AW139
Artington Cl, Orp. BR6 245 EQ105
Artington Wk, Guil. GU2 280 AW137
Artisan Cl, E6 25 N10
Artisan Cres, St.Alb. AL3 64 CC19
Artizan St, E1 19 P8
Sch Arts Ed Sch London, The,
W4 off Bath Rd 180 CS77
Arundel Av, Epsom KT17 239 CV110
Morden SM4 221 CZ98
South Croydon CR2 242 DU110
Arundel Cl, E15 13 K1
SW11 202 DE85
Bexley DA5 208 EZ86
Cheshunt EN8 88 DW28
Croydon CR0 223 DP104
Hampton Hill TW12 198 CB92
Hemel Hempstead HP2 63 BP19
Arundel Ct, N12 120 DE51
Harrow HA2 138 CA63
Slough SL3 174 AX77
Arundel Dr, Borwd. WD6 100 CQ43
Harrow HA2 138 BZ63
Orpington BR6 246 EV106
Woodford Green IG8 124 EG52
Arundel Gdns, N21 121 DN46
W11 14 G10
Edgware HA8 118 CR52
Ilford IG3 148 EU61
Arundel Gt Ct, WC2 18 D10
Arundel Gro, N16 9 N2
St. Albans AL3 65 CD15
Arundel Pl, N1 8 E5
Arundel Rd, Abb.L. WD5 81 BU32
Cockfosters EN4 102 DE41
Croydon CR0 224 DR100
Dartford DA1 190 FJ84
Dorking RH4 285 CG136
Hounslow TW4 178 BW83
Kingston upon Thames KT1 220 CP96
Romford RM3 128 FM53
Sutton SM2 239 CZ108
Uxbridge UB8 156 BH68
Arundel Sq, N7 8 E5
Arundel St, WC2 18 D10
Arundel Ter, SW13 181 CV79
Arvon Rd, N5 8 F2
Asbaston Ter, Ilf. IG1
off Buttsbury Rd 147 EQ64
Ascalon Ho, SW8
off Ascalon St 41 L5
Ascalon St, SW8 41 L5
Ascension Rd, Rom. RM5 127 FC51
Ascent, NW9
off Boulevard Dr 119 CT54
● Ascent Pk, Harl. CM20 58 EU10
Ascham Dr, E4
off Rushcroft Rd 123 EB52
Ascham End, E17 123 DY53
Ascham St, NW5 7 L2
Aschurch Rd, Croy. CR0 224 DT101
Ascot Cl, Els. WD6 100 CN43
Ilford IG6 125 ES51
Northolt UB5 138 CA64
Ascot Gdns, Enf. EN3 104 DW37
Hornchurch RM12 150 FL63
Southall UB1 158 BZ71
Ascot Ms, Wall. SM6 241 DJ109
Ascot Rd, E6 25 J2
N15 144 DR57
N18 122 DU49
SW17 202 DG93
Feltham TW14 196 BN88
Gravesend DA12 213 GH90
Orpington BR5 227 ET98
Watford WD18 97 BS43
Ascots La, Welw.G.C. AL7 51 CY14
Ascott Av, W5 180 CL75
Ascot Ter, Gt Amwell SG12
off Yearling Cl 55 DZ08
Ashanti Ms, E8 10 F3
Ashbeam Cl, Gt Warley
CM13 129 FW51
Ashbourne, St.Alb. AL2 82 BZ31
Ashbourne Av, E18 146 EH56
N20 120 DF47
NW11 141 CZ57
Bexleyheath DA7 188 EY80
Harrow HA2 139 CD61
Ashbourne Cl, N12 120 DB49
W5 160 CN71
Coulsdon CR5 257 DJ118
Ashbourne Ct, E5
off Daubeney Rd 145 DY63
Ashbourne Gdns, Hert. SG13 54 DS11
Ashbourne Gro, NW7 118 CR50
SE22 204 DT85
W4 180 CS78
Ashbourne Ho, Slou. SL1 174 AS75
Coll Ashbourne Indep 6th
Form Coll, W8 27 L4
Ashbourne Par, W5
off Ashbourne Rd 160 CM70
Ashbourne Ri, Orp. BR6 245 ER105
Ashbourne Rd, W5 160 CM71
Broxbourne EN10 71 DZ21
Mitcham CR4 202 DG93
Romford RM3 128 FJ49
Ashbourne Sq, Nthwd. HA6 115 BS51
Ashbourne Ter, SW19 202 DA94
Ashbourne Way, NW11 141 CZ57
Ashbridge Rd, E11 146 EE59
Ashbridge St, NW8 16 C5
Ashbrook Rd, N19 143 DK60
Dagenham RM10 149 FB62
Old Windsor SL4 194 AV87
Ashburn Gdns, SW7 27 N8
Ashburnham Av, Har. HA1 139 CF58
Ashburnham Cl, N2 142 DD55
Sevenoaks TN13
off Fiennes Way 279 FJ127
Watford WD19 115 BU48
Ashburnham Dr, Wat. WD19 115 BU48
Ashburnham Gdns, Har. HA1 139 CF58
Upminster RM14 150 FP60
Ashburnham Gro, SE10 46 D5
Ashburnham Pk, Esher KT10 236 CC105
Ashburnham Pl, SE10 46 D5
Sch Ashburnham Prim Sch,
SW10 40 A4
Ashburnham Retreat, SE10 46 D5
Ashburnham Rd, NW10 14 A2
SW10 39 P5
Belvedere DA17 189 FC77
Richmond TW10 199 CH90
Ashburnham Twr, SW10
off Blantyre St 40 A4
Ashburn Pl, SW7 27 N8
Ashburton Av, Croy. CR0 224 DV102
Ilford IG3 147 ES63
Ashburton Cl, Croy. CR0 224 DU102
Ashburton Ct, Pnr. HA5 138 BX55
Ashburton Gdns, Croy.
CR0 224 DU103
Sch Ashburton Jun & Inf Sch,
Croy. CR0 off Long La 224 DV100
Ashburton Rd, E16 23 P8
Croydon CR0 224 DU102
Ruislip HA4 137 BU61
Ashburton Ter, E13 13 N10
Ashburton Triangle, N5
off Drayton Pk 143 DN63
Ashbury Cl, Hat. AL10 66 CS18
Ashbury Cres, Guil. GU4 265 BC132
Ashbury Dr, Uxb. UB10 137 BP61
Ashbury Gdns, Rom. RM6 148 EX57
Ashbury Pl, SW19 202 DC93
Ashbury Rd, SW11 40 G10
Ashby Av, Chess. KT9 238 CN107
Ashby Cl, Horn. RM11
off Holme Rd 150 FN60
Ashby Gdns, St.Alb. AL1 65 CD24
Ashby Gro, N1 9 K6
Ashby Ho, N1 9 K6
Ashby Ms, SE4 45 N9
SW2 off Prague Pl 203 DL85
Ashby Rd, N15 144 DU57
SE4 45 P9
Watford WD24 97 BU38
Ashby St, EC1 19 H3
Ashby Wk, Croy. CR0 224 DQ100
Ashby Way, Sipson UB7 176 BN80
Ashchurch Gro, W12 181 CU75
Ashchurch Pk Vil, W12 181 CU76
Ashchurch Ter, W12 181 CU76
Ash Cl, SE20 224 DW96
Abbots Langley WD5 81 BR32
Brookmans Park AL9 86 DA25
Carshalton SM5 222 DF103
Edgware HA8 118 CQ49
Harefield UB9 114 BK53
New Malden KT3 220 CR96
Petts Wood BR5 227 ER99
Pilgrim's Hatch CM15 130 FT43
Pyrford GU22 250 BG115
Romford RM5 127 FB52
Sidcup DA14 208 EV90
Slough SL3 175 BB76
South Merstham RH1 273 DJ130
Stanmore HA7 117 CG51
Swanley BR8 229 FC96
Tadworth KT20 270 CQ131
Watford WD25 97 BV35
Woking GU22 248 AY120
Ashcombe, Welw.G.C. AL8 51 CY05
Ashcombe Av, Surb. KT6 219 CK101
Ashcombe Cl, Ashf. TW15 196 BK90
Ashcombe Gdns, Edg. HA8 118 CN49
Ashcombe Ho, Enf. EN3 105 DX41
Ashcombe Pk, NW2 140 CS62
Ashcombe Rd, SW19 202 DA92
Carshalton SM5 240 DG107
Dorking RH4 269 CG134
Merstham RH1 273 DJ127
Sch Ashcombe Sch, The, Dor.
RH4 off Ashcombe Rd 269 CH134
Ashcombe Sq, N.Mal. KT3 220 CQ97
Ashcombe St, SW6 39 L9
Ashcombe Ter, Tad. KT20 255 CV120
Ash Copse, Brick.Wd AL2 82 BZ31
Ash Ct, N11 off Cline Rd 121 DJ51
Epsom KT19 238 CQ105
Ashcroft, Pnr. HA5 116 CA51
Shalford GU4 280 AY141
Ashcroft Av, Sid. DA15 208 EU86
Ashcroft Ct, N20 120 DD47
Broxbourne EN10
off Winford Dr 71 DZ22
Burnham SL1 152 AH68
Ashcroft Cres, Sid. DA15 208 EU86
Ashcroft Dr, Denh. UB9 135 BF58
Ashcroft Pk, Cob. KT11 236 BY112
Ashcroft Pl, Lthd. KT22 253 CJ121
Ashcroft Ri, Couls. CR5 257 DL116
Ashcroft Rd, E3 21 L3
Chessington KT9 220 CM104
Ashcroft Sq, W6 26 A9
Ashdale, Bkhm KT23 268 CC126
Ashdale Cl, Stai. TW19 196 BL89
Twickenham TW2 198 CC87
Ashdale Gro, Stan. HA7 117 CF51
Ashdale Rd, SE12 206 EH88
Ashdales, St.Alb. AL1 65 CD24
Ashdale Way, Twick. TW2
off Ashdale Cl 198 CC87
Ashdene, SE15 44 E6
Pinner HA5 138 BW55
Ashdene Cl, Ashf. TW15 197 BQ94
Ashdon Cl, Hutt. CM13
off Poplar Dr 131 GC44
Ashdon Cl, South Ockendon RM15
off Afton Dr 171 FV72
Woodford Green IG8 124 EH51
Ashdon Rd, NW10 160 CS67
Bushey WD23 98 BX41
Ashdown Cl, Beck. BR3 225 EB96
Bexley DA5 209 FC87
Reigate RH2 288 DB138
Woking GU22
off Guildford Rd 248 AY118
Ashdown Ct, E17 123 EC54
Ashdown Cres, NW5 6 G3
Cheshunt EN8 89 DY28
Ashdown Dr, Borwd. WD6 100 CM40
Ashdown Gdns, S.Croy. CR2 258 DV115
Ashdown Pl, T.Ditt. KT7 219 CG100
Ashdown Rd, Enf. EN3 104 DW41
Epsom KT17 239 CT113
Kingston upon Thames KT1 220 CL96
Reigate RH2 288 DB138
Uxbridge UB10 156 BN68
Ashdown Wk, E14 34 B8
Romford RM7 127 FB54
Ashdown Way, SW17 202 DG89
Amersham HP6 77 AR37
Ash Dr, Hat. AL10 67 CU21
Redhill RH1 289 DH136
Ashen, E6 25 L8
Jct Ashen Cross, Slou. SL3 155 BB71
Ashenden, SE17 31 J8
Ashendene Rd, Bayford SG13 69 DL20
Ashenden Rd, E5 11 K2
Guildford GU2 280 AT135
Ashenden Wk, Farn.Com. SL2 133 AR63
Ashen Dr, Dart. DA1 209 FG86
Ashen Gro, SW19 202 DA90
Ashentree Ct, EC4 18 F9
Ashen Vale, S.Croy. CR2 243 DX109
● Asheridge Business Cen,
Chesh. HP5 76 AN29
Asheridge Rd, Chesh. HP5 76 AM28
Asher Loftus Way, N11 120 DF51
Asher Way, E1 32 D2
Ashfield Av, Bushey WD23 98 CB44
Feltham TW13 197 BV88
Ashfield Cl, Ashtd. KT21 254 CL119
Beckenham BR3 205 EA94
Richmond TW10 200 CL88
Sch Ashfield Jun Sch,
Bushey WD23
off School La 116 CB45
Ashfield La, Chis. BR7 207 EQ93
Ashfield Par, N14 121 DK46
Ashfield Rd, N4 144 DQ58
N14 121 DJ48
W3 161 CT74
Chesham HP5 76 AR29
Ashfields, Loug. IG10 107 EM40
Reigate RH2 272 DB132
Watford WD25 97 BT35
Ashfield St, E1 20 E7
Ashfield Yd, E1 20 G7
ASHFORD, TW15 196 BM92
⇌ Ashford 196 BL91
Ashford Av, N8 143 DL56
Ashford TW15 197 BP93
Brentwood CM14 130 FV48
Hayes UB4 158 BX72
Ashford Cl, E17 145 DZ58
Ashford TW15 196 BL91
Sch Ashford C of E Prim Sch, Ashf.
TW15 off School Rd 197 BP93
Ashford Cres, Ashf. TW15 196 BL90
Enfield EN3 104 DW40
Ashford Gdns, Cob. KT11 252 BX116
Ashford Grn, Wat. WD19 116 BX50
H Ashford Hosp, Ashf. TW15 196 BL89
● Ashford Ind Est, Ashf.
TW15 197 BQ91
Ashford La, Dorney SL4 172 AH75
Maidenhead SL6 172 AG75
Ashford Ms, N17 122 DU53
Sch Ashford Pk Prim Sch,
Ashf. TW15
off Station Cres 196 BK91
Ashford Rd, E6 167 EN65
E18 124 EH54
NW2 4 C1
Ashford TW15 197 BQ94
Feltham TW13 197 BT90
Iver SL0 155 BC66
Staines-upon-Thames TW18 216 BK95
Ashford St, N1 19 N2
Ash Grn, Denh. UB9 156 BH65
Ash Gro, E8 10 F9
N10 143 DH56
N13 122 DQ48
NW2 4 D1
SE20 224 DW96
W5 180 CL75
Amersham HP6 77 AN36
Enfield EN1 122 DS45
Feltham TW14 197 BS88
Guildford GU2 264 AU134
Harefield UB9 114 BK53
Hayes UB3 157 BR73
Hemel Hempstead HP3 62 BM24
Hounslow TW5 178 BX81
Southall UB1 158 CA71
Staines-upon-Thames TW18 196 BJ93
Stoke Poges SL2 154 AT66
Wembley HA0 139 CG63
West Drayton UB7 156 BM73
West Wickham BR4 225 EC103
Ashgrove Rd, Ashf. TW15 197 BQ92
Bromley BR1 205 ED93
Ilford IG3 147 ET60
Sevenoaks TN13 278 FG127
Ash Gros, Saw. CM21 58 FA05
Sch Ashgrove Sch, Brom.
BR1 off Widmore Rd 226 EH96
Ash Hill Cl, Bushey WD23 116 CB46
Ash Hill Dr, Pnr. HA5 138 BW55
Ash Ho, SE1
off Longfield Est 32 B9
● Ash Ind Est,
Harl. CM19 73 EM16
Ashingdon Cl, E4 123 EC48
Ashington Ho, E1
off Barnsley St 20 F4
Ashington Rd, SW6 39 H8

Ash - Aus

Ash Island, E.Mol. KT8 219 CD97
Ashlake Rd, SW16 203 DL91
Ashland Pl, W1 16 G6
Ash La, Horn. RM11
off Wiltshire Av 150 FM56
Romford RM1 127 FG51
Windsor SL4 173 AK82
Ashlar Pl, SE18 37 N9
Ashlea Rd, Chal.St.P. SL9 112 AX54
Ashleigh Av, Egh. TW20 195 BC94
Ashleigh Cl, Amer. HP7 77 AS39
Horley RH6 290 DF148
Ashleigh Cotts, Dor. RH5 285 CH144
Ashleigh Ct, Wal.Abb. EN9
off Lamplighters Cl 90 EG34
Wat. WD17 off Loates La 98 BW41
Ashleigh Gdns, Sutt. SM1 222 DB103
Upminster RM14 151 FR62
Ashleigh Ms, SE15 44 B10
Ashleigh Pt, SE23
off Dacres Rd 205 DX90
Ashleigh Rd, SE20 224 DV97
SW14 180 CS83
Ashley Av, Epsom KT18 238 CR113
Ilford IG6 125 EP54
Morden SM4 222 DA99
● Ashley Cen, Epsom KT18 238 CR113
Ashley Cl, NW4 119 CW54
Bookham KT23 268 BZ125
Hemel Hempstead HP3 62 BM22
Pinner HA5 115 BV54
Sevenoaks TN13 279 FH124
Walton-on-Thames KT12 217 BT102
Welwyn Garden City AL8 51 CW07
Sch Ashley C of E Prim Sch, Walt.
KT12 off Ashley Rd 217 BU102
Ashley Ct, Epsom KT18 238 CR113
Hatfield AL10 67 CU17
Woking GU21 248 AT118
Ashley Cres, N22 121 DN54
SW11 41 H10
Ashley Dr, Bans. SM7 240 DA114
Borehamwood WD6 100 CQ43
Isleworth TW7 179 CE79
Penn HP10 110 AC45
Twickenham TW2 198 CB87
Walton-on-Thames KT12 217 BU104
Ashley Gdns, N13 122 DQ49
SW1 29 M7
Orpington BR6 245 ES106
Richmond TW10 199 CK90
Shalford GU4 281 AZ141
Wembley HA9 140 CL61
ASHLEY GREEN, Chesh. HP5 60 AS24
Ashley Grn Rd, Chesh. HP5 76 AR27
Ashley Gro, Loug. IG10
off Staples Rd 106 EL41
Ashley La, NW4 119 CW54
NW7 119 CW54
Croydon CR0 241 DP105
ASHLEY PARK, Walt. KT12 217 BT104
Ashley Pk Av, Walt. KT12 217 BT103
Ashley Pk Cres, Walt. KT12 217 BT102
Ashley Pk Rd, Walt. KT12 217 BU103
Ashley Pl, SW1 29 L7
Ashley Ri, Walt. KT12 235 BU105
Ashley Rd, E4 123 EA50
E7 166 EJ66
N17 144 DU55
N19 143 DL60
SW19 202 DB93
Enfield EN3 104 DW40
Epsom KT18 238 CR114
Hampton TW12 218 CA95
Hertford SG14 53 DN10
Richmond TW9
off Jocelyn Rd 180 CL83
St. Albans AL1 65 CJ20
Sevenoaks TN13 279 FH123
Thames Ditton KT7 219 CF100
Thornton Heath CR7 223 DM98
Uxbridge UB8 156 BH68
Walton-on-Thames KT12 217 BU102
Westcott RH4 284 CC137
Woking GU21 248 AT118
Ashleys, Rick. WD3 113 BF45
Ashley Sq, Epsom KT18 238 CR113
Ashley Wk, NW7 119 CW52
Ashling Rd, Croy. CR0 224 DU102
Ashlin Rd, E15 13 H1
Ashlone Rd, SW15 38 B10
Ashlyn Cl, Bushey WD23 98 BY42
Ashlyn Gro, Horn. RM11 150 FK55
Ashlyns Ct, Berk. HP4 60 AV20
Ashlyns La, Ong. CM5 75 FG23
Ashlyns Pk, Cob. KT11 236 BY113
Ashlyns Rd, Berk. HP4 60 AV20
Epping CM16 91 ET30
Sch Ashlyns Sch, Berk. HP4
off Chesham Rd 60 AW21
Ashlyns Way, Chess. KT9 237 CK107
Ashmead, N14 103 DJ43
Ashmead Dr, Denh. UB9 136 BG61
Ashmead Gate, Brom. BR1 226 EJ95
Ashmead Ho, E9
off Kingsmead Way 11 M2
Ashmead La, Denh. UB9 136 BG61
Ashmead Ms, SE8
off Ashmead Rd 46 A8
Ashmead Pl, Amer. HP7 94 AW39
Sch Ashmead Prim Sch, SE8 46 A8
Ashmead Rd, SE8 46 A8
Feltham TW14 197 BU88
Ashmeads Ct, Shenley WD7 83 CK33
Ashmere Av, Beck. BR3 225 ED96
Ashmere Cl, Sutt. SM3 239 CW106
Ashmere Gro, SW2 183 DL84
Ash Ms, Epsom KT18 238 CS113
Ashmill St, NW1 16 C6
Ashmole Pl, SW8 42 D3
Sch Ashmole Prim Sch, SW8 42 D3
Sch Ashmole Sch, N14
off Cecil Rd 121 DJ46
Ashmole St, SW8 42 D3
Ashmore Cl, SE15 44 B5
Ashmore Ct, Houns. TW5
off Wheatlands 178 CA79
Ashmore Gdns, Hem.H. HP3 63 BP21
Northfleet DA11 212 GD91
Ashmore Gro, Well. DA16 187 ER83
Ashmore La, Kes. BR2 244 EH111
Ashmore Rd, W9 15 H4
Ashmount Cres, Slou. SL1 173 AN75
Sch Ashmount Prim Sch, N19
off Ashmount Rd 143 DJ59
Ashmount Rd, N15 144 DT57
N19 143 DJ59
Ashmount Ter, W5 179 CK77
Ashmour Gdns, Rom. RM1 127 FD54
Ashneal Gdns, Har. HA1 139 CD62
Ashness Gdns, Grnf. UB6 159 CH65
Ashness Rd, SW11 202 DF85
Ash Platt, The, Seal TN14, TN15 279 FL121
Ash Platt Rd, Seal TN15 279 FL121
Ash Ride, Enf. EN2 103 DN35
Ashridge Cl, Bov. HP3 79 AZ28
Harrow HA3 139 CJ58
Ashridge Cres, SE18 187 EQ80
Ashridge Dr, Brick.Wd AL2 82 BY30
Watford WD19 116 BW50
Ashridge Gdns, N13 121 DK50
Pinner HA5 138 BY56
Ashridge Ri, Berk. HP4 60 AT18
Ashridge Rd, Chesh. HP5 78 AW31
Ashridge Way, Mord. SM4 221 CZ97
Sunbury-on-Thames TW16 197 BU93
Ash Rd, E15 13 K2
Croydon CR0 225 EA103
Dartford DA1 210 FK88
Gravesend DA12 213 GJ91
Hawley DA2 210 FM91
Orpington BR6 245 ET108
Shepperton TW17 216 BN98
Sutton SM3 221 CY101
Westerham TN16 277 ER125
Woking GU22 248 AX120
Ash Row, Brom. BR2 227 EN101
ASHTEAD, KT21 254 CL118
⇌ Ashtead 253 CK117
Ashtead Common, Ashtd. KT21 253 CJ115
Ashtead Gap, Lthd. KT22 253 CH116
H Ashtead Hosp, Ashtd.
KT21 254 CL119
ASHTEAD PARK, Ashtd. KT21 254 CN118
Ashtead Rd, E5 144 DU59
Ashtead Wds Rd, Ashtd. KT21 253 CJ117
Ashton Cl, Hersham KT12 235 BV107
Sutton SM1 240 DA105
Ashton Ct, E4
off Connington Cres 124 EE48
Romford RM6 148 EY58
Ashton Gdns, Houns. TW4 178 BZ84
Romford RM6 148 EY58
Sch Ashton Ho Sch, Islw. TW7
off Eversley Cres 179 CD81
Ashton Rd, E15 12 G3
Enfield EN3 105 DY36
Romford RM3 128 FK52
Woking GU21 248 AT117
Ashton St, E14 22 F10
Ashtree Av, Mitch. CR4 222 DD96
Ash Tree Cl, Croy. CR0 225 DY100
Ashtree Cl, Orp. BR6 245 EP105
Ash Tree Cl, Surb. KT6 220 CL102
Ashtree Ct, St.Alb. AL1
off Granville Rd 65 CF20
Waltham Abbey EN9
off Farthingale La 90 EG34
Ash Tree Dell, NW9 140 CQ57
Ash Tree Fld, Harl. CM20 57 EN13
Ash Tree Rd, Wat. WD24 97 BV36
Ash Tree Way, Croy. CR0 225 DY99
Ashtree Way, Hem.H. HP1 62 BG21
Ashurst Cl, SE20 224 DV95
Dartford DA1 189 FF83
Kenley CR8 258 DR115
Leatherhead KT22 253 CG121
Northwood HA6 115 BS52
Ashurst Dr, Box H. KT20 270 CP130
Ilford IG2, IG6 147 EP58
Shepperton TW17 216 BL99
Ashurst Pl, Dor. RH4 269 CJ134
Ashurst Rd, N12 120 DE50
Barnet EN4 102 DF43
Tadworth KT20 255 CV121
Ashurst Wk, Croy. CR0 224 DV103
Ash Vale, Map.Cr. WD3 113 BD50
Ashvale Dr, Upmin. RM14 151 FS61
Ashvale Gdns, Rom. RM5 127 FD50
Upminster RM14 151 FS61
Ashvale Rd, SW17 202 DF92
Ashview Cl, Ashf. TW15 196 BL93
Ashview Gdns, Ashf. TW15 196 BL92
Ashville Rd, E11 145 ED61
Ash Wk, SW2 203 DM88
South Ockendon RM15 171 FX69
Wembley HA0 139 CJ63
Ashwater Rd, SE12 206 EG88
● Ashway Cen, The, Kings.T.
KT2 off Elm Cres 220 CL95
Ashwell Cl, E6 25 H8
Ashwell Pl, Wat. WD24 97 BU37
Ashwells Manor Dr, Penn
HP10 110 AC47
Ashwells Rd, Pilg.Hat. CM15 130 FS41
Ashwell St, St.Alb. AL3 65 CD19
Ashwells Way, Ch.St.G. HP8 112 AW47
Ashwick Cl, Cat. CR3 274 DU125
Ashwindham Ct, Wok. GU21
off Raglan Rd 248 AT118
Ashwin St, E8 10 A4
Ashwood, Warl. CR6 258 DW120
Ashwood Av, Rain. RM13 169 FH70
Uxbridge UB8 156 BN72
Ashwood Dr, Chesh. HP5 76 AP30
Ashwood Gdns, Hayes UB3
off Cranford Dr 177 BT77
New Addington CR0 243 EB107
Ashwood Ms, St.Alb. AL1
off Prospect Rd 65 CD22
Ashwood Pk, Fetch. KT22 252 CC124
Woking GU22 249 BA118
Ashwood Pl, Bean DA2
off Bean La 211 FV90
Ashwood Rd, E4 123 ED48
Englefield Green TW20 194 AV93
Potters Bar EN6 86 DB33
Woking GU22 249 AZ118
Ashworth Cl, SE5 43 L8
Ashworth Pl, Guil. GU2 264 AT134
Harlow CM17 74 EX15
Ashworth Rd, W9 15 M2
Asker Ho, N7
off Tufnell Pk Rd 143 DL63
Askern Cl, Bexh. DA6 188 EX84
Aske St, N1 19 N2
Askew Cres, W12 181 CT75
Askew Fm La, Grays RM17 192 FY78
Askew Rd, W12 161 CT74
Northwood HA6 115 BR47
Askham Ct, W12 161 CU74
Askham Rd, W12 161 CU74
Askill Dr, SW15 201 CY85
Askwith Rd, Rain. RM13 169 FD69
Asland Rd, E15 13 J9
Aslett St, SW18 202 DB87
Asmara Rd, NW2 4 F2
Asmar Cl, Couls. CR5 257 DL115
Asmuns Hill, NW11 142 DA57
Asmuns Pl, NW11 141 CZ57
Asolando Dr, SE17 31 K9
Aspasia Cl, St.Alb. AL1 65 CF21
Aspdin Rd, Nthflt DA11 212 GD90
Aspect Ct, SW6 39 P8
Aspects, Sutt. SM1 240 DB106
Aspects Ct, Slou. SL1
off Windsor Rd 174 AS75
Aspen Cl, N19
off Hargrave Pk 143 DJ61
W5 180 CM75
Bricket Wood AL2 82 BY30
Guildford GU4 265 BD131
Orpington BR6 246 EU106
Slough SL2 off Birch Gro 153 AP71
Staines-upon-Thames TW18 195 BF90
Stoke D'Abernon KT11 252 BY116
Swanley BR8 229 FD95
West Drayton UB7 156 BM74
Aspen Copse, Brom. BR1 227 EM96
Aspen Ct, Brwd. CM13 131 GA48
Hayes UB3 177 BS77
Virginia Water GU25 214 AY98
Aspen Dr, Wem. HA0 139 CG63
Aspen Gdns, W6 181 CV78
Ashford TW15 197 BQ92
Mitcham CR4 222 DG99
Aspen Grn, Erith DA18 188 EZ76
Aspen Gro, Pnr. HA5 137 BT55
Upminster RM14 150 FN63
Aspen Ho, NW3 6 F4
Warlingham CR6
off East Parkside 259 EB115
Aspen La, Nthlt. UB5 158 BY69
Aspenlea Rd, W6 38 C2
Aspen Pk Dr, Wat. WD25 97 BV35
Aspens Pl, Hem.H. HP1 61 BF23
Aspen Sq, Wey. KT13 217 BR104
Aspen Vale, Whyt. CR3
off Whyteleafe Hill 258 DT118
Aspen Way, E14 34 B1
Banstead SM7 239 CX114
Enfield EN3 105 DX35
Feltham TW13 197 BV90
South Ockendon RM15 171 FX69
Welwyn Garden City AL7 52 DC10
Aspern Gro, NW3 6 D3
Aspfield Row, Hem.H. HP1 62 BH18
Aspinall Rd, SE4 45 K10
Aspinden Rd, SE16 32 F8
Aspley Rd, SW18 202 DB85
Asplins Rd, N17 122 DU53
Asprey Ct, Cat. CR3 258 DT123
Asprey Gro, Cat. CR3 258 DU124
Asprey Ms, Beck. BR3 225 DZ99
Asprey Pl, Brom. BR1
off Chislehurst Rd 226 EL96
Asquith Cl, Dag. RM8 148 EW60
Assam St, E1 20 C8
Assata Ms, N1 9 H4
Assembly Pas, E1 21 H6
Assembly Wk, Cars. SM5 222 DE101
Assher Rd, Hersham KT12 218 BY104
Assheton Rd, Beac. HP9 111 AK51
Assurance Cotts, Belv. DA17
off Heron Hill 188 EZ78
Astall Cl, Har. HA3 117 CE53
Astbury Business Pk, SE15
off Station Pas 44 G6
Astbury Ho, SE11 30 E7
Astbury Rd, SE15 44 G6
Astede Pl, Ashtd. KT21 254 CM118
Astell St, SW3 28 D10
Aster Ct, E5 144 DW61
Asters, The, Chsht EN7 88 DR28
Aste St, E14 34 E5
Asteys Row, N1 9 H7
Asthall Gdns, Ilf. IG6 147 EQ56
Astleham Rd, Shep. TW17 216 BL97
Astle St, SW11 40 G8
Astley, Grays RM17 192 FZ79
Astley Av, NW2 4 B2
Sch Astley Cooper Sch, The, Hem.H.
HP2 off St. Agnells La 62 BN15
Astley Ho, SE1
off Rowcross St 32 B10
Astley Rd, Hem.H. HP1 62 BJ20
● Astolat Ind Est, Peasm.
GU3 280 AV142
Aston Av, Har. HA3 139 CJ59
Aston Cl, Ashtd. KT21 253 CJ118
Bushey WD23 98 CC44
Sidcup DA14 208 EU90
Watford WD24 98 BW40
Aston Ct, N4 off Queens Dr 144 DQ61
Aston Gra, Hert. SG14 54 DR07
Aston Grn, Houns. TW4 178 BW82
Aston Ho, SW8 41 N7
Sch Aston Ho Sch, Jun Sch,
W5 off Aston Rd 159 CK72
Sen Sch, W5
off Montpelier Rd 159 CK71
Aston Mead, Wind. SL4 173 AL80
Aston Ms, Rom. RM6 148 EW59
Aston Pl, SW16
off Averil Gro 203 DP93
Aston Rd, SW20 221 CW96
W5 159 CK72
Claygate KT10 237 CE106
Astons Rd, Nthwd. HA6 115 BQ48
Aston St, E14 21 L8
Aston Ter, SW12
off Cathles Rd 203 DH86
Astonville St, SW18 202 DA88
Aston Way, Epsom KT18 255 CT115
Potters Bar EN6 86 DD32
Astor Av, Rom. RM7 149 FC58
Astor Cl, Add. KT15 234 BK105
Kingston upon Thames KT2 200 CP93
Astoria, NW9
off Boulevard Dr 119 CT54
Astoria Ct, Pur. CR8
off High St 241 DN111
Astoria Wk, SW9 183 DN83
● Astra Business Cen,
Red. RH1 288 DG144
● Astra Cen, Harl. CM20 57 ET11
Astra Cl, Horn. RM12 169 FH65
Astra Dr, Grav. DA12 213 GL92
Astrop Ms, W6 26 A6
Astrop Ter, W6 26 A6
Astwick Av, Hat. AL10 67 CT15
Astwood Ms, SW7 27 N8
Asylum Arch Rd, Red. RH1 288 DF137
Asylum Rd, SE15 44 F4
Atalanta Cl, Pur. CR8 241 DN110
Atalanta St, SW6 38 D6
Atbara Ct, Tedd. TW11 199 CH93
Atbara Rd, Tedd. TW11 199 CH93
Atcham Rd, Houns. TW3 178 CC84
Atcost Rd, Bark. IG11 168 EU71
Atheldene Rd, SW18 202 DB88
Sch Athelney Prim Sch, SE6
off Athelney St 205 EA90
Athelney St, SE6 205 EA90
Athelstan Cl, Rom. RM3 128 FM53
Athelstane Gro, E3 21 N1
Athelstane Ms, N4
off Stroud Grn Rd 143 DN60
Athelstan Gdns, NW6 4 F7
Athelstan Ho, E9
off Kingsmead Way 11 N2
Sch Athelstan Ho Sch, Hmptn.
TW12 off Percy Rd 218 CA95
Athelstan Rd, Hem.H. HP3 62 BM23
Kingston upon Thames KT1 220 CM98
Romford RM3 128 FM53
Athelstan Wk N, Welw.G.C. AL7 51 CY10
Athelstan Wk S, Welw.G.C. AL7 51 CX10
Athelstan Way, Orp. BR5 228 EU95
Athelstone Rd, Har. HA3 117 CD54
Athena Cl, Har. HA2
off Byron Hill Rd 139 CE61
Kingston upon Thames KT1 220 CM97
Athena Ct, SE1 off Long La 31 N5
Athenaeum Ct, N5 9 K1
Athenaeum Pl, N10 143 DH55
Athenaeum Rd, N20 120 DC46
Athena Pl, Nthwd. HA6
off The Drive 115 BT53
Athenia Cl, Goffs Oak EN7 87 DN29
Athenlay Rd, SE15 205 DX85
Athens Gdns, W9 15 J5
Atherden Rd, E5 144 DW63
Atherfield Rd, Reig. RH2 288 DC137
Atherfold Rd, SW9 42 A10
Atherley Way, Houns. TW4 198 BZ87
Atherstone Ct, W2 15 M6
Atherstone Ms, SW7 27 P8
Atherton Cl, Shalf. GU4 280 AY140
Stanwell TW19 196 BK86
Atherton Ct, Eton SL4
off Meadow La 173 AR80
Atherton Dr, SW19 201 CX91
Atherton Gdns, Grays RM16 193 GJ77
Atherton Hts, Wem. HA0 159 CJ65
Atherton Ms, E7 13 M4
Atherton Pl, Har. HA2 139 CD55
Southall UB1 158 CA73
Atherton Rd, E7 13 M3
SW13 181 CU80
Ilford IG5 124 EL54
Atherton St, SW11 40 D8
Athlone, Clay. KT10 237 CE107
Athlone Cl, E5 10 F2
Radlett WD7 99 CG36
Athlone Rd, SW2 203 DM87
Athlone Sq, Wind. SL4
off Ward Royal 173 AQ81
Athlone St, NW5 7 H4
Athlon Rd, Wem. HA0 159 CK68
Athol Cl, Pnr. HA5 115 BV53
Athole Gdns, Enf. EN1 104 DS43
Athol Gdns, Pnr. HA5 115 BV53
Atholl Ho, W9 15 N3
Atholl Rd, Ilf. IG3 148 EU59
Athol Rd, Erith DA8 189 FC78
Athol Sq, E14 22 F9
Athol Way, Uxb. UB10 156 BN69
Atkin Cl, Ruis HA4 137 BU58
Atkins Cl, Bigg.H. TN16 244 EJ112
Wok. GU21
off Greythorne Rd 248 AU118
Atkins Dr, W.Wick. BR4 225 ED103
Atkinson Cl, Bushey WD23 117 CE45
Orp. BR6 off Martindale Av 246 EU106
Atkinson Ho, SW11
off Austin Rd 40 G7
Atkinson Rd, E16 24 D7
Atkins Rd, E10 145 EB58
SW12 203 DK87
Atlanta Boul, Rom. RM1 149 FE58
Atlanta Bldg, SE13
off Deals Gateway 46 C7
Atlantic, E16 off Seagull La 23 N10
Atlantic Cl, Swans. DA10 212 FY85
Atlantic Rd, SW9 183 DN84
Atlantis Av, E16 25 P10
Atlantis Cl, Bark. IG11 168 EV69
● Atlas Business Cen, NW2 141 CV61
Atlas Cres, Edg. HA8 118 CP47
Atlas Gdns, SE7 36 C8
Atlas Ms, E8 10 B4
N7 8 D5
Atlas Rd, E13 23 P1
N11 121 DH51
NW10 160 CS69
Dartford DA1
off Cornwall Rd 190 FM83
Wembley HA9 140 CQ63
● Atlas Trade Pk, Erith DA8 189 FD78
Atley Rd, E3 12 A9
● Atlip Cen, Wem. HA0
off Atlip Rd 160 CL67
Atlip Rd, Wem. HA0 160 CL67
Atney Rd, SW15 181 CY84
Atria Rd, Nthwd. HA6 115 BU50
● Atrium, The, Uxb. UB8
off Harefield Rd 156 BJ66
Attenborough Cl, Wat. WD19 116 BY48
Atterbury Cl, West. TN16 277 ER126
Atterbury Rd, N4 143 DN58
Atterbury St, SW1 29 P9
Attewood Av, NW10 140 CS62
Attewood Rd, Nthlt. UB5 158 BY65
Attfield Cl, N20 120 DD47
Attimore Cl, Welw.G.C. AL8 51 CV10
Attimore Rd, Welw.G.C. AL8 51 CV10
Attle Cl, Uxb. UB10 156 BN68
Attlee Cl, Hayes UB4 157 BV69
Thornton Heath CR7 224 DQ100
Attlee Ct, Grays RM17 192 GA76
Attlee Dr, Dart. DA1 210 FN85
Attlee Rd, SE28 168 EV73
Hayes UB4 157 BU69
Attlee Ter, E17 145 EB56
Attneave St, WC1 18 E3
Attwood Cl, S.Croy. CR2 242 DV114
Atwater Cl, SW2 203 DN88
Atwell Cl, E10
off Belmont Pk Rd 145 EB58
Atwell Pl, T.Ditt. KT7 219 CF102
Atwell Rd, SE15 44 D9
Atwood, Bkhm KT23 252 BY124
Atwood Av, Rich. TW9 180 CN82
Sch Atwood Prim Sch, S.Croy.
CR2 off Limpsfield Rd 242 DU113
Atwood Rd, W6 181 CV77
Atwoods All, Rich. TW9 180 CN81
Auber Cl, Hodd. EN11 55 DZ14
Aubert Ct, N5 143 DP63
Aubert Pk, N5 143 DP63
Aubert Rd, N5 143 DP63
Aubrey Av, Lon.Col. AL2 83 CJ26
Aubrey Beardsley Ho, SW1
off Vauxhall Br Rd 29 M9
Aubrey Moore Pt, E15 12 F10
Aubrey Pl, NW8 15 N1
Aubrey Rd, E17 145 EA55
N8 143 DL57
W8 27 H2
Aubreys Rd, Hem.H. HP1 61 BE21
Aubrey Wk, W8 27 H3
Aubrietia Cl, Rom. RM3 128 FL53
Auburn Cl, SE14 45 L5
Aubyn Hill, SE27 204 DQ91
Aubyn Sq, SW15 181 CU84
Auckland Av, Rain. RM13 169 FF69
Auckland Cl, SE19 224 DT95
Enfield EN1 104 DV37
Tilbury RM18 193 GG82
Auckland Gdns, SE19 224 DS95
Auckland Hill, SE27 204 DQ91
Auckland Ri, SE19 224 DS95
Auckland Rd, E10 145 EB62
SE19 224 DT95
SW11 182 DE84
Caterham CR3 258 DS122
Ilford IG1 147 EP60
Kingston upon Thames KT1 220 CM98
Potters Bar EN6 85 CY32
Auckland St, SE11 42 C1
Auden Dr, Borwd. WD6 100 CN43
Auden Pl, NW1 6 G8
Sutton SM3
off Wordsworth Dr 239 CW105
Audleigh Pl, Chig. IG7 125 EN51
Audley Cl, N10 121 DH52
SW11 41 H10
Addlestone KT15 234 BH106
Borehamwood WD6 100 CN41
Audley Ct, E18 146 EF56
Pinner HA5
off Rickmansworth Rd 116 BW54
Audley Dr, E16 36 A2
Warlingham CR6 258 DW115
Audley Firs, Hersham KT12 236 BW105
Audley Gdns, Ilf. IG3 147 ET61
Loughton IG10 107 EQ40
Waltham Abbey EN9 89 EC34
Audley Pl, Sutt. SM2 240 DB108
Sch Audley Prim Sch, Cat. CR3
off Whyteleafe Rd 258 DT121
Audley Rd, NW4 141 CV58
W5 160 CM71
Enfield EN2 103 DP40
Richmond TW10 200 CM85
Audley Sq, W1 29 H2
Audley Wk, Orp. BR5 228 EW100
Audrey Cl, Beck. BR3 225 EB100
Audrey Gdns, Wem. HA0 139 CH61
Audrey Rd, Ilf. IG1 147 EP62
Audrey St, E2 10 C10
Audric Cl, Kings.T. KT2 220 CN95
Audwick Cl, Chsht EN8 89 DX28
Augur Cl, Stai. TW18 195 BF92
Augurs La, E13 24 B2
Augusta Cl, W.Mol. KT8
off Freeman Dr 218 BZ97
Augusta Rd, Twick. TW2 198 CC89
Augusta St, E14 22 C8
August End, Geo.Grn SL3 154 AY72
Augustine Cl, Colnbr. SL3 175 BE83
Augustine Ct, Wal.Abb. EN9
off Beaulieu Dr 89 EB33
Whyteleafe CR3
off Godstone Rd 258 DU119
Augustine Rd, W14 26 C7
Gravesend DA12 213 GJ87
Harrow HA3 116 CB53
Orpington BR5 228 EX97
August La, Albury GU5 282 BK144
Augustus Cl, W12
off Goldhawk Rd 181 CV75
Brentford TW8 179 CJ80
St. Albans AL3 64 CA22
Stanmore HA7 117 CK48
Augustus Ct, SE1 31 N8
Augustus Ho, NW1
off Augustus St 17 L2
Augustus La, Orp. BR6 228 EU103
Augustus Rd, SW19 201 CY88
Augustus St, NW1 17 K1
Aulay Lawrence Ct, N9
off Menon Dr 122 DV48
Aultone Way, Cars. SM5 222 DF104
Sutton SM1 222 DB103
Aultone Yd, Cars. SM5 222 DF104
Aulton Pl, SE11 42 F1
Aurelia Gdns, Croy. CR0 223 DM99
Aurelia Rd, Croy. CR0 223 DL100
Auriel Av, Dag. RM10 169 FD65
Auriga Ms, N1 9 M2
Auriol Cl, Wor.Pk. KT4
off Auriol Pk Rd 220 CS104
Auriol Dr, Grnf. UB6 159 CD66
Uxbridge UB10 156 BN65
Sch Auriol Jun Sch, Ewell
KT19 off Vale Rd 239 CT105
Auriol Pk Rd, Wor.Pk. KT4 220 CS104
Auriol Rd, W14 26 E9
Aurora Ct, Edg. HA8
off Fortune Ave 118 CP53
Grav. DA12 off Canal Rd 213 GJ86
Aurum Cl, Horl. RH6 291 DH149
Austell Gdns, NW7 118 CS48
Austen Apts, SE20
off Croydon Rd 224 DV96
Austen Cl, SE28 168 EV74
Greenhithe DA9 211 FW85
Loughton IG10 107 ER41
Tilbury RM18
off Coleridge Rd 193 GJ82
Austen Gdns, Dart. DA1 190 FM84
Austen Ho, NW6 15 J2
Austen Rd, Erith DA8 189 FB80
Guildford GU1 281 AZ135
Harrow HA2 138 CB61

Austenway, Chal.St.P. SL9 134 AX55
Austen Way, Slou. SL3 175 AZ79
Austenwood Cl, Chal.St.P. SL9 112 AW54
Austenwood La, Chal.St.P. SL9 112 AX54
Austin Av, Brom. BR2 226 EL99
Austin Cl, SE23 205 DZ87
Coulsdon CR5 257 DP118
Twickenham TW1 199 CJ85
Austin Ct, E6 off Kings Rd 166 EJ67
Austin Friars, EC2 19 M8
Austin Friars Pas, EC2 19 M8
Austin Friars Sq, EC2 19 M8
Austin Rd, SW11 40 G7
Hayes UB3 177 BT75
Northfleet DA11 213 GF88
Orpington BR5 228 EU100
Austin's La, Uxb. UB10 137 BQ62
Austins Mead, Bov. HP3 79 BB28
Austins Pl, Hem.H. HP2
off St. Mary's Rd 62 BK19
Austin St, E2 20 A3
Austin Waye, Uxb. UB8 156 BJ67
Austral Cl, Sid. DA15 207 ET90
Austral Dr, Horn. RM11 150 FK59
Australia Rd, W12 161 CV73
Slough SL1 154 AV74
Austral St, SE11 30 G8
Austyn Gdns, Surb. KT5 220 CP102
Austyns Pl, Ewell KT17 239 CU109
Autumn Cl, SW19 202 DC93
Enfield EN1 104 DU39
Slough SL1 153 AM74
Autumn Dr, Sutt. SM2 240 DB109
Autumn Glades, Hem.H. HP3 63 BQ22
Autumn Gro, Brom. BR1 206 EH93
Welwyn Garden City AL7 52 DB11
Autumn St, E3 12 B9
Auxiliaries Way, Uxb. UB9 135 BF57
Avalon Cl, SW20 221 CY96
W13 159 CG71
Enfield EN2 103 DN40
Orpington BR6 228 EX104
Watford WD25 82 BY32
Avalon Ct, Bushey WD23 98 CA40
Avalon Rd, SW6 39 L6
W13 159 CG70
Orpington BR6 228 EW103
Avante Ct, Kings.T. KT1 219 CK97
Avard Gdns, Orp. BR6 245 EQ105
Avarn Rd, SW17 202 DF93
Avebury, Slou. SL1 153 AN74
Avebury Ct, N1
off Avebury St 9 L9
Hemel Hempstead HP2 62 BN17
Avebury Pk, Surb. KT6 219 CK101
Avebury Rd, E11
off Southwest Rd 145 ED60
SW19 221 CZ95
Orpington BR6 227 ER104
Avebury St, N1 9 L9
AVELEY, S.Ock. RM15 171 FR73
Aveley Bypass, S.Ock. RM15 170 FQ73
Aveley Cl, Aveley RM15 171 FR74
Erith DA8 189 FF79
Sch Aveley Prim Sch, Aveley
RM15 off Stifford Rd 171 FS74
Aveley Rd, Rom. RM1 149 FD56
Upminster RM14 170 FP65
Aveline St, SE11 42 E1
Aveling Cl, Pur. CR8 241 DM113
Aveling Pk Rd, E17 123 EA54
Avelon Rd, Rain. RM13 169 FG67
Romford RM5 127 FD51
Ave Maria La, EC4 19 H9
Avenell Rd, N5 143 DP62
Avening Rd, SW18
off Brathway Rd 202 DA87
Avening Ter, SW18 202 DA86
Avenons Rd, E13 23 N5
Avenue, The, E4 123 ED51
E11 (Leytonstone) 146 EF61
E11 (Wanstead) 146 EH58
N3 120 DA54
N8 143 DN55
N10 121 DJ54
N11 121 DH49
N17 122 DS54
NW6 4 E7
NW10 off Hillside 160 CR67
SE10 46 G4
SW4 202 DG85
SW11 202 DE87
SW18 202 DE87
W4 180 CS76
W13 159 CH73
Amersham HP7 77 AQ38
Barnet EN5 101 CY41
Beckenham BR3 225 EB95
Bexley DA5 208 EX87
Brentwood CM13 129 FW51
Brockham RH3 270 CN134
Bromley BR1 226 EK97
Bushey WD23 98 BZ42
Carshalton SM5 240 DG108
Cheam SM3 239 CW108
Chobham GU24 232 AT109
Claygate KT10 237 CE107
Coulsdon CR5 257 DK115
Cowley UB8 156 BK70
Cranford TW5 177 BU81
Croydon CR0 224 DS104
Datchet SL3 174 AV81
Egham TW20 195 BB91
Epsom KT17 239 CV108
Farnham Common SL2 133 AP64
Gravesend DA11 213 GG88
Greenhithe DA9 191 FV84
Hampton TW12 198 BZ93
Harrow HA3 117 CF53
Hatch End HA5 116 CA52
Hemel Hempstead HP1 61 BE19
Hertford SG14 53 DP07
Hoddesdon EN11 71 DZ19
Horley RH6 290 DF149
Hornchurch RM12 150 FJ61
Hounslow TW3 198 CB85
Ickenham UB10 136 BN63
Isleworth TW7 179 CD79
Keston BR2 226 EK104
Leatherhead KT22 237 CF112
Loughton IG10 106 EK44
Nazeing EN9 90 EJ25
New Haw KT15 234 BG110
Northwood HA6 115 BQ51
Old Windsor SL4 194 AV85
Orpington BR6 227 ET103
Pinner HA5 138 BZ58
Potters Bar EN6 85 CZ30
Radlett WD7 83 CG33
Avenue, The, Richmond TW9 180 CM82
Romford RM1 149 FD56
St. Paul's Cray BR5 208 EV94
South Nutfield RH1 289 DL137
Staines-upon-Thames TW18 216 BH95
Sunbury-on-Thames TW16 217 BV95
Surbiton KT5 220 CM100
Sutton SM2 239 CZ109
Tadworth KT20 255 CV122
Twickenham TW1 199 CJ85
Watford WD17 97 BU40
Wembley HA9 140 CM61
West Drayton UB7 176 BL76
West Wickham BR4 225 EC101
Westerham TN16 261 EM122
Whyteleafe CR3 258 DU119
Worcester Park KT4 221 CT103
Worplesdon GU3 264 AS127
Wraysbury TW19 174 AX83
Avenue App, Kings L. WD4 80 BN30
Avenue Cl, N14 103 DJ44
NW8 6 D9
Hounslow TW5 177 BU81
Romford RM3 128 FM52
Tadworth KT20 255 CV122
West Drayton UB7 176 BK76
Avenue Ct, Tad. KT20
off The Avenue 255 CV123
Avenue Cres, W3 180 CP75
Hounslow TW5 177 BV80
Avenue Dr, Slou. SL3 155 AZ71
Avenue Elmers, Surb. KT6 220 CL99
Avenue Gdns, SE25 224 DU97
SW14 180 CS83
W3 180 CP75
Horley RH6 291 DJ149
Hounslow TW5 177 BU80
Teddington TW11 199 CF94
Avenue Gate, Loug. IG10 106 EJ44
● Avenue Ind Est, E4 123 DZ51
Romford RM3 128 FK54
Avenue Ms, N10 143 DH55
Avenue Pk Rd, SE27 203 DP89
Sch Avenue Prim Sch, E12
off Meanley Rd 146 EL64
Cheam SM2 off Avenue Rd 240 DA110
Avenue Ri, Bushey WD23 98 CA43
Tra Avenue Road 225 DX96
Avenue Rd, E7 146 EH64
N6 143 DJ59
N12 120 DC49
N14 121 DH45
N15 144 DR57
NW3 6 A6
NW8 6 B7
NW10 161 CT68
SE20 224 DW95
SE25 224 DU96
SW16 223 DK96
SW20 221 CV96
W3 180 CP75
Banstead SM7 256 DB115
Beckenham BR3 224 DW95
Belvedere DA17 189 FC77
Bexleyheath DA7 188 EY83
Brentford TW8 179 CJ78
Caterham CR3 258 DR122
Chadwell Heath RM6 148 EV59
Cobham KT11 252 BX116
Epsom KT18 238 CR114
Erith DA8 189 FC80
Feltham TW13 197 BT90
Hampton TW12 218 CB95
Harold Wood RM3 128 FM52
Hoddesdon EN11 71 ED19
Isleworth TW7 179 CF81
Kingston upon Thames KT1 220 CL97
New Malden KT3 220 CS98
Pinner HA5 138 BY55
St. Albans AL1 65 CE19
Sevenoaks TN13 279 FJ123
Southall UB1 178 BZ75
Staines-upon-Thames TW18 195 BD92
Sutton SM2 240 DA110
Tatsfield TN16 260 EL120
Teddington TW11 199 CG94
Theydon Bois CM16 107 ER36
Wallington SM6 241 DJ108
Warley CM14 130 FW49
Woodford Green IG8 124 EJ51
Avenue Rd Est, E11
off High Rd Leytonstone 145 ED63
Avenue S, Surb. KT5 220 CM101
Avenue Ter, N.Mal. KT3
off Kingston Rd 220 CQ97
Watford WD19 98 BY44
Averil Ct, Tap. SL6 152 AJ72
Averil Gro, SW16 203 DP93
Averill St, W6 38 C3
Avern Gdns, W.Mol. KT8 218 CB98
Avern Rd, W.Mol. KT8 218 CB99
Avery Fm Row, SW1 29 J9
Avery Gdns, Ilf. IG2 147 EM57
AVERY HILL, SE9 207 EQ86
★ Avery Hill Pk, SE9 207 EQ86
Avery Hill Rd, SE9 207 ER86
Avery Row, W1 17 J10
Avey La, High Beach IG10 106 EH39
Waltham Abbey EN9 105 ED36
Avia Cl, Hem.H. HP3 62 BK24
Avian Ave, Frog. AL2 83 CE28
Aviary Cl, E16 23 M7
Aviary Rd, Wok. GU22 250 BG116
Aviation Dr, NW9 119 CT54
● Aviator Pk, Add. KT15 216 BK104
Aviemore Cl, Beck. BR3 225 DZ99
Aviemore Way, Beck. BR3 225 DY99
Sch Avigdor Hirsch Torah
Temimah Prim Sch,
NW2 off Parkside 141 CV63
Avignon Rd, SE4 45 K10
Avington Cl, Guil. GU1
off London Rd 264 AY134
Avington Ct, SE1
off Old Kent Rd 31 P9
Avington Gro, SE20 204 DW94
Avion Cres, NW9 119 CU53
Avior Dr, Nthwd. HA6 115 BT49
Avis Gro, Croy. CR0 243 DY110
Avis Sq, E1 21 K8
Avoca Rd, SW17 202 DG91
Avocet Cl, SE1 32 C10
St. Albans AL3 64 CC17
Avocet Ms, SE28 187 ER76
Avon Cl, Add. KT15 234 BG107
Gravesend DA12 213 GK89
Hayes UB4 158 BW70
Slough SL1 153 AL73
Sutton SM1 240 DC105
Avon Cl, Watford WD25 82 BW34
Worcester Park KT4 221 CU103
Avon Ct, Buck.H. IG9
off Chequers 124 EH46
Greenford UB6
off Braund Av 158 CB70
Avondale Av, N12 120 DB50
NW2 140 CS62
Barnet EN4 120 DF46
Esher KT10 219 CG104
Staines-upon-Thames TW18 195 BF94
Worcester Park KT4 221 CT102
Avondale Cl, Hersham KT12
off Pleasant Pl 236 BW106
Horley RH6 290 DF146
Loughton IG10 125 EM45
Avondale Ct, E11 146 EE60
E16 23 K6
E18 124 EH53
Avondale Cres, Enf. EN3 105 DY41
Ilford IG4 146 EK57
Avondale Dr, Hayes UB3 157 BU74
Loughton IG10 125 EM45
Avondale Gdns, Houns. TW4 198 BZ85
Avondale Ho, SE1
off Avondale Sq 44 C1
Avondale Pk Gdns, W11 26 E1
Sch Avondale Pk Prim Sch, W11 26 E1
Avondale Pk Rd, W11 14 E10
Avondale Ri, SE15 44 A10
Avondale Rd, E16 23 K6
E17 145 EA59
N3 120 DC53
N13 121 DN47
N15 143 DP57
SE9 206 EL89
SW14 180 CR83
SW19 202 DB92
Ashford TW15 196 BK90
Bromley BR1 206 EE93
Harrow HA3 139 CF55
South Croydon CR2 242 DQ107
Welling DA16 188 EW82
Avondale Sq, SE1 44 C1
Avon Grn, S.Ock. RM15 171 FV72
Sch Avon Ho Sch, Wdf.Grn. IG8
off High Rd Woodford Grn 124 EG49
Avonley Rd, SE14 45 H5
Avonmead, Wok. GU21
off Silversmiths Way 248 AW118
Avon Ms, Pnr. HA5 116 BZ53
Avonmore Av, Guil. GU1 265 AZ133
Avonmore Gdns, W14
off Avonmore Rd 26 G9
Avonmore Pl, W14 26 F8
Sch Avonmore Prim Sch, W14 26 F8
Avonmore Rd, W14 26 G8
Avonmor Ms, Ripley GU23 250 BH122
Avonmouth Rd, Dart. DA1 210 FK85
Avonmouth St, SE1 31 J6
Avon Path, S.Croy. CR2 242 DQ107
Avon Pl, SE1 31 K5
Avon Rd, E17 145 ED55
SE4 46 A10
Greenford UB6 158 CA70
Sunbury-on-Thames TW16 197 BT94
Upminster RM14 151 FR58
Avon Sq, Hem.H. HP2 62 BM15
Avonstowe Cl, Orp. BR6 227 EQ104
Avontar Rd, S.Ock. RM15 171 FV70
Avon Way, E18 146 EG55
Avonwick Rd, Houns. TW3 178 CB82
Avril Way, E4 123 EC50
Avro, NW9 off Boulevard Dr 119 CT54
Avro Way, Wall. SM6 241 DL108
Weybridge KT13 234 BL110
Awlfield Av, N17 122 DR53
Awliscombe Rd, Well. DA16 187 ET82
Axes La, Red. RH1 289 DJ141
Axe St, Bark. IG11 167 EQ67
Axholme Av, Edg. HA8 118 CN53
Axiom Apts, Rom. RM1
off Mercury Gdns 149 FF56
● Axis Cen, Lthd. KT22 253 CF119
Axis Ct, SE10 47 J2
SE16 off East La 32 D4
● Axis Pk, Langley SL3 175 BB78
Axminster Cres, Well. DA16 188 EW81
Axminster Rd, N7 143 DL62
Axon Pl, Ilf. IG1 147 EQ61
Axtaine Rd, Orp. BR5 228 EX101
Axtane, Sthflt DA13 212 FZ94
Axtane Cl, Sutt.H. DA4 230 FQ96
Axwood, Epsom KT18 254 CQ115
Aybrook St, W1 16 G7
Aycliffe Cl, Brom. BR1 227 EM98
Aycliffe Dr, Hem.H. HP2 62 BL16
Sch Aycliffe Dr Prim Sch, Hem.H.
HP2 off Aycliffe Dr 62 BL16
Aycliffe Rd, W12 161 CT74
Borehamwood WD6 100 CL39
Ayebridges Av, Egh. TW20 195 BC94
Aylands Cl, Wem. HA9 140 CL61
Aylands Rd, Enf. EN3 104 DW36
Sch Aylands Sch, Enf. EN3
off Keswick Dr 104 DW36
Aylesbury Cl, E7 13 M4
Aylesbury Ct, Sutt. SM1
off Benhill Wd Rd 222 DC104
Aylesbury Cres, Slou. SL1 153 AR72
Aylesbury End, Beac. HP9 111 AL54
Aylesbury Est, SE17 43 M1
Aylesbury Rd, SE17 43 M1
Bromley BR2 226 EG97
Aylesbury St, EC1 18 G5
NW10 140 CR62
Aylesford Av, Beck. BR3 225 DY99
Aylesford St, SW1 29 N10
Aylesham Cen, SE15 44 C7
Aylesham Cl, NW7 119 CU52
Aylesham Rd, Orp. BR6 227 ET101
Ayles Rd, Hayes UB4 157 BV69
Aylestone Av, NW6 4 C8
Aylesworth Av, Slou. SL2
off Doddsfield Rd 153 AN69
Aylesworth Spur, Old Wind.
SL4 194 AV87
Aylets Fld, Harl. CM18 73 ES19
Aylett Rd, SE25 224 DV98
Isleworth TW7 179 CE82
Upminster RM14 150 FQ61
Ayley Cft, Enf. EN1 104 DU43
Ayliffe Cl, Kings.T. KT1
off Cambridge Gdns 220 CN96
Aylmer Cl, Stan. HA7 117 CG49
Aylmer Dr, Stan. HA7 117 CG49
Aylmer Par, N2 142 DF57
Aylmer Rd, E11 146 EF60
N2 142 DE57
Aylmer Rd, W12 180 CS75
Dagenham RM8 148 EY62
Ayloffe Rd, Dag. RM9 168 EZ65
Sch Ayloff Prim Sch, Elm Pk
RM12 off South End Rd 149 FH63
Ayloffs Cl, Horn. RM11 150 FL57
Ayloffs Wk, Horn. RM11 150 FK57
Aylsham Dr, Uxb. UB10 137 BR62
Aylsham La, Rom. RM3 128 FJ49
Aylsham Rd, Hodd. EN11 71 EC15
Aylton Est, SE16 33 H5
Sch Aylward First & Mid Sch, Stan.
HA7 off Pangbourne Dr 117 CK50
Aylward Gdns, Chesh. HP5 76 AN30
Aylward Rd, SE23 205 DX89
SW20 221 CZ96
Sch Aylward Sch, N18
off Windmill Rd 122 DR49
Aylwards Ri, Stan. HA7 117 CG49
Aylward St, E1 20 G8
Aylwyn Est, SE1 31 P6
Aymer Cl, Stai. TW18 215 BE95
Aymer Dr, Stai. TW18 215 BE95
Aynhoe Rd, W14 26 D8
Aynho St, Wat. WD18 97 BV43
Aynscombe Angle, Orp. BR6 228 EV101
Aynscombe La, SW14 180 CQ83
Aynscombe Path, SW14
off Thames Bk 180 CQ82
Aynsley Gdns, Harl. CM17 74 EW15
AYOT GREEN, Welw. AL6 51 CU07
Ayot Grn, Welw. AL6 51 CU06
Ayot Greenway, St.Alb. AL4 50 CN06
Ayot Little Grn, Ayot St.P. AL6 51 CT06
Ayot Path, Borwd. WD6 100 CN37
Ayot St. Peter Rd, Welw. AL6 51 CT05
Ayr Ct, W3 160 CN71
Ayres Cl, E13 23 P3
Ayres St, SE1 31 K4
Ayr Grn, Rom. RM1 127 FE52
Ayron Rd, S.Ock. RM15 171 FV70
Ayrsome Rd, N16 144 DS62
Ayrton Gould Ho, E2 21 K2
Ayrton Rd, SW7 28 A6
Ayr Way, Rom. RM1 127 FE52
Aysgarth Ct, Sutt. SM1
off Sutton Common Rd 222 DB104
Aysgarth Rd, SE21 204 DS86
Aytoun Pl, SW9 42 D9
Aytoun Rd, SW9 42 D9
Azalea Cl, W7 159 CF74
Ilford IG1 147 EP64
London Colney AL2 83 CH27
Azalea Ct, Pur. CR8
off Whytecliffe Rd S 241 DP111
Wok. GU22 248 AX119
Woodford Green IG8
off The Bridle Path 124 EE52
Azalea Dr, Swan. BR8 229 FD98
Azalea Ho, Felt. TW13
off Bedfont La 197 BV88
Azalea Wk, Pnr. HA5 137 BV57
Azalea Way, Geo.Grn SL3
off Blinco La 154 AY72
Azania Ms, NW5 7 J4
Azenby Rd, SE15 44 A8
Sch Azhar Academy Girl's Sch, E7 13 N4
Azile Everitt Ho, SE18
off Blendon Ter 187 EQ78
Azof St, SE10 35 K9
Azura Ct, E15 off Warton Rd 12 F8
Azure Ct, NW9 140 CN57
Azure Pl, Houns. TW3
off Holly Rd 178 CB84

B

Baalbec Rd, N5 9 H3
Baas Hill, Brox. EN10 71 DX21
Baas Hill Cl, Brox. EN10 71 DY21
Baas La, Brox. EN10 71 DY21
Babbacombe Cl, Chess. KT9 237 CK106
Babbacombe Gdns, Ilf. IG4 146 EL56
Babbacombe Rd, Brom. BR1 226 EG95
Baber Br Caravan Site,
Felt. TW14 198 BW85
Baber Dr, Felt. TW14 198 BW86
Babington Ct, WC1
off Ormond Cl 18 B6
Sch Babington Ho Sch, Chis.
BR7 off Grange Dr 207 EM93
Babington Ri, Wem. HA9 160 CN65
Babington Rd, NW4 141 CV56
SW16 203 DK92
Dagenham RM8 148 EW64
Hornchurch RM12 149 FH60
Babmaes St, SW1 29 N1
Babylon La, Lwr Kgswd KT20 272 DA127
Bacchus Wk, N1 19 N1
Bachelors Acre, Wind. SL4 173 AR81
Bachelor's La, Wok. GU23 250 BN124
Baches St, N1 19 M3
Back, The, Pott.End HP4 61 BB16
Back All, Dor. RH4 285 CH136
Back Ch La, E1 20 C10
Back Grn, Hersham KT12 236 BW107
Back Hill, EC1 18 E5
Backhouse Pl, SE17 31 P9
Back La, N8 143 DL57
NW3 off Heath St 142 DC63
Bexley DA5 208 FA87
Brentford TW8 179 CK79
Buckhurst Hill IG9 124 EK47
Chalfont St. Giles HP8 112 AU48
Chenies WD3 95 BB38
East Clandon GU4 266 BK130
Edgware HA8 118 CQ53
Godden Green TN15 279 FN124
Hertford SG13 70 DQ18
Ide Hill TN14 278 FC126
Letchmore Heath WD25 99 CE39
Nazeing EN9 72 EJ23
North Stifford RM16 171 FW74
Purfleet RM19 191 FS76
Richmond TW10 199 CJ90
Romford RM6
off Station Rd 148 EX59
Sheering CM22 58 FA06
Tewin AL6 52 DE05
Backley Gdns, SE25 224 DU100
Back of High St, Chobham
GU24 off High St 232 AS111
Back Path, Red. RH1 274 DQ133
Back Rd, Sid. DA14 208 EU91
Backs, The, Chesh. HP5 76 AQ31
Back St, Harl. CM17
off Broadway Av 58 EW11
Bacon Gro, SE1 32 A7
Bacon La, NW9 140 CP56
Edgware HA8 118 CN53
Bacon Link, Rom. RM5 127 FB51
Sch Bacon's Coll, SE16 33 L4
Bacons Dr, Cuffley EN6 87 DL29
Bacons La, N6 142 DG60
Bacons Mead, Denh. UB9 136 BG61
Bacon St, E1 20 B4
E2 20 B4
Bacon Ter, Dag. RM8
off Fitzstephen Rd 148 EV64
Bacton, NW5 6 F2
Bacton St, E2 21 H2
Badburgham Ct, Wal.Abb. EN9 90 EF33
Baddeley Cl, Enf. EN3 105 EA37
Baddow Cl, Dag. RM10 168 FA67
Woodford Green IG8 124 EK51
Baddow Wk, N1 9 J8
Baden Cl, Stai. TW18 196 BG94
Baden Dr, E4 105 EB42
Horley RH6 290 DE147
Baden Pl, SE1 31 L4
Baden Powell Cl, Dag. RM9 168 EY67
Surbiton KT6 220 CM103
Sch Baden-Powell Prim Sch,
E5 off Ferron Rd 144 DV62
Baden Powell Rd, Sev. TN13 278 FE121
Baden Rd, N8 143 DK56
Guildford GU2 264 AU132
Ilford IG1 147 EP64
Bader Cl, Ken. CR8 258 DR115
Welwyn Garden City AL7 52 DC09
Bader Gdns, Slou. SL1 173 AN75
Bader Wk, Nthflt DA11 212 GE90
Bader Way, SW15 201 CU86
Rainham RM13 169 FG65
Badger Cl, Felt. TW13 197 BV90
Guildford GU2 264 AV131
Hounslow TW4 178 BW83
Ilford IG2 147 EQ59
Badgers Cl, Ashf. TW15 196 BM92
Borehamwood WD6
off Kingsley Av 100 CM40
Enfield EN2 103 DP41
Harrow HA1 139 CD58
Hayes UB3 157 BS73
Hertford SG13 54 DV09
Woking GU21 248 AW118
Badgers Copse, Orp. BR6 227 ET103
Worcester Park KT4 221 CT103
Badgers Cft, N20 119 CY46
SE9 207 EN90
Broxbourne EN10 71 DY21
Hemel Hempstead HP2 63 BR21
BADGERS DENE, Grays RM17 192 FZ77
Badgers Hill, Vir.W. GU25 214 AW99
Badgers Hole, Croy. CR0 243 DX105
Badgers La, Warl. CR6 258 DW120
BADGERS MOUNT, Sev. TN14 247 FB110
Badgers Mt, Orsett RM16 193 GF75
Badgers Ri, Bad.Mt TN14 246 FA110
Badgers Rd, Bad.Mt TN14 247 FB110
Badgers Wk, Chorl. WD3 95 BF42
New Malden KT3 220 CS96
Purley CR8 241 DK111
Whyteleafe CR3 258 DT119
Badgers Wd, Chaldon CR3 274 DQ125
Farnham Common SL2 133 AQ64
Badger Way, Hat. AL10 67 CV20
Badingham Dr, Fetch. KT22 253 CE123
Badlis Rd, E17 123 EA54
Badlow Cl, Erith DA8 189 FE80
Badma Cl, N9 off Hudson Way 122 DW48
Badminton Cl, Borwd. WD6 100 CN40
Harrow HA1 139 CE56
Northolt UB5 158 CA65
Badminton Ms, E16 35 P2
Badminton Pl, Brox. EN10 71 DY20
Badminton Rd, SW12 202 DG86
Badric Ct, SW11 40 B9
Badsworth Rd, SE5 43 J5
Baffin Way, E14 34 F1
Bafton Gate, Brom. BR2 226 EH102
Bagden Hill, Westh. RH5 269 CD130
Bagley Cl, West Dr. UB7 176 BL75
Bagley's La, SW6 39 M7
Bagleys Spring, Rom. RM6 148 EY56
Bagot Cl, Ashtd. KT21 254 CM116
Bagshot Ct, SE18
off Prince Imperial Rd 187 EN81
Bagshot Rd, Enf. EN1 122 DT45
Englefield Green TW20 194 AW94
Bagshot St, SE17 43 P1
Bahram Rd, Epsom KT19 238 CR110
Baildon St, SE8 45 P5
Bailey Cl, E4 123 EC49
N11 121 DK52
SE28 167 ES74
Purfleet RM19
off Gabion Av 191 FR77
Windsor SL4 173 AN82
Bailey Cres, Chess. KT9 237 CK108
Bailey Ho, SE18
off Berber Par 186 EL81
Bailey Ms, SW2 203 DN85
W4 off Herbert Gdns 180 CP79
Bailey Pl, N16 off Gillett St 9 P3
SE26 205 DX93
Bailey Rd, Westc. RH4 284 CC137
Baillie Cl, Rain. RM13 169 FH70
Baillie Rd, Guil. GU1 281 AZ135
Baillies Wk, W5
off Liverpool Rd 179 CK75
Bainbridge Cl, Ham TW10
off Latchmere Cl 200 CL92
Bainbridge Rd, Dag. RM9 148 EZ63
Bainbridge St, WC1 17 P8
Baines Cl, S.Croy. CR2
off Brighton Rd 242 DR106
Baines Wk, Chesh. HP5
off High St 76 AP31
Bainton Mead, Wok. GU21 248 AU117
Baird Av, Sthl. UB1 158 CB73
Baird Cl, E10 off Marconi Rd 145 EA60
NW9 140 CQ58
Bushey WD23
off Ashfield Av 98 CB44
Slough SL1 173 AP75

Baird Gdns, SE19 204 DS91
Baird Rd, Enf. EN1 104 DV42
Baird St, EC1 19 K4
Bairny Wd App, Wdf.Grn. IG8
off Broadway Cl 124 EH51
Bairstow Cl, Borwd. WD6 100 CL39
Baizdon Rd, SE3 47 J9
Bakeham La, Eng.Grn TW20 194 AW94
Bakehouse Ms, Hmptn. TW12 198 CA94
Bakehouse Rd, Horl. RH6 290 DF146
Baker Boy La, Croy. CR0 243 DZ112
Baker Cres, Dart. DA1 210 FJ87
Baker Hill Cl, Nthflt DA11 213 GF91
Baker La, Mitch. CR4 222 DG96
Baker Pas, NW10 off Baker Rd 160 CS67
Baker Pl, Epsom KT19 238 CQ107
Baker Rd, NW10 160 CS67
SE18 186 EL80
Bakers Av, E17 145 EB58
Bakers Cl, Ken. CR8 242 DQ114
St. Albans AL1 65 CG21
Bakers Ct, SE25 224 DS97
Bakerscroft, Chsht EN8 89 DX28
Bakers End, SW20 221 CY96
Bakers Fld, N7 143 DK63
Bakers Gdns, Cars. SM5 222 DE103
Bakers Gro, Welw.G.C. AL7 52 DC08
Bakers Hall Ct, EC3
off Great Tower St 31 P1
Bakers Hill, E5 144 DW60
New Barnet EN5 102 DB40
Bakers La, N6 142 DF58
Epping CM16 91 ET30
High Wych CM21 57 ET05
Bakers Mead, Gdse. RH9 274 DW130
Baker's Ms, W1 16 G8
Bakers Ms, Orp. BR6 245 ET107
Bakers Orchard, Woob.Grn
HP10 132 AE58
Bakers Pas, NW3 5 P1
Baker's Rents, E2 20 A3
Bakers Rd, Chsht EN7 88 DV30
Uxbridge UB8 156 BK66
Bakers Row, E15 13 J10
Baker's Row, EC1 18 E5
⊖ Baker Street 16 F6
Baker St, NW1 16 F5
W1 16 F6
Enfield EN1 104 DR41
Hertford SG13 54 DS09
Potters Bar EN6 101 CY35
Weybridge KT13 234 BN105
Bakers Wk, Saw. CM21 58 EY05
Bakers Wd, Denh. UB9 135 BD60
Baker's Yd, EC1 18 E5
Uxbridge UB8
off Bakers Rd 156 BK66
Bakery Cl, SW9 42 D6
Roydon CM19 72 EJ15
Bakery Path, Edg. HA8
off Station Rd 118 CP51
Bakery Pl, SW11
off Altenburg Gdns 182 DF84
Bakewell Way, N.Mal. KT3 220 CS96
Balaams La, N14 121 DK47
Balaam St, E13 23 P4
Balaclava Rd, SE1 32 B9
Surbiton KT6 219 CJ101
Bala Grn, NW9
off Snowdon Dr 140 CS58
Balcary Gdns, Berk. HP4 60 AS20
Balcaskie Rd, SE9 207 EM85
Balchen Rd, SE3 186 EK82
Balchier Rd, SE22 204 DV86
Balchins La, Westc. RH4 284 CA138
Balcombe Cl, Bexh. DA6 188 EX84
Balcombe Gdns, Horl. RH6 291 DJ149
Balcombe Rd, Horl. RH6 291 DH147
Balcombe St, NW1 16 E5
Balcon Ct, W5 off Boileau Rd 160 CM72
Balcon Way, Borwd. WD6 100 CQ39
Balcorne St, E9 11 H7
Balder Ri, SE12 206 EH89
Balderton St, W1 17 H9
Baldocks Rd, They.B. CM16 107 ES35
Baldock St, E3 22 C1
Ware SG12 55 DX06
Baldock Way, Borwd. WD6 100 CM39
Baldry Gdns, SW16 203 DL93
Baldwin Cres, SE5 43 J6
Guildford GU4 265 BC132
Baldwin Gdns, Houns. TW3
off Chamberlain Gdns 178 CC81
Baldwin Rd, SW11 202 DG86
Beaconsfield HP9 111 AP54
Burnham SL1 152 AJ69
Baldwins, Welw.G.C. AL7 52 DB09
Baldwin's Gdns, EC1 18 E6
Baldwins Hill, Loug. IG10 107 EM40
Baldwins La, Crox.Grn WD3 96 BN42
Baldwins Shore, Eton SL4 173 AR79
Baldwin St, EC1 19 L3
Baldwin Ter, N1 9 J10
Baldwyn Gdns, W3 160 CQ73
Baldwyns Pk, Bex. DA5 209 FD89
Baldwyns Rd, Bex. DA5 209 FD89
Balearic Apts, E16
off Western Gateway 35 P1
Bale Rd, E1 21 L6
Coll Bales Coll, W10 14 D3
Balfern Gro, W4 180 CS78
Balfern St, SW11 40 D7
Balfe St, N1 18 B1
Balfont Cl, S.Croy. CR2 242 DU113
Balfour Av, W7 159 CF74
Woking GU22 248 AY122
● Balfour Business Cen,
Sthl. UB2 178 BX76
Balfour Gro, N20 120 DF48
Balfour Ho, Ilf. IG1 off High Rd 147 ER61
W10 14 D6
Balfour Ms, N9 122 DU48
W1 29 H2
Bovingdon HP3 79 AZ27
Balfour Pl, SW15 181 CV84
W1 29 H1
Balfour Rd, N5 9 J1
SE25 224 DU98
SW19 202 DB94
W3 160 CQ71
W13 179 CG75
Balfour Rd, Bromley BR2 226 EK99
Carshalton SM5 240 DF108
Grays RM17 192 GC77
Harrow HA1 139 CD57
Hounslow TW3 178 CB83
Ilford IG1 147 EP61
Southall UB2 178 BX76
Weybridge KT13 234 BN105
Balfour St, SE17 31 L8
Hertford SG14 54 DQ08
Balfron Twr, E14 22 E8
Balgonie Rd, E4 123 ED46
Balgores Cres, Rom. RM2 149 FH55
Balgores La, Rom. RM2 149 FH55
Balgores Sq, Rom. RM2 149 FH56
Balgowan Cl, N.Mal. KT3 220 CS99
Sch Balgowan Prim Sch, Beck.
BR3 off Balgowan Rd 225 DY96
Balgowan Rd, Beck. BR3 225 DY97
Balgowan St, SE18 187 ET77
BALHAM, SW12 202 DF88
⇌ Balham 203 DH88
⊖ Balham 203 DH88
Balham Continental Mkt,
SW12 off Shipka Rd 203 DH88
Balham Gro, SW12 202 DG87
Balham High Rd, SW12 202 DG88
SW17 202 DG89
Balham Hill, SW12 203 DH87
Balham New Rd, SW12 203 DH87
Balham Pk Rd, SW12 202 DF88
Balham Rd, N9 122 DU47
Balham Sta Rd, SW12 203 DH88
Balkan Wk, E1 32 E1
Balladier Wk, E14 22 C7
Ballamore Rd, Brom. BR1 206 EG90
Ballance Rd, E9 11 K4
Ballands N, The, Fetch. KT22 253 CE122
Ballands S, The, Fetch. KT22 253 CE123
Ballantine St, SW18 182 DC84
Ballantyne Cl, SE9 206 EL91
Ballantyne Dr, Kgswd KT20 255 CZ121
Ballard Cl, Kings.T. KT2 200 CR94
Ballard Grn, Wind. SL4 173 AL80
Ballards Cl, Dag. RM10 169 FB67
Ballards Fm Rd, Croy. CR0 242 DU107
South Croydon CR2 242 DU107
Ballards Grn, Tad. KT20 255 CY119
Ballards La, N3 120 DA53
N12 120 DA53
Oxted RH8 276 EJ129
Ballards Ms, Edg. HA8 118 CN51
Ballards Ri, S.Croy. CR2 242 DU107
Ballards Rd, NW2 141 CU61
Dagenham RM10 169 FB67
Ballards Way, Croy. CR0 242 DV107
South Croydon CR2 242 DU107
Ballast Quay, SE10 35 H10
Ballater Cl, Wat. WD19 116 BW49
Ballater Rd, SW2 183 DL84
South Croydon CR2 242 DT106
Ball Ct, EC3 off Castle Ct 19 M9
Ballenger Ct, Wat. WD18 97 BV41
Ballina St, SE23 205 DX87
Ballin Ct, E14 off Stewart St 34 F5
Ballingdon Rd, SW11 202 DG86
Ballinger Ct, Berk. HP4 60 AV20
Ballinger Pt, E3 22 C2
Ballinger Way, Nthlt. UB5 158 BY70
Balliol Av, E4 123 ED49
Balliol Rd, N17 122 DS53
W10 14 B8
Welling DA16 188 EV82
Balloch Rd, SE6 205 ED88
Ballogie Av, NW10 140 CS63
Ballota Ct, Edg. HA8
off Fortune Ave 118 CP53
Ballow Cl, SE5 43 N5
Balls Pk, Hert. SG13 54 DT11
Balls Pond Pl, N1 9 M4
Balls Pond Rd, N1 9 M4
Balmain Cl, W5 159 CK74
Balmer Rd, E3 21 N1
Balmes Rd, N1 9 M8
Balmoral Apts, W2
off Praed St 16 C7
Balmoral Av, N11 120 DG50
Beckenham BR3 225 DY98
Balmoral Cl, SW15 201 CX86
Park Street AL2 82 CC28
Slough SL1 153 AL72
Balmoral Ct, Wor.Pk. KT4 221 CV103
Balmoral Cres, W.Mol. KT8 218 CA97
Balmoral Dr, Borwd. WD6 100 CR43
Hayes UB4 157 BT71
Southall UB1 158 BZ70
Woking GU22 249 BC116
Balmoral Gdns, W13 179 CG76
Bexley DA5 208 EZ87
Ilford IG3 147 ET60
South Croydon CR2 242 DR110
Windsor SL4 173 AR83
Balmoral Gro, N7 8 C5
Balmoral Ms, W12 181 CT76
Balmoral Rd, E7 146 EJ63
E10 145 EB61
NW2 161 CV65
Abbots Langley WD5 81 BU32
Enfield EN3 105 DX36
Harrow HA2 138 CA63
Hornchurch RM12 150 FK62
Kingston upon Thames KT1 220 CM98
Pilgrim's Hatch CM15 130 FV44
Romford RM2 149 FH56
Sutton at Hone DA4 210 FP94
Watford WD24 98 BW38
Worcester Park KT4 221 CV104
Balmoral Way, Sutt. SM2 240 DA110
Balmore Cl, E14 22 F8
Balmore Cres, Barn. EN4 102 DG43
Balmore St, N19 143 DH61
Balmuir Gdns, SW15 181 CW84
Balnacraig Av, NW10 140 CS63
Balniel Gate, SW1 29 P10
Balquhain Cl, Ashtd. KT21 253 CK117
Balsams Cl, Hert. SG13 54 DR11
Baltic Apts, E16
off Western Gateway 35 P1
Baltic Cl, SW19 202 DD94
Baltic Ct, SE16 33 K4
Baltic Pl, N1 9 P9
Baltic Quay, SE16 33 M8
Baltic St E, EC1 19 J5
Baltic St W, EC1 19 J5
Baltic Wf, Grav. DA11 213 GG86
Baltimore Ho, SW18 182 DC84
Baltimore Pl, Well. DA16 187 ET82
Baltimore Wharf, E14 34 D6
Balvaird Pl, SW1 41 P1
Balvernie Gro, SW18 201 CZ87
Bamber Ho, Bark. IG11
off St. Margarets 167 EQ67
Bamber Rd, SE15 44 A6
Bamboo Ct, E5 144 DW61
Bamborough Gdns, W12 26 B5
Bamford Av, Wem. HA0 160 CM67
Bamford Rd, Bark. IG11 167 EQ65
Bromley BR1 205 EC92
Bamford Way, Rom. RM5 127 FB50
Bampfylde Cl, Wall. SM6 223 DJ104
Bampton Dr, NW7 119 CU52
Bampton Rd, SE23 205 DX90
Romford RM3 128 FL52
Bampton Way, Wok. GU21 248 AU118
Banavie Gdns, Beck. BR3 225 EC95
Banbury Av, Slou. SL1 153 AM71
Banbury Cl, Enf. EN2
off Holtwhites Hill 103 DP39
Banbury Ct, WC2 18 A10
Sutton SM2 240 DA108
● Banbury Enterprise Cen,
Croy. CR0 off Factory La 223 DP103
Banbury Rd, E9 11 J7
E17 123 DX52
Banbury St, SW11 40 D8
Watford WD18 97 BU43
Banbury Vil, Grav. DA13 212 FZ94
Banbury Wk, Nthlt. UB5
off Brabazon Rd 158 CA68
Banchory Rd, SE3 186 EH80
Bancroft Av, N2 142 DE57
Buckhurst Hill IG9 124 EG47
Bancroft Chase, Horn. RM12 149 FF61
Bancroft Cl, Ashf. TW15
off Feltham Hill Rd 196 BN92
Bancroft Ct, SW8 42 A6
Northolt UB5 158 BW67
Reigate RH2 272 DB134
Bancroft Gdns, Har. HA3 116 CC53
Orpington BR6 227 ET102
Bancroft Rd, E1 21 H3
Harrow HA3 116 CC54
Reigate RH2 272 DA134
Sch Bancroft's Sch, Wdf.Grn. IG8
off High Rd Woodford Grn 124 EG48
Banders Ri, Guil. GU1 265 BC133
Band La, Egh. TW20 195 AZ92
Bandon Cl, Uxb. UB10 156 BM67
Sch Bandon Hill Prim Sch, Wall.
SM6 off Sandy La S 241 DK107
Bandon Ri, Wall. SM6 241 DK106
Banes Down, Lwr Naze. EN9 72 EE22
Banfield Ct, Lon.Col. AL2 83 CH26
Banfield Rd, SE15 184 DV83
Sch Bangabandhu Prim Sch, E2 21 H3
Bangalore St, SW15 181 CW83
Bangor Cl, Nthlt. UB5 138 CB64
Bangors Cl, Iver SL0 155 BE72
Bangors Rd N, Iver SL0 155 BD67
Bangors Rd S, Iver SL0 155 BE71
Banim St, W6 181 CV76
Banister Ms, NW6 5 L6
Banister Rd, W10 14 D2
⊖ Bank 19 L9
DLR Bank 19 L9
Bank, The, N6
off Cholmeley Pk 143 DH60
Bank Av, Mitch. CR4 222 DD96
Bank Ct, Dart. DA1
off High St 210 FL86
Hemel Hempstead HP1 62 BJ21
Bank End, SE1 31 K2
Bankfoot, Bad.Dene RM17 192 FZ77
Bankfoot Rd, Brom. BR1 206 EE91
Bankhurst Rd, SE6 205 DZ87
Bank La, SW15 200 CS85
Kingston upon Thames KT2 200 CL94
Bank Ms, Sutt. SM1
off Sutton Ct Rd 240 DC107
Bank Mill, Berk. HP4 60 AY19
Bank Mill La, Berk. HP4 60 AY20
★ Bank of England, EC2 19 L9
★ Bank of England Mus, EC2 19 M9
Bank Pl, Brwd. CM14
off High St 130 FW47
Bank Rd, Penn HP10 110 AC47
Banks Ho, SE1 31 J7
Banksian Wk, Islw. TW7 179 CE81
Banksia Rd, N18 122 DW50
Bankside, SE1 31 J1
Dunton Green TN13 278 FE121
Enfield EN2 103 DP39
Northfleet DA11 212 GC86
South Croydon CR2 242 DT107
Southall UB1 158 BX74
Woking GU21
off Wyndham Rd 248 AV118
Bankside Av, SE13 185 EB83
Northolt UB5 off Townson Av 157 BU68
Bankside Cl, N4 144 DQ58
Bexley DA5 209 FD91
Biggin Hill TN16 260 EJ118
Carshalton SM5 240 DE107
Harefield UB9 114 BG51
Isleworth TW7 179 CF84
Bankside Dr, T.Ditt. KT7 219 CH102
★ Bankside Gall, SE1 31 H1
Bankside Lofts, SE1 31 H2
Pier Bankside Pier 31 J1
Bankside Rd, Ilf. IG1 147 EQ64
Bankside Way, SE19
off Lunham Rd 204 DS93
Banks La, Bexh. DA6 188 EZ84
Bank's La, Eff. KT24 251 BV122
Banks La, Epp. CM16 92 EY32
Banks Rd, Borwd. WD6 100 CQ40
Banks Spur, Slou. SL1
off Cooper Way 173 AP75
Bank St, E14 34 B3
Gravesend DA12 213 GH86
Sevenoaks TN13 279 FH125
Banks Way, E12 147 EN63
Guildford GU4 265 AZ131
Banks Yd, Houns. TW5 178 BZ79
Bankton Rd, SW2 183 DN84
Bankwell Rd, SE13 186 EE84
Bann Cl, S.Ock. RM15 171 FV73
Banner Cl, Purf. RM19
off Brimfield Rd 191 FR77
Bannerman Ho, SW8 42 C3
Banner St, EC1 19 K5
Banning St, SE10 47 J1
Bannister Cl, SW2 203 DN88
Greenford UB6 139 CD64
Slough SL3 174 AY75
Bannister Dr, Hutt. CM13 131 GC44
Bannister Gdns, Orp. BR5
off Main Rd 228 EW97
Bannister Ho, E9 11 J3
Harrow HA3
off Headstone Dr 139 CE55
Bannister's Rd, Guil. GU2 280 AT136
Sch Bannockburn Prim Sch, SE18
off Plumstead High St 187 ET77
Bannockburn Rd, SE18 187 ES77
Bannow Cl, Epsom KT19 238 CS105
★ Banqueting Ho, SW1 30 A3
BANSTEAD, SM7 256 DB115
⇌ Banstead 239 CY114
Sch Banstead Comm Jun Sch, Bans.
SM7 off The Horseshoe 255 CZ115
Banstead Ct, W12
off Hilary Rd 161 CT73
Jct Banstead Crossroads,
Bans. SM7 239 CZ114
Banstead Gdns, N9 122 DS48
Sch Banstead Inf Sch, Bans. SM7
off The Horseshoe 255 CZ115
Banstead Rd, Bans. SM7 239 CX112
Carshalton SM5 240 DE107
Caterham CR3 258 DR121
Epsom KT17 239 CV110
Purley CR8 241 DN111
Banstead Rd S, Sutt. SM2 240 DD110
Banstead St, SE15 44 G10
Banstead Way, Wall. SM6 241 DL106
Banstock Rd, Edg. HA8 118 CP51
Banting Dr, N21 103 DM43
Banton Cl, Enf. EN1
off Central Av 104 DV40
Bantry Rd, Slou. SL1 173 AM75
Bantry St, SE5 43 M5
Banwell Rd, Bex. DA5
off Woodside La 208 EX86
Banyard Rd, SE16 32 F7
Banyards, Horn. RM11 150 FL56
Bapchild Pl, Orp. BR5
off Okemore Gdns 228 EW98
Baptist Gdns, NW5 6 G4
Barandon Wk, W11 14 D10
Barataria Pk, Ripley GU23 249 BF121
Barbara Brosnan Ct, NW8 16 A1
Barbara Castle Cl, SW6 39 H3
Barbara Cl, Shep. TW17 217 BP99
Barbara Hucklesby Cl, N22
off The Sandlings 121 DP54
Sch Barbara Speake Stage Sch,
W3 off East Acton La 160 CS73
Barbauld Rd, N16 144 DS62
Barbel Cl, Wal.Cr. EN8 89 EA34
Barber Cl, N21 121 DN45
Barberry Cl, Rom. RM3 128 FJ52
Barberry Rd, Hem.H. HP1 62 BG20
Barber's All, E13 24 A2
BARBICAN, EC2 19 J7
⇌ Barbican 19 H6
⊖ Barbican 19 H6
★ Barbican Arts & Conf Cen,
EC2 19 K6
Barbican Rd, Grnf. UB6 158 CB72
Barb Ms, W6 26 B7
Barbon Cl, WC1 18 B6
Barbot Cl, N9 122 DU48
Barchard St, SW18 202 DB85
Barchester Cl, W7 159 CF74
Uxbridge UB8 156 BJ70
Barchester Rd, Har. HA3 117 CD54
Slough SL3 175 AZ75
Barchester St, E14 22 C7
Barclay Cl, SW6 39 J5
Fetcham KT22 252 CB123
Hertford Heath SG13 54 DV11
Watford WD18 97 BU44
Barclay Ct, Hodd. EN11 71 EA18
Slough SL1 173 AQ75
Barclay Oval, Wdf. Grn.
IG8 124 EG49
Barclay Path, E17 145 EC57
Sch Barclay Prim Sch, E10
off Canterbury Rd 145 ED58
Barclay Rd, E11 146 EE60
E13 24 C5
E17 145 EC57
N18 122 DR51
SW6 39 J5
Croydon CR0 224 DR104
Barclay Way, W.Thur. RM20 191 FT78
Barcombe Av, SW2 203 DL89
Barcombe Cl, Orp. BR5 227 ET97
Barden Cl, Hare. UB9 114 BJ52
Barden St, SE18 187 ES80
Bardeswell Cl, Brwd. CM14 130 FW47
Bardfield Av, Rom. RM6 148 EX55
Bardney Rd, Mord. SM4 222 DB98
Bardolph Av, Croy. CR0 243 DZ109
Bardolph Rd, N7 143 DL63
Richmond TW9
off St. Georges Rd 180 CM83
Bardon Wk, Wok. GU21
off Bampton Way 248 AV117
Bard Rd, W10 26 C1
Bards Cor, Hem.H. HP1
off Laureate Way 62 BH19
Bardsey Pl, E1 20 G5
Bardsey Wk, N1 9 K5
Bardsley Cl, Croy. CR0 224 DT104
Bardsley La, SE10 46 E3
Bardwell Ct, St.Alb. AL1 65 CD21
Bardwell Rd, St.Alb. AL1 65 CD21
Barfett St, W10 14 G4
Barfield, Sutt.H. DA4 230 FP95
Barfield Av, N20 120 DE47
Barfield Rd, E11 146 EF60
Bromley BR1 227 EN97
Barfields, Bletch. RH1 273 DP133
Loughton IG10 107 EN42
Barfields Gdns, Loug. IG10
off Barfields 107 EN42
Barfields Path, Loug. IG10 107 EN42
Barfleur La, SE8 33 N9
Barfolds, N.Mymms AL9
off Dixons Hill Rd 67 CW23
Barford Cl, NW4 119 CU53
Barford St, N1 8 F9
Barforth Rd, SE15 184 DV83
Barfreston Way, SE20 224 DV95
Bargate Cl, SE18 187 ET78
New Malden KT3 221 CU101
Bargate Ct, Guil. GU2
off Chapelhouse Cl 264 AS134
Barge Ct, Green. DA9 191 FW84
Barge Ho Rd, E16 37 N3
Barge Ho St, SE1 30 F2
Barge La, E3 11 M9
Bargery Rd, SE6 205 EB88
Barge Wk, E.Mol. KT8 219 CD97
Kingston upon Thames KT1,
KT2 219 CK95
Walton-on-Thames KT12 218 BX97
Bargrove Av, Hem.H. HP1 62 BG21
Bargrove Cl, SE20 204 DU94
Bargrove Cres, SE6
off Elm La 205 DZ89
Barham Av, Els. WD6 100 CM41
Barham Cl, Brom. BR2 226 EL102
Chislehurst BR7 207 EP92
Gravesend DA12 213 GM88
Romford RM7 127 FB54
Wembley HA0 159 CH65
Weybridge KT13 235 BQ105
Sch Barham Prim Sch, Wem.
HA0 off Danethorpe Rd 159 CJ65
Barham Rd, SW20 201 CU94
Chislehurst BR7 207 EP92
Dartford DA1 210 FN87
South Croydon CR2 242 DQ105
Baring Cl, SE12 206 EG89
Baring Cres, Beac. HP9 110 AJ52
Sch Baring Prim Sch, SE12
off Linchmere Rd 206 EG87
Baring Rd, SE12 206 EG87
Beaconsfield HP9 110 AJ52
Cockfosters EN4 102 DD41
Croydon CR0 224 DU102
Baring St, N1 9 L9
Baritone Ct, E15 off Church St 13 L9
Barkantine Shop Par, The,
E14 34 A5
Bark Burr Rd, Grays RM16 192 FZ75
Barker Cl, Cher. KT16 215 BE101
New Malden KT3
off England Way 220 CP98
Northwood HA6 115 BT52
Richmond TW9 180 CP82
Barker Dr, NW1 7 M7
Barker Ms, SW4 183 DH84
Barker Rd, Cher. KT16 215 BE101
Barker St, SW10 39 N2
Barker Wk, SW16 203 DK90
Barkham Rd, N17 122 DR52
Barkham Ter, SE1 30 F6
Bark Hart Rd, Orp. BR6 228 EV102
BARKING, IG11 167 EP67
⇌ Barking 167 EQ66
Barking 167 EQ66
⊖ Barking 167 EQ66
Sch Barking Abbey Sch,
Lwr Sch, Bark. IG11
off Longbridge Rd 147 ES64
Upr Sch, Bark. IG11
off Sandringham Rd 167 ET65
Barking & Dagenham Civic Cen,
Dag. RM10 149 FB61
● Barking Business Cen,
Bark. IG11 168 EU69
Coll Barking Coll, Rush Grn RM7
off Dagenham Rd 149 FD61
H Barking Hosp, Bark. IG11 167 ET66
● Barking Ind Pk, Bark. IG11 167 ET67
Barking Rd, E6 24 D1
E13 24 A3
E16 23 L7
BARKINGSIDE, Ilf. IG6 147 EP55
⊖ Barkingside 147 ER56
Bark Pl, W2 15 L10
Barkston Gdns, SW5 27 L10
Barkston Path, Borwd. WD6 100 CN37
Barkway Ct, N4 off Queens Dr 144 DQ61
Barkway Dr, Orp. BR6 245 EN105
Barkwood Cl, Rom. RM7 149 FC57
Barkworth Rd, SE16 44 F1
Barlborough St, SE14 45 H4
Barlby Gdns, W10 14 C5
Sch Barlby Prim Sch, W10 14 D5
Barlby Rd, W10 14 C6
Barlee Cres, Uxb. UB8 156 BJ71
Barle Gdns, S.Ock. RM15 171 FV72
Barley Brow, Wat. WD25 81 BV31
Barley Cl, Bushey WD23 98 CB43
Wembley HA0 139 CK63
Barleycorn Way, E14 21 N10
Hornchurch RM11 150 FM58
Barley Cft, Harl. CM18 73 ER19
Hemel Hempstead HP2 63 BQ20
Hertford SG14 54 DR07
Barleycroft Grn, Welw.G.C. AL8 51 CW09
Barleycroft Rd, Welw.G.C. AL8 51 CW10
Barley Flds, Woob.Grn HP10 132 AE55
Barleyfields Cl, Rom. RM6 148 EV59
Barley Ho, NW7
off Morphou Rd 119 CY50
Barley La, Ilf. IG3 148 EU60
Romford RM6 148 EV58
Sch Barley La Prim Sch, Chad.Hth
RM6 off Huxley Dr 148 EV59
Barleymead, Horl. RH6
off Oatlands 291 DJ147
Barley Mow Caravan Pk,
St.Alb. AL4 66 CM22
Barley Mow Ct, Bet. RH3 270 CQ134
Barley Mow La, St.Alb. AL4 66 CL23
Barley Mow Pas, EC1 19 H7
W4 180 CR78
Barley Mow Rd, Eng.Grn TW20 194 AW92
Barley Mow Way, Shep. TW17 216 BN98
Barley Ponds Cl, Ware SG12 55 DZ06
Barley Ponds Rd, Ware SG12 55 DZ06
● Barley Shotts Business Pk,
W10 off Acklam Rd 14 G6
Barlow Cl, Hat. AL10 66 CR16
Wallington SM6 241 DL108
Barlow Dr, SE18 186 EL81
Barlow Ho, SE16
off Rennie Est 32 F9
Barlow Pl, W1 29 K1
Barlow Rd, NW6 5 H4
W3 160 CP74
Hampton TW12 198 CA94
Barlow St, SE17 31 M8
Barlow Way, Rain. RM13 169 FD71
Barmeston Rd, SE6 205 EB89
Barmor Cl, Har. HA2 116 CB54
Barmouth Av, Perivale UB6 159 CF68
Barmouth Rd, SW18 202 DC86
Croydon CR0 225 DX103
Barnabas Ct, N21
off Cheyne Wk 103 DN43
Barnabas Rd, E9 11 K3
Barnaby Cl, Har. HA2 138 CC61
Barnaby Pl, SW7 28 A9
Barnaby Way, Chig. IG7 125 EP48
Barnacre Cl, Uxb. UB8 156 BK72
Barnacres Rd, Hem.H. HP3 80 BM25
Barnard Acres, Lwr Naze. EN9 72 EE23
Barnard Cl, SE18 37 M8
Chislehurst BR7 227 ER95

Barnard Cl, Sunbury-on-Thames TW16
off Oak Gro 197 BV94
Wallington SM6 241 DK108
Barnard Ct, Wok. GU21 248 AS118
Barnard Gdns, Hayes UB4 157 BV70
New Malden KT3 221 CU98
Barnard Grn, Welw.G.C. AL7 51 CZ10
Barnard Gro, E15 13 L7
Barnard Hill, N10 120 DG54
Barnard Ms, SW11 182 DE84
Barnardo Dr, Ilf. IG6 147 EQ56
Barnardo Gdns, E1 21 J10
Barnardo St, E1 21 J9
Barnardos Village, Ilf. IG6 147 EQ55
Barnard Rd, SW11 182 DE84
Enfield EN1 104 DV40
Mitcham CR4 222 DG97
Warlingham CR6 259 EB119
Barnard's Inn, EC1
off Holborn 18 F8
Barnards Pl, S.Croy. CR2 241 DP109
Barnard Way, Hem.H. HP3 62 BL21
Barnato Cl, W.Byf. KT14 234 BL112
Barnby Sq, E15 13 J8
Barnby St, E15 13 J8
NW1 17 M1
Barn Cl, Ashf. TW15 197 BP92
Banstead SM7 256 DD115
Epsom KT18
off Woodcote Side 254 CP115
Farnham Common SL2 133 AP63
Hemel Hempstead HP3 62 BM23
Northolt UB5 158 BW68
Radlett WD7 99 CG35
Tadworth KT20 270 CM132
Welwyn Garden City AL8 51 CW09
Barn Cres, Pur. CR8 242 DR113
Stanmore HA7 117 CJ51
Barncroft Cl, Loug. IG10 107 EN43
Uxbridge UB8 157 BP71
Barncroft Grn, Loug. IG10 107 EN43
Sch Barn Cft Prim Sch, E17
off Brunel Rd 145 DY58
Sch Barncroft Prim Sch, Hem.H.
HP2 off Washington Av 62 BK15
Barncroft Rd, Berk. HP4 60 AT20
Loughton IG10 107 EN43
Barncroft Way, St.Alb. AL1 65 CG21
Barndicott, Welw.G.C. AL7 52 DC09
Barneby Cl, Twick. TW2
off Rowntree Rd 199 CE88
BARNEHURST, Bexh. DA7 189 FD83
⇌ Barnehurst 189 FC82
Barnehurst Av, Bexh. DA7 189 FC81
Erith DA8 189 FC81
Barnehurst Cl, Erith DA8 189 FC81
Sch Barnehurst Inf Sch,
Northumb.Hth DA8
off Barnehurst Cl 189 FC81
Sch Barnehurst Jun Sch,
Northumb.Hth DA8
off Barnehurst Cl 189 FC81
Barnehurst Rd, Bexh. DA7 189 FC82
Barn Elms Pk, SW15 38 B9
Sch Barn End Cen, Wilm. DA2
off High Rd 210 FJ90
Barn End Dr, Dart. DA2 210 FJ90
Barn End La, Dart. DA2 210 FJ92
BARNES, SW13 181 CU82
⇌ Barnes 181 CU83
Barnes Av, SW13 181 CU80
Chesham HP5 76 AQ30
Southall UB2 178 BZ77
⇌ Barnes Bridge 180 CS82
Barnes Br, SW13 180 CS82
W4 180 CS82
Barnesbury Ho, SW4 203 DK85
Barnes Cl, E12 146 EK63
★ Barnes Common, SW13 181 CU83
Barnes Ct, E16 24 D6
Barnet EN5 102 DB42
Woodford Green IG8 124 EK50
BARNES CRAY, Dart. DA1 189 FH84
Barnes Cray Cotts, Dart. DA1
off Maiden La 209 FG85
Barnes Cray Rd, Dart. DA1 189 FG84
Barnesdale Cres, Orp. BR5 228 EU100
Barnes End, N.Mal. KT3 221 CU99
Barnes High St, SW13 181 CT82
H Barnes Hosp, SW14 180 CS83
Barnes Ho, Bark. IG11
off St. Marys 167 ER67
Barnes La, Kings L. WD4 80 BH27
Barnes Pikle, W5 159 CK73
Sch Barnes Prim Sch, SW13
off Cross St 181 CT83
Barnes Ri, Kings L. WD4 80 BM27
Barnes Rd, N18 122 DW49
Godalming GU7 280 AS143
Ilford IG1 147 EQ64
Barnes St, E14 21 L9
Barnes Ter, SE8 45 P1
Barnes Wallis Cl, Eff. KT24 268 BX127
Barnes Wallis Dr, Wey. KT13 234 BL111
Barnes Way, Iver SL0 155 BF73
Wal.Abb. EN9 90 EG32
BARNET, EN4 & EN5 101 CZ41
Coll Barnet & Southgate Coll,
Grahame Pk campus, NW9
off Grahame Pk Way 119 CT53
Southgate campus, N14
off High St 121 DK47
Wood St campus, Barn. EN5 101 CZ42
Barnet Bypass, Barn. EN5 100 CS41
Borehamwood WD6 100 CS41
Barnet Dr, Brom. BR2 226 EL103
BARNET GATE, Barn. EN5 101 CT44
Barnet Gate La, Barn. EN5 101 CT44
Barnet Gro, E2 20 C2
Barnet Hill, Barn. EN5 102 DA42
H Barnet Hosp, Barn. EN5 101 CX42
Barnet La, N20 119 CZ46
Barnet EN5 101 CZ44
Elstree WD6 99 CK44
★ Barnet Mus, Barn. EN5
off Wood St 101 CY42
Barnet Rd, Barn. EN5 101 CV43
London Colney AL2 84 CL27
Potters Bar EN6 102 DA35
Barnett Cl, Erith DA8 189 FF82
Leatherhead KT22 253 CH119
Wonersh GU5 281 BC143
Barnett La, Won. GU5 281 BB144
● Barnet Trd Est, High Barn.
EN5 101 CZ41
Barnett Row, Jacobs Well
GU4 264 AX129
Barnetts Ct, Har. HA2
off Leathsail Rd 138 CB62
Barnetts Shaw, Oxt. RH8 275 ED127
Barnett St, E1 20 E8
Barnetts Way, Oxt. RH8 275 ED127
Sch Barnett Wd Inf Sch, Ashtd.
KT21 off Barnett Wd La 253 CK117
Barnett Wd La, Ashtd. KT21 253 CJ119
Leatherhead KT22 253 CH120
Barnet Way, NW7 118 CR45
Barnet Wd Rd, Brom. BR2 226 EJ103
Barney Cl, SE7 36 C10
Barn Fld, NW3 6 E3
Barnfield, Bans. SM7 240 DB114
Epping CM16 92 EU28
Gravesend DA11 213 GG89
Hemel Hempstead HP3 62 BM23
Horley RH6 290 DG149
Iver SL0 155 BE72
New Malden KT3 220 CS100
Slough SL1 153 AK74
Barnfield Av, Croy. CR0 224 DW103
Kingston upon Thames KT2 199 CK91
Mitcham CR4 223 DH98
Barnfield Cl, N4
off Crouch Hill 143 DL59
SW17 202 DC90
Coulsdon CR5 258 DQ119
Greenhithe DA9 211 FT86
Hoddesdon EN11 71 EA15
Lower Nazeing EN9 72 EF22
Swanley BR8 229 FC101
Barnfield Gdns, SE18
off Barnfield Rd 187 EP79
Kingston upon Thames KT2 200 CL91
Barnfield Pl, E14 34 B9
Sch Barnfield Prim Sch, Edg.
HA8 off Silkstream Rd 118 CQ53
Barnfield Rd, SE18 187 EP79
W5 159 CJ70
Belvedere DA17 188 EZ79
Edgware HA8 118 CQ53
Orpington BR5 228 EX97
St. Albans AL4 65 CJ17
Sevenoaks TN13 278 FD123
South Croydon CR2 242 DS109
Tatsfield TN16 260 EK120
Welwyn Garden City AL7 51 CY11
Barnfield Way, Oxt. RH8 276 EG133
Barnfield Wd Cl, Beck. BR3 225 ED100
Barnfield Wd Rd, Beck. BR3 225 ED100
Barnham Dr, SE28 167 ET74
Barnham Rd, Grnf. UB6 158 CC69
Barnham St, SE1 31 P4
Barnhill, Pnr. HA5 138 BW57
Barn Hill, Roydon CM19 72 EH19
Wembley HA9 140 CP61
Barnhill Av, Brom. BR2 226 EF99
Sch Barnhill Comm High Sch,
Hayes UB4
off Yeading La 158 BW69
Barnhill La, Hayes UB4 157 BV69
Barnhill Rd, Hayes UB4 157 BV70
Wembley HA9 140 CQ62
Barnhurst Path, Wat. WD19 116 BW50
Barningham Way, NW9 140 CR58
Barn Lea, Mill End WD3 114 BG46
Barnlea Cl, Felt. TW13 198 BY89
Barnmead, Chobham GU24 232 AT110
Barn Mead, Harl. CM18 73 ER17
Theydon Bois CM16 107 ES36
Toot Hill CM5 93 FE29
Barnmead Gdns, Dag. RM9 148 EZ64
Barn Meadow, Epp.Upl. CM16
off Upland Rd 91 ET25
Barn Meadow La, Bkhm KT23 252 BZ124
Barnmead Rd, Beck. BR3 225 DY95
Dagenham RM9 148 EZ64
Barnock Cl, Dart. DA1 209 FE87
Barn Ri, Wem. HA9 140 CN60
BARNSBURY, N1 8 D6
Barnsbury Cl, N.Mal. KT3 220 CQ98
Barnsbury Cres, Surb. KT5 220 CQ102
Barnsbury Est, N1 8 D9
Barnsbury Gro, N7 8 D5
Sch Barnsbury Inf Sch, Wok.
GU22 off Hawthorn Rd 248 AX121
Sch Barnsbury Jun Sch, Wok.
GU22 off Almond Av 248 AX121
Barnsbury La, Surb. KT5 220 CP103
Barnsbury Pk, N1 8 E6
Barnsbury Rd, N1 8 E10
Barnsbury Sq, N1 8 E7
Barnsbury St, N1 8 E7
Barnsbury Ter, N1 8 D7
Barns Ct, Harl. CM19 73 EN20
Waltham Abbey EN9 90 EG32
Barnscroft, SW20 221 CV97
Barnsdale Av, E14 34 B8
Barnsdale Cl, Borwd. WD6 100 CM39
Barnsdale Rd, W9 15 H4
Barnsfield Pl, Uxb. UB8 156 BJ66
Barnside Ct, Welw.G.C. AL8 51 CW09
Barnsley Rd, Rom. RM3 128 FM52
Barnsley St, E1 20 F4
Barnstaple La, SE13
off Lewisham High St 185 EC84
Barnstaple Path, Rom. RM3 128 FJ50
Barnstaple Rd, Rom. RM3 128 FJ50
Ruislip HA4 138 BW62
Barnston Wk, N1 9 J8
Barnston Way, Hutt. CM13 131 GC43
Barn St, N16 144 DS61
Barnsway, Kings L. WD4 80 BL28
Barnway, Eng.Grn TW20 194 AW92
Barn Way, Wem. HA9 140 CN60
Barnwell Rd, SW2 203 DN85
Dartford DA1 190 FM83
Barnwood Cl, N20 119 CZ46
W9 15 L5
Guildford GU2 264 AS132
Ruislip HA4 137 BR61
Barnwood Rd, Guil. GU2 264 AS133
Barnyard, The, Walt.Hill KT20 255 CU124
Baron Cl, N11 120 DG50
Sutton SM2 240 DB110
Baroness Rd, E2 20 B2
Baronet Gro, N17 122 DU53
Baronet Rd, N17 122 DU53
Baron Gdns, Ilf. IG6 147 EQ55
Baron Gro, Mitch. CR4 222 DE98
Baron Ho, SW19
off Chapter Way 222 DD95
Baron Rd, Dag. RM8 148 EX60
Barons, The, Twick. TW1 199 CH86
⊖ Barons Court 26 E10
Barons Ct, Wall. SM6
off Whelan Way 223 DK104
Barons Ct Rd, W14 26 E10
Baronsfield Rd, Twick. TW1 199 CH86
Barons Gate, Barn. EN4 102 DE44
Barons Hurst, Epsom KT18 254 CQ116
Barons Keep, W14 26 E10
Barons Mead, Har. HA1 139 CE56
Baronsmead Rd, SW13 181 CU81
Baronsmede, W5 180 CM75
Baronsmere Rd, N2 142 DE56
Barons Pl, SE1 30 F5
Baron St, N1 8 E10
Barons Wk, Croy. CR0 225 DY100
Barons Way, Egh. TW20 195 BD93
Reigate RH2 288 DA138
Baron Wk, E16 23 L6
Mitcham CR4 222 DE98
Baroque Ct, Houns. TW3
off Prince Regent Rd 178 CC83
Barque Ms, SE8 46 A2
Barrack La, Wind. SL4 173 AR82
Barrack Path, Wok. GU21 248 AT118
Barrack Rd, Guil. GU2 264 AU132
Hounslow TW4 178 BX84
Barrack Row, Grav. DA11 213 GH86
Barracks, The, Add. KT15 216 BH104
Barracks Hill, Colesh. HP7 111 AM45
Barracks La, Barn. EN5
off High St 101 CY41
Barra Cl, Hem.H. HP3 63 BP23
Barra Hall Circ, Hayes UB3 157 BS72
Barra Hall Rd, Hayes UB3 157 BS73
Barrards Way, Seer Grn HP9 111 AQ51
Barrass Cl, Enf. EN3 105 EA37
Barratt Av, N22 121 DM54
● Barratt Ind Pk, E3 22 E5
● Barratt Ind Est,
Southall UB1 178 CA75
Barratt Way, Har. HA3
off Tudor Rd 139 CD55
Barrenger Rd, N10 120 DF53
Barrens Brae, Wok. GU22 249 BA118
Barrens Cl, Wok. GU22 249 BA118
Barrens Pk, Wok. GU22 249 BA118
Barrett Cl, Rom. RM3 127 FH52
Barrett Rd, E17 145 EC56
Fetcham KT22 252 CC124
Barretts Grn Rd, NW10 160 CQ68
Barretts Gro, N16 9 P2
Barretts Rd, Dunt.Grn TN13 263 FD120
Barrett St, W1 17 H9
Barrhill Rd, SW2 203 DL89
Barricane, Wok. GU21 248 AV119
Barrie Cl, Couls. CR5 257 DJ115
Barriedale, SE14 45 M8
Barrie Est, W2 16 A10
Barrier App, SE7 36 E7
Barrier Pt Rd, E16 36 C3
Barrier Pt Twr, E16
off Barrier Pt Rd 36 C4
Barringer Sq, SW17 202 DG91
Barrington Cl, NW5 6 G2
Ilford IG5 125 EM53
Loughton IG10 107 EQ42
Barrington Ct, W3
off Cheltenham Pl 180 CP75
Dorking RH4
off Barrington Rd 285 CG137
Hutton CM13 131 GC44
N10 off Colney Hatch La 120 DG54
Barrington Dr, Fetch. KT22 269 CD125
Harefield UB9 114 BG52
Barrington Grn, Loug. IG10 107 EQ42
Barrington Lo, Wey. KT13 235 BQ106
Barrington Ms, Welw.G.C. AL7 52 DB10
Barrington Pk Gdns, Ch.St.G.
HP8 112 AX46
Sch Barrington Prim Sch, Bexh.
DA7 off Barrington Rd 188 EX82
Barrington Rd, E12 167 EN65
N8 143 DK57
SW9 183 DP83
Bexleyheath DA7 188 EX82
Dorking RH4 285 CG137
Loughton IG10 107 EQ41
Purley CR8 241 DJ112
Sutton SM3 222 DA102
Barrington Vil, SE18 187 EN81
Barrow Av, Cars. SM5 240 DF108
Barrow Cl, N21 121 DP48
Barrowdene Cl, Pnr. HA5
off Paines La 116 BY54
Barrowell Grn, N21 121 DP47
Barrowfield Cl, N9 122 DV48
Barrow Gdns, Red. RH1 273 DH132
Barrowgate Rd, W4 180 CQ78
Barrow Grn Rd, Oxt. RH8 275 EC128
Barrow Hedges Cl, Cars. SM5 240 DE108
Sch Barrow Hedges Prim Sch,
Cars. SM5 off Harbury Rd 240 DE108
Barrow Hedges Way, Cars.
SM5 240 DE108
Barrow Hill, Wor.Pk. KT4 220 CS103
Barrow Hill Cl, Wor.Pk. KT4 220 CS103
Barrow Hill Est, NW8 16 C1
Sch Barrow Hill Jun Sch, NW8 16 C1
Barrow Hill Rd, NW8 16 C1
Barrow La, Chsht EN7 88 DT30
Barrow Pt Av, Pnr. HA5 116 BY54
Barrow Pt La, Pnr. HA5 116 BY54
Barrow Rd, SW16 203 DK93
Croydon CR0 241 DN106
Barrowsfield, S.Croy. CR2 242 DT112
Barrows Rd, Harl. CM19 73 EM15
Barrow Wk, Brent. TW8 179 CJ79
Barr Rd, Grav. DA12 213 GM89
Potters Bar EN6 86 DC33
Barrsbrook Fm Rd, Cher. KT16 215 BE102
Barrsbrook Hall, Cher. KT16 215 BE102
Barrs Rd, NW10 160 CR66
Barr's Rd, Tap. SL6 152 AH72
Barry Av, N15 144 DT58
Bexleyheath DA7 188 EY80
Windsor SL4 173 AQ80
Barry Cl, Grays RM16 193 GG75
Orpington BR6 227 ES104
St. Albans AL2 82 CB25
Barry Ho, SE16
off Rennie Est 32 F10
Barry Rd, E6 25 H8
NW10 160 CQ66
SE22 204 DU86
Bars, The, Guil. GU1 280 AX135
Barset Rd, SE15 44 G10
Barson Cl, SE20 204 DW94
Barston Rd, SE27 204 DQ89
Barstow Cres, SW2 203 DM88
Bartel Cl, Hem.H. HP3 63 BR22
Bartelotts Rd, Slou. SL2 153 AK70
Barter St, WC1 18 B7
Barters Wk, Pnr. HA5
off High St 138 BY55
Barth Ms, SE18 187 ES77
Bartholomew Cl, EC1 19 J7
SW18 182 DC84
Bartholomew Ct, E14
off Newport Av 35 H1
Dorking RH4 off South St 285 CG137
Bartholomew Dr, Harold Wd
RM3 128 FK54
Bartholomew Ho, W10
off Appleford Rd 14 F5
Bartholomew La, EC2 19 M9
Bartholomew Pl, EC1 19 J7
Bartholomew Rd, NW5 7 M5
Bartholomew Sq, E1 20 F4
EC1 19 K4
Bartholomew St, SE1 31 L7
Bartholomew Vil, NW5 7 L5
Bartholomew Way, Swan. BR8 229 FE97
Barth Rd, SE18 187 ES77
Bartle Av, E6 166 EL68
Bartle Rd, W11 14 D9
Bartlett Cl, E14 22 B8
Bartlett Ct, EC4 18 F8
Bartlett Ms, E14
off East Ferry Rd 34 D10
Bartlett Rd, Grav. DA11 213 GG88
Westerham TN16 277 EQ126
Bartletts, Chal.St.P. SL9 112 AY52
Bartletts Mead, Hert. SG14 54 DR06
Bartletts Pas, EC4 18 F8
Bartlett St, S.Croy. CR2 242 DR106
Bartlow Gdns, Rom. RM5 127 FD53
Barton, The, Cob. KT11 236 BX112
Barton Av, Rom. RM7 149 FB60
Barton Cl, E6 25 K8
E9 11 H2
NW4 141 CU57
SE15 44 F10
Addlestone KT15 234 BG107
Bexleyheath DA6 208 EY85
Chigwell IG7 125 EQ47
Shepperton TW17 217 BP100
Barton Ct, Whyt. CR3 258 DU119
Barton Grn, N.Mal. KT3 220 CR96
Barton Ho, E3 off Bow Rd 22 C2
N1 9 H6
SW6 39 M10
Barton Meadows, Ilf. IG6 147 EQ56
Barton Pl, Guil. GU4
off London Rd 265 BB131
Barton Rd, W14 38 E1
Bramley GU5 281 BA144
Hornchurch RM12 149 FG60
Sidcup DA14 208 EY93
Slough SL3 175 AZ75
Sutton at Hone DA4 230 FP95
Bartons, The, Els. WD6 99 CK44
Barton St, SW1 30 A6
Bartonway, NW8 6 A9
Barton Way, Borwd. WD6 100 CN40
Croxley Green WD3 97 BP43
Bartram Cl, Uxb. UB8 157 BP70
Bartram Rd, SE4 205 DY85
Bartrams La, Barn. EN4 102 DC38
Bartrop Cl, Goffs Oak EN7 88 DR28
Barts Cl, Beck. BR3 225 EA99
Barville Cl, SE4
off St. Norbert Rd 185 DY84
● Barwell Business Pk,
Chess. KT9 237 CK108
Barwell Cres, Bigg.H. TN16 244 EJ113
Barwell La, Chess. KT9 237 CJ108
Barwick Dr, Uxb. UB8 157 BP71
Barwick Ho, W3 180 CQ75
Barwick Rd, E7 146 EH63
Barwood Av, W.Wick. BR4 225 EB102
Bascombe Gro, Dart. DA1 209 FE87
Bascombe St, SW2 203 DN86
Basden Gro, Felt. TW13 198 CA89
Basedale Rd, Dag. RM9 168 EV66
Baseing Cl, E6 25 M10
Basevi Way, SE8 46 C2
Basford Way, Wind. SL4 173 AK83
Bashley Rd, NW10 160 CR70
Basil Av, E6 25 H2
Basildene Rd, Houns. TW4 178 BX82
Basildon Av, Ilf. IG5 125 EN53
Basildon Cl, Sutt. SM2 240 DB109
Watford WD18 97 BQ44
Basildon Rd, SE2 188 EU78
Basildon Sq, Hem.H. HP2 62 BM16
Basil Gdns, SE27 204 DQ92
Croydon CR0
off Primrose La 225 DX102
Basil Ms, Harl. CM17
off Square St 58 EW14
Basilon Rd, Bexh. DA7 188 EY82
Basil St, SW3 28 E6
Basin App, E14 21 M9
E16 37 P1
Basing Cl, T.Ditt. KT7 219 CF101
Basing Ct, SE15 44 B7
Basingdon Way, SE5 184 DR84
Basing Dr, Bex. DA5 208 EZ86
Basingfield Rd, T.Ditt. KT7 219 CF101
Basinghall Av, EC2 19 L7
Basinghall Gdns, Sutt. SM2 240 DB109
Basinghall St, EC2 19 L8
Basing Hill, NW11 141 CZ60
Wembley HA9 140 CM61
Basing Ho, Bark. IG11
off St. Margarets 167 ER67
Basing Ho Yd, E2 19 P2
Basing Pl, E2 19 P2
Basing Rd, Bans. SM7 239 CZ114
Mill End WD3 113 BF46
Basing St, W11 14 G8
Basing Way, N3 142 DA55
Thames Ditton KT7 219 CF101
Basire St, N1 9 J8
Baskerville Gdns, NW10 140 CS63
Baskerville Rd, SW18 202 DE87
Basket Gdns, SE9 206 EL85
Baslow Cl, Har. HA3 117 CD53
Baslow Wk, E5 145 DX63
Basnett Rd, SW11 41 H10
Basque Ct, SE16 33 J4
Bassano St, SE22 204 DT85
Bassant Rd, SE18 187 ET79
Bass Ct, E15 off Plaistow Gro 13 L9
Bassein Pk Rd, W12 181 CT75
Basset Cl, New Haw KT15 234 BH110
Bassett Cl, Sutt. SM2 240 DB109
Bassett Dr, Reig. RH2 272 DA133
Bassett Flds, N.Wld Bas. CM16 93 FD25
Bassett Gdns, Islw. TW7 178 CC80
North Weald Bassett CM16 93 FB26
Bassett Ho, Dag. RM9 168 EV67
SW19 off Durnsford Rd 202 DB92
Bassett Rd, W10 14 D8
Bassett Rd, Uxbridge UB8
off Oxford Rd 156 BJ66
Woking GU22 249 BC116
Bassetts Cl, Orp. BR6 245 EP105
Bassett St, NW5 6 G3
Bassetts Way, Orp. BR6 245 EP105
Bassett Way, Grnf. UB6 158 CB72
Slough SL2
off Pemberton Rd 153 AL70
Bassil Rd, Hem.H. HP2 62 BK21
Bassingbourne Cl, Brox. EN10 71 DZ20
Bassingburn Wk, Welw.G.C. AL7 51 CZ10
Bassingham Rd, SW18 202 DC87
Wembley HA0 159 CK65
Bassishaw Highwalk, EC2
off Aldermanbury Sq 19 K7
Basswood Cl, SE15
off Candle Gro 184 DV83
Bastable Av, Bark. IG11 167 ES68
Bastion Highwalk, EC2 19 J7
● Bastion Ho, EC2
off London Wall 19 J7
Bastion Rd, SE2 188 EU78
Baston Manor Rd, Brom. BR2 226 EH104
Baston Rd, Brom. BR2 226 EH102
Sch Baston Sch, Hayes BR2
off Baston Rd 226 EH103
Bastwick St, EC1 19 J4
Basuto Rd, SW6 39 J7
⇌ Bat & Ball 279 FJ121
Jct Bat & Ball Junct, Sev.
TN14 279 FH121
Bat & Ball Rd, Sev. TN14 279 FJ121
Batavia Cl, Sun. TW16 218 BW95
Batavia Ms, SE14 45 M5
Batavia Rd, SE14 45 M5
Sunbury-on-Thames TW16 217 BV95
Batchelor St, N1 8 E10
Batchelors Way, Amer. HP7 77 AR39
Chesham HP5 76 AP29
Batchwood Dr, St.Alb. AL3 64 CC17
Batchwood Gdns, St.Alb. AL3 65 CD17
Batchwood Grn, Orp. BR5 228 EU97
Batchwood Hall, St.Alb. AL3 64 CB17
Sch Batchwood Sch, St.Alb.
AL3 off Townsend Dr 65 CD17
Batchwood Vw, St.Alb. AL3 64 CC16
BATCHWORTH, Rick. WD3 114 BM47
BATCHWORTH HEATH, Rick.
WD3 114 BN49
Batchworth Heath Hill, Rick.
WD3 114 BN49
Batchworth Hill, Rick. WD3 114 BM48
Batchworth La, Nthwd. HA6 115 BS50
Jct Batchworth Rbt, Rick. WD3 114 BK46
Bateman Cl, Bark. IG11
off Glenny Rd 167 EQ65
Bateman Ct, Croy. CR0
off Harry Cl 224 DQ100
Bateman Ho, SE17 42 G3
Bateman Rd, E4 123 EA51
Croxley Green WD3 96 BN44
Bateman's Bldgs, W1 17 N9
Batemans Ms, Warley CM14
off Vaughan Williams Way 130 FV49
Bateman's Row, EC2 19 P4
Bateman St, W1 17 N9
● Bates Business Cen,
Harold Wd. RM3
off Church Rd 128 FN52
Bates Cl, Geo.Grn SL3 154 AY72
Bates Cres, SW16 203 DJ94
Croydon CR0 241 DN106
● Bates Ind Est, Harold Wd
RM3 128 FP52
Bateson St, SE18 187 ES77
Bateson Way, Wok. GU21 233 BC114
Bates Rd, Rom. RM3 128 FN52
Bate St, E14 21 P10
Bates Wk, Add. KT15 234 BJ108
● B.A.T. Export Ho, Wok. GU21 248 AY117
Batford Cl, Welw.G.C. AL7 52 DB10
Bath Cl, SE15 44 F5
Bath Ct, EC1 18 E5
EC1 (St. Luke's Est)
off St. Luke's Est 19 L3
Bathgate Rd, SW19 201 CX90
Bath Ho, SE1 off Bath Ter 31 K6
Bath Ho Rd, Croy. CR0 223 DL102
Bath Pas, Kings.T. KT1
off St. James Rd 219 CK96
Bath Pl, EC2 19 N3
Barnet EN5 101 CZ41
Bath Rd, E7 166 EK65
N9 122 DV47
W4 180 CS77
Colnbrook SL3 175 BB79
Dartford DA1 209 FH87
Harlington UB3 177 BQ81
Hounslow TW3, TW4, TW5,
TW6 178 BX82
Romford RM6 148 EY58
Slough SL1 153 AP74
Taplow SL6 152 AF72
West Drayton UB7 176 BK81
Baths Rd, Brom. BR2 226 EK98
Bath St, EC1 19 K3
Gravesend DA11 213 GH86
Bath Ter, SE1 31 J7
Bathurst Av, SW19
off Brisbane Av 222 DB95
Bathurst Cl, Iver SL0 175 BF75
Bathurst Gdns, NW10 161 CV68
Bathurst Ms, W2 16 A10
Bathurst Rd, Hem.H. HP2 62 BK17
Ilford IG1 147 EP60
Bathurst St, W2 16 A10
Bathurst Wk, Iver SL0 175 BE75
Bathway, SE18 37 M8
Batley Cl, Mitch. CR4 222 DF101
Batley Pl, N16 144 DT62
Batley Rd, N16
off Stoke Newington High St 144 DT62
Enfield EN2 104 DQ39
Batman Cl, W12 161 CV74
Baton Cl, Purf. RM19 191 FR77
Batoum Gdns, W6 26 B6
Batsford Ho, SW19
off Durnsford Rd 202 DB91
Batson Ho, E1
off Fairclough St 20 D9

Batson St, W12 181 CU75
Batsworth Rd, Mitch. CR4 222 DD97
Batten Av, Wok. GU21 248 AS119
Battenburg Wk, SE19
off Brabourne Cl 204 DS92
Batten Cl, E6 25 K9
Batten St, SW11 40 D10
Batterdale, Hat. AL9 67 CW17
Battersby Rd, SE6 205 ED89
BATTERSEA, SW11 40 F6
Battersea Br, SW3 40 B4
SW11 40 B4
Battersea Br Rd, SW11 40 C5
● Battersea Business Cen, SW11 *off Lavender Hill* 182 DG83
Battersea Ch Rd, SW11 40 B6
★ Battersea Dogs & Cats Home, SW8 41 K5
Battersea High St, SW11 40 B7
★ Battersea Park, SW11 40 F4
⇌ Battersea Park 41 J6
Battersea Pk Rd, SW8 41 J6
SW11 40 C9
Battersea Pk Sch, SW11 40 F7
Battersea Ri, SW11 202 DE85
Battersea Sq, SW11
off Battersea High St 40 B7
Battery Rd, SE28 187 ES75
Battis, The, Rom. RM1
off South St 149 FE57
Battishill Gdns, N1
off Waterloo Ter 8 G7
Battishill St, N1 8 G7
Battlebridge Ct, N1 8 B10
Battle Br La, SE1
off Tooley St 31 N3
Battlebridge La, Merst. RH1 273 DH130
Battle Br Rd, NW1 18 A1
Battle Cl, SW19 202 DC93
Battledean Rd, N5 8 G2
Battlefield Rd, St.Alb. AL1 65 CF18
Battlemead Cl, Maid. SL6 152 AC68
Battle Rd, Belv. DA17 189 FC77
Erith DA8 189 FC77
BATTLERS GREEN, Rad. WD7 99 CE37
Battlers Grn Dr, Rad. WD7 99 CE37
Batts Hill, Red. RH1 272 DE132
Reigate RH2 272 DD132
Batty St, E1 20 D8
Batwa Ho, SE16 44 F1
Baudwin Rd, SE6 206 EE89
Baugh Rd, Sid. DA14 208 EW92
Baulk, The, SW18 202 DA87
Bavant Rd, SW16 223 DL96
Bavaria Rd, N19 143 DL61
Bavdene Ms, NW4
off The Burroughs 141 CV56
Bavent Rd, SE5 43 K9
Bawdale Rd, SE22 204 DT85
Bawdsey Av, Ilf. IG2 147 ET56
Bawtree Cl, Sutt. SM2 240 DC110
Bawtree Rd, SE14 45 L4
Uxbridge UB8 156 BK65
Bawtry Rd, N20 120 DF48
Baxendale, N20 120 DC47
Baxendale St, E2 20 C2
Baxter Av, Red. RH1 272 DE134
Baxter Cl, Brom. BR1
off Stoneleigh Rd 227 EP97
Slough SL1 174 AS76
Southall UB2 178 CB75
Uxbridge UB10 157 BP69
Baxter Gdns, Noak Hill RM3
off North End 128 FJ47
Baxter Ho, E3
off Bromley High St 22 C2
Baxter Rd, E16 24 D8
N1 9 M5
N18 122 DV49
NW10 160 CS70
Ilford IG1 147 EP64
Baxter Wk, SW16 203 DK89
Bayards, Warl. CR6 258 DW118
Bay Cl, Horl. RH6 290 DE145
Bay Ct, W5 180 CL76
Baycroft Cl, Pnr. HA5 138 BW55
Baydon Ct, Brom. BR2 226 EF97
Bayes Cl, SE26 204 DW92
Bayeux, Tad. KT20 255 CX122
Bayeux Ho, SE7
off Springfield Gro 186 EJ79
Bayfield Rd, SE9 186 EK84
Horley RH6 290 DE147
BAYFORD, Hert. SG13 69 DM18
⇌ Bayford 69 DN18
BAYFORDBURY, Hert. SG13 53 DM13
Bayford Cl, Hem.H. HP2 63 BQ15
Hertford SG13 54 DQ11
Bayford Grn, Bayford SG13 69 DN18
Bayford La, Bayford SG13 53 DM14
Bayford Ms, E8 10 F7
Bayford Prim Sch, Bayford SG13 *off Ashendene Rd* 69 DM18
Bayford Rd, NW10 14 C3
Bayford St, E8 10 F7
Baygrove Ms, Hmptn W. KT1 219 CJ95
Bayham Pl, NW1 7 L10
Bayham Rd, W4 180 CR76
W13 159 CH73
Morden SM4 222 DB98
Sevenoaks TN13 279 FJ123
Bayham St, NW1 7 L9
Bayhorne La, Horl. RH6 291 DJ150
Bayhurst Dr, Nthwd. HA6 115 BT51
★ Bayhurst Wood Country Pk, Uxb. UB9 136 BM56
Bayleaf Cl, Hmptn H. TW12 199 CD92
Bayley Cres, Burn. SL1 152 AG71
Bayleys Mead, Hutt. CM13 131 GC47
Bayley St, WC1 17 N7
Bayley Wk, SE2
off Woolwich Rd 188 EY78
Baylie Ct, Hem.H. HP2
off Baylie La 62 BL18
Baylie La, Hem.H. HP2 62 BL18
Baylis Ct Sch, Slou. SL1
off Gloucester Av 153 AR71
Baylis Ms, Twick. TW1 199 CG87
Baylis Par, Slou. SL1
off Oatlands Dr 154 AS72
Baylis Pl, Brom. BR1 226 EL97
Baylis Rd, SE1 30 E5
Slough SL1 153 AR73
Bayliss Av, SE28 168 EX73
Bayliss Cl, N21 103 DL43
Southall UB1 158 CB72
Bayliss Ct, Guil. GU1
off Mary Rd 280 AW135
Bayly Rd, Dart. DA1 210 FN86
Bay Manor La, Grays RM20 191 FT79
Baymans Wd, Shenf. CM15 130 FY47
Bayne Cl, E6 25 K9
Bayne Hill Cl, Seer Grn HP9 111 AR52
Baynes Cl, Enf. EN1 104 DU40
Baynes Ms, NW3 6 B4
Baynes St, NW1 7 M7
Baynham Cl, Bex. DA5 208 EZ86
Baynton Rd, Wok. GU22 249 BB120
Bayonne Rd, W6 38 E3
Bays Fm Ct, West Dr. UB7 176 BJ80
Bayshill Ri, Nthlt. UB5 158 CB65
Bayston Rd, N16 144 DT62
BAYSWATER, W2 15 M9
⊖ Bayswater 15 L10
Bayswater Rd, W2 16 B10
Baythorne St, E3 21 P6
Bay Tree Av, Lthd. KT22 253 CG120
Baytree Cen, Brwd. CM14 *off High St* 130 FW47
Bay Tree Cl, Brom. BR1 226 EJ95
Baytree Cl, Chsht EN7 88 DT27
Bay Tree Cl, Ilf. IG6
off Hazel La 125 EP52
Baytree Cl, Park St AL2 82 CB27
Sidcup DA15 207 ET88
Bay Tree Ct, Burn. SL1 152 AJ69
Baytree Ho, E4 *off Dells Cl* 123 EB45
Baytree Ms, SE17 31 L8
Baytree Rd, SW2 183 DM84
Bay Trees, Oxt. RH8 276 EH133
Baytree Wk, Wat. WD17 97 BT38
Baywood Sq, Chig. IG7 126 EV49
Bazalgette Cl, N.Mal. KT3 220 CR99
Bazalgette Ct, W6
off Great W Rd 181 CU78
Bazalgette Gdns, N.Mal. KT3 220 CR99
Bazely St, E14 22 E10
Bazile Rd, N21 103 DN44
Beacham Cl, SE7 186 EK78
Beachborough Rd, Brom. BR1 205 EC91
Beachcroft Av, Sthl. UB1 158 BZ74
Beachcroft Rd, E11 146 EE62
Beachcroft Way, N19 143 DK60
Beach Gro, Felt. TW13 198 CA89
Beach's Ho, Stai. TW18 196 BG92
Beachy Rd, E3 12 A7
Beacon Cl, Bans. SM7 255 CX116
Beaconsfield HP9 110 AG54
Chalfont St. Peter SL9 112 AY52
Uxbridge UB8 136 BK64
Beacon Dr, Bean DA2 211 FV90
Beaconfield Av, Epp. CM16 91 ET29
Beaconfield Rd, Epp. CM16 91 ET29
Beaconfields, Sev. TN13 278 FF126
Beaconfield Way, Epp. CM16 91 ET29
Beacon Gate, SE14 45 J9
Beacon Gro, Cars. SM5 240 DG105
Beacon Hill, N7 8 A2
Penn HP10 110 AD48
Purfleet RM19 190 FP78
Woking GU21 248 AW118
● Beacon Hill Ind Est, Purf. RM19 190 FP78
Beacon Hill Sch, S.Ock. RM15 *off Erriff Dr* 171 FU71
Post 16 Provision, S.Ock. RM15 *off Fortin Cl* 171 FU73
Beacon Ri, Sev. TN13 278 FG126
Beacon Rd, SE13 205 ED86
Erith DA8 189 FH80
London Heathrow Airport TW6 196 BN86
Ware SG12 55 EA05
Beacon Rd Rbt, Lon.Hthrw Air. TW6 197 BP86
Beacons, The, Hat. AL10
off Beaconsfield Cl 67 CW17
Loughton IG10 107 EN38
Beacon Sch, The, Bans. SM7 *off Picquets Way* 255 CY117
Chesham Bois HP6
off Amersham Rd 77 AP35
Beacons Cl, E6 25 H7
BEACONSFIELD, HP9 110 AJ53
⇌ Beaconsfield 111 AL52
Beaconsfield Cl, N11 120 DG49
SE3 47 N2
W4 180 CQ78
Hatfield AL10 67 CW17
Beaconsfield Common La, Slou. SL2 133 AQ57
Beaconsfield Gdns, Clay. KT10 237 CE108
Beaconsfield High Sch, Beac. HP9 *off Wattleton Rd* 111 AL54
Beaconsfield Par, SE9
off Beaconsfield Rd 206 EL91
Beaconsfield Pl, Epsom KT17 238 CS112
Beaconsfield Prim Sch, Sthl. UB1 *off Beaconsfield Rd* 178 BY75
Beaconsfield Rd, E10 145 EC61
E16 23 L5
E17 145 DZ58
N9 122 DU49
N11 120 DG48
N15 144 DS56
NW10 161 CT65
SE3 47 M3
SE9 206 EL89
SE17 43 M1
W4 180 CR76
W5 179 CJ75
Bexley DA5 209 FE88
Bromley BR1 226 EK97
Claygate KT10 237 CE108
Croydon CR0 224 DR100
Enfield EN3 105 DX37
Epsom KT18 254 CR119
Hatfield AL10 67 CW17
Hayes UB4 158 BW74
New Malden KT3 220 CR96
St. Albans AL1 65 CE20
Slough SL2 153 AQ68
Southall UB1 158 BX74
Surbiton KT5 220 CM101
Twickenham TW1 199 CH86
Woking GU22 249 AZ120
Beaconsfield Sch, The, Beac. HP9 *off Wattleton Rd* 111 AL54
Beaconsfield Ter, Rom. RM6 148 EX58
Beaconsfield Ter Rd, W14 26 E7
Beaconsfield Wk, E6 25 M9
SW6 39 H7
Beacontree Av, E17 123 ED53
Beacontree Rd, E11 146 EF59
Beacon Way, Bans. SM7 255 CX116
Rickmansworth WD3 114 BG45
★ Beacon Wd Country Pk, Dart. DA2 211 FV91
Beadles La, Oxt. RH8 275 ED130
Beadlow Cl, Cars. SM5
off Olveston Wk 222 DD100
Beadman Pl, SE27
off Norwood High St 203 DP91
Beadman St, SE27 203 DP91
Beadnell Rd, SE23 205 DX88
Beadon Rd, W6 26 A9
Bromley BR2 226 EG98
Beads Hall La, Pilg.Hat. CM15 130 FV42
Beaford Gro, SW20 221 CY97
Beagle Cl, Felt. TW13 197 BV91
Radlett WD7 99 CF37
Beagles Cl, Orp. BR5 228 EX103
Beak St, W1 17 M10
Beal Cl, Well. DA16 188 EU81
Beale Cl, N13 121 DP50
Beale Pl, E3 11 N10
Beale Rd, E3 11 N9
Beales La, Wey. KT13 216 BN104
Beales Rd, Bkhm KT23 268 CB127
Beal High Sch, Ilf. IG4
off Woodford Br Rd 146 EL56
Bealings End, Beac. HP9 111 AK50
Beal Rd, Ilf. IG1 147 EN61
Beam Av, Dag. RM10 169 FB67
Beames Rd, NW10 160 CR67
Beaminster Gdns, Ilf. IG6 125 EP54
Beaminster Ho, SW8
off Dorset Rd 42 C4
Beamish Cl, N.Wld Bas. CM16 93 FC25
Beamish Dr, Bushey Hth WD23 116 CC46
Beamish Ho, SE16
off Rennie Est 32 G9
Beamish Rd, N9 122 DU46
Orpington BR5 228 EW101
Beam Prim Sch, Dag. RM10 *off Oval Rd N* 169 FC68
Beamway, Dag. RM10 169 FD66
BEAN, Dart. DA2 211 FV90
Beanacre Cl, E9 11 P4
Beane Cft, Grav. DA12 213 GM88
Beane River Vw, Hert. SG14 54 DQ09
Beane Rd, Hert. SG14 53 DP09
Bean Interchange, Dart. DA2 211 FU89
Bean La, Bean DA2 211 FV89
Bean Prim Sch, Bean DA2 *off School La* 211 FW91
Bean Rd, Bexh. DA6 188 EX84
Greenhithe DA9 211 FV85
Beanshaw, SE9 207 EN91
Beansland Gro, Rom. RM6 126 EY54
Bear All, EC4 18 G8
Bear Cl, Rom. RM7 149 FB58
Beardell St, SE19 204 DT93
Beardow Gro, N14 103 DJ44
Beard Rd, Kings.T. KT2 200 CM92
Beardsfield, E13 13 N9
Beard's Hill, Hmptn. TW12 218 CA95
Beard's Hill Cl, Hmptn. TW12
off Beard's Hill 218 CA95
Beardsley Ter, Dag. RM8
off Fitzstephen Rd 148 EV64
Beardsley Way, W3 180 CR75
Beards Rd, Ashf. TW15 197 BS93
Bearfield Rd, Kings.T. KT2 200 CL94
Bear Gdns, SE1 31 J2
Bearing Cl, Chig. IG7 126 EU49
Bearing Way, Chig. IG7 126 EU49
Bear La, SE1 31 H2
Bear Rd, Felt. TW13 198 BX92
Bears Den, Kgswd KT20 255 CZ122
Bears Rails Pk, Old Wind. SL4 194 AT87
Bearstead Ri, SE4 205 DZ85
Bearsted Ter, Beck. BR3 225 EA95
Bear St, WC2 17 P10
Bearswood End, Beac. HP9 111 AL51
Bearwood Cl, Add. KT15
off Ongar Pl 234 BG107
Potters Bar EN6 86 DD31
Beasleys Ait La, Sun. TW16 217 BT100
Beasleys Yd, Uxb. UB8
off Warwick Pl 156 BJ66
Beaton Cl, SE15 44 B6
Greenhithe DA9 191 FV84
Beatrice Av, SW16 223 DM97
Wembley HA9 140 CL64
Beatrice Cl, E13 23 N4
Pinner HA5 137 BU56
Beatrice Ct, Buck.H. IG9 124 EK47
Beatrice Gdns, Nthflt DA11 212 GE89
Beatrice Pl, W8 27 L7
Beatrice Rd, E17 145 EA57
N4 143 DN59
N9 122 DW45
SE1 32 D9
Oxted RH8 276 EE129
Richmond TW10
off Albert Rd 200 CM85
Southall UB1 158 BZ74
Beatrice Tate Sch, E2 20 F2
Beatrice Wilson Flats, Sev. TN13
off Rockdale Rd 279 FH125
Beatrix Potter Prim Sch, SW18 *off Magdalen Rd* 202 DC88
Beatson Wk, SE16 33 L2
Beattie Cl, Bkhm KT23 252 BZ124
Feltham TW14 197 BT88
Beattock Ri, N10 143 DH56
Beatty Av, Guil. GU1 265 BA133
Beatty Rd, N16 144 DS63
Stanmore HA7 117 CJ51
Waltham Cross EN8 89 DZ34
Beatty St, NW1 7 L10
Beattyville Gdns, Ilf. IG6 147 EN55
Beauchamp Cl, W4
off Beaumont Rd 180 CQ76
Beauchamp Ct, Stan. HA7
off Hardwick Cl 117 CJ50
Beauchamp Gdns, Mill End WD3 114 BG46
Beauchamp Pl, SW3 28 D6
Beauchamp Rd, E7 166 EH66
SE19 224 DR95
SW11 182 DE84
East Molesey KT8 218 CB99
Sutton SM1 240 DA106
Twickenham TW1 199 CG87
West Molesey KT8 218 CB99
Beauchamps, Welw.G.C. AL7 52 DB10
Beauchamp St, EC1 18 E7
Beauchamp Ter, SW15
off Dryburgh Rd 181 CV83
Beauclare Cl, Lthd. KT22
off Delderfield 253 CK121
Beauclerc Inf Sch, Sun. TW16 *off French St* 218 BW97
Beauclerc Rd, W6 181 CV76
Beauclerk Cl, Felt. TW13 197 BV88
Beaudesert Ms, West Dr. UB7 176 BL75
Beaufort, E6 25 M8
Beaufort Av, Har. HA3 139 CG56
Beaufort Cl, E4
off Higham Sta Av 123 EB51
SW15 201 CV87
W5 160 CM71
Chafford Hundred RM16
off Clifford Rd 192 FZ76
North Weald Bassett CM16 92 FA27
Reigate RH2 271 CZ133
Romford RM7 149 FC56
Woking GU22 249 BC116
Beaufort Comm Prim Sch, Wok. GU21
off Kirkland Av 248 AT116
Beaufort Ct, SW6 39 J2
Richmond TW10 199 CJ91
Beaufort Dr, NW11 142 DA56
Beaufort Gdns, NW4 141 CW58
SW3 28 D6
SW16 203 DM94
Hounslow TW5 178 BY81
Ilford IG1 147 EN60
Beaufort Ms, SW6 39 H2
Beaufort Pk, NW11 142 DA56
Beaufort Pl, Bray SL6 172 AD75
Beaufort Rd, W5 160 CM71
Kingston upon Thames KT1 220 CL98
Reigate RH2 271 CZ133
Richmond TW10 199 CJ91
Ruislip HA4
off Lysander Rd 137 BR61
Twickenham TW1 199 CJ87
Woking GU22 249 BC116
Beauforts, Eng.Grn TW20 194 AW92
Beaufort St, SW3 40 B3
Beaufort Way, Epsom KT17 239 CU108
Beaufoy Rd, N17 122 DS52
Beaufoy Wk, SE11 30 D9
Beaulieu Av, E16 36 A2
SE26 204 DV91
Beaulieu Cl, NW9 140 CS56
SE5 43 M10
Datchet SL3 174 AV81
Hounslow TW4 198 BZ85
Mitcham CR4 222 DG95
Twickenham TW1 199 CK87
Watford WD19 116 BW46
Beaulieu Dr, Pnr. HA5 138 BX58
Waltham Abbey EN9 89 EB32
Beaulieu Gdns, N21 122 DQ45
Beaulieu Pl, W4 180 CQ76
Beauly Way, Rom. RM1 127 FE53
Beaumanor Gdns, SE9 207 EN91
Beaumaris Dr, Wdf.Grn. IG8 124 EK52
Beaumaris Gdns, SE19 204 DQ94
Beaumaris Grn, NW9
off Goldsmith Av 140 CS58
Beaumaris Twr, W3 180 CP75
Beaumayes Cl, Hem.H. HP1 62 BH21
Beaumont Av, W14 26 G10
Harrow HA2 138 CB58
Richmond TW9 180 CM83
St. Albans AL1 65 CH18
Wembley HA0 139 CJ64
Beaumont Cl, N2 142 DE56
Kingston upon Thames KT2 200 CN94
Romford RM2 128 FJ54
Beaumont Cres, W14 26 G10
Rainham RM13 169 FG65
Beaumont Dr, Ashf. TW15 197 BR92
Northfleet DA11 212 GE87
Worcester Park KT4 221 CV102
Beaumont Gdns, NW3 142 DA62
Hutton CM13
off Bannister Dr 131 GC44
Beaumont Gate, Rad. WD7 99 CG35
Beaumont Gro, E1 21 J5
Beaumont Ms, W1 17 H6
Pinner HA5 138 BY55
Beaumont Pk Dr, Roydon CM19 72 EH15
Beaumont Pl, W1 17 M4
Barnet EN5 101 CZ39
Isleworth TW7 199 CF85
Watford WD18 97 BU43
Beaumont Prim Sch, E10
off Burchell Rd 145 EB60
Purley CR8 *off Old Lo La* 241 DN114
Beaumont Ri, N19 143 DK60
Beaumont Rd, E10 145 EB59
E13 24 B3
SE19 204 DQ93
SW19 201 CY87
W4 180 CQ76
Broxbourne EN10 70 DR24
Petts Wood BR5 227 ER100
Purley CR8 241 DN113
Slough SL2 153 AR70
Windsor SL4 173 AQ82
Beaumonts, Red. RH1 288 DF143
Beaumont Sch, St.Alb. AL4 *off Oakwood Dr* 65 CJ19
Beaumont Sq, E1 21 J6
Beaumont St, W1 17 H6
Beaumont Vw, Chsht EN7 88 DR26
Beaumont Wk, NW3 6 F6
● Beaumont Wks, St.Alb. AL1 *off Hedley Rd* 65 CH20
Beauvais Ter, Nthlt. UB5 158 BX69
Beauval Rd, SE22 204 DT86
Beaverbank Rd, SE9 207 ER88
Beaverbrook Rbt, Lthd. KT22 253 CK123
Beaver Cl, SE20
off Lullington Rd 204 DU94
Hampton TW12 218 CB95
Morden SM4 221 CW101
Beaver Gro, Nthlt. UB5
off Jetstar Way 158 BY69
● Beaver Ind Pk, Sthl. UB2 178 BW76
Beaver Rd, Ilf. IG6 126 EW50
Beavers Cl, Guil. GU3 264 AS133
Beavers Comm Prim Sch, Houns. TW4 *off Arundel Rd* 178 BW83
Beavers Cres, Houns. TW4 178 BW84
Beavers La, Houns. TW4 178 BW83
Beaverwood Rd, Chis. BR7 207 ES93
Beaverwood Sch for Girls, Chis. BR7 *off Beaverwood Rd* 207 ES93
Beavor Gro, W6 *off Beavor La* 181 CU78
Beavor La, W6 181 CU77
Beazley Cl, Ware SG12 55 DY05
Bebbington Rd, SE18 187 ES77
Beblets Cl, Orp. BR6 245 ET106
Beccles Dr, Bark. IG11 167 ES65
Beccles St, E14 21 P10
Bec Cl, Ruis. HA4 138 BX62
Beck Cl, SE13 46 C7
Beck Ct, Beck. BR3 225 DX97
BECKENHAM, BR3 225 EA95
● Beckenham Business Cen, Beck. BR3 205 DY93
Beckenham Gdns, N9 122 DS48
Beckenham Gro, Brom. BR2 225 ED96
⇌ Beckenham Hill 205 EC92
Beckenham Hill Rd, SE6 205 EB92
Beckenham BR3 205 EB92
Beckenham Hosp, Beck. BR3 225 DZ96
⇌ Beckenham Junction 225 EA95
Beckenham Junction 225 EA95
Beckenham La, Brom. BR2 226 EE96
Beckenham Pl Pk, Beck. BR3 205 EB94
Beckenham Road 225 DY95
Beckenham Rd, Beck. BR3 225 DX95
West Wickham BR4 225 EB101
Beckenshaw Gdns, Bans. SM7 256 DE115
Beckers, The, N16 144 DU63
Becket Av, E6 25 L2
Becket Cl, SE25 224 DU100
Great Warley CM13 129 FW51
Becket Fold, Har. HA1
off Courtfield Cres 139 CF57
Becket Ho, Brwd. CM14 130 FW47
Becket Rd, N18 122 DW49
Beckets Sq, Berk. HP4
off Bridle Way 60 AU17
Becket St, SE1 31 L6
Beckett Av, Ken. CR8 257 DP115
Beckett Chase, Slou. SL3
off Olivia Dr 175 AZ78
Beckett Cl, NW10 160 CR65
SW16 203 DK89
Belvedere DA17
off Tunstock Way 188 EY76
Beckett Ho, SW9 42 B9
Beckett Rd, Couls. CR5 257 DK122
Becketts, Hert. SG14 53 DN10
Beckett's Av, St.Alb. AL3 64 CC17
Becketts Cl, Bex. DA5 209 FC88
Feltham TW14 197 BV86
Orpington BR6 227 ET104
Becketts Pl, Hmptn W. KT1 219 CK95
Beckett Wk, Beck. BR3 205 DY93
Beckford Cl, W14 27 H9
Beckford Dr, Orp. BR5 227 ER101
Beckford Pl, SE17 43 K1
Beckford Prim Sch, NW6 5 H3
Beckford Rd, Croy. CR0 224 DT100
Beckham Ho, SE11
off Marylee Way 30 D9
Beckingham Rd, Guil. GU2 264 AU132
Beckings Way, Flack.Hth HP10 132 AC56
Beck La, Beck. BR3 225 DX97
Becklow Gdns, W12 181 CU75
Becklow Ms, W12
off Becklow Rd 181 CT75
Becklow Rd, W12 181 CU75
Beckman Cl, Halst. TN14 263 FC115
Beckmead Sch, Beck. BR3
off Monks Orchard Rd 225 EA102
Beck River Pk, Beck. BR3 225 DZ95
Beck Rd, E8 10 E8
Becks Rd, Sid. DA14 208 EU90
BECKTON, E6 25 M7
Beckton 25 L7
Beckton Alps, E6 25 L5
Beckton Park 25 K10
Beckton Pk Rbt, E16 25 J10
Beckton Retail Pk, E6 25 L6
Beckton Rd, E16 23 M6
Beckton Triangle Retail Pk, E6 25 M4
Beck Way, Beck. BR3 225 DZ97
Beckway Rd, SW16 223 DK96
Beckway St, SE17 31 M9
Beckwell Rd, Slou. SL1 173 AQ75
Beckwith Rd, SE24 204 DR86
Beclands Rd, SW17 202 DG93
Becmead Av, SW16 203 DK91
Harrow HA3 139 CH57
Becondale Rd, SE19 204 DS92
BECONTREE, Dag. RM8 148 EY62
⊖ Becontree 168 EW66
Becontree Av, Dag. RM8 148 EV63
BECONTREE HEATH, Dag. RM8 148 FA60
Becontree Prim Sch, Dag. RM8 *off Stevens Rd* 148 EV62
Becquerel Ct, SE10 35 M7
Bective Pl, SW15
off Bective Rd 181 CZ84
Bective Rd, E7 146 EG63
SW15 181 CZ84
Becton Pl, Erith DA8 189 FB80
Bedale Rd, Enf. EN2 104 DQ38
Romford RM3 128 FN50
Bedale St, SE1 31 L3
Bedale Wk, Dart. DA2 210 FP88
BEDDINGTON, Croy. CR0 223 DK103
BEDDINGTON CORNER, Mitch. CR4 222 DG101
Beddington Cross, Croy. CR0 223 DL102
Beddington Fm Rd, Croy. CR0 223 DL102
Beddington Gdns, Cars. SM5 240 DG107
Wallington SM6 241 DH107
Beddington Grn, Orp. BR5 227 ET95
Beddington Gro, Wall. SM6 241 DK106
Beddington Inf Sch, Wall. SM6 *off Croydon Rd* 241 DJ105
Beddington Lane 223 DJ100
Beddington La, Croy. CR0 223 DJ99
● Beddington La Ind Est, Croy. CR0 223 DJ100
Beddington Pk Prim Sch, Bedd. CR0
off Derry Rd 223 DK104
Beddington Path, Orp. BR5 227 ET95
Beddington Rd, Ilf. IG3 147 ET59
Orpington BR5 227 ES96
● Beddington Trd Pk, Croy. CR0 223 DL102
Beddlestead La, Warl. CR6 260 EF117
Bede Cl, Pnr. HA5 116 BX53
Bedelsford Sch, Kings.T. KT1 *off Grange Rd* 220 CL97
Bedens Rd, Sid. DA14 208 EY93
Bede Rd, Rom. RM6 148 EW58
Bedevere Rd, N9 122 DU48

Bedfont Cl, Felt. TW14 197 BQ86
Mitcham CR4 222 DG96
Bedfont Ct, Stai. TW19 176 BH84
Bedfont Ct Est, Stai. TW19 176 BG83
Bedfont Grn Cl, Felt. TW14 197 BQ88
Sch **Bedfont Inf & Nurs & Jun Schs**, E.Bed. TW14 *off Hatton Rd* 197 BS86
Bedfont La, Felt. TW13, TW14 197 BT87
Bedfont Rd, Felt. TW13, TW14 197 BS89
Stanwell TW19 196 BL86
Bedford Av, WC1 17 P7
Amersham HP6 94 AW39
Barnet EN5 101 CZ43
Hayes UB4 157 BV72
Slough SL1 153 AM72
Bedfordbury, WC2 18 A10
Bedford Cl, N10 120 DG52
W4 180 CS79
Chenies WD3 95 BB38
Woking GU21 248 AW115
Bedford Cor, W4 180 CS77
Bedford Ct, WC2 30 A1
Bedford Cres, Enf. EN3 105 DY35
Bedford Dr, Farn.Com. SL2 133 AP64
Bedford Gdns, W8 27 J3
Hornchurch RM12 150 FJ61
Bedford Hill, SW12 203 DH88
SW16 203 DH88
Bedford Ho, SW4 183 DL84
Guildford GU1 *off Bedford Rd* 280 AW135
Bedford Ms, N2 142 DE55
SE6 205 EB89
BEDFORD PARK, W4 180 CR76
Bedford Pk, Croy. CR0 224 DQ102
Bedford Pk Cor, W4 *off Bath Rd* 180 CS77
Bedford Pk Rd, St.Alb. AL1 65 CE20
Bedford Pas, SW6 38 F4
Bedford Pl, WC1 18 A6
Croydon CR0 224 DR102
Bedford Rd, E6 167 EN67
E17 123 EA54
E18 124 EG54
N2 142 DE55
N8 143 DK58
N9 122 DV45
N15 144 DS56
N22 121 DL53
NW7 118 CS47
SW4 183 DL83
W4 180 CR76
W13 159 CH73
Dartford DA1 210 FN87
Grays RM17 192 GB78
Guildford GU1 280 AW135
Harrow HA1 138 CC58
Ilford IG1 147 EP62
Northfleet DA11 213 GF89
Northwood HA6 115 BQ48
Orpington BR6 228 EV103
Ruislip HA4 137 BT63
St. Albans AL1 65 CE21
Sidcup DA15 207 ES90
Twickenham TW2 199 CD90
Worcester Park KT4 221 CW103
Bedford Row, WC1 18 D6
Bedford Sq, WC1 17 P7
Bedford St, WC2 18 A10
Berkhamsted HP4 60 AX19
Watford WD24 97 BV39
Bedford Ter, SW2 *off Lyham Rd* 203 DL85
Bedford Way, WC1 17 P5
Bedgebury Ct, E17 *off Hawker Pl* 123 EC54
Bedgebury Gdns, SW19 201 CY89
Bedgebury Rd, SE9 186 EK84
Bedivere Rd, Brom. BR1 206 EG90
Bedlam Ms, SE11 30 E8
Bedlam Way, Houns. TW3 178 BZ84
Bedlow Way, Croy. CR0 241 DM105
BEDMOND, Abb.L. WD5 81 BS27
Bedmond Hill, Pimlico HP3 81 BS25
Bedmond La, Abb.L. WD5 81 BV25
St. Albans AL2, AL3 64 BX24
Bedmond Rd, Abb.L. WD5 81 BT29
Hemel Hempstead HP3 63 BS23
Sch **Bedmond Village Prim & Nurs Sch**, Bedmond WD5 *off Meadow Way* 81 BT28
Sch **Bedonwell Inf Sch**, Belv. DA17 *off Bedonwell Rd* 188 EY79
Sch **Bedonwell Jun Sch**, Belv. DA17 *off Bedonwell Rd* 188 EY79
Bedonwell Rd, SE2 188 EY79
Belvedere DA17 188 FA79
Bexleyheath DA7 188 FA79
Bedser Cl, SE11 42 D2
Thornton Heath CR7 224 DQ97
Woking GU21 249 BA116
Bedser Dr, Grnf. UB6 139 CD64
Bedster Gdns, W.Mol. KT8 218 CB96
Bedwardine Rd, SE19 204 DS94
Bedwell Av, Essen. AL9 68 DG18
Bedwell Cl, Welw.G.C. AL7 51 CY10
Bedwell Gdns, Hayes UB3 177 BS78
Bedwell Pk, Essen. AL9 68 DF18
Bedwell Rd, N17 122 DS53
Belvedere DA17 188 FA78
Beeby Rd, E16 24 A7
Beech Av, N20 120 DE46
W3 160 CS74
Brentford TW8 179 CH80
Brentwood CM13 131 FZ48
Buckhurst Hill IG9 124 EH47
Effingham KT24 268 BX129
Enfield EN2 103 DN35
Radlett WD7 83 CG33
Ruislip HA4 137 BV60
Sidcup DA15 208 EU87
South Croydon CR2 242 DR111
Swanley BR8 229 FF98
Tatsfield TN16 260 EK119
Upminster RM14 150 FP62
Beech Bottom, St.Alb. AL3 65 CD17
Beech Cl, N9 104 DU44
SE8 45 P3
SW15 201 CU87
SW19 201 CW93
Beech Cl, Ashford TW15 197 BR92
Byfleet KT14 234 BL112
Carshalton SM5 222 DF103
Cobham KT11 236 CA112
Dorking RH4 285 CF135
Effingham KT24 268 BX128
Hatfield AL10 67 CU19
Hersham KT12 236 BW105
Hornchurch RM12 149 FH62
Beech Cl, Loughton IG10 107 EP41
Stanwell TW19 *off St. Mary's Cres* 196 BK87
Sunbury-on-Thames TW16 *off Harfield Rd* 218 BX96
Ware SG12 55 DX08
West Drayton UB7 176 BN76
Beech Cl Ct, Cob. KT11 236 BZ111
Beech Copse, Brom. BR1 227 EM96
South Croydon CR2 242 DS106
Beech Ct, SE9 206 EL86
Ilford IG1 147 EN62
Beech Cres, Box H. KT20 270 CQ130
Beechcroft, Ashtd. KT21 254 CM119
Chislehurst BR7 207 EN94
Beechcroft Av, NW11 141 CZ59
Bexleyheath DA7 189 FD81
Croxley Green WD3 97 BQ44
Harrow HA2 138 CA59
Kenley CR8 258 DR115
New Malden KT3 220 CQ95
Beechcroft Cl, Houns. TW5 178 BY80
Orpington BR6 245 ER105
Beechcroft Gdns, Wem. HA9 140 CM62
Beechcroft Lo, Sutt. SM2 *off Devonshire Rd* 240 DC108
Beechcroft Manor, Wey. KT13 217 BR104
Beechcroft Rd, E18 124 EH54
SW14 180 CQ83
SW17 202 DE89
Bushey WD23 98 BY43
Chesham HP5 76 AN30
Chessington KT9 238 CM105
Orpington BR6 245 ER105
Beechdale, N21 121 DM47
Beechdale Rd, SW2 203 DM86
Beech Dell, Kes. BR2 245 EM105
Beechdene, Tad. KT20 255 CV122
Beech Dr, N2 142 DF55
Berkhamsted HP4 60 AW20
Borehamwood WD6 100 CM40
Kingswood KT20 255 CZ122
Reigate RH2 272 DD134
Ripley GU23 250 BG124
Sawbridgeworth CM21 58 EW07
Beechen Cliff Way, Islw. TW7 *off Henley Cl* 179 CF81
Beechen Gro, Pnr. HA5 138 BZ55
Watford WD17 98 BW42
Beechen La, Lwr Kgswd KT20 271 CZ125
Beechenlea La, Swan. BR8 229 FH97
Beechen Wd, Map.Cr. WD3 113 BD49
Beeches, The, Amer. HP6 77 AN36
Banstead SM7 256 DB116
Beaconsfield HP9 110 AH54
Bramley GU5 281 AZ144
Brentwood CM14 130 FV48
Chorleywood WD3 95 BF43
Fetcham KT22 253 CE124
Hounslow TW3 178 CB81
Park Street AL2 83 CE27
Swanley BR8 209 FF94
Tilbury RM18 193 GH82
Beeches Av, Cars. SM5 240 DE108
Beeches Cl, SE20 224 DW95
Kingswood KT20 256 DA123
Beeches Dr, Farn.Com. SL2 133 AP64
Beeches Pk, Beac. HP9 111 AK53
Beeches Rd, SW17 202 DE90
Farnham Common SL2 133 AP64
Sutton SM3 221 CY102
Beeches Wk, Cars. SM5 240 DD109
Beeches Way, B.End SL8 132 AD61
Beeches Wd, Kgswd KT20 256 DA122
Beech Fm Rd, Warl. CR6 259 EC120
Beechfield, Bans. SM7 240 DB113
Hoddesdon EN11 55 EA13
Kings Langley WD4 80 BM30
Sawbridgeworth CM21 58 EZ05
Beechfield Cl, Borwd. WD6 100 CL40
Beechfield Cotts, Brom. BR1 *off Widmore Rd* 226 EJ96
Beechfield Gdns, Rom. RM7 149 FC59
Beechfield Rd, N4 144 DQ58
SE6 205 DZ88
Bromley BR1 226 EJ96
Erith DA8 189 FE80
Hemel Hempstead HP1 62 BH21
Ware SG12 55 DZ05
Welwyn Garden City AL7 51 CY11
Sch **Beechfield Sch**, Wat. WD24 *off Gammons La* 97 BU37
Beechfield Wk, Wal.Abb. EN9 105 ED35
Beech Gdns, EC2 *off White Lyon Ct* 19 J6
W5 180 CL75
Dagenham RM10 169 FB66
Woking GU21 248 AY115
Beech Gro, Add. KT15 234 BH105
Amersham HP7 77 AQ39
Aveley RM15 170 FQ74
Bookham KT23 268 CA127
Caterham CR3 274 DS126
Croydon CR0 243 DY110
Epsom KT18 255 CV117
Guildford GU2 264 AT134
Ilford IG6 125 ES51
Mayford GU22 248 AX123
Mitcham CR4 223 DK98
New Malden KT3 220 CR97
Beech Hall, Ott. KT16 233 BC108
Beech Hall Cres, E4 123 ED52
Beech Hall Rd, E4 123 EC52
Beech Hill, Barn. EN4 102 DD38
Woking GU22 248 AX123
Beech Hill Av, Barn. EN4 102 DC39
Beech Hill Ct, Berk. HP4 60 AX18
Beech Hill Gdns, Wal.Abb. EN9 106 EH37
Beechhill Rd, SE9 207 EN85
Beech Holt, Lthd. KT22 253 CJ122
Beech Ho, NW3 *off Maitland Pk Vil* 6 F4
Croydon CR0 243 EB107
Beech Ho Rd, Croy. CR0 224 DR104
Beech Hurst Cl, Chis. BR7 227 EQ95
Beech Hyde La, Wheat. AL4 50 CM07
Beech La, Buck.H. IG9 124 EH47
Guildford GU2 280 AW137
Jordans HP9 112 AS52
Beech Lawn, Guil. GU1 281 AZ135
Beech Lawns, N12 120 DD50
Beech Lo, Stai. TW18 *off Farm Cl* 195 BE92
Beechmeads, Cob. KT11 236 BX113
Beechmont Av, Vir.W. GU25 214 AX99
Beechmont Cl, Brom. BR1 206 EE92
Beechmont Rd, Sev. TN13 279 FH129
Beechmore Gdns, Sutt. SM3 221 CX103
Beechmore Rd, SW11 40 F7
Beechmount Av, W7 159 CD71
Beecholme, Bans. SM7 239 CY114
Beecholme Av, Mitch. CR4 223 DH95
Beecholme Est, E5 144 DV62
Sch **Beecholme Prim Sch**, Mitch. CR4 *off Edgehill Rd* 223 DH95
Beecholm Ms, Chsht EN8 89 DX28
Beech Pk, Amer. HP6 94 AV39
Beechpark Way, Wat. WD17 97 BS37
Beech Pl, Epp. CM16 91 ET31
St. Albans AL3 65 CD17
Beech Rd, N11 121 DL51
SW16 223 DL96
Biggin Hill TN16 260 EH118
Dartford DA1 210 FK88
Epsom KT17 255 CT115
Feltham TW14 197 BS87
Merstham RH1 273 DJ126
Orpington BR6 246 EU108
Reigate RH2 272 DA131
St. Albans AL3 65 CE17
Sevenoaks TN13 *off Victoria Rd* 279 FH125
Slough SL3 174 AY75
Watford WD24 97 BU37
Weybridge KT13 *off St. Marys Rd* 235 BR105
Beechrow, Ham TW10 200 CL91
Beech St, EC2 19 J6
Romford RM7 149 FC56
Beechtree Av, Eng.Grn TW20 194 AV93
Beech Tree Cl, N1 8 E6
Stanmore HA7 117 CJ50
Beech Tree Glade, E4 124 EF46
Beechtree La, St.Alb. AL3 63 BV22
Beech Tree La, Stai. TW18 *off Staines Rd* 216 BH96
Beech Tree Pl, Sutt. SM1 *off St. Nicholas Way* 240 DB106
Beech Vale, Wok. GU22 *off Hill Vw Rd* 249 AZ118
Beechvale Cl, N12 120 DE50
Beech Wk, NW7 118 CS51
Dartford DA1 189 FG84
Epsom KT17 239 CU111
Hoddesdon EN11 71 DZ17
Beech Way, NW10 160 CR66
Beechway, Bex. DA5 208 EX86
Beech Way, Epsom KT17 255 CT115
Beechway, Guil. GU1 265 BB133
Beech Way, S.Croy. CR2 243 DX113
Twickenham TW2 198 CA90
Beech Waye, Ger.Cr. SL9 135 AZ59
Beechwood Av, N3 141 CZ55
Amersham HP6 94 AW38
Chorleywood WD3 95 BB42
Coulsdon CR5 257 DH115
Greenford UB6 158 CB69
Harrow HA2 138 CB62
Hayes UB3 157 BR73
Kingswood KT20 256 DA121
Orpington BR6 245 ES106
Potters Bar EN6 86 DB33
Richmond TW9 180 CN81
Ruislip HA4 137 BT61
St. Albans AL1 65 CH18
Staines-upon-Thames TW18 196 BH93
Sunbury-on-Thames TW16 197 BU93
Thornton Heath CR7 223 DP98
Uxbridge UB8 156 BN72
Weybridge KT13 235 BS105
Beechwood Circle, Har. HA2 *off Beechwood Gdns* 138 CB62
Beechwood Cl, NW7 118 CR50
Amersham HP6 94 AW39
Cheshunt EN7 88 DS26
Hertford SG13 54 DT09
Knaphill GU21 248 AS117
Long Ditton KT6 219 CJ101
Weybridge KT13 235 BS105
Beechwood Ct, Cars. SM5 240 DF105
Sunbury-on-Thames TW16 197 BU93
Beechwood Cres, Bexh. DA7 188 EX83
Beechwood Dr, Cob. KT11 236 CA111
Keston BR2 244 EK105
Woodford Green IG8 124 EF50
Beechwood Gdns, NW10 *off St. Annes Gdns* 160 CM69
Caterham CR3 258 DU122
Harrow HA2 138 CB62
Ilford IG5 147 EM57
Rainham RM13 169 FH71
Slough SL1 174 AS75
Beechwood Gro, W3 160 CS73
Long Ditton KT6 219 CJ101
Beechwood La, Warl. CR6 259 DX119
Beechwood Manor, Wey. KT13 235 BS105
Beechwood Ms, N9 122 DU47
Beechwood Pk, E18 146 EG55
Chorleywood WD3 95 BF42
Hemel Hempstead HP3 61 BF24
Leatherhead KT22 253 CJ123
Beechwood Ri, Chis. BR7 207 EP91
Watford WD24 97 BV36
Beechwood Rd, E8 10 A4
N8 143 DK56
Beaconsfield HP9 110 AJ53
Caterham CR3 258 DU122
Knaphill GU21 248 AS117
Slough SL2 153 AR71
South Croydon CR2 242 DS109
Virginia Water GU25 214 AU101
Sch **Beechwood Sch**, SW16 *off Leigham Ct Rd* 203 DL90
Slough SL2 *off Long Readings La* 153 AP69
Beechwoods Ct, SE19 *off Crystal Palace Par* 204 DT92
Beechwood Vil, Red. RH1 288 DG144
Beechworth Cl, NW3 142 DA61
Beecot La, Walt. KT12 218 BW103
Beecroft La, SE4 *off Beecroft Rd* 205 DY85
Beecroft Ms, SE4 *off Beecroft Rd* 205 DY85
Beecroft Rd, SE4 205 DY85
Beehive Cl, E8 10 A6
Elstree WD6 99 CK44
Uxbridge UB10 *off Honey Hill* 156 BM66
Beehive Ct, Rom. RM3 *off Arundel Rd* 128 FM52
Beehive Grn, Welw.G.C. AL7 52 DA11
Beehive La, Ilf. IG1, IG4 147 EM58
Welwyn Garden City AL7 52 DA12
Beehive Pas, EC3 19 N9
Beehive Pl, SW9 183 DN83
Beehive Rd, Goffs Oak EN7 87 DP28
Staines-upon-Thames TW18 195 BF92
Beehive Way, Reig. RH2 288 DB138
Beeken Dene, Orp. BR6 *off Isabella Dr* 245 EQ105
Beel Cl, Amer. HP7 94 AW39
Beeleigh Rd, Mord. SM4 222 DB98
Beesfield La, Fnghm DA4 230 FN101
Beeston Cl, E8 10 C2
Watford WD19 116 BX49
Beeston Dr, Chsht EN8 89 DX27
Beeston Pl, SW1 29 K7
Beeston Rd, Barn. EN4 102 DD44
Beeston Way, Felt. TW14 198 BW86
Beethoven Rd, Els. WD6 99 CJ44
Beethoven St, W10 14 F2
Beeton Cl, Pnr. HA5 116 CA52
Begbie Rd, SE3 186 EJ81
Beggars Bush La, Wat. WD18 97 BR43
Jct **Beggar's Hill**, Epsom KT17 239 CT107
Beggars Hill, Epsom KT17 239 CT108
Beggars Hollow, Enf. EN2 104 DR37
Beggars La, Abin.Ham. RH5 283 BT137
Westerham TN16 277 ER125
Beggars Roost La, Sutt. SM1 240 DA107
Begonia Cl, E6 25 H6
Begonia Pl, Hmptn. TW12 *off Gresham Rd* 198 CA93
Begonia Wk, W12 *off Du Cane Rd* 161 CT72
Beira St, SW12 203 DH87
Sch **Beis Chinuch Lebonos Girls Sch**, N4 *off Woodberry Gro* 144 DQ59
Sch **Beis Malka Girls' Sch**, N16 *off Alkham Rd* 144 DT60
Sch **Beis Rochel D'Satmar Girls' Sch**, N16 *off Amhurst Pk* 144 DS59
Sch **Beis Yaakov Prim Sch**, NW9 *off Edgware Rd* 140 CR55
Bejun Ct, New Barn. EN5 *off Station App* 102 DC42
Beken Ct, Wat. WD25 *off First Av* 98 BW35
Bekesbourne St, E14 21 L9
Bekesbourne Twr, Orp. BR5 228 EX102
★ **Bekonscot Model Village**, Beac. HP9 111 AK51
Belcher Rd, Hodd. EN11 *off Amwell St* 71 EA16
Belchers La, Naze.Gate EN9 72 EJ24
● **Belcon Ind Est**, Hodd. EN11 71 EB17
Belcroft Cl, Brom. BR1 206 EF94
Beldam Haw, Halst. TN14 246 FA112
Beldham Gdns, W.Mol. KT8 218 CB97
Belfairs Dr, Rom. RM6 148 EW59
Belfairs Grn, Wat. WD19 116 BX50
Belfast Av, Slou. SL1 153 AQ72
Belfast Rd, N16 144 DT61
SE25 224 DV98
Belfield Gdns, Harl. CM17 74 EW16
Belfield Rd, Epsom KT19 238 CR109
Belfont Wk, N7 8 B1
Belford Gro, SE18 37 L9
Belford Rd, Borwd. WD6 100 CM38
Belfort Rd, SE15 45 H8
Belfour Ter, N3 *off Squires La* 120 DB54
Belfry Av, Hare. UB9 114 BG53
Belfry Cl, SE16 32 F10
Bromley BR1 227 EP98
Belfry La, Rick. WD3 114 BJ46
Belfry Shop Cen, Red. RH1 272 DF133
Belgrade Rd, N16 9 P1
Hampton TW12 218 CB95
Belgrave Av, Rom. RM2 150 FJ55
Watford WD18 97 BT43
Belgrave Cl, N14 *off Prince George Av* 103 DJ43
NW7 118 CR50
W3 *off Avenue Rd* 180 CP75
Hersham KT12 235 BV105
Orpington BR5 228 EW98
St. Albans AL4 65 CJ16
Belgrave Ct, E14 33 P1
Belgrave Cres, Sun. TW16 217 BV95
Belgrave Dr, Kings L. WD4 81 BQ28
Belgrave Gdns, N14 103 DK43
NW8 5 M9
Stanmore HA7 *off Copley Rd* 117 CJ50
Belgrave Hts, E11 146 EG60
Belgrave Manor, Wok. GU22 248 AY119
Belgrave Ms, Uxb. UB8 156 BK70
Belgrave Ms N, SW1 28 G5
Belgrave Ms S, SW1 29 H6
Belgrave Ms W, SW1 28 G6
Belgrave Pl, SW1 29 H6
Belgrave Rd, E10 145 EC60
E11 146 EG61
E13 24 B4
E17 145 EA57
SE25 224 DT98
SW1 29 L9
SW13 181 CT80
Hounslow TW4 178 BZ83
Ilford IG1 147 EM60
Mitcham CR4 222 DD97
Slough SL1 154 AS73
Sunbury-on-Thames TW16 217 BV95
Belgrave Sq, SW1 28 G6
Belgrave St, E1 21 K9
Belgrave Ter, Wdf.Grn. IG8 124 EG48
Tra **Belgrave Walk** 222 DD97
Belgrave Wk, Mitch. CR4 222 DD97
Belgrave Yd, SW1 29 J7
BELGRAVIA, SW1 28 G7
Belgravia Cl, Barn. EN5 101 CZ41
Belgravia Gdns, Brom. BR1 206 EE93
Belgravia Ho, SW4 203 DK86
Belgravia Ms, Kings.T. KT1 219 CK98
Belgrove St, WC1 18 A2
Belham Rd, Kings L. WD4 80 BM28
Belham Wk, SE5 *off Mary Datchelor Cl* 43 M6
Belhaven Ct, Borwd. WD6 100 CM39
Belhus Chase, Aveley RM15 171 FR71
Sch **Belhus Chase Sch**, Aveley RM15 *off Nethan Dr* 171 FR73
Belhus Pk, Aveley RM15 171 FS73
Belinda Rd, SW9 183 DP83
Belitha Vil, N1 8 D6
Jct **Bell, The**, E17 145 EA55
Bellamy Cl, E14 34 A4
W14 39 H1
Edgware HA8 118 CQ48
Uxbridge UB10 136 BN62
Watford WD17 97 BU39
Bellamy Dr, Stan. HA7 117 CH53
Bellamy Ho, SW17 *off Garratt La* 202 DD91
Hounslow TW5 178 CA79
Bellamy Rd, E4 123 EB51
Cheshunt EN8 89 DY29
Enfield EN2 104 DR40
Bellamy St, SW12 203 DH87
Bel La, Felt. TW13 *off Butts Cotts* 198 BZ90
Bellarmine Cl, SE28 187 ET75
Bellasis Av, SW2 203 DL89
Bell Av, Rom. RM3 127 FH53
West Drayton UB7 176 BM77
Bell Br Rd, Cher. KT16 215 BF102
Bellchambers Cl, Lon.Col. AL2 83 CJ26
Bell Cl, Beac. HP9 111 AM53
Bedmond WD5 81 BT27
Greenhithe DA9 211 FT85
Pinner HA5 116 BW54
Ruislip HA4 137 BT62
Slough SL2 154 AV71
Bellclose Rd, West Dr. UB7 176 BL75
BELL COMMON, Epp. CM16 91 ER32
Bell Common, Epp. CM16 91 ES32
Bell Common Tunnel, Epp. CM16 91 ER33
Bell Ct, Surb. KT5 *off Barnsbury La* 220 CP103
Bell Cres, Couls. CR5 *off Maple Way* 257 DH121
Bell Dr, SW18 201 CY87
Bellefield Rd, Orp. BR5 228 EV99
Bellefields Rd, SW9 183 DM83
Bellegrove Cl, Well. DA16 187 ET82
Bellegrove Par, Well. DA16 *off Bellegrove Rd* 187 ET83
Bellegrove Rd, Well. DA16 187 ER82
Sch **Bellenden Prim Sch**, SE15 44 C10
Bellenden Rd, SE15 44 B8
Coll **Bellerbys Coll**, SE8 46 B3
Bellestaines Pleasaunce, E4 123 EA47
Sch **Belleville Prim Sch**, SW11 *off Webbs Rd* 202 DF85
Belleville Rd, SW11 202 DF85
Belle Vue, Grnf. UB6 159 CD67
Belle Vue Cl, Stai. TW18 216 BG95
Belle Vue Est, NW4 *off Bell La* 141 CW56
Belle Vue La, Bushey Hth WD23 117 CD46
Bellevue Ms, N11 120 DG50
Bellevue Par, SW17 *off Bellevue Rd* 202 DE88
Belle Vue Pk, Th.Hth. CR7 224 DQ97
Bellevue Pl, E1 20 G5
Slough SL1 174 AT76
Belle Vue Rd, E17 123 ED54
Bellevue Rd, N11 120 DG49
Belle Vue Rd, NW4 141 CW56
Bellevue Rd, SW13 181 CU82
SW17 202 DE88
W13 159 CH70
Bexleyheath DA6 208 EZ85
Belle Vue Rd, Downe BR6 *off Standard Rd* 245 EN110
Bellevue Rd, Horn. RM11 150 FM60
Kingston upon Thames KT1 220 CL97
Romford RM5 127 FC51
Belle Vue Rd, Ware SG12 55 DZ06
Bellevue Ter, Hare. UB9 114 BG52
Bellew St, SW17 202 DC90
Bell Fm Av, Dag. RM10 149 FC62
Sch **Bell Fm Jun Sch**, Hersham KT12 *off Hersham Rd* 236 BW105
Bellfield, Croy. CR0 243 DY109
Slough SL1 173 AM75
Bellfield Av, Har. HA3 116 CC51
Bellfield Cl, SE3 47 P4
Bellfield Ct, Guil. GU1 264 AW130
BELLFIELDS, Guil. GU1 264 AW131
Bellfields Rd, Guil. GU1 264 AX132
Bellflower Cl, E6 24 G6
Bellflower Path, Rom. RM3 128 FJ52
Bell Gdns, E17 *off Markhouse Rd* 145 DZ57
Orpington BR5 228 EW99
Bellgate, Hem.H. HP2 62 BL17
Bellgate Ms, NW5 *off York Ri* 143 DH62
Sch **Bellgate Prim Sch**, Hem.H. HP2 *off Fletcher Way* 62 BL18
BELL GREEN, SE6 205 DZ90
Bell Grn, SE26 205 DZ90
Bovingdon HP3 79 BB27
Bell Grn La, SE26 205 DY92
Bellhaven, E15 13 H4
Bell Hill, Croy. CR0 *off Surrey St* 224 DQ103
Bellhouse La, Pilg.Hat. CM14 130 FS43
Bellhouse Rd, Rom. RM7 149 FC60
Bellina Ms, NW5 7 K1
● **Bell Ind Est**, W4 *off Cunnington St* 180 CQ77
Bellingdon Rd, Chesh. HP5 76 AP31
BELLINGHAM, SE6 205 EB90
⇌ **Bellingham** 205 EB90
Bellingham Ct, Bark. IG11 *off Renwick Rd* 168 EV69
Bellingham Dr, Reig. RH2 271 CZ134
Bellingham Grn, SE6 205 EA90
Bellingham Rd, SE6 205 EB90
● **Bellingham Trd Est**, SE6 *off Franthorne Way* 205 EB90
Bell Inn Yd, EC3 19 M9
Bell La, E1 20 A7
E16 35 N2
NW4 141 CX56
Amersham HP6, HP7 94 AV39
Bedmond WD5 81 BT27
Berkhamsted HP4 60 AS18
Brookmans Park AL9 86 DA25
Broxbourne EN10 71 DY21
Enfield EN3 105 DX38
Eton Wick SL4 173 AM77
Fetcham KT22 253 CD123
Hertford SG14 54 DR09
Hoddesdon EN11 71 EA17
London Colney AL2 84 CL29
Twickenham TW1 *off The Embankment* 199 CG88
Wembley HA9 *off Magnet Rd* 139 CK61
Bell La Cl, Fetch. KT22 253 CD123

Bell La Comb Sch, Lt.Chal. HP6 off Bell La 94 AV38
Bell La Prim Sch, NW4 off Bell La 141 CX56
Bellmaker Ct, E3 22 A6
Bellman Av, Grav. DA12 213 GL88
Bellmarsh Rd, Add. KT15 234 BH105
Bell Rd, Saw. CM21 58 EY05
Bell Meadow, SE19 off Dulwich Wd Av 204 DS91
Godstone RH9 274 DV132
Bellmount Wd Av, Wat. WD17 97 BS39
Bello Cl, SE24 203 DP87
Bellot Gdns, SE10 35 K10
Bellot St, SE10 35 K10
Bell Par, Wind. SL4 off St. Andrews Av 173 AM82
Bellridge Pl, Knot.Grn HP9 110 AH49
Bellring Cl, Belv. DA17 188 FA79
Bell Rd, E.Mol. KT8 219 CD99
Enfield EN1 104 DR39
Hounslow TW3 178 CB84
Bells All, SW6 39 J9
Bells Gdn Est, SE15 44 C5
Bells Hill, Barn. EN5 101 CX43
Bell's Hill, Stoke P. SL2 154 AU67
Bells Hill Grn, Stoke P. SL2 154 AU66
Bells La, Horton SL3 175 BB83
Bell St, NW1 16 C6
SE18 186 EL81
Reigate RH2 272 DA134
Sawbridgeworth CM21 58 EY05
Bellswood La, Iver SL0 155 BB71
Belltrees Gro, SW16 203 DM92
Bell Vw, St.Alb. AL4 65 CK20
Windsor SL4 173 AM83
Bell Vw Cl, Wind. SL4 173 AM82
Bell Water Gate, SE18 37 M6
Bell Weir Cl, Stai. TW19 195 BB89
Bellwether La, Outwood RH1 289 DP143
Bell Wf La, EC4 31 K1
Bellwood Rd, SE15 185 DX84
Bell Yd, WC2 18 E8
Bell Yd Ms, SE1 31 P5
Belmarsh Rd, SE28 off Western Way 187 ES75
BELMONT, Har. HA3 117 CG54
BELMONT, Sutt. SM2 240 DB111
⇌ Belmont 240 DA110
Belmont, Mill Hill Prep Sch, NW7 off The Ridgeway 119 CU48
Belmont, Slou. SL2 153 AN71
Weybridge KT13 off Egerton Rd 235 BQ107
Belmont Av, N9 122 DU46
N13 121 DL50
N17 144 DQ55
Barnet EN4 102 DF43
Guildford GU2 264 AT131
New Malden KT3 221 CU99
Southall UB2 178 BY76
Upminster RM14 150 FM61
Welling DA16 187 ES83
Wembley HA0 160 CM67
Belmont Circle, Har. HA3 117 CH53
Belmont Cl, E4 123 ED50
N20 120 DB46
SW4 183 DJ83
Cockfosters EN4 102 DF42
Uxbridge UB8 156 BK65
Woodford Green IG8 124 EH49
Belmont Cotts, Colnbr. SL3 off High St 175 BC80
Belmont Ct, NW11 141 CZ57
Belmont First & Mid Schs, Har.Wld HA3 off Hibbert Rd 117 CF54
Belmont Gro, SE13 46 G10
W4 off Belmont Ter 180 CR77
Belmont Hall Ct, SE13 off Belmont Gro 185 ED83
Belmont Hill, SE13 185 ED83
St. Albans AL1 65 CD21
Belmont Inf Sch, N22 off Rusper Rd 144 DQ55
Belmont Jun Sch, N22 off Rusper Rd 144 DQ55
Belmont La, Chis. BR7 207 EQ92
Stanmore HA7 117 CJ52
Belmont Ms, SW19 off Chapman Sq 201 CX89
Belmont Pk, SE13 185 ED84
Belmont Pk Cl, SE13 185 ED84
Belmont Pk Rd, E10 145 EB58
Belmont Pk Sch, E10 off Leyton Grn Rd 145 EC58
Belmont Prim Sch, W4 off Belmont Rd 180 CR77
Erith DA8 off Belmont Rd 188 FA80
Belmont Ri, Sutt. SM2 239 CZ107
Belmont Rd, N15 144 DQ56
N17 144 DQ56
SE25 224 DV99
SW4 183 DJ83
W4 off Chiswick High Rd 180 CR77
Beckenham BR3 225 DZ96
Bushey WD23 98 BY43
Chesham HP5 76 AP29
Chislehurst BR7 207 EP92
Erith DA8 188 FA80
Grays RM17 192 FZ78
Harrow HA3 139 CF55
Hemel Hempstead HP3 62 BL24
Hornchurch RM12 150 FK62
Ilford IG1 147 EQ62
Leatherhead KT22 253 CG122
Reigate RH2 288 DC135
Sutton SM2 240 DA110
Twickenham TW2 199 CD89
Uxbridge UB8 156 BK66
Wallington SM6 241 DH106
Belmont St, NW1 7 H6
Belmont Ter, W4 180 CR77
Belmor, Els. WD6 100 CN43
Belmore Av, Hayes UB4 157 BU72
Woking GU22 249 BD116
Belmore La, N7 7 P3
Belmore Prim Sch, Hayes UB4 off Owen Rd 157 BV69
Belmore St, SW8 41 N6
Beloe Cl, SW15 181 CU83
Belper Ct, E5 off Pedro St 145 DX63
Belsham Cl, Chesh. HP5 76 AP28
Belsham St, E9 10 G4
BELSIZE, Rick. WD3 79 BF33
Belsize Av, N13 121 DM51
NW3 6 B4
W13 179 CH76
Belsize Cl, Hem.H. HP3 62 BN21
St. Albans AL4 65 CJ15
Belsize Ct, NW3 6 B2
Sutt. SM1 240 DB105
Belsize Cres, NW3 6 B3
Belsize Gro, NW3 6 D4
Belsize La, NW3 6 A5
Belsize Ms, NW3 6 B4
BELSIZE PARK, NW3 6 C5
⊖ Belsize Park 6 D3
Belsize Pk, NW3 6 A5
Belsize Pk Gdns, NW3 6 B4
Belsize Pk Ms, NW3 6 B4
Belsize Pl, NW3 6 B4
Belsize Rd, NW6 5 P7
Harrow HA3 117 CD52
Hemel Hempstead HP3 62 BN21
Belsize Sq, NW3 6 B4
Belsize Ter, NW3 6 B4
Belson Rd, SE18 37 J8
Belswains Grn, Hem.H. HP3 off Belswains La 62 BL23
Belswains La, Hem.H. HP3 80 BM25
Belswains Prim Sch, Hem.H. HP3 off Barnfield 62 BM24
Beltana Dr, Grav. DA12 213 GL91
Beltane Dr, SW19 201 CX90
Belthorn Cres, SW12 203 DJ87
Beltinge Rd, Rom. RM3 150 FM55
Beltona Gdns, Chsht EN8 89 DX27
Belton Rd, E7 166 EH66
E11 146 EE63
N17 144 DS55
NW2 161 CU65
Berkhamsted HP4 60 AU18
Sidcup DA14 208 EU91
Belton Way, E3 22 A6
Beltran Rd, SW6 39 L9
Beltwood Rd, Belv. DA17 189 FC77
BELVEDERE, DA17 189 FB77
⇌ Belvedere 188 FA76
Belvedere, The, SW10 39 P7
Belvedere Av, SW19 201 CY92
Ilford IG5 125 EP54
Belvedere Bldgs, SE1 31 H5
● Belvedere Business Pk, Belv. DA17 189 FB75
Belvedere Cl, Amer. HP6 94 AT36
Esher KT10 236 CB106
Gravesend DA12 213 GJ88
Guildford GU2 264 AV132
Teddington TW11 199 CE92
Weybridge KT13 234 BN106
Belvedere Ct, N1 9 N8
N2 142 DD57
Belvedere Dr, SW19 201 CY92
Belvedere Gdns, St.Alb. AL2 82 CA27
West Molesey KT8 218 BZ99
Belvedere Gro, SW19 201 CY92
Belvedere Ho, Felt. TW13 197 BU88
Belvedere Ind Est, Belv. DA17 189 FC76
Belvedere Inf Sch, Belv. DA17 off Mitchell Cl 189 FB76
Belvedere Jun Sch, Belv. DA17 off Mitchell Cl 189 FB76
Belvedere Ms, SE3 47 P5
SE15 184 DW83
Belvedere Pl, SE1 31 H5
SW2 183 DM84
Belvedere Rd, E10 145 DY60
SE1 30 D4
SE2 168 EX74
SE19 204 DT94
W7 179 CF76
Bexleyheath DA7 188 EZ83
Biggin Hill TN16 261 EM118
Brentwood CM14 130 FT48
Belvederes, The, Reig. RH2 288 DB137
Belvedere Sq, SW19 201 CY92
Belvedere Strand, NW9 119 CT54
Belvedere Way, Har. HA3 140 CL58
Belvoir Cl, SE9 206 EL90
Belvoir Ho, SW1 off Vauxhall Br Rd 29 M8
Belvoir Rd, SE22 204 DU87
● Belvue Business Cen, Nthlt. UB5 158 CB66
Belvue Cl, Nthlt. UB5 158 CA66
Belvue Rd, Nthlt. UB5 158 CA66
Belvue Sch, Nthlt. UB5 off Rowdell Rd 158 CA67
Bembridge Cl, NW6 4 E6
Bembridge Ct, Slou. SL1 off Park St 174 AT75
Bembridge Gdns, Ruis. HA4 137 BR61
Bembridge Pl, Wat. WD25 81 BU33
Bemersyde Pt, E13 24 A3
Bemerton Est, N1 8 B7
Bemerton St, N1 8 C8
Bemish Rd, SW15 181 CX83
Bempton Dr, Ruis. HA4 137 BV61
Bemsted Rd, E17 145 DZ55
Benares Rd, SE18 187 ET77
Benbow Cl, St.Alb. AL1 65 CH22
Benbow Rd, W6 181 CV76
Benbow St, SE8 46 B2
Benbow Waye, Uxb. UB8 156 BJ71
Benbrick Rd, Guil. GU2 280 AU135
Benbury Cl, Brom. BR1 205 EC92
Bence, The, Egh. TW20 215 BB97
Bench Fld, S.Croy. CR2 242 DT107
Benchleys Rd, Hem.H. HP1 61 BF21
Bench Manor Cres, Chal.St.P. SL9 112 AW54
Bencombe Rd, Pur. CR8 241 DN114
Bencroft, Chsht EN7 88 DU26
Bencroft Rd, SW16 203 DJ94
Hemel Hempstead HP2 62 BL20
Bencurtis Pk, W.Wick. BR4 225 ED104
Bendall Ms, NW1 16 D6
Bendemeer Rd, SW15 38 C10
Bendish Pt, SE28 187 EQ75
Bendish Rd, E6 166 EL66
Bendmore Av, SE2 188 EU78
Bendon Valley, SW18 202 DB87
Bendysh Rd, Bushey WD23 98 BY41
Benedict Cl, Belv. DA17 off Tunstock Way 188 EY76
Orpington BR6 227 ES104
Benedict Dr, Felt. TW14 197 BR87
Benedictine Gate, Wal.Cr. EN8 89 DY27
Benedict Prim Sch, Mitch. CR4 off Church Rd 222 DD97
Benedict Rd, SW9 42 D10
Mitcham CR4 222 DD97
Benedicts Wf, Bark. IG11 off Town Quay 167 EP67
Benedict Way, N2 142 DC55
Benenden Grn, Brom. BR2 226 EG99
Benen-Stock Rd, Stai. TW19 195 BF85
Benets Rd, Horn. RM11 150 FN60
Benett Gdns, SW16 223 DL96
Benfleet Cl, Cob. KT11 236 BY112
Sutton SM1 222 DC104
Benfleet Way, N11 120 DG47
Benford Rd, Hodd. EN11 71 DZ19
Bengal Ct, EC3 off Birchin La 19 M9
Bengal Rd, Ilf. IG1 147 EP63
Bengarth Dr, Har. HA3 117 CD54
Bengarth Rd, Nthlt. UB5 158 BX67
BENGEO, Hert. SG14 54 DQ07
Bengeo Gdns, Rom. RM6 148 EW58
Bengeo Meadows, Hert. SG14 54 DR06
Bengeo Ms, Hert. SG14 54 DQ06
Bengeo Prim Sch, Hert. SG14 off The Avenue 54 DQ06
Bengeo St, Hert. SG14 54 DQ08
Bengeworth Rd, SE5 43 J10
Harrow HA1 139 CG61
Ben Hale Cl, Stan. HA7 117 CH49
Benham Cl, SW11 182 DD83
Chesham HP5 76 AP29
Chessington KT9 237 CJ107
Coulsdon CR5 257 DP118
Benham Gdns, Houns. TW4 198 BZ85
Benham Rd, W7 159 CE71
Benhams Cl, Horl. RH6 290 DG146
Benhams Dr, Horl. RH6 290 DG146
Benhams Pl, NW3 off Holly Wk 142 DC63
Benhill Av, Sutt. SM1 240 DB105
Benhill Rd, SE5 43 M5
Sutton SM1 222 DC104
Benhill Wd Rd, Sutt. SM1 222 DC104
BENHILTON, Sutt. SM1 222 DB103
Benhilton Gdns, Sutt. SM1 222 DB104
Benhurst Av, Horn. RM12 149 FH62
Benhurst Cl, S.Croy. CR2 243 DX110
Benhurst Ct, SW16 203 DN92
Benhurst Gdns, S.Croy. CR2 242 DW110
Benhurst La, SW16 203 DN92
Benhurst Prim Sch, Elm Pk RM12 off Benhurst Av 149 FH62
Beningfield Dr, Lon.Col. AL2 83 CH27
Benington Ct, N4 off Brownswood Rd 144 DQ61
Benin St, SE13 205 ED87
Benison Ct, Slou. SL1 off Hencroft St S 174 AT76
Benjafield Cl, N18 122 DV49
Benjamin Cl, E8 10 D9
Hornchurch RM11 149 FG58
Benjamin La, Wexham SL3 154 AV70
Benjamin Ms, SW12 203 DJ87
Benjamin St, EC1 18 G6
Ben Jonson Ho, EC2 off The Barbican 19 K6
Ben Jonson Prim Sch, E1 21 M5
Ben Jonson Rd, E1 21 K7
Benledi Rd, E14 22 G8
Benlow Wks, Hayes UB3 off Silverdale Rd 177 BU75
Benn Cl, Oxt. RH8 276 EG134
Bennelong Cl, W12 161 CV73
Bennerley Rd, SW11 202 DE85
Bennet Ms, N19 off Wedmore St 143 DK62
Bennets Ctyd, SW19 off Watermill Way 222 DC95
Bennetsfield Rd, Uxb. UB11 157 BP74
Bennet's Hill, EC4 19 H10
Bennet St, SW1 29 L2
Bennett Cl, Cob. KT11 235 BU113
Hampton Wick KT1 219 CJ95
Hounslow TW4 198 BY85
Northwood HA6 115 BT52
Welling DA16 188 EU82
Welwyn Garden City AL7 51 CZ13
Bennett Gro, SE13 46 D7
Bennett Ho, SW1 off Page St 29 P8
Bennett Pk, SE3 47 L10
Bennett Rd, E13 24 C5
N16 9 N1
SW9 42 F9
Romford RM6 148 EY58
Bennetts, Chesh. HP5 76 AR30
Bennetts Av, Croy. CR0 225 DY103
Greenford UB6 159 CE67
Bennetts Castle La, Dag. RM8 148 EW63
Bennetts Cl, N17 122 DT51
Colney Heath AL4 66 CR23
Mitcham CR4 223 DH95
Slough SL1 153 AN74
Bennetts Copse, Chis. BR7 206 EL93
BENNETTS END, Hem.H. HP3 62 BM23
Bennetts End Cl, Hem.H. HP3 62 BM21
Bennetts End Rd, Hem.H. HP3 62 BM21
Bennetts Fm Pl, Bkhm KT23 268 BZ125
Bennetts Fld, Bushey WD23 98 BY43
Bennetts Gate, Hem.H. HP3 off Kimps Way 62 BN23
Bennett St, W4 180 CS79
Bennetts Way, Croy. CR0 225 DY103
Bennetts Yd, SW1 29 P7
Uxbridge UB8 off High St 156 BJ66
Bennett Way, Lane End DA2 211 FR91
West Clandon GU4 266 BG129
Benning Cl, Wind. SL4 173 AK83
Benning Dr, Dag. RM8 148 EY60
Benningfield Gdns, Berk. HP4 60 AY17
Benningholme Rd, Edg. HA8 118 CS51
Bennington Dr, Borwd. WD6 100 CM39
Bennington Rd, N17 122 DS53
Woodford Green IG8 124 EE52
Bennions Cl, Horn. RM12 off Franklin Rd 170 FK65
Bennison Dr, Harold Wd RM3 128 FK54
Benn St, E9 11 M4
Benn's Wk, Rich. TW9 off Rosedale Rd 180 CL84
Benrek Cl, Ilf. IG6 125 EQ53
Bensbury Cl, SW15 201 CV87
Bensham Cl, Th.Hth. CR7 224 DQ98
Bensham Gro, Th.Hth. CR7 224 DQ96
Bensham La, Croy. CR0 223 DP101
Thornton Heath CR7 223 DP98
Bensham Manor Rd, Th.Hth. CR7 224 DQ98
Bensham Manor Sch, Th.Hth. CR7 off Ecclesbourne Rd 224 DQ99
Bensington Ct, Felt. TW14 197 BR86
Benskin Rd, Wat. WD18 97 BU43
Benskins La, Noak Hill RM4 128 FK46
Bensley Cl, N11 120 DF50
Ben Smith Way, SE16 32 D6
Benson Av, E6 24 D1
Benson Cl, Houns. TW3 178 CA84
Slough SL2 154 AU74
Uxbridge UB8 156 BL71
Benson Ct, SW8 off Hartington Rd 42 A6
Enfield EN3 off Harston Dr 105 EA38
Benson Prim Sch, Croy. CR0 off West Way 225 DY104
Benson Quay, E1 32 G1
Benson Rd, SE23 204 DW88
Croydon CR0 223 DN104
Grays RM17 192 GB79
Bentall Cen, The, Kings.T. KT1 219 CK96
Bentfield Gdns, SE9 off Aldersgrove Av 206 EJ90
Benthall Gdns, Ken. CR8 258 DQ117
Benthal Prim Sch, N16 off Benthal Rd 144 DU62
Benthal Rd, N16 144 DU61
Bentham Av, Wok. GU21 249 BC115
Bentham Ct, N1 9 J7
Bentham Ho, SE1 off Falmouth Rd 31 L6
Bentham Rd, E9 11 J5
SE28 168 EV73
Bentham Wk, NW10 140 CQ64
Ben Tillet Cl, Bark. IG11 168 EU66
Ben Tillett Cl, E16 37 J3
Bentinck Cl, NW8 off Prince Albert Rd 16 D1
Gerrards Cross SL9 134 AX57
Bentinck Ms, W1 17 H8
Bentinck Rd, West Dr. UB7 156 BK74
Bentinck St, W1 17 H8
Bentley Ct, SE13 off Whitburn Rd 185 EC84
Bentley Dr, NW2 141 CZ62
Harlow CM17 74 EW16
Ilford IG2 147 EQ58
Weybridge KT13 234 BN109
BENTLEY HEATH, Barn. EN5 101 CZ35
Bentley Heath La, Barn. EN5 85 CY34
Bentley Ms, Enf. EN1 104 DR44
Bentley Pk, Burn. SL1 153 AK68
★ Bentley Priory Open Space, Stan. HA7 117 CF49
Bentley Rd, N1 9 P5
Hertford SG14 53 DL08
Slough SL1 153 AN74
Bentleys, Hat.Hth CM22 59 FH05
Bentley St, Grav. DA12 213 GJ86
Bentley Way, Stan. HA7 117 CG50
Woodford Green IG8 124 EG48
Bentley Wd High Sch for Girls, Stan. HA7 off Bridges Rd 117 CF50
Benton Rd, Ilf. IG1 147 ER60
Watford WD19 116 BX50
Bentons La, SE27 204 DQ91
Bentons Ri, SE27 204 DR92
Bentry Cl, Dag. RM8 148 EY61
Bentry Rd, Dag. RM8 148 EY61
Bentsbrook Cl, N.Holm. RH5 285 CH140
Bentsbrook Pk, N.Holm. RH5 285 CH140
Bentsbrook Rd, N.Holm. RH5 285 CH140
Bentsley Cl, St.Alb. AL4 65 CJ16
Bentworth Prim Sch, W12 off Bentworth Rd 161 CV72
Bentworth Rd, W12 161 CV72
Benville Ho, SW8 42 D5
Benwell Ct, Sun. TW16 217 BU95
Benwell Rd, N7 8 E1
Benwick Cl, SE16 32 F8
Benworth St, E3 21 P2
Benyon Path, S.Ock. RM15 off Tyssen Pl 171 FW69
Benyon Prim Sch, S.Ock. RM15 off Tyssen Pl 171 FW68
Benyon Rd, N1 9 M8
Benyon Wf, E8 9 P8
Beomonds Row, Cher. KT16 off Heriot Rd 216 BG101
Beormund Sch, SE1 31 M5
Berberis Cl, Guil. GU1 264 AW132
Berberis Ho, Felt. TW13 off Highfield Rd 197 BU89
Berberis Wk, West Dr. UB7 176 BL77
Berber Par, SE18 186 EL81
Berber Pl, E14 22 A10
Berber Rd, SW11 202 DF85
Berberry Cl, Edg. HA8 off Larkspur Gro 118 CQ49
Berceau Wk, Wat. WD17 97 BS39
Bercta Rd, SE9 207 EQ89
Berdan Ct, Enf. EN3 off George Lovell Dr 105 EA37
Bere Cl, Green. DA9 211 FW85
Berecroft, Harl. CM18 73 ER20
Beredens La, Gt Warley CM13 151 FT55
Berefeld, Hem.H. HP2 62 BK18
Berengers Ct, Rom. RM6 148 EZ59
Berengers Pl, Dag. RM9 168 EV65
Berenger Twr, SW10 40 A4
Berenger Wk, SW10 off Blantyre St 40 A4
Berens Rd, NW10 14 C3
Orpington BR5 228 EX99
Berens Way, Chis. BR7 227 ET98
Beresford Av, N20 120 DF47
W7 159 CD71
Slough SL2 154 AW74
Surbiton KT5 220 CP102
Twickenham TW1 199 CJ86
Wembley HA0 160 CM67
Beresford Dr, Brom. BR1 226 EL97
Woodford Green IG8 124 EJ49
Beresford Gdns, Enf. EN1 104 DS42
Hounslow TW4 198 BZ85
Romford RM6 148 EY57
Beresford Rd, E4 124 EE46
E17 123 EB53
N2 142 DE55
N5 9 L3
N8 143 DN57
Dorking RH4 285 CH136
Harrow HA1 139 CD57
Kingston upon Thames KT2 220 CM95
Mill End WD3 113 BF46
New Malden KT3 220 CQ98
Northfleet DA11 212 GE87
St. Albans AL1 65 CH21
Southall UB1 158 BX74
Beresford Rd, Sutton SM2 239 CZ108
Beresford Sq, SE18 37 N8
Beresford St, SE18 37 N7
Beresford Ter, N5 9 K3
Berestede Rd, W6 181 CT78
Bere St, E1 21 K10
Bergenia Ho, Felt. TW13 off Bedfont La 197 BV88
Bergen Sq, SE16 33 M6
Berger Cl, Petts Wd BR5 227 ER100
Berger Prim Sch, E9 11 J4
Berger Rd, E9 11 J4
Berghem Ms, W14 26 D7
Berghers Hill, Woob.Grn HP10 132 AF59
Bergholt Av, Ilf. IG4 146 EL57
Bergholt Cres, N16 144 DS59
Bergholt Ms, NW1 7 M7
Berglen Ct, E14 21 L9
Bericot Way, Welw.G.C. AL7 52 DC09
Bering Sq, E14 34 B10
Bering Wk, E16 24 E9
Berisford Ms, SW18 202 DB86
Berkeley Av, Bexh. DA7 188 EX81
Chesham HP5 76 AN30
Greenford UB6 159 CE65
Hounslow TW4 177 BU82
Ilford IG5 125 EN54
Romford RM5 127 FC52
Berkeley Cl, Abb.L. WD5 81 BT32
Chesham HP5 off Berkeley Av 76 AN30
Elstree WD6 100 CN43
Hornchurch RM11 150 FP61
Kingston upon Thames KT2 200 CL94
Petts Wood BR5 227 ES101
Potters Bar EN6 85 CY32
Ruislip HA4 137 BU62
Staines-upon-Thames TW19 195 BD89
Ware SG12 54 DW05
Berkeley Ct, N14 103 DJ44
Croxley Green WD3 off Mayfare 97 BR43
Guildford GU1 off London Rd 264 AY134
Wallington SM6 223 DJ104
Weybridge KT13 217 BR103
Berkeley Cres, Barn. EN4 102 DD43
Dartford DA1 210 FM88
Berkeley Dr, Horn. RM11 150 FN60
West Molesey KT8 218 BZ97
Berkeley Gdns, N21 122 DR45
W8 27 K3
Claygate KT10 237 CG107
Walton-on-Thames KT12 217 BT101
West Byfleet KT14 233 BF114
Berkeley Ho, E3 21 P3
Berkeley Ms, W1 16 F8
Berkeley Pl, SW19 201 CX93
Epsom KT18 254 CR115
Berkeley Prim Sch, Heston TW5 off Cranford La 178 BX80
Berkeley Rd, E12 146 EL64
N8 143 DK57
N15 144 DR58
NW9 140 CN56
SW13 181 CU81
Loudwater HP10 110 AC53
Uxbridge UB10 157 BQ66
Berkeleys, The, Fetch. KT22 253 CE124
Berkeley Sq, W1 29 K1
Berkeley St, W1 29 K1
Berkeley Twr, E14 33 P2
Berkeley Wk, N7 off Durham Rd 143 DM61
Berkeley Waye, Houns. TW5 178 BX80
Berkerley Ms, Sun. TW16 218 BW97
Berkhampstead Rd, Belv. DA17 188 FA78
Chesham HP5 76 AQ30
BERKHAMSTED, HP4 60 AW17
⇌ Berkhamsted 60 AW18
Berkhamsted Av, Wem. HA9 160 CM65
Berkhamsted Bypass, Berk. HP4 60 AV21
Hemel Hempstead HP1 61 BB23
★ Berkhamsted Castle, Berk. HP4 60 AX18
Berkhamsted Collegiate Sch, Castle Campus, Berk. HP4 off Castle St 60 AW19
Kings Campus, Berk. HP4 off Kings Rd 60 AV19
Prep Sch, Berk. HP4 off Kings Rd 60 AV19
Berkhamsted Hill, Berk. HP4 60 AY17
Berkhamsted La, Essen. AL9 68 DF20
Berkhamsted Pl, Berk. HP4 60 AW17
Berkhamsted Rd, Hem.H. HP1 61 BD17
Berkley Av, Wal.Cr. EN8 89 DX34
Berkley Cl, St.Alb. AL4 65 CJ16
Berkley Ct, Berk. HP4 off Mill St 60 AW19
Berkley Cres, Grav. DA12 off Milton Rd 213 GJ86
Berkley Gro, NW1 6 F7
Berkley Rd, NW1 6 F7
Beaconsfield HP9 111 AK49
Gravesend DA12 213 GH86
Berks Hill, Chorl. WD3 95 BC43
Berkshire Av, Slou. SL1 153 AP72
Berkshire Cl, Cat. CR3 258 DR122
Berkshire Gdns, N13 121 DN51
N18 122 DV50
Berkshire Rd, E9 11 P4
Berkshire Sq, Mitch. CR4 off Berkshire Way 223 DL98
Berkshire Way, Horn. RM11 150 FN57
Mitcham CR4 223 DL98
Bermans Cl, Hutt. CM13 131 GB47
Bermans Way, NW10 140 CS63
Bermer Rd, Wat. WD24 98 BW39
BERMONDSEY, SE1 32 A7
⊖ Bermondsey 32 D6
Bermondsey Sq, SE1 31 P6
Bermondsey St, SE1 31 N3
● Bermondsey Trd Est, SE16 off Rotherhithe New Rd 32 G10
Bermondsey Wall E, SE16 32 D5
Bermondsey Wall W, SE16 32 C4
Bermuda Rd, Til. RM18 193 GG82
Bernal Cl, SE28 off Haldane Rd 168 EX73
Bernard Ashley Dr, SE7 186 EH78
Bernard Av, W13 179 CH76
Bernard Cassidy St, E16 23 M6
Bernard Gdns, SW19 201 CZ92
Bernard Gro, Wal.Abb. EN9 off Beaulieu Dr 89 EB33
Bernard Rd, N15 144 DT57

Bernard Rd, Romford RM7 149 FC59
Wallington SM6 241 DH105
Bernards Cl, Ilf. IG6 125 EQ51
Bernard Shaw Ho, NW10
off Knatchbull Rd 160 CR67
Sch Bernards Heath Inf Sch, St.Alb.
AL1 off Sandridge Rd 65 CF18
Sch Bernards Heath Jun Sch,
St.Alb. AL3 off Watson Av 65 CE17
Bernard St, WC1 18 A5
Gravesend DA12 213 GH86
St. Albans AL3 65 CD19
Bernays Cl, Stan. HA7 117 CJ51
Bernays Gro, SW9 183 DM84
Bernel Dr, Croy. CR0 225 DZ104
Berne Rd, Th.Hth. CR7 224 DQ99
Berners Cl, Slou. SL1 153 AL73
Berners Dr, W13 159 CG72
Broxbourne EN10
off Berners Way 71 DZ23
St. Albans AL1 65 CD23
Bernersmede, SE3 47 N10
Berners Ms, W1 17 M7
Berners Pl, W1 17 M8
Berners Rd, N1 8 F10
N22 121 DN53
Berners St, W1 17 M7
Berners Way, Brox. EN10 71 DZ23
Berney Rd, Croy. CR0 224 DR101
Bernhardt Cres, NW8 16 C4
Bernhart Cl, Edg. HA8 118 CQ52
Bernice Cl, Rain. RM13 170 FJ70
Bernville Way, Har. HA3 140 CM57
Bernwell Rd, E4 124 EE48
Berricot Grn, Tewin AL6 52 DE08
Berridge Grn, Edg. HA8 118 CN52
Berridge Ms, NW6 5 J2
Berridge Rd, SE19 204 DS92
Berries, The, Sand. AL4 65 CG16
Berriman Rd, N7 143 DM62
Berrington Dr, E.Hors. KT24 251 BT124
Berrington Ms, Slou. SL1 153 AN74
Berriton Rd, Har. HA2 138 BZ60
Berry Av, Wat. WD24 97 BU36
Berrybank Cl, E4
off Greenbank Cl 123 EC47
Berry Cl, N21 121 DP46
Dagenham RM10 148 FA64
Hornchurch RM12
off Airfield Way 150 FJ64
Rickmansworth WD3 114 BH45
Berry Ct, Houns. TW4
off Raglan Cl 198 BZ85
Berrydale Rd, Hayes UB4 158 BY70
Berryfield, Slou. SL2 154 AW72
Berryfield Cl, E17 145 EB56
Bromley BR1 226 EL95
Berry Fld Pk, Amer. HP6 77 AP37
Berryfield Rd, SE17 31 H10
Jct Berrygrove Interchange,
Wat. WD25 98 CA38
Berry Gro La, Wat. WD25 98 CA39
Sch Berrygrove Prim Sch, Wat.
WD25 off Fourth Av 98 BX35
Berryhill, SE9 187 EP84
Berry Hill, Stan. HA7 117 CK49
Taplow SL6 152 AD71
Berry Hill Ct, Tap. SL6 152 AD71
Berryhill Gdns, SE9 187 EP84
BERRYLANDS, Surb. KT5 220 CM99
⇌ Berrylands 220 CN98
Berrylands, SW20 221 CW97
Orpington BR6 228 EW104
Surbiton KT5 220 CN99
Berrylands Rd, Surb. KT5 220 CM100
Berry La, SE21 204 DR91
Hersham KT12
off Burwood Rd 236 BX106
Rickmansworth WD3 114 BH46
Berryman Cl, Dag. RM8
off Bennetts Castle La 148 EW62
Berrymans La, SE26 205 DX91
Berrymead, Hem.H. HP2 62 BM19
Berry Meade, Ashtd. KT21 254 CM117
Berry Meade Cl, Ashtd. KT21
off Berry Meade 254 CM117
Berrymead Gdns, W3 160 CQ74
Sch Berrymede Inf Sch, W3
off Park Rd N 180 CP75
Sch Berrymede Jun Sch, W3
off Osborne Rd 180 CP75
Berrymede Rd, W4 180 CR76
Berry Pl, EC1 19 H3
Berryscroft Ct, Stai. TW18 196 BJ94
Berryscroft Rd, Stai. TW18 196 BJ94
BERRY'S GREEN, West. TN16 261 EP116
Berry's Grn Rd, Berry's Grn
TN16 261 EP116
Berry's Hill, Berry's Grn TN16 261 EP115
Berry's La, Byfleet KT14 234 BK111
Berry St, EC1 19 H4
Berry Wk, Ashtd. KT21 254 CM119
Berry Way, W5 180 CL76
Rickmansworth WD3 114 BH45
Bersham La, Bad.Dene RM17 192 FZ77
Bertal Rd, SW17 202 DD91
Bertelli Pl, Felt. TW13 197 BV88
Berther Rd, Horn. RM11 150 FK59
Berthold Ms, Wal.Abb. EN9 89 EB33
Berthon St, SE8 46 B4
Bertie Rd, NW10 161 CU65
SE26 205 DX93
Bertram Cotts, SW19 202 DA94
Bertram Rd, NW4 141 CU58
Enfield EN1 104 DU42
Kingston upon Thames KT2 200 CN94
Bertram St, N19 143 DH61
Bertram Way, Enf. EN1 104 DT42
Bertrand St, SE13 46 C10
Bertrand Way, SE28 168 EV73
Bert Rd, Th.Hth. CR7 224 DQ99
Berwick Av, Hayes UB4 158 BX72
Slough SL1 153 AP73
Berwick Cl, Beac. HP9 111 AP54
Stanmore HA7 117 CF51
Twickenham TW2 198 CA87
Waltham Cross EN8 89 EA34
Berwick Cres, Sid. DA15 207 ES86
Berwick Gdns, Sutt. SM1 222 DC104
Berwick La, Stanfd.Riv. CM5 109 FF36
Berwick Pl, Welw.G.C. AL7 51 CX12
Berwick Pond Cl, Rain. RM13 170 FK68
Berwick Pond Rd, Rain. RM13 170 FL68
Upminster RM14 170 FM66
Berwick Rd, E16 24 C9
N22 121 DP53
Borehamwood WD6 100 CM38
Rainham RM13 170 FK68
Welling DA16 188 EV81
Berwick St, W1 17 N9
Berwick Way, Orp. BR6 228 EU102
Sevenoaks TN14 279 FH121
Berwyn Av, Houns. TW3 178 CB81
Berwyn Rd, SE24 203 DP88
Richmond TW10 180 CP84
Beryl Av, E6 25 H6
Beryl Ho, SE18 off Spinel Cl 187 ET78
Beryl Rd, W6 38 C1
Berystede, Kings.T. KT2 200 CP94
Besant Ct, N1 9 M3
Besant Pl, SE22
off Hayes Gro 184 DT84
Besant Rd, NW2 141 CY63
Besant Wk, N7
off Newington Barrow Way 143 DM61
Besant Way, NW10 140 CQ64
Besley St, SW16 203 DJ93
Bessant Dr, Rich. TW9 180 CP81
Bessborough Gdns, SW1 29 P10
Bessborough Pl, SW1 29 N10
Bessborough Rd, SW15 201 CU88
Harrow HA1 139 CD60
Bessborough St, SW1 29 N10
BESSELS GREEN, Sev. TN13 278 FC124
Bessels Grn Rd, Sev. TN13 278 FD123
Bessels Meadow, Sev. TN13 278 FD124
Bessels Way, Sev. TN13 278 FC124
Bessemer Cl, Slou. SL3 175 AZ78
Sch Bessemer Gra Prim Sch,
SE5 off Dylways 184 DR84
Bessemer Rd, SE5 43 K9
Welwyn Garden City AL7,
AL8 51 CY05
Bessie Lansbury Cl, E6 25 L9
Bessingby Rd, Ruis. HA4 137 BU61
Bessingham Wk, SE4
off Aldersford Cl 205 DX85
Besson St, SE14 45 H6
Bessy St, E2 21 H2
Bestobell Rd, Slou. SL1 153 AQ72
Bestwood St, SE8 33 K9
Beswick Ms, NW6 5 M3
Betam Rd, Hayes UB3 177 BR75
Beta Pl, SW4 off Santley St 183 DM84
Beta Rd, Chobham GU24 232 AT110
Woking GU22 249 BB116
Beta Way, Egh. TW20 215 BC95
BETCHWORTH, RH3 270 CR134
⇌ Betchworth 270 CR132
Betchworth Cl, Sutt. SM1
off St. Barnabas Rd 240 DD106
Betchworth Fort Pk, Tad. KT20 270 CP131
Betchworth Rd, Ilf. IG3 147 ES61
Betchworth Way, New Adgtn
CR0 243 EC109
Betenson Av, Sev. TN13 278 FF122
Betham Rd, Grnf. UB6 159 CD69
Bethany Cl, Horn. RM12 150 FJ61
Bethany Pl, Wok. GU21 248 AX118
Bethany Waye, Felt. TW14 197 BS87
Bethecar Rd, Har. HA1 139 CE57
Bethell Av, E16 23 L4
Ilford IG1 147 EN59
Bethel Rd, Sev. TN13 279 FJ123
Welling DA16 188 EW83
Bethersden Cl, Beck. BR3 205 DZ94
Sch Beth Jacob Gram Sch for Girls,
NW4 off Stratford Rd 141 CX56
H Bethlem Royal Hosp, Beck.
BR3 225 EA101
BETHNAL GREEN, E2 20 E2
⇌ Bethnal Green 20 E4
⊖ Bethnal Green 20 G3
Bethnal Grn Est, E2 20 G3
Bethnal Grn Rd, E1 20 A4
E2 20 A4
Sch Bethnal Grn Tech Coll, E2 20 B3
Sch Beths Gram Sch, Bex.
DA5 off Hartford Rd 209 FB86
Bethune Av, N11 120 DF49
Bethune Rd, N16 144 DR59
NW10 160 CR70
Bethwin Rd, SE5 43 H4
Betjeman Cl, Chsht EN7
off Rosedale Way 88 DU28
Coulsdon CR5 257 DM117
Pinner HA5 138 CA56
Betjeman Ct, West Dr. UB7 156 BK74
Betjeman Gdns, Chorl. WD3 95 BD42
Betjeman Way, Hem.H. HP1 62 BH18
Betley Ct, Walt. KT12 217 BV104
Betony Cl, Croy. CR0
off Primrose La 225 DX102
Betony Rd, Rom. RM3 128 FJ51
Betoyne Av, E4 124 EE49
BETSHAM, Grav. DA13 212 FY91
Betsham Rd, Erith DA8 189 FF80
Southfleet DA13 211 FX92
Swanscombe DA10 212 FY87
Betstyle Rd, N11 121 DH49
Betterton Dr, Sid. DA14 208 EY89
Betterton Rd, Rain. RM13 169 FE69
Betterton St, WC2 18 A9
Bettles Cl, Uxb. UB8 156 BJ68
Bettoney Vere, Bray SL6 172 AC75
Bettons Pk, E15 13 K9
Bettridge Rd, SW6 39 H9
Betts Cl, Beck. BR3 225 DY96
Betts La, Naze. EN9 72 EJ21
Betts Ms, E17 145 DZ58
Betts St, E1 32 E1
Betts Way, SE20 224 DV95
Long Ditton KT6 219 CH102
Sch Betty Layward Prim Sch,
N16 off Clissold Rd 144 DR62
Betula Cl, Ken. CR8 258 DR115
Betula Wk, Rain. RM13 170 FK69
Between Sts, Cob. KT11 235 BU114
Beulah Av, Th.Hth. CR7
off Beulah Rd 224 DQ96
Beulah Cl, Edg. HA8 118 CP48
Beulah Cres, Th.Hth. CR7 224 DQ96
Beulah Gro, Croy. CR0 224 DQ100
Beulah Hill, SE19 203 DP93
Sch Beulah Inf & Nurs Sch, Th.Hth.
CR7 off Furze Rd 224 DQ97
Sch Beulah Jun Sch, Th.Hth.
CR7 off Beulah Rd 224 DQ97
Beulah Path, E17
off Addison Rd 145 EB57
Beulah Rd, E17 145 EB57
SW19 201 CZ94
Epping CM16 92 EU29
Hornchurch RM12 150 FJ62
Sutton SM1 240 DA105
Thornton Heath CR7 224 DQ97
Beulah Wk, Wold. CR3 259 DY120
Beult Rd, Dart. DA1 189 FG83
Bevan Av, Bark. IG11 168 EU66
Bevan Cl, Hem.H. HP3 62 BK22
Bevan Ct, Croy. CR0 241 DN106
Bevan Hill, Chesh. HP5 76 AP29
Bevan Ho, Grays RM16
off Laird Av 192 GD75
Bevan Pk, Epsom KT17 239 CT111
Bevan Pl, Swan. BR8 229 FF98
Bevan Rd, SE2 188 EV78
Barnet EN4 102 DF42
Bevans Cl, Green. DA9 211 FW86
Bevan St, N1 9 K9
Bevan Way, Horn. RM12 150 FM63
Bev Callender Cl, SW8 41 J10
Bevenden St, N1 19 M2
Bevercote Wk, Belv. DA17
off Osborne Rd 188 EZ79
Beveridge Rd, NW10 160 CS66
Beverley Av, SW20 221 CT95
Hounslow TW4 178 BZ84
Sidcup DA15 207 ET87
Beverley Cl, N21 122 DQ46
SW11 off Maysoule Rd 182 DD84
SW13 181 CT82
Addlestone KT15 234 BK106
Broxbourne EN10 71 DY21
Chessington KT9 237 CJ105
Enfield EN1 104 DS42
Epsom KT17 239 CW111
Hornchurch RM11 150 FM59
Weybridge KT13 217 BS103
Beverley Cotts, SW15
off Kingston Vale 200 CS90
Beverley Ct, N14 121 DJ45
N20 off Farnham Cl 120 DC45
SE4 45 P10
Beverley Cres, Wdf.Grn. IG8 124 EH53
Beverley Dr, Edg. HA8 140 CP55
Beverley Gdns, NW11 141 CY59
SW13 181 CT83
Cheshunt EN7 88 DT30
Hornchurch RM11 150 FM59
St. Albans AL4 65 CK16
Stanmore HA7 117 CG53
Welwyn Garden City AL7 52 DC09
Wembley HA9 140 CM60
Worcester Park KT4
off Green La 221 CU102
Beverley Hts, Reig. RH2 272 DB132
Beverley Hyrst, Croy. CR0 224 DT103
Beverley La, SW15 201 CT90
Kingston upon Thames KT2 200 CS94
Beverley Ms, E4
off Beverley Rd 123 ED51
Beverley Path, SW13 181 CT82
Beverley Rd, E4 123 ED51
E6 24 F2
SE20 off Wadhurst Cl 224 DV96
SW13 181 CT83
W4 181 CT78
Bexleyheath DA7 189 FC82
Bromley BR2 226 EL103
Dagenham RM9 148 EY63
Kingston upon Thames KT1 219 CJ95
Mitcham CR4 223 DK98
New Malden KT3 221 CU98
Ruislip HA4 137 BU61
Southall UB2 178 BY77
Sunbury-on-Thames TW16 217 BT95
Whyteleafe CR3 258 DS116
Worcester Park KT4 221 CW103
● Beverley Trd Est, Mord.
SM4 off Garth Rd 221 CX101
Beverley Way, SW20 221 CT95
New Malden KT3 221 CT95
Beverly, NW8 16 C3
Beversbrook Rd, N19 143 DK62
Beverstone Rd, SW2 203 DM85
Thornton Heath CR7 223 DN98
Beverston Ms, W1 16 E7
Bevil Ct, Hodd. EN11
off Molesworth 55 EA14
Bevill Allen Cl, SW17 202 DF92
Bevill Cl, SE25 224 DU97
Bevin Cl, SE16 33 L2
Bevin Ct, WC1 18 D2
Bevington Path, SE1
off Tanner St 32 A5
Sch Bevington Prim Sch, W10 14 F6
Bevington Rd, W10 14 F6
Beckenham BR3 225 EB96
Bevington St, SE16 32 D5
Bevin Rd, Hayes UB4 157 BU69
Bevin Sq, SW17 202 DF90
Bevin Way, WC1 18 E2
Bevis Cl, Dart. DA2 210 FQ87
Bevis Marks, EC3 19 P8
Bewcastle Gdns, Enf. EN2 103 DL42
Bew Ct, SE22 off Lordship La 204 DU87
Bewdley St, N1 8 E6
Bewick Ms, SE15 44 E5
Bewick St, SW8 41 K9
Bewley Cl, Chsht EN8 89 DX31
Bewley St, E1 20 F10
SW19 202 DC93
Bewlys Rd, SE27 203 DP92
Bexhill Cl, Felt. TW13 198 BY89
Bexhill Dr, Grays RM17 192 FY79
Bexhill Rd, N11 121 DK50
SE4 205 DZ87
SW14 180 CQ83
Bexhill Wk, E15 13 K9
BEXLEY, DA5 208 FA86
⇌ Bexley 208 FA88
Coll Bexley Cen for Music & Dance,
Sid. DA15 off Station Rd 208 EU90
Bexley Cl, Dart. DA1 209 FE85
Coll Bexley Coll, Holly Hill Campus,
Belv. DA17 off Holly Hill Rd 189 FB78
Sidcup Campus, Sid.
DA14 off Main Rd 207 ET91
Tower Rd Campus, Belv.
DA17 off Tower Rd 189 FC77
Bexley Gdns, N9 122 DR48
Chadwell Heath RM6 148 EV57
Sch Bexley Gram Sch, Well. DA16
off Danson La 188 EV84
BEXLEYHEATH, DA6 & DA7 208 EZ85
⇌ Bexleyheath 188 EY82
Sch Bexleyheath Sch, Bexh.
DA6 off Graham Rd 188 FA83
Bexley High St, Bex. DA5 208 FA87
Bexley La, Dart. DA1 209 FE85
Sidcup DA14 208 EW90
Bexley Rd, SE9 207 EP85
Erith DA8 189 FC80
Bexley St, Wind. SL4 173 AQ81
Beyers Gdns, Hodd. EN11 55 EA14
Beyers Prospect, Hodd. EN11 55 EA13
Beyers Ride, Hodd. EN11 55 EA13
Beynon Rd, Cars. SM5 240 DF106
Bézier Apts, EC1 19 M4
Bianca Ct, NW7
off Marchant Cl 118 CS51
Bianca Rd, SE15 44 C3
Bibsworth Rd, N3 119 CZ54
Bibury Cl, SE15 43 P3
Bicester Rd, Rich. TW9 180 CN83
Bickenhall St, W1 16 F6
Bickersteth Rd, SW17 202 DF93
Bickerton Rd, N19 143 DJ61
BICKLEY, Brom. BR1 227 EM97
⇌ Bickley 226 EL97
Bickley Cres, Brom. BR1 226 EL98
Bickley Pk Rd, Brom. BR1 226 EL97
Sch Bickley Pk Sch, Nurs &
Pre-Prep, Brom. BR1
off Page Heath La 226 EK97
Sch Bickley Prim Sch, Brom.
BR1 off Nightingale La 226 EJ96
Bickley Rd, E10 145 EB59
Bromley BR1 226 EK96
Bickley St, SW17 202 DE92
Bicknell Cl, Guil. GU1 264 AW133
Bicknell Rd, SE5 184 DQ83
Bickney Way, Fetch. KT22 252 CC122
Bicknoller Cl, Sutt. SM2 240 DB110
Bicknoller Rd, Enf. EN1 104 DT39
Bicknor Rd, Orp. BR6 227 ES101
Bidborough Cl, Brom. BR2 226 EF99
Bidborough St, WC1 18 A3
Biddenden Way, SE9 207 EN91
Istead Rise DA13 212 GE94
Biddenham Turn, Wat. WD25 98 BW35
Bidder St, E16 23 J6
Biddestone Rd, N7 8 C1
Biddles Cl, Slou. SL1 153 AL74
Biddulph Rd, W9 15 L3
South Croydon CR2 242 DQ109
Bideford Av, Perivale UB6 159 CH68
Bideford Cl, Edg. HA8 118 CN53
Feltham TW13 198 BZ90
Romford RM3 128 FJ53
Bideford Gdns, Enf. EN1 122 DS45
Bideford Rd, Brom. BR1 206 EF90
Enfield EN3 105 DZ38
Ruislip HA4 137 BV62
Welling DA16 188 EV80
Bideford Spur, Slou. SL2 153 AP69
Bidhams Cres, Tad. KT20 255 CW121
Bidwell Gdns, N11 121 DJ52
Bidwell St, SE15 44 F7
★ Big Ben (The Clock Tower),
SW1 30 B5
Bigbury Cl, N17 122 DS52
Big Common La, Bletch. RH1 273 DP133
Biggerstaff Rd, E15 12 E8
Biggerstaff St, N4 143 DN61
Biggin Av, Mitch. CR4 222 DF95
BIGGIN HILL, West. TN16 260 EH116
Biggin Hill, SE19 203 DP94
● Biggin Hill Business Pk,
West. TN16 260 EK115
Biggin Hill Cl, Kings.T. KT2 199 CJ92
Sch Biggin Hill Prim Sch, Bigg.H.
TN16 off Old Tye Av 260 EL116
Biggin La, Grays RM16 193 GH79
Biggin Way, SE19 203 DP94
Bigginwood Rd, SW16 203 DP94
Biggs Gro Rd, Chsht EN7 88 DR27
Biggs Row, SW15
off Felsham Rd 181 CX83
Biggs Sq, E9 off Felstead St 11 P5
Big Hill, E5 144 DV60
Sch Bigland Grn Prim Sch, E1 20 E9
Bigland St, E1 20 E9
Bignell Rd, SE18 187 EP78
Jct Bignell's Cor, S.Mimms EN6 85 CU34
Bignold Rd, E7 13 P1
Bigwood Rd, NW11 142 DB57
Biko Cl, Uxb. UB8
off Sefton Way 156 BJ72
Billet Cl, Rom. RM6 148 EX55
Billet La, Berk. HP4 60 AU18
Hornchurch RM11 150 FK60
Iver SL0 155 BB69
Slough SL3 155 BB73
Billet Rd, E17 123 DX54
Romford RM6 148 EV55
Staines-upon-Thames TW18 196 BG90
Billets Hart Cl, W7 179 CE75
● Billet Wks, E17 123 DZ53
Bill Faust Ho, E1
off Tarling St 20 G9
Bill Hamling Cl, SE9 207 EM89
Billingford Cl, SE4 185 DX84
Billing Pl, SW10 39 M4
Billing Rd, SW10 39 M4
Billings Cl, Dag. RM9
off Ellerton Rd 168 EW66
🔒 Billingsgate Mkt, E14 34 D2
Billing St, SW10 39 M4
Billington Ms, W3
off High St 160 CP74
Billington Rd, SE14 45 J5
Billinton Hill, Croy. CR0 224 DR103
Billiter Sq, EC3 19 P10
Billiter St, EC3 19 P9
Bill Nicholson Way, N17
off High Rd 122 DT52
Billockby Cl, Chess. KT9 238 CM107
Billson St, E14 34 F9
Billy Lows La, Pot.B. EN6 86 DA31
Bilsby Gro, SE9 206 EK91
Bilton Cl, Poyle SL3 175 BE82
Bilton Rd, Erith DA8 189 FG80
Perivale UB6 159 CH67
Bilton Twrs, W1
off Great Cumberland Pl 16 F9
Bilton Way, Enf. EN3 105 DY39
Hayes UB3 177 BV75
Bina Gdns, SW5 27 N9
Bincote Rd, Enf. EN2 103 DM41
Binden Rd, W12 181 CT76
Bindon Grn, Mord. SM4 222 DB98
Binfield Rd, SW4 42 B7
Byfleet KT14 234 BL112
South Croydon CR2 242 DT106
Bingfield St, N1 8 B8
Bingham Cl, Hem.H. HP1 61 BF18
South Ockendon RM15 171 FV72
Bingham Ct, N1 9 H6
Bingham Dr, Stai. TW18 196 BK94
Woking GU21 248 AT118
Bingham Pl, W1 16 G6
Bingham Pt, SE18 37 P9
Bingham Rd, Burn. SL1 152 AG71
Croydon CR0 224 DU102
Bingham St, N1 9 L4
Bingley Rd, E16 24 C8
Greenford UB6 158 CC71
Hoddesdon EN11 71 EC17
Sunbury-on-Thames TW16 197 BU94
Binley Ho, SW15
off Highcliffe Dr 201 CU86
Binne Ho, SE1 off Bath Ter 31 J7
Binney St, W1 17 H10
Binnie Rd, Dart. DA1 190 FM82
Binns Rd, W4 180 CS78
Binns Ter, W4 off Binns Rd 180 CS78
Binscombe Cres, Gdmg. GU7 280 AS144
Binsey Wk, SE2 168 EW74
Binstead Cl, Hayes UB4 158 BY71
Binyon Cres, Stan. HA7 117 CF50
Birbetts Rd, SE9 207 EM89
Birchall La, Cole Grn SG14 52 DF12
Birchall Wd, Welw.G.C. AL7 52 DC10
Bircham Path, SE4
off Aldersford Cl 205 DX85
Birchanger Rd, SE25 224 DU99
Birch Av, N13 122 DQ48
Caterham CR3 258 DR124
Leatherhead KT22 253 CF120
West Drayton UB7 156 BM72
Birch Circle, Gdmg. GU7 280 AT143
Birch Cl, E16 23 K6
N19 143 DJ61
SE15 44 D9
Amersham HP6 77 AS37
Banstead SM7 239 CY114
Brentford TW8 179 CH80
Buckhurst Hill IG9 124 EK48
Eynsford DA4 230 FK104
Hounslow TW3 179 CD83
Iver SL0 155 BD68
New Haw KT15 234 BK109
Romford RM7 149 FB55
Send GU23 265 BF124
Sevenoaks TN13 279 FH123
South Ockendon RM15 171 FX69
Teddington TW11 199 CG92
Woking GU21 248 AW119
Birch Copse, Brick.Wd AL2 82 BY30
Birch Ct, Nthwd. HA6
off Rickmansworth Rd 115 BQ51
Rom. RM6 148 EW58
Welwyn Garden City AL7 52 DA12
Birch Cres, Horn. RM11 150 FL56
South Ockendon RM15 171 FX69
Uxbridge UB10 156 BM67
Birchcroft Cl, Chaldon CR3 274 DQ125
Birchdale, Ger.Cr. SL9 134 AX60
Birchdale Cl, W.Byf. KT14 234 BJ111
Birchdale Gdns, Rom. RM6 148 EX59
Birchdale Rd, E7 146 EJ64
Birchdene Dr, SE28 188 EU75
Birchdown Ho, E3 22 C3
Birch Dr, Hat. AL10 67 CU19
Maple Cross WD3 113 BD50
Birchen Cl, NW9 140 CR61
Birchend Cl, S.Croy. CR2 242 DR107
Birchen Gro, NW9 140 CR61
Bircherley Ct, Hert. SG14
off Priory St 54 DR09
🔒 Bircherley Grn Shop Cen, Hert.
SG14 off Green St 54 DR09
Bircherley St, Hert. SG14 54 DR09
Birches, The, E12
off Station Rd 146 EL63
N21 103 DM44
SE7 186 EH79
Beaconsfield HP9 110 AH53
Brentwood CM13 130 FY48
Bushey WD23 98 CC43
East Horsley KT24 267 BS126
Hemel Hempstead HP3 61 BF23
North Weald Bassett CM16 93 FB26
Orpington BR6 245 EN105
Swanley BR8 229 FE96
Waltham Abbey EN9
off Honey La 90 EF34
Woking GU22
off Heathside Rd 249 AZ118
Birches Cl, Epsom KT18 254 CS115
Mitcham CR4 222 DF97
Pinner HA5 138 BY57
Birches La, Goms. GU5 283 BQ141
Birchfield, N.Stfd RM16 171 FX74
Birchfield Cl, Add. KT15 234 BH105
Coulsdon CR5 257 DM116
Birchfield Gro, Epsom KT17 239 CW110
Birchfield Rd, Chsht EN8 88 DV29
Birchfield St, E14 22 A10
Birch Gdns, Amer. HP7 77 AS39
Dagenham RM10 149 FC62
Birchgate Ms, Tad. KT20
off Bidhams Cres 255 CW121
BIRCH GREEN, Hert. SG14 53 DJ11
Birch Grn, NW9 off Clayton Fld 118 CS52
Hemel Hempstead HP1 61 BF19
Hertford SG14 53 DJ12
Staines-upon-Thames TW18 196 BG91
Birch Gro, E11 146 EE62
SE12 206 EF87
W3 160 CN74
Cobham KT11 236 BW114
Kingswood KT20 255 CY124
Potters Bar EN6 86 DA32
Shepperton TW17 217 BS96
Slough SL2 153 AP71
Welling DA16 188 EU84
Windsor SL4 173 AK81
Woking GU22 249 BD115
Birchgrove Ho, Rich. TW9 180 CP80
Birch Hill, Croy. CR0 243 DX106
Birchington Cl, Bexh. DA7 189 FB81
Orpington BR5
off Hart Dyke Rd 228 EW102
Birchington Ho, E5 10 E2
Birchington Rd, N8 143 DK58
NW6 5 K8
Surbiton KT5 220 CM101
Windsor SL4 173 AN82
Birchin La, EC3 19 M9
Birchlands Av, SW12 202 DF87
Birch La, Flaun. HP3 79 BB33
Purley CR8 241 DL111
Birch Leys, Hem.H. HP2
off Hunters Oak 63 BQ15

Birchmead, Orp. BR6 227 EN103
Watford WD17 97 BT38
Birchmead Av, Pnr. HA5 138 BW56
Birchmead Cl, St.Alb. AL3 65 CD17
● Birchmere Business Pk, SE28 188 EU75
Birchmere Row, SE3 47 M9
Birchmore Wk, N5 144 DQ62
Birch Pk, Har. HA3 116 CC52
Birch Pl, Green. DA9 211 FS86
Birch Rd, Felt. TW13 198 BX92
Godalming GU7 280 AT143
Romford RM7 149 FB55
Birch Row, Brom. BR2 227 EN101
Birch Tree Av, W.Wick. BR4 244 EF106
Birch Tree Gro, Ley Hill HP5 78 AV30
Birch Tree Wk, Wat. WD17 97 BT37
Birch Tree Way, Croy. CR0 224 DV103
Birch Vale, Cob. KT11 236 CA112
Birch Vw, Epp. CM16 92 EV29
Birch Wk, Borwd. WD6 100 CN39
Erith DA8 189 FC79
Ilf. IG3 off Craigen Gdns 147 ES63
Mitcham CR4 223 DH95
West Byfleet KT14 234 BG112
Birch Way, Chesh. HP5 76 AR29
Hatfield AL10 off Crawford Rd 67 CV16
Birchway, Hayes UB3 157 BU74
Birch Way, Lon.Col. AL2 83 CK27
Redhill RH1 289 DH136
Warlingham CR6 259 DY118
BIRCHWOOD, Hat. AL10 67 CU16
Birchwood, Shenley WD7 84 CN34
Waltham Abbey EN9 off Roundhills 90 EE34
Birchwood Av, N10 142 DG55
Beckenham BR3 225 DZ98
Hatfield AL10 67 CU16
Sidcup DA14 208 EV89
Wallington SM6 222 DG104
Sch Birchwood Av Prim Sch, Hat. AL10 off Birchwood Av 67 CV16
Birchwood Cl, Gt Warley CM13 129 FW51
Hatfield AL10 67 CU16
Horley RH6 291 DH147
Morden SM4 222 DB98
Birchwood Ct, N13 121 DP50
Edgware HA8 118 CQ54
Birchwood Dr, NW3 142 DB62
Dartford DA2 209 FE91
West Byfleet KT14 234 BG112
Birchwood Gro, Hmptn. TW12 198 CA93
Birchwood La, Chaldon CR3 273 DP125
Esher KT10 237 CD110
Knockholt Pound TN14 262 EZ115
Leatherhead KT22 237 CD110
Birchwood Pk Av, Swan. BR8 229 FE97
Sch Birchwood Prim Sch, Swan. BR8 off Russett Way 229 FD95
Birchwood Rd, SW17 203 DH92
Dartford DA2 209 FE92
Petts Wood BR5 227 ER98
Swanley BR8 229 FC95
West Byfleet KT14 234 BG112
Birchwood Ter, Swan. BR8 off Birchwood Rd 229 FC95
Birchwood Way, Park St AL2 82 CB28
Birdbrook Cl, Dag. RM10 169 FC66
Hutton CM13 131 GB44
Birdbrook Rd, SE3 186 EJ83
Birdcage Wk, SW1 29 M5
Harlow CM20 57 EQ14
Coll Bird Coll, Sid. DA14 off Birkbeck Rd 208 EU90
Birdcroft Rd, Welw.G.C. AL8 51 CW09
Birdham Cl, Brom. BR1 226 EL99
Birdhouse La, Downe BR6 261 EN115
Birdhurst Av, S.Croy. CR2 242 DR105
Birdhurst Gdns, S.Croy. CR2 242 DR105
Birdhurst Ri, S.Croy. CR2 242 DS106
Birdhurst Rd, SW18 182 DC84
SW19 202 DE93
South Croydon CR2 242 DS106
Birdie Way, Hert. SG13 54 DV08
Bird in Bush Rd, SE15 44 D4
Bird-in-Hand La, Brom. BR1 226 EK96
Bird-in-Hand Ms, SE23 off Dartmouth Rd 204 DW89
Bird-in-Hand Pas, SE23 off Dartmouth Rd 204 DW89
Bird in Hand Yd, NW3 5 P1
Bird La, Gt Warley CM13 151 FX55
Harefield UB9 114 BJ54
Upminster RM14 151 FR57
Birds Cl, Welw.G.C. AL7 52 DB11
Birds Fm Av, Rom. RM5 127 FB53
Birdsfield La, E3 11 N8
Birds Hill Dr, Oxshott KT22 237 CD113
Birds Hill Ri, Oxshott KT22 237 CD113
Birds Hill Rd, Oxshott KT22 237 CD112
Bird St, W1 17 H9
Birdswood Dr, Wok. GU21 248 AS119
Bird Wk, Twick. TW2 198 BZ88
Birdwood Av, Dart. DA1 190 FM82
SE13 205 ED86
Birdwood Cl, S.Croy. CR2 243 DX111
Teddington TW11 199 CE91
Birfield Rd, Loud. HP10 110 AC53
⇌ Birkbeck 224 DW97
Tram Birkbeck 224 DW97
Birkbeck Av, W3 160 CQ73
Greenford UB6 158 CC67
Uni Birkbeck Coll, Main Bldg, WC1 17 P5
Clore Management Cen, WC1 17 P5
Gordon Ho & Ingold Laboratories, WC1 17 N4
Gordon Sq, WC1 17 P4
Russell Sq, WC1 17 P6
Birkbeck Gdns, Wdf.Grn. IG8 124 EF47
Birkbeck Gro, W3 180 CR75
Birkbeck Hill, SE21 203 DP89
Birkbeck Ms, E8 10 A3
W3 160 CR74
Birkbeck Pl, SE21 204 DQ88
Sch Birkbeck Prim Sch, Sid. DA14 off Alma Rd 208 EV90
Birkbeck Rd, E8 10 A3
N8 143 DL56
N12 120 DC50
Birkbeck Rd, N17 122 DT53
NW7 119 CT50
SW19 202 DB92
W3 160 CR74
W5 179 CJ77
Beckenham BR3 224 DW96
Enfield EN2 104 DR39
Hutton CM13 131 GD44
Ilford IG2 147 ER57
Romford RM7 149 FD60
Sidcup DA14 208 EU90
Birkbeck St, E2 20 F3
Birkbeck Way, Grnf. UB6 158 CC67
Birkdale Av, Pnr. HA5 138 CA55
Romford RM3 128 FM52
Birkdale Cl, SE16 44 E1
SE28 168 EX72
Orpington BR6 227 ER101
Birkdale Gdns, Croy. CR0 243 DX105
Watford WD19 116 BX48
Birkdale Rd, SE2 188 EU77
W5 160 CL70
Birkenhead Av, Kings.T. KT2 220 CM96
Birkenhead St, WC1 18 B2
Birken Ms, Nthwd. HA6 115 BP50
Birkett Way, Ch.St.G. HP8 94 AX41
Birkhall Rd, SE6 205 ED88
Birkheads Rd, Reig. RH2 272 DA133
Birklands La, St.Alb. AL1 83 CH25
Birkwood Cl, SW12 203 DK87
Birley Rd, N20 120 DC47
Slough SL1 153 AR72
Birley St, SW11 40 G9
Birling Rd, Erith DA8 189 FD80
Birnam Cl, Send M. GU23 250 BG124
Birnam Rd, N4 143 DM61
Birnbeck Cl, NW11 141 CZ57
Birnbeck Ct, NW11 off Finchley Rd 141 CZ57
Birrell Ho, SW9 42 C9
Birse Cres, NW10 140 CS63
Birstall Grn, Wat. WD19 116 BX49
Birstall Rd, N15 144 DS57
Birtley Path, Borwd. WD6 100 CL39
Biscayne Av, E14 34 F1
Biscay Rd, W6 38 C1
Biscoe Cl, Houns. TW5 178 CA79
Biscoe Way, SE13 185 ED83
Bisenden Rd, Croy. CR0 224 DS103
Bisham Cl, Cars. SM5 222 DF102
Bisham Gdns, N6 142 DG60
Bishop Butt Cl, Orp. BR6 227 ET104
Bishop Cen, Tap. SL6 152 AF72
Sch Bishop Challoner Cath Collegiate Sch, E1 21 H9
Sch Bishop Challoner Sch, Short. BR2 off Bromley Rd 225 ED96
Sch Bishop David Brown Sch, The, Sheer. GU21 off Albert Dr 233 BD113
Sch Bishop Douglass Sch, N2 off Hamilton Rd 142 DC55
Bishop Duppa's Pk, Shep. TW17 217 BR101
Bishop Fox Way, W.Mol. KT8 218 BZ98
Sch Bishop Gilpin C of E Prim Sch, SW19 off Lake Rd 201 CZ92
Sch Bishop John Robinson Prim Sch, SE28 off Hoveton Rd 168 EW73
Sch Bishop Justus C of E Sch, Brom. BR2 off Magpie Hall La 226 EL101
Bishop Ken Rd, Har. HA3 117 CF54
Bishop Kings Rd, W14 26 F8
Sch Bishop Perrin C of E Prim Sch, Whitton TW2 off Hospital Br Rd 198 CB88
Bishop Ramsey Cl, Ruis. HA4 137 BT59
Sch Bishop Ramsey C of E Sch, Ruis. HA4 off Hume Way 137 BU59
Sch Bishop Ridley C of E Prim Sch, Well. DA16 off Northumberland Av 187 ES84
Bishop Rd, N14 121 DH45
Bishop's Av, E13 166 EH67
SW6 38 D8
Bishops Av, Brom. BR1 226 EJ96
Elstree WD6 100 CM43
Northwood HA6 115 BS49
Romford RM6 148 EW58
Bishops Av, The, N2 142 DD59
Bishops Br, W2 15 P8
Bishops Br Rd, W2 15 M9
Bishops Cl, E17 145 EB56
Bishop's Cl, N19 143 DJ62
Bishops Cl, SE9 207 EQ89
W4 180 CQ78
Barnet EN5 101 CX44
Bishop's Cl, Couls. CR5 257 DN118
Bishops Cl, Enf. EN1 off Central Av 104 DV40
Hatfield AL10 67 CT18
Richmond TW10 199 CK90
St. Albans AL4 65 CG16
Bishop's Cl, Sutt. SM1 222 DA104
Bishops Cl, Uxb. UB10 156 BN68
Bishop's Ct, EC4 18 G8
WC2 18 E8
Bishops Ct, Abb.L. WD5 81 BT31
Cheshunt EN8 off Churchgate 88 DV30
Greenhithe DA9 211 FS85
Bishops Dr, Felt. TW14 197 BR86
Northolt UB5 158 BY67
Bishops Fm Cl, Oakley Grn SL4 172 AH82
Bishopsfield, Harl. CM18 73 ES18
Sch Bishopsford Comm Sch, Mord. SM4 off Lilleshall Rd 222 DD100
Bishopsford Rd, Mord. SM4 222 DC101
Bishops Garth, St.Alb. AL4 off Bishops Cl 65 CG16
Bishopsgate, EC2 19 N9
Bishopsgate Arc, EC2 19 P7
Bishopsgate Chyd, EC2 19 N7
Coll Bishopsgate Inst, EC2 19 P7
Bishopsgate Rd, Eng.Grn TW20 194 AT90
Sch Bishopsgate Sch, Egh. TW20 off Bishopsgate Rd 194 AU90
Bishops Grn, Brom. BR1 off Upper Pk Rd 226 EJ95
Bishops Gro, N2 142 DD58
Hampton TW12 198 BZ91
Bishop's Hall, Kings.T. KT1 219 CK96
Bishops Hall Rd, Pilg.Hat. CM15 130 FV44
Sch Bishopshalt Sch, Hlgdn UB8 off Royal La 156 BM69
Sch Bishop's Hatfield Girls' Sch, Hat. AL10 off Woods Av 67 CU18
Bishops Hill, Walt. KT12 217 BU101
Bishops Ho, SW8 off South Lambeth Rd 42 B5
Bishopsmead, SE5 off Camberwell Rd 43 K5
Bishops Mead, Hem.H. HP1 62 BH22
Bishopsmead Cl, E.Hors. KT24 off Ockham Rd S 267 BS128
Epsom KT19 238 CR110
Bishopsmead Dr, E.Hors. KT24 267 BT129
Bishopsmead Par, E.Hors. KT24 off Ockham Rd S 267 BS129
Bishops Orchard, Farn.Royal SL2 153 AP69
Bishop's Pk, SW6 38 C8
Bishop's Pk Rd, SW6 38 D8
Bishops Pk Rd, SW16 223 DL95
Bishops Pl, Sutt. SM1 off Lind Rd 240 DC106
● Bishop Sq, Hat. AL10 66 CS17
Bishops Ri, Hat. AL10 67 CT22
Bishops Rd, N6 142 DG58
SW6 38 G5
Bishop's Rd, SW11 40 D4
Bishops Rd, W7 179 CE75
Croydon CR0 223 DP101
Hayes UB3 157 BQ71
Slough SL1 174 AU75
Bishops Sq, E1 19 P6
Bishops Ter, SE11 30 F8
Bishopsthorpe Rd, SE26 205 DX91
Sch Bishop Stopford's Sch, Enf. EN1 off Brick La 104 DV40
Bishop St, N1 9 J8
Bishops Wk, Chis. BR7 227 EQ95
Croydon CR0 243 DX106
Bishop's Wk, Pnr. HA5 off High St 138 BY55
Bishops Wk, Woob.Grn HP10 132 AE58
Bishops Way, E2 10 F10
Egham TW20 195 BD93
Bishops Wd, Wok. GU21 248 AT117
H Bishops Wood Hosp, Nthwd. HA6 115 BP51
Bishopswood Rd, N6 142 DF59
Sch Bishop Thomas Grant Catholic Sch, SW16 off Belltrees Gro 203 DM92
Bishop Wk, Shenf. CM15 131 FZ47
Sch Bishop Wand C of E Sch, The, Sun. TW16 off Laytons La 217 BT96
Bishop Wilfred Wd Cl, SE15 44 D8
Sch Bishop Winnington-Ingram C of E Prim Sch, Ruis. HA4 off Southcote Ri 137 BR59
Biskra, Wat. WD17 97 BU39
Bisley Cl, Wal.Cr. EN8 89 DX33
Worcester Park KT4 221 CW102
Bisley Ho, SW19 201 CX89
Bispham Rd, NW10 160 CM69
Bisson Rd, E15 12 F10
Bisterne Av, E17 145 ED55
● Bittacy Busines Cen, NW7 119 CY52
Bittacy Cl, NW7 119 CX51
Bittacy Ct, NW7 off Bittacy Hill 119 CY52
Bittacy Hill, NW7 119 CX51
Bittacy Pk Av, NW7 119 CX51
Bittacy Ri, NW7 119 CW51
Bittacy Rd, NW7 119 CX51
Bittams La, Cher. KT16 233 BE105
Bittern Cl, Chsht EN7 88 DQ25
Hayes UB4 158 BX71
Hemel Hempstead HP3 80 BM25
Bitterne Dr, Wok. GU21 248 AT117
Bittern Ho, West Dr. UB7 off Wraysbury Dr 156 BK73
Bittern Pl, N22 121 DM54
Bittern St, SE1 31 J5
Bittoms, The, Kings.T. KT1 219 CK97
Bixley Cl, Sthl. UB2 178 BZ77
Black Acre Cl, Amer. HP7 77 AS39
Blackacre Rd, They.B. CM16 107 ES37
Blackall St, EC2 19 N4
Blackberry Cl, Guil. GU1 264 AV131
Shepperton TW17 off Cherry Way 217 BS98
Blackberry Fm Cl, Houns. TW5 178 BY80
Blackberry Fld, Orp. BR5 228 EU95
Blackbird Hill, NW9 140 CQ61
Blackbirds La, Ald. WD25 99 CD35
Blackbird Yd, E2 20 B2
Blackborne Rd, Dag. RM10 168 FA65
Blackborough Cl, Reig. RH2 272 DC134
Blackborough Rd, Reig. RH2 288 DC135
Black Boy La, N15 144 DQ57
Black Boy Wd, Brick.Wd AL2 82 CA30
Blackbridge Rd, Wok. GU22 248 AX119
BLACKBROOK, Dor. RH5 286 CL141
Blackbrook La, Brom. BR1, BR2 227 EN97
Blackbrook Rd, Dor. RH5 285 CK140
Black Bull Yd, EC1 off Hatton Wall 18 E6
Blackburn, The, Bkhm KT23 off Little Bookham St 252 BZ124
Blackburne's Ms, W1 16 G10
Blackburn Rd, NW6 5 L5
● Blackburn Trd Est, Stanw. TW19 196 BM86
Blackburn Way, Houns. TW4 198 BY85
Blackbury Cl, Pot.B. EN6 86 DC31
Blackbush Av, Rom. RM6 148 EX57
Blackbush Cl, Sutt. SM2 240 DB108
Blackbush Spring, Harl. CM20 58 EU14
Black Cut, St.Alb. AL1 65 CE21
Blackdale, Chsht EN7 88 DU27
Blackdown Av, Wok. GU22 249 BE115
Blackdown Cl, N2 120 DC54
Woking GU22 249 BC116
Blackdown Ter, SE18 off Prince Imperial Rd 187 EM80
Black Eagle Cl, West. TN16 277 EQ127
Black Eagle Dr, Nthflt DA11 212 GA85
Black Eagle Sq, West. TN16 off High St 277 EQ127
Blackett Cl, Stai. TW18 215 BE96
Blackett St, SW15 181 CX83
Blacketts Wd Dr, Chorl. WD3 95 BB43
Black Fan Cl, Enf. EN2 104 DQ39
Black Fan Rd, Welw.G.C. AL7 52 DB09
BLACKFEN, Sid. DA15 207 ET87
Blackfen Par, Sid. DA15 off Blackfen Rd 208 EU86
Blackfen Rd, Sid. DA15 207 ES85
Sch Blackfen Sch for Girls, Sid. DA15 off Blackfen Rd 208 EV86
Blackford Cl, S.Croy. CR2 241 DP109
Blackford Rd, Wat. WD19 116 BX50
Blackford's Path, SW15 off Roehampton High St 201 CU87
⇌ Blackfriars 19 H10
Blackfriars Br, EC4 18 G10
SE1 18 G10
Blackfriars Ct, EC4 18 G10
⇌ Blackfriars for Bankside & South Bank 30 G1
Black Friars La, EC4 18 G10
RB Blackfriars Millennium Pier 18 F10
Blackfriars Pas, EC4 18 G10
Blackfriars Rd, SE1 30 G5
Black Gates, Pnr. HA5 off Moss La 138 BZ55
Black Grn Wd Cl, Park St AL2 82 CB29
Blackhall La, Sev. TN15 279 FK123
BLACKHEATH, SE3 47 K7
BLACKHEATH, Guil. GU4 281 BE142
★ Blackheath, SE3 47 M7
⇌ Blackheath 47 K10
Blackheath Av, SE10 47 H5
Sch Blackheath Bluecoat C of E Sch, SE3 off Old Dover Rd 186 EH80
● Blackheath Business Est, SE10 46 E7
Coll Blackheath Conservatoire of Music & The Arts, SE3 47 L10
Blackheath Gro, SE3 47 L9
Wonersh GU5 281 BB143
Sch Blackheath High Sch, Jun Dept, SE3 47 M9
Sen Dept, SE3 47 N4
Blackheath Hill, SE10 46 D7
H Blackheath Hosp, The, SE3 186 EE83
Blackheath La, Albury GU5 282 BH140
Guildford GU4, GU5 281 BD143
Sch Blackheath Nurs & Prep Sch, SE3 47 N6
BLACKHEATH PARK, SE3 186 EF84
Blackheath Pk, SE3 47 M10
Blackheath Ri, SE13 46 E9
Blackheath Rd, SE10 46 C6
Blackheath Vale, SE3 47 K8
Blackheath Village, SE3 47 L9
Blackhills, Esher KT10 236 CA109
Blackhorse Av, Chesh. HP5 76 AR33
Blackhorse Cl, Amer. HP6 77 AS38
Black Horse Cl, Wind. SL4 173 AK82
Black Horse Ct, SE1 31 M6
Blackhorse Cres, Amer. HP6 77 AS38
Tram Blackhorse Lane 224 DU101
Blackhorse La, E17 145 DX55
Croydon CR0 224 DU101
North Weald Bassett CM16 93 FD25
Reigate RH2 272 DB129
South Mimms EN6 84 CS30
● Blackhorse Ms, E17 off Blackhorse La 145 DX55
Black Horse Pl, Uxb. UB8 off Waterloo Rd 156 BJ67
⇌ Blackhorse Road 145 DX56
⊖ Blackhorse Road 145 DX56
Jct Blackhorse Rd, E17 145 DX56
Blackhorse Rd, E17 145 DX56
SE8 45 M2
Sidcup DA14 208 EU91
Woking GU22 248 AS122
Blackhouse Fm, Egh. TW20 off Coldharbour La 215 BC97
Black Lake Cl, Egh. TW20 215 BA95
Blacklands Dr, Hayes UB4 157 BQ70
Blacklands Meadow, Nutfld RH1 273 DL133
Blacklands Rd, SE6 205 EC91
Blacklands Ter, SW3 28 E9
Blackley Cl, Wat. WD17 97 BT37
Black Lion Ct, Harl. CM17 58 EW11
Black Lion Hill, Shenley WD7 84 CL32
Black Lion La, W6 181 CU77
Black Lion Ms, W6 off Black Lion La 181 CU77
Blackmans Cl, Dart. DA1 210 FJ88
Blackmans La, Warl. CR6 244 EE114
Blackmead, Rvrhd TN13 278 FE121
Blackmoor La, Wat. WD18 97 BR43
Blackmore Av, Sthl. UB1 159 CD74
Blackmore Cl, Grays RM17 192 GB78
Blackmore Ct, Wal.Abb. EN9 90 EG33
Blackmore Cres, Wok. GU21 249 BB115
Blackmore Dr, NW10 160 CP66
Blackmore Rd, Buck.H. IG9 124 EL45
Blackmores, Harl. CM19 73 EP15
Blackmores Gro, Tedd. TW11 199 CG93
Blackmore Way, Uxb. UB8 156 BK65
Blackness La, Kes. BR2 244 EK109
Woking GU22 248 AY119
★ Black Park Country Pk, Slou. SL3 155 AZ67
Black Pk Rd, Slou. SL3 155 AZ68
Black Path, E10 145 DX59
Blackpond La, Slou. SL2 153 AP66
Blackpool Gdns, Hayes UB4 157 BS70
Blackpool Rd, SE15 44 E9
Black Prince Cl, Byfleet KT14 234 BM114
Jct Black Prince Interchange, Bex. DA5 209 FB86
Black Prince Rd, SE1 30 C9
SE11 30 D9
Black Rod Cl, Hayes UB3 177 BT76
Blackshaw Rd, SW17 202 DC91
Blackshots La, Grays RM16 192 GD75
Blacksmith Cl, Ashtd. KT21 254 CM119
Blacksmith La, Chilw. GU4 281 BC139
Blacksmith Row, Slou. SL3 175 BA77
Blacksmiths Cl, Gt Amwell SG12 55 EA08
Romford RM6 148 EW58
Blacksmiths Hill, S.Croy. CR2 242 DU113
Blacksmiths La, Cher. KT16 216 BG101
Denham UB9 135 BC61
Orpington BR5 228 EW99
Rainham RM13 169 FF67
St. Albans AL3 64 CB20
Staines-upon-Thames TW18 216 BH97
Blacksmiths Way, High Wych CM21 58 EU06
Blacks Rd, W6 26 A9
Blackstock Ms, N4 off Blackstock Rd 143 DP61
Blackstock Rd, N4 143 DP61
N5 143 DP61
Blackstone Cl, Red. RH1 288 DE135
Blackstone Est, E8 10 D7
Blackstone Hill, Red. RH1 288 DE135
Blackstone Ho, SW1 off Churchill Gdns 41 L1
Blackstone Rd, NW2 4 B2
Black Swan Ct, Ware SG12 off Baldock St 55 DX06
Black Swan Yd, SE1 31 N4
Black's Yd, Sev. TN13 off Bank St 279 FJ125
Blackthorn Av, West Dr. UB7 176 BN77
Blackthorn Cl, Reig. RH2 288 DC136
St. Albans AL4 65 CJ17
Watford WD25 81 BV32
Blackthorn Ct, Houns. TW5 178 BY80
Blackthorn Dell, Slou. SL3 174 AW76
Blackthorne Av, Croy. CR0 224 DW101
Blackthorne Cl, Hat. AL10 67 CT21
Blackthorne Cres, Colnbr. SL3 175 BE83
Blackthorne Dr, E4 123 ED49
Blackthorne Rd, Bigg.H. TN16 260 EK116
Bookham KT23 268 CC126
Colnbrook SL3 175 BE83
Blackthorn Gro, Bexh. DA7 188 EX83
Blackthorn Rd, Ilf. IG1 147 ER64
Reigate RH2 288 DC136
Welwyn Garden City AL7 52 DA10
Blackthorn St, E3 22 B5
Blackthorn Way, Warley CM14 130 FX50
Blacktree Ms, SW9 183 DN83
DLR Blackwall 34 F1
Blackwall La, SE10 35 K10
Blackwall Pier, E14 35 J1
● Blackwall Trd Est, E14 23 H7
Blackwall Tunnel, E14 34 G1
Blackwall Tunnel App, SE10 35 J5
Blackwall Tunnel Northern App, E3 12 B10
E14 22 E2
Blackwall Way, E14 34 F1
Blackwater Cl, E7 13 M1
Rainham RM13 169 FD71
Blackwater La, Hem.H. HP3 63 BS23
Blackwater Rd, Sutt. SM1 off High St 240 DB105
Blackwater St, SE22 204 DT85
Blackwell Cl, E5 145 DX63
N21 103 DL43
Harrow HA3 117 CD52
Blackwell Dr, Wat. WD19 98 BW44
Blackwell Gdns, Edg. HA8 118 CN48
Blackwell Hall La, Chesh. HP5 78 AW33
Blackwell Rd, Kings L. WD4 80 BN29
Blackwood Av, N18 off Harbet Rd 123 DX50
Blackwood Cl, W.Byf. KT14 234 BJ112
Blackwood Ct, Brox. EN10 off Groom Rd 89 DZ26
Blackwood St, SE17 31 L10
Blade Ct, Rom. RM7 off Oldchurch Rd 149 FE58
Blade Ms, SW15 181 CZ84
Bladen Cl, Wey. KT13 235 BR107
Blades Cl, Lthd. KT22 253 CK120
Blades Ct, SW15 181 CZ84
Bladindon Dr, Bex. DA5 208 EW87
Bladon Cl, Guil. GU1 265 BA133
Bladon Gdns, Har. HA2 138 CB58
Blagdens Cl, N14 121 DJ47
Blagdens La, N14 121 DK47
Blagdon Rd, SE13 205 EB86
New Malden KT3 221 CT98
Blagdon Wk, Tedd. TW11 199 CJ93
Blagrove Cres, Ruis HA4 137 BV58
Blagrove Rd, W10 14 F7
Blair Av, NW9 140 CS59
Esher KT10 218 CC103
Blair Cl, N1 9 K4
Hayes UB3 177 BU77
Sidcup DA15 207 ES85
Blairderry Rd, SW2 203 DL89
Blair Dr, Sev. TN13 279 FH123
Blairhead Dr, Wat. WD19 115 BV48
Blair Ho, SW9 42 C8
Sch Blair Peach Prim Sch, Sthl. UB1 off Beaconsfield Rd 158 BX74
Blair Rd, Slou. SL1 154 AS74
Blair St, E14 22 F9
Blake Apts, N8 off New River Av 143 DM55
Blake Av, Bark. IG11 167 ES67
Blakeborough Dr, Harold Wd RM3 128 FL54
Blake Cl, W10 14 B6
Carshalton SM5 222 DE101
Hayes UB4 157 BR68
Rainham RM13 169 FF67
St. Albans AL1 65 CG23
Welling DA16 187 ES81
Blakeden Dr, Clay. KT10 237 CF107
Blakefield Gdns, Couls. CR5 257 DM118
Blake Gdns, SW6 39 L6
Dartford DA1 190 FM84
Blake Hall Cres, E11 146 EG60
Blake Hall Rd, E11 146 EG59
Blakehall Rd, Cars. SM5 240 DF107
Blake Hall Rd, Ong. CM5 93 FG25
Blake Ho, Beck. BR3 205 EA93
Blakemere Rd, Welw.G.C. AL8 51 CX07
Blake Ms, Rich. TW9 off High Pk Rd 180 CN81
Blakemore Gdns, SW13 off Lonsdale Rd 181 CV79
Blakemore Rd, SW16 203 DL90
Thornton Heath CR7 223 DM99
Blakemore Way, Belv. DA17 188 EY76
Blakeney Av, Beck. BR3 225 DZ95
Blakeney Cl, E8 10 C2
N20 120 DC46
NW1 7 N7
Epsom KT19 238 CR111
Blakeney Rd, Beck. BR3 205 DZ94
Blakenham Rd, SW17 202 DF91
Blaker Ct, SE7 off Fairlawn 186 EJ80
Blake Rd, E16 23 L5
N11 121 DJ52
Croydon CR0 224 DS103
Mitcham CR4 222 DE97
Blaker Rd, E15 12 E9
Blakes Av, N.Mal. KT3 221 CT99
Blakes Ct, Saw. CM21 off Church St 58 EY05
Blake's Grn, W.Wick. BR4 225 EC102
Blakes La, E.Clan. GU4 266 BL132
New Malden KT3 221 CT99
West Horsley KT24 266 BM131
Blakesley Av, W5 159 CJ72
Blakesley Ho, E12 off Grantham Rd 147 EN62
Blakesley Wk, SW20 off Kingston Rd 221 CZ96
Blakes Rd, SE15 43 P4
Blakes Ter, N.Mal. KT3 221 CU99

Blake St, SE8 46 A2
Blakesware Gdns, N9 122 DR45
Blakes Way, Til. RM18
off Coleridge Rd 193 GJ82
Blakewood Cl, Felt. TW13 198 BW91
Blanchard Cl, SE9 206 EL90
Blanchard Dr, Wat. WD18
off Cassio Pl 97 BS42
Blanchard Gro, Enf. EN3 105 EB38
Blanchard Ms, Harold Wd RM3 128 FM52
Blanchards Hill, Guil. GU4 264 AY128
Blanchard Way, E8 10 D5
Blanch Cl, SE15 44 G5
Blanchedowne, SE5 184 DR84
Blanche La, S.Mimms EN6 85 CT34
Sch **Blanche Nevile Sch**, N10
off Burlington Rd 142 DG55
Blanche St, E16 23 L5
Blanchland Rd, Mord. SM4 222 DB99
Blanchmans Rd, Warl. CR6 259 DY118
Blandfield Rd, SW12 202 DG86
Blandford Av, Beck. BR3 225 DY96
Twickenham TW2 198 CB88
Blandford Cl, N2 142 DC56
Croydon CR0 223 DL104
Romford RM7 149 FB56
Slough SL3 174 AX76
Woking GU22 249 BB117
Blandford Ct, Slou. SL3
off Blandford Rd S 174 AX76
Blandford Cres, E4 123 EC45
Blandford Rd, W4 180 CS76
W5 179 CK75
Beckenham BR3 224 DW96
St. Albans AL1 65 CG20
Southall UB2 178 CA77
Teddington TW11 199 CD92
Blandford Rd N, Slou. SL3 174 AX76
Blandford Rd S, Slou. SL3 174 AX76
Blandford Sq, NW1 16 D5
Blandford St, W1 16 F8
Blandford Waye, Hayes UB4 158 BW72
Bland St, SE9 186 EK84
Blaney Cres, E6 25 N3
Blanford Ms, Reig. RH2 272 DD133
Blanford Rd, Reig. RH2 288 DC135
Blanmerle Rd, SE9 207 EP88
Blann Cl, SE9 206 EK86
Blantyre St, SW10 40 A4
Blantyre Twr, SW10 40 A4
Blantyre Wk, SW10
off Blantyre St 40 A4
Blashford, NW3 6 E6
Blashford St, SE13 205 ED87
Blasker Wk, E14 34 B10
Blattner Cl, Els. WD6 100 CL42
Blawith Rd, Har. HA1 139 CE56
Blaxland Ter, Chsht EN8
off Davison Dr 89 DX28
Blaydon Cl, N17 122 DV52
Ruislip HA4 137 BS59
Blaydon Wk, N17 122 DV52
Blays Cl, Eng.Grn TW20 194 AW93
Blays La, Eng.Grn TW20 194 AV94
Bleak Hill La, SE18 187 ET79
Blean Gro, SE20 204 DW94
Bleasdale Av, Perivale UB6 159 CG68
Blechynden St, W10 14 D10
Bleddyn Cl, Sid. DA15 208 EW86
Bledlow Cl, NW8 16 B5
SE28 168 EW73
Bledlow Ri, Grnf. UB6 158 CC68
Bleeding Heart Yd, EC1 18 F7
Blegberry Gdns, Berk. HP4 60 AS19
Blegborough Rd, SW16 203 DJ93
Blemundsbury, WC1
off Dombey St 18 C6
Blencarn Cl, Wok. GU21 248 AT116
Blendon Dr, Bex. DA5 208 EX86
Blendon Path, Brom. BR1
off Hope Pk 206 EF94
Blendon Rd, Bex. DA5 208 EX86
Blendon Ter, SE18 187 EQ78
Blendworth Pt, SW15
off Wanborough Dr 201 CV88
Blenheim Av, Ilf. IG2 147 EN58
Blenheim Cen, The, Houns. TW3 178 CB82
Blenheim Cen, SE20 204 DW94
Blenheim Cl, N21 122 DQ46
SE12 206 EH88
SW20 221 CW97
Dartford DA1 210 FJ86
Greenford UB6
off Leaver Gdns 159 CD68
Romford RM7 149 FC56
Sawbridgeworth CM21 58 EW07
Slough SL3 155 AZ74
Upminster RM14 151 FS60
Wallington SM6 241 DJ108
Watford WD19 116 BX45
West Byfleet KT14
off Madeira Rd 233 BF113
Blenheim Ct, N19 143 DL61
Bromley BR2 *off Durham Av* 226 EF98
Sidcup DA14 207 ER90
Sutton SM2
off Wellesley Rd 240 DC107
Waltham Cross EN8
off Eleanor Cross Rd 89 DZ34
Woodford Green IG8
off Navestock Cres 124 EJ53
Blenheim Cres, W11 14 E10
Ruislip HA4 137 BR61
South Croydon CR2 242 DQ108
Blenheim Dr, Well. DA16 187 ET81
Blenheim Gdns, NW2 4 B4
SW2 203 DM86
Aveley RM15 170 FP74
Kingston upon Thames KT2 200 CP94
South Croydon CR2 242 DU112
Wallington SM6 241 DJ107
Wembley HA9 140 CL62
Woking GU22 248 AV119
Blenheim Gro, SE15 44 B9
Sch **Blenheim High Sch**, Epsom KT19 *off Longmead Rd* 238 CR110
Blenheim Ms, Shenley WD7 84 CL33
Blenheim Pk Rd, S.Croy. CR2 242 DQ109
Blenheim Pas, NW8 5 N10
Blenheim Pl, Tedd. TW11 199 CF92
Sch **Blenheim Prim Sch**, Orp. BR6 *off Blenheim Rd* 228 EW103
Blenheim Ri, N15 144 DT56
Blenheim Rd, E6 24 E2
E15 146 EE63
E17 145 DX55
NW8 5 N10
Blenheim Rd, SE20
off Maple Rd 204 DW94
SW20 221 CW97
W4 180 CS76
Abbots Langley WD5 81 BU33
Barnet EN5 101 CX41
Bromley BR1 226 EL98
Dartford DA1 210 FJ86
Epsom KT19 238 CR111
Harrow HA2 138 CB58
Northolt UB5 158 CB65
Orpington BR6 228 EW103
Pilgrim's Hatch CM15 130 FU44
St. Albans AL1 65 CF19
Sidcup DA15 208 EW88
Slough SL3 174 AX77
Sutton SM1 222 DA104
Blenheim Sq, N.Wld Bas. CM16 92 FA27
Blenheim St, W1 17 J9
Blenheim Ter, NW8 5 N10
Blenheim Way, Islw. TW7 179 CG81
North Weald Bassett CM16 92 FA27
● **Blenheim Ct**, Welw.G.C. AL7 51 CZ08
Blenkarne Rd, SW11 202 DF86
Blenkin Cl, St.Alb. AL3 64 CC16
Bleriot Rd, Houns. TW5 178 BW80
Blessbury Rd, Edg. HA8 118 CQ53
Sch **Blessed Dominic RC Prim Sch**, NW9 *off Lanacre Av* 119 CT54
Sch **Blessed Sacrament RC Prim Sch**, N1 8 C9
Blessington Cl, SE13 185 ED83
Blessington Rd, SE13 185 ED83
Blessing Way, Bark. IG11 168 EW68
BLETCHINGLEY, Red. RH1 274 DQ132
Coll **Bletchingley Adult Ed Cen**, Bletch. RH1
off Stychens La 274 DQ133
Bletchingley Cl, Merst. RH1 273 DJ129
Thornton Heath CR7 223 DP98
Bletchingley Rd, Gdse. RH9 274 DU131
Merstham RH1 273 DJ129
Nutfield RH1 273 DN133
Bletchley Ct, N1 19 L1
Bletchley St, N1 19 K1
Bletchmore Cl, Harling. UB3 177 BR78
Bletsoe Wk, N1 9 K10
Blewbury Ho, SE2
off Yarnton Way 188 EX75
Bligh Rd, Grav. DA11 213 GG86
Bligh's Ct, Sev. TN13
off Bligh's Wk 279 FH125
Bligh's Rd, Sev. TN13
off High St 279 FJ125
Bligh's Wk, Sev. TN13 279 FH125
Blincoe Cl, SW19 201 CX89
Blinco La, Geo.Grn SL3 154 AY72
Blind La, Bans. SM7 256 DE115
Betchworth RH3 286 CQ137
High Beach IG10 106 EE40
Waltham Abbey EN9 90 EJ33
Blindman's La, Chsht EN8 89 DX30
Bliss Cres, SE13 46 D8
Blissett St, SE10 46 E6
Bliss Ho, Enf. EN1 104 DT38
Bliss Ms, W10 14 F2
Blisworth Cl, Hayes UB4 158 BY70
Blithbury Rd, Dag. RM9 168 EV65
Blithdale Rd, SE2 188 EU77
Blithfield St, W8 27 L7
Blockhouse Rd, Grays RM17 192 GC79
Blockley Rd, Wem. HA0 139 CH61
Bloemfontein Av, W12 161 CV74
Bloemfontein Rd, W12 161 CV73
Bloemfontein Way, W12
off Bloemfontein Rd 161 CV74
Blomfield Ct, SW11 40 B7
Blomfield Ms, W2 15 N7
Blomfield Rd, W9 15 N6
Blomfield St, EC2 19 M7
Blomfield Vil, W2 15 M7
Blomville Rd, Dag. RM8 148 EY62
Blondell Cl, Harm. UB7 176 BK79
Blondel St, SW11 40 G8
Blondin Av, W5 179 CJ77
Blondin St, E3 12 A10
Bloomburg St, SW1 29 M9
Bloomfield Cl, Knap. GU21 248 AS118
Bloomfield Ct, E10
off Brisbane Rd 145 EB62
Bloomfield Cres, Ilf. IG2 147 EP58
Bloomfield Pl, W1 17 K10
Bloomfield Rd, N6 142 DG58
SE18 187 EP78
Bromley BR2 226 EK99
Cheshunt EN7 88 DQ25
Kingston upon Thames KT1 220 CL98
Bloomfield Ter, SW1 29 H10
Westerham TN16 277 ES125
Bloom Gro, SE27 203 DP90
Bloomhall Rd, SE19 204 DR92
Bloom Pk Rd, SW6 38 G5
BLOOMSBURY, WC1 17 P7
Bloomsbury Cl, NW7 119 CU52
W5 160 CM73
Epsom KT19 238 CR110
Bloomsbury Ct, WC1 18 B7
Guildford GU1
off St. Lukes Sq 281 AZ135
Pinner HA5 138 BZ55
Bloomsbury Ho, SW4 203 DK86
Bloomsbury Ms, Wdf.Grn. IG8 *off Waltham Rd* 124 EL51
Bloomsbury Pl, SW18 202 DC85
WC1 18 B6
Bloomsbury Sq, WC1 18 B7
Bloomsbury St, WC1 17 P7
Bloomsbury Way, WC1 18 A8
Blore Cl, SW8 41 N7
Blore Ct, W1 17 N9
Blossom Cl, W5 180 CL75
Dagenham RM9 168 EZ67
South Croydon CR2 242 DT106
Blossom Dr, Orp. BR6 227 ET103
Sch **Blossom Ho Sch**, SW20
off The Drive 201 CW94
Blossom La, Enf. EN2 104 DQ39
Blossom St, E1 19 P6
Blossom Way, Uxb. UB10 156 BM66
West Drayton UB7 176 BN77
Blossom Waye, Houns. TW5 178 BY80
Blount St, E14 21 M8
Bloxam Gdns, SE9 206 EL85
Bloxhall Rd, E10 145 DZ60
Bloxham Cres, Hmptn. TW12 198 BZ94
Bloxworth Cl, Wall. SM6 223 DJ104
Blucher Rd, SE5 43 K5
Blucher St, Chesh. HP5 76 AP31
Blue Anchor All, Rich. TW9
off Kew Rd 180 CL84
Blue Anchor La, SE16 32 D8
West Tilbury RM18 193 GL77
Blue Anchor Yd, E1 20 C10
Blue Ball La, Egh. TW20 195 AZ92
Blue Ball Yd, SW1 29 L3
Blue Barn La, Wey. KT13 234 BN111
Bluebell Av, E12 146 EK64
Bluebell Cl, E9 10 G8
SE26 204 DT91
Hemel Hempstead HP1
off Sundew Rd 61 BE21
Hertford SG13 54 DU09
Northolt UB5 158 BZ65
Orpington BR6 227 EQ103
Park Street AL2 82 CC27
Rush Green RM7 149 FE61
Wallington SM6 223 DH102
Bluebell Ct, Wok. GU22 248 AX119
Bluebell Dr, Bedmond WD5 81 BT27
Cheshunt EN7 88 DR28
Bluebell La, E.Hors. KT24 267 BS129
Bluebell Way, Hat. AL10 51 CT14
Ilford IG1 167 EP65
Blueberry Cl, St.Alb. AL3 65 CD16
Woodford Green IG8 124 EG51
Blueberry Gdns, Couls. CR5 257 DM116
Blueberry La, Knock. TN14 262 EW116
Bluebird La, Dag. RM10 168 FA66
Bluebird Way, SE28 187 ER75
Bricket Wood AL2 82 BY30
Bluebridge Av, Brook.Pk AL9 85 CY27
Bluebridge Rd, Brook.Pk AL9 85 CY26
Blue Cedars, Bans. SM7 239 CX114
Blue Cedars Pl, Cob. KT11 236 BX112
Bluecoat Ct, Hert. SG14
off Railway St 54 DR09
Bluecoats Av, Hert. SG14 54 DR09
Bluecoat Yd, Ware SG12 55 DX06
Bluefield Cl, Hmptn. TW12 198 CA92
Sch **Blue Gate Flds Inf & Jun Schs**, E1 20 G10
Bluegates, Ewell KT17 239 CU108
Bluehouse Gdns, Oxt. RH8 276 EG128
Blue Ho Hill, St.Alb. AL3 64 CA20
Bluehouse La, Oxt. RH8 276 EG127
Bluehouse Rd, E4 124 EE48
Blue Leaves Av, Couls. CR5 257 DK121
Bluelion Pl, SE1 31 N6
Bluemans, N.Wld Bas. CM16 75 FD24
Bluemans End, N.Wld Bas. CM16 75 FD24
Blueprint Apts, SW12
off Balham Gro 203 DH87
Sch **Blue Sch, The**, Islw. TW7
off North St 179 CG83
Bluett Rd, Lon.Col. AL2 83 CK27
Bluewater 211 FU88
Bluewater Ho, SW18
off Smugglers Way 182 DB84
Bluewater Parkway, Bluewater DA9 211 FS87
Bluewater Shop Cen, Green. DA9 211 FT87
Blumfield Ct, Slou. SL1 153 AK70
Blumfield Cres, Slou. SL1 153 AK70
Blundel La, Stoke D'Ab. KT11 236 CB114
Blundell Av, Horl. RH6 290 DF148
Blundell Cl, E8 10 C2
St. Albans AL3 65 CD16
Blundell Rd, Edg. HA8 118 CR53
Blundell St, N7 8 B6
Blunden Cl, Dag. RM8 148 EW60
Blunden Dr, Slou. SL3 175 BB77
Blunesfield, Pot.B. EN6 86 DD31
Blunt Rd, S.Croy. CR2 242 DR106
Blunts Av, Sipson UB7 176 BN80
Blunts La, St.Alb. AL2 82 BW27
Blunts Rd, SE9 207 EN85
Blurton Rd, E5 11 H1
Blyth Cl, E14 34 G8
Borehamwood WD6 100 CM39
Twickenham TW1
off Grimwood Rd 199 CF86
Blythe Cl, SE6 205 DZ87
Iver SL0 155 BF72
Blythe Hill, SE6 205 DZ87
Orpington BR5 227 ET95
Blythe Hill La, SE6 205 DZ87
Blythe Hill Pl, SE23
off Brockley Pk 205 DY87
Blythe Ms, W14 26 C6
Blythe Rd, W14 26 E8
Hoddesdon EN11 71 ED19
Blythe St, E2 20 E2
Blytheswood Pl, Hem.H. HP3 62 BG23
Blytheswood Pl, SW16
off Curtis Fld Rd 203 DM91
Blythe Vale, SE6 205 DZ88
Blyth Rd, E17 145 DZ59
SE28 168 EW73
Bromley BR1 226 EF95
Hayes UB3 177 BS75
Blyth's Wf, E14 33 M1
Blythswood Rd, Ilf. IG3 148 EU60
Blyth Wk, Upmin. RM14 151 FS58
Blythway, Welw.G.C. AL7 51 CZ06
Blyth Wd Pk, Brom. BR1
off Blyth Rd 226 EF95
Blythwood Rd, N4 143 DL59
Pinner HA5 116 BX53
Blyton Cl, Beac. HP9 111 AK51
Sch **Bnois Jerusalem Sch**, N16 *off Amhurst Pk* 144 DS59
Boades Ms, NW3 *off New End* 142 DD63
Boadicea Cl, Slou. SL1 153 AK74
Boadicea St, N1 8 C9
Boakes Cl, NW9 140 CQ56
Boakes Meadow, Shore. TN14 247 FF111
Boar Cl, Chig. IG7 126 EU50
Boardman Av, E4 105 EB43
Boardman Cl, Barn. EN5 101 CY43
Board Sch Rd, Wok. GU21 249 AZ116
Boardwalk Pl, E14 34 E2
Boar Hill, Dor. RH5 285 CF142
Boarlands Cl, Slou. SL1 153 AM73
Boarlands Path, Slou. SL1
off Brook Path 153 AM73
Boar's Head Yd, Brent. TW8
off Brent Way 179 CK80
Boars Rd, Harl. CM17 58 FA14
Boatemah Wk, SW9
off Peckford Pl 42 E9
Boathouse Wk, SE15 44 B4
Richmond TW9 180 CL81
Boat Lifter Way, SE16 33 M8
Bob Anker Cl, E13 23 P2
Bobbin Cl, SW4 41 L10
Bobby Moore Way, N10 120 DF52
Bob Dunn Way, Dart. DA1 190 FJ84
Bob Marley Way, SE24
off Mayall Rd 183 DN84
Bobs La, Rom. RM1 127 FG52
Bocketts La, Lthd. KT22 253 CF124
Bockhampton Rd, Kings.T. KT2 200 CM94
Bocking St, E8 10 E8
Boddicott Cl, SW19 201 CY89
Boddington Gdns, W3 180 CN75
Bodell Cl, Grays RM16 192 GB76
Bodiam Cl, Enf. EN1 104 DR40
Bodiam Rd, SW16 203 DK94
Bodiam Way, NW10 160 CM69
Bodicea Ms, Houns. TW4 198 BZ87
Bodle Av, Swans. DA10 212 FY87
Bodley Cl, Epp. CM16 91 ET30
New Malden KT3 220 CS99
Bodley Manor Way, SW2
off Hambridge Way 203 DN87
Bodley Rd, N.Mal. KT3 220 CR100
Bodmin Av, Slou. SL2 153 AN71
Bodmin Cl, Har. HA2 138 BZ62
Orpington BR5 228 EW102
Bodmin Gro, Mord. SM4 222 DB99
Bodmin St, SW18 202 DA88
Bodnant Gdns, SW20 221 CU97
Bodney Rd, E8 10 E3
Bodwell Cl, Hem.H. HP1 61 BF19
Boeing Way, Sthl. UB2 177 BV76
Boevey Path, Belv. DA17 188 EZ79
Bogey La, Orp. BR6 245 EN108
Bognor Gdns, Wat. WD19 116 BW50
Bognor Rd, Well. DA16 188 EX81
Bohemia, Hem.H. HP2 62 BL19
Bohemia Pl, E8 10 F4
Bohn Rd, E1 21 L6
Bohun Gro, Barn. EN4 102 DE44
Boileau Par, W5
off Boileau Rd 160 CM72
Boileau Rd, SW13 181 CU80
W5 160 CM72
Bois Av, Amer. HP6 77 AP36
Bois Hall Rd, Add. KT15 234 BK105
Bois Hill, Chesh. HP5 76 AS34
Bois La, Amer. HP6 77 AR35
Bois Moor Rd, Chesh. HP5 76 AQ33
Boissy Cl, St.Alb. AL4 66 CL21
Bolberry Rd, Coll.Row RM5 127 FD50
Bolden St, SE8 46 C8
Bolderwood Way, W.Wick. BR4 225 EB103
Boldmere Rd, Pnr. HA5 138 BW59
Boleyn Av, Enf. EN1 104 DV39
Epsom KT17 239 CV110
Boleyn Cl, E17 145 EA56
Chafford Hundred RM16
off Clifford Rd 192 FZ76
Hemel Hempstead HP2
off Parr Cres 63 BQ15
Loughton IG10
off Roding Gdns 106 EL44
Staines-upon-Thames TW18
off Chertsey La 195 BE92
Boleyn Ct, Brox. EN10 71 DY21
Buckhurst Hill IG9 124 EG46
Boleyn Dr, Ruis. HA4 138 BX61
St. Albans AL1 65 CD22
West Molesey KT8 218 BZ97
Boleyn Gdns, Brwd. CM13 131 GA48
Dagenham RM10 169 FC66
West Wickham BR4 225 EB103
Boleyn Gro, W.Wick. BR4 225 EC103
Boleyn Rd, E6 166 EK68
E7 13 P7
N16 9 P3
Boleyn Row, Epp. CM16 92 EV29
Boleyn Wk, Lthd. KT22 253 CF120
Boleyn Way, Barn. EN5 102 DC41
Ilford IG6 125 EQ51
Swanscombe DA10 212 FY87
Bolina Rd, SE16 33 H10
Bolingbroke Gro, SW11 182 DE84
Bolingbroke Rd, W14 26 D6
Bolingbroke Wk, SW11 40 B5
Bolingbroke Way, Hayes UB3 157 BR74
Bolingbrook, St.Alb. AL4 65 CG16
Bolliger Ct, NW10
off Park Royal Rd 160 CQ70
Bollo Br Rd, W3 180 CP76
Bollo La, W3 180 CP75
W4 180 CQ77
Bolney Gate, SW7 28 C5
Bolney St, SW8 42 C5
Bolney Way, Felt. TW13 198 BY90
Bolsover Gro, Merst. RH1 273 DL129
Bolsover St, W1 17 K5
Bolstead Rd, Mitch. CR4 223 DH95
Bolster Gro, N22 121 DK52
Bolt Cellar La, Epp. CM16 91 ES29
Bolt Ct, EC4 18 F9
Bolters La, Bans. SM7 239 CZ114
Bolters Rd, Horl. RH6 290 DG146
Bolters Rd S, Horl. RH6 290 DF146
Boltmore Cl, NW4 141 CX55
Bolton Av, Wind. SL4 173 AQ83
Bolton Cl, SE20 *off Selby Rd* 224 DU96
Chessington KT9 237 CK107
Bolton Cres, SE5 42 F3
Windsor SL4 173 AQ83
Bolton Dr, Mord. SM4 222 DC101
Bolton Gdns, NW10 14 C1
SW5 27 L10
Bromley BR1 206 EF93
Teddington TW11 199 CG93
Bolton Gdns Ms, SW10 27 N10
Bolton Rd, E15 13 M5
N18 122 DT50
NW8 5 M9
NW10 160 CS67
W4 180 CQ80
Chessington KT9 237 CK107
Harrow HA1 138 CC56
Windsor SL4 173 AQ83
Boltons, The, SW10 27 N10
Wembley HA0 139 CF63
Woodford Green IG8 124 EG49
Boltons Cl, Wok. GU22 250 BG116
Boltons La, Harling. UB3 177 BQ80
Woking GU22 250 BG116
Boltons Pl, SW5 27 N10
Bolton St, W1 29 K2
Bolton Wk, N7 *off Durham Rd* 143 DM61
Bombay St, SE16 32 E8
★ **Bomber Command Mem**, W1 29 J4
Bombers La, West. TN16 261 ER119
Bomer Cl, Sipson UB7 176 BN80
Bomore Rd, W11 14 D10
Bonar Pl, Chis. BR7 206 EL94
Bonar Rd, SE15 44 C5
Bonaventure Ct, Grav. DA12 213 GM91
Bonchester Cl, Chis. BR7 207 EN94
Bonchurch Cl, Sutt. SM2 240 DB108
Bonchurch Rd, W10 14 E6
W13 159 CH74
Bond Cl, Iver SL0 155 BB66
Knockholt Pound TN14 262 EX115
West Drayton UB7 156 BM72
Bond Ct, EC4 19 L9
Bondfield Av, Hayes UB4 157 BU69
Bondfield Rd, E6 25 H7
Bondfield Wk, Dart. DA1 190 FM84
Bond Gdns, Wall. SM6 241 DJ105
Bonding Yd Wk, SE16 33 M5
Sch **Bond Prim Sch**, Mitch. CR4 *off Bond Rd* 222 DF96
Bond Rd, Mitch. CR4 222 DE96
Surbiton KT6 220 CM103
Warlingham CR6 259 DX118
Bonds La, Mid Holm. RH5 285 CH142
⊖ **Bond Street** 17 H9
Bond St, E15 13 J2
W4 180 CS77
W5 159 CK73
Englefield Green TW20 194 AV92
Grays RM17 192 GC79
Bondway 42 B2
Bondway, SW8 42 B3
Bonehurst Rd, Horl. RH6 288 DG144
Salfords RH1 288 DG142
Bone Mill La, Gdse. RH9
off Eastbourne Rd 275 DY134
Boneta Rd, SE18 37 J7
Bonfield Rd, SE13 185 EC84
Bonham Cl, Belv. DA17 188 EZ78
Bonham Gdns, Dag. RM8 148 EX61
Bonham Rd, SW2 203 DM85
Dagenham RM8 148 EX61
Bonham Way, Nthflt. DA11 212 GC88
Bonheur Rd, W4 180 CR75
Bonhill St, EC2 19 M5
Boniface Gdns, Har. HA3 116 CB52
Boniface Rd, Uxb. UB10 137 BP62
Boniface Wk, Har. HA3 116 CB52
Bonington Ho, Enf. EN1
off Ayley Cft 104 DU43
Bonington Rd, Horn. RM12 150 FK64
Bonita Ms, SE4 45 J10
Bonks Hill, Saw. CM21 58 EX06
Bon Marche Ter Ms, SE27
off Gipsy Rd 204 DS91
Bonner Ct, Chsht EN8
off Coopers Wk 89 DX28
Bonner Hill Rd, Kings.T. KT1 220 CM97
Sch **Bonner Prim Sch**, E2 21 H1
Bonner Rd, E2 10 G10
Bonners Cl, Wok. GU22 248 AY122
Bonnersfield Cl, Har. HA1 139 CF58
Bonnersfield La, Har. HA1 139 CG58
Bonner St, E2 21 H1
Bonner Wk, Grays RM16
off Clifford Rd 192 FZ76
Bonnett Ms, Horn. RM11 150 FL60
Bonneville Gdns, SW4 203 DJ86
Sch **Bonneville Prim Sch**, SW4
off Bonneville Gdns 203 DJ86
Bonney Gro, Chsht EN7 88 DU30
Sch **Bonneygrove Prim Sch**, Chsht EN7 *off Dark La* 88 DU30
Bonney Way, Swan. BR8 229 FE96
Bonnington Ho, N1
off Killick St 18 C1
Bonningtons, Brwd. CM13 131 GB48
Bonnington Sq, SW8 42 C2
Bonnington Twr, Brom. BR2 226 EL100
Sch **Bonnygate Prim Sch**, S.Ock. RM15 *off Arisdale Av* 171 FV71
Bonny's Rd, Reig. RH2 287 CX135
Bonny St, NW1 7 L7
Bonser Rd, Twick. TW1 199 CF89
Bonsey Cl, Wok. GU22 248 AY121
Bonsey La, Wok. GU22 248 AY121
Bonseys La, Chobham GU24 233 AZ110
Bonsor Dr, Kgswd KT20 255 CY122
Bonsor St, SE5 43 N5
Sch **Bonus Pastor Cath Coll**, Lwr Sch, Brom. BR1
off Churchdown 206 EE91
Upr Sch, Brom. BR1
off Winlaton Rd 206 EE91
Bonville Gdns, NW4
off Handowe Cl 141 CU56
Bonville Rd, Brom. BR1 206 EF92
Bookbinders' Cotts, N20
off Manor Dr 120 DF48
Booker Cl, E14 21 P7
Booker Rd, N18 122 DU50
⇌ **Bookham** 252 BZ123
Bookham Ct, Lthd. KT23
off Church Rd 252 BZ123
Mitcham CR4 222 DD97
Bookham Gro, Bkhm KT23 268 CB126
● **Bookham Ind Est**, Bkhm KT23 252 BZ123
Bookham Rd, Down. KT11 252 BW119
Book Ms, WC2 17 P9
Boone Ct, N9 122 DW48
Boones Rd, SE13 186 EE84
Boone St, SE13 186 EE84
Boord St, SE10 35 K6
Boot All, St.Alb. AL1
off Market Pl 65 CD20
Boothby Rd, N19 143 DK61
Booth Cl, E9 10 F9
SE28 168 EV73
Booth Dr, Stai. TW18 196 BK93
Booth Ho, Brent. TW8
off London Rd 179 CJ80
Booth La, EC4 19 J10
Boothman Ho, Har. HA3 139 CK55
Booth Rd, E16 36 D3
NW9 118 CS54
Croydon CR0
off Waddon New Rd 223 DP103
Booths Cl, N.Mymms AL9 67 CX24
Booth's Ct, Hutt. CM13 131 GB44
Booth's Pl, W1 17 M7
Boot St, N1 19 N3

Bordars Rd, W7 159 CE71
Bordars Wk, W7 159 CE71
Borden Av, Enf. EN1 104 DR44
Border Cres, SE26 204 DV92
Border Gdns, Croy. CR0 243 EB105
Bordergate, Mitch. CR4 222 DE95
Border Rd, SE26 204 DV92
Borderside, Slou. SL2 154 AU72
Borders La, Loug. IG10 107 EN42
Bordesley Rd, Mord. SM4 222 DB98
Bordon Wk, SW15 201 CU87
Boreas Wk, N1 19 H1
Boreham Av, E16 23 N9
Boreham Cl, E11
off Hainault Rd 145 EC60
Boreham Holt, Els. WD6 100 CM42
Boreham Rd, N22 122 DQ54
BOREHAMWOOD, WD6 100 CP41
● Borehamwood Ind Pk, Borwd. WD6 100 CR40
Borehamwood Shop Pk, Borwd. WD6 100 CN41
Borgard Rd, SE18 37 J8
Borham Ms, Hodd. EN11 55 EA13
Borkwood Pk, Orp. BR6 245 ET105
Borkwood Way, Orp. BR6 245 ES105
Borland Cl, Green. DA9
off Steele Av 211 FU85
Borland Rd, SE15 184 DW84
Teddington TW11 199 CH93
Bornedene, Pot.B. EN6 85 CY31
Borneo St, SW15 181 CW83
⊖ Borough 31 K5
Borough Gra, S.Croy. CR2 242 DU112
BOROUGH, THE, SE1 31 J5
Borough, The, Brock. RH3 286 CN135
Borough High St, SE1 31 J5
Borough Hill, Croy. CR0 223 DP104
★ Borough Mkt, SE1 31 L3
Borough Rd, SE1 30 G6
Isleworth TW7 179 CE81
Kingston upon Thames KT2 220 CN95
Mitcham CR4 222 DE96
Tatsfield TN16 260 EK121
Borough Sq, SE1 31 J5
Borough Way, Pot.B. EN6 85 CY32
Borrell Cl, Brox. EN10 71 DZ20
Borrett Cl, SE17 43 J1
Borrodaile Rd, SW18 202 DB86
Borromeo Way, Brwd. CM14 130 FV46
Borrowdale Av, Har. HA3 117 CG54
Borrowdale Cl, N2 120 DC54
Egham TW20
off Derwent Rd 195 BB94
Ilford IG4 146 EL56
South Croydon CR2 242 DT113
Borrowdale Ct, Enf. EN2 104 DQ39
Hemel Hempstead HP2 62 BL17
Borrowdale Dr, S.Croy. CR2 242 DT112
Borthwick Ms, E15 13 J1
Borthwick Rd, E15 13 J1
NW9 off West Hendon Bdy 141 CT58
Borthwick St, SE8 46 A1
Borwick Av, E17 145 DZ55
Bosanquet Cl, Uxb. UB8 156 BK70
Bosanquet Rd, Hodd. EN11 71 EC15
Bosbury Rd, SE6 205 EC90
Boscastle Rd, NW5 143 DH62
Boscobel Cl, Brom. BR1 227 EM96
Boscobel Pl, SW1 29 H8
Boscobel St, NW8 16 B5
Bosco Cl, Orp. BR6 245 ET105
Boscombe Av, E10 145 ED59
Grays RM17 192 GD77
Hornchurch RM11 150 FK60
Boscombe Circ, NW9
off Warmwell Av 118 CR54
Boscombe Cl, E5 11 L2
Egham TW20 215 BC95
Boscombe Gdns, SW16 203 DL93
Boscombe Rd, SW17 202 DG93
SW19 222 DB95
W12 161 CU74
Worcester Park KT4 221 CW102
Bose Cl, N3 119 CY53
Bosgrove, E4 123 EC46
Boshers Gdns, Egh. TW20 195 AZ93
Boss Ho, SE1 32 A4
Boss St, SE1 32 A4
Bostall Heath, SE2 188 EW78
Bostall Hill, SE2 188 EU78
Bostall La, SE2 188 EV78
Bostall Manorway, SE2 188 EV77
Bostall Pk Av, Bexh. DA7 188 EY80
Bostall Rd, Orp. BR5 208 EV94
Bostal Row, Bexh. DA7
off Harlington Rd 188 EZ83
Bostock Ho, Houns. TW5 178 CA79
Boston Gdns, W4 180 CS79
W7 179 CG77
Brentford TW8 179 CG77
Boston Gro, Ruis. HA4 137 BQ58
Slough SL1 153 AQ72
⊖ Boston Manor 179 CG77
★ Boston Manor Ho, Brent. TW8 179 CH78
Boston Manor Rd, Brent. TW8 179 CH77
Boston Pk Rd, Brent. TW8 179 CJ78
Boston Pl, NW1 16 E5
Boston Rd, E6 24 G2
E17 145 EA58
W7 159 CE74
Croydon CR0 223 DM100
Edgware HA8 118 CQ52
Bostonthorpe Rd, W7 179 CE75
Boston Vale, W7 179 CG77
Bosun Cl, E14 34 B4
Bosville Av, Sev. TN13 278 FG123
Bosville Dr, Sev. TN13 278 FG123
Bosville Rd, Sev. TN13 278 FG123
Boswell Cl, Orp. BR5
off Killewarren Way 228 EW100
Shenley WD7 84 CL32
Boswell Ct, WC1 18 B6
Boswell Path, Hayes UB3
off Croyde Av 177 BT77
Boswell Rd, Th.Hth. CR7 224 DQ98
Boswell Row, Cat. CR3
off Croydon Rd 258 DU122
Boswell St, WC1 18 B6
Bosworth Cl, E17 123 DZ53
Bosworth Ct, Slou. SL1 152 AJ73
Bosworth Cres, Rom. RM3 128 FJ51
Bosworth Ho, Erith DA8
off Saltford Cl 189 FE78
Bosworth Rd, N11 121 DK51
W10 14 F5
Barnet EN5 102 DA41
Dagenham RM10 148 FA63
BOTANY BAY, Enf. EN2 103 DK36
Botany Bay La, Chis. BR7 227 EQ97
Botany Cl, Barn. EN4 102 DE42
Botany Rd, Nthflt DA11 192 GA83
Botany Way, Purf. RM19 190 FP78
Boteley Cl, E4 123 ED47
Botery's Cross, Red. RH1 273 DP133
Botham Cl, Edg. HA8 118 CQ52
Botham Dr, Slou. SL1 174 AS76
Botha Rd, E13 24 B6
Bothwell Cl, E16 23 M7
Bothwell Rd, New Adgtn CR0 243 EC110
Bothwell St, W6 38 D3
BOTLEY, Chesh. HP5 78 AV30
Botley La, Chesh. HP5 78 AU30
Botley Rd, Chesh. HP5 78 AT30
Hemel Hempstead HP2 62 BN15
Botolph All, EC3 19 N10
Botolph La, EC3 31 M1
Botsford Rd, SW20 221 CY96
Bottom Ho Fm La, Ch.St.G. HP8 112 AT45
Bottom La, Chesh. HP5 78 AT34
Kings Langley WD4 96 BH35
Seer Green HP9 111 AP51
Bottrells Cl, Ch.St.G. HP8 112 AT47
Bottrells La, Ch.St.G. HP8 112 AT47
Coleshill HP7 111 AP46
Bott Rd, Hawley DA2 210 FM91
Botts Ms, W2 15 K9
Botts Pas, W2 15 K9
Botwell Common Rd, Hayes UB3 157 BR73
Botwell Cres, Hayes UB3 157 BS72
Botwell Ho RC Prim Sch, Hayes UB3 off Botwell La 177 BT75
Botwell La, Hayes UB3 157 BS74
Boucher Cl, Tedd. TW11 199 CF92
Boucher Dr, Nthflt DA11 213 GF90
Bouchier Wk, Rain. RM13
off Deere Av 169 FG65
Boughton Av, Brom. BR2 226 EF101
● Boughton Business Pk, Amer. HP6 94 AV39
Boughton Hall Av, Send GU23 249 BF124
Boughton Rd, SE28 187 ES76
Boughton Way, Amer. HP6 94 AW38
Boulcott St, E1 21 K9
Boulevard, The, SW6 39 P7
SW17 off Balham High Rd 202 DG89
SW18 off Smugglers Way 182 DB84
Greenhithe DA9
off Ingress Pk Av 191 FW84
Watford WD18 97 BR43
Welwyn Garden City AL7 51 CZ07
Wembley HA9
off Engineers Way 140 CN63
Woodford Green IG8 125 EN51
Boulevard Dr, NW9 119 CT54
Boulmer Rd, Uxb. UB8 156 BJ69
Boulogne Rd, Croy. CR0 224 DQ100
Boulter Cl, Brom. BR1 227 EP97
Boulter Gdns, Rain. RM13 169 FG65
Boulters Cl, Maid. SL6 152 AC70
Slough SL1
off Amerden Way 173 AN75
Boulters Ct, Maid. SL6 152 AC70
Boulters Gdns, Maid. SL6 152 AC70
Boulters La, Maid. SL6 152 AC70
Boulters Lock Island, Maid. SL6 152 AC69
Boulthurst Way, Oxt. RH8 276 EH132
Boulton Ho, Brent. TW8
off Green Dragon La 180 CL78
Boulton Rd, Dag. RM8 148 EY62
Boultwood Rd, E6 25 H9
Bounce, The, Hem.H. HP2 62 BK18
BOUNCE HILL, Rom. RM4 109 FH39
Bounces La, N9 122 DV47
Bounces Rd, N9 122 DV46
Boundaries Rd, SW12 202 DF89
Feltham TW13 198 BW88
Boundary, The, Lt.Berk. SG13 69 DJ19
Boundary Av, E17 145 DZ59
● Boundary Business Cen, Wok. GU21 249 BA115
● Boundary Business Ct, Mitch. CR4 222 DD97
Boundary Cl, SE20
off Haysleigh Gdns 224 DU96
Barnet EN5 101 CZ39
Ilford IG3 off Loxford La 147 ES63
Kingston upon Thames KT1 220 CP97
Southall UB2 178 CA78
Boundary Ct, Epp. CM16 91 ER32
N18 122 DT51
Welwyn Garden City AL7
off Boundary La 51 CZ13
Boundary Dr, Hert. SG14 54 DR07
Hutton CM13 131 GE45
Boundary La, E13 24 E3
SE17 43 K3
Welwyn Garden City AL7 51 CY12
Boundary Pk, Wey. KT13 217 BS103
Boundary Pas, E2 20 A4
Boundary Pl, Woob.Grn HP10 132 AD55
Boundary Rd, E13 24 D1
E17 145 DZ59
N9 104 DW44
N22 143 DP55
NW8 5 M9
SW19 202 DD93
Ashford TW15 196 BJ92
Barking IG11 167 EQ68
Carshalton SM5 241 DH107
Chalfont St. Peter SL9 112 AX52
High Wycombe HP10 110 AC54
Pinner HA5 138 BX58
Romford RM1 149 FG58
St. Albans AL1 65 CE18
Sidcup DA15 207 ES85
Taplow SL6 152 AE70
Upminster RM14 150 FN62
Wallington SM6 241 DH107
Wembley HA9 140 CL62
Woking GU21 249 BA116
Boundary Row, SE1 30 G4
Boundary St, E2 20 A3
Erith DA8 189 FF80
Boundary Way, Croy. CR0 243 EA106
Boundary Way, Hemel Hempstead HP2 63 BQ18
Watford WD25 81 BV32
Woking GU21 249 BA115
Boundary Yd, Wok. GU21
off Boundary Rd 249 BA116
Boundfield Rd, SE6 206 EE90
⊖ Bounds Green 121 DK51
● Bounds Grn Ind Est, N11 121 DH51
Bounds Grn Inf Sch, N11
off Bounds Grn Rd 121 DK52
Bounds Grn Jun Sch, N11
off Bounds Grn Rd 121 DL52
Bounds Grn Rd, N11 121 DJ51
N22 121 DJ51
Bourbon La, W12 26 C3
Bourchier Cl, Sev. TN13 279 FH126
Bourchier St, W1 17 N10
Bourdon Pl, W1 17 K10
Bourdon Rd, SE20 224 DW96
Bourdon St, W1 17 K10
Bourke Cl, NW10 160 CS65
SW4 203 DL86
Bourke Hill, Chipstead CR5 256 DF118
Bourlet Cl, W1 17 L7
Bourn Av, N15 144 DR56
Barnet EN4 102 DD43
Uxbridge UB8 156 BN70
Bournbrook Rd, SE3 186 EK83
Bourne, The, N14 121 DK46
Bovingdon HP3 79 BA27
Ware SG12 55 DX05
Bourne Av, N14 121 DL47
Chertsey KT16 216 BG97
Hayes UB3 177 BQ76
Ruislip HA4 138 BW64
Windsor SL4 173 AQ84
Bournebridge Cl, Hutt. CM13 131 GE45
Bournebridge La, Stap.Abb. RM4 126 EZ45
● Bourne Business Pk, Add. KT15 234 BK105
Bourne Cl, Brox. EN10 71 DZ20
Chilworth GU4 281 BB140
Isleworth TW7 179 CE83
Thames Ditton KT7 219 CF103
Ware SG12 55 DX05
West Byfleet KT14 234 BH113
Bourne Ct, Ruis. HA4 137 BV64
Bourne Dr, Mitch. CR4 222 DD96
BOURNE END, Hem.H. HP1 61 BC22
Bourne End, Horn. RM11 150 FN59
Bourne End La, Hem.H. HP1 61 BC22
● Bourne End Mills, Hem.H. HP1 61 BB22
Bourne End Rd, Maid. SL6 132 AD62
Northwood HA6 115 BS49
Bourne Est, EC1 18 E6
Bournefield Rd, Whyt. CR3
off Godstone Rd 258 DT118
Bourne Gdns, E4 123 EB49
Bourne Gro, Ashtd. KT21 253 CK119
Bournehall Av, Bushey WD23 98 CA43
Bournehall La, Bushey WD23 98 CA44
★ Bourne Hall Mus & Lib, Epsom KT17 239 CT109
Bournehall Prim Sch, Bushey WD23 off Bournehall Av 98 CB43
Bournehall Rd, Bushey WD23 98 CA44
Bourne Hill, N13 121 DL46
Bourne Hill Cl, N13
off Bourne Hill 121 DM47
● Bourne Ind Pk, Dart. DA1 209 FE85
Bourne La, Cat. CR3 258 DR121
Bourne Mead, Bex. DA5 209 FD85
Bournemead, Bushey WD23 98 CB44
Bournemead Av, Nthlt. UB5 157 BU68
Bournemead Cl, Nthlt. UB5 157 BU68
Bourne Meadow, Egh. TW20 215 BB98
Bournemead Way, Nthlt. UB5 157 BV68
Bourne Ms, Gdse. RH9 274 DW130
Bournemouth Cl, SE15 44 D9
Bournemouth Rd, SE15 44 D9
SW19 222 DA95
Bourne Pk Cl, Ken. CR8 258 DS115
Bourne Pl, W4 180 CR78
Chertsey KT16 216 BH102
Bourne Prim Sch, Ruis. HA4 off Cedar Av 158 BW65
Bourne Rd, E7 146 EF62
N8 143 DL58
Berkhamsted HP4 60 AT18
Bexley DA5 209 FB86
Bromley BR2 226 EK98
Bushey WD23 98 CA43
Dartford DA1 209 FC86
Godalming GU7 280 AT143
Gravesend DA12 213 GM89
Slough SL1 173 AQ75
South Merstham RH1 273 DJ130
Virginia Water GU25 214 AX99
Bourneside, Vir.W. GU25 214 AU101
Bourneside Cres, N14 121 DK46
Bourneside Gdns, SE6 205 EC92
Bourneside Rd, Add. KT15 234 BK105
Bourne St, SW1 28 G9
Croydon CR0
off Waddon New Rd 223 DP103
Bourne Ter, W2 15 L6
Bourne Vale, Brom. BR2 226 EG101
Bournevale Rd, SW16 203 DL91
Bourne Vw, Grnf. UB6 159 CF65
Kenley CR8 258 DR115
Bourne Way, Add. KT15 234 BJ106
Bromley BR2 226 EF103
Epsom KT19 238 CQ105
Sutton SM1 239 CZ106
Swanley BR8 229 FC97
Woking GU22 248 AX122
Bournewood Rd, SE18 188 EU80
Orpington BR5 228 EV101
Bournville Rd, SE6 205 EA87
Bournwell Cl, Barn. EN4 102 DF41
Bourton Cl, Hayes UB3 157 BU74
Bousfield Prim Sch, SW5 27 N10
Bousfield Rd, SE14 45 J8
Bousley Ri, Ott. KT16 233 BD108
Boutcher C of E Prim Sch, SE1 32 A8
Boutflower Rd, SW11 182 DE84
Boutique Hall, SE13
off Lewisham Cen 185 EC84
Bouton Pl, N1
off Waterloo Ter 8 G7
Bouverie Gdns, Har. HA3 139 CK58
Purley CR8 241 DL114
Bouverie Ms, N16 144 DS61
Bouverie Pl, W2 16 B8
Bouverie Rd, N16 144 DS61
Bouverie Rd, Chipstead CR5 256 DG118
Harrow HA1 138 CC59
Bouverie St, EC4 18 F9
Bouverie Way, Slou. SL3 174 AY78
Bouvier Rd, Enf. EN3 104 DW38
BOVENEY, Wind. SL4 173 AK79
Boveney Cl, Slou. SL1
off Amerden Way 173 AN75
Boveney New Rd, Eton Wick SL4 173 AL77
Boveney Rd, SE23 205 DX87
Dorney SL4 172 AJ77
Boveney Wd La, Burn. SL1 132 AJ62
Bovey Way, S.Ock. RM15 171 FV71
Bovill Rd, SE23 205 DX87
BOVINGDON, Hem.H. HP3 79 BA28
Bovingdon Av, Wem. HA9 160 CN65
Bovingdon Cl, N19
off Brookside Rd 143 DJ61
Bovingdon Cres, Wat. WD25 82 BX34
Bovingdon La, NW9 118 CS53
Bovingdon Prim Sch, Bov. HP3 off High St 79 BB27
Bovingdon Rd, SW6 39 L7
Bovingdon Sq, Mitch. CR4
off Leicester Av 223 DL98
BOW, E3 21 M1
Bow Arrow La, Dart. DA1, DA2 210 FN86
Bowater Cl, NW9 140 CR57
SW2 203 DL86
Bowater Gdns, Sun. TW16 217 BV96
Bowater Pl, SE3 186 EH80
Bowater Ridge, St.Geo.H. KT13 235 BR110
Bowater Rd, SE18 36 F7
Wembley HA9 140 CP62
Bow Br Est, E3 22 C2
DLR Bow Church 22 B3
Bow Chyd, EC4 19 K9
Bow Common La, E3 21 N5
Bowden Cl, Felt. TW14 197 BS88
Bowden Dr, Horn. RM11 150 FL60
H Bowden Ho, Har.Hill HA1 139 CE61
Bowden St, SE11 42 F1
Bowditch, SE8 33 N10
Bowdon Rd, E17 145 EA59
Bowen Dr, SE21 204 DS90
Bowen Rd, Har. HA1 138 CC59
Bowen St, E14 22 D8
Bowens Wd, Croy. CR0 243 DZ109
Bowen Way, Couls. CR5 257 DK122
Bower Av, SE10 47 K5
Bower Cl, Nthlt. UB5 158 BW68
Romford RM5 127 FD52
Bower Ct, Epp. CM16 92 EU32
Woking GU22
off Princess Rd 249 BB116
Bowerdean St, SW6 39 L7
Bower Fm Rd, Hav.at.Bow. RM4 127 FC48
BOWER HILL, Epp. CM16 92 EU31
Bower Hill, Epp. CM16 92 EU32
Bower Hill Cl, S.Nutfld RH1 289 DL137
● Bower Hill Ind Est, Epp. CM16 92 EU32
Bower Hill La, S.Nutfld RH1 289 DK135
Bower La, Eyns. DA4 230 FL103
Bowerman Av, SE14 45 M3
Bowerman Rd, Grays RM16 193 GG77
Bower Pk Sch, Rom. RM1
off Havering Rd 127 FE51
Bower Rd, Swan. BR8 209 FG94
Bowers Av, Nthflt DA11 213 GF91
Bowers Cl, Guil. GU4
off Cotts Wd Dr 265 BA129
Bowers Fm Dr, Guil. GU4 265 BA130
Bowers La, Guil. GU4 265 BA129
Bowers Rd, Shore. TN14 247 FF111
Bower St, E1 21 J9
Bowers Wk, E6 25 H8
Bower Ter, Epp. CM16 92 EU32
Bower Vale, Epp. CM16 92 EU32
Bower Way, Slou. SL1 153 AM73
Bowery Ct, Dag. RM10
off St. Mark's Pl 169 FB65
Bowes Cl, Sid. DA15 208 EV86
Bowes-Lyon Cl, Wind. SL4
off Ward Royal 173 AQ81
Bowes-Lyon Ms, St.Alb. AL3 65 CD20
BOWES PARK, N22 121 DL51
⇌ Bowes Park 121 DL51
Bowes Prim Sch, N11
off Bowes Rd 121 DK50
Bowes Rd, N11 121 DH50
N13 121 DL50
W3 160 CS73
Dagenham RM8 148 EW63
Staines-upon-Thames TW18 195 BE92
Walton-on-Thames KT12 217 BV103
Bowfell Rd, W6 38 B3
Bowford Av, Bexh. DA7 188 EY81
Bowgate, St.Alb. AL1 65 CE19
Bowhay, Hutt. CM13 131 GA47
Bowhill Cl, SW9 42 F4
Bowie Cl, SW4 203 DK87
Bowland Rd, SW4 183 DK84
Woodford Green IG8 124 EJ51
Bowland Yd, SW1 28 F5
Bow La, EC4 19 K9
N12 120 DC53
Morden SM4 221 CY100
Bowl Ct, EC2 19 P5
Bowlers Grn, Magd.Lav. CM5 75 FF21
Bowlers Orchard, Ch.St.G. HP8 112 AU48
Bowles Grn, Enf. EN1 104 DV36
Bowley Cl, SE19 204 DT93
Bowley La, SE19 204 DT92
Bowling Cl, Uxb. UB10
off Birch Cres 156 BM67
Bowling Ct, Wat. WD18 97 BU42
Bowling Grn Cl, SW15 201 CV87
Bowling Grn La, EC1 18 F4
Bowling Grn Pl, SE1 31 L4
Bowling Grn Rd, Chobham GU24 232 AS109
Bowling Grn Row, SE18 37 J7
Bowling Grn St, SE11 42 E2
Bowling Grn Wk, N1 19 N2
Bowling Rd, Ware SG12 55 DY06
Bowls, The, Chig. IG7 125 ES49
Bowls Cl, Stan. HA7 117 CH50
Bowman Av, E16 23 M10
Bowman Ms, SW18 201 CZ88
Bowmans Cl, W13 159 CH74
Burnham SL1 152 AH67
Potters Bar EN6 86 DD32
Bowmans Ct, Hem.H. HP2 62 BK18
Bowmans Grn, Wat. WD25 98 BX36
Bowmansgreen Prim Sch, Lon.Col. AL2 off Telford Rd 83 CJ27
Bowmans Lea, SE23 204 DW87
Bowmans Meadow, Wall. SM6 223 DH104
Bowmans Ms, E1 20 C10
Bowman's Ms, N7
off Seven Sisters Rd 143 DL62
Bowmans Pl, N7
off Holloway Rd 143 DL62
Bowmans Rd, Dart. DA1 209 FF87
● Bowman Trd Est, NW9 140 CN56
Bowmead, SE9 207 EM89
Bowmont Cl, Hutt. CM13 131 GB44
Bowmore Wk, NW1 7 P6
Bown Cl, Til. RM18 193 GH82
Bowness Cl, E8 10 A5
Bowness Cres, SW15 200 CS92
Bowness Dr, Houns. TW4 178 BY84
Bowness Rd, SE6 205 EB87
Bexleyheath DA7 189 FB82
Bowness Way, Horn. RM12 149 FG64
Bowood Rd, SW11 182 DG84
Enfield EN3 105 DX40
Bowring Grn, Wat. WD19 116 BW50
⊖ Bow Road 22 A2
Bow Rd, E3 21 P3
Bowrons Av, Wem. HA0 159 CK66
Bowry Dr, Wrays. TW19 195 AZ86
Bow Sch, E3 22 B1
Bowsher Ct, Ware SG12 55 DY06
Bowsley Ct, Felt. TW13
off Highfield Rd 197 BU89
Bowsprit, The, Cob. KT11 252 BW115
Bowsprit Pt, E14 34 A6
Bow St, E15 13 J3
WC2 18 B9
Bowstridge La, Ch.St.G. HP8 112 AW51
● Bow Triangle Business Cen, E3 22 B3
Bowyer Cl, E6 25 K6
Bowyer Ct, E4
off The Ridgeway 123 EC46
Bowyer Cres, Denh. UB9 135 BF58
Bowyer Dr, Slou. SL1 153 AL74
Bowyer Pl, SE5 43 K4
Bowyers, Hem.H. HP2 62 BK18
Bowyers Cl, Ashtd. KT21 254 CM118
Bowyer St, SE5 43 J4
Boxall Rd, SE21 204 DS86
Box Elder Cl, Edg. HA8 118 CQ50
Boxfield, Welw.G.C. AL7 52 DB12
Boxford Cl, S.Croy. CR2 243 DX112
Boxgrove Av, Guil. GU1 265 BA132
Boxgrove La, Guil. GU1 265 BA133
Boxgrove Prim Sch, SE2
off Boxgrove Rd 188 EW76
Guildford GU1
off Boxgrove La 265 BB133
Boxgrove Rd, SE2 188 EW76
Guildford GU1 265 BA133
BOX HILL, Tad. KT20 270 CP131
Boxhill, Hem.H. HP2 62 BK18
⇌ Boxhill & Westhumble 269 CH131
Boxhill Rd, Box H. KT20 270 CP131
Dorking RH4 270 CL133
Box Hill Sch, Mick. RH5
off Old London Rd 269 CH127
Boxhill Way, Strood Grn RH3 286 CP138
Box La, Bark. IG11 168 EV68
Hemel Hempstead HP3 61 BE24
Hoddesdon EN11 71 DX16
Boxley Rd, Mord. SM4 222 DC98
Boxley St, E16 36 A3
BOXMOOR, Hem.H. HP1 62 BH22
Boxmoor Ho Sch, Hem.H. HP3 off Box La 61 BF23
Boxmoor Prim Sch, Hem.H. HP1 off Cowper Rd 62 BG21
Boxmoor Rd, Har. HA3 139 CH56
Romford RM5 127 FC50
Boxoll Rd, Dag. RM9 148 EZ63
Box Ridge Av, Pur. CR8 241 DM112
Boxted Cl, Buck.H. IG9 124 EL46
Boxted Rd, Hem.H. HP1 61 BF18
Box Tree Cl, Chesh. HP5 76 AR33
Boxtree La, Har. HA3 116 CC53
Boxtree Rd, Har. HA3 117 CD52
Boxtree Wk, Orp. BR5 228 EX102
Box Tree Wk, Red. RH1 288 DC136
Box Wk, Lthd. KT24 267 BS132
Boxwell Rd, Berk. HP4 60 AV19
Boxwood Cl, West Dr. UB7
off Hawthorne Cres 176 BM75
Boxwood Way, Warl. CR6 259 DX117
Boxworth Cl, N12 120 DD50
Boxworth Gro, N1 8 D8
Boyard Rd, SE18 37 N10
Boyce Cl, Borwd. WD6 100 CL39
Boyce St, SE1 30 D3
Boyce Way, E13 23 N4
Boycroft Av, NW9 140 CQ58
Boyd Av, Sthl. UB1 158 BZ74
Boyd Cl, Kings.T. KT2 200 CN94
Boydell Ct, NW8 6 A7
Boyd Rd, SW19 202 DD93
Boyd St, E1 20 C9
Boyes Cres, Lon.Col. AL2 83 CH26
Boyfield St, SE1 31 H5
Boyland Rd, Brom. BR1 206 EF92
Boyle Av, Stan. HA7 117 CG51
Boyle Cl, Uxb. UB10 156 BM68
Boyle Fm Island, T.Ditt. KT7 219 CG100
Boyle Fm Rd, T.Ditt. KT7 219 CG100
Boyle St, W1 17 L10
Boyne Av, NW4 141 CX56
Boyne Rd, SE13 46 F10
Dagenham RM10 148 FA62
Boyne Ter Ms, W11 26 G2
Boyseland Ct, Edg. HA8 118 CQ47
Boyson Rd, SE17 43 L2
Boyton Cl, E1 21 H4
N8 143 DL55
Boyton Rd, N8 143 DL55
Brabant Ct, EC3 19 N10
Brabant Rd, N22 121 DM54
Brabazon Av, Wall. SM6 241 DL108
Brabazon Rd, Houns. TW5 178 BW80
Northolt UB5 158 CA68
Brabazon St, E14 22 C8
Brabiner Gdns, Croy. CR0 243 ED110
Brabourne Cl, SE19 204 DS92
Brabourne Cres, Bexh. DA7 188 EZ79
Brabourne Hts, NW7 118 CS48
Brabourne Ri, Beck. BR3 225 EC99
Brabourn Gro, SE15 44 G9
Brace Cl, Chsht EN7 87 DP25
Bracer Ho, N1 off Nuttall St 9 P10
Bracewell Av, Grnf. UB6 139 CF64
Bracewell Rd, W10 14 A7
Bracewood Gdns, Croy. CR0 224 DT104

Bracey Ms, N4 off Bracey St 143 DL61
Bracey St, N4 143 DL61
Bracken, The, E4
off Hortus Rd 123 EC47
Bracken Av, SW12 202 DG86
Croydon CR0 225 EB104
Brackenbridge Dr, Ruis. HA4 138 BX62
Brackenbury Gdns, W6 181 CV76
Sch Brackenbury Prim Sch,
W6 off Dalling Rd 181 CV76
Brackenbury Rd, N2 142 DC55
W6 181 CV76
Bracken Cl, E6 25 J7
Bookham KT23 252 BZ124
Borehamwood WD6 100 CP39
Farnham Common SL2 133 AR63
Sunbury-on-Thames TW16 197 BT93
Twickenham TW2 198 CA87
Woking GU22 249 AZ118
Bracken Ct, Hat. AL10 51 CT14
Brackendale, N21 121 DM47
Potters Bar EN6 86 DA33
Brackendale Cl, Houns. TW3 178 CB81
Brackendale Gdns, Upmin.
RM14 150 FQ63
Brackendene, Brick.Wd AL2 82 BZ30
Dartford DA2 209 FE91
Brackendene Cl, Wok. GU21 249 BA115
Bracken Dr, Chig. IG7 125 EP51
Bracken End, Islw. TW7 199 CD85
Brackenfield Cl, E5 144 DV62
Brackenforde, Slou. SL3 174 AW75
Bracken Gdns, SW13 181 CU82
Brackenhill, Berk. HP4 60 AY18
Cobham KT11 236 CA111
Ruis. HA4 138 BY63
Bracken Hill Cl, Brom. BR1 226 EF95
Bracken Hill La, Brom. BR1 226 EF95
● Bracken Ind Est, Ilf. IG6 125 ET53
Bracken Ms, E4 off Hortus Rd 123 EC46
Romford RM7 148 FA58
Bracken Path, Epsom KT18 238 CP113
Brackens, The, Enf. EN1 122 DS45
Hemel Hempstead HP2
off Heather Way 62 BK19
Orpington BR6 246 EU106
Brackens Dr, Warley CM14 130 FW50
Brackenside, Horl. RH6
off Stockfield 291 DH147
Bracken Way, Chobham GU24 232 AT110
Guildford GU3 264 AS132
Brackenwood, Sun. TW16 217 BU95
Brackley, Wey. KT13 235 BR106
Brackley Av, SE15 184 DV83
Brackley Cl, Wall. SM6 241 DL108
Brackley Rd, W4 180 CS78
Beckenham BR3 205 DZ94
Brackley Sq, Wdf.Grn. IG8 124 EK52
Brackley St, EC1 19 J6
Brackley Ter, W4 180 CS78
Bracklyn Cl, N1 9 L10
Bracklyn Ct, N1 9 L10
Bracklyn St, N1 9 L10
Bracknell Cl, N22 121 DN53
Bracknell Gdns, NW3 5 L1
Bracknell Gate, NW3 5 L2
Bracknell Pl, Hem.H. HP2 62 BM16
Bracknell Way, NW3 5 L1
Bracondale, Esher KT10 236 CC107
Bracondale Rd, SE2 188 EU77
H Bracton Cen, The, Dart.
DA2 209 FF89
Bracton La, Dart. DA2 209 FF89
Bradbery, Map.Cr. WD3 113 BD50
Bradbourne Pk Rd, Sev. TN13 278 FG123
Bradbourne Rd, Bex. DA5 208 FA87
Grays RM17 192 GB79
Sevenoaks TN13 279 FH122
Bradbourne St, SW6 39 K8
Bradbourne Vale Rd, Sev.
TN13 278 FF122
Bradbury Cl, Borwd. WD6 100 CP39
Southall UB2 178 BZ77
Bradbury Ct, SW20
off Clifton Pk Av 221 CW96
Bradbury Gdns, Fulmer SL3 134 AX63
Bradbury Ms, N16 9 P3
Bradbury St, N16 9 P3
Bradd Cl, S.Ock. RM15 171 FW69
Braddock Cl, Coll.Row RM5 127 FC51
Isleworth TW7 179 CF83
Braddon Rd, Rich. TW9 180 CM83
Braddyll St, SE10 47 J1
Bradenham Av, Well. DA16 188 EU84
Bradenham Cl, SE17 43 L2
Bradenham Rd, Har. HA3 139 CH56
Hayes UB4 157 BS69
Bradenhurst Cl, Cat. CR3 274 DT126
Braden St, W9 15 L5
Bradfield Cl, Guil. GU4 265 BA131
Woking GU22 248 AY118
Bradfield Dr, Bark. IG11 148 EU64
Bradfield Ho, SW8
off Wandsworth Rd 41 N8
Bradfield Rd, E16 35 P4
Ruislip HA4 138 BY64
Bradford Cl, N17 122 DT51
SE26 off Coombe Rd 204 DV91
Bromley BR2 227 EM102
Bradford Dr, Epsom KT19 239 CT107
Bradford Rd, W3
off Warple Way 180 CS75
Heronsgate WD3 113 BC45
Ilford IG1 147 ER60
Slough SL1 153 AN72
Bradfords Cl, Buck.H. IG9 124 EK49
Bradgate, Cuffley EN6 87 DK27
Bradgate Cl, Cuffley EN6 87 DK28
Bradgate Rd, SE6 205 EA86
Brading Cres, E11 146 EH61
Brading Rd, SW2 203 DM87
Croydon CR0 223 DM100
Brading Ter, W12 181 CV76
Bradiston Rd, W9 15 H2
Bradleigh Av, Grays RM17 192 GC77
Bradley Cl, N1 8 F10
N7 8 B5
Belmont SM2
off Station Rd 240 DA110
Bradley Gdns, W13 159 CH72
Bradley Ho, E3
off Bromley High St 22 D1
SE16 off Nelldale Rd 32 F8
Bradley La, Dor. RH5 269 CG132
Bradley Lynch Ct, E2
off Morpeth St 21 J2
Bradley Ms, SW17 202 DF88
Bradley Rd, N22 121 DM54
SE19 204 DQ93
Bradley Rd, Enfield EN3 105 DY38
Slough SL1 153 AR73
Waltham Abbey EN9 105 EC36
Bradley Stone Rd, E6 25 J7
Bradman Row, Edg. HA8
off Pavilion Way 118 CQ52
Bradmead, SW8 41 K5
Bradmore Ct, Enf. EN3
off Enstone Rd 105 DY41
Bradmore Grn, Brook.Pk AL9 85 CY26
Coulsdon CR5
off Coulsdon Rd 257 DM118
Bradmore La, Brook.Pk AL9 85 CW27
Bradmore Pk Rd, W6 181 CV76
Bradmore Way, Brook.Pk AL9 85 CY26
Coulsdon CR5 257 DL117
Bradshaw Cl, SW19 202 DA93
Windsor SL4 173 AL81
Bradshaw Dr, NW7 119 CX52
Bradshawe Waye, Uxb. UB8 156 BL71
Bradshaw Rd, Wat. WD24 98 BW39
Bradshaws, Hat. AL10 67 CT22
Bradshaws Cl, SE25 224 DU97
Bradstock Rd, E9 11 K5
Epsom KT17 239 CU106
Bradstone Brook, Shalf. GU4 281 BA141
Brad St, SE1 30 F3
Bradstowe Ho, Har. HA1
off Junction Rd 139 CE58
Bradwell Av, Dag. RM10 148 FA61
Bradwell Cl, E18 146 EF56
Hornchurch RM12 169 FH65
Bradwell Ct, Whyt. CR3
off Godstone Rd 258 DU119
Bradwell Grn, Hutt. CM13 131 GC44
Bradwell Ms, N18
off Lyndhurst Rd 122 DU49
Bradwell Rd, Buck.H. IG9 124 EL46
Bradwell St, E1 21 K3
Brady Av, Loug. IG10 107 EQ40
Brady Ct, Dag. RM8 148 EX60
Brady Dr, Brom. BR1 227 EN97
Bradymead, E6 25 M8
Sch Brady Prim Sch, Rain. RM13
off Wennington Rd 170 FJ71
Brady St, E1 20 E5
Braemar Av, N22 121 DL53
NW10 140 CR62
SW19 202 DA89
Bexleyheath DA7 189 FC84
South Croydon CR2 242 DQ109
Thornton Heath CR7 223 DN97
Wembley HA0 159 CK66
Braemar Cl, SE16 32 E10
Braemar Gdns, NW9 118 CR53
Hornchurch RM11 150 FN58
Sidcup DA15 207 ER90
Slough SL1 173 AN75
West Wickham BR4 225 EC102
Braemar Rd, E13 23 M5
N15 144 DS57
Brentford TW8 179 CK79
Worcester Park KT4 221 CV104
Braemer Ho, W9 15 N3
Braeside, Beck. BR3 205 EA92
New Haw KT15 234 BH111
Braeside Av, SW19 221 CY95
Sevenoaks TN13 278 FF124
Braeside Cl, Pnr. HA5 116 CA52
Sevenoaks TN13 278 FF123
Braeside Cres, Bexh. DA7 189 FC84
Braeside Rd, SW16 203 DJ94
Sch Braeside Sch, Jun Sch, Buck.H.
IG9 off Palmerston Rd 124 EJ47
Sen Sch, Buck.H. IG9
off High Rd 124 EH46
Braes Mead, S.Nutfld RH1 289 DL135
Braes St, N1 9 H6
Braesyde Cl, Belv. DA17 188 EZ77
Brafferton Rd, Croy. CR0 242 DQ105
Braganza St, SE17 30 G10
Bragg Cl, Dag. RM8
off Porters Av 168 EV65
Bragmans La, Flaun. HP3 79 BB34
Sarratt WD3 79 BE33
Braham St, E1 20 B9
Braid, The, Chesh. HP5 76 AS30
Braid Av, W3 160 CS72
Braid Cl, Felt. TW13 198 BZ89
Braid Ct, W4 off Lawford Rd 180 CQ80
Braidwood Pas, EC1
off Cloth St 19 J6
Braidwood Rd, SE6 205 ED88
Braidwood St, SE1 31 N3
Brailsford Cl, Mitch. CR4 202 DE94
Brailsford Rd, SW2 203 DN85
Brain Cl, Hat. AL10 67 CV18
Sch Braintcroft Prim Sch, NW2
off Warren Rd 141 CT61
Brainton Av, Felt. TW14 197 BV87
Braintree Av, Ilf. IG4 146 EL56
● Braintree Ind Est, Ruis.
HA4 137 BV63
Braintree Rd, Dag. RM10 148 FA62
Ruislip HA4 137 BV63
Braintree St, E2 20 G4
Braithwaite Av, Rom. RM7 148 FA59
Braithwaite Gdns, Stan. HA7 117 CJ53
Braithwaite Ho, EC1 19 K4
Braithwaite Rd, Enf. EN3 105 DZ41
Braithwaite St, E1 20 A5
Braithwaite Twr, W2 16 A6
Brakefield Rd, Sthflt DA13 212 GB93
Brakey Hill, Bletch. RH1 274 DS134
Brakynbery, Nthch HP4 60 AS16
Bramah Grn, SW9 42 F6
Bramalea Cl, N6 142 DG58
Bramall Cl, E15 13 L2
Bramall Ct, N7 8 C4
Bramber Ct, Brent. TW8
off Sterling Pl 180 CL77
Slough SL1 153 AN74
Bramber Ho, Kings.T. KT2
off Kingsgate Rd 220 CL95
Bramber Rd, N12 120 DE50
W14 38 G2
Bramber Way, Warl. CR6 259 DZ116
Brambleacres Cl, Sutt. SM2 240 DA108
Bramble Av, Bean DA2 211 FW90
Bramble Banks, Cars. SM5 240 DG109
Bramblebury Rd, SE18 187 EQ78
Bramble Cl, N15 144 DU56
Beckenham BR3 225 EC99
Chalfont St. Peter SL9
off Garners Rd 112 AY51
Chigwell IG7 125 EQ46
Croydon CR0 243 EA105
Guildford GU3 264 AS132
Oxted RH8 276 EH133
Bramble Cl, Redhill RH1 288 DG136
SE19 224 DR95
Shepperton TW17
off Halliford Cl 217 BR97
Stanmore HA7 117 CK52
Uxbridge UB8 156 BM71
Watford WD25 81 BU34
Bramble Cft, Erith DA8 189 FC77
Brambledene Cl, Wok. GU21 248 AW118
Brambledown, Stai. TW18 216 BG95
Brambledown Cl, W.Wick. BR4 226 EE99
Brambledown Rd, Cars. SM5 240 DG108
South Croydon CR2 242 DS108
Wallington SM6 241 DH108
Bramblefield Cl, Long. DA3 231 FX97
Bramble Gdns, W12 161 CT73
Bramblehall La, Tad. KT20 270 CM132
Bramble La, Amer. HP7 77 AS41
Hampton TW12 198 BZ93
Hoddesdon EN11 71 DY17
Sevenoaks TN13 279 FH128
Upminster RM14 170 FQ67
Bramble Mead, Ch.St.G. HP8 112 AV48
Bramble Ri, Cob. KT11 252 BW115
Harlow CM20 57 EQ14
Bramble Rd, Hat. AL10 66 CR18
Brambles, The, Chsht EN8 89 DX31
Chigwell IG7 off Clayside 125 EQ51
St. Albans AL1 65 CD22
West Drayton UB7 176 BL77
Brambles Cl, Cat. CR3 258 DS122
Isleworth TW7 179 CG80
Brambles Fm Dr, Uxb. UB10 156 BN69
Sch Brambletye Jun Sch, Red. RH1
off Brambletye Pk Rd 288 DG136
Brambletye Pk Rd, Red. RH1 288 DG135
Bramble Wk, Epsom KT18 238 CP114
Bramble Way, Ripley GU23 249 BF124
Bramblewood, Merst. RH1 273 DH129
Bramblewood Cl, Cars. SM5 222 DE102
Brambling Cl, Bushey WD23 98 BY42
Green. DA9 211 FU86
Brambling Ri, Hem.H. HP2 62 BL17
Bramblings, The, E4 123 ED49
Bramcote Av, Mitch. CR4 222 DF98
Bramcote Ct, Mitch. CR4
off Bramcote Av 222 DF98
Bramcote Gro, SE16 32 G10
Bramcote Rd, SW15 181 CV84
Bramdean Cres, SE12 206 EG88
Bramdean Gdns, SE12 206 EG88
Bramerton Rd, Beck. BR3 225 DZ97
Bramerton St, SW3 40 C2
Bramfield, Wat. WD25
off Garston La 82 BY34
Bramfield Ct, N4
off Queens Dr 144 DQ61
Bramfield La, Waterf. SG14 53 DL05
Bramfield Rd, SW11 202 DE86
Hertford SG14 53 DL06
Bramford Ct, N14 121 DK47
Bramford Rd, SW18 182 DC84
Bramham Gdns, SW5 27 L10
Chessington KT9 237 CK105
Bramhope La, SE7 186 EH79
Bramlands Cl, SW11 182 DE83
Bramleas, Wat. WD18 97 BT42
Bramley Av, Couls. CR5 257 DJ115
● Bramley Business Cen,
Bramley GU5
off Station Rd 281 AZ144
Bramley Cl, E17 123 DY54
N14 103 DH43
NW7 118 CS48
Chertsey KT16 216 BH102
Eastcote HA5 137 BT55
Hayes UB3 157 BU73
Istead Rise DA13 213 GF94
Orpington BR6 227 EP102
Redhill RH1
off Abinger Dr 288 DE136
South Croydon CR2 241 DP106
Staines-upon-Thames TW18 196 BJ93
Swanley BR8 229 FE98
Twickenham TW2 198 CC86
Woodford Green IG8
off Orsett Ter 124 EJ52
Bramley Ct, Wat. WD25
off Orchard Av 81 BV31
Welling DA16 188 EV81
Bramley Cres, SW8 41 P4
Ilford IG2 147 EN58
Bramley Gdns, Wat. WD19 116 BW50
Bramley Gro, Ashtd. KT21 254 CL119
Bramley Hill, S.Croy. CR2 241 DP106
Bramley Ho, SW15
off Tunworth Cres 201 CT86
W10 14 D9
Bramley Ho Ct, Enf. EN2 104 DR37
Bramley Hyrst, S.Croy. CR2 242 DQ105
Bramley Par, N14 103 DJ42
Bramley Pl, Dart. DA1 189 FG84
Bramley Rd, N14 103 DH43
W5 179 CJ76
W10 14 D10
Cheam SM2 239 CX109
Sutton SM1 240 DD106
Sch Bramley Sch, Walt.Hill
KT20 off Chequers La 271 CU125
Bramley Shaw, Wal.Abb. EN9 90 EF33
Bramley Wk, Horl. RH6 291 DJ148
Bramley Way, Ashtd. KT21 254 CM117
Hounslow TW4 198 BZ85
St. Albans AL4 65 CJ21
West Wickham BR4 225 EB103
Brammas Cl, Slou. SL1 173 AQ76
Brampton Cl, E5 144 DV61
Cheshunt EN7 88 DU28
Brampton Gdns, N15 144 DQ57
Hersham KT12 236 BW106
Brampton Gro, NW4 141 CV56
Harrow HA3 139 CG56
Wembley HA9 140 CN60
Brampton La, NW4 141 CW56
Sch Brampton Manor Sch, E6 24 E4
Brampton Pk Rd, N22 143 DN55
Sch Brampton Prim Sch, E6 24 G3
Bexleyheath DA7
off Brampton Rd 188 EX82
Brampton Rd, E6 24 F4
N15 144 DQ57
NW9 140 CN56
SE2 188 EW79
Bexleyheath DA7 188 EX80
Croydon CR0 224 DT101
Hillingdon UB10 157 BP68
St. Albans AL1 65 CG19
Watford WD19 115 BU48
Brampton Ter, Borwd. WD6 100 CN38
Bramshaw Gdns, Wat. WD19 116 BX50
Bramshaw Ri, N.Mal. KT3 220 CS100
Bramshaw Rd, E9 11 K5
Bramshill Cl, Chig. IG7
off Tine Rd 125 ES50
Bramshill Gdns, NW5 143 DH62
Bramshill Rd, NW10 161 CT68
Bramshot Av, SE7 47 P1
Bramshot Way, Wat. WD19 115 BU47
Bramston Cl, Ilf. IG6 125 ET51
Bramston Rd, NW10 161 CU68
SW17 202 DC90
Bramwell Cl, Sun. TW16 218 BX96
Bramwell Ho, SE1
off Harper Rd 31 K7
SW1 41 L1
Bramwell Ms, N1 8 D8
Bramwell Way, E16 36 D3
Brancaster Dr, NW7 119 CT52
Brancaster La, Pur. CR8 242 DQ112
Brancaster Pl, Loug. IG10 107 EM41
Brancaster Rd, E12 147 EM63
SW16 203 DL90
Ilford IG2 147 ER58
Brancepeth Gdns, Buck.H. IG9 124 EG47
Branch Cl, Hat. AL10 67 CW16
Branch Hill, NW3 142 DC62
Branch Pl, N1 9 M8
Branch Rd, E14 21 L10
Ilford IG6 126 EV50
Park Street AL2 83 CD27
St. Albans AL3 64 CB19
Branch St, SE15 43 P5
Brancker Rd, Har. HA3 139 CK55
Brancroft Way, Enf. EN3 105 DY39
Brand Cl, N4 143 DP60
Brandesbury Sq, Wdf.Grn. IG8 125 EN51
Sch Brandlehow Prim Sch, SW15
off Brandlehow Rd 181 CZ84
Brandlehow Rd, SW15 181 CZ84
Brandon Cl, Chaff.Hun. RM16 192 FZ75
Cheshunt EN7 88 DS26
Brandon Est, SE17 43 H3
Brandon Gros Av, S.Ock. RM15 171 FW69
Brandon Mead, Chesh. HP5 76 AM29
Brandon Ms, EC2
off The Barbican 19 L7
Brandon Rd, E17 145 EC55
N7 8 A6
Dartford DA1 210 FN87
Southall UB2 178 BZ78
Sutton SM1 240 DB105
Brandon St, SE17 31 J9
Gravesend DA11 213 GH87
Brandram Ms, SE13 186 EE83
Brandram Rd, SE13 186 EE83
Brandreth Ct, Har. HA1
off Sheepcote Rd 139 CF58
Brandreth Rd, E6 25 K8
SW17 203 DH89
Brandries, The, Wall. SM6 223 DK104
BRANDS HILL, Slou. SL3 175 BB79
Brandsland, Reig. RH2 288 DB138
Brands Rd, Slou. SL3 175 BB79
Brand St, SE10 46 E5
Brandville Gdns, Ilf. IG6 147 EP56
Brandville Rd, West Dr. UB7 176 BL75
Brandy Way, Sutt. SM2 240 DA108
Sch Branfil Inf Sch, Upmin.
RM14 off Cedar Av 150 FN63
Sch Branfil Jun Sch, Upmin.
RM14 off Cedar Av 150 FN63
Branfill Rd, Upmin. RM14 150 FP61
Brangbourne Rd, Brom. BR1 205 EC92
Brangton Rd, SE11 42 D1
Brangwyn Cres, SW19 222 DD95
Branksea St, SW6 38 E5
Branksome Av, N18 122 DT51
Branksome Cl, Hem.H. HP2 62 BN19
Teddington TW11 199 CD91
Walton-on-Thames KT12 218 BX103
Branksome Rd, SW2 203 DL85
SW19 222 DA95
Branksome Way, Har. HA3 140 CL58
New Malden KT3 220 CQ95
Bransby Rd, Chess. KT9 238 CL107
Branscombe Gdns, N21 121 DN45
Branscombe St, SE13 46 D10
Bransdale Cl, NW6 5 K8
Bransell Cl, Swan. BR8 229 FC100
Bransgrove Rd, Edg. HA8 118 CM53
Branston Cres, Petts Wd BR5 227 ER102
Branstone Rd, Rich. TW9 180 CM81
Branton Rd, Green. DA9 211 FT86
Brants Wk, W7 159 CE70
Brantwood Av, Erith DA8 189 FC80
Isleworth TW7 179 CG84
Brantwood Cl, E17 145 EB55
West Byfleet KT14
off Brantwood Gdns 234 BG113
Brantwood Ct, W.Byf. KT14
off Brantwood Dr 233 BF113
Brantwood Dr, W.Byf. KT14 233 BF113
Brantwood Gdns, Enf. EN2 103 DL42
Ilford IG4 146 EL56
West Byfleet KT14 233 BF113
Brantwood Rd, N17 122 DT51
SE24 204 DQ85
Bexleyheath DA7 189 FB82
South Croydon CR2 242 DQ109
Brantwood Way, Orp. BR5 228 EW97
Brasenose Dr, SW13 38 A3
Brasher Cl, Grnf. UB6 139 CD64
Brassett Pt, E15 13 K9
Brassey Cl, Felt. TW14 197 BU88
Oxted RH8 276 EG129
Brassey Hill, Oxt. RH8 276 EG130
Brassey Rd, NW6 5 H4
Oxted RH8 276 EF130
Brassey Sq, SW11 40 G10
Brassie Av, W3 160 CS72
Brass Tally All, SE16 33 K5
BRASTED, West. TN16 262 EW124
Brasted Cl, SE26 204 DW91
Bexleyheath DA6 208 EX85
Orpington BR6 227 ET103
Sutton SM2 240 DA110
Brasted Hill, Knock. TN14 262 EU120
Brasted Hill Rd, Brasted TN16 262 EV121
Brasted La, Knock. TN14 262 EU119
Brasted Rd, Erith DA8 189 FE80
Westerham TN16 277 ES126
Brathway Rd, SW18 202 DA87
Bratley St, E1 20 C5
Brattle Wd, Sev. TN13 279 FH129
Braund Av, Grnf. UB6 158 CB70
Braundton Av, Sid. DA15 207 ET88
Braunston Dr, Hayes UB4 158 BY70
Bravington Cl, Shep. TW17 216 BM99
Bravington Pl, W9 14 G4
Bravington Rd, W9 14 G4
Bravingtons Wk, N1 18 B1
Brawlings La, Chal.St.P. SL9 113 BA49
Brawne Ho, SE17 43 H3
Braxfield Rd, SE4 185 DY84
Braxted Pk, SW16 203 DM93
BRAY, Maid. SL6 172 AC76
Bray, NW3 6 D6
Brayards Rd, SE15 44 E9
Brayards Rd Est, SE15
off Firbank Rd 44 F8
Braybank, Bray SL6 172 AC75
Braybourne Cl, Uxb. UB8 156 BJ65
Braybourne Dr, Islw. TW7 179 CF80
Braybrooke Gdns, SE19
off Fox Hill 204 DS94
Braybrook St, W12 161 CT71
Brayburne Av, SW4 41 M9
Bray Cl, Borwd. WD6 100 CQ39
Bray SL6 172 AC76
Bray Ct, Maid. SL6 172 AC77
Braycourt Av, Walt. KT12 217 BV101
Bray Cres, SE16 33 J4
Braydon Rd, N16 144 DT60
Bray Dr, E16 23 M10
Brayfield Rd, Bray SL6 172 AC75
Brayfield Ter, N1 8 E7
Brayford Sq, E1 21 H8
Bray Gdns, Wok. GU22 249 BE116
Bray Pas, E16 23 N10
Bray Pl, SW3 28 E9
Bray Rd, NW7 119 CX51
Guildford GU2 280 AV135
Stoke D'Abernon KT11 252 BY116
BRAYS GROVE, Harl. CM18 74 EU17
Sch Brays Gro Comm Coll, Harl.
CM18 off Tracyes Rd 74 EV17
Brays Mead, Harl. CM18 73 ET17
Bray Springs, Wal.Abb. EN9
off Roundhills 90 EE34
Brayton Gdns, Enf. EN2 103 DK42
Braywood Av, Egh. TW20 195 AZ93
Sch Braywood C of E First Sch,
Oakley Grn SL4
off Oakley Grn Rd 172 AE82
Braywood Rd, SE9 187 ER84
Brazier Cres, Nthlt. UB5 158 BZ70
Braziers Fld, Hert. SG13 54 DT09
Brazil Cl, Bedd. CR0 223 DL101
Breach Barn Mobile Home Pk,
Wal.Abb. EN9 90 EH29
Breach Barns La, Wal.Abb.
EN9 90 EF30
Breach La, Dag. RM9 168 FA69
Little Berkhamsted SG13 69 DJ18
Breach Rd, Grays RM20 191 FT79
Bread & Cheese La, Chsht EN7 88 DR25
Bread St, EC4 19 K9
Breakfield, Couls. CR5 257 DL116
Breakmead, Welw.G.C. AL7 52 DB10
Breakneck Hill, Green. DA9 211 FV85
Breakspear Av, St.Alb. AL1 65 CF21
Breakspeare Cl, Abb.L. WD5 81 BT30
Breakspeare Cl, Wat. WD24 97 BV38
Breakspeare Rd, Abb.L. WD5 81 BS31
Sch Breakspeare Sch, Abb.L. WD5
off Gallows Hill La 81 BS31
Sch Breakspear Inf & Jun Schs,
Ickhm UB10
off Bushey Rd 136 BN61
Breakspear Path, Hare. UB9 136 BJ55
Breakspear Pl, Abb.L. WD5
off Hanover Gdns 81 BT30
Breakspear Rd, Ruis. HA4 137 BP59
Breakspear Rd N, Hare. UB9 136 BN57
Breakspear Rd S, Ickhm UB9,
UB10 136 BM62
Breakspears Dr, Orp. BR5 228 EU95
Breakspears Ms, SE4 46 A9
Breakspears Rd, SE4 46 A10
Breakspear Way, Hem.H. HP2 63 BQ20
Breaks Rd, Hat. AL10 67 CV18
Bream Cl, N17 144 DV56
Bream Gdns, E6 25 L3
Breamore Cl, SW15 201 CU88
Breamore Rd, Ilf. IG3 147 ET61
Bream's Bldgs, EC4 18 E8
Bream St, E3 12 B7
Breamwater Gdns, Rich. TW10 199 CH90
Brearley Cl, Edg. HA8 118 CQ52
Uxbridge UB8 156 BL65
Sch Breaside Prep Sch, Brom.
BR1 off Orchard Rd 226 EK95
Breasley Cl, SW15 181 CV84
Brechin Pl, SW7 27 P9
Brecken Cl, St.Alb. AL4 65 CG16
Sch Brecknock Prim Sch, NW1 7 P4
Brecknock Rd, N7 7 N2
N19 143 DJ63
Brecknock Rd Est, N19 7 M1
Breckonmead, Brom. BR1
off Wanstead Rd 226 EJ96
Brecon Cl, Mitch. CR4 223 DL97
Worcester Park KT4 221 CW103
Brecon Grn, NW9
off Goldsmith Av 140 CS58
Brecon Ms, N7 7 N3
Brecon Rd, W6 38 F3
Enfield EN3 104 DW42
Brede Cl, E6 25 L2
Bredgar, SE13 205 EC85
Bredgar Rd, N19 143 DJ61
Bredhurst Cl, SE20 204 DW93
Bredinghurst, SE22 204 DU87
Sch Bredinghurst Sch, SE15
off Stuart Rd 185 DX84
Bredon Rd, Croy. CR0 224 DT101
Bredune, Ken. CR8 258 DR115
Bredward Cl, Burn. SL1 152 AH69
Breech La, Walt.Hill KT20 255 CU124
Breer St, SW6 39 L10
Breezers Hill, E1 32 D1
Breeze Ter, Chsht EN8
off Collet Cl 89 DX28
Brember Rd, Har. HA2 138 CC61
Bremer Ms, E17 145 EB56
Bremer Rd, Stai. TW18 196 BG90
Bremner Av, Horl. RH6 290 DF147
Bremner Cl, Swan. BR8 229 FG98
Bremner Rd, SW7 27 P5

Brenchley Av, Grav. DA11 213 GH92
Brenchley Cl, Brom. BR2 226 EF100
Chislehurst BR7 227 EN95
Brenchley Gdns, SE23 204 DW86
Brenchley Rd, Orp. BR5 227 ET95
Bren Ct, Enf. EN3
off Colgate Pl 105 EA37
Brendans Cl, Horn. RM11 150 FL60
Brenda Rd, SW17 202 DF89
Brenda Ter, Swans. DA10
off Manor Rd 212 FY87
Brende Gdns, W.Mol. KT8 218 CB98
Brendon Av, NW10 140 CS63
Brendon Cl, Erith DA8 189 FE81
Esher KT10 236 CC107
Harlington UB3 177 BQ80
Brendon Ct, Rad. WD7 83 CH34
Brendon Dr, Esher KT10 236 CC107
Brendon Gdns, Har. HA2 138 CB63
Ilford IG2 147 ES57
Brendon Gro, N2 120 DC54
Brendon Rd, SE9 207 ER89
Dagenham RM8 148 EZ60
Brendon St, W1 16 D8
Brendon Way, Enf. EN1 122 DS45
Brenley Cl, Mitch. CR4 222 DG97
Brenley Gdns, SE9 186 EK84
Brennan Rd, Til. RM18 193 GH82
Brent, The, Dart. DA1, DA2 210 FN87
Brent Adult Coll, NW10
off Morland Gdns 160 CR67
Brent Cl, Bex. DA5 208 EY88
Dartford DA2 210 FP86
Brentcot Cl, W13 159 CH70
Brent Cres, NW10 160 CM68
Brent Cross 141 CX59
Brent Cross Gdns, NW4
off Cooper Rd 141 CX58
Brent Cross Interchange, The, NW2 141 CX59
Brent Cross Shop Cen, NW4 141 CW59
Brentfield, NW10 160 CP66
Brentfield Cl, NW10 160 CR65
Brentfield Gdns, NW2
off Hendon Way 141 CX59
Brentfield Ho, NW10
off Stonebridge Pk 160 CR66
Brentfield Prim Sch, NW10
off Meadow Garth 160 CR65
Brentfield Rd, NW10 160 CR65
Dartford DA1 210 FN86
BRENTFORD, TW8 179 CK79
⇌ Brentford 179 CJ79
● Brentford Business Cen, Brent. TW8 179 CH80
Brentford Cl, Hayes UB4 158 BX70
★ Brentford FC, Brent. TW8 179 CK79
Brentford Sch for Girls, Brent. TW8
off Boston Manor Rd 179 CK79
Brent Grn, NW4 141 CW57
Brent Grn Wk, Wem. HA9 140 CQ62
Brenthall Twrs, Harl. CM17 74 EW17
Brentham Way, W5 159 CK70
Brenthouse Rd, E9 10 G6
Brenthurst Rd, NW10 141 CT64
Brent Knoll Sch, SE23
off Mayow Rd 205 DX90
Brentlands Dr, Dart. DA1 210 FN88
Brent La, Dart. DA1 210 FM87
Brent Lea, Brent. TW8 179 CJ80
Brentmead Cl, W7 159 CE73
Brentmead Gdns, NW10 160 CM68
Brentmead Pl, NW11
off North Circular Rd 141 CX58
● Brent New Enterprise Cen, NW10 off Cobbold Rd 161 CT65
Brenton St, E14 21 M8
Brent Pk, NW10 140 CR64
Brent Pk Rd, NW4 141 CV59
NW9 141 CU60
Brent Pl, Barn. EN5 102 DA43
Brent Prim Sch, The, Dart. DA2 off London Rd 210 FQ87
Brent Rd, E16 23 P8
SE18 187 EP80
Brentford TW8 179 CJ79
South Croydon CR2 242 DV109
Southall UB2 178 BW76
Brent Side, Brent. TW8 179 CJ79
Brentside Cl, W13 159 CG70
● Brentside Executive Cen, Brent. TW8 179 CH79
Brentside High Sch, W7
off Greenfield Av 159 CE70
Brentside Prim Sch, W7
off Kennedy Rd 159 CE70
Brent S Shop Pk, NW2 141 CW60
Brent St, NW4 141 CW56
Brent Ter, NW2 141 CW61
Brentvale Av, Sthl. UB1 159 CD74
Wembley HA0 160 CM67
Brent Vw Rd, NW9 141 CU59
Brentwaters Business Pk, Brent. TW8 off The Ham 179 CJ80
Brent Way, N3 120 DA51
Brentford TW8 179 CK80
Dartford DA2 210 FP86
Wembley HA9 160 CP65
Brentwick Gdns, Brent. TW8 180 CL77
BRENTWOOD, CM13 - CM15 130 FW47
⇌ Brentwood 130 FW48
Brentwood Bypass, Brwd. CM14, CM15 129 FR49
Brentwood Cl, SE9 207 EQ88
Brentwood Comm Hosp & Minor Injuries Unit, Brwd. CM15 130 FY46
Brentwood Co High Sch, Brwd. CM14
off Seven Arches Rd 130 FX48
Brentwood Ct, Add. KT15 234 BH105
Brentwood Ho, SE18
off Shooters Hill Rd 186 EK80
★ Brentwood Mus, Brwd. CM14 130 FW49
Brentwood Pl, Brwd. CM15 130 FX46
Brentwood Prep Sch, Brwd. CM15
off Middleton Hall La 130 FY46
Brentwood Rd, Brwd. CM13 131 GA49
Grays RM16 193 GH77
Romford RM1, RM2 149 FF58
Brentwood Sch, Brwd. CM15 off Ingrave Rd 130 FX47
Brentwood Ursuline Conv High Sch, Brwd. CM14
off Queens Rd 130 FX47
Brereton Ct, Hem.H. HP3 62 BL22
Brereton Rd, N17 122 DT52
Bressay Dr, NW7 119 CU52
Bressenden Pl, SW1 29 K6
Bressey Av, Enf. EN1 104 DU39
Bressey Gro, E18 124 EF54
Bretlands Rd, Cher. KT16 215 BE103
Breton Ho, EC2
off The Barbican 19 K6
Brett Cl, N16 144 DS61
Northolt UB5
off Broomcroft Av 158 BX69
Brett Ct, N9 122 DW47
Cheshunt EN8
off Coopers Wk 89 DX28
Brett Cres, NW10 160 CR66
Brettell St, SE17 43 M1
Brettenham Av, E17 123 EA53
Brettenham Prim Sch, N18
off Brettenham Rd 122 DU49
Brettenham Rd, E17 123 EA54
N18 122 DU49
Brett Gdns, Dag. RM9 168 EY66
Brettgrave, Epsom KT19 238 CQ110
Brett Ho Cl, SW15
off Putney Heath La 201 CX86
Brett Pas, E8 10 F3
Brett Pl, Wat. WD24 97 BU37
Brett Rd, E8 10 F3
Barnet EN5 101 CW43
Brevet Cl, Purf. RM19 191 FR77
Brewer's Fld, Dart. DA2 210 FJ91
Brewer's Grn, SW1 29 N6
Brewers Hall Gdns, EC2 19 K7
Brewers La, Rich. TW9 199 CK85
Brewer St, W1 17 M10
Bletchingley RH1 274 DQ131
★ Brewery, The, EC1 19 K6
● Brewery, The, Rom. RM1 149 FE57
Brewery Cl, Wem. HA0 139 CG64
Brewery La, Byfleet KT14 234 BL113
Hoddesdon EN11 71 EA17
Sevenoaks TN13
off High St 279 FJ125
Twickenham TW1 199 CF87
Brewery Rd, N7 8 A6
SE18 187 ER78
Bromley BR2 226 EL102
Hoddesdon EN11 71 EA17
Woking GU21 248 AX117
Brewery Sq, EC1 18 G4
SE1 32 A3
Brewery Wk, Rom. RM1 149 FE57
Brewhouse La, E1 32 F3
SW15 181 CY83
Hertford SG14 54 DQ09
Brewhouse Rd, SE18 37 K8
Brew Ho Rd, Strood Grn RH3
off Tanners Meadow 286 CP138
Brewhouse Wk, SE16 33 L3
Brewhouse Yd, EC1 19 H4
Gravesend DA12
off Queen St 213 GH86
Brewood Rd, Dag. RM8 168 EV65
Brewster Gdns, W10 14 A6
Brewster Ho, E14 21 N10
Brewster Rd, E10 145 EB60
Brian Av, S.Croy. CR2 242 DS112
Brian Cl, Horn. RM12 149 FH63
Briane Rd, Epsom KT19 238 CQ110
Brian Rd, Rom. RM6 148 EW57
Briant Est, SE1 30 E7
Briant Ho, SE1 30 D7
Briants Cl, Pnr. HA5 116 BZ54
Briant St, SE14 45 J6
Briar Av, SW16 203 DM94
Briarbank Rd, W13 159 CG72
Briar Banks, Cars. SM5 240 DG109
Briarcliff, Hem.H. HP1 61 BE19
Briar Cl, N2 142 DB55
N13 122 DQ48
Buckhurst Hill IG9 124 EK47
Cheshunt EN8 88 DW29
Hampton TW12 198 BZ92
Isleworth TW7 199 CF85
Potten End HP4 61 BA16
Taplow SL6 152 AH72
Warlingham CR6 259 EA116
West Byfleet KT14 234 BH111
Briar Ct, Sutt. SM3 239 CW105
Briar Cres, Nthlt. UB5 158 CB65
Briardale Gdns, NW3 142 DA62
Briarfield Av, N3 120 DB54
Briarfield Cl, Bexh. DA7 188 FA82
Briar Gdns, Brom. BR2 226 EF102
Briar Gro, S.Croy. CR2 242 DU113
Briar Hill, Pur. CR8 241 DL111
Briaris Cl, N17 122 DV52
Briar La, Cars. SM5 240 DG109
Croydon CR0 243 EB105
Briarleas Gdns, Upmin. RM14 151 FS59
Briarley Cl, Brox. EN10 71 DZ22
Briar Pas, SW16 223 DL97
Briar Pl, SW16 223 DM97
Briar Rd, NW2 141 CW63
SW16 223 DL97
Bexley DA5 209 FD90
Harrow HA3 139 CJ57
Romford RM3 128 FJ52
St. Albans AL4 65 CJ17
Send GU23 249 BB123
Shepperton TW17 216 BM99
Twickenham TW2 199 CE88
Watford WD25 81 BU34
Briars, The, Bushey Hth WD23 117 CE45
Cheshunt EN8 89 DY31
Harlow CM18 73 ES18
Hertford SG13 54 DU09
Sarratt WD3 96 BH36
Slough SL3 175 AZ78
Briars Cl, Hat. AL10 67 CU18
Briars Ct, Oxshott KT22 237 CD114
Briars La, Hat. AL10 67 CU18
Briars Wk, Rom. RM3 128 FL54
Briarswood, Goffs Oak EN7 88 DS28
Briars Wd, Hat. AL10 67 CT18
Horley RH6 291 DJ147
Briarswood Way, Orp. BR6 245 ET106
Briar Wk, SW15 181 CV84
W10 14 E4
Edgware HA8 118 CQ52
Briar Wk, West Byfleet KT14 234 BG112
Briarway, Berk. HP4 60 AW20
Briar Way, Guil. GU4 265 BB130
Slough SL2 153 AQ71
West Drayton UB7 176 BN75
Briarwood, Bans. SM7 256 DA115
Briarwood Cl, NW9 140 CQ58
Feltham TW13 197 BS90
Briar Wd Cl, Brom. BR2
off Gravel Rd 226 EL104
Briarwood Cl, Wor.Pk. KT4
off The Avenue 221 CU102
Briarwood Dr, Nthwd. HA6 115 BU54
Briarwood Rd, SW4 203 DK85
Epsom KT17 239 CU107
Briary Cl, NW3 6 C6
Briary Ct, E16 23 M9
Sidcup DA14 208 EV92
Briary Gdns, Brom. BR1 206 EH92
Briary Gro, Edg. HA8 118 CP54
Briary La, N9 122 DT48
Brick Ct, EC4 18 E9
Grays RM17
off Columbia Wf Rd 192 GA79
Brickcroft, Brox. EN10 89 DY26
Brickcroft Hoppit, Harl. CM17 58 EX14
Brickenden Ct, Wal.Abb. EN9 90 EF33
BRICKENDON, Hert. SG13 70 DQ19
BRICKENDONBURY, Hert. SG13 54 DR14
Brickendon Grn, Brickendon SG13 70 DQ19
Brickendon La, Hert. SG13 70 DQ18
Brickett Rd, St.Alb. AL1 65 CD20
Brickett Cl, Ruis. HA4 137 BQ57
BRICKET WOOD, St.Alb. AL2 82 BZ29
⇌ Bricket Wood 82 CA30
Brick Fm Cl, Rich. TW9 180 CP81
Brickfield, Hat. AL10 67 CU21
Brickfield Av, Hem.H. HP3 63 BP21
Brickfield Cl, E9 10 F5
Brentford TW8 179 CJ80
Brickfield Cotts, SE18 187 ET79
Brickfield Fm Gdns, Orp. BR6 245 EQ105
Brickfield La, Barn. EN5 101 CT44
Burnham SL1 152 AG67
Harlington UB3 177 BR79
Hookwood RH6 290 DD150
Brickfield Rd, SW19 202 DB91
Coopersale CM16 92 EX29
Outwood RH1 289 DN142
Thornton Heath CR7 223 DP95
Brickfields, Har. HA2 139 CD61
Brickfields, The, Ware SG12 54 DV05
● Brickfields Ind Est, Hem.H. HP2 63 BP16
Brickfields La, Cooper. CM16
off Brickfield Rd 92 EX29
Brickfields Way, West Dr. UB7 176 BM76
Brick Kiln Cl, Wat. WD19 98 BY44
Brick Kiln La, Oxt. RH8 276 EJ131
Brick Knoll Pk, St.Alb. AL1 65 CJ21
Brickland Ct, N9
off The Broadway 122 DU47
Brick La, E1 20 B4
E2 20 B3
Enfield EN1, EN3 104 DV40
Nthlt. UB5 158 BZ69
Stanmore HA7 117 CK52
● Bricklayer's Arms Distribution Cen, SE1 31 P9
Bricklayer's Arms Rbt, SE1 31 L8
Brickmakers La, Hem.H. HP3 63 BP21
Brick St, W1 29 J3
Brickwall Cl, Ayot St.P. AL6 51 CU07
Brickwall La, Ruis. HA4 137 BS60
Brickwood Cl, SE26 204 DV90
Brickwood Rd, Croy. CR0 224 DS103
Brickyard La, Wotton RH5 284 BW141
Brideale Cl, SE15 44 B3
Bride Ct, EC4 18 G9
Bride La, EC4 18 G9
Bridel Ms, N1 8 G9
Brides Pl, N1 9 N7
Bride St, N7 8 D5
Bridewain St, SE1 32 A6
Bridewell Pl, E1 32 F3
EC4 18 G9
Bridford Ms, W1 17 K6
Bridge, The, SW8 41 J5
Harrow HA3 139 CE55
Kings Langley WD4 81 BP29
Bridge Acad, E2 10 B9
Bridge App, NW1 6 G6
Bridge Av, W6 181 CW78
W7 159 CD71
Upminster RM14 150 FN61
Bridge Barn La, Wok. GU21 248 AW117
● Bridge Business Cen, Sthl. UB2 178 CA75
Bridge Cl, W10 14 D9
Brentwood CM13 131 FZ49
Byfleet KT14 234 BM112
Dartford DA2 191 FR83
Enfield EN1 104 DV40
Romford RM7 149 FE58
Slough SL1 153 AM73
Staines-upon-Thames TW18 195 BE91
Teddington TW11 199 CF91
Walton-on-Thames KT12 217 BT101
Woking GU21 248 AW117
Bridge Cotts, Upmin. RM14 151 FU64
Bridge Ct, E14
off Newport Av 23 H10
Grays RM17 off Bridge Rd 192 GB79
Har. HA2 138 CC61
Welwyn Garden City AL7 51 CZ09
Woking GU21 248 AX117
Bridge Dr, N13 121 DM49
Bridge End, E17 123 EC53
Bridge End Cl, Kings.T. KT2
off Clifton Rd 220 CN95
Bridgefield Cl, Bans. SM7 255 CW115
Bridgefield Rd, Sutt. SM1 240 DA107
Bridgefields, Welw.G.C. AL7 51 CZ08
Bridgefoot, SE1 42 A1
Ware SG12 off High St 55 DX06
Bridgefoot La, Pot.B. EN6 85 CX33
Bridge Gdns, N16 9 L1
Ashford TW15 197 BQ94
East Molesey KT8 219 CD98
Bridge Gate, N21 122 DQ45
● Bridgegate Cen, Welw.G.C. AL7 off Martinfield 51 CZ08
Bridgeham Cl, Wey. KT13
off Mayfield Rd 234 BN106
Bridgeham Way, Smallfield RH6 291 DP148
Bridge Hill, Epp. CM16 91 ET33
Bridgehill Cl, Guil. GU2 264 AU133
Bridgehill Cl, Wembley HA0 159 CK67
Bridge Ho, NW3
off Adelaide Rd 6 G6
SW8 off St. George Wf 42 A1
Bridge Ho Quay, E14 34 F3
● Bridge Ind Est, Horl. RH6 291 DH148
Bridgeland Rd, E16 23 P10
Bridgelands Cl, Beck. BR3 205 DZ94
Bridge La, NW11 141 CY57
SW11 40 D7
Virginia Water GU25 214 AY99
Bridgeman Dr, Wind. SL4 173 AN82
Bridgeman Rd, N1 8 C7
Teddington TW11 199 CG93
Bridgeman St, NW8 16 C1
Bridge Meadows, SE14 45 J2
Bridge Ms, Wok. GU21
off Bridge Barn La 248 AX117
Bridgend Rd, SW18 182 DC84
Enfield EN1 104 DW35
Bridgenhall Rd, Enf. EN1 104 DT39
Bridgen Rd, Bex. DA5 208 EY86
Bridge Pk, SW18 202 DA85
Guildford GU4 265 BC131
Bridge Pl, SW1 29 K8
Amersham HP6 77 AS38
Croydon CR0 224 DR101
Watford WD17
off Lower High St 98 BX43
Bridgepoint Pl, N6
off Hornsey La 143 DJ60
Bridgeport Pl, E1 32 D2
Bridger Cl, Wat. WD25 82 BX33
Bridge Rd, E6 167 EM66
E15 13 H7
E17 145 DZ59
N9 off Fore St 122 DU48
N22 121 DL53
NW10 160 CS65
Beckenham BR3 205 DZ94
Bexleyheath DA7 188 EY82
Chertsey KT16 216 BH101
Chessington KT9 238 CL106
East Molesey KT8 219 CE98
Epsom KT17 239 CT112
Erith DA8 189 FF81
Grays RM17 192 GB78
Hounslow TW3 179 CD82
Hunton Bridge WD4 81 BQ33
Isleworth TW7 179 CD83
Orpington BR5 228 EV100
Rainham RM13 169 FF70
Southall UB2 178 BZ75
Sutton SM2 240 DB107
Twickenham TW1 199 CH86
Uxbridge UB8 156 BJ68
Wallington SM6 241 DJ106
Welwyn Garden City AL7, AL8 51 CW08
Wembley HA9 140 CN62
Weybridge KT13 234 BM105
Bridge Rd E, Welw.G.C. AL7 51 CY08
Bridge Rd Prim Sch, Croy. CR0
off Cross Rd 224 DR102
Bridge Sch, The, Prim Dept, N7 7 P4
Sec Dept, N7 7 P1
Bridges Cl, Horl. RH6 291 DK148
Bridges Ct, SW11 40 A10
Bridges Dr, Dart. DA1 210 FP85
Bridges La, Croy. CR0 241 DL105
Bridges Pl, SW6 39 H6
Bridges Rd, SW19 202 DB93
Stanmore HA7 117 CF50
Bridges Rd Ms, SW19
off Bridges Rd 202 DB93
Bridge St, SW1 30 A5
W4 180 CR77
Berkhamsted HP4 60 AX19
Colnbrook SL3 175 BD80
Guildford GU1 280 AW135
Hemel Hempstead HP1 62 BJ21
Leatherhead KT22 253 CG122
Pinner HA5 138 BX55
Richmond TW9 199 CK85
Staines-upon-Thames TW18 195 BE91
Walton-on-Thames KT12 217 BT102
Bridge Ter, E15 13 H7
SE13 off Mercator Rd 185 ED84
Bridgetown Cl, SE19
off Georgetown Cl 204 DS92
Bridge Vw, W6 26 A10
Greenhithe DA9 191 FV84
Bridgeview Ct, Ilf. IG6 125 ER51
Bridgewater Cl, Chis. BR7 227 ES97
Bridgewater Ct, Slou. SL3 175 BA78
Bridgewater Gdns, Edg. HA8 118 CM54
Bridgewater Hill, Nthch HP4 60 AT16
Bridgewater Rd, E15
off Warton Rd 12 E9
Berkhamsted HP4 60 AU17
Wembley HA0 159 CJ66
Weybridge KT13 235 BR107
Bridgewater Sch, Berk. HP4 off Bridle Way 60 AU17
Bridgewater Sq, EC2 19 J6
Bridgewater St, EC2 19 J6
Bridgewater Ter, Wind. SL4 173 AR81
Bridgewater Way, Bushey WD23 98 CB44
Windsor SL4
off Bridgewater Ter 173 AR81
Bridge Way, N11
off Pymmes Grn Rd 121 DJ48
NW11 141 CZ57
Bridgeway, Bark. IG11 167 ET66
Bridge Way, Chipstead CR5 256 DE119
Cobham KT11 235 BT113
Twickenham TW2 198 CC87
Uxbridge UB10 137 BP64
Bridgeway, Wem. HA0 160 CL66
Bridgeway St, NW1 17 M1
Bridge Wf, Cher. KT16 216 BJ101
Bridge Wf Rd, Islw. TW7
off Church St 179 CH83
Bridgewood Cl, SE20 204 DV94
Bridgewood Rd, SW16 203 DK94
Worcester Park KT4 239 CU105
● Bridge Wks, Uxb. UB8 156 BJ70
Bridge Yd, SE1 31 M2
Bridgford St, SW18 202 DC90
Bridgman Rd, W4 180 CQ76
Bridgwater Cl, Rom. RM3 128 FK50
Bridgwater Rd, Rom. RM3 128 FJ50
Ruislip HA4 137 BU63
Bridgwater Wk, Rom. RM3 128 FK50
Bridle Cl, Enf. EN3 105 DZ37
Epsom KT19 238 CR106
Hoddesdon EN11 55 EA13
Kingston upon Thames KT1 219 CK98
Bridle Cl, St. Albans AL3 65 CE18
Sunbury-on-Thames TW16
off Forge La 217 BU97
Bridle End, Epsom KT17 239 CT114
Bridle La, W1 17 M10
Cobham KT11 252 CB115
Leatherhead KT22 252 CB115
Loudwater WD3 96 BK41
Twickenham TW1 199 CH86
Bridle Ms, Barn. EN5
off High St 101 CZ42
Bridle Path, Bedd. CR0 223 DM104
Watford WD17 97 BV40
Bridle Path, The, Epsom KT17 239 CV110
Woodford Green IG8 124 EE52
Bridlepath Way, Felt. TW14 197 BS88
Bridle Rd, Clay. KT10 237 CH107
Croydon CR0 225 EA104
Epsom KT17 239 CT113
Pinner HA5 138 BW58
Bridle Rd, The, Pur. CR8 241 DL110
Bridle Way, Berk. HP4 60 AU17
Croydon CR0 243 EA106
Great Amwell SG12 55 EA09
Hoddesdon EN11 55 EA14
Orpington BR6 245 EQ105
Bridle Way, The, Croy. CR0 243 DY110
Bridleway, The, Wall. SM6 241 DJ105
Bridleway Cl, Epsom KT17 239 CW110
Bridle Way N, Hodd. EN11 55 EA13
Bridle Way S, Hodd. EN11 55 EA14
Bridlington Cl, Bigg.H. TN16 260 EH119
Bridlington Rd, N9 122 DV45
Watford WD19 116 BX48
Bridlington Spur, Slou. SL1 173 AP76
Bridport Av, Rom. RM7 149 FB58
Bridport Pl, N1 9 M10
Bridport Rd, N18 122 DS50
Greenford UB6 158 CB67
Thornton Heath CR7 223 DN97
Bridport Ter, SW8 41 N7
Bridport Way, Slou. SL2 153 AP70
Bridstow Pl, W2 15 K8
Brief St, SE5 42 G8
Brier Lea, Lwr Kgswd KT20 271 CZ126
Brierley, New Adgtn CR0 243 EB107
Brierley Av, N9 122 DW46
Brierley Cl, SE25 224 DU98
Hornchurch RM11 150 FJ58
Brierley Rd, E11 145 ED63
SW12 203 DJ89
Brierly Cl, Guil. GU2 264 AU132
Brierly Gdns, E2 21 H1
Brier Rd, Tad. KT20 255 CV119
Briery Ct, Chorl. WD3 96 BG42
Hemel Hempstead HP2 62 BN19
Briery Fld, Chorl. WD3 96 BG42
Briery Way, Amer. HP6 77 AS37
Hemel Hempstead HP2 62 BN18
Brigade Cl, Har. HA2 139 CD61
Brigade Pl, Cat. CR3 258 DQ122
Brigade St, SE3 47 L9
Brigadier Av, Enf. EN2 104 DQ39
Brigadier Hill, Enf. EN2 104 DQ38
Briggeford Cl, E5 144 DU61
BRIGGENS PARK, Ware SG12 56 EJ11
Briggs Cl, Mitch. CR4 223 DH95
Bright Cl, Belv. DA17 188 EX77
Brightfield Rd, SE12 206 EF85
Bright Hill, Guil. GU1 280 AX136
Brightlands, Nthflt DA11 212 GE91
Brightlands Rd, Reig. RH2 272 DC132
Brightling Rd, SE4 205 DZ86
Brightlingsea Pl, E14 21 N10
Brightman Rd, SW18 202 DD88
Brighton Av, E17 145 DZ57
Brighton Cl, Add. KT15 234 BJ106
Uxbridge UB10 157 BP66
Brighton Dr, Nthlt. UB5 158 CA65
Brighton Gro, SE14 45 L6
Brighton Rd, E6 25 M2
N2 120 DC54
N16 144 DS63
Addlestone KT15 234 BJ105
Banstead SM7 239 CZ114
Coulsdon CR5 257 DJ119
Horley RH6 290 DF149
Purley CR8 242 DQ110
Redhill RH1 288 DF135
South Croydon CR2 242 DQ106
Surbiton KT6 219 CJ100
Sutton SM2 240 DB109
Tadworth KT20 255 CY119
Watford WD24 97 BU38
Brighton Spur, Slou. SL2 153 AP70
Brighton Ter, SW9 183 DM84
Redhill RH1 off Hooley La 288 DF135
Brights Av, Rain. RM13 169 FH70
Brightside, The, Enf. EN3 105 DX39
Brightside Av, Stai. TW18 196 BJ94
Brightside Rd, SE13 205 ED86
Bright St, E14 22 D8
Brightview Cl, Brick.Wd AL2 82 BY29
Brightwell Cl, Croy. CR0
off Sumner Rd 223 DN102
Brightwell Cres, SW17 202 DF92
Brightwell Rd, Wat. WD18 97 BU43
Brightwen Gro, Stan. HA7 117 CG47
Brigidine Sch Windsor, Wind. SL4 off King's Rd 173 AR83
Brig Ms, SE8 46 A3
Brigstock Rd, Belv. DA17 189 FB77
Coulsdon CR5 257 DH115
Thornton Heath CR7 223 DN99
Brill Pl, NW1 17 P1
Brimfield Rd, Purf. RM19 191 FR77
Brim Hill, N2 142 DC56
Brimpsfield Cl, SE2 188 EV76
BRIMSDOWN, Enf. EN3 105 DY41
⇌ Brimsdown 105 DY41
Brimsdown Av, Enf. EN3 105 DY40
● Brimsdown Ind Est, Enf. EN3 105 DY39
Brimsdown Inf & Jun Schs, Enf. EN3 off Green St 105 DX41
Brimshot La, Chobham GU24 232 AS109
Brimstone Cl, Orp. BR6 246 EW108
Brimstone Ho, E15
off Victoria St 13 J6
Brimstone La, Dor. RH5 286 CM143
Brimstone Wk, Berk. HP4 60 AT17
Brindishe Prim Sch, SE12
off Wantage Rd 206 EF85
Brindle Gate, Sid. DA15 207 ES88
Brindle La, Forty Grn HP9 110 AG51
Brindles, Horn. RM11 150 FL56
Brindles, The, Bans. SM7 255 CZ117
Brindles Cl, Hutt. CM13 131 GC47

Brindley Cl, Bexh. DA7 189 FB83
Wembley HA0 159 CJ67
Brindley Ho, SW2
off New Pk Rd 203 DL87
Brindley St, SE14 45 N7
Brindley Way, Brom. BR1 206 EG92
Hemel Hempstead HP3
off London Rd 80 BM25
Southall UB1 158 CB73
Brindwood Rd, E4 123 DZ48
Brinkburn Cl, SE2 188 EU77
Edgware HA8 118 CP54
Brinkburn Gdns, Edg. HA8 140 CN55
Brinkley, Kings.T. KT1
off Burritt Rd 220 CN96
Brinkley Rd, Wor.Pk. KT4 221 CV103
Brinklow Ct, St.Alb. AL3 64 CB23
Brinklow Cres, SE18 187 EP80
Brinklow Ho, W2 15 K6
Brinkworth Rd, Ilf. IG5 146 EL55
Brinkworth Way, E9 11 P4
Brinley Cl, Chshl EN8 88 DW31
Brinsdale Rd, NW4 141 CX56
Brinsley Ho, E1 off Tarling St 20 G9
Brinsley Rd, Har. HA3 117 CD54
Brinsmead, Frog. AL2 83 CD27
Brinsmead Rd, Rom. RM3 128 FN54
Brinsworth Cl, Twick. TW2 199 CD89
Brinton Wk, SE1 30 G3
Brion Pl, E14 22 E7
Brisbane Av, SW19 222 DB95
Brisbane Ho, Til. RM18 193 GF81
Brisbane Rd, E10 145 EB61
W13 179 CG75
Ilford IG1 147 EP59
Brisbane St, SE5 43 L5
Briscoe Cl, E11 146 EF61
Hoddesdon EN11 71 DZ15
Briscoe Rd, SW19 202 DD93
Hoddesdon EN11 71 DZ15
Rainham RM13 170 FJ68
Briset Rd, SE9 186 EK83
Briset St, EC1 18 G6
Briset Way, N7 143 DM61
Brisson Cl, Esher KT10 236 BZ107
Bristol Cl, Houns. TW4
off Harvey Rd 198 CA87
Stanwell TW19 196 BL86
Wallington SM6 241 DL108
Bristol Gdns, SW15
off Portsmouth Rd 201 CW87
W9 15 M5
Bristol Ho, SE11
off Lambeth Wk 30 E7
Bristol Ms, W9 15 M5
Bristol Pk Rd, E17 145 DY56
Bristol Rd, E7 166 EJ65
Gravesend DA12 213 GK90
Greenford UB6 158 CB67
Morden SM4 222 DC99
Bristol Way, Slou. SL1 154 AS74
Briston Gro, N8 143 DL58
Briston Ms, NW7 119 CU52
Bristowe Cl, SW2 203 DN86
Bristow Rd, SE19 204 DS92
Bexleyheath DA7 188 EY81
Croydon CR0 241 DL105
Hounslow TW3 178 CC83
★ Britain at War Experience, SE1 31 N3
Britannia Bldg, N1
off Ebenezer St 19 L2
● Britannia Business Pk, Wal.Cr. EN8 89 DZ34
Britannia Cl, SW4
off Bowland Rd 183 DK84
Erith DA8 189 FF79
Northolt UB5 158 BX69
Britannia Ct, Kings.T. KT2
off Skerne Wk 219 CK95
Britannia Dr, Grav. DA12 213 GM92
Britannia Gate, E16 35 P2
● Britannia Ind Est, Colnbr. SL3 175 BD82
Britannia La, Twick. TW2 198 CC87
Britannia Rd, E14 34 B9
N12 120 DC48
SW6 39 L5
Chesham HP5 76 AQ29
Ilford IG1 147 EP62
Surbiton KT5 220 CM101
Waltham Cross EN8 89 DZ34
Warley CM14 130 FW50
Britannia Row, N1 9 H8
Britannia St, WC1 18 C2
Sch Britannia Village Prim Sch, E16 36 A3
Britannia Wk, N1 19 L2
Britannia Way, NW10 160 CP70
SW6 39 M5
Stanwell TW19 196 BK87
★ British Dental Assoc Mus, W1 17 J7
British Gro, W4 181 CT78
British Gro N, W4
off Middlesex Ct 181 CT78
British Gro Pas, W4 181 CT78
British Gro S, W4
off British Gro Pas 181 CT78
British Legion Rd, E4 124 EF47
★ British Lib, NW1 17 P2
★ British Lib Newspapers, NW9 140 CS55
★ British Med Assoc, WC1 17 P4
★ British Mus, The, WC1 17 P7
Coll British Sch of Osteopathy, SE1 31 K5
British St, E3 21 P3
Coll British Transport Pol Training Sch, Walt.Hill KT20 255 CU123
off Sandlands Gro 255 CU123
Briton Cl, S.Croy. CR2 242 DS111
Briton Cres, S.Croy. CR2 242 DS111
Briton Hill Rd, S.Croy. CR2 242 DS110
Coll BRIT Sch for Performing Arts & Tech, The, Croy. CR0
off The Crescent 224 DR100
Brittain Rd, Dag. RM8 148 EY62
Hersham KT12 236 BX106
Brittains La, Sev. TN13 278 FF123
Brittany Ho, Enf. EN2
off Chantry Cl 104 DQ38
Brittany Pt, SE11 30 E9
Britten Cl, NW11 142 DB60
Elstree WD6
off Rodgers Cl 99 CK44
Brittenden Cl, Orp. BR6 245 ES107
Brittenden Par, Grn St Grn BR6
off Glentrammon Rd 245 ET107
Britten Dr, Sthl. UB1 158 CA72
Brittens Cl, Guil. GU2 264 AU129
Britten St, SW3 40 C1
Brittidge Rd, NW10
off Paulet Way 160 CS66
Britton Av, St.Alb. AL3 65 CD20
Britton Cl, SE6
off Brownhill Rd 205 ED87
Sch Brittons Sch, Rain. RM13
off Ford La 169 FF66
Britton St, EC1 18 G5
Britwell Dr, Berk. HP4 60 AY17
Britwell Est, Slou. SL2 153 AM70
Britwell Gdns, Burn. SL1 153 AK69
Britwell Rd, Burn. SL1 153 AK69
Brixham Cres, Ruis. HA4 137 BU60
Brixham Gdns, Ilf. IG3 147 ES64
Brixham Rd, Well. DA16 188 EX81
Brixham St, E16 37 K3
BRIXTON, SW2 183 DL84
⇌ Brixton 183 DN84
⊖ Brixton 183 DN84
Brixton Hill, SW2 203 DL87
Brixton Hill Pl, SW2 203 DL87
Brixton Oval, SW2 183 DN84
Brixton Rd, SW9 42 E5
Watford WD24 97 BV39
Brixton Sta Rd, SW9 183 DN84
🔒 Brixton Village Mkt, SW9
off Coldharbour La 183 DN84
Brixton Water La, SW2 203 DM85
Broad Acre, Brick.Wd AL2 82 BY30
Broadacre, Stai. TW18 196 BG92
Broadacre Cl, Uxb. UB10 137 BP62
Broad Acres, Gdmg. GU7 280 AS143
Broadacres, Guil. GU3 264 AS132
Broad Acres, Hat. AL10 67 CT15
Broadbent Cl, N6 143 DH60
Broadbent St, W1 17 J10
Broadberry Ct, N18 122 DV50
Broadbridge Cl, SE3 47 N4
Broadbridge La, Smallfield RH6 291 DN148
Broad Cl, Hersham KT12 218 BX104
Broad Common Est, N16
off Osbaldeston Rd 144 DU60
Broadcoombe, S.Croy. CR2 242 DW108
Broad Ct, WC2 18 B9
Welwyn Garden City AL7 51 CY09
Broadcroft, Hem.H. HP2 62 BK18
Broadcroft Av, Stan. HA7 117 CK54
Broadcroft Rd, Petts Wd BR5 227 ER101
Broad Ditch Rd, Sthflt DA13 212 GC94
Broadeaves Cl, S.Croy. CR2 242 DS106
Broadfield, Harlow CM20 57 ES14
● Broadfield Cl, Croy. CR0
off Progress Way 223 DM103
Broadfield Cl, NW2 141 CW62
Romford RM1 149 FF57
Tadworth KT20 255 CW120
Broadfield Ct, Bushey Hth WD23 117 CE47
Sch Broadfield Inf Sch, Hem.H. HP2 off Broadfield Rd 62 BM20
Sch Broadfield Jun Sch, Hem.H. HP2 off Windmill Rd 62 BM20
Broadfield La, NW1 8 A6
Broadfield Pl, Welw.G.C. AL8 51 CV10
Broadfield Rd, SE6 206 EE87
Hemel Hempstead HP2 62 BM20
Peaslake GU5 283 BR142
Broadfields, E.Mol. KT8 219 CD100
Goffs Oak EN7 87 DP29
Harrow HA2 116 CB54
High Wych CM21 58 EV06
Broadfields Av, N21 121 DN45
Edgware HA8 118 CP49
Sch Broadfields Co Prim Sch, Harl. CM20 off Freshwaters 57 ES14
Broadfields Hts, Edg. HA8 118 CP49
Broadfields La, Wat. WD19 115 BV46
Sch Broadfields Prim Sch, Edg. HA8 off Broadfields Av 118 CN47
Broadfield Sq, Enf. EN1 104 DV40
Broadfields Way, NW10 141 CT64
Broadfield Way, Ald. WD25 98 CB36
Buck.H. IG9 124 EJ48
Broadford, Shalf. GU4 280 AX141
Broadford La, Chobham GU24 232 AT112
● Broadford Pk, Shalf. GU4 280 AX141
Sch Broadford Prim Sch, Harold Hill RM3 off Faringdon Av 128 FK51
Broadford Rd, Peasm. GU3 280 AW142
BROADGATE, EC2 19 M6
Broadgate, E13 166 EJ68
Waltham Abbey EN9 90 EF33
Broadgate Circle, EC2 19 N6
Broadgate Rd, E16 24 E8
Broadgates Av, Barn. EN4 102 DB39
Broadgates Rd, SW18
off Ellerton Rd 202 DD88
BROAD GREEN, Croy. CR0 223 DN100
Broad Grn, Bayford SG13 69 DM15
Broad Grn Av, Croy. CR0 223 DP101
Broadgreen Rd, Chsht EN7 88 DR26
Broad Grn Wd, Bayford SG13 69 DM15
Broadham Grn Rd, Oxt. RH8 275 ED132
Broadham Pl, Oxt. RH8 275 ED131
Broadhead Strand, NW9 119 CT53
Broadheath Dr, Chis. BR7 207 EM92
Broad Highway, Cob. KT11 236 BX114
Broadhinton Rd, SW4 41 K10
Broadhurst, Ashtd. KT21 254 CL116
Broadhurst Av, Edg. HA8 118 CP49
Ilford IG3 147 ET63
Broadhurst Cl, NW6 5 N5
Richmond TW10
off Lower Gro Rd 200 CM85
Broadhurst Gdns, NW6 5 L5
Chigwell IG7 125 EQ49
Reigate RH2 288 DB137
Ruislip HA4 138 BW61
Broadhurst Wk, Rain. RM13 169 FG65
Broadis Way, Rain. RM13 169 FD68
Broadlake Cl, Lon.Col. AL2 83 CK27
Broadlands, Bad.Dene RM17
off Bankfoot 192 FZ78
Hanworth TW13 198 BZ90
Horley RH6 291 DJ147
Broadlands Av, SW16 203 DL89
Chesham HP5 76 AQ31
Enfield EN3 104 DV41
Shepperton TW17 217 BQ100
Broadlands Cl, N6 142 DG59
SW16 203 DL89
Enfield EN3 104 DV41
Waltham Cross EN8 89 DX34
Broadlands Dr, Warl. CR6 258 DW119
Broadlands Rd, N6 142 DF59
Broadlands Rd, Bromley BR1 206 EH91
Broadlands Way, N.Mal. KT3 221 CT100
Broad La, EC2 19 N6
N8 off Tottenham La 143 DM57
N15 144 DT56
Beaconsfield HP9 132 AH55
Dartford DA2 209 FG91
Hampton TW12 198 CA93
Wooburn Green HP10 132 AG58
Broad Lawn, SE9 207 EN89
Broadlawns Ct, Har. HA3 117 CF53
Broadleaf Gro, Welw.G.C. AL8 51 CV06
BROADLEY COMMON, Wal.Abb. EN9 72 EL20
Broadley Gdns, Shenley WD7
off Queens Way 84 CL32
Broadley Rd, Harl. CM19 73 EM19
Broadley St, NW8 16 B6
Broadley Ter, NW1 16 D5
Waltham Abbey EN9 72 EL21
Broadmark Rd, Slou. SL2 154 AV73
Broadmayne, SE17 31 K10
Broadmead, SE6 205 EA90
Ashtead KT21 254 CM117
Horley RH6 291 DJ147
Broadmead Av, Wor.Pk. KT4 221 CU101
Broadmead Cl, Hmptn. TW12 198 CA93
Pinner HA5 116 BY52
Sch Broadmead Junior, Inf & Nurs Sch, Croy. CR0
off Sydenham Rd 224 DR101
Broadmead Rd, Hayes UB4 158 BY70
Northolt UB5 158 BY70
Woking GU22, GU23 249 BB122
Woodford Green IG8 124 EG51
Broadmeads, Send GU23
off Broadmead Rd 249 BB122
Ware SG12 55 DX06
Sch Broadmere Comm Prim Sch, Sheer. GU21
off Devonshire Av 233 BD113
BROADMOOR, Dor. RH5 284 CA143
Broadmoor, Dor. RH5 284 CA143
Broad Oak, Slou. SL2 153 AQ70
Sunbury-on-Thames TW16 197 BT93
Woodford Green IG8 124 EH50
Broadoak Av, Enf. EN3 105 DX35
Broad Oak Cl, E4 123 EA50
Orpington BR5 228 EU96
Broadoak Cl, Sutt.H. DA4 210 FN93
Broadoak Ct, SW9
off Gresham Rd 183 DN83
Broad Oak Ct, Slou. SL2 153 AQ70
BROADOAK END, Hert. SG14 53 DM07
Broad Oak La, Hert. SG14 53 DM07
Broad Oak Manor, Hert. SG14 53 DM07
Broadoak Rd, Erith DA8 189 FD80
Broadoaks, Epp. CM16 91 ET31
Broadoaks Cres, W.Byf. KT14 234 BH114
Broadoaks Way, Brom. BR2 226 EF99
Broad Platts, Slou. SL3 174 AX76
Broad Ride, Egh. TW20 214 AU96
Broad Rd, Swans. DA10 212 FY86
Broad Sanctuary, SW1 29 P5
Broadstone Pl, W1 16 G7
Broadstone Rd, Horn. RM12 149 FG61
Broad St, Chesh. HP5 76 AQ30
Dagenham RM10 168 FA66
Hemel Hempstead HP2 62 BK19
Rydeshill GU3 264 AS132
Teddington TW11 199 CF93
Broad St Av, EC2 19 N7
Broad St Pl, EC2 19 M7
Broadstrood, Loug. IG10 107 EN38
Broad Vw, NW9 140 CN58
Broadview Av, Grays RM16 192 GD75
Broadview Ho, Enf. EN3
off Tysoe Av 105 DZ36
Broadview Rd, SW16 203 DJ94
Chesham HP5 76 AP27
Broadwalk, E18 146 EF55
Broad Wk, N21 121 DM47
NW1 17 J3
SE3 186 EJ83
W1 28 G2
Caterham CR3 258 DT122
Coulsdon CR5 256 DG123
Croydon CR0 243 DY110
Epsom KT18 255 CX119
Harlow CM20 57 ER14
Broadwalk, Har. HA2 138 CA57
Broad Wk, Houns. TW5 178 BX81
Orpington BR6 228 EX104
Richmond TW9 180 CM80
Sevenoaks TN15 279 FL128
Broad Wk, The, W8 27 M1
East Molesey KT8 219 CF97
Broadwalk, The, Nthwd. HA6 115 BQ54
Broadwalk Ct, W8 27 K2
Broad Wk La, NW11 141 CZ59
Broad Wk N, The, Brwd. CM13 131 GA49
🔒 Broadwalk Shop Cen, Edg. HA8 118 CN51
Broad Wk S, The, Brwd. CM13 131 GA49
Broadwall, SE1 30 F2
Broadwater, Berk. HP4 60 AW18
Potters Bar EN6 86 DB30
Broadwater Cl, Hersham KT12 235 BU106
Woking GU21 233 BD112
Wraysbury TW19 195 AZ87
Broadwater Cres, Welw.G.C. AL7 51 CX10
Broad Water Cres, Wey. KT13 217 BQ104
Broadwater Fm Est, N17 122 DR54
Sch Broadwater Fm Prim Sch, N17 off Moira Cl 122 DR54
Broadwater Gdns, Hare. UB9 136 BH56
Orpington BR6 245 EP105
Broadwater La, Hare. UB9 136 BH56
● Broadwater Pk, Denh. UB9 136 BG58
Broadwater Pk, Maid. SL6 172 AE78
Broadwater Pl, Wey. KT13
off Oatlands Dr 217 BS103
Sch Broadwater Prim Sch, SW17
off Broadwater Rd 202 DE91
Broadwater Ri, Guil. GU1 265 BA134
Broadwater Rd, N17 122 DS53
SE28 187 ER76
SW17 202 DE91
Welwyn Garden City AL7 51 CY10
Broadwater Rd N, Hersham KT12 235 BT106
Broadwater Rd S, Hersham KT12 235 BT106
Sch Broadwater Sch, Farnc. GU7 off Summers Rd 280 AU143
Broadway, E15 13 H7
SW1 29 N6
W7 159 CG74
Broadway, W13 159 CG74
Barking IG11 167 EQ67
Bexleyheath DA6, DA7 188 EY84
Grays RM17 192 GC79
Nthwd. HA6 off Joel St 115 BU54
Potters Bar EN6
off Darkes La 85 CZ32
Rainham RM13 169 FG70
Romford RM2 149 FG55
Staines-upon-Thames TW18
off Kingston Rd 196 BH93
Swanley BR8 229 FC100
Tilbury RM18 193 GF82
Broadway, The, E4 123 EC51
E13 24 A1
N8 143 DL58
N9 122 DU47
N14 off Winchmore Hill Rd 121 DK46
N22 121 DN54
NW7 118 CS50
SW13 off The Terrace 180 CS82
SW19 201 CZ93
W5 159 CK73
W7 off Cherington Rd 159 CE74
Amersham HP7 77 AP40
Beaconsfield HP9
off Penn Rd 111 AK52
Cheam SM3 239 CY107
Chesham HP5 76 AP31
Croydon CR0
off Croydon Rd 241 DL105
Dagenham RM8 148 EZ61
Farnham Common SL2 153 AQ65
Greenford UB6 158 CC70
Hatfield AL9 67 CW17
Hornchurch RM12 149 FH63
Laleham TW18 216 BJ97
Loughton IG10 107 EQ42
New Haw KT15 234 BG110
Pinner HA5 116 BZ52
Southall UB1 158 BX73
Stanmore HA7 117 CJ50
Sutton SM1 off Manor La 240 DC106
Thames Ditton KT7
off Hampton Ct Way 219 CE102
Watford WD17 98 BW41
Wealdstone HA3 117 CE54
Wembley HA9 off East La 140 CL62
Woking GU21 249 AZ117
Woodford Green IG8 124 EH51
Wycombe End HP9 111 AL54
Broadway Av, Croy. CR0 224 DR99
Harlow CM17 58 EV11
Twickenham TW1 199 CH86
Broadway Cl, Amer. HP7 77 AP40
South Croydon CR2 242 DV114
Woodford Green IG8 124 EH51
Broadway Ct, SW19 201 CZ93
Amersham HP7 77 AP40
Broadway E, Denh. UB9 136 BG59
Broadway Est, Til. RM18 193 GF81
Broadway Gdns, Mitch. CR4 222 DE98
🔒 Broadway Mkt, SW17 202 DF91
Broadway Mkt, E8 10 D9
Broadway Mkt Ms, E8 10 D9
Broadway Ms, E5 144 DT59
N13 off Elmdale Rd 121 DM50
N21 121 DP46
Broadway Par, N8 143 DL58
Hayes UB3
off Coldharbour La 157 BU74
Hornchurch RM12
off The Broadway 149 FH63
Broadway Pl, SW19
off Hartfield Rd 201 CZ93
🔒 Broadway Shop Cen, W6 26 B9
Broadway Wk, E14 34 B6
Broadwick St, W1 17 M10
Broadwood, Grav. DA11 213 GH92
Broadwood Av, Ruis. HA4 137 BS58
Broadwood Rd, Couls. CR5 257 DK121
Broadwood Ter, W8
off Pembroke Rd 27 H8
Broad Yd, EC1 18 G5
Brocas Cl, NW3 6 D6
Brocas St, Eton SL4 173 AR80
Brocas Ter, Eton SL4 173 AQ80
Brockbridge Ho, SW15
off Tangley Gro 201 CT86
Brockdene Dr, Kes. BR2 244 EK105
Brockdish Av, Bark. IG11 147 ET64
Brockenhurst, W.Mol. KT8 218 BZ100
Brockenhurst Av, Wor.Pk. KT4 220 CS102
Brockenhurst Cl, Wok. GU21 233 AZ114
Brockenhurst Gdns, NW7 118 CS50
Ilford IG1 147 EQ64
Brockenhurst Ms, N18 122 DU49
Brockenhurst Rd, Croy. CR0 224 DV101
Brockenhurst Way, SW16 223 DK96
Brocket Cl, Chig. IG7
off Brocket Way 125 ET50
Brocket Pk, Lmsfd AL8 50 CS10
Brocket Rd, Grays RM16 193 GG76
Hoddesdon EN11 71 EA17
Welwyn Garden City AL8 51 CT11
Brockett Cl, Welw.G.C. AL8 51 CV09
Brocket Way, Chig. IG7 125 ES50
Brock Grn, S.Ock. RM15
off Cam Grn 171 FV72
BROCKHAM, Bet. RH3 286 CP136
Brockham Cl, SW19 201 CZ92
Brockham Cres, New Adgtn CR0 243 ED108
Brockham Dr, SW2
off Fairview Pl 203 DM87
Ilford IG2 147 EP58
Brockham Grn, Brock. RH3 286 CP135
Brockham Hill Pk, Box H. KT20 270 CQ131
Brockhamhurst Rd, Bet. RH3 286 CN141
Brockham Keep, Horl. RH6
off Langshott La 291 DJ147
Brockham La, Brock. RH3 270 CN134
Sch Brockham Sch, Brock. RH3 off Wheelers La 286 CP136
Brockham St, SE1 31 K6
Brockhill, Wok. GU21 248 AU117
Brockhurst Cl, Stan. HA7 117 CF51
Brockhurst Rd, Chesh. HP5 76 AQ29
Brockill Cres, SE4 185 DY84
Brocklebank Ct, Whyt. CR3 258 DU118
Brocklebank Ho, E16
off Glenister St 37 M3
● Brocklebank Ind Est, SE7 35 P8
Brocklebank Rd, SE7 36 A9
SW18 202 DC87
Brocklehurst St, SE14 45 K4
Brocklesbury Cl, Wat. WD24 98 BW41
Brocklesby Rd, SE25 224 DV98
Brockles Mead, Harl. CM19 73 EQ19
BROCKLEY, SE4 205 DY85
⇌ Brockley 45 M10
⊖ Brockley 45 M10
Brockley Av, Stan. HA7 118 CL48
Brockley Cl, Stan. HA7 118 CL49
Brockley Combe, Wey. KT13 235 BR105
Brockley Cres, Rom. RM5 127 FC52
Brockley Cross, SE4 45 N10
Brockley Footpath, SE15 184 DW84
Brockley Gdns, SE4 45 N8
Brockley Gro, SE4 205 DZ85
Hutton CM13 131 GA46
Brockley Hall Rd, SE4 205 DY86
Brockley Hill, Stan. HA7 117 CJ46
Brockley Ms, SE4 205 DY85
Brockley Pk, SE23 205 DY87
Stanmore HA7 118 CL48
Sch Brockley Prim Sch, SE4
off Brockley Rd 205 DZ85
Brockley Ri, SE23 205 DY86
Brockley Rd, SE4 45 M10
Brockleyside, Stan. HA7 117 CK49
Brockley Vw, SE23 205 DY87
Brockley Way, SE4 205 DX85
Brockman Ri, Brom. BR1 205 ED91
Brock Pl, E3 22 C5
Brock Rd, E13 24 B6
Brocks Dr, Sutt. SM3 221 CY104
Brockshot Cl, Brent. TW8 179 CK79
Brocksparkwood, Brwd. CM13 131 GB48
Brock St, SE15 44 G10
Brockswood La, Welw.G.C. AL8 51 CU08
Brockton Cl, Rom. RM1 149 FF56
Brock Way, Vir.W. GU25 214 AW99
Brockway Cl, E11 146 EE60
Guildford GU1 265 BB132
Brockweir, E2 20 G1
Brockwell Av, Beck. BR3 225 EB99
Brockwell Cl, Orp. BR5 227 ET99
★ Brockwell Park, SE24 203 DP86
Brockwell Pk Gdns, SE24 203 DN87
Brockwell Pk Row, SW2 203 DN86
Broderick Gro, Bkhm KT23
off Lower Shott 268 CA126
Brodewater Rd, Borwd. WD6 100 CP40
Brodia Rd, N16 144 DS62
Brodick Ho, E3 11 N10
Brodie Ho, SE1
off Coopers Rd 32 B10
Brodie Rd, E4 123 EC46
Enfield EN2 104 DQ38
Guildford GU1 280 AY135
Brodie St, SE1 32 B10
Brodlove La, E1 21 J10
Brodrick Gro, SE2 188 EV77
Brodrick Rd, SW17 202 DE89
Brograve Gdns, Beck. BR3 225 EB96
Broke Ct, Guil. GU4
off Speedwell Cl 265 BC131
Broke Fm Dr, Orp. BR6 246 EW109
Broken Furlong, Eton SL4 173 AP78
Brokengate La, Denh. UB9 135 BC60
Broken Wf, EC4 19 J10
Brokes Cres, Reig. RH2 272 DA132
Brokesley St, E3 21 N3
Brokes Rd, Reig. RH2 272 DA132
Broke Wk, E8 10 B8
Bromar Rd, SE5 43 P10
Bromborough Grn, Wat. WD19 116 BW50
Bromefield, Stan. HA7 117 CJ53
Bromefield Ct, Wal.Abb. EN9 90 EG33
Bromehead Rd, E1 20 G8
Bromehead St, E1 20 G8
Bromell's Rd, SW4 183 DJ84
Brome Rd, SE9 187 EM83
Bromet Cl, Wat. WD17 97 BT38
Sch Bromet Prim Sch, Wat. WD19 off Oxhey Rd 116 BX45
Bromfelde Rd, SW4 41 P10
Bromfelde Wk, SW4 41 P9
Bromfield St, N1 8 F10
Bromford Cl, Oxt. RH8 276 EG133
Bromhall Rd, Dag. RM8, RM9 168 EV65
Bromhedge, SE9 207 EM90
Bromholm Rd, SE2 188 EV76
Bromleigh Cl, Chsht EN8 89 DY28
Bromleigh Ct, SE23 204 DV89
BROMLEY, BR1 & BR2 226 EF96
BROMLEY, E3 22 D5
Bromley, Grays RM17 192 FZ79
Coll Bromley Adult Ed Coll, Kentwood Cen, SE20
off Kingsdale Rd 205 DX94
Poverest Cen, Orp. BR5
off Poverest Rd 228 EU99
Widmore Cen, Brom. BR1
off Nightingale La 226 EJ97
Bromley Av, Brom. BR1 206 EE94
⊖ Bromley-by-Bow 22 D4
Bromley Cl, Harl. CM20 58 EV11
Coll Bromley Coll of Further & Higher Ed, Anerley, SE20
off Hawthorn Gro 224 DW95
Beckenham Learning Cen, Beck. BR3 off Beckenham Rd 225 DZ95
Rookery La Campus, Brom. BR2 off Rookery La 226 EK100
BROMLEY COMMON, Brom. BR2 227 EM101
Bromley Common, Brom. BR2 226 EJ98
Bromley Cres, Brom. BR2 226 EF97
Ruislip HA4 137 BT63
Bromley Gdns, Brom. BR2 226 EF97
Bromley Gro, Brom. BR2 225 ED96
Bromley Hall Rd, E14 22 E6
Sch Bromley High Sch GDST, Brom. BR1 off Blackbrook La 227 EN98
Bromley High St, E3 22 C2
Bromley Hill, Brom. BR1 206 EE92
● Bromley Ind Cen, Brom. BR1 226 EJ97
Bromley La, Chis. BR7 207 EQ94
★ Bromley Mus, Orp. BR6 228 EV101
⇌ Bromley North 226 EG95
⊖ Bromley North 226 EG95
BROMLEY PARK, Brom. BR1 226 EE95
Bromley Pk, Brom. BR1
off London Rd 226 EF95
Bromley Pl, W1 17 L6
Bromley Rd, E10 145 EB58
E17 123 EA54

Bromley Rd, N17 122 DT53
N18 122 DR48
SE6 205 EB88
Beckenham BR3 225 EB95
Chislehurst BR7 227 EP95
Downham BR1 205 EC91
Shortlands BR2 225 EC96
Bromley Rd Inf Sch, Beck. BR3 off Bromley Rd 225 EB95
● Bromley Rd Retail Pk, SE6 off Bromley Rd 205 EB89
⇌ Bromley South 226 EG97
Bromley St, E1 21 K7
BROMPTON, SW3 28 C7
Brompton Arc, SW3 28 E5
Brompton Cl, SE20 off Selby Rd 224 DU96
Hounslow TW4 198 BZ85
Brompton Dr, Erith DA8 189 FH80
Brompton Gro, N2 142 DE56
★ Brompton Oratory, SW7 28 C7
Brompton Pk Cres, SW6 39 L3
Brompton Pl, SW3 28 D6
Brompton Rd, SW1 28 D6
SW3 28 C8
SW7 28 D6
Brompton Sq, SW3 28 C6
Brompton Ter, SE18 off Prince Imperial Rd 187 EN81
Bromwich Av, N6 142 DG61
Bromyard Av, W3 160 CS74
Bromyard Ho, SE15 44 E4
W3 160 CS74
Bromycroft Rd, Slou. SL2 153 AN69
BRONDESBURY, NW2 4 E6
⊖ Brondesbury 4 G6
Brondesbury Ct, NW2 4 C5
Brondesbury Ms, NW6 5 J7
BRONDESBURY PARK, NW6 4 B7
⊖ Brondesbury Park 4 E8
Brondesbury Pk, NW2 161 CV65
NW6 4 E7
Brondesbury Rd, NW6 4 G10
Brondesbury Vil, NW6 5 H10
Bronsart Rd, SW6 38 E5
Bronsdon Way, Denh. UB9 135 BF61
Bronson Rd, SW20 221 CX96
Bronte Cl, E7 off Bective Rd 146 EG63
Erith DA8 189 FB80
Ilford IG2 147 EN57
Slough SL1 174 AS75
Tilbury RM18 193 GJ82
Bronte Ct, Borwd. WD6 off Chaucer Gro 100 CN42
Bronte Gro, Dart. DA1 190 FM84
Bronte Ho, NW6 15 K2
Bronte Sch, Grav. DA11 off Pelham Rd 213 GG87
Bronte Vw, Grav. DA12 213 GJ88
Bronti Cl, SE17 43 K1
Bronze Age Way, Belv. DA17 189 FC76
Erith DA8 189 FC76
Bronze St, SE8 46 B4
BROOK, Guil. GU5 282 BL142
Brook Av, Dag. RM10 169 FB66
Edgware HA8 118 CP51
Wembley HA9 140 CN62
Brookbank, Enf. EN1 104 DV37
Wooburn Green HP10 132 AC60
Brookbank Av, W7 159 CD71
Brookbank Rd, SE13 185 EA83
● Brook Business Cen, Uxb. UB8 off St. Johns Rd 156 BH68
Brook Cl, NW7 119 CY52
SW17 202 DG89
SW20 221 CV97
W3 160 CN74
Borehamwood WD6 100 CP41
Dorking RH4 269 CJ134
Epsom KT19 238 CS109
Romford RM2 127 FF53
Ruislip HA4 137 BS59
Stanwell TW19 196 BM87
Brook Comm Prim Sch, E8 10 D3
Brook Ct, Bark. IG11 off Spring Pl 167 EQ68
Buckhurst Hill IG9 124 EH46
Brook Cres, E4 123 EA49
N9 122 DV49
Slough SL1 153 AL72
Brookdale, N11 121 DJ49
Brookdale Av, Upmin. RM14 150 FN62
Brookdale Cl, Upmin. RM14 150 FP62
Brookdale Rd, E17 145 EA55
SE6 205 EB86
Bexley DA5 208 EY86
Brookdene Av, Wat. WD19 115 BV45
Brookdene Dr, Nthwd. HA6 115 BT52
Brookdene Rd, SE18 187 ET77
Brook Dr, SE11 30 F7
Harrow HA1 138 CC56
Radlett WD7 83 CF33
Ruislip HA4 137 BS58
Brooke Av, Har. HA2 138 CC62
Brooke Cl, Bushey WD23 116 CC45
Brooke Ct, W10 14 F1
Brookehowse Rd, SE6 205 EB90
Brook End, Saw. CM21 58 EX05
Brookend Rd, Sid. DA15 207 ES88
Brooke Rd, E5 144 DU62
E17 145 EC56
N16 144 DT62
Grays RM17 192 GA78
Brooker Rd, Wal.Abb. EN9 89 EC34
Brookers Cl, Ashtd. KT21 253 CJ117
Brooke's Ct, EC1 18 E6
Brookes Mkt, EC1 18 F6
Brooke St, EC1 18 E7
● Brooke Trading Est, Rom. RM1 149 FF59
Brooke Way, Bushey WD23 116 CC45
Brook Fm Rd, Cob. KT11 252 BX115
Brookfield, N6 142 DG62
Godalming GU7 280 AU143
Thornwood CM16 92 EW25
Woking GU21 248 AV116
Brookfield Adult Learning Cen, Uxb. UB8 off Park Rd 156 BL65
Brookfield Av, E17 145 EC56
NW7 119 CV51
W5 159 CK70
Brookfield Av, Sutton SM1 240 DD105
● Brookfield Cen, Chsht EN8 89 DX27
Brookfield Cl, NW7 119 CV51
Ashtead KT21 254 CL120
Hutton CM13 131 GC44
Ottershaw KT16 233 BD107
Redhill RH1 288 DG140
Brookfield Ct, Grnf. UB6 158 CC69
Harrow HA3 139 CK57
Brookfield Cres, NW7 119 CV51
Harrow HA3 140 CL57
Brookfield Gdns, Chsht EN8 89 DX27
Claygate KT10 237 CF107
Brookfield Ho Sch, Wdf.Grn. IG8 off Alders Av 124 EE51
Brookfield La E, Chsht EN8 89 DX27
Brookfield La W, Chsht EN8 88 DV28
Brookfield Pk, NW5 143 DH62
Brookfield Path, Wdf.Grn. IG8 124 EE51
Brookfield Pl, Cob. KT11 252 BY115
Brookfield Prim Sch, N19 off Chester Rd 143 DH61
Sutton SM3 off Ridge Rd 221 CY102
● Brookfield Retail Pk, Chsht EN8 89 DX26
Brookfield Rd, E9 11 M5
N9 122 DU48
W4 180 CR75
Wooburn Green HP10 132 AD60
Brookfields, Enf. EN3 105 DX42
Sawbridgeworth CM21 58 EX05
Brookfields Av, Mitch. CR4 222 DE99
Brook Gdns, E4 123 EB49
SW13 181 CT83
Kingston upon Thames KT2 220 CQ95
Brook Gate, W1 28 F1
Brook Grn, W6 26 D8
Chobham GU24 off Brookleys 232 AT110
Brook Hill, Far.Grn GU5 282 BK143
Oxted RH8 275 EC130
Brookhill Cl, SE18 187 EP78
East Barnet EN4 102 DE43
Brookhill Rd, SE18 187 EP78
Barnet EN4 102 DE43
Brookhouse Dr, Woob.Grn HP10 132 AC60
Brookhouse Gdns, E4 124 EE49
Brookhurst Rd, Add. KT15 234 BH107
● Brook Ind Est, Hayes UB4 158 BX74
Brooking Cl, Dag. RM8 148 EW62
Brooking Rd, E7 13 P2
Brookland Cl, NW11 142 DA56
Brookland Garth, NW11 142 DB56
Brookland Hill, NW11 142 DA56
Brookland Inf & Jun Schs, NW11 off Hill Top 142 DB56
Brookland Inf Sch, Chsht EN8 off Elm Dr 89 DY28
Brookland Jun Sch, Chsht EN8 off Elm Dr 89 DY28
Brookland Ri, NW11 142 DA56
BROOKLANDS, Wey. KT13 234 BM109
Brooklands, Dart. DA1 210 FL88
Brooklands App, Rom. RM1 149 FD56
Brooklands Av, SW19 202 DB89
Sidcup DA15 207 ER89
Brooklands Cl, Cob. KT11 252 BY115
Romford RM7 off Marshalls Rd 149 FD56
Sunbury-on-Thames TW16 217 BS95
Brooklands Coll, Ashford Campus, Ashf. TW15 off Church Rd 196 BM91
Weybridge Campus, Wey. KT13 off Heath Rd 234 BM107
Brooklands Ct, New Haw KT15 234 BK110
St. Albans AL1 65 CE20
Weybridge KT13 235 BP108
Brooklands Dr, Perivale UB6 159 CJ67
Weybridge KT13 234 BM110
Brooklands Gdns, Horn. RM11 150 FJ57
Potters Bar EN6 85 CY32
● Brooklands Ind Pk, Wey. KT13 234 BL110
Brooklands La, Rom. RM7 149 FD56
Weybridge KT13 234 BM107
★ Brooklands Mus, Wey. KT13 234 BN109
Brooklands Pk, SE3 47 N10
Brooklands Pas, SW8 41 N6
Brooklands Pl, Hmptn. TW12 198 CB92
Brooklands Prim Sch, SE3 47 P10
Brooklands Rd, Rom. RM7 149 FD56
Thames Ditton KT7 219 CF102
Weybridge KT13 235 BP107
Brooklands Sch, Reig. RH2 off Wray Pk Rd 272 DB132
Brooklands Way, Red. RH1 272 DE132
Brook La, SE3 186 EH82
Albury GU5 282 BL142
Berkhamsted HP4 60 AV18
Bexley DA5 208 EX86
Bromley BR1 206 EG93
Sawbridgeworth CM21 58 EX05
Send GU23 249 BE122
● Brook La Business Cen, Brent. TW8 off Brook La N 179 CK78
Brooklane Fld, Harl. CM18 74 EV18
Brook La N, Brent. TW8 179 CK78
Brooklea Cl, NW9 118 CS53
Brookleys, Chobham GU24 232 AT110
Brooklyn Av, SE25 224 DV98
Loughton IG10 106 EL42
Brooklyn Cl, Cars. SM5 222 DE103
Woking GU22 248 AY119
Brooklyn Ct, Wok. GU22 off Brooklyn Rd 248 AY119
Brooklyn Gro, SE25 224 DV98
Brooklyn Pas, W12 26 A5
Brooklyn Rd, SE25 224 DV98
Bromley BR2 226 EK99
Woking GU22 248 AY118
Brooklyn Way, West Dr. UB7 176 BK76
Brookmans Av, Brook.Pk AL9 85 CY26
Brookmans Cl, Upmin. RM14 151 FS59
BROOKMANS PARK, Hat. AL9 85 CY26
⇌ Brookmans Park 85 CX27
Brookmans Pk Dr, Upmin. RM14 151 FS57
Brookmans Pk Prim Sch, Brook.Pk AL9 off Bradmore Way 85 CY26
● Brookmarsh Ind Est, SE10 46 C4
Brook Mead, Epsom KT19 238 CS107
Brookmead Av, Brom. BR1 227 EM99
Brookmead Cl, Orp. BR5 228 EV101
● Brookmead Ind Est, Croy. CR0 223 DJ100
Brook Meadow, N12 120 DB49
Brook Meadow Cl, Wdf.Grn. IG8 124 EE51
Brookmeadow Way, Wal.Abb. EN9 off Breach Barn Mobile Home Pk 90 EH30
Brookmead Rd, Croy. CR0 223 DJ100
Brookmeads Est, Mitch. CR4 222 DE99
Brookmead Way, Orp. BR5 228 EV100
Brook Ms, N13 121 DN50
Chig. IG7 125 EP48
Brook Ms N, W2 15 P10
Brookmill Cl, Wat. WD19 off Brookside Rd 115 BV45
Brookmill Rd, SE8 46 B6
Brook Par, Chig. IG7 off High Rd 125 EP48
Brook Pk, Dart. DA1 210 FN89
Brook Pk Cl, N21 103 DP44
Brook Path, Loug. IG10 106 EL42
Slough SL1 153 AM73
Brook Pl, Barn. EN5 102 DA43
● Brook Retail Pk, Ruis. HA4 138 BX64
Brook Ri, Chig. IG7 125 EN48
Brook Rd, N8 143 DL56
N22 143 DM55
NW2 141 CU61
Borehamwood WD6 100 CN40
Brentwood CM14 130 FT48
Buckhurst Hill IG9 124 EG47
Chilworth GU4 281 BC140
Epping CM16 92 EU33
Ilford IG2 147 ES58
Loughton IG10 106 EL43
Merstham RH1 273 DJ129
Northfleet DA11 212 GE88
Redhill RH1 288 DF135
Romford RM2 127 FF53
Sawbridgeworth CM21 58 EX06
Surbiton KT6 220 CL103
Swanley BR8 229 FD97
Thornton Heath CR7 224 DQ98
Twickenham TW1 199 CG86
Waltham Cross EN8 89 DZ34
Brook Rd S, Brent. TW8 179 CK79
Brooks Av, E6 25 J4
Brooksbank St, E9 11 J5
Brooksby Ms, N1 8 F6
Brooksby St, N1 8 F7
Brooksby's Wk, E9 11 J2
Brooks Cl, SE9 207 EN89
Weybridge KT13 234 BN110
Brooks Ct, Hert. SG14 53 DM08
Brookscroft, Croy. CR0 243 DY110
Brookscroft Rd, E17 123 EB53
Brooksfield, Welw.G.C. AL7 52 DB08
Brookshill, Har. HA3 117 CD50
Brookshill Av, Har. HA3 117 CD50
Brookshill Dr, Har. HA3 117 CD50
Brookshill Gate, Har.Wld HA3 117 CD50
Brookside, Ilf. IG3 off Barley La 148 EU58
Brookside, N21 103 DM44
Carshalton SM5 240 DG106
Chertsey KT16 215 BE101
Colnbrook SL3 175 BC80
East Barnet EN4 102 DE44
Harlow CM19 73 EM17
Hatfield AL10 66 CR18
Hertford SG13 54 DS09
Hoddesdon EN11 71 DZ17
Hornchurch RM11 150 FL57
Ilford IG6 125 EQ51
Jacobs Well GU4 264 AX129
Orpington BR6 227 ET101
South Mimms EN6 85 CU32
Uxbridge UB10 156 BM66
Waltham Abbey EN9 off Broomstick Hall Rd 90 EE32
Wat. WD24 off North Western Ave 98 BX36
Brookside Av, Ashf. TW15 196 BJ92
Wraysbury TW19 174 AY83
Brookside Cl, Barn. EN5 101 CY44
Feltham TW13 197 BU90
Kenton HA3 139 CK57
South Harrow HA2 138 BY63
Brookside Cres, Cuffley EN6 87 DL27
Worcester Park KT4 off Green La 221 CU102
Brookside Gdns, Enf. EN1 104 DV37
Brookside Inf & Jun Schs, Harold Hill RM3 off Dagnam Pk Dr 128 FL50
Brookside Prim Sch, Hayes UB4 off Perth Av 158 BW69
Brookside Rd, N9 122 DV49
N19 143 DJ61
NW11 141 CY58
Hayes UB4 158 BW73
Istead Rise DA13 213 GF94
Watford WD19 115 BV45
Brookside S, E.Barn. EN4 120 DG45
Brookside Wk, N3 119 CY54
N12 120 DA51
NW4 141 CY56
NW11 141 CY56
Brookside Way, Croy. CR0 225 DX100
Brooks La, W4 180 CN79
Brook's Ms, W1 17 J10
Brook Sq, SE18 off Barlow Dr 186 EL81
Brooks Rd, E13 13 N9
W4 180 CN78
BROOK STREET, Brwd. CM14 130 FS49
Brook St, N17 off High Rd 122 DT54
W1 17 H10
W2 16 B10
Belvedere DA17 189 FB78
Brentwood CM14 130 FS50
Erith DA8 189 FB79
Kingston upon Thames KT1 220 CL96
Windsor SL4 173 AR82
Brooksville Av, NW6 4 F9
Brooks Way, Orp. BR5 228 EW96
Brook Vale, Erith DA8 189 FB81
Brook Valley, Mid Holm. RH5 285 CH142
Brookview Rd, SW16 203 DJ92
Brookville Rd, SW6 38 G5
Brook Wk, N2 120 DD53
Edgware HA8 118 CR51
Brookway, SE3 186 EG83
Brook Way, Chig. IG7 125 EN48
Leatherhead KT22 253 CG118
Rainham RM13 169 FH71
Brookwood, Horl. RH6 off Stockfield 291 DH147
Brookwood Av, SW13 181 CT83
Brookwood Cl, Brom. BR2 226 EF98
Brookwood Rd, SW18 201 CZ88
Hounslow TW3 178 CB81
Broom Av, Orp. BR5 228 EV96
Broom Cl, Brom. BR2 226 EL100
Cheshunt EN7 88 DU27
Esher KT10 236 CB106
Hatfield AL10 67 CT21
Teddington TW11 199 CK94
Broomcroft Av, Nthlt. UB5 158 BW69
Broomcroft Cl, Wok. GU22 249 BD116
Broomcroft Dr, Wok. GU22 249 BD115
Broome Cl, Headley KT18 270 CQ126
Broome Ho, E5 10 E2
Broome Pl, Aveley RM15 171 FR74
Broome Rd, Hmptn. TW12 198 BZ94
Broomer Pl, Chsht EN8 88 DW29
Broome Way, SE5 43 L5
Broom Fm Est, Wind. SL4 172 AJ83
Broomfield, E17 145 DZ59
Guildford GU2 264 AS133
Harlow CM20 58 EV12
Park Street AL2 82 CC27
Staines-upon-Thames TW18 196 BG93
Sunbury-on-Thames TW16 217 BU95
Broomfield Av, N13 121 DM50
Broxbourne EN10 89 DY26
Loughton IG10 107 EM44
Broomfield Cl, Guil. GU3 264 AS132
Romford RM5 127 FD52
Broomfield Ct, Wey. KT13 235 BP107
Broomfield Gate, Slou. SL2 153 AP70
Broomfield Ho Sch, Kew TW9 off Broomfield Rd 180 CM81
Broomfield La, N13 121 DM49
Broomfield Pk, Westc. RH4 284 CC137
Broomfield Pl, W13 159 CH74
Broomfield Ride, Oxshott KT22 237 CD112
Broomfield Ri, Abb.L. WD5 81 BR32
Broomfield Rd, N13 121 DL50
W13 159 CH74
Beckenham BR3 225 DY97
Bexleyheath DA6 208 FA85
New Haw KT15 234 BH111
Richmond TW9 180 CM81
Romford RM6 148 EX59
Sevenoaks TN13 278 FF122
Surbiton KT5 220 CM102
Swanscombe DA10 212 FY86
Teddington TW11 off Melbourne Rd 199 CJ93
Broomfields, Esher KT10 236 CC106
Broomfield Sch, N14 off Wilmer Way 121 DK50
Broomfield St, E14 22 B7
Broom Gdns, Croy. CR0 225 EA104
Broom Gro, Wat. WD17 97 BU38
Broomgrove Gdns, Edg. HA8 118 CN53
Broomgrove Rd, SW9 42 D9
Broom Hall, Oxshott KT22 237 CD114
Broomhall End, Wok. GU21 off Broomhall La 248 AY116
Broomhall La, Wok. GU21 248 AY116
Broomhall Rd, S.Croy. CR2 242 DR109
Woking GU21 248 AY116
Broom Hill, Hem.H. HP1 61 BE21
Stoke Poges SL2 154 AU66
Broomhill Ct, Wdf.Grn. IG8 off Broomhill Rd 124 EG51
Broomhill Ri, Bexh. DA6 208 FA85
Broomhill Rd, SW18 202 DA85
Dartford DA1 209 FH86
Ilford IG3 148 EU61
Orpington BR6 228 EU101
Woodford Green IG8 124 EG51
Broomhills, Sthflt DA13 off Betsham Rd 212 FY91
Welwyn Garden City AL7 52 DA08
Broomhill Wk, Wdf.Grn. IG8 124 EF52
Broom Ho, Slou. SL3 175 AZ77
Broomhouse La, SW6 39 J9
Broomhouse Rd, SW6 39 J8
Broomlands La, Oxt. RH8 276 EJ125
Broom La, Chobham GU24 232 AS109
Broomleys, St.Alb. AL4 65 CK17
Broomloan La, Sutt. SM1 222 DA103
Broom Lock, Tedd. TW11 199 CJ93
Broom Mead, Bexh. DA6 208 FA85
Broom Pk, Tedd. TW11 199 CK94
Broom Rd, Croy. CR0 225 EA104
Teddington TW11 199 CJ93
Brooms Cl, Welw.G.C. AL8 51 CX06
● Broomsleigh Business Pk, SE26 off Worsley Br Rd 205 DZ92
Broomsleigh St, NW6 5 H3
Broomstick Hall Rd, Wal.Abb. EN9 90 EE33
Broomstick La, Chesh. HP5 78 AU30
Broom Water, Tedd. TW11 199 CJ93
Broom Water W, Tedd. TW11 199 CJ92
Broom Way, Wey. KT13 235 BS105
Broomwood Cl, Bex. DA5 209 FD89
Croydon CR0 225 DX99
Broomwood Gdns, Pilg.Hat. CM15 130 FU44
Broomwood Hall Sch, SW12 off Nightingale La 202 DG87
Broomwood Rd, SW11 202 DF86
Orpington BR5 228 EV96
Broseley Gdns, Rom. RM3 128 FL49
Broseley Gro, SE26 205 DY92
Broseley Rd, Rom. RM3 128 FL49
Brosse Way, Brom. BR2 226 EL101
Broster Gdns, SE25 224 DT97
Brougham Rd, E8 10 C8
W3 160 CQ72
Brougham St, SW11 40 F8
Brough Cl, SW8 42 B5
Kingston upon Thames KT2 199 CK92
Broughinge Rd, Borwd. WD6 100 CP40
Broughton Av, N3 141 CY55
Richmond TW10 199 CH90
Broughton Dr, SW9 183 DN84
Broughton Gdns, N6 143 DJ58
Broughton Rd, SW6 39 L7
W13 159 CH73
Orpington BR6 227 ER103
Otford TN14 263 FG116
Thornton Heath CR7 223 DN100
Broughton Rd App, SW6 39 L8
Broughton St, SW8 41 J8
Broughton Way, Rick. WD3 114 BG45
Brouncker Rd, W3 180 CQ75
Brow, The, Ch.St.G. HP8 112 AX48
Redhill RH1 off Spencer Way 288 DG139
Watford WD25 81 BV33
Brow Cl, Orp. BR5 off Brow Cres 228 EX101
Brow Cres, Orp. BR5 228 EW102
Browells La, Felt. TW13 197 BV89
Brownacres Towpath, Wey. KT13 217 BP102
Brown Cl, Wall. SM6 241 DK108
Browne Cl, Brwd. CM14 130 FV46
Romford RM5 127 FB50
Woking GU22 249 BB120
Brownell Pl, W7 179 CF75
Brownfields, Welw.G.C. AL7 51 CZ08
Brownfields Ct, Welw.G.C. AL7 off Brownfields 52 DA08
Brownfield St, E14 22 D9
Browngraves Rd, Harling. UB3 177 BQ80
Brown Hart Gdns, W1 17 H10
Brownhill Rd, SE6 205 EB87
Browning Av, W7 159 CF72
Sutton SM1 240 DE105
Worcester Park KT4 221 CV102
Browning Cl, E17 145 EC56
W9 15 P5
Collier Row RM5 126 EZ52
Hampton TW12 198 BZ91
Welling DA16 187 ES81
Browning Ct, Borwd. WD6 off Chaucer Gro 100 CN42
Browning Ms, W1 17 J7
Browning Rd, E11 146 EF59
E12 167 EM65
Dartford DA1 190 FM84
Enfield EN2 104 DR38
Fetcham KT22 269 CD125
Browning St, SE17 31 K10
Browning Wk, Til. RM18 off Coleridge Rd 193 GJ82
Browning Way, Houns. TW5 178 BX81
Brownlea Gdns, Ilf. IG3 148 EU61
Brownlow Cl, Barn. EN4 102 DD43
Brownlow Ms, WC1 18 D5
Brownlow Rd, E7 off Woodford Rd 146 EG63
E8 10 B8
N3 120 DB52
N11 121 DL51
NW10 160 CS66
W13 159 CG74
Berkhamsted HP4 60 AW18
Borehamwood WD6 100 CN42
Croydon CR0 242 DS105
Redhill RH1 272 DE134
Brownlow St, WC1 18 D7
Brownrigg Rd, Ashf. TW15 196 BN91
Brown Rd, Grav. DA12 213 GL88
Brown's Bldgs, EC3 19 P9
Brownsea Wk, NW7 119 CX51
Browns La, NW5 7 J3
Effingham KT24 268 BX127
Brownspring Dr, SE9 207 EP91
Browns Rd, E17 145 EA55
Surbiton KT5 220 CM101
Brown's Sch, Orp. BR6 off Hawstead La 246 EZ106
Browns Spring, Pott.End HP4 61 BC16
Brown St, W1 16 E8
Brownswell Rd, N2 120 DD54
Brownswood Rd, N4 143 DP62
Beaconsfield HP9 111 AK51
Broxash Rd, SW11 202 DG86
BROXBOURNE, EN10 71 DZ21
⇌ Broxbourne 71 EA20
Broxbourne Av, E18 146 EH56
Broxbournebury Ms, Brox. EN10 off White Stubbs La 70 DW21
● Broxbourne Business Cen, Chsht EN8 off Fairways 89 DX26
Broxbourne C of E Prim Sch, Brox. EN10 off Mill La 71 DZ21
Broxbourne Common, Brox. EN10 70 DU19
Broxbourne Rd, E7 146 EG62
Orpington BR6 227 ET101
Broxbourne Sch, The, Brox. EN10 off High Rd 71 DZ21
Broxburn Dr, S.Ock. RM15 171 FV73
Broxburn Par, S.Ock. RM15 off Broxburn Dr 171 FV73
Broxhill Rd, Hav.at.Bow. RM4 127 FH48
Broxholme Cl, SE25 off Whitehorse La 224 DR98
Broxholm Rd, SE27 203 DN90
Brox La, Ott. KT16 233 BD109
Brox Ms, Ott. KT16 off Brox Rd 233 BC107
Brox Rd, Ott. KT16 233 BC107
Broxted Ms, Hutt. CM13 off Bannister Dr 131 GC44
Broxted Rd, SE6 205 DZ89
Broxwood Way, NW8 6 D9
Bruce Av, Horn. RM12 150 FK61
Shepperton TW17 217 BQ100
★ Bruce Castle Mus, N17 122 DS53
Bruce Castle Rd, N17 122 DT53
Bruce Cl, W10 14 D6
Byfleet KT14 234 BK113
Slough SL1 153 AN74
Welling DA16 188 EV81
Bruce Dr, S.Croy. CR2 243 DX109
Bruce Gdns, N20 120 DF48
⇌ Bruce Grove 122 DT54
Bruce Gro, N17 off High Rd 122 DT54
Bruce Gro, N17 122 DS53
Orpington BR6 228 EU102
Watford WD24 98 BW38
Bruce Gro Prim Sch, N17 off Sperling Rd 122 DT54
Bruce Hall Ms, SW17 202 DG91
Bruce Rd, E3 22 C3
NW10 160 CR66
SE25 224 DR98
Barnet EN5 off St. Albans Rd 101 CY41
Harrow HA3 117 CE54
Mitcham CR4 202 DG94
Bruce's Wf Rd, Grays RM17 192 GA79
Bruce Wk, Wind. SL4 173 AK82
Bruce Way, Wal.Cr. EN8 89 DX33
Bruckner St, W10 14 F3
Brudenell, Wind. SL4 173 AM83
Brudenell Cl, Amer. HP6 94 AT38
Brudenell Rd, SW17 202 DF90
Bruffs Meadow, Nthlt. UB5 158 BY65
Bruford Ct, SE8 46 B3
Bruges Pl, NW1 7 M7
Brumana Cl, Wey. KT13 235 BP107
Brumfield Rd, Epsom KT19 238 CQ106
Brummel Cl, Bexh. DA7 189 FC83
★ Brunei Gall, WC1 17 P6
⊖ Brunel 154 AT74

Brunel Cl, SE19 204 DT93
Hounslow TW5 177 BV80
Northolt UB5 158 BZ69
Romford RM1 149 FE56
Tilbury RM18 193 GH83
Brunel Est, W2 15 J7
Brunel Ho, N16
off Stamford Hill 144 DT60
Brwd. CM14 130 FW48
Brunel Ms, W10 14 D2
★ Brunel Mus & Engine Ho, SE16 32 G4
Brunel Pl, Sthl. UB1 158 CB72
Brunel Rd, E17 145 DY58
SE16 32 G5
W3 160 CS71
Woodford Green IG8 125 EM50
Uni Brunel Science Pk, Uxb. UB8 156 BL69
Brunel St, E16 23 L9
Uni Brunel Uni, Runnymede Campus, Eng.Grn TW20 off Coopers Hill La 194 AW90
Uxbridge Campus, Uxb. UB8 off Kingston La 156 BK69
Brunel Wk, N15 144 DS56
Twickenham TW2 off Stephenson Rd 198 CA87
Brunel Way, Slou. SL1 154 AT74
Brune St, E1 20 A7
Brunlees Ho, SE1 off Bath Ter 31 J7
Brunner Cl, NW11 142 DB57
Brunner Ct, Ott. KT16 233 BC106
Brunner Rd, E17 145 DY57
W5 159 CK70
Bruno Pl, NW9 140 CQ61
Brunswick, WC1 18 A4
Brunswick Av, N11 120 DG48
Upminster RM14 151 FS59
Brunswick Cl, Bexh. DA6 188 EX84
Pinner HA5 138 BY58
Thames Ditton KT7 219 CF102
Twickenham TW2 199 CD90
Walton-on-Thames KT12 218 BW103
Brunswick Ct, EC1 off Tompion St 18 G3
SE1 31 P5
SW1 off Regency St 29 P9
Barnet EN4 102 DD43
Upminster RM14 off Waycross Rd 151 FS59
Brunswick Cres, N11 120 DG48
Brunswick Gdns, W5 160 CL69
W8 27 K3
Ilford IG6 125 EQ52
Brunswick Gro, N11 120 DG48
Cobham KT11 236 BW113
● Brunswick Ind Pk, N11 121 DH49
Brunswick Ms, SW16 off Potters La 203 DK93
W1 16 F8
BRUNSWICK PARK, N11 120 DF48
Brunswick Pk, SE5 43 M6
Brunswick Pk Gdns, N11 120 DG47
Sch Brunswick Pk Prim Sch, N14 off Osidge La 120 DG47
SE5 43 M5
Brunswick Pk Rd, N11 120 DG47
Brunswick Pl, N1 19 M3
NW1 17 H4
SE19 204 DU94
Brunswick Quay, SE16 33 K7
Brunswick Rd, E10 145 EC60
E14 off Blackwall Tunnel Northern App 22 F9
N15 144 DS57
W5 159 CK70
Bexleyheath DA6 188 EX84
Enfield EN3 105 EA38
Kingston upon Thames KT2 220 CN95
Sutton SM1 240 DB105
Brunswick Sq, N17 122 DT51
WC1 18 B5
Brunswick St, E17 145 EC57
Brunswick Vil, SE5 43 N6
Brunswick Wk, Grav. DA12 213 GK87
Brunswick Way, N11 121 DH49
Brunton Pl, E14 21 M9
Brushfield St, E1 19 P6
Brushmakers Ct, Chesh. HP5 off Higham Rd 76 AP30
Brushrise, Wat. WD24 97 BU36
Brushwood Cl, E14 22 D6
Brushwood Dr, Chorl. WD3 95 BC42
Sch Brushwood Jun Sch, Chesh. HP5 off Brushwood Rd 76 AS29
Brushwood Rd, Chesh. HP5 76 AR29
Brussels Rd, SW11 182 DD84
Bruton Cl, Chis. BR7 207 EM94
Bruton La, W1 29 K1
Bruton Pl, W1 29 K1
Bruton Rd, Mord. SM4 222 DC99
Bruton St, W1 29 K1
Bruton Way, W13 159 CG71
Bryan Av, NW10 161 CV66
Bryan Cl, Sun. TW16 197 BU94
Bryan Rd, SE16 33 N4
Bryan's All, SW6 39 L8
Bryanston Av, Twick. TW2 198 CB88
Bryanston Cl, Sthl. UB2 178 BZ77
Bryanstone Av, Guil. GU2 264 AU131
Bryanstone Cl, Guil. GU2 264 AT131
Bryanstone Ct, Sutt. SM1 off Oakhill Rd 240 DC105
Bryanstone Gro, Guil. GU2 264 AT130
Bryanstone Rd, N8 143 DK57
Waltham Cross EN8 89 DZ34
Bryanston Ms E, W1 16 E7
Bryanston Ms W, W1 16 E7
Bryanston Pl, W1 16 E7
Bryanston Rd, Til. RM18 193 GJ82
Bryanston Sq, W1 16 E7
Bryanston St, W1 16 E9
Bryant Av, Rom. RM3 128 FK53
Slough SL2 153 AR71
Bryant Cl, Barn. EN5 101 CZ43
Bryant Ct, E2 10 A10
W3 160 CR74
Bryant Rd, Nthlt. UB5 158 BW69
Bryant Row, Noak Hill RM3 off Long Meadow 128 FJ47
Bryant St, E15 13 H7
Bryantwood Rd, N7 8 E2
Brycedale Cres, N14 121 DK49
Bryce Rd, Dag. RM8 148 EW63
Brydale Ho, SE16 33 J8
Bryden Cl, SE26 205 DY92
Brydges Pl, WC2 30 A1
Brydges Rd, E15 13 H2
Brydon Wk, N1 8 B8
Bryer Ct, EC2 off Bridgewater St 19 J6
Bryer Pl, Wind. SL4 173 AK83
Bryett Rd, N7 143 DL62
Brymay Cl, E3 22 B1
Brympton Cl, Dor. RH4 285 CG138
Brynford Cl, Wok. GU21 248 AY115
Brynmaer Rd, SW11 40 E7
Bryn-y-Mawr Rd, Enf. EN1 104 DT42
Bryony Cl, Loug. IG10 107 EP42
Uxbridge UB8 156 BM71
Bryony Rd, W12 161 CU73
Guildford GU1 265 BB131
Bryony Way, Sun. TW16 197 BT93
Coll BSix, Brooke Ho 6th Form Coll, E5 off Kenninghall Rd 144 DV62
Bubblestone Rd, Otford TN14 263 FH116
Buccleuch Rd, Datchet SL3 174 AU80
Buchanan Cl, N21 103 DM43
Aveley RM15 170 FQ74
Buchanan Ct, Borwd. WD6 100 CQ40
Buchanan Gdns, NW10 161 CV68
Buchan Cl, Uxb. UB8 156 BJ69
Buchan Rd, SE15 45 H10
Bucharest Rd, SW18 202 DC87
Buckbean Path, Rom. RM3 off Clematis Cl 128 FJ52
Buckden Cl, N2 off Southern Rd 142 DF56
SE12 206 EF86
Bucketsland La, Borwd. WD6 100 CR38
Buckfast Ct, W13 off Romsey Rd 159 CG73
Buckfast Rd, Mord. SM4 222 DB98
Buckfast St, E2 20 D3
Buckham Thorns Rd, West. TN16 277 EQ126
Buck Hill Wk, W2 28 B1
Buckhold Rd, SW18 202 DA86
Buckhurst Av, Cars. SM5 222 DE102
Sevenoaks TN13 279 FJ125
Buckhurst Cl, Red. RH1 272 DE132
BUCKHURST HILL, IG9 124 EH45
⊖ Buckhurst Hill 124 EK47
Sch Buckhurst Hill Comm Prim Sch, Buck.H. IG9 off Lower Queens Rd 124 EL47
Buckhurst La, Sev. TN13 279 FJ125
Buckhurst Rd, West. TN16 261 EN121
Buckhurst St, E1 20 F5
Buckhurst Way, Buck.H. IG9 124 EK49
Buckingham Arc, WC2 30 B1
Buckingham Av, N20 120 DC45
Feltham TW14 197 BV86
Perivale UB6 159 CG67
Slough SL1 153 AQ72
Thornton Heath CR7 223 DN95
Welling DA16 187 ES84
West Molesey KT8 218 CB97
Buckingham Av E, Slou. SL1 153 AQ72
Buckingham Chambers, SW1 off Greencoat Pl 29 M8
Buckingham Cl, W5 159 CJ71
Enfield EN1 104 DS40
Guildford GU1 265 AZ133
Hampton TW12 198 BZ92
Hornchurch RM11 150 FK58
Petts Wood BR5 227 ES101
Sch Buckingham Coll Prep Sch, Pnr. HA5 off Rayners La 138 BZ59
Sch Buckingham Coll Sch, Har. HA1 off Hindes Rd 139 CE57
Buckingham Ct, NW4 141 CU55
Loughton IG10 107 EN40
Buckingham Dr, Chis. BR7 207 EP92
Buckingham Gdns, Edg. HA8 118 CM52
Slough SL1 174 AT75
Thornton Heath CR7 223 DN96
West Molesey KT8 218 CB96
Buckingham Gate, SW1 29 L5
London Gatwick Airport RH6 291 DJ152
Buckingham Gro, Uxb. UB10 156 BN68
Buckingham La, SE23 205 DY87
Buckingham Lo, N10 143 DJ56
Hoddesdon EN11 off Taverners Way 71 EA17
Buckingham Ms, N1 9 P5
NW10 161 CT68
SW1 29 L6
★ Buckingham Palace, SW1 29 K5
Buckingham Palace Rd, SW1 29 J9
Buckingham Pl, SW1 29 L6
Sch Buckingham Prim Sch, Hmptn. TW12 off Buckingham Rd 198 BZ92
Buckingham Rd, E10 145 EB62
E11 146 EJ57
E15 13 L2
E18 124 EF53
N1 9 N5
N22 121 DL53
NW10 161 CT68
Borehamwood WD6 100 CR42
Edgware HA8 118 CM52
Gravesend DA11 off Dover Rd 212 GD87
Hampton TW12 198 BZ91
Harrow HA1 139 CD57
Ilford IG1 147 ER61
Kingston upon Thames KT1 220 CM98
Mitcham CR4 223 DL99
Richmond TW10 199 CK89
Watford WD24 98 BW37
Uni Buckinghamshire Chilterns Uni Coll, Chalfont Campus, Ch.St.G. HP8 off Gorelands La 113 BA47
Buckingham St, WC2 30 B1
Buckingham Way, Wall. SM6 241 DJ109
BUCKLAND, Bet. RH3 271 CU133
Buckland Av, Slou. SL3 174 AV77
Buckland Cl, NW7 119 CU49
Buckland Ct Gdns, Bet. RH3 271 CU133
Buckland Cres, NW3 6 A6
Windsor SL4 173 AM81
Buckland Gate, Wexham SL3 154 AV68
Buckland La, Bet. RH3 271 CU130
Tadworth KT20 271 CT129
Sch Buckland Prim Sch, Laleham TW18 off Berryscroft Rd 196 BJ94
Buckland Ri, Pnr. HA5 116 BW53
Buckland Rd, E10 145 EC61
Chessington KT9 238 CM106
Lower Kingswood KT20 271 CZ128
Orpington BR6 245 ES105
Reigate RH2 271 CX133
Sutton SM2 239 CW110
Bucklands, The, Rick. WD3 114 BG45
Bucklands Rd, Tedd. TW11 199 CJ93
Buckland St, N1 19 M1
Buckland Wk, W3 160 CQ74
Morden SM4 222 DC98
Buckland Way, Wor.Pk. KT4 221 CW102
Buck La, NW9 140 CR57
Bucklebury, NW1 17 L4
Bucklebury Cl, Holy. SL6 172 AC78
Buckleigh Av, SW20 221 CY97
Buckleigh Rd, SW16 203 DK93
Buckleigh Way, SE19 224 DT95
Buckler Ct, N7 off Eden Gro 8 D3
Buckler Gdns, SE9 off Southold Ri 207 EM90
Bucklers All, SW6 39 H3
Bucklersbury, EC4 19 L9
Bucklersbury Pas, EC4 19 L9
Bucklers Cl, Brox. EN10 71 DZ22
Bucklers Ct, Warley CM14 130 FW50
Bucklers Way, Cars. SM5 222 DF104
Buckles Ct, Belv. DA17 off Fendyke Rd 188 EX76
Buckles La, S.Ock. RM15 171 FW71
Buckle St, E1 20 B8
Buckles Way, Bans. SM7 255 CY116
Buckley Cl, SE23 204 DV87
Dartford DA1 189 FF82
Buckley Rd, NW6 5 H7
Buckley St, SE1 30 E3
Buckmaster Cl, SW9 42 E10
Buckmaster Rd, SW11 182 DE84
Bucknalls Cl, Wat. WD25 82 BY32
Bucknalls Dr, Brick.Wd AL2 82 BZ31
Bucknalls La, Wat. WD25 82 BX32
Bucknall St, WC2 17 P8
Bucknall Way, Beck. BR3 225 EB98
Bucknell Cl, SW2 183 DM84
Buckner Rd, SW2 183 DM84
Bucknills Cl, Epsom KT18 238 CP114
Buckrell Rd, E4 123 ED47
Bucks All, Hert. SG13 69 DK19
Bucks Av, Wat. WD19 116 BY45
Bucks Cl, W.Byf. KT14 234 BH114
Bucks Cross Rd, Nthflt DA11 213 GF90
Orpington BR6 246 EY106
BUCKS HILL, Kings L. WD4 80 BK34
Bucks Hill, Kings L. WD4 80 BK34
Buckstone Cl, SE23 204 DW86
Buckstone Rd, N18 122 DU51
Buck St, NW1 7 K7
Buckters Rents, SE16 33 L3
Buckthorne Ho, Chig. IG7 126 EV49
Buckthorne Rd, SE4 205 DY86
Buckton Rd, Borwd. WD6 100 CM38
Buck Wk, E17 off Wood St 145 ED56
Buckwell Pl, Sev. TN13 279 FJ129
Budd Cl, N12 120 DB49
Buddcroft, Welw.G.C. AL7 52 DB08
Buddings Circle, Wem. HA9 140 CQ62
Budd's All, Twick. TW1 199 CJ85
Budebury Rd, Stai. TW18 196 BG92
Bude Cl, E17 145 DZ57
Budge La, Mitch. CR4 222 DF101
Budgen Dr, Red. RH1 272 DG131
Budge Row, EC4 19 L10
Budge's Wk, W2 27 N2
Budgin's Hill, Orp. BR6 246 EW112
Budleigh Cres, Well. DA16 188 EW81
Budoch Ct, Ilf. IG3 148 EU61
Budoch Dr, Ilf. IG3 148 EU61
Buer Rd, SW6 38 F9
Buff Av, Bans. SM7 240 DB114
Buffers La, Lthd. KT22 off Kingston Rd 253 CG119
Buffins, Tap. SL6 152 AE69
Bug Hill, Wold. CR3 259 DX120
Bugsby's Way, SE7 35 P9
SE10 35 L8
Buick Ho, Kings.T. KT2 220 CN96
Building 22, SE18 off Carriage St 37 P7
Building 36, SE18 off Marlborough Rd 187 EQ76
Building 45, SE18 off Hopton Rd 37 P6
Building 47, SE18 off Marlborough Rd 187 EQ76
Building 48, SE18 off Marlborough Rd 187 EQ76
Building 49, SE18 off Argyll Rd 187 EQ76
Building 50, SE18 off Argyll Rd 187 EQ76
Coll Building Crafts Coll, E15 12 G7
Bulbourne Cl, Berk. HP4 60 AT17
Hemel Hempstead HP1 62 BG21
Bulganak Rd, Th.Hth. CR7 224 DQ98
Bulinga St, SW1 29 P9
Bulkeley Av, Wind. SL4 173 AP82
Bulkeley Cl, Eng.Grn TW20 194 AW91
Bullace Cl, Hem.H. HP1 62 BG19
Bullace La, Dart. DA1 210 FL86
Bullace Row, SE5 43 K6
Bull All, Well. DA16 off Welling High St 188 EV83
Bullards Pl, E2 21 J2
Bullbanks Rd, Belv. DA17 189 FC77
Bullbeggars La, Berk. HP4 61 AZ20
Godstone RH9 274 DW132
Woking GU21 248 AV116
Bull Cl, Grays RM16 192 FZ75
Jct Bull Dog, The, Ashf. TW15 196 BL89
Bullen Ho, E1 20 F5
BULLEN'S GREEN, St.Alb. AL4 66 CS22
Bullens Grn La, Coln.Hth AL4 66 CS23
Bullen St, SW11 40 C8
Buller Cl, SE15 44 C5
Buller Rd, N17 122 DU54
N22 121 DN54
NW10 14 D3
Barking IG11 167 ES66
Thornton Heath CR7 224 DR96
Bullers Cl, Sid. DA14 208 EY92
Bullers Wd Dr, Chis. BR7 206 EL94
Sch Bullers Wd Sch, Chis. BR7 off St. Nicolas La 226 EL95
Bullescroft Rd, Edg. HA8 118 CN48
Bullfinch Cl, Horl. RH6 290 DE147
Sevenoaks TN13 278 FD122
Bullfinch Dene, Sev. TN13 278 FD122
Bullfinch La, Sev. TN13 278 FD122
Bullfinch Rd, S.Croy. CR2 243 DX110
Bullhead Rd, Borwd. WD6 100 CQ41
Bull Hill, Hort.Kir. DA4 230 FQ98
Leatherhead KT22 253 CG121
Bullied Way, SW1 29 K9
Bull Inn Ct, WC2 30 B1
Bullivant Cl, Green. DA9 211 FU85
Bullivant St, E14 22 E9
Bull La, N18 122 DS50
Chislehurst BR7 207 ER94
Dagenham RM10 149 FB62
Gerrards Cross SL9 134 AX55
Sutton Green GU4 265 AZ126
Bullocks La, Hert. SG13 54 DQ11
Bull Plain, Hert. SG14 54 DR09
Bull Rd, E15 13 L10
Bullrush Cl, Cars. SM5 222 DE103
Croydon CR0 224 DS100
Hatfield AL10 67 CV19
Bullrush Gro, Uxb. UB8 156 BJ70
Bull's All, SW14 180 CR82
● Bulls Br Centre, Hayes UB3 off The Parkway 177 BV76
● Bullsbridge Ind Est, Sthl. UB2 177 BV77
Bulls Br Rd, Sthl. UB2 177 BV76
Bullsbrook Rd, Hayes UB4 158 BW74
BULLS CROSS, Wal.Cr. EN7 104 DT35
Bulls Cross, Enf. EN2 104 DU37
Bulls Cross Ride, Wal.Cr. EN7 104 DU35
Bulls Gdns, SW3 28 D8
Bull's Head Pas, EC3 19 N9
Bullsland Gdns, Chorl. WD3 95 BB44
Bullsland La, Chorl. WD3 95 BB44
Gerrards Cross SL9 113 BB45
Bulls La, Hat. AL9 67 CZ24
BULLSMOOR, Enf. EN1 104 DV37
Bullsmoor Cl, Wal.Cr. EN8 104 DW35
Bullsmoor Gdns, Wal.Cr. EN8 104 DV35
Bullsmoor La, Enf. EN1, EN3 104 DW35
Waltham Cross EN7 104 DU35
Bullsmoor Ride, Wal.Cr. EN8 104 DW35
Bullsmoor Way, Wal.Cr. EN8 104 DV35
Bull Stag Grn, Hat. AL9 67 CW15
Bullwell Cres, Chsht EN8 89 DY29
Bull Yd, SE15 44 D7
Gravesend DA12 off High St 213 GH86
Bulmer Gdns, Har. HA3 139 CK59
Bulmer Ms, W11 27 J2
Bulmer Pl, W11 27 J2
Bulmer Wk, Rain. RM13 170 FJ68
Bulow Est, SW6 39 M7
Bulstrode Av, Houns. TW3 178 BZ82
Bulstrode Cl, Chipper. WD4 79 BE29
Bulstrode Ct, Ger.Cr. SL9 134 AX58
Bulstrode Gdns, Houns. TW3 178 BZ83
Bulstrode La, Chipper. WD4 79 BE29
Felden HP3 80 BG27
Bulstrode Pl, W1 17 H7
Slough SL1 174 AT76
Bulstrode Rd, Houns. TW3 178 CA83
Bulstrode St, W1 17 H8
Bulstrode Way, Ger.Cr. SL9 134 AX57
Bulwer Ct Rd, E11 145 ED60
Bulwer Gdns, Barn. EN5 102 DC42
Bulwer Rd, E11 145 ED59
N18 122 DS49
Barnet EN5 102 DB42
Bulwer St, W12 26 B3
BUMBLE'S GREEN, Wal.Abb. EN9 72 EG24
Bumbles Grn La, Naze.Gate EN9 90 EH25
Bunbury Way, Epsom KT17 255 CV116
Bunby Rd, Stoke P. SL2 154 AT66
BUNCE COMMON, Reig. RH2 286 CR141
Bunce Common Rd, Leigh RH2 286 CR141
Bunce Dr, Cat. CR3 258 DR123
Buncefield La, Hem.H. HP2 63 BR20
● Buncefield Terminal, Hem.H. HP2 63 BR18
Bunces Cl, Eton Wick SL4 173 AP78
Bunces La, Wdf.Grn. IG8 124 EF52
Bundys Way, Stai. TW18 195 BF93
Bungalow Rd, SE25 224 DS98
Woking GU23 251 BQ124
Bungalows, The, SW16 203 DH94
Wallington SM6 241 DH106
Bunhill Row, EC1 19 L4
Bunhouse Pl, SW1 28 G10
Bunkers Hill, NW11 142 DC59
Belvedere DA17 188 FA77
Sidcup DA14 208 EZ90
Bunkers La, Hem.H. HP3 80 BN25
Bunning Way, N7 8 B6
Bunnsfield, Welw.G.C. AL7 52 DC08
Bunns La, NW7 119 CT51
Bunn's La, Chesh. HP5 78 AU34
Bunsen St, E3 11 L10
Bunten Meade, Slou. SL1 153 AP74
Buntingbridge Rd, Ilf. IG2 147 ER57
Bunting Cl, N9 off Dunnock Cl 123 DX46
Mitcham CR4 222 DF99
Bunton St, SE18 37 M7
Bunyan Ct, EC2 off The Barbican 19 J6
Bunyan Rd, E17 145 DY55
Bunyard Dr, Wok. GU21 233 BC114
Bunyons Cl, Gt Warley CM13 129 FW51
Buonaparte Ms, SW1 29 N10
Burbage Cl, SE1 31 L7
Cheshunt EN8 89 DY31
Hayes UB3 157 BR72
Sch Burbage Prim Sch, N1 9 N10
Burbage Rd, SE21 204 DR86
SE24 204 DQ86
Burberry Cl, N.Mal. KT3 220 CS96
Harefield UB9 114 BJ54
Burbery Cl, Hare.UB9 114 BJ54
Burbidge Rd, Shep. TW17 216 BN98
Burbridge Way, N17 122 DT54
Burcham St, E14 22 D8
Burcharbro Rd, SE2 188 EX79
Burchell Ct, Bushey WD23 off Catsey La 116 CC45
Burchell Rd, E10 145 EB60
SE15 44 F7
Burcher Gale Gro, SE15 43 P4
Burchets Hollow, Peasl. GU5 283 BR144
Burchetts Way, Shep. TW17 217 BP100
Burchett Way, Rom. RM6 148 EZ58
Burch Rd, Nthflt DA11 213 GF86
Burchwall Cl, Rom. RM5 127 FC52
Burcote, Wey. KT13 235 BR107
Burcote Rd, SW18 202 DD88
Burcott Gdns, Add. KT15 234 BJ107
Burcott Rd, Pur. CR8 241 DN114
Burden Cl, Brent. TW8 179 CJ78
Burdenshott Hill, Worp. GU3 264 AU125
Burdenshott Av, Rich. TW10 180 CP84
Burdenshott Rd, Wok. GU22 264 AU125
Worplesdon GU3 264 AU125
Burden Way, E11 146 EH61
Burden Way, Guildford GU2 264 AV129
Burder Cl, N1 9 P4
Burder Rd, N1 9 P4
Burdett Av, SW20 221 CU95
Burdett Cl, W7 off Cherington Rd 159 CF74
Sidcup DA14 208 EY92
Sch Burdett Coutts C of E Prim Sch, SW1 29 N7
Burdett Ms, NW3 6 A5
W2 15 L8
Burdett Rd, E3 21 M4
E14 21 M4
Croydon CR0 224 DR100
Richmond TW9 180 CM82
Burdetts Rd, Dag. RM9 168 EZ67
Burdett St, SE1 30 E6
Burdock Cl, Croy. CR0 225 DX102
Burdock Rd, N17 144 DU55
Burdon La, Sutt. SM2 239 CY108
Burdon Pk, Sutt. SM2 239 CZ109
Burfield Cl, SW17 202 DD91
Hatfield AL10 67 CU16
Burfield Dr, Warl. CR6 258 DW119
Burfield Rd, Chorl. WD3 95 BB43
Old Windsor SL4 194 AU86
Burford Cl, Dag. RM8 148 EW62
Ilford IG6 147 EQ56
Uxbridge UB10 136 BL63
Burford Gdns, N13 121 DM48
Hoddesdon EN11 71 EB16
Slough SL1 off Buttermere Av 152 AJ71
Burford La, Epsom KT17 239 CW111
Burford Ms, Hodd. EN11 off Burford St 71 EA16
Burford Pl, Hodd. EN11 71 EA16
Burford Rd, E6 24 G2
E15 12 G7
SE6 205 DZ89
Brentford TW8 180 CL78
Bromley BR1 226 EL98
Sutton SM1 222 DA103
Worcester Park KT4 221 CT101
Burford St, Hodd. EN11 71 EA17
Burford Wk, SW6 39 M5
Burford Way, New Adgtn CR0 243 EC107
Burford Wf Apts, E15 12 G8
Burgage La, Ware SG12 55 DX06
Burgate Cl, Dart. DA1 189 FF83
Burges Cl, Horn. RM11 150 FM58
Burges Ct, E6 167 EN66
Burges Gro, SW13 181 CV80
Burges Rd, E6 166 EL66
Burgess Av, NW9 140 CR58
● Burgess Business Pk, SE5 43 M4
Burgess Cl, Chsht EN7 88 DQ25
Feltham TW13 198 BY91
Burgess Ct, Borwd. WD6 off Belford Rd 100 CM38
Burgess Hill, NW2 142 DA63
Burgess Ms, SW19 202 DB93
Burgess Rd, E15 13 J1
Sutton SM1 240 DB105
Burgess St, E14 22 A7
Burgess Wd Gro, Beac. HP9 110 AH53
Burgess Wd Rd, Beac. HP9 110 AH53
Burgess Wd Rd S, Beac. HP9 132 AH55
Burge St, SE1 31 M7
Burges Way, Stai. TW18 196 BG92
Burgett Rd, Slou. SL1 173 AP76
Burghfield, Epsom KT17 255 CT115
Burghfield Rd, Istead Rise DA13 213 GF94
BURGH HEATH, Tad. KT20 255 CX119
Burgh Heath Rd, Epsom KT17 238 CS114
★ Burgh Ho (Hampstead Mus), NW3 off New End Sq 142 DD63
Burghill Rd, SE26 205 DY91
Burghley Av, Borwd. WD6 100 CQ43
New Malden KT3 220 CR95
Burghley Hall Cl, SW19 201 CY87
Burghley Ho, SW19 201 CY90
Burghley Pl, Mitch. CR4 222 DF99
Burghley Rd, E11 146 EE60
N8 143 DN55
NW5 7 K2
SW19 201 CX91
Chafford Hundred RM16 191 FW76
Burghley Twr, W3 161 CT73
Burgh Mt, Bans. SM7 255 CZ115
Burgh St, N1 9 H10
Burgh Wd, Bans. SM7 255 CY115
Burgon St, EC4 19 H9
Burgos Cl, Croy. CR0 241 DN107
Burgos Gro, SE10 46 C6
Burgoyne Hatch, Harl. CM20 off Momples Rd 58 EU14
Burgoyne Rd, N4 143 DP58
SE25 224 DT98
SW9 42 C10
Sunbury-on-Thames TW16 197 BT93
Burgundy Cft, Welw.G.C. AL7 51 CZ11
Burgundy Ho, Enf. EN2 off Bedale Rd 104 DQ38
Burgundy Pl, W12 off Bourbon La 26 C3
Burham Cl, SE20 off Maple Rd 204 DW94
Burhill, Hersham KT12 235 BU109
Sch Burhill Comm Inf Sch, Hersham KT12 off Pleasant Pl 236 BX107
Burhill Gro, Pnr. HA5 116 BY54
Burhill Rd, Hersham KT12 236 BW107
Burke Cl, SW15 180 CS84
Burke Ho, SW11 off Maysoule Rd 182 DD84
Burkes Cl, Beac. HP9 132 AH55
Burkes Cres, Beac. HP9 111 AK53
Burkes Par, Beac. HP9 off Station Rd 111 AK52
Burkes Rd, Beac. HP9 110 AJ54
Burke St, E16 23 M7
Burket Cl, Sthl. UB2 178 BZ77
Burland Rd, SW11 202 DF85
Brentwood CM15 130 FX46
Romford RM5 127 FC51
Burlea Cl, Hersham KT12 235 BV106
Burleigh Av, Sid. DA15 207 ET85
Wallington SM6 222 DG104
Burleigh Cl, Add. KT15 234 BH106
Romford RM7 149 FB56

Burleigh Gdns, N14 121 DJ46
Ashford TW15 197 BQ92
Woking GU21 249 AZ116
Burleigh Ho, W10 14 D6
Burleigh Mead, Hat. AL9 67 CW16
Burleigh Pk, Cob. KT11 236 BY112
Burleigh Pl, SW15 201 CX85
Burleigh Prim Sch, Chshnt EN8 *off Blindman's La* 89 DX29
Burleigh Rd, Add. KT15 234 BH105
Cheshunt EN8 89 DY32
Enfield EN1 104 DS42
Hemel Hempstead HP2 63 BQ21
Hertford SG13 54 DU08
St. Albans AL1 65 CH20
Sutton SM3 221 CY102
Uxbridge UB10 157 BP67
Burleigh St, WC2 18 C10
Burleigh Wk, SE6 205 EC88
Burleigh Way, Cuffley EN6 87 DL30
Enfield EN2 *off Church St* 104 DR41
Burley Cl, E4 123 EA50
SW16 223 DK96
Burley Hill, Harl. CM17 74 EX16
Burley Orchard, Cher. KT16 216 BG100
Burley Rd, E16 24 C7
Burlingham Cl, Guil. GU4 *off Gilliat Dr* 265 BD132
Burlings La, Knock. TN14 261 ET118
Burlington Arc, W1 29 L1
Burlington Av, Rich. TW9 180 CN81
Romford RM7 149 FB58
Slough SL1 174 AS75
Burlington Cl, E6 25 H8
W9 15 H5
Feltham TW14 197 BR87
Orpington BR6 227 EP103
Pinner HA5 137 BV55
Burlington Danes Acad, W12 *off Wood La* 161 CV72
Burlington Gdns, W1 29 L1
W3 160 CQ74
W4 180 CQ78
Romford RM6 148 EY59
Burlington Inf & Nurs Sch, N.Mal. KT3 *off Burlington Rd* 221 CT98
Burlington Jun Sch, N.Mal. KT3 *off Burlington Rd* 221 CT98
Burlington La, W4 180 CS80
Burlington Ms, SW15 201 CZ85
W3 160 CQ74
Burlington Pl, SW6 38 F9
Reigate RH2 272 DA134
Woodford Green IG8 124 EG48
Burlington Ri, E.Barn. EN4 120 DE46
Burlington Rd, N10 *off Tetherdown* 142 DG55
N17 122 DU53
SW6 38 F8
W4 180 CQ78
Burnham SL1 152 AH70
Enfield EN2 104 DR39
Isleworth TW7 179 CD81
New Malden KT3 221 CU98
Slough SL1 174 AS75
Thornton Heath CR7 224 DQ96
Burman Cl, Dart. DA2 210 FQ87
Burma Rd, N16 144 DR63
Longcross KT16 214 AT104
Burmester Rd, SW17 202 DC90
Burnaby Cres, W4 180 CP79
Burnaby Gdns, W4 180 CQ79
Burnaby Rd, Nthflt DA11 212 GE87
Burnaby St, SW10 39 N5
Burnbrae Cl, N12 120 DB51
Burnbury Rd, SW12 203 DJ88
Burn Cl, Add. KT15 234 BK105
Oxshott KT22 252 CC115
Burncroft Av, Enf. EN3 104 DW40
Burndell Way, Hayes UB4 158 BX71
Burne Jones Ho, W14 26 G9
Burnell Av, Rich. TW10 199 CJ92
Welling DA16 188 EU82
Burnell Gdns, Stan. HA7 117 CK53
Burnell Rd, Sutt. SM1 240 DB105
Burnell Wk, SE1 32 B10
Great Warley CM13 129 FW51
Burnels Av, E6 25 L3
Burness Cl, N7 8 C4
Uxbridge UB8 156 BK68
Burne St, NW1 16 C6
Burnet Av, Guil. GU1 265 BB131
Burnet Cl, Hem.H. HP3 62 BL21
Burnet Gro, Epsom KT19 238 CQ113
Burnett Cl, E9 11 H3
Burnett Ho, SE13 46 F9
Burnett Pk, Harl. CM19 73 EP20
Burnett Rd, Erith DA8 190 FK79
Ilford IG6 125 EP52
Burnett Sq, Hert. SG14 53 DM08
Burnetts Rd, Wind. SL4 173 AL81
Burney Av, Surb. KT5 220 CM99
Burney Cl, Fetch. KT22 268 CC125
Burney Dr, Loug. IG10 107 EP40
Burney Ho, Lthd. KT22 *off Highbury Dr* 253 CG121
Burney Rd, Westh. RH5 269 CG131
Burney St, SE10 46 F4
Burnfoot Av, SW6 38 F7
Burnfoot Ct, SE22 204 DV88
BURNHAM, Slou. SL1 152 AJ68
⇌ Burnham 153 AK72
Burnham, NW3 6 C6
Burnham Av, Beac. HP9 133 AN55
Uxbridge UB10 137 BQ63
Burnham Cl, NW7 119 CU52
SE1 32 B9
Enfield EN1 104 DS38
Wealdstone HA3 139 CG56
Windsor SL4 173 AK82
Burnham Ct, NW4 141 CW56
Burnham Cres, E11 146 EJ56
Dartford DA1 190 FJ84
Burnham Dr, Reig. RH2 272 DA133
Worcester Park KT4 221 CX103
Burnham Gdns, Croy. CR0 224 DT101
Hayes UB3 177 BR76
Hounslow TW4 177 BV81
Burnham Gram Sch, Burn. SL1 *off Hogfair La* 153 AK70
Burnham Hts, Slou. SL1 *off Goldsworthy Way* 152 AJ72
Burnham La, Slou. SL1 153 AL72
Burnham Rd, E4 123 DZ50
Beaconsfield HP9 133 AL58
Dagenham RM9 168 EV66
Dartford DA1 190 FJ84
Morden SM4 222 DB99
Romford RM7 149 FD55
St. Albans AL1 65 CG20
Sidcup DA14 208 EY89
Burnhams Gro, Epsom KT19 238 CP111
Burnhams Rd, Bkhm KT23 252 BY124
Burnham St, E2 20 G2
Kingston upon Thames KT2 220 CN95
Burnham Upr Sch, Burn. SL1 *off Opendale Rd* 152 AH71
Burnham Wk, Slou. SL2 133 AN64
Burnham Way, SE26 205 DZ92
W13 179 CH77
Burnhill Cl, SE15 44 F4
Burnhill Rd, Beck. BR3 225 EA96
Burnley Cl, Wat. WD19 116 BW50
Burnley Rd, NW10 141 CU64
SW9 42 C8
Grays RM20 191 FT81
Burnsall St, SW3 28 D10
Burns Av, Chad.Hth RM6 148 EW59
Feltham TW14 197 BU86
Sidcup DA15 208 EV86
Southall UB1 158 CA73
Burns Cl, E17 145 EC56
SW19 202 DD93
Carshalton SM5 240 DG109
Erith DA8 189 FF81
Hayes UB4 157 BT71
Welling DA16 187 ET81
Burns Dr, Bans. SM7 239 CY114
Burnside, Ashtd. KT21 254 CM118
Hertford SG14 53 DN10
Hoddesdon EN11 71 DZ17
St. Albans AL1 65 CH22
Sawbridgeworth CM21 58 EX05
Burnside Av, E4 123 DZ51
Burnside Cl, SE16 33 K2
Barnet EN5 102 DA41
Hatfield AL10 *off Homestead Rd* 67 CU15
Twickenham TW1 199 CG86
Burnside Cres, Wem. HA0 159 CK67
Burnside Rd, Dag. RM8 148 EW61
Burnside Ter, Harl. CM17 58 EZ12
Burns Pl, Til. RM18 193 GH81
Burns Rd, NW10 161 CT67
SW11 40 E8
W13 179 CH75
Wembley HA0 159 CK68
Burns Ter, Esher KT10 *off Farm Rd* 218 CB103
Burns Way, Houns. TW5 178 BX82
Hutton CM13 131 GD45
Burnt Ash Hts, Brom. BR1 206 EH92
Burnt Ash Hill, SE12 206 EF86
Burnt Ash La, Brom. BR1 206 EG93
Burnt Ash Prim Sch, Brom. BR1 *off Rangefield Rd* 206 EG92
Burnt Ash Rd, SE12 206 EF85
Burnt Common Cl, Ripley GU23 265 BF125
Burnt Common La, Ripley GU23 266 BG125
Burnt Fm Ride, Enf. EN2 87 DP34
Waltham Cross EN7 87 DP31
Burnt Ho La, Hawley DA2 210 FL91
Burnthwaite Rd, SW6 39 H5
Burnt Mill, Harl. CM20 57 EQ13
Burnt Mill Cl, Harl. CM20 *off Burnt Mill La* 57 EQ12
● Burnt Mill Ind Est, Harl. CM20 57 EQ12
Burnt Mill La, Harl. CM20 57 EQ12
Burnt Mill Rbt, Harl. CM20 57 ER12
Burnt Mill Sch, Harl. CM20 *off First Av* 57 ES13
BURNT OAK, Edg. HA8 118 CQ52
⊖ Burnt Oak 118 CQ53
Burnt Oak Bdy, Edg. HA8 118 CN52
Burnt Oak Flds, Edg. HA8 118 CQ53
Burnt Oak Jun Sch, Sid. DA15 *off Burnt Oak La* 208 EU88
Burnt Oak La, Sid. DA15 208 EU86
Burntwood, Brwd. CM14 130 FW48
Burntwood Av, Horn. RM11 150 FK58
Burntwood Cl, SW18 202 DD88
Caterham CR3 258 DU121
Burntwood Gra Rd, SW18 202 DD88
Burntwood Gro, Sev. TN13 279 FH127
Burntwood La, SW17 202 DE89
Caterham CR3 258 DU121
Burntwood Rd, Sev. TN13 279 FH128
Burntwood Sch, SW17 *off Burntwood La* 202 DD89
Burntwood Vw, SE19 *off Bowley La* 204 DT92
Burn Wk, Burn. SL1 152 AH70
Burnway, Horn. RM11 150 FL59
Buross St, E1 20 F9
BURPHAM, Guil. GU1 265 BB130
Burpham, Guil. GU4 265 BC129
Burpham Cl, Hayes UB4 158 BX71
★ Burpham Court Fm Pk, Guil. GU4 265 AZ128
Burpham La, Guil. GU4 265 BA129
Burpham Prim Sch, Burpham GU4 *off Burpham La* 265 BA130
Burrage Gro, SE18 187 EQ77
Burrage Pl, SE18 187 EP78
Burrage Rd, SE18 187 EQ79
Redhill RH1 272 DG132
Burrard Rd, E16 24 A8
NW6 5 J2
Burr Cl, E1 32 C2
Bexleyheath DA7 188 EZ83
London Colney AL2 *off Waterside* 84 CL27
Burrell, The, Westc. RH4 284 CC137
Burrell Cl, Croy. CR0 225 DY100
Edgware HA8 118 CP47
Burrell Row, Beck. BR3 *off High St* 225 EA96
Burrell St, SE1 30 G2
Burrells Wf Sq, E14 34 C10
Burrell Twrs, E10 145 EA59
Burren Ct, N18 *off Baxter Rd* 122 DV49
Burrfield Dr, Orp. BR5 228 EX99
Burr Hill La, Chobham GU24 232 AS109
Burritt Rd, Kings.T. KT1 220 CN96
Burroughs, The, NW4 141 CV57
Burroughs Gdns, NW4 141 CV56
Burroughs Par, NW4 *off The Burroughs* 141 CV56
Burroway Rd, Slou. SL3 175 BB76
Burrow Cl, Chig. IG7 *off Burrow Rd* 125 ET50
Burrowfield, Welw.G.C. AL7 51 CX11
Burrow Grn, Chig. IG7 125 ET50
BURROWHILL, Wok. GU24 232 AS108
Burrow Rd, SE22 184 DS84
Chigwell IG7 125 ET50
Burrows Chase, Wal.Abb. EN9 105 ED36
Burrows Cl, Bkhm KT23 252 BZ124
Guildford GU2 264 AT133
Penn HP10 110 AC45
Burrows Cross, Shere GU5 283 BQ141
Burrows La, Goms. GU5 283 BQ140
Burrows Ms, SE1 30 G4
Burrows Rd, NW10 14 A2
Burrow Wk, SE21 204 DQ87
Burr Rd, SW18 202 DA87
Bursdon Cl, Sid. DA15 207 ET89
Burses Way, Hutt. CM13 131 GB45
Bursland Rd, Enf. EN3 105 DX42
Burslem Av, Ilf. IG6 126 EU51
Burslem St, E1 20 D9
Burstead Cl, Cob. KT11 236 BX113
Bursted Wd Prim Sch, Bexh. DA7 *off Swanbridge Rd* 189 FB82
Burstock Rd, SW15 181 CY84
Burston Dr, Park St AL2 82 CC28
Burston Rd, SW15 201 CX85
Burston Vil, SW15 *off St. John's Av* 201 CX85
BURSTOW, Horl. RH6 291 DN152
● Burstow Business Cen, Horl. RH6 291 DP146
Burstow Prim Sch, Smallfield RH6 *off Wheelers La* 291 DP148
Burstow Rd, SW20 221 CY95
Burtenshaw Rd, T.Ditt. KT7 219 CG101
Burtley Cl, N4 144 DQ60
Burton Av, Wat. WD18 97 BU42
Burton Cl, Chess. KT9 237 CK108
Horley RH6 290 DG149
Thornton Heath CR7 224 DR97
Burton Ct, SW3 *off Franklin's Row* 28 F10
Burton Dr, Enf. EN3 105 EA37
Burton Gdns, Houns. TW5 178 BZ81
Burton Gro, SE17 43 L1
Burtonhole Cl, NW7 119 CX49
Burtonhole La, NW7 119 CY49
Burton La, SW9 42 F8
Goffs Oak EN7 88 DS29
Burton Ms, SW1 29 H9
Burton Pl, WC1 17 P3
Burton Rd, E18 146 EH55
NW6 5 H7
SW9 42 G8
Kingston upon Thames KT2 200 CL94
Loughton IG10 107 EQ42
Burtons La, Ch.St.G. HP8 95 AZ43
Rickmansworth WD3 95 AZ43
Burtons Rd, Hmptn H. TW12 198 CB91
Burton St, WC1 17 P3
Burtons Way, Ch.St.G. HP8 94 AW40
Burton Way, Wind. SL4 173 AL83
Burtwell La, SE27 204 DR91
Burwash Ct, Orp. BR5 *off Rookery Gdns* 228 EW99
Burwash Ho, SE1 31 M5
Burwash Rd, SE18 187 ER78
Burway Cl, S.Croy. CR2 242 DS107
Burway Cres, Cher. KT16 216 BG97
Burwell Av, Grnf. UB6 159 CE65
Burwell Cl, E1 20 F9
Burwell Rd, E10 145 DY60
Burwell Wk, E3 22 B4
Burwood Av, Brom. BR2 226 EH103
Kenley CR8 241 DP114
Pinner HA5 138 BW57
Burwood Cl, Guil. GU1 265 BD133
Hersham KT12 236 BW107
Reigate RH2 272 DD134
Surbiton KT6 220 CN102
Burwood Gdns, Rain. RM13 169 FF69
BURWOOD PARK, Walt. KT12 235 BT106
Burwood Pk, Cob. KT11 235 BS112
Burwood Pk Rd, Hersham KT12 235 BV105
Burwood Pl, W2 16 D8
Barnet EN4 102 DC39
Burwood Rd, Hersham KT12 235 BV107
Burwood Sch, Orp. BR6 *off Avalon Rd* 228 EX103
Bury, The, Chesh. HP5 76 AP31
Hemel Hempstead HP1 62 BJ19
Bury Av, Hayes UB4 157 BS68
Ruislip HA4 137 BQ58
Bury Cl, SE16 33 K2
Woking GU21 248 AX116
Bury Ct, EC3 19 P8
Burycroft, Welw.G.C. AL8 51 CY06
Burydell La, Park St AL2 83 CD27
Bury Fm, Amer. HP7 *off Gore Hill* 77 AQ40
Bury Flds, Guil. GU2 280 AW136
Buryfield Ter, Ware SG12 *off Priory St* 54 DW06
Buryfield Way, Ware SG12 54 DW05
BURY GREEN, Wal.Cr. EN7 88 DV31
Bury Grn, Hem.H. HP1 62 BJ19
Bury Grn Rd, Chshnt EN7 88 DU31
Bury Gro, Mord. SM4 222 DB99
Bury Hill, Hem.H. HP1 62 BH19
Bury Hill Cl, Hem.H. HP1 62 BJ19
Buryholme, Brox. EN10 71 DZ23
Bury La, Chesh. HP5 76 AP31
Epping CM16 91 ES31
Rickmansworth WD3 114 BK46
Woking GU21 248 AW116
Bury Meadows, Rick. WD3 114 BK46
Bury Ms, Rick. WD3 *off Bury La* 114 BK46
Bury Pl, WC1 18 A7
Bury Ri, Hem.H. HP3 79 BD25
Bury Rd, E4 106 EE43
N22 143 DN55
Dagenham RM10 149 FB64
Epping CM16 91 ES31
Harlow CM17 58 EW11
Hatfield AL10 67 CW17
Hemel Hempstead HP1 62 BJ19
Burys Ct Sch, Leigh RH2 *off Flanchford Rd* 287 CX140
Buryside Cl, Ilf. IG2 147 ET56
Bury St, EC3 19 P9
N9 122 DU46
SW1 29 M2
Bury St, Guildford GU2 280 AW136
Ruislip HA4 137 BQ57
Bury St W, N9 122 DR45
Bury Wk, SW3 28 C9
Busbridge Ho, E14 22 B7
Busby Ms, NW5 *off Busby Pl* 7 N4
Busby Pl, NW5 7 N4
Busch Cl, Islw. TW7 179 CH81
Bushbaby Cl, SE1 31 N7
Bushbarns, Chsht EN7 88 DU29
Bushberry Rd, E9 11 M4
Bushbury La, Bet. RH3 286 CN139
Bushby Av, Brox. EN10 71 DZ22
Bush Cl, Add. KT15 234 BJ106
Ilford IG2 147 ER57
Bush Cotts, SW18 *off Putney Br Rd* 202 DA85
Bush Ct, W12 26 D4
Bushell Cl, SW2 203 DM89
Bushell Grn, Bushey Hth WD23 117 CD47
Bushell St, E1 32 D3
Bushell Way, Chis. BR7 207 EN92
Bush Elms Rd, Horn. RM11 149 FG59
Bushetts Gro, Merst. RH1 273 DH129
BUSHEY, WD23 116 CA45
Bushey 98 BX44
Bushey Acad, The, Bushey WD23 *off London Rd* 98 BZ44
Bushey & Oxhey Inf Sch, Bushey WD23 *off Aldenham Rd* 98 BY43
Bushey Av, E18 146 EF55
Petts Wood BR5 227 ER101
Bushey Cl, E4 123 EC48
Kenley CR8 258 DS116
Uxbridge UB10 137 BP61
Welwyn Garden City AL7 52 DB10
Bushey Ct, SW20 221 CV96
Bushey Cft, Harl. CM18 73 ES17
Oxted RH8 275 EC130
Bushey Down, SW12 *off Bedford Hill* 203 DH89
Bushey Grn, Welw.G.C. AL7 52 DB10
Bushey Gro Rd, Bushey WD23 98 BX42
Bushey Hall Dr, Bushey WD23 98 BY42
Bushey Hall Pk, Bushey WD23 98 BY42
Bushey Hall Rd, Bushey WD23 98 BX42
BUSHEY HEATH, Bushey WD23 117 CE46
Bushey Heath Prim Sch, Bushey WD23 *off The Rutts* 117 CD46
Bushey Hill Rd, SE5 43 P7
Bushey La, Sutt. SM1 240 DA105
Bushey Lees, Sid. DA15 *off Fen Gro* 207 ET86
Bushey Ley, Welw.G.C. AL7 52 DB10
Bushey Manor Jun Sch, Bushey WD23 *off Grange Rd* 98 BY44
BUSHEY MEAD, SW20 221 CX97
Bushey Meads Sch, Bushey WD23 *off Coldharbour La* 98 CC43
Bushey Mill Cres, Wat. WD24 98 BW37
Bushey Mill La, Bushey WD23 98 BZ40
Watford WD24 98 BW37
Bushey Rd, E13 24 E1
N15 144 DS58
SW20 221 CV97
Croydon CR0 225 EA103
Hayes UB3 177 BS77
Sutton SM1 240 DB105
Uxbridge UB10 136 BN61
Bushey Shaw, Ashtd. KT21 253 CH117
Bushey Vw Wk, Wat. WD24 98 BX40
Bushey Way, Beck. BR3 225 ED100
Bush Fair, Harl. CM18 73 ET17
Bushfield Cl, Edg. HA8 118 CP47
Bushfield Cres, Edg. HA8 118 CP47
Bushfield Dr, Red. RH1 288 DG139
Bushfield Rd, Bov. HP3 79 BC25
Bushfields, Loug. IG10 107 EN43
Bushfield Wk, Swans. DA10 212 FY86
Bush Gro, NW9 140 CQ59
Stanmore HA7 117 CK53
Bushgrove Rd, Dag. RM8 148 EX63
Bush Hall La, Hat. AL9 67 CX15
Bush Hill, N21 122 DQ45
BUSH HILL PARK, Enf. EN1 104 DS43
⇌ Bush Hill Park 104 DT44
Bush Hill Pk Prim Sch, Enf. EN1 *off Main Av* 104 DU43
Bush Hill Rd, N21 104 DR44
Harrow HA3 140 CM58
Bush Ho, SE18 *off Berber Par* 186 EL80
Harlow CM18 *off Bush Fair* 73 ET17
● Bush Ind Est, N19 143 DJ62
NW10 160 CR70
Bush La, EC4 19 L10
Send GU23 249 BD124
Bushmead Cl, N15 *off Duffield Dr* 144 DT56
Bushmoor Cres, SE18 187 EQ80
Bushnell Rd, SW17 203 DH89
Bush Rd, E8 10 E9
E11 146 EF59
SE8 33 K8
Buckhurst Hill IG9 124 EK49
Richmond TW9 180 CM79
Shepperton TW17 216 BM99
Bushway, Dag. RM8 148 EX63
Bushwood, E11 146 EF60
Bushwood Cl, N.Mymms AL9 *off Dellsome La* 67 CV23
Bushwood Dr, SE1 32 B9
Bushwood Rd, Rich. TW9 180 CN79
Bushy Cl, Rom. RM1 127 FD51
BUSHY HILL, Guil. GU1 265 BC132
Bushy Hill Dr, Guil. GU1 265 BB132
Bushy Hill Jun Sch, Guil. GU1 *off Sheeplands Av* 265 BD133
★ Bushy Park, Tedd. TW11 219 CF95
Bushy Pk, Hmptn H. TW12 219 CF95
Teddington TW11 219 CF95
Bushy Pk Gdns, Tedd. TW11 199 CD92
Bushy Pk Rd, Tedd. TW11 199 CH94
Bushy Rd, Fetch. KT22 252 CB122
Teddington TW11 199 CF93
Business Acad Bexley, The, Prim Sch, Erith DA18 *off Yarnton Way* 188 EY75
Sec Sch, Erith DA18 *off Yarnton Way* 188 EY75
● Business Centre, Rom. RM3 *off Faringdon Ave* 128 FK52
★ Business Design Cen, N1 8 F9
● Business Pk 8, Lthd. KT22 *off Barnett Wd La* 253 CH119
● Business Village, The, Slou. SL2 154 AV74
Buslins La, Chesh. HP5 76 AL28
Butcher Row, E1 21 K10
E14 21 K10
Butchers La, Sev. TN15 231 FX103
Butchers Ms, Hayes UB3 *off Hemmen La* 157 BT73
Butchers Rd, E16 23 P8
Butcher Wk, Swans. DA10 212 FY87
Bute Av, Rich. TW10 200 CL89
Bute Ct, Wall. SM6 241 DJ106
Bute Gdns, W6 26 C9
Wallington SM6 241 DJ106
Bute Gdns W, Wall. SM6 241 DJ106
Bute Ho Prep Sch for Girls, W6 26 C8
Bute Ms, NW11 *off Northway* 142 DB57
Bute Rd, Croy. CR0 223 DN102
Ilford IG6 147 EP57
Wallington SM6 241 DJ105
Bute St, SW7 28 A8
Bute Wk, N1 9 L5
Butler Av, Har. HA1 139 CD59
Butler Cl, Edg. HA8 *off Scott Rd* 118 CP54
Butler Ct, Wem. HA0 *off Harrow Rd* 139 CG63
Butler Fm Cl, Rich. TW10 199 CK91
Butler Ho, Grays RM17 *off Argent St* 192 GB79
Butler Pl, SW1 29 N6
Butler Rd, NW10 161 CT66
Dagenham RM8 148 EV63
Harrow HA1 138 CC59
Butlers & Colonial Wf, SE1 32 B4
Butlers Cl, Amer. HP6 77 AN37
Hounslow TW4 178 BZ83
Windsor SL4 173 AK82
Butlers Ct, Wal.Cr. EN8 89 DY32
Butlers Ct Rd, Beac. HP9 111 AK54
Butlers Ct Sch, Beac. HP9 *off Wattleton Rd* 111 AK54
BUTLERS CROSS, Beac. HP9 112 AT49
Butlers Dene Rd, Wold. CR3 259 DZ120
Butlers Dr, E4 105 EC38
Butlers Hill, W.Hors. KT24 267 BP130
Butler St, E2 21 H2
Uxbridge UB10 157 BP70
Butlers Wf, SE1 32 A3
Butler Wk, Grays RM17 *off Palmers Dr* 192 GD77
Buttell Cl, Grays RM17 192 GD78
Buttercross La, Epp. CM16 92 EU30
Buttercup Cl, Hat. AL10 51 CT14
Northolt UB5 158 BY65
Romford RM3 *off Copperfields Way* 128 FK53
Buttercup Sq, Stanw. TW19 *off Diamedes Av* 196 BK88
Butterfield, Woob.Grn HP10 132 AD59
Butterfield Cl, N17 122 DQ51
SE16 32 E5
Twickenham TW1 199 CF86
Butterfield Ho, SE18 *off Berber Par* 186 EL80
Butterfield La, St.Alb. AL1 65 CE24
Butterfields, E17 145 EC57
Butterfield Sq, E6 25 J9
Butterfly La, SE9 207 EP86
Elstree WD6 99 CG41
Butterfly Wk, Warl. CR6 258 DW120
Butterfly Wk Shop Cen, SE5 43 K7
Butter Hill, Cars. SM5 222 DG104
Dorking RH4 *off South St* 285 CG136
Wallington SM6 222 DG104
Butteridges Cl, Dag. RM9 168 EZ67
Butterly Av, Dart. DA1 210 FM89
Buttermere Av, Slou. SL1 152 AJ71
Buttermere Cl, E15 13 H1
SE1 32 A9
Feltham TW14 197 BT88
Morden SM4 221 CX100
St. Albans AL1 65 CH21
Buttermere Dr, SW15 201 CY85
Buttermere Gdns, Pur. CR8 242 DR113
Buttermere Pl, Wat. WD25 *off Linden Lea* 81 BU33
Buttermere Rd, Orp. BR5 228 EX98
Buttermere Wk, E8 10 B5
Buttermere Way, Egh. TW20 *off Keswick Rd* 195 BB94
Buttersweet Ri, Saw. CM21 58 EY06
Butterwick, W6 26 B9
Watford WD25 98 BY36
Butterwick La, St.Alb. AL4 66 CN22
Butterworth Gdns, Wdf.Grn. IG8 124 EG51
Buttery Ms, N14 121 DL48
Buttesland St, N1 19 M2
Buttfield Cl, Dag. RM10 169 FB65
Butt Fld Vw, St.Alb. AL1 64 CC24
Buttlehide, Map.Cr. WD3 113 BD50
Buttmarsh Cl, SE18 37 P10
Buttondene Cres, Brox. EN10 71 EB22
Button Rd, Grays RM17 192 FZ77
Buttonscroft Cl, Th.Hth. CR7 224 DQ97
Button St, Swan. BR8 230 FJ96
Butts, The, Brent. TW8 179 CK79
Broxbourne EN10 71 DY24
Otford TN14 263 FH116
Sunbury-on-Thames TW16 *off Elizabeth Gdns* 218 BW97
Buttsbury Rd, Ilf. IG1 147 EQ64
Butts Cotts, Felt. TW13 198 BZ90
Butts Cres, Han. TW13 198 CA90
Butts End, Hem.H. HP1 62 BG18
Butts Grn Rd, Horn. RM11 150 FK58
Buttsmead, Nthwd. HA6 115 BQ52
Butts Piece, Nthlt. UB5 *off Longhook Gdns* 157 BV68
Butts Rd, Brom. BR1 206 EE92
Woking GU21 248 AY117
Buxhall Cres, E9 11 N4
Buxlow Prep Sch, Wem. HA9 *off Castleton Gdns* 140 CL62
Buxted Rd, E8 10 A6
N12 120 DE50
SE22 184 DS84
Buxton Av, Cat. CR3 258 DS121
Buxton Cl, N9 122 DW47
Epsom KT19 238 CP111
St. Albans AL4 65 CK17
Woodford Green IG8 124 EK51
Buxton Ct, N1 19 K2
Buxton Cres, Sutt. SM3 239 CY105
Buxton Dr, E11 146 EE56
New Malden KT3 220 CR96
Buxton Gdns, W3 160 CP73
Buxton Ho, SW11 *off Maysoule Rd* 182 DD84

Buxton La, Cat. CR3 258 DR120
Buxton Ms, SW4 41 P8
Buxton Path, Wat. WD19 116 BW48
Buxton Pl, Cat. CR3 258 DR120
Buxton Rd, E4 123 ED45
E6 24 G2
E15 13 J3
E17 145 DY56
N19 143 DK60
NW2 161 CV65
SW14 180 CS83
Ashford TW15 196 BK92
Erith DA8 189 FD80
Grays RM16 192 GE75
Ilford IG2 147 ES58
Theydon Bois CM16 107 ES36
Thornton Heath CR7 223 DP99
Waltham Abbey EN9 90 EG32
Buxton St, E1 20 B5
● Buzzard Creek Ind Est, Bark. IG11 167 ET71
Byam St, SW6 39 N9
Byards Cft, SW16 223 DK95
Byatt Wk, Hmptn. TW12 off Victors Dr 198 BY93
Bybend Cl, Farn.Royal SL2 153 AP67
Bychurch End, Tedd. TW11 199 CF92
Bycliffe Ter, Grav. DA11 213 GF87
Bycroft Rd, Sthl. UB1 158 CA70
Bycroft St, SE20 off Penge La 205 DX94
Byculla Av, Enf. EN2 103 DP41
Byculla Rd, Enf. EN2 103 DP41
Byde St, Hert. SG14 54 DQ08
Bye, The, W3 160 CS72
Byegrove Ct, SW19 off Byegrove Rd 202 DD94
Byegrove Rd, SW19 202 DD93
Byers Cl, Pot.B. EN6 86 DC34
Byewaters, Wat. WD18 97 BQ44
Byeway, The, SW14 180 CQ83
Bye Way, The, Har. HA3 117 CE53
Byeway, The, Rick. WD3 114 BL47
Byeways, Twick. TW2 198 CB90
Byeways, The, Surb. KT5 220 CN99
Byfeld Gdns, SW13 181 CU81
Byfield, Welw.G.C. AL8 51 CY06
Byfield Cl, SE16 33 M4
Byfield Pas, Islw. TW7 179 CG83
Byfield Rd, Islw. TW7 179 CG83
BYFLEET, W.Byf. KT14 234 BM113
⇌ Byfleet & New Haw 234 BK110
● Byfleet Ind Est, Wat. WD18 115 BP46
Sch Byfleet Prim Sch, Byfleet KT14 off Kings Head La 234 BK111
Byfleet Rd, Byfleet KT14 234 BN112
Cobham KT11 235 BS113
New Haw KT15 234 BK108
● Byfleet Tech Cen, Byfleet KT14 234 BK111
Byford Cl, E15 13 K7
Bygrove, New Adgtn CR0 243 EB107
Sch Bygrove Prim Sch, E14 22 C9
Bygrove St, E14 22 C9
Byland Cl, N21 121 DM45
Morden SM4 off Bolton Dr 222 DD101
Bylands, Wok. GU22 249 BA119
Bylands Cl, SE2 188 EV76
SE16 33 K2
Byne Rd, SE26 204 DW93
Carshalton SM5 222 DE103
Bynes Rd, S.Croy. CR2 242 DR108
Byng Dr, Pot.B. EN6 86 DA31
Bynghams, Harl. CM19 73 EM17
Byng Pl, WC1 17 N5
Byng Rd, Barn. EN5 101 CX41
Byng St, E14 34 A4
Bynon Av, Bexh. DA7 188 EY83
Bypass Rd, Lthd. KT22 253 CH120
Byre, The, N14 103 DH44
Byrefield Rd, Guil. GU2 264 AT131
Byre Rd, N14 102 DG44
Byrne Cl, Croy. CR0 223 DP100
Byrne Ho, SW2 off Kett Gdns 203 DM85
Byrne Rd, SW12 203 DH88
Byron Av, E12 166 EL65
E18 146 EF55
NW9 140 CP56
Borehamwood WD6 100 CN43
Coulsdon CR5 257 DL115
Hounslow TW4 177 BU82
New Malden KT3 221 CU99
Sutton SM1 240 DD105
Watford WD24 98 BX39
Byron Av E, Sutt. SM1 240 DD105
Byron Cl, E8 10 C8
SE26 205 DY91
SE28 168 EW74
SW16 203 DL93
Hampton TW12 198 BZ91
Knaphill GU21 248 AS117
Waltham Cross EN7 off Allard Cl 88 DT27
Walton-on-Thames KT12 218 BY102
Byron Ct, W9 15 K4
Enfield EN2 103 DP40
Harrow HA1 139 CE58
Windsor SL4 173 AN83
Sch Byron Ct Prim Sch, Wem. HA0 off Spencer Rd 139 CJ61
Byron Dr, N2 142 DD58
Erith DA8 189 FB80
Byron Gdns, Sutt. SM1 240 DD105
Tilbury RM18 193 GJ81
Byron Hill Rd, Har. HA2 139 CD60
Byron Ho, Beck. BR3 205 EA93
Slough SL3 175 BB78
Byron Ms, NW3 6 D2
W9 15 K4
Byron Pl, Lthd. KT22 253 CH122
Sch Byron Prim Sch, Couls. CR5 off St. Davids 257 DM117
Byron Rd, E10 145 EB60
E17 145 EA55
NW2 141 CV61
NW7 119 CU50
W5 160 CM74
Addlestone KT15 234 BL105
Dartford DA1 190 FP84
Harrow HA1 139 CE58
Hutton CM13 131 GD45
South Croydon CR2 242 DV110
Wealdstone HA3 117 CF54
Wembley HA0 139 CJ62
Byron St, E14 22 E8
Byron Ter, N9 104 DW44
SE7 186 EJ80
Byron Way, Hayes UB4 157 BS70
Byron Way, Northolt UB5 158 BY69
Romford RM3 128 FJ53
West Drayton UB7 176 BM77
Bysouth Cl, N15 144 DR56
Ilford IG5 125 EP53
By the Mt, Welw.G.C. AL7 51 CX10
By the Wd, Wat. WD19 116 BX47
Bythorn St, SW9 183 DM83
Byton Rd, SW17 202 DF93
Byttom Hill, Mick. RH5 269 CJ127
Byward Av, Felt. TW14 198 BW86
Byward St, EC3 31 P1
Bywater Pl, SE16 33 M2
Bywater St, SW3 28 E10
Byway, The, Epsom KT19 239 CT105
Potters Bar EN6 86 DA33
Sutton SM2 240 DD109
Byways, Berk. HP4 60 AY18
Burnham SL1 152 AG71
Byways, The, Ashtd. KT21 off Skinners La 253 CK118
Bywell Pl, W1 17 L7
Bywood Av, Croy. CR0 224 DW100
Bywood Cl, Bans. SM7 255 CZ117
Kenley CR8 257 DP115
By-Wood End, Chal.St.P. SL9 113 AZ50
Byworth Wk, N19 off Courtauld Rd 143 DL60

C

Cabbell Pl, Add. KT15 234 BJ105
Cabbell St, NW1 16 C7
Cabell Rd, Guil. GU2 264 AS133
Caberfeigh Cl, Red. RH1 272 DD134
Cabinet Way, E4 123 DZ51
Cable Ho Ct, Wok. GU21 248 AY115
Cable Pl, SE10 46 F6
Cable St, E1 20 C10
● Cable Trade Pk, SE7 36 C9
Cabot Pl, E14 34 B2
Cabot Sq, E14 34 B2
Cabot Way, E6 off Parr Rd 166 EK67
Cabrera Av, Vir.W. GU25 214 AW100
Cabrera Cl, Vir.W. GU25 214 AX100
Cabul Rd, SW11 40 C9
Cacket's Cotts, Cudham TN14 261 ES115
Cackets La, Cudham TN14 261 ER115
Cactus Cl, SE15 43 P8
Cactus Wk, W12 off Du Cane Rd 161 CT72
Cadbury Cl, Islw. TW7 179 CG81
Sunbury-on-Thames TW16 197 BS94
Cadbury Rd, Sun. TW16 197 BS94
Cadbury Way, SE16 32 B7
Caddington Cl, Barn. EN4 102 DE43
Caddington Rd, NW2 141 CY62
Caddis Cl, Stan. HA7 117 CF52
Caddy Cl, Egh. TW20 195 BA92
Cade La, Sev. TN13 279 FJ128
Cadell Cl, E2 20 B1
Cade Rd, SE10 46 G6
Cader Rd, SW18 202 DC86
Cadet Dr, SE1 32 B10
Cadet Pl, SE10 35 J10
Cadiz Rd, Dag. RM10 169 FC66
Cadiz St, SE17 43 K1
Cadley Ter, SE23 204 DW89
Cadlocks Hill, Halst. TN14 246 EZ110
Cadman Cl, SW9 off Langton Rd 42 G5
Cadmer Cl, N.Mal. KT3 220 CS98
Cadmore Ct, Hert. SG14 off The Ridgeway 53 DM07
Cadmore La, Chsht EN8 89 DX28
Cadmus Cl, SW4 off Aristotle Rd 183 DK83
Cadnam Pt, SW15 off Dilton Gdns 201 CV88
Cadogan Av, Dart. DA2 211 FR87
Cadogan Cl, E9 11 P6
Beckenham BR3 off Albemarle Rd 225 ED95
Harrow HA2 138 CB63
Teddington TW11 199 CE92
Cadogan Ct, Sutt. SM2 240 DB107
Cadogan Gdns, E18 146 EH55
N3 120 DB53
N21 103 DN43
SW3 28 F8
Cadogan Gate, SW1 28 F8
Cadogan La, SW1 28 G7
Pier Cadogan Pier 40 D3
Cadogan Pl, SW1 28 F6
Kenley CR8 258 DQ117
Cadogan Rd, SE18 37 P6
Surbiton KT6 219 CK99
Cadogan Sq, SW1 28 F7
Cadogan St, SW3 28 E9
Cadogan Ter, E9 11 N5
Cadoxton Av, N15 144 DT58
Cadwallon Rd, SE9 207 EP89
Caedmon Rd, N7 143 DM63
Caenshill Pl, Wey. KT13 234 BN108
Caenshill Rd, Wey. KT13 234 BN108
Caenwood Cl, Wey. KT13 234 BN107
Caen Wd Rd, Ashtd. KT21 253 CJ118
Caerleon Cl, Clay. KT10 237 CH108
Sidcup DA14 208 EW92
Caerleon Ter, SE2 off Blithdale Rd 188 EV77
Caernarvon Cl, Hem.H. HP2 62 BK20
Hornchurch RM11 150 FN60
Mitcham CR4 223 DL97
Caernarvon Dr, Ilf. IG5 125 EN53
Caesars Wk, Mitch. CR4 222 DF99
Caesars Way, Shep. TW17 217 BR100
Cage Pond Rd, Shenley WD7 84 CM33
Cages Wd Dr, Farn.Com. SL2 133 AP63
Cage Yd, Reig. RH2 off High St 272 DA134
Cahill St, EC1 19 K5
Cahir St, E14 34 C9
Caillard Rd, Byfleet KT14 234 BL111
Cain Cl, St.Alb. AL1 65 CF22
Cains La, Felt. TW14 197 BS85
Caird St, W10 14 F3
Cairn Av, W5 159 CK74
Cairncross Ms, N8 off Felix Av 143 DL58
Cairndale Cl, Brom. BR1 206 EF94
Cairnfield Av, NW2 140 CS62
Cairngorm Cl, Tedd. TW11 off Vicarage Rd 199 CG92
Cairngorm Pl, Slou. SL2 153 AR70
Cairns Av, Wdf.Grn. IG8 124 EL51
Cairns Cl, Dart. DA1 210 FK85
St. Albans AL4 65 CK21
Cairns Ms, SE18 off Bell St 186 EL81
Cairns Rd, SW11 202 DE85
Cairn Way, Stan. HA7 117 CF51
Cairo New Rd, Croy. CR0 223 DP103
Cairo Rd, E17 145 EA56
Caishowe Rd, Borwd. WD6 100 CP39
Caister Cl, Hem.H. HP2 62 BL21
Caistor Ms, SW12 off Caistor Rd 203 DH87
Caistor Pk Rd, E15 13 M9
Caistor Rd, SW12 203 DH87
Caithness Dr, Epsom KT18 238 CR114
Caithness Gdns, Sid. DA15 207 ET86
Caithness Rd, W14 26 C8
Mitcham CR4 203 DH94
Calabria Rd, N5 8 G4
Calais Cl, Chsht EN7 88 DR26
Calais Gate, SE5 off Cormont St 42 G6
Calais St, SE5 43 H6
Calbourne Av, Horn. RM12 149 FH64
Calbourne Rd, SW12 202 DF87
Calbroke Ct, Slou. SL2 off Calbroke Rd 153 AM69
Calbroke Rd, Slou. SL2 153 AM70
Calcott Cl, Brwd. CM14 130 FV46
Calcott Wk, SE9 206 EK91
Calcroft Av, Green. DA9 211 FW85
Calcutta Rd, Til. RM18 193 GF82
Caldbeck, Wal.Abb. EN9 89 ED34
Caldbeck Av, Wor.Pk. KT4 221 CU103
Caldecot Av, Chsht EN7 88 DT29
Caldecote Gdns, Bushey WD23 99 CE44
Caldecote La, Bushey WD23 117 CF45
Caldecot Rd, SE5 43 K8
Caldecott Way, E5 145 DX62
Caldecot Way, Brox. EN10 71 DZ22
Calder Av, Brook.Pk AL9 86 DB26
Perivale UB6 159 CF68
Calder Cl, Enf. EN1 104 DS41
Calder Ct, Rom. RM1 149 FD56
Slough SL3 175 AZ78
Calder Gdns, Edg. HA8 140 CN55
Calderon Pl, W10 14 A7
Calderon Rd, E11 145 EC63
Calder Rd, Mord. SM4 222 DC99
Caldervale Rd, SW4 203 DK85
Calder Way, Colnbr. SL3 175 BF83
Calderwood, Grav. DA12 213 GL92
Calderwood Pl, Barn. EN4 102 DB39
Calderwood St, SE18 37 M8
Caldicot Grn, NW9 140 CS58
Sch Caldicott Sch, Farn.Royal SL2 off Crown La 153 AP66
Caldon Ho, Nthlt. UB5 off Waxlow Way 158 BZ70
Caldwell Gdns Est, SW9 42 E6
Caldwell Rd, Wat. WD19 116 BX49
Caldwell St, SW9 42 D5
Caldy Rd, Belv. DA17 189 FB76
Caldy Wk, N1 9 J6
Caleb St, SE1 31 J4
Caledon Cl, Beac. HP9 111 AK52
Caledonian Cl, Ilf. IG3 148 EV60
Caledonian Ct, Nthlt. UB5 off Taywood Rd 158 BY70
⊖ Caledonian Road 8 B4
Caledonian Rd, N1 18 B1
N7 8 C4
⇌ Caledonian Road & Barnsbury 8 D6
Caledonian Sq, NW1 7 N4
Caledonian Way, Gat. RH6 off Queen's Gate 291 DH151
Caledonian Wf, E14 34 G9
Caledonia Rd, Stai. TW19 196 BL88
Caledonia St, N1 18 B1
Caledon Pl, Guil. GU4 off Darfield Rd 265 BA131
Caledon Rd, E6 166 EL67
Beaconsfield HP9 111 AL52
London Colney AL2 83 CK26
Wallington SM6 240 DG105
Cale St, SW3 28 C10
Caletock Way, SE10 35 L10
Calfstock La, Fnghm DA4 230 FL98
Calico Row, SW11 39 P10
Calidore Cl, SW2 203 DM86
California Bldg, SE13 off Deals Gateway 46 C6
California Cl, Sutt. SM2 240 DA110
California La, Bushey Hth WD23 117 CD46
California Rd, N.Mal. KT3 220 CP98
Caliph Cl, Grav. DA12 213 GM90
Callaby Ter, N1 9 M5
Callaghan Cl, SE13 186 EE84
Callander Rd, SE6 205 EB89
Callan Gro, S.Ock. RM15 171 FV73
Callard Av, N13 121 DP50
Callcott Rd, NW6 4 G7
Callcott St, W8 27 J2
Callendar Rd, SW7 28 A6
Callender Ct, Croy. CR0 off Harry Cl 224 DQ100
Calley Down Cres, New Adgtn CR0 243 ED110
Callingham Cl, E14 21 P7
Callingham Pl, Beac. HP9 111 AL52
Callis Fm Cl, Stanw. TW19 off Bedfont Rd 196 BL86
Callisons Pl, SE10 35 K10
Callis Rd, E17 145 DZ58
Callisto Ct, Hem.H. HP2 off Jupiter Dr 62 BM17
Callow Fld, Pur. CR8 241 DN113
Callow Hill, Vir.W. GU25 214 AW97
Callowland Cl, Wat. WD24 97 BV38
Callow St, SW3 39 P2
Calluna Ct, Wok. GU22 off Heathside Rd 249 AZ118
Calmington Rd, SE5 43 P1
Calmont Rd, Brom. BR1 205 ED93
Calmore Cl, Horn. RM12 150 FJ64
Calne Av, Ilf. IG5 125 EP53
Calonne Rd, SW19 201 CX91
Calshot Av, Chaff.Hun. RM16 192 FZ75
Calshot Rd, Lon.Hthrw Air. TW6 176 BN82
Calshot St, N1 8 C10
Calshot Way, Enf. EN2 103 DP41
London Heathrow Airport TW6 off Calshot Rd 177 BP82
Calthorpe Gdns, Edg. HA8 118 CL50
Sutton SM1 222 DC104
Calthorpe St, WC1 18 D4
Calton Av, SE21 204 DS85
Calton Av, Hertford SG14 53 DM08
Calton Ct, Hert. SG14 off Calton Av 53 DM09
Calton Rd, New Barn. EN5 102 DC44
Calverley Cl, Beck. BR3 205 EB93
Calverley Ct, Epsom KT19 off Kingston Rd 238 CR105
Calverley Cres, Dag. RM10 148 FA61
Calverley Gdns, Har. HA3 139 CK59
Calverley Gro, N19 143 DK60
Calverley Rd, Epsom KT17 239 CU107
Calvert Av, E2 19 P3
Calvert Cl, Belv. DA17 188 FA77
Epsom KT19 238 CP110
Sidcup DA14 208 EY93
Calvert Cres, Dor. RH4 off Calvert Rd 269 CH134
Calvert Dr, Dart. DA2 209 FD89
Calverton, SE5 43 M2
Sch Calverton Prim Sch, E16 24 F9
Calverton Rd, E6 167 EN67
Calvert Rd, SE10 47 L1
Barnet EN5 101 CX40
Dorking RH4 269 CH134
Effingham KT24 267 BV128
Calvert's Bldgs, SE1 31 L3
Calvert St, NW1 6 G8
Calvin Cl, Orp. BR5 228 EX97
Calvin St, E1 20 A5
Calydon Rd, SE7 186 EH78
Calypso Cres, SE15 44 A4
Calypso Way, SE16 33 N7
Camac Rd, Twick. TW2 199 CD88
Camarthen Grn, NW9 140 CS57
Cambalt Rd, SW15 201 CX85
Sch Cambell Inf Sch, Dag. RM9 off Langley Cres 168 EX66
Sch Cambell Jun Sch, Dag. RM9 off Langley Cres 168 EX66
Camberley Av, SW20 221 CV96
Enfield EN1 104 DS42
Camberley Cl, Sutt. SM3 221 CX104
Camberley Rd, Lon.Hthrw Air. TW6 176 BN83
Cambert Way, SE3 186 EH84
CAMBERWELL, SE5 43 K5
● Camberwell Business Cen, SE5 43 L5
Camberwell Ch St, SE5 43 L7
Uni Camberwell Coll of Arts, Peckham Rd, SE5 43 P6
Wilson Rd, SE5 43 N7
Jct Camberwell Grn, SE5 43 K6
Camberwell Grn, SE5 43 L6
Camberwell Gro, SE5 43 M7
Camberwell New Rd, SE5 42 E3
Camberwell Pas, SE5 43 K6
Camberwell Rd, SE5 43 K3
Camberwell Sta Rd, SE5 43 J7
Cambeys Rd, Dag. RM10 149 FB64
Camborne Av, W13 179 CH75
Romford RM3 128 FL52
Camborne Cl, Lon.Hthrw Air. TW6 off Camborne Rd 176 BN83
Camborne Dr, Hem.H. HP2 62 BL16
Camborne Ms, SW18 off Camborne Rd 202 DA87
W11 14 E9
Camborne Rd, SW18 202 DA87
Croydon CR0 224 DU101
London Heathrow Airport TW6 176 BN83
Morden SM4 221 CX99
Sidcup DA14 208 EW90
Sutton SM2 240 DA108
Welling DA16 187 ET82
Camborne Way, Houns. TW5 178 CA81
London Heathrow Airport TW6 off Camborne Rd 176 BN83
Romford RM3 128 FL52
Cambourne Av, N9 123 DX45
Cambray Rd, SW12 203 DJ88
Orpington BR6 227 ET101
Cambria Cl, Houns. TW3 178 CA84
Sidcup DA15 207 ER88
Cambria Ct, Felt. TW14 197 BV87
Cambria Cres, Grav. DA12 213 GL91
Cambria Gdns, Stai. TW19 196 BL87
Cambria Ho, SE26 off High Level Dr 204 DU91
Erith DA8 off Larner Rd 189 FE80
Cambrian Av, Ilf. IG2 147 ES57
Cambrian Cl, SE27 203 DP90
Cambrian Grn, NW9 140 CS57
Cambrian Gro, Grav. DA11 213 GG87
Cambrian Rd, E10 145 EA59
Richmond TW10 200 CM86
Cambrian Way, Hem.H. HP2 62 BL17
Cambria Rd, SE5 43 J10
Cambria St, SW6 39 M5
Cambridge Av, NW6 5 K10
Burnham SL1 152 AH68
Greenford UB6 139 CF64
New Malden KT3 221 CT96
Romford RM2 150 FJ55
Slough SL1 153 AM72
Welling DA16 187 ET84
Cambridge Barracks Rd, SE18 37 K9
Cambridge Circ, WC2 17 P9
Cambridge Cl, E17 145 DZ58
N22 121 DN53
NW10 off Lawrence Way 140 CQ62
SW20 221 CV95
Cheshunt EN8 88 DW29
East Barnet EN4 120 DG46
Harmondsworth UB7 176 BK79
Hounslow TW4 178 BY84
Woking GU21 248 AT118
Cambridge Cotts, Rich. TW9 180 CN79
Cambridge Cres, E2 20 E1
Teddington TW11 199 CG92
Cambridge Dr, SE12 206 EG85
Potters Bar EN6 85 CX31
Ruislip HA4 138 BW61
Cambridge Gdns, N10 120 DG53
N13 121 DN50
N17 122 DR52
N21 122 DR45
NW6 5 K10
W10 14 F8
Enfield EN1 104 DU40
Grays RM16 193 GG77
Kingston upon Thames KT1 220 CN96
Cambridge Gate, NW1 17 K3
Cambridge Gate Ms, NW1 17 K3
Cambridge Grn, SE9 207 EP88
Cambridge Gro, SE20 224 DV95
W6 181 CV77
Cambridge Gro Rd, Kings.T. KT1 220 CN96
⇌ Cambridge Heath 10 E10
Cambridge Heath Rd, E1 20 F6
E2 20 F6
Cambridge Ho, Wind. SL4 off Ward Royal 173 AQ81
Cambridge Lo Mobile Home Pk, Horl. RH6 290 DG145
Cambridge Mans, SW11 40 E7
Cambridge Par, Enf. EN1 off Great Cambridge Rd 104 DU39
Cambridge Pk, E11 146 EG59
Twickenham TW1 199 CK87
Cambridge Pk Rd, E11 off Cambridge Pk 146 EG59
Cambridge Pl, W8 27 M5
Cambridge Rd, E4 123 ED46
E11 146 EF58
NW6 15 J2
SE20 224 DV97
SW11 40 E7
SW13 181 CT82
SW20 221 CU95
W7 179 CF75
Ashford TW15 197 BQ94
Barking IG11 167 EQ66
Beaconsfield HP9 110 AJ53
Bromley BR1 206 EG94
Carshalton SM5 240 DE107
Hampton TW12 198 BZ94
Harlow CM20 58 EW09
Harrow HA2 138 CA57
Hounslow TW4 178 BY84
Ilford IG3 147 ES60
Kingston upon Thames KT1, KT2 220 CM96
Mitcham CR4 223 DJ97
New Malden KT3 220 CS98
Richmond TW9 180 CN80
St. Albans AL1 65 CH21
Sidcup DA14 207 ES91
Southall UB1 158 BZ74
Teddington TW11 199 CF91
Twickenham TW1 199 CK86
Uxbridge UB8 156 BK65
Walton-on-Thames KT12 217 BV100
Watford WD18 98 BW42
West Molesey KT8 218 BZ98
Cambridge Rd N, W4 180 CP78
Cambridge Rd S, W4 180 CP78
Cambridge Row, SE18 187 EP78
Sch Cambridge Sch, W6 off Cambridge Gro 181 CV77
Cambridge Sq, W2 16 C8
Redhill RH1 288 DG137
Cambridge St, SW1 29 K9
Cambridge Ter, N13 121 DN50
NW1 17 K3
Berkhamsted HP4 60 AX19
Cambridge Ter Ms, NW1 17 K3
Coll Cambridge Tutors Coll, Croy. CR0 off Water Twr Hill 242 DS105
Cambstone Cl, N11 120 DG47
Cambus Cl, Hayes UB4 158 BY71
Cambus Rd, E16 23 P6
Camdale Rd, SE18 187 ET80
★ Camden Arts Cen, NW3 5 N3
Camden Av, Felt. TW13 198 BW89
Hayes UB4 158 BW73
Camden Cl, Chad.St.M. RM16 193 GH77
Chislehurst BR7 207 EQ94
Gravesend DA11 212 GC88
Camden Gdns, NW1 7 K7
Sutton SM1 240 DB106
Thornton Heath CR7 223 DP97
Camden Gro, Chis. BR7 207 EP93
Camden High St, NW1 7 K8
Camden Hill Rd, SE19 204 DS93
Camdenhurst St, E14 21 M8
Sch Camden Jun Sch, Cars. SM5 off Camden Rd 240 DF105
Camden La, N7 7 P3
★ Camden Lock Mkt & Waterbuses, NW1 7 J7
Camden Lock Pl, NW1 7 J7
Camden Ms, NW1 7 M6
Camden Pk Rd, NW1 7 N4
Chislehurst BR7 207 EM94
Camden Pas, N1 8 G10
⇌ Camden Road 7 L7
Camden Rd, E11 146 EH58
E17 145 DZ58
N7 7 L7
NW1 7 N4
Bexley DA5 208 EZ88
Carshalton SM5 240 DF105
Grays RM16 192 FY76
Sevenoaks TN13 279 FH122
Sutton SM1 240 DA106
Camden Row, SE3 47 K9
Sch Camden Sch for Girls, NW5 7 M5
Camden Sq, NW1 7 N6
SE15 44 A6
Camden St, NW1 7 L8
Camden Ter, NW1 7 N5
CAMDEN TOWN, NW1 7 L9
⊖ Camden Town 7 K8
Camden Wk, N1 8 G9
Camden Way, Chis. BR7 207 EM94
Thornton Heath CR7 223 DP97
Camelford Wk, W11 14 E9
Camel Gro, Kings.T. KT2 199 CK92
Camellia Cl, Rom. RM3 128 FL53
Camellia Ct, Wdf.Grn. IG8 off The Bridle Path 124 EE52
Camellia Ho, Felt. TW13 off Tilley Rd 197 BV88
Camellia Pl, Twick. TW2 198 CB87
Camellia St, SW8 42 A5
Camelot Cl, SE28 187 ER75
SW19 202 DA91
Biggin Hill TN16 260 EJ116
Camelot Ct, Bushey WD23 off Hartswood Cl 98 CA40
Camelot Ho, NW1 7 P4
Sch Camelot Prim Sch, SE15 44 E3
Camelot St, SE15 44 E3
Camel Rd, E16 36 F2
Camera Pl, SW10 40 A3
Cameron Cl, N18 122 DV49

Cameron Cl, N20
off Myddelton Pk 120 DE47
N22 121 DM52
Bexley DA5 209 FD90
Warley CM14 130 FW49
Cameron Ct, Ware SG12 55 DX05
Cameron Cres, Edg. HA8 118 CP53
Cameron Dr, Dart. DA1 190 FN82
Wal.Cr. EN8 89 DX34
Cameron Ho, SE5
off Comber Gro 43 J5
Sch Cameron Ho Sch, SW3 40 B2
Cameron Pl, E1 20 F8
SW16 203 DN89
Cameron Rd, SE6 205 DZ89
Bromley BR2 226 EG98
Chesham HP5 76 AQ30
Croydon CR0 223 DP100
Ilford IG3 147 ES60
Cameron Sq, Mitch. CR4 222 DE95
Camerton Cl, E8 10 B5
Camfield, Welw.G.C. AL7 51 CZ13
Camfield Pl, Essen. AL9 68 DD21
● Camgate Cen, Stanw. TW19 196 BM86
Cam Grn, S.Ock. RM15 171 FV72
Camilla Cl, Bkhm KT23 268 CB125
Sunbury-on-Thames TW16 197 BT93
Camilla Dr, Westh. RH5 269 CG130
Camilla Rd, SE16 32 E9
Camille Cl, SE25 224 DU97
Camlan Rd, Brom. BR1 206 EF91
Camlet St, E2 20 A4
Camlet Way, Barn. EN4 102 DA40
St. Albans AL3 64 CB19
Camley St, NW1 7 P10
★ Camley St Natural Pk, NW1 7 P10
Camm Av, Wind. SL4 173 AL83
Camm Gdns, Kings.T. KT1
off Church Rd 220 CM96
Thames Ditton KT7 219 CE101
Camms Ter, Dag. RM10 149 FC64
Camomile Av, Mitch. CR4 222 DF95
Camomile Rd, Rush Grn RM7 149 FD61
Camomile St, EC3 19 N8
Camomile Way, West Dr. UB7 156 BL72
CAMP, THE, St.Alb. AL1 65 CH21
Campana Rd, SW6 39 J6
Campbell Av, Ilf. IG6 147 EQ56
Woking GU22 249 AZ121
Campbell Cl, SE18
off Moordown 187 EN81
SW16 203 DK91
Byfleet KT14 234 BK112
Harlow CM17
off Carters Mead 74 EV16
Romford RM1 127 FE51
Ruislip HA4 137 BU58
Twickenham TW2 199 CD89
Campbell Ct, N17 122 DT53
SE22 off Lordship La 204 DU87
Campbell Cft, Edg. HA8 118 CN50
Campbell Dr, Beac. HP9 110 AJ51
Campbell Gordon Way, NW2 141 CV63
Campbell Rd, E3 22 B2
E6 166 EL67
E15 13 L1
E17 145 DZ56
N17 122 DU53
W7 159 CE73
Caterham CR3 258 DR121
Croydon CR0 223 DP101
East Molesey KT8
off Hampton Ct Rd 219 CF97
Gravesend DA11 213 GF88
Twickenham TW2 199 CD89
Weybridge KT13 234 BN108
Campbell Wk, N1 8 B8
Campdale Rd, N7 143 DK62
Campden Cres, Dag. RM8 148 EV63
Wembley HA0 139 CH61
Campden Gro, W8 27 K4
Campden Hill, W8 27 J4
Campden Hill Ct, W8 27 K4
Campden Hill Gdns, W8 27 H2
Campden Hill Gate, W8 27 J4
Campden Hill Pl, W11 27 H2
Campden Hill Rd, W8 27 K5
Campden Hill Sq, W8 27 H2
Campden Hill Twrs, W11 27 J2
Campden Ho Cl, W8 27 J4
Campden Rd, S.Croy. CR2 242 DS106
Uxbridge UB10 136 BM62
Campden St, W8 27 J3
Campden Way, Dag. RM8 148 EV63
Campen Cl, SW19 201 CY89
Camp End Rd, Wey. KT13 235 BR110
Camperdown St, E1 20 B9
Campfield Rd, SE9 206 EK87
Hertford SG14 53 DP09
St. Albans AL1 65 CG21
Camphill Ct, W.Byf. KT14 234 BG112
● Camphill Ind Est, W.Byf. KT14 234 BH111
Camphill Rd, W.Byf. KT14 234 BG112
Campine Cl, Chsht EN8
off Welsummer Way 89 DX28
Campion Cl, E6 25 K10
Croydon CR0 242 DS105
Denham UB9 136 BG62
Harrow HA3 140 CM58
Hillingdon UB8 156 BM71
Northfleet DA11 212 GE91
Rush Green RM7 149 FD61
Watford WD25 81 BU33
Campion Ct, Grays RM17 192 GD79
Wembley HA0 off Elmore Cl 160 CL68
Campion Dr, Tad. KT20 255 CV120
Campion Gdns, Wdf.Grn. IG8 124 EG50
Campion Pl, SE28 168 EV74
Campion Rd, E10 145 EB59
SW15 181 CW84
Hatfield AL10 67 CT15
Hemel Hempstead HP1 61 BE21
Isleworth TW7 179 CF81
Campions, Epp. CM16 92 EU28
Loughton IG10 107 EN38
Campions, The, Borwd. WD6 100 CN38
Sch Campion Sch, The, Horn. RM11 off Wingletye La 150 FM56
Campions Cl, Borwd. WD6 100 CP37
Campions Ct, Berk. HP4 60 AU20
Campion Ter, NW2 141 CX62
Campion Way, Edg. HA8 118 CQ49
Cample La, S.Ock. RM15 171 FU73
Camplin Rd, Har. HA3 140 CL57
Camplin St, SE14 45 K4
Sch Camp Prim & Nurs Sch, St.Alb. AL1 off Camp Rd 65 CH21
Camp Rd, SW19 201 CV92
Gerrards Cross SL9 134 AX59
St. Albans AL1 65 CJ21
Woldingham CR3 259 DY120
Campsbourne, The, N8
off High St 143 DL56
Campsbourne Rd, N8 143 DL55
Sch Campsbourne Sch & Children's Cen, N8
off Nightingale La 143 DL55
Campsey Gdns, Dag. RM9 168 EV66
Campsey Rd, Dag. RM9 168 EV66
Campsfield Rd, N8 143 DL55
Campshill Pl, SE13
off Campshill Rd 205 EC85
Campshill Rd, SE13 205 EC85
Campus, The, Loug. IG10 107 EP42
Welw.G.C. AL8 51 CX08
Campus Ave, Dag. RM9 148 EU63
Campus Rd, E17 145 DZ58
Campus Way, NW4 141 CV56
Camp Vw, SW19 201 CV92
Camp Vw Rd, St.Alb. AL1 65 CH21
Cam Rd, E15 12 G8
Camrose Av, Edg. HA8 118 CM53
Erith DA8 189 FB79
Feltham TW13 197 BV91
Camrose Cl, Croy. CR0 225 DY101
Morden SM4 222 DA98
Camrose St, SE2 188 EU78
Canada Av, N18 122 DQ51
Redhill RH1 288 DG138
Canada Cres, W3 160 CQ71
Canada Dr, Red. RH1 288 DG138
Canada Est, SE16 33 H6
Canada Fm Rd, Long. DA3 231 FU99
South Darenth DA4 231 FU98
Canada Gdns, SE13 205 EC85
Canada La, Brox. EN10 89 DY25
Canada Rd, W3 160 CQ70
Byfleet KT14 234 BK111
Cobham KT11 236 BW113
Erith DA8 189 FH80
Slough SL1 174 AV75
Canadas, The, Brox. EN10 89 DY25
Canada Sq, E14 34 C2
Canada St, SE16 33 J5
⊖ Canada Water 33 H5
⊖ Canada Water 33 H5
Canada Way, W12 161 CV73
Canadian Av, SE6 205 EB88
Canadian Mem Av, Egh. TW20 214 AT96
Canal App, SE8 45 L1
Canal Bk Ms, Wok. GU21
off Vale Fm Rd 248 AY117
Canal Basin, Grav. DA12 213 GK86
Canal Boul, NW1 7 N4
Canal Bldg, N1
off Shepherdess Wk 9 K10
Canal Cl, E1 21 L4
W10 14 D4
Canal Ct, Berk. HP4 60 AY20
● Canal Est, Langley SL3 175 BA75
Canal Gro, SE15 44 D2
● Canal Ind Pk, Grav. DA12 213 GK86
Canal Path, E2 10 A9
Canal Rd, Grav. DA12 213 GJ86
● Canalside, Berk. HP4 60 AT17
Canal Side, Hare. UB9 114 BG52
Canalside, Red. RH1 273 DH131
Canalside Gdns, Sthl. UB2 178 BY77
Canal St, SE5 43 L3
Canal Wk, N1 9 M9
NW10 off West End Cl 160 CQ66
SE26 204 DW92
Croydon CR0 224 DS100
Canal Way, N1 9 K10
NW1 16 D2
NW8 16 C3
NW10 161 CT70
W2 15 M6
W9 15 H6
W10 15 H6
Harefield UB9 114 BG51
Canal Way Wk, W10 14 C4
Canal Wf, Slou. SL3 175 BA75
⊖ Canary Wharf 34 C3
DLR Canary Wharf 34 B2
RB Canary Wharf Pier 33 P2
Canberra Cl, NW4 141 CU55
Dagenham RM10 169 FD66
Hornchurch RM12 150 FJ63
St. Albans AL3 65 CF16
Canberra Cres, Dag. RM10 169 FD66
Canberra Dr, Hayes UB4 158 BW69
Northolt UB5 158 BW69
Canberra Pl, Rich. TW9 180 CN83
Sch Canberra Prim Sch, W12
off Australia Rd 161 CV73
Canberra Rd, E6
off Barking Rd 167 EM67
SE7 186 EJ79
W13 159 CG74
Bexleyheath DA7 188 EX79
London Heathrow Airport TW6 176 BN83
Canberra Sq, Til. RM18 193 GG82
Canbury Av, Kings.T. KT2 220 CM95
● Canbury Business Pk, Kings.T. KT2 off Elm Cres 220 CL95
Canbury Ms, SE26
off Wells Pk Rd 204 DU90
Canbury Pk Rd, Kings.T. KT2 220 CL95
Canbury Pas, Kings.T. KT2 219 CK95
Canbury Path, Orp. BR5 228 EU98
Sch Canbury Sch, Kings.T. KT2
off Kingston Hill 200 CP93
Cancell Rd, SW9 42 F6
Candahar Rd, SW11 40 C9
Cander Way, S.Ock. RM15 171 FV73
Candlefield Cl, Hem.H. HP3
off Candlefield Rd 62 BN23
Candlefield Rd, Hem.H. HP3 62 BN23
Candlefield Wk, Hem.H. HP3
off Candlefield Rd 62 BN23
Candle Gro, SE15 184 DV83
Candlemakers Apts, SW11 40 A10
Candlemas La, Beac. HP9 111 AL53
Candlemas Mead, Beac. HP9 111 AL53
Candlemas Oaks, Beac. HP9 111 AL53
Candler Ms, Twick. TW1 199 CG87
Candler St, N15 144 DR58
Candlerush Cl, Wok. GU22 249 BB117
Candlestick La, Wal.Cr. EN7
off Park La 88 DV27
Candle St, E1 21 L6
Candover Cl, Harm. UB7 176 BK80
Candover Rd, Horn. RM12 149 FH60
Candover St, W1 17 L7
Candy Cft, Bkhm KT23 268 CB125
Candy St, E3 11 P8
Cane Hill, Harold Wd RM3
off Bennison Dr 128 FK54
Caneland Ct, Wal.Abb. EN9 90 EF34
Canes La, Hast. CM17 74 EX21
North Weald Bassett CM16 74 FA23
Canewdon Cl, Wok. GU22 248 AY119
Caney Ms, NW2 141 CX61
Canfield Dr, Ruis. HA4 137 BV64
Canfield Gdns, NW6 5 N5
Canfield Pl, NW6 5 N5
Canfield Rd, Rain. RM13 169 FF67
Woodford Green IG8 124 EL52
Canford Av, Nthlt. UB5 158 BY67
Canford Cl, Enf. EN2 103 DN40
Canford Dr, Add. KT15 216 BH103
Canford Gdns, N.Mal. KT3 220 CR100
Canford Pl, Tedd. TW11 199 CH93
Canford Rd, SW11 202 DG85
Cangels Cl, Hem.H. HP1 61 BF22
Canham Rd, SE25 224 DS97
W3 180 CS75
Can Hatch, Tad. KT20 255 CY118
Canmore Gdns, SW16 203 DJ94
Sch Cann Hall Prim Sch, E11
off Cann Hall Rd 146 EF62
Cann Hall Rd, E11 13 J1
Canning Cres, N22 121 DM53
Canning Cross, SE5 43 N9
Canning Pas, W8 27 N6
Canning Pl, W8 27 N6
Canning Pl Ms, W8 27 N5
Canning Rd, E15 23 J1
E17 145 DY56
N5 143 DP62
Croydon CR0 224 DT103
Harrow HA3 139 CF55
Cannington Rd, Dag. RM9 168 EW65
CANNING TOWN, E16 23 N8
⊖ Canning Town 23 K8
DLR Canning Town 23 K8
Canning Town 23 K8
Jct Canning Town, E16 23 K8
Cannizaro Rd, SW19 201 CW93
Cannock Ct, E17 123 EC54
Cannonbury Av, Pnr. HA5 138 BX58
Cannon Cl, SW20 221 CW97
Hampton TW12 198 CB93
Cannon Ct, EC1
off Brewhouse Yd 19 H4
Cannon Cres, Chobham GU24 232 AS111
Cannon Dr, E14 34 A1
Cannon Gate, Slou. SL2
off Uxbridge Rd 154 AW73
Cannon Gro, Fetch. KT22 253 CE121
Cannon Hill, N14 121 DK48
NW6 5 K2
Cannon Hill Cl, Bray SL6 172 AC77
Cannon Hill La, SW20 221 CY97
Cannon La, NW3 142 DD62
Pinner HA5 138 BY60
Sch Cannon La First & Mid Schs, Pnr. HA5
off Cannonbury Av 138 BX58
Cannon Ms, Wal.Abb. EN9 89 EB33
Cannon Mill Av, Chesh. HP5 76 AR33
Cannon Pl, NW3 142 DD62
SE7 37 H10
Cannon Rd, N14 121 DL48
Bexleyheath DA7 188 EY81
Watford WD18 98 BW43
Cannonside, Fetch. KT22 253 CE122
Cannons Meadow, Tewin AL6 52 DE06
⇌ Cannon Street 31 L1
⊖ Cannon Street 31 L1
Cannon St, EC4 19 J9
St. Albans AL3 65 CD19
Cannon St Rd, E1 20 E8
● Cannon Trd Est, Wem. HA9 140 CP63
Cannon Way, Fetch. KT22 253 CE121
West Molesey KT8 218 CA98
● Cannon Wf Business Cen, SE8 33 L9
● Cannon Workshops, E14 34 A1
Canon All, EC4
off St. Paul's Chyd 19 H9
Canon Av, Rom. RM6 148 EW57
Sch Canon Barnett Prim Sch, E1 20 B8
Canon Beck Rd, SE16 33 H4
Canonbie Rd, SE23 204 DW87
CANONBURY, N1 9 H5
⊖ Canonbury 9 J3
Canonbury Cres, N1 9 J6
Canonbury Gro, N1 9 J6
Canonbury La, N1 8 G6
Canonbury Pk N, N1 9 J5
Canonbury Pk S, N1 9 J5
Canonbury Pl, N1 9 H5
Sch Canonbury Prim Sch, N1 9 H5
Canonbury Rd, N1 8 G5
Enfield EN1 104 DS39
Canonbury Sq, N1 9 H6
Canonbury St, N1 9 J6
Canonbury Vil, N1 9 H6
Canonbury Yd, N1 9 K8
Canonbury Yd W, N1 9 H5
Canon Mohan Cl, N14
off Farm La 103 DH44
Sch Canon Palmer Cath High Sch, Ilf. IG3
off Aldborough Rd S 147 ES60
Canon Rd, Brom. BR1 226 EJ97
Canon Row, SW1 30 A5
Canons Brook, Harl. CM19 73 EN15
Canons Cl, N2 142 DD59
Edgware HA8 118 CM51
Radlett WD7 99 CH35
Reigate RH2 271 CZ133
Jct Canons Cor, Edg. HA8 118 CL49
Canons Ct, Edg. HA8 118 CM51
Canons Dr, Edg. HA8 118 CL51
Canons Gate, Chsht EN8 89 DZ26
Harlow CM20 57 EN14
Sch Canons High Sch, Edg. HA8 off Shaldon Rd 118 CM54
Canon's Hill, Couls. CR5 257 DN117
Canons La, Tad. KT20 255 CY118
Canonsleigh Rd, Dag. RM9 168 EV66
CANONS PARK, Edg. HA8 118 CL52
⊖ Canons Park 118 CL52
Canons Pk Cl, Edg. HA8
off Donnefield Av 118 CL52
Canons Rd, Ware SG12 54 DW05
Canon St, N1 9 J9
Canons Wk, Croy. CR0 225 DX104
Canopus Way, Nthwd. HA6 115 BU49
Staines-upon-Thames TW19 196 BL87
Canopy La, Harl. CM17 58 EW14
Canrobert St, E2 20 E2
Cantelowes Rd, NW1 7 P5
Canterbury Av, Ilf. IG1 146 EL59
Sidcup DA15 208 EW89
Slough SL2 153 AQ70
Upminster RM14 151 FT60
Canterbury Cl, E6 25 J8
Amersham HP7 77 AS39
Beckenham BR3 225 EB95
Chigwell IG7 125 ET48
Dartford DA1 210 FN87
Greenford UB6 158 CB72
Northwood HA6 115 BT51
Worcester Park KT4 221 CX103
Canterbury Ct, Dor. RH4
off Station Rd 285 CG135
Canterbury Cres, SW9 183 DN83
Canterbury Gro, SE27 203 DP90
Canterbury Ho, E3 off Bow Rd 22 C2
SE1 30 D6
Borehamwood WD6 100 CN40
Erith DA8 off Arthur St 189 FF80
Canterbury Ms, Oxshott KT22 236 CC113
Windsor SL4 173 AN82
Canterbury Par, S.Ock. RM15 171 FW69
Canterbury Pl, SE17 31 H9
Canterbury Rd, E10 145 EC59
NW6 15 J1
Borehamwood WD6 100 CN40
Croydon CR0 223 DM101
Feltham TW13 198 BY90
Gravesend DA12 213 GJ89
Guildford GU2 264 AT132
Harrow HA1, HA2 138 CB57
Morden SM4 222 DC99
Watford WD17 97 BV40
Canterbury Ter, NW6 5 J10
Canterbury Way, Crox.Grn WD3 97 BQ41
Great Warley CM13 129 FW51
Purfleet RM19 191 FS80
Cantium Retail Pk, SE1 44 C2
Cantley Gdns, SE19 224 DT95
Ilford IG2 147 EQ58
Cantley Rd, W7 179 CG76
Canto Ct, EC1 off Old St 19 K4
Canton St, E14 22 A9
Cantrell Rd, E3
off Bow Common La 21 P5
Cantwell Rd, SE18 187 EP80
Canute Gdns, SE16 33 J8
Canvey St, SE1 31 H2
Capability Way, Green. DA9 191 FW84
Cape Cl, Bark. IG11 167 EP65
Capel Av, Wall. SM6 241 DM106
Capel Cl, N20 120 DC48
Bromley BR2 226 EL102
Capel Ct, EC2 19 M9
SE20 224 DW95
Capel Cres, Stan. HA7 117 CG47
Capel Gdns, Ilf. IG3 147 ET63
Pinner HA5 138 BZ56
Capella Rd, Nthwd. HA6 115 BT50
Capell Av, Chorl. WD3 95 BC43
Capell Rd, Chorl. WD3 95 BC43
Capell Way, Chorl. WD3 95 BD43
Coll Capel Manor Coll, Regent's Pk, NW1 17 H3
Coll Capel Manor Coll & Gdns, Enf. EN1 off Bullsmoor La 104 DU35
Sch Capel Manor Prim Sch, Enf. EN1 off Bullsmoor La 104 DV35
Capel Pl, Dart. DA2 210 FJ91
Capel Pt, E7 146 EH63
Capel Rd, E7 146 EH63
E12 146 EJ63
Barnet EN4 102 DE44
Enfield EN1 104 DV36
Watford WD19 98 BY44
Capel Vere Wk, Wat. WD17 97 BS39
Capener's Cl, SW1 28 G5
Capern Rd, SW18
off Cargill Rd 202 DC88
Cape Rd, N17
off High Cross Rd 144 DU55
St. Albans AL1 65 CH20
Cape Yd, E1 32 D2
H Capio Nightingale Hosp, NW1 16 D6
● Capital Business Cen, Mitch. CR4 222 DF99
S.Croy. CR2 242 DR108
Wembley HA0 159 CK68
● Capital Business Pk, Borwd. WD6 100 CQ41
Sch Capital City Acad, NW10
off Doyle Gdns 161 CV67
Coll Capital Coll (CIFE) London Sch of Insurance, WC1 18 C6
Capital E Apts, E16
off Western Gateway 35 P1
Capital Interchange Way, Brent. TW8 180 CN78
● Capital Pk, Old Wok. GU22 249 BB121
● Capital Pl, Harl. CM19
off Lovet Rd 73 EN16
● Capitol Ind Pk, NW9 140 CQ55
Capitol Sq, Epsom KT17
off Church St 238 CS113
Capitol Way, NW9 140 CQ55
Capland St, NW8 16 B4
Caple Par, NW10
off Harley Rd 160 CS68
Caple Rd, NW10 161 CT68
Capon Cl, Brwd. CM14 130 FV46
Caponfield, Welw.G.C. AL7 52 DB11
Cappell La, Stans.Abb. SG12 55 ED10
Capper St, WC1 17 M5
Caprea Cl, Hayes UB4
off Triandra Way 158 BX71
Capri Rd, Croy. CR0 224 DT102
● Capstan Cen, Til. RM18 192 GD80
Capstan Cl, Rom. RM6 148 EV58
Capstan Ct, Dart. DA2 190 FQ84
Capstan Dr, Rain. RM13 169 FG70
Capstan Ms, Grav. DA11 212 GE87
Capstan Ride, Enf. EN2 103 DN40
Capstan Rd, SE8 33 N8
Capstan Sq, E14 34 F5
Capstan's Wf, Wok. GU21 248 AT118
Capstan Way, SE16 33 M3
Capstone Rd, Brom. BR1 206 EF91
● Capswood Business Cen, Denh. UB9 135 BB60
Captain Cook Cl, Ch.St.G. HP8 112 AU49
Captains Cl, Chesh. HP5 76 AN27
Captains Wk, Berk. HP4 60 AX20
Capthorne Av, Har. HA2 138 BY60
Capuchin Cl, Stan. HA7 117 CH51
Capulet Ms, E16 35 P2
Capulet Sq, E3 22 D3
Capworth St, E10 145 EA60
Caractacus Cottage Vw, Wat. WD18 115 BU45
Caractacus Grn, Wat. WD18 97 BT44
Caradoc Cl, W2 15 J8
Caradoc St, SE10 35 J10
Caradon Cl, E11 146 EE60
Woking GU21 248 AV118
Caradon Way, N15 144 DR56
Caravan La, Rick. WD3 114 BL45
Caravel Cl, E14 34 A6
Grays RM16 192 FZ76
Caravelle Gdns, Nthlt. UB5
off Javelin Way 158 BX69
Caravel Ms, SE8 46 A2
Caraway Cl, E13 24 A6
Caraway Pl, Guil. GU2 264 AU129
Wallington SM6 223 DH104
Carberry Rd, SE19 204 DS93
Carbery Av, W3 180 CM75
Carbis Cl, E4 123 ED46
Carbis Rd, E14 21 N8
Carbone Hill, Newgate St SG13 87 DK26
Northaw EN6 87 DJ27
Carbuncle Pas Way, N17 122 DU54
Carburton St, W1 17 K6
Carbury Cl, Horn. RM12 170 FJ65
Cardale St, E14 34 E5
Cardamom Cl, Guil. GU2 264 AU130
Carde Cl, Hert. SG14 53 DM08
Carden Rd, SE15 184 DV83
Cardiff Cl, Rom. RM5 127 FD52
Cardiff Rd, W7 179 CG76
Enfield EN3 104 DV42
Watford WD18 97 BV44
Cardiff St, SE18 187 ES80
Cardiff Way, Abb.L. WD5 81 BU32
Cardigan Cl, Slou. SL1 153 AM73
Woking GU21 248 AS118
Cardigan Gdns, Ilf. IG3 148 EU61
Cardigan Rd, E3 11 P10
SW13 181 CU82
SW19 off Haydons Rd 202 DC93
Richmond TW10 200 CL86
Cardigan St, SE11 30 E10
Cardigan Wk, N1
off Ashby Gro 9 K6
Cardinal Av, Borwd. WD6 100 CP41
Kingston upon Thames KT2 200 CL92
Morden SM4 221 CY100
Cardinal Bourne St, SE1 31 M7
Cardinal Bldg, Hayes UB3
off Station Rd 177 BT76
Cardinal Cap All, SE1
off New Globe Wk 31 J1
Cardinal Cl, Chsht EN7 88 DT26
Chislehurst BR7 227 ER95
Edgware HA8 118 CR52
Morden SM4 221 CY101
South Croydon CR2 242 DU113
Worcester Park KT4 239 CU105
Cardinal Ct, Borwd. WD6 100 CP41
Cardinal Cres, N.Mal. KT3 220 CQ96
Cardinal Dr, Ilf. IG6 125 EQ51
Walton-on-Thames KT12 218 BX102
Cardinal Gro, St.Alb. AL3 64 CB22
Cardinal Hinsley Cl, NW10 161 CU68
Sch Cardinal Hinsley Mathematics & Computing Coll, NW10
off Harlesden Rd 161 CU67
Sch Cardinal Newman Catholic Prim Sch, Hersham KT12
off Arch Rd 218 BX104
Cardinal Pl, SW15 181 CX84
Park St. AL2 83 CD25
Cardinal Rd, Chaff.Hun. RM16 192 FY76
Feltham TW13 197 BV88
Ruislip HA4 138 BX60
Sch Cardinal Rd Inf & Nurs Sch, Felt. TW13 off Cardinal Rd 197 BV88
Cardinals Wk, Hmptn. TW12 198 CC94
Sunbury-on-Thames TW16 197 BS93
Taplow SL6 152 AJ72
Cardinals Way, N19 143 DK60
Sch Cardinal Vaughan Mem Sch, W14 26 E4
Cardinal Wk, SW1
off Palace St 29 L6
Cardinal Way, Har. HA3 139 CE55
Rainham RM13 170 FK68
Sch Cardinal Wiseman Sch, The, Grnf. UB6
off Greenford Rd 158 CC71
Cardine Ms, SE15 44 E4
Cardingham, Wok. GU21 248 AU117
Cardington Sq, Houns. TW4 178 BX84
Cardington St, NW1 17 L2
Cardinham Rd, Orp. BR6 245 ET105
Cardozo Rd, N7 8 B2
Cardrew Av, N12 120 DD50
Cardrew Cl, N12 120 DD50
Cardross St, W6 181 CV76
Sch Cardwell Prim Sch, SE18 37 J8
Cardwell Rd, N7 143 DL63
Cardwells Keep, Guil. GU2 264 AU131
Cardy Rd, Hem.H. HP1 62 BH21
Carew Cl, N7 143 DM61
Chafford Hundred RM16 192 FY76
Coulsdon CR5 257 DP119
Carew Ct, Sutt. SM2 240 DB109
Sch Carew Manor Sch, Wall. SM6 off Church Rd 223 DK104
Carew Rd, N17 122 DU54
W13 179 CJ75
Ashford TW15 197 BQ93
Mitcham CR4 222 DG96
Northwood HA6 115 BS51
Thornton Heath CR7 223 DP97
Wallington SM6 241 DJ107
Carew St, SE5 43 H8
Carew Way, Orp. BR5 228 EW102
Watford WD19 116 BZ48
Carey Cl, Wind. SL4 173 AP83
Carey Ct, Bexh. DA6 209 FB85
Carey Gdns, SW8 41 N7
Carey La, EC2 19 J9
Carey Pl, SW1 29 N9
Carey Rd, Dag. RM9 148 EY63
Careys Cft, Berk. HP4 60 AU16
Carey's Fld, Dunt.Grn TN13 263 FE120

Carey St, WC2 18 D9
Careys Wd, Smallfield RH6 291 DP148
Carey Way, Wem. HA9 140 CP63
Carfax Pl, SW4 183 DK84
Carfax Rd, Hayes UB3 177 BT78
Hornchurch RM12 149 FF63
Carfree Cl, N1 8 F6
Cargill Rd, SW18 202 DB88
Cargo Forecourt Rd, Gat. RH6 290 DD152
Cargo Rd, Gat. RH6 290 DD152
Cargreen Pl, SE25
off Cargreen Rd 224 DT98
Cargreen Rd, SE25 224 DT98
Carholme Rd, SE23 205 DZ88
Carisbrook Cl, Enf. EN1 104 DT39
Carisbrook, N10 120 DG56
Carisbrooke Av, Bex. DA5 208 EX88
Watford WD24 98 BX39
Carisbrooke Cl, Horn. RM11 150 FN60
Hounslow TW4 198 BY87
Stanmore HA7 117 CK54
Carisbrooke Ct, Slou. SL1 154 AT73
Carisbrooke Gdns, SE15 44 B4
Carisbrooke Ho, Kings.T. KT2
off Kingsgate Rd 220 CL95
Carisbrooke Rd, E17 145 DY56
Bromley BR2 226 EJ98
Mitcham CR4 223 DK98
St. Albans AL2 82 CB26
Carisbrook Rd, Pilg.Hat. CM15 130 FV44
Carker's La, NW5 7 J2
Carlbury Cl, St.Alb. AL1 65 CH21
Carl Ekman Ho, Grav. DA11 212 GD87
Carleton Av, Wall. SM6 241 DK109
Carleton Cl, Esher KT10 219 CD102
Carleton Pl, Hort.Kir. DA4 230 FQ98
Carleton Rd, N7 7 N2
Cheshunt EN8 89 DX28
Dartford DA1 210 FN87
Carlile Cl, E3 21 P1
Carlina Gdns, Wdf.Grn. IG8 124 EH50
Carlingford Gdns, Mitch. CR4 202 DF94
Carlingford Rd, N15 143 DP55
NW3 142 DD63
Morden SM4 221 CX100
Carlisle Av, EC3 19 P9
W3 160 CS72
St. Albans AL1, AL3 65 CD18
Carlisle Cl, Kings.T. KT2 220 CN95
Pinner HA5 138 BY59
Carlisle Gdns, Har. HA3 139 CK59
Ilford IG1 146 EL58
Sch Carlisle Inf Sch, Hmptn. TW12 off Broad La 198 CB93
Carlisle La, SE1 30 D7
Carlisle Ms, NW8 16 B6
Carlisle Pl, N11 121 DH49
SW1 29 L7
Carlisle Rd, E10 145 EA61
N4 143 DN59
NW6 4 E8
NW9 140 CQ55
Dartford DA1 210 FN86
Hampton TW12 198 CB94
Romford RM1 149 FF57
Slough SL1 153 AR73
Sutton SM1 239 CZ106
Carlisle St, W1 17 N9
Carlisle Wk, E8 10 A5
Carlisle Way, SW17 202 DG92
Carlos Pl, W1 29 H1
Carlow St, NW1 7 L10
Carlton Av, N14 103 DK43
Feltham TW14 198 BW86
Greenhithe DA9 211 FS86
Harrow HA3 139 CH57
Hayes UB3 177 BS77
South Croydon CR2 242 DS108
Carlton Av E, Wem. HA9 140 CL60
Carlton Av W, Wem. HA0 139 CH61
Carlton Cl, NW3 142 DA61
Borehamwood WD6 100 CR42
Chessington KT9 237 CK107
Edgware HA8 118 CN50
Northolt UB5
off Whitton Av W 138 CC64
Upminster RM14 150 FP61
Woking GU21 233 AZ114
Carlton Ct, SW9 42 G6
Ilford IG6 147 ER55
Uxbridge UB8 156 BK71
Carlton Cres, Sutt. SM3 239 CY105
Carlton Dr, SW15 201 CY85
Ilford IG6 147 ER55
Carlton Gdns, SW1 29 N3
W5 159 CJ72
Carlton Grn, Red. RH1 272 DE131
Carlton Gro, SE15 44 E6
Carlton Hill, NW8 5 N9
Carlton Ho, Felt. TW14 197 BT87
Carlton Ho Ter, SW1 29 N3
Carlton Par, Orp. BR6 228 EV101
Sevenoaks TN13
off St. John's Hill 279 FJ122
Carlton Pk Av, SW20 221 CW96
Carlton Pl, Nthwd. HA6 115 BP50
Weybridge KT13
off Castle Vw Rd 235 BP105
Sch Carlton Prim Sch, NW5 7 H3
Carlton Rd, E11 146 EF60
E12 146 EK63
E17 123 DY53
N4 143 DN59
N11 120 DG50
SW14 180 CQ83
W4 180 CR75
W5 159 CJ73
Erith DA8 189 FB79
Grays RM16 193 GF75
New Malden KT3 220 CS96
Redhill RH1 272 DF131
Reigate RH2 272 DD132
Romford RM2 149 FG57
Sidcup DA14 207 ET92
Slough SL2 154 AV73
South Croydon CR2 242 DR107
Sunbury-on-Thames TW16 197 BT94
Walton-on-Thames KT12 217 BV101
Welling DA16 188 EV83
Woking GU21 233 BA114
Carlton Sq, E1 21 J4
Carlton St, SW1 29 N1
Carlton Ter, E11 146 EH57
N18 122 DR48
SE26 204 DW90
Carlton Twr Pl, SW1 28 F6
Carlton Twrs, Cars. SM5 222 DF104
Carlton Tye, Horl. RH6 291 DJ148
Carlton Vale, NW6 15 K1
Sch Carlton Vale Inf Sch, NW6 15 H2
Carlton Vil, SW15
off St. John's Av 201 CX85
Carlwell St, SW17 202 DE92
Carlyle Av, Brom. BR1 226 EK97
Southall UB1 158 BZ73
Carlyle Cl, N2 142 DC58
West Molesey KT8 218 CB96
Carlyle Ct, SW10
off Chelsea Harbour 39 P6
Carlyle Gdns, Sthl. UB1 158 BZ73
Carlyle Lo, New Barn. EN5
off Richmond Rd 102 DC43
Carlyle Ms, E1 21 K4
Carlyle Pl, SW15 181 CX84
Carlyle Rd, E12 146 EL63
NW10 160 CR67
SE28 168 EV73
W5 179 CJ78
Croydon CR0 224 DU103
Staines-upon-Thames TW18 195 BF94
★ Carlyle's Ho, SW3 40 C3
Carlyle Sq, SW3 40 B1
Carly Ms, E2 20 C3
Carlyon Av, Har. HA2 138 BZ63
Carlyon Cl, Wem. HA0 160 CL67
Carlyon Rd, Hayes UB4 158 BW72
Wembley HA0 160 CL68
Carlys Cl, Beck. BR3 225 DX96
Carmalt Gdns, SW15 181 CW84
Hersham KT12 236 BW106
Carmarthen Pl, SE1 31 N4
Carmarthen Rd, Slou. SL1 154 AS73
Carmel Cl, Wok. GU22 248 AY118
Carmel Ct, W8 27 L4
Wembley HA9 140 CP61
Carmelite Cl, Har. HA3 116 CC53
Carmelite Rd, Har. HA3 116 CC53
Carmelite St, EC4 18 F10
Carmelite Wk, Har. HA3 116 CC53
Carmelite Way, Har. HA3 116 CC54
Carmel Way, Rich. TW9 180 CP82
Carmen Ct, Borwd. WD6
off Belford Rd 100 CM38
Carmen St, E14 22 C8
Carmichael Av, Green. DA9 191 FW84
Carmichael Cl, SW11
off Darien Rd 182 DD83
Ruislip HA4 137 BU63
Carmichael Ms, SW18 202 DD87
Carmichael Rd, SE25 224 DU99
Carminia Rd, SW17 203 DH89
Carnaby Rd, Brox. EN10 71 DY20
Carnaby St, W1 17 L9
Carnach Grn, S.Ock. RM15 171 FV73
Carnac St, SE27 204 DR91
Carnanton Rd, E17 123 ED53
Carnarvon Av, Enf. EN1 104 DT41
Carnarvon Dr, Hayes UB3 177 BQ76
Carnarvon Rd, E10 145 EC58
E15 13 L4
E18 124 EF53
Barnet EN5 101 CY41
Carnation Cl, Rush Grn RM7 149 FE61
Carnation St, SE2 188 EV78
Carnbrook Ms, SE3
off Carnbrook Rd 186 EK83
Carnbrook Rd, SE3 186 EK83
Carnecke Gdns, SE9 206 EL85
Carnegie Cl, Enf. EN3 105 EB38
Surbiton KT6
off Fullers Av 220 CM103
Carnegie Pl, SW19 201 CX90
Carnegie Rd, St.Alb. AL3 65 CD16
Carnegie St, N1 8 C9
CARNELES GREEN, Brox. EN10 70 DV22
Carnet Cl, Dart. DA1 209 FE87
Carnforth Cl, Epsom KT19 238 CP107
Carnforth Gdns, Horn. RM12 149 FG64
Carnforth Rd, SW16 203 DK94
Carnie Lo, SW17
off Manville Rd 203 DH90
Carnoustie Cl, SE28 168 EX72
Carnoustie Dr, N1 8 C7
Carnwath Rd, SW6 182 DA83
Caro La, Hem.H. HP3 62 BN23
Carol Cl, NW4 141 CX56
Carolina Cl, E15 13 J3
Carolina Rd, Th.Hth. CR7 223 DP96
Caroline Cl, N10 121 DH54
SW16 203 DM90
W2 27 M1
Croydon CR0 242 DS105
Isleworth TW7 179 CD80
West Drayton UB7 176 BK75
Caroline Ct, Ashf. TW15 197 BP93
Stanmore HA7 117 CG51
Caroline Gdns, E2
off Kingsland Rd 19 P2
SE15 44 E4
Caroline Pl, SW11 41 H9
W2 15 M10
Harlington UB3 177 BS80
Watford WD19 98 BY44
Caroline Pl Ms, W2 27 M1
Caroline Rd, SW19 201 CZ94
Caroline St, E1 21 K9
Caroline Ter, SW1 28 G9
Caroline Wk, W6 38 E3
Carol St, NW1 7 L8
Carolyn Cl, Wok. GU21 248 AT119
Carolyn Dr, Orp. BR6 228 EU104
● Carolyn Ho, Croy. CR0
off Dingwall Rd 224 DR103
Caroon Dr, Sarratt WD3 96 BH36
Carpenders Av, Wat. WD19 116 BY48
CARPENDERS PARK, Wat. WD19 116 BZ47
⇌ Carpenders Park 116 BX48
Carpenter Cl, Epsom KT17 239 CT109
Carpenter Gdns, N21 121 DP47
Carpenter Path, Hutt. CM13 131 GD43
Carpenters Arms La, Thnwd CM16 92 EV25
Carpenters Arms Path, SE9
off Eltham High St 207 EM86
Carpenters Cl, Barn. EN5 102 DB44
Carpenters Ct, Twick. TW2 199 CE89
Carpenters Ms, N7 8 B3
Carpenters Pl, SW4 183 DK84
Sch Carpenters Prim Sch, E15 12 F8
Carpenters Rd, E15 12 F7
Enfield EN1 104 DW36
Carpenter St, W1 29 J1
Carpenters Wd Dr, Chorl. WD3 95 BB42
Carpenter Way, Pot.B. EN6 86 DC33
Carrack Ho, Erith DA8
off Saltford Cl 189 FE78
Carrara Cl, SW9 183 DP84
Carrara Ms, E8 10 C3
Carrara Wf, SW6 38 F10
Carr Cl, Stan. HA7 117 CG51
Carre Ms, SE5 43 H7
Carr Gro, SE18 37 H8
Carriage Dr E, SW11 40 G4
Carriage Dr N, SW11 41 H3
Carriage Dr S, SW11 40 E6
Carriage Dr W, SW11 40 E5
Carriage Ms, Ilf. IG1 147 EQ61
Carriage Pl, N16 144 DR62
SW16 203 DJ92
Carriages, The, Ware SG12
off Station Rd 55 DY07
Carriage St, SE18 37 P7
Carriageway, The, Brasted TN16 262 EX124
Carrick Cl, Islw. TW7 179 CG83
Carrick Dr, Ilf. IG6 125 EQ53
Sevenoaks TN13 279 FH123
Carrick Gdns, N17 122 DS52
Carrick Gate, Esher KT10 218 CC104
Carrick Ms, SE8 46 A2
Carriden Ct, Hert. SG14
off The Ridgeway 53 DM07
Carrill Way, Belv. DA17 188 EX77
Carrington Av, Borwd. WD6 100 CP43
Hounslow TW3 198 CB85
Carrington Cl, Arkley EN5 101 CU43
Borehamwood WD6 100 CQ43
Croydon CR0 225 DY101
Kingston upon Thames KT2 200 CQ92
Redhill RH1 272 DF133
Carrington Gdns, E7
off Woodford Rd 146 EG63
Carrington Pl, Esher KT10 236 CB105
Carrington Rd, Dart. DA1 210 FM86
Richmond TW10 180 CN84
Slough SL1 154 AS73
Carrington Sq, Har. HA3 116 CC52
Carrington St, W1 29 J3
Carrol Cl, NW5 7 J1
Carroll Av, Guil. GU1 265 BB134
Carroll Cl, E15 13 K3
Carroll Hill, Loug. IG10 107 EM41
Carronade Ct, N7
off Eden Gro 8 D3
Carronade Pl, SE28 187 EQ76
Carron Cl, E14 22 D8
Carroun Rd, SW8 42 C4
Carroway La, Grnf. UB6 159 CD69
Carrow Rd, Dag. RM9 168 EV66
Walton-on-Thames KT12 218 BX104
Carr Rd, E17 123 DZ54
Northolt UB5 158 CA65
Carrs La, N21 104 DQ43
Carr St, E14 21 M7
CARSHALTON, SM5 240 DD105
⇌ Carshalton 240 DF105
CARSHALTON BEECHES, Cars. SM5 240 DD109
⇌ Carshalton Beeches 240 DF107
Sch Carshalton Boys Sports Coll, Cars. SM5
off Winchcombe Rd 222 DE103
Coll Carshalton Coll, Cars. SM5
off Nightingale Rd 222 DF104
Carshalton Gro, Sutt. SM1 240 DD105
Sch Carshalton High Sch for Girls, Cars. SM5 off West St 222 DF104
CARSHALTON ON THE HILL, Cars. SM5 240 DG109
Carshalton Pk Rd, Cars. SM5 240 DF106
Carshalton Pl, Cars. SM5 240 DG105
Carshalton Rd, Bans. SM7 240 DF114
Carshalton SM5 240 DC106
Mitcham CR4 222 DG98
Sutton SM1 240 DC106
Carsington Gdns, Dart. DA1 210 FK89
Carslake Rd, SW15 201 CW86
Carson Rd, E16 23 P5
SE21 204 DQ89
Cockfosters EN4 102 DF42
Carson Ter, W11 26 E2
Carstairs Rd, SE6 205 EC90
Carston Cl, SE12 206 EF85
Carswell Cl, Hutt. CM13 131 GD44
Ilford IG4 146 EK56
Carswell Rd, SE6 205 EC87
Cartbridge Cl, Send GU23
off Send Rd 249 BB123
Cartel Cl, Purf. RM19 191 FR77
Carter Cl, NW9 140 CR58
Romford RM5 127 FB52
Windsor SL4 173 AN82
Carter Dr, Rom. RM5 127 FB52
Carteret St, SW1 29 N5
Carteret Way, SE8 33 M9
Sch Carterhatch Inf Sch, Enf. EN1 off Carterhatch La 104 DV39
Sch Carterhatch Jun Sch, Enf. EN1 off Carterhatch La 104 DV39
Carterhatch La, Enf. EN1 104 DU40
Carterhatch Rd, Enf. EN3 104 DW40
Carter Ho, SW11
off Petergate 182 DC84
Carter La, EC4 19 H9
Carter Pl, SE17 43 K1
Carter Rd, E13 166 EH67
SW19 202 DD93
Carters Cl, Guil. GU1 264 AY130
Worcester Park KT4 221 CX103
Carters Cotts, Red. RH1 288 DE136
Cartersfield Rd, Wal.Abb. EN9 89 EC34
CARTERS GREEN, Harl. CM17 59 FD13
Carters Hill, Undrvr TN15 279 FP127
Carters Hill Cl, SE9 206 EJ88
Carters La, SE23 205 DY89
Epping Green CM16 73 EP24
Woking GU22 249 BC120
Carters Mead, Harl. CM17 74 EV16
Cartersmead Cl, Horl. RH6 291 DH147
Carters Rd, Epsom KT17 255 CT115
Carters Row, Nthflt DA11 213 GF88
Carter St, SE17 43 J2
Carters Yd, SW18 202 DA85
Carter Wk, Penn HP10 110 AC47
Carthagena Est, Brox. EN10 71 EC20
Carthew Rd, W6 181 CV76
Carthew Vil, W6 181 CV76
Carthouse La, Wok. GU21 232 AS114
Carthusian St, EC1 19 J6
Cartier Circle, E14 34 D3
Carting La, WC2 30 B1
Cart La, E4 123 ED45
Cart Lodge Ms, Croy. CR0 224 DS102
Cartmel, NW1 17 L2
Cartmel Cl, N17
off Heybourne Rd 122 DV52
Cartmel Cl, Reigate RH2 272 DE133
Cartmel Ct, Nthlt. UB5 158 BY65
Cartmel Gdns, Mord. SM4 222 DC99
Cartmel Rd, Bexh. DA7 188 FA81
Carton St, W1 16 F8
Cart Path, Wat. WD25 82 BW33
Cartridge Pl, SE18 37 P7
Cartwright Gdns, WC1 18 A3
Cartwright Rd, Dag. RM9 168 EZ66
Cartwright St, E1 20 B10
Cartwright Way, SW13 181 CV80
Carve Ley, Welw.G.C. AL7 52 DB10
Carver Cl, W4 180 CQ76
Carver Rd, SE24 204 DQ86
Carville Cres, Brent. TW8 180 CL77
Cary Rd, E11 146 EE63
Carysfort Rd, N8 143 DK57
N16 144 DR62
Cary Wk, Rad. WD7 83 CH34
Casby Ho, SE16 32 C6
Cascade Av, N10 143 DJ56
Cascade Cl, Buck.H. IG9
off Cascade Rd 124 EK47
Orpington BR5 228 EW97
Cascade Rd, Buck.H. IG9 124 EK47
Cascades, Croy. CR0 243 DZ110
Cascades Twr, E14 33 P3
Caselden Cl, Add. KT15 234 BJ106
Casella Rd, SE14 45 J5
Casewick Rd, SE27 203 DP91
Casey Cl, NW8 16 C3
Casimir Rd, E5 144 DV62
Casino Av, SE24 204 DQ85
Caspian Cl, Purf. RM19 190 FN77
Caspian Ct, E3 off Violet Rd 22 C6
Caspian St, SE5 43 L4
Caspian Wk, E16 24 E9
Caspian Way, Purf. RM19 190 FN78
Swanscombe DA10 212 FY85
Caspian Wf, E3 off Violet Rd 22 C6
Cassander Pl, Pnr. HA5
off Holly Gro 116 BY53
Cassandra Cl, Nthlt. UB5 139 CD63
Cassandra Gate, Chsht EN8 89 DZ27
Cassel Ct, Stan. HA7
off Brightwen Gro 117 CG47
Casselden Rd, NW10 160 CR66
H Cassel Hosp, The, Ham TW10 199 CK91
Cassidy Rd, SW6 39 J5
Cassilda Rd, SE2 188 EU77
Cassilis Rd, E14 34 B5
Twickenham TW1 199 CH85
Cassini Apts, E16
off Fords Pk Rd 23 N8
Cassiobridge, Wat. WD18 97 BR42
Cassiobridge Rd, Wat. WD18 97 BS42
Cassiobury Av, Felt. TW14 197 BT86
Cassiobury Ct, Wat. WD17 97 BS40
Cassiobury Dr, Wat. WD17 97 BT40
Sch Cassiobury Inf & Nurs Sch, Wat. WD17
off Bellmount Wd Av 97 BS39
Sch Cassiobury Jun Sch, Wat. WD17 off Bellmount Wd Av 97 BS39
★ Cassiobury Park, Wat. WD18 97 BS41
Cassiobury Pk, Wat. WD18 97 BS41
Cassiobury Pk Av, Wat. WD18 97 BS41
Cassiobury Rd, E17 145 DX57
Cassio Pl, Wat. WD18 97 BS42
Cassio Rd, Wat. WD18 97 BV41
Cassis Ct, Loug. IG10 107 EQ42
Cassius Dr, St.Alb. AL3 64 CB22
Cassland Rd, E9 11 H6
Thornton Heath CR7 224 DR98
Casslee Rd, SE6 205 DZ87
Cassocks Sq, Shep. TW17 217 BR100
Casson St, E1 20 C7
Castalne Cl, Swan. BR8 209 FF94
Castalia Sq, E14
off Roserton St 34 E5
Castano Ct, Abb.L. WD5 81 BS31
Castellain Rd, W9 15 N5
Castellan Av, Rom. RM2 149 FH55
Castellane Cl, Stan. HA7 117 CF52
Castello Av, SW15 201 CW85
Castell Rd, Loug. IG10 107 EQ39
CASTELNAU, SW13 181 CU79
Castelnau, SW13 181 CV79
Castelnau Gdns, SW13
off Arundel Ter 181 CV79
Castelnau Pl, SW13
off Castelnau 181 CV79
Castelnau Row, SW13
off Lonsdale Rd 181 CV79
Casterbridge, NW6 5 M8
Casterbridge Rd, SE3 186 EG83
Casterton St, E8 10 F5
Castile Gdns, Kings L. WD4 80 BM29
Castile Rd, SE18 37 M8
Sch Castilion Prim Sch, SE28
off Copperfield Rd 168 EW72
Castille Ct, Wal.Cr. EN8 89 DZ34
Castillon Rd, SE6 206 EE89
Castlands Rd, SE6 205 DZ89
Castle Av, E4 123 ED50
Datchet SL3 174 AU79
Epsom KT17 239 CU109
Rainham RM13 169 FE66
West Drayton UB7 156 BL73
Castlebar Hill, W5 159 CH71
Castlebar Ms, W5 159 CJ71
⇌ Castle Bar Park 159 CF71
Castlebar Pk, W5 159 CH70
Castlebar Rd, W5 159 CJ71
Sch Castlebar Sch, W13
off Hathaway Gdns 159 CF71
Castle Baynard St, EC4 19 H10
Castlebrook Cl, SE11 30 G8
Castle Cl, E9 11 L3
SW19 201 CX90
W3 180 CP75
Bletchingley RH1 274 DQ133
Bromley BR2 226 EE97
Bushey WD23 98 CB44
Hoddesdon EN11 55 EC14
Reigate RH2 288 DB138
Romford RM3 128 FJ48
Sunbury-on-Thames TW16
off Percy Bryant Rd 197 BS94
Castlecombe Dr, SW19 201 CX87
Sch Castlecombe Prim Sch, SE9
off Castlecombe Rd 206 EL92
Castlecombe Rd, SE9 206 EL91
Castle Cor, Bletch. RH1
off Overdale 274 DQ133
Castle Ct, EC3 19 M9
SE26 205 DY91
Castle Ct, SW15 181 CY83
Castledine Rd, SE20 204 DV94
Castle Dr, Horl. RH6 291 DJ150
Ilford IG4 146 EL58
Reigate RH2 288 DA138
Castle Fm, Wind. SL4 173 AK82
Castle Fm Rd, Shore. TN14 247 FF109
Castlefield Rd, Reig. RH2 272 DA133
Castleford Av, SE9 207 EP88
Castleford Cl, N17 122 DT51
Borehamwood WD6 100 CM38
Castle Gdns, Dor. RH4 270 CM134
Castlegate, Rich. TW9 180 CM83
Castle Gateway, Berk. HP4 60 AW17
Castle Grn, Wey. KT13 217 BS104
Castle Gro Rd, Chobham GU24 232 AS113
Castlehaven Rd, NW1 7 J7
Castle Hill, Berk. HP4 60 AW17
Guildford GU1 280 AX136
Longfield DA3 231 FX99
Windsor SL4 173 AR81
Castle Hill Av, Berk. HP4 60 AW18
New Addington CR0 243 EB109
Castle Hill Cl, Berk. HP4 60 AV18
Sch Castle Hill Prim Sch, Chess. KT9 off Buckland Rd 238 CM105
Chessington KT9
off Moor La 238 CM106
New Addington CR0
off Dunley Dr 243 EC107
Castle Hill Rd, Egh. TW20 194 AV91
Castle La, SW1 29 M6
Castleleigh Ct, Enf. EN2 104 DR43
Castlemaine Av, Epsom KT17 239 CV109
South Croydon CR2 242 DT106
Castlemaine Twr, SW11 40 F8
Castlemain St, E1 20 E6
Castlemead, SE5 43 K5
Castle Mead, Hem.H. HP1 62 BH22
Castle Ms, N12 off Castle Rd 120 DC50
NW1 7 J5
SW17 202 DE91
Hampton TW12
off Station Rd 218 CB95
Weybridge KT13 217 BS104
Castle Par, Epsom KT17
off Ewell Bypass 239 CU108
Castle Pl, NW1 7 K5
W4 off Windmill Rd 180 CS77
Castle Pt, E13 24 D1
Castlereagh St, W1 16 D8
Castle Rd, N12 120 DC50
NW1 7 J5
Chipstead CR5 256 DE120
Dagenham RM9 168 EV67
Enfield EN3 105 DY39
Epsom KT18 254 CP115
Eynsford DA4 247 FH107
Grays RM17 192 FZ79
Hoddesdon EN11 55 EB14
Isleworth TW7 179 CF82
Northolt UB5 158 CB65
St. Albans AL1 65 CH20
Shoreham TN14 247 FG108
Southall UB2 178 BZ76
Swanscombe DA10 212 FZ86
Weybridge KT13 217 BS104
Woking GU21 233 AZ114
Castle Sq, Bletch. RH1 274 DQ133
Guildford GU1 280 AX136
Castle St, E6 166 EJ68
Berkhamsted HP4 60 AW19
Bletchingley RH1 273 DP133
Greenhithe DA9 211 FU85
Guildford GU1 280 AX136
Hertford SG14 54 DQ10
Kingston upon Thames KT1 220 CL96
Slough SL1 174 AT76
Swanscombe DA10 212 FZ86
Castleton Av, Bexh. DA7 189 FD81
Wembley HA9 140 CL63
Castleton Cl, Bans. SM7 256 DA115
Croydon CR0 225 DY100
Castleton Dr, Bans. SM7 256 DA115
Castleton Gdns, Wem. HA9 140 CL62
Castleton Rd, E17 123 ED54
SE9 206 EK91
Ilford IG3 148 EU60
Mitcham CR4 223 DK98
Ruislip HA4 138 BX60
Castletown Rd, W14 38 F1
Castle Vw, Epsom KT18 238 CP114
Castleview Cl, N4 144 DQ60
Castleview Gdns, Ilf. IG1 146 EL58
Castleview Rd, Slou. SL3 174 AW77
Castle Vw Rd, Wey. KT13 235 BP105
Sch Castleview Sch, Slou. SL3
off Woodstock Av 174 AX77
Castle Wk, Reig. RH2
off London Rd 272 DA134
Sunbury-on-Thames TW16
off Elizabeth Gdns 218 BW97
Castle Way, SW19 201 CX90
Epsom KT17 off Castle Av 239 CU109
Feltham TW13 198 BW91
Castlewood Dr, SE9 187 EM82
Castlewood Rd, N15 144 DU58
N16 144 DU59
Cockfosters EN4 102 DD41
Castle Yd, N6 off North Rd 142 DG59
SE1 31 H2
Richmond TW10 off Hill St 199 CK85
Castor La, E14 34 C1
Catalina Av, Chaff.Hun. RM16 192 FZ75
Catalina Rd, Lon.Hthrw Air. TW6 off Cromer Rd 176 BN82
Catalin Ct, Wal.Abb. EN9
off Howard Cl 89 ED33
Catalonia Apts, Wat. WD18
off Linden Av 97 BT42
Catalpa Cl, Guil. GU1
off Cedar Way 264 AW132
Catalpa Ct, SE13
off Hither Grn La 205 ED86
Cater Gdns, Guil. GU3 264 AT132
CATERHAM, CR3 258 DU123
⇌ Caterham 258 DU124
Caterham Av, Ilf. IG5 125 EM54
Caterham Bypass, Cat. CR3 258 DV120
Caterham Cl, Cat. CR3 258 DS120

Caterham Ct, Wal.Abb. EN9 90 EF34
Caterham Dene Hosp, Cat. CR3 258 DT123
Caterham Dr, Couls. CR5 257 DP118
Caterham High Sch, Ilf. IG5 off Caterham Av 125 EM54
CATERHAM-ON-THE-HILL, Cat. CR3 258 DT122
Caterham Rd, SE13 185 EC83
Caterham Sch, Cat. CR3 off Harestone Valley Rd 274 DT126
Catesby St, SE17 31 M9
CATFORD, SE6 205 EB88
Catford 205 EA87
Catford Bridge 205 EA87
Catford Bdy, SE6 205 EB87
Catford Gyratory, SE6 205 EB87
Catford Hill, SE6 205 DZ89
Catford Ms, SE6 off Holbeach Rd 205 EB87
Catford Rd, SE6 205 EA88
Cathall Rd, E11 145 ED62
Catham Cl, St.Alb. AL1 65 CH22
Catharine Cl, Chaff.Hun. RM16 192 FZ75
Cathay St, SE16 32 F5
Cathay Wk, Nthlt. UB5 off Brabazon Rd 158 CA68
Cathcart Dr, Orp. BR6 227 ES103
Cathcart Hill, N19 143 DJ62
Cathcart Rd, SW10 39 M2
Cathcart St, NW5 7 J4
Cathedral Cl, Guil. GU2 280 AV135
Cathedral Ct, St.Alb. AL3 64 CB22
Cathedral Hill, Guil. GU2 264 AU133
● Cathedral Hill Ind Est, Guil. GU2 off Cathedral Hill 264 AU133
★ Cathedral of the Holy Spirit Guildford, Guil. GU2 264 AV134
Cathedral Piazza, SW1 29 L7
Cathedral Pl, Brwd. CM14 130 FX47
Cathedral Sch of St. Saviour & St. Mary Overie, The, SE1 31 K4
Cathedral St, SE1 31 L2
Cathedral Vw, Guil. GU2 264 AT134
Cathedral Wk, SW1 29 L6
Catherall Rd, N5 144 DQ62
Catherine Cl, Byfleet KT14 234 BL114
Hemel Hempstead HP2 off Parr Cres 63 BQ15
Loughton IG10 off Roding Gdns 107 EM44
Pilgrim's Hatch CM15 130 FU43
Catherine Ct, N14 off Conisbee Ct 103 DJ43
Catherine Dr, Rich. TW9 180 CL84
Sunbury-on-Thames TW16 197 BT93
Catherine Gdns, Houns. TW3 179 CD84
Catherine Griffiths Ct, EC1 18 F4
Catherine Gro, SE10 46 C6
Catherine Ho, N1 off Phillipp St 9 P9
Catherine Howard Ct, SE9 off Avery Hill Rd 207 ER86
Weybridge KT13 off Old Palace Rd 217 BP104
Catherine of Aragon Ct, SE9 off Avery Hill Rd 207 EQ86
Catherine Parr Ct, SE9 off Avery Hill Rd 207 ER86
Catherine Pl, SW1 29 L6
Harrow HA1 139 CF57
Catherine Rd, Enf. EN3 105 DY36
Romford RM2 149 FH57
Surbiton KT6 219 CK99
Catherine's Cl, West Dr. UB7 off Money La 176 BK76
Catherine St, WC2 18 C10
St. Albans AL3 65 CD19
Catherine Wheel All, E1 19 P7
Catherine Wheel Rd, Brent. TW8 179 CK80
Catherine Wheel Yd, SW1 29 L3
Catherwood Ct, N1 off Murray Gro 19 L1
Cat Hill, Barn. EN4 102 DE44
Cathles Rd, SW12 203 DH86
Cathnor Rd, W12 181 CV75
Cathrow Ms, Hodd. EN11 55 EA14
Catisfield Rd, Enf. EN3 105 DY37
Catkin Cl, Hem.H. HP1 62 BH19
Catlin Cres, Shep. TW17 217 BR99
Catlin Gdns, Gdse. RH9 274 DV130
Catling Cl, SE23 204 DW90
Catlins La, Pnr. HA5 137 BV55
Catlin St, SE16 44 D1
Hemel Hempstead HP3 62 BH23
Cator Cl, New Adgtn CR0 244 EE111
Cator Cres, New Adgtn CR0 243 ED111
Cator La, Beck. BR3 225 DZ96
Cato Rd, SW4 183 DK83
Cator Pk Sch, Beck. BR3 off Lennard Rd 205 DY94
Cator Rd, SE26 205 DX93
Carshalton SM5 240 DF106
Cator St, SE15 44 A3
Cato St, W1 16 D7
Catsey La, Bushey WD23 116 CC45
Catsey Wds, Bushey WD23 116 CC45
Catterick Cl, N11 120 DG51
Catterick Way, Borwd. WD6 100 CM39
Cattistock Rd, SE9 206 EL92
CATTLEGATE, Enf. EN2 87 DL33
Cattlegate Hill, Northaw EN6 87 DK31
Cattlegate Rd, Enf. EN2 87 DL34
Northaw EN6 87 DK31
Cattley Cl, Barn. EN5 101 CY42
Cattlins Cl, Chsht EN7 88 DS29
Catton St, WC1 18 C7
Cattsdell, Hem.H. HP2 62 BL18
Caughley Ho, SE11 off Lambeth Wk 30 E7
Caulfield Rd, E6 167 EM66
SE15 44 F8
W3 180 CQ76
Causeway, The, N2 142 DE56
SW18 182 DB84
SW19 201 CX92
Bray SL6 172 AC75
Carshalton SM5 222 DG104
Chessington KT9 238 CL105
Claygate KT10 237 CF108
Causeway, The, Feltham TW14 177 BU84
Hounslow TW4 177 BU84
Potters Bar EN6 86 DC31
Staines-upon-Thames TW18 195 BC91
Sutton SM2 240 DC109
Teddington TW11 off Broad St 199 CF93
Causeway Cl, Pot.B. EN6 86 DD31
● Causeway Corporate Cen, Stai. TW18 195 BB91
Causeway Ct, Wok. GU21 off Bingham Dr 248 AT118
Causeyware Rd, N9 122 DV45
Causton Rd, N6 143 DH59
Causton Sq, Dag. RM10 168 FA66
Causton St, SW1 29 P9
Cautherly La, Gt Amwell SG12 55 DZ10
Cautley Av, SW4 203 DJ85
Cavalier Cl, Rom. RM6 148 EX56
Cavalier Gdns, Hayes UB3 157 BR72
Cavalier Ho, W5 off Uxbridge Rd 159 CJ73
Cavalry Barracks, Houns. TW4 178 BX83
Cavalry Cres, Houns. TW4 178 BX84
Windsor SL4 173 AQ83
Cavalry Gdns, SW15 201 CY85
Cavalry Sq, SW3 28 F10
Cavan Dr, St.Alb. AL3 65 CD15
Cavan Pl, Pnr. HA5 116 BZ53
Cavaye Pl, SW10 39 P1
Cavell Cres, Dart. DA1 190 FN84
Harold Wood RM3 128 FL54
Cavell Dr, Enf. EN2 103 DN40
Cavell Rd, N17 122 DR52
Cheshunt EN7 88 DT27
Cavell St, E1 20 F6
Cavell Way, Epsom KT19 238 CN111
Cavendish Av, N3 120 DA54
NW8 16 B1
W13 159 CG71
Erith DA8 189 FC79
Harrow HA1 139 CD63
Hornchurch RM12 169 FH65
New Malden KT3 221 CV99
Ruislip HA4 137 BV64
Sevenoaks TN13 278 FG122
Sidcup DA15 208 EU87
Welling DA16 187 ET83
Woodford Green IG8 124 EH53
Cavendish Cl, N18 122 DV50
NW6 4 G5
NW8 16 B2
Amersham HP6 94 AV39
Hayes UB4 157 BS71
Sunbury-on-Thames TW16 197 BT93
Taplow SL6 152 AG72
Cavendish Coll, WC1 17 N6
Cavendish Ct, EC3 19 P8
Croxley Green WD3 off Mayfare 97 BR43
Sunbury-on-Thames TW16 197 BT93
Cavendish Cres, Els. WD6 100 CN42
Hornchurch RM12 169 FH65
Cavendish Dr, E11 145 ED60
Claygate KT10 237 CE106
Edgware HA8 118 CM51
Cavendish Gdns, SW4 203 DJ86
Aveley RM15 190 FQ75
Barking IG11 147 ES64
Ilford IG1 147 EN60
Redhill RH1 272 DG133
Romford RM6 148 EY57
Cavendish Ms N, W1 17 K6
Cavendish Ms S, W1 17 K7
Cavendish Par, SW4 off Clapham Common S Side 203 DH86
Cavendish Pl, NW2 4 D5
W1 17 K8
Bromley BR1 227 EM97
Cavendish Prim Sch, W4 off Edensor Rd 180 CS80
Cavendish Rd, E4 123 EC51
N4 143 DN58
N18 122 DV50
NW6 4 F7
SW12 203 DH86
SW19 202 DD94
W4 180 CQ81
Barnet EN5 101 CW41
Chesham HP5 76 AR32
Croydon CR0 223 DP102
New Malden KT3 221 CT99
Redhill RH1 272 DG134
Saint Albans AL1 65 CF20
Sunbury-on-Thames TW16 197 BT93
Sutton SM2 240 DC108
Weybridge KT13 235 BQ108
Woking GU22 248 AX119
Cavendish Sch, The, NW1 7 K8
Hemel Hempstead HP1 off Warners End Rd 62 BH19
Cavendish Sq, W1 17 K8
Longfield DA3 231 FX97
Cavendish St, N1 19 L1
Cavendish Ter, Felt. TW13 197 BU89
Cavendish Wk, Epsom KT19 238 CP111
Cavendish Way, Hat. AL10 67 CT18
West Wickham BR4 225 EB102
Cavenham Cl, Wok. GU22 248 AY119
Cavenham Gdns, Horn. RM11 150 FJ57
Ilford IG1 147 ER62
Caverleigh Way, Wor.Pk. KT4 221 CU102
Cave Rd, E13 24 B1
Richmond TW10 199 CJ91
Caversham Av, N13 121 DN48
Sutton SM3 221 CY103
Caversham Ct, N11 120 DG48
Caversham Flats, SW3 40 E2
Caversham Rd, N15 144 DQ56
NW5 7 L4
Kingston upon Thames KT1 220 CM96
Caversham St, SW3 40 E2
Caverswall St, W12 14 A8
Caveside Cl, Chis. BR7 227 EN95
Cavill's Wk, Chig. IG7 126 EW47
Romford RM4 126 EX47
Cawcott Dr, Wind. SL4 173 AL81
Cawdor Av, S.Ock. RM15 171 FU73
Cawdor Cres, W7 179 CG77
Cawley Hatch, Harl. CM19 73 EM15
Cawnpore St, SE19 204 DS92
Cawsey Way, Wok. GU21 248 AY117
Caxton Av, Add. KT15 234 BG107
● Caxton Cen, St.Alb. AL3 65 CF15
Caxton Dr, Uxb. UB8 156 BK68
Caxton Gdns, Guil. GU2 264 AV133
Caxton Gro, E3 22 A2
Caxton Hill, Hert. SG13 54 DT09
Caxton Hill Ext Rd, Hert. SG13 54 DT09
Caxton La, Oxt. RH8 276 EL131
Caxton Ms, Brent. TW8 off The Butts 179 CK79
● Caxton Pt Trading Est, Hayes UB3 177 BS75
Caxton Ri, Red. RH1 272 DG133
Caxton Rd, N22 121 DM54
SW19 202 DC92
W12 26 C4
Hoddesdon EN11 55 EB13
Southall UB2 178 BX76
Caxtons Ct, Guil. GU1 265 BA132
Caxton St, SW1 29 M6
Caxton St N, E16 23 L9
Caxton Way, Rom. RM1 149 FE56
Watford WD18 97 BR44
Cayenne Ct, SE1 32 B3
Cayford Ho, NW3 6 D2
Caygill Cl, Brom. BR2 226 EF98
Cayley Prim Sch, E14 21 L8
Cayley Rd, Sthl. UB2 off McNair Rd 178 CB76
Cayton Pl, EC1 19 L3
Cayton Rd, Couls. CR5 257 DJ122
Greenford UB6 159 CE68
Cayton St, EC1 19 L3
Cazenove Mans, N16 off Cazenove Rd 144 DU61
Cazenove Rd, E17 123 EA53
N16 144 DT61
Cearns Ho, E6 166 EK67
Cearn Way, Couls. CR5 257 DM115
Cecil Av, Bark. IG11 167 ER66
Enfield EN1 104 DT42
Grays RM16 192 FZ75
Hornchurch RM11 150 FL55
Wembley HA9 140 CM64
Cecil Cl, W5 159 CK71
Ashford TW15 197 BQ93
Chessington KT9 237 CK105
Cecil Ct, WC2 29 P1
Barnet EN5 101 CX41
Cecil Cres, Hat. AL10 67 CV16
Cecile Pk, N8 143 DL58
Cecilia Cl, N2 142 DC55
★ Cecilia Colman Gall, NW8 6 B10
Cecilia Rd, E8 10 C2
Cecil Manning Cl, Perivale UB6 159 CG67
Cecil Pk, Pnr. HA5 138 BY56
Cecil Pl, Mitch. CR4 222 DF99
Cecil Rd, E11 146 EE62
E13 13 P8
E17 123 EA53
N10 121 DH54
N14 121 DJ46
NW9 140 CS55
NW10 160 CS67
SW19 202 DB94
W3 160 CQ71
Ashford TW15 197 BQ94
Cheshunt EN8 89 DX32
Croydon CR0 223 DM100
Enfield EN2 104 DR42
Gravesend DA11 213 GF88
Harrow HA3 139 CE55
Hertford SG13 54 DQ12
Hoddesdon EN11 71 EC15
Hounslow TW3 178 CC82
Ilford IG1 147 EP63
Iver SL0 155 BE72
Potters Bar EN6 85 CU32
Romford RM6 148 EX59
St. Albans AL1 65 CF20
Sutton SM1 239 CZ107
Cecil Rd Prim & Nurs Sch, Grav. DA11 off Cecil Rd 213 GF88
★ Cecil Sharp Ho, NW1 7 H8
Cecil St, Wat. WD24 97 BV38
Cecil Way, Brom. BR2 226 EG102
Slough SL2 153 AM70
Cedar Av, Barn. EN4 120 DE45
Cobham KT11 252 BW115
Enfield EN3 104 DW40
Gravesend DA12 213 GJ91
Hayes UB3 157 BU72
Romford RM6 148 EY57
Ruislip HA4 158 BW65
Sidcup DA15 208 EU87
Twickenham TW2 198 CB86
Upminster RM14 150 FN63
Waltham Cross EN8 89 DX33
West Drayton UB7 156 BM74
Cedar Chase, Tap. SL6 152 AD70
Cedar Cl, E3 11 P8
SE21 204 DQ88
SW15 200 CR91
Borehamwood WD6 100 CP42
Bromley BR2 226 EL104
Buckhurst Hill IG9 124 EK47
Carshalton SM5 240 DF107
Chesham HP5 76 AS30
Dorking RH4 285 CH136
East Molesey KT8 off Cedar Rd 219 CE98
Epsom KT17 239 CT114
Esher KT10 236 BZ108
Hertford SG14 53 DP09
Hutton CM13 131 GD45
Ilford IG1 147 ER64
Iver SL0 off Thornbridge Rd 155 BC66
Potters Bar EN6 86 DA30
Reigate RH2 288 DC136
Romford RM7 149 FC56
Sawbridgeworth CM21 58 EY06
Staines-upon-Thames TW18 216 BJ97
Swanley BR8 229 FC96
Ware SG12 55 DX07
Warlingham CR6 259 DY119
Cedar Copse, Brom. BR1 227 EM96
Cedar Ct, E11 off Grosvenor Rd 146 EH57
N1 9 K6
SE7 off Fairlawn 186 EJ79
SE9 206 EL86
SW19 201 CX90
Egham TW20 195 BA91
Epping CM16 92 EU31
St. Albans AL4 65 CK20
Cedar Cres, Brom. BR2 226 EL104
Cedarcroft Rd, Chess. KT9 238 CM105
Cedar Dr, N2 142 DE56
Chesham HP5 76 AN30
Fetcham KT22 253 CE123
Loughton IG10 107 EP40
Pinner HA5 116 CA51
Sutton at Hone DA4 230 FP96
Cedar Gdns, Chobham GU24 232 AT110
Cedar Gdns, Sutton SM2 240 DC107
Upminster RM14 150 FQ62
Woking GU21 off St. John's Rd 248 AV118
Cedar Grn, Hodd. EN11 71 EA18
Cedar Gro, W5 180 CL76
Amersham HP7 77 AR39
Bexley DA5 208 EW86
Southall UB1 158 CA71
Weybridge KT13 235 BQ105
Cedar Hts, Rich. TW10 200 CL88
Cedar Hill, Epsom KT18 254 CQ116
Cedar Ho, SW6 off Lensbury Ave 39 P8
Croy. CR0 243 EB107
Sunbury-on-Thames TW16 197 BT94
Cedarhurst, Brom. BR1 206 EE94
Cedarhurst Dr, SE9 206 EJ85
Cedar Lawn Av, Barn. EN5 101 CY43
Cedar Lo, Chsht EN8 off High St 89 DX28
Cedar Ms, SW15 off Cambalt Rd 201 CX85
Cedar Mt, SE9 206 EK88
Cedarne Rd, SW6 39 L5
Cedar Pk, Cat. CR3 258 DS121
Chigwell IG7 off High Rd 125 EP49
Cedar Pk Gdns, SW19 201 CV93
Rom. RM6 148 EX59
Cedar Pk Rd, Enf. EN2 104 DQ38
Cedar Pl, SE7 36 C10
Northwood HA6 115 BQ51
Cedar Ri, N14 120 DG45
South Ockendon RM15 off Sycamore Way 171 FX70
Cedar Rd, N17 122 DT53
NW2 141 CW63
Berkhamsted HP4 60 AX20
Bromley BR1 226 EJ96
Cobham KT11 235 BV114
Croydon CR0 224 DS103
Dartford DA1 210 FK88
East Molesey KT8 219 CE98
Enfield EN2 103 DP38
Erith DA8 189 FG81
Feltham TW14 197 BR88
Grays RM16 193 GG76
Hatfield AL10 67 CU19
Hornchurch RM12 150 FJ62
Hounslow TW4 178 BW82
Hutton CM13 131 GD44
Romford RM7 149 FC56
Sutton SM2 240 DC107
Teddington TW11 199 CG92
Watford WD19 98 BW44
Weybridge KT13 234 BN105
Woking GU22 248 AV120
Cedars, Bans. SM7 240 DF114
Cedars, The, E15 13 M8
W13 159 CJ72
Bookham KT23 268 CC126
Brockham RH3 270 CN134
Buckhurst Hill IG9 124 EG46
Byfleet KT14 234 BM112
Guildford GU1 265 BA131
Leatherhead KT22 254 CL121
Reigate RH2 272 DD134
Slough SL2 153 AM69
Teddington TW11 off Adelaide Rd 199 CF93
Cedars Av, E17 145 EA57
Mitcham CR4 222 DG98
Rickmansworth WD3 114 BJ46
Cedars Cl, NW4 141 CX55
SE13 185 ED83
Chalfont St. Peter SL9 112 AY50
Cedars Ct, N9 122 DT47
Cedars Dr, Uxb. UB10 156 BM68
Cedars Manor Sch, Har. HA3 off Whittlesea Rd 116 CC53
Cedars Ms, SW4 183 DH84
Cedars Prim Sch, The, Cran. TW5 off High St 177 BV80
Cedars Rd, E15 13 K4
N21 121 DP47
SW4 183 DH83
SW13 181 CT82
W4 180 CQ78
Beckenham BR3 225 DY96
Croydon CR0 223 DL104
Hampton Wick KT1 219 CJ95
Morden SM4 222 DA98
Cedars Wk, Chorl. WD3 off Badgers Wk 95 BF42
Cedar Ter, Rich. TW9 180 CL84
Cedar Ter Rd, Sev. TN13 279 FJ123
Cedar Tree Gro, SE27 203 DP92
Cedarville Gdns, SW16 203 DM93
Cedar Vista, Kew TW9 180 CL82
Cedar Wk, Clay. KT10 237 CF107
Hemel Hempstead HP3 62 BK22
Kenley CR8 258 DQ116
Kingswood KT20 255 CY120
Waltham Abbey EN9 89 ED34
Welwyn Garden City AL7 52 DB10
Cedar Way, NW1 7 N7
Berkhamsted HP4 60 AX20
Guildford GU1 264 AW132
Slough SL3 174 AY78
Sunbury-on-Thames TW16 197 BS94
● Cedar Way Ind Est, N1 off Cedar Way 7 N7
Cedarwood Dr, St.Alb. AL4 65 CK20
Cedar Wd Dr, Wat. WD25 97 BV35
Cedra Ct, N16 144 DU60
Cedric Av, Rom. RM1 149 FE55
Cedric Rd, SE9 207 EQ90
Celadon Cl, Enf. EN3 105 DY41
Celandine Cl, E14 22 A7
South Ockendon RM15 171 FW70
Celandine Dr, E8 10 B6
SE28 168 EV74
Celandine Gro, N14 103 DJ43
Celandine Rd, Hersham KT12 236 BY105
Celandine Way, E15 23 K2
Celbridge Ms, W2 15 M8
Celedon Cl, Grays RM16 192 FY75
Celestial Gdns, SE13 185 ED84
Celia Cres, Ashf. TW15 196 BK93
Celia Rd, N19 7 M1
Cell Barnes Cl, St.Alb. AL1 65 CH22
Cell Barnes La, St.Alb. AL1 65 CH23
Cell Fm Av, Old Wind. SL4 194 AV85
Celtic Av, Brom. BR2 226 EE97
Celtic Rd, Byfleet KT14 234 BL114
Celtic St, E14 22 D6
Cement Block Cotts, Grays RM17 192 GC79
Cemetery Hill, Hem.H. HP1 62 BJ21
Cemetery La, SE7 186 EL79
Lower Nazeing EN9 90 EF25
Shepperton TW17 217 BP101
Cemetery Rd, E7 13 L2
N17 122 DS52
SE2 188 EV80
Cemmaes Ct Rd, Hem.H. HP1 62 BJ20
Cemmaes Meadow, Hem.H. HP1 62 BJ20
Cenacle Cl, NW3 142 DA62
★ Cenotaph, The, SW1 30 A4
● Centaurs Business Cen, Islw. TW7 179 CG79
Centaur St, SE1 30 D6
Centaurus Sq, Frog. AL2 83 CE27
Centaury Ct, Grays RM17 192 GD79
● Centenary Ind Est, Enf. EN3 105 DZ42
Centenary Rd, Enf. EN3 105 DZ42
Centenary Wk, Loug. IG10 106 EH41
Centenary Way, Amer. HP6 94 AT38
Centennial Av, Els. WD6 117 CH45
Centennial Ct, Els. WD6 117 CJ45
● Centennial Pk, Els. WD6 117 CJ45
Central Av, E11 145 ED61
N2 120 DD54
N9 122 DS48
SW11 40 E5
Aveley RM15 190 FQ75
Enfield EN1 104 DV40
Gravesend DA12 213 GH89
Grays RM20 191 FT77
Harlow CM20 57 ER14
Hayes UB3 157 BU73
Hounslow TW3 178 CC84
Pinner HA5 138 BZ58
Tilbury RM18 193 GG81
Wallington SM6 241 DL106
Waltham Cross EN8 89 DY33
Welling DA16 187 ET82
West Molesey KT8 218 BZ98
● Central Business Cen, NW10 off Great Cen Way 140 CS64
Central Circ, NW4 off Hendon Way 141 CV57
★ Central Criminal Ct (Old Bailey), EC4 19 H8
Central Dr, Horn. RM12 150 FL62
St. Albans AL4 65 CJ19
Slough SL1 153 AM73
Welwyn Garden City AL7 51 CZ07
Centrale 224 DQ103
Centrale Shop Cen, Croy. CR0 224 DQ103
Central Foundation Boys' Sch, EC2 19 M4
Central Foundation Girls' Sch, Lwr Sch, E3 21 M2
Upr Sch, E3 21 P3
Central Gdns, Mord. SM4 222 DB99
Central Hill, SE19 204 DR92
Central Ho, E15 12 D10
Barking IG11 off Cambridge Rd 167 EQ66
Central Middlesex Hosp, NW10 160 CQ69
Central Par, E17 off Hoe St 145 EA56
Feltham TW14 198 BW87
Hounslow TW5 off Heston Rd 178 CA80
New Addington CR0 243 EC110
Perivale UB6 159 CG69
Surbiton KT6 220 CL100
Central Pk Av, Dag. RM10 149 FB62
● Central Pk Est, Houns. TW4 198 BX85
Central Pk Prim Sch, E6 24 F1
Central Pk Rd, E6 24 D1
Central Pl, SE25 off Portland Rd 224 DV98
Central Prim Sch, Wat. WD17 off Derby Rd 98 BW42
Central Rd, Dart. DA1 210 FL85
Harlow CM20 58 EU11
Morden SM4 222 DA100
Wembley HA0 139 CH64
Worcester Park KT4 221 CU103
Central St. Martins Coll of Art & Design, Back Hill Site, EC1 18 F5
Byam Shaw Sch of Art, N19 off Elthorne Rd 143 DK61
King's Cross N1 8 A9
Central Sch Footpath, SW14 180 CQ83
Central Sch of Ballet, EC1 18 F5
Central Sch of Speech & Drama, NW3 6 A6
Central Sq, NW11 142 DB58
Wembley HA9 off Station Gro 140 CL64
West Molesey KT8 218 BZ98
Central St, EC1 19 J3
Central Wk, Epsom KT19 off Station App 238 CR113
Central Way, NW10 160 CQ69
SE28 168 EU74
Carshalton SM5 240 DE108
Feltham TW14 197 BU85
Oxted RH8 275 ED127
Central West, Grnf. UB6 158 CC70
● Centrapark, Welw.G.C. AL7 51 CY08
Centre, The, Felt. TW13 off High St 197 BV88
Centre, The, Walt. KT12 217 BT102
Centre Av, W3 160 CR74
W10 14 B3
Epping CM16 91 ET32
Centre Cl, Epp. CM16 91 ET32
Centre Common Rd, Chis. BR7 207 EQ93
Centre Ct Shop Cen, SW19 201 CZ93
Centre Dr, Epp. CM16 91 ET32
Centre Grn, Epp. CM16 off Centre Av 91 ET32
● Centrepoint, WC1 17 P8
Centre Pt, SE1 32 C10
Centre Rd, E7 146 EG61
E11 146 EG61
Dagenham RM10 169 FB68
Windsor SL4 172 AJ80
Centre St, E2 20 E1
Centre Way, E17 123 EC52
N9 122 DW47
Centreway Apts, Ilf. IG1 off High Rd 147 EQ61
Centric Cl, NW1 7 J8
Centrillion Pt, Croy. CR0 off Masons Av 242 DQ105

Centrium, Wok. GU22 248 AY117
Centurion Bldg, SW8 41 J3
Centurion Cl, N7 8 C6
Centurion Ct, SE18 37 K9
Hackbridge SM6
off Wandle Rd 223 DH104
Romford RM1 149 FD55
St. Albans AL1
off Camp Rd 65 CG21
Centurion La, E3 11 P10
Centurion Sq, SE18 186 EL81
Centurion Way, Erith DA18 188 FA76
Purfleet RM19 190 FM77
Century Cl, NW4 141 CX57
St. Albans AL3 64 CC19
Century Ct, Wok. GU21 249 AZ116
Century Gdns, S.Croy. CR2 242 DU113
Century Ms, E5 10 G1
Century Pk, Wat. WD17 98 BW43
Century Rd, E17 145 DY55
Hoddesdon EN11 71 EA16
Staines-upon-Thames TW18 195 BC92
Ware SG12 55 DX05
Century Yd, SE23 204 DW89
Cephas Av, E1 21 H4
Cephas St, E1 20 G5
Ceres Rd, SE18 187 ET77
Cerise Rd, SE15 44 D7
Cerne Cl, Hayes UB4 158 BW73
Cerne Rd, Grav. DA12 213 GL91
Morden SM4 222 DC100
Cerney Ms, W2 16 A10
Cerotus Pl, Cher. KT16 215 BF101
Cervantes Ct, W2 15 M9
Northwood HA6
off Green La 115 BT52
Cervia Way, Grav. DA12 213 GM90
Cester St, E2 10 C9
Cestreham Cres, Chesh. HP5 76 AR29
Ceylon Rd, W14 26 D7
Chabot Dr, SE15 184 DV83
Chace Av, Pot.B. EN6 86 DD32
Sch Chace Comm Sch, Enf.
EN1 off Churchbury La 104 DS39
Chacombe Pl, Beac. HP9 111 AK50
Chadacre Av, Ilf. IG5 147 EM55
Chadacre Rd, Epsom KT17 239 CV107
Chadbourn St, E14 22 D7
Chad Cres, N9 122 DW48
Chadd Dr, Brom. BR1 226 EL97
Chadd Grn, E13 13 N9
Chadfields, Til. RM18 193 GG80
Chadhurst Cl, N.Holm. RH5
off Wildcroft Dr 285 CK139
Chadview Ct, Chad.Hth RM6 148 EX59
Chadville Gdns, Rom. RM6 148 EX57
Chadway, Dag. RM8 148 EW60
Chadwell, Ware SG12 54 DW07
Chadwell Av, Chsht EN8 88 DW28
Romford RM6 148 EV59
Chadwell Bypass, Grays RM16 193 GF78
CHADWELL HEATH, Rom.
RM6 148 EX58
⇌ Chadwell Heath 148 EX59
Sch Chadwell Heath Foundation
Sch, The, Chad.Hth RM6
off Christie Gdns 148 EV58
● Chadwell Heath Ind Pk,
Dag. RM8 148 EY60
Chadwell Heath La, Rom.
RM6 148 EV57
Chadwell Hill, Grays RM16 193 GH78
Chadwell La, N8 143 DM55
Sch Chadwell Prim Sch, Chad.Hth
RM6 off High Rd 148 EW59
Chadwell Ri, Ware SG12 54 DW07
Chadwell Rd, Grays RM17 192 GC77
CHADWELL ST. MARY,
Grays RM16 193 GJ76
Sch Chadwell St. Mary Prim Sch,
Chad.St.M. RM16
off River Vw 193 GH77
Chadwell St, EC1 18 F2
Chadwick Av, E4 123 ED49
N21 103 DM42
SW19 202 DA93
Chadwick Cl, SW15 201 CT87
W7 off Westcott Cres 159 CF71
Northfleet DA11 212 GE89
Teddington TW11 199 CG93
Chadwick Dr, Harold Wd RM3 128 FK54
Chadwick Ms, W4
off Thames Rd 180 CP79
Chadwick Pl, Long Dit. KT6 219 CJ101
Chadwick Rd, E11 146 EE59
NW10 161 CT67
SE15 44 A9
Ilford IG1 147 EP62
Chadwick St, SW1 29 P7
Chadwick Way, SE28 168 EX73
Chadwin Rd, E13 24 A6
Chadworth Way, Clay. KT10 237 CD106
Chaffers Mead, Ashtd. KT21 254 CM116
Chaffinch Av, Croy. CR0 225 DX100
● Chaffinch Business Pk,
Beck. BR3 225 DX98
Chaffinch Cl, N9 123 DX46
Croydon CR0 225 DX99
Surbiton KT6 220 CN104
Chaffinches Grn, Hem.H. HP3 62 BN24
Chaffinch La, Wat. WD18 115 BT45
Chaffinch Rd, Beck. BR3 225 DY95
Chaffinch Way, Horl. RH6 290 DE147
CHAFFORD HUNDRED,
Grays RM16 191 FX76
⇌ Chafford Hundred 191 FV77
Sch Chafford Hundred Business &
Enterprise Coll, Chaff.Hun.
RM16 off Mayflower Rd 191 FW78
Sch Chafford Hundred Prim Sch,
Grays RM16
off Mayflower Rd 191 FW78
Sch Chafford Sch, The, Rain.
RM13 off Lambs La S 170 FJ71
Chafford Wk, Rain. RM13 170 FJ68
Chafford Way, Rom. RM6 148 EW56
Chagford St, NW1 16 E5
Chailey Av, Enf. EN1 104 DT40
Chailey Cl, Houns. TW5
off Springwell Rd 178 BX81
Chailey Pl, Hersham KT12 236 BY105
Chailey St, E5 144 DW62
Chalbury Wk, N1 8 D10
Chalcombe Rd, SE2 188 EV76
Chalcot Cl, Sutt. SM2 240 DA108
Chalcot Cres, NW1 6 F8
Chalcot Gdns, NW3 6 E5
Chalcot Ms, SW16 203 DL90
Chalcot Rd, NW1 6 G7
Sch Chalcot Sch, NW1 7 J6
Chalcot Sq, NW1 6 G7
Chalcott Gdns, Long Dit. KT6 219 CJ102
Chalcroft Rd, SE13 206 EE85
CHALDON, Cat. CR3 257 DN124
Chaldon Cl, Red. RH1 288 DE136
Chaldon Common Rd, Chaldon
CR3 258 DQ124
Chaldon Path, Th.Hth. CR7 223 DP98
Chaldon Rd, SW6 38 E4
Caterham CR3 258 DR124
Chaldon Way, Couls. CR5 257 DL117
Chale Rd, SW2 203 DL86
Chalet Cl, Berk. HP4 60 AT19
Bexley DA5 209 FD91
Chalet Est, NW7 119 CU49
Chale Wk, Sutt. SM2
off Hulverston Cl 240 DB109
⇌ Chalfont & Latimer 94 AW39
⊖ Chalfont & Latimer 94 AW39
Chalfont Av, Amer. HP6 94 AX39
Wembley HA9 160 CP65
Chalfont Cen for Epilepsy,
Chal.St.P. SL9 112 AY49
Chalfont Cl, Hem.H. HP2 63 BP15
CHALFONT COMMON,
Ger.Cr. SL9 113 AZ49
Chalfont Ct, NW9 141 CT55
Chalfont Grn, N9 122 DS48
● Chalfont Gro, Chal.St.P. SL9 112 AV51
Chalfont La, Chorl. WD3 95 BB43
Gerrards Cross SL9 113 BC51
West Hyde WD3 113 BC51
Chalfont Ms, SW19
off Augustus Rd 201 CZ88
Uxb. UB10 157 BP66
● Chalfont Pk, Chal.St.P. SL9 135 AZ55
Chalfont Rd, N9 122 DS48
SE25 224 DT97
Chalfont St. Giles HP8 113 BB48
Gerrards Cross SL9 113 BB48
Hayes UB3 177 BU75
Maple Cross WD3 113 BD49
Seer Green HP9 111 AR50
CHALFONT ST. GILES, HP8 112 AV47
Sch Chalfont St. Giles Inf Sch
& Nurs, Ch.St.G. HP8
off School La 112 AV48
Sch Chalfont St. Giles Jun Sch,
Ch.St.G. HP8
off Parsonage Rd 112 AV48
CHALFONT ST. PETER,
Ger.Cr. SL9 113 AZ53
Sch Chalfont St. Peter C of E Sch,
Chal.St.P. SL9
off Penn Rd 112 AX53
Sch Chalfont St. Peter Inf Sch,
Chal.St.P. SL9
off Lovel End 112 AW52
H Chalfonts & Gerrards Cross
Hosp, Chal.St.P. SL9 112 AX53
Sch Chalfonts Comm Coll,
Chal.St.P. SL9 off Narcot La 112 AW52
Chalfont Sta Rd, Amer. HP7 94 AW40
Chalfont Wk, Pnr. HA5
off Willows Cl 116 BW54
Chalfont Way, W13 179 CH76
Chalford Cl, W.Mol. KT8 218 CA98
Chalforde Gdns, Rom. RM2 149 FH56
Chalford Flats, Woob.Grn HP10 132 AE57
Chalford Rd, SE21 204 DR91
Chalford Wk, Wdf.Grn. IG8 124 EK53
Chalgrove, Welw.G.C. AL7 52 DD08
Chalgrove Av, Mord. SM4 222 DA99
Chalgrove Cres, Ilf. IG5 124 EL54
Chalgrove Gdns, N3 141 CY55
Sch Chalgrove Prim Sch, N3
off Chalgrove Gdns 141 CY55
Chalgrove Rd, N17 122 DV53
Sutton SM2 240 DD108
Chalice Cl, Wall. SM6
off Lavender Vale 241 DK107
Chalice Way, Green. DA9 211 FS85
Chalk Ct, Grays RM17 192 GA79
Chalk Dale, Welw.G.C. AL7 52 DB08
Chalk Dell, Rick. WD3
off Orchard Way 114 BG45
Chalkdell Flds, St.Alb. AL4 65 CG16
Chalkdell Hill, Hem.H. HP2 62 BL20
Chalkenden Cl, SE20 204 DV94
Jct Chalkers Cor, SW14 180 CP83
⊖ Chalk Farm 6 F6
Chalk Fm Rd, NW1 6 G6
Chalk Hill, Chesh. HP5 76 AP29
Coleshill HP7 111 AM45
Watford WD19 98 BX44
Sch Chalkhill Prim Sch, Wem.
HA9 off Barnhill Rd 140 CP62
Chalk Hill Rd, W6 26 C9
Chalkhill Rd, Wem. HA9 140 CP62
Chalklands, Wem. HA9 140 CQ62
Chalk La, Ashtd. KT21 254 CM119
Barnet EN4 102 DF42
East Horsley KT24 267 BT130
Epsom KT18 254 CR115
Harlow CM17 58 FA14
Chalkley Cl, Mitch. CR4 222 DF96
Chalkmill Dr, Enf. EN1 104 DV41
Chalk Paddock, Epsom KT18 254 CR115
Chalk Pit Av, Orp. BR5 228 EW97
Chalkpit La, Bet. RH3 270 CP133
Bookham KT23 268 BZ128
Chalk Pit La, Burn. SL1 152 AH66
Chalkpit La, Dor. RH4 285 CG135
Oxted RH8 275 EC125
Woldingham CR3 275 EC125
Chalk Pit Rd, Bans. SM7 256 DA117
Epsom KT18 254 CQ119
Chalkpit Ter, Dor. RH4 269 CG134
Chalk Pit Way, Sutt. SM1 240 DC106
Chalkpit Wd, Oxt. RH8 275 ED127
Chalk Rd, E13 24 B6
Chalkstone Cl, Well. DA16 188 EU81
Chalkstream Way, Woob.Grn
HP10 off Glory Mill La 132 AE56
Chalkwell Pk Av, Enf. EN1 104 DS42
Chalky Bk, Grav. DA11 213 GG91
Chalky La, Chess. KT9 237 CK109
Challacombe Cl, Hutt. CM13 131 GB46
Challenge Cl, NW10 160 CS67
Gravesend DA12 213 GM91
Challenge Ct, Lthd. KT22 253 CH119
Twickenham TW2
off Langhorn Dr 199 CE87
Challenge Rd, Ashf. TW15 197 BQ90
Challice Way, SW2 203 DM88
Challinor, Harl. CM17 74 EY15
Challin St, SE20 224 DW95
Challis Rd, Brent. TW8 179 CK78
Challock Cl, Bigg.H. TN16 260 EJ116
Challoner Cl, N2 120 DD54
Challoner Cres, W14 38 G1
Challoners Cl, E.Mol. KT8 219 CD98
Challoner St, W14 26 G10
Chalmers Ct, Crox.Grn WD3 96 BM44
Chalmers Ho, SW11
off York Rd 182 DC83
Chalmers Rd, Ashf. TW15 197 BP91
Banstead SM7 256 DD115
Chalmers Rd E, Ashf. TW15 197 BP91
Chalmers Wk, SE17 43 H3
Chalmers Way, Felt. TW14 197 BV85
Twick. TW1 179 CH84
Chaloner Ct, SE1 31 L4
Chalsey Rd, SE4 185 DZ84
Chalton Dr, N2 142 DC58
Chalton St, NW1 17 P2
CHALVEY, Slou. SL1 173 AQ76
Chalvey Gdns, Slou. SL1 174 AS75
Chalvey Gro, Slou. SL1 173 AP75
Chalvey Pk, Slou. SL1 174 AS75
Chalvey Rd E, Slou. SL1 174 AS75
Chalvey Rd W, Slou. SL1 173 AR75
Chamberlain Cl, SE28
off Broadwater Rd 187 ER76
Harlow CM17 74 EW15
Ilford IG1
off Richmond Rd 147 EQ62
Chamberlain Cotts, SE5 43 M7
Chamberlain Cres, W.Wick.
BR4 225 EB102
Chamberlain Gdns, Houns.
TW3 178 CC81
Chamberlain La, Pnr. HA5 137 BU56
Chamberlain Pl, E17 145 DY55
Chamberlain Rd, N2 120 DC54
W13 off Midhurst Rd 179 CG75
Chamberlain St, NW1 6 F7
Chamberlain Wk, Felt. TW13
off Burgess Cl 198 BY91
Chamberlain Way, Pnr. HA5 137 BV55
Surbiton KT6 220 CL101
Chamberlayne Av, Wem. HA9 140 CL61
Chamberlayne Rd, NW10 14 C2
Chambers Av, Sid. DA14 208 EY93
Chambersbury La, Hem.H. HP3 80 BN25
Sch Chambersbury Prim Sch, Hem.H.
HP3 off Hill Common 62 BN23
● Chambers Business Pk,
West Dr. UB7 176 BN79
Chambers Cl, Green. DA9 211 FU85
Chambers Gdns, N2 120 DD53
Chambers Gro, Welw.G.C. AL7 51 CY12
Chambers Ho, SW16
off Pringle Gdns 203 DJ91
Chambers La, NW10 161 CV66
Chambers Manor Ms, Epp.Upl.
CM16 91 EP26
Chambers Pl, S.Croy. CR2
off Rolleston Rd 242 DR108
Chambers Rd, N7 143 DL63
Chambers St, SE16 32 C4
Hertford SG14 54 DQ09
Chamber St, E1 20 B10
Chambers Wk, Stan. HA7 117 CH50
Chambon Pl, W6 off Beavor La 181 CU77
Chambord St, E2 20 B3
Chamers Ct, W12
off Heathstan Rd 161 CU72
Champa Cl, N17 122 DT54
Champion Cres, SE26 205 DY91
Champion Down, Eff. KT24
off Norwood Cl 268 BY128
Champion Gro, SE5 43 M10
Champion Hill, SE5 43 M10
Champion Hill Est, SE5 184 DS83
Champion Pk, SE5 43 L9
Champion Pk Est, SE5 43 M10
Champion Rd, SE26 205 DY91
Upminster RM14 150 FP61
Champions Grn, Hodd. EN11 55 EA14
Champions Way, NW4 119 CV53
NW7 119 CV53
Hoddesdon EN11 55 EA14
Champness Cl, SE27 204 DR91
Champness Rd, Bark. IG11 167 ET65
Champney Cl, Horton SL3 175 BA83
Champneys Cl, Sutt. SM2 239 CZ108
Chance Cl, Grays RM16 192 FZ76
Chancellor Gdns, S.Croy. CR2 241 DP109
Chancellor Gro, SE21 204 DQ89
Chancellor Pas, E14 34 B3
Chancellor Pl, NW9 119 CT54
Chancellors Ct, WC1
off Orde Hall St 18 C6
Chancellors Rd, W6 38 A1
Sch Chancellor's Sch,
Brook.Pk AL9
off Pine Gro 86 DB25
Chancellors St, W6 38 A1
Chancellors Wf, W6 38 A1
Chancellor Way, Sev. TN13 278 FG122
Chancelot Rd, SE2 188 EV77
Chancel St, SE1 30 G2
Chancery Cl, St.Alb. AL4 65 CK15
Chancery Ct, Dart. DA1 210 FN87
Egham TW20
off The Chantries 195 BA92
● Chancerygate Business Cen,
Slou. SL3 174 AY75
● Chancery Gate Business Cen,
Sthl. UB2 178 BW76
Chancerygate Cl, Ruis. HA4 138 BY64
Chancerygate Way, Ruis. HA4 138 BY63
⊖ Chancery Lane 18 E7
Chancery La, WC2 18 E8
Beckenham BR3 225 EB96
Chancery Ms, SW17 202 DE89
Chance St, E1 20 A4
E2 20 A4
Chanctonbury Chase, Red.
RH1 273 DH134
Chanctonbury Cl, SE9 207 EP90
Chanctonbury Gdns, Sutt.
SM2 240 DB108
Chanctonbury Way, N12 119 CZ49
Chandler Av, E16 23 N6
Chandler Cl, Hmptn. TW12 218 CA95
Chandler Ct, Th.Hth. CR7
off Bensham La 223 DP99
Chandler Rd, Loug. IG10 107 EP39
Chandlers Cl, Felt. TW14 197 BT87
Jct Chandlers Cor, Rain. RM13 170 FJ69
CHANDLERS CROSS,
Rick. WD3 96 BM38
Chandlers Dr, Erith DA8 189 FD77
Sch Chandlers Fld Prim Sch,
W.Mol. KT8 off High St 218 CA99
Chandler's La, Chan.Cr. WD3 96 BL37
Chandlers Ms, E14 34 A4
Greenhithe DA9 191 FW84
Chandlers Rd, St.Alb. AL4 65 CJ17
Chandler St, E1 32 F2
Chandlers Way, SW2 203 DN87
Hertford SG14 53 DN09
Romford RM1 149 FE57
Chandler Way, SE15 43 P3
Dorking RH5 285 CJ138
Chandon Lo, Sutt. SM2
off Devonshire Rd 240 DC108
Chandos Av, E17 123 EA54
N14 121 DJ48
N20 120 DC46
W5 179 CJ77
Chandos Cl, Amer. HP6 94 AW38
Buckhurst Hill IG9 124 EH47
Chandos Ct, N14 121 DK47
Stan. HA7 117 CH51
Chandos Cres, Edg. HA8 118 CM52
Chandos Gdns, Couls. CR5 257 DP119
Chandos Pl, WC2 30 A1
Chandos Rd, E15 12 G2
N2 120 DD54
N17 122 DS54
NW2 4 A3
NW10 160 CS70
Borehamwood WD6 100 CM40
Harrow HA1 138 CC57
Pinner HA5 138 BW59
Staines-upon-Thames TW18 195 BD92
Chandos St, W1 17 K7
Chandos Way, NW11 142 DB60
Change All, EC3 19 M9
Chanlock Path, S.Ock. RM15
off Carnach Grn 171 FV73
Channel Cl, Houns. TW5 178 CA81
Channel Gate Rd, NW10
off Old Oak La 161 CT69
Channel Ho, E14 21 L7
SE16 off Canada St 33 J5
Channel Islands Est, N1 9 K5
● Channelsea Ho Business Cen,
E15 23 H1
Channelsea Rd, E15 12 G8
Channing Cl, Horn. RM11 150 FM59
Channings, Horsell GU21 248 AY115
Sch Channing Sch for Girls, Jun Sch,
N6 off Highgate High St 143 DH60
Sen Sch, N6
off Highgate High St 143 DH60
Chantilly Way, Epsom KT19 238 CP110
Chanton Dr, Epsom KT17 239 CW110
Sutton SM2 239 CW110
Chantress Cl, Dag. RM10 169 FC67
Chantrey Cl, Ashtd. KT21 253 CJ119
Chantrey Rd, SW9 183 DM83
Chantreywood, Brwd. CM13 131 GA48
Chantries, The, Egh. TW20 195 BA92
Chantry, The, E4
off The Ridgeway 123 EC46
Harlow CM20 58 EU13
Uxbridge UB8 156 BM69
Chantry Cl, NW7
off Hendon Wd La 101 CT44
SE2 off Felixstowe Rd 188 EW76
W9 15 H5
Enfield EN2 104 DQ38
Harrow HA3 140 CM57
Horley RH6 290 DF147
Kings Langley WD4 80 BN29
Sidcup DA14
off Ellenborough Rd 208 EY92
Sunbury-on-Thames TW16 197 BU94
West Drayton UB7 156 BK73
Windsor SL4 173 AN81
Chantry Cotts, Chilw. GU4 281 BB140
Chantry Ct, Cars. SM5 222 DE104
Hatfield AL10 67 CT19
Chantry Cres, NW10 161 CT65
Chantry Ho, Rain. RM13
off Chantry Way 169 FD68
Chantry Hurst, Epsom KT18 254 CR115
Chantry La, Brom. BR2
off Bromley Common 226 EK99
Hatfield AL10 67 CT19
London Colney AL2 83 CK26
Shere GU5 282 BM139
Chantry Pl, Har. HA3 116 CB53
Sch Chantry Prim Sch, Grav.
DA12 off Ordnance Rd 213 GJ86
Chantry Rd, Cher. KT16 216 BJ101
Chessington KT9 238 CM106
Chilworth GU4 281 BB140
Harrow HA3 116 CB53
Sch Chantry Sch, The, Yiew.
UB7 off Falling La 156 BL73
Chantry Sq, W8
off St. Mary's Pl 27 L7
Chantry St, N1 9 H9
Chantry Vw Rd, Guil. GU1 280 AX137
Chantry Way, Mitch. CR4
off Church Rd 222 DD97
Chant Sq, E15 13 H7
Chant St, E15 13 H7
Chapel Av, Add. KT15 234 BH105
Chapel Cl, NW10 141 CT64
Brookmans Park AL9 86 DD27
Dartford DA1 209 FE85
Grays RM20 191 FV79
Watford WD25 81 BT34
Chapel Cotts, Hem.H. HP2 62 BK18
Chapel Ct, N2 142 DE55
SE1 31 L4
SE18 187 ET79
Dorking RH4 285 CG135
Chapel Cft, Chipper. WD4 80 BG31
Chapel Cfts, Nthch HP4 60 AS17
Chapel End, Chal.St.P. SL9 112 AX54
Hoddesdon EN11 71 EA18
Sch Chapel End Inf & Jun Schs,
E17 off Beresford Rd 123 EB53
Chapel Fm Rd, SE9 207 EM90
Chapel Fld, Harl. CM17 74 EW17
Chapelfields, Stans.Abb. SG12 55 ED10
Chapel Gate Ms, SW4
off Bedford Rd 183 DL83
Chapel Gro, Add. KT15 234 BH105
Epsom KT18 255 CW119
Chapel Hill, Dart. DA1 209 FE85
Effingham KT24
off The Street 268 BX127
Chapelhouse Cl, Guil. GU2 264 AS134
Chapel Ho St, E14 34 D10
Chapelier Ho, SW18
off Eastfields Av 182 DA84
Chapel La, Bkhm KT23 268 CC128
Chigwell IG7 125 ET48
Chapel La, Harlow CM17 74 EW17
Letty Green SG14 53 DH13
Pinner HA5 138 BX55
Romford RM6 148 EX59
Stoke Poges SL2 154 AV66
Uxbridge UB8 156 BN72
Westcott RH4 284 CC137
Westhumble RH5 269 CD130
Chapel Mkt, N1 8 E10
Chapel Ms, Wdf.Grn. IG8 125 EN51
Chapel Mill Rd, Kings.T. KT1 220 CM97
Chapelmount Rd, Wdf.Grn.
IG8 125 EM51
Chapel Pk Rd, Add. KT15 234 BH105
Chapel Path, E11 146 EG58
Chapel Pl, EC2 19 N3
N1 8 F10
N17 off White Hart La 122 DT52
W1 17 J9
St. Albans AL1 65 CD23
Chapel Rd, SE27 203 DP91
W13 159 CH74
Bexleyheath DA7 188 FA84
Epping CM16 91 ET30
Hounslow TW3 178 CB83
Ilford IG1 147 EN62
Oxted RH8 276 EJ130
Redhill RH1 272 DF134
Smallfield RH6 291 DP148
Tadworth KT20 255 CW123
Twickenham TW1 199 CH87
Warlingham CR6 259 DX118
Chapel Row, Hare. UB9 114 BJ53
Chapels Cl, Slou. SL1 153 AL74
Chapel Side, W2 15 L10
Chapel Sq, Vir.W. GU25 214 AY98
Chapel Stones, N17 122 DT53
Chapel St, NW1 16 C7
SW1 29 H6
Berkhamsted HP4 60 AW19
Enfield EN2 104 DQ41
Guildford GU1
off Castle St 280 AX136
Hemel Hempstead HP2 62 BK19
Slough SL1 174 AT75
Uxbridge UB8
off Trumper Way 156 BJ67
Woking GU21 249 AZ117
Chapel Ter, Loug. IG10
off Forest Rd 106 EL42
Chapel Vw, S.Croy. CR2 242 DV107
Chapel Wk, Croy. CR0
off Whitgift Cen 224 DQ103
Chapel Wk, NW4 141 CV56
Bexley DA5 209 FE89
Coulsdon CR5 257 DK122
Dartford DA2 209 FE89
Chapel Way, N7
off Sussex Way 143 DM62
Bedmond WD5 81 BT27
Epsom KT18 255 CW119
Chapel Yd, SW18
off Wandsworth High St 202 DA85
Chaplaincy Gdns,
Horn. RM11 150 FL60
Chaplin Cl, SE1 30 F4
Chaplin Ct, Sutt.H. DA4 210 FN93
Chaplin Cres, Sun. TW16 197 BS93
Chaplin Ms, Slou. SL3 175 AZ78
Chaplin Rd, E15 13 K10
N17 144 DT55
NW2 161 CU65
Dagenham RM9 168 EY66
Wembley HA0 159 CJ65
Chaplin Sq, N12 120 DD52
Chapman Cl, West Dr. UB7 176 BM76
Chapman Ct, Dart. DA1 190 FM82
Chapman Ctyd, Chsht EN8 89 DX30
Chapman Cres, Har. HA3 140 CL57
● Chapman Pk Ind Est,
NW10 161 CT65
Chapman Pl, N4 143 DP61
Chapman Rd, E9 11 P5
Belvedere DA17 188 FA78
Croydon CR0 223 DN102
Chapmans Cl, Sund. TN14 262 EY124
Chapmans Cres, Chesh. HP5 76 AN29
Chapman's La, SE2 188 EW77
Belvedere DA17 188 EX77
Chapmans La, Orp. BR5 228 EX96
Chapman Sq, SW19 201 CX89
Chapmans Rd, Sund. TN14 262 EY124
Chapman St, E1 20 E10
Chapone Pl, W1 17 N9
Chapter Chambers, SW1
off Chapter St 29 N9
Chapter Cl, W4 180 CQ76
Uxbridge UB10 156 BM66
Chapter Ct, Egh. TW20
off The Chantries 195 BA92
Chapter Ho Ct, EC4 19 J9
Chapter Ms, Wind. SL4 173 AR80
Chapter Rd, NW2 141 CU64
SE17 43 H1
Chapter St, SW1 29 N9
Chapter Way, SW19 222 DC95
Hampton TW12 198 CA91
Chara Pl, W4 180 CR79
Charcot Ho, SW15
off Highcliffe Dr 201 CT86
Charcot Rd, NW9 118 CS54
Charcroft Gdns, Enf. EN3 105 DX42
Chardin Rd, W4
off Elliott Rd 180 CS77
Chardins Cl, Hem.H. HP1 61 BF19
Chardmore Rd, N16 144 DU60
Chard Rd, Lon.Hthrw Air. TW6
off Heathrow Tunnel App 177 BP82
Chardwell Cl, E6 25 J8
Charecroft Way, W12 26 C5
W14 26 C5
Charfield Ct, W9 15 L5
Charford Rd, E16 23 P7
Chargate Cl, Hersham KT12 235 BT107
Chargeable La, E13 23 M4
Chargeable St, E16 23 M4
Chargrove Cl, SE16 33 K4
Charing Cl, Orp. BR6 245 ET105
⇌ Charing Cross 30 A2
⊖ Charing Cross 30 A2
Charing Cross, SW1 29 P2

H Charing Cross Hosp, W6 38 C2
Charing Cross Rd, WC2 17 P8
Chariot Cl, E3 12 A9
Chariotts Pl, Wind. SL4 off Victoria St 173 AR81
Charkham Ms, N.Mymms AL9 67 CW24
Charlbert St, NW8 6 C10
Charlbury Av, Stan. HA7 117 CK50
Charlbury Cl, Rom. RM3 128 FJ51
Charlbury Cres, Rom. RM3 128 FJ51
Charlbury Gdns, Ilf. IG3 147 ET61
Charlbury Gro, W5 159 CJ72
Charlbury Ho, E12 off Grantham Rd 147 EN62
Charlbury Rd, Uxb. UB10 136 BM62
Charlcot Ms, Slou. SL1 153 AL73
Charldane Rd, SE9 207 EP90
Charlecote Gro, SE26 204 DV90
Charlecote Rd, Dag. RM8 148 EY62
Charlemont Rd, E6 25 K4
Charles Babbage Cl, Chess. KT9 237 CJ108
Charles Barry Cl, SW4 41 M10
Charles Burton Ct, E5 11 L1
Charles Ch Wk, Ilf. IG1 147 EM58
Charles Cl, Sid. DA14 208 EV91
Charles Cobb Gdns, Croy. CR0 241 DN106
Charles Coveney Rd, SE15 44 A6
Charles Cres, Har. HA1 139 CD59
Sch Charles Darwin Sch, Bigg.H. TN16 off Jail La 261 EM116
Charles Dickens Ho, E2 20 E3
★ Charles Dickens Mus, WC1 18 D4
Sch Charles Dickens Prim Sch, SE1 31 J5
Charles Dickens Ter, SE20 off Maple Rd 204 DW94
Sch Charles Edward Brooke C of E Girls' Sch, Lwr Sch, SE5 42 G7
Upr Sch, SW9 43 H6
Charlesfield, SE9 206 EJ90
Charlesfield Rd, Horl. RH6 290 DF147
Charles Flemwell Ms, E16 35 P3
Charles Gdns, Slou. SL2 154 AV72
Charles Gardner Ct, N1 19 M2
Charles Grinling Wk, SE18 37 L8
Charles Gro, N14 121 DJ46
Charles Haller St, SW2 off Tulse Hill 203 DN87
Charles Hocking Ho, W3 off Bollo Br Rd 180 CQ75
Charles Ho, N17 off Love La 122 DT52
Chertsey KT16 off Guildford St 215 BF102
Windsor SL4 off Ward Royal 173 AQ81
Charles La, NW8 16 B1
Charles Mackenzie Ho, SE16 off Linsey St 32 C8
Charlesmere Gdns, SE28 off Battery Rd 187 ES75
Charles Nex Ms, SE21 204 DQ89
Charles Pl, E4 123 ED45
NW1 17 M3
Charles Rd, E7 off Lens Rd 166 EJ66
SW19 222 DA95
W13 159 CG72
Badgers Mount TN14 247 FB110
Dagenham RM10 169 FD65
Romford RM6 148 EX59
Staines-upon-Thames TW18 196 BK93
Charles Rowan Ho, WC1 18 E3
Charles II Pl, SW3 off King's Rd 40 E1
Charles II St, SW1 29 N2
Charles Sevright Dr, NW7 119 CX50
Charles Sq, N1 19 M3
Charles Sq Est, N1 19 M3
Charles St, SW13 180 CS82
W1 29 J2
Berkhamsted HP4 60 AV19
Chertsey KT16 215 BF102
Croydon CR0 224 DQ104
Enfield EN1 104 DT43
Epping CM16 92 EU32
Grays RM17 192 GB79
Greenhithe DA9 211 FT85
Hemel Hempstead HP1 62 BJ21
Hounslow TW3 178 BZ82
Uxbridge UB10 157 BP70
Windsor SL4 173 AQ81
Charleston Cl, Felt. TW13 197 BU90
Charleston St, SE17 31 K9
Charles Townsend Ho, EC1 18 F4
Charles Whincup Rd, E16 36 A2
Charlesworth Cl, Hem.H. HP3 62 BK22
Charlesworth Pl, SW13 off Eleanor Gro 181 CT83
Charleville Circ, SE26 204 DU92
Charleville Ms, Islw. TW7 off Railshead Rd 179 CH84
Charleville Rd, W14 38 F1
Jct Charlie Brown's Rbt, E18 124 EJ54
Charlie Chaplin Wk, SE1 off Waterloo Br 30 D3
Charlieville Rd, Erith DA8 off Northumberland Pk 189 FC80
Charlmont Rd, SW17 202 DF93
Charlock Way, Guil. GU1 265 BB131
Watford WD18 97 BT44
Charlotte Av, Slou. SL2 154 AT73
Charlotte Cl, Wat. WD19 116 BW45
Ashtd. KT21 254 CL118
Bexleyheath DA6 208 EY85
Ilford IG6 off Connor Cl 125 EQ53
St. Albans AL4 66 CL20
Charlotte Ct, N8 143 DK58
W6 off Invermead Cl 181 CU77
Esher KT10 236 CC106
Charlotte Despard Av, SW11 41 H7
Charlotte Gdns, Rom. RM5 127 FB51
Charlotte Gro, Smallfield RH6 291 DN147
Charlotte Ms, W1 17 M6
W10 14 C9
W14 26 E8
Rain. RM13 170 FJ68
Charlotte Pk Av, Brom. BR1 226 EL97
Charlotte Pl, NW9 off Uphill Dr 140 CQ57
SW1 29 L9
W1 17 M7
Charlotte Pl, Grays RM20 191 FV79
Charlotte Rd, EC2 19 N4
SW13 181 CT81
Dagenham RM10 169 FB65
Wallington SM6 241 DJ107
Charlotte Row, SW4 183 DJ83
Sch Charlotte Sharman Prim Sch, SE11 30 G7
Charlotte Sq, Rich. TW10 off Greville Rd 200 CM86
Charlotte St, W1 17 M6
Charlotte Ter, N1 8 D9
CHARLOTTEVILLE, Guil. GU1 280 AY137
Charlow Cl, SW6 39 N9
CHARLTON, SE7 186 EJ79
⇌ Charlton 36 B10
Charlton, Wind. SL4 172 AJ82
★ Charlton Athletic FC, SE7 36 D10
Charlton Av, Hersham KT12 235 BV105
Charlton Ch La, SE7 36 C10
Charlton Cl, Hodd. EN11 71 EA17
Slough SL1 173 AP75
Uxbridge UB10 137 BP61
Charlton Cres, Bark. IG11 167 ET68
Charlton Dene, SE7 186 EJ80
Charlton Dr, Bigg.H. TN16 260 EK117
Charlton Gdns, Couls. CR5 257 DJ118
● Charlton Gate, SE7 off Anchor And Hope La 36 C9
Charlton Kings, Wey. KT13 217 BS104
Charlton Kings Rd, NW5 7 N2
Charlton La, SE7 36 E10
Shepperton TW17 217 BS98
Sch Charlton Manor Prim Sch, SE7 off Indus Rd 186 EK80
Charlton Mead La, Hodd. EN11 71 EC18
Charlton Mead La S, Hodd. EN11 off Charlton Mead La 71 ED18
Charlton Pk La, SE7 186 EK80
Charlton Pk Rd, SE7 186 EK79
Charlton Pl, N1 8 G10
Windsor SL4 off Charlton 172 AJ82
Charlton Rd, N9 123 DX46
NW10 160 CS67
SE3 186 EG80
SE7 186 EH80
Harrow HA3 139 CK56
Shepperton TW17 217 BQ97
Wembley HA9 140 CM60
Charlton Row, Wind. SL4 off Charlton 172 AJ82
Sch Charlton Sch, SE7 off Charlton Pk Rd 186 EL79
Charlton Sq, Wind. SL4 off Charlton 172 AJ82
Charlton St, Grays RM20 191 FX79
Charlton Wk, Wind. SL4 off Charlton 172 AJ82
Charlton Way, SE3 47 J7
Hoddesdon EN11 71 EA17
Windsor SL4 172 AJ82
Charlwood, Croy. CR0 243 DZ109
Charlwood Cl, Bkhm KT23 252 CB124
Harrow HA3 off Kelvin Cres 117 CE51
Charlwood Dr, Oxshott KT22 253 CD115
Charlwood Ho, SW1 off Vauxhall Br Rd 29 N9
Richmond TW9 180 CP80
Charlwood Pl, SW1 29 M9
Reigate RH2 271 CZ134
Charlwood Rd, SW15 181 CX83
Horley RH6 290 DB152
Charlwood St, SW1 29 M9
Charlwood Ter, SW15 181 CX84
Charman Ho, SW8 off Hemans St 42 A4
Charman Rd, Red. RH1 272 DE134
Charm Cl, Horl. RH6 290 DE147
Charmian Av, Stan. HA7 139 CK55
Charminster Av, SW19 222 DA96
Charminster Ct, Surb. KT6 off Lovelace Gdns 219 CK101
Charminster Rd, SE9 206 EK91
Worcester Park KT4 221 CX102
Charmouth Ct, St.Alb. AL1 65 CG17
Charmouth Ho, SW8 off Dorset Rd 42 C4
Charmouth Rd, St.Alb. AL1 65 CG18
Welling DA16 188 EW81
Charmwood La, Orp. BR6 246 EV109
Charne, The, Otford TN14 263 FG117
Charnock, Swan. BR8 229 FE98
Charnock Rd, E5 144 DV62
Charnwood Av, SW19 222 DA96
Charnwood Cl, N.Mal. KT3 220 CS98
Charnwood Dr, E18 146 EH55
Charnwood Gdns, E14 34 B8
Charnwood Pl, N20 120 DC48
Charnwood Rd, SE25 224 DR99
Enfield EN1 104 DV36
Uxbridge UB10 156 BN68
Charnwood St, E5 144 DU61
Charrington Court Rom, Rom. RM1 149 FE58
Charrington Pl, St.Alb. AL1 65 CF21
Charrington Rd, Croy. CR0 off Drayton Rd 223 DP103
Charrington St, NW1 7 N10
Charsley Cl, Amer. HP6 94 AW39
Charsley Rd, SE6 205 EB89
Charta Rd, Egh. TW20 195 BC92
Chart Cl, Brom. BR2 226 EE95
Croydon CR0 224 DW100
Dorking RH5 285 CK138
Mitcham CR4 222 DF98
Chart Downs, Dor. RH5 285 CJ138
Charter Av, Ilf. IG2 147 ER60
Charter Cl, St.Alb. AL1 off Bricket Rd 65 CE20
Slough SL1 174 AT76
Charter Ct, N.Mal. KT3 220 CS97
Charter Cres, Houns. TW4 178 BY84
Charter Dr, Amer. HP6 94 AT38
Bexley DA5 208 EY87
★ Charterhouse, EC1 19 H5
Charterhouse Av, Wem. HA0 139 CJ63
Charterhouse Bldgs, EC1 19 H5
Charterhouse Dr, Sev. TN13 278 FG123
Charterhouse Ms, EC1 19 H6
Charterhouse Rd, E8 10 C1
Orpington BR6 228 EU104
Charterhouse Sq, EC1 19 H6
Sch Charterhouse Sq Sch, EC1 19 J6
Charterhouse St, EC1 18 F7
Charteris Rd, N4 143 DN60
NW6 5 H9
Woodford Green IG8 124 EH52
● Charter Pl, Uxb. UB8 156 BK66
Charter Pl, Wat. WD17 98 BW42
Charter Pl, Stai. TW18 196 BG93
Charter Rd, Kings.T. KT1 220 CP97
Slough SL1 153 AL73
Charter Rd, The, Wdf.Grn. IG8 124 EE51
Sch Charter Sch, The, SE24 off Red Post Hill 204 DR85
Charters Cl, SE19 204 DS92
Charters Cross, Harl. CM18 73 ER18
Charter Sq, Kings.T. KT1 220 CP96
Charter Way, N3 141 CZ56
N14 103 DJ44
Chartfield Av, SW15 201 CV85
Chartfield Pl, Wey. KT13 235 BP106
Chartfield Rd, Reig. RH2 288 DC135
Chartfield Sq, SW15 201 CX85
Chart Gdns, Dor. RH5 285 CJ139
Chartham Ct, SW9 183 DN83
Chartham Gro, SE27 off Royal Circ 203 DP90
Chartham Rd, SE25 224 DV97
Chart Hills Cl, SE28 off Fairway Dr 168 EY72
Chart La, Dor. RH4 285 CH136
Reigate RH2 272 DB134
Chart La S, Dor. RH5 285 CJ138
Chartley Av, NW2 140 CS62
Stanmore HA7 117 CF51
Charton Cl, Belv. DA17 188 EZ79
Chartridge Cl, Barn. EN5 101 CU43
Bushey WD23 98 CC44
Chartridge La, Chesh. HP5 76 AM29
Chartridge Way, Hem.H. HP2 63 BQ20
Chart St, N1 19 M2
Chartway, Reig. RH2 272 DB133
Sevenoaks TN13 279 FJ124
★ Chartwell, West. TN16 277 ET131
Chartwell Cl, SE9 207 EQ89
Croydon CR0 224 DR102
Greenford UB6 158 CB67
Waltham Abbey EN9 90 EE33
Chartwell Ct, NW2 141 CU62
Chartwell Dr, Orp. BR6 245 ER106
Chartwell Gdns, Sutt. SM3 239 CY105
Chartwell Gate, Beac. HP9 111 AK53
Chartwell Pl, Epsom KT18 238 CS114
Harrow HA2 139 CD61
Sutton SM3 239 CZ105
Chartwell Rd, Nthwd. HA6 115 BT51
Chartwell Way, SE20 224 DV95
Chartwood Pl, Dor. RH4 off South St 285 CG136
Charville La, Hayes UB4 157 BS68
Charville La W, Uxb. UB10 157 BP69
Sch Charville Prim Sch, Hayes UB4 off Bury Av 157 BS68
Charwood, SW16 203 DN91
Charwood Cl, Shenley WD7 84 CL33
Chasden Rd, Hem.H. HP1 61 BF17
Chase, The, E12 146 EK63
SW4 41 J10
SW16 203 DM94
SW20 221 CY95
Ashtead KT21 253 CJ118
Bexleyheath DA7 189 FB83
Brentwood (Cromwell Rd) CM14 130 FV49
Brentwood (Seven Arches Rd) CM14 130 FX48
Brentwood (Woodman Rd) CM14 130 FX50
Bromley BR1 226 EH97
Chadwell Heath RM6 148 EY58
Chesham HP5 76 AP29
Chigwell IG7 125 EQ49
Coulsdon CR5 241 DJ114
East Horsley KT24 267 BT126
Eastcote HA5 138 BW58
Edgware HA8 118 CP53
Goffs Oak EN7 87 DP28
Grays RM20 191 FX79
Great Amwell SG12 55 EA09
Guildford GU2 280 AU135
Harlow CM17 58 EW14
Hemel Hempstead HP2 off Turners Hill 62 BL21
Hornchurch RM12 149 FE62
Ingrave CM13 131 GC50
Kingswood KT20 256 DA122
Loughton IG10 124 EJ45
Oxshott KT22 252 CC115
Penn HP10 110 AC46
Pinner HA5 138 BZ56
Radlett WD7 99 CF35
Reigate RH2 288 DD135
Romford RM1 149 FE55
Rush Green RM7 149 FD62
Stanmore HA7 117 CG50
Sunbury-on-Thames TW16 217 BV95
Upminster RM14 151 FS62
Uxbridge UB10 136 BN64
Wallington SM6 241 DL106
Watford WD18 97 BS42
Wooburn Green HP10 132 AF59
Sch Chase Br Prim Sch, Twick. TW2 off Kneller Rd 199 CE86
Chase Cl, Colesh. HP7 77 AN43
Penn HP10 110 AC46
Chase Ct Gdns, Enf. EN2 104 DQ41
CHASE CROSS, Rom. RM1 127 FE51
Chase Cross Rd, Rom. RM5 127 FC52
Chase End, Epsom KT19 238 CR112
H Chase Fm Hosp, Enf. EN2 103 DN38
Chasefield Cl, Guil. GU4 265 BA131
Chasefield Rd, SW17 202 DF91
Chase Gdns, E4 123 EA49
Twickenham TW2 199 CD86
Chase Grn, Enf. EN2 104 DQ41
Pot.B. EN6 87 DL29
Chase Grn Av, Enf. EN2 103 DP40
Chase Hill, Enf. EN2 104 DQ41
Chase Ho Gdns, Horn. RM11 off Great Nelmes Chase 150 FM57
Chase La, Chig. IG7 126 EU48
Ilford IG6 147 ER57
Sch Chase La Prim Sch, E4 off York Rd 123 DZ50
Chaseley Dr, W4 180 CP78
South Croydon CR2 242 DR110
Chaseley St, E14 21 L9
Chasemore Cl, Mitch. CR4 222 DF101
Chasemore Gdns, Croy. CR0 241 DN106
Chase Ridings, Enf. EN2 103 DN40
Chase Rd, N14 103 DJ44
NW10 160 CR70
W3 160 CR70
Brentwood CM14 130 FW48
Epsom KT19 238 CR112
Chase Side, N14 102 DG44
Chase Side, Enfield EN2 104 DQ41
Chase Side Av, SW20 221 CY95
Enfield EN2 104 DQ40
Chaseside Cl, Rom. RM1 127 FE51
Chase Side Cres, Enf. EN2 104 DQ39
Chaseside Gdns, Cher. KT16 216 BH101
Chase Side Pl, Enf. EN2 off Chase Side 104 DQ40
Sch Chase Side Prim Sch, Enf. EN2 off Trinity St 104 DQ40
Chase Sq, Grav. DA11 off High St 213 GH86
Chaseville Par, N21 103 DM43
Chaseville Pk Rd, N21 103 DL43
Chase Way, N14 121 DH47
Chaseways, Saw. CM21 58 EW07
Chasewood Av, Enf. EN2 103 DP40
Chasewood Pk, Har. HA1 139 CE62
Chastilian Rd, Dart. DA1 209 FF87
Chaston Pl, NW5 off Grafton Ter 6 G3
Chatelet Cl, Horl. RH6 291 DH147
Chater Ho, E2 off Roman Rd 21 J2
Sch Chater Infants' Sch, Wat. WD18 off Southsea Av 97 BU42
Sch Chater Jun Sch, Wat. WD18 off Addiscombe Rd 97 BV42
Chatfield, Slou. SL2 153 AN71
Chatfield Ct, Cat. CR3 258 DR122
Chatfield Dr, Guil. GU4 265 BC132
Chatfield Rd, SW11 182 DC83
Croydon CR0 223 DP102
Chatham Av, Brom. BR2 226 EF101
Chatham Cl, NW11 142 DA57
SE18 37 P6
Sutton SM3 221 CZ101
Chatham Hill Rd, Sev. TN14 279 FJ121
Chatham Ms, Guil. GU2 264 AU131
Chatham Pl, E9 10 G4
Chatham Rd, E17 145 DY55
E18 off Grove Hill 124 EF54
SW11 202 DF86
Kingston upon Thames KT1 220 CN96
Orpington BR6 off Gladstone Rd 245 EQ106
Chatham St, SE17 31 L8
Chatham Way, Brwd. CM14 130 FW47
Chatsfield, Epsom KT17 239 CU110
Chatsfield Pl, W5 160 CL72
Chatsworth Av, NW4 119 CW54
SW20 221 CY95
Bromley BR1 206 EH91
Sidcup DA15 208 EU88
Wembley HA9 140 CM64
Chatsworth Cl, NW4 119 CW54
Borehamwood WD6 100 CN41
West Wickham BR4 226 EF103
Chatsworth Ct, W8 27 J8
Stanmore HA7 off Marsh La 117 CJ50
Chatsworth Cres, Houns. TW3 179 CD84
Chatsworth Dr, Enf. EN1 122 DU45
Chatsworth Est, E5 off Elderfield Rd 145 DX63
Chatsworth Gdns, W3 160 CP73
Harrow HA2 138 CB60
New Malden KT3 221 CT99
Sch Chatsworth Inf & Nurs Sch, Houns. TW3 off Heath Rd 178 CC84
Sch Chatsworth Inf Sch, Sid. DA15 off Burnt Oak La 208 EU88
Sch Chatsworth Jun Sch, Houns. TW3 off Heath Rd 178 CC84
Chatsworth Ms, Wat. WD24 97 BU38
Chatsworth Par, Petts Wd BR5 off Queensway 227 EQ99
Chatsworth Pl, Mitch. CR4 222 DF97
Oxshott KT22 237 CD112
Teddington TW11 199 CG91
Chatsworth Ri, W5 160 CM70
Chatsworth Rd, E5 144 DW62
E15 13 L3
NW2 4 E5
W4 180 CQ79
W5 160 CM70
Croydon CR0 242 DR105
Dartford DA1 210 FJ85
Hayes UB4 157 BV70
Sutton SM3 239 CX106
Chatsworth Way, SE27 203 DP90
Chatteris Av, Rom. RM3 128 FJ51
Chattern Hill, Ashf. TW15 197 BP91
Chattern Rd, Ashf. TW15 197 BQ91
Chatterton Ms, N4 off Chatterton Rd 143 DP62
Chatterton Rd, N4 143 DP62
Bromley BR2 226 EK98
Chatto Rd, SW11 202 DF85
Chaucer Av, Hayes UB4 157 BU71
Hounslow TW4 177 BV82
Richmond TW9 180 CN82
Weybridge KT13 234 BN108
Chaucer Cl, N11 121 DJ50
Banstead SM7 239 CY114
Berkhamsted HP4 60 AT18
Saint Albans AL1 65 CF18
Tilbury RM18 193 GJ82
Windsor SL4 173 AR83
Chaucer Ct, N16 9 N1
Guildford GU2 off Lawn Rd 280 AW137
Chaucer Dr, SE1 32 B9
Chaucer Gdns, Sutt. SM1 222 DA104
Chaucer Grn, Croy. CR0 224 DV101
Chaucer Gro, Borwd. WD6 100 CN42
Chaucer Ho, SW1 41 L1
Sutton SM1 222 DA104
Chaucer Pk, Dart. DA1 210 FM87
Chaucer Rd, E7 13 P5
E11 146 EG58
E17 123 EC54
SE24 203 DN85
W3 160 CQ74
Ashford TW15 196 BL91
Northfleet DA11 212 GD90
Romford RM3 127 FH52
Sidcup DA15 208 EW88
Sutton SM1 240 DA105
Welling DA16 187 ES81
Chaucer Way, SW19 202 DD93
Addlestone KT15 234 BG107
Dartford DA1 190 FN84
Hoddesdon EN11 55 EA13
Slough SL1 154 AT74
CHAULDEN, Hem.H. HP1 61 BE21
Chaulden Ho Gdns, Hem.H. HP1 61 BF21
Sch Chaulden Inf & Nurs Sch, Hem.H. HP1 off School Row 61 BF21
Sch Chaulden Jun Sch, Hem.H. HP1 off School Row 61 BF21
Chaulden La, Hem.H. HP1 61 BD22
Chaulden Ter, Hem.H. HP1 61 BF21
Chauncey Cl, N9 122 DU48
Chauncy Av, Pot.B. EN6 86 DC33
Chauncy Ct, Hert. SG14 off Bluecoats Av 54 DR09
Sch Chauncy Sch, The, Ware SG12 off Park Rd 54 DV05
Chaundrye Cl, SE9 207 EM86
Chauntler Cl, E16 24 B10
Chauntry Cl, Maid. SL6 152 AC73
Chavecroft Ter, Epsom KT18 255 CW119
Chave Rd, Dart. DA2 210 FL90
Chaville Way, N3 120 DA53
Chaworth Cl, Ott. KT16 233 BC107
Chaworth Rd, Ott. KT16 233 BC107
CHEAM, Sutt. SM3 239 CX107
⇌ Cheam 239 CY108
Cheam Cl, Tad. KT20 off Waterfield 255 CW121
Sch Cheam Common Infants' Sch, Wor.Pk. KT4 off Balmoral Rd 221 CV103
Sch Cheam Common Jun Sch, Wor.Pk. KT4 off Kingsmead Av 221 CV103
Cheam Common Rd, Wor.Pk. KT4 221 CV103
Sch Cheam Flds Prim Sch, Cheam SM3 off Stoughton Av 239 CY106
Sch Cheam High Sch, Cheam SM3 off Chatsworth Rd 239 CY105
Cheam Mans, Sutt. SM3 239 CY108
Sch Cheam Pk Fm Infants' Sch, Sutt. SM3 off Molesey Dr 221 CY104
Sch Cheam Pk Fm Jun Sch, Sutt. SM3 off Kingston Av 221 CY104
Cheam Pk Way, Sutt. SM3 239 CY107
Cheam Rd, E.Ewell SM2 239 CX110
Epsom KT17 239 CU109
Sutton SM1 239 CZ107
Cheam St, SE15 44 F10
Jct Cheam Village, Sutt. SM3 239 CY107
Cheapside, EC2 19 K9
N13 off Taplow Rd 122 DQ49
Woking GU21 232 AX114
Cheapside La, Denh. UB9 135 BF61
Chearsley, SE17 off Deacon Way 31 K8
Chedburgh, Welw.G.C. AL7 52 DD08
Cheddar Cl, N11 120 DF51
Cheddar Rd, Lon.Hthrw Air. TW6 off Cromer Rd 176 BN82
Cheddar Waye, Hayes UB4 157 BV72
Cheddington Rd, N18 122 DS48
Chedworth Cl, E16 23 L8
Cheelson Rd, S.Ock. RM15 171 FW68
Cheeseman Cl, Hmptn. TW12 198 BY93
Cheesemans Ter, W14 38 G1
Cheffins Rd, Hodd. EN11 55 DZ14
Cheldon Av, NW7 119 CX52
Chelford Rd, Brom. BR1 205 ED92
Chelmer Cres, Bark. IG11 168 EV68
Chelmer Dr, Hutt. CM13 131 GE44
South Ockendon RM15 171 FW73
Chelmer Rd, E9 11 K2
Grays RM16 193 GG78
Upminster RM14 151 FR58
Chelmsford Av, Rom. RM5 127 FD52
Chelmsford Cl, E6 25 J9
W6 38 D2
Sutton SM2 240 DA109
Chelmsford Dr, Upmin. RM14 150 FM62
Chelmsford Gdns, Ilf. IG1 146 EL59
Chelmsford Rd, E11 145 ED60
E17 145 EA58
E18 124 EF53
N14 121 DJ45
Hatfield Heath CM22 59 FH05
Hertford SG14 53 DN10
Shenfield CM15 131 FZ44
Chelmsford Sq, NW10 4 A9
CHELSEA, SW3 40 A2
Sch Chelsea Acad, SW10 39 P5
H Chelsea & Westminster Hosp, SW10 39 P3
★ Chelsea Antique Mkt, SW3 40 B2
Chelsea Br, SW1 41 J2
SW8 41 J2
Chelsea Br Rd, SW1 28 G10
Chelsea Cloisters, SW3 28 D9
Chelsea Cl, NW10 off Winchelsea Rd 160 CR67
Edgware HA8 118 CN54
Hampton Hill TW12 198 CC93
Worcester Park KT4 221 CU101
Uni Chelsea Coll of Art & Design, SW1 30 A10
Chelsea Cres, SW10 39 P7
Chelsea Embk, SW3 40 D3
Chelsea Flds, Hodd. EN11 55 EB13
★ Chelsea FC, SW6 39 L4
Chelsea Gdns, SW1 off Chelsea Br Rd 41 H1
W13 off Hathaway Gdns 159 CF71
Harlow CM17 74 EY16
Sutton SM3 239 CY105
Chelsea Harbour, SW10 39 P7
● Chelsea Harbour Design Cen, SW10 off Harbour Av 39 P6
Chelsea Harbour Dr, SW10 39 P6
Riv Chelsea Harbour Pier 40 A7
Chelsea Manor Ct, SW3 40 D2
Chelsea Manor Gdns, SW3 40 D2
Chelsea Manor St, SW3 40 C1
Chelsea Ms, E11 146 EG58
Horn. RM11 off St. Leonards Way 149 FH60
Chelsea Pk Gdns, SW3 40 A2
★ Chelsea Physic Gdn, SW3 40 E2
Chelsea Reach Twr, SW10 40 A4
Chelsea Sq, SW3 28 B10
Chelsea Twrs, SW3 40 D1
Chelsea Village, SW6 39 M4
Chelsea Vista, SW6 39 P7
Chelsea Way, Brwd. CM14 130 FW46
Chelsea Wf, SW10 40 A5
CHELSFIELD, Orp. BR6 246 EW106
⇌ Chelsfield 246 EV106
Chelsfield Av, N9 123 DX45
Chelsfield Gdns, SE26 204 DW90
Chelsfield Grn, N9 off Chelsfield Av 123 DX45
Chelsfield Hill, Orp. BR6 246 EW109
Chelsfield La, Maypole BR6 246 FA108
Orpington BR5, BR6 228 EX101
Sevenoaks TN14 247 FC109
H Chelsfield Pk Hosp, Chels. BR6 246 EZ106

Sch **Chelsfield Prim Sch**, Chels. BR6 *off Warren Rd* 246 EY106
Chelsfield Rd, Orp. BR5 228 EW100
CHELSHAM, Warl. CR6 259 EA117
Chelsham Cl, Warl. CR6 259 DY118
Chelsham Common, Warl. CR6 259 EA116
Chelsham Common Rd, Warl. CR6 259 EA117
Chelsham Ct Rd, Warl. CR6 259 ED118
Chelsham Rd, SW4 41 P10
South Croydon CR2 242 DR107
Warlingham CR6 259 EA117
Chelsing Ri, Hem.H. HP2 63 BQ21
Chelston App, Ruis. HA4 137 BU61
Chelston Rd, Ruis. HA4 137 BU60
Chelsworth Cl, Rom. RM3 *off Chelsworth Dr* 128 FM53
Chelsworth Dr, SE18 187 ER79
Romford RM3 128 FL52
Cheltenham Av, Twick. TW1 199 CG87
Cheltenham Cl, Grav. DA12 213 GJ92
New Malden KT3 *off Northcote Rd* 220 CQ97
Northolt UB5 158 CB65
Cheltenham Gdns, E6 24 G1
Loughton IG10 106 EL44
Cheltenham Pl, W3 160 CP74
Harrow HA3 140 CL56
Cheltenham Rd, E10 145 EC58
SE15 184 DW84
Orpington BR6 228 EU104
Cheltenham Ter, SW3 28 F10
Cheltenham Vil, Stai. TW19 195 BF86
Chelverton Rd, SW15 181 CX84
Chelveston, Welw.G.C. AL7 52 DD08
Chelwood, N20 *off Oakleigh Rd N* 120 DD47
Chelwood Av, Hat. AL10 67 CU16
Chelwood Cl, E4 105 EB44
Coulsdon CR5 257 DJ119
Epsom KT17 239 CT112
Northwood HA6 115 BQ52
Chelwood Gdns, Rich. TW9 180 CN82
Chelwood Gdns Pas, Rich. TW9 *off Chelwood Gdns* 180 CN82
Chelwood Wk, SE4 185 DY84
Chenappa Cl, E13 23 M3
Chenduit Way, Stan. HA7 117 CF50
Chene Dr, St.Alb. AL3 65 CD18
Chene Ms, St.Alb. AL3 65 CD18
Cheney Row, E17 123 DZ53
Cheneys Rd, E11 146 EE62
Cheney St, Pnr. HA5 138 BW57
CHENIES, Rick. WD3 95 BB38
Chenies, The, Dart. DA2 209 FE91
Petts Wood BR6 227 ES100
Chenies Av, Amer. HP6 94 AW39
Chenies Bottom, Chenies WD3 95 BA37
Chenies Ct, Hem.H. HP2 *off Datchet Cl* 63 BP15
Chenies Hill, Flaun. HP3 79 BB34
★ **Chenies Manor**, Rick. WD3 95 BA38
Chenies Ms, WC1 17 N5
Chenies Par, Amer. HP7 94 AW40
Chenies Pl, NW1 7 N10
Barn. EN5 101 CU43
Chenies Rd, Chorl. WD3 95 BD40
Sch **Chenies Sch**, Chenies WD3 *off Latimer Rd* 95 BB38
Chenies St, WC1 17 N6
Chenies Way, Wat. WD18 115 BS45
Cheniston Cl, W.Byf. KT14 234 BG113
Cheniston Gdns, W8 27 L6
Chennells, Hat. AL10 67 CT19
Sch **Chennestone Prim Sch**, Sun. TW16 *off Manor La* 217 BV96
Chepstow Av, Horn. RM12 150 FL62
Chepstow Cl, SW15 201 CY86
Chepstow Cres, W11 15 J10
Ilford IG3 147 ES58
Chepstow Gdns, Sthl. UB1 158 BZ72
Chepstow Pl, W2 15 K10
Chepstow Ri, Croy. CR0 224 DS104
Chepstow Rd, W2 15 K8
W7 179 CG76
Croydon CR0 224 DS104
Chepstow Vil, W11 15 H10
Chequers, Buck.H. IG9 124 EH46
Hatfield AL9 51 CX13
Welwyn Garden City AL7 51 CX11
Chequers Cl, NW9 140 CS55
Horley RH6 290 DG147
Orpington BR5 227 ET98
Walton on the Hill KT20 271 CU125
Chequers Dr, Horl. RH6 290 DG147
Chequers Fld, Welw.G.C. AL7 51 CX12
Chequers Gdns, N13 121 DP50
Chequers Hill, Amer. HP7 77 AR40
Chequers La, Dag. RM9 168 EZ70
Walton on the Hill KT20 271 CU125
Watford WD25 82 BW30
Chequers Orchard, Iver SL0 155 BF72
Chequers Par, SE9 *off Eltham High St* 207 EM86
Chequers Pl, Dor. RH4 285 CH136
Chequers Rd, Brwd. CM14 128 FM46
Loughton IG10 107 EN43
Romford RM3 128 FL47
🔒 **Chequers Sq**, Uxb. UB8 *off The Mall Pavilions* 156 BJ66
Chequer St, EC1 19 K5
St. Albans AL1 65 CD20
Chequers Wk, Wal.Abb. EN9 90 EF33
Chequers Way, N13 122 DQ50
Chequers Yd, Dor. RH4 *off Chequers Pl* 285 CH136
Chequer Tree Cl, Knap. GU21 248 AS116
Cherbury Cl, SE28 168 EX72
Cherbury Ct, N1 19 M1
Cherbury St, N1 19 M1
Cherchefelle Ms, Stan. HA7 117 CH50
Cherimoya Gdns, W.Mol. KT8 *off Kelvinbrook* 218 CB97
Cherington Rd, W7 159 CF74
Cheriton Av, Brom. BR2 226 EF99
Ilford IG5 125 EM54
Cheriton Cl, W5 159 CJ71
Barnet EN4 102 DF41
St. Albans AL4 65 CK16
Cheriton Ct, Walt. KT12 218 BW102
Cheriton Dr, SE18 187 ER80
Cheriton Ho, E5 *off Pembury Rd* 10 E2
Cheriton Lo, Ruis. HA4 *off Pembroke Rd* 137 BT60
Cheriton Sq, SW17 202 DG89
Cherkley Hill, Lthd. KT22 269 CJ126
Cherries, The, Slou. SL2 154 AV72
Cherry Acre, Chal.St.P. SL9 112 AX49
Cherry Av, Brwd. CM13 131 FZ48
Slough SL3 174 AX75
Southall UB1 158 BX74
Swanley BR8 229 FD97
Cherry Blossom Cl, N13 121 DP50
Harlow CM17 58 EW11
Cherry Bounce, Hem.H. HP1 62 BK18
Cherry Cl, E17 145 EB57
NW9 119 CT54
SW2 203 DN87
W5 179 CK76
Banstead SM7 239 CX114
Carshalton SM5 222 DF103
Morden SM4 221 CY98
Ruislip HA4 137 BT62
Cherrycot Hill, Orp. BR6 245 ER105
Cherrycot Ri, Orp. BR6 245 EQ105
Cherry Cres, Brent. TW8 179 CH80
Cherry Cft, Crox.Grn WD3 96 BN44
Welwyn Garden City AL8 51 CX05
Cherrycroft Gdns, Pnr. HA5 *off Westfield Pk* 116 BZ52
Cherrydale, Wat. WD18 97 BT42
Cherrydown Av, E4 123 DZ48
Cherrydown Cl, E4 123 DZ48
Cherrydown Rd, Sid. DA14 208 EX89
Cherrydown Wk, Rom. RM7 127 FB54
Cherry Dr, Forty Grn HP9 110 AH51
Cherry Gdns, Dag. RM9 148 EZ64
Northolt UB5 158 CB66
Sch **Cherry Gdn Sch**, SE16 32 D8
Cherry Gdn St, SE16 32 E5
Cherry Garth, Brent. TW8 179 CK77
Cherry Grn Cl, Red. RH1 289 DH136
Cherry Gro, Hayes UB3 157 BV74
Uxbridge UB8 157 BP71
Cherry Hill, Har. HA3 117 CE51
Loudwater WD3 96 BH41
New Barnet EN5 102 DB44
St. Albans AL2 82 CA25
Cherry Hill Gdns, Croy. CR0 241 DM105
Cherry Hills, Wat. WD19 116 BY50
Cherry Hollow, Abb.L. WD5 81 BT31
Cherrylands Cl, NW9 140 CQ61
Cherry La, Amer. HP7 77 AN40
West Drayton UB7 176 BM77
Sch **Cherry La Prim Sch**, West Dr. UB7 *off Sipson Rd* 176 BM77
Jct **Cherry La Rbt**, West Dr. UB7 177 BP77
Cherry Laurel Wk, SW2 *off Beechdale Rd* 203 DM86
Cherry Orchard, SE7 *off Charlton Rd* 186 EJ79
Amer. HP6 77 AS37
Ashtead KT21 254 CP118
Hemel Hempstead HP1 62 BG18
Staines-upon-Thames TW18 196 BG92
Stoke Poges SL2 154 AV66
West Drayton UB7 176 BL75
Cherry Orchard Cl, Orp. BR5 228 EW99
Cherry Orchard Est, SE7 186 EJ80
Cherry Orchard Gdns, Croy. CR0 *off Oval Rd* 224 DR103
West Molesey KT8 218 BZ97
Sch **Cherry Orchard Prim Sch**, SE7 *off Rectory Fld Cres* 186 EJ80
Cherry Orchard Rd, Brom. BR2 226 EL103
Croydon CR0 224 DR103
West Molesey KT8 218 CA97
Cherry Ri, Ch.St.G. HP8 112 AX47
Cherry Rd, Enf. EN3 104 DW38
Cherry St, Rom. RM7 149 FD57
Woking GU21 248 AY118
Cherry Tree Av, Guil. GU2 264 AT134
London Colney AL2 83 CK26
Staines-upon-Thames TW18 196 BH93
West Drayton UB7 156 BM72
Cherry Tree Cl, E9 11 H8
Grays RM17 192 GC79
Rainham RM13 169 FG68
Wembley HA0 139 CG63
Cherry Tree Ct, NW9 *off Boakes Cl* 140 CQ56
SE7 *off Fairlawn* 186 EJ79
Coulsdon CR5 257 DM118
Cherry Tree Dr, SW16 203 DL90
South Ockendon RM15 171 FX70
Cherry Tree Grn, Hert. SG14 53 DM07
South Croydon CR2 242 DV114
Cherrytree La, Chal.St.P. SL9 112 AX54
Cherry Tree La, Dart. DA2 209 FF90
Epsom KT19 *off Christ Ch Rd* 238 CN112
Fulmer SL3 155 AZ65
Harlow CM20 57 EP14
Hemel Hempstead HP2 63 BQ17
Heronsgate WD3 113 BC46
Iver SL0 156 BG67
Potters Bar EN6 86 DB34
Rainham RM13 169 FE69
Cherry Tree Ms, Hodd. EN11 *off Cherry Tree Rd* 71 EA16
Sch **Cherry Tree Prim Sch**, Wat. WD24 *off Berry Av* 97 BU36
Cherry Tree Ri, Buck.H. IG9 124 EJ49
Cherry Tree Rd, E15 13 J2
N2 142 DF56
Beaconsfield HP9 110 AH54
Farnham Royal SL2 153 AQ66
Hoddesdon EN11 71 EA16
Watford WD24 97 BV36
Cherrytrees, Couls. CR5 257 DK121
Sch **Cherry Trees Sch, The**, E3 22 B3
Cherry Tree Wk, EC1 19 K5
Beckenham BR3 225 DZ98
Chesham HP5 76 AR29
West Wickham BR4 244 EF105
Cherry Tree Way, E13 24 E4
Penn HP10 110 AC46
Stanmore HA7 117 CH51
Cherry Wk, Brom. BR2 226 EG102
Grays RM16 193 GG76
Kew. TW9 180 CM81
Loudwater WD3 96 BJ40
Rainham RM13 169 FF68
Cherry Way, Epsom KT19 238 CR107
Hatfield AL10 67 CU21
Horton SL3 175 BC83
Shepperton TW17 217 BR98
Cherrywood Av, Eng.Grn TW20 194 AV93
Cherrywood Cl, E3 21 M2
Kingston upon Thames KT2 200 CN94
Cherry Wd Cl, Seer Grn HP9 111 AR50
Cherrywood Dr, SW15 201 CX85
Northfleet DA11 212 GE90
Cherrywood La, Mord. SM4 221 CY98
Cherrywood Lo, SE13 *off Oakwood Cl* 205 ED86
Cherry Wd Way, W5 *off Hanger Vale La* 160 CN71
Cherston Gdns, Loug. IG10 107 EN42
Cherston Rd, Loug. IG10 107 EN42
CHERTSEY, KT16 216 BG102
⇌ **Chertsey** 215 BF102
Chertsey Br Rd, Cher. KT16 216 BK101
Chertsey Cl, Ken. CR8 257 DP115
Chertsey Cres, New Adgtn CR0 243 EC110
Chertsey Dr, Sutt. SM3 221 CY103
Chertsey La, Cher. KT16 215 BE95
Epsom KT19 238 CN112
Staines-upon-Thames TW18 195 BE92
Chertsey Meads, Cher. KT16 216 BK102
★ **Chertsey Mus**, Cher. KT16 *off Windsor St* 216 BG100
Chertsey Rd, E11 145 ED61
Addlestone KT15 216 BH103
Ashford TW15 197 BR94
Byfleet KT14 234 BK111
Chobham GU24 232 AY110
Feltham TW13 197 BS92
Ilford IG1 147 ER63
Shepperton TW17 216 BN101
Sunbury-on-Thames TW16 197 BR94
Twickenham TW1, TW2 199 CF86
Woking GU21 233 BA113
Chertsey St, SW17 202 DG92
Guildford GU1 280 AX135
Cherubs, The, Farn.Com. SL2 153 AQ65
Chervil Cl, Felt. TW13 197 BU90
Chervil Ms, SE28 168 EV74
Cherwell Cl, Crox.Grn WD3 96 BN43
Slough SL3 *off Tweed Rd* 175 BB79
Cherwell Ct, Epsom KT19 238 CQ105
Teddington TW11 199 CK94
Cherwell Gro, S.Ock. RM15 171 FV73
Cherwell Ho, NW8 *off Church St Est* 16 B5
Cherwell Way, Ruis. HA4 137 BQ58
Cheryls Cl, SW6 39 M6
Cheselden Rd, Guil. GU1 280 AY135
Cheseman St, SE26 204 DV90
Chesfield Rd, Kings.T. KT2 200 CL94
CHESHAM, HP5 76 AQ31
⊖ **Chesham** 76 AQ31
Chesham Av, Petts Wd BR5 227 EP100
CHESHAM BOIS, Amer. HP6 77 AQ36
Sch **Chesham Bois C of E Comb Sch**, Amer. HP6 *off Bois La* 77 AS35
Chesham Cl, SW1 28 G7
Romford RM7 149 FD56
Sutton SM2 239 CY110
Chesham Ct, Nthwd. HA6 *off Frithwood Av* 115 BT51
Chesham Cres, SE20 224 DW96
Sch **Chesham High Sch**, Chesh. HP5 *off White Hill* 76 AR30
H **Chesham Hosp**, Chesh. HP5 76 AQ32
Chesham La, Ch.St.G. HP8 112 AY48
Chalfont St. Peter SL9 112 AY49
Chesham Ms, SW1 28 G6
Guildford GU1 *off Chesham Rd* 281 AZ135
Sch **Chesham Pk Comm Coll**, Chesh. HP5 *off Chartridge La* 76 AN30
Chesham Pl, SW1 28 G7
Sch **Chesham Prep Sch**, Chesh. HP5 *off Orchard Leigh* 78 AU27
Chesham Rd, SE20 224 DW96
SW19 202 DD92
Amersham HP6 77 AQ38
Ashley Green HP5 60 AT24
Berkhamsted HP4 60 AV21
Bovingdon HP3 78 AY27
Guildford GU1 280 AY135
Kingston upon Thames KT1 220 CN95
Chesham St, NW10 140 CR62
SW1 28 G7
Chesham Ter, W13 179 CH75
Chesham Way, Wat. WD18 97 BS44
Cheshire Cl, E17 123 EB53
SE4 45 N8
Hornchurch RM11 150 FN57
Mitcham CR4 223 DL97
Ottershaw KT16 233 BC107
Cheshire Ct, EC4 18 F9
Slough SL1 *off Sussex Pl* 174 AV75
Cheshire Dr, Lvsdn WD25 81 BT34
Cheshire Gdns, Chess. KT9 237 CK107
Cheshire Ho, N18 122 DV49
Cheshire Rd, N22 121 DM52
Cheshire St, E2 20 B4
Chesholm Rd, N16 144 DS62
CHESHUNT, Wal.Cr. EN8 89 DX31
⇌ **Cheshunt** 89 DZ30
H **Cheshunt Comm Hosp**, Chsht EN8 89 DY31
Cheshunt Pk, Chsht EN7 88 DV26
Cheshunt Rd, E7 166 EH65
Belvedere DA17 188 FA78
Sch **Cheshunt Sch**, Chsht EN8 *off College Rd* 88 DW30
Cheshunt Wash, Chsht EN8 89 DY27
Chesil Ct, E2 10 G10
Chesilton Rd, SW6 38 G6
Chesil Way, Hayes UB4 157 BT69
Chesley Gdns, E6 24 F1
Chesney Cres, New Adgtn CR0 243 EC108
Chesney St, SW11 40 G7
Chesnut Est, N17 144 DT55
Chesnut Gro, N17 144 DT55
Chesnut Rd, N17 144 DT55
Chessbury Cl, Chesh. HP5 *off Missenden Rd* 76 AP32
Chessbury Rd, Chesh. HP5 76 AN32
● **Chess Business Pk**, Chesh. HP5 76 AQ33
Chess Cl, Latimer HP5 94 AX36
Loudwater WD3 96 BK42
Chessell Cl, Th.Hth. CR7 223 DP98
Chessfield Pk, Amer. HP6 94 AY39
Chess Hill, Loud. WD3 96 BK42
Chessholme Ct, Sun. TW16 197 BS94
Chessholme Rd, Ashf. TW15 197 BQ93
CHESSINGTON, KT9 238 CL107
Chessington Av, N3 141 CY55
Bexleyheath DA7 188 EY80
Chessington Cl, Epsom KT19 238 CQ107
Sch **Chessington Comm Coll**, Chess. KT9 *off Garrison La* 237 CK108
Chessington Ct, N3 *off Charter Way* 141 CZ55
Pinner HA5 138 BZ56
Chessington Hall Gdns, Chess. KT9 237 CK108
Chessington Hill Pk, Chess. KT9 238 CN106
Chessington Lo, N3 141 CZ55
Chessington Mans, E10 *off Albany Rd* 145 EA59
⇌ **Chessington North** 238 CL106
Chessington Rd, Epsom KT17, KT19 239 CT109
⇌ **Chessington South** 237 CK108
● **Chessington Trade Pk**, Chess. KT9 238 CN105
Chessington Way, W.Wick. BR4 225 EB103
★ **Chessington World of Adventures**, Chess. KT9 237 CJ110
Chess La, Loud. WD3 96 BK42
CHESSMOUNT, Chesh. HP5 76 AR33
Chessmount Ri, Chesh. HP5 76 AR33
Chesson Rd, W14 38 G2
Chess Vale Ri, Crox.Grn WD3 96 BM44
Chess Valley Wk, Chesh. HP5 94 AU35
Rickmansworth WD3 96 BL44
Chess Way, Chorl. WD3 96 BG41
Chesswood Way, Pnr. HA5 116 BX54
Chester Av, Rich. TW10 200 CM86
Twickenham TW2 198 BZ88
Upminster RM14 151 FS61
Chester Cl, SW1 29 H5
SW13 181 CV83
Ashford TW15 197 BR92
Chafford Hundred RM16 192 FY76
Dorking RH4 269 CJ134
Guildford GU2 264 AT132
Loughton IG10 107 EQ39
Potters Bar EN6 86 DB29
Richmond TW10 200 CM86
Sutton SM1 222 DA103
Uxbridge UB8 157 BP72
Chester Cl N, NW1 17 K2
Chester Cl S, NW1 17 K3
Chester Cotts, SW1 28 G9
Chester Ct, NW1 *off Albany St* 17 K3
SE5 43 L5
Chester Cres, E8 10 B3
Chester Dr, Har. HA2 138 BZ58
Chesterfield Cl, Orp. BR5 228 EX98
Chesterfield Dr, Dart. DA1 209 FH85
Esher KT10 219 CG103
Sevenoaks TN13 278 FD122
Chesterfield Gdns, N4 143 DP57
SE10 46 G5
W1 29 J2
Chesterfield Gro, SE22 204 DT85
Chesterfield Hill, W1 29 J1
Chesterfield Ms, N4 143 DP57
Ashford TW15 196 BL91
Chesterfield Rd, E10 145 EC58
N3 120 DA51
W4 180 CQ79
Ashford TW15 196 BL91
Barnet EN5 101 CX43
Enfield EN3 105 DY37
Epsom KT19 238 CR108
Sch **Chesterfield Sch**, Enf. EN3 *off Chesterfield Rd* 105 DY37
Chesterfield St, W1 29 J2
Chesterfield Wk, SE10 47 H6
Chesterfield Way, SE15 44 G5
Hayes UB3 177 BU75
Chesterford Gdns, NW3 5 M1
Chesterford Ho, SE18 *off Shooters Hill Rd* 186 EK81
Chesterford Rd, E12 147 EM64
Chester Gdns, W13 159 CH72
Enfield EN3 104 DV44
Morden SM4 222 DC100
Chester Gate, NW1 17 J3
Chester Gibbons Grn, Lon.Col. AL2 83 CK26
Chester Grn, Loug. IG10 107 EQ39
Chester Ms, E17 *off Chingford Rd* 123 EA54
SW1 29 J6
Chester Path, Loug. IG10 107 EQ39
Chester Pl, NW1 17 J2
Chester Rd, E7 166 EK66
E11 146 EH58
E16 23 K5
E17 145 DX57
N9 122 DV46
N17 144 DR55
N19 143 DH61
NW1 17 H3
SW19 201 CW93
Borehamwood WD6 100 CQ41
Chigwell IG7 125 EN48
Effingham KT24 267 BV128
Hounslow TW4 177 BV83
Ilford IG3 147 ET60
London Heathrow Airport TW6 176 BN83
Loughton IG10 107 EP40
Northwood HA6 115 BS52
Sidcup DA15 207 ES85
Slough SL1 153 AR72
Watford WD18 97 BU43
Chester Row, SW1 28 G9
Chesters, Horl. RH6 290 DE146
Chesters, The, N.Mal. KT3 220 CS95
Chester Sq, SW1 29 J8
Chester Sq Ms, SW1 29 J7
Chester St, E2 20 D4
SW1 29 H6
Chester Ter, NW1 17 J2
Chesterton Cl, SW18 202 DA85
Chesham HP5 *off Milton Rd* 76 AP29
Greenford UB6 158 CB68
Chesterton Dr, Merst. RH1 273 DL128
Staines-upon-Thames TW19 196 BM88
Chesterton Grn, Beac. HP9 111 AL52
Chesterton Ho, SW11 *off Ingrave St* 40 B10
Sch **Chesterton Prim Sch**, SW11 40 G7
Chesterton Rd, E13 23 P2
W10 14 D7
Chesterton Sq, W8 27 H8
Chesterton Ter, E13 23 N2
Kingston upon Thames KT1 220 CN96
Chesterton Way, Til. RM18 193 GJ82
Chester Way, SE11 30 F9
Chesthunte Rd, N17 122 DQ53
Chestnut All, SW6 39 H3
Chestnut Av, E7 146 EH63
N8 143 DL57
SW14 *off Thornton Rd* 180 CR83
SW17 203 DJ90
Bluewater DA9 211 FT87
Brentford TW8 179 CK77
Brentwood CM14 130 FS45
Chestnut Av, Buckhurst Hill IG9 124 EK48
Chesham HP5 76 AR29
East Molesey KT8 219 CF97
Edgware HA8 118 CL51
Epsom KT19 238 CS105
Esher KT10 219 CD101
Grays RM16 192 GB75
Guildford GU2 280 AW138
Hampton TW12 198 CA94
Hornchurch RM12 149 FF61
Northwood HA6 115 BT54
Rickmansworth WD3 96 BG43
Slough SL3 174 AY75
Teddington TW11 219 CF96
Virginia Water GU25 214 AT98
Wembley HA0 139 CH64
West Drayton UB7 156 BM73
West Wickham BR4 244 EE106
Westerham TN16 260 EK122
Weybridge KT13 235 BQ108
Whiteley Village KT12 235 BS109
Chestnut Av N, E17 145 EC56
Chestnut Av S, E17 145 EC56
Chestnut Cl, N14 103 DJ43
N16 144 DR61
SE6 205 EC92
SE14 45 N6
SW16 203 DN91
Addlestone KT15 234 BK106
Amersham HP6 77 AR37
Ashford TW15 197 BP91
Buckhurst Hill IG9 124 EK48
Carshalton SM5 222 DF102
Chalfont St. Peter SL9 113 AZ52
Englefield Green TW20 194 AW93
Hayes UB3 157 BS73
Hornchurch RM12 *off Lancaster Dr* 150 FJ63
Hunsdon SG12 56 EK06
Kingswood KT20 256 DA123
Northfleet DA11 *off Burch Rd* 213 GF86
Orpington BR6 246 EU106
Potten End HP4 61 BB17
Redhill RH1 *off Haigh Cres* 289 DH136
Ripley GU23 250 BG124
Sidcup DA15 208 EU88
Sunbury-on-Thames TW16 197 BT93
West Drayton UB7 177 BP80
Chestnut Copse, Oxt. RH8 276 EG132
Chestnut Ct, SW6 39 H3
Amersham HP6 77 AS37
Surbiton KT6 *off Penners Gdns* 220 CL101
Chestnut Cres, Whiteley Vill. KT12 *off Chestnut Av* 235 BS109
Chestnut Dr, E11 146 EG58
Berkhamsted HP4 60 AX20
Bexleyheath DA7 188 EX83
Englefield Green TW20 194 AX93
Harrow HA3 117 CF52
Pinner HA5 138 BX58
St. Albans AL4 65 CH18
Windsor SL4 173 AL84
Chestnut Glen, Horn. RM12 149 FF61
Chestnut Gro, SE20 204 DV94
SW12 202 DG87
W5 179 CK76
Barnet EN4 102 DF43
Brentwood CM14 130 FW47
Dartford DA2 209 FD91
Hoddesdon EN11 55 EB13
Ilford IG6 125 ES51
Isleworth TW7 179 CG84
Mitcham CR4 223 DK98
New Malden KT3 220 CR97
South Croydon CR2 242 DV108
Staines-upon-Thames TW18 196 BJ93
Wembley HA0 139 CH64
Woking GU22 248 AY120
Sch **Chestnut Gro Sch**, SW12 *off Chestnut Gro* 202 DG88
Chestnut Ho, NW3 *off Maitland Pk Vil* 6 F4
Chestnut La, N20 119 CY46
Amersham HP6 77 AR36
Harlow CM20 57 EP14
Sevenoaks TN13 279 FH124
Weybridge KT13 235 BP106
Sch **Chestnut La Sch**, Amer. HP6 *off Chestnut La* 77 AS36
Chestnut Manor Cl, Stai. TW18 196 BH92
Chestnut Mead, Red. RH1 *off Oxford Rd* 272 DE133
Chestnut Ms, Chal.St.P. SL9 *off Gold Hill E* 112 AX54
Chestnut Pk, Bray SL6 172 AE77
Chestnut Pl, SE26 204 DT91
Ashtead KT21 254 CL119
Epsom KT17 239 CU111
Weybridge KT13 235 BP106
Chestnut Ri, SE18 187 ER79
Bushey WD23 116 CB45
Chestnut Rd, SE27 203 DP90
SW20 221 CX96
Ashford TW15 197 BP91
Beaconsfield HP9 110 AH54
Dartford DA1 210 FK88
Enfield EN3 105 DY36
Guildford GU1 264 AX134
Horley RH6 290 DG146
Kingston upon Thames KT2 200 CL94
Twickenham TW2 199 CE89
Chestnut Row, N3 *off Nether St* 120 DA52
Chestnuts, Hutt. CM13 131 GB46
Chestnuts, The, Abridge RM4 108 EV41
Hemel Hempstead HP3 61 BF24
Hertford SG13 54 DR10
Horley RH6 291 DH146
Walton-on-Thames KT12 217 BU103
Sch **Chestnuts Prim Sch**, N15 *off Black Boy La* 144 DQ57
Chestnut Wk, Byfleet KT14 *off Royston Rd* 234 BL112
Chalfont St. Peter SL9 112 AY52
Epping Green CM16 *off Epping Rd* 73 EP24
Sevenoaks TN15 279 FL129

Chestnut Wk, Shepperton TW17 217 BS99
Watford WD24 97 BU37
Whiteley Village KT12
off Octagon Rd 235 BS109
Woodford Green IG8 124 EG50
Chestnut Way, Felt. TW13 197 BV90
Cheston Av, Croy. CR0 225 DY103
Chestwood Gro, Uxb. UB10 156 BM66
Cheswick Cl, Dart. DA1 189 FF84
Chesworth Cl, Erith DA8 189 FE81
Chettle Cl, SE1 31 L6
Chettle Ct, N8 143 DN58
Chetwode Dr, Epsom KT18 255 CX118
Chetwode Rd, SW17 202 DF90
Tadworth KT20 255 CW119
Chetwood Wk, E6 25 H7
Chetwynd Av, E.Barn. EN4 120 DF46
Chetwynd Dr, Uxb. UB10 156 BM68
Chetwynd Rd, NW5 143 DH63
Chevalier Cl, Stan. HA7 118 CL49
Cheval Pl, SW7 28 D6
Cheval St, E14 34 A6
Cheveley Cl, Rom. RM3
off Chelsworth Dr 128 FM53
Cheveley Gdns, Burn. SL1 152 AJ68
Chevely Cl, Cooper. CM16 92 EX29
Cheveney Wk, Brom. BR2
off Marina Cl 226 EG97
CHEVENING, Sev. TN14 262 EZ119
Jct Chevening Cross, Chev. TN14 262 FA120
Chevening Cross Rd, Chev. TN14 262 FA120
Chevening La, Knock.P. TN14 262 EY115
Chevening Rd, NW6 4 E9
SE10 47 M1
SE19 204 DR93
Chevening TN14 262 EZ119
Chipstead TN13 278 FB121
Sundridge TN14 262 EY123
Chevenings, The, Sid. DA14 208 EW90
Sch Chevening St. Botolph's C of E Prim Sch, Sev. TN13
off Chevening Rd 278 FB122
Cheverton Rd, N19 143 DK60
Chevet St, E9 11 L3
Chevington Pl, Horn. RM12
off Chevington Way 150 FK64
Chevington Way, Horn. RM12 150 FK63
Cheviot Cl, Bans. SM7 256 DB115
Bexleyheath DA7 189 FE82
Bushey WD23 98 CC44
Enfield EN1 104 DR40
Harlington UB3 177 BR80
Sutton SM2 240 DD109
Cheviot Gdns, NW2 141 CX61
SE27 203 DP91
Cheviot Gate, NW2 141 CY61
Cheviot Rd, SE27 203 DN92
Hornchurch RM11 149 FG60
Slough SL3 175 BA78
Cheviots, Hat. AL10 67 CU21
Hemel Hempstead HP2 62 BM17
Cheviot Way, Ilf. IG2 147 ES56
Chevron Cl, E16 23 P8
Chevy Rd, Sthl. UB2 178 CC75
Chewton Rd, E17 145 DY56
Cheyham Gdns, Sutt. SM2 239 CX110
Cheyham Way, Sutt. SM2 239 CY110
Cheyne Av, E18 146 EF55
Twickenham TW2 198 BZ88
Cheyne Cl, NW4 141 CW57
Amersham HP6 77 AR36
Bromley BR2 226 EL104
Gerrards Cross SL9 134 AY60
Ware SG12 55 DX05
Cheyne Ct, SW3 40 E2
Banstead SM7 off Park Rd 256 DB115
Cheyne Gdns, SW3 40 D2
Cheyne Hill, Surb. KT5 220 CM98
Cheyne Ms, SW3 40 D2
Chesham HP5 76 AR30
Cheyne Pk Dr, W.Wick. BR4 225 EC104
Cheyne Path, W7 159 CF71
Cheyne Pl, SW3 40 E2
Cheyne Rd, Ashf. TW15 197 BR93
Cheyne Row, SW3 40 C3
Cheyne Wk, N21 103 DP43
NW4 141 CW58
SW3 40 D3
SW10 40 A4
Chesham HP5 76 AR31
Croydon CR0 224 DU103
Horley RH6 290 DG149
Longfield DA3
off Cavendish Sq 231 FX97
Cheyneys Av, Edg. HA8 117 CK51
Chichele Gdns, Croy. CR0 242 DS105
Chichele Rd, NW2 4 C2
Oxted RH8 276 EE128
Chicheley Gdns, Har. HA3 116 CC52
Chicheley Rd, Har. HA3 116 CC52
Chicheley St, SE1 30 D4
Chichester Av, Ruis. HA4 137 BR61
Chichester Cl, E6 25 H9
SE3 186 EJ80
Aveley RM15 170 FQ74
Chafford Hundred RM16 191 FX77
Dorking RH4 269 CH134
Hampton TW12 off Maple Cl 198 BZ93
Chichester Ct, NW1 7 L6
Epsom KT17 239 CT109
Slough SL1 174 AV75
Stanmore HA7 140 CL55
Chichester Dr, Pur. CR8 241 DM112
Sevenoaks TN13 278 FF125
Chichester Gdns, Ilf. IG1 146 EL59
Chichester Ms, SE27 203 DN91
Chichester Rents, WC2 18 E8
Chichester Ri, Grav. DA12 213 GK91
Chichester Rd, E11 146 EE62
N9 122 DU46
NW6 15 J1
W2 15 M6
Croydon CR0 224 DS104
Dorking RH4 269 CH133
Greenhithe DA9 211 FT85
Chichester Row, Amer. HP6 77 AR38
Chichester St, SW1 41 M1
Chichester Way, E14 34 G8
Chichester Way, Feltham TW14 197 BV87
Watford WD25 82 BY33
Chichester Wf, Erith DA8 189 FE78
Chicksand St, E1 20 B7
Chiddingfold, N12 120 DA48
Chiddingstone Av, Bexh. DA7 188 EZ80
Chiddingstone Cl, Sutt. SM2 240 DA110
Chiddingstone St, SW6 39 K8
Chieftan Dr, Purf. RM19 190 FM77
Chieveley Rd, Bexh. DA7 189 FB84
Chiffinch Gdns, Nthflt DA11 212 GE90
Chignell Pl, W13
off Broadway 159 CG74
CHIGWELL, IG7 125 EP48
⊖ Chigwell 125 EP49
Chigwell Gra, Chig. IG7 125 EQ46
Chigwell Hill, E1 32 E1
Chigwell Hurst Ct, Pnr. HA5 138 BX55
Chigwell La, Loug. IG10 107 EQ43
Chigwell Pk, Chig. IG7 125 EP49
Chigwell Pk Dr, Chig. IG7 125 EN48
Sch Chigwell Prim Sch, Chig. IG7 off High Rd 125 EQ47
Chigwell Ri, Chig. IG7 125 EN47
Chigwell Rd, E18 146 EH55
Woodford Green IG8 124 EJ54
CHIGWELL ROW, Chig. IG7 126 EU47
Sch Chigwell Row Inf Sch, Chig. IG7 off Lambourne Rd 126 EV47
Sch Chigwell Sch, Chig. IG7
off High Rd 125 EQ47
Chigwell Vw, Rom. RM5
off Lodge La 126 FA51
Chilberton Dr, S.Merst. RH1 273 DJ130
Chilbrook Rd, Down. KT11 251 BU118
Chilcombe Ho, SW15
off Fontley Way 201 CU87
Chilcot Cl, E14 22 D9
Chilcote La, Lt.Chal. HP7 94 AV39
Chilcott Cl, Wem. HA0 139 CJ63
Chilcott Rd, Wat. WD24 97 BS36
Childebert Rd, SW17 203 DH89
Sch Childeric Prim Sch, SE14 45 M5
Childeric Rd, SE14 45 M5
Childerley, Kings.T. KT1
off Burritt Rd 220 CN97
Childerley St, SW6 38 E6
Childers, The, Wdf.Grn. IG8 125 EM50
Childers St, SE8 45 M2
Child La, SE10 35 M7
Sch Children's Ho Upr Sch, The, N1 9 N3
H Children's Trust, The, Tad. KT20 255 CX121
Childs Av, Hare. UB9 114 BJ54
Childs Cl, Horn. RM11 150 FJ58
Childs Cres, Swans. DA10 211 FX86
Childs Hall Cl, Bkhm KT23
off Childs Hall Rd 268 BZ125
Childs Hall Dr, Bkhm KT23 268 BZ125
Childs Hall Rd, Bkhm KT23 268 BZ125
CHILDS HILL, NW2 142 DA61
Sch Childs Hill Prim Sch, NW2
off Dersingham Rd 141 CY62
Childs Hill Wk, NW2 141 CZ62
Childs La, SE19
off Westow St 204 DS93
Child's Ms, SW5
off Child's Pl 27 L9
Child's Pl, SW5 27 K9
Child's St, SW5 27 K9
Child's Wk, SW5 27 K9
Childs Way, NW11 141 CZ57
Childwick Ct, Hem.H. HP3
off Rumballs Rd 62 BN23
Chilham Cl, Bex. DA5 208 EZ87
Hemel Hempstead HP2 62 BL21
Perivale UB6 159 CG68
Chilham Rd, SE9 206 EL91
Chilham Way, Brom. BR2 226 EG101
Chillerton Rd, SW17 202 DG92
Chillingford Ho, SW17
off Blackshaw Rd 202 DC91
Chillington Dr, SW11 182 DC84
Chillingworth Gdns, Twick. TW1 off Tower Rd 199 CF90
Chillingworth Rd, N7 8 E3
Chilmans Dr, Bkhm KT23 268 CB125
Chilmark Gdns, Merst. RH1 273 DL129
New Malden KT3 221 CT101
Chilmark Rd, SW16 223 DK96
Chilmead La, Nutfld RH1 273 DK132
Chilsey Grn Rd, Cher. KT16 215 BE100
Chiltern Av, Amer. HP6 77 AR38
Bushey WD23 98 CC44
Twickenham TW2 198 CA88
● Chiltern Business Village, Uxb. UB8 156 BH68
Chiltern Cl, Berk. HP4 60 AT18
Bexleyheath DA7 189 FE81
Borehamwood WD6 100 CM40
Bushey WD23 98 CB44
Croydon CR0 224 DS104
Goffs Oak EN7 87 DP27
Ickenham UB10 137 BP61
Staines-upon-Thames TW18 196 BG92
Watford WD18 97 BT42
Woking GU22 248 AW122
Worcester Park KT4
off Cotswold Way 221 CW103
● Chiltern Commerce Cen, Chesh. HP5
off Asheridge Rd 76 AN29
Chiltern Cor, Berk. HP4
off Durrants Rd 60 AU18
● Chiltern Ct, Chesh. HP5
off Asheridge Rd 76 AN29
Chiltern Ct, N10 120 DG54
Uxb. UB8 157 BP70
Chiltern Dene, Enf. EN2 103 DM42
Chiltern Dr, Mill End WD3 113 BF45
Surbiton KT5 220 CP99
Chiltern Gdns, NW2 141 CX62
Bromley BR2 226 EF98
Hornchurch RM12 150 FJ62
Chiltern Hts, Amer. HP7 94 AU39
Chiltern Hill, Chal.St.P. SL9 112 AY53
Chiltern Hills Rd, Beac. HP9 110 AJ53
★ Chiltern Open Air Mus, Ch.St.G. HP8 113 AZ47
Chiltern Par, Amer. HP6 77 AQ37
Chiltern Pk, Chal.St.P. SL9 112 AY53
Chiltern Pk Av, Berk. HP4 60 AU17
Chiltern Pl, E5 144 DV61
Chiltern Rd, E3 22 B5
Amersham HP6 77 AP35
Burnham SL1 152 AH71
Ilford IG2 147 ES56
Northfleet DA11 212 GE90
Chiltern Rd, Pinner HA5 138 BW57
St. Albans AL4 65 CJ16
Sutton SM2 240 DB109
Chilterns, Hat. AL10 67 CU21
Hemel Hempstead HP2 62 BL18
Chilterns, The, Nthch HP4
off Stoney Cl 60 AT17
Sutton SM2 off Gatton Cl 240 DB109
Chiltern St, W1 16 G6
Chiltern Vw Rd, Uxb. UB8 156 BJ68
Chiltern Way, Wdf.Grn. IG8 124 EG48
Chilthorne Cl, SE6
off Ravensbourne Pk Cres 205 DZ87
Chilton Av, W5 179 CK77
Chilton Cl, Penn HP10 110 AC45
Chilton Ct, Hert. SG14
off The Ridgeway 53 DM07
Walton-on-Thames KT12 235 BU105
Chilton Grn, Welw.G.C. AL7 52 DC09
Chilton Gro, SE8 33 K9
● Chiltonian Ind Est, SE12 206 EF86
Chilton Rd, Chesh. HP5 76 AQ29
Edgware HA8 118 CN51
Grays RM16 193 GG76
Richmond TW9 180 CN83
Chiltons, The, E18
off Grove Hill 124 EG54
Chiltons Cl, Bans. SM7
off High St 256 DB115
Chilton St, E2 20 B4
Chilvers Cl, Twick. TW2 199 CE89
Chilver St, SE10 35 M10
Chilwell Gdns, Wat. WD19 116 BW49
Chilwick Rd, Slou. SL2 153 AM69
CHILWORTH, Guil. GU4 281 BC140
⇌ Chilworth 281 BE140
Sch Chilworth C of E Inf Sch, Chilw. GU4 off Dorking Rd 281 BD140
Chilworth Ct, SW19 201 CX88
Chilworth Gdns, Sutt. SM1 222 DC104
Chilworth Gate, Brox. EN10
off Silverfield 71 DZ22
Cheshunt EN8
off Davison Dr 89 DX28
Chilworth Ms, W2 15 P9
Chilworth Rd, Albury GU5 282 BG139
Chilworth St, W2 15 P9
Chimes Av, N13 121 DN50
Chime Sq, St.Alb. AL3 65 CE19
Chimes Shop Cen, The, Uxb. UB8 156 BK66
Chimney La, Woob.Grn HP10
off Glory Mill La 132 AE56
China Hall Ms, SE16 33 H7
China Ms, SW2 203 DM87
★ Chinatown, W1
off Gerrard St 17 P10
Chinbrook Cres, SE12 206 EH90
Chinbrook Est, SE9 206 EK90
Chinbrook Rd, SE12 206 EH90
Chinchilla Dr, Houns. TW4 178 BW82
Chindit Cl, Brox. EN10 71 DY20
Chindits La, Warley CM14 130 FW50
Chine, The, N10 143 DJ56
N21 103 DP44
Dorking RH4 off High St 285 CH135
Wembley HA0 139 CH64
Chine Fm Pl, Knock.P. TN14 262 EX116
Ching Ct, WC2 18 A9
Chingdale Rd, E4 124 EE48
CHINGFORD, E4 123 EB46
⇌ Chingford 124 EE45
⊖ Chingford 124 EE45
Chingford Av, E4 123 EB48
Sch Chingford C of E Inf Sch, E4 off Kings Rd 123 ED46
Sch Chingford C of E (VC) Jun Sch, E4 off Cambridge Rd 123 ED46
Sch Chingford Foundation Sch, E4 off Nevin Dr 123 EC46
CHINGFORD GREEN, E4 124 EF46
Sch Chingford Hall Comm Prim Sch, E4 off Burnside Av 123 DZ51
CHINGFORD HATCH, E4 123 EC49
● Chingford Ind Cen, E4 123 DY50
Chingford La, Wdf.Grn. IG8 124 EE49
Chingford Mt Rd, E4 123 EA49
Chingford Rd, E4 123 EA51
E17 123 EB53
Chingley Cl, Brom. BR1 206 EE93
Ching Way, E4 123 DZ51
Chinnery Cl, Enf. EN1 104 DT39
Chinnor Cres, Grnf. UB6 158 CB68
Chinthurst La, Guil. GU4, GU5 280 AY141
Chinthurst Ms, Couls. CR5 256 DG116
Chinthurst Pk, Shalf. GU4 280 AY142
Sch Chinthurst Sch, Tad. KT20
off Tadworth St 255 CW123
Chipka St, E14 34 E5
Chipley St, SE14 45 L3
Chipmunk Chase, Hat. AL10 66 CR16
Chipmunk Gro, Nthlt. UB5
off Argus Way 158 BY69
Chippendale All, Uxb. UB8
off Chippendale Waye 156 BK66
Chippendale Ho, SW1 41 K1
Chippendale St, E5 145 DX62
Chippendale Waye, Uxb. UB8 156 BK66
Chippenham Av, Wem. HA9 140 CP64
Chippenham Cl, Pnr. HA5 137 BT56
Romford RM3 128 FK50
Chippenham Gdns, NW6 15 J3
Romford RM3 128 FK50
Chippenham Ms, W9 15 J5
Chippenham Rd, W9 15 J5
Romford RM3 128 FK51
Chippenham Wk, Rom. RM3
off Chippenham Rd 128 FK51
CHIPPERFIELD, Kings L. WD4 80 BG31
Chipperfield Cl, Upmin. RM14 151 FS60
Chipperfield Rd, Bov. HP3 79 BB27
Hemel Hempstead HP3 62 BJ24
Kings Langley WD4 80 BK30
Orpington BR5 228 EU95
CHIPPING BARNET, Barn. EN5 101 CY42
Chipping Cl, Barn. EN5
off St. Albans Rd 101 CY41
Chippingfield, Harl. CM17 58 EW12
CHIPSTEAD, Couls. CR5 256 DF118
CHIPSTEAD, Sev. TN13 278 FC122
⇌ Chipstead 256 DF118
Chipstead, Chal.St.P. SL9 112 AW53
Chipstead Av, Th.Hth. CR7 223 DP98
CHIPSTEAD BOTTOM, Couls. CR5 256 DE121
Chipstead Cl, SE19 204 DT94
Coulsdon CR5 256 DG116
Redhill RH1 288 DF136
Sutton SM2 240 DB109
Chipstead Ct, Knap. GU21
off Creston Av 248 AS117
Chipstead Gdns, NW2 141 CV61
Chipstead La, Chipstead CR5 256 DB124
Lower Kingswood KT20 271 CZ125
Sevenoaks TN13 278 FC122
Chipstead Pk, Sev. TN13 278 FD122
Chipstead Pk Cl, Sev. TN13 278 FC122
Chipstead Pl Gdns, Sev. TN13 278 FC122
Chipstead Rd, Bans. SM7 255 CZ117
Erith DA8 189 FE80
Lon.Hthrw Air. TW6 176 BN83
Chipstead Sta Par, Chipstead CR5 off Station App 256 DF118
Chipstead St, SW6 39 K7
Sch Chipstead Valley Prim Sch, Couls. CR5
off Chipstead Valley Rd 256 DG116
Chipstead Valley Rd, Couls. CR5 257 DH116
Chipstead Way, Bans. SM7 256 DF115
Chip St, SW4 183 DK83
Chirk Cl, Hayes UB4 158 BY70
Chirton Wk, Wok. GU21 248 AU118
Sch Chisenhale Prim Sch, E3 11 L10
Chisenhale Rd, E3 11 L10
Chisholm Rd, Croy. CR0 224 DS103
Richmond TW10 200 CM86
Chisledon Wk, E9 11 P4
CHISLEHURST, BR7 207 EN94
⇌ Chislehurst 227 EN96
Sch Chislehurst & Sidcup Gram Sch, Sid. DA15
off Hurst Rd 208 EV89
Chislehurst Av, N12 120 DC52
★ Chislehurst Caves, Chis. BR7 off Caveside Cl 227 EN95
Sch Chislehurst C of E Prim Sch, Chis. BR7 off School Rd 207 EQ94
Chislehurst Rd, Brom. BR1 226 EK96
Chislehurst BR7 226 EK96
Orpington BR5, BR6 227 ES98
Richmond TW10 200 CL86
Sidcup DA14 208 EU92
CHISLEHURST WEST, Chis. BR7 207 EM92
Chislet Cl, Beck. BR3 205 EA94
Chisley Rd, N15 144 DS58
Chiswell Ct, Wat. WD24 98 BW38
CHISWELL GREEN, St.Alb. AL2 82 CA26
Chiswell Grn La, St.Alb. AL2 82 BX25
Chiswell Sq, SE3
off Brook La 186 EH82
Chiswell St, EC1 19 K6
SE5 43 M4
CHISWICK, W4 180 CR79
⇌ Chiswick 180 CQ80
Sch Chiswick & Bedford Pk Prep Sch, W4 off Priory Av 180 CS77
Chiswick Br, SW14 180 CQ82
W4 180 CQ82
Chiswick Cl, Croy. CR0 223 DM104
Chiswick Common Rd, W4 180 CR77
Sch Chiswick Comm Sch, W4
off Burlington La 180 CR80
Chiswick Ct, Pnr. HA5 138 BZ55
Chiswick Grn Studios, W4
off Evershed Wk 180 CQ77
Chiswick High Rd, W4 180 CR77
Brentford TW8 180 CM78
★ Chiswick Ho, W4 180 CS79
Chiswick Ho Grds, W4 180 CR79
Chiswick La, W4 180 CS78
Chiswick La S, W4 181 CT78
Chiswick Mall, W4 181 CT79
W6 181 CT79
⊖ Chiswick Park 180 CQ77
● Chiswick Pk, W4 180 CP77
Chiswick Pier, W4 181 CT80
Chiswick Quay, W4 180 CQ81
Chiswick Rd, N9 122 DU47
W4 180 CQ77
Jct Chiswick Rbt, W4 180 CN78
Chiswick Sq, W4
off Hogarth Rbt 180 CS79
Chiswick Staithe, W4 180 CQ81
Chiswick Ter, W4
off Acton La 180 CQ77
Chiswick Village, W4 180 CP78
Chiswick War Mem Homes, W4
Burlington La 180 CR80
Chiswick Wf, W4 181 CT79
Chittenden Cl, Hodd. EN11
off Founders Rd 55 EB14
Chittenden Cotts, Wisley GU23 250 BL116
Chitterfield Gate, Sipson UB7 176 BN80
Chitty's Common, Guil. GU2 264 AT130
Chitty's La, Dag. RM8 148 EX61
Chitty St, W1 17 M6
Chittys Wk, Guil. GU3 264 AT130
Chivalry Rd, SW11 202 DE85
Chivenor Gro, Kings.T. KT2 199 CK92
Chivenor Pl, St.Alb. AL4 65 CJ22
Chivers Rd, E4 123 EB48
Choats Manor Way, Dag. RM9 168 EZ69
Choats Rd, Bark. IG11 168 EW68
Dagenham RM9 168 EW68
CHOBHAM, Wok. GU24 232 AT111
Sch Chobham Academy Sec Sch, E20
off Founders Rd 12 F3
● Chobham Business Pk, Chobham GU24 232 AX110
Chobham Cl, Ott. KT16 233 BB107
★ Chobham Common National Nature Reserve, Wok. GU24 232 AS105
Chobham Gdns, SW19 201 CX89
Chobham La, Longcr. KT16 214 AV102
Chobham Pk La, Chobham GU24 232 AU110
Chobham Rd, E15 12 G3
Horsell GU21 232 AW113
Ottershaw KT16 233 BA108
Woking GU21 248 AY116
Sch Chobham St. Lawrence C of E Prim Sch, Chobham GU24
off Bagshot Rd 232 AS111
Choice Vw, Ilf. IG1
off Axon Pl 147 EQ61
Choir Grn, Knap. GU21 248 AS117
Cholmeley Cres, N6 143 DH59
Cholmeley Pk, N6 143 DH60
Cholmley Gdns, NW6 5 J2
Cholmley Rd, T.Ditt. KT7 219 CH100
Cholmondeley Av, NW10 161 CU68
Cholmondeley Wk, Rich. TW9 199 CJ85
Choppins Ct, E1 32 F2
Chopwell Cl, E15 13 H7
CHORLEYWOOD, Rick. WD3 95 BE43
⇌ Chorleywood 95 BE42
⊖ Chorleywood 95 BE42
CHORLEYWOOD BOTTOM, Rick. WD3 95 BD44
Chorleywood Bottom, Chorl. WD3 95 BD43
Chorleywood Cl, Rick. WD3 114 BK45
Chorleywood Common, Chorl. WD3 95 BE42
Chorleywood Cres, Orp. BR5 227 ET96
Chorleywood Ho Dr, Chorl. WD3 95 BE41
Chorleywood Lo La, Chorl. WD3 95 BF41
Sch Chorleywood Prim Sch, Chorl. WD3 off Stag La 95 BC44
Chorleywood Rd, Rick. WD3 96 BG42
Choumert Gro, SE15 44 C9
Choumert Ms, SE15 44 C9
Choumert Rd, SE15 44 A10
Choumert Sq, SE15 44 C9
Chow Sq, E8 10 A2
Chrislaine Cl, Stanw. TW19 196 BK86
Chrisp St, E14 22 C7
Christabel Cl, Islw. TW7 179 CE83
Christchurch Av, N12 120 DC51
NW6 4 F6
Erith DA8 189 FD79
Harrow HA3 139 CH56
Rainham RM13 169 FF68
Teddington TW11 199 CG92
Wembley HA0 160 CL65
Sch Christ Ch Bentinck C of E Prim Sch, NW1 16 D6
Sch Christchurch (Brixton) C of E Prim Sch, SW9 42 F6
Christchurch Cl, N12
off Summers La 120 DD52
SW19 202 DD94
Enfield EN2 104 DQ40
St. Albans AL3 64 CC19
Sch Christ Ch C of E Inf Sch, Vir.W. GU25 off Christchurch Rd 214 AV97
Sch Christ Ch C of E Jun Sch, W5 off New Bdy 159 CK73
Ottershaw KT16
off Fletcher Rd 233 BD107
Sch Christ Ch C of E Prim Sch, Regent's Pk, NW1 17 K2
Hampstead, NW3
off Christchurch Hill 142 DD62
SE23 off Perry Vale 205 DX89
SW3 40 E2
Sch Christchurch C of E Prim Sch, SW11 40 D10
Sch Christ Ch C of E Prim Sch, Barn. EN5 off Byng Rd 101 CX40
Surbiton KT5
off Pine Gdns 220 CN100
Sch Christ Ch C of E Prim Sch & Nurs, Ware SG12
off New Rd 55 DY06
Sch Christ Ch C of E Prim Sch, Purley, Pur. CR8
off Montpelier Rd 241 DP110
Sch Christ Ch C of E Sch, E1 20 B6
Chorleywood WD3
off Rickmansworth Rd 95 BF41
Christchurch Ct, NW6 4 E6
Christchurch Cres, Grav. DA12
off Christchurch Rd 213 GJ87
Radlett WD7 99 CG36
Sch Christ Ch Erith C of E Prim Sch, Erith DA8
off Lesney Pk Rd 189 FD79
Christchurch Gdns, Epsom KT19 238 CP111
Harrow HA3 139 CG56
Christchurch Grn, Wem. HA0 160 CL65
Christchurch Hill, NW3 142 DD62
Christchurch La, Barn. EN5 101 CY40
Christ Ch Mt, Epsom KT19 238 CP112
Sch Christ Ch New Malden Prim Sch, N.Mal. KT3
off Elm Rd 220 CR97
New Malden KT3
off Lime Gro 220 CS97
Christchurch Pk, Sutt. SM2 240 DC108
Christ Ch Pas, EC1 19 H8
Christchurch Pas, NW3 142 DC62
Barnet EN5 101 CY41
Christ Ch Path, Hayes UB3 177 BQ76
Christchurch Pl, Epsom KT19 238 CP111
Hertford SG14
off Port Vale 54 DQ09
Sch Christ Ch Prim Sch, NW6 4 G7
SE10 35 K10
SE18 off Shooters Hill 187 EN81
Sch Christchurch Prim Sch, Ilf. IG1 off Wellesley Rd 147 EQ60
Christchurch Rd, N8 143 DL58
SW2 203 DM88
SW14 200 CP85
SW19 222 DD95
Christ Ch Rd, Beck. BR3
off Fairfield Rd 225 EA96
Christchurch Rd, Dart. DA1 210 FJ87
Christ Ch Rd, Epsom KT19 238 CL112
Christchurch Rd, Grav. DA12 213 GJ88
Hemel Hempstead HP2 62 BK19
Ilford IG1 147 EP60
Purley CR8 241 DP110
Sidcup DA15 207 ET91
Christ Ch Rd, Surb. KT5 220 CM100
Christchurch Rd, Til. RM18 193 GG81
Virginia Water GU25 214 AU97
Christchurch Sq, E9 10 G9
Sch Christ Ch (Streatham) C of E Prim Sch, SW2
off Cotherstone Rd 203 DM88
Christchurch St, SW3 40 E2
Christchurch Ter, SW3 40 E2
Christchurch Way, SE10 35 K9
Woking GU21
off Church St E 249 AZ117
Christian Cl, Hodd. EN11 55 DZ13
Christian Ct, SE16 33 N3
Christian Flds, SW16 203 DN94
Christian Flds Av, Grav. DA12 213 GJ91
Christian Sq, Wind. SL4
off Ward Royal 173 AQ81
Christian St, E1 20 D8
Christie Cl, Bkhm KT23 268 BZ125
Broxbourne EN10 71 DZ21
Guildford GU1
off Waterside Rd 264 AX131

Christie Ct, N19
off Hornsey Rd 143 DL61
Watford WD18 97 BU43
Christie Dr, Croy. CR0 224 DU99
Christie Gdns, Rom. RM6 148 EV58
Christie Ho, W12
off Du Cane Rd 161 CV72
Christie Rd, E9 11 L5
Waltham Abbey EN9
off Deer Pk Way 105 EB35
Christies Av, Bad.Mt TN14 246 FA110
Coll Christie's Ed, W1 17 K6
Christie Wk, Cat. CR3 258 DR122
Christina Sq, N4 143 DP60
Christina St, EC2 19 N4
Christine Worsley Cl, N21
off Highfield Rd 121 DP47
Christmas Hill, Guil. GU4, GU5 281 AZ141
Christmas La, Farn.Com. SL2 133 AQ62
Christopher Av, W7 179 CG76
Christopher Cl, SE16 33 J4
Hornchurch RM12
off Chevington Way 150 FK63
Sidcup DA15 207 ET85
Christopher Ct, Hem.H. HP3
off Seaton Rd 62 BK23
Tadworth KT20 off High St 255 CW123
Christopher Gdns, Dag.
RM9 off Wren Rd 148 EX64
Sch Christopher Hatton Prim Sch,
EC1 18 E5
Christopher Pl, NW1 17 P3
Christopher Pl Shop Cen,
St.Alb. AL3 off Market Pl 65 CD20
Christopher Rd, Sthl. UB2 177 BV77
Christopher's Ms, W11 26 F2
Christopher St, EC2 19 M5
Sch Christ's Coll Finchley, N2
off East End Rd 142 DB55
Sch Christ's Coll, Guildford, Guil.
GU1 off Larch Av 264 AW131
Sch Christ's Sch, Rich. TW10
off Queens Rd 200 CN85
Sch Christ the King RC Prim Sch,
N4 off Tollington Pk 143 DM61
Coll Christ the King 6th Form Coll,
SE13 47 H10
Christy Rd, Bigg.H. TN16 260 EJ115
Chryssell Rd, SW9 42 F5
Chrystie La, Bkhm KT23 268 CB126
Chubworthy St, SE14 45 L3
Chucks La, Walt.Hill KT20 255 CV124
Chudleigh Cres, Ilf. IG3 147 ES63
Chudleigh Gdns, Sutt. SM1 222 DC104
Chudleigh Rd, NW6 4 B7
SE4 205 DZ85
Romford RM3 128 FL49
Twickenham TW2 199 CF87
Chudleigh St, E1 21 J8
Chudleigh Way, Ruis. HA4 137 BU60
Chulsa Rd, SE26 204 DV92
Chumleigh Gdns, SE5
off Chumleigh St 43 N2
Chumleigh St, SE5 43 N2
Chumleigh Wk, Surb. KT5 220 CM98
Church All, Ald. WD25 98 CC38
Croydon CR0 223 DN102
Gravesend DA11
off High St 213 GH86
Church App, SE21 204 DR90
Cudham TN14
off Cudham La S 261 EQ115
Egham TW20 215 BC97
Stanwell TW19 196 BK86
Church Av, E4 123 ED51
NW1 7 K5
SW14 180 CR83
Beckenham BR3 225 EA95
Northolt UB5 158 BZ66
Pinner HA5 138 BY58
Ruislip HA4 137 BR60
Sidcup DA14 208 EU92
Southall UB2 178 BY76
Churchbury Cl, Enf. EN1 104 DS40
Churchbury La, Enf. EN1 104 DR41
Churchbury Rd, SE9 206 EK87
Enfield EN1 104 DR40
Church Cl, N20 120 DE48
W8 27 L4
Addlestone KT15 234 BH105
Cuffley EN6 87 DL29
Edgware HA8 118 CQ50
Eton SL4 173 AR79
Fetcham KT22 253 CD124
Hayes UB4 157 BR71
Horsell GU21 248 AX116
Hounslow TW3 off Bath Rd 178 BZ83
Little Berkhamsted SG13
off Church Rd 69 DJ19
Loughton IG10 107 EM40
Lower Kingswood KT20
off Buckland Rd 271 CZ127
Northwood HA6 115 BT52
Radlett WD7 99 CG36
Staines-upon-Thames TW18
off The Broadway 216 BJ97
Uxbridge UB8 156 BH68
West Drayton UB7 176 BL76
Church Cor, SW17
off Mitcham Rd 202 DF92
Church Ct, Reig. RH2 272 DB134
Richmond TW9
off George St 199 CK85
Church Cres, E9 11 J6
N3 119 CZ53
N10 143 DH56
N20 120 DE48
St. Albans AL3 64 CC19
Sawbridgeworth CM21 58 EZ05
South Ockendon RM15 171 FW69
Church Cft, St.Alb. AL4 65 CJ22
Churchcroft Cl, SW12 202 DG87
Churchdown, Brom. BR1 206 EE91
Church Dr, NW9 140 CR60
Bray SL6 172 AC75
Harrow HA2 138 BZ58
West Wickham BR4 226 EE104
Church Elm La, Dag. RM10 168 FA65
CHURCH END, N3 119 CZ53
CHURCH END, NW10 160 CS65
Church End, E17 145 EB56
NW4 141 CV55
Harlow CM19 73 EN17
Church Entry, EC4 19 H9
Church Est Almshouses, Rich.
TW9 off St. Mary's Gro 180 CM84
Church Fm Cl, Swan. BR8 229 FC100
★ Church Farm Ho Mus,
NW4 141 CV55
Church Fm La, Sutt. SM3 239 CY107
Church Fm Way, Ald. WD25 98 CB38
Church Fld, Dart. DA2 210 FK89
Epping CM16 92 EU29
Churchfield, Harl. CM20 58 EU13
Church Fld, Rad. WD7 99 CG36
Sevenoaks TN13 278 FE122
Churchfield Av, N12 120 DC51
Churchfield Cl, Har. HA2 138 CC56
Hayes UB3 157 BT73
Churchfield Ms, Slou. SL2 154 AU72
Churchfield Path, Chsht EN8 88 DW29
Churchfield Pl, Shep. TW17
off Chertsey Rd 217 BP101
Weybridge KT13 234 BN105
Sch Churchfield Prim Sch,
N9 off Latymer Rd 122 DT46
Churchfield Rd, W3 160 CQ74
W7 179 CE75
W13 159 CH74
Chalfont St. Peter SL9 112 AX53
Reigate RH2 271 CZ133
Tewin AL6 52 DC06
Walton-on-Thames KT12 217 BU102
Welling DA16 188 EU83
Weybridge KT13 234 BN105
Churchfields, E18 124 EG53
SE10 46 E4
Broxbourne EN10 71 EA21
Guildford GU4
off Burpham La 265 BA129
Hertford SG13 54 DR10
Horsell GU21 248 AY116
Loughton IG10 106 EL42
West Molesey KT8 218 CA97
Churchfields Av, Felt. TW13 198 BZ90
Weybridge KT13 235 BP105
Sch Churchfields Infants' Sch,
E18 off Churchfields 124 EG53
Sch Churchfields Jun Sch, E18
off Churchfields 124 EG53
Churchfields La, Brox. EN10
off Station Rd 71 EA20
Sch Churchfields Prim Sch, Beck.
BR3 off Churchfields Rd 225 DX96
Churchfields Rd, Beck. BR3 225 DX96
Watford WD24 97 BT36
Church Gdns, W5 179 CK75
Dorking RH4 285 CG135
Wembley HA0 139 CG63
Church Garth, N19
off Pemberton Gdns 143 DK61
Church Gate, SW6 38 F10
Churchgate, Chsht EN8 88 DV30
Sch Churchgate C of E Prim Sch,
Harl. CM17
off Hobbs Cross Rd 58 EZ12
Churchgate Gdns, Harl. CM17
off Sheering Rd 58 EZ11
Churchgate Rd, Chsht EN8 88 DV29
Churchgate St, Harl. CM17 58 EY11
Church Grn, SW9 42 F8
Hayes UB3 157 BT72
Hersham KT12 236 BW107
St. Albans AL1
off Hatfield Rd 65 CD19
Church Gro, SE13 185 EB84
Amersham HP6 94 AY39
Kingston upon Thames KT1 219 CJ95
Wexham SL3 154 AW71
Church Hill, E17 145 EA56
N21 121 DM45
SE18 37 K7
SW19 201 CZ92
Bedmond WD5 81 BT26
Carshalton SM5 240 DF106
Caterham CR3 258 DT124
Crayford DA2 189 FE84
Cudham TN14 261 EQ115
Dartford DA2 210 FK90
Epping CM16 92 EU29
Greenhithe DA9 211 FS85
Harefield UB9 136 BJ55
Harrow HA1 139 CE60
Hertford Heath SG13 54 DV11
Horsell GU21 248 AX116
Lemsford AL8 51 CU10
Loughton IG10 106 EL41
Merstham RH1 273 DH126
Nutfield RH1 273 DM133
Orpington BR6 228 EU101
Purley CR8 241 DL110
Pyrford GU22 249 BF117
Shere GU5 282 BN139
Tatsfield TN16 260 EK122
Sch Church Hill Prim Sch, Barn.
EN4 off Burlington Ri 120 DF45
Church Hill Rd, E17 145 EB56
Barnet EN4 120 DF45
Surbiton KT6 220 CL99
Sutton SM3 239 CX105
Church Hill Wd, Orp. BR5 227 ET99
Church Hollow, Purf. RM19 190 FN78
Church Hyde, SE18
off Old Mill Rd 187 ES79
Churchill Av, Har. HA3 139 CH58
Uxbridge UB10 157 BP69
Churchill Cl, Dart. DA1 210 FP88
Feltham TW14 197 BT88
Fetcham KT22 253 CE123
Uxbridge UB10 157 BP69
Warlingham CR6 258 DW117
Sch Churchill C of E Prim Sch,
West. TN16 off Rysted La 277 EQ125
Churchill Ct, SE18
off Rushgrove St 37 K9
W5 160 CM70
Northolt UB5 138 CA64
Staines-upon-Thames TW18
off Chestnut Gro 196 BH93
Churchill Cres, N.Mymms AL9
off Dixons Hill Rd 67 CW23
Churchill Dr, Knot.Grn HP9 110 AJ50
Weybridge KT13 217 BQ104
Churchill Gdns, SW1 41 L1
W3 160 CN72
Sch Churchill Gdns Prim Sch,
SW1 41 M1
Churchill Gdns Rd, SW1 41 K1
Churchill Ms, Wdf.Grn. IG8
off High Rd Woodford Grn 124 EF51
★ Churchill Mus & Cabinet
War Rooms, SW1 29 P4
Churchill Pl, E14 34 D2
Harrow HA1
off Sandridge Cl 139 CE56
Churchill Rd, E16 24 C9
NW2 161 CV65
NW5 143 DH63
Churchill Rd, Edgware HA8 118 CM51
Epsom KT19 238 CN111
Gravesend DA11 213 GF88
Grays RM17 192 GD79
Guildford GU1 280 AY135
Horton Kirby DA4 230 FQ98
St. Albans AL1 65 CG18
Slough SL3 175 AZ77
Smallfield RH6 291 DP148
South Croydon CR2 242 DQ109
Churchill Ter, E4 123 EA49
Churchill Wk, E9 11 H2
Churchill Way, Bigg.H. TN16 244 EK113
Bromley BR1
off Ethelbert Rd 226 EG97
Sunbury-on-Thames TW16 197 BU92
Church Island, Stai. TW18 195 BD91
Churchlands Way,
Wor.Pk. KT4 221 CX103
Church La, E11 146 EE60
E17 145 EB56
N2 142 DD55
N8 143 DM56
N9 122 DU47
N17 122 DS53
NW9 140 CQ61
SW17 203 DH91
SW19 221 CZ95
W5 179 CJ75
Abridge RM4 108 EY40
Albury GU5 282 BH139
Aldenham WD25 98 CB38
Bayford SG13 69 DM17
Berkhamsted HP4 60 AW19
Bletchingley RH1 274 DR133
Bovingdon HP3 79 BB27
Bray SL6 172 AC75
Bromley BR2 226 EL102
Broxbourne EN10 70 DW22
Burstow RH6 291 DL153
Chaldon CR3 257 DN123
Chalfont St. Peter SL9 112 AX53
Chelsham CR6 259 EC116
Cheshunt EN8 88 DV29
Chessington KT9 238 CM107
Chislehurst BR7 227 EQ95
Colney Heath AL4 66 CP22
Coulsdon CR5 256 DG122
Dagenham RM10 169 FB65
Enfield EN1 104 DR41
Godstone RH9 275 DX132
Great Warley CM13 151 FW58
Harrow HA3 117 CF53
Hatfield AL9 67 CW18
Headley KT18 254 CQ124
Hutton CM13 131 GE46
Kings Langley WD4 80 BN29
Loughton IG10 107 EM41
Mill End WD3 114 BG46
Nork SM7 255 CX117
North Ockendon RM14 151 FV64
North Weald Bassett CM16 93 FB26
Northaw EN6 86 DG30
Oxted RH8 276 EE129
Pinner HA5 138 BY55
Purfleet RM19 190 FN78
Richmond TW10 200 CL88
Romford RM1 149 FE56
Sarratt WD3 95 BF38
Send GU23 265 BB126
Sheering CM22 59 FD07
Shere GU5 282 BN139
Stapleford Abbotts RM4 109 FC42
Stoke Poges SL2 154 AT69
Teddington TW11 199 CF92
Thames Ditton KT7 219 CF100
Twickenham TW1 199 CG88
Uxbridge UB8 156 BH68
Wallington SM6 223 DK104
Warlingham CR6 259 DX117
Wennington RM13 170 FK72
Westerham TN16 260 EK122
Wexham SL3 154 AW71
Weybridge KT13 234 BN105
Windsor SL4 173 AR81
Worplesdon GU3 264 AS127
Church La Av, Couls. CR5 257 DH122
Church La Dr, Couls. CR5 257 DH122
CHURCH LANGLEY, Harl. CM17 58 EY14
Sch Church Langley Comm
Prim Sch, Ch.Lang. CM17
off Church Langley Way 74 EW15
Jct Church Langley Rbt,
Harl. CM17 74 EV15
Church Langley Way, Harl.
CM17 74 EW15
Churchley Rd, SE26 204 DV91
Church Leys, Harl. CM18 73 ET16
Church Manor Est, SW9 42 F5
Church Manorway, SE2 187 ET77
Erith DA8 189 FD76
Church Manorway Ind Est,
Erith DA8 189 FC76
Churchmead, SE5
off Camberwell Rd 43 K5
Church Mead, Roydon CM19 56 EH14
Churchmead Cl, E.Barn. EN4 102 DE44
Sch Churchmead C of E Sch,
Datchet SL3 off Priory Way 174 AV80
Church Meadow, Long Dit.
KT6 219 CJ103
Churchmead Rd, NW10 161 CU65
Church Ms, Add. KT15 234 BJ105
Church Mill Gra, Harl. CM17 58 EY12
Churchmore Rd, SW16 223 DJ95
Church Mt, N2 142 DD57
Church Paddock Ct, Wall. SM6 223 DK104
● Church Pk Ind Est, Craw.
RH11 290 DE154
Church Pas, EC2
off Gresham St 19 K8
Barnet EN5 off Wood St 101 CZ42
Surbiton KT6 220 CL99
Church Path, E11 146 EG57
E17 off St. Mary Rd 145 EB56
N5 9 H2
N12 120 DC50
N17 off White Hart La 122 DS52
N20 120 DC49
NW10 160 CS66
SW14 180 CR83
SW19 222 DA96
W4 180 CQ76
W7 159 CE74
Bray SL6 172 AC75
Cobham KT11 235 BV114
Coulsdon CR5 257 DN118
Grays RM17 192 GA79
Great Amwell SG12 55 DZ09
Church Path, Greenhithe DA9 211 FT85
Mitcham CR4 222 DE97
Northfleet DA11 212 GC86
Southall UB1 158 CA74
Southall Green UB2 178 BZ76
Swanley BR8 off School La 229 FH95
Woking GU21 off High St 249 AZ117
Church Pl, SW1 29 M1
W5 off Church Gdns 179 CK75
Ickenham UB10 137 BQ62
Mitcham CR4 222 DE97
Twickenham TW1
off Church St 199 CG88
Church Ri, SE23 205 DX88
Chessington KT9 238 CM107
Church Rd, E10 145 EB61
E12 146 EL64
E17 123 DY54
N1 9 K5
N6 142 DG58
N17 122 DS53
NW4 141 CV56
NW10 160 CS65
SE19 224 DS95
SW13 181 CT82
SW19 (Wimbledon) 201 CY90
W3 180 CQ75
W7 159 CE73
Addlestone KT15 234 BG106
Ashford TW15 196 BM90
Ashtead KT21 253 CK117
Barking IG11 167 EQ65
Bexleyheath DA7 188 EZ82
Biggin Hill TN16 260 EK117
Bookham KT23 252 BZ123
Bourne End SL8 132 AD62
Brasted TN16 262 EV124
Bromley BR2 226 EG96
Buckhurst Hill IG9 124 EH46
Burstow RH6 291 DN151
Byfleet KT14 234 BM113
Caterham CR3 258 DT123
Chelsfield BR6 246 EY106
Claygate KT10 237 CF107
Cowley UB8 156 BK70
Cranford TW5 177 BV78
Crockenhill BR8 229 FD101
Croydon CR0 223 DP104
East Molesey KT8 219 CD98
Egham TW20 195 BA92
Enfield EN3 104 DW44
Epsom KT17 238 CS112
Erith DA8 189 FC78
Farnborough BR6 245 EQ106
Farnham Royal SL2 153 AQ69
Feltham TW13 198 BX92
Gravesend DA12, DA13 213 GJ94
Greenhithe DA9 211 FS85
Guildford GU1 280 AX135
Halstead TN14 246 EY111
Ham TW10 200 CM92
Harefield UB9 136 BJ55
Harlow CM17 74 EW18
Harold Wood RM3 128 FN53
Hayes UB3 157 BT72
Hemel Hempstead HP3 63 BQ21
Hertford SG14 53 DP08
Heston TW5 178 CA80
High Beach IG10 106 EH40
High Wycombe HP10 110 AD47
Horley RH6 290 DF149
Horsell GU21 248 AY116
Ilford IG2 147 ER58
Isleworth TW7 179 CD81
Iver SL0 155 BC69
Kenley CR8 258 DR115
Keston BR2 244 EK108
Kingston upon Thames KT1 220 CM96
Leatherhead KT22 253 CH122
Leigh RH2 287 CU141
Little Berkhamsted SG13 69 DJ19
Long Ditton KT6 219 CJ103
Lowfield Heath RH11 290 DE154
Mitcham CR4 222 DD96
Noak Hill RM4 128 FK46
Northolt UB5 158 BZ66
Northwood HA6 115 BT52
Old Windsor SL4 194 AV85
Penn HP10 110 AC47
Potten End HP4 61 BB16
Potters Bar EN6 86 DB30
Purley CR8 241 DL110
Redhill RH1 288 DE136
Reigate RH2 288 DA136
Richmond TW9, TW10 200 CL85
St. John's GU21 248 AU119
Seal TN15 279 FM121
Seer Green HP9 111 AR51
Shepperton TW17 217 BP101
Shortlands BR2 226 EE97
Sidcup DA14 208 EU91
Southall UB2 178 BZ76
Stanmore HA7 117 CH50
Sutton SM3 239 CY107
Sutton at Hone DA4 210 FL94
Swanley BR8 230 FK95
Swanscombe DA10 212 FZ86
Teddington TW11 199 CE91
Tilbury RM18 193 GF81
Wallington SM6 223 DJ104
Warlingham CR6 258 DW117
Watford WD17 97 BU39
Welling DA16 188 EV82
Welwyn Garden City AL8 51 CX09
West Drayton UB7 176 BK76
West Ewell KT19 238 CR108
West Tilbury RM18 193 GL79
Whyteleafe CR3 258 DT118
Woldingham CR3 259 DX122
Worcester Park KT4 220 CS102
Church Rd Merton, SW19 222 DD95
Church Row, NW3 5 N1
Chislehurst BR7 207 EQ94
Church Row Ms, Ware SG12
off Church St 55 DX06
Church Side, Epsom KT18 238 CP113
Churchside Cl, Bigg.H. TN16 260 EJ117
Church Sq, Shep. TW17 217 BP101
Church Street 223 DP103
Church St, E15 13 K8
E16 37 N3
N9 122 DS47
NW8 16 B6
W2 16 B6
W4 180 CS79
Amersham HP7 77 AP40
Betchworth RH3 286 CS135
Bovingdon HP3 79 BB27
Burnham SL1 152 AJ70
Church St, Chalvey SL1 173 AQ75
Chesham HP5 76 AP31
Cobham KT11 251 BV115
Croydon CR0 224 DQ103
Dagenham RM10 169 FB65
Dorking RH4 285 CG136
Effingham KT24 268 BX127
Enfield EN2 104 DR41
Epsom KT17 238 CS113
Esher KT10 236 CB105
Essendon AL9 68 DE17
Ewell KT17 239 CU109
Gravesend DA11 213 GH86
Grays RM17 192 GC79
Hampton TW12 218 CC95
Hatfield AL9 67 CW17
Hemel Hempstead HP2 62 BK18
Hertford SG14 54 DR09
Isleworth TW7 179 CH83
Kingston upon Thames KT1 219 CK96
Leatherhead KT22 253 CH122
Old Woking GU22 249 BC121
Reigate RH2 272 DA134
Rickmansworth WD3 114 BL46
St. Albans AL3 65 CD19
Sawbridgeworth CM21 58 EY05
Seal TN15 279 FN121
Shoreham TN14 247 FF111
Slough SL1 174 AT76
Southfleet DA13 212 GA92
Staines-upon-Thames TW18 195 BE91
Sunbury-on-Thames TW16 217 BV97
Sutton SM1 off High St 240 DB106
Twickenham TW1 199 CG88
Waltham Abbey EN9 89 EC33
Walton-on-Thames KT12 217 BU102
Ware SG12 55 DX06
Watford WD18 98 BW42
Weybridge KT13 234 BN105
Windsor SL4
off Castle Hill 173 AR81
Church St E, Wok. GU21 249 AZ117
Church St Est, NW8 16 B5
Church St N, E15 13 K8
Church St Pas, E15 13 K8
Church St W, Wok. GU21 248 AY117
Church Stretton Rd, Houns.
TW3 198 CC85
Church Ter, NW4 141 CV55
SE13 186 EE83
SW8 41 P8
Richmond TW10 199 CK85
Windsor SL4 173 AL82
CHURCH TOWN, Gdse. RH9 275 DX131
● Church Trd Est, Erith DA8 189 FG80
Church Vale, N2 142 DF55
SE23 204 DW89
Church Vw, Aveley RM15 190 FQ75
Broxbourne EN10 71 DZ20
Swanley BR8 off Lime Rd 229 FD97
Upminster RM14 150 FN61
Church Vw Cl, Horl. RH6 290 DF149
Church Vw Gro, SE26 205 DX93
Churchview Rd, Twick. TW2 199 CD88
Church Vil, Sev. TN13
off Maidstone Rd 278 FE122
Church Wk, N6 142 DG62
N16 9 M2
NW2 141 CZ62
NW4 141 CW55
NW9 140 CR61
SW13 181 CU81
SW15 201 CV85
SW16 223 DJ96
SW20 221 CW97
Bletchingley RH1 274 DR133
Brentford TW8 179 CJ79
Burnham SL1 152 AH70
Bushey WD23 off High St 98 CA44
Caterham CR3 258 DU124
Chertsey KT16 216 BG101
Dartford DA2 210 FK90
Enfield EN2 104 DR41
Eynsford DA4 230 FL104
Gravesend DA12 213 GK88
Hayes UB3 157 BT72
Horley RH6
off Woodroyd Av 290 DF149
Leatherhead KT22 253 CH122
Outwood RH1 289 DP142
Reigate RH2
off Reigate Rd 272 DC134
Richmond TW9
off Red Lion St 199 CK85
Sawbridgeworth CM21 58 EZ05
Thames Ditton KT7 219 CF100
Walton-on-Thames KT12 217 BU102
Weybridge KT13
off Beales La 216 BN104
Church Wk Shop Cen, Cat.
CR3 off Church Wk 258 DU124
Churchward Ho, W14
off Ivatt Pl 39 H1
Church Way, N20 120 DD48
Churchway, NW1 17 P2
Church Way, Barn. EN4 102 DF42
Edgware HA8 118 CN51
Oxted RH8 276 EF132
South Croydon CR2 242 DT110
Churchwell Path, E9 10 G4
Churchwood Gdns, Wdf.Grn.
IG8 124 EG49
Churchyard, The, Bray SL6
off Church Dr 172 AC75
Churchyard Row, SE11 31 H8
Church Yd Wk, W2 16 A6
Churston Av, E13 166 EH67
Churston Cl, SW2
off Tulse Hill 203 DP88
Churston Dr, Mord. SM4 221 CX99
Churston Gdns, N11 121 DJ51
Churton Pl, SW1 29 M9
Churton St, SW1 29 M9
Chuters Cl, Byfleet KT14 234 BL112
Chuters Gro, Epsom KT17 239 CT112
Chyne, The, Ger.Cr. SL9 135 AZ57
Chyngton Cl, Sid. DA15 207 ET90
Cibber Rd, SE23 205 DX89
Cicada Rd, SW18 202 DC85
Cicely Rd, SE15 44 D7
Cillocks Cl, Hodd. EN11 71 EA16

Cimba Wd, Grav. DA12 213 GL91
Cinderella Path, NW11
off North End Rd 142 DB60
Cinderford Way, Brom. BR1 206 EE91
Cinder Path, Wok. GU22 248 AW119
Cinnabar Wf, E1 32 D3
Cinnamon Cl, SE15 44 A4
Croydon CR0 223 DL101
Windsor SL4 173 AM81
Cinnamon Gdns, Guil. GU2 264 AU129
Cinnamon Row, SW11 39 P10
Cinnamon St, E1 32 F3
Cintra Pk, SE19 204 DT94
CIPPENHAM, Slou. SL1 173 AM75
Cippenham Cl, Slou. SL1 153 AM73
Cippenham Inf Sch, Slou.
SL1 off Dennis Way 153 AK73
Cippenham Jun Sch, Cipp.
SL1 off Elmshott La 153 AL73
Cippenham La, Slou. SL1 153 AM73
Circle, The, NW2 140 CS62
NW7 118 CR50
SE1 32 A4
Tilbury RM18
off Toronto Rd 193 GG81
Circle Gdns, SW19 222 DA96
Byfleet KT14 234 BM113
Circle Rd, Whiteley Vill. KT12 235 BS110
Circuits, The, Pnr. HA5 138 BW56
Circular Rd, N17 144 DT55
Circular Way, SE18 187 EM79
Circus Lo, NW8 16 A2
Circus Ms, W1 16 E6
Circus Pl, EC2 19 M7
Circus Rd, NW8 16 A2
Circus Space, N1 19 N3
Circus St, SE10 46 E5
Cirencester St, W2 15 L6
Cirrus Cl, Wall. SM6 241 DL108
Cirrus Cres, Grav. DA12 213 GL92
Cissbury Ring N, N12 119 CZ50
Cissbury Ring S, N12 119 CZ50
Cissbury Rd, N15 144 DR57
Citadel Pl, SE11 30 C10
Citizen Ho, N7
off Harvist Est 143 DN63
Citizen Rd, N7 143 DN63
● C.I. Twr, N.Mal. KT3 220 CS97
Citron Ter, SE15
off Nunhead La 184 DV83
City & Guilds of London
Art Sch, SE11 42 F1
City & Islington Coll, Adult
Learning Cen, N19
off Junction Rd 143 DJ61
Cen for Applied Sciences, EC1 18 G2
Cen for Business, Arts & Tech,
N7 8 B1
Cen for Health, Social & Child
Care, N7 off Holloway Rd 143 DL63
Cen for Lifelong Learning,
N4 off Blackstock Rd 143 DP61
City & Islington 6th
Form Coll, EC1 18 G2
● City Business Cen, SE16
off Lower Rd 32 G5
City Business Coll, EC1 19 H3
City Coll, The, N1 19 L2
● City Cross Business Pk,
SE10 35 K8
● City Forum, EC1 19 J2
City Gdn Row, N1 19 H1
City Gate Ho, Ilf. IG2 147 EN58
City House, Croy. CR0 223 DP101
City Learning Cen, NW10 4 C9
City Lit, Keeley Ho, WC2 18 C9
Stukeley St, WC2 18 B8
City Mill River Towpath, E15
off Blaker Rd 12 E9
City of London Acad
(Islington), N1 9 J9
City of London Acad
(Southwark), SE1 32 D10
City of London Freemen's Sch,
Ashtd. KT21
off Park La 254 CN119
City of London Sch, EC4 19 J10
City of London Sch for Girls,
EC2 19 K6
★ City of Westminster Archives
Cen, SW1 29 P6
City of Westminster Coll,
Cockpit Thea, NW8 16 C5
Cosway St Cen, NW1 16 D6
Maida Vale Cen, W9 15 L3
Paddington Grn Cen, W2 16 A6
Queens Pk Cen, W9 15 J3
● City Pk, Welw.G.C. AL7 52 DA08
● City Pt, EC2 19 L6
City Rd, EC1 18 G1
⇌ City Thameslink 18 G9
City Twr, E14 34 D6
City Uni, Cass Business Sch,
EC1 19 L5
Halls of Res & Saddlers Sports
Cen, EC1 19 J4
Northampton Sq Campus,
EC1 18 G3
Walter Sickert Hall, N1 19 J2
City Uni - Inns of Ct Sch of Law,
Atkin Bldg, WC1 18 D6
Gray's Inn Pl, WC1 18 D7
Princeton St, WC1 18 D6
City Uni - St. Bartholomew Sch
of Nursing & Midwifery, E1 20 F7
City Vw, Ilf. IG1
off Axon Pl 147 EQ61
City Vw Apts, N1 9 J7
Cityview Ct, SE22 204 DU87
City Wk, SE1 31 N5
Civic Cl, St.Alb. AL1 65 CD20
Civic Offices, St.Alb. AL1 65 CD20
Civic Sq, Harl. CM20
off South Gate 73 ER15
Tilbury RM18 193 GG82
Civic Way, Ilf. IG6 147 EQ56
Ruislip HA4 138 BX64
Clabon Ms, SW1 28 E7
Clacket La, West. TN16 260 EL124
Clack La, Ruis. HA4 137 BQ60
Clack St, SE16 33 H5
Clacton Rd, E6 24 E2
E17 145 DY58
N17 off Sperling Rd 122 DT54
Claddagh Ct, N18
off Baxter Rd 122 DV49
Claigmar Gdns, N3 120 DB53
Claire Causeway, Dart. DA2 191 FS84
Claire Ct, N12 120 DC48
Bushey Heath WD23 117 CD46
Pinner HA5
off Westfield Pk 116 BZ52
Claire Gdns, Stan. HA7 117 CJ50
Claire Pl, E14 34 B6
Clairvale, Horn. RM11 150 FL59
Clairvale Rd, Houns. TW5 178 BX81
Clairview Rd, SW16 203 DH92
Clairville Ct, Reig. RH2 272 DD134
Clairville Gdns, W7 159 CE74
Clairville Pt, SE23 205 DX90
Clammas Way, Uxb. UB8 156 BJ71
Clamp Hill, Stan. HA7 117 CD49
Clancarty Rd, SW6 39 K9
⇌ Clandon 266 BH129
Clandon Av, Egh. TW20 195 BC94
Clandon Cl, W3 180 CP75
Epsom KT17 239 CT107
Clandon C of E Inf Sch, W.Clan.
GU4 off The Street 266 BG131
Clandon Gdns, N3 142 DA55
★ Clandon Park, Guil. GU4 266 BG132
Clandon Pk, W.Clan. GU4 266 BG132
Clandon Rd, Guil. GU1 280 AY135
Ilford IG3 147 ES61
Send GU23 265 BF125
West Clandon GU4 265 BF125
Clandon St, SE8 46 B8
Clanricarde Gdns, W2 27 K1
Clapgate Rd, Bushey WD23 98 CB44
CLAPHAM, SW4 183 DH83
★ Clapham Common, SW4 182 DG84
⊖ Clapham Common 183 DJ84
Clapham Common, SW4 183 DJ84
Clapham Common N Side,
SW4 183 DH84
Clapham Common S Side,
SW4 203 DH85
Clapham Common W Side,
SW4 182 DG84
Clapham Cres, SW4 183 DK84
Clapham Est, SW11 182 DE84
⇌ Clapham High Street 183 DK83
Clapham High St, SW4 183 DK84
⇌ Clapham Junction 182 DD84
Clapham Junction 182 DD84
Clapham Manor Prim Sch,
SW4 off Belmont Rd 183 DJ83
Clapham Manor St, SW4 41 M10
⊖ Clapham North 183 DL83
CLAPHAM PARK, SW4 203 DK86
Clapham Pk Est, SW4 203 DK86
Clapham Pk Rd, SW4 183 DK84
Clapham Rd, SW9 42 D6
Clapham Rd Est, SW4 41 P10
⊖ Clapham South 203 DH86
Clap La, Dag. RM10 149 FB62
Claps Gate La, E6 25 N4
⇌ Clapton 144 DV61
Clapton App, Woob.Grn HP10 132 AD55
Clapton Common, E5 144 DT59
Clapton Girls' Tech Coll, E5 10 G1
CLAPTON PARK, E5 145 DY63
Clapton Pk Est, E5
off Blackwell Cl 145 DX63
Clapton Pas, E5 10 G2
Clapton Sq, E5 10 F2
Clapton Ter, E5
off Clapton Common 144 DU60
Clapton Way, E5 144 DU63
Clara Grant Sch, E3 22 B5
Clara Pl, SE18 37 M8
Clare Cl, N2 142 DC55
Elstree WD6 100 CM44
West Byfleet KT14 234 BG113
Clare Cor, SE9 207 EP87
Clare Cotts, Bletch. RH1 273 DP133
Clare Ct, Aveley RM15 190 FQ75
Northwood HA6 115 BS50
Woldingham CR3 259 EA123
Clare Cres, Lthd. KT22 253 CG118
Claredale, Wok. GU22 248 AY119
Claredale St, E2 20 D1
Clare Dr, Farn.Com. SL2 133 AP63
Clare Gdns, E7 13 N1
W11 14 F9
Barking IG11 167 ET65
Egham TW20
off Mowbray Cres 195 BA92
Clare Hill, Esher KT10 236 CB107
Clare Ho, E3 11 N8
Clare Ho Prim Sch, Beck.
BR3 off Oakwood Av 225 EC96
Clare La, N1 9 K7
Clare Lawn Av, SW14 200 CR85
Clare Mkt, WC2 18 C9
Clare Ms, SW6 39 L5
Claremont, Brick.Wd AL2 82 CA31
Cheshunt EN7 88 DT29
Claremont Av, Esher KT10 236 BZ107
Harrow HA3 140 CL57
Hersham KT12 236 BX105
New Malden KT3 221 CU99
Sunbury-on-Thames TW16 217 BV95
Woking GU22 248 AY119
Claremont Cl, E16 37 M3
N1 18 F1
SW2 off Christchurch Rd 203 DM88
Grays RM16 off Premier Av 192 GC76
Hersham KT12 236 BW106
Orpington BR6 245 EN105
South Croydon CR2 258 DV115
Claremont Ct, Dor. RH4 285 CH137
Surbiton KT6
off St. James Rd 219 CK100
Claremont Cres, Crox.Grn WD3 97 BQ43
Dartford DA1 189 FE84
Claremont Dr, Esher KT10 236 CB108
Shepperton TW17 217 BP100
Woking GU22 248 AY119
Claremont End, Esher KT10 236 CB107
Claremont Fan Ct Sch, Esher
KT10 off Claremont Dr 236 CB108
Claremont Gdns, Ilf. IG3 147 ES61
Surbiton KT6 220 CL99
Upminster RM14 151 FR60
Claremont Gro, W4
off Edensor Gdns 180 CS80
Woodford Green IG8 124 EJ51
Claremont High Sch, Kenton
HA3 off Claremont Av 140 CL57
★ Claremont Landscape Gdn,
Esher KT10 236 BZ108
Claremont La, Esher KT10 236 CB105
CLAREMONT PARK, Esher
KT10 236 CB108
Claremont Pk, N3 119 CY53
Claremont Pk Rd,
Esher KT10 236 CB107
Claremont Pl, Grav. DA11
off Cutmore St 213 GH87
Claremont Prim Sch, NW2
off Claremont Rd 141 CX61
Claremont Rd, E7 146 EH64
E11 off Grove Grn Rd 145 ED62
E17 123 DY54
N6 143 DJ59
NW2 141 CX62
W9 14 F1
W13 159 CG71
Barnet EN4 102 DD37
Bromley BR1 226 EL98
Claygate KT10 237 CE108
Croydon CR0 224 DU102
Harrow HA3 117 CE54
Hornchurch RM11 149 FG58
Redhill RH1 272 DG131
Staines-upon-Thames TW18 195 BD92
Surbiton KT6 220 CL100
Swanley BR8 209 FE94
Teddington TW11 199 CF92
Twickenham TW1 199 CH86
West Byfleet KT14 234 BG112
Windsor SL4 173 AQ82
Claremont Sq, N1 18 E1
Claremont St, E16 37 M3
N18 122 DU51
SE10 46 D4
Claremont Way, NW2 141 CW60
● Claremont Way Ind Est,
NW2 141 CW60
Claremount Cl, Epsom
KT18 255 CW117
Claremount Gdns, Epsom
KT18 255 CW117
Clarence Av, SW4 203 DK86
Bromley BR1 226 EL98
Ilford IG2 147 EN58
New Malden KT3 220 CQ96
Upminster RM14 150 FN61
Clarence Cl, Barn. EN4 102 DD43
Bushey Heath WD23 117 CF45
Hersham KT12 236 BW105
Clarence Ct, Egh. TW20
off Clarence St 195 AZ93
Horley RH6 291 DK147
Clarence Cres, SW4 203 DK86
Sidcup DA14 208 EV90
Windsor SL4 173 AQ81
Clarence Dr, Eng.Grn TW20 194 AW91
Clarence Gdns, NW1 17 K3
Clarence Gate, Wdf.Grn. IG8 125 EN51
Clarence Gate Gdns, NW1
off Glentworth St 16 F5
★ Clarence Ho, SW1 29 M4
Clarence La, SW15 200 CS86
Clarence Lo, Hodd. EN11
off Taverners Way 71 EA17
Clarence Ms, E5 10 F2
SE16 33 J3
SW12 203 DH87
Clarence Pl, E5 10 F2
Gravesend DA12 213 GH87
Clarence Rd, E5 144 DV63
E12 146 EK64
E16 23 K5
E17 123 DX54
N15 144 DQ57
N22 121 DL52
NW6 4 G7
SE8 46 C3
SE9 206 EL89
SW19 202 DB93
W4 180 CN78
Berkhamsted HP4 60 AW19
Bexleyheath DA6 188 EY84
Biggin Hill TN16 261 EM118
Bromley BR1 226 EK97
Croydon CR0 224 DR101
Enfield EN3 104 DV43
Grays RM17 192 GA79
Hersham KT12 235 BV105
Pilgrim's Hatch CM15 130 FV44
Redhill RH1 288 DD137
Richmond TW9 180 CM81
St. Albans AL1 65 CF20
Sidcup DA14 208 EV90
Sutton SM1 240 DB105
Teddington TW11 199 CF93
Wallington SM6 241 DH106
Windsor SL4 173 AP81
Clarence Row, Grav. DA12 213 GH87
Clarence St, Egh. TW20 195 AZ93
Kingston upon Thames KT1 220 CL96
Richmond TW9 180 CL84
Southall UB2 178 BX76
Staines-upon-Thames TW18 195 BE91
Clarence Ter, NW1 16 F4
Hounslow TW3 178 CB84
Clarence Wk, SW4 42 A8
Redhill RH1 288 DD137
Clarence Way, NW1 7 J6
Horley RH6 291 DK147
South Ockendon RM15 171 FX72
Clarence Way Est, NW1 7 K6
Clarenden Pl, Dart. DA2 209 FD92
Clarendon Cl, E9 11 H7
W2 16 C10
Hemel Hempstead HP2 62 BK19
Orpington BR5 228 EU97
Clarendon Ct, Slou. SL2 154 AV73
Clarendon Cres, Twick. TW2 199 CD90
Clarendon Cross, W11 26 F1
Clarendon Dr, SW15 181 CW84
Clarendon Flds, Chan.Cr.
WD3 96 BM38
Clarendon Gdns, NW4 141 CU55
W9 15 P5
Dartford DA2 211 FR87
Ilford IG1 147 EM60
Wembley HA9 140 CL63
Clarendon Gate, Ott. KT16 233 BD107
Clarendon Grn, Orp. BR5 228 EU98
Clarendon Gro, NW1 17 N2
Mitcham CR4 222 DF97
Orpington BR5 228 EU97
Clarendon Ho, Kings.T. KT2
off Cowleaze Rd 220 CL95
Clarendon Ms, W2 16 C9
Ashtead KT21 254 CL119
Clarendon Ms, Bexley DA5 209 FB88
Borehamwood WD6
off Clarendon Rd 100 CN41
Clarendon Path, Orp. BR5 228 EU97
Clarendon Pl, W2 16 C10
Sevenoaks TN13
off Clarendon Rd 278 FG125
Clarendon Prim Sch, Ashf.
TW15 off Knapp Rd 196 BM91
Clarendon Ri, SE13 185 EC83
Clarendon Rd, E11 145 ED60
E17 145 EB58
E18 146 EG55
N8 143 DM55
N15 143 DP56
N18 122 DU51
N22 121 DM54
SW19 202 DE94
W5 160 CL69
W11 14 E10
Ashford TW15 196 BM91
Borehamwood WD6 100 CN41
Cheshunt EN8 89 DX29
Croydon CR0 223 DP103
Gravesend DA12 213 GJ86
Harrow HA1 139 CE58
Hayes UB3 177 BT75
Redhill RH1 272 DF133
Sevenoaks TN13 278 FG124
Wallington SM6 241 DJ107
Watford WD17 97 BV40
Clarendon Sch, Hmptn.
TW12 off Hanworth Rd 198 CB93
Clarendon St, SW1 41 K1
Clarendon Ter, W9 15 P4
Clarendon Wk, W11 14 E9
Clarendon Way, N21 104 DQ44
Chislehurst BR7 227 ET97
Orpington BR5 227 ET97
Clarens St, SE6 205 DZ89
Clare Pk, Amer. HP7 77 AS40
Clare Pl, SW15
off Minstead Gdns 201 CT87
Clare Pt, NW2
off Claremont Rd 141 CX60
Clare Rd, E11 145 ED58
NW10 161 CU66
SE14 45 N7
Greenford UB6 159 CD65
Hounslow TW4 178 BZ83
Stanwell TW19 196 BL87
Taplow SL6 152 AJ72
Clares, The, Cat. CR3 258 DU124
Clare St, E2 20 F1
Claret Gdns, SE25 224 DS98
Clareville Gro, SW7 27 P9
Clareville Gro Ms, SW7
off Clareville St 27 P9
Clareville Rd, Cat. CR3 258 DU124
Orpington BR5 227 EQ103
Clareville St, SW7 27 P9
Clare Way, Bexh. DA7 188 EY81
Sevenoaks TN13 279 FJ127
Clare Wd, Lthd. KT22 253 CH118
Clarewood Wk, SW9 183 DP84
Clarges Ms, W1 29 J2
Clarges St, W1 29 K2
Claribel Rd, SW9 42 G8
Clarice Way, Wall. SM6 241 DL109
Claridge Rd, Dag. RM8 148 EX60
Clarinda Ho, Green. DA9 191 FW84
Clarissa Rd, Rom. RM6 148 EX59
Clarissa St, E8 10 A9
Clark Cl, Erith DA8 189 FG81
Clarkebourne Dr, Grays RM17 192 GD79
Clarke Cl, Croy. CR0 224 DQ100
Clarke Ct, W6 off Great W Rd 181 CU78
Clarke Grn, Wat. WD25 97 BU35
Clarke Ms, N9 off Plevna Rd 122 DV48
Clarke Path, N16 144 DU60
Clarkes Av, Wor.Pk. KT4 221 CX102
Clarkes Dr, Uxb. UB8 156 BL71
Clarke's Ms, W1 17 H6
Clarkes Rd, Hat. AL10 67 CV17
Clarke Way, Wat. WD25 97 BU35
Clarkfield, Mill End WD3 114 BH46
Clark Gro, Ilf. IG3 147 ES63
Clark Lawrence Ct, SW11
off Winstanley Rd 182 DD83
Clarks La, Epp. CM16 91 ET31
Halstead TN14 246 EZ112
Warlingham CR6 260 EF123
Westerham TN16 260 EK123
Clarks Mead, Bushey WD23 116 CC45
Clarkson Ct, Hat. AL10 66 CS17
Clarkson Rd, E16 23 L8
Clarkson Row, NW1 17 L1
Clarksons, The, Bark. IG11 167 EQ68
Clarkson St, E2 20 E2
Clarks Pl, EC2 19 N8
Clarks Rd, Ilf. IG1 147 ER61
Clark St, E1 20 F7
Clark Way, Houns. TW5 178 BX80
Classon Cl, West Dr. UB7 176 BL75
Claston Cl, Dart. DA1 189 FE84
CLATTERFORD END, Ong. CM5 93 FG30
Claude Rd, E10 145 EC61
E13 166 EH67
SE15 44 E9
Claude St, E14 34 A8
Claudia Jones Way, SW2 203 DL86
Claudian Pl, St.Alb. AL3 64 CA22
Claudian Way, Grays RM16 193 GH76
Claudia Pl, SW19 201 CY88
Claudius Cl, Stan. HA7 117 CK48
Claughton Rd, E13 24 D1
Claughton Way, Hutt. CM13 131 GD44
Clauson Av, Nthlt. UB5 138 CB64
Clavell St, SE10 46 E2
Claverdale Rd, SW2 203 DM87
Claverhambury Rd, Wal.Abb.
EN9 90 EF29
Clavering Av, SW13 181 CV79
Clavering Cl, Twick. TW1 199 CG91
Clavering Pl, SW12 202 DG86
Clavering Rd, E12 146 EK60
● Claverings Ind Est, N9 123 DX47
Clavering Way, Hutt. CM13
off Poplar Dr 131 GC44
Claverley Gro, N3 120 DA52
Claverley Vil, N3 120 DB52
Claverton Cl, Bov. HP3 79 BA28
Claverton St, SW1 41 M1
Clave St, E1 32 G3
Claxton Gro, W6 38 D1
Claxton Path, SE4
off Hainford Cl 185 DX84
Clay Acre, Chesh. HP5 76 AR30
Clay Av, Mitch. CR4 223 DH96
Claybank Gro, SE13 46 C10
Claybourne Ms, SE19
off Church Rd 204 DS94
Claybridge Rd, SE12 206 EJ91
Claybrook Cl, N2 142 DD55
Claybrook Rd, W6 38 D2
Clayburn Gdns, S.Ock. RM15 171 FV73
Claybury, Bushey WD23 116 CB45
Claybury Bdy, Ilf. IG5 146 EL55
Claybury Hall, Wdf.Grn. IG8 125 EM52
Claybury Rd, Wdf.Grn. IG8 124 EL52
Clay Cor, Cher. KT16
off Eastworth Rd 216 BH102
Claycots Prim Sch, Slou.
SL2 off Monksfield Way 153 AN70
Claycroft, Welw.G.C. AL7 52 DB08
Claydon, SE17
off Deacon Way 31 J8
Claydon Dr, Croy. CR0 241 DL105
Claydon End, Chal.St.P. SL9 134 AY55
Claydon La, Chal.St.P. SL9 134 AY55
Claydon Rd, Wok. GU21 248 AU116
Claydown Ms, SE18 37 M10
Clayfarm Rd, SE9 207 EQ89
Clayfields, Penn HP10 110 AC45
CLAYGATE, Esher KT10 237 CE108
⇌ Claygate 237 CD107
Claygate Cl, Horn. RM12 149 FG63
Claygate Cres, New Adgtn CR0 243 EC107
Claygate La, Esher KT10 219 CG103
Thames Ditton KT7 219 CG102
Waltham Abbey EN9 89 ED30
Claygate Lo Cl, Clay. KT10 237 CE108
Claygate Prim Sch, Clay.
KT10 off Foley Rd 237 CE108
Claygate Rd, W13 179 CH76
Dorking RH4 285 CH138
CLAYHALL, Ilf. IG5 125 EM54
Clayhall Av, Ilf. IG5 146 EL55
Clayhall La, Old Wind. SL4 194 AT85
Reigate RH2 287 CX138
Clayhanger, Guil. GU4 265 BC132
CLAY HILL, Enf. EN2 104 DQ37
Clay Hill, Enf. EN2 104 DQ37
Clayhill, Surb. KT5 220 CN99
Clayhill Cl, Leigh RH2 287 CU141
Clayhill Cres, SE9 206 EK91
Clayhill Rd, Leigh RH2 287 CT142
Claylands Pl, SW8 42 E4
Claylands Rd, SW8 42 D3
Clay La, Bushey Hth WD23 117 CE45
Edgware HA8 118 CN46
Guildford GU4 264 AY128
Headley KT18 254 CP124
South Nutfield RH1 289 DJ135
Stanwell TW19 196 BM87
Claymill Ho, SE18 187 EQ78
Claymills Ms, Hem.H. HP3 62 BN23
Claymore, Hem.H. HP2 62 BL16
Claymore Cl, Mord. SM4 222 DA101
Claymore Ct, E17
off Billet Rd 123 DY53
Clay Path, E17
off Bedford Rd 123 EA54
Claypit Hill, Wal.Abb. EN9 106 EJ36
Claypole Dr, Houns. TW5 178 BY81
Claypole Rd, E15 12 F10
Claypond Av, Brent. TW8 180 CL77
Clayponds Gdns, W5 179 CK77
Clayponds Hosp, W5 180 CL77
Clayponds La, Brent. TW8 180 CL78
Clay Rd, The, Loug. IG10 106 EL39
Clayside, Chig. IG7 125 EQ51
Clay's La, Loug. IG10 107 EN39
Clay St, W1 16 F7
Beaconsfield HP9 110 AJ48
Clayton Av, Upmin. RM14 150 FP64
Wembley HA0 160 CL66
● Clayton Business Cen,
Hayes UB3 177 BS75
Clayton Cl, E6 25 K8
Clayton Cres, N1 8 B9
Brentford TW8 179 CK78
Clayton Cft Rd, Dart. DA2 209 FG89
Clayton Dr, SE8 33 L10
Guildford GU2 264 AT131
Hemel Hempstead HP3 63 BR22
Clayton Fld, NW9 118 CS52
Clayton Mead, Gdse. RH9 274 DV130
Clayton Ms, SE10 46 G6
Clayton Rd, SE15 44 D7
Chessington KT9 237 CJ105
Epsom KT17 238 CS113
Hayes UB3 177 BS75
Isleworth TW7 179 CE83
Romford RM7 149 FC60
Clayton St, SE11 42 E2
Clayton Ter, Hayes UB4
off Jollys La 158 BX71
Clayton Wk, Amer. HP7 94 AW39
Clayton Way, Uxb. UB8 156 BK70
Clay Tye Rd, Upmin. RM14 151 FW63
Claywood Cl, Orp. BR6 227 ES101
Claywood La, Bean DA2 211 FX90
Clayworth Cl, Sid. DA15 208 EV86
Cleall Av, Wal.Abb. EN9
off Quaker La 89 EC34
Cleanthus Cl, SE18 187 EP81
Cleanthus Rd, SE18 187 EP81
Clearbrook Way, E1 21 H8
Cleardene, Dor. RH4 285 CH136
Cleardown, Wok. GU22 249 BB118
Cleares Pasture, Burn. SL1 152 AH69
Clearmount, Chobham GU24 232 AS107
Clears, The, Reig. RH2 271 CY132
Clearwater Pl, Long Dit. KT6 219 CJ100
Clearwater Ter, W11 26 D4
Clearwell Dr, W9 15 L5
Cleave Av, Hayes UB3 177 BS77
Orpington BR6 245 ES107
Cleaveland Rd, Surb. KT6 219 CK99
Cleave Prior, Chipstead CR5 256 DE119
Cleaverholme Cl, SE25 224 DV100
Cleaver Sq, SE11 30 F10
Cleaver St, SE11 30 F10
Cleeve, The, Guil. GU1 265 BA134
Cleeve Ct, Felt. TW14
off Kilross Rd 197 BS88
Cleeve Hill, SE23 204 DV88
Cleeve Pk Gdns, Sid. DA14 208 EV89
Cleeve Pk Sch, Sid. DA14
off Bexley La 208 EW90
Cleeve Rd, Lthd. KT22 253 CF120
● Cleeve Studios, E2
off Boundary St 20 A3
Cleeve Way, SW15 201 CT86
Sutton SM1 222 DB102
Clegg St, E1 32 F2
E13 13 P10

Cleland Path, Loug. IG10 107 EP39
Cleland Rd, Chal.St.P. SL9 112 AX54
Clematis Cl, Rom. RM3 128 FJ52
Clematis Gdns, Wdf.Grn. IG8 124 EG50
Clematis St, W12 161 CT73
Clem Attlee Ct, SW6 38 G3
Clem Attlee Par, SW6
off North End Rd 39 H3
Clemence Rd, Dag. RM10 169 FC67
Clemence St, E14 21 N7
Clement Av, SW4 183 DK84
Clement Cl, NW6 4 B7
W4 180 CR76
Purley CR8
off Croftleigh Av 257 DP116
Clement Danes Ho, W12
off Du Cane Rd 161 CV72
Clement Gdns, Hayes UB3 177 BS77
Clementhorpe Rd, Dag. RM9 168 EW65
Clementina Rd, E10 145 DZ60
Clementine Churchill Hosp,
Har. HA1 139 CF62
Clementine Cl, W13
off Balfour Rd 179 CH75
Clementine Wk, Wdf.Grn. IG8
off Salway Cl 124 EG52
Clementine Way, Hem.H. HP1 62 BH22
Clement Rd, SW19 201 CY92
Beckenham BR3 225 DX96
Cheshunt EN8 89 DY27
Clements Av, E16 23 N10
Clements Cl, N12 120 DB49
Slough SL1 174 AV75
Clements Ct, Houns. TW4 178 BX84
Ilford IG1
off Clements La 147 EP62
Watford WD25 98 BW35
Clements Ho, Lthd. KT22 253 CG119
Clement's Inn, WC2 18 D9
Clement's Inn Pas, WC2 18 D9
Clements La, EC4 19 M10
Ilford IG1 147 EP62
Clements Mead, Lthd. KT22 253 CG119
Clements Pl, Brent. TW8 179 CK78
Clements Rd, E6 167 EM66
SE16 32 D7
Chorleywood WD3 95 BD43
Ilford IG1 147 EP62
Walton-on-Thames KT12 217 BV103
Clements St, Ware SG12 55 DY06
Clement St, Swan. BR8 210 FK93
Clement Way, Upmin. RM14 150 FM62
Clemson Ms, Epsom KT17 239 CT112
Clenches Fm La, Sev. TN13 278 FG126
Clenches Fm Rd, Sev. TN13 278 FG126
Clendon Way, SE18
off Polthorne Gro 187 ER77
Clennam St, SE1 31 K4
Clensham Ct, Sutt. SM1
off Sutton Common Rd 222 DA103
Clensham La, Sutt. SM1 222 DA103
Clenston Ms, W1 16 E8
Cleopatra Cl, Stan. HA7 117 CK48
★ Cleopatra's Needle, WC2 30 C2
Clephane Rd, N1 9 L5
Clere St, EC2 19 M4
Clerics Wk, Shep. TW17
off Gordon Rd 217 BR100
CLERKENWELL, EC1 18 G5
Clerkenwell Cl, EC1 18 F4
Clerkenwell Grn, EC1 18 F5
Clerkenwell Parochial C of E
Prim Sch, EC1 18 E2
Clerkenwell Rd, EC1 18 E5
Clerks Cft, Bletch. RH1 274 DR133
Clerks Piece, Loug. IG10 107 EM41
Clermont Rd, E9 10 G8
Clevedon, Wey. KT13 235 BQ106
Clevedon Cl, N16
off Smalley Cl 144 DT62
Clevedon Gdns, Hayes UB3 177 BR76
Hounslow TW5 177 BV81
Clevedon Rd, SE20 225 DX95
Kingston upon Thames KT1 220 CN96
Twickenham TW1 199 CK86
Clevehurst Cl, Stoke P. SL2 154 AT65
Cleveland Av, SW20 221 CZ96
W4 181 CT77
Hampton TW12 198 BZ94
Cleveland Cl, Walt. KT12 217 BV104
Wooburn Green HP10 132 AE55
Cleveland Cres, Borwd.
WD6 100 CQ43
Cleveland Dr, Stai. TW18 216 BH96
Cleveland Gdns, N4 144 DQ57
NW2 141 CX61
SW13 181 CT82
W2 15 N9
Worcester Park KT4 220 CS103
Cleveland Gro, E1 20 G5
Cleveland Inf & Jun Schs,
Ilf. IG1 off Cleveland Rd 147 EP63
Cleveland Ms, W1 17 L6
Cleveland Pk, Stai. TW19 196 BL86
Cleveland Pk Av, E17 145 EA56
Cleveland Pk Cres, E17 145 EA56
Cleveland Pl, SW1 29 M2
Cleveland Ri, Mord. SM4 221 CX101
Cleveland Rd, E18 146 EG55
N1 9 M7
N9 122 DV45
SW13 181 CT82
W4 off Antrobus Rd 180 CQ76
W13 159 CH71
Hemel Hempstead HP2 63 BP18
Ilford IG1 147 EP62
Isleworth TW7 179 CG84
New Malden KT3 220 CS98
Uxbridge UB8 156 BK68
Welling DA16 187 ET82
Worcester Park KT4 220 CS103
Cleveland Row, SW1 29 L3
Cleveland Sq, W2 15 N9
Cleveland St, W1 17 L5
Cleveland Ter, W2 15 P8
Cleveland Way, E1 20 G5
Hemel Hempstead HP2 63 BP18
Cleveley Cl, SE7 36 F8
Cleveley Cres, W5 160 CL68
Cleveleys Rd, E5 144 DV62
Cleverly Est, W12 161 CU74
Cleve Rd, NW6 5 K6
Sidcup DA14 208 EX90
Cleves Av, Brwd. CM14 130 FV46
Epsom KT17 239 CV109
Cleves Cl, Cob. KT11 235 BV114
Loughton IG10 106 EL44
Cleves Ct, Wind. SL4 173 AM83
Cleves Cres, New Adgtn CR0 243 EC111
Cleves Prim Sch, E6
off Arragon Rd 166 EK67
Cleves Rd, E6 166 EK67
Hemel Hempstead HP2 63 BP15
Richmond TW10 199 CJ90
Cleves Sch, Wey. KT13
off Oatlands Av 235 BT105
Cleves Wk, Ilf. IG6 125 EQ52
Cleves Way, Hmptn. TW12 198 BZ94
Ruislip HA4 138 BX60
Sunbury-on-Thames TW16 197 BT93
Cleves Wd, Wey. KT13 235 BS105
Clewer Av, Wind. SL4 173 AN82
Clewer Ct Rd, Wind. SL4 173 AP80
Clewer Cres, Har. HA3 117 CD53
Clewer Flds, Wind. SL4 173 AQ81
CLEWER GREEN, Wind. SL4 173 AM82
Clewer Grn C of E First Sch,
Wind. SL4 off Hatch La 173 AN83
Clewer Hill Rd, Wind. SL4 173 AL82
Clewer Ho, SE2
off Wolvercote Rd 188 EX75
CLEWER NEW TOWN,
Wind. SL4 173 AN82
Clewer New Town, Wind. SL4 173 AN82
Clewer Pk, Wind. SL4 173 AN80
CLEWER VILLAGE, Wind. SL4 173 AM80
Clichy Est, E1 21 H7
Clifden Ms, E5 11 K1
Clifden Rd, E5 11 H2
Brentford TW8 179 CK79
Twickenham TW1 199 CF88
Cliff End, Pur. CR8 241 DP112
Cliffe Rd, S.Croy. CR2 242 DR106
Cliffe Wk, Sutt. SM1
off Turnpike La 240 DC106
Clifford Av, SW14 180 CP83
Chislehurst BR7 207 EM93
Ilford IG5 125 EP53
Wallington SM6 241 DJ105
Clifford Cl, Nthlt. UB5 158 BY67
Clifford Dr, SW9 183 DP84
Clifford Gdns, NW10 14 A1
Hayes UB3 177 BR77
Clifford Gro, Ashf. TW15 196 BN91
Clifford Haigh Ho, SW6
off Fulham Palace Rd 181 CX80
Clifford Manor Rd, Guil. GU4 280 AY138
Clifford Rd, E16 23 L5
E17 123 EC54
N9 104 DW44
SE25 224 DU98
Barnet EN5 102 DB41
Chafford Hundred RM16 192 FZ75
Hounslow TW4 178 BX83
Richmond TW10 199 CK89
Wembley HA0 159 CK67
Clifford's Inn Pas, EC4 18 E9
Clifford St, W1 29 L1
Clifford Way, NW10 141 CT63
Cliff Pl, S.Ock. RM15 171 FX69
Cliff Reach, Bluewater DA9 211 FS87
Cliff Richard Ct, Chsht EN8
off High St 89 DX28
Cliff Rd, NW1 7 P4
Cliff Ter, SE8 46 B8
Cliffview Rd, SE13 185 EA83
Cliff Vil, NW1 7 P4
Cliff Wk, E16 23 M6
Clifton Av, E17 145 DX55
N3 119 CZ53
W12 161 CT74
Feltham TW13 198 BW90
Stanmore HA7 117 CH54
Sutton SM2 240 DB111
Wembley HA9 160 CM65
Clifton Cl, Add. KT15 216 BH103
Caterham CR3 258 DR123
Cheshunt EN8 89 DY29
Horley RH6 291 DK148
Orpington BR6 245 EQ106
Clifton Ct, N4
off Biggerstaff St 143 DN61
NW8 16 A4
Woodford Green IG8
off Snakes La W 124 EG51
Clifton Cres, SE15 44 F5
Clifton Est, SE15 44 D7
Clifton Gdns, N15 144 DT58
NW11 141 CZ58
W4 off Dolman Rd 180 CR77
W9 15 N5
Enfield EN2 103 DL42
Uxbridge UB10 157 BP68
Clifton Gro, E8 10 C4
Gravesend DA11 213 GH87
Clifton Hatch, Harl. CM18
off Trotters Rd 74 EU18
Clifton Hill, NW8 5 N9
Clifton Hill Sch, Cat. CR3
off Chaldon Rd 258 DR123
Clifton Lawns, Amer. HP6 77 AQ35
Clifton Lo Boys' Prep Sch,
W5 off Mattock La 159 CK73
Clifton Marine Par, Grav. DA11 213 GF86
Clifton Pk Av, SW20 221 CW96
Clifton Pl, SE16 33 H4
W2 16 B10
Banstead SM7 256 DA115
Clifton Prim Sch, Sthl.
UB2 off Clifton Rd 178 BY77
Clifton Ri, SE14 45 M5
Windsor SL4 173 AK81
Clifton Rd, E7 166 EK65
E16 23 K6
N1 9 K5
N3 120 DC53
N8 143 DK58
N22 121 DJ53
NW10 161 CU68
SE25 224 DS98
SW19 201 CX93
W9 15 P4
Amersham HP6 77 AP35
Coulsdon CR5 257 DH115
Gravesend DA11 213 GG86
Greenford UB6 158 CC70
Harrow HA3 140 CM57
Hornchurch RM11 149 FG58
Ilford IG2 147 ER58
Isleworth TW7 179 CD82
Kingston upon Thames KT2 200 CM94
London Heathrow Airport
TW6 off Inner Ring E 177 BP83
Loughton IG10 106 EL42
Sidcup DA14 207 ES91
Slough SL1 174 AV75
Southall UB2 178 BY77
Teddington TW11 199 CE91
Clifton Rd, Wallington SM6 241 DH106
Watford WD18 97 BV43
Welling DA16 188 EW83
Cliftons La, Reig. RH2 271 CX131
Clifton's Rbt, SE12 206 EH86
Clifton St, EC2 19 N6
St. Albans AL1 65 CE19
Clifton Ter, N4 143 DN61
Clifton Vil, W9 15 M6
Cliftonville, Dor. RH4 285 CH137
Clifton Wk, E6 25 H8
W6 off Galena Rd 181 CV77
Dartford DA2
off Osbourne Rd 210 FP86
Clifton Way, SE15 44 F5
Borehamwood WD6 100 CN39
Hutton CM13 131 GD46
Wembley HA0 160 CL67
Woking GU21 248 AT117
Climb, The, Rick. WD3 96 BH44
Clinch Ct, E16 23 P7
Cline Rd, N11 121 DJ51
Guildford GU1 281 AZ136
Clinger Ct, N1 9 N9
★ Clink Prison Mus, SE1 31 L2
Clink St, SE1 31 K2
Clinton Av, E.Mol. KT8 218 CC98
Welling DA16 187 ET84
Clinton Cl, Wey. KT13 217 BP104
Clinton Cres, Ilf. IG6 125 ES51
Clinton End, Hem.H. HP2 63 BQ20
Clinton Rd, E3 21 L3
E7 13 P1
N15 144 DR56
Leatherhead KT22 253 CJ123
Clinton Ter, Sutt. SM1
off Manor La 240 DC105
Clipper Boul, Dart. DA2 191 FS83
Clipper Boul W, Dart. DA2 191 FR83
Clipper Cl, SE16 33 J4
Clipper Cres, Grav. DA12 213 GM91
Clipper Pk, Til. RM18 192 GD80
Clipper Way, SE13 185 EC84
Clippesby Cl, Chess. KT9 238 CM108
Clipstone Ms, W1 17 L5
Clipstone Rd, Houns. TW3 178 CA83
Clipstone St, W1 17 K6
Clissold Cl, N2 142 DF55
Clissold Ct, N4 144 DQ61
Clissold Cres, N16 144 DR62
Clissold Rd, N16 144 DR62
Clitheroe Av, Har. HA2 138 CA60
Clitheroe Gdns, Wat. WD19 116 BX48
Clitheroe Rd, SW9 42 B9
Romford RM5 127 FC50
Clitherow Av, W7 179 CG76
Clitherow Pas, Brent. TW8 179 CJ78
Clitherow Rd, Brent. TW8 179 CH78
Clitterhouse Cres, NW2 141 CW60
Clitterhouse Rd, NW2 141 CW60
Clive Av, N18
off Claremont St 122 DU51
Dartford DA1 209 FF86
Clive Cl, Pot.B. EN6 85 CZ31
Clive Ct, W9 15 P4
Slough SL1 173 AR75
★ Cliveden, Maid. SL6 132 AD64
Cliveden Cl, N12 120 DC49
Shenfield CM15 131 FZ45
Cliveden Gages, Tap. SL6 152 AE65
Cliveden Pl, SW1 28 G8
Shepperton TW17 217 BP100
Cliveden Rd, SW19 221 CZ95
Burnham SL1 152 AE65
Taplow SL6 152 AE65
Clivedon Ct, W13 159 CH71
Clivedon Rd, E4 124 EE50
Clive Par, Nthwd. HA6
off Maxwell Rd 115 BS52
Clive Pas, SE21 off Clive Rd 204 DR90
Clive Rd, SE21 204 DR90
SW19 202 DE93
Belvedere DA17 188 FA77
Enfield EN1 104 DU42
Esher KT10 236 CB105
Feltham TW14 197 BU86
Gravesend DA11 213 GH86
Great Warley CM13 129 FW52
Romford RM2 149 FH57
Twickenham TW1 199 CF91
Clivesdale Dr, Hayes UB3 157 BV74
Clive Way, Enf. EN1 104 DU42
Watford WD24 98 BW39
Cloak La, EC4 19 K10
⇌ Clock House 225 DY96
Clockhouse Av, Bark. IG11 167 EQ67
Clockhouse Cl, SW19 201 CW90
Clock Ho Cl, Byfleet KT14 234 BM112
Clockhouse Ct, Guil. GU1
off Palm Gro 264 AW130
Clockhouse Junct, N13 121 DM50
Clockhouse La, Ashf. TW15 196 BN91
Feltham TW14 197 BP89
Grays RM16 171 FX74
Romford RM5 127 FB52
Clock Ho La, Sev. TN13 278 FG123
Clockhouse La E, Egh. TW20 195 BB94
Clockhouse La W, Egh. TW20 195 BA94
Clock Ho Mead, Oxshott KT22 236 CB114
Clockhouse Ms, Chorl. WD3
off Chorleywood Ho Dr 95 BE41
● Clockhouse Pl, Felt. TW14 197 BQ88
Clockhouse Pl, SW15 201 CY85
Clockhouse Prim Sch,
Coll.Row RM5
off Clockhouse La 127 FB51
Clock Ho Rd, Beck. BR3 225 DY97
Clockhouse Rbt,
Felt. TW14 197 BP88
★ Clockmakers' Museum, The
(Guildhall Lib), EC2 19 K8
Clock Twr Ms, N1 9 K9
SE28 168 EV73
W7 off Uxbridge Rd 159 CE74
Clock Twr Rd, Islw. TW7 179 CF83
Clock Twr Rbt, Harl. CM17 74 EV16
Clock Vw Cres, N7 8 A4
Cloister Cl, Rain. RM13 169 FH70
Teddington TW11 199 CH92
Cloister Gdns, SE25 224 DV100
Edgware HA8 118 CQ50
Cloister Garth, Berk. HP4 60 AW19
St. Albans AL1 65 CE24
Cloister Rd, NW2 141 CZ62
W3 160 CQ71
Cloisters, The, Bushey WD23 98 CB44
Guildford GU1
off London Rd 265 BA131
Rickmansworth WD3 114 BL45
Cloisters, The, Welwyn Garden City
AL8 51 CX09
Windsor SL4 173 AN82
Woking GU22 249 BB121
Cloisters Av, Brom. BR2 227 EM99
● Cloisters Business Cen,
SW8 off Battersea Pk Rd 41 K5
Cloisters Ct, Rick. WD3
off The Cloisters 114 BL45
Cloisters Mall, Kings.T. KT1
off Union St 219 CK96
Cloister Wk, Hem.H. HP2
off Townsend 62 BK18
Clonard Way, Pnr. HA5 116 CA51
Clonbrock Rd, N16 144 DS63
Cloncurry St, SW6 38 D8
Clonmel Cl, Har. HA2 139 CD61
Clonmell Rd, N17 144 DR55
Clonmel Rd, SW6 39 H5
Teddington TW11 199 CD91
Clonmel Way, Burn. SL1 152 AH69
Clonmore St, SW18 201 CZ88
Cloonmore Av, Orp. BR6 245 ET105
Clorane Gdns, NW3 142 DA62
Clore Shalom Sch, Shenley
WD7 off Hugo Gryn Way 84 CL30
Clore Tikva Sch, Ilf. IG6
off Fullwell Av 125 EQ54
Close, The, E4
off Beech Hall Rd 123 EC52
N14 121 DK47
N20 119 CZ47
SE3 47 H9
Beckenham BR3 225 DY98
Berry's Green TN16 261 EP116
Bexley DA5 208 FA86
Brentwood CM14 130 FW48
Brookmans Park AL9 85 CY26
Bushey WD23 98 CB43
Carshalton SM5 240 DE109
Dartford DA2 210 FJ90
East Barnet EN4 102 DF44
Eastcote HA5 138 BW59
Grays RM16 192 GC75
Harrow HA2 116 CC54
Hillingdon UB10 156 BN67
Horley RH6 291 DJ150
Isleworth TW7 179 CD82
Iver SL0 155 BC69
Mitcham CR4 222 DF98
New Malden KT3 220 CQ96
Petts Wood BR5 227 ES100
Potters Bar EN6 86 DA32
Purley (Pampisford Rd) CR8 241 DP110
Purley (Russ.Hill) CR8 241 DM110
Radlett WD7 83 CF33
Rayners Lane HA5 138 BZ59
Reigate RH2 288 DB135
Richmond TW9 180 CP83
Rickmansworth WD3 114 BJ46
Romford RM6 148 EY58
Sevenoaks TN13 278 FE124
Sidcup DA14 208 EV91
Slough SL1
off St. George's Cres 153 AK73
Strood Green RH3 286 CP138
Sutton SM3 221 CZ101
Uxbridge UB10 156 BL66
Virginia Water GU25 214 AW99
Ware SG12 55 DY06
Wembley (Barnhill Rd) HA9 140 CQ62
Wembley (Lyon Pk Av) HA0 160 CL65
West Byfleet KT14 234 BG113
Wonersh GU5 281 BB144
Closemead Cl, Nthwd. HA6 115 BQ51
Cloth Ct, EC1 19 H7
Cloth Fair, EC1 19 H7
Clothier St, E1 19 P8
Cloth St, EC1 19 J6
Clothworkers Rd, SE18 187 ER80
Cloudberry Rd, Rom. RM3 128 FK51
Cloudesdale Rd, SW17 203 DH89
Cloudesley Cl, Sid. DA14 207 ET92
Cloudesley Pl, N1 8 E9
Cloudesley Rd, N1 8 E8
Bexleyheath DA7 188 EZ81
Erith DA8 189 FF81
Cloudesley Sq, N1 8 E9
Cloudesley St, N1 8 F9
Clouston Cl, Wall. SM6 241 DL106
Clova Rd, E7 13 M4
Clove Cres, E14 22 F10
Clove Hitch Quay, SW11 39 P10
Clovelly Av, NW9 141 CT56
Uxbridge UB10 137 BQ63
Warlingham CR6 258 DV118
Clovelly Cl, Pnr. HA5 137 BV55
Uxbridge UB10 137 BQ63
Clovelly Ct, Horn. RM11 150 FM61
Clovelly Gdns, SE19 224 DT95
Enfield EN1 122 DS45
Romford RM7 127 FB53
Clovelly Pl, Green. DA9
off Carmichael Ave 191 FW84
Clovelly Rd, N8 143 DK56
W4 180 CQ75
W5 179 CJ75
Bexleyheath DA7 188 EY79
Hounslow TW3 178 CA82
Clovelly Way, E1 21 H8
Harrow HA2 138 BZ61
Orpington BR6 227 ET100
Clover Cl, E11 off Norman Rd 145 ED61
Clover Ct, Edg. HA8
off Springwood Cres 118 CQ47
Grays RM17 off Churchill Rd 192 GD79
Woking GU22 248 AX118
Cloverdale Gdns, Sid. DA15 207 ET86
Clover Fld, Harl. CM18 74 EU18
Cloverfield, Welw.G.C. AL7 51 CZ06
Clover Fld, The, Bushey WD23 98 BZ44
Cloverfields, Horl. RH6 291 DH147
Clover Hill, Couls. CR5 257 DH121
Cloverland, Hat. AL10 67 CT21
Clover Lea, Gdmg. GU7 280 AS143
Clover Leas, Epp. CM16 91 ET30
Cloverleys, Loug. IG10 106 EK43
Clover Ms, SW3 40 E2
Clover Rd, Guil. GU2 264 AS132
Clovers, The, Nthflt DA11 212 GE91
Clover Way, Hat. AL10 67 CT15
Hemel Hempstead HP1 62 BH19
Wallington SM6 222 DG102
Clove St, E13 23 N5
Clowders Rd, SE6 205 DZ90
Clowser Cl, Sutt. SM1
off Turnpike La 240 DC106
Cloysters Grn, E1 32 C2
Cloyster Wd, Edg. HA8 117 CK52
Club Gdns Rd, Brom. BR2 226 EG101
Club Row, E1 20 A4
E2 20 A4
Clump, The, Rick. WD3 96 BG43
Clump Av, Box H. KT20 270 CQ131
Clumps, The, Ashf. TW15 197 BR91
Clunas Gdns, Rom. RM2 128 FK54
Clunbury Av, Sthl. UB2 178 BZ78
Clunbury Ct, Berk. HP4
off Manor St 60 AX19
Clunbury St, N1 19 M1
Cluny Est, SE1 31 N6
Cluny Ms, SW5 27 J9
Cluny Pl, SE1 31 N6
Cluse Ct, N1 9 J10
Clutterbucks, Sarratt WD3 96 BG36
Clutton St, E14 22 D7
Clydach Rd, Enf. EN1 104 DT42
Clyde Av, S.Croy. CR2 258 DV115
Clyde Circ, N15 144 DS56
Clyde Cl, Red. RH1 272 DG133
Clyde Cres, Upmin. RM14 151 FS58
Clyde Pl, E10 145 EB59
Clyde Rd, N15 144 DS56
N22 121 DK53
Croydon CR0 224 DT102
Hoddesdon EN11 71 ED19
Stanwell TW19 196 BK88
Sutton SM1 240 DA106
Wallington SM6 241 DJ106
Clydesdale, Enf. EN3 105 DX42
Clydesdale Av, Stan. HA7 139 CK55
Clydesdale Cl, Borwd. WD6 100 CR43
Isleworth TW7 179 CF83
Clydesdale Gdns, Rich. TW10 180 CP84
Clydesdale Ho, Erith DA18
off Kale Rd 188 EY75
Clydesdale Rd, W11 14 G8
Hornchurch RM11 149 FF59
Clydesdale Wk, Brox. EN10
off Tarpan Way 89 DZ25
Clyde Sq, Hem.H. HP2 62 BM15
Clyde St, SE8 45 P3
Clyde Ter, SE23 204 DW89
Hertford SG13 54 DU09
Clyde Vale, SE23 204 DW89
Clyde Way, Rom. RM1 127 FE53
Clydon Cl, Erith DA8 189 FE79
Clyfford Rd, Ruis. HA4 137 BT63
Clyfton Cl, Brox. EN10 71 DZ23
Clymping Dene, Felt. TW14 197 BV87
Clyston Rd, Wat. WD18 97 BT44
Clyston St, SW8 41 N8
Clyve Way, Stai. TW18 215 BE95
Coach All, Woob.Grn HP10 132 AF60
Coach & Horses Yd, W1 17 K10
Coach Ho La, N5 8 G1
SW19 201 CX91
Coach Ho Ms, SE14 45 J8
Coachhouse Ms, SE20 204 DV94
Coach Ho Ms, SE23 205 DX86
Redhill RH1 off Mill St 288 DF135
Coach Ho Yd, SW18
off Ebner St 182 DB84
Coachlads Av, Guil. GU2 264 AT134
Coachmaker Ms, SW4
off Fenwick Pl 183 DL83
W4 off Berrymede Rd 180 CR76
Coach Ms, St.Alb. AL1 65 CH20
Coach Rd, Brock. RH3 270 CL134
Ottershaw KT16 233 BC107
Coach Yd Ms, N19 143 DL60
Coade Ct, SW4 off Paradise Rd 42 A8
Coal Ct, Grays RM17
off Columbia Wf Rd 192 GA79
Coaldale Wk, SE21
off Lairdale Cl 204 DQ87
Coalecroft Rd, SW15 181 CW84
Coalmans Way, Burn. SL1 152 AH72
Coalport Cl, Harl. CM17 74 EW16
Coalport Ho, SE11
off Walnut Tree Wk 30 E8
Coal Post Cl, Grn St Grn
BR6 off Lynne Cl 245 ET107
Coal Rd, Til. RM18 193 GL77
Coast Hill, Westc. RH4 284 BZ139
Coast Hill La, Westc. RH4 284 CA138
Coaters La, Woob.Grn HP10 132 AE56
Coates Av, SW18 202 DE86
Coates Cl, Th.Hth. CR7 224 DQ97
Coates Dell, Wat. WD25 82 BY33
Coates Hill Rd, Brom. BR1 227 EN96
Coates Rd, Els. WD6 117 CK45
Coate St, E2 20 D1
Coates Wk, Brent. TW8 180 CL78
Coates Way, Wat. WD25 82 BX33
Coates Way JMI & Nurs Sch,
Wat. WD25 off Coates Way 82 BY33
Coat Wicks, Seer Grn HP9 111 AQ51
Cobalt Cl, Beck. BR3 225 DX98
Cobb Cl, Borwd. WD6 100 CQ43
Datchet SL3 174 AX81
Cobbett Cl, Enf. EN3 104 DW36
Cobbett Rd, SE9 186 EL83
Guildford GU2 264 AS133
Twickenham TW2 198 CA88
Cobbetts Av, Ilf. IG4 146 EK57
Cobbetts Cl, Wok. GU21 248 AV117
Cobbetts Hill, Wey. KT13 235 BP107
Cobbett St, SW8 42 D5
Cobb Grn, Wat. WD25 81 BV32
Cobbins, The, Wal.Abb. EN9 90 EE33
Cobbinsbank, Wal.Abb. EN9
off Farm Hill Rd 89 ED33
Cobbinsend Rd, Wal.Abb. EN9 90 EK29
Cobbins Way, Harl. CM17 58 EY11
Cobble La, N1 8 G6
Cobble Ms, N5 144 DQ62
N6 off Highgate W Hill 142 DG60
Cobblers Cl, Farn.Royal SL2 153 AP68
Cobblers Wk, E.Mol. KT8 219 CG95
Hampton TW12 198 CC94
Kingston upon Thames KT2 219 CG95
Teddington TW11 219 CG95
Cobbles, The, Brwd. CM15 130 FY47
Upminster RM14 151 FT59
Cobblestone Pl, Croy. CR0
off Oakfield Rd 224 DQ102
● Cobbold Est, NW10 161 CT65
Cobbold Ms, W12
off Cobbold Rd 181 CT75

Cobbold Rd, E11 146 EF62
NW10 161 CT65
W12 180 CS75
Cobb Rd, Berk. HP4 60 AT19
Cobb's Ct, EC4
off Pilgrim St 19 H9
Cobb's Rd, Houns. TW4 178 BZ84
Cobb St, E1 20 A7
Cobb Terr Ms, E6
off Sandford Rd 25 J2
Cobden Cl, Uxb. UB8 156 BJ67
Cobden Hill, Rad. WD7 99 CH36
Cobden Ms, SE26 204 DV92
Cobden Rd, E11 146 EE62
SE25 224 DU99
Orpington BR6 245 ER105
Sevenoaks TN13 279 FJ123
COBHAM, KT11 251 BV115
Cobham, Grays RM16 192 GB75
⇌ Cobham & Stoke D'Abernon 252 BY117
Cobham Av, N.Mal. KT3 221 CU99
Cobham Cl, SW11 202 DE86
Bromley BR2 226 EL101
Edgware HA8 118 CP54
Enfield EN1 104 DU41
Greenhithe DA9 211 FV86
Sidcup DA15 off Park Mead 208 EV86
Slough SL1 173 AM75
Wallington SM6 241 DL107
H Cobham Comm Hosp, Cob. KT11 235 BV113
Cobham Gate, Cob. KT11 235 BV114
Cobham Gra, Cob. KT11
off Between Sts 235 BV114
Cobham Ho, Bark. IG11
off St. Margarets 167 EQ67
Erith DA8 off Boundary St 189 FF80
Cobham Ms, NW1 7 N6
Cobham Pk, Cob. KT11 251 BV116
Cobham Pk Rd, Cob. KT11 251 BV117
Cobham Pl, Bexh. DA6 208 EX85
Cobham Rd, E17 123 EC53
N22 143 DP55
Fetcham KT22 253 CE122
Hounslow TW5 178 BW80
Ilford IG3 147 ES61
Kingston upon Thames KT1 220 CN95
Stoke D'Abernon KT11 252 CA118
Ware SG12 55 DZ05
Cobham St, Grav. DA11 213 GG87
Cobham Ter, Green. DA9
off Bean Rd 211 FV85
Cobham Way, E.Hors. KT24 267 BS126
Cobill Cl, Horn. RM11 150 FJ56
Cobland Rd, SE12 206 EJ91
Cobmead, Hat. AL10 67 CV16
Coborn Rd, E3 21 N1
Coborn St, E3 21 P2
Sch Cobourg Prim Sch, SE5 44 A2
Cobourg Rd, SE5 44 A2
Cobourg St, NW1 17 M3
Cobsdene, Grav. DA12 213 GK93
Cobs Way, New Haw KT15 234 BJ110
Cobtree Ct, Sthl. UB1 158 CC72
Coburg Cl, SW1 29 M8
Coburg Cres, SW2 203 DM88
Coburg Gdns, Ilf. IG5 124 EK54
Coburg Rd, N22 143 DM55
Cochrane Dr, Dart, DA1 210 FK86
Cochrane Ms, NW8 16 B1
Cochrane Rd, SW19 201 CZ94
Cochrane St, NW8 16 B1
Cockayne Way, SE8 33 M10
Cockbush Av, Hert. SG13 54 DU08
Cockerell Rd, E17 145 DY59
Cockerhurst Rd, Shore. TN14 247 FD107
Cocker Rd, Enf. EN1 104 DV36
Cockett Rd, Slou. SL3 174 AY76
COCKFOSTERS, Barn. EN4 102 DE42
⊖ Cockfosters 102 DG42
Cockfosters Par, Barn. EN4
off Cockfosters Rd 102 DG42
Cockfosters Rd, Barn. EN4 102 DF40
Cock Grn, Harl. CM19 73 EP17
Cock Hill, E1 19 P7
Cock La, EC1 18 G7
Broxbourne EN10 70 DU20
Fetcham KT22 252 CC122
Hoddesdon EN11 71 DY19
Cockle Way, Shenley WD7 84 CL33
Cockmannings La, Orp. BR5 228 EX102
Cockmannings Rd, Orp. BR5 228 EX101
Cockpit Steps, SW1 29 P5
Cockpit Yd, WC1 18 D6
Cockrobin La, Harl. CM20 57 EN08
Ware SG12 57 EN05
Cocks Cres, N.Mal. KT3 221 CT98
Cocksett Av, Orp. BR6 245 ES107
Cockshot Hill, Reig. RH2 288 DB136
Cockshot Rd, Reig. RH2 288 DB135
Cockspur Ct, SW1 29 P2
Cockspur St, SW1 29 P2
Cocksure La, Sid. DA14 208 FA90
Cock's Yd, Uxb. UB8
off Bakers Rd 156 BK66
● Coda Cen, The, SW6 38 E5
Code St, E1 20 B5
Codham Hall La, Gt Warley CM13 151 FV56
Codicote Dr, Wat. WD25 82 BX34
Codicote Rd, Welw. AL6 50 CL05
Wheathampstead AL4 50 CL05
Codling Cl, E1 32 D2
Codling Way, Wem. HA0 139 CK63
CODMORE, Chesh. HP5 76 AS29
Codmore Cres, Chesh. HP5 76 AS30
Codmore Wd Rd, Chesh. HP5 78 AW33
Codrington Ct, Wok. GU21
off Raglan Rd 248 AT118
Codrington Cres, Grav. DA12 213 GJ92
Codrington Gdns, Grav. DA12 213 GK92
Codrington Hill, SE23 205 DY87
Codrington Ms, W11 14 F9
Cody Cl, Har. HA3 139 CK55
Wallington SM6
off Alcock Cl 241 DK108
Cody Rd, E16 23 H5
● Cody Rd Business Cen, E16 23 H5
Coe Av, SE25 224 DU100
Coe's All, Barn. EN5
off Wood St 101 CY42
Coe Spur, Slou. SL1 173 AP75
Coffey St, SE8 46 B4
Coftards, Slou. SL2 154 AW72
Cogan Av, E17 123 DY53
Cohen Cl, Chsht EN8 89 DY31
Coin St, SE1 30 E2
Coity Rd, NW5 7 H4
Cokers La, SE21
off Perifield 204 DQ88
Coke's Fm La, Ch.St.G. HP8 94 AV41
Coke's La, Amer. HP7 94 AW41
Chalfont St. Giles HP8 94 AU42
Coke St, E1 20 C8
Colas Ms, NW6 5 K8
Colbeck Ms, SW7 27 M9
Colbeck Rd, Har. HA1 138 CC59
Colberg Pl, N16 144 DS59
Colborne Way, Wor.Pk. KT4 221 CW104
Colbrook Av, Hayes UB3 177 BR76
Colbrook Cl, Hayes UB3 177 BR76
Colburn Av, Cat. CR3 258 DT124
Pinner HA5 116 BY51
Colburn Cres, Guil. GU4
off Sutherland Dr 265 BA131
Colburn Way, Sutt. SM1 222 DD104
Colby Ms, SE19 204 DS92
Colby Rd, SE19 204 DS92
Walton-on-Thames KT12
off Winchester Rd 217 BU102
Colchester Av, E12 147 EM62
Colchester Dr, Pnr. HA5 138 BX57
Colchester Rd, E10 145 EC59
E17 145 EA58
Edgware HA8 118 CQ52
Northwood HA6 115 BU54
Romford RM3 128 FK53
Colchester St, E1 20 B8
Colclough Ct, Croy. CR0
off Simpson Cl 224 DQ100
Colcokes Rd, Bans. SM7 256 DA116
Cold Arbor Rd, Sev. TN13 278 FD124
Coldbath Sq, EC1 18 E4
Coldbath St, SE13 46 D7
COLDBLOW, Bex. DA5 209 FC89
Cold Blow Cres, Bex. DA5 209 FD88
Cold Blow La, SE14 45 K3
Cold Blows, Mitch. CR4 222 DF97
Coldershaw Rd, W13 159 CG74
Coldfall Av, N10 120 DF54
Sch Coldfall Prim Sch, N10
off Coldfall Av 120 DF54
Coldham Gro, Enf. EN3 105 DY37
Cold Harbour, E14 34 F3
Coldharbour Cl, Egh. TW20 215 BC97
Coldharbour Crest, SE9
off Great Harry Dr 207 EN90
Coldharbour La, SE5 183 DN84
SW9 183 DN84
Bletchingley RH1 274 DT134
Bushey WD23 98 CB44
Dorking RH4, RH5 285 CG138
Egham TW20 215 BC97
Hayes UB3 157 BU73
Purley CR8 241 DN110
Rainham RM13 169 FE72
Woking GU22 249 BF115
● Coldharbour La Ind Est, SE5 off Coldharbour La 43 K9
● Coldharbour Pinnacles Est, Harl. CM19 73 EM16
Coldharbour Pl, SE5 43 L8
Coldharbour Rd, Croy. CR0 241 DN106
Harlow CM19 73 EM16
Northfleet DA11 212 GE89
West Byfleet KT14 233 BF114
Woking GU22 249 BF115
Coldharbour Way, Croy. CR0 241 DN106
Coldmoreham Yd, Amer. HP7 77 AM39
Coldshott, Oxt. RH8 276 EG133
Coldstream Gdns, SW18 201 CZ86
Coldstream Rd, Cat. CR3 258 DQ121
Cole Av, Chad.St.M. RM16 193 GJ77
Colebeck Ms, N1 9 H5
Colebert Av, E1 20 G4
Colebrook, Ott. KT16 233 BD107
Colebrook Cl, NW7 119 CX52
SW15 201 CX87
Colebrooke Av, W13 159 CH72
Colebrooke Dr, E11 146 EH59
Colebrooke Pl, N1 9 H9
Colebrooke Rd, Red. RH1 272 DE132
Colebrooke Row, N1 18 G1
Colebrook Gdns, Loug. IG10 107 EP40
Colebrook Ho, E14 22 B8
Colebrook La, Loug. IG10 107 EP40
Colebrook Path, Loug. IG10 107 EP40
Colebrook Pl, Ott. KT16 233 BB108
Colebrook Ri, Brom. BR2 226 EE96
Colebrook Rd, SW16 223 DL95
Colebrook St, Erith DA8 189 FF78
Colebrook Way, N11 121 DH50
Coleby Path, SE5 43 M5
Colechurch Ho, SE1
off Avondale Sq 44 C1
Cole Cl, SE28 168 EV74
Coledale Dr, Stan. HA7 117 CJ53
Coleford Rd, SW18 202 DC85
Cole Gdns, Houns. TW5 177 BU80
Sch Colegrave Prim Sch, E15 13 H3
Colegrave Rd, E15 12 G2
COLE GREEN, Hert. SG14 52 DG12
Cole Grn Bypass, Hert. SG14 52 DF12
Cole Grn La, Welw.G.C. AL7 52 DB11
Cole Grn Way, Hert. SG14 53 DK12
Colegrove Rd, SE15 44 B3
Coleherne Ct, SW5 39 M1
Coleherne Ms, SW10 39 L1
Coleherne Rd, SW10 39 L1
Colehill Gdns, SW6 38 E7
Colehill La, SW6 38 E7
Colekitchen La, Goms. GU5 283 BR136
Coleman Cl, SE25 224 DU96
Coleman Flds, N1 9 K8
COLEMAN GREEN, St.Alb. AL4 50 CM10
Coleman Grn La, Wheat. AL4 50 CM10
Coleman Rd, SE5 43 N4
Belvedere DA17 188 FA77
Dagenham RM9 168 EY65
Colemans Heath, SE9 207 EP90
Coleman's La, Lwr Naze. EN9 89 ED26
Colemans La, Ong. CM5 93 FH30
Coleman St, EC2 19 L8
Colenorton Cres, Eton Wick SL4 173 AL77
Colenso Dr, NW7 119 CU52
Colenso Rd, E5 144 DW63
Ilford IG2 147 ES60
Cole Pk Gdns, Twick. TW1 199 CG86
Cole Pk Rd, Twick. TW1 199 CG86
Cole Pk Vw, Twick. TW1
off Hill Vw Rd 199 CG86
Colepits Wd Rd, SE9 207 EQ85
Sch Coleraine Pk Prim Sch, N17 off Glendish Rd 122 DV53
Coleraine Rd, N8 143 DN55
SE3 47 L3
Coleridge Av, E12 166 EL65
Sutton SM1 240 DE105
Coleridge Cl, SW8 41 K9
Cheshunt EN7 88 DT27
Coleridge Cres, Colnbr. SL3 175 BE81
Coleridge Dr, Ruis HA4 137 BV58
Coleridge Gdns, NW6 5 N7
SW10 39 M4
Coleridge Ho, SW1 41 L1
Coleridge La, N8 143 DL58
Sch Coleridge Prim Sch, N8
off Crouch End Hill 143 DK59
Coleridge Rd, E17 145 DZ56
N4 143 DN61
N8 143 DK58
N12 120 DC50
Ashford TW15 196 BL91
Croydon CR0 224 DW101
Dartford DA1 190 FN84
Romford RM3 127 FH52
Tilbury RM18 193 GJ82
Coleridge Sq, SW10 39 N4
W13 159 CG72
Coleridge Wk, NW11 142 DA56
Hutton CM13 131 GC45
Coleridge Way, Borwd. WD6 100 CN42
Hayes UB4 157 BU72
Orpington BR6 228 EU100
West Drayton UB7 176 BM77
Cole Rd, Twick. TW1 199 CG86
Watford WD17 97 BV39
Colesburg Rd, Beck. BR3 225 DZ97
Coles Cres, Har. HA2 138 CB61
Colescroft Hill, Pur. CR8 257 DN115
Colesdale, Cuffley EN6 87 DL30
Coles Grn, Bushey Hth WD23 116 CC46
Loughton IG10 107 EN39
Coles Grn Ct, NW2 141 CU61
Coles Grn Rd, NW2 141 CU60
COLESHILL, Amer. HP7 77 AM43
Coles Hill, Hem.H. HP1 62 BG18
Sch Coleshill C of E Inf Sch, Colesh. HP7
off Village Rd 77 AM44
Coleshill Flats, SW1
off Pimlico Rd 29 H9
Coleshill La, Winch.Hill HP7 110 AJ45
Coleshill Rd, Tedd. TW11 199 CE93
Coles La, Brasted TN16 262 EW123
Colesmead Rd, Red. RH1 272 DF131
COLES MEADS, Red. RH1 272 DF131
Colestown St, SW11 40 D8
Cole St, SE1 31 K5
Colet Cl, N13 121 DP51
Colet Gdns, W14 26 D10
Colet Rd, Hutt. CM13 131 GC43
Colets Orchard, Otford TN14 263 FH116
Coley Av, Wok. GU22 249 BA118
Coley St, WC1 18 D5
Colfe Rd, SE23 205 DY88
Sch Colfe's Sch, SE12
off Horn Pk La 206 EH86
Colgate Pl, Enf. EN3 105 EA37
Colgrove, Welw.G.C. AL8 51 CW10
Colham Av, West Dr. UB7 156 BL74
Colham Grn Rd, Uxb. UB8 156 BN71
Sch Colham Manor Prim Sch, Hlgdn UB8 off Violet Av 156 BN72
Colham Mill Rd, West Dr. UB7 176 BK75
Colham Rd, Uxb. UB8 156 BM70
Jct Colham Rbt, Uxb. UB8 156 BN73
Colina Ms, N15 143 DP56
Colina Rd, N15 143 DP57
Colin Cl, NW9 140 CS56
Croydon CR0 225 DZ104
Dartford DA2 210 FP86
West Wickham BR4 226 EF104
Colin Cres, NW9 141 CT56
⊖ Colindale 140 CS55
Colindale Av, NW9 140 CR55
St. Albans AL1 65 CF22
● Colindale Business Pk, NW9 140 CQ55
Sch Colindale Prim Sch, NW9
off Poolsford Rd 141 CT56
Colindeep Gdns, NW4 141 CU57
Colindeep La, NW4 140 CS55
NW9 140 CS55
Colin Dr, NW9 141 CT57
Colinette Rd, SW15 181 CW84
Colin Gdns, NW9 141 CT57
Colin Par, NW9
off Edgware Rd 140 CS56
Colin Pk Rd, NW9 140 CS56
Colin Rd, NW10 161 CU65
Caterham CR3 258 DU123
Colinsdale, N1 8 G9
Colinton Rd, Ilf. IG3 148 EV61
Colin Way, Slou. SL1 173 AP76
Coliston Pas, SW18
off Coliston Rd 202 DA87
Coliston Rd, SW18 202 DA87
Collamore Av, SW18 202 DE88
Collapit Cl, Har. HA1 138 CB57
Collard Av, Loug. IG10 107 EQ40
Collard Cl, Ken. CR8 258 DS120
Collard Grn, Loug. IG10 107 EQ40
Collard Pl, NW1 7 J6
College App, SE10 46 F3
College Av, Egh. TW20 195 BB93
Epsom KT17 239 CT114
Grays RM17 192 GB77
Harrow HA3 117 CE53
Slough SL1 174 AS76
College Cl, E9 10 G2
N18 122 DT50
Grays RM17 192 GC78
Harrow HA3 117 CE52
Loug. IG10 107 EP42
North Mymms AL9 85 CX28
Twickenham TW2 199 CD88
Ware SG12 55 DX07
College Ct, Chsht EN8 88 DW30
College Cres, NW3 6 A5
Redhill RH1 272 DG131
Windsor SL4 173 AP82
College Cross, N1 8 F7
College Dr, Ruis. HA4 137 BU59
Thames Ditton KT7 219 CE101
College Gdns, E4 123 EB45
College Gdns, N18 122 DT50
SE21 204 DS88
SW17 202 DE89
Enfield EN2 104 DR39
Ilford IG4 146 EL57
New Malden KT3 221 CT99
College Gate, Harl. CM20 73 EQ15
College Grn, SE19 204 DS94
College Gro, NW1 7 N9
College Hill, EC4 19 K10
College Hill Rd, Har. HA3 117 CF53
College La, NW5 143 DH63
Hatfield AL10 66 CS20
Woking GU22 248 AW119
College Ms, SW1 30 A6
SW18 off St. Ann's Hill 202 DB85
★ College of Arms, EC4 19 H10
Coll College of Law, The, Bloomsbury Cen, WC1 17 N6
Moorgate Cen, EC1 19 L5
Guildford GU3
off Portsmouth Rd 280 AW138
Coll College of N E London, The, Tottenham Cen, N15
off High Rd 144 DT56
Tottenham Grn Cen, N15
off Town Hall App Rd 144 DT56
Coll College of N W London, Kilburn Cen, NW6 5 J8
Wembley Pk Cen, Wem. HA9 off North End Rd 140 CN62
Willesden Cen, NW10
off Dudden Hill La 141 CT64
College Pk Cl, SE13 185 ED84
College Pk Rd, N17 122 DT51
Sch College Pk Sch, W2 15 L9
College Pl, E17 146 EE56
NW1 7 M9
SW10 39 N4
Greenhithe DA9 191 FW84
St. Albans AL3 64 CC20
College Pt, E15 13 L4
College Rd, E17 145 EC57
N17 122 DT51
N21 121 DN47
NW10 14 A1
SE19 204 DT92
SE21 204 DS87
SW19 202 DD93
W13 159 CH72
Abbots Langley WD5 81 BT31
Bromley BR1 206 EG94
Cheshunt EN8 88 DV30
Croydon CR0 224 DR103
Enfield EN2 104 DR40
Epsom KT17 239 CU114
Grays RM17 192 GC77
Guildford GU1 280 AX135
Harrow on the Hill HA1 139 CE58
Harrow Weald HA3 117 CE53
Hertford Heath SG13 54 DW13
Hoddesdon EN11 71 DZ15
Isleworth TW7 179 CF81
Northfleet DA11 212 GB85
St. Albans AL1 65 CH21
Slough SL1 153 AM74
Swanley BR8 229 FE95
Wembley HA9 139 CK60
Woking GU22 249 BB116
College Row, E9 11 J3
College Slip, Brom. BR1 226 EG95
College Sq, Harl. CM20
off College Gate 73 ER15
College St, EC4 19 K10
St. Albans AL3 65 CD20
College Ter, E3 21 N2
N3 off Hendon La 119 CZ54
College Vw, SE9 206 EK88
College Wk, Kings.T. KT1
off Grange Rd 220 CL97
College Way, Ashf. TW15 196 BM91
Hayes UB3 157 BU73
Northwood HA6 115 BR51
Welwyn Garden City AL8 51 CX08
College Yd, NW5 7 K1
Watford WD24
off Gammons La 97 BV38
Collent St, E9 11 H5
Coller Cres, Lane End DA2 211 FS91
Colless Rd, N15 144 DT57
Collet Cl, Chsht EN8 89 DX28
Collet Gdns, Chsht EN8
off Collet Cl 89 DX28
Collett Ho, N16
off Stamford Hill 144 DT60
Collett Rd, SE16 32 D7
Hemel Hempstead HP1 62 BJ20
Ware SG12 55 DX05
Sch Collett Sch, The, Hem.H. HP1 off Lockers Pk La 62 BH19
Collett Way, Sthl. UB2 158 CB74
Colley Hill La, Hedg. SL2 134 AT62
Colley Ho, Uxb. UB8 156 BK67
Colleyland, Chorl. WD3 95 BD42
Colley La, Reig. RH2 271 CY132
Colley Manor Dr, Reig. RH2 271 CX133
Colley Way, Reig. RH2 271 CY131
Collier Cl, E6 25 N10
Epsom KT19 238 CN107
Collier Dr, Edg. HA8 118 CN54
COLLIER ROW, Rom. RM5 126 FA53
Collier Row La, Rom. RM5 127 FB52
Collier Row Rd, Rom. RM5 126 EZ53
Colliers, Cat. CR3 274 DU125
Colliers Cl, Wok. GU21 248 AV117
Colliers Shaw, Kes. BR2 244 EK105
Collier St, N1 18 C1
Colliers Water La, Th.Hth. CR7 223 DN99
COLLIER'S WOOD, SW19 202 DD94
⊖ Colliers Wood 202 DD94
Collier Way, Guil. GU4 265 BD132
Collindale Av, Erith DA8 189 FB79
Sidcup DA15 208 EU88
Collingbourne Rd, W12 161 CV74
Collingham Gdns, SW5 27 M9
Collingham Pl, SW5 27 L9
Collingham Rd, SW5 27 M8
Sch Collingham Sch, SW5 27 M9
Collings Cl, N22 121 DM51
Collington Cl, Nthflt DA11
off Beresford Rd 212 GE87
Collington St, SE10 47 H1
Collingtree Rd, SE26 204 DW91
Collingwood Av, N10 142 DG55
Surbiton KT5 220 CQ102
Collingwood Cl, SE20 224 DV95
Horley RH6 291 DH147
Twickenham TW2 198 CA86
Collingwood Cres, Guil. GU1 265 BA133
Collingwood Dr, Lon.Col. AL2 83 CK25
Collingwood Pl, Walt. KT12 217 BU104
Collingwood Rd, E17 145 EA58
N15 144 DS56
Mitcham CR4 222 DE96
Rainham RM13 169 FF68
Sutton SM1 222 DA104
Uxbridge UB8 157 BP70
Sch Collingwood Sch, Jun Dept, Wall. SM6 off Maldon Rd 241 DH106
Sen Dept, Wall. SM6
off Springfield Rd 241 DH106
Collingwood St, E1 20 F4
Collins Av, Stan. HA7 118 CL54
Collins Dr, Ruis. HA4 138 BW61
Collins Meadow, Harl. CM19 73 EP15
Collinson Ct, Enf. EN3
off The Generals Wk 105 DY37
Collinson St, SE1 31 J5
Collinson Wk, SE1 31 J5
Collins Rd, N5 144 DQ63
Collins Sq, SE3 47 L9
Collins St, SE3 47 K9
Collins Way, Hutt. CM13 131 GE43
Collinswood Rd, Farn.Com. SL2 133 AN60
Collin's Yd, N1 8 G9
Collinwood Av, Enf. EN3 104 DW41
Collinwood Gdns, Ilf. IG5 147 EM57
Collis All, Twick. TW2
off The Green 199 CE88
Collison Pl, N16 144 DS61
Sch Collis Prim Sch, Tedd. TW11 off Fairfax Rd 199 CH93
Colls Rd, SE15 44 G6
Collum Grn Rd, Slou. SL2 133 AR62
Collyer Av, Croy. CR0 241 DL105
Collyer Pl, SE15 44 C7
Collyer Rd, Croy. CR0 241 DL105
London Colney AL2 83 CJ27
Colman Cl, Epsom KT18 255 CW117
Colman Rd, E16 24 C7
Colmans Hill, Peasl. GU5 283 BS144
Colman Way, Red. RH1 272 DE132
Colmar Cl, E1 21 J4
Colmer Pl, Har. HA3 117 CD52
Colmer Rd, SW16 223 DL95
Colmore Ms, SE15 44 F7
Colmore Rd, Enf. EN3 104 DW42
COLNBROOK, Slou. SL3 175 BD80
Colnbrook Bypass, Slou. SL3 175 BF80
West Drayton UB7 175 BF80
Colnbrook Cl, Lon.Col. AL2 84 CL27
Sch Colnbrook C of E Prim Sch, Colnbr. SL3 off High St 175 BD80
Colnbrook Ct, Slou. SL3 175 BF81
Sch Colnbrook Sch, S.Oxhey WD19 off Hayling Rd 116 BW48
Colnbrook St, SE1 30 G7
Colndale Rd, Colnbr. SL3 175 BE82
Colne Av, Mill End WD3 114 BG47
Watford WD19 97 BV44
West Drayton UB7 176 BJ77
Colne Bk, Horton SL3 175 BC83
Colnebridge Cl, Stai. TW18
off Clarence St 195 BE91
Colne Br Retail Pk, Wat. WD17 off Lower High St 98 BX43
Colne Cl, S.Ock. RM15 171 FW73
Colne Ct, Epsom KT19 238 CQ105
Colnedale Rd, Uxb. UB8 136 BK64
Colne Dr, Rom. RM3 128 FM51
Walton-on-Thames KT12 218 BX104
Colne Gdns, Lon.Col. AL2 84 CL27
Colne Ho, Bark. IG11 167 EP65
Colne Mead, Mill End WD3
off Uxbridge Rd 114 BG47
Colne Orchard, Iver SL0 155 BF72
Colne Pk Caravan Site, West Dr. UB7 176 BJ77
Colne Reach, Stai. TW19 195 BF85
Colne Rd, E5 11 L1
N21 122 DR45
Twickenham TW1, TW2 199 CE88
Colne St, E13 23 N3
Colne Valley, Upmin. RM14 151 FS58
Colne Valley Retail Pk, Wat. WD17 98 BX43
Colne Way, Hem.H. HP2 62 BM15
Staines-upon-Thames TW19 195 BB90
Watford WD24, WD25 98 BW36
Colne Way Ct, Wat. WD24
off North Western Ave 98 BX36
Colney Flds Shop Pk, Lon.Col. AL2 84 CM28
Colney Hatch La, N10 120 DG52
N11 120 DF51
COLNEY HEATH, St.Alb. AL4 66 CR22
Colney Heath La, St.Alb. AL4 66 CL20
Sch Colney Heath Sch, Coln.Hth AL4 off High St 66 CQ22
Colney Rd, Dart. DA1 210 FM86
COLNEY STREET, St.Alb. AL2 83 CE31
● Coln Ind Est, Colnbr. SL3 175 BF81
Cologne Rd, SW11 182 DD84
Sch Coloma Conv Girls' Sch, Croy. CR0 off Upper Shirley Rd 225 DX104
Colombo Rd, Ilf. IG1 147 EQ60
Colombo St, SE1 30 G3
Colomb St, SE10 47 K1
Colonels La, Cher. KT16 216 BG100
Colonels Wk, Enf. EN2 103 DP40
Colonial Av, Twick. TW2 198 CC85
● Colonial Business Pk, Wat. WD24 off Colonial Way 98 BW39
Colonial Dr, W4 180 CQ77
Colonial Rd, Felt. TW14 197 BS87
Slough SL1 174 AU75
Colonial Way, Wat. WD24 98 BX39
Colonnade, The, SE8 33 N9
Colonnade, WC1 18 A5
● Colonnade Wk, SW1 29 J9
Colonsay, Hem.H. HP3 63 BQ22
Colony Ms, N1
off Mildmay Gro N 9 M3
Colorado Apts, N8
off Great Amwell La 143 DM55
Colorado Bldg, SE13
off Deals Gateway 46 C7
Colosseum Ter, NW1
off Albany St 17 K4
Colson Gdns, Loug. IG10 107 EN42
Colson Grn, Loug. IG10
off Colson Rd 107 EP42
Colson Path, Loug. IG10 107 EN41
Colson Rd, Croy. CR0 224 DS103
Loughton IG10 107 EP42
Colson Way, SW16 203 DJ91
Colsterworth Rd, N15 144 DT56

Colston Av, Cars. SM5 240 DE105
Colston Cl, Cars. SM5
off West St 240 DF105
Colston Cres, Goffs Oak EN7 87 DP27
Colston Rd, E7 166 EK65
SW14 180 CQ84
Colt Hatch, Harl. CM20 57 EP13
Colthurst Cres, N4 144 DQ61
Colthurst Dr, N9 122 DV48
Colthurst Gdns, Hodd. EN11 71 ED15
Coltishall Rd, Horn. RM12 170 FJ65
Coltman St, E14 21 M7
Colt Ms, Enf. EN3 105 EA37
Coltness Cres, SE2 188 EV78
Colton Gdns, N17 144 DQ55
Colton Rd, Har. HA1 139 CE57
Coltsfoot, Welw.G.C. AL7 52 DB11
Coltsfoot, The, Hem.H. HP1 61 BE21
Coltsfoot Ct, Grays RM17 192 GD79
Coltsfoot Dr, Guil. GU1 265 BA131
West Drayton UB7 156 BL72
Coltsfoot La, Oxt. RH8 276 EF133
Coltsfoot Path, Rom. RM3 128 FJ52
Columbas Dr, NW3 142 DD60
Columbia Av, Edg. HA8 118 CP53
Ruislip HA4 137 BV60
Worcester Park KT4 221 CT101
Columbia Pt, SE16 33 H6
Sch Columbia Prim Sch, E2 20 B2
Columbia Rd, E2 20 A2
E13 23 M6
Broxbourne EN10 89 DY26
Columbia Sq, SW14
off Upper Richmond Rd W 180 CQ84
Columbia Wf Rd, Grays RM17 192 GA79
Columbine Av, E6 24 G7
South Croydon CR2 241 DP108
Columbine Way, SE13 46 E9
Romford RM3 128 FL53
Columbus Ct, SE16
off Rotherhithe St 33 H3
Columbus Ctyd, E14 34 A2
Columbus Gdns, Nthwd. HA6 115 BU53
Columbus Sq, Erith DA8 189 FF79
Colva Wk, N19 off Chester Rd 143 DH61
Colvestone Cres, E8 10 A3
Sch Colvestone Prim Sch, E8 10 A3
Colview Ct, SE9
off Mottingham La 206 EK88
Colville Est, N1 9 N9
Colville Gdns, W11 15 H9
Colville Hos, W11 14 G8
Colville Ms, W11 15 H9
Colville Pl, W1 17 M7
Sch Colville Prim Sch, W11 15 H9
Colville Rd, E11 145 EC62
E17 123 DY54
N9 122 DV46
W3 180 CP76
W11 15 H9
Colville Sq, W11 14 G9
Colville Ter, W11 14 G9
Colvin Cl, SE26 204 DW92
Colvin Gdns, E4 123 EC48
E11 146 EH56
Ilford IG6 125 EQ53
Waltham Cross EN8 105 DX35
Colvin Rd, E6 166 EL66
Thornton Heath CR7 223 DN99
Colwall Gdns, Wdf.Grn. IG8 124 EG50
Colwell Rd, SE22 204 DT85
Colwick Cl, N6 143 DK59
Colwith Rd, W6 38 B3
Colwood Gdns, SW19 202 DD94
Colworth Gro, SE17 31 K9
Colworth Rd, E11 146 EE58
Croydon CR0 224 DU102
Colwyn Av, Perivale UB6 159 CF68
Colwyn Cl, SW16 203 DJ92
Colwyn Cres, Houns. TW3 178 CC81
Colwyn Grn, NW9
off Snowdon Dr 140 CS58
Colwyn Ho, SE1
off Briant Est 30 E7
Colwyn Rd, NW2 141 CV62
Colyer Cl, N1 8 D10
SE9 207 EP89
Colyer Rd, Nthflt DA11 212 GC89
Colyers Cl, Erith DA8 189 FD81
Colyers La, Erith DA8 189 FC81
Colyers Wk, Erith DA8
off Colyers La 189 FE81
Colyton Cl, Well. DA16 188 EX81
Wembley HA0 159 CJ65
Woking GU21 248 AW118
Colyton La, SW16 203 DN92
Colyton Rd, SE22 204 DV85
Colyton Way, N18 122 DU50
Combe, The, NW1 17 K3
Combe Av, SE3 47 M4
Combe Bk Dr, Sund. TN14 262 EY122
Sch Combe Bk Sch, Sund. TN14
off Combe Bk Dr 262 EY123
Combe Bottom, Guil. GU5 282 BM137
Combedale Rd, SE10 35 N10
Combe La, Guil. GU5 283 BP135
Combemartin Rd, SW18 201 CY87
Combe Ms, SE3 47 L4
Comber Cl, NW2 141 CV62
Comber Gro, SE5 43 J6
Sch Comber Gro Prim Sch, SE5 43 J5
Comber Ho, SE5
off Comber Gro 43 K5
Combermere Cl, Wind. SL4 173 AP82
Combermere Rd, SW9 42 C10
Morden SM4 222 DB100
Combe Rd, Gdmg. GU7 280 AS143
Watford WD18 97 BT44
Comberton Rd, E5 144 DV61
Combeside, SE18 187 ET80
Combe St, Hem.H. HP1 62 BJ20
Combwell Cres, SE2 188 EU76
Comely Bk Rd, E17 145 EC57
Comeragh Cl, Wok. GU22 248 AU119
Comeragh Ms, W14 26 F10
Comeragh Rd, W14 38 E1
Comer Cres, Sthl. UB2
off Windmill Av 178 CC75
Comerford Rd, SE4 185 DY84
Comer Ho, Barn. EN5
off Station Rd 102 DC42
Comet Cl, E12 146 EK63
Purfleet RM19 190 FN77
Watford WD25 81 BT34
Comet Pl, SE8 46 A5
Comet Rd, Hat. AL10 67 CT18
Stanwell TW19 196 BK87
Comet St, SE8 46 A5
Comet Way, Hat. AL9, AL10 66 CS19
Comforts Fm Av, Oxt. RH8 276 EF133
Comfort St, SE15 43 N3
Comfrey Ct, Grays RM17 192 GD79
Commander Av, NW9 141 CU55
● Commerce Pk Croydon,
Croy. CR0 223 DM103
Commerce Rd, N22 121 DM53
Brentford TW8 179 CJ80
● Commerce Trade Pk,
Croy. CR0 223 DM104
Commerce Way, Croy. CR0 223 DM103
Commercial Pl, Grav. DA12 213 GJ86
Commercial Rd, E1 20 C8
E14 21 M9
N17 122 DS51
N18 122 DS50
Guildford GU1 280 AX135
Staines-upon-Thames TW18 196 BG93
Commercial St, E1 20 A5
Commercial Way, NW10 160 CP68
SE15 44 A5
Woking GU21 249 AZ117
Commerell Pl, SE10 35 L10
Commerell St, SE10 35 K10
Commodity Quay, E1 32 B1
Commodore Ho, SW18 182 DC84
Commodore St, E1 21 L5
Common, The, E15 13 L4
W5 160 CL73
Ashtead KT21 253 CK116
Berkhamsted HP4 61 AZ17
Chipperfield WD4 80 BG32
Hatfield AL10 67 CU17
Kings Langley WD4 80 BN28
Penn HP10 110 AC46
Richmond TW10 199 CK90
Shalford GU4 280 AY141
Southall UB2 178 BW77
Stanmore HA7 117 CE47
West Drayton UB7 176 BJ77
Wonersh GU5 281 BB143
Common Cl, Wok. GU21 232 AX114
Commondale, SW15 38 A9
Commonfield Rd, Bans. SM7 240 DA114
Commonfields, Harl. CM20 57 ES13
Common Gdns, Pott.End HP4 61 BB17
Common Gate Rd, Chorl. WD3 95 BD43
Common La, Burn. SL1 133 AK62
Claygate KT10 237 CG108
Dartford DA2 209 FG89
Eton SL4 173 AQ78
Kings Langley WD4 80 BM28
Letchmore Heath WD25 99 CE39
New Haw KT15 234 BJ109
Radlett WD7 99 CE39
Commonmeadow La, Ald.
WD25 82 CB33
Common Mile Cl, SW4 203 DK85
Common Rd, SW13 181 CU83
Chorleywood WD3 95 BD42
Claygate KT10 237 CG107
Dorney SL4 172 AJ77
Eton Wick SL4 173 AM78
Ingrave CM13 131 GC50
Langley SL3 175 BA77
Leatherhead KT23 252 BY121
Redhill RH1 288 DF136
Stanmore HA7 117 CD49
Waltham Abbey EN9 72 EK22
Commons, The, Welw.G.C. AL7 52 DA12
Commonside, Bkhm KT23 252 CA122
Epsom KT18 254 CN115
Keston BR2 244 EJ105
Commonside Cl, Couls. CR5 257 DP120
Sutton SM2 240 DB111
Commonside E, Mitch. CR4 222 DF97
Commonside Rd, Harl. CM18 73 ES19
Commonside W, Mitch. CR4 222 DF97
Commons La, Hem.H. HP2 62 BL19
Commons Wd Caravan Club,
Welw.G.C. AL7 52 DA13
Sch Commonswood Sch, Welw.G.C.
AL7 off The Commons 52 DB12
Commonwealth Av, W12 161 CV73
Hayes UB3 157 BR72
Commonwealth Rd, N17 122 DU52
Caterham CR3 258 DU123
Commonwealth Way, SE2 188 EV78
COMMONWOOD, Kings L. WD4 80 BH34
Common Wd, Farn.Com. SL2 133 AQ63
Commonwood La, Kings L.
WD4 96 BH35
Common Wd La, Penn HP10 110 AD46
Community Cl, Houns. TW5 177 BV81
Uxbridge UB10 137 BQ62
Coll Community Coll Hackney,
London Flds, E8 10 F7
Shoreditch Campus, N1 19 P2
Coll Community Ed Lewisham,
Brockley Cen, SE23
off Brockley Ri 205 DY88
Granville Pk Adult Learning Cen,
SE13 46 F10
Grove Pk Cen, SE12
off Pragnell Rd 206 EH89
Holbeach Cen, SE6
off Doggett Rd 205 EA87
Community La, N7 7 N2
Coll Community Learning & Skills
Service Friday Hill Cen, E4
off Simmons La 124 EE47
Community Rd, E15 13 H3
Greenford UB6 158 CC67
Community Wk, Esher KT10
off High St 236 CC105
Community Way, Crox.Grn
WD3 off Barton Way 97 BP43
Como Rd, SE23 205 DY89
Como St, Rom. RM7 149 FD57
Compass Bldg, Hayes UB3
off Station Rd 177 BT76
Compass Cl, Ashf. TW15 197 BQ94
Edgware HA8 118 CM49
Compass Hill, Rich. TW10 199 CK86
Compass Ho, SW18
off Smugglers Way 182 DB84
Compass La, Brom. BR1
off North St 226 EG95
Compass Pt, Nthch HP4
off Chapel Cfts 60 AS17
Compayne Gdns, NW6 5 L6
Comport Grn, New Adgtn CR0 244 EE112
Compter Pas, EC2 off Wood St 19 K8
Compton Av, E6 166 EK68
N1 8 G5
N6 142 DE59
Hutton CM13 131 GC46
Romford RM2 149 FH55
Wembley HA0 139 CJ63
Compton Cl, E3 22 B6
NW1 17 K3
NW11 141 CX62
SE15 44 C5
W13 159 CG72
Edgware HA8 118 CQ52
Esher KT10 236 CC106
Compton Ct, SE19 204 DS92
Slough SL1
off Brook Cres 153 AL72
Compton Cres, N17 122 DQ52
W4 180 CQ79
Chessington KT9 238 CL107
Northolt UB5 158 BX67
Compton Gdns, Add. KT15
off Monks Cres 234 BH106
St. Albans AL2 82 CB26
Compton Ho, SW11
off Parkham St 40 C6
Compton Pas, EC1 19 H4
Compton Pl, WC1 18 A4
Erith DA8 189 FF79
Watford WD19 116 BY48
Compton Ri, Pnr. HA5 138 BY57
Compton Rd, N1 9 H5
N21 121 DN46
NW10 14 C3
SW19 201 CZ93
Croydon CR0 224 DV102
Hayes UB3 157 BS73
Sch Compton Sch, The, N12
off Summers La 120 DE51
Compton St, EC1 18 G4
Compton Ter, N1 8 G5
Comreddy Cl, Enf. EN2 103 DP39
Comus Pl, SE17 31 N9
Comyne Rd, Wat. WD24 97 BT36
Comyn Rd, SW11 182 DE84
Comyns, The, Bushey Hth
WD23 116 CC46
Comyns Cl, E16 23 L6
Comyns Rd, Dag. RM9 168 FA66
Conant Ms, E1 20 C10
Conaways Cl, Epsom KT17 239 CU110
Concanon Rd, SW2 183 DM84
Concert Hall App, SE1 30 D3
● Concord Business Cen,
W3 off Concord Rd 160 CP71
Concord Cl, Nthlt. UB5 158 BY69
Concorde Cl, Houns. TW3 178 CB82
Uxbridge UB10 156 BL68
Concorde Ct, Wind. SL4
off Green La 173 AN82
Concorde Dr, E6 25 J7
Hemel Hempstead HP2 62 BK20
Concorde Way, SE16 33 J9
Slough SL1 173 AQ75
Concord Rd, W3 160 CP70
Enfield EN3 104 DW43
Concord Ter, Har. HA2
off Coles Cres 138 CB61
Concourse, The, N9 off
Edmonton Grn Shop Cen 122 DU47
NW9 119 CT53
Concrete Cotts, Wisley
GU23 off Wisley La 250 BL116
Condell Rd, SW8 41 M7
Conder St, E14 21 L8
Condor Ct, Guil. GU2
off Millmead Ter 280 AW136
Condor Path, Nthlt. UB5
off Brabazon Rd 158 CA68
Condor Rd, Stai. TW18 216 BH97
Condor Wk, Horn. RM12
off Heron Flight Av 169 FH66
Condover Cres, SE18 187 EP80
Condray Pl, SW11 40 C5
Sch Conductive Ed Cen, N10
off Muswell Hill 143 DH55
Conduit, The, Bletch. RH1 274 DS129
Conduit Av, SE10 47 H6
Conduit Ct, WC2 18 A10
Conduit La, N18 122 DW50
Croydon CR0 242 DU106
Enfield EN3 off Morson Rd 105 DY44
Hoddesdon EN11 71 EA17
South Croydon CR2 242 DU106
Conduit La E, Hodd. EN11 71 EB17
Conduit Ms, SE18 37 P10
W2 16 A9
Conduit Pas, W2 16 A9
Conduit Pl, W2 16 A9
Conduit Rd, SE18 37 P10
Conduit St, W1 17 K10
Conduit Way, NW10 160 CQ66
Conegar Ct, Slou. SL1 154 AS74
Conewood St, N5 143 DP62
Coney Acre, SE21 204 DQ88
Coneyberry, Reig. RH2 288 DC138
Coney Burrows, E4 124 EE47
Coneybury, Bletch. RH1 274 DS134
Coneybury Cl, Warl. CR6 258 DV119
Coney Cl, Hat. AL10 67 CV19
Coneydale, Welw.G.C. AL8 51 CX07
Coney Gro, Uxb. UB8 156 BN69
Coneygrove Path, Nthlt. UB5
off Arnold Rd 158 BY65
CONEY HALL, W.Wick. BR4 226 EF104
Coney Hill Rd, W.Wick. BR4 226 EE103
Coney Way, SW8 42 D3
Conference Cl, E4
off Greenbank Cl 123 EC47
Conference Rd, SE2 188 EW77
Conford Dr, Shalf. GU4 280 AY141
Congleton Gro, SE18 187 EQ78
Congo Dr, N9 122 DW48
Congo Rd, SE18 187 ER78
Congress Ho, Har. HA1
off Lyon Rd 139 CF58
Congress Rd, SE2 188 EW77
Congreve Rd, SE9 187 EM83
Waltham Abbey EN9 90 EE33
Congreve St, SE17 31 N8
Congreve Wk, E16 24 E7
Conical Cor, Enf. EN2 104 DQ40
Coniers Way, Guil. GU4 265 BB131
Conifer Av, Rom. RM5 127 FB50
Conifer Cl, Orp. BR6 245 ER105
Reigate RH2 272 DA132
Waltham Cross EN7 88 DT29
Conifer Dr, Warley CM14 130 FX50
Conifer Gdns, SW16 203 DL90
Enfield EN1 104 DS44
Sutton SM1 222 DB103
Conifer La, Egh. TW20 195 BC92
Conifer Pk, Epsom KT17 238 CS111
Conifers, Wey. KT13 235 BS105
Conifers, The, Hem.H. HP3 61 BF23
Watford WD25 98 BW35
Conifers Cl, Tedd. TW11 199 CH94
Conifer Way, Hayes UB3 157 BU73
Swanley BR8 229 FC95
Wembley HA0 139 CJ62
Coniger Rd, SW6 39 J8
Coningesby Dr, Wat. WD17 97 BS39
Coningham Ms, W12 161 CU74
Coningham Rd, W12 181 CV75
Coningsby Av, NW9 118 CS54
Coningsby Bk, St.Alb. AL1 64 CC24
Coningsby Cl, N.Mymms AL9 67 CX24
Coningsby Cotts, W5
off Coningsby Rd 179 CK75
Coningsby Dr, Pot.B. EN6 86 DD33
Coningsby Gdns, E4 123 EB51
Coningsby La, Fifield SL6 172 AC81
Coningsby Rd, N4 143 DP59
W5 179 CJ75
South Croydon CR2 242 DQ109
Conington Rd, SE13 46 D8
Conisbee Ct, N14 103 DJ43
Sch Conisborough Coll, SE6
off Bellingham Rd 205 EC90
Conisborough Cres, SE6 205 EC90
Coniscliffe Cl, Chis. BR7 227 EN95
Coniscliffe Rd, N13 122 DQ48
Conista Ct, Wok. GU21
off Roundthorn Way 248 AT116
Coniston Av, Bark. IG11 167 ES66
Perivale UB6 159 CH69
Purfleet RM19 190 FQ79
Upminster RM14 150 FQ63
Welling DA16 187 ES83
Coniston Cl, N20 120 DC48
SW13 181 CT80
SW20 221 CX100
W4 180 CQ81
Barking IG11
off Coniston Av 167 ES66
Bexleyheath DA7 189 FC81
Dartford DA1 209 FH88
Erith DA8 189 FE80
Hemel Hempstead HP3 63 BQ21
Coniston Ct, NW7
off Langstone Way 119 CY52
Wallington SM6 241 DH105
Weybridge KT13 235 BP107
Coniston Cres, Slou. SL1 152 AJ71
Conistone Way, N7 8 B6
Coniston Gdns, N9 122 DW46
NW9 140 CR57
Ilford IG4 146 EL56
Pinner HA5 137 BU56
Sutton SM2 240 DD107
Wembley HA9 139 CJ60
Coniston Ho, SE5 43 J4
Coniston Rd, N10 121 DH54
N17 122 DU51
Bexleyheath DA7 189 FC81
Bromley BR1 206 EE93
Coulsdon CR5 257 DJ116
Croydon CR0 224 DU101
Kings Langley WD4 80 BM28
Twickenham TW2 198 CB86
Woking GU22 249 BB120
Coniston Wk, E9 11 H2
Coniston Way, Chess. KT9 220 CL104
Egham TW20 195 BB94
Hornchurch RM12 149 FG64
Reigate RH2 272 DE133
Conlan St, W10 14 E4
Conley Rd, NW10 160 CS65
Conley St, SE10 35 K10
Connaught Av, E4 123 ED45
SW14 180 CQ83
Ashford TW15 196 BL91
East Barnet EN4 120 DF46
Enfield EN1 104 DS40
Grays RM16 192 GB75
Hounslow TW4 198 BY85
Loughton IG10 106 EK42
Connaught Br, E16 36 E3
● Connaught Business Cen,
NW9 off Hyde Est Rd 141 CT57
Mitcham CR4 222 DF99
Connaught Cl, E10 145 DY61
W2 16 C9
Enfield EN1 104 DS40
Hemel Hempstead HP2 62 BN18
Sutton SM1 222 DD103
Uxbridge UB8 157 BQ70
Connaught Ct, E17
off Orford Rd 145 EB56
Buckhurst Hill IG9
off Chequers 124 EH46
Connaught Dr, NW11 142 DA56
Weybridge KT13 234 BN111
Connaught Gdns, N10 143 DH57
N13 121 DP49
Berkhamsted HP4 60 AT16
Morden SM4 222 DC98
Connaught Hts, Uxb. UB10
off Uxbridge Rd 157 BQ70
Connaught Hill, Loug. IG10 106 EK42
Sch Connaught Ho Sch, W2 16 E9
Connaught La, Ilf. IG1 147 EQ61
Connaught Ms, NW3 6 C1
SE18 37 M10
Ilford IG1
off Connaught Rd 147 ER61
Connaught Pl, W2 16 E10
Connaught Rd, E4 124 EE45
E11 145 ED60
E16 36 F2
E17 145 EA57
N4 143 DN59
NW10 160 CS67
SE18 37 M10
W13 159 CH73
Barnet EN5 101 CX44
Harrow HA3 117 CF53
Hornchurch RM12 150 FK62
Ilford IG1 147 ER61
New Malden KT3 220 CS98
Richmond TW10
off Albert Rd 200 CM85
St. Albans AL3 64 CC18
Slough SL1 174 AV75
Sutton SM1 222 DD103
Teddington TW11 199 CD92
Jct Connaught Rbt, E16 24 E10
Sch Connaught Sch for Girls,
E11 off Connaught Rd 146 EE60
Annexe, E11
off Madeira Rd 146 EE61
Connaught Sq, W2 16 E9
Connaught St, W2 16 C9
Connaught Way, N13 121 DP49
Connect La, Barkingside IG6 125 EQ54
Connell Cres, W5 160 CM70
Connemara Cl, Borwd. WD6 100 CQ44
Connicut La, Lthd. KT23 268 CB128
Connington Cres, E4 123 ED48
Connop Rd, Enf. EN3 105 DX38
Connor Cl, E11 146 EE60
Ilford IG6 125 EP53
Connor Ct, SW11
off Alfreda St 41 J7
Connor Rd, Dag. RM9 148 EZ63
Connor St, E9 11 J8
Conolly Rd, W7 159 CE74
Conquerors Hill, Wheat. AL4 50 CL07
Conquest Rd, Add. KT15 234 BG106
Conrad Cl, Grays RM16 192 GB75
Conrad Dr, Wor.Pk. KT4 221 CW102
Conrad Gdns, Grays RM16 192 GA75
Conrad Ho, N16 9 N2
Consfield Av, N.Mal. KT3 221 CU98
Consort Cl, Warley CM14 130 FW50
Consort Ms, Islw. TW7 199 CD85
Consort Rd, SE15 44 E8
Consort Way, Horl. RH6 290 DG148
Consort Way E, Horl. RH6 291 DH149
Cons St, SE1 30 F4
Constable Av, E16 36 A2
Constable Cl, N11
off Friern Barnet La 120 DF50
NW11 142 DB58
Hayes UB4 157 BQ68
Constable Cres, N15 144 DU57
Constable Gdns, Edg. HA8 118 CN53
Isleworth TW7 199 CD85
Constable Ho, E14
off Cassilis Rd 34 B5
NW3 6 F6
Enf. EN1 off Ayley Cft 104 DU43
Constable Ms, Brom. BR1 226 EH96
Dagenham RM8
off Stonard Rd 148 EV63
Constable Rd, Nthflt DA11 212 GE90
Constable Wk, SE21 204 DS90
Constance Cl, SW15 200 CR91
Constance Cres, Brom. BR2 226 EF101
Constance Gro, Dart. DA1 210 FK86
Constance Rd, Croy. CR0 223 DP101
Enfield EN1 104 DS44
Sutton SM1 240 DC105
Twickenham TW2 198 CB87
Constance St, E16 36 G3
Constantine Pl, Hlgdn UB10 156 BM67
Constantine Rd, NW3 6 D1
Constitution Cres, Grav. DA12
off South Hill Rd 213 GJ88
Constitution Hill, SW1 29 J4
Gravesend DA12 213 GJ88
Woking GU22 248 AY119
Constitution Ri, SE18 187 EN81
Consul Av, Dag. RM9 169 FC69
Rain. RM13 169 FD69
Consul Gdns, Swan. BR8 209 FG94
Content St, SE17 31 K9
Contessa Cl, Orp. BR6 245 ES106
Control Twr Rd, Lon.Hthrw Air.
TW6 176 BN83
Convair Wk, Nthlt. UB5
off Kittiwake Rd 158 BX69
Convent Cl, Barn. EN5 101 CZ40
Beck. BR3 205 EC94
Convent Ct, Wind. SL4 173 AN82
Convent Gdns, W5 179 CJ77
W11 14 F9
Convent Hill, SE19 204 DQ93
Convent La, Cob. KT11 235 BS111
Coll Convent of Jesus & Mary
Language Coll, NW10
off Crownhill Rd 161 CT67
Sch Convent of Jesus & Mary
RC Inf Sch, NW2 4 A5
Convent Rd, Ashf. TW15 196 BN92
Windsor SL4 173 AN82
Convent Way, Sthl. UB2 178 BW77
Conway Cl, Beck. BR3 225 DY95
Loudwater HP10 110 AC53
Rainham RM13 169 FG66
Stanmore HA7 117 CG51
Conway Cres, Perivale UB6 159 CE68
Romford RM6 148 EW59
Conway Dr, Ashf. TW15 197 BQ93
Hayes UB3 177 BQ76
Sutton SM2 240 DB107
Conway Gdns, Enf. EN2 105 DS38
Grays RM17 192 GB80
Mitcham CR4 223 DK98
Wembley HA9 139 CJ59
Conway Gro, W3 160 CR71
Conway Ms, W1 17 L6
Sch Conway Prim Sch, SE18
off Gallosson Rd 187 ES77
Conway Rd, N14 121 DL48
N15 143 DP57
NW2 141 CW61
SE18 187 ER77
SW20 221 CW95
Feltham TW13 198 BX92
Hounslow TW4 198 BZ87
London Heathrow Airport
TW6 off Inner Ring E 177 BP83
Taplow SL6 152 AH72
Conway St, E13 23 N5
W1 17 L5
Conway Wk, Hmptn. TW12
off Fearnley Cres 198 BZ93
Conybeare, NW3 6 D6
Conybury Cl, Wal.Abb. EN9 90 EG32
Cony Cl, Chsht EN7 88 DS26
Conyers, Harl. CM20 57 EQ13
Conyers Cl, Hersham KT12 236 BX106
Woodford Green IG8 124 EE51
Conyers Rd, SW16 203 DK92
Conyer St, E3 21 L1
Conyers Way, Loug. IG10 107 EP41
Cooden Cl, Brom. BR1 206 EH94
Cook Ct, SE16
off Rotherhithe St 33 H3
Cooke Cl, Chaff.Hun. RM16 192 FY76
Cookes Cl, E11 146 EF61
Cookes La, Sutt. SM3 239 CY107
Cooke St, Bark. IG11 167 EQ67
Cookham Cl, Sthl. UB2 178 CB75
Cookham Cres, SE16 33 J4

Cookham Dene Cl, Chis. BR7 227 ER95
Cookham Hill, Orp. BR6 228 FA104
Cookham Rd, Sid. DA14 208 FA94
Swanley BR8 228 FA95
Cookhill Rd, SE2 188 EV75
Cook Rd, Dag. RM9 168 EX67
Cooks Cl, E14 off Cabot Sq 34 B2
Chalfont St. Peter SL9 112 AY51
Romford RM5 127 FC53
Cooks Ferry, N18 123 DY50
Cooks Ferry Rbt, N18
off Advent Way 123 DX50
Cook's Hole Rd, Enf. EN2 103 DP38
Cooks Mead, Bushey WD23 98 CB44
Cookson Gro, Erith DA8 189 FB80
Cook Sq, Erith DA8 189 FF80
Cook's Rd, E15 12 C10
Cooks Rd, SE17 42 G2
Cooks Spinney, Harl. CM20 58 EU13
Cooks Vennel, Hem.H. HP1 62 BG18
Cooks Way, Hat. AL10 67 CV20
Coolfin Rd, E16 23 P9
Coolgardie Av, E4 123 EC50
Chigwell IG7 125 EN48
Coolgardie Rd, Ashf. TW15 197 BQ92
Coolhurst Rd, N8 143 DK58
Cool Oak La, NW9 140 CS59
Coomassie Rd, W9 14 G4
COOMBE, Kings.T. KT2 200 CQ94
Coombe, The, Bet. RH3 270 CR131
Coombe Av, Croy. CR0 242 DS105
Sevenoaks TN14 263 FH120
Coombe Bk, Kings.T. KT2 220 CS95
Coombe Boys' Sch, N.Mal.
KT3 off College Gdns 221 CU99
Coombe Cliff CETS Cen, Croy.
CR0 off Coombe Rd 242 DR105
Coombe Cl, Edg. HA8 118 CM54
Hounslow TW3 178 CA84
Coombe Cor, N21 121 DP46
Coombe Cres, Hmptn. TW12 198 BY94
Coombe Dr, Add. KT15 233 BF107
Kingston upon Thames KT2 200 CR94
Ruislip HA4 137 BV60
Coombe End, Kings.T. KT2 200 CR94
Coombefield Cl, N.Mal. KT3 220 CS99
Coombe Gdns, SW20 221 CU96
Berkhamsted HP4 60 AT18
New Malden KT3 221 CT98
Coombe Girls' Sch, N.Mal.
KT3 off Clarence Av 220 CR96
Coombe Hts, Kings.T. KT2 200 CS94
Coombe Hill Ct, Wind. SL4 173 AK84
Coombe Hill Glade, Kings.T.
KT2 200 CS94
Coombe Hill Inf & Jun Schs,
Kings.T. KT2
off Coombe La W 220 CR95
Coombe Hill Rd, Kings.T. KT2 200 CS94
Mill End WD3 114 BG45
Coombe Ho Chase, N.Mal.
KT3 220 CR95
Coombehurst Cl, Barn. EN4 102 DF40
Coombelands La, Add. KT15 234 BG107
Coombe Lane 242 DW106
Coombe La, SW20 221 CT95
Coombe La, SW20 221 CU95
Croydon CR0 242 DV106
Whiteley Village KT12 235 BT109
Coombe La W, Kings.T. KT2 200 CS94
Coombe Lea, Brom. BR1 226 EL97
Coombe Lo, SE7 186 EJ79
Coombe Neville, Kings.T. KT2 200 CR94
Coombe Pk, Kings.T. KT2 200 CR92
Coombe Ridings, Kings.T. KT2 200 CQ92
Coombe Ri, Kings.T. KT2 220 CQ95
Shenfield CM15 131 FZ46
Coombe Rd, N22 121 DN53
NW10 140 CR62
SE26 204 DV91
W4 180 CS78
W13 off Northcroft Rd 179 CH76
Bushey WD23 116 CC45
Croydon CR0 242 DR105
Gravesend DA12 213 GJ89
Hampton TW12 198 BZ93
Kingston upon Thames KT2 220 CN95
New Malden KT3 220 CS96
Romford RM3 150 FM55
Coomber Way, Croy. CR0 223 DK101
Coombes Rd, Dag. RM9 168 EZ67
London Colney AL2 83 CH26
Coombe Vale, Ger.Cr. SL9 134 AY60
Coombe Wk, Sutt. SM1 222 DB104
Coombe Way, Byfleet KT14 234 BM112
Coombewood Dr, Rom. RM6 148 EZ58
Coombe Wd Hill, Pur. CR8 242 DQ112
Coombe Wd Rd, Kings.T. KT2 200 CQ92
Coombfield Dr, Lane End DA2 211 FR91
Coombs St, N1 19 H1
Coomer Ms, SW6 39 H3
Coomer Pl, SW6 39 H3
Coomer Rd, SW6 39 H3
Cooms Wk, Edg. HA8
off East Rd 118 CQ53
Cooperage Cl, N17 122 DT51
Co-operative Ho, SE15 44 D10
Cooper Av, E17 123 DX53
Cooper Cl, SE1 30 F5
Greenhithe DA9 211 FS85
Smallfield RH6 291 DN148
Cooper Cres, Cars. SM5 222 DF104
Cooper Rd, NW4 141 CX58
NW10 141 CT64
Croydon CR0 241 DN105
Guildford GU1 280 AY136
COOPERSALE, Epp. CM16 92 EX29
Coopersale & Theydon Garnon
C of E Prim Sch, Epp. CM16
off Brickfield Rd 92 EX29
Coopersale Cl, Wdf.Grn. IG8
off Navestock Cres 124 EJ52
Coopersale Common, Cooper.
CM16 92 EX28
Coopersale Hall Sch, Epp.
CM16 off Flux's La 92 EV34
Coopersale La, Epp. CM16 108 EU37
Coopersale Rd, E9 11 K2
Coopersale St, Epp. CM16 92 EW32
Coopers Cl, E1 20 G5
Chigwell IG7 126 EV47
Coopers Cl, Dagenham RM10 169 FB65
South Darenth DA4 231 FR95
Staines-upon-Thames TW18 195 BE92
Coopers' Company & Coborn
Sch, Upmin. RM14
off St. Mary's La 151 FR61
Coopers Ct, Gidea Pk RM2
off Kidman Cl 150 FJ55
Hertford SG14
off The Folly 54 DR09
Cooper's Ct, Ware SG12 55 DY06
Coopers Cres, Borwd. WD6 100 CQ39
Coopers Dr, Dart. DA2 209 FE89
Coopers Gate, Coln.Hth AL4 66 CP22
Coopers Grn La, Hat. AL10 50 CS13
St. Albans AL4 66 CL17
Welwyn Garden City AL8 50 CQ14
Coopers Hill La, Egh. TW20 194 AY91
Coopers Hill Rd, Red. RH1 273 DM133
Coopers La, E10 145 EB60
NW1 7 P10
Cooper's La, SE12 206 EH89
Coopers La, Pot.B. EN6 86 DD31
Staines-upon-Thames TW18 195 BF91
Cooper's La Prim Sch,
SE12 off Pragnell Rd 206 EH89
Coopers La Rd, Pot.B. EN6 86 DE31
Coopers Ms, Beck. BR3 225 EA96
Watford WD25
off High Elms La 82 BW31
Coopers Rd, SE1 44 B1
Northfleet DA11 212 GE88
Potters Bar EN6 86 DC30
Swanscombe DA10 212 FZ86
Cooper's Row, EC3 20 A10
Coopers Row, Iver SL0 155 BC70
Coopers Shaw Rd, Til. RM18 193 GK80
Coopers Tech Coll, Chis.
BR7 off Hawkwood La 227 EQ95
Cooper St, E16 23 M7
Coopers Wk, E15 13 J3
Cheshunt EN8 89 DX28
Coopers Yd, N1 8 G6
Cooper's Yd, SE19 204 DS93
Cooper Way, Berk. HP4
off Robertson Rd 60 AX19
Slough SL1 173 AP76
Coote Gdns, Dag. RM8 148 EZ62
Coote Rd, Bexh. DA7 188 EZ81
Dagenham RM8 148 EZ62
Copeland Dr, E14 34 B8
Copeland Ho, SE11 30 D7
Copeland Rd, E17 145 EB57
SE15 44 D9
Copeman Cl, SE26 204 DW92
Copeman Rd, Hutt. CM13 131 GD45
Copenhagen Gdns, W4 180 CQ75
Copenhagen Pl, E14 21 N9
Copenhagen Prim Sch, N1 8 C9
Copenhagen St, N1 8 B9
Copenhagen Way, Walt. KT12 217 BV104
Cope Pl, W8 27 J7
Copers Cope Rd, Beck. BR3 205 DZ93
Cope St, SE16 33 J8
Copford Cl, Wdf.Grn. IG8 124 EL51
Copford Wk, N1 9 J8
Copgate Path, SW16 203 DM93
Copinger Wk, Edg. HA8
off North Rd 118 CP53
Copland Av, Wem. HA0 139 CK64
Copland Cl, Wem. HA0 139 CJ64
Copland Comm Sch & Tech Cen,
Wem. HA9 off Cecil Av 140 CM64
Copland Ms, Wem. HA0 160 CL65
Copland Rd, Wem. HA0 160 CL65
Copleigh Dr, Kgswd KT20 255 CY120
Copleston Ms, SE15 44 A10
Copleston Pas, SE15 44 A10
Copleston Rd, SE15 184 DT83
Copley Cl, SE17 43 H3
W7 159 CF71
Redhill RH1 272 DE132
Woking GU21 248 AS119
Copley Dene, Brom. BR1 226 EK95
Copley Pk, SW16 203 DM93
Copley Rd, Stan. HA7 117 CJ50
Copley St, E1 21 J7
Copley Way, Tad. KT20 255 CX120
Copmans Wick, Chorl. WD3 95 BD43
Coppard Gdns, Chess. KT9 237 CJ107
Copped Hall, SE21
off Glazebrook Cl 204 DR89
Epping CM16 91 EN32
Coppelia Rd, SE3 186 EF84
Coppen Rd, Dag. RM8 148 EZ59
Copperas St, SE8 46 C3
Copper Beech Cl, Grav. DA12 213 GK87
Hemel Hempstead HP3 61 BF23
Ilford IG5 125 EN53
Orpington BR5 228 EW99
Windsor SL4 173 AK81
Woking GU22 248 AV121
Copperbeech Cl, NW3
off Akenside Rd 6 A3
Copper Beech Ct, Loug. IG10 107 EN39
Copper Beeches, Islw. TW7 179 CD81
Copper Beech Rd, S.Ock.
RM15 171 FW69
★ Copper Box, E20 12 B5
Copper Cl, N17 122 DV52
SE19 off Auckland Rd 204 DT94
Copperdale Rd, Hayes UB3 177 BU75
Copperfield, Chig. IG7 125 ER51
Copperfield Av, Uxb. UB8 156 BN71
Copperfield Cl, S.Croy. CR2 242 DQ111
Copperfield Ct, Lthd. KT22
off Kingston Rd 253 CG121
Pinner HA5
off Copperfield Way 138 BZ56
Copperfield Dr, N15 144 DT56
Copperfield Gdns, Brwd.
CM14 130 FV46
Copperfield Ms, N18 122 DS50
Copperfield Ri, Add. KT15 233 BF106
Copperfield Rd, E3 21 M5
SE28 168 EW72
Copperfields, Beac. HP9 111 AL50
Dartford DA1
off Spital St 210 FL86
Fetcham KT22 252 CC122
Welwyn Garden City AL7
off Forresters Dr 52 DC10
Copperfield St, SE1 31 H4
Copperfields Way, Rom. RM3 128 FK53
Copperfield Ter, Slou. SL2
off Mirador Cres 154 AV73
Copperfield Way, Chis. BR7 207 EQ93
Pinner HA5 138 BZ56
Coppergate Cl, Brom. BR1 226 EH95
Coppergate Ct, Wal.Abb. EN9
off Farthingale La 90 EG34
Coppergate Ms, Surb. KT6 219 CJ100
Copperkins Gro, Amer. HP6 77 AP36
Copperkins La, Amer. HP6 77 AM35
Copper Mead Cl, NW2 141 CW62
Copper Ms, W4 180 CQ76
Copper Mill Dr, Islw. TW7 179 CF82
Coppermill La, E17 144 DW58
Copper Mill La, SW17 202 DC91
Coppermill La, Hare. UB9 113 BE52
Rickmansworth WD3 113 BE52
Coppermill Prim Sch, E17
off Edward Rd 145 DX57
Coppermill Rd, Wrays. TW19 175 BC84
Copper Ridge, Chal.St.P. SL9 113 AZ50
Copper Row, SE1 32 A3
Copperwood, Hert. SG13 54 DT09
Coppetts Centre, N12 120 DF52
Coppetts Cl, N12 120 DE52
Coppetts Rd, N10 120 DG54
Coppetts Wd Hosp, N10 120 DF53
Coppetts Wd Prim Sch,
N10 off Coppetts Rd 120 DG53
Coppice, The, Ashf. TW15
off School Rd 197 BP93
Bexley DA5 209 FD90
Enfield EN2 103 DP42
Hemel Hempstead HP2 63 BP19
Seer Green HP9 111 AR51
Watford WD19 98 BW44
West Drayton UB7 156 BL72
Coppice Cl, SW20 221 CW97
Beckenham BR3 225 EB98
Hatfield AL10 67 CT22
Ruislip HA4 137 BR58
Stanmore HA7 117 CF51
Coppice Dr, SW15 201 CV86
Wraysbury TW19 194 AX87
Coppice End, Wok. GU22 249 BE116
Coppice Fm Rd, Penn HP10 110 AC45
Coppice Hatch, Harl. CM18 73 ER17
Coppice La, Reig. RH2 271 CZ132
Coppice Path, Chig. IG7 126 EV49
Coppice Prim Sch, Chig.
IG7 off Manford Way 126 EU50
Coppice Row, They.B. CM16 107 EM36
Coppice Wk, N20 120 DA48
Coppice Way, E18 146 EF56
Hedgerley SL2 133 AR61
Coppies Gro, N11 120 DG49
Copping Cl, Croy. CR0 242 DS105
Coppings, The, Hodd. EN11
off Danemead 55 EA14
Coppins, The, Har. HA3 117 CE51
New Addington CR0 243 EB107
Welwyn Garden City AL8 51 CU11
Coppins Cl, Berk. HP4 60 AS19
Coppins La, Iver SL0 155 BF71
Coppock Cl, SW11 40 C9
Coppsfield, W.Mol. KT8
off Hurst Rd 218 CA97
Copse, The, E4 124 EF46
Amersham HP7 77 AQ38
Beaconsfield HP9 110 AJ51
Bushey WD23 98 BY41
Caterham CR3 274 DU126
Fetcham KT22 252 CB123
Hemel Hempstead HP1 61 BE18
Hertford SG13 54 DU09
South Nutfield RH1 289 DL136
Tatsfield TN16 260 EJ120
Warlingham CR6 259 DY117
Copse Av, W.Wick. BR4 225 EB104
Copse Cl, SE7 186 EH79
Chilworth GU4 281 BC140
Northwood HA6 115 BQ54
Slough SL1 153 AM74
West Drayton UB7 176 BK76
Copse Edge Av, Epsom KT17 239 CT113
Copse Glade, Surb. KT6 219 CK102
COPSE HILL, SW20 201 CV94
Copse Hill, SW20 201 CV94
Harlow CM19 73 EP18
Purley CR8 241 DL113
Sutton SM2 240 DB108
Copse La, Horl. RH6 291 DJ147
Jordans HP9 112 AS52
Copsem Dr, Esher KT10 236 CB107
Copsem La, Esher KT10 236 CB107
Oxshott KT22 236 CC111
Copsem Way, Esher KT10 236 CC107
Copsen Wd, Oxshott KT22 236 CC111
Copse Rd, Cob. KT11 235 BV113
Redhill RH1 288 DC136
Woking GU21 248 AT118
Copse Vw, S.Croy. CR2 243 DX109
Copse Way, Chesh. HP5 76 AN27
Copse Wd, Iver SL0 155 BD67
Copsewood Cl, Sid. DA15 207 ES86
Copse Wd Ct, Reig. RH2
off Green La 272 DE132
Copsewood Rd, Wat. WD24 97 BV39
Copse Wd Way, Nthwd. HA6 115 BQ52
Copshall Cl, Harl. CM18 73 ES19
Copsleigh Av, Red. RH1 288 DG141
Copsleigh Cl, Salf. RH1 288 DG140
Copsleigh Way, Red. RH1 288 DG140
Coptain Ho, SW18
off Eastfields Av 182 DA84
Coptefield Dr, Belv. DA17 188 EX76
Coptfold Rd, Brwd. CM14 130 FW47
Copthall Av, EC2 19 M8
Copthall Bldgs, EC2 19 L8
Copthall Cl, EC2 19 L8
Chalfont St. Peter SL9 113 AZ52
Copthall Cor, Chal.St.P. SL9 112 AY52
Copthall Ct, EC2 19 L8
Copthall Dr, NW7 119 CU52
Copthall Gdns, NW7 119 CU52
Twickenham TW1 199 CF88
COPTHALL GREEN,
Wal.Abb. EN9 90 EK33
Copthall La, Chal.St.P. SL9 112 AY52
Copthall Rd E, Uxb. UB10 136 BN61
Copthall Rd W, Uxb. UB10 136 BN61
Copthall Sch, NW7
off Pursley Rd 119 CV52
Copthall Way, New Haw KT15 233 BF110
Copt Hill La, Kgswd KT20 255 CY120
Copthorn Av, Brox. EN10 71 DZ21
Copthorne Av, SW12 203 DK87
Bromley BR2 227 EM103
Ilford IG6 125 EP51
Copthorne Chase, Ashf. TW15 196 BM91
Copthorne Cl, Crox.Grn WD3 96 BM43
Shepperton TW17 217 BQ100
Copthorne Gdns, Horn. RM11 150 FN57
Copthorne Ms, Hayes UB3 177 BS77
Copthorne Pl, Eff.Junct. KT24 251 BU122
Copthorne Ri, S.Croy. CR2 242 DR113
Copthorne Rd, Crox.Grn WD3 96 BM44
Leatherhead KT22 253 CH120
Coptic St, WC1 18 A7
Copwood Cl, N12 120 DD49
Coral Apts, E16
off Western Gateway 35 P1
Coral Cl, Rom. RM6 148 EW56
Coral Gdns, Hem.H. HP2 62 BM19
Coraline Cl, Sthl. UB1 158 BZ69
Coralline Wk, SE2 188 EW75
Coral Row, SW11 39 P10
Corals Mead, Welw.G.C. AL7 51 CX10
Coral St, SE1 30 F5
Coram Cl, Berk. HP4 60 AW20
Coram Grn, Hutt. CM13 131 GD44
★ Coram's Flds, WC1 18 B5
Coram St, WC1 18 A5
Coran Cl, N9 123 DX45
Corban Rd, Houns. TW3 178 CA83
Corbar Cl, Barn. EN4 102 DD38
Corbden Cl, SE15 44 B6
Corben Ms, SW8 off Clyston St 41 M8
Corbet Cl, Wall. SM6 222 DG102
Corbet Ct, EC3 19 M9
Corbet Pl, E1 20 A6
Corbet Rd, Epsom KT17 238 CS110
Corbets Av, Upmin. RM14 150 FP64
CORBETS TEY, Upmin. RM14 170 FQ65
Corbets Tey Rd, Upmin. RM14 150 FP63
Corbets Tey Sch, Upmin.
RM14 off Harwood Hall La 150 FQ64
Corbett Cl, Croy. CR0 243 ED112
Corbett Gro, N22 121 DL52
Corbett Rd, E11 146 EJ58
E17 145 EC55
Corbetts La, SE16 32 G9
Corbetts Pas, SE16 32 G9
Corbicum, E11 146 EE59
Corbidge Ct, SE8 46 C2
Corbiere Ct, SW19
off Thornton Rd 201 CX93
Corbiere Ho, N1 9 N8
Corbin Ho, E3 22 D2
Corbins La, Har. HA2 138 CB62
Corbould Cl, Cars. SM5 240 DF107
Corbridge Cres, E2 10 E10
Corbridge Ms, Rom. RM1 149 FF57
Corby Cl, Eng.Grn TW20 194 AW93
St. Albans AL2 82 CA25
Corby Cres, Enf. EN2 103 DL42
Corby Dr, Eng.Grn TW20 194 AV93
Corbylands Rd, Sid. DA15 207 ES87
Corbyn St, N4 143 DL60
Corby Rd, NW10 160 CR68
Corby Way, E3 22 A5
Corcorans, Pilg.Hat. CM15 130 FV44
Cordelia Cl, SE24 183 DP84
Cordelia Ct, NW7
off Marchant Cl 118 CS51
Cordelia Gdns, Stai. TW19 196 BL87
Cordelia Rd, Stai. TW19 196 BL87
Cordelia St, E14 22 C8
Cordell Cl, Chsht EN8 89 DY28
Cordell Ho, N15 144 DU57
Corder Cl, St.Alb. AL3 64 CA23
Corderoy Pl, Cher. KT16 215 BE100
Cordingley Rd, Ruis. HA4 137 BR61
Cording St, E14 22 D7
Cordons Cl, Chal.St.P. SL9 112 AX53
Cordrey Gdns, Couls. CR5 257 DL115
Cordwainers at London Coll
of Fashion, EC1 19 J5
Cordwainers Wk, E13 13 P10
Cord Way, E14 34 B6
Cordwell Rd, SE13 206 EE85
Corefield Cl, N11
off Benfleet Way 120 DG47
Corelli Rd, SE3 186 EL82
Corfe Av, Har. HA2 138 CA63
Corfe Cl, Ashtd. KT21 253 CJ118
Borehamwood WD6 100 CR41
Hayes UB4 158 BW72
Hemel Hempstead HP2 62 BL21
Hounslow TW4 198 BY87
Corfe Gdns, Slou. SL1
off Avebury 153 AN74
Corfe Ho, SW8
off Dorset Rd 42 C4
Corfe Twr, W3 180 CP75
Corfield Rd, N21 103 DM43
Corfield St, E2 20 F3
Corfton Rd, W5 160 CL72
Coriander Av, E14 22 G9
Coriander Cres, Guil. GU2 264 AU129
Cories Cl, Dag. RM8 148 EX61
Corinium Cl, Wem. HA9 140 CM63
Corinium Gate, St.Alb. AL3 64 CA22
● Corinium Ind Est, Amer.
HP6 94 AT38
Corinne Rd, N19 7 M1
Corinthian Manorway,
Erith DA8 189 FD77
Corinthian Rd, Erith DA8 189 FD77
Corinthian Way, Stanw. TW19
off Clare Rd 196 BK87
Corker Wk, N7 143 DM61
Cork Ho, SW19 off Plough La 202 DB92
Corkran Rd, Surb. KT6 219 CK101
Corkscrew Hill, W.Wick. BR4 225 ED103
Cork Sq, E1 32 E2
Cork St, W1 29 L1
Cork St Ms, W1 29 L1
Cork Tree Retail Pk, E4 123 DY50
Cork Tree Way, E4 123 DY50
Corlett St, NW1 16 C6
Cormongers La, Nutfld RH1 273 DK131
Cormont Rd, SE5 42 G7
Cormorant Cl, E17 123 DX53
Cormorant Ct, SE21
off Elmworth Gro 204 DR89
Cormorant Ho, Enf. EN3
off Alma Rd 105 DX43
Cormorant Pl, Sutt. SM1
off Sandpiper Rd 239 CZ106
Cormorant Rd, E7 13 M2
Cormorant Wk, Horn. RM12
off Heron Flight Av 169 FH65
Cornbury Ho, SE8 off Evelyn St 45 P2
Cornbury Rd, Edg. HA8 117 CK52
Corncroft, Hat. AL10 67 CV16
Cornelia Dr, Hayes UB4 158 BW70
Cornelia Pl, Erith DA8
off Queen St 189 FE79
Cornelia St, N7 8 D5
Cornell Cl, Sid. DA14 208 EY93
Cornell Ct, Enf. EN3 105 DY41
Cornell Way, Rom. RM5 126 FA50
Corner, The, W.Byf. KT14 234 BG113
Corner Fm Cl, Tad. KT20 255 CW122
Cornerfield, Hat. AL10 67 CV15
Corner Fielde, SW2
off Streatham Hill 203 DL88
Corner Grn, SE3 47 N9
Corner Hall, Hem.H. HP3 62 BJ22
Corner Hall Av, Hem.H. HP3 62 BK22
Corner Ho St, WC2 30 A2
Corner Mead, NW9 119 CT52
Corner Meadow, Harl. CM18 74 EU19
Corners, Welw.G.C. AL7 52 DA07
Cornerside, Ashf. TW15 197 BQ94
Corner Vw, N.Mymms AL9 67 CW24
Corney Reach Way, W4 180 CS80
Corney Rd, W4 180 CS79
Cornfield Cl, Uxb. UB8 156 BK68
Cornfield Rd, Bushey WD23 98 CB42
Reigate RH2 288 DC135
Cornfields, Gdmg. GU7 280 AT143
Cornfields, The, Hem.H. HP1 62 BH21
Cornflower La, Croy. CR0 225 DX102
Cornflower Ter, SE22 204 DV86
Cornflower Way, Hat. AL10 66 CS15
Romford RM3 128 FL53
Cornford Cl, Brom. BR2 226 EG99
Cornford Gro, SW12 203 DH89
Cornhill, EC3 19 M9
Cornhill Cl, Add. KT15 216 BH103
Cornhill Dr, Enf. EN3 105 DY37
Corn Ho, NW7 off Peacock Cl 119 CY50
Cornish Ct, N9 122 DV45
Cornish Gro, SE20 204 DV94
Cornish Ho, SE17 42 G3
Brentford TW8
off Green Dragon La 180 CM78
Corn Mead, Welw.G.C. AL8 51 CW06
Cornmill, Wal.Abb. EN9 89 EB33
Corn Mill Dr, Orp. BR6 227 ET101
Cornmill Ms, Wal.Abb. EN9
off Highbridge St 89 EB33
Cornmow Dr, NW10 141 CT64
Cornshaw Rd, Dag. RM8 148 EX60
Cornsland, Brwd. CM14 130 FX48
Cornsland Cl, Upmin. RM14 150 FQ55
Cornsland Ct, Brwd. CM14 130 FW48
Cornthwaite Rd, E5 144 DW62
Cornwall Av, E2 20 G3
N3 120 DA52
N22 121 DL53
Byfleet KT14 234 BM114
Claygate KT10 237 CF108
Slough SL2 153 AQ70
Southall UB1 158 BZ71
Welling DA16 187 ES83
Cornwall Cl, Bark. IG11 167 ET65
Eton Wick SL4 173 AL78
Hornchurch RM11 150 FN56
Waltham Cross EN8 89 DY33
Cornwall Cres, W11 14 E10
Cornwall Dr, Orp. BR5 208 EW94
Cornwall Gdns, NW10 161 CV65
SW7 27 M7
Cornwall Gdns Wk, SW7 27 M7
Cornwall Gate, Purf. RM19
off Fanns Ri 190 FN77
Cornwall Gro, W4 180 CS78
Cornwallis Av, N9 122 DV47
SE9 207 ER89
Cornwallis Cl, Cat. CR3 258 DQ122
Erith DA8 189 FF79
Cornwallis Ct, SW8 42 A6
Cornwallis Gro, N9 122 DV47
Cornwallis Rd, E17 145 DX56
N9 122 DV47
N19 143 DL61
SE18 187 EQ77
Dagenham RM9 148 EX63
Cornwallis Sq, N19 143 DL61
Cornwallis Wk, SE9 187 EM83
Cornwall Ms S, SW7 27 N7
Cornwall Ms W, SW7 27 M7
Cornwall Pl, E4 105 EB42
Cornwall Rd, N4 143 DN59
N15 144 DR57
N18 122 DU50
SE1 30 E2
Croydon CR0 223 DP103
Dartford DA1 190 FM83
Harrow HA1 138 CC58
Pilgrim's Hatch CM15 130 FV43
Pinner HA5 116 BZ52
Ruislip HA4 137 BT62
St. Albans AL1 65 CE22
Sutton SM2 239 CZ108
Twickenham TW1 199 CG87
Uxbridge UB8 156 BK65
Cornwall Sq, SE11 30 F10
Cornwall St, E1 20 F10
Cornwall Ter, NW1 16 F5
Cornwall Ter Ms, NW1 16 F5
Cornwall Way, Stai. TW18 195 BE93
Corn Way, E11 145 ED62
Cornwell Av, Grav. DA12 213 GJ90
Cornwell Rd, Old Wind. SL4 194 AU86
Cornwood Cl, N2 142 DD57
Cornwood Dr, E1 20 G8
Cornworthy Rd, Dag. RM8 148 EW64
Corona Rd, SE12 206 EG87
Coronation Av, N16
off Victorian Rd 144 DT62
George Green SL3 154 AY72
Windsor SL4 174 AT81
Coronation Cl, Bex. DA5 208 EX86
Ilford IG6 147 EQ56
Coronation Dr, Horn. RM12 149 FH63
Coronation Hill, Epp. CM16 91 ET30
Coronation Rd, E13 24 D3
NW10 160 CN70
Hayes UB3 177 BT77
Ware SG12 55 DX05
Coronation Wk, Twick. TW2 198 CA88
Coronet, The, Horl. RH6 291 DJ150
Coronet St, N1 19 N3
★ Coronet Thea, SE1 31 H7
Corporation Av, Houns. TW4 178 BY84
Corporation Row, EC1 18 F4
Corporation St, E15 23 K1
N7 8 A3
Corpus Christi Prim Sch,
N.Mal. KT3
off Chestnut Gro 220 CQ97
Corpus Christi RC Prim Sch,
SW2 off Trent Rd 203 DM85
Annexe, SW2 off Trent Rd 203 DM85
Corrance Rd, SW2 183 DL84
Corran Way, S.Ock. RM15 171 FV73
Corri Av, N14 121 DK49
Corrib Dr, Sutt. SM1 240 DE106

Corrie Gdns, Vir.W. GU25 214 AW101
Corrie Rd, Add. KT15 234 BK105
Woking GU22 249 BC120
Corrigan Av, Couls. CR5 240 DG114
Corrigan Cl, NW4 141 CW55
Corringham Ct, NW11
off Corringham Rd 142 DA59
St. Albans AL1
off Lemsford Rd 65 CF19
Corringham Rd, NW11 142 DA59
Wembley HA9 140 CN61
Corringway, NW11 142 DB59
W5 160 CN70
Corris Grn, NW9 140 CS58
Corry Dr, SW9 183 DP84
Corsair Cl, Stai. TW19 196 BK87
Corsair Rd, Stai. TW19 196 BL87
Corscombe Cl, Kings.T. KT2 200 CQ92
Corsehill St, SW16 203 DJ93
Corsham St, N1 19 M3
Corsica St, N5 8 G4
Corsley Way, E9
off Silk Mills Sq 11 P4
Cortayne Rd, SW6 39 H8
Cortina Dr, Dag. RM9 169 FC69
Cortis Rd, SW15 201 CV86
Cortis Ter, SW15 201 CV86
Cortland Cl, Dart. DA1 209 FE86
Woodford Green IG8 124 EJ53
Corunna Rd, SW8 41 M6
Corunna Ter, SW8 41 L6
Corve La, S.Ock. RM15 171 FV73
Corvette Sq, SE10 47 H2
Corwell Gdns, Uxb. UB8 157 BQ72
Corwell La, Uxb. UB8 157 BQ72
Cory Dr, Hutt. CM13 131 GB45
Coryton Path, W9 15 H4
Cory Wright Way, Wheat. AL4 50 CL06
Cosbycote Av, SE24 204 DQ85
Cosdach Av, Wall. SM6 241 DK108
Cosedge Cres, Croy. CR0 241 DN106
Cosgrove Cl, N21 122 DQ47
Hayes UB4 off Kingsash Dr 158 BY70
Cosmo Pl, WC1 18 B6
Cosmopolitan Ct, Enf. EN1
off Main Ave 104 DU43
Cosmur Cl, W12 181 CT76
Cossall Wk, SE15 44 E8
Cossar Ms, SW2 203 DN86
Cosser St, SE1 30 E6
Costa St, SE15 44 C9
Costead Manor Rd, Brwd.
CM14 130 FV46
Costell's Meadow, West. TN16 277 ER126
Costins Wk, Berk. HP4
off Robertson Rd 60 AX19
Sch Coston Prim Sch, Grnf.
UB6 off Oldfield La S 158 CC69
Costons Av, Grnf. UB6 159 CD69
Costons La, Grnf. UB6 159 CD69
Coston Wk, SE4
off Hainford Cl 185 DX84
Cosway St, NW1 16 D6
Cotall St, E14 22 B8
Coteford Cl, Loug. IG10 107 EP40
Pinner HA5 137 BU57
Sch Coteford Inf Sch, Eastcote
HA5 off Fore St 137 BU58
Sch Coteford Jun Sch, Eastcote
HA5 off Fore St 137 BT57
Coteford St, SW17 202 DF91
Cotelands, Croy. CR0 224 DS104
Cotesbach Rd, E5 144 DW62
Cotesmore Gdns, Dag. RM8 148 EW63
Cotesmore Rd, Hem.H. HP1 61 BE21
Cotford Rd, Th.Hth. CR7 224 DQ98
Cotham St, SE17 31 K9
Cotherstone, Epsom KT19 238 CR110
Cotherstone Rd, SW2 203 DM88
Cotland Acres, Red. RH1 288 DD136
Cotlandswick, Lon.Col. AL2 83 CJ26
Cotleigh Av, Bex. DA5 208 EX89
Cotleigh Rd, NW6 5 J6
Romford RM7 149 FD58
Cotman Cl, NW11 142 DC58
SW15 201 CX86
Cotmandene, Dor. RH4 285 CH136
Cotmandene Cres, Orp. BR5 228 EU96
Cotman Gdns, Edg. HA8 118 CN54
Cotman Ms, Dag. RM8 148 EW64
Cotmans Cl, Hayes UB3 157 BU74
Coton Dr, Uxb. UB10 136 BQ61
Coton Rd, Well. DA16 188 EU83
Cotsford Av, N.Mal. KT3 220 CQ99
Cotsmoor, St.Alb. AL1
off Granville Rd 65 CF20
Cotswold, Hem.H. HP2
off Mendip Way 62 BL17
Cotswold Av, Bushey WD23 98 CC44
Cotswold Cl, Bexh. DA7 189 FE82
Hinchley Wood KT10 219 CF104
Kingston upon Thames KT2 200 CP93
St. Albans AL4
off Chiltern Rd 65 CJ15
Slough SL1 173 AP76
Staines-upon-Thames TW18 196 BG92
Uxbridge UB8 156 BJ67
Cotswold Ct, EC1 19 J4
N11 120 DG49
Cotswold Gdns, E6 24 F2
NW2 141 CX61
Hutton CM13 131 GE45
Ilford IG2 147 ER59
Cotswold Gate, NW2 141 CY60
Cotswold Grn, Enf. EN2
off Cotswold Way 103 DM42
Cotswold Ms, SW11 40 B7
Cotswold Ri, Orp. BR6 227 ET100
Cotswold Rd, Hmptn. TW12 198 CA93
Northfleet DA11 212 GE90
Romford RM3 128 FM54
Sutton SM2 240 DB110
Cotswolds, Hat. AL10 67 CU20
Cotswold St, SE27
off Norwood High St 203 DP91
Cotswold Way, Enf. EN2 103 DM42
Worcester Park KT4 221 CW103
Cottage Av, Brom. BR2 226 EL102
Cottage Cl, Crox.Grn WD3 96 BM44
Harrow HA2 139 CE61
Ottershaw KT16 233 BC107
Ruislip HA4 137 BR60
Watford WD17 97 BT40
Cottage Fm Way, Egh. TW20
off Green Rd 215 BC97
Cottage Fld Cl, Sid. DA14 208 EW88
Cottage Gdns, Chsht EN8 88 DW29
Cottage Grn, SE5 43 M4
Cottage Gro, SW9 183 DL83
Cottage Gro, Surbiton KT6 219 CK100
Cottage Pk Rd, Hedg. SL2 133 AR61
Cottage Pl, SW3 28 C6
Cottage Rd, N7 8 C3
Epsom KT19 238 CR108
Cottage St, E14 22 D10
Cottage Wk, N16
off Brooke Rd 144 DT62
Cottenham Dr, NW9 141 CT55
SW20 201 CV94
Cottenham Par, SW20
off Durham Rd 221 CV96
COTTENHAM PARK, SW20 221 CV95
Cottenham Pk Rd, SW20 201 CV94
Cottenham Pl, SW20 201 CV94
Cottenham Rd, E17 145 DZ56
Cotterells, Hem.H. HP1 62 BJ21
Cotterells Hill, Hem.H. HP1 62 BJ20
Cotterill Rd, Surb. KT6 220 CL103
Cottesbrooke Cl, Colnbr. SL3 175 BD81
Cottesbrook St, SE14 45 L4
Cottesloe Ms, SE1 30 F6
Cottesmore Av, Ilf. IG5 125 EN54
Cottesmore Gdns, W8 27 M6
Cottimore Av, Walt. KT12 217 BV102
Cottimore Cres, Walt. KT12 217 BV101
Cottimore La, Walt. KT12 218 BW102
Cottimore Ter, Walt. KT12 217 BV101
Cottingham Chase, Ruis. HA4 137 BU62
Cottingham Rd, SE20 205 DX94
SW8 42 D3
Cottington Rd, Felt. TW13 198 BX91
Cottington St, SE11 30 F10
Cottle Way, SE16 32 F5
Cotton Av, W3 160 CR72
Cotton Cl, E11 146 EE61
Dagenham RM9
off Flamstead Rd 168 EW66
Cotton Dr, Hert. SG13 54 DV08
Cotton Fld, Hat. AL10 67 CV16
Cottongrass Cl, Croy. CR0
off Cornflower La 225 DX102
Cottonham Cl, N12
off Fenstanton Ave 120 DD50
Cotton Hill, Brom. BR1 205 ED91
Cotton La, Dart. DA2 210 FQ86
Greenhithe DA9 210 FQ85
Cottonmill Cres, St.Alb. AL1 65 CD21
Cottonmill La, St.Alb. AL1 65 CE23
Cotton Rd, Pot.B. EN6 86 DC31
Cotton Row, SW11 39 P10
Cottons App, Rom. RM7 149 FD57
Cottons Ct, Rom. RM7 149 FD57
Cottons Gdns, E2 19 P2
Cottons La, SE1 31 M2
Cotton St, E14 22 E10
Cottrell Ct, SE10
off Greenroof Way 35 M8
Cottrill Gdns, E8 10 E4
Cotts Cl, W7
off Westcott Cres 159 CF72
Cotts Wd Dr, Guil. GU4 265 BA129
Couchmore Av, Esher KT10 219 CE103
Ilford IG5 125 EM54
Coulgate St, SE4 185 DY83
COULSDON, CR5 257 DJ116
Sch Coulsdon C of E Prim Sch,
Couls. CR5
off Bradmore Grn 257 DM118
Coll Coulsdon Coll, Couls. CR5
off Placehouse La 257 DN119
Coulsdon Common, Cat. CR3 258 DQ121
Coulsdon Ct Rd, Couls. CR5 257 DM116
Coulsdon La, Chipstead CR5 256 DF119
● Coulsdon N Ind Est, Couls.
CR5 257 DK116
Coulsdon Pl, Cat. CR3 258 DR122
Coulsdon Ri, Couls. CR5 257 DL117
Coulsdon Rd, Cat. CR3 258 DQ121
Coulsdon CR5 257 DM115
⇌ Coulsdon South 257 DK116
⇌ Coulsdon Town 257 DL115
Coulser Cl, Hem.H. HP1 62 BG17
Coulson Cl, Dag. RM8 148 EW59
Coulson Ct, Lon.Col. AL2 83 CK27
Coulson St, SW3 28 E10
Coulson Way, Burn. SL1 152 AH71
Coulter Cl, Cuffley EN6 87 DK27
Hayes UB4
off Berrydale Rd 158 BY70
Coulter Rd, W6 181 CV76
Coulton Av, Nthflt DA11 212 GE87
Council Av, Nthflt DA11 212 GC86
Council Cotts, Wisley GU23
off Wisley La 250 BK115
Councillor St, SE5 43 J5
Counter Ct, SE1
off Borough High St 31 L3
Counters Cl, Hem.H. HP1 62 BG20
Counter St, SE1
off Tooley St 31 N2
Sch Countess Anne C of E Prim Sch,
Hat. AL10 off School La 67 CW17
Countess Cl, Hare. UB9 114 BJ54
Countess Rd, NW5 7 L2
Countisbury Av, Enf. EN1 122 DT45
Countisbury Gdns, Add. KT15 234 BH106
Country Way, Han. TW13 197 BV94
Sunbury-on-Thames TW16 197 BV94
County Gate, SE9 207 EQ90
New Barnet EN5 102 DB44
County Gro, SE5 43 J6
★ County Hall, SE1 30 C4
County Rd, E6 25 N7
Thornton Heath CR7 223 DP96
County St, SE1 31 K7
Coupland Pl, SE18 187 EQ78
Courage Cl, Horn. RM11 150 FJ58
Courage Wk, Hutt. CM13 131 GD44
Courcy Rd, N8 143 DN55
Courier Rd, Dag. RM9 169 FC70
Courland Gro, SW8 41 P7
Courland Gro Hall, SW8 41 P8
Courland Rd, Add. KT15 216 BH104
Courland St, SW8 41 P7
Course, The, SE9 207 EN90
Coursers Rd, Coln.Hth AL4 84 CN27
Court, The, Ruis. HA4 138 BY63
Warlingham CR6 259 DY118
Courtauld Cl, SE28 168 EU74
★ Courtauld Inst of Art, WC2 18 C10
Courtauld Rd, N19 143 DK60
Courtaulds, Chipper. WD4 80 BH30
Court Av, Belv. DA17 188 EZ78
Coulsdon CR5 257 DN118
Romford RM3 128 FN52
Court Bushes Rd, Whyt. CR3 258 DU120
Court Cl, Har. HA3 139 CK55
Maidenhead SL6 172 AC77
Court Cl, Twickenham TW2 198 CB90
Wallington SM6 241 DK108
Court Cl Av, Twick. TW2 198 CB90
Court Cres, Chess. KT9 237 CK106
Slough SL1 153 AR72
Swanley BR8 229 FE98
Court Downs Rd, Beck. BR3 225 EB96
Court Dr, Croy. CR0 241 DM105
Maidenhead SL6 152 AC68
Stanmore HA7 118 CL49
Sutton SM1 240 DE105
Uxbridge UB10 156 BM67
Courtenay Av, N6 142 DE58
Harrow HA3 116 CC53
Sutton SM2 240 DA109
Courtenay Dr, Beck. BR3 225 ED96
Chafford Hundred RM16
off Clifford Rd 192 FZ76
Courtenay Gdns, Har. HA3 116 CC54
Upminster RM14 150 FQ60
Courtenay Ms, E17
off Cranbrook Ms 145 DY57
Courtenay Pl, E17 145 DY57
Courtenay Rd, E11 146 EF62
E17 145 DX56
SE20 205 DX94
Wembley HA9 139 CK62
Woking GU21 249 BA116
Worcester Park KT4 221 CW104
Courtenay Sq, SE11 42 E1
Courtenay St, SE11 30 E10
Courtens Ms, Stan. HA7 117 CJ52
Court Fm Av, Epsom KT19 238 CR106
Court Fm Cl, Slou. SL1
off Weekes Dr 153 AP74
Court Fm La, Oxt. RH8 276 EE128
Court Fm Pk, Warl. CR6 258 DU116
Court Fm Rd, SE9 206 EK89
Northolt UB5 158 CA66
Warlingham CR6 258 DU118
Courtfield, W5
off Castlebar Hill 159 CJ71
Courtfield Av, Har. HA1 139 CF57
Courtfield Cl, Brox. EN10 71 EA20
Courtfield Cres, Har. HA1 139 CF57
Courtfield Gdns, SW5 27 M8
W13 159 CG72
Denham UB9 136 BG62
Ruislip HA4 137 BT61
Courtfield Ms, SW5 27 N9
Courtfield Ri, W.Wick. BR4 225 ED104
Courtfield Rd, SW7 27 M9
Ashford TW15 197 BP93
Court Gdns, N7 8 F5
Courtgate Cl, NW7 119 CT51
Court Grn Hts, Wok. GU22 248 AW120
Court Haw, Bans. SM7 256 DE115
Court Hill, Chipstead CR5 256 DE118
South Croydon CR2 242 DS112
Courthill Rd, SE13 185 EC84
Courthope Rd, NW3 6 F1
SW19 201 CY92
Greenford UB6 159 CD68
Courthope Vil, SW19 201 CY94
Court Ho Gdns, N3 120 DA51
Courthouse Rd, N12 120 DB51
Courtland Av, E4 124 EF47
NW7 118 CR48
SW16 203 DM94
Ilford IG1 147 EM61
Courtland Dr, Chig. IG7 125 EP48
Courtland Gro, SE28 168 EX73
Sch Courtland Prim Sch, NW7
off Courtland Av 118 CS47
Courtland Rd, E6
off Harrow Rd 166 EL67
Courtlands, Rich. TW10 180 CN84
Courtlands Av, SE12 206 EH85
Bromley BR2 226 EF102
Esher KT10 236 BZ107
Hampton TW12 198 BZ93
Richmond TW9 180 CP82
Slough SL3 174 AX77
Courtlands Cl, Ruis. HA4 137 BT59
South Croydon CR2 242 DT110
Watford WD24 97 BS35
Courtlands Cres, Bans. SM7 256 DA115
Courtlands Dr, Epsom KT19 238 CS107
Watford WD17, WD24 97 BS37
Courtlands Rd, Surb. KT5 220 CN101
Court La, SE21 204 DS86
Burnham SL1 153 AK69
Dorney SL4 172 AG76
Epsom KT19 238 CQ113
Iver SL0 156 BG74
Court La Gdns, SE21 204 DS87
Court Lawns, Penn HP10 110 AC46
Courtleas, Cob. KT11 236 CA113
Courtleet Dr, Erith DA8 189 FB81
Courtleigh Av, Barn. EN4 102 DD38
Courtleigh Gdns, NW11 141 CY56
Court Lo Rd, Horl. RH6 290 DE147
Courtman Rd, N17 122 DQ52
Court Mead, Nthlt. UB5 158 BZ69
Courtmead Cl, SE24 204 DQ86
Courtnell St, W2 15 J8
Courtney Cl, SE19 204 DS93
Courtney Cres, Cars. SM5 240 DF108
Courtney Pl, Cob. KT11 236 BZ112
Croydon CR0 223 DN104
Courtney Rd, N7 8 E2
SW19 202 DE94
Croydon CR0 223 DN104
Grays RM16 193 GJ75
London Heathrow Airport
TW6 176 BN83
Courtney Way, Lon.Hthrw Air.
TW6 176 BN83
Court Par, Wem. HA0 139 CH62
Courtrai Rd, SE23 205 DY86
Court Rd, SE9 206 EL89
SE25 224 DT96
Banstead SM7 256 DA116
Caterham CR3 258 DR123
Godstone RH9 274 DW131
Lane End DA2 211 FS92
Maidenhead SL6 152 AC69
Orpington BR6 228 EV101
Southall UB2 178 BZ77
Uxbridge UB10 137 BP64
Courtside, N8 143 DK58
Court St, E1 20 E6
Bromley BR1 226 EG96
Court Way, NW9 140 CS56
W3 160 CQ71
Ilford IG6 147 EQ55
Romford RM3 128 FL54
Twickenham TW2 199 CF87
Courtway, Wdf.Grn. IG8 124 EJ50
Courtway, The, Wat. WD19 116 BY47
Courtwood Dr, Sev. TN13 278 FG124
Court Wd Gro, Croy. CR0 243 DZ111
Courtwood La, Croy. CR0 243 DZ110
Sch Courtwood Prim Sch, Croy.
CR0 off Courtwood La 243 DZ110
Court Yd, SE9 206 EL86
Courtyard, The, N1 8 D6
Brentwood CM15 130 FV45
Hertingfordbury SG14 53 DM10
Keston BR2 244 EL107
Shendish HP3 80 BK26
Courtyard Ho, SW6
off Lensbury Av 39 P8
Courtyard Ms, Green. DA9 211 FU86
Orp. BR5 off Dorchester Cl 208 EU94
Rain. RM13 169 FF67
● Courtyards, The, Wat.
WD18 115 BR45
Courtyards, The, Slou. SL3
off Waterside Dr 175 BA75
Cousin La, EC4 31 L1
Cousins Cl, West Dr. UB7 156 BL73
Couthurst Rd, SE3 186 EH79
Coutts Av, Chess. KT9 238 CL106
Coutts Cres, NW5 142 DG62
Couzins Wk, Dart. DA1 190 FN82
Coval Gdns, SW14 180 CP84
Coval La, SW14 180 CP84
Coval Pas, SW14 off Coval Rd 180 CQ84
Coval Rd, SW14 180 CP84
Covelees Wall, E6 25 M8
Covell Ct, SE8
off Reginald Sq 46 B5
Covenbrook, Brwd. CM13 131 GB48
★ Covent Garden, WC2 18 B10
⊖ Covent Garden 18 A10
Covent Gdn Mkt, WC2 18 B10
Coventry Cl, E6 25 J9
NW6 5 K9
Coventry Rd, E1 20 F4
E2 20 F4
SE25 224 DU98
Ilford IG1 147 EP60
Coventry St, W1 29 N1
Coverack Cl, N14 103 DJ44
Croydon CR0 225 DY101
Coverdale, Hem.H. HP2
off Wharfedale 62 BL17
Coverdale Cl, Stan. HA7 117 CH50
Coverdale Ct, Enf. EN3
off Raynton Rd 105 DY37
Coverdale Gdns, Croy. CR0
off Park Hill Ri 224 DT104
Coverdale Rd, N11 120 DG51
NW2 4 D6
W12 161 CV74
Coverdales, The, Bark. IG11 167 EQ68
Coverdale Way, Slou. SL2 153 AL70
Coverley Cl, E1 20 D6
Great Warley CM13
off Wilmot Grn 129 FW51
Covert, The, Nthwd. HA6 115 BQ53
Petts Wood BR6 227 ES100
Coverton Rd, SW17 202 DE92
Covert Rd, Ilf. IG6 125 ET51
Coverts, The, Hutt. CM13 131 GA46
Coverts Rd, Clay. KT10 237 CF109
Covert Way, Barn. EN4 102 DC40
Covesfield, Grav. DA11 213 GF87
Covet Wd Cl, Orp. BR5 227 ET100
Covey Cl, SW19 222 DB96
Covey Rd, Wor.Pk. KT4 221 CX103
Covington Gdns, SW16 203 DP94
Covington Way, SW16 203 DM93
Cowan Cl, E6 25 H7
Cowbridge, Hert. SG14 54 DQ09
Cowbridge La, Bark. IG11 167 EP66
Cowbridge Rd, Har. HA3 140 CM56
Cowcross St, EC1 18 G6
Cowdenbeath Path, N1 8 C8
Cowden Rd, Orp. BR6 227 ET101
Cowden St, SE6 205 EA91
Cowdray Rd, Uxb. UB10 157 BQ67
Cowdray Way, Horn. RM12 149 FF63
Cowdrey Cl, Enf. EN1 104 DS40
Cowdrey Ct, Dart. DA1 209 FH87
Cowdrey Rd, SW19 202 DB92
Cowdry Rd, E9
off East Cross Route 11 N5
Cowen Av, Har. HA2 138 CC61
Cowgate Rd, Grnf. UB6 159 CD68
Cowick Rd, SW17 202 DF91
Cowings Mead, Nthlt. UB5 158 BY66
Cowland Av, Enf. EN3 104 DW42
Cow La, Bushey WD23 98 CA44
Greenford UB6 159 CD68
Watford WD25 98 BW36
Cow Leaze, E6 25 M8
Cowleaze Rd, Kings.T. KT2 220 CL95
Cowles, Chsht EN7 88 DT27
COWLEY, Uxb. UB8 156 BJ70
Cowley Av, Cher. KT16 215 BF101
Greenhithe DA9 211 FT85
● Cowley Business Pk,
Cowley UB8 156 BJ69
Cowley Cl, S.Croy. CR2 242 DW109
Cowley Cres, Hersham KT12 236 BW105
Uxbridge UB8 156 BJ71
Cowley Est, SW9 42 E6
Cowley Hill, Borwd. WD6 100 CP37
Sch Cowley Hill Prim Sch, Borwd.
WD6 off Winstre Rd 100 CP39
Cowley La, Cher. KT16 215 BF101
Cowley Mill Rd, Uxb. UB8 156 BH68
Cowley Pl, NW4 141 CW57
Cowley Retail Pk,
Cowley UB8 156 BK73
Cowley Rd, E11 146 EH57
SW9 42 F7
SW14 180 CS83
W3 161 CT74
Ilford IG1 147 EM59
Romford RM3 127 FH52
Uxbridge UB8 156 BJ68
Sch Cowley St. Laurence C of E
Prim Sch, Cowley UB8
off Worcester Rd 156 BK71
Cowley St, SW1 30 A6
Cowling Cl, W11 26 E2
Cowlins, Harl. CM17 58 EX11
Cowper Av, E6 166 EL66
Sutton SM1 240 DD105
Tilbury RM18 193 GH81
Cowper Cl, Brom. BR2 226 EK98
Chertsey KT16 215 BF100
Welling DA16 208 EU85
Cowper Ct, Wat. WD24 97 BU37
Cowper Cres, Hert. SG14 53 DP07
Cowper Gdns, N14 103 DJ44
Wallington SM6 241 DJ107
Cowper Rd, N14 121 DH46
N16 9 N2
N18 122 DU50
SW19 202 DC93
W3 160 CR74
W7 159 CF73
Belvedere DA17 188 FA77
Berkhamsted HP4 60 AV19
Bromley BR2 226 EK98
Chesham HP5 76 AP29
Hemel Hempstead HP1 62 BH21
Kingston upon Thames KT2 200 CM92
Rainham RM13 169 FG70
Slough SL2 153 AN70
Welwyn Garden City AL7 51 CZ11
Cowpers Ct, EC3
off Birchin La 19 M9
Cowper St, EC2 19 M4
Cowper Ter, W10 14 C7
Cowslip Cl, Uxb. UB10 156 BL66
Cowslip La, Mick. RH5 269 CG129
Woking GU21 248 AV115
Cowslip Rd, E18 124 EH54
Cowslips, Welw.G.C. AL7 52 DC10
Cowthorpe Rd, SW8 41 P6
Cox Cl, Shenley WD7 84 CM32
Coxdean, Epsom KT18 255 CW119
Coxe Pl, Wealds. HA3 139 CG56
Coxfield Cl, Hem.H. HP2 62 BL21
Cox La, Chess. KT9 238 CM105
Epsom KT19 238 CP106
Coxley Ri, Pur. CR8 242 DQ113
Coxmount Rd, SE7 36 E10
Coxon Dr, Chaff.Hun. RM16 192 FY76
Coxson Way, SE1 32 A5
Cox's Wk, SE21 204 DU88
Coxwell Rd, SE18 187 ER78
SE19 204 DS94
Coxwold Path, Chess. KT9
off Garrison La 238 CL108
Cozens La E, Brox. EN10 71 DZ23
Cozens La W, Brox. EN10 71 DY22
Cozens Rd, Ware SG12 55 DZ06
Crabbe Cres, Chesh. HP5 76 AR29
Crabbs Cft Cl, Orp. BR6
off Ladycroft Way 245 EQ106
Crab Hill, Beck. BR3 205 ED94
Crab Hill La, S.Nutfld RH1 289 DM138
Crab La, Ald. WD25 98 CB35
Crabtree Av, Rom. RM6 148 EX56
Wembley HA0 160 CL68
Crabtree Cl, E2 20 A1
Beaconsfield HP9 110 AH54
Bookham KT23 268 CC126
Bushey WD23 98 CB43
Hemel Hempstead HP3 62 BK22
Jct Crabtree Cor, Egh. TW20 215 BB95
Crabtree Ct, Hem.H. HP3
off Crabtree La 62 BL22
Crabtree Dr, Lthd. KT22 253 CJ124
Crabtree Hill, Lamb.End RM4 126 EZ45
Crabtree La, SW6 38 C4
Bookham KT23 268 CC126
Headley KT18 270 CQ126
Hemel Hempstead HP3 62 BK22
Westhumble RH5 269 CF130
● Crabtree Manorway Ind Est,
Belv. DA17 189 FB76
Crabtree Manorway N, Belv.
DA17 189 FC75
Crabtree Manorway S, Belv.
DA17 189 FC76
● Crabtree Office Village, Egh.
TW20 off Eversley Way 215 BC96
Crabtree Rd, Egh. TW20 215 BC96
Crabtree Wk, Brox. EN10 71 DY19
Crace St, NW1
off Drummond Cres 17 N2
Crackley Meadow, Hem.H. HP2 63 BP15
Cracknell Cl, Enf. EN1 104 DV37
Craddock Rd, Enf. EN1 104 DT41
Craddocks Av, Ashtd. KT21 254 CL117
Craddocks Cl, Ashtd. KT21 254 CN116
Craddocks Par, Ashtd. KT21 254 CL117
Craddock St, NW5 6 G5
Cradhurst Cl, Westc. RH4 284 CC137
Cradley Rd, SE9 207 ER88
Cragg Av, Rad. WD7 99 CF36
Craigavon Rd, Hem.H. HP2 62 BM16
Craigdale Rd, Horn. RM11 149 FF58
Craig Dr, Uxb. UB8 157 BP72
Craigen Av, Croy. CR0 224 DV102
Craigen Gdns, Ilf. IG3 147 ES63
Craigerne Rd, SE3 186 EH80
Craig Gdns, E18 124 EF54
Craigholm, SE18 187 EN82
Craiglands, St.Alb. AL1 65 CK16
Craigmore Twr, Wok. GU22
off Guildford Rd 248 AY119
Craig Mt, Rad. WD7 99 CH35
Craigmuir Pk, Wem. HA0 160 CM67
Craignair Rd, SW2 203 DN87
Craignish Av, SW16 223 DM96
Craig Pk Rd, N18 122 DV50
Craig Rd, Rich. TW10 199 CJ91
Craigs Ct, SW1 30 A2
Craigs Wk, Chsht EN8
off Davison Dr 89 DX28
Craigton Rd, SE9 187 EM84
Craigweil Av, Rad. WD7 99 CH35
Craigweil Cl, Stan. HA7 117 CK50
Craigweil Dr, Stan. HA7 117 CK50
Craigwell Av, Felt. TW13 197 BU90
Craigwell Cl, Stai. TW18 215 BE95
Craik Ct, NW6 15 H1
Crail Row, SE17 31 M9
Crakell Rd, Reig. RH2 288 DC135
Cramer Ct, N.Mal. KT3
off Warwick Rd 220 CQ97
Cramer St, W1 17 H7
Crammerville Wk, Rain. RM13 169 FH70
Crammond Cl, W6 38 E2
● Crammond Pk, Harl. CM19 73 EN16
Cramond Ct, Felt. TW14 197 BS88
Crampshaw La, Ashtd. KT21 254 CM119
Sch Crampton Prim Sch, SE17 31 H10
Crampton Rd, SE20 204 DW93
Cramptons Rd, Sev. TN14 263 FH120

Crampton St, SE17 31 J9
Cranberry Cl, Nthlt. UB5
 off Parkfield Av 158 BX68
Cranberry La, E16 23 J5
Cranborne Av, Sthl. UB2 178 CA77
 Surbiton KT6 220 CN104
Cranborne Cl, Hert. SG13 54 DQ12
 Potters Bar EN6 85 CY31
Cranborne Cres, Pot.B. EN6 85 CY31
Cranborne Gdns, Upmin.
 RM14 150 FP61
 Welwyn Garden City AL7 51 CZ10
● Cranborne Ind Est, Pot.B.
 EN6 85 CY30
Sch Cranborne Prim Sch, Pot.B.
 EN6 off Laurel Flds 85 CZ31
Cranborne Rd, Bark. IG11 167 ER67
 Cheshunt EN8 89 DX32
 Hatfield AL10 67 CV17
 Hoddesdon EN11 71 EB16
 Potters Bar EN6 85 CY31
Cranborne Waye, Hayes UB4 158 BW73
Cranbourn All, WC2
 off Cranbourn St 17 P10
Cranbourne Av, E11 146 EH56
 Windsor SL4 173 AM82
Cranbourne Cl, SW16 223 DL97
 Hersham KT12 236 BW107
 Horley RH6 291 DH146
 Slough SL1 153 AQ74
Cranbourne Dr, Hodd. EN11 55 EB13
 Pinner HA5 138 BX57
Cranbourne Gdns, NW11 141 CY57
 Ilford IG6 147 EQ55
Cranbourne Pas, SE16 32 E5
Sch Cranbourne Prim Sch, Hodd.
 EN11 off Bridle Way N 55 EB13
Cranbourne Rd, E12
 off High St N 146 EL64
 E15 12 F1
 N10 121 DH54
 Northwood HA6 137 BT55
 Slough SL1 153 AQ74
Cranbourn St, WC2 17 P10
CRANBROOK, Ilf. IG1 147 EM60
Cranbrook Cl, Brom. BR2 226 EG100
Sch Cranbrook Coll, Ilf. IG1
 off Mansfield Rd 147 EN61
Cranbrook Dr, Esher KT10 218 CC102
 Romford RM2 149 FH56
 St. Albans AL4 66 CL20
 Twickenham TW2 198 CB88
Cranbrook Ho, E5
 off Pembury Rd 10 E2
 Erith DA8 off Boundary St 189 FF80
Cranbrook La, N11 121 DH49
Cranbrook Ms, E17 145 DY57
Cranbrook Pk, N22 121 DM53
Sch Cranbrook Prim Sch, Ilf.
 IG1 off The Drive 147 EM59
Cranbrook Ri, Ilf. IG1 147 EM59
Cranbrook Rd, SE8 46 B7
 SW19 201 CY94
 W4 180 CS78
 Barnet EN4 102 DD44
 Bexleyheath DA7 188 EZ81
 Hounslow TW4 178 BZ84
 Ilford IG1, IG2, IG6 147 EN59
 Thornton Heath CR7 224 DQ96
Cranbrook St, E2 21 K1
Cranbury Rd, SW6 39 M8
Crandale Ho, E5
 off Pembury Rd 10 E2
Crandon Wk, S.Darenth DA4
 off Gorringe Av 231 FS96
Crane Av, W3 160 CQ73
 Isleworth TW7 199 CG85
Cranebank Ms, Twick. TW1 179 CG84
Cranebrook, Twick. TW2
 off Manor Rd 198 CC89
Crane Cl, Dag. RM10 168 FA65
 Harrow HA2 138 CC62
Crane Ct, EC4 18 F9
 W13 off Gurnell Gro 159 CF70
 Epsom KT19 238 CQ105
Cranefield Dr, Wat. WD25 82 BY32
Craneford Cl, Twick. TW2 199 CF87
Craneford Way, Twick. TW2 199 CE87
Crane Gdns, Hayes UB3 177 BT77
Crane Gro, N7 8 F4
Crane Ho, SE15 44 A7
Cranell Grn, S.Ock. RM15 171 FV74
Crane Lo Rd, Houns. TW5 177 BV79
Crane Mead, Ware SG12 55 DY07
● Crane Mead Business Pk,
 Ware SG12 55 DY07
Sch Crane Pk Prim Sch, Han.
 TW13 off Norman Av 198 BZ89
Crane Pk Rd, Twick. TW2 198 CB89
Crane Rd, Twick. TW2 199 CE88
Cranesbill Cl, NW9
 off Annesley Av 140 CR55
 SW16 223 DK96
Cranes Dr, Surb. KT5 220 CL98
Cranes Pk, Surb. KT5 220 CL98
Cranes Pk Av, Surb. KT5 220 CL98
Cranes Pk Cres, Surb. KT5 220 CM98
Crane St, SE10 46 G1
 SE15 44 A6
Craneswater, Hayes UB3 177 BT80
Craneswater Pk, Sthl. UB2 178 BZ78
Cranes Way, Borwd. WD6 100 CQ43
Crane Way, Twick. TW2 198 CC87
Cranfield Cl, SE27
 off Norwood High St 204 DQ90
Cranfield Ct, Wok. GU21
 off Martindale Rd 248 AU118
Cranfield Cres, Cuffley EN6 87 DL29
Cranfield Dr, NW9 118 CS52
Cranfield Rd, SE4 45 N10
Cranfield Rd E, Cars. SM5 240 DG109
Cranfield Rd W, Cars. SM5 240 DF109
Cranfield Row, SE1 30 F6
CRANFORD, Houns. TW5 177 BU80
Cranford Av, N13 121 DL50
 Staines-upon-Thames TW19 196 BL87
Cranford Cl, SW20 221 CV95
 Purley CR8 242 DQ113
 Staines-upon-Thames TW19 196 BL87
Sch Cranford Comm Coll, Cran.
 TW5 off High St 177 BV79
Cranford Cotts, E1
 off Cranford St 21 K10
Cranford Ct, Hert. SG14
 off The Ridgeway 53 DM08
Cranford Dr, Hayes UB3 177 BT77
 Slough SL1 173 AM75
Sch Cranford Inf & Nurs Sch, Cran.
 TW4 off Berkeley Av 177 BV82
Sch Cranford Jun Sch, Cran.
 TW4 off Woodfield Rd 177 BV82
Cranford La, Hayes UB3 177 BR79
 Heston TW5 178 BX80
 London Heathrow Airport
 TW6 177 BT83
 London Heathrow Airport
 N TW6 177 BT81
Cranford Ms, Brom. BR2 226 EL99
Sch Cranford Pk Prim Sch, Harling.
 UB3 off Phelps Way 177 BT77
Cranford Pk Rd, Hayes UB3 177 BT77
Cranford Ri, Esher KT10 236 CC106
Cranford Rd, Dart. DA1 210 FL88
Cranford St, E1 21 K10
Cranford Way, N8 143 DM57
CRANHAM, Upmin. RM14 151 FS59
Cranham Gdns, Upmin. RM14 151 FS60
Cranham Hall Ms,
 Upmin. RM14 151 FS62
Cranham Rd, Horn. RM11 149 FH58
Cranhurst Rd, NW2 4 B4
Cranleigh Cl, SE20 224 DV96
 Bexley DA5 209 FB86
 Cheshunt EN7 88 DU28
 Orpington BR6 228 EU104
 South Croydon CR2 242 DU112
Cranleigh Ct, Mitch. CR4
 off Phipps Br Rd 222 DD97
Cranleigh Dr, Swan. BR8 229 FE98
Cranleigh Gdns, N21 103 DN43
 SE25 224 DS97
 Barking IG11 167 ER66
 Harrow HA3 140 CL57
 Kingston upon Thames KT2 200 CM93
 Loughton IG10 107 EM44
 South Croydon CR2 242 DU112
 Southall UB1 158 BZ72
 Sutton SM1 222 DB103
● Cranleigh Gdns Ind Est, Sthl.
 UB1 off Cranleigh Gdns 158 BZ71
Cranleigh Ms, SW11 40 D9
Cranleigh Rd, N15 144 DQ57
 SW19 222 DA97
 Esher KT10 218 CC102
 Feltham TW13 197 BT91
 Wonersh GU5 281 BB144
Cranleigh St, NW1 17 M1
Cranley Cl, Guil. GU1 265 BA134
Cranley Dene, Guil. GU1 265 BA134
Cranley Dene Ct, N10 142 DG56
Cranley Dr, Ilf. IG2 147 EQ59
 Ruislip HA4 137 BT61
Cranley Gdns, N10 143 DJ56
 N13 121 DM48
 SW7 27 P10
 Wallington SM6 241 DJ108
Cranley Ms, SW7 27 P10
Cranley Par, SE9
 off Beaconsfield Rd 206 EL91
Cranley Pl, SW7 28 A9
Cranley Rd, E13 24 A6
 Guildford GU1 265 AZ134
 Hersham KT12 235 BS106
 Ilford IG2 147 EQ58
Cranmer Av, W13 179 CH76
Cranmer Cl, Mord. SM4 221 CX100
 Potters Bar EN6 86 DB30
 Ruislip HA4 138 BX60
 Stanmore HA7 117 CJ52
 Warlingham CR6 259 DY117
 Weybridge KT13 234 BN108
Cranmer Ct, SW3 28 D9
 SW4 183 DK83
 Hampton Hill TW12
 off Cranmer Rd 198 CB92
Sch Cranmere Prim Sch, Esher
 KT10 off The Drive 218 CC102
Cranmer Fm Cl, Mitch. CR4 222 DF98
Cranmer Gdns, Dag. RM10 149 FC63
 Warlingham CR6 259 DY117
Cranmer Ho, SW11
 off Surrey La 40 C6
Sch Cranmer Prim Sch, Mitch.
 CR4 off Cranmer Rd 222 DF98
Cranmer Rd, E7 146 EH63
 SW9 42 F4
 Croydon CR0 223 DP104
 Edgware HA8 118 CP48
 Hampton Hill TW12 198 CB92
 Hayes UB3 157 BR72
 Kingston upon Thames KT2 200 CL92
 Mitcham CR4 222 DF98
 Sevenoaks TN13 278 FE123
Cranmer Ter, SW17 202 DD92
Cranmore Av, Islw. TW7 178 CC80
Cranmore Cotts, Lthd. KT24 267 BP129
Cranmore Ct, St.Alb. AL1 65 CF19
Cranmore La, W.Hors. KT24 267 BP129
Cranmore Rd, Brom. BR1 206 EE90
 Chislehurst BR7 207 EM92
Sch Cranmore Sch, W.Hors.
 KT24 off Epsom Rd 267 BQ130
Cranmore Way, N10 143 DJ56
Cranston Cl, Houns. TW3 178 BY82
 Reigate RH2 288 DB135
 Uxbridge UB10 137 BR61
Cranston Est, N1 19 M1
Cranston Gdns, E4 123 EB50
Cranston Pk Av, Upmin. RM14 150 FP63
Cranston Rd, SE23 205 DY88
Cranstoun Cl, Guil. GU3 264 AT130
Cranswick Rd, SE16 32 F10
Crantock Rd, SE6 205 EB89
Cranwell Cl, E3 22 C5
 St. Albans AL4 65 CJ22
Cranwell Gro, Shep. TW17 216 BM98
Cranwells La, Farn.Com. SL2 133 AQ62
Cranwich Av, N21 122 DR45
Cranwich Rd, N16 144 DR59
Cranwood St, EC1 19 L3
Cranworth Cres, E4 123 ED46
Cranworth Gdns, SW9 42 E7
Craster Rd, SW2 203 DM87
Crathie Rd, SE12 206 EH86
Cravan Av, Felt. TW13 197 BU89
Craven Av, W5 159 CJ73
 Southall UB1 158 BZ71
Craven Cl, N16 144 DU59
 Hayes UB4 157 BU72
Craven Gdns, SW19 202 DA92
Craven Gdns, Barking IG11 167 ES68
 Collier Row RM5 126 FA50
 Harold Wood RM3 128 FQ51
 Ilford IG6 125 ER54
Craven Hill, W2 15 P10
Craven Hill Gdns, W2 15 N10
Craven Hill Ms, W2 15 P10
Craven Ms, SW11
 off Taybridge Rd 182 DG83
Craven Pk, NW10 160 CS67
Craven Pk Ms, NW10 160 CS66
Craven Pk Rd, N15 144 DT58
 NW10 160 CS67
Craven Pas, WC2 30 A2
Craven Rd, NW10 160 CR67
 W2 15 P10
 W5 159 CJ73
 Croydon CR0 224 DV102
 Kingston upon Thames KT2 220 CM95
 Orpington BR6 228 EX104
Cravens, The, Smallfield RH6 291 DN148
Craven St, WC2 30 A2
Craven Ter, W2 15 P10
Craven Wk, N16 144 DU59
Crawford Av, Dart. DA1 210 FK86
 Wem. HA0 139 CK64
Crawford Cl, Islw. TW7 179 CE82
Crawford Compton Cl, Horn.
 RM12 170 FJ65
Crawford Est, SE5 43 K8
Crawford Gdns, N13 121 DP48
 Northolt UB5 158 BZ69
Crawford Ms, W1 16 E7
Crawford Pas, EC1 18 E5
Crawford Pl, W1 16 D8
Sch Crawford Prim Sch, SE5 43 K7
Crawford Rd, SE5 43 K7
 Hatfield AL10 67 CU16
Crawfords, Swan. BR8 209 FE94
Crawford St, NW10
 off Fawood Av 160 CR66
 W1 16 E7
Crawley Dr, Hem.H. HP2 62 BM16
Crawley Rd, E10 145 EB60
 N22 122 DQ54
 Enfield EN1 122 DS45
Crawshaw Rd, Ott. KT16 233 BD107
Crawshay Cl, Sev. TN13 278 FG123
Crawshay Ct, SW9 42 F6
Crawthew Gro, SE22 184 DT84
Cray Av, Ashtd. KT21 254 CL116
 Orpington BR5 228 EV99
Craybrooke Rd, Sid. DA14 208 EV91
Crayburne, Sthflt DA13 212 FZ92
Craybury End, SE9 207 EQ89
Cray Cl, Dart. DA1 189 FG84
Craydene Rd, Erith DA8 189 FF81
● Crayfields Business Pk,
 Orp. BR5 228 EW95
● Crayfields Ind Pk,
 Orp. BR5 228 EW96
CRAYFORD, Dart. DA1 209 FD85
⇌ Crayford 209 FE86
Crayford Cl, E6 24 G8
● Crayford Creek, Dart.
 DA1 off Thames Rd 189 FH83
Crayford High St, Dart. DA1 189 FE84
● Crayford Ind Est, Dart, DA1 209 FF85
Crayford Rd, N7 143 DK63
 Dartford DA1 209 FF85
Crayford Way, Dart. DA1 209 FF85
Crayke Hill, Chess. KT9 238 CL108
Craylands, Orp. BR5 228 EW97
Craylands La, Swans. DA10 211 FX85
Sch Craylands Sch, The, Swans.
 DA10 off Craylands La 211 FX85
Craylands Sq, Swans. DA10 211 FX85
Crayle St, Slou. SL2 153 AN69
Craymill Sq, Dart. DA1 189 FF82
Crayonne Cl, Sun. TW16 217 BS95
Cray Riverway, Dart. DA1 209 FF85
 Sid. DA14 208 EX92
Cray Rd, Belv. DA17 188 FA79
 Sidcup DA14 208 EW94
 Swanley BR8 229 FB100
● Crayside Ind Est,
 Cray. DA1 189 FH84
Cray Valley Rd, Orp. BR5 228 EU99
Cray Vw Cl, Orp. BR5
 off Mill Brook Rd 228 EW98
Crealock Gro, Wdf.Grn. IG8 124 EF50
Crealock St, SW18 202 DB86
Creasey Cl, Horn. RM11 149 FH61
Creasy Cl, Abb.L. WD5 81 BT31
Creasy Est, SE1 31 N7
Crebor St, SE22 204 DU86
Crecy Ct, SE11 off Hotspur St 30 E10
Credenhall Dr, Brom. BR2 227 EM102
Credenhill St, SW16 203 DJ93
Crediton Hill, NW6 5 L2
Crediton Rd, E16 23 N8
 NW10 4 C9
Crediton Way, Clay. KT10 237 CG106
Credon Rd, E13 166 EJ68
 SE16 32 F10
Credo Way, Grays RM20 191 FV79
Creechurch La, EC3 19 P9
Creechurch Pl, EC3 19 P9
Creed Ct, EC4 off Ludgate Sq 19 H9
Creed La, EC4 19 H9
Creed's Fm Yd, Epp. CM16 91 ES32
Creek, The, Grav. DA11 212 GB85
 Sunbury-on-Thames TW16 217 BU99
CREEKMOUTH, Bark. IG11 168 EU70
Creek Rd, SE8 46 A3
 SE10 46 A3
 Barking IG11 167 ET69
 East Molesey KT8 219 CE98
Creekside, SE8 46 C5
 Rainham RM13 169 FF70
Creek Way, Rain. RM13 169 FE71
Creeland Gro, SE6 205 DZ88
Cree Way, Rom. RM1 127 FE52
Crefeld Cl, W6 38 D3
Creffield Rd, W3 160 CM73
 W5 160 CM73
Creighton Av, E6 166 EK68
 N2 142 DE55
 N10 120 DG54
 St. Albans AL1 65 CD24
Creighton Cl, W12 161 CU73
Creighton Rd, N17 122 DS52
 NW6 4 D10
 W5 179 CK76
Cremer St, E2 20 A1
Cremorne Br, SW6
 off Townmead Rd 39 P7
 SW11 off Lombard Rd 182 DD82
Cremorne Est, SW10 40 A4
Cremorne Gdns, Epsom KT19 238 CR109
Cremorne Rd, SW10 39 P5
 Northfleet DA11 213 GF87
Crescent, EC3 20 A10
Crescent, The, E17 145 DY57
 N11 120 DF49
 NW2 141 CV62
 SW13 181 CT82
 SW19 202 DA90
 W3 160 CS72
 Abbots Langley WD5 81 BT30
 Aldenham WD25 98 CB37
 Ashford TW15 196 BM92
 Barnet EN5 102 DB41
 Beckenham BR3 225 EA95
 Belmont SM2 240 DA111
 Bexley DA5 208 EW87
 Bricket Wood AL2 82 CA30
 Caterham CR3 259 EA123
 Chertsey KT16
 off Western Av 216 BG97
 Croxley Green WD3 97 BP44
 Croydon CR0 224 DR99
 Egham TW20 194 AY93
 Epping CM16 91 ET32
 Epsom KT18 238 CN114
 Greenhithe DA9 211 FW85
 Guildford GU2 264 AU132
 Harlington UB3 177 BQ80
 Harlow CM17 58 EW09
 Harrow HA2 139 CD60
 Horley RH6 291 DH150
 Ilford IG2 147 EN58
 Leatherhead KT22 253 CH122
 Loughton IG10 106 EK43
 New Malden KT3 220 CQ96
 Northfleet DA11 213 GF89
 Reigate RH2 off Chartway 272 DB134
 Sevenoaks TN13 279 FK121
 Shepperton TW17 217 BT101
 Sidcup DA14 207 ET91
 Slough SL1 174 AS75
 Southall UB1 178 BZ75
 Surbiton KT6 220 CL99
 Sutton SM1 240 DD105
 Upminster RM14 151 FS59
 Watford WD18 98 BW42
 Wembley HA0 139 CH61
 West Molesey KT8 218 CA98
 West Wickham BR4 226 EE100
 Weybridge KT13 216 BN104
Crescent Arc, SE10 46 E3
Crescent Av, Grays RM17 192 GD78
 Hornchurch RM12 149 FF61
Crescent Cotts, Sev. TN13 263 FE120
Crescent Ct, Grays RM17 192 GD78
 Surb. KT6 219 CK99
Crescent Dr, Petts Wd BR5 227 EP100
 Shenfield CM15 130 FY46
Crescent E, Barn. EN4 102 DC38
Crescent Gdns, SW19 202 DA90
 Ruislip HA4 137 BV58
 Swanley BR8 229 FC96
Crescent Gro, SW4 183 DJ84
 Mitcham CR4 222 DE98
Crescent Ho, SE13
 off Ravensbourne Pl 46 C8
Crescent La, SW4 203 DK85
Crescent Ms, N22 121 DL53
Crescent Par, Uxb. UB10
 off Uxbridge Rd 156 BN69
Crescent Pl, SW3 28 C8
Sch Crescent Prim Sch, The,
 Croy. CR0 224 DR99
Crescent Ri, N22 121 DK53
 Barnet EN4 102 DE43
Crescent Rd, E4 124 EE45
 E6 166 EJ67
 E10 145 EB61
 E13 13 P8
 E18 124 EJ54
 N3 119 CZ53
 N8 143 DK59
 N9 122 DU46
 N11 120 DF49
 N15 off Carlingford Rd 143 DP55
 N22 121 DK53
 SE18 37 N10
 SW20 221 CX95
 Aveley RM15 190 FQ75
 Barnet EN4 102 DE43
 Beckenham BR3 225 EB96
 Bletchingley RH1 274 DQ133
 Bromley BR1 206 EG94
 Caterham CR3 258 DU124
 Dagenham RM10 149 FB63
 Enfield EN2 103 DP41
 Erith DA8 189 FF79
 Hemel Hempstead HP2 62 BK20
 Kingston upon Thames KT2 200 CN94
 Reigate RH2 288 DA136
 Shepperton TW17 217 BQ99
 Sidcup DA15 207 ET90
 Warley CM14 130 FV49
Crescent Row, EC1 19 J5
Crescent Stables, SW15 201 CY85
Crescent St, N1 8 D6
Crescent Vw, Loug. IG10 106 EK44
Crescent Wk, Aveley RM15 190 FQ75
Crescent Way, N12 120 DE51
 SE4 185 EA83
 SW16 203 DM94
 Aveley RM15 171 FR74
 Horley RH6 290 DG150
 Orpington BR6 245 ES106
Crescent W, Barn. EN4 102 DC38
Crescent Wd Rd, SE26 204 DU90
Cresford Rd, SW6 39 L7
Crespigny Rd, NW4 141 CV58
Cressage Cl, Sthl. UB1 158 CA70
Cressall Cl, Lthd. KT22 253 CH120
Cressall Mead, Lthd. KT22 253 CH120
Cress End, Rick. WD3 114 BG47
Cresset Cl, Stans.Abb. SG12 55 EC12
Cresset Rd, E9 11 H5
Cresset St, SW4 183 DK83
Cressfield Cl, NW5 7 H2
Cressida Rd, N19 143 DJ60
Cressingham Gro, Sutt. SM1 240 DC105
Cressingham Rd, SE13 46 F10
 Edgware HA8 118 CR51
Cressinghams, The, Epsom
 KT18 238 CR113
Cressington Cl, N16 9 P2
Cress Ms, Brom. BR1 205 ED92
Cress Rd, Slou. SL1 173 AP75
Cresswell Gdns, SW5 27 N10
Cresswell Pk, SE3 47 L10
Cresswell Pl, SW10 27 N10
Cresswell Rd, SE25 224 DU98
 Chesham HP5 76 AR34
 Feltham TW13 198 BY91
 Twickenham TW1 199 CK86
Cresswell Way, N21 121 DN45
Cressy Ct, E1 21 H6
 W6 181 CV76
Cressy Ho, E1
 off Hannibal Rd 21 H6
Cressy Pl, E1 21 H6
Cressy Rd, NW3 6 E2
Crest, The, N13 121 DN49
 NW4 141 CW57
 Beaconsfield HP9 110 AG54
 Goffs Oak EN7
 off Orchard Way 87 DP27
 Sawbridgeworth CM21 58 EX05
 Surbiton KT5 220 CN99
Cresta Dr, Wdhm KT15 233 BF110
Crest Av, Grays RM17 192 GB80
Crestbrook Av, N13 121 DP48
Crestbrook Pl, N13 121 DP48
Crest Cl, Bad.Mt TN14 247 FB111
Crest Dr, Enf. EN3 104 DW38
Crestfield St, WC1 18 B2
Crest Gdns, Ruis. HA4 138 BW62
Crest Hill, Peasl. GU5 283 BR142
Cresthill Av, Grays RM17 192 GC77
Creston Av, Knap. GU21 248 AS116
Creston Way, Wor.Pk. KT4 221 CX102
Crest Pk, Hem.H. HP2 63 BQ19
Crest Rd, NW2 141 CT61
 Bromley BR2 226 EF101
 South Croydon CR2 242 DV108
Crest Vw, Green. DA9
 off Woodland Way 191 FU84
 Pinner HA5 138 BX56
Crest Vw Dr, Petts Wd BR5 227 EP99
Crestway, SW15 201 CV86
Crestwood Way, Houns. TW4 198 BZ85
Creswell Dr, Beck. BR3 225 EB99
Creswick Ct, Welw.G.C. AL7 51 CX10
Sch Creswick Prim & Nurs Sch,
 Welw.G.C. AL7
 off Chequers 51 CY12
Creswick Rd, W3 160 CP73
Creswick Wk, E3 22 A2
 NW11 141 CZ56
Crete Hall Rd, Grav. DA11 212 GD86
Creton St, SE18 37 M7
Creukhorne Rd, NW10 160 CS66
Crewdson Rd, SW9 42 E5
 Horley RH6 291 DH148
Crewe Curve, Berk. HP4 60 AT16
Crewe Pl, NW10 161 CT69
Crewe's Av, Warl. CR6 258 DW116
Crewe's Cl, Warl. CR6 258 DW116
Crewe's Fm La, Warl. CR6 259 DX116
Crewe's La, Warl. CR6 259 DX116
CREWS HILL, Enf. EN2 103 DP35
⇌ Crews Hill 87 DM34
Crews St, E14 34 A8
Crewys Rd, NW2 141 CZ61
 SE15 44 F9
Crib St, Ware SG12 55 DX05
Crichton Av, Wall. SM6 241 DK106
Crichton Rd, Cars. SM5 240 DF107
Crichton St, SW8 41 L8
Crick Ct, Bark. IG11
 off Spring Pl 167 EQ68
Cricketers Arms Rd, Enf. EN2 104 DQ40
Cricketers Cl, N14 121 DJ45
 Chessington KT9 237 CK105
 Erith DA8 189 FE78
 St. Albans AL3
 off Stonecross 65 CE19
Cricketers Ct, SE11 30 G9
Cricketers Ms, SW18
 off East Hill 202 DB85
Cricketers Ter, Cars. SM5
 off Wrythe La 222 DE104
Cricketers Wk, SE26
 off Doctors Cl 204 DW92
Cricketfield Rd, E5 10 F1
Cricket Fld Rd, Uxb. UB8 156 BK67
Cricketfield Rd, West Dr. UB7 176 BJ77
Cricket Grn, Mitch. CR4 222 DF97
Sch Cricket Grn Sch, Mitch.
 CR4 off Lower Grn W 222 DE97
Cricket Grd Rd, Chis. BR7 227 EP95
Cricket Hill, S.Nutfld RH1 289 DM136
Cricket La, Beck. BR3 205 DY93
Crickett's Hill, Shere GU5 282 BN139
Cricket Way, Wey. KT13 217 BS103
Cricklade Av, SW2 203 DL89
 Romford RM3 128 FK51
CRICKLEWOOD, NW2 141 CX62
⇌ Cricklewood 141 CX63
Cricklewood Bdy, NW2 141 CW62
Cricklewood La, NW2 4 D1
Cridland St, E15 13 L9
Crieff Ct, Tedd. TW11 199 CJ94
Crieff Rd, SW18 202 DC86
Criffel Av, SW2 203 DK89
Crimp Hill, Eng.Grn TW20 194 AU90
Crimp Hill Rd, Old Wind. SL4 194 AU88
Crimscott St, SE1 31 P7
Crimsworth Rd, SW8 41 P6
Crinan St, N1 8 B10
Cringle St, SW8 41 L4
Cripplegate St, EC2 19 J6
Cripps Grn, Hayes UB4
 off Stratford Rd 157 BV70
Crispe Ho, Bark. IG11
 off Dovehouse Mead 167 ER68
Crispen Rd, Felt. TW13 198 BY91
Crispian Cl, NW10 140 CS63
Crispin Cl, Ashtd. KT21 254 CM118
 Beaconsfield HP9 110 AJ51
 Croydon CR0
 off Harrington Cl 223 DL103
Crispin Cres, Croy. CR0 223 DK104
Crispin Ms, NW11 141 CZ57
Crispin Pl, E1 20 A6
Crispin Rd, Edg. HA8 118 CQ51
Crispin St, E1 20 A7
Crispin Way, Farn.Com. SL2 133 AR63
 Uxbridge UB8 156 BM70
Crisp Rd, W6 38 A1
Criss Cres, Chal.St.P. SL9 112 AW54
Criss Gro, Chal.St.P. SL9 112 AW54
Cristowe Rd, SW6 39 H8
Critchley Av, Dart, DA1 210 FK86
Criterion Ms, N19 143 DK61
 SE24 off Shakespeare Rd 203 DP85
Jct Crittall's Cor, Sid. DA14 208 EV94
Critten La, Dor. RH5 268 BX132
Crockenhall Way, Istead Rise
 DA13 212 GE94

CROCKENHILL, Swan. BR8 229 FD101
Crockenhill La, Eys. DA4 229 FG101
Sch Crockenhill Prim Sch, Crock. BR8 off Stones Cross Rd 229 FC100
Crockenhill Rd, Orp. BR5 228 EX99
Swanley BR8 228 EZ100
Crockerton Rd, SW17 202 DF89
Crockery La, E.Clan. GU4 266 BL129
Crockford Cl, Add. KT15 234 BJ105
Crockford Pk Rd, Add. KT15 234 BJ106
CROCKHAM HILL, Eden. TN8 277 EQ133
Sch Crockham Hill C of E Prim Sch, Crock.H. TN8 off Main Rd 277 EQ133
Crockham Way, SE9 207 EN91
Crocknorth Rd, Dor. RH5 267 BU133
East Horsley KT24 267 BT132
Crocus Cl, Croy. CR0 off Cornflower La 225 DX102
Crocus Fld, Barn. EN5 101 CZ44
Croffets, Tad. KT20 255 CX121
Croft, The, E4 124 EE47
NW10 161 CT68
W5 160 CL71
Barnet EN5 101 CX42
Broxbourne EN10 71 DY23
Fetcham KT22 253 CE123
Hounslow TW5 178 BY79
Loughton IG10 107 EN40
Pinner HA5 138 BZ59
Ruislip HA4 138 BW63
St. Albans AL2 82 CA25
Swanley BR8 229 FC97
Welwyn Garden City AL7 51 CZ12
Wembley HA0 139 CJ64
Croft Av, Dor. RH4 269 CH134
West Wickham BR4 225 EC102
Croft Cl, NW7 118 CS48
Belvedere DA17 188 EZ78
Chalfont St. Peter SL9 112 AX54
Chipperfield WD4 80 BG30
Chislehurst BR7 207 EM91
Harlington UB3 177 BQ80
Uxbridge UB10 156 BN66
Croft Cor, Old Wind. SL4 194 AV85
Croft Ct, Borwd. WD6 100 CR41
Croftdown Rd, NW5 142 DG62
Croft End Cl, Chess. KT9 off Ashcroft Rd 220 CM104
Croft End Rd, Chipper. WD4 80 BG30
Crofters, The, Wind. SL4 194 AU86
Crofters Cl, Islw. TW7 off Ploughmans End 199 CD85
Redhill RH1 289 DH136
Stanwell TW19 off Park Rd 196 BK86
Crofters Ct, SE8 off Croft St 33 L9
Crofters Mead, Croy. CR0 243 DZ109
Crofters Rd, Nthwd. HA6 115 BS49
Crofters Way, NW1 7 N8
Croft Fld, Chipper. WD4 80 BG30
Hatfield AL10 67 CU18
Croft Gdns, W7 179 CG75
Ruislip HA4 137 BS60
Crofthill Rd, Slou. SL2 153 AP70
Croft La, Chipper. WD4 80 BG30
Croftleigh Av, Pur. CR8 257 DN116
Croft Lo Cl, Wdf.Grn. IG8 124 EH51
Croft Meadow, Chipper. WD4 80 BG30
Croft Ms, N12 120 DC48
Crofton, Ashtd. KT21 254 CL118
Crofton Av, W4 180 CR80
Bexley DA5 208 EX87
Orpington BR6 227 EQ103
Walton-on-Thames KT12 218 BW104
Crofton Cl, Ott. KT16 233 BC108
Croftongate Way, SE4 205 DY85
Crofton Gro, E4 123 ED49
Sch Crofton Inf Sch, Orp. BR5 off Towncourt La 227 ER101
Sch Crofton Jun Sch, Orp. BR5 off Towncourt La 227 ER101
Crofton La, Orp. BR5, BR6 227 ER101
⇌ Crofton Park 205 DZ85
Crofton Pk Rd, SE4 205 DZ86
Crofton Rd, E13 24 A4
SE5 43 P7
Grays RM16 192 GE76
Orpington BR6 227 EN104
Crofton Ter, E5 off Studley Cl 11 L2
Richmond TW9 180 CM84
Crofton Way, Barn. EN5 off Wycherley Cres 102 DB44
Enfield EN2 103 DN40
Croft Rd, SW16 223 DN95
SW19 202 DC94
Bromley BR1 206 EG93
Chalfont St. Peter SL9 112 AY54
Enfield EN3 105 DY39
Sutton SM1 240 DE106
Ware SG12 54 DW05
Westerham TN16 277 EP126
Woldingham CR3 259 DZ122
Crofts, The, Hem.H. HP3 63 BP21
Shepperton TW17 217 BS98
Croftside, SE25 off Sunny Bk 224 DU97
Crofts La, N22 121 DN52
Crofts Path, Hem.H. HP3 63 BP22
Crofts Rd, Har. HA1 139 CG58
Crofts St, E1 32 C1
Croft St, SE8 33 L9
Croft Wk, Brox. EN10 71 DY23
Croftway, NW3 5 K1
Richmond TW10 199 CH90
Croft Way, Sev. TN13 278 FF125
Sidcup DA15 207 ES90
Crogsland Rd, NW1 6 G6
Croham Cl, S.Croy. CR2 242 DS108
Croham Manor Rd, S.Croy. CR2 242 DS106
Croham Mt, S.Croy. CR2 242 DS108
Croham Pk Av, S.Croy. CR2 242 DT106
Croham Rd, S.Croy. CR2 242 DR106
Croham Valley Rd, S.Croy. CR2 242 DT107
Croindene Rd, SW16 223 DL95
Cromartie Rd, N19 143 DK59
Cromarty Rd, Edg. HA8 118 CP47
Crombie Cl, Ilf. IG4 147 EM57
Crombie Rd, Sid. DA15 207 ER88
Cromer Cl, Uxb. UB8 157 BQ72
CROMER HYDE, Welw.G.C. AL8 50 CS10
Cromer Hyde La, Lmsfd AL8 50 CR10
Crome Rd, NW10 160 CS65
Cromer Pl, Orp. BR6 off Andover Rd 227 ER102
Cromer Rd, E10 145 ED59
N17 122 DU54
SE25 224 DV97
Cromer Rd, SW17 202 DG93
Chadwell Heath RM6 148 EY58
Hornchurch RM11 150 FK59
London Heathrow Airport TW6 176 BN83
New Barnet EN5 102 DC42
Romford RM7 149 FC58
Watford WD24 98 BW38
Woodford Green IG8 124 EG49
Sch Cromer Rd Prim Sch, New Barn. EN5 off Cromer Rd 102 DC41
Cromer St, WC1 18 B3
Cromer Ter, E8 10 C2
Cromer Vil Rd, SW18 201 CZ86
Cromford Cl, Orp. BR6 227 ES104
Cromford Path, E5 off Overbury St 145 DX63
Cromford Rd, SW18 202 DA85
Cromford Way, N.Mal. KT3 220 CR95
Cromlix Cl, Chis. BR7 227 EP96
Crompton Pl, Enf. EN3 off Brunswick Rd 105 EA38
Crompton St, W2 16 A5
Cromwell Av, N6 143 DH60
W6 181 CV78
Bromley BR2 226 EH98
Cheshunt EN7 88 DU30
New Malden KT3 221 CT99
Cromwell Cl, N2 142 DD56
W3 off High St 160 CQ74
Bromley BR2 226 EH98
Chalfont St. Giles HP8 112 AW48
St. Albans AL4 65 CK15
Walton-on-Thames KT12 217 BV102
Cromwell Cres, SW5 27 J8
Cromwell Dr, Slou. SL1 154 AS72
Cromwell Gdns, SW7 28 B7
Cromwell Gro, W6 26 B6
Caterham CR3 258 DQ121
Cromwell Highwalk, EC2 off Silk St 19 K6
H Cromwell Hosp, The, SW5 27 L8
● Cromwell Ind Est, E10 145 DY60
Cromwell Ms, SW7 28 B8
Cromwell Pl, N6 143 DH60
SW7 28 B8
SW14 180 CQ83
W3 off Grove Pl 160 CQ74
Cromwell Road 220 CL95
Cromwell Rd, E7 166 EJ66
E17 145 EC57
N3 120 DC54
N10 120 DG52
SW5 27 K8
SW7 28 A8
SW9 42 G6
SW19 202 DA92
Beckenham BR3 225 DY96
Borehamwood WD6 100 CL39
Caterham CR3 258 DQ121
Cheshunt EN7 88 DV28
Croydon CR0 224 DR101
Feltham TW13 197 BV88
Grays RM17 192 GA77
Hayes UB3 157 BR72
Hertford SG13 54 DT08
Hounslow TW3 178 CA84
Kingston upon Thames KT2 220 CL95
Redhill RH1 272 DF133
Teddington TW11 199 CG93
Walton-on-Thames KT12 217 BV102
Ware SG12 55 DZ06
Warley CM14 130 FV49
Wembley HA0 160 CL68
Worcester Park KT4 220 CR104
Cromwells Ct, Slou. SL3 155 AZ74
Cromwells Mere, Rom. RM1 off Havering Rd 127 FD51
Cromwell St, Houns. TW3 178 CA84
Cromwell Twr, EC2 19 K6
Cromwell Wk, Red. RH1 272 DF134
Crondace Rd, SW6 39 K7
Crondall Ct, N1 19 N1
Crondall Ho, SW15 off Fontley Way 201 CU88
Crondall St, N1 19 M1
Cronin St, SE15 44 A5
Cronks Hill, Red. RH1 288 DC135
Reigate RH2 288 DC135
Cronks Hill Cl, Red. RH1 288 DD136
Cronks Hill Rd, Red. RH1 288 DD136
Jct Crooked Billet, E17 123 EB52
Crooked Billet, SW19 201 CW93
Jct Crooked Billet Rbt, Stai. TW18 196 BG91
Crooked Billet Yd, E2 19 P2
Crooked La, Grav. DA12 213 GH86
Crooked Mile, Wal.Abb. EN9 89 EC33
Jct Crooked Mile Rbt, Wal.Abb. EN9 89 EC33
Crooked Usage, N3 141 CY55
Crooked Way, Lwr Naze. EN9 72 EE22
Crooke Rd, SE8 33 L10
Crookham Rd, SW6 38 G7
Crookhams, Welw.G.C. AL7 52 DA07
Crook Log, Bexh. DA6 188 EX83
Sch Crook Log Prim Sch, Bexh. DA6 off Crook Log 188 EX84
Crookston Rd, SE9 187 EN83
Croombs Rd, E16 24 C7
Crooms Hill, SE10 46 F4
Crooms Hill Gro, SE10 46 F4
Crop Common, Hat. AL10 off Stonecross Rd 67 CV16
Cropley Ct, N1 9 L10
Cropley St, N1 9 L10
Croppath Rd, Dag. RM10 148 FA63
Cropthorne Ct, W9 15 P3
Crosby Cl, Beac. HP9 133 AM55
Feltham TW13 198 BY91
St. Albans AL4 65 CJ23
Crosby Ct, SE1 31 L4
Crosby Rd, E7 13 P5
Dagenham RM10 169 FB68
Crosby Row, SE1 31 L5
Crosby Sq, EC3 19 N9
Crosby Wk, E8 10 A5
SW2 203 DN87
Crosier Cl, SE3 186 EL81
Crosier Rd, Ickhm UB10 137 BQ63
Crosier Way, Ruis. HA4 137 BS62
Crosland Pl, SW11 off Taybridge Rd 182 DG83
Crossacres, Wok. GU22 249 BE115
Cross Av, SE10 47 H3
Crossbow Rd, Chig. IG7 125 ET50
Crossbrook, Hat. AL10 66 CS19
Crossbrook Rd, SE3 186 EL82
Crossbrook St, Chsht EN8 89 DX31
Cross Cl, SE15 44 E8
Cross Deep, Twick. TW1 199 CF89
Cross Deep Gdns, Twick. TW1 199 CF89
Crossett Grn, Hem.H. HP3 63 BQ22
Crossfield Cl, Berk. HP4 60 AT19
Crossfield Pl, Wey. KT13 235 BP108
Crossfield Rd, N17 144 DQ55
NW3 6 B5
Hoddesdon EN11 71 EB15
Crossfields, Loug. IG10 107 EP43
St. Albans AL3 64 CB23
Crossfield St, SE8 46 A4
Crossford St, SW9 42 B9
Crossgate, Edg. HA8 118 CN48
Greenford UB6 159 CH65
DLR Crossharbour 34 D6
Crossing Rd, Epp. CM16 92 EU32
Cross Keys Cl, N9 off Balham Rd 122 DU47
W1 17 H7
Sevenoaks TN13 278 FG127
Cross Keys Sq, EC1 19 J7
Cross Lances Rd, Houns. TW3 178 CB84
Crossland Rd, Red. RH1 272 DG134
Thornton Heath CR7 223 DP100
Crosslands, Cher. KT16 215 BE104
Crosslands Av, W5 160 CM74
Southall UB2 178 BZ78
Crosslands Rd, Epsom KT19 238 CR107
Cross La, EC3 off Great Tower St 31 N1
N8 143 DM56
Beaconsfield HP9 133 AM55
Bexley DA5 208 EZ87
Hertford SG14 53 DP09
Ottershaw KT16 233 BB107
Cross La E, Grav. DA12 213 GH89
Cross Las, Chal.St.P. SL9 112 AY50
Guildford GU1 281 AZ135
Cross Las Cl, Chal.St.P. SL9 off Cross Las 113 AZ50
Cross La W, Grav. DA11 213 GH89
Crosslet St, SE17 31 M8
Crosslet Vale, SE10 46 C7
Crossley Cl, Bigg.H. TN16 260 EK115
Crossleys, Ch.St.G. HP8 112 AW49
Crossley St, N7 8 E4
Crossmead, SE9 207 EM88
Watford WD19 97 BV44
Crossmead Av, Grnf. UB6 158 CA69
Cross Meadow, Chesh. HP5 76 AM29
Crossmount Ho, SE5 43 J4
Crossness La, SE28 168 EX73
★ Crossness Pumping Sta, SE2 168 EY72
Crossness Rd, Bark. IG11 167 ET69
Cross Oak, Wind. SL4 173 AN82
Crossoak La, Red. RH1 289 DH144
Cross Oak Rd, Berk. HP4 60 AU20
Crossoaks La, Borwd. WD6 100 CR35
South Mimms EN6 84 CS34
Crosspath, The, Rad. WD7 99 CG35
Cross Rd, E4 123 ED46
N11 121 DH50
N22 121 DN52
SE5 43 P8
SW19 202 DA94
Belmont SM2 240 DA110
Bromley BR2 226 EL103
Chadwell Heath RM6 148 EW59
Croydon CR0 224 DR102
Dartford DA1 210 FJ86
Enfield EN1 104 DS42
Feltham TW13 198 BY91
Harrow HA1 139 CD56
Hawley DA2 210 FM91
Hertford SG14 54 DQ08
Kingston upon Thames KT2 200 CM94
Northfleet DA11 213 GF86
Orpington BR5 228 EV99
Purley CR8 241 DP113
Romford RM7 148 FA55
Sidcup DA14 off Sidcup Hill 208 EV91
South Harrow HA2 138 CB62
Sutton SM2 240 DD106
Tadworth KT20 255 CW122
Uxbridge UB8 156 BJ66
Waltham Cross EN8 89 DY33
Watford WD19 98 BY44
Wealdstone HA3 117 CG54
Weybridge KT13 217 BR104
Woodford Green IG8 125 EM51
Cross Rds, High Beach IG10 106 EH40
Crossroads, The, Eff. KT24 268 BX128
Cross St, N1 8 G8
SW13 180 CS82
Erith DA8 off Bexley Rd 189 FE78
Hampton Hill TW12 198 CC92
Harlow CM20 73 ER15
St. Albans AL3 off Spencer St 65 CD20
Uxbridge UB8 156 BJ66
Ware SG12 55 DY06
Watford WD17 98 BW41
Cross Ter, Wal.Abb. EN9 off Stonyshotts 90 EE34
Crossthwaite Av, SE5 184 DR84
Crosstrees Ho, E14 off Cassilis Rd 34 B6
Crosswall, EC3 20 A10
Crossway, N12 120 DD51
N16 9 P3
NW9 141 CT56
Cross Way, NW10 161 CU66
Crossway, SE28 168 EW72
SW20 221 CW98
W13 159 CG70
Chesham HP5 76 AS30
Dagenham RM8 148 EW62
Enfield EN1 122 DS45
Harlow CM17 58 EX14
Hayes UB3 157 BU74
Petts Wood BR5 227 ER98
Pinner HA5 115 BV54
Ruislip HA4 138 BW63
Walton-on-Thames KT12 217 BV103
Welwyn Garden City AL8 51 CW05
Woodford Green IG8 124 EJ49
Crossway, The, N22 121 DP52
SE9 206 EK89
Cross Way, The, Har. HA3 117 CE54
Crossway, The, Uxb. UB10 156 BM68
CROSSWAYS, Dart. DA2 191 FR84
Crossways, N21 104 DQ44
Beaconsfield HP9 111 AM54
Berkhamsted HP4 60 AT20
Effingham KT24 268 BX127
Crossways, Egham TW20 195 BD93
Hemel Hempstead HP3 63 BP20
Romford RM2 149 FH55
Shenfield CM15 131 GA44
South Croydon CR2 243 DY108
Sunbury-on-Thames TW16 197 BT94
Sutton SM2 240 DD109
Tatsfield TN16 260 EJ120
Crossways, The, Couls. CR5 257 DM119
Guildford GU2 280 AU135
Hounslow TW5 178 BZ80
South Merstham RH1 273 DJ130
Wembley HA9 140 CN61
Crossways Boul, Dart. DA2 190 FQ84
Greenhithe DA9 191 FT84
● Crossways Business Pk, Dart. DA2 190 FQ84
Crossways La, Reig. RH2 272 DC128
Crossways Rd, Beck. BR3 225 EA98
Mitcham CR4 223 DH97
Coll Crossways Sixth Form, SE4 45 L9
Crosswell Cl, Shep. TW17 217 BQ96
Crosthwaite Way, Slou. SL1 153 AK71
Croston St, E8 10 D8
Crothall Cl, N13 121 DM48
Crouch Av, Bark. IG11 168 EV68
Crouch Cl, Beck. BR3 205 EA93
Crouch Ct, Harl. CM20 57 EQ13
Crouch Cft, SE9 207 EN90
CROUCH END, N8 143 DJ58
Crouch End Hill, N8 143 DK59
Crouchfield, Hem.H. HP1 62 BH21
Hertford SG14 54 DQ06
Crouch Hall Rd, N8 143 DK58
⊖ Crouch Hill 143 DM59
Crouch Hill, N4 143 DL58
N8 143 DL58
Crouch La, Goffs Oak EN7 88 DQ28
Crouchman Cl, Grays RM16 192 GB75
Crouchman's Cl, SE26 204 DT90
Crouch Oak La, Add. KT15 234 BJ105
Crouch Rd, NW10 160 CR66
Grays RM16 193 GG78
Crouch Valley, Upmin. RM14 151 FS59
Crowborough Cl, Warl. CR6 259 DY117
Crowborough Dr, Warl. CR6 259 DY118
Crowborough Path, Wat. WD19 116 BX49
Crowborough Rd, SW17 202 DG93
Crowcroft Cl, Guil. GU2 off Henderson Av 264 AV130
Crowden Way, SE28 168 EW73
Crowder Cl, N12 120 DC53
Crowder St, E1 20 E10
Crow Dr, Halst. TN14 263 FC115
Crowfoot Cl, E9 11 P3
SE28 167 ES74
CROW GREEN, Brwd. CM15 130 FT41
Crow Grn La, Pilg.Hat. CM15 130 FU43
Crow Grn Rd, Pilg.Hat. CM15 130 FT43
Crowhurst Cl, SW9 42 F8
Crowhurst Mead, Gdse. RH9 274 DW130
Crowhurst Way, Orp. BR5 228 EW99
Crowland Av, Hayes UB3 177 BS77
Crowland Gdns, N14 121 DL45
Sch Crowland Prim Sch, N15 off Crowland Rd 144 DU57
Crowland Rd, N15 144 DT57
Thornton Heath CR7 224 DR98
Crowlands Av, Rom. RM7 149 FB58
Sch Crowlands Inf & Jun Schs, Rom. RM7 off London Rd 149 FC58
Crowland Ter, N1 9 L6
Crowland Wk, Mord. SM4 222 DB100
Crow La, Rom. RM7 148 EZ59
Crowley Cres, Croy. CR0 241 DN106
Crowline Wk, N1 off Clephane Rd 9 K4
Crowmarsh Gdns, SE23 off Tyson Rd 204 DW87
Crown Arc, Kings.T. KT1 off Union St 219 CK96
Crown Ash Hill, West. TN16 244 EH114
Crown Ash La, Warl. CR6 260 EG116
Westerham TN16 260 EG116
Crownbourne Ct, Sutt. SM1 off St. Nicholas Way 240 DB105
● Crown Business Est, Chesh. HP5 off Berkhampstead Rd 76 AQ30
Crown Cl, E3 12 A8
N22 off Winkfield Rd 121 DN53
NW6 5 L4
NW7 119 CT47
Buckhurst Hill IG9 124 EH46
Colnbrook SL3 175 BC80
Hayes UB3 177 BT75
Orpington BR6 246 EU105
Sheering CM22 59 FC07
Walton-on-Thames KT12 218 BW101
● Crown Cl Business Cen, E3 12 A9
Crown Ct, EC2 19 K9
SE12 206 EH86
WC2 18 B9
Crown Dale, SE19 203 DP93
Crowndale Rd, NW1 7 L10
Crownfield, Brox. EN10 71 EA21
Crownfield Av, Ilf. IG2 147 ES57
Sch Crownfield Inf Sch, Coll.Row RM7 off White Hart La 126 FA54
Sch Crownfield Jun Sch, Coll.Row RM7 off White Hart La 126 FA54
Crownfield Rd, E15 12 G2
Crownfields, Sev. TN13 279 FH125
Crown Gate, Harl. CM20 73 ER15
Crowngate Ho, E3 21 P1
Jct Crown Gate Rbt, Harl. CM18 73 ER15
Crown Grn Ms, Wem. HA9 140 CL61
Crown Hts, Guil. GU1 280 AY137
Crown Hill, Croy. CR0 off Church St 224 DQ103
Epping CM16 91 EM33
Waltham Abbey EN9 91 EM33
Crownhill Rd, NW10 161 CT67
Woodford Green IG8 124 EL52
Crown Ho, N.Mal. KT3 off Kingston Rd 220 CQ98
Crown La, N14 121 DJ46
SW16 203 DN92
Bromley BR2 226 EK99
Chislehurst BR7 227 EQ95
Farnham Royal SL2 153 AN68
High Wycombe HP11 110 AF48
Morden SM4 222 DB97
Virginia Water GU25 214 AX100
Crown La Gdns, SW16 203 DN92
Sch Crown La Prim Sch, SW16 off Crown La 203 DP92
Crown La Spur, Brom. BR2 226 EK100
Crown Meadow, Colnbr. SL3 175 BB80
Crownmead Way, Rom. RM7 149 FB56
Crown Ms, E13 off Waghorn Rd 166 EJ67
W6 181 CU77
Crown Mill, Mitch. CR4 222 DE99
Crown Office Row, EC4 18 E10
Crown Pas, SW1 29 M3
Kingston upon Thames KT1 off Church St 219 CK96
Watford WD18 off The Crescent 98 BW42
Crown Pl, EC2 19 N6
NW5 7 K4
SE16 44 F1
Crown Pt Par, SE19 off Beulah Hill 203 DP93
Crown Reach, SW1 41 P1
Crown Ri, Cher. KT16 215 BF102
Watford WD25 82 BW34
Crown Rd, N10 120 DG52
Borehamwood WD6 100 CN39
Enfield EN1 104 DV42
Grays RM17 192 GA79
Ilford IG6 147 ER56
Morden SM4 222 DB98
New Malden KT3 220 CQ95
Orpington BR6 246 EU106
Ruislip HA4 138 BX64
Shoreham TN14 247 FF110
Sutton SM1 240 DB105
Twickenham TW1 199 CH86
Virginia Water GU25 214 AW100
Crown Sq, Wok. GU21 off Commercial Way 249 AZ117
Crownstone Rd, SW2 203 DN85
Crown St, SE5 43 K4
W3 160 CP74
Brentwood CM14 130 FW47
Dagenham RM10 169 FC65
Egham TW20 195 BA92
Harrow HA2 139 CD60
Crown Ter, Rich. TW9 180 CM84
Crown Trading Est, Hayes UB3 177 BS75
Crowntree Cl, Islw. TW7 179 CF79
Crown Wk, Uxb. UB8 off The Mall Pavilions 156 BJ66
Crown Wk, Hem.H. HP3 62 BL24
Wembley HA9 140 CM62
Crown Way, West Dr. UB7 156 BM74
Crown Wds La, SE9 187 EP82
SE18 187 EP82
Sch Crown Wds Sch, SE9 off Riefield Rd 207 EQ85
Crown Wds Way, SE9 207 ER85
Crown Wks, E2 20 E1
Crown Yd, Houns. TW3 off High St 178 CC83
Crow Piece La, Farn.Royal SL2 153 AM66
Crowshott Av, Stan. HA7 117 CJ53
Crows Rd, E15 23 H2
Barking IG11 167 EP65
Epping CM16 91 ET30
Crowstone Rd, Grays RM16 192 GC75
Crowther Av, Brent. TW8 180 CL77
Crowther Cl, SW6 39 H3
Crowther Rd, SE25 224 DU98
Crowthorne Cl, SW18 201 CZ88
Crowthorne Rd, W10 14 C9
Croxdale Rd, Borwd. WD6 100 CM40
Croxden Cl, Edg. HA8 140 CM55
Croxden Wk, Mord. SM4 222 DC100
Croxford Gdns, N22 121 DP52
Croxford Way, Rom. RM7 off Horace Av 149 FD60
⊖ Croxley 97 BP44
Croxley Cl, Orp. BR5 228 EV96
CROXLEY GREEN, Rick. WD3 96 BN43
Croxley Grn, Orp. BR5 228 EV95
● Croxley Green Business Pk, Wat. WD18 97 BR44
Croxley Hall Wds, Crox.Grn WD3 114 BM45
Croxley Rd, W9 15 H3
Croxley Vw, Wat. WD18 97 BS44
Croxted Cl, SE21 204 DQ87
Croxted Ms, SE24 204 DQ86
Croxted Rd, SE21 204 DQ87
SE24 204 DQ87
Croxteth Ho, SW8 41 N8
Croxton, Kings.T. KT1 off Burritt Rd 220 CN96
Croyde Av, Grnf. UB6 158 CC69
Hayes UB3 177 BS77
Croyde Cl, Sid. DA15 207 ER87
CROYDON, CR0 224 DR102
Coll Croydon Coll, Croy. CR0 off College Rd 224 DR103
Croydon Gro, Croy. CR0 223 DP102
Sch Croydon High Sch, S.Croy. CR2 off Old Farleigh Rd 242 DW110
Croydon La, Bans. SM7 240 DB114
Croydon La S, Bans. SM7 240 DB114
Croydon Rd, E13 23 M5
SE20 224 DV96
Beckenham BR3 225 DY98
Beddington CR0 241 DL105
Bromley BR2 226 EF104
Caterham CR3 258 DU122
Keston BR2 226 EJ104
London Heathrow Airport TW6 177 BP82
Mitcham CR4 222 DG98
Mitcham Common CR0 222 DG98
Reigate RH2 272 DB134
Wallington SM6 241 DH105
Warlingham CR6 259 ED122
West Wickham BR4 226 EE104
Westerham TN16 261 EM123
● Croydon Rd Ind Est, Beck. BR3 225 DX98
● Croydon Valley Trade Pk, Croy. CR0 off Beddington Fm Rd 223 DL101
Croyland Rd, N9 122 DU46
Croylands Dr, Surb. KT6 220 CL101
Croysdale Av, Sun. TW16 217 BU97
Crozier Dr, S.Croy. CR2 242 DV110
Crozier Ho, SE3 off Ebdon Way 186 EH83
Crozier Ter, E9 11 K3

Crucible Cl, Rom. RM6 148 EV58
Crucifix La, SE1 31 N4
Cruden Ho, SE17 42 G3
Cruden Rd, Grav. DA12 213 GM90
Cruden St, N1 9 H9
Cruick Av, S.Ock. RM15 171 FW73
Cruikshank Rd, E15 13 K1
Cruikshank St, WC1 18 E2
Crummock Cl, Slou. SL1 152 AJ72
Crummock Gdns, NW9 140 CS57
Crumpsall St, SE2 188 EW77
Crundale Av, NW9 140 CN57
Crundal Twr, Orp. BR5 228 EW102
Crunden Rd, S.Croy. CR2 242 DR108
Crusader Cl, Purf. RM19
off Centurion Way 190 FN77
Crusader Gdns, Croy. CR0 224 DS104
● Crusader Industrial Est, N4 off Hermitage Rd 144 DQ58
Crusader Way, Wat. WD18 97 BT44
Crushes Cl, Hutt. CM13 131 GE44
Crusoe Ms, N16 144 DR61
Crusoe Rd, Erith DA8 189 FD78
Mitcham CR4 202 DF94
Crutched Friars, EC3 19 P10
Crutches La, Jordans HP9 112 AS51
Crutchfield La, Hkwd RH6 290 DA145
Walton-on-Thames KT12 217 BV103
Crutchley Rd, SE6 206 EE89
Crystal Av, Horn. RM12 150 FL63
Crystal Ct, SE19
off College Rd 204 DT92
Crystal Ho, SE18
off Spinel Cl 187 ET78
⇌ Crystal Palace 204 DU93
Crystal Palace 204 DU93
★ Crystal Palace FC, SE25 224 DS98
★ Crystal Palace Nat Sports Cen, SE19 204 DU93
Crystal Palace Par, SE19 204 DU93
★ Crystal Palace Pk, SE19 204 DT92
Crystal Palace Pk Rd, SE26 204 DU92
Crystal Palace Rd, SE22 184 DU84
Crystal Palace Sta Rd, SE19 204 DU93
Crystal Ter, SE19 204 DR93
Crystal Vw Ct, Brom. BR1 205 ED91
Crystal Way, Dag. RM8 148 EW60
Harrow HA1 139 CF57
Crystal Wf, N1 19 H1
Cuba Dr, Enf. EN3 104 DW40
Cuba St, E14 34 A4
Cubitt Bldg, SW1 41 J1
Cubitt Sq, Sthl. UB2
off Windmill Av 158 CC74
Cubitt Steps, E14 34 B2
Cubitt St, WC1 18 D3
Cubitts Yd, WC2 18 B10
Cubitt Ter, SW4 41 M10
CUBITT TOWN, E14 34 F6
Sch Cubitt Town Inf & Jun Schs, E14 34 F7
Cublands, Hert. SG13 54 DV09
Cuckmans Dr, St.Alb. AL2 82 CA25
Cuckmere Way, Orp. BR5 228 EX102
Cuckoo Av, W7 159 CE70
Cuckoo Dene, W7 159 CD71
Cuckoo Hall La, N9 122 DW45
Sch Cuckoo Hall Prim Sch, N9
off Cuckoo Hall La 123 DX45
Cuckoo Hill, Pnr. HA5 138 BW55
Cuckoo Hill Dr, Pnr. HA5 138 BW55
Cuckoo Hill Rd, Pnr. HA5 138 BW56
Cuckoo La, W7 159 CE73
Cuckoo Pound, Shep. TW17 217 BS99
Cucumber La, Essen. AL9 68 DF20
Hertford SG13 68 DF20
Cudas Cl, Epsom KT19 239 CT105
Cuddington, SE17 31 J8
Cuddington Av, Wor.Pk. KT4 221 CT104
Cuddington Cl, Tad. KT20 255 CW120
Sch Cuddington Comm Prim Sch, Wor.Pk. KT4
off Salisbury Rd 221 CT104
Sch Cuddington Cft Prim Sch, Cheam SM2 off West Dr 239 CX109
Cuddington Glade, Epsom KT19 238 CN112
Cuddington Pk Cl, Bans. SM7 239 CZ113
Cuddington Way, Sutt. SM2 239 CX112
CUDHAM, Sev. TN14 261 ER115
Cudham Cl, Belmont SM2 240 DA110
Sch Cudham C of E Prim Sch, Bigg.H. TN16 off Jail La 261 EN116
Cudham Dr, New Adgtn CR0 243 EC110
Cudham La N, Cudham TN14 245 ER112
Orpington BR6 245 ES110
Cudham La S, Sev. TN14 261 EQ115
Cudham Pk Rd, Cudham TN14 245 ES110
Cudham Rd, Downe BR6 245 EN111
Tatsfield TN16 260 EL120
Cudham St, SE6 205 EC87
Cudworth St, E1 20 F4
Cuff Cres, SE9 206 EK86
CUFFLEY, Pot.B. EN6 87 DM29
⇌ Cuffley 87 DM29
Cuffley Av, Wat. WD25 82 BX34
Cuffley Ct, Hem.H. HP2 63 BQ15
Cuffley Hill, Goffs Oak EN7 87 DN29
Sch Cuffley Sch, Cuffley EN6
off Theobalds Rd 87 DM30
Cuff Pt, E2 20 A2
Cugley Rd, Dart. DA2 210 FQ87
Culford Gdns, SW3 28 F9
Culford Gro, N1 9 N5
Culford Ms, N1 9 N4
Culford Rd, N1 9 N6
Grays RM16 192 GC75
Culgaith Gdns, Enf. EN2 103 DL42
Cullen Sq, S.Ock. RM15 171 FW73
Cullen Way, NW10 160 CQ70
Cullera Cl, Nthwd. HA6 115 BT51
Cullerne Cl, Ewell KT17 239 CT110
Cullesden Rd, Ken. CR8 257 DP115
Culling Rd, SE16 32 G6
Cullings Ct, Wal.Abb. EN9 90 EF33
Cullington Cl, Har. HA3 139 CG56
Cullingworth Rd, NW10 141 CU64
Culloden Cl, SE16 44 D1
Sch Culloden Prim Sch, E14 22 F9
Culloden Rd, Enf. EN2 103 DP40
Culloden St, E14 22 F8
Cullum St, EC3 19 N10
Culmington Rd, W13 179 CJ75
South Croydon CR2 242 DQ109
Culmore Rd, SE15 44 F5
Culmstock Rd, SW11 202 DG85
Culpeper Cl, Ilf. IG6 125 EP51
Culpepper Cl, N18 122 DV50
Culross Cl, N15 144 DQ56
Culross St, W1 28 G1
Culsac Rd, Surb. KT6 220 CL103
Culverden Rd, SW12 203 DJ89
Watford WD19 115 BV48
Culver Dr, Oxt. RH8 276 EE130
Culver Gro, Stan. HA7 117 CJ54
Culverhay, Ashtd. KT21 254 CL116
Culverhouse Gdns, SW16 203 DM90
Culverlands Cl, Stan. HA7 117 CH49
Culverley Rd, SE6 205 EB88
Culver Rd, St.Alb. AL1 65 CE19
Culvers Av, Cars. SM5 222 DF103
Culvers Ct, Grav. DA12 213 GM88
Culvers Cft, Seer Grn HP9 111 AQ51
Sch Culvers Ho Prim Sch, Mitch. CR4 off Orchard Av 222 DG102
Culvers Retreat, Cars. SM5 222 DF102
Culverstone Cl, Brom. BR2 226 EF100
Culvers Way, Cars. SM5 222 DF103
Culvert La, Uxb. UB8 156 BH68
Culvert Pl, SW11 40 G9
Culvert Rd, N15 144 DS57
SW11 40 F7
Culworth St, NW8 16 C1
Culzean Cl, SE27
off Chatsworth Way 203 DP90
Cumberland Av, NW10 160 CP69
Gravesend DA12 213 GJ87
Guildford GU2 264 AU129
Hornchurch RM12 150 FL62
Slough SL2 153 AQ70
Welling DA16 187 ES83
● Cumberland Business Pk, NW10 160 CN69
Cumberland Cl, E8 10 A5
SW20 off Lansdowne Rd 201 CX94
Amersham HP7 94 AV39
Epsom KT19 238 CS110
Hemel Hempstead HP3 63 BS24
Hertford SG14 53 DP06
Hornchurch RM12 150 FL62
Ilford IG6 125 EQ53
Twickenham TW1
off Westmorland Cl 199 CH86
Cumberland Ct, Hodd. EN11 71 EA16
Welling DA16
off Bellegrove Rd 187 ES82
Cumberland Cres, W14 26 F8
Cumberland Dr, Bexh. DA7 188 EY80
Chessington KT9 220 CM104
Dartford DA1 210 FM87
Esher KT10 219 CG103
Cumberland Gdns, NW4 119 CX54
WC1 18 D2
Cumberland Gate, W1 16 E10
Cumberland Ho, NW10 161 CU70
SE28 187 EQ75
Cumberland Mkt, NW1 17 K2
Cumberland Mkt Est, NW1 17 K2
Cumberland Ms, SE11 42 F1
Cumberland Mills Sq, E14 34 G10
● Cumberland Pk, NW10 161 CU69
Cumberland Pk, W3 160 CQ73
Cumberland Pl, NW1 17 J2
SE6 206 EF88
Sunbury-on-Thames TW16 217 BU98
Cumberland Rd, E12 146 EK63
E13 24 A6
E17 123 DY54
N9 122 DW46
N22 121 DM54
SE25 224 DV100
SW13 181 CT81
W3 160 CQ73
W7 179 CF75
Ashford TW15 196 BK90
Bromley BR2 226 EE98
Chafford Hundred RM16 192 FY75
Harrow HA1 138 CB57
Richmond TW9 180 CN80
Stanmore HA7 140 CM55
Cumberlands, Ken. CR8 258 DR115
Sch Cumberland Sch, E13 24 C4
Cumberland St, SW1 29 K10
Staines-upon-Thames TW18 195 BD92
Cumberland Ter, NW1 17 J1
Cumberland Ter Ms, NW1 17 J1
Cumberland Vil, W3
off Cumberland Rd 160 CQ73
Cumberlow Av, SE25 224 DU97
Cumberlow Pl, Hem.H. HP2 63 BQ21
Cumbernauld Gdns, Sun. TW16 197 BT92
Cumberton Rd, N17 122 DR53
Cumbrae Cl, Slou. SL2
off St. Pauls Av 154 AU74
Cumbrae Gdns, Long Dit. KT6 219 CK103
Cumbrian Av, Bexh. DA7 189 FE81
Cumbrian Gdns, NW2 141 CX61
Cumbrian Way, Uxb. UB8 156 BK67
Cum Cum Hill, Hat. AL9 68 DD21
★ Cuming Mus, SE17
off Walworth Rd 31 J9
Cumley Rd, Toot Hill CM5 93 FE30
Cummings Hall La, Noak Hill RM3 128 FJ48
Cumming St, N1 18 C1
Cumnor Gdns, Epsom KT17 239 CU107
Sch Cumnor Ho Sch, S.Croy. CR2 off Pampisford Rd 241 DP109
Cumnor Ri, Ken. CR8 258 DQ117
Cumnor Rd, Sutt. SM2 240 DC107
Cunard Ct, Stan. HA7
off Brightwen Gro 117 CG47
Cunard Cres, N21 104 DR44
Cunard Pl, EC3 19 P9
Cunard Rd, NW10 160 CR69
Cunard Wk, SE16 33 K8
Cundalls Rd, Ware SG12 55 DY05
Cundy Rd, E16 24 C9
Cundy St, SW1 29 H9
Cundy St Est, SW1 29 H9
Cunliffe Cl, Headley KT18 254 CP124
Cunliffe Rd, Epsom KT19 239 CT105
Cunliffe St, SW16 203 DJ93
Cunningham Av, Enf. EN3 105 DY36
Guildford GU1 265 BA133
Hatfield AL10 66 CR17
St. Albans AL1 65 CF22
Cunningham Cl, Rom. RM6 148 EW57
Cunningham Cl, West Wickham BR4 225 EB103
Cunningham Ct, E10
off Oliver Rd 145 EB62
Sch Cunningham Hill Inf Sch, St.Alb. AL1 off Cell Barnes La 65 CG21
Sch Cunningham Hill Jun Sch, St.Alb. AL1
off Cell Barnes La 65 CG22
Cunningham Hill Rd, St.Alb. AL1 65 CF22
Cunningham Pk, Har. HA1 138 CC57
Cunningham Pl, NW8 16 A4
Cunningham Ri, N.Wld Bas. CM16 93 FC25
Cunningham Rd, N15 144 DU56
Banstead SM7 256 DD115
Cheshunt EN8 89 DY27
Cunnington St, W4 180 CQ76
Cupar Rd, SW11 41 H6
CUPID GREEN, Hem.H. HP2 62 BN16
Cupid Grn La, Hem.H. HP2 62 BN15
Cupola Cl, Brom. BR1 206 EH92
Curates Wk, Dart. DA2 210 FK90
Curchin Cl, Bigg.H. TN16 244 EJ112
Cureton St, SW1 29 P9
Curfew Bell Rd, Cher. KT16 215 BF101
Curfew Yd, Wind. SL4
off Thames St 173 AR81
Curie Gdns, NW9 118 CS54
Curlew Cl, SE28 168 EX73
Berkhamsted HP4 60 AW20
South Croydon CR2 243 DX111
Curlew Ct, W13
off Gurnell Gro 159 CF70
Brox. EN10 71 DZ23
Surbiton KT6 220 CM104
Curlew Gdns, Guil. GU4 265 BD132
Curlew Ho, Enf. EN3
off Allington Ct 105 DX43
Curlews, The, Grav. DA12 213 GK89
Curlew St, SE1 32 A4
Curlew Ter, Ilf. IG5
off Tiptree Cres 147 EN55
Curlew Way, Hayes UB4 158 BX71
Curling Cl, Couls. CR5 257 DM120
Curling La, Bad.Dene RM17 192 FZ78
Curling Vale, Guil. GU2 280 AU136
Curness St, SE13 185 EC84
Curnick's La, SE27
off Chapel Rd 204 DQ91
Curnock Est, NW1 7 L9
● Curo Pk, Frog. AL2 83 CE27
Curran Av, Sid. DA15 207 ET85
Wallington SM6 222 DG104
Curran Cl, Uxb. UB8 156 BJ70
Currey Rd, Grnf. UB6 159 CD65
Curricle St, W3 160 CS74
Currie Hill Cl, SW19 201 CZ91
Curries La, Slou. SL1 133 AK64
Currie St, Hert. SG13 54 DS09
Curry Ri, NW7 119 CX51
Cursitor St, EC4 18 E8
Curtain Pl, EC2 19 P4
Curtain Rd, EC2 19 N5
Curteys, Harl. CM17 58 EX10
Curthwaite Gdns, Enf. EN2 103 DK42
Curtis Cl, Mill End WD3 114 BG46
Curtis Dr, W3 160 CR72
Curtis Fld Rd, SW16 203 DM91
Curtis Gdns, Dor. RH4 285 CG135
Curtis Ho, N11 121 DH50
Curtis La, Wem. HA0
off Station Gro 140 CL64
Curtismill Cl, Orp. BR5 228 EV97
Curtis Mill Grn, Nave. RM4 109 FF42
Curtis Mill La, Nave. RM4 109 FF42
Curtismill Way, Orp. BR5 228 EV97
Curtis Rd, Dor. RH4 285 CF135
Epsom KT19 238 CQ105
Hemel Hempstead HP3 63 BQ21
Hornchurch RM11 150 FM60
Hounslow TW4 198 BZ87
Curtiss Dr, Lvsdn WD25 81 BT34
Curtis St, SE1 32 A8
Curtis Way, SE1 32 A8
SE28 off Tawney Rd 168 EV73
Berkhamsted HP4 60 AX20
Curvan Cl, Epsom KT17 239 CT110
Curve, The, W12 161 CU73
Curwen Av, E7
off Woodford Rd 146 EH63
Sch Curwen Prim Sch, E13 23 N1
Curwen Rd, W12 181 CU75
Curzon Av, Beac. HP9 111 AK51
Enfield EN3 105 DX43
Hazlemere HP15 110 AC45
Stanmore HA7 117 CG53
Curzon Cl, Haz. HP15 110 AC45
Orpington BR6 245 ER105
Weybridge KT13
off Curzon Rd 234 BN105
Curzon Cres, NW10 161 CT66
Barking IG11 167 ET68
Curzon Dr, Grays RM17 192 GC80
Curzon Gate, W1 28 G3
Curzon Pl, Pnr. HA5 138 BW57
Curzon Rd, N10 121 DH54
W5 159 CH70
Thornton Heath CR7 223 DN100
Weybridge KT13 234 BN105
Curzon Sq, W1 29 H3
Curzon St, W1 29 H3
Cusack Cl, Twick. TW1
off Waldegrave Rd 199 CF91
Cussons Cl, Chsht EN7 88 DU29
CUSTOM HOUSE, E16 24 F8
DLR Custom House for ExCeL 24 B10
Custom Ho Reach, SE16 33 N5
Custom Ho Wk, EC3 31 N1
Cut, The, SE1 30 F4
Slough SL2 153 AN70
Cutcombe Rd, SE5 43 K9
Cuthberga Cl, Bark. IG11
off George St 167 EQ66
Cuthbert Ct, Whyt. CR3
off Godstone Rd 258 DU119
Cuthbert Gdns, SE25 224 DS97
Cuthbert Rd, E17 145 EC55
N18 off Fairfield Rd 122 DU50
Croydon CR0 223 DP103
Cuthberts Cl, Chsht EN7 88 DT29
Cuthbert St, W2 16 A6
Cut Hills, Egh. TW20 214 AV95
Virginia Water GU25 214 AU96
Cuthill Wk, SE5 43 L7
Cutlers Gdns, E1 19 P8
Cutlers Gdns Arc, EC2
off Devonshire Sq 19 P8
Cutlers Sq, E14 34 B9
Cutlers Ter, N1 9 N4
Cutler St, E1 19 P8
Cutmore, Bark. IG11
off Ripple Rd 167 EQ66
Cutmore Dr, Coln.Hth AL4 66 CP22
Cutmore St, Grav. DA11 213 GH87
Cutter La, SE10 35 K4
Cutthroat All, Rich. TW10
off Ham St 199 CJ89
Cutthroat La, Hodd. EN11 71 DZ15
Cutting, The, Red. RH1 288 DF136
Cuttsfield Ter, Hem.H. HP1 61 BF21
★ Cutty Sark, SE10 46 E2
Cutty Sark Ct, Green. DA9
off Low Cl 211 FU85
DLR Cutty Sark for Maritime Greenwich 46 E3
Cutty Sark Gdns, SE10 46 F2
Cuxton Cl, Bexh. DA6 208 EY85
Cwmbran Ct, Hem.H. HP2 62 BM16
Cyclamen Cl, Hmptn. TW12
off Gresham Rd 198 CA93
Cyclamen Rd, Swan. BR8 229 FD98
Cyclamen Way, Epsom KT19 238 CP106
Cyclops Ms, E14 34 A8
Cygnet Av, Felt. TW14 198 BW87
Cygnet Cl, NW10 140 CR64
Borehamwood WD6 100 CQ39
Northwood HA6 115 BQ52
Woking GU21 248 AV116
Cygnet Gdns, Nthflt DA11 213 GF89
Cygnets, The, Felt. TW13 198 BY91
Staines-upon-Thames TW18
off Edgell Rd 195 BF92
Cygnets Cl, Red. RH1 272 DG132
Cygnet St, E1 20 B4
Cygnet Vw, Grays RM20 191 FT77
Cygnet Way, Hayes UB4 158 BX71
● Cygnus Business Cen, NW10 161 CT65
Cygnus Ct, Pur. CR8
off Brighton Rd 241 DN111
Cymbeline Ct, Har. HA1
off Gayton Rd 139 CF58
Cynthia St, N1 18 D1
Cyntra Pl, E8 10 F7
Cypress Av, Enf. EN2 103 DN35
Twickenham TW2 198 CC87
Welwyn Garden City AL7 52 DC10
Cypress Cl, E5 144 DU61
Waltham Abbey EN9 89 ED34
Cypress Ct, Vir.W. GU25 214 AY98
Cypress Gdns, SE4 205 DY85
Cypress Gro, Ilf. IG6 125 ES51
Sch Cypress Inf Sch, SE25
off Cypress Rd 224 DS96
Sch Cypress Jun Sch, SE25
off Cypress Rd 224 DS96
Cypress Path, Rom. RM3 128 FK52
Cypress Pl, W1 17 M5
Cypress Rd, SE25 224 DS96
Guildford GU1 264 AW132
Harrow HA3 117 CD54
Cypress Tree Cl, Sid. DA15 207 ET88
Cypress Wk, Eng.Grn TW20 194 AV93
Watford WD25
off Cedar Wd Dr 97 BV35
Cypress Way, Bans. SM7 239 CX114
DLR Cyprus 25 M10
Cyprus Av, N3 119 CY54
Cyprus Cl, N4
off Atterbury Rd 143 DP58
Cyprus Gdns, N3 119 CY54
Cyprus Pl, E2 21 H1
E6 25 M10
Cyprus Rd, N3 119 CZ54
N9 122 DT47
Jct Cyprus Rbt, E16 25 M10
Cyprus St, E2 20 G1
Cyrena Rd, SE22 204 DT86
Sch Cyril Jackson Prim Sch, N Bldg, E14 21 P10
S Bldg, E14 33 P1
Cyril Mans, SW11 40 F7
Cyril Rd, Bexh. DA7 188 EY82
Orpington BR6 228 EU101
Cyrils Way, St.Alb. AL1
off Maynard Dr 65 CD23
Cyrus St, EC1 19 H4
Czar St, SE8 46 A2

D

Dabbling Cl, Erith DA8 189 FH80
Dabbs Hill La, Nthlt. UB5 138 CB64
D'Abernon Chase, Lthd. KT22 237 CG114
D'Abernon Cl, Esher KT10 236 CA105
D'Abernon Dr, Stoke D'Ab. KT11 252 BY116
Dabin Cres, SE10 46 E6
Dacca St, SE8 45 P2
Dace Rd, E3 12 A8
Dacorum Way, Hem.H. HP1 62 BJ20
Dacre Av, Aveley RM15 171 FR74
Ilford IG5 125 EN54
Dacre Cl, Chig. IG7 125 EQ49
Greenford UB6 158 CB68
Dacre Cres, Aveley RM15 171 FR74
Dacre Gdns, SE13 186 EE84
Borehamwood WD6 100 CR43
Chigwell IG7 125 EQ49
● Dacre Ind Est, Chsht EN8
off Fieldings Rd 89 DZ29
Dacre Pk, SE13 186 EE83
Dacre Pl, SE13 186 EE83
Dacre Rd, E11 146 EF60
E13 166 EH67
Croydon CR0 223 DL101
Dacres Est, SE23 205 DX90
Dacres Rd, SE23 205 DX90
Dacre St, SW1 29 N6
Dade Way, Sthl. UB2 178 BZ78
Dads Wd, Harl. CM20 73 EQ15
Daerwood Cl, Brom. BR2 227 EM102
Daffodil Av, Pilg.Hat. CM15 130 FV43
Daffodil Cl, Croy. CR0 225 DX102
Hatfield AL10 51 CT14
Daffodil Gdns, Ilf. IG1 147 EP64
Daffodil Pl, Hmptn. TW12
off Gresham Rd 198 CA93
Daffodil St, W12 161 CT73
Dafforne Rd, SW17 202 DG90
Dagden Rd, Shalf. GU4 280 AY140
DAGENHAM, RM8 - RM10 168 FA65
Dagenham Av, Dag. RM9
off Cook Rd 168 EY67
⇌ Dagenham Dock 168 EZ68
⊖ Dagenham East 149 FC64
⊖ Dagenham Heathway 168 EZ65
Dagenham Leisure Pk, Dag. RM9 168 EY67
Sch Dagenham Pk Comm Sch, Dag. RM10 off School Rd 169 FB67
Dagenham Rd, E10 145 DZ60
Dagenham RM10 149 FC63
Rainham RM13 169 FD66
Romford RM7 149 FD62
Dagger La, Els. WD6 99 CG44
Daggs Dell Rd, Hem.H. HP1 61 BE18
Dagley Fm Pk Homes, Shalf. GU4 280 AX140
Dagley La, Shalf. GU4 280 AY140
Dagmar Av, Wem. HA9 140 CM63
Dagmar Ct, E14
off New Union Cl 34 F6
Dagmar Gdns, NW10 14 C1
Dagmar Ms, Sthl. UB2
off Dagmar Rd 178 BY76
Dagmar Pas, N1 9 H8
Dagmar Rd, N4 143 DN59
N15 off Cornwall Rd 144 DR56
N22 121 DK53
SE5 43 N7
SE25 224 DS99
Dagenham RM10 169 FC66
Kingston upon Thames KT2 220 CM95
Southall UB2 178 BY76
Windsor SL4 173 AR82
Dagmar Ter, N1 9 H8
Dagnall Cres, Uxb. UB8 156 BJ71
Dagnall Pk, SE25 224 DS100
Dagnall Rd, SE25 224 DS99
Dagnall St, SW11 40 F8
Dagnam Pk Cl, Rom. RM3 128 FN50
Dagnam Pk Dr, Rom. RM3 128 FL50
Dagnam Pk Gdns, Rom. RM3 128 FN51
Dagnam Pk Sq, Rom. RM3 128 FP51
Dagnan Rd, SW12 203 DH87
Dagonet Gdns, Brom. BR1 206 EG90
Dagonet Rd, Brom. BR1 206 EG90
Dahlia Cl, Chsht EN7 88 DQ25
Dahlia Dr, Swan. BR8 229 FF96
Dahlia Gdns, Ilf. IG1 167 EP65
Mitcham CR4 223 DK98
Dahlia Rd, SE2 188 EV77
Dahomey Rd, SW16 203 DJ93
Daiglen Dr, S.Ock. RM15 171 FU73
Sch Daiglen Sch, The, Buck.H. IG9 off Palmerston Rd 124 EJ47
Daimler Way, Wall. SM6 241 DL108
Daines Cl, E12 147 EM62
South Ockendon RM15 171 FU70
Dainford Cl, Brom. BR1 205 ED92
Dainton Cl, Brom. BR1 226 EH95
Daintry Cl, Har. HA3 139 CG56
Daintry Lo, Nthwd. HA6 115 BT52
Daintry Way, E9 11 N4
Sch Dair Ho Sch, Farn.Royal SL2
off Beaconsfield Rd 153 AQ67
Dairsie Rd, SE9 187 EN83
Dairy Cl, NW10 161 CU67
SW6 39 H7
Bromley BR1
off Plaistow La 206 EH94
Grnf. UB6 159 CD68
Sutton at Hone DA4 210 FP94
Thornton Heath CR7 224 DQ96
Westcott RH4 284 CC137
Dairy Fm La, Hare. UB9 114 BJ54
Dairy Fm Pl, SE15 44 G7
Dairyglen Av, Chsht EN8 89 DY31
Dairy La, SE18 37 J9
Crockham Hill TN8 277 EN134
Dairyman Cl, NW2 141 CY62
Dairyman's Wk, Guil. GU4 265 BB129
Sch Dairy Meadow Prim Sch, Sthl. UB2 off Swift Rd 178 BZ76
Dairy Ms, N2 off East End Rd 142 DE56
SW9 183 DL83
Rom. RM6 148 EX59
Dairy Wk, SW19 201 CY91
Dairy Way, Abb.L. WD5 81 BT29
Daisy Cl, NW9 140 CQ61
Croydon CR0 225 DX102
Daisy Dobbins Wk, N19
off Hillrise Rd 143 DL59
Daisy Dr, Hat. AL10 67 CT15
Daisy La, SW6 39 J10
Daisy Meadow, Egh. TW20 195 BA92
Daisy Rd, E16 23 J4
E18 124 EH54
Dakin Pl, E1 21 L7
Dakota Bldg, SE13
off Deals Gateway 46 B7
Dakota Cl, Wall. SM6 241 DM108
Dakota Gdns, E6 25 H5
Northolt UB5
off Argus Way 158 BY69
Dalberg Rd, SW2 183 DN84
Dalberg Way, SE2
off Lanridge Rd 188 EX76
Dalby Rd, SW18 182 DC84
Dalbys Cres, N17 122 DS51
Dalby St, NW5 7 J5
Dalcross Rd, Houns. TW4 178 BY82
Dale, The, Kes. BR2 244 EK105
Waltham Abbey EN9 90 EE34
Dale Av, Edg. HA8 118 CM53
Hounslow TW4 178 BY83
Dalebury Rd, SW17 202 DE89
Dale Cl, SE3 47 N10
Addlestone KT15 234 BH106
Bookham KT23 268 CC125
Dartford DA1 209 FF86
New Barnet EN5 102 DB44
Pinner HA5 115 BV53
South Ockendon RM15 171 FU72
Dale Ct, Saw. CM21
off The Crest 58 EX06
Slough SL1 173 AQ75
Wat. WD25 off High Rd 81 BU33
Dale Dr, Hayes UB4 157 BT70
Dale End, Dart. DA1
off Dale Rd 209 FF86
Dale Gdns, Wdf.Grn. IG8 124 EH49
Dalegarth Gdns, Pur. CR8 242 DR113
Dale Grn Rd, N11 121 DH48
Dale Gro, N12 120 DC50
Daleham Av, Egh. TW20 195 BA93
Daleham Dr, Uxb. UB8 157 BP72
Daleham Gdns, NW3 6 A3
Daleham Ms, NW3 6 B4

Dalehead, NW1 17 L1
Dalemain Ms, E16 35 P2
Dale Pk Av, Cars. SM5 222 DF103
Dale Pk Rd, SE19 224 DQ95
Dale Rd, NW5 7 H2
SE17 43 H3
Dartford DA1 209 FF86
Greenford UB6 158 CB71
Purley CR8 241 DN112
Southfleet DA13 212 GA91
Sunbury-on-Thames TW16 197 BT94
Sutton SM1 239 CZ105
Swanley BR8 229 FC96
Walton-on-Thames KT12 217 BT101
Dale Row, W11 14 F9
Daleside, Ger.Cr. SL9 134 AY60
Orpington BR6 246 EU106
Daleside Cl, Orp. BR6 246 EU107
Daleside Dr, Pot.B. EN6 85 CZ32
Daleside Gdns, Chig. IG7 125 EQ48
Daleside Rd, SW16 203 DH92
Epsom KT19 238 CR107
Dales Path, Borwd. WD6
off Farriers Way 100 CR43
Dales Rd, Borwd. WD6 100 CR43
Dalestone Ms, Rom. RM3 127 FH51
Dale St, W4 180 CS78
Dale Vw, Erith DA8 189 FF82
Headley KT18 254 CP123
Woking GU21 248 AU118
Dale Vw Av, E4 123 EC47
Dale Vw Cres, E4 123 EC47
Dale Vw Gdns, E4 123 ED48
Daleview Rd, N15 144 DS58
Dale Wk, Dart. DA2 210 FQ88
Dalewood, Welw.G.C. AL7 52 DD10
Dalewood Cl, Horn. RM11 150 FM59
Dalewood Gdns, Wor.Pk. KT4 221 CV103
Dale Wd Rd, Orp. BR6 227 ES101
Daley St, E9 11 K4
Daley Thompson Way, SW8 41 J9
Dalgarno Gdns, W10 14 A6
Dalgarno Way, W10 14 A5
Dalgleish St, E14 21 M9
Daling Way, E3 11 M9
Dalkeith Gro, Stan. HA7 117 CK50
Dalkeith Rd, SE21 204 DQ88
Ilford IG1 147 EQ62
Dallas Rd, NW4 141 CU59
SE26 204 DV90
W5 160 CM71
Sutton SM3 239 CY107
Dallas Ter, Hayes UB3 177 BT76
Dallega Cl, Hayes UB3 157 BR73
Dallinger Rd, SE12 206 EF86
Dalling Rd, W6 181 CV76
Dallington Cl, Hersham KT12 236 BW107
Dallington Sch, EC1 19 H4
Dallington Sq, EC1
off Dallington St 19 H4
Dallington St, EC1 19 H4
Dallin Rd, SE18 187 EP80
Bexleyheath DA6 188 EX84
Dalmain Prim Sch, SE23
off Grove Cl 205 DY88
Dalmain Rd, SE23 205 DX88
Dalmally Pas, Croy. CR0
off Morland Rd 224 DT101
Dalmally Rd, Croy. CR0 224 DT101
Dalmeny Av, N7 8 A2
SW16 223 DN96
Dalmeny Cl, Wem. HA0 159 CJ65
Dalmeny Cres, Houns. TW3 179 CD84
Dalmeny Rd, N7 7 P1
Carshalton SM5 240 DG108
Erith DA8 189 FB81
New Barnet EN5 102 DC44
Worcester Park KT4 221 CV104
Dalmeyer Rd, NW10 161 CT65
Dalmore Av, Clay. KT10 237 CF107
Dalmore Rd, SE21 204 DQ89
Dalroy Cl, S.Ock. RM15 171 FU72
Dalrymple Cl, N14 121 DK45
Dalrymple Rd, SE4 185 DY84
DALSTON, E8 10 C6
Dalston Gdns, Stan. HA7 118 CL53
Dalston Junction 10 A5
Dalston Kingsland 9 P4
Dalston La, E8 10 A4
Dalton Av, Mitch. CR4 222 DE96
Dalton Cl, Hayes UB4 157 BR70
Orpington BR6 227 ES104
Purley CR8 242 DQ112
Dalton Grn, Slou. SL3 175 AZ79
Dalton Rd, Har.Wld HA3 117 CD54
Daltons Rd, Chels. BR6 229 FB104
Swanley BR8 229 FC102
Dalton St, SE27 203 DP89
St. Albans AL3 65 CD19
Dalton Way, Wat. WD17 98 BX43
Dalwood St, SE5 43 N6
Daly Dr, Brom. BR1 227 EN97
Dalyell Rd, SW9 42 C10
Damascene Wk, SE21
off Lovelace Rd 204 DQ88
Damask Ct, Sutt. SM1
off Cleeve Way 222 DB102
Damask Cres, E16 23 J4
Damask Grn, Hem.H. HP1 61 BE21
Dame Alice Owen's Sch, Pot.B.
EN6 off Dugdale Hill La 85 CY33
Damer Ter, SW10 39 P5
Dames Rd, E7 146 EG62
Dame St, N1 9 J10
Dameswick Vw, St.Alb. AL2 82 CA27
Dame Tipping C of E Prim Sch,
Hav.at.Bow. RM4
off North Rd 127 FE48
Damien St, E1 20 F8
Damigos Rd, Grav. DA12 213 GM88
Damon Cl, Sid. DA14 208 EV90
Damory Ho, SE16
off Abbeyfield Rd 32 G8
Damphurst La, Dor. RH5 284 BZ139
Damson Ct, Swan. BR8 229 FD98
Damson Dr, Hayes UB3 157 BU73
Damson Gro, Slou. SL1 173 AQ75
Damson Ho, SW16
off Hemlock Cl 223 DK96
Damson Way, Cars. SM5 240 DF110
St. Albans AL4 65 CJ18
Damsonwood Rd, Sthl. UB2 178 CA76
Danbrook Rd, SW16 223 DL95
Danbury Cl, Pilg.Hat. CM15 130 FT43
Romford RM6 148 EX55
Danbury Cres, S.Ock. RM15 171 FV72
Danbury Ms, Wall. SM6 241 DH105
Danbury Rd, Loug. IG10 124 EL45
Rainham RM13 169 FF67
Danbury St, N1 9 H10
Danbury Way, Wdf.Grn. IG8 124 EJ51
Danby St, SE15 44 A10
Dancer Rd, SW6 38 G7
Richmond TW9 180 CN83
DANCERS HILL, Barn. EN5 101 CW35
Dancers Hill Rd, Barn. EN5 101 CY36
Dancers La, Barn. EN5 101 CW35
Dandelion Cl, Rush Grn RM7 149 FE61
Dando Cres, SE3 186 EH83
Dandridge Cl, SE10 35 M10
Slough SL3 174 AX77
Dandridge Dr, B.End SL8
off Millside 132 AC60
Danebury, New Adgtn CR0 243 EB107
Danebury Av, SW15 200 CS86
Daneby Rd, SE6 205 EB90
Dane Cl, Amer. HP7 94 AT41
Bexley DA5 208 FA87
Orpington BR6 245 ER106
Dane Ct, Wok. GU22 249 BF115
Danecourt Gdns, Croy. CR0 224 DT104
Danecroft Rd, SE24 204 DQ85
Danegrove Prim Sch,
Years 2-6, Barn. EN4
off Windsor Dr 102 DE44
Reception & Year 1, E.Barn.
EN4 off Ridgeway Av 102 DF44
Danehill Wk, Sid. DA14
off Hatherley Rd 208 EU90
Daneholes Rbt, Grays
RM16 192 GD76
Danehurst Cl, Egh. TW20 194 AY93
Danehurst Gdns, Ilf. IG4 146 EL57
Danehurst St, SW6 38 E6
Daneland, Barn. EN4 102 DF44
Danemead, Hodd. EN11 55 EA14
Danemead Gro, Nthlt. UB5 138 CB64
Danemere St, SW15 38 B10
Dane Pl, E3 11 N10
Dane Rd, N18 122 DW49
SW19 222 DC95
W13 159 CJ74
Ashford TW15 197 BQ93
Ilford IG1 147 EQ64
Otford TN14 263 FE117
Southall UB1 158 BY73
Warlingham CR6 259 DX117
Danes, The, Park St AL2 82 CC28
Danesbury Pk, Hert. SG14 54 DR08
Danesbury Rd, Felt. TW13 197 BV88
Danes Cl, Nthflt DA11 212 GC90
Oxshott KT22 236 CC114
Danescombe, SE12 206 EG88
Danes Ct, Wem. HA9
off North End Rd 140 CP62
Danescourt Cres, Sutt. SM1 222 DC103
Danescroft, NW4 141 CX57
Danescroft Av, NW4 141 CX57
Danescroft Gdns, NW4 141 CX57
Danesdale Rd, E9 11 L5
Danesfield, SE5 43 N2
Ripley GU23 249 BF123
Danesfield Cl, Walt. KT12 217 BV104
Danesfield Manor Sch, Walt.
KT12 off Rydens Av 218 BW103
Danes Gate, Har. HA1 139 CE55
Daneshill, Red. RH1 272 DE133
Danes Hill, Wok. GU22 249 BA118
Daneshill Cl, Red. RH1 272 DE133
Danes Hill Sch, Main Sch,
Oxshott KT22
off Leatherhead Rd 237 CD114
Pre-Prep Dept, Oxshott
KT22 off Steels La 236 CC113
Danes Rd, Rom. RM7 149 FC59
Danesrood, Guil. GU1
off Lower Edgeborough Rd 281 AZ135
Dane St, WC1 18 C7
Danes Way, Oxshott KT22 237 CD114
Pilgrim's Hatch CM15 130 FU43
Daneswood Av, SE6 205 EC90
Daneswood Cl, Wey. KT13 235 BP106
Danethorpe Rd, Wem. HA0 159 CK65
Danetree Cl, Epsom KT19 238 CQ108
Danetree Jun Sch, W.Ewell
KT19 off Danetree Rd 238 CQ108
Danetree Rd, Epsom KT19 238 CQ108
Danette Gdns, Dag. RM10 148 EZ61
Daneville Rd, SE5 43 L7
Dangan Rd, E11 146 EG58
Daniel Bolt Cl, E14 22 D6
Daniel Cl, N18 122 DW49
SW17 202 DE93
Chafford Hundred RM16 192 FY75
Grays RM16 193 GH76
Hounslow TW4 198 BZ87
Daniel Gdns, SE15 44 A4
Daniells, Welw.G.C. AL7 52 DA08
Daniell Way, Croy. CR0 223 DL102
Daniel Pl, NW4 141 CV58
Daniel Rd, W5 160 CM73
Daniels La, Warl. CR6 259 DZ116
Daniels Rd, SE15 184 DW83
Daniel Way, Bans. SM7 240 DB114
Dan Leno Wk, SW6 39 L5
Dan Mason Dr, W4 180 CR82
Danses Cl, Guil. GU4 265 BD132
Dansey Pl, W1 17 N10
Dansington Rd, Well. DA16 188 EU84
Danson Cres, Well. DA16 188 EV83
Danson Interchange,
Sid. DA15 208 EW86
Danson La, Well. DA16 188 EU84
Danson Mead, Well. DA16 188 EW83
★ Danson Park, Well. DA16 188 EW84
Danson Pk, Bexh. DA6 188 EW84
Danson Prim Sch, Well.
DA16 off Danson La 188 EU84
Danson Rd, Bex. DA5 208 EX85
Bexleyheath DA6 208 EX85
Danson Underpass, Sid.
DA15 off Danson Rd 208 EW85
Dante Pl, SE11 31 H8
Dante Rd, SE11 30 G8
Danube Apts, N8
off Great Amwell La 143 DM55
Danube Cl, N9 122 DW48
Danube St, SW3 28 D10
Danvers Rd, N8 143 DK56
Danvers St, SW3 40 B3
Danvers Way, Cat. CR3 258 DQ123
Danyon Cl, Rain. RM13 170 FJ68
Danziger Way, Borwd. WD6 100 CQ39
Dapdune Ct, Guil. GU1 264 AW134
Dapdune Rd, Guil. GU1 264 AX134
Dapdune Wf, Guil. GU1 264 AW134
Daphne Gdns, E4
off Gunners Gro 123 EC48
Daphne Jackson Rd, Guil.
GU2 280 AS135
Daphne St, SW18 202 DC86
Daplyn St, E1 20 C6
Darblay Cl, Sand. AL4 50 CM10
D'Arblay St, W1 17 M9
Darby Cl, Cat. CR3 258 DQ122
Darby Cres, Sun. TW16 218 BW96
Darby Dr, Wal.Abb. EN9 89 EC33
Darby Gdns, Sun. TW16 218 BW96
Darcy Av, Wall. SM6 241 DJ105
Darcy Cl, N20 120 DD47
Cheshunt EN8 89 DY31
Coulsdon CR5 257 DP119
D'Arcy Cl, Hutt. CM13 131 GB45
D'Arcy Dr, Har. HA3 139 CK56
Darcy Gdns, Dag. RM9 168 EZ67
D'Arcy Gdns, Har. HA3 140 CL56
Darcy Ho, E8 10 E8
D'Arcy Pl, Ashtd. KT21 254 CM117
Bromley BR2 226 EG98
Darcy Rd, SW16 223 DL96
D'Arcy Rd, Ashtd. KT21 254 CM117
Darcy Rd, Islw. TW7
off London Rd 179 CG81
D'Arcy Rd, Sutt. SM3 239 CX105
Dare Gdns, Dag. RM8 148 EY62
Darell Prim Sch, Rich.
TW9 off Darell Rd 180 CN83
Darell Rd, Rich. TW9 180 CN83
Darent Cl, Chipstead TN13 278 FC122
DARENTH, Dart. DA2 210 FQ91
Darenth Comm Prim Sch, Dart.
DA2 off Green St Grn Rd 211 FT93
Darenth Gdns, West. TN16 277 ER126
Darenth Hill, Dart. DA2 210 FQ92
Darenth Interchange, Dart.
DA2 210 FP90
Darenth La, Dunt.Grn TN13 278 FE121
South Ockendon RM15 171 FU72
Darenth Pk Av, Dart. DA2 211 FR89
Darenth Rd, N16 144 DT59
Darenth DA2 210 FP91
Dartford DA1 210 FM87
Welling DA16 188 EU81
Darenth Way, Horl. RH6 290 DF145
Shoreham TN14 247 FG111
Darenth Wd Rd, Dart. DA2 211 FS89
● Darent Ind Pk, Erith DA8 190 FJ79
Darent Mead, Sutt.H. DA4 230 FP95
Darent Valley Hosp,
Dart. DA2 211 FS88
Darent Valley Path, Dart.
DA1, DA2, DA4 210 FM89
Sevenoaks TN13, TN14 263 FG115
Darfield Rd, SE4 205 DZ85
Guildford GU4 265 BA131
Darfield Way, W10 14 C10
Darfur St, SW15 181 CX83
Dargate Cl, SE19
off Chipstead Cl 204 DT94
Dariel Cl, Slou. SL1 173 AM75
Darien Rd, SW11 182 DD83
Darkes La, Pot.B. EN6 86 DA32
Darkhole Ride, Wind. SL4 172 AH84
Dark Ho Wk, EC3
off Grant's Quay Wf 31 M1
Dark La, Chsht EN7 88 DU31
Great Warley CM14 129 FU52
Puttenham GU3 282 BM139
Ware (Musley La) SG12 55 DY05
Darlands Dr, Barn. EN5 101 CX43
Darlan Rd, SW6 39 H5
Darlaston Rd, SW19 201 CX94
Darley Cl, Add. KT15 234 BJ106
Croydon CR0 225 DY100
Darley Cft, Park St AL2 82 CB28
Darley Dene Inf Sch, Add.
KT15 off Garfield Rd 234 BJ106
Darley Dr, N.Mal. KT3 220 CR96
Darley Gdns, Mord. SM4 222 DB100
Darley Rd, N9 122 DT46
SW11 202 DF86
Darling Rd, SE4 46 A10
Darling Row, E1 20 F5
Darlington Cl, Amer. HP6
off King George V Rd 77 AR38
Darlington Gdns, Rom. RM3 128 FK50
Darlington Path, Rom. RM3
off Darlington Gdns 128 FK50
Darlington Rd, SE27 203 DP92
Darlton Cl, Dart. DA1 189 FF83
Darmaine Cl, S.Croy. CR2 242 DQ108
Darnaway Pl, E14 22 F7
Darndale Cl, E17 123 DZ54
Darnets Fld, Otford TN14 263 FF117
Darnhills, Rad. WD7 99 CG35
Darnicle Hill, Chsht EN7 87 DM25
Darnley Ho, E14 21 M8
Darnley Pk, Wey. KT13 217 BP104
Darnley Rd, E9 10 F5
Gravesend DA11 213 GG88
Grays RM17 off Stanley Rd 192 GB79
Woodford Green IG8 124 EG53
Darnley St, Grav. DA11 213 GG87
Darnley Ter, W11 26 D2
Darns Hill, Swan. BR8 229 FC101
Darrell Cl, Slou. SL3 175 AZ77
Darrell Rd, SE22 204 DU85
Darren Cl, N4 143 DM59
Darrick Wd Inf Sch, Orp.
BR6 off Lovibonds Av 245 EP105
Darrick Wd Jun Sch, Orp.
BR6 off Lovibonds Av 245 EP105
Darrick Wd Rd, Orp. BR6 227 ER103
Darrick Wd Sch, Orp. BR6
off Lovibonds Av 227 EP104
Darrington Rd, Borwd. WD6 100 CL39
Darris Cl, Hayes UB4 158 BY70
Darsley Dr, SW8 41 P6
Dart, The, Hem.H. HP2 62 BN15
Dart Cl, Slou. SL3 175 BB79
Upminster RM14 151 FR58
Dartfields, Rom. RM3 128 FK51
DARTFORD, DA1 & DA2; DA4 210 FJ87
Dartford 210 FL86
Dartford Adult Ed Cen, Dart.
DA1 off Highfield Rd 210 FK87
Dartford Av, N9 104 DW44
Dartford Bypass, Bex. DA5 209 FE88
Dartford DA2 209 FH89
Dartford Gdns, Chad.Hth RM6
off Heathfield Pk Dr 148 EV57
Dartford Gram Sch, Dart.
DA1 off West Hill 210 FJ86
Dartford Gram Sch for Girls,
Dart. DA1
off Shepherds La 210 FJ87
★ Dartford Heath, Dart. DA1 209 FG88
Dartford Heath, Bex. DA5 209 FF88
Dartford Heath Retail Pk,
Dart, DA1 210 FJ88
Dartford Ho, SE1
off Longfield Est 32 B9
★ Dartford Mus, Dart. DA1 210 FL87
Dartford Rd, Bex. DA5 209 FC88
Dartford DA1 209 FG86
Farningham DA4 230 FP95
Sevenoaks TN13 279 FJ124
Dartford St, SE17 43 K2
Dartford Tech Coll, Dart.
DA1 off Heath La 210 FJ87
Dartford Tunnel, Dart. DA1 191 FR83
Purfleet RM19 191 FR83
Dartford Tunnel App Rd,
Dart. DA1 210 FN86
Dart Grn, S.Ock. RM15 171 FV72
Dartmoor Wk, E14 34 B8
Dartmouth Av, Wok. GU21 233 BC114
Dartmouth Cl, W11 15 H8
Dartmouth Grn, Wok. GU21 233 BD114
Dartmouth Gro, SE10 46 F7
Dartmouth Hill, SE10 46 F7
Dartmouth Ho, Kings.T. KT2
off Kingsgate Rd 220 CL95
DARTMOUTH PARK, NW5 143 DH62
Dartmouth Pk Av, NW5 143 DH62
Dartmouth Pk Hill, N19 143 DH60
NW5 143 DH60
Dartmouth Pk Rd, NW5 143 DH63
Dartmouth Path, Wok. GU21 233 BD114
Dartmouth Pl, SE23
off Dartmouth Rd 204 DW89
W4 180 CS79
Dartmouth Rd, E16 23 N8
NW2 4 C4
NW4 141 CU58
SE23 204 DW90
SE26 204 DW90
Bromley BR2 226 EG101
Ruislip HA4 137 BU62
Dartmouth Row, SE10 46 F8
Dartmouth St, SW1 29 N5
Dartmouth Ter, SE10 46 G7
Dartnell Av, W.Byf. KT14 234 BH112
Dartnell Cl, W.Byf. KT14 234 BH112
Dartnell Ct, W.Byf. KT14 234 BJ112
Dartnell Cres, W.Byf. KT14 234 BH112
DARTNELL PARK, W.Byf. KT14 234 BJ113
Dartnell Pk Rd, W.Byf. KT14 234 BJ111
Dartnell Pl, W.Byf. KT14 234 BH112
Dartnell Rd, Croy. CR0 224 DT101
Dartrey Twr, SW10
off Blantyre St 40 A4
Dartrey Wk, SW10
off Blantyre St 40 A4
Dart St, W10 14 F2
Dartview Cl, Grays RM17 192 GE77
Darvel Cl, Wok. GU21 248 AU116
Darvell Dr, Chesh. HP5 76 AN29
Darvells Yd, Chorl. WD3 95 BD41
Darville Rd, N16 144 DT62
Darvills La, Slou. SL1 173 AR75
Darwell Cl, E6 25 L1
Darwen Pl, E2 10 E9
Darwin Cl, N11 121 DH48
Orpington BR6 245 ER106
St. Albans AL3 65 CE16
Darwin Ct, SE17 31 M9
Guildford GU1 264 AX130
Darwin Dr, Sthl. UB1 158 CB72
Darwin Gdns, Wat. WD19 116 BW50
Darwin Rd, N22 121 DP53
W5 179 CJ78
Slough SL3 175 AZ75
Tilbury RM18 193 GF81
Welling DA16 187 ET83
Darwin St, SE17 31 M8
Daryngton Dr, Grnf. UB6 159 CD68
Guildford GU1 265 BB134
Dashes, The, Harl. CM20 57 ES14
Dashwood Cl, Bexh. DA6 208 FA85
Slough SL3 174 AW77
West Byfleet KT14 234 BJ112
Dashwood Lang Rd, Add.
KT15 234 BK105
Dashwood Rd, N8 143 DM58
Gravesend DA11 213 GG89
Dassett Rd, SE27 203 DP92
Datchelor Pl, SE5
off Camberwell Church St 43 M7
DATCHET, Slou. SL3 174 AW81
Datchet 174 AV81
Datchet Cl, Hem.H. HP2 63 BP15
Datchet Pl, Datchet SL3 174 AV81
Datchet Rd, SE6 205 DZ90
Horton SL3 175 AZ83
Old Windsor SL4 174 AU84
Slough SL3 174 AT77
Windsor SL4 173 AR80
Datchet St. Mary's C of E
Prim Sch, Datchet SL3
off The Green 174 AV81
Datchworth Ct, N4
off Queens Dr 144 DQ62
Datchworth Turn, Hem.H. HP2 63 BQ20
Date St, SE17 43 L1
Daubeney Gdns, N17 122 DQ52
Daubeney Pl, Hmptn. TW12
off High St 218 CC95
Daubeney Prim Sch, E5 11 L1
Daubeney Rd, E5 11 L1
N17 122 DQ52
Daubeney Twr, SE8 33 N9
Dault Rd, SW18 202 DC86
Davall Ho, Grays RM17
off Argent St 192 GB79
Davema Cl, Chis. BR7 227 EN95
Davenant Foundation Sch,
Loug. IG10
off Chester Rd 107 EQ38
Davenant Rd, N19 143 DK61
Croydon CR0
off Duppas Hill Rd 241 DP105
Davenant St, E1 20 D7
Davenham Av, Nthwd. HA6 115 BT49
Davenies Sch, Beac. HP9
off Station Rd 111 AL53
Davenport, Ch.Lang. CM17 74 EY16
Davenport Cl, Tedd. TW11 199 CG93
Davenport Ho, SE11
off Walnut Tree Wk 30 E8
Davenport Rd, SE6 205 EB86
Sidcup DA14 208 EX89
Daventer Dr, Stan. HA7 117 CF52
Daventry Av, E17 145 EA58
Daventry Cl, Colnbr. SL3 175 BF81
Daventry Gdns, Rom. RM3 128 FJ50
Daventry Grn, Rom. RM3
off Hailsham Rd 128 FJ50
Daventry Rd, Rom. RM3 128 FJ50
Daventry St, NW1 16 C6
Davern Cl, SE10 35 L9
Davey Cl, N7 8 D5
N13 121 DM50
Davey Rd, E9 12 A6
Davey St, SE15 44 B3
David Av, Grnf. UB6 159 CE69
David Cl, Harling. UB3 177 BR80
David Dr, Rom. RM3 128 FN51
Davidge Pl, Knot.Grn HP9 110 AJ50
Davidge St, SE1 30 G5
David Lee Pt, E15 13 K9
David Livingstone Prim Sch,
Th.Hth. CR7
off Northwood Rd 224 DQ95
David Ms, SE10 46 E4
W1 16 F6
David Rd, Colnbr. SL3 175 BF82
Dagenham RM8 148 EY61
Davidson Gdns, SW8 42 A5
Davidson La, Har. HA1
off Grove Hill 139 CF59
Davidson Prim Sch, Croy.
CR0 off Dartnell Rd 224 DT101
Davidson Rd, Croy. CR0 224 DT100
Davidson Terraces, E7
off Windsor Rd 146 EH64
Davidson Way, Rom. RM7 149 FE58
Davids Rd, SE23 204 DW88
David St, E15 13 H4
David's Way, Ilf. IG6 125 ES52
David Twigg Cl, Kings.T. KT2 220 CL95
Davies Cl, Croy. CR0 224 DU100
Rainham RM13 170 FJ69
Davies Laing & Dick
Indep Coll, W1 17 H8
Davies La, E11 146 EE61
Davies La Prim Sch, E11
off Davies La 146 EF61
Davies Ms, W1 17 J10
Davies St, W1 17 J10
Hertford SG13 54 DS09
Davies Wk, Islw. TW7 179 CD81
Davies Way, Loud. HP10 110 AC54
Da Vinci Lo, SE10 35 M7
Davington Gdns, Dag. RM8 148 EV64
Davington Rd, Dag. RM8 168 EV65
Davinia Cl, Wdf.Grn. IG8
off Deacon Way 125 EM51
Davis Av, Nthflt DA11 212 GE88
Davis Cl, Sev. TN13 279 FJ122
Davis Ct, St.Alb. AL1 65 CE20
Davison Cl, Chsht EN8 89 DX28
Epsom KT19 238 CP111
Davison Dr, Chsht EN8 89 DX28
Davison Rd, Slou. SL3 175 AZ78
Davis Rd, W3 161 CT74
Aveley RM15 171 FR74
Chafford Hundred RM16 192 FZ76
Chessington KT9 238 CN105
Weybridge KT13 234 BM110
● Davis Rd Ind Pk, Chess.
KT9 238 CN105
Davis St, E13 24 B1
Davisville Rd, W12 181 CU75
Davis Way, Sid. DA14 208 EY93
Davos Cl, Wok. GU22 248 AY119
Davys Cl, Wheat. AL4 50 CL08
Davys Pl, Grav. DA12 213 GL93
Dawell Dr, Bigg.H. TN16 260 EJ117
Dawes Av, Horn. RM12 150 FK62
Isleworth TW7 199 CG85
Dawes Cl, Chesh. HP5 76 AP32
Greenhithe DA9 211 FT85
Dawes Ct, Esher KT10 236 CB105
Dawes E Rd, Burn. SL1 152 AJ70
DAWESGREEN, Reig. RH2 287 CT140
Dawes Ho, SE17 31 L9
Dawes La, Sarratt WD3 95 BE37
Dawes Moor Cl, Slou. SL2 154 AW72
Dawes Rd, SW6 38 E4
Uxbridge UB10 156 BL68
Dawes St, SE17 31 M10
Dawley, Welw.G.C. AL7 51 CZ06
Dawley Av, Uxb. UB8 157 BQ71
Dawley Ct, Hem.H. HP2 62 BM16
Dawley Grn, S.Ock. RM15 171 FU72
Dawley Par, Hayes UB3 157 BQ73
Dawley Ride, Colnbr. SL3 175 BE81
Dawley Rd, Hayes UB3 157 BR73
Uxbridge UB8 157 BQ73
Dawlish Av, N13 121 DL49
SW18 202 DB89
Perivale UB6 159 CG68
Dawlish Dr, Ilf. IG3 147 ES63
Pinner HA5 138 BY57
Ruislip HA4 137 BU61
Dawlish Prim Sch, E10
off Jesse Rd 145 EC60
Dawlish Rd, E10 145 EC61
N17 144 DU55
NW2 4 D4
Dawlish Wk, Rom. RM3 128 FJ53
Dawnay Gdns, SW18 202 DD89
Dawnay Rd, SW18 202 DC89
Bookham KT23 268 CB126
Dawnay Sch, The, Bkhm
KT23 off Griffin Way 268 CA126
Dawn Cl, Houns. TW4 178 BY83
Dawn Cres, E15 13 H8
Dawn Redwood Cl, Horton
SL3 175 BA83
Dawpool Rd, NW2 141 CT61
Daws Hill, E4 105 EC41
Daws La, NW7 119 CT50
Dawson Av, Bark. IG11 167 ES66
Orpington BR5 228 EV96
Dawson Cl, SE18 187 EQ77
Hayes UB3 157 BR71
Windsor SL4 173 AN82
Dawson Dr, Rain. RM13 169 FH66
Swanley BR8 209 FE94
Dawson Gdns, Bark. IG11 167 ET66
Dawson Hts Est, SE22 204 DU87
Dawson Pl, W2 15 J10
Dawson Rd, NW2 4 B2
Byfleet KT14 234 BK111
Kingston upon Thames KT1 220 CM97

Dawson St, E2 20 B1
Dawson Ter, N9 122 DW45
Daws Pl, Red. RH1 273 DJ131
Dax Ct, Sun. TW16
off Thames St 218 BW97
Daybrook Rd, SW19 222 DB96
Day Dr, Dag. RM8 148 EX60
Daye Mead, Welw.G.C. AL7 52 DB12
Daylesford Av, SW15 181 CU84
Daylesford Gro, Slou. SL1 173 AM75
Daylop Dr, Chig. IG7 126 EV48
Daymer Gdns, Pnr. HA5 137 BV56
Daymerslea Ridge, Lthd. KT22 253 CJ121
Days Acre, S.Croy. CR2 242 DT110
Daysbrook Rd, SW2 203 DM89
Days Cl, Hat. AL10 67 CT18
Dayseys Hill, Outwood RH1 289 DN143
Days La, Pilg.Hat. CM15 130 FU42
Sidcup DA15 207 ES87
Sch Days La Prim Sch, Sid.
DA15 off Days La 207 ET86
Days Mead, Hat. AL10 67 CT18
Dayspring, Guil. GU2 264 AV130
Dayton Dr, Erith DA8 190 FK78
Dayton Gro, SE15 44 G6
Deacon Cl, Down. KT11 251 BV119
Purley CR8 241 DL109
St. Albans AL1
off Creighton Av 65 CD24
Deacon Fld, Guil. GU2
off Cathedral Hill 264 AU133
Deacon Ms, N1 9 M7
Deacon Pl, Cat. CR3 258 DQ123
Deacon Rd, NW2 141 CU64
Kingston upon Thames KT2 220 CM95
Deacons Cl, Els. WD6 100 CN42
Pinner HA5 115 BV54
Deaconsfield Rd, Hem.H. HP3 62 BK23
Deacons Hts, Els. WD6 100 CN44
Deacons Hill, Wat. WD19 98 BW44
Deacons Hill Rd, Els. WD6 100 CM42
Deacons Leas, Orp. BR6 245 ER105
Deacons Ri, N2 142 DD57
Deacons Wk, Hmptn. TW12
off Bishops Gro 198 BZ91
● Deacon Trd Est, E4
off Cabinet Way 123 DZ51
Deacon Way, SE17 31 J8
Woodford Green IG8 125 EM52
Deadfield La, Hert. SG14 52 DF13
Deadhearn La, Ch.St.G. HP8 112 AY46
Deadman's Ash La, Sarratt WD3 96 BH36
Deakin Cl, Wat. WD18
off Chenies Way 115 BS45
Deal Av, Slou. SL1 153 AM72
Deal Ms, W5 179 CK77
Deal Porters Way, SE16 33 H6
Deal Rd, SW17 202 DG93
Deals Gateway, SE13 46 B6
Deal St, E1 20 C6
Dealtry Rd, SW15 181 CW84
Deal Wk, SW9 42 E5
Deanacre Cl, Chal.St.P. SL9 112 AY51
Dean Av, Hodd. EN11 71 DX17
DEAN BOTTOM, Dart. DA4 231 FV97
Dean Bradley St, SW1 30 A7
Dean Cl, E9 11 H2
SE16 33 K3
Uxbridge UB10 156 BM66
Windsor SL4 173 AK83
Woking GU22 249 BE115
Dean Ct, SW8
off Thorncroft St 42 A5
Wembley HA0 139 CH62
Deancroft Rd, Chal.St.P. SL9 112 AY51
Deancross St, E1 20 G9
Dean Dr, Stan. HA7 118 CL54
Deane Av, Ruis. HA4 138 BW64
Deane Cft Rd, Pnr. HA5 137 BV58
Deanery Cl, N2 142 DE56
Deanery Ms, W1 29 H2
Deanery Rd, E15 13 J5
Crockham Hill TN8 277 EQ134
Deanery St, W1 29 H2
Sch Deanesfield Prim Sch, Ruis.
HA4 off Queens Wk 138 BX63
Deane Way, Ruis. HA4 137 BV58
Dean Farrar St, SW1 29 N6
Dean Fld, Bov. HP3 79 BA27
Dean Gdns, E17 145 ED56
W13 off Northfield Av 159 CH74
Deanhill Ct, SW14 180 CP84
Deanhill Rd, SW14 180 CP84
Dean Ho, E1 off Tarling St 20 G9
N16 off Stamford Hill 144 DT60
Dean La, EC4
off New Fetter La 18 F8
Redhill RH1 257 DH123
Dean Moore Cl, St.Alb. AL1 65 CD21
Dean Oak La, Leigh RH2 287 CW144
Dean Rd, NW2 4 A5
SE28 168 EU73
Croydon CR0 242 DR105
Hampton TW12 198 CA92
Hounslow TW3 198 CB85
Dean Ryle St, SW1 30 A8
Deansbrook Cl, Edg. HA8 118 CQ51
Sch Deansbrook Inf Sch, NW7
off Hale Dr 118 CQ51
Sch Deansbrook Jun Sch,
NW7 off Hale Dr 118 CQ51
Deansbrook Rd, Edg. HA8 118 CQ52
Deans Bldgs, SE17 31 L9
Deans Cl, W4 180 CP79
Abbots Langley WD5 81 BR32
Amersham HP6 94 AT37
Dean's Cl, Croy. CR0 224 DT104
Deans Cl, Edg. HA8 118 CQ51
Stoke Poges SL2 154 AV67
Walton on the Hill KT20 255 CV124
Deans Ct, EC4 19 H9
Deanscroft Av, NW9 140 CQ61
Deans Dr, N13 121 DP51
Edgware HA8 118 CR50
● Deans Factory Est, Rain.
RM13 off Lambs La N 170 FK70
Deansfield, Cat. CR3 274 DT125
Sch Deansfield Prim Sch, SE9
off Dairsie Rd 187 EN83
Deans Gdns, St.Alb. AL4 65 CG16
Dean's Gate Cl, SE23 205 DX90
Deans La, W4 off Deans Cl 180 CP79
Edgware HA8 118 CQ51
Nutfield RH1 273 DN133
Walton on the Hill KT20 255 CV124
Deans Ms, W1 17 K8
Deans Rd, W7 159 CF74
South Merstham RH1 273 DJ130
Sutton SM1 222 DB104
Warley CM14 130 FV49
Dean Stanley St, SW1 30 A7
Dean St, E7 13 N2
W1 17 N8
Deans Wk, Couls. CR5 257 DN118
Deansway, N2 142 DD56
N9 122 DS48
Chesham HP5 76 AP29
Deans Way, Edg. HA8 118 CQ50
Deansway, Hem.H. HP3 62 BM23
Dean's Yd, SW1 29 P6
Dean Trench St, SW1 30 A7
Dean Wk, Bkhm KT23 268 CB126
Edgware HA8
off Deansbrook Rd 118 CQ51
Deanway, Ch.St.G. HP8 112 AU48
Dean Way, Sthl. UB2 178 CB75
Dean Wd Rd, Jordans HP9 111 AR52
Dearne Cl, Stan. HA7 117 CG50
De'Arn Gdns, Mitch. CR4 222 DE97
Dearsley Ho, Rain. RM13 169 FD68
Dearsley Rd, Enf. EN1 104 DU41
Deason St, E15 12 F9
De Barowe Ms, N5 9 H1
DEBDEN, Loug. IG10 107 ER41
⊖ Debden 107 EQ42
Debden Cl, NW9 off Kenley Av 118 CS54
Kingston upon Thames
KT2 199 CK92
Woodford Green IG8 124 EJ52
DEBDEN GREEN, Loug. IG10 107 EQ38
Debden Grn, Loug. IG10 107 EP38
Debden La, Loug. IG10 107 EP38
Sch Debden Pk High Sch, Loug.
IG10 off Willingale Rd 107 ER40
Debden Rd, Loug. IG10 107 EP38
Debden Wk, Horn. RM12 169 FH65
De Beauvoir, N1
off Tottenham Rd 9 P5
De Beauvoir Cres, N1 9 N8
De Beauvoir Est, N1 9 M8
Sch De Beauvoir Prim Sch, N1 9 P5
De Beauvoir Rd, N1 9 N6
De Beauvoir Sq, N1 9 P7
DE BEAUVOIR TOWN, N1 9 M8
Debenham Rd, Chsht EN7 88 DV27
Debnams Rd, SE16 32 G9
De Bohun Av, N14 103 DH44
Sch De Bohun Prim Sch, N14
off Green Rd 103 DH43
Deborah Cl, Islw. TW7 179 CE81
Deborah Cres, Ruis. HA4 137 BR59
Debrabant Cl, Erith DA8 189 FD79
De Brome Rd, Felt. TW13 198 BW88
De Burgh Gdns, Tad. KT20 255 CX119
De Burgh Pk, Bans. SM7 256 DB115
Deburgh Rd, SW19 202 DC94
Decies Way, Stoke P. SL2 154 AU67
Decima St, SE1 31 N6
Deck Cl, SE16 33 K4
Decoy Av, NW11 141 CY57
De Crespigny Pk, SE5 43 L8
Dedswell Dr, W.Clan. GU4 266 BG128
DEDWORTH, Wind. SL4 173 AL81
Dedworth Dr, Wind. SL4 173 AL81
Sch Dedworth Grn First Sch,
Wind. SL4 off Smiths La 173 AL82
Sch Dedworth Mid Sch, Wind.
SL4 off Smiths La 173 AL82
Dedworth Rd, Wind. SL4 173 AL82
Dee, The, Hem.H. HP2 62 BM15
Dee Cl, Upmin. RM14 151 FS58
Deeley Rd, SW8 41 N6
Deena Cl, W3 160 CM72
Slough SL1 153 AL73
Deep Acres, Amer. HP6 77 AN36
Deepdale, SW19 201 CX91
Deepdale Av, Brom. BR2 226 EF98
Deepdale Cl, N11 120 DG51
Deepdene, W5 160 CM70
Potters Bar EN6 85 CX31
Deepdene Av, Croy. CR0 224 DT104
Dorking RH4, RH5 269 CJ134
Deepdene Av Rd, Dor. RH4 269 CJ134
Deepdene Cl, E11 146 EG56
Deepdene Ct, N21 103 DP44
Bromley BR2 226 EE97
Deepdene Dr, Dor. RH5 285 CJ135
Deepdene Gdns, SW2 203 DM87
Dorking RH4 285 CH135
Deepdene Pk Rd, Dor. RH5 285 CJ135
Deepdene Path, Loug. IG10 107 EN42
Deepdene Pt, SE23
off Dacres Rd 205 DX90
Deepdene Rd, SE5 184 DR84
Loughton IG10 107 EN42
Welling DA16 188 EU83
Deepdene Vale, Dor. RH4 285 CJ135
Deepdene Wd, Dor. RH5 285 CJ136
Deep Fld, Datchet SL3 174 AV80
Deepfields, Horl. RH6 290 DF146
Deepfield Way, Couls. CR5 257 DL116
Deep Pool La, Chobham GU24 232 AV114
Deeprose Cl, Guil. GU2 264 AV130
Deepwell Cl, Islw. TW7 179 CG81
Deepwood La, Grnf. UB6 159 CD69
Deerbarn Rd, Guil. GU2 264 AV133
Deerbrook Rd, SE24 203 DP88
Deer Cl, Hert. SG13 54 DT09
Deercote Ct, Chsht EN8
off Glen Luce 89 DX31
Deerdale Rd, SE24 184 DQ84
Deere Av, Rain. RM13 169 FG65
Deerfield Cl, NW9 141 CT57
Ware SG12 55 DX05
Deerhurst Cl, Felt. TW13 197 BU91
Deerhurst Cres, Hmptn H.
TW12 198 CC92
Deerhurst Rd, NW2 4 D5
SW16 203 DM92
Deerings Dr, Pnr. HA5 137 BU57
Deerings Rd, Reig. RH2 272 DB134
Deerleap Gro, E4 105 EB43
Deerleap La, Sev. TN14 246 EX113
Deerleap Rd, Westc. RH4 284 CB137
Deer Mead Ct, Rom. RM1
off Junction Rd 149 FF57
Dee Rd, Rich. TW9 180 CM84
Windsor SL4 172 AJ80
Deer Pk, Harl. CM19 73 EN18
Deer Pk Cl, Kings.T. KT2 200 CP94
Deer Pk Gdns, Mitch. CR4 222 DD97
Deer Pk Rd, SW19 222 DB96
Deer Pk Wk, Chesh. HP5 76 AS28
Deer Pk Way, Wal.Abb. EN9 105 EB36
West Wickham BR4 226 EF103
Deers Fm Cl, Wisley GU23 250 BL116
Deerswood Av, Hat. AL10 67 CV20
Deerswood Cl, Cat. CR3 258 DU124
Deeside Rd, SW17 202 DD90
Dee St, E14 22 F8
Deeves Hall La, Pot.B. EN6 84 CS33
Dee Way, Epsom KT19 238 CS110
Romford RM1 127 FE53
Defence Cl, SE28 167 ES74
H Defence Medical Rehab Cen
Headley Ct, Epsom KT18 254 CP123
Coll Defence Sch of Languages,
Seer Grn HP9 off Wilton Pk 111 AP54
Defiance Wk, SE18 37 J7
Defiant Way, Wall. SM6 241 DL108
Defoe Av, Rich. TW9 180 CN80
Defoe Cl, SE16 33 N5
SW17 202 DE93
Erith DA8 off Selkirk Dr 189 FF81
Defoe Ho, EC2
off The Barbican 19 J6
Defoe Par, Grays RM16 193 GH76
Defoe Pl, EC2
off The Barbican 19 K6
SW17 off Lessingham Av 202 DF91
Defoe Rd, N16 144 DS61
Defoe Way, Rom. RM5 126 FA51
De Frene Rd, SE26 205 DX91
De Gama Pl, E14
off Maritime Quay 34 B10
Degema Rd, Chis. BR7 207 EP92
Dehar Cres, NW9 141 CU59
★ De Havilland Aircraft Heritage
Cen, St.Alb. AL2 84 CP29
De Havilland Cl, Hat. AL10 67 CT17
Dehavilland Cl, Nthlt. UB5 158 BX69
De Havilland Ct, Ilf. IG1
off Piper Way 147 ER60
Shenley WD7
off Armstrong Gdns 84 CL32
De Havilland Dr, SE18 187 EP79
Weybridge KT13 234 BL111
Sch De Havilland Prim Sch, Hat.
AL10 off Travellers La 67 CU20
De Havilland Rd, Edg. HA8 118 CP54
Hounslow TW5 178 BW80
De Havilland Way, Abb.L. WD5 81 BT32
Stanwell TW19 196 BK86
Deimos Dr, Hem.H. HP2 62 BN17
Dekker Rd, SE21 204 DS86
Delabole Rd, Merst. RH1 273 DL129
Delacourt Rd, SE3
off Old Dover Rd 186 EH80
Delafield Ho, E1 20 D9
Delafield Rd, SE7 36 B10
Grays RM17 192 GD78
Delaford Cl, Iver SL0 155 BF72
Delaford Rd, SE16 32 F10
Delaford St, SW6 38 F4
Delagarde Rd, West. TN16 277 EQ126
Delahay Ri, Berk. HP4 60 AV17
Delamare Cres, Croy. CR0 224 DW100
Delamare Rd, Chsht EN8 89 DZ30
Delamere Ct, E17
off Hawker Pl 123 EC54
Delamere Gdns, NW7 118 CR51
Delamere Rd, SW20 221 CX95
W5 160 CL74
Borehamwood WD6 100 CP39
Hayes UB4 158 BX73
Reigate RH2 288 DB138
Delamere St, W2 15 N6
Delamere Ter, W2 15 M6
Delancey Pas, NW1 7 K9
Delancey St, NW1 7 J9
Delaporte Cl, Epsom KT17 238 CS112
De Lapre Cl, Orp. BR5 228 EX101
De Lara Way, Wok. GU21 248 AX118
Delargy Cl, Grays RM16 193 GH76
De Laune St, SE17 42 G1
Delaware Rd, W9 15 L4
Delawyk Cres, SE24 204 DQ86
Delcombe Av, Wor.Pk. KT4 221 CW102
Delderfield, Lthd. KT22 253 CK120
Delft Way, SE22
off East Dulwich Gro 204 DS85
Delhi Rd, Enf. EN1 122 DT45
Delhi St, N1 8 B9
Delia St, SW18 202 DB87
Delisle Rd, SE28 167 ES74
Delius Cl, Els. WD6 99 CJ44
Delius Gro, E15 12 G10
Dell, The, SE2 188 EU78
SE19 224 DT95
Bexley DA5 209 FE88
Brentford TW8 179 CJ79
Chalfont St. Peter SL9 112 AY51
Feltham TW14 197 BV87
Great Warley CM13 129 FV51
Greenhithe DA9 211 FV85
Hertford SG13 54 DQ12
Horley RH6 291 DH147
Northwood HA6 115 BS47
Penn HP10 110 AC46
Pinner HA5 116 BX54
Radlett WD7 99 CG36
Reigate RH2 272 DA133
St. Albans AL1 65 CG18
Tadworth KT20 255 CW121
Waltham Abbey EN9
off Greenwich Way 105 EC36
Wembley HA0 139 CH64
Woking GU21 248 AW118
Woodford Green IG8 124 EH48
Della Path, E5 144 DV62
Dellbow Rd, Felt. TW14 197 BV85
Dell Cl, E15 13 H8
Chesham HP5 76 AM29
Farnham Common SL2 133 AQ64
Fetcham KT22 253 CE123
Mickleham RH5 269 CJ127
Wallington SM6 241 DJ105
Woodford Green IG8 124 EH48
Dellcott Cl, Welw.G.C. AL8 51 CV08
Dellcut Rd, Hem.H. HP2 62 BN18
Dell Fm Rd, Ruis. HA4 137 BR57
Dellfield, Chesh. HP5 76 AN29
St. Albans AL1 65 CF21
Dellfield Av, Berk. HP4 60 AV17
Dellfield Cl, Beck. BR3 225 EC95
Berkhamsted HP4 60 AU17
Radlett WD7 99 CE35
Watford WD17 97 BU40
Dellfield Cres, Uxb. UB8 156 BJ70
Dellfield Par, Cowley UB8 156 BJ70
Dellfield Rd, Hat. AL10 67 CU18
Dell La, Epsom KT17 239 CU106
Dell Lees, Seer Grn HP9 111 AQ51
Dellmeadow, Abb.L. WD5 81 BS30
Dell Meadow, Hem.H. HP3 62 BL24
Dell Orchard, Winch.Hill HP7
off Fagnall La 110 AJ45
Dellors Cl, Barn. EN5 101 CX43
Dellow Cl, Ilf. IG2 147 ER59
Dellow St, E1 20 F10
Dell Ri, Park St AL2 82 CB26
Dell Rd, Enf. EN3 104 DW38
Epsom KT17 239 CU107
Grays RM17 192 GB77
Watford WD24 97 BU37
West Drayton UB7 176 BM76
Dells, The, Hem.H. HP3 63 BP21
Dells Cl, E4 123 EB45
Teddington TW11
off Middle La 199 CF93
Dellside, Hare. UB9 136 BJ57
Dell Side, Wat. WD24 97 BU37
Dell's Ms, SW1 29 M9
Dellsome La, Coln.Hth AL4 66 CS23
North Mymms AL9 67 CV23
Dellswood Cl, Hert. SG13 54 DS10
Dells Wd Cl, Hodd. EN11 55 DZ14
Dell Wk, N.Mal. KT3 220 CS96
Dell Way, W13 159 CJ72
Dellwood, Rick. WD3 114 BH46
Dellwood Gdns, Ilf. IG5 147 EN55
Delmar Av, Hem.H. HP2 63 BR21
Delmare Cl, SW9 183 DM84
Delmeade Rd, Chesh. HP5 76 AN32
Delme Cres, SE3 186 EH82
Delmey Cl, Croy. CR0 224 DT104
Deloraine St, SE8 46 A7
Delorme St, W6 38 C3
Delta Bungalows, Horl. RH6
off Michael Cres 290 DG150
● Delta Cen, Wem. HA0
off Mount Pleasant 160 CM67
Delta Cl, Chobham GU24 232 AT110
Worcester Park KT4 220 CS104
Delta Ct, NW2 141 CU61
Delta Dr, Horl. RH6
off Cheyne Wk 290 DG150
Delta Gain, Wat. WD19 116 BX47
Delta Gro, Nthlt. UB5 158 BX69
Delta Ho, N1 off Nile St 19 L2
● Delta Pk Ind Est, Enf. EN3 105 DZ40
Delta Rd, Chobham GU24 232 AT110
Hutton CM13 131 GD44
Woking GU21 249 BA116
Worcester Park KT4 220 CS104
Delta St, E2 20 C2
Delta Way, Egh. TW20 215 BC95
De Luci Rd, Erith DA8 189 FC78
Sch De Lucy Prim Sch, SE2
off Cookhill Rd 188 EV75
De Lucy St, SE2 188 EV77
Delvan Cl, SE18
off Ordnance Rd 187 EN80
Delvers Mead, Dag. RM10 149 FC63
Delverton Rd, SE17 43 H1
Delves, Tad. KT20 255 CX121
Delvino Rd, SW6 39 J7
De Mandeville Gate, Enf. EN1
off Southbury Rd 104 DU42
De Mel Cl, Epsom KT19 238 CP112
Demesne Rd, Wall. SM6 241 DK106
Demeta Cl, Wem. HA9 140 CQ62
De Montfort Par, SW16
off Streatham High Rd 203 DL90
De Montfort Rd, SW16 203 DL90
De Morgan Rd, SW6 39 M10
Dempster Cl, Long Dit. KT6 219 CJ102
Dempster Rd, SW18 202 DC85
Denbar Par, Rom. RM7
off Mawney Rd 149 FC56
Denberry Dr, Sid. DA14 208 EV90
Denbigh Cl, W11 15 H10
Chislehurst BR7 207 EM93
Hemel Hempstead HP2 62 BL21
Hornchurch RM11 150 FN56
Ruislip HA4 137 BT61
Southall UB1 158 BZ72
Sutton SM1 239 CZ106
Denbigh Dr, Hayes UB3 177 BQ75
Denbigh Gdns, Rich. TW10 200 CM85
Denbigh Ms, SW1 29 L9
Denbigh Pl, SW1 29 L10
Denbigh Rd, E6 24 E3
W11 15 H10
W13 159 CH73
Hounslow TW3 178 CB82
Southall UB1 158 BZ72
Denbigh St, SW1 29 L9
Denbigh Ter, W11 15 H10
Denbridge Rd, Brom. BR1 227 EM96
Denby Gra, Harl. CM17 74 EY15
Denby Rd, Cob. KT11 236 BW113
Den Cl, Beck. BR3 225 ED97
Dendridge Cl, Enf. EN1 104 DV37
Dene, The, W13 159 CH71
Abinger Hammer RH5 283 BV141
Croydon CR0 243 DX105
Sevenoaks TN13 279 FH126
Sutton SM2 239 CZ111
Wembley HA9 140 CL63
West Molesey KT8 218 BZ99
Dene Av, Houns. TW3 178 BZ83
Sidcup DA15 208 EV87
Dene Cl, E10 145 EB61
SE4 185 DY83
Bromley BR2 226 EF102
Coulsdon CR5 256 DE119
Dartford DA2 209 FE91
Guildford GU1 265 BB132
Horley RH6 290 DE146
Worcester Park KT4 221 CT103
Dene Ct, Stan. HA7 117 CJ50
Denecroft Cres, Uxb. UB10 157 BP67
Denecroft Gdns, Grays RM17 192 GD76
Dene Dr, Orp. BR6 228 EV104
Denefield Dr, Ken. CR8 258 DR115
Dene Gdns, Stan. HA7 117 CJ50
Thames Ditton KT7 219 CG103
Sch Deneholm Prim Sch, Grays
RM16 off Culford Rd 192 GC75
Dene Holm Rd, Nthflt DA11 212 GD90
Denehurst Gdns, NW4 141 CW58
W3 160 CP74
Richmond TW10 180 CN84
Twickenham TW2 199 CD87
Woodford Green IG8 124 EH49
Dene Path, S.Ock. RM15 171 FU72
Dene Pl, Wok. GU21 248 AV118
Dene Rd, N11 120 DF46
Ashtead KT21 254 CM119
Buckhurst Hill IG9 124 EK46
Dartford DA1 210 FM87
Guildford GU1 280 AY135
Northwood HA6 115 BS51
Denes, The, Hem.H. HP3
off Barnacres Rd 62 BM24
Dene St, Dor. RH4 285 CH136
Dene St Gdns, Dor. RH4 285 CH136
Denewood, New Barn. EN5 102 DC43
Denewood Cl, Wat. WD17 97 BT37
Denewood Ms, Wat. WD17 97 BT37
Denewood Rd, N6 142 DF58
Denfield, Dor. RH4 285 CH138
Denford St, SE10 35 L10
Dengie Wk, N1 9 J8
DENHAM, Uxb. UB9 136 BG62
⇌ Denham 136 BG59
★ Denham Aerodrome,
Uxb. UB9 135 BD57
Denham Av, Denh. UB9 135 BF61
Denham Cl, Denh. UB9 136 BG62
Hemel Hempstead HP2 62 BN15
Welling DA16 188 EW83
Denham Ct Dr, Denh. UB9 136 BH63
Denham Cres, Mitch. CR4 222 DF98
Denham Dr, Ilf. IG2 147 EQ58
Denham Gdn Village,
Denh. UB9 135 BF58
⇌ Denham Golf Club 135 BD59
DENHAM GREEN, Uxb. UB9 135 BE58
Denham Grn Cl, Denh. UB9 136 BG59
Denham Grn La, Denh. UB9 135 BE57
Denham La, Chal.St.P. SL9 113 BA53
Denham Lo, Denh. UB9 156 BJ65
● Denham Media Pk,
Denh. UB9 136 BG57
Denham Rd, N20 120 DF48
Denham UB9 155 BE65
Egham TW20 195 BA91
Epsom KT17 239 CT112
Feltham TW14 198 BW86
Iver SL0 155 BD67
Jct Denham Rbt, Uxb. UB9 136 BG63
Denham St, SE10 35 N10
Sch Denham Village Inf Sch, Denh.
UB9 off Cheapside La 135 BF61
Denham Wk, Chal.St.P. SL9 113 AZ51
Denham Way, Bark. IG11 167 ES67
Borehamwood WD6 100 CR39
Denham UB9 136 BG62
Maple Cross WD3 113 BE50
Denholme Rd, W9 15 H2
Denholme Wk, Rain. RM13
off Ryder Gdns 169 FF65
Denholm Gdns, Guil. GU4 265 BA131
Denison Cl, N2 142 DC55
Denison Rd, SW19 202 DD93
W5 159 CJ70
Feltham TW13 197 BT91
Deniston Av, Bex. DA5 208 EY88
Denis Way, SW4 41 P10
Denleigh Gdns, N21 121 DN46
Thames Ditton KT7 219 CE100
Denman Dr, NW11 142 DA57
Ashford TW15 197 BP93
Claygate KT10 237 CG106
Denman Dr N, NW11 142 DA57
Denman Dr S, NW11 142 DA57
Denman Pl, W1
off Great Windmill St 29 N1
Denman Rd, SE15 44 A7
Denman St, W1 29 N1
Denmark Av, SW19 201 CY94
Denmark Ct, Mord. SM4 222 DA99
Denmark Gdns, Cars. SM5 222 DF104
Denmark Gro, N1 8 E10
⇌ Denmark Hill 43 L9
Denmark Hill, SE5 43 L7
Denmark Hill Dr, NW9 141 CT56
Denmark Hill Est, SE5 184 DR84
Denmark Pl, E3 22 B2
WC2 17 P8
Denmark Rd, N8 143 DN56
NW6 15 H1
SE5 43 J7
SE25 224 DU99
SW19 201 CX93
W13 159 CH73
Bromley BR1 226 EH95
Carshalton SM5 222 DF104
Guildford GU1 280 AY135
Kingston upon Thames KT1 220 CL97
Twickenham TW2 199 CD90
Denmark St, E11
off High Rd Leytonstone 146 EE62
E13 24 A6
N17 122 DV53
WC2 17 P9
Watford WD17 97 BV40
Denmark Ter, N2
off Fortis Grn 142 DF55
Denmark Wk, SE27 204 DQ91
Denmead Cl, Ger.Cr. SL9 134 AY59
Denmead Ho, SW15
off Highcliffe Dr 201 CT86
Denmead Rd, Croy. CR0 223 DP102
Sch Denmead Sch, Hmptn. TW12
off Wensleydale Rd 198 CB94
Dennan Rd, Surb. KT6 220 CM102
Dennard Way, Farnboro. BR6 245 EP105
Denner Rd, E4 123 EA47
Denne Ter, E8 10 B9
Dennett Rd, Croy. CR0 223 DN102
Dennetts Gro, SE14 45 J8
Dennettsland Rd, Crock.H. TN8 277 EQ134
Dennetts Rd, SE14 45 H7
Denning Av, Croy. CR0 241 DN105
Denning Cl, NW8 15 P2
Hampton TW12 198 BZ93
Denning Ms, SW12 202 DG86
Denning Pt, E1 20 A8
Denning Rd, NW3 142 DD63
Dennington Cl, E5
off Detmold Rd 144 DV61
Dennington Pk Rd, NW6 5 K4
Denningtons, The, Wor.Pk. KT4 220 CS103
Dennis Av, Wem. HA9 140 CM64
Dennis Cl, Ashf. TW15 197 BR94
Redhill RH1 272 DE132
Dennises La, S.Ock. RM15 171 FU66
Upminster RM14 171 FS67
Dennis Gdns, Stan. HA7 117 CJ50
Dennis La, Stan. HA7 117 CH48
Dennison Pt, E15 12 F7
Dennis Pk Cres, SW20 221 CY95
Dennis Reeve Cl, Mitch. CR4 222 DF95
Dennis Rd, E.Mol. KT8 218 CC98

Dennis Rd, Gravesend DA11 213 GG90
Dennis Way, Guil. GU1 264 AY129
Slough SL1 153 AK73
Denny Av, Wal.Abb. EN9 89 ED34
Denny Cl, E6 24 G7
Denny Cres, SE11 30 F9
Denny Gdns, Dag. RM9
off Canonsleigh Rd 168 EV66
Denny Gate, Chsht EN8 89 DZ27
Denny Rd, N9 122 DV46
Slough SL3 175 AZ77
Dennys La, Berk. HP4 60 AT21
Denny St, SE11 30 F10
De Novo Pl, St.Alb. AL1
off Granville Rd 65 CF20
Den Rd, Brom. BR2 225 ED97
Densham Dr, Pur. CR8 241 DN114
Densham Rd, E15 13 K8
Densley Cl, Welw.G.C. AL8 51 CX07
Densole Cl, Beck. BR3 225 DY95
Densworth Gro, N9 122 DW47
Dent Cl, S.Ock. RM15 171 FU72
DENTON, Grav. DA12 213 GL87
Denton, NW1 7 H5
Denton Cl, Barn. EN5 101 CW43
Redhill RH1 288 DG139
Denton Ct Rd, Grav. DA12 213 GL87
Denton Gro, Walt. KT12 218 BX103
Denton Rd, N8 143 DM57
N18 122 DS49
Bexley DA5 209 FE89
Dartford DA1 209 FE88
Twickenham TW1 199 CK86
Welling DA16 188 EW80
Denton St, SW18 202 DB86
Gravesend DA12 213 GL87
Denton Ter, Bex. DA5
off Denton Rd 209 FE89
Denton Way, E5 145 DX62
Woking GU21 248 AT118
Dents Gro, Lwr Kgswd KT20 271 CZ128
Dents Rd, SW11 202 DF86
Denvale Wk, Wok. GU21 248 AU118
Denver Cl, Petts Wd BR6 227 ES100
● **Denver Ind Est**, Rain. RM13 169 FF71
Denver Rd, N16 144 DS59
Dartford DA1 209 FG87
Denyer St, SW3 28 D9
Denziloe Av, Uxb. UB10 157 BP69
Denzil Rd, NW10 141 CT64
Guildford GU2 280 AV135
Deodar Rd, SW15 181 CY84
Deodora Cl, N20 120 DE48
★ **Department for Environment, Food & Rural Affairs (Defra)**, SW1 30 A7
★ **Department for Transport (DfT)**, SW1 29 P8
★ **Department of Energy & Climate Change (DECC)** SW1 30 A3
★ **Department of Health**, SW1 30 A4
De Paul Way, Brwd. CM14 130 FV46
Depot App, NW2 141 CX63
Depot Rd, W12 14 B10
Epsom KT17 238 CS113
Hounslow TW3 179 CD83
DEPTFORD, SE8 45 P1
⇌ **Deptford** 46 A4
DLR **Deptford Bridge** 46 B6
Deptford Br, SE8 46 B6
Deptford Bdy, SE8 46 A6
Deptford Ch St, SE8 46 B3
Deptford Ferry Rd, E14 34 B9
Deptford Grn, SE8 46 B3
Sch **Deptford Grn Sch**, Lwr Sch, SE14 45 M4
Upr Sch, SE14 45 N4
Deptford High St, SE8 46 A3
Sch **Deptford Pk Prim Sch**, SE8 33 M10
Deptford Strand, SE8 33 P9
● **Deptford Trd Est**, SE8 45 L2
Deptford Wf, SE8 33 N8
De Quincey Ho, SW1
off Lupus St 41 L1
De Quincey Ms, E16 35 P2
De Quincey Rd, N17 122 DR53
Derby Arms Rd, Epsom KT18 255 CT117
Derby Av, N12 120 DC50
Harrow HA3 117 CD53
Romford RM7 149 FC58
Upminster RM14 150 FM62
Derby Cl, Epsom KT18 255 CV119
Derby Ct, E5 *off Overbury St* 145 DX63
Derby Gate, SW1 30 A4
Derby Hill, SE23 204 DW89
Derby Hill Cres, SE23 204 DW89
Derby Ho, SE11
off Walnut Tree Wk 30 E8
Derby Rd, E7 166 EJ66
E9 11 J8
E18 124 EF53
N18 122 DW50
SW14 180 CP84
SW19 202 DA94
Croydon CR0 223 DP103
Enfield EN3 104 DV43
Grays RM17 192 GB78
Greenford UB6 158 CB67
Guildford GU2 264 AT134
Hoddesdon EN11 71 ED19
Hounslow TW3 178 CB84
Surbiton KT5 220 CN102
Sutton SM1 239 CZ107
Uxbridge UB8 156 BJ68
Watford WD17 98 BW41
Derby Rd Br, Grays RM17 192 GB79
● **Derby Rd Ind Est**, Houns. TW3 *off Derby Rd* 178 CB84
Derbyshire St, E2 20 D3
Derby Sq, The, Epsom KT19
off High St 238 CR113
Derby Stables Rd, Epsom KT18 254 CS117
Derby St, W1 29 H3
Dereham Pl, EC2 19 P3
Romford RM5 127 FB51
Dereham Rd, Bark. IG11 167 ET65
Derehams Av, Loud. HP10 110 AC52
Derehams La, Loud. HP10 110 AC53
Derek Av, Epsom KT19 238 CN106
Wallington SM6 241 DH105
Wembley HA9 160 CP66
Derek Cl, Ewell KT19 238 CP106
Derek Walcott Cl, SE24
off Shakespeare Rd 183 DP84
Derham Gdns, Upmin. RM14 150 FQ62
Deri Av, Rain. RM13 169 FH70
Dericote St, E8 10 D8
Deridene Cl, Stanw. TW19 196 BL86
Derifall Cl, E6 25 K6
Dering Pl, Croy. CR0 242 DQ105
Dering Rd, Croy. CR0 242 DQ105
Dering St, W1 17 J9
Dering Way, Grav. DA12 213 GM87
Derinton Rd, SW17 202 DF91
Derley Rd, Sthl. UB2 178 BW76
Dermody Gdns, SE13 205 ED85
Dermody Rd, SE13 205 ED85
Deronda Rd, SE24 203 DP88
De Ros Pl, Egh. TW20 195 BA93
Deroy Cl, Cars. SM5 240 DF107
Derrick Av, S.Croy. CR2 242 DQ110
Derrick Gdns, SE7
off Anchor And Hope La 36 C7
Derrick Rd, Beck. BR3 225 DZ97
Derry Av, S.Ock. RM15 171 FU72
Derrydown, Wok. GU22 248 AW121
DERRY DOWNS, Orp. BR5 228 EX100
Derry Downs, Orp. BR5 228 EW100
Derry Leys, Hat. AL10 66 CS16
Derry Rd, Croy. CR0 223 DL104
Derry St, W8 27 L5
Dersingham Av, E12 147 EN64
Sch **Dersingham Inf Sch**, E12
off Dersingham Av 147 EN64
Dersingham Rd, NW2 141 CY62
Derwent Av, N18 122 DR50
NW7 118 CR50
NW9 140 CS57
SW15 200 CS91
Barnet EN4 120 DF46
Pinner HA5 116 BY51
Uxbridge UB10 136 BN62
Derwent Cl, Add. KT15 234 BK106
Amersham HP7 94 AV39
Claygate KT10 237 CE107
Dartford DA1 209 FH88
Feltham TW14 197 BT88
Watford WD25 82 BW34
Derwent Cres, N20 120 DC48
Bexleyheath DA7 188 FA82
Stanmore HA7 117 CJ54
Derwent Dr, Hayes UB4 157 BS71
Petts Wood BR5 227 ER101
Purley CR8 242 DR113
Slough SL1 152 AJ71
Derwent Gdns, Ilf. IG4 146 EL56
Wembley HA9 139 CJ59
Derwent Gro, SE22 184 DT84
Derwent Par, S.Ock. RM15 171 FU72
Derwent Ri, NW9 140 CS58
Derwent Rd, N13 121 DM49
SE20 224 DU96
SW20 221 CX100
W5 179 CJ76
Egham TW20 195 BB94
Hemel Hempstead HP3 63 BQ21
Southall UB1 158 BZ72
Twickenham TW2 198 CB86
Derwent St, SE10 35 J10
Derwent Wk, Wall. SM6 241 DH108
Sch **Derwentwater Prim Sch**, W3 *off Shakespeare Rd* 160 CQ74
Derwentwater Rd, W3 160 CQ74
Derwent Way, Horn. RM12 149 FH64
Derwent Yd, W5
off Northfield Av 179 CJ76
De Salis Rd, Uxb. UB10 157 BQ70
Desborough Cl, W2 15 M6
Hertford SG14 53 DP06
Shepperton TW17 216 BN101
Welwyn Garden City AL7 52 DB12
Desborough Ho, W14
off North End Rd 39 H2
Desborough St, W2 15 L6
Desenfans Rd, SE21 204 DS86
● **Deseronto Trd Est**, Slou. SL3 174 AY75
Desford Ct, Ashf. TW15
off Desford Way 196 BM89
Desford Ms, E16 23 K5
Desford Rd, E16 23 K5
Desford Way, Ashf. TW15 196 BM89
★ **Design Mus**, SE1 32 B3
Desmond Rd, Wat. WD24 97 BT36
Desmond St, SE14 45 M3
Desmond Tutu Dr, SE23
off St. Germans Rd 205 DY88
De Soissons Cl, Welw.G.C. AL8 51 CV11
Despard Rd, N19 143 DJ60
Sch **De Stafford Sch**, Cat. CR3
off Burntwood La 258 DT121
Desvignes Dr, SE13 205 ED86
De Tany Ct, St.Alb. AL1 65 CD21
Detillens La, Oxt. RH8 276 EG129
Detling Cl, Horn. RM12 150 FJ64
Detling Rd, Brom. BR1 206 EG92
Erith DA8 189 FD80
Northfleet DA11 212 GD88
Detmold Rd, E5 144 DW61
Deva Cl, St.Alb. AL3 64 CA22
Devalls Cl, E6 25 M10
Devana End, Cars. SM5 222 DF104
Devane Way, SE27 203 DP90
Devas Rd, SW20 221 CW95
Devas St, E3 22 D4
Devenay Rd, E15 13 L7
Devenish Rd, SE2 188 EU75
Deventer Cres, SE22 204 DS85
Deveraux Cl, Beck. BR3 225 EC99
De Vere Cl, Wall. SM6 241 DL108
De Vere Gdns, W8 27 N5
Ilford IG1 147 EM61
Deverell St, SE1 31 L7
De Vere Ms, W8 27 N6
Devereux Ct, WC2 18 E9
Devereux Dr, Wat. WD17 97 BS38
Devereux La, SW13 181 CV80
Devereux Rd, SW11 202 DF86
Grays RM16 192 FZ76
Windsor SL4 173 AR82
De Vere Wk, Wat. WD17 97 BS40
Deverill Ct, SE20 224 DW95
Deverills Way, Slou. SL3 175 BC77
Deveron Gdns, S.Ock. RM15 171 FU71
Deveron Way, Rom. RM1 127 FE53
Devey Cl, Kings.T. KT2 200 CS94
Devils La, Egh. TW20 195 BD94
Devil's La, Hert. SG13 69 DP21
Devitt Cl, Ashtd. KT21 254 CN116
Devizes St, N1 9 M9
Devoil Cl, Guil. GU4 265 BB130
Devoke Way, Walt. KT12 218 BX103
Devon Av, Slou. SL1 153 AQ72
Devon Av, Twickenham TW2 198 CC88
Devon Bk, Guil. GU2
off Portsmouth Rd 280 AW137
Devon Cl, N17 144 DT55
Buckhurst Hill IG9 124 EH47
Kenley CR8 258 DT116
Perivale UB6 159 CJ67
Devon Ct, Buck.H. IG9
off Chequers 124 EH46
St. Albans AL1 65 CE21
Sutton at Hone DA4 230 FP95
Devon Cres, Red. RH1 272 DD134
Devoncroft Gdns, Twick. TW1 199 CG87
Devon Gdns, N4 143 DP58
Devonhurst Pl, W4
off Heathfield Ter 180 CR78
Devonia Gdns, N18 122 DQ51
Devonia Rd, N1 9 H10
Devon Mans, SE1
off Tooley St 32 A4
Devon Mead, Hat. AL10
off Chipmunk Chase 66 CR16
Devonport Gdns, Ilf. IG1 147 EM58
Devonport Ms, W12
off Devonport Rd 161 CV74
Devonport Rd, W12 181 CV75
Devonport St, E1 21 J9
Devon Ri, N2 142 DD56
Devon Rd, Bark. IG11 167 ES67
Hersham KT12 236 BW105
South Merstham RH1 273 DJ130
Sutton SM2 239 CY109
Sutton at Hone DA4 230 FP95
Watford WD24 98 BX39
Devons Est, E3 22 D3
Devonshire Av, Amer. HP6 77 AP37
Box Hill KT20 270 CQ131
Dartford DA1 209 FH86
Sutton SM2 240 DC108
Woking GU21 233 BC114
● **Devonshire Business Cen**, Pot.B. EN6 85 CY30
● **Devonshire Business Pk**, Borwd. WD6 100 CR41
Devonshire Cl, E15 13 K1
N13 121 DN49
W1 17 J6
Amersham HP6 77 AQ37
Farnham Royal SL2 153 AP68
Devonshire Cres, NW7 119 CX52
Devonshire Dr, SE10 46 C5
Long Ditton KT6 219 CK102
Devonshire Gdns, N17 122 DQ51
N21 122 DQ45
W4 180 CQ80
Devonshire Grn, Farn.Royal SL2 153 AP68
Devonshire Gro, SE15 44 F3
Devonshire Hill La, N17 122 DQ51
Sch **Devonshire Hill Prim Sch**, N17 *off Weir Hall Rd* 122 DR51
Devonshire Ho, SE1
off Bath Ter 31 J6
Sutton SM2
off Devonshire Av 240 DC108
Sch **Devonshire Ho Prep Sch**, NW3 5 P2
Devonshire Ms, SW10
off Park Wk 40 A2
W4 180 CS78
Devonshire Ms N, W1 17 J6
Devonshire Ms S, W1 17 J6
Devonshire Ms W, W1 17 J5
Devonshire Pas, W4 180 CS78
Devonshire Pl, NW2 142 DA62
W1 17 H5
W8 27 L7
Devonshire Pl Ms, W1 17 H5
Sch **Devonshire Prim Sch**, Sutt. SM2 *off Devonshire Av* 240 DC108
Devonshire Rd, E16 24 B8
E17 145 EA58
N9 122 DW46
N13 121 DM49
N17 122 DQ51
NW7 119 CX52
SE9 206 EL89
SE23 204 DW88
SW19 202 DE94
W4 180 CS78
W5 179 CJ76
Bexleyheath DA6 188 EY84
Carshalton SM5 240 DG105
Croydon CR0 224 DR101
Eastcote HA5 138 BW58
Feltham TW13 198 BY90
Gravesend DA12 213 GH88
Grays RM16 192 FY77
Harrow HA1 139 CD58
Hatch End HA5 116 BZ53
Hornchurch RM12 150 FJ61
Ilford IG2 147 ER59
Orpington BR6 228 EU101
Southall UB1 158 CA71
Sutton SM2 240 DC108
Weybridge KT13 234 BN105
Devonshire Row, EC2 19 P7
Devonshire Row Ms, W1 17 K5
Devonshire Sq, EC2 19 P8
Bromley BR2 226 EH98
Devonshire St, W1 17 H6
W4 180 CS78
Devonshire Ter, W2 15 P9
Devonshire Way, Croy. CR0 225 DY103
Hayes UB4 157 BV72
DLR **Devons Road** 22 C4
Devons Rd, E3 22 B6
Devon St, SE15 44 F3
Devon Way, Chess. KT9 237 CJ106
Epsom KT19 238 CP106
Uxbridge UB10 156 BM68
Devon Waye, Houns. TW5 178 BZ80
De Walden St, W1 17 H7
Dewar Spur, Slou. SL3 175 AZ79
Dewar St, SE15 184 DU83
Dewberry Gdns, E6 24 G6
Dewberry St, E14 22 E7
Dewey La, SW2 *off Tulse Hill* 203 DN86
Dewey Path, Horn. RM12 170 FJ65
Dewey Rd, N1 8 E10
Dagenham RM10 169 FB65
Dewey St, SW17 202 DF92
Dewgrass Gro, Wal.Cr. EN8 105 DX35
Dewhurst Rd, W14 26 C6
Cheshunt EN8 88 DW29
Sch **Dewhurst St. Mary C of E Prim Sch**, Chsht EN8
off Churchgate 88 DW29
Dewlands, Gdse. RH9 274 DW131
Dewlands Av, Dart. DA2 210 FP87
Dewlands Ct, NW4 119 CX54
Dewsbury Cl, Pnr. HA5 138 BY58
Romford RM3 128 FL51
Dewsbury Ct, W4
off Chiswick Rd 180 CQ77
Dewsbury Gdns, Rom. RM3 128 FK51
Worcester Park KT4 221 CU104
Dewsbury Rd, NW10 141 CU64
Romford RM3 128 FK51
Dewsbury Ter, NW1 7 K8
Dexter Cl, Grays RM17 192 GA76
St. Albans AL1 65 CG21
Dexter Ct, SW6
off Parsons Grn La 39 J7
Dexter Ho, Erith DA18
off Kale Rd 188 EY76
Dexter Rd, Barn. EN5 101 CX44
Harefield UB9 114 BJ54
Deyncourt Gdns, Upmin. RM14 150 FQ61
Deyncourt Rd, N17 122 DQ53
Deynecourt Gdns, E11 146 EJ56
D'Eynsford Rd, SE5 43 L6
Dhonan Ho, SE1
off Longfield Est 32 B8
Diadem Ct, W1 17 N9
Dial Cl, Green. DA9 211 FW85
Dialmead, Ridge EN6
off Crossoaks La 85 CT34
Dial Wk, The, W8 27 M4
Diamedes Av, Stanw. TW19 196 BK87
Diameter Rd, Petts Wd BR5 227 EP101
Diamond Cl, Dag. RM8 148 EW60
Grays RM16 192 FZ76
Diamond Rd, Ruis. HA4 138 BX63
Slough SL1 174 AU75
Watford WD24 97 BU38
Diamond St, NW10 160 CR66
SE15 43 P5
Diamond Ter, SE10 46 F6
Diamond Way, SE8 46 B4
Diana Cl, E18 124 EH53
SE8 45 P2
Chafford Hundred RM16 192 FZ76
George Green SL3 154 AY72
Sidcup DA14 208 EY89
Diana Gdns, Surb. KT6 220 CM103
Diana Ho, SW13 181 CT81
★ **Diana Princess of Wales Mem**, W2 28 C4
Diana Rd, E17 145 DZ55
Diana Wk, Horl. RH6
off High St 291 DH148
Dianne Way, Barn. EN4 102 DE43
Dianthus Cl, SE2
off Carnation St 188 EV78
Chertsey KT16 215 BE101
Dianthus Ct, Wok. GU22 248 AX118
Diban Av, Horn. RM12 149 FH63
Diban Ct, Horn. RM12 149 FH63
Dibden Hill, Ch.St.G. HP8 112 AW49
Dibden La, Ide Hill TN14 278 FE126
Dibden St, N1 9 H8
Dibdin Cl, Sutt. SM1 222 DA104
Dibdin Ho, W9 5 L10
Dibdin Rd, Sutt. SM1 222 DA104
Diceland Rd, Bans. SM7 255 CZ116
Dicey Av, NW2 4 A2
Dickens Av, N3 120 DC53
Dartford DA1 190 FN84
Tilbury RM18 193 GH81
Uxbridge UB8 157 BP72
Dickens Cl, Chsht EN7 88 DU26
Erith DA8 189 FB80
Hayes UB3 *off Croyde Av* 177 BS77
Richmond TW10 200 CL89
St. Albans AL3 65 CD19
Dickens Ct, Hat. AL10 67 CV16
Dickens Dr, Add. KT15 233 BF107
Chislehurst BR7 207 EQ93
Dickens Est, SE1 32 C5
SE16 32 C5
Dickens Ho, NW6 15 J2
Dickens La, N18 122 DS50
Dickens Ms, EC1 18 G6
Dickenson Cl, N9 122 DU46
Dickenson Rd, N8 143 DL59
Feltham TW13 198 BW92
Dickensons La, SE25 224 DU99
Dickensons Pl, SE25 224 DU100
Dickenson Way, Ware SG12 55 DX05
Dickens Pl, Colnbr. SL3 175 BE81
Dickens Ri, Chig. IG7 125 EN48
Dickens Rd, E6 166 EK68
Gravesend DA12 213 GL88
Dickens Sq, SE1 31 K6
Dickens St, SW8 41 K8
Dickens Way, Rom. RM1 149 FE56
Dickenswood Cl, SE19 203 DP94
Dickerage La, N.Mal. KT3 220 CQ97
Dickerage Rd, Kings.T. KT1 220 CQ95
New Malden KT3 220 CQ95
● **Dicker Mill Est**, Hert. SG13 54 DR08
Dickinson Av, Crox.Grn WD3 96 BN44
Dickinson Ct, EC1
off Brewhouse Yd 19 H5
Dickinson Quay, Hem.H. HP3 80 BL25
Dickinson Sq, Crox.Grn WD3 96 BN44
Dickson, Chsht EN7 88 DT27
Dickson Fold, Pnr. HA5 138 BX56
Dickson Rd, SE9 186 EL83
Dick Turpin Way, Felt. TW14 177 BT84
Didsbury Cl, E6
off Barking Rd 167 EM67
Dieppe Cl, W14 27 H10
Digby Cres, N4 144 DQ61
Digby Gdns, Dag. RM10 168 FA67
Digby Pl, Croy. CR0 224 DT104
Digby Rd, E9 11 J3
Barking IG11 167 ET66
Digby St, E2 21 H3
Digby Wk, Horn. RM12
off Pembrey Way 170 FJ65
Digby Way, Byfleet KT14
off High Rd 234 BM112
Dig Dag Hill, Chsht EN7 88 DT27
Digdens Ri, Epsom KT18 254 CQ115
Diggon St, E1 21 J7
Dighton Ct, SE5 43 J3
Dighton Rd, SW18 202 DC85
Dignum St, N1 8 E10
Digswell Cl, Borwd. WD6 100 CN38
Digswell Hill, Welw. AL6 51 CU06
Digswell Ho, Welw.G.C. AL8 51 CX05
Digswell Ho Ms, Welw.G.C. AL8 51 CX05
Digswell La, Welw. AL6 51 CZ05
Digswell Pl, Welw.G.C. AL8 51 CW06
Digswell Ri, Welw.G.C. AL8 51 CX07
Digswell Rd, Welw.G.C. AL8 51 CY06
Digswell St, N7 8 F4
Dilhorne Cl, SE12 206 EH90
Sch **Dilkes Prim Sch**, S.Ock. RM15 *off Garron La* 171 FT72
Dilke St, SW3 40 F2
● **Dilloway Yd**, Sthl. UB2
off The Green 178 BY75
Dillwyn Cl, SE26 205 DY91
Dilston Cl, Nthlt. UB5
off Yeading La 158 BW69
Dilston Gro, SE16 32 G8
Dilston Rd, Lthd. KT22 253 CG119
Dilton Gdns, SW15 201 CU88
Dilwyn Ct, E17
off Hillyfield 123 DY54
Dimes Pl, W6 *off King St* 181 CV77
Dimmock Dr, Grnf. UB6 139 CD64
Dimmocks La, Sarratt WD3 96 BH36
Dimond Cl, E7 13 P1
Dimsdale Dr, NW9 140 CQ60
Enfield EN1 104 DU44
Slough SL2 133 AM63
Dimsdale St, Hert. SG14 54 DQ09
Dimsdale Wk, E13 13 P9
Dimson Cres, E3 22 A4
Dinant Link Rd, Hodd. EN11 71 EA16
Dingle, The, Uxb. UB10 157 BP68
Dingle Cl, Barn. EN5 101 CT44
Dingle Gdns, E14 34 B1
Dingle Rd, Ashf. TW15 197 BP92
Dingley La, SW16 203 DK89
Dingley Pl, EC1 19 K3
Dingley Rd, EC1 19 J3
Dingwall Av, Croy. CR0 224 DQ103
Dingwall Gdns, NW11 142 DA58
Dingwall Rd, SW18 202 DC87
Carshalton SM5 240 DF109
Croydon CR0 224 DR103
Dinmont St, E2 10 E10
Dinmore, Bov. HP3 79 AZ28
Dinsdale Cl, Wok. GU22 249 AZ118
Dinsdale Gdns, SE25 224 DS98
New Barnet EN5 102 DB43
Dinsdale Rd, SE3 47 L2
Dinsmore Rd, SW12 203 DH87
Dinton Rd, SW19 202 DD93
Kingston upon Thames KT2 200 CM94
Dione Rd, Hem.H. HP2
off Saturn Way 62 BM17
Diploma Av, N2 142 DE56
Diploma Ct, N2
off Diploma Av 142 DE56
Dirdene Cl, Epsom KT17 239 CT112
Dirdene Gdns, Epsom KT17 239 CT112
Dirdene Gro, Epsom KT17 238 CS112
Dirleton Rd, E15 13 L8
Dirtham La, Eff. KT24 267 BU127
Disbrowe Rd, W6 38 E3
● **Discovery Business Pk**, SE16
off St. James's Rd 32 D7
Discovery Dock Apts E, E14 34 C4
Discovery Dock Apts W, E14 34 C4
Sch **Discovery Prim Sch & Children's Cen**, SE28
off Battery Rd 167 ET74
Discovery Wk, E1 32 E1
Dishforth La, NW9 118 CS53
Disney Ms, N4 143 DP57
Disney Pl, SE1 31 K4
Disney St, SE1 31 K4
Dison Cl, Enf. EN3 105 DX39
Disraeli Cl, SE28 168 EW74
W4 *off Acton La* 180 CR76
Disraeli Ct, Slou. SL3
off Sutton Pl 175 BB79
Disraeli Gdns, SW15
off Fawe Pk Rd 181 CZ84
Disraeli Pk, Beac. HP9 111 AK50
Disraeli Rd, E7 13 P4
NW10 160 CQ68
SW15 181 CY84
W5 159 CK74
Diss St, E2 20 A2
Distaff La, EC4 19 J10
Distillery La, W6 38 B1
Distillery Rd, W6 38 B1
Distillery Wk, Brent. TW8 180 CL79
Distin St, SE11 30 E9
District Rd, Wem. HA0 139 CH64
Ditch All, SE10 46 D7
Ditchburn St, E14 34 F1
Ditches La, Cat. CR3 257 DM122
Coulsdon CR5 257 DL120
Ditches Ride, The, Loug. IG10 107 EN37
Ditchfield Rd, Hayes UB4 158 BY70
Hoddesdon EN11 55 EA14
Dittisham Rd, SE9 206 EL91
Ditton Cl, T.Ditt. KT7 219 CG101
Dittoncroft Cl, Croy. CR0 242 DS105
Ditton Gra Cl, Long Dit. KT6 219 CK102
Ditton Gra Dr, Long Dit. KT6 219 CK102
Ditton Hill, Long Dit. KT6 219 CJ102
Ditton Hill Rd, Long Dit. KT6 219 CJ102
Ditton Lawn, T.Ditt. KT7 219 CG102
Ditton Pk, Slou. SL3 174 AX78
Ditton Pk Rd, Slou. SL3 174 AY79
Ditton Pl, SE20 224 DV95
Ditton Reach, T.Ditt. KT7 219 CH100
Ditton Rd, Bexh. DA6 208 EX85
Datchet SL3 174 AX81
Slough SL3 175 AZ79
Southall UB2 178 BZ78
Surbiton KT6 220 CL102
Sch **Divine Saviour RC Prim Sch, The**, Abb.L. WD5
off Broomfield Ri 81 BR32
Divine Way, Hayes UB3 157 BR72
Divis Way, SW15
off Dover Pk Dr 201 CV86
Divot Pl, Hert. SG13 54 DV08
Dixon Clark Ct, N1 8 G5
Dixon Cl, E6 25 K8
Dixon Dr, Wey. KT13 234 BM110
Dixon Ho, W10 14 C9
Dixon Pl, W.Wick. BR4 225 EB102
Dixon Rd, SE14 45 M6
SE25 224 DS97
Dixon's All, SE16 32 E5
Dixon's Ct, Ware SG12
off Crane Mead 55 DY06

Dixons Hill Cl, N.Mymms AL9 85 CV25
Dixons Hill Rd, N.Mymms AL9 85 CU25
Dixon Way, NW10
off Church Rd 160 CS66
Dobbin Cl, Har. HA3 117 CG54
Dobb's Weir, Hodd. EN11 71 EC18
Dobb's Weir Rd, Hodd. EN11 71 ED18
Roydon CM19 71 ED18
Dobell Path, SE9
off Dobell Rd 207 EM85
Dobell Rd, SE9 207 EM85
Doble Ct, S.Croy. CR2 242 DU111
Dobree Av, NW10 161 CV66
Dobson Cl, NW6 6 A7
Dobson Rd, Grav. DA12 213 GL92
Doby Ct, EC4 19 K10
Dockers Tanner Rd, E14 34 A7
Dockett Eddy, Cher. KT16 216 BL102
Dockett Eddy La, Shep. TW17 216 BM102
Dockhead, SE1 32 B5
Dock Hill Av, SE16 33 K4
Dockland St, E16 37 L3
Dockley Rd, SE16 32 C7
● Dockley Rd Ind Est, SE16
off Rouel Rd 32 C7
Dock Rd, E16 35 M1
Barking IG11 167 EQ68
Brentford TW8 179 CK80
Grays RM17 192 GD79
Tilbury RM18 193 GF82
Dockside Rd, E16 24 F10
Dock St, E1 20 C10
Dockwell Cl, Felt. TW14 177 BU84
Sch Doctor Challoner's Gram Sch,
Amer. HP6 off Chesham Rd 77 AQ38
Sch Doctor Challoner's High Sch,
Lt.Chal. HP7 off Coke's La 94 AV40
Doctor Johnson Av, SW17 203 DH90
★ Doctor Johnson's Ho, EC4 18 F9
Doctors Cl, SE26 204 DW92
Doctors Commons Rd,
Berk. HP4 60 AV20
Doctors La, Chaldon CR3 257 DN123
Sch Doctor Triplett's C of E
Prim Sch, Hayes UB3
off Hemmen La 157 BT72
Docwra's Bldgs, N1 9 N4
Dodbrooke Rd, SE27 203 DN90
Dodd Ho, SE16
off Rennie Est 32 F9
Doddinghurst Rd, Brwd.
CM15 130 FW44
Doddington Gro, SE17 42 G2
Doddington Pl, SE17 42 G2
Dodd's Cres, W.Byf. KT14 234 BH114
Doddsfield Rd, Slou. SL2 153 AN69
Dodds La, Ch.St.G. HP8 112 AU47
Piccotts End HP2 62 BJ16
Dodd's La, Wok. GU22 234 BG114
Dodds Pk, Brock. RH3 286 CP136
Dodsley Pl, N9 122 DW48
Dodson St, SE1 30 F5
Dod St, E14 21 P8
Dodwood, Welw.G.C. AL7 52 DB10
Doebury Wk, SE18
off Prestwood Cl 188 EU79
Doel Cl, SW19 202 DC94
Doggett Rd, SE6 205 EA87
Doggetts Cl, E.Barn. EN4 102 DE43
Doggetts Fm Rd, Denh. UB9 135 BC59
Doggetts Way, St.Alb. AL1 64 CC22
Doggetts Wd Cl, Ch.St.G. HP8 94 AV42
Doggetts Wd La, Ch.St.G. HP8 94 AV41
Doghurst Av, Harling. UB3 177 BP80
Doghurst Dr, West Dr. UB7 177 BP80
Doghurst La, Chipstead CR5 256 DF120
Dog Kennel Grn, Ran.Com.
RH5 268 BX133
Dog Kennel Hill, SE22 184 DS83
Dog Kennel Hill Est, SE22 184 DS83
Sch Dog Kennel Hill Prim Sch,
SE22 43 P10
Dog Kennel La, Chorl. WD3 95 BF42
Hatfield AL10 67 CU17
Dog La, NW10 140 CS63
Dognell Grn, Welw.G.C. AL8 51 CV08
Dogwood Cl, Nthflt DA11 212 GE91
Doherty Rd, E13 23 P4
● Dokal Ind Est, Sthl. UB2
off Hartington Rd 178 BY76
Dolben St, SE1 30 G3
Dolby Rd, SW6 38 G9
Dolland St, SE11 42 D1
Dollis Av, N3 119 CZ53
Dollis Brook Wk, Barn. EN5 101 CY44
Dollis Cres, Ruis. HA4 138 BW60
DOLLIS HILL, NW2 141 CV62
⊖ Dollis Hill 141 CU64
Dollis Hill Av, NW2 141 CV62
Dollis Hill La, NW2 141 CV62
Sch Dollis Inf Sch, NW7
off Pursley Rd 119 CW52
Sch Dollis Jun Sch, NW7
off Pursley Rd 119 CW52
● Dollis Ms, N3 120 DA53
Dollis Pk, N3 119 CZ53
Dollis Rd, N3 119 CY52
NW7 119 CY52
Dollis Valley Dr, Barn. EN5 101 CZ44
Dollis Valley Grn Wk, N20
off Totteridge La 120 DC47
Barnet EN5 101 CY44
Dollis Valley Way, Barn. EN5 101 CZ44
Dolman Cl, N3
off Avondale Rd 120 DC54
Dolman Rd, W4 180 CR77
Dolman St, SW4 183 DM84
Dolphin App, Rom. RM1 149 FF56
Dolphin Cl, SE16 33 J4
SE28 168 EX72
Surbiton KT6 219 CK100
Dolphin Ct, NW11 141 CY58
Slough SL1 174 AV75
Staines-upon-Thames TW18 196 BG90
Dolphin Ct N, Stai. TW18 196 BG90
● Dolphin Est, Sun. TW16 217 BS95
Dolphin Ho, SW6
off Lensbury Ave 39 P8
SW18 off Smugglers Way 182 DB84
Dolphin La, E14 34 C1
Dolphin Pt, Purf. RM19 191 FS78
Dolphin Rd, Nthlt. UB5 158 BZ68
Slough SL1 174 AV75
Sunbury-on-Thames TW16 217 BS95
Dolphin Rd N, Sun. TW16 217 BS95
Dolphin Rd S, Sun. TW16 217 BR95
Dolphin Rd W, Sun. TW16 217 BR95
Dolphin Sq, SW1 41 M1
W4 180 CS80
Dolphin St, Kings.T. KT1 220 CL95
Dolphin Twr, SE8 45 P3
Dolphin Way, Purf. RM19 191 FS78
Dolphin Yd, St.Alb. AL1 65 CD20
Ware SG12 off East St 55 DX06
Dombey St, WC1 18 C6
Jct Dome, The, Wat. WD25 98 BW36
Dome Hill, Cat. CR3 274 DS127
Dome Hill Pk, SE26 204 DT91
Dome Hill Peak, Cat. CR3 274 DS126
Domett Cl, SE5 184 DR84
Dome Way, Red. RH1 272 DF133
Domfe Pl, E5 off Rushmore Rd 144 DW63
Domingo St, EC1 19 J4
Dominica Cl, E13 24 D1
Dominic Ct, Wal.Abb. EN9 89 EB33
● Dominion Business Pk,
N9 off Goodwin Rd 123 DX47
Dominion Cl, Houns. TW3 179 CD82
Dominion Dr, Rom. RM5 127 FB51
Dominion Ho, W13 159 CH73
Dominion Rd, Croy. CR0 224 DT101
Southall UB2 178 BY76
Dominion St, EC2 19 M6
★ Dominion Thea, W1 17 P8
Dominion Way, Rain. RM13 169 FG69
Domonic Dr, SE9 207 EP91
Domus Ct, Edg. HA8
off Fortune Ave 118 CP52
Domville Cl, N20 120 DD47
Donald Biggs Dr, Grav. DA12 213 GK87
Donald Dr, Rom. RM6 148 EW57
Donald Rd, E13 166 EH67
Croydon CR0 223 DM100
Donaldson Rd, NW6 5 H9
SE18 187 EN81
Donald Wds Gdns, Surb. KT5 220 CP103
Donato Dr, SE15 43 N3
Doncaster Dr, Nthlt. UB5 138 BZ64
Doncaster Gdns, N4 144 DQ58
Northolt UB5 138 BZ64
Doncaster Grn, Wat. WD19 116 BW50
Doncaster Rd, N9 122 DV45
Doncaster Way, Upmin. RM14 150 FM62
Doncel Ct, E4 123 ED45
Doncella Cl, Chaff.Hun. RM16 191 FX76
Donegal St, N1 18 D1
Doneraile St, SW6 38 D8
Dongola Rd, E1 21 L6
E13 24 A3
N17 144 DS55
Dongola Rd W, E13 24 A3
Sch Donhead Wimbledon Coll
Prep Sch, SW19
off Edge Hill 201 CX94
Donington Av, Ilf. IG6 147 EQ57
Donkey All, SE22 204 DU87
Donkey La, Abin.Com. RH5 284 BX143
Enfield EN1 104 DU40
Farningham DA4 230 FP103
Horley RH6 291 DK152
West Drayton UB7 176 BJ77
Donkin Ho, SE16
off Rennie Est 32 F9
Donnay Cl, Ger.Cr. SL9 134 AX58
Donne Ct, SE24 204 DQ86
Donnefield Av, Edg. HA8 118 CL52
Donne Gdns, Wok. GU22 249 BE115
Donne Pl, SW3 28 D8
Mitcham CR4 223 DH98
Donne Rd, Dag. RM8 148 EW61
Donnington Ct, NW10 161 CV66
Sch Donnington Prim Sch,
NW10 off Uffington Rd 161 CV66
Donnington Rd, NW10 161 CV66
Dunton Green TN13 263 FD120
Harrow HA3 139 CK57
Worcester Park KT4 221 CU103
Donnybrook Rd, SW16 203 DJ94
Donovan Av, N10 121 DH54
Donovan Cl, Epsom KT19 238 CR110
Donovan Ct, SW10
off Drayton Gdns 40 A1
Donovan Pl, N21 103 DM43
Don Phelan Cl, SE5 43 M6
Don Way, Rom. RM1 127 FE52
Doods Pk Rd, Reig. RH2 272 DC133
Doods Pl, Reig. RH2 272 DC133
Doods Rd, Reig. RH2 272 DC133
Doods Way, Reig. RH2 272 DD133
Doone Cl, Tedd. TW11 199 CG93
Doon St, SE1 30 E3
Dorado Gdns, Orp. BR6 228 EX104
Doral Way, Cars. SM5 240 DF106
Dorando Cl, W12 161 CV73
Doran Dr, Red. RH1 272 DD134
Doran Gdns, Red. RH1 272 DD134
Doran Gro, SE18 187 ES80
Doran Wk, E15 12 F7
Dora Rd, SW19 202 DA92
Dora St, E14 21 N8
Dora Way, SW9 42 F9
Dorcas Ct, St.Alb. AL1 65 CE21
Dorchester Av, N13 122 DQ49
Bexley DA5 208 EX88
Harrow HA2 138 CC58
Hoddesdon EN11 71 EA15
Dorchester Cl, Dart. DA1 210 FM87
Northolt UB5 138 CB64
Orpington BR5 208 EU94
Dorchester Ct, N14 121 DH45
SE24 204 DQ85
Croxley Green WD3
off Mayfare 97 BQ43
Woking GU22 249 BA116
Dorchester Dr, SE24 204 DQ85
Feltham TW14 197 BS86
Dorchester Gdns, E4 123 EA49
NW11 142 DA56
Dorchester Gro, W4 180 CS78
Dorchester Ho, Rich. TW9 180 CP80
Dorchester Ms, N.Mal. KT3
off Elm Rd 220 CR98
Twickenham TW1 199 CJ87
Sch Dorchester Prim Sch,
Wor.Pk. KT4
off Dorchester Rd 221 CW102
Dorchester Rd, Grav. DA12 213 GK90
Morden SM4 222 DB101
Northolt UB5 138 CB64
Weybridge KT13 217 BP104
Dorchester Rd, Worcester Park
KT4 221 CW102
Dorchester Way, Har. HA3 140 CM58
Dorchester Waye, Hayes UB4 158 BW72
Dorcis Av, Bexh. DA7 188 EY82
Dordrecht Rd, W3 160 CS74
Dore Av, E12 147 EN64
Doreen Av, NW9 140 CR60
Dore Gdns, Mord. SM4 222 DB101
Dorell Cl, Sthl. UB1 158 BZ71
Dorey Ho, Brent. TW8
off London Rd 179 CJ80
Doria Dr, Grav. DA12 213 GL90
Dorian Rd, Horn. RM12 149 FG60
Doria Rd, SW6 39 H8
Doric Dr, Kgswd KT20 255 CZ120
Doric Way, NW1 17 N2
Dorie Ms, N12 120 DB49
Dorien Rd, SW20 221 CX96
Dorin Ct, Warl. CR6 258 DV119
Dorincourt, Wok. GU22 249 BE115
Doris Ashby Cl, Perivale UB6 159 CG67
Doris Av, Erith DA8 189 FC81
Doris Rd, E7 13 P6
Ashford TW15 197 BR93
DORKING, RH4 & RH5 285 CH137
⇌ Dorking 269 CJ134
Coll Dorking Adult Learning Cen,
Dor. RH4 off Dene St 285 CH136
★ Dorking & District Mus,
Dor. RH4 285 CG136
● Dorking Business Pk,
Dor. RH4 285 CG135
Dorking Cl, SE8 45 N2
Worcester Park KT4 221 CX103
⇌ Dorking Deepdene 269 CJ134
Dorking Gdns, Rom. RM3 128 FK50
H Dorking Gen Hosp, Dor.
RH4 285 CG137
Dorking Glen, Rom. RM3 128 FK49
Dorking Ri, Rom. RM3 128 FK49
Dorking Rd, Abin.Ham. RH5 283 BS139
Bookham KT23 268 CB126
Chilworth GU4, GU5 281 BF139
Epsom KT18 254 CN116
Gomshall GU5 283 BR139
Leatherhead KT22 253 CH122
Romford RM3 128 FK49
Tadworth KT20 255 CX123
Dorking Wk, Rom. RM3 128 FK49
⇌ Dorking West 285 CG135
Dorkins Way, Upmin. RM14 151 FS59
Dorlcote Rd, SW18 202 DD87
Dorling Dr, Epsom KT17 239 CT112
Dorly Cl, Shep. TW17 217 BS99
Dorman Pl, N9 122 DU47
Dormans Cl, Nthwd. HA6 115 BR52
Dorman Wk, NW10 140 CQ64
Dorman Way, NW8 6 A8
● Dorma Trd Pk, E10 145 DX60
Dormay St, SW18 202 DB85
Dormer Cl, E15 13 L4
Barnet EN5 101 CX43
Dormers Av, Sthl. UB1 158 CA72
Dormers Ri, Sthl. UB1 158 CB72
DORMER'S WELLS, Sthl. UB1 158 CB73
Sch Dormers Wells High Sch, Sthl.
UB1 off Dormers Wells La 158 CA72
Sch Dormers Wells Inf & Jun
Schs, Sthl. UB1
off Dormers Wells La 158 CB73
Dormers Wells La, Sthl. UB1 158 CA72
Dormie Cl, St.Alb. AL3 64 CC18
Dormywood, Ruis. HA4 137 BT57
Dornberg Cl, SE3 47 P4
Dornberg Rd, SE3
off Banchory Rd 186 EH80
Dorncliffe Rd, SW6 38 F8
Dornels, Slou. SL2 154 AW72
DORNEY, Wind. SL4 172 AH76
Dorney, NW3 6 D6
★ Dorney Ct, Wind. SL4 172 AG77
Dorney End, Chesh. HP5 76 AN30
Dorney Gro, Wey. KT13 217 BP103
DORNEY REACH, Maid. SL6 172 AF76
Dorney Reach Rd, Dorney R.
SL6 172 AF76
Dorney Ri, Orp. BR5 227 ET98
Sch Dorney Sch, Dorney R.
SL6 off Harcourt Cl 172 AF76
Dorney Way, Houns. TW4 198 BY85
Dorney Wd Rd, Burn. SL1 133 AK63
Dornfell St, NW6 5 H3
Dornford Gdns, Couls. CR5 258 DQ119
Dornton Rd, SW12 203 DH89
South Croydon CR2 242 DR106
Dorothy Av, Wem. HA0 160 CL66
Sch Dorothy Barley Inf Sch, Dag.
RM8 off Davington Rd 148 EV64
Sch Dorothy Barley Jun Sch, Dag.
RM8 off Ivinghoe Rd 148 EV64
Dorothy Evans Cl, Bexh. DA7 189 FB84
Dorothy Gdns, Dag. RM8 148 EV63
Dorothy Rd, SW11 182 DF83
Dorrell Pl, SW9
off Brixton Rd 183 DN84
Dorriens Cft, Berk. HP4 60 AT16
Dorrien Wk, SW16 203 DK89
Dorrington Ct, SE25 224 DS96
Dorrington Gdns, Horn. RM12 150 FK60
Dorrington Pt, E3 22 C2
Dorrington St, EC1 18 E6
Dorrington Way, Beck. BR3 225 EC99
Dorrit Cres, Guil. GU3 264 AS132
Dorrit Ms, N18 122 DS49
Dorrit St, SE1 31 K4
Dorrit Way, Chis. BR7 207 EQ93
Dorrofield Cl, Crox.Grn WD3 97 BQ43
Dors Cl, NW9 140 CR60
Dorset Av, Hayes UB4 157 BS69
Romford RM1 149 FD55
Southall UB2 178 CA77
Welling DA16 187 ET84
Dorset Bldgs, EC4 18 G9
Dorset Cl, NW1 16 E6
Berkhamsted HP4 60 AT18
Hayes UB4 157 BS69
Dorset Ct, Nthlt. UB5
off Taywood Rd 158 BY70
Dorset Cres, Grav. DA12 213 GL91
Dorset Dr, Edg. HA8 118 CM51
Woking GU22 249 BB117
Dorset Est, E2 20 B2
Dorset Gdns, Mitch. CR4 223 DM98
Dorset Ho, Enf. EN3 105 DX37
Dorset Ms, N3 120 DA53
SW1 29 J6
Dorset Ri, EC4 18 G9
Dorset Rd, E7 166 EJ66
Dorset Rd, N15 144 DR56
N22 121 DL53
SE9 206 EL89
SW8 42 B4
SW19 222 DA95
W5 179 CJ76
Ashford TW15 196 BK90
Beckenham BR3 225 DX97
Harrow HA1 138 CC58
Mitcham CR4 222 DE96
Sutton SM2 240 DA110
Windsor SL4 173 AQ82
Sch Dorset Rd Inf Sch, SE9
off Dorset Rd 206 EL89
Dorset Sq, NW1 16 E5
Epsom KT19 238 CR110
Dorset St, W1 16 F7
Sevenoaks TN13
off High St 279 FJ125
Dorset Way, Byfleet KT14 234 BK110
Twickenham TW2 199 CD88
Uxbridge UB10 156 BM68
Dorset Waye, Houns. TW5 178 BZ80
Dorton Cl, SE15 43 P5
Coll Dorton Coll of Further Ed,
Seal TN15 off Seal Dr 279 FM122
Dorton Dr, Sev. TN15 279 FM122
Sch Dorton Ho Sch, Seal TN15
off Wildernesse Av 279 FM122
Dorton Way, Ripley GU23 250 BH121
Dorville Cres, W6 181 CV76
Dorville Rd, SE12 206 EF85
Dothill Rd, SE18 187 ER80
Douai Gro, Hmptn. TW12 218 CC95
Sch Douay Martyrs Sch, The, Ickhm
UB10 off Edinburgh Dr 137 BP63
Doubleday Rd, Loug. IG10 107 EQ41
Doughty Ms, WC1 18 C5
Doughty St, WC1 18 C4
Douglas Av, E17 123 EA53
New Malden KT3 221 CV98
Romford RM3 128 FL54
Watford WD24 98 BX37
Wembley HA0 160 CL66
Douglas Cl, Barn. EN4 102 DD38
Chaff.Hun. RM16 192 FY76
Ilford IG6 125 EP52
Jacobs Well GU4 264 AX128
Stanmore HA7 117 CG50
Wallington SM6 241 DL108
Douglas Ct, Cat. CR3 258 DQ122
Westerham TN16 261 EL117
Douglas Cres, Hayes UB4 158 BW70
Douglas Dr, Croy. CR0 225 EA104
Douglas Gdns, Berk. HP4 60 AT18
Douglas Ho, Chsht EN8
off Coopers Wk 89 DX28
Douglas La, Wrays. TW19 195 AZ85
Douglas Ms, NW2 141 CY62
Banstead SM7
off North Acre 255 CZ116
Douglas Path, E14 34 F10
Douglas Rd, E4 124 EE45
E16 23 P7
N1 9 J6
N22 121 DN53
NW6 4 G8
Addlestone KT15 216 BH104
Esher KT10 218 CB103
Hornchurch RM11 149 FF58
Hounslow TW3 178 CB83
Ilford IG3 148 EU58
Kingston upon Thames KT1 220 CP96
Reigate RH2 272 DA133
Slough SL2 153 AR71
Stanwell TW19 196 BK86
Surbiton KT6 220 CM103
Welling DA16 188 EV81
Douglas Sq, Mord. SM4 222 DA100
Douglas St, SW1 29 N9
Douglas Ter, E17
off Penrhyn Av 123 DZ53
Douglas Way, SE8 45 P5
Welwyn Garden City AL7 52 DC09
Doug Siddons Ct, Grays
RM17 off Elm Rd 192 GC79
Doulton Cl, Harl. CM17 74 EY16
Doulton Ho, SE11
off Lambeth Wk 30 D7
Doulton Ms, NW6 5 M4
Doultons, The, Stai. TW18 196 BG94
Dounesforth Gdns, SW18 202 DB88
Dounsell Ct, Pilg.Hat. CM15
off Ongar Rd 130 FU44
Douro Pl, W8 27 M6
Douro St, E3 12 A10
Douthwaite Sq, E1 32 D2
Dove App, E6 24 G7
Dove Cl, NW7 119 CT52
Chafford Hundred RM16 192 FY76
Northolt UB5
off Wayfarer Rd 158 BX70
South Croydon CR2 243 DX111
Wallington SM6 241 DM108
Dovecot Cl, Pnr. HA5 137 BV57
Dovecote Av, N22 143 DN55
Dovecote Barns, Purf. RM19 191 FR79
Dovecote Cl, Wey. KT13 217 BP104
Dovecote Gdns, SW14
off Avondale Rd 180 CR83
Dovecote Ho, SE16
off Canada St 33 J5
Dove Ct, EC2 19 L9
Beaconsfield HP9 111 AK52
Hatfield AL10 67 CU20
Dovedale Av, Har. HA3 139 CJ58
Ilford IG5 125 EN54
Dovedale Cl, Guil. GU4
off Weylea Av 265 BA131
Harefield UB9 114 BJ54
Welling DA16 188 EU81
Dovedale Ri, Mitch. CR4 202 DF94
Dovedale Rd, SE22 204 DV85
Dartford DA2 210 FQ88
Dovedon Cl, N14 121 DL47
Dove Ho Cres, Slou. SL2 153 AL69
Dovehouse Cft, Harl. CM20 58 EU13
Dove Ho Gdns, E4 123 EA47
Dovehouse Grn, Wey. KT13
off Rosslyn Pk 235 BR105
Dovehouse Mead, Bark. IG11 167 ER68
Dovehouse St, SW3 28 C10
Dove La, Pot.B. EN6 86 DB34
Dove Ms, SW5 27 N9
Doveney Cl, Orp. BR5 228 EW97
Dove Pk, Chorl. WD3 95 BB44
Pinner HA5 116 CA52
Dover Cl, NW2 off Brent Ter 141 CX61
Romford RM5 127 FC54
Dovercourt Av, Th.Hth. CR7 223 DN98
Dovercourt Est, N1 9 M5
Dovercourt Gdns, Stan. HA7 118 CL50
Dovercourt La, Sutt. SM1 222 DC104
Dovercourt Rd, SE22 204 DS86
Doverfield, Goffs Oak EN7 88 DQ29
Doverfield Rd, SW2 203 DL86
Guildford GU4 265 BA131
Dover Flats, SE1 31 P9
Dover Gdns, Cars. SM5 222 DF104
Dover Ho, SE5 off Cormont Rd 42 G7
Dover Ho Rd, SW15 181 CU84
Doveridge Gdns, N13 121 DP49
Dove Rd, N1 9 L4
Dove Row, E2 10 C9
Dover Pk Dr, SW15 201 CV86
Dover Patrol, SE3
off Kidbrooke Way 186 EH82
Dover Rd, E12 146 EJ61
N9 122 DW47
SE19 204 DR93
Northfleet DA11 212 GD87
Romford RM6 148 EY58
Slough SL1 153 AM72
Sch Dover Rd Comm Prim Sch,
Nthflt DA11
off Dover Rd E 212 GE88
Dover Rd E, Grav. DA11 212 GE87
Jct Dovers Cor, Rain. RM13 169 FG69
● Dovers Cor Ind Est,
Rain. RM13 169 FF70
DOVERSGREEN, Reig. RH2 288 DB139
Dovers Grn Rd, Reig. RH2 288 DB139
Sch Dovers Grn Sch, Reig.
RH2 off Rushetts Rd 288 DC138
Doversmead, Knap. GU21 248 AS116
Dover St, W1 29 K1
Dover Way, Crox.Grn WD3 97 BQ42
Dover Yd, W1 29 K2
Doves Cl, Brom. BR2 226 EL103
Doves Yd, N1 8 F9
Dovet Ct, SW8 42 C6
Doveton Rd, S.Croy. CR2 242 DR106
Doveton St, E1 20 G4
Dove Wk, SW1 28 G10
Hornchurch RM12
off Heron Flight Av 169 FH65
Dowanhill Rd, SE6 205 ED88
Dowd Cl, N11
off Nurserymans Rd 120 DG47
Dowdeswell Cl, SW15 180 CS84
Dowding Pl, Stan. HA7 117 CG51
Dowding Rd, Bigg.H. TN16 260 EK115
Uxbridge UB10 156 BM66
Dowding Wk, Nthflt DA11 212 GE90
Dowding Way, Horn. RM12 169 FH66
Leavesden WD25 81 BT34
Waltham Abbey EN9 105 ED36
Dowdney Cl, NW5 7 M3
Dower Av, Wall. SM6 241 DH109
Dower Cl, Knot.Grn HP9 110 AJ50
Dower Ct, Edg. HA8
off Penniwell Cl 118 CM49
Dower Pk, Wind. SL4 173 AL84
Dowgate Hill, EC4 19 L10
Dowland St, W10 14 F2
Dowlans Cl, Bkhm KT23 268 CA127
Dowlans Rd, Bkhm KT23 268 CB127
Dowlas Est, SE5 43 N4
Dowlas St, SE5 43 N4
Dowlerville Rd, Orp. BR6 245 ET107
Dowley Wd, Welw.G.C. AL7 52 DB10
Dowling Ct, Hem.H. HP3 62 BK23
Dowman Cl, SW19
off Nelson Gro Rd 222 DB95
Downage, NW4 141 CW55
Downage, The, Grav. DA11 213 GG89
Downalong, Bushey Hth WD23 117 CD46
Downbank Av, Bexh. DA7 189 FD81
Downbarns Rd, Ruis. HA4 138 BX62
Downbury Ms, SW18
off Merton Rd 202 DA86
Down Cl, Nthlt. UB5 157 BV68
Sch Downderry Prim Sch, Brom.
BR1 off Downderry Rd 206 EE91
Downderry Rd, Brom. BR1 205 ED90
DOWNE, Orp. BR6 245 EM111
Downe Av, Cudham TN14 245 EQ112
Downe Cl, Horl. RH6 290 DE146
Welling DA16 188 EW80
Downedge, St.Alb. AL3 64 CB19
Downe Ho, SE7
off Springfield Gro 186 EJ79
Sch Downe Manor Prim Sch,
Nthlt. UB5
off Down Way 157 BV69
Downend, SE18 off Moordown 187 EP80
Sch Downe Prim Sch, Downe
BR6 off High Elms Rd 245 EN111
Downer Dr, Sarratt WD3 96 BG36
Downer Meadow, Gdmg. GU7 280 AS143
Downe Rd, Cudham TN14 245 EQ114
Keston BR2 244 EK109
Mitcham CR4 222 DF96
Downes Cl, Twick. TW1
off St. Margarets Rd 199 CH86
Downes Ct, N21 121 DN46
Downes Rd, St.Alb. AL4 65 CH16
Downfield, Wor.Pk. KT4 221 CT102
Downfield Cl, W9 15 L5
Hertford Heath SG13 54 DW11
Sch Downfield JMI Sch, Chsht
EN8 off Downfield Rd 89 DY31
Downfield Rd, Chsht EN8 89 DY31
Hertford Heath SG13 54 DW09
Downfields, Welw.G.C. AL8 51 CV11
Downhall Rd, Hat.Hth CM22 59 FH08
Down Hall Rd, Kings.T. KT2 219 CK95
Downhall Rd, Match.Grn CM17 59 FH08
DOWNHAM, Brom. BR1 206 EF92
Downham Cl, Rom. RM5 126 FA52
Downham La, Brom. BR1 205 ED92
Downham Rd, N1 9 L7
Downham Way, Brom. BR1 205 ED92
Downhills Av, N17 144 DR55
Downhills Pk Rd, N17 144 DQ55
Sch Downhills Prim Sch, N15
off Philip La 144 DR56
Downhills Way, N17 144 DQ55
★ Down Ho - Darwin Mus,
Orp. BR6 245 EN112
Downhurst Av, NW7 118 CR50
Downing Av, Guil. GU2 280 AT135
Downing Cl, Har. HA2 138 CC55
Downing Ct, Borwd. WD6
off Bennington Dr 100 CM39
Downing Dr, Grnf. UB6 159 CD67
Downing Path, Slou. SL2 153 AL70
Downing Rd, Dag. RM9 168 EZ67

Downings, E6 25 M8
Downings Rds Moorings, SE1
off Mill St 32 C4
Downing St, SW1 30 A4
Downings Wd, Map.Cr. WD3 113 BD50
Downland Cl, N20 120 DC46
Coulsdon CR5 241 DH114
Epsom KT18 255 CV118
Downland Gdns, Epsom KT18 255 CV118
Downlands, Wal.Abb. EN9 90 EE34
Downlands Rd, Pur. CR8 241 DL113
Downland Way, Epsom KT18 255 CV118
Downleys Cl, SE9 206 EL89
Downman Rd, SE9 186 EL83
Down Pl, W6 181 CV77
Water Oakley SL4 172 AG79
Down Rd, Guil. GU1 265 BB134
Teddington TW11 199 CH93
Downs, The, SW20 201 CX94
Harlow CM20 73 ES15
Hatfield AL10 67 CU20
Leatherhead KT22 269 CJ125
Downs Av, Chis. BR7 207 EM92
Dartford DA1 210 FN87
Epsom KT18 238 CS114
Pinner HA5 138 BZ58
Downs Br Rd, Beck. BR3 225 ED95
Downsbury Ms, SW18
off Merton Rd 202 DA85
Downs Ct, Sutt. SM2 240 DB111
Downs Ct Rd, Pur. CR8 241 DP112
Sch Downsell Prim Sch, E15
off Downsell Rd 145 ED63
Downsell Rd, E15 12 F1
Sch Downsend Sch,
Lthd. KT22
off Leatherhead Rd 253 CK120
Downsfield, Hat. AL10
off Sandifield 67 CV21
Downsfield Rd, E17 145 DY58
Downshall Av, Ilf. IG3 147 ES58
Sch Downshall Prim Sch,
Seven Kings IG3
off Meads La 147 ES59
Downs Hill, Beck. BR3 205 ED94
Southfleet DA13 212 GC94
Downs Hill Rd, Epsom KT18 238 CS114
Downshire Hill, NW3 6 B1
Downs Ho Rd, Epsom KT18 255 CT118
DOWNSIDE, Cob. KT11 251 BV118
Downside, Cher. KT16 215 BF102
Epsom KT18 238 CS114
Hemel Hempstead HP2 62 BL19
Sunbury-on-Thames TW16 217 BU95
Twickenham TW1 199 CF90
Downside Br Rd, Cob. KT11 251 BV115
Downside Cl, SW19 202 DC93
Downside Common, Down.
KT11 251 BV118
Downside Common Rd,
Down. KT11 251 BV118
Downside Cres, NW3 6 D3
W13 159 CG70
Downside Orchard, Wok.
GU22 off Park Rd 249 BA117
Downside Rd, Down. KT11 251 BV116
Guildford GU4 281 BB135
Sutton SM2 240 DD107
Downside Wk, Brent. TW8
off Sidney Gdns 179 CJ79
Northolt UB5 158 BZ69
Downsland Dr, Brwd. CM14 130 FW48
Downs La, E5 off Downs Rd 144 DV63
Hatfield AL10 67 CU20
Leatherhead KT22 253 CH123
Downs Pk Rd, E5 10 D2
E8 10 B2
Sch Downs Prim Sch & Nurs,
The, Harl. CM20
off The Hides 73 ES15
Downs Rd, E5 144 DU63
Beckenham BR3 225 EB96
Coulsdon CR5 257 DK118
Dorking RH5 269 CJ128
Enfield EN1 104 DS42
Epsom KT18 254 CS115
Istead Rise DA13 212 GD91
Purley CR8 241 DP111
Slough SL3 174 AX75
Sutton SM2 240 DB110
Thornton Heath CR7 224 DQ95
Downs Side, Sutt. SM2 239 CZ111
Down St, W1 29 J3
West Molesey KT8 218 CA99
Down St Ms, W1 29 J3
Downs Vw, Dor. RH4 269 CJ134
Isleworth TW7 179 CF81
Tadworth KT20 255 CV121
Downsview Av, Wok. GU22 249 AZ121
Downsview Cl, Down. KT11 251 BV119
Downs Vw Cl, Orp. BR6 246 EW110
Downsview Cl, Swan. BR8 229 FF97
Downsview Ct, Guil. GU1
off Hazel Av 264 AW130
Downsview Gdns, SE19 203 DP94
Dorking RH4 285 CH137
Sch Downsview Prim Sch,
SE19 off Biggin Way 204 DQ94
Swanley BR8 off Beech Av 229 FG97
Downsview Rd, SE19 204 DQ94
Downs Vw Rd, Bkhm KT23 268 CC126
Downsview Rd, Sev. TN13 278 FF125
Sch Downsview Sch, E5
off Downs Rd 144 DV63
Downs Way, Bkhm KT23 268 CC126
Epsom KT18 255 CT116
Downsway, Guil. GU1 265 BD134
Orpington BR6 245 ES106
Downs Way, Oxt. RH8 276 EE127
Downsway, S.Croy. CR2 242 DS111
Downs Way, Tad. KT20 255 CV121
Downsway, Whyt. CR3 258 DT116
Downsway, The, Sutt. SM2 240 DC109
Downs Way Cl, Tad. KT20 255 CU121
Sch Downs Way Sch, Oxt.
RH8 off Downs Way 276 EE128
Downs Wd, Epsom KT18 255 CV117
Downswood, Reig. RH2 272 DE131
Downton Av, SW2 203 DL89
Downtown Rd, SE16 33 M4
Down Way, Nthlt. UB5 157 BV69
Dowrey St, N1 8 E8
Dowry Wk, Wat. WD17 97 BT38
Dowsett Rd, N17 122 DT54
Dowson Cl, SE5 184 DR84
Doyce St, SE1 31 J4
Doyle Cl, Erith DA8 189 FE81
Doyle Gdns, NW10 161 CU67
Doyle Rd, SE25 224 DU98
Doyle Way, Til. RM18
off Coleridge Rd 193 GJ82
D'Oyley St, SW1 28 G8
D'Oyly Carte Island, Wey.
KT13 217 BP102
Doynton St, N19 143 DH61
Draco Gate, SW15 38 A10
Draco St, SE17 43 J2
Dragonfly Cl, E13 24 B2
Dragon La, Wey. KT13 234 BN110
Dragon Rd, SE15 43 N3
Hatfield AL10 66 CS17
Dragoon Rd, SE8 45 N1
Dragor Rd, NW10 160 CQ70
Drake Av, Cat. CR3 258 DQ122
Slough SL3 174 AX77
Staines-upon-Thames TW18 195 BF92
Drake Cl, SE16 33 K4
Barking IG11 168 EU70
Warley CM14 130 FX50
Drake Ct, SE19 204 DT92
W12 26 A5
Harrow HA2 138 BZ60
Drake Cres, SE28 168 EW72
Drakefell Rd, SE4 45 J9
SE14 45 J9
Drakefield Rd, SW17 202 DG90
Drake Ho, SW8
off St. George Wf 42 A1
Drakeley Ct, N5 143 DP63
Drake Ms, Brom. BR2 226 EJ98
Hornchurch RM12
off Fulmar Rd 169 FG66
Drake Rd, SE4 46 A10
Chafford Hundred RM16 192 FY76
Chessington KT9 238 CN106
Croydon CR0 223 DM101
Harrow HA2 138 BZ61
Horley RH6 290 DE148
Mitcham CR4 222 DG100
Drakes, The, Denh. UB9
off Patrons Way E 135 BF58
Drakes Cl, Chsht EN8 89 DX28
Esher KT10 236 CA106
Drakes Ctyd, NW6 5 H6
Drakes Dr, Nthwd. HA6 115 BP53
St. Albans AL1 65 CH23
Drakes Dr Mobile Home Pk,
St.Alb. AL1 off Drakes Dr 65 CH22
Drakes Meadow, Harl. CM17 58 EY11
Drakes Rd, Amer. HP7 77 AR39
Drake St, WC1 18 C7
Enfield EN2 104 DR39
Drakes Wk, E6 167 EM67
Drakes Way, Hat. AL10 67 CV20
Woking GU22 248 AX122
Drakewood Rd, SW16 203 DK94
Draper Cl, Belv. DA17 188 EZ77
Isleworth TW7 179 CD82
Draper Ct, Horn. RM12 150 FL61
Draper Ho, SE1 31 H8
Draper Pl, N1 off Dagmar Ter 9 H8
Drapers' Ct, SW11 41 H6
Drapers' Cres, Whiteley Vill.
KT12 off Octagon Rd 235 BT110
Drapers Rd, E15 12 F1
N17 144 DT55
Enfield EN2 103 DP40
Drappers Way, SE16 32 D8
Draven Cl, Brom. BR2 226 EF101
Drawdock Rd, SE10 35 H3
Drawell Cl, SE18 187 ES78
Drax Av, SW20 201 CV94
Draxmont, SW19 201 CY93
Draycot Rd, E11 146 EH58
Surbiton KT6 220 CN102
Draycott Av, SW3 28 D8
Harrow HA3 139 CH58
Draycott Cl, NW2 141 CX62
SE5 43 L5
Harrow HA3 139 CH58
Draycott Ms, SW6 39 H8
Draycott Pl, SW3 28 E9
Draycott Ter, SW3 28 F8
Dray Ct, Guil. GU2
off The Chase 280 AV135
Drayford Cl, W9 15 H4
Dray Gdns, SW2 203 DM85
Draymans Ms, SE15 44 A9
Draymans Way, Islw. TW7 179 CF83
Drayside Ms, Sthl. UB2 178 BZ75
Drayson Cl, Wal.Abb. EN9 90 EE32
Drayson Ms, W8 27 K5
Drayton Av, W13 159 CG73
Loughton IG10 107 EM44
Orpington BR6 227 EP102
Potters Bar EN6 85 CY32
Drayton Br Rd, W7 159 CF73
W13 159 CF73
Drayton Cl, Fetch. KT22 253 CE124
Hounslow TW4 198 BZ85
Ilford IG1 147 ER60
Drayton Ford, Rick. WD3 114 BG48
Drayton Gdns, N21 121 DP45
SW10 27 P10
W13 159 CG73
West Drayton UB7 176 BL75
⇌ Drayton Green 159 CF72
Drayton Grn, W13 159 CG73
Sch Drayton Grn Prim Sch, W13
off Drayton Gro 159 CG73
Drayton Grn Rd, W13 159 CH73
Drayton Gro, W13 159 CG73
Sch Drayton Ho Sch, Guil.
GU1 off Austen Rd 281 AZ135
Sch Drayton Manor High Sch,
W7 off Drayton Br Rd 159 CF73
⇌ Drayton Park 8 F2
Drayton Pk, N5 8 E3
Drayton Pk Ms, N5 8 E2
Sch Drayton Pk Prim Sch, N5 8 F2
Drayton Rd, E11 145 ED60
N17 122 DS54
NW10 161 CT67
W13 159 CG73
Borehamwood WD6 100 CN42
Croydon CR0 223 DP103
Drayton Waye, Har. HA3 139 CH58
Dreadnought Cl, SW19 222 DD96
Dreadnought St, SE10
off Boord St 35 K6
Drenon Sq, Hayes UB3 157 BT73
Dresden Cl, NW6 5 M4
Dresden Ho, SE11
off Lambeth Wk 30 D8
Dresden Rd, N19 143 DJ60
Dresden Way, Wey. KT13 235 BQ106
Dressington Av, SE4 205 EA86
Drew Av, NW7 119 CY51
Drew Gdns, Grnf. UB6 159 CF65
Drew Meadow, Farn.Com. SL2 133 AQ63
Drew Pl, Cat. CR3 258 DR123
Sch Drew Prim Sch, E16 36 G3
Drew Rd, E16 36 G3
Drews Pk, Knot.Grn HP9 110 AH49
Drewstead Rd, SW16 203 DK89
Drey, The, Chal.St.P. SL9 112 AY50
Driffield Rd, E3 11 M10
Drift, The, Brom. BR2 226 EK104
Jct Drift Br, Epsom KT17 255 CW115
Drift La, Cob. KT11 252 BZ115
Drift Rd, Lthd. KT24 251 BT124
Winkfield SL4 172 AD84
Drift Way, Colnbr. SL3 175 BC81
Richmond TW10 200 CM88
Driftway, The, Bans. SM7 255 CW115
Hemel Hempstead HP2 62 BM20
Leatherhead KT22
off Downs La 253 CH123
Mitcham CR4 222 DG95
Driftwood Av, St.Alb. AL2 82 CA26
Driftwood Dr, Ken. CR8 257 DP117
Drill Hall Rd, Cher. KT16 216 BG101
Dorking RH4
off Westcott Rd 285 CG136
Drinkwater Rd, Har. HA2 138 CB61
Drive, The, E4 123 ED45
E17 145 EB56
E18 146 EG56
N3 120 DA52
N6 142 DF57
N11 121 DJ51
NW10 off Longstone Av 161 CT67
NW11 141 CY59
SW6 38 F8
SW16 223 DM97
SW20 201 CW94
W3 160 CQ72
Amersham HP7 77 AR38
Artington GU3 280 AV138
Ashford TW15 197 BR94
Banstead SM7 255 CY117
Barking IG11 167 ET66
Beckenham BR3 225 EA96
Bexley DA5 208 EW86
Brookmans Park AL9 86 DA25
Buckhurst Hill IG9 124 EJ45
Chalfont St. Peter SL9 112 AY52
Chislehurst BR7 227 ET97
Cobham KT11 236 BY114
Collier Row RM5 127 FC53
Coulsdon CR5 241 DL114
Datchet SL3 174 AV81
Edgware HA8 118 CN50
Enfield EN2 104 DR39
Epsom KT19 239 CT107
Erith DA8 189 FB80
Esher KT10 218 CC102
Feltham TW14 198 BW87
Fetcham KT22 253 CE122
Goffs Oak EN7 87 DP28
Gravesend DA12 213 GK91
Great Warley CM13 130 FW50
Guildford GU2
off Beech Gro 264 AT134
Harlow CM20 57 ES14
Harold Wood RM3 128 FL53
Harrow HA2 138 CA59
Headley KT18 254 CN124
Hertford SG14 54 DQ07
High Barnet EN5 101 CY41
Hoddesdon EN11 71 EA15
Horley RH6 291 DH149
Hounslow TW3 179 CD82
Ilford IG1 147 EM60
Isleworth TW7 179 CD82
Kingston upon Thames KT2 200 CQ94
Loughton IG10 106 EL41
Morden SM4 222 DD99
New Barnet EN5 102 DC44
Newgate Street SG13 69 DL24
Northwood HA6 115 BS54
Onslow Village GU2 280 AT136
Orpington BR6 227 ET103
Potters Bar EN6 85 CZ33
Radlett WD7 83 CG34
Rickmansworth WD3 96 BJ44
Sawbridgeworth CM21 58 EY05
Scadbury Park BR7 227 ES95
Sevenoaks TN13 279 FH124
Sidcup DA14 208 EV90
Slough SL3 174 AY75
Surbiton KT6 220 CL101
Sutton SM2 239 CZ112
Thornton Heath CR7 224 DR98
Tyrrell's Wood KT22 254 CN124
Uxbridge UB10 136 BL63
Virginia Water GU25 215 AZ99
Wallington SM6 241 DJ110
Watford WD17 97 BR37
Wembley HA9 140 CQ61
West Wickham BR4 225 ED101
Woking GU22 248 AV120
Wraysbury TW19 194 AX85
Drive Mead, Couls. CR5 241 DL114
Drive Rd, Couls. CR5 257 DM119
Drive Spur, Kgswd KT20 256 DB121
Driveway, The, E17 145 EA58
Cuffley EN6 87 DL28
Drodges Cl, Bramley GU5 281 AZ143
Droitwich Cl, SE26 204 DU90
Dromey Gdns, Har. HA3 117 CF52
Dromore Rd, SW15 201 CY86
Dronfield Gdns, Dag. RM8 148 EW64
Droop St, W10 14 E4
Drop La, Brick.Wd AL2 82 CB30
Sch Dropmore Inf Sch, Burn.
SL1 off Littleworth Rd 132 AJ62
Dropmore Pk, Burn. SL1 132 AH62
Dropmore Rd, Burn. SL1 152 AJ67
Drove Rd, Dor. RH5 284 BW135
Guildford GU4 282 BG136
Drovers Mead, Warley CM14 130 FV49
Drovers Pl, SE15 44 F4
Drovers Rd, S.Croy. CR2 242 DR106
Drovers Way, N7 8 A4
Hatfield AL10 67 CV15
St. Albans AL3 65 CD20
Seer Green HP9 111 AQ51
Droveway, Loug. IG10 107 EP40
Drove Way, The, Istead Rise
DA13 212 GE94
Druce Rd, SE21 204 DS86
Drudgeon Way, Bean DA2 211 FV90
Druids Cl, Ashtd. KT21 254 CM120
Druid St, SE1 31 P4
Druids Way, Brom. BR2 225 ED98
Drumaline Ridge, Wor.Pk. KT4 220 CS103
Drummond Av, Rom. RM7 149 FD56
Drummond Cl, Erith DA8 189 FE81
Drummond Cres, NW1 17 N2
Drummond Dr, Stan. HA7 117 CF52
Drummond Gdns, Epsom
KT19 238 CP111
Drummond Gate, SW1 29 P10
Drummond Ho, Wind. SL4
off Balmoral Gdns 173 AR83
Drummond Pl, Twick. TW1 199 CH86
Drummond Rd, E11 146 EH58
SE16 32 E6
Croydon CR0 224 DQ103
Guildford GU1 264 AX134
Romford RM7 149 FD56
Drummonds, The, Buck.H. IG9 124 EH47
Epping CM16 92 EU30
Drummonds Pl, Rich. TW9 180 CL84
Drummond St, NW1 17 L4
Drum St, E1 20 B8
Drury Cres, Croy. CR0 223 DN103
Drury La, WC2 18 B9
Hunsdon SG12 56 EK06
Drury Rd, Har. HA1 138 CC59
Drury Way, NW10 140 CR64
● Drury Way Ind Est, NW10 140 CQ64
Dryad St, SW15 181 CX83
Dryburgh Gdns, NW9 140 CN55
Dryburgh Rd, SW15 181 CV83
Drycroft, Welw.G.C. AL7 51 CY13
Drydell La, Chesh. HP5 76 AM31
Dryden Av, W7 159 CF72
Dryden Cl, SW4 203 DK85
Ilford IG6 125 ET51
Dryden Ct, SE11 30 F9
Dryden Pl, Til. RM18
off Fielding Av 193 GH81
Dryden Rd, SW19 202 DC93
Enfield EN1 104 DS44
Harrow HA3 117 CF53
Welling DA16 187 ES81
Dryden St, WC2 18 B9
Dryden Twrs, Rom. RM3 127 FH52
Dryden Way, Orp. BR6 228 EU102
Dryfield Cl, NW10 160 CQ65
Dryfield Rd, Edg. HA8 118 CQ51
Dryfield Wk, SE8 46 A2
Dryhill La, Sund. TN14 278 FB123
Dryhill Rd, Belv. DA17 188 EZ79
Dryland Av, Orp. BR6 245 ET105
Drylands Rd, N8 143 DL58
Drynham Pk, Wey. KT13 217 BS104
Drysdale Av, E4 123 EB45
Drysdale Cl, Nthwd. HA6
off Northbrook Dr 115 BS52
Drysdale Pl, N1 19 P2
Drysdale St, N1 19 P3
Duarte Pl, Grays RM16 192 FZ76
Dublin Av, E8 10 D8
Dubrae Cl, St.Alb. AL3 64 CA22
Du Burstow Ter, W7 179 CE75
Ducal St, E2 20 B3
Du Cane Ct, SW17 202 DG88
Du Cane Rd, W12 161 CT72
Duchess Cl, N11 121 DH50
Sutton SM1 240 DC105
Duchess Ct, Wey. KT13 217 BR104
Duchess Gro, Buck.H. IG9 124 EH47
Duchess Ms, W1 17 K7
Duchess of Bedford's Wk, W8 27 J5
Duchess of Kent Cl, Guil.
GU2 264 AV130
Duchess St, W1 17 K7
Slough SL1 153 AL74
Duchess Wk, Sev. TN15 279 FL125
Duchy Pl, SE1 30 F2
Duchy Rd, Barn. EN4 102 DD38
Duchy St, SE1 30 F2
Ducie Ho, SE7
off Springfield Gro 186 EJ79
Ducie St, SW4 183 DM84
Duckett Ms, N4 143 DP58
Duckett Rd, N4 143 DP58
Ducketts Mead, Roydon
CM19 56 EH14
Ducketts Rd, Dart. DA1 209 FF85
Duckett St, E1 21 L6
Ducking Stool Ct, Rom. RM1 149 FE56
Duck La, W1 17 N9
Thornwood CM16 92 EW26
Duck Lees La, Enf. EN3 105 DY42
Duckling La, Saw. CM21
off Vantorts Rd 58 EY05
Ducks Hill, Nthwd. HA6 114 BN54
Ducks Hill Rd, Nthwd. HA6 115 BP54
Ruislip HA4 115 BP54
DUCKS ISLAND, Barn. EN5 101 CX44
Ducks Wk, Twick. TW1 199 CJ85
Du Cros Dr, Stan. HA7 117 CK51
Du Cros Rd, W3 off The Vale 160 CS74
Dudden Hill La, NW10 141 CT63
Duddington Cl, SE9 206 EK91
Dudley Av, Har. HA3 139 CJ55
Waltham Cross EN8 89 DX32
Dudley Cl, Add. KT15 216 BJ104
Bovingdon HP3 79 BA27
Chafford Hundred RM16 192 FY75
Dudley Ct, NW11 141 CZ56
Slough SL1 off Upton Rd 174 AU76
Dudley Dr, Mord. SM4 221 CY101
Ruislip HA4 137 BV64
Dudley Gdns, W13 179 CH75
Harrow HA2 139 CD60
Romford RM3 128 FK51
Dudley Gro, Epsom KT18 238 CQ114
Dudley Ho, W2
off North Wf Rd 16 A7
Dudley Ms, SW2
off Bascombe St 203 DN86
Dudley Pl, Hayes UB3 177 BR77
Stanw. TW19 196 BM86
Dudley Rd, E17 123 EA54
N3 120 DB54
NW6 4 F10
SW19 202 DA93
Ashford TW15 196 BM92
Feltham TW14 197 BQ88
Harrow HA2 138 CC61
Ilford IG1 147 EP63
Kingston upon Thames KT1 220 CM97
Northfleet DA11 212 GE87
Richmond TW9 180 CM82
Romford RM3 128 FK51
Southall UB2 178 BX75
Walton-on-Thames KT12 217 BU100
Dudley St, W2 16 A7
Dudlington Rd, E5 144 DW61
Dudmaston Ms, SW3 28 B10
Dudrich Cl, N11 120 DF51
Dudrich Ms, SE22 204 DT85
Dudsbury Rd, Dart. DA1 209 FG86
Sidcup DA14 208 EV93
Dudset La, Houns. TW5 177 BU81
Duffell Ho, SE11 30 D10
Dufferin Av, EC1 19 L5
Dufferin St, EC1 19 K5
Duffield Cl, Grays (Daniel Cl)
RM16 192 FY75
Grays (Davis Rd) RM16 192 FZ76
Harrow HA1 139 CF57
Duffield Dr, N15 144 DT56
Duffield La, Stoke P. SL2 154 AT65
Duffield Pk, Stoke P. SL2 154 AU69
Duffield Rd, Walt.Hill KT20 255 CV124
Duffins Orchard, Ott. KT16 233 BC108
Duff St, E14 22 C9
Dufour's Pl, W1 17 M9
Dugard Way, SE11 30 G8
Dugdale Hill La, Pot.B. EN6 85 CY33
Dugdales, Crox.Grn WD3 96 BN42
Duggan Dr, Chis. BR7 206 EL92
Dugolly Av, Wem. HA9 140 CP62
Duke Ct, Har. HA2
off Station Rd 138 CB57
Duke Gdns, Ilf. IG6
off Duke Rd 147 ER56
Duke Humphrey Rd, SE3 47 K6
Duke of Cambridge Cl, Twick.
TW2 199 CD86
Duke of Edinburgh Rd, Sutt.
SM1 222 DD103
Duke of Wellington Av, SE18 37 P7
Duke of Wellington Pl, SW1 29 H4
Duke of York Sq, SW3 28 F9
Duke of York St, SW1 29 M2
Duke Pl, Slou. SL1
off Montague Rd 154 AT73
Duke Rd, W4 180 CR78
Ilford IG6 147 ER56
Dukes Av, N3 120 DB53
N10 143 DJ55
W4 180 CR78
Edgware HA8 118 CM51
Grays RM17 192 GA75
Harrow HA1 139 CE56
Hounslow TW4 178 BY84
Kingston upon Thames KT2 199 CJ91
New Malden KT3 221 CT97
North Harrow HA2 138 BZ58
Northolt UB5 158 BY66
Richmond TW10 199 CJ91
Theydon Bois CM16 107 ES35
Dukes Cl, Ashf. TW15 197 BQ91
Gerrards Cross SL9 134 AX60
Hampton TW12 198 BZ92
North Weald Bassett CM16 93 FB27
● Dukes Ct, Wok. GU21 249 AZ117
Dukes Ct, E6 167 EN67
Dukes Dr, Slou. SL2 133 AM64
Dukes Gate, W4 180 CQ77
Dukes Grn Av, Felt. TW14 197 BU85
Dukes Head Yd, N6
off Highgate High St 143 DH60
Dukes Hill, Wold. CR3 259 DY120
Duke Shore Pl, E14 33 N1
Duke Shore Wf, E14 33 M1
Dukes Kiln Dr, Ger.Cr. SL9 134 AW60
Dukes La, W8 27 K4
Gerrards Cross SL9 134 AY59
Dukes Lo, Nthwd. HA6 115 BS50
Duke's Meadows, W4 180 CR81
Dukes Ms, N10 143 DH55
Duke's Ms, W1 17 H8
Dukes Orchard, Bex. DA5 209 FC88
● Dukes Pk, Harl. CM20 57 ET12
Duke's Pas, E17 145 EC56
Dukes Pl, EC3 19 P9
Dukes Ride, Ger.Cr. SL9 134 AY60
North Holmwood RH5 285 CK139
Uxbridge UB10 136 BL63
Dukes Rd, E6 167 EN67
W3 160 CN71
Duke's Rd, WC1 17 P3
Dukes Rd, Hersham KT12 236 BX106
Dukesthorpe Rd, SE26 205 DX91
Duke St, SW1 29 M2
W1 17 H8
Hoddesdon EN11 71 EA16
Richmond TW9 179 CK84
Sutton SM1 240 DD105
Watford WD17 98 BW41
Windsor SL4 173 AP80
Woking GU21 249 AZ117
Duke St Hill, SE1 31 M2
Dukes Valley, Ger.Cr. SL9 134 AV61
Dukes Way, Berk. HP4 60 AU17
Uxbridge UB8
off Waterloo Rd 156 BJ67
West Wickham BR4 226 EE104
Dukes Wd Av, Ger.Cr. SL9 134 AY60
Dukes Wd Dr, Ger.Cr. SL9 134 AW60
Duke's Yd, W1 17 H10
Dulas St, N4 143 DM60
Dulcie Cl, Green. DA9 211 FT86
Dulford St, W11 14 E10
Dulka Rd, SW11 202 DF85
Dulshott Grn, Epsom KT17
off Church St 238 CS113
Sch Dulverton Prim Sch, SE9
off Dulverton Rd 207 ER89
Dulverton Rd, SE9 207 EQ89
Romford RM3 128 FK51
Ruislip HA4 137 BU60
South Croydon CR2 242 DW110
DULWICH, SE21 204 DS87
Sch Dulwich Coll, SE21
off College Rd 204 DS89
★ Dulwich Coll Picture Gall,
SE21 204 DS87
Sch Dulwich Coll Prep Sch,
SE21 off Alleyn Pk 204 DS90
Dulwich Common, SE21 204 DS88
SE22 204 DS88
H Dulwich Comm Hosp,
SE22 184 DS84
Sch Dulwich Hamlet Jun Sch,
SE21 off Dulwich Village 204 DS86
Dulwich Lawn Cl, SE22
off Colwell Rd 204 DT85
Dulwich Oaks, The, SE21 204 DS90

Dulwich Ri Gdns, SE22
off Lordship La 204 DT85
Dulwich Rd, SE24 203 DN85
Dulwich Village, SE21 204 DS86
Sch Dulwich Village C of E Inf Sch, SE21
off Dulwich Village 204 DS86
Dulwich Way, Crox.Grn WD3 96 BN43
Dulwich Wd Av, SE19 204 DS91
Dulwich Wd Pk, SE19 204 DS91
Dumas Way, Wat. WD18 97 BS42
Dumbarton Av, Wal.Cr. EN8 89 DX34
Dumbarton Rd, SW2 203 DL86
Dumbleton Cl, Kings.T. KT1 220 CP95
Dumbletons, The, Map.Cr. WD3 113 BE49
Dumbreck Rd, SE9 187 EM84
Dumfries Cl, Wat. WD19 115 BT48
Dumont Rd, N16 144 DS62
Dumpton Pl, NW1 6 G7
Dumsey Eyot, Cher. KT16 216 BK101
Dumville Dr, Gdse. RH9 274 DV131
Dunally Pk, Shep. TW17 217 BR101
Dunbar Av, SW16 223 DN96
Beckenham BR3 225 DY98
Dagenham RM10 148 FA62
Dunbar Cl, Hayes UB4 157 BU71
Slough SL2 154 AU72
Dunbar Ct, Sutt. SM1 240 DD106
Walton-on-Thames KT12 218 BW103
Dunbar Gdns, Dag. RM10 148 FA64
Dunbar Rd, E7 13 P5
N22 121 DN53
New Malden KT3 220 CQ98
Dunbar St, SE27 204 DQ90
Dunblane Cl, Edg. HA8 118 CP47
Dunblane Rd, SE9 186 EL83
Dunboe Pl, Shep. TW17 217 BQ101
Dunboyne Pl, Old Wind. SL4 174 AU84
Dunboyne Rd, NW3 6 E2
Dunbridge Ho, SW15
off Highcliffe Dr 201 CT86
Dunbridge St, E2 20 D4
Duncan Cl, Barn. EN5 102 DC42
Welwyn Garden City AL7 51 CY10
Duncan Dr, Guil. GU1 265 BA133
Duncan Gdns, Stai. TW18 196 BG93
Duncan Gro, W3 160 CS72
Duncannon Cres, Wind. SL4 173 AK83
Duncannon Pl, Green. DA9 191 FW84
Duncannon St, WC2 30 A1
Duncan Rd, E8 10 E8
Richmond TW9 180 CL84
Tadworth KT20 255 CY119
Duncan St, N1 8 G10
Duncans Yd, West. TN16
off Market Sq 277 ER126
Duncan Ter, N1 18 G1
Duncan Way, Bushey WD23 98 BZ40
Dunch St, E1 20 F9
Duncombe Cl, Amer. HP6 77 AS38
Hertford SG14 54 DQ07
Duncombe Ct, Stai. TW18 195 BF94
Duncombe Hill, SE23 205 DY87
Sch Duncombe Prim Sch, N19 off Sussex Way 143 DL60
Duncombe Rd, N19 143 DK60
Hertford SG14 54 DQ08
Northchurch HP4 60 AS17
Sch Duncombe Sch, Hert. SG14
off Warren Pk Rd 54 DQ08
Duncrievie Rd, SE13 205 ED86
Duncroft, SE18 187 ES80
Windsor SL4 173 AM83
Duncroft Cl, Reig. RH2 271 CZ133
Dundalk Rd, SE4 185 DY83
Dundas Gdns, W.Mol. KT8 218 CB97
Dundas Ms, Enf. EN3 105 EA37
Dundas Rd, SE15 44 G8
Dundee Ho, W9 15 N2
Dundee Rd, E13 24 A1
SE25 224 DV99
Slough SL1 153 AM72
Dundee St, E1 32 E3
Dundee Way, Enf. EN3 105 DY41
Dundee Wf, E14 33 N1
Dundela Gdns, Wor.Pk. KT4 239 CV105
Dundonald Cl, E6 25 H8
Sch Dundonald Prim Sch, SW19
off Dundonald Rd 201 CZ94
Tra Dundonald Road 201 CZ94
Dundonald Rd, NW10 4 C9
SW19 201 CY94
Dundrey Cres, Merst. RH1 273 DL129
Dunedin Dr, Cat. CR3 274 DS125
Dunedin Ho, E16
off Manwood St 37 K3
Dunedin Rd, E10 145 EB62
Ilford IG1 147 EQ60
Rainham RM13 169 FF69
Dunedin Way, Hayes UB4 158 BW70
Dunelm Gro, SE27 204 DQ91
Dunelm St, E1 21 J8
Dunfee Way, W.Byf. KT14 234 BL112
Dunfield Gdns, SE6 205 EB91
Dunfield Rd, SE6 205 EB92
Dunford Ct, Pnr. HA5
off Cornwall Rd 116 BZ52
Dunford Rd, N7 8 D1
Dungarvan Av, SW15 181 CU84
Dungates La, Buckland RH3 271 CU133
Dunham Ms, Hat. AL10 67 CW17
Dunheved Cl, Th.Hth. CR7 223 DN100
Dunheved Rd N, Th.Hth. CR7 223 DN100
Dunheved Rd S, Th.Hth. CR7 223 DN100
Dunheved Rd W, Th.Hth. CR7 223 DN100
Dunhill Pt, SW15
off Dilton Gdns 201 CV88
Dunholme Grn, N9 122 DT48
Dunholme La, N9 122 DT48
Dunholme Rd, N9 122 DT48
Dunkeld Rd, SE25 224 DR98
Dagenham RM8 148 EV61
Dunkellin Gro, S.Ock. RM15 171 FU71
Dunkellin Way, S.Ock. RM15 171 FU72
Dunkery Rd, SE9 206 EK91
Dunkin Rd, Dart. DA1 190 FN84
Dunkirk Cl, Grav. DA12 213 GJ92
Dunkirks Ms, Hert. SG13
off Queens Rd 54 DR11
Dunkirk St, SE27 204 DQ91
Dunlace Rd, E5 11 H2
Dunleary Cl, Houns. TW4 198 BZ87
Dunley Dr, New Adgtn CR0 243 EB108
Dunlin Cl, Red. RH1 288 DE139
Dunlin Ct, Enf. EN3
off Teal Cl 104 DW36
Dunlin Ho, W13 159 CF70
Dunlin Ri, Guil. GU4 265 BD132
Dunlin Rd, Hem.H. HP2 62 BL15
Dunloe Av, N17 144 DR55
Dunloe St, E2 20 A1
Dunlop Cl, Dart. DA1 190 FL83
Tilbury RM18
off Dunlop Rd 193 GF82
Dunlop Pl, SE16 32 B7
Dunlop Rd, Til. RM18 193 GF81
Dunmail Dr, Pur. CR8 242 DS114
Dunmore Pt, E2 20 A3
Dunmore Rd, NW6 4 E9
SW20 221 CW95
Dunmow Cl, Felt. TW13 198 BX91
Loughton IG10 106 EL44
Romford RM6 148 EW57
Dunmow Dr, Rain. RM13 169 FF67
Dunmow Ho, Dag. RM9 168 EV67
Dunmow Rd, E15 13 H1
Dunmow Wk, N1 9 J8
Dunnage Cres, SE16 33 M8
Dunnets, Knap. GU21 248 AS117
Dunning Cl, S.Ock. RM15 171 FU72
Dunningford Cl, Horn. RM12 149 FF64
Sch Dunningford Prim Sch, Elm Pk RM12
off Upper Rainham Rd 149 FF64
Dunn Mead, NW9 119 CT52
Dunnock Cl, N9 123 DX46
Borehamwood WD6 100 CN42
Dunnock Ct, SE21
off Elmworth Gro 204 DR89
Dunnock Rd, E6 25 H8
Dunns Pas, WC1 18 B8
Dunn St, E8 10 A2
Dunny La, Chipper. WD4 79 BE32
Dunnymans Rd, Bans. SM7 255 CZ115
Dunollie Pl, NW5 7 M2
Dunollie Rd, NW5 7 L2
Dunoon Rd, SE23 204 DW87
Dunottar Cl, Red. RH1 288 DD136
Sch Dunottar Sch, Reig. RH2
off High Trees Rd 288 DD135
Dunraven Av, Red. RH1 289 DH141
Dunraven Dr, Enf. EN2 103 DN40
Dunraven Rd, W12 161 CU74
Sch Dunraven Sch, Lwr Sch, SW16
off Mount Nod Rd 203 DM90
Upr Sch, SW16
off Leigham Ct Rd 203 DM90
Dunraven St, W1 16 F10
Dunsany Rd, W14 26 C7
Dunsborough Pk, Ripley GU23 250 BJ120
Dunsbury Cl, Sutt. SM2
off Nettlecombe Cl 240 DB109
Dunsdon Av, Guil. GU2 280 AV135
Dunsfold Ri, Couls. CR5 241 DK113
Dunsfold Way, New Adgtn CR0 243 EB108
Dunsford Way, SW15 201 CV86
Dunsmore Cl, Bushey WD23 99 CD44
Hayes UB4 158 BX70
Dunsmore Rd, Walt. KT12 217 BV100
Dunsmore Way, Bushey WD23 99 CD44
Dunsmure Rd, N16 144 DS60
Dunspring La, Ilf. IG5 125 EP54
Dunstable Cl, Rom. RM3
off Dunstable Rd 128 FK51
Dunstable Ms, W1 17 H6
Dunstable Rd, Rich. TW9 180 CL84
Romford RM3 128 FK51
West Molesey KT8 218 BZ98
Dunstall Grn, Chobham GU24 232 AW109
Dunstall Rd, SW20 201 CV93
Dunstalls, Harl. CM19 73 EN19
Dunstall Way, W.Mol. KT8 218 CB97
● Dunstall Welling Est, Well. DA16 off Leigh Pl 188 EV82
Dunstan Cl, N2 142 DC55
Dunstan Ct, Whyt. CR3
off Godstone Rd 258 DU119
Dunstan Ho, E1
off Stepney Grn 21 H6
Dunstan Rd, NW11 141 CZ60
Coulsdon CR5 257 DK117
Dunstans Gro, SE22 204 DV86
Dunstans Rd, SE22 204 DU87
Dunster Av, Mord. SM4 221 CX102
Dunster Cl, Barn. EN5 101 CX42
Harefield UB9 114 BH53
Romford RM5 127 FC54
Dunster Ct, EC3 19 N10
Borehamwood WD6
off Kensington Way 100 CR41
Dunster Cres, Horn. RM11 150 FN61
Dunster Dr, NW9 140 CQ60
Dunster Gdns, NW6 5 H6
Slough SL1 off Avebury 153 AN73
Dunsters Mead, Welw.G.C. AL7 52 DA11
Dunsterville Way, SE1 31 M5
Dunster Way, Har. HA2 138 BY62
Wallington SM6
off Helios Rd 222 DG102
Dunston Rd, E8 10 A9
SW11 41 H9
Dunston St, E8 10 A8
Dunton Cl, Surb. KT6 220 CL102
DUNTON GREEN, Sev. TN13 263 FC119
⇌ Dunton Green 263 FF119
Sch Dunton Grn Prim Sch, Dunt.Grn TN13
off London Rd 263 FE120
Dunton Rd, E10 145 EB59
SE1 32 A10
Romford RM1 149 FE56
Duntshill Rd, SW18 202 DB88
Dunvegan Cl, W.Mol. KT8 218 CB98
Dunvegan Rd, SE9 187 EM84
Dunwich Rd, Bexh. DA7 188 EZ81
Dunworth Ms, W11 14 G8
Duplex Ride, SW1 28 F5
Dupont Rd, SW20 221 CX96
Duppas Av, Croy. CR0
off Violet La 241 DP105
Duppas Cl, Shep. TW17 217 BR99
Duppas Hill La, Croy. CR0
off Duppas Hill Rd 241 DP105
Duppas Hill Rd, Croy. CR0 241 DP105
Duppas Hill Ter, Croy. CR0 223 DP104
Duppas Rd, Croy. CR0 223 DN104
Dupre Cl, Chaff.Hun. RM16 192 FY76
Dupre Cl, Slough SL1 173 AL75
Dupre Cres, Beac. HP9 111 AP54
Dupree Rd, SE7 36 A10
Du Pre Wk, Woob.Grn HP10
off Stratford Dr 132 AD59
Dura Den Cl, Beck. BR3 205 EB94
Durand Cl, Cars. SM5 222 DF102
Durand Gdns, SW9 42 D6
Sch Durand Prim Sch, SW9 42 D6
Cowley Rd Annexe, SW9 42 F7
Durands Wk, SE16 33 M4
Durand Way, NW10 160 CQ66
Durant Rd, Swan. BR8 209 FG93
Durants Pk Av, Enf. EN3 105 DX42
Durants Rd, Enf. EN3 104 DW42
Sch Durants Sch, Enf. EN3
off Pitfield Way 104 DW39
Durant St, E2 20 C2
Durban Gdns, Dag. RM10 169 FC66
Durban Rd, E15 23 J2
E17 123 DZ53
N17 122 DS51
SE27 204 DQ91
Beckenham BR3 225 DZ96
Ilford IG2 147 ES60
Durban Rd E, Wat. WD18 97 BU42
Durban Rd W, Wat. WD18 97 BU42
Durbin Rd, Chess. KT9 238 CL105
Sch Durdans Pk Prim Sch, Sthl. UB1 off King Georges Dr 158 BZ71
Durdans Rd, Sthl. UB1 158 BZ72
Durell Gdns, Dag. RM9 148 EX64
Durell Rd, Dag. RM9 148 EX64
Durfey Pl, SE5 43 M4
Durfold Dr, Reig. RH2 272 DC134
Durford Cres, SW15 201 CU88
Durham Av, Brom. BR2 226 EF98
Hounslow TW5 178 BZ78
Romford RM2 150 FJ56
Slough SL1 153 AN72
Woodford Green IG8 124 EK50
Durham Cl, SW20
off Durham Rd 221 CV96
Guildford GU2 264 AT132
Sawbridgeworth CM21 58 EW06
Stanstead Abbotts SG12 55 EB10
Durham Hill, Brom. BR1 206 EF91
Durham Ho St, WC2 30 B1
Durham Pl, SW3 40 E1
Ilford IG1 off Eton Rd 147 EQ63
Durham Ri, SE18 187 EQ78
Durham Rd, E12 146 EK63
E16 23 K5
N2 142 DE55
N7 143 DM61
N9 122 DU47
SW20 221 CV95
W5 179 CK76
Borehamwood WD6 100 CQ41
Bromley BR2 226 EF97
Dagenham RM10 149 FC64
Feltham TW14 198 BW87
Harrow HA1 138 CB57
Sidcup DA14 208 EV92
Durham Row, E1 21 K7
Durham St, SE11 42 C1
Durham Ter, W2 15 L8
Durham Wf Dr, Brent. TW8 179 CJ80
Durham Yd, E2 20 E2
Duriun Way, Erith DA8 189 FH80
Durleston Pk Dr, Bkhm KT23 268 CC125
Durley Av, Pnr. HA5 138 BY59
Durley Gdns, Orp. BR6 246 EV105
Durley Rd, N16 144 DS59
Durlston Rd, E5 144 DU61
Kingston upon Thames KT2 200 CL93
Durndale La, Nthflt DA11 213 GF91
Durnell Way, Loug. IG10 107 EN41
Durnford St, N15 144 DS57
SE10 46 F3
Durning Rd, SE19 204 DR92
Durnsford Av, SW19 202 DA89
Durnsford Ct, Enf. EN3
off Enstone Rd 105 DY41
Durnsford Rd, N11 121 DK53
SW19 202 DA89
Durrants Cl, Rain. RM13 170 FJ68
Durrants Dr, Crox.Grn WD3 97 BQ42
Durrants Hill Rd, Hem.H. HP3 62 BK23
Durrants La, Berk. HP4 60 AT18
Durrants Path, Chesh. HP5 76 AN27
Durrants Rd, Berk. HP4 60 AT18
Durrant Way, Orp. BR6 245 ER106
Swanscombe DA10 212 FY87
Durrell Rd, SW6 38 G7
Durrell Way, Shep. TW17 217 BR100
Durrington Av, SW20 221 CW95
Durrington Pk Rd, SW20 201 CW94
Durrington Rd, E5 11 L1
Durrington Twr, SW8 41 M8
Dursley Cl, SE3 186 EJ82
Dursley Gdns, SE3 186 EK81
Dursley Rd, SE3 186 EJ82
Sch Durston Ho Sch, W5
off Castlebar Rd 159 CK72
Durward St, E1 20 E6
Durweston Ms, W1 16 F6
Durweston St, W1 16 F6
Dury Falls Cl, Horn. RM11 150 FM60
Dury Rd, Barn. EN5 101 CZ39
Dutch Barn Cl, Stanw. TW19 196 BK86
Dutch Elm Av, Wind. SL4 174 AT80
Dutch Gdns, Kings.T. KT2 200 CP93
Dutch Yd, SW18
off Wandsworth High St 202 DA85
Dutton St, SE10 46 E6
Dutton Way, Iver SL0 155 BE72
Duxberry Cl, Brom. BR2
off Southborough La 226 EL99
Duxford Cl, Horn. RM12 169 FH65
Duxford Ho, SE2
off Wolvercote Rd 188 EX75
Duxhurst La, Reig. RH2 288 DB144
Duxons Turn, Hem.H. HP2
off Maylands Av 63 BP19
Dwight Ct, SW6 38 F8
Dwight Rd, Wat. WD18 115 BR45
Sch Dycorts Sch, Harold Hill RM3 off Settle Rd 128 FN49
Dye Ho La, E3 12 B9
Dyer Ct, Enf. EN3
off Manton Rd 105 EA37
Dyer's Bldgs, EC1 18 E7
Dyers Fld, Smallfield RH6 291 DP148
Dyers Hall Rd, E11 146 EE60
Dyers La, SW15 181 CV84
Dyers Way, Rom. RM3 127 FH52
Dyke Dr, Orp. BR5 228 EW102
Dykes Path, Wok. GU21
off Bentham Av 249 BC115
Dykes Way, Brom. BR2 226 EF97
Dykewood Cl, Bex. DA5 209 FE90
Dylan Cl, Els. WD6 117 CK45
Dylan Rd, SE24 183 DP84
Belvedere DA17 188 FA76
Dylways, SE5 184 DR84
Dymchurch Cl, Ilf. IG5 125 EN54
Orpington BR6 245 ES105
Dymes Path, SW19
off Queensmere Rd 201 CX89
Dymock St, SW6 39 L10
Dymoke Grn, St.Alb. AL4 65 CG16
Dymoke Rd, Horn. RM11 149 FF59
Dymokes Way, Hodd. EN11 55 EA14
Dymond Est, SW17
off Glenburnie Rd 202 DE90
Dyneley Rd, SE12 206 EJ91
Dyne Rd, NW6 4 F7
Dynevor Rd, N16 144 DS62
Richmond TW10 200 CL85
Dynham Rd, NW6 5 J6
Dyott St, WC1 18 A8
Dyrham La, Barn. EN5 101 CU36
Dysart Av, Kings.T. KT2 199 CJ92
Sch Dysart Sch, Surb. KT6
off Ewell Rd 220 CM101
Dysart St, EC2 19 M5
Dyson Cl, Wind. SL4 173 AP83
Dyson Rd, E11 146 EE58
E15 13 M5
Dysons Cl, Wal.Cr. EN8 89 DX33
Dysons Rd, N18 122 DV50

E

Eade Rd, N4 144 DQ59
Eagans Cl, N2 142 DD55
Eagle Av, Rom. RM6 148 EY58
Eagle Cl, SE16 44 G1
Amersham HP6 94 AT37
Enfield EN3 104 DW42
Hornchurch RM12 169 FH65
Wallington SM6 241 DL107
Waltham Abbey EN9 90 EG34
Eagle Ct, EC1 18 G6
N18 122 DT51
Hertford SG13 54 DV08
Eagle Dr, NW9 118 CS54
Eagle Hts, SW11
off Bramlands Cl 40 C10
Eagle Hill, SE19 204 DR93
Eagle Ho Ms, SW4
off Narbonne Av 203 DJ85
Sch Eagle Ho Sch, Mitch. CR4 off London Rd 222 DF96
Eagle La, E11 146 EG56
Eagle Lo, NW11 141 CZ59
Eagle Ms, N1 9 N5
Eagle Pl, SW1 29 M1
SW7 27 P10
Eagle Rd, Guil. GU1 280 AX135
Lon.Hthrw Air. TW6 177 BT83
Slough SL1 153 AM73
Wembley HA0 159 CK66
Eagles, The, Denh. UB9
off Patrons Way E 135 BF58
Eagles Dr, Tats. TN16 260 EK118
Eaglesfield Rd, SE18 187 EP80
Eagles Rd, Green. DA9 191 FV84
Eagle St, WC1 18 C7
Eagle Ter, Wdf.Grn. IG8 124 EH52
● Eagle Trd Est, Mitch. CR4 222 DF100
Eagle Way, Gt Warley CM13 129 FV51
Hatfield AL10 67 CU20
Northfleet DA11 212 GA85
Eagle Wf Rd, N1 9 K10
Eagling Cl, E3 22 B3
Sch Ealdham Prim Sch, SE9
off Ealdham Sq 186 EJ84
Ealdham Sq, SE9 186 EJ84
EALING, W5 159 CJ73
Coll Ealing & W London Coll, W5 off Ealing Grn 159 CK74
⇌ Ealing Broadway 159 CK73
⊖ Ealing Broadway 159 CK73
Ealing Bdy Shop Cen, W5 159 CK73
Coll Ealing City Learning Cen, W3 off Gunnersbury La 180 CN75
Ealing Cl, Borwd. WD6 100 CR39
Sch Ealing Coll Upr Sch, W13
off The Avenue 159 CH72
★ Ealing Common, W5 160 CL74
⊖ Ealing Common 160 CM74
Ealing Common, W5 160 CM73
Ealing Grn, W5 159 CK74
H Ealing Hosp NHS Trust, Sthl. UB1 179 CD75
Coll Ealing Indep Coll, W5
off New Bdy 159 CJ73
Ealing Pk Gdns, W5 179 CJ77
Ealing Rd, Brent. TW8 179 CK78
Northolt UB5 158 CA66
Wembley HA0 159 CK67
Ealing Village, W5 160 CL72
Eamont Cl, Ruis. HA4 137 BP59
Eamont St, NW8 6 C10
Eardemont Cl, Dart. DA1 189 FF84
Eardley Cres, SW5 39 K1
Eardley Pt, SE18 37 P9
Sch Eardley Prim Sch, SW16
off Cunliffe St 203 DJ93
Eardley Rd, SW16 203 DJ92
Belvedere DA17 188 FA78
Sevenoaks TN13 279 FH124
Earhart Way, Houns. TW4 177 BU83
Earl Cl, N11 121 DH50
Earldom Rd, SW15 181 CW84
Earle Gdns, Kings.T. KT2 200 CL93
Earleswood, Cob. KT11 236 BX112
Earlham Gro, E7 13 L3
N22 121 DM52
Sch Earlham Prim Sch, E7 13 M3
N22 off Earlham Gro 121 DN52
Earlham St, WC2 17 P9
Earl Ri, SE18 187 ER77
Earl Rd, SW14 180 CQ84
Northfleet DA11 212 GE89
Earlsbrook Rd, Red. RH1 288 DF136
Earlsbury Gdns, Edg. HA8 118 CN49
EARLS COURT, SW5 27 H10
⊖ Earl's Court 27 K9
★ Earls Court Exhib Cen, SW5 27 J10
Earls Ct Gdns, SW5 27 L9
Earls Ct Rd, SW5 27 K8
W8 27 K8
Earls Ct Sq, SW5 27 L10
Earls Cres, Har. HA1 139 CE56
Earlsdown Ho, Bark. IG11
off Wheelers Cross 167 ER68
Earlsferry Way, N1 8 B7
EARLSFIELD, SW18 202 DC88
⇌ Earlsfield 202 DC88
Earlsfield, Holy. SL6 172 AC77
Earlsfield Ho, Kings.T. KT2
off Kingsgate Rd 219 CK95
Sch Earlsfield Prim Sch, SW18
off Tranmere Rd 202 DC89
Earlsfield Rd, SW18 202 DC88
Earlshall Rd, SE9 187 EM84
Earls Ho, Rich. TW9 180 CP80
Earls La, Slou. SL1 153 AM74
South Mimms EN6 84 CS32
Earlsmead, Har. HA2 138 BZ63
Sch Earlsmead First & Mid Sch, S.Har. HA2 off Arundel Dr 138 BZ63
Sch Earlsmead Prim Sch, N15
off Broad La 144 DT57
Earlsmead Rd, N15 144 DT57
NW10 14 A2
Earl's Path, Loug. IG10 106 EJ40
Earls Ter, W8 27 H7
Earlsthorpe Ms, SW12 202 DG86
Earlsthorpe Rd, SE26 205 DX91
Earlstoke St, EC1 18 G2
Earlston Gro, E9 10 F9
Earl St, EC2 19 N6
Watford WD17 98 BW41
Earls Wk, W8 27 J7
Dagenham RM8 148 EV63
EARLSWOOD, Red. RH1 288 DF136
⇌ Earlswood 288 DF136
Earlswood Av, Th.Hth. CR7 223 DN99
Earlswood Gdns, Ilf. IG5 147 EN55
Sch Earlswood Inf & Nurs Sch, Red. RH1
off St. John's Rd 288 DG135
Earlswood Rd, Red. RH1 288 DF135
Earlswood St, SE10 47 K1
Early Ms, NW1 7 K8
Earnshaw St, WC2 17 P8
Earsby St, W14 26 F8
Easby Cres, Mord. SM4 222 DB100
Easebourne Rd, Dag. RM8 148 EW64
Easedale Dr, Horn. RM12 149 FG64
Easedale Ho, Islw. TW7
off Summerwood Rd 199 CF85
Eashing Pt, SW15
off Wanborough Dr 201 CV88
Easington Pl, Guil. GU1
off Maori Rd 281 AZ135
Easington Way, S.Ock. RM15 171 FU71
Easley's Ms, W1 17 H8
EASNEYE, Ware SG12 55 EC06
● East 10 Enterprise Pk, E10
off Argall Way 145 DY60
Coll East 15 Acting Sch, Loug. IG10 off Rectory La 107 EP41
EAST ACTON, W3 160 CR74
⊖ East Acton 161 CT72
East Acton La, W3 160 CS73
Sch East Acton Prim Sch, W3
off East Acton La 160 CS73
East Arbour St, E1 21 J8
East Av, E12 166 EL66
E17 145 EB56
Hayes UB3 177 BT75
Southall UB1 158 BZ73
Wallington SM6 241 DM106
Whiteley Village KT12
off Octagon Rd 235 BT110
East Bk, N16 144 DS59
Eastbank Cl, E17
off Grosvenor Pk Rd 145 EB57
Eastbank Rd, Hmptn H. TW12 198 CC92
EAST BARNET, Barn. EN4 102 DE44
East Barnet Rd, Barn. EN4 102 DE44
Sch East Barnet Sch, Barn. EN4 off Chestnut Gro 102 DF44
EAST BEDFONT, Felt. TW14 197 BS88
Coll East Berkshire Coll, Langley Campus, Langley SL3
off Station Rd 175 BA76
Windsor Campus, Wind. SL4
off St. Leonards Rd 173 AQ82
Eastbourne Av, W3 160 CR72
Eastbourne Gdns, SW14 180 CQ83
Eastbourne Ms, W2 15 P8
Eastbourne Rd, E6 25 M2
E15 13 K9
N15 144 DS58
SW17 202 DG93
W4 180 CQ79
Brentford TW8 179 CJ78
Feltham TW13 198 BX89
Godstone RH9 274 DW132
Slough SL1 153 AM72
Eastbourne Ter, W2 15 P8
Eastbournia Av, N9 122 DV48
Eastbridge, Slou. SL2 174 AV75
Eastbrook Av, N9 122 DW45
Dagenham RM10 149 FC63
Eastbrook Cl, Dag. RM10 149 FC63
Wok. GU21 249 BA116
Sch Eastbrook Comp Sch, Dag. RM10 off Dagenham Rd 149 FC63
Eastbrook Dr, Rom. RM7 149 FE62
Sch Eastbrook Prim Sch, Hem.H. HP2 off St. Agnells La 62 BN15
Eastbrook Rd, SE3 186 EH80
Waltham Abbey EN9 90 EE33
Eastbrook Way, Hem.H. HP2 62 BL20
EAST BURNHAM, Slou. SL2 153 AN67
East Burnham La, Farn.Royal SL2 153 AN67
East Burrowfield, Welw.G.C. AL7 51 CX11
EASTBURY, Nthwd. HA6 115 BS49
Eastbury Av, Bark. IG11 167 ES67
Enfield EN1 104 DS39
Northwood HA6 115 BS50
Sch Eastbury Comp Sch, Bark. IG11 off Rosslyn Rd 167 ES65
Eastbury Ct, Bark. IG11 167 ES67
St. Albans AL1 65 CF19
Eastbury Fm Cl, Nthwd. HA6 115 BS49
Sch Eastbury Fm JMI Sch & Nurs, Nthwd. HA6
off Bishops Av 115 BT49
Eastbury Gro, W4 180 CS78
★ Eastbury Manor Ho, Bark. IG11 167 ET67
Eastbury Pl, Nthwd. HA6 115 BT50

Eastbury Prim Sch, Bark. IG11 *off Dawson Av* 167 ET66
Eastbury Rd, E6 25 L5
Kingston upon Thames KT2 200 CL94
Northwood HA6 115 BS51
Petts Wood BR5 227 ER100
Romford RM7 149 FD58
Watford WD19 115 BV45
Eastbury Sq, Bark. IG11 167 ET67
Eastbury Ter, E1 21 J5
Eastcastle St, W1 17 L8
Eastcheap, EC3 19 M10
East Churchfield Rd, W3 160 CR74
East Ch Rd, Lon.Hthrw Air. TW6 177 BS82
EAST CLANDON, Guil. GU4 266 BL131
East Cl, W5 160 CN70
Barnet EN4 102 DG42
Greenford UB6 158 CC68
Rainham RM13 169 FH70
St. Albans AL2 82 CB25
Eastcombe Av, SE7 186 EH79
East Common, Ger.Cr. SL9 134 AY58
EASTCOTE, Pnr. HA5 138 BW58
⊖ Eastcote 138 BW59
Eastcote, Orp. BR6 227 ET102
Eastcote Av, Grnf. UB6 139 CG64
Harrow HA2 138 CB61
West Molesey KT8 218 BZ99
Eastcote High Rd, Eastcote Vill. HA5 137 BU58
● Eastcote Ind Est, Ruis. HA4 138 BW59
Eastcote La, Har. HA2 138 CA62
Northolt UB5 158 CA66
Eastcote La N, Nthlt. UB5 158 BZ65
Eastcote Pl, Pnr. HA5 137 BV58
Eastcote Prim Sch, Well. DA16 *off Eastcote Rd* 187 ER83
Eastcote Rd, Harrow HA2 138 CC62
Pinner HA5 138 BX57
Ruislip HA4 137 BS59
Welling DA16 187 ER82
Eastcote St, SW9 42 C9
Eastcote Vw, Pnr. HA5 138 BW56
EASTCOTE VILLAGE, Pnr. HA5 137 BV57
Eastcott Cl, Kings.T. KT2 200 CQ92
Eastcourt, Sun. TW16 218 BW96
East Ct, Wem. HA0 139 CJ61
Eastcourt Sch, Ilf. IG3 *off Eastwood Rd* 148 EU60
East Cres, N11 120 DF49
Enfield EN1 104 DT43
Windsor SL4 173 AM81
East Cres Rd, Grav. DA12 213 GJ86
Eastcroft, Slou. SL2 153 AP70
Eastcroft Rd, Epsom KT19 238 CS108
East Cross Route, E3 11 P6
E9 11 M5
⇌ East Croydon 224 DR103
East Croydon 224 DR103
Eastdean Av, Epsom KT18 238 CP113
East Dene Dr, Harold Hill RM3 128 FK50
Eastdown Pk, SE13 185 ED84
East Dr, NW9 141 CU55
Carshalton SM5 240 DE109
Oaklands AL4 66 CL19
Orpington BR5 228 EV100
Sawbridgeworth CM21 58 EY06
Stoke Poges SL2 154 AS69
Virginia Water GU25 214 AU101
Watford WD25 97 BV35
East Duck Lees La, Enf. EN3 105 DY42
EAST DULWICH, SE22 204 DU86
⇌ East Dulwich 184 DS84
East Dulwich Gro, SE22 204 DS86
East Dulwich Rd, SE15 184 DT84
SE22 184 DT84
EAST END GREEN, Hert. SG14 53 DK13
East End Rd, N2 142 DC55
N3 120 DA54
East End Way, Pnr. HA5 138 BY55
East Entrance, Dag. RM10 169 FB68
Eastergate, Beac. HP9 110 AJ51
Eastern Av, E11 146 EJ58
Aveley RM15 170 FQ74
Chertsey KT16 216 BG97
Ilford IG2, IG4 146 EL58
Pinner HA5 138 BX59
Romford RM6 148 EW56
Waltham Cross EN8 89 DY33
West Thurrock RM20 191 FT79
Eastern Av E, Rom. RM1, RM2, RM3 149 FD55
● Eastern Av Retail Pk, Rom. RM7 149 FC56
Eastern Av W, Rom. RM1, RM5, RM6, RM7 148 EY56
Eastern Dr, B.End SL8 132 AC59
Eastern Gateway, E16 36 D1
● Eastern Ind Est, Erith DA18 188 FA75
Eastern Pathway, Horn. RM12 170 FJ67
Eastern Perimeter Rd, Lon.Hthrw Air. TW6 177 BT83
Eastern Quay Apts, E16 *off Rayleigh Rd* 36 B2
Eastern Rd, E13 166 EH68
E17 145 EC57
N2 142 DF55
N22 121 DL53
SE4 185 EA84
Grays RM17 192 GD77
Romford RM1 149 FE57
Eastern Rbt, Ilf. IG1 147 EQ61
Eastern Vw, Bigg.H. TN16 260 EJ117
Easternville Gdns, Ilf. IG2 147 EQ58
Eastern Way, SE2 168 EX74
SE28 188 EU75
Belvedere DA17 189 FB75
Erith DA18 168 EX74
Grays RM17 192 GA79
● Easter Pk, Rain. RM13 169 FE73
EAST EWELL, Sutt. SM2 239 CX110
East Ferry Rd, E14 34 D8
Eastfield Av, Wat. WD24 98 BX39
Eastfield Cl, Slou. SL1 *off St. Laurence Way* 174 AU76
Eastfield Cotts, Hayes UB3 177 BR78
Eastfield Ct, St.Alb. AL4 *off Southfield Way* 65 CK17
Eastfield Gdns, Dag. RM10 148 FA63
Eastfield Par, Pot.B. EN6 86 DD32
Eastfield Prim Sch, Enf. EN3 *off Eastfield Rd* 105 DX38
Eastfield Rd, E17 145 EA56
N8 143 DL55
Brentwood CM14 130 FX47
Burnham SL1 152 AG71
Dagenham RM9, RM10 148 FA63
Eastfield Rd, Enfield EN3 105 DX38
Redhill RH1 289 DJ135
Waltham Cross EN8 89 DY32
Eastfields, Pnr. HA5 138 BW57
Eastfields Av, SW18 182 DA84
Eastfields Rd, W3 160 CQ71
Mitcham CR4 222 DG96
Eastfield St, E14 21 M7
EAST FINCHLEY, N2 142 DD56
⊖ East Finchley 142 DE56
East Flint, Hem.H. HP1 61 BF19
East Gdns, SW17 202 DE93
Woking GU22 249 BC117
Eastgate, Bans. SM7 239 CY114
East Gate, Harl. CM20 57 EQ14
● Eastgate Business Pk, E10 145 DY60
Eastgate Cl, SE28 168 EX72
Eastgate Gdns, Guil. GU1 280 AY135
Eastglade, Nthwd. HA6 115 BS50
Pinner HA5 138 BY55
East Gorse, Croy. CR0 243 DY112
East Grn, Hem.H. HP3 80 BM25
East Hall La, Wenn. RM13 170 FK72
East Hall Rd, Orp. BR5 228 EY101
EAST HAM, E6 24 F1
⊖ East Ham 166 EL66
Eastham Cl, Barn. EN5 101 CY43
Eastham Cres, Brwd. CM13 131 GA49
● East Ham Ind Est, E6 24 G5
East Ham Manor Way, E6 25 L8
East Ham Mkt Hall, E6 *off Myrtle Rd* 166 EL67
★ East Ham Nature Reserve & Visitor Cen, E6 25 K4
East Harding St, EC4 18 F8
East Heath Rd, NW3 142 DD62
East Hill, SW18 202 DB85
Biggin Hill TN16 260 EH118
Dartford DA1 210 FM87
Oxted RH8 276 EE129
South Croydon CR2 242 DS110
South Darenth DA4 230 FQ95
Wembley HA9 140 CN61
Woking GU22 249 BC116
East Hill Dr, Dart. DA1 210 FM87
East Hill Rd, Oxt. RH8 276 EE129
Eastholm, NW11 142 DB56
East Holme, Erith DA8 189 FD81
Eastholme, Hayes UB3 157 BU74
EAST HORSLEY, Lthd. KT24 267 BS127
East India 23 H10
East India Dock Rd, E14 21 P9
East India Way, Croy. CR0 224 DT102
East Kent Av, Nthflt DA11 212 GC86
Eastlake Ho, NW8 *off Frampton St* 16 B5
Eastlake Rd, SE5 43 H9
Eastlands Cl, Oxt. RH8 275 ED127
Eastlands Cres, SE21 204 DT86
Eastlands Way, Oxt. RH8 275 ED127
East La, SE16 32 C5
Abbots Langley WD5 81 BU29
Kingston upon Thames KT1 *off High St* 219 CK97
South Darenth DA4 231 FR96
Watford WD25 81 BU29
Wembley HA0, HA9 139 CK62
West Horsley KT24 267 BQ125
● East La Business Pk, Wem. HA9 139 CK62
Eastlea Av, Wat. WD25 98 BY37
Eastlea Comm Sch, E16 23 K4
Eastlea Ms, E16 23 K5
Eastleigh Av, Har. HA2 138 CB61
Eastleigh Cl, NW2 140 CS62
Sutton SM2 240 DB108
Eastleigh Rd, E17 123 DZ54
Bexleyheath DA7 189 FC82
Eastleigh Wk, SW15 201 CU87
Eastleigh Way, Felt. TW14 197 BU88
East Lo La, Enf. EN2 103 DK36
East Mall, Rom. RM1 *off Mercury Gdns* 149 FE57
Eastman Dental Hosp, WC1 18 C3
Eastman Rd, W3 160 CR74
Eastman Way, Epsom KT19 238 CP110
Hemel Hempstead HP2 62 BN17
East Mascalls, SE7 *off Mascalls Rd* 186 EJ79
East Mead, Ruis. HA4 138 BX62
Welwyn Garden City AL7 52 DB12
Eastmead, Wok. GU21 248 AV117
Eastmead Av, Grnf. UB6 158 CB69
Eastmead Cl, Brom. BR1 226 EL96
East Meads, Guil. GU2 280 AT135
Eastmearn Rd, SE21 204 DQ89
East Ms, E15 *off East Rd* 13 N9
East Mill, Grav. DA11 213 GF86
East Milton Rd, Grav. DA12 213 GK87
East Mimms, Hem.H. HP2 62 BL19
EAST MOLESEY, KT8 219 CD98
Eastmont Rd, Esher KT10 219 CE103
Eastmoor Pl, SE7 36 E7
Eastmoor St, SE7 36 E7
East Mt St, E1 20 F7
Eastney Rd, Croy. CR0 223 DP102
Eastney St, SE10 46 G1
Eastnor, Bov. HP3 79 BA28
Eastnor Cl, Reig. RH2 287 CZ137
Eastnor Rd, SE9 207 EQ88
Reigate RH2 288 DA136
Easton Gdns, Borwd. WD6 100 CR42
Easton St, WC1 18 E3
Eastor, Welw.G.C. AL7 52 DA06
East Pk, Harl. CM17 58 EV12
Sawbridgeworth CM21 58 EY06
East Pk Cl, Rom. RM6 148 EX57
East Parkside, SE10 35 L5
Warlingham CR6 259 EA116
East Pas, EC1 19 H6
East Pier, E1 32 E3
East Pl, SE27 *off Pilgrim Hill* 204 DQ91
East Pt, SE1 32 C10
East Poultry Av, EC1 18 G7
⊖ East Putney 201 CY85
East Ramp, Lon.Hthrw Air. TW6 177 BP81
East Ridgeway, Cuffley EN6 87 DK29
East Rd, E15 13 N9
N1 19 L3
SW3 40 G1
SW19 202 DC93
Barnet EN4 120 DG46
Chadwell Heath RM6 148 EY57
Edgware HA8 118 CP53
Enfield EN3 104 DW38
Feltham TW14 197 BR87
Harlow CM20 58 EV11
East Rd, Kingston upon Thames KT2 220 CL95
Reigate RH2 271 CZ133
Rush Green RM7 149 FD59
Welling DA16 188 EV82
West Drayton UB7 176 BM77
Weybridge KT13 235 BR108
East Rochester Way, SE9 187 ES84
Bexley DA5 208 EX86
Sidcup DA15 187 ES84
East Row, E11 146 EG58
W10 14 E5
Eastry Av, Brom. BR2 226 EF100
Eastry Rd, Erith DA8 188 FA80
East Shalford La, Guil. GU4 280 AY139
EAST SHEEN, SW14 180 CR84
East Sheen Av, SW14 180 CR84
East Sheen Prim Sch, SW14 *off Upper Richmond Rd W* 180 CS84
Eastside Ms, E3 22 A1
Eastside Rd, NW11 141 CZ56
East Smithfield, E1 32 B1
East St, SE17 31 K10
Barking IG11 167 EQ66
Bexleyheath DA7 188 FA84
Bookham KT23 268 CB125
Brentford TW8 179 CJ80
Bromley BR1 226 EG96
Chertsey KT16 216 BG101
Chesham HP5 76 AP32
Epsom KT17 238 CS113
Grays RM17 192 GC79
Hemel Hempstead HP2 62 BK20
South Stifford RM20 192 FY79
Ware SG12 55 DX06
East Surrey College, Gatton Pt N, Red. RH1 *off Claremont Rd* 272 DG130
Gatton Pt S, Red. RH1 *off College Cres* 272 DG131
East Surrey Gro, SE15 44 A5
East Surrey Hosp, Red. RH1 288 DG138
★ East Surrey Mus, Cat. CR3 258 DU124
East Tenter St, E1 20 B9
East Ter, Grav. DA12 213 GJ86
East Thurrock Rd, Grays RM17 192 GB79
East Twrs, Pnr. HA5 138 BX57
East Vale, W3 *off The Vale* 161 CT74
East Vw, E4 123 EC50
Barnet EN5 101 CZ41
Essendon AL9 68 DF17
Eastview Av, SE18 187 ES80
★ East Village London, E20 12 E3
Eastville Av, NW11 141 CZ58
East Wk, E.Barn. EN4 120 DG45
Harlow CM20 57 ER14
Hayes UB3 157 BU74
Reigate RH2 272 DB134
Eastway, E9 11 N4
East Way, E11 146 EH57
Eastway, Beac. HP9 110 AG54
East Way, Brom. BR2 226 EG101
Croydon CR0 225 DY103
Eastway, Epsom KT19 238 CQ112
Gatwick RH6 291 DH152
East Way, Guil. GU2 264 AT134
Hayes UB3 157 BU74
Eastway, Mord. SM4 221 CX99
East Way, Ruis. HA4 137 BU60
Eastway, Wall. SM6 241 DJ105
Eastway Cres, Har. HA2 *off Eliot Dr* 138 CB61
Eastwell Cl, Beck. BR3 225 DY95
EASTWICK, Harl. CM20 57 EP11
Eastwick Ct, SW19 *off Victoria Dr* 201 CX88
Eastwick Cres, Mill End WD3 113 BF47
Eastwick Dr, Bkhm KT23 252 CA123
Eastwick Hall La, Harl. CM20 57 EN09
EAST WICKHAM, Well. DA16 188 EU80
East Wickham Inf Sch, Well. DA16 *off Wickham St* 187 ET81
East Wickham Jun Sch, Well. DA16 *off Wickham St* 188 EU81
Eastwick Inf Sch, Bkhm KT23 *off Eastwick Dr* 252 CB124
Eastwick Jun Sch, Bkhm KT23 *off Eastwick Dr* 252 CB124
Eastwick Lo Rbt, Harl. CM20 57 EQ11
Eastwick Pk Av, Bkhm KT23 252 CB124
Eastwick Rd, Bkhm KT23 268 CB125
Harlow CM20 57 EM11
Hersham KT12 235 BV106
Hunsdon SG12 56 EK08
Stanstead Abbotts SG12 56 EF12
Eastwick Row, Hem.H. HP2 62 BN21
East Wood Apts, Ald.WD25 *off Wall Hall Dr* 98 CB36
Eastwood Cl, E18 *off George La* 124 EG54
N7 8 D2
N17 122 DV52
Eastwood Ct, Hem.H. HP2 62 BN19
Eastwood Dr, Rain. RM13 169 FH72
Eastwood Rd, E18 124 EG54
N10 120 DG54
Bramley GU5 281 AZ144
Ilford IG3 148 EU59
West Drayton UB7 176 BN75
East Woodside, Bex. DA5 208 EY88
Eastwood St, SW16 203 DJ93
Eastworth Rd, Cher. KT16 216 BG102
Eatington Rd, E10 145 ED57
Eaton Av, Slou. SL1 152 AJ73
Eaton Cl, SW1 28 G9
Stanmore HA7 117 CH49
Eaton Ct, Guil. GU1 265 BA132
Eaton Dr, SW9 183 DP84
Kingston upon Thames KT2 200 CN94
Romford RM5 127 FB52
Eaton Gdns, Brox. EN10 71 DY22
Dagenham RM9 168 EY66
Eaton Gate, SW1 28 G8
Northwood HA6 115 BQ51
Eaton Ho, E14 *off Westferry Circ* 33 P1
Eaton La, SW1 29 K7
Eaton Ms N, SW1 28 G8
Eaton Ms S, SW1 29 H8
Eaton Ms W, SW1 29 H8
Eaton Pk, Cob. KT11 236 BY114
Eaton Pk Rd, N13 121 DN47
Cobham KT11 236 BY114
Eaton Pl, SW1 28 G7
Eaton Ri, E11 146 EJ57
W5 159 CK72
Eaton Rd, NW4 141 CW57
Enfield EN1 104 DS41
Hemel Hempstead HP2 63 BP17
Hounslow TW3 179 CD84
St. Albans AL1 65 CH20
Sidcup DA14 208 EX89
Sutton SM2 240 DD107
Upminster RM14 151 FS61
Eaton Row, SW1 29 J6
Eatons Mead, E4 123 EA47
Eaton Sq, SW1 29 J6
Longfield DA3 *off Bramblefield Cl* 231 FX97
Eaton Ter, SW1 28 G8
Eaton Ter Ms, SW1 28 G8
Eatonville Rd, SW17 202 DF89
Eatonville Vil, SW17 *off Eatonville Rd* 202 DF89
Eaton Way, Borwd. WD6 100 CM39
Eaves Cl, Add. KT15 234 BJ107
Ebbas Way, Epsom KT18 254 CP115
Ebb Ct, E16 *off Albert Basin Way* 167 EQ73
Ebberns Rd, Hem.H. HP3 62 BK23
Ebbett Ct, W3 *off Victoria Rd* 160 CR71
Ebbisham Cl, Dor. RH4 *off Nower Rd* 285 CG136
Ebbisham Dr, SW8 42 C2
Ebbisham La, Walt.Hill KT20 255 CT121
Ebbisham Rd, Epsom KT18 238 CP114
Worcester Park KT4 221 CW103
● Ebbsfleet Business Pk, Nthflt. DA11 212 GA85
Ebbsfleet Gateway, Nthflt DA11 212 GA88
⇌ Ebbsfleet International 212 GA86
Ebbsfleet Rd, NW2 4 E2
Ebbsfleet Wk, Nthflt DA11 212 GB86
Ebdon Way, SE3 186 EH83
Ebenezer Ho, SE11 30 F9
Ebenezer St, N1 19 L2
Ebenezer Wk, SW16 223 DJ95
Ebley Cl, SE15 44 A3
Ebner St, SW18 202 DB85
Ebor Cotts, SW15 200 CS90
Ebor St, E1 20 A4
Ebrington Rd, Har. HA3 139 CK58
Ebsworth Cl, Maid. SL6 152 AC68
Ebsworth St, SE23 205 DX87
Eburne Rd, N7 143 DL62
Ebury App, Rick. WD3 *off Ebury Rd* 114 BK46
Ebury Br, SW1 29 J10
Ebury Br Est, SW1 29 J10
Ebury Br Rd, SW1 41 H1
Ebury Cl, Kes. BR2 226 EL104
Northwood HA6 115 BQ50
Ebury Ms, SE27 203 DP90
SW1 29 H8
Ebury Ms E, SW1 29 J8
Ebury Rd, Rick. WD3 114 BK46
Watford WD17 98 BW41
Ebury Sq, SW1 29 H9
Ebury St, SW1 29 J8
Ebury Way Cycle Path, The, Rick. WD3 115 BP45
Watford WD18 115 BP45
Ecclesbourne Cl, N13 121 DN50
Ecclesbourne Gdns, N13 121 DN50
Ecclesbourne Prim Sch, Th.Hth. CR7 *off Bensham La* 224 DQ99
Ecclesbourne Rd, N1 9 K7
Thornton Heath CR7 224 DQ99
Eccles Hill, N.Holm. RH5 285 CJ140
Eccles Rd, SW11 182 DF84
Eccleston Br, SW1 29 K8
Eccleston Cl, Cockfos. EN4 102 DF42
Orpington BR6 227 ER102
Eccleston Cres, Rom. RM6 148 EU59
Ecclestone Ct, Wem. HA9 *off St. John's Rd* 140 CL64
Ecclestone Pl, Wem. HA9 140 CM64
Eccleston Ms, SW1 29 H7
Eccleston Pl, SW1 29 J8
Eccleston Rd, W13 159 CG73
Eccleston Sq, SW1 29 K9
Eccleston Sq Ms, SW1 29 L9
Eccleston St, SW1 29 J7
Echelforde Dr, Ashf. TW15 196 BN91
Echelford Prim Sch, The, Ashf. TW15 *off Park Rd* 197 BP92
Echo Hts, E4 123 EB46
Echo Pit Rd, Guil. GU1 280 AY138
Echo Sq, Grav. DA12 *off Old Rd E* 213 GJ89
Eckford St, N1 8 E10
Eckington Ho, N15 144 DR58
Eckstein Rd, SW11 182 DE84
Eclipse Ho, N22 *off Station Rd* 121 DM54
Eclipse Rd, E13 24 A6
Ecob Cl, Guil. GU3 264 AT130
Ecole Française de Londres, W6 26 D8
Ecton Rd, Add. KT15 234 BH105
Ector Rd, SE6 206 EE89
Edbrooke Rd, W9 15 J4
Eddington Cres, Welw.G.C. AL7 51 CX12
Eddinton Cl, New Adgtn. CR0 243 EC107
Eddiscombe Rd, SW6 39 H8
Eddy Cl, Rom. RM7 149 FB58
Eddystone Rd, SE4 205 DY85
Eddystone Twr, SE8 33 M9
Eddystone Wk, Stai. TW19 196 BL87
Eddy St, Berk. HP4 60 AU18
Ede Cl, Houns. TW3 178 BZ83
Edenbridge Cl, SE16 44 F1
Orpington BR5 228 EX98
Edenbridge Rd, E9 11 K7
Enfield EN1 104 DS44
Eden Cl, NW3 142 DA61
W8 27 K6
Bexley DA5 209 FD91
Enfield EN3 105 EA38
New Haw KT15 234 BH110
Slough SL3 175 BA78
Wembley HA0 159 CK67
Edencourt Rd, SW16 203 DH93
Edencroft, Bramley GU5 281 AZ144
Edendale Rd, Bexh. DA7 189 FD81
Edenfield Gdns, Wor.Pk. KT4 221 CT104
Eden Grn, S.Ock. RM15 171 FV71
Eden Gro, E17 145 EB57
N7 8 D3
NW10 *off St. Andrews Rd* 161 CV65
Eden Gro Rd, Byfleet KT14 234 BL113
Edenhall Cl, Hem.H. HP2 63 BR21
Romford RM3 128 FJ50
Edenhall Glen, Rom. RM3 128 FJ50
Edenhall Rd, Rom. RM3 128 FJ50
Edenham High Sch, Croy. CR0 *off Orchard Way* 225 DZ101
Edenham Way, W10 14 G6
Eden Ho, SE16 *off Canada St* 33 J5
Edenhurst Av, SW6 38 G10
Eden Ms, SW17 *off Huntspill St* 202 DC90
EDEN PARK, Beck. BR3 225 EA99
⇌ Eden Park 225 EA99
Eden Pk Av, Beck. BR3 225 DY98
Eden Pl, Grav. DA12 *off Lord St* 213 GH87
Eden Rd, E17 145 EB57
SE27 203 DP92
Beckenham BR3 225 DY98
Bexley DA5 209 FC91
Croydon CR0 242 DR105
Edenside Rd, Bkhm KT23 252 BZ124
Edensor Gdns, W4 180 CS80
Edensor Rd, W4 180 CS80
Eden St, Kings.T. KT1 219 CK96
Edenvale, Goffs Oak EN7 88 DV29
Edenvale Cl, Mitch. CR4 *off Edenvale Rd* 202 DG94
Edenvale Rd, Mitch. CR4 202 DG94
Edenvale St, SW6 39 M9
Eden Wk, Kings.T. KT1 *off Eden Wk Shop Cen* 220 CL96
Eden Wk Shop Cen, Kings.T. KT1 220 CL96
Eden Way, E3 *off Old Ford Rd* 11 P9
Beckenham BR3 225 DZ99
Warlingham CR6 259 DY118
Ederline Av, SW16 223 DM97
Edes Flds, Reig. RH2 287 CY136
★ EDF Energy London Eye, SE1 30 C4
Edgar Cl, Swan. BR8 229 FF97
Edgar Ho, E11 146 EG59
NW7 *off Morphou Rd* 119 CY50
Edgar Kail Way, SE22 184 DS84
Edgarley Ter, SW6 38 E7
Edgar Myles Ho, E16 *off Malmesbury Rd* 23 L6
Edgar Rd, E3 22 D2
Hounslow TW4 198 BZ87
Romford RM6 148 EX59
South Croydon CR2 242 DR109
Tatsfield TN16 260 EK121
West Drayton UB7 156 BL73
Edgars Ct, Welw.G.C. AL7 51 CY10
Edgar Wallace Cl, SE15 43 P4
Edgbaston Dr, Shenley WD7 84 CL32
Edgbaston Rd, Wat. WD19 115 BV48
Edgeborough Way, Brom. BR1 206 EK94
Edgebury, Chis. BR7 207 EP91
Edgebury Prim Sch, Chis. BR7 *off Belmont La* 207 EQ91
Edgebury Wk, Chis. BR7 207 EQ91
● Edge Business Cen, NW2 141 CV61
Edge Cl, Wey. KT13 234 BN108
Edgecombe Ho, SW19 201 CY88
Edgecoombe, S.Croy. CR2 242 DW108
Edgecoombe Cl, Kings.T. KT2 200 CR94
Edgecote Cl, W3 *off Cheltenham Pl* 160 CQ74
Edgecot Gro, N15 144 DS57
Edgefield Av, Bark. IG11 167 ET66
Edgefield Cl, Dart. DA1 210 FP88
Redhill RH1 288 DG139
Edge Gro Sch, Ald. WD25 *off High Cross* 98 CC37
Edge Hill, SE18 187 EP79
SW19 201 CX94
Edge Hill Av, N3 142 DA56
Edge Hill Ct, SW19 201 CX94
Edgehill Ct, Walt. KT12 *off St. Johns Dr* 218 BW102
Edgehill Gdns, Dag. RM10 148 FA63
Edgehill Rd, W13 159 CJ71
Chislehurst BR7 207 EQ90
Mitcham CR4 223 DH95
Purley CR8 241 DN110
Edgeley, Bkhm KT23 252 BY124
Edgeley Caravan Pk, Far.Grn GU5 282 BL143
Edgeley La, SW4 *off Edgeley Rd* 183 DK83
Edgeley Rd, SW4 41 N10
Edgell Cl, Vir.W. GU25 215 AZ97
Edgell Rd, Stai. TW18 195 BF92
Edgel St, SW18 *off Ferrier St* 182 DB84
Edge Pt Cl, SE27 203 DP92
Edge St, W8 27 K2
Edgewood Dr, Orp. BR6 245 ET106
Edgewood Grn, Croy. CR0 225 DX102
Edgeworth Av, NW4 141 CU57
Edgeworth Cl, NW4 141 CU57
Whyteleafe CR3 258 DU118
Edgeworth Cres, NW4 141 CU57
Edgeworth Rd, SE9 186 EJ84
Cockfosters EN4 102 DE42
Edgington Rd, SW16 203 DK93
Edgington Way, Sid. DA14 208 EW94
Edgson Ho, SW1 *off Ebury Br Rd* 29 J10
EDGWARE, HA8 118 CP50
⊖ Edgware 118 CP51
⊖ Edgware 118 CN51
Edgwarebury Gdns, Edg. HA8 118 CN50
Edgwarebury La, Edg. HA8 118 CN49
Elstree WD6 118 CL45
Edgware Comm Hosp, Edg. HA8 118 CP52
Edgware Ct, Edg. HA8 *off High St* 118 CN51
Edgware Inf Sch, Edg. HA8 *off High St* 118 CN51
Edgware Jun Sch, Edg. HA8 *off Heming Rd* 118 CN51
⊖ Edgware Road 16 C7
Edgware Rd, NW2 141 CV60
NW9 140 CR55
W2 16 D8
Edgware Rd Sub, W2 *off Edgware Rd* 16 C7
Edgware Way, Edg. HA8 118 CM49
Edinburgh Av, Mill End WD3 96 BG44
Slough SL1 153 AN71

Edinburgh Cl, E2 20 G1
Pinner HA5 138 BX59
Uxbridge UB10 137 BP63
Edinburgh Ct, SW20 221 CX99
Kingston upon Thames KT1
off Watersplash Cl 220 CL97
Edinburgh Cres, Wal.Cr. EN8 89 DY33
Edinburgh Dr, Abb.L. WD5 81 BU32
Ickenham UB10 137 BP63
Staines-upon-Thames TW18 196 BK93
Edinburgh Gdns, Wind. SL4 173 AR83
Edinburgh Gate, SW1 28 E4
Denham UB9 135 BF58
Harlow CM20 57 ER12
Edinburgh Ho, W9 15 M2
Edinburgh Ms, Til. RM18 193 GH82
Edinburgh Pl, Harl. CM20 58 EU11
Sch Edinburgh Prim Sch, E17
off Edinburgh Rd 145 DZ57
Edinburgh Rd, E13 166 EH68
E17 145 EA57
N18 122 DU50
W7 179 CF75
Sutton SM1 222 DC103
Edinburgh Way, Harl. CM20 57 ER12
Edington Rd, SE2 188 EV76
Enfield EN3 104 DW40
Edison Av, Horn. RM12 149 FF61
Edison Cl, E17 off Exeter Rd 145 EA57
Hornchurch RM12
off Edison Av 149 FF60
St. Albans AL4 65 CJ21
West Drayton UB7 176 BM75
Edison Ct, SE10 35 M8
Watford WD18 97 BU44
Edison Dr, Sthl. UB1 158 CB72
Wembley HA9 140 CL62
Edison Gro, SE18 187 ET80
Edison Rd, N8 143 DK58
Bromley BR2 226 EG96
Enfield EN3 105 DZ40
Welling DA16 187 ET81
Edis St, NW1 6 G8
Edith Cavell Cl, N19
off Hillrise Rd 143 DL59
Edith Cavell Way, SE18 186 EL81
Edith Gdns, Surb. KT5 220 CP101
Edith Gro, SW10 39 N3
Edithna St, SW9 42 B10
Edith Nesbit Wk, SE9 206 EL85
Sch Edith Neville Prim Sch,
NW1 17 N1
Edith Rd, E6 166 EK66
E15 13 H2
N11 121 DK52
SE25 224 DR99
SW19 202 DB93
W14 26 E9
Orpington BR6 246 EU106
Romford RM6 148 EX58
Edith Row, SW6 39 M6
Edith St, E2 10 C10
Edith Summerskill Ho, SW6 39 H3
Edith Ter, SW10 39 N4
Edith Vil, SW15
off Bective Rd 181 CY84
W14 26 G9
Edith Yd, SW10 39 P4
Edlyn Cl, Berk. HP4 60 AT18
Edmansons Cl, N17 122 DS53
Edmeston Cl, E9 11 M4
Edmond Beaufort Dr, St.Alb.
AL3 65 CD18
Edmonds Ct, W.Mol. KT8
off Avern Rd 218 CB99
EDMONTON, N9 122 DU49
Sch Edmonton Co Sch, Lwr Sch,
N9 off Little Bury St 122 DS46
Upr Sch, Enf. EN1
off Great Cambridge Rd 122 DT45
⇌ Edmonton Green 122 DU47
⊖ Edmonton Green 122 DU47
Edmonton Grn, N9
off The Green 122 DU47
Edmonton Grn Mkt, N9
off Edmonton Grn Shop Cen 122 DV47
Edmonton Grn Shop Cen,
N9 122 DV47
● Edmonton Trade Pk, N18
off Eley Rd 122 DW50
Edmund Ct, Beac. HP9
off North Dr 132 AG55
Edmund Gro, Felt. TW13 198 BZ89
Edmund Halley Way, SE10 35 J5
Edmund Hurst Dr, E6 25 N7
Edmund Rd, Chaff.Hun. RM16 191 FX75
Mitcham CR4 222 DE97
Orpington BR5 228 EW100
Rainham RM13 169 FE68
Welling DA16 188 EU83
Edmunds Av, Orp. BR5 228 EX97
Edmunds Cl, Hayes UB4 158 BW71
Edmunds Ms, Kings L. WD4 80 BN29
Edmunds Rd, Hert. SG14 53 DM08
Edmunds Twr, Harl. CM19 73 EQ15
Edmund St, SE5 43 L4
Edmunds Wk, N2 142 DE56
Edmunds Way, Slou. SL2 154 AV71
Sch Edmund Waller Prim Sch,
SE14 45 J8
Edna Rd, SW20 221 CX96
Edna St, SW11 40 C7
Edrich Ho, SW4 42 A7
Edric Ho, SW1 off Page St 29 P8
Edrick Rd, Edg. HA8 118 CQ51
Edrick Wk, Edg. HA8 118 CQ51
Edric Rd, SE14 45 J4
Edridge Cl, Bushey WD23 98 CC43
Hornchurch RM12 150 FK64
Edridge Rd, Croy. CR0 224 DQ104
Edson Cl, Wat. WD25 81 BT33
Edulf Rd, Borwd. WD6 100 CP39
Edward Amey Cl, Wat. WD25 98 BW36
Edward Av, E4 123 EB51
Morden SM4 222 DD99
Sch Edward Betham C of E
Prim Sch, Grnf. UB6
off Oldfield La S 158 CC68
Edward Cl, N9 122 DT45
NW2 4 D1
Abbots Langley WD5 81 BT32
Edward Cl, Chafford Hundred
RM16 191 FX76
Hampton Hill TW12
off Edward Rd 198 CC92
Romford RM2 150 FJ55
St. Albans AL1 65 CF21
Edward Ct, E16 23 N6
Hemel Hempstead HP3 62 BK24
Staines-upon-Thames TW18 196 BJ93
Waltham Abbey EN9 90 EF33
Edwardes Pl, W8 27 H7
Edwardes Sq, W8 27 J6
Edward Gro, Barn. EN4 102 DD43
Edward Ho, Red. RH1
off Royal Earlswood Pk 288 DG137
Edward Ms, NW1 17 K1
Edward Pauling Ho, Felt. TW14
off Westmacott Dr 197 BT87
Sch Edward Pauling Prim Sch, Felt.
TW13 off Redford Cl 197 BS89
Edward Pl, SE8 45 P3
Edward Rd, E17 145 DX56
SE20 205 DX94
Barnet EN4 102 DD43
Biggin Hill TN16 260 EL118
Bromley BR1 206 EH94
Chislehurst BR7 207 EP92
Coulsdon CR5 257 DK115
Croydon CR0 224 DS101
Feltham TW14 197 BR85
Hampton Hill TW12 198 CC92
Harrow HA2 138 CC55
Northolt UB5 158 BW68
Romford RM6 148 EY58
Edward's Av, Ruis. HA4 157 BV65
Edwards Cl, Hutt. CM13 131 GE44
Worcester Park KT4 221 CX103
Edwards Cotts, N1 8 G5
Edwards Ct, Slou. SL1 174 AS75
Waltham Cross EN8
off Turners Hill 89 DX31
Edwards Dr, N11
off Gordon Rd 121 DK52
Edward II Av, Byfleet KT14 234 BM114
Edwards Gdns, Swan. BR8 229 FD98
Edwards La, N16 144 DR61
Edwards Ms, N1 8 F6
W1 16 G9
Edward Sq, N1 8 C9
SE16 33 M2
Edwards Rd, Belv. DA17 188 FA77
Edward St, E16 23 N5
SE8 45 N4
SE14 45 M4
Edward's Way, SE4
off Adelaide Av 205 EA85
Edwards Way, Hutt. CM13 131 GE44
Edwards Yd, Wem. HA0
off Mount Pleasant 160 CL67
Edward Temme Av, E15 13 L7
Edward Tyler Rd, SE12 206 EH89
Edward Way, Ashf. TW15 196 BM89
Sch Edward Wilson Prim Sch,
W2 15 L6
Edwina Gdns, Ilf. IG4 146 EL57
Edwin Av, E6 25 L1
Edwin Cl, Bexh. DA7 188 EZ79
Rainham RM13 169 FF69
West Horsley KT24 267 BR125
Edwin Hall Pl, SE13
off Hither Grn La 205 ED86
Sch Edwin Lambert Sch, Horn.
RM11 off Malvern Rd 149 FG59
Edwin Pl, Croy. CR0
off Cross Rd 224 DR102
Edwin Rd, Dart. DA2 209 FH90
Edgware HA8 118 CR51
Twickenham TW1, TW2 199 CF88
West Horsley KT24 267 BQ125
Edwin's Mead, E9
off Lindisfarne Way 145 DY63
Edwin St, E1 21 H4
E16 23 N7
Gravesend DA12 213 GH87
Edwin Ware Ct, Pnr. HA5
off Crossway 116 BW54
Edwyn Cl, Barn. EN5 101 CW44
Edwyn Ho, SW18
off Neville Gill Cl 202 DB86
Eel Brook Cl, SW6 39 L6
Eel Brook Studios, SW6 39 K5
Eel Pie Island, Twick. TW1 199 CG88
Effie Pl, SW6 39 K5
Effie Rd, SW6 39 K5
EFFINGHAM, Lthd. KT24 268 BY127
Effingham Cl, Sutt. SM2 240 DB108
Effingham Common, Eff.
KT24 251 BU123
Effingham Common Rd, Eff.
KT24 251 BU123
Effingham Ct, Wok. GU22
off Constitution Hill 248 AY119
Effingham Hill, Dor. RH5 268 BX132
⇌ Effingham Junction 251 BU123
Effingham Pl, Eff. KT24 268 BX127
Effingham Rd, N8 143 DN57
SE12 206 EE85
Croydon CR0 223 DM101
Long Ditton KT6 219 CH101
Reigate RH2 288 DB135
Effort St, SW17 202 DE92
Effra Par, SW2 203 DN85
Effra Rd, SW2 183 DN84
SW19 202 DB93
Egan Cl, Ken. CR8 258 DR120
Egan Way, Hayes UB3 157 BS73
Egbert St, NW1 6 G8
Egbury Ho, SW15
off Tangley Gro 201 CT86
Egdean Wk, Sev. TN13 279 FJ123
Egeremont Rd, SE13 46 D8
Egerton Av, Swan. BR8 209 FF94
Egerton Cl, Dart. DA1 209 FH88
Pinner HA5 137 BU56
Egerton Ct, Guil. GU2
off Egerton Rd 264 AS134
Egerton Cres, SW3 28 D8
Egerton Dr, SE10 46 C6
Egerton Gdns, NW4 141 CV56
NW10 4 A9
SW3 28 C7
W13 159 CH72
Ilford IG3 147 ET62
Egerton Gdns Ms, SW3 28 D7
Egerton Pl, SW3 28 D7
Weybridge KT13 235 BQ107
Egerton Rd, N16 144 DT59
SE25 224 DS97
Berkhamsted HP4 60 AU17
Egerton Rd, Guildford GU2 264 AS134
New Malden KT3 221 CT98
Slough SL2 153 AL70
Twickenham TW2 199 CE87
Wembley HA0 160 CM66
Weybridge KT13 235 BQ107
Sch Egerton-Rothesay Nurs &
Pre-Prep Sch, Berk. HP4
off Charles St 60 AV19
Sch Egerton-Rothesay Sch, Berk.
HP4 off Durrants La 60 AT19
Egerton Ter, SW3 28 D7
Egerton Way, Hayes UB3 177 BP80
Eggardon Ct, Nthlt. UB5
off Lancaster Rd 158 CC65
Egg Fm La, Kings L. WD4 81 BP30
Egg Hall, Epp. CM16 92 EU29
Eggesfield Cl, Berk. HP4 60 AS17
EGHAM, TW20 195 BA93
⇌ Egham 195 BA92
● Egham Business Village,
Egh. TW20 215 BC96
Egham Bypass, Egh. TW20 195 AZ92
Egham Cl, SW19 201 CY89
Sutton SM3 221 CY103
Egham Cres, Sutt. SM3 221 CX104
Egham Hill, Egh. TW20 194 AX93
EGHAM HYTHE, Stai. TW18 195 BE93
★ Egham Mus, Egh. TW20 195 BA92
Egham Rd, E13 24 B6
Eghams Cl, Knot.Grn HP9 110 AJ51
Eghams Wd Rd, Beac. HP9 110 AH51
EGHAM WICK, Egh. TW20 194 AU94
Eglantine La, Dart. DA4 230 FN101
Eglantine Rd, SW18 202 DC85
Egleston Rd, Mord. SM4 222 DB100
Egley Dr, Wok. GU22 248 AX122
Egley Rd, Wok. GU22 248 AX122
Eglington Ct, SE17 43 J2
Eglington Rd, E4 123 ED45
Eglinton Hill, SE18 187 EP79
Sch Eglinton Prim Sch & Early
Years Cen, SE18
off Paget Ri 187 EN80
Eglinton Rd, SE18 187 EN79
Swanscombe DA10 212 FZ86
Eglise Rd, Warl. CR6 259 DY117
Egliston Ms, SW15 181 CW83
Egliston Rd, SW15 181 CW83
Eglon Ms, NW1 6 F7
Egmont Av, Surb. KT6 220 CM102
Egmont Ms, Epsom KT19 238 CR105
Egmont Pk Rd, Walt.Hill KT20 271 CU125
Egmont Rd, N.Mal. KT3 221 CT98
Surbiton KT6 220 CM102
Sutton SM2 240 DC108
Walton-on-Thames KT12 217 BV101
Egmont St, SE14 45 K5
Egmont Way, Tad. KT20 255 CY119
Egremont Gdns, Slou. SL1 153 AN74
Egremont Ho, SE13 46 D8
Egremont Rd, SE27 203 DN90
Egret Ct, Enf. EN3
off Teal Cl 104 DW36
Egret Way, Hayes UB4 158 BX71
EGYPT, Slou. SL2 133 AQ63
Egypt La, Farn.Com. SL2 133 AP61
Eider Cl, E7 13 L2
Hayes UB4 off Cygnet Way 158 BX71
Eight Acres, Burn. SL1 152 AH70
Eighteenth Rd, Mitch. CR4 223 DL98
Eighth Av, E12 147 EM63
Hayes UB3 157 BU74
Eileen Rd, SE25 224 DR99
Eindhoven Cl, Cars. SM5 222 DG102
Eisenhower Dr, E6 25 H7
Elaine Gro, NW5 6 G2
Elam Cl, SE5 43 H9
Elam St, SE5 43 H8
Eland Pl, Croy. CR0
off Eland Rd 223 DP104
Eland Rd, SW11 40 F10
Croydon CR0 223 DP104
Sch Elangeni Sch, Amer. HP6
off Woodside Av 77 AS36
Elan Rd, S.Ock. RM15 171 FU71
Elba Pl, SE17 31 K8
Elberon Av, Croy. CR0 223 DJ100
Elbe St, SW6 39 N8
Elborough Rd, SE25 224 DU99
Elborough St, SW18 202 DA88
Elbow La, Hert.Hth SG13 70 DV17
Elbow Meadow, Colnbr. SL3 175 BF81
Elbury Dr, E16 23 P9
Elcho St, SW11 40 C5
Elcot Av, SE15 44 E4
● Eldenwall Est, Dag. RM8 148 EZ60
Elder Av, N8 143 DL57
Elderbek Cl, Chsht EN7 88 DU28
Elderberry Cl, Ilf. IG6
off Hazel La 125 EP52
Elderberry Gro, SE27
off Linton Gro 204 DQ91
Elderberry Rd, W5 180 CL75
Elderberry Way, E6 25 K2
Watford WD25 97 BV35
Elder Cl, N20 120 DB47
Guildford GU4 265 BA131
Sidcup DA15 207 ET88
West Drayton UB7 156 BL73
Elder Ct, Bushey Hth WD23 117 CE47
Elderfield, Harl. CM17 58 EX11
Welwyn Garden City AL7 52 DB10
Elderfield Pl, SW17 203 DH91
Elderfield Rd, E5 11 H1
Stoke Poges SL2 154 AT65
Elderfield Wk, E11 146 EH57
Elderflower Way, E15 13 J6
Elder Gdns, SE27 204 DQ91
Elder Oak Cl, SE20 224 DV95
Elder Pl, S.Croy. CR2 241 DP107
Elder Rd, SE27 204 DQ92
Eldersley Cl, Red. RH1 272 DF132
Elderslie Cl, Beck. BR3 225 EB99
Elderslie Rd, SE9 207 EN85
Elder St, E1 20 A6
Elderton Rd, SE26 205 DY91
Eldertree Pl, Mitch. CR4
off Eldertree Way 223 DJ95
Eldertree Way, Mitch. CR4 223 DH95
Elder Wk, N1 9 H8
SE13 off Bankside Av 185 EC83
Elder Way, Langley SL3 175 AZ75
North Holmwood RH5 285 CJ140
Rainham RM13 170 FK69
Elderwood Pl, SE27 204 DQ92
Eldon Av, Borwd. WD6 100 CN40
Croydon CR0 224 DW103
Hounslow TW5 178 CA80
Eldon Ct, Rom. RM1
off Slaney Rd 149 FE57
Eldon Gro, NW3 6 B2
Sch Eldon Inf Sch, N9
off Eldon Rd 122 DW46
Sch Eldon Jun Sch, N9
off Eldon Rd 122 DW46
Eldon Pk, SE25 224 DV98
Eldon Rd, E17 145 DZ56
N9 122 DW47
N22 121 DP53
W8 27 M7
Caterham CR3 258 DR121
Hoddesdon EN11 71 ED19
Eldon St, EC2 19 M7
Eldon Way, NW10 160 CP68
Eldred Dr, Orp. BR5 228 EW103
Eldred Gdns, Upmin. RM14 151 FS59
Eldred Rd, Bark. IG11 167 ES67
Eldrick Ct, Felt. TW14 197 BR88
Eldridge Cl, Felt. TW14 197 BU88
Eldridge Ct, Dag. RM10
off St. Mark's Pl 169 FB65
Eleanor Av, Epsom KT19 238 CR110
St. Albans AL3 65 CD18
Eleanor Cl, N15 144 DT55
SE16 33 J4
Eleanor Cres, NW7 119 CX49
Eleanor Cross Rd, Wal.Cr. EN8 89 DY34
Eleanore Pl, St.Alb. AL3 65 CD18
Eleanor Gdns, Barn. EN5 101 CX43
Dagenham RM8 148 EZ62
Eleanor Gro, SW13 180 CS83
Ickenham UB10 137 BP62
Sch Eleanor Palmer Prim Sch,
NW5 7 L1
Eleanor Rd, E8 10 E5
E15 13 M5
N11 121 DL51
Chalfont St. Peter SL9 112 AW53
Hertford SG14 54 DQ08
Waltham Cross EN8 89 DY33
Sch Eleanor Smith Sch, E13 24 A1
Eleanor St, E3 22 A3
Eleanor Wk, SE18 37 J9
Greenhithe DA9 191 FW84
Eleanor Way, Wal.Cr. EN8 89 DZ34
Warley CM14 130 FX50
Electra Av, Lon.Hthrw Air.
TW6 177 BT83
● Electra Business Pk, E16 23 H6
Electric Av, SW9 183 DN84
Enfield EN3 105 DZ36
Electric La, SW9 183 DN84
Electric Par, E18
off George La 124 EG54
Surbiton KT6 219 CK100
Elektron Ho, E14 23 H10
Element Ho, Enf. EN3
off Tysoe Av 105 DZ36
⇌ Elephant & Castle 31 J8
⊖ Elephant & Castle 31 J8
Elephant & Castle, SE1 31 H7
Elephant & Castle Shop Cen,
SE1 off Elephant & Castle 31 J8
Elephant La, SE16 32 G4
Elephant Rd, SE17 31 J8
Elers Rd, W13 179 CJ75
Hayes UB3 177 BR77
Eleven Acre Ri, Loug. IG10 107 EM41
● Eley Est, N18 122 DW50
Eley Rd, N18 123 DX50
Eley Rd Retail Pk, N18 123 DX50
Elfindale Rd, SE24 204 DQ85
Elfin Gro, Tedd. TW11
off Broad St 199 CF92
Elford Cl, SE3 186 EH84
Elfort Rd, N5 143 DN63
Elfrida Cres, SE6 205 EA91
Sch Elfrida Prim Sch, SE6
off Elfrida Cres 205 EB91
Elfrida Rd, Wat. WD18 98 BW43
Elf Row, E1 21 H10
Elfwine Rd, W7 159 CE71
Elgal Cl, Orp. BR6 245 EP106
Elgar Av, NW10 160 CR65
SW16 223 DL97
W5 180 CL75
Surbiton KT5 220 CP101
Elgar Cl, E13 off Bushey Rd 166 EJ68
SE8 46 A5
Buckhurst Hill IG9 124 EK47
Elstree WD6 117 CJ45
Uxbridge UB10 136 BN61
Elgar Gdns, Til. RM18 193 GH81
Elgar St, SE16 33 M6
Elgin Av, W9 15 L3
W12 181 CU75
Ashford TW15 197 BQ93
Harrow HA3 117 CH54
Romford RM3 128 FP52
Elgin Cl, W12 181 CV75
Elgin Cres, W11 14 G9
Caterham CR3 258 DU122
London Heathrow Airport TW6
off Eastern Perimeter Rd 177 BS82
Elgin Dr, Nthwd. HA6 115 BS52
Elgin Gdns, Guil. GU1 265 BA133
Elgin Ho, Rom. RM6 148 EZ58
Elgin Ms, W11 14 F9
Elgin Ms N, W9 15 M2
Elgin Ms S, W9 15 M2
Elgin Pl, Wey. KT13 235 BQ107
Elgin Rd, N22 121 DJ54
Broxbourne EN10 71 DZ24
Cheshunt EN8 88 DW30
Croydon CR0 224 DT102
Ilford IG3 147 ES60
Sutton SM1 222 DC104
Wallington SM6 241 DJ107
Weybridge KT13 234 BN106
Elgiva La, Chesh. HP5 76 AP31
Elgood Av, Nthwd. HA6 115 BU51
Elgood Cl, W11 26 E1
Elham Cl, Brom. BR1 206 EK94
Elham Ho, E5 off Pembury Rd 10 E3
Elia Ms, N1 18 G1
Elias Pl, SW8 42 E3
Elia St, N1 18 G1
Elibank Rd, SE9 187 EN84
Elim Est, SE1 31 N6
Elim St, SE1 31 M6
Elim Way, E13 23 M3
Eliot Bk, SE23 204 DV89
Sch Eliot Bk Prim Sch, SE26
off Thorpewood Av 204 DV89
Eliot Cotts, SE3 47 K9
Eliot Ct, N15
off Tynemouth Rd 144 DT56
Eliot Dr, Har. HA2 138 CB61
Eliot Gdns, SW15 181 CU84
Eliot Hill, SE13 46 F9
Eliot Ms, NW8 15 P1
Eliot Pk, SE13 46 F9
Eliot Pl, SE3 47 J9
Eliot Rd, Dag. RM9 148 EX63
Dartford DA1 210 FP85
Eliot Vale, SE3 47 H9
Elizabethan Cl, Stanw. TW19 196 BK87
Elizabethan Way, Stanw. TW19 196 BK87
Elizabeth Av, N1 9 K8
Amersham HP6 94 AV39
Enfield EN2 103 DP41
Ilford IG1 147 ER61
Staines-upon-Thames TW18 196 BJ93
Elizabeth Blackwell Ho, N22
off Progress Way 121 DN53
Elizabeth Br, SW1 29 J9
Elizabeth Cl, E14 22 C9
W9 15 P4
Barnet EN5 101 CX41
Hertford SG14
off Welwyn Rd 53 DM09
Lower Nazeing EN9 71 ED23
Romford RM7 127 FB53
Sutton SM1 239 CZ105
Tilbury RM18 193 GH82
Welwyn Garden City AL7 52 DC09
Elizabeth Clyde Cl, N15 144 DS56
Elizabeth Cotts, Kew TW9 180 CM81
Elizabeth Ct, SW1 29 P7
Godalming GU7 280 AS144
Gravesend DA11
off St. James's Rd 213 GG86
Horley RH6 290 DG148
Kingston upon Thames KT2
off Lower Kings Rd 220 CL95
St. Albans AL4
off Villiers Cres 65 CK17
Watford WD17 97 BT38
Woodford Green IG8
off Navestock Cres 124 EJ52
Elizabeth Dr, Bans. SM7 256 DC118
Theydon Bois CM16 107 ES36
Elizabeth Est, SE17 43 L2
Elizabeth Fry Pl, SE18 186 EL81
Elizabeth Fry Rd, E8 10 F7
Elizabeth Gdns, W3 161 CT74
Isleworth TW7 179 CG84
Stanmore HA7 117 CJ51
Sunbury-on-Thames TW16 218 BW97
Sch Elizabeth Garrett Anderson
Language Coll, N1 8 D10
Elizabeth Ho, Bans. SM7 256 DC118
Rom. RM2 150 FJ56
Elizabeth Huggins Cotts,
Grav. DA11 213 GG89
Elizabeth Ms, NW3 6 D5
Elizabeth Pl, N15 144 DR56
Elizabeth Ride, N9 122 DV45
Elizabeth Rd, E6 166 EK67
N15 144 DS57
Godalming GU7 280 AS144
Grays RM16 192 FZ76
Pilgrim's Hatch CM15 130 FV44
Rainham RM13 169 FH71
Sch Elizabeth Selby Inf Sch, E2 20 D2
Elizabeth Sq, SE16 33 L1
Elizabeth St, SW1 29 H8
Greenhithe DA9 211 FS85
Elizabeth Ter, SE9 207 EM86
Elizabeth Way, SE19 204 DR94
Feltham TW13 198 BW91
Harlow CM19, CM20 73 EM16
Orpington BR5 228 EW99
Stoke Poges SL2 154 AT67
Elizabeth Wheeler Ho, Brom.
BR1 off The Mall 226 EG97
Eliza Cook Cl, Green. DA9
off Watermans Way 191 FV84
Elkanette Ms, N20 120 DC47
Elkington Pt, SE11 30 E9
Elkington Rd, E13 24 A5
Elkins, The, Rom. RM1 127 FE54
Elkins Gdns, Guil. GU4 265 BA131
Elkins Rd, Hedg. SL2 134 AS61
Elkstone Rd, W10 14 G6
Ella Cl, Beck. BR3 225 EA96
Ellacott Ms, SW16 203 DK89
Ellaline Rd, W6 38 C3
Ella Ms, NW3 6 E1
Ellanby Cres, N18 122 DV49
Elland Cl, Barn. EN5 102 DD43
Elland Rd, SE15 184 DW84
Walton-on-Thames KT12 218 BX103
Ella Rd, N8 143 DL59
Ellement Cl, Pnr. HA5 138 BX57
Ellenborough Pl, SW15 181 CU84
Ellenborough Rd, N22 122 DQ53
Sidcup DA14 208 EX92
Ellenbridge Way, S.Croy. CR2 242 DS109
ELLENBROOK, Hat. AL10 66 CR19
Ellenbrook Cl, Wat. WD24
off Hatfield Rd 97 BV39
Ellenbrook Cres, Hat. AL10
off Ellenbrook La 66 CR18
Ellenbrook La, Hat. AL10 66 CS19
Ellen Cl, Brom. BR1 226 EK97
Hemel Hempstead HP2 62 BM19
Ellen Ct, N9 122 DW47
Ellen St, E1 20 D9
Ellen Webb Dr, Wealds. HA3 139 CE55
Ellen Wilkinson Ho, E2
off Usk St 21 J2
Sch Ellen Wilkinson Prim Sch,
E6 24 G7
Sch Ellen Wilkinson Sch for Girls,
The, W3 off Queens Dr 160 CM72
Elleray Rd, Tedd. TW11 199 CF93
Ellerby St, SW6 38 D7
Ellerdale Cl, NW3 5 N1
Ellerdale Rd, NW3 5 P1
Ellerdale St, SE13 185 EB84
Ellerdine Rd, Houns. TW3 178 CC84
Ellerker Gdns, Rich. TW10 200 CL86
Ellerman Av, Twick. TW2 198 BZ88
Ellerman Rd, Til. RM18 193 GF82
Ellerslie, Grav. DA12 213 GK87
Ellerslie Gdns, NW10 161 CU67
Ellerslie Rd, W12 161 CV74
● Ellerslie Sq Ind Est, SW2 203 DL85
Ellerton, NW6 5 H3
Ellerton Gdns, Dag. RM9 168 EW66
Ellerton Rd, SW13 181 CU81
SW18 202 DD88
SW20 201 CU94
Dagenham RM9 168 EW66
Surbiton KT6 220 CM103

Ellery Rd, SE19 204 DR94
Ellery St, SE15 44 E9
Elles Av, Guil. GU1 265 BB134
Ellesborough Cl, Wat. WD19 116 BW50
Ellesmere Av, NW7 118 CR48
Beckenham BR3 225 EB96
Ellesmere Cl, E11 146 EF57
Datchet SL3 174 AU79
Ruislip HA4 137 BQ59
Ellesmere Dr, S.Croy. CR2 242 DV114
Ellesmere Gdns, Ilf. IG4 146 EL57
Ellesmere Gro, Barn. EN5 101 CZ43
Ellesmere Pl, Walt. KT12 235 BS106
Ellesmere Rd, E3 11 L10
NW10 141 CU64
W4 180 CR79
Berkhamsted HP4 60 AX19
Greenford UB6 158 CC70
Twickenham TW1 199 CJ86
Weybridge KT13 235 BR107
Ellesmere St, E14 22 C8
Ellice Rd, Oxt. RH8 276 EF129
Ellies Ms, Ashf. TW15 196 BL89
Elliman Av, Slou. SL2 154 AS73
Ellingfort Rd, E8 10 F6
Ellingham Cl, Hem.H. HP2 62 BN18
Sch Ellingham Prim Sch, Chess. KT9 *off Ellingham Rd* 237 CK108
Ellingham Rd, E15 145 ED63
W12 181 CU75
Chessington KT9 237 CK107
Hemel Hempstead HP2 62 BM19
Ellington Ct, N14 121 DK47
Tap. SL6 *off Ellington Rd* 152 AC72
Ellington Gdns, Tap. SL6 152 AC72
Ellington Ho, SE1 31 K6
Ellington Rd, N10 143 DH56
Feltham TW13 197 BT91
Hounslow TW3 178 CB82
Taplow SL6 152 AC72
Ellington St, N7 8 E5
Ellington Way, Epsom KT18 255 CV117
Elliot Cl, E15 13 J7
Elliot Rd, NW4 141 CV58
Stanmore HA7 117 CG51
Elliott Av, Ruis. HA4 137 BV61
Elliott Cl, Welw.G.C. AL7 51 CX12
Wembley HA9 140 CM62
Elliott Gdns, Rom. RM3 127 FH53
Shepperton TW17 216 BN98
Elliott Rd, SW9 42 G5
W4 180 CS77
Bromley BR2 226 EK98
Thornton Heath CR7 223 DP98
Sch Elliott Sch, SW15 *off Pullman Gdns* 201 CW86
Elliotts Cl, Cowley UB8 156 BJ71
Elliotts La, Brasted TN16 262 EW124
Elliott's Pl, N1 9 H9
Elliott Sq, NW3 6 D6
Elliotts Row, SE11 30 G8
Elliott St, Grav. DA12 213 GK87
Ellis Av, Chal.St.P. SL9 113 AZ53
Onslow Village GU2 280 AT136
Rainham RM13 169 FG71
Slough SL1 174 AS75
Ellis Cl, NW10 *off High Rd* 161 CV65
SE9 207 EQ89
Coulsdon CR5 257 DM120
Edgware HA8 118 CS51
Hoddesdon EN11 55 DZ13
Ruislip HA4 137 BU58
Swanley BR8 229 FD98
Elliscombe Rd, SE7 186 EJ78
Ellis Ct, W7 159 CF71
Ellis Fm Cl, Wok. GU22 248 AX122
Ellisfield Dr, SW15 201 CT87
Ellis Flds, St.Alb. AL3 65 CE17
Ellis Ho, St.Alb. AL1 65 CF21
Ellison Cl, Wind. SL4 173 AM83
Ellison Gdns, Sthl. UB2 178 BZ77
Ellison Ho, SE13 46 E8
Ellison Rd, SW13 181 CT82
SW16 203 DK94
Sidcup DA15 207 ER88
Ellis Rd, Couls. CR5 257 DM120
Mitcham CR4 222 DF100
Southall UB2 158 CC74
Ellis St, SW1 28 F8
Elliston Ho, SE18 37 L9
Ellis Way, Dart. DA1 210 FM89
Ellmore Cl, Rom. RM3 127 FH53
Ellora Rd, SW16 203 DK92
Ellsworth St, E2 20 E2
Ellwood Ct, W9 15 L5
Ellwood Gdns, Wat. WD25 81 BV34
Ellwood Ri, Ch.St.G. HP8 112 AW47
Ellwood Rd, Beac. HP9 110 AH54
Elmar Grn, Slou. SL2 153 AN69
Elmar Rd, N15 144 DR56
Elm Av, W5 160 CL74
Carshalton SM5 240 DF110
Ruislip HA4 137 BU60
Upminster RM14 150 FP62
Watford WD19 116 BY45
Elmbank, N14 121 DL45
Elmbank Av, Barn. EN5 101 CW42
Englefield Green TW20 194 AV93
Guildford GU2 280 AU135
Elm Bk Dr, Brom. BR1 226 EK96
Elm Bk Gdns, SW13 180 CS82
Elmbank Way, W7 159 CD71
Elmbourne Dr, Belv. DA17 189 FB77
Elmbourne Rd, SW17 202 DG90
Elmbridge, Harl. CM17 58 EZ12
Elmbridge Av, Surb. KT5 220 CP99
Elmbridge Cl, Ruis. HA4 137 BU58
Elmbridge Dr, Ruis. HA4 137 BT57
Elmbridge La, Wok. GU22 249 AZ119
★ **Elmbridge Mus**, Wey. KT13 234 BN105
Elmbridge Rd, Ilf. IG6 126 EU51
Elmbridge Wk, E8 10 D6
Elmbrook Cl, Sun. TW16 217 BV95
Elmbrook Gdns, SE9 186 EL84
Elmbrook Rd, Sutt. SM1 239 CZ105
Elm Cl, E11 146 EH58
N19 143 DJ61
NW4 141 CX57
SW20 221 CW98
Amersham HP6 77 AQ38
Box Hill KT20 270 CQ130
Buckhurst Hill IG9 124 EK47
Carshalton SM5 222 DF102
Dartford DA1 210 FJ88
Epping Green CM16 73 EP24
Farnham Common SL2 153 AQ65
Harrow HA2 138 CB58
Hayes UB3 157 BU72
Leatherhead KT22 253 CH122
Elm Cl, Ripley GU23 250 BG124
Romford RM7 127 FB54
South Croydon CR2 242 DS107
Stanwell TW19 196 BK88
Surbiton KT5 220 CQ101
Twickenham TW2 198 CB89
Waltham Abbey EN9 89 ED34
Warlingham CR6 259 DX117
Woking GU21 248 AX115
ELM CORNER, Wok. GU23 250 BN119
Elmcote Way, Crox.Grn WD3 96 BM44
Elm Ct, EC4 18 E10
Mitcham CR4 *off Armfield Cres* 222 DF96
Sunbury-on-Thames TW16 197 BT94
Elmcourt Rd, SE27 203 DP89
Sch Elm Ct Sch, SE27 *off Elmcourt Rd* 204 DQ89
Elm Cres, W5 160 CL74
Kingston upon Thames KT2 220 CL95
Elmcroft, N8 143 DM57
Elm Cft, Datchet SL3 174 AW81
Elmcroft, Lthd. KT23 252 CA124
Elmcroft Av, E11 146 EH57
N9 104 DV44
NW11 141 CZ59
Sidcup DA15 207 ET86
Elmcroft Cl, E11 146 EH56
W5 159 CK72
Chessington KT9 220 CL104
Feltham TW14 197 BT86
Elmcroft Cres, NW11 141 CY59
Harrow HA2 138 CA55
Elmcroft Dr, Ashf. TW15 196 BN92
Chessington KT9 220 CL104
Elmcroft Gdns, NW9 140 CN57
Elmcroft Rd, Orp. BR6 228 EU101
Elmcroft St, E5 144 DW63
Elmdale Rd, N13 121 DM50
Elmdene, Surb. KT5 220 CQ102
Elmdene Av, Horn. RM11 150 FM57
Elmdene Cl, Beck. BR3 225 DZ99
Elmdene Ct, Wok. GU22 *off Constitution Hill* 248 AY118
Elmdene Ms, Nthwd. HA6 115 BQ51
Elmdene Rd, SE18 187 EP78
Elmdon Pl, Guil. GU1 *off Buckingham Cl* 265 AZ133
Elmdon Rd, Houns. TW4 178 BX82
London Heathrow Airport TW6 177 BT83
South Ockendon RM15 171 FU71
Elm Dr, Chsht EN8 89 DY28
Chobham GU24 232 AT110
Harrow HA2 138 CB58
Hatfield AL10 67 CU19
Leatherhead KT22 253 CH122
St. Albans AL4 65 CJ20
Sunbury-on-Thames TW16 218 BW96
Swanley BR8 229 FD96
Elmer Av, Hav.at.Bow. RM4 127 FE48
Elmer Cl, Enf. EN2 103 DM41
Rainham RM13 169 FG66
Elmer Cotts, Fetch. KT22 253 CG123
Elmer Gdns, Edg. HA8 118 CP52
Isleworth TW7 179 CD83
Rainham RM13 169 FG66
Elmer Ms, Fetch. KT22 253 CG123
Elmer Rd, SE6 205 EC87
Elmers Ct, Beac. HP9 *off Post Office La* 111 AK52
Elmers Dr, Tedd. TW11 *off Kingston Rd* 199 CH93
ELMERS END, Beck. BR3 225 DY97
⇌ **Elmers End** 225 DX98
Tram **Elmers End** 225 DX98
Elmers End Rd, SE20 224 DW96
Beckenham BR3 224 DW96
Elmerside Rd, Beck. BR3 225 DY98
Elmers Rd, SE25 224 DU101
Elm Fm Caravan Pk, Lyne KT16 215 BC101
Elmfield, Bkhm KT23 252 CA123
Elmfield Av, N8 143 DL57
Mitcham CR4 222 DG95
Teddington TW11 199 CF92
Elmfield Cl, Grav. DA11 213 GH88
Harrow HA1 139 CE61
Potters Bar EN6 85 CY33
Elmfield Pk, Brom. BR1 226 EG97
Elmfield Rd, E4 123 EC47
E17 145 DX58
N2 142 DD55
SW17 202 DG89
Bromley BR1 226 EG97
Potters Bar EN6 85 CY33
Southall UB2 178 BY76
Elmfield Way, W9 15 J6
South Croydon CR2 242 DT109
Elm Friars Wk, NW1 7 P7
Elm Gdns, N2 142 DC55
Claygate KT10 237 CF107
Enfield EN2 104 DR38
Epsom KT18 255 CW119
Mitcham CR4 223 DK98
North Weald Bassett CM16 93 FB26
Welwyn Garden City AL8 51 CV09
Elmgate Av, Felt. TW13 197 BV90
Elmgate Gdns, Edg. HA8 118 CR50
Elm Grn, W3 160 CS72
Hemel Hempstead HP1 61 BE18
Elmgreen Cl, E15 13 K8
Elm Gro, N8 143 DL58
NW2 141 CX63
SE15 44 B8
SW19 201 CY94
Berkhamsted HP4 60 AV19
Caterham CR3 258 DS122
Epsom KT18 238 CQ114
Erith DA8 189 FD80
Harrow HA2 138 CA59
Hornchurch RM11 150 FL58
Kingston upon Thames KT2 220 CL95
Orpington BR6 227 ET102
Sutton SM1 240 DB105
Watford WD24 97 BU37
West Drayton UB7 156 BM73
Woodford Green IG8 124 EF50
Elmgrove Cres, Har. HA1 139 CF57
Sch Elmgrove First Sch, Kenton HA3 *off Kenmore Av* 139 CG56
Elmgrove Gdns, Har. HA1 139 CG57
Sch Elmgrove Mid Sch, Kenton HA3 *off Kenmore Av* 139 CG56
Elm Gro Par, Wall. SM6 *off Butter Hill* 222 DG104
Elm Gro Rd, SW13 181 CU82
W5 180 CL75
Cobham KT11 252 BX116
Elmgrove Rd, Croy. CR0 224 DV101
Harrow HA1 139 CF57
Weybridge KT13 234 BN105
Elm Hall Gdns, E11 146 EH58
Elm Hatch, Harl. CM18 *off St. Andrews Meadow* 73 ET16
Elmhurst, Belv. DA17 188 EY79
Elmhurst Av, N2 142 DD55
Mitcham CR4 203 DH94
Elmhurst Cl, Bushey WD23 98 BY42
Elmhurst Ct, Guil. GU1 *off Lower Edgeborough Rd* 281 AZ135
Elmhurst Dr, E18 124 EG54
Dorking RH4 285 CH138
Hornchurch RM11 150 FJ60
Elmhurst Mans, SW4 41 N10
Sch Elmhurst Prim Sch, E7 *off Upton Pk Rd* 166 EH66
Elmhurst Rd, E7 166 EH66
N17 122 DS54
SE9 206 EL89
Enfield EN3 104 DW37
Slough SL3 175 BA76
Sch Elmhurst Sch, S.Croy. CR2 *off South Pk Hill Rd* 242 DR106
Elmhurst St, SW4 41 N10
Elmhurst Vil, SE15 *off Cheltenham Rd* 184 DW84
Elmhurst Way, Loug. IG10 125 EM45
Elmington Cl, Bex. DA5 209 FB86
Elmington Est, SE5 43 M4
Elmington Rd, SE5 43 L6
Elmira St, SE13 185 EB83
Elm La, SE6 205 DZ89
Woking GU23 251 BP118
Elm Lawn Cl, Uxb. UB8 156 BL66
Elm Lawns Cl, St.Alb. AL1 *off Avenue Rd* 65 CE19
Elmlea Dr, Hayes UB3 157 BS72
Elmlee Cl, Chis. BR7 207 EM93
Elmley Cl, E6 25 H7
Elmley St, SE18 187 ER77
Elm Ms, Rich. TW10 200 CM86
Elmore Cl, Wem. HA0 160 CL68
Elmore Rd, E11 145 EC62
Chipstead CR5 256 DF121
Enfield EN3 105 DX39
Elmores, Loug. IG10 107 EN41
Elmore St, N1 9 K6
Elm Par, Horn. RM12 149 FH63
Sidcup DA14 *off Main Rd* 208 EU91
ELM PARK, Horn. RM12 149 FH64
⊖ **Elm Park** 149 FH63
Elm Pk, SW2 203 DM86
Stanmore HA7 117 CH50
Elm Pk Av, N15 144 DT57
Hornchurch RM12 149 FG63
Elm Pk Ct, Pnr. HA5 138 BW55
Elm Pk Gdns, NW4 141 CX57
SW10 40 A1
South Croydon CR2 242 DW110
Elm Pk La, SW3 40 A1
Elm Pk Mans, SW10 39 P2
Elm Pk Rd, E10 145 DY60
N3 119 CZ52
N21 122 DQ45
SE25 224 DT97
SW3 40 A2
Pinner HA5 116 BW54
Elm Pl, SW7 28 A10
Ashford TW15 *off Limes Cl* 196 BN92
Elm Quay Ct, SW8 41 N2
Elm Rd, E7 13 M4
E11 145 ED61
E17 145 EC57
N22 121 DP53
SW14 180 CQ83
Aveley RM15 170 FQ74
Barnet EN5 101 CZ42
Beckenham BR3 225 DZ96
Chessington KT9 238 CL105
Claygate KT10 237 CF107
Dartford DA1 210 FK88
Epsom KT17 239 CT107
Erith DA8 189 FG81
Feltham TW14 197 BR88
Godalming GU7 280 AT143
Gravesend DA12 213 GJ90
Grays RM17 192 GC79
Greenhithe DA9 211 FS86
Horsell GU21 248 AX115
Kingston upon Thames KT2 220 CM95
Leatherhead KT22 253 CH122
New Malden KT3 220 CR98
Orpington BR6 246 EU108
Penn HP10 110 AD46
Purley CR8 241 DP113
Redhill RH1 272 DE134
Romford RM7 127 FB54
Sidcup DA14 208 EU91
Thornton Heath CR7 224 DR98
Wallington SM6 222 DG102
Warlingham CR6 259 DX117
Wembley HA9 140 CL64
Westerham TN16 277 ES125
Windsor SL4 173 AP83
Woking GU21 248 AX118
Elm Rd W, Sutt. SM3 221 CZ101
Elm Row, NW3 142 DC62
Elmroyd Av, Pot.B. EN6 85 CZ33
Elmroyd Cl, Pot.B. EN6 85 CZ33
Elms, The, SW13 181 CT83
Hertford SG13 54 DU09
Loughton IG10 106 EF40
Warlingham CR6 258 DW115
Elms Av, N10 143 DH55
NW4 141 CX57
Elms Cl, Horn. RM11 149 FH59
Elmscott Gdns, N21 104 DQ44
Elmscott Rd, Brom. BR1 206 EE92
Elms Ct, Wem. HA0 139 CF63
Elms Cres, SW4 203 DJ86
Elmscroft Gdns, Pot.B. EN6 85 CZ32
Elmsdale Rd, E17 145 DZ56
Elms Fm Rd, Horn. RM12 150 FJ64
Elms Gdns, Dag. RM9 148 EZ63
Wembley HA0 139 CG63
Elmshaw Rd, SW15 201 CU85
Elmshorn, Epsom KT17 255 CW116
Elmshott La, Slou. SL1 153 AL73
Elmshurst Cres, N2 142 DD56
Elmside, Guil. GU2 280 AU135
New Addington CR0 243 EB107
Elmside Rd, Wem. HA9 140 CN62
Elms La, Wem. HA0 139 CG63
Elmsleigh Av, Har. HA3 139 CH56
🔒 **Elmsleigh Cen, The**, Stai. TW18 195 BF91
Elmsleigh Ct, Sutt. SM1 222 DB104
Elmsleigh Rd, Stai. TW18 195 BF92
Twickenham TW2 199 CD89
Elmslie Cl, Epsom KT18 238 CQ114
Woodford Green IG8 125 EM51
Elmslie Pt, E3 21 P7
Elms Ms, W2 16 A10
Elms Pk Av, Wem. HA0 139 CG63
Elms Rd, SW4 203 DJ85
Chalfont St. Peter SL9 112 AY52
Harrow HA3 117 CE52
Ware SG12 55 EA05
ELMSTEAD, Chis. BR7 206 EK92
Elmstead Av, Chis. BR7 207 EM92
Wembley HA9 140 CL60
Elmstead Cl, N20 120 DA47
Epsom KT19 238 CS106
Sevenoaks TN13 278 FE122
Elmstead Cres, Well. DA16 188 EW79
Elmstead Gdns, Wor.Pk. KT4 221 CU104
Elmstead Glade, Chis. BR7 207 EM93
Elmstead La, Chis. BR7 207 EM92
Elmstead Rd, Erith DA8 189 FE81
Ilford IG3 147 ES61
West Byfleet KT14 234 BG113
⇌ **Elmstead Woods** 206 EL93
Elmstone Rd, SW6 39 J6
Elm St, WC1 18 D5
Elmsway, Ashf. TW15 196 BM92
Elmswell Ct, Hert. SG14 *off The Ridgeway* 53 DM08
Elmswood, Bkhm KT23 252 BZ124
Chigwell IG7 *off Copperfield* 125 ER51
Elmsworth Av, Houns. TW3 178 CB82
Elm Ter, NW2 142 DA62
SE9 207 EN86
Grays RM20 191 FV79
Harrow HA3 117 CD52
Elm Tree Av, Esher KT10 219 CD101
Elm Tree Cl, NW8 16 A2
Ashford TW15 *off Convent Rd* 197 BP92
Elmtree Cl, Byfleet KT14 234 BL113
Elm Tree Cl, Cher. KT16 215 BE103
Horley RH6 290 DG147
Northolt UB5 158 BZ68
Elm Tree Ct, SE7 *off Fairlawn* 186 EJ79
Elmtree Hill, Chesh. HP5 76 AP30
Elm Tree Rd, NW8 16 A2
Elmtree Rd, Tedd. TW11 199 CE91
Sch Elmtree Sch, Chesh. HP5 *off Elmtree Hill* 76 AP30
Elm Tree Wk, Chorl. WD3 95 BF42
Elm Wk, NW3 142 DA61
SW20 221 CW98
Orpington BR6 227 EM104
Radlett WD7 99 CF36
Romford RM2 149 FG55
Elm Way, N11 120 DG51
NW10 140 CS63
Brentwood CM14 130 FU48
Epsom KT19 238 CR106
Rickmansworth WD3 114 BH46
Worcester Park KT4 221 CW104
Elmwood, Saw. CM21 58 EZ06
Welwyn Garden City AL8 51 CV10
Elmwood Av, N13 121 DL50
Borehamwood WD6 100 CP42
Feltham TW13 197 BU89
Harrow HA3 139 CG57
Elmwood Cl, Ashtd. KT21 253 CK117
Epsom KT17 239 CU108
Wallington SM6 222 DG103
Elmwood Ct, SW11 41 J6
Ashtead KT21 *off Elmwood Cl* 253 CK117
Wembley HA0 139 CG62
Elmwood Cres, NW9 140 CQ56
Elmwood Dr, Bex. DA5 208 EY87
Epsom KT17 239 CU107
Elmwood Gdns, W7 159 CE72
Elmwood Gro, Hem.H. HP3 62 BM23
Sch Elmwood Inf Sch, Croy. CR0 *off Lodge Rd* 223 DP100
Sch Elmwood Jun Sch, Croy. CR0 *off Lodge Rd* 223 DP101
Elmwood Pk, Ger.Cr. SL9 134 AY60
Sch Elm Wd Prim Sch, SE27 *off Carnac St* 204 DR90
Elmwood Rd, SE24 204 DR85
W4 180 CQ79
Croydon CR0 223 DP101
Mitcham CR4 222 DF97
Redhill RH1 272 DG130
Slough SL2 154 AV73
Elmworth Gro, SE21 204 DR89
Elnathan Ms, W9 15 M5
Elphinstone Rd, E17 123 DZ54
Elphinstone St, N5 143 DP63
Elppin Ct, Brox. EN10 71 DZ20
Elrick Cl, Erith DA8 *off Queen St* 189 FE79
Elrington Rd, E8 10 C5
Woodford Green IG8 124 EG50
Elruge Cl, West Dr. UB7 176 BK76
Elsa Rd, Well. DA16 188 EV82
Elsa St, E1 21 L7
Elsdale St, E9 11 H5
Elsden Ms, E2 21 H1
Elsden Rd, N17 122 DT53
Elsdon Rd, Wok. GU21 248 AU117
Elsenham, The, Chsht EN8 88 DW28
Elsenham Rd, E12 147 EM64
Elsenham St, SW18 201 CZ88
Elsham Rd, E11 146 EE62
W14 26 E5
Elsham Ter, W14 26 E5
Elsiedene Rd, N21 122 DQ45
Elsiemaud Rd, SE4 205 DZ85
Elsie Rd, SE22 184 DT84
Elsinge Rd, Enf. EN1 104 DV36
Elsinore Av, Stai. TW19 196 BL87
Elsinore Gdns, NW2 141 CY62
Elsinore Rd, SE23 205 DY88
Elsinore Way, Rich. TW9 180 CP83
Sch Elsley Prim Sch, Wem. HA9 *off Tokyngton Av* 160 CM65
Elsley Rd, SW11 40 F10
Sch Elsley Sch, SW11 40 G10
Elsons Ms, Welw.G.C. AL7 52 DB09
Elspeth Rd, SW11 182 DF84
Wembley HA0 140 CL64
Elsrick Av, Mord. SM4 222 DA99
Elstan Way, Croy. CR0 225 DY101
Elstead Ct, Sutt. SM3 *off Stonecot Hill* 221 CY102
Elstead Ho, Mord. SM4 *off Green La* 222 DA100
Elsted St, SE17 31 M9
Elstow Cl, SE9 207 EN85
Ruislip HA4 138 BX59
Elstow Gdns, Dag. RM9 168 EY67
Elstow Rd, Dag. RM9 168 EY66
ELSTREE, Borwd. WD6 99 CK43
★ **Elstree Aerodrome**, Borwd. WD6 99 CF41
⇌ **Elstree & Borehamwood** 100 CM42
● **Elstree Business Cen**, Borwd. WD6 100 CR41
Elstree Cl, Horn. RM12 169 FH66
Elstree Gdns, N9 122 DV46
Belvedere DA17 188 EY77
Ilford IG1 147 EQ64
Elstree Hill, Brom. BR1 206 EE94
Elstree Hill N, Els. WD6 99 CK44
Elstree Hill S, Els. WD6 117 CJ45
Elstree Pk, Borwd. WD6 100 CR44
Elstree Rd, Bushey Hth WD23 117 CD45
Elstree WD6 99 CG44
Elstree Way, Borwd. WD6 100 CP41
Elswick Rd, SE13 46 C10
Elswick St, SW6 39 N8
Elsworth Cl, Felt. TW14 197 BS88
Elsworthy, T.Ditt. KT7 219 CE100
Elsworthy Ri, NW3 6 D6
Elsworthy Rd, NW3 6 D7
Elsworthy Ter, NW3 6 D7
Elsynge Rd, SW18 202 DD85
ELTHAM, SE9 206 EK86
⇌ **Eltham** 207 EM85
⊖ **Eltham** 207 EM85
Eltham Av, Slou. SL1 173 AL75
Slough (east section) SL1 173 AM75
Sch Eltham C of E Prim Sch, SE9 *off Roper St* 207 EM85
Sch Eltham Coll Jun Sch, SE9 *off Mottingham La* 206 EK88
Sch Eltham Coll Sen Sch, SE9 *off Grove Pk Rd* 206 EK89
Eltham Grn, SE9 206 EJ85
Eltham Grn Rd, SE9 186 EJ84
Sch Eltham Grn Sch, SE9 *off Queenscroft Rd* 206 EK86
Eltham High St, SE9 207 EM86
Eltham Hill, SE9 206 EK85
Sch Eltham Hill Tech Coll for Girls, SE9 *off Eltham Hill* 206 EL86
★ **Eltham Palace**, SE9 206 EL87
Eltham Palace Rd, SE9 206 EJ86
Eltham Pk Gdns, SE9 187 EN84
Eltham Rd, SE9 206 EJ85
SE12 206 EF85
Elthiron Rd, SW6 39 K7
Elthorne Av, W7 179 CF75
Elthorne Ct, Felt. TW13 198 BW88
Sch Elthorne Pk High Sch, W7 *off Westlea Rd* 179 CF76
Elthorne Pk Rd, W7 179 CF75
Elthorne Rd, N19 143 DK61
NW9 140 CR59
Uxbridge UB8 156 BK68
Elthorne Way, NW9 140 CR58
Elthruda Rd, SE13 205 ED86
Eltisley Rd, Ilf. IG1 147 EP63
Elton Av, Barn. EN5 101 CZ43
Greenford UB6 159 CF65
Wembley HA0 139 CH64
Elton Cl, Kings.T. KT1 199 CJ94
Elton Ho, E3 11 P8
Elton Pk, Wat. WD17 97 BV40
Elton Pl, N16 9 N2
Elton Rd, Hert. SG14 54 DQ08
Kingston upon Thames KT2 220 CM95
Purley CR8 241 DJ112
Elton Way, Wat. WD25 98 CB40
Eltringham St, SW18 182 DC84
Eluna Apts, E1 *off Wapping La* 32 F1
Elvaston Ms, SW7 27 P6
Elvaston Pl, SW7 27 N7
Elveden Cl, Wok. GU22 250 BH117
Elveden Pl, NW10 160 CN68
Elveden Rd, NW10 160 CN68
Elvedon Rd, Cob. KT11 235 BV111
Feltham TW13 197 BT90
Elvendon Rd, N13 121 DL51
Elver Gdns, E2 20 D2
Elverson Ms, SE8 46 C9
DLR **Elverson Road** 46 D9
Elverson Rd, SE8 46 D8
Elverton St, SW1 29 N8
Elvet Av, Rom. RM2 150 FJ56
Elvin Dr, N.Stfd RM16 171 FX74
Elvington Grn, Brom. BR2 226 EF99
Elvington La, NW9 118 CS53
Elvino Rd, SE26 205 DY92
Elvis Rd, NW2 4 A4
Elwell Cl, Egh. TW20 *off Mowbray Cres* 195 BA92
Elwick Rd, S.Ock. RM15 171 FW72
Elwill Way, Beck. BR3 225 EC98
Elwin St, E2 20 C2
Elwood, Harl. CM17 74 EY16
Elwood Cl, Barn. EN5 102 DC42
Elwood Ct, N9 122 DV46
Elwood St, N5 143 DP62
Elwyn Gdns, SE12 206 EG87
Ely Av, Slou. SL1 153 AQ71
Ely Cl, Amer. HP7 77 AS39
Erith DA8 189 FF82
Hatfield AL10 67 CT17
New Malden KT3 221 CT96
Ely Ct, EC1 18 F7
Ely Gdns, Borwd. WD6 100 CR43
Dagenham RM10 149 FC62
Ilford IG1 146 EL59
Elyne Rd, N4 143 DN58
Ely Pl, EC1 18 F7
Guildford GU2 *off Canterbury Rd* 264 AT132
Woodford Green IG8 125 EN51
Ely Rd, E10 145 EC59
Croydon CR0 224 DR99
Hounslow West TW4 178 BW83
London Heathrow Airport TW6 *off Eastern Perimeter Rd* 177 BT82
St. Albans AL1 65 CH21

Elysian Av, Orp. BR5 227 ES100
Elysian Pl, S.Croy. CR2 242 DQ108
Elysium Bldg, The, SE8 33 K10
Elysium Pl, SW6 38 G9
Elysium St, SW6 38 G9
Elystan Cl, Wall. SM6 241 DH109
Elystan Pl, SW3 28 D10
Elystan St, SW3 28 C9
Elystan Wk, N1 8 E9
Emanuel Av, W3 160 CQ72
Emanuel Dr, Hmptn. TW12 198 BZ92
[Sch] Emanuel Sch, SW11
off Battersea Ri 202 DE85
⊖ Embankment 30 B2
Embankment, SW15 38 C9
Embankment, The, Twick. TW1 199 CG88
Wraysbury TW19 194 AW87
Embankment Gdns, SW3 40 F2
[Pier] Embankment Pier 30 C2
Embankment Pl, WC2 30 B2
Embassy Ct, Sid. DA14 208 EV90
Welling DA16
off Welling High St 188 EV83
Embassy Gdns, Beck. BR3
off Blakeney Rd 225 DZ95
Emba St, SE16 32 D5
● Ember Cen, Walt. KT12 218 BY103
Ember Cl, Add. KT15 234 BK106
Petts Wood BR5 227 EQ101
Embercourt Rd, T.Ditt. KT7 219 CE100
Ember Fm Av, E.Mol. KT8 219 CD100
Ember Fm Way, E.Mol. KT8 219 CD100
Ember Gdns, T.Ditt. KT7 219 CE101
Ember La, E.Mol. KT8 219 CD101
Esher KT10 219 CD101
Ember Rd, Slou. SL3 175 BB76
Emberson Way, N.Wld Bas.
CM16 93 FC26
Emberton, SE5 43 N2
Emberton Ct, EC1
off Tompion St 18 G3
Embleton Rd, SE13 185 EB83
Watford WD19 115 BU48
Embleton Wk, Hmptn. TW12
off Fearnley Cres 198 BZ93
Embry Cl, Stan. HA7 117 CG49
Embry Dr, Stan. HA7 117 CG51
Embry Way, Stan. HA7 117 CG50
Emden Cl, West Dr. UB7 176 BN75
Emden St, SW6 39 M6
Emerald Cl, E16 24 G9
Emerald Ct, Slou. SL1 174 AS75
Emerald Gdns, Dag. RM8 148 FA60
Emerald Rd, NW10 160 CR67
Emerald Sq, Sthl. UB2 178 BX76
Emerald St, WC1 18 C6
Emerson Apts, N8
off Chadwell La 143 DM55
Emerson Ct, Woob.Grn HP10 132 AE57
Emerson Dr, Horn. RM11 150 FK59
Emerson Gdns, Har. HA3 140 CM58
EMERSON PARK, Horn. RM11 150 FL58
⇌ Emerson Park 150 FL59
[Sch] Emerson Pk Sch, Horn.
RM11 off Wych Elm Rd 150 FP59
Emerson Rd, Ilf. IG1 147 EN59
Emersons Av, Swan. BR8 209 FF94
Emerson St, SE1 31 J2
Emerton Cl, Bexh. DA6 188 EY84
Emerton Ct, Nthch HP4
off Emerton Garth 60 AS16
Emerton Garth, Nthch HP4 60 AS16
Emerton Rd, Lthd. KT22 252 CC120
Emery Hill St, SW1 29 M7
Emery St, SE1 30 F6
Emes Rd, Erith DA8 189 FC80
Emilia Cl, Enf. EN3 104 DV43
Emily Davison Dr, Epsom
KT18 255 CV118
Emily Duncan Pl, E7 146 EH63
Emily Jackson Cl, Sev. TN13 279 FH124
★ Emirates Air Line, E16/SE10 35 L3
Emley Rd, Add. KT15 216 BG104
Emlyn Gdns, W12 180 CS75
Emlyn La, Lthd. KT22 253 CG122
Emlyn Rd, W12 180 CS75
Horley RH6 290 DE147
Redhill RH1 288 DG136
Emma Ho, Rom. RM1
off Market Link 149 FE56
Emmanuel Cl, Guil. GU2 264 AU131
[Sch] Emmanuel C of E Prim Sch,
NW6 5 K2
Emmanuel Lo, Chsht EN8 88 DW30
Emmanuel Rd, SW12 203 DJ88
Northwood HA6 115 BT52
Emma Rd, E13 23 M1
Emma's Cres, Stans.Abb.
SG12 55 EB11
Emma St, E2 10 E10
Emmaus Way, Chig. IG7 125 EN50
Emmett Cl, Shenley WD7 84 CL33
Emmetts Cl, Wok. GU21 248 AW117
Emminster, NW6 off Abbey Rd 5 L8
Emmott Av, Ilf. IG6 147 EQ57
Emmott Cl, E1 21 M5
NW11 142 DC58
Emms Pas, Kings.T. KT1 219 CK96
Emperor Cl, Berk. HP4 60 AT16
Emperor's Gate, SW7 27 M7
Empire Av, N18 122 DQ50
Empire Centre, Wat. WD24 98 BW39
Empire Ct, Wem. HA9 140 CP62
Empire Ms, SW16 203 DL92
Empire Par, N18
off Empire Av 122 DR51
Empire Rd, Perivale UB6 159 CJ67
Empire Sq, N7 143 DL62
SE1 31 L5
SE20 off High St 205 DX94
Empire Sq E, SE1
off Empire Sq 31 L5
Empire Sq S, SE1
off Empire Sq 31 L5
Empire Sq W, SE1
off Empire Sq 31 L5
Empire Vil, Red. RH1 288 DG144
Empire Wk, Green. DA9 191 FW84
Empire Way, Wem. HA9 140 CM63
Empire Wf Rd, E14 34 G9
Empress App, SW6 39 J1
⊖ Empress Approach Bus
Terminus 39 J2
Empress Av, E4 123 EB52
E12 146 EJ61
Ilford IG1 147 EM61
Woodford Green IG8 124 EF52
Empress Dr, Chis. BR7 207 EP93
Empress Ms, SE5 43 J8
Empress Pl, SW6 39 J1
Empress Rd, Grav. DA12 213 GL87
Empress St, SE17 43 K2
Empson St, E3 22 D4
Emsworth Cl, N9 122 DW46
Emsworth Rd, Ilf. IG6 125 EP54
Emsworth St, SW2 203 DM89
Emu Rd, SW8 41 H9
Ena Rd, SW16 223 DL97
Enborne Grn, S.Ock. RM15 171 FU71
Enbrook St, W10 14 F3
Endale Cl, Cars. SM5 222 DF103
Endeavour Rd, Chsht EN8 89 DY27
[Sch] Endeavour Sch, The, Brwd.
CM15 off Hogarth Av 131 FZ48
Endeavour Way, SW19 202 DB91
Barking IG11 168 EU68
Croydon CR0 223 DK101
Endell St, WC2 18 A8
Enderby St, SE10 47 H1
Enderley Cl, Har. HA3 117 CE53
Enderley Rd, Har. HA3 117 CE53
Endersby Rd, Barn. EN5 101 CW43
Enders Cl, Enf. EN2 103 DN39
Endersleigh Gdns, NW4 141 CU56
Endlebury Rd, E4 123 EB47
Endlesham Rd, SW12 202 DG87
Endsleigh Cl, S.Croy. CR2 242 DW110
Endsleigh Gdns, WC1 17 N4
Hersham KT12 236 BW106
Ilford IG1 147 EM61
Surbiton KT6 219 CJ100
● Endsleigh Ind Est, Sthl.
UB2 178 BZ77
Endsleigh Pl, WC1 17 P4
Endsleigh Rd, W13 159 CG73
South Merstham RH1 273 DJ129
Southall UB2 178 BY77
Endsleigh St, WC1 17 N4
Endway, Surb. KT5 220 CN101
Endwell Rd, SE4 45 M9
Endymion Ct, Hat. AL10
off Endymion Rd 67 CW17
Endymion Ms, Hat. AL10
off Endymion Rd 67 CW17
Endymion Rd, N4 143 DN59
SW2 203 DM86
Hatfield AL10 67 CW17
Energen Cl, NW10 160 CS65
ENFIELD, EN1 - EN3 104 DT41
⇌ Enfield Chase 104 DQ41
Enfield Cl, Uxb. UB8 156 BK68
[Coll] Enfield Coll, Enf. EN3
off Hertford Rd 104 DW41
[Sch] Enfield Co Sch, Lwr Sch, Enf.
EN2 off Rosemary Av 104 DS39
Upr Sch, Enf. EN2
off Holly Wk 104 DR41
● Enfield Enterprise Cen, Enf.
EN3 off Queensway 104 DW43
[Sch] Enfield Gram Sch, Lwr Sch,
Enf. EN1 off Baker St 104 DR40
Upr Sch, Enf. EN2
off Market Pl 104 DR41
ENFIELD HIGHWAY, Enf. EN3 104 DW41
ENFIELD LOCK, Enf. EN3 105 DZ37
⇌ Enfield Lock 105 DY37
Enfield Lock, Enf. EN3 105 EA38
Enfield Retail Pk, Enf. EN1 104 DV41
Enfield Rd, N1 9 P7
W3 180 CP75
Brentford TW8 179 CK78
Enfield EN2 103 DK42
Lon.Hthrw Air. TW6
off Eastern Perimeter Rd 177 BS82
[Jct] Enfield Rd Rbt, Lon.Hthrw Air.
TW6 177 BS82
ENFIELD TOWN, Enf. EN2 104 DR40
⇌ Enfield Town 104 DS42
Enfield Wk, Brent. TW8 179 CK78
ENFIELD WASH, Enf. EN3 105 DX38
Enford St, W1 16 E6
Engadine Cl, Croy. CR0 224 DT104
Engadine St, SW18 201 CZ88
Engate St, SE13 185 EC84
Engayne Gdns, Upmin. RM14 150 FP60
[Sch] Engayne Prim Sch, Upmin.
RM14 off Severn Dr 151 FS58
Engel Pk, NW7 119 CW51
Engineer Cl, SE18 187 EN79
Engineers Way, Wem. HA9 140 CN63
Engineer's Wf, Nthlt. UB5 158 BZ70
Englands La, NW3 6 E5
Loughton IG10 107 EN40
England Way, N.Mal. KT3 220 CP98
Englefield Cl, Croy. CR0 224 DQ100
Enfield EN2 103 DN40
Englefield Green TW20
off Alexandra Rd 194 AW93
Orpington BR5 227 ET99
Englefield Cres, Orp. BR5 227 ET98
ENGLEFIELD GREEN, Egh.
TW20 194 AV92
Englefield Grn, Eng.Grn TW20 194 AW91
[Sch] Englefield Grn Inf Sch, Eng.Grn
TW20 off Barley Mow Rd 194 AW92
Englefield Path, Orp. BR5 227 ET98
Englefield Rd, N1 9 L5
Orpington BR5 228 EU98
Engleheart Dr, Felt. TW14 197 BT86
Engleheart Rd, SE6 205 EB87
Englehurst, Eng.Grn TW20 194 AW93
Englemere Pk, Oxshott KT22 236 CB114
Englewood Rd, SW12 203 DH86
Engliff La, Wok. GU22 249 BF116
English Gdns, Wrays. TW19 174 AX84
English Grds, SE1
off Tooley St 31 N3
[Sch] English Martyrs' Cath
Prim Sch, SE17 31 M9
[Sch] English Martyrs RC Prim Sch,
E1 20 B9
English St, E3 21 N4
Enid Cl, Brick.Wd AL2 82 BZ31
Enid St, SE16 32 B6
Enmore Av, SE25 224 DU99
Enmore Gdns, SW14 200 CR85
Enmore Rd, SE25 224 DU99
SW15 181 CW84
Southall UB1 158 CA70
Ennerdale Av, Horn. RM12 149 FG64
Ennerdale Av, Stanmore HA7 139 CJ55
Ennerdale Cl, Felt. TW14 197 BT88
St. Albans AL1 65 CH22
Sutton SM1 239 CZ105
Ennerdale Cres, Slou. SL1 152 AJ71
Ennerdale Dr, NW9 140 CS57
Watford WD25 82 BW33
Ennerdale Gdns, Wem. HA9 139 CJ60
Ennerdale Ho, E3 21 N4
Ennerdale Rd, Bexh. DA7 188 FA81
Richmond TW9 180 CM82
Ennersdale Rd, SE13 205 ED85
Ennismore Av, W4 181 CT77
Greenford UB6 159 CE65
Guildford GU1 265 AZ134
Ennismore Gdns, SW7 28 C5
Thames Ditton KT7 219 CE100
Ennismore Gdns Ms, SW7 28 C6
Ennismore Ms, SW7 28 C6
Ennismore St, SW7 28 C6
Ennis Rd, N4 143 DN60
SE18 187 EQ79
Ensign Cl, Lon.Hthrw Air. TW6 177 BS83
Purley CR8 241 DN110
Stanwell TW19 196 BK88
Ensign Dr, N13 122 DQ48
Ensign Ho, SW8
off St. George Wf 42 A2
SW18 182 DC83
Ensign St, E1 20 C10
Ensign Way, Stanw. TW19 196 BK88
Wallington SM6 241 DL108
Enslin Rd, SE9 207 EN86
Ensor Ms, SW7 28 A10
Enstone Rd, Enf. EN3 105 DY41
Uxbridge UB10 136 BM62
Enterdent, The, Gdse. RH9 275 DX133
Enterdent Rd, Gdse. RH9 274 DW134
● Enterprise Cen, The,
Pot.B. EN6 85 CY30
Enterprise Cl, Croy. CR0 223 DN102
● Enterprise Distribution Cen,
Til. RM18 193 GG84
● Enterprise Est, Guil. GU1 264 AY130
Enterprise Ho, E9 10 G7
● Enterprise Ind Est, SE16 32 G10
Enterprise Way, NW10 161 CU69
SW18 182 DA84
Hemel Hempstead HP2 63 BQ18
Teddington TW11 199 CF92
Enterprize Way, SE8 33 N8
Entertainment Av, SE10
off Millennium Way 35 J3
Envoy Av, Lon.Hthrw Air. TW6 177 BT83
[Jct] Envoy Av Rbt, Lon.Hthrw Air.
TW6 177 BT83
Eothen Cl, Cat. CR3 258 DU124
Epirus Ms, SW6 39 J4
Epirus Rd, SW6 39 H4
EPPING, CM16 91 ES31
⊖ Epping 92 EU31
Epping Cl, E14 34 B8
Romford RM7 149 FB55
★ Epping Forest, Epp. CM16
& Loug. IG10 106 EJ39
[Coll] Epping Forest Coll, Loug.
IG10 off Borders La 107 EP42
★ Epping Forest District Mus,
Wal.Abb. EN9 off Sun St 89 EC33
[Coll] Epping Forest Fld Cen,
High Beach IG10
off Wake Rd 106 EJ38
Epping Glade, E4 105 EC44
EPPING GREEN, Epp. CM16 73 EN24
EPPING GREEN, Hert. SG13 69 DK21
Epping Grn, Hem.H. HP2 62 BN15
Epping Grn Rd, Epp.Grn CM16 73 EN21
Epping La, Stap.Taw. RM4 108 EV40
Epping Long Grn, Epp.Grn
CM16 73 EM24
Epping New Rd, Buck.H. IG9 124 EH47
Loughton IG10 106 EH43
Epping Pl, N1 8 F5
Epping Rd, Epp. CM16 107 EM36
Epping Green CM16 91 ER27
North Weald Bassett CM16 92 EW28
North Weald Bassett North
CM16 75 FD24
Ongar CM5 75 FF24
Roydon CM19 72 EK18
Toot Hill CM5 93 FC30
Waltham Abbey EN9 72 EK18
EPPING UPLAND, Epp. CM16 91 EQ25
[Sch] Epping Upland C of E Prim Sch,
Epp.Grn CM16
off Carters La 73 EP24
Epping Way, E4 105 EB44
Epple Rd, SW6 39 H6
EPSOM, KT17 - KT19 238 CQ114
⇌ Epsom 238 CR113
[Coll] Epsom Adult Ed Cen, Epsom
KT17 off Church St 238 CS113
[Sch] Epsom & Ewell High Sch,
W.Ewell KT19
off Ruxley La 238 CQ106
● Epsom Business Pk, Epsom
KT17 238 CS111
Epsom Cl, Bexh. DA7 189 FB83
Northolt UB5 138 BZ64
[Coll] Epsom Coll, Epsom KT17
off College Rd 239 CU114
⇌ Epsom Downs 255 CV115
Epsom Downs, Epsom KT18 255 CT118
● Epsom Downs Metro Cen,
Tad. KT20 off Waterfield 255 CV120
★ Epsom Downs Racecourse,
Epsom KT18 255 CT118
Epsom Gap, Lthd. KT22 253 CH115
[H] Epsom Gen Hosp, Epsom
KT18 254 CQ115
Epsom La N, Epsom KT18 255 CV118
Tadworth KT20 255 CV118
Epsom La S, Tad. KT20 255 CW121
[Sch] Epsom Prim Sch, Epsom
KT19 off Pound La 238 CR111
Epsom Rd, E10 145 EC58
Ashtead KT21 254 CM118
Croydon CR0 241 DN105
Epsom KT17 239 CT110
Guildford GU1, GU4 265 BE133
Ilford IG3 147 ET58
Leatherhead KT22 253 CH121
Morden SM4 221 CZ101
Sutton SM3 221 CZ101
West Horsley KT24 267 BP130
Epsom Sq, Lon.Hthrw Air. TW6
off Eastern Perimeter Rd 177 BT82
● Epsom Trade Pk,
Epsom KT19 238 CR111
Epsom Way, Horn. RM12 150 FM63
Epstein Rd, SE28 168 EU74
Epworth Rd, Islw. TW7 179 CH80
Epworth St, EC2 19 M5
Equana Apts, SE8 33 L10
Equinox Ho, Bark. IG11 167 EQ65
Equity Ms, W5 159 CK74
Equity Sq, E2 20 B3
Erasmus St, SW1 29 P9
Erbin Ct, N9 off Galahad Rd 122 DU47
Erconwald St, W12 161 CT72
Erebus Dr, SE28 187 EQ76
Eresby Dr, Beck. BR3 225 EA102
Eresby Pl, NW6 5 J7
Erica Cl, Slou. SL1 153 AL73
Erica Ct, Swan. BR8
off Azalea Dr 229 FE98
Woking GU22 248 AX118
Erica Gdns, Croy. CR0 243 EB105
Erica St, W12 161 CU73
Eric Clarke La, Bark. IG11 25 P4
Eric Cl, E7 13 N1
Ericcson Cl, SW18 202 DA85
Eric Fletcher Ct, N1
off Essex Rd 9 K6
Eric Rd, E7 13 N1
NW10 161 CT65
Romford RM6 148 EX59
Ericson Ho, N16
off Stamford Hill 144 DS60
Eric Steele Ho, St.Alb. AL2 82 CB27
Eric St, E3 21 N4
Eridge Grn Cl, Orp. BR5 228 EW102
Eridge Rd, W4 180 CR76
Erin Cl, Brom. BR1 206 EE94
Ilford IG3 148 EU58
Erin Ct, NW2 4 B4
Erindale, SE18 187 ER79
Erindale Ter, SE18 187 ER79
Eriswell Cres, Hersham KT12 235 BS107
Eriswell Rd, Hersham KT12 235 BT105
ERITH, DA8; DA18 189 FD79
⇌ Erith 189 FE78
[H] Erith & District Hosp,
Erith DA8 189 FD79
Erith Ct, Purf. RM19 190 FN77
Erith Cres, Rom. RM5 127 FC53
Erith High St, Erith DA8 189 FE78
★ Erith Lib & Mus,
Erith DA8
off Walnut Tree Rd 189 FE78
Erith Riverside, Erith DA8 189 FE79
Erith Rd, Belv. DA17 188 FA78
Bexleyheath DA7 189 FB84
Erith DA8 189 FB84
[Sch] Erith Sch, Erith DA8
off Avenue Rd 189 FD80
Erkenwald Cl, Cher. KT16 215 BE101
Erlanger Rd, SE14 45 K8
Erlesmere Gdns, W13 179 CG76
Ermine Cl, Chsht EN7 88 DV31
Hounslow TW4 178 BW82
St. Albans AL3 64 CA21
Ermine Ho, N17
off Moselle St 122 DT52
Ermine Ms, E2 10 A9
Ermine Rd, N15 144 DT58
SE13 185 EB83
Ermine Side, Enf. EN1 104 DU43
Ermington Rd, SE9 207 EQ89
Ermyn Cl, Lthd. KT22 253 CK121
Ermyn Way, Lthd. KT22 253 CK121
Ernald Av, E6 166 EL68
Ernan Cl, S.Ock. RM15 171 FU71
Ernan Rd, S.Ock. RM15 171 FU71
Erncroft Way, Twick. TW1 199 CF86
Ernest Av, SE27 203 DP91
[Sch] Ernest Bevin Coll, SW17
off Beechcroft Rd 202 DE89
Ernest Cl, Beck. BR3 225 EA99
Ernest Gdns, W4 180 CP79
Ernest Gro, Beck. BR3 225 DZ99
Ernest Rd, Horn. RM11 150 FL58
Kingston upon Thames KT1 220 CP96
Ernest Sq, Kings.T. KT1 220 CP96
Ernest St, E1 21 K5
Ernle Rd, SW20 201 CV94
Ernshaw Pl, SW15
off Carlton Dr 201 CY85
★ Eros, W1 29 N1
Eros Ho, SE6
off Brownhill Rd 205 EB87
Erpingham Rd, SW15 181 CW83
Erridge Rd, SW19 222 DA96
Erriff Dr, S.Ock. RM15 171 FT71
Errington Cl, Grays RM16
off Cedar Rd 193 GH76
Hatfield AL10 66 CS17
Errington Dr, Wind. SL4 173 AN81
Errington Rd, W9 15 H4
Errol Gdns, Hayes UB4 157 BV70
New Malden KT3 221 CU98
Erroll Rd, Rom. RM1 149 FF56
Errol St, EC1 19 K5
Erskine Cl, Sutt. SM1 222 DE104
Erskine Cres, N17 144 DV56
Erskine Hill, NW11 142 DA57
Erskine Ho, SE7
off Springfield Gro 186 EJ79
Erskine Ms, NW3 6 F7
Erskine Rd, E17 145 DZ56
NW3 6 F7
Sutton SM1 240 DD105
Watford WD19 116 BW48
Erwood Rd, SE7 37 H10
Esam Way, SW16 203 DN92
Esbies Est, Saw. CM21 58 EZ05
Escomb Ct, Whyt. CR3
off Godstone Rd 258 DU119
Escombe Dr, Guil. GU2 264 AV129
Escott Gdns, SE9 206 EL91
Escott Pl, Ott. KT16 233 BC107
Escot Way, Barn. EN5 101 CW43
[Coll] ESCP-EAP European Sch of
Management, NW3 5 K1
Escreet Gro, SE18 37 L8
Esdaile Gdns, Upmin. RM14 151 FR59
Esdaile La, Hodd. EN11 71 EA18
ESHER, KT10 236 CB105
⇌ Esher 219 CD103
Esher Av, Rom. RM7 149 FC58
Sutton SM3 221 CX104
Walton-on-Thames KT12 217 BU101
Esher Bypass, Chess. KT9 237 CH108
Cobham KT11 235 BU112
Esher KT10 237 CH108
[Sch] Esher Ch Sch, Esher KT10
off Milbourne La 236 CC106
Esher Cl, Bex. DA5 208 EY88
Esher Cl, Esher KT10 236 CB106
[Sch] Esher C of E High Sch,
Esher KT10 off More La 218 CA104
[Coll] Esher Coll, T.Ditt. KT7
off Weston Grn Rd 219 CE101
Esher Common, Esher
KT10 236 CC110
Esher Cres, Lon.Hthrw Air. TW6
off Eastern Perimeter Rd 177 BS82
Esher Gdns, SW19 201 CX89
Esher Grn, Esher KT10 236 CB105
[Coll] Esher Grn Adult Learning Cen,
Esher KT10 off Esher Grn 236 CB105
Esher Grn Dr, Esher KT10 218 CB104
Esher Ms, Mitch. CR4 222 DF97
Esher Pk Av, Esher KT10 236 CC105
Esher Pl Av, Esher KT10 236 CB105
Esher Rd, E.Mol. KT8 219 CD100
Hersham KT12 236 BX106
Ilford IG3 147 ES62
Eskdale, NW1 17 L1
London Colney AL2 84 CM27
Eskdale Av, Chesh. HP5 76 AQ30
Northolt UB5 158 BZ67
Eskdale Cl, Dart. DA2 210 FQ89
Wembley HA9 139 CK61
Eskdale Ct, Hem.H. HP2
off Lonsdale 62 BL17
Eskdale Gdns, Pur. CR8 242 DR114
Eskdale Rd, Bexh. DA7 188 FA82
Uxbridge UB8 156 BH68
Eskley Gdns, S.Ock. RM15 171 FV70
Eskmont Ridge, SE19 204 DS94
Esk Rd, E13 23 P4
Esk Way, Rom. RM1 127 FD52
Esmar Cres, NW9 141 CU59
Esme Ho, SW15 181 CT84
Esmeralda Rd, SE1 32 D9
Esmond Cl, Rain. RM13
off Dawson Dr 169 FH66
Esmond Gdns, W4
off South Par 180 CR77
Esmond Rd, NW6 5 H9
W4 180 CR77
Esmond St, SW15 181 CY84
Esparto St, SW18 202 DB87
Essendene Cl, Cat. CR3 258 DS123
[Sch] Essendene Lo Sch, Cat.
CR3 off Essendene Rd 258 DS123
Essendene Rd, Cat. CR3 258 DS123
Essenden Rd, Belv. DA17 188 FA78
South Croydon CR2 242 DS108
[Sch] Essendine Prim Sch, W9 15 K3
Essendine Rd, W9 15 K4
ESSENDON, Hat. AL9 68 DE17
[Sch] Essendon C of E Prim Sch,
Essen. AL9 off School La 68 DF17
Essendon Gdns, Welw.G.C. AL7 51 CZ09
Essendon Hill, Essen. AL9 68 DE17
Essendon Pl, Essen. AL9 68 DE19
Essendon Rd, Hert. SG13 68 DG15
Essex Av, Islw. TW7 179 CE83
Slough SL2 153 AQ71
Essex Cl, E17 145 DY56
Addlestone KT15 234 BJ105
Morden SM4 221 CX101
Romford RM7 149 FB56
Ruislip HA4 138 BX60
Essex Ct, EC4 18 E9
SW13 181 CT82
Essex Gdns, N4 143 DP58
Hornchurch RM11 150 FM57
Essex Gro, SE19 204 DR93
Essex Ho, E14 22 C8
Essex La, Kings L. WD4 81 BS33
Essex Lo, N10 120 DG54
Essex Pk, N3 120 DB51
Essex Pk Ms, W3 160 CS74
Essex Pl, W4 180 CQ77
Essex Pl Sq, W4
off Chiswick High Rd 180 CR77
[Sch] Essex Prim Sch, E12
off Sheridan Rd 147 EM64
⇌ Essex Road 9 J7
Essex Rd, E4 124 EE46
E10 145 EC58
E12 146 EL64
E17 145 DY58
E18 124 EH54
N1 9 J7
NW10 160 CS66
W3 160 CQ73
W4 off Belmont Ter 180 CR77
Barking IG11 167 ER66
Borehamwood WD6 100 CN41
Chadwell Heath RM6 148 EW59
Chesham HP5 76 AQ29
Dagenham RM10 149 FC64
Dartford DA1 210 FK86
Enfield EN2 104 DR42
Gravesend DA11 213 GG88
Grays RM20 191 FU79
Hoddesdon EN11 71 EC18
Longfield DA3 231 FX96
Romford RM7 149 FB56
Watford WD17 97 BU40
Essex Rd S, E11 145 ED59
Essex St, E7 13 N2
WC2 18 E10
St. Albans AL1 65 CE19
Essex Twr, SE20 224 DV95
Essex Vil, W8 27 J5
Essex Way, Epp. CM16 92 EV32
Great Warley CM13 129 FW51
Hoddesdon EN11 71 EC17
Ongar CM5 93 FF29
Essex Wf, E5 144 DW61
Essian St, E1 21 L6
Essoldo Way, Edg. HA8 140 CM55
Estate Way, E10 145 DZ60
Estcourt Rd, SE25 224 DV100
SW6 38 G4
Watford WD17 98 BW41
Estella Av, N.Mal. KT3 221 CV98
Estelle Rd, NW3 6 F1
Esterbrooke St, SW1 29 N9
Este Rd, SW11 40 C10
Estfeld Cl, Hodd. EN11 55 EB14
Esther Cl, N21 121 DN45
Esther Ms, Brom. BR1 226 EH95
Esther Rd, E11 146 EE59
Estoria Cl, SW2 203 DN87
★ Estorick Collection of Modern
Italian Art, N1 9 H5
Estreham Rd, SW16 203 DK93
Estridge Cl, Houns. TW3 178 CA84
Estuary Cl, Bark. IG11 168 EV69
Eswyn Rd, SW17 202 DF91
Etchingham Pk Rd, N3 120 DB52

Etchingham Rd, E15 145 EC63
Eternit Wk, SW6 38 B6
Etfield Gro, Sid. DA14 208 EV92
Ethel Bailey Cl, Epsom KT19 238 CN112
Ethelbert Cl, Brom. BR1 226 EG97
Ethelbert Gdns, Ilf. IG2 147 EM57
Ethelbert Rd, SW20 221 CX95
Bromley BR1 226 EG97
Erith DA8 189 FC80
Hawley DA2 210 FL91
Orpington BR5 228 EX97
Ethelbert St, SW12 203 DH88
Ethelburga Rd, Rom. RM3 128 FM53
Ethelburga St, SW11 40 D6
Ethelburga Twr, SW11 40 D6
Etheldene Av, N10 143 DJ56
Ethelden Rd, W12 161 CV74
Ethelred Cl, Welw.G.C. AL7 51 CZ10
Ethelred Ct, Whyt. CR3
off Godstone Rd 258 DU119
Ethelred Est, SE11 30 D9
Ethel Rd, E16 24 A9
Ashford TW15 196 BL92
Ethel St, SE17 31 J9
Ethel Ter, Orp. BR6 246 EW109
Ethelwine Pl, Abb.L. WD5
off The Crescent 81 BT30
Etheridge Grn, Loug. IG10 107 EQ41
Etheridge Rd, NW4 141 CW59
Loughton IG10 107 EP40
Etherley Rd, N15 144 DQ57
Etherow St, SE22 204 DU86
Etherstone Grn, SW16 203 DN91
Etherstone Rd, SW16 203 DN91
Ethnard Rd, SE15 44 E3
Ethorpe Cl, Ger.Cr. SL9 134 AY57
Ethorpe Cres, Ger.Cr. SL9 134 AY57
Ethronvi Rd, Bexh. DA7 188 EY83
Etloe Rd, E10 145 EA61
Etna Rd, St.Alb. AL3 65 CD19
ETON, Wind. SL4 173 AQ80
Eton Av, N12 120 DC52
NW3 6 C6
Barnet EN4 102 DE44
Hounslow TW5 178 BZ79
New Malden KT3 220 CR99
Wembley HA0 139 CH63
Eton Cl, SW18 202 DB87
Datchet SL3 174 AU79
Sch Eton Coll, Eton SL4
off High St 173 AR79
Eton Coll Rd, NW3 6 F5
Eton Ct, NW3 6 B6
Eton SL4 173 AR80
Staines-upon-Thames TW18 195 BF92
Wembley HA0 139 CJ63
Sch Eton End PNEU Sch, Datchet
SL3 off Eton Rd 174 AU79
Eton Garages, NW3 6 D5
Eton Gro, NW9 140 CN55
SE13 186 EE83
Eton Hall, NW3 6 F5
Sch Eton Ho The Manor Sch, SW4
off Clapham Common
N Side 183 DH84
Eton Pl, NW3 6 G6
Sch Eton Porny C of E First Sch,
Eton SL4 off High St 173 AR79
Eton Ri, NW3 6 F5
Eton Rd, NW3 6 E6
Datchet SL3 174 AT78
Hayes UB3 177 BT80
Ilford IG1 147 EQ64
Orpington BR6 246 EV105
Eton Sq, Eton SL4 173 AR80
Eton St, Rich. TW9 200 CL85
Eton Vil, NW3 6 F5
Eton Way, Dart. DA1 190 FJ84
ETON WICK, Wind. SL4 173 AM77
Sch Eton Wick C of E First Sch,
Eton Wick SL4
off Sheepcote Rd 173 AN78
Eton Wick Rd, Wind. SL4 173 AL77
Etta St, SE8 45 M2
Etton Cl, Horn. RM12 150 FL61
Ettrick St, E14 22 F8
Etwell Pl, Surb. KT5 220 CM100
Eucalyptus Ms, SW16
off Estreham Rd 203 DK93
Euclid Way, Grays RM20 191 FT78
Euesden Cl, N9 122 DV48
Eugene Cl, Rom. RM2 150 FJ56
Eugenia Rd, SE16 33 H9
Eugenie Ms, Chis. BR7 227 EP95
Eunice Gro, Chesh. HP5 76 AR32
Eureka Gdns, Epp.Grn CM16 73 EN21
Eureka Rd, Kings.T. KT1
off Washington Rd 220 CN96
Coll Eurocentres, Lee Grn, SE3
off Meadowcourt Rd 186 EF84
London Cen, SW1 29 K9
Euro Cl, NW10 161 CU65
Coll Europa Cen for Modern
Languages, Horn. RM11
off The Walk 150 FM61
Europa Pk Rd, Guil. GU1 264 AW133
Europa Pl, EC1 19 J3
Europa Rd, Hem.H. HP2
off Jupiter Dr 62 BM17
● Europa Trade Est, Erith DA8 189 FD78
● Europa Trade Pk, E16 23 J5
Europe Rd, SE18 37 K7
Eustace Bldg, SW8 41 J3
Eustace Pl, SE18 37 J8
Eustace Rd, E6 24 G2
SW6 39 J4
Guildford GU4 265 BD132
Romford RM6 148 EX59
⇌ Euston 17 M2
⊖ Euston 17 M2
⊖ Euston 17 M2
⊖ Euston 17 N3
Euston Av, Wat. WD18 97 BT43
Euston Cen, NW1
off Triton Sq 17 L4
Euston Gro, NW1 17 N3
Euston Rd, N1 18 A2
NW1 17 K5
Croydon CR0 223 DN102
⊖ Euston Square 17 M4
Euston Sq, NW1 17 N3
Euston Sta Colonnade, NW1 17 N3
Euston St, NW1 17 M4
● Euston Twr, NW1 17 L4
Evan Cook Cl, SE15 44 G7
Evandale Rd, SW9 42 F8
Evangelist Rd, NW5 7 K1
Evans Av, Wat. WD25 97 BT35
● Evans Business Cen, NW2 141 CU62
Evans Cl, E8 10 B5
Croxley Green WD3 96 BN43
Greenhithe DA9 211 FU85
Evansdale, Rain. RM13
off New Zealand Way 169 FF69
Evans Gro, Felt. TW13 198 CA89
St. Albans AL4 65 CJ16
Evans Rd, SE6 206 EE89
Evanston Av, E4 123 EC52
Evanston Gdns, Ilf. IG4 146 EL58
Evans Wf, Hem.H. HP3 62 BL24
Eva Rd, Rom. RM6 148 EW59
H Evelina Children's Hosp,
SE1 30 C6
Evelina Rd, SE15 44 G10
SE20 205 DX94
Eveline Lowe Est, SE16 32 C7
Sch Eveline Lowe Prim Sch,
SE1 44 D1
Eveline Rd, Mitch. CR4 222 DF95
Evelyn Av, NW9 140 CR56
Ruislip HA4 137 BT58
Titsey RH8 260 EJ124
Evelyn Cl, Twick. TW2 198 CB87
Woking GU22 248 AX120
Evelyn Cotts, Dor. RH5 284 BX143
Evelyn Ct, N1 19 L1
Evelyn Cres, Sun. TW16 217 BT95
Evelyn Denington Rd, E6 25 H5
Evelyn Dr, Pnr. HA5 116 BX52
Evelyn Fox Ct, W10 14 B7
Evelyn Gdns, SW7 40 A1
Godstone RH9 274 DW130
Richmond TW9 180 CL84
Sch Evelyn Grace Acad, SE24 183 DP84
Evelyn Gro, W5 160 CM74
Southall UB1 158 BZ72
Evelyn Rd, E16 35 P2
E17 145 EC56
SW19 202 DB92
W4 180 CR76
Cockfosters EN4 102 DF42
Ham TW10 199 CJ90
Richmond TW9 180 CL83
Evelyns Cl, Uxb. UB8 156 BN72
Evelyn Sharp Cl, Rom. RM2
off Amery Gdns 150 FK55
Evelyn St, SE8 33 L9
Evelyn Ter, Rich. TW9 180 CL83
Evelyn Wk, N1 19 L1
Great Warley CM13
off Essex Way 129 FW51
Evelyn Way, Epsom KT19 238 CN111
Stoke D'Abernon KT11 252 BZ116
Sunbury-on-Thames TW16 217 BT95
Wallington SM6 241 DK105
Evelyn Yd, W1 17 N8
Evening Hill, Beck. BR3 205 EC94
Evensyde, Wat. WD18 97 BR44
Evenwood Cl, SW15 201 CY85
Everard Av, Brom. BR2 226 EG102
Slough SL1 174 AS75
Everard Cl, St.Alb. AL1 65 CD22
Everard La, Cat. CR3
off Tillingdown Hill 258 DU122
Everard Way, Wem. HA9 140 CL62
Everatt Cl, SW18
off Amerland Rd 201 CZ86
Everdon Rd, SW13 181 CU79
Everest Cl, Nthflt DA11 212 GE90
Everest Ct, Wok. GU21
off Langmans Way 248 AS116
Everest Pl, E14 22 E6
Swanley BR8 229 FD98
Everest Rd, SE9 206 EL85
Stanwell TW19 196 BK87
Everest Way, Hem.H. HP2 62 BN19
Everett Cl, Bushey Hth WD23 117 CE46
Cheshunt EN7 88 DQ25
Pinner HA5 137 BT55
Everett Wk, Belv. DA17
off Osborne Rd 188 EZ78
Everglade, Bigg.H. TN16 260 EK118
Everglade Strand, NW9 119 CT53
Evergreen Cl, SE20 204 DW94
Evergreen Ct, Stanw. TW19
off Evergreen Way 196 BK87
Evergreen Oak Av, Wind. SL4 174 AU83
Evergreen Sq, E8 10 A6
Evergreen Wk, Hem.H. HP3 62 BL22
Evergreen Way, Hayes UB3 157 BT73
Stanwell TW19 196 BK87
Everilda St, N1 8 D9
Evering Rd, E5 144 DT62
N16 144 DT62
Everington Rd, N10 120 DF54
Everington St, W6 38 D2
Everitt Rd, NW10 160 CR69
Everlands Cl, Wok. GU22 248 AY118
Everlasting La, St.Alb. AL3 64 CC19
Everleigh St, N4 143 DM60
Eve Rd, E11 13 J1
E15 23 K1
N17 144 DS55
Isleworth TW7 179 CG84
Woking GU21 249 BB115
Eversfield Gdns, NW7 118 CS51
Eversfield Rd, Reig. RH2 272 DB134
Richmond TW9 180 CM82
Evershed Wk, W4 180 CQ76
Eversholt Ct, Barn. EN5
off Lyonsdown Rd 102 DC43
Eversholt St, NW1 7 M10
Evershot Rd, N4 143 DM60
Eversleigh Gdns, Upmin.
RM14 151 FR60
Eversleigh Rd, E6 166 EK67
N3 119 CZ52
SW11 40 G9
Barnet EN5 102 DC43
Eversley Av, Bexh. DA7 189 FD82
Wembley HA9 140 CN61
Eversley Cl, N21 103 DM44
Loughton IG10 107 EQ41
Eversley Cres, N21 103 DM44
Isleworth TW7 179 CD81
Ruislip HA4 137 BS61
Eversley Cross, Bexh. DA7 189 FE82
Eversley Mt, N21 103 DM44
Eversley Pk, SW19 201 CV92
Eversley Pk Rd, N21 103 DM44
Sch Eversley Prim Sch, N21
off Chaseville Pk Rd 103 DM43
Eversley Rd, SE7 186 EH79
SE19 204 DR94
Surbiton KT5 220 CM98
Eversley Way, Croy. CR0 243 EA105
Egham TW20 215 BC96
Everthorpe Rd, SE15 184 DT83
Everton Bldgs, NW1 17 L3
Everton Dr, Stan. HA7 140 CM55
Everton Rd, Croy. CR0 224 DU102
Evesham Av, E17 123 EA54
Evesham Cl, Grnf. UB6 158 CB68
Reigate RH2 271 CZ133
Sutton SM2 240 DA108
Evesham Ct, W13
off Tewkesbury Rd 159 CG74
Evesham Grn, Mord. SM4 222 DB100
Evesham Rd, E15 13 L8
N11 121 DJ50
Gravesend DA12 213 GK89
Morden SM4 222 DB100
Reigate RH2 271 CZ134
Evesham Rd N, Reig. RH2 271 CZ133
Evesham St, W11 26 C1
Evesham Wk, SE5 43 L8
SW9 42 E7
Evesham Way, SW11 41 H10
Ilford IG5 147 EN55
Evette Ms, Ilf. IG5 125 EN53
Evreham Rd, Iver SL0 155 BE72
Evron Pl, Hert. SG14
off Fore St 54 DR09
Evry Rd, Sid. DA14 208 EW93
Ewald Rd, SW6 38 G9
Ewanrigg Ter, Wdf.Grn. IG8 124 EJ50
Ewan Rd, Harold Wd RM3 128 FK54
Ewart Gro, N22 121 DN53
Ewart Pl, E3 11 N10
Ewart Rd, SE23 205 DX87
Ewe Cl, N7 8 B4
Ewelands, Horl. RH6 291 DJ147
EWELL, Epsom KT17 239 CU110
Ewell Bypass, Epsom KT17 239 CU108
Sch Ewell Castle Sch, Ewell
KT17 off Church St 239 CU109
Ewell Ct Av, Epsom KT19 238 CS106
Ewell Downs Rd, Epsom KT17 239 CU111
⇌ Ewell East 239 CV110
Sch Ewell Gro Inf & Nurs Sch,
Ewell KT17 off West St 239 CT109
Ewell Ho Gro, Epsom KT17 239 CT110
Ewellhurst Rd, Ilf. IG5 124 EL54
Ewell Pk Gdns, Epsom KT17 239 CU108
Ewell Pk Way, Ewell KT17 239 CU107
Ewell Rd, Long Dit. KT6 219 CH101
Surbiton KT6 220 CL100
Sutton SM3 239 CY107
⇌ Ewell West 238 CS109
Ewelme Rd, SE23 204 DW88
Ewen Cres, SW2 203 DN87
Ewer St, SE1 31 J3
Ewhurst Av, S.Croy. CR2 242 DT109
Ewhurst Cl, E1 21 H7
Sutton SM2 239 CW109
Ewhurst Ct, Mitch. CR4
off Phipps Br Rd 222 DD97
Ewhurst Rd, SE4 205 DZ86
Exbury Rd, SE6 205 EA89
Excalibur Ct, N9
off Galahad Rd 122 DU48
Excel Ct, WC2 29 P1
★ ExCeL London, E16 36 B1
ExCeL Marina, E16 36 A1
Excelsior Cl, Kings.T. KT1
off Washington Rd 220 CN96
Excelsior Gdns, SE13 46 E9
ExCeL Waterfront, E16 36 B1
Exchange, The, E1
off Commercial St 20 A5
Croy. CR0 off Scarbrook Rd 224 DQ104
Exchange Arc, EC2 19 P6
Exchange Cl, N11
off Benfleet Way 120 DG47
Exchange Ct, WC2 30 B1
Exchange Ho, N8 143 DL58
Exchange Pl, EC2 19 N6
Exchange Rd, Wat. WD18 97 BV42
🔒 Exchange Shop cen, SW15 181 CX84
Exchange Sq, EC2 19 N6
Exchange St, Rom. RM1 149 FE57
Exchange Wk, Pnr. HA5 138 BY59
Exeforde Av, Ashf. TW15 196 BN91
Exeter Cl, E6 25 J8
Watford WD24 98 BW40
Exeter Ct, Surb. KT6
off Maple Rd 220 CL99
Exeter Gdns, Ilf. IG1 146 EL60
Exeter Ho, SW15
off Putney Heath 201 CW86
Exeter Ms, NW6 5 L5
SW6 39 J4
Exeter Pl, Guil. GU2 264 AT132
Exeter Rd, E16 23 P7
E17 145 EA57
N9 122 DW47
N14 121 DH46
NW2 4 F5
Croydon CR0 224 DS101
Dagenham RM10 169 FB65
Enfield EN3 105 DX41
Feltham TW13 198 BZ90
Gravesend DA12 213 GK90
Harrow HA2 138 BY61
London Heathrow Airport
TW6 177 BS83
Welling DA16 187 ET82
Exeter St, WC2 18 B10
Exeter Way, SE14 45 N5
London Heathrow Airp. TW6 177 BS82
Exford Gdns, SE12 206 EH88
Exford Rd, SE12 206 EH89
Exhibition Cl, W12 26 A1
Exhibition Rd, SW7 28 B5
Exmoor Cl, Ilf. IG6 125 EQ53
Exmoor St, W10 14 D5
Exmouth Mkt, EC1 18 E4
Exmouth Ms, NW1 17 M3
Exmouth Pl, E8 10 E7
Exmouth Rd, E17 145 DZ57
Grays RM17 192 GB79
Hayes UB4 157 BS69
Ruislip HA4 138 BW62
Welling DA16 188 EW81
Exmouth St, E1 21 H8
Exning Rd, E16 23 L5
Exon Apts, Rom. RM1
off Mercury Gdns 149 FE56
Exon St, SE17 31 N9
Explorer Av, Stai. TW19 196 BL88
Explorer Dr, Wat. WD18 97 BT44
Express Dr, Ilf. IG3 148 EV60
Exton Gdns, Dag. RM8 148 EW64
Exton Rd, NW10 160 CQ66
Exton St, SE1 30 E3
Eyebright Cl, Croy. CR0
off Primrose La 225 DX102
Eyhurst Av, Horn. RM12 149 FG62
Eyhurst Cl, NW2 141 CU61
Kingswood KT20 255 CZ123
Eyhurst Pk, Tad. KT20 256 DC123
Eyhurst Spur, Kgswd KT20 255 CZ124
Eylewood Rd, SE27 204 DQ92
Eynella Rd, SE22 204 DT87
Eynham Rd, W12 14 A7
EYNSFORD, Dart. DA4 230 FL103
★ Eynsford Castle, Dart. DA4 230 FL103
Eynsford Cl, Petts Wd BR5 227 EQ101
Eynsford Cres, Bex. DA5 208 EW88
Eynsford Rd, Fnghm DA4 230 FM102
Greenhithe DA9 211 FW85
Ilford IG3 147 ES61
Swanley BR8 229 FD100
Eynsham Dr, SE2 188 EU77
Eynswood Dr, Sid. DA14 208 EV92
Eyot Gdns, W6 181 CT78
Eyot Grn, W4 181 CT78
Eyre Cl, Rom. RM2 149 FH56
Eyre Ct, NW8 6 A10
Eyre Grn, Slou. SL2 153 AN69
Eyre St Hill, EC1 18 E5
Eyston Dr, Wey. KT13 234 BN110
Eythorne Ct, Epsom KT17
off Windmill La 239 CT112
Eythorne Rd, SW9 42 F6
Eywood Rd, St.Alb. AL1 64 CC22
Ezra St, E2 20 B2

F

Faber Gdns, NW4 141 CU57
Fabian Rd, SW6 39 H4
Fabian St, E6 25 H5
Fackenden La, Shore. TN14 247 FH113
Factory La, N17 122 DT54
Croydon CR0 223 DN102
Factory Rd, E16 36 G3
Northfleet DA11 212 GC86
Factory Sq, SW16 203 DL93
Factory Yd, W7 159 CE74
Faesten Way, Bex. DA5 209 FE90
Faggotters La, High Laver CM5 75 FF15
Matching Tye CM17 59 FE13
Faggotts Cl, Rad. WD7 99 CJ35
Faggs Rd, Felt. TW14 197 BU85
Fagnall La, Winch.Hill HP7 110 AJ45
Fagus Av, Rain. RM13 170 FK69
Faints Cl, Chsht EN7 88 DS29
Fairacre, Hem.H. HP3 62 BM24
New Malden KT3 220 CS97
Fairacres, SW15 181 CU84
Fair Acres, Brom. BR2 226 EG99
Fairacres, Cob. KT11 236 BX112
Croydon CR0 243 DZ109
Redhill RH1 289 DJ142
Ruislip HA4 137 BT59
Tadworth KT20 255 CW121
Windsor SL4 173 AK82
Fairacres Cl, Pot.B. EN6 85 CZ33
● Fairacres Ind Est,
Wind. SL4 172 AJ82
Fairbairn Cl, Pur. CR8 241 DN113
Fairbairn Grn, SW9 42 F6
Fairbank Av, Orp. BR6 227 EP103
Fairbank Est, N1 19 M1
Fairbanks Rd, N17 144 DT55
Fairborne Way, Guil. GU2 264 AU131
Fairbourne, Cob. KT11 236 BX113
Fairbourne Cl, Wok. GU21 248 AU118
Fairbourne La, Cat. CR3 258 DQ122
Fairbourne Rd, N17 144 DS55
Fairbridge Rd, N19 143 DK61
Fairbrook Cl, N13 121 DN50
Fairbrook Rd, N13 121 DN51
Fairburn Cl, Borwd. WD6 100 CN39
Fairburn Ct, SW15 201 CY85
Fairburn Ho, N16
off Stamford Hill 144 DS60
W14 off Ivatt Pl 39 H1
Fairby Ho, SE1 32 B8
Fairby Rd, SE12 206 EH85
● Faircharm Trd Est, SE8 46 C4
Fairchild Cl, SW11 40 B9
Fairchildes Av, New Adgtn CR0 243 ED112
Fairchildes La, Warl. CR6 243 ED114
Sch Fairchildes Prim Sch,
New Adgtn CR0
off Fairchildes Av 244 EE112
Fairchild Pl, EC2 19 P5
Fairchild St, EC2 19 P5
Fair Cl, Bushey WD23
off Claybury 116 CB45
Fairclough Cl, Nthlt. UB5 158 BZ70
Fairclough St, E1 20 D9
Faircroft, Slou. SL2 153 AP70
Faircross Av, Bark. IG11 167 EQ65
Romford RM5 127 FD52
Faircross Par, Bark. IG11 167 ES65
Faircross Way, St.Alb. AL1 65 CG18
Fairdale Gdns, SW15 181 CV84
Hayes UB3 157 BU74
Fairdene Rd, Couls. CR5 257 DK117
Fairey Av, Hayes UB3 177 BT77
Fairfax Av, Epsom KT17 239 CV109
Redhill RH1 272 DE133
Fairfax Cl, Oxt. RH8 275 ED130
Walton-on-Thames KT12 217 BV102
Fairfax Ct, Dart. DA1 210 FN86
Fairfax Gdns, SE3 186 EK81
Fairfax Ms, E16 36 A2
SW15 181 CW84
Amersham HP7 77 AN40
Fairfax Pl, NW6 5 P7
W14 26 F7
Fairfax Rd, N8 143 DN56
NW6 5 P7
W4 180 CS76
Grays RM17 192 GB78
Hertford SG13 54 DT08
Teddington TW11 199 CG93
Tilbury RM18 193 GF81
Woking GU22 249 BB120
⊖ Fairfield 220 CL96
Fairfield App, Wrays. TW19 194 AX86
Fairfield Av, NW4 141 CV58
Datchet SL3 174 AW80
Edgware HA8 118 CP51
Horley RH6 290 DG149
Ruislip HA4 137 BQ59
Staines-upon-Thames TW18 195 BF91
Twickenham TW2 198 CB88
Upminster RM14 150 FQ62
Fairfield Av, Watford WD19 116 BW48
Fairfield Cl, N12 120 DC49
Datchet SL3 174 AX80
Dorking RH4
off Fairfield Dr 269 CH134
Enfield EN3
off Scotland Grn Rd N 105 DY42
Ewell KT19 238 CS106
Guildford GU2 264 AU133
Hatfield AL10 67 CW15
Hornchurch RM12 149 FG60
Mitcham CR4 202 DE94
Northwood HA6
off Thirlmere Gdns 115 BP50
Radlett WD7 99 CE37
Sidcup DA15 207 ET86
Fairfield Cotts, Lthd. KT23 268 CB125
Fairfield Ct, NW10 161 CU67
Northwood HA6
off Windsor Cl 115 BU54
Fairfield Cres, Edg. HA8 118 CP51
Fairfield Dr, SW18 202 DB85
Broxbourne EN10 71 DZ24
Dorking RH4 269 CH134
Harrow HA2 138 CC55
Perivale UB6 159 CJ67
Fairfield E, Kings.T. KT1 220 CL96
Fairfield Gdns, N8 143 DL57
Fairfield Gro, SE7 186 EK78
★ Fairfield Halls, Croy. CR0 224 DR104
Sch Fair Fld Jun Sch, Rad.
WD7 off Watford Rd 99 CE36
Fairfield La, Farn.Royal SL2 153 AP68
Fairfield N, Kings.T. KT1 220 CL96
Fairfield Pk, Cob. KT11 236 BX114
Fairfield Path, Croy. CR0 224 DR104
Fairfield Pathway,
Horn. RM12 170 FJ66
Fairfield Pl, Kings.T. KT1 220 CL97
Fairfield Ri, Guil. GU2 264 AT133
Fairfield Rd, E3 12 A10
E17 123 DY54
N8 143 DL57
N18 122 DU49
W7 179 CG76
Beckenham BR3 225 EA96
Bexleyheath DA7 188 EZ82
Brentwood CM14 130 FW48
Bromley BR1 206 EG94
Burnham SL1 152 AJ69
Croydon CR0 224 DS104
Epping CM16 92 EV29
Hoddesdon EN11 71 EA15
Ilford IG1 167 EP65
Kingston upon Thames KT1 220 CL96
Leatherhead KT22 253 CH121
Petts Wood BR5 227 ER100
Southall UB1 158 BZ72
Uxbridge UB8 156 BK65
West Drayton UB7 156 BL74
Woodford Green IG8 124 EG51
Wraysbury TW19 194 AX86
Fairfields, Cher. KT16 216 BG102
Gravesend DA12 213 GL92
Fairfields Cl, NW9 140 CQ57
Fairfields Cres, NW9 140 CQ56
Fairfield S, Kings.T. KT1 220 CL97
Sch Fairfields Prim Sch, Chsht
EN7 off Rosedale Way 88 DU27
Fairfield Sq, Grav. DA11 213 GG86
Fairfields Rd, Houns. TW3 178 CC83
Fairfield St, SW18 202 DB85
● Fairfield Trade Pk, Kings.T.
KT1 220 CM97
Fairfield Wk, Chsht EN8 89 DY28
Leatherhead KT22
off Fairfield Rd 253 CH121
Fairfield Way, Barn. EN5 102 DA43
Coulsdon CR5 241 DK114
Epsom KT19 238 CS106
Fairfield W, Kings.T. KT1 220 CL96
Fairfolds, Wat. WD25 98 BY36
Fairfoot Rd, E3 22 A5
Fairford Av, Bexh. DA7 189 FD81
Croydon CR0 225 DX99
Fairford Cl, Croy. CR0 225 DY99
Reigate RH2 272 DC132
Romford RM3 128 FP51
West Byfleet KT14 233 BF114
Fairford Ct, Sutt. SM2
off Grange Rd 240 DB108
Fairford Gdns, Wor.Pk. KT4 221 CT104
Fairford Ho, SE11 30 F9
Fairford Way, Rom. RM3 128 FP51
Fairgreen, Barn. EN4 102 DF41
Fair Grn, Saw. CM21
off The Square 58 EY05
Fairgreen E, Barn. EN4 102 DF41
Fairgreen Par, Mitch. CR4
off London Rd 222 DF97
Fairgreen Rd, Th.Hth. CR7 223 DP99
Fairham Av, S.Ock. RM15 171 FU73
Fairhaven, Egh. TW20 195 AZ92
Fairhaven Av, Croy. CR0 225 DX100
Fairhaven Cres, Wat. WD19 115 BU48
Fairhaven Rd, Red. RH1 272 DG130
Fairhazel Gdns, NW6 5 M5
Fairhill, Hem.H. HP3 62 BM24
Fairholme, Felt. TW14 197 BR87
Fairholme Av, Rom. RM2 149 FG57
Fairholme Cl, N3 141 CY56
Fairholme Cres, Ashtd. KT21 253 CJ117
Hayes UB4 157 BT70
Fairholme Gdns, N3 141 CY55
Upminster RM14 151 FT59
Sch Fairholme Prim Sch, Felt.
TW14 off Peacock Av 197 BR88
Fairholme Rd, W14 38 F1
Ashford TW15 196 BL92
Croydon CR0 223 DN101
Harrow HA1 139 CF57
Ilford IG1 147 EM59
Sutton SM1 239 CZ107
Fairholt Cl, N16 144 DS60
Fairholt Rd, N16 144 DR60
Fairholt St, SW7 28 D6
Fairkytes Av, Horn. RM11 150 FK60
Fairland Rd, E15 13 L5
Fairlands Av, Buck.H. IG9 124 EG47
Sutton SM1 222 DA103
Thornton Heath CR7 223 DM98

Fairlands Ct, SE9
off North Pk 207 EN86
Fair La, Chipstead CR5 272 DC125
Fairlawn, SE7 186 EJ79
Bookham KT23 252 BZ124
Weybridge KT13 235 BS106
Fairlawn Av, N2 142 DE56
W4 180 CQ77
Bexleyheath DA7 188 EX82
Fairlawn Cl, N14 103 DJ44
Claygate KT10 237 CF107
Feltham TW13 198 BZ91
Kingston upon Thames KT2 200 CQ93
Fairlawn Ct, SE7
off Fairlawn 186 EJ80
Fairlawn Dr, Red. RH1 288 DE136
Woodford Green IG8 124 EG52
● Fairlawn Enterprise Pk, Salf. RH1 288 DG143
Fairlawnes, Wall. SM6
off Maldon Rd 241 DH106
Fairlawn Gdns, Sthl. UB1 158 BZ73
Fairlawn Gro, W4 180 CQ77
Banstead SM7 240 DD113
Fairlawn Pk, SE26 205 DY92
Windsor SL4 173 AL84
Woking GU21 232 AY114
Sch Fairlawn Prim Sch, SE23
off Honor Oak Rd 204 DW87
Fairlawn Rd, SW19 201 CZ94
Banstead SM7 240 DD110
Carshalton SM5 240 DC111
Fairlawns, Brwd. CM14 130 FU48
Horley RH6 291 DH149
Pinner HA5 116 BW54
Sunbury-on-Thames TW16 217 BU97
Twickenham TW1 199 CJ86
Watford WD17 97 BT38
Woodham KT15 233 BF111
Fairlawns Cl, Horn. RM11 150 FM59
Staines-upon-Thames TW18 196 BH93
Fairlead Ho, E14
off Cassilis Rd 34 B6
Fairlea Pl, W5 159 CK70
Fair Leas, Chesh. HP5 76 AN29
Fairley Way, Chsht EN7 88 DV28
Fairlie Ct, E3
off Stroudley Wk 22 C2
Fairlie Gdns, SE23 204 DW87
Fairlie Rd, Slou. SL1 153 AN72
Fairlight Av, E4 123 ED47
NW10 160 CS68
Windsor SL4 173 AR82
Woodford Green IG8 124 EG51
Fairlight Cl, E4 123 ED47
Worcester Park KT4 239 CW105
Fairlight Dr, Uxb. UB8 156 BK65
Fairlight Rd, SW17 202 DD91
⊖ Fairlop 125 ER53
Fairlop Cl, Horn. RM12 169 FH65
Fairlop Gdns, Ilf. IG6 125 EQ52
Sch Fairlop Prim Sch, Ilf. IG6
off Colvin Gdns 125 EQ53
Fairlop Rd, E11 145 ED59
Ilford IG6 125 EQ54
Fairmark Dr, Uxb. UB10 156 BN65
Fairmead, Brom. BR1 227 EM98
Surbiton KT5 220 CP102
Woking GU21 248 AW118
Fairmead Cl, Brom. BR1 227 EM98
Hounslow TW5 178 BX80
New Malden KT3 220 CR97
Fairmead Cres, Edg. HA8 118 CQ48
Fairmead Gdns, Ilf. IG4 146 EL57
Fairmead Ho, E9
off Kingsmead Way 11 M1
Fairmead Rd, N19 143 DK62
Croydon CR0 223 DM102
Loughton IG10 106 EH42
Fairmeads, Cob. KT11 236 BZ113
Loughton IG10 107 EP40
Fairmeadside, Loug. IG10 106 EJ43
FAIRMILE, Cob. KT11 236 BZ112
Fairmile Av, SW16 203 DK92
Cobham KT11 236 BY114
Fairmile Ct, Cob. KT11 236 BY112
Fairmile Ho, Tedd. TW11
off Twickenham Rd 199 CG91
Fairmile La, Cob. KT11 236 BX112
Fairmile Pk Copse, Cob. KT11 236 BZ112
Fairmile Pk Rd, Cob. KT11 236 BZ113
Fairmont Av, E14 34 G2
Fairmont Cl, Belv. DA17 188 EZ78
Fairmount Rd, SW2 203 DM86
Fairoak Cl, Ken. CR8 257 DP115
Oxshott KT22 237 CD112
Petts Wood BR5 227 EP101
Fairoak Dr, SE9 207 ER85
Fairoak Gdns, Rom. RM1 127 FE54
Fairoak Gro, Enf. EN3 105 DX37
Fair Oak La, Chess. KT9 237 CF111
Oxshott KT22 237 CF111
Fair Oak Pl, Ilf. IG6 125 EQ54
Fairseat Cl, Bushey Hth WD23 117 CE47
Fairs Rd, Lthd. KT22 253 CG119
Fairstead Wk, N1 9 J8
Fairstone Ct, Horl. RH6
off Tanyard Way 291 DH147
Fair St, SE1 31 P4
Hounslow TW3 off High St 178 CC83
Fairthorn Rd, SE7 35 P10
Fairtrough Rd, Orp. BR6 246 EV112
Fairview, Epsom KT17 239 CW111
Erith DA8 off Guild Rd 189 FF80
Potters Bar EN6
off Hawkshead Rd 86 DB29
Ruislip HA4
off The Fairway 138 BW63
Fairview Av, Hutt. CM13 131 GE45
Rainham RM13 170 FK68
Wembley HA0 159 CK65
Woking GU22 248 AY118
● Fairview Business Cen, Hayes UB3 off Clayton Rd 177 BT75
Fairview Cl, E17 123 DY53
Chigwell IG7 125 ES49
Woking GU22
off Fairview Av 249 AZ118
Fairview Ct, NW4 119 CX54
Ashford TW15 196 BN92
Fairview Cres, Har. HA2 138 CA60
Fairview Dr, Chig. IG7 125 ES49
Orpington BR6 245 ER105
Shepperton TW17 216 BM99
Watford WD17 97 BS36
Fairview Gdns, Wdf.Grn. IG8 124 EH53
● Fairview Ind Est, Amer. HP6 94 AT38
Oxted RH8 276 EG133
● Fairview Ind Pk, Rain. RM13 169 FD71
Fairview Pl, SW2 203 DM87
Fairview Rd, N15 144 DT57
SW16 223 DM95
Chigwell IG7 125 ES49
Enfield EN2 103 DN39
Epsom KT17 239 CT111
Istead Rise DA13 212 GD94
Slough SL2 153 AM70
Sutton SM1 240 DD106
Taplow SL6 152 AG72
Fairview Way, Edg. HA8 118 CN49
Fairwater Av, Well. DA16 188 EU84
Fairwater Dr, New Haw KT15 234 BK109
Fairway, SW20 221 CW97
Bexleyheath DA6 208 EY85
Carshalton SM5 240 DC111
Chertsey KT16 216 BH102
Guildford GU1 265 BD133
Hemel Hempstead HP3 62 BM24
Petts Wood BR5 227 ER99
Sawbridgeworth CM21 58 EY05
Virginia Water GU25 214 AV100
Ware SG12 54 DW07
Woodford Green IG8 124 EJ50
Fairway, The, N13 122 DQ48
N14 103 DH44
NW7 118 CR48
W3 160 CS72
Abbots Langley WD5 81 BR32
Bromley BR1 227 EM99
Burnham SL1 152 AJ68
Flackwell Heath HP10 132 AC56
Gravesend DA11 213 GG89
Harlow CM18 73 ET17
Leatherhead KT22 253 CG118
New Barnet EN5 102 DB44
New Malden KT3 220 CR95
Northolt UB5 158 CC65
Northwood HA6 115 BS49
Ruislip HA4 138 BX62
Upminster RM14 150 FQ59
Uxbridge UB10 156 BM68
Wembley HA0 139 CH62
West Molesey KT8 218 CB97
Weybridge KT13 234 BN111
Fairway Av, NW9 140 CP55
Borehamwood WD6 100 CP40
West Drayton UB7 156 BJ74
Fairway Cl, NW11 142 DC59
Croydon CR0 225 DY99
Epsom KT19 238 CQ105
Hounslow TW4 198 BW85
Park Street AL2 82 CC27
West Drayton UB7
off Fairway Av 156 BK74
Woking GU22 248 AU119
Fairway Ct, NW7 118 CR48
Hemel Hempstead HP3
off Fairway 62 BM24
Fairway Dr, SE28 168 EX72
Dartford DA2 210 FP87
Greenford UB6 158 CB66
Fairway Gdns, Beck. BR3 225 ED100
Ilford IG1 147 EQ64
Sch Fairway Prim Sch, The, NW7 off The Fairway 118 CR47
Fairways, Ashf. TW15 197 BP93
Cheshunt EN8 89 DX26
Kenley CR8 258 DQ117
Stanmore HA7 118 CL54
Teddington TW11 199 CK94
Waltham Abbey EN9 90 EE34
Fairways, The, Red. RH1 288 DD137
● Fairways Business Pk, E10 off Lammas Rd 145 DY61
Fairweather Cl, N15 144 DS56
Fairweather Rd, N16 144 DU58
Fairwell La, W.Hors. KT24 267 BP128
Fairwyn Rd, SE26 205 DY91
Faithfield, Bushey WD23
off Aldenham Rd 98 BY44
Faithorn Cl, Chesh. HP5 76 AN30
Fakenham Cl, NW7 119 CU52
Northolt UB5
off Goodwood Dr 158 CA65
Fakruddin St, E1 20 D5
Falaise, Egh. TW20 194 AY92
Falcon Av, Brom. BR1 226 EL98
Grays RM17 192 GB79
Falconberg Ct, W1 17 P8
Falconberg Ms, W1 17 N8
Sch Falconbrook Prim Sch, SW11 40 B10
● Falcon Business Cen, Mitch. CR4 222 DF99
Romford RM3 128 FL52
Falcon Cl, W4
off Sutton La S 180 CQ79
Dartford DA1 210 FM85
Hatfield AL10 67 CU20
Northwood HA6 115 BS52
Sawbridgeworth CM21 58 EW06
Waltham Abbey EN9
off Kestrel Rd 90 EG34
Falcon Ct, EC4 18 E9
SE21 off Elmworth Gro 204 DR89
Woking GU21 233 BC113
Falcon Cres, Enf. EN3 105 DX43
Falcon Dr, Stanw. TW19 196 BK86
Falconer Ct, N17
off Compton Cres 122 DQ52
Falconer Rd, Bushey WD23 98 BZ44
Ilford IG6 126 EV50
Sch Falconer Sch, Bushey WD23 off Falconer Rd 98 BZ43
Falconers Pk, Saw. CM21 58 EX06
Falconer Wk, N7
off Newington Barrow Way 143 DM61
● Falcon Est, Felt. TW14 197 BV85
Falcon Gro, SW11 40 C10
Falcon Ho, W13 159 CF70
Falconhurst, Oxshott KT22 253 CD115
Falcon La, SW11 182 DE83
Falcon Ms, Grav. DA11 212 GE88
● Falcon Pk Ind Est, NW10 140 CS64
Falcon Ridge, Berk. HP4 60 AW20
Falcon Rd, SW11 40 C9
Enfield EN3 105 DX43
Guildford GU1 280 AX135
Hampton TW12 198 BZ94
Falcons Cl, Bigg.H. TN16 260 EK117
Falcons Cft, Woob.Moor HP10 132 AE55
Sch Falcons Sch for Boys, The, W4 off Burnaby Gdns 180 CQ79
Sch Falcons Sch for Girls, The, W5 off Gunnersbury Av 160 CM74
Falcon St, E13 23 N4
Falcon Ter, SW11 182 DE83
Falcon Way, E11 146 EG56
E14 34 D8
NW9 118 CS54
Feltham TW14 197 BV85
Harrow HA3 140 CL57
Hornchurch RM12 169 FG66
Sunbury-on-Thames TW16 217 BS96
Watford WD25 82 BY34
Welwyn Garden City AL7 51 CY07
Falcon Wf, SW11 40 A9
FALCONWOOD, Well. DA16 187 ER83
⇌ Falconwood 187 EQ84
Jct Falconwood, SE9 187 EQ84
Falconwood, Bushey WD23 98 BZ44
East Horsley KT24 251 BT124
Egham TW20 194 AY92
Falcon Wd, Lthd. KT22 253 CF120
Falconwood Av, Well. DA16 187 ER82
Falconwood Par, Well. DA16 187 ES84
Falconwood Rd, Croy. CR0 243 EA108
Falcourt Cl, Sutt. SM1 240 DB106
Falkirk Cl, Horn. RM11 150 FN60
Falkirk Gdns, Wat. WD19 116 BX50
Falkirk Ho, W9 15 M2
Falkirk St, N1 19 P1
Falkland Av, N3 120 DA52
N11 120 DG49
Falkland Gdns, Dor. RH4
off Harrow Rd W 285 CG137
Falkland Gro, Dor. RH4 285 CG137
Falkland Ho, SE6
off Bromley Rd 205 EC91
Falkland Pk Av, SE25 224 DS97
Falkland Pl, NW5 7 L2
Falkland Rd, N8 143 DN56
NW5 7 L2
Barnet EN5 101 CY40
Dorking RH4 285 CG137
Sch Falkner Ho Sch, SW7 27 P9
Fallaize Av, Ilf. IG1
off Riverdene Rd 147 EP63
Falling La, West Dr. UB7 156 BL73
Falloden Way, NW11 142 DA56
Fallow Cl, Chig. IG7 125 ET50
Fallow Ct, SE16 44 D1
Fallow Ct Av, N12 120 DC52
Fallowfield, N4
off Six Acres Est 143 DM61
Bean DA2 211 FV90
Stanmore HA7 117 CG48
Welwyn Garden City AL7 51 CZ06
Fallowfield Cl, Hare. UB9 114 BJ53
Fallowfield Ct, Stan. HA7 117 CG48
Fallow Flds, Loug. IG10 124 EJ45
Fallowfields Dr, N12 120 DE51
Fallowfield Wk, Hem.H. HP1
off Tollpit End 62 BG17
Fallowfield Way, Horl. RH6 291 DH147
Fallow Ri, Hert. SG13 54 DS09
Fallows Cl, N2 120 DC54
Fallsbrook Rd, SW16 203 DJ94
Falman Cl, N9 122 DU46
Falmer Rd, E17 145 EB55
N15 144 DQ57
Enfield EN1 104 DS42
Falmouth Av, E4 123 ED50
Falmouth Cl, N22 121 DM52
SE12 206 EF85
Falmouth Ct, St.Alb. AL3 65 CD18
Falmouth Gdns, Ilf. IG4 146 EL57
Falmouth Ho, SE11
off Seaton Cl 30 F10
Kingston upon Thames KT2
off Kingsgate Rd 219 CK95
Falmouth Rd, SE1 31 K6
Hersham KT12 236 BW105
Slough SL1 153 AN72
Falmouth St, E15 13 H3
Falmouth Way, E17
off Gosport Rd 145 DZ57
Falstaff Cl, Cray. DA1 209 FE87
Falstaff Gdns, St.Alb. AL1 64 CB23
Falstaff Ms, Hmptn H. TW12
off Hampton Rd 199 CD92
Falstone, Wok. GU21 248 AV118
Fambridge Cl, SE26 205 DZ91
Fambridge Ct, Rom. RM7 149 FD57
Fambridge Rd, Dag. RM8 148 FA60
Famet Av, Pur. CR8 242 DQ113
Famet Cl, Pur. CR8 242 DQ113
Famet Gdns, Ken. CR8
off Godstone Rd 242 DQ113
Famet Wk, Pur. CR8 242 DQ113
Fancourt Ms, Brom. BR1 227 EN97
Fane St, W14 39 H2
Fangrove Pk, Lyne KT16 215 BB102
Fanhams Rd, Ware SG12 55 DY05
★ Fan Mus, SE10 46 F4
Fanns Ri, Purf. RM19 190 FN77
Fann St, EC1 19 J5
EC2 19 J5
Fanshawe, The, Dag. RM9
off Gale St 168 EX66
Fanshawe Av, Bark. IG11 167 EQ65
Fanshawe Ct, Hert. SG14
off Byde St 54 DQ08
Fanshawe Cres, Dag. RM9 148 EY64
Hornchurch RM11 150 FK58
Ware SG12 54 DW05
Fanshawe Rd, Grays RM16 193 GG76
Richmond TW10 199 CJ91
Fanshawe St, Hert. SG14 53 DP08
Fanshaws La, Brickendon SG13 70 DQ18
Fanshaw St, N1 19 N2
Jct Fantail, The, Orp. BR6 245 EM105
Fantail Cl, SE28
off Greenhaven Dr 168 EW72
Fantasia Ct, Warley CM14 130 FV50
Fanthorpe St, SW15 38 B10
Faraday Av, Sid. DA14 208 EU89
Faraday Cl, N7 8 D5
Slough SL2 153 AP71
Watford WD18 97 BR44
Faraday Ct, Wat. WD18 97 BU44
Faraday Ho, Enf. EN3
off Innova Science Pk 105 DZ37
Faraday Lo, SE10
off Renaissance Wk 35 M6
★ Faraday Mus, W1 29 L1
Faraday Pl, W.Mol. KT8 218 CA98
Faraday Rd, E15 13 L5
Faraday Rd, SW19 202 DA93
W3 160 CQ73
W10 14 E6
Guildford GU1 264 AW133
Slough SL2 153 AP71
Southall UB1 158 CB73
Welling DA16 188 EU83
West Molesey KT8 218 CA98
Faraday Way, SE18 36 E7
Croydon CR0
off Ampere Way 223 DM102
Orpington BR5 228 EV98
Fareham Rd, Felt. TW14 198 BW87
Fareham St, W1 17 N8
Far End, Hat. AL10 67 CV21
Farewell Pl, Mitch. CR4 222 DE95
Faringdon Av, Brom. BR2 227 EP100
Romford RM3 128 FJ53
Faringford Cl, Pot.B. EN6 86 DD31
Faringford Rd, E15 13 J7
Farington Acres, Wey. KT13 217 BR104
Faris Barn Dr, Wdhm KT15 233 BF112
Faris La, Wdhm KT15 233 BF111
Farjeon Rd, SE3 186 EK81
Farland Rd, Hem.H. HP2 62 BN21
FARLEIGH, Warl. CR6 243 DZ114
Farleigh Av, Brom. BR2 226 EF100
Farleigh Border, Croy. CR0 243 DY112
Farleigh Ct, Guil. GU2
off Chapelhouse Cl 264 AS134
Farleigh Ct Rd, Warl. CR6 243 DZ114
Farleigh Dean Cres, Croy. CR0 243 EB111
Farleigh Pl, N16 144 DT63
Sch Farleigh Prim Sch, Warl. CR6 off Farleigh Rd 259 DY117
Farleigh Rd, N16 144 DT63
New Haw KT15 234 BG111
Warlingham CR6 259 DX118
Farleton Cl, Wey. KT13 235 BR107
Farley Common, West. TN16 277 EP126
Farleycroft, West. TN16 277 EQ126
Farley Dr, Ilf. IG3 147 ES60
FARLEY GREEN, Guil. GU5 282 BK144
Farley Heath, Albury GU5 282 BJ144
Farley La, West. TN16 277 EP127
Farley Ms, SE6 205 EC87
Farley Nurs, West. TN16 277 EQ127
Farley Pk, Oxt. RH8 275 ED130
Farley Pl, SE25 224 DU98
Farley Rd, SE6 205 EB87
Gravesend DA12 213 GM88
South Croydon CR2 242 DV108
Farleys Cl, W.Hors. KT24 267 BQ126
Farlington Pl, SW15
off Roehampton La 201 CV87
Farlow Cl, Nthflt DA11 213 GF90
Farlow Rd, SW15 181 CX83
Farlton Rd, SW18 202 DB87
Farman Gro, Nthlt. UB5
off Wayfarer Rd 158 BX69
Farm Av, NW2 141 CY62
SW16 203 DL91
Harrow HA2 138 BZ59
Swanley BR8 229 FC97
Wembley HA0 159 CJ65
Farmborough Cl, Har. HA1 139 CD59
Farm Cl, SW6 39 K4
Amersham HP6 94 AX39
Barnet EN5 101 CW43
Borehamwood WD6 99 CK38
Buckhurst Hill IG9 124 EJ48
Byfleet KT14 234 BM112
Cheshunt EN8 88 DW30
Chipstead CR5 256 DF120
Cuffley EN6 87 DK27
Dagenham RM10 169 FC66
East Horsley KT24 267 BT128
Fetcham KT22 253 CD124
Guildford GU1 264 AX131
Hertford SG14 53 DN09
Holyport SL6 172 AC78
Hutton CM13 131 GC45
Lyne KT16 215 BA100
Roydon CM19 56 EH14
Shenley WD7 84 CL30
Shepperton TW17 216 BN101
Southall UB1 158 CB73
Staines-upon-Thames TW18 195 BE92
Sutton SM2 240 DD108
Uxbridge UB10 137 BP61
Wallington SM6 241 DJ110
Welwyn Garden City AL8 51 CW09
West Wickham BR4 226 EE104
Farmcote Rd, SE12 206 EG88
Farm Ct, NW4 141 CU55
Farm Cres, Lon.Col. AL2 83 CG26
Slough SL2 154 AV71
Farmcroft, Grav. DA11 213 GG89
Farmdale Rd, SE10 35 P10
Carshalton SM5 240 DE108
Farm Dr, Croy. CR0 225 DZ103
Purley CR8 241 DK112
Farm End, E4 106 EE43
Northwood HA6
off Drakes Dr 115 BP53
Farmer Rd, E10 145 EB60
Farmers Cl, Wat. WD25 81 BV33
Farmers Ct, Wal.Abb. EN9
off Winters Way 90 EG33
Farmers Pl, Chal.St.P. SL9 112 AW54
Farmers Rd, SE5 43 H4
Staines-upon-Thames TW18 195 BE92
Farmer St, W8 27 J2
Farmers Way, Seer Grn HP9 111 AQ51
Farmery Ct, Berk. HP4 60 AY17
Farm Fld, Wat. WD17 97 BS38
Farmfield Dr, Charl. RH6 290 DB150
H Farmfield Hosp, Horl. RH6 290 DB150
Farmfield Rd, Brom. BR1 206 EE92
Farm Flds, S.Croy. CR2 242 DS111
Farm Gro, Knot.Grn HP9 110 AJ50
Farm Hill Rd, Wal.Abb. EN9 89 ED33
Farm Ho Cl, Brox. EN10 89 DZ25
Farmhouse Cl, Wok. GU22 249 BD115
Farmhouse La, Hem.H. HP2 62 BN18
Farmhouse Rd, SW16 203 DJ94
Farmilo Rd, E17 145 DZ59
Farmington Av, Sutt. SM1 222 DD104
Farmlands, Enf. EN2 103 DN39
Pinner HA5 137 BU56
Farmlands, The, Nthlt. UB5 158 BZ65
Farmland Wk, Chis. BR7 207 EP92
Farm La, N14 102 DG44
SW6 39 K3
Addlestone KT15 234 BG107
Ashtead KT21 254 CN116
Carshalton SM5 240 DF110
Croydon CR0 225 DZ103
East Horsley KT24 267 BT128
Farm La, Epsom KT18 254 CP119
Hoddesdon EN11 71 EC15
Jordans HP9 111 AR52
Loudwater WD3 96 BH41
Purley CR8 241 DJ110
Send GU23 249 BC123
Slough SL1 153 AR73
● Farm La Trd Cen, SW6 39 J3
Farm Lea, Woob.Grn HP10 132 AF56
Farmleigh, N14 121 DJ45
Farmleigh Gro, Hersham KT12 235 BT106
Farm Pl, W8 27 J2
Berkhamsted HP4 60 AT18
Dartford DA1 189 FG84
Farm Rd, N21 121 DP46
NW10 160 CR67
Chorleywood WD3 95 BA42
Edgware HA8 118 CP51
Esher KT10 218 CB102
Hoddesdon EN11 71 EC16
Hounslow TW4 198 BY88
Morden SM4 222 DB99
Northwood HA6 115 BQ50
Orsett RM16 193 GF75
Rainham RM13 170 FJ69
St. Albans AL1 65 CH19
Sevenoaks TN14 279 FJ121
Staines-upon-Thames TW18 196 BH93
Sutton SM2 240 DD108
Taplow SL6 152 AF56
Warlingham CR6 259 DY119
Woking GU22 249 BB120
Farmstead Rd, SE6 205 EB91
Harrow HA3 117 CD53
Farm St, W1 29 J1
Farm Vale, Bex. DA5 209 FB86
Farm Vw, Cob. KT11 252 BX116
Lower Kingswood KT20 271 CZ127
Farm Wk, NW11 141 CZ57
Guildford GU2
off Wilderness Rd 280 AT136
Horley RH6
off Court Lo Rd 290 DF148
Farm Way, Buck.H. IG9 124 EJ49
Bushey WD23 98 CB42
Farmway, Dag. RM8 148 EW63
Farm Way, Hat. AL10 67 CV15
Hornchurch RM12 149 FH63
Northwood HA6 115 BS49
Staines-upon-Thames TW19 195 BF86
Worcester Park KT4 221 CW104
Farm Yd, Wind. SL4 173 AR80
Farnaby Dr, Sev. TN13 278 FF126
Farnaby Rd, SE9 186 EJ84
Bromley BR1, BR2 205 ED94
Farnan Av, E17 123 EA54
Farnan Rd, SW16 203 DL92
FARNBOROUGH, Orp. BR6 245 EP106
Farnborough Av, E17 145 DY55
South Croydon CR2 243 DX108
Farnborough Cl, Wem. HA9 140 CP61
Farnborough Common, Orp. BR6 227 EM104
Farnborough Cres, Brom. BR2 off Saville Row 226 EF102
South Croydon CR2 243 DY109
Farnborough Hill, Orp. BR6 245 ER106
Farnborough Ho, SW15
off Fontley Way 201 CU88
Sch Farnborough Prim Sch, Farnboro. BR6
off Farnborough Hill 245 EQ106
Farnborough Way, Orp. BR6 245 EQ105
Farnburn Av, Slou. SL1 153 AP71
⇌ Farncombe 280 AT144
Sch Farncombe C of E Inf Sch, Farnc. GU7 off Grays Rd 280 AS144
Farncombe St, SE16 32 D5
Godalming GU7 280 AS144
Farndale Av, N13 121 DP48
Farndale Ct, SE18 186 EL80
Farndale Cres, Grnf. UB6 158 CC69
Farnell Ms, SW5 27 L10
Weybridge KT13
off Thames St 217 BP104
Farnell Pl, W3 160 CP73
Farnell Rd, Islw. TW7 179 CD83
Staines-upon-Thames TW18 196 BG90
Farnes Dr, Rom. RM2 128 FJ54
Farney Fld, Peasl. GU5 283 BR142
Farnham Cl, N20 120 DC45
Bovingdon HP3 79 BA28
Sawbridgeworth CM21 58 EW06
FARNHAM COMMON, Slou. SL2 153 AQ65
Sch Farnham Common Inf Sch, Farn.Com. SL2
off Beaconsfield Rd 133 AQ63
Sch Farnham Common Jun Sch, Farn.Com. SL2
off Sherbourne Wk 133 AQ63
Farnham Gdns, SW20 221 CV96
Sch Farnham Grn Prim Sch, Seven Kings IG3
off Royal Cl 148 EU58
Farnham La, Slou. SL2 153 AN68
Farnham Pk La, Farn.Royal SL2 153 AQ66
Farnham Pl, SE1 31 H3
Farnham Rd, Guil. GU1, GU2 280 AT137
Ilford IG3 147 ET59
Romford RM3 128 FK50
Slough SL1, SL2 153 AQ71
Welling DA16 188 EW82
H Farnham Rd Hosp, Guil. GU2 280 AV136
FARNHAM ROYAL, Slou. SL2 153 AQ68
Farnham Royal, SE11 42 D1
FARNINGHAM, Dart. DA4 230 FN100
Farningham Cres, Cat. CR3
off Commonwealth Rd 258 DU123
Farningham Hill Rd, Fnghm DA4 230 FJ99
⇌ Farningham Road 230 FP96
Farningham Rd, N17 122 DU52
Caterham CR3 258 DU123
Farnley, Wok. GU21 248 AT117
Farnley Rd, E4 124 EE45
SE25 224 DR98
Farnol Rd, Dart. DA1 190 FN84
Farnsworth Ct, SE10
off West Parkside 35 M7
Farnworth Ho, E14
off Manchester Rd 34 F8
Faro Cl, Brom. BR1 227 EN96
Faroe Rd, W14 26 D7
Farorna Wk, Enf. EN2 103 DN39
Farquhar Rd, SE19 204 DT92
SW19 202 DA90

Farquharson Rd, Croy. CR0 224 DQ102
Farquhar St, Hert. SG14 54 DQ08
Farraline Rd, Wat. WD18 97 BV42
Farrance Rd, Rom. RM6 148 EY58
Farrance St, E14 21 P9
Farrans Ct, Har. HA3 139 CH59
Farrant Av, N22 121 DN54
Farrant Cl, Orp. BR6 246 EU108
Farrant Way, Borwd. WD6 100 CL39
Farr Av, Bark. IG11 168 EU68
Farrell Ho, E1 21 H9
Farren Rd, SE23 205 DY89
Farrer Ms, N8 *off Farrer Rd* 143 DJ56
Farrer Rd, N8 143 DJ56
Harrow HA3 140 CL57
Farrer's Pl, Croy. CR0 243 DX105
Farriday Cl, St.Alb. AL3 65 CE16
Farrier Cl, Brom. BR1 226 EK97
Sunbury-on-Thames TW16 217 BU98
Uxbridge UB10 156 BN72
Farrier Pl, Sutt. SM1 222 DA104
Farrier Rd, Nthlt. UB5 158 CA68
Farriers, Gt Amwell SG12 55 EA09
Farriers Cl, Bov. HP3 79 BB28
Epsom KT17 238 CS111
Gravesend DA12 213 GM88
Farriers Ct, Sutt. SM3
off Forge La 239 CY108
Watford WD25 81 BV32
Farriers End, Brox. EN10 89 DZ26
Farriers Ms, SE15 44 G10
Farriers Rd, Epsom KT17 238 CS112
Farrier St, NW1 7 K6
Farriers Way, Borwd. WD6 100 CQ44
Chesham HP5 76 AN28
Farrier Wk, SW10 39 N2
⇌ Farringdon 18 F6
⊖ Farringdon 18 F6
Farringdon Ho, Rich. TW9 180 CP80
Farringdon La, EC1 18 F5
Farringdon Rd, EC1 18 E4
Farringdon St, EC4 18 G8
Farringford Cl, St.Alb. AL2 82 CA26
Farrington Ave, Bushey WD23 98 CB43
Orpington BR5 228 EV97
Farrington Pl, Chis. BR7 207 ER94
Northwood HA6 115 BT49
Sch Farringtons Sch, Chis.
BR7 *off Perry St* 207 ER94
Farrins Rents, SE16 33 L3
Farrow La, SE14 45 H4
Farrow Pl, SE16 33 L6
Farr Rd, Enf. EN2 104 DR39
Farrs All, Rick. WD3
off High St 114 BK46
Farthingale Ct, Wal.Abb. EN9 90 EG34
Farthingale La, Wal.Abb. EN9 90 EG34
Farthingale Wk, E15 12 G7
Farthing All, SE1 32 C5
Farthing Cl, Dart. DA1 190 FM84
Watford WD18 98 BW43
Farthing Ct, NW7 119 CY52
Farthing Flds, E1 32 F2
Farthing Grn La, Stoke P. SL2 154 AU68
Farthings, Knap. GU21 248 AS116
Farthings, The, Amer. HP6
off Milton Lawns 77 AR36
Hemel Hempstead HP1 62 BH20
Kingston upon Thames KT2 220 CN95
Farthings Cl, E4 124 EE48
Pinner HA5 137 BV58
Farthing St, Downe BR6 245 EM108
Farthing Way, Couls. CR5 257 DK117
Farwell Rd, Sid. DA14 208 EV90
Farwig La, Brom. BR1 226 EF95
Fashion St, E1 20 A7
Fashoda Rd, Brom. BR2 226 EK98
Fassett Rd, E8 10 D4
Kingston upon Thames KT1 220 CL98
Fassett Sq, E8 10 C4
Fassnidge Way, Uxb. UB8
off Oxford Rd 156 BJ66
Fauconberg Rd, W4 180 CQ79
Faulkner Cl, Dag. RM8 148 EX59
Faulkner Ms, E17 123 DY53
Faulkner's All, EC1 18 G6
Faulkners Rd, Hersham KT12 236 BW106
Faulkner St, SE14 45 H6
Fauna Cl, Rom. RM6 148 EW59
Stanmore HA7 117 CK49
Faunce St, SE17 42 G2
Favart Rd, SW6 39 K6
Faverolle Grn, Chsht EN8 89 DX28
Faversham Av, E4 124 EE46
Enfield EN1 104 DR44
Faversham Cl, Chig. IG7 126 EV47
Faversham Rd, SE6 205 DZ87
Beckenham BR3 225 DZ96
Morden SM4 222 DB100
Sch Fawbert & Barnard Infants' Sch,
Saw. CM21 *off Knight St* 58 EY05
Sch Fawbert & Barnard's
Prim Sch, Harl. CM17
off London Rd 58 EW12
Fawcett Cl, SW11 40 B9
SW16 203 DN91
Fawcett Est, E5 144 DU60
Fawcett Rd, NW10 161 CT67
Croydon CR0 224 DQ104
Windsor SL4 173 AP81
Fawcett St, SW10 39 N2
Fawcus Cl, Clay. KT10 237 CE107
Fawe Pk Rd, SW15 181 CZ84
Fawe St, E14 22 D7
Fawke Common, Undrvr TN15 279 FP127
Fawke Common Rd, Sev.
TN15 279 FP126
Fawkes Av, Dart. DA1 210 FM89
Sch Fawkham C of E Prim Sch,
Long. DA3 *off Valley Rd* 231 FV102
FAWKHAM GREEN, Long.
DA3 231 FV104
Fawkham Grn Rd, Fawk.Grn
DA3 231 FV104
Fawkham Ho, SE1
off Longfield Est 32 B9
H Fawkham Manor Hosp,
Fawk. DA3 231 FW102
Fawkham Rd, Long. DA3 231 FX97
Fawkon Wk, Hodd. EN11 71 EA17
Fawley Rd, NW6 5 L3
Fawnbrake Av, SE24 203 DP85
Fawn Ct, Hat. AL9 67 CW16
Fawn Rd, E13 166 EJ68
Chigwell IG7 125 ET50
Fawns Manor Cl, Felt. TW14 197 BQ88
Fawns Manor Rd, Felt. TW14 197 BR88
Fawood Av, NW10 160 CR66
Fawsley Cl, Colnbr. SL3 175 BE80
Fawters Cl, Hutt. CM13 131 GD44
Fayerfield, Pot.B. EN6 86 DD31
Faygate Cres, Bexh. DA6 208 FA85
Faygate Rd, SW2 203 DM89
Fay Grn, Abb.L. WD5 81 BR33
Fayland Av, SW16 203 DJ92
Fayland Est, SW16 203 DJ92
Faymore Gdns, S.Ock. RM15 171 FU72
Feacey Down, Hem.H. HP1 62 BG18
Fearn Cl, E.Hors. KT24 267 BS129
Fearney Mead, Mill End WD3 114 BG46
Fearnley Cres, Hmptn. TW12 198 BY92
Fearnley Rd, Welw.G.C. AL8 51 CW10
Fearnley St, Wat. WD18 97 BV42
Fearns Mead, Warley CM14
off Bucklers Ct 130 FW50
Fearon St, SE10 35 N10
Featherbed La, Croy. CR0 243 DZ108
Hemel Hempstead HP3 62 BJ24
Romford RM4 126 EY45
Warlingham CR6 243 ED113
Feather Dell, Hat. AL10 67 CT18
Feathers La, Wrays. TW19 195 BA89
Feathers Pl, SE10 47 H2
Featherstone Av, SE23 204 DV89
Featherstone Gdns, Borwd.
WD6 100 CQ42
Sch Featherstone High Sch, Sthl.
UB2 *off Montague Waye* 178 BY76
● Featherstone Ind Est,
Sthl. UB2 178 BY75
Sch Featherstone Prim Sch, Sthl.
UB2 *off Western Rd* 178 BW77
Featherstone Rd, NW7 119 CV51
Southall UB2 178 BY76
Featherstone St, EC1 19 L4
Featherstone Ter, Sthl. UB2 178 BY76
Featley Rd, SW9 42 G10
Federal Rd, Perivale UB6 159 CJ68
Federal Way, Wat. WD24 98 BW38
Federation Rd, SE2 188 EV77
Fee Fm Rd, Clay. KT10 237 CF108
Feenan Highway, Til. RM18 193 GH80
Feeny Cl, NW10 141 CT63
Felbridge Av, Stan. HA7 117 CG53
Felbridge Cl, SW16 203 DN91
Sutton SM2 240 DB109
Felbridge Ho, SE22
off Pytchley Rd 184 DS83
Felbrigge Rd, Ilf. IG3 147 ET61
Felcott Cl, Hersham KT12 218 BW104
Felcott Rd, Hersham KT12 218 BW104
Felday Hos, Holm.St.M. RH5 283 BV144
Felday Rd, SE13 205 EB86
Abinger Hammer RH5 283 BT140
FELDEN, Hem.H. HP3 62 BG24
Felden Cl, Pnr. HA5 116 BY52
Watford WD25 82 BX34
Felden Dr, Felden HP3 62 BG24
Felden La, Felden HP3 62 BG24
Felden St, SW6 38 G6
Feldman Cl, N16 144 DU60
Feldspar Ct, Enf. EN3
off Enstone Rd 105 DY41
Felgate Ms, W6 181 CV77
Felhampton Rd, SE9 207 EP89
Felhurst Cres, Dag. RM10 149 FB63
Felicia Way, Grays RM16 193 GH77
Felipe Rd, Chaff.Hun. RM16 191 FW76
Felix Av, N8 143 DL58
Felix Dr, W.Clan. GU4 266 BG128
Felix La, Shep. TW17 217 BS100
Felix Pl, SW2 *off Talma Rd* 203 DN85
Felix Rd, W13 159 CG73
Walton-on-Thames KT12 217 BU100
Felixstowe Ct, E16 37 P3
Felixstowe Rd, N9 122 DU49
N17 144 DT55
NW10 161 CV69
SE2 188 EV76
Felland Way, Reig. RH2 288 DC138
Fellbrigg Rd, SE22 204 DT85
Fellbrook, Rich. TW10 199 CH90
Fellmongers Path, SE1 31 P5
Fellmongers Yd, Croy. CR0
off Surrey St 224 DQ104
Fellowes Cl, Hayes UB4
off Paddington Cl 158 BX70
Fellowes La, Coln.Hth AL4 66 CS23
Fellowes Rd, Cars. SM5 222 DE104
Fellows Ct, E2 20 A1
Croy. CR0 224 DT101
Fellows Rd, NW3 6 B6
Fell Rd, Croy. CR0 224 DQ104
Felltram Ms, SE7 35 P10
Felltram Way, SE7 35 P10
Fell Wk, Edg. HA8
off East Rd 118 CQ53
Felmersham Cl, SW4 183 DK84
Felmingham Rd, SE20 224 DW96
Felmongers, Harl. CM20 58 EV12
● Felnex Trd Est, Wall. SM6 222 DG103
Felsberg Rd, SW2 203 DL86
Fels Cl, Dag. RM10 149 FB62
Fels Fm Av, Dag. RM10 149 FC62
Felsham Rd, SW15 181 CX83
Felspar Cl, SE18 187 ET78
Felstead Av, Ilf. IG5 125 EN53
Felstead Cl, N13 121 DN50
Hutton CM13 131 GC44
Felstead Gdns, E14 46 E1
Felstead Rd, E11 146 EG59
Epsom KT19 238 CR111
Loughton IG10 124 EL45
Orpington BR6 228 EU103
Romford RM5 127 FC51
Waltham Cross EN8 89 DY32
Felstead St, E9 11 P5
Felsted Rd, E16 24 E9
FELTHAM, TW13 & TW14 197 BV89
⇌ Feltham 197 BV88
Feltham Av, E.Mol. KT8 219 CE98
Felthambrook Way, Felt. TW13 197 BV90
● Feltham Business Complex,
Felt. TW13 197 BV89
Coll Feltham City Learning Cen,
Felt. TW13
off Browells La 198 BW89
Coll Feltham Comm Coll, Felt.
TW13 *off Browells La* 198 BW89
FELTHAMHILL, Felt. TW13 197 BU92
Sch Feltham Hill Inf & Nurs Sch,
Felt. TW13
off Bedfont Rd 197 BT90
Sch Feltham Hill Jun Sch,
Felt. TW13
off Ashford Rd 197 BT90
Feltham Hill Rd, Ashf. TW15 197 BP92
Feltham Rd, Ashf. TW15 197 BP91
Feltham Rd, Mitcham CR4 222 DF96
Redhill RH1 288 DF139
Feltham Wk, Red. RH1 288 DF139
● Feltimores Pk, Harl. CM17 58 FA12
Felton Cl, Borwd. WD6 100 CL38
Broxbourne EN10 89 DZ25
Petts Wood BR5 227 EP100
Sch Feltonfleet Sch, Cob.
KT11 *off Byfleet Rd* 235 BS113
Felton Gdns, Bark. IG11
off Sutton Rd 167 ES67
Felton Lea, Sid. DA14 207 ET92
Felton Rd, W13
off Camborne Av 179 CJ75
Barking IG11
off Sutton Rd 167 ES68
Felton St, N1 9 M9
Fencepiece Rd, Chig. IG7 125 EQ50
Ilford IG6 125 EQ50
Fenchurch Av, EC3 19 N9
Fenchurch Bldgs, EC3 19 P9
Fenchurch Pl, EC3 19 P10
⇌ Fenchurch Street 19 P10
Fenchurch St, EC3 19 N10
Fen Cl, Shenf. CM15 131 GC42
Fen Ct, EC3 19 N9
Fendall Rd, Epsom KT19 238 CQ106
Fendall St, SE1 31 P7
Fendt Cl, E16 23 M9
Fendyke Rd, Belv. DA17 188 EX76
Fenelon Pl, W14 27 H9
Fenemore Rd, Ken. CR8 258 DR119
Fengates Rd, Red. RH1 272 DE134
Fen Gro, Sid. DA15 207 ET86
Fenham Rd, SE15 44 D5
Fenland Ho, E5
off Mount Pleasant Hill 144 DW61
Fen La, SW13 181 CV81
North Ockendon RM14 151 FW64
Fenman Ct, N17 122 DV53
Fenman Gdns, Ilf. IG3 148 EV60
Fenn Cl, Brom. BR1 206 EG93
Fennel Cl, E16 23 K4
Croydon CR0
off Primrose La 225 DX102
Guildford GU1 265 BB131
Fennells, Harl. CM19 73 EQ20
Fennells Mead, Epsom KT17 239 CT109
Fennel St, SE18 187 EN79
Fenner Cl, SE16 32 F8
Fenner Ho, Walt. KT12 235 BU105
Fenner Rd, Grays RM16 191 FW77
Fenners Marsh, Grav. DA12 213 GM88
Fenner Sq, SW11
off Thomas Baines Rd 182 DD83
Fennings, The, Amer. HP6 77 AR36
Fenning St, SE1 31 N4
Fenn St, E9 11 H3
Fenns Way, Wok. GU21 248 AY115
Fennycroft Rd, Hem.H. HP1 62 BG17
Fensomes All, Hem.H. HP2
off Queensway 62 BK19
Fensomes Cl, Hem.H. HP2
off Broad St 62 BK19
Fenstanton Av, N12 120 DD50
Sch Fenstanton Prim Sch,
SW2 *off Abbots Pk* 203 DN88
Fen St, E16 23 M10
Fens Way, Swan. BR8 209 FG93
Fenswood Cl, Bex. DA5 208 FA85
Fentiman Rd, SW8 42 B3
Fentiman Way, Har. HA2 138 CB61
Hornchurch RM11 150 FL60
Fenton Av, Stai. TW18 196 BJ93
Fenton Cl, E8 10 B4
SW9 42 C8
Chislehurst BR7 207 EM92
Redhill RH1 272 DG134
Fenton Gra, Harl. CM17 74 EW16
★ Fenton Ho, NW3 142 DC62
Fenton Ho, Houns. TW5 178 CA79
Fenton Rd, N17 122 DQ52
Chafford Hundred RM16 192 FY76
Redhill RH1 272 DG134
Fenton St, E1
off Commercial Rd 20 F8
Fentons Av, E13 24 A1
Fentum Rd, Guil. GU2 264 AU132
Fenwick Cl, SE18 187 EN79
Woking GU21 248 AV118
Fenwick Gro, SE15 184 DU83
Fenwick Path, Borwd. WD6 100 CM38
Fenwick Pl, SW9 183 DL83
South Croydon CR2 241 DP108
Fenwick Rd, SE15 184 DU83
Ferdinand Pl, NW1 7 H6
Ferdinand St, NW1 7 H5
Ferguson Av, Grav. DA12 213 GJ91
Romford RM2 128 FJ54
Surbiton KT5 220 CM99
Ferguson Cl, E14 34 A9
Bromley BR2 225 ED97
Ferguson Ct, Rom. RM2 128 FK54
Ferguson Dr, W3 160 CR72
Fergus Rd, N5 9 H3
Ferme Pk Rd, N4 143 DL57
N8 143 DL57
Fermor Rd, SE23 205 DY88
Fermoy Rd, W9 14 G5
Greenford UB6 158 CB70
Fern Av, Mitch. CR4 223 DK98
Fernbank, Buck.H. IG9 124 EH46
Fernbank Av, Horn. RM12 150 FJ63
Walton-on-Thames KT12 218 BY101
Wembley HA0 139 CF63
Fernbank Ms, SW12 203 DH86
Fernbank Rd, Add. KT15 234 BG106
Fernbrook Av, Sid. DA15
off Blackfen Rd 207 ES85
Fernbrook Cres, SE13 206 EE86
Fernbrook Dr, Har. HA2 138 CB59
Fernbrook Rd, SE13 206 EE86
Ferncliff Rd, E8 10 C2
Fern Cl, N1 9 N10
Broxbourne EN10 71 DZ23
Erith DA8
off Hollywood Way 189 FH81
Warlingham CR6 259 DY118
Fern Ct, Rom. RM7
off Cottons App 149 FD57
Ferncroft Av, N12 120 DE51
NW3 142 DA62
Ruislip HA4 138 BW61
Ferndale, Brom. BR1 226 EJ96
Guildford GU3 264 AS132
Ferndale Av, E17 145 ED57
Chertsey KT16 215 BE104
Hounslow TW4 178 BY83
Ferndale Cl, Bexh. DA7 188 EY81
Ferndale Ct, SE3 47 M4
Ferndale Cres, Uxb. UB8 156 BJ69
Ferndale Pk, Bray SL6 172 AE79
Ferndale Rd, E7 166 EH66
E11 146 EE61
N15 144 DT58
SE25 224 DV99
SW4 183 DL84
SW9 183 DM83
Ashford TW15 196 BK92
Banstead SM7 255 CZ116
Enfield EN3 105 DY37
Gravesend DA12 213 GH89
Romford RM5 127 FC54
Woking GU21 249 AZ116
Ferndale St, E6 25 N10
Ferndale Ter, Har. HA1 139 CF56
Ferndale Way, Orp. BR6 245 ER106
Ferndell Av, Bex. DA5 209 FD90
Fern Dells, Hat. AL10 67 CT19
Fern Dene, W13
off Templewood 159 CH71
Ferndene, Brick.Wd AL2 82 BZ31
Ferndene Rd, SE24 184 DQ84
Fernden Ri, Gdmg. GU7 280 AS144
Fernden Way, Rom. RM7 149 FB58
Ferndown, Horl. RH6 290 DF146
Hornchurch RM11 150 FM58
Northwood HA6 115 BU54
Ferndown Av, Orp. BR6 227 ER102
Ferndown Cl, Guil. GU1 281 BA135
Pinner HA5 116 BY52
Sutton SM2 240 DD107
Ferndown Ct, Guil. GU1 264 AW133
Ferndown Gdns, Cob. KT11 236 BW113
Ferndown Lo, E14
off Manchester Rd 34 F7
Ferndown Rd, SE9 206 EK87
Watford WD19 116 BW48
Fern Dr, Hem.H. HP3 62 BL21
Taplow SL6 152 AH72
Fernecroft, St.Alb. AL1 65 CD23
Fernery, The, Stai. TW18 195 BE92
Fernes Cl, Uxb. UB8 156 BJ72
Ferney Ct, Byfleet KT14
off Ferney Rd 234 BK112
Ferney Meade Way, Islw. TW7 179 CG82
Ferney Rd, Byfleet KT14 234 BK112
Cheshunt EN7 88 DR26
East Barnet EN4 120 DG45
Fern Gro, Felt. TW14 197 BV87
Welwyn Garden City AL8 51 CX05
Ferngrove Cl, Fetch. KT22 253 CE122
Fernhall Dr, Ilf. IG4 146 EK57
Fernhall La, Wal.Abb. EN9 90 EK31
Fernham Rd, Th.Hth. CR7 224 DQ97
Fernhead Rd, W9 15 H2
Fernheath Way, Dart. DA2 209 FD92
Fernhill, Oxshott KT22 237 CD114
Fernhill Cl, Wok. GU22 248 AW120
Fernhill Ct, E17 123 ED54
Fernhill Gdns, Kings.T. KT2 199 CK92
Fern Hill La, Harl. CM18 73 ES19
Fernhill La, Wok. GU22 248 AW120
Fernhill Pk, Wok. GU22 248 AW120
Sch Fern Hill Prim Sch,
Kings.T. KT2
off Richmond Rd 200 CL93
Fernhill Rd, Horl. RH6 291 DK152
Fernhills, Hunt.Br. WD4 81 BR33
Fernhill St, E16 37 K3
Fernholme Rd, SE15 205 DX85
Fernhurst Cl, Beac. HP9 111 AM53
Fernhurst Gdns, Edg. HA8 118 CN51
Fernhurst Rd, SW6 38 F6
Ashford TW15 197 BQ91
Croydon CR0 224 DU101
Fernie Cl, Chig. IG7 126 EU50
Fernihough Cl, Wey. KT13 234 BN111
Fernlands Cl, Cher. KT16 215 BE104
Fern La, Houns. TW5 178 BZ78
Fernlea, Bkhm KT23 252 CB124
Fernlea Pl, Cob. KT11 236 BX112
Fernlea Rd, SW12 203 DH88
Mitcham CR4 222 DG96
Fernleigh Cl, W9 15 H2
Croydon CR0 241 DN105
Walton-on-Thames KT12 217 BV104
Fernleigh Ct, Har. HA2 116 CB54
Wembley HA9 140 CL61
Fernleigh Rd, N21 121 DN47
Fernley Cl, Eastcote HA5 137 BU56
Fernleys, St.Alb. AL4 65 CJ17
Ferns, The, Beac. HP9 111 AM54
Hatfield AL10
off Campion Rd 67 CT15
St. Albans AL3 65 CD16
Fernsbury St, WC1 18 E3
Ferns Cl, Enf. EN3 105 DY36
South Croydon CR2 242 DV110
Fernshaw Rd, SW10 39 N3
Fernside, NW11 142 DA61
Buckhurst Hill IG9 124 EH46
Slough SL3 154 AV73
Fernside Av, NW7 118 CR48
Feltham TW13 197 BV91
Fernside La, Sev. TN13 279 FJ129
Fernside Rd, SW12 202 DF88
Fernsleigh Cl, Chal.St.P. SL9 112 AY51
Ferns Rd, E15 13 L5
Fern St, E3 22 B5
Fernthorpe Rd, SW16 203 DJ93
Ferntower Rd, N5 9 L2
Fern Twrs, Cat. CR3 274 DU125
Fernville La, Hem.H. HP2 62 BK20
Fern Wk, SE16 44 D1
Ashford TW15
off Ferndale Rd 196 BK92
Fern Way, Wat. WD25 97 BU35
Fernways, Ilf. IG1
off Cecil Rd 147 EP63
Fernwood, SW19
off Albert Dr 201 CZ88
Fernwood Av, SW16 203 DK91
Wembley HA0 139 CJ64
Fernwood Cl, Brom. BR1 226 EJ96
Fernwood Cres, N20 120 DF48
Ferny Hill, Barn. EN4 102 DF38
Ferranti Cl, SE18 36 F7
Ferraro Cl, Houns. TW5 178 CA79
Ferrers Av, Wall. SM6 241 DK105
West Drayton UB7 176 BK75
Ferrers Cl, Slou. SL1 153 AL74
Ferrers Rd, SW16 203 DK92
Ferrestone Rd, N8 143 DM56
Ferrey Ms, SW9 42 F9
Ferriby Cl, N1 8 E6
● Ferrier Ind Est, SW18 182 DB84
Ferrier Pt, E16 23 N7
Ferrier St, SW18 182 DB84
Ferriers Way, Epsom KT18 255 CW119
Ferring Cl, Har. HA2 138 CC60
Ferrings, SE21 204 DS89
Ferris Av, Croy. CR0 225 DZ104
Ferris Rd, SE22 184 DU84
Ferron Rd, E5 144 DV62
Ferro Rd, Rain. RM13 169 FG70
Ferrour Ct, N2 142 DD55
Ferry Av, Stai. TW18 195 BE94
Ferrybridge Ho, SE11 30 D7
Ferryhills Cl, Wat. WD19 116 BW48
Ferry Ho, E5
off Harrington Hill 144 DW60
Ferry La, N17 144 DU56
SW13 181 CT79
Brentford TW8 180 CL79
Chertsey KT16 216 BH98
Guildford GU2
off Portsmouth Rd 280 AW138
Laleham TW18 216 BJ97
Rainham RM13 169 FE72
Richmond TW9 180 CM79
Shepperton TW17 216 BN102
Wraysbury TW19 195 BB89
● Ferry La Ind Est, E17 145 DX55
Sch Ferry La Prim Sch, N17
off Jarrow Rd 144 DV56
Ferryman's Quay, SW6 39 N9
Ferrymead Av, Grnf. UB6 158 CA69
Ferrymead Dr, Grnf. UB6 158 CA68
Ferrymead Gdns, Grnf. UB6 158 CC68
Ferrymoor, Rich. TW10 199 CH90
Ferry Pl, SE18 37 M7
Ferry Quays, Brent. TW8
off Ferry La 180 CL79
Ferry Rd, SW13 181 CU80
Bray SL6 172 AC75
Teddington TW11 199 CH92
Thames Ditton KT7 219 CH100
Tilbury RM18 193 GG83
Twickenham TW1 199 CH88
West Molesey KT8 218 CA97
Ferry Sq, Brent. TW8 179 CK79
Shepperton TW17 217 BP101
Ferry St, E14 34 E10
Feryby Rd, Grays RM16 193 GH76
Feryngs Cl, Harl. CM17
off Watlington Rd 58 EX11
Fesants Cft, Harl. CM20 58 EV12
Festing Rd, SW15 38 C10
Festival Cl, Bex. DA5 208 EX88
Erith DA8 *off Betsham Rd* 189 FF80
Uxbridge UB10 157 BP67
Festival Ct, Sutt. SM1
off Cleeve Way 222 DB101
Festival Path, Wok. GU21 248 AT119
Riv Festival Pier 30 C2
Festival Wk, Cars. SM5 240 DF106
Festoon Way, E16 24 E10
FETCHAM, Lthd. KT22 253 CD123
Fetcham Common La, Fetch.
KT22 252 CB121
Fetcham Downs, Fetch. KT22 269 CE126
Fetcham Pk Dr, Fetch. KT22 253 CE123
Sch Fetcham Village Inf Sch, Fetch.
KT22 *off School La* 253 CD122
Fetherstone Cl, Pot.B. EN6 86 DD32
Fetherton Ct, Bark. IG11
off Spring Pl 167 EQ68
Fetter La, EC4 18 F9
Ffinch St, SE8 46 A4
Fiddicroft Av, Bans. SM7 240 DB114
● Fiddlebridge Ind Cen, Hat.
AL10 *off Lemsford Rd* 67 CT17
Fiddlebridge La, Hat. AL10 67 CT17
Fiddlers Cl, Green. DA9 191 FV84
FIDDLERS HAMLET, Epp. CM16 92 EW32
Fidgeon Cl, Brom. BR1 227 EN97
Fidler Pl, Bushey WD23
off Ashfield Av 98 CB44
Field Cl, E4 123 EB51
NW2 141 CU61
Abridge RM4 108 EV41
Bromley BR1 226 EJ96
Buckhurst Hill IG9 124 EJ48
Chesham HP5 76 AS28
Chessington KT9 237 CJ106
Guildford GU4 265 BD132
Harlington UB3 177 BQ80
Hounslow TW4 177 BV81
Ruislip HA4 137 BQ60
Sandridge AL4 65 CG16
South Croydon CR2 242 DV114
West Molesey KT8 218 CB99
Fieldcommon La, Walt. KT12 218 BZ101
Field Ct, WC1 18 D7
Gravesend DA11 213 GF89
Oxted RH8 276 EE127
Field End, Barn. EN5 101 CV42
Coulsdon CR5 241 DK114
Northolt UB5 158 BX65
Ruislip HA4 158 BW65
Fieldend, Twick. TW1 199 CF91
Field End Cl, Wat. WD19 116 BY45
Sch Field End Inf & Jun Schs, Ruis.
HA4 *off Field End Rd* 138 BX61
Field End Ms, Wat. WD19
off Field End Cl 116 BY45
Fieldend Rd, SW16 223 DJ95
Field End Rd, Pnr. HA5 137 BV58
Ruislip HA4 138 BY63
Fielders Cl, Enf. EN1
off Woodfield Cl 104 DS42
Harrow HA2 138 CC60
Fielders Grn, Guil. GU1 265 AZ134
Fielders Way, Shenley WD7 84 CL33
Fieldfare Rd, SE28 168 EW73
Fieldgate La, Mitch. CR4 222 DE97
Fieldgate St, E1 20 D7
Fieldhouse Cl, E18 124 EG53
Fieldhouse Rd, SW12 203 DJ88
Fieldhurst, Slou. SL3 175 AZ78
Fieldhurst Cl, Add. KT15 234 BH106
Sch Field Inf Sch, Wat. WD18
off Neal St 98 BW43
Fielding Av, Til. RM18 193 GH81
Twickenham TW2 198 CC90
Sch Fielding Co Prim Sch, W13
off Wyndham Rd 179 CH76
Fielding Gdns, Slou. SL3 174 AW75

Fielding Ho, NW6 15 K2
Fielding La, Brom. BR2 226 EJ98
Fielding Ms, SW13
  off Castelnau 181 CV79
Fielding Rd, W4 180 CR76
  W14 26 D6
Fieldings, The, SE23 204 DW88
  Banstead SM7 255 CZ117
  Horley RH6 291 DJ147
  Woking GU21 248 AT116
Fieldings Rd, Chsht EN8 89 DZ29
Fielding St, SE17 43 J2
Fielding Wk, W13 179 CH76
Fielding Way, Hutt. CM13 131 GC44
[Sch] Field Jun Sch, Wat. WD18
  off Watford Fld Rd 98 BW43
Field La, Brent. TW8 179 CJ80
  Godalming GU7
  off The Oval 280 AT144
  Teddington TW11 199 CG92
Field Mead, NW7 118 CS52
  NW9 118 CS52
Fieldpark Gdns, Croy. CR0 225 DY102
Field Pl, Gdmg. GU7 280 AS144
  New Malden KT3 221 CT100
Field Pt, E7 *off Station Rd* 146 EG63
Field Rd, E7 146 EF63
  N17 144 DR55
  W6 38 E1
  Aveley RM15 170 FQ74
  Denham UB9 135 BE63
  Feltham TW14 197 BV86
  Hemel Hempstead HP2 62 BN21
  Watford WD19 98 BY44
Fields, The, Slou. SL1 173 AR75
Fields Ct, Pot.B. EN6 86 DD33
Fields End La, Hem.H. HP1 61 BE18
Fieldsend Rd, Sutt. SM3 239 CY106
Fields Est, E8 10 D7
Fieldside Cl, Orp. BR6
  off State Fm Av 245 EQ105
Fieldside Rd, Brom. BR1 205 ED92
Fields Pk Cres, Rom. RM6 148 EX57
Field St, WC1 18 C2
Fieldview, SW18 202 DD88
Field Vw, Egh. TW20 195 BC92
  Feltham TW13 197 BR91
Fieldview, Horl. RH6
  off Stockfield 291 DH147
Field Vw Cl, Rom. RM7 148 FA55
Fieldview Ct, Slou. SL1 153 AQ71
  Staines-upon-Thames TW18
  off Burges Way 196 BG93
Field Vw Ri, Brick.Wd AL2 82 BY29
Field Vw Rd, Pot.B. EN6 86 DA33
[Tra] Fieldway 243 EB108
Field Way, NW10 160 CQ66
Fieldway, Amer. HP7 77 AP41
  Berkhamsted HP4 60 AY21
Field Way, Bov. HP3 79 BA27
  Chalfont St. Peter SL9 112 AX52
Fieldway, Dag. RM8 148 EV63
Field Way, Grnf. UB6 158 CB67
  Hoddesdon EN11 55 EC13
Fieldway, New Adgtn CR0 243 EB107
  Petts Wood BR5 227 ER100
Field Way, Rick. WD3 114 BH46
  Ripley GU23 265 BF125
  Ruislip HA4 137 BQ60
Fieldway, Stans.Abb. SG12 55 EB11
Field Way, Uxb. UB8 156 BK70
Fieldway Cres, N5 8 F3
Fiennes Cl, Dag. RM8 148 EW60
Fiennes Way, Sev. TN13 279 FJ127
Fiesta Dr, Dag. RM9 169 FC70
Fifehead Cl, Ashf. TW15 196 BL93
Fife Rd, E16 23 N7
  N22 121 DP52
  SW14 200 CQ85
  Kingston upon Thames KT1 220 CL96
Fife Ter, N1 8 D10
Fife Way, Lthd. KT23 268 CA125
FIFIELD, Maid. SL6 172 AD81
Fifield La, Wink. SL4 172 AD84
Fifield Path, SE23
  off Bampton Rd 205 DX90
Fifield Rd, Maid. SL6 172 AD80
Fifth Av, E12 147 EM63
  W10 14 E3
  Grays RM20 191 FU79
  Harlow CM20 57 ER13
  Hayes UB3 157 BT74
  Watford WD25 98 BX35
Fifth Cross Rd, Twick. TW2 199 CD89
Fifth Way, Wem. HA9 140 CP63
Figges Rd, Mitch. CR4 202 DG94
Figgswood, Couls. CR5 257 DJ122
Fig St, Sev. TN14 278 FF129
Fig Tree Cl, NW10
  off Craven Pk 160 CS67
Figtree Hill, Hem.H. HP2 62 BK19
Filbert Cl, Hat. AL10 67 CT21
Filby Rd, Chess. KT9 238 CM107
Filey Av, N16 144 DU60
Filey Cl, Bigg.H. TN16 260 EH119
  Sutton SM2 240 DC108
Filey Spur, Slou. SL1 173 AP75
Filey Waye, Ruis. HA4 137 BU61
Filigree Ct, SE16 33 M3
Fillebrook Av, Enf. EN1 104 DS40
Fillebrook Rd, E11 145 ED60
Fillingham Way, Hat. AL10 66 CS16
Filmer La, Sev. TN14 279 FL121
Filmer Rd, SW6 38 G6
  Windsor SL4 173 AK82
Filston La, Sev. TN14 247 FE113
Filston Rd, Erith DA8
  off Riverdale Rd 189 FC78
Filton Cl, NW9 118 CS54
Finborough Rd, SW10 39 L2
  SW17 202 DF93
Finchale Rd, SE2 188 EU76
Fincham Cl, Uxb. UB10 137 BQ62
Finch Av, SE27 204 DR91
Finch Cl, NW10 140 CR64
  Barnet EN5 102 DA43
  Hatfield AL10
  off Eagle Way 67 CU20
Finchdale, Hem.H. HP1 62 BG20
Finchdean Ho, SW15
  off Tangley Gro 201 CT87
Finch Dr, Felt. TW14 198 BX87
Finch End, Penn HP10 110 AC47
Finches, The, Hert. SG13 54 DV09
Finches Av, Crox.Grn WD3 96 BM41
Finches Ri, Guil. GU1 265 BC132
Finch Gdns, E4 123 EA50
Finch Grn, Chorl. WD3 95 BF42
Finchingfield Av, Wdf.Grn. IG8 124 EJ52
Finch La, EC3 19 M9
  Amersham HP7 94 AV40
  Bushey WD23 98 CA43
  Knotty Green HP9 110 AJ50
FINCHLEY, N3 120 DB53
[Sch] Finchley Catholic High Sch,
  N12 *off Woodside La* 120 DB48
⊖ Finchley Central 120 DA53
Finchley Cl, Dart. DA1 210 FN86
Finchley Ct, N3 120 DB51
Finchley La, NW4 141 CW56
[H] Finchley Mem Hosp, N12 120 DC52
Finchley Pk, N12 120 DC49
Finchley Pl, NW8 6 A10
⊖ Finchley Road 5 N4
Finchley Rd, NW2 142 DA62
  NW3 5 N4
  NW8 6 A9
  NW11 141 CZ58
  Grays RM17 192 GB79
⊖ Finchley Road & Frognal 5 N3
Finchley Way, N3 120 DA52
Finch Ms, SE15 44 A6
Finchmoor, Harl. CM18 73 ER18
Finch Rd, Berk. HP4 60 AU19
  Guildford GU1 264 AX134
Finden Rd, E7 146 EH64
Findhorn Av, Hayes UB4 157 BV71
Findhorn St, E14 22 F8
Findlay Dr, Guil. GU3 264 AT130
Findon Cl, SW18 202 DA86
  Harrow HA2 138 CB62
Findon Ct, Add. KT15 233 BF106
Findon Gdns, Rain. RM13 169 FG71
Findon Rd, N9 122 DV46
  W12 181 CU75
Fine Bush La, Hare. UB9 137 BP58
Fingal St, SE10 35 M10
Finglesham Cl, Orp. BR5
  off Westwell Cl 228 EX102
Finians Cl, Uxb. UB10 156 BM66
Finland Quay, SE16 33 L7
Finland Rd, SE4 185 DY83
Finland St, SE16 33 M6
Finlay Gdns, Add. KT15 234 BJ105
Finlays Cl, Chess. KT9 238 CN106
Finlay St, SW6 38 C7
Finnart Cl, Wey. KT13 235 BQ105
Finnart Ho Dr, Wey. KT13
  off Vaillant Rd 235 BQ105
Finney La, Islw. TW7 179 CG81
Finnis St, E2 20 F3
Finnymore Rd, Dag. RM9 168 EY66
FINSBURY, EC1 18 F2
Finsbury Av, EC2 19 M7
Finsbury Av Sq, EC2
  off Eldon St 19 M7
Finsbury Circ, EC2 19 M7
Finsbury Cotts, N22 121 DL52
Finsbury Ct, Wal.Cr. EN8
  off Parkside 89 DY34
Finsbury Est, EC1 18 F3
Finsbury Ho, N22 121 DL53
Finsbury Mkt, EC2 19 N5
FINSBURY PARK, N4 143 DN60
★ Finsbury Park, N4 143 DP59
⇌ Finsbury Park 143 DN61
⊖ Finsbury Park 143 DN61
Finsbury Park 143 DN61
Finsbury Pk Av, N4 144 DQ58
Finsbury Pk Rd, N4 143 DP61
Finsbury Pavement, EC2 19 M6
Finsbury Rd, N22 121 DM53
Finsbury Sq, EC2 19 M6
Finsbury St, EC2 19 L6
● Finsbury Twr, EC1 19 L5
Finsbury Way, Bex. DA5 208 EZ86
Finsen Rd, SE5 184 DQ83
Finstock Rd, W10 14 C8
[Sch] Finton Ho Sch, SW17
  off Trinity Rd 202 DF89
Finucane Dr, Orp. BR5 228 EW101
Finucane Gdns, Rain. RM13 169 FG65
Finucane Ri, Bushey Hth WD23 116 CC47
Finway Ct, Wat. WD18
  off Whippendell Rd 97 BT43
Finway Rd, Hem.H. HP2 63 BP16
Fiona Cl, Bkhm KT23 252 CA124
Firbank Cl, E16 24 E6
  Enfield EN2
  off Gladbeck Way 104 DQ42
Firbank Dr, Wat. WD19 116 BY45
  Woking GU21 248 AV119
Firbank La, Wok. GU21 248 AV119
Firbank Pl, Eng.Grn TW20 194 AV93
Firbank Rd, SE15 44 F8
  Romford RM5 127 FB50
  St. Albans AL3 65 CF16
Fir Cl, Walt. KT12 217 BU101
Fircroft Cl, Stoke P. SL2 154 AU65
  Woking GU22 249 AZ118
Fircroft Ct, Wok. GU22
  off Fircroft Cl 249 AZ118
Fircroft Gdns, Har. HA1 139 CE62
[Sch] Fircroft Prim Sch, SW17
  off Fircroft Rd 202 DF90
Fircroft Rd, SW17 202 DF89
  Chessington KT9 238 CM105
  Englefield Green TW20 194 AW94
Fir Dene, Orp. BR6 227 EM104
Firdene, Surb. KT6 220 CQ102
Fire Bell All, Surb. KT6 220 CL100
Firecrest Dr, NW3 142 DB62
Firefly Gdns, E6 24 G5
Firemans Run, S.Darenth
  DA4 *off East Hill* 230 FQ95
★ Firepower, SE18 37 P6
Fire Sta All, Barn. EN5
  off Christchurch La 101 CY40
Firethorn Cl, Edg. HA8
  off Larkspur Gro 118 CQ49
Firfield Rd, Add. KT15 234 BG105
Firfields, Wey. KT13 235 BP107
Fir Gra Av, Wey. KT13 235 BP106
Fir Gro, N.Mal. KT3 221 CT100
Firgrove, St.John's GU21 248 AU119
Fir Gro Rd, SW9 42 F8
Firham Pk Av, Rom. RM3 128 FN52
Firhill Rd, SE6 205 EA91
Firlands, Horl. RH6
  off Stockfield 291 DH147
Firlands, Weybridge KT13 235 BS107
Firle Ct, Epsom KT17
  off Dirdene Gdns 239 CT112
Firmans Ct, E17 145 ED56
Firmingers Rd, Orp. BR6 247 FB106
Firmin Rd, Dart. DA1 210 FJ85
Fir Pk, Harl. CM19 73 EP18
Fir Rd, Felt. TW13 198 BX92
  Sutton SM3 221 CZ102
Firs, The, E6 166 EL66
  E17 *off Leucha Rd* 145 DY57
  N20 120 DD46
  W5 159 CK71
  Artington GU3 280 AV138
  Bexley DA5 209 FD88
  Bookham KT23 252 CC124
  Caterham CR3
  off Chatfield Ct 258 DR122
  Cheshunt EN7 88 DS27
  Pilgrim's Hatch CM15 130 FU44
  St. Albans AL1 65 CH24
  Tadworth KT20 271 CZ126
  Welwyn Garden City AL8 51 CW05
Firs Av, N10 142 DG55
  N11 120 DG51
  SW14 180 CQ84
  Windsor SL4 173 AM83
Firsby Av, Croy. CR0 225 DX102
Firsby Rd, N16 144 DT60
Firs Cl, N10 142 DG55
  SE23 205 DX87
  Claygate KT10 237 CE107
  Dorking RH4 285 CG138
  Hatfield AL10 67 CV19
  Iver SL0
  off Thornbridge Rd 155 BC67
  Mitcham CR4 223 DH96
Firscroft, N13 122 DQ48
Firsdene Cl, Ott. KT16
  off Slade Rd 233 BD107
Firs Dr, Houns. TW5 177 BV80
  Loughton IG10 107 EN39
  Slough SL3 155 AZ74
Firs End, Chal.St.P. SL9 134 AY55
[Sch] Firs Fm Prim Sch, N13
  off Rayleigh Rd 122 DR48
Firsgrove Cres, Warley CM14 130 FV49
Firsgrove Rd, Warley CM14 130 FV49
Firside Gro, Sid. DA15 207 ET88
Firs La, N13 122 DQ48
  N21 122 DQ47
  Potters Bar EN6 86 DB33
Firs Pk, The, Hat. AL9 68 DA23
Firs Pk Av, N21 122 DR46
Firs Pk Gdns, N21 122 DQ46
Firs Rd, Ken. CR8 257 DP115
First Av, E12 146 EL63
  E13 23 N2
  E17 145 EA57
  N18 122 DW49
  NW4 141 CW56
  SW14 180 CS83
  W3 161 CT74
  W10 14 G4
  Amersham HP7 77 AQ40
  Bexleyheath DA7 188 EW80
  Dagenham RM10 169 FB68
  Enfield EN1 104 DT44
  Epsom KT19 238 CS109
  Grays RM20 191 FU79
  Harlow CM17, CM20 57 ER14
  Hayes UB3 157 BT74
  Lower Kingswood KT20 271 CY125
  Northfleet DA11 212 GE88
  Romford RM6 148 EW57
  Waltham Abbey EN9 *off Breach*
  Barn Mobile Home Pk 90 EH30
  Walton-on-Thames KT12 217 BV100
  Watford WD25 98 BW35
  Wembley HA9 139 CK61
  West Molesey KT8 218 BZ98
First Cl, W.Mol. KT8 218 CC97
First Cres, Slou. SL1 153 AQ71
First Cross Rd, Twick. TW2 199 CE89
First Dr, NW10 160 CQ66
● First Quarter, Epsom KT19 238 CS110
First Slip, Lthd. KT22 253 CG118
First St, SW3 28 D8
Firstway, SW20 221 CW96
First Way, Wem. HA9 140 CP63
Firs Wk, Nthwd. HA6 115 BR51
  Woodford Green IG8 124 EG50
Firsway, Guil. GU2 264 AT133
Firswood Av, Epsom KT19 239 CT106
Firs Wd Cl, Pot.B. EN6 86 DF32
Firth Gdns, SW6 38 E7
Fir Tree Av, Mitch. CR4 222 DG96
  Stoke Poges SL2 154 AT70
  West Drayton UB7 176 BN76
Fir Tree Cl, SW16 203 DJ92
  W5 160 CL72
  Epsom KT17 255 CW115
  Esher KT10 236 CC106
  Ewell KT19 239 CT105
  Grays RM17 192 GD79
  Hemel Hempstead HP3 62 BN21
  Leatherhead KT22 253 CJ123
  Orpington BR6 245 ET106
  Romford RM1 149 FD55
Firtree Ct, Els. WD6 100 CM42
Fir Tree Gdns, Croy. CR0 243 EA105
Fir Tree Gro, Cars. SM5 240 DF108
Fir Tree Hill, Chan.Cr. WD3 96 BM38
Fir Tree Pl, Ashf. TW15
  off Percy Av 196 BN92
Fir Tree Rd, Bans. SM7 239 CW114
  Epsom KT17 255 CV116
  Guildford GU1 264 AX131
  Hounslow TW4 178 BY84
  Leatherhead KT22 253 CJ123
Fir Trees, Abridge RM4 108 EV41
Fir Trees Cl, SE16 33 M3
Fir Tree Wk, Dag. RM10
  off Wheel Fm Dr 149 FC62
  Enfield EN1 104 DR41
  Reigate RH2 272 DD134
Firwood Av, St.Alb. AL4 66 CL20
Firwood Cl, Wok. GU21 248 AS119
Firwood Rd, Vir.W. GU25 214 AS100
Fisgard Ct, Grav. DA12
  off Admirals Way 213 GK86
Fisher Cl, E9 11 K2
  Croydon CR0 224 DT102
  Enfield EN3 105 EB37
  Greenford UB6 158 CA69
  Hersham KT12 235 BV105
  Kings Langley WD4 80 BN29
Fisher Ct, Warley CM14 130 FV50
Fisher Ho, N1 8 E9
Fisherman Cl, Rich. TW10 199 CJ91
Fishermans Dr, SE16 33 K4
Fishermans Hill, Nthflt DA11 212 GB85
Fisherman's Wk, E14 34 A2
Fishermans Wk, SE28
  off Tugboat St 187 ES75
Fishermans Way, Hodd. EN11 71 ED15
Fisher Rd, Har. HA3 117 CF54
Fishers, Horl. RH6
  off Ewelands 291 DJ147
Fishers Cl, SW16 203 DK90
  Bushey WD23 98 BY41
  Waltham Cross EN8 89 EA34
Fishers Ct, SE14 45 J6
Fishersdene, Clay. KT10 237 CG108
Fishers Grn La, Wal.Abb. EN9 89 EB29
Fishers Hatch, Harl. CM20 57 ES14
● Fisher's Ind Est, Wat. WD18 98 BW43
Fishers La, W4 180 CR77
  Epping CM16 91 ES32
Fisher St, E16 23 N6
  WC1 18 B7
Fishers Way, Belv. DA17 169 FC74
Fisherton St, NW8 16 A5
Fishery Pas, Hem.H. HP1
  off Fishery Rd 62 BG22
Fishery Rd, Hem.H. HP1 62 BG22
  Maidenhead SL6 152 AC74
Fishguard Spur, Slou. SL1 174 AV75
Fishguard Way, E16 37 P4
Fishing Temple, Stai. TW18 215 BF95
Fishlock Ct, SW4
  off Paradise Rd 42 A8
Fishponds Rd, SW17 202 DE91
  Keston BR2 244 EK106
Fishpool St, St.Alb. AL3 64 CB20
Fish St Hill, EC3 19 M10
Fisk Cl, Sun. TW16 197 BT93
Fiske Ct, N17 122 DU53
  Bark. IG11 167 ER68
Fitzalan Rd, N3 141 CY55
  Claygate KT10 237 CE108
Fitzalan St, SE11 30 E8
Fitzgeorge Av, W14 26 E9
  New Malden KT3 220 CR95
Fitzgerald Av, SW14 180 CS83
Fitzgerald Cl, E11
  off Fitzgerald Rd 146 EG57
Fitzgerald Ho, E14 22 D9
  SW9 42 E9
  Hayes UB3 157 BV74
Fitzgerald Rd, E11 146 EG57
  SW14 180 CR83
  Thames Ditton KT7 219 CG100
Fitzhardinge St, W1 16 G8
Fitzherbert Ho, Rich. TW10
  off Kingsmead 200 CM86
Fitzhugh Gro, SW18 202 DD86
Fitzilian Av, Rom. RM3 128 FM53
Fitzjames Av, W14 26 F9
  Croydon CR0 224 DU103
Fitzjohn Av, Barn. EN5 101 CY43
Fitzjohn Cl, Guil. GU4 265 BC131
Fitzjohn's Av, NW3 6 A3
[Sch] Fitzjohn's Prim Sch, NW3 6 A2
Fitzmaurice Ho, SE16
  off Rennie Est 32 F9
Fitzmaurice Pl, W1 29 K2
Fitzneal St, W12 161 CT72
Fitzrobert Pl, Egh. TW20 195 BA93
Fitzroy Cl, N6 142 DF60
Fitzroy Ct, W1 17 M5
Fitzroy Cres, W4 180 CR80
Fitzroy Gdns, SE19 204 DS94
Fitzroy Ms, W1 17 L5
Fitzroy Pk, N6 142 DF60
Fitzroy Pl, Reig. RH2 272 DD134
Fitzroy Rd, NW1 6 F8
Fitzroy Sq, W1 17 L5
Fitzroy St, W1 17 L5
Fitzroy Yd, NW1 6 G8
Fitzsimmons Ct, NW10
  off Knatchbull Rd 160 CR67
Fitzstephen Rd, Dag. RM8 148 EV64
Fitzwarren Gdns, N19 143 DJ60
Fitzwilliam Av, Rich. TW9 180 CM82
Fitzwilliam Cl, N20 120 DG46
Fitzwilliam Ct, Borwd. WD6
  off Eaton Way 100 CM39
  Harl. CM17 58 EY11
Fitzwilliam Ms, E16 35 N2
Fitzwilliam Rd, SW4 41 L10
Fitzwygram Cl, Hmptn H.
  TW12 198 CC92
Five Acre, NW9 119 CT53
Fiveacre Cl, Th.Hth. CR7 223 DN100
Five Acres, Chesh. HP5 76 AR33
  Harlow CM18 73 ES18
  Kings Langley WD4 80 BM29
  London Colney AL2 83 CK25
  Wooburn Green HP10 132 AF56
Five Acres Av, Brick.Wd AL2 82 BZ29
Five Ash Rd, Grav. DA11 213 GF87
Five Bell All, E14 21 P9
[Sch] Five Elms Prim Sch, Dag.
  RM9 *off Wood La* 148 EZ62
Five Elms Rd, Brom. BR2 226 EH104
  Dagenham RM9 148 EZ62
Five Flds Cl, Wat. WD19 116 BZ48
Five Oaks, Add. KT15 233 BF107
Five Oaks La, Chig. IG7 126 EY51
Five Oaks Ms, Brom. BR1 206 EG90
[Jct] Five Points, Iver SL0 155 BB69
Fives Ct, SE11 30 G8
[Jct] Fiveways, Croy. CR0 241 DN105
[Jct] Five Ways Cor, NW4 119 CV53
Fiveways Rd, SW9 42 F8
Five Wents, Swan. BR8 229 FG96
Fladbury Rd, N15 144 DR58
Fladgate Rd, E11 146 EE58
Flag Cl, Croy. CR0 225 DX102
Flagon Ct, Croy. CR0
  off Lower Coombe St 242 DQ105
Flags, The, Hem.H. HP2 63 BP20
Flagstaff Cl, Wal.Abb. EN9 89 EB33
Flagstaff Ho, SW8
  off St. George Wf 42 A2
Flagstaff Rd, Wal.Abb. EN9 89 EB33
Flag Wk, Pnr. HA5 137 BU58
Flambard Rd, Har. HA1 139 CH58
Flamborough Cl, Bigg.H. TN16 260 EH119
Flamborough Rd, Ruis. HA4 137 BU62
Flamborough Spur, Slou. SL1 173 AN75
Flamborough St, E14 21 L8
Flamborough Wk, E14 21 L9
Flamingo Cl, Hat. AL10 66 CR17
Flamingo Gdns, Nthlt. UB5
  off Jetstar Way 158 BY69
Flamingo Wk, Horn. RM12 169 FG65
FLAMSTEAD END, Wal.Cr. EN7 88 DU28
[Sch] Flamstead End Prim Sch,
  Chsht EN7
  off Longfield La 88 DU27
Flamstead End Rd, Chsht EN8 88 DV28
Flamstead Gdns, Dag. RM9
  off Flamstead Rd 168 EW66
Flamstead Rd, Dag. RM9 168 EW66
Flamsted Av, Wem. HA9 160 CN65
Flamsteed Rd, SE7 186 EL78
Flanchford Rd, W12 181 CT76
  Reigate RH2 271 CX134
Flanders Ct, Egh. TW20 195 BC92
Flanders Cres, SW17 202 DF94
Flanders Rd, E6 25 K1
  W4 180 CS77
Flanders Way, E9 11 J4
Flandrian Cl, Enf. EN3 105 EA38
Flank St, E1 20 C10
Flannery Ct, SE16
  off Drummond Rd 32 E6
Flash La, Enf. EN2 103 DP37
Flask Cotts, NW3
  off New End Sq 142 DD63
Flask Wk, NW3 5 P1
Flatfield Rd, Hem.H. HP3 62 BN22
Flather Cl, SW16
  off Blegborough Rd 203 DJ92
Flat Iron Sq, SE1
  off Union St 31 K3
FLAUNDEN, Hem.H. HP3 79 BB33
Flaunden Bottom, Chesh. HP5 94 AY36
  Flaunden HP3 94 AY35
Flaunden Hill, Flaun. HP3 79 AZ33
Flaunden La, Hem.H. HP3 79 BB32
  Rickmansworth WD3 79 BD33
Flaunden Pk, Flaun. HP3 79 BA32
Flavell Ms, SE10 35 K10
Flavian Cl, St.Alb. AL3 64 BZ22
Flaxen Cl, E4 *off Flaxen Rd* 123 EB48
Flaxen Rd, E4 123 EB48
Flaxley Rd, Mord. SM4 222 DB100
Flaxman Ct, W1 17 N9
Flaxman Rd, SE5 43 H9
Flaxman Ter, WC1 17 P3
Flaxton Rd, SE18 187 ER81
Flecker Cl, Stan. HA7 117 CF50
Fleece Dr, N9 122 DU49
[Sch] Fleecefield Prim Sch, N18
  off Brettenham Rd 122 DU49
Fleece Rd, Long Dit. KT6 219 CJ102
Fleece Wk, N7 8 B4
Fleeming Cl, E17
  off Pennant Ter 123 DZ54
Fleeming Rd, E17 123 DZ54
Fleet Av, Dart. DA2 210 FQ88
  Upminster RM14 151 FR58
Fleet Cl, Ruis. HA4 137 BQ58
  Upminster RM14 151 FR58
  West Molesey KT8 218 BZ99
Fleetdale Par, Dart. DA2
  off Fleet Av 210 FQ88
[Sch] Fleetdown Inf Sch, Dart.
  DA2 *off Lunedale Rd* 210 FQ89
[Sch] Fleetdown Jun Sch, Darenth
  DA2 *off Lunedale Rd* 210 FQ89
Fleet La, W.Mol. KT8 218 BZ100
Fleet Pl, EC4
  off Limeburner La 18 G8
[Sch] Fleet Prim Sch, NW3 6 E2
Fleet Rd, NW3 6 D2
  Dartford DA2 210 FQ88
  Northfleet DA11 212 GC90
Fleetside, W.Mol. KT8 218 BZ100
Fleet Sq, WC1 18 D3
Fleet St, EC4 18 E9
Fleet St Hill, E1 20 C5
FLEETVILLE, St.Alb. AL1 65 CG20
[Sch] Fleetville Inf & Nurs Sch, St.Alb.
  AL1 *off Woodstock Rd S* 65 CH20
[Sch] Fleetville Jun Sch, St.Alb.
  AL1 *off Hatfield Rd* 65 CG20
Fleetway, Egh. TW20 215 BC97
● Fleetway Business Pk,
  Perivale UB6 159 CH68
Fleetwood Cl, E16 24 E6
  Chalfont St. Giles HP8 112 AU49
  Chessington KT9 237 CK108
  Croydon CR0 224 DT104
  Tadworth KT20 255 CW120
Fleetwood Ct, E6 25 J6
  West Byfleet KT14 234 BG113
Fleetwood Gro, W3
  off East Acton La 160 CS73
Fleetwood Rd, NW10 141 CU64
  Kingston upon Thames KT1 220 CP97
  Slough SL2 154 AT74
Fleetwood Sq, Kings.T. KT1 220 CP97
Fleetwood St, N16
  off Stoke Newington Ch St 144 DS61
Fleetwood Way, Wat. WD19 116 BW49
Fleming Cl, W9 15 J5
  Cheshunt EN7 88 DU26
Fleming Ct, W2 16 A6
  Croydon CR0 241 DN106
  Nthflt. DA11 212 GC88
Fleming Cres, Hert. SG14
  off Tudor Way 53 DN09
Fleming Dr, N21 103 DM43
Fleming Gdns, Harold Wd RM3
  off Bartholomew Dr 128 FK54
  Tilbury RM18
  off Fielding Av 193 GJ81
Fleming Mead, Mitch. CR4 202 DE94
Fleming Rd, SE17 43 H2
  Chafford Hundred RM16 191 FW77
  Southall UB1 158 CB72
  Waltham Abbey EN9 105 EB35
Flemings, Gt Warley CM13 129 FW51
Fleming Wk, NW9
  off Pasteur Cl 118 CS54
Fleming Way, SE28 168 EX73
  Isleworth TW7 179 CF83
Flemish Flds, Cher. KT16 216 BG101
Flemming Av, Ruis. HA4 137 BV60
Flempton Rd, E10 145 DY59
Fletcher Cl, E6 25 N10
  Ottershaw KT16 233 BE107
  St. John's GU21 248 AT118
Fletcher La, E10 145 EC59
Fletcher Path, SE8 46 B5
Fletcher Rd, W4 180 CQ76
  Chigwell IG7 125 ET50
  Ottershaw KT16 233 BD107
Fletchers Cl, Brom. BR2 226 EH98
Fletcher St, E1 20 D10
Fletcher Way, Hem.H. HP2 62 BJ18
Fletching Rd, E5 144 DW62
  SE7 186 EJ79

Fletton Rd, N11 121 DL52
Fleur de Lis St, E1 19 P5
Fleur Gates, SW19 201 CX87
Flexley Wd, Welw.G.C. AL7 51 CZ06
Flex Meadow, Harl. CM19 72 EL16
Flexmere Gdns, N17 122 DR53
Flexmere Rd, N17 122 DR53
Flight App, NW9 119 CT54
Flimwell Cl, Brom. BR1 206 EE92
Flinders Cl, St.Alb. AL1 65 CG22
Flint Cl, E15 13 L6
Banstead SM7 240 DB114
Bookham KT23 268 CC126
Green Street Green BR6
off Lynne Cl 245 ET107
Redhill RH1 272 DF133
Flint Down Cl, Orp. BR5 228 EU95
Flint Hill, Dor. RH4 285 CH138
Flint Hill Cl, Dor. RH4 285 CH139
Flintlock Cl, Stai. TW19 176 BG84
Flintmill Cres, SE3 186 EL82
Flinton St, SE17 31 P10
Flint St, SE17 31 M9
Grays RM20 191 FV79
Flint Way, St.Alb. AL3 64 CC15
Flitcroft St, WC2 17 P8
Floathaven Cl, SE28 168 EU74
Floats, The, Rvrhd TN13 278 FE121
Flock Mill Pl, SW18 202 DB88
Flockton St, SE16 32 C5
Flodden Rd, SE5 43 J7
Flood La, Twick. TW1
off Church La 199 CG88
Flood Pas, SE18 37 J7
Flood St, SW3 40 D1
Flood Wk, SW3 40 D2
Flora Cl, E14 22 C9
Stanmore HA7 118 CL48
Flora Gdns, W6 181 CV77
Croydon CR0 243 EC111
Romford RM6 148 EW58
Sch Flora Gdns Prim Sch, W6
off Dalling Rd 181 CV77
Flora Gro, St.Alb. AL1 65 CF21
Flora Ho, E3 *off Garrison Rd* 12 A9
Floral Ct, Ashtd. KT21
off Rosedale 253 CJ118
Floral Dr, Lon.Col. AL2 83 CK26
Floral Pl, N1
off Northampton Gro 9 L3
Floral St, WC2 18 A10
Flora St, Belv. DA17 188 EZ78
Florence Av, Enf. EN2 104 DQ41
Morden SM4 222 DC99
New Haw KT15 234 BG111
Florence Cantwell Wk, N19
off Hillrise Rd 143 DL59
Florence Cl, Grays RM20 192 FY79
Harlow CM17 74 EW17
Hornchurch RM12 150 FL61
Walton-on-Thames KT12
off Florence Rd 217 BV101
Watford WD25 97 BU35
Florence Ct, W9
off Maida Vale 15 P3
Florence Dr, Enf. EN2 104 DQ41
Florence Elson Cl, E12 147 EN63
Florence Gdns, W4 180 CQ79
Romford RM6 *off Roxy Av* 148 EW59
Staines-upon-Thames TW18 196 BH94
Florence Nightingale Ho, N1
off Nightingale Rd 9 K5
★ Florence Nightingale Mus,
SE1 30 C5
Florence Rd, E6 166 EJ67
E13 23 N1
N4 143 DN60
SE2 188 EW76
SE14 45 P7
SW19 202 DB93
W4 180 CR76
W5 160 CL73
Beckenham BR3 225 DX96
Bromley BR1 226 EG95
Feltham TW13 197 BV88
Kingston upon Thames KT2 200 CM94
South Croydon CR2 242 DR109
Southall UB2 178 BX77
Walton-on-Thames KT12 217 BV101
Florence St, E16 23 M4
N1 8 G7
NW4 141 CW56
Florence Ter, SE14 45 P6
SW15 *off Roehampton Vale* 200 CS90
Florence Way, SW12 202 DF88
Uxbridge UB8 156 BJ66
Florence White Ct, N9
off Colthurst Dr 122 DV48
Florey Sq, N21
off Highlands Av 103 DM43
Florfield Pas, E8 10 F5
Florfield Rd, E8 10 F5
Florian Av, Sutt. SM1 240 DD105
Florian Rd, SW15 181 CY84
Florida Cl, Bushey Hth WD23 117 CD47
Florida Ct, Brom. BR2
off Westmoreland Rd 226 EF98
Florida Rd, Shalf. GU4 280 AY140
Thornton Heath CR7 223 DP95
Florida St, E2 20 C3
Florin Ct, EC1 19 J6
SE1 *off Tanner St* 32 A5
Floris Pl, SW4 41 L10
Floriston Av, Uxb. UB10 157 BQ66
Floriston Cl, Stan. HA7 117 CH53
Floriston Ct, Nthlt. UB5 138 CB64
Floriston Gdns, Stan. HA7 117 CH53
Floss St, SW15 38 B9
Flower & Dean Wk, E1 20 B7
Flower Cres, Ott. KT16 233 BB107
Flowerfield, Otford TN14 263 FF117
Flowerhill Way, Istead Rise
DA13 212 GE94
Flower La, NW7 119 CT50
Godstone RH9 275 DY128
Flower Ms, NW11 141 CY58
Flower Pot Cl, N15
off St. Ann's Rd 144 DT58
Flowers Av, Ruis HA4 137 BU58
Flowers Cl, NW2 141 CU62
Flowersmead, SW17 202 DG89
Flowers Ms, N19
off Archway Rd 143 DJ61
Flower Wk, Guil. GU2 280 AW137
Flower Wk, The, SW7 27 N5
Floyd Rd, SE7 36 C10
Floyds La, Wok. GU22 250 BG116
Floyer Cl, Rich. TW10 200 CM85
Fludyer St, SE13 186 EE84
Flux's La, Epp. CM16 92 EU33
Flyer's Way, The, West. TN16 277 ER126
● Flyers Way Ind Est, West.
TN16 *off The Flyer's Way* 277 ER126
Fogerty Cl, Enf. EN3 105 EB37
Fold Cft, Harl. CM20 57 EN14
Foley Cl, Beac. HP9 110 AJ51
Foley Ho, E1 *off Tarling St* 20 G9
Foley Ms, Clay. KT10 237 CE108
Foley Rd, Bigg.H. TN16 260 EK118
Claygate KT10 237 CE108
Foley St, W1 17 L7
Foley Wd, Clay. KT10 237 CF108
Folgate St, E1 19 P6
Foliot Ho, N1
off Priory Grn Est 8 C10
Foliot St, W12 161 CT72
Folkes La, Upmin. RM14 151 FT57
Folkestone Ct, Slou. SL3 175 BA78
Folkestone Rd, E6 25 M1
E17 145 EB56
N18 122 DU49
Folkingham La, NW9 118 CR53
Folkington Cor, N12 119 CZ50
Follet Dr, Abb.L. WD5 81 BT31
Follett Cl, Old Wind. SL4 194 AV86
Follett St, E14 22 E9
Folly, The, Hert. SG14 54 DR09
Folly Av, St.Alb. AL3 64 CC19
Folly Cl, Rad. WD7 99 CF36
Follyfield Rd, Bans. SM7 240 DA114
Folly La, E4 123 DZ52
E17 123 DY53
St. Albans AL3 64 CC19
South Holmwood RH5 285 CH144
Folly Ms, W11 14 G9
Folly Pathway, Rad. WD7 99 CF35
Folly Vw, Stans.Abb. SG12 55 EB10
Folly Wall, E14 34 F5
Fontaine Rd, SW16 203 DM94
Fontarabia Rd, SW11 182 DG84
Fontayne Av, Chig. IG7 125 EQ49
Rainham RM13 169 FE66
Romford RM1 127 FE54
Fontenelle, SE5 43 N6
Fontenoy Rd, SW12 203 DH89
Fonteyne Gdns, Wdf.Grn. IG8 124 EJ54
Fonthill Cl, SE20
off Selby Rd 224 DU96
Fonthill Ms, N4 143 DM61
Fonthill Rd, N4 143 DM60
Font Hills, N2 120 DC54
● Fontigarry Fm Business Pk,
Reig. RH2 288 DC143
Fontley Way, SW15 201 CU87
Fontmell Cl, Ashf. TW15 196 BN92
St. Albans AL3 65 CE18
Fontmell Pk, Ashf. TW15 196 BM92
Fontwell Cl, Har. HA3 117 CE52
Northolt UB5 158 CA65
Fontwell Dr, Brom. BR2 227 EN99
Fontwell Pk Gdns, Horn.
RM12 150 FL63
Foord Cl, Dart. DA2 211 FS89
Football La, Har. HA1 139 CE60
Footbury Hill Rd, Orp. BR6 228 EU101
Footpath, The, SW15 201 CU85
FOOTS CRAY, Sid. DA14 208 EV93
Foots Cray High St, Sid. DA14 208 EW93
Foots Cray La, Sid. DA14 208 EW88
Footscray Rd, SE9 207 EN86
Forbench Cl, Ripley GU23 250 BH122
Forbes Av, Pot.B. EN6 86 DD33
Forbes Cl, NW2 141 CU62
Hornchurch RM11
off St. Leonards Way 149 FH60
Forbes Ct, SE19 204 DS92
Forbe's Ride, Wind. SL4 172 AG84
Forbes St, E1 20 D9
Forbes Way, Ruis. HA4 137 BV61
Forburg Rd, N16 144 DU60
FORCE GREEN, West. TN16 261 ER124
Force Grn La, West. TN16 261 ER124
Fordbridge Cl, Cher. KT16 216 BH102
Fordbridge Pk, Sun. TW16 217 BT100
Fordbridge Rd, Ashf. TW15 196 BM92
Shepperton TW17 217 BS100
Sunbury-on-Thames TW16 217 BS100
Jct Fordbridge Rbt,
Ashf. TW15 196 BL93
Ford Cl, E3 11 M10
Ashford TW15 196 BL93
Bushey WD23 98 CC42
Harrow HA1 139 CD59
Rainham RM13 169 FF66
Shepperton TW17 216 BN98
Thornton Heath CR7 223 DP100
Fordcroft Rd, Orp. BR5 228 EV99
Forde Av, Brom. BR1 226 EJ97
Fordel Rd, SE6 205 ED88
Ford End, Denh. UB9 135 BF61
Woodford Green IG8 124 EH51
Fordham Cl, Barn. EN4 102 DE41
Hornchurch RM11 150 FN59
Worcester Park KT4 221 CV102
Fordham Rd, Barn. EN4 102 DD41
Fordham St, E1 20 D8
Fordhook Av, W5 160 CM73
Fordingley Rd, W9 15 H3
Fordington Ho, SE26
off Sydenham Hill Est 204 DV90
Fordington Rd, N6 142 DF57
Ford La, Iver SL0 156 BG72
Rainham RM13 169 FF66
Fordmill Rd, SE6 205 EA89
Ford Rd, E3 11 N10
Ashford TW15 196 BM91
Chertsey KT16 216 BH102
Dagenham RM9, RM10 168 EZ66
Northfleet DA11 212 GB85
Old Woking GU22 249 BB120
Fords Gro, N21 122 DQ46
Fords Pk Rd, E16 23 N8
Ford Sq, E1 20 F7
Ford St, E3 11 M9
E16 23 L8
Fordwater Rd, Cher. KT16 216 BH102
● Fordwater Trd Est, Cher.
KT16 216 BJ102
Fordwich Cl, Hert. SG14 53 DN09
Orpington BR6 227 ET101
Fordwich Hill, Hert. SG14 53 DN09
Fordwich Ri, Hert. SG14 53 DN09
Fordwich Rd, Welw.G.C. AL8 51 CW10
Fordwych Rd, NW2 4 G3
Fordyce Cl, Horn. RM11 150 FM59
Fordyce Ho, SW16
off Colson Way 203 DJ91
Fordyce Rd, SE13 205 EC86
Fordyke Rd, Dag. RM8 148 EZ61
Forebury, The, Saw. CM21 58 EY05
Forebury Av, Saw. CM21 58 EZ05
Forebury Cres, Saw. CM21 58 EZ05
Forefield, St.Alb. AL2 82 CA27
★ Foreign & Commonwealth
Office, SW1 29 P4
Foreign St, SE5 43 H8
Foreland Ct, NW4 119 CY53
Forelands Pl, Saw. CM21
off Bell St 58 EY05
Foreland St, SE18
off Plumstead Rd 187 ER77
Forelands Way, Chesh. HP5 76 AQ32
Foremark Cl, Ilf. IG6 125 ET50
Foreshore, SE8 33 P9
Forest, The, E11 146 EE56
Forest App, E4 124 EE45
Woodford Green IG8 124 EF52
Forest Av, E4 124 EE45
Chigwell IG7 125 EN50
Hemel Hempstead HP3 62 BK22
● Forest Business Pk, E10 145 DX59
Forest Cl, E11 146 EF57
NW6 4 E7
Chislehurst BR7 227 EN95
East Horsley KT24 267 BT125
Slough SL2 154 AV71
Waltham Abbey EN9 106 EH37
Woking GU22 249 BD115
Woodford Green IG8 124 EH48
Forest Ct, E4 124 EF46
E11 146 EE56
Forest Cres, Ashtd. KT21 254 CN116
Forest Cft, SE23 204 DV89
FORESTDALE, Croy. CR0 243 EA109
Forestdale, N14 121 DK49
Forestdale Cen, The, Croy.
CR0 *off Holmbury Gro* 243 DZ108
Sch Forestdale Prim Sch, Croy.
CR0 *off Pixton Way* 243 DZ109
Forest Dr, E12 146 EK62
Keston BR2 244 EL105
Kingswood KT20 255 CZ121
Sunbury-on-Thames TW16 197 BT94
Theydon Bois CM16 107 ES36
Woodford Green IG8 123 ED52
Forest Dr E, E11 145 ED59
Forest Dr W, E11 145 EC59
Forest Edge, Buck.H. IG9 124 EJ49
Forester Rd, SE15 184 DV84
Foresters Cl, Chsht EN7 88 DS27
Wallington SM6 241 DK108
Woking GU21 248 AT118
Foresters Cres, Bexh. DA7 189 FB84
Foresters Dr, E17 145 ED56
Wallington SM6 241 DK108
Sch Foresters Prim Sch, Wall.
SM6 *off Redford Av* 241 DK107
Forest Gdns, N17 122 DT54
FOREST GATE, E7 13 N3
⇌ Forest Gate 13 P2
Forest Gate, NW9 140 CS56
Sch Forest Gate Comm Sch, E7 13 P2
Forest Glade, E4 124 EE49
E11 146 EE58
North Weald Bassett CM16 92 EY27
Forest Gro, E8 10 A5
Thnwd. CM16 92 EW26
Forest Hts, Buck.H. IG9 124 EG47
FOREST HILL, SE23 205 DX88
⇌ Forest Hill 204 DW89
⊖ Forest Hill 204 DW89
Jct Forest Hill, SE23 204 DW89
● Forest Hill Business Cen,
SE23 *off Clyde Vale* 204 DW89
● Forest Hill Ind Est, SE23
off Perry Vale 204 DW89
Forest Hill Rd, SE22 204 DV85
SE23 204 DV85
Sch Forest Hill Sch, SE23
off Dacres Rd 205 DX90
Forestholme Cl, SE23 204 DW89
● Forest Ind Pk, Ilf. IG6 125 ES53
Forest La, E7 13 N3
E15 13 K4
Chigwell IG7 125 EN50
Leatherhead KT24 251 BT124
Forest Mt Rd, Wdf.Grn. IG8 123 ED52
Forest Pt, E7 *off Windsor Rd* 146 EH64
Fore St, EC2 19 K7
N9 122 DU50
N18 122 DT51
Harlow CM17 58 EW11
Hatfield AL9 67 CW17
Hertford SG14 54 DR09
Pinner HA5 137 BU57
Fore St Av, EC2 19 L7
Forest Ridge, Beck. BR3 225 EA97
Keston BR2 244 EL105
Forest Ri, E17 145 ED57
Forest Rd, E7 146 EG63
E8 10 A5
E11 145 ED59
E17 144 DW56
N9 122 DV46
N17 144 DW56
Cheshunt EN8 89 DX29
Enfield EN3 105 DY36
Erith DA8 189 FG81
Feltham TW13 198 BW89
Ilford IG6 125 ES53
Leatherhead KT24 251 BU123
Loughton IG10 106 EK41
Richmond TW9 180 CN80
Romford RM7 149 FB55
Sutton SM3 222 DA102
Watford WD25 81 BV33
Windsor SL4 173 AK82
Woking GU22 249 BD115
Woodford Green IG8 124 EG48
Sch Forest Sch, E17
off College Pl 146 EE56
Forest Side, E4 124 EF45
E7 146 EH63
Buckhurst Hill IG9 124 EJ46
Epping CM16 91 ER33
Waltham Abbey EN9 106 EJ36
Worcester Park KT4 221 CT102
Forest St, E7 13 N2
● Forest Trd Est, E17 145 DX55
Forest Vw, E4 123 ED45
E11 146 EF59
Forest Vw Av, E10 145 ED57
Forest Vw Rd, E12 146 EL63
E17 123 EC53
Loughton IG10 106 EK42
Forest Wk, N10 121 DH53
Bushey WD23 *off Millbrook Rd* 98 BZ39
Forest Way, N19
off Hargrave Pk 143 DJ61
Ashtead KT21 254 CM117
Loughton IG10 106 EL41
Orpington BR5 227 ET99
Sidcup DA15 207 ER87
Waltham Abbey EN9 106 EK35
Woodford Green IG8 124 EH49
● Forest Wks, E17
off Forest Rd 145 DX55
Forfar Rd, N22 121 DP53
SW11 41 H6
Forge, The, Northaw EN6 86 DE30
Forge Av, Couls. CR5 257 DN120
Forge Br La, Couls. CR5 257 DH121
Forge Cl, Brom. BR2 226 EG102
Chipperfield WD4 80 BG31
Harlington UB3 177 BR79
Forge Dr, Clay. KT10 237 CG108
Farnham Common SL2 153 AQ65
Forge End, Amer. HP7 77 AP40
St. Albans AL2 82 CA26
Woking GU21 248 AY117
Forgefield, Bigg.H. TN16
off Main Rd 260 EK116
Forge La, Felt. TW13 198 BY92
Gravesend DA12 213 GM89
Horton Kirby DA4 230 FQ98
Northwood HA6 115 BS52
Richmond TW10
off Petersham Rd 200 CL88
Sunbury-on-Thames TW16 217 BU97
Sutton SM3 239 CY108
Sch Forge La Prim Sch, Han.
TW13 *off Forge La* 198 BY92
Forge Ms, Croy. CR0
off Addington Village Rd 243 EA106
Forge Pl, NW1 7 H5
Horley RH6 290 DE150
Forge Steading, Bans. SM7
off Salisbury Rd 256 DB115
Forge Sq, E14 *off Westferry Rd* 34 C9
Forge Way, Shore. TN14 247 FF111
Forlong Path, Nthlt. UB5
off Cowings Mead 158 BY65
Forman Pl, N16
off Farleigh Rd 144 DT63
Formation, The, E16 37 N4
Formby Av, Stan. HA7 139 CJ55
Formby Cl, Slou. SL3 175 BC77
Sch Former Elmgreen Sch,
SE27 204 DQ91
Formosa St, W9 15 N5
Formunt Cl, E16 23 M7
Forres Cl, Hodd. EN11 71 EA15
Forres Gdns, NW11 142 DA58
Sch Forres Prim Sch, Hodd.
EN11 *off Stanstead Rd* 55 EB14
Forrester Path, SE26 204 DW91
Forresters Dr, Welw.G.C. AL7 52 DC10
Forrest Gdns, SW16 223 DM97
Forrest Pl, Shere GU5
off Wellers Ct 282 BN139
Forris Av, Hayes UB3 157 BT74
Forset St, W1 16 D8
Forstal Cl, Brom. BR2
off Ridley Rd 226 EG97
Forster Cl, Wdf.Grn. IG8 123 ED52
Sch Forster Pk Prim Sch, SE6
off Boundfield Rd 206 EE90
Forster Rd, E17 145 DY58
N17 144 DT55
SW2 203 DL87
Beckenham BR3 225 DY97
Croydon CR0
off Windmill Rd 224 DQ101
Guildford GU2 264 AU130
Forsters Cl, Rom. RM6 148 EZ58
Forster's Way, SW18 202 DB88
Forsters Way, Hayes UB4 157 BV72
Forston St, N1 9 L10
Forsyte Cres, SE19 224 DS95
Forsyth Ct, Dag. RM10
off St. Mark's Pl 169 FB65
Forsyth Gdns, SE17 43 H2
Forsyth Ho, SW1
off Tachbrook St 29 M10
Forsythia Cl, Ilf. IG1 147 EP64
Forsythia Gdns, Slou. SL3 174 AY76
Forsythia Pl, Guil. GU1
off Larch Av 264 AW132
Forsyth Path, Wok. GU21 233 BD113
Forsyth Pl, Enf. EN1 104 DS43
Forsyth Rd, Wok. GU21 233 BC114
Forterie Gdns, Ilf. IG3 148 EU62
Fortescue Av, E8 10 F7
Twickenham TW2 198 CC90
Fortescue Rd, SW19 202 DD94
Edgware HA8 118 CR53
Weybridge KT13 234 BM105
Fortess Gro, NW5 7 L2
Fortess Rd, NW5 7 K2
Fortess Wk, NW5 7 K2
Fortess Yd, NW5 7 K1
Forthbridge Rd, SW11 182 DG84
Forth Rd, Upmin. RM14 151 FR58
Fortin Cl, S.Ock. RM15 171 FU73
Fortin Path, S.Ock. RM15 171 FU73
Fortin Way, S.Ock. RM15 171 FU73
Fortis Cl, E16 24 C9
FORTIS GREEN, N2 142 DF56
Fortis Grn, N2 142 DE56
N10 142 DE56
Fortis Grn Av, N2 142 DF55
Fortis Grn Rd, N10 142 DG55
Fortismere Av, N10 142 DG55
Sch Fortismere Sch, N10
off Tetherdown 142 DG55
Coll Fortismere Sch 6th Form Cen,
N10 *off Tetherdown* 142 DG55
Fort La, Reig. RH2 272 DB130
Fortnam Rd, N19 143 DK61
★ Fortnum & Mason, W1 29 L2
Fortnums Acre, Stan. HA7 117 CF51
● Fortress Distribution Pk,
Til. RM18 193 GG84
Fort Rd, SE1 32 B9
Box Hill KT20 270 CP131
Guildford GU1 280 AY137
Halstead TN14 263 FC115
Northolt UB5 158 CA66
Tilbury RM18 193 GH84
Fortrose Cl, E14 23 H8
Fortrose Gdns, SW2 203 DL88
Fortrye Cl, Nthflt DA11 212 GE89
Fort St, E1 19 P7
E16 36 B3
Fortuna Cl, N7 8 D4
Fortune Ave, Edg. HA8 118 CP52
Fortune Gate Rd, NW10 160 CS67
Fortune Grn Rd, NW6 5 J1
Fortune La, Els. WD6 99 CK44
Fortune Pl, SE1 44 B1
Fortunes, The, Harl. CM18 73 ET17
Fortunes Mead, Nthlt. UB5 158 BY65
Fortune St, EC1 19 K5
Fortune Wk, SE28
off Broadwater Rd 187 ER76
Fortune Way, NW10 161 CU69
Forty Acre La, E16 23 N7
Forty Av, Wem. HA9 140 CM62
Forty Cl, Wem. HA9 140 CM61
Forty Footpath, SW14 180 CQ83
Fortyfoot Rd, Lthd. KT22 253 CJ121
FORTY GREEN, Beac. HP9 110 AH50
Forty Grn Rd, Knot.Grn HP9 110 AH51
★ Forty Hall & Mus, Enf. EN2 104 DT38
FORTY HILL, Enf. EN2 104 DS37
Forty Hill, Enf. EN2 104 DT38
Sch Forty Hill C of E Prim Sch,
Enf. EN2 *off Forty Hill* 104 DU37
Forty La, Wem. HA9 140 CP61
★ Forum, The, NW5 7 K2
Forum, The, W.Mol. KT8 218 CB98
Forum Cl, E3 12 A9
Forum Ho, Wem. HA9 140 CN63
Forum Magnum Sq, SE1 30 C4
Forum Pl, Hat. AL10 67 CU17
Forumside, Edg. HA8
off Station Rd 118 CN51
Forum Way, Edg. HA8 118 CN51
Forval Cl, Mitch. CR4 222 DF99
Forward Dr, Har. HA3 139 CF56
Fosbery Ct, Enf. EN3
off Sten Cl 105 EA37
Fosbury Ms, W2 27 M1
Foscote Ms, W9 15 K5
Foscote Rd, NW4 141 CV58
Foskett Ms, E8 10 B2
Foskett Rd, SW6 38 G9
Foss Av, Croy. CR0 241 DN106
Sch Fossdene Prim Sch, SE7
off Victoria Way 186 EH78
Fossdene Rd, SE7 186 EH78
Fossdyke Cl, Hayes UB4 158 BY71
Fosse Way, W13 159 CG71
West Byfleet KT14
off Brantwood Dr 233 BF113
Fossil Rd, SE13 185 EA83
Fossington Rd, Belv. DA17 188 EX77
Foss Rd, SW17 202 DD91
Fossway, Dag. RM8 148 EW61
Foster Av, Wind. SL4 173 AL83
Foster Cl, Chsht EN8 89 DX30
Fosterdown, Gdse. RH9 274 DV129
Foster La, EC2 19 J8
Foster Rd, E13 23 N4
W3 160 CS73
W4 180 CR78
Hemel Hempstead HP1 62 BG22
Fosters Cl, E18 124 EH53
Chislehurst BR7 207 EM92
Fosters Path, Slou. SL2 153 AM70
Sch Foster's Prim Sch, Well.
DA16 *off Westbrooke Rd* 188 EW83
Foster St, NW4 141 CW56
Harlow CM17 74 EY17
Foster Wk, NW4 *off Foster St* 141 CW56
Fothergill Cl, E13 13 N10
Fothergill Dr, N21 103 DL43
Fotheringay Gdns, Slou. SL1 153 AN73
Fotheringham Rd, Enf. EN1 104 DT42
Fotherley Rd, Mill End WD3 113 BF47
Foubert's Pl, W1 17 L9
Foulden Rd, N16 144 DT63
Foulden Ter, N16
off Foulden Rd 144 DT63
Sch Foulds Prim Sch, Barn.
EN5 *off Byng Rd* 101 CX41
Foulis Ter, SW7 28 B10
Foulser Rd, SW17 202 DF90
Foulsham Rd, Th.Hth. CR7 224 DQ97
● Foundation Units,
Guil. GU1 264 AY130
Founder Cl, E6 25 N9
Founders Cl, Nthlt. UB5 158 BZ69
Founders Ct, EC2 19 L8
Founders Gdns, SE19 204 DQ94
Founders Rd, Hodd. EN11 55 EB14
★ Foundling Mus, WC1 18 B4
Foundry Cl, SE16 33 L2
Foundry Ct, Slou. SL2 154 AT74
Foundry Gate, Wal.Cr. EN8
off York Rd 89 DY33
Foundry La, Horton SL3 175 BB83
Foundry Ms, NW1 17 M4
Hounslow TW3
off New Rd 178 CB84
Foundry Pl, E1 20 G6
Founes Dr, Chaff.Hun. RM16 192 FY76
Fountain Cl, E5
off Lower Clapton Rd 144 DV62
SE18 37 N10
Uxbridge UB8 157 BQ71
Fountain Ct, EC4 18 E10
Borwd. WD6 100 CN40
Eynsford DA4
off Pollyhaugh 230 FL103
Fountain Dr, SE19 204 DT91
Carshalton SM5 240 DF109
Hertford SG13 54 DT8
Fountain Fm, Harl. CM18 73 ET17
Fountain Gdns, Wind. SL4 173 AR83
Fountain Grn Sq, SE16 32 D5
Fountain Ho, SW6
off The Boulevard 39 P8
SW8 *off St. George Wf* 42 B1
Fountain La, Sev. TN15 279 FP122
Fountain Ms, N5
off Highbury Gra 9 J1
NW3 6 E4
Fountain Pl, SW9 42 F7
Waltham Abbey EN9 89 EC34
Fountain Rd, SW17 202 DD92
Redhill RH1 288 DE136
Thornton Heath CR7 224 DQ96
Fountains, The, Loug. IG10
off Fallow Flds 124 EK45
Fountains Av, Felt. TW13 198 BZ90
Fountains Cl, Felt. TW13 198 BZ89

Fountains Cres, N14 121 DL45
Fountain Sq, SW1 29 J8
Fountain Wk, Nthflt DA11 212 GE86
Fountayne Rd, N15 144 DU56
N16 144 DU61
Fount St, SW8 41 P5
Fouracre Path, SE25 224 DS100
Fouracres, SW12
off Little Dimocks 203 DH89
Four Acres, Cob. KT11 236 BY113
Fouracres, Enf. EN3 105 DY39
Four Acres, Guil. GU1 265 BC132
Welwyn Garden City AL7 51 CZ11
Four Acres, The, Saw. CM21 58 EZ06
Fouracres Dr, Hem.H. HP3 62 BM22
Fouracres Wk, Hem.H. HP3 62 BM22
Fourdinier Way, Hem.H. HP3 62 BK23
Four Hills Est, Enf. EN2 104 DQ38
Fourland Wk, Edg. HA8 118 CQ51
Fournier St, E1 20 A6
Four Oaks, Chesh. HP5 76 AN27
Four Seasons Cl, E3 12 A10
● **Four Seasons Cres**, Sutt. SM3 221 CZ103
Four Swannes Prim Sch, Wal.Cr. EN8 *off King Edward Rd* 89 DY33
Fourth Av, E12 147 EM63
W10 14 E3
Grays RM20 191 FU79
Harlow CM19, CM20 73 EM15
Hayes UB3 157 BT74
Romford RM7 149 FD60
Watford WD25 98 BX35
Fourth Cross Rd, Twick. TW2 199 CD89
Fourth Dr, Couls. CR5 257 DK116
Fourth Way, Wem. HA9 140 CQ63
Four Trees, St.Alb. AL2 64 CB24
Four Tubs, The, Bushey WD23 117 CD45
Fourways, Bayford SG13 69 DN18
St. Albans AL4
off Hatfield Rd 66 CM20
Fourways Mkt, N.Mymms AL9 *off Dixons Hill Rd* 67 CW24
Four Wents, Cob. KT11 235 BV113
Four Wents, The, E4
off Kings Rd 123 ED47
Fowey Av, Ilf. IG4 146 EK57
Fowey Cl, E1 32 E2
Fowler Cl, SW11 182 DD83
Fowler Rd, E7 146 EG63
N1 9 H7
Ilford IG6 126 EV51
Mitcham CR4 222 DG96
Fowlers Cl, Sid. DA14
off Thursland Rd 208 EY92
Fowlers Mead, Chobham GU24 *off Windsor Rd* 232 AS110
Fowlers Wk, W5 159 CK70
Fowley Cl, Wal.Cr. EN8 89 DZ34
Fowley Mead Pk, Wal.Cr. EN8 89 EA34
Fownes St, SW11 40 D10
Foxacre, Cat. CR3
off Town End Cl 258 DS122
Fox All, Wat. WD18
off Lower High St 98 BW43
Fox & Knot St, EC1 19 H6
Foxberry Rd, SE4 185 DY83
Foxberry Wk, Nthflt DA11
off Rowmarsh Cl 212 GD91
Foxboro Rd, Red. RH1 272 DG132
Foxborough Cl, Slou. SL3 175 BA78
Foxborough Gdns, SE4 205 EA86
Foxborough Sch, Langley SL3 *off Common Rd* 175 BA78
Foxbourne Rd, SW17 202 DG89
Fox Burrow Rd, Chig. IG7 126 EX50
Foxburrows Av, Guil. GU2 264 AT134
Foxbury Av, Chis. BR7 207 ER93
Foxbury Cl, Brom. BR1 206 EH93
Orpington BR6 246 EU106
Foxbury Dr, Orp. BR6 246 EU107
Foxbury Rd, Brom. BR1 206 EG93
Fox Cl, E1 21 H4
E16 23 N7
Bushey WD23 98 CB42
Elstree WD6 99 CK44
Orpington BR6 246 EU106
Romford RM5 127 FB50
Weybridge KT13 235 BR106
Woking GU22 249 BD115
Foxcombe, New Adgtn CR0 243 EB107
Foxcombe Cl, E6 *off Boleyn Rd* 166 EK68
Foxcombe Rd, SW15
off Alton Rd 201 CU88
Foxcote, SE5 43 P1
Fox Covert, Fetch. KT22 253 CD124
Foxcroft, St.Alb. AL1 65 CG22
Foxcroft Rd, SE18 187 EP81
Foxdell, Nthwd. HA6 115 BR51
Foxdells, Birch Grn SG14 53 DJ12
Foxdell Way, Chal.St.P. SL9 112 AY50
Foxdene Cl, E18 146 EH55
Foxearth Cl, Bigg.H. TN16 260 EL118
Foxearth Rd, S.Croy. CR2 242DW110
Foxearth Spur, S.Croy. CR2 242DW109
Foxenden Rd, Guil. GU1 280 AY135
Foxes Cl, Hert. SG13 54 DV09
Foxes Dale, SE3 47 N10
Bromley BR2 225 ED97
Foxes Dr, Wal.Cr. EN7 88 DU29
Foxes Grn, Orsett RM16 193 GG75
Foxes La, Cuffley EN6 87 DL28
North Mymms AL9 67 CY23
Foxes Path, Sutt.Grn GU4 265 AZ126
Foxfield Cl, Nthwd. HA6 115 BT51
Foxfield Prim Sch, SE18
off Sandbach Pl 187 EQ78
Foxfield Rd, Orp. BR6 227 ER103
Foxglove Cl, N9 122 DW46
Hatfield AL10 67 CV19
Hoddesdon EN11
off Castle Cl 55 EC14
Sidcup DA15 208 EU86
Southall UB1 158 BY73
Stanwell TW19 196 BK88
Foxglove Gdns, E11 146 EJ56
Guildford GU4 265 BC132
Purley CR8 241 DL111
Foxglove La, Chess. KT9 238 CN105
Foxglove Path, SE28
off Crowfoot Cl 167 ES74
Foxglove Rd, Rush Grn RM7 149 FE61
South Ockendon RM15 171 FW71
Foxgloves, The, Hem.H. HP1 61 BE21
Foxglove St, W12 161 CT73
Foxglove Way, Wall. SM6 223 DH102
Foxgrove, N14 121 DL48
Fox Gro, Walt. KT12 217 BV101
Foxgrove Av, Beck. BR3 205 EB94
Foxgrove Dr, Wok. GU21 249 BA115
Foxgrove Path, Wat. WD19 116 BX50
Foxgrove Rd, Beck. BR3 205 EB94
Foxhall Rd, Upmin. RM14 150 FQ64
Foxham Rd, N19 143 DK62
Foxhanger Gdns, Wok. GU22
off Oriental Rd 249 BA116
Foxherne, Slou. SL3 174 AW75
Fox Hill, SE19 204 DT94
Foxhill, Wat. WD24 97 BU36
Fox Hill Gdns, SE19 204 DT94
Foxhills, Wok. GU21 248AW117
Foxhills Cl, Ott. KT16 233 BB107
Foxhills Ms, Cher. KT16 215 BB104
Foxhills Rd, Ott. KT16 233 BA105
Foxhole Rd, SE9 206 EL85
Foxholes, Wey. KT13 235 BR106
Foxholes Av, Hert. SG13 54 DT09
● **Foxholes Business Pk**, Hert. SG13 54 DT09
Fox Hollow Cl, SE18 187 ES78
Fox Hollow Dr, Bexh. DA7 188 EX83
Foxhollow Dr, Farn.Com. SL2 133 AQ64
Foxhollows, Hat. AL10 67 CV16
London Colney AL2 83 CJ26
Foxholt Gdns, NW10 160 CQ66
Foxhome Cl, Chis. BR7 207 EN93
Foxhounds La, Grav. DA13 212 GA90
Fox Ho, SW11 *off Maysoule Rd* 182 DD84
Chertsey KT16
off Fox La N 215 BF102
Fox Ho Rd, Belv. DA17 189 FB77
Foxlake Rd, Byfleet KT14 234BM112
Foxlands Cl, Wat. WD25 81 BU34
Foxlands Cres, Dag. RM10 149 FC64
Foxlands La, Dag. RM10 149 FC64
Foxlands Rd, Dag. RM10 149 FC64
Fox La, N13 121 DM48
W5 160 CL70
Bookham KT23 252 BY124
Caterham CR3 257 DP121
Keston BR2 244 EJ106
Reigate RH2 272 DB131
Fox La N, Cher. KT16 215 BF102
Fox La S, Cher. KT16
off Guildford St 215 BF102
Foxlees, Wem. HA0 139 CG63
Foxley Cl, E8 10 C2
Loughton IG10 107 EP40
Redhill RH1 288 DG139
Foxley Ct, Sutt. SM2 240 DC108
Foxley Gdns, Pur. CR8 241 DP113
Foxley Hill Rd, Pur. CR8 241 DN112
Foxley Ho, E3
off Bromley High St 22 D2
Foxley La, Pur. CR8 241 DK111
Foxley Rd, SW9 42 F4
Kenley CR8 241 DP114
Thornton Heath CR7 223 DP98
Foxleys, Wat. WD19 116 BY48
Foxley Sq, SW9 42 G6
Foxmead Cl, Enf. EN2 103 DM41
Foxmoor Ct, Denh. UB9
off Broadway E 136 BG58
Foxmore St, SW11 40 E7
Foxon Cl, Cat. CR3 258 DS121
Foxon La, Cat. CR3 258 DR121
Foxon La Gdns, Cat. CR3 258 DS121
Fox Prim Sch, W8 27 J2
Fox Rd, E16 23 L7
Slough SL3 174 AX77
Fox's Path, Mitch. CR4 222 DE96
Foxton Gro, Mitch. CR4 222 DD96
Foxton Rd, Grays RM20 191 FX79
Hoddesdon EN11 71 DZ17
Foxwarren, Clay. KT10 237 CF109
Foxwell Ms, SE4 45 M10
Foxwell St, SE4 45 M10
Fox Wd, Walt. KT12 235 BT108
Foxwood Chase, Wal.Abb. EN9 105 EC35
Foxwood Cl, NW7 118 CS49
Feltham TW13 197 BV90
Foxwood Grn Cl, Enf. EN1 104 DS44
Foxwood Gro, Nthflt DA11 212 GE88
Pratt's Bottom BR6 246EW110
Foxwood Rd, SE3 186 EF84
Bean DA2 211 FV90
Foyle Dr, S.Ock. RM15 171 FU71
Foyle Rd, N17 122 DU53
SE3 47 L3
Frailey Cl, Wok. GU22 249 BB116
Frailey Hill, Wok. GU22 249 BB116
Framewood Rd, Slou. SL2, SL3 154 AW66
Framfield Cl, N12 120 DA48
Framfield Ct, Enf. EN1 104 DS44
Framfield Rd, N5 8 G2
W7 159 CE72
Mitcham CR4 202 DG94
Framlingham Cl, E5
off Detmold Rd 144 DW61
Framlingham Cres, SE9 206 EL91
Frampton Cl, Sutt. SM2 240 DA108
Frampton Ct, Denh. UB9
off Denham Grn La 135 BF58
Frampton Pk Est, E9 10 G6
Frampton Pk Rd, E9 10 G5
Frampton Rd, Epp. CM16 92 EU28
Hounslow TW4 198 BY85
Potters Bar EN6 86 DC30
Frampton St, NW8 16 A5
Hertford SG14 54 DR09
Francemary Rd, SE4 205 EA85
Frances & Dick James Ct, NW7
off Langstone Way 119 CY52
Frances Av, Chaff.Hun. RM16 191 FW77
Maidenhead SL6 152 AC70
Frances Bardsley Sch for Girls, Rom. RM1
off Brentwood Rd 149 FH58
Frances Gdns, S.Ock. RM15 171 FT72
Frances King Sch of English, South Kensington, SW7 27 P8
Victoria, SW1 29 K6
Frances Rd, E4 123 EA51
Windsor SL4 173 AR82
Frances St, SE18 37 J8
Chesham HP5 76 AQ30
Franche Ct Rd, SW17 202 DC90
Franchise St, Chesh. HP5 76 AQ30
Francis Av, Bexh. DA7 188 FA82
Francis Av, Feltham TW13 197 BU90
Ilford IG1 147 ER61
St. Albans AL3 64 CC17
Francis Bacon Maths & Computing Coll, St.Alb. AL1 *off Drakes Dr* 65 CH23
Francis Barber Cl, SW16
off Well Cl 203 DM91
Francis Bentley Ms, SW4
off Old Town 183 DJ83
Franciscan Prim Sch, SW17
off Franciscan Rd 202 DG92
Franciscan Rd, SW17 202 DF92
Francis Chichester Way, SW11 41 H7
Francis Cl, E14 34 G8
Epsom KT19 238 CR105
Shepperton TW17 216 BN98
Francisco Cl, Chaff.Hun. RM16 191 FW77
Francis Combe Acad, Wat. WD25
off Horseshoe La 82 BW32
Francis Ct, Guil. GU2 264 AV132
Francis Gro, SW19 201 CZ93
Francis Holland Sch, Marylebone, NW1 16 E4
Belgravia, SW1 29 H9
Francis Pl, N6
off Holmesdale Rd 143 DH59
Francis Rd, E10 145 EC60
N2 142 DF56
Caterham CR3 258 DR122
Croydon CR0 223 DP101
Dartford DA1 210 FK85
Harrow HA1 139 CG57
Hounslow TW4 178 BX82
Ilford IG1 147 ER61
Orpington BR5 228 EX97
Perivale UB6 159 CH68
Pinner HA5 138 BW57
Wallington SM6 241 DJ107
Ware SG12 55 DX05
Watford WD18 97 BV42
Francis St, E15 13 J3
SW1 29 L8
Ilford IG1 147 ER61
Francis Ter, N19 143 DJ62
Francis Ter Ms, N19
off Francis Ter 143 DJ62
Francis Wk, N1 8 C8
Francis Way, Slou. SL1 153 AK73
Francklyn Gdns, Edg. HA8 118 CN48
Francombe Gdns, Rom. RM1 149 FG58
Franconia Rd, SW4 203 DJ85
Frank Bailey Wk, E12
off Gainsborough Av 147 EN64
Frank Barnes Sch for Deaf Children, NW3 6 B7
Frank Burton Cl, SE7
off Victoria Way 186 EH78
Frank Dixon Cl, SE21 204 DS88
Frank Dixon Way, SE21 204 DS88
Frankfurt Rd, SE24 204 DQ85
Frankham St, SE8 46 A5
Frankland Cl, SE16 32 F7
Croxley Green WD3 114 BN45
Woodford Green IG8 124 EJ50
Frankland Rd, E4 123 EA50
SW7 28 A7
Croxley Green WD3 97 BP44
Franklands Dr, Add. KT15 233 BF108
Franklin Av, Chsht EN7 88 DV30
Slough SL2 153 AP70
Watford WD18 97 BU44
Franklin Cl, N20 120 DC45
SE13 46 C7
SE27 203 DP90
Colney Heath AL4 66 CS22
Hemel Hempstead HP3 62 BL23
Kingston upon Thames KT1 220 CN97
Franklin Ct, Guil. GU2
off Humbolt Cl 264 AT134
Franklin Cres, Mitch. CR4 223 DJ98
Franklin Ho, NW9 141 CT59
Enf. EN3
off Innova Science Pk 105 DZ37
Franklin Pas, SE9 186 EL83
Franklin Pl, SE13 46 C7
Franklin Rd, SE20 204 DW94
Bexleyheath DA7 188 EY81
Dartford DA2 209 FE89
Gravesend DA12 213 GK92
Hornchurch RM12 170 FJ65
Watford WD17 97 BV40
Franklins, Map.Cr. WD3 113 BE49
Franklins Ms, Har. HA2 138 CC61
Franklin Sq, W14 39 H1
Franklin's Row, SW3 28 F10
Franklin St, E3 22 D2
N15 144 DS58
Frank Lunnon Cl, B.End SL8 132 AC60
Franklyn Cres, Wind. SL4 173 AK83
Franklyn Gdns, Ilf. IG6 125 ER51
Franklyn Rd, NW10 161 CT66
Walton-on-Thames KT12 217 BU100
Frank Martin Ct, Wal.Cr. EN7 88 DU30
Frank Ms, SE16 32 E9
Franks Av, N.Mal. KT3 220 CQ98
Franksfield, Peasl. GU5 283 BS144
Franks La, Hort.Kir. DA4 230 FN98
Franks Rd, Guil. GU2 264 AU131
Frank St, E13 23 P5
Frank Sutton Way, Slou. SL1 153 AR73
Frankswood Av, Petts Wd BR5 227 EP99
West Drayton UB7 156 BM72
Frank Towell Ct, Felt. TW14 197 BU87
Franlaw Cres, N13 122 DQ49
Franmil Rd, Horn. RM12 149 FG60
Fransfield Gro, SE26 204 DV90
Frant Cl, SE20 204 DW94
Franthorne Way, SE6 205 EB89
Frant Rd, Th.Hth. CR7 223 DP99
Fraser Cl, E6 24 G8
Bexley DA5 209 FC88
Fraser Ct, W12
off Heathstan Rd 161 CU72
Fraser Gdns, Dor. RH4 285 CG135
Fraser Ho, Brent. TW8
off Green Dragon La 180 CM78
Fraser Rd, E17 145 EB57
N9 122 DV48
Cheshunt EN8 89 DY28
Erith DA8 189 FC78
Perivale UB6 159 CH67
Fraser St, W4 180 CS78
Frating Cres, Wdf.Grn. IG8 124 EG51
Frays Av, West Dr. UB7 176 BK75
Frays Cl, West Dr. UB7 176 BK76
Frayslea, Uxb. UB8 156 BJ68
Frays Waye, Uxb. UB8 156 BJ67
Frazer Av, Ruis. HA4 138 BW64
Frazer Cl, Rom. RM1 149 FF59
Frazier St, SE1 30 E5
Frean St, SE16 32 C6
Freda Corbett Cl, SE15 44 C4
Frederica Rd, E4 123 ED45
Frederica St, N7 8 C6
Frederick Andrews Ct, Grays RM17 192 GD79
Frederick Bremer Sch, E17 *off Fulbourne Rd* 123 EC54
Frederick Cl, W2 16 D10
Sutton SM1 239 CZ105
Frederick Ct, NW2 141 CY62
Frederick Cres, SW9 42 G5
Enfield EN3 104 DW40
Frederick Gdns, Croy. CR0 223 DP100
Sutton SM1 239 CZ106
Frederick Pl, N8
off Crouch Hall Rd 143 DL58
SE18 37 N10
Frog. AL2 *off Curo Pk* 83 CE28
Frederick Rd, SE17 43 H2
Rainham RM13 169 FD68
Sutton SM1 239 CZ106
Frederick's Pl, EC2 19 L9
Fredericks Pl, N12 120 DC49
Frederick Sq, SE16 33 L1
Frederick's Row, EC1 18 G2
Frederick St, WC1 18 C3
Frederick Ter, E8 10 A7
Frederick Vil, W7
off Lower Boston Rd 159 CE74
Frederic Ms, SW1 28 F5
Frederic St, E17 145 DY57
Fredley Pk, Mick. RH5 269 CJ129
Fredora Av, Hayes UB4 157 BT70
Fred White Wk, N7 8 B4
Fred Wigg Twr, E11 146 EF61
Freeborne Gdns, Rain. RM13 169 FG65
Freedom Cl, E17 145 DY56
Freedom Rd, N17 122 DR54
Freedom St, SW11 40 F8
Freedown La, Sutt. SM2 240 DC113
Freegrove Rd, N7 8 B3
Freehold Ind Centre, Houns. TW4
off Amberley Way 198 BW85
Freeland Pk, NW4 119 CY54
Freeland Rd, W5 160 CM73
Freelands Av, S.Croy. CR2 243 DX109
Freelands Gro, Brom. BR1 226 EH95
Freelands Rd, Brom. BR1 226 EH95
Cobham KT11 235 BV114
Freeland Way, Erith DA8
off Slade Grn Rd 189 FG81
Freeling St, N1 8 C7
Freeman Cl, Nthlt. UB5 158 BY66
Shepperton TW17 217 BS98
Freeman Ct, N7
off Tollington Way 143 DL62
SW16 223 DL96
Chesham HP5 *off Barnes Av* 76 AQ30
Freeman Dr, W.Mol. KT8 218 BZ97
Freeman Rd, Grav. DA12 213 GL90
Morden SM4 222 DD99
Freemans Acre, Hat. AL10
off Cunningham Av 66 CR17
Freemans Cl, Stoke P. SL2 154 AT65
Freemans La, Hayes UB3 157 BS73
Freemantle Av, Enf. EN3 105 DX43
Freemantles Sch, Wok. GU22
off Smarts Heath Rd 248AW122
Freemantle St, SE17 31 N10
Freeman Way, Horn. RM11 150 FL58
★ **Freemason's Hall** (United Grand Lo of England), WC2 18 B8
Freemasons Pl, Croy. CR0
off Freemasons Rd 224 DS102
Freemasons Rd, E16 24 A7
Croydon CR0 224 DS102
Free Prae Rd, Cher. KT16 216 BG102
Freesia Cl, Orp. BR6 245 ET106
Freethorpe Cl, SE19 224 DR95
Free Trade Wf, E1 21 J10
Freezeland Way, Hlgdn UB10 157 BP65
FREEZYWATER, Wal.Cr. EN8 105 DY35
Freezywater St. George's Prim Sch, Enf. EN3
off Hertford Rd 105 DX36
★ **Freightliners Fm**, N7 8 D4
● **Freightmaster Est**, Rain. RM13 189 FG76
Freke Rd, SW11 182 DG83
Fremantle Ho, Til. RM18 193 GF81
Fremantle Rd, Belv. DA17 188 FA77
Ilford IG6 125 EQ54
Fremont St, E9 10 G8
French Apts, The, Pur. CR8
off Lansdowne Rd 241 DN112
Frenchaye, Add. KT15 234 BJ106
Frenches, The, Red. RH1 272 DG132
Frenches Ct, Red. RH1
off Frenches Rd 272 DG132
Frenches Rd, Red. RH1 272 DG132
French Gdns, Cob. KT11 236BW114
French Horn La, Hat. AL10 67 CV17
Frenchlands Gate, E.Hors. KT24 267 BS127
French Ordinary Ct, EC3 19 P10
French Pl, E1 19 P4
French Row, St.Alb. AL3
off Market Pl 65 CD20
French's Cl, Stans.Abb. SG12 55 EB11
French St, Sun. TW16 218 BW96
Westerham TN16 277 ES128
French's Wells, Wok. GU21 248 AV117
Frenchum Gdns, Slou. SL1 153 AL74
Frendsbury Rd, SE4 185 DY84
Frensham, Chsht EN7 88 DT27
Frensham Cl, Sthl. UB1 158 BZ70
Frensham Ct, Mitch. CR4 222 DD97
Frensham Dr, SW15 201 CU89
New Addington CR0 243 EC108
Frensham Rd, SE9 207 ER89
Kenley CR8 241 DP114
Frensham St, SE15 44 D3
Frensham Wk, Farn.Com. SL2 133 AQ64
Frensham Way, Epsom KT17 255CW116
Frere St, SW11 40 D8
Freshborough Ct, Guil. GU1
off Lower Edgeborough Rd 281 AZ135
Freshfield Av, E8 10 A7
Freshfield Cl, SE13
off Mercator Rd 185 ED84
Freshfield Dr, N14 121 DH45
Freshfields, Croy. CR0 225 DZ101
Freshfields Av, Upmin. RM14 150 FP64
Freshford St, SW18 202 DC90
Freshmount Gdns, Epsom KT19 238 CP111
Freshwater Cl, SW17 202 DG93
Freshwater Rd, SW17 202 DG93
Dagenham RM8 148 EX60
Freshwaters, Harl. CM20
off School La 57 ES14
Freshwell Av, Rom. RM6 148 EW56
Fresh Wf, Bark. IG11 167 EP67
● **Fresh Wf Est**, Bark. IG11
off Fresh Wf 167 EP67
Freshwood Cl, Beck. BR3 225 EB95
Freshwood Way, Wall. SM6 241 DH109
Freston Gdns, Barn. EN4 102 DG43
Freston Pk, N3 119 CZ54
Freston Rd, W10 14 C10
W11 26 D1
Freta Rd, Bexh. DA6 208 EZ85
Fretherne Rd, Welw.G.C. AL8 51 CX09
Fretwell Ho, N14
off Chase Side 121 DK46
★ **Freud Mus**, NW3 6 A4
Frewin Rd, SW18 202 DD88
Friar Ms, SE27 203 DP90
Friar Rd, Hayes UB4 158 BX70
Orpington BR5 228 EU99
Friars, The, Chig. IG7 125 ES49
Harlow CM19 73 EN17
Friars Av, N20 120 DE48
SW15 201 CT90
Shenfield CM15 131 GA46
Friars Cl, E4 123 EC48
SE1 30 G3
Ilford IG1 147 ER60
Northolt UB5
off Broomcroft Av 158 BX69
Shenfield CM15 131 FZ45
Friarscroft, Brox. EN10 71 EA20
Friars Fld, Nthch HP4
off Herons Elm 60 AS16
Friars Gdns, W3
off St. Dunstans Av 160 CR72
Friars Gate, Guil. GU2 280 AU136
Friars Gate Cl, Wdf.Grn. IG8 124 EG49
Friars La, Hat.Hth CM22 59 FH06
Richmond TW9 199 CK85
Friars Mead, E14 34 E7
Friars Ms, SE9 207 EN85
Friars Orchard, Fetch. KT22 253 CD121
Friars Pl La, W3 160 CR73
Friars Prim Sch, SE1 31 H4
Friars Ri, Wok. GU22 249 BA118
Friars Rd, E6 166 EK67
Virginia Water GU25 214 AX98
Friars Stile Pl, Rich. TW10
off Friars Stile Rd 200 CL86
Friars Stile Rd, Rich. TW10 200 CL86
Friar St, EC4 19 H9
Friars Wk, N14 121 DH46
SE2 188 EX78
Friars Way, W3 160 CR72
Bushey WD23 98 BZ39
Chertsey KT16 216 BG100
Kings Langley WD4 80 BN30
Friars Wd, Croy. CR0 243 DY109
Friary, The, Old Wind. SL4 194 AW86
Waltham Cross EN8 89 DZ33
Friary Br, Guil. GU1 280AW135
Friary Cl, N12 120 DE50
Friary Ct, SW1 29 M3
Woking GU21 248 AT118
Friary Est, SE15 44 D3
Friary Island, Wrays. TW19 194 AW86
Friary La, Wdf.Grn. IG8 124 EG49
Friary Pk Est, W3
off Friary Rd 160 CR72
Friary Pas, Guil. GU1
off Friary St 280AW136
Friary Rd, N12 120 DD49
SE15 44 D3
W3 160 CR72
Wraysbury TW19 194 AW86
Friary Shop Cen, The, Guil. GU1 *off Onslow St* 280AW135
Friary St, Guil. GU1 280AW136
Friary Way, N12 120 DE49
FRIDAY HILL, E4 123 ED47
Friday Hill, E4 124 EE47
Friday Hill E, E4 124 EE48
Friday Hill W, E4 124 EE47
Friday Rd, Erith DA8 189 FD78
Mitcham CR4 202 DF94
FRIDAY STREET, Dor. RH5 284 BZ143
Friday St, EC4 19 J9
Abinger Common RH5 284 BZ143
Frideswide Pl, NW5 7 L3
Friendly Pl, SE13 46 D7
Friendly St, SE8 46 A8
Friendly St Ms, SE8 46 A8
Friends Av, Chsht EN8 89 DX31
Friendship Wk, Nthlt. UB5
off Wayfarer Rd 158 BX69
Friendship Way, E15 12 F8
Friends Rd, Croy. CR0 224 DR104
Purley CR8 241 DP112
Friend St, EC1 18 G2
Friends Wk, Stai. TW18 195 BF92
Uxbridge UB8
off Bakers Rd 156 BK66
FRIERN BARNET, N11 120 DE49
Friern Barnet La, N11 120 DE49
N20 120 DE49
Friern Barnet Rd, N11 120 DF50
Friern Barnet Sch, N11
off Hemington Av 120 DF50
Friern Br Retail Pk, N11 121 DH51
Friern Cl, Chsht EN7 88 DS26
Friern Ct, N20 120 DD48
Friern Mt Dr, N20 120 DC45
Friern Pk, N12 120 DC50
Friern Rd, SE22 204 DU86
Friern Watch Av, N12 120 DC49
Frigate Ms, SE8 46 A2
Frimley Av, Horn. RM11 150 FN60
Wallington SM6 241 DL106
Frimley Cl, SW19 201 CY89
New Addington CR0 243 EC108
Frimley Ct, Sid. DA14 208 EV92
Frimley Cres, New Adgtn CR0 243 EC108
Frimley Dr, Slou. SL1 173 AM75
Frimley Gdns, Mitch. CR4 222 DE97
Frimley Rd, Chess. KT9 238 CL106
Hemel Hempstead HP1 61 BE19
Ilford IG3 147 ES62
Frimley Way, E1 21 J4
Fringewood Cl, Nthwd. HA6 115 BP53
Frinstead Gro, Orp. BR5 228 EX98
Frinstead Ho, W10 14 C10
Frinsted Rd, Erith DA8 189 FD80
Frinton Cl, Wat. WD19 115 BV47
Frinton Dr, Wdf.Grn. IG8 123 ED52

Frinton Ms, Ilf. IG2 147 EN58
Frinton Rd, E6 24 E3
N15 144 DS58
SW17 202 DG93
Romford RM5 126 EZ52
Sidcup DA14 208 EY89
Friston Path, Chig. IG7 125 ES50
Friston St, SW6 39 L9
Friswell Pl, Bexh. DA6 188 FA84
Fritham Cl, N.Mal. KT3 220 CS100
Frith Ct, NW7 119 CY52
Frithe, The, Slou. SL2 154 AV72
Frith Knowle, Hersham KT12 235 BV106
Frith La, NW7 119 CY52
Sch **Frith Manor Prim Sch**, N12
off Lullington Garth 119 CZ50
Frith Rd, E11 145 EC63
Croydon CR0 224 DQ103
Frithsden Copse, Pott.End HP4 61 AZ15
Frithsden Rd, Berk. HP4 60 AY17
Friths Dr, Reig. RH2 272 DB131
Frith St, W1 17 N9
Frithville Gdns, W12 26 A2
Frithwald Rd, Cher. KT16 215 BF101
Frithwood Av, Nthwd. HA6 115 BS51
Sch **Frithwood Prim Sch**, Nthwd.
HA6 *off Carew Rd* 115 BT51
Frizlands La, Dag. RM10 149 FB63
Frobisher Cl, Bushey WD23 98 CA44
Kenley CR8 *off Hayes La* 258 DQ117
Pinner HA5 138 BX59
Frobisher Cres, EC2
off The Barbican 19 K6
Staines-upon-Thames TW19 196 BL87
Frobisher Gdns, Chaff.Hun.
RM16 192 FY76
Guildford GU1 265 BA133
Staines-upon-Thames TW19 196 BL87
Frobisher Ms, Enf. EN2 104 DR42
Frobisher Pas, E14 34 B2
Frobisher Pl, SE15 44 G7
Frobisher Rd, E6 25 K8
N8 143 DN56
Erith DA8 189 FF80
St. Albans AL1 65 CJ22
Frobisher St, SE10 47 K2
Frobisher Way, Grav. DA12 213 GL92
Greenhithe DA9 191 FV84
Hatfield AL10 66 CR15
Froggy La, Denh. UB9 135 BD62
Froghall La, Chig. IG7 125 ER49
FROGHOLE, Eden. TN8 277 ER133
Froghole La, Eden. TN8 277 ER132
Frog La, Sutt.Grn GU4 264 AY125
Frogley Rd, SE22 184 DT84
Frogmoor La, Rick. WD3 114 BK47
FROGMORE, St.Alb. AL2 83 CE28
Frogmore, SW18 202 DA85
St. Albans AL2 83 CD27
Frogmore Av, Hayes UB4 157 BS69
Frogmore Cl, Slou. SL1 173 AN75
Sutton SM3 221 CX104
Frogmore Dr, Wind. SL4 174 AS81
● **Frogmore Est**, Grays
RM20 191 FU78
Frogmore Gdns, Hayes UB4 157 BS70
Sutton SM3 239 CY105
Frogmore Home Pk,
St.Alb. AL2 83 CD27
● **Frogmore Ind Est**, N5 9 J1
NW10 160 CQ69
Frogmore Rd, Hem.H. HP3 62 BK23
Frognal, NW3 5 N4
Frognal Av, Har. HA1 139 CF56
Sidcup DA14 208 EU92
Frognal Cl, NW3 5 N2
Jct **Frognal Cor**, Sid. DA14 207 ET93
Frognal Ct, NW3 5 P4
Frognal Gdns, NW3 5 N1
Frognal La, NW3 5 L2
Frognal Par, NW3
off Frognal Ct 5 P4
Frognal Pl, Sid. DA14 208 EU93
Frognal Ri, NW3 142 DC63
Frognal Way, NW3 5 N1
Froissart Rd, SE9 206 EK85
Frome Rd, N22 143 DP55
Fromer Rd, Woob.Grn HP10 132 AD59
Frome Sq, Hem.H. HP2
off Waveney 62 BM15
Frome St, N1 9 J10
Fromondes Rd, Sutt. SM3 239 CY106
Front, The, Pott.End HP4 61 BB16
Front La, Upmin. RM14 151 FS59
Frostic Wk, E1 20 B7
Froude St, SW8 41 K9
Frowick Cl, N.Mymms AL9 67 CW23
Frowyke Cres, S.Mimms EN6 85 CU32
Fruen Rd, Felt. TW14 197 BT87
Fruiterers Pas, EC4
off Southwark Br 31 K1
Fryatt Rd, N17 122 DR52
Fry Cl, Rom. RM5 126 FA50
Fryday Gro Ms, SW12 203 DJ87
Fryent Cl, NW9 140 CN58
Fryent Cres, NW9 140 CS58
Fryent Flds, NW9 140 CS58
Fryent Gro, NW9 140 CS58
Sch **Fryent Prim Sch**, NW9
off Church La 140 CQ59
Fryent Way, NW9 140 CN57
Fryer Cl, Chesh. HP5 76 AR33
Fryern Wd, Chaldon CR3 258 DQ124
Frying Pan All, E1 20 A7
Frymley Vw, Wind. SL4 173 AK81
Fry Rd, E6 166 EK66
NW10 161 CT67
Fryston Av, Couls. CR5 241 DH114
Croydon CR0 224 DU103
Fryth Mead, St.Alb. AL3 64 CB19
Fuchsia Cl, Rush Grn RM7 149 FE61
Fuchsia St, SE2 188 EV78
Fulbeck Dr, NW9 118 CS53
Fulbeck Wk, Edg. HA8
off Burrell Cl 118 CP47
Fulbeck Way, Har. HA2 116 CC54
Fulbourne Cl, Red. RH1
off Dennis Cl 272 DE132
Fulbourne Rd, E17 123 EC53
Fulbourne St, E1 20 E6
Fulbrook Av, New Haw KT15 234 BG111
Fulbrook La, S.Ock. RM15 171 FT73
Fulbrook Ms, N19
off Junction Rd 143 DJ63
Fulbrook Rd, N19
off Junction Rd 143 DJ63
Fulford Gro, Wat. WD19 115 BV47
Fulford Rd, Cat. CR3 258 DR121
Epsom KT19 238 CR108
Fulford St, SE16 32 F5
FULHAM, SW6 38 E8
Fulham Br, SW15 181 CY83
⊖ **Fulham Broadway** 39 K4
Fulham Bdy, SW6 39 K4
Fulham Bdy Retail Cen,
SW6 *off Fulham Bdy* 39 K4
Fulham Cl, Uxb. UB10 157 BQ71
Fulham Ct, SW6 39 J6
Sch **Fulham Cross Girls' Sch**,
SW6 38 E4
★ **Fulham FC**, SW6 38 C7
Fulham High St, SW6 38 F9
★ **Fulham Palace**, SW6 38 E9
Fulham Palace Rd, SW6 38 D4
W6 26 B10
Fulham Pk Gdns, SW6 38 G9
Fulham Pk Rd, SW6 38 G8
Sch **Fulham Prep Sch**,
Pre-Prep, SW6 38 F9
Prep, W14 38 F2
Sch **Fulham Prim Sch**, SW6 39 J3
Fulham Rd, SW3 40 A1
SW6 39 L5
SW10 40 A1
Fulkes Cotts, Lthd. KT24 267 BP128
Fullarton Cres, S.Ock. RM15 171 FT72
Fullbrooks Av, Wor.Pk. KT4 221 CT102
Sch **Fullbrook Sch**, New Haw
KT15 *off Selsdon Rd* 234 BG111
Fuller Cl, E2 20 C4
Bushey WD23 117 CD45
Orpington BR6 245 ET106
Fuller Gdns, Wat. WD24 97 BV37
Fullerian Cres, Wat. WD18 97 BT42
Fuller Rd, Dag. RM8 148 EV62
Watford WD24 97 BV37
Fullers Av, Surb. KT6 220 CM103
Woodford Green IG8 124 EF52
Fullers Cl, Chesh. HP5 76 AP32
Romford RM5 127 FC52
Waltham Abbey EN9 90 EG33
Fullers Fm Rd, W.Hors. KT24 267 BP134
★ **Fuller's Griffin Brewery**,
W4 181 CT79
Fullers Hill, Chesh. HP5 76 AM34
Hyde Heath HP6 76 AM34
Westerham TN16
off Market Sq 277 ER126
Fullers La, Rom. RM5 127 FC52
Fullers Mead, Harl. CM17 74 EW16
Fullers Rd, E18 124 EF53
Fuller St, NW4 141 CW56
Fullers Way N, Surb. KT6 220 CM104
Fullers Way S, Chess. KT9 238 CL105
Fullers Wd, Croy. CR0 243 EA106
Fullers Wd La, S.Nutfld RH1 273 DJ134
Fuller Ter, Ilf. IG1
off Oaktree Gro 147 ER64
Fullerton Cl, Byfleet KT14 234 BM114
Fullerton Dr, Byfleet KT14 234 BL114
Fullerton Rd, SW18 202 DC85
Byfleet KT14 234 BM114
Carshalton SM5 240 DE109
Croydon CR0 224 DT101
Fullerton Way, Byfleet KT14 234 BL114
Fuller Way, Crox.Grn WD3 96 BN43
Hayes UB3 177 BT78
Fullmer Way, Wdhm KT15 233 BF110
Fullwell Av, Ilf. IG5, IG6 125 EM53
FULLWELL CROSS, Ilf. IG6 125 ER53
Fullwell Cross Rbt, Ilf. IG6
off High St 125 ER54
Sch **Fullwood Prim Sch**, Barkingside
IG6 *off Burford Cl* 147 EQ56
Fullwoods Ms, N1 19 M2
Fulmar Cl, Surb. KT5 220 CM100
Fulmar Cres, Hem.H. HP1 62 BG21
Fulmar Rd, Horn. RM12 169 FG66
Fulmead St, SW6 39 M7
FULMER, Slou. SL3 134 AX63
Fulmer Cl, Hmptn. TW12 198 BY92
Fulmer Common Rd, Fulmer
SL3 155 AZ65
Iver SL0 155 AZ65
Fulmer Dr, Ger.Cr. SL9 134 AY61
Sch **Fulmer Inf Sch**, Fulmer
SL3 *off Alderbourne La* 134 AY63
Fulmer La, Fulmer SL3 134 AY62
Gerrards Cross SL9 135 BB60
Fulmer Ri, Fulmer SL3 155 AZ65
Fulmer Rd, E16 24 E7
Fulmer SL3 134 AY63
Gerrards Cross SL9 134 AY59
Fulmer Way, W13 179 CH76
Gerrards Cross SL9 134 AY58
Fulready Rd, E10 145 ED57
Fulstone Cl, Houns. TW4 178 BZ84
Fulthorp Rd, SE3 47 M8
Fulton Ct, Borwd. WD6 100 CM38
Enfield EN3
off Harston Dr 105 EA38
Fulton Ms, W2 15 N10
Fulton Rd, Wem. HA9 140 CN62
Fulvens, Peasl. GU5 283 BS143
Fulvens Cotts, Peasl. GU5 283 BS142
⇌ **Fulwell** 199 CD91
Fulwell Pk Av, Twick. TW2 198 CB89
Fulwell Rd, Tedd. TW11 199 CD91
Fulwich Rd, Dart. DA1 210 FM86
Fulwood Av, Wem. HA0 160 CM67
Fulwood Cl, Hayes UB3 157 BT72
Fulwood Gdns, Twick. TW1 199 CF86
Fulwood Pl, WC1 18 D7
Fulwood Wk, SW19 201 CY88
Furber St, W6 181 CV76
Furham Feild, Pnr. HA5 116 CA52
Furley Rd, SE15 44 D5
Furlong Cl, Wall. SM6 223 DH102
Furlong Rd, N7 8 F4
Westcott RH4 284 CC137
Furlongs, Hem.H. HP1 62 BG19
Furlongs, The, Esher KT10 218 CB104
Furlong Way, Gat. RH6 290 DF151
off Racecourse Way
Great Amwell SG12 55 DZ09
Furlough, The, Wok. GU22
off Pembroke Rd 249 BA117
Furmage St, SW18 202 DB87
Furneaux Av, SE27 203 DP92
Furner Cl, Dart. DA1 189 FF83
Furness, Wind. SL4 172 AJ82
Furness Cl, Grays RM16 193 GH78
Furness Pl, Wind. SL4
off Furness 172 AJ82
Sch **Furness Prim Sch**, NW10
off Palermo Rd 161 CU68
Furness Rd, NW10 161 CU68
SW6 39 M8
Furness Rd, Harrow HA2 138 CB59
Morden SM4 222 DB101
Furness Row, Wind. SL4
off Furness 172 AJ82
Sch **Furness Sch**, Hext. BR8
off Rowhill Rd 209 FF93
Furness Sq, Wind. SL4
off Furness 172 AJ82
Furness Wk, Wind. SL4
off Furness 172 AJ82
Furness Way, Horn. RM12 149 FG64
Windsor SL4 172 AJ82
Furnival Av, Slou. SL2 153 AP71
Furnival Cl, Vir.W. GU25 214 AX100
Furnival St, EC4 18 E8
Furrowfield, Hat. AL10
off Stonecross Rd 67 CV16
Furrow La, E9 11 H3
Furrows, The, Hare. UB9 136 BJ57
Walton-on-Thames KT12 218 BW103
Furrows Pl, Cat. CR3 258 DT123
Fursby Av, N3 120 DA51
Furse Av, St.Alb. AL4 65 CG17
Further Acre, NW9 119 CT54
Furtherfield, Abb.L. WD5 81 BS32
Furtherfield Cl, Croy. CR0 223 DN100
Further Grn Rd, SE6 206 EE87
Furtherground, Hem.H. HP2 62 BL21
Furzebushes La, St.Alb. AL2 82 BY25
Furze Cl, Horl. RH6 291 DK148
Redhill RH1 272 DF133
Watford WD19 116 BW50
FURZEDOWN, SW17 202 DG92
Furzedown Cl, Egh. TW20 194 AY93
Furzedown Dr, SW17 203 DH92
Furzedown Hall, SW17
off Spalding Rd 203 DH92
Sch **Furzedown Prim Sch**, SW17
off Beclands Rd 202 DG93
Furzedown Rd, SW17 203 DH92
Sutton SM2 240 DC111
Furze Fm Cl, Rom. RM6 126 EY54
Furzefield, Chsht EN8 88 DV28
Furze Fld, Oxshott KT22 237 CD113
Furzefield Cl, Chis. BR7 207 EP93
Furzefield Ct, Pot.B. EN6 85 CY31
Furzefield Cres, Reig. RH2 288 DC136
Sch **Furzefield Prim Comm Sch**,
Merst. RH1
off Delabole Rd 273 DK128
Furzefield Rd, SE3 186 EH79
Beaconsfield HP9 110 AJ53
Reigate RH2 288 DC136
Welwyn Garden City AL7 51 CY10
Furzeground Way, Uxb. UB11 157 BQ74
Furze Gro, Kgswd KT20 255 CZ121
Furzeham Rd, West Dr. UB7 176 BL75
Furze Hill, Kgswd KT20 255 CZ120
Purley CR8 241 DL111
Redhill RH1
off Linkfield La 272 DE133
Furzehill Par, Borwd. WD6
off Shenley Rd 100 CN41
Furzehill Rd, Borwd. WD6 100 CN42
Furzehill Sq, St.M.Cray BR5 228 EV98
Sch **Furze Inf Sch**, Chad.Hth
RM6 *off Bennett Rd* 148 EY58
Furze La, Gdmg. GU7 280 AT143
Purley CR8 241 DL111
Furzen Cl, Slou. SL2 153 AN69
Furzen Cres, Hat. AL10 67 CT21
Furze Rd, Add. KT15 233 BF107
Hemel Hempstead HP1 61 BE21
Thornton Heath CR7 224 DQ97
Furze St, E3 22 B6
Furze Vw, Chorl. WD3 95 BC44
Furzewood, Sun. TW16 217 BU95
Fuschia Ct, Wdf.Grn. IG8
off The Bridle Path 124 EE52
Fusedale Way, S.Ock. RM15 171 FT73
Fusiliers Way, Houns. TW4 178 BW83
Fuzzens Wk, Wind. SL4 173 AL82
Fyefoot La, EC4
off Queen Victoria St 19 J10
Fyfe Apts, N8
off Chadwell La 143 DM55
Fyfe Way, Brom. BR1
off Widmore Rd 226 EG96
Fyfield, N4
off Six Acres Est 143 DN61
Fyfield Cl, Brom. BR2 225 ED98
Fyfield Ct, E7 13 N4
Fyfield Dr, S.Ock. RM15 171 FT73
Fyfield Rd, E17 145 ED55
SW9 42 F10
Enfield EN1 104 DS41
Rainham RM13 169 FF67
Woodford Green IG8 124 EJ52
Fynes St, SW1 29 N8

G

Gabion Av, Purf. RM19 191 FR77
Gable Cl, Abb.L. WD5 81 BS32
Dartford DA1 209 FG85
Pinner HA5 116 CA52
Gable Ct, SE26
off Lawrie Pk Av 204 DV91
Gables, The, Bans. SM7 255 CZ117
Guildford GU2 264 AV131
Hemel Hempstead HP2
off Chapel St 62 BK19
Oxshott KT22 236 CC112
Wembley HA9 140 CN62
Gables Av, Ashf. TW15 196 BM92
Borehamwood WD6 100 CM41
Gables Cl, SE5 43 N6
SE12 206 EG88
Chalfont St. Peter SL9 112 AY49
Datchet SL3 174 AU79
Kingfield GU22
off Kingfield Rd 249 AZ120
Gables Ct, Kgfld GU22
off Kingfield Rd 249 AZ120
Pur. CR8 *off Godstone Rd* 241 DP112
Gables Way, Bans. SM7 255 CZ117
Gabriel Cl, Chaff.Hun. RM16 191 FW76
Feltham TW13 198 BX91
Romford RM5 127 FC52
Gabriel Gdns, Grav. DA12 213 GL92
Gabrielle Cl, Wem. HA9 140 CM62
Gabrielle Ct, NW3 6 B5
Gabrielle Ho, Ilf. IG2
off Perth Rd 147 EN58
Gabriel Ms, NW2 141 CZ61
Gabriel's Ms, Beck. BR3 225 DX95
Gabriel Spring Rd, Fawk.Grn
DA3 231 FR103
Gabriel Spring Rd (East),
Fawk.Grn DA3 231 FS103
Gabriel St, SE23 205 DX87
Gabriel's Wf, SE1 30 E2
Gadbrook Rd, Bet. RH3 286 CS139
Gad Cl, E13 24 A2
Gaddesden Av, Wem. HA9 160 CM65
Gaddesden Cres, Wat. WD25 82 BX34
Gaddesden Gro, Welw.G.C.
AL7 *off Widford Rd* 52 DC09
Gade Av, Wat. WD18 97 BS42
Gade Bk, Crox.Grn WD3 97 BR42
GADEBRIDGE, Hem.H. HP1 61 BF18
Gadebridge La, Hem.H. HP1 62 BJ18
Gadebridge Rd, Hem.H. HP1 62 BG18
Gadebury Hts, Hem.H. HP1 62 BJ20
Gade Cl, Hayes UB3 157 BV74
Hemel Hempstead HP1 62 BH17
Watford WD18 97 BS42
Gadesden Rd, Epsom KT19 238 CQ107
Gadeside, Wat. WD25 97 BS35
Gade Twr, Hem.H. HP3 80 BN25
Gade Valley Cl, Kings L. WD4 80 BN28
Sch **Gade Valley JMI Sch**,
Hem.H. HP1
off Gadebridge Rd 62 BH19
Gade Vw Gdns, Kings L. WD4 81 BQ32
Gadeview Rd, Hem.H. HP3 62 BK24
Gadsbury Cl, NW9 141 CT58
Gadsden Cl, Upmin. RM14 151 FS58
Gadswell Cl, Wat. WD25 98 BX36
Gadwall Cl, E16 24 A8
Gadwall Way, SE28 187 ER75
Gage Ms, S.Croy. CR2 242 DQ106
Gage Rd, E16 23 K6
Gage St, WC1 18 B6
Gainford St, N1 8 E8
Gainsboro Gdns, Grnf. UB6 139 CE64
Gainsborough Av, E12 147 EN64
Dartford DA1 210 FJ85
St. Albans AL1 65 CF19
Tilbury RM18 193 GG81
Gainsborough Cl, Beck. BR3 205 EA94
Esher KT10 219 CE102
Sch **Gainsborough Comm Sch**,
E9 12 A4
Gainsborough Ct, N12 120 DB50
W12 26 A5
Bromley BR2 226 EJ98
Walton-on-Thames KT12 235 BU105
Gainsborough Dr, Nthflt DA11 212 GD90
South Croydon CR2 242 DU113
Gainsborough Gdns, NW3 142 DD62
NW11 141 CZ59
Edgware HA8 118 CM54
Isleworth TW7 199 CD85
Gainsborough Ho, E14 34 B5
Enfield EN1 *off Ayley Cft* 104 DU43
Gainsborough Ms, SE26
off Panmure Rd 204 DV90
Gainsborough Pl, Chig. IG7 125 ET48
Cobham KT11 252 BY115
Sch **Gainsborough Prim Sch**,
E15 23 K3
Gainsborough Rd, E11 146 EE59
E15 23 J3
N12 120 DB50
W4 181 CT77
Dagenham RM8 148 EV63
Epsom KT19 238 CQ110
Hayes UB4 157 BQ68
New Malden KT3 220 CR101
Rainham RM13 169 FG67
Richmond TW9 180 CM83
Woodford Green IG8 124 EL51
Gainsborough Sq, Bexh. DA6
off Regency Way 188 EX83
Gainsborough St, E9 11 P5
Gainsborough Studios, N1 9 L9
Gainsford Rd, E17 145 DZ56
Gainsford St, SE1 32 A4
Gainswood, Welw.G.C. AL7 51 CY10
Gairloch Rd, SE5 43 P8
Gaisford St, NW5 7 L4
Gaist Av, Cat. CR3 258 DU122
Gaitskell Ct, SW11 40 B8
Gaitskell Ho, Borwd. WD6 100 CR42
Gaitskell Rd, SE9 207 EQ88
Gaitskell Way, SE1
off Weller St 31 J4
Galahad Cl, Slou. SL1 173 AN75
Galahad Rd, N9 122 DU48
Bromley BR1 206 EG90
Galata Rd, SW13 181 CU80
Galatea Sq, SE15 44 E10
Galaxy, E14 *off Crews St* 34 A8
Galba Ct, Brent. TW8
off Augustus Cl 179 CK80
Galbraith St, E14 34 E6
Galdana Av, Barn. EN5 102 DC41
Galeborough Av, Wdf.Grn. IG8 123 ED52
Gale Cl, Hmptn. TW12 198 BY93
Mitcham CR4 222 DD97
Gale Cres, Bans. SM7 256 DA117
Galena Ho, SE18
off Grosmont Rd 187 ET78
Galena Rd, W6 181 CV77
Galen Cl, Epsom KT19 238 CN111
Galen Pl, WC1 18 B7
Galesbury Rd, SW18 202 DC86
Gales Cl, Guil. GU4
off Gilliat Dr 265 BD132
Gales Gdns, E2 20 F3
Gale St, E3 22 B6
Dagenham RM9 168 EX67
Gales Way, Wdf.Grn. IG8 124 EL52
Galey Grn, S.Ock. RM15
off Bovey Way 171 FV71
Galgate Cl, SW19 201 CY88
Gallants Fm Rd, E.Barn. EN4 120 DE45
Galleon Boul, Dart. DA2 191 FR84
Galleon Cl, SE16 33 H4
Erith DA8 189 FD77
Galleon Ho, SW8
off St. George Wf 42 A2
Galleon Ms, Grav. DA11
off Maritime Gate 212 GE87
Galleon Rd, Chaff.Hun. RM16 191 FW77
Galleons Dr, Bark. IG11 168 EU69
Galleons La, Geo.Grn SL3 154 AX71
Galleons Vw, E14
off Stewart St 34 F5
Galleria, The, Hat. AL10 66 CS18
Galleries, The, Brwd. CM14 130 FV50
Gallery Ct, Egh. TW20
off The Chantries 195 BA92
Gallery Gdns, Nthlt. UB5 158 BX68
Gallery Rd, SE21 204 DR88
Galley, The, E16 37 P1
Galley Grn, Hailey SG13 55 EA13
Galley Hill, Hem.H. HP1 61 BF18
Waltham Abbey EN9 90 EF30
Galley Hill Rd, Nthflt DA11 212 FZ85
Swanscombe DA10 212 FZ85
● **Galley Hill Trade Pk**,
Swans. DA10 212 FY85
Galley La, Barn. EN5 101 CV41
Galleymead Rd, Colnbr. SL3 175 BF81
Galleywall Rd, SE16 32 E9
Galleywood Cres, Rom. RM5 127 FD51
Galliard Cl, N9 104 DW44
Sch **Galliard Prim Sch**, N9
off Galliard Rd 104 DU44
Galliard Rd, N9 122 DU46
Gallia Rd, N5 9 H3
Gallica Ct, Sutt. SM1
off Cleeve Way 222 DB102
Gallions Cl, Bark. IG11 168 EU69
Sch **Gallions Mt Prim Sch**,
SE18 *off Purrett Rd* 187 ET78
Sch **Gallions Prim Sch**, E6 25 N8
DLR **Gallions Reach** 25 P10
Gallions Reach Shop Pk,
E6 167 EQ71
Gallions Rd, E16 37 P1
SE7 36 B9
Jct **Gallions Rbt**, E16 25 N10
Gallions Vw Rd, SE28
off Goldfinch Rd 187 ES75
Gallon Cl, SE7 36 D9
Gallop, The, S.Croy. CR2 242 DV108
Sutton SM2 240 DC108
Gallops, The, Esher KT10 218 CB104
Tadworth KT20 271 CV126
Gallosson Rd, SE18 187 ES77
Galloway Chase, Slou. SL2 154 AU73
Galloway Cl, Brox. EN10 89 DZ26
Galloway Dr, Dart. DA1 209 FE87
Galloway Path, Croy. CR0 242 DR105
Galloway Rd, W12 161 CU74
Jct **Gallows Cor**, Harold Wd
RM3 128 FK53
Gallows Hill, Kings L. WD4 81 BQ31
Gallows Hill La, Abb.L. WD5 81 BQ32
Gallus Cl, N21 103 DM44
Gallus Sq, SE3 186 EH83
Gallys Rd, Wind. SL4 173 AK82
Galpins Rd, Th.Hth. CR7 223 DM98
Galsworthy Av, E14 21 M7
Romford RM6 148 EV59
Galsworthy Cl, SE28 168 EV74
Galsworthy Cres, SE3
off Merriman Rd 186 EJ81
Galsworthy Rd, NW2 141 CY63
Chertsey KT16 216 BG101
Kingston upon Thames KT2 200 CP94
Tilbury RM18 193 GJ81
Galsworthy Ter, N16 144 DS62
Galton St, W10 14 E4
Galva Cl, Barn. EN4 102 DG42
Galvani Way, Croy. CR0
off Ampere Way 223 DM102
Galveston Rd, SW15 201 CZ85
Galvin Rd, Slou. SL1 153 AQ74
Galvins Cl, Guil. GU2 264 AU131
Galway Cl, SE16 44 F1
Galway Ho, EC1 19 K3
Galway St, EC1 19 K3
Gambetta St, SW8 41 K9
Gambia St, SE1 31 H3
Gambier Ho, EC1 19 K2
Gambles La, Ripley GU23 250 BJ124
Gambole Rd, SW17 202 DE91
Games Ho, SE7
off Springfield Gro 186 EJ79
Games Rd, Barn. EN4 102 DF41
Gamlen Rd, SW15 181 CX84
Gammon Cl, Hem.H. HP3 62 BN21
Gammons Fm Cl, Wat. WD24 97 BT36
Gammons La, Brox. EN10 88 DT25
Watford WD24 97 BV38
Gamuel Cl, E17 145 EA58
Gander Grn Cres, Hmptn.
TW12 218 CA95
Gander Grn La, Sutt.
SM1, SM3 221 CY103
Ganders Ash, Wat. WD25 81 BU33
Gandhi Cl, E17 145 EA58
Gandolfi St, SE15 43 N3
Gangers Hill, Gdse. RH9 275 EA127
Woldingham CR3 275 EA127
Ganghill, Guil. GU1 265 BA132
Ganley Ct, SW11
off Newcomen Rd 182 DD83
Ganley Rd, SW11 40 B10
Gant Ct, Wal.Abb. EN9 90 EF34
Ganton St, W1 17 L10
Ganton Wk, Wat. WD19 116 BX49
GANTS HILL, Ilf. IG2 147 EN57
⊖ **Gants Hill** 147 EN58
Jct **Gants Hill**, Ilf. IG2
off Eastern Av 147 EN58
Gantshill Cres, Ilf. IG2 147 EN57
Ganwick, Barn. EN5 102 DA36
GANWICK CORNER,
Barn. EN5 102 DB35
Ganymede Pl, Hem.H. HP2
off Jupiter Dr 62 BM18
Gap Rd, SW19 202 DA92
Garage Rd, W3 160 CN72
Garand Ct, N7 8 D2
Garbrand Wk, Epsom KT17 239 CT109
Garbutt Pl, W1 17 H6
Garbutt Rd, Upmin. RM14 150 FQ61
Garden Av, Bexh. DA7 188 FA83
Hatfield AL10 67 CU22
Mitcham CR4 203 DH94
Garden City, Edg. HA8 118 CN51
Garden Cl, E4 123 EA50
SE12 206 EH90
SW15 201 CV87
Addlestone KT15 234 BK105
Arkley EN5 101 CW42
Ashford TW15 197 BQ93
Banstead SM7 256 DA115
Hampton TW12 198 BZ92
Leatherhead KT22 253 CJ124

Garden Cl, New Malden KT3 220 CS98
Northolt UB5 158 BY67
Ruislip HA4 137 BS61
St. Albans AL1 65 CH19
Wallington SM6 241 DL106
Watford WD17 97 BT40
Garden Cotts, Orp. BR5
off Main Rd 228 EW96
Garden Ct, EC4 18 E10
N12 120 DB50
Richmond TW9 180 CM81
Stanmore HA7 117 CJ50
Welwyn Garden City AL7 51 CY08
West Molesey KT8
off Avern Rd 218 CB98
● Garden Ct Business Cen,
Welw.G.C. AL7
off Garden Ct 51 CZ08
Garden End, Amer. HP6 77 AS37
Gardeners Cl, N11 120 DG47
SE9 206 EL90
Gardeners Rd, Croy. CR0 223 DP102
Gardeners Wk, Bkhm KT23 268 CB126
Garden Fld La, Berk. HP4 61 AZ21
Sch Garden Flds JMI Sch, St.Alb.
AL3 off Townsend Dr 65 CD17
H Garden Hosp, The, NW4 141 CW55
Sch Garden Ho Sch, SW3 28 F10
Gardenia Rd, Brom. BR1 227 EN97
Enfield EN1 104 DS44
Gardenia Way, Wdf.Grn. IG8 124 EG50
Garden La, SW2
off Christchurch Rd 203 DM88
Bromley BR1 206 EH93
Garden Ms, W2 27 K1
Slough SL1
off Littledown Rd 154 AT74
★ Garden Museum, SE1 30 C7
Garden Pl, E8 10 B8
Dartford DA2 210 FK90
Sch Garden Prim Sch, Mitch.
CR4 off Abbotts Rd 223 DK97
Garden Reach, Ch.St.G. HP8 94 AX41
Garden Rd, NW8 15 P2
SE20 224 DW95
Abbots Langley WD5 81 BS31
Bromley BR1 206 EH94
Richmond TW9 180 CN83
Sevenoaks TN13 279 FK122
Walton-on-Thames KT12 217 BV100
Garden Row, SE1 30 G7
Northfleet DA11 213 GF90
Gardens, The, E5 144 DT59
SE22 184 DU84
Beckenham BR3 225 EC96
Brookmans Park AL9 85 CY27
Esher KT10 236 CA105
Feltham TW14 197 BR85
Harrow HA1 138 CC58
Pinner HA5 138 BZ58
Watford WD17 97 BT40
Garden St, E1 21 K7
Sch Garden Suburb Inf Sch,
NW11 off Childs Way 141 CZ57
Sch Garden Suburb Jun Sch,
NW11 off Childs Way 141 CZ57
Garden Ter, SW1 29 N10
Garden Ter Rd, Harl. CM17 58 EW11
Garden Wk, EC2 19 N3
Beckenham BR3 225 DZ95
Coulsdon CR5 257 DH123
Garden Way, NW10 160 CQ65
Loughton IG10 107 EN38
Gardiner Av, NW2 4 A2
Gardiner Cl, Dag. RM8 148 EX63
Enfield EN3 105 DX44
Orpington BR5 228 EW96
Gardiners, The, Harl. CM17 74 EV15
Gardner Cl, E11 146 EH58
Gardner Ct, EC1
off Brewery Sq 18 G4
N5 9 J1
Gardner Gro, Felt. TW13 198 BZ89
● Gardner Ind Est, Beck. BR3 205 DY92
Gardner Pl, Felt. TW14 197 BV86
Gardner Rd, E13 24 A4
Guildford GU1 264 AW134
Gardners La, EC4 19 J10
Gardnor Rd, NW3 off Flask Wk 142 DD63
Gard St, EC1 19 H2
Garendon Gdns, Mord. SM4 222 DB101
Garendon Rd, Mord. SM4 222 DB101
Gareth Cl, Wor.Pk. KT4 221 CX103
Gareth Dr, N9 122 DU47
Gareth Gro, Brom. BR1 206 EG91
Garfield Ms, SW11
off Garfield Rd 183 DH83
Garfield Pl, Wind. SL4
off Russell St 173 AR81
Sch Garfield Prim Sch, N11
off Springfield Rd 121 DJ50
SW19 off Garfield Rd 202 DC93
Garfield Rd, E4 123 ED46
E13 23 M5
SW11 182 DG83
SW19 202 DC92
Addlestone KT15 234 BJ106
Enfield EN3 104 DW42
Twickenham TW1 199 CG88
Garfield St, Wat. WD24 97 BV38
Garford St, E14 34 A1
Garganey Wk, SE28 168 EX73
Garibaldi Rd, Red. RH1 288 DF135
Garibaldi St, SE18 187 ES77
Garland Cl, Chsht EN8 89 DY31
Hemel Hempstead HP2 62 BK19
Garland Ct, SE17
off Wansey St 31 K9
Garland Dr, Houns. TW3 178 CC82
Garland Ho, N16 144 DR62
Kingston upon Thames KT2
off Kingsgate Rd 220 CL95
Garland Rd, SE18 187 ER80
Bromley BR1 227 EP97
Stanmore HA7 118 CL53
Ware SG12 55 DY06
Garlands Ct, Croy. CR0 242 DR105
Garlands Rd, Lthd. KT22 253 CH121
Redhill RH1 288 DF135
Garland Way, Cat. CR3 258 DR122
Hornchurch RM11 150 FL56
Garlichill Rd, Epsom KT18 255 CV117
Garlick Hill, EC4 19 K10
Garlic St, Dor. RH5 268 BZ133
Garlies Rd, SE23 205 DY90
Garlinge Rd, NW2 4 G5
Garman Cl, N18 122 DR50
Garman Rd, N17 122 DW52
Garnault Ms, EC1 18 F3
Garnault Pl, EC1 18 F3
Garnault Rd, Enf. EN1 104 DT38
Garner Cl, Dag. RM8 148 EX60
Garner Dr, Brox. EN10 89 DY26
Garner Rd, E17 123 EC53
Garners Cl, Chal.St.P. SL9 112 AY51
Garners End, Chal.St.P. SL9 112 AY51
Garners Rd, Chal.St.P. SL9 112 AY51
Garner St, E2 20 D1
Garnet Cl, Slou. SL1 173 AN75
Garnet Rd, NW10 160 CS65
Thornton Heath CR7 224 DR98
Garnet St, E1 32 G1
Garnett Cl, SE9 187 EM83
Watford WD24 98 BX37
Garnett Dr, Brick.Wd AL2 82 BZ29
Garnett Rd, NW3 6 E2
Garnett Way, E17
off McEntee Av 123 DY53
Garnet Wk, E6 25 H6
Garnham Cl, N16
off Garnham St 144 DT61
Garnham St, N16 144 DT61
Garnies Cl, SE15 44 A4
Garnon Mead, Cooper. CM16 92 EX28
Garrad's Rd, SW16 203 DK90
Garrard Cl, Bexh. DA7 188 FA83
Chislehurst BR7 207 EP92
Garrard Rd, Bans. SM7 256 DA116
Slough SL2 153 AL70
Garrard Wk, NW10
off Garnet Rd 160 CS65
Garratt Cl, Croy. CR0 241 DL105
Garratt Ho, N16
off Stamford Hill 144 DS60
Garratt La, SW17 202 DD91
SW18 202 DB85
Sch Garratt Pk Sch, SW18
off Waldron Rd 202 DC90
Garratt Rd, Edg. HA8 118 CN52
Garratts Cl, Hert. SG14 54 DQ09
Garratts La, Bans. SM7 255 CZ116
Garratts Rd, Bushey WD23 116 CC45
Garratt Ter, SW17 202 DE91
Garrett Cl, W3 160 CR71
Chesham HP5 76 AQ33
Garrett St, EC1 19 K4
Garrick Av, NW11 141 CY58
Garrick Cl, SW18 182 DC84
W5 160 CL70
Hersham KT12 235 BV105
Richmond TW9
off Old Palace La 199 CK85
Staines-upon-Thames TW18 196 BG94
Garrick Ct, Edg. HA8 118 CM49
Garrick Cres, Croy. CR0 224 DS103
Garrick Dr, NW4 119 CW54
SE28 187 ER76
Garrick Gdns, W.Mol. KT8 218 CA97
Garrick Pk, NW4 119 CX54
Garrick Rd, NW9 141 CT58
Greenford UB6 158 CB70
Richmond TW9 180 CN82
● Garrick Rd Ind Est, NW9 141 CT57
Garricks Ho, Kings.T. KT1 219 CK96
Garrick St, WC2 18 A10
Gravesend DA11
off Barrack Row 213 GH86
Garrick Way, NW4 141 CX56
Garrick Yd, WC2
off St. Martin's La 18 A10
Garrison Cl, SE18
off Red Lion La 187 EN80
Hounslow TW4 198 BZ85
Garrison La, Chess. KT9 237 CK108
Garrison Par, Purf. RM19
off Comet Cl 190 FN77
Garrison Rd, E3 11 P9
Garrolds Cl, Swan. BR8 229 FD96
Garron La, S.Ock. RM15 171 FT72
Garrowsfield, Barn. EN5 101 CZ43
Garry Cl, Rom. RM1 127 FE52
Garry Way, Rom. RM1 127 FE52
Garsdale Cl, N11 120 DG51
Garside Cl, SE28 187 ER76
Hampton TW12 198 CB93
Garsington Ms, SE4 185 DZ83
Garsmouth Way, Wat. WD25 98 BX36
Garson Cl, Esher KT10
off Garson Rd 236 BZ107
Garson Gro, Chesh. HP5 76 AN29
Garson La, Wrays. TW19 194 AX87
Garson Mead, Esher KT10 236 BZ106
Garson Rd, Esher KT10 236 BZ107
GARSTON, Wat. WD25 98 BW35
⇌ Garston 98 BX35
Garston Cres, Wat. WD25 82 BW34
Garston Dr, Wat. WD25 82 BW34
Garston Gdns, Ken. CR8
off Godstone Rd 258 DR115
Garston La, Ken. CR8 242 DR114
Watford WD25 82 BX34
Sch Garston Manor Sch, Wat.
WD25 off Horseshoe La 82 BW32
Garston Pk Par, Wat. WD25 82 BX34
Garstons, The, Bkhm KT23 268 CA125
Garter Way, SE16 33 J5
Garth, The, N12 120 DB50
Abbots Langley WD5 81 BR33
Cobham KT11 236 BY113
Hampton Hill TW12 198 CB93
Harrow HA3 140 CM58
Garth Cl, W4 180 CR78
Kingston upon Thames KT2 200 CM92
Morden SM4 221 CX101
Ruislip HA4 138 BX60
Garth Ct, W4 180 CR78
Garth Ho, NW2
off Granville Rd 141 CZ61
Garthland Dr, Barn. EN5 101 CV43
Garth Ms, W5
off Greystoke Gdns 160 CL70
Garthorne Rd, SE23 205 DX87
Garth Rd, NW2 141 CZ61
W4 180 CR79
Kingston upon Thames KT2 200 CM92
Morden SM4 221 CW100
Sevenoaks TN13 279 FJ128
South Ockendon RM15 171 FW70
● Garth Rd Ind Cen,
Mord. SM4 221 CX101
Garthside, Ham TW10 200 CL92
Garthway, N12 120 DE51
Gartlet Rd, Wat. WD17 98 BW41
Gartmoor Gdns, SW19 201 CZ88
Gartmore Rd, Ilf. IG3 147 ET60
Garton Bk, Bans. SM7 256 DA117
Garton Pl, SW18 202 DC86
Gartons Cl, Enf. EN3 104 DW43
Gartons Way, SW11 182 DC83
Garvary Rd, E16 24 B9
Garvin Av, Beac. HP9 111 AL52
Garvin Ms, Beac. HP9 111 AL53
Garvock Dr, Sev. TN13 278 FG126
Garway Rd, W2 15 L9
Garwood Cl, N17 122 DV53
Gary Ct, Croy. CR0 223 DP101
Gascoigne Gdns, Wdf.Grn.
IG8 124 EE52
Gascoigne Pl, E2 20 A3
Sch Gascoigne Prim Sch, Bark.
IG11 off Gascoigne Rd 167 EQ67
Gascoigne Rd, Bark. IG11 167 EQ67
New Addington CR0 243 EC110
Weybridge KT13 217 BP104
Gascons Gro, Slou. SL2 153 AN70
Gascony Av, NW6 5 J7
Gascony Pl, W12
off Bourbon La 26 C3
Gascoyne Cl, Rom. RM3 128 FK52
South Mimms EN6 85 CU32
Gascoyne Dr, Dart. DA1 189 FF82
Gascoyne Rd, E9 11 K6
Gascoyne Way, Hert.
SG13, SG14 54 DQ09
Gaselee St, E14 34 F1
Gaskarth Rd, SW12 203 DH86
Edgware HA8 118 CQ53
Gaskell Rd, N6 142 DF58
Gaskell St, SW4 42 A8
Gaskin St, N1 8 G8
Gaspar Cl, SW5 27 M8
Gaspar Ms, SW5 27 M8
Gassiot Rd, SW17 202 DF91
Gassiot Way, Sutt. SM1 222 DD104
Gasson Rd, Swans. DA10 212 FY86
Gastein Rd, W6 38 D2
Gaston Bell Cl, Rich. TW9 180 CM83
Gaston Br Rd, Shep. TW17 217 BS99
Gaston Rd, Mitch. CR4 222 DG97
Gaston Way, Shep. TW17 217 BR99
★ Gasworks Gall, SE11 42 D2
Gas Wks La, Brox. EN10 71 EA19
Gataker St, SE16 32 F6
Gatcombe Ho, SE22
off Pytchley Rd 184 DS83
Gatcombe Ms, W5 160 CM73
Gatcombe Rd, E16 35 P2
N19 143 DK62
Gatcombe Way, Barn. EN4 102 DF41
Gate Cl, Borwd. WD6 100 CQ39
Gatecroft, Hem.H. HP3 62 BM22
Gate End, Nthwd. HA6 115 BU52
Gateforth St, NW8 16 C5
Gatehill Rd, Nthwd. HA6 115 BT52
Gatehope Dr, S.Ock. RM15 171 FT72
Gatehouse, The, Rom. RM1 149 FE57
Gatehouse Cl, Kings.T. KT2 200 CQ94
Windsor SL4
off St. Leonards Rd 173 AP83
Sch Gatehouse Sch, E2 11 J10
Gate Ho Sq, SE1 31 K2
Gateley Rd, SW9 183 DM83
Gate Lo, Har. HA3
off Weston Dr 117 CH53
Gate Ms, SW7 28 D5
Gater Dr, Enf. EN2 104 DR39
Gatesborough St, EC2 19 N4
Gatesden Cl, Fetch. KT22 252 CC123
Gatesden Rd, Fetch. KT22 252 CC123
Gates Grn Rd, Kes. BR2 244 EG105
West Wickham BR4 226 EF104
Gateshead Rd, Borwd. WD6 100 CM39
Gateside Rd, SW17 202 DF90
Gatestone Rd, SE19 204 DS93
Gate St, WC2 18 C8
Gate Studios, Borwd. WD6 100 CN42
Gateway, SE17 43 K2
Gate Way, Wey. KT13
off Palace Dr 217 BP104
Gateway, The, Wat. WD18 97 BS43
Woking GU21 233 BB114
Sch Gateway Acad, The, Grays
RM16 off Marshfoot Rd 193 GG79
● Gateway Business Cen,
SE26 205 DY93
SE28 off Tom Cribb Rd 187 ER76
Gateway Cl, Nthwd. HA6 115 BQ51
Gateway Ct, Ilf. IG2 147 EN58
● Gateway Ind Est, NW10 161 CT69
Gateway Ms, E8 10 A2
N11 off Ringway 121 DJ51
Sch Gateway Prim Sch, NW8 16 B4
Sch Gateway Prim Sch, The,
Dart. DA2 off Milestone Rd 210 FP86
● Gateway Retail Pk, E6 25 P5
Gateway Rd, E10 145 EB62
Gateways, Guil. GU1 265 BA134
Gateways, The, SW3 28 D9
Goffs Oak EN7 88 DR28
Gatewick Cl, Slou. SL1 154 AS74
Gatfield Gro, Felt. TW13 198 CA89
Gathorne Rd, N22 121 DN54
Gathorne St, E2 21 K1
Gatley Av, Epsom KT19 238 CP106
Gatley Dr, Guil. GU4 265 AZ131
Gatliff Cl, SW1
off Ebury Br Rd 41 J1
Gatliff Rd, SW1 41 H1
Gatling Rd, SE2 188 EU78
Gatonby St, SE15 44 B6
Gatting Cl, Edg. HA8 118 CQ52
Gatting Way, Uxb. UB8 156 BL65
GATTON, Reig. RH2 272 DF128
Gatton Bottom, Merst. RH1 273 DH127
Reigate RH2 272 DE128
Gatton Cl, Reig. RH2 272 DC131
Sutton SM2 240 DB109
Gatton Pk, Reig. RH2 272 DF129
Gatton Pk Rd, Red. RH1 272 DD132
Reigate RH2 272 DD132
Sch Gatton Prim Sch, SW17
off Gatton Rd 202 DE91
Gatton Rd, SW17 202 DE91
Reigate RH2 272 DC131
Gattons Way, Sid. DA14 208 EZ91
Gatward Cl, N21 103 DP44
Gatward Grn, N9 122 DT47
★ Gatwick Airport (London),
Gat. RH6 290 DD153
⇌ Gatwick Airport 291 DH152
● Gatwick Business Pk,
Hkwd RH6 290 DC149
Gatwick Gate, Craw. RH11 290 DD154
● Gatwick Gate Ind Est,
Lwfld Hth RH11 290 DE154
● Gatwick Metro Cen,
Horl. RH6 291 DH147
Gatwick Rd, SW18 201 CZ87
Gatwick RH6 290 DG154
Gravesend DA12 213 GH90
Jct Gatwick Rd Rbt,
Horl. RH6 290 DG154
Gatwick Way, Gat. RH6 290 DF151
Hornchurch RM12
off Haydock Cl 150 FM63
Gauden Cl, SW4 41 N10
Gauden Rd, SW4 41 N9
Gaumont App, Wat. WD17 97 BV41
Gaumont Ter, W12
off Lime Gro 26 A4
Gauntlet Cl, Nthlt. UB5 158 BY66
Gauntlett Ct, Wem. HA0 139 CH64
Gauntlett Rd, Sutt. SM1 240 DD106
Gaunt St, SE1 31 H6
Gautrey Rd, SE15 45 H8
Gautrey Sq, E6 25 K9
● Gavel Cen, The, St.Alb.
AL3 off Porters Wd 65 CF16
Gavell Rd, Cob. KT11 235 BU113
Gavel St, SE17 31 M8
Gavenny Path, S.Ock. RM15 171 FT72
Gaverick Ms, E14 34 A8
Gaveston Cl, Byfleet KT14 234 BM113
Gaveston Dr, Berk. HP4 60 AV17
Gavestone Cres, SE12 206 EH87
Gavestone Rd, SE12 206 EH87
Gaveston Rd, Lthd. KT22 253 CG120
Slough SL2 153 AL69
Gaviller Pl, E5
off Clarence Rd 144 DV63
Gavina Cl, Mord. SM4 222 DE99
Gavin St, SE18 187 ES77
Gaviots Cl, Ger.Cr. SL9 135 AZ60
Gaviots Grn, Ger.Cr. SL9 134 AY60
Gaviots Way, Ger.Cr. SL9 134 AY59
Gawain Wk, N9 off Galahad Rd 122 DU48
Gawber St, E2 21 H2
Gawdrey Cl, Chesh. HP5
off Five Acres 76 AR33
Gawsworth Cl, E15 13 K2
Gawthorne Ct, E3
off Mostyn Gro 22 A1
Gawton Cres, Couls. CR5 257 DJ121
Gay Cl, NW2 141 CV64
Gaydon Ho, W2 15 M6
Gaydon La, NW9 118 CS53
Gayfere Rd, Epsom KT17 239 CU106
Ilford IG5 147 EM55
Gayfere St, SW1 30 A7
Gayford Rd, W12 181 CT75
Gay Gdns, Dag. RM10 149 FC63
Gayhurst, SE17 43 M2
Sch Gayhurst Comm Sch, E8 10 D6
Gayhurst Rd, E8 10 C6
Sch Gayhurst Sch, Sen Sch,
Chal.St.P. SL9
off Bull La 134 AW56
Jun Sch, Ger.Cr. SL9
off Maltmans La 134 AW56
Gayler Cl, Bletch. RH1 274 DT133
Gaylor Rd, Nthlt. UB5 138 BZ64
Tilbury RM18 192 GE81
Gaynes Ct, Upmin. RM14 150 FP63
Gaynesford Rd, SE23 205 DX89
Carshalton SM5 240 DF108
Gaynes Hill Rd, Wdf.Grn. IG8 124 EL51
Gaynes Pk, Cooper. CM16 92 EY31
Gaynes Pk Rd, Upmin. RM14 150 FN63
Gaynes Rd, Upmin. RM14 150 FP61
Sch Gaynes Sch, Upmin. RM14
off Brackendale Gdns 150 FQ64
Gay Rd, E15 12 G10
Gaysham Av, Ilf. IG2 147 EN57
Gaysham Hall, Ilf. IG5 147 EP55
Gay St, SW15 181 CX83
Gayton Cl, Amer. HP6 77 AS35
Ashtead KT21 254 CL118
Gayton Ct, Har. HA1 139 CF58
Gayton Cres, NW3 142 DD63
Gayton Ho, E3 22 B5
Gayton Rd, NW3 6 A1
SE2 off Florence Rd 188 EW76
Harrow HA1 139 CF58
Gayville Rd, SW11 202 DF86
Gaywood Av, Chsht EN8 89 DX30
Gaywood Cl, SW2 203 DM88
Gaywood Est, SE1 30 G7
Gaywood Rd, E17 145 EA55
Ashtead KT21 254 CM118
Gaywood St, SE1 31 H7
Gaza St, SE17 42 G1
Gazelle Glade, Grav. DA12 213 GM92
Gazelle Ho, E15 13 J4
Gean Ct, N11 off Cline Rd 121 DJ51
Gean Wk, Hat. AL10 67 CU21
Sch Gearies Infants' Sch, Ilf.
IG2 off Waremead Rd 147 EP57
Sch Gearies Jun Sch, Ilf. IG2
off Gantshill Cres 147 EP57
Geariesville Gdns, Ilf. IG6 147 EP56
Gearing Cl, SW17 202 DG91
Geary Cl, Smallfield RH6 291 DP150
Geary Ct, N9
off The Broadway 122 DU47
Geary Dr, Brwd. CM14, CM15 130 FW46
Geary Rd, NW10 141 CU64
Geary St, N7 8 D3
Geddes Pl, Bexh. DA6
off Market Pl 188 FA84
Geddes Rd, Bushey WD23 98 CC42
Geddings Rd, Hodd. EN11 71 EB17
Geddington Ct, Wal.Cr. EN8
off Eleanor Way 89 EA34
Gedeney Rd, N17 122 DQ53
Gedling Ho, SE22
off Quorn Rd 184 DT83
Gedling Pl, SE1 32 B6
Geere Rd, E15 13 M9
Gees Ct, W1 17 H9
Gee St, EC1 19 J4
Geffrye Ct, N1 19 P1
Geffrye Est, N1 19 P1
★ Geffrye Mus, E2 19 P1
Geffrye St, E2 10 A10
Geisthorp Ct, Wal.Abb. EN9 90 EG33
Geldart Rd, SE15 44 E5
Geldeston Rd, E5 144 DU61
Gellatly Rd, SE14 45 H8
Gell Cl, Uxb. UB10 136 BM62
Gelsthorpe Rd, Rom. RM5 127 FB52
● Gemini Business Pk, E6 167 ER71
Gemini Ct, Pur. CR8
off Brighton Rd 241 DN111
Gemini Gro, Nthlt. UB5
off Javelin Way 158 BY69
Gemini Ho, E3
off Garrison Rd 12 A9
● Gemini Project, SE14 45 K1
Gemmell Cl, Pur. CR8 241 DM114
Genas Cl, Ilf. IG6 125 EP53
General Gordon Pl, SE18 37 N8
Generals Wk, The, Enf. EN3 105 DY37
General Wolfe Rd, SE10 47 H6
● Genesis Business Pk, NW10 160 CP68
Wok. GU21 249 BC115
Genesis Cl, Stanw. TW19 196 BM88
Genesta Rd, SE18 187 EP79
Geneva Cl, Shep. TW17 217 BS96
Geneva Dr, SW9 183 DN84
Geneva Gdns, Rom. RM6 148 EY57
Geneva Rd, Kings.T. KT1 220 CL98
Thornton Heath CR7 224 DQ99
Genever Cl, E4 123 EA50
Genista Rd, N18 122 DV50
Genoa Av, SW15 201 CW85
Genoa Rd, SE20 224 DW95
Genotin Ms, Horn. RM12 150 FJ64
Genotin Rd, Enf. EN1 104 DR41
Genotin Ter, Enf. EN1
off Genotin Rd 104 DR41
Gentian Row, SE13 46 E7
Gentlemans Row, Enf. EN2 104 DQ41
Gentry Gdns, E13 23 P4
Genyn Rd, Guil. GU2 280 AV136
Geoff Cade Way, E3 22 A6
Geoffrey Av, Rom. RM3 128 FN51
Geoffrey Cl, SE5 43 J9
Geoffrey Gdns, E6 24 G1
Geoffrey Rd, SE4 45 N10
Sch George Abbot Sch, Guil.
GU1 off Woodruff Av 265 BB132
George Avey Ct, N.Wld Bas.
CM16 93 FB26
George Beard Rd, SE8 33 N9
George Belt Ho, E2 21 J2
Sch George Carey C of E
Prim Sch, Bark. IG11 168 EU70
George Comberton Wk, E12
off Gainsborough Av 147 EN64
George Ct, WC2 30 B1
George Cres, N10 120 DG52
George Crook's Ho, Grays
RM17 off New Rd 192 GB79
George Downing Est, N16 144 DT61
George Eliot Ho, SW1
off Vauxhall Br Rd 29 M9
Sch George Eliot Inf Sch, NW8 6 A8
Sch George Eliot Jun Sch, NW8 6 A8
George Elliston Ho, SE1
off Old Kent Rd 44 C1
George V Av, Pnr. HA5 138 CA55
George V Cl, Pnr. HA5 138 CA55
Watford WD18 97 BT42
George V Way, Perivale UB6 159 CH67
Sarratt WD3 96 BG36
George Gange Way, Wealds.
HA3 139 CE55
GEORGE GREEN, Slou. SL3 154 AX72
George Grn Dr, Geo.Grn SL3 155 AZ71
George Grn Rd, Geo.Grn SL3 154 AX72
Sch George Green's Sch, E14 34 F10
George Gros Rd, SE20 224 DU95
George Hudson Twr, E15
off High St 22 D1
★ George Inn, SE1 31 L3
George Inn Yd, SE1 31 L3
Georgelands, Ripley GU23 250 BH121
George La, E18 124 EG54
SE13 205 EC86
Bromley BR2 226 EH102
Jct George La Rbt, E18 124 EG54
George Lansbury Ho, N22
off Progress Way 121 DN53
George Loveless Ho, E2 20 B2
George Lovell Dr, Enf. EN3 105 EA37
George Lowe Ct, W2 15 L6
George Mathers Rd, SE11 30 G8
George Ms, NW1 17 L3
SW9 42 E9
Enfield EN2 off Church St 104 DR41
Sch George Mitchell Sch, E10
off Farmer Rd 145 EB60
George Rd, E4 123 EA51
Godalming GU7 280 AS144
Guildford GU1 264 AX134
Kingston upon Thames KT2 200 CP94
New Malden KT3 221 CT98
George Row, SE16 32 C5
Georges Cl, Orp. BR5 228 EW97
Georges Dr, Flack.Hth HP10 132 AC56
Pilgrim's Hatch CM15 130 FT43
Georges Mead, Els. WD6 99 CK44
Sch George Spicer Prim Sch, Enf.
EN1 off Southbury Rd 104 DT41
George Sq, SW19
off Mostyn Rd 221 CZ97
George's Rd, N7 8 D3
Georges Rd, Tats. TN16 260 EK120
Georges Sq, SW6 39 H2
Georges Ter, Cat. CR3
off Coulsdon Rd 258 DR122
George Street 224 DQ103
George St, E16 23 L9
W1 16 F8
W7 off Uxbridge Rd 159 CE74
Barking IG11 167 EQ66
Berkhamsted HP4 60 AY19
Chesham HP5 76 AQ30
Croydon CR0 224 DR103
Grays RM17 192 GA79
Hemel Hempstead HP2 62 BK19
Hertford SG14 54 DQ09
Hounslow TW3 178 BZ82
Richmond TW9 199 CK85
Romford RM1 149 FF58
St. Albans AL3 64 CC20
Southall UB2 178 BY77
Staines-upon-Thames TW18 195 BF91
Uxbridge UB8 156 BK66
Watford WD18 98 BW42
Sch George St Prim Sch, Hem.H.
HP2 off George St 62 BK19
George's Wd Rd, Brook.Pk AL9 86 DA26
George Taylor Ct, N9
off Colthurst Dr 122 DV48
George Tilbury Ho, Grays
RM16 193 GH75

Sch George Tomlinson Prim Sch,
E11 off Vernon Rd 146 EE60
Georgetown Cl, SE19 204 DS92
Georgette Pl, SE10 46 F5
Georgeville Gdns, Ilf. IG6 147 EP56
Georgewood Rd, Hem.H. HP3 80 BM25
George Wyver Cl, SW19
off Beaumont Rd 201 CY87
George Yd, EC3 19 M9
W1 17 H10
Georgiana St, NW1 7 L8
Georgian Cl, Brom. BR2 226 EH101
Staines-upon-Thames TW18 196 BH91
Stanmore HA7 117 CG52
Uxbridge UB10 136 BL63
Georgian Ct, SW16
off Gleneldon Rd 203 DL91
Wembley HA9 160 CN65
Georgian Way, Har. HA1 139 CD61
Georgia Rd, N.Mal. KT3 220 CQ98
Thornton Heath CR7 223 DP95
Georgina Gdns, E2 20 B2
Geraint Rd, Brom. BR1 206 EG91
Gerald Game Br, Hodd. EN11 71 EC17
Geraldine Rd, SW18 202 DC85
W4 180 CN79
Geraldine St, SE11 30 G7
Gerald Ms, SW1 29 H8
Gerald Rd, E16 23 L4
SW1 29 H8
Dagenham RM8 148 EZ61
Gravesend DA12 213 GL87
Geralds Gro, Bans. SM7 239 CX114
Gerard Av, Houns. TW4 198 CA87
Gerard Ct, NW2 4 C2
Gerard Gdns, Rain. RM13 169 FE68
Gerard Pl, E9 11 J6
Gerard Rd, SW13 181 CT81
Harrow HA1 139 CG58
Gerards Cl, SE16 44 G1
Gerards Pl, SW4
off Clapham Pk Rd 183 DK84
Gerda Rd, SE9 207 EQ89
Gerdview Dr, Dart. DA2 210 FJ91
Germains Cl, Chesh. HP5 76 AP32
Germain St, Chesh. HP5 76 AP32
Germander Way, E15 23 K3
Sch German Sch, The, Rich.
TW10 off Petersham Rd 199 CK88
Gernigan Ho, SW18 202 DD86
Gernon Cl, Rain. RM13
off Jordans Way 170 FK68
Gernon Rd, E3 21 L1
Geron Way, NW2 141 CV60
Gerpins La, Upmin. RM14 170 FM68
Gerrard Cres, Brwd. CM14 130 FV48
Gerrard Gdns, Pnr. HA5 137 BU57
Gerrard Ho, SE14 45 H5
Gerrard Pl, W1 17 P10
Gerrard Rd, N1 9 H10
Gerrards Cl, N14 103 DJ43
GERRARDS CROSS, SL9 134 AX58
⇌ Gerrards Cross 134 AY57
Sch Gerrards Cross C of E Sch,
The, Ger.Cr. SL9
off Moreland Dr 135 AZ59
Gerrards Cross Rd, Stoke P.
SL2 154 AU66
Gerrards Mead, Bans. SM7 255 CZ116
Gerrard St, W1 17 N10
Gerridge St, SE1 30 F5
Gerry Raffles Sq, E15 13 H5
Gertrude Rd, Belv. DA17 188 FA77
Gertrude St, SW10 39 P3
Gervaise Cl, Slou. SL1 153 AM74
Gervase Cl, Wem. HA9 140 CQ62
Gervase Rd, Edg. HA8 118 CQ53
Gervase St, SE15 44 F4
Gews Cor, Chsht EN8 89 DX29
Ghent St, SE6 205 EA89
Ghent Way, E8 10 B4
Giant Arches Rd, SE24 204 DQ87
Giant Tree Hill, Bushey Hth
WD23 117 CD46
Gibbard Ms, SW19 201 CX92
Gibb Cft, Harl. CM18 73 ES19
Gibbfield Cl, Rom. RM6 148 EY55
Gibbins Rd, E15 12 F7
Gibbon Rd, SE15 45 H9
W3 160 CS73
Kingston upon Thames KT2 220 CL95
Gibbons Cl, Borwd. WD6 100 CL39
Gibbons La, Dart. DA1 210 FK86
Gibbons Ms, NW11 141 CZ57
Gibbons Rents, SE1
off Bermondsey St 31 N3
Gibbons Rd, NW10 160 CR65
Gibbon Wk, SW15 181 CU84
Gibbs Av, SE19 204 DR92
Gibbs Brook La, Oxt. RH8 275 ED133
Gibbs Cl, SE19 204 DR92
Cheshunt EN8 89 DX29
Gibbs Couch, Wat. WD19 116 BX48
Gibbs Grn, W14 27 H10
Edgware HA8 118 CQ50
Sch Gibbs Grn Sch, W14 27 H10
Gibbs Rd, N18 122 DW49
Gibbs Sq, SE19 204 DR92
Gibney Ter, Brom. BR1
off Durham Hill 206 EF91
Gibraltar Cl, Gt Warley CM13 129 FW51
Gibraltar Cres, Epsom KT19 238 CS110
Gibraltar Ho, Brwd. CM13 129 FW51
Gibraltar Wk, E2 20 B3
● Gibson Business Cen,
N17 off High Rd 122 DT52
Gibson Cl, E1 21 H4
N21 103 DN44
Chessington KT9 237 CJ107
Isleworth TW7 179 CD83
North Weald Bassett CM16
off Beamish Cl 93 FC25
Northfleet DA11 213 GF90
Gibson Ct, Rom. RM1
off Regarth Av 149 FE58
Slough SL3 175 AZ78
Gibson Gdns, N16 144 DT61
Gibson Ms, Twick. TW1
off Richmond Rd 199 CJ87
Gibson Pl, Stanw. TW19 196 BJ86
Gibson Rd, SE11 30 D9
Dagenham RM8 148 EW60
Sutton SM1 240 DB106
Uxbridge UB10 136 BM63
Gibson's Hill, SW16 203 DN93
Gibson Sq, N1 8 F8
Gibson St, SE10 47 J1
Gidd Hill, Couls. CR5 256 DG116
Gidea Av, Rom. RM2 149 FG55
Gidea Cl, Rom. RM2 149 FG55
South Ockendon RM15
off Tyssen Pl 171 FW69
GIDEA PARK, Rom. RM2 149 FG55
⇌ Gidea Park 150 FJ56
Sch Gidea Pk Coll, Gidea Pk
RM2 off Balgores La 149 FG55
Sch Gidea Pk Prim Sch, Gidea Pk
RM2 off Lodge Av 149 FG55
Gideon Cl, Belv. DA17 189 FB77
Gideon Ms, W5 179 CK75
Gideon Rd, SW11 40 G10
Gidian Ct, Park St AL2 83 CD27
Giesbach Rd, N19 143 DJ61
Giffard Rd, N18 122 DS50
Giffard Way, Guil. GU2 264 AU131
Giffin St, SE8 46 A4
Gifford Gdns, W7 159 CD71
Gifford Pl, Warley CM14 130 FX50
Sch Gifford Prim Sch, Nthlt.
UB5 off Greenhill Gdns 158 BZ68
Gifford Rd, NW10 160 CS66
Giffordside, Grays RM16 193 GH78
Gifford St, N1 8 B7
Gift La, E15 13 L8
Giggs Hill, Orp. BR5 228 EU96
Giggs Hill Gdns, T.Ditt. KT7 219 CG102
Giggs Hill Rd, T.Ditt. KT7 219 CG101
Gilbert Cl, SE18 187 EM81
Swanscombe DA10 211 FX86
Sch Gilbert Colvin Prim Sch,
Ilf. IG5 off Strafford Av 125 EN54
Gilbert Gro, Edg. HA8 118 CR53
Gilbert Ho, EC2
off The Barbican 19 K6
SE8 46 B3
SW1 41 K1
Gilbert Pl, WC1 18 A7
Gilbert Rd, SE11 30 F9
SW19 202 DC94
Belvedere DA17 188 FA76
Bromley BR1 206 EG94
Chafford Hundred RM16 191 FW76
Harefield UB9 114 BK54
Pinner HA5 138 BX56
Romford RM1 149 FF56
Gilbert Scott Cl, Amer. HP7 77 AP40
Sch Gilbert Scott Jun & Inf
Comm Schs, S.Croy. CR2
off Farnborough Av 243 DY108
Gilbert Sq, Har. HA2
off Station Rd 138 CB57
Gilbert St, E15 13 J1
W1 17 H9
Enfield EN3 104 DW37
Hounslow TW3 off High St 178 CC83
Gilbert Way, Berk. HP4 60 AU19
Croydon CR0
off Beddington Fm Rd 223 DL102
Slough SL3 175 AZ78
Gilbert White Cl, Perivale
UB6 159 CG67
Gilbey Cl, Uxb. UB10 137 BP63
Gilbey Rd, SW17 202 DE91
Gilbeys Yd, NW1 7 H7
Gilbey Wk, Woob.Grn HP10
off Stratford Dr 132 AD59
Gilbourne Rd, SE18 187 ET79
Gilda Av, Enf. EN3 105 DY43
Gilda Cres, N16 144 DU60
Gildea Cl, Pnr. HA5 116 CA52
Gildea St, W1 17 K7
Gilden Cl, Harl. CM17 58 EY11
Gilden Cres, NW5 6 G3
Gildenhill Rd, Swan. BR8 210 FJ94
Gilden Way, Harl. CM17 58 EW12
Gilders, Saw. CM21 58 EX05
Gildersome St, SE18
off Nightingale Vale 187 EN79
Gilders Rd, Chess. KT9 238 CM107
Giles Cl, Rain. RM13 170 FK68
Giles Coppice, SE19 204 DT91
Giles Fld, Grav. DA12 213 GM88
Giles Travers Cl, Egh. TW20 215 BC97
Gilfrid Cl, Uxb. UB8 157 BP72
Gilhams Av, Bans. SM7 239 CX112
Gilkes Cres, SE21 204 DS86
Gilkes Pl, SE21 204 DS86
Gillam Way, Rain. RM13 169 FG65
Gillan Grn, Bushey Hth WD23 116 CC47
Gillards Ms, E17
off Gillards Way 145 EA56
Gillards Way, E17 145 EA56
Gill Av, E16 23 P9
Guildford GU2 280 AS135
Gill Cl, Wat. WD18 97 BQ44
Gill Cres, Nthflt DA11 213 GF90
Gillender St, E3 22 E4
E14 22 E4
Sch Gillespie Prim Sch, N5
off Gillespie Rd 143 DP62
Gillespie Rd, N5 143 DN62
Gillett Av, E6 166 EL68
Jct Gillette Cor, Islw. TW7 179 CG80
Gillett Pl, N16 9 P3
Gillett Rd, Th.Hth. CR7 224 DR98
Gillett Sq, N16 9 P3
Gillett St, N16 9 P3
Gillfoot, NW1 17 L1
Gillham Ter, N17 122 DU51
Gillian Gro, Pur. CR8 241 DN110
Gillian Av, St.Alb. AL1 64 CC24
Gillian Cres, Rom. RM2 128 FJ54
Gillian Pk Rd, Sutt. SM3 221 CZ102
Gillian St, SE13 205 EB85
Gilliat Cl, Iver SL0
off Grange Way 155 BF72
Gilliat Dr, Guil. GU4 265 BD132
Gilliat Rd, Slou. SL1 154 AS73
Gilliat's Grn, Chorl. WD3 95 BD42
Gillies St, NW5 7 H3
Gilling Ct, NW3 6 D4
Gillingham Rd, NW2 141 CY62
Gillingham Row, SW1 29 L8
Gillingham St, SW1 29 K8
Gillison Wk, SE16
off Tranton Rd 32 D6
Gillman Dr, E15 13 L9
Gillmans Rd, Orp. BR5 228 EV102
Gills Hill, Rad. WD7 99 CF35
Gills Hill La, Rad. WD7 99 CF36
Gills Hollow, Rad. WD7 99 CF36
Gill's Rd, S.Darenth DA2, DA4 231 FS95
Gillsted Ct, St.Alb. AL3
off Repton Grn 65 CD17
Gill St, E14 21 P10
Gillum Cl, E.Barn. EN4 120 DF46
Gilmais, Bkhm KT23 268 CC125
Gilman Cres, Wind. SL4 173 AK83
Gilmore Cl, Slou. SL3 174 AW75
Uxbridge UB10 136 BN62
Gilmore Cres, Ashf. TW15 196 BN92
Gilmore Rd, SE13 185 ED84
Gilmour Cl, Wal.Cr. EN7 104 DU35
Gilpin Av, SW14 180 CR84
Gilpin Cl, W2 16 A6
Mitcham CR4 222 DE96
Gilpin Cres, N18 122 DT50
Twickenham TW2 198 CB87
Gilpin Rd, E5 145 DY63
Ware SG12 55 DY07
Gilpin's Gallop, Stans.Abb.
SG12 55 EB11
Gilpins Ride, Berk. HP4 60 AX18
Gilpin Way, Harling. UB3 177 BR80
Gilroy Cl, Rain. RM13 169 FF65
Gilroy Rd, Hem.H. HP2 62 BK19
Gilroy Way, Orp. BR5 228 EV101
Gilsland, Wal.Abb. EN9 106 EE35
Gilsland Pl, Th.Hth. CR7
off Gilsland Rd 224 DR98
Gilsland Rd, Th.Hth. CR7 224 DR98
Gilson Pl, N10 120 DF52
Gilstead Rd, SW6 39 M8
Gilston La, Gilston Pk CM20 57 EQ09
GILSTON PARK, Harl. CM20 57 EP08
Gilston Rd, SW10 39 P1
Gilton Rd, SE6 206 EE90
Giltspur St, EC1 19 H8
Gilwell Cl, E4
off Antlers Hill 105 EB42
Gilwell La, E4 105 EC42
Gilwell Pk, E4 105 EC41
Gimcrack Hill, Lthd. KT22
off Dorking Rd 253 CH123
Ginsburg Yd, NW3
off Heath St 142 DC63
Gippeswyck Cl, Pnr. HA5
off Uxbridge Rd 116 BX53
⇌ Gipsy Hill 204 DS92
Gipsy Hill, SE19 204 DS91
Gipsy La, SW15 181 CU83
Grays RM17 192 GC79
Gipsy Rd, SE27 204 DQ91
Welling DA16 188 EX81
Gipsy Rd Gdns, SE27 204 DQ91
Giralda Cl, E16 24 E7
Giraud St, E14 22 C8
Girdlers Rd, W14 26 D8
Girdlestone Wk, N19 143 DJ61
Girdwood Rd, SW18 201 CY87
Girling Way, Felt. TW14 177 BU83
Girona Cl, Chaff.Hun. RM16 191 FW76
Gironde Rd, SW6 39 H5
Girton Av, NW9 140 CN55
Girton Cl, Nthlt. UB5 158 CC65
Girton Ct, Chsht EN8 89 DY30
Girton Gdns, Croy. CR0 225 EA104
Girton Rd, SE26 205 DX92
Northolt UB5 158 CC65
Girton Vil, W10 14 D8
Girton Way, Crox.Grn WD3 97 BQ43
Gisborne Gdns, Rain. RM13 169 FF69
Gisbourne Cl, Wall. SM6 223 DK104
Gisburne Way, Wat. WD24 97 BU37
Gisburn Rd, N8 143 DM56
Gissing Wk, N1 8 F7
Gittens Cl, Brom. BR1 206 EF91
Given Wilson Wk, E13 23 M1
Giverny Ho, SE16
off Canada St 33 J5
GIVONS GROVE, Lthd. KT22 269 CJ126
Givons Gro, Lthd. KT22 269 CH125
Jct Givons Gro Rbt, Lthd.
KT22 269 CH125
Glacier Way, Wem. HA0 159 CK68
Gladbeck Way, Enf. EN2 103 DP42
Gladding Rd, E12 146 EK63
Cheshunt EN7 87 DP25
Glade, The, N21 103 DM44
SE7 186 EJ80
Bromley BR1 226 EK96
Coulsdon CR5 257 DN119
Croydon CR0 225 DX99
Enfield EN2 103 DN41
Epsom KT17 239 CU106
Fetcham KT22 252 CA122
Gerrards Cross SL9 134 AX60
Hutton CM13 131 GA46
Ilford IG5 125 EM53
Kingswood KT20 256 DA121
Penn HP10 110 AC46
Sevenoaks TN13 279 FH123
Staines-upon-Thames TW18 196 BH94
Sutton SM2 239 CY109
Upminster RM14 150 FQ64
Welwyn Garden City AL8 51 CW07
West Byfleet KT14 233 BE113
West Wickham BR4 225 EB104
Woodford Green IG8 124 EH48
● Glade Business Cen,
Grays RM20 191 FT78
Glade Cl, Long Dit. KT6 219 CK103
Glade Ct, Ilf. IG5 125 EM53
Uxbridge UB8 156 BJ65
Glade Gdns, Croy. CR0 225 DY101
Glade La, Sthl. UB2 178 CB75
Glade Ms, Guil. GU1 281 AZ135
Sch Glade Prim Sch, Ilf. IG5
off Atherton Rd 125 EM54
Glades, The, Grav. DA12 213 GK93
Hemel Hempstead HP1 61 BE19
Gladeside, N21 103 DM44
Croydon CR0 225 DX100
St. Albans AL4 65 CK17
Gladeside Cl, Chess. KT9 237 CK108
Gladeside Ct, Warl. CR6 258 DV120
Gladesmere Ct, Wat. WD24 97 BV36
Sch Gladesmore Comm Sch,
N15 off Crowland Rd 144 DU57
Gladesmore Rd, N15 144 DT58
Glade Spur, Kgswd KT20 256 DB121
Glades Shop Cen, The,
Brom. BR1 226 EG96
Gladeswood Rd, Belv. DA17 189 FB77
Gladeway, The, Wal.Abb. EN9 89 ED33
Gladiator St, SE23 205 DY86
Glading Ter, N16 144 DT62
Gladioli Cl, Hmptn. TW12
off Gresham Rd 198 CA93
Gladsdale Dr, Pnr. HA5 137 BU56
Gladsmuir Cl, Walt. KT12 218 BW103
Gladsmuir Rd, N19 143 DJ60
Barnet EN5 101 CY40
Gladstone Av, E12 166 EL66
N22 121 DN54
Feltham TW14 197 BU86
Twickenham TW2 199 CD87
Gladstone Ct, SW1
off Regency St 29 P9
SW8 off Havelock Ter 41 K6
SW19 202 DA94
Gladstone Gdns, Houns. TW3 178 CC81
Gladstone Ms, N22
off Pelham Rd 121 DN54
NW6 4 G6
SE20 204 DW94
Gladstone Par, NW2
off Edgware Rd 141 CV60
Gladstone Pk Gdns, NW2 141 CV62
Sch Gladstone Pk Prim Sch, NW10
off Sherrick Grn Rd 141 CV64
Gladstone Pl, E3 11 P10
Barnet EN5 101 CX42
Gladstone Rd, SW19 202 DA94
W4 off Acton La 180 CR76
Ashtead KT21 253 CK118
Buckhurst Hill IG9 124 EH46
Chesham HP5 76 AQ31
Croydon CR0 224 DR101
Dartford DA1 210 FM86
Hoddesdon EN11 71 EB16
Kingston upon Thames KT1 220 CN97
Orpington BR6 245 EQ106
Southall UB2 178 BY75
Surbiton KT6 219 CK103
Ware SG12 54 DW05
Watford WD17 98 BW41
Gladstone St, SE1 30 G6
Gladstone Ter, SE27
off Bentons La 204 DQ91
Gladstone Way, Slou. SL1 173 AN75
Wealdstone HA3 139 CE55
Gladwell Rd, N8 143 DM58
Bromley BR1 206 EG93
Gladwin Way, Harl. CM20 57 ER13
Gladwyn Rd, SW15 38 C10
Gladys Rd, NW6 5 K6
Glaisher St, SE8 46 B2
Glaisyer Way, Iver SL0 155 BC68
Glamis Cl, Chsht EN7 88 DU29
Glamis Cres, Hayes UB3 177 BQ76
Glamis Dr, Horn. RM11 150 FL60
Glamis Pl, E1 21 H10
Hemel Hempstead HP2 62 BL19
Glamis Rd, E1 21 H10
Glamis Way, Nthlt. UB5 158 CC65
Glamorgan Cl, Mitch. CR4 223 DL97
Glamorgan Rd, Kings.T. KT1 199 CJ94
Glan Avon Ms, Harl. CM17 74 EW16
Glanford Way, Chad.Hth RM6 148 EV57
Glanfield, Hem.H. HP2
off Bathurst Rd 62 BL17
Glanfield Rd, Beck. BR3 225 DZ98
Glanleam Rd, Stan. HA7 117 CK49
Glanmead, Shenf. CM15 130 FY46
Glanmor Rd, Slou. SL2 154 AV73
Glanthams Cl, Shenf. CM15 130 FY47
Glanthams Rd, Shenf. CM15 131 FZ47
Glanty, The, Egh. TW20 195 BB91
Glanville Dr, Horn. RM11 150 FM60
Glanville Ms, Stan. HA7 117 CG50
Glanville Rd, SW2 203 DL85
Bromley BR2 226 EH97
Glasbrook Av, Twick. TW2 198 BZ88
Glasbrook Rd, SE9 206 EK87
Glaserton Rd, N16 144 DS59
Glasford St, SW17 202 DF93
Glasgow Ho, W9 15 M1
Glasgow Rd, E13 24 A1
N18 122 DV50
Slough SL1 153 AN72
Glasgow Ter, SW1 41 L1
Glasier Ct, E15 13 K6
Glaskin Ms, E9 11 M5
Glasse Cl, W13 159 CG73
Glasshill St, SE1 31 H4
Glasshouse Cl, Uxb. UB8 157 BP71
Glasshouse Flds, E1 21 J10
Glasshouse St, W1 29 M1
Glasshouse Wk, SE11 30 B10
Glasshouse Yd, EC1 19 J5
Glasslyn Rd, N8 143 DK57
Glassmill La, Brom. BR2 226 EF96
Glass St, E2 20 F4
Glass Yd, SE18 37 M6
Glastonbury Av, Wdf.Grn. IG8 124 EK52
Glastonbury Cl, Orp. BR5 228 EW102
Glastonbury Ho, SW1 29 J10
Glastonbury Pl, E1 20 G9
Glastonbury Rd, N9 122 DU46
Morden SM4 222 DA101
Glastonbury St, NW6 5 H3
Glaucus St, E3 22 C6
Glazbury Rd, W14 26 F9
Glazebrook Cl, SE21 204 DR89
Glazebrook Rd, Tedd. TW11 199 CF94
Gleave Cl, St.Alb. AL1 65 CH19
Glebe, The, SE3 47 J10
SW16 203 DK91
Chislehurst BR7 227 EQ95
Harlow CM20 off School La 57 ES14
Horley RH6 290 DF148
Kings Langley WD4 80 BN29
Leigh RH2 287 CU141
Magdalen Laver CM5 75 FD18
Watford WD25 82 BW33
West Drayton UB7 176 BM77
Worcester Park KT4 221 CT102
Glebe Av, Enf. EN2 103 DP41
Harrow HA3 140 CL55
Mitcham CR4 222 DE96
Ruislip HA4 157 BV65
Uxbridge UB10 137 BQ63
Woodford Green IG8 124 EG51
Glebe Cl, W4 180 CS78
Bookham KT23 268 CA126
Chalfont St. Peter SL9 112 AX52
Essendon AL9 68 DF17
Hemel Hempstead HP3 62 BL24
Hertford SG14 54 DR07
South Croydon CR2 242 DT111
Taplow SL6 172 AF75
Uxbridge UB10 137 BQ63
Glebe Cotts, Brasted TN16 262 EV123
Essendon AL9 68 DF17
Sutton SM1 off Vale Rd 240 DB105
West Clandon GU4 266 BH132
Glebe Ct, W7 159 CD73
Coulsdon CR5 257 DH115
Guildford GU1 265 AZ134
Mitcham CR4 222 DF97
Sevenoaks TN13 off Oak La 279 FH126
Stanmore HA7 117 CJ50
Glebe Cres, NW4 141 CW56
Harrow HA3 140 CL55
Glebefield, The, Sev. TN13 278 FF123
Sch Glebe First & Mid Sch, Kenton
HA3 off D'Arcy Gdns 140 CL56
Glebe Gdns, Byfleet KT14 234 BK114
New Malden KT3 220 CS101
Glebe Ho Dr, Brom. BR2 226 EH102
Glebe Hyrst, SE19 204 DS91
South Croydon CR2 242 DT112
Glebeland, Hat. AL10
off St. Etheldredas Dr 67 CW18
Glebeland Gdns, Shep. TW17 217 BQ100
Glebelands, Chig. IG7 126 EV48
Claygate KT10 237 CF109
Dartford DA1 189 FF84
Harlow CM20 57 ET12
Penn HP10 110 AC47
West Molesey KT8 218 CB99
Glebelands Av, E18 124 EG54
Ilford IG2 147 ER59
Glebelands Cl, N12 120 DD53
Glebelands Rd, Felt. TW14 197 BU87
Glebe La, Abin.Com. RH5 284 BX143
Barnet EN5 101 CU43
Harrow HA3 140 CL56
Sevenoaks TN13 279 FH126
Glebe Ms, Sid. DA15 207 ET85
Glebe Path, Mitch. CR4 222 DE97
Glebe Pl, SW3 40 C2
Horton Kirby DA4 230 FQ98
Sch Glebe Prim Sch, Ickhm
UB10 off Sussex Rd 137 BQ63
Glebe Rd, E8 10 A7
N3 120 DC53
N8 143 DM56
NW10 161 CT65
SW13 181 CU82
Ashtead KT21 253 CK118
Bromley BR1 226 EG95
Carshalton SM5 240 DF107
Chalfont St. Peter SL9 112 AW53
Dagenham RM10 169 FB65
Dorking RH4 285 CF136
Egham TW20 195 BC93
Gravesend DA11 213 GF88
Hayes UB3 157 BT74
Hertford SG14 54 DR07
Merstham RH1 257 DH124
Old Windsor SL4 194 AV85
Rainham RM13 170 FJ69
Staines-upon-Thames TW18 196 BH93
Stanmore HA7 117 CJ50
Sutton SM2 239 CY109
Uxbridge UB8 156 BJ68
Warlingham CR6 259 DX117
Sch Glebe Sch, W.Wick. BR4
off Hawes La 225 ED103
Glebe Side, Twick. TW1 199 CF86
Glebe Sq, Mitch. CR4 222 DF97
Glebe St, W4 180 CS78
Glebe Ter, W4 off Glebe St 180 CS78
Glebe Way, Amer. HP6 77 AR36
Erith DA8 189 FE79
Hanworth TW13 198 CA90
Hornchurch RM11 150 FL59
South Croydon CR2 242 DT112
West Wickham BR4 225 EC103
Glebeway, Wdf.Grn. IG8 124 EJ50
Gledhow Gdns, SW5 27 N9
Gledhow Wd, Kgswd KT20 256 DB121
Gledstanes Rd, W14 38 F1
Gledwood Av, Hayes UB4 157 BT71
Gledwood Cres, Hayes UB4 157 BT71
Gledwood Dr, Hayes UB4 157 BT71
Gledwood Gdns, Hayes UB4 157 BT71
Gleed Av, Bushey Hth WD23 117 CD47
Gleeson Dr, Orp. BR6 245 ET106
Gleeson Ms, Add. KT15 234 BJ105
Glegg Pl, SW15 181 CX84
Glen, The, Add. KT15 233 BF106
Bromley BR2 226 EE96
Croydon CR0 225 DX104
Eastcote HA5 137 BV57
Enfield EN2 103 DP42
Hemel Hempstead HP2 62 BM15
Northwood HA6 115 BR52
Orpington BR6 227 EM104
Pinner HA5 138 BY59
Rainham RM13 170 FJ70
Slough SL3 174 AW77
Southall UB2 178 BZ78
Wembley HA9 139 CK63
Glenaffric Av, E14 34 F9
Glen Albyn Rd, SW19 201 CX89
Glenalla Rd, Ruis. HA4 137 BT59
Glenalmond Rd, Har. HA3 140 CL56
Glenalvon Way, SE18 36 G8
Glena Mt, Sutt. SM1 240 DC105
Sch Glenarm Coll, Ilf. IG1
off Coventry Rd 147 EP61
Glenarm Rd, E5 10 G2
Glen Av, Ashf. TW15 196 BN91
Glenavon Cl, Clay. KT10 237 CG108
Glenavon Gdns, Slou. SL3 174 AW77
Glenavon Rd, E15 13 K6
Glenbarr Cl, SE9 187 EP83
Glenbow Rd, Brom. BR1 206 EE93
Glenbrook N, Enf. EN2 103 DM42
Sch Glenbrook Prim Sch, SW4
off Clarence Av 203 DK86
Glenbrook Rd, NW6 5 J3
Glenbrook S, Enf. EN2 103 DM42
Glenbuck Ct, Surb. KT6
off Glenbuck Rd 220 CL100
Glenbuck Rd, Surb. KT6 219 CK100
Glenburnie Rd, SW17 202 DF90
Glencairn Dr, W5 159 CH70
Glencairne Cl, E16 24 E6
Glencairn Rd, SW16 223 DL95
Glen Cl, Kgswd KT20 255 CY123
Shepperton TW17 216 BN98
Glencoe Av, Ilf. IG2 147 ER59
Glencoe Dr, Dag. RM10 148 FA63
Glencoe Rd, Bushey WD23 98 CA44
Hayes UB4 158 BY71
Weybridge KT13 216 BN104
Glencorse Grn, Wat. WD19 116 BX49
Glen Ct, Stai. TW18 195 BF94
Glen Cres, Wdf.Grn. IG8 124 EH51
Glendale, Hem.H. HP1 62 BH20
Swanley BR8 229 FF99
Glendale Av, N22 121 DN52
Edgware HA8 118 CM49

Glendale Av, Romford RM6 148 EW59
Glendale Cl, SE9 187 EN83
Shenfield CM15 130 FY45
Woking GU21 248 AW118
Glendale Dr, SW19 201 CZ92
Guildford GU4 265 BB130
Glendale Gdns, Wem. HA9 139 CK60
Glendale Ms, Beck. BR3 225 EB95
Glendale Ri, Ken. CR8 257 DP115
Glendale Rd, Erith DA8 189 FC77
Northfleet DA11 212 GE91
Glendale Wk, Chsht EN8 89 DY30
Glendale Way, SE28 168 EW73
Glendall St, SW9 183 DM84
Glendarvon St, SW15 38 D10
Glendean Ct, Enf. EN3
off Tysoe Av 105 DZ36
Glendene Av, E.Hors. KT24 267 BS126
Glendevon Cl, Edg. HA8 118 CP48
Glendish Rd, N17 122 DU53
Glendor Gdns, NW7 118 CR49
Glendower Cres, Orp. BR6 228 EU100
Glendower Gdns, SW14
off Glendower Rd 180 CR83
Glendower Pl, SW7 28 A8
Sch **Glendower Prep Sch**, SW7 28 A8
Glendower Rd, E4 123 ED46
SW14 180 CR83
Glendown Rd, SE2 188 EU78
Glendun Rd, W3 160 CS73
Gleneagle Ms, SW16
off Ambleside Av 203 DK92
Gleneagle Rd, SW16 203 DK92
Gleneagles, Stan. HA7 117 CH51
Gleneagles Cl, SE16 44 E1
Orpington BR6 227 ER102
Romford RM3 128 FM52
Stanwell TW19 196 BK86
Watford WD19 116 BX49
Gleneagles Grn, Orp. BR6
off Tandridge Dr 227 ER102
Gleneagles Twr, Sthl. UB1 158 CC72
Gleneldon Ms, SW16 203 DL91
Gleneldon Rd, SW16 203 DL91
Glenelg Rd, SW2 203 DL85
Glenesk Rd, SE9 187 EN83
Sch **Glenesk Sch**, E.Hors. KT24
off Ockham Rd N 267 BR125
Glenester Cl, Hodd. EN11 55 EA14
Glen Faba, Roydon CM19 72 EE16
Glen Faba Rd, Roydon CM19 72 EF17
Glenfarg Rd, SE6 205 ED88
Glenferrie Rd, St.Alb. AL1 65 CG20
Glenfield Cl, Brock. RH3 286 CP138
Glenfield Cres, Ruis. HA4 137 BR59
Glenfield Rd, SW12 203 DJ88
W13 179 CH75
Ashford TW15 197 BP93
Banstead SM7 256 DB115
Brockham RH3 286 CP138
Glenfields, Stoke P. SL2 154 AT67
Glenfield Ter, W13 179 CH75
Glenfinlas Way, SE5 43 H4
Glenforth St, SE10 35 M10
Glengall Gro, E14 34 E6
Glengall Rd, NW6 5 H9
SE15 44 B2
Bexleyheath DA7 188 EY83
Edgware HA8 118 CP48
Woodford Green IG8 124 EG51
Glengall Ter, SE15 44 B2
Glen Gdns, Croy. CR0 223 DP104
Glengarnock Av, E14 34 F9
Glengarry Rd, SE22 204 DS85
Glenham Dr, Ilf. IG2 147 EP57
Glenhaven Av, Borwd. WD6 100 CN41
Glenhead Cl, SE9 187 EP83
Glenheadon Cl, Lthd. KT22
off Glenheadon Ri 253 CK123
Glenheadon Ri, Lthd. KT22 253 CK123
Glenhill Cl, N3 120 DA54
Glen Ho, E16 *off Storey St* 37 M3
Glenhouse Rd, SE9 207 EN85
Glenhurst Av, NW5 142 DG63
Bexley DA5 208 EZ88
Ruislip HA4 137 BQ59
Glenhurst Ct, SE19 204 DT92
Glenhurst Ri, SE19 204 DQ94
Glenhurst Rd, N12 120 DD50
Brentford TW8 179 CJ79
Glenilla Rd, NW3 6 C4
Glenister Gdns, Hayes UB3 177 BV75
Glenister Ho, Hayes UB3 157 BV74
Glenister Pk Rd, SW16 203 DK94
Glenister Rd, SE10 35 L10
Chesham HP5 76 AQ28
Glenister St, E16 37 M3
Glenkerry Ho, E14 22 E8
Glenlea Path, SE9
off Well Hall Rd 207 EM85
Glenlea Rd, SE9 207 EM85
Glenlion Ct, Wey. KT13 217 BR104
Glenloch Rd, NW3 6 C4
Enfield EN3 104 DW40
Glen Luce, Chsht EN8 89 DX31
Glenluce Rd, SE3 47 N3
Glenlyn Av, St.Alb. AL1 65 CH21
Glenlyon Rd, SE9 207 EN85
Glenmere Av, NW7 119 CU52
Glenmere Row, SE12 206 EG86
Glen Ms, E17 *off Glen Rd* 145 DZ57
Glenmill, Hmptn. TW12 198 BZ92
Glenmire Ter, Stans.Abb. SG12 55 ED11
Glenmore Cl, Add. KT15 216 BH104
Glenmore Gdns, Abb.L. WD5
off Stewart Cl 81 BU32
Glenmore Rd, NW3 6 C4
Welling DA16 187 ET81
Glenmore Way, Bark. IG11 168 EU69
Glenmount Path, SE18
off Raglan Rd 187 EQ78
Glenn Av, Pur. CR8 241 DP111
Glennie Rd, SE27 203 DN90
Glenny Rd, Bark. IG11 167 EQ65
Glenorchy Cl, Hayes UB4 158 BY71
Glenparke Rd, E7 166 EH65
Glen Ri, Wdf.Grn. IG8 124 EH51
Glen Rd, E13 24 C4
E17 145 DZ57
Chessington KT9 220 CL104
Glen Rd End, Wall. SM6 241 DH109
Glenrosa Gdns, Grav. DA12 213 GM92
Glenrosa St, SW6 39 N8
Glenrose Ct, Sid. DA14 208 EV92
Glenroy St, W12 14 A8
Glensdale Rd, SE4 185 DZ83
Glenshee Cl, Nthwd. HA6
off Rickmansworth Rd 115 BQ51
Glenshiel Rd, SE9 207 EN85
Glenside, Chig. IG7 125 EP51
Glenside Cl, Ken. CR8 258 DR115
Glenside Cotts, Slou. SL1 174 AT76
Glentanner Way, SW17 202 DD90
Glen Ter, E14 34 E4
Glentham Gdns, SW13 181 CV79
Glentham Rd, SW13 181 CU79
Glenthorne Av, Croy. CR0 224 DV102
Glenthorne Cl, Sutt. SM3 222 DA102
Uxbridge UB10 156 BN69
Glenthorne Gdns, Ilf. IG6 147 EN55
Sutton SM3 222 DA102
Sch **Glenthorne High Sch**, Sutt. SM3
off Sutton Common Rd 222 DA102
Glenthorne Ms, W6
off Glenthorne Rd 181 CV77
Glenthorne Rd, E17 145 DY57
N11 120 DF50
W6 26 A8
Kingston upon Thames KT1 220 CM98
Glenthorpe Rd, Mord. SM4 221 CX99
Glenton Cl, Rom. RM1 127 FE51
Glenton Rd, SE13 186 EE84
Glenton Way, Rom. RM1 127 FE52
Glentrammon Av, Orp. BR6 245 ET107
Glentrammon Cl, Orp. BR6 245 ET107
Glentrammon Gdns, Orp. BR6 245 ET107
Glentrammon Rd, Orp. BR6 245 ET107
Glentworth Pl, Slou. SL1 153 AQ74
Glentworth St, NW1 16 F5
Glenure Rd, SE9 207 EN85
Glenview, SE2 188 EX79
Glen Vw, Grav. DA12 213 GJ88
Glenview Gdns, Hem.H. HP1
off Glenview Rd 62 BH20
Glenview Rd, Brom. BR1 226 EK96
Hemel Hempstead HP1 62 BH20
Glenville Av, Enf. EN2 104 DQ38
Glenville Gro, SE8 45 P5
Glenville Ms, SW18 202 DB87
Glenville Rd, Kings.T. KT2 220 CN95
Glen Wk, Islw. TW7 199 CD85
Glen Way, Wat. WD17 97 BS38
Glenwood, Brox. EN10 71 DZ19
Dorking RH5 285 CJ138
Welwyn Garden City AL7 52 DD10
Glenwood Av, NW9 140 CS60
Rainham RM13 169 FG70
Glenwood Cl, Har. HA1 139 CF57
Glenwood Ct, E18
off Clarendon Rd 146 EG55
Glenwood Dr, Rom. RM2 149 FG56
Glenwood Gdns, Ilf. IG2 147 EN57
Glenwood Gro, NW9 140 CQ60
Glenwood Rd, N15 143 DP57
NW7 118 CS48
SE6 205 DZ88
Epsom KT17 239 CU107
Hounslow TW3 179 CD83
Glenwood Way, Croy. CR0 225 DX100
Glenworth Av, E14 34 G9
Glevum Cl, St.Alb. AL3 64 BZ22
Gliddon Dr, E5 144 DU63
Gliddon Rd, W14 26 E9
Glimpsing Grn, Erith DA18 188 EY76
Glisson Rd, Uxb. UB10 156 BN68
Gload Cres, Orp. BR5 228 EX103
Global App, E3 22 D1
Sch **Globe Acad**, SE1 31 L7
Globe Ct, Hert. SG14
off Bengeo St 54 DQ07
● **Globe Ind Est**, Grays RM17 192 GC78
Globe Pond Rd, SE16 33 L3
Sch **Globe Prim Sch**, E2 21 H2
Globe Rd, E1 21 H2
E2 20 G1
E15 13 L3
Hornchurch RM11 149 FG58
Woodford Green IG8 124 EJ51
Globe Rope Wk, E14 34 E9
Globe St, SE1 31 K6
Globe Ter, E2 20 G2
Globe Town, E2 21 J1
Globe Vw, EC4
off High Timber St 19 J10
Globe Wf, SE16 33 K1
Globe Yd, W1 17 J9
Glory Cl, Woob.Grn HP10 132 AF56
Glory Hill La, Beac. HP9 132 AE55
Glory Mead, Dor. RH4 285 CH139
Glory Mill La, Woob.Grn HP10 132 AE56
Glossop Rd, S.Croy. CR2 242 DR109
Gloster Rd, N.Mal. KT3 220 CS98
Woking GU22 249 BA120
Gloucester Arc, SW7 27 N8
Gloucester Av, NW1 7 H8
Grays RM16 192 GC75
Hornchurch RM11 150 FN56
Sidcup DA15 207 ES89
Slough SL1 153 AQ71
Waltham Cross EN8 89 DY33
Welling DA16 187 ET84
Gloucester Circ, SE10 46 F4
Gloucester Cl, NW10 160 CR66
Thames Ditton KT7 219 CG102
Gloucester Ct, EC3
off Byward St 31 P1
Croxley Green WD3 97 BP41
Denham UB9 136 BG59
Hatfield AL10
off De Havilland Cl 67 CT17
Richmond TW9 180 CN80
Tilbury RM18 *off Dock Rd* 193 GF82
Gloucester Cres, NW1 7 J8
Staines-upon-Thames TW18 196 BK93
Gloucester Dr, N4 143 DP61
NW11 142 DA56
Staines-upon-Thames TW18 195 BC90
Gloucester Gdns, NW11 141 CZ59
W2 15 M8
Cockfosters EN4 102 DG42
Ilford IG1 146 EL59
Sutton SM1 222 DB103
Gloucester Gate, NW1 7 J10
Gloucester Gate Ms, NW1 7 J10
Gloucester Gro, Edg. HA8 118 CR53
Gloucester Ho, NW6 15 K1
Gloucester Ms, E10
off Gloucester Rd 145 EA59
W2 15 P9
Gloucester Ms W, W2 15 N9
Gloucester Par, Sid. DA15 208 EU85
Gloucester Pl, NW1 16 E4
W1 16 F6
Windsor SL4 173 AR82
Gloucester Pl Ms, W1 16 F7
Sch **Gloucester Prim Sch**, SE15 44 A4
⊖ **Gloucester Road** 27 P8
Gloucester Rd, E10 145 EA59
E11 146 EH57
E12 147 EM62
E17 123 DX54
N17 122 DR54
N18 122 DT50
SW7 27 N6
W3 180 CQ75
W5 179 CJ75
Barnet EN5 102 DC43
Belvedere DA17 188 EZ78
Croydon CR0 224 DR100
Dartford DA1 209 FH87
Enfield EN2 104 DQ38
Feltham TW13 198 BW88
Gravesend DA12 213 GJ91
Guildford GU2 264 AT132
Hampton TW12 198 CB94
Harrow HA1 138 CB57
Hounslow TW4 178 BY84
Kingston upon Thames KT1 220 CP96
Pilgrim's Hatch CM15 130 FV43
Redhill RH1 272 DF133
Richmond TW9 180 CN80
Romford RM1 149 FE58
Teddington TW11 199 CE92
Twickenham TW2 198 CC88
Gloucester Sq, E2 10 C9
W2 16 B9
Woking GU21, GU22
off Church St E 249 AZ117
Gloucester St, SW1 41 L1
Gloucester Ter, W2 15 N8
Gloucester Wk, W8 27 K4
Woking GU21 249 AZ117
Gloucester Way, EC1 18 F3
Glover Cl, SE2 188 EW77
Cheshunt EN7
off Allwood Rd 88 DT27
Glover Dr, N18 122 DW51
Glover Rd, Pnr. HA5 138 BX58
Glovers Cl, Bigg.H. TN16 260 EH116
Hertford SG13 54 DQ11
Glovers Gro, Ruis. HA4 137 BP59
Glovers La, Hast. CM17 74 EY20
Glovers Rd, Reig. RH2 288 DB135
Gloxinia Rd, Sthflt DA13 212 GB93
Gloxinia Wk, Hmptn. TW12 198 CA93
Glycena Rd, SW11 40 F10
Glyn Av, Barn. EN4 102 DD42
Glyn Cl, SE25 224 DS96
Epsom KT17 239 CU109
Glyn Ct, SW16 203 DN90
Stanmore HA7 117 CH51
Glyn Davies Cl, Dunt.Grn TN13 263 FE120
Glyndebourne Pk, Orp. BR6 227 EP103
Glynde Ms, SW3 28 D7
Glynde Rd, Bexh. DA7 188 EX83
Glynde St, SE4 205 DZ86
Glyndon Rd, SE18 187 EQ77
Glyn Dr, Sid. DA14 208 EV91
Glynfield Rd, NW10 160 CS66
Glynne Rd, N22 121 DN54
Glyn Rd, E5 11 K2
Enfield EN3 104 DW42
Worcester Park KT4 221 CX103
Glyn St, SE11 42 C1
Glynswood, Chal.St.P. SL9 113 AZ52
Glynswood Pl, Nthwd. HA6 115 BP52
Sch **Glyn Tech Sch**, Ewell KT17
off The Kingsway 239 CT111
Glynwood Ct, SE23 204 DW89
Goaters All, SW6 38 G5
GOATHURST COMMON,
Sev. TN14 278 FB130
Goat La, Enf. EN1 104 DT38
Surbiton KT6 219 CJ103
Goat Rd, Mitch. CR4 222 DG101
Goatsfield Rd, Tats. TN16 260 EJ120
Goatswood La, Nave. RM4 127 FH45
Goat Wf, Brent. TW8 180 CL79
Gobions Av, Rom. RM5 127 FD52
Gobions Way, Pot.B. EN6
off Swanley Bar La 86 DB28
Goblins Grn, Welw.G.C. AL7 51 CX10
Godalming Av, Wall. SM6 241 DL106
Godalming Rd, E14 22 C7
Godbold Rd, E15 23 J3
Goddard Cl, Guil. GU2 264 AU130
Shepperton TW17
off Magdalene Rd 216 BM97
Goddard Dr, Bushey WD23 98 CC43
Goddard Pl, N19 143 DJ62
Goddard Rd, Beck. BR3 225 DX98
Goddards Cl, Lt.Berk. SG13 69 DJ19
Goddards Way, Ilf. IG1 147 ER60
GODDEN GREEN, Sev. TN15 279 FN125
H **Godden Grn Clinic**,
Godden Grn TN15 279 FP125
GODDINGTON, Orp. BR6 228 EW104
Goddington Chase, Orp. BR6 246 EV105
Goddington La, Orp. BR6 228 EU104
Godfrey Av, Nthlt. UB5 158 BY67
Twickenham TW2 199 CD87
Godfrey Hill, SE18 37 H9
Godfrey Ho, EC1 19 L3
Godfrey Pl, E2 *off Austin St* 20 A3
Godfrey Rd, SE18 37 J9
Godfrey St, E15 12 F10
SW3 28 D10
Godfrey Way, Houns. TW4 198 BY87
Goding St, SE11 42 B1
Godley Cl, SE14 45 H7
Godley Rd, SW18 202 DD88
Byfleet KT14 234 BM113
Godliman St, EC4 19 J9
Godman Rd, SE15 44 E9
Grays RM16 193 GG76
Sch **Godolphin & Latymer Sch**,
The, W6 *off Iffley Rd* 181 CV77
Godolphin Cl, N13 121 DP51
Sutton SM2 239 CZ111
Sch **Godolphin Inf Sch**, Slou.
SL1 *off Warrington Av* 153 AQ72
Sch **Godolphin Jun Sch**, Slou.
SL1 *off Oatlands Dr* 153 AR72
Godolphin Pl, W3 160 CR73
Godolphin Rd, W12 181 CV75
Seer Green HP9 111 AQ51
Slough SL1 153 AR73
Weybridge KT13 235 BR107
Godric Cres, New Adgtn CR0 243 ED110
Godson Rd, Croy. CR0 223 DN104
Godson St, N1 8 E10
Godson Yd, NW6
off Kilburn Pk Rd 15 J3
GODSTONE, RH9 274 DV131
Godstone Bypass, Gdse. RH9 274 DW129
Godstone Grn, Gdse. RH9 274 DV131
Godstone Grn Rd, Gdse. RH9 274 DV131
Godstone Hill, Gdse. RH9 274 DV127
Jct **Godstone Interchange**,
Gdse. RH9 274 DW128
Godstone Rd, Bletch. RH1 274 DR133
Caterham CR3 258 DU124
Kenley CR8 242 DR114
Oxted RH8 275 EA131
Purley CR8 241 DN112
Sutton SM1 240 DC105
Twickenham TW1 199 CG86
Whyteleafe CR3 258 DT116
Sch **Godstone Village Sch**, Gdse.
RH9 *off Ivy Mill La* 274 DV132
Godstow Rd, SE2 188 EW75
Godwin Cl, E4 105 EC38
N1 9 K10
Epsom KT19 238 CQ107
Godwin Ct, NW1 7 M10
Godwin Ho, NW6
off Tollgate Gdns 5 L10
Sch **Godwin Jun Sch**, E7
off Cranmer Rd 146 EH63
Sch **Godwin Prim Sch**, Dag.
RM9 *off Finnymore Rd* 168 EY66
Godwin Rd, E7 146 EH63
Bromley BR2 226 EJ97
Coll **Goethe Institut**, SW7 28 B6
Goffers Rd, SE3 47 J7
Goffs Cres, Goffs Oak EN7 87 DP29
Goffs La, Goffs Oak EN7 88 DU29
GOFFS OAK, Wal.Cr. EN7 88 DQ29
Goffs Oak Av, Goffs Oak EN7 87 DP28
Sch **Goffs Oak Prim Sch**, Goffs Oak
EN7 *off Millcrest Rd* 87 DP28
Goffs Rd, Ashf. TW15 197 BR93
Sch **Goffs Sch**, Chsht EN7
off Goffs La 88 DU29
Gogmore Fm Cl, Cher. KT16 215 BF101
Gogmore La, Cher. KT16 216 BG101
Goidel Cl, Wall. SM6 241 DK105
Golborne Gdns, W10 14 F5
Golborne Ms, W10 14 E7
Golborne Rd, W10 14 F7
Goldace, Grays RM17 192 FZ79
Golda Cl, Barn. EN5 101 CX44
Goldbeaters Gro, Edg. HA8 118 CS51
Sch **Goldbeaters Prim Sch**, Edg.
HA8 *off Thirleby Rd* 118 CR53
Goldcliff Cl, Mord. SM4 222 DA101
Gold Cl, Brox. EN10 71 DY20
Goldcrest Cl, E16 24 E6
SE28 168 EW73
Horley RH6 290 DD147
Goldcrest Ms, W5 159 CK71
Goldcrest Way, Bushey WD23 116 CC46
New Addington CR0 243 ED109
Purley CR8 241 DK110
Goldcroft, Hem.H. HP3 62 BN22
Golden Ct, Islw. TW7 179 CD82
Richmond TW9
off George St 199 CK85
Golden Cres, Hayes UB3 157 BT74
Golden Cross Ms, W11 14 G8
Golden Dell, Welw.G.C. AL7 51 CZ13
★ **Golden Hinde**, SE1 31 L2
Golden Jubilee Br, SE1 30 C3
WC2 30 B2
Golden La, EC1 19 J5
Golden La Est, EC1 19 J5
Golden Lion Ct, N9 *off The Grn* 122 DU47
Golden Manor, W7 159 CE73
Golden Oak Cl, Farn.Com. SL2 153 AQ65
Golden Plover Cl, E16 24 A8
Golden Sq, W1 17 M10
Golden Yd, NW3
off Heath St 142 DC63
Golders Cl, Edg. HA8 118 CP50
Golders Gdns, NW11 141 CY59
GOLDERS GREEN, NW11 142 DA59
⊖ **Golders Green** 142 DA59
⊖ **Golders Green** 142 DA60
Golders Grn Cres, NW11 141 CZ59
Golders Grn Rd, NW11 141 CY58
Sch **Golders Hill Sch**, NW11
off Finchley Rd 142 DA59
Golders Manor Dr, NW11 141 CX58
Golders Pk Cl, NW11 142 DA60
Golders Ri, NW4 141 CX57
Golders Way, NW11 141 CZ59
Goldfinch Cl, Orp. BR6 246 EU106
Goldfinch Gdns, Guil. GU4 265 BD133
Goldfinch Rd, SE28 187 ER76
South Croydon CR2 243 DY110
Goldfinch Way, Borwd. WD6 100 CN42
Goldfort Wk, Wok. GU21
off Langmans Way 248 AS116
Goldhawk Ms, W12
off Devonport Rd 181 CV75
⊖ **Goldhawk Road** 26 A5
Goldhawk Rd, W6 181 CT77
W12 181 CU76
Goldhaze Cl, Wdf.Grn. IG8 124 EK52
Gold Hill, Edg. HA8 118 CR51
Gold Hill E, Chal.St.P. SL9 112 AX54
Gold Hill N, Chal.St.P. SL9 112 AW53
Gold Hill W, Chal.St.P. SL9 112 AW53
Goldhurst Ter, NW6 5 N7
H **Golding Leigh Hosp**, SE2 188 EW79
Golding Cl, Chess. KT9
off Coppard Gdns 237 CJ107
Golding Ct, Ilf. IG1 147 EN62
Goldingham Av, Loug. IG10 107 EQ40
Golding Rd, Sev. TN13 279 FJ122
Goldings, Hert. SG14 53 DN06
Goldings, The, Wok. GU21 248 AT116
Goldings Cres, Hat. AL10 67 CV17
Goldings Hill, Loug. IG10 107 EN39
Goldings Ho, Hat. AL10 67 CV17
Goldings La, Waterf. SG14 53 DN06
Goldings Ri, Loug. IG10 107 EN39
Goldings Rd, Loug. IG10 107 EN39
Golding St, E1 20 D9
Golding Ter, SW11
off Longhedge St 41 H8
Goldington Cl, Hodd. EN11 55 DZ14
Goldington Cres, NW1 7 N10
Goldington St, NW1 7 N10
Gold La, Edg. HA8 118 CR51
Goldman Cl, E2 20 C4
Goldmark Ho, SE3
off Lebrun Sq 186 EH83
Goldney Rd, W9 15 J5
Goldrill Dr, N11 120 DG47
Goldrings Rd, Oxshott KT22 236 CC113
Goldring Way, Lon.Col. AL2 83 CH27
Goldsboro Rd, SW8 41 P6
Goldsborough Cres, E4 123 EC47
H **Goldsborough Indep Hosp**,
Red. RH1 288 DG138
Goldsdown Cl, Enf. EN3 105 DY40
Goldsdown Rd, Enf. EN3 105 DX40
Goldsel Rd, Swan. BR8 229 FD99
Goldsmid St, SE18 187 ES78
Goldsmith, Grays RM17 192 FZ79
Goldsmith Av, E12 166 EL65
NW9 141 CT58
W3 160 CR73
Romford RM7 148 FA59
Goldsmith Cl, W3 160 CR74
Biggin Hill TN16 260 EL117
Harrow HA2 138 CB60
Goldsmith La, NW9 140 CP56
Goldsmith Rd, E10 145 EA60
E17 123 DX54
N11 120 DF50
SE15 44 C6
W3 160 CR74
Goldsmiths Bottom, Sev.
TN14 278 FE127
Goldsmiths Cl, Wok. GU21 248 AW118
Uni **Goldsmiths Coll**, SE14 45 M6
★ **Goldsmiths' Hall**, EC2 19 J8
Goldsmith's Pl, NW6 5 L9
Goldsmith's Row, E2 20 C1
Goldsmith's Sq, E2 10 D10
Goldsmith St, EC2 19 K8
Goldsmith Way, St.Alb. AL3 64 CC19
Goldstone Cl, Ware SG12
off High Oak Rd 55 DX05
Goldstone Fm Vw, Lthd. KT23 268 CA127
Goldsworth Orchard, Wok.
GU21 *off St. John's Rd* 248 AU118
GOLDSWORTH PARK, Wok.
GU21 248 AU117
Goldsworth Pk, Wok. GU21 248 AU117
● **Goldsworth Pk Trd Est**,
Wok. GU21 248 AU116
Sch **Goldsworth Prim Sch**, Wok.
GU21 *off Bridge Barn La* 248 AW118
Goldsworth Rd, Wok. GU21 248 AW118
● **Goldsworth Rd Ind Est**, Wok.
GU21 *off Goldsworth Rd* 248 AX117
Goldsworthy Gdns, SE16 33 H9
Goldsworthy Way, Slou. SL1 152 AJ72
Goldwell Ho, SE22
off Quorn Rd 184 DS83
Goldwell Rd, Th.Hth. CR7 223 DM98
Goldwin Cl, SE14 45 H6
Golding Cl, E16 23 P9
Golf Cl, Bushey WD23 98 BX41
Stanmore HA7 117 CJ52
Thornton Heath CR7
off Kensington Av 223 DN95
Woking GU22 233 BE114
Golf Club Dr, Kings.T. KT2 200 CR94
Golf Club Rd, Brook.Pk AL9 86 DA26
Weybridge KT13 235 BP109
Woking GU22 248 AU120
Golfe Rd, Ilf. IG1 147 ER62
Golf Ho Rd, Oxt. RH8 276 EJ129
Golf Links Av, Grav. DA11 213 GH92
Golf Ride, Enf. EN2 103 DN35
Golf Rd, W5 160 CM72
Bromley BR1 227 EN97
Kenley CR8 258 DR118
Golf Side, Sutt. SM2 239 CY111
Twickenham TW2 199 CD90
Golfside Cl, N20 120 DE48
New Malden KT3 220 CS96
Gollogly Ter, SE7 186 EJ78
Gombards, St.Alb. AL3 65 CD19
Gombards All, St.Alb. AL3
off Worley Rd 65 CD19
Gomer Gdns, Tedd. TW11 199 CG93
Gomer Pl, Tedd. TW11 199 CG93
Gomm Rd, SE16 32 G7
Gomms Wd Cl, Forty Grn HP9 110 AH51
GOMSHALL, Guil. GU5 283 BR139
⇌ **Gomshall** 283 BR139
Gomshall Av, Wall. SM6 241 DL106
Gomshall Gdns, Ken. CR8 258 DS115
Gomshall La, Shere GU5 282 BN139
Gomshall Rd, Sutt. SM2 239 CW110
Gondar Gdns, NW6 4 G2
Gonnerston, St.Alb. AL3 64 CB19
Gonson St, SE8 46 C3
Gonston Cl, SW19 201 CY89
Gonville Av, Crox.Grn WD3 97 BP44
Gonville Cres, Nthlt. UB5 158 CB65
Sch **Gonville Prim Sch**, Th.Hth.
CR7 *off Gonville Rd* 223 DM99
Gonville Rd, Th.Hth. CR7 223 DM99
Gonville St, SW6 38 F10
Gooch Ho, E5 144 DV62
Goodacre Cl, Pot.B. EN6 86 DB32
Goodall Rd, E11 145 EC62
Goodchild Rd, N4 144 DQ60
Gooden Ct, Har. HA1 139 CE62
Goodenough Cl, Couls. CR5 257 DN120
Goodenough Rd, SW19 201 CZ94
Goodenough Way, Couls.
CR5 257 DM120
Gooderham Ho, Grays RM16 193 GH75
Goodey Rd, Bark. IG11 167 ET66
Goodge Pl, W1 17 M7
⊖ **Goodge Street** 17 M6
Goodge St, W1 17 M7
Goodhall Cl, Stan. HA7 117 CG51
Goodhall St, NW10 160 CS69
Goodhart Pl, E14 21 M10
Goodhart Way, W.Wick. BR4 226 EE101
Goodhew Rd, Croy. CR0 224 DU100
Gooding Cl, N.Mal. KT3 220 CQ98
Goodinge Cl, N7 8 A4
Goodison Cl, Bushey WD23 98 CC43
Goodlake Ct, Denh. UB9 135 BF59
GOODLEY STOCK, West. TN16 277 EP130
Goodley Stock Rd, West. TN16 277 EP129
Goodley Stock Rd, Crock.H.
TN8 277 EP131
Westerham TN16 277 EP128
Goodman Cres, SW2 203 DK89
Croy. CR0 223 DP100
Goodman Pk, Slou. SL2 154 AW74
Goodman Pl, Stai. TW18 195 BF91
Goodman Rd, E10 145 EC59
Goodmans Ct, E1 20 A10
Wembley HA0 139 CK63
Goodman's Stile, E1 20 C8
Goodman's Yd, E1 20 A10

GOODMAYES, Ilf. IG3 148 EV61
⇌ **Goodmayes** 148 EV60
Goodmayes Av, Ilf. IG3 148 EU60
H **Goodmayes Hosp**, Ilf. IG3 148 EU57
Goodmayes La, Ilf. IG3 148 EU63
Sch **Goodmayes Prim Sch**, Ilf. IG3 *off Airthrie Rd* 148 EV60
Goodmayes Retail Pk, Rom. RM6 148 EV60
Goodmayes Rd, Ilf. IG3 148 EU60
Goodmead Rd, Orp. BR6 228 EU101
Goodrich Cl, Wat. WD25 97 BU35
Sch **Goodrich Prim Sch**, SE22 *off Dunstans Rd* 204 DU86
Goodrich Rd, SE22 204 DT86
Sch **Good Shepherd Prim Sch**, Downham BR1 *off Moorside Rd* 206 EF91
Sch **Good Shepherd RC Prim Sch**, New Adgtn CR0 *off Dunley Dr* 243 EB108
Sch **Good Shepherd RC Prim Sch, The**, W12 *off Gayford Rd* 181 CT75
Goodson Rd, NW10 160 CS66
Goods Way, NW1 8 A10
Goodway Gdns, E14 22 G8
Goodwill Dr, Har. HA2 138 CA60
Goodwin Cl, SE16 32 B7
Mitcham CR4 222 DD97
Goodwin Ct, Barn. EN4 102 DE44
Waltham Cross EN8 89 DY28
Goodwin Dr, Sid. DA14 208 EX90
Goodwin Gdns, Croy. CR0 241 DP107
Goodwin Meadows, Woob.Grn HP10 132 AE57
Goodwin Rd, N9 122 DW46
W12 181 CU75
Croydon CR0 241 DP106
Slough SL2 153 AM69
Goodwins Ct, WC2 18 A10
Goodwin St, N4 *off Fonthill Rd* 143 DN61
Goodwood Av, Enf. EN3 104 DW37
Hornchurch RM12 150 FL63
Hutton CM13 131 GE44
Watford WD24 97 BS35
Goodwood Cl, Hodd. EN11 71 DZ16
Morden SM4 222 DA98
Stanmore HA7 117 CJ50
Goodwood Cres, Grav. DA12 213 GJ93
Goodwood Dr, Nthlt. UB5 158 CA65
Goodwood Path, Borwd. WD6 100 CN40
Goodwood Rd, SE14 45 L5
Redhill RH1 272 DF132
Goodworth Rd, Red. RH1 273 DH132
Goodwyn Av, NW7 118 CS50
Sch **Goodwyn Sch**, NW7 *off Hammers La* 119 CU50
Goodwyns Pl, Dor. RH4 285 CH138
Goodwyns Rd, Dor. RH4 285 CH139
Goodwyns Vale, N10 120 DG53
Goodyers Av, Rad. WD7 83 CF33
Goodyers Gdns, NW4 141 CX57
Goosander Way, SE28 187 ER76
Goose Acre, Chesh. HP5 78 AT30
Gooseacre, Welw.G.C. AL7 51 CZ11
Gooseacre La, Har. HA3 139 CK57
Goosecroft, Hem.H. HP1 61 BF19
Goosefields, Rick. WD3 96 BJ44
GOOSE GREEN, Hodd. EN11 70 DW17
Goose Grn, Cob. KT11 251 BU119
Farnham Royal SL2 153 AP68
Gomshall GU5 283 BQ139
Goose Grn Cl, Orp. BR5 228 EU96
Sch **Goose Grn Prim Sch**, SE22 *off Tintagel Cres* 184 DT84
Goose La, Wok. GU22 248 AV122
Gooseley La, E6 25 L2
Goosens Cl, Sutt. SM1 *off Turnpike La* 240 DC106
Goose Rye Rd, Worp. GU3 264 AT125
Goose Sq, E6 25 J9
Gooshays Dr, Rom. RM3 128 FL50
Gooshays Gdns, Rom. RM3 128 FL51
Gophir La, EC4 19 L10
Gopsall St, N1 9 M9
Goral Mead, Rick. WD3 114 BK46
Goran Ct, N9 *off Bedevere Rd* 122 DU48
Gordon Av, E4 124 EE51
SW14 180 CS84
Hornchurch RM12 149 FF61
South Croydon CR2 242 DQ110
Stanmore HA7 117 CH51
Twickenham TW1 199 CG85
Sch **Gordonbrock Prim Sch**, SE4 *off Gordonbrock Rd* 205 EA85
Gordonbrock Rd, SE4 205 EA85
Gordon Cl, E17 145 EA58
N19 143 DJ61
Chertsey KT16 215 BE104
St. Albans AL1 *off Kitchener Cl* 65 CH21
Staines-upon-Thames TW18 196 BH93
Gordon Cres, Croy. CR0 224 DS102
Hayes UB3 177 BU76
Gordondale Rd, SW19 202 DA89
Gordon Dr, Cher. KT16 215 BE104
Shepperton TW17 217 BR100
Gordon Gdns, Edg. HA8 118 CP54
Gordon Gro, SE5 43 H9
⇌ **Gordon Hill** 103 DP39
Gordon Hill, Enf. EN2 104 DQ39
H **Gordon Hosp**, SW1 29 N9
Gordon Ho, E1 20 G10
Gordon Ho Rd, NW5 7 H1
Sch **Gordon Infants' Sch**, Ilf. IG1 *off Golfe Rd* 147 ER62
Gordon Pl, W8 27 K4
Gravesend DA12 *off East Ter* 213 GJ86
Sch **Gordon Prim Sch**, SE9 *off Craigton Rd* 187 EM84
Gordon Prom, Grav. DA12 213 GJ86
Gordon Prom E, Grav. DA12 213 GJ86
Gordon Rd, E4 124 EE45
E11 146 EG58
E15 12 F1
E18 124 EH53
N3 119 CZ52
N9 122 DV47
N11 121 DK52
SE15 44 E7
W4 180 CP79
W5 159 CJ73
W13 159 CH73
Ashford TW15 196 BL90
Barking IG11 167 ES67
Beckenham BR3 225 DZ97
Belvedere DA17 189 FC77
Gordon Rd, Carshalton SM5 240 DF107
Caterham CR3 258 DR121
Chesham HP5 76 AQ32
Claygate KT10 237 CE107
Dartford DA1 210 FK87
Enfield EN2 104 DQ39
Grays RM16 193 GF75
Harrow HA3 139 CE55
Hounslow TW3 178 CC84
Ilford IG1 147 ER62
Kingston upon Thames KT2 220 CM95
Northfleet DA11 212 GE87
Redhill RH1 272 DG131
Richmond TW9 180 CM82
Romford RM6 148 EZ58
Sevenoaks TN13 279 FH125
Shenfield CM15 131 GA46
Shepperton TW17 217 BR100
Sidcup DA15 207 ES85
Southall UB2 178 BY77
Staines-upon-Thames TW18 195 BC91
Surbiton KT5 220 CM101
Waltham Abbey EN9 89 EA34
West Drayton UB7 156 BL73
Windsor SL4 173 AM82
Gordon Sq, WC1 17 P5
Gordon St, E13 23 P3
WC1 17 N4
Gordons Way, Oxt. RH8 275 ED128
Gordon Way, Barn. EN5 101 CZ42
Bromley BR1 226 EG95
Chalfont St. Giles HP8 112 AV48
Gore, The, Burn. SL1 152 AG69
Gore Cl, Hare. UB9 136 BH56
Gore Ct, NW9 140 CN57
Gorefield Pl, NW6 5 J10
Gore Hill, Amer. HP7 77 AP43
Gorelands La, Ch.St.G. HP8 113 AZ47
Gorell Rd, Beac. HP9 111 AP54
Gore Rd, E9 11 H9
SW20 221 CW96
Burnham SL1 152 AH69
Dartford DA2 210 FQ90
Goresbrook Rd, Dag. RM9 168 EV67
Goresbrook Village, Dag. RM9 *off Goresbrook Rd* 168 EV67
Gore St, SW7 27 P6
GORHAMBURY, St.Alb. AL3 64 BY18
★ **Gorhambury**, St.Alb. AL3 64 BW19
Gorhambury Dr, St.Alb. AL3 64 BW19
Gorham Dr, St.Alb. AL1 65 CE23
Gorham Pl, W11 26 E1
Goring Cl, Rom. RM5 127 FC53
Goring Gdns, Dag. RM8 148 EW63
Goring Rd, N11 121 DL51
Dagenham RM10 169 FD65
Staines-upon-Thames TW18 195 BD92
Gorings Sq, Stai. TW18 195 BE91
Goring St, EC3 19 P8
Goring Way, Grnf. UB6 158 CC68
Gorle Cl, Wat. WD25 81 BU34
Gorleston Rd, N15 144 DR57
Gorleston St, W14 26 F8
Gorman Rd, SE18 37 K8
Gorringe Av, S.Darenth DA4 231 FR96
Gorringe Pk Av, Mitch. CR4 202 DF94
Sch **Gorringe Pk Prim Sch**, Mitch. CR4 *off Sandy La* 222 DG95
Gorse Cl, E16 23 N9
Hatfield AL10 67 CT21
Tadworth KT20 255 CV120
Gorse Ct, Guil. GU4 265 BC132
Gorse Hill, Fnghm DA4 230 FL100
Gorse Hill La, Vir.W. GU25 214 AX98
Gorse Hill Rd, Vir.W. GU25 214 AX98
Gorselands Cl, W.Byf. KT14 234 BJ111
Gorse La, Chobham GU24 232 AS108
Gorse Meade, Slou. SL1 153 AN74
Gorse Ri, SW17 202 DG92
Gorse Rd, Croy. CR0 243 EA105
Orpington BR5 228 FA103
Gorse Wk, West Dr. UB7 156 BL72
Gorseway, Hat. AL10 51 CT14
Romford RM7 149 FD61
Gorst Rd, NW10 160 CQ70
SW11 202 DF86
Gorsuch Pl, E2 20 A2
Gorsuch St, E2 20 A2
Gosberton Rd, SW12 202 DG88
Gosbury Hill, Chess. KT9 238 CL105
Gosden Cl, Bramley GU5 280 AY143
Gosden Common, Bramley GU5 280 AY143
Gosden Hill Rd, Guil. GU4 265 BC130
Sch **Gosden Ho Sch**, Bramley GU5 *off Gosden Common* 280 AY143
Gosfield Rd, Dag. RM8 148 FA61
Epsom KT19 238 CR112
Gosfield St, W1 17 L6
Gosford Gdns, Ilf. IG4 147 EM57
Gosforth La, Wat. WD19 116 BW48
Gosforth Path, Wat. WD19 115 BU48
Goshawk Gdns, Hayes UB4 157 BS69
Goshawk Way, Felt. TW14 197 BV85
Goslar Way, Wind. SL4 173 AP82
Goslett Ct, Bushey WD23 *off Bournehall Av* 98 CA43
Goslett Yd, WC2 17 P9
Gosling Cl, Grnf. UB6 158 CA69
Gosling Grn, Slou. SL3 174 AY76
Gosling Rd, Slou. SL3 174 AY76
Gosling Way, SW9 42 F7
Gospatrick Rd, N17 122 DQ52
GOSPEL OAK, NW5 7 H1
⇔ **Gospel Oak** 7 H1
Sch **Gospel Oak Prim Sch**, NW3 6 G1
Gosport Dr, Horn. RM12 170 FJ65
Gosport Rd, E17 145 DZ57
Gosport Wk, N17 *off Yarmouth Cres* 144 DV57
Gossage Rd, SE18 187 ER78
Uxbridge UB10 156 BM66
Gossamers, The, Wat. WD25 98 BY36
Gosse Cl, Hodd. EN11 55 DZ14
Gosselin Rd, Hert. SG14 54 DQ07
Gosset St, E2 20 B2
Goss Hill, Dart. DA2 210 FJ93
Swanley BR8 210 FJ93
Gosshill Rd, Chis. BR7 227 EN96
Gossington Cl, Chis. BR7 *off Beechwood Ri* 207 EP91
Gossoms End, Berk. HP4 60 AU18
Gossoms Ryde, Berk. HP4 60 AU18
Gosterwood St, SE8 45 M2
Gostling Rd, Twick. TW2 198 CA88
Goston Gdns, Th.Hth. CR7 223 DN97
Goswell Arches, Wind. SL4 *off Goswell Rd* 173 AR81
Goswell Hill, Wind. SL4 *off Peascod St* 173 AR81
Goswell Rd, EC1 19 J5
Windsor SL4 173 AR81
Gothic Cl, Dart. DA1 210 FK90
Gothic Ct, Hayes UB3 *off Sipson La* 177 BR79
Gothic Rd, Twick. TW2 199 CD89
Gottfried Ms, NW5 *off Fortess Rd* 143 DJ63
Goudhurst Rd, Brom. BR1 206 EE92
Gouge Av, Nthflt DA11 212 GE88
Gough Rd, E15 13 L1
Enfield EN1 104 DV40
Gough Sq, EC4 18 F8
Gough St, WC1 18 D4
Gough Wk, E14 22 A9
Gould Cl, N.Mymms AL9 67 CV24
Gould Ct, SE19 204 DS92
Guildford GU4 265 BD132
Goulden Ho App, SW11 40 C8
Goulding Gdns, Th.Hth. CR7 223 DP96
Gould Rd, Felt. TW14 197 BS87
Twickenham TW2 199 CE88
Goulds Grn, Uxb. UB8 157 BP72
Gould Ter, E8 10 F3
Goulston St, E1 20 A8
Goulton Rd, E5 10 F2
Gourley Pl, N15 144 DS57
Gourley St, N15 144 DS57
Gourock Rd, SE9 207 EN85
Govan St, E2 10 D9
Gover Ct, SW4 *off Paradise Rd* 42 B8
Government Row, Enf. EN3 105 EA38
Governors Av, Denh. UB9 135 BF57
Governors Cl, Amer. HP6 94 AT37
Govett Av, Shep. TW17 217 BQ99
Govier Cl, E15 13 K7
Gowan Av, SW6 38 E7
Gowan Rd, NW10 161 CV65
Gowar Fld, S.Mimms EN6 85 CU32
Gower, The, Egh. TW20 215 BB97
Gower Cl, SW4 203 DJ86
Gower Ct, WC1 17 N4
Sch **Gower Ho Sch**, NW9 *off Blackbird Hill* 140 CQ61
Gower Ms, WC1 17 N7
Gower Pl, WC1 17 M4
Gower Rd, E7 13 P5
Horley RH6 290 DE148
Isleworth TW7 179 CF79
Weybridge KT13 235 BR107
Gowers, The, Amer. HP6 77 AS36
Harlow CM20 58 EU13
Gowers La, Orsett RM16 193 GF75
Gower St, WC1 17 M4
Gower's Wk, E1 20 C8
Gowings Grn, Slou. SL1 173 AL75
Gowland Pl, Beck. BR3 225 DZ96
Gowlett Rd, SE15 184 DU83
Gowlland Cl, Croy. CR0 224 DU101
Gowrie Pl, Cat. CR3 258 DQ122
Gowrie Rd, SW11 182 DG83
Graburn Way, E.Mol. KT8 219 CD97
Grace Av, Bexh. DA7 188 EZ82
Shenley WD7 83 CK33
● **Grace Business Cen**, Mitch. CR4 222 DF100
Gracechurch St, EC3 19 M10
Grace Cl, SE9 206 EK90
Borehamwood WD6 100 CR39
Edgware HA8 118 CQ52
Ilford IG6 125 ET51
Grace Ct, Slou. SL1 153 AQ74
Gracedale Rd, SW16 203 DH92
Gracefield Gdns, SW16 203 DL90
Grace Jones Cl, E8 10 C5
Grace Ms, Beck. BR3 205 EA93
Grace Path, SE26 204 DW91
Grace Pl, E3 22 D3
Grace Rd, Croy. CR0 224 DQ100
Grace's All, E1 20 C10
Graces Ms, SE5 43 M8
Graces Rd, SE5 43 N8
Grace St, E3 22 D3
Gracious La, Sev. TN13 278 FG130
Gracious La End, Sev. TN14 278 FF130
Gracious Pond Rd, Chobham GU24 232 AT108
Gradient, The, SE26 204 DU91
Graduate Pl, SE1 *off Long La* 31 N6
Graeme Rd, Enf. EN1 104 DR40
Graemesdyke Av, SW14 180 CP83
Graemesdyke Rd, Berk. HP4 60 AU20
Grafton Cl, W13 159 CG72
George Green SL3 154 AY72
Hounslow TW4 198 BY88
St. Albans AL4 *off Princess Diana Dr* 65 CK21
West Byfleet KT14 *off Madeira Rd* 233 BF113
Worcester Park KT4 220 CS104
Grafton Ct, Felt. TW14 197 BR88
Grafton Cres, NW1 7 J5
Grafton Gdns, N4 144 DQ58
Dagenham RM8 148 EY61
Grafton Ho, E3 22 A3
Sch **Grafton Inf & Jun Schs**, Dag. RM8 *off Grafton Rd* 148 EZ61
Grafton Ms, W1 17 L5
Grafton Pk Rd, Wor.Pk. KT4 220 CS103
Grafton Pl, NW1 17 N3
Sch **Grafton Prim Sch**, N7 *off Eburne Rd* 143 DL62
Grafton Rd, NW5 7 J4
W3 160 CQ73
Croydon CR0 223 DN102
Dagenham RM8 148 EY61
Enfield EN2 103 DM41
Harrow HA1 138 CC57
New Malden KT3 220 CS97
Worcester Park KT4 220 CR104
Graftons, The, NW2 *off Hermitage La* 142 DA62
Grafton Sq, SW4 183 DJ83
Grafton St, W1 29 K1
Grafton Ter, NW5 6 F3
Grafton Way, W1 17 L5
WC1 17 L5
West Molesey KT8 218 BZ98
Grafton Yd, NW5 7 K5
Graham Av, W13 179 CH75
Broxbourne EN10 71 DY20
Mitcham CR4 222 DG95
Graham Cl, Croy. CR0 225 EA103
Hutton CM13 131 GC43
St. Albans AL1 65 CD23
Grahame Pk Est, NW9 118 CS53
Grahame Pk Way, NW7 119 CT52
NW9 119 CT54
Graham Gdns, Surb. KT6 220 CL102
Graham Rd, E8 10 C4
E13 23 N4
N15 143 DP55
NW4 141 CV58
SW19 201 CZ94
W4 180 CR76
Bexleyheath DA6 188 FA84
Hampton TW12 198 CA91
Harrow HA3 139 CE55
Mitcham CR4 222 DG95
Purley CR8 241 DN113
Graham St, N1 19 H1
Graham Ter, SW1 28 G9
Grainger Cl, Nthlt. UB5 *off Lancaster Rd* 138 CC64
Grainger Rd, N22 122 DQ53
Isleworth TW7 179 CF82
Grainge's Yd, Uxb. UB8 *off Cross St* 156 BJ66
Grainstore, The, E16 24 A10
Gramer Cl, E11 *off Norman Rd* 145 ED61
Sch **Grammar Sch for Girls Wilmington, The**, Dart. DA2 *off Parsons La* 209 FH90
Grampian Cl, Harling. UB3 177 BR80
Orpington BR6 *off Clovelly Way* 227 ET100
Sutton SM2 240 DC108
Grampian Gdns, NW2 141 CY60
Grampian Ho, N9 *off Edmonton Grn Shop Cen* 122 DV47
Grampian Way, Slou. SL3 175 BA78
Gramsci Way, SE6 205 EB90
Granard Av, SW15 201 CV85
● **Granard Business Cen**, NW7 *off Bunns La* 118 CS51
Sch **Granard Prim Sch**, SW15 *off Cortis Rd* 201 CV86
Granard Rd, SW12 202 DF87
Granaries, The, Wal.Abb. EN9 90 EE34
Granary, The, Roydon CM19 56 EH14
Stanstead Abbotts SG12 55 EC12
Granary Cl, N9 122 DW45
Horley RH6 *off Waterside* 290 DG146
Granary Ct, E15 13 H4
Granary Mans, SE28 187 EQ75
Granary Rd, E1 20 E5
Granary Sq, N1 8 F5
Granary St, NW1 7 N9
Granby Pk Rd, Chsht EN7 88 DT28
Granby Pl, SE1 30 E5
Granby Rd, SE9 187 EM82
Gravesend DA11 212 GD85
Granby St, E2 20 B4
Granby Ter, NW1 17 L1
Grand Arc, N12 *off Ballards La* 120 DC50
Grand Av, EC1 19 H6
N10 142 DG56
Surbiton KT5 220 CP99
Wembley HA9 140 CN64
Grand Av E, Wem. HA9 140 CP64
Sch **Grand Av Prim & Nurs Sch**, Surb. KT5 *off Grand Av* 220 CQ100
Grand Dep Rd, SE18 187 EN78
Grand Dr, SW20 221 CW96
Southall UB2 178 CC75
Granden Rd, SW16 223 DL96
Grandfield Av, Wat. WD17 97 BT39
Grandis Cotts, Ripley GU23 250 BH122
Grandison Rd, SW11 202 DF85
Worcester Park KT4 221 CW103
Grand Junct Isle, Sun. TW16 *off Lower Hampton Rd* 218 BY96
Grand Junct Wf, N1 19 J1
Grand Par, N4 *off Green Las* 143 DP58
Wembley HA9 *off Forty Av* 140 CN61
Grand Par Ms, SW15 201 CY85
Grand Stand Rd, Epsom KT18 255 CT117
Grand Union Canal Wk, W7 179 CE76
Grand Union Centre, W10 *off West Row* 14 D4
Grand Union Cres, E8 10 D7
Grand Union Enterprise Pk, Sthl. UB2 *off Bridge Rd* 178 CA75
Grand Union Hts, Wem. HA0 159 CK67
● **Grand Union Ind Est**, NW10 160 CP68
Grand Union Wk, NW1 7 K7
Wembley HA0 *off Water Rd* 160 CM67
Grand Union Way, Kings L. WD4 81 BP29
Southall UB2 178 CA75
Grand Vw Av, Bigg.H. TN16 260 EJ117
Grand Wk, E1 21 M4
Granfield St, SW11 40 B7
Grange, The, N20 120 DC46
SE1 32 A6
SW19 201 CX93
W14 *off Lisgar Ter* 26 G9
Abbots Langley WD5 81 BS31
Chobham GU24 232 AS110
Croydon CR0 225 DZ103
Old Windsor SL4 194 AV85
South Darenth DA4 231 FR95
Walton-on-Thames KT12 217 BV103
Wembley HA0 160 CN66
Worcester Park KT4 220 CR104
Grange Av, N12 120 DC50
N20 119 CY45
SE25 224 DS96
East Barnet EN4 120 DE46
Stanmore HA7 117 CH54
Twickenham TW2 199 CE89
Woodford Green IG8 124 EG51
Grangecliffe Gdns, SE25 224 DS96
Grange Cl, Bletch. RH1 274 DR133
Chalfont St. Peter SL9 112 AY53
Edgware HA8 118 CQ50
Guildford GU2 264 AV130
Hayes UB3 157 BS71
Hemel Hempstead HP2 62 BN21
Hertford SG14 53 DP09
Hounslow TW5 178 BZ79
Ingrave CM13 131 GC50
Leatherhead KT22 253 CK120
Merstham RH1 273 DH128
Sidcup DA15 208 EU90
Watford WD17 97 BU39
West Molesey KT8 218 CB98
Westerham TN16 277 EQ126
Woodford Green IG8 124 EG52
Wraysbury TW19 194 AY86
Sch **Grange Comm Inf Sch, The**, New Haw KT15 *off The Avenue* 234 BG110
Grange Ct, WC2 18 D9
Chigwell IG7 125 EQ47
Loughton IG10 106 EK43
Northolt UB5 158 BW68
Staines-upon-Thames TW18 *off Gresham Rd* 196 BG92
Waltham Abbey EN9 89 EC34
Walton-on-Thames KT12 217 BU103
Grangecourt Rd, N16 144 DS60
Grange Cres, SE28 168 EW72
Chigwell IG7 125 ER50
Dartford DA2 210 FP86
Grangedale Cl, Nthwd. HA6 115 BS53
Grange Dr, Chis. BR7 206 EL93
Merstham RH1 273 DH128
Orpington BR6 *off Rushmore Hill* 246 EW109
Woking GU21 232 AY114
Wooburn Green HP10 132 AD60
Grange End, Smallfield RH6 291 DN148
Grange Est, The, N2 120 DD54
Grange Farm Cl, Har. HA2 138 CC61
Grange Farm La, Chig. IG7 125 EQ46
Grange Flds, Chal.St.P. SL9 112 AY53
Grangefields Rd, Jacobs Well GU4 264 AX128
Sch **Grange First Sch**, S.Har. HA2 *off Welbeck Rd* 138 CB60
Grange Gdns, N14 121 DK46
NW3 142 DB62
SE25 224 DS96
Banstead SM7 240 DB113
Farnham Common SL2 133 AR64
Pinner HA5 138 BZ56
Ware SG12 55 DY07
Grange Gro, N1 9 H4
GRANGE HILL, Chig. IG7 125 ER51
⊖ **Grange Hill** 125 ER49
Grange Hill, SE25 224 DS96
Edgware HA8 118 CQ50
Grangehill Pl, SE9 *off Westmount Rd* 187 EM83
Grangehill Rd, SE9 187 EM84
Grange Ho, Bark. IG11 *off St. Margarets* 167 ER67
Erith DA8 189 FG82
Grange La, SE21 204 DT89
Letchmore Heath WD25 99 CD39
Roydon CM19 72 EJ15
Grange Mans, Epsom KT17 239 CT108
Grange Meadow, Bans. SM7 240 DB113
Sch **Grange Mid Sch**, S.Har. HA2 *off Welbeck Rd* 138 CB60
Grangemill Rd, SE6 205 EA90
Grangemill Way, SE6 205 EA89
Grangemount, Lthd. KT22 253 CK120
GRANGE PARK, N21 103 DP43
⇌ **Grange Park** 103 DP43
Grange Pk, W5 160 CL74
Woking GU21 248 AY115
Grange Pk Av, N21 103 DP44
Sch **Grange Pk Inf & Jun Schs**, Hayes UB4 *off Lansbury Dr* 157 BT70
Grange Pk Pl, SW20 201 CV94
Sch **Grange Pk Prep Sch**, N21 *off The Chine* 103 DP44
Sch **Grange Pk Prim Sch**, N21 *off Worlds End La* 103 DN42
Grange Pk Rd, E10 145 EB60
Thornton Heath CR7 224 DR98
Grange Pl, NW6 5 J7
Staines-upon-Thames TW18 216 BJ96
Walton-on-Thames KT12 217 BU103
Sch **Grange Prim Sch**, E13 23 M3
SE1 31 N7
W5 *off Church Pl* 179 CK75
Grange Rd, E10 145 EA60
E13 23 L3
E17 145 DY57
N6 142 DG58
N17 122 DU51
N18 122 DU51
NW10 161 CV65
SE1 31 P6
SE19 224 DR98
SE25 224 DR98
SW13 181 CU81
W4 180 CP78
W5 159 CK74
Aveley RM15 170 FQ74
Bushey WD23 98 BY43
Caterham CR3 274 DU125
Chalfont St. Peter SL9 112 AY53
Chessington KT9 238 CL105
Edgware HA8 118 CR51
Egham TW20 195 AZ92
Elstree WD6 100 CM43
Gravesend DA11 213 GG87
Grays RM17 192 GB79
Guildford GU2 264 AV129
Harrow HA1 139 CG58
Hayes UB3 157 BS72
Hersham KT12 236 BY105
Ilford IG1 147 EP63
Kingston upon Thames KT1 220 CL97
Leatherhead KT22 253 CK120
New Haw KT15 234 BG110
Orpington BR6 227 EQ103
Romford RM3 127 FH51
Sevenoaks TN13 278 FG127
South Croydon CR2 242 DQ110
South Harrow HA2 139 CD61
Southall UB1 178 BY75
Sutton SM2 240 DA108
Thornton Heath CR7 224 DR98
West Molesey KT8 218 CB98
Woking GU21 232 AY114
Granger Way, Rom. RM1 149 FG58
Grange St, N1 9 M9
St. Albans AL3 65 CD19
Grange Vale, Sutt. SM2 240 DB108
Grange Vw Rd, N20 120 DC46
Grange Wk, SE1 31 P6
Grange Wk Ms, SE1 31 P7
Grangeway, N12 120 DB49
NW6 5 J7
Grange Way, Erith DA8 189 FH80
Iver SL0 155 BF72
Grangeway, Smallfield RH6 291 DN148
Woodford Green IG8 124 EJ49

Grangeway, The, N21 103 DP44
Grangeway Gdns, Ilf. IG4 146 EL57
Grangeways Cl, Nthflt DA11 213 GF91
Grangewood, Bex. DA5 208 EZ88
Potters Bar EN6 86 DB30
Wexham SL3 154 AW71
Grangewood Av, Grays RM16 192 GE76
Rainham RM13 170 FJ70
Grangewood Cl, Brwd. CM13
off Knight's Way 131 GA48
Pinner HA5 137 BU57
Grangewood Dr, Sun. TW16
off Spelthorne Gro 197 BT94
Sch Grangewood Indep Sch,
E7 off Chester Rd 166 EK66
Grangewood La, Beck. BR3 205 DZ93
Sch Grangewood Sch, Eastcote
HA5 off Fore St 137 BT57
Grangewood St, E6 166 EJ67
Grangewood Ter, SE25
off Grange Rd 224 DR96
Grange Yd, SE1 32 A7
Granham Gdns, N9 122 DT47
Granite Apts, E15 13 H4
Granite St, SE18 187 ET78
Granleigh Rd, E11 146 EE61
Gransden Av, E8 10 F7
Gransden Rd, W12
off Wendell Rd 181 CT75
Grant Av, Slou. SL1 154 AS72
Grantbridge St, N1 9 H10
Grantchester Cl, Har. HA1 139 CF62
Grant Cl, N14 121 DJ45
N17 122 DS54
Shepperton TW17 217 BP100
Grant Ct, E4
off The Ridgeway 123 EC46
Grantham Cl, Edg. HA8 118 CL48
Grantham Gdns, Rom. RM6 148 EZ58
Ware SG12 55 DY05
Grantham Grn, Borwd. WD6 100 CQ43
Grantham Ms, Berk. HP4 60 AX19
Grantham Pl, W1 29 J3
Grantham Rd, E12 147 EN63
SW9 42 B9
W4 180 CS80
Grantley Cl, Shalf. GU4 280 AY141
Grantley Gdns, Guil. GU2 264 AU133
Grantley Pl, Esher KT10 236 CB106
Grantley Rd, Guil. GU2 264 AU133
Hounslow TW4 178 BW82
Grantley St, E1 21 J3
Grantock Rd, E17 123 ED53
Granton Av, Upmin. RM14 150 FM61
Sch Granton Prim Sch, SW16
off Granton Rd 203 DJ94
Granton Rd, SW16 223 DJ95
Ilford IG3 148 EU60
Sidcup DA14 208 EW93
Grant Pl, Croy. CR0 224 DT102
Grant Rd, SW11 182 DD84
Croydon CR0 224 DT102
Harrow HA3 139 CF55
Grants Cl, NW7 119 CW52
Grants La, Oxt. RH8 276 EJ132
Grant's Quay Wf, EC3 31 M1
Grant St, E13 23 N3
N1 8 E10
Grantully Rd, W9 15 L3
Grant Way, Islw. TW7 179 CG79
Grantwood Cl, Red. RH1
off Bushfield Dr 289 DH139
Granville Av, N9 122 DW48
Feltham TW13 197 BU89
Hounslow TW3 198 CA85
Slough SL2 153 AR71
Granville Cl, Byfleet KT14
off Church Rd 234 BM113
Croydon CR0 224 DS103
Weybridge KT13 235 BQ107
Granville Ct, N1 9 M8
Granville Dene, Bov. HP3 79 BA27
Granville Gdns, SW16 223 DM95
W5 160 CM74
Hoddesdon EN11 55 EA13
Granville Gro, SE13 185 EC83
Granville Ms, Sid. DA14 208 EU91
Granville Pk, SE13 46 F10
Granville Pl, N12 120 DC52
SW6 39 L5
W1 16 G9
Pinner HA5 138 BX55
Granville Pt, NW2 141 CZ61
Granville Rd, E17 145 EB58
E18 124 EH54
N4 143 DM58
N12 120 DB52
N13 121 DM51
N22 121 DP53
NW2 141 CZ61
NW6 15 J1
SW18 202 DA87
SW19 off Russell Rd 202 DA94
Barnet EN5 101 CW42
Epping CM16 92 EV29
Gravesend DA11 213 GF87
Hayes UB3 177 BT77
Ilford IG1 147 EP60
Northchurch HP4 60 AS17
Oxted RH8 276 EF129
St. Albans AL1 65 CF20
Sevenoaks TN13 278 FG124
Sidcup DA14 208 EU91
Uxbridge UB10 157 BP65
Watford WD18 98 BW42
Welling DA16 188 EW83
Westerham TN16 277 EQ126
Weybridge KT13 235 BQ107
Woking GU22 249 AZ120
Sch Granville Sch, The, Sev. TN13
off Bradbourne Pk Rd 278 FG123
Granville Sq, SE15 43 P4
WC1 18 D3
Granville St, WC1 18 D3
Grape St, WC2 18 A8
Graphite Apts, N1
off Provost St 19 L1
Graphite Sq, SE11 30 C10
Grapsome Cl, Chess. KT9
off Nigel Fisher Way 237 CJ108
Grasdene Rd, SE18 188 EU80
Grasgarth Cl, W3 160 CQ73
Grasholm Way, Slou. SL3 175 BC77
Grasmere Av, SW15 200 CR91
SW19 222 DA97
W3 160 CQ73
Hounslow TW3 198 CB86
Orpington BR6 227 EP104
Ruislip HA4 137 BQ59
Slough SL2 154 AU73
Wembley HA9 139 CK59
Grasmere Cl, Egh. TW20
off Keswick Rd 195 BB94
Feltham TW14 197 BT88
Guildford GU1 265 BB133
Hemel Hempstead HP3 63 BP22
Loughton IG10 107 EM40
Watford WD25 81 BV32
Grasmere Ct, N22 121 DM51
Grasmere Gdns, Har. HA3 117 CG54
Ilford IG4 147 EM57
Orpington BR6 227 EP104
Grasmere Pt, SE15 44 G4
Sch Grasmere Prim Sch, N16 9 M1
Grasmere Rd, E13 13 N10
N10 121 DH53
N17 122 DU51
SE25 224 DV100
SW16 203 DM92
Bexleyheath DA7 189 FC81
Bromley BR1 226 EF95
Orpington BR6 227 EP104
Purley CR8 241 DP111
St. Albans AL1 65 CH22
Grasmere Way, Byfleet KT14 234 BM112
Grassbanks, Dart. DA1 210 FM88
Grassfield Cl, Couls. CR5 257 DH119
Grasshaven Way, SE28 167 ET74
Grassingham End, Chal.St.P.
SL9 112 AY52
Grassingham Rd, Chal.St.P.
SL9 112 AY52
Grassington Cl, N11 120 DG50
Bricket Wood AL2 82 CA30
Grassington Rd, Sid. DA14 208 EU91
Grasslands, Smallfield RH6 291 DN148
Grassmere, Horl. RH6 291 DH147
Grassmere Rd, Horn. RM11 150 FM56
Grassmount, SE23 204 DV89
Purley CR8 241 DJ110
Grass Pk, N3 119 CZ53
Grass Warren, Tewin AL6 52 DE06
Grassway, Wall. SM6 241 DJ105
Grassy Cl, Hem.H. HP1 62 BG19
Grassy La, Sev. TN13 279 FH126
Grasvenor Av, Barn. EN5 102 DA44
Sch Grasvenor Av Inf Sch, Barn.
EN5 off Grasvenor Av 102 DA44
Gratton Dr, Wind. SL4 173 AL84
Gratton Rd, W14 26 E7
Gratton Ter, NW2 141 CX62
Gravel Cl, Chig. IG7 126 EU47
Graveley, Kings.T. KT1
off Willingham Way 220 CN96
Graveley Av, Borwd. WD6 100 CQ42
Graveley Ct, Hem.H. HP2 63 BQ21
Graveley Dell, Welw.G.C. AL7 52 DB10
Tram Gravel Hill 243 DY108
Gravel Hill, N3 119 CZ54
Bexleyheath DA6 209 FB85
Chalfont St. Peter SL9 112 AY53
Croydon CR0 243 DX107
Hemel Hempstead HP1 62 BH20
High Beach IG10 106 EG38
Leatherhead KT22
off North St 253 CH121
Uxbridge UB8 136 BK64
Gravel Hill Cl, Bexh. DA6 209 FB85
Sch Gravel Hill Prim Sch,
Bexh. DA6
off Watling St 189 FB84
Gravel Hill Ter, Hem.H. HP1 62 BG21
Gravel La, E1 20 A8
Chigwell IG7 126 EU46
Hemel Hempstead HP1 62 BG21
Gravelly Hill, Cat. CR3 274 DS128
Gravelly Ride, SW19 201 CV91
Gravel Path, Berk. HP4 60 AX19
Hemel Hempstead HP1 62 BG20
Gravel Pit La, SE9 207 EQ85
Gravelpits La, Goms. GU5 283 BQ139
Gravel Pit Way, Orp. BR6 228 EU103
Gravel Rd, Brom. BR2 226 EL103
Sutton at Hone DA4 210 FP94
Twickenham TW2 199 CE88
Gravelwood Cl, Chis. BR7 207 EQ90
Gravely Way, Penn HP10 110 AF45
Gravenel Gdns, SW17
off Nutwell St 202 DE92
Graveney Gro, SE20 204 DW94
Graveney Rd, SW17 202 DE91
Sch Graveney Sch, SW17
off Welham Rd 203 DH92
GRAVESEND, DA11 - DA13 213 GJ85
⇌ Gravesend 213 GG87
Coll Gravesend Adult Ed Cen,
Grav. DA11 o
off Darnley Rd 213 GG86
Sch Gravesend Gram Sch, Grav.
DA12 off Church Wk 213 GK87
Sch Gravesend Gram Sch for Girls,
Grav. DA11 off Pelham Rd 213 GG88
Gravesend Rd, W12 161 CU73
H Gravesham Comm Hosp,
The, Grav. DA11 213 GG86
Gravesham Ct, Grav. DA12
off Clarence Row 213 GH87
★ Gravesham Mus, Grav.
DA11 213 GH86
● Graves Yd Ind Est, Well. DA16
off Upper Wickham La 188 EV82
Gravetts La, Guil. GU3 264 AS131
Gray Av, Dag. RM8 148 EZ60
Grayburn Cl, Ch.St.G. HP8 112 AU47
Gray Cl, Add. KT15
off Monks Cres 234 BH106
Gray Gdns, Rain. RM13 169 FG65
Grayham Cres, N.Mal. KT3 220 CR98
Grayham Rd, N.Mal. KT3 220 CR98
Grayland Cl, Brom. BR1 226 EK95
Graylands, They.B. CM16 107 ER37
Woking GU21 248 AY116
Graylands Cl, Slou. SL1 153 AM74
Woking GU21 248 AY116
Grayling Cl, E16 23 K4
Grayling Ct, Berk. HP4
off Admiral Way 60 AT17
Grayling Rd, N16 144 DR61
Graylings, The, Abb.L. WD5 81 BR33
Grayling Sq, E2 20 D2
Gray Pl, Ott. KT16
off Clarendon Gate 233 BD107
GRAYS, RM16 & RM17; RM20 192 GA78
⇌ Grays 192 GA79
Sch Grays Conv High Sch, Grays
RM17 off College Av 192 GB77
Grayscroft Rd, SW16 203 DK94
Grays End Cl, Grays RM17 192 GA76
Sch Gray's Fm Prim Sch, Orp.
BR5 off Grays Fm Rd 228 EV95
Grays Fm Rd, Orp. BR5 228 EV95
Graysfield, Welw.G.C. AL7 52 DA12
Grayshott Rd, SW11 40 G9
★ Gray's Inn, WC1 18 D6
Gray's Inn Pl, WC1 18 D7
Gray's Inn Rd, WC1 18 C3
Gray's Inn Sq, WC1 18 E6
Grays La, Ashf. TW15 197 BP91
Gray's La, Ashtd. KT21 254 CM119
Epsom KT18 254 CN120
Grayson Ho, EC1 19 K3
Grays Pk Rd, Stoke P. SL2 154 AU68
Grays Pl, Slou. SL2 154 AT74
Grays Rd, Gdmg. GU7 280 AT144
Slough SL1 154 AT74
Uxbridge UB10 156 BL67
Westerham TN16 261 EP121
Sch Grays Sch Media Arts Coll,
The, Grays RM17
off Hathaway Rd 192 GB76
Grays Shop Cen, Grays
RM17 off High St 192 GA79
Gray St, SE1 30 F5
Grays Wk, Chesh. HP5 76 AP29
Hutton CM13 131 GD45
Grays Wd, Horl. RH6 291 DJ148
Grayswood Gdns, SW20
off Farnham Gdns 221 CV96
Grayswood Pt, SW15
off Norley Vale 201 CU88
Gray's Yd, W1 17 H9
Graywood Ct, N12 120 DC52
Sch Grazebrook Prim Sch,
N16 off Lordship Rd 144 DR61
Grazebrook Rd, N16 144 DR61
Grazeley Cl, Bexh. DA6 209 FC85
Grazeley Ct, SE19
off Gipsy Hill 204 DS92
Grazings, The, Hem.H. HP2 62 BM18
Greatacre, Chesh. HP5 76 AR30
Great Acre Ct, SW4
off Clapham Pk Rd 183 DK84
GREAT AMWELL, Ware SG12 55 DZ10
Great Amwell La, N8 143 DM55
Great Arthur Ho, EC1 19 J5
Great Auger St, Harl. CM17 58 EX14
Great Bell All, EC2 19 L8
Great Benty, West Dr. UB7 176 BL77
Great Bois Wd, Amer. HP6
off Manor Dr 77 AQ36
GREAT BOOKHAM, Lthd.
KT23 268 CB125
★ Great Bookham Common,
Lthd. KT23 252 BZ121
Great Braitch La, Hat. AL10 51 CT14
Great Brays, Harl. CM18 74 EU16
Great Break, Welw.G.C. AL7 52 DB10
Great Brownings, SE21 204 DT91
Great Bushey Dr, N20 120 DB46
Great Cambridge Ind Est,
Enf. EN1 104 DU43
Jct Great Cambridge Junct,
N18 122 DR49
Great Cambridge Rd, N9 122 DS46
N17 122 DR50
N18 122 DR50
Cheshunt EN8 88 DW34
Enfield EN1 104 DU42
Turnford EN10 89 DY26
Great Castle St, W1 17 K8
Great Cen Av, Ruis. HA4 138 BW64
Great Cen St, NW1 16 E6
Great Cen Way, NW10 140 CS64
Wembley HA9 140 CQ63
Great Chapel St, W1 17 N8
Great Chart St, SW11 182 DD84
Great Chertsey Rd, W4 180 CQ82
Feltham TW13 198 CA90
Great Ch La, W6 26 D10
Great Coll St, SW1 30 A6
Great Conduit, Welw.G.C. AL7 52 DC08
Great Cross Av, SE10 47 J5
Great Cullings, Rom. RM7 149 FE61
Great Cumberland Ms, W1 16 E9
Great Cumberland Pl, W1 16 E8
Great Dell, Welw.G.C. AL8 51 CX07
Great Dover St, SE1 31 K5
Greatdown Rd, W7 159 CF70
● Great Eastern Enterprise Cen,
E14 34 C5
Great Eastern Rd, E15 12 G6
WalthamCross EN8
off Great Cambridge Rd 88 DW33
Warley CM14 130 FW49
Great Eastern St, EC2 19 N3
Great Eastern Wk, EC2 19 P7
Great Ellshams, Bans. SM7 256 DA116
Great Elms Rd, Brom. BR2 226 EJ98
Hemel Hempstead HP3 62 BM24
Great Fld, NW9 118 CS53
Greatfield Av, E6 25 J4
Greatfield Cl, N19
off Warrender Rd 143 DJ63
SE4 185 EA84
Greatfields Dr, Uxb. UB8 156 BN71
Greatfields Rd, Bark. IG11 167 ER67
Great Fleete Way, Bark. IG11
off Choats Rd 168 EW68
Greatford Dr, Guil. GU1 265 BD134
Great Galley Cl, Bark. IG11 168 EV69
Great Ganett, Welw.G.C. AL7 52 DB11
Great Gdns Rd, Horn. RM11 149 FH58
Great Gatton Cl, Croy. CR0 225 DY101
Great George St, SW1 29 P5
Great Goodwin Dr, Guil. GU1 265 BB132
Great Gregories La, Epp. CM16 91 ES33
Great Gro, Bushey WD23 98 CB42
Great Gros, Goffs Oak EN7 88 DS28
Great Guildford St, SE1 31 J2
Great Hall, SW11
off Battersea Pk Rd 41 H6
Greatham Rd, Bushey WD23 98 BX41
● Greatham Rd Ind Est,
Bushey WD23 98 BX41
Greatham Wk, SW15 201 CU88
Great Harry Dr, SE9 207 EN90
Great Heart, Hem.H. HP2 62 BL18
Great Heath, Hat. AL10 67 CV15
GREAT HIVINGS, Chesh. HP5 76 AP27
Great Hivings, Chesh. HP5 76 AN27
Greathurst End, Bkhm KT23 252 BZ124
Great James St, WC1 18 C5
Great Julians, Rick. WD3 96 BN42
Great Lake Ct, Horl. RH6
off Tanyard Way 291 DH147
Great Ley, Welw.G.C. AL7 51 CY11
Great Leylands, Harl. CM18 74 EU16
Great Marlborough St, W1 17 L9
Great Maze Pond, SE1 31 M4
Great Meadow, Brox. EN10 71 EA22
Great Molewood, Hert. SG14 53 DP06
Great Nelmes Chase, Horn.
RM11 150 FM57
Greatness La, Sev. TN14 279 FJ121
Greatness Rd, Sev. TN14 279 FJ121
Great Newport St, WC2
off Charing Cross Rd 17 P10
Great New St, EC4
off New Fetter La 18 F8
Great N Leisure Pk, N12 120 DD52
Great N Rd, N2 142 DE56
N6 142 DE56
Barnet EN5 101 CZ38
Hatfield AL9, AL10 67 CZ23
New Barnet EN5 102 DA43
Potters Bar EN6 86 DB27
Welwyn Garden City AL8 51 CU10
Great N Way, NW4 119 CW54
Great Oak Ct, Hunsdon SG12 56 EK08
Great Oaks, Chig. IG7 125 EQ49
Hutton CM13 131 GB44
Great Oaks Pk, Guil. GU4 265 BB129
Greatorex St, E1 20 C6
Great Ormond St, WC1 18 B6
H Great Ormond St Hosp for
Children, The, WC1 18 B5
Great Owl Rd, Chig. IG7 125 EN48
Great Palmers, Hem.H. HP2 62 BM15
Great Pk, Kings L. WD4 80 BM30
Great Pk Cl, Uxb. UB10 156 BN66
GREAT PARNDON, Harl. CM19 73 EP17
Great Percy St, WC1 18 D2
Great Peter St, SW1 29 N7
Great Pettits Ct, Rom. RM1 127 FE54
Great Plumtree, Harl. CM20 57 ET13
⊖ Great Portland Street 17 K5
Great Portland St, W1 17 K6
Great Pulteney St, W1 17 M10
Great Quarry, Guil. GU1 280 AX137
Great Queen St, WC2 18 B9
Dartford DA1 210 FM87
Great Rd, Hem.H. HP2 62 BM19
Great Ropers La, Gt Warley
CM13 129 FU51
Great Russell St, WC1 17 P8
Great St. Helens, EC3 19 N8
Great St. Thomas Apostle, EC4 19 K10
Great Scotland Yd, SW1 30 A3
Great Slades, Pot.B. EN6 85 CZ33
Great Smith St, SW1 29 P6
Great South-West Rd, Felt.
TW14 197 BQ87
Hounslow TW4 177 BT84
Great Spilmans, SE22 204 DS85
Great Stockwood Rd, Chsht
EN7 88 DR26
Great Strand, NW9 119 CT53
Great Sturgess Rd, Hem.H. HP1 61 BF20
Great Suffolk St, SE1 31 H3
Great Sutton St, EC1 19 H5
Great Swan All, EC2 19 L8
Great Tattenhams, Epsom
KT18 255 CV118
Great Thrift, Petts Wd BR5 227 EQ98
Great Till Cl, Otford TN14 263 FE116
Great Titchfield St, W1 17 L8
Great Twr St, EC3 19 N10
Great Trinity La, EC4 19 K10
Great Turnstile, WC1 18 D7
GREAT WARLEY, Brwd. CM14 129 FV53
Great Warley St, Gt Warley
CM13 129 FU53
Great Western Rd, W2 15 J7
W9 15 H5
W11 15 J7
● Great W Ho, Brent. TW8 179 CJ79
Great W Rd, W4 180 CP78
W6 181 CT78
Brentford TW8 180 CP78
Hounslow TW5 178 BX82
Isleworth TW7 179 CF80
Great Whites Rd, Hem.H. HP3 62 BM22
Great Winchester St, EC2 19 M8
Great Windmill St, W1 17 N10
Greatwood, Chis. BR7 207 EN94
Greatwood Cl, Ott. KT16 233 BC109
Great Woodcote Dr, Pur. CR8 241 DK110
Great Woodcote Pk, Pur. CR8 241 DK110
Great Yd, SE1 31 P4
Greaves Cl, Bark. IG11 167 ER66
Greaves Pl, SW17 202 DE91
Greaves Twr, SW10 39 P4
Grebe Av, Hayes UB4
off Cygnet Way 158 BX72
Grebe Cl, E7 13 M2
E17 123 DY52
Barking IG11 168 EU70
Grebe Ct, Sutt. SM1 239 CZ106
Grebe Crest, Grays RM20 191 FU77
Grecian Cres, SE19 203 DP93
Greding Wk, Hutt. CM13 131 GB47
Greek Ct, W1 17 P9
★ Greek Orthodox Cath
of the Divine Wisdom
(St. Sophia),
W2 15 K10
Greek St, W1 17 P9
Greek Yd, WC2 18 A10
Green, The, E4 123 EC46
E11 146 EH58
E15 13 K5
N9 122 DU47
N14 121 DK48
N17 122 DQ51
N21 121 DN45
SW14 180 CQ83
SW19 201 CX92
W3 160 CS72
W5 off High St 159 CK73
Amersham HP7 77 AR38
Bexleyheath DA7 188 FA81
Bovingdon HP3 79 BA29
Bromley BR1
off Downham Way 206 EG90
Burgh Heath KT20 255 CY119
Burnham SL1 152 AH70
Carshalton SM5
off High St 240 DG105
Green, The, Chalfont St. Giles HP8
off High St 112 AW47
Chalvey SL1 173 AR75
Cheshunt EN8 88 DW28
Claygate KT10 237 CF107
Croxley Green WD3 96 BN44
Croydon CR0 243 DZ109
Dartford DA2 211 FR89
Datchet SL3 174 AV80
Englefield Green TW20 194 AW91
Epsom KT17 239 CU111
Feltham TW13 197 BV89
Fetcham KT22 253 CD124
Harefield UB9 114 BJ53
Havering-atte-Bower RM4 127 FE48
Hayes UB3 off Wood End 157 BS72
Hayes BR2 226 EG101
Hounslow TW5 178 CA79
Ickenham UB10 137 BQ61
Letchmore Heath WD25 99 CE39
London Colney AL2 83 CK27
Matching Tye CM17 59 FE12
Morden SM4 221 CY98
New Malden KT3 220 CQ97
Otford TN14 263 FH116
Potten End HP4 61 BB17
Pratt's Bottom BR6
off Rushmore Hill 246 EW110
Richmond TW9 199 CK85
Ripley GU23 250 BH121
St. Albans. AL3 64 CB22
St. Paul's Cray BR5
off The Avenue 208 EV94
Sarratt WD3 96 BG35
Seal TN15 off Church Rd 279 FM121
Sevenoaks TN13 279 FK122
Shepperton TW17 217 BS98
Sidcup DA14 208 EU91
South Ockendon RM15 171 FW69
Southall UB2 178 BY76
Sutton SM1 222 DB104
Theydon Bois CM16 107 ES37
Twickenham TW2 199 CE88
Waltham Abbey EN9 89 EC34
Warlingham CR6 259 DX117
Welling DA16 187 ES84
Welwyn Garden City AL7 52 DA11
Wembley HA0 139 CG61
Wennington RM13 170 FL73
West Drayton UB7 176 BK76
West Tilbury RM18 193 GL79
Westerham TN16 277 ER126
Whiteley Village KT12
off Octagon Rd 235 BS110
Woldingham CR3 259 EA123
Wooburn Green HP10 132 AE58
Woodford Green IG8 124 EG50
Wraysbury TW19 194 AY86
Greenacre, Dart. DA1 210 FK89
Knaphill GU21
off Mead Ct 248 AS116
Windsor SL4 173 AL82
Greenacre Cl, Barn. EN5 101 CZ38
Northolt UB5 138 BZ64
Swanley BR8 229 FE98
Greenacre Ct, Eng.Grn TW20 194 AW93
Greenacre Gdns, E17 145 EC56
Greenacre Pl, Hackbr. SM6
off Park Rd 223 DH103
Greenacres, N3 119 CY54
SE9 207 EN86
Barnet EN4 102 DD42
Bookham KT23 252 CB124
Bushey Heath WD23 117 CD47
Green Acres, Croy. CR0 224 DT104
Greenacres, Dart. DA2 210 FP86
Epping CM16 91 ET29
Green Acres, Hem.H. HP2 63 BR21
Greenacres, Lwr Kgswd KT20 271 CZ128
Oxted RH8 276 EE127
Green Acres, Welw.G.C. AL7 51 CZ12
Greenacres Av, Uxb. UB10 136 BM62
Sch Greenacre Sch, Bans.
SM7 off Sutton La 240 DB113
Greenacres Cl, Orp. BR6 245 EQ105
Rainham RM13 170 FL69
Greenacres Dr, Stan. HA7 117 CH52
Sch Greenacres Prim Sch, SE9
off Witherston Way 207 EN89
Greenacre Sq, SE16 33 K4
Greenacre Wk, N14 121 DK48
Greenall Cl, Chsht EN8 89 DY30
Green Arbour Ct, EC1 18 G8
Green Av, NW7 118 CR49
W13 179 CH76
Greenaway Av, N18 123 DX51
Greenaway Gdns, NW3 5 L1
Green Bk, E1 32 E3
N12 120 DB49
Greenbank, Chsht EN8 88 DV28
Greenbank Av, Wem. HA0 139 CG64
Greenbank Cl, E4 123 EC47
Romford RM3 128 FK48
Greenbank Ct, Islw. TW7
off Lanadron Cl 179 CF82
Greenbank Cres, NW4 141 CY56
Greenbank Rd, Wat. WD17 97 BR36
Greenbanks, Dart. DA1 210 FL89
St. Albans AL1 65 CF22
Upminster RM14 151 FS60
Greenbay Rd, SE7 186 EK80
Greenberry St, NW8 16 C1
Greenbrook Av, Barn. EN4 102 DC39
Greenbury Cl, Chorl. WD3 95 BC41
● Green Business Cen,
Stai. TW18
off The Glanty 195 BC91
Green Cl, NW9 140 CQ58
NW11 142 DC59
Bromley BR2 226 EE97
Brookmans Park AL9 85 CY26
Carshalton SM5 222 DF103
Cheshunt EN8 89 DY32
Epping Green CM16 73 EP24
Feltham TW13 198 BY92
Taplow SL6 152 AG72
Greencoates, Hert. SG13 54 DS10
Greencoat Pl, SW1 29 M8
Greencoat Row, SW1 29 M7
Sch Green C of E Prim Sch, The,
N17 off Somerset Rd 144 DT55
Green Common La, Woob.Grn
HP10 132 AG59
Greencourt Av, Croy. CR0 224 DV103
Edgware HA8 118 CP53
Greencourt Gdns, Croy. CR0 224 DV102
Greencourt Rd, Petts Wd BR5 227 ER99
Green Ct Rd, Swan. BR8 229 FD99
Green Cres, Flack.Hth HP10 132 AC56

Greencrest Pl, NW2 *off Dollis Hill La* 141 CU62
Greencroft, Edg. HA8 118 CQ50
Guildford GU1 265 BB134
Green Cft, Hat. AL10 *off Talbot Rd* 67 CU15
Greencroft Av, Ruis. HA4 138 BW61
Greencroft Cl, E6 24 G7
Greencroft Gdns, NW6 5 L7
Enfield EN1 104 DS41
Greencroft Rd, Houns. TW5 178 BZ81
Green Curve, Bans. SM7 239 CZ114
Green Dale, SE5 184 DR84
SE22 204 DS85
Green Dale Cl, SE22 *off Green Dale* 204 DS85
Greendale Ms, Slou. SL2 154 AU73
Greendale Wk, Nthflt DA11 212 GE90
Green Dell Way, Hem.H. HP3 63 BP20
Green Dene, E.Hors. KT24 267 BT131
Green Dragon Ct, SE1 31 L2
Green Dragon La, N21 103 DP44
Brentford TW8 180 CL78
Sch **Green Dragon Prim Sch**, Brent. TW8 *off North Rd* 180 CL79
Green Dragon Yd, E1 20 C7
Green Dr, Maid. SL6 152 AE65
Ripley GU23 249 BF123
Slough SL3 174 AY77
Southall UB1 158 CA74
Green E Rd, Jordans HP9 112 AS52
Greene Fielde End, Stai. TW18 196 BK94
Greene Fld Rd, Berk. HP4 60 AW19
Green End, N21 121 DP47
Chessington KT9 238 CL105
● **Green End Business Cen**, Sarratt WD3 96 BG37
Green End Gdns, Hem.H. HP1 62 BG21
Green End La, Hem.H. HP1 61 BF20
Greenend Rd, W4 180 CS75
Green End Rd, Hem.H. HP1 62 BG21
Greener Ct, Enf. EN3 *off Martini Dr* 105 EA37
Greenes Ct, Berk. HP4 *off Lower Kings Rd* 60 AW18
Greene Wk, Berk. HP4 60 AX20
Green Fm Cl, Orp. BR6 245 ET106
Greenfell Mans, SE8 46 C2
Greenfern Av, Slou. SL1 152 AJ72
Green Ferry Way, E17 145 DX56
Greenfield, Hat. AL9 67 CX15
Welwyn Garden City AL8 51 CX06
Greenfield Av, Surb. KT5 220 CP101
Watford WD19 116 BX47
Greenfield Dr, N2 142 DF56
Bromley BR1 226 EJ96
Greenfield End, Chal.St.P. SL9 112 AY51
Greenfield Gdns, NW2 141 CY61
Dagenham RM9 168 EX67
Petts Wood BR5 227 ER101
Greenfield Link, Couls. CR5 257 DL115
Greenfield Rd, E1 20 D7
N15 144 DS57
Dagenham RM9 168 EW67
Dartford DA2 209 FD92
Greenfields, Cuffley EN6 *off South Dr* 87 DL30
Loughton IG10 107 EN42
Sch **Greenfield Sch**, Wok. GU22 *off Brooklyn Rd* 248 AY119
Greenfields Cl, Gt Warley CM13 129 FW51
Horley RH6 290 DE146
Loughton IG10 107 EN42
Sch **Greenfields Prim Sch**, S.Oxhey WD19 *off Ellesborough Cl* 116 BW50
Greenfields Rd, Horl. RH6 290 DE146
Greenfield St, Wal.Abb. EN9 89 EC34
Greenfield Way, Har. HA2 138 CB55
GREENFORD, UB6 158 CB69
⇌ **Greenford** 159 CD67
⊖ **Greenford** 159 CD67
Greenford Av, W7 159 CE70
Southall UB1 158 BZ73
Greenford Gdns, Grnf. UB6 158 CB69
● **Greenford Grn Business Pk**, Grnf. UB6 159 CE67
Sch **Greenford High Sch**, Sthl. UB1 *off Lady Margaret Rd* 158 CA69
Greenford Pk, Grnf. UB6 159 CD66
Greenford Rd, Grnf. UB6 158 CC71
Harrow HA1 139 CE64
Southall UB1 158 CC74
Sutton SM1 240 DB105
Jct **Greenford Rbt**, Grnf. UB6 159 CD68
Green Gdns, Orp. BR6 245 EQ106
Greengate, Grnf. UB6 159 CH65
Greengate St, E13 24 A1
Green Glade, They.B. CM16 107 ES37
Green Glades, Horn. RM11 150 FM58
Greenhalgh Wk, N2 142 DC56
Greenham Cl, SE1 30 E5
Greenham Cres, E4 123 DZ51
Greenham Rd, N10 120 DG54
Greenham Wk, Wok. GU21 248 AW118
Greenhaven Dr, SE28 168 EV72
Greenhayes Av, Bans. SM7 240 DA114
Greenhayes Cl, Reig. RH2 272 DC134
Greenhayes Gdns, Bans. SM7 256 DA115
● **Greenheath Business Cen**, E2 *off Three Colts La* 20 F4
Greenheys Cl, Nthwd. HA6 115 BS53
Greenheys Dr, E18 146 EF55
Greenheys Pl, Wok. GU22 *off White Rose La* 249 AZ118
Greenhill, NW3 6 A1
Green Hill, SE18 187 EM78
Buckhurst Hill IG9 124 EJ46
Downe BR6 244 EL112
Greenhill, Sutt. SM1 222 DC103
Wembley HA9 140 CP61
Greenhill Av, Cat. CR3 258 DV121
Greenhill Cres, Wat. WD18 97 BS44
Greenhill Gdns, Guil. GU4 265 BC131
Northolt UB5 158 BZ68
Greenhill Gro, E12 146 EL63
Green Hill La, Warl. CR6 259 DY117
Greenhill Par, New Barn. EN5 *off Great N Rd* 102 DB43
Greenhill Pk, NW10 160 CS67
New Barnet EN5 102 DB43
Greenhill Rd, NW10 160 CS67
Harrow HA1 139 CE58
Northfleet DA11 213 GF89
Greenhills, Harl. CM20 73 ES15
Greenhills Cl, Rick. WD3 96 BH43
Greenhill's Rents, EC1 18 G6
Greenhills Ter, N1 9 M5
Greenhill Ter, SE18 37 K10
Greenhill Ter, Northolt UB5 158 BZ68
Greenhill Way, Croy. CR0 243 DX111
Harrow HA1 139 CE58
Wembley HA9 140 CP61
GREENHITHE, DA9 211 FV85
Greenhithe Cl, Sid. DA15 207 ES87
⇌ **Greenhithe for Bluewater** 211 FU85
Greenholm Rd, SE9 207 EP85
Green Hundred Rd, SE15 44 D3
Greenhurst La, Oxt. RH8 276 EG132
Greenhurst Rd, SE27 203 DN92
Greening St, SE2 188 EW77
Green Knight Ct, N9 *off Galahad Rd* 122 DU48
Greenlake Ter, Stai. TW18 195 BF94
Greenland Cres, Sthl. UB2 178 BW76
Greenland Ms, SE8 45 K1
Riv **Greenland Pier** 33 N7
Greenland Pl, NW1 7 K8
Greenland Quay, SE16 33 K8
Greenland Rd, NW1 7 K8
Barnet EN5 101 CW44
Greenlands, Ott. KT16 215 BC104
Greenlands La, NW4 119 CV53
Greenlands Rd, Stai. TW18 196 BG91
Weybridge KT13 217 BP104
Greenland St, NW1 7 K8
Greenland Way, Croy. CR0 223 DK101
Green La, E4 106 EE41
NW4 141 CX57
SE9 207 EN89
SE20 205 DX94
SW16 203 DM94
W7 179 CE75
Addlestone KT15 216 BG104
Amersham HP6 77 AS38
Ashtead KT21 253 CJ117
Bletchingley RH1 274 DS131
Bovingdon HP3 79 AZ28
Broxbourne EN10 71 EB23
Burnham SL1 153 AK66
Byfleet KT14 234 BM112
Caterham CR3 258 DQ122
Chertsey KT16 215 BE103
Chesham HP5 78 AV33
Chesham Bois HP6 77 AR35
Chessington KT9 238 CL109
Chigwell IG7 125 ER47
Chipstead CR5 274 DA125
Chislehurst BR7 207 EP91
Chobham GU24 232 AT110
Cobham KT11 236 BY112
Croxley Green WD3 96 BM43
Dagenham RM8 148 EU60
Datchet SL3 174 AV81
Edgware HA8 118 CN50
Egham TW20 195 BB91
Farnham Common SL2 133 AP64
Feltham TW13 198 BY92
Fifield SL6 172 AC81
Godalming GU7 280 AS142
Guildford GU1 265 BB134
Harrow HA1 139 CE62
Hemel Hempstead HP2 63 BQ21
Hersham KT12 235 BV107
Hounslow TW4 177 BV83
Ilford IG1, IG3 147 EQ61
Leatherhead KT22 253 CK121
Lower Kingswood KT20 271 CZ126
Mayford GU24 *off Copper Beech Cl* 248 AV121
Morden SM4 222 DB100
New Malden KT3 220 CQ99
Northwood HA6 115 BT52
Ockham GU23 251 BP124
Outwood RH1 289 DL141
Panshanger AL7 52 DD10
Pilgrim's Hatch CM15 130 FV43
Purley CR8 241 DJ111
Redhill RH1 272 DE132
Reigate RH2 271 CZ134
St. Albans AL3 65 CD16
Shamley Green GU5 282 BG144
Shepperton TW17 217 BQ100
Shipley Bridge RH6 291 DM152
South Ockendon RM15 171 FR69
Staines-upon-Thames TW18 215 BE95
Stanmore HA7 117 CH49
Sunbury-on-Thames TW16 197 BT94
Thornton Heath CR7 223 DN95
Thorpe TW20 215 BD95
Threshers Bush CM17 74 FA16
Upminster RM14 171 FR68
Uxbridge UB8 157 BQ71
Waltham Abbey EN9 90 EJ34
Warley CM14 129 FU52
Warlingham CR6 259 DY116
Watford WD19 116 BW46
West Clandon GU4 266 BG127
West Molesey KT8 218 CB99
White Bushes RH1 288 DG139
Windsor SL4 173 AP82
Worcester Park KT4 221 CU102
Green La Av, Hersham KT12 236 BW106
Green La Cl, Amer. HP6 77 AR36
Byfleet KT14 234 BM112
Chertsey KT16 215 BE103
Green La Gdns, Th.Hth. CR7 224 DQ96
Sch **Green La Prim & Nurs Sch**, Wor.Pk. KT4 *off Green La* 221 CV101
Green Las, N4 144 DQ60
N8 143 DP55
N13 121 DM51
N15 143 DP55
N16 144 DQ62
N21 121 DP46
Epsom KT19 238 CS109
Hatfield AL10 51 CT13
Lemsford AL8 51 CT11
Sch **Green Las Prim Sch**, Hat. AL10 *off Green Las* 51 CT14
Green La W, Wok. GU23 266 BN125
Greenlaw Ct, W5 159 CK72
Greenlaw Gdns, N.Mal. KT3 221 CT101
Greenlawn La, Brent. TW8 179 CK77
Green Lawns, Ruis. HA4 138 BW60
Greenlaw St, SE18 37 L7
Green Leaf Av, Wall. SM6 241 DK105
Greenleaf Cl, SW2 203 DN87
Greenleafe Dr, Ilf. IG6 147 EP55
Sch **Greenleaf Prim Sch**, E17 *off Greenleaf Rd* 145 DZ55
Greenleaf Rd, E6 *off Redclyffe Rd* 166 EJ67
E17 145 DZ55
Greenleaf Way, Har. HA3 139 CF55
● **Greenlea Pk**, SW19 202 DD94
Green Leas, Sun. TW16 197 BT93
Greenleas, Wal.Abb. EN9 105 ED35
Green Leas Cl, Sun. TW16 197 BT94
Greenleaves Ct, Ashf. TW15 *off Redleaves Av* 197 BP93
Greenleigh Av, St.P.Cray BR5 228 EV98
Greenlink Wk, Rich. TW9 180 CP81
Green Man Ct, Eastwick CM20 *off Eastwick Hall La* 57 EN11
Green Man Gdns, W13 159 CG73
Green Man La, W13 159 CG74
Feltham TW14 177 BU84
Green Manor Way, Grav. DA11 192 FZ84
Green Man Pas, W13 159 CH73
Green Man Rd, Ong. CM5 75 FD19
Jct **Green Man Rbt**, E11 146 EF59
Greenman St, N1 9 J7
Green Mead, Esher KT10 *off Winterdown Gdns* 236 BZ107
Greenmead Cl, SE25 224 DU99
Green Meadow, Pot.B. EN6 86 DA30
Greenmeads, Wok. GU22 248 AY122
Sch **Greenmead Sch**, SW15 *off St. Margaret's Cres* 201 CV85
Green Moor Link, N21 121 DP45
Greenmoor Rd, Enf. EN3 104 DW40
Green N Rd, Jordans HP9 112 AS51
Greenoak Pl, Cockfos. EN4 102 DF40
Greenoak Ri, Bigg.H. TN16 260 EJ118
Greenoak Way, SW19 201 CX91
Greenock Rd, SW16 223 DK95
W3 180 CP76
Slough SL1 153 AN72
Greenock Way, Rom. RM1 127 FE52
Greeno Cres, Shep. TW17 216 BN99
⊖ **Green Park** 29 L3
Green Pk, Harl. CM20 73 ES15
Staines-upon-Thames TW18 195 BE90
★ **Green Park, The**, SW1 29 K3
Green Pk Ct, Rom. RM1 *off Kew Cl* 127 FE51
Greenpark Ct, Wem. HA0 159 CJ66
Green Pk Way, Grnf. UB6 159 CE67
Green Pl, SE10 35 J4
Dartford DA1 209 FE85
Green Pt, E15 13 K5
Green Pond Cl, E17 145 DZ55
Green Pond Rd, E17 145 DY55
Green Ride, Epp. CM16 107 EP35
Loughton IG10 106 EG43
Green Rd, N14 103 DH44
N20 120 DC48
Thorpe TW20 215 BB98
Greenroof Way, SE10 35 M7
Greensand Cl, S.Merst. RH1 273 DK128
Green Sand Rd, Red. RH1 272 DG133
Greensand Way, Bet. RH3 286 CM136
Dorking RH5 286 CM136
Godstone RH9 274 DV134
South Nutfield RH1 289 DP135
Sch **Green Sch, The**, Islw. TW7 *off London Rd* 179 CG81
Greens Cl, The, Loug. IG10 107 EN40
Green's Ct, W1 17 N10
Green's End, SE18 37 N8
Greenshank Cl, E17 *off Banbury Rd* 123 DY52
Greenshaw, Brwd. CM14 130 FV46
Sch **Greenshaw High Sch**, Sutt. SM1 *off Grennell Rd* 222 DD103
● **Greenshields Ind Est**, E16 35 P3
Greenside, Bex. DA5 208 EY88
Borehamwood WD6 100 CN38
Dagenham RM8 148 EW60
Slough SL2 153 AN71
Swanley BR8 229 FD96
Greenside Cl, N20 120 DD47
SE6 205 ED89
Guildford GU4 265 BC131
Ilf. IG6 125 EQ51
Greenside Dr, Ashtd. KT21 253 CH118
Sch **Greenside Prim Sch**, W12 *off Westville Rd* 181 CU75
Greenside Rd, W12 181 CU76
Croydon CR0 223 DN101
Greenside Wk, Bigg.H. TN16 *off Kings Rd* 260 EH118
Greenslade Av, Ashtd. KT21 254 CP119
Sch **Greenslade Prim Sch**, SE18 *off Erindale* 187 ER79
Greenslade Rd, Bark. IG11 167 ER66
Greensleeves Cl, St.Alb. AL4 65 CJ21
Greensleeves Dr, Warley CM14 130 FV50
Greenstead, Saw. CM21 58 EY06
Greenstead Av, Wdf.Grn. IG8 124 EJ52
Greenstead Cl, Hutt. CM13 131 GE45
Woodford Green IG8 *off Greenstead Gdns* 124 EJ51
Greenstead Gdns, SW15 201 CU85
Woodford Green IG8 124 EJ51
Greensted Ct, Whyt. CR3 *off Godstone Rd* 258 DU119
GREENSTED GREEN, Ong. CM5 93 FH28
Greensted Rd, Loug. IG10 124 EL45
Ongar CM5 93 FG28
Greenstone Ms, E11 146 EG58
GREEN STREET, Borwd. WD6 100 CP37
Green St, E7 166 EH65
E13 166 EJ67
W1 16 F10
Borehamwood WD6 100 CN36
Enfield EN3 104 DW40
Harlow CM17 58 EX14
Hatfield AL9 67 CZ21
Hertford SG14 54 DR09
Rickmansworth WD3 95 BC40
Shenley WD7 100 CN36
Sunbury-on-Thames TW16 217 BU95
GREEN STREET GREEN, Dart. DA2 211 FU93
GREEN STREET GREEN, Orp. BR6 245 ES107
Sch **Green St Grn Prim Sch**, Grn St Grn BR6 *off Vine Rd* 245 ET107
Green St Grn Rd, Dart. DA1, DA2 210 FP88
Greensward, Bushey WD23 98 CB44
Green Ter, EC1 18 F3
Green Tiles La, Denh. UB9 135 BF58
Green Trees, Epp. CM16 92 EU31
Green Vale, W5 160 CM72
Bexleyheath DA6 208 EX85
Greenvale, Welw.G.C. AL7 52 DA10
Sch **Greenvale Prim Sch**, S.Croy. CR2 *off Sandpiper Rd* 243 DX111
Greenvale Rd, SE9 187 EM84
Sch **Greenvale Sch**, SE6 *off Waters Rd* 206 EE90
Green Valley, Woob.Grn HP10 110 AE54
Green Verges, Stan. HA7 117 CK52
Green Vw, Chess. KT9 238 CM108
Greenview Av, Beck. BR3 225 DY100
Croydon CR0 225 DY100
Greenview Cl, W3 160 CS74
Green Vw Cl, Bov. HP3 79 BA29
Greenview Cl, Ashf. TW15 *off Church Rd* 196 BM91
Greenview Dr, SW20 221 CW97
Green Wk, NW4 141 CX57
SE1 31 N7
Buckhurst Hill IG9 124 EL45
Dartford DA1 189 FF84
Hampton TW12 *off Orpwood Cl* 198 BZ93
Ruislip HA4 137 BT60
Southall UB2 178 CA78
Woodford Green IG8 124 EL51
Green Wk, The, E4 123 EC46
Greenwatt Way, Slou. SL1 173 AR76
Greenway, N14 121 DL47
N20 120 DA47
Green Way, SE9 206 EK85
Greenway, SW20 221 CW98
Berkhamsted HP4 60 AU19
Green Way, Bkhm KT23 252 CB123
Bromley BR2 226 EL100
Burnham SL1 152 AH69
Greenway, Chesh. HP5 76 AP28
Chislehurst BR7 207 EN92
Dagenham RM8 148 EW61
Harlow CM19 72 EL15
Hayes UB4 157 BV70
Hemel Hempstead HP2 63 BP20
Hutton CM13 131 GA45
Kenton HA3 140 CL57
Pinner HA5 115 BV54
Green Way, Red. RH1 272 DE132
Greenway, Rom. RM3 128 FP51
Green Way, Sun. TW16 217 BU98
Greenway, Tats. TN16 260 EJ120
Wallington SM6 241 DJ105
Woodford Green IG8 124 EJ50
Greenway, The, NW9 118 CR54
Chalfont St. Peter SL9 134 AX55
Enfield EN3 105 DX35
Epsom KT18 254 CN115
Harrow Weald HA3 117 CE53
Hounslow TW4 178 BZ84
Ickenham UB10 137 BQ61
Mill End WD3 114 BG45
Orpington BR5 228 EV100
Oxted RH8 276 EH133
Pinner HA5 138 BZ58
Potters Bar EN6 86 DA33
Slough SL1 153 AK74
Uxbridge UB8 156 BJ68
Greenway Av, E17 145 ED56
● **Greenway Business Cen**, Harl. CM19 72 EL15
Greenway Cl, N4 144 DQ61
N11 120 DG51
N15 *off Copperfield Dr* 144 DT56
N20 120 DA47
NW9 118 CR54
West Byfleet KT14 234 BG113
Greenway Dr, Stai. TW18 216 BK95
Sch **Greenway First & Nurs Sch**, Berk. HP4 *off Crossways* 60 AU19
Greenway Gdns, NW9 118 CR54
Croydon CR0 225 DZ104
Greenford UB6 158 CA69
Harrow HA3 117 CE54
Greenway Par, Chesh. HP5 76 AP28
Greenways, Abb.L. WD5 81 BS32
Beckenham BR3 225 EA96
Egham TW20 194 AY92
Esher KT10 237 CE105
Goffs Oak EN7 87 DP29
Hertford SG14 53 DN09
Walton on the Hill KT20 271 CV125
Woking GU22 *off Pembroke Rd* 249 BA117
Greenways, The, Twick. TW1 *off South Western Rd* 199 CG86
Greenways Ct, Horn. RM11 150 FK58
Greenwell Cl, Gdse. RH9 274 DV130
Greenwell St, W1 17 K5
Green W Rd, Jordans HP9 112 AS52
GREENWICH, SE10 46 G4
⇌ **Greenwich** 46 D4
DLR **Greenwich** 46 D4
Greenwich Av, Brwd. CM14 130 FV45
● **Greenwich Cen Business Pk**, SE10 46 D4
Greenwich Ch St, SE10 46 F3
Coll **Greenwich Comm Coll**, Burrage Cen, SE18 *off Burrage Gro* 187 EQ77
Haimo Cen, SE9 *off Haimo Rd* 206 EK85
London Leisure Coll, SE7 36 E10
New London Cen, SE3 *off Telemann Sq* 186 EH83
Plumstead Cen, SE18 *off Plumstead Rd* 187 EQ77
Greenwich Ct, Wal.Cr. EN8 *off Parkside* 89 DY34
Greenwich Cres, E6 24 G7
Greenwich Foot Tunnel, E14 46 F1
SE10 46 F1
Greenwich Hts, SE18 186 EL80
★ **Greenwich Heritage Cen**, SE18 37 N6
Greenwich High Rd, SE10 46 C6
Greenwich Ho, SE13 *off Hither Grn La* 205 ED86
● **Greenwich Ind Est**, SE7 36 A9
🔒 **Greenwich Mkt**, SE10 46 F3
★ **Greenwich Pk**, SE10 47 J4
Greenwich Pk St, SE10 47 H1
GREENWICH PENINSULA 35 J5
Riv **Greenwich Pier** 46 E2
Greenwich Quay, SE8 46 C3
Coll **Greenwich Sch of Management**, SE10 46 E4
🔒 **Greenwich Shop Pk**, SE7 35 P9
Greenwich S St, SE10 46 D6
Greenwich Vw Pl, E14 34 C7
Greenwich Way, Wal.Abb. EN9 105 EC36
Greenwood, The, Guil. GU1 265 BA134
Greenwood Av, Chsht EN7 88 DV31
Dagenham RM10 149 FB63
Enfield EN3 105 DY40
Greenwood Cl, Amer. HP6 77 AS37
Bushey Heath WD23 *off Langmead Dr* 117 CE45
Cheshunt EN7 88 DV31
Morden SM4 221 CY98
Greenwood Cl, Petts Wood BR5 227 ES100
Seer Green HP9 *off Farmers Way* 111 AR51
Sidcup DA15 208 EU89
Thames Ditton KT7 219 CG102
Woodham KT15 233 BF111
Greenwood Ct, SW1 29 L10
Greenwood Dr, E4 *off Avril Way* 123 EC50
Redhill RH1 288 DG139
Watford WD25 81 BV34
Greenwood Gdns, N13 121 DP48
Caterham CR3 274 DU125
Ilford IG6 125 EQ52
Oxted RH8 276 EG134
Shenley WD7 84 CL33
Greenwood Ho, Grays RM17 *off Argent St* 192 GB79
Greenwood La, Hmptn H. TW12 198 CB92
Greenwood Pk, Kings.T. KT2 200 CS94
Greenwood Pl, NW5 7 K2
Sch **Greenwood Prim Sch**, Nthlt. UB5 *off Wood End Way* 139 CD64
Greenwood Rd, E8 10 D5
E13 13 M10
Bexley DA5 209 FD91
Chigwell IG7 126 EV49
Croydon CR0 223 DP101
Isleworth TW7 179 CE83
Mitcham CR4 223 DK97
Thames Ditton KT7 219 CG102
Woking GU21 248 AS120
Greenwoods, The, S.Har. HA2 138 CC62
Greenwood Ter, NW10 160 CR67
Greenwood Way, Sev. TN13 278 FF125
Green Wrythe Cres, Cars. SM5 222 DE102
Green Wrythe La, Cars. SM5 222 DD100
Sch **Green Wrythe Prim Sch**, Cars. SM5 *off Green Wrythe La* 222 DD100
Greenyard, Wal.Abb. EN9 89 EC33
Greer Rd, Har. HA3 116 CC53
Greet St, SE1 30 F3
Greg Cl, E10 145 EC58
Gregories Fm La, Beac. HP9 111 AK53
Gregories Rd, Beac. HP9 110 AH53
Gregor Ms, SE3 47 P5
Gregory Av, Pot.B. EN6 86 DC33
Gregory Cl, Brom. BR2 226 EE98
Woking GU21 248 AW117
Gregory Cres, SE9 206 EK87
Gregory Dr, Old Wind. SL4 194 AV86
Gregory Ms, Wal.Abb. EN9 *off Beaulieu Dr* 89 EB32
Gregory Pl, W8 27 L4
Gregory Rd, Hedg. SL2 133 AR61
Romford RM6 148 EX56
Southall UB2 178 CA76
Gregson Cl, Borwd. WD6 100 CQ39
Gregson's Ride, Loug. IG10 107 EN38
Sch **Greig City Acad**, N8 *off High St* 143 DL56
Greig Cl, N8 143 DL57
Greig Ter, SE17 43 H2
Grenaby Av, Croy. CR0 224 DR101
Grenaby Rd, Croy. CR0 224 DR101
Grenada Rd, SE7 186 EJ80
Grenade St, E14 21 P10
Grenadier Cl, St.Alb. AL4 65 CJ21
Grenadier Pl, Cat. CR3 258 DQ122
Grenadier St, E16 37 L3
Grenadine Cl, Chsht EN7 88 DT27
Grena Gdns, Rich. TW9 180 CM84
Grenard Cl, SE15 44 C5
Grena Rd, Rich. TW9 180 CM84
Grendon Cl, Horl. RH6 290 DF146
Grendon Gdns, Wem. HA9 140 CN61
Grendon Ho, N1 *off Priory Grn Est* 18 C1
Grendon St, NW8 16 C4
Grenfell Av, Horn. RM12 149 FF60
Grenfell Cl, Borwd. WD6 100 CQ39
Grenfell Gdns, Har. HA3 140 CL59
Grenfell Ho, SE5 *off Comber Gro* 43 J5
Grenfell Rd, W11 14 D10
Beaconsfield HP9 111 AL52
Mitcham CR4 202 DF93
Grenfell Twr, W11 14 D10
Grenfell Wk, W11 14 D10
Grennell Cl, Sutt. SM1 222 DD103
Grennell Rd, Sutt. SM1 222 DC103
Grenoble Gdns, N13 121 DN51
Grenside Rd, Wey. KT13 217 BP104
Grenville Av, Brox. EN10 71 DZ21
Grenville Cl, N3 119 CZ53
Burnham SL1 152 AH68
Cobham KT11 236 BX113
Surbiton KT5 220 CQ102
Waltham Cross EN8 89 DX32
Grenville Ct, SE19 *off Lymer Av* 204 DT92
Grenville Gdns, Wdf.Grn. IG8 124 EJ53
Grenville Ms, N19 143 DL60
Hampton TW12 198 CB92
Grenville Pl, NW7 118 CR50
SW7 27 N7
Grenville Rd, N19 143 DL60
Chafford Hundred RM16 191 FV78
New Addington CR0 243 EC109
Grenville St, WC1 18 B5
Gresford Cl, St.Alb. AL4 65 CK20
Gresham Av, N20 120 DF49
Warlingham CR6 259 DY118
Gresham Cl, Bex. DA5 208 EY86
Brentwood CM14 130 FW48
Enfield EN2 104 DQ41
Oxted RH8 276 EF128
Gresham Ct, Berk. HP4 60 AV20
Gresham Dr, Rom. RM6 148 EV57
Gresham Gdns, NW11 141 CY60
Gresham Pl, N19 143 DK61
Sch **Gresham Prim Sch**, S.Croy. CR2 *off Limpsfield Rd* 242 DU112
Gresham Rd, E6 25 K1
E16 24 B9
NW10 140 CR64
SE25 224 DU98
SW9 183 DN83
Beckenham BR3 225 DY96

Gresham Rd, Brentwood CM14 130 FW48
Edgware HA8 118 CM51
Hampton TW12 198 CA93
Hounslow TW3 178 CC81
Oxted RH8 276 EF128
Slough SL1 153 AN72
Staines-upon-Thames TW18 195 BF92
Uxbridge UB10 156 BN68
Gresham St, EC2 19 J8
Gresham Way, SW19 202 DA90
Gresley Cl, E17 145 DY58
N15 144 DR56
Welwyn Garden City AL8 51 CY08
Gresley Ct, Pot.B. EN6 86 DC30
Gresley Rd, N19 143 DJ60
Gressenhall Rd, SW18 201 CZ86
Gresse St, W1 17 N7
Gresswell Cl, Sid. DA14 208 EU90
Greswell St, SW6 38 C7
Greta Bk, W.Hors. KT24 267 BQ126
Gretton Rd, N17 122 DS52
Greville Av, S.Croy. CR2 243 DX110
Greville Cl, Ashtd. KT21 254 CL119
Guildford GU2 264 AS134
North Mymms AL9 67 CV24
Twickenham TW1 199 CH87
Greville Ct, E5
off Napoleon Rd 144 DV62
Bookham KT23 268 CC125
Greville Hall, NW6 5 L10
Greville Ms, NW6 5 L9
Greville Pk Av, Ashtd. KT21 254 CL118
Greville Pk Rd, Ashtd. KT21 254 CL118
Greville Pl, NW6 5 M10
Greville Prim Sch, The, Ashtd. KT21 *off Stonny Cft* 254 CM117
Greville Rd, E17 145 EC56
NW6 5 L10
Richmond TW10 200 CM86
Greville St, EC1 18 F7
Grey Alders, Bans. SM7 239 CW114
Greycaine Rd, Wat. WD24 98 BX37
Grey Cl, NW11 142 DC58
Greycoat Gdns, SW1
off Greycoat St 29 N7
Grey Coat Hosp Sch, Lwr Sch, SW1 29 N7
Upr Sch, SW1 29 N9
Greycoat Pl, SW1 29 N7
Greycoat St, SW1 29 N7
Greycot Rd, Beck. BR3 205 EA92
Grey Ct Sch, Rich. TW10
off Ham St 199 CJ90
Grey Eagle St, E1 20 A6
Greyfell Cl, Stan. HA7
off Coverdale Cl 117 CH50
Greyfields Cl, Pur. CR8 241 DP113
Greyfriars, Hutt. CM13 131 GB45
Greyfriars Pas, EC1 19 H8
Greyfriars Rd, Ripley GU23 250 BG124
Greygoose Pk, Harl. CM19 73 EN18
Greyhound Hill, NW4 141 CU55
Greyhound La, SW16 203 DK93
Orsett RM16 193 GG75
South Mimms EN6 85 CU33
Greyhound Rd, N17 144 DS55
NW10 161 CV69
W6 38 D2
W14 38 D2
Sutton SM1 240 DC106
Greyhound Ter, SW16 223 DJ95
Greyhound Way, Dart. DA1 209 FE86
Greyladies Gdns, SE10 46 F7
Greys Pk Cl, Kes. BR2 244 EJ106
Greystead Rd, SE23 204 DW87
Greystoke Av, Pnr. HA5 138 CA55
Greystoke Cl, Berk. HP4 60 AU20
Greystoke Dr, Ruis. HA4 137 BP58
Greystoke Gdns, W5 160 CL70
Enfield EN2 103 DK42
Greystoke Pk Ter, W5 159 CK69
Greystoke Pl, EC4 18 E8
Greystoke Rd, Slou. SL2 153 AM71
Greystone Cl, S.Croy. CR2 242 DW111
Greystone Gdns, Har. HA3 139 CJ58
Ilford IG6 125 EQ54
Greystone Path, E11
off Grove Rd 146 EF59
Greystones Cl, Red. RH1 288 DD136
Greystones Dr, Reig. RH2 272 DC132
Greyswood Av, N18 123 DX51
Greyswood St, SW16 203 DH93
Greythorne Rd, Wok. GU21 248 AU118
Grey Twrs Av, Horn. RM11 150 FK60
Grey Twrs Gdns, Horn. RM11
off Grey Twrs Av 150 FK60
Grice Av, Bigg.H. TN16 244 EH113
Gridiron Pl, Upmin. RM14 150 FP62
Grierson Rd, SE23 205 DX87
Grieves Rd, Nthflt DA11 213 GF90
Griffetts Yd, Chesh. HP5
off Bellingdon Rd 76 AP30
Griffin Av, Upmin. RM14 151 FS58
● **Griffin Cen**, Felt. TW14 197 BV86
Griffin Cl, NW10 141 CV64
Slough SL1 173 AQ75
Griffin Ct, Ashtd. KT21
off The Warren 254 CL119
Bookham KT23
off Griffin Way 268 CB126
Northfleet DA11 212 GA85
Griffin Manor Way, SE28 187 ER76
Griffin Rd, N17 122 DS54
SE18 187 ER78
Griffins, The, Grays RM16 192 GB75
Griffins Cl, N21 122 DR45
Griffin Wk, Green. DA9
off Church Rd 211 FT85
Griffin Way, Bkhm KT23 268 CA126
Sunbury-on-Thames TW16 217 BU96
Griffith Cl, Dag. RM8
off Gibson Rd 148 EW60
Griffiths Cl, Wor.Pk. KT4 221 CV103
Griffiths Rd, SW19 202 DA94
Griffiths Way, St.Alb. AL1 64 CC22
Griffon Way, Lvsdn WD25 81 BT34
Grifon Rd, Chaff.Hun. RM16 191 FW76
Griggs App, Ilf. IG1 147 EQ61
Griggs Cl, Ilf. IG3 147 ES63
Griggs Gdns, Horn. RM12
off Tylers Cres 150 FJ64
Griggs Pl, SE1 31 P7
Griggs Rd, E10 145 EC58
Grilse Cl, N9 122 DV49
Grimsby Gro, E16 37 P4
Grimsby Rd, Slou. SL1 173 AM75
Grimsby St, E2 20 B5
Grimsdells La, Amer. HP6 77 AR37
Grimsdyke Cres, Barn. EN5 101 CW41
Grimsdyke First & Mid Sch, Hatch End HA5
off Sylvia Av 116 BZ51
Grimsdyke Rd, Pnr. HA5 116 BY52
Grimsel Path, SE5 43 H4
Grimshaw Cl, N6 142 DG59
Grimshaw Way, Rom. RM1 149 FF57
Grimstone Cl, Rom. RM5 127 FB51
Grimston Rd, SW6 38 G9
St. Albans AL1 65 CF21
Grimthorpe Cl, St.Alb. AL3 65 CD17
Grimthorpe Ho, EC1 18 G4
Grimwade Av, Croy. CR0 224 DU104
Grimwade Cres, SE15 44 G10
Grimwood Rd, Twick. TW1 199 CF87
Grindall Cl, Croy. CR0 241 DP105
Grindal St, SE1 30 E5
Grindcobbe, St.Alb. AL1 65 CD23
Grindleford Av, N11 120 DG47
Grindley Gdns, Croy. CR0 224 DT100
Grinling Gibbons Prim Sch, SE8 45 P3
Grinling Pl, SE8 46 A3
Grinstead Rd, SE8 45 L1
Grisedale Cl, Pur. CR8 242 DS114
Grisedale Gdns, Pur. CR8 242 DS114
Grittleton Av, Wem. HA9 160 CP65
Grittleton Rd, W9 15 J4
Grizedale Ter, SE23 204 DV89
Grobars Av, Wok. GU21 248 AW115
Grocer's Hall Ct, EC2 19 L9
Grogan Cl, Hmptn. TW12 198 BZ93
Groombridge Cl, Hersham KT12 235 BV106
Welling DA16 208 EU85
Groombridge Rd, E9 11 J7
Groom Cl, Brom. BR2 226 EH98
Groom Cres, SW18 202 DD87
Groomfield Cl, SW17 202 DG91
Groom Pl, SW1 29 H6
Groom Rd, Brox. EN10 89 DZ26
Grooms Cotts, Chesh. HP5 78 AV30
Grooms Dr, Pnr. HA5 137 BU57
Groom Wk, Guil. GU1 264 AY131
Grosmont Rd, SE18 187 ET78
Grosse Way, SW15 201 CV86
Grosvenor Av, N5 9 J3
SW14 180 CS83
Carshalton SM5 240 DF107
Harrow HA2 138 CB58
Hayes UB4 157 BS68
Kings Langley WD4 81 BQ28
Richmond TW10 200 CL85
Grosvenor Br, SW1 41 K2
Grosvenor Cl, Horl. RH6 290 DG150
Iver SL0 155 BD69
Loughton IG10 107 EP39
Grosvenor Cotts, SW1 28 G8
Grosvenor Ct, N14 121 DJ45
NW6 4 D8
Croxley Green WD3
off Mayfare 97 BR43
Guildford GU4 265 BB130
Slough SL1 154 AS72
Sutton SM2
off Brighton Rd 240 DC107
Grosvenor Cres, NW9 140 CN56
SW1 29 H5
Dartford DA1 210 FK85
Uxbridge UB10 157 BP66
Grosvenor Cres Ms, SW1 28 G5
Grosvenor Dr, Horn. RM11 150 FJ60
Loughton IG10 107 EP39
Maidenhead SL6 152 AC71
Grosvenor Est, SW1 29 P8
Grosvenor Gdns, E6 24 E2
N10 143 DJ55
N14 103 DK43
NW2 4 B3
NW11 141 CZ58
SW1 29 J6
SW14 180 CS83
Kingston upon Thames KT2 199 CK93
Upminster RM14 151 FR60
Wallington SM6 241 DJ108
Woodford Green IG8 124 EG51
Grosvenor Gdns Ms E, SW1 29 K6
Grosvenor Gdns Ms N, SW1 29 J7
Grosvenor Gdns Ms S, SW1 29 K7
Grosvenor Gate, W1 28 F1
Grosvenor Hill, SW19 201 CY93
W1 17 J10
Grosvenor Ms, Epsom KT18 254 CR119
Reigate RH2 288 DB137
Grosvenor Pk, SE5 43 J3
Grosvenor Pk Rd, E17 145 EA57
Grosvenor Path, Loug. IG10 107 EP39
Grosvenor Pl, SW1 29 H5
Weybridge KT13
off Vale Rd 217 BR104
Woking GU21
off Burleigh Gdns 249 AZ116
Grosvenor Ri E, E17 145 EB57
Grosvenor Rd, E6 166 EK67
E7 166 EH65
E10 145 EC60
E11 146 EG57
N3 119 CZ52
N9 122 DV46
N10 121 DH53
SE25 224 DU98
SW1 41 J2
W4 180 CP78
W7 159 CG74
Belvedere DA17 188 FA79
Bexleyheath DA6 208 EX85
Borehamwood WD6 100 CN41
Brentford TW8 179 CK79
Broxbourne EN10 71 DZ20
Dagenham RM8 148 EZ60
Epsom KT18 254 CR119
Hounslow TW3 178 BZ83
Ilford IG1 147 EQ62
Northwood HA6 115 BT50
Petts Wood BR5 227 ES100
Richmond TW10 200 CL85
Romford RM7 149 FD59
St. Albans AL1 65 CE21
Southall UB2 178 BZ76
Staines-upon-Thames TW18 196 BG94
Twickenham TW1 199 CG87
Grosvenor Rd, Wallington SM6 241 DH107
Watford WD17 98 BW42
West Wickham BR4 225 EB102
Grosvenor Sq, W1 17 H10
Kings Langley WD4
off Grosvenor Av 81 BQ28
Grosvenor St, W1 17 J10
Grosvenor Ter, SE5 43 H4
Hemel Hempstead HP1 62 BG21
Grosvenor Vale, Ruis. HA4 137 BT61
Grosvenor Way, E5 144 DW61
Grosvenor Wf Rd, E14 34 G9
Grote's Bldgs, SE3 47 K9
Grote's Pl, SE3 47 J9
Groton Rd, SW18 202 DB89
Grotto, The, Ware SG12 55 DX07
Grotto Pas, W1 17 H6
Grotto Rd, Twick. TW1 199 CF89
Weybridge KT13 217 BP104
Ground La, Hat. AL10 67 CV16
Grove, The, SE22 204 DU88
Grove, The, E15 13 J4
N3 120 DA53
N4 143 DM59
N6 142 DG60
N8 143 DK57
N13 121 DN50
N14 103 DJ43
NW9 140 CR57
NW11 141 CY59
W5 159 CK74
Addlestone KT15 234 BH106
Amersham HP6 77 AR36
Bexleyheath DA6 188 EX84
Biggin Hill TN16 260 EK118
Brentwood CM14 130 FT49
Brookmans Park AL9 86 DA27
Caterham CR3 257 DP121
Chipperfield WD4 80 BJ30
Coulsdon CR5 257 DK115
Edgware HA8 118 CP49
Egham TW20 195 BA92
Enfield EN2 103 DN40
Epsom KT17 238 CS113
Esher KT10 218 CB102
Ewell KT17 239 CT110
Gravesend DA12 213 GH87
Greenford UB6 158 CC72
Horley RH6 291 DH149
Isleworth TW7 179 CE81
Latimer HP5 94 AX36
Potters Bar EN6 86 DC32
Radlett WD7 83 CG34
Sidcup DA14 208 EY91
Slough SL1 174 AU75
Stanmore HA7 117 CG47
Swanley BR8 229 FF97
Swanscombe DA10 212 FZ85
Teddington TW11 199 CG91
Twickenham TW1
off Bridge Rd 199 CH86
Upminster RM14 150 FP63
Uxbridge UB10 136 BN64
Walton-on-Thames KT12 217 BV101
Watford WD17 97 BQ37
West Wickham BR4 225 EB104
Woking GU21 249 AZ116
Grove Av, N3 120 DA52
N10 121 DJ54
W7 159 CE72
Epsom KT17 238 CS113
Pinner HA5 138 BY56
Sutton SM1 240 DA107
Twickenham TW1 199 CF88
Grove Bk, Wat. WD19 116 BX46
Grovebarns, Stai. TW18 196 BG93
Grovebury Cl, Erith DA8 189 FD79
Grovebury Gdns, Park St AL2 82 CC27
Grovebury Rd, SE2 188 EV75
Grove Cl, N14 121 DJ45
SE23 205 DX88
Bromley BR2 226 EG103
Chalfont St. Peter SL9
off Grove La 112 AW53
Epsom KT19 238 CP110
Feltham TW13 198 BY91
Kingston upon Thames KT1 220 CM98
Old Windsor SL4 194 AV87
Slough SL1 *off Alpha St S* 174 AU76
Uxbridge UB10 136 BN64
Grove Cor, Bkhm KT23
off Lower Shott 268 CA126
Grove Cotts, SW3 40 D2
Grove Ct, Barn. EN5
off High St 101 CZ41
Beaconsfield HP9
off Station Rd 111 AK53
East Molesey KT8
off Walton Rd 219 CD99
Egham TW20 195 BA92
Send GU23 *off Send Rd* 249 BD123
Waltham Abbey EN9 89 EB33
Grove Cres, E18 124 EF54
NW9 140 CQ56
Croxley Green WD3 96 BN42
Feltham TW13 198 BY91
Kingston upon Thames KT1 220 CL97
Walton-on-Thames KT12 217 BV101
Grove Cres Rd, E15 13 H5
Grovedale Cl, Chsht EN7 88 DT30
Grovedale Rd, N19 143 DK61
Grove Dws, E1 20 G6
Grove End, E18
off Grove Hill 124 EF54
NW5 *off Chetwynd Rd* 143 DH63
Chalfont St. Peter SL9 112 AW53
Grove End Gdns, NW8
off Grove End Rd 16 A1
Grove End La, Esher KT10 219 CD102
Grove End Rd, NW8 16 A1
Grove Fm Ct, Mitch. CR4
off Brookfields Av 222 DF98
Grove Fm Pk, Nthwd. HA6 115 BR50
Grove Fm Retail Pk, Chad.Hth RM6 148 EW59
Grove Footpath, Surb. KT5 220 CL98
Grove Gdns, NW4 141 CU56
NW8 16 D3
Dagenham RM10 149 FC62
Enfield EN3 105 DX39
Teddington TW11 199 CG91
Grove Grn Rd, E11 145 EC62
Grove Hall Ct, NW8 15 P2
Grove Hall Rd, Bushey WD23 98 BY42
Grove Heath, Ripley GU23 250 BJ124
Grove Heath Ct, Ripley GU23 250 BJ124
Grove Heath N, Ripley GU23 250 BH122
Grove Heath Rd, Ripley GU23 250 BJ123
Groveherst Rd, Dart. DA1 190 FM83
GROVEHILL, Hem.H. HP2 62 BL16
Grove Hill, E18 124 EF54
Chalfont St. Peter SL9 112 AW52
Harrow HA1 139 CE59
Grove Hill Rd, SE5 43 N10
Harrow HA1 139 CE59
Grovehill Rd, Red. RH1 272 DE134
Grove Ho, Chsht EN8 88 DW30
Grove Ho Rd, N8 143 DL56
Groveland Av, SW16 203 DM94
Groveland Ct, EC4 19 K9
Groveland Rd, Beck. BR3 225 DZ97
Grovelands, Horl. RH6
off The Grove 291 DH149
Park Street AL2 82 CB27
West Molesey KT8 218 CA98
● **Grovelands Business Cen**, Hem.H. HP2 63 BQ18
Grovelands Cl, SE5 43 N9
Harrow HA2 138 CB62
Grovelands Ct, N14 121 DK45
Grovelands Rd, N13 121 DM49
N15 144 DU58
Orpington BR5 208 EU94
Purley CR8 241 DL112
Grovelands Sch, Walt. KT12 *off Terrace Rd* 217 BV100
Grovelands Way, Grays RM17 192 FZ78
Groveland Way, N.Mal. KT3 220 CQ99
Grove La, SE5 43 L7
Chalfont St. Peter SL9 112 AW53
Chesham HP5 78 AV27
Chigwell IG7 125 ET48
Coulsdon CR5 240 DG113
Epping CM16 *off High St* 92 EU30
Kingston upon Thames KT1 220 CL98
Uxbridge UB8 156 BM70
Grove La Ter, SE5
off Grove La 43 N10
Grove Lea, Hat. AL10 67 CU21
Groveley Rd, Sun. TW16 197 BT92
Grove Mkt Pl, SE9 207 EM86
Grove Mead, Hat. AL10 67 CT18
Grove Meadow, Welw.G.C. AL7 52 DC09
Grove Ms, W6 26 A6
W11 14 G9
Grove Mill, Mitch. CR4 222 DE99
Grove Mill La, Wat. WD17 97 BP37
Grove Mill Pl, Cars. SM5 222 DG104
GROVE PARK, SE12 206 EG89
GROVE PARK, W4 180 CP80
⇌ **Grove Park** 206 EG90
Grove Park 206 EH90
Grove Pk, E11 146 EH58
NW9 140 CQ56
SE5 43 N9
Grove Pk Av, E4 123 EB52
Grove Pk Br, W4 180 CQ80
Grove Pk Gdns, W4 180 CP79
Grove Pk Ms, W4 180 CQ80
Grove Pk Prim Sch, W4
off Nightingale Cl 180 CQ79
Grove Pk Rd, N15 144 DS56
SE9 206 EJ90
W4 180 CP80
Rainham RM13 169 FG67
Grove Pk Sch, NW9
off Grove Pk 140 CQ56
Grove Pk Ter, W4 180 CP79
Grove Pas, E2 10 E10
Teddington TW11 199 CG92
Grove Path, Chsht EN7 88 DU31
Grove Pl, NW3
off Christchurch Hill 142 DD62
SW12 203 DH86
W3 160 CQ74
Banstead SM7 240 DF112
Barking IG11
off Clockhouse Av 167 EQ67
North Mymms AL9
off Dixons Hill Rd 67 CW24
Watford WD25 98 CB39
Weybridge KT13 235 BQ106
Grove Prim Sch, Chad.Hth RM6 *off Chadwell Heath La* 148 EW57
Grover Cl, Hem.H. HP2 62 BK19
Grove Rd, E3 11 K10
E4 123 EB49
E11 146 EF59
E17 145 EB58
E18 124 EF54
N11 121 DH50
N12 120 DD50
N15 144 DS57
NW2 4 A4
SW13 181 CT82
SW19 202 DC94
W3 160 CQ74
W5 159 CK73
Amersham HP6 94 AT37
Ashtead KT21 254 CM118
Beaconsfield HP9 111 AK53
Belvedere DA17 188 EZ79
Bexleyheath DA7 189 FC84
Borehamwood WD6 100 CN39
Brentford TW8 179 CJ78
Burnham SL1 153 AL67
Chertsey KT16 215 BF100
Cockfosters EN4 102 DE41
East Molesey KT8 219 CD98
Edgware HA8 118 CN51
Epsom KT17 238 CS113
Grays RM17 192 GC79
Guildford GU1 265 BC134
Hemel Hempstead HP1 62 BG22
Horley RH6 290 DE147
Hounslow TW3 178 CB84
Isleworth TW7 179 CE81
Mill End WD3 114 BG47
Mitcham CR4 223 DH96
Northfleet DA11 212 GB85
Northwood HA6 115 BR50
Oxted RH8
off Southlands La 275 EC134
Pinner HA5 138 BZ57
Redhill RH1
off Lower Br Rd 272 DF134
Richmond TW10 200 CM86
Romford RM6 148 EV59
St. Albans AL1 65 CD21
Seal TN15 279 FN122
Sevenoaks TN14 279 FJ121
Shepperton TW17 217 BQ100
Surbiton KT6 219 CK99
Sutton SM1 240 DB107
Tatsfield TN16 260 EJ120
Thornton Heath CR7 223 DN98
Twickenham TW2 199 CD90
Grove Rd, Uxbridge UB8 156 BK66
Ware SG12 55 DZ05
Windsor SL4 173 AQ82
Woking GU21 249 AZ116
Grove Rd Prim Sch, Houns. TW3
off Cromwell Rd 178 CA84
Grove Rd W, Enf. EN3 104 DW37
Grover Rd, Wat. WD19 116 BX45
Groves Cl, B.End SL8 132 AC60
South Ockendon RM15 171 FT73
Grove Shaw, Kgswd KT20 255 CY124
Groveside, Bkhm KT23 268 CA127
Groveside Cl, W3 160 CN72
Bookham KT23 268 CA127
Carshalton SM5 222 DE103
Groveside Rd, E4 124 EE47
Grovestile Waye, Felt. TW14 197 BR87
Grove St, N18 122 DT51
SE8 33 N8
Groves Way, Chesh. HP5 76 AM29
Grove Ter, NW5 143 DH62
Teddington TW11 199 CG91
Grove Ter Ms, NW5
off Grove Ter 143 DH62
Grove Vale, SE22 184 DS84
Chislehurst BR7 207 EN93
Grove Vil, E14 22 D10
Grove Wk, Hert. SG14 54 DQ07
Groveway, SW9 42 D7
Grove Way, Chorl. WD3 95 BB42
Groveway, Dag. RM8 148 EX63
Grove Way, Esher KT10 218 CC101
Uxbridge UB8 156 BK66
Wembley HA9 140 CP64
Grovewood, Rich. TW9 180 CN81
Grove Wd Cl, Brom. BR1 227 EN97
Grovewood Cl, Chorl. WD3 95 BB43
Grove Wd Hill, Couls. CR5 241 DK114
Grovewood Pl, Wdf.Grn. IG8 125 EM51
Grubbs La, Hat. AL9 68 DA22
Grub St, Oxt. RH8 276 EJ128
Grummant Rd, SE15 44 A6
Grundy St, E14 22 C9
Gruneisen Rd, N3 120 DB52
● **Gryphon Ind Pk, The**, Port.Wd AL3 65 CF15
GSA Conservatoire, Guil. GU2 *off Millmead Ter* 280 AW136
Guardian Angels RC Prim Sch, E3 21 M4
Guardian Av, N.Stfd RM16 191 FX75
● **Guardian Business Cen**, Rom. RM3
off Faringdon Ave 128 FK52
Guardian Cl, Horn. RM11 149 FH60
Guards Av, Cat. CR3 258 DQ122
Guards Club Rd, Maid. SL6 152 AC72
Guardsman Cl, Warley CM14 130 FX50
★ **Guards Mus**, SW1 29 M5
Guards Rd, Wind. SL4 172 AJ82
Guards Wk, Wind. SL4
off Guards Rd 172 AJ82
Gubbins La, Rom. RM3 128 FM52
Gubyon Av, SE24 203 DP85
Guerin Sq, E3 21 N2
Guernsey Cl, Guil. GU4
off Cotts Wd Dr 265 BA129
Hounslow TW5 178 CA81
Guernsey Fm Dr, Wok. GU21 248 AX115
Guernsey Gro, SE24 204 DQ87
Guernsey Ho, N1 9 K5
Enfield EN3
off Eastfield Rd 105 DX38
Guernsey Rd, E11 145 ED60
Guessens Ct, Welw.G.C. AL8 51 CW09
Guessens Gro, Welw.G.C. AL8 51 CW09
Guessens Rd, Welw.G.C. AL8 51 CW09
Guessens Wk, Welw.G.C. AL8 51 CW08
Guibal Rd, SE12 206 EH87
Guildcroft, Guil. GU1 265 BA134
Guildersfield Rd, SW16 203 DL94
GUILDFORD, GU1 - GU5 280 AU135
⇌ **Guildford** 280 AW135
Guildford 280 AX135
Guildford Adult Learning Cen, Guil. GU1
off Sydenham Rd 280 AY135
Guildford & Godalming Bypass, Guil. GU2, GU3 280 AS136
Guildford Av, Felt. TW13 197 BT89
● **Guildford Business Pk**, Guil. GU2 264 AV133
Guildford Bypass, Guil. GU1, GU2, GU4 265 AZ131
★ **Guildford Castle**, Guil. GU1 280 AX136
Guildford Coll, Stoke Pk Campus, Guil. GU1
off Stoke Rd 264 AX133
Guildford Co Sch, Guil. GU2 *off Farnham Rd* 280 AV136
Guildford Gdns, Rom. RM3 128 FL51
Guildford Gro, SE10 46 D6
Guildford Gro Prim Sch, Guil. GU2 *off Southway* 264 AS134
Guildford High Sch, Guil. GU1 *off London Rd* 264 AY134
★ **Guildford House Gall**, Guil. GU1 *off High St* 280 AX135
● **Guildford Ind Est**, Guil. GU2 264 AU133
Guildford La, Albury GU5 282 BH139
Woking GU22 248 AX120
Guildford Lo Dr, E.Hors. KT24 267 BT129
★ **Guildford Mus**, Guil. GU1 280 AX136
Guildford Nuffield Hosp, Guil. GU2 264 AS134
GUILDFORD PARK, Guil. GU2 280 AV135
Guildford Pk Av, Guil. GU2 280 AV135
Guildford Pk Rd, Guil. GU2 280 AV135
Guildford Rd, E6 25 J9
E17 123 EC53
SW8 42 B6
Bookham KT23 268 BZ127
Chertsey KT16 215 BE102
Croydon CR0 224 DR100
Dorking RH5 284 BW140
Fetcham KT22 253 CG122
Godalming GU7 280 AU144
Guildford GU3, GU4 264 AX127
Ilford IG3 147 ES61
Leatherhead KT24 268 BW129
Mayford GU22 248 AX122
Romford RM3 128 FL51
St. Albans AL1 65 CH21
Westcott RH4 284 CA138
Woking GU22 248 AY119
Guildford St, Cher. KT16 216 BG101

Guildford St, Staines-upon-Thames TW18 196 BG93
Guildford Way, Wall. SM6 241 DL106
★ **Guildhall, The**, EC2 19 L8
★ **Guildhall Art Gall** (Guildhall Lib), EC2 19 K8
Guildhall Bldgs, EC2 19 L8
Guildhall Sch of Music & Drama, EC2 19 K6
Hall of Res, EC1 19 L6
Guildhall Yd, EC2 19 K8
Guildhouse St, SW1 29 L8
Guildown Av, N12 120 DB49
Guildford GU2 280 AV137
Guildown Rd, Guil. GU2 280 AV137
Guild Rd, SE7 186 EK78
Erith DA8 189 FF80
Guildsway, E17 123 DZ53
● **Guildway, The**, Guil. GU3 280 AW140
Guileshill La, Ock. GU23 250 BL123
Guilford Av, Surb. KT5 220 CM99
Guilford Pl, WC1 18 C5
Guilfords, Harl. CM17 58 EX10
Guilford St, WC1 18 B5
Guinery Gro, Hem.H. HP3 62 BM24
Guinevere Gdns, Wal.Cr. EN8 89 DY31
Guinness Cl, E9 11 L7
Hayes UB3 177 BR76
Guinness Ct, E1 20 B9
Woking GU21
off Iveagh Rd 248 AT118
Guinness Sq, SE1 31 N8
Guinness Trust Bldgs, SE1
off Snowsfields 31 N4
SE11 30 G10
SW3 28 E9
SW9 183 DP84
W6 *off Fulham Palace Rd* 26 B10
Guinness Trust Est, N16 144 DS60
Guion Rd, SW6 39 H8
Gulland Wk, N1
off Nightingale Rd 9 K5
Gullbrook, Hem.H. HP1 62 BG20
Gullet Wd Rd, Wat. WD25 97 BU35
Gulliver Cl, Nthlt. UB5 158 BZ67
Gulliver Rd, Sid. DA15 207 ES89
Gulliver St, SE16 33 N6
Gull Wk, Horn. RM12
off Heron Flight Av 169 FH66
Gulphs, The, Hert. SG13 54 DR10
Gulston Wk, SW3 28 F9
Gumbrell Ms, Red. RH1 273 DH132
Gumleigh Rd, W5 179 CJ77
Gumley Gdns, Islw. TW7 179 CG83
Gumley Ho RC Conv Sch, Islw. TW7 *off St. John's Rd* 179 CG83
Gumley Rd, Grays RM20 191 FX79
Gumping Rd, Orp. BR5 227 EQ103
Gundulph Rd, Brom. BR2 226 EJ97
Gunfleet Cl, Grav. DA12 213 GL87
Gun Hill, W.Til. RM18 193 GK79
Gunmakers La, E3 11 M9
Gunnell Cl, SE26 204 DU92
Croydon CR0 224 DU100
Gunner Dr, Enf. EN3 105 EA37
Gunner La, SE18 187 EN78
GUNNERSBURY, W4 180 CP77
Gunnersbury 180 CP78
Gunnersbury 180 CP78
Gunnersbury Av, W3 180 CN76
W4 180 CN76
W5 160 CM74
Gunnersbury Catholic Sch for Boys, Brent. TW8
off The Ride 179 CJ78
Gunnersbury Cl, W4
off Grange Rd 180 CP78
Gunnersbury Ct, W3 180 CP75
Gunnersbury Cres, W3 180 CN75
Gunnersbury Dr, W5 180 CM75
Gunnersbury Gdns, W3 180 CN75
Gunnersbury La, W3 180 CN76
Gunnersbury Ms, W4
off Chiswick High Rd 180 CP78
★ **Gunnersbury Park**, W3 180 CM77
Gunnersbury Pk, W3 180 CM76
Gunnersbury Pk, W3 180 CM77
W5 180 CM77
★ **Gunnersbury Park Mus**, W3 180 CN76
Gunners Gro, E4 123 EC48
Gunners Rd, SW18 202 DD89
● **Gunnery Ter**, SE18 187 EQ77
Gunning Rd, Grays RM17 192 GD78
Gunning St, SE18 187 ES77
Gunn Rd, Swans. DA10 212 FY86
Gunpowder Sq, EC4 18 F8
Gunstor Rd, N16 144 DS63
Gun St, E1 20 A7
Gunter Gro, SW10 39 N3
Edgware HA8 118 CR53
Gunters Mead, Esher KT10 236 CC110
Gunterstone Rd, W14 26 E9
Gunthorpe St, E1 20 B7
Gunton Rd, E5 144 DV62
SW17 202 DG93
Gunwhale Cl, SE16 33 K3
Gunyard Ms, SE18 186 EL80
Gurdon Rd, SE7 47 P1
Gurnard Cl, West Dr. UB7 156 BK73
Gurnell Gro, W13 159 CF70
Gurnells Rd, Seer Grn HP9 111 AQ50
Gurney Cl, E15 13 K2
E17 123 DX53
Barking IG11 167 EP65
Beaconsfield HP9 110 AJ53
Gurney Ct Rd, St.Alb. AL1 65 CF18
Gurney Cres, Croy. CR0 223 DM102
Gurney Dr, N2 142 DC57
Gurney Rd, E15 13 J2
SW6 39 N10
Carshalton SM5 240 DG105
Northolt UB5 157 BV69
Gurney's Cl, Red. RH1 288 DF135
Guru Gobind Singh Khalsa Coll, Chig. IG7 *off Roding La* 125 EM46
Guru Nanak Marg, Grav. DA12 213 GJ87
Guru Nanak Prim Sch, Hayes UB4 *off Springfield Rd* 158 BW74
Guru Nanak Sec Sch, Hayes UB4
off Springfield Rd 158 BW74
Guthrie St, SW3 28 C10
Gutteridge La, Stap.Abb. RM4 109 FC44
Gutter La, EC2 19 K8
Guyatt Gdns, Mitch. CR4
off Ormerod Gdns 222 DG96
Guy Barnett Gro, SE3
off Casterbridge Rd 186 EG83
Guy Rd, Wall. SM6 223 DK104
Guyscliff Rd, SE13 205 EC85
Guysfield Cl, Rain. RM13 169 FG67
Guysfield Dr, Rain. RM13 169 FG67
Guy's Hosp, SE1 31 M4
Guy St, SE1 31 M4
Gwalior Rd, SW15
off Felsham Rd 181 CX83
Gwendolen Av, SW15 201 CX85
Gwendolen Cl, SW15 201 CW85
Gwendolen Ho, Stai. TW19
off Yeoman Dr 196 BL88
Gwendoline Av, E13 166 EH67
Gwendoline Ct, Wal.Cr. EN8 89 DZ34
Gwendwr Rd, W14 26 F10
Gwen Morris Ho, SE5 43 K5
Gwent Cl, Wat. WD25 82 BX34
Gwillim Cl, Sid. DA15 208 EU85
Gwydor Rd, Beck. BR3 225 DX98
Gwydyr Rd, Brom. BR2 226 EF97
Gwyn Cl, SW6 39 N5
Gwyn Jones Prim Sch, E11
off Hainault Rd 145 ED59
Gwynne Av, Croy. CR0 225 DX101
Gwynne Cl, W4
off Pumping Sta Rd 181 CT79
Windsor SL4 173 AL81
Gwynne Ct, Guil. GU2
off Railton Rd 264 AV130
Gwynne Pk Av, Wdf.Grn. IG8 125 EM51
Gwynne Pl, WC1 18 D3
Gwynne Rd, SW11 40 A8
Caterham CR3 258 DR123
Gwynn Rd, Nthflt DA11 212 GC89
Gwynns Wk, Hert. SG13 54 DS09
Gyfford Wk, Chsht EN7 88 DV31
Gylcote Cl, SE5 184 DR84
Gyles Pk, Stan. HA7 117 CJ53
Gyllyngdune Gdns, Ilf. IG3 147 ET61
Gypsy Cl, Gt Amwell SG12 55 DZ11
Gypsy Cor, W3 160 CQ71
Gypsy La, Gt Amwell SG12 55 DZ11
Hunton Bridge WD4 97 BR35
Stoke Poges SL2 134 AS63
Welwyn Garden City AL7 51 CZ13
Gypsy Moth Av, Hat. AL10 66 CS16

H

Haarlem Rd, W14 26 C7
Haberdasher Est, N1
off Haberdasher St 19 M2
Haberdasher Pl, N1 19 M2
Haberdashers' Aske's Boys' Sch, Els. WD6
off Butterfly La 99 CH41
Haberdashers' Aske's Crayford Acad, Cray. DA1
off Iron Mill La 189 FG84
Haberdashers' Aske's Hatcham Coll, SE14 45 L6
Pepys Rd, SE14 45 L9
Haberdashers' Aske's Knights Acad, Brom. BR1
off Launcelot Rd 206 EG91
Haberdashers' Aske's Sch for Girls, Els. WD6
off Aldenham Rd 99 CH42
Haberdasher St, N1 19 M2
Habgood Rd, Loug. IG10 106 EL41
Habitat Cl, SE15 44 F9
Haccombe Rd, SW19
off Haydons Rd 202 DC93
HACKBRIDGE, Wall. SM6 223 DH103
Hackbridge 223 DH103
Hackbridge Grn, Wall. SM6 222 DG103
Hackbridge Pk Gdns, Cars. SM5 222 DG103
Hackbridge Prim Sch, Wall. SM6 *off Hackbridge Rd* 222 DG103
Hackbridge Rd, Wall. SM6 222 DG103
Hackett La, Saw. CM21 57 ET05
Hacketts La, Wok. GU22 233 BF114
Hackford Rd, SW9 42 E5
Hackford Wk, SW9 42 D7
Hackforth Cl, Barn. EN5 101 CV43
Hackhurst La, Abin.Ham. RH5 283 BT138
Hackington Cres, Beck. BR3 205 EA93
HACKNEY, E8 10 E5
Hackney Central 10 E4
★ **Hackney City Fm**, E2 20 C1
Hackney Cl, Borwd. WD6 100 CR43
Hackney Downs 10 E4
Hackney Gro, E8
off Reading La 10 F5
★ **Hackney Marsh**, E9 145 DY62
★ **Hackney Mus**, E8 10 F5
Hackney Rd, E2 20 A3
HACKNEY WICK, E9 12 A4
Hackney Wick 12 A5
Hackworth Ho, N16
off Stamford Hill 144 DS60
Hackworth Pt, E3 22 B3
Hacon Sq, E8 10 F6
HACTON, Rain. RM13 150 FM64
Hacton Dr, Horn. RM12 150 FK63
Hacton La, Horn. RM12 150 FM62
Upminster RM14 150 FM64
Hacton Prim Sch, Horn. RM12 *off Chepstow Av* 150 FL63
Hadar Cl, N20 120 DA46
Hadden Rd, SE28 187 ES76
Hadden Way, Grnf. UB6 159 CD65
Haddestoke Gate, Chsht EN8 89 DZ26
Haddington Rd, Brom. BR1 205 ED90
Haddo Ho, SE10 *off Haddo St* 46 D3
Haddon Cl, Borwd. WD6 100 CN40
Enfield EN1 104 DU44
Hemel Hempstead HP3 62 BN21
New Malden KT3 221 CT99
Weybridge KT13 217 BR104
Haddonfield, SE8 33 K9
Haddon Gro, Sid. DA15 208 EU87
Haddon Rd, Chorl. WD3 95 BC43
Orpington BR5 228 EW99
Sutton SM1 240 DB105
Haddo St, SE10 46 E3
Haden Ct, N4 *off Lennox Rd* 143 DN61
Haden La, N11 121 DJ49
Hadfield Cl, Sthl. UB1
off Adrienne Av 158 BZ69
Hadfield Rd, Stanw. TW19 196 BK86
Hadlands Cl, Bov. HP3 79 AZ26
Hadleigh Cl, E1 20 G4
SW20 221 CZ96
Hadleigh Cl, Shenley WD7 83 CK30
Hadleigh Ct, Brox. EN10 71 DZ22
Hadleigh Dr, Sutt. SM2 240 DA109
Hadleigh Rd, N9 122 DV45
Hadleigh St, E2 21 H3
Hadleigh Wk, E6 25 H8
HADLEY, Barn. EN5 101 CZ40
Hadley Cl, N21 103 DN44
Elstree WD6 100 CM43
Hadley Common, Barn. EN5 102 DA40
Hadley Ct, N16 144 DU60
Hadley Gdns, W4 180 CR78
Southall UB2 178 BZ78
Hadley Gra, Harl. CM17 74 EW16
Hadley Grn, Barn. EN5 101 CZ40
Hadley Grn Rd, Barn. EN5 101 CZ40
Hadley Grn W, Barn. EN5 101 CZ40
Hadley Gro, Barn. EN5 101 CY40
Hadley Hts, Barn. EN5
off Hadley Rd 102 DB40
Hadley Highstone, Barn. EN5 101 CZ39
Hadley Pl, Wey. KT13 234 BN108
Hadley Ridge, Barn. EN5 101 CZ41
Hadley Rd, Belv. DA17 188 EZ77
Enfield EN2 103 DL38
Hadley Wood EN4 103 DH38
Mitcham CR4 223 DK98
New Barnet EN5 102 DB42
Hadley St, NW1 7 J5
Hadley Way, N21 103 DN44
HADLEY WOOD, Barn. EN4 102 DE38
Hadley Wood 102 DC38
Hadley Wd Prim Sch, Had.Wd EN4 *off Courtleigh Av* 102 DC38
Hadley Wd Ri, Ken. CR8 257 DP115
Hadlow Coll Mottingham Cen, SE12
off Mottingham La 206 EJ88
Hadlow Ct, Slou. SL1 153 AQ73
Hadlow Pl, SE19 204 DU94
Hadlow Rd, Sid. DA14 208 EU91
Welling DA16 188 EW80
Hadlow Way, Istead Rise DA13 212 GE94
Hadrian Cl, E3 12 A9
St. Albans AL3 64 BZ22
Staines-upon-Thames TW19 196 BL87
Hadrian Ct, Sutt. SM2
off Stanley Rd 240 DB108
Hadrian Est, E2 20 D1
Hadrian Ms, N7 8 D6
Hadrians Ride, Enf. EN1 104 DT43
Hadrian St, SE10 35 J10
Hadrian Way, Stanw. TW19 196 BL87
Hadyn Pk Rd, W12 181 CU75
Hafer Rd, SW11 182 DF84
Hafton Rd, SE6 206 EE88
Hagden La, Wat. WD18 97 BT43
Haggard Rd, Twick. TW1 199 CH87
HAGGERSTON, E2 10 B10
Haggerston 10 A8
Haggerston Rd, E8 10 A7
Borehamwood WD6 100 CL38
Haggerston Sch, E2 10 B10
Haggerston Studios, E8
off Kingsland Rd 10 A8
Hag Hill La, Tap. SL6 152 AG72
Hag Hill Ri, Tap. SL6 152 AG72
Hagsdell La, Hert. SG13 54 DR10
Hagsdell Rd, Hert. SG13 54 DR10
Hague Prim Sch, E2 20 F4
Hague St, E2 20 D3
Ha-Ha Rd, SE18 187 EM79
Haig Cl, St.Alb. AL1 65 CH21
Haig Dr, Slou. SL1 173 AP75
Haig Gdns, Grav. DA12 213 GJ87
Haigh Cres, Red. RH1 289 DH136
Haig Pl, Mord. SM4
off Green La 222 DA100
Haig Rd, Bigg.H. TN16 260 EL117
Grays RM16 193 GG76
Stanmore HA7 117 CJ50
Uxbridge UB8 157 BP71
Haig Rd E, E13 24 C2
Haig Rd W, E13 24 C2
Haigville Gdns, Ilf. IG6 147 EP56
Hailes Cl, SW19 202 DC93
HAILEY, Hert. SG13 55 DZ13
Hailey Av, Hodd. EN11 55 EA13
Haileybury, Hert. SG13
off College Rd 55 DX13
Haileybury Av, Enf. EN1 104 DT44
Haileybury Rd, Orp. BR6 246 EU105
Hailey Cl, Hailey SG13 55 DY13
Hailey Hall Sch, Hert. SG13 *off Hailey La* 55 DZ13
Hailey La, Hailey SG13 55 DX14
Hailey Rd, Erith DA18 188 FA75
Hailsham Av, SW2 203 DM89
Hailsham Cl, Rom. RM3 128 FJ50
Surbiton KT6 219 CK101
Hailsham Dr, Har. HA1 139 CD55
Hailsham Gdns, Rom. RM3 128 FJ50
Hailsham Rd, SW17 202 DG93
Romford RM3 128 FJ50
Hailsham Ter, N18 122 DQ50
Haimo Prim Sch, SE9
off Haimo Rd 206 EK85
Haimo Rd, SE9 206 EK85
HAINAULT, Ilf. IG6 125 ES52
Hainault 125 ES52
● **Hainault Business Pk**, Ilf. IG6 126 EW50
Hainault Ct, E17 145 ED56
★ **Hainault Forest Country Pk**, Chig. IG7 126 EW47
Hainault Forest High Sch, Ilf. IG6 *off Harbourer Rd* 126 EV50
Hainault Gore, Rom. RM6 148 EY57
Hainault Gro, Chig. IG7 125 EQ49
Hainault Rd, E11 145 EC60
Chadwell Heath RM6 148 EZ58
Chigwell IG7 125 EP48
Little Heath RM6 148 EV55
Romford RM5 127 FC54
Hainault St, SE9 207 EP88
Ilford IG1 147 EP61
Haines Cl, N1 9 N7
Haines Ct, Wey. KT13 235 BR106
Haines Wk, Mord. SM4
off Dorchester Rd 222 DB101
Haines Way, Wat. WD25 81 BU34
Hainford Cl, SE4 185 DX84
Haining Cl, W4
off Wellesley Rd 180 CN78
Hainthorpe Rd, SE27 203 DP90
Hainton Cl, E1 20 F9
Halberd Ms, E5 144 DV61
Halbutt Gdns, Dag. RM9 148 EZ62
Halbutt St, Dag. RM9 148 EZ63
Halcomb St, N1 9 N9
Halcot Av, Bexh. DA6 209 FB85
Halcrow St, E1 20 F7
Halcyon Way, Horn. RM11 150 FM60
Haldane Cl, N10 121 DH52
Enfield EN3 105 EB38
Haldane Gdns, Grav. DA11 212 GC88
Haldane Pl, SW18 202 DB88
Haldane Rd, E6 24 G2
SE28 168 EX73
SW6 39 H4
Southall UB1 158 CC73
Haldan Rd, E4 123 EC51
Haldens, Welw.G.C. AL7 51 CZ06
Haldon Cl, Chig. IG7
off Arrowsmith Rd 125 ES50
Haldon Rd, SW18 201 CZ85
Hale, The, E4 123 ED52
N17 144 DU55
Hale Cl, E4 123 EC48
Edgware HA8 118 CQ50
Orpington BR6 245 EQ105
Hale Dr, NW7 118 CQ51
HALE END, E4 123 ED51
Hale End, Rom. RM3 127 FH51
Woking GU22 248 AV121
Hale End Cl, Ruis. HA4 137 BU58
Hale End Rd, E4 123 ED51
E17 123 ED53
Woodford Green IG8 123 ED52
Halefield Rd, N17 122 DU53
Hale Gdns, N17 144 DU55
W3 160 CN74
Hale Gro Gdns, NW7 118 CR50
Hale La, NW7 118 CR50
Edgware HA8 118 CP50
Otford TN14 263 FE117
Hale Path, SE27 203 DP91
Hale Pit Rd, Bkhm KT23 268 CC126
Hale Rd, E6 25 H5
N17 144 DU55
Hertford SG13 54 DR10
Hales Oak, Bkhm KT23 268 CC126
Halesowen Rd, Mord. SM4 222 DB101
Hales Pk, Hem.H. HP2 63 BQ19
Hales Pk Cl, Hem.H. HP2 63 BQ19
Hales Prior, N1
off Calshot St 18 C1
Hales St, SE8 46 A5
Hale St, E14 22 C10
Staines-upon-Thames TW18 195 BE91
Haleswood, Cob. KT11 235 BV114
Haleswood Rd, Hem.H. HP2 62 BN19
Halesworth Cl, E5
off Theydon Rd 144 DW61
Romford RM3 128 FL52
Halesworth Rd, SE13 46 C10
Romford RM3 128 FL51
Hale Wk, W7 159 CE71
Haley Rd, NW4 141 CW58
Half Acre, Brent. TW8 179 CK79
Halfacre Hill, Chal.St.P. SL9 112 AY53
Half Acre Rd, W7 159 CE74
Halfhide La, Chsht EN8 89 DX27
Turnford EN10 89 DY26
Halfhides, Wal.Abb. EN9 89 ED33
Half Moon Ct, EC1 19 J7
Half Moon Cres, N1 8 D10
Half Moon La, SE24 204 DQ86
Epping CM16 91 ET31
Half Moon Meadow, Hem.H. HP2 63 BQ15
Half Moon Ms, St.Alb. AL1
off London Rd 65 CD20
Half Moon Pas, E1
off Alie St 20 B9
Half Moon St, W1 29 K2
Half Moon Yd, St.Alb. AL1
off London Rd 65 CD20
Halford Cl, Edg. HA8 118 CP54
Halford Ct, Hat. AL10 66 CS17
Halford Rd, E10 145 ED57
SW6 39 K3
Richmond TW10 200 CL85
Uxbridge UB10 136 BN64
Halfpenny Cl, Chilw. GU4 281 BD140
Halfpenny La, Chilw. GU4 281 BC136
Halfway Ct, Purf. RM19 190 FN77
Halfway Grn, Walt. KT12 217 BV104
Halfway Ho La, Amer. HP6 76 AL33
Halfway St, Sid. DA15 207 ER87
Haliburton Rd, Twick. TW1 199 CG85
Haliday Wk, N1 9 M4
Halidon Cl, E9 10 G2
Halidon Ri, Rom. RM3 128 FP51
Halifax Cl, Brick.Wd AL2 82 BZ30
Leavesden WD25 81 BT34
Teddington TW11 199 CE93
Halifax Rd, Enf. EN2 104 DQ40
Greenford UB6 158 CB67
Heronsgate WD3 113 BC45
Halifax St, SE26 204 DV91
Halifax Way, Welw.G.C. AL7 52 DE09
Halifield Dr, Belv. DA17 188 EY76
Haling Down Pas, S.Croy. CR2 242 DQ109
Haling Gro, S.Croy. CR2 242 DQ108
Haling Manor High Sch, S.Croy. CR2 *off Kendra Hall Rd* 241 DP108
Haling Pk, S.Croy. CR2 241 DQ107
Haling Pk Gdns, S.Croy. CR2 241 DP107
Haling Pk Rd, S.Croy. CR2 241 DP106
Haling Rd, S.Croy. CR2 242 DR107
Halings La, Denh. UB9 135 BE56
Halkin Arc, SW1 28 G6
Halkingcroft, Slou. SL3 174 AW75
Halkin Ms, SW1 28 G6
Halkin Pl, SW1 28 G6
Halkin St, SW1 29 H5
Hall, The, SE3 47 N10
Hallam Cl, Chis. BR7 207 EM92
Watford WD24 98 BW40
Hallam Gdns, Pnr. HA5 116 BY52
Hallam Ms, W1 17 K6
Hallam Rd, N15 143 DP56
SW13 181 CV83
Hallam St, W1 17 K5
Halland Way, Nthwd. HA6 115 BR51
Hallane Ho, SE27
off Elder Rd 204 DQ92
Hall Av, N18 122 DR51
Aveley RM15 170 FQ74
Hall Cl, W5 160 CL71
Godalming GU7 280 AS144
Mill End WD3 114 BG46
Hall Ct, Datchet SL3 174 AV80
Teddington TW11 199 CF92
Hall Cres, Aveley RM15 190 FQ75
Hall Dene Cl, Guil. GU1 265 BC133
Hall Dr, SE26 204 DW92
W7 159 CE72
Harefield UB9 114 BJ53
Halley Gdns, SE13 185 ED84
Halley Prim Sch, E14 21 M7
Halley Rd, E7 166 EJ65
E12 166 EK65
Waltham Abbey EN9 105 EB36
Halleys App, Wok. GU21 248 AU118
Halleys Ct, Wok. GU21
off Halleys App 248 AU118
Halleys Ridge, Hert. SG14 53 DN10
Halley St, E14 21 L7
Halleys Wk, Add. KT15 234 BJ108
Hall Fm Cl, Stan. HA7 117 CH49
Hall Fm Dr, Twick. TW2 199 CD87
Hallfield Est, W2 15 N8
Hallfield Inf & Jun Schs, W2 15 M9
Hallford Way, Dart. DA1 210 FJ85
Hall Gdns, E4 123 DZ49
Colney Heath AL4 66 CR23
Hall Gate, NW8 15 P2
Hall Grn La, Hutt. CM13 131 GC45
HALL GROVE, Welw.G.C. AL7 52 DB11
Hall Gro, Welw.G.C. AL7 52 DB11
Hall Heath Cl, St.Alb. AL1 65 CH18
Hall Hill, Oxt. RH8 275 ED131
Seal TN15 279 FP123
Halliards, The, Walt. KT12
off Felix Rd 217 BU100
Halliday Cl, Shenley WD7 84 CL32
Halliday Ho, E1
off Christian St 20 D9
Halliday Sq, Sthl. UB2 159 CD74
Halliford Cl, Shep. TW17 217 BR98
Halliford Rd, Shep. TW17 217 BS99
Sunbury-on-Thames TW16 217 BS99
Halliford Sch, Shep. TW17
off Russell Rd 217 BQ101
Halliford St, N1 9 K6
Halliloo Valley Rd, Wold. CR3 259 DZ119
Hallingbury Ct, E17 145 EB55
Halling Hill, Harl. CM20 57 ET13
Hallings Wf Studios, E15 12 G8
Hallington Cl, Wok. GU21 248 AV117
Halliwell Rd, SW2 203 DM86
Halliwick Rd, N10 120 DG53
Hall La, E4 123 DY50
Hall La, E4 123 DY50
NW4 119 CU53
Harlington UB3 177 BR80
Shenfield CM15 131 FZ44
South Ockendon RM15 171 FX68
Upminster RM14 150 FQ60
● **Hallmark Trd Cen**, Wem. HA9 140 CQ63
Hall Meadow, Burn. SL1 152 AJ68
Hallmead Rd, Sutt. SM1 222 DB104
Hall Mead Sch, Upmin. RM14
off Marlborough Gdns 151 FR60
Hallmores, Brox. EN10 71 EA19
Hall Oak Wk, NW6 5 H4
Hallowell Av, Croy. CR0 241 DL105
Hallowell Cl, Mitch. CR4 222 DG97
Hallowell Gdns, Th.Hth. CR7 224 DQ96
Hallowell Rd, Nthwd. HA6 115 BS52
Hallowes Cl, Guil. GU2 264 AV129
Hallowes Cres, Wat. WD19 115 BU48
Hallowfield Way, Mitch. CR4 222 DD97
Hallows Gro, Sun. TW16 197 BT92
Hall Pk, Berk. HP4 60 AY20
Hall Pk Gate, Berk. HP4 60 AY21
Hall Pk Hill, Berk. HP4 60 AY21
Hall Pk Rd, Upmin. RM14 150 FQ64
★ **Hall Pl**, Bex. DA5 209 FC86
Hall Pl, W2 16 A5
Woking GU21 249 BA116
Hall Pl Cl, St.Alb. AL1 65 CE19
Hall Pl Cres, Bex. DA5 209 FC85
Hall Pl Dr, Wey. KT13 235 BS106
Hall Pl Gdns, St.Alb. AL1 65 CE19
Hall Rd, E6 167 EM67
E15 145 ED63
NW8 15 P3
Aveley RM15 190 FQ75
Chadwell Heath RM6 148 EW58
Dartford DA1 190 FM84
Gidea Park RM2 149 FH55
Hemel Hempstead HP2 63 BP18
Isleworth TW7 199 CD85
Northfleet DA11 212 GC90
Wallington SM6 241 DH109
Hall Sch, The, Jun Sch, NW3 6 B5
Sen Sch, NW3 6 B5
Hall Sch Wimbledon, Jun Sch, SW15 *off Stroud Cres* 201 CU90
Sen Sch, SW20
off The Downs 221 CX95
HALLS GREEN, Harl. CM19 72 EJ18
Hallside Rd, Enf. EN1 104 DT38
Hallsland Way, Oxt. RH8 276 EF133
Hall St, EC1 19 H2
N12 120 DC50
Hallsville Prim Sch, E16 23 N9
Hallsville Rd, E16 23 L9
Hallswelle Par, NW11
off Finchley Rd 141 CZ57
Hallswelle Rd, NW11 141 CZ57
Hall Ter, Aveley RM15 191 FR75
Romford RM3 128 FN52
Hall Twr, W2 16 B6
Hall Vw, SE9 206 EK89
Hall Way, Pur. CR8 241 DP113
Hallwood Cres, Shenf. CM15 130 FY45
Hallywell Cres, E6 25 K7
Halons Rd, SE9 207 EN87
Halpin Pl, SE17 31 M9
Halsbrook Rd, SE3 186 EK83
Halsbury Cl, Stan. HA7 117 CH49
Halsbury Rd, W12 161 CV74
Halsbury Rd E, Nthlt. UB5 138 CC63
Halsbury Rd W, Nthlt. UB5 138 CB64
Halse Dr, Slou. SL2 133 AM64
Halsend, Hayes UB3 157 BV74
Halsey Dr, Hem.H. HP1 61 BF18
Halsey Ms, SW3 28 E8
Halsey Pk, Lon.Col. AL2 84 CM27
Halsey Pl, Wat. WD24 97 BV38
Halsey Rd, Wat. WD18 97 BV41
Halsey St, SW3 28 E8

Halsham Cres, Bark. IG11 167 ET65
Halsmere Rd, SE5 43 H6
HALSTEAD, Sev. TN14 246 EZ113
Halstead Cl, Croy. CR0
off Charles St 224 DQ104
Halstead Comm Prim Sch,
Halst. TN14 off Otford La 246 EZ112
Halstead Ct, N1 19 L1
Halstead Gdns, N21 122 DR46
Halstead Hill, Goffs Oak EN7 88 DS29
Halstead La, Knock.P. TN14 246 EZ114
Halstead Prep Sch, Wok.
GU21 off Woodham Ri 233 BA114
Halstead Rd, E11 146 EG57
N21 122 DQ46
Enfield EN1 104 DS42
Erith DA8 189 FE81
Halstead Way, Hutt. CM13 131 GC44
Halston Cl, SW11 202 DF86
Halstow Prim Sch, SE10 47 N1
Halstow Rd, NW10 14 C3
SE10 35 N10
Halsway, Hayes UB3 157 BU74
Halter Cl, Borwd. WD6 100 CR43
Halton Cl, N11 120 DF51
Park Street AL2 82 CC28
Halton Cross St, N1 9 H8
Halton Pl, N1 9 J8
Halton Rd, N1 9 H6
Grays RM16 193 GH76
Kenley CR8 258 DS120
Halt Robin La, Belv. DA17
off Halt Robin Rd 189 FB77
Halt Robin Rd, Belv. DA17 188 FA77
Haltside, Hat. AL10 66 CS19
Halwick Cl, Hem.H. HP1 62 BH21
Halyard Ct, Rom. RM1
off Western Rd 149 FE57
Halyard Ho, E14
off New Union Cl 34 F6
HAM, Rich. TW10 199 CK90
Ham, The, Brent. TW8 179 CJ80
Hamara Ghar, E13 166 EJ67
Hambalt Rd, SW4 203 DJ85
Hamble Cl, Ruis. HA4 137 BS61
Woking GU21 248 AU117
Hamble Ct, Tedd. TW11 199 CK94
Hambledon Cl, Uxb. UB8 157 BP70
Hambledon Gdns, SE25 224 DT97
Hambledon Hill, Epsom KT18 254 CQ116
Hambledon Ho, Mord. SM4
off Yenston Cl 222 DA100
Hambledon Pl, SE21 204 DS88
Bookham KT23 252 CA123
Hambledon Rd, SW18 201 CZ87
Caterham CR3 258 DR123
Hambledon Vale, Epsom KT18 254 CQ116
Hambledown Rd, Sid. DA15 207 ER87
Hamble La, S.Ock. RM15 171 FT71
Hamble St, SW6 39 M10
Hambleton Cl, Wor.Pk. KT4 221 CW103
Hamble Wk, Nthlt. UB5
off Brabazon Rd 158 CA68
Woking GU21 248 AU118
Hambley Ho, SE16
off Manor Est 32 E9
Hamblings Cl, Shenley WD7 83 CK33
Hambridge Way, SW2 203 DN87
Hambro Av, Brom. BR2 226 EG102
Hambrook Rd, SE25 224 DV97
Hambro Rd, SW16 203 DK93
Hambrough Prim Sch,
Sthl. UB1 off South Rd 158 BZ74
Hambrough Rd, Sthl. UB1 158 BY74
Hamburgh Ct, Chsht EN8 89 DX28
Ham Cl, Rich. TW10 199 CJ90
Ham Common, Rich. TW10 200 CL91
Ham Cft Cl, Felt. TW13 197 BU90
Hamden Cres, Dag. RM10 149 FB62
Hamel Cl, Har. HA3 139 CK55
Hamelin St, E14 22 E9
Hamels Dr, Hert. SG13 54 DV08
Hamer Cl, Bov. HP3 79 BA28
Hamerton Rd, Nthflt DA11 212 GB85
Hameway, E6 25 L4
Ham Fm Rd, Rich. TW10 199 CK91
Hamfield Cl, Oxt. RH8 275 EC127
Ham Flds, Rich. TW10 199 CG90
Hamfrith Rd, E15 13 L4
Ham Gate Av, Rich. TW10 199 CK90
Hamhaugh Island, Shep.
TW17 216 BN103
★ Ham Ho, Rich. TW10 199 CJ88
Hamilton Av, N9 122 DU45
Cobham KT11 235 BU113
Hoddesdon EN11 71 EA15
Ilford IG6 147 EP56
Romford RM1 127 FD54
Surbiton KT6 220 CP102
Sutton SM3 221 CY103
Woking GU22 249 BE115
Hamilton Cl, N17 144 DT55
NW8 16 A3
SE16 33 M5
Bricket Wood AL2 82 CA30
Chertsey KT16 215 BF102
Cockfosters EN4 102 DE42
Epsom KT19 238 CQ112
Feltham TW13 197 BT92
Guildford GU2 264 AU129
Horley RH6 290 DG149
Purley CR8 241 DP112
South Mimms EN6 85 CU33
Teddington TW11 199 CH93
Hamilton Ct, W5 160 CM73
W9 15 N2
Bookham KT23
off Eastwick Pk Av 268 CB125
Hatfield AL10 off Cooks Way 67 CV20
Hounslow TW3
off Hanworth Rd 178 CB84
Hamilton Cres, N13 121 DN49
Harrow HA2 138 BZ62
Hounslow TW3 198 CB85
Warley CM14 130 FW49
Hamilton Dr, Guil. GU2 264 AU129
Romford RM3 128 FL54
Hamilton Gdns, NW8 15 P2
Burnham SL1 152 AH69
Hamilton Gordon Ct, Guil.
GU1 off Langley Cl 264 AW133
Hamilton Ho, SW8
off St. George Wf 42 A2
Hamilton La, N5 9 H1
Hamilton Mead, Bov. HP3 79 BA27
Hamilton Ms, SW18
off Merton Rd 202 DA88
W1 29 J4
Hamilton Pk, N5 9 H1
Hamilton Pk W, N5 8 G1
Hamilton Pl, N19 143 DK62
W1 29 H3
Guildford GU2 264 AU129
Kingswood KT20 255 CZ122
Sunbury-on-Thames TW16 197 BV94
Hamilton Rd, E15 23 K3
E17 123 DY54
N2 142 DC55
N9 122 DU45
NW10 141 CU64
NW11 141 CX59
SE27 204 DR91
SW19 202 DB94
W4 180 CS75
W5 160 CL73
Berkhamsted HP4 60 AV19
Bexleyheath DA7 188 EY82
Brentford TW8 179 CK79
Cockfosters EN4 102 DE42
Feltham TW13 197 BT91
Harrow HA1 139 CE57
Hayes UB3 157 BV73
Hunton Bridge WD4 81 BQ33
Ilford IG1 147 EP63
Romford RM2 149 FH57
St. Albans AL1 65 CG19
Sidcup DA15 208 EU91
Slough SL1 153 AN72
Southall UB1 158 BZ74
Thornton Heath CR7 224 DR97
Twickenham TW2 199 CE88
Uxbridge UB8 156 BK71
Watford WD19 115 BV48
● Hamilton Rd Ind Est, SE27 204 DR91
Hamilton Rd Ms, SW19
off Hamilton Rd 202 DB94
Hamilton Sq, N12 120 DD51
SE1 31 M4
Hamilton St, SE8 46 A4
Watford WD18 98 BW43
Hamilton Ter, NW8 15 P2
Hamilton Wk, Erith DA8 189 FF80
Hamilton Way, N3 120 DA51
N13 121 DP49
Farnham Common SL2 133 AQ64
Wallington SM6 241 DK109
Ham Island, Old Wind. SL4 174 AX84
Ham La, Eng.Grn TW20 194 AV91
Old Windsor SL4 174 AX84
Hamlea Cl, SE12 206 EG85
Hamlet, The, SE5 184 DR83
Potten End HP4 61 BA16
Hamlet Cl, SE13 186 EE84
Bricket Wood AL2 82 BZ30
Romford RM5 126 FA52
Hamlet Est, Erith DA8 189 FD78
Hamlet Gdns, W6 181 CU77
Hamlet Hill, Roydon CM19 72 EG19
Hamlet Ho, Erith DA8
off Waterhead Cl 189 FE80
Hamlet Ms, SE21
off Thurlow Pk Rd 204 DR88
Hamleton Ter, Dag. RM9
off Flamstead Rd 168 EW66
Hamlet Rd, SE19 204 DT94
Romford RM5 126 FA52
Hamlet Sq, NW2 141 CY62
Hamlets Way, E3 21 N4
Hamlet Way, SE1 31 M4
★ Hamleys, W1 17 L10
Hamlin Cres, Pnr. HA5 138 BW57
Hamlin Rd, Sev. TN13 278 FE121
Hamlyn Cl, Edg. HA8 118 CL48
Hamlyn Gdns, SE19 204 DS94
Hamlyn Ho, Felt. TW13
off High St 197 BV88
Hammarskjold Rd, Harl.
CM20 57 EQ14
Hamm Ct, Wey. KT13 216 BL103
Hammelton Grn, SW9 42 G6
Hammelton Rd, Brom. BR1 226 EF95
HAMMERFIELD, Hem.H. HP1 62 BG20
Hammerfield Dr, Abin.Ham.
RH5 283 BT140
Hammer La, Hem.H. HP2 62 BM19
Hammer Par, Wat. WD25 81 BU33
Hammers Gate, St.Alb. AL2 82 CA25
Hammers La, NW7 119 CU50
Hammersley La, Penn HP10,
HP13 110 AC49
HAMMERSMITH, W6 26 B10
⊖ Hammersmith 26 B9
⊖ Hammersmith 26 B9
Hammersmith & W London
Coll, W14 26 E10
Hammersmith Br, SW13 181 CV79
W6 181 CV79
Hammersmith Br Rd, W6 38 A1
Hammersmith Bdy, W6 26 B9
Hammersmith Bdy, W6 26 B9
Hammersmith Flyover, W6 26 B10
Hammersmith Gro, W6 26 A7
Hammersmith Hosp, W12 161 CV72
Hammersmith Rd, W6 26 C9
W14 26 C9
Hammersmith Ter, W6 181 CU78
Hammerton Cl, Bex. DA5 209 FE90
Hammet Cl, Hayes UB4 158 BX71
Hammett St, EC3 20 A10
Hamm Moor La, Add. KT15 234 BL106
Hammond Av, Mitch. CR4 223 DH96
Hammond Cl, Barn. EN5 101 CY43
Cheshunt EN7 88 DS26
Greenford UB6
off Lilian Board Way 139 CD64
Hampton TW12 218 CA95
Woking GU21 248 AW115
Hammond Ct, SE11
off Hotspur St 30 E10
Chsht EN7
off Stocksbridge Cl 88 DS26
Hammond End, Farn.Com.
SL2 133 AP63
Hammond Ho, SE14
off Lubbock St 45 H5
Hammond JMI & Nurs Sch,
Hem.H. HP2
off Cambrian Way 62 BM17
Hammond Rd, Enf. EN1 104 DV40
Southall UB2 178 BY76
Hammond Rd, Woking GU21 248 AW115
Hammonds Cl, Dag. RM8 148 EW62
Hammonds La, Gt Warley
CM13 129 FV51
Hammond's La, Hat. AL10 50 CQ13
Sandridge AL4 50 CN12
HAMMOND STREET,
Wal.Cr. EN7 88 DR26
Hammond St, NW5 7 L4
Hammondstreet Rd, Chsht EN7 88 DR26
Hammond Way, SE28
off Oriole Way 168 EV73
Hamond Cl, S.Croy. CR2 241 DP109
Hamonde Cl, Edg. HA8 118 CP47
Hamond Sq, N1 9 N10
Ham Pk Rd, E7 13 L6
E15 13 L6
Hampden Av, Beck. BR3 225 DY96
Chesham HP5 76 AN30
Hampden Cl, NW1 17 P1
North Weald Bassett CM16 92 FA27
Stoke Poges SL2 154 AU69
Hampden Cres, Chsht EN7 88 DV31
Warley CM14 130 FW49
Hampden Gurney C of E
Prim Sch, W1 16 D8
Hampden Gurney St, W1 16 E9
Hampden Hill, Beac. HP9 110 AH53
Ware SG12 55 DZ06
Hampden Hill Cl, Ware SG12 55 DZ05
Hampden La, N17 122 DT53
Hampden Pl, Frog. AL2 83 CE29
Hampden Rd, N8 143 DN56
N10 120 DG52
N17 122 DU53
N19 off Holloway Rd 143 DK61
Beckenham BR3 225 DY96
Chalfont St. Peter SL9 112 AX53
Grays RM17 192 GB78
Harrow HA3 116 CC53
Kingston upon Thames KT1 220 CN97
Romford RM5 127 FB52
Slough SL3 175 AZ76
Hampden Sq, N14
off Osidge La 121 DH46
Hampden Way, N14 121 DH47
Watford WD17 97 BS36
Hampermill La, Wat. WD19 115 BT47
Hampshire Av, Slou. SL1 153 AQ71
Hampshire Cl, N18 122 DV50
Hampshire Ct, Add. KT15
off Garfield Rd 234 BJ106
Hampshire Hog La, W6
off King St 181 CV77
Hampshire Rd, N22 121 DM52
Hornchurch RM11 150 FN56
Hampshire Sch, The,
Pre-Prep, SW7 28 C5
Prep, W2 15 N10
Hampshire St, NW5 7 N4
Hampson Way, SW8 42 C6
HAMPSTEAD, NW3 142 DD63
⊖ Hampstead 142 DC63
Hampstead Av, Wdf.Grn. IG8 125 EN52
Hampstead Cl, SE28 168 EV74
Bricket Wood AL2 82 BZ31
Hampstead Gdns, NW11 142 DA58
Chadwell Heath RM6 148 EV57
HAMPSTEAD GARDEN SUBURB,
N2 142 DC57
Hampstead Garden Suburb Inst,
The, N2 off Beaumont Cl 142 DE56
Hampstead Grn, NW3 6 C2
Hampstead Gro, NW3 142 DC62
★ Hampstead Heath, NW3 142 DD61
⊖ Hampstead Heath 6 D1
Hampstead Hts, N2 142 DC56
Hampstead High St, NW3 142 DC63
Hampstead Hill Gdns, NW3 6 B1
Hampstead La, N6 142 DD59
NW3 142 DD59
Dorking RH4 285 CG137
Hampstead Ms, Beck. BR3 225 EB98
Hampstead Parochial C of E
Prim Sch, NW3 5 P1
Hampstead Rd, NW1 7 L10
Dorking RH4 285 CG137
Hampstead Sch, NW2 4 F1
Hampstead Sq, NW3 142 DC62
Hampstead Wk, E3
off Waterside Cl 11 P8
Hampstead Way, NW11 142 DC60
HAMPTON, TW12 218 CB95
⇌ Hampton 218 CA95
● Hampton Business Pk,
Felt. TW13 198 BY90
Hampton Cl, N11 121 DH50
NW6 15 J3
SW20 201 CW94
Borehamwood WD6 100 CQ43
Chafford Hundred RM16 191 FW76
Hampton Comm Coll, Hmptn.
TW12 off Hanworth Rd 198 CA92
⇌ Hampton Court 219 CE98
Hampton Ct, N1 8 G5
Hampton Ct Av, E.Mol. KT8 219 CD99
Hampton Ct Cres, E.Mol. KT8 219 CD97
★ Hampton Court Palace & Pk,
E.Mol. KT8 219 CE97
Hampton Ct Par, E.Mol. KT8
off Creek Rd 219 CE98
Hampton Ct Pk, E.Mol.
(Home Pk) KT8 219 CG98
Kingston upon Thames
(Home Pk) KT1 219 CG98
Hampton Ct Rd, E.Mol. KT8 219 CF97
Hampton TW12 218 CC96
Kingston upon Thames KT1 219 CF97
Hampton Ct Way, E.Mol. KT8 219 CE100
Esher KT10 219 CE103
Thames Ditton KT7 219 CE103
Hampton Cres, Grav. DA12 213 GL89
Hampton Gdns, Saw. CM21 58 EV08
Hampton Gro, Epsom KT17 239 CT111
HAMPTON HILL, Hmptn.
TW12 198 CC93
● Hampton Hill Business Pk,
Hmptn. TW12
off Wellington Rd 198 CC92
Hampton Hill Jun Sch,
Hmptn H. TW12
off St. James's Av 198 CC92
Hampton Ho, SW8
off Ascalon St 41 L5
Hampton Inf Sch, Hmptn.
TW12 off Ripley Rd 198 CA94
Hampton Jun Sch, Hmptn.
TW12 off Percy Rd 218 CA95
Hampton La, Felt. TW13 198 BY91
Hampton Lo, Sutt. SM2
off Cavendish Rd 240 DC107
Hampton Mead, Loug. IG10 107 EP41
Hampton Ms, NW10
off Minerva Rd 160 CR69
Hampton Ri, Har. HA3 140 CL58
Hampton Rd, E4 123 DZ50
E7 146 EH64
E11 145 ED60
Croydon CR0 224 DQ100
Hampton Hill TW12 199 CD92
Ilford IG1 147 EP63
Redhill RH1 288 DF139
Teddington TW11 199 CD92
Twickenham TW2 199 CD90
Worcester Park KT4 221 CU103
Hampton Rd E, Han. TW13 198 BZ90
Hampton Rd W, Felt. TW13 198 BY89
Hampton Sch, Hmptn.
TW12 off Hanworth Rd 198 CA92
Hampton St, SE1 31 H9
SE17 31 H9
HAMPTON WICK, Kings.T. KT1 219 CH95
⇌ Hampton Wick 219 CJ95
Hampton Wick Inf & Nurs Sch,
Hmptn W. TW11
off Normansfield Av 199 CK94
Ham Ridings, Rich. TW10 200 CM92
HAMSEY GREEN, Warl. CR6 258 DW116
Hamsey Grn Gdns, Warl. CR6 258 DV116
Hamsey Grn Inf Sch, Warl.
CR6 off Tithepit Shaw La 258 DV116
Hamsey Grn Jun Sch, Warl.
CR6 off Tithepit Shaw La 258 DV116
Hamsey Way, S.Croy. CR2 258 DV115
Hamshades Cl, Sid. DA15 207 ET90
Hamstel Rd, Harl. CM20 57 EP14
Ham St, Rich. TW10 199 CJ89
Ham Vw, Croy. CR0 225 DY100
Ham Yd, W1 17 N10
Hanah Ct, SW19 201 CX94
Hanameel St, E16 35 P2
Hana Ms, E5 10 F1
Hanbury Cl, NW4 141 CW55
Burnham SL1 152 AG71
Cheshunt EN8 89 DX29
Ware SG12 55 DY06
Hanbury Ct, Har. HA1 139 CF58
Hanbury Dr, E11
off High Rd Leytonstone 146 EF59
N21 103 DM43
Biggin Hill TN16 244 EH113
Hanbury La, Essen. AL9 68 DE17
Hanbury Ms, N1 9 K9
Hanbury Path, Wok. GU21 233 BD114
Hanbury Rd, N17 122 DV54
W3 180 CP75
Hanbury St, E1 20 A6
Hanbury Wk, Bex. DA5 209 FE90
Hancock Ct, Borwd. WD6 100 CQ39
Hancock Rd, E3 22 E3
SE19 204 DR93
Hancroft Rd, Hem.H. HP3 62 BM22
Hancross Cl, Brick.Wd AL2 82 BY30
Handa Cl, Hem.H. HP3 63 BP23
Handa Wk, N1 9 K4
Hand Ct, WC1 18 D7
Handcroft Rd, Croy. CR0 223 DP101
Handel Cl, Edg. HA8 118 CM51
Handel Cres, Til. RM18 193 GG80
Handel Pl, NW10 160 CR65
Handel St, WC1 18 A4
Handel Way, Edg. HA8 118 CN52
Handen Rd, SE12 206 EE85
Handford Ct, Wat. WD25 82 BX34
Handforth Rd, SW9 42 E4
Ilford IG1
off Winston Way 147 EP62
Handinhand La, Tad. KT20 270 CQ130
Hand La, Saw. CM21 58 EW06
Handley Gate, Brick.Wd AL2 82 BZ29
Handley Gro, NW2 141 CX62
Handley Page Rd, Wall. SM6 241 DM108
Handley Page Way, Coln.St AL2 83 CF30
Handley Rd, E9 11 H8
Handleys Ct, Hem.H. HP2
off Selden Hill 62 BK22
Handowe Cl, NW4 141 CU56
Handpost Hill, Northaw EN6 87 DH28
Handpost Lo Gdns, Hem.H.
HP2 63 BR21
HANDSIDE, Welw.G.C. AL8 51 CV10
Handside Cl, Welw.G.C. AL8 51 CW09
Worcester Park KT4 221 CX102
Handside Grn, Welw.G.C. AL8 51 CW08
Handside La, Welw.G.C. AL8 51 CV11
Hands Wk, E16 23 P8
Handsworth Av, E4 123 ED51
Handsworth Prim Sch, E4
off Handsworth Av 123 ED51
Handsworth Rd, N17 144 DR55
Handsworth Way, Wat.
WD19 115 BU48
Handtrough Way, Bark. IG11
off Fresh Wf 167 EP68
Hanford Cl, SW18 202 DA88
Hanford Rd, Aveley RM15 170 FQ74
Hanford Row, SW19 201 CW93
Hangar Ruding, Wat. WD19 116 BZ48
Hanger Cl, Hem.H. HP1 62 BH21
Hanger Ct, Knap. GU21 248 AS117
Hanger Grn, W5 160 CN70
Hanger Hill, Wey. KT13 235 BP107
⊖ Hanger Lane 160 CM69
Hanger La, W5 160 CL69
Hanger La, W5 160 CM70
Hanger Vale La, W5 160 CM72
Hanger Vw Way, W3 160 CN72
Hanging Hill La, Hutt. CM13 131 GB48
Hanging Sword All, EC4 18 F9
Hangrove Hill, Downe BR6 245 EP113
Hankey Pl, SE1 31 M5
Hankins La, NW7 118 CS48
Hanley Cl, Wind. SL4 173 AK81
Hanley Gdns, N4 143 DL60
Hanley Pl, Beck. BR3 205 EA94
Hanley Rd, N4 143 DL60
Hanmer Wk, N7
off Newington Barrow Way 143 DM62
Hannaford Wk, E3 22 D4
Hannah Cl, NW10 140 CQ63
Beckenham BR3 225 EC97
Hannah Ct, N13 121 DM47
Hannah Mary Way, SE1 32 D9
Hannah Ms, Wall. SM6 241 DJ108
Hannards Way, Ilf. IG6 126 EV50
Hannay La, N8 143 DK59
Hannay Wk, SW16 203 DK89
Hannell Rd, SW6 38 E4
Hannen Rd, SE27
off Norwood High St 203 DP90
Hannibal Rd, E1 21 H6
Stanwell TW19 196 BK87
Hannibal Way, Croy. CR0 241 DM107
Hannington Rd, SW4 183 DH83
Hanno Cl, Wall. SM6 241 DK108
Hanover Av, E16 35 N2
Feltham TW13 197 BU88
Hanover Circle, Hayes UB3 157 BQ72
Hanover Cl, Eng.Grn TW20 194 AV93
Merstham RH1 273 DJ128
Richmond TW9 180 CN80
Slough SL1 174 AU76
Sutton SM3 239 CZ105
Windsor SL4
off Hanover Way 173 AM81
Hanover Ct, SE19
off Anerley Rd 204 DT94
W12 off Uxbridge Rd 161 CU74
Dorking RH4 285 CF136
Guildford GU1
off Riverside 264 AX132
Hoddesdon EN11
off Jersey Cl 71 EA16
Waltham Abbey EN9
off Quaker La 89 EC34
Woking GU22
off Midhope Rd 248 AY119
Hanover Dr, Chis. BR7 207 EQ91
Hanover Gdns, SE11 42 E3
Abbots Langley WD5 81 BT30
Ilford IG6 125 EQ52
Hanover Gate, NW1 16 D3
Slough SL1
off Cippenham La 153 AN74
Hanover Gate Mans, NW1 16 D4
Hanover Grn, Hem.H. HP1 62 BG22
Hanover Ho, Surb. KT6
off Lenelby Rd 220 CN102
Hanover Mead, Bray SL6 172 AC76
Hanover Pk, SE15 44 C7
Hanover Pl, E3 21 N3
WC2 18 B9
Warley CM14 130 FV50
Hanover Prim Sch, N1 9 H10
Hanover Rd, N15 144 DT56
NW10 4 B8
SW19 202 DC94
Hanover Sq, W1 17 K9
Hanover Steps, W2
off St. Georges Flds 16 D9
Hanover St, W1 17 K9
Croydon CR0
off Abbey Rd 223 DP104
Hanover Ter, Islw. TW7
off London Rd 179 CG81
NW1 16 D3
Hanover Ter Ms, NW1 16 D3
Hanover Wk, Hat. AL10 67 CT21
Weybridge KT13 217 BS104
Hanover Way, Bexh. DA6 188 EX83
Windsor SL4 173 AM82
● Hanover W Ind Est, NW10 160 CR68
Hanover Yd, N1 9 H10
Hansa Cl, Sthl. UB2 178 BW76
Hansard Ms, W14 26 D4
Hansart Way, Enf. EN2
off The Ridgeway 103 DN39
Hanscomb Ms, SW4
off Bromell's Rd 183 DJ84
Hans Cres, SW1 28 E6
Hanselin Cl, Stan. HA7 117 CF50
Hansells Mead, Roydon CM19 72 EG15
Hansen Dr, N21 103 DM43
Hanshaw Dr, Edg. HA8 118 CR53
Hansler Gro, E.Mol. KT8 219 CD98
Hansler Rd, SE22 204 DT85
Hansol Rd, Bexh. DA6 208 EY85
Hanson Cl, SW12 203 DH87
SW14 180 CQ83
Beckenham BR3 205 EB93
Guildford GU4 265 AZ131
Loughton IG10 107 EQ40
West Drayton UB7 176 BM76
Hanson Dr, Loug. IG10 107 EQ40
Hanson Gdns, Sthl. UB1 178 BY75
Hanson Grn, Loug. IG10 107 EQ40
Hanson St, W1 17 L6
Hans Pl, SW1 28 F6
Hans Rd, SW3 28 E6
Hans St, SW1 28 F7
Hanway Pl, W1 17 N8
Hanway Rd, W7 159 CD72
Hanway St, W1 17 N8
HANWELL, W7 159 CF74
⇌ Hanwell 159 CE73
HANWORTH, Felt. TW13 198 BX91
Hanworth La, Cher. KT16 215 BF102
Hanworth Rd, Felt. TW13 197 BV88
Hampton TW12 198 CB93
Hounslow TW3, TW4 178 CB83
Redhill RH1 288 DF139
Sunbury-on-Thames TW16 197 BU94
Hanworth Ter, Houns. TW3 178 CB84
● Hanworth Trd Est, Felt.
TW13 198 BY90
Hanyards End, Cuffley EN6 87 DL28
Hanyards La, Cuffley EN6 87 DK28
Hapgood Cl, Grnf. UB6 139 CD64
Harads Pl, E1 32 D1
Harbans Ct, Colnbr. SL3
off Old Bath Rd 175 BE81
Harben Rd, NW6 5 P6
Harberson Rd, E15 13 L8
SW12 203 DH88
Harberton Rd, N19 143 DJ60
Harberts Rd, Harl. CM19 73 EP16
Harbet Rd, E4 123 DX50
N18 123 DX50
W2 16 B7
Harbex Cl, Bex. DA5 209 FB87
Harbinger Prim Sch, E14 34 C9
Harbinger Rd, E14 34 C9
Harbledown Pl, Orp. BR5
off Okemore Gdns 228 EW98
Harbledown Rd, SW6 39 J6
South Croydon CR2 242 DU111
Harbord Cl, SE5 43 L8
Harbord St, SW6 38 C6
Harborne Cl, Wat. WD19 116 BW50
Harborough Av, Sid. DA15 207 ES87
Harborough Cl, Slou. SL1 153 AK74
Harborough Rd, SW16 203 DM91
Harbour Av, SW10 39 P6
Harbour Cl, Mitch. CR4 222 DG95
Harbourer Cl, Ilf. IG6 126 EV50
Harbourer Rd, Ilf. IG6 126 EV50
Harbour Ex Sq, E14 34 D5

Harbourfield Rd, Bans. SM7 256 DB115
Harbour Reach, SW6
off The Boulevard 39 P7
Harbour Rd, SE5 43 J10
Harbour Yd, SW10 39 P7
Harbridge Av, SW15 201 CT87
Harbury Rd, Cars. SM5 240 DE109
Harbut Rd, SW11 182 DD84
Harcamlow Way, Ware SG12 56 EH10
Harcombe Rd, N16 144 DS62
Harcourt, Wrays. TW19 194 AY86
Harcourt Av, E12 147 EM63
Edgware HA8 118 CQ48
Sidcup DA15 208 EW86
Wallington SM6 241 DH105
Harcourt Cl, Dorney R. SL6 172 AF76
Egham TW20 195 BC93
Isleworth TW7 179 CG83
Harcourt Fld, Wall. SM6 241 DH105
Harcourt Lo, Wall. SM6
off Croydon Rd 241 DH105
Harcourt Ms, Rom. RM2 149 FF57
Harcourt Rd, E15 23 L1
N22 121 DK53
SE4 185 DY84
SW19 off Russell Rd 202 DA94
Bexleyheath DA6 188 EY84
Bushey WD23 98 CC43
Dorney Reach SL6 172 AF76
Thornton Heath CR7 223 DM100
Wallington SM6 241 DH105
Windsor SL4 173 AL81
Harcourt St, W1 16 D7
Harcourt Ter, SW10 39 M1
Hardcastle Cl, Croy. CR0 224 DU100
Hardcourts Cl, W.Wick. BR4 225 EB104
Hardell Cl, Egh. TW20 195 BA92
Hardel Ri, SW2 203 DP89
Hardel Wk, SW2
off Papworth Way 203 DN87
Harden Fm Cl, Couls. CR5 257 DJ121
Harden Rd, Nthflt DA11 213 GF90
Hardens Manorway, SE7 36 E7
Harders Rd, SE15 44 E8
Hardess St, SE24
off Herne Hill Rd 184 DQ83
Hardie Cl, NW10 140 CR64
Hardie Rd, Dag. RM10 149 FC62
Harding Cl, SE17 43 J2
Croydon CR0 224 DT104
Watford WD25 82 BW33
Harding Dr, Dag. RM8 148 EY60
Hardinge Cl, Uxb. UB8 157 BP72
Hardinge Cres, SE18 187 EQ76
Hardinge Rd, N18 122 DS50
NW10 161 CV67
Hardinge St, E1 21 H9
Harding Ho, Hayes UB3 157 BU72
Harding Rd, Bexh. DA7 188 EZ82
Chesham HP5 76 AR30
Epsom KT18 254 CS119
Grays RM16 193 GG76
Hardings, Welw.G.C. AL7 52 DC08
Hardings Cl, Hem.H. HP3 62 BH23
Iver SL0 155 BD69
Harding's Cl, Kings.T. KT2 220 CM95
Hardings La, SE20 205 DX93
Harding Spur, Slou. SL3
off Shaw Gdns 175 AZ78
Hardings Row, Iver SL0 155 BC69
Hardingstone Ct, Wal.Cr. EN8
off Eleanor Way 89 DZ34
Hardley Cres, Horn. RM11 150 FK56
Hardman Rd, SE7 36 A10
Kingston upon Thames KT2 220 CL96
Hardwick Cl, Oxshott KT22 252 CC115
Stanmore HA7 117 CJ50
Hardwick Cres, Dart. DA2 210 FP86
Hardwicke Av, Houns. TW5 178 CA81
Hardwicke Gdns, Amer. HP6 77 AS38
Hardwicke Ho, E3
off Bromley High St 22 C2
Hardwicke Ms, WC1 18 D3
Hardwicke Pl, Lon.Col. AL2 83 CK27
Hardwicke Rd, N13 121 DL51
W4 180 CQ77
Reigate RH2 272 DA133
Richmond TW10 199 CJ91
Hardwicke St, Bark. IG11 167 EQ67
Hardwick Grn, W13 159 CH71
Hardwick Ho, Brom. BR2
off Masons Hill 226 EH98
Hardwick La, Lyne KT16 215 BC101
Hardwick Pl, SW16
off Farmhouse Rd 203 DJ94
Hardwick Rd, Red. RH1 288 DD136
Hardwick's Sq, SW18 202 DA85
Hardwick St, EC1 18 F3
Hardwidge St, SE1 31 N4
Hardy Av, E16 35 P2
Northfleet DA11 212 GE89
Ruislip HA4 137 BV64
Hardy Cl, SE16 33 K5
Barnet EN5 101 CY44
Horley RH6 290 DE148
North Holmwood RH5 285 CH141
Pinner HA5 138 BX59
Slough SL1 153 AN74
Hardy Ct, SW18
off Furmage St 202 DB87
Borehamwood WD6
off Chaucer Gro 100 CN42
Hardy Gro, Dart. DA1 190 FN84
Hardy Ms, Uxb. UB8 156 BJ67
Hardy Pas, N22
off Berners Rd 121 DN54
Hardy Rd, E4 123 DZ51
SE3 47 M3
SW19 202 DB94
Hemel Hempstead HP2 62 BM19
Hardy's Ms, E.Mol. KT8 219 CE98
Hardy Way, Enf. EN2 103 DN39
Hare & Billet Rd, SE3 46 G7
Harebell, Welw.G.C. AL7 51 CY13
Harebell Cl, Hert. SG13 54 DV09
Harebell Dr, E6 25 M7
Harebell Hill, Cob. KT11 236 BX114
Harebell Way, Rom. RM3 128 FK52
Harebreaks, The, Wat. WD24 97 BV38
Harecastle Cl, Hayes UB4 158 BY70
Hare Ct, EC4 18 E9
Harecourt Rd, N1 9 J4
Hare Cres, Wat. WD25 81 BU32
Harecroft, Dor. RH4 285 CJ139
Fetcham KT22 252 CB123
Haredale Rd, SE24 184 DQ84
Haredon Cl, SE23 204 DW87
HAREFIELD, Uxb. UB9 114 BL53
Harefield, Esher KT10 237 CE105
Harefield, Harlow CM20 58 EU14
Harefield Acad, The, Hare.
UB9 off Northwood Way 114 BK53
Harefield Av, Sutt. SM2 239 CY109
Harefield Cl, Enf. EN2 103 DN39
Harefield Hosp, Hare. UB9 114 BJ53
Harefield Inf Sch, Hare.
UB9 off High St 114 BJ53
Harefield Jun Sch, Hare.
UB9 off Park La 114 BJ53
Harefield Ms, SE4 45 N10
Harefield Pl, St.Alb. AL4 65 CK17
Harefield Rd, N8 143 DK57
SE4 185 DZ83
SW16 203 DM94
Rickmansworth WD3 114 BK50
Sidcup DA14 208 EX89
Uxbridge UB8 156 BK65
Hare Hall La, Rom. RM2 149 FH56
Harehatch La, Slou. SL2 133 AL60
Hare Hill, Add. KT15 233 BF107
Hare Hill Cl, Pyrford GU22 250 BG115
Harelands Cl, Wok. GU21 248 AW117
Harelands La, Wok. GU21 248 AW117
Hare La, Clay. KT10 237 CE107
Hatfield AL10 67 CU20
Hare Marsh, E2 20 C4
Harenc Sch, Sid. DA14
off Rectory La 208 EW92
Harendon, Tad. KT20 255 CW121
Harepark Cl, Hem.H. HP1 61 BF19
Harepit Cl, S.Croy. CR2 241 DP108
Hare Pl, EC4 18 F9
Hare Row, E2 10 F10
Hares Bk, New Adgtn CR0 243 ED110
Haresfield Rd, Dag. RM10 168 FA65
Haresfoot Sch, Berk. HP4
off Chesham Rd 60 AV22
Harestone Dr, Cat. CR3 258 DT124
Harestone Hill, Cat. CR3 274 DT126
Harestone La, Cat. CR3 274 DS125
Harestone Marie Curie Cen,
Cat. CR3 274 DT125
Harestone Valley Rd, Cat. CR3 274 DT126
HARE STREET, Harl. CM19 73 EP16
Hare St, SE18 37 M7
Harlow CM19 73 EP15
Hare St Comm Prim Sch & Nurs,
Harl. CM19 off Little Gro Fld 73 EQ15
Hare St Springs, Harl. CM19 73 EP15
Hare Ter, Grays RM20
off Mill La 191 FX78
Hare Wk, N1 19 P1
Hareward Rd, Guil. GU4 265 BC132
Harewood, Rick. WD3 96 BH43
Harewood Av, NW1 16 D5
Northolt UB5 158 BY66
Harewood Cl, Nthlt. UB5 158 BZ66
Reigate RH2 272 DC132
Harewood Ct, Warl. CR6 259 DY118
Harewood Dr, Ilf. IG5 125 EM54
Harewood Gdns, S.Croy. CR2 258 DV115
Harewood Hill, They.B. CM16 107 ES35
Harewood Pl, W1 17 K9
Slough SL1 174 AU76
Harewood Rd, SW19 202 DE93
Chalfont St. Giles HP8 94 AW41
Isleworth TW7 179 CF80
Pilgrim's Hatch CM15 130 FV44
South Croydon CR2 242 DS107
Watford WD19 115 BV48
Harewood Row, NW1 16 D6
Harewood Ter, Sthl. UB2 178 BZ77
Harfield Gdns, SE5 43 N10
Harfield Rd, Sun. TW16 218 BX96
Harford Cl, E4 123 EB45
Harford Dr, Wat. WD17 97 BS38
Harford Ms, N19 143 DK62
Harford Rd, E4 123 EB45
Harford St, E1 21 L5
Harford Wk, N2 142 DD57
Harfst Way, Swan. BR8 229 FC95
Hargood Cl, Har. HA3 140 CL58
Hargood Rd, SE3 186 EJ81
Hargrave Pk, N19 143 DJ61
Hargrave Pk Prim Sch,
N19 off Hargrave Pk 143 DJ61
Hargrave Pl, N7 7 N3
Hargrave Rd, N19 143 DJ61
Hargreaves Av, Chsht EN7 88 DV30
Hargreaves Cl, Chsht EN7 88 DV31
Hargwyne St, SW9 183 DM83
Hari Cl, Nthlt. UB5 138 CB64
Haringey Pk, N8 143 DL58
Haringey Pas, N4 143 DP58
N8 143 DN56
Haringey Rd, N8 143 DL56
Haringey 6th Form Cen,
N17 off College Rd 122 DT51
Harington Ter, N9 122 DR48
N18 122 DR48
Harkett Cl, Har. HA3
off Byron Rd 117 CF54
Harkett Ct, Har. HA3 117 CF54
Harkness, Chsht EN7 88 DU29
Harkness Cl, Epsom KT17 255 CW116
Romford RM3 128 FM50
Harkness Ct, Sutt. SM1
off Cleeve Way 222 DC102
Harkness Ho, E1
off Christian St 20 D9
Harkness Rd, Burn. SL1 152 AH71
Hemel Hempstead HP2 62 BK19
Harland Av, Croy. CR0 224 DT104
Sidcup DA15 207 ER90
Harland Cl, SW19 222 DB97
Harland Rd, SE12 206 EG88
Harlands Gro, Orp. BR6 245 EP105
Harlech Gdns, Houns. TW5 178 BW79
Pinner HA5 138 BX59
Harlech Rd, N14 121 DL48
Abbots Langley WD5 81 BU31
Harlech Twr, W3 180 CP75
Harlequin, The, Wat. WD17 98 BW42
Harlequin Av, Brent. TW8 179 CG79
Harlequin Cl, Bark. IG11 168 EU70
Hayes UB4 off Cygnet Way 158 BX71
Isleworth TW7 199 CE85
Harlequin Ho, Erith DA18
off Kale Rd 188 EY76
Harlequin Rd, Tedd. TW11 199 CH94
★ Harlequins RL, Twick. TW2 199 CE87
Harlescott Rd, SE15 185 DX84
HARLESDEN, NW10 160 CS68
Harlesden 160 CR68
Harlesden 160 CR68
Harlesden Cl, Rom. RM3 128 FM52
Harlesden Gdns, NW10 161 CT67
Harlesden La, NW10 161 CU67
Harlesden Prim Sch,
NW10 off Acton La 160 CS68
Harlesden Rd, NW10 161 CU67
Romford RM3 128 FM51
St. Albans AL1 65 CG20
Harlesden Wk, Rom. RM3 128 FM52
Harleston Cl, E5
off Theydon Rd 144 DW61
Harley Cl, Wem. HA0 159 CK65
Harley Ct, E11
off Blake Hall Rd 146 EG59
St. Albans AL4
off Villiers Cres 65 CK16
Harley Cres, Har. HA1 139 CD56
Harleyford, Brom. BR1 226 EH95
Harleyford Rd, SE11 42 C2
Harleyford St, SE11 42 E3
Harley Gdns, SW10 39 P1
Orpington BR6 245 ES105
Harley Gro, E3 21 P2
Harley Pl, W1 17 J7
Harley Rd, NW3 6 B7
NW10 160 CS68
Harrow HA1 139 CD56
Harley St, W1 17 J7
Harley St Clinic, The, W1 17 J6
Harling Ct, SW11 40 E8
Harlinger St, SE18 36 G6
Harlings, Hert.Hth SG13 54 DW13
HARLINGTON, Hayes UB3 177 BQ79
Harlington Cl, Harling. UB3 177 BQ80
Harlington Comm Sch,
Harling. UB3
off Pinkwell La 177 BR77
Harlington Cor, Hayes
UB3 off Bath Rd 177 BR81
Harlington Rd, Bexh. DA7 188 EY83
Uxbridge UB8 157 BP71
Harlington Rd E, Felt.
TW13, TW14 197 BV87
Harlington Rd W, Felt. TW14 197 BV86
HARLOW, CM17 - CM20 73 ER15
Harlow 57 ER14
Harlowbury Prim Sch, Old Harl.
CM17 off Watlington Rd 58 EX11
● Harlow Business Cen,
Harl. CM19 73 EN16
● Harlow Business Pk,
Harl. CM19 72 EL15
Harlow Coll, Harl. CM20
off Velizy Av 57 ES14
Harlow Common, Harl. CM17 74 EW18
Harlow Ct, Hem.H. HP2 62 BN16
Harlow Flds Sch, Harl.
CM18 off Tendring Rd 73 ES17
Harlow Gdns, Rom. RM5 127 FC51
● Harlow Ind Cen, Harl. CM20 58 EV10
Harlow Mkt, Harl. CM20
off East Gate 57 ER14
Harlow Mill 58 EW10
Harlow Potter St Bypass,
Harl. CM17, CM20 74 EV15
Harlow PRU, Harl. CM20
off Mowbray Rd 58 EU12
Harlow Retail Pk,
Harl. CM20 57 ET11
Harlow Rd, N13 122 DR48
Harlow CM20 58 EW08
Matching Tye CM17 59 FC12
Old Harlow CM17 58 FA09
Rainham RM13 169 FF67
Roydon CM19 72 EJ15
Sawbridgeworth CM21 58 EW08
Sheering CM22 58 FA09
Harlow Town 57 ER12
HARLOW TYE, Harl. CM17 59 FC12
Harlton Ct, Wal.Abb. EN9 90 EF34
Harlyn Dr, Pnr. HA5 137 BV55
Harlyn Prim Sch, Pnr.
HA5 off Tolcarne Dr 137 BV55
Harman Av, Grav. DA11 213 GH92
Woodford Green IG8 124 EF52
Harman Cl, E4 123 ED49
NW2 141 CY62
SE1 off Avondale Sq 44 C1
Harman Dr, NW2 141 CY62
Sidcup DA15 207 ET86
Harman Pl, Pur. CR8 241 DP111
Harman Ri, Ilf. IG3 147 ES63
Harman Rd, Enf. EN1 104 DT43
Harmer Rd, Swans. DA10 212 FZ86
Harmer St, Grav. DA12 213 GJ86
Harmonds Wd Cl, Brox. EN10 71 DY19
HARMONDSWORTH, West Dr.
UB7 176 BK79
Harmondsworth La, West Dr.
UB7 176 BL79
Harmondsworth Prim Sch,
Harm. UB7 off School Rd 176 BK79
Harmondsworth Rd, West Dr.
UB7 176 BL78
Harmony Cl, NW11 141 CY57
Hatfield AL10 67 CU16
Wallington SM6 241 DL109
Harmony Pl, SE1 32 B10
Harmony Ter, Har. HA2
off Goldsmith Cl 138 CB60
Harmony Way, NW4 141 CW56
Harmood Gro, NW1 7 J6
Harmood Pl, NW1 7 J6
Harmood St, NW1 7 J5
Harms Gro, Guil. GU4 265 BC131
Harmsworth Ms, SE11 30 G7
Harmsworth St, SE17 42 G1
Harmsworth Way, N20 119 CZ46
Harness Way, St.Alb. AL4 65 CK17
Harnetts Cl, Swan. BR8 229 FD100
Harold Av, Belv. DA17 188 EZ78
Hayes UB3 177 BT76
Harold Cl, Harl. CM19 73 EM16
Harold Ct, Wal.Cr. EN8
off Alexandra Way 89 DZ34
Harold Ct Prim Sch, Harold Wd
RM3 off Church Rd 128 FN52
Harold Ct Rd, Rom. RM3 128 FP51
Harold Cres, Wal.Abb. EN9 89 EC32
Harold Est, SE1 31 P7
Harold Gibbons Ct, SE7 186 EJ79
HAROLD HILL, Rom. RM3 128 FL50
● Harold Hill Ind Est,
Rom. RM3 128 FK52
Harold Laski Ho, EC1 18 G3
HAROLD PARK, Rom. RM3 128 FN52
Harold Pl, SE11
off Kennington La 42 E1
Harold Rd, E4 123 EC49
E11 146 EE60
E13 166 EH67
N8 143 DM57
Harold Rd, N15 144 DT57
NW10 160 CR69
SE19 204 DS93
Hawley DA2 210 FM91
Sutton SM1 240 DD105
Woodford Green IG8 124 EG53
Haroldslea, Horl. RH6 291 DK150
Haroldslea Cl, Horl. RH6 291 DJ150
Haroldslea Dr, Horl. RH6 291 DJ150
Harolds Rd, Harl. CM19 72 EL16
Haroldstone Rd, E17 145 DX57
Harold Vw, Rom. RM3 128 FM54
HAROLD WOOD, Rom. RM3 128 FL54
Harold Wood 128 FM53
Harold Wd Hall, Rom. RM3 128 FK53
Harold Wd Prim Sch,
Harold Wd RM3
off Recreation Av 150 FN55
Harp All, EC4 18 G8
● Harp Business Cen, NW2 141 CT61
Harpenden Rd, E12 146 EJ61
SE27 203 DP90
St. Albans AL3 65 CD17
Harpenmead Pt, NW2 141 CZ61
Harperbury Hosp,
Shenley WD7 83 CJ31
Harper Cl, N14
off Alexandra Ct 103 DJ43
Chafford Hundred RM16 191 FW78
Harper La, Rad. WD7 83 CG32
Harper Ms, SW17 202 DC90
Harper Rd, E6 25 J9
SE1 31 J6
Harpers Yd, N17 122 DT53
Harpesford Av, Vir.W. GU25 214 AV99
Harp Island Cl, NW10 140 CR61
Harp La, EC3 31 N1
Harpley Sch, E1 21 J4
Harpley Sq, E1 21 H3
Harpour Rd, Bark. IG11 167 EQ65
Harp Rd, W7 159 CF70
Harpsden St, SW11 40 G7
Harpsfield Bdy, Hat. AL10 67 CT17
Harps Oak La, Merst. RH1 272 DF125
Harpswood Cl, Couls. CR5 257 DJ122
Harptree Way, St.Alb. AL1 65 CG18
Harpur Ms, WC1 18 C6
Harpurs, Tad. KT20 255 CX122
Harpur St, WC1 18 C6
Harraden Rd, SE3 186 EJ81
Harrap Chase, Bad.Dene RM17 192 FZ78
Harrap St, E14 22 F10
Harrier Av, E11
off Eastern Av 146 EH58
Harrier Cl, Horn. RM12 169 FH65
Harrier Ms, SE28 187 ER76
Harrier Rd, NW9 118 CS54
Harriers Cl, W5 160 CL73
Harrier Way, E6 25 K7
Waltham Abbey EN9 90 EG34
Harries Cl, Chesh. HP5
off Deansway 76 AP30
Harriescourt, Wal.Abb. EN9 90 EG32
Harries Rd, Hayes UB4 158 BW70
Harriet Cl, E8 10 C8
Harriet Gdns, Croy. CR0 224 DU103
Harriet St, SW1 28 F5
Harriet Tubman Cl, SW2 203 DN87
Harriet Wk, SW1 28 F5
Harriet Walker Way, Rick. WD3 113 BF45
HARRINGAY, N8 143 DN57
Harringay 143 DN58
Harringay Gdns, N8 143 DP56
Harringay Green Lanes 143 DP58
Harringay Rd, N15 143 DP57
Harrington Cl, NW10 140 CR62
Croydon CR0 223 DL103
Leigh RH2 287 CU141
Windsor SL4 173 AM84
Harrington Ct, W10
off Dart St 14 G2
Croydon CR0 off Altyre Rd 224 DR103
Hertford Heath SG13
off Trinity Rd 54 DW12
Harrington Cres, N.Stfd RM16 171 FX74
Harrington Gdns, SW7 27 M9
Harrington Hill, E5 144 DV60
Harrington Hill Prim Sch,
E5 off Harrington Hill 144 DV60
Harrington Ho, NW1 17 L2
Harrington Road 224 DW97
Harrington Rd, E11 146 EE60
SE25 224 DU98
SW7 28 A8
Harrington Sq, NW1 17 L1
Harrington St, NW1 17 L2
Harrington Way, SE18 36 F6
Harriott Cl, SE10 35 L9
Harriotts Cl, Ashtd. KT21
off Harriotts La 253 CJ120
Harriotts La, Ashtd. KT21 253 CJ119
Harris Acad Bermondsey,
SE16 32 B8
Harris Acad Crystal Palace,
SE19 off Maberley Rd 224 DT95
Harris Acad Falconwood,
Well. DA16 off The Green 187 ES84
Harris Acad Merton, Mitch.
CR4 off Wide Way 223 DK97
Harris Acad Peckham,
SE15 44 B7
Harris Acad S Norwood, SE25
off South Norwood Hill 224 DT97
Harris Boys' Acad E Dulwich,
SE22 off Peckham Rye 204 DV85
Harris Cl, Enf. EN2 103 DP39
Hounslow TW3 178 CA81
Northfleet DA11 212 GE90
Romford RM3 128 FL52
Harris Gdns, Slou. SL1 173 AQ75
Harris Girls' Acad E Dulwich,
SE22 off Homestall Rd 204 DW85
Harris La, Shenley WD7 84 CN34
Harrison Cl, N20 120 DE46
Hutton CM13 131 GD43
Northwood HA6 115 BQ51
Reigate RH2 288 DB135
Harrison Dr, Brom. BR1 227 EP98
North Weald Bassett CM16 93 FB26
Harrison Rd, NW10 160 CR67
Dagenham RM10 169 FB65
Waltham Abbey EN9 105 EC35
Harrisons Ri, Croy. CR0 223 DP104
Harrison St, WC1 18 B3
Harrisons Wf, Purf. RM19 190 FN78
Harrison Wk, Chsht EN8 89 DX30
Harrison Way, Sev. TN13 278 FG122
Shepperton TW17 217 BP99
Harrison Way, Slough SL1 153 AK74
Harris Rd, Bexh. DA7 188 EY81
Dagenham RM9 148 EZ64
Watford WD25 97 BU35
Harris's La, Ware SG12 54 DW05
Harris St, E17 145 DZ59
SE5 43 M5
Harris Way, Sun. TW16 217 BS95
Harrod Ct, NW9 140 CQ56
Harrodian Sch, The, SW13
off Lonsdale Rd 181 CT80
★ Harrods, SW1 28 E6
Harrogate Ct, Slou. SL3 175 BA78
Harrogate Rd, Wat. WD19 116 BW48
Harrold Rd, Dag. RM8 148 EV64
● Harrovian Business Village,
Har. HA1
off Bessborough Rd 139 CD59
HARROW, HA1 - HA3 139 CD59
Harrow 139 CE58
Harrow & Wealdstone 139 CE56
Harrow & Wealdstone 139 CE56
Harrow & Wealdstone 139 CE56
★ Harrow Arts Cen, Pnr. HA5 116 CB52
Harrow Av, Enf. EN1 104 DT44
Harroway Manor, Fetch. KT22 253 CF122
Harroway Rd, SW11 40 B9
Harrowbond Rd, Harl. CM17 58 EW14
Harrow Bottom Rd, Vir.W.
GU25 215 AZ100
Harrowby Gdns, Nthflt DA11 212 GE89
Harrowby St, W1 16 D8
Harrow Cl, Add. KT15 216 BH103
Chessington KT9 237 CK108
Dorking RH4 285 CG137
Hornchurch RM11 149 FH60
Harrow Coll, Harrow-on-the-Hill
Campus, Har. HA1
off Lowlands Rd 139 CE59
Harrow Weald Campus, Har.Wld
HA3 off Brookshill 117 CE51
Harrow Cres, Rom. RM3 127 FH52
Harrowdene Cl, Wem. HA0 139 CK63
Harrowdene Gdns, Tedd. TW11 199 CG93
Harrowdene Rd, Wem. HA0 139 CK62
Harrow Dr, N9 122 DT46
Hornchurch RM11 149 FH60
Harrowes Meade, Edg. HA8 118 CN48
Harrow Flds Gdns, Har. HA1 139 CE62
Harrow Fire Training Cen,
Pnr. HA5 off Pinner Rd 138 CA56
Harrow Gdns, Orp. BR6 246 EV105
Warlingham CR6 259 DZ115
Harrow Gate Gdns, Dor. RH4
off Horsham Rd 285 CH138
Harrowgate Rd, E9 11 L5
Harrow Grn, E11 146 EE62
Harrow High Sch, Har.
HA1 off Gayton Rd 139 CG58
Harrowlands Pk, Dor. RH4 285 CH137
Harrow La, E14 34 E1
Godalming GU7 280 AS144
Harrow Manorway, SE2 168 EW74
Harrow Mkt, Slou. SL3 175 BA76
★ Harrow Mus, Har. HA2 138 CB55
HARROW ON THE HILL,
Har. HA1 139 CE61
Harrow on the Hill 139 CE58
Harrow on the Hill 139 CE58
Harrow Pk, Har. HA1 139 CE61
Harrow Pas, Kings.T. KT1
off Market Pl 219 CK96
Harrow Pl, E1 19 P8
Harrow Rd, E6 166 EL67
E11 146 EE62
NW10 14 C3
W2 15 L7
W9 15 J5
W10 14 F4
Barking IG11 167 ES67
Harrow Rd, Cars. SM5 240 DE106
Feltham TW14 196 BN88
Ilford IG1 147 EQ63
Knockholt Pound TN14 262 EY115
Slough SL3 175 AZ76
Tokyngton HA9 140 CM64
Warlingham CR6 259 DZ115
Wembley HA0 139 CJ64
Harrow Rd E, Dor. RH4 285 CH138
Harrow Rd W, Dor. RH4 285 CG138
Harrow Sch, Har.Hill HA1
off High St 139 CE60
Harrowsley Ct, Horl. RH6
off Tanyard Way 291 DH147
Harrowsley Grn La, Horl. RH6 291 DJ149
Harrow Vw, Har. HA1, HA2 139 CD56
Hayes UB3 157 BU72
Uxbridge UB10 157 BQ69
Harrow Vw Rd, W5 159 CH70
Harrow Way, Shep. TW17 217 BQ96
Watford WD19 116 BY48
HARROW WEALD, Har. HA3 117 CD53
Harrow Weald Pk, Har. HA3 117 CD51
Harry Cl, Croy. CR0 224 DQ100
Harry Day Ms, SE27 204 DQ90
Harry Gosling Prim Sch, E1 20 D9
Harry's Pl, S.Ock. RM15 171 FX71
Harry Zeital Way, E5
off Mount Pleasant Hill 144 DW61
Harston Dr, Enf. EN3 105 EA38
Harston Wk, E3 22 E4
Hart Cl, Bletch. RH1 274 DT134
Croydon CR0 223 DP104
Hart Cor, Grays RM20 191 FX78
Hart Cres, Chig. IG7 125 ET50
Hartcroft Cl, Hem.H. HP3 63 BP21
Hart Dyke Cres, Swan. BR8
off Hart Dyke Rd 229 FD97
Hart Dyke Rd, Orp. BR5 228 EW102
Swanley BR8 229 FD97
Harte Rd, Houns. TW3 178 BZ82
Hartfield Av, Els. WD6 100 CN43
Northolt UB5 157 BV68
Hartfield Cl, Els. WD6 100 CN43
Hartfield Ct, Ware SG12 55 DX05
Hartfield Cres, SW19 201 CZ94
West Wickham BR4 226 EG104
Hartfield Gro, SE20 224 DV95
Hartfield Pl, Nthflt DA11 212 GD87
Hartfield Rd, SW19 201 CZ94
Chessington KT9 237 CK106

Hartfield Rd, West Wickham
BR4 244 EG105
Hartfield Ter, E3 22 B1
Hartford Av, Har. HA3 139 CG55
Hartforde Rd, Borwd. WD6 100 CN40
Hartford Rd, Bex. DA5 208 FA86
Epsom KT19 238 CN107
Hart Gdns, Dor. RH4
off Hart Rd 285 CH135
Hart Gro, W5 160 CN74
Southall UB1 158 CA71
Harthall La, Hem.H. HP3 81 BS26
Kings Langley WD4 81 BP28
Hartham Cl, N7 8 B3
Isleworth TW7 179 CG81
Hartham La, Hert. SG14 54 DQ09
Hartham Rd, N7 8 A2
N17 122 DT54
Isleworth TW7 179 CF81
Harting Rd, SE9 206 EL91
Hartington Cl, Farnboro. BR6 245 EQ106
Harrow HA1 139 CE63
Reigate RH2 272 DA132
Hartington Ct, W4 180 CP80
Hartington Rd, E16 24 A9
E17 145 DY58
SW8 42 A5
W4 180 CP80
W13 159 CH73
Southall UB2 178 BY76
Twickenham TW1 199 CH87
Hartismere Rd, SW6 39 H4
Hartlake Rd, E9 11 K5
Hartland Cl, N21
off Elmscott Gdns 104 DQ44
Edgware HA8 118 CN47
New Haw KT15 234 BJ110
Slough SL1 153 AR74
Hartland Dr, Edg. HA8 118 CN47
Ruislip HA4 137 BV62
Hartland Rd, E15 13 L7
N11 120 DF50
NW1 7 J6
NW6 4 G10
Addlestone KT15 234 BG108
Cheshunt EN8 89 DX30
Epping CM16 92 EU31
Hampton Hill TW12 198 CB91
Hornchurch RM12 149 FG61
Isleworth TW7 179 CG83
Morden SM4 222 DA101
Hartlands Cl, Bex. DA5 208 EZ86
Hartland Way, Croy. CR0 225 DY103
Morden SM4 221 CZ101
Hartlepool Ct, E16 37 P3
Hartley Av, E6 166 EL67
NW7 119 CT50
Hartley Cl, NW7 119 CT50
Bromley BR1 227 EM96
Stoke Poges SL3 154 AW67
Hartley Copse, Old Wind. SL4 194 AU86
Hartley Down, Pur. CR8 241 DM114
Hartley Fm Est, Pur. CR8 257 DM115
HARTLEY GREEN, Long. DA3 231 FX99
Hartley Hill, Pur. CR8 257 DM115
Hartley Ho, SE1
off Longfield Est 32 B8
Hartley Old Rd, Pur. CR8 241 DM114
Hartley Prim Sch, E6
off Hartley Av 166 EL67
Hartley Rd, E11 146 EF60
Croydon CR0 223 DP101
Welling DA16 188 EW80
Westerham TN16 277 ER125
Hartley St, E2 21 H2
Hartley Way, Pur. CR8 257 DM115
Hartmann Rd, E16 36 F2
Hartmoor Ms, Enf. EN3 105 DX37
Hartnoll St, N7 8 D2
Harton Cl, Brom. BR1 226 EK95
Harton Rd, N9 122 DV47
Harton St, SE8 46 A6
Hartopp Pt, SW6
off Pellant Rd 38 F4
Hart Rd, Byfleet KT14 234 BL113
Dorking RH4 285 CH135
Harlow CM17 58 EW10
St. Albans AL1 65 CD21
Hartsbourne Av, Bushey Hth
WD23 116 CC47
Hartsbourne Cl, Bushey Hth
WD23 117 CD47
Hartsbourne Prim Sch,
Bushey WD23
off Hartsbourne Rd 117 CD47
Hartsbourne Rd, Bushey Hth
WD23 117 CD47
Hartsbourne Way, Hem.H. HP2 63 BQ21
Harts Cl, Bushey WD23 98 CA40
Hartscroft, Croy. CR0 243 DY109
Harts Gdns, Guil. GU2 264 AV131
Harts Gro, Wdf.Grn. IG8 124 EG50
Hartshill Cl, Uxb. UB10 156 BN65
Hartshill Rd, Nthflt DA11 213 GF89
Hartshill Wk, Wok. GU21 248 AV116
Hartshorn All, EC3 19 P9
Hartshorn Gdns, E6 25 L4
Hartslands Rd, Sev. TN13 279 FJ123
Harts La, SE14 45 L5
Barking IG11 167 EP65
Hartslock Dr, SE2 188 EX75
Hartsmead Rd, SE9 207 EM89
Hartspiece Rd, Red. RH1 288 DG136
Hartspring La, Bushey WD23 98 CA40
Watford WD25 98 CA39
Hart Sq, Mord. SM4 222 DA100
Hart St, EC3 19 P10
Brentwood CM14 130 FW47
Hartsway, Enf. EN3 104 DW42
Hartswood, Wat. WD25 98 CA39
Hartswood, N.Holm. RH5 285 CK139
off Wildcroft Dr
Hartswood Av, Reig. RH2 288 DA138
Hartswood Cl, Bushey WD23 98 CA40
Warley CM14 130 FY49
Hartswood Gdns, W12 181 CT76
Hartswood Grn, Bushey Hth
WD23 117 CD47
Hartswood Rd, W12 181 CT75
Warley CM14 130 FY49
Hartsworth Cl, E13 23 M1
Hartville Rd, SE18 187 ES77
Hartwell Cl, SW2
off Challice Way 203 DM88
Penn HP10 110 AC45
Hartwell Dr, E4 123 EC51
Beaconsfield HP9 111 AK52
Hartwell St, E8 10 A4
Harvard Hill, W4 180 CP79
Harvard La, W4 180 CQ78
Harvard Rd, SE13 205 EC85
W4 180 CP78
Isleworth TW7 179 CE81
Harvard Wk, Horn. RM12 149 FG63
Harvel Cl, Orp. BR5 228 EU97
Harvel Cres, SE2 188 EX78
Harvest Bk Rd, W.Wick. BR4 226 EF104
Harvest Ct, St.Alb. AL4
off Harvesters 65 CJ16
Shepperton TW17 216 BN98
Harvest End, Wat. WD25 98 BX36
Harvester Rd, Epsom KT19 238 CR110
Harvesters, St.Alb. AL4 65 CK16
Harvesters Cl, Islw. TW7 199 CD85
Harvest Hill, B.End SL8 132 AD61
Harvest La, Loug. IG10 124 EK45
Thames Ditton KT7 219 CG100
Harvest Mead, Hat. AL10 67 CV17
Harvest Rd, Bushey WD23 98 CB42
Englefield Green TW20 194 AX92
Feltham TW13 197 BU91
Harvestside, Horl. RH6 291 DJ147
Harvest Way, Swan. BR8 229 FD101
Harvey, Grays RM16 192 GB75
Harvey Cen, Harl. CM20 73 EQ15
Harvey Cen App, Harl. CM20 73 ER15
Harvey Dr, Hmptn. TW12 218 CB95
Harveyfields, Wal.Abb. EN9 89 EC34
Harvey Gdns, E11 146 EF60
SE7 36 D10
Loughton IG10 107 EP41
Harvey Ho, Brent. TW8
off Green Dragon La 180 CL78
Harvey Orchard, Beac. HP9 110 AJ52
Harvey Rd, E11 146 EF60
N8 143 DM57
SE5 43 L6
Croxley Green WD3 96 BN44
Guildford GU1 280 AY136
Hounslow TW4 198 BZ87
Ilford IG1 147 EP64
London Colney AL2 83 CJ26
Northolt UB5 158 BW66
Slough SL3 175 BB76
Uxbridge UB10 156 BN68
Walton-on-Thames KT12 217 BT101
Harvey Rd Prim Sch, Crox.Grn
WD3 *off Harvey Rd* 96 BN44
Harveys La, Rom. RM7 149 FD61
Harvey St, N1 9 M9
Harvill Rd, Sid. DA14 208 EX92
Harvil Rd, Hare. UB9 136 BK58
Ickenham UB10 136 BL60
Harvington Sch, W5
off Castlebar Rd 159 CK72
Harvington Wk, E8 10 D6
Harvist Est, N7 143 DM63
Harvist Rd, NW6 14 D2
Harwater Dr, Loug. IG10 107 EM40
Harwell Cl, Ruis. HA4 137 BR60
Harwell Pas, N2 142 DF56
Harwich Rd, Slou. SL1 153 AN72
Harwood Av, Brom. BR1 226 EH96
Hornchurch RM11 150 FL55
Mitcham CR4 222 DE97
Harwood Cl, N12 120 DE51
Tewin AL6 52 DE05
Welwyn Garden City AL8 51 CY05
Wembley HA0 139 CK62
Harwood Dr, Uxb. UB10 156 BM67
Harwood Gdns, Old Wind. SL4 194 AV87
Harwood Hall La, Upmin.
RM14 170 FP65
Harwood Hill, Welw.G.C. AL8 51 CY06
Harwood Hill JMI & Nurs Sch,
Welw.G.C. AL8
off Harwood Hill 51 CY05
Harwood Pk, Red. RH1 288 DG143
Harwood Rd, SW6 39 K5
Harwoods, The, Ware SG12 54 DV05
Harwoods Rd, Wat. WD18 97 BU42
Harwoods Yd, N21
off Wades Hill 121 DN45
Harwood Ter, SW6 39 L6
Hascombe Ter, SE5 43 L8
Hasedines Rd, Hem.H. HP1 62 BG19
Haselbury Rd, N9 122 DS49
N18 122 DS49
Haseldine Meadows, Hat. AL10 67 CT19
Haseldine Rd, Lon.Col. AL2 83 CK26
Haseley End, SE23
off Tyson Rd 204 DW87
Haselrigge Rd, SW4 183 DK84
Haseltine Prim Sch, SE26
off Haseltine Rd 205 DZ91
Haseltine Rd, SE26 205 DZ91
Haselwood Dr, Enf. EN2 103 DP42
Haskard Rd, Dag. RM9 148 EX63
Hasker St, SW3 28 D8
Haslam Av, Sutt. SM3 221 CY102
Haslam Cl, N1 8 F6
Uxbridge UB10 137 BQ61
Haslam Ct, N11
off Waterfall Rd 121 DH49
Haslam St, SE15 44 B5
Haslemere Av, NW4 141 CX58
SW18 202 DB89
W7 179 CG76
W13 179 CG76
Barnet EN4 120 DF46
Hounslow TW5 178 BW82
Mitcham CR4 222 DD96
Haslemere Business Cen,
Enf. EN1 104 DV43
Haslemere Cl, Hmptn. TW12 198 BZ92
Wallington SM6 241 DL106
Haslemere Gdns, N3 141 CZ55
Haslemere Heathrow Est,
Houns. TW4 177 BU82
Haslemere Ind Est, SW18 202 DB89
Haslemere Prim Sch, Mitch.
CR4 *off Haslemere Av* 222 DD96
Haslemere Rd, N8 143 DK59
N21 121 DP47
Bexleyheath DA7 188 EZ82
Ilford IG3 147 ET61
Thornton Heath CR7 223 DP99
Windsor SL4 173 AN81
Hasler Cl, SE28 168 EV73
Haslett Rd, Shep. TW17 217 BS96
Haslewood Av, Hodd. EN11 71 EA17
Hasluck Gdns, New Barn. EN5 102 DC44
Hasmonean High Sch, Boys,
NW4 *off Holders Hill Rd* 119 CX54
Girls, NW7 *off Page St* 119 CU53
Hasmonean Prim Sch,
NW4 *off Shirehall La* 141 CX57
Hassard St, E2 20 B1
Hassendean Rd, SE3 186 EH79
Hassett Rd, E9 11 K4
Hassocks Cl, SE26 204 DV90
Hassocks Rd, SW16 223 DK95
Hassock Wd, Kes. BR2 244 EK105
Hassop Rd, NW2 141 CX63
Hassop Wk, SE9 206 EL91
Hasted Cl, Green. DA9 211 FW86
Hasted Rd, SE7 36 E10
Hastings Av, Ilf. IG6 147 EQ56
Hastings Cl, SE15 44 C5
Barnet EN5 102 DC42
Grays RM17 192 FY79
Wembley HA0 139 CJ63
Hastings Dr, Surb. KT6 219 CJ100
Hastings Ho, SE18 37 K9
Hastings Pl, Croy. CR0
off Hastings Rd 224 DT102
Hastings Rd, N11 121 DJ50
N17 144 DR55
W13 159 CH73
Bromley BR2 226 EL102
Croydon CR0 224 DT102
Romford RM2 149 FH57
Hastings St, SE18 187 EQ76
WC1 18 A3
Hastings Way, Bushey WD23 98 BY42
Croxley Green WD3 97 BP42
HASTINGWOOD, Harl. CM17 74 EZ19
Hastingwood Business Cen,
Hast. CM17 74 EZ18
Hastingwood Interchange,
Harl. CM17 74 EW20
Hastingwood Rd, Hast. CM17 74 EX20
Magdalen Laver CM5 75 FB19
Hastingwood Trd Est, N18 123 DX51
Hastoe Cl, Hayes UB4 158 BY70
Hasty Cl, Mitch. CR4
off Slade Way 222 DG95
Hat & Mitre Ct, EC1 19 H5
Hatch, The, Enf. EN3 105 DX39
Windsor SL4 172 AJ80
Hatcham Ms Business Cen,
SE14 45 K6
Hatcham Pk Ms, SE14 45 K6
Hatcham Pk Rd, SE14 45 K6
Hatcham Rd, SE15 44 G3
Hatchard Rd, N19 143 DK61
Hatch Cl, Add. KT15 216 BH104
Hatchcroft, NW4 141 CV55
HATCH END, Pnr. HA5 116 BY52
Hatch End 116 BZ52
Hatch End High Sch, Har.
HA3 *off Headstone La* 116 CB53
Hatchers Ms, SE1 31 P5
Hatchett Rd, Felt. TW14 197 BQ88
Hatch Fm Ms, Add. KT15 216 BJ103
Hatch Gdns, Tad. KT20 255 CX120
Hatchgate, Horl. RH6 290 DF149
Hatchgate Gdns, Burn. SL1 153 AK69
Hatch Gro, Rom. RM6 148 EY56
Hatchingtan, The, Worp. GU3 264 AW126
Hatchlands Ho & Pk,
Guil. GU4 266 BM131
Hatchlands Rd, Red. RH1 272 DE134
Hatch La, E4 123 ED49
Cobham KT11 251 BP119
Coulsdon CR5 256 DG115
Harmondsworth UB7 176 BK80
Ockham GU23 251 BP120
Redhill RH1 289 DM142
Windsor SL4 173 AN83
Hatch Pl, Kings.T. KT2 200 CM92
Hatch Rd, SW16 223 DL96
Pilgrim's Hatch CM15 130 FU43
Hatch Side, Chig. IG7 125 EN50
Hatchwood Cl, Wdf.Grn. IG8
off Sunset Av 124 EF49
Hatcliffe Cl, SE3 47 L10
Hatcliffe St, SE10 35 L10
Hatfeild Cl, Mitch. CR4 222 DD98
Hatfeild Mead, Mord. SM4 222 DA99
Hatfeild Prim Sch, Mord. SM4
off Lower Morden La 221 CY100
HATFIELD, AL9 & AL10 67 CV17
Hatfield 67 CW17
Hatfield Av, Hat. AL10 66 CS15
Hatfield Business Pk,
Hat. AL10 66 CR15
Hatfield Cl, SE14 45 J5
Hornchurch RM12 150 FK64
Hutton CM13 131 GD45
Ilford IG6 147 EP55
Sutton SM2 240 DA109
West Byfleet KT14 234 BH112
Hatfield Cres, Hem.H. HP2 62 BM16
HATFIELD GARDEN VILLAGE,
Hat. AL10 51 CU14
Hatfield Ho & Pk, Hat. AL9 67 CX18
HATFIELD HYDE, Welw.G.C. AL7 51 CZ12
Hatfield Ms, Dag. RM9 168 EY66
Hatfield Pk, Hat. AL9 67 CX18
Hatfield Rd, E15 13 K2
W4 180 CR75
W13 159 CG74
Ashtead KT21 254 CM119
Chafford Hundred RM16 191 FX77
Dagenham RM9 168 EY65
Hatfield AL9 52 DE14
Potters Bar EN6 86 DC30
St. Albans AL1, AL4 65 CF20
Slough SL1 174 AU75
Watford WD24 97 BV39
Hatfields, SE1 30 F2
Loughton IG10 107 EP41
Hatfield Tunnel, Hat. AL10 67 CT17
Hathaway Cl, Brom. BR2 227 EM102
Ilford IG6 125 EP51
Ruislip HA4
off Stafford Rd 137 BT63
Stanmore HA7 117 CG50
Hathaway Ct, St.Alb. AL4 66 CL20
Hathaway Cres, E12 167 EM65
Hathaway Gdns, W13 159 CF71
Grays RM17
off Hathaway Rd 192 GA76
Romford RM6 148 EX57
Hathaway Prim Sch, W13
off Hathaway Gdns 159 CF71
Hathaway Rd, Croy. CR0 223 DP101
Grays RM17 192 GB77
Hatherleigh Cl, NW7 119 CX52
Chessington KT9 237 CK106
Morden SM4 222 DA98
Hatherleigh Gdns, Pot.B. EN6 86 DD32
Hatherleigh Rd, Ruis. HA4 137 BU61
Hatherleigh Way, Rom. RM3 128 FK53
Hatherley Cres, Sid. DA14 208 EU89
Hatherley Gdns, E6 24 F4
N8 143 DL58
Hatherley Gro, W2 15 L8
Hatherley Ms, E17 145 EA56
Hatherley Rd, E17 145 DZ56
Richmond TW9 180 CM81
Sidcup DA14 208 EU91
Hatherley St, SW1 29 M9
Hathern Gdns, SE9 207 EN91
Hatherop Rd, Hmptn. TW12 198 BZ94
Hathersage Ct, N1 9 M2
Hathersham Cl, Smallfield
RH6 291 DN147
Hathersham La, Smallfield
RH6 289 DK144
Hatherwood, Lthd. KT22 253 CK121
Hathorne Cl, SE15 44 F8
Hathway St, SE15 45 H9
Hathway Ter, SE14
off Hathway St 45 J9
Hatley Av, Ilf. IG6 147 EQ56
Hatley Cl, N11 120 DF50
Hatley Rd, N4 143 DM61
Hatteraick St, SE16 33 H4
Hattersfield Cl, Belv. DA17 188 EZ77
Hatters La, Wat. WD18 97 BR44
HATTON, Felt. TW14 177 BT84
Hatton Av, Slou. SL2 153 AR70
Hatton Cl, SE18 187 ER80
Chafford Hundred RM16 191 FX76
Northfleet DA11 212 GE90
Hatton Cross 177 BT84
Hatton Cross 177 BT84
Hatton Cross, Felt. TW14 177 BT84
Hatton Cross Rbt,
Lon.Hthrw Air. TW6 177 BS83
Hatton Gdn, EC1 18 F6
Hatton Gdns, Mitch. CR4 222 DF99
Hatton Grn, Felt. TW14 177 BU84
Hatton Gro, West Dr. UB7 176 BK75
Hatton Ho, E1 20 D10
Hatton Ms, Green. DA9 191 FW84
Hatton Pl, EC1 18 F5
Hatton Rd, Chsht EN8 89 DX29
Croydon CR0 223 DN102
Feltham TW14 197 BS85
London Heathrow Airport
TW6 177 BT84
Hatton Row, NW8 16 B5
Hatton Sch, Wdf.Grn.
IG8 *off Roding La S* 146 EK55
Hatton St, NW8 16 B5
Hatton Wk, Enf. EN2
off London Rd 104 DR42
Hatton Wall, EC1 18 E6
Haul Rd, NW1 8 A10
Haunch of Venison Yd, W1 17 J9
Hauteville Ct Gdns, W6
off Stamford Brook Av 181 CT76
Havana Cl, Rom. RM1
off Exchange St 149 FE57
Havana Rd, SW19 202 DA89
Havannah St, E14 34 B5
Havant Rd, E17 145 EC55
Havelock Cl, W12
off India Way 161 CV73
Havelock Pl, Har. HA1 139 CE58
Havelock Prim Sch, Sthl.
UB2 *off Havelock Rd* 178 BZ76
Havelock Rd, N17 122 DU54
SW19 202 DC92
Belvedere DA17 188 EZ77
Bromley BR2 226 EJ98
Croydon CR0 224 DT102
Dartford DA1 209 FH87
Gravesend DA11 213 GF88
Harrow HA3 139 CE55
Kings Langley WD4 80 BN28
Southall UB2 178 BZ76
Havelock St, N1 8 B8
Ilford IG1 147 EP61
Havelock Ter, SW8 41 K5
Havelock Wk, SE23 204 DW88
Haven, The, SE26 204 DV92
Grays RM16 193 GF78
Richmond TW9 180 CN83
Sunbury-on-Thames TW16 197 BU94
Havenbury Ind Est, Dor.
RH4 *off Station Rd* 285 CG135
Haven Cl, SE9 207 EM90
SW19 201 CX90
Esher KT10 219 CE103
Hatfield AL10 67 CT17
Hayes UB4 157 BS71
Istead Rise DA13 213 GF94
Sidcup DA14 208 EW93
Swanley BR8 229 FF96
Haven Ct, Esher KT10
off Portsmouth Rd 219 CE103
Haven Dr, Epsom KT19 238 CP110
Havengore Av, Grav. DA12 213 GL87
Haven Grn, W5 159 CK72
Haven Grn Ct, W5 159 CK72
Havenhurst Ri, Enf. EN2 103 DN40
Haven La, W5 160 CL72
Haven Ms, N1 8 F7
Haven Pl, W5 159 CK73
Esher KT10 219 CE103
Grays RM16 192 GC75
Haven Rd, Ashf. TW15 197 BP91
Havensfield, Chipper. WD4 80 BH31
Haven St, NW1 7 J7
Haven Way, Epsom KT19 238 CP111
Havenwood, Wem. HA9 140 CP62
Havenwood Cl, Gt Warley
CM13 *off Wilmot Grn* 129 FW51
Havercroft Cl, St.Alb. AL3 64 CB22
Haverfield Gdns, Rich. TW9 180 CN80
Haverfield Rd, E3 21 L2
Haverford Way, Edg. HA8 118 CM53
Haverhill Rd, E4 123 EC46
SW12 203 DJ88
HAVERING-ATTE-BOWER,
Rom. RM4 127 FE48
**Havering Coll of Further &
Higher Ed**, Ardleigh Grn
Campus, Horn. RM11
off Ardleigh Grn Rd 150 FL56
Quarles Campus, Harold Hill
RM3 *off Tring Gdns* 128 FL49
Havering Dr, Rom. RM1 149 FE56
Havering Gdns, Rom. RM6 148 EW57
Havering Music Sch, Horn.
RM11 *off The Walk* 150 FM61
HAVERING PARK, Rom. RM5 126 FA50
Havering Rd, Rom. RM1 149 FD55
Havering 6th Form Coll, Horn.
RM11 *off Wingletye La* 150 FM60
Havering St, E1 21 J9
Havering Way, Bark. IG11 168 EV69
Havers Av, Hersham KT12 236 BX106
Haversfield Est, Brent. TW8 180 CL78
Haversham Cl, Twick. TW1 199 CK86
Haversham Pl, N6 142 DF61
Haverstock Ct, Orp. BR5 228 EU96
Haverstock Hill, NW3 6 D3
Haverstock Pl, N1
off Haverstock St 19 H2
Haverstock Rd, NW5 6 G3
Haverstock Sch, NW3 6 G5
Haverstock St, N1 19 H1
Haverthwaite Rd, Orp. BR6 227 ER103
Havil St, SE5 43 N5
Havisham Pl, SE19 203 DP93
Hawarden Gro, SE24 204 DQ87
Hawarden Hill, NW2 141 CU62
Hawarden Rd, E17 145 DX56
Caterham CR3 258 DQ121
Haward Rd, Hodd. EN11 71 EC15
Hawbridge Rd, E11 145 ED60
Hawes Cl, Nthwd. HA6 115 BT52
Hawes Down Inf Sch, W.Wick.
BR4 *off The Mead* 225 ED102
Hawes Down Jun Sch, W.Wick.
BR4 *off The Mead* 225 ED102
Hawes La, E4 105 EC38
West Wickham BR4 225 EC102
Hawes Rd, N18 122 DV51
Bromley BR1 226 EH95
Tadworth KT20
off Hatch Gdns 255 CX120
Hawes St, N1 9 H7
Haweswater Dr, Wat. WD25 82 BW33
Haweswater Ho, Islw. TW7
off Summerwood Rd 199 CF85
Hawfield Bk, Orp. BR6 228 EX104
Hawfield Gdns, Park St AL2 83 CD26
Hawgood St, E3 22 B7
Hawk Cl, Wal.Abb. EN9 90 EG34
Hawkdene, E4 105 EB44
**Hawkedale Inf - A Foundation
Sch**, Sun. TW16
off Stratton Rd 217 BT97
Hawkenbury, Harl. CM19 73 EN17
Hawke Pk Rd, N22 143 DP55
Hawke Pl, SE16 33 K4
Hawke Rd, SE19 204 DS93
Hawker Pl, E17 123 EC54
Hawker Rd, Croy. CR0 241 DN107
Hawkesbury Cl, Ilf. IG6 126 EV49
Hawkesbury Rd, SW15 201 CV85
Hawkes Cl, Grays RM17
off New Rd 192 GB79
Langley SL3 175 BB76
Hawkes Ct, Chesh. HP5 76 AQ30
Hawkesfield Rd, SE23 205 DY89
Hawkesley Cl, Twick. TW1 199 CG91
Hawke's Pl, Sev. TN13 278 FG127
Hawkes Rd, Felt. TW14 197 BU87
Mitcham CR4 222 DE95
Hawkesworth Cl, Nthwd. HA6 115 BS52
Hawke Twr, SE14 45 L3
Hawkewood Rd, Sun. TW16 217 BU97
Hawkhirst Rd, Ken. CR8 258 DR115
Hawkhurst, Cob. KT11 236 CA114
Hawkhurst Gdns, Chess. KT9 238 CL105
Romford RM5 127 FD51
Hawkhurst Rd, SW16 223 DK95
Hawkhurst Way, N.Mal. KT3 220 CR99
West Wickham BR4 225 EB103
Hawkinge Wk, Orp. BR5 228 EV97
Hawkinge Way, Horn. RM12 170 FJ65
Hawkins Av, Grav. DA12 213 GJ91
Hawkins Cl, NW7
off Hale La 118 CR50
Borehamwood WD6
off Banks Rd 100 CQ40
Harrow HA1 139 CD59
Hawkins Dr, Chaff.Hun. RM16 191 FX75
Hawkins Rd, NW10 160 CS66
Teddington TW11 199 CH93
Hawkins Ter, SE7 37 H10
Hawkins Way, SE6 205 EA92
Bovingdon HP3 79 BA26
Hawkley Gdns, SE27 203 DP89
Hawkridge, NW5 7 H4
Hawkridge Cl, Rom. RM6 148 EW59
Hawkridge Dr, Grays RM17 192 GD78
Hawksbrook La, Beck. BR3 225 EB100
Hawkshaw Cl, SW2
off Tierney Rd 203 DL87
Hawkshead, NW1 17 L2
Hawkshead Cl, Brom. BR1 206 EE94
Hawkshead La, N.Mymms AL9 85 CW28
Hawkshead Rd, NW10 161 CT66
W4 180 CS75
Potters Bar EN6 86 DB29
Hawks Hill, B.End SL8 132 AC61
Hawk's Hill, Lthd. KT22 253 CF123
Hawks Hill, N.Wld Bas. CM16 92 FA27
Hawkshill, St.Alb. AL1 65 CG21
Hawkshill Cl, Esher KT10 236 CA107
Hawks Hill Cl, Fetch. KT22 253 CF123
Hawkshill Dr, Felden HP3 61 BE23
Hawkshill Rd, Slou. SL2 153 AN69
Hawkshill Way, Esher KT10 236 BZ107
Hawkslade Rd, SE15 205 DX85
Hawksley Rd, N16 144 DS62
Hawksmead Cl, Enf. EN3 105 DX35
Hawks Ms, SE10 46 F5
Hawksmoor, Shenley WD7 84 CN33
Hawksmoor Cl, E6 24 G8
SE18 187 ES78
Hawksmoor Grn, Hutt. CM13 131 GD43
Hawksmoor Ms, E1 20 E10
Hawksmoor Prim Sch,
SE28 *off Bentham Rd* 168 EV74
Hawksmoor St, W6 38 D3
Hawksmouth, E4 123 EB45
Hawks Rd, Kings.T. KT1 220 CM96
Hawkstone Est, SE16 33 H9
Hawkstone Rd, SE16 33 H9
Hawksview, Cob. KT11 236 BZ113
Hawksway, Stai. TW18 195 BF90
Hawkswell Cl, Wok. GU21 248 AT117
Hawkswell Wk, Wok. GU21
off Lockfield Dr 248 AS117
Hawkswood Gro, Fulmer SL3 155 AZ65
Hawkswood La, Ger.Cr. SL9 135 AZ64
Hawk Ter, Ilf. IG5
off Tiptree Cres 147 EN55

Hawkwell Ct, E4
off Colvin Gdns 123 EC48
Hawkwell Ho, Dag. RM8 148 FA60
Hawkwell Wk, N1 9 K8
Hawkwood Cres, E4 105 EB44
Hawkwood Dell, Bkhm KT23 268 CA126
Hawkwood La, Chis. BR7 227 EQ95
Hawkwood Mt, E5 144 DV60
Hawkwood Ri, Bkhm KT23 268 CA126
Hawlands Dr, Pnr. HA5 138 BY59
HAWLEY, Dart. DA2 210 FM92
Hawley Cl, Hmptn. TW12 198 BZ93
Hawley Cres, NW1 7 K7
Sch Hawley Inf Sch, NW1 7 K7
Hawley Ms, NW1 7 J6
Hawley Mill, Dart. DA2 210 FN91
Hawley Rd, N18 123 DX50
NW1 7 K6
Dartford DA1, DA2 210 FL89
HAWLEY'S CORNER,
West. TN16 261 EN121
Hawley St, NW1 7 J7
Hawley Ter, Dart. DA2 210 FN92
Hawley Vale, Dart. DA2 210 FN92
Hawley Way, Ashf. TW15 196 BN92
Haws La, Stai. TW19 196 BG86
Hawstead La, Orp. BR6 246 EZ106
Hawstead Rd, SE6 205 EB86
Hawsted, Buck.H. IG9 124 EH45
Hawthorn Av, E3 11 N8
N13 121 DL50
Brentwood CM13 131 FZ48
Kew TW9 180 CL82
Rainham RM13 169 FH70
Thornton Heath CR7 223 DP95
● Hawthorn Cen, The
Har. HA1 off Elmgrove Rd 139 CF56
Hawthorn Cl, Abb.L. WD5 81 BU32
Banstead SM7 239 CY114
Gravesend DA12 213 GH91
Hampton TW12 198 CA92
Hertford SG14 53 DN08
Hounslow TW5 177 BV80
Iver SL0 155 BD68
Petts Wood BR5 227 ER100
Redhill RH1
off Bushfield Dr 288 DG139
Watford WD17 97 BT38
Woking GU22 248 AY120
Hawthorn Cres, SW17 202 DG92
South Croydon CR2 242 DW111
Hawthornden Cl, N12
off Fallowfields Dr 120 DE51
Hawthorndene Cl, Brom.
BR2 226 EF103
Hawthorndene Rd, Brom.
BR2 226 EF103
Hawthorn Dr, Denh. UB9 156 BJ65
Harrow HA2 138 BZ58
West Wickham BR4 244 EE105
Hawthorne Av, Bigg.H. TN16 260 EK115
Carshalton SM5 240 DG108
Cheshunt EN7 88 DV31
Harrow HA3 139 CG58
Mitcham CR4 222 DD96
Ruislip HA4 137 BV58
Hawthorne Cl, N1 9 N4
Bromley BR1 227 EM97
Cheshunt EN7 88 DV31
Sutton SM1
off Aultone Way 222 DC103
Hawthorne Ct, Nthwd. HA6
off Ryefield Cres 115 BU54
Walton-on-Thames KT12
off Ambleside Av 218 BX103
Hawthorne Cres, Slou. SL1 154 AS71
West Drayton UB7 176 BM75
Hawthorne Fm Av, Nthlt. UB5 158 BY67
Hawthorne Gro, NW9 140 CQ59
Hawthorne La, Hem.H. HP1 61 BF19
Hawthorne Ms, Grnf. UB6 158 CC72
Hawthorne Pl, Epsom KT17 238 CS112
Hayes UB3 157 BT73
Hawthorne Rd, E17 145 EA55
Bromley BR1 226 EL97
Radlett WD7 83 CG34
Staines-upon-Thames TW18 195 BC92
Hawthornes, Hat. AL10 67 CT20
Hawthorne Way, N9 122 DS47
Guildford GU4 265 BB130
Stanwell TW19 196 BK87
Hawthorn Gdns, W5 179 CK76
Hawthorn Gro, SE20 204 DV94
Barnet EN5 101 CT44
Enfield EN2 104 DR38
Hawthorn Hatch, Brent. TW8 179 CH80
Hawthorn La, Farn.Com. SL2 153 AP65
Sevenoaks TN13 278 FF122
Hawthorn Ms, NW7
off Holders Hill Rd 119 CY53
Hawthorn Pl, Erith DA8 189 FC78
Guildford GU4
off Merrow St 265 BD132
Penn HP10 110 AC47
Hawthorn Rd, N8 143 DK55
N18 122 DT51
NW10 161 CU66
Bexleyheath DA6 188 EZ84
Brentford TW8 179 CH80
Buckhurst Hill IG9 124 EK49
Dartford DA1 210 FK88
Feltham TW13 197 BU88
Hoddesdon EN11 71 EB15
Ripley GU23 250 BG124
Sutton SM1 240 DE107
Wallington SM6 241 DH108
Woking GU22 248 AX120
Hawthorns, Harl. CM18 73 ET19
Welwyn Garden City AL8 51 CX07
Woodford Green IG8 124 EG48
Hawthorns, The, Berk. HP4 60 AU18
Chalfont St. Giles HP8 94 AW40
Colnbrook SL3 175 BF81
Epsom KT17
off Kingston Rd 239 CT107
Hemel Hempstead HP3 61 BF24
Loughton IG10 107 EN42
Maple Cross WD3 113 BD50
Oxted RH8 276 EG133
Ridge EN6 84 CS33
Sch Hawthorns Sch, The, Bletch.
RH1 off Pendell Rd 273 DP131
Hawthorn Wk, W10 14 E4
Hawthorn Way, Chesh. HP5 76 AR29
New Haw KT15 234 BJ110
Redhill RH1 289 DH136
St. Albans AL2 64 CA24
Shepperton TW17 217 BR98
Hawtrees, Rad. WD7 99 CF35
Hawtrey Av, Nthlt. UB5 158 BX68
Hawtrey Cl, Slou. SL1 174 AV75
Hawtrey Dr, Ruis. HA4 137 BU59
Hawtrey Rd, NW3 6 C7
Windsor SL4 173 AQ82
Haxted Rd, Brom. BR1
off North Rd 226 EH95
Haybourn Mead, Hem.H. HP1 62 BH21
Hayburn Way, Horn. RM12 149 FF60
Hay Cl, E15 13 K6
Borehamwood WD6 100 CQ40
Haycroft Cl, Couls. CR5
off Caterham Dr 257 DP118
Haycroft Gdns, NW10 161 CU67
Haycroft Rd, SW2 203 DL85
Surbiton KT6 220 CL104
Hay Currie St, E14 22 D8
Hayday Rd, E16 23 N6
Hayden Ct, Felt. TW13 197 BS91
New Haw KT15 234 BH111
Hayden Rd, Wal.Abb. EN9 105 EC35
Haydens Cl, Orp. BR5 228 EV100
Haydens Pl, W11 14 G8
Haydens Rd, Harl. CM20 73 EQ15
Hayden Way, Rom. RM5 127 FC54
Haydn Av, Pur. CR8 241 DN114
Haydns Ms, W3 160 CQ72
Haydock Av, Nthlt. UB5 158 CA65
Haydock Cl, Horn. RM12 150 FM63
Haydock Grn, Nthlt. UB5
off Haydock Av 158 CA65
Haydon Cl, NW9 140 CQ56
Enfield EN1
off Mortimer Dr 104 DS44
Romford RM3 127 FH52
Haydon Dell, Bushey WD23 98 BZ44
Haydon Dr, Pnr. HA5 137 BU56
Haydon Pk Rd, SW19 202 DB92
Haydon Pl, Guil. GU1 280 AX135
Haydon Rd, Dag. RM8 148 EW61
Watford WD19 98 BY44
Sch Haydon Sch, Eastcote
HA5 off Wiltshire La 137 BT55
⇌ Haydons Road 202 DC92
Haydons Rd, SW19 202 DB92
Haydon St, EC3 20 A10
Haydon Wk, E1 20 B9
Haydon Way, SW11 182 DD84
HAYES, UB3 & UB4 157 BS72
HAYES, Brom. BR2 226 EG103
⇌ Hayes 226 EF102
Hayes, The, Epsom KT18 254 CR119
⇌ Hayes & Harlington 177 BT76
Hayes Barton, Wok. GU22 249 BD116
🔒 Hayes Br Retail Pk,
Hayes UB4 158 BW73
Hayes Bypass, Hayes
UB3, UB4 158 BX70
Hayes Chase, W.Wick. BR4 226 EE99
Hayes Cl, Brom. BR2 226 EG103
Grays RM20 191 FW79
Hayes Ct, SW2 203 DL88
Hayes Cres, NW11 141 CZ57
Sutton SM3 239 CX105
Hayes Dr, Rain. RM13 169 FH66
HAYES END, Hayes UB3 157 BQ71
Hayes End Cl, Hayes UB4 157 BR70
Hayes End Dr, Hayes UB4 157 BR70
Hayesend Ho, SW17
off Blackshaw Rd 202 DC91
Hayes End Rd, Hayes UB4 157 BR70
Hayesford Pk Dr, Brom. BR2 226 EF99
Hayes Gdn, Brom. BR2 226 EG103
Hayes Gro, SE22 184 DT84
Hayes Hill, Brom. BR2 226 EE102
Hayes Hill Rd, Brom. BR2 226 EF102
Hayes La, Beck. BR3 225 EC97
Bromley BR2 226 EG99
Kenley CR8 242 DQ114
Hayes Mead Rd, Brom. BR2 226 EE102
● Hayes Metro Cen,
Hayes UB4 158 BW73
Hayes Pk, Hayes UB4 157 BS70
Sch Hayes Pk Sch, Hayes
UB4 off Raynton Dr 157 BT70
Hayes Pl, NW1 16 D5
Sch Hayes Prim Sch, Hayes
BR2 off George La 226 EH102
Sch Hayes Prim Sch, The,
Ken. CR8 off Hayes La 257 DP116
Hayes Rd, Brom. BR2 226 EG98
Greenhithe DA9 211 FS87
Southall UB2 177 BV77
Sch Hayes Sch, Hayes BR2
off West Common Rd 226 EH103
Hayes St, Brom. BR2 226 EH102
HAYES TOWN, Hayes UB3 177 BS75
Hayes Wk, Brox. EN10
off Landau Way 89 DZ25
Potters Bar EN6 86 DB33
Smallfield RH6 291 DN147
Hayes Way, Beck. BR3 225 EC98
Hayes Wd Av, Brom. BR2 226 EH102
Hayfield Cl, Bushey WD23 98 CB42
Hayfield Pas, E1 21 H5
Hayfield Rd, Orp. BR5 228 EU99
Hayfields, Horl. RH6
off Ryelands 291 DJ147
Hayfield Yd, E1 21 H5
Haygarth Pl, SW19 201 CX92
Hay Grn, Horn. RM11 150 FN58
Haygreen Cl, Kings.T. KT2 200 CP93
Hay Hill, W1 29 K1
Hayland Cl, NW9 140 CR56
Hay La, NW9 140 CR56
Fulmer SL3 134 AX63
Sch Hay La Sch, NW9
off Grove Pk 140 CQ56
Hayles St, SE11 30 G8
Haylett Gdns, Kings.T. KT1
off Anglesea Rd 219 CK98
Hayley Cl, Chaff.Hun. RM16 191 FW76
Hayling Av, Felt. TW13 197 BU90
Hayling Cl, N16 9 P2
Slough SL1 153 AP74
Hayling Rd, Wat. WD19 115 BV47
Haymaker Cl, Uxb. UB10 156 BM66
Hayman Cres, Hayes UB4 157 BR68
Hayman St, N1 9 H7
Haymarket, SW1 29 N1
Haymarket Arc, SW1 29 N1
Haymeads, Welw.G.C. AL8 51 CY06
Haymeads Dr, Esher KT10 236 CC107
Haymer Gdns, Wor.Pk. KT4 221 CU104
Haymerle Rd, SE15 44 C3
Sch Haymerle Sch, SE15 44 C3
Hay Ms, NW3 6 F5
Haymill Cl, Perivale UB6 159 CF69
Haymill Rd, Slou. SL1, SL2 153 AK70
Hayne Rd, Beck. BR3 225 DZ96
Haynes Cl, N11 120 DG48
N17 122 DV52
SE3 186 EE83
Ripley GU23 250 BH122
Slough SL3 175 AZ78
Welwyn Garden City AL7 52 DA10
Haynes Dr, N9 122 DV48
Haynes La, SE19 204 DS93
Haynes Mead, Berk. HP4 60 AU17
Haynes Pk Ct, Horn. RM11 150 FJ57
Haynes Rd, Horn. RM11 150 FK57
Northfleet DA11 213 GF90
Wembley HA0 160 CL66
Hayne St, EC1 19 H6
Haynt Wk, SW20 221 CY97
Hayre Dr, Sthl. UB2 178 BX78
Hayse Hill, Wind. SL4 173 AK81
🔒 Hay's Galleria, SE1 31 N2
Hay's La, SE1 31 N3
Haysleigh Gdns, SE20 224 DU96
Hay's Ms, W1 29 J1
Haysoms Cl, Rom. RM1 149 FE56
Haystall Cl, Hayes UB4 157 BS68
Hay St, E2 10 D9
Hays Wk, Sutt. SM2 239 CX110
Hayter Ct, E11 146 EH61
Hayter Rd, SW2 203 DL85
Hayton Cl, E8 10 B5
Haywain, Oxt. RH8 275 ED130
Hayward Cl, SW19 222 DB95
Dartford DA1 209 FD85
Hayward Copse, Loud. WD3 96 BK42
Hayward Dr, Dart. DA1 210 FM89
★ Hayward Gall, SE1 30 D2
Hayward Gdns, SW15 201 CW86
Hayward Rd, N20 120 DC47
Thames Ditton KT7 219 CG102
Haywards Cl, Chad.Hth RM6 148 EV57
Hutton CM13 131 GE44
Haywards Mead, Eton Wick
SL4 173 AM78
Hayward's Pl, EC1 18 G5
Haywood Cl, Pnr. HA5 116 BX54
Haywood Ct, Wal.Abb. EN9 90 EF34
Haywood Dr, Chorl. WD3 95 BF43
Hemel Hempstead HP3 61 BF23
Haywood Pk, Chorl. WD3 95 BF43
Haywood Ri, Orp. BR6 245 ES105
Haywood Rd, Brom. BR2 226 EK98
Hazel Av, Guil. GU1 264 AW130
West Drayton UB7 176 BN76
Hazelbank, Crox.Grn WD3 97 BQ44
Surbiton KT5 220 CQ102
Hazelbank Ct, Cher. KT16 216 BJ102
Hazelbank Rd, SE6 205 ED89
Chertsey KT16 216 BJ102
Hazelbourne Rd, SW12 203 DH86
Hazelbrouck Gdns, Ilf. IG6 125 ER52
Hazelbury Av, Abb.L. WD5 81 BQ32
Hazelbury Cl, SW19 222 DA96
Hazelbury Grn, N9 122 DS48
Sch Hazelbury Inf Sch, N9
off Haselbury Rd 122 DS48
Sch Hazelbury Jun Sch, N9
off Haselbury Rd 122 DS48
Hazelbury La, N9 122 DS48
Hazel Cl, N13 122 DR48
N19 143 DJ61
NW9 118 CS54
SE15 44 D9
Brentford TW8 179 CH80
Croydon CR0 225 DX101
Englefield Green TW20 194 AV93
Hornchurch RM12 149 FH62
Mitcham CR4 223 DK98
Reigate RH2 288 DC136
Twickenham TW2 198 CC87
Waltham Cross EN7 88 DS26
Hazel Ct, Shenley WD7 84 CM33
Hazelcroft, Pnr. HA5 116 CA51
Hazelcroft Cl, Uxb. UB10 156 BM66
Hazeldean Rd, NW10 160 CR66
Hazeldell Link, Hem.H. HP1 61 BF21
Hazeldell Rd, Hem.H. HP1 61 BF21
Hazeldene, Add. KT15 234 BJ106
Waltham Cross EN8 89 DY32
Hazeldene Ct, Ken. CR8 258 DR115
Hazeldene Dr, Pnr. HA5 138 BW55
Hazeldene Gdns, Uxb. UB10 157 BQ67
Hazeldene Rd, Ilf. IG3 148 EV61
Welling DA16 188 EW82
Hazeldon Rd, SE4 205 DY85
Hazel Dr, Erith DA8 189 FH81
Ripley GU23 265 BF125
South Ockendon RM15 171 FW69
Hazeleigh, Brwd. CM13 131 GB48
Hazeleigh Gdns, Wdf.Grn. IG8 124 EL50
Hazel End, Swan. BR8 229 FE99
Hazel Gdns, Edg. HA8 118 CP49
Grays RM16 192 GE76
Sawbridgeworth CM21 58 EZ06
Hazelgreen Cl, N21 121 DP46
Hazel Gro, SE26 205 DX91
Enfield EN1
off Dimsdale Dr 104 DU44
Feltham TW13 197 BU88
Hatfield AL10 67 CT21
Orpington BR6 227 EP103
Romford RM6 148 EY55
Staines-upon-Thames TW18 196 BH93
Watford WD25
off Cedar Wd Dr 97 BV35
Welwyn Garden City AL7 52 DB08
Wembley HA0
off Carlyon Rd 160 CL67
Hazel Gro Est, SE26 205 DX91
Hazel Ho, NW3
off Maitland Pk Rd 6 F4
Hazelhurst, Beck. BR3 225 ED95
Horley RH6 291 DJ147
Hazelhurst Cl, Guil. GU4
off Weybrook Dr 265 BB129
Hazelhurst Ct, SE6
off Beckenham Hill Rd 205 EC92
Hazelhurst Rd, SW17 202 DC91
Burnham SL1 152 AJ68
Hazel La, Ilf. IG6 125 EP52
Richmond TW10 200 CL89
Hazell Cres, Rom. RM5 127 FB53
Hazell Pk, Amer. HP7 77 AR39
Hazells Rd, Grav. DA13 212 GD92
Hazellville Rd, N19 143 DK59
Hazell Way, Stoke P. SL2 154 AT65
Hazel Mead, Barn. EN5 101 CV43
Epsom KT17 239 CU110
Hazelmere Cl, Felt. TW14 197 BR86
Leatherhead KT22 253 CH119
Northolt UB5 158 BZ68
Hazelmere Dr, Nthlt. UB5 158 BZ68
Hazelmere Gdns, Horn. RM11 149 FH57
Hazelmere Rd, NW6 5 H8
Northolt UB5 158 BZ69
Petts Wood BR5 227 EQ98
St. Albans AL4 65 CJ17
Hazelmere Wk, Nthlt. UB5 158 BZ68
Hazelmere Way, Brom. BR2 226 EG100
Hazel Ms, N8 143 DN55
Hazel Ri, Horn. RM11 150 FJ58
Hazel Rd, E15 13 J2
NW10 14 A2
Berkhamsted HP4 60 AX20
Dartford DA1 210 FK89
Erith DA8 189 FG81
Park Street AL2 82 CB28
Reigate RH2 288 DC136
West Byfleet KT14 234 BG114
Hazels, The, Welw. AL6 52 DE05
Hazeltree La, Nthlt. UB5 158 BY69
Hazel Tree Rd, Wat. WD24 97 BV37
Hazel Wk, Brom. BR2 227 EN100
North Holmwood RH5
off Lake Vw 285 CJ139
Hazel Way, E4 123 DZ51
SE1 32 A8
Chipstead CR5 256 DF119
Fetcham KT22 252 CC122
Hazelway Cl, Fetch. KT22 252 CC123
HAZELWOOD, Sev. TN14 245 ER111
Hazelwood, Dor. RH4 285 CH137
Loughton IG10 106 EK43
Hazelwood Av, Mord. SM4 222 DB98
Hazelwood Cl, W5 180 CL75
Chesham HP5 76 AR29
Harrow HA2 138 CB56
Hazelwood Ct, NW10
off Neasden La N 140 CS62
Hazelwood Cres, N13 121 DN49
Hazelwood Cft, Surb. KT6 220 CL100
Hazelwood Dr, Pnr. HA5 115 BV54
St. Albans AL4 65 CJ19
Hazelwood Gdns, Pilg.Hat.
CM15 130 FU44
Hazelwood Gro, S.Croy. CR2 242 DV113
Hazelwood Hts, Oxt. RH8 276 EG131
Sch Hazelwood Inf Sch, N13
off Hazelwood La 121 DN49
Sch Hazelwood Jun Sch, N13
off Hazelwood La 121 DN49
Hazelwood La, N13 121 DN49
Abbots Langley WD5 81 BQ32
Chipstead CR5 256 DF119
Hazelwood Pk Cl, Chig. IG7 125 ES50
Hazelwood Rd, E17 145 DY57
Croxley Green WD3 97 BQ44
Cudham TN14 245 ER112
Enfield EN1 104 DT44
Knaphill GU21 248 AS118
Oxted RH8 276 EH132
Sch Hazelwood Sch, Lmpfld
RH8 off Wolfs Hill 276 EG131
Hazlebury Rd, SW6 39 L8
Hazledean Rd, Croy. CR0 224 DR103
Hazledene Rd, W4 180 CQ79
Hazlemere Gdns, Wor.Pk. KT4 221 CV102
Hazlemere Rd, Penn HP10 110 AC45
Slough SL2 154 AW74
Hazlewell Rd, SW15 201 CV85
Hazlewood Cl, E5 145 DY62
Hazlewood Cres, W10 14 F5
Hazlewood Ms, SW9 42 A10
Hazlewood Twr, W10 14 F5
Hazlitt Cl, Felt. TW13 198 BY91
Hazlitt Ms, W14 26 E7
Hazlitt Rd, W14 26 E7
Hazon Way, Epsom KT19 238 CQ112
Heacham Av, Uxb. UB10 137 BQ62
Headcorn Pl, Th.Hth. CR7
off Headcorn Rd 223 DM98
Headcorn Rd, N17 122 DT52
Bromley BR1 206 EF92
Thornton Heath CR7 223 DM98
Headfort Pl, SW1 29 H5
Headingley Cl, Chsht EN7 88 DT26
Ilford IG6 125 ET51
Shenley WD7 84 CL32
Headingley Dr, Beck. BR3 205 EA93
Headington Pl, Slou. SL2 154 AT74
Headington Rd, SW18 202 DC88
Headlam Rd, SW4 203 DK86
Headlam St, E1 20 F5
Headlands Dr, Berk. HP4 60 AX18
HEADLEY, Epsom KT18 270 CQ125
Headley App, Ilf. IG2 147 EN57
Headley Av, Wall. SM6 241 DM106
Headley Chase, Warley CM14 130 FW49
Headley Cl, Epsom KT19 238 CN107
Headley Common, Gt Warley
CM13 off Warley Gap 129 FV52
Headley Common Rd, Headley
KT18 270 CR127
Tadworth KT20 270 CR127
Headley Ct, SE26 204 DV92
Headley Dr, Epsom KT18 255 CV119
Ilford IG2 147 EP58
New Addington CR0 243 EB108
Headley Gro, Tad. KT20 255 CV120
★ Headley Heath, Epsom
KT18 270 CP128
Headley Heath App, Box H.
KT20 270 CP130
Mickleham RH5 270 CP130
Headley La, Mick. RH5 269 CJ129
Headley Rd, Lthd. KT22 253 CK123
Tyrrell's Wood KT18 254 CN123
Woodcote KT18 254 CP118
Head's Ms, W11 15 J9
HEADSTONE, Har. HA2 138 CC56
Headstone Dr, Har. HA1, HA3 139 CE55
Headstone Gdns, Har. HA2 138 CC56
⊖ Headstone Lane 116 CB53
Headstone La, Har. HA2, HA3 138 CB56
Headstone Rd, Har. HA1 139 CE57
Head St, E1 21 J9
Headway, The, Epsom KT17 239 CT109
Headway Cl, Rich. TW10
off Locksmeade Rd 199 CJ91
Heald St, SE14 46 A6
Healey Rd, Wat. WD18 97 BT44
Healey St, NW1 7 J5
Healy Dr, Orp. BR6 245 ET105
Heanor Ct, E5 off Pedro St 145 DX63
Heards La, Shenf. CM15 131 FZ41
Hearle Way, Hat. AL10 66 CS16
Hearne Ct, Ch.St.G. HP8
off Gordon Way 112 AV48
Hearne Rd, W4 180 CN79
Hearnes Cl, Seer Grn HP9 111 AR50
Hearnes Meadow, Seer Grn
HP9 111 AR50
Hearn Ri, Nthlt. UB5 158 BX67
Hearn Rd, Rom. RM1 149 FF58
Hearn's Bldgs, SE17 31 M9
Hearnshaw St, E14 21 M7
Hearn's Rd, Orp. BR5 228 EW98
Hearn St, EC2 19 P5
Hearnville Rd, SW12 202 DG88
🔒 Heart, The, Walt. KT12
off New Zealand Av 217 BU102
H Heart Hosp, The, W1 17 H7
Sch Heartlands High Sch, N22 121 DL54
Heath, The, W7
off Lower Boston Rd 159 CE74
Chaldon CR3 258 DQ124
Hatfield Heath CM22 59 FG05
Radlett WD7 83 CG33
Heathacre, Colnbr. SL3
off Park St 175 BE81
Heatham Pk, Twick. TW2 199 CF87
Heath Av, Bexh. DA7 188 EX79
St. Albans AL3 65 CD18
Heathbourne Rd, Bushey Hth
WD23 117 CE47
Stanmore HA7 117 CE47
Heathbridge, Wey. KT13 234 BN108
Sch Heathbrook Prim Sch, SW8 41 L9
Heath Brow, NW3
off North End Way 142 DC62
Hemel Hempstead HP1 62 BJ22
● Heath Business Cen, The,
Salf. RH1 288 DG143
Heath Cl, NW11 142 DB59
W5 160 CM70
Banstead SM7 240 DB114
Harlington UB3 177 BR80
Hemel Hempstead HP1 62 BJ21
Orpington BR5
off Sussex Rd 228 EW100
Potters Bar EN6 86 DB30
Romford RM2 149 FG55
South Croydon CR2 241 DP107
Stanwell TW19 196 BJ86
Heathclose, Swan. BR8
off Moreton Cl 229 FE96
Heath Cl, Vir.W. GU25 214 AX98
Heathclose Av, Dart. DA1 209 FH87
Heathclose Rd, Dart. DA1 209 FG88
Heathcock Ct, WC2
off Exchange Ct 30 B1
Heathcote, Tad. KT20 255 CX121
Heathcote Av, Hat. AL10 67 CU16
Ilford IG5 125 EM54
Heathcote Ct, Ilf. IG5
off Heathcote Av 125 EM54
Heathcote Gdns, Harl. CM17 74 EY15
Heathcote Gro, E4 123 EC48
Heathcote Pt, E9 11 J5
Heathcote Rd, Epsom KT18 238 CR114
Twickenham TW1 199 CH86
Sch Heathcote Sch, E4
off Normanton Pk 124 EE47
Heathcote St, WC1 18 C4
Heathcote Way, West Dr. UB7 156 BK74
Heath Cotts, Pot.B. EN6
off Heath Rd 86 DB30
Heath Ct, SE9 207 EQ88
Hertford SG14 53 DM08
Hounslow TW4 178 BZ84
Uxbridge UB8 156 BL66
Heathcroft, NW11 142 DB60
W5 160 CM70
Welwyn Garden City AL7 52 DC09
Heathcroft Av, Sun. TW16 197 BT94
Heathcroft Gdns, E17 123 ED53
Heathdale Av, Houns. TW4 178 BY83
Heathdene, Tad. KT20
off Brighton Rd 255 CY119
Heathdene Dr, Belv. DA17 189 FB77
Heathdene Manor, Wat. WD17
off Grandfield Ave 97 BT39
Heathdene Rd, SW16 203 DM94
Wallington SM6 241 DH108
Heathdown Rd, Wok. GU22 249 BD115
Heath Dr, NW3 5 L1
SW20 221 CW98
Potters Bar EN6 86 DA30
Romford RM2 127 FG53
Send GU23 249 BB123
Sutton SM2 240 DC109
Theydon Bois CM16 107 ES35
Walton on the Hill KT20 271 CU125
Heathedge, SE26 204 DV89
Heath End Rd, Bex. DA5 209 FE88
Heather Av, Rom. RM1 127 FD54
Heatherbank, SE9 187 EM82
Chislehurst BR7 227 EN96
Heatherbank Cl, Cob. KT11 236 BX111
Dartford DA1 209 FE86
Heather Cl, E6 25 N9
N7 143 DM62
SE13 205 ED86
SW8 41 J10
Abbots Langley WD5 81 BU32
Guildford GU2 264 AV132
Hampton TW12 218 BZ95
Isleworth TW7
off Harvesters Cl 199 CD85
Kingswood KT20 255 CY122
New Haw KT15 234 BH110
Pilgrim's Hatch CM15 130 FU43
Redhill RH1 273 DH130
Romford RM1 127 FF55
Uxbridge UB8 156 BM71
Woking GU21 248 AW115
Heatherdale Cl, Kings.T. KT2 200 CN93
Heatherdene, W.Hors. KT24 267 BR125
Heatherdene Cl, N12 120 DC53
Mitcham CR4 222 DE98
Heatherden Grn, Iver SL0 155 BC67
Heather Dr, Dart. DA1 209 FG87
Enfield EN2 103 DP40
Romford RM1 127 FD54
Heather End, Swan. BR8 229 FD98
Heatherfield La, Wey. KT13 235 BS106
Heatherfields, New Haw KT15 234 BH110
Heatherfold Way, Pnr. HA5 137 BT55
Heather Gdns, NW11 141 CY58
Romford RM1 127 FD54
Sutton SM2 240 DA107

Heather Gdns, Waltham Abbey EN9 105 EC36
Heather Glen, Rom. RM1 127 FD54
Heatherlands, Horl. RH6
off Stockfield 291 DH147
Sunbury-on-Thames TW16 197 BU93
Heather La, Wat. WD24 97 BT35
West Drayton UB7 156 BL72
Heatherlea Gro, Wor.Pk. KT4 221 CV102
Heatherley Dr, Ilf. IG5 146 EL55
Coll Heatherley's Sch of Fine Art, SW10 39 P5
Heathermount, Guil. GU3
off Broad St 264 AS132
Heather Pk Dr, Wem. HA0 160 CN66
Heather Pl, Esher KT10
off Park Rd 236 CB105
Heather Ri, Bushey WD23 98 BZ40
Heather Rd, E4 123 DZ51
NW2 141 CT61
SE12 206 EG89
Welwyn Garden City AL8 51 CW11
Heathers, The, Stai. TW19 196 BM86
Heatherset Cl, Esher KT10 236 CC106
Heatherset Gdns, SW16 203 DM94
Heatherside Cl, Bkhm KT23 268 BZ125
Heatherside Dr, Vir.W. GU25 214 AU100
Heatherside Gdns, Farn.Com. SL2 133 AR62
Heatherside Rd, Epsom KT19 238 CR108
Sidcup DA14 off Wren Rd 208 EW90
Heathersland, Dor. RH4 285 CJ139
Sch Heatherton Ho Sch, Amer. HP6 off Copperkins La 77 AQ36
Heatherton Pk, Amer. HP6 77 AP36
Heatherton Ter, N3 120 DB54
Heathervale Caravan Pk, New Haw KT15 234 BJ110
Heathervale Rd, New Haw KT15 234 BH110
Heathervale Way, New Haw KT15 234 BJ110
Heather Wk, W10 14 F4
Edgware HA8 118 CP50
Twickenham TW2
off Hedley Rd 198 CA87
Whiteley Village KT12
off Octagon Rd 235 BT110
Heather Way, Chobham GU24 232 AS108
Hemel Hempstead HP2 62 BK19
Potters Bar EN6 85 CZ32
Romford RM1 127 FD54
South Croydon CR2 243 DX109
Stanmore HA7 117 CF51
Heatherwood Cl, E12 146 EJ61
Heatherwood Dr, Hayes UB4 157 BR68
Heath Fm Ct, Wat. WD17 97 BR37
Heath Fm La, St.Alb. AL3 65 CE18
Heathfield, E4 123 EC48
Chislehurst BR7 207 EQ93
Cobham KT11 236 CA114
Heathfield Av, SW18
off Heathfield Rd 202 DD87
South Croydon CR2 243 DY109
Heathfield Cl, E16 24 E6
Keston BR2 244 EJ106
Potters Bar EN6 86 DB30
Watford WD19 116 BW45
Woking GU22 249 BA118
Heathfield Ct, SE14 45 H4
St. Albans AL1
off Avenue Rd 65 CE19
Heathfield Dr, Mitch. CR4 222 DE95
Redhill RH1 288 DE139
Heathfield Gdns, NW11 141 CX58
SE3 47 J9
SW18 202 DD86
W4 180 CQ78
Croydon CR0
off Coombe Rd 242 DQ105
Heathfield La, Chis. BR7 207 EP93
Heathfield N, Twick. TW2 199 CF87
Sch Heathfield Nurs & Inf & Jun Schs, Twick. TW2
off Cobbett Rd 198 CA88
Heathfield Pk, NW2 4 A5
Heathfield Pk Dr, Chad.Hth RM6 148 EV57
Heathfield Ri, Ruis. HA4 137 BQ59
Heathfield Rd, SW18 202 DC86
W3 180 CP75
Bexleyheath DA6 188 EZ84
Bromley BR1 206 EF94
Burnham SL1 132 AG62
Bushey WD23 98 BY42
Croydon CR0 242 DR105
Hersham KT12 236 BY105
Keston BR2 244 EJ106
Sevenoaks TN13 278 FF122
Woking GU22 249 BA118
Sch Heathfield Sch, Pnr. HA5
off Beaulieu Dr 138 BX59
Heathfields Cl, Ashtd. KT21 253 CJ118
Heathfields Ct, Houns. TW4
off Heathlands Way 198 BY85
Heathfield S, Twick. TW2 199 CF87
Heathfield Sq, SW18 202 DD87
Heathfield St, W11 26 E1
Heathfield Ter, SE18 187 ET79
W4 180 CQ78
Heathfield Vale, S.Croy. CR2 243 DX109
Heath Gdns, Twick. TW1 199 CF88
Heathgate, NW11 142 DB58
Hertford Heath SG13 54 DV13
Heathgate Pl, NW3
off Agincourt Rd 6 F2
Heath Gro, SE20 off Maple Rd 204 DW94
Sunbury-on-Thames TW16 197 BT94
Heath Hill, Dor. RH4 285 CH136
Heath Hurst Rd, NW3 6 C1
Heathhurst Rd, S.Croy. CR2 242 DS109
Heathland Rd, N16 144 DS60
Heathlands, Tad. KT20 255 CX122
Sch Heathland Sch, The, Houns. TW4 off Wellington Rd S 198 BZ86
Heathlands Cl, Sun. TW16 217 BT96
Twickenham TW1 199 CF89
Woking GU21 232 AY114
Heathlands Dr, St.Alb. AL3 65 CE18
Heathlands Ri, Dart. DA1 209 FH86
Sch Heathlands Sch, St.Alb. AL3 off Heathlands Dr 65 CE17
Heathlands Way, Houns. TW4 198 BY85
Heath La, SE3 47 H9
Albury GU5 282 BL141
Dartford (Lower) DA1 210 FJ88
Dartford (Upper) DA1 209 FG89
Hemel Hempstead HP1 62 BJ22
Hertford Heath SG13 54 DW13
Heathlee Rd, SE3 186 EF84
Dartford DA1 209 FE86
Heathley End, Chis. BR7 207 EQ93
Heathmans Rd, SW6 39 H7
Heath Mead, SW19 201 CX90
Sch Heathmere Prim Sch, SW15 off Alton Rd 201 CU88
Heath Ms, Ripley GU23 250 BH123
Heath Pk Ct, Rom. RM2
off Heath Pk Rd 149 FG57
Heath Pk Dr, Brom. BR1 226 EL97
Heath Pk Rd, Rom. RM2 149 FG57
Heath Pas, NW3 142 DB61
Heath Ridge Grn, Cob. KT11 236 CA113
Heath Ri, SW15 201 CX86
Bromley BR2 226 EF100
Ripley GU23 250 BH123
Virginia Water GU25 214 AX98
Westcott RH4 284 CC138
Heath Rd, SW8 41 K9
Beaconsfield HP9 132 AG55
Bexley DA5 209 FC88
Caterham CR3 258 DR123
Dartford DA1 209 FF86
Grays RM16 193 GG75
Harrow HA1 138 CC59
Hounslow TW3 178 CB84
Oxshott KT22 236 CC112
Potters Bar EN6 86 DA30
Romford RM6 148 EX59
St. Albans AL1 65 CE19
Thornton Heath CR7 224 DQ97
Twickenham TW1, TW2 199 CF88
Uxbridge UB10 157 BQ70
Watford WD19 116 BX45
Weybridge KT13 234 BN106
Woking GU21 249 AZ115
Heathrow, Goms. GU5 283 BQ139
★ Heathrow Airport (London), Houns. TW6 177 BP81
● Heathrow Causeway Centre, Houns. TW4 177 BV83
Heathrow Cl, West Dr. UB7 176 BH81
⇌ Heathrow Express Terminal 4 197 BP85
⇌ Heathrow Express Terminal 5 176 BJ83
⇌ Heathrow Express Terminals 1 & 3 177 BP83
● Heathrow Int Trd Est, Houns. TW4 177 BV83
Sch Heathrow Prim Sch, Sipson UB7 off Harmondsworth La 176 BM79
⊖ Heathrow Terminal 5 176 BJ83
⊖ Heathrow Terminal 4 197 BP85
⊖ Heathrow Terminals 1 & 3 177 BP83
Heathrow Tunnel App, Lon.Hthrw Air. TW6 177 BP83
Heathrow Vehicle Tunnel, Lon.Hthrw Air. TW6 177 BP81
Heaths Cl, Enf. EN1 104 DS40
Heath Side, NW3 142 DD63
Heathside, NW11 142 DA60
Colney Heath AL4 66 CP23
Esher KT10 219 CE104
Hounslow TW4 198 BZ87
Heath Side, Petts Wd BR5 227 EQ102
Heathside, St.Alb. AL1 65 CE18
Weybridge KT13 235 BP106
Heathside Av, Bexh. DA7 188 EY81
Heathside Cl, Esher KT10 219 CE104
Ilford IG2 147 ER57
Northwood HA6 115 BR50
Heathside Ct, Tad. KT20 255 CV123
Heathside Cres, Wok. GU22 249 AZ117
Heathside Gdns, Wok. GU22 249 BA117
Heathside Pk Rd, Wok. GU22 249 AZ118
Heathside Pl, Epsom KT18 255 CX118
Sch Heathside Prep Sch, Lwr Sch, NW3
off Heath St 142 DC63
Upr Sch, NW3 off New End 142 DD63
Heathside Rd, Nthwd. HA6 115 BR49
Woking GU22 249 AZ118
Sch Heathside Sch, Wey. KT13 off Brooklands La 234 BM106
Heathstan Rd, W12 161 CU72
Heath St, NW3 142 DC62
Dartford DA1 210 FK87
Heath Vw, N2 142 DC56
East Horsley KT24 267 BT125
Heathview Av, Dart. DA1 209 FE86
Heath Vw Cl, N2 142 DC56
Heathview Ct, SW19 201 CX89
Heathview Cres, Dart. DA1 209 FG88
Heathview Dr, SE2 188 EX79
Heathview Gdns, SW15 201 CW87
Grays RM16 192 GC75
Heathview Rd, Grays RM16 192 GC75
Thornton Heath CR7 223 DN98
Heath Vil, SE18 187 ET78
SW18 off Cargill Rd 202 DC88
Heathville Rd, N19 143 DL59
Heathwall St, SW11 40 F10
Heathway, SE3 47 N5
Chaldon CR3 274 DQ125
Croydon CR0 225 DZ104
Dagenham RM9, RM10 168 FA66
East Horsley KT24 251 BT124
Heath Way, Erith DA8 189 FC81
Heathway, Iver SL0 155 BD68
Southall UB2 178 BW77
Woodford Green IG8 124 EJ49
● Heathway Ind Est, Dag. RM10 off Manchester Way 169 FB63
Heathwood Gdns, SE7 36 G9
Swanley BR8 229 FC96
Heathwood Pt, SE23
off Dacres Rd 205 DX90
Heathwood Wk, Bex. DA5 209 FE88
Heaton Av, Rom. RM3 127 FH52
Heaton Cl, E4 123 EC48
Romford RM3 128 FJ52
Heaton Ct, Chsht EN8 89 DX29
Heaton Gra Rd, Rom. RM2 127 FF54
Heaton Rd, SE15 44 D10
Mitcham CR4 202 DG94
Heaton Way, Rom. RM3 128 FJ52
Heavens Lea, B.End SL8 132 AC61
Heaven Tree Cl, N1 9 K3
Heaver Rd, SW11 40 B10
Sch Heavers Fm Prim Sch, SE25 off Dinsdale Gdns 224 DT99
Heavitree Cl, SE18 187 ER78
Heavitree Rd, SE18 187 ER78
Heayfield, Welw.G.C. AL7 52 DC08
Hebden Ct, E2 10 A9
Hebden Ter, N17 122 DS51
Hebdon Rd, SW17 202 DE90
Sch Heber Prim Sch, SE22 off Heber Rd 204 DT86
Heber Rd, NW2 4 C2
SE22 204 DT86
Hebron Rd, W6 181 CV76
Hecham Cl, E17 123 DY54
Heckets Ct, Esher KT10 236 CC111
Heckfield Pl, SW6 39 J5
Heckford Cl, Wat. WD18 97 BQ44
Heckford St, E1 21 K10
Hector Cl, N9 122 DU47
Hector St, SE18 187 ES77
Heddington Gro, N7 8 C2
Heddon Cl, Islw. TW7 179 CG84
Heddon Ct Av, Barn. EN4 102 DF43
Heddon Ct Par, Barn. EN4
off Cockfosters Rd 102 DG43
Heddon Rd, Cockfos. EN4 102 DF43
Heddon St, W1 17 L10
Hedgebrooms, Welw.G.C. AL7 52 DC08
Hedge Hill, Enf. EN2 103 DP39
Hedge La, N13 121 DP48
Hedge Lea, Woob.Grn HP10 132 AD55
Hedgeley, Ilf. IG4 147 EM56
Hedgemans Rd, Dag. RM9 168 EX66
Hedgemans Way, Dag. RM9 168 EY65
Hedge Pl Rd, Green. DA9 211 FT86
HEDGERLEY, Slou. SL2 133 AR60
Hedgerley Ct, Wok. GU21 248 AW117
Hedgerley Gdns, Grnf. UB6 158 CC68
Hedgerley Grn, Hedg. SL2 134 AT58
Hedgerley Hill, Hedg. SL2 133 AR62
Hedgerley La, Beac. HP9 133 AN56
Gerrards Cross SL9 134 AV59
Hedgerley SL2 134 AS58
Hedgerow, Chal.St.P. SL9 112 AY51
Hedge Row, Hem.H. HP1 62 BG18
Hedgerow La, Arkley EN5 101 CV43
Hedgerows, Hutt. CM13 131 GE44
Sawbridgeworth CM21 58 EZ05
Hedgerows, The, Nthflt DA11 212 GE89
Hedgerow Wk, Chsht EN8 89 DX30
Hedgers Cl, Loug. IG10
off Newmans La 107 EN42
Hedgers Gro, E9 11 L5
Hedger St, SE11 30 G8
Hedges, The, St.Alb. AL3 64 CC16
Hedges Cl, Hat. AL10 67 CV17
Hedgeside, Pott.End HP4 61 BA16
Hedgeside Rd, Nthwd. HA6 115 BQ50
Hedge Wk, SE6 205 EB92
Hedgeway, Guil. GU2 280 AU136
Hedgewood Gdns, Ilf. IG5 147 EN56
Sch Hedgewood Sch, Hayes UB4 off Weymouth Rd 157 BS69
Hedgley St, SE12 206 EF85
Hedingham Cl, N1 9 J7
Horley RH6 291 DJ147
Hedingham Ho, Kings.T. KT2
off Kingsgate Rd 220 CL95
Hedingham Rd, Chaff.Hun. RM16 191 FW78
Dagenham RM8 148 EV64
Hornchurch RM11 150 FN60
Hedley Av, Grays RM20 191 FW80
Hedley Cl, Rom. RM1
off High St 149 FE57
Hedley Ho, E14 off Stewart St 34 F6
Hedley Rd, St.Alb. AL1 65 CH20
Twickenham TW2 198 CA87
Hedley Row, N5 9 M2
Hedley Vw, Loud. HP10 110 AD54
Hedsor Hill, B.End SL8 132 AC62
Hedsor La, Burn. SL1 132 AG61
Wooburn Green HP10 132 AG61
Hedsor Pk, Tap. SL6 132 AD63
Hedsor Wf, B.End SL8 132 AC62
Hedworth Av, Wal.Cr. EN8 89 DX33
Heenan Cl, Bark. IG11
off Glenny Rd 167 EQ65
Heene Rd, Enf. EN2 104 DR39
Heideck Gdns, Hutt. CM13
off Victors Cres 131 GB47
Heidegger Cres, SW13
off Wyatt Dr 181 CV80
Heigham Rd, E6 166 EK66
Heighams, Harl. CM19 73 EM18
Heighton Gdns, Croy. CR0 241 DP106
Heights, The, SE7 186 EJ78
Beckenham BR3 205 EC94
Hemel Hempstead HP2
off Saturn Way 62 BM18
Loughton IG10 107 EM40
Nazeing EN9 90 EH25
Northolt UB5 138 BZ64
Weybridge KT13 234 BN110
Heights Cl, SW20 201 CV94
Banstead SM7 255 CY116
Heiron St, SE17 43 H3
Helby Rd, SW4 203 DK86
Helder Gro, SE12 206 EF87
Helder St, S.Croy. CR2 242 DR107
Heldmann Cl, Houns. TW3 179 CD84
Helegan Cl, Orp. BR6 245 ET105
Helena Cl, Barn. EN4 102 DD38
Helena Ho, Red. RH1 288 DG137
Helena Pl, E9 10 F9
Helena Rd, E13 23 M1
E17 145 EA57
NW10 141 CV64
W5 159 CK71
Windsor SL4 173 AR82
Helena Sq, SE16 33 L1
Helen Av, Felt. TW14 197 BV87
Helen Cl, N2 142 DC55
Dartford DA1 209 FH87
West Molesey KT8 218 CB98
Helen Rd, Horn. RM11 150 FK55
Helens Gate, Chsht EN8 89 DZ26
Helenslea Av, NW11 141 CZ60
Helen's Pl, E2 20 G2
Helen St, SE18 37 P8
Helford Cl, Ruis. HA4 137 BS61
Helford Wk, Wok. GU21 248 AU118
Helford Way, Upmin. RM14 151 FR58
Helgiford Gdns, Sun. TW16 197 BS94
Heligan Ho, SE16
off Canada St 33 J5
Helions Rd, Harl. CM19 73 EP15
Helios Rd, Wall. SM6 222 DG102
● Heliport Ind Est, SW11
off Bridges Ct 39 P9
Helix Gdns, SW2 203 DM86
Helix Rd, SW2 203 DM86
Helleborine, Bad.Dene RM17 192 FZ78
Hellen Way, Wat. WD19 116 BW49
Hellings St, E1 32 D3
Hellyer Way, B.End SL8 132 AC60
Helm, The, E16
off Albert Basin Way 37 P1
Helm Cl, Epsom KT19 238 CN112
Helme Cl, SW19 201 CZ92
Helmet Row, EC1 19 K4
Helmore Rd, Bark. IG11 167 ET66
Helmsdale, Wok. GU21
off Winnington Way 248 AV118
Helmsdale Cl, Hayes UB4 158 BY70
Romford RM1 127 FE52
Helmsdale Rd, SW16 223 DJ95
Romford RM1 127 FE52
Helmsley Pl, E8 10 E7
Helperby Rd, NW10 160 CS66
Helsinki Sq, SE16 33 M6
Helston Cl, Pnr. HA5 116 BZ52
Helston Gro, Hem.H. HP2 62 BK16
Helston La, Wind. SL4 173 AN81
Helston Pl, Abb.L. WD5
off Shirley Rd 81 BT32
Helvellyn Cl, Egh. TW20 195 BB94
Helvetia St, SE6 205 DZ89
Hemans Est, SW8 41 P5
Hemans St, SW8 41 P4
Hemberton Rd, SW9 42 A10
HEMEL HEMPSTEAD, HP1 - HP3 62 BK21
⇌ Hemel Hempstead 62 BG23
◆ Hemel Hempstead 62 BJ20
H Hemel Hempstead Gen Hosp, Hem.H. HP2 62 BK21
● Hemel Hempstead Ind Est, Hem.H. HP2 63 BP17
Hemel Hempstead Rd, Hem.H. HP3 63 BR22
Redbourn AL3 63 BQ15
St. Albans AL3 64 CA21
Sch Hemel Hempstead Sch, The, Hem.H. HP1
off Heath La 62 BJ21
Hemery Rd, Grnf. UB6 139 CD64
Hemingford Cl, N12 120 DD50
Hemingford Rd, N1 8 D9
Sutton SM3 239 CW105
Watford WD17 97 BS36
Heming Rd, Edg. HA8 118 CP52
Hemington Av, N11 120 DF50
Hemingway Cl, NW5 7 H1
Hemlock Cl, SW16 223 DK96
Kgswd KT20 255 CY123
Hemlock Rd, W12 161 CT73
Hemmen La, Hayes UB3 157 BT72
Hemming Cl, Hmptn. TW12 218 CA95
Hemmings, The, Berk. HP4 60 AT20
Hemmings Cl, Sid. DA14 208 EV89
Hemmings Mead, Epsom KT19 238 CP107
Hemming St, E1 20 D5
Hemming Way, Slou. SL2 153 AP69
Watford WD25 97 BU35
Hemnall Ms, Epp. CM16
off Hemnall St 92 EU30
Hemnall St, Epp. CM16 91 ET31
Hempshaw Av, Bans. SM7 256 DF116
Hempson Av, Slou. SL3 174 AW76
Hempstall, Welw.G.C. AL7 52 DB11
Hempstead Cl, Buck.H. IG9 124 EG47
Hempstead La, Pott.End HP4 61 BC17
Hempstead Rd, E17 123 ED54
Bovingdon HP3 79 BA27
Kings Langley WD4 80 BM26
Watford WD17 97 BT39
Hemp Wk, SE17 31 M8
Hemsby Rd, Chess. KT9 238 CM107
Hemsley Rd, Kings L. WD4 81 BP29
Hemstal Rd, NW6 5 J6
Hemsted Rd, Erith DA8 189 FE80
Hemswell Dr, NW9 118 CS53
Hemsworth Ct, N1 9 N9
Hemsworth St, N1 9 N10
Hemus Pl, SW3 40 D1
Hemwood Rd, Wind. SL4 173 AK83
Henage La, Wok. GU22 249 BC120
Hen & Chicken Ct, EC4 18 E9
Henbane Path, Rom. RM3
off Clematis Cl 128 FK52
Henbit Cl, Tad. KT20 255 CV119
Henbury Way, Wat. WD19 116 BX48
Henchley Dene, Guil. GU4 265 BD131
Henchman St, W12 161 CT72
Hencroft St N, Slou. SL1 174 AT75
Hencroft St S, Slou. SL1 174 AT76
Hendale Av, NW4 141 CU55
Henderson Av, Guil. GU2 264 AV130
Henderson Cl, NW10 160 CQ65
Hornchurch RM11 149 FH61
St. Albans AL3 64 CC16
Henderson Dr, NW8 16 A4
Dartford DA1 190 FM84
Henderson Gro, Bigg.H. TN16 244 EJ112
Henderson Pl, Bedmond WD5 81 BT27
Epping Green SG13 69 DJ21
Henderson Rd, E7 166 EJ65
N9 122 DV46
SW18 202 DE87
Croydon CR0 224 DR100
Hayes UB4 157 BU69
Hendham Rd, SW17 202 DE89
HENDON, NW4 141 CV56
⇌ Hendon 141 CU58
Hendon Av, N3 119 CY53
⊖ Hendon Central 141 CW57
Hendon Gdns, Rom. RM5 127 FC51
Hendon Gro, Epsom KT19 238 CN109
Hendon Hall Ct, NW4
off Parson St 141 CX55
Hendon La, N3 141 CY55
Hendon Pk Row, NW11 141 CZ58
Sch Hendon Prep Sch, NW4
off Tenterden Gro 141 CX55
Hendon Rd, N9 122 DU47
Sch Hendon Sch, NW4
off Golders Ri 141 CX57
Hendon Way, NW2 141 CZ62
NW4 141 CV58
Stanwell TW19 196 BK86
Hendon Wd La, NW7 101 CT44
Hendren Cl, Grnf. UB6 139 CD64
Hendre Rd, SE1 31 P9
Hendrick Av, SW12 202 DF86
Heneage Cres, New Adgtn CR0 243 EC110
Heneage La, EC3 19 P9
Heneage St, E1 20 B6
Henfield Cl, N19 143 DJ60
Bexley DA5 208 FA86
Henfield Rd, SW19 221 CZ95
Henfold La, Dor. RH5 286 CL144
Hengelo Gdns, Mitch. CR4 222 DD98
Hengist Rd, SE12 206 EH87
Erith DA8 189 FB80
Hengist Way, Brom. BR2 226 EE98
Wallington SM6 241 DK108
Hengrave Rd, SE23 205 DX87
Hengrove Ct, Bex. DA5 208 EY88
Hengrove Cres, Ashf. TW15 196 BK90
Henhurst Rd, Cobham DA12 213 GK94
Henley Av, Sutt. SM3 221 CY104
Henley Bk, Guil. GU2 280 AU136
Henley Cl, SE16
off St. Marychurch St 32 G4
Greenford UB6 158 CC68
Isleworth TW7 179 CF81
Henley Ct, N14 121 DJ45
Woking GU22 249 BA120
Henley Cross, SE3 186 EH83
Henley Deane, Nthflt DA11 212 GE91
Henley Dr, SE1 32 B8
Kingston upon Thames KT2 201 CT94
Henley Gdns, Pnr. HA5 137 BV55
Romford RM6 148 EY57
Henley Prior, N1
off Collier St 18 C1
Henley Rd, E16 37 K4
N18 122 DS49
NW10 4 B8
Ilford IG1 147 EQ63
Slough SL1 153 AL72
Henley St, SW11 41 H8
Henley Way, Felt. TW13 198 BX92
Henlow Pl, Rich. TW10 199 CK89
Jct Henlys Cor, N3 141 CZ56
Jct Henlys Rbt, Houns. TW5 178 BW81
Henman Way, Brwd. CM14 130 FV46
Henneker Cl, Rom. RM5 127 FC51
Hennel Cl, SE23 204 DW90
Hennessy Ct, Wok. GU21 233 BC113
Hennessy Rd, N9 122 DW47
Henniker Gdns, E6 24 F2
Henniker Ms, SW3 40 A2
Henniker Pt, E15 13 J3
Henniker Rd, E15 12 G3
Henningham Rd, N17 122 DR53
Henning St, SW11 40 C7
Sch Henrietta Barnett Sch, The, NW11 off Central Sq 142 DB57
Henrietta Barnett Wk, NW11 142 DA58
Henrietta Cl, SE8 46 B2
Henrietta Ms, WC1 18 B4
Henrietta Pl, W1 17 J9
Henrietta St, E15 12 F2
WC2 18 B10
Henriques St, E1 20 D8
Henry Addlington Cl, E6 25 N7
Sch Henry Cavendish Prim Sch, SW12 off Hydethorpe Rd 203 DJ88
Henry Cl, Enf. EN2 104 DS38
Sch Henry Compton Sch, SW6 38 E6
Henry Cooper Way, SE9 206 EK90
Henry Darlot Dr, NW7 119 CX50
Henry DeGrey Cl, Grays RM17 192 FZ77
Henry Dent Cl, SE5 184 DR83
Henry Dickens Ct, W11 26 D2
Henry Doulton Dr, SW17 203 DH91
Sch Henry Fawcett Prim Sch, SE11 42 E2
Sch Henry Grn Prim Sch, Dag. RM8 off Green La 148 EX61
Henry Jackson Rd, SW15 181 CX83
Henry Macaulay Av, Kings.T. KT2 219 CK95
Sch Henry Maynard Infants' Sch, E17 off Maynard Rd 145 EC57
Sch Henry Maynard Jun Sch, E17 off Addison Rd 145 EC57
Sch Henry Moore Prim Sch, Harl. CM17 off Kiln La 74 EX17
Henry Peters Dr, Tedd. TW11
off Somerset Gdns 199 CE92
Henry Rd, E6 166 EL68
N4 144 DQ60
Barnet EN4 102 DD43
Slough SL1 173 AR75
Henry's Av, Wdf.Grn. IG8 124 EF50
Henryson Rd, SE4 205 EA85
Henry St, Brom. BR1 226 EH95
Grays RM17
off East Thurrock Rd 192 GC79
Hemel Hempstead HP3 62 BK24
Henry's Wk, Ilf. IG6 125 ER52
Henry Tate Ms, SW16 203 DN92
Henry Wells Sq, Hem.H. HP2
off Aycliffe Dr 62 BL16
Henry Wise Ho, SW1
off Vauxhall Br Rd 29 M9
Hensford Gdns, SE26
off Wells Pk Rd 204 DV91
Henshall Pt, E3 22 C2
Henshall St, N1 9 M5
Henshawe Rd, Dag. RM8 148 EX62
Henshaw St, SE17 31 L8
Hensley Pt, E9 11 K5
Henslowe Rd, SE22 204 DU85
Henslow Way, Wok. GU21 233 BD114
Henson Av, NW2 4 A2
Henson Cl, Orp. BR6 227 EP103
Henson Path, Har. HA3 139 CK55
Henson Pl, Nthlt. UB5 158 BW67
Henstridge Pl, NW8 6 C10
Hensworth Rd, Ashf. TW15 196 BK92
Henty Cl, SW11 40 D5
Henty Wk, SW15 201 CV85
Henville Rd, Brom. BR1 226 EH95
Sch Henwick Prim Sch, SE9
off Henwick Rd 186 EK83
Henwick Rd, SE9 186 EK83
Henwood Side, Wdf.Grn. IG8
off Love La 125 EM51
Hepburn Cl, Chaff.Hun. RM16 191 FX77
Hepburn Ct, S.Mimms EN6 85 CU32
Hepburn Gdns, Brom. BR2 226 EE102
Hepburn Ms, SW11
off Webbs Rd 202 DF85
Hepple Cl, Islw. TW7 179 CH82
Hepplestone Cl, SW15 201 CV86
Hepscott Rd, E9 12 A5
Hepworth Ct, SW1 41 H1
Barking IG11 148 EU64
Hepworth Gdns, Bark. IG11 148 EU64

Hepworth Rd, SW16 203 DL94
Hepworth Wk, NW3 6 D3
Hepworth Way, Walt. KT12 217 BT102
Heracles Cl, Park St AL2 82 CC28
Herald Gdns, Wall. SM6 223 DH104
Herald's Pl, SE11 30 G8
Herald St, E2 20 F4
Herald Wk, Dart. DA1
off Temple Hill Sq 210 FM85
Herbal Hill, EC1 18 F5
Herbert Cres, SW1 28 F6
Knaphill GU21 248 AS118
Herbert Gdns, NW10 161 CV68
W4 180 CP79
Romford RM6 148 EX59
St. Albans AL2 82 CB29
Herbert Ms, SW2
off Bascombe St 203 DN86
Herbert Morrison Ho, SW6 38 G3
Herbert Morrison Prim Sch, SW8 42 A5
Herbert Pl, SE18
off Plumstead Common Rd 187 EP79
Isleworth TW7 179 CD81
Herbert Rd, E12 146 EL63
E17 145 DZ59
N11 121 DL52
N15 144 DT57
NW9 141 CU58
SE18 187 EN80
SW19 201 CZ94
Bexleyheath DA7 188 EY82
Bromley BR2 226 EK99
Hornchurch RM11 150 FL59
Ilford IG3 147 ES61
Kingston upon Thames KT1 220 CM97
Southall UB1 158 BZ74
Swanley BR8 209 FH93
Swanscombe DA10 212 FZ86
Herbert St, E13 23 P1
NW5 6 G4
Hemel Hempstead HP2
off St. Mary's Rd 62 BK19
Herbert Ter, SE18 187 EP80
Herbrand St, WC1 18 A4
Hercies Rd, Uxb. UB10 156 BM66
Hercules Pl, N7 143 DL62
Hercules Rd, SE1 30 D7
Hercules St, N7 143 DL62
Hercules Way, Lvsdn WD25 81 BT34
Hereford Av, Barn. EN4 120 DF46
Hereford Cl, Epsom KT18 238 CR113
Guildford GU2 264 AT132
Staines-upon-Thames TW18 216 BH95
Hereford Copse, Wok. GU22 248 AV119
Hereford Ct, Sutt. SM2
off Worcester Rd 240 DA108
Hereford Gdns, SE13
off Longhurst Rd 206 EE85
Ilford IG1 146 EL59
Pinner HA5 138 BY57
Twickenham TW2 198 CC88
Hereford Ho, NW6 15 K1
Hereford Ms, W2 15 K9
Hereford Pl, SE14 45 N4
Hereford Retreat, SE15 44 C3
Hereford Rd, E3 21 P1
E11 146 EH57
W2 15 K8
W3 160 CP73
W5 179 CJ76
Feltham TW13 198 BW88
Hereford Sq, SW7 27 P9
Hereford St, E2 20 C4
Hereford Way, Chess. KT9 237 CJ106
Herent Dr, Ilf. IG5 146 EL56
Hereward Av, Pur. CR8 241 DN111
Hereward Cl, Wal.Abb. EN9 89 ED32
Hereward Gdns, N13 121 DN50
Hereward Grn, Loug. IG10 107 EQ39
Hereward Ho Sch, NW3 6 C6
Hereward Prim Sch, Loug. IG10 *off Colebrook La* 107 EQ39
Hereward Rd, SW17 202 DF91
Herga Ct, Har. HA1 139 CE62
Watford WD17 97 BU40
Herga Rd, Har. HA3 139 CF56
Herington Gro, Hutt. CM13 131 GA45
Herington Ho Sch, Hutt. CM13 *off Mount Av* 131 GB44
Heriot Av, E4 123 EA47
Heriot Rd, NW4 141 CW57
Chertsey KT16 216 BG101
Heriots Cl, Stan. HA7 117 CG49
Heritage Av, NW9 119 CT54
Heritage Cl, SW9 183 DP83
Sunbury-on-Thames TW16 217 BU95
Uxbridge UB8 156 BJ70
Heritage Hill, Kes. BR2 244 EJ106
Heritage Ho, N14
off Chase Side 121 DK46
Heritage Ho Sch, Chesh. HP5 *off Cameron Rd* 76 AR30
Heritage Lawn, Horl. RH6 291 DJ147
Heritage Pl, SW18
off Earlsfield Rd 202 DC88
Heritage Vw, Har. HA1 139 CF62
Heritage Wk, Chorl. WD3
off Chenies Rd 95 BE41
Herkomer Cl, Bushey WD23 98 CB44
Herkomer Rd, Bushey WD23 98 CA43
Herlwyn Av, Ruis. HA4 137 BS62
Herlwyn Gdns, SW17 202 DF91
Herm Cl, Islw. TW7 178 CC80
Hermes Cl, W9 15 J5
Hermes St, N1 18 E1
Hermes Wk, Nthlt. UB5
off Hotspur Rd 158 CA68
Herm Ho, Enf. EN3
off Eastfield Rd 105 DX38
Hermiston Av, N8 143 DL57
Hermitage, The, SE13 46 F8
SE23 204 DW88
SW13 181 CT81
Feltham TW13 197 BT90
Richmond TW10 199 CK85
Uxbridge UB8 156 BL65
Hermitage Cl, E18 146 EF56
SE2 *off Felixstowe Rd* 188 EW76
Claygate KT10 237 CG107
Enfield EN2 103 DP40
Shepperton TW17 216 BN98
Slough SL3 174 AW76
Hermitage Ct, E18 146 EG56
NW2 *off Hermitage La* 142 DA62
Potters Bar EN6
off Southgate Rd 86 DC33
Hermitage Gdns, NW2 142 DA62
SE19 204 DQ93
Hermitage La, N18 122 DR50
NW2 142 DA62
SE25 224 DU100
SW16 203 DM94
Croydon CR0 224 DU100
Windsor SL4 173 AN83
Hermitage Path, SW16 223 DL95
Hermitage Prim Sch, E1 32 D3
Uxbridge UB8 *off Belmont Rd* 156 BK66
Hermitage Rd, N4 143 DP59
N15 143 DP59
SE19 204 DQ94
Kenley CR8 258 DQ116
Woking GU21 248 AT119
Hermitage Row, E8 10 D3
Hermitage Sch, The, St.John's GU21 *off Oakwood Rd* 248 AS119
Hermitage St, W2 16 A7
Hermitage Wk, E18 146 EF56
Hermitage Wall, E1 32 D3
Hermitage Waterside, E1 32 C2
Hermitage Way, Stan. HA7 117 CG53
Hermitage Wds Cres, Wok. GU21 248 AS119
Hermit Pl, NW6 5 L9
Hermit Rd, E16 23 L6
Hermit St, EC1 18 G2
Hermon Gro, Hayes UB3 157 BU74
Hermon Hill, E11 146 EG57
E18 146 EG57
Herndon Cl, Egh. TW20 195 BA91
Herndon Rd, SW18 202 DC85
Herne Cl, NW10
off North Circular Rd 140 CR64
Hayes UB3 157 BT72
Herne Ct, Bushey WD23
off Richfield Rd 116 CC45
HERNE HILL, SE24 204 DQ85
Herne Hill 203 DP86
Herne Hill, SE24 204 DQ86
Herne Hill Ho, SE24
off Railton Rd 203 DP86
Herne Hill Rd, SE24 43 H10
Herne Hill Sch, SE24
off Herne Hill Rd 204 DQ85
Herne Ms, N18 122 DU49
Herne Pl, SE24 203 DP85
Herne Rd, Bushey WD23 98 CB44
Surbiton KT6 219 CK103
Hernes Cl, Stai. TW18
off Staines Rd 216 BH95
Herneshaw, Hat. AL10 67 CT20
Herns La, Welw.G.C. AL7 52 DB08
Herns Way, Welw.G.C. AL7 52 DA07
Herold Cl, Rain. RM13 169 FG67
Heron Cl, E17 123 DZ54
NW10 160 CS65
Buckhurst Hill IG9 124 EG46
Guildford GU2 264 AV131
Hemel Hempstead HP3 80 BM25
Rickmansworth WD3 114 BK47
Sawbridgeworth CM21 58 EX06
Sutton SM1
off Sandpiper Rd 239 CZ106
Uxbridge UB8 156 BK65
Heron Ct, E5 *off Big Hill* 144 DV60
Bromley BR2 226 EJ98
Heron Cres, Sid. DA14 207 ES90
Heron Dale, Add. KT15 234 BK106
Herondale, S.Croy. CR2 243 DX109
Herondale Av, SW18 202 DD88
Heron Dr, N4 144 DQ61
Slough SL3 175 BB77
Stanstead Abbotts SG12 55 EC12
Heronfield, Eng.Grn TW20 194 AV93
Potters Bar EN6 86 DC30
Heron Flight Av, Horn. RM12 169 FG66
Herongate Rd, E12 146 EJ61
Cheshunt EN8 89 DY27
Swanley BR8 209 FE93
Heron Hill, Belv. DA17 188 EZ77
Heron Ho, W13 *off Gurnell Gro* 159 CF70
Heron Mead, Enf. EN3 105 EA38
Heron Ms, Ilf. IG1
off Balfour Rd 147 EP61
Heron Pl, SE16 33 M2
Harefield UB9 114 BG51
Heron Quay, E14 34 A3
Heron Quays 34 B3
Heron Rd, SE24 184 DQ84
Croydon CR0 *off Tunstall Rd* 224 DS103
Twickenham TW1 179 CG84
Heronry, The, Hersham KT12 235 BU107
Herons, The, E11 146 EF58
Herons Cft, Wey. KT13 235 BQ107
Herons Elm, Nthch HP4 60 AS16
Heronsforde, W13 159 CJ72
HERONSGATE, Rick. WD3 113 BD45
Heronsgate, Edg. HA8 118 CN50
Heronsgate Prim Sch, SE28 *off Whinchat Rd* 187 ER76
Heronsgate Rd, Chorl. WD3 95 BB44
Heronslea, Wat. WD25 98 BW36
Heronslea Dr, Stan. HA7 118 CL50
Heron's Pl, Islw. TW7 179 CH83
Heron Sq, Rich. TW9
off Bridge St 199 CK85
Herons Ri, New Barn. EN4 102 DE42
Herons Way, St.Alb. AL1 65 CH23
Herons Wd, Harl. CM20 57 EP13
Heronswood, Wal.Abb. EN9 90 EE34
Heronswood Ct, Horl. RH6
off Tanyard Way 291 DH147
Heronswood Pl, Welw.G.C. AL7 51 CZ10
Heronswood Rd, Welw.G.C. AL7 52 DA09
● **Heron Trd Est**, W3
off Alliance Rd 160 CP70
Heron Wk, Nthwd. HA6 115 BS49
Woking GU21
off Blackmore Cres 233 BC114
Heron Way, Felt. TW14 177 BU84
Grays RM20 191 FV78
Hatfield AL10 67 CU19
Wallington SM6 241 DK108
Heronway, Hutt. CM13 131 GA46
Heron Way, Upmin. RM14 151 FS60
Heronway, Wdf.Grn. IG8 124 EJ49
Herrick Rd, N5 144 DQ62
Herrick St, SW1 29 P8
Herries St, W10 14 F1
Herringham Prim Sch, Chad.St.M. RM16
off St. Mary's Rd 193 GH77
Herringham Rd, SE7 36 D7
Herrings La, Cher. KT16 216 BG100
Herrongate Cl, Enf. EN1 104 DT40
Her Royal Highness Princess Christian's Hosp, Wind. SL4 173 AQ81
Hersant Cl, NW10 161 CU67
Herschel Gram Sch, Slou. SL1 *off Northampton Av* 153 AQ73
Herschell Ms, SE5
off Bicknell Rd 184 DQ83
Herschell Rd, SE23 205 DX87
Herschel Pk Dr, Slou. SL1 174 AT75
Herschel St, Slou. SL1 174 AT75
HERSHAM, Walt. KT12 236 BX107
Hersham 218 BY104
Hersham Bypass, Walt. KT12 235 BV106
Hersham Cen, The, Walt. KT12 236 BX106
Hersham Cl, SW15 201 CU87
Hersham Gdns, Hersham KT12 236 BW105
Hersham Rd, Walt. KT12 236 BW105
HERTFORD, SG13 & SG14 53 DP10
Hertford Av, SW14 200 CR85
Hertford Cl, Barn. EN4 102 DD41
CroxleyGreen WD3 97 BP42
Hertford Co Hosp, Hert. SG14 53 DP09
Hertford Ct, N13
off Green Las 121 DN48
Hertford East 54 DS09
HERTFORD HEATH, Hert. SG13 54 DV12
Hertford Heath Prim Sch, Hert.Hth SG13
off Woodland Rd 54 DW12
Hertford Ho, Nthlt. UB5
off Taywood Rd 158 BZ70
★ **Hertford Mus**, Hert. SG14 54 DR09
Hertford North 53 DP09
● **Hertford Pl**, Rick. WD3 113 BF48
Hertford Regional Coll, Broxbourne Cen, Turnf. EN10 *off High Rd* 89 DZ25
Ware Cen, Ware SG12
off Scotts Rd 55 DX07
Hertford Rd, N1 9 P8
N2 142 DE55
N9 122 DV47
Barking IG11 167 EP66
Barnet EN4 102 DC41
Enfield EN3 104 DW41
Great Amwell SG12 55 DZ11
Hatfield AL9 67 CW16
Hertford SG14 52 DB06
Hertford Heath SG13 54 DW13
Hoddesdon EN11 71 DY15
Ilford IG2 147 ES58
Marden Hill SG14 52 DG06
Tewin AL6 52 DE05
Waltham Cross EN8 105 DX37
Ware SG12 54 DW07
Welwyn AL6 52 DB06
Hertford St. Andrew's C of E Prim Sch, Hert. SG14
off Calton Av 53 DM08
Hertfordshire Co Hall, Hert. SG13 54 DQ10
Hertford Sq, Mitch. CR4
off Hertford Way 223 DL98
Hertford St, W1 29 J2
Hertford Wk, Belv. DA17
off Hoddesdon Rd 188 FA78
Hertford Way, Mitch. CR4 223 DL98
HERTINGFORDBURY, Hert. SG14 53 DL10
Hertingfordbury Cowper Prim Sch, Hert. SG14
off Birch Grn 53 DJ11
Hertingfordbury Rd, Hert. SG14 53 DL11
Hertslet Rd, N7 143 DM62
● **Hertsmere Ind Pk**, Borwd. WD6 100 CR41
Hertsmere Jewish Prim Sch, Rad. WD7 *off Watling St* 99 CJ38
Hertsmere Rd, E14 34 A1
Hertswood Ct, Barn. EN5
off Hillside Gdns 101 CY42
Hertswood Sch, Lwr Sch, Borwd. WD6
off Cowley Hill 100 CQ39
Upr Sch, Borwd. WD6
off Thrift Fm La 100 CQ40
Hervey Cl, N3 120 DA53
Hervey Pk Rd, E17 145 DY56
Hervey Rd, SE3 186 EH81
Hervines Ct, Amer. HP6 77 AQ37
Hervines Rd, Amer. HP6 77 AP37
Hesa Rd, Hayes UB3 157 BU72
Hesewall Cl, SW4 41 M9
Hesiers Hill, Warl. CR6 260 EE117
Hesiers Rd, Warl. CR6 260 EE117
Hesketh Av, Dart. DA2 210 FP88
Hesketh Pl, W11 26 E1
Hesketh Rd, E7 146 EG62
Heslop Rd, SW12 202 DF88
Hesper Ms, SW5 27 L10
Hesperus Cres, E14 34 C9
Hessel Rd, W13 179 CG75
Hessel St, E1 20 E9
Hesselyn Dr, Rain. RM13 169 FH66
Hessle Gro, Epsom KT17 239 CT111
Hestercombe Av, SW6 38 F8
Hester Ct, Dag. RM10
off St. Mark's Pl 168 FA65
Hesterman Way, Croy. CR0 223 DL102
Hester Rd, N18 122 DU50
SW11 40 C5
Hester Ter, Rich. TW9
off Chilton Rd 180 CN83
Hestia Ho, SE1
off Royal Oak Yd 31 N5
HESTON, Houns. TW5 178 BZ80
Heston Av, Houns. TW5 178 BY80
● **Heston Centre, The**, Houns. TW5
off International Ave 178 BW78
Heston Comm Sch, Heston TW5 *off Heston Rd* 178 CA80
Heston Gra, Houns. TW5 178 BZ79
Heston Gra La, Houns. TW5 178 BZ79
● **Heston Ind Mall**, Houns. TW5 178 BZ80
Heston Inf & Nurs Sch, Heston TW5 *off Heston Rd* 178 CA80
Heston Jun Sch, Heston TW5 *off Heston Rd* 178 CA80
Heston Rd, Houns. TW5 178 CA80
Redhill RH1 288 DF138
Heston St, SE14 46 A6
Heston Wk, Red. RH1 288 DF138
Heswell Grn, Wat. WD19
off Fairhaven Cres 115 BU48
Hetchleys, Hem.H. HP1 62 BG17
Hetherington Cl, Slou. SL2 153 AM69
Hetherington Rd, SW4 183 DL84
Hetherington Rd, Shepperton TW17 217 BQ96
Hetherington Way, Uxb. UB10 136 BL63
Hethersett Cl, Reig. RH2 272 DC131
Hetley Gdns, SE19 204 DT94
Hetley Rd, W12 161 CV74
Heton Gdns, NW4 141 CU56
Heusden Way, Ger.Cr. SL9 135 AZ60
Hevelius Cl, SE10 35 L10
Hever Ct Rd, Grav. DA12 213 GH93
Hever Cft, SE9 207 EN91
Hever Gdns, Brom. BR1 227 EN96
Heverham Rd, SE18 187 ES77
Hevers Av, Horl. RH6 290 DF147
Hevers Cor, Horl. RH6
off Horley Row 290 DF147
Heversham Rd, Bexh. DA7 188 FA82
Hevingham Dr, Chad.Hth RM6 148 EW57
Hewens Cl, Hayes End UB4
of Hewens Rd 157 BG70
Hewens Rd, Hayes UB4 157 BQ70
Uxbridge UB10 157 BQ70
Hewer St, W10 14 D6
Hewers Way, Tad. KT20 255 CV120
Hewett Cl, Stan. HA7 117 CH49
Hewett Pl, Swan. BR8 229 FD98
Hewett Rd, Dag. RM8 148 EX64
Hewetts Quay, Bark. IG11 167 EP67
Hewett St, EC2 19 P5
Hewins Cl, Wal.Abb. EN9
off Broomstick Hall Rd 90 EE32
Hewish Rd, N18 122 DS49
Hewison St, E3 11 P10
Hewitt Av, N22 121 DP54
Hewitt Cl, Croy. CR0 225 EA104
Hewitt Rd, N8 143 DN57
Hewitts Rd, Orp. BR6 246 EZ108
Hewlett Rd, E3 11 M10
Hexagon, The, N6 142 DF60
● **Hexagon Business Cen**, Hayes UB4 158 BW73
Hexal Rd, SE6 206 EE90
Hexham Gdns, Islw. TW7 179 CG80
Northolt. UB5 138 BZ64
Hexham Rd, SE27 204 DQ89
Barnet EN5 102 DB42
Morden SM4 222 DB102
HEXTABLE, Swan. BR8 209 FG94
Hextable Inf Sch, Hext. BR8 *off St. Davids Rd* 209 FF93
Hextable Jun Sch, Hext. BR8 *off Rowhill Rd* 209 FF93
Hextable Sch, Hext. BR8
off Egerton Av 229 FF95
Hextalls La, Bletch. RH1 274 DR128
Hexton Ct, N4
off Brownswood Rd 144 DQ61
Heybourne Cres, NW9 118 CS53
Heybourne Rd, N17 122 DV52
Heybridge Av, SW16 203 DL94
Heybridge Ct, Hert. SG14
off The Ridgeway 53 DM08
Heybridge Dr, Ilf. IG6 125 ER54
Heybridge Way, E10 145 DY59
Heydons Cl, St.Alb. AL3 65 CD18
Heyford Av, SW8 42 B4
SW20 221 CZ97
Heyford Rd, Mitch. CR4 222 DE96
Radlett WD7 99 CF37
Heyford Ter, SW8
off Heyford Av 42 B4
Heyford Way, Hat. AL10 67 CW16
Heygate St, SE17 31 J9
Heylyn Sq, E3 21 P2
Heymede, Lthd. KT22 253 CJ123
Heynes Rd, Dag. RM8 148 EW63
Heysham Dr, Wat. WD19 116 BW50
Heysham La, NW3 142 DB62
Heysham Rd, N15 144 DR58
Heythorp Cl, Wok. GU21 248 AT117
Heythorp St, SW18 201 CZ88
Heythrop Coll, W8 27 L6
Heythrop Dr, Ickhm UB10 136 BM63
Heywood Av, NW9 118 CS53
Heyworth Rd, E5 144 DV63
E15 13 L2
Hibbert Av, Wat. WD24 98 BX38
Hibbert Lo, Chal.St.P. SL9
off Gold Hill E 112 AX54
Hibbert Rd, E17 145 DZ59
Harrow HA3 117 CF54
Hibberts All, Wind. SL4
off Bachelors Acre 173 AR81
Hibbert St, SW11 182 DC83
Hibberts Way, Ger.Cr. SL9 134 AY55
Hibbs Cl, Swan. BR8 229 FD96
Hibernia Dr, Grav. DA12 213 GM90
Hibernia Gdns, Houns. TW3 178 CA84
Hibernia Pt, SE2
off Wolvercote Rd 188 EX75
Hibernia Rd, Houns. TW3 178 CA84
Hibiscus Cl, Edg. HA8
off Campion Way 118 CQ49
Hibiscus Ho, Felt. TW13
off High St 197 BV88
Hichisson Rd, SE15 204 DW85
Hicken Rd, SW2 203 DM85
Hickeys Almshouses, Rich. TW9 *off St. Mary's Gro* 180 CM84
Hickin Cl, SE7 36 E9
Hickin St, E14 34 E6
Hickling Rd, Ilf. IG1 147 EP64
Hickman Av, E4 123 EC51
Hickman Cl, E16 24 E7
Broxbourne EN10 71 DX20
Hickman Rd, Rom. RM6 148 EW59
Hickmans Cl, Gdse. RH9 274 DW132
Hickmore Wk, SW4 41 M10
Hickory Cl, N9 122 DU45
Hicks Av, Grnf. UB6 159 CD68
Hicks Cl, SW11 40 C10
Hicks St, SE8 33 L10
Hidalgo Ct, Hem.H. HP2 62 BM18
Hidcote Cl, Wok. GU22 249 BB116
Hidcote Gdns, SW20 221 CV97
Hide, E6 25 M8
Hideaway, The, Abb.L. WD5 81 BU31
Hide Pl, SW1 29 N9
Hide Rd, Har. HA1 139 CD56
Hides, The, Harl. CM20 57 ER14
Hides St, N7 8 D4
Hide Twr, SW1 29 N9
Higgins Rd, Chsht EN7 88 DR27
Higgins Wk, Hmptn. TW12
off Abbott Cl 198 BY93
High, The, Harl. CM20 73 ER15
Highacre, Dor. RH4 285 CH139
High Acres, Abb.L. WD5 81 BR32
Enfield EN2 *off Old Pk Vw* 103 DN41
HIGHAM HILL, E17 123 DY54
Higham Hill Rd, E17 123 DY54
Higham Mead, Chesh. HP5 76 AQ30
Higham Ms, Nthlt. UB5
off Taywood Rd 158 BZ70
Higham Pl, E17 145 DY55
Higham Rd, N17 144 DR55
Chesham HP5 76 AP30
Woodford Green IG8 124 EG51
Highams Ct, E4 *off Friars Cl* 123 ED48
● **Highams Lo Business Cen**, E17 145 DX55
HIGHAMS PARK, E4 123 ED50
Highams Park 123 ED51
● **Highams Pk Ind Est**, E4 123 EC51
Highams Pk Sch, E4
off Handsworth Av 123 ED51
Higham Sta Av, E4 123 EB51
Higham St, E17 145 DY55
Higham Vw, N.Wld Bas. CM16 93 FB26
Highbanks Cl, Well. DA16 188 EV80
Highbanks Rd, Pnr. HA5 116 CB51
Highbank Way, N8 143 DN58
HIGH BARNET, Barn. EN5 101 CX40
High Barnet 102 DA42
High Barn Rd, Dor. RH5 268 BX134
Effingham KT24 268 BX129
Highbarns, Hem.H. HP3 80 BN25
Highbarrow Cl, Pur. CR8 241 DM110
Highbarrow Rd, Croy. CR0 224 DU101
HIGH BEACH, Loug. IG10 106 EG39
High Beech, S.Croy. CR2 242 DS108
High Beech C of E Prim Sch, Loug. IG10 *off Mott St* 106 EG39
High Beeches, Bans. SM7 239 CW114
Gerrards Cross SL9 134 AX60
Orpington BR6 246 EU107
Sidcup DA14 208 EY92
Weybridge KT13 235 BS107
High Beeches Cl, Pur. CR8 241 DK110
High Beech Rd, Loug. IG10 106 EL42
High Bois La, Amer. HP6 77 AR35
High Br, SE10 47 H1
Highbridge Cl, Rad. WD7 83 CF33
● **Highbridge Est**, Uxb. UB8 156 BJ66
Highbridge Rd, Bark. IG11 167 EP67
Highbridge St, Wal.Abb. EN9 89 EA33
High Br Wf, SE10 46 G1
Highbrook Rd, SE3 186 EK83
High Broom Cres, W.Wick. BR4 225 EB101
HIGHBURY, N5 9 J3
Highbury & Islington 8 F5
Highbury & Islington 8 F5
Highbury & Islington 8 F5
Highbury Av, Hodd. EN11 71 EA15
Thornton Heath CR7 223 DN96
Highbury Cl, N.Mal. KT3 220 CQ98
West Wickham BR4 225 EB103
Highbury Cor, N5 8 G4
Highbury Cres, N5 8 F3
Highbury Dr, Lthd. KT22 253 CG121
Highbury Est, N5 9 K3
Highbury Flds Sch, N5 8 G2
Annexe, N5 9 J2
Highbury Gdns, Ilf. IG3 147 ES61
Highbury Gra, N5 9 H1
Highbury Gro, N5 9 H4
Highbury Gro Sch, N5 9 J3
Highbury Hill, N5 9 H2
Highbury New Pk, N5 9 H4
Highbury Pk, N5 9 H1
Highbury Pl, N5 8 G4
Highbury Quad, N5 143 DP62
Highbury Quad Prim Sch, N5 9 K1
Highbury Rd, SW19 201 CY92
Highbury Sq, N14
off Burleigh Gdns 121 DJ46
Highbury Stadium Sq, N5
off Avenell Rd 143 DP62
Highbury Sta Rd, N1 8 F5
Highbury Ter, N5 8 G3
Highbury Ter Ms, N5 8 G3
High Canons, Borwd. WD6 100 CQ37
High Cedar Dr, SW20 201 CV94
High Clandon, E.Clan. GU4 266 BL133
Highclere, Guil. GU1 265 BA132
Highclere Cl, Ken. CR8 258 DQ115
Highclere Ct, St.Alb. AL1
off Avenue Rd 65 CE19
Highclere Dr, Hem.H. HP3 62 BN24
Highclere Rd, N.Mal. KT3 220 CR97
Highclere St, SE26 205 DY91
Highcliffe Dr, SW15 201 CT86
Highcliffe Gdns, Ilf. IG4 146 EL57
High Cl, Rick. WD3 96 BJ43
Highcombe, SE7 186 EH79
Highcombe Cl, SE9 206 EK88
High Coombe Pl, Kings.T. KT2 200 CR94
High Coppice, Amer. HP7 77 AQ39
Highcotts La, Guil. GU4 265 BF126
Highcroft, NW9 140 CS57
Highcroft Av, Wem. HA0 160 CN66
Highcroft Ct, Bkhm KT23 252 CA123
Highcroft Gdns, NW11 141 CZ58
Highcroft Rd, N19 143 DL59
Felden HP3 80 BG25
High Cross, Ald. WD25 99 CD37
● **High Cross Cen, The**, N15 144 DU56
High Cross Rd, N17 144 DU55
Highcross Rd, Sthflt DA13 211 FX92
Highcross Way, SW15 201 CU88
Highdaun Dr, SW16 223 DM98
High Dells, Hat. AL10 67 CT19
Highdown, Wor.Pk. KT4 220 CS103
Highdown Cl, Bans. SM7 255 CZ116
Highdown La, Sutt. SM2 240 DB111
Highdown Rd, SW15 201 CV86
High Dr, N.Mal. KT3 220 CQ95
Oxshott KT22 237 CD114
Woldingham CR3 259 DZ122
High Elms, Chig. IG7 125 ES49
Upminster RM14 151 FS60
Woodford Green IG8 124 EG50
High Elms Cl, Nthwd. HA6 115 BR51
High Elms La, Wat. WD25 81 BV31
High Elms Rd, Downe BR6 245 EP110
HIGHER DENHAM, Uxb. UB9 135 BB59
Higher Dr, Bans. SM7 239 CX112
Leatherhead KT24 267 BS127

Higher Dr, Purley CR8 241 DN113
Higher Grn, Epsom KT17 239 CU113
HIGHFIELD, Hem.H. HP2 62 BL18
Highfield, Bans. SM7 256 DE117
Bushey Heath WD23 117 CE47
Chalfont St. Giles HP8 112 AX47
Harlow CM18 74 EU16
Kings Langley WD4 80 BL28
Shalford GU4 280 AY142
Watford WD19 116 BZ48
Highfield Av, NW9 140 CQ57
NW11 141 CX59
Erith DA8 189 FB79
Greenford UB6 139 CE64
Orpington BR6 245 ET106
Pinner HA5 138 BZ57
Wembley HA9 140 CL62
Highfield Cl, N22 121 DN53
NW9 140 CQ57
SE13 205 ED86
Amersham HP6 77 AR37
Englefield Green TW20
off Highfield Rd 194 AW93
Long Ditton KT6 219 CJ102
Northwood HA6 115 BS53
Oxshott KT22 237 CD111
Romford RM5 127 FC51
West Byfleet KT14 234 BG113
Highfield Ct, N14 103 DJ44
Highfield Cres, Horn. RM12 150 FM61
Northwood HA6 115 BS53
Highfield Dr, Brom. BR2 226 EE98
Broxbourne EN10 71 DY21
Caterham CR3 258 DU122
Epsom KT19 239 CT108
Ickenham UB10 136 BL63
West Wickham BR4 225 EB103
Highfield Gdns, NW11 141 CY58
Grays RM16 192 GD75
Highfield Grn, Epp. CM16 91 ES31
Highfield Hill, SE19 204 DR94
Sch Highfield Inf Sch, Short. BR2 off Highfield Dr 226 EE98
Sch Highfield Jun Sch, Short. BR2 off South Hill Rd 226 EE98
Highfield La, Hem.H. HP2 62 BM18
Tyttenhanger AL4 66 CL23
Highfield Link, Rom. RM5 127 FC51
Highfield Manor, St.Alb. AL4 66 CL24
Highfield Ms, NW6 5 L6
Highfield Pk Dr, St.Alb. AL1, AL4 65 CH23
Highfield Pl, Epp. CM16 91 ES31
Sch Highfield Prim Sch, N21
off Highfield Rd 122 DQ46
Hillingdon UB10
off Charville La W 157 BP69
Highfield Rd, N21 121 DP47
NW11 141 CY58
W3 160 CP71
Berkhamsted HP4 60 AX20
Bexleyheath DA6 208 EZ85
Biggin Hill TN16 260 EJ117
Bromley BR1 227 EM98
Bushey WD23 98 BY43
Caterham CR3 258 DU122
Chertsey KT16 216 BG102
Chesham HP5 76 AP29
Cheshunt EN7 88 DS26
Chislehurst BR7 227 ET97
Dartford DA1 210 FK87
Englefield Green TW20 194 AX93
Feltham TW13 197 BU89
Hertford SG13 54 DR11
Hornchurch RM12 150 FM61
Isleworth TW7 179 CF81
Northwood HA6 115 BS53
Purley CR8 241 DM110
Romford RM5 127 FC52
Sunbury-on-Thames TW16 217 BT98
Surbiton KT5 220 CQ101
Sutton SM1 240 DE106
Walton-on-Thames KT12 217 BU102
West Byfleet KT14 234 BG113
Windsor SL4 173 AM83
Woodford Green IG8 124 EL52
Highfield Rd N, Dart. DA1 210 FK86
Highfields, Ashtd. KT21 253 CK119
Cuffley EN6 87 DL28
East Horsley KT24 267 BS128
Fetcham KT22 253 CD124
Radlett WD7 99 CF35
Highfields Gro, N6 142 DF60
Highfield Twr, Rom. RM5 127 FD50
Highfield Way, Horn. RM12 150 FM61
Potters Bar EN6 86 DB32
Rickmansworth WD3 96 BH44
High Firs, Rad. WD7 99 CF35
Swanley BR8 229 FE98
Sch High Firs Prim Sch, Swan. BR8
off Court Cres 229 FF98
High Foleys, Clay. KT10 237 CH108
High Gables, Loug. IG10 106 EK43
High Garth, Esher KT10 236 CC107
HIGHGATE, N6 142 DG61
⊖ Highgate 143 DH58
H Highgate Acute Mental Health Cen, N19 143 DH61
Highgate Av, N6 143 DH58
★ Highgate Cem, N6 142 DG60
Highgate Cl, N6 142 DG59
Highgate Edge, N2 142 DE57
Highgate Gro, Saw. CM21 58 EX05
Highgate High St, N6 142 DG60
Highgate Hill, N6 143 DH60
N19 143 DH60
Highgate Ho, SE26
off Sydenham Hill Est 204 DU90
Sch Highgate Jun Sch, N6
off Bishopswood Rd 142 DF59
Sch Highgate Prim Sch, N6
off North Hill 142 DF58
Highgate Rd, NW5 143 DH63
Sch Highgate Sch, N6
off North Rd 142 DG59
Highgate Spinney, N8
off Crescent Rd 143 DK58
Highgate Wk, SE23 204 DW89
Highgate W Hill, N6 142 DG61
Sch Highgate Wd Sch, N8
off Montenotte Rd 143 DJ57
High Gro, SE18 187 ER80
Bromley BR1 226 EJ95
Highgrove, Pilg.Hat. CM15 130 FV44
High Gro, St.Alb. AL3 65 CD18
Welwyn Garden City AL8 51 CW08
Highgrove Cl, N11
off Balmoral Av 120 DG50
Chislehurst BR7 226 EL95
Highgrove Ms, Cars. SM5 222 DF104
Grays RM17 192 GC78
Highgrove Rd, Dag. RM8 148 EW64
Highgrove Way, Ruis. HA4 137 BU58
High Hill, E5
off Mount Pleasant La 144 DV60
High Hill Ferry, E5
off Big Hill 144 DV60
High Hill Rd, Warl. CR6 259 EC115
High Holborn, WC1 18 B8
High Ho Est, Harl. CM17 58 EZ11
High Ho La, Orsett RM16 193 GJ75
West Tilbury RM18 193 GK77
Highland Av, W7 159 CE72
Brentwood CM15 130 FW46
Dagenham RM10 149 FC62
Loughton IG10 106 EL44
Highland Cotts, Wall. SM6 241 DH105
Highland Ct, E18 124 EH53
Highland Cft, Beck. BR3 205 EB92
Highland Dr, Bushey WD23 116 CC45
Hemel Hempstead HP3 63 BP20
Highland Pk, Felt. TW13 197 BT91
Highland Rd, SE19 204 DS93
Amersham HP7 77 AR39
Badgers Mount TN14 247 FB111
Bexleyheath DA6 208 FA85
Bromley BR1, BR2 226 EF95
Lower Nazeing EN9 72 EE22
Northwood HA6 115 BT54
Purley CR8 241 DN114
Highlands, Ashtd. KT21 253 CJ119
Farnham Common SL2 133 AP64
Hatfield AL9 67 CW15
Watford WD19 116 BW46
Highlands, The, Barn. EN5 102 DB43
East Horsley KT24 267 BS125
Edgware HA8 118 CP54
Potters Bar EN6 86 DC30
Rickmansworth WD3 114 BH45
Highlands Av, N21 103 DM43
W3 160 CQ73
Leatherhead KT22 253 CJ122
Highlands Cl, N4
off Mount Vw Rd 143 DL59
Chalfont St. Peter SL9 113 AZ52
Hounslow TW3 178 CB81
Leatherhead KT22 253 CH122
Highlands End, Chal.St.P. SL9 113 AZ52
Highlands Gdns, Ilf. IG1 147 EM60
Highlands Heath, SW15 201 CW87
Highlands Hill, Swan. BR8 229 FG96
Highlands La, Chal.St.P. SL9 113 AZ51
Woking GU22 248 AY122
Highlands Pk, Lthd. KT22 253 CK123
Seal TN15 279 FL121
Sch Highlands Prim Sch, Ilf. IG1 off Lennox Gdns 147 EM60
Highlands Rd, Barn. EN5 102 DA43
Leatherhead KT22 253 CH122
Orpington BR5 228 EV101
Reigate RH2 272 DD133
Seer Green HP9 111 AQ50
Sch Highlands Sch, N21
off Worlds End La 103 DN42
High La, W7 159 CD72
Caterham CR3 259 DZ119
Sheering CM22 59 FE09
Warlingham CR6 259 DZ118
HIGH LAVER, Ong. CM5 75 FH17
High Lawns, Har. HA1 139 CE62
Highlea Cl, NW9 118 CS53
High Leigh Barns, Hodd. EN11 71 DY17
High Level Dr, SE26 204 DU91
Highlever Rd, W10 14 B7
Sch High March Sch, Beac. HP9 off Ledborough La 111 AK51
Highmead, SE18 187 ET80
High Mead, Chig. IG7 125 EQ47
Harrow HA1 139 CE57
West Wickham BR4 225 ED103
Highmead Cres, Wem. HA0 160 CM66
High Meadow Cl, Dor. RH4 285 CH137
Pinner HA5 138 BW56
Highmeadow Cres, NW9 140 CR57
High Meadow Pl, Cher. KT16 215 BF100
High Meadows, Chig. IG7 125 ER50
High Meads Rd, E16 24 E8
High Molewood, Hert. SG14 53 DP07
Highmoor, Amer. HP7 77 AR39
Highmore Rd, SE3 47 K4
High Mt, NW4 141 CU58
High Oak Rd, Ware SG12 55 DX05
High Oaks, Enf. EN2 103 DM38
St. Albans AL3 64 CC15
High Oaks Rd, Welw.G.C. AL8 51 CV08
Highover Pk, Amer. HP7 77 AR40
High Pk Av, E.Hors. KT24 267 BT126
Richmond TW9 180 CN81
High Pk Rd, Rich. TW9 180 CN81
High Pastures, Sheering CM22 59 FD06
High Path, SW19 222 DB95
High Path Rd, Guil. GU1 265 BC134
High Pewley, Guil. GU1 280 AY136
High Pine Cl, Wey. KT13 235 BQ106
High Pines, Warl. CR6 258 DW119
High Pt, N6 142 DG59
SE9 207 EP90
Weybridge KT13 234 BN106
High Ridge, Cuffley EN6 87 DL27
Highridge Cl, Epsom KT18 254 CS115
High Ridge Cl, Hem.H. HP3 80 BK25
Highridge La, Bet. RH3 286 CP140
High Ridge Rd, Hem.H. HP3 80 BK25
High Rd, N2 142 DE56
N11 121 DH50
N12 120 DC51
N15 144 DT58
N17 122 DT53
N20 120 DC45
N22 143 DN55
NW10 (Willesden) 161 CV65
Broxbourne EN10 71 DZ20
Buckhurst Hill IG9 124 EH47
Bushey Heath WD23 117 CD46
Byfleet KT14 234 BM112
Chadwell Heath RM6 148 EV60
Chigwell IG7 125 EM50
Chipstead CR5 256 DF121
High Rd, Cowley UB8 156 BJ71
Eastcote HA5 137 BV56
Epping CM16 91 ER32
Essendon AL9 68 DE17
Harrow Weald HA3 117 CE52
Ilford IG1 147 EP62
Leavesden WD25 97 BT35
Loughton IG10 124 EJ45
North Weald Bassett CM16 93 FB27
Reigate RH2 272 DD126
Seven Kings IG3 147 ET60
Thornwood CM16 92 EV28
Wembley HA0, HA9 139 CK64
Wilmington DA2 210 FJ90
High Rd Ickenham, Uxb. UB10 137 BP62
High Rd Leyton, E10 145 EB60
E15 145 EC62
High Rd Leytonstone, E11 13 J1
E15 146 EE63
High Rd Turnford, Brox. EN10 89 DY25
High Rd Woodford Grn, E18 124 EF52
Woodford Green IG8 124 EF52
High Rd Wormley, Turnf. EN10 71 DY24
Highshore Rd, SE15 44 B8
Sch Highshore Sch, SE15 44 B7
High Silver, Loug. IG10 106 EK42
High Standing, Chaldon CR3 274 DQ125
Highstead Cres, Erith DA8 189 FE81
Highstone Av, E11 146 EG58
High St, E11 146 EG57
E13 13 N10
E15 12 E10
E17 145 DZ57
N8 143 DL56
N14 121 DK46
NW7 119 CV49
NW10 (Harlesden) 161 CT68
SE20 204 DV93
SE25 (S.Norwood) 224 DT98
W3 160 CP74
W5 159 CK73
Abbots Langley WD5 81 BS31
Addlestone KT15 234 BH105
Amersham HP7 77 AM38
Aveley RM15 171 FR74
Banstead SM7 256 DA115
Barkingside IG6 125 EQ54
Barnet EN5 101 CY41
Bean DA2 211 FV90
Beckenham BR3 225 EA96
Bedmond WD5 81 BT27
Berkhamsted HP4 60 AW19
Bletchingley RH1 274 DQ133
Bookham KT23 268 CB125
Bovingdon HP3 79 BA27
Brasted TN16 262 EV124
Bray SL6 172 AC75
Brentford TW8 179 CJ80
Brentwood CM14 130 FV47
Bromley BR1 226 EG96
Burnham SL1 152 AJ69
Bushey WD23 98 CA44
Carshalton SM5 240 DG105
Caterham CR3 258 DS123
Chalfont St. Giles HP8 112 AW48
Chalfont St. Peter SL9 112 AY53
Chalvey SL1 173 AQ76
Cheam SM3 239 CY107
Chesham HP5 76 AQ31
Cheshunt EN8 89 DX29
Chipstead TN13 278 FC122
Chislehurst BR7 207 EP93
Chobham GU24 232 AS111
Claygate KT10 237 CF107
Cobham KT11 235 BV114
Colnbrook SL3 175 BC80
Colney Heath AL4 66 CP22
Cowley UB8 156 BJ70
Cranford TW5 177 BV80
Croydon CR0 224 DQ103
Dartford DA1 210 FL86
Datchet SL3 174 AV81
Dorking RH4 285 CH136
Downe BR6 245 EN111
Edgware HA8 118 CN51
Egham TW20 195 BA92
Elstree WD6 99 CK44
Epping CM16 91 ET31
Epsom KT19 238 CR113
Esher KT10 236 CB105
Eton SL4 173 AR79
Ewell KT17 239 CT109
Eynsford DA4 230 FL103
Farnborough BR6 245 EP106
Farningham DA4 230 FM100
Feltham TW13 197 BT90
Godstone RH9 274 DV131
Gravesend DA11 213 GH86
Grays RM17 192 GA79
Green Street Green BR6 245 ET108
Greenhithe DA9 191 FV84
Guildford GU1, GU2 280 AX135
Hampton TW12 198 CC93
Hampton Wick KT1 219 CJ95
Harefield UB9 114 BJ54
Harlington UB3 177 BS78
Harlow CM17 58 EW11
Harmondsworth UB7 176 BK79
Harrow HA1, HA2 139 CE60
Hemel Hempstead HP1 62 BJ18
Hoddesdon EN11 71 EA19
Horley RH6 291 DH148
Hornchurch RM11, RM12 150 FK60
Horsell GU21 248 AV115
Hounslow TW3 178 CC83
Hunsdon SG12 56 EK06
Iver SL0 155 BE72
Kings Langley WD4 80 BN29
Kingston upon Thames KT1 219 CK96
Langley SL3 175 AZ78
Leatherhead KT22 253 CH122
Limpsfield RH8 276 EG128
London Colney AL2 83 CJ25
Merstham RH1 273 DH128
New Malden KT3 220 CS97
Northchurch HP4 60 AS17
Northfleet DA11 212 GB86
Northwood HA6 115 BT53
Nutfield RH1 273 DM133
Old Woking GU22 249 BB121
Orpington BR6 228 EU102
Otford TN14 263 FF116
Oxshott KT22 237 CD113
Oxted RH8 275 ED130
Pinner HA5 138 BY55
Ponders End EN3 104 DW43
Potters Bar EN6 86 DC33
Purfleet RM19 190 FN78
Purley CR8 241 DN111
High St, Redhill RH1 272 DF134
Reigate RH2 272 DA134
Rickmansworth WD3 114 BK46
Ripley GU23 250 BJ121
Romford RM1 149 FE57
Roydon CM19 56 EH14
Ruislip HA4 137 BS59
St. Albans AL3 65 CD20
St. Mary Cray BR5 228 EW98
Seal TN15 279 FL121
Sevenoaks TN13 279 FJ125
Shepperton TW17 217 BP100
Shoreham TN14 247 FF110
Slough SL1 174 AU75
Southall UB1 158 BZ74
Staines-upon-Thames TW18 195 BF91
Stanstead Abbotts SG12 55 EC11
Stanwell TW19 196 BK86
Sutton SM1 240 DB105
Swanley BR8 229 FF98
Swanscombe DA10 212 FZ85
Tadworth KT20 255 CW123
Taplow SL6 152 AE70
Teddington TW11 199 CG92
Thames Ditton KT7 219 CG101
Thornton Heath CR7 224 DQ98
Uxbridge UB8 156 BK67
Waltham Cross EN8 89 DY34
Walton-on-Thames KT12 217 BU102
Ware SG12 55 DX06
Watford WD17 97 BV41
Wealdstone HA3 139 CE55
Wembley HA9 140 CM63
West Molesey KT8 218 CA98
West Wickham BR4 225 EB102
Westerham TN16 277 EQ127
Weybridge KT13 234 BN105
Whitton TW2 198 CC87
Windsor SL4 173 AR81
Woking GU21 248 AY117
Wraysbury TW19 194 AY86
Yiewsley UB7 156 BK74
High St Colliers Wd, SW19 202 DD94
High St Grn, Hem.H. HP2 62 BN18
⊖ High Street Kensington 27 L5
High St Ms, SW19 201 CY92
High St N, E6 166 EL67
E12 146 EL64
High St S, E6 167 EM68
High St Wimbledon, SW19 201 CX92
High Timber St, EC4 19 J10
High Tor Cl, Brom. BR1 206 EH94
High Tor Vw, SE28 167 ES74
High Tree Cl, Add. KT15 233 BF106
Sawbridgeworth CM21 58 EX06
High Tree Ct, W7 159 CE73
High Trees, SW2 203 DN88
Barnet EN4 102 DE43
Croydon CR0 225 DY102
Dartford DA2 210 FP86
High Trees Cl, Cat. CR3 258 DT123
High Trees Ct, Brwd. CM14
off Warley Mt 130 FW49
High Trees Rd, Reig. RH2 288 DD135
Highview, Cat. CR3 258 DS124
High Vw, Ch.St.G. HP8 112 AX47
Chorleywood WD3 96 BG42
Gomshall GU5 283 BQ139
Hatfield AL10 67 CT20
Highview, Knap. GU21
off Mulgrave Way 248 AS117
Northolt UB5 158 BY69
High Vw, Pnr. HA5 138 BW56
Sutton SM2 239 CZ111
Watford WD18 97 BT44
Highview Av, Edg. HA8 118 CQ49
High Vw Av, Grays RM17 192 GC78
Highview Av, Wall. SM6 241 DM106
High Vw Caravan Pk, Kings L. WD4 81 BR28
High Vw Cl, SE19 224 DT96
Loughton IG10 106 EJ43
Highview Cl, Pot.B. EN6 86 DC33
Highview Cres, Hutt. CM13 131 GC44
Highview Gdns, N3 141 CY56
N11 121 DJ50
Edgware HA8 118 CQ49
High Vw Gdns, Grays RM17 192 GC78
Highview Gdns, Pot.B. EN6 86 DC33
St. Albans AL4 65 CJ15
Upminster RM14 150 FP61
Highview Ho, Rom. RM6 148 EY56
Highview Path, Bans. SM7 256 DA115
High View Pl, Amer. HP7 77 AQ40
Sch High Vw Prim Sch, SW11
off Plough Rd 182 DD84
Wallington SM6
off The Chase 241 DL106
High Vw Rd, E18 146 EF55
SE19 204 DR93
Highview Rd, W13 159 CG71
High Vw Rd, Guil. GU2 280 AS137
Highview Rd, Sid. DA14 208 EV91
Highway, The, E1 32 D1
E14 32 D1
Beaconsfield HP9
off Station Rd 111 AK52
Orpington BR6 246 EW106
Stanmore HA7 117 CF53
Sutton SM2 240 DC109
Highway Ct, Beac. HP9
off Station Rd 111 AK52
Sch Highway Prim Sch, The, Orp. BR6 off The Highway 246 EW106
High Wickfield, Welw.G.C. AL7 52 DC10
Highwold, Chipstead CR5 256 DG118
Highwood, Brom. BR2 225 ED97
Highwood Av, N12 120 DC49
Bushey WD23 98 BZ39
Highwood Cl, SE22 204 DU88
Brentwood CM14 130 FV45
Kenley CR8 258 DQ117
Orpington BR6 227 EQ103
Highwood Dr, Orp. BR6 227 EQ103
Highwood Gdns, Ilf. IG5 147 EM57
Highwood Gro, NW7 118 CR50
High Woodhall La, Hem.H. HP3 80 BN25
HIGHWOOD HILL, NW7 119 CU47
Highwood Hill, NW7 119 CT47
Highwood La, Loug. IG10 107 EN43
Sch Highwood Prim Sch, Bushey WD23 off Bushey Mill La 98 BY39
Highwood Rd, N19 143 DL62
High Wd Rd, Hodd. EN11 71 DZ15
Highwoods, Cat. CR3 274 DS125
Leatherhead KT22 253 CJ121
High Worple, Har. HA2 138 BZ59
Highworth Rd, N11 121 DK51
HIGH WYCH, Saw. CM21 58 EV06
Sch High Wych C of E Prim Sch, High Wych CM21
off High Wych Rd 58 EU06
High Wych Rd, Saw. CM21 58 EV06
Hilary Av, Mitch. CR4 222 DG97
Hilary Cl, SW6 39 L4
Erith DA8 189 FC81
Hornchurch RM12 150 FK64
Hilary Rd, W12 161 CT72
Hilbert Rd, Sutt. SM3 221 CX104
Hilborough Way, Orp. BR6 245 ER106
Hilbury, Hat. AL10 67 CT19
Hilbury Cl, Amer. HP6 77 AQ35
Hilda Lockert Wk, SW9
off Fiveways Rd 42 G9
Hilda May Av, Swan. BR8 229 FE97
Hilda Rd, E6 166 EK66
E16 23 K5
Hilda Ter, SW9 42 F8
Hilda Vale Cl, Orp. BR6 245 EN105
Hilda Vale Rd, Orp. BR6 245 EN105
Hildenborough Gdns, Brom. BR1 206 EE93
Hilden Dr, Erith DA8 189 FH80
Hildenlea Pl, Brom. BR2 226 EE96
Hildenley Cl, Merst. RH1
off Malmstone Av 273 DK128
Hildens, The, Westc. RH4 284 CB138
Hilders, The, Ashtd. KT21 254 CP117
Hildreth St, SW12 203 DH88
Hildreth St Ms, SW12
off Hildreth St 203 DH88
Hildyard Rd, SW6 39 K2
Hiley Rd, NW10 14 A1
Hilfield La, Ald. WD25 99 CD41
Hilfield La S, Bushey WD23 99 CF44
Hilgay, Guil. GU1 265 AZ134
Hilgay Cl, Guil. GU1 265 AZ134
Hilgrove Rd, NW6 5 P7
Hiliary Gdns, Stan. HA7 117 CJ54
Hiljon Cres, Chal.St.P. SL9 112 AY53
Hill, The, Cat. CR3 258 DT124
Harlow CM17 58 EW11
Northfleet DA11 212 GC86
Hillars Heath Rd, Couls. CR5 257 DL115
Hillary Av, Nthflt DA11 212 GE90
Hillary Cres, Walt. KT12 218 BW102
Hillary Dr, Islw. TW7 179 CF84
Hillary Ri, Barn. EN5 102 DA42
Hillary Rd, Hem.H. HP2 62 BN19
Slough SL3 174 AY75
Southall UB2 178 CA76
Hill Av, Amer. HP6 77 AQ38
Hill Barn, S.Croy. CR2 242 DS111
Hillbeck Cl, SE15 44 G4
Hillbeck Way, Grnf. UB6 159 CD67
Hillborne Cl, Hayes UB3 177 BU78
Hillborough Av, Sev. TN13 279 FK122
Hillborough Cl, SW19 202 DC94
Hillbrook Gdns, Wey. KT13 234 BN108
Sch Hillbrook Prim Sch, SW17
off Hillbrook Rd 202 DG91
Hillbrook Rd, SW17 202 DF90
Hill Brow, Brom. BR1 226 EK95
Dartford DA1 209 FF86
Hillbrow, N.Mal. KT3 221 CT97
Hillbrow Cl, Bex. DA5 209 FD91
Hillbrow Cotts, Gdse. RH9 274 DW132
Hillbrow Ct, Gdse. RH9 274 DW132
Hillbrow Rd, Brom. BR1 206 EE94
Esher KT10 236 CC105
Hillbury Av, Har. HA3 139 CH57
Hillbury Cl, Warl. CR6 258 DV118
Hillbury Cres, Warl. CR6 258 DW118
Hillbury Gdns, Warl. CR6 258 DW118
Hillbury Rd, SW17 203 DH90
Warlingham CR6 258 DU117
Whyteleafe CR3 258 DU117
Hill Cl, NW2 141 CV62
NW11 142 DA58
Barnet EN5 101 CW43
Chislehurst BR7 207 EP92
Cobham KT11 236 CA112
Harrow HA1 139 CE62
Istead Rise DA13 212 GE94
Purley CR8 242 DQ113
Stanmore HA7 117 CH49
Woking GU21 248 AX116
Wooburn Green HP10 132 AF56
Hill Common, Hem.H. HP3 62 BN24
Hillcote Av, SW16 203 DN94
Hill Ct, Gdmg. GU7 280 AS144
Northolt UB5 138 CA64
Hillcourt Av, N12 120 DB51
Hillcourt Est, N16 144 DR60
Hillcourt Rd, SE22 204 DV86
Hill Cres, N20 120 DB47
Bexley DA5 209 FC88
Harrow HA1 139 CG57
Hornchurch RM11 150 FJ58
Surbiton KT5 220 CM99
Worcester Park KT4 221 CW103
Hillcrest, N6 142 DG59
N21 121 DP45
SE24 184 DR84
Hatfield AL10 67 CU18
Hill Crest, Pot.B. EN6 86 DC34
Hillcrest, St.Alb. AL3 64 CB22
Hill Crest, Sev. TN13 278 FG122
Sidcup DA15 208 EU87
Hillcrest, Wey. KT13 235 BP105
Hillcrest Av, NW11 141 CY57
Chertsey KT16 233 BE105
Edgware HA8 118 CP49
Grays RM20 191 FU79
Pinner HA5 138 BX56
Hillcrest Caravan Pk, Box H. KT20 270 CP131
Hillcrest Cl, SE26 204 DU91
Beckenham BR3 225 DZ99
Epsom KT18 255 CT115
Goffs Oak EN7 88 DQ29
Hillcrest Ct, Sutt. SM2
off Eaton Rd 240 DD107
Hillcrest Dr, Green. DA9
off Riverview Rd 211 FU85
Hillcrest Gdns, N3 141 CY56
NW2 141 CU62
Esher KT10 219 CF104
Hillcrest Par, Couls. CR5 241 DH114
Hillcrest Rd, E17 123 ED54
E18 124 EF54
W3 160 CN74
W5 160 CL71
Biggin Hill TN16 260 EK116
Bromley BR1 206 EG92
Dartford DA1 209 FF87
Guildford GU2 264 AT133
Hornchurch RM11 149 FG59

Hillcrest Rd, Loughton IG10 106 EK44
Orpington BR6 228 EU103
Purley CR8 241 DM110
Shenley WD7 84 CN33
Toot Hill CM5 93 FE30
Whyteleafe CR3 258 DT117
Hillcrest Vw, Beck. BR3 225 DZ100
Hillcrest Way, Epp. CM16 92 EU31
Hillcrest Waye, Ger.Cr. SL9 135 AZ59
Hillcroft, Loug. IG10 107 EN40
Hill Cft, Rad. WD7 83 CG33
Hillcroft Av, Pnr. HA5 138 BZ58
Purley CR8 241 DJ113
Coll Hillcroft Coll, Surb. KT6 off South Bk 220 CL100
Hillcroft Cres, W5 160 CL72
Ruislip HA4 138 BX62
Watford WD19 115 BV46
Wembley HA9 140 CM63
Sch Hillcroft Prim Sch, Cat. CR3 off Chaldon Rd 258 DS123
Hillcroft Rd, E6 25 N6
Chesham HP5 76 AR29
Penn HP10 110 AC46
Hillcroome Rd, Sutt. SM2 240 DD107
Hillcross Av, Mord. SM4 221 CZ99
Sch Hillcross Prim Sch, Mord. SM4 off Ashridge Way 221 CZ98
Hilldale Rd, Sutt. SM1 239 CZ105
Hilldeane Rd, Pur. CR8 241 DN109
Hilldene Av, Rom. RM3 128 FJ51
Hilldene Cl, Rom. RM3 128 FK50
Sch Hilldene Prim Sch, Rom. RM3 off Grange Rd 128 FJ51
Hilldown Rd, SW16 203 DL94
Bromley BR2 226 EE102
Hemel Hempstead HP1 62 BG18
Hill Dr, NW9 140 CQ60
SW16 223 DM97
Leatherhead KT22 253 CF119
Hilldrop Cres, N7 7 P3
Hilldrop Est, N7 7 N2
Hilldrop La, N7 7 P3
Hilldrop Rd, N7 7 N2
Bromley BR1 206 EG93
HILL END, Uxb. UB9 114 BH51
Hillend, SE18 187 EN81
Hill End, Orp. BR6 off The Approach 227 ET103
Hill End La, St.Alb. AL4 65 CJ23
Hill End Rd, Hare. UB9 114 BH51
Hillersdon, Slou. SL2 154 AV71
Hillersdon Av, SW13 181 CU82
Edgware HA8 118 CM50
Hillery Cl, SE17 31 M9
Hilley Fld La, Fetch. KT22 252 CC122
Hill Fm App, Woob.Grn HP10 132 AE55
Hill Fm Av, Wat. WD25 81 BU33
Hill Fm Cl, Wat. WD25 81 BU33
● Hill Fm Ind Est, Wat. WD25 81 BT33
Hill Fm La, Ch.St.G. HP8 112 AT46
Hill Fm Rd, W10 14 B6
Chalfont St. Peter SL9 112 AY52
Chesham HP5 76 AR34
Taplow SL6 152 AE68
Uxbridge UB10 off Austin's La 137 BR63
Hillfield, Hat. AL10 67 CV15
Hillfield Av, N8 143 DL57
NW9 140 CS57
Morden SM4 222 DE100
Wembley HA0 160 CL66
Hillfield Cl, Guil. GU1 265 BC132
Harrow HA2 138 CC56
Redhill RH1 272 DG134
Hillfield Ct, NW3 6 C3
Hemel Hempstead HP2 62 BL20
Hillfield Ms, N8 143 DM56
Hillfield Pk, N10 143 DH56
N21 121 DN47
Hillfield Pk Ms, N10 143 DH56
Hillfield Pl, Dunt.Grn TN13 263 FE120
Hillfield Rd, NW6 5 H3
Chalfont St. Peter SL9 112 AY52
Dunton Green TN13 263 FE120
Hampton TW12 198 BZ94
Hemel Hempstead HP2 62 BK20
Redhill RH1 272 DG134
Hillfield Sq, Chal.St.P. SL9 112 AY52
Hillfoot Av, Rom. RM5 127 FC53
Hillfoot Rd, Rom. RM5 127 FC53
Hillford Pl, Red. RH1 288 DG140
Hillgate Pl, SW12 203 DH87
W8 27 J2
Hillgate St, W8 27 J2
Hill Gate Wk, N6 143 DJ58
Hillground Gdns, S.Croy. CR2 241 DP110
Hillgrove, Chal.St.P. SL9 113 AZ53
Hill Gro, Felt. TW13 off Watermill Way 198 BZ89
Romford RM1 149 FE55
● Hillgrove Business Pk, Lwr Naze. EN9 71 EC22
Hill Hall, They.Mt CM16 108 EZ35
Hill Ho, E5 144 DV60
Hillhouse, Wal.Abb. EN9 90 EF33
Hill Ho Av, Stan. HA7 117 CF52
Hill Ho Cl, N21 121 DN45
Chalfont St. Peter SL9 off Rickmansworth La 112 AY52
Sch Hillhouse C of E Prim Sch, Wal.Abb. EN9 off Ninefields 90 EF33
Hill Ho Dr, Chad.St.M. RM16 193 GH78
Hampton TW12 218 CA95
Hillhouse Dr, Reig. RH2 288 DB136
Hill Ho Dr, Wey. KT13 234 BN111
Sch Hill Ho Int Jun Sch, SW1 28 F7
Hill Ho Ms, Brom. BR2 226 EF96
Hill Ho Rd, SW16 203 DM92
Hillhouse Rd, Dart. DA2 210 FQ87
Hillhurst Gdns, Cat. CR3 258 DS120
Hilliard Rd, Nthwd. HA6 115 BT53
Hilliards Ct, E1 32 F2
Hilliards Rd, Uxb. UB8 156 BK72
Hillier Cl, New Barn. EN5 102 DB44
Hillier Gdns, Croy. CR0 241 DN106
Hillier Pl, Chess. KT9 237 CK107
Hillier Rd, SW11 202 DF86
Guildford GU1 265 BA134
Hilliers Av, Uxb. UB8 156 BN69
Hilliers La, Croy. CR0 223 DL104
Hillier Way, Slou. SL3 175 BA77
Hillingdale, Bigg.H. TN16 260 EH118
HILLINGDON, Uxb. UB8 156 BN69
⊖ Hillingdon 136 BN64
Hillingdon Av, Sev. TN13 279 FJ121
Staines-upon-Thames TW19 196 BL88
Jct Hillingdon Circ, Uxb. UB10 136 BM64
Hillingdon Hill, Uxb. UB10 156 BL69
H Hillingdon Hosp, Uxb. UB8 156 BM71
Sch Hillingdon Manor Sch, Lwr & Mid Schs, Hayes End UB8 off Harlington Rd 157 BP71
Sch Hillingdon Prim Sch, Hlgdn UB10 off Uxbridge Rd 157 BP69
Hillingdon Ri, Sev. TN13 279 FK122
Hillingdon Rd, Bexh. DA7 189 FC82
Gravesend DA11 213 GG89
Uxbridge UB10 156 BL67
Watford WD25 81 BU34
Hillingdon St, SE17 43 H3
Hillington Gdns, Wdf.Grn. IG8 124 EK54
Hill La, Kgswd KT20 255 CY121
Ruislip HA4 137 BQ60
Hill Ley, Hat. AL10 67 CT18
Hill Leys, Cuffley EN6 87 DL28
Hillman Cl, Horn. RM11 150 FK55
Uxbridge UB8 136 BL64
Hillman Dr, W10 14 B5
Hillman St, E8 10 F5
Hillmarton Rd, N7 8 A2
Hillmead, Berk. HP4 60 AU20
Hillmead Ct, Tap. SL6 152 AF71
Hillmead Dr, SW9 183 DP84
Hill Meadow, Colesh. HP7 77 AM43
Sch Hill Mead Prim Sch, SW9 off Hillmead Dr 183 DP84
Hillmont Rd, Esher KT10 219 CE104
Hillmore Gro, SE26 205 DX92
Hillmount, Wok. GU22 off Constitution Hill 248 AY119
Hill Path, SW16 off Valley Rd 203 DM92
Hill Pl, Farn.Com. SL2 153 AP66
Hillpoint, Loud. WD3 96 BJ43
Hillreach, SE18 37 J10
Hill Ri, N9 104 DV44
NW11 142 DB56
SE23 204 DV88
Chalfont St. Peter SL9 112 AX54
Cuffley EN6 87 DK27
Dorking RH4 269 CG134
Esher KT10 219 CH103
Greenford UB6 158 CC66
Lane End DA2 211 FR92
Potters Bar EN6 86 DC34
Richmond TW10 199 CK85
Rickmansworth WD3 96 BH44
Ruislip HA4 137 BQ60
Slough SL3 175 BA79
Upminster RM14 150 FN61
Hillrise, Walt. KT12 217 BT101
Hillrise Av, Wat. WD24 98 BX38
Hill Ri Cres, Chal.St.P. SL9 112 AY54
Hillrise Rd, N19 143 DL59
Romford RM5 127 FC51
Hill Rd, N10 120 DF53
NW8 15 P1
Brentwood CM14 130 FU48
Carshalton SM5 240 DE107
Dartford DA2 210 FL89
Fetcham KT22 252 CB122
Harrow HA1 139 CG57
Mitcham CR4 223 DH95
Northwood HA6 115 BR51
Pinner HA5 138 BY57
Purley CR8 241 DM112
Sutton SM1 240 DB106
Theydon Bois CM16 107 ES37
Wembley HA0 139 CH62
Hillsboro Rd, SE22 204 DS85
Hillsborough Grn, Wat. WD19 115 BU48
Hills Chace, Warley CM14 130 FW49
Hillsgrove Cl, Well. DA16 188 EW80
Sch Hillsgrove Prim Sch, Well. DA16 off Sidmouth Rd 188 EW80
Hillside, NW9 140 CR56
NW10 160 CQ67
SW19 201 CX93
Banstead SM7 255 CY115
Chesham HP5 76 AN28
Erith DA8 189 FD77
Farningham DA4 230 FM101
Grays RM17 192 GD77
Harefield UB9 136 BJ57
Harlow CM17 74 EW17
Hatfield AL10 67 CU18
Hoddesdon EN11 71 DZ16
Lane End DA2 211 FS92
New Barnet EN5 102 DC43
Slough SL1 174 AS75
Virginia Water GU25 214 AW100
Ware SG12 54 DW07
Welwyn Garden City AL7 52 DB12
Woking GU22 248 AX120
Hillside, The, Orp. BR6 246 EV109
Hillside Av, N11 120 DF51
Borehamwood WD6 100 CP42
Cheshunt EN8 89 DX31
Gravesend DA12 213 GK89
Purley CR8 241 DP113
Wembley HA9 140 CM63
Woodford Green IG8 124 EJ50
Hillside Cl, NW8 5 M10
Abbots Langley WD5 81 BS32
Banstead SM7 255 CY116
Brockham RH3 286 CN135
Chalfont St. Giles HP8 112 AV48
Chalfont St. Peter SL9 112 AY51
Morden SM4 221 CY98
Woodford Green IG8 124 EJ50
Hillside Ct, St.Alb. AL1 off Hillside Rd 65 CE19
Swanley BR8 229 FG98
Hillside Cres, Chsht EN8 89 DX31
Enfield EN2 104 DR38
Harrow HA2 138 CC60
Northwood HA6 115 BU53
Stanstead Abbotts SG12 55 EB11
Watford WD19 98 BY44
Hillside Dr, Edg. HA8 118 CN51
Gravesend DA12 213 GK89
Hillside Gdns, E17 145 ED55
N6 142 DG58
SW2 203 DN89
Addlestone KT15 233 BF106
Amersham HP7 77 AS40
Barnet EN5 101 CY42
Berkhamsted HP4 60 AX20
Brockham RH3 270 CN134
Edgware HA8 118 CM49
Harrow HA3 140 CL59
Northwood HA6 115 BU52
Wallington SM6 241 DJ108
Hillside Gate, St.Alb. AL1 65 CE19
Hillside Gro, N14 121 DK45
NW7 119 CU52
Sch Hillside Inf & Jun Schs, Nthwd. HA6 off Northwood Way 115 BU52
Hillside La, Brom. BR2 226 EG103
Great Amwell SG12 55 EA10
Hillside Pas, SW2 203 DM89
Sch Hillside Prim Sch, Orp. BR5 off Dyke Dr 228 EW101
Hillside Ri, Nthwd. HA6 115 BU52
Hillside Rd, N15 144 DS59
SW2 203 DN89
W5 160 CL71
Ashtead KT21 254 CM117
Bromley BR2 226 EF97
Bushey WD23 98 BY43
Chorleywood WD3 95 BC43
Coulsdon CR5 257 DM118
Croydon CR0 241 DP106
Dartford DA1 209 FG86
Epsom KT17 239 CV110
Northwood HA6 115 BU52
Pinner HA5 115 BV52
Radlett WD7 99 CH35
St. Albans AL1 65 CE19
Sevenoaks TN13 279 FK123
Southall UB1 158 CA70
Surbiton KT5 220 CM99
Sutton SM2 239 CZ108
Tatsfield TN16 260 EL119
Whyteleafe CR3 258 DU118
Hillside Ter, Hert. SG13 54 DQ11
Hillside Wk, Brwd. CM14 130 FU48
Hills La, Nthwd. HA6 115 BS53
Hillsleigh Rd, W8 27 H2
Hillsmead Way, S.Croy. CR2 242 DU113
Hills Ms, W5 160 CL73
Hills Pl, W1 17 L9
Hillspur Cl, Guil. GU2 264 AT133
Hillspur Rd, Guil. GU2 264 AT133
Hills Rd, Buck.H. IG9 124 EH46
Hillstowe St, E5 144 DW61
Hill St, W1 29 H2
Richmond TW9 199 CK85
St. Albans AL3 64 CC20
● Hillswood Business Pk, Cher. KT16 233 BC105
Hillswood Dr, Cher. KT16 233 BC105
Hillthorpe Cl, Pur. CR8 241 DM110
HILLTOP, Chesh. HP5 76 AR28
Hill Top, NW11 142 DB56
Hilltop, Loug. IG10 107 EN40
Hill Top, Mord. SM4 222 DA100
Sutton SM3 221 CZ101
Hilltop Av, NW10 160 CQ66
Hilltop Cl, Chsht EN7 88 DT26
Guildford GU3 264 AT130
Leatherhead KT22 253 CJ123
Hill Top Cl, Loug. IG10 107 EN41
Sch Hilltop First Sch, Wind. SL4 off Clewer Hill Rd 173 AL83
Hilltop Gdns, NW4 119 CV54
Dartford DA1 210 FM85
Orpington BR6 227 ES103
Hilltop La, Chaldon CR3 273 DN126
Redhill RH1 273 DN126
Hill Top Pl, Loug. IG10 107 EN41
Hilltop Ri, Bkhm KT23 268 CC126
Hilltop Rd, NW6 5 K6
Berkhamsted HP4 60 AW20
Grays RM20 191 FV79
Kings Langley WD4 81 BR27
Reigate RH2 288 DB136
Whyteleafe CR3 258 DS117
Hill Top Vw, Wdf.Grn. IG8 125 EM51
Hilltop Wk, Wold. CR3 259 DY120
Hilltop Way, Stan. HA7 117 CG48
Hillview, SW20 201 CV94
Hill Vw, Berk. HP4 60 AU17
Dorking RH4 285 CJ135
Hillview, Mitch. CR4 223 DL98
Whyteleafe CR3 258 DT117
Hillview Av, Har. HA3 140 CL57
Hornchurch RM11 150 FJ58
Hillview Cl, Pnr. HA5 116 BZ51
Purley CR8 241 DP111
Hill Vw Cl, Tad. KT20 255 CW121
Hillview Cl, Wem. HA9 140 CM61
Hillview Cl, Wok. GU22 249 AZ118
Hillview Cres, Guil. GU2 264 AT132
Ilford IG1 147 EM58
Orpington BR6 227 ES102
Hill Vw Dr, SE28 167 ES74
Hillview Dr, Red. RH1 288 DG135
Hill Vw Dr, Well. DA16 187 ES82
Hillview Gdns, NW4 141 CX56
Hill Vw Gdns, NW9 140 CR57
Hillview Gdns, Chsht EN8 89 DX27
Harrow HA2 138 CA55
Hillview Rd, NW7 119 CX49
Chislehurst BR7 207 EN92
Hill Vw Rd, Clay. KT10 237 CG108
Hillview Rd, Orp. BR6 227 ET102
Pinner HA5 116 BZ52
Sutton SM1 222 DC104
Hill Vw Rd, Twick. TW1 199 CG86
Woking GU22 249 AZ118
Wraysbury TW19 194 AX86
Hillway, N6 142 DG61
NW9 140 CS60
Amersham HP7 77 AP41
Hill Waye, Ger.Cr. SL9 135 AZ58
Hillwood Cl, Hutt. CM13 131 GB46
Hillwood Gro, Hutt. CM13 131 GB46
Hillworth Rd, SW2 203 DN87
Hillyard Rd, W7 159 CE71
Hillyard St, SW9 42 D7
Hillyfield, E17 123 DY54
Hilly Fld, Harl. CM18 73 ET19
Hillyfield Cl, E9 11 M3
Sch Hillyfield Prim Sch, E17 off Higham Hill Rd 145 DY55
Hillyfields, Loug. IG10 107 EN40
Hilly Flds, Welw.G.C. AL7 52 DC08
Hilly Flds Cres, SE4 185 EA83
Hilmay Dr, Hem.H. HP1 62 BH21
Hilperton Rd, Slou. SL1 174 AS75
Hilsea Pt, SW15 off Wanborough Dr 201 CV88
Hilsea St, E5 144 DW63
Hilton Av, N12 120 DD50
Hilton Cl, Uxb. UB8 156 BH68
Hilton Ct, Horl. RH6 off Clarence Way 291 DK147
Riv Hilton Docklands Nelson Dock Pier 33 N2
Hilton Way, S.Croy. CR2 258 DV115
Hilversum Cres, SE22 off East Dulwich Gro 204 DS85
Himalayan Way, Wat. WD18 97 BT43
Himley Rd, SW17 202 DE92
Hinchley Cl, Esher KT10 219 CF104
Hinchley Dr, Esher KT10 219 CF104
Hinchley Manor, Esher KT10 219 CF104
Hinchley Way, Esher KT10 219 CG104
HINCHLEY WOOD, Esher KT10 219 CF104
⇌ Hinchley Wood 219 CF104
Sch Hinchley Wd Prim Sch, Hinch.Wd KT10 off Claygate La 219 CG103
Sch Hinchley Wd Sch & 6th Form Cen, Hinch.Wd KT10 off Claygate La 219 CG103
Hinckley Rd, SE15 184 DU84
Hind Cl, Chig. IG7 125 ET50
Hind Ct, EC4 18 F9
Hind Cres, Erith DA8 189 FD79
Hinde Ms, W1 off Marylebone La 17 H8
Hindes Rd, Har. HA1 139 CD57
Hinde St, W1 17 H8
Hind Gro, E14 22 A9
Hindhead Cl, N16 144 DS60
Uxbridge UB8 157 BP71
Hindhead Gdns, Nthlt. UB5 158 BY67
Hindhead Grn, Wat. WD19 116 BW50
Hindhead Pt, SW15 off Wanborough Dr 201 CV88
Hindhead Way, Wall. SM6 241 DL106
Hind Ho, N7 off Harvist Est 143 DN63
Hinde Ho, E8 10 A1
Hindmans Rd, SE22 204 DU85
Hindmans Way, Dag. RM9 168 EZ70
Hindmarsh Cl, E1 20 D10
Hindon Ct, SW1 29 L8
Hindrey Rd, E5 10 E2
Hindsley's Pl, SE23 204 DW89
Hind Ter, Grays RM20 off Mill La 191 FX78
Hine Cl, Couls. CR5 257 DJ122
Epsom KT19 238 CP111
Hinkler Rd, Har. HA3 139 CK55
Hinkley Cl, Hare. UB9 136 BJ56
Hinksey Cl, Slou. SL3 175 BB76
Hinksey Path, SE2 188 EX76
Hinstock Rd, SE18 187 EQ79
Hinton Av, Houns. TW4 178 BX84
Hinton Cl, SE9 206 EL88
Hinton Rd, N18 122 DS49
SE24 183 DP83
Slough SL1 153 AL73
Uxbridge UB8 156 BJ67
Wallington SM6 241 DJ107
Hintons, Harl. CM19 73 EM19
Hipkins Pl, Brox. EN10 71 DY20
Hipley Ct, Guil. GU1 281 BA135
Hipley St, Wok. GU22 249 BB121
Hippodrome Ms, W11 26 E1
Hippodrome Pl, W11 26 F1
Hirst Ct, SW1 41 J1
Hirst Cres, Wem. HA9 140 CL62
Hispano Ms, Enf. EN3 105 EA37
Hitcham La, Burn. SL1 152 AG69
Taplow SL6 152 AG69
Hitcham Rd, E17 145 DZ59
Burnham SL1 152 AF70
Taplow SL6 152 AF72
Hitchcock Cl, Shep. TW17 216 BM97
Hitchcock La, E20 12 F5
Hitchen Hatch La, Sev. TN13 278 FG124
Hitchens Cl, Hem.H. HP1 61 BF19
Hitchin Cl, Rom. RM3 128 FJ49
Hitchings Way, Reig. RH2 288 DA138
Hitchin Sq, E3 11 M10
Hithe Gro, SE16 33 H7
Hitherbaulk, Welw.G.C. AL7 51 CY11
Hitherbroom Rd, Hayes UB3 157 BU74
Hitherbury Cl, Guil. GU2 280 AW137
Hither Fm Rd, SE3 186 EJ83
Sch Hitherfield Prim Sch, SW16 off Hitherfield Rd 203 DN90
Hitherfield Rd, SW16 203 DM89
Dagenham RM8 148 EY61
HITHER GREEN, SE13 206 EE86
⇌ Hither Green 206 EE86
Hither Grn La, SE13 205 EC85
Sch Hither Grn Prim Sch, SE13 off Beacon Rd 205 ED86
Hitherlands, SW12 203 DH89
Hither Meadow, Chal.St.P. SL9 off Lower Rd 112 AY54
Hithermoor Rd, Stai. TW19 196 BG85
Hitherway, Welw.G.C. AL8 51 CY05
Hitherwell Dr, Har. HA3 117 CD53
Hitherwood Cl, Horn. RM12 off Swanbourne Dr 150 FK63
Reigate RH2 272 DD132
Hitherwood Dr, SE19 204 DT91
Hive, The, Nthflt DA11 off Fishermans Hill 212 GB85
Hive Cl, Brwd. CM14 130 FU47
Bushey Heath WD23 117 CD47
Hive La, Nthflt DA11 212 GB86
Hive Rd, Bushey Hth WD23 117 CD47
Hivings Hill, Chesh. HP5 76 AN28
Hivings Pk, Chesh. HP5 76 AP28
Hixberry La, St.Alb. AL4 65 CK21
★ H.M.S. Belfast, SE1 31 P2
★ H.M.S. President, EC4 30 F1
★ H.M. Treasury, SW1 30 A4
Hoadly Rd, SW16 203 DK90
Hobart Cl, N20 off Oakleigh Rd N 120 DE47
Hayes UB4 158 BX70
Hobart Dr, Hayes UB4 158 BX70
Hobart Gdns, Th.Hth. CR7 224 DR97
Hobart La, Hayes UB4 158 BX70
Hobart Pl, SW1 29 J6
Richmond TW10 off Chisholm Rd 200 CM86
Hobart Rd, Dag. RM9 148 EX63
Hayes UB4 158 BX70
Ilford IG6 125 EQ54
Tilbury RM18 193 GG81
Worcester Park KT4 221 CV104
Hobart Wk, St.Alb. AL3 off Valley Rd 65 CF16
Hobbans Fm Shop, Ong. CM5 75 FH23
Sch Hobbayne Prim Sch, W7 off Greenford Av 159 CF72
Hobbayne Rd, W7 159 CD72
Hobbes Wk, SW15 201 CV85
Hobbs Cl, Chsht EN8 89 DX29
St. Albans AL4 66 CL21
West Byfleet KT14 234 BH113
Hobbs Cross, Harl. CM17 58 FA14
● Hobbs Cross Business Cen, They.Gar. CM16 108 EX36
Hobbs Cross Rd, Harl. CM17 58 EY12
Theydon Garnon CM16 108 EW35
Hobbs Grn, N2 142 DC55
Hobbs Hill Rd, Hem.H. HP3 62 BL24
Sch Hobbs Hill Wd Prim Sch, Hem.H. HP3 off Peascroft Rd 63 BP22
Hobbs Ms, Ilf. IG3 off Ripley Rd 147 ET61
Hobbs Pl Est, N1 9 N9
Hobbs Rd, SE27 204 DQ91
Hobbs Way, Welw.G.C. AL8 51 CW10
Hobby Horse Cl, Chsht EN7 off Great Stockwood Rd 88 DR26
Hobby St, Enf. EN3 105 DX43
Hobday St, E14 22 C8
Hobill Wk, Surb. KT5 220 CM100
Hoblands End, Chis. BR7 207 ES93
Sch Hobletts Manor Inf & Nurs Sch, Hem.H. HP2 off Adeyfield Rd 62 BN19
Sch Hobletts Manor Jun Sch, Hem.H. HP2 off Adeyfield Rd 62 BN19
Hobletts Rd, Hem.H. HP2 62 BM19
Hobsons Cl, Hodd. EN11 55 DZ14
Hobsons Pl, E1 20 C6
Hobtoe Rd, Harl. CM20 57 EN14
Hobury St, SW10 39 P3
Hockenden La, Swan. BR8 229 FB96
Hockeridge Bottom, Berk. HP4 60 AT21
Hockering Gdns, Wok. GU22 249 BA117
Hockering Rd, Wok. GU22 249 BA118
Hocker St, E2 20 A3
Hocklands, Welw.G.C. AL7 52 DC08
Hockley Av, E6 166 EL68
Hockley Ct, E18 off Churchfields 124 EG53
Hockley Dr, Rom. RM2 127 FH54
Hockley La, Stoke P. SL2 154 AV67
Hockley Ms, Bark. IG11 167 ES68
Hocroft Av, NW2 141 CZ62
Hocroft Rd, NW2 141 CZ63
Hocroft Wk, NW2 141 CZ62
Hodder Dr, Perivale UB6 159 CF68
HODDESDON, EN11 71 DZ18
Jct Hoddesdon, Hodd. EN11 71 DX16
Hoddesdon Bypass, Brox. EN10 71 DX19
Hertford SG13 55 DY14
Hoddesdon EN11 55 DY14
● Hoddesdon Ind Cen, Hodd. EN11 71 EC15
Hoddesdon Rd, Belv. DA17 188 FA78
Broxbourne EN10 89 DX27
Stanstead Abbotts SG12 55 EC11
Hodds Wd Rd, Chesh. HP5 76 AQ33
Hodes Row, NW3 6 F1
Hodford Rd, NW11 141 CZ61
Hodgemoor Vw, Ch.St.G. HP8 112 AT48
Hodges Cl, Chaff.Hun. RM16 191 FX78
Hodges Way, Wat. WD18 97 BU44
Hodgkin Cl, SE28 off Fleming Way 168 EX73
Hodgkins Ms, Stan. HA7 117 CH50
Hodgson Gdns, Guil. GU4 off Sutherland Dr 265 BA131
Hodings Rd, Harl. CM20 57 EP14
Hodister Cl, SE5 43 K5
Hodnet Gro, SE16 33 J8
Hodsoll Ct, Orp. BR5 228 EX100
Hodson Cl, Har. HA2 138 BZ62
Hodson Cres, Orp. BR5 228 EX100
Hodson Pl, Enf. EN3 105 EA38
HOE, Guil. GU5 283 BS143
Hoe, The, Wat. WD19 116 BX47
Sch Hoe Br Sch, Old Wok. GU22 off Old Woking Rd 249 BC119
Hoebrook Cl, Wok. GU22 248 AX121
Hoecroft, Lwr Naze. EN9 72 EF22
Hoe La, Abin.Ham. RH5 283 BT143
Abridge RM4 108 EV43
Enfield EN1, EN3 104 DU38
Nazeing EN9 72 EF22
Peaslake GU5 283 BR144
Ware SG12 55 DX09
Hoe Meadow, Beac. HP9 110 AJ51
Hoestock Rd, Saw. CM21 58 EX05
Hoe St, E17 145 EA56
Hoffmann Gdns, S.Croy. CR2 242 DU108
Hoffman Sq, N1 off Chart St 19 M2
Hofland Rd, W14 26 D6
Hoford Rd, Grays RM16 193 GK76
Linford SS17 193 GL75
West Tilbury RM18 193 GK77
Hogan Ms, W2 16 A6
Hogan Way, E5 144 DU61
Hogarth Av, Ashf. TW15 197 BQ93
Brentwood CM15 130 FY48
● Hogarth Business Pk, W4 180 CS79
Hogarth Cl, E16 24 E6
W5 160 CL71
Slough SL1 153 AL73
Uxbridge UB8 156 BJ69
Hogarth Ct, EC3 19 P10
SE19 off Fountain Dr 204 DT91
Bushey WD23 off Steeplands 116 CB45
Hogarth Cres, SW19 222 DD95
Croydon CR0 224 DQ101
Hogarth Gdns, Houns. TW5 178 CA80
Hogarth Hill, NW11 141 CZ56
Hogarth Ho, Enf. EN1 off Ayley Cft 104 DU43
Hogarth La, W4 180 CS79
Hogarth Pl, SW5 27 L9
Sch Hogarth Prim Sch, Brwd. CM15 off Riseway 131 FZ48
Hogarth Reach, Loug. IG10 107 EM43
Hogarth Rd, SW5 27 L9
Dagenham RM8 148 EV64
Edgware HA8 118 CN54
Jct Hogarth Rbt, W4 181 CT79
Hogarth Rbt Flyover, W4 off Burlington La 180 CS79
★ Hogarth's Ho, W4 off Hogarth La 180 CS79
Hogarth Way, Hmptn. TW12 218 CC95
Hogback Wd Rd, Beac. HP9 110 AH51
Hogden La, Lthd. KT23 268 CA129
Ranmore Common RH5 268 BZ132
Hogfair La, Burn. SL1 152 AJ69

Hogg End La, Hem.H. HP2 63 BR17
St. Albans AL3 63 BT17
Hogges Cl, Hodd. EN11
off Conduit La 71 EA17
Hogg La, Els. WD6 99 CG42
Grays RM16, RM17 192 GA76
Hog Hill Rd, Rom. RM5 126 EZ52
Hog Pits, Flaun. HP3 79 BB32
HOGPITS BOTTOM,
Hem.H. HP3 79 BA31
Hogpits Bottom, Flaun. HP3 79 BA32
Hogs Back, Guil. GU3 280 AS137
Hogscross La, Chipstead CR5 256 DF123
Hogsdell La, Hert.Hth SG13 54 DV11
Hogshead Pas, E1 32 F1
Hogshill La, Cob. KT11 235 BV114
Hogs La, Grav. DA11 212 GD90
Hogsmill La, Kings.T. KT1 220 CM97
Hogsmill Way, Epsom KT19 238 CQ106
Hogs Orchard, Swan. BR8 229 FH95
Hogtrough Hill, Brasted TN16 261 ET120
Hogtrough La, Gdse. RH9 275 EA128
Oxted RH8 275 EB128
Redhill RH1 289 DJ135
Holbeach Cl, NW9 118 CS53
Holbeach Gdns, Sid. DA15 207 ES86
Holbeach Ms, SW12 203 DH88
Sch Holbeach Prim Sch, SE6
off Doggett Rd 205 EA87
Holbeach Rd, SE6 205 EA87
Holbeck La, Chsht EN7 88 DT26
Holbeck Row, SE15 44 D5
Holbein Gate, Nthwd. HA6 115 BS50
Holbein Ms, SW1 28 G10
Holbein Pl, SW1 28 G9
Holbein Ter, Barn. EN5
off Ivere Dr 102 DB44
Dag. RM8
off Marlborough Rd 148 EW63
Holberton Gdns, NW10 161 CV69
HOLBORN, WC2 18 C8
⊖ Holborn 18 B8
Holborn, EC1 18 E7
Holborn Circ, EC1 18 F7
Holborn Cl, St.Alb. AL4 65 CK15
Coll Holborn Coll, SE7 36 F8
Holborn Pl, WC1 18 C7
Holborn Rd, E13 24 A5
Holborn Viaduct, EC1 18 F7
Holborn Way, Mitch. CR4 222 DF96
Holbreck Pl, Wok. GU22
off Heathside Rd 249 AZ118
Holbrook Cl, N19
off Dartmouth Pk Hill 143 DH60
Enfield EN1 104 DT39
Shalford GU4 280 AY142
Holbrooke Ct, N7 143 DL63
Holbrooke Pl, Rich. TW10 199 CK85
Holbrook Gdns, Ald. WD25 98 CB36
Holbrook La, Chis. BR7 207 ER94
Holbrook Meadow, Egh. TW20 195 BC93
Holbrook Rd, E15 23 L1
Holbrook Way, Brom. BR2 227 EM100
Holburne Cl, SE3 186 EJ81
Holburne Gdns, SE3 186 EK81
Holburne Rd, SE3 186 EJ81
Holcombe Cl, West. TN16 277 ER126
Holcombe Hill, NW7 119 CU48
Holcombe Rd, N17 144 DT55
Ilford IG1 147 EN59
Holcombe St, W6 181 CV78
Holcon Ct, Red. RH1 272 DG131
Holcote Cl, Belv. DA17
off Blakemore Way 188 EY76
Holcroft Rd, E9 11 H6
HOLDBROOK, Wal.Cr. EN8 89 EA34
Holdbrook Ct, Wal.Cr. EN8
off Queens Way 89 DZ34
Holdbrook N, Wal.Cr. EN8 89 DZ33
Sch Holdbrook Prim Sch,
Wal.Cr. EN8
off Longcroft Dr 89 DZ34
Holdbrook S, Wal.Cr. EN8
off Queens Way 89 DZ34
Holdbrook Way, Rom. RM3 128 FM54
Holden Av, N12 120 DB50
NW9 140 CQ60
Holdenby Rd, SE4 205 DY85
Holden Cl, Dag. RM8 148 EV62
Hertford SG13 54 DS09
Holden Gdns, Warley CM14 130 FX50
Holdenhurst Av, N12 120 DB52
Holden Pl, Cob. KT11 235 BV114
Holden Pt, E15 13 H4
Holden Rd, N12 120 DB50
HOLDENS, Welw.G.C. AL7 52 DA06
Holden St, SW11 40 G9
Holden Way, Upmin. RM14 151 FR59
Holder Cl, N3 120 DB52
Holdernesse Cl, Islw. TW7 179 CG81
Holdernesse Rd, SW17 202 DF90
Holderness Way, SE27 203 DP92
HOLDERS HILL, NW4 119 CX54
Holders Hill Av, NW4 119 CX54
Holders Hill Circ, NW7
off Dollis Rd 119 CY52
Holders Hill Cres, NW4 119 CX54
Holders Hill Dr, NW4 141 CX55
Holders Hill Gdns, NW4 119 CY54
Holders Hill Rd, NW4 119 CX54
NW7 119 CX54
Holdings, The, Hat. AL9 67 CW16
Holecroft, Wal.Abb. EN9 90 EE34
Hole Fm La, Gt Warley CM13 151 FV55
Holegate St, SE7 36 E7
Hole Hill, Westc. RH4 284 CA136
Holford Ho, SE16
off Manor Est 32 E9
Holford Ms, WC1 18 E1
Holford Pl, WC1 18 D2
Holford Rd, NW3 142 DC62
Guildford GU1 265 BC134
Holford St, WC1 18 E2
Holford Way, SW15 201 CU86
Holford Yd, WC1 18 D1
Holgate Av, SW11 182 DD83
Holgate Gdns, Dag. RM10 148 FA64
Holgate Rd, Dag. RM10 148 FA64
HOLLAND, Oxt. RH8 276 EG134
Holland Av, SW20 221 CT95
Sutton SM2 240 DA109
Holland Cl, Brom. BR2 226 EF103
Epsom KT19 238 CQ111
New Barnet EN5 120 DD45
Redhill RH1 272 DF134
Romford RM7 149 FC57
Stanmore HA7 117 CH50
Holland Ct, E17 *off Evelyn Rd* 145 EC56
NW7 119 CU51
Borhamwood WD6
off Chaucer Gro 100 CN42
Holland Cres, Oxt. RH8 276 EG133
Holland Dr, SE23 205 DY90
Holland Gdns, W14 26 F6
Brentford TW8 180 CL79
Egham TW20 215 BF96
Watford WD25 98 BW35
Holland Gro, SW9 42 F5
Sch Holland Ho Sch, Edg.
HA8 *off Broadhurst Av* 118 CP49
Sch Holland Jun Sch, Oxt.
RH8 *off Holland Rd* 276 EG134
Holland La, Oxt. RH8 276 EG133
★ Holland Pk, W8 26 G4
⊖ Holland Park 26 G3
Holland Pk, W11 26 F3
Holland Pk Av, W11 26 D4
Ilford IG3 147 ES58
Holland Pk Gdns, W14 26 E3
Holland Pk Ms, W11 26 F3
Holland Pk Rd, W14 26 G7
Holland Pk Rbt, W11 26 D4
Sch Holland Pk Sch, W8 27 H4
Holland Pas, N1 9 J8
Holland Pl, W8 27 L4
Holland Ri Ho, SW9 42 D5
Holland Rd, E6 167 EM67
E15 23 K2
NW10 161 CU67
SE25 224 DU99
W14 26 D4
Oxted RH8 276 EG133
Wembley HA0 159 CK65
Hollands, The, Felt. TW13 198 BX91
Woking GU22
off Montgomery Rd 248 AY118
Worcester Park KT4 221 CT102
Hollands Cft, Hunsdon SG12 56 EK06
Holland St, SE1 31 H2
W8 27 K5
Holland Town Est, SW9
off Mandela St 42 F5
Holland Vil Rd, W14 26 E4
Holland Wk, N19
off Duncombe Rd 143 DK60
W8 27 H3
Stanmore HA7 117 CG50
Holland Way, Brom. BR2 226 EF103
Harlow CM17 *off Tatton St* 58 EW14
Hollar Rd, N16
off Stoke Newington High St 144 DT62
Hollen St, W1 17 N8
Holles Cl, Hmptn. TW12 198 CA93
Holles St, W1 17 K8
Holley Rd, W3 180 CS75
Hollickwood Av, N12 120 DF51
Sch Hollickwood Prim Sch,
N10 *off Sydney Rd* 121 DH52
Holliday Sq, SW11
off Fowler Cl 182 DD83
Holliday St, Berk. HP4 60 AX19
Hollidge Way, Dag. RM10 169 FB65
Hollies, The, Smallfield RH6 291 DP149
Hollier Ct, Hat. AL10
off Cranborne Rd 67 CV17
Holliers Way, Hat. AL10 67 CU18
Hollies, The, E11 146 EG57
N20 *off Oakleigh Pk N* 120 DD46
Bovingdon HP3 79 BA29
Gravesend DA12 213 GK93
Harrow HA3 139 CG56
Oxted RH8 276 EH133
Welwyn Garden City AL8 51 CV13
Hollies Av, Sid. DA15 207 ET89
West Byfleet KT14 233 BF113
Hollies Cl, SW16 203 DN93
Twickenham TW1 199 CF89
Hollies Ct, Add. KT15 234 BJ106
Hollies End, NW7 119 CV50
Hollies Rd, W5 179 CJ77
Hollies Way, SW12
off Bracken Av 202 DG87
Potters Bar EN6 86 DC31
Holligrave Rd, Brom. BR1 226 EG95
Hollingbourne Av, Bexh. DA7 188 EZ80
Hollingbourne Gdns, W13 159 CH71
Hollingbourne Rd, SE24 204 DQ85
Hollingbourne Twr, Orp. BR5 228 EX102
Hollingsworth Ms, Wat. WD25
off Bramble Cl 81 BU34
Hollingsworth Rd, Croy. CR0 242 DV107
Hollington Cres, N.Mal. KT3 221 CT100
Hollington Rd, E6 25 J3
N17 122 DU54
Hollingworth Cl, W.Mol. KT8 218 BZ98
Hollingworth Rd, Petts Wd
BR5 227 EP100
Hollingworth Way, West. TN16 277 ER126
Hollins Ho, N7
off Tufnell Pk Rd 143 DL63
Hollis Pl, Grays RM17
off Ward Av 192 GA77
Hollman Gdns, SW16 203 DP93
Hollow, The, Wdf.Grn. IG8 124 EF49
HOLLOWAY, N7 8 B2
Holloway Cl, West Dr. UB7 176 BL78
Holloway Dr, Vir.W. GU25 214 AY98
Holloway Hill, Cher. KT16 215 BC104
Holloway La, Chenies WD3 95 BD36
West Drayton UB7 176 BL79
⊖ Holloway Road 8 D2
Holloway Rd, E6 25 K3
E11 146 EE62
N7 8 F4
N19 143 DK61
Sch Holloway Sch, N7 7 P2
Holloways La, N.Mymms AL9 67 CX23
Holloway St, Houns. TW3 178 CB83
Hollow Cl, Guil. GU2
off Lynwood 280 AV135
Hollow Cotts, Purf. RM19 190 FN78
Hollowfield Av, Grays RM17 192 GD77
Hollowfield Wk, Nthlt. UB5 158 BY65
Hollow Hill La, Iver SL0 155 BB73
Hollow La, Vir.W. GU25 214 AY97
Wotton RH5 284 BX140
Hollows, The, Brent. TW8 180 CM79
Hollow Wk, Kew TW9
off Royal Botanic Gdns 180 CL80
Hollow Way La, Amer. HP6 77 AS35
Hollow Way La, Chesham HP5 77 AS35
Holly Av, New Haw KT15 234 BG110
Stanmore HA7 118 CL54
Walton-on-Thames KT12 218 BX102
Hollybank Cl, Hmptn. TW12 198 CA92
Hollybank Rd, W.Byf. KT14 234 BG114
Holly Bk Rd, Wok. GU22 248 AV121
Hollyberry La, NW3
off Holly Wk 142 DC63
Hollybrake Cl, Chis. BR7 207 ER94
Hollybush Av, St.Alb. AL2 64 CA24
Hollybush Cl, E11 146 EG57
Harrow HA3 117 CE53
Potten End HP4 61 BD16
Sevenoaks TN13 279 FJ124
Watford WD19 116 BW45
Hollybush Ct, Sev. TN13 279 FJ124
Hollybush Gdns, E2 20 F2
Hollybush Hill, E11 146 EF58
Holly Bush Hill, NW3 142 DC63
Hollybush Hill, Stoke P. SL2 154 AU66
Hollybush La, Amer. HP6 77 AR37
Denham UB9 135 BE63
Holly Bush La, Hmptn. TW12 198 BZ94
Hollybush La, Hem.H. HP1 61 BF19
Iver SL0 155 BB73
Orpington BR6 246 FA107
Ripley GU23 250 BK119
Holly Bush La, Sev. TN13 279 FJ123
Hollybush La, Welw.G.C. AL7 51 CZ13
Hollybush Pl, E2 20 F2
Sch Hollybush Prim Sch, Hert.
SG14 *off Fordwich Ri* 53 DN09
Hollybush Rd, Chesh. HP5 76 AN27
Gravesend DA12 213 GJ89
Kingston upon Thames KT2 200 CL92
Holly Bush Steps, NW3
off Heath St 142 DC63
Hollybush St, E13 24 B2
Holly Bush Vale, NW3
off Heath St 142 DC63
Hollybush Way, Chsht EN7 88 DU28
Holly Cl, Beck. BR3 225 EC98
Buckhurst Hill IG9 124 EK48
Englefield Green TW20 194 AV93
Farnham Common SL2 133 AQ63
Feltham TW13 198 BY92
Hatfield AL10 67 CT19
Longcross KT16 214 AU104
Wallington SM6 241 DH108
Woking GU21 248 AV119
Hollycombe, Eng.Grn TW20 194 AW91
Holly Cottage Ms, Uxb. UB8
off Pield Heath Rd 156 BN71
Holly Ct, SE10 35 M7
Romford RM1
off Dolphin App 149 FF56
Sutton SM2
off Worcester Rd 240 DA108
Holly Cres, Beck. BR3 225 DZ99
Windsor SL4 173 AK82
Woodford Green IG8 123 ED52
Holly Cft, Hert. SG14 53 DN08
Hollycroft Av, NW3 142 DA62
Wembley HA9 140 CM61
Hollycroft Cl, Sipson UB7 176 BN79
South Croydon CR2 242 DS106
Hollycroft Gdns, Sipson UB7 176 BN79
Hollycross Rd, Ware SG12 55 DZ07
Hollydale Cl, Nthlt. UB5
off Dorchester Rd 138 CB63
Hollydale Dr, Brom. BR2 227 EM104
Sch Hollydale Prim Sch, SE15 45 H9
Hollydale Rd, SE15 44 G7
Hollydell, Hert. SG13 54 DQ11
Hollydene, SE15 44 E6
Hollydown Way, E11 145 ED62
Holly Dr, E4 123 EB45
Berkhamsted HP4 60 AX20
Brentford TW8 179 CG79
Potters Bar EN6 86 DB33
South Ockendon RM15 171 FX70
Windsor SL4 194 AS85
Holly Fm Rd, Sthl. UB2 178 BY78
Holly Fld, Harl. CM19 73 EQ18
Hollyfield, Hat. AL10 67 CU21
Hollyfield Av, N11 120 DF50
Hollyfield Rd, Surb. KT5 220 CM101
Hollyfields, Brox. EN10 89 DY26
Sch Hollyfield Sch & 6th Form
Cen, The, Surb. KT6
off Surbiton Hill Rd 220 CL99
Holly Gdns, Bexh. DA7 189 FC84
West Drayton UB7 176 BM75
Holly Gate, Add. KT15 234 BH105
Holly Grn, Wey. KT13 217 BR104
Holly Gro, NW9 140 CQ59
SE15 44 B8
Bushey WD23 117 CD45
Pinner HA5 116 BY53
Hollygrove Cl, Houns. TW3 178 BZ84
Holly Gro Rd, Bramfld SG14 53 DH07
Hollyhedge Rd, Cob. KT11 235 BV114
Holly Hedges La, Bov. HP3 79 BC30
Rickmansworth WD3 79 BC30
Holly Hedge Ter, SE13 205 ED85
Holly Hill, N21 103 DM44
NW3 142 DC63
Holly Hill Dr, Bans. SM7 256 DA117
Holly Hill Pk, Bans. SM7 256 DA117
Holly Hill Rd, Belv. DA17 189 FB78
Erith DA8 189 FB78
Hollyhock Cl, Hem.H. HP1 61 BE18
Holly Ho, Brwd. CM15
off Sawyers Hall La 130 FX46
H Holly Ho Hosp, Buck.H. IG9 124 EH47
● Holly Ind Pk, Wat. WD24 98 BW39
Holly La, Bans. SM7 256 DA116
Ilford IG3 *off Goodmayes La* 148 EU61
Holly La E, Bans. SM7 256 DA116
Holly La W, Bans. SM7 256 DA117
Holly Lea, Jacobs Well GU4 264 AX128
Holly Lo, Lwr Kgswd KT20 271 CY126
Holly Lo Gdns, N6 142 DG61
Hollymead, Cars. SM5 222 DF104
Hollymead Rd, Chipstead
CR5 256 DG118
Hollymeoak Rd, Couls. CR5 257 DH119
Holly Ms, SW10 39 P1
Hollymoor La, Epsom KT19 238 CR110
Holly Mt, NW3
off Holly Bush Hill 142 DC63
Hollymount Cl, SE10 46 E6
Sch Hollymount Prim Sch, SW20
off Cambridge Rd 221 CW95
Holly Pk, N3 141 CZ55
N4 143 DM59
Holly Pk Est, N4
off Blythwood Rd 143 DL59
Holly Pk Gdns, N3 142 DA55
Sch Holly Pk Prim Sch, N11
off Bellevue Rd 120 DG50
Holly Pk Rd, N11 120 DG50
W7 159 CF74
Holly Pl, NW3 *off Holly Wk* 142 DC63
Holly Rd, E11
off Green Man Rbt 146 EF59
W4 *off Dolman Rd* 180 CR77
Dartford DA1 210 FK88
Enfield EN3 105 DX36
Hampton Hill TW12 198 CC93
Hounslow TW3 178 CB84
Orpington BR6 246 EU108
Reigate RH2 288 DB136
Twickenham TW1 199 CG88
Holly St, E8 10 B6
Holly Ter, N6
off Highgate W Hill 142 DG60
N20 *off Swan La* 120 DC47
Hollytree Av, Swan. BR8 229 FE96
Hollytree Cl, SW19 201 CX88
Chalfont St. Peter SL9 112 AY50
Holly Tree Cl, Ley Hill HP5 78 AV31
Holly Tree Rd, Cat. CR3
off Elm Gro 258 DS122
Sch Holly Trees Prim Sch,
Warley CM14
off Vaughan Williams Way 130 FV49
Hollyview Cl, NW4 141 CU58
Holly Village, N6
off Swains La 143 DH61
Holly Wk, NW3 5 N1
Enfield EN2 104 DQ41
Richmond TW9 180 CL82
Welwyn Garden City AL8 51 CW05
Holly Way, Mitch. CR4 223 DK98
Hollywood Ct, Els. WD6
off Deacons Hill Rd 100 CM42
Hollywood Gdns, Hayes UB4 157 BV72
Hollywood Ms, SW10 39 N2
Hollywood Rd, E4 123 DY50
SW10 39 N1
Hollywoods, Croy. CR0 243 DZ109
Hollywood Way, Erith DA8 189 FH81
Woodford Green IG8 123 ED52
Holman Ho, E2 *off Roman Rd* 21 J2
Holman Rd, SW11 40 A9
Epsom KT19 238 CQ106
Holmbank Dr, Shep. TW17 217 BS98
Holmbridge Gdns, Enf. EN3 105 DX42
Holmbrook Dr, NW4 141 CX57
Holmbury Ct, SW17 202 DF90
SW19 202 DE94
Holmbury Dr, N.Holm. RH5 285 CJ139
Holmbury Gdns, Hayes UB3 157 BT74
Holmbury Gro, Croy. CR0 243 DZ108
Holmbury Keep, Horl. RH6
off Langshott La 291 DJ147
Holmbury Pk, Brom. BR1 206 EL94
Holmbury Vw, E5 144 DV60
Holmbush Rd, SW15 201 CY86
Holm Cl, Wdhm KT15 233 BE112
Holmcote Gdns, N5 9 J3
Holmcroft, Walt.Hill KT20 271 CV125
Holmcroft Way, Brom. BR2 227 EM99
Holmdale Cl, Borwd. WD6 100 CM40
Holmdale Gdns, NW4 141 CX57
Holmdale Rd, NW6 5 J3
Chislehurst BR7 207 EQ92
Holmdale Ter, N15 144 DS59
Holmdene Av, NW7 119 CU51
SE24 204 DQ85
Harrow HA2 138 CB55
Holmdene Cl, Beck. BR3 225 EC96
Holmead Rd, SW6 39 M5
Holmebury Cl, Bushey Hth
WD23 117 CE47
Holme Chase, Wey. KT13 235 BQ107
Holme Cl, Chsht EN8 89 DY31
Hatfield AL10 67 CT15
Holme Ct, Islw. TW7
off Twickenham Rd 179 CG83
Holmedale, Slou. SL2 154 AW73
Holmefield Ct, NW3 6 D4
Holme Lacey Rd, SE12 206 EF86
Holme Lea, Wat. WD25 82 BW34
Holme Oak Av, Rain. RM13 169 FD68
Holme Pk, Borwd. WD6 100 CM40
Holme Pl, Hem.H. HP2
off Crest Pk 63 BQ19
Holme Rd, E6 166 EL67
Hatfield AL10 67 CT15
Hornchurch RM11 150 FN60
Holmes Av, E17 145 DZ55
NW7 119 CY50
Holmes Cl, SE22 184 DU84
Purley CR8 241 DM113
Woking GU22 249 AZ121
Holmes Ct, SW4
off Paradise Rd 42 A8
Gravesend DA12 213 GM88
Holmesdale, Wal.Cr. EN8 105 DX35
Holmesdale Av, SW14 180 CP83
Redhill RH1 273 DJ131
Holmesdale Cl, SE25 224 DT97
Guildford GU1 265 BB133
Sch Holmesdale Comm Inf Sch,
Reig. RH2 *off Alma Rd* 272 DB132
Holmesdale Hill, S.Darenth
DA4 230 FQ95
Holmesdale Manor, Red. RH1 272 DG132
Holmesdale Pk, Nutfld RH1 273 DM134
Holmesdale Rd, N6 143 DH59
SE25 224 DR99
Bexleyheath DA7 188 EX82
Croydon CR0 224 DR99
North Holmwood RH5 285 CH140
Reigate RH2 272 DA133
Richmond TW9 180 CM81
Sevenoaks TN13 279 FJ123
South Darenth DA4 230 FQ95
South Nutfield RH1 289 DM136
Teddington TW11 199 CJ94
Holmesdale Ter, N.Holm.
RH5 285 CH140
Holmesley Rd, SE23 205 DY86
Holmes Meadow, Harl. CM19 73 EP21
Holmes Pl, SW10 39 P2
Holmes Rd, NW5 7 J4
SW19 202 DC94
Twickenham TW1 199 CF89
Holmes Ter, SE1 30 E4
HOLMETHORPE, Red. RH1 273 DH132
Holmethorpe Av, Red. RH1 273 DH131
● Holmethorpe Ind Est,
Red. RH1 273 DH131
Holme Way, Stan. HA7 117 CF51
Holmewood Gdns, SW2 203 DM87
Holmewood Rd, SE25 224 DS97
SW2 203 DL87
Holmfield Av, NW4 141 CX57
Holm Gro, Uxb. UB10 156 BN66
Holmhurst Rd, Belv. DA17 189 FB78
Holmlea Rd, Datchet SL3 174 AX81
Holmlea Wk, Datchet SL3 174 AW81
Holmleigh Av, Dart. DA1 190 FJ84
Sch Holmleigh Prim Sch, N16
off Dunsmure Rd 144 DT60
Holmleigh Rd, N16 144 DS60
Holmleigh Rd Est, N16
off Holmleigh Rd 144 DS60
Holmoak Cl, Pur. CR8 241 DM110
Holm Oak Cl, SW15 201 CZ86
Holm Oak Ms, SW4 203 DL85
Holm Oak Pk, Wat. WD18 97 BT43
Holmsdale Cl, Iver SL0 155 BF72
Holmsdale Gro, Bexh. DA7 189 FE82
Holmshaw Cl, SE26 205 DY91
Holmshill La, Borwd. WD6 100 CS36
Holmside Ri, Wat. WD19 115 BV48
Holmside Rd, SW12 202 DG86
Holmsley Cl, N.Mal. KT3 221 CT100
Holmsley Ho, SW15
off Tangley Gro 201 CT87
Holms St, E2 10 C10
Holmstall Av, Edg. HA8 140 CQ55
Holm Wk, SE3 47 P9
Holmwood Av, Shenf. CM15 131 GA44
South Croydon CR2 242 DT113
Holmwood Cl, Add. KT15 234 BG106
East Horsley KT24 267 BS128
Harrow HA2 138 CC55
Northolt UB5 158 CB65
Sutton SM2 239 CX109
Holmwood Gdns, N3 120 DA54
Wallington SM6 241 DH107
Holmwood Gro, NW7 118 CR50
Holmwood Rd, Chess. KT9 237 CK106
Enfield EN3 105 DX36
Ilford IG3 147 ES61
Sutton SM2 239 CW110
Holmwood Vw Rd, Mid Holm.
RH5 *off Horsham Rd* 285 CH142
Holmwood Vil, SE7 35 P10
Holne Chase, N2 142 DC58
Morden SM4 221 CZ100
Holness Rd, E15 13 L5
Holroyd Cl, Clay. KT10 237 CF109
Holroyd Rd, SW15 181 CW84
Claygate KT10 237 CF109
Holsart Cl, Tad. KT20 255 CV122
Holstein Av, Wey. KT13 234 BN105
Holstein Way, Erith DA18 188 EY76
Holst Ho, W12 *off Du Cane Rd* 161 CV72
Holstock Rd, Ilf. IG1 147 EQ61
Holsworth Cl, Har. HA2 138 CC57
Holsworthy Sq, WC1 18 D5
Holsworthy Way, Chess. KT9 237 CJ106
Holt, The, Hem.H. HP2
off Turners Hill 62 BL21
Ilford IG6 125 EQ51
Morden SM4 *off London Rd* 222 DA98
Wallington SM6 241 DJ105
Welwyn Garden City AL7 52 DD10
Holt Cl, N10 142 DG56
SE28 168 EV73
Chigwell IG7 125 ET50
Elstree WD6 100 CM42
Holton St, E1 21 J4
Holt Rd, E16 37 H3
Romford RM3 128 FL52
Wembley HA0 139 CH62
Holtsmere Cl, Wat. WD25 98 BW35
Sch Holtsmere End Inf & Nurs Sch,
Hem.H. HP2 *off Shenley Rd* 63 BP15
Sch Holtsmere End Jun Sch, Hem.H.
HP2 *off Shenley Rd* 63 BP15
HOLTSPUR, Beac. HP9 110 AF54
Holtspur Av, Woob.Grn HP10 132 AE56
Holtspur Cl, Beac. HP9 110 AG54
Holtspur La, Woob.Grn HP10 132 AE57
Sch Holtspur Sch, Holt. HP9
off Cherry Tree Rd 110 AG54
Holtspur Top La, Beac. HP9 110 AG54
Holtspur Way, Beac. HP9 110 AG54
Holt Way, Chig. IG7 125 ET50
Holtwhite Av, Enf. EN2 104 DQ40
Holtwhites Hill, Enf. EN2 103 DP39
Holtwood Rd, Oxshott KT22 236 CC113
Holwell Caravan Site, Hat. AL9 52 DE14
Holwell Hyde, Welw.G.C. AL7 52 DC11
Holwell Hyde La, Welw.G.C.
AL7 52 DC12
Holwell La, Hat. AL9 52 DE14
Holwell Pl, Pnr. HA5 138 BY56
Sch Holwell Prim Sch, Welw.G.C.
AL7 *off Holwell Rd* 51 CZ10
Holwell Rd, Welw.G.C. AL7 51 CY10
Holwood Cl, Walt. KT12 218 BW103
Holwood Pk Av, Orp. BR6 245 EM105
Holwood Pl, SW4 183 DK84
Holy Acre, Roydon CM19
off Roydon Mill Pk 56 EG14
Holybourne Av, SW15 201 CU87
Sch Holy Cross Cath Prim Sch,
SE6 *off Culverley Rd* 205 EC88
SW6 39 J6
Harlow CM18
off Tracyes Rd 74 EU17
South Ockendon RM15
off Daiglen Dr 171 FV72
Sch Holy Cross Conv Sch, Chal.St.P.
SL9 *off Gold Hill E* 112 AX53
Holy Cross Hill, Brox. EN10 70 DU24
Sch Holy Cross Prep Sch, Kings.T.
KT2 *off George Rd* 200 CQ94
Sch Holy Cross Sch, The, N.Mal.
KT3 *off Sandal Rd* 220 CS99
Sch Holy Family Catholic Prim Sch,
Add. KT15 *off Ongar Hill* 234 BG106
Langley SL3 *off High St* 175 AZ78
Sch Holy Family RC Prim Sch,
E14 22 C10
SE3 *off Tudway Rd* 186 EJ84
Welwyn Garden City AL7
off Crookhams 52 DA06
Sch Holy Family Tech Coll, E17
off Shernhall St 145 EC55
Wiseman Ho Site, E17
off Shernhall St 145 EC56
HOLYFIELD, Wal.Abb. EN9 89 ED28
Holyfield, Wal.Abb. EN9 89 EC29
Sch Holy Ghost RC Prim Sch,
SW12 *off Nightingale Sq* 202 DG87
Holyhead Cl, E3 22 B3
E6 25 J6
Holyhead Ms, Slou. SL1 153 AL72

Sch **Holy Innocents Cath Prim Sch**, Orp. BR6 *off Mitchell Rd* 227 ET104
Holyoake Av, Wok. GU21 248 AW117
Holyoake Ct, SE16 33 M4
Holyoake Cres, Wok. GU21 248 AW117
Holyoake Ter, Sev. TN13 278 FG124
Holyoake Wk, N2 142 DC55
W5 159 CJ70
Holyoak Rd, SE11 30 G8
HOLYPORT, Maid. SL6 172 AC78
Holyport Rd, SW6 38 B4
Holyrood Av, Har. HA2 138 BY63
Holyrood Cres, St.Alb. AL1 65 CD24
Holyrood Gdns, Edg. HA8 140 CP55
Grays RM16 193 GJ77
Holyrood Ms, E16 35 P2
Sch **Holy Rood RC Prim Sch**, Wat. WD17 *off Greenbank Rd* 97 BR36
Holyrood Rd, New Barn. EN5 102 DC44
Holyrood St, SE1
off Bermondsey St 31 N3
Sch **Holy Trinity & St. Silas C of E Prim Sch**, NW1 7 J6
Sch **Holy Trinity C of E Jun Sch**, Wall. SM6 *off Bute Rd* 241 DJ105
Sch **Holy Trinity C of E Jun Sch Guildford**, Guil. GU1
off Addison Rd 281 AZ136
Sch **Holy Trinity C of E Prim Sch**, E8 10 A5
N2 *off Eagans Cl* 142 DD55
NW3 5 P5
SE23 *off Dartmouth Rd* 204 DW89
Jun, SW1 28 G8
SW2 *off Upper Tulse Hill* 203 DM87
Inf, SW3 28 F8
SW19 *off Effra Rd* 202 DB93
Dartford DA1
off Chatsworth Rd 210 FJ85
Gravesend DA12
off Trinity Rd 213 GJ87
Northwood HA6
off Rickmansworth Rd 115 BQ51
Richmond TW10
off Carrington Rd 180 CN84
Waltham Cross EN8
off Crossbrook St 89 DX32
Sch **Holy Trinity Lamorbey C of E Prim Sch**, Sid. DA15
off Burnt Oak La 208 EU88
Holy Wk, Brox. EN10
off St. Catharines Rd 71 EA19
Hoddesdon EN11
off High St 71 EA18
HOLYWELL, Wat. WD18 97 BS44
Holywell Cl, SE3 47 P2
SE16 32 F10
Orpington BR6 246 EU105
Staines-upon-Thames TW19 196 BL88
Holywell Hill, St.Alb. AL1 64 CC21
● **Holywell Ind Est**, Wat. WD18 115 BR45
Holywell La, EC2 19 P4
Sch **Holywell Prim Sch**, Wat. WD18 *off Tolpits La* 97 BT44
Holywell Rd, Wat. WD18 97 BU43
Holywell Row, EC2 19 N5
Holywell Way, Stai. TW19 196 BL88
Homan Ct, N12 120 DC49
Home Barn Ct, Eff. KT24
off The Street 268 BX127
Home Cl, Brox. EN10 71 DZ24
Carshalton SM5 222 DF103
Fetcham KT22 253 CD121
Harlow CM20 73 ET15
Northolt UB5 158 BZ69
Virginia Water GU25 214 AX100
Homecroft Gdns, Loug. IG10 107 EP42
Homecroft Rd, N22 121 DP53
SE26 204 DW92
Homedean Rd, Chipstead TN13 278 FC122
Home Fm, Orp. BR6 246 FA106
Home Fm Cl, Bet. RH3 286 CS135
Esher KT10 236 CB107
Ottershaw KT16 233 BA108
Shepperton TW17 217 BS98
Tadworth KT20 255 CX117
Thames Ditton KT7 219 CF101
Home Fm Gdns, Walt. KT12 218 BW103
● **Home Fm Ind Est**, Stans.Abb. SG12 56 EF10
Homefarm Rd, W7 159 CE72
Home Fm Rd, N.Mymms AL9 85 CV26
Rickmansworth WD3 114 BN49
Home Fm Way, Stoke P. SL3 154 AW67
Homefield, Bov. HP3 79 BB28
Home Fld, Pott.End HP4 61 BB16
Homefield, Wal.Abb. EN9 90 EG32
Walton-on-Thames KT12 236 BX105
Homefield Av, Ilf. IG2 147 ES57
Homefield Cl, NW10 160 CQ65
Epping CM16 92 EU30
Hayes UB4 158 BW70
Horley RH6
off Tanyard Way 291 DH147
Leatherhead KT22 253 CJ121
St. Paul's Cray BR5 228 EV98
Swanley BR8 229 FF97
Woodham KT15 233 BE112
Homefield Fm Rd, Sutt.H. DA4 230 FM96
Homefield Gdns, N2 142 DD55
Mitcham CR4 222 DC96
Tadworth KT20 255 CW120
Homefield Ms, Beck. BR3 225 EA95
Homefield Pk, Sutt. SM1 240 DB107
Homefield Pl, Croy. CR0 224 DT103
Sch **Homefield Prep Sch**, Sutt. SM1 *off Western Rd* 240 DA106
Homefield Ri, Orp. BR6 228 EU102
Homefield Rd, SW19 201 CX93
W4 181 CT77
Bromley BR1 226 EJ95
Bushey WD23 98 CA43
Chorleywood WD3 95 BD42
Coulsdon CR5 257 DP119
Edgware HA8 118 CR51
Hemel Hempstead HP2 62 BN20
Radlett WD7 99 CF37
Sevenoaks TN13 278 FE122
Walton-on-Thames KT12 218 BY101
Ware SG12 55 DY05
Warlingham CR6 258 DW119
Wembley HA0 139 CG63
Homefield St, N1 19 N1
Homefirs Ho, Wem. HA9 140 CM62
Home Gdns, Dag. RM10 149 FC62
Dartford DA1 210 FL86
Home Hill, Swan. BR8 209 FF94
Homeland Dr, Sutt. SM2 240 DB109
Homelands, Lthd. KT22 253 CJ121
Homelands Dr, SE19 204 DS94
Home Lea, Orp. BR6 245 ET106
Homeleigh Ct, Chsht EN8 88 DV29
Homeleigh Rd, SE15 205 DX85
Home Ley, Welw.G.C. AL7 51 CY10
Homemead, SW12 203 DH89
Home Mead, Stan. HA7 117 CJ53
Homemead Cl, Grav. DA12 213 GH87
Homemead Ct, Grav. DA12
off Homemead Cl 213 GH87
Home Meadow, Bans. SM7 256 DA116
Farnham Royal SL2 153 AQ68
Welwyn Garden City AL7 51 CZ09
Home Meadow Ms, SE22 204 DU85
Homemead Rd, Brom. BR2 227 EM99
Croydon CR0 223 DJ100
★ **Home Office**, SW1 29 P7
Home Orchard, Dart. DA1 210 FL86
Home Pk, E.Mol. (Hampton Ct Pk) KT8 219 CH98
Kingston upon Thames (Hampton Ct Pk) KT1 219 CH98
Oxted RH8 276 EG131
● **Home Pk Ind Est**, Kings L. WD4 81 BP30
Home Pk Mill Link Rd, Kings L. WD4 81 BP31
Home Pk Par, Kings.T. KT1
off High St 219 CK96
Home Pk Rd, SW19 202 DA90
Home Pk Wk, Kings.T. KT1 219 CK98
Homer Cl, Bexh. DA7 189 FC81
Homer Dr, E14 34 A9
Homerfield, Welw.G.C. AL8 51 CW08
Sch **Homer First Sch**, Wind. SL4 *off Testwood Rd* 173 AK81
Home Rd, SW11 40 C8
Homer Rd, E9 11 M5
Croydon CR0 225 DX100
Homer Row, W1 16 D7
Homersham Rd, Kings.T. KT1 220 CN96
Homers Rd, Wind. SL4 173 AK81
Homer St, W1 16 D7
Homerswood La, Welw. AL6 51 CU05
Sch **Homerswood Prim Sch**, Welw.G.C. AL8 *off Kirklands* 51 CX05
HOMERTON, E9 11 M3
⊖ **Homerton** 11 J4
Homerton Gro, E9 11 J3
Homerton High St, E9 11 H3
Homerton Rd, E9 11 M2
Homerton Row, E9 11 H3
Homerton Ter, E9 11 H4
H **Homerton Uni Hosp**, E9 11 J2
Homesdale Cl, E11 146 EG57
Homesdale Rd, Brom. BR1, BR2 226 EJ98
Caterham CR3 258 DR123
Petts Wood BR5 227 ES101
Homesfield, NW11 142 DA57
Homestall Rd, SE22 204 DW85
Homestead, The, N11 121 DH49
Dartford DA1 210 FJ86
Homestead Cl, Park St AL2 82 CC27
Homestead Ct, Welw.G.C. AL7 51 CZ11
Homestead Gdns, Clay. KT10 237 CE106
Homestead La, Welw.G.C. AL7 51 CZ12
Homestead Paddock, N14 103 DH43
Homestead Pk, NW2 141 CT62
Homestead Rd, SW6 38 G5
Caterham CR3 258 DR123
Dagenham RM8 148 EZ61
Hatfield AL10 67 CU15
Orpington BR6 246 EV108
Rickmansworth WD3
off Park Rd 114 BK45
Staines-upon-Thames TW18 196 BH93
Homesteads, The, Hunsdon SG12 *off Hunsdon Rd* 56 EK07
Homestead Way, New Adgtn CR0 243 EC111
Homewaters Av, Sun. TW16 217 BT95
Home Way, Mill End WD3 113 BF46
Homeway, Rom. RM3 128 FP51
Homewillow Cl, N21 103 DP44
Homewood, Geo.Grn SL3 154 AX72
Homewood Av, Cuffley EN6 87 DL27
Homewood Cl, Hmptn. TW12 198 BZ93
Homewood Cres, Chis. BR7 207 ES93
Sch **Homewood Indep Sch**, Park St AL2 *off Hazel Rd* 82 CB28
Homewood La, Northaw EN6 87 DJ27
Homewood Rd, St.Alb. AL1 65 CH17
Homildon Ho, SE26
off Sydenham Hill Est 204 DU90
Honduras St, EC1 19 J4
Honeybourne Rd, NW6 5 L2
Honeybourne Way, Petts Wd BR5 227 ER102
Honey Brook, Wal.Abb. EN9 90 EE33
Honeybrook Rd, SW12 203 DJ87
Honey Cl, Dag. RM10 169 FB65
Honeycrock La, Red. RH1 288 DG141
Honeycroft, Loug. IG10 107 EN42
Welwyn Garden City AL8 51 CW10
Honeycroft Dr, St.Alb. AL4 65 CJ22
Honeycroft Hill, Uxb. UB10 156 BL66
Honeycross Rd, Hem.H. HP1 61 BE21
Honeyden Rd, Sid. DA14 208 EY93
Honey Hill, Uxb. UB10 156 BM66
Honey La, EC2 19 K9
Hertford SG14 *off Fore St* 54 DR09
Waltham Abbey EN9 106 EG35
Honeyman Cl, NW6 4 C6
Honeymeade, Saw. CM21 58 EW08
● **Honeypot Business Cen**, Stan. HA7 118 CL53
Honeypot Cl, NW9 140 CM56
Honeypot La, NW9 140 CM55
Brentwood CM14 130 FU48
Stanmore HA7 140 CM55
Waltham Abbey EN9 90 EJ34
Honeypots Rd, Wok. GU22 248 AX122
Honeysett Rd, N17
off Reform Row 122 DT54
Honeysuckle Bottom, E.Hors. KT24 267 BS134
Honeysuckle Cl, Hert. SG13 54 DU09
Horley RH6 291 DJ147
Iver SL0 155 BC72
Pilgrim's Hatch CM15 130 FV43
Romford RM3 128 FJ51
Southall UB1 158 BY73
Honeysuckle Fld, Chesh. HP5 76 AQ30
Honeysuckle Gdns, Croy. CR0 225 DX101
Hatfield AL10 67 CV19
Honeysuckle La, N.Holm. RH5 *off Treelands* 285 CJ139
Sch **Honeywell Inf & Jun Schs**, SW11 *off Honeywell Rd* 202 DF86
Honeywell Rd, SW11 202 DF86
Honeywood Cl, Pot.B. EN6 86 DE33
★ **Honeywood Heritage Cen**, Cars. SM5 240 DF106
Honeywood Rd, NW10 161 CT68
Isleworth TW7 179 CG84
Honeywood Wk, Cars. SM5 240 DF105
Sch **Honilands Prim Sch**, Enf. EN1 *off Lovell Rd* 104 DV36
Honister Cl, Stan. HA7 117 CH53
Honister Gdns, Stan. HA7 117 CH52
Honister Hts, Pur. CR8 242 DR114
Honister Pl, Stan. HA7 117 CH53
Honiton Gdns, NW7 119 CX52
SE15 *off Gibbon Rd* 45 H9
Honiton Ho, Enf. EN3
off Exeter Rd 105 DX41
Honiton Rd, NW6 4 G10
Romford RM7 149 FD58
Welling DA16 187 ET82
Honley Rd, SE6 205 EB87
Honnor Gdns, Islw. TW7 179 CD82
Honnor Rd, Stai. TW18 196 BK94
HONOR OAK, SE23 204 DW86
HONOR OAK PARK, SE4 205 DY86
⇌ **Honor Oak Park** 205 DX86
⊖ **Honor Oak Park** 205 DX86
Honor Oak Pk, SE23 204 DW86
Honor Oak Ri, SE23 204 DW86
Honor Oak Rd, SE23 204 DW88
Honor St, Harl. CM17 58 EX14
Hoo, The, Harl. CM17 58 EW10
Hood Av, N14 103 DH44
SW14 200 CQ85
Orpington BR5 228 EV99
Hood Cl, Croy. CR0 223 DP102
Hoodcote Gdns, N21 121 DP45
Hood Ct, EC4 18 F9
Hood Rd, SW20 201 CT94
Rainham RM13 169 FE67
Hood Wk, Rom. RM7 127 FB53
HOOK, Chess. KT9 238 CL105
Hook, The, New Barn. EN5 102 DD44
Hooke Rd, E.Hors. KT24 267 BT125
Hookers Rd, E17 145 DX55
Hook Fm Rd, Brom. BR2 226 EK99
Hookfield, Epsom KT19 238 CQ113
Harlow CM18 73 ES17
Hookfields, Nthflt DA11 212 GE90
Hook Gate, Enf. EN1 104 DV36
HOOK GREEN, Dart. DA2 209 FG91
HOOK GREEN, Grav. DA13 212 FZ93
Hook Grn La, Dart. DA2 209 FF90
Hook Grn Rd, Sthflt DA13 212 FY94
HOOK HEATH, Wok. GU22 248 AV120
Hook Heath Av, Wok. GU22 248 AV119
Hook Heath Gdns, Wok. GU22 248 AT121
Hook Heath Rd, Wok. GU22 248 AW121
Hook Hill, S.Croy. CR2 242 DS110
Hook Hill La, Wok. GU22 248 AV121
Hook Hill Pk, Wok. GU22 248 AV121
Hooking Grn, Har. HA2 138 CB57
Jct **Hook Junct**, Surb. KT6 219 CK104
Hook La, Northaw EN6 86 DF32
Romford RM4 108 EZ44
Shere GU5 282 BN141
Welling DA16 207 ET85
Sch **Hook La Prim Sch**, Well. DA16 *off Faraday Rd* 188 EU83
Hook Ri N, Surb. KT6 220 CN104
Hook Ri S, Surb. KT6 220 CN104
● **Hook Ri S Business Cen**, Surb. KT6 220 CN104
● **Hook Ri S Ind Pk**, Surb. KT6 220 CM104
Hook Rd, Chess. KT9 237 CK106
Epsom KT19 238 CR111
Surbiton KT6 220 CL104
Hooks Cl, SE15 44 F7
Hooks Hall Dr, Dag. RM10 149 FC62
Hookstone Way, Wdf.Grn. IG8 124 EK52
Hook Wk, Edg. HA8 118 CQ51
HOOKWOOD, Horl. RH6 290 DC150
Hookwood Cor, Oxt. RH8
off Hookwood Pk 276 EH128
Hookwood Cotts, Headley KT18 254 CQ123
Hookwood Pk, Oxt. RH8 276 EH128
Hookwood Rd, Orp. BR6 246 EW111
Hool Cl, NW9 140 CQ57
HOOLEY, Couls. CR5 256 DG122
Hooley La, Red. RH1 288 DF135
Hooper Dr, Uxb. UB8 157 BP71
Hooper Rd, E16 23 P9
Hooper's Ct, SW3 28 E5
Hoopers Ms, W3 160 CQ74
Hooper's Ms, Bushey WD23 116 CB46
Hooper St, E1 20 C10
Hoopers Yd, NW6 4 G8
Sevenoaks TN13 279 FJ126
Hoop La, NW11 141 CZ59
Hope Cl, N1 9 K4
SE12 206 EH90
Brentford TW8 180 CL78
Chadwell Heath RM6 148 EW56
Sutton SM1 240 DC106
Woodford Green IG8
off West Gro 124 EJ51
Hopedale Rd, SE7 186 EH79
Hopefield Av, NW6 4 F10
Hope Gdns, W3 *off Park Rd N* 180 CP75
Hope Grn, Wat. WD25 81 BU33
Hope La, SE9 207 EP89
Hope Pk, Brom. BR1 206 EF94
Hope Rd, Swans. DA10 212 FZ86
Hopes Cl, Houns. TW5
off Old Cote Dr 178 CA79
Hope St, SW11 182 DD83
Hope Ter, Grays RM20 191 FX78
Hopetown St, E1 20 B7
Hopewell Cl, Chaff.Hun. RM16 191 FX78
Hopewell Dr, Grav. DA12 213 GM92
Hopewell St, SE5 43 M5
Hopewell Yd, SE5 43 M5
Hope Wf, SE16
off St. Marychurch St 32 G4
Hopfield, Horsell GU21 248 AY116
Hopfield Av, Byfleet KT14 234 BL112
Hopgarden La, Sev. TN13 278 FG128
Hop Gdns, WC2 30 A1
Hop Gdn Way, Wat. WD25 82 BW31
Hopgood St, W12 26 B4
Hopground Cl, St.Alb. AL1 65 CG22
Hopkin Cl, Guil. GU2 264 AV130
Hopkins Cl, N10 120 DG52
Hopkins Cl, Romford RM2 150 FJ55
Hopkins Ms, E15 13 M9
Hopkinsons Pl, NW1 6 F8
Hopkins Rd, E10 145 EB59
Hopkins St, W1 17 M9
Hoppers Rd, N13 121 DN47
N21 121 DN47
Hoppett Rd, E4 124 EE48
Hoppety, The, Tad. KT20 255 CX122
Hopping La, N1 9 H5
Hoppingwood Av, N.Mal. KT3 220 CS97
Hoppit Rd, Wal.Abb. EN9 89 EB32
Hoppner Rd, Hayes UB4 157 BQ68
Hop St, SE10 35 M8
Hopton Ct, Guil. GU2
off Chapelhouse Cl 264 AS134
Hopton Gdns, N.Mal. KT3 221 CU100
Hopton Rd, SE18 37 P6
SW16 203 DL92
Hopton's Gdns, SE1 31 H2
Hopton St, SE1 31 H2
Hoptree Cl, N12
off Woodside Pk Rd 120 DB49
Hopwood Cl, SW17 202 DC90
Watford WD17 97 BR36
Hopwood Rd, SE17 43 M2
Hopwood Wk, E8 10 D6
Horace Av, Rom. RM7 149 FC60
Horace Bldg, SW8
off Queenstown Rd 41 J4
Horace Rd, E7 146 EH63
Ilford IG6 147 EQ55
Kingston upon Thames KT1 220 CM97
Horatio Ct, SE16
off Rotherhithe St 33 H3
Horatio Pl, E14 34 F4
SW19 222 DA95
Horatio St, E2 20 B1
Horatius Way, Croy. CR0 241 DM107
Horbury Cres, W11 27 J1
Horbury Ms, W11 27 H1
Horder Rd, SW6 38 F7
Hordle Gdns, St.Alb. AL1 65 CF21
● **Horizon Business Cen**, N9
off Goodwin Rd 123 DX46
● **Horizon Business Village**, Wey. KT13 234 BN112
Horizon Ho, Enf. EN3
off Tysoe Av 105 DZ36
Sch **Horizon Sch**, N16 9 P1
● **Horizon Trade Pk**, N11
off Ringway 121 DJ51
Horizon Way, SE7 36 B9
Horksley Gdns, Hutt. CM13
off Bannister Dr 131 GC44
Horle Wk, SE5 42 G8
HORLEY, RH6 290 DG148
⇌ **Horley** 291 DH149
Horley Cl, Bexh. DA6 208 FA85
Sch **Horley Inf Sch**, Horl. RH6
off Lumley Rd 290 DG148
Horley Lo La, Red. RH1 288 DF143
Horley Rd, SE9 206 EL91
Redhill RH1 288 DF136
Horley Row, Horl. RH6 290 DF147
Hormead Rd, W9 14 G5
Hornbeam Av, Upmin. RM14 150 FN63
Hornbeam Chase, S.Ock. RM15 171 FX69
Hornbeam Cl, NW7 119 CT48
SE11 30 E8
Barking IG11 168 EU69
Borehamwood WD6 100 CN39
Brentwood CM13 131 GB48
Buckhurst Hill IG9
off Hornbeam Rd 124 EK48
Hertford SG14 53 DP08
Ilford IG1 147 ER64
Northolt UB5 138 BZ64
Theydon Bois CM16 107 ES37
Hornbeam Cres, Brent. TW8 179 CH80
Hornbeam Gdns, N.Mal. KT3 221 CU100
Slough SL1 *off Upton Rd* 174 AU76
Hornbeam Gro, E4 124 EE48
Hornbeam Ho, NW3 6 F4
Hornbeam La, E4 106 EE43
Bexleyheath DA7 189 FC82
Essendon AL9 68 DE22
Hornbeam Rd, Buck.H. IG9 124 EK48
Guildford GU1 264 AW131
Hayes UB4 158 BW71
Reigate RH2 288 DB137
Theydon Bois CM16 107 ER37
Hornbeams, Brick.Wd AL2 82 BZ30
Hornbeams, The, Harl. CM20 57 EQ13
Hornbeams Av, Enf. EN1 104 DW35
Hornbeam Sq, E3 11 N8
Hornbeams Ri, N11 120 DG51
Hornbeam Ter, Cars. SM5 222 DE102
Hornbeam Wk, Rich. TW10 200 CM90
Whiteley Village KT12
off Octagon Rd 235 BT109
Hornbeam Way, Brom. BR2 227 EN100
Waltham Cross EN7 88 DT29
Hornbill Cl, Uxb. UB8 156 BK72
Hornblower Cl, SE16 33 L8
Hornbuckle Cl, Har. HA2 139 CD61
Hornby Cl, NW3 6 B6
Horncastle Cl, SE12 206 EG87
Horncastle Rd, SE12 206 EG87
HORNCHURCH, RM11 & RM12 150 FJ61
⊖ **Hornchurch** 150 FK62
Hornchurch Cl, Kings.T. KT2 199 CK91
Hornchurch Hill, Whyt. CR3 258 DT117
Hornchurch Rd, Horn. RM11, RM12 149 FG60
Horndean Cl, SW15
off Bessborough Rd 201 CU88
Horndon Cl, Rom. RM5 127 FC53
Horndon Grn, Rom. RM5 127 FC53
Horndon Rd, Rom. RM5 127 FC53
Horner La, Mitch. CR4 222 DD96
Horner Sq, E1
off Commercial St 20 A6
Horne Rd, Shep. TW17 216 BN98
Hornets, The, Wat. WD18 97 BV42
Horne Way, SW15 38 A9
Hornfair Rd, SE7 186 EJ79
Hornford Way, Rom. RM7 149 FE59
Hornhatch, Chilw. GU4 281 BB140
Hornhatch Cl, Chilw. GU4 281 BB140
Hornhatch La, Guil. GU4 281 BA140
Hornhill Rd, Ger.Cr. SL9 113 BB50
Maple Cross WD3 113 BD50
Horniman Dr, SE23 204 DV88
★ **Horniman Mus**, SE23 204 DV88
Sch **Horniman Prim Sch**, SE23
off Horniman Dr 204 DV88
Horning Cl, SE9 206 EL91
Horn La, SE10 35 N9
W3 160 CQ73
Woodford Green IG8 124 EG51
Horn Link Way, SE10 35 N8
Hornminster Glen, Horn. RM11 150 FN61
Horn Pk Cl, SE12 206 EH85
Horn Pk La, SE12 206 EH85
Sch **Horn Pk Prim Sch**, SE12
off Alnwick Rd 206 EH87
Sch **Hornsby Ho Sch**, SW12
off Hearnville Rd 202 DG88
Hornsby La, Orsett RM16 193 GG75
Horns Cl, Hert. SG13 54 DQ11
Horns Cft Cl, Bark. IG11
off Thornhill Gdns 167 ES66
Horns End Pl, Pnr. HA5 138 BW56
HORNSEY, N8 143 DM55
⇌ **Hornsey** 143 DM56
Hornsey La, N6 143 DH60
Hornsey La Est, N19 143 DK59
Hornsey La Gdns, N6 143 DJ59
Hornsey Pk Rd, N8 143 DM55
Hornsey Ri, N19 143 DK59
Hornsey Ri Gdns, N19 143 DK59
Hornsey Rd, N7 143 DM61
N19 143 DL60
Sch **Hornsey Sch for Girls**, N8 *off Inderwick Rd* 143 DM57
Hornsey St, N7 8 D2
Hornsfield, Welw.G.C. AL7 52 DC08
HORNS GREEN, Sev. TN14 261 ES117
Hornshay St, SE15 45 H3
Horns Mill Rd, Hert. SG13 54 DQ12
Horns Rd, Hert. SG13 54 DQ10
Ilford IG2, IG6 147 EQ57
Hornton Pl, W8 27 K5
Hornton St, W8 27 K4
Horsa Gdns, Hat. AL10 66 CR16
Horsa Rd, SE12 206 EJ87
Erith DA8 189 FC80
Horse & Dolphin Yd, W1 17 P10
Horsebridges Cl, Dag. RM9 168 EY67
Horsecroft, Bans. SM7
off Lyme Regis Rd 255 CZ117
Horsecroft Cl, Orp. BR6 228 EV102
Horsecroft Pl, Harl. CM19 72 EL16
Horsecroft Rd, Edg. HA8 118 CR52
Harlow CM19 72 EL16
Hemel Hempstead HP1 62 BG22
Horse Fair, Kings.T. KT1 219 CK96
Horseferry Pl, SE10 46 E3
Horseferry Rd, E14 21 L10
SW1 29 N7
Horse Guards Av, SW1 30 A3
★ **Horse Guards Par**, SW1 29 P3
Horse Guards Rd, SW1 29 P3
Horse Hill, Chesh. HP5 78 AX32
Horsehill, Horl. RH6 290 DA146
Horse La, Ware SG12 55 DX05
Horse Leaze, E6 25 M8
Horselers, Hem.H. HP3 62 BN23
HORSELL, Wok. GU21 248 AW116
Horsell Birch, Wok. GU21 248 AV115
Sch **Horsell C of E Jun Sch**, Horsell GU21 *off Meadway Dr* 248 AW116
Horsell Common, Wok. GU21 232 AX114
Horsell Common Rd, Wok. GU21 232 AW114
Horsell Ct, Cher. KT16
off Stepgates 216 BH101
Horsell Moor, Wok. GU21 248 AX117
Horsell Pk, Wok. GU21 248 AX116
Horsell Pk Cl, Wok. GU21 248 AX116
Horsell Ri, Wok. GU21 248 AX115
Horsell Ri Cl, Wok. GU21 248 AX115
Horsell Rd, N5 8 E3
Orpington BR5 228 EV95
Horsell Vale, Wok. GU21 248 AY115
Sch **Horsell Village Sch, The**, Horsell GU21 *off Church Hill* 248 AX116
Horsell Way, Wok. GU21 248 AW116
Horselydown La, SE1 32 A4
Horseman Side, Nave.S. CM14 127 FH45
Horsemans Ride, St.Alb. AL2 82 CA26
Horsemongers Ms, SE1 31 K5
Horsemoor Cl, Slou. SL3 175 BA77
Horsenden Av, Grnf. UB6 139 CE64
Horsenden Cres, Grnf. UB6 139 CF64
Horsenden La N, Grnf. UB6 159 CF65
Horsenden La S, Perivale UB6 159 CG67
Sch **Horsenden Prim Sch**, Grnf. UB6 *off Horsenden La N* 159 CF65
Horse Ride, SW1 29 N3
Dorking RH5 285 CD144
Leatherhead KT24 267 BR130
Tadworth KT20 271 CY125
Horse Rd, E7 *off Centre Rd* 146 EH62
Horseshoe, The, Bans. SM7 255 CZ115
Coulsdon CR5 241 DK113
Hemel Hempstead HP3 63 BQ22
● **Horseshoe Business Pk**, Brick.Wd AL2 82 CA30
Horseshoe Cl, E14 34 E10
NW2 141 CV61
Waltham Abbey EN9 90 EG34
Horse Shoe Ct, EC1
off Brewhouse Yd 19 H4
Horseshoe Cres, Beac. HP9 111 AL54
Horse Shoe Cres, Nthlt. UB5 158 CA68
Horseshoe Dr, Uxb. UB8 156 BN72
Horse Shoe Grn, Sutt. SM1
off Aultone Way 222 DB103
Horseshoe Hill, Burn. SL1 132 AJ63
Waltham Abbey EN9 90 EJ33
Horseshoe La, N20 119 CX46
Enfield EN2
off Chase Side 104 DQ41
Watford WD25 81 BV32
Horseshoe La E, Guil. GU1 265 BB133
Horseshoe La W, Guil. GU1 265 BB133
Horseshoe Ms, SW2
off Acre La 183 DL84
Horseshoe Ridge, Wey. KT13 235 BQ111
Horse Yd, N1 9 H8
Horsfeld Gdns, SE9 206 EL85
Horsfeld Rd, SE9 206 EK85
Horsfield Cl, Dart. DA2 210 FQ87
Horsford Rd, SW2 203 DM85

Horsham Av, N12 120 DE50
Horsham Rd, Abin.Ham. RH5 283 BT142
Bexleyheath DA6 208 FA85
Dorking RH4 285 CG137
Feltham TW14 197 BQ86
Guildford GU4, GU5 280 AY142
Holmwood RH5 285 CH140
Horshams, Harl. CM19 off Little Gro Fld 73 EQ15
⇌ Horsley 267 BS125
Horsley Cl, Epsom KT19 238 CR113
Horsleydown Old Stairs, SE1 32 A3
Horsley Dr, Kings.T. KT2 199 CK92
New Addington CR0 243 EC108
Horsley Rd, E4 123 EC47
Bromley BR1 off Palace Rd 226 EH95
Cobham KT11 251 BV119
Horsleys, Map.Cr. WD3 113 BD50
Horsley St, SE17 43 L2
Horsmonden Cl, Orp. BR6 227 ES101
Horsmonden Rd, SE4 205 DZ85
Hortensia Rd, SW10 39 N3
Horticultural Pl, W4 180 CR78
HORTON, Epsom KT19 238 CP110
HORTON, Slou. SL3 175 BA83
Horton Av, NW2 4 F1
Horton Br Rd, West Dr. UB7 156 BM74
Horton Cl, Maid. SL6 152 AC70
West Drayton UB7 156 BM74
★ Horton Country Pk, Epsom KT19 238 CM110
Horton Cres, Epsom KT19 238 CP110
Horton Footpath, Epsom KT19 238 CQ111
Horton Gdns, Epsom KT19 238 CQ111
Horton Hill, Epsom KT19 238 CQ111
Horton Ho, SW8 42 C4
● Horton Ind Pk, West Dr. UB7 156 BM74
HORTON KIRBY, Dart. DA4 231 FR98
Sch Horton Kirby C of E Prim Sch, Hort.Kir. DA4 off Horton Rd 230 FQ97
Horton La, Epsom KT19 238 CP110
Horton Par, West Dr. UB7 off Horton Rd 156 BL74
★ Horton Park Children's Fm, Epsom KT19 238 CN110
● Horton Pl, West. TN16 off Hortons Way 277 ER126
Horton Rd, E8 10 E4
Colnbrook SL3 175 BA81
Dartford DA4 230 FQ97
Datchet SL3 174 AV80
Poyle SL3 175 BE83
Staines-upon-Thames TW19 196 BG85
West Drayton UB7 156 BN74
Horton St, SE13 46 D10
Hortons Way, West. TN16 277 ER126
Horton Twr, Orp. BR5 228 EW98
Horton Way, Croy. CR0 225 DX99
Farningham DA4 230 FM101
Hortus Rd, E4 123 EC47
Southall UB2 178 BZ75
Horvath Cl, Wey. KT13 235 BR105
Horwood Cl, Rick. WD3 off Thellusson Way 114 BG45
Horwood Ct, Wat. WD24 98 BX37
Hosack Rd, SW17 202 DF89
Hoser Av, SE12 206 EG89
Hosey Common La, West. TN16 277 ES130
Hosey Common Rd, Eden. TN8 277 EQ133
Westerham TN16 277 ER130
HOSEY HILL, West. TN16 277 ES127
Hosey Hill, West. TN16 277 ER127
Hosier La, EC1 18 G7
Hoskins Cl, E16 24 D8
Hayes UB3 177 BT78
Hoskins Rd, Oxt. RH8 276 EE129
Hoskins St, SE10 47 H1
Hoskins Wk, Oxt. RH8 276 EE129
Hospital Br Rd, Twick. TW2 198 CB87
Hospital Hill, Chesh. HP5 76 AQ32
H Hospital of St. John & St. Elizabeth, NW8 16 A1
Hospital Rd, E9 11 H2
Hounslow TW3 178 CA83
Sevenoaks TN13 279 FJ121
Hospital Way, SE13 205 ED87
Hotham Cl, Sutt.H. DA4 210 FP94
Swanley BR8 229 FH95
West Molesey KT8 off Garrick Gdns 218 CA97
Sch Hotham Prim Sch, SW15 off Charlwood Rd 181 CX84
Hotham Rd, SW15 181 CW83
SW19 202 DC94
Hotham Rd Ms, SW19 off Haydons Rd 202 DC94
Hotham St, E15 13 J8
Hothfield Pl, SE16 33 H7
● Hotspur Ind Est, N17 122 DV51
Hotspur Rd, Nthlt. UB5 158 CA68
Hotspur St, SE11 30 E10
Houblon Rd, Rich. TW10 200 CL85
Houblons Hill, Cooper. CM16 92 EW31
Houghton Cl, E8 10 B5
Hampton TW12 198 BY93
Houghton Rd, N15 off West Grn Rd 144 DT56
Houghton Sq, SW9 42 A9
Houghton St, WC2 18 D9
Houlder Cres, Croy. CR0 241 DP107
Hound Ho Rd, Shere GU5 282 BN141
Houndsden Rd, N21 103 DM44
Houndsditch, EC3 19 P8
Sch Houndsfield Prim Sch, N9 off Ripon Rd 122 DV45
Houndsfield Rd, N9 122 DV45
HOUNSLOW, TW3 - TW6 178 BZ84
⇌ Hounslow 198 CB85
Hounslow Av, Houns. TW3 198 CB85
● Hounslow Business Pk, Houns. TW3 off Alice Way 178 CB84
⊖ Hounslow Central 178 CA83
⊖ Hounslow East 178 CC82
Hounslow Gdns, Houns. TW3 198 CB85
★ Hounslow Heath, TW4 198 BY86
Sch Hounslow Heath Inf & Nur Sch, Houns. TW4 off Martindale Rd 178 BY83
Sch Hounslow Heath Jun Sch, Houns. TW4 off Selwyn Cl 178 BY83
Sch Hounslow Manor Sch, Houns. TW3 off Prince Regent Rd 178 CC83
Hounslow Rd, Feltham TW14 197 BV88
Hanworth TW13 198 BX90
Twickenham TW2 198 CC86
Sch Hounslow Town Prim Sch, Houns. TW3 off Pears Rd 178 CC83
HOUNSLOW WEST, Houns. TW4 178 BX83
⊖ Hounslow West 178 BY82
Housden Cl, Wheat. AL4 50 CL08
Housefield Way, St.Alb. AL4 65 CJ23
House La, Sand. AL4 65 CK16
Houseman Way, SE5 43 M5
★ Houses of Parliament, SW1 30 B5
Housewood End, Hem.H. HP1 62 BH17
HOUSHAM TYE, Harl. CM17 59 FD13
Houston Pl, Esher KT10 off Lime Tree Av 219 CE102
Houston Rd, SE23 205 DY89
Long Ditton KT6 219 CH100
Hove Av, E17 145 DZ57
Hove Cl, Grays RM17 192 GA79
Hutton CM13 131 GC47
Hoveden Rd, NW2 4 E2
Hove Gdns, Sutt. SM1 222 DB102
Hoveton Rd, SE28 168 EW72
Hoveton Way, Ilf. IG6 125 EP52
Howard Agne Cl, Bov. HP3 79 BA27
Howard Av, Bex. DA5 208 EW88
Epsom KT17 239 CU110
Slough SL2 153 AR71
Howard Bldg, SW8 41 J3
Howard Business Pk, Wal.Abb. EN9 off Howard Cl 89 ED34
🔒 Howard Cen, The, Welw.G.C. AL8 51 CX09
Howard Cl, N11 120 DG47
NW2 141 CY63
W3 160 CP72
Ashtead KT21 254 CM118
Bushey Heath WD23 117 CE45
Hampton TW12 198 CC93
Leatherhead KT22 253 CJ123
Loughton IG10 106 EL44
St. Albans AL1 65 CJ22
Sunbury-on-Thames TW16 197 BT93
Waltham Abbey EN9 89 ED34
Walton on the Hill KT20 271 CT125
Watford WD24 97 BU37
West Horsley KT24 267 BR125
Howard Ct, Reig. RH2 272 DC133
Howard Cres, Seer Grn HP9 111 AQ50
Howard Dr, Borwd. WD6 100 CR42
Howard Gdns, Guil. GU1 265 BA133
● Howard Ind Est, Chesh. HP5 76 AQ29
Howard Ms, N5 9 H1
Slough SL3 off Laburnum Gro 175 BB79
Sch Howard of Effingham Sch, Eff. KT24 off Lower Rd 268 BX127
Howard Pl, Reig. RH2 272 DA132
Sch Howard Prim Sch, Croy. CR0 off Dering Pl 242 DQ105
Howard Ridge, Burpham GU4 265 BA130
Howard Rd, E6 167 EM68
E11 146 EE62
E17 145 EA55
N15 144 DS58
N16 9 M1
NW2 4 C1
SE20 224 DW95
SE25 224 DU99
Barking IG11 167 ER67
Bookham KT23 268 CB127
Bromley BR1 206 EG94
Chafford Hundred RM16 191 FW76
Chesham HP5 76 AP28
Coulsdon CR5 257 DJ115
Dartford DA1 210 FN86
Dorking RH4 285 CG136
Effingham Junction KT24 251 BU122
Ilford IG1 147 EP63
Isleworth TW7 179 CF83
New Malden KT3 220 CS97
North Holmwood RH5 off Holmesdale Rd 285 CJ140
Reigate RH2 288 DB135
Seer Green HP9 111 AQ50
Southall UB1 158 CB72
Surbiton KT5 220 CM100
Upminster RM14 150 FQ61
Howards Cl, Pnr. HA5 115 BV54
Woking GU22 249 BA120
Howards Crest Cl, Beck. BR3 225 EC96
Howards Dr, Hem.H. HP1 61 BF17
Howards Gate, Farn.Royal SL2 off Farnham Rd 153 AQ69
Howardsgate, Welw.G.C. AL8 51 CX08
Howards La, SW15 201 CV85
Addlestone KT15 233 BE107
Howards Rd, E13 23 N2
Woking GU22 249 AZ120
Howards Thicket, Ger.Cr. SL9 134 AW61
Howard St, T.Ditt. KT7 219 CH101
Howards Wd Dr, Ger.Cr. SL9 134 AX61
Howard Wk, N2 142 DC56
Howard Way, Barn. EN5 101 CX43
Harlow CM20 74 EU15
Howarth Rd, SE2 188 EU78
Howberry Cl, Edg. HA8 117 CK51
Howberry Rd, Edg. HA8 117 CK51
Stanmore HA7 117 CK51
Thornton Heath CR7 224 DR95
Howbury La, Erith DA8 189 FG82
Howbury Rd, SE15 44 G10
Howcroft Cres, N3 120 DA52
Howcroft La, Grnf. UB6 159 CD69
Howden Cl, SE28 168 EX73
Howden Rd, SE25 224 DT96
Howden St, SE15 44 C10
Howe Cl, Rom. RM7 126 FA53
Shenley WD7 84 CL32
Howe Dell, Hat. AL10 67 CV18
Sch Howe Dell Prim Sch, Hat. AL10 off The Runway 66 CS16
Sch Howe Dell Sch, Hat. AL10 off The Runway 66 CS16
Howe Dr, Beac. HP9 111 AK50
Caterham CR3 258 DR122
Howell Cl, Rom. RM6 148 EX57
Howell Hill Cl, Epsom KT17 239 CW111
Howell Hill Gro, Epsom KT17 239 CW110
Howell Wk, SE1 31 H9
Howerd Way, SE18 186 EL81
Howe Rd, Hem.H. HP3 62 BN22
Howes Cl, N3 142 DA55
Howfield Grn, Hodd. EN11 55 DZ14
Howfield Pl, N17 144 DT55
Howgate Rd, SW14 180 CR83
Howick Pl, SW1 29 M7
Howicks Grn, Welw.G.C. AL7 52 DA12
Howie St, SW11 40 C5
Howitt Cl, N16 off Allen Rd 144 DS63
NW3 6 D4
Howitt Rd, NW3 6 C4
Howitts Cl, Esher KT10 236 CA107
Howland Est, SE16 33 H6
Howland Garth, St.Alb. AL1 64 CC24
Howland Ms E, W1 17 M6
Howlands, Welw.G.C. AL7 52 DB12
Howlands Ho, Welw.G.C. AL7 52 DA12
Howland St, W1 17 L6
Howland Way, SE16 33 M5
How La, Chipstead CR5 256 DG117
Howletts La, Ruis. HA4 137 BQ57
Howletts Rd, SE24 204 DQ86
Howley Pl, W2 15 P6
Howley Rd, Croy. CR0 223 DP104
Hows Cl, Uxb. UB8 156 BJ67
Howse Rd, Wal.Abb. EN9 off Deer Pk Way 105 EB35
Howsman Rd, SW13 181 CU79
Hows Mead, N.Wld Bas. CM16 75 FD24
Howson Rd, SE4 185 DY84
Howson Ter, Rich. TW10 200 CL86
Hows Rd, Uxb. UB8 156 BJ67
Hows St, E2 10 A10
Howton Pl, Bushey Hth WD23 117 CD46
HOW WOOD, St.Alb. AL2 82 CC27
⇌ How Wood 82 CC28
How Wd, Park St AL2 82 CB28
Sch How Wd Prim Sch, Park St AL2 off Spooners Dr 82 CC27
HOXTON, N1 19 N1
⊖ Hoxton 19 P1
Hoxton Mkt, N1 19 N3
Hoxton Sq, N1 19 N3
Hoxton St, N1 19 P3
Hoylake Cl, Slou. SL1 173 AL75
Hoylake Cres, Ickhm UB10 136 BN60
Hoylake Gdns, Mitch. CR4 223 DJ97
Romford RM3 128 FN53
Ruislip HA4 137 BV60
Watford WD19 116 BX49
Hoylake Rd, W3 160 CS72
Hoyland Cl, SE15 44 E4
Hoyle Rd, SW17 202 DE92
Hoy St, E16 23 L9
Hoy Ter, Grays RM20 191 FX78
★ H.Q.S. Wellington, Master Mariners' Hall, WC2 18 E10
Hubbard Dr, Chess. KT9 237 CJ107
Hubbard Rd, SE27 204 DQ91
Hubbards Chase, Horn. RM11 150 FN57
Hubbards Cl, Horn. RM11 150 FN57
Uxbridge UB8 157 BP72
Hubbard's Hall Est, Harl. CM17 58 EY14
Hubbards Rd, Chorl. WD3 95 BD43
Hubbard St, E15 13 J9
● Hubbinet Ind Est, Rom. RM7 149 FC55
Hubert Day Cl, Beac. HP9 off Seeleys Rd 111 AK52
Hubert Gro, SW9 183 DL83
Hubert Rd, E6 24 E2
Brentwood CM14 130 FV48
Rainham RM13 169 FF69
Slough SL3 174 AX76
Hucknall Cl, Rom. RM3 128 FM51
Huddart St, E3 21 P6
Huddleston Cl, E2 10 G10
Huddleston Cres, Merst. RH1 273 DK128
Huddlestone Rd, E7 146 EF63
NW2 161 CV65
Huddleston Rd, N7 7 N1
Hudson Apts, N8 off Chadwell La 143 DM55
Hudson Av, Denh. UB9 135 BF58
Hudson Cl, E15 13 N8
W12 off Canada Way 161 CV73
St. Albans AL1 65 CD23
Watford WD24 97 BT36
Hudson Ct, E14 off Maritime Quay 34 B10
SW19 202 DB94
Guildford GU2 off Cobbett Rd 264 AT133
Hudson Gdns, Grn St Grn BR6 off Superior Dr 245 ET107
Hudson Ho, Epsom KT19 238 CR113
Hudson Pl, SE18 187 EQ78
Slough SL3 175 AZ78
Hudson Rd, Bexh. DA7 188 EZ82
Harlington UB3 177 BR79
Hudsons, Tad. KT20 255 CX121
Hudsons Ct, Pot.B. EN6 86 DA31
Hudson's Pl, SW1 29 K8
Hudson Way, N9 122 DW48
NW2 off Gratton Ter 141 CX62
Huggens College, Nthflt. DA11 212 GB85
Huggin Ct, EC4 19 K10
Huggin Hill, EC4 19 K10
Huggins La, N.Mymms AL9 67 CV23
Huggins Pl, SW2 203 DM88
Hughan Rd, E15 13 H2
Hugh Dalton Av, SW6 38 G3
Hughenden Av, Har. HA3 139 CH57
Hughenden Gdns, Nthlt. UB5 158 BW69
Hughenden Rd, St.Alb. AL4 65 CH17
Slough SL1 153 AR72
Worcester Park KT4 221 CU101
Hughendon Ter, E15 off Westdown Rd 145 EC63
Hughes Cl, N12 120 DC50
Hughes Rd, Ashf. TW15 197 BQ94
Grays RM16 193 GG76
Hayes UB3 157 BV73
Hughes Ter, SW9 off Styles Gdns 43 H10
Hughes Wk, Croy. CR0 off St. Saviours Rd 224 DQ101
Hugh Gaitskell Cl, SW6 38 G3
Hugh Herland Ho, Kings.T. KT1 220 CL97
Hugh Ms, SW1 29 K9
Sch Hugh Myddelton Prim Sch, EC1 18 F3
Hugh's Twr, Harl. CM20 57 ER14
Hugh St, SW1 29 K9
Hugo Cl, Wat. WD18 off Malkin Way 97 BS42
Hugo Gdns, Rain. RM13 169 FF65
Hugo Gryn Way, Shenley WD7 84 CL31
Hugon Rd, SW6 39 L10
Hugo Rd, N19 143 DJ63
Huguenot Pl, E1 20 B6
SW18 202 DC85
Huguenot Sq, SE15 44 E10
HULBERRY, Dart. DA4 229 FG103
Hullbridge Ms, N1 9 L8
Hull Cl, SE16 33 K4
Cheshunt EN7 88 DR26
Slough SL1 173 AQ75
Sutton SM2 off Yarbridge Cl 240 DB110
Hulletts La, Pilg.Hat. CM15 130 FT43
Hull Gro, Harl. CM19 73 EN20
Hull Pl, E16 off Fishguard Way 167 EQ74
Hull St, EC1 19 J3
Hulme Pl, SE1 31 K5
Hulse Av, Bark. IG11 167 ER65
Romford RM7 127 FB53
Hulse Ter, Ilf. IG1 off Buttsbury Rd 147 EQ64
Hulsewood Cl, Dart. DA2 209 FH90
Hulton Cl, Lthd. KT22 253 CJ123
Hulverston Cl, Sutt. SM2 240 DB110
Humber Av, S.Ock. RM15 171 FT72
Humber Cl, West Dr. UB7 156 BK74
Humber Dr, W10 14 C5
Upminster RM14 151 FR58
Humber Rd, NW2 141 CV61
SE3 47 L2
Dartford DA1 210 FK85
Humberstone Rd, E13 24 C3
Humberton Cl, E9 11 L3
Humber Way, Slou. SL3 175 BA77
Humbolt Cl, Guil. GU2 264 AS134
Humbolt Rd, W6 38 E3
Hume Av, Til. RM18 193 GG83
Hume Cl, Til. RM18 193 GG83
Hume Ms, Til. RM18 off Hume Cl 193 GG83
Humes Av, W7 179 CE76
Hume Ter, E16 24 C7
Hume Way, Ruis. HA4 137 BU58
Hummer Rd, Egh. TW20 195 BA91
Humphrey Cl, Fetch. KT22 252 CC122
Ilford IG5 125 EM53
Humphrey St, SE1 32 A10
Humphries Cl, Dag. RM9 148 EZ63
Hundred Acre, NW9 119 CT54
Hundred Acres La, Amer. HP7 77 AR40
Hungerdown, E4 123 EC46
Hungerford Av, Slou. SL2 154 AS71
Hungerford Br, SE1 30 B2
WC2 30 B2
Hungerford La, WC2 30 A2
Sch Hungerford Prim Sch, N7 7 P4
Hungerford Rd, N7 7 P4
Hungerford Sq, Wey. KT13 off Rosslyn Pk 235 BR105
Hungerford St, E1 20 F8
Hungry Hill, Ripley GU23 250 BK124
Hungry Hill La, Send GU23 250 BK124
HUNSDON, Ware SG12 56 EJ06
Hunsdon, Welw.G.C. AL7 52 DD09
HUNSDONBURY, Ware SG12 56 EJ08
Hunsdon Cl, Dag. RM9 168 EY65
Hunsdon Dr, Sev. TN13 279 FH123
Sch Hunsdon JMI Sch, Hunsdon SG12 off High St 56 EK06
Hunsdon Pound, Stans.Abb. SG12 56 EL12
Hunsdon Rd, SE14 45 J4
Stanstead Abbotts SG12 56 EE11
Hunslett St, E2 21 H1
Hunstanton Cl, Colnbr. SL3 175 BC80
Hunston Rd, Mord. SM4 222 DB102
Hunt Cl, W11 26 D2
St. Albans AL4 off Villiers Cres 65 CK17
Hunter Av, Shenf. CM15 131 GA44
Hunter Cl, SE1 31 M7
SW12 202 DG88
Borehamwood WD6 100 CQ43
Potters Bar EN6 86 DB33
Wallington SM6 241 DL108
Huntercombe Cl, Tap. SL6 152 AH72
Huntercombe La N, Slou. SL1 152 AJ71
Taplow SL6 152 AJ71
Huntercombe La S, Tap. SL6 152 AH74
H Huntercombe Manor, Tap. SL6 152 AJ73
Huntercombe Spur, Slou. SL1 152 AJ73
Huntercrombe Gdns, Wat. WD19 116 BW50
Hunter Dr, Horn. RM12 150 FJ63
Hunter Ho, Felt. TW13 197 BU88
Hunter Rd, SW20 221 CW95
Guildford GU1 280 AY135
Ilford IG1 147 EP64
Thornton Heath CR7 224 DR97
Hunters, The, Beck. BR3 225 EC95
Hunters Cl, Bex. DA5 209 FE90
Bovingdon HP3 79 BA29
Chesham HP5 76 AN30
Epsom KT19 off Marshalls Cl 238 CQ113
Hunters Ct, Rich. TW9 199 CK85
Huntersfield Cl, Reig. RH2 272 DB131
Hunters Gate, Nutfld RH1 273 DM133
Watford WD25 off Hunters La 81 BU33
Hunters Gro, Har. HA3 139 CJ56
Hayes UB3 157 BU74
Orpington BR6 245 EP105
Romford RM5 127 FB50
Sch Hunters Hall Prim Sch, Dag. RM10 off Alibon Rd 149 FB64
Hunters Hall Rd, Dag. RM10 148 FA63
Hunters Hill, Ruis. HA4 138 BW62
Hunters La, Wat. WD25 81 BT33
Hunters Meadow, SE19 off Dulwich Wd Av 204 DS91
Hunters Oak, Hem.H. HP2 63 BP15
Hunters Pk, Berk. HP4 60 AY18
Hunters Reach, Wal.Cr. EN7 88 DT29
Hunters Ride, Brick.Wd AL2 82 CA31
Hunters Rd, Chess. KT9 220 CL104
Hunters Sq, Dag. RM10 148 FA63
Hunter St, WC1 18 B4
Hunters Wk, Knock.P. TN14 246 EY114
Hunters Way, Croy. CR0 242 DS105
Enfield EN2 103 DN39
Slough SL1 173 AL75
Welwyn Garden City AL7 51 CZ12
Hunter Wk, E13 13 N10
Borehamwood WD6 off Hunter Cl 100 CQ43
Hunting Cl, Esher KT10 236 CA105
Huntingdon Cl, Brox. EN10 71 DY24
Mitcham CR4 223 DL97
Huntingdon Cl, Northolt UB5 158 CA65
Huntingdon Gdns, W4 180 CQ80
Worcester Park KT4 221 CW104
Huntingdon Rd, N2 142 DE55
N9 122 DW46
Redhill RH1 272 DF134
Woking GU21 248 AT117
Huntingdon St, E16 23 M9
N1 8 C7
Huntingfield, Croy. CR0 243 DZ108
Huntingfield Rd, SW15 181 CU84
Huntingfield Way, Egh. TW20 195 BD94
Hunting Gate, Hem.H. HP2 62 BL16
Hunting Gate Cl, Enf. EN2 103 DN41
Hunting Gate Dr, Chess. KT9 238 CL108
Hunting Gate Ms, Sutt. SM1 222 DB104
Twickenham TW2 off Colne Rd 199 CE88
Huntings Rd, Dag. RM10 168 FA65
Huntington Pl, Langley SL3 175 BB76
Huntland Cl, Rain. RM13 169 FH71
Huntley Av, Nthflt DA11 212 GB86
Huntley Cl, Stanw. TW19 off Cambria Gdns 196 BL87
Huntley Ho, Walt. KT12 off Octagon Rd 235 BT109
Huntley St, WC1 17 M5
Huntley Way, SW20 221 CU96
Huntly Dr, N3 120 DA51
Huntly Rd, SE25 224 DS98
HUNTON BRIDGE, Kings L. WD4 81 BP33
Hunton Br Hill, Hunt.Br. WD4 81 BQ33
Jct Hunton Br Interchange, Wat. WD17 97 BQ35
Hunton St, E1 20 C5
Hunt Rd, Nthflt DA11 212 GE90
Southall UB2 178 CA76
Hunt's Cl, SE3 47 P8
Hunt's Ct, WC2 29 P1
Hunts La, E15 22 E1
Taplow SL6 152 AE68
Huntsman Rd, Ilf. IG6 126 EU51
Huntsmans Cl, Felt. TW13 197 BV91
Fetcham KT22 off The Green 253 CD124
Warlingham CR6 258 DW119
Huntsmans Dr, Upmin. RM14 150 FQ64
Huntsman St, SE17 31 M9
Hunts Mead, Enf. EN3 105 DX41
Hunts Mead Cl, Chis. BR7 207 EM94
Huntsmill Rd, Hem.H. HP1 61 BE21
Huntsmoor Rd, Epsom KT19 238 CR106
Huntspill St, SW17 202 DC90
Hunts Slip Rd, SE21 204 DS90
Huntswood La, Slou. SL1 152 AE66
Taplow SL6 152 AE66
Huntsworth Ms, NW1 16 E5
Hurdwick Pl, NW1 off Harrington Sq 7 L10
Hurley Cl, Walt. KT12 217 BV103
Hurley Ct, SW17 off Mitcham Rd 202 DG93
Hurley Cres, SE16 33 K4
Hurley Gdns, Guil. GU4 265 AZ130
Hurley Ho, SE11 30 F9
Hurley Rd, Grnf. UB6 158 CB72
Hurlfield, Dart. DA2 210 FJ90
Hurlford, Wok. GU21 248 AU117
Sch Hurlingham & Chelsea Sch, SW6 39 K10
● Hurlingham Business Pk, SW6 182 DA83
★ Hurlingham Club, SW6 181 CZ83
Hurlingham Ct, SW6 38 G10
Hurlingham Gdns, SW6 38 G10
★ Hurlingham Park, SW6 39 H10
🔒 Hurlingham Retail Pk, SW6 off Carnwath Rd 182 DB83
Hurlingham Rd, SW6 38 G9
Bexleyheath DA7 188 EZ80
Sch Hurlingham Sch, SW15 off Putney Br Rd 181 CZ84
Hurlingham Sq, SW6 182 DA83
Hurlock St, N5 143 DP62
Hurlstone Rd, SE25 224 DR99
Hurn Ct Rd, Houns. TW4 178 BX82
Hurnford Cl, S.Croy. CR2 242 DS110
Huron Cl, Grn St Grn BR6 off Winnipeg Dr 245 ET107
Huron Rd, SW17 202 DG89
Broxbourne EN10 89 DY26
Uni Huron Uni USA in London, WC1 18 A6
Hurren Cl, SE3 47 J10
Hurricane Rd, Wall. SM6 241 DL108
● Hurricane Trd Cen, NW9 119 CU53
Hurricane Way, Abb.L. WD5 off Abbey Dr 81 BU32
North Weald Bassett CM16 92 EZ27
Slough SL3 175 BB78
Hurry Cl, E15 13 K7
Hursley Rd, Chig. IG7 125 ET50
Hurst Av, E4 123 EA49
N6 143 DJ58
Hurstbourne, Clay. KT10 237 CF107
Hurstbourne Gdns, Bark. IG11 167 ES65
Hurstbourne Ho, SW15 off Tangley Gro 201 CT86
Hurstbourne Rd, SE23 205 DY88
Hurst Cl, E4 123 EA48
NW11 142 DB58
Bromley BR2 226 EF102
Chessington KT9 238 CN106
Headley KT18 254 CQ124
Northolt UB5 158 BZ65
Welwyn Garden City AL7 52 DC10
Woking GU22 248 AW120
Hurstcourt Rd, Sutt. SM1 222 DB103
Hurst Cft, Guil. GU1 280 AY137
Hurstdene Av, Brom. BR2 226 EF102
Staines-upon-Thames TW18 196 BH93
Hurstdene Gdns, N15 144 DS59
Hurst Dr, Wal.Cr. EN8 89 DX34
Walton on the Hill KT20 271 CU126
Sch Hurst Dr Prim Sch, Wal.Cr. EN8 off Hurst Dr 89 DX34
Hurst Est, SE2 188 EX78
Hurstfield, Brom. BR2 226 EG99
Hurstfield Cres, Hayes UB4 157 BS70
Hurstfield Dr, Tap. SL6 152 AH72
Hurstfield Rd, W.Mol. KT8 218 CA97
HURST GREEN, Oxt. RH8 276 EG132
⇌ Hurst Green 276 EF132
Hurst Grn Cl, Oxt. RH8 276 EG132
Hurst Grn Rd, Oxt. RH8 276 EF132
Sch Hurst Grn Sch, Oxt. RH8 off Wolfs Wd 276 EG132
Hurst Gro, Walt. KT12 217 BT102

Hurstlands, Oxt. RH8 276 EG132
Hurstlands Cl, Horn. RM11 150 FJ59
Hurstlands Dr, Orp. BR6 228 EW104
Hurst La, SE2 188 EX78
East Molesey KT8 218 CC98
Egham TW20 215 BA96
Headley KT18 254 CQ124
Hurstleigh Cl, Red. RH1 272 DF132
Hurstleigh Dr, Red. RH1 272 DF132
Hurstleigh Gdns, Ilf. IG5 125 EM53
Hurstlings, Welw.G.C. AL7 52 DB10
Hurstmead Ct, Edg. HA8 118 CP49
Sch Hurstmere Sch, Sid. DA15 off Hurst Rd 208 EW88
Hurst Pk Av, Horn. RM12 off Crystal Av 150 FL63
Sch Hurst Pk Prim Sch, W.Mol. KT8 off Hurst Rd 218 CA97
Hurst Pl, Nthwd. HA6 115 BP53
Sch Hurst Prim Sch, Bex. DA5 off Dorchester Av 208 EX87
Hurst Ri, Barn. EN5 102 DA41
Hurst Rd, E17 145 EB55
N21 121 DN46
Bexley DA5 208 EX88
Buckhurst Hill IG9 124 EK46
Croydon CR0 242 DR106
East Molesey KT8 218 CA97
Epsom KT19 238 CR111
Erith DA8 189 FC80
Headley KT18 254 CR123
Horley RH6 290 DE147
Sidcup DA15 208 EU89
Slough SL1 153 AK71
Walton on the Hill KT20 254 CR123
Walton-on-Thames KT12 218 BW99
West Molesey KT8 218 BY97
Hurst Springs, Bex. DA5 208 EY88
Hurst St, SE24 203 DP86
Hurst Vw Rd, S.Croy. CR2 242 DS108
Hurst Way, Pyrford GU22 233 BE114
Sevenoaks TN13 279 FJ127
South Croydon CR2 242 DS107
Hurstway Wk, W11 14 D10
Hurstwood Av, E18 146 EH56
Bexley DA5 208 EY88
Bexleyheath DA7 189 FE81
Erith DA8 189 FE81
Pilgrim's Hatch CM15 130 FV43
Hurstwood Ct, Upmin. RM14 150 FP60
Hurstwood Dr, Brom. BR1 227 EM97
Hurstwood Rd, NW11 141 CY56
Hurtwood Rd, Walt. KT12 218 BZ101
Hurworth Av, Slou. SL3 174 AW76
Huskards, Upmin. RM14 150 FP61
Huson Cl, NW3 6 C6
Hussain Cl, Har. HA1 139 CF63
Hussars Cl, Houns. TW4 178 BY83
Husseywell Cres, Brom. BR2 226 EG102
Hutchingsons Rd, New Adgtn CR0 243 EC111
Hutchings Rd, Beac. HP9 111 AK50
Hutchings St, E14 34 A5
Hutchings Wk, NW11 142 DB56
Hutchins Cl, E15 12 F7
Hornchurch RM12 150 FL62
Hutchinson Ter, Wem. HA9 139 CK62
Hutchins Rd, SE28 168 EU73
Hutchins Way, Horl. RH6 290 DF146
Hutson Ter, Purf. RM19 off London Rd Purfleet 191 FR79
HUTTON, Brwd. CM13 131 GD44
Sch Hutton All Saints' C of E Prim Sch, Hutt. CM13 off Claughton Way 131 GD44
Hutton Cl, Grnf. UB6 off Mary Peters Dr 139 CD64
Hertford SG14 53 DN09
Walton-on-Thames KT12 235 BV106
Woodford Green IG8 124 EH51
Hutton Dr, Hutt. CM13 131 GD45
Hutton Gdns, Har. HA3 116 CC52
Hutton Gate, Hutt. CM13 131 GB45
Hutton Gro, N12 120 DB50
Hutton La, Har. HA3 116 CC52
Hutton Ms, SW15 201 CV85
HUTTON MOUNT, Brwd. CM13 131 GB46
Hutton Pl, Hutt. CM13 131 GB44
Hutton Rd, Shenf. CM15 131 FZ45
Hutton Row, Edg. HA8 118 CQ52
Hutton St, EC4 18 F9
Hutton Village, Hutt. CM13 131 GE45
Hutton Wk, Har. HA3 116 CC52
Huxbear St, SE4 205 DZ85
Huxley Cl, Nthlt. UB5 158 BY67
Uxbridge UB8 156 BK70
Wexham SL3 154 AV70
Huxley Dr, Rom. RM6 148 EV59
Huxley Gdns, NW10 160 CM69
Huxley Par, N18 122 DR50
Huxley Pl, N13 121 DP49
Huxley Rd, E10 145 EC61
N18 122 DR49
Welling DA16 187 ET83
Huxley Sayze, N18 122 DR50
Huxley St, W10 14 E3
Huxtable Gdns, Maid. SL6 172 AD79
Hyacinth Cl, Hmptn. TW12 off Gresham Rd 198 CA93
Ilford IG1 167 EP65
Hyacinth Ct, Pnr. HA5 off Tulip Ct 138 BW55
Hyacinth Dr, Uxb. UB10 156 BL66
Hyacinth Rd, SW15 201 CU88
Hyburn Cl, Brick.Wd AL2 82 BZ30
Hemel Hempstead HP3 63 BP21
Hycliffe Gdns, Chig. IG7 125 EQ49
HYDE, THE, NW9 141 CT56
Hyde, The, NW9 140 CS57
Ware SG12 54 DV05
Hyde Av, Pot.B. EN6 86 DB33
Hyde Cl, E13 13 P10
Ashford TW15 off Hyde Ter 197 BS93
Barnet EN5 101 CZ41
Chafford Hundred RM16 191 FX76
Romford RM1 127 FD51
Hyde Ct, N20 120 DD48
Waltham Cross EN8 off Parkside 89 DY34
Hyde Cres, NW9 140 CS57
Hyde Dr, St.P.Cray BR5 228 EV98
Hyde Est Rd, NW9 141 CT57
Hyde Fm Ms, SW12 203 DK88
Hydefield Cl, N21 122 DR46
Hydefield Ct, N9 122 DS47
Hyde Grn, Beac. HP9 111 AM52
Hyde Gro, Dart. DA1 190 FN82
● Hyde Ho, NW9 140 CS57
Hyde La, SW11 40 C6
Bovingdon HP3 79 BA27
Frogmore AL2 83 CE28
Hemel Hempstead HP3 81 BR26
Ockham GU23 250 BN120
Park Street AL2 82 CC28
Hyde Mead, Lwr Naze. EN9 72 EE23
Hyde Meadows, Bov. HP3 79 BA28
Hyde Ms, Rom. RM1 off Hyde Cl 127 FE51
★ Hyde Park, W2 28 C2
Hyde Pk, SW7 28 C2
W1 28 C2
Hyde Pk Av, N21 122 DQ47
⊖ Hyde Park Corner 28 G4
Hyde Pk Cor, W1 29 H4
Hyde Pk Cres, W2 16 C9
Hyde Pk Gdns, N21 122 DQ46
W2 16 B10
Hyde Pk Gdns Ms, W2 16 B10
Hyde Pk Gate, SW7 27 P5
Hyde Pk Gate Ms, SW7 27 P5
Hyde Pk Pl, W2 16 D10
Hyde Pk Sq, W2 16 C9
Hyde Pk Sq Ms, W2 16 C9
Hyde Pk St, W2 16 C9
Sch Hyde Prim Sch, The, NW9 off Hyde Cres 141 CT57
Hyderabad Way, E15 13 J6
Hyde Rd, N1 9 M9
Bexleyheath DA7 188 EZ82
Richmond TW10 off Albert Rd 200 CM85
South Croydon CR2 242 DS113
Watford WD17 97 BU40
Hyder Rd, Grays RM16 193 GJ76
Hydeside Gdns, N9 122 DT47
Hydes Pl, N1 8 G6
Hyde St, SE8 46 A3
Hyde Ter, Ashf. TW15 197 BS93
Hydethorpe Av, N9 122 DT47
Hydethorpe Rd, SW12 203 DJ88
Hyde Vale, SE10 46 F5
Hyde Valley, Welw.G.C. AL7 51 CZ11
Hyde Wk, Mord. SM4 222 DA101
Hyde Way, N9 122 DT47
Hayes UB3 177 BT77
Welwyn Garden City AL7 51 CY09
Hydro Ho, Cher. KT16 off Bridge Wf 216 BJ101
Hyland Cl, Horn. RM11 149 FH59
Sch Hyland Ho Sch, E17 off Forest Rd 123 ED54
Hylands Cl, Epsom KT18 254 CQ115
Hylands Ms, Epsom KT18 254 CQ115
Hylands Rd, E17 123 ED54
Epsom KT18 254 CQ115
Hyland Way, Horn. RM11 149 FH59
Hylle Cl, Wind. SL4 173 AL81
Hylton St, SE18 187 ET77
Hyndewood, SE23 205 DX90
Hyndford Cres, Green. DA9 off Ingress Pk Av 211 FW85
Hyndman St, SE15 44 E3
Hynton Rd, Dag. RM8 148 EW61
Hyperion Ct, Hem.H. HP2 62 BM17
Hyperion Ho, E3 21 L1
Hyperion Pl, Epsom KT19 238 CR109
Hyperion Wk, Horl. RH6 291 DH150
Hyrons Cl, Amer. HP6 77 AS38
Hyrons La, Amer. HP6 77 AR38
Hyrstdene, S.Croy. CR2 241 DP105
Hyson Rd, SE16 32 F10
Hythe, The, Stai. TW18 195 BE92
Hythe Av, Bexh. DA7 188 EZ80
Hythe Cl, N18 122 DU49
Orpington BR5 off Sandway Rd 228 EW98
HYTHE END, Stai. TW19 195 BB90
Hythe End Rd, Wrays. TW19 195 BA89
Hythe Fld Av, Egh. TW20 195 BD93
Hythe Pk Rd, Egh. TW20 195 BC92
Hythe Path, Th.Hth. CR7 224 DR97
Hythe Rd, NW10 161 CU70
Staines-upon-Thames TW18 195 BD92
Thornton Heath CR7 224 DR96
● Hythe Rd Ind Est, NW10 161 CU69
Sch Hythe Sch, The, Stai. TW18 off Thorpe Rd 195 BD92
Hythe St, Dart. DA1 210 FL86
Hythe St Lwr, Dart. DA1 210 FL85
Hyver Hill, NW7 100 CR44

I

Sch Ian Mikardo High Sch, E3 22 D3
Ian Sq, Enf. EN3 off Lansbury Rd 105 DX39
Ibbetson Path, Loug. IG10 107 EP41
Ibbotson Av, E16 23 M8
Ibbott St, E1 21 H4
Iberian Av, Wall. SM6 241 DK105
Ibex Ho, E15 13 K4
Ibis La, W4 180 CQ81
Ibis Way, Hayes UB4 off Cygnet Way 158 BX72
Ibscott Cl, Dag. RM10 169 FC65
Ibsley Gdns, SW15 201 CU88
Ibsley Way, Cockfos. EN4 102 DE43
Sch Ibstock Pl Sch, SW15 off Clarence La 200 CS86
★ ICC London, E16 36 B1
Icehouse Wd, Oxt. RH8 276 EE131
Iceland Rd, E3 12 B9
Iceland Wf, SE16 33 L8
Iceni Ct, E3 11 P9
Ice Wf, N1 8 B10
Ice Wf Marina, N1 off New Wf Rd 8 B10
Ickburgh Est, E5 144 DV61
Ickburgh Rd, E5 144 DV62
Sch Ickburgh Sch, E5 off Ickburgh Rd 144 DV62
ICKENHAM, Uxb. UB10 137 BQ62
⊖ Ickenham 137 BQ63
Ickenham Cl, Ruis. HA4 137 BR61
Ickenham Rd, Ickhm UB10 137 BQ61
Ruislip HA4 137 BR60
Ickleton Rd, SE9 206 EL91
Icklingham Gate, Cob. KT11 236 BW112
Icklingham Rd, Cob. KT11 236 BW112
Icknield Cl, St.Alb. AL3 64 BZ22
Icknield Dr, Ilf. IG2 147 EP57
Ickworth Pk Rd, E17 145 DY56
Icona Pt, E15 off Warton Rd 12 E8
Idaho Bldg, SE13 off Deals Gateway 46 C7
Ida Rd, N15 144 DR57
Ida St, E14 22 E9
Iden Cl, Brom. BR2 226 EE97
Idlecombe Rd, SW17 202 DG93
Idmiston Rd, E15 13 L3
SE27 204 DQ90
Worcester Park KT4 221 CT101
Idmiston Sq, Wor.Pk. KT4 221 CT101
Idol La, EC3 31 N1
Idonia St, SE8 45 P4
Idris Ct, N9 off Galahad Rd 122 DU48
Iffley Cl, Uxb. UB8 156 BK66
Iffley Rd, W6 181 CV76
IFIELD, Grav. DA13 213 GH94
Ifield Cl, Red. RH1 288 DE137
Ifield Rd, SW10 39 M2
Sch Ifield Sch, Grav. DA12 off Cedar Av 213 GJ92
Ifield Way, Grav. DA12 213 GK93
Ifold Rd, Red. RH1 288 DG136
Ifor Evans Pl, E1 21 K5
Ightham Rd, Erith DA8 188 FA80
Igraine Ct, N9 off Galahad Rd 122 DU48
Ikona Ct, Wey. KT13 235 BQ106
Ilbert St, W10 14 D3
Ilchester Gdns, W2 15 L10
Ilchester Pl, W14 26 G6
Ilchester Rd, Dag. RM8 148 EV64
Ildersly Gro, SE21 204 DR89
Sch Ilderton Prim Sch, SE16 44 G1
Ilderton Rd, SE15 44 G2
SE16 32 F10
Ilex Cl, Eng.Grn TW20 194 AV94
Sunbury-on-Thames TW16 off Oakington Dr 218 BW96
Ilex Ct, Berk. HP4 60 AV19
Ilex Ho, N4 143 DM59
Ilex Rd, NW10 161 CT65
Ilex Way, SW16 203 DN92
ILFORD, IG1 - IG6 147 EQ62
⇌ Ilford 147 EN62
Sch Ilford Co High Sch, Ilf. IG6 off Fremantle Rd 125 EP54
Ilford Hill, Ilf. IG1 147 EN62
Sch Ilford Jewish Prim Sch, Barkingside IG6 off Carlton Dr 147 ER55
Ilford La, Ilf. IG1 147 EP62
Sch Ilford Ursuline High Sch, Ilf. IG1 off Morland Rd 147 EP61
Sch Ilford Ursuline Prep Sch, Ilf. IG1 off Coventry Rd 147 EN61
Ilfracombe Cres, Horn. RM12 150 FJ63
Ilfracombe Gdns, Rom. RM6 148 EV59
Ilfracombe Rd, Brom. BR1 206 EF90
Iliffe St, SE17 31 H10
Iliffe Yd, SE17 31 H10
Ilkeston Ct, E5 off Overbury St 145 DX63
Ilkley Cl, SE19 204 DR93
Ilkley Rd, E16 24 C7
Watford WD19 116 BX50
Illingworth, Wind. SL4 173 AL84
Illingworth Cl, Mitch. CR4 222 DD97
Illingworth Way, Enf. EN1 104 DS42
Ilmington Rd, Har. HA3 139 CK58
Ilminster Gdns, SW11 182 DE84
Imber Cl, N14 121 DJ45
Esher KT10 219 CD102
● Imber Ct Trd Est, E.Mol. KT8 219 CD100
Imber Gro, Esher KT10 219 CD101
Imber Pk Rd, Esher KT10 219 CD102
Imber St, N1 9 L9
Imer Pl, T.Ditt. KT7 219 CF101
Sch Immanuel & St. Andrew C of E Prim Sch, SW16 off Buckleigh Rd 203 DL93
Sch Immanuel Coll, Bushey WD23 off Elstree Rd 117 CE45
Sch Immanuel Sch, Rom. RM1 off Havering Rd 127 FD50
Imperial Av, N16 144 DT62
● Imperial Business Est, Grav. DA11 213 GF86
Imperial Cl, NW2 141 CV64
Harrow HA2 138 CA58
Uni Imperial Coll London, Charing Cross Campus, W6 38 C1
Hammersmith Campus, W12 off Du Cane Rd 161 CU72
St. Mary's Campus, W2 16 B8
S. Kensington Campus, SW7 28 A6
Imperial Coll Rd, SW7 28 A7
Imperial Ct, NW8 6 D10
Chislehurst BR7 227 EN95
Imperial Cres, SW6 39 N8
Weybridge KT13 217 BQ104
Imperial Dr, Grav. DA12 213 GM92
Harrow HA2 138 CA59
Imperial Gdns, Mitch. CR4 223 DH97
Imperial Ms, E6 24 E1
Imperial Pk, Ruis. HA4 138 BY64
● Imperial Pk, Wat. WD24 98 BW39
Imperial Pl, Chis. BR7 off Forest Cl 227 EN95
● Imperial Retail Pk, Grav. DA11 213 GG86
Imperial Rd, N22 121 DL53
SW6 39 M6
Feltham TW14 197 BS87
Windsor SL4 173 AN83
Imperial Sq, SW6 39 M6
Imperial St, E3 22 E3
● Imperial Trd Est, Rain. RM13 170 FJ70
★ Imperial War Mus, SE1 30 F7
Imperial Way, Chis. BR7 207 EQ90
Croxley Green WD3 115 BP45
Croydon CR0 241 DM107
Harrow HA3 140 CL58
Hemel Hempstead HP3 62 BL24
Watford WD24 98 BW39
Imperial Wf, SW6 39 N8
⇌ Imperial Wf, SW6 39 P7
Impington, Kings.T. KT1 off Willingham Way 220 CN96
● Impresa Pk, Hodd. EN11 71 EC16
● Imprimo Pk, Loug. IG10 107 EQ42
Imre Cl, W12 161 CV74
Inca Dr, SE9 207 EP87
Inca Ter, N15 off Milton Rd 143 DP55
Ince Rd, Hersham KT12 235 BS107
Coll Inchbald Sch of Design, Garden Design Faculty, SW1 29 K9
Interior Design Faculty, SW1 28 G8
Inchmery Rd, SE6 205 EB89
Inchwood, Croy. CR0 243 EB105
Indells, Hat. AL10 67 CT19
Independence Ho, SW19 off Chapter Way 222 DD95
Sch Independent Jewish Day Sch, The, NW4 off Green La 141 CX57
Independent Pl, E8 10 B2
Independents Rd, SE3 47 L10
Inderwick Rd, N8 143 DM57
Indescon Ct, E14 34 B5
Index Apts, Rom. RM1 off Mercury Gdns 149 FF56
Indiana Bldg, SE13 off Deals Gateway 46 B7
India Pl, WC2 18 C10
India Rd, Slou. SL1 174 AV75
India St, EC3 20 A9
India Way, W12 161 CV73
Indigo Ms, E14 22 F9
N16 144 DR62
Indigo Wk, N2 142 DF56
N6 142 DF56
Indus Rd, SE7 186 EJ80
Industry Ter, SW9 off Canterbury Cres 183 DN83
Inforum Ms, SE15 44 D4
Ingal Rd, E13 23 N5
Ingate Pl, SW8 41 K7
Ingatestone Rd, E12 146 EJ60
SE25 224 DV98
Woodford Green IG8 124 EG52
Ingelow Rd, SW8 41 J9
Ingels Mead, Epp. CM16 91 ET29
Ingersoll Rd, W12 161 CV74
Enfield EN3 104 DW38
Ingestre Ct, W1 off Ingestre Pl 17 M10
Ingestre Pl, W1 17 M9
Ingestre Rd, E7 146 EG63
NW5 143 DH63
Ingham Cl, S.Croy. CR2 243 DX109
Ingham Rd, NW6 5 J1
South Croydon CR2 242 DW109
Inglebert St, EC1 18 E2
Ingleboro Dr, Pur. CR8 242 DR113
Ingleborough St, SW9 42 E8
Ingleby Dr, Har. HA1 139 CD62
Ingleby Gdns, Chig. IG7 126 EV48
Ingleby Rd, N7 off Bryett Rd 143 DL62
Dagenham RM10 169 FB65
Grays RM16 193 GH76
Ilford IG1 147 EP60
Ingleby Way, Chis. BR7 207 EN92
Wallington SM6 241 DK109
Ingle Cl, Pnr. HA5 138 BY55
Ingledew Rd, SE18 187 ER78
Inglefield, Pot.B. EN6 86 DA30
Ingleglen, Farn.Com. SL2 133 AP64
Hornchurch RM11 150 FN59
Inglehurst, New Haw KT15 234 BH110
Inglehurst Gdns, Ilf. IG4 147 EM57
Inglemere Rd, SE23 205 DX90
Mitcham CR4 202 DF94
Ingle Ms, EC1 18 E2
Ingles, Welw.G.C. AL8 51 CX06
Inglesham Wk, E9 11 P4
Ingleside, Colnbr. SL3 175 BE81
Ingleside Cl, Beck. BR3 205 EA94
Ingleside Gro, SE3 47 M3
Inglethorpe St, SW6 38 C6
Ingleton Av, Well. DA16 208 EU85
Ingleton Rd, N18 122 DU51
Carshalton SM5 240 DE109
Ingleton St, SW9 42 E8
Ingleway, N12 120 DD51
Inglewood, Cher. KT16 215 BF104
Croydon CR0 243 DY109
Woking GU21 248 AV118
Inglewood Cl, E14 34 B8
Hornchurch RM12 150 FK63
Ilford IG6 125 ET51
Inglewood Copse, Brom. BR1 226 EL96
Inglewood Gdns, St.Alb. AL2 off North Orbital Rd 83 CE25
Inglewood Ms, Surb. KT6 220 CN102
Inglewood Rd, NW6 5 K3
Bexleyheath DA7 189 FD84
Inglis Barracks, NW7 119 CX50
Inglis Rd, W5 160 CM73
Croydon CR0 224 DT102
Inglis St, SE5 43 H7
Ingoldsby Rd, Grav. DA12 213 GL88
Ingram Av, NW11 142 DC59
Ingram Cl, SE11 30 D8
Stanmore HA7 117 CJ50
Ingram Ho, E3 11 L10
Ingram Rd, N2 142 DE56
Dartford DA1 210 FL88
Grays RM17 192 GD77
Thornton Heath CR7 224 DQ95
Ingrams Cl, Hersham KT12 236 BW106
Ingram Way, Grnf. UB6 159 CD67
Ingrave Ho, Dag. RM9 168 EV67
Ingrave Rd, Brwd. CM13, CM14, CM15 130 FX47
Romford RM1 149 FD56
Ingrave St, SW11 40 B10
Ingrebourne Ave, Rom. RM3 128 FK49
Ingrebourne Gdns, Upmin. RM14 150 FQ60
Sch Ingrebourne Prim Sch, Harold Hill RM3 off Taunton Rd 128 FJ49
Ingrebourne Rd, Rain. RM13 169 FH70
Ingrebourne Valley Grn Way, Horn. RM12 150 FK64
Ingress Gdns, Green. DA9 211 FX85
Ingress Pk, Green. DA9 off Ingress Pk Av 191 FW84
Ingress Pk Av, Green. DA9 191 FV84
Ingress St, W4 off Devonshire Rd 180 CS78
Ingreway, Rom. RM3 128 FP52
Inholms La, Dor. RH5 285 CH140
Inigo Jones Rd, SE7 186 EL80
Inigo Pl, WC2 18 A10
Inkerman Rd, NW5 7 J4
Eton Wick SL4 173 AM77
Knaphill GU21 248 AS118
St. Albans AL1 65 CE21
Inkerman Ter, W8 off Allen St 27 K7
Chesham HP5 76 AQ33
Inkerman Way, Wok. GU21 248 AS118
Inks Grn, E4 123 EC50
Inkster Ho, SW11 off Ingrave St 40 C10
Inkwell Cl, N12 120 DC48
Inman Rd, NW10 160 CS67
SW18 202 DC87
Inmans Row, Wdf.Grn. IG8 124 EG49
Inner Circle, NW1 16 G3
Innerd Ct, Croy. CR0 off Pawson's Rd 224 DQ100
Inner Pk Rd, SW19 201 CX88
Inner Ring E, Lon.Hthrw Air. TW6 177 BP83
Inner Ring W, Lon.Hthrw Air. TW6 176 BN83
Inner Temple, EC4 off Fleet St 18 F9
Inner Temple La, EC4 18 E9
Innes Cl, SW20 221 CY96
Innes Ct, Hem.H. HP3 62 BK22
Innes Gdns, SW15 201 CV86
Innes St, SE15 43 P4
Innes Yd, Croy. CR0 off Whitgift St 224 DQ104
Inniskilling Rd, E13 24 D1
● Innova Business Pk, Enf. EN3 105 DZ36
● Innova Science Pk, Enf. EN3 105 DZ37
Innovation Cl, Wem. HA0 160 CL67
Innova Way, Enf. EN3 105 DZ36
Inskip Cl, E10 145 EB61
Inskip Dr, Horn. RM11 150 FL60
Inskip Rd, Dag. RM8 148 EX60
Insley Ho, E3 off Bow Rd 22 C2
Uni Institute of Cancer Research, The, Sutton Site, Sutt. SM2 off Cotswold Rd 240 DC110
★ Institute of Contemporary Arts (I.C.A.), SW1 29 P3
Uni Institute of Ed, WC1 17 P5
Institute Pl, E8 10 E3
Institute Rd, Cooper. CM16 92 EX29
Taplow SL6 152 AF72
Westcott RH4 off Guildford Rd 284 CC137
Instone Rd, Dart. DA1 210 FK87
Integer Gdns, E11 145 ED59
● Interchange E Ind Est, E5 off Grosvenor Way 144 DW61
International Av, Houns. TW5 178 BW78
Sch International Comm Sch, NW1 17 H5
Sch International Sch of London, W3 off Gunnersbury Av 180 CN77
● International Trd Est, Southall. UB2 177 BV76
International Way, E20 12 E4
Grav. DA10, DA11 212 GA87
Sunbury-on-Thames TW16 217 BS95
Inveraray Pl, SE18 off Old Mill Rd 187 ER79
Inver Cl, E5 off Theydon Rd 144 DW61
Inverclyde Gdns, Rom. RM6 148 EX56
Inver Ct, W2 15 M9
W6 off Invermead Cl 181 CU76
Inveresk Gdns, Wor.Pk. KT4 221 CT104
Inverforth Cl, NW3 off North End Way 142 DC61
Inverforth Rd, N11 121 DH50
Inverine Rd, SE7 186 EH78
Invermead Cl, W6 181 CU77
Invermore Pl, SE18 187 EQ77
Inverness Av, Enf. EN1 104 DS39
Inverness Dr, Ilf. IG6 125 ES51
Inverness Gdns, W8 27 L3
Inverness Ms, E16 167 EQ74
W2 15 M10
Inverness Pl, W2 15 M10
Inverness Rd, N18 122 DV50
Hounslow TW3 178 BZ84
Southall UB2 178 BY77
Worcester Park KT4 221 CX102
Inverness St, NW1 7 J8
Inverness Ter, W2 15 M10
Inverton Rd, SE15 185 DX84
Invicta Cl, E3 22 B7
Chislehurst BR7 207 EN92
Feltham TW14 197 BT88
Invicta Gro, Nthlt. UB5 158 BZ69
Invicta Plaza, SE1 30 G2
Sch Invicta Prim Sch, SE3 47 P3
Invicta Rd, SE3 47 P4
Dartford DA2 210 FP86
Inville Rd, SE17 43 M1
Inwen Ct, SE8 45 M1
Inwood Av, Couls. CR5 257 DN120
Hounslow TW3 178 CC83
● Inwood Business Pk, Houns. TW3 off Whitton Rd 178 CB84
Inwood Cl, Croy. CR0 225 DY103
Inwood Ct, Walt. KT12 218 BW103
Inwood Ho, SE22 off Pytchley Rd 184 DS83
Inwood Rd, Houns. TW3 178 CB84
Inworth St, SW11 40 D8
Inworth Wk, N1 9 J8
● IO Cen, SE18 off Armstrong Rd 187 EQ76
Barking IG11 167 ET70
Hatfield AL10 66 CS16
Waltham Abbey EN9 105 EA35
Iona Cl, SE6 205 EA87
Morden SM4 222 DB101
Iona Cres, Slou. SL1 153 AL72
Ionian Bldg, E14 21 L10
Ionian Way, Hem.H. HP2 off Jupiter Dr 62 BM18
Ionia Wk, Grav. DA12 213 GM90
Ion Sq, E2 20 C1
● IO Trade Centre Croydon, Bedd. CR0 241 DM105
Ipswich Rd, SW17 202 DG93
Slough SL1 153 AN73
Sch Iqua Slough Islamic Prim Sch, Slou. SL3 154 AV73
Ira Ct, SE27 off Norwood Rd 203 DP89
Ireland Cl, E6 25 J7
Ireland Pl, N22 121 DL52
Ireland Yd, EC4 19 H9
Irene Rd, SW6 39 J7
Orpington BR6 227 ET101
Stoke D'Abernon KT11 236 CA114
Ireton Av, Walt. KT12 217 BS103
Ireton Cl, N10 120 DG52
Ireton Pl, Grays RM17 off Russell Rd 192 GA77
Ireton St, E3 22 A4

Iris Av, Bex. DA5 208 EY85
Iris Cl, E6 25 H6
Croydon CR0 225 DX102
Pilgrim's Hatch CM15 130 FV43
Surbiton KT6 220 CM101
Iris Ct, Pnr. HA5 138 BW55
Iris Cres, Bexh. DA7 188 EZ79
Iris Path, Rom. RM3
off Clematis Cl 128 FJ52
Iris Rd, W.Ewell KT19 238 CP106
Iris Wk, Edg. HA8 off Ash Cl 118 CQ49
Irkdale Av, Enf. EN1 104 DT39
Iron Br Cl, NW10 140 CS64
Southall UB2 158 CC74
Ironbridge Rd N, Uxb. UB11 176 BN75
Ironbridge Rd S, West Dr. UB7 176 BN75
Iron Dr, Hert. SG13 54 DV08
Iron Mill La, Dart. DA1 189 FE84
Iron Mill Pl, SW18
off Garratt La 202 DB86
Dartford DA1 189 FF84
Iron Mill Rd, SW18 202 DB86
Ironmonger La, EC2 19 L9
Ironmonger Pas, EC1 19 K4
Ironmonger Row, EC1 19 K3
Ironmongers Pl, E14 34 B9
IRONS BOTTOM, Reig. RH2 288 DA142
Ironsbottom, Horl. RH6 290 DA146
Sidlow RH2 288 DB141
Ironside Cl, SE16 33 J4
Ironside Rd, Brent. TW8 179 CJ80
Irons Way, Rom. RM5 127 FC52
Iron Wks, E3 12 A8
Irvine Av, Har. HA3 139 CG55
Irvine Cl, E14 22 D6
N20 120 DE47
Irvine Gdns, S.Ock. RM15 171 FT72
Irvine Pl, Vir.W. GU25 214 AY99
Irvine Way, Orp. BR6 227 ET101
Irving Av, Nthlt. UB5 158 BX67
Irving Gro, SW9 42 C9
Irving Ms, N1 9 J5
Irving Rd, W14 26 D6
Irving St, WC2 29 P1
Irving Wk, Swans. DA10 212 FY87
Irving Way, NW9 141 CT57
Swanley BR8 229 FD96
Irwell Est, SE16
off Neptune St 32 G5
Irwin Av, SE18 187 ES80
Irwin Cl, Uxb. UB10 136 BN62
Irwin Gdns, NW10 161 CV67
Irwin Rd, Guil. GU2 280 AU135
Isaac Way, SE1 31 K4
Isabel Ct, Hodd. EN11 71 EB15
Isabel Gate, Chsht EN8 89 DZ26
Isabel Hill Cl, Hmptn. TW12
off Upper Sunbury Rd 218 CB95
Isabella Cl, N14 121 DJ45
Isabella Ct, Rich. TW10
off Grove Rd 200 CM86
Isabella Dr, Orp. BR6 245 EQ105
Isabella Ms, N1 9 N4
Isabella Pl, Kings.T. KT2 200 CM92
Isabella Rd, E9 11 H3
Isabella St, SE1 30 G3
Isabelle Cl, Goffs Oak EN7 88 DQ29
Isabel St, SW9 42 D6
Isambard Cl, Uxb. UB8
off Station Rd 156 BK70
Isambard Ms, E14 34 F7
Isambard Pl, SE16 33 H3
Isbell Gdns, Rom. RM1 127 FE52
Isbells Dr, Reig. RH2 288 DB135
Isel Way, SE22
off East Dulwich Gro 204 DS85
Isenburg Way, Hem.H. HP2 62 BK15
Isham Rd, SW16 223 DL96
Isis Cl, SW15 181 CW84
Ruislip HA4 137 BQ58
Isis Dr, Upmin. RM14 151 FS58
Isis Ho, N18 122 DT51
Cher. KT16 off Bridge Wf 216 BJ101
● Isis Reach, Belv. DA17 169 FB74
Isis St, SW18 202 DC89
Sch Islamia Prim Sch, NW6 4 F8
Coll Islamic Coll for Advanced Studies, NW10
off High Rd 161 CV65
Island, The, West Dr. UB7 176 BH81
Wraysbury TW19 195 BA90
Island Apts, N1
off Coleman Flds 9 K8
Island Cen Way, Enf. EN3 105 EA37
Island Cl, Stai. TW18 195 BE91
Island Fm Av, W.Mol. KT8 218 BZ99
Island Fm Rd, W.Mol. KT8 218 BZ99
DLR Island Gardens 34 E9
Island Ho, E3 22 E2
Island Rd, SE16 33 J9
Mitcham CR4 202 DF94
Island Row, E14 21 N9
Isla Rd, SE18 187 EQ79
Islay Gdns, Houns. TW4 198 BX85
Islay Wk, N1 9 K5
Isledon Rd, N7 143 DN62
Islehurst Cl, Chis. BR7 227 EN95
Islet Pk, Maid. SL6 152 AC68
Islet Pk Dr, Maid. SL6 152 AC68
ISLEWORTH, TW7 179 CF83
⇌ Isleworth 179 CF82
Sch Isleworth & Syon Sch for Boys, Islw. TW7 off Ridgeway Rd 179 CE80
● Isleworth Business Complex, Islw. TW7 off St. John's Rd 179 CF82
Isleworth Prom, Twick. TW1 179 CH84
Sch Isleworth Town Prim Sch, Islw. TW7 off Twickenham Rd 179 CG82
ISLINGTON, N1 8 E9
Sch Islington Arts & Media Sch, N4 off Turle Rd 143 DM60
Coll Islington City Learning Cen, N5 9 J3
Islington Grn, N1 8 G9
Islington High St, N1 18 F1
Islington Pk Ms, N1 8 G6
Islington Pk St, N1 8 F6
Islip Gdns, Edg. HA8 118 CR52
Northolt UB5 158 BY66
Islip Manor Rd, Nthlt. UB5 158 BY66
Islip St, NW5 7 L3
Ismailia Rd, E7 166 EH66
★ Ismaili Cen, SW7 28 B8
Isom Cl, E13 24 B3
Issa Rd, Houns. TW3 178 BZ84
Issigonis Ho, W3
off Cowley Rd 161 CT74
ISTEAD RISE, Grav. DA13 212 GE94
Istead Ri, Grav. DA13 213 GF94
Sch Italia Conti Acad of Thea Arts, EC1 19 J5
Coll Italia Conti Arts Cen, Guil. GU1 off Epsom Rd 265 BD133
Itchingwood Common Rd, Oxt. RH8 276 EJ133
Ivanhoe Cl, Uxb. UB8 156 BK71
Ivanhoe Dr, Har. HA3 139 CG55
Ivanhoe Rd, SE5 184 DT83
Hounslow TW4 178 BX83
Ivatt Pl, W14 39 H1
Ivatt Way, N17 143 DP55
Iveagh Av, NW10 160 CN68
Iveagh Cl, E9 11 K8
NW10 160 CN68
Northwood HA6 115 BP53
Iveagh Ct, Hem.H. HP2 62 BK19
Iveagh Rd, Guil. GU2 280 AV135
Woking GU21 248 AT118
Iveagh Ter, NW10
off Iveagh Av 160 CN68
Ivedon Rd, Well. DA16 188 EW82
Ive Fm Cl, E10 145 EA61
Ive Fm La, E10 145 EA61
Iveley Rd, SW4 41 L9
IVER, SL0 155 BF72
⇌ Iver 175 BF75
Iverdale Cl, Iver SL0 155 BC73
Ivere Dr, New Barn. EN5 102 DB44
IVER HEATH, Iver SL0 155 BD69
Sch Iver Heath Inf Sch & Nurs, Iver SL0 off Slough Rd 155 BD69
Sch Iver Heath Jun Sch, Iver SL0 off St. Margarets Cl 155 BE68
Iverhurst Cl, Bexh. DA6 208 EX85
Iver La, Iver SL0 156 BH71
Uxbridge UB8 156 BH71
Iver Lo, Iver SL0 155 BF71
Iverna Ct, W8 27 K6
Iverna Gdns, W8 27 K6
Feltham TW14 197 BR85
Iver Rd, Iver SL0 156 BG72
Pilgrim's Hatch CM15 130 FV44
Iverson Rd, NW6 5 H5
Ivers Way, New Adgtn CR0 243 EB108
Sch Iver Village Inf Sch, Iver SL0 off West Sq 155 BF72
Sch Iver Village Jun Sch, Iver SL0 off High St 155 BE72
Ives Gdns, Rom. RM1
off Sims Cl 149 FF56
Ives Rd, E16 23 J7
Hertford SG14 53 DP08
Slough SL3 175 AZ76
Ives St, SW3 28 D8
Ivestor Ter, SE23 204 DW87
Ivimey St, E2 20 D2
Ivinghoe Cl, Enf. EN1 104 DS40
St. Albans AL4
off Highview Gdns 65 CJ15
Watford WD25 98 BX35
Ivinghoe Rd, Bushey WD23 117 CD45
Dagenham RM8 148 EV64
Mill End WD3 114 BG45
Ivins Rd, Beac. HP9 110 AG54
Ivor Cl, Guil. GU1 281 AZ135
Ivor Gro, SE9 207 EP88
Ivor Pl, NW1 16 E5
Ivor St, NW1 7 L7
Ivory Cl, St.Alb. AL4 65 CJ22
Ivory Ct, Felt. TW13 197 BU88
Hemel Hempstead HP3 62 BL23
Ivorydown, Brom. BR1 206 EG91
Ivory Sq, SW11
off Gartons Way 182 DC83
Ivy Bower Cl, Green. DA9
off Riverview Rd 211 FV85
Ivybridge, Brox. EN10 71 EA19
Ivybridge Cl, Twick. TW1 199 CG86
Uxbridge UB8 156 BL69
Ivybridge Est, Islw. TW7 199 CF85
Ivybridge Ho, SE22
off Pytchley Rd 184 DS83
Ivybridge La, WC2 30 B1
Sch Ivybridge Prim Sch, Islw. TW7
off Summerwood Rd 199 CF86
IVY CHIMNEYS, Epp. CM16 91 ES32
Sch Ivy Chimneys Prim Sch, Epp. CM16
off Ivy Chimneys Rd 91 ET32
Ivy Chimneys Rd, Epp. CM16 91 ES32
Ivychurch Cl, SE20 204 DW94
Ivychurch La, SE17 32 A10
Ivy Cl, Chesh. HP5 76 AP30
Dartford DA1 210 FN87
Gravesend DA12 213 GJ90
Harrow HA2 138 BZ63
Pinner HA5 138 BW59
Sunbury-on-Thames TW16 218 BW96
Ivy Cotts, E14 22 D10
Ivy Ct, SE16 44 D1
Ivy Cres, W4 180 CQ77
Slough SL1 153 AM73
Sch Ivydale Prim Sch, SE15
off Ivydale Rd 185 DX84
Ivydale Rd, SE15 185 DX83
Carshalton SM5 222 DF103
Ivyday Gro, SW16 203 DM90
Ivydene, W.Mol. KT8 218 BZ99
Ivydene Cl, Red. RH1 289 DH139
Sutton SM1 240 DC105
Ivy Gdns, N8 143 DL58
Mitcham CR4 223 DK97
Ivy Ho La, Berk. HP4 60 AY19
Sevenoaks TN14 263 FD118
Ivyhouse Rd, Dag. RM9 168 EX65
Ivy Ho Rd, Uxb. UB10 137 BP62
Ivy La, Houns. TW4 178 BZ84
Knockholt Pound TN14 262 EY116
Woking GU22 249 BB118
Ivy Lea, Rick. WD3
off Springwell Av 114 BG46
Ivy Lo La, Rom. RM3 128 FP53
Ivy Mill Cl, Gdse. RH9 274 DV132
Ivy Mill La, Gdse. RH9 274 DU132
Ivymount Rd, SE27 203 DN90
Ivy Rd, E16 23 N8
E17 145 EA58
N14 121 DJ45
NW2 141 CW63
Ivy Rd, SE4 185 DZ84
SW17 off Tooting High St 202 DE92
Hounslow TW3 178 CB84
Surbiton KT6 220 CN102
Ivy St, N1 9 N10
Ivy Ter, Hodd. EN11 71 EC15
Ivy Wk, Dag. RM9 168 EY65
Hatfield AL10 66 CS15
Ixworth Pl, SW3 28 C10
Izane Rd, Bexh. DA6 188 EZ84

J

J31 Pk, Grays RM20 191 FU78
Jacaranda Cl, N.Mal. KT3 220 CS97
Jacaranda Gro, E8 10 B7
Sch Jack & Jill Sch, Hmptn. TW12 off Nightingale Rd 198 CA93
Jackass La, Kes. BR2 244 EH107
Tandridge RH8 275 DZ131
Jack Barnett Way, N22 121 DM54
Jack Clow Rd, E15 23 K1
Jack Cornwell St, E12 147 EN63
Jack Dash Way, E6 24 G5
Jackdaws, Welw.G.C. AL7 52 DC09
Jackets La, Hare. UB9 114 BN52
Northwood HA6 115 BP53
Jacketts Fld, Abb.L. WD5 81 BT31
Jack Goodchild Way, Kings.T. KT1 off Kingston Rd 220 CP97
Jack Jones Way, Dag. RM9 168 EZ67
Jacklin Grn, Wdf.Grn. IG8 124 EG49
Jackman Ms, NW2 140 CS62
Jackmans La, Wok. GU21 248 AU119
Jackman St, E8 10 E9
JACKS HATCH, Epp. CM16 73 EN21
Jacks La, Hare. UB9 114 BG53
Jackson Cl, E9 11 H7
Epsom KT18 238 CR114
Greenhithe DA9
off Cowley Av 211 FU85
Hornchurch RM11 150 FM56
Slough SL3 174 AY76
Jackson Ct, E11
off Brading Cres 146 EH60
Dagenham RM10
off St. Mark's Pl 168 FA65
Jackson Rd, N7 8 D1
Barking IG11 167 ER67
Barnet EN4 102 DE44
Bromley BR2 226 EL103
Jacksons Dr, Chsht EN7 88 DU28
Jacksons La, N6 142 DG59
Jacksons Pl, Croy. CR0
off Cross Rd 224 DR102
Jackson St, SE18 187 EN79
Jacksons Way, Croy. CR0 225 EA104
Jackson Way, Epsom KT19
off Lady Harewood Way 238 CN109
Southall UB2 178 CB75
Jack Stevens Cl, Harl. CM17
off Potter St 74 EW17
Sch Jack Taylor Sch, NW8 5 N8
Sch Jack Tizard Sch, W12
off South Africa Rd 161 CV74
Jack Walker Ct, N5 9 H1
Jacob Cl, Wind. SL4 173 AL81
Jacob Ct, Enf. EN3
off Baddeley Cl 105 EA37
Jacob Ho, Erith DA18
off Kale Rd 188 EX75
Jacob Ms, Stan. HA7 117 CG47
Jacobs Av, Harold Wd RM3 128 FL54
Jacobs Cl, Dag. RM10 149 FB62
Jacobs Ho, E13 24 C2
Jacobs Ladder, Hat. AL9
off The Broadway 67 CW18
Jacobs La, Hort.Kir. DA4 230 FQ97
Jacob St, SE1 32 B4
JACOBS WELL, Guil. GU4 264 AY129
Jacob's Well Ms, W1 17 H8
Jacob's Well Rd, Jacobs Well GU4 264 AX129
Jacqueline Cl, Nthlt. UB5 158 BY67
Jade Cl, E16 24 F9
NW2 141 CX59
Dagenham RM8 148 EW60
Jaffe Rd, Ilf. IG1 147 EQ60
Jaffray Pl, SE27 203 DP91
Jaffray Rd, Brom. BR2 226 EK98
Jaggard Way, SW12 202 DF87
Jagger Cl, Dart. DA2 210 FQ87
Jago Cl, SE18 187 EQ79
Jago Wk, SE5 43 L5
Jail La, Bigg.H. TN16 260 EK116
Jake's Vw, Park St AL2 82 CC27
Sch Jamahiriya Sch, SW3 40 C2
Jamaica Rd, SE1 32 B5
SE16 32 E6
Thornton Heath CR7 223 DP100
Jamaica St, E1 21 H8
Sch James Allen's Girls' Sch, SE22
off East Dulwich Gro 204 DS85
Sch James Allen's Prep Sch, Pre-Prep Sch, SE21
off Dulwich Village 204 DR86
Mid Sch, SE22
off East Dulwich Gro 204 DS85
James Av, NW2 4 B2
Dagenham RM8 148 EZ60
James Bedford Cl, Pnr. HA5 116 BW54
James Boswell Cl, SW16
off Samuel Johnson Cl 203 DN91
James Clavell Sq, SE18 37 P6
James Cl, E13 13 P10
NW11 off Woodlands 141 CY58
Bushey WD23 98 BY43
Romford RM2 149 FG57
James Collins Cl, W9 14 G5
James Ct, N1 9 K7
Sch James Dixon Prim Sch, SE20
off William Booth Rd 224 DU95
James Dudson Ct, NW10 160 CQ66
Sch James Elliman Prim Sch, Slou. SL2 off Elliman Av 154 AT73
James Gdns, N22 121 DP52
James Hammett Ho, E2 20 B1
James Ho, W10
off Appleford Rd 14 F5
James Joyce Wk, SE24
off Shakespeare Rd 183 DP84
James La, E10 145 ED59
E11 145 ED58
James Lee Sq, Enf. EN3
off Harston Dr 105 EA38
James Martin Cl, Denh. UB9 136 BG58
James Meadow, Slou. SL3 175 AZ79
James Newman Ct, SE9
off Great Harry Dr 207 EN90
Sch James Oglethorpe Prim Sch, The, Upmin. RM14
off Ashvale Gdns 151 FT61
Jameson Cl, W3 off Acton La 180 CQ75
Jameson Ct, E2 20 G1
St. Albans AL1
off Avenue Rd 65 CF19
Jameson Ho, SE11
off Glasshouse Wk 30 C10
Jameson St, W8 27 K2
James Pl, N17 122 DT53
James Riley Pt, E15 12 F8
James Rd, Dart. DA1 209 FG87
Peasmarsh GU3 280 AW142
James's Cotts, Rich. TW9 180 CN80
James St, W1 17 H8
WC2 18 B10
Barking IG11 167 EQ66
Enfield EN1 104 DT43
Epping CM16 91 ET28
Hounslow TW3 179 CD83
Windsor SL4 173 AR81
James Ter, SW14
off Mullins Path 180 CR83
Jameston Lo, Ruis. HA4
off Pembroke Rd 137 BT60
Jamestown Rd, NW1 7 J8
Jamestown Way, E14 35 H1
James Voller Way, E1 20 G9
James Watt Way, Erith DA8 189 FE79
James Way, Wat. WD19 116 BX49
Sch James Wolfe Prim Sch, SE10 46 E4
James Yd, E4 123 ED51
Jamieson Ho, Houns. TW4 198 BZ87
Jamnagar Cl, Stai. TW18 195 BF93
Jamuna Cl, E14 21 M7
Jane Cl, Hem.H. HP2 63 BP15
Jane Seymour Ct, SE9
off Avery Hill Rd 207 ER87
Jane St, E1 20 E8
Janet St, E14 34 B6
Janeway Pl, SE16 32 E5
Janeway St, SE16 32 D5
Janice Ms, Ilf. IG1
off Oakfield Rd 147 EP62
Janmead, Hutt. CM13 131 GB45
Janoway Hill La, Wok. GU21 248 AW119
Jansen Wk, SW11 off Hope St 182 DD84
Janson Cl, E15 13 J2
NW10 140 CR62
Janson Rd, E15 13 J2
Jansons Rd, N15 144 DS55
Japan Cres, N4 143 DM60
Sch Japanese Sch, The, W3
off Creffield Rd 160 CN73
Japan Rd, Rom. RM6 148 EX58
Japonica Cl, Wok. GU21 248 AW118
Jardine Rd, E1 21 K10
Jarman Cl, Hem.H. HP3 62 BL22
Jarman Ho, E1 20 G7
🔒 Jarman Pk, Hem.H. HP2 62 BM21
Jarman Way, Hem.H. HP2 62 BM21
Jarrah Cotts, Purf. RM19 191 FR79
Jarrett Cl, SW2 203 DP88
Jarrow Cl, Mord. SM4 222 DB99
Jarrow Rd, N17 144 DV56
SE16 32 G9
Romford RM6 148 EW58
Jarrow Way, E9 11 M1
Jarvis Cleys, Chsht EN7 88 DT26
Jarvis Cl, Bark. IG11
off Westbury Rd 167 ER67
Barnet EN5 101 CX43
Jarvis Rd, SE22
off Melbourne Gro 184 DS84
South Croydon CR2 242 DR107
Jarvis Way, Harold Wd RM3 128 FL54
Jasmin Cl, Nthwd. HA6 115 BT53
Jasmine Cl, Ilf. IG1 147 EP64
Orpington BR6 227 EP103
Redhill RH1
off Spencer Way 288 DG139
Southall UB1 158 BY73
Woking GU21 248 AT116
Jasmine Dr, Hert. SG13 54 DU09
Jasmine Gdns, Croy. CR0 225 EB104
Harrow HA2 138 CA61
Hatfield AL10 67 CU16
Jasmine Gro, SE20 224 DV95
Jasmine Rd, Rush Grn RM7 149 FE61
Jasmine Sq, E3 11 N9
Jasmine Ter, West Dr. UB7 176 BN75
Jasmine Wk, Chesh. HP5 76 AN30
Jasmine Way, E.Mol. KT8
off Hampton Ct Way 219 CE98
Jasmin Ho, Ilf. IG2
off Perth Rd 147 EN58
Jasmin Rd, Epsom KT19 238 CP106
Jasmin Way, Hem.H. HP1
off Larkspur Cl 61 BE19
Jason Cl, Brwd. CM14 130 FT49
Redhill RH1 288 DE139
Weybridge KT13 235 BQ106
Jason Ct, W1
off Marylebone La 17 H8
Jasons Dr, Guil. GU4 265 BC131
Jasons Hill, Chesh. HP5 78 AV30
Jason Wk, SE9 207 EN91
Jasper Ave, W7 179 CF75
Jasper Cl, Enf. EN3 104 DW38
Jasper Pas, SE19 204 DT93
Jasper Rd, E16 24 F9
SE19 204 DT92
Jasper Wk, N1 19 L2
Javelin Way, Nthlt. UB5 158 BX69
Jaycroft, Enf. EN2
off The Ridgeway 103 DN39
Jay Gdns, Chis. BR7 207 EM91
Jay Ms, SW7 27 P5
Jays Cl, Brick.Wd AL2 82 CA31
Jays Covert, Couls. CR5 256 DG119
Jazzfern Ter, Wem. HA0
off Maybank Av 139 CG64
Jean Batten Cl, Wall. SM6 241 DM108
Jebb Av, SW2 203 DL86
Jebb St, E3 22 B1
Jedburgh Rd, E13 24 C2
Jedburgh St, SW11 182 DG84
Jeddo Rd, W12 181 CT75
Jeeva Mans, N16
off Shacklewell La 10 B1
Jefferson Cl, W13 179 CH76
Ilford IG2 147 EP57
Slough SL3 175 BA77
Jefferson Plaza, E3 22 E4
Jefferson Wk, SE18
off Kempt St 187 EN79
Jeffreys Pl, NW1 7 L6
Jeffreys Rd, SW4 42 A8
Enfield EN3 105 DZ41
Jeffreys St, NW1 7 K6
Jeffreys Wk, SW4 42 A8
Jeffries Ho, NW10 160 CQ67
Jeffries Pas, Guil. GU1
off High St 280 AX135
Jeffries Rd, Ware SG12 55 DY06
West Horsley KT24 267 BQ130
Jeffs Cl, Hmptn. TW12 198 CB93
Jeffs Rd, Sutt. SM1 239 CZ105
Jeger Av, E2 10 A9
Jeken Rd, SE9 186 EJ84
Jelf Rd, SW2 203 DN85
Jellicoe Av, Grav. DA12 213 GJ90
Jellicoe Av W, Grav. DA12
off Kitchener Av 213 GJ90
Jellicoe Cl, Slou. SL1 173 AP75
Jellicoe Gdns, Stan. HA7 117 CF51
Jellicoe Ho, SW8
off St. George Wf 42 A2
Jellicoe Rd, E13 23 P5
N17 122 DR52
Watford WD18 97 BU44
Jemma Knowles Cl, SW2
off Neil Wates Cres 203 DN88
Jemmett Cl, Kings.T. KT2 220 CP95
Jengar Cl, Sutt. SM1 240 DB105
Jenkins Av, Brick.Wd AL2 82 BY30
Jenkins Cl, Nthflt DA11 213 GF90
Jenkins La, E6 25 M1
Barking IG11 25 P1
Jenkinson Ho, E2 off Usk St 21 J2
Jenkins Rd, E13 24 B5
Jenner Av, W3 160 CR71
Jenner Cl, Sid. DA14 208 EU91
Jenner Pl, SW13 181 CV79
Jenner Rd, N16 144 DT61
Guildford GU1 280 AY135
Jenner Way, Epsom KT19
off Monro Pl 238 CN109
Jennery La, Burn. SL1 152 AJ69
Jennett Rd, Croy. CR0 223 DN104
Jennifer Rd, Brom. BR1 206 EF90
Jennings Cl, RM8 148 EY60
Long Ditton KT6 219 CJ101
New Haw KT15
off Woodham La 234 BJ109
Jennings Fld, Flack.Hth HP10 132 AC56
Jennings Rd, SE22 204 DT86
St. Albans AL1 65 CG19
Jennings Way, Barn. EN5 101 CW41
Hemel Hempstead HP3 62 BL22
Horley RH6 291 DK148
Jenningtree Rd, Erith DA8 189 FH80
Jenningtree Way, Belv. DA17 189 FC75
Jenny Hammond Cl, E11
off Newcomen Rd 146 EF62
Sch Jenny Hammond Prim Sch, E11 off Worsley Rd 146 EE63
Jenny Path, Rom. RM3 128 FK52
Jennys Way, Couls. CR5 257 DJ122
Jenson Way, SE19 204 DT94
Jenton Av, Bexh. DA7 188 EY81
Jephson Rd, E7 166 EJ66
Jephson St, SE5 43 L7
Jephtha Rd, SW18 202 DA86
Jeppos La, Mitch. CR4 222 DF98
Jepps Cl, Chsht EN7 88 DS27
Jepson Ho, SW6
off Pearscroft Rd 39 M7
Jerdan Pl, SW6 39 K4
Jeremiah Ct, Red. RH1 273 DJ131
Jeremiah St, E14 22 C9
Jeremys Grn, N18 122 DV49
Jermyn St, SW1 29 L2
Jerningham Av, Ilf. IG5 125 EP54
Jerningham Rd, SE14 45 L6
Jerome Cres, NW8 16 C4
Jerome Dr, St.Alb. AL3 64 CA22
Jerome Pl, Kings.T. KT1
off Wadbrook St 219 CK96
Jerome St, E1 20 A6
Jerome Twr, W3 180 CP75
Jerounds, Harl. CM19 73 EP17
Sch Jerounds Comm Inf Sch, Harl. CM19 off Pyenest Rd 73 EP18
Sch Jerounds Comm Jun Sch, Harl. CM19 off Pyenest Rd 73 EP18
Jerrard St, N1 19 P1
SE13 46 D10
Jersey Av, Stan. HA7 117 CH54
Jersey Cl, Cher. KT16 215 BF104
Guildford GU4
off Weybrook Dr 265 BB129
Hoddesdon EN11 71 EA16
Jersey Ct, SW6 off Dairy Cl 39 H7
Jersey Dr, Petts Wd BR5 227 ER100
JERSEY FARM, St.Alb. AL4 65 CJ15
Jersey Ho, N1 9 K5
Enfield EN3
off Eastfield Rd 105 DX38
Jersey La, St.Alb. AL4 65 CH18
Jersey Par, Houns. TW5 178 CB81
Jersey Rd, E11 145 ED60
E16 24 C8
SW17 203 DH93
W7 179 CG75
Hounslow TW3, TW5 178 CB81
Ilford IG1 147 EP63
Isleworth TW7 179 CE79
Rainham RM13 169 FG66
Jersey St, E2 20 F3
Jerusalem Pas, EC1 18 G5
Jervis Av, Enf. EN3 105 DY35
Jervis Ct, W1 17 K9
Jervis Rd, SW6 39 H3
Jerviston Gdns, SW16 203 DN93
Jesmond Av, Wem. HA9 160 CM65
Jesmond Cl, Mitch. CR4 223 DH97
Jesmond Rd, Croy. CR0 224 DT101
Jesmond Way, Stan. HA7 118 CL50
Jessam Av, E5 144 DV60
Jessamine Pl, Dart. DA2 210 FQ87
Jessamine Rd, W7 159 CE74
Jessamy Rd, Wey. KT13 217 BP103
Jessel Dr, Loug. IG10 107 EQ39
Jessel Ho, SW1 off Page St 29 P8
Jesse Rd, E10 145 EC60
Jesses La, Peasl. GU5 283 BQ144
Jessett Cl, Erith DA8
off West St 189 FD77
Jessica Rd, SW18 202 DC86
Jessie Blythe La, N19 143 DL59

Jessiman Ter, Shep. TW17 216 BN99
Jessop Av, Sthl. UB2 178 BZ77
Jessop Ct, N1 off Graham St 19 H1
Jessop Prim Sch, SE24 off Lowden Rd 184 DQ84
Jessop Rd, SE24 off Milkwood Rd 183 DP84
Jessop Sq, E14 34 A3
Jessops Way, Croy. CR0 223 DJ100
Jessup Cl, SE18 187 EQ77
Jethou Ho, N1 off Nightingale Rd 9 K5
Jetstar Way, Nthlt. UB5 158 BY69
Jetty Wk, Grays RM17 192 GA79
Jevington Way, SE12 206 EH88
Jewel Rd, E17 145 EA55
Jewels Hill, Bigg.H. TN16 244 EG112
★ Jewel Twr (Hos of Parliament), SW1 30 A6
★ Jewish Mus, NW1 7 J9
Jewry St, EC3 20 A9
Jew's Row, SW18 182 DB84
Jews Wk, SE26 204 DV91
Jeymer Av, NW2 141 CV64
Jeymer Dr, Grnf. UB6 158 CC67
Jeypore Pas, SW18 off Jeypore Rd 202 DC86
Jeypore Rd, SW18 202 DC87
JFK Ho, Bushey WD23 off Royal Connaught Dr 98 BZ42
JFS, Har. HA3 off The Mall 140 CN58
Jigger Mast Ho, SE18 37 K6
Jillian Cl, Hmptn. TW12 198 CA94
Jim Bradley Cl, SE18 37 M8
Jim Desormeaux Bungalows, Harl. CM20 off School La 57 ES13
Jim Griffiths Ho, SW6 off Clem Attlee Ct 39 H3
Jim O'Neill Wk, Ruis. HA4 off Sidmouth Dr 137 BU62
Jim Veal Dr, N7 8 B4
Jinnings, The, Welw.G.C. AL7 52 DA12
Joan Cres, SE9 206 EK87
Joan Gdns, Dag. RM8 148 EY61
Joan Rd, Dag. RM8 148 EY61
Joan St, SE1 30 G3
Jocelyn Rd, Rich. TW9 180 CL83
Jocelyns, Harl. CM17 58 EW11
Jocelyn St, SE15 44 C6
Jocketts Hill, Hem.H. HP1 61 BF20
Jocketts Rd, Hem.H. HP1 61 BF21
Jockey's Flds, WC1 18 D6
Jodane St, SE8 33 N9
Jodies Ct, St.Alb. AL4 65 CJ18
Jodrell Cl, Islw. TW7 179 CG81
Jodrell Rd, E3 11 P8
Jodrell Way, W.Thur. RM20 191 FT78
Joel St, Nthwd. HA6 137 BU55
Pinner HA5 137 BU55
Johanna Prim Sch, SE1 30 E5
Johanna St, SE1 30 E5
John Adam St, WC2 30 B2
John Aird Ct, W2 15 P6
John Archer Way, SW18 202 DD86
John Ashby Cl, SW2 203 DL86
John Austin Cl, Kings.T. KT2 off Queen Elizabeth Rd 220 CM95
John Ball Prim Sch, SE3 47 K9
John Barnes Wk, E15 13 L4
John Betts Prim Sch, W6 off Paddenswick Rd 181 CV76
John Bradshaw Rd, N14 121 DK46
John Bramston Prim Sch, Ilf. IG6 off Newcastle Av 126 EU51
John Burns Dr, Bark. IG11 167 ES66
John Burns Prim Sch, SW11 41 H9
Johnby Cl, Enf. EN3 105 DY37
John Campbell Rd, N16 9 P3
John Carpenter St, EC4 18 G10
John Cobb Rd, Wey. KT13 234 BN108
John Cornwell VC Ho, E12 147 EN63
John Ct, Hodd. EN11 off Molesworth 55 EA14
John Donne Prim Sch, SE15 44 E7
John Drinkwater Cl, E11 off Browning Rd 146 EF59
John Eliot Cl, Lwr Naze. EN9 72 EE21
John Fearon Wk, W10 14 F2
John Felton Rd, SE16 32 C5
John Fisher Sch, The, Pur. CR8 off Peaks Hill 241 DL110
John Fisher St, E1 20 C10
John F. Kennedy Post 16 (Beckton) Annexe, E16 24 E6
John F. Kennedy RC Sch, Hem.H. HP1 off Hollybush La 61 BF19
John F. Kennedy Sch, E15 13 H8
John Gale Ct, Ewell KT17 off West St 239 CT109
John Gooch Dr, Enf. EN2 103 DP39
John Harrison Ho, E1 off Philpot St 20 F8
John Harrison Way, SE10 35 L7
John Horner Ms, N1 9 J10
John Howard Cen, E9 11 K3
John Islip St, SW1 30 A9
John Keats Ho, N22 121 DM52
John Keble C of E Prim Sch, NW10 off Crownhill Rd 161 CT67
John Kelly Boys' Tech Coll, NW2 off Crest Rd 141 CU62
John Kelly Girls' Tech Coll, NW2 off Crest Rd 141 CU62
John Kennedy Ct, N1 off Newington Grn Rd 9 M4
John Kennedy Ho,SE16 33 H8
John Loughborough Sch, The, N17 off Holcombe Rd 122 DU54
John Lyon Rbt, Har. HA1 139 CG61
John Lyon Sch, The, Har. HA2 off Middle Rd 139 CD60
John Maurice Cl, SE17 31 L8
John McKenna Wk, SE16 32 D6
John Mills Ct, Denh. UB9 135 BF58
John Milton Pas, EC4 off Bread St 19 K9
John Newton Ct, Well. DA16 188 EV83
John Parker Cl, Dag. RM10 169 FB66
John Parker Sq, SW11 off Thomas Baines Rd 182 DD83
John Paul II RC Sch, SW19 off Princes Way 201 CX87
John Penn St, SE13 46 D7
John Perrin Pl, Har. HA3 140 CL59
John Perryn Prim Sch, W3 off Long Dr 160 CS72
John Perry Prim Sch, Dag. RM10 off Charles Rd 169 FD65
John Princes St, W1 17 K8
John Rennie Wk, E1 32 F2
John Roan Sch, The, SE3 47 K4
John Roll Way, SE16 32 D6
John Ruskin Prim Sch, SE5 43 J3
John Ruskin 6th Form Coll, S.Croy. CR2 off Selsdon Pk Rd 243 DY108
John Ruskin St, SE5 42 G4
John Russell Cl, Guil. GU2 264 AU131
Johns Av, NW4 141 CW56
Johns Cl, Ashf. TW15 197 BQ91
John Scurr Prim Sch, E1 20 G5
Johnsdale, Oxt. RH8 276 EF129
John Silkin La, SE8 33 K9
Johns La, Mord. SM4 222 DC99
John's Ms, WC1 18 D5
John Smith Av, SW6 38 G4
John Smith Ms, E14 22 G10
Johnson Cl, E8 10 C8
Northfleet DA11 212 GD90
Johnson Ct, Hem.H. HP3 62 BL22
Johnson Ho, E2 20 D2
Johnson Rd, NW10 160 CR67
Bromley BR2 226 EK99
Croydon CR0 224 DR101
Hounslow TW5 178 BW80
Johnsons Av, Bad.Mt TN14 247 FB110
Johnsons Cl, Cars. SM5 222 DF104
Johnson's Ct, EC4 off Fleet St 18 F9
Johnsons Ct, Seal TN15 off School La 279 FM121
Johnsons Dr, Hmptn. TW12 218 CC95
Johnson's Pl, SW1 41 L1
Johnson St, E1 21 H9
Southall UB2 178 BW76
Johnsons Way, NW10 160 CP70
Greenhithe DA9 211 FW86
Johnsons Yd, Uxb. UB8 off Redford Way 156 BJ66
John Spencer Sq, N1 9 H5
John's Pl, E1 20 F8
Johns Rd, Tats. TN16 260 EK120
John Stainer Prim Sch, SE4 off St. Asaph Rd 185 DY83
John's Ter, Croy. CR0 224 DR102
Romford RM3 128 FP51
Johnston Cl, SW9 42 D7
Johnston Ct, E10 off Oliver Rd 145 EB62
Johnstone Rd, E6 25 K3
Johnston Grn, Guil. GU2 264 AU130
Johnston Rd, Wdf.Grn. IG8 124 EG50
Johnston Ter, NW2 off Kara Way 141 CX62
Johnston Wk, Guil. GU2 264 AU130
John St, E15 13 L9
SE25 224 DU98
WC1 18 D5
Enfield EN1 104 DT43
Grays RM17 192 GC79
Hounslow TW3 178 BY82
Johns Wk, Whyt. CR3 258 DU119
John's Way, S.Ock. RM15 171 FX72
John Tate Rd, Hert. SG13 54 DT10
John Trundle Ct, EC2 off The Barbican 19 J6
John Walsh Twr, E11 146 EF61
John Warner Sch, The, Hodd. EN11 off Stanstead Rd 55 EB14
John Watkin Cl, Epsom KT19 238 CP109
John Wesley Cl, E6 25 K2
John William Cl, Chaff.Hun. RM16 191 FX78
John Williams Cl, SE14 45 J3
Kingston upon Thames KT2 off Henry Macaulay Av 219 CK95
John Wilson St, SE18 37 L7
John Woolley Cl, SE13 186 EE84
Joiner's Arms Yd, SE5 43 L7
Joiners Cl, Chal.St.P. SL9 113 AZ52
Ley Hill HP5 78 AV30
Joiners La, Chal.St.P. SL9 112 AY53
Joiners Pl, N5 9 L1
Joiner St, SE1 31 M3
Joiners Way, Chal.St.P. SL9 112 AY52
Joiners Yd, N1 off Caledonia St 18 B1
Joinville Pl, Add. KT15 234 BK105
Jolles Ho, E3 off Bromley High St 22 D2
Jolliffe Rd, Red. RH1 273 DJ126
Jollys La, Har. HA2 139 CD60
Hayes UB4 158 BX71
Jonathan Ct, W4 off Windmill Rd 180 CS77
Jonathan St, SE11 30 C10
Jones Ho, N16 off Stamford Hill 144 DS60
Jones Rd, E13 24 B5
Goffs Oak EN7 87 DP30
Jones St, W1 29 J1
Jones Wk, Rich. TW10 off Lower Gro Rd 200 CM86
Jones Way, Hedg. SL2 133 AR61
Jonquil Cl, Welw.G.C. AL7 52 DB11
Jonquil Gdns, Hmptn. TW12 off Partridge Rd 198 CA93
Jonson Cl, Hayes UB4 157 BU71
Mitcham CR4 223 DH98
Jordan Cl, Har. HA2 138 BZ62
South Croydon CR2 242 DT111
Watford WD25 97 BT35
Jordan Ct, SW15 off Charlwood Rd 181 CX84
Jordan Rd, Perivale UB6 159 CH67
JORDANS, Beac. HP9 112 AT52
Jordans Cl, Dag. RM10 149 FB63
Guildford GU1 off Beatty Av 265 BA133
Isleworth TW7 179 CE81
Redhill RH1 288 DG139
Stanwell TW19 196 BJ87
Jordans La, Jordans HP9 112 AS53
Jordans Ms, Twick. TW2 199 CE89
Jordans Rd, Rick. WD3 114 BG45
Jordans Sch, Jordans HP9 off Puers La 112 AT51
Jordans Way, Brick.Wd AL2 82 BZ30
Jordans HP9 112 AT51
Rainham RM13 170 FK68
Jo Richardson Comm Sch, The, Dag. RM9 off Gale St 168 EX67
Joseph Av, W3 160 CR72
Joseph Clarke Sch, E4 off Vincent Rd 123 ED51
Joseph Conrad Ho, SW1 off Tachbrook St 29 M9
Joseph Hardcastle Cl, SE14 45 K4
Joseph Hood Prim Sch, SW20 off Whatley Av 221 CY97
Josephine Av, SW2 203 DM85
Lower Kingswood KT20 271 CZ126
Josephine Cl, Lwr Kgswd KT20 271 CZ127
Joseph Locke Way, Esher KT10 218 CA103
Joseph Powell Cl, SW12 203 DJ86
Joseph Ray Rd, E11 146 EE61
Joseph's Rd, Guil. GU1 264 AX133
Joseph St, E3 21 P5
Joseph Trotter Cl, EC1 off Myddelton St 18 F3
Joshua Cl, N10 121 DH52
South Croydon CR2 241 DP108
Joshua St, E14 22 E8
Joshua Wk, Wal.Cr. EN8 off Longcroft Dr 89 EA34
Josling Cl, Grays RM17 192 FZ79
Joslings Cl, W12 161 CV73
Joslin Rd, Purf. RM19 190 FQ78
Joslyn Cl, Enf. EN3 105 EA38
Joubert St, SW11 40 E8
Journeys End, Stoke P. SL2 154 AS71
Jowett St, SE15 44 B5
Joyce Av, N18 122 DT50
Joyce Ct, Wal.Abb. EN9 89 ED34
Joyce Dawson Way, SE28 off Thamesmere Dr 168 EU73
Joyce Dawson Way Shop Arc, SE28 off Thamesmere Dr 168 EU73
Joyce Grn La, Dart. DA1 190 FL81
Joyce Grn Wk, Dart. DA1 190 FM84
Joyce Lattimore Ct, N9 off Colthurst Dr 122 DV48
Joyce Page Cl, SE7 186 EK79
Joyce Wk, SW2 203 DN86
JOYDENS WOOD, Bex. DA5 209 FC92
Joydens Wd Inf Sch, Bex. DA5 off Park Way 209 FE90
Joydens Wd Jun Sch, Wilm. DA2 off Birchwood Dr 209 FE91
Joydens Wd Rd, Bex. DA5 209 FD91
Joydon Dr, Rom. RM6 148 EV58
Joyes Cl, Rom. RM3 128 FK49
Joyners Cl, Dag. RM9 148 EZ63
Joyners Fld, Harl. CM18 73 EQ19
Joy Rd, Grav. DA12 213 GJ88
Jubb Powell Ho, N15 144 DS58
Jubilee Arch, Wind. SL4 off High St 173 AR81
Jubilee Av, E4 123 EC51
London Colney AL2 83 CK26
Romford RM7 149 FB57
Twickenham TW2 198 CC88
Ware SG12 55 DZ05
Jubilee Cl, NW9 140 CR58
NW10 160 CS68
Greenhithe DA9 211 FW86
Kingston upon Thames KT1 off High St 219 CJ95
Pinner HA5 116 BW54
Romford RM7 149 FB57
Stanwell TW19 196 BJ87
Jubilee Ct, Hat. AL10 67 CV15
Staines-upon-Thames TW18 196 BG91
Waltham Abbey EN9 90 EF33
Jubilee Cres, N9 122 DU46
Addlestone KT15 234 BK106
Gravesend DA12 213 GL89
Jubilee Dr, Ruis. HA4 138 BX63
★ Jubilee Gdns, SE1 30 C3
Jubilee Gdns, Sthl. UB1 158 CA72
Jubilee International High Sch, Add. KT15 off School La 234 BG106
Jubilee La, W5 off Haven La 160 CL72
Jubilee Mkt Hall, WC2 18 B10
Jubilee Par, Wdf.Grn. IG8 off Snakes La E 124 EJ51
Jubilee Pl, SW3 28 D10
Jubilee Prim Sch, N16 off Filey Av 144 DU60
SE28 off Crossway 168 EW73
SW2 off Tulse Hill 203 DN86
Jubilee Ri, Seal TN15 279 FM121
Jubilee Rd, Grays RM20 191 FV79
Orpington BR6 246 FA107
Perivale UB6 159 CH67
Sutton SM3 239 CX108
Watford WD24 97 BU38
Jubilee St, E1 20 G8
Jubilee Ter, Bet. RH3 286 CP138
Dorking RH4 285 CH135
Jubilee Trust, SE10 off Egerton Dr 46 D5
Jubilee Wk, Kings L. WD4 80 BN30
Watford WD19 115 BV49
Jubilee Way, SW19 222 DB95
Chessington KT9 238 CN105
Datchet SL3 174 AW80
Feltham TW14 197 BT88
Sidcup DA14 208 EU89
Judd Apts, N8 off Great Amwell La 143 DM55
Judd St, WC1 18 A3
Jude St, E16 23 L9
Judeth Gdns, Grav. DA12 213 GL92
Judge Heath La, Hayes UB3 157 BQ72
Uxbridge UB8 157 BQ72
Judges Hill, Northaw EN6 86 DE29
Judge St, Wat. WD24 97 BV38
Judge Wk, Clay. KT10 237 CE107
Judith Av, Rom. RM5 127 FB51
Juer St, SW11 40 D5
Jug Hill, Bigg.H. TN16 off Hillcrest Rd 260 EK116
Juglans Rd, Orp. BR6 228 EU102
Jules Thorn Av, Enf. EN1 104 DT41
Julia Gdns, Bark. IG11 168 EX68
Julia Garfield Ms, E16 36 B2
Juliana Cl, N2 142 DC55
Julian Av, W3 160 CP73
Julian Cl, New Barn. EN5 102 DB41
Woking GU21 248 AW118
Julian Hill, Har. HA1 139 CE61
Weybridge KT13 234 BN108
Julian Ho, SE21 off Kingswood Est 204 DS91
Julian Pl, E14 34 D10
Julian Rd, Orp. BR6 246 EU107
Julians Cl, Sev. TN13 278 FG127
Julian's Prim Sch, SW16 off Leigham Ct Rd 203 DN91
Julians Way, Sev. TN13 278 FG127
Julian Tayler Path, SE23 204 DV89
Julia St, NW5 6 G1
Julien Rd, W5 179 CJ76
Coulsdon CR5 257 DK115
Juliet Ct, NW7 off Marchant Cl 118 CS51
Juliette Cl, Aveley RM15 190 FN75
Juliette Rd, E13 23 M1
Juliette Way, Aveley RM15 190 FM75
Julius Caesar Way, Stan. HA7 117 CK49
Julius Nyerere Cl, N1 8 C9
Junction, The, Grays RM20 191 FT77
Junction App, SE13 46 E10
SW11 182 DE83
Junction Av, W10 14 B3
Junction Ms, W2 16 C8
Junction Pl, W2 16 B8
Junction Rd, E13 166 EH68
N9 122 DU46
N17 144 DU55
N19 143 DJ63
W5 179 CJ77
Ashford TW15 197 BQ92
Brentford TW8 179 CJ77
Dartford DA1 210 FK86
Dorking RH4 285 CG136
Harrow HA1 139 CE58
Romford RM1 149 FF56
South Croydon CR2 242 DR106
Warley CM14 130 FW49
Junction Rd E, Rom. RM6 off Kenneth Rd 148 EY59
Junction Rd W, Rom. RM6 148 EY59
Junction Shop Cen, The, SW11 off St. John's Hill 182 DE84
Junction, Wembley Retail Pk, The, Wem. HA9 140 CP63
June Cl, Couls. CR5 241 DH114
June La, Red. RH1 289 DH141
Junewood Cl, Wdhm KT15 233 BF111
Juniper Av, Brick.Wd AL2 82 CA31
Juniper Cl, Barn. EN5 101 CX43
Biggin Hill TN16 260 EL117
Broxbourne EN10 89 DZ25
Chesham HP5 76 AN30
Chessington KT9 238 CM107
Feltham TW13 197 BV90
Guildford GU1 264 AV129
Oxted RH8 276 EH133
Reigate RH2 288 DC136
Rickmansworth WD3 114 BK48
Wembley HA9 140 CM64
Juniper Ct, Nthwd. HA6 off Neal Cl 115 BU53
Slou. SL1 off Nixey Cl 174 AU75
Juniper Cres, NW1 7 H7
Juniper Dr, SW18 182 DC84
Juniper Gdns, SW16 off Leonard Rd 223 DJ95
Shenley WD7 84 CL33
Sunbury-on-Thames TW16 197 BT93
Juniper Gate, Rick. WD3 114 BK47
Juniper Grn, Hem.H. HP1 61 BE20
Juniper Gro, Wat. WD17 97 BU38
Juniper La, E6 25 H7
High Wycombe HP10 132 AD56
Juniper Pl, Shalf. GU4 280 AX141
Juniper Rd, Ilf. IG1 147 EN63
Reigate RH2 288 DC136
Juniper St, E1 20 G10
Juniper Ter, Shalf. GU4 280 AX141
Juniper Wk, Brock. RH3 286 CQ136
Swanley BR8 229 FD96
Juniper Way, Hayes UB3 157 BR73
Romford RM3 128 FL53
Juno Ho, E3 off Garrison Rd 12 A9
Juno Rd, Hem.H. HP2 off Saturn Way 62 BM17
Juno Way, SE14 45 K2
Jupiter Ct, Slou. SL1 153 AL73
Jupiter Dr, Hem.H. HP2 62 BM18
Jupiter Dr Prim Sch, Hem.H. HP2 off Jupiter Dr 62 BM18
Jupiter Way, N7 8 D4
Jupp Rd, E15 12 G7
Jupp Rd W, E15 12 F8
Jury St, Grav. DA11 off Princes St 213 GH86
Justice Wk, SW3 40 C3
Justin Cl, Brent. TW8 179 CK80
Justines Pl, E2 21 K2
Justin Pl, N22 121 DM52
Justin Rd, E4 123 DZ51
Jute La, Enf. EN3 105 DY40
Jutland Cl, N19 143 DL60
Jutland Gdns, Couls. CR5 257 DM120
Jutland Pl, Egh. TW20 195 BC92
Jutland Rd, E13 23 P5
SE6 205 EC87
Jutsums Av, Rom. RM7 149 FB58
Jutsums La, Rom. RM7 149 FB58
Juxon Cl, Har. HA3 116 CB53
Juxon St, SE11 30 D8

K

Kaduna Cl, Pnr. HA5 137 BU57
Kaine Pl, Croy. CR0 225 DY101
Kaizen Prim Sch, E13 24 A5
Kale Rd, Erith DA18 188 EY75
Kambala Rd, SW11 40 B9
Kandlewood, Hutt. CM13 131 GB45
Kangley Br Rd, SE26 205 DZ93
Kaplan Dr, N21 103 DL43
Kapuvar Cl, SE15 44 D9
Kara Way, NW2 141 CX63
Karen Cl, Brwd. CM15 130 FW45
Rainham RM13 169 FE68
Karen Ct, SE4 45 P10
Bromley BR1 226 EF95
Karen Ter, E11 off Montague Rd 146 EF61
Karenza Ct, Wem. HA9 off Lulworth Av 139 CJ59
Kariba Cl, N9 122 DW48
Karina Cl, Chig. IG7 125 ES50
Karma Way, Har. HA2 138 CA60
Karoline Gdns, Grnf. UB6 off Oldfield La N 159 CD68
Kashgar Rd, SE18 187 ET78
Kashmir Cl, New Haw KT15 234 BK109
Kashmir Rd, SE7 186 EK80
Kassala Rd, SW11 40 F6
Katella Trd Est, Bark. IG11 167 ES69
Kates Cl, Barn. EN5 101 CU43
Katescroft, Welw.G.C. AL7 51 CY13
Katharine St, Croy. CR0 224 DQ104
Katherine Cl, N4 144 DQ59
SE16 33 J3
Addlestone KT15 234 BG107
Katherine Cl, Hemel Hempstead HP3 62 BL23
Penn HP10 110 AC47
Katherine Gdns, SE9 186 EK84
Ilford IG6 125 EQ52
Katherine Ms, Whyt. CR3 258 DT117
Katherine Pl, Abb.L. WD5 81 BU32
Katherine Rd, E6 166 EK66
E7 146 EJ64
Twickenham TW1 off London Rd 199 CG88
KATHERINES, Harl. CM19 73 EM18
Katherines Hatch, Harl. CM19 off Brookside 73 EN17
Katherines Prim Sch, Harl. CM19 off Brookside 73 EN17
Katherine Sq, W11 26 E2
Katherines Way, Harl. CM19 73 EN18
Kathleen Av, W3 160 CQ71
Wembley HA0 160 CL66
Kathleen Rd, SW11 182 DF83
Katrine Sq, Hem.H. HP2 62 BK16
Kavanaghs Rd, Brwd. CM14 130 FU48
Kavanaghs Ter, Brwd. CM14 130 FV48
Kavsan Pl, Houns. TW5 177 BU80
Kayani Av, N4 144 DQ59
Kaye Ct, Guil. GU1 264 AW131
Kaye Don Way, Wey. KT13 234 BN111
Kayemoor Rd, Sutt. SM2 240 DE108
Kay Rd, SW9 42 B9
Kays Ter, E18 off Walpole Rd 124 EF53
Kay St, E2 10 D10
Welling DA16 188 EV81
Kay Wk, St.Alb. AL4 65 CK20
Kay Way, SE10 46 D4
Kaywood Cl, Slou. SL3 174 AW76
Kean Cres, Dag. RM8 148 EY60
Kean St, WC2 18 C9
Kearton Cl, Ken. CR8 258 DQ117
Keary Rd, Swans. DA10 212 FY87
Keate's La, Eton SL4 173 AR79
Keatley Grn, E4 123 DZ51
Keats Av, E16 36 A2
Redhill RH1 272 DG132
Romford RM3 127 FH52
Keats Cl, E11 off Nightingale La 146 EH57
NW3 6 C1
SE1 32 A9
SW19 202 DD93
Borhamwood WD6 100 CN42
Chigwell IG7 125 EQ51
Enfield EN3 105 DX43
Hayes UB4 157 BU71
Keats Gdns, Til. RM18 193 GH82
Keats Gro, NW3 6 B1
★ Keats Ho, NW3 6 C1
Keats Ho, SW1 41 M2
Beckenham BR3 205 EA93
Keats Pl, EC2 19 L7
Keats Rd, E10 145 EB59
Belvedere DA17 189 FC76
Welling DA16 187 ES81
Keats Wk, Hutt. CM13 off Byron Rd 131 GD45
Keats Way, Croy. CR0 224 DW100
Greenford UB6 158 CB71
West Drayton UB7 176 BM77
Kebbell Ter, E7 146 EH64
Keble Cl, Nthlt. UB5 138 CC64
Worcester Park KT4 221 CT102
Keble Ct, Borwd. WD6 off Gateshead Rd 100 CM39
Keble Pl, SW13 off Somerville Av 181 CV79
Keble Sch, N21 off Wades Hill 121 DN45
Keble St, SW17 202 DC91
Keble Ter, Abb.L. WD5 81 BT32
Kebony Cl, West Dr. UB7 176 BN75
Kechill Gdns, Brom. BR2 226 EG101
Kedelston Ct, E5 off Redwald Rd 145 DY63
Kedeston Ct, Sutt. SM1 off Hurstcourt Rd 222 DB102
Kedleston Dr, Orp. BR5 227 ET100
Kedleston Wk, E2 20 F2
Keedonwood Rd, Brom. BR1 206 EE92
Keefield, Harl. CM19 73 EP20
Keel Cl, N18 off Amersham Ave 122 DS51
SE16 33 K3
Barking IG11 168 EW68
Keel Ct, E14 off Newport Av 23 H10
Keel Dr, Slou. SL1 173 AQ75
Keele Cl, Wat. WD24 98 BW40
Keeler Cl, Wind. SL4 173 AL83
Keeley Rd, Croy. CR0 224 DQ103
Keeley St, WC2 18 C9
Keeling Ho, E2 20 E1
Keeling Rd, SE9 206 EK85
Keely Cl, Barn. EN4 102 DE43
Keemor Cl, SE18 187 EN80
Keensacre, Iver SL0 155 BD68
Keens Cl, SW16 203 DK92
Keens La, Guil. GU3 264 AT130
Keens Pk Rd, Guil. GU3 264 AT130
Keens Rd, Croy. CR0 242 DQ105
Keen Students Sch, E1 20 D6
Keens Yd, N1 9 H5
Keep, The, SE3 47 N9
Kingston upon Thames KT2 200 CM93
Keepers Cl, Guil. GU4 265 BD131
Keepers Fm Cl, Wind. SL4 173 AL82
Keepers Ms, Tedd. TW11 199 CJ93
Keepers Wk, Vir.W. GU25 214 AX99
Keep La, N11 off Gardeners Cl 120 DG47
Keetons Rd, SE16 32 E6
Keevil Dr, SW19 201 CX87
Keighley Cl, N7 8 B1
Keighley Rd, Rom. RM3 128 FL52
Keightley Dr, SE9 207 EQ88
Keilder Cl, Uxb. UB10 156 BN68
Keildon Rd, SW11 182 DF84
Keir, The, SW19 201 CW92
Keir Hardie Est, E5 off Springfield 144 DV60
Keir Hardie Ho, W6 38 B2
Keir Hardie Prim Sch, E16 23 N7
Keir Hardie Way, Bark. IG11 168 EU66
Hayes UB4 157 BU69

Keith Av, Sutt.H. DA4 210 FP93
Keith Connor Cl, SW8 41 J10
Keith Gro, W12 181 CU75
Keith Pk Cres, Bigg.H. TN16 244 EH112
Keith Pk Rd, Uxb. UB10 156 BM66
Keith Rd, E17 123 DZ53
Barking IG11 167 ER68
Hayes UB3 177 BS76
Keiths Rd, Hem.H. HP3 62 BN21
Keith Way, Horn. RM11 150 FL59
Kelbrook Rd, SE3 186 EL83
Kelburn Way, Rain. RM13
off Dominion Way 169 FG69
Kelby Path, SE9 207 EP90
Kelbys, Welw.G.C. AL7 52 DC08
Kelceda Cl, NW2 141 CU61
Kelday Hts, E1 20 F9
Kelf Gro, Hayes UB3 157 BT72
Kelfield Gdns, W10 14 B8
Kelfield Ms, W10 14 C7
Kelland Cl, N8 143 DK57
Kelland Rd, E13 23 P4
Kellaway Rd, SE3 186 EJ82
Keller Cres, E12 146 EK63
Kellerton Rd, SE13 206 EE85
Kellett Rd, SW2 183 DN84
Kelling Gdns, Croy. CR0 223 DP101
Kellino St, SW17 202 DF91
Kellner Rd, SE28 187 ET76
Kell St, SE1 31 H6
Kelly Av, SE15 44 A5
Kelly Cl, NW10 140 CR62
Shepperton TW17 217 BS96
Kelly Ct, Borwd. WD6 100 CQ40
Kelly Ms, W9 15 H5
Kelly Rd, NW7 119 CY51
Kelly St, NW1 7 K5
Kelly Way, Rom. RM6 148 EY57
Kelman Cl, SW4 41 P9
Waltham Cross EN8 89 DX31
Kelmore Gro, SE22 184 DU84
Kelmscott Cl, E17 123 DZ54
Watford WD18 97 BU43
Kelmscott Cres, Wat. WD18 97 BU43
Kelmscott Gdns, W12 181 CU76
Kelmscott Pl, Ashtd. KT21 253 CJ117
Kelmscott Rd, SW11 202 DE85
Kelmscott Sch, E17
off Markhouse Rd 145 DZ58
Kelpatrick Rd, Slou. SL1 153 AK72
Kelross Pas, N5
off Kelross Rd 144 DQ63
Kelross Rd, N5 143 DP63
Kelsall Cl, SE3 186 EH82
Kelsall Ms, Rich. TW9 180 CP81
Kelsey Cl, Horl. RH6
off Court Lo Rd 290 DF148
Kelsey Gate, Beck. BR3 225 EB96
Kelsey La, Beck. BR3 225 EA97
Kelsey Pk Av, Beck. BR3 225 EB96
Kelsey Pk Rd, Beck. BR3 225 EA96
Kelsey Pk Sports Coll, Beck.
BR3 *off Manor Way* 225 EA97
Kelsey Rd, Orp. BR5 228 EV96
Kelsey Sq, Beck. BR3 225 EA96
Kelsey St, E2 20 D4
Kelsey Way, Beck. BR3 225 EA97
Kelshall, Wat. WD25 98 BY36
Kelshall Ct, N4
off Brownswood Rd 144 DQ61
Kelsie Way, Ilf. IG6 125 ES52
Kelso Dr, Grav. DA12 213 GM91
Kelson Ho, E14 34 F6
Kelso Pl, W8 27 M6
Kelso Rd, Cars. SM5 222 DC101
Kelston Rd, Ilf. IG6 125 EP54
Kelvedon Av, Hersham KT12 235 BS108
Kelvedon Cl, Hutt. CM13 131 GE44
Kingston upon Thames KT2 200 CM93
Kelvedon Ho, SW8 42 B6
Kelvedon Rd, SW6 39 H5
Kelvedon Wk, Rain. RM13
off Ongar Way 169 FE66
Kelvedon Way, Wdf.Grn. IG8 125 EM51
Kelvin Av, N13 121 DM51
Leatherhead KT22 253 CF119
Teddington TW11 199 CE93
Kelvinbrook, W.Mol. KT8 218 CB97
Kelvin Cl, Epsom KT19 238 CN107
Kelvin Cres, Har. HA3 117 CE52
Kelvin Dr, Twick. TW1 199 CH86
Kelvin Gdns, Croy. CR0 223 DL101
Southall UB1 158 CA72
Kelvin Gro, SE26 204 DV90
Chessington KT9 219 CK104
Kelvin Gro Prim Sch,
SE26 *off Kirkdale* 204 DV90
Kelvington Cl, Croy. CR0 225 DY101
Kelvington Rd, SE15 205 DX85
● Kelvin Ind Est, Grnf. UB6 158 CB66
Kelvin Par, Orp. BR6 227 ES102
Kelvin Rd, N5 9 H1
Tilbury RM18 193 GG82
Welling DA16 188 EU83
Kember St, N1 8 C7
Kemble Cl, Pot.B. EN6 86 DD33
Weybridge KT13 235 BR105
Kemble Cotts, Add. KT15
off Emley Rd 234 BG105
Kemble Dr, Brom. BR2 226 EL104
Kemble Par, Pot.B. EN6
off High St 86 DC32
Kemble Rd, N17 122 DU53
SE23 205 DX88
Croydon CR0 223 DN104
Kembleside Rd, Bigg.H. TN16 260 EJ118
Kemble St, WC2 18 C9
Kemerton Rd, SE5 184 DQ83
Beckenham BR3 225 EB96
Croydon CR0 224 DT101
Kemeys St, E9 11 L3
Kemishford, Wok. GU22 248 AU123
Kemnal Rd, Chis. BR7 207 ER91
Kemnal Tech Coll,
Sid. DA14
off Sevenoaks Way 208 EV94
Kemp Ct, SW8 42 A5
Kempe Cl, St.Alb. AL1 64 CC24
Slough SL3 175 BC77
Kempe Rd, NW6 14 C1
Enfield EN1 104 DV36
Kemp Gdns, Croy. CR0 224 DQ100
Kemp Ho, W1 *off Berwick St* 17 N10
Kempis Way, SE22
off East Dulwich Gro 204 DS85
Kemplay Rd, NW3 6 A1
Kemp Pl, Bushey WD23 98 CA44
Kemp Rd, Dag. RM8 148 EX60
Kemprow, Ald. WD25 99 CD36
Kemp's Ct, W1 17 M9
Kemps Dr, E14 22 B10
Northwood HA6 115 BT52
Kempsford Gdns, SW5 39 K1
Kempsford Rd, SE11 30 F9
Kemps Gdns, SE13
off Thornford Rd 205 EC85
Kempshott Rd, SW16 203 DK94
Kempson Rd, SW6 39 K6
Kempthorne Rd, SE8 33 M8
Kempton Av, Horn. RM12 150 FM63
Northolt UB5 158 CA65
Sunbury-on-Thames TW16 217 BV95
Kempton Cl, Erith DA8 189 FC79
Uxbridge UB10 137 BQ63
Kempton Ct, E1 20 E6
Sunbury-on-Thames TW16 217 BV95
Kempton Park 197 BV94
★ Kempton Park Racecourse,
Sun. TW16 198 BW94
Kempton Rd, E6 167 EM67
Hampton TW12 218 BZ96
Kempton Wk, Croy. CR0 225 DY100
Kempt St, SE18 187 EN79
Kemsing Cl, Bex. DA5 208 EY87
Bromley BR2 226 EF103
Thornton Heath CR7 224 DQ98
Kemsing Rd, SE10 35 N10
Kemsley, SE13 205 EC85
Kemsley Chase, Farn.Royal
SL2 153 AR67
Kemsley Cl, Green. DA9 211 FV86
Northfleet DA11 213 GF91
Kemsley Rd, Tats. TN16 260 EK119
Kenbury Cl, Uxb. UB10 136 BN62
Kenbury Gdns, SE5 43 J8
Kenbury St, SE5 43 J8
Kenchester Cl, SW8 42 B5
Kencot Cl, Erith DA18 188 EZ75
● Kencot Cl Business Pk,
Erith DA18 188 EZ75
Kendal, Purf. RM19 190 FQ78
Kendal Av, N18 122 DR49
W3 160 CN70
Barking IG11 167 ES66
Epping CM16 92 EU30
Kendal Cl, N20 120 DE47
SW9 42 G4
Feltham TW14
off Ambleside Dr 197 BT88
Hayes UB4 157 BS68
Reigate RH2 272 DD133
Slough SL2 154 AU73
Woodford Green IG8 124 EF47
Kendal Cft, Horn. RM12 149 FG64
Kendal Dr, Slou. SL2 154 AU73
Kendale, Grays RM16 193 GH76
Hemel Hempstead HP3 63 BP21
Kendale Rd, Brom. BR1 206 EE92
Kendal Gdns, N18 122 DR49
Sutton SM1 222 DC103
Kendal Ho, N1 8 D10
Kendall Av, Beck. BR3 225 DY96
South Croydon CR2 242 DR109
Kendall Av S, S.Croy. CR2 242 DQ110
Kendall Cl, Welw.G.C. AL7 51 CY13
Kendall Ct, SW19 202 DD93
Borehamwood WD6
off Gregson Cl 100 CQ39
Kendall Gdns, Grav. DA11 213 GF87
Kendall Pl, W1 16 G7
Kendall Rd, SE18 186 EL81
Beckenham BR3 225 DY96
Isleworth TW7 179 CG82
Kendalmere Cl, N10 121 DH53
Kendal Par, N18
off Great Cambridge Rd 122 DR49
Kendal Pl, SW15 201 CZ85
Kendal Rd, NW10 141 CU63
Waltham Abbey EN9 105 EC35
Kendals Cl, Rad. WD7 99 CE36
Kendal Steps, W2
off St. Georges Flds 16 D9
Kendal St, W2 16 D9
Kender Prim Sch, SE14 45 H6
Kender St, SE14 45 H5
Kendoa Rd, SW4 183 DK84
Kendon Cl, E11 146 EH57
Kendor Av, Epsom KT19 238 CQ111
Kendra Hall Rd, S.Croy. CR2 241 DP108
Kendrey Gdns, Twick. TW2 199 CE86
Kendrick Ms, SW7 28 A8
Kendrick Pl, SW7 28 A9
Kendrick Rd, Slou. SL3 174 AV76
Kenelm Cl, Har. HA1 139 CG62
Kenerne Dr, Barn. EN5 101 CY43
Kenford Cl, Wat. WD25 81 BV32
Kenia Wk, Grav. DA12 213 GM90
Kenilford Rd, SW12 203 DH87
Kenilworth Av, E17 123 EA54
SW19 202 DA92
Harrow HA2 138 BZ63
Romford RM3 128 FP50
Stoke D'Abernon KT11 236 CB114
Kenilworth Cl, Bans. SM7 256 DB116
Borehamwood WD6 100 CQ41
Hemel Hempstead HP2 62 BL21
Slough SL1 174 AT76
Kenilworth Ct, SW15
off Lower Richmond Rd 181 CY83
Watford WD17 97 BU39
Kenilworth Cres, Enf. EN1 104 DS39
Kenilworth Dr, Borwd. WD6 100 CQ41
Croxley Green WD3 97 BP42
Walton-on-Thames KT12 218 BX104
Kenilworth Gdns, SE18 187 EP82
Hayes UB4 157 BT71
Hornchurch RM12 150 FJ62
Ilford IG3 147 ET61
Loughton IG10 107 EM44
Southall UB1 158 BZ69
Staines-upon-Thames TW18 196 BJ92
Watford WD19 116 BW50
Kenilworth Prim Sch, Borwd.
WD6 *off Kenilworth Dr* 100 CR41
Kenilworth Rd, E3 11 L10
NW6 5 H8
SE20 225 DX95
W5 160 CL74
Ashford TW15 196 BK90
Edgware HA8 118 CQ48
Kenilworth Rd, Epsom KT17 239 CU107
Petts Wood BR5 227 EQ100
KENLEY, CR8 258 DQ116
Kenley 242 DQ114
Kenley, N17 122 DR54
Kenley Av, NW9 118 CS54
Kenley Cl, Barn. EN4 102 DE42
Bexley DA5 208 FA87
Caterham CR3 258 DR120
Chislehurst BR7 227 ES97
Kenley Gdns, Horn. RM12 150 FM61
Thornton Heath CR7 223 DP98
Kenley La, Ken. CR8 242 DQ114
Kenley Prim Sch, Whyt.
CR3 *off New Barn La* 258 DS116
Kenley Rd, SW19 221 CZ96
Kingston upon Thames KT1 220 CP96
Twickenham TW1 199 CG86
Kenley Wk, W11 26 E1
Sutton SM3 239 CX105
Kenlor Rd, SW17 202 DD92
Kenmare Dr, N17 122 DT54
Mitcham CR4 202 DF94
Kenmare Gdns, N13 121 DP49
Kenmare Rd, Th.Hth. CR7 223 DN100
Kenmere Gdns, Wem. HA0 160 CN67
Kenmere Rd, Well. DA16 188 EW82
Kenmont Gdns, NW10 161 CV69
Kenmont Prim Sch, NW10
off Valliere Rd 161 CV69
Kenmore Av, Har. HA3 139 CG56
Kenmore Cl, Rich. TW9
off Kent Rd 180 CN80
Kenmore Cres, Hayes UB4 157 BT69
Kenmore Gdns, Edg. HA8 118 CP54
Kenmore Pk First & Mid Schs,
Kenton HA3
off Moorhouse Rd 140 CL55
Kenmore Rd, Har. HA3 139 CK55
Kenley CR8 241 DP114
Kenmure Rd, E8 10 F3
Kenmure Yd, E8 10 F3
Kennacraig Cl, E16 35 P3
Kennard Rd, E15 12 G7
N11 120 DF50
Kennards Ct, Amer. HP6 77 AS38
Kennard St, E16 37 J3
SW11 40 G7
Kenneally, Wind. SL4 172 AJ82
Kenneally Cl, Wind. SL4
off Kenneally 172 AJ82
Kenneally Pl, Wind. SL4
off Kenneally 172 AJ82
Kenneally Row, Wind. SL4
off Kenneally 172 AJ82
Kenneally Wk, Wind. SL4
off Kenneally 172 AJ82
Kennedy Av, Enf. EN3 104 DW44
Hoddesdon EN11 71 DZ17
Kennedy Cl, E13 23 P1
Cheshunt EN8 89 DX28
Farnham Common SL2 153 AQ65
London Colney AL2 83 CK26
Mitcham CR4 222 DG96
Petts Wood BR5 227 ER102
Pinner HA5 116 BZ51
Kennedy Gdns, Sev. TN13 279 FJ123
Kennedy Ho, SE11
off Vauxhall Wk 30 C10
Kennedy Path, W7 *off Harp Rd* 159 CF70
Kennedy Rd, W7 159 CE71
Barking IG11 167 ES67
Kennedy Wk, SE17
off Flint St 31 M9
Kennel Cl, Fetch. KT22 252 CC124
Kennel La, Fetch. KT22 252 CC122
Hookwood RH6 290 DD149
Kennelwood Cres, New Adgtn
CR0 243 ED111
Kennelwood La, Hat. AL10 67 CV17
Kennet Cl, SW11
off Maysoule Rd 182 DD84
Upminster RM14 151 FS58
Kennet Grn, S.Ock. RM15 171 FV73
Kenneth Av, Ilf. IG1 147 EP63
Kenneth Cres, NW2 141 CV64
Kenneth Gdns, Stan. HA7 117 CG51
Kenneth More Rd, Ilf. IG1
off Oakfield Rd 147 EP62
Kennet Ho, NW8 16 B6
Kenneth Rd, Bans. SM7 256 DD115
Romford RM6 148 EX59
Kenneth Robbins Ho, N17 122 DV52
Kennet Rd, W9 15 H4
Dartford DA1 189 FG83
Isleworth TW7 179 CF83
Kennet Sq, Mitch. CR4 222 DE95
Kennet St, E1 32 D2
Kennett Ct, Swan. BR8 229 FE97
Kennett Dr, Hayes UB4 158 BY71
Kennett Rd, Slou. SL3 175 BB76
Kennet Wf La, EC4 19 K10
Kenninghall, N18 122 DV50
Kenninghall Rd, E5 144 DU62
N18 122 DW50
Kenning Rd, Hodd. EN11 71 EA15
Kenning St, SE16 33 H4
Kennings Way, SE11 30 F10
Kenning Ter, N1 9 N8
KENNINGTON, SE11 42 E3
Kennington 30 G10
Kennington Grn, SE11 42 E1
Kennington La, SE11 30 F10
Kennington Oval, SE11 42 D2
● Kennington Pk, SW9 42 F4
Kennington Pk Est, SE11 42 E3
Kennington Pk Gdns, SE11 42 G2
Kennington Pk Pl, SE11 42 F1
Kennington Pk Rd, SE11 42 F2
Kennington Rd, SE1 30 E6
SE11 30 E7
Kenningtons Prim Sch,
Aveley RM15
off Tamar Dr 170 FQ72
Kennoldes, SE21 204 DR89
Kenny Dr, Cars. SM5 240 DF109
Kenrick Pl, W1 16 G6
Kenrick Sq, Bletch. RH1 274 DS133
KENSAL GREEN, NW10 14 B2
Kensal Green 14 B2
Kensal Green 14 B2
★ Kensal Green Cem, W10 14 A3
KENSAL RISE, NW6 14 C1
Kensal Rise 14 B1
Kensal Ri Prim Sch, NW6 14 C1
Kensal Rd, W10 14 F4
KENSAL TOWN, W10 14 E4
Kensal Wf, W10 14 D4
KENSINGTON, W8 27 H3
Kensington & Chelsea Coll,
Hortensia Cen, SW10 39 N4
Marlborough Cen, SW3 28 D9
Wornington Cen, W10 14 F6
Kensington Av, E12 166 EL65
Thornton Heath CR7 223 DN95
Watford WD18 97 BT42
Kensington Av Prim Sch, Th.Hth.
CR7 *off Kensington Av* 223 DN95
Kensington Ch Ct, W8 27 L5
Kensington Ch St, W8 27 K2
Kensington Ch Wk, W8 27 L4
Kensington Cl, N11 120 DG50
St. Albans AL1 65 CG22
Kensington Coll of Business,
WC2 18 C8
Kensington Ct, NW7
off Grenville Pl 118 CR50
W8 27 M5
Kensington Ct Gdns, W8
off Kensington Ct Pl 27 M6
Kensington Ct Ms, W8 27 M5
Kensington Ct Pl, W8 27 M6
Kensington Dr, Wdf.Grn. IG8 124 EK53
★ Kensington Gdns, W2 27 P3
Kensington Gdns, Ilf. IG1 147 EM61
Kingston upon Thames KT1
off Portsmouth Rd 219 CK97
Kensington Gdns Sq, W2 15 L9
Kensington Gate, W8 27 N6
Kensington Gore, SW7 28 A5
Kensington Grn, W8 27 L7
Kensington Hall Gdns, W14 26 G10
Kensington High St, W8 27 J6
W14 26 G7
Kensington Ho, West Dr. UB7
off Park Lo Av 176 BM75
Kensington Mall, W8 27 K2
Kensington (Olympia) 26 E6
Kensington (Olympia) 26 E6
Kensington (Olympia) 26 E6
★ Kensington Palace, W8 27 M3
Kensington Palace Gdns, W8 27 L2
Kensington Pk, Stap.Abb. RM4 127 FE45
Kensington Pk Gdns, W11 26 G1
Kensington Pk Ms, W11 14 G9
Kensington Pk Rd, W11 14 G10
Kensington Path, E10
off Balmoral Rd 145 EB61
Kensington Pl, W8 27 J3
Kensington Prim Sch, E12
off Kensington Av 167 EM65
Kensington Rd, SW7 28 B5
W8 27 M5
Northolt UB5 158 CA69
Pilgrim's Hatch CM15 130 FU44
Romford RM7 149 FC58
Kensington Sq, W8 27 L5
Kensington Ter, S.Croy. CR2 242 DR108
Kensington Village, W14 27 H9
Kensington Way, Borwd. WD6 100 CR41
Brentwood CM14 130 FW46
Kent Av, W13 159 CH71
Dagenham RM9 168 FA70
Slough SL1 153 AQ71
Welling DA16 207 ET85
Kent Cl, Borwd. WD6 100 CR38
Mitcham CR4 223 DL98
Orpington BR6 245 ES107
Staines-upon-Thames TW18 196 BK93
Uxbridge UB8 156 BJ65
Kent Dr, Cockfos. EN4 102 DG42
Hornchurch RM12 150 FK63
Teddington TW11 199 CE92
Kentford Way, Nthlt. UB5 158 BY67
Kent Gdns, W13 159 CH71
Ruislip HA4 137 BV58
Kent Gate Way, Croy. CR0 243 EA106
KENT HATCH, Eden. TN8 277 EP131
Kent Hatch Rd, Crock.H. TN8 277 EM131
Oxted RH8 276 EJ129
Kent House 225 DY95
Kent Ho La, Beck. BR3 205 DY92
Kent Ho Rd, SE26 225 DX95
Beckenham BR3 205 DY92
Kentish Bldgs, SE1 31 L3
Kentish La, Hat. AL9 86 DC25
Kentish Rd, Belv. DA17 188 FA77
KENTISH TOWN, NW5 7 L4
Kentish Town 7 L3
Kentish Town 7 L3
Kentish Town C of E
Prim Sch, NW5 7 L3
Kentish Town Rd, NW1 7 K7
NW5 7 K7
Kentish Town West 7 H5
Kentish Way, Brom. BR1 226 EG96
● Kent Kraft Ind Est,
Nthflt DA11 212 FZ85
Kentlea Rd, SE28 187 ES75
Kentmere Rd, SE18 187 ES77
KENTON, Har. HA3 139 CH57
Kenton 139 CH58
Kenton 139 CH58
Kenton Av, Har. HA1 139 CF59
Southall UB1 158 CA73
Sunbury-on-Thames TW16 218 BY96
Kenton Ct, W14 26 G7
Kenton Gdns, Har. HA3 139 CJ57
St. Albans AL1 65 CF21
Kenton La, Har. HA3 139 CJ55
Kenton Pk Av, Har. HA3 139 CK56
Kenton Pk Cl, Har. HA3 139 CJ56
Kenton Pk Cres, Har. HA3 139 CK56
Kenton Pk Par, Har. HA3 139 CJ57
Kenton Pk Rd, Har. HA3 139 CJ56
Kenton Rd, E9 11 J5
Harrow HA1, HA3 139 CK57
Kentons La, Wind. SL4 173 AL82
Kenton St, WC1 18 A4
Kenton Way, Hayes UB4
off Exmouth Rd 157 BS69
Woking GU21 248 AT117
● Kent Pk Ind Est, SE15 44 E2
Kent Pas, NW1 16 E4
Kent Rd, N21 122 DR46
W4 180 CQ76
Dagenham RM10 149 FB64
Dartford DA1 210 FK86
East Molesey KT8 218 CC98
Gravesend DA11 213 GG88
Grays RM17 192 GC79
Kingston upon Thames KT1
off The Bittoms 219 CK97
Longfield DA3 231 FX96
Orpington BR5 228 EV100
Richmond TW9 180 CN80
West Wickham BR4 225 EB102
Woking GU22 249 BB116
Kents Av, Hem.H. HP3 62 BK24
Kents La, N.Wld Bas. CM16 75 FD21
Kents Pas, Hmptn. TW12 218 BZ95
Kent St, E2 10 B10
E13 24 B3
Kent Ter, NW1 16 D3
Kent Vw, Aveley RM15 190 FQ75
Kent Vw Gdns, Ilf. IG3 147 ES61
Kent Way, Surb. KT6 220 CL104
Kentwell Cl, SE4 185 DY84
Kentwode Grn, SW13 181 CU80
Kentwyns Ri, S.Nutfld RH1 289 DM135
Kent Yd, SW7 28 D5
Kenver Av, N12 120 DD51
Kenward Rd, SE9 206 EJ85
Kenway, Rain. RM13 170 FJ69
Romford RM5 127 FC54
Ken Way, Wem. HA9 140 CQ61
Kenway Cl, Rain. RM13 170 FJ69
Kenway Dr, Amer. HP7 94 AV39
Kenway Rd, SW5 27 L9
Kenway Wk, Rain. RM13 170 FK69
Kenwood Av, N14 103 DK43
SE14 45 H6
Kenwood Cl, NW3 142 DD60
Sipson UB7 176 BN79
Kenwood Dr, Beck. BR3 225 EC97
Hersham KT12 235 BV107
Mill End WD3 113 BF47
Kenwood Gdns, E18 146 EH55
Ilford IG2 147 EN56
★ Kenwood Ho, NW3 142 DE60
Kenwood Pk, Wey. KT13 235 BR107
Kenwood Ridge, Ken. CR8 257 DP117
Kenwood Rd, N6 142 DF58
N9 122 DU46
Kenworth Cl, Wal.Cr. EN8 89 DX33
Kenworth Ho, Enf. EN1
off Great Cambridge Rd 104 DU43
Kenworthy Rd, E9 11 L3
Kenwyn Dr, NW2 140 CS62
Kenwyn Rd, SW4 183 DK84
SW20 221 CW95
Dartford DA1 210 FK85
Kenya Rd, SE7 186 EK80
Kenyngton Dr, Sun. TW16 197 BU92
Kenyngton Manor Prim Sch,
Sun. TW16 *off Bryony Way* 197 BU93
Kenyngton Pl, Har. HA3 139 CJ57
Kenyon Pl, Welw.G.C. AL7
off Twelve Acres 51 CY12
Kenyons, W.Hors. KT24 267 BP128
Kenyon St, SW6 38 C6
Keogh Rd, E15 13 K4
Kepler Rd, SW4 183 DL84
Keppel Rd, E6 167 EM66
Dagenham RM9 148 EY63
Dorking RH4 269 CH134
Keppel Row, SE1 31 J3
Keppel Spur, Old Wind. SL4 194 AV87
Keppel St, WC1 17 P6
Windsor SL4 173 AR82
Kerbela St, E2 20 C4
Kerbey St, E14 22 D8
Kerdistone Cl, Pot.B. EN6 86 DB30
Kerem Sch, N2
off Norrice Lea 142 DD57
Kerfield Cres, SE5 43 L7
Kerfield Pl, SE5 43 L7
Kernow Cl, Horn. RM12 150 FL61
Kerr Cl, S.Croy. CR2 243 DY108
Kerri Cl, Barn. EN5 101 CW42
Kerridge Ct, N1 9 P4
Kerril Cft, Harl. CM20 57 EN14
Kerrill Av, Couls. CR5 257 DN119
Kerrison Pl, W5 159 CK74
Kerrison Rd, E15 12 G8
SW11 40 C10
W5 159 CK74
Kerrison Vil, W5
off Kerrison Pl 159 CK74
Kerry Av, Aveley RM15 190 FM75
Stanmore HA7 117 CK49
Kerry Av N, Stan. HA7 117 CK49
Kerry Cl, E16 24 A9
N13 121 DM47
Upminster RM14 151 FT59
Kerry Ct, SW6 *off Dairy Cl* 39 H7
Stanmore HA7 117 CK49
Kerry Dr, Upmin. RM14 151 FT59
Kerry Ho, E1 *off Sidney St* 20 G8
Kerry Path, SE14 45 N3
Kerry Rd, SE14 45 N3
Kerry Ter, Wok. GU21 249 BB116
Kersey Dr, S.Croy. CR2 242 DW112
Kersey Gdns, SE9 206 EL91
Romford RM3 128 FL52
Kersfield Rd, SW15 201 CX86
Kershaw Cl, SW18 202 DC86
Chafford Hundred RM16 191 FW77
Hornchurch RM11 150 FK59
Kershaw Rd, Dag. RM10 148 FA62
Kersley Ms, SW11 40 E7
Kersley Rd, N16 144 DS62
Kersley St, SW11 40 E8
Kerstin Cl, Hayes UB3 157 BT73
Kerswell Cl, N15 144 DS57
Kerwick Cl, N7 8 B6
Keslake Rd, NW6 14 C1
Kessock Cl, N17 144 DV57
Kesters Rd, Chesh. HP5 76 AR32
Kesteven Cl, Ilf. IG6 125 ET51
Kestlake Rd, Bex. DA5
off East Rochester Way 208 EW86
KESTON, BR2 244 EJ106
Keston Av, Couls. CR5 257 DN119
Keston BR2 244 EJ106
New Haw KT15 234 BG111
Keston Cl, N18 122 DR48
Welling DA16 188 EW80
Keston C of E Prim Sch,
Kes. BR2 *off Lakes Rd* 244 EK106
Keston Gdns, Kes. BR2 244 EJ105
Keston Mark, Kes. BR2 226 EL104
Keston Ms, Wat. WD17
off Nascot Rd 97 BV40
Keston Pk Cl, Kes. BR2 227 EM104
Keston Prim Sch, Couls.
CR5 *off Keston Av* 257 DN119
Keston Rd, N17 144 DR55
SE15 184 DU83
Thornton Heath CR7 223 DN100
Kestral Ct, Wall. SM6
off Carew Rd 241 DJ106
Kestrel Av, E6 24 G7
SE24 203 DP85
Staines-upon-Thames TW18 195 BF90
Kestrel Cl, NW9 118 CS54
NW10 140 CR64

Kestrel Cl, Berkhamsted HP4 60 AW20
Epsom KT19 238 CN111
Guildford GU4 265 BD132
Hornchurch RM12 169 FH66
Ilford IG6 126 EW49
Kingston upon Thames KT2 199 CK91
Watford WD25 82 BY34
Kestrel Grn, Hat. AL10 67 CU19
Kestrel Ho, EC1 19 J2
SW8 off St. George Wf 42 A2
W13 159 CF70
Enfield EN3 off Alma Rd 105 DY43
Kestrel Path, Slou. SL2 153 AL70
Kestrel Pl, SE14
off Milton Ct Rd 45 M3
Kestrel Rd, Wal.Abb. EN9 90 EG34
Kestrels, The, Brick.Wd AL2 82 BZ31
Denh.UB9 off Patrons Way E 135 BF57
Kestrel Way, Felt. TW14 197 BV85
Hayes UB3 177 BR75
New Addington CR0 243 ED109
Welwyn Garden City AL7 51 CZ07
Woking GU21 248 AV115
Keswick Av, SW15 200 CS92
SW19 222 DA96
Hornchurch RM11 150 FK60
Keswick Bdy, SW15
off Upper Richmond Rd 201 CZ85
Keswick Cl, St.Alb. AL1 65 CH21
Sutton SM1 240 DC105
Keswick Ct, Slou. SL2
off Stoke Rd 154 AT73
Keswick Dr, Enf. EN3 104 DW36
Keswick Gdns, Ilf. IG4 146 EL57
Purfleet RM19 190 FQ79
Ruislip HA4 137 BR58
Wembley HA9 140 CL63
Keswick Ms, W5 160 CL74
Keswick Rd, SW15 201 CY85
Bexleyheath DA7 188 FA82
Egham TW20 195 BB94
Leatherhead KT22, KT23 268 CC125
Orpington BR6 227 ET102
Twickenham TW2 198 CC86
West Wickham BR4 226 EE103
Kettering Rd, Enf. EN3
off Beaconsfield Rd 105 DX37
Romford RM3 128 FL52
Kettering St, SW16 203 DJ93
Kett Gdns, SW2 203 DM85
Kettlebaston Rd, E10 145 DZ60
Kettlewell Cl, N11 120 DG51
Woking GU21 232 AX114
Kettlewell Ct, Swan. BR8 229 FF96
Kettlewell Dr, Wok. GU21 232 AY114
Kettlewell Hill, Wok. GU21 232 AY114
Ketton Grn, Merst. RH1
off Malmstone Av 273 DK128
Kevan Dr, Send GU23 249 BE124
Kevan Ho, SE5 43 J5
Kevelioc Rd, N17 122 DQ53
Kevin Cl, Houns. TW4 178 BX82
Kevington Cl, Orp. BR5 227 ET98
Kevington Dr, Chis. BR7 227 ET98
Orpington BR5 227 ET98
KEW, Rich. TW9 180 CN79
Kew Bridge 180 CM78
Kew Br, Brent. TW8 180 CM78
Kew Br, Brent. TW8 180 CM79
Richmond TW9 180 CM79
Kew Br Arches, Rich. TW9
off Kew Br 180 CM79
Kew Br Ct, W4 180 CN78
● Kew Br Distribution Cen,
Brent. TW8 180 CM78
Kew Br Rd, Brent. TW8 180 CM79
★ Kew Bridge Steam Mus,
Brent. TW8 180 CM78
Kew Cl, Rom. RM1 127 FE51
Uxbridge UB8 156 BK68
Kew Coll, Kew TW9
off Cumberland Rd 180 CN80
Kew Cres, Sutt. SM3 221 CY104
Kewferry Dr, Nthwd. HA6 115 BP50
Kewferry Rd, Nthwd. HA6 115 BQ51
Kew Foot Rd, Rich. TW9 180 CL84
Kew Gardens 180 CM81
Kew Gardens 180 CM81
Kew Gdns Rd, Rich. TW9 180 CM80
Kew Grn, Rich. TW9 180 CM80
Kew Grn, Rich. TW9 180 CN80
Kew Meadows Path, Rich.
TW9 180 CP82
★ Kew Observatory, Rich.
TW9 179 CH83
★ Kew Palace (Royal Botanic Gdns),
Rich. TW9 180 CL80
Kew Retail Pk, Rich. TW9 180 CP81
Kew Riverside Prim Sch, Rich.
TW9 off Courtlands Av 180 CP82
Kew Rd, Rich. TW9 180 CN79
Key Cl, E1 20 F5
Keyes Rd, NW2 4 D2
Dartford DA1 190 FM84
Keyfield Ter, St.Alb. AL1 65 CD21
Keyham Ho, W2 15 J7
Keymer Cl, Bigg.H. TN16 260 EK116
Keymer Rd, SW2 203 DM89
Keynes Cl, N2 142 DF55
Keynsham Av, Wdf.Grn. IG8 124 EE49
Keynsham Gdns, SE9 206 EL85
Keynsham Rd, SE9 206 EK85
Morden SM4 222 DB102
Keynsham Wk, Mord. SM4 222 DB102
Keynton Cl, Hert. SG14 53 DM08
Keys, The, Gt Warley CM13
off Eagle Way 129 FW51
Keyse Rd, SE1 32 A7
Keysers Est, Brox. EN10 71 EB21
Keysers Rd, Brox. EN10 71 EA22
Keysham Av, Houns. TW5
off The Avenue 177 BU81
Keys Ho, Enf. EN3
off Beaconsfield Rd 105 DX37
Keys Meadow Prim Sch,
Enf. EN3 off Tysoe Av 105 DZ36
Keystone Cres, N1 18 B1
Keywood Dr, Sun. TW16 197 BU93
Keyworth Cl, E5 145 DY63
Keyworth Pl, SE1 31 H6
Keyworth Prim Sch, SE17 42 G1
Keyworth St, SE1 31 H6
Kezia Ms, SE8 33 L10
Kezia St, SE8 45 L1
Khalsa Av, Grav. DA12 213 GJ87
Khalsa Ct, N22 121 DP53
Khalsa Prim Sch, Slou.
SL2 off Wexham Rd 154 AU72
Khama Rd, SW17 202 DE91
Khartoum Pl, Grav. DA12 213 GJ86
Khartoum Rd, E13 24 A3
SW17 202 DD91
Ilford IG1 147 EP64
Khyber Rd, SW11 40 C9
★ Kia Oval, The (Surrey CCC),
SE11 42 D2
Kibes La, Ware SG12 55 DX06
Kibworth St, SW8 42 C5
Kidborough Down, Bkhm
KT23 268 CA127
KIDBROOKE, SE3 186 EH83
Kidbrooke 186 EH83
Kidbrooke Gdns, SE3 47 N8
Kidbrooke Gro, SE3 47 P6
Kidbrooke Interchange,
SE3 186 EJ83
Kidbrooke La, SE9 186 EL84
Kidbrooke Pk Cl, SE3 186 EH81
Kidbrooke Pk Prim Sch,
SE3 off Hargood Rd 186 EJ81
Kidbrooke Pk Rd, SE3 186 EH81
Kidbrooke Sch, SE3
off Corelli Rd 186 EK82
Kidbrooke Way, SE3 186 EH82
Kidderminster Pl, Croy. CR0
off Kidderminster Rd 223 DP102
Kidderminster Rd, Croy. CR0 223 DP102
Slough SL2 153 AN69
Kidderpore Av, NW3 142 DA63
Kidderpore Gdns, NW3 142 DA63
Kidd Pl, SE7 37 H10
Kidman Cl, Gidea Pk RM2 150 FJ55
Kidworth Cl, Horl. RH6 290 DF147
Kielder Cl, Ilf. IG6 125 ET51
Kiffen St, EC2 19 M4
Kilberry Cl, Islw. TW7 179 CD81
Kilbride Ct, Hem.H. HP2
off Aycliffe Dr 62 BM16
KILBURN, NW6 5 J10
Kilburn 4 F5
Kilburn Br, NW6 5 K9
Kilburn Gate, NW6 5 L10
Kilburn High Road 5 K9
Kilburn High Rd, NW6 5 H6
Kilburn La, W9 14 D3
W10 14 D3
Kilburn Park 5 J10
Kilburn Pk Jun Sch, NW6 15 H1
Kilburn Pk Rd, NW6 15 J3
Kilburn Pl, NW6 5 K9
Kilburn Priory, NW6 5 L9
Kilburn Sq, NW6 5 J8
Kilburn Vale, NW6 5 L9
Kilby Cl, Wat. WD25 98 BX35
Kilby Ct, SE10 off Child La 35 M7
Kilcorral Cl, Epsom KT17 239 CU114
Kildare Cl, Ruis. HA4 138 BW60
Kildare Gdns, W2 15 K8
Kildare Rd, E16 23 N6
Kildare Ter, W2 15 K8
Kildare Wk, E14 22 A9
Kildonan Cl, Wat. WD17 97 BT39
Kildoran Rd, SW2 203 DL85
Kildowan Rd, Ilf. IG3 148 EU60
Kilfillan Gdns, Berk. HP4 60 AU20
Kilgour Rd, SE23 205 DY86
Kilkie St, SW6 39 N9
Killarney Rd, SW18 202 DC86
Killasser Ct, Tad. KT20 255 CW123
Killburns Mill Cl, Wall. SM6
off London Rd 223 DH103
Killearn Rd, SE6 205 ED88
Killester Gdns, Wor.Pk. KT4 239 CV105
Killewarren Way, Orp. BR5 228 EW100
Killick Cl, Dunt.Grn TN13 278 FE121
Killick Ms, Sutt. SM3 239 CY107
Killick St, N1 8 C10
Killieser Av, SW2 203 DL89
Killigrew Inf & Nurs Sch,
St.Alb. AL2 off West Av 82 CB25
Killigrew Jun Sch, St.Alb.
AL2 off West Av 82 CB25
Killip Cl, E16 23 M8
Killowen Av, Nthlt. UB5 138 CC64
Killowen Cl, Tad. KT20 255 CX122
Killowen Rd, E9 11 J5
Killy Hill, Chobham GU24 232 AS108
Killyon Rd, SW8 41 M8
Killyon Ter, SW8 41 M9
Kilmaine Rd, SW6 38 F5
Kilmarnock Gdns, Dag. RM8
off Lindsey Rd 148 EW62
Kilmarnock Pk, Reig. RH2 272 DB133
Kilmarnock Rd, Wat. WD19 116 BX49
Kilmarsh Rd, W6 26 A8
Kilmartin Av, SW16 223 DM97
Kilmartin Rd, Ilf. IG3 148 EU61
Kilmartin Way, Horn. RM12 149 FH64
Kilmington Cl, Hutt. CM13 131 GB47
Kilmington Rd, SW13 181 CU79
Kilmiston Av, Shep. TW17 217 BQ100
Kilmorey Gdns, Twick. TW1 199 CH85
Kilmorey Rd, Twick. TW1 179 CH84
Kilmorie Prim Sch, SE23
off Kilmorie Rd 205 DY89
Kilmorie Rd, SE23 205 DY88
Kiln Av, Amer. HP6 94 AW38
Kiln Cl, Harling. UB3 177 BR79
Potten End HP4 61 BB17
Kiln Ct, Beac. HP9 132 AG55
Kilncroft, Hem.H. HP3 63 BP22
Kilndown, Grav. DA12 213 GK93
Kilner St, E14 22 A7
Kilnfield, Welw.G.C. AL7 51 CZ06
Kiln Flds, Woob.Grn HP10 132 AE61
Kiln Grd, Hem.H. HP3 62 BN22
Kiln Ho Cl, Ware SG12 55 DY05
Kiln La, B.End SL8 132 AC60
Brockham RH3 286 CP135
Church Langley CM17 74 EW16
Epsom KT17 238 CS111
Hedgerley SL2 133 AQ60
Horley RH6 290 DG146
Ley Hill HP5 78 AV31
Ripley GU23 250 BH124
Wooburn Green HP10 132 AC60
Kiln Ms, SW17 202 DD92
Kiln Pl, NW5 7 H2
Kiln Rd, N.Wld Bas. CM16 92 FA27
Kilnside, Clay. KT10 237 CG108
Kiln Wk, Red. RH1 288 DG139
Kiln Way, Bad.Dene RM17 192 FZ78
Northwood HA6 115 BS51
Kilnwood, Halst. TN14 246 EZ113
Kiln Wd La, Hav.at.Bow. RM4 127 FD50
Kilpatrick Way, Hayes UB4 158 BY71
Kilravock St, W10 14 E3
Kilross Rd, Felt. TW14 197 BR88
Kilrue La, Hersham KT12 235 BT105
Kilrush Ter, Wok. GU21 249 BA116
Kilsby Wk, Dag. RM9
off Rugby Rd 168 EV65
Kilsha Rd, Walt. KT12 217 BV100
Kilsmore La, Chsht EN8 89 DX28
Kilvinton Dr, Enf. EN2 104 DR38
Kilworth Av, Shenf. CM15 131 GA44
Kilworth Cl, Welw.G.C. AL7 52 DB11
Kimbell Gdns, SW6 38 E7
Kimbell Pl, SE3
off Tudway Rd 186 EJ84
Kimber Cl, Wind. SL4 173 AM83
Kimber Ct, Guil. GU4
off Gilliat Dr 265 BD132
Kimberley Av, E6 166 EL68
SE15 44 F9
Ilford IG2 147 ER59
Romford RM7 149 FC58
Kimberley Cl, Horl. RH6 290 DE148
Slough SL3 175 AZ77
Kimberley Dr, Sid. DA14 208 EX89
Kimberley Gdns, N4 143 DP57
Enfield EN1 104 DT41
● Kimberley Ind Est, E17 123 DZ53
Kimberley Pl, Pur. CR8
off Brighton Rd 241 DN111
Kimberley Ride, Cob. KT11 236 CB113
Kimberley Rd, E4 124 EE46
E11 145 ED61
E16 23 L4
E17 123 DZ53
N17 122 DU54
N18 122 DV51
NW6 4 F8
SW9 42 B9
Beckenham BR3 225 DX96
Croydon CR0 223 DP100
St. Albans AL3 64 CC19
Kimberley Wk, Walt. KT12
off Cottimore La 217 BV101
Kimberley Way, E4 124 EE46
Kimber Pl, Houns. TW4
off Meadow Cl 198 CA87
Kimber Rd, SW18 202 DA87
Kimbers Dr, Burn. SL1 153 AK69
Kimble Cl, Wat. WD18 97 BS44
Kimble Cres, Bushey WD23 116 CC45
Kimble Rd, SW19 202 DD93
Kimbolton Cl, SE12 206 EF86
Kimbolton Grn, Borwd. WD6 100 CQ42
Kimbolton Row, SW3 28 C9
Kimmeridge Gdns, SE9 206 EL91
Kimmeridge Rd, SE9 206 EL91
Kimps Way, Hem.H. HP3 62 BN23
Kimpton Av, Brwd. CM15 130 FV45
Kimpton Cl, Hem.H. HP2 63 BP15
Kimpton Ho, SW15
off Fontley Way 201 CU87
● Kimpton Link Business Cen,
Sutt. SM3 off Kimpton Rd 221 CZ103
Kimpton Pk Way, Sutt. SM3 221 CZ103
Kimpton Pl, Wat. WD25 82 BX34
Kimpton Rd, SE5 43 L6
Sutton SM3 221 CZ103
Kimptons Cl, Pot.B. EN6 85 CX33
Kimptons Mead, Pot.B. EN6 85 CX32
● Kimpton Trade & Business
Cen, Sutt. SM3 221 CZ103
Kinburn Dr, Egh. TW20 194 AY92
Kinburn St, SE16 33 J4
Kincaid Rd, SE15 44 E5
Kincardine Gdns, W9 15 J5
Kinch Gro, Wem. HA9 140 CM59
Kincraig Dr, Sev. TN13 278 FG124
Kinder Cl, SE28 168 EX73
Kinderscout, Hem.H. HP3 62 BN22
Kindersley Way, Abb.L. WD5 81 BQ31
Kinder St, E1 20 E9
Kinderton Cl, N14 121 DJ46
Kinefold Ho, N7 8 A4
● Kinetic Business Cen,
Borwd. WD6 100 CM41
Kinetic Cres, Enf. EN3 105 DZ36
Kinfauns Av, Horn. RM11 150 FJ58
Kinfauns Rd, SW2 203 DN89
Ilford IG3 148 EU60
Kingaby Gdns, Rain. RM13 169 FG66
King Acre Ct, Stai. TW18 195 BE90
King Alfred Av, SE6 205 EA90
King Alfred Rd, Rom. RM3 128 FM54
King Alfred Sch, The, NW11
off North End Rd 142 DB60
King & Queen Cl, SE9
off St. Keverne Rd 206 EL91
King & Queen St, SE17 31 K9
King & Queen Wf, SE16 33 J2
King Arthur Cl, SE15 44 G5
King Arthur Ct, Chsht EN8 89 DX31
King Athelstan Prim Sch,
Kings.T. KT1 off Villiers Rd 220 CM97
King Charles Cen, Surb.
KT5 off Hollyfield Rd 220 CM101
King Charles Cres, Surb. KT5 220 CM101
King Charles Rd, Shenley WD7 84 CL32
Surbiton KT5 220 CM99
King Charles St, SW1 29 P4
King Charles Ter, E1
off Sovereign Cl 32 F1
King Charles Wk, SW19
off Princes Way 201 CY88
Kingcup Cl, Croy. CR0 225 DX101
King David La, E1 20 G10
Kingdom St, W2 15 N7
Kingdon Rd, NW6 5 K4
King Edward Av, Dart. DA1 210 FK86
Rainham RM13 170 FK68
King Edward Ct, Wem. HA9
off Elm Rd 140 CL64
Windsor SL4 173 AR81
King Edward Dr, Chess. KT9
off Kelvin Gro 220 CL104
Grays RM16 192 GE75
King Edward Ms, SW13 181 CU81
King Edward Rd, E10 145 EC60
E17 145 DY55
Barnet EN5 102 DA42
Brentwood CM14 130 FW48
Greenhithe DA9 211 FU85
Romford RM1 149 FF58
Shenley WD7 84 CM33
Waltham Cross EN8 89 DY33
Watford WD19 98 BY44
King Edward VII Av, Wind. SL4 174 AS80
King Edward VII Hosp,
Wind. SL4 173 AQ83
King Edward VII's Hosp
for Officers, W1 17 H6
King Edward's Gdns, W3 160 CN74
King Edwards Gro, Tedd. TW11 199 CH93
King Edward's Pl, W3 160 CN74
King Edwards Rd, E9 10 F8
N9 122 DV45
Barking IG11 167 ER67
King Edward's Rd, Enf. EN3 105 DX42
King Edwards Rd, Ruis. HA4 137 BR60
Ware SG12 55 DY05
King Edward St, EC1 19 J8
Hemel Hempstead HP3 62 BJ24
Slough SL1 173 AR75
King Edward III Ms, SE16 32 F5
King Edward Wk, SE1 30 F6
King Fahad Acad, The, W3
off Bromyard Av 160 CS73
Girls Upr Sch, W5
off Little Ealing La 179 CJ77
Kingfield Cl, Wok. GU22 249 AZ120
Kingfield Dr, Wok. GU22 249 AZ120
Kingfield Gdns, Wok. GU22 249 AZ120
Kingfield Grn, Wok. GU22 249 AZ120
Kingfield Rd, W5 159 CK70
Woking GU22 248 AY120
Kingfield Sch, Wok. GU22
off Kingfield Rd 249 BA120
Kingfield St, E14 34 F9
Kingfisher Av, E11
off Eastern Av 146 EH58
Kingfisher Cl, SE28 168 EW73
Broxbourne EN10 71 EA20
Harrow Weald HA3 117 CF52
Hersham KT12 236 BY106
Hutton CM13 131 GA45
Northwood HA6 115 BP53
Orpington BR5 228 EX98
Stanstead Abbotts SG12
off Lawrence Av 55 EC12
Kingfisher Ct, SW19
off Queensmere Rd 201 CY89
Enfield EN2 off Mount Vw 103 DM38
Sheerwater GU21
off Blackmore Cres 233 BC114
Surbiton KT6 off Ewell Rd 220 CM101
Sutton SM1
off Sandpiper Rd 239 CZ106
Woking GU22
off Vale Fm Rd 248 AX117
Kingfisher Dr, Green. DA9 211 FU85
Guildford GU4 265 BC132
Hemel Hempstead HP3 80 BM25
Redhill RH1 272 DG131
Richmond TW10 199 CH91
Staines-upon-Thames TW18 195 BF91
Kingfisher Gdns, S.Croy. CR2 243 DX111
Kingfisher Height, Grays
RM17 192 GA78
Kingfisher Ho, SW18 182 DC83
Kingfisher Lure, Kings L. WD4 81 BP29
Loudwater WD3 96 BH42
Kingfisher Ms, SE13 185 EB84
Kingfisher Pl, N22
off Clarendon Rd 121 DM54
Kingfisher Rd, Upmin. RM14 151 FT60
Kingfishers, Denh.UB9
off Patrons Way E 135 BF58
Kingfisher Sq, SE8 45 P3
Kingfisher St, E6 25 H6
Kingfisher Wk, NW9 118 CS54
Kingfisher Way, NW10 140 CR64
Beckenham BR3 225 DX99
King Frederik IX Twr, SE16 33 N6
King Gdns, Croy. CR0 241 DP106
King George Av, E16 24 E8
Bushey WD23 98 CB44
Ilford IG2 147 ER57
Walton-on-Thames KT12 218 BX102
King George Cl, Rom. RM7 149 FC55
Sunbury-on-Thames TW16 197 BS92
King George Cres, Wem. HA0 139 CK64
King George V 37 M3
King George V Dock, E16 37 J2
King George V Rd, Amer. HP6 77 AR38
King George Hosp, Ilf. IG3 148 EV57
King George Rd, Wal.Abb. EN9 89 EC34
Ware SG12 55 DY05
King Georges Av, Wat. WD18 97 BS43
King Georges Dr, New Haw
KT15 234 BG110
Southall UB1 158 BZ71
King George VI Av, Mitch. CR4 222 DF98
Westerham TN16 260 EK116
King George Sq, Rich. TW10 200 CM86
King Georges Rd, Pilg.Hat.
CM15 130 FV44
● King George's Trd Est,
Chess. KT9 238 CN105
King George St, SE10 46 F5
Kingham Cl, SW18 202 DC87
W11 26 E4
King Harold Ct, Wal.Abb.
EN9 off Sun St 89 EC33
King Harold Sch, Wal.Abb.
EN9 off Broomstick Hall Rd 90 EE33
King Harolds Way, Bexh. DA7 188 EX80
King Harry La, St.Alb. AL3 64 CA21
King Harry St, Hem.H. HP2 62 BK21
King Henry Ms, Har. HA2 139 CE60
Orpington BR6
off Osgood Av 245 ET106
King Henrys Ct, Wal.Abb.
EN9 off Deer Pk Way 105 EC36
King Henry's Drive 243 EB109
King Henry's Dr, New Adgtn
CR0 243 EC109
King Henry's Ms, Enf. EN3 105 EA37
King Henry's Reach, W6 38 B2
King Henry's Rd, NW3 6 D7
Kingston upon Thames KT1 220 CP97
King Henry St, N16 9 N2
King Henry's Wk, N1 9 N4
Epp. CM16 off Boleyn Row 92 EV29
King Henry Ter, E1 32 F1
Kinghorn St, EC1 19 J7
King James Av, Cuffley EN6 87 DL29
King James Ct, SE1 31 H5
King James St, SE1 31 H5
King John Ct, EC2 19 P4
King Johns Cl, Wrays. TW19 194 AW86
King John St, E1 21 K7
King Johns Wk, SE9 206 EK88
Kinglake Ct, Wok. GU21
off Raglan Rd 248 AS118
Kinglake Est, SE17 31 P10
Kinglake St, SE17 43 N1
Kinglet Cl, E7 13 N4
● Kingley Pk, Kings L. WD4 81 BP29
Kingly Ct, W1 17 M10
Kingly St, W1 17 L9
Kingsand Rd, SE12 206 EG89
Kings Arbour, Sthl. UB2 178 BY78
Kings Arms Ct, E1 20 C7
Kings Arms Yd, EC2 19 L8
Kingsash Dr, Hayes UB4 158 BY70
Kings Av, N10 142 DG55
N21 121 DP46
King's Av, SW4 203 DK87
SW12 203 DK88
Kings Av, W5 159 CK72
Bromley BR1 206 EF93
Buckhurst Hill IG9 124 EK47
Byfleet KT14 234 BK112
Carshalton SM5 240 DE108
Greenford UB6 158 CB72
Hemel Hempstead HP3 62 BM24
Hounslow TW3 178 CB81
New Malden KT3 220 CS98
Redhill RH1 288 DE136
Romford RM6 148 EZ58
Sunbury-on-Thames TW16 197 BT92
Watford WD18 97 BT42
Woodford Green IG8 124 EH51
King's Av Prim Sch, SW4
off King's Av 203 DL85
King's Av Sch Early Years Cen,
SW4 off Park Hill 203 DL85
Kings Bench St, SE1 31 H4
Kings Bench Wk, EC4 18 F9
Kingsbridge Av, W3 180 CM75
Kingsbridge Circ, Rom. RM3 128 FL51
Kingsbridge Cl, Rom. RM3 128 FL51
Kingsbridge Ct, E14
off Dockers Tanner Rd 34 B7
Kingsbridge Cres, Sthl. UB1 158 BZ71
Kingsbridge Dr, NW7 119 CX52
Kingsbridge Rd, W10 14 B8
Barking IG11 167 ER68
Morden SM4 221 CX101
Romford RM3 128 FL51
Southall UB2 178 BZ77
Walton-on-Thames KT12 217 BV101
Kingsbridge Way, Hayes UB4 157 BS69
Kingsbrook, Lthd. KT22
off Ryebrook Rd 253 CG118
KINGSBURY, NW9 140 CP58
Kingsbury 140 CN57
Kingsbury Av, St.Alb. AL3 64 CC19
Kingsbury Circle, NW9 140 CN57
Kingsbury Cres, Stai. TW18 195 BD91
Kingsbury Dr, Old Wind. SL4 194 AV86
Kingsbury Grn Prim Sch,
NW9 off Old Kenton La 140 CQ57
Kingsbury High Sch,
Lwr Sch, NW9
off Bacon La 140 CQ56
Upr Sch, NW9
off Princes Av 140 CP56
Kingsbury Ms, St.Alb. AL3 64 CB19
Kingsbury Rd, N1 9 P4
NW9 140 CP57
Kingsbury Ter, N1 9 P4
● Kingsbury Trd Est, NW9 140 CQ58
★ Kingsbury Watermill,
St.Alb. AL3 64 CB19
Kings Butts, SE9
off Strongbow Cres 207 EM85
Kings Chace Vw, Enf. EN2
off Crofton Way 103 DN40
Kings Chase, Brwd. CM14 130 FW48
East Molesey KT8 218 CC97
Kingsclere Cl, SW15 201 CU87
Kingsclere Ct, Barn. EN5
off Gloucester Rd 102 DC43
Kingsclere Pl, Enf. EN2 104 DQ40
Kingscliffe Gdns, SW19 201 CZ88
Kings Cl, E10 145 EB59
NW4 141 CX56
Beaconsfield HP9 132 AG55
Chalfont St. Giles HP8 112 AV47
Chipperfield WD4 80 BH31
Dartford DA1 189 FE84
Northwood HA6 115 BT51
Staines-upon-Thames TW18 196 BK94
Thames Ditton KT7 219 CG100
Walton-on-Thames KT12 217 BV102
King's Cl, Wat. WD18
off Lady's Cl 98 BW42
Kings Coll, Guil. GU2
off Southway 264 AS134
King's Coll - Denmark Hill
Campus, SE5
off Champion Hill 184 DR83
King's Coll - Guy's Campus,
SE1 31 L6
King's Coll - Hampstead
Campus, NW3
off Kidderpore Av 142 DA63
King's Coll - Maughan Lib &
Information Services Cen,
WC2 18 E8
King's Coll - Strand Campus,
WC2 18 D10
King's Coll - Waterloo Campus,
SE1 30 E3
King's Coll Hosp, SE5 43 L9
Kings Coll Rd, NW3 6 C6
Ruislip HA4 137 BT58
King's Coll Sch, SW19
off Southside Common 201 CW93
Kingscote Rd, W4 180 CR76
Croydon CR0 224 DV101
New Malden KT3 220 CR97
Kingscote Sch, Ger.Cr.
SL9 off Oval Way 134 AY55
Kingscote St, EC4 18 G10
Kings Ct, E13 166 EH67
W6 off Hamlet Gdns 181 CU77
Berkhamsted HP4
off Lower Kings Rd 60 AW18
Borehamwood WD6
off Bennington Dr 100 CM39
Tadworth KT20 255 CW122
Wembley HA9 140 CP61
Kings Ct First Sch, Old Wind.
SL4 off Ashbrook Rd 194 AV87
Kingscourt Rd, SW16 203 DK90
Kings Ct S, SW3
off Chelsea Manor Gdns 40 D1
Kings Cres, N4 144 DQ62
Kings Cres Est, N4 144 DQ61
Kingscroft, Welw.G.C. AL7 52 DB08

Kingscroft Jun Sch, Stai. TW18 off Park Av 196 BG93
Kingscroft Rd, NW2 4 F4
Banstead SM7 256 DD115
Leatherhead KT22 253 CH120
KING'S CROSS, N1 7 P8
⇌ King's Cross 18 A1
King's Cross Br, N1 18 B2
Kings Cross La, S.Nutfld RH1 289 DL136
King's Cross Rd, WC1 18 D2
⊖ King's Cross St. Pancras 18 A1
Kingsdale Ct, Wal.Abb. EN9 off Lamplighters Cl 90 EG34
Kingsdale Foundation Sch, SE21 off Alleyn Pk 204 DS90
Kingsdale Gdns, W11 26 D3
Kingsdale Rd, SE18 187 ET80
SE20 205 DX94
Berkhamsted HP4 60 AU20
Kingsdene, Tad. KT20 255 CV121
Kingsdon La, Harl. CM17 74 EW16
Kingsdown Av, W3 160 CS73
W13 179 CH75
South Croydon CR2 241 DP109
Kingsdown Cl, SE16 44 F1
W10 14 D9
Gravesend DA12 off Farley Rd 213 GM88
Kingsdowne Rd, Surb. KT6 220 CL101
Kingsdown Rd, E11 146 EE62
N19 143 DL61
Epsom KT17 239 CU113
Sutton SM3 239 CY106
Kingsdown Way, Brom. BR2 226 EG101
Kings Dr, Edg. HA8 118 CM49
Gravesend DA12 213 GH90
Surbiton KT5 220 CN101
Teddington TW11 199 CD92
Thames Ditton KT7 219 CH100
Wembley HA9 140 CP61
Kings Dr, The, Hersham KT12 235 BT110
Kingsend, Ruis. HA4 137 BR60
KINGS FARM, Grav. DA12 213 GJ90
Kings Fm Av, Rich. TW10 180 CN84
King's Fm Prim Sch, Grav. DA12 off Cedar Av 213 GJ91
Kings Fm Rd, Chorl. WD3 95 BD44
Kingsfield, Albury GU5 282 BL144
Hoddesdon EN11 71 EA15
Windsor SL4 173 AK81
Kingsfield Av, Har. HA2 138 CB56
● Kingsfield Business Cen, Red. RH1 288 DG135
Kingsfield Ct, Wat. WD19 116 BX45
Kingsfield Dr, Enf. EN3 105 DX35
Kingsfield Ho, SE9 206 EK90
Kingsfield Rd, Har. HA1 139 CD59
Watford WD19 116 BX45
Kingsfield Ter, Dart. DA1 210 FK85
Kingsfield Way, Enf. EN3 105 DX35
Redhill RH1 288 DG135
Kingsford Comm Sch, E6 25 J8
Kingsford St, NW5 6 E3
Kingsford Way, E6 25 K7
Kings Gdns, NW6 5 K7
Ilford IG1 147 ER60
Upminster RM14 151 FS59
King's Garth Ms, SE23 off London Rd 204 DW89
Kings Gate, Add. KT15 234 BH105
Kingsgate, St.Alb. AL3 off King Harry La 64 CB22
Wembley HA9 140 CQ62
Kingsgate Av, N3 142 DA55
Kingsgate Cl, Bexh. DA7 188 EY81
Orpington BR5 off Main Rd 228 EW97
Kingsgate Est, N1 9 P5
Kingsgate Pl, NW6 5 J7
Kingsgate Prim Sch, NW6 5 J6
Kingsgate Rd, NW6 5 J6
Kingston upon Thames KT2 220 CL95
Kings Grn, Loug. IG10 106 EL41
Kingsground, SE9 206 EL87
Kings Gro, SE15 44 F5
Romford RM1 149 FG57
Kings Hall Ms, SE13 46 F10
Kings Hall Rd, Beck. BR3 205 DY94
Kings Head Hill, E4 123 EB45
Kings Head La, Byfleet KT14 234 BK111
Kings Head Yd, SE1 31 L3
Kings Highway, SE18 187 ES79
Kingshill, SE17 31 K9
Kings Hill, Loug. IG10 106 EL40
Kingshill Av, Har. HA3 139 CH56
Hayes UB4 157 BS69
Northolt UB5 157 BU69
Romford RM5 127 FC51
St. Albans AL4 65 CG17
Worcester Park KT4 221 CU101
Kingshill Cl, Hayes UB4 157 BU69
Kingshill Dr, Har. HA3 139 CH55
Kingshill Way, Berk. HP4 60 AU21
Kingshold Est, E9 10 G8
Kingshold Rd, E9 11 H7
Kingsholm Gdns, SE9 186 EK84
King's Ho, SW8 42 B4
King's Ho Sch, Jun Dept, Rich. TW10 off Kings Rd 200 CM85
Sen Dept, Rich. TW10 off Kings Rd 200 CM85
Kingshurst Rd, SE12 206 EG87
● Kingside, SE18 36 G7
King's Keep, SW15 off Westleigh Av 201 CX85
Kings Keep, Kings.T. KT1 off Beaufort Rd 220 CL98
KINGSLAND, N1 9 N5
Kingsland, NW8 6 D9
Harlow CM18 73 EQ17
Potters Bar EN6 85 CZ33
Kingsland Basin, N1 9 P8
Kingsland Grn, E8 9 P4
Kingsland High St, E8 10 A4
Kingsland Pas, E8 9 P4
Kingsland Rd, E2 19 P2
E8 9 P8
E13 24 C3
Hemel Hempstead HP1 62 BG22
Kingsland Shop Cen, E8 10 A4
Kings La, Chipper. WD4 80 BG31
Englefield Green TW20 194 AU92
Kings La, Sutton SM1 240 DD107
KINGS LANGLEY, WD4 80 BM30
⇌ Kings Langley 81 BQ30
Kings Langley Bypass, Hem.H. HP1, HP3 62 BG23
Kings Langley WD4 80 BK28
Kings Langley Prim Sch, Kings L. WD4 off Common La 80 BM28
Kings Langley Sch, Kings L. WD4 off Love La 80 BL28
Kingslawn Cl, SW15 201 CV85
Kingslea, Lthd. KT22 253 CG120
Kingsleigh Cl, Brent. TW8 179 CK79
Kingsleigh Pl, Mitch. CR4 222 DF97
Kingsleigh Wk, Brom. BR2 off Stamford Dr 226 EF98
Kingsley Av, W13 159 CG72
Banstead SM7 256 DA115
Borehamwood WD6 100 CM40
Cheshunt EN8 88 DV29
Dartford DA1 210 FN85
Englefield Green TW20 194 AV93
Hounslow TW3 178 CC82
Southall UB1 158 CA73
Sutton SM1 240 DD105
Kingsley Cl, N2 142 DC57
Dagenham RM10 149 FB63
Horley RH6 290 DF146
Kingsley Ct, Edg. HA8 118 CP47
Welwyn Garden City AL7 51 CZ13
Kingsley Dr, Wor.Pk. KT4 off Badgers Copse 221 CT103
Kingsley Flats, SE1 31 N8
Kingsley Gdns, E4 123 EA50
Hornchurch RM11 150 FK56
Ottershaw KT16 233 BD107
Kingsley Grn, St.Alb. WD7 83 CJ31
Kingsley Gro, Reig. RH2 288 DA137
Kingsley High Sch, Har. HA3 off Whittlesea Rd 116 CC52
Kingsley Ms, E1 32 F1
W8 27 M7
Chislehurst BR7 207 EP93
Kingsley Path, Slou. SL2 153 AK70
Kingsley Pl, N6 142 DG59
Kingsley Prim Sch, Croy. CR0 off Thomson Cres 223 DN102
Kingsley Rd, E7 13 P6
E17 123 EC54
N13 121 DN49
NW6 5 H8
SW19 202 DB92
Croydon CR0 223 DN102
Harrow HA2 138 CC63
Horley RH6 290 DF146
Hounslow TW3 178 CC82
Hutton CM13 131 GD45
Ilford IG6 125 EQ53
Loughton IG10 107 ER41
Orpington BR6 245 ET107
Pinner HA5 138 BZ56
Kingsley St, SW11 40 F10
Kingsley Wk, Grays RM16 193 GG77
Kingsley Way, N2 142 DC58
Kingsley Wd Dr, SE9 207 EM90
Kings Lo, Ruis. HA4 off Pembroke Rd 137 BS60
Kingslyn Cres, SE19 224 DS95
Kings Lynn Cl, Rom. RM3 off Kings Lynn Dr 128 FK51
Kings Lynn Dr, Rom. RM3 128 FK51
Kings Lynn Path, Rom. RM3 off Kings Lynn Dr 128 FK51
Kings Mall, W6 26 A9
Kingsman Par, SE18 37 K7
Kingsman St, SE18 37 K7
Kingsmead, Barn. EN5 102 DA42
Biggin Hill TN16 260 EK116
Cuffley EN6 87 DL28
Richmond TW10 200 CM86
St. Albans AL4 65 CK17
Sawbridgeworth CM21 58 EY06
Kings Mead, Smallfield RH6 291 DP148
South Nutfield RH1 289 DL136
Kingsmead, Wal.Cr. EN8 89 DX28
Kingsmead Av, N9 122 DV46
NW9 140 CR59
Mitcham CR4 223 DJ97
Romford RM1 149 FE58
Sunbury-on-Thames TW16 218 BW97
Surbiton KT6 220 CN103
Worcester Park KT4 221 CV104
Kingsmead Cl, Epsom KT19 238 CR108
Roydon CM19 72 EH16
Sidcup DA15 208 EU89
Teddington TW11 199 CH93
Kingsmead Dr, Nthlt. UB5 158 BZ66
Kingsmead Est, E9 11 M2
Kingsmead Hill, Roydon CM19 72 EH16
Kingsmead Ho, E9 off Kingsmead Way 11 M1
Kings Meadow, Kings L. WD4 80 BN28
Kings Mead Pk, Clay. KT10 237 CE108
Kingsmead Prim Sch, E9 11 M1
Kingsmead Rd, SW2 203 DN89
Kingsmead Sch, Enf. EN1 off Southbury Rd 104 DU41
Kingsmead Way, E9 11 M1
Kingsmere Cl, SW15 off Felsham Rd 181 CX83
Kingsmere Pk, NW9 140 CP60
Kingsmere Pl, N16 144 DR60
Kingsmere Rd, SW19 201 CX89
Kings Ms, SW4 off King's Av 203 DL85
King's Ms, WC1 18 D5
Kings Ms, Chig. IG7 125 EQ47
● Kingsmill Business Pk, Kings.T. KT1 220 CM97
Kingsmill Ct, Hat. AL10 off Drakes Way 67 CV20
Kingsmill Gdns, Dag. RM9 148 EZ64
Kings Mill La, Red. RH1 289 DK138
Kingsmill Rd, Dag. RM9 148 EZ64
Kingsmill Ter, NW8 6 B10
KINGSMOOR, Harl. CM19 73 EQ20
Kingsmoor Inf Sch, Harl. CM18 off Ployters Rd 73 EQ19
Kingsmoor Jun Sch, Harl. CM18 off Ployters Rd 73 EQ19
Kingsmoor Rd, Harl. CM19 73 EP18
Kingsnympton Pk, Kings.T. KT2 200 CP93
Kings Oak, Rom. RM7 148 FA55
Kings Oak Hosp, The, Enf. EN2 103 DN38
King Solomon Acad, NW1 16 C6
King Solomon High Sch, Ilf. IG6 off Forest Rd 125 ER54
King's Orchard, SE9 206 EL86
Kings Paddock, Hmptn. TW12 218 CC95
Kings Par, Cars. SM5 off Wrythe La 222 DE104
Kings Pk, Colnbr. SL3 175 BD80
Kingspark Ct, E18 146 EG55
● Kings Pk Ind Est, Kings L. WD4 81 BP29
King's Pas, E11 146 EE59
Kings Pas, Kings.T. KT1 off Market Pl 219 CK96
★ Kings Pl, N1 8 B10
Kings Pl, SE1 31 J5
W4 180 CQ78
Buckhurst Hill IG9 124 EJ47
Loughton IG10 124 EK45
King Sq, EC1 19 J3
Kings Quarter Apts, N1 off Copenhagen St 8 B9
King's Quay, SW10 39 P6
● King's Reach Twr, SE1 30 F2
Kings Ride Gate, Rich. TW10 180 CN84
Kingsridge, SW19 201 CY89
Kingsridge Gdns, Dart. DA1 210 FK86
Kings Rd, E4 123 ED46
E6 166 EJ67
E11 146 EE59
King's Rd, N17 122 DT53
Kings Rd, N18 122 DU50
N22 121 DM53
NW10 161 CV66
SE25 224 DU97
King's Rd, SW3 28 D10
SW6 39 M5
SW10 39 M5
Kings Rd, SW14 180 CR83
SW19 202 DA93
W5 159 CK71
Barking IG11 off North St 167 EQ66
Barnet EN5 101 CW41
Berkhamsted HP4 60 AU20
Biggin Hill TN16 260 EJ116
Brentwood CM14 130 FW48
Chalfont St. Giles HP8 112 AX47
Egham TW20 195 BA91
Feltham TW13 198 BW88
Guildford GU1 264 AX134
Harrow HA2 138 BZ61
King's Rd, Hert. SG13 54 DU08
Kings Rd, Horl. RH6 290 DG148
Kingston upon Thames KT2 200 CL94
London Colney AL2 83 CJ26
Long Ditton KT6 219 CJ102
Mitcham CR4 222 DG97
New Haw KT15 234 BH110
Orpington BR6 245 ET105
Richmond TW10 200 CM85
Romford RM1 149 FG57
St. Albans AL3 64 CB19
Shalford GU4 280 AY141
Slough SL1 174 AS76
Sutton SM2 240 DA110
Teddington TW11 199 CD92
Twickenham TW1 199 CH86
King's Rd, Uxb. UB8 156 BK68
Kings Rd, Wal.Cr. EN8 89 DY34
Walton-on-Thames KT12 217 BV103
West Drayton UB7 176 BM75
King's Rd, Wind. SL4 173 AR82
Kings Rd, Wok. GU21 249 BA116
Kings Rd Bungalows, Har. HA2 off Kings Rd 138 BZ62
King's Scholars' Pas, SW1 29 L7
King Stable Ct, Wind. SL4 off King Stable St 173 AR80
King Stable St, Eton SL4 173 AR80
King Stairs Cl, SE16 32 F4
King's Ter, NW1 7 L9
Kings Ter, Islw. TW7 off South St 179 CG83
Kingsthorpe Rd, SE26 205 DX91
⇌ Kingston 220 CL95
Kingston Av, E.Hors. KT24 267 BS126
Feltham TW14 197 BS86
Leatherhead KT22 253 CH121
Sutton SM3 221 CY104
West Drayton UB7 156 BM73
Kingston Br, Kings.T. KT1 219 CK96
● Kingston Business Cen, Chess. KT9 220 CL104
Kingston Bypass, SW15 200 CS93
SW20 200 CS93
Esher KT10 219 CG104
New Malden KT3 221 CU96
Surbiton KT5, KT6 220 CL104
Kingston Cl, Nthlt. UB5 158 BZ66
Romford RM6 148 EY55
Teddington TW11 199 CH93
Kingston Coll, Kings.T. KT1 off Kingston Hall Rd 219 CK97
Sch of Art & Design, Kings.T. KT2 off Richmond Rd 220 CL95
Kingston Ct, Nthflt DA11 212 GB85
Kingston Cres, Ashf. TW15 196 BJ92
Beckenham BR3 225 DZ95
Kingston Gdns, Croy. CR0 223 DL104
Kingston Gram Sch, Kings.T. KT2 off London Rd 220 CM96
Kingston Hall Rd, Kings.T. KT1 219 CK97
Kingston Hill, Kings.T. KT2 200 CQ93
Kingston Hill Av, Rom. RM6 126 EY54
Kingston Hill Pl, Kings.T. KT2 200 CQ91
Kingston Hosp, Kings.T. KT2 220 CP95
● Kingston Ho Est, Long Dit. KT6 219 CH100
Kingston Ho Gdns, Lthd. KT22 off Upper Fairfield Rd 253 CH121
Kingston La, Lthd. KT24 266 BM127
Teddington TW11 199 CG92
Uxbridge UB8 156 BL69
West Drayton UB7 176 BM75
Kingston Lo, N.Mal. KT3 off Kingston Rd 220 CS98
★ Kingston Mus & Heritage Cen, Kings.T. KT1 220 CL96
Kingston Pk Est, Kings.T. KT2 200 CP93
Kingston Pl, Har. HA3 off Richmond Gdns 117 CF52
Kingston Ri, New Haw KT15 234 BG110
Kingston Rd, N9 122 DU47
SW15 201 CU88
SW19 221 CZ95
SW20 221 CW96
Ashford TW15 196 BL93
Barnet EN4 102 DD43
Epsom KT17, KT19 238 CS106
Kingston Rd, Ilford IG1 147 EP63
Kingston upon Thames KT1 220 CP97
Leatherhead KT22 253 CG117
New Malden KT3 220 CR98
Romford RM1 149 FF56
Southall UB2 178 BZ75
Staines-upon-Thames TW18 196 BJ93
Surbiton KT5 220 CP103
Teddington TW11 199 CH92
Worcester Park KT4 220 CP103
Kingston Sq, SE19 204 DR92
Leatherhead KT22 off Kingston Rd 253 CG119
Kingston Uni, Clayhills Halls of Res, Surb. KT5 off Clayhill 220 CN99
Kingston Hill, Kings.T. KT2 off Kingston Hill 200 CR92
Kingston Vale, SW15 off Kingston Vale 200 CR91
Knights Pk, Kings.T. KT1 off Grange Rd 220 CL97
Penrhyn Rd, Kings.T. KT1 off Penrhyn Rd 220 CL98
Roehampton Vale, SW15 off Friars Av 201 CT90
Seething Wells Halls of Res, Surb. KT6 off Portsmouth Rd 219 CJ100
KINGSTON UPON THAMES, KT1 & KT2 220 CL96
KINGSTON VALE, SW15 200 CS91
Kingston Vale, SW15 200 CR91
Kingstown St, NW1 6 G8
King St, E13 23 N5
EC2 19 K9
N2 142 DD55
N17 122 DT53
SW1 29 M3
W3 160 CP74
W6 181 CU77
WC2 18 A10
Chertsey KT16 216 BG102
Chesham HP5 76 AP32
Gravesend DA12 213 GH86
Richmond TW9 199 CK85
Southall UB2 178 BY76
Twickenham TW1 199 CG88
Watford WD18 98 BW42
King St Ms, N2 off King St 142 DD55
King's Wk, Kings.T. KT2 219 CK95
Kings Wk, Grays RM17 192 GA79
S.Croy. CR2 242 DV114
Kings Wk Shop Mall, SW3 off King's Rd 28 E10
Kings Wardrobe Apts, EC4 off Carter La 19 H9
Kings Warren, Oxshott KT22 236 CC111
Kingswater Pl, SW11 off Battersea Ch Rd 40 C5
Kingsway, N12 120 DC51
SW14 180 CP83
WC2 18 C8
Chalfont St. Peter SL9 134 AY55
Kings Way, Croy. CR0 241 DM106
Kingsway, Cuffley EN6 87 DL30
Enfield EN3 104 DV43
Farnham Common SL2 153 AP65
Kings Way, Har. HA1 139 CE56
Kingsway, Hayes UB3 157 BQ71
Iver SL0 155 BE72
New Malden KT3 221 CW98
Petts Wood BR5 227 ES99
Staines-upon-Thames TW19 196 BK88
Watford WD25 82 BW34
Wembley HA9 140 CL63
West Wickham BR4 226 EE104
Woking GU21 248 AX118
Woodford Green IG8 124 EJ50
Kingsway, The, Epsom KT17 239 CT111
Kingsway Av, S.Croy. CR2 242 DW109
Woking GU21 248 AX118
● Kingsway Business Pk, Hmptn. TW12 218 BZ95
Kingsway Cres, Har. HA2 138 CC56
Kingsway Infants' Sch, Wat. WD25 off North App 81 BU34
Kingsway Jun Sch, Wat. WD25 off Briar Rd 81 BU34
Kingsway Ms, Farn.Com. SL2 153 AQ65
Kingsway Pl, EC1 18 F4
Kingsway Rd, Sutt. SM3 239 CY108
Kingswear Rd, NW5 143 DH62
Ruislip HA4 137 BU61
Kingswell Ride, Cuffley EN6 87 DL30
● Kingsway Business Pk, Wok. GU21 233 BC114
Kings Wf, E8 9 P8
KINGSWOOD, Tad. KT20 255 CY123
KINGSWOOD, Wat. WD25 81 BV34
⇌ Kingswood 255 CZ121
Kingswood Av, NW6 4 E9
Belvedere DA17 188 EZ77
Bromley BR2 226 EE97
Hampton TW12 198 CB93
Hounslow TW3 178 BZ81
South Croydon CR2 258 DV115
Swanley BR8 229 FF98
Thornton Heath CR7 223 DN99
Kingswood Cen, The, NW9 140 CN56
Kingswood Cl, N20 102 DC44
SW8 42 B5
Ashford TW15 197 BQ91
Dartford DA1 210 FJ85
Enfield EN1 104 DS43
Englefield Green TW20 194 AX91
Guildford GU1 265 BC133
New Malden KT3 221 CT100
Orpington BR6 227 ER101
Surbiton KT6 220 CL101
Weybridge KT13 235 BP108
Kingswood Ct, SE13 off Hither Grn La 205 ED86
Kingswood Creek, Wrays. TW19 194 AX85
Kingswood Dr, SE19 204 DS91
Carshalton SM5 222 DF102
Sutton SM2 240 DB109
Kingswood Est, SE21 204 DS91
Kingswood Gra, Lwr Kgswd KT20 272 DA128
Kingswood Ho Sch, Epsom KT19 off West Hill 238 CQ113
Kingswood La, S.Croy. CR2 242 DW113
Warlingham CR6 258 DW115
Kingswood Ms, N15 off Harringay Rd 143 DP57
Kingswood Pk, N3 119 CZ54
Kings Wood Pk, Epp. CM16 92 EV29
Kingswood Pl, SE13 186 EE84
Kingswood Prim Sch, SE27 off Gipsy Rd 204 DR92
Lower Kingswood KT20 off Buckland Rd 271 CZ128
Kingswood Ri, Eng.Grn TW20 194 AX92
Kingswood Rd, E11 146 EE59
SE20 204 DW93
SW2 203 DL86
SW19 201 CZ94
W4 180 CQ76
Bromley BR2 225 ED98
Dunton Green TN13 263 FE120
Ilford IG3 148 EU60
Tadworth KT20 255 CV121
Watford WD25 81 BV34
Wembley HA9 140 CN62
King's Wd Sch, Harold Hill RM3 off Settle Rd 128 FN49
Kingswood Ter, W4 off Kingswood Rd 180 CQ76
Kingswood Way, S.Croy. CR2 242 DW113
Wallington SM6 241 DL106
Kingsworth Cl, Beck. BR3 225 DY99
Kingsworthy Cl, Kings.T. KT1 220 CM97
King's Yd, SW15 off Stanbridge Rd 38 B10
Kingthorpe Rd, NW10 160 CR66
Kingthorpe Ter, NW10 160 CR65
Kingwell Rd, Barn. EN4 102 DD38
Kingweston Cl, NW2 141 CY62
King William Ct, Wal.Abb. EN9 off Kendal Rd 105 EC35
King William IV Gdns, SE20 off St. John's Rd 204 DW93
King William La, SE10 47 J1
King William St, EC4 31 M1
King William Wk, SE10 46 F2
Kingwood City Learning Cen, The, SW6 38 E6
Kingwood Rd, SW6 38 D6
Kinlet Rd, SE18 187 EQ81
Kinloch Dr, NW9 140 CS59
Kinloch St, N7 143 DM62
Kinloss Ct, N3 off Kinloss Gdns 141 CZ56
Kinloss Gdns, N3 141 CZ56
Kinloss Rd, Cars. SM5 222 DC101
Kinnaird Av, W4 180 CQ80
Bromley BR1 206 EF93
Kinnaird Cl, Brom. BR1 206 EF93
Slough SL1 152 AJ72
Kinnaird Ho, N6 143 DK59
Kinnaird Way, Wdf.Grn. IG8 125 EM51
Kinnear Apts, N8 off Chadwell La 143 DM55
Kinnear Rd, W12 181 CT75
Kinnersley Manor, Reig. RH2 288 DC142
Kinnersley Wk, Reig. RH2 288 DB139
Kinnerton Pl N, SW1 28 F5
Kinnerton Pl S, SW1 28 F5
Kinnerton St, SW1 28 G5
Kinnerton Yd, SW1 28 F5
Kinnoul Rd, W6 38 E2
Kinross Av, Wor.Pk. KT4 221 CU103
Kinross Cl, Edg. HA8 118 CP47
Harrow HA3 140 CM57
Sunbury-on-Thames TW16 197 BT92
Kinross Dr, Sun. TW16 197 BT92
Kinross Ter, E17 123 DZ54
Kinsale Rd, SE15 184 DU83
Kinsella Gdns, SW19 201 CV92
Kinsey Ho, SE21 off Kingswood Est 204 DS91
Kintore Way, SE1 32 A8
Kintyre Cl, SW16 223 DM96
Kinveachy Gdns, SE7 36 G9
Kinver Ho, N19 off Elthorne Rd 143 DK61
Kinver Rd, SE26 204 DW91
Kipings, Tad. KT20 255 CX122
Kipling Av, Til. RM18 193 GH81
Kipling Cl, Warley CM14 130 FV50
Kipling Dr, SW19 202 DD93
Kipling Est, SE1 31 M5
Kipling Pl, Stan. HA7 117 CF51
Kipling Rd, Bexh. DA7 188 EY81
Dartford DA1 210 FP85
Kipling St, SE1 31 M5
Kipling Ter, N9 122 DR48
Kipling Twrs, Rom. RM3 127 FH52
KIPPINGTON, Sev. TN13 278 FG126
Kippington Cl, Sev. TN13 278 FF124
Kippington Dr, SE9 206 EK88
Kippington Ho, Sev. TN13 off Kippington Rd 278 FG126
Kippington Rd, Sev. TN13 278 FG124
Kirby Cl, Epsom KT19 239 CT106
Ilford IG6 125 ES51
Loughton IG10 124 EL45
Northwood HA6 115 BT51
Romford RM3 128 FN50
Kirby Est, SE16 32 E6
West Dr. UB7 off Trout Rd 156 BK73
Kirby Gro, SE1 31 N4
Kirby Rd, Dart. DA2 210 FQ87
Woking GU21 248 AW117
Kirby St, EC1 18 F6
Kirby Way, Uxb. UB8 156 BM70
Walton-on-Thames KT12 218 BW100
Kirchen Rd, W13 159 CH73
Kirkby Cl, N11 off Coverdale Rd 120 DG51
Kirkcaldy Grn, Wat. WD19 off Trevose Way 116 BW48
Kirk Ct, Sev. TN13 278 FG123
Kirkdale, SE26 204 DV89
Kirkdale Rd, E11 146 EE60
Kirkefields, Guil. GU2 264 AU131
Kirkfield Cl, W13 off Broomfield Rd 159 CH74
Kirkham Rd, E6 25 H8
Kirkham St, SE18 187 ES79
Kirkland Av, Ilf. IG5 125 EN54
Woking GU21 248 AS116
Kirkland Cl, Sid. DA15 207 ES86
Kirkland Dr, Enf. EN2 103 DP39
Kirklands, Welw.G.C. AL8 51 CX05
Kirkland Wk, E8 10 A5
Kirk La, SE18 187 EQ79
Kirkleas Rd, Surb. KT6 220 CL102
Kirklees Rd, Dag. RM8 148 EW64
Thornton Heath CR7 223 DN99
Kirkley Rd, SW19 222 DA95
Kirkly Cl, S.Croy. CR2 242 DS109
Kirkman Pl, W1 17 N7
Kirkmichael Rd, E14 22 F8
Kirk Ri, Sutt. SM1 222 DB104
Kirk Rd, E17 145 DZ58
Kirkside Rd, SE3 47 N2
Kirkstall Av, N17 144 DR56

Kirkstall Gdns, SW2 203 DK88
Kirkstall Rd, SW2 203 DK88
Kirkstead Ct, E5
off Mandeville St 145 DY63
Kirksted Rd, Mord. SM4 222 DB102
Kirkstone Lo, Islw. TW7
off Summerwood Rd 199 CF85
Kirkstone Way, Brom. BR1 206 EE94
Kirk St, WC1 18 C5
Kirkton Rd, N15 144 DS56
Kirkwall Pl, E2 21 H2
Kirkwall Spur, Slou. SL1 154 AS71
Kirkwood Rd, SE15 44 F8
Kirn Rd, W13 off Kirchen Rd 159 CH73
Kirrane Cl, N.Mal. KT3 221 CT99
Kirsty Cl, Dor. RH5 285 CJ138
Kirtle Rd, Chesh. HP5 76 AQ31
Kirtley Ho, N16
off Stamford Hill 144 DS60
Kirtley Rd, SE26 205 DY91
Kirtling St, SW8 41 L4
Kirton Cl, W4 180 CR77
Hornchurch RM12 170 FJ65
Kirton Gdns, E2 20 B3
Kirton Rd, E13 166 EJ68
Kirton Wk, Edg. HA8 118 CQ52
Kirwyn Way, SE5 43 H4
Sch Kisharon Day Sch, NW11
off Finchley Rd 141 CZ58
Kitcat Ter, E3 22 B2
Kitchen Ct, E10
off Brisbane Rd 145 EB61
Kitchener Av, Grav. DA12 213 GJ90
Kitchener Cl, St.Alb. AL1 65 CH21
Kitchener Rd, E7 166 EH65
E17 123 EB53
N2 142 DE55
N17 144 DR55
Dagenham RM10 169 FB65
Thornton Heath CR7 224 DR97
Kitcheners Mead, St.Alb. AL3 64 CC20
Jct Kitchenride Cor, Cher.
KT16 233 BA105
Kite Fld, Nthch HP4 60 AS16
Kite Pl, E2 20 D2
Kite Yd, SW11 40 E7
Kitley Gdns, SE19 224 DT95
Kitsbury Rd, Berk. HP4 60 AV19
Kitsbury Ter, Berk. HP4 60 AV19
Kitsmead La, Longcr. KT16 214 AX103
Kitson Rd, SE5 43 K4
SW13 181 CU81
Kitson Way, Harl. CM20 57 EQ14
Kitswell Way, Rad. WD7 83 CF33
Kitten La, Stans.Abb. SG12 56 EE11
Kitters Grn, Abb.L. WD5
off High St 81 BS31
Kittiwake Cl, S.Croy. CR2 243 DY110
Kittiwake Pl, Sutt. SM1
off Sandpiper Rd 239 CZ106
Kittiwake Rd, Nthlt. UB5 158 BX69
Kittiwake Way, Hayes UB4 158 BX71
Kitto Rd, SE14 45 J9
KITT'S END, Barn. EN5 101 CY37
Kitt's End Rd, Barn. EN5 101 CX36
Kittywake Ho, Slou. SL1 154 AS74
Kiver Rd, N19 143 DK61
Klea Av, SW4 203 DJ86
Kleine Wf, N1 9 P9
Knapdale Cl, SE23 204 DV89
Knapmill Rd, SE6 205 EA89
Knapmill Way, SE6 205 EB89
Knapp Cl, NW10 160 CS65
Knapp Rd, E3 22 A5
Ashford TW15 196 BM91
Knapton Ms, SW17
off Seely Rd 202 DG93
Knaresborough Dr, SW18 202 DB88
Knaresborough Pl, SW5 27 L8
Knatchbull Rd, NW10 160 CR67
SE5 43 J7
Knaves Beech, Loud. HP10 110 AD53
● Knaves Beech Business Cen,
H.Wyc. HP10
off Boundary Rd 110 AC54
● Knaves Beech Ind Est,
Loud. HP10 110 AC54
Knaves Beech Way, Loud.
HP10 110 AC54
Knaves Hollow, Woob.Moor
HP10 110 AD54
Knebworth Av, E17 123 EA53
Knebworth Cl, Barn. EN5 102 DB42
Knebworth Path, Borwd. WD6 100 CR42
Knebworth Rd, N16 144 DS63
Knee Hill, SE2 188 EW77
Knee Hill Cres, SE2 188 EW77
Knella Grn, Welw.G.C. AL7 52 DA09
Knella Rd, Welw.G.C. AL7 51 CY10
Kneller Gdns, Islw. TW7 199 CD85
Kneller Rd, SE4 185 DY84
New Malden KT3 220 CS101
Twickenham TW2 198 CC86
Knevett Ter, Houns. TW3 178 CA84
Knight Cl, Dag. RM8 148 EW61
Knight Ct, E4
off The Ridgeway 123 EC46
Knighten St, E1 32 E3
Knighthead Pt, E14 34 A6
Knightland Rd, E5 144 DV61
Knighton Cl, Rom. RM7 149 FD58
South Croydon CR2 241 DP108
Woodford Green IG8 124 EH49
Knighton Dr, Wdf.Grn. IG8 124 EG49
Knighton Grn, Buck.H. IG9
off High Rd 124 EH47
Knighton La, Buck.H. IG9 124 EH47
Knighton Pk Rd, SE26 205 DX92
Knighton Rd, E7 146 EG62
Otford TN14 263 FF116
Redhill RH1 288 DG136
Romford RM7 149 FC58
Knighton Way La, Denh. UB9 156 BH65
Knightrider Ct, EC4
off Knightrider St 19 J10
Knightrider St, EC4 19 J10
Knights Av, W5 180 CL75
⊖ Knightsbridge 28 E5
Knightsbridge, SW1 28 F5
SW7 28 D5
Knightsbridge Apts, The, SW7
off Knightsbridge 28 E5
Knightsbridge Ct, Langley
SL3 off High St 175 BA77
Knightsbridge Cres, Stai.
TW18 196 BH93
Knightsbridge Gdns, Rom.
RM7 149 FD57
Knightsbridge Grn, SW1 28 E5
Knightsbridge Way, Hem.H.
HP2 62 BL20
Knights Cl, E9 11 H3
Egham TW20 195 BD93
West Molesey KT8 218 BZ99
Windsor SL4 173 AK81
Knightscote Cl, Hare. UB9 114 BK54
Knights Ct, Kings.T. KT1 220 CL97
Romford RM6 148 EY58
Knights Fld, Eyns. DA4 230 FL104
Knightsfield, Welw.G.C. AL8 51 CY06
Knights Hill, SE27 203 DP92
Knights Hill Sq, SE27 203 DP91
Knights La, N9 122 DU48
Knights Manor Way,
Dart. DA1 210 FM86
Knights Ms, Sutt. SM2
off York Rd 240 DA108
Knights Orchard, Hem.H. HP1 61 BF18
Knights Pk, Kings.T. KT1 220 CL97
Knights Pl, Red. RH1
off Noke Dr 272 DG133
Knight's Pl, Twick. TW2
off May Rd 199 CE88
Knights Pl, Wind. SL4
off Frances Rd 173 AQ82
Knights Ridge, Orp. BR6
off Stirling Dr 246 EV106
Knights Rd, E16 35 P4
Stanmore HA7 117 CJ49
Knight St, Saw. CM21 58 EY05
Knights Wk, SE11 30 G9
Abridge RM4 108 EV41
Knight's Way, Brwd. CM13 131 GA48
Knights Way, Ilf. IG6 125 EQ51
Knightswood, Wok. GU21 248 AT118
Knightswood Cl, Edg. HA8 118 CQ47
Knightswood Rd, Rain. RM13 169 FG68
Knightwood Cl, Reig. RH2 288 DA136
Knightwood Cres, N.Mal. KT3 220 CS100
Knipp Hill, Cob. KT11 236 BZ113
Knivet Rd, SW6 39 J3
Knobfield, Abin.Ham. RH5 283 BT143
KNOCKHALL, Green. DA9 211 FW85
Knockhall Chase, Green. DA9 211 FV85
Sch Knockhall Comm Prim Sch,
Green. DA9
off Eynsford Rd 211 FW85
Knockhall Rd, Green. DA9 211 FW86
KNOCKHOLT, Sev. TN14 262 EU116
⇌ Knockholt 246 EY109
Knockholt Cl, Sutt. SM2 240 DB110
Knockholt Main Rd, Knock.P.
TN14 262 EY115
KNOCKHOLT POUND,
Sev. TN14 262 EX115
Knockholt Rd, SE9 206 EK85
Halstead TN14 246 EZ113
Knole, The, SE9 207 EN91
Istead Rise DA13 212 GE94
Sch Knole Acad
(Knole East), Sev. TN13
off Seal Hollow Rd 279 FL121
(Knole West), Sev. TN13
off Bradbourne Vale Rd 278 FG121
Knole Cl, Croy. CR0 224 DW100
Knole Gate, Sid. DA15
off Woodside Cres 207 ES90
★ Knole Ho & Pk, Sev. TN15 279 FL126
Knole La, Sev. TN13 279 FJ126
Knole Rd, Dart. DA1 209 FG87
Sevenoaks TN13 279 FK123
Knole Way, Sev. TN13 279 FJ125
Knoll, The, W13 159 CJ71
Beckenham BR3 225 EB95
Bromley BR2 226 EG103
Chertsey KT16 215 BF102
Cobham KT11 236 CA113
Hertford SG13 54 DV08
Leatherhead KT22 253 CJ121
Knoll Ct, SE19 204 DS92
Knoll Cres, Nthwd. HA6 115 BS53
Knoll Dr, N14 120 DG45
Knolles Cres, N.Mymms AL9 67 CV24
Knollmead, Surb. KT5 220 CQ102
Sch Knollmead Prim Sch,
Surb. KT5
off Knollmead 220 CQ103
Knoll Pk Rd, Cher. KT16 215 BF102
Knoll Ri, Orp. BR6 227 ET102
Knoll Rd, SW18 202 DC85
Bexley DA5 208 FA87
Dorking RH4 285 CG138
Sidcup DA14 208 EV92
Jct Knoll Rbt, Lthd. KT22 253 CJ121
Knolls, The, Epsom KT17 255 CW116
Knolls Cl, Wor.Pk. KT4 221 CV104
Knollys Cl, SW16 203 DN90
Knollys Rd, SW16 203 DN90
Knolton Way, Slou. SL2 154 AW72
Knotley Way, W.Wick. BR4 225 EB103
Knottisford St, E2 21 H2
Knottocks Cl, Beac. HP9 110 AJ50
Knottocks Dr, Beac. HP9 110 AJ50
Knottocks End, Beac. HP9 111 AK50
Knotts Grn Ms, E10 145 EB58
Knotts Grn Rd, E10 145 EB58
Knotts Pl, Sev. TN13 278 FG124
KNOTTY GREEN, Beac. HP9 110 AJ49
Knowle, The, Hodd. EN11 71 EA18
Tadworth KT20 255 CW121
Knowle Av, Bexh. DA7 188 EY80
Knowle Cl, SW9 42 E10
Knowle Gdns, W.Byf. KT14
off Madeira Rd 233 BF113
Knowle Grn, Stai. TW18 196 BG92
Knowle Gro, Vir.W. GU25 214 AW101
Knowle Gro Cl, Vir.W. GU25 214 AW101
Knowle Hill, Vir.W. GU25 214 AV101
Knowle Pk, Cob. KT11 252 BY115
Knowle Pk Av, Stai. TW18 196 BH93
Sch Knowle Pk Inf Sch, Stai.
TW18 off Knowle Grn 196 BG92
Knowle Rd, Brom. BR2 226 EL103
Twickenham TW2 199 CE88
Knowles Cl, West Dr. UB7 156 BL74
Knowles Ct, Har. HA1 139 CF58
Knowles Hill Cres, SE13 205 ED85
Knowles Ho, SW18
off Neville Gill Cl 202 DB86
Knowles Wk, SW4 41 M10
Knowl Hill, Wok. GU22 249 BB119
Knowl Pk, Els. WD6 100 CL43
Knowlton Grn, Brom. BR2 226 EF99
Knowl Way, Els. WD6 100 CL42
Knowsley Av, Sthl. UB1 158 CA74
Knowsley Rd, SW11 40 E9
Knoxfield Caravan Pk, Dart.
DA2 211 FS90
Knox Rd, E7 13 M5
Guildford GU2 264 AU129
Knox St, W1 16 E6
Knoyle St, SE14 45 L3
Knutsford Av, Wat. WD24 98 BX38
Sch Knutsford Prim Sch, Wat.
WD24 off Knutsford Av 98 BX38
Sch Kobi Nazrul Prim Sch, E1 20 D8
Kohat Rd, SW19 202 DB92
Koh-i-noor Av, Bushey WD23 98 CA44
Koonowla Cl, Bigg.H. TN16 260 EK115
Kooringa, Warl. CR6 258 DV119
Korda Cl, Shep. TW17 216 BM97
Kossuth St, SE10 35 J10
Kotan Dr, Stai. TW18 195 BC90
Kotree Way, SE1 32 D9
Kramer Ms, SW5 39 K1
Kreedman Wk, E8 10 C3
Kreisel Wk, Rich. TW9 180 CM79
Kuala Gdns, SW16 223 DM95
● Kubrick Business Est, E7
off Woodgrange Rd 146 EH63
Kuhn Way, E7 13 P2
Kwesi Ms, SE27 203 DN92
Kydbrook Cl, Petts Wd BR5 227 EQ101
Kylemore Cl, E6 off Parr Rd 166 EK68
Kylemore Rd, NW6 5 J6
Kymberley Rd, Har. HA1 139 CE58
Kyme Rd, Horn. RM11 149 FF58
Kynance Cl, Rom. RM3 128 FJ48
Kynance Gdns, Stan. HA7 117 CJ53
Kynance Ms, SW7 27 N7
Kynance Pl, SW7 27 N7
Kynaston Av, N16
off Dynevor Rd 144 DT62
Thornton Heath CR7 224 DQ99
Kynaston Cl, Har. HA3 117 CD52
Kynaston Cres, Th.Hth. CR7 224 DQ99
Kynaston Rd, N16 144 DS62
Bromley BR1 206 EG92
Enfield EN2 104 DR39
Orpington BR5 228 EV101
Thornton Heath CR7 224 DQ99
Kynaston Wd, Har. HA3 117 CD52
Kynersley Cl, Cars. SM5
off William St 222 DF104
Kyngeshene Gdns, Guil. GU1 281 BA135
Kynoch Rd, N18 122 DW49
Kyrle Rd, SW11 202 DG85
Kytes Dr, Wat. WD25 82 BX33
Kytes Est, Wat. WD25 82 BX33
Kyverdale Rd, N16 144 DT61

L

Laburnham Cl, Barn. EN5 101 CZ41
Upminster RM14 151 FU59
Laburnham Gdns, Upmin.
RM14 151 FT59
Laburnum Av, N9 122 DS47
N17 122 DR52
Dartford DA1 210 FJ88
Hornchurch RM12 169 FF62
Sutton SM1 222 DE104
Swanley BR8 229 FC97
West Drayton UB7 156 BM73
Laburnum Cl, E4 123 DZ51
N11 120 DG51
SE15 44 G5
Cheshunt EN8 89 DX31
Guildford GU1 264 AW131
Sheering CM22 59 FC07
Wembley HA0 160 CN66
Laburnum Ct, E2 10 A9
Stanmore HA7 117 CJ49
Laburnum Cres, Sun. TW16
off Batavia Rd 217 BV95
Laburnum Gdns, N21 122 DQ47
Croydon CR0 225 DX101
Laburnum Gro, N21 122 DQ47
NW9 140 CQ59
Hounslow TW3 178 BZ84
New Malden KT3 220 CR96
Northfleet DA11 212 GD87
Ruislip HA4 137 BR58
St. Albans AL2 82 CB25
Slough SL3 175 BB79
South Ockendon RM15 171 FW69
Southall UB1 158 BZ70
Laburnum Ho, Dag. RM10
off Bradwell Av 148 FA61
Laburnum Pl, Eng.Grn TW20 194 AV93
Laburnum Rd, SW19 202 DC94
Chertsey KT16 216 BG102
Coopersale CM16 92 EW29
Epsom KT18 238 CS113
Hayes UB3 177 BT77
Hoddesdon EN11 71 EB15
Mitcham CR4 222 DG96
Woking GU22 248 AX120
Laburnum St, E2 10 A9
Laburnum Wk, Horn. RM12 150 FJ64
Laburnum Way, Brom. BR2 227 EN101
Goffs Oak EN7
off Millcrest Rd 87 DP28
Staines-upon-Thames TW19 196 BM88
Lacebark Cl, Sid. DA15 207 ET87
Lacewing Cl, E13 23 P2
Lacey Av, Couls. CR5 257 DN120
Lacey Cl, N9 122 DU47
Egham TW20 195 BD94
Lacey Dr, Couls. CR5 257 DN120
Dagenham RM8 148 EV63
Edgware HA8 118 CL49
Hampton TW12 218 BZ95
Lacey Grn, Couls. CR5 257 DN120
Lacey Ms, E3 22 B1
Lackford Rd, Chipstead CR5 256 DF118
Lackington St, EC2 19 M6
Lackmore Rd, Enf. EN1 104 DW35
Lacock Cl, SW19 202 DC93
Lacock Ct, W13
off Singapore Rd 159 CG74
Lacon Rd, SE22 184 DU84
Lacrosse Way, SW16 223 DK95
Lacy Rd, SW15 181 CX84
Ladas Rd, SE27 204 DQ91
Ladbroke Ct, Red. RH1 272 DG132
Ladbroke Cres, W11 14 F9
Ladbroke Gdns, W11 14 G10
⊖ Ladbroke Grove 14 F8
Ladbroke Gro, W10 14 D4
W11 14 F9
Redhill RH1 272 DG133
Ladbroke Ms, W11 26 F3
Ladbroke Rd, W11 26 F2
Enfield EN1 104 DT44
Epsom KT18 238 CR114
Horley RH6 290 DG146
Redhill RH1 272 DG133
Ladbroke Sq, W11 26 G1
Ladbroke Ter, W11 27 H1
Ladbroke Wk, W11 27 H2
Ladbrook Cl, Pnr. HA5 138 BZ57
Ladbrooke Cl, Pot.B. EN6 86 DA32
Ladbrooke Cres, Sid. DA14 208 EX90
Ladbrooke Dr, Pot.B. EN6 86 DA32
Sch Ladbrooke JMI Sch, Pot.B. EN6
off Watkins Ri 86 DB32
Ladbrooke Rd, Slou. SL1 173 AQ76
Ladbrook Rd, SE25 224 DR97
Ladderstile Ride, Kings.T. KT2 200 CP92
Ladderswood Way, N11 121 DJ50
Ladds Way, Swan. BR8 229 FD98
Ladies Gro, St.Alb. AL3 64 CB18
Ladlands, SE22 204 DU87
Lady Aylesford Av, Stan. HA7 117 CH50
Sch Lady Bankes Inf & Jun Schs,
Hlgdn HA4 off Dawlish Dr 137 BU61
Lady Booth Rd, Kings.T. KT1 220 CL96
Sch Lady Boswell's C of E Prim Sch,
Sev. TN13 off Plymouth Dr 279 FJ125
Lady Cooper Ct, Berk. HP4
off Benningfield Gdns 60 AY17
Lady Craig Ct, Uxb. UB8
off Harlington Rd 157 BP71
Ladycroft Gdns, Orp. BR6 245 EQ106
Ladycroft Rd, SE13 185 EB83
Ladycroft Wk, Stan. HA7 117 CK53
Ladycroft Way, Orp. BR6 245 EQ106
Ladyday Pl, Slou. SL1
off Glentworth Pl 153 AQ74
Lady Dock Path, SE16 33 L5
Ladyegate Cl, Dor. RH5 285 CK135
Ladyegate Rd, Dor. RH5 285 CJ136
Sch Lady Eleanor Holles Sch, The,
Hmptn. TW12
off Hanworth Rd 198 CB92
Jun Dept, Hmptn. TW12
off Uxbridge Rd 198 CB92
Ladyfield Cl, Loug. IG10 107 EP42
Ladyfields, Loug. IG10 107 EP42
Northfleet DA11 213 GF91
Lady Forsdyke Way, Epsom
KT19 238 CN109
Ladygate La, Ruis. HA4 137 BP58
Ladygrove, Croy. CR0 243 DY109
Lady Gro, Welw.G.C. AL7 51 CY12
Ladygrove Dr, Guil. GU4 265 BA129
Lady Harewood Way, Epsom
KT19 238 CN109
Lady Hay, Wor.Pk. KT4 221 CT103
Sch Lady Margaret Prim Sch,
Sthl. UB1
off Lady Margaret Rd 158 BZ71
Lady Margaret Rd, N19 7 M1
NW5 7 L2
Southall UB1 158 BZ71
Sch Lady Margaret Sch, SW6 39 J7
Ladymead, Guil. GU1 264 AW133
Lady Meadow, Kings L. WD4 80 BK27
Ladymead Retail Pk, Guil.
GU1 264 AW133
Lady's Cl, Wat. WD18 97 BV42
Ladyshot, Harl. CM20 58 EU14
Ladysmith Av, E6 166 EL68
Ilford IG2 147 ER59
Ladysmith Cl, NW7 119 CU52
Ladysmith Rd, E16 23 L3
N17 122 DU54
N18 122 DV50
SE9 207 EN86
Enfield EN1 104 DS41
Harrow HA3 117 CE54
St. Albans AL3 65 CD19
Lady Somerset Rd, NW5 7 K1
Ladythorpe Cl, Add. KT15
off Church Rd 234 BH105
Ladywalk, Map.Cr. WD3 113 BE50
LADYWELL, SE13 205 EA85
⇌ Ladywell 205 EB85
Ladywell Cl, SE4
off Adelaide Av 185 EA84
Ladywell Hts, SE4 205 DZ86
Ladywell Prospect, Saw. CM21 58 FA06
Ladywell Rd, SE13 205 EA85
Ladywell St, E15 13 L9
Ladywood Av, Petts Wd BR5 227 ES99
Ladywood Cl, Rick. WD3 96 BH41
Ladywood Rd, Hert. SG14 53 DM09
Lane End DA2 211 FS92
Surbiton KT6 220 CN103
Lady Yorke Pk, Iver SL0 155 BD65
Lafone Av, Felt. TW13
off Alfred Rd 198 BW88
Lafone St, SE1 32 A4
Lagado Ms, SE16 33 K3
Lagger, The, Ch.St.G. HP8 112 AV48
Lagger Cl, Ch.St.G. HP8 112 AV48
Laglands Cl, Reig. RH2 272 DC132
Lagonda Av, Ilf. IG6 125 ET51
Lagonda Way, Dart. DA1 190 FJ84
Lagoon Rd, Orp. BR5 228 EV99
Laidlaw Dr, N21 103 DM42
Laidon Sq, Hem.H. HP2 62 BK16
Laing Cl, Ilf. IG6 125 ER51
Laing Dean, Nthlt. UB5 158 BW67
Laing Ho, SE5
off Comber Gro 43 J5
Laings Av, Mitch. CR4 222 DF96
Lainlock Pl, Houns. TW3 178 CB81
Lainson St, SW18 202 DA87
Lairdale Cl, SE21 204 DQ88
Laird Av, Grays RM16 192 GD75
Laird Ho, SE5 43 J5
Lairs Cl, N7 8 B4
Lait Ho, Beck. BR3 225 EA95
Laitwood Rd, SW12 203 DH88
Lakanal, SE5 off Sceaux Gdns 43 P6
Lake, The, Bushey Hth WD23 116 CC46
Lake Av, Brom. BR1 206 EG93
Rainham RM13 170 FK68
Slough SL1 153 AR73
● Lake Business Cen, N17
off Tariff Rd 122 DU52
Lake Cl, SW19 off Lake Rd 201 CZ92
Byfleet KT14 234 BK112
Dagenham RM8 148 EW62
Lakedale Rd, SE18 187 ES79
Lake Dr, Bushey Hth WD23 116 CC47
Lake End Ct, Tap. SL6
off Taplow Rd 152 AH72
Lake End Rd, Dorney SL4 172 AH76
Taplow SL6 152 AH73
Lakefield Cl, SE20
off Limes Av 204 DV94
Lakefield Rd, N22 121 DP54
Lakefields Cl, Rain. RM13 170 FK68
Lake Gdns, Dag. RM10 148 FA64
Richmond TW10 199 CH89
Wallington SM6 223 DH104
Lakehall Gdns, Th.Hth. CR7 223 DP99
Lakehall Rd, Th.Hth. CR7 223 DP99
Lake Ho Rd, E11 146 EG62
Lakehurst Rd, Epsom KT19 238 CS106
Lakeland Cl, Chig. IG7 126 EV49
Harrow HA3 117 CD51
Lake La, Horl. RH6 289 DJ144
Lakenheath, N14 103 DK44
Lake Ri, Grays RM20 191 FU77
Romford RM1 149 FF55
Lake Rd, E10 145 EB59
SW19 201 CZ92
Croydon CR0 225 DZ103
Lower Nazeing EN9 72 EE21
Romford RM6 148 EX56
Virginia Water GU25 214 AV98
Laker Pl, SW15 201 CY86
Lakers Ri, Bans. SM7 256 DE116
Lakes Cl, Chilw. GU4 281 BB140
Lakes Ct, Stans.Abb. SG12 55 EB11
Lakeside 191 FV76
Lakeside, Grays RM20 191 FV77
Lakeside, W13 off Edgehill Rd 159 CJ72
Beckenham BR3 225 EB97
Enfield EN2 103 DK42
Rainham RM13 170 FL68
Redhill RH1 272 DG132
Wallington SM6
off Derek Av 223 DH104
Weybridge KT13 217 BS103
Woking GU21 248 AS119
Lakeside Av, SE28 168 EU74
Ilford IG4 146 EK56
Lakeside Cl, SE25 224 DU96
Chigwell IG7 125 ET49
Ruislip HA4 137 BR56
Sidcup DA15 208 EW85
Woking GU21 248 AS119
Lakeside Ct, N4 143 DP61
Elstree WD6 100 CN43
Lakeside Cres, Barn. EN4 102 DF43
Brentwood CM14 130 FX48
Weybridge KT13
off Churchill Dr 217 BQ104
Lakeside Dr, NW10 160 CM69
Bromley BR2 226 EL104
Chobham GU24 232 AS113
Esher KT10 236 CC107
Stoke Poges SL2 154 AS67
Lakeside Gra, Wey. KT13 217 BQ104
● Lakeside Ind Est, Colnbr.
SL3 176 BG79
Lakeside Pl, Lon.Col. AL2 83 CK27
Lakeside Retail Pk, Grays
RM20 191 FU77
Lakeside Rd, N13 121 DM49
W14 26 C6
Cheshunt EN8 88 DW28
Slough SL3 175 BF80
Sch Lakeside Sch, Welw.G.C. AL8
off Lemsford La 51 CV11
Lakeside Way, Wem. HA9 140 CM63
Lakes La, Beac. HP9 111 AM54
Lakes Rd, Kes. BR2 244 EJ106
Lakeswood Rd, Petts Wd BR5 227 EP100
Lake Vw, Edg. HA8 118 CM50
Kings Langley WD4 81 BP28
North Holmwood RH5 285 CJ139
Potters Bar EN6 86 DC33
Lakeview Ct, SW19
off Victoria Dr 201 CY89
Lakeview Est, E3 11 K10
Lakeview Rd, SE27 203 DN92
Lake Vw Rd, Sev. TN13 278 FG122
Lakeview Rd, Well. DA16 188 EV84
Lakis Cl, NW3 off Flask Wk 142 DC63
LALEHAM, Stai. TW18 216 BJ97
Laleham Av, NW7 118 CR48
Laleham Cl, Stai. TW18
off Worple Rd 216 BH95
Sch Laleham C of E Prim Sch,
Laleham TW18
off The Broadway 216 BJ96
Laleham Ct, Wok. GU21 248 AY116
Sch Laleham Lea Prep Sch, Pur.
CR8 off Peaks Hill 241 DL110
Laleham Pk, Stai. TW18 216 BJ98
Laleham Reach, Cher. KT16 216 BH96
Laleham Rd, SE6 205 EC86
Shepperton TW17 216 BM98
Staines-upon-Thames TW18 195 BF92
Lalor St, SW6 38 E8
Lamb All, St.Alb. AL3
off Market Pl 65 CD20
Lambarde Av, SE9 207 EN91
Lambarde Dr, Sev. TN13 278 FG123
Lambarde Rd, Sev. TN13 278 FG122
Lambardes Cl, Pr.Bot. BR6 246 EW110
Lamb Cl, Hat. AL10 67 CV19
Northolt UB5 158 BY69
Tilbury RM18
off Coleridge Rd 193 GJ82
Watford WD25 82 BW34
Lamberhurst Cl, Orp. BR5 228 EX102
Lamberhurst Rd, SE27 203 DN91
Dagenham RM8 148 EZ60
Lambert Av, Rich. TW9 180 CP83
Slough SL3 174 AY75
Lambert Cl, Bigg.H. TN16 260 EK116
Lambert Ct, Bushey WD23 98 BX42
Lambert Jones Ms, EC2
off The Barbican 19 J6
Lamberton Ct, Borwd. WD6
off Blyth Cl 100 CN39
Lambert Rd, E16 24 A8
N12 120 DC50
SW2 203 DL85
Banstead SM7 240 DA114
Lamberts Pl, Croy. CR0 224 DR102
Lamberts Rd, Surb. KT5 220 CL99
Lambert St, N1 8 E7
Lambert Wk, Wem. HA9 139 CK62
Lambert Way, N12 120 DC50
LAMBETH, SE1 30 C6

Sch Lambeth Acad, SW4
off Elms Rd 203 DJ85
Lambeth Br, SE1 30 B8
SW1 30 B8
Coll Lambeth Coll, Adare Cen,
SW16 off Adare Wk 203 DM89
Brixton Cen, SW2
off Brixton Hill 203 DM85
Clapham Cen, SW4 off Clapham
Common S Side 203 DJ85
Vauxhall Cen, SW8 41 P6
Lambeth High St, SE1 30 C9
Lambeth Hill, EC4 19 J10
H Lambeth Hosp, SW9 42 B10
⊖ Lambeth North 30 E5
★ Lambeth Palace, SE1 30 C7
Lambeth Palace Rd, SE1 30 C7
Lambeth Pier, SE1 30 B7
Lambeth Rd, SE1 30 D7
SE11 30 D7
Croydon CR0 223 DN101
Lambeth Twrs, SE11 30 E7
Lambeth Wk, SE1 30 D8
SE11 30 D8
Lambfold Ho, N7 8 A4
Lambkins Ms, E17 145 EC56
Lamb La, E8 10 E7
Lamble St, NW5 6 G2
Lambley Rd, Dag. RM9 168 EV65
Lambly Hill, Vir.W. GU25 214 AY97
Lambolle Pl, NW3 6 D5
Lambolle Rd, NW3 6 C5
Lambourn Chase, Rad. WD7 99 CF36
Lambourn Cl, W7 179 CF75
South Croydon CR2 241 DP109
Lambourne Av, SW19 201 CZ91
Lambourne Cl, Chig. IG7 126 EV48
Lambourne Ct, Wdf.Grn. IG8
off Navestock Cres 124 EJ53
Lambourne Cres, Chig. IG7 126 EV47
Woking GU21 233 BD113
Lambourne Dr, Cob. KT11 252 BX115
Hutton CM13 131 GE45
LAMBOURNE END, Rom.
RM4 108 EX44
Lambourne Gdns, E4 123 EA47
Barking IG11 167 ET66
Enfield EN1 104 DT40
Hornchurch RM12 150 FK61
Lambourne Gro, SE16 33 J9
Lambourne Pl, SE3
off Shooters Hill Rd 186 EH81
Sch Lambourne Prim Sch, Abridge
RM4 off Hoe La 108 EV42
Lambourne Rd, E11 145 EC59
Barking IG11 167 ES66
Chigwell IG7 125 ES49
Ilford IG3 147 ES61
Lambourne Sq, Lamb.End RM4 126 EW46
Lambourn Gro, Kings.T. KT1 220 CP96
Lambourn Rd, SW4 41 K10
Lambrook Ter, SW6 38 E6
Lamb's Bldgs, EC1 19 L5
Lambs Cl, N9
off Winchester Rd 122 DU47
Cuffley EN6 87 DM29
Lambs Conduit Pas, WC1 18 C6
Lamb's Conduit St, WC1 18 C5
Lambscroft Av, SE9 206 EJ90
Lambscroft Way, Chal.St.P.
SL9 112 AY54
Lambs La N, Rain. RM13 170 FJ70
Lambs La S, Rain. RM13 169 FH71
Lambs Meadow, Wdf.Grn.
IG8 124 EK54
Lambs Ms, N1 8 G9
Lamb's Pas, EC1 19 L6
Lambs Ter, N9 122 DR47
Lamb St, E1 20 A6
Lambs Wk, Enf. EN2 104 DQ40
Lambton Av, Wal.Cr. EN8 89 DX32
Lambton Ms, N19
off Lambton Rd 143 DL60
Lambton Pl, W11 15 H10
Lambton Rd, N19 143 DL60
SW20 221 CW95
Lamb Wk, SE1 31 N5
Lambyn Cft, Horl. RH6 291 DJ147
Lamerock Rd, Brom. BR1 206 EF91
Lamerton Rd, Ilf. IG6 125 EP54
Lamerton St, SE8 46 A3
Lamford Cl, N17 122 DR52
Lamington St, W6 181 CV77
Lamlash St, SE11 30 G8
Lammas Av, Mitch. CR4 222 DG96
Lammas Cl, Stai. TW18 195 BE90
Lammas Ct, Stai. TW19 195 BD89
Windsor SL4 173 AQ82
Lammas Dr, Stai. TW18 195 BD90
Lammas Grn, SE26 204 DV90
Lammas La, Esher KT10 236 CA106
Lammasmead, Brox. EN10 71 DZ23
Lammas Pk, W5 179 CJ75
Lammas Pk Gdns, W5 179 CJ75
Lammas Pk Rd, W5 159 CJ74
Lammas Rd, E9 11 K7
E10 145 DY61
Richmond TW10 199 CJ91
Slough SL1 153 AK71
Watford WD18 98 BW43
Sch Lammas Sch, The, E10
off Seymour Rd 145 DZ60
Lammas Way, Loud. HP10 110 AC54
Lammermoor Rd, SW12 203 DH87
Lammtarra Pl, Epsom KT17
off Windmill La 239 CT112
Lamont Rd, SW10 39 P3
Lamont Rd Pas, SW10
off Lamont Rd 40 A3
LAMORBEY, Sid. DA15 207 ET88
Lamorbey Cl, Sid. DA15 207 ET88
Lamorna Av, Grav. DA12 213 GJ90
Lamorna Cl, E17 123 EC54
Orpington BR6 228 EU101
Radlett WD7 83 CH34
Lamorna Gro, Stan. HA7 117 CK53
Lampard Gro, N16 144 DT60
Lampern Sq, E2 20 D2
Lampeter Cl, NW9 140 CS58
Woking GU22 248 AY118
Lampeter Sq, W6 38 E3
Lampits, Hodd. EN11 71 EB17
Lamplighter Cl, E1 20 G5
Lamplighters Cl, Dart. DA1 210 FM86
Waltham Abbey EN9 90 EG34
Lampmead Rd, SE12 206 EE85
Lamp Office Ct, WC1 18 C5
Lamport Cl, SE18 37 K8
LAMPTON, Houns. TW3 178 CB81
Lampton Av, Houns. TW3 178 CB81
Lampton Ho Cl, SW19 201 CX91
Lampton Pk Rd, Houns. TW3 178 CB82
Lampton Rd, Houns. TW3 178 CB82
Sch Lampton Sch, Houns. TW3
off Lampton Av 178 CA81
Lamsey Rd, Hem.H. HP3 62 BK22
Lamson Rd, Rain. RM13 169 FF70
Lanacre Av, NW9 119 CT53
Lanadron Cl, Islw. TW7 179 CF82
Lanark Cl, W5 159 CJ71
Lanark Ms, W9 15 N3
Lanark Pl, W9 15 P4
Lanark Rd, W9 15 N3
Lanark Sq, E14 34 D6
Lanata Wk, Hayes UB4
off Ramulis Dr 158 BX70
Lanbury Rd, SE15 185 DX84
Lancashire Ct, W1 17 K10
Lancaster Av, E18 146 EH56
SE27 203 DP89
SW19 201 CX92
Barking IG11 167 ES66
Barnet EN4 102 DD38
Guildford GU1 281 AZ136
Mitcham CR4 223 DL99
Slough SL2 153 AQ70
Lancaster Cl, N1 9 P7
N17 122 DU52
NW9 119 CT52
Ashford TW15 196 BL91
Bromley BR2 226 EF98
Egham TW20 194 AX92
Kingston upon Thames KT2 199 CK92
Pilgrim's Hatch CM15 130 FU43
Stanwell TW19 196 BL86
Woking GU21 249 BA116
Lancaster Cotts, Rich. TW10
off Lancaster Pk 200 CL86
Lancaster Ct, SE27 203 DP89
SW6 39 J5
W2 27 P1
Banstead SM7 239 CZ114
Walton-on-Thames KT12 217 BU101
Lancaster Dr, E14 34 F3
NW3 6 C5
Bovingdon HP3 79 AZ27
Hornchurch RM12 149 FH64
Loughton IG10 106 EL44
Lancaster Gdns, SW19 201 CY92
W13 179 CH75
Bromley BR1 226 EL99
Kingston upon Thames KT2 199 CK92
⊖ Lancaster Gate 16 A10
Lancaster Gate, W2 27 P1
Lancaster Gro, NW3 6 B5
Lancaster Ho, Islw. TW7 179 CF80
★ Lancaster Ho, SW1 29 L4
Sch Lancasterian Prim Sch, N17
off King's Rd 122 DT53
Lancaster Ms, SW18
off East Hill 202 DB85
W2 15 P10
Richmond TW10
off Richmond Hill 200 CL86
Lancaster Pk, Rich. TW10 200 CL85
Lancaster Pl, SW19 201 CX92
WC2 18 C10
Hounslow TW4 178 BW82
Ilford IG1 off Staines Rd 147 EQ63
Twickenham TW1 199 CG86
Lancaster Rd, E7 13 P6
E11 146 EE61
E17 123 DX54
N4 143 DN59
N11 121 DK51
N18 122 DT50
NW10 141 CT64
SE25 224 DT96
SW19 201 CX92
W11 14 E9
Barnet EN4 102 DD43
Chafford Hundred RM16 191 FX78
Enfield EN2 104 DR39
Harrow HA2 138 CA57
North Weald Bassett CM16 92 FA26
Northolt UB5 158 CC65
St. Albans AL1 65 CF18
Southall UB1 158 BY73
Uxbridge UB8 156 BK65
Lancaster St, SE1 31 H5
Lancaster Ter, W2 16 A10
Lancaster Wk, W2 28 A4
Hayes UB3 157 BQ72
Lancaster Way, Abb.L. WD5 81 BT31
Worcester Park KT4 221 CV101
Lancaster W, W11
off Grenfell Rd 14 D10
Lancastrian Rd, Wall. SM6 241 DL108
Lancefield St, W10 14 G2
Lancell St, N16 144 DS62
Lancelot Av, Wem. HA0 139 CK63
Lancelot Cl, Slou. SL1 173 AN75
Lancelot Ct, Bushey WD23
off Hartswood Cl 98 CA40
Lancelot Cres, Wem. HA0 139 CK63
Lancelot Gdns, E.Barn. EN4 120 DG45
Lancelot Pl, SW7 28 E5
Lancelot Rd, Ilf. IG6 125 ES51
Welling DA16 188 EU84
Wembley HA0 139 CK64
Lance Rd, Har. HA1 138 CC59
Lancer Sq, W8 27 L4
Lancey Cl, SE7 36 F8
Lanchester Rd, N6 142 DF57
Lanchester Way, SE14 45 H6
Lancing Gdns, N9 122 DT46
Lancing Rd, W13
off Drayton Grn Rd 159 CH73
Croydon CR0 223 DM100
Feltham TW13 197 BT89
Ilford IG2 147 ER58
Orpington BR6 228 EU103
Romford RM3 128 FL52
Lancing St, NW1 17 N3
Lancing Way, Crox.Grn WD3 97 BP43
Lancresse Cl, Uxb. UB8 156 BK65
Lancresse Ct, N1 9 N8
Landale Gdns, Dart. DA1 210 FJ87
Landau Way, Brox. EN10 89 DZ26
Erith DA8 190 FK78
Landcroft Rd, SE22 204 DT86
Landells Rd, SE22 204 DT86
Landen Pk, Horl. RH6 290 DE146
Lander Rd, Grays RM17 192 GD78
Landford Cl, Rick. WD3 114 BL47
Landford Rd, SW15 181 CW83
Landgrove Rd, SW19 202 DA92
Landmann Ho, SE16 32 F9
Landmann Way, SE14 45 K2
● Landmark Commercial Cen,
N18 122 DS51
Landmark East Twr, E14 34 A4
Landmark Hts, E5 11 L1
Landmark West Twr, E14 34 A3
Landmead Rd, Chsht EN8 89 DY29
Landon Pl, SW1 28 E6
Landons Cl, E14 34 F2
Landon Wk, E14 22 D10
Landon Way, Ashf. TW15
off Courtfield Rd 197 BP93
Landor Rd, SW9 183 DL83
Landor Wk, W12 181 CU75
Landra Gdns, N21 103 DP44
● Land Registry, Croy. CR0 224 DQ102
Landridge Dr, Enf. EN1 104 DV38
Landridge Rd, SW6 38 F8
Landrock Rd, N8 143 DL58
Landscape Rd, Warl. CR6 258 DV119
Woodford Green IG8 124 EH52
Landsdown Cl, New Barn.
EN5 102 DC42
Landseer Av, E12 147 EN64
Northfleet DA11 212 GD90
Landseer Cl, SW19
off Thorburn Way 222 DD95
Edgware HA8 118 CN54
Hornchurch RM11 149 FH60
Landseer Rd, N19 143 DL62
Enfield EN1 104 DU43
New Malden KT3 220 CR101
Sutton SM1 240 DA107
Lands End, Els. WD6 99 CK44
Landstead Rd, SE18 187 ER80
Landway, The, Orp. BR5 228 EW97
Lane, The, NW8 5 N10
SE3 47 P10
Chertsey KT16 216 BG97
Virginia Water GU25 214 AY97
Lane Av, Green. DA9 211 FW86
Lane Cl, NW2 141 CV62
Addlestone KT15 234 BG106
LANE END, Dart. DA2 211 FR92
Lane End, Berk. HP4 60 AT19
Bexleyheath DA7 189 FB83
Epsom KT18 238 CP114
Harlow CM17 74 EY15
Hatfield AL10 67 CT21
Lanefield Wk, Welw.G.C. AL8 51 CW09
Lane Gdns, Bushey Hth WD23 117 CE45
Claygate KT10 237 CF108
Lane Ms, E12
off Colchester Av 147 EM62
Lanercost Cl, SW2 203 DN89
Lanercost Gdns, N14 121 DL45
Lanercost Rd, SW2 203 DN89
Lanes Av, Nthflt DA11 213 GG90
Lanesborough Pl, SW1 29 H4
Sch Lanesborough Sch, Guil. GU1
off Maori Rd 265 AZ134
Laneside, Chis. BR7 207 EP92
Edgware HA8 118 CQ50
Laneside Av, Dag. RM8 148 EZ59
Laneway, SW15 201 CV85
Lane Wd Cl, Amer. HP7 94 AT39
Lanfranc Rd, E3 21 L1
Lanfrey Pl, W14 38 G1
Langaller La, Fetch. KT22 252 CB122
Langbourne Av, N6 142 DG61
Langbourne Pl, E14 34 C10
Sch Langbourne Prim Sch, SE21
off Lyall Av 204 DS90
Langbourne Way, Clay. KT10 237 CG107
Langbrook Rd, SE3 186 EK83
Lang Cl, Fetch. KT22 252 CB123
Langcroft Cl, Cars. SM5 222 DF104
Langdale, NW1 17 L2
Langdale Av, Mitch. CR4 222 DF97
Langdale Cl, SE17 43 J2
SW14 180 CP84
Dagenham RM8 148 EW60
Orpington BR6
off Grasmere Rd 227 EP104
Woking GU21 248 AW116
Langdale Ct, Hem.H. HP2
off Wharfedale 62 BL17
Langdale Cres, Bexh. DA7 188 FA80
Langdale Dr, Hayes UB4 157 BS68
Langdale Gdns, Horn. RM12 149 FG64
Perivale UB6 159 CH69
Waltham Cross EN8 105 DX35
Langdale Rd, SE10 46 E5
Thornton Heath CR7 223 DN98
Langdale St, E1 20 E9
Langdale Wk, Nthflt DA11
off Landseer Av 212 GE90
Langdon Ct, EC1 off City Rd 19 H1
NW10 160 CS67
Langdon Cres, E6 167 EN68
Langdon Dr, NW9 140 CQ60
DLR Langdon Park 22 D7
Langdon Pk, Tedd. TW11 199 CJ94
Langdon Pk Rd, N6 143 DJ59
Sch Langdon Pk Sch, E14 22 D8
Langdon Pl, SW14 180 CQ83
Langdon Rd, E6 167 EN67
Bromley BR2 226 EH97
Morden SM4 222 DC99
Sch Langdon Sch, E6
off Sussex Rd 167 EP67
Langdons Ct, Sthl. UB2 178 CA76
Langdon Shaw, Sid. DA14 207 ET92
Langdon Wk, Mord. SM4 222 DC99
Langdon Way, SE1 32 D9
Langfield Cl, Lwr Naze. EN9 72 EE22
Langford Cl, E8 10 C2
N15 144 DS58
NW8 5 P10
W3 180 CP75
St. Albans AL4 65 CJ18
Langford Ct, NW8 15 N1
Langford Cres, Cockfos. EN4 102 DF42
Langford Grn, SE5 184 DS83
Hutton CM13 131 GC44
Langford Ho, SE off Evelyn St 846 A2
Langford Ms, N1 8 F6
SW11 off St. John's Hill 182 DD84
Langford Pl, NW8 15 P1
Sidcup DA14 208 EU90
Sch Langford Prim Sch, SW6 39 M8
Langford Rd, SW6 39 M8
Cockfosters EN4 102 DE42
Woodford Green IG8 124 EJ51
Langfords, Buck.H. IG9 124 EK47
Langfords Way, Croy. CR0 243 DY111
Langham Cl, N15
off Langham Rd 143 DP55
Bromley BR2 226 EL103
St. Albans AL4 65 CK15
Langham Ct, Horn. RM11 150 FK59
Langham Dene, Ken. CR8 257 DP115
Langham Dr, Rom. RM6 148 EV58
Langham Gdns, N21 103 DN43
W13 159 CH73
Edgware HA8 118 CQ52
Richmond TW10 199 CJ91
Wembley HA0 139 CJ61
Langham Ho Cl, Rich. TW10 199 CK91
Langham Pk Pl, Brom. BR2 226 EF98
Langham Pl, N15 143 DP55
W1 17 K7
W4 180 CS79
Egham TW20 195 AZ92
Langham Rd, N15 143 DP55
SW20 221 CW95
Edgware HA8 118 CQ51
Teddington TW11 199 CH92
Langham St, W1 17 K7
Langhedge Cl, N18 122 DT51
Langhedge La, N18 122 DT50
● Langhedge La Ind Est,
N18 122 DT51
Langholm Cl, SW12 203 DK87
Langholme, Bushey WD23 116 CC46
Langhorn Dr, Twick. TW2 199 CE87
Langhorne Ho, SE7
off Springfield Gro 186 EJ79
Langhorne Rd, Dag. RM10 168 FA66
Langland Ct, Nthwd. HA6 115 BQ52
Langland Cres, Stan. HA7 140 CL55
Langland Dr, Pnr. HA5 116 BY52
Langland Gdns, NW3 5 M2
Croydon CR0 225 DZ103
Langlands Dr, Lane End DA2 211 FS92
Langlands Ri, Epsom KT19 238 CQ113
Langler Rd, NW10 14 B1
LANGLEY, Slou. SL3 175 BA76
⇌ Langley 175 BA75
Sch Langley Acad, Langley SL3
off Langley Rd 174 AY76
Langley Av, Hem.H. HP3 62 BL23
Ruislip HA4 137 BV60
Surbiton KT6 219 CK102
Worcester Park KT4 221 CX103
Langley Broom, Slou. SL3 175 AZ78
LANGLEYBURY, Kings L. WD4 81 BP34
Langleybury Flds,
Kings L. WD4 80 BM34
Langleybury La, Kings L. WD4 97 BP37
● Langley Business Cen, Langley
SL3 175 BA75
Langley Cl, Epsom KT18 254 CR119
Guildford GU1 264 AW133
Romford RM3 128 FK52
Jct Langley Cor, Fulmer SL3 155 AZ65
● Langley Ct, Beck. BR3 225 EB99
Langley Ct, WC2 18 A9
Langley Cres, E11 146 EJ59
Dagenham RM9 168 EW66
Edgware HA8 118 CQ48
Hayes UB3 177 BT80
Kings Langley WD4 80 BN30
St. Albans AL3 64 CC18
Langley Dr, E11 146 EH59
W3 160 CP74
Brentwood CM14 130 FU48
Langley Gdns, Brom. BR2
off Great Elms Rd 226 EJ98
Dagenham RM9 168 EW66
Petts Wood BR5 227 EP100
Sch Langley Gram Sch, Langley
SL3 off Reddington Dr 175 AZ77
Langley Gro, N.Mal. KT3 220 CS96
Langley Hill, Kings L. WD4 80 BM29
Langley Hill Cl, Kings L. WD4 80 BN29
Langley La, SW8 42 B2
Abbots Langley WD5 81 BT31
Headley KT18 270 CP125
Langley Lo La, Kings L. WD4 80 BN31
Sch Langley Manor Sch, Langley
SL3 off St. Mary's Rd 154 AY74
Langley Meadow, Loug. IG10 107 ER40
Langley Oaks Av, S.Croy. CR2 242 DU110
Langley Pk, NW7 118 CS51
★ Langley Park Country Pk,
Slou. SL3 155 BA70
Langley Pk Rd, Iver SL0 155 BC72
Slough SL3 175 BA75
Sutton SM1, SM2 240 DC106
Sch Langley Pk Sch for Boys,
Beck. BR3
off Hawksbrook La 225 EB100
Sch Langley Pk Sch for Girls, Beck.
BR3 off Hawksbrook La 225 EC100
Langley Quay, Langley SL3 175 BA75
Langley Rd, SW19 221 CZ95
Abbots Langley WD5 81 BS31
Beckenham BR3 225 DY98
Chipperfield WD4 80 BH30
Isleworth TW7 179 CF82
Slough SL3 174 AW75
South Croydon CR2 243 DX109
Staines-upon-Thames TW18 195 BF93
Surbiton KT6 220 CL101
Watford WD17 97 BU39
Welling DA16 188 EW79
Langley Row, Barn. EN5 101 CZ39
Langley St, WC2 18 A9
LANGLEY VALE, Epsom KT18 254 CR120
Langley Vale Rd, Epsom KT18 254 CR118
Langley Wk, Wok. GU22 248 AY119
Langley Way, Wat. WD17 97 BS40
West Wickham BR4 225 ED102
Langmans La, Wok. GU21 248 AV118
Langmans Way, Wok. GU21 248 AS116
Langmead Dr, Bushey Hth
WD23 117 CD46
Langmead St, SE27
off Beadman St 203 DP91
Langmore Ct, Bexh. DA6
off Regency Way 188 EX83
Langport Ct, Walt. KT12 218 BW102
Langridge Ms, Hmptn. TW12
off Oak Av 198 BZ93
Langroyd Rd, SW17 202 DF89
Langshott, Horl. RH6 291 DH146
Langshott Cl, Wdhm KT15 233 BE111
Sch Langshott Inf Sch, Horl. RH6
off Smallfield Rd 291 DJ148
Langshott La, Horl. RH6 291 DJ147
Langside Av, SW15 181 CU84
Langside Cres, N14 121 DK48
Langstone Ley, Welw.G.C. AL7 52 DB09
Langstone Way, NW7 119 CX52
Langston Hughes Cl, SE24
off Shakespeare Rd 183 DP84
Langston Rd, Loug. IG10 107 EQ43
Lang St, E1 20 G4
Langthorn Ct, EC2 19 L8
Langthorne Ct, Brom. BR1 205 EC91
Langthorne Cres, Grays RM17 192 GC77
Langthorne Rd, E11 145 ED62
Langthorne St, SW6 38 C5
Langton Av, E6 25 L2
N20 120 DC45
Epsom KT17 239 CT111
Langton Cl, WC1 18 D3
Addlestone KT15 216 BH104
Slough SL1 153 AK74
Woking GU21 248 AT117
Langton Gro, Nthwd. HA6 115 BQ50
Langton Ho, SW16
off Colson Way 203 DJ91
Langton Pl, SW18
off Merton Rd 202 DA88
Langton Ri, SE23 204 DV87
Langton Rd, NW2 141 CW62
SW9 43 H5
Harrow HA3 116 CC52
Hoddesdon EN11 71 DZ17
West Molesey KT8 218 CC98
Sch Langtons Inf & Jun Schs, Horn.
RM11 off Westland Av 150 FL60
Langton's Meadow, Farn.Com.
SL2 153 AQ65
Langton St, SW10 39 P3
Langton Way, SE3 47 M6
Croydon CR0 242 DS105
Egham TW20 195 BC93
Grays RM16 193 GJ77
Langtree Ave, Slou. SL1 173 AM75
Langtry Ct, Islw. TW7
off Lanadron Cl 179 CF82
Langtry Pl, SW6 39 K2
Langtry Rd, NW8 5 L9
Northolt UB5 158 BX68
Langtry Wk, NW8 5 N8
Langwood Chase, Tedd. TW11 199 CJ93
Langwood Cl, Ashtd. KT21 254 CN117
Langwood Gdns, Wat. WD17 97 BU39
Langworth Cl, Dart. DA2 210 FK90
Langworth Dr, Hayes UB4 157 BU72
Lanherne Ho, SW20 201 CX94
Lanhill Rd, W9 15 J4
Lanier Rd, SE13 205 EC86
Lanigan Dr, Houns. TW3 198 CB85
Lankaster Gdns, N2 120 DD53
Lankers Dr, Har. HA2 138 BZ58
Lankester Sq, Oxt. RH8 275 ED128
Lankton Cl, Beck. BR3 225 EC95
Lannock Rd, Hayes UB3 157 BS74
Lannoy Pt, SW6
off Pellant Rd 38 F4
Lannoy Rd, SE9 207 EQ88
Lanrick Copse, Berk. HP4 60 AY18
Lanrick Rd, E14 23 H8
Lanridge Rd, SE2 188 EX76
Lansbury Av, N18 122 DR50
Barking IG11 168 EU66
Feltham TW14 197 BV86
Romford RM6 148 EY57
Lansbury Cl, NW10 140 CQ64
Lansbury Cres, Dart. DA1 210 FN85
Lansbury Dr, Hayes UB4 157 BT71
Lansbury Est, E14 22 C8
Lansbury Gdns, E14 22 G8
Tilbury RM18 193 GG81
Sch Lansbury Lawrence Prim Sch,
E14 22 C9
Lansbury Rd, Enf. EN3 105 DX39
Lansbury Way, N18 122 DS50
Lanscombe Wk, SW8 42 A6
Lansdell Rd, Mitch. CR4 222 DG96
Lansdown, Guil. GU1 265 BA134
Lansdown Cl, Walt. KT12 218 BW102
Woking GU21 248 AT119
Lansdowne Av, Bexh. DA7 188 EX80
Orpington BR6 227 EP102
Slough SL1 154 AS74
Lansdowne Cl, SW20 201 CX94
Surbiton KT5 220 CP103
Twickenham TW1 199 CF88
Watford WD25 98 BX35
Coll Lansdowne Coll, W2 27 K1
Lansdowne Copse, Wor.Pk.
KT4 221 CU103
Lansdowne Ct, Pur. CR8 241 DP110
Slough SL1 154 AS74
Worcester Park KT4 221 CU103
Lansdowne Cres, W11 26 F1
Lansdowne Dr, E8 10 D5
Lansdowne Gdns, SW8 42 A6
Lansdowne Grn, SW8 41 P5
Lansdowne Gro, NW10 140 CS63
Lansdowne Hill, SE27 203 DP90
Lansdowne La, SE7 186 EK79
Lansdowne Ms, SE7 186 EK78
W11 26 G2
Lansdowne Pl, SE1 31 M6
SE19 204 DT94
Sch Lansdowne Prim Sch, Til.
RM18 off Alexandra Rd 193 GF82
Lansdowne Ri, W11 26 F1
Lansdowne Rd, E4 123 EA47
E11 146 EF61
E17 145 EA57
E18 146 EG55
N3 119 CZ52
N10 121 DJ54
N17 122 DT53
SW20 201 CW94
W11 14 F10
Bromley BR1 206 EG94
Chesham HP5 76 AQ29
Croydon CR0 224 DR103
Epsom KT19 238 CQ108
Harrow HA1 139 CE59
Hounslow TW3 178 CB83
Ilford IG3 147 ET60
Purley CR8 241 DN112
Sevenoaks TN13 279 FK122
Staines-upon-Thames TW18 196 BH94
Stanmore HA7 117 CJ51
Tilbury RM18 193 GF82
Uxbridge UB8 157 BP72
Lansdowne Row, W1 29 K2
Sch Lansdowne Sch, SW9 42 C10
Lansdowne Sq, Nthflt DA11 213 GF86

Lansdowne Ter, WC1 18 B5
Lansdowne Wk, W11 26 F2
Lansdowne Way, SW8 41 P6
Lansdowne Wd Cl, SE27 203 DP90
Lansdown Pl, Nthflt DA11 213 GF88
Lansdown Rd, E7 166 EJ66
Chalfont St. Peter SL9 112 AX53
Sidcup DA14 208 EV90
Lansfield Av, N18 122 DU49
Lanson Bldg, SW8 41 J4
Lantern Cl, SW15 181 CU84
Orpington BR6 245 EP105
Wembley HA0 139 CK64
Lantern Way, West Dr. UB7 176 BL75
Lanthorn Cl, Brox. EN10 71 DY19
Lant St, SE1 31 J4
Lanvanor Rd, SE15 44 G8
Lapford Cl, W9 15 H4
Lapis Cl, NW10 160 CN69
Lapis Ms, E15 12 F9
La Plata Gro, Brwd. CM14 130 FV48
Lapponum Wk, Hayes UB4
off Lochan Cl 158 BY70
Lapraik Gro, Ch.St.G. HP8 112 AW48
Lapse Wd Wk, SE26 204 DV89
Lapstone Gdns, Har. HA3 139 CJ58
Lapwing Cl, Erith DA8 189 FH80
Hemel Hempstead HP2 62 BL16
South Croydon CR2 243 DY110
Lapwing Ct, Surb. KT6
off Chaffinch Cl 220 CN104
Lapwing Gro, Guil. GU4 265 BD132
Lapwing Pl, Wat. WD25 82 BW32
Lapwings, The, Grav. DA12 213 GK89
Lapwing Ter, E7
off Hampton Rd 146 EK64
Lapwing Twr, SE8 45 N3
Lapwing Way, Abb.L. WD5 81 BU31
Hayes UB4 158 BX72
Lapworth Ct, Orp. BR6 228 EW103
Lara Cl, SE13 205 EC86
Chessington KT9 238 CL108
Larbert Rd, SW16 223 DJ95
Larby Pl, Epsom KT17 238 CS110
Larch Av, W3 160 CS74
Bricket Wood AL2 82 BY30
Guildford GU1 264 AW132
Larch Cl, E13 24 C4
N11 120 DG52
N19 off Bredgar Rd 143 DJ61
SE8 45 P3
SW12 203 DH89
Cheshunt EN7 off The Firs 88 DS27
Kingswood KT20 256 DC121
Penn HP10 110 AC45
Redhill RH1 288 DC136
Slough SL2 153 AP71
Warlingham CR6 259 DY119
Larch Cres, Epsom KT19 238 CP107
Hayes UB4 158 BW70
Larch Dene, Orp. BR6 227 EN103
Larch Dr, W4
off Gunnersbury Av 180 CN78
Larches, The, N13 122 DQ48
Amersham HP6 94 AV38
Bushey WD23 98 BY43
Northwood HA6
off Rickmansworth Rd 115 BQ51
St. Albans AL4 65 CK16
Uxbridge UB10 157 BP69
Woking GU21 248 AY116
Larches Av, SW14 180 CR84
Enfield EN1 104 DW35
Larch Grn, NW9
off Clayton Fld 118 CS53
Larch Gro, Sid. DA15 207 ET88
Larchlands, The, Penn HP10 110 AD46
Larchmoor Pk, Stoke P. SL2 134 AU64
Larch Ri, Berk. HP4 60 AU18
Larch Rd, E10 145 EA61
NW2 141 CW63
Dartford DA1 210 FK87
Larch Tree Way, Croy. CR0 225 EA104
Larch Wk, Swan. BR8 229 FD96
Larch Way, Brom. BR2 227 EN101
Larchwood Av, Rom. RM5 127 FB51
Larchwood Cl, Bans. SM7 255 CY116
Romford RM5 127 FC51
Larchwood Dr, Eng.Grn TW20 194 AV93
Larchwood Gdns, Pilg.Hat.
CM15 130 FU44
Larchwood Ho, Chig. IG7 126 EV49
Larchwood Prim Sch, Pilg.Hat.
CM15 off Larchwood Gdns 130 FU44
Larchwood Rd, SE9 207 EP89
Hemel Hempstead HP2 62 BM18
Larcombe Cl, Croy. CR0 242 DT105
Larcom St, SE17 31 K9
Larden Rd, W3 160 CS74
La Retraite RC Girls' Sch,
SW12 off Atkins Rd 203 DJ87
Largewood Av, Surb. KT6 220 CN103
Largo Wk, Erith DA8
off Selkirk Dr 189 FE81
Larissa St, SE17 31 M10
Lark Av, Stai. TW18 195 BF90
Larkbere Rd, SE26 205 DY91
Lark Cl, Warley CM14 130 FV49
Larken Cl, Bushey WD23
off Larken Dr 116 CC46
Larken Dr, Bushey WD23 116 CC46
Larkfield, Cob. KT11 235 BU113
Larkfield Av, Har. HA3 139 CH55
Larkfield Cl, Brom. BR2 226 EF103
Larkfield Ct, Smallfield RH6
off Cooper Cl 291 DN148
Larkfield Rd, Rich. TW9 180 CL84
Sevenoaks TN13 278 FC123
Sidcup DA14 207 ET90
Larkfields, Nthflt DA11 212 GE90
Larkhall Cl, Hersham KT12 236 BW107
Larkhall La, SW4 41 N9
Larkhall Prim Sch, SW4 41 P9
Larkhall Ri, SW4 41 M10
Larkham Cl, Felt. TW13 197 BS90
Larkhill Ter, SE18
off Prince Imperial Rd 187 EN80
Larkin Cl, Couls. CR5 257 DM117
Hutton CM13 131 GC45
Larkings La, Stoke P. SL2 154 AV67
Larkins Rd, Lon.Gat.Air. RH6 290 DD152
Lark Ri, E.Hors. KT24 267 BS131
Hatfield AL10 67 CU20
Lark Row, E2 10 G9
Larksfield, Eng.Grn TW20 194 AW94
Horley RH6 291 DH147
Larksfield Gro, Enf. EN1 104 DV39
Larks Gro, Bark. IG11 167 ES66
Larkshall Ct, Rom. RM7 127 FC54
Larkshall Cres, E4 123 EC49
Larkshall Rd, E4 123 EC50
Larkspur Cl, E6 24 G6
N17 122 DR52
NW9 140 CP57
Hemel Hempstead HP1 61 BE19
Orpington BR6 228 EW103
Ruislip HA4 137 BQ59
South Ockendon RM15 171 FW69
Larkspur Gro, Edg. HA8 118 CQ49
Larkspur Way, Epsom KT19 238 CQ106
North Holmwood RH5 285 CK139
Larks Ridge, St.Alb. AL2 82 CA27
Larks Ri, Chesh. HP5 76 AR33
Larkswood, Harl. CM17 74 EW17
Larkswood Cl, Erith DA8 189 FG81
Larkswood Ct, E4 123 ED50
Larkswood Leisure Pk, E4
off New Rd 123 EC49
Larkswood Prim Sch, E4
off New Rd 123 EB49
Larkswood Ri, Pnr. HA5 138 BW56
St. Albans AL4 65 CJ15
Larkswood Rd, E4 123 EA49
Lark Way, Cars. SM5 222 DE101
Larkway Cl, NW9 140 CR56
Larmans Rd, Enf. EN3 104 DW36
Larmenier & Sacred Heart
Prim Sch, W6 26 D9
Larnach Rd, W6 38 C3
Larner Ct, W12
off Heathstan Rd 161 CU72
Larne Rd, Ruis. HA4 137 BT59
Larner Rd, Erith DA8 189 FE80
La Roche Cl, Slou. SL3 174 AW76
Larpent Av, SW15 201 CW85
Larsen Dr, Wal.Abb. EN9 89 ED34
Larwood Cl, Grnf. UB6 139 CD64
La Sainte Union Cath Sch,
NW5 off Highgate Rd 142 DG62
La Salette Cath Prim Sch, Rain.
RM13 off Dunedin Rd 169 FF69
Lascar Cl, Houns. TW3 178 BZ83
Lascelles Av, Har. HA1 139 CD59
Lascelles Cl, E11 145 ED61
Pilgrim's Hatch CM15 130 FU43
Lascelles Rd, Slou. SL3 174 AV76
Lascotts Rd, N22 121 DM51
Las Palmas Est, Shep. TW17 217 BQ101
Lassa Rd, SE9 206 EL85
Lassell St, SE10 47 H1
Lasseter Pl, SE3 47 K2
Lasswade Rd, Cher. KT16 215 BF101
Latchett Rd, E18 124 EH53
Latchford Pl, Chig. IG7 126 EV49
Hemel Hempstead HP1 62 BG21
Latching Cl, Rom. RM3
off Troopers Dr 128 FK49
Latchingdon Ct, E17 145 DX56
Latchingdon Gdns, Wdf.Grn.
IG8 124 EL51
Latchmere Cl, Rich. TW10 200 CL92
Latchmere Inf Sch, Kings.T.
KT2 off Latchmere Rd 200 CM93
Latchmere Jun Sch, Kings.T.
KT2 off Latchmere Rd 200 CM93
Latchmere La, Kings.T. KT2 200 CM93
Latchmere Pas, SW11 40 D9
Latchmere Rd, SW11 40 E8
Kingston upon Thames KT2 200 CL94
Latchmere St, SW11 40 E8
Latchmoor Av, Chal.St.P. SL9 134 AX56
Latchmoor Gro, Chal.St.P.
SL9 134 AX56
Latchmoor Way, Chal.St.P.
SL9 134 AX56
Lateward Rd, Brent. TW8 179 CK79
Latham Cl, E6 25 H8
Biggin Hill TN16 260 EJ116
Dartford DA2 211 FS89
Twickenham TW1 199 CG87
Latham Gra, Upmin. RM14 150 FQ61
Latham Ho, E1 21 K8
Latham Rd, Bexh. DA6 208 FA85
Twickenham TW1 199 CF87
Lathams Way, Croy. CR0 223 DM102
Lathkill Cl, Enf. EN1 122 DU45
Lathom Jun Sch, E6
off Lathom Rd 166 EL66
Lathom Rd, E6 167 EM66
LATIMER, Chesh. HP5 94 AY36
Latimer, SE17 43 N1
Latimer Av, E6 167 EM67
Latimer Cl, Amer. HP6 94 AW39
Hemel Hempstead HP2 62 BN15
Pinner HA5 116 BW53
Watford WD18 115 BS45
Woking GU22 249 BB116
Worcester Park KT4 239 CV105
Latimer Ct, Earls. RH1 288 DF136
Waltham Cross EN8 89 DZ34
Latimer Dr, Horn. RM12 150 FK62
Latimer Gdns, Pnr. HA5 116 BW53
Welwyn Garden City AL7 52 DB09
Latimer Ind Est, W10 14 B8
Latimer Pl, W10 14 B8
Latimer Road 14 D10
Latimer Rd, E7 146 EH63
N15 144 DS58
SW19 202 DB93
W10 14 A7
Barnet EN5 102 DB41
Chenies WD3 95 BB38
Chesham HP5 94 AU36
Croydon CR0
off Abbey Rd 223 DP104
Teddington TW11 199 CF92
Latimer Way, Knot.Grn HP9 110 AJ49
Latitude Apts, N16 144 DS60
Latitude Ct, E16
off Albert Basin Way 167 EQ73
Latium Cl, St.Alb. AL1 65 CD21
Latona Dr, Grav. DA12 213 GM92
Latona Rd, SE15 44 C3
La Tourne Gdns, Orp. BR6 227 EQ104
Lattimer Pl, W4 180 CS79
Lattimore Rd, St.Alb. AL1 65 CE21
LATTON BUSH, Harl. CM18 74 EU18
Latton Cl, Esher KT10 236 CB105
Walton-on-Thames KT12 218 BY101
Latton Common, Harl. CM17 74 EV18
Latton Common Rd, Harl.
CM18 74 EU18
Latton Grn, Harl. CM18 73 ET19
Latton Grn Prim Sch, Harl.
CM18 off Riddings La 73 ET19
Latton Hall Cl, Harl. CM20 58 EU14
Latton Ho, Harl. CM18 74 EV18
Latton St, Harl. CM20 58 EU14
Latton St, Potter Street CM17 74 EW18
Latymer All Saints C of E
Prim Sch, N9
off Hydethorpe Av 122 DT47
Latymer Cl, Wey. KT13 235 BQ105
Latymer Ct, W6 26 D9
Latymer Rd, N9 122 DT46
Latymer Sch, The, N9
off Haselbury Rd 122 DS47
Latymer Upr Sch, W6
off King St 181 CU77
Latymer Way, N9 122 DR47
Laubin Cl, Twick. TW1 179 CH84
Lauder Cl, Nthlt. UB5 158 BX68
Lauderdale Dr, Rich. TW10 199 CK90
Lauderdale Pl, EC2
off The Barbican 19 J6
Lauderdale Rd, W9 15 L3
Hunton Bridge WD4 81 BQ33
Lauderdale Twr, EC2 19 J6
Laud St, SE11 30 C10
Croydon CR0 224 DQ104
Laugan Wk, SE17 off East St 31 K10
Laughton Ct, Borwd. WD6
off Banks Rd 100 CR40
Laughton Rd, Nthlt. UB5 158 BX67
Launcelot Prim Sch, Downham
BR1 off Launcelot Rd 206 EG91
Launcelot Rd, Brom. BR1 206 EG91
Launcelot St, SE1 30 E5
Launceston, Chorl. WD3 95 BB44
Launceston Cl, Rom. RM3 128 FJ53
Launceston Gdns, Perivale
UB6 159 CJ67
Launceston Pl, W8 27 N6
Launceston Rd, Perivale UB6 159 CJ67
Launch St, E14 34 E6
Launders Gate, W3 180 CP75
Launders La, Rain. RM13 170 FM69
Laundress La, N16 144 DU62
Laundry La, N1 9 J7
Lower Nazeing EN9 90 EE25
Laundry Ms, SE23 205 DY87
Laundry Rd, W6 38 E3
Guildford GU1 280 AW135
Launton Dr, Bexh. DA6 188 EX84
Laura Cl, E11 146 EJ57
Enfield EN1 104 DS43
Lauradale Rd, N2 142 DF56
Laura Dr, Swan. BR8 209 FG94
Laurance Haines Prim &
Nurs Sch, Wat. WD18
off Vicarage Rd 97 BU44
Laura Pl, E5 10 G1
Laureate Way, Hem.H. HP1 62 BG18
Laurel Apts, SE17
off Townsend St 31 N8
Laurel Av, Eng.Grn TW20 194 AV92
Gravesend DA12 213 GJ89
Potters Bar EN6 85 CZ32
Slough SL3 174 AY75
Twickenham TW1 199 CF88
Laurel Bk, Felden HP3 61 BF23
Laurel Bk Gdns, SW6 39 H8
Laurel Bk Rd, Enf. EN2 104 DQ39
Laurel Bk Vil, W7
off Lower Boston Rd 159 CE74
Laurel Cl, N19
off Hargrave Pk 143 DJ61
SW17 202 DE92
Colnbrook SL3 175 BE80
Dartford DA1
off Willow Rd 210 FJ88
Hemel Hempstead HP2 62 BM19
Hutton CM13 131 GB43
Ilford IG6 125 EQ51
Sidcup DA14 208 EU90
Watford WD19 116 BX45
Woking GU21 233 BD113
Laurel Ct, Amer. HP6 77 AQ36
Cuffley EN6
off Station Rd 87 DM29
Laurel Cres, Croy. CR0 225 EA104
Romford RM7 149 FE60
Woking GU21 233 BC113
Laurel Dr, N21 121 DN45
Oxted RH8 276 EF131
South Ockendon RM15 171 FX70
Laurel Flds, Pot.B. EN6 85 CZ31
Laurel Gdns, E4 123 EB45
NW7 118 CR48
W7 159 CE74
Bromley BR1 226 EL98
Hounslow TW4 178 BY84
New Haw KT15 234 BH110
Laurel Gro, SE20 204 DV94
SE26 205 DX91
Laurel La, Horn. RM12
off Station La 150 FL61
West Drayton UB7 176 BL77
Laurel Lo La, Barn. EN5 101 CW36
Laurel Manor, Sutt. SM2 240 DC108
Laurel Pk, Har. HA3 117 CF52
Laurel Rd, SW13 181 CU82
SW20 221 CV95
Chalfont St. Peter SL9 112 AX53
Hampton Hill TW12 199 CD92
St. Albans AL1 65 CF20
Laurels, The, Bans. SM7 255 CZ117
Cobham KT11 252 BY115
Dartford DA2 210 FJ90
Potten End HP4 61 BB17
Waltham Cross EN7 88 DS27
Weybridge KT13 217 BR104
Laurels, Brom. BR1 226 EH95
Saint Albans AL2 82 CA28
Laurelsfield, St.Alb. AL3 64 CB23
Laurels Rd, Iver SL0 155 BD68
Laurel St, E8 10 B5
Laurel Vw, N12 120 DB48
Laurel Way, E18 146 EF56
N20 120 DA48
Laurence Ms, W12
off Askew Rd 181 CU75
Laurence Pountney Hill, EC4 19 L10
Laurence Pountney La, EC4 19 L10
Laurie Gro, SE14 45 M6
Laurie Rd, W7 159 CE71
Laurier Rd, NW5 143 DH62
Croydon CR0 224 DT101
Lauries Cl, Hem.H. HP1 61 BB22
Laurie Wk, Rom. RM1
off Market Pl 149 FE56
Laurimel Cl, Stan. HA7 117 CH51
Laurino Pl, Bushey Hth WD23 116 CC47
Lauriston Prim Sch, E9 11 J8
Lauriston Rd, E9 11 J8
SW19 201 CX93
Lausanne Rd, N8 143 DN56
Lausanne Rd, SE15 45 H7
Lauser Rd, Stanw. TW19 196 BJ87
Laustan Cl, Guil. GU1 265 BC134
Lavell St, N16 9 M1
Lavender Av, NW9 140 CQ60
Mitcham CR4 222 DE95
Pilgrim's Hatch CM15 130 FV43
Worcester Park KT4 221 CW104
Lavender Cl, E4 123 EA49
SW3 40 B3
Bromley BR2 226 EL100
Carshalton SM5 240 DG105
Chaldon CR3 274 DQ125
Cheshunt EN7 88 DT27
Coulsdon CR5 257 DJ119
Harlow CM20 57 ES14
Hatfield AL10 66 CS15
Leatherhead KT22 253 CJ123
Redhill RH1 289 DH139
Romford RM3 128 FK52
Lavender Ct, W.Mol. KT8
off Molesham Way 218 CB97
Lavender Cres, St.Alb. AL3 64 CC18
Lavender Dr, Uxb. UB8 156 BM71
Lavender Gdns, SW11 182 DF84
Enfield EN2 103 DP39
Harrow Weald HA3 117 CE51
Lavender Gate, Oxshott KT22 236 CB113
Lavender Gro, E8 10 B7
Mitcham CR4 222 DE95
Lavender Hill, SW11 182 DE84
Enfield EN2 103 DN39
Swanley BR8 229 FD97
Lavender Pk Rd, W.Byf. KT14 234 BG112
Lavender Pl, Ilf. IG1 147 EP64
Lavender Prim Sch, Enf. EN2
off Lavender Rd 104 DS39
Lavender Ri, West Dr. UB7 176 BN75
Lavender Rd, SE16 33 L2
SW11 40 B10
Carshalton SM5 240 DG105
Croydon CR0 223 DM100
Enfield EN2 104 DR39
Epsom KT19 238 CP106
Sutton SM1 240 DD105
Uxbridge UB8 156 BM71
Woking GU22 249 BB116
Lavender St, E15 13 J4
Lavender Sweep, SW11 182 DF84
Lavender Ter, SW11 40 D10
Lavender Vale, Wall. SM6 241 DK107
Lavender Wk, SW11 182 DF84
Hemel Hempstead HP2 62 BK18
Mitcham CR4 222 DG97
Lavender Way, Croy. CR0 225 DX100
Lavengro Rd, SE27 204 DQ89
Lavenham Rd, SW18 201 CZ89
Lavernock Rd, Bexh. DA7 188 FA82
Laverock Sch, Oxt. RH8
off Bluehouse La 276 EE128
Lavers Rd, N16 144 DS62
Laverstoke Gdns, SW15 201 CU87
Laverton Ms, SW5 27 M9
Laverton Pl, SW5 27 M9
Lavidge Rd, SE9 206 EL89
Lavina Gro, N1 8 C10
Lavington Cl, E9 11 N4
Lavington Rd, W13 159 CH74
Croydon CR0 223 DM104
Lavington St, SE1 31 H3
Lavinia Av, Wat. WD25 82 BX34
Lavinia Rd, Dart. DA1 210 FM86
Lavrock La, Rick. WD3 114 BM45
Lawbrook La, Guil. GU5 283 BQ144
Lawdale Jun Sch, E2 20 D2
Lawdons Gdns, Croy. CR0 241 DP105
Lawford Av, Chorl. WD3 95 BC44
Lawford Cl, Chorl. WD3 95 BC44
Hornchurch RM12 150 FJ63
Lawford Gdns, Dart. DA1 210 FJ85
Kenley CR8 258 DQ116
Lawford Rd, N1 9 N7
NW5 7 L5
W4 180 CQ80
Law Ho, Bark. IG11 168 EU68
Lawkland, Farn.Royal SL2 153 AQ69
Lawless St, E14 22 D10
Lawley Rd, N14 121 DH45
Lawley St, E5 144 DW63
Lawn, The, Harl. CM20 58 EV12
Southall UB2 178 CA78
Lawn Av, West Dr. UB7 176 BJ75
Lawn Cl, N9 122 DT45
Bromley BR1 206 EH93
Datchet SL3 174 AW80
New Malden KT3 220 CS96
Ruislip HA4 137 BT62
Swanley BR8 229 FC96
Lawn Cres, Rich. TW9 180 CM82
Lawn Fm Gro, Rom. RM6 148 EY56
Lawn Gdns, W7 159 CE74
Lawn Ho Cl, E14 34 E4
Lawn La, SW8 42 B2
Hemel Hempstead HP3 62 BK22
Lawn Pk, Sev. TN13 279 FH127
Lawn Prim Sch, Nthflt DA11
off High St 212 GC86
Lawn Rd, NW3 6 E2
Beckenham BR3 205 DZ94
Gravesend DA11 212 GC86
Guildford GU2 280 AW137
Uxbridge UB8 156 BJ66
Lawns, The, E4 123 EA50
SE3 47 K10
SE19 224 DR95
Colnbrook SL3 175 BE81
Hemel Hempstead HP1 61 BE19
Pinner HA5 116 CB52
St. Albans AL3 64 CC19
Shenley WD7 84 CL33
Sidcup DA14 208 EV91
Sutton SM2 239 CY108
Welwyn Garden City AL8 51 CX06
Lawns, Brwd. CM14
off Uplands Rd 130 FY50
Lawns Ct, Wem. HA9
off The Avenue 140 CM61
Lawns Cres, Grays RM17 192 GD79
Lawns Dr, The, Brox. EN10 71 DZ21
Lawnside, SE3 186 EF84
Lawnsmead, Won. GU5 281 BB144
Lawns Way, Rom. RM5 127 FC52
Lawn Ter, SE3 47 K10
Lawn Vale, Pnr. HA5 116 BX54
Lawrance Gdns, Chsht EN8 89 DX28
Lawrance Rd, St.Alb. AL3 64 CC16
Lawrance Sq, Nthflt DA11 213 GF90
Lawrence Av, E12 147 EN63
E17 123 DX53
Lawrence Av, N13 121 DP49
NW7 118 CS49
NW10 160 CR67
New Malden KT3 220 CR100
Stanstead Abbotts SG12 55 EC11
Lawrence Bldgs, N16 144 DT62
Lawrence Campe Cl, N20 120 DD48
Lawrence Cl, E3 22 A1
N15 144 DS55
W12 off Australia Rd 161 CV73
Guildford GU4
off Ladygrove Dr 265 BB129
Hertford SG14 53 DL08
Lawrence Ct, NW7 118 CS50
Lawrence Cres, Dag. RM10 149 FB62
Edgware HA8 118 CN54
Lawrence Dr, Uxb. UB10 137 BQ63
Lawrence Gdns, NW7 119 CT48
Tilbury RM18 193 GH80
Lawrence Hall, E13 24 A4
Lawrence Hall End, Welw.G.C.
AL7 51 CY12
Lawrence Hill, E4 123 EA47
Lawrence Hill Gdns, Dart. DA1 210 FJ86
Lawrence Hill Rd, Dart. DA1 210 FJ86
Lawrence La, EC2 19 K9
Buckland RH3 271 CV131
Lawrence Moorings, Saw.
CM21 58 EZ06
Lawrence Orchard, Chorl. WD3 95 BD43
Lawrence Pl, N1 8 B8
Lawrence Rd, E6 166 EK67
E13 166 EH67
N15 144 DS56
N18 122 DV49
SE25 224 DT98
W5 179 CJ77
Erith DA8 189 FB80
Hampton TW12 198 BZ94
Hayes UB4 157 BQ68
Hounslow TW4 178 BW84
Pinner HA5 138 BX57
Richmond TW10 199 CJ91
Romford RM2 149 FH57
West Wickham BR4 244 EG105
Lawrence St, E16 23 M7
NW7 119 CT49
SW3 40 C3
Lawrence Trading Est,
Grays RM17
off Askew Fm La 192 FY79
Lawrence Way, NW10 140 CQ62
Slough SL1 153 AK71
Lawrence Weaver Cl, Mord. SM4
off Green La 222 DA100
Lawrie Ho, SW19
off Plough La 202 DB92
Lawrie Pk Av, SE26 204 DV92
Lawrie Pk Cres, SE26 204 DV92
Lawrie Pk Gdns, SE26 204 DV91
Lawrie Pk Rd, SE26 204 DV93
Laws Cl, SE25 224 DR98
Lawson Cl, E16 24 D7
SW19 201 CX90
Ilford IG1 147 ER64
Lawson Ct, N11 off Ringway 121 DJ51
Lawson Est, SE1 31 L7
Lawson Gdns, Dart. DA1 210 FK85
Pinner HA5 137 BV55
Lawson Rd, Dart. DA1 190 FK84
Enfield EN3 104 DW39
Southall UB1 158 BZ70
Lawson Wk, Cars. SM5 240 DF110
Law St, SE1 31 M6
Lawton Rd, E3 21 M3
E10 145 EC60
Cockfosters EN4 102 DD41
Loughton IG10 107 EP41
Laxcon Cl, NW10 140 CQ64
Laxey Rd, Orp. BR6 245 ET107
Laxley Cl, SE5 43 H4
Laxton Gdns, Merst. RH1 273 DK128
Shenley WD7 84 CL32
Laxton Pl, NW1 17 K4
Layard Rd, SE16 32 F8
Enfield EN1 104 DT39
Thornton Heath CR7 224 DR96
Layard Sq, SE16 32 F8
Layborne Av, Noak Hill RM3
off North End 128 FJ47
Laybrook, St.Alb. AL4 65 CG16
Layburn Cres, Slou. SL3 175 BB79
Laycock Prim Sch, N1 8 G5
Laycock St, N1 8 F5
Layer Gdns, W3 160 CN73
Layfield Cl, NW4 141 CV59
Layfield Cres, NW4 141 CV59
Layfield Rd, NW4 141 CV59
Layhams Rd, Kes. BR2 244 EF106
West Wickham BR4 225 ED104
Layhill, Hem.H. HP2 62 BK18
Laymarsh Cl, Belv. DA17 188 EZ76
Laymead Cl, Nthlt. UB5 158 BY65
Laystall St, EC1 18 E5
Layters Av, Chal.St.P. SL9 112 AW54
Layters Av S, Chal.St.P. SL9 112 AW54
Layters Cl, Chal.St.P. SL9 112 AW54
Layters End, Chal.St.P. SL9 112 AW54
LAYTER'S GREEN, Ger.Cr.
SL9 112 AV54
Layters Grn La, Chal.St.P. SL9 134 AU55
Layter's Grn Mobile Home Pk,
Chal.St.P. SL9
off Layters Grn La 112 AV54
Layters Way, Ger.Cr. SL9 134 AX56
Layton Ct, Wey. KT13 235 BP105
Layton Cres, Croy. CR0 241 DN106
Layton Pl, Kew TW9 180 CN81
Layton Rd, Brent. TW8 179 CK78
Hounslow TW3 178 CB84
Laytons Bldgs, SE1 31 K4
Laytons La, Sun. TW16 217 BT96
Layton St, Welw.G.C. AL7 51 CY12
Layzell Wk, SE9
off Mottingham La 206 EK88
Lazar Wk, N7 off Briset Way 143 DM61
Lazell Gdns, Bet. RH3 286 CQ140
Lazenby Ct, WC2 18 A10
Lea, The, Egh. TW20 215 BB95
Leabank Cl, Har. HA1 139 CE62
Leabank Sq, E9 12 A4

Leabank Vw, N15 144 DU58
Leabourne Rd, N16 144 DU58
LEA BRIDGE, E5 145 DX62
Lea Br Rd, E5 144 DW62
E10 145 DY60
E17 145 ED56
Lea Bushes, Wat. WD25 98 BY35
Leachcroft, Chal.St.P. SL9 112 AV53
Leach Gro, Lthd. KT22 253 CJ122
Lea Cl, Bushey WD23 98 CB43
Twickenham TW2 198 BZ87
Lea Ct, N15 off Broad La 144 DU56
Lea Cres, Ruis. HA4 137 BT63
Leacroft, Slou. SL1 173 AM75
Staines-upon-Thames TW18 196 BH91
Leacroft Av, SW12 202 DF87
Leacroft Cl, N21 121 DP47
Kenley CR8 258 DQ116
Staines-upon-Thames TW18 196 BH91
West Drayton UB7 156 BL72
Leacroft Rd, Iver SL0 155 BD72
Leadale Av, E4 123 EA47
Leadale Rd, N15 144 DU58
N16 144 DU58
Leadbeaters Cl, N11
off Goldsmith Rd 120 DF50
Leadbetter Dr, Wat. WD25 97 BR36
Leaden Cl, Loug. IG10 107 EP41
Leadenhall Mkt, EC3 19 N9
Leadenhall Pl, EC3 19 N9
Leadenhall St, EC3 19 N9
Leadenham Ct, E3 22 A5
Leader Av, E12 147 EN64
Leadings, The, Wem. HA9 140 CQ62
Leaf Cl, Nthwd. HA6 115 BR52
Thames Ditton KT7 219 CE99
Leaf Gro, SE27 203 DN92
Leafield Cl, SW16 203 DP93
Woking GU21
off Winnington Way 248 AV118
Leafield La, Sid. DA14 208 EZ91
Leafield Rd, SW20 221 CZ97
Sutton SM1 222 DA103
Leaford Cres, Wat. WD24 97 BT37
Leaforis Rd, Wal.Cr. EN7 88 DU28
Leaf Way, St.Alb. AL1 65 CD23
Leafy Gro, Croy. CR0 243 DY111
Keston BR2 244 EJ106
Leafy Oak Rd, SE12 206 EJ90
Leafy Way, Croy. CR0 224 DT103
Hutton CM13 131 GD46
Lea Gdns, Wem. HA9 140 CL63
Leagrave St, E5 144 DW62
Lea Hall Gdns, E10
off Lea Hall Rd 145 EA60
Lea Hall Rd, E10 145 EA60
Leahoe Gdns, Hert. SG13 54 DQ10
Leaholme Gdns, Slou. SL1 152 AJ71
Leaholme Way, Ruis. HA4 137 BP58
Leahurst Rd, SE13 205 ED85
Lea Interchange, E9 12 B2
Leake St, SE1 30 D4
Lealand Rd, N15 144 DT58
Leamington Av, E17 145 EA57
Bromley BR1 206 EJ92
Morden SM4 221 CZ98
Orpington BR6 245 ES105
Leamington Cl, E12 146 EL64
Bromley BR1 206 EJ91
Hounslow TW3 198 CC85
Romford RM3 128 FM51
Leamington Ct, SE3 47 K2
Leamington Cres, Har. HA2 138 BY62
Leamington Gdns, Ilf. IG3 147 ET61
Leamington Pk, W3 160 CR71
Leamington Pl, Hayes UB4 157 BT70
Leamington Rd, Rom. RM3 128 FN50
Southall UB2 178 BX77
Leamington Rd Vil, W11 15 H7
Leamore St, W6 181 CV77
Lea Mt, Goffs Oak EN7 88 DS28
Leamouth Rd, E6 24 G8
E14 23 H9
Leander Ct, SE8 46 A7
Leander Dr, Grav. DA12 213 GM91
Leander Gdns, Wat. WD25 98 BY37
Leander Rd, SW2 203 DM86
Northolt UB5 158 CA68
Thornton Heath CR7 223 DM98
Leapale La, Guil. GU1 280 AX135
Leapale Rd, Guil. GU1 280 AX135
● Lea Pk Trd Estates, E10
off Warley Cl 145 DZ60
Learner Dr, Har. HA2 138 CA61
Lea Rd, Beck. BR3
off Fairfield Rd 225 EA96
Enfield EN2 104 DR39
Grays RM16 193 GG78
Hoddesdon EN11 71 EC15
Sevenoaks TN13 279 FJ127
Southall UB2 178 BY77
Waltham Abbey EN9 89 EA34
Watford WD24 97 BV38
Learoyd Gdns, E6 25 L10
Leas, The, Bushey WD23 98 BZ39
Hemel Hempstead HP3 62 BN24
Staines-upon-Thames TW18
off Raleigh Ct 196 BG91
Upminster RM14 151 FR59
Leas Cl, Chess. KT9 238 CM108
Leas Dale, SE9 207 EN90
Leas Dr, Iver SL0 155 BE72
Leas Grn, Chis. BR7 207 ET93
Leaside, Bkhm KT23 252 CA123
Hemel Hempstead HP2 63 BQ21
Leaside Av, N10 142 DG55
Leaside Ct, Uxb. UB10 157 BP69
Leaside Rd, E5 144 DW60
Leaside Wk, Ware SG12
off East St 55 DX06
Leas La, Warl. CR6 259 DX118
Leasowes Rd, E10 145 EA60
Lea Sq, E3 11 P9
Leas Rd, Guil. GU1 280 AW135
Warlingham CR6 259 DX118
Leasway, Brwd. CM14 130 FX48
Upminster RM14 150 FQ62
Leathart Cl, Horn. RM12
off Dowding Way 169 FH66
Leatherbottle Grn, Erith DA18 188 EZ76
Leather Bottle La, Belv. DA17 188 EY77
Leather Cl, Mitch. CR4 222 DG96
Leatherdale St, E1 21 J3
Leather Gdns, E15 13 K9
LEATHERHEAD, KT22 - KT24 253 CF121
Leatherhead 253 CG121
Leatherhead Bypass Rd, Lthd.
KT22 253 CJ120
Leatherhead Cl, N16 144 DT60
LEATHERHEAD COMMON, Lthd.
KT22 253 CF119
Leatherhead Hosp, Lthd.
KT22 253 CJ122
★ Leatherhead Mus of Local
History, Lthd. KT22 253 CH122
Leatherhead Rd, Ashtd. KT21 253 CK121
Bookham KT22, KT23 268 CB126
Chessington KT9 237 CJ111
Leatherhead KT22 253 CK121
Oxshott KT22 237 CD114
● Leatherhead Trade Pk, Lthd.
KT22 253 CG121
Leatherhead Trinity Sch, Lthd.
KT22 off Woodvill Rd 253 CH120
Leatherhead KT22
off Fortyfoot Rd 253 CJ122
Leather La, EC1 18 F7
Gomshall GU5 283 BQ139
Hornchurch RM11
off North St 150 FK60
Leather Mkt, The, SE1 31 N5
Leathermarket Ct, SE1 31 N5
Leathermarket St, SE1 31 N5
Leather Rd, SE16 33 J9
Leathersellers Cl, Barn. EN5
off The Avenue 101 CY42
Leathsail Rd, Har. HA2 138 CB62
Leathwaite Rd, SW11 182 DF84
Leathwell Rd, SE8 46 D8
Lea Vale, Dart. DA1 189 FD84
● Lea Valley Business Pk, E10
off Lammas Rd 145 DY61
Lea Valley High Sch, Enf. EN3
off Bullsmoor La 104 DW35
Lea Valley Prim Sch, N17
off Somerford Gro 122 DU52
Lea Valley Rd, E4 105 DY43
Enfield EN3 105 DY43
● Lea Valley Trd Est, N18 123 DX50
Lea Valley Viaduct, E4 123 DX50
N18 123 DX50
Lea Valley Wk, E3 22 E1
E5 145 DY62
E9 11 P2
E10 145 DY62
E14 22 A8
E15 12 B8
E17 122 DW53
N9 123 DY46
N15 144 DU58
N16 144 DU58
N17 122 DW53
N18 122 DW53
Broxbourne EN10 71 EB21
Enfield EN3 105 DZ41
Hatfield AL9 68 DA15
Hertford SG13, SG14 53 DP11
Hoddesdon EN11 71 ED18
Waltham Abbey EN9 89 DZ30
Waltham Cross EN8 89 DZ30
Ware SG12 54 DW06
Welwyn Garden City
AL7, AL8 51 CW13
Leaveland Cl, Beck. BR3 225 EA98
Leaver Gdns, Grnf. UB6 159 CD68
Leavesden Ct, Abb.L. WD5 81 BU31
LEAVESDEN GREEN, Wat.
WD25 81 BS34
Leavesden Grn, Wat. WD25 97 BT35
Leavesden Grn JMI Sch, Lvsdn
WD25 off High Rd 81 BU34
Leavesden Rd, Stan. HA7 117 CG51
Watford WD24 97 BV38
Weybridge KT13 235 BP106
LEAVES GREEN, Kes. BR2 244 EK109
Leaves Grn Cres, Kes. BR2 244 EJ111
Leaves Grn Rd, Kes. BR2 244 EK111
Leaview, Wal.Abb. EN9 89 EB33
Lea Vw Ho, E5
off Springfield 144 DV60
Leaway, E10 145 DX60
Leazes Av, Chaldon CR3 257 DN123
Leazes La, Cat. CR3 257 DN123
Lebanon Av, Felt. TW13 198 BX92
Lebanon Cl, Wat. WD17 97 BR36
Lebanon Ct, Twick. TW1 199 CH87
Lebanon Dr, Cob. KT11 236 CA113
Lebanon Gdns, SW18 202 DA86
Biggin Hill TN16 260 EK117
Lebanon Pk, Twick. TW1 199 CH87
Lebanon Road 224 DS103
Lebanon Rd, SW18 202 DA85
Croydon CR0 224 DS102
Lebrun Sq, SE3 186 EH83
Lechford Rd, Horl. RH6 290 DG149
Lechmere App, Wdf.Grn. IG8 124 EJ54
Lechmere Av, Chig. IG7 125 EQ49
Woodford Green IG8 124 EK54
Lechmere Rd, NW2 161 CV65
Leckford Rd, SW18 202 DC89
Leckhampton Pl, SW2
off Scotia Rd 203 DN87
Leckwith Av, Bexh. DA7 188 EY79
Lecky St, SW7 28 A10
Leclair Ho, SE3
off Gallus Sq 186 EH83
Leconfield Av, SW13 181 CT83
Leconfield Rd, N5 9 L1
Leconfield Wk, Horn. RM12
off Airfield Way 170 FJ65
Le Corte Cl, Kings L. WD4 80 BM29
Lectern La, St.Alb. AL1 65 CD24
Leda Av, Enf. EN3 105 DX39
Leda Rd, SE18 37 J7
Ledborough Gate, Beac. HP9 111 AM51
Ledborough La, Beac. HP9 111 AK52
Ledborough Wd, Beac. HP9 111 AL51
Ledbury Est, SE15 44 E4
Ledbury Ho, SE22
off Pytchley Rd 184 DS83
Ledbury Ms N, W11 15 J10
Ledbury Ms W, W11 15 J10
Ledbury Pl, Croy. CR0 242 DR105
Ledbury Rd, W11 15 H8
Croydon CR0 242 DQ105
Reigate RH2 271 CZ133
Ledbury St, SE15 44 D4
Ledger Cl, Guil. GU1 265 BB132
Ledger Dr, Add. KT15 233 BF106
Ledger La, Fifield SL6 172 AD82
Ledgers Rd, Slou. SL1 173 AR75
Warlingham CR6 259 EA116
Ledrington Rd, SE19 204 DU93
Ledway Dr, Wem. HA9 140 CM59
LEE, SE12 186 EE84
Lee 206 EG86
Lee, The, Nthwd. HA6 115 BT50
Lee Av, Rom. RM6 148 EY58
Lee Br, SE13 185 EC83
Leechcroft Av, Sid. DA15 207 ET85
Swanley BR8 229 FF97
Leechcroft Rd, Wall. SM6 222 DG104
Leech La, Headley KT18 270 CQ126
Leatherhead KT22 270 CQ126
Lee Ch St, SE13 186 EE84
Lee Cl, E17 123 DX53
Barnet EN5 102 DC42
Hertford SG13 54 DQ11
Stanstead Abbotts SG12 55 EC11
Lee Conservancy Rd, E9 11 P3
Leecroft Rd, Barn. EN5 101 CY43
Leeds Cl, Orp. BR6 228 EX103
Leeds Pl, N4 143 DM60
Leeds Rd, Ilf. IG1 147 ER60
Slough SL1 154 AS73
Leeds St, N18 122 DU50
Lee Fm Cl, Chesh. HP5 78 AU30
Leefern Rd, W12 181 CU75
Leefe Way, Cuffley EN6 87 DK28
Lee Gdns Av, Horn. RM11 150 FN60
Leegate, SE12 206 EF85
Leegate Cl, Wok. GU21
off Sythwood 248 AV116
Lee Grn, SE12 206 EF85
off Lee High Rd 206 EF85
Lee Grn, Orp. BR5 228 EU99
Lee Grn La, Epsom KT18 254 CP124
Lee Gro, Chig. IG7 125 EN47
Lee High Rd, SE12 185 ED83
SE13 185 ED83
Leeke St, WC1 18 C2
Leeland Rd, W13 159 CG74
Leeland Ter, W13 159 CG74
Leeland Way, NW10 140 CS63
Lee Manor Prim Sch, SE13
off Leahurst Rd 206 EE86
Leeming Rd, Borwd. WD6 100 CM39
Lee Pk, SE3 186 EF84
Lee Pk Way, N9 123 DX49
N18 123 DX49
Leerdam Dr, E14 34 F7
Lee Rd, NW7 119 CX52
SE3 47 L10
SW19 222 DB95
Enfield EN1 104 DU44
Perivale UB6 159 CJ67
Lees, The, Croy. CR0 225 DZ103
Lees Av, Nthwd. HA6 115 BT53
Leeside, Barn. EN5 101 CY43
Potters Bar EN6
off Wayside 86 DD32
● Leeside Business Cen, Enf.
EN3 105 DZ40
Leeside Ct, SE16 33 J2
Leeside Cres, NW11 141 CZ58
● Leeside Ind Est, N17
off Garman Rd 122 DW52
Leeside Rd, N17 122 DV51
Leeson Gdns, Eton Wick SL4
off Victoria Rd 173 AL77
Leeson Rd, SE24 183 DN84
Leesons Hill, Chis. BR7 227 ES97
Orpington BR5 228 EU97
Leesons Prim Sch, St.P.Cray
BR5 off Leesons Hill 228 EV97
Leesons Way, Orp. BR5 227 ET96
Lees Pl, W1 16 G10
Lees Rd, Uxb. UB8 157 BP70
Lee St, E8 10 A8
Horley RH6 290 DE148
Lee Ter, SE3 186 EE83
SE13 186 EE83
Lee Valley Cycle Route, Harl.
CM19 72 EF15
Hoddesdon EN11 56 EE13
Waltham Abbey EN9 71 ED20
Ware SG12 55 EB09
★ Lee Valley Hockey Cen &
Tennis Cen, E20 12 C1
★ Lee Valley Pk, E10 89 DZ31
Lee Valley Pathway, E9 145 DZ62
E10 144 DW59
E17 144 DW59
Waltham Abbey EN9 89 EA31
● Lee Valley Technopark,
N17 144 DU55
★ Lee Valley VeloPark, E20 12 D2
★ Lee Valley White Water Cen,
Waltham Cross EN9 89 EA33
Lee Vw, Enf. EN2 103 DP39
Leeward Gdns, SW19 201 CZ93
Leeway, SE8 33 N10
Leeway Cl, Hatch End HA5 116 BZ52
Leewood Cl, SE12
off Upwood Rd 206 EF86
Leewood Pl, Swan. BR8 229 FD98
Leewood Way, Eff. KT24 268 BW127
Le Fay Ct, N9 off Galahad Rd 122 DU48
Lefevre Wk, E3 12 A10
Lefroy Rd, W12 181 CT75
Legard Rd, N5 143 DP63
Legatt Rd, SE9 206 EK85
Leggatt Rd, E15 12 F10
Leggatts Cl, Wat. WD24 97 BT36
Leggatts Pk, Pot.B. EN6 86 DD29
Leggatts Ri, Wat. WD25 97 BU35
Leggatts Way, Wat. WD24 97 BT36
Leggatts Wd Av, Wat. WD24 97 BV36
Legge St, SE13 205 EC85
Leggfield Ter, Hem.H. HP1 61 BF20
Leghorn Rd, NW10 161 CT68
SE18 187 ER78
Legion Cl, N1 8 F5
Legion Ct, Mord. SM4 222 DA100
Legion Rd, Grnf. UB6 158 CC67
Legion Ter, E3 11 P9
Legion Way, N12 120 DE52
Legon Av, Rom. RM7 149 FC60
Legra Av, Hodd. EN11 71 EA17
Legrace Av, Houns. TW4 178 BX82
Leicester Av, Mitch. CR4 223 DL98
Leicester Cl, Wor.Pk. KT4 239 CW105
Leicester Ct, WC2 17 P10
Leicester Gdns, Ilf. IG3 147 ES59
Leicester Ms, N2 142 DE55
Leicester Pl, WC2 17 P10
Leicester Rd, E11 146 EH57
N2 142 DE55
Barnet EN5 102 DB43
Leicester Rd, Croydon CR0 224 DS101
Tilbury RM18 193 GF81
Leicester Square 17 P10
Leicester Sq, WC2 29 P1
Leicester St, WC2 17 P10
LEIGH, Reig. RH2 287 CU141
Leigh, The, Kings.T. KT2 200 CS93
Leigham Av, SW16 203 DL90
Leigham Cl, SW16 203 DM90
Leigham Ct, Wall. SM6
off Clyde Rd 241 DJ107
Leigham Ct Rd, SW16 203 DL89
Leigham Dr, Islw. TW7 179 CE80
Leigham Vale, SW2 203 DN90
SW16 203 DM90
Leigh Av, Ilf. IG4 146 EK56
Leigh Cl, Add. KT15 233 BF108
New Malden KT3 220 CQ98
● Leigh Cl Ind Est, N.Mal. KT3
off Leigh Cl 220 CR98
Leigh Common, Welw.G.C. AL7 51 CY11
Leigh Cor, Cob. KT11
off Leigh Hill Rd 252 BW115
Leigh Ct, SE4
off Lewisham Way 46 A8
Borehamwood WD6
off Banks Rd 100 CR40
Harrow HA2 139 CE60
Leigh Ct Cl, Cob. KT11 236 BW114
Leigh Cres, New Adgtn CR0 243 EB108
Leigh Dr, Rom. RM3 128 FK49
Leigh Gdns, NW10 14 A1
Leigh Hill Rd, Cob. KT11 236 BW114
Leigh Hunt Dr, N14 121 DK46
Leigh Hunt St, SE1 31 J4
Leigh Orchard Cl, SW16 203 DM90
Leigh Pk, Datchet SL3 174 AV80
Leigh Pl, EC1 18 E6
Cobham KT11 252 BW115
Dartford DA2 210 FN92
Feltham TW13 198 BW88
Welling DA16 188 EU82
Leigh Pl La, Gdse. RH9 275 DY132
Leigh Pl Rd, Reig. RH2 287 CU140
Leigh Rd, E6 167 EN65
E10 145 EC59
N5 8 G1
Betchworth RH3 286 CQ140
Cobham KT11 235 BV113
Gravesend DA11 213 GH89
Hounslow TW3 179 CD84
Slough SL1 153 AP73
Leigh Rodd, Wat. WD19 116 BZ48
Leigh Sq, Wind. SL4 173 AK82
Leigh St, WC1 18 A4
Leigh Tech Acad, The, Dart.
DA1 off Green St Grn Rd 210 FP88
Leigh Ter, Orp. BR5
off Saxville Rd 228 EV97
Leighton Av, E12 147 EN64
Pinner HA5 138 BY55
Leighton Buzzard Rd, Hem.H.
HP1 62 BJ19
Leighton Cl, Edg. HA8 118 CN54
Leighton Cres, NW5 7 M2
Leighton Gdns, NW10 161 CV68
South Croydon CR2 242 DV113
Tilbury RM18 193 GG80
Leighton Gro, NW5 7 M3
★ Leighton Ho Mus, W14 27 H6
Leighton Pl, NW5 7 L3
Leighton Rd, NW5 7 N3
W13 179 CG75
Enfield EN1 104 DT43
Harrow Weald HA3 117 CD54
Leighton St, Croy. CR0 223 DP102
Leighton Way, Epsom KT18 238 CR114
Leila Parnell Pl, SE7 186 EJ79
Leinster Av, SW14 180 CQ83
Leinster Gdns, W2 15 N9
Leinster Ms, W2 15 N10
Barnet EN5 101 CY41
Leinster Pl, W2 15 N9
Leinster Rd, N10 143 DH56
Leinster Sq, W2 15 K10
Leinster Ter, W2 15 N10
Leiston Spur, Slou. SL1 154 AS72
Leisure La, W.Byf. KT14 234 BH112
Leisure Way, N12 120 DD52
Leith Cl, NW9 140 CR60
Slough SL1 154 AU74
Leithcote Gdns, SW16 203 DM91
Leithcote Path, SW16 203 DM90
Leith Hill, Orp. BR5 228 EU95
Leith Hill Grn, Orp. BR5
off Leith Hill 228 EU95
Leith Hill Rd, Abin.Com. RH5 284 BY144
Leith Pk Rd, Grav. DA12 213 GH88
Leith Rd, N22 121 DP53
Epsom KT17 238 CS112
Leith Twrs, Sutt. SM2 240 DB108
Leith Vw, N.Holm. RH5 285 CJ140
Leith Yd, NW6 5 J8
Lela Av, Houns. TW4 178 BW82
Lelitia Cl, E8 10 C9
Leman St, E1 20 B9
Lemark Cl, Stan. HA7 117 CJ50
Le May Av, SE12 206 EH90
Le May Cl, Horl. RH6 290 DG147
Lemmon Rd, SE10 47 J2
Lemna Rd, E11 146 EE59
Lemonfield Dr, Wat. WD25 82 BY32
Lemon Gro, Felt. TW13 197 BU88
Lemonwell Ct, SE9
off Lemonwell Dr 207 EQ85
Lemonwell Dr, SE9 207 EQ85
LEMSFORD, Welw.G.C. AL8 51 CT10
Lemsford Cl, N15 144 DU57
Lemsford Ct, N4
off Brownswood Rd 144 DQ61
Borehamwood WD6 100 CQ42
Lemsford La, Welw.G.C. AL8 51 CV10
Lemsford Rd, Hat. AL10 67 CT17
Lemsford AL8 51 CT10
St. Albans AL1 65 CF20
Lemsford Village, Lmsfd AL8 51 CU10
Lemuel St, SW18 202 DB86
Lena Cres, N9 122 DW47
Lena Gdns, W6 26 B7
Lena Gdns Prim Sch, W6 26 B6
Lena Kennedy Cl, E4 123 EB51
Lenanton Steps, E14 34 B4
Lendal Ter, SW4 183 DK83
Lenelby Rd, Surb. KT6 220 CN102
Len Freeman Pl, SW6 38 G3
Lenham Rd, SE12 186 EF84
Bexleyheath DA7 188 EZ79
Sutton SM1 240 DB105
Thornton Heath CR7 224 DR96
Lenmore Av, Grays RM17 192 GC76
Lennard Av, W.Wick. BR4 226 EE103
Lennard Cl, W.Wick. BR4 226 EE103
Lennard Rd, SE20 204 DW93
Beckenham BR3 205 DX93
Bromley BR2 227 EM102
Croydon CR0 224 DQ102
Dunton Green TN13 263 FE120
Lennard Row, Aveley RM15 171 FR74
Lennon Rd, NW2 4 A3
Lennox Av, Grav. DA11 213 GF86
Lennox Cl, Chaff.Hun. RM16 191 FW77
Romford RM1 149 FF58
Lennox Gdns, NW10 141 CT63
SW1 28 E7
Croydon CR0 241 DP105
Ilford IG1 147 EM60
Lennox Gdns Ms, SW1 28 E7
Lennox Rd, E17 145 DZ58
N4 143 DM61
Gravesend DA11 213 GF86
Lennox Rd E, Grav. DA11 213 GG87
Lenor Cl, Bexh. DA6 188 EY84
Lensbury Av, SW6 39 P8
Lensbury Cl, Chsht EN8 89 DY28
Lensbury Way, SE2 188 EW76
Lens Rd, E7 166 EJ66
Len Taylor Cl, Hayes UB4
off Welwyn Way 157 BS70
Lenten Cl, Peasl. GU5 283 BR142
Lent Grn, Burn. SL1 152 AH70
Lent Grn La, Burn. SL1 152 AH70
Lenthall Av, Grays RM17 192 GA75
Lenthall Ho, SW1 41 M1
Lenthall Rd, E8 10 B6
Loughton IG10 107 ER42
Lenthorp Rd, SE10 35 L10
Lentmead Rd, Brom. BR1 206 EF90
Lenton Path, SE18 187 ER79
Lenton Ri, Rich. TW9 180 CL83
Lenton St, SE18 187 ER77
Lenton Ter, N4
off Fonthill Rd 143 DN61
LENT RISE, Slou. SL1 152 AH72
Lent Ri Comb Sch, Burn. SL1
off Coulson Way 152 AH71
Lent Ri Rd, Burn. SL1 152 AH72
Taplow SL6 152 AH72
Leo Baeck Coll, N3
off East End Rd 120 DA54
Leof Cres, SE6 205 EB92
Leominster Rd, Mord. SM4 222 DC100
Leominster Wk, Mord. SM4 222 DC100
Leonard Av, Mord. SM4 222 DC99
Otford TN14 263 FH116
Romford RM7 149 FD60
Swanscombe DA10 212 FY87
Leonard Pl, N16 off Allen Rd 144 DS63
Leonard Rd, E4 123 EA51
E7 13 N1
N9 122 DT48
SW16 223 DJ95
Southall UB2 178 BX76
Leonard Robbins Path, SE28
off Tawney Rd 168 EV73
Leonard St, E16 37 H3
EC2 19 M4
Leonard Way, Brwd. CM14 130 FS49
Leonora Tyson Ms, SE21 204 DR89
Leontine Cl, SE15 44 D5
Leopards Ct, EC1 18 E6
Leopold Av, SW19 201 CZ92
Leopold Ms, E9 10 G8
Leopold Prim Sch, NW10
off Hawkshead Rd 161 CT66
Leopold Rd, E17 145 EA57
N2 142 DD55
N18 122 DV50
NW10 160 CS66
SW19 201 CZ91
W5 160 CM74
Leopold St, E3 21 P6
Leopold Ter, SW19 201 CZ92
Leo St, SE15 44 F4
Leo Yd, EC1 19 H5
Le Personne Rd, Cat. CR3 258 DR122
Lepoc Rd, SW4 203 DK85
Leret Way, Lthd. KT22 253 CH121
Leroy St, SE1 31 N8
Lerry Cl, W14 39 H2
Lerwick Dr, Slou. SL1 154 AS71
Lesbourne Rd, Reig. RH2 288 DB135
Lescombe Cl, SE23 205 DY90
Lescombe Rd, SE23 205 DY90
Lesley Cl, Bex. DA5 209 FB87
Istead Rise DA13 213 GF94
Swanley BR8 229 FD97
Leslie Gdns, Sutt. SM2 240 DA108
Leslie Gro, Croy. CR0 224 DS102
Leslie Gro Pl, Croy. CR0
off Leslie Gro 224 DS102
Leslie Pk Rd, Croy. CR0 224 DS102
Leslie Rd, E11 12 F1
E16 24 A9
N2 142 DD55
Chobham GU24 232 AS110
Dorking RH4 269 CK134
Leslie Smith Sq, SE18
off Nightingale Vale 187 EN79
★ Lesnes Abbey (ruins), Erith
DA18 188 EX77
Lesney Fm Est, Erith DA8 189 FD80
Lesney Pk, Erith DA8 189 FD79
Lesney Pk Rd, Erith DA8 189 FD79
Lessar Av, SW4 203 DJ85
Lessingham Av, SW17 202 DF91
Ilford IG5 147 EN55
Lessing St, SE23 205 DY87
Lessington Av, Rom. RM7 149 FC58
Lessness Av, Bexh. DA7 188 EX80
LESSNESS HEATH, Belv.
DA17 189 FB78
Lessness Heath Prim Sch,
Belv. DA17
off Erith Rd 188 FA78
Lessness Pk, Belv. DA17 188 EZ78
Lessness Rd, Belv. DA17
off Stapley Rd 188 FA78
Morden SM4 222 DC100
Lester Av, E15 23 K3
Lestock Cl, SE25 224 DU97
Leston Cl, Rain. RM13 169 FH69
Leswin Pl, N16 144 DT62
Leswin Rd, N16 144 DT62
Letchfield, Ley Hill HP5 78 AV31
Letchford Gdns, NW10 161 CU69
Letchford Ms, NW10
off Letchford Gdns 161 CU69
Letchford Ter, Har. HA3 116 CB53

LETCHMORE HEATH, Wat. WD25 99 CD38
Letchmore Rd, Rad. WD7 99 CG36
Letchworth Av, Felt. TW14 197 BT87
Letchworth Cl, Brom. BR2 226 EG99
Watford WD19 116 BX50
Letchworth Dr, Brom. BR2 226 EG99
Letchworth St, SW17 202 DF91
Lethbridge Cl, SE13 46 E7
Letter Box La, Sev. TN13 279 FJ129
Letterstone Rd, SW6 38 G5
Lettice St, SW6 38 G7
Lett Rd, E15 12 G7
Lettsom St, SE5 43 N8
Lettsom Wk, E13 13 N10
LETTY GREEN, Hert. SG14 53 DH13
Leucha Rd, E17 145 DY57
Levana Cl, SW19 201 CY88
Levehurst Ho, SE27
off Elder Rd 204 DQ92
Levehurst Way, SW4 42 B8
Leven Cl, Wal.Cr. EN8 89 DX33
Watford WD19 116 BX50
Levendale Rd, SE23 205 DY89
Leven Dr, Wal.Cr. EN8 89 DX33
Leven Rd, E14 22 F7
Leven Way, Hayes UB3 157 BS72
Hemel Hempstead HP2 62 BK16
Leveret Cl, New Adgtn CR0 243 ED111
Watford WD25 81 BU34
Leverett St, SW3 28 D8
Leverholme Gdns, SE9 207 EN90
Leverson St, SW16 203 DJ93
Lever Sq, Grays RM16 193 GG77
LEVERSTOCK GREEN, Hem.H. HP3 63 BQ21
Sch Leverstock Grn C of E Prim Sch, Hem.H. HP2 off Green La 63 BR21
Leverstock Grn Rd, Hem.H. HP2, HP3 63 BQ21
Leverstock Grn Way, Hem.H. HP3 63 BQ20
Lever St, EC1 19 H3
Sch Leverton Inf & Nurs Sch, Wal.Abb. EN9 off Honey La 90 EF34
Sch Leverton Jun Sch, Wal.Abb. EN9 off Honey La 90 EF34
Leverton Pl, NW5 7 K3
Leverton St, NW5 7 L3
Leverton Way, Wal.Abb. EN9 89 EC33
Leveson Rd, Grays RM16 193 GH76
Levett Gdns, Ilf. IG3 147 ET63
Levett Rd, Bark. IG11 167 ES65
Leatherhead KT22 253 CH120
Levine Gdns, Bark. IG11 168 EX68
Levison Way, N19
off Grovedale Rd 143 DK61
Levylsdene, Guil. GU1 265 BD134
Lewen Cl, Croy. CR0 224 DR102
Lewes Cl, Grays RM17 192 GA79
Northolt UB5 158 CA65
Lewes Ct, Slou. SL1
off Chalvey Gro 173 AQ75
Lewesdon Cl, SW19 201 CX88
Lewes Rd, N12 120 DE50
Bromley BR1 226 EK96
Romford RM3 128 FJ49
Leweston Pl, N16 144 DT59
Lewes Way, Crox.Grn WD3 97 BQ42
Lewey Ho, E3 21 P5
Lewgars Av, NW9 140 CQ58
Lewing Cl, Orp. BR6
off Place Fm Av 227 ES102
Lewington Ct, Enf. EN3
off Hertford Rd 105 DX37
Lewin Rd, SW14 180 CR83
SW16 203 DK93
Bexleyheath DA6 188 EY84
Lewins Rd, Chal.St.P. SL9 134 AX55
Epsom KT18 238 CP114
Lewins Way, Slou. SL1 153 AM73
Lewin Ter, Felt. TW14 197 BR87
Lewis Av, E17 123 EA53
Lewis Cl, N14 121 DJ45
Addlestone KT15 234 BJ105
Harefield UB9 114 BJ54
Shenfield CM15 131 FZ45
Lewis Cres, NW10 140 CQ64
Lewis Gdns, N2 120 DD54
N16 144 DT58
Lewis Gro, SE13 185 EC83
LEWISHAM, SE13 185 EB84
⇌ Lewisham 46 D10
DLR Lewisham 46 E10
⊖ Lewisham 46 E10
Sch Lewisham Br Prim Sch, SE13
off Elmira St 185 EB83
Lewisham Cen, SE13 185 EC83
Coll Lewisham City Learning Cen, SE23 off Mayow Rd 205 DX90
Coll Lewisham Coll, Deptford Campus, SE8 46 B6
Lewisham Way Campus, SE4 46 A9
Lewisham Ct, Enf. EN3
off Hodson Pl 105 EA38
Lewisham High St, SE13 46 F10
Lewisham Hill, SE13 46 F9
Lewisham Pk, SE13 205 EB86
Lewisham Rd, SE13 46 D7
Lewisham St, SW1 29 P5
Lewisham Way, SE4 45 N6
SE14 45 N6
Lewis La, Chal.St.P. SL9 112 AY53
Lewis Pl, E8 10 C3
Lewis Rd, Horn. RM11 150 FJ58
Mitcham CR4 222 DD96
Richmond TW10
off Red Lion St 199 CK85
Sidcup DA14 208 EW90
Southall UB1 178 BY75
Sutton SM1 240 DB105
Swanscombe DA10 212 FY86
Welling DA16 188 EW83
Lewis St, NW1 7 K5
Lewiston Cl, Wor.Pk. KT4 221 CV101
Lewis Way, Dag. RM10 169 FB65
Leworth Pl, Wind. SL4
off Bachelors Acre 173 AR81
Lexden Dr, Rom. RM6 148 EV58
Lexden Rd, W3 160 CP73
Mitcham CR4 223 DK98
Lexham Ct, Grnf. UB6
off Oldfield La N 159 CD67
Lexham Gdns, W8 27 L8
Amersham HP6 77 AQ37
Lexham Gdns Ms, W8 27 M7
Lexham Ho, Bark. IG11
off St. Margarets 167 ER67
Lexham Ms, W8 27 K8
Lexham Wk, W8 27 M7
Lexicon Apts, Rom. RM1
off Mercury Gdns 149 FE56
Lexington Apts, EC1 19 L4
Lexington Bldg, E3
off Fairfield Rd 22 B1
Lexington Cl, Borwd. WD6 100 CM41
Lexington Ct, Pur. CR8 242 DQ110
Lexington Ho, West Dr. UB7
off Park Lo Ave 176 BM75
Lexington Pl, Kings.T. KT1 199 CK94
Lexington St, W1 17 M9
Lexington Way, Barn. EN5 101 CX42
Upminster RM14 151 FT58
Lexton Gdns, SW12 203 DK88
Leybome Av, W13 179 CH75
Leyborne Pk, Rich. TW9 180 CN81
Leybourne Av, Byfleet KT14 234 BM113
Leybourne Cl, Brom. BR2 226 EG100
Byfleet KT14 234 BM113
Leybourne Rd, E11 146 EF60
NW1 7 K7
NW9 140 CN57
Uxbridge UB10 157 BQ67
Leybourne St, NW1 7 J7
Leybridge Ct, SE12 206 EG85
Leyburn Cl, E17 145 EB56
Leyburn Cres, Rom. RM3 128 FL52
Leyburn Gdns, Croy. CR0 224 DS103
Leyburn Gro, N18 122 DU51
Leyburn Rd, N18 122 DU51
Romford RM3 128 FL52
Leycroft Cl, Loug. IG10 107 EN43
Leycroft Gdns, Erith DA8 189 FH81
Leydenhatch La, Swan. BR8 229 FC95
Leyden St, E1 20 A7
Leydon Cl, SE16 33 K3
Leyfield, Wor.Pk. KT4 220 CS102
Leyhill Cl, Swan. BR8 229 FE99
Ley Hill Rd, Bov. HP3 78 AX30
Sch Ley Hill Sch, Ley Hill HP5
off Jasons Hill 78 AV30
Leyland Av, Enf. EN3 105 DY40
St. Albans AL1 65 CD22
Leyland Cl, Chsht EN8 88 DW28
Leyland Ct, N11
off Oakleigh Rd S 121 DH49
Leyland Gdns, Wdf.Grn. IG8 124 EJ50
Leyland Rd, SE12 206 EG85
Leylands La, Stai. TW19 195 BF85
Leylang Rd, SE14 45 K4
Sch Ley Pk Prim Sch, Brox. EN10
off Cozens La E 71 DZ22
Leys, The, N2 142 DC56
Amersham HP6 77 AP35
Harrow HA3 140 CM58
St. Albans AL4 65 CK17
Leys Av, Dag. RM10 169 FC66
Leys Cl, Dag. RM10 169 FC66
Harefield UB9 114 BK53
Harrow HA1 139 CD57
Leysdown, Welw.G.C. AL7 52 DD09
Leysdown Av, Bexh. DA7 189 FC84
Leysdown Rd, SE9 206 EL89
Leysfield Rd, W12 181 CU75
Leys Gdns, Barn. EN4 102 DG43
Sch Leys Prim Sch, The, Dag. RM10
off Leys Av 169 FC66
Leyspring Rd, E11 146 EF60
Leys Rd, Hem.H. HP3 62 BL22
Oxshott KT22 237 CD112
Leys Rd E, Enf. EN3 105 DY39
Leys Rd W, Enf. EN3 105 DY39
Ley St, Ilf. IG1, IG2 147 EP61
Leyswood Dr, Ilf. IG2 147 ES57
Leythe Rd, W3 180 CQ75
LEYTON, E11 145 EB60
⊖ Leyton 145 EC62
● Leyton Business Cen, E10 145 EA61
Leyton Cross Rd, Dart. DA2 209 FF90
Leyton Gra, E10 145 EA61
Leyton Gra Est, E10
off Leyton Gra 145 EA61
Leyton Grn Rd, E10 145 EC58
● Leyton Ind Village, E10 145 DX59
⇌ Leyton Midland Road 145 EC60
★ Leyton Orient FC, E10 145 EB62
Leyton Pk Rd, E10 145 EC62
Leyton Rd, E15 12 G3
SW19 202 DC94
Coll Leyton 6th Form Coll, E10
off Essex Rd 145 ED58
LEYTONSTONE, E11 145 ED59
⊖ Leytonstone 146 EE60
⇌ Leytonstone High Road 146 EE61
Leytonstone Rd, E15 13 J3
Sch Leytonstone Sch, E11
off Colworth Rd 146 EE58
Ley Wk, Welw.G.C. AL7 52 DC09
Leywick St, E15 13 J10
Leywood Cl, Amer. HP7 77 AR40
Lezayre Rd, Orp. BR6 245 ET107
Lianne Gro, SE9 206 EJ90
Liardet St, SE14 45 M3
Liberia Rd, N5 9 H4
★ Liberty, W1 17 L9
Liberty, The, Rom. RM1 149 FE57
Liberty Av, SW19 222 DD95
● Liberty Cen, Wem. HA0
off Mount Pleasant 160 CM67
Liberty Cl, N18 122 DT49
Hertford SG13 54 DQ11
Worcester Park KT4 221 CW102
Liberty Hall Rd, Add. KT15 234 BG106
Liberty Ho, Cher. KT16
off Guildford St 215 BF102
Liberty La, Add. KT15 234 BG106
Liberty Ms, SW12 203 DH86
Sch Liberty Prim Sch, Mitch. CR4
off Western Rd 222 DE96
Liberty Ri, Add. KT15 234 BG107
Liberty St, SW9 42 D7
Liberty Wk, St.Alb. AL1 65 CJ21
Libra Rd, E3 11 P9
E13 13 N10
Library Ct, N17 off High Rd 144 DT55
Library Hill, Brwd. CM14
off Coptfold Rd 130 FX47
Library Pl, E1 20 F10
Library St, SE1 30 G5
Library Way, Twick. TW2
off Nelson Rd 198 CC87
Lichfield Cl, Barn. EN4 102 DF41
Lichfield Ct, Rich. TW9
off Sheen Rd 200 CL85
Lichfield Gdns, Rich. TW9 180 CL84
Lichfield Gro, N3 120 DA53
Lichfield Pl, St.Alb. AL1
off Avenue Rd 65 CF19
Lichfield Rd, E3 21 M2
E6 24 E3
N9 122 DU47
NW2 141 CY63
Dagenham RM8 148 EV63
Hounslow TW4 178 BW83
Northwood HA6 137 BU55
Richmond TW9 180 CM81
Woodford Green IG8 124 EE49
Lichfield Ter, Upmin. RM14 151 FS61
Lichfield Way, Brox. EN10 71 DZ22
South Croydon CR2 243 DX110
Lichlade Cl, Orp. BR6 245 ET105
Lickey Ho, W14
off North End Rd 39 H2
Lidbury Rd, NW7 119 CY51
Lidcote Gdns, SW9 42 E9
Liddall Way, West Dr. UB7 156 BM74
Liddell, Wind. SL4 172 AJ83
Liddell Cl, Har. HA3 139 CK55
Liddell Gdns, NW10 4 A10
Liddell Pl, Wind. SL4
off Liddell 172 AJ82
Liddell Rd, NW6 5 J4
Liddell Sq, Wind. SL4
off Liddell 172 AJ82
Liddell Way, Wind. SL4
off Liddell 172 AJ83
Lidding Rd, Har. HA3 139 CK57
Liddington Hall Dr, Rydes. GU3 264 AS131
Liddington New Rd, Rydes. GU3 264 AS131
Liddington Rd, E15 13 L8
Liddon Rd, E13 24 A3
Bromley BR1 226 EJ97
Liden Cl, E17 145 DZ59
Lidfield Rd, N16 9 L1
Lidgate Rd, SE15 44 A5
Lidgould Gr, Ruis. HA4 137 BU58
Lidiard Rd, SW18 202 DC89
Lidlington Pl, NW1 17 L1
Lido Ho, W13
off Northfield Av 159 CH74
Lido Sq, N17 122 DR53
Lidstone Cl, Wok. GU21 248 AV117
Lidstone Ct, Geo.Grn SL3 154 AX72
Lidyard Rd, N19 143 DJ60
Lieutenant Ellis Way, Wal.Cr. EN7, EN8 88 DT31
Coll Lifelong Learning, The Shadwell Cen, E1 21 J10
★ Lifetimes Mus (Croydon Cen Lib), Croy. CR0 224 DQ104
Liffler Rd, SE18 187 ES78
Liffords Pl, SW13 181 CT82
Lifford St, SW15 181 CX84
Lightcliffe Rd, N13 121 DN49
Lighter Cl, SE16 33 M8
Lighterman Ms, E1 21 K8
Lighterman's Ms, Grav. DA11 212 GE87
Lightermans Rd, E14 34 B5
Lightermans Way, Green. DA9 191 FW84
Lightfoot Rd, N8 143 DL57
Lightley Cl, Wem. HA0 160 CM67
Lightswood Cl, Chsht EN7 88 DR27
Ligonier St, E2 20 A4
Lilac Av, Enf. EN1 104 DW36
Woking GU22 248 AX120
Lilac Cl, E4 123 DZ51
Cheshunt EN7 88 DV31
Guildford GU1 264 AW130
Pilgrim's Hatch CM15
off Magnolia Way 130 FV43
Lilac Ct, Slou. SL2 153 AM69
Lilac Gdns, W5 179 CK76
Croydon CR0 225 EA104
Hayes UB3 157 BS72
Romford RM7 149 FE60
Swanley BR8 229 FD97
Lilac Ms, N8 off Courcy Rd 143 DN55
Lilac Pl, SE11 30 C9
West Drayton UB7 156 BM73
Lilac Rd, Hodd. EN11 71 EB15
Lilac St, W12 161 CU73
Lilah Ms, Brom. BR2
off Beckenham La 226 EE96
Lila Pl, Swan. BR8 229 FE98
Lilbourne Dr, Hert. SG13 54 DU08
Lilburne Gdns, SE9 206 EL85
Lilburne Rd, SE9 206 EL85
Lilburne Wk, NW10 160 CQ65
Lile Cres, W7 159 CE71
Lilestone St, NW8 16 C4
Lilford Rd, SE5 42 G8
Lilian Barker Cl, SE12 206 EG85
Sch Lilian Baylis Tech Sch, SE11 42 D1
Lilian Board Way, Grnf. UB6 139 CD64
Lilian Cl, N16 144 DS62
Lilian Cres, Hutt. CM13 131 GC47
Lilian Gdns, Wdf.Grn. IG8 124 EH53
Lilian Rd, SW16 223 DJ95
Lillechurch Rd, Dag. RM8 168 EV65
Lilleshall Rd, Mord. SM4 222 DD100
Lilley Cl, E1 32 D3
Brentwood CM14 130 FT49
Lilley Dr, Kgswd KT20 256 DB122
Lilley La, NW7 118 CR50
Lilley Mead, Red. RH1 273 DJ131
Lilley Way, Slou. SL1 153 AL74
Lillian Av, W3 180 CN75
Lillian Rd, SW13 181 CU79
Lilliards Cl, Hodd. EN11 55 EB13
Lillie Rd, SW6 38 D3
Biggin Hill TN16 260 EK118
Lillieshall Rd, SW4 183 DH83
Lillie Yd, SW6 39 J2
Lillingston Ho, N7
off Harvist Est 143 DN63
Lillington Gdns Est, SW1 29 M9
Lilliots La, Lthd. KT22
off Kingston Rd 253 CG119
Lilliput Av, Nthlt. UB5 158 BZ67
Lilliput Rd, Rom. RM7 149 FD59
Lillyfee Fm La, Woob.Grn HP10 132 AG57
Lilly La, Hem.H. HP2 63 BR16
Lily Cl, W14 26 E9
Lily Dr, West Dr. UB7 176 BK77
Lily Gdns, Wem. HA0 159 CJ68
Lily Pl, EC1 18 F6
Lily Rd, E17 145 EA58
Lilyville Rd, SW6 38 G6
Limbourne Av, Dag. RM8 148 EZ59
Limburg Rd, SW11 182 DF84
Lime Av, Brwd. CM13 131 FZ48
Northfleet DA11 212 GD87
Lime Av, Upminster RM14 150 FN63
West Drayton UB7 156 BM73
Windsor SL4 174 AT80
Limeburner La, EC4 18 G9
Limebush Cl, New Haw KT15 234 BJ109
Lime Cl, E1 32 D2
Bromley BR1 226 EL98
Buckhurst Hill IG9 124 EK48
Carshalton SM5 222 DF103
Harrow HA3 117 CF54
Pinner HA5 137 BT55
Reigate RH2 288 DB137
Romford RM7 149 FC56
South Ockendon RM15 171 FW69
Ware SG12 55 DY05
Watford WD19 116 BX45
West Clandon GU4 266 BH128
Lime Ct, Mitch. CR4 222 DD96
Lime Cres, Sun. TW16 218 BW96
Limecroft Cl, Epsom KT19 238 CR108
Limedene Cl, Pnr. HA5 116 BX53
Lime Gro, E4 123 DZ51
N20 119 CZ46
W12 26 A4
Addlestone KT15 234 BG105
Guildford GU1 264 AV130
Hayes UB3 157 BR73
Ilford IG6 125 ET51
New Malden KT3 220 CR97
Orpington BR6 227 EP103
Ruislip HA4 137 BV59
Sidcup DA15 207 ET86
Twickenham TW1 199 CF86
Warlingham CR6 259 DY118
West Clandon GU4 266 BG128
Woking GU22 248 AY121
Limeharbour, E14 34 D5
LIMEHOUSE, E14 21 M10
⇌ Limehouse 21 L9
DLR Limehouse 21 L9
Limehouse Causeway, E14 21 P10
Limehouse Link, E14 33 P1
Limehouse Lo, E5
off Mount Pleasant Hill 144 DW61
Limekiln Dr, SE7 186 EH79
Limekiln Pl, SE19 204 DT94
Lime Meadow Av, S.Croy. CR2 242 DU113
Lime Pit La, Dunt.Grn TN13 263 FC117
Lime Quarry Ms, Guil. GU1 265 BD133
Limerick Cl, SW12 203 DJ87
Limerick Gdns, Upmin. RM14 151 FT59
Limerick Ms, N2 142 DE55
Lime Rd, Epp. CM16 91 ET31
Richmond TW9 180 CM84
Swanley BR8 229 FD97
Lime Row, Erith DA18
off Northwood Pl 188 EZ76
Limerston St, SW10 39 P2
Limes, The, SW18 202 DA86
W2 27 K1
Amersham HP6 77 AP35
Brentwood CM13 131 FZ48
Bromley BR2 226 EL103
Hornchurch RM11 150 FK55
Horsell GU21 248 AX115
Purfleet RM19
off Tank Hill Rd 190 FN78
St. Albans AL1 65 CE18
Welwyn Garden City AL7 52 DA11
Windsor SL4 172 AJ82
Limes Av, E11 146 EH56
N12 120 DC49
NW7 118 CS51
NW11 141 CY59
SE20 204 DV94
SW13 181 CT82
Carshalton SM5 222 DF102
Chigwell IG7 125 EQ50
Croydon CR0 223 DN104
Horley RH6 291 DH150
Limes Av, The, N11 121 DH50
Limes Cl, Ashf. TW15 196 BN92
Leatherhead KT22
off Linden Gdns 253 CJ120
Limes Ct, Brwd. CM15
off Sawyers Hall La 130 FX46
Hoddesdon EN11
off Conduit La 71 EA17
Limesdale Gdns, Edg. HA8 118 CQ54
Sch Limes Fm Inf & Nurs & Jun Schs, Chig. IG7
off Limes Av 125 ER50
Limes Fld Rd, SW14
off First Av 180 CS83
Limesford Rd, SE15 185 DX84
Limes Gdns, SW18 202 DA86
Limes Gro, SE13 185 EC84
Limes Ms, Egh. TW20
off Limes Rd 195 AZ92
Limes Pl, Croy. CR0 224 DR101
Limes Rd, Beck. BR3 225 EB96
Cheshunt EN8 89 DX32
Croydon CR0 224 DR100
Egham TW20 195 AZ92
Weybridge KT13 234 BN105
Limes Row, Farnboro. BR6 245 EP106
Limestone Wk, Erith DA18 188 EX76
Lime St, E17 145 DY56
EC3 19 N10
Lime St Pas, EC3 19 N9
Limes Wk, SE15 184 DV84
W5 179 CK75
Lime Ter, W7 off Manor Ct Rd 159 CE73
Lime Tree Av, Bluewater DA9 211 FU88
Esher KT10 219 CD102
Thames Ditton KT7 219 CD102
Lime Tree Cl, E18 146 EJ56
Limetree Cl, SW2 203 DM88
Lime Tree Cl, Bkhm KT23 252 CA124
Lime Tree Ct, Ashtd. KT21
off Greville Pk Rd 254 CL118
London Colney AL2 83 CH26
Lime Tree Gro, Croy. CR0 225 DZ104
Lime Tree Pl, Mitch. CR4 223 DH95
St. Albans AL1 65 CF21
Lime Tree Rd, Houns. TW5 178 CB81
Limetree Wk, SW17
off Hawthorn Cres 202 DG92
Lime Tree Wk, Amer. HP7 94 AT39
Bushey Heath WD23 117 CE46
Enfield EN2 104 DQ38
Rickmansworth WD3 96 BH43
Sevenoaks TN13 279 FH125
Virginia Water GU25 214 AY98
West Wickham BR4 244 EF105
Lime Wk, E15 13 K8
Denham UB9 136 BJ64
Hemel Hempstead HP3 62 BM22
Lime Wk, Shere GU5 282 BM139
Sch Lime Wk Prim Sch, Hem.H. HP3
off Lime Wk 62 BM22
Limeway Ter, Dor. RH4 269 CG134
Limewood Cl, E17 145 DZ56
W13 159 CH72
Beckenham BR3 225 EC99
Limewood Ct, Ilf. IG4 147 EM57
Limewood Rd, Erith DA8 189 FC80
Lime Wks Rd, Merst. RH1 273 DJ126
LIMPSFIELD, Oxt. RH8 276 EG128
Limpsfield Av, SW19 201 CX89
Thornton Heath CR7 223 DM99
LIMPSFIELD CHART, Oxt. RH8 276 EL130
Sch Limpsfield C of E Inf Sch, Oxt. RH8 off Westerham Rd 276 EJ129
Sch Limpsfield Gra Sch, Oxt. RH8
off Bluehouse La 276 EG127
Limpsfield Rd, S.Croy. CR2 242 DU112
Warlingham CR6 258 DW116
Linacre Cl, SE15 44 F10
Linacre Ct, W6 26 D10
Linacre Rd, NW2 161 CV65
Linale Ho, N1 off Murray Gro 19 L1
Linberry Wk, SE8 33 M9
Lince La, Westc. RH4 285 CD136
Linces Way, Welw.G.C. AL7 52 DB11
Linchfield Rd, Datchet SL3 174 AW81
Linchmere Rd, SE12 206 EF87
Lincoln Av, N14 121 DJ48
SW19 201 CX90
Romford RM7 149 FD60
Twickenham TW2 198 CB89
Lincoln Cl, SE25
off Woodside Grn 224 DV100
Erith DA8 189 FF82
Greenford UB6 158 CC67
Harrow HA2 138 BZ57
Horley RH6 290 DF149
Hornchurch RM11 150 FN57
Welwyn Garden City AL7 52 DD08
Lincoln Ct, N16 144 DR59
Berkhamsted HP4 60 AV19
Borehamwood WD6 100 CR43
Denham UB9 135 BF58
Lincoln Cres, Enf. EN1 104 DS43
Lincoln Dr, Crox.Grn WD3 97 BP42
Watford WD19 116 BW48
Woking GU22 249 BE115
Lincoln Gdns, Ilf. IG1 146 EL59
Lincoln Grn Rd, Orp. BR5 227 ET99
Lincoln Hatch La, Burn. SL1 152 AJ70
Lincoln Ms, N15 144 DQ56
NW6 4 G8
SE21 204 DR88
Lincoln Pk, Amer. HP7 77 AS39
Lincoln Rd, E7 166 EK65
E13 24 A5
E18 off Grove Rd 124 EG53
N2 142 DE55
SE25 224 DV97
Chalfont St. Peter SL9 112 AY53
Dorking RH4 269 CJ134
Enfield EN1, EN3 104 DU43
Erith DA8 189 FF82
Feltham TW13 198 BZ90
Guildford GU2 264 AT132
Harrow HA2 138 BZ57
Mitcham CR4 223 DL99
New Malden KT3 220 CQ97
Northwood HA6 137 BT55
Sidcup DA14 208 EV92
Wembley HA0 159 CK65
Worcester Park KT4 221 CV102
Lincolns, The, NW7 119 CT48
Lincolns Cl, St.Alb. AL4 65 CJ15
Lincolns Fld, Epp. CM16 91 ET29
Lincolnshott, Sthflt DA13 212 GB92
★ Lincoln's Inn, WC2 18 D8
Lincoln's Inn Flds, WC2 18 C8
Lincoln St, E11 146 EE61
SW3 28 E9
Lincoln Wk, Epsom KT19 238 CR110
Lincoln Way, Crox.Grn WD3 97 BP42
Enfield EN1 104 DV43
Slough SL1 153 AK73
Sunbury-on-Thames TW16 217 BS95
Lincombe Rd, Brom. BR1 206 EF90
Lindal Cres, Enf. EN2 103 DL42
Lindale Cl, Vir.W. GU25 214 AT98
Lindales, The, N17
off Brantwood Rd 122 DT51
Lindal Rd, SE4 205 DZ85
Lindbergh, Welw.G.C. AL7 52 DC09
Lindbergh Rd, Wall. SM6 241 DL108
Linden Av, NW10 14 C1
Coulsdon CR5 257 DH116
Dartford DA1 210 FJ88
Enfield EN1 104 DU39
Hounslow TW3 198 CB85
Ruislip HA4 137 BU60
Thornton Heath CR7 223 DP98
Watford WD18 97 BS42
Wembley HA9 140 CM64
Sch Linden Br Sch, Wor.Pk. KT4
off Grafton Rd 220 CS104
Linden Chase, Sev. TN13 279 FH122
Linden Cl, N14 103 DJ44
Iver SL0 155 BD68
New Haw KT15 234 BG111
Orpington BR6 246 EU106
Purfleet RM19 190 FQ79
Ruislip HA4 137 BU60
Stanmore HA7 117 CH50
Tadworth KT20 255 CX120
Thames Ditton KT7 219 CF101
Waltham Cross EN7 88 DV30
Linden Ct, W12 26 A2
Englefield Green TW20 194 AV93
Leatherhead KT22 253 CH121
Linden Cres, Grnf. UB6 159 CF65
Kingston upon Thames KT1 220 CM96
St. Albans AL1 65 CJ20
Woodford Green IG8 124 EH51
Linden Dr, Chaldon CR3 258 DQ124
Chalfont St. Peter SL9 112 AY53
Farnham Royal SL2 153 AQ66
Lindenfield, Chis. BR7 227 EP96
Linden Gdns, W2 27 K1

Linden Gdns, W4 180 CR78
Enfield EN1 104 DU39
Leatherhead KT22 253 CJ121
Linden Glade, Hem.H. HP1 62 BG21
Linden Gro, SE15 184 DV83
SE26 204 DW93
New Malden KT3 220 CS97
Teddington TW11
off Waldegrave Rd 199 CF92
Walton-on-Thames KT12 217 BT103
Warlingham CR6 259 DY118
Linden Ho, Slou. SL3 175 BB78
Linden Lawns, Wem. HA9 140 CM63
Linden Lea, N2 142 DC57
Dorking RH4 285 CJ138
Watford WD25 81 BU33
Linden Leas, W.Wick. BR4 225 ED103
Sch Linden Lo Sch, SW19
off Princes Way 201 CY88
Linden Mans, N6
off Hornsey La 143 DH60
Linden Ms, N1 9 M3
W2 27 K1
Linden Pas, W4
off Linden Gdns 180 CR78
Linden Pit Path, Lthd. KT22 253 CH121
Linden Pl, Epsom KT17
off East St 238 CS112
Leatherhead KT24
off Station App 267 BS126
Mitcham CR4 222 DE98
Linden Ri, Warley CM14 130 FX50
Linden Rd, E17
off High St 145 DZ57
N10 143 DH56
N11 120 DF47
N15 144 DQ56
Guildford GU1 264 AX134
Hampton TW12 198 CA94
Leatherhead KT22 253 CH121
Weybridge KT13 235 BQ109
Lindens, The, N12 120 DD50
W4 180 CQ81
Hemel Hempstead HP3 61 BF23
Loughton IG10 107 EM43
New Addington CR0 243 EC107
Lindens Cl, Eff. KT24 268 BY128
Linden Sq, Hare. UB9 114 BG51
Sevenoaks TN13
off London Rd 278 FE122
Linden St, Rom. RM7 149 FD56
Linden Wk, N19
off Hargrave Pk 143 DJ61
Linden Way, N14 103 DJ44
Purley CR8 241 DJ110
Ripley GU23 249 BF124
Shepperton TW17 217 BQ99
Woking GU22 249 AZ121
Lindeth Cl, Stan. HA7 117 CH51
Lindfield Gdns, NW3 5 M2
Guildford GU1 265 AZ133
Lindfield Rd, W5 159 CJ70
Croydon CR0 224 DT100
Romford RM3 128 FL50
Lindfield St, E14 22 A8
Lindhill Cl, Enf. EN3 105 DX39
Lindie Gdns, Uxb. UB10 156 BL66
Lindisfarne Cl, Grav. DA12 213 GL89
Lindisfarne Rd, SW20 201 CU94
Dagenham RM8 148 EW62
Lindisfarne Way, E9 11 M1
Lindley Est, SE15 44 C4
Lindley Pl, Kew TW9 180 CN81
Lindley Rd, E10 145 EB61
Godstone RH9 274 DW130
Walton-on-Thames KT12 218 BX104
Lindley St, E1 20 G6
Lindlings, Hem.H. HP1 61 BE21
Lindo Cl, Chesh. HP5 76 AP30
Sch Lindon Bennett Sch,
Han. TW13
off Main St 198 BX92
Lindore Rd, SW11 182 DF84
Lindores Rd, Cars. SM5 222 DC101
Lindo St, SE15 45 H9
Lind Rd, Sutt. SM1 240 DC106
Lindrop St, SW6 39 N8
Lindsay Cl, Chess. KT9 238 CL108
Epsom KT19 238 CQ113
Stanwell TW19 196 BK85
Lindsay Ct, SW11 40 B7
Lindsay Dr, Har. HA3 140 CL58
Shepperton TW17 217 BR100
Lindsay Pl, Wal.Cr. EN7 88 DV30
Lindsay Rd, Hmptn H. TW12 198 CB91
New Haw KT15 234 BG110
Worcester Park KT4 221 CV103
Lindsay Sq, SW1 29 P10
Lindsell St, SE10 46 E6
Lindsey Cl, Brwd. CM14 130 FU49
Bromley BR1 226 EK97
Mitcham CR4 223 DL98
Lindsey Gdns, Felt. TW14 197 BR87
Lindsey Ms, N1 9 K6
Lindsey Rd, Dag. RM8 148 EW63
Denham UB9 136 BG62
Lindsey St, EC1 19 H6
Epping CM16 91 ER28
Lindsey Way, Horn. RM11 150 FJ57
Lind St, SE8 46 B8
Lindum Pl, St.Alb. AL3 64 BZ22
Lindum Rd, Tedd. TW11 199 CJ94
Lindvale, Wok. GU21 248 AY115
Lindway, SE27 203 DP92
Lindwood Cl, E6 25 H7
Linfield Cl, NW4 141 CW55
Hersham KT12 235 BV106
Linfield Ct, Hert. SG14 53 DM08
Linfields, Amer. HP7 94 AW40
LINFORD, S.le H. SS17 193 GM75
Linford Cl, Harl. CM19 73 EP17
Linford End, Harl. CM19 73 EQ17
Linford Rd, E17 145 EC55
Grays RM16 193 GH78
West Tilbury RM18 193 GJ77
Linford St, SW8 41 L6
Lingards Rd, SE13 185 EC84
Lingey Cl, Sid. DA15 207 ET89
Lingfield Av, Dart. DA2 210 FP87
Kingston upon Thames KT1 220 CL98
Upminster RM14 150 FM62
Lingfield Cl, Enf. EN1 104 DS44
Northwood HA6 115 BS52
Lingfield Cres, SE9 187 ER84
Lingfield Gdns, N9 122 DV45
Coulsdon CR5 257 DP119
Lingfield Rd, SW19 201 CX92
Gravesend DA12 213 GH89
Worcester Park KT4 221 CW104
Lingfield Way, Wat. WD17 97 BT38
Lingham St, SW9 42 B8
Lingholm Way, Barn. EN5 101 CX43
Lingmere Cl, Chig. IG7 125 EQ47
Lingmoor Dr, Wat. WD25 82 BW33
Ling Rd, E16 23 P6
Erith DA8 189 FC79
Lingrove Gdns, Buck.H. IG9 124 EH48
Lings Coppice, SE21 204 DR89
Lingwell Rd, SW17 202 DE90
Lingwood Gdns, Islw. TW7 179 CE80
Lingwood Rd, E5 144 DU59
Linhope St, NW1 16 E4
Linington Av, Chesh. HP5 78 AU30
Link, The, SE9 207 EN90
W3 160 CP72
Eastcote HA5 138 BW59
Enfield EN3 105 DY39
Northolt UB5
off Eastcote La 138 BZ64
Slough SL2 154 AV72
Wembley HA0
off Nathans Rd 139 CJ60
Link Av, Wok. GU22 249 BD115
Link Cl, Hat. AL10 67 CV18
Link Dr, Hat. AL10 67 CV18
Linkfield, Brom. BR2 226 EG100
Welwyn Garden City AL7 51 CY13
West Molesey KT8 218 CA97
Linkfield Cor, Red. RH1
off Hatchlands Rd 272 DE133
Linkfield Gdns, Red. RH1
off Hatchlands Rd 272 DE134
Linkfield La, Red. RH1 272 DE133
Linkfield Rd, Islw. TW7 179 CF82
Linkfield St, Red. RH1 272 DE134
Link La, Wall. SM6 241 DK107
Linklea Cl, NW9 118 CS52
Sch Link Prim Sch, The, Croy. CR0
off Croydon Rd 241 DL105
Link Rd, N11 120 DG49
Addlestone KT15
off Weybridge Rd 234 BL105
Chenies WD3 95 BA37
Dagenham RM9 169 FB68
Datchet SL3 174 AW80
Feltham TW14 197 BT87
Hemel Hempstead HP1, HP2 62 BJ17
Wallington SM6 222 DG102
Watford WD24 98 BX40
Links, The, E17 145 DY56
Cheshunt EN8 89 DX26
Walton-on-Thames KT12 217 BU103
Welwyn Garden City AL8
off Applecroft Rd 51 CV09
Links Av, Hert. SG13 54 DV08
Morden SM4 222 DA98
Romford RM2 127 FH54
Links Brow, Fetch. KT22 253 CE124
Links Cl, Ashtd. KT21 253 CJ117
Linkscroft Av, Ashf. TW15 197 BP93
Links Dr, N20 120 DA46
Elstree WD6 100 CM41
Radlett WD7 83 CF33
Sch Link Sec Sch, The, Bedd. CR0
off Croydon Rd 241 DM105
Links Gdns, SW16 203 DN94
Links Grn Way, Cob. KT11 236 CA114
Linkside, N12 119 CZ51
Chigwell IG7 125 EQ50
New Malden KT3 220 CS96
Linkside Cl, Enf. EN2 103 DM41
Linkside Gdns, Enf. EN2 103 DM41
Links Pl, Ashtd. KT21 253 CK117
Sch Links Prim Sch, SW17
off Frinton Rd 202 DG93
Links Rd, NW2 141 CT61
SW17 202 DF93
W3 160 CN72
Ashford TW15 196 BL92
Ashtead KT21 253 CJ118
Bramley GU5 280 AY144
Epsom KT17 239 CU113
Flackwell Heath HP10 132 AC56
West Wickham BR4 225 EC102
Woodford Green IG8 124 EG50
Links Side, Enf. EN2 103 DN41
Link St, E9 11 H4
Links Vw, N3 119 CZ52
Dartford DA1 210 FJ88
St. Albans AL3 64 CB18
Links Vw Av, Brock. RH3 270 CN134
Links Vw Cl, Stan. HA7 117 CG51
Links Vw Rd, Croy. CR0 225 EA104
Hampton Hill TW12 198 CC92
Linksway, NW4 119 CX54
Links Way, Beck. BR3 225 EA100
Bookham KT23 268 BY128
Croxley Green WD3 97 BQ41
Linksway, Nthwd. HA6 115 BQ53
Linkswood Rd, Burn. SL1 152 AJ68
Links Yd, E1 20 C6
Link Wk, Hat. AL10 67 CV17
Linkway, N4 144 DQ59
SW20 221 CV97
Link Way, Brom. BR2 226 EL101
Linkway, Dag. RM8 148 EW63
Link Way, Denh. UB9 136 BG58
Linkway, Guil. GU2 264 AT133
Harlow CM20
off North Gate 57 EQ14
Link Way, Horn. RM11 150 FL60
Pinner HA5 116 BX53
Linkway, Rich. TW10 199 CH89
Link Way, Stai. TW18 196 BH93
Linkway, Wok. GU22 249 BC117
Linkway, The, Barn. EN5 102 DB44
Sutton SM2 240 DC109
Linkway Rd, Brwd. CM14 130 FT48
Linkwood Wk, NW1 7 P6
Linley Cres, Rom. RM7 149 FB55
Linley Rd, N17 122 DS54
★ Linley Sambourne Ho, W8 27 K5
Linnell Cl, NW11 142 DB58
Linnell Dr, NW11 142 DB58
Linnell Rd, N18 122 DU50
SE5 43 P8
Redhill RH1 288 DG135
Linnet Cl, N9 123 DX46
SE28 168 EW73
Bushey WD23 116 CC45
Linnet Cl, South Croydon CR2 243 DX110
Linnet Gro, Guil. GU4
off Partridge Way 265 BD132
Linnet Ms, SW12 202 DG87
Linnet Rd, Abb.L. WD5 81 BU31
Linnett Cl, E4 123 EC49
Linnet Ter, Ilf. IG5
off Tiptree Cres 147 EN55
Linnet Wk, Hat. AL10
off Lark Ri 67 CU20
Linnet Way, Purf. RM19 190 FP78
Linom Rd, SW4 183 DL84
Linscott Rd, E5 10 G1
Linsdell Rd, Bark. IG11 167 EQ67
Linsey Cl, Hem.H. HP3 62 BN24
Linsey St, SE16 32 C8
Linslade Cl, Houns. TW4
off Heathlands Way 198 BY85
Pinner HA5 137 BV55
Linslade Rd, Orp. BR6 246 EU107
Linstead St, NW6 5 J6
Linstead Way, SW18 201 CY87
Linsted Ct, SE9 207 ES86
Linster Gro, Borwd. WD6 100 CQ43
Lintaine Cl, W6 38 F3
Linthorpe Av, Wem. HA0 159 CJ65
Linthorpe Rd, N16 144 DS59
Cockfosters EN4 102 DE41
Linton Av, Borwd. WD6 100 CM39
Linton Cl, Mitch. CR4 222 DF101
Welling DA16 188 EV81
Linton Ct, Rom. RM1 127 FE54
Linton Gdns, E6 24 G8
Linton Glade, Croy. CR0 243 DY109
Linton Gro, SE27 203 DP92
Sch Linton Mead Prim Sch, SE28
off Central Way 168 EV73
Linton Rd, Bark. IG11 167 EQ66
Lintons Cl, Hodd. EN11
off Essex Rd 71 EB16
Lintons La, Epsom KT17 238 CS112
Linton St, N1 9 K9
Lintott Ct, Stanw. TW19 196 BK86
Linver Rd, SW6 39 H8
Linwood, Saw. CM21 58 EY05
Linwood Cl, SE5 44 A9
Linwood Cres, Enf. EN1 104 DU39
Linzee Rd, N8 143 DL56
Lion Av, Twick. TW1
off Lion Rd 199 CF88
● Lion Business Pk, Grav.
DA12 213 GM87
Lion Cl, SE4 205 EA86
Shepperton TW17 216 BL97
Lion Ct, Borwd. WD6 100 CQ39
Lionel Gdns, SE9 206 EK85
Lionel Ms, W10 14 E6
Lionel Oxley Ho, Grays RM17
off New Rd 192 GB79
Sch Lionel Prim Sch, Brent. TW8
off Lionel Rd N 180 CL77
Lionel Rd, SE9 206 EK85
Lionel Rd N, Brent. TW8 180 CL77
Lionel Rd S, Brent. TW8 180 CM78
● Liongate Enterprise Pk,
Mitch. CR4 222 DD98
Lion Gate Gdns, Rich. TW9 180 CM83
Lion Gate Ms, SW18 202 DA87
Lion Grn Rd, Couls. CR5 257 DK115
Lion La, Red. RH1 272 DF133
Lion Mills, E2 20 D1
Lion Pk Av, Chess. KT9 238 CN105
Lion Plaza, EC2 *off Lothbury* 19 L8
Lion Rd, E6 25 K7
N9 122 DU47
Bexleyheath DA6 188 EZ84
Croydon CR0 224 DQ99
Twickenham TW1 199 CF88
Lions Cl, SE9 206 EJ90
Lion Way, Brent. TW8 179 CK80
Lion Wf Rd, Islw. TW7 179 CH83
Lion Yd, SW4 183 DK84
off Tremadoc Rd
Liphook Cl, Horn. RM12
off Petworth Way 149 FF63
Liphook Cres, SE23 204 DW87
Liphook Rd, Wat. WD19 116 BX49
Lippitts Hill, High Beach IG10 106 EE39
Lipsham Cl, Bans. SM7 240 DD113
Lipton Cl, SE28
off Aisher Rd 168 EW73
Lipton Rd, E1 21 J9
Lisbon Av, Twick. TW2 198 CC89
Lisbon Cl, E17 123 DZ54
Lisburne Rd, NW3 6 E1
Lisford St, SE15 44 B6
Lisgar Ter, W14 26 G8
Liskeard Cl, Chis. BR7 207 EQ93
Liskeard Gdns, SE3 47 P7
Liskeard Lo, Cat. CR3 274 DU126
Lisle Cl, SW17 203 DH91
Lisle Pl, Grays RM17 192 GA76
Lisle St, WC2 17 P10
● Lismirrane Ind Pk, Els. WD6 99 CG44
Lismore, Hem.H. HP3 63 BQ22
Lismore Circ, NW5 6 G2
off Wellesley Rd
Lismore Cl, Islw. TW7 179 CG82
Lismore Pk, Slou. SL2 154 AT72
Lismore Rd, N17 144 DR55
South Croydon CR2 242 DS107
Lismore Wk, N1 9 K4
Lissant Cl, Long Dit. KT6 219 CK101
Lissenden Gdns, NW5 142 DG63
Lissoms Rd, Chipstead CR5 256 DG118
Lisson Grn Est, NW8 16 C3
LISSON GROVE, NW8 16 B4
Lisson Gro, NW1 16 C4
NW8 16 B3
Lisson St, NW1 16 C6
Lister Av, Rom. RM3 128 FK54
Lister Cl, W3 160 CR71
Mitcham CR4 222 DE95
Sch Lister Comm Sch, E13
off St. Marys Rd 166 EH68
Lister Ct, NW9 118 CS54
Lister Dr, Nthflt. DA11 212 GC88
Lister Gdns, N18 122 DQ50
H Lister Hosp, The, SW1 41 J1
Lister Rd, E11 146 EE60
Tilbury RM18 193 GG82
Lister Wk, SE28
off Haldane Rd 168 EX73
Liston Rd, N17 122 DU53
SW4 183 DJ83
Liston Way, Wdf.Grn. IG8
off Navestock Cres 124 EJ52
Listowel Cl, SW9 42 F4
Listowel Rd, Dag. RM10 148 FA62
Listria Pk, N16 144 DS61
Litcham Spur, Slou. SL1 153 AR72
Litchfield Av, E15 13 J5
Morden SM4 221 CZ101
Litchfield Gdns, NW10 161 CU65
Cobham KT11 235 BU114
Litchfield Rd, Sutt. SM1 240 DC105
Litchfield St, WC2 17 P10
Litchfield Way, NW11 142 DB57
Guildford GU2 280 AT136
Lithos Rd, NW3 5 M4
Litten Cl, Col.Row. RM5 126 FA51
Little Acre, Beck. BR3 225 EA97
Bookham KT23 252 BZ124
St. Albans AL3 65 CD17
Little Acres, Ware SG12 55 DX07
Little Albany St, NW1 17 K4
Little Argyll St, W1 17 L9
Little Aston Rd, Rom. RM3 128 FM52
Little Belhus Cl, S.Ock. RM15 171 FU70
Little Benty, West Dr. UB7 176 BK78
LITTLE BERKHAMSTED,
Hert. SG13 69 DH18
Little Berkhamsted La, Lt.Berk.
SG13 69 DH20
Little Birch Cl, New Haw
KT15 234 BK109
Little Birches, Sid. DA15 207 ES89
Little Boltons, The, SW5 27 M10
SW10 27 M10
LITTLE BOOKHAM, Lthd.
KT23 268 BY125
Little Bookham Common, Bkhm
KT23 252 BY122
Little Bookham St, Bkhm
KT23 252 BZ124
Little Bornes, SE21 204 DS91
Little Borough, Brock. RH3 286 CN135
Little Brays, Harl. CM18 74 EU16
Little Br Rd, Berk. HP4 60 AX19
Little Britain, EC1 19 J8
Littlebrook Av, Slou. SL2 153 AL70
Littlebrook Cl, Croy. CR0 225 DX100
Littlebrook Gdns, Chsht EN8 88 DW30
Jct Littlebrook Interchange, Dart.
DA1 190 FP84
Littlebrook Manor Way, Dart.
DA1 210 FN85
Little Brook Rd, Roydon CM19 72 EJ15
Little Brownings, SE23 204 DV89
Little Buntings, Wind. SL4 173 AM83
Little Burrow, Welw.G.C. AL7 51 CX11
Littlebury Rd, SW4 41 N10
Little Bury St, N9 122 DR46
Little Bushey La, Bushey WD23 99 CD44
Little Bushey La Footpath, Bushey
WD23 *off Little Bushey La* 117 CD45
Little Catherells, Hem.H. HP1 61 BE18
Little Cattins, Harl. CM19 73 EM19
Little Cedars, N12 120 DC49
LITTLE CHALFONT, Amer. HP7 94 AW40
LITTLE CHALFONT, Ch.St.G.
HP8 94 AW40
Sch Little Chalfont Prim Sch,
Lt.Chal. HP6
off Oakington Av 94 AY39
Little Chapels Way, Slou. SL1 153 AN74
Little Chester St, SW1 29 H6
Little Cloisters, SW1
off College Ms 30 A6
Little Coll La, EC4
off College St 19 L10
Little Coll St, SW1 30 A6
Little Collins, Outwood RH1 289 DP144
Littlecombe, SE7 186 EH79
Littlecombe Cl, SW15 201 CX86
Little Common, Stan. HA7 117 CG48
Little Common La, Bletch.
RH1 273 DP132
Littlecote Cl, SW19 201 CX87
Littlecote Pl, Pnr. HA5 116 BY53
Little Cottage Pl, SE10 46 D4
Little Ct, W.Wick. BR4 226 EE103
Littlecourt Rd, Sev. TN13 278 FG124
Little Cranmore La, W.Hors.
KT24 267 BP128
Littlecroft, SE9 187 EN83
Istead Rise DA13 212 GE94
Littlecroft Rd, Egh. TW20 195 AZ92
Littledale, SE2 188 EU79
Dartford DA2 210 FQ90
Little Dean's Yd, SW1 30 A6
Little Dell, Welw.G.C. AL8 51 CX07
Little Dimocks, SW12 203 DH89
Little Dormers, Ger.Cr. SL9 135 AZ56
Little Dorrit Ct, SE1 31 K4
Littledown Rd, Slou. SL1 154 AT74
Little Dragons, Loug. IG10 106 EK42
LITTLE EALING, W5 179 CJ77
Little Ealing La, W5 179 CJ77
Sch Little Ealing Prim Sch, W5
off Weymouth Av 179 CJ76
Little E Fld, Couls. CR5 257 DK121
Little Edward St, NW1 17 K2
Little Elms, Harling. UB3 177 BR80
Little Essex St, WC2 18 E10
Little Ferry Rd, Twick. TW1
off Ferry Rd 199 CH88
Littlefield Cl, N19
off Tufnell Pk Rd 143 DJ63
Kingston upon Thames KT1
off Fairfield W 220 CL96
Littlefield Rd, Edg. HA8 118 CQ52
Littleford La, Guil. GU4, GU5 281 BE142
Little Friday Rd, E4 124 EE47
Little Ganett, Welw.G.C. AL7 52 DB11
Little Gaynes Gdns, Upmin.
RM14 150 FP63
Little Gaynes La, Upmin.
RM14 150 FM63
Little Gearies, Ilf. IG6 147 EP56
Little George St, SW1 30 A5
Little Gerpins La, Upmin.
RM14 170 FM67
Little Gra, Grnf. UB6
off Perivale La 159 CG69
Little Graylings, Abb.L. WD5 81 BS33
Little Grn, Rich. TW9 179 CK84
Little Greencroft, Chesh. HP5 76 AN27
Sch Little Grn Jun Sch, Crox.Grn
WD3 *off Lincoln Dr* 97 BP41
Little Grn La, Cher. KT16 215 BE104
Croxley Green WD3 97 BP41
Little Grn St, NW5 7 J1
Little Gregories La, They.B.
CM16 107 ER35
Little Gro, Bushey WD23 98 CB42
Littlegrove, E.Barn. EN4 102 DE44
Little Gro Av, Chsht EN7 88 DS27
Little Gro Fld, Harl. CM19 73 EQ15
Little Halliards, Walt. KT12
off Felix Rd 217 BU100
Little Hardings, Welw.G.C. AL7 52 DC08
Little Hayes, Kings L. WD4 80 BN29
Jct Little Heath, Rom. RM6 148 EV56
Little Heath, SE7 186 EL79
Chadwell Heath RM6 148 EV56
Little Heath La, Berk. HP4 61 BB21
Chobham GU24 232 AS109
Littleheath La, Cob. KT11 236 CA114
Sch Little Heath Prim Sch, Pot.B.
EN6 *off School Rd* 86 DC30
Little Heath Rd, Bexh. DA7 188 EZ81
Chobham GU24 232 AS109
Littleheath Rd, S.Croy. CR2 242 DV108
Sch Little Heath Sch, Rom. RM6
off Hainault Rd 148 EV56
Little Henleys, Hunsdon SG12 56 EK06
Little Hide, Guil. GU1 265 BB132
Little Highwood Way,
Borehamwood. CM14 130 FV46
Little Hill, Herons. WD3 95 BC44
Little Hivings, Chesh. HP5 76 AN27
★ Little Holland Ho, Cars.
SM5 240 DE108
Little How Cft, Abb.L. WD5 81 BQ31
LITTLE ILFORD, E12 146 EL64
Little Ilford La, E12 147 EM63
Sch Little Ilford Sch, E12
off Browning Rd 147 EM64
Littlejohn Rd, W7 159 CF72
Orpington BR5 228 EU100
Little Julians Hill, Sev. TN13 278 FG128
Little Kiln, Gdmg. GU7 280 AS143
Little Lake, Welw.G.C. AL7 52 DB12
Little Ley, Welw.G.C. AL7 51 CY12
Jct Little London, Chig. IG7 107 ET42
Little London, Albury GU5 282 BL141
Little London Cl, Uxb. UB8 157 BP71
Little London Ct, SE1
off Mill St 32 B5
Little Marlborough St, W1
off Foubert's Pl 17 L9
Little Martins, Bushey WD23 98 CB43
Littlemead, Esher KT10 237 CD105
Little Mead, Hat. AL10 67 CV15
Woking GU21 248 AT116
Littlemede, SE9 207 EM90
Little Mimms, Hem.H. HP2 62 BK19
Little Moreton Cl, W.Byf. KT14 234 BH112
Littlemore Rd, Ilf. IG1 147 ER62
Littlemore Rd, SE2 188 EU75
Little Moss La, Pnr. HA5 116 BY54
Little Mundells, Welw.G.C. AL7 51 CZ07
Little Newport St, WC2 17 P10
Little New St, EC4 18 F8
Little Oaks Cl, Shep. TW17 216 BM98
Little Orchard, Hem.H. HP2 62 BN18
Woking GU21 233 BA114
Woodham KT15 233 BF111
Little Orchard Cl, Abb.L. WD5 81 BR32
Pinner HA5
off Barrow Pt La 116 BY54
Little Orchard Way, Shalf.
GU4 280 AY141
Little Oxhey La, Wat. WD19 116 BX50
Little Pk, Bov. HP3 79 BA28
Little Pk Dr, Felt. TW13 198 BX89
Little Pk Gdns, Enf. EN2 104 DQ41
LITTLE PARNDON, Harl. CM20 57 EP14
Sch Little Parndon Prim Sch,
Harl. CM20 *off Park Mead* 57 EP14
Little Pipers Cl, Goffs Oak EN7 87 DP29
Little Plucketts Way, Buck.H.
IG9 124 EJ46
Little Portland St, W1 17 L8
Littleport Spur, Slou. SL1 154 AS72
Little Potters, Bushey WD23 117 CD45
Little Pynchons, Harl. CM18 73 ET18
Little Queens Rd, Tedd. TW11 199 CF93
Little Queen St, Dart. DA1 210 FM87
Sch Little Reddings Prim Sch,
Bushey WD23
off Harcourt Rd 98 CB43
Little Redlands, Brom. BR1 226 EL96
Little Reeves Av, Amer. HP7 94 AT39
Little Ridge, Welw.G.C. AL7 52 DA09
Little Riding, Wok. GU22 249 BB116
Little Rivers, Welw.G.C. AL7 52 DA08
Little Rd, Croy. CR0
off Lower Addiscombe Rd 224 DS102
Hayes UB3 177 BT75
Hemel Hempstead HP2 62 BM19
Little Roke Av, Ken. CR8 241 DP114
Little Roke Rd, Ken. CR8 242 DQ114
Littlers Cl, SW19
off Runnymede 222 DD95
Little Russell St, WC1 18 A7
Little Russets, Hutt. CM13
off Hutton Village 131 GE45
Little St. James's St, SW1 29 L3
Little St. Leonards, SW14 180 CQ83
Little Sanctuary, SW1 29 P5
Little Shardeloes, Amer. HP7 77 AN39
Little Smith St, SW1 29 P6
Little Somerset St, E1 20 A9
Little Spring, Chesh. HP5 76 AP28
Sch Little Spring Prim Sch, Chesh.
HP5 *off Greenway* 76 AP28
Sch Little Stanmore First & Mid Sch,
Edg. HA8 *off St. Davids Dr* 118 CM53
Little Stock Rd, Chsht EN7 88 DR26
Littlestone Cl, Beck. BR3 205 EA93
Little Strand, NW9 119 CT54
Little Stream Cl, Nthwd. HA6 115 BS50
Little St, Guil. GU2 264 AV130
Waltham Abbey EN9
off Greenwich Way 105 EC36
Little Sutton La, Slou. SL3 175 BC78
Little Thistle, Welw.G.C. AL7 52 DC12
Little Thrift, Petts Wd BR5 227 EQ98
LITTLE THURROCK, Grays
RM17 192 GD76
Sch Little Thurrock Prim Sch,
Grays RM17
off Rectory Rd 192 GD76
Little Titchfield St, W1 17 L7
LITTLETON, Guil. GU3 280 AU140
LITTLETON, Shep. TW17 217 BP97
Littleton Av, E4 124 EF46
Sch Littleton C of E Inf Sch,
Littleton TW17
off Rectory Cl 216 BN97
Littleton Cres, Har. HA1 139 CF61
Littleton Ho, SW1
off Lupus St 41 L1
Littleton La, Littleton GU3 280 AU139
Reigate RH2 287 CX136

Littleton La, Shepperton TW17 216 BK101
Littleton Rd, Ashf. TW15 197 BQ94
Harrow HA1 139 CF61
Littleton St, SW18 202 DC89
Little Trinity La, EC4 19 K10
Little Tumners Ct, Gdmg. GU7 280 AS144
Little Turnstile, WC1 18 C8
★ Little Venice (Waterbuses), W2 15 N6
Little Wade, Welw.G.C. AL7 51 CZ12
Little Wk, Harl. CM20 73 EQ15
Little Warren Cl, Guil. GU4 281 BB136
Littlewick Common, Knap. GU21 248 AS115
Littlewick Rd, Wok. GU21 232 AW114
Little Widbury, Ware SG12 55 DZ06
Little Widbury La, Ware SG12 55 DZ06
Little Windmill Hill, Chipper. WD4 79 BE32
Littlewood, SE13 205 EC85
Little Wd, Sev. TN13 279 FJ122
Littlewood Cl, W13 179 CH76
Little Wd Cl, Orp. BR5 228 EU95
LITTLE WOODCOTE, Cars. SM5 240 DG111
Little Woodcote Est, Cars. SM5 240 DG111
Wallington SM6 240 DG111
Little Woodcote La, Cars. SM5 241 DH112
Purley CR8 241 DH112
Wallington SM6 241 DH112
Little Woodlands, Wind. SL4 173 AM83
Littleworth Av, Esher KT10 237 CD106
Littleworth Common Rd, Esher KT10 219 CD104
Littleworth La, Esher KT10 237 CD105
Littleworth Pl, Esher KT10 237 CD105
Littleworth Rd, Burn. SL1 133 AK61
Esher KT10 237 CE105
Little Youngs, Welw.G.C. AL8 51 CW09
Litton Ct, Loud. HP10 110 AC53
Livermere Rd, E8 10 A8
Liverpool Gro, SE17 43 K1
Liverpool Rd, E10 145 EC58
E16 23 K6
N1 8 F7
N7 8 E4
W5 179 CK75
Kingston upon Thames KT2 200 CN94
St. Albans AL1 65 CE20
Slough SL1 153 AP72
Thornton Heath CR7 224 DQ97
Watford WD18 97 BV43
⇌ Liverpool Street 19 N7
⊖ Liverpool Street 19 N7
Liverpool St, EC2 19 N7
Liveryman Wk, Green. DA9 off Capability Way 191 FW84
Livesey Cl, SE28 187 EQ76
Kingston upon Thames KT1 220 CM97
Livesey Pl, SE15 44 D2
Livingstone Ct, E10 off Matlock Rd 145 EC58
Barnet EN5 off Christchurch La 101 CY40
Livingstone Gdns, Grav. DA12 213 GK92
H Livingstone Hosp, Dart. DA1 210 FM87
Livingstone Pl, E14 46 E1
Sch Livingstone Prim Sch, New Barn. EN4 off Baring Rd 102 DD41
Livingstone Rd, E17 145 EB58
N13 121 DL51
SW11 off Winstanley Rd 182 DD83
Caterham CR3 258 DR122
Gravesend DA12 213 GK92
Hounslow TW3 178 CC84
Southall UB1 158 BX73
Thornton Heath CR7 224 DQ96
Livingstone Ter, Rain. RM13 169 FE67
Livingstone Wk, SW11 182 DD83
Hemel Hempstead HP2 62 BM16
Sch Livity Sch, SW2 off Mandrell Rd 203 DL85
Livonia St, W1 17 M9
Lizard St, EC1 19 K3
Lizban St, SE3 186 EH80
Llanbury Cl, Chal.St.P. SL9 112 AY52
Llanelly Rd, NW2 141 CZ61
Llanover Rd, SE18 187 EN79
Wembley HA9 139 CK62
Llanthony Rd, Mord. SM4 222 DD100
Llanvanor Rd, NW2 141 CZ61
Llewellyn St, SE16 32 D5
Lloyd Av, SW16 223 DL95
Coulsdon CR5 240 DG114
Lloyd Baker St, WC1 18 D3
Lloyd Ct, Pnr. HA5 138 BX57
Lloyd Ms, Enf. EN3 105 EA38
Tra Lloyd Park 242 DT105
Lloyd Pk, E17 123 EA54
Lloyd Pk Av, Croy. CR0 242 DT105
Lloyd Rd, E6 167 EM67
E17 145 DX56
Dagenham RM9 168 EZ65
Worcester Park KT4 221 CW104
Lloyd's Av, EC3 19 P9
★ Lloyd's of London, EC3 19 N9
Lloyds Pl, SE3 47 K9
Lloyd Sq, WC1 18 E2
Lloyd's Row, EC1 18 F3
Lloyd St, WC1 18 E2
Lloyds Way, Beck. BR3 225 DY99
Lloyd Vil, SE4 46 A8
Sch Lloyd Williamson Sch, W10 14 E6
Loampit Hill, SE13 46 B9
Jct Loampit Vale, SE13 46 E10
Loampit Vale, SE13 46 D10
Loanda Cl, E8 10 A8
Loates La, Wat. WD17 98 BW41
Loats Rd, SW2 203 DL86
Lobelia Cl, E6 24 G6
Local Board Rd, Wat. WD17 98 BX43
Locarno Rd, W3 160 CQ74
Greenford UB6 158 CC70
Lochaber Rd, SE13 186 EE84
Lochaline St, W6 38 B2
Lochan Cl, Hayes UB4 158 BY70
Loch Cres, Edg. HA8 118 CM49
Lochinvar Cl, Slou. SL1 173 AP75
Lochinvar St, SW12 203 DH87
Sch Lochinver Ho Sch, Pot.B. EN6 off Heath Rd 86 DB30
Lochmere Cl, Erith DA8 189 FB79
Lochnagar St, E14 22 F7
Lochnell Rd, Berk. HP4 60 AT17
Lock Av, Maid. SL6 152 AC69
Lock Bldg, The, E15 12 E10
Lock Chase, SE3 186 EE83
Lock Cl, Sthl. UB2 off Navigator Dr 178 CC75
Woodham KT15 233 BE113
Locke Cl, Rain. RM13 169 FF65
Locke Gdns, Slou. SL3 174 AW75
Locke Ho, N16 off Stamford Hill 144 DS60
Locke King Cl, Wey. KT13 234 BN108
Locke King Rd, Wey. KT13 234 BN108
Lockers Pk La, Hem.H. HP1 62 BH20
Sch Lockers Pk Sch, Hem.H. HP1 off Lockers Pk La 62 BH20
Lockesfield Pl, E14 34 D10
Lockesley Dr, Orp. BR5 227 ET100
Lockesley Sq, Surb. KT6 off Lovelace Gdns 219 CK100
Lockestone, Wey. KT13 234 BM107
Lockestone Cl, Wey. KT13 234 BM107
Locket Rd, Har. HA3 139 CE55
Locket Rd Ms, Har. HA3 139 CE55
Lockets Cl, Wind. SL4 173 AL81
Locke Way, Wok. GU21 off The Broadway 249 AZ117
Lockfield Av, Enf. EN3 105 DY40
Lockfield Dr, Wok. GU21 248 AT118
Lockgate Cl, E9 11 N2
Lockhart Cl, N7 8 C4
Enfield EN3 104 DV43
Lockhart Rd, Cob. KT11 236 BW113
Watford WD17 off Church Rd 97 BU39
Lockhart St, E3 21 P5
Lock Ho, NW1 off Oval Rd 7 H7
● Lock Ho Ind Est, Hert. SG13 54 DS08
Lockhursthatch La, Far.Grn GU5 282 BM144
Lockhurst St, E5 145 DX63
Lockie Pl, SE25 224 DU97
Lockier Wk, Wem. HA9 139 CK62
Lockington Rd, SW8 41 K6
Lock Island, Shep. TW17 216 BN103
Lock La, Wok. GU22 250 BH116
Lockley Cres, Hat. AL10 67 CV16
Lock Mead, Maid. SL6 152 AC69
Lockmead Rd, N15 144 DU58
SE13 46 F10
Lock Ms, NW1 7 N4
Lockner Holt, Chilw. GU4 281 BF141
Lock Path, Dorney SL4 173 AL79
Lock Rd, Guil. GU1 264 AX131
Richmond TW10 199 CJ91
Lockside, E14 off Northey St 21 M10
Locks La, Mitch. CR4 222 DF95
Locksley Dr, Wok. GU21 off Robin Hood Rd 248 AT118
Locksley Est, E14 21 N8
Locksley St, E14 21 N7
Locksmeade Rd, Rich. TW10 199 CJ91
Locksons Cl, E14 22 C7
Lockswood Cl, Barn. EN4 102 DF42
Lockton St, W10 14 C10
Lockwell Rd, Dag. RM10 148 EZ62
Lockwood Cl, SE26 205 DX91
Lockwood Ho, E5 off Mount Pleasant Hill 144 DW61
SE11 off Kennington Oval 42 E3
● Lockwood Ind Pk, N17 144 DV55
Lockwood Path, Wok. GU21 233 BD113
Lockwood Pl, E4 123 EA51
Lockwood Sq, SE16 32 E6
🔒 Lockwood Wk, Rom. RM1 off Western Rd 149 FE57
Lockwood Way, E17 123 DX54
Chessington KT9 238 CN106
Lockyer Est, SE1 31 M4
Lockyer Ms, Enf. EN3 105 EB38
Lockyer Rd, Purf. RM19 190 FQ79
Lockyer St, SE1 31 M5
Locomotive Dr, Felt. TW14 197 BU88
Locton Grn, E3 11 P8
Loddiges Rd, E9 10 G6
Loddon Spur, Slou. SL1 154 AS73
Loder Cl, Wok. GU21 233 BD113
Loder St, SE15 44 G6
Lodge Av, SW14 180 CS83
Croydon CR0 223 DN104
Dagenham RM8, RM9 168 EU67
Dartford DA1 210 FJ86
Elstree WD6 100 CM43
Harrow HA3 140 CL56
Romford RM2 149 FG56
Jct Lodge Av Junct, Bark. IG11 168 EU67
Lodgebottom Rd, Lthd. KT22 270 CM127
Lodge Cl, N18 122 DQ50
Chigwell IG7 126 EU48
Edgware HA8 118 CM51
Englefield Green TW20 194 AX92
Epsom KT17 off Howell Hill Gro 239 CW110
Fetcham KT22 253 CD122
Hertford SG14 54 DQ07
Hutton CM13 131 GE45
Isleworth TW7 179 CH81
North Holmwood RH5 285 CJ140
Orpington BR6 228 EV102
Slough SL1 173 AQ75
Stoke D'Abernon KT11 252 BZ115
Uxbridge UB8 156 BJ70
Wallington SM6 222 DG102
Lodge Ct, Horn. RM12 150 FL61
Wembley HA0 140 CL64
Lodge Cres, Orp. BR6 228 EV102
Waltham Cross EN8 89 DX34
Lodge Dr, N13 121 DN49
Hatfield AL9 67 CX15
Loudwater WD3 96 BJ42
Lodge End, Crox.Grn WD3 97 BR42
Radlett WD7 83 CH34
Lodgefield, Welw.G.C. AL7 51 CY06
Lodge Gdns, Beck. BR3 225 DZ99
Lodge Hall, Harl. CM18 73 ES19
Lodge Hill, SE2 188 EV80
Ilford IG4 146 EL56
Purley CR8 257 DN115
Welling DA16 188 EV80
Lodgehill Pk Cl, Har. HA2 138 CB61
Lodge La, N12 120 DC50
Bexley DA5 208 EX86
Chalfont St. Giles HP8 95 AZ41
Grays RM16, RM17 192 GA75
New Addington CR0 243 EA107
Redhill RH1 288 DE143
Lodge La, Romford RM5 126 FA52
South Holmwood RH5 286 CL144
Waltham Abbey EN9 105 ED35
Westerham TN16 277 EQ127
Lodge Pl, Sutt. SM1 240 DB106
Lodge Rd, NW4 141 CW56
NW8 16 B3
Bromley BR1 206 EH94
Croydon CR0 223 DP100
Epping CM16 off Crown Hill 91 EN34
Fetcham KT22 252 CC122
Wallington SM6 241 DH106
Sch Lodge Sch, Commonweal Lo, Pur. CR8 off Woodcote La 241 DK112
Downside Lo, Pur. CR8 off Woodcote La 241 DK111
Lodge Vil, Wdf.Grn. IG8 124 EF52
Lodge Wk, Warl. CR6 259 EA116
Lodge Way, Ashf. TW15 196 BL89
Shepperton TW17 217 BQ96
Windsor SL4 173 AL83
Lodore Gdns, NW9 140 CS57
Lodore Grn, Uxb. UB10 136 BL62
Lodore St, E14 22 E9
Loewen Rd, Grays RM16 193 GG76
Lofthouse Pl, Chess. KT9 237 CJ107
Loftie St, SE16 32 D5
Lofting Rd, N1 8 E7
Loftus Rd, W12 161 CV74
Barking IG11 167 EQ65
Logan Cl, Enf. EN3 105 DX39
Hounslow TW4 178 BZ83
Logan Ct, Rom. RM1 off Logan Ms 149 FE57
Logan Ms, W8 27 J8
Romford RM1 149 FE57
Logan Pl, W8 27 J8
Logan Rd, N9 122 DV47
Wembley HA9 140 CL61
Loggetts, The, SE21 204 DS90
Logmore La, Dor. RH4 284 CB138
Logs Hill, Brom. BR1 206 EL94
Chislehurst BR7 206 EL94
Logs Hill Cl, Chis. BR7 226 EL95
Lohmann Ho, SE11 off Kennington Oval 42 E2
Lois Dr, Shep. TW17 217 BP99
Lolesworth Cl, E1 20 A7
Lollards Cl, Amer. HP6 77 AQ37
Lollard St, SE11 30 D8
Lollesworth La, W.Hors. KT24 267 BQ126
Loman Path, S.Ock. RM15 171 FT72
Loman St, SE1 31 H4
Lomas Cl, Croy. CR0 243 EC108
Lomas Dr, E8 10 B6
Lomas St, E1 20 D6
Lombard Av, Enf. EN3 104 DW39
Ilford IG3 147 ES60
● Lombard Business Pk, SW19 222 DB96
Lombard Ct, EC3 19 M10
W3 off Crown St 160 CP74
Lombard La, EC4 18 F9
Lombard Rd, N11 121 DH50
SW11 40 A9
SW19 222 DB96
Jct Lombard Rbt, Croy. CR0 223 DM101
Lombards, The, Horn. RM11 150 FM59
Lombard St, EC3 19 M9
Horton Kirby DA4 230 FQ99
Lombard Wall, SE7 36 A7
Lombardy Cl, Hem.H. HP2 63 BR21
Ilford IG6 off Hazel La 125 EP52
Woking GU21 off Nethercote Av 248 AT117
Lombardy Dr, Berk. HP4 60 AX20
Lombardy Pl, W2 27 L1
🔒 Lombardy Retail Pk, Hayes UB3 157 BV73
Lombardy Way, Borwd. WD6 100 CL39
Lomond Cl, N15 144 DS56
Wembley HA0 160 CM66
Lomond Gdns, S.Croy. CR2 243 DY108
Lomond Gro, SE5 43 L4
Lomond Rd, Hem.H. HP2 62 BK16
Loncin Mead Av, New Haw KT15 234 BJ109
Loncroft Rd, SE5 43 P2
Londesborough Rd, N16 144 DS63
Londinium Twr, E1 off Mansell St 20 B10
Sch London Acad, Edg. HA8 off Spur Rd 118 CM49
Coll London Acad of Computing & Electronics, SW17 off Upper Tooting Rd 202 DF90
Coll London Acad of Management Sciences, Ilf. IG1 off Cranbrook Rd 147 EN61
Coll London Acad of Music & Dramatic Art, W14 26 D10
★ London Aquarium, SE1 30 C4
★ London Aquatics Cen, E20 12 E7
★ London Biggin Hill Airport, West. TN16 244 EK113
★ London Brass Rubbing Cen (St. Martin-in-the-Fields Ch), WC2 30 A1
⇌ London Bridge 31 N3
⊖ London Bridge 31 N3
London Br, EC4 31 M2
SE1 31 M2
Riv London Bridge City Pier 31 N2
★ London Bridge Experience & The London Tombs, The, SE1 31 M2
H London Br Hosp, SE1 31 M2
London Br St, SE1 31 L3
Coll London Business Sch, NW1 16 E4
★ London Canal Mus, The, N1 off New Wf Rd 8 B10
🔒 London Cen Mkts, EC1 18 G6
★ London Cen Mosque, NW8 16 D2
H London Chest Hosp, E2 11 H10
★ London City Airport, E16 36 G2
DLR London City Airport 36 G2
Coll London City Coll, SE1 30 E3
H London Clinic, The, W1 17 H5
★ London Coliseum, WC2 30 A1
Coll London Coll of Beauty Therapy, W1 17 L9
Uni London Coll of Communication, SE1 31 H7
Uni London Coll of Fashion, Curtain Rd, EC2 19 P4
John Princes St, W1 17 K8
Lime Gro, W12 26 A4
Mare St, E8 10 F6
LONDON COLNEY, St.Alb. AL2 84 CL26
London Colney Bypass, Lon.Col. AL2 83 CK25
Sch London Colney JMI Sch, Lon.Col. AL2 off Alexander Rd 83 CK26
Jct London Colney Rbt, St.Alb. AL2 65 CJ24
★ London Dungeon, SE1 31 M3
Coll London Electronics Coll, SW5 27 L10
London End, Beac. HP9 111 AM54
Riv London Eye Millennium Pier 30 C4
⇌ London Fields 10 E7
London Flds, E8 10 E6
London Flds E Side, E8 10 E7
Sch London Flds Prim Sch, E8 10 E8
London Flds W Side, E8 10 D6
★ London Film Mus, SE1 30 C4
★ London Fire Brigade Mus, SE1 31 J4
London Fruit Ex, E1 off Brushfield St 20 A7
★ London Gatwick Airport, Gat. RH6 290 DD153
✈ London Gatwick Airport 291 DH152
★ London Heathrow Airport, Houns. TW6 177 BP81
✈ London Heathrow Airport Central 177 BP83
✈ London Heathrow Airport Terminal 4 197 BQ85
H London Indep Hosp, E1 21 J6
● London Ind Est, E6 25 M6
London La, E8 10 F6
Bromley BR1 206 EF94
East Horsley KT24 267 BU131
Shere GU5 282 BN138
London Master Bakers Almshouses, E10 off Lea Br Rd 145 EB58
★ London Met Archives, EC1 18 F4
Uni London Met Uni - London City Campus, Calcutta Ho, E1 20 B8
Central Ho, E1 20 C8
Commercial Rd, E1 20 D8
Goulston St, E1 20 A8
Jewry St, EC3 20 A9
Moorgate, EC2 19 M7
Students Union, E1 20 B8
Tower Hill, EC3 20 A10
Whitechapel High St, E1 20 B8
Uni London Met Uni - London N Campus, Carleton Gra Hall of Res, N7 7 P1
Dept of Architecture, N7 8 F4
Eden Gro, N7 8 D2
Harglenis, N7 8 E2
James Leicester Hall of Res, N7 8 B4
Ladbroke Ho, N5 9 H2
Learning Cen, N7 8 D1
Science Cen, N7 8 E1
Stapleton Ho, N7 8 D2
The Arc Hall of Res, N7 off Holloway Rd 143 DL63
Tower Bldg, N7 8 E2
Tufnell Pk Hall of Res, N7 off Huddleston Rd 143 DJ62
London Ms, W2 16 B9
Sch London Nautical Sch, SE1 30 F2
Sch London Oratory Sch, The, SW6 39 L4
★ London Palladium, W1 17 L9
★ London Peace Pagoda, SW11 40 F4
★ London Regatta Cen, E16 36 F1
London Rd, E13 13 N10
SE1 30 G6
SE23 204 DV88
SW16 223 DM95
SW17 222 DF96
Abridge RM4 107 ET42
Amersham HP7 77 AQ40
Ashford TW15 196 BH90
Aveley RM15 170 FM74
Barking IG11 167 EP66
Beaconsfield HP9 111 AM54
Beddington Corner CR4 222 DG101
Berkhamsted HP4 60 AY20
Borehamwood WD6 84 CN34
Brentwood CM14 130 FS49
Bromley BR1 206 EF94
Bushey WD23 98 BY44
Caterham CR3 258 DR123
Chadwell Heath RM6, RM7 148 FA58
Chalfont St. Giles HP8 112 AW47
Crayford DA1 209 FD85
Croydon CR0 223 DP101
Datchet SL3 174 AV80
Dorking RH4, RH5 269 CJ133
Dunton Green TN13 263 FD118
Enfield EN2 104 DR41
Englefield Green TW20 214 AV95
Ewell KT17 239 CT109
Farningham DA4 230 FL100
Feltham TW14 196 BH90
Gatwick RH6 290 DF150
Grays RM17, RM20 191 FW79
Greenhithe DA9 211 FS86
Guildford GU1, GU4 265 BB129
Halstead TN14 247 FB112
Harrow HA1 139 CE61
Hemel Hempstead HP1, HP3 62 BK24
Hertford SG13 54 DT10
High Wycombe HP10 110 AD54
Hounslow TW3 178 CC83
Isleworth TW7 179 CF82
Kingston upon Thames KT2 220 CM96
Mitcham CR4 222 DF96
Morden SM4 222 DA99
Northfleet DA11 212 GD86
Old Harlow CM17 74 EV16
Potter Street CM17 74 EW18
Redhill RH1 272 DG132
Reigate RH2 272 DA134
Rickmansworth WD3 114 BM47
St. Albans AL1 65 CH24
Sawbridgeworth CM21 74 EW15
Send GU23 265 BC128
Sevenoaks TN13 278 FF123
Shenley WD7 84 CM33
Slough SL3 175 AZ78
Staines-upon-Thames TW18 195 BF91
Stanford Rivers CM5 109 FH36
Stanmore HA7 117 CJ50
Stapleford Tawney RM4 109 FC40
Stone DA2 210 FP87
Sutton SM3 221 CX104
London Rd, Swanley BR8 229 FC95
Swanscombe DA10 211 FV85
Thornton Heath CR7 223 DN99
Thornwood CM17 74 EV23
Tilbury RM18 193 GG82
Twickenham TW1 199 CG85
Virginia Water GU25 214 AU97
Wallington SM6 241 DH105
Ware SG12 55 DY07
Wembley HA9 160 CL65
Westerham TN16 261 EQ123
● London Rd Business Pk, St.Alb. AL1 65 CF22
London Rd E, Amer. HP7 94 AT42
⇌ London Road (Guildford) 264 AY134
London Rd N, Merst. RH1 273 DH125
London Rd Purfleet, Purf. RM19 190 FN78
Jct London Rd Rbt, Twick. TW1 199 CG86
London Rd S, Merst. RH1 272 DG130
London Rd W, Amer. HP7 77 AQ40
London Rd W Thurrock, Grays RM20 191 FS79
Uni London Sch of Economics & Political Science, WC2 18 D9
Coll London Sch of Flying, Borwd. WD6 off Hogg La 99 CF42
Uni London Sch of Hygiene & Tropical Medicine, WC1 17 P6
Uni London Sch of Jewish Studies, NW4 off Albert Rd 141 CX56
Coll London Sch of Theology, Nthwd. HA6 off Green La 115 BR51
Londons Cl, Upmin. RM14 150 FQ64
🔒 London Silver Vaults, WC2 18 E7
Uni London S Bk Uni, SE1 31 H6
Caxton Ho, SE1 30 G6
● London Sq, Guil. GU1 264 AY134
London Stile, W4 off Wellesley Rd 180 CN78
★ London Stone, EC4 19 L10
London St, EC3 19 P10
W2 16 A9
Chertsey KT16 216 BG101
Coll London Studio Cen, N1 8 B10
★ London Television Cen, SE1 30 E2
London Ter, E2 20 C1
Coll London Theological Seminary, N3 off Hendon La 119 CY54
★ London Transport Mus, WC2 18 B10
🔒 London Trocadero, The, W1 29 N1
London Wall, EC2 19 K7
London Wall Bldgs, EC2 19 M7
★ London Wetland Cen, SW13 181 CV80
Londrina Ct, Berk. HP4 60 AX19
Londrina Ter, Berk. HP4 60 AX19
Lone Oak, Smallfield RH6 291 DP150
Lonesome La, Reig. RH2 288 DB138
Sch Lonesome Prim Sch, Mitch. CR4 off Grove Rd 223 DH96
Lonesome Way, SW16 223 DH95
Long Acre, WC2 18 A10
Longacre, Harl. CM17 58 EV11
Long Acre, Orp. BR6 228 EX103
Longacre Pl, Cars. SM5 off Beddington Gdns 240 DG107
Longacre Rd, E17 123 ED53
Longacres, St.Alb. AL4 65 CK20
Longaford Way, Hutt. CM13 131 GC46
Long Arrotts, Hem.H. HP1 62 BH18
Long Banks, Harl. CM18 73 ER19
Long Barn Cl, Wat. WD25 81 BU32
Longbeach Rd, SW11 182 DF83
Longberrys, NW2 141 CZ62
Longboat Row, Sthl. UB1 158 BZ72
Long Bottom La, Beac. HP9 111 AR52
Longbourn, Wind. SL4 173 AN83
Longbourne Grn, Gdmg. GU7 280 AS143
Longbourne Way, Cher. KT16 215 BF100
Longboyds, Cob. KT11 235 BV114
Longbridge Ho, E16 37 N1
Longbridge Rd, Bark. IG11 167 EQ66
Dagenham RM8 148 EU63
Horley RH6 290 DF150
Jct Longbridge Rbt, Horl. RH6 290 DE149
Longbridge Vw, Chipstead CR5 256 DF120
Longbridge Wk, Horl. RH6 290 DF150
Longbridge Way, SE13 205 EC85
Cowley UB8 156 BH68
London Gatwick Airport RH6 290 DF150
Longbury Cl, Orp. BR5 228 EV97
Longbury Dr, Orp. BR5 228 EV97
Longchamp Cl, Horl. RH6 291 DJ148
Long Chaulden, Hem.H. HP1 61 BE20
Longcliffe Path, Wat. WD19 115 BU48
Long Cl, Farn.Com. SL2 153 AP66
Sch Long Cl Sch, Slou. SL3 off Upton Ct Rd 174 AU76
Long Copse Cl, Bkhm KT23 252 CB123
Long Ct, Purf. RM19 190 FN77
Longcourt Ms, E11 146 EJ56
Longcroft, SE9 207 EM90
Watford WD19 115 BV45
Longcroft Av, Bans. SM7 240 DC114
Longcroft Dr, Wal.Cr. EN8 89 DZ34
Longcrofte Rd, Edg. HA8 117 CK52
Longcroft Gdns, Welw.G.C. AL8 51 CX10
Longcroft Grn, Welw.G.C. AL8 off Stanborough Rd 51 CX10
Longcroft La, Hem.H. HP3 79 BC28
Welwyn Garden City AL8 51 CX10
Longcroft Ri, Loug. IG10 107 EN43
Longcroft Rd, Map.Cr. WD3 113 BD50
Longcrofts, Wal.Abb. EN9 off Roundhills 90 EE34
LONGCROSS, Cher. KT16 214 AU104
⇌ Longcross 214 AT102
Longcross Rd, Longcr. KT16 214 AY104
Long Deacon Rd, E4 124 EE46
Longdean Pk, Hem.H. HP3 62 BN24
Sch Longdean Sch, Hem.H. HP3 off Rumballs Rd 63 BP23
LONG DITTON, Surb. KT6 219 CJ102

Sch Long Ditton Inf & Nurs Sch, Long Dit. KT6 off Ditton Hill Rd 219 CJ102
Sch Long Ditton St. Mary's C of E Jun Sch, Long Dit. KT7 off Sugden Rd 219 CH102
Longdon Ct, Rom. RM1 149 FF57
Longdon Wd, Kes. BR2 244 EL105
Longdown La N, Epsom KT17 239 CU114
Longdown La S, Epsom KT17 239 CU114
Longdown Rd, SE6 205 EA91
Epsom KT17 239 CU114
Guildford GU4 281 BB137
Long Dr, W3 160 CS72
Burnham SL1 152 AJ69
Greenford UB6 158 CB67
Ruislip HA4 138 BX63
Long Dyke, Guil. GU1 265 BB132
Long Elmes, Har. HA3 116 CB53
Long Elms, Abb.L. WD5 81 BR33
Long Elms Cl, Abb.L. WD5 81 BR33
Long Fallow, St.Alb. AL2 82 CA27
Longfellow Dr, Hutt. CM13 131 GC45
Longfellow Rd, E17 145 DZ58
Worcester Park KT4 221 CU103
Longfellow Way, SE1 32 B9
Long Fld, NW9 118 CS52
Longfield, Brom. BR1 226 EF95
Harlow CM18 74 EU17
Hedgerley SL2 133 AR61
Hemel Hempstead HP3 63 BP22
Loughton IG10 106 EJ43
Longfield Av, E17 145 DY56
NW7 119 CU52
W5 159 CJ73
Enfield EN3 104 DW37
Hornchurch RM11 149 FF59
Wallington SM6 222 DG102
Wembley HA9 140 CL60
Longfield Cres, SE26 204 DW90
Tadworth KT20 255 CW120
Longfield Dr, SW14 200 CP85
Amersham HP6 77 AP38
Mitcham CR4 202 DE94
Longfield Est, SE1 32 B9
Sch Longfield First & Mid Schs, Har. HA2 off Dukes Av 138 CA58
Longfield La, Chsht EN7 88 DU27
Longfield Rd, W5 159 CJ73
Chesham HP5 76 AM29
Dorking RH4 285 CF137
Longfield St, SW18 202 DA87
Longfield Wk, W5 159 CJ72
LONGFORD, Sev. TN13 263 FD120
LONGFORD, West Dr. UB7 176 BH81
Longford Av, Felt. TW14 197 BS86
Southall UB1 158 CA73
Staines-upon-Thames TW19 196 BL88
Longford Cl, Hmptn H. TW12 198 CA91
Hanworth TW13 198 BY90
Hayes UB4 158 BX73
Sch Longford Comm Sch, Felt. TW14 off Tachbrook Rd 197 BT87
Longford Ct, E5 off Pedro St 145 DX63
NW4 141 CX56
Epsom KT19 238 CQ105
Longford Gdns, Hayes UB4 158 BX73
Sutton SM1 222 DC104
Longford Ho, E1 off Jubilee St 20 G8
Longford Rd, Twick. TW2 198 CA88
Longford Rbt, Stai. TW19 176 BG81
Longford St, NW1 17 K4
Longford Wk, SW2 off Papworth Way 203 DN87
Longford Way, Stai. TW19 196 BL88
Long Furlong Dr, Slou. SL2 153 AN70
Long Gore, Gdmg. GU7 280 AS142
Long Grn, Chig. IG7 125 ES49
Nazeing Gate EN9 90 EH25
Long Gro, Harold Wd RM3 128 FL54
Seer Green HP9 111 AQ51
Long Gro Cl, Brox. EN10 71 DY19
Long Gro Rd, Epsom KT19 238 CQ111
Longhayes Av, Rom. RM6 148 EX56
Longhayes Ct, Rom. RM6 off Longhayes Av 148 EX56
Longheath Dr, Bkhm KT23 252 BY124
Longheath Gdns, Croy. CR0 224 DW99
Longhedge Ho, SE26 204 DT91
Long Hedges, Houns. TW3 178 CA81
Longhedge St, SW11 41 H8
Long Hill, Wold. CR3 259 DX121
Longhill Rd, SE6 205 ED89
Longhook Gdns, Nthlt. UB5 157 BU68
Longhope Cl, SE15 44 A3
Long Ho, Harl. CM18 off Bush Fair 73 ET17
Longhouse Rd, Grays RM16 193 GH76
Longhurst Rd, SE13 205 ED85
Croydon CR0 224 DV100
East Horsley KT24 267 BS129
Long John, Hem.H. HP3 62 BM22
Longland Br, Sheering CM22 59 FC07
Longland Ct, SE1 32 C10
Longland Dr, N20 120 DB48
LONGLANDS, Chis. BR7 207 EQ90
Longlands, Hem.H. HP2 62 BN20
Longlands Av, Couls. CR5 240 DG114
Longlands Cl, Chsht EN8 89 DX32
Longlands Ct, W11 15 H10
Mitcham CR4 off Summerhill Way 222 DG95
Longlands Pk Cres, Sid. DA15 207 ES90
Sch Longlands Prim Sch, Sid. DA15 off Woodside Rd 207 ES90
Sch Longlands Prim Sch & Nurs, Turnf. EN10 off Nunsbury Dr 89 DZ25
Longlands Rd, Sid. DA15 207 ES90
Welwyn Garden City AL7 51 CY11
Long La, EC1 19 H6
N2 120 DC54
N3 120 DB52
SE1 31 L5
Bexleyheath DA7 188 EX80
Bovingdon HP3 79 AZ31
Croydon CR0 224 DW99
Grays RM16 192 GA75
Heronsgate WD3 95 BC44
Mill End WD3 113 BF47
Long La, Stanwell TW19 196 BM87
Uxbridge UB10 156 BN69
Longleat Ho, SW1 off Rampayne St 29 N10
Longleat Ms, Orp. BR5 off High St 228 EW98
Longleat Rd, Enf. EN1 104 DS43
Longleat Way, Felt. TW14 197 BR87
Longlees, Map.Cr. WD3 113 BC50
Longleigh La, SE2 188 EW79
Bexleyheath DA7 188 EW79
Longlents Ho, NW10 160 CR67
Long Ley, Harl. CM20 73 ET15
Welwyn Garden City AL7 52 DC09
Longley Av, Wem. HA0 160 CM67
Longley Ct, SW8 42 A6
Longley Ms, Grays RM16 193 GF75
Longley Rd, SW17 202 DE93
Croydon CR0 223 DP101
Harrow HA1 138 CC57
Long Leys, E4 123 EB51
Longley St, SE1 32 C9
Longley Way, NW2 141 CW62
Long Lo Dr, Walt. KT12 218 BW104
Longman Ct, Hem.H. HP3 80 BL25
Longmans Cl, Wat. WD18 97 BQ44
Long Mark Rd, E16 24 E7
Longmarsh La, SE28 167 ES74
Longmarsh Vw, Sutt.H. DA4 230 FP95
Long Mead, NW9 119 CT53
Longmead, Chis. BR7 227 EN96
Guildford GU1 265 BC134
Hatfield AL10 67 CV15
Windsor SL4 173 AL81
● Longmead Business Cen, Epsom KT19 238 CR111
● Longmead Business Pk, Epsom KT19 238 CR111
Longmead Cl, Cat. CR3 258 DS122
Shenfield CM15 130 FY46
Longmead Dr, Sid. DA14 208 EX89
Longmeade, Grav. DA12 213 GM88
Longmead Ho, SE27 off Elder Rd 204 DQ92
● Longmead Ind Est, Epsom KT19 238 CS111
Longmead La, Slou. SL1 153 AK66
Long Meadow, NW5 7 N3
Longmeadow, Bkhm KT23 268 BZ125
Long Meadow, Chesh. HP5 76 AQ28
Hutton CM13 131 GC47
Noak Hill RM3 128 FJ48
Riverhead TN13 278 FD121
Long Meadow Cl, W.Wick. BR4 225 EC101
Longmeadow Rd, Sid. DA15 207 ES88
Sch Longmead Prim Sch, West Dr. UB7 off Laurel La 176 BL77
Longmead Rd, SW17 202 DF92
Epsom KT19 238 CR111
Hayes UB3 157 BT73
Thames Ditton KT7 219 CE101
Longmere Gdns, Tad. KT20 255 CW119
Long Mimms, Hem.H. HP2 62 BL19
Long Moor, Chsht EN8 89 DY29
Longmoore St, SW1 29 L9
Longmoor Pt, SW15 off Norley Vale 201 CU88
Longmore Av, Barn. EN4, EN5 102 DC44
Longmore Cl, Map.Cr. WD3 113 BF49
Longmore Gdns, Welw.G.C. AL7 51 CZ09
Longmore Rd, Hersham KT12 236 BY105
Longnor Rd, E1 21 K3
Long Orchard Dr, Penn HP10 110 AC47
Long Pk, Amer. HP6 77 AQ36
Long Pk Cl, Amer. HP6 77 AQ36
Long Pk Way, Amer. HP6 77 AQ35
Long Pond Rd, SE3 47 K7
Longport Cl, Ilf. IG6 126 EU51
Long Reach, Ock. GU23 250 BN123
West Horsley KT24 267 BP125
Long Reach Ct, Bark. IG11 167 ER68
Longreach Rd, Bark. IG11 167 ET70
Erith DA8 189 FH80
Long Readings La, Slou. SL2 153 AP70
Long Ride, The, Hat. AL9 67 CZ18
Longridge, Rad. WD7 83 CH34
Longridge Gro, Wok. GU22 233 BF114
Longridge Ho, SE1 31 K7
Longridge La, Sthl. UB1 158 CB73
Longridge Rd, SW5 27 J9
Long Ridings Av, Hutt. CM13 131 GB43
Sch Long Ridings Prim Sch, Hutt. CM13 off Long Ridings Av 131 GB43
Long Rd, SW4 183 DH84
Longs Cl, Wok. GU22 250 BG116
Long's Ct, WC2 17 N10
Longs Ct, Rich. TW9 off Crown Ter 180 CM84
Longsdon Way, Cat. CR3 258 DU124
Longshaw, Lthd. KT22 253 CG119
Sch Longshaw Prim Sch, E4 off Longshaw Rd 123 ED48
Longshaw Rd, E4 123 ED48
Longshore, SE8 33 N9
Longside Cl, Egh. TW20 215 BC95
Long Spring, Port.Wd AL3 65 CF16
Longspring, Wat. WD24 97 BV38
Longspring Wd, Sev. TN14 278 FF130
Longstaff Cres, SW18 202 DA86
Longstaff Rd, SW18 202 DA86
Longstone Av, NW10 161 CT66
Longstone Ct, SE1 31 K5
Longstone Rd, SW17 203 DH92
Iver SL0 155 BC68
Long St, E2 20 A2
Waltham Abbey EN9 90 EL32
Longthornton Rd, SW16 223 DJ96
Longthorpe Ct, W6 off Invermead Cl 181 CU76
Longton Av, SE26 204 DU91
Longton Gro, SE26 204 DV91
Longton Ho, SE11 off Lambeth Wk 30 D8
Longtown Cl, Rom. RM3 128 FJ50
Longtown Rd, Rom. RM3 128 FJ50
Longview, Beac. HP9 132 AF55
Long Vw, Berk. HP4 60 AU17
Longview Way, Rom. RM5 127 FD53
Longville Rd, SE11 30 G8
Long Wk, SE1 31 P6
SE18 187 EP79
SW13 180 CS82
Chalfont St. Giles HP8 94 AX41
Epsom KT18 255 CX119
New Malden KT3 220 CQ97
Waltham Abbey EN9 89 EA30
West Byfleet KT14 234 BJ114
Long Wk, West Horsley KT24 266 BN128
Long Wk, The, Wind. SL4 173 AR83
Longwalk Rd, Uxb. UB11 157 BP74
Longwood, Harl. CM18 73 ER20
Longwood Av, Slou. SL3 175 BB78
● Longwood Business Pk, Sun. TW16 217 BT99
Longwood Cl, Upmin. RM14 150 FQ64
Longwood Dr, SW15 201 CU86
Long Wd Dr, Jordans HP9 112 AT51
Longwood Gdns, Ilf. IG5, IG6 147 EM56
Longwood La, Amer. HP7 77 AR39
Longwood Rd, Hert. SG14 53 DM08
Kenley CR8 258 DR116
Sch Longwood Sch, Bushey WD23 off Bushey Hall Dr 98 BZ42
Longworth Cl, SE28 168 EX72
Longworth Dr, Maid. SL6 152 AC70
Long Yd, WC1 18 C5
Loning, The, NW9 140 CS56
Enfield EN3 104 DW38
Lonsdale, Hem.H. HP2 62 BL17
Lonsdale Av, E6 24 E3
Hutton CM13 131 GD44
Romford RM7 149 FC58
Wembley HA9 140 CL64
Lonsdale Cl, E6 24 G4
SE9 206 EK90
Edgware HA8 118 CM50
Pinner HA5 116 BY52
Uxbridge UB8 157 BQ71
Lonsdale Cres, Dart. DA2 210 FQ88
Ilford IG2 147 EP58
Lonsdale Dr, Enf. EN2 103 DL43
Lonsdale Gdns, Th.Hth. CR7 223 DM98
Lonsdale Ms, W11 15 H9
Richmond TW9 off Elizabeth Cotts 180 CN81
Lonsdale Pl, N1 8 F7
Dorking RH4 off Lonsdale Rd 285 CH135
Lonsdale Rd, E11 146 EF59
NW6 4 G10
SE25 224 DV98
SW13 181 CU79
W4 181 CT77
W11 15 H9
Bexleyheath DA7 188 EZ82
Dorking RH4 285 CH135
Southall UB2 178 BX76
Weybridge KT13 234 BN108
Lonsdale Sq, N1 8 F7
Lonsdale Way, Maid. SL6 172 AC78
Loobert Rd, N15 144 DS55
Looe Gdns, Ilf. IG6 147 EP55
Loom La, Rad. WD7 99 CG37
Loom Pl, Rad. WD7 99 CG36
Loop Rd, Chis. BR7 207 EQ93
Epsom KT18 off Woodcote Side 254 CQ116
Waltham Abbey EN9 89 EB32
Woking GU22 249 AZ121
Lopen Rd, N18 122 DS49
Loraine Cl, Enf. EN3 104 DW43
Loraine Gdns, Ashtd. KT21 254 CL117
Loraine Rd, N7 143 DM63
W4 180 CP79
Lorane Ct, Wat. WD17 97 BU40
Lord Amory Way, E14 34 E4
Lord Av, Ilf. IG5 147 EM56
Lord Chancellor Wk, Kings.T. KT2 220 CQ95
Lord Chatham's Ride, Sev. TN14 262 EX117
Lord Darby Ms, Cudham TN14 261 ER115
Lordell Pl, SW19 201 CW93
Lorden Wk, E2 20 C3
Lord Gdns, Ilf. IG5 146 EL56
Lord Hills Br, W2 15 M7
Lord Hills Rd, W2 15 M6
Lord Holland La, SW9 42 F8
Lord Knyvett Cl, Stanw. TW19 196 BK86
Lord Knyvetts Ct, Stanw. TW19 off De Havilland Way 196 BL86
Lord Mayors Dr, Farn.Com. SL2 133 AN64
Lord Napier Pl, W6 off Oil Mill La 181 CU78
Lord N St, SW1 30 A7
Lord Roberts Ms, SW6 39 L5
Lord Roberts Ter, SE18 187 EN78
★ Lord's (Marylebone CC & Mus, Middlesex CCC), NW8 16 B2
Lordsbury Fld, Wall. SM6 241 DJ110
Lord's Cl, SE21 204 DQ89
Lords Cl, Felt. TW13 198 BY89
Shenley WD7 84 CL32
Lordsgrove Cl, Tad. KT20 off Whitegate Way 255 CV120
Lordship Cl, Hutt. CM13 131 GD46
Lordship Gro, N16 144 DR61
Lordship La, N17 122 DQ53
N22 121 DN54
SE22 204 DT86
Lordship La Est, SE22 204 DU88
Sch Lordship La Prim Sch, N22 off Lordship La 122 DQ53
Lordship Pk, N16 144 DQ61
Lordship Pk Ms, N16 144 DQ61
Lordship Pl, SW3 40 C3
Lordship Rd, N16 144 DR61
Cheshunt EN7 88 DV30
Northolt UB5 158 BY66
Lordship Ter, N16 144 DR61
Lordsmead Rd, N17 122 DS53
Lord St, E16 37 H3
Gravesend DA12 213 GH87
Hoddesdon EN11 70 DV17
Watford WD17 98 BW41
Lord's Vw, NW8 16 B3
Lords Wd, Welw.G.C. AL7 52 DC09
Lordswood Cl, Bexh. DA6 208 EY85
Lane End DA2 211 FS91
Lord Warwick St, SE18 37 J7
Lorenzo Ho, Ilf. IG3 148 EU58
Lorenzo St, WC1 18 C2
Sch Loreto Coll, St.Alb. AL1 off Hatfield Rd 65 CE20
Loretto Gdns, Har. HA3 140 CL56
Lorian Cl, N12 120 DB49
Lorian Dr, Reig. RH2 272 DC133
Loriners Cl, Cob. KT11 235 BU114
Loring Rd, N20 120 DE47
SE14 45 M6
Berkhamsted HP4 60 AW20
Isleworth TW7 179 CF82
Windsor SL4 173 AM81
Loris Rd, W6 26 B7
Lorn Ct, SW9 42 E8
Lorne, The, Bkhm KT23 268 CA126
Lorne Av, Croy. CR0 225 DX101
Lorne Cl, NW8 16 D3
Slough SL1 173 AP76
Lorne Gdns, E11 146 EJ56
W11 26 D4
Croydon CR0 225 DX101
Lorne Rd, E7 146 EH63
E17 145 EA57
N4 143 DM60
Harrow HA3 117 CF54
Richmond TW10 off Albert Rd 200 CM85
Warley CM14 130 FW49
Lorn Rd, SW9 42 D8
Lorraine Pk, Har. HA3 117 CE52
Lorrimore Rd, SE17 43 H2
Lorrimore Sq, SE17 43 H2
Lorton Cl, Grav. DA12 213 GL89
Loseberry Rd, Clay. KT10 237 CD106
Sch Loseley Flds Prim Sch, Farnc. GU7 off Green La 280 AS143
★ Loseley Ho & Pk, Guil. GU3 280 AS140
Loseley Pk, Littleton GU3 280 AS140
Loseley Rd, Gdmg. GU7 280 AS143
Losfield Rd, Wind. SL4 173 AL81
Lossie Dr, Iver SL0 155 BB73
Lothair Rd, W5 179 CK75
Lothair Rd N, N4 143 DP58
Lothair Rd S, N4 143 DN59
Lothair St, SW11 off Grant Rd 182 DE83
Lothbury, EC2 19 L8
Lothian Av, Hayes UB4 157 BV71
Lothian Cl, Wem. HA0 139 CG63
Lothian Rd, SW9 43 H6
Lothian Wd, Tad. KT20 255 CV122
Lothrop St, W10 14 E2
Lots Rd, SW10 39 N5
Lotus Cl, SE21 204 DQ90
Lotus Rd, Bigg.H. TN16 261 EM118
Loubet St, SW17 202 DF93
Loudhams Rd, Amer. HP7 94 AW39
Loudhams Wd La, Ch.St.G. HP8 94 AX40
Loudoun Av, Ilf. IG6 147 EP57
Loudoun Rd, NW8 5 P10
LOUDWATER, H.Wyc. HP10 110 AD53
LOUDWATER, Rick. WD3 96 BK41
Loudwater Cl, Sun. TW16 217 BU98
Loudwater Dr, Loud. WD3 96 BJ42
Loudwater Hts, Loud. WD3 96 BH41
Loudwater La, Rick. WD3 96 BK42
Loudwater Ridge, Loud. WD3 96 BJ42
Loudwater Rd, Sun. TW16 217 BU98
Loughborough Est, SW9 42 F9
Loughborough Junction 43 H10
Loughborough Pk, SW9 183 DP84
Sch Loughborough Prim Sch, SW9 42 G9
Loughborough Rd, SW9 42 E8
Loughborough St, SE11 30 D10
Lough Rd, N7 8 D4
LOUGHTON, IG10 107 EM43
Loughton 106 EL43
Loughton Business Cen, Loug. IG10 107 EQ42
Loughton Ct, Wal.Abb. EN9 90 EH33
Loughton La, They.B. CM16 107 ER38
● Loughton Seedbed Cen, Loug. IG10 off Langston Rd 107 ER42
Loughton Way, Buck.H. IG9 124 EK46
Louisa Cl, E9 11 K8
Louisa Gdns, E1 21 J5
Louisa Ho, SW15 180 CS84
Ilford IG3 148 EU58
Louisa St, E1 21 J5
Louise Aumonier Wk, N19 off Hillrise Rd 143 DL59
Louise Bennett Cl, SE24 off Shakespeare Rd 183 DP84
Louise Ct, E11 146 EH57
Louise Gdns, Rain. RM13 169 FE69
Louise Rd, E15 13 K4
Louise Wk, Bov. HP3 79 BA28
Louis Gdns, Chis. BR7 207 EM91
Louis Ms, N10 121 DH53
Louisville Cl, Stans.Abb. SG12 55 EC11
Louisville Rd, SW17 202 DG90
Louvaine Rd, SW11 182 DD84
Louvain Rd, Green. DA9 211 FS87
Louvain Way, Wat. WD25 81 BV32
Lovage App, E6 25 H7
Lovat Cl, NW2 141 CT62
Lovat La, EC3 31 N1
Lovatt Cl, Edg. HA8 118 CP51
Lovatt Dr, Ruis. HA4 137 BT57
Lovatts, Crox.Grn WD3 96 BN42
Lovat Wk, Houns. TW5 off Cranford La 178 BY80
Loveday Rd, W13 159 CH74
Love Grn La, Iver SL0 155 BD71
Lovegrove Cl, S.Croy. CR2 242 DR110
Lovegrove Dr, Slou. SL2 153 AM70
Lovegrove St, SE1 44 D1
Lovegrove Wk, E14 34 E3
Love Hill La, Slou. SL3 155 BA73
Lovejoy La, Wind. SL4 173 AK83
Lovekyn Cl, Kings.T. KT2 off Queen Elizabeth Rd 220 CM96
Lovelace Av, Brom. BR2 227 EN100
Lovelace Cl, Eff.Junct. KT24 251 BU123
Lovelace Dr, Wok. GU22 249 BF115
Lovelace Gdns, Bark. IG11 148 EU63
Hersham KT12 236 BW106
Surbiton KT6 219 CK101
Lovelace Grn, SE9 187 EM83
Lovelace Ho, W13 159 CH73
Sch Lovelace Prim Sch, Chess. KT9 off Mansfield Rd 237 CJ106
Lovelace Rd, SE21 204 DQ89
Barnet EN4 120 DE45
Surbiton KT6 219 CJ101
Lovelands La, Lwr Kgswd KT20 272 DB127
Love La, EC2 19 K8
N17 122 DT52
SE18 37 M9
SE25 224 DV97
Abbots Langley WD5 81 BT30
Aveley RM15 190 FQ75
Bexley DA5 208 EZ86
Godstone RH9 274 DW132
Gravesend DA12 213 GJ87
Iver SL0 155 BD72
Kings Langley WD4 80 BL29
Mitcham CR4 222 DE97
Love La, Morden SM4 222 DA101
Pinner HA5 138 BY55
Surbiton KT6 219 CK103
Sutton SM3 239 CY107
Walton on the Hill KT20 271 CT126
Woodford Green IG8 125 EM51
Lovel Av, Well. DA16 188 EU82
Lovel Cl, Hem.H. HP1 62 BG20
Lovel End, Chal.St.P. SL9 112 AW52
Lovelinch Cl, SE15 45 H3
Lovell Ho, E8 10 C8
Lovell Pl, SE16 33 M6
Lovell Rd, Enf. EN1 104 DV35
Richmond TW10 199 CJ90
Southall UB1 158 CB72
Lovell Wk, Rain. RM13 169 FG65
Lovel Mead, Chal.St.P. SL9 112 AW52
Lovelock Cl, Ken. CR8 258 DQ117
Lovel Rd, Chal.St.P. SL9 112 AW52
Loveridge Ms, NW6 5 H5
Loveridge Rd, NW6 5 H5
Lovering Rd, Chsht EN7 88 DQ26
Lovers La, Green. DA9 191 FX84
Lovers Wk, N3 120 DA52
NW7 119 CZ51
SE10 47 J3
Lover's Wk, W1 28 G2
Lovet Rd, Harl. CM19 73 EN16
Lovett Dr, Cars. SM5 222 DC101
Lovett Rd, Hare. UB9 136 BJ55
London Colney AL2 83 CG26
Staines-upon-Thames TW18 195 BB91
Lovett's Pl, SW18 off Old York Rd 182 DB84
Lovett Way, NW10 140 CQ64
Love Wk, SE5 43 L8
Lovibonds Av, Orp. BR6 245 EP105
West Drayton UB7 156 BM72
Lowbell La, Lon.Col. AL2 84 CL27
Lowbrook Rd, Ilf. IG1 147 EP64
Lowburys, Dor. RH4 285 CH139
Low Cl, Green. DA9 211 FU85
Low Cross Wd La, SE21 204 DT90
Lowdell Cl, West Dr. UB7 156 BL72
Lowden Rd, N9 122 DV46
SE24 183 DP84
Southall UB1 158 BY73
Lowe, The, Chig. IG7 126 EU50
Lowe Av, E16 23 P7
Lowe Cl, Chig. IG7 126 EU50
Lowell St, E14 21 M9
Lowen Rd, Rain. RM13 169 FD68
Lower Addiscombe Rd, Croy. CR0 224 DS102
Lower Addison Gdns, W14 26 D5
Lower Adeyfield Rd, Hem.H. HP2 62 BK19
Lower Alderton Hall La, Loug. IG10 107 EN43
LOWER ASHTEAD, Ashtd. KT21 253 CJ119
Lower Barn, Hem.H. HP3 62 BM23
Lower Barn Rd, Pur. CR8 242 DR112
Lower Bedfords Rd, Rom. RM1 127 FE51
Lower Belgrave St, SW1 29 J7
Lower Bobbingworth Grn, Ong. CM5 75 FG24
LOWER BOIS, Chesh. HP5 76 AR34
Lower Boston Rd, W7 159 CE74
Lower Br Rd, Red. RH1 272 DF134
Lower Britwell Rd, Slou. SL2 153 AK70
Lower Broad St, Dag. RM10 168 FA67
Lower Bury La, Epp. CM16 91 ES31
Lower Camden, Chis. BR7 207 EM94
Lower Ch Hill, Green. DA9 211 FS85
Lower Ch St, Croy. CR0 off Waddon New Rd 223 DP103
Lower Cippenham La, Slou. SL1 153 AN74
Lower Clabdens, Ware SG12 55 DZ06
LOWER CLAPTON, E5 11 H1
Lower Clapton Rd, E5 10 G3
Lower Clarendon Wk, W11 off Lancaster Rd 14 E9
Lower Common S, SW15 181 CV83
Lower Coombe St, Croy. CR0 242 DQ105
Lower Ct Rd, Epsom KT19 238 CQ111
Lower Cft, Swan. BR8 229 FF98
Lower Dagnall St, St.Alb. AL3 64 CC20
Lower Derby Rd, Wat. WD17 off Water La 98 BW42
Lower Downs Rd, SW20 221 CX95
Lower Drayton Pl, Croy. CR0 off Drayton Rd 223 DP103
Lower Dr, Beac. HP9 111 AK50
Lower Dunnymans, Bans. SM7 off Upper Sawley Wd 239 CZ114
Lower Edgeborough Rd, Guil. GU1 281 AZ135
LOWER EDMONTON, N9 122 DU46
Lower Emms, Hem.H. HP2 off Hunters Oak 63 BQ15
Lower Fm Rd, Eff. KT24 251 BV124
LOWER FELTHAM, Felt. TW13 197 BS90
Lowerfield, Welw.G.C. AL7 52 DA10
Lower George St, Rich. TW9 199 CK85
Lower Gravel Rd, Brom. BR2 226 EL102
LOWER GREEN, Esher KT10 218 CA103
Lower Grn, Tewin AL6 52 DE05
Lower Grn Gdns, Wor.Pk. KT4 221 CU102
Lower Grn Rd, Esher KT10 218 CB103
Lower Grn W, Mitch. CR4 222 DE97
Lower Grosvenor Pl, SW1 29 J6
Lower Gro Rd, Rich. TW10 200 CM86
Lower Guild Hall, Bluewater DA9 off Bluewater Shop Cen 211 FT87
Lower Hall La, E4 123 DY50
Lower Hampton Rd, Sun. TW16 218 BW97
Lower Ham Rd, Kings.T. KT2 199 CK93
Lower Hatfield Rd, Hert. SG13 69 DK15
Lower Higham Rd, Grav. DA12 213 GM88
Lower High St, Wat. WD17 98 BX43
Lower Hill Rd, Epsom KT19 238 CP112
LOWER HOLLOWAY, N7 8 C2
● Lower Hook Business Pk, Orp. BR6 245 EM108
Lower James St, W1 17 M10
Lower John St, W1 17 M10
Lower Kenwood Av, Enf. EN2 103 DK43
Lower Kings Rd, Berk. HP4 60 AW19
Kingston upon Thames KT2 220 CL95
LOWER KINGSWOOD, Tad. KT20 272 DA127
Lower Lea Crossing, E14 23 J10
E16 23 J10

Lower Lees Rd, Slou. SL2 153 AN69
Lower Maidstone Rd, N11
off Telford Rd 121 DJ51
Lower Mall, W6 181 CV78
Lower Mardyke Av, Rain. RM13 169 FC68
Lower Marsh, SE1 30 E5
Lower Marsh La, Kings.T. KT1 220 CM98
Lower Mast Ho, SE18 37 K6
Lower Mead, Iver SL0 155 BD69
Lowermead, Red. RH1 272 DF132
Lower Meadow, Chsht EN8 89 DX27
Harlow CM18 73 ES19
Lower Merton Ri, NW3 6 D6
Lower Morden La, Mord. SM4 221 CW100
Lower Mortlake Rd, Rich. TW9 180 CL84
LOWER NAZEING, Wal.Abb. EN9 72 EE23
Lower Noke Cl, Brwd. CM14 128 FL47
Lower Northfield, Bans. SM7 239 CZ114
Lower Paddock Rd, Wat. WD19 98 BY44
Lower Pk Rd, N11 121 DJ50
Belvedere DA17 188 FA76
Chipstead CR5 256 DE118
Loughton IG10 106 EK43
Lower Paxton Rd, St.Alb. AL1 65 CE21
Lower Peryers, E.Hors. KT24 267 BS128
Lower Pillory Down, Cars. SM5 240 DG113
● Lower Pl Business Cen, NW10 off Steele Rd 160 CQ68
Lower Plantation, Loud. WD3 96 BJ41
Lower Queens Rd, Buck.H. IG9 124 EK47
Lower Range Rd, Grav. DA12 213 GL87
Lower Richmond Rd, SW14 180 CP83
SW15 181 CW83
Richmond TW9 180 CN83
Lower Riding, Beac. HP9 110 AH53
Lower Rd, SE1 30 E4
SE8 32 G6
SE16 33 J8
Belvedere DA17 188 FA76
Chorleywood WD3 95 BC42
Denham UB9 135 BC59
Erith DA8 189 FD77
Gerrards Cross SL9 112 AY53
Great Amwell SG12 55 DZ08
Harrow HA2 139 CD61
Hemel Hempstead HP3 80 BN25
Kenley CR8 241 DP113
Leatherhead KT22, KT23, KT24 253 CD123
Loughton IG10 107 EN40
Mountnessing CM13, CM15 131 GD41
Northfleet DA11 192 FY84
Orpington BR5 228 EV101
Redhill RH1 288 DD136
Sutton SM1 240 DC105
Swanley BR8 209 FF94
Lower Robert St, WC2 off John Adam St 30 B1
🛍 Lower Rose Gall, Bluewater DA9 off Bluewater Shop Cen 211 FU87
Lower Sales, Hem.H. HP1 61 BF21
Lower Sandfields, Send GU23 249 BD124
Lower Sand Hills, Long Dit. KT6 219 CJ101
Lower Sawley Wd, Bans. SM7 off Upper Sawley Wd 239 CZ114
Lower Shott, Bkhm KT23 268 CA126
Cheshunt EN7 88 DT26
Lower Sloane St, SW1 28 G9
Lower Sq, Islw. TW7 179 CH83
Lower Sta Rd, Cray. DA1 209 FE86
Lower Strand, NW9 119 CT54
Lower St, Shere GU5 282 BN139
Lower Sunbury Rd, Hmptn. TW12 218 BZ96
Lower Swaines, Epp. CM16 91 ES30
LOWER SYDENHAM, SE26 205 DX91
⇌ Lower Sydenham 205 DZ92
● Lower Sydenham Ind Est, SE26 off Kangley Br Rd 205 DZ92
Lower Tail, Wat. WD19 116 BY48
Lower Talbot Wk, W11 off Talbot Wk 161 CY72
Lower Teddington Rd, Kings.T. KT1 219 CK95
Lower Ter, NW3 142 DC62
Lower Thames St, EC3 31 M1
🛍 Lower Thames Wk, Bluewater DA9 off Bluewater Shop Cen 211 FT88
Lower Tub, Bushey WD23 117 CD45
Lower Wd Rd, Clay. KT10 237 CG107
Lower Woodside, Hat. AL9 67 CZ22
Lower Yott, Hem.H. HP2 62 BM21
Lowestoft Cl, E5 off Theydon Rd 144 DW61
Lowestoft Dr, Slou. SL1 152 AJ72
Lowestoft Ms, E16 37 P4
Lowestoft Rd, Wat. WD24 97 BV39
Loweswater Cl, Wat. WD25 82 BW33
Wembley HA9 139 CK61
★ Lowewood Mus, Hodd. EN11 71 EA18
Lowfield, Saw. CM21 58 EX06
● Lowfield Heath Ind Est, Craw. RH11 290 DE154
Lowfield La, Hodd. EN11 71 EA17
Lowfield Rd, NW6 5 J6
W3 160 CQ72
Lowfield St, Dart. DA1 210 FL89
Low Hall Cl, E4 123 EA45
Low Hall La, E17 145 DY58
Low Hill Rd, Roydon CM19 72 EF17
Lowick Rd, Har. HA1 139 CE56
Lowlands, Hat. AL9 67 CW15
Lowlands Dr, Stanw. TW19 196 BK85
Lowlands Gdns, Rom. RM7 149 FB58
Lowlands Rd, Aveley RM15 170 FP74
Harrow HA1 139 CE59
Pinner HA5 138 BW59
Lowman Rd, N7 8 D1
Lowndes Av, Chesh. HP5 76 AP30
Lowndes Cl, SW1 29 H7
Lowndes Ct, W1 17 L9
Bromley BR1 off Queens Rd 226 EG96
Lowndes Ms, SW16 off Broadlands Ave 203 DL89
Lowndes Pl, SW1 28 G7
Lowndes Sq, SW1 28 F5
Lowndes St, SW1 28 F6
Lowood Ct, SE19 204 DT92
Lowood St, E1 20 F10
Low Rd, Hat. AL9 68 DF15
Lowry Cl, Erith DA8 189 FD77
Lowry Cres, Mitch. CR4 222 DE96
Lowry Ho, E14 off Cassilis Rd 34 B5
Lowry Rd, Dag. RM8 148 EV63
Lowshoe La, Rom. RM5 127 FB53
Lowson Gro, Wat. WD19 116 BY45
LOW STREET, Til. RM18 193 GM79
Low St La, E.Til. RM18 193 GM78
Lowswood Cl, Nthwd. HA6 115 BQ53
Lowther Cl, Els. WD6 100 CM43
Lowther Dr, Enf. EN2 103 DL42
Lowther Gdns, SW7 28 A6
Lowther Hill, SE23 205 DY87
Sch Lowther Prim Sch, SW13 off Stillingfleet Rd 181 CU79
Lowther Rd, E17 123 DY54
N7 8 E3
SW13 181 CT81
Kingston upon Thames KT2 220 CM95
Stanmore HA7 140 CM55
Lowthorpe, Wok. GU21 off Shilburn Way 248 AU118
Lowth Rd, SE5 43 J7
LOXFORD, Ilf. IG1 147 EQ64
Loxford Av, E6 166 EK68
Loxford La, Ilf. IG1, IG3 147 EQ64
Loxford Rd, Bark. IG11 167 EP65
Caterham CR3 274 DT125
Sch Loxford Sch of Science & Tech, Ilf. IG1 off Loxford La 147 ER64
Loxford Ter, Bark. IG11 off Fanshawe Av 167 EQ65
Loxford Way, Cat. CR3 274 DT125
Loxham Rd, E4 123 EA52
Loxham St, WC1 18 B3
Loxley Cl, SE26 205 DX92
Byfleet KT14 234 BL114
Loxley Ct, Ware SG12 55 DY06
Loxley Rd, SW18 202 DD88
Berkhamsted HP4 60 AS17
Hampton TW12 198 BZ91
Loxton Rd, SE23 205 DX88
Loxwood Cl, Felt. TW14 197 BR88
Hemel Hempstead HP3 61 BF23
Orpington BR5 228 EX103
Loxwood Rd, N17 144 DS55
Sch Loyola Prep Sch, Buck.H. IG9 off Palmerston Rd 124 EJ46
Coll L.S.O. St. Luke's, EC1 19 K4
Sch Lubavitch Girls Prim Sch, N16 off Stamford Hill 144 DT59
Sch Lubavitch Ho Boys' Sch, E5 off Clapton Common 144 DT59
Lubbock Rd, Chis. BR7 207 EM94
Lubbock St, SE14 45 H5
Lucan Dr, Stai. TW18 196 BK94
Lucan Pl, SW3 28 C9
Lucan Rd, Barn. EN5 101 CY41
Lucas Av, E13 166 EH67
Harrow HA2 138 CA61
Lucas Cl, NW10 off Pound La 161 CU66
Lucas Ct, SW11 41 H7
Harrow HA2 138 CA60
Waltham Abbey EN9 90 EF33
Lucas Cres, Green. DA9 off Ingress Pk Av 211 FW85
Lucas Gdns, N2 120 DC54
Lucas Rd, SE20 204 DW93
Grays RM17 192 GA76
Lucas Sq, NW11 off Hampstead Way 142 DA58
Lucas St, SE8 46 A8
Sch Lucas Vale Prim Sch, SE8 46 A7
Lucern Cl, Chsht EN7 88 DS27
Lucerne Cl, N13 121 DL49
Woking GU22 248 AY119
Lucerne Ct, Erith DA18 off Middle Way 188 EY76
Lucerne Gro, E17 145 ED56
Lucerne Ms, W8 27 K2
Lucerne Rd, N5 143 DP63
Orpington BR6 227 ET102
Thornton Heath CR7 223 DP99
Lucerne Way, Rom. RM3 128 FK51
Lucey Rd, SE16 32 C7
Lucey Way, SE16 32 D7
Lucida Ct, Wat. WD18 off Whippendell Rd 97 BS43
Lucie Av, Ashf. TW15 197 BP93
Lucien Rd, SW17 202 DG91
SW19 202 DB89
Lucknow St, SE18 187 ES80
Lucks Hill, Hem.H. HP1 61 BE20
Lucorn Cl, SE12 206 EF86
Lucton Ms, Loug. IG10 107 EP42
Luctons Av, Buck.H. IG9 124 EJ46
Lucy Cres, W3 160 CQ71
Lucy Gdns, Dag. RM8 148 EY62
Luddesdon Rd, Erith DA8 188 FA80
Luddington Av, Vir.W. GU25 215 AZ96
Ludford Cl, Croy. CR0 off Warrington Rd 241 DP105
Ludgate Bdy, EC4 18 G9
Ludgate Circ, EC4 18 G9
Ludgate Hill, EC4 18 G9
Ludgate Sq, EC4 19 H9
Ludham Cl, SE28 off Rollesby Way 168 EW72
Ilford IG6 125 EQ53
Ludlow Cl, Brom. BR2 off Aylesbury Rd 226 EG97
Harrow HA2 138 BZ63
Ludlow Ct, Dag. RM10 off St. Mark's Pl 168 FA65
Ludlow Mead, Wat. WD19 115 BV48
Ludlow Pl, Grays RM17 192 GB76
Ludlow Rd, W5 159 CJ70
Feltham TW13 197 BU91
Guildford GU2 280 AV135
Ludlow St, EC1 19 J4
Ludlow Way, N2 142 DC56
Croxley Green WD3 97 BQ42
Ludovick Wk, SW15 180 CS84
Ludwick Cl, Welw.G.C. AL7 51 CZ11
Ludwick Grn, Welw.G.C. AL7 51 CZ10
Ludwick Ms, SE14 45 M4
Ludwick Way, Welw.G.C. AL7 51 CZ09
Luff Cl, Wind. SL4 173 AL83
Luffield Rd, SE2 188 EV76
Luffman Rd, SE12 206 EH90
Lugard Rd, SE15 44 F8
Lugg App, E12 147 EN62
Luke Ho, E1 20 E9
Luke St, EC2 19 N4
Lukin Cres, E4 123 ED48
Lukin St, E1 21 H9
Lukintone Cl, Loug. IG10 106 EL44
Lullarook Cl, Bigg.H. TN16 260 EJ116
Lullingstone Av, Swan. BR8 229 FF97
Lullingstone Cl, Orp. BR5 208 EV94
Lullingstone Cres, Orp. BR5 208 EU94
Lullingstone La, SE13 205 ED86
Eynsford DA4 230 FJ104
★ Lullingstone Park Visitor Cen, Dart. DA4 247 FG107
Lullingstone Rd, Belv. DA17 188 EZ79
★ Lullingstone Roman Vil, Dart. DA4 229 FH104
Lullington Garth, N12 119 CZ50
Borehamwood WD6 100 CP43
Bromley BR1 206 EE94
Lullington Rd, SE20 204 DU94
Dagenham RM9 168 EY66
Lulot Gdns, N19 143 DH61
Lulworth, NW1 7 M7
SE17 31 L10
Lulworth Av, Goffs Oak EN7 87 DP29
Hounslow TW5 178 CB80
Wembley HA9 139 CJ59
Lulworth Cl, Har. HA2 138 BZ62
Lulworth Cres, Mitch. CR4 222 DE96
Lulworth Dr, Pnr. HA5 138 BX59
Romford RM5 127 FB50
Lulworth Gdns, Har. HA2 138 BY61
Lulworth Ho, SW8 42 C4
Lulworth Rd, SE9 206 EL89
SE15 44 F8
Welling DA16 187 ET82
Lulworth Waye, Hayes UB4 158 BW72
Lumbards, Welw.G.C. AL7 52 DA06
Lumen Rd, Wem. HA9 139 CK61
Lumiere Ct, SW17 202 DG89
Luminoscity Ct, W13 off Drayton Grn Rd 159 CH73
Lumley Cl, Belv. DA17 188 FA79
Lumley Ct, WC2 30 B1
Horley RH6 290 DG147
Lumley Flats, SW1 off Holbein Pl 28 G10
Lumley Gdns, Sutt. SM3 239 CY106
Lumley Rd, Horl. RH6 290 DG147
Sutton SM3 239 CY107
Lumley St, W1 17 H9
Luna Ho, SE16 32 D4
Luna Pl, St.Alb. AL1 65 CG20
Lunar Cl, Bigg.H. TN16 260 EK116
Luna Rd, Th.Hth. CR7 224 DQ97
Lundin Wk, Wat. WD19 116 BX49
Lund Pt, E15 12 E8
Lundy Dr, Hayes UB3 177 BS77
Lundy Wk, N1 9 K5
Lunedale Rd, Dart. DA2 210 FQ88
Lunedale Wk, Dart. DA2 off Lunedale Rd 210 FQ88
Lunghurst Rd, Wold. CR3 259 DZ120
Lunham Rd, SE19 204 DS93
Lupin Cl, SW2 off Palace Rd 203 DP89
Croydon CR0 off Primrose La 225 DX102
Rush Green RM7 149 FD61
West Drayton UB7 off Magnolia St 176 BK78
Lupin Cres, Ilf. IG1 off Bluebell Way 167 EP65
Lupino Ct, SE11 30 D9
Lupin Pt, SE1 32 B5
Luppit Cl, Hutt. CM13 131 GA46
Lupton Cl, SE12 206 EH91
Lupton St, NW5 7 L1
Lupus St, SW1 41 M1
Luralda Gdns, E14 34 F10
Lurgan Av, W6 38 D2
Lurline Gdns, SW11 41 H6
Luscombe Ct, Brom. BR2 226 EE96
Luscombe Way, SW8 42 A4
Lushes Ct, Loug. IG10 off Lushes Rd 107 EP43
Lushes Rd, Loug. IG10 107 EP43
Lushington Dr, Cob. KT11 235 BV114
Lushington Rd, NW10 161 CV68
SE6 205 EB92
Lushington Ter, E8 10 D3
Lusted Hall La, Tats. TN16 260 EJ120
Lusted Rd, Sev. TN13 263 FE120
Lusteds Cl, Dor. RH4 off Glory Mead 285 CJ139
Luther Cl, Edg. HA8 118 CQ47
Luther King Cl, E17 145 DY58
Luther Ms, Tedd. TW11 off Luther Rd 199 CF92
Luther Rd, Tedd. TW11 199 CF92
Luton Pl, SE10 46 F5
Luton Rd, E13 23 N5
E17 145 DZ55
Sidcup DA14 208 EW90
Luton St, NW8 16 B5
Lutton Ter, NW3 142 DC63
Luttrell Av, SW15 201 CV85
Lutwyche Rd, SE6 205 DZ89
Lutyens Cl, Eff. KT24 268 BX127
Lutyens Ho, SW1 off Churchill Gdns 41 L1
Luxborough La, Chig. IG7 124 EL48
Luxborough St, W1 16 G6
Luxborough Twr, W1 off Luxborough St 16 G6
Luxembourg Ms, E15 13 J3
Luxemburg Gdns, W6 26 C8
Luxfield Rd, SE9 206 EL88
Luxford Pl, Saw. CM21 58 EZ06
Luxford St, SE16 33 J9
Luxmore St, SE4 45 P7
Luxor St, SE5 43 H9
Luxted Rd, Downe BR6 245 EN112
Lyall Av, SE21 204 DS90
Lyall Ms, SW1 28 G7
Lyall Ms W, SW1 28 G7
Lyall St, SW1 28 G7
Lyal Rd, E3 21 M1
Lycaste Cl, St.Alb. AL1 65 CF21
Sch Lycée Français Charles de Gaulle, SW7 28 A8
Lycett Pl, W12 off Becklow Rd 181 CU75
Lych Gate, Wat. WD25 82 BX33
Lych Gate Rd, Orp. BR6 228 EU102
Lych Gate Wk, Hayes UB3 157 BT73
Lych Way, Wok. GU21 248 AX116
Lyconby Gdns, Croy. CR0 225 DY101
Lycrome La, Chesh. HP5 76 AR28
Lycrome Rd, Chesh. HP5 76 AS28
Lydd Cl, Sid. DA14 207 ES90
Lydden Ct, SE9 207 ES86
Lydden Gro, SW18 202 DB87
Lydden Rd, SW18 202 DB87
Lydd Rd, Bexh. DA7 188 EZ80
Lydeard Rd, E6 167 EM66
Lydele Cl, Wok. GU21 249 AZ115
Lydford Av, Slou. SL2 153 AR71
Lydford Cl, N16 9 P2
Lydford Rd, N15 144 DR57
NW2 4 B5
W9 15 H4
Lydger Cl, Wok. GU22 249 BB120
Lydhurst Av, SW2 203 DM89
Lydia Ms, N.Mymms AL9 67 CW24
Lydia Rd, Erith DA8 189 FF79
Lydney Cl, SW19 off Princes Way 201 CY89
Lydon Rd, SW4 183 DJ83
Lydsey Cl, Slou. SL2 153 AN69
Lydstep Rd, Chis. BR7 207 EN91
Lye, The, Tad. KT20 255 CW122
LYE GREEN, Chesh. HP5 78 AT27
Lye Grn Rd, Chesh. HP5 76 AR30
Lye La, Brick.Wd AL2 82 CA30
Lyell Pl E, Wind. SL4 off Lyell Rd 172 AJ83
Lyell Pl W, Wind. SL4 off Lyell Rd 172 AJ83
Lyell Rd, Wind. SL4 172 AJ83
Lyell Wk E, Wind. SL4 off Lyell Rd 172 AJ83
Lyell Wk W, Wind. SL4 off Lyell Rd 172 AJ83
Lyfield, Oxshott KT22 236 CB114
Lyford Rd, SW18 202 DD87
Lyford St, SE18 37 H9
Lygean Av, Ware SG12 55 DY06
Lygon Ho, SW6 38 E6
Lygon Pl, SW1 29 J7
Lyham Cl, SW2 203 DL86
Lyham Rd, SW2 203 DL85
Lyle Cl, Mitch. CR4 222 DG101
Lyle Pk, Sev. TN13 279 FH123
Lymbourne Cl, Sutt. SM2 240 DA110
Lymden Gdns, Reig. RH2 288 DB135
Lyme Fm Rd, SE12 186 EG84
Lyme Gro, E9 10 G6
Lymer Av, SE19 204 DT92
Lyme Regis Rd, Bans. SM7 255 CZ117
Lyme Rd, Well. DA16 188 EV81
Lymescote Gdns, Sutt. SM1 222 DA103
Lyme St, NW1 7 L7
Lyme Ter, NW1 7 L7
Lyminge Cl, Sid. DA14 207 ET91
Lyminge Gdns, SW18 202 DE88
Lymington Av, N22 121 DN54
Lymington Cl, E6 25 J6
SW16 223 DK96
Lymington Ct, Sutt. SM1 off All Saints Rd 222 DC104
Lymington Dr, Ruis. HA4 137 BR61
Lymington Gdns, Epsom KT19 239 CT106
Lymington Rd, NW6 5 L4
Dagenham RM8 148 EX60
Lyminster Cl, Hayes UB4 off West Quay Dr 158 BY71
Lympstone Gdns, SE15 44 D4
Lynbridge Gdns, N13 121 DP49
Lynbrook Cl, Rain. RM13 169 FD68
Lynbrook Gro, SE15 43 P4
Lynceley Gra, Epp. CM16 92 EU29
Lynch, The, Hodd. EN11 71 EB17
Uxbridge UB8 156 BJ66
Lynch Cl, SE3 47 L9
Uxbridge UB8 off Cross Rd 156 BJ66
Lynchen Cl, Houns. TW5 off The Avenue 177 BU81
Lynch Hill La, Slou. SL2 153 AL70
Sch Lynch Hill Prim Sch, Slou. SL2 off Garrard Rd 153 AM69
Lynchmere Pl, Guil. GU2 off Peak Rd 264 AU131
Lynch Wk, SE8 45 P2
Lyncott Cres, SW4 183 DH84
Lyncroft Av, Pnr. HA5 138 BY57
Lyncroft Gdns, NW6 5 K2
W13 179 CJ75
Epsom KT17 239 CT109
Hounslow TW3 178 CC84
Lyndale, NW2 141 CZ63
Lyndale Av, NW2 141 CZ62
Lyndale Cl, SE3 47 L3
Lyndale Ct, W.Byf. KT14 off Parvis Rd 234 BG113
● Lyndale Est, Grays RM20 191 FV79
Lyndale Rd, Red. RH1 272 DF131
Lynden Hyrst, Croy. CR0 224 DT103
Lynden Way, Swan. BR8 229 FC97
Lyndhurst Av, N12 120 DF51
NW7 118 CS51
SW16 223 DK96
Pinner HA5 115 BV53
Southall UB1 158 CB74
Sunbury-on-Thames TW16 217 BU97
Surbiton KT5 220 CP102
Twickenham TW2 198 BZ88
Lyndhurst Cl, NW10 140 CR62
Bexleyheath DA7 189 FB83
Croydon CR0 224 DT104
Orpington BR6 245 EP105
Woking GU21 248 AX115
Lyndhurst Ct, E18 off Churchfields 124 EG53
Sutton SM2 off Overton Rd 240 DA108
Lyndhurst Dr, E10 145 EC59
Hornchurch RM11 150 FJ60
New Malden KT3 220 CS100
Sevenoaks TN13 278 FE124
Lyndhurst Gdns, N3 119 CY53
NW3 6 B2
Barking IG11 167 ES65
Enfield EN1 104 DS42
Ilford IG2 147 ER58
Pinner HA5 115 BV53
Lyndhurst Gro, SE15 43 P8
Lyndhurst Ho, SW15 off Ellisfield Dr 201 CU87
Sch Lyndhurst Ho Prep Sch, NW3 6 B2
Sch Lyndhurst Prim Sch, SE5 43 M8
Lyndhurst Ri, Chig. IG7 125 EN49
Lyndhurst Rd, E4 123 EC52
N18 122 DU49
N22 121 DM51
NW3 6 B2
Bexleyheath DA7 189 FB83
Chesham HP5 76 AP28
Coulsdon CR5 256 DG116
Greenford UB6 158 CB70
Reigate RH2 288 DA137
Lyndhurst Rd, Thornton Heath CR7 223 DN98
Lyndhurst Sq, SE15 44 B7
Lyndhurst Ter, NW3 6 A2
Lyndhurst Wk, Borwd. WD6 100 CM39
Lyndhurst Way, SE15 44 B6
Chertsey KT16 215 BE104
Hutton CM13 131 GC46
Sutton SM2 240 DA108
Lyndon Av, Pnr. HA5 116 BY51
Sidcup DA15 207 ET85
Wallington SM6 222 DG104
Lyndon Rd, Belv. DA17 188 FA77
Lyndon Yd, SW17 202 DB91
Lyndwood Dr, Old Wind. SL4 194 AU86
LYNE, Cher. KT16 215 BA102
Sch Lyne & Long Cross C of E Inf Sch, Lyne KT16 off Lyne La 215 BB103
Lyne Cl, Vir.W. GU25 215 AZ100
Lyne Cres, E17 123 DZ53
Lyne Crossing Rd, Lyne KT16 215 BA100
Lyne Gdns, Bigg.H. TN16 260 EL118
Lynegrove Av, Ashf. TW15 197 BQ92
Lyneham Dr, NW9 118 CS53
Lyneham Wk, E5 off Boscombe Cl 11 L2
Pinner HA5 137 BT55
Lyne La, Egh. TW20 215 BA99
Lyne KT16 215 BA100
Virginia Water GU25 215 BA100
Lyne Rd, Vir.W. GU25 214 AX100
Lynette Av, SW4 203 DH86
Lynett Rd, Dag. RM8 148 EX61
Lyne Way, Hem.H. HP1 61 BF18
Lynford Cl, Barn. EN5 101 CT43
Edgware HA8 118 CQ52
Lynford Gdns, Edg. HA8 118 CP48
Ilford IG3 147 ET61
Lyngarth Cl, Bkhm KT23 268 CC125
Lyngfield Pk, Maid. SL6 172 AD79
Lynhurst Cres, Uxb. UB10 157 BQ66
Lynhurst Rd, Uxb. UB10 157 BQ66
Lynmere Rd, Well. DA16 188 EV82
Lyn Ms, E3 21 N3
N16 9 P1
Lynmouth Av, Enf. EN1 104 DT44
Morden SM4 221 CX101
Lynmouth Dr, Ruis. HA4 137 BV61
Lynmouth Gdns, Houns. TW5 178 BX81
Perivale UB6 159 CH67
Lynmouth Ri, Orp. BR5 228 EV98
Lynmouth Rd, E17 145 DY58
N2 142 DF55
N16 144 DT60
Perivale UB6 159 CH67
Welwyn Garden City AL7 51 CZ09
Lynn Cl, Ashf. TW15 197 BR92
Harrow HA3 117 CD54
Lynne Cl, Grn St Grn BR6 245 ET107
South Croydon CR2 242 DW111
Lynne Wk, Esher KT10 236 CC106
Lynne Way, Nthlt. UB5 158 BX68
Lynn Ms, E11 off Lynn Rd 146 EE61
Lynn Rd, E11 146 EE61
SW12 203 DH87
Ilford IG2 147 ER59
Lynn St, Enf. EN2 104 DR39
Lynn Wk, Reig. RH2 288 DB137
Lynross Cl, Rom. RM3 128 FM54
Lynscott Way, S.Croy. CR2 241 DP109
Lynsted Cl, Bexh. DA6 209 FB85
Bromley BR1 226 EJ96
Lynsted Ct, Beck. BR3 off Churchfields Rd 225 DY96
Lynsted Gdns, SE9 186 EK83
Lynton Av, N12 120 DD49
NW9 141 CT56
W13 159 CG72
Orpington BR5 228 EV98
Romford RM7 126 FA53
St. Albans AL1 65 CJ21
Lynton Cl, NW10 140 CS64
Chessington KT9 238 CL105
Isleworth TW7 179 CF84
Lynton Cres, Ilf. IG2 147 EP58
Lynton Crest, Pot.B. EN6 off Strafford Gate 86 DA32
Lynton Est, SE1 32 C9
Lynton Gdns, N11 121 DK51
Enfield EN1 122 DS45
Lynton Mead, N20 120 DA48
Lynton Par, Chsht EN8 off Turners Hill 89 DX30
Lynton Rd, E4 123 EB50
N8 143 DK57
NW6 5 H9
SE1 32 B9
W3 160 CN73
Chesham HP5 76 AP28
Croydon CR0 223 DN100
Gravesend DA11 213 GG88
Harrow HA2 138 BY61
New Malden KT3 220 CR99
Lynton Rd S, Grav. DA11 213 GG88
Lynton Ter, W3 160 CP72
Lynton Wk, Hayes UB4 157 BS69
Lynwood, Guil. GU2 280 AV135
Lynwood Av, Couls. CR5 257 DH115
Egham TW20 194 AY93
Epsom KT17 239 CT114
Slough SL3 174 AX76
Lynwood Cl, E18 124 EJ53
Harrow HA2 138 BY62
Romford RM5 127 FB51
Woking GU21 233 BD113
Lynwood Dr, Nthwd. HA6 115 BS53
Romford RM5 127 FB51
Worcester Park KT4 221 CU103
Lynwood Gdns, Croy. CR0 241 DM105
Southall UB1 158 BZ72
Lynwood Gro, N21 121 DN46
Orpington BR6 227 ES101
Lynwood Hts, Rick. WD3 96 BH43
Lynwood Rd, SW17 202 DF90
W5 160 CL70
Epsom KT17 239 CT114
Redhill RH1 272 DG132
Thames Ditton KT7 219 CF103
Lynx Hill, E.Hors. KT24 267 BT128
Lynx Way, E16 24 E10

Lyo - Mal

● Lyon Business Pk, Bark. IG11 167 ES68
Lyon Ho, Har. HA1 *off Lyon Rd* 139 CF58
Lyon Meade, Stan. HA7 117 CJ53
Lyon Pk Av, Wem. HA0 160 CL65
Sch Lyon Pk Inf & Jun Schs, Wem. HA0 *off Vincent Rd* 160 CM66
Lyon Rd, SW19 222 DC95
Harrow HA1 139 CF58
Romford RM1 149 FF59
Walton-on-Thames KT12 218 BY103
Lyons Ct, Dor. RH4 285 CH136
Lyonsdene, Lwr Kgswd KT20 271 CZ127
Lyonsdown Av, New Barn. EN5 102 DC44
Lyonsdown Rd, New Barn. EN5 102 DC44
Sch Lyonsdown Sch, New Barn. EN5 *off Richmond Rd* 102 DC43
Lyons Dr, Guil. GU2 264 AU129
Lyons Pl, NW8 16 A4
Lyon St, N1 8 C7
Lyons Wk, W14 26 E8
Lyon Way, Grnf. UB6 159 CE67
St. Albans AL4 66 CN20
Lyoth Rd, Orp. BR5 227 EQ103
Lyrical Way, Hem.H. HP1 62 BH18
Lyric Dr, Grnf. UB6 158 CB70
★ Lyric Hammersmith, W6 26 A9
Lyric Ms, SE26 204 DW91
Lyric Rd, SW13 181 CT81
Lyric Sq, W6 *off King St* 26 A9
Lysander Cl, Bov. HP3 79 AZ27
Lysander Ct, N.Wld Bas. CM16 93 FB26
Lysander Gdns, Surb. KT6 *off Ewell Rd* 220 CM100
Lysander Gro, N19 143 DK60
Lysander Ho, E2 20 E1
Lysander Ms, N19 143 DJ60
Lysander Rd, Croy. CR0 241 DM107
Ruislip HA4 137 BR61
Lysander Way, Abb.L. WD5 81 BU32
Orpington BR6 227 EQ104
Welwyn Garden City AL7 52 DD08
Lys Hill Gdns, Hert. SG14 53 DP07
Lysias Rd, SW12 202 DG86
Lysia St, SW6 38 C5
Lysley Pl, Brook.Pk AL9 86 DC27
Lysons Wk, SW15 201 CU85
Lyster Ms, Cob. KT11 235 BV113
Lytchet Rd, Brom. BR1 206 EH94
Lytchet Way, Enf. EN3 104 DW39
Lytchgate Cl, S.Croy. CR2 242 DS108
Lytcott Dr, W.Mol. KT8 *off Freeman Dr* 218 BZ98
Lytcott Gro, SE22 204 DT85
Lyte St, E2 10 G10
Lytham Av, Wat. WD19 116 BX50
Lytham Cl, SE28 168 EY72
Lytham Gro, W5 160 CM69
Lytham St, SE17 43 L1
Lyttelton Cl, NW3 6 C7
Lyttelton Rd, E10 145 EB62
N2 142 DC57
Lyttleton Rd, N8 143 DN55
Lytton Av, N13 121 DN47
Enfield EN3 105 DY38
Lytton Cl, N2 142 DD58
Loughton IG10 107 ER41
Northolt UB5 158 BZ66
Lytton Gdns, Wall. SM6 241 DK105
Welwyn Garden City AL8 51 CX09
Lytton Gro, SW15 201 CX85
Lytton Pk, Cob. KT11 236 BZ112
Lytton Rd, E11 146 EE59
Barnet EN5 102 DC42
Grays RM16 193 GG77
Pinner HA5 116 BY52
Romford RM2 149 FH57
Woking GU22 249 BB116
Lytton Strachey Path, SE28 *off Titmuss Av* 168 EV73
Lyttons Way, Hodd. EN11 55 EA14
Lyveden Rd, SE3 186 EH80
SW17 202 DE93
Lywood Cl, Tad. KT20 255 CW122

M

Mabbotts, Tad. KT20 255 CX121
Mabbutt Cl, Brick.Wd AL2 82 BY30
Mabel Rd, Swan. BR8 209 FG93
Mabel St, Wok. GU21 248 AX117
Maberley Cres, SE19 204 DU94
Maberley Rd, SE19 224 DT95
Beckenham BR3 225 DX97
Mabeys Wk, High Wych CM21 58 EV06
Mabledon Pl, WC1 17 P3
Mablethorpe Rd, SW6 38 E5
Mabley St, E9 11 L4
McAdam Cl, Hodd. EN11 71 EA15
McAdam Dr, Enf. EN2 103 DP40
McArdle Way, Colnbr. SL3 175 BD80
Macaret Cl, N20 120 DB45
MacArthur Cl, E7 13 P5
Erith DA8 189 FE78
Wembley HA9 160 CP65
MacArthur Ter, SE7 186 EK79
Macaulay Av, Esher KT10 219 CE103
Sch Macaulay C of E Prim Sch, SW4 *off Victoria Ri* 183 DH83
Macaulay Ct, SW4 183 DH83
Macaulay Rd, E6 166 EK68
SW4 183 DH83
Caterham CR3 258 DS122
Macaulay Sq, SW4 183 DJ84
Macaulay Way, SE28 *off Booth Cl* 168 EV73
McAuley Cl, SE1 30 E6
SE9 207 EP85
Macauley Ms, SE13 46 F7
McAuliffe Dr, Slou. SL2 133 AM63
Macbean St, SE18 37 M7
Macbeth St, W6 181 CV78
McCabe Ct, E16 23 L7
McCall Cl, SW4 42 A8
McCall Cres, SE7 186 EL78
McCall Ho, N7 *off Tufnell Pk Rd* 143 DL62
McCarthy Rd, Felt. TW13 198 BX92
Macclesfield Br, NW1 6 D10
Macclesfield Rd, EC1 19 J2
SE25 224 DV99
Macclesfield St, W1 17 P10
McClintock Pl, Enf. EN3 105 EB37
McCoid Way, SE1 31 J5
McCrone Ms, NW3 6 B4
McCudden Rd, Dart. DA1 *off Cornwall Rd* 190 FM83
McCullum Rd, E3 11 N9
McDermott Cl, SW11 40 C10
McDermott Rd, SE15 44 C10
Macdonald Av, Dag. RM10 149 FB62
Hornchurch RM11 150 FL56
● McDonald Business Pk, Hem.H. HP2 63 BP17
Macdonald Cl, Amer. HP6 77 AR35
McDonald Ct, Hat. AL10 67 CU20
Macdonald Rd, E7 13 N1
E17 123 EC54
N11 120 DF50
N19 143 DJ61
Macdonald Way, Horn. RM11 150 FL56
Macdonnell Gdns, Wat. WD25 97 BT35
McDonough Cl, Chess. KT9 238 CL105
McDougall Rd, Berk. HP4 60 AX19
McDowall Cl, E16 23 M7
McDowall Rd, SE5 43 J7
Macdowall Rd, Guil. GU2 264 AV129
Macduff Rd, SW11 41 H6
Mace Cl, E1 32 E2
Mace Ct, Grays RM17 192 GE79
Mace La, Cudham TN14 245 ER113
McEntee Av, E17 123 DY53
Macers Ct, Brox. EN10 71 DZ24
Macers La, Brox. EN10 71 DZ24
Mace St, E2 21 J1
McEwen Way, E15 13 H8
Macey Ho, SW11 *off Surrey La* 40 D7
Macfarland Gro, SE15 43 P4
MacFarlane La, Islw. TW7 179 CF79
Macfarlane Rd, W12 26 A2
Macfarren Pl, NW1 17 H5
McGrath Rd, E15 13 L3
McGredy, Chsht EN7 88 DV29
Macgregor Rd, E16 24 D6
McGregor Rd, W11 14 G8
Machell Rd, SE15 44 G10
Macintosh Cl, Chsht EN7 88 DR26
McIntosh Cl, Rom. RM1 149 FE55
Wallington SM6 241 DL108
McIntosh Rd, Rom. RM1 149 FE55
Mackay Rd, SW4 41 K10
McKay Rd, SW20 201 CV94
● McKay Trd Est, Colnbr. SL3 175 BE82
McKellar Cl, Bushey Hth WD23 116 CC47
Mackennal St, NW8 16 D1
Mackenzie Cl, W12 *off Australia Rd* 161 CV73
Mackenzie Rd, N7 8 C4
Beckenham BR3 224 DW96
McKenzie Rd, Brox. EN10 71 DZ20
Mackenzie St, Slou. SL1 154 AT74
Mackenzie Wk, E14 34 B3
McKenzie Way, Epsom KT19 238 CN110
Mackenzie Way, Grav. DA12 213 GK93
McKerrell Rd, SE15 44 D7
Mackeson Rd, NW3 6 E1
Mackie Rd, SW2 203 DN87
Mackies Hill, Peasl. GU5 283 BR144
Mackintosh La, E9 11 K3
Macklin St, WC2 18 B8
Mackrells, Red. RH1 288 DC137
Mackrow Wk, E14 22 E10
Macks Rd, SE16 32 D8
Mackworth St, NW1 17 L2
Maclaren Ms, SW15 181 CW84
Maclean Rd, SE23 205 DY86
Maclennan Av, Rain. RM13 170 FK69
Macleod Cl, Grays RM17 192 GD77
Macleod Rd, N21 103 DL43
McLeod Rd, SE2 188 EV77
McLeod's Ms, SW7 27 M7
Macleod St, SE17 43 K1
Maclise Rd, W14 26 E7
Macmahon Cl, Chobham GU24 232 AS110
McMillan Cl, Grav. DA12 213 GJ91
Macmillan Gdns, Dart. DA1 190 FN84
McMillan St, SE8 46 A3
McMillan Student Village, SE8 46 B3
Macmillan Ct, Grnf. UB6 *off Ruislip Rd E* 158 CC70
Macmillan Way, SW17 203 DH91
McNair Rd, Sthl. UB2 178 CB75
McNeil Rd, SE5 43 N9
McNicol Dr, NW10 160 CQ68
Macoma Rd, SE18 187 ER79
Macoma Ter, SE18 187 ER79
Maconochies Rd, E14 34 C10
Macon Way, Upmin. RM14 151 FT59
Macquarie Way, E14 34 D9
McRae La, Mitch. CR4 222 DF101
Macroom Rd, W9 15 H2
Mac's Pl, EC4 18 F8
★ Madame Tussauds, NW1 16 G5
Madan Cl, West. TN16 277 ES125
Sch Madani Girls Sch, E1 20 E8
Madan Rd, West. TN16 277 ER125
Madans Wk, Epsom KT18 238 CR114
Mada Rd, Orp. BR6 227 EP104
Maddams St, E3 22 C5
Madden Cl, Swans. DA10 211 FX86
Maddison Cl, N2 *off Long La* 120 DC54
Teddington TW11 199 CF93
Maddocks Cl, Sid. DA14 208 EY92
Maddock Way, SE17 42 G3
Maddox La, Bkhm KT23 252 BY123
Maddox Pk, Bkhm KT23 252 BY123
Maddox Rd, Harl. CM20 57 ES14
Hemel Hempstead HP2 63 BP20
Maddox St, W1 17 K10
Madeira Av, Brom. BR1 206 EE94
Madeira Cl, W.Byf. KT14 *off Brantwood Gdns* 234 BG113
Madeira Cres, W.Byf. KT14 *off Brantwood Gdns* 234 BG113
Madeira Gro, Wdf.Grn. IG8 124 EJ51
Madeira Rd, E11 145 ED60
N13 121 DP49
SW16 203 DL92
Mitcham CR4 222 DF98
West Byfleet KT14 233 BF113
Madeira Wk, Brwd. CM15 130 FY48
Reigate RH2 272 DD133
Windsor SL4 173 AR81
Madeleine Cl, Rom. RM6 148 EW58
Madeleine Terr, SE5 44 A7
Madeley Cl, Amer. HP6 77 AR36
Madeley Rd, W5 160 CL72
Madeline Gro, Ilf. IG1 147 ER64
Madeline Rd, SE20 224 DU95
Madells, Epp. CM16 91 ET31
Madford Retail Pk, Hert. SG13 54 DS09
Madge Gill Way, E6 *off Ron Leighton Way* 166 EL67
Madgeways Cl, Gt Amwell SG12 55 DZ09
Madgeways La, Gt Amwell SG12 55 DZ10
Madinah Rd, E8 10 C3
Madingley, Kings.T. KT1 *off St. Peters Rd* 220 CN96
Madison Bldg, SE10 *off Blackheath Rd* 46 C6
Madison Cl, Sutt. SM2 240 DD108
Madison Ct, Dag. RM10 *off St. Mark's Pl* 169 FB65
Madison Cres, Bexh. DA7 188 EW80
Madison Gdns, Bexh. DA7 188 EW80
Bromley BR2 226 EF97
Madison Hts, Houns. TW3 178 CC83
Madison Way, Sev. TN13 278 FF123
Madoc Cl, NW2 141 CZ61
Madras Pl, N7 8 E4
Madras Rd, Ilf. IG1 147 EP63
Madresfield Ct, Shenley WD7 *off Russet Dr* 84 CL32
Madrid Rd, SW13 181 CU81
Guildford GU2 280 AV135
Madrigal La, SE5 43 H5
Madron St, SE17 31 P10
Maesmaur Rd, Tats. TN16 260 EK121
Mafeking Av, E6 166 EK68
Brentford TW8 180 CL79
Ilford IG2 147 ER59
Mafeking Rd, E16 23 L4
N17 122 DU54
Enfield EN1 104 DT41
Wraysbury TW19 195 BB89
Magazine Pl, Lthd. KT22 253 CH122
Magazine Rd, Cat. CR3 257 DP122
Magdala Av, N19 143 DH61
Magdala Rd, Islw. TW7 179 CG83
South Croydon CR2 *off Napier Rd* 242 DR108
Magdalen Cl, Byfleet KT14 234 BL114
Magdalen Cres, Byfleet KT14 234 BL114
Magdalene Cl, SE15 44 E9
Magdalene Gdns, E6 25 L4
N20 120 DF46
Magdalene Rd, Shep. TW17 216 BM98
Magdalen Gdns, Hutt. CM13 131 GE44
Magdalen Gro, Orp. BR6 246 EV105
MAGDALEN LAVER, Ong. CM5 75 FE17
Magdalen Ms, NW3 5 N4
Magdalen Pas, E1 20 B10
Magdalen Rd, SW18 202 DC88
Magdalen St, SE1 *off Bermondsey St* 31 N3
Magee St, SE11 42 E2
Magellan Boul, E16 167 EQ73
Magellan Pl, E14 *off Maritime Quay* 34 B9
Maggie Blakes Causeway, SE1 *off Shad Thames* 32 A3
Magna Carta La, Wrays. TW19 194 AX88
★ Magna Carta Monument, Egh. TW20 194 AX89
Sch Magna Carta Sch, The, Stai. TW18 *off Thorpe Rd* 195 BD93
Magna Rd, Eng.Grn TW20 194 AV93
Magnaville Rd, Bushey Hth WD23 117 CE45
● Magnet Est, Grays RM20 191 FW78
Magnet Rd, Wem. HA9 139 CK61
West Thurrock RM20 191 FW79
Magnin Cl, E8 10 D8
Magnolia Av, Abb.L. WD5 81 BU32
Magnolia Cl, E10 145 EA61
Hertford SG13 54 DU09
Kingston upon Thames KT2 200 CP93
Park Street AL2 83 CD27
Magnolia Ct, Felt. TW13 *off Highfield Rd* 197 BU88
Harrow HA3 140 CM59
Horley RH6 290 DG148
Uxbridge UB10 157 BP65
Wallington SM6 *off Parkgate Rd* 241 DH106
Magnolia Dr, Bans. SM7 255 CZ116
Bigg.H. TN16 260 EK116
Magnolia Gdns, Edg. HA8 118 CQ49
Slough SL3 174 AW76
Magnolia Pl, SW4 203 DK85
W5 159 CK71
Magnolia Rd, W4 180 CP79
Magnolia St, West Dr. UB7 176 BK77
Magnolia Way, Epsom KT19 238 CQ106
North Holmwood RH5 285 CK139
Pilgrim's Hatch CM15 130 FV43
Wooburn Green HP10 *off Glory Mill La* 132 AE56
Magnum Cl, Rain. RM13 170 FJ70
Magnum Ho, Kings.T. KT2 *off London Rd* 220 CN95
Magnus Ct, N9 *off Bedevere Rd* 122 DU48
Magpie All, EC4 18 F9
Magpie Cl, E7 13 M2
NW9 *off Eagle Dr* 118 CS54
Coulsdon CR5 *off Ashbourne Cl* 257 DJ118
Enfield EN1 104 DU39
Magpie Hall Cl, Brom. BR2 226 EL100
Magpie Hall La, Brom. BR2 227 EM99
Magpie Hall Rd, Bushey Hth WD23 117 CE47
Magpie La, Colesh. HP7 111 AM45
Little Warley CM13 129 FW54
Magpie Pl, SE14 *off Milton Ct Rd* 45 M3
Watford WD25 82 BW32
Magpies, The, Epp.Grn CM16 73 EN24
Magpie Wk, Hat. AL10 *off Lark Ri* 67 CU20
Magpie Way, Slou. SL2 *off Pemberton Rd* 153 AL70
Magri Wk, E1 20 G7
Maguire Dr, Rich. TW10 199 CJ91
Maguire St, SE1 32 B4
● Mahatma Gandhi Ind Est, SE24 *off Milkwood Rd* 183 DP84
Mahlon Av, Ruis. HA4 137 BV64
Mahogany Cl, SE16 33 M3
Mahon Cl, Enf. EN1 104 DT39
Maida Av, E4 123 EB45
W2 15 P6
MAIDA HILL, W9 15 J4
Maida Rd, Belv. DA17 188 FA76
MAIDA VALE, W9 15 M4
Maida Vale 15 M2
Maida Vale, W9 15 N3
Maida Vale Rd, Dart. DA1 209 FG85
Maida Way, E4 123 EB45
Maiden Erlegh Av, Bex. DA5 208 EY88
Maidenhead Rd, Wind. SL4 173 AK80
Maidenhead St, Hert. SG14 54 DR09
Maiden La, NW1 7 P6
SE1 31 K2
WC2 30 B1
Dartford DA1 189 FG83
Maiden Pl, NW5 143 DJ62
Maiden Rd, E15 13 K6
Maiden's Br, Enf. EN2 104 DU37
Maidensfield, Welw.G.C. AL8 51 CX06
Maidenshaw Rd, Epsom KT19 238 CR112
Maidenstone Hill, SE10 46 E6
Maids of Honour Row, Rich. TW9 *off The Green* 199 CK85
Maidstone Av, Rom. RM5 127 FC54
Maidstone Bldgs Ms, SE1 31 K3
Maidstone Ho, E14 22 C8
Maidstone Rd, N11 121 DJ51
Grays RM17 192 GA79
Seal TN15 279 FN121
Sevenoaks TN13 278 FE122
Sidcup DA14 208 EX93
Swanley BR8 229 FB95
Main Av, Enf. EN1 104 DT43
Northwood HA6 115 BQ48
Main Dr, Ger.Cr. SL9 134 AW57
Iver SL0 175 BE76
Wembley HA9 139 CK62
Main Par, Chorl. WD3 *off Whitelands Av* 95 BC42
Main Par Flats, Chorl. WD3 *off Whitelands Av* 95 BC42
Main Ride, Egh. TW20 194 AS93
Mainridge Rd, Chis. BR7 207 EN91
Main Rd, Crock. BR8 229 FD100
Crockham Hill TN8 277 EQ134
Farningham DA4 230 FL100
Hextable BR8 209 FF94
Knockholt TN14 262 EV117
Longfield DA3 231 FX96
Orpington BR5 228 EW95
Romford RM1, RM2, RM7 149 FF56
Sidcup DA14 207 ES90
Sundridge TN14 262 EX124
Sutton at Hone DA4 210 FP93
Westerham TN16 244 EJ113
Windsor SL4 172 AJ80
Main St, Felt. TW13 198 BX92
Maisie Webster Cl, Stanw. TW19 *off Lauser Rd* 196 BK87
Maismore St, SE15 44 D3
Maisonettes, The, Sutt. SM1 239 CZ106
Maitland Cl, Houns. TW4 178 BZ83
Walton-on-Thames KT12 218 BY103
West Byfleet KT14 234 BG113
Maitland Cl Est, SE10 46 D5
Maitland Pk Est, NW3 6 F4
Maitland Pk Rd, NW3 6 F5
Maitland Pk Vil, NW3 6 F4
Maitland Pl, E5 10 G1
Maitland Rd, E15 13 L5
SE26 205 DX93
Maize Cft, Horl. RH6 291 DJ147
Maizey Ct, Pilg.Hat. CM15 *off Danes Way* 130 FU43
Majendie Rd, SE18 187 ER78
Majestic Way, Mitch. CR4 222 DF96
Major Cl, SW9 43 H10
Major Draper Rd, SE18 37 P7
Sch Majorie McClure Sch, Chis. BR7 *off Hawkwood La* 227 EQ96
Major Rd, E15 12 F2
SE16 32 D6
Majors Fm Rd, Slou. SL3 174 AX80
Makepeace Av, N6 142 DG61
Makepeace Rd, E11 146 EG56
Northolt UB5 158 BY68
Makins St, SW3 28 D9
Malabar St, E14 34 A5
Malacca Fm, W.Clan. GU4 266 BH127
Malam Ct, SE11 30 E9
Malam Gdns, E14 22 C10
Malan Cl, Bigg.H. TN16 260 EL117
Malan Sq, Rain. RM13 169 FH65
Malbrook Rd, SW15 181 CV84
Malcolm Cl, SE20 *off Oakfield Rd* 204 DW94
Malcolm Ct, Stan. HA7 117 CJ50
Malcolm Cres, NW4 141 CU58
Malcolm Dr, Surb. KT6 220 CL102
Malcolm Gdns, Hkwd RH6 290 DD150
Malcolm Pl, E2 20 G4
Sch Malcolm Prim Sch, SE20 *off Malcolm Rd* 204 DW94
Malcolm Rd, E1 20 G4
SE20 204 DW94
SE25 224 DU100
SW19 201 CY93
Coulsdon CR5 257 DK115
Uxbridge UB10 136 BM63
Malcolms Way, N14 103 DJ43
Malcolm Way, E11 146 EG57
Malden Av, SE25 224 DV98
Greenford UB6 139 CE64
Malden Cl, Amer. HP6 94 AT38
Malden Ct, N.Mal. KT3 221 CV97
Malden Cres, NW1 7 H5
Malden Flds, Bushey WD23 98 BX42
Malden Grn Av, Wor.Pk. KT4 221 CT102
Malden Grn Ms, Wor.Pk. KT4 *off Malden Rd* 221 CU102
Malden Hill, N.Mal. KT3 221 CT97
Malden Hill Gdns, N.Mal. KT3 221 CT97
Jct Malden Junct, N.Mal. KT3 221 CT99
Malden Manor 220 CS101
Sch Malden Manor Prim & Nurs Sch, N.Mal. KT3 *off Lawrence Av* 220 CS101
Malden Pk, N.Mal. KT3 221 CT100
Sch Malden Parochial C of E Prim Sch, Wor.Pk. KT4 *off The Manor Drive* 220 CS102
Malden Pl, NW5 6 G3
Malden Rd, NW5 6 F3
Borehamwood WD6 100 CN41
New Malden KT3 220 CS99
Sutton SM3 239 CX105
Watford WD17 97 BU40
Worcester Park KT4 221 CT101
MALDEN RUSHETT, Chess. KT9 237 CH111
Malden Way, N.Mal. KT3 221 CT99
Maldon Cl, E15 13 J3
N1 9 J8
SE5 43 N10
Maldon Ct, Wall. SM6 241 DJ106
Maldon Rd, N9 122 DT48
W3 160 CQ73
Romford RM7 149 FC59
Wallington SM6 241 DH106
Maldon Wk, Wdf.Grn. IG8 124 EJ51
Malet Cl, Egh. TW20 195 BD93
Malet Pl, WC1 17 N5
Malet St, WC1 17 N5
Maley Av, SE27 203 DP89
Malford Ct, E18 124 EG54
Malford Gro, E18 146 EF56
Malfort Rd, SE5 43 P10
Malham Cl, N11 *off Catterick Cl* 120 DG51
Malham Rd, SE23 205 DX88
Malham Ter, N18 *off Dysons Rd* 122 DV51
Malin Ct, Hem.H. HP3 62 BJ23
Malins Cl, Barn. EN5 101 CV43
Malkin Dr, Beac. HP9 110 AJ52
Church Langley CM17 74 EY16
Malkin Way, Wat. WD18 97 BS42
Mall, The, Brom. BR1 226 EG97
Croydon CR0 224 DQ103
Romford RM1 149 FF56
Mall, The, N14 121 DL48
SW1 29 M4
SW14 200 CQ85
W5 160 CL73
Harrow HA3 140 CM58
Hornchurch RM11 149 FH60
Park Street AL2 82 CC27
Surbiton KT6 219 CK99
Swanley BR8 *off London Rd* 229 FE97
Mallams Ms, SW9 42 F10
Mallard Cl, E9 11 P4
NW6 5 K9
W7 179 CE75
Burnham SL1 152 AH68
Dartford DA1 210 FM85
Horley RH6 290 DG146
New Barnet EN5 *off The Hook* 102 DD44
Redhill RH1 272 DG131
Twickenham TW2 *off Stephenson Rd* 198 CA87
Upminster RM14 151 FT59
Mallard Dr, Slou. SL1 153 AM73
Mallard Path, SE28 *off Goosander Way* 187 ER76
Mallard Pl, Twick. TW1 199 CG90
Mallard Pt, E3 22 C3
Mallard Rd, Abb.L. WD5 81 BU31
South Croydon CR2 243 DX110
Mallards, E11 146 EG59
Mallards, The, Denh. UB9 *off Patrons Way E* 135 BF58
Hem.H. HP3 80 BM25
Staines-upon-Thames TW18 216 BH96
Mallards Reach, Wey. KT13 217 BR103
Mallards Ri, Harl. CM17 74 EX15
Mallards Rd, Bark. IG11 168 EU69
Woodford Green IG8 124 EH52
Mallard Wk, Beck. BR3 225 DX99
Sidcup DA14 208 EW92
Mallard Way, NW9 140 CQ59
Hutton CM13 131 GB45
Northwood HA6 115 BQ52
Wallington SM6 241 DJ109
Watford WD25 98 BY37
Mall Bexleyheath, The, Bexleyheath DA6 188 FA84
Mall Chambers, W8 *off Kensington Mall* 27 K2
Mallet Dr, Nthlt. UB5 138 BZ64
Mallet Rd, SE13 205 ED86
Mall Ex, The, Ilf. IG1 147 EP61
★ Mall Galleries, SW1 29 P2
Malling, SE13 205 EC85
Malling Cl, Croy. CR0 224 DW100
Malling Gdns, Mord. SM4 222 DC100
Malling Way, Brom. BR2 226 EF101
Mallinson Cl, Horn. RM12 150 FJ64
Mallinson Rd, SW11 202 DE85
Croydon CR0 223 DK104
Mallion Ct, Wal.Abb. EN9 90 EF33
Mallord St, SW3 40 B2
Mallory Cl, E14 22 D6
SE4 185 DY84
Mallory Gdns, E.Barn. EN4 120 DG45
Mallory St, NW8 16 D4
Mallow Cl, Croy. CR0 *off Marigold Way* 225 DX102
Northfleet DA11 212 GE91
Tadworth KT20 255 CV119
● Mallow Ct, Welw.G.C. AL7 52 DA08
Mallow Ct, Grays RM17 192 GD79
Mallow Cres, Guil. GU4 265 BB131
Mallow Cft, Hat. AL10 *off Oxlease Dr* 67 CV19
Mallow Mead, NW7 119 CY52
Mallows, The, Uxb. UB10 137 BP62
Mallows Grn, Harl. CM19 73 EN19
Mallow St, EC1 19 L4
Mallow Wk, Goffs Oak EN7 88 DR28
Mall Pavilions, The, Uxb. UB8 156 BJ66
Mall Rd, W6 181 CV78
Sch Mall Sch, The, Twick. TW2 *off Hampton Rd* 199 CD90
Mall Shop, Dag. RM10 *off Heathway* 168 FA65
Mall Walthamstow, The, E17 145 DZ56
Mall Wood Green, The, N22 121 DN54
Mallys Pl, S.Darenth DA4 230 FQ95
Malmains Cl, Beck. BR3 225 ED99
Malmains Way, Beck. BR3 225 EC98
Malm Cl, Rick. WD3 114 BK47
Malmesbury, E2 20 G1
Malmesbury Cl, Pnr. HA5 137 BT56
Sch Malmesbury Prim Sch, E3 21 P2
Morden SM4 *off Malmesbury Rd* 222 DC100

Malmesbury Rd, E3 21 N2
E16 23 K6
E18 124 EF53
Morden SM4 222 DC101
Malmesbury Ter, E16 23 L6
Malmes Cft, Hem.H. HP3 63 BQ22
Malmsdale, Welw.G.C. AL8 51 CX05
Malmsmead Ho, E9
off Kingsmead Way 11 M2
Malmstone Av, Merst. RH1 273 DJ128
Sch Malorees Inf & Jun Schs, NW6 4 D7
Malory Cl, Beck. BR3 225 DY96
Malory Ct, N9
off Galahad Rd 122 DU48
Malpas Dr, Pnr. HA5 138 BX57
Malpas Rd, E8 10 E4
SE4 45 N9
Dagenham RM9 168 EX65
Grays RM16 193 GJ76
Slough SL2 154 AV73
Malta Rd, E10 145 EA60
Tilbury RM18 193 GF82
Malta St, EC1 19 H4
Maltby Cl, Orp. BR6 228 EU102
Maltby Dr, Enf. EN1 104 DV38
Maltby Rd, Chess. KT9 238 CN107
Maltby St, SE1 32 A5
Malt Hill, Egh. TW20 194 AY92
Malt Ho Cl, Old Wind. SL4 194 AV87
Malthouse Dr, W4 180 CS79
Feltham TW13 198 BX92
Malthouse Pas, SW13
off The Terrace 180 CS82
Malthouse Pl, Rad. WD7 83 CG34
Malt Ho Pl, Rom. RM1
off Exchange St 149 FE57
Malthouse Sq, Beac. HP9 133 AM55
Malthus Path, SE28
off Byron Cl 168 EW74
Malting Ho, E14 21 N10
Malting Mead, Hat. AL10
off Endymion Rd 67 CW17
● Maltings, The, Saw. CM21 58 FA05
Stanstead Abbotts SG12 55 ED11
Maltings, The, St.Alb. AL1 65 CD20
Maltings, The, Byfleet KT14 234 BM113
Hunton Bridge WD4 81 BQ33
Orpington BR6 227 ET102
Oxted RH8 276 EF131
Romford RM1 149 FF59
Staines-upon-Thames TW18
off Church St 195 BE91
Worcester Park KT4
off Sherbrooke Way 221 CV101
Maltings Cl, E3 22 E3
SW13 off Cleveland Gdns 180 CS82
Maltings Dr, Epp. CM16 92 EU29
Maltings La, Epp. CM16 92 EU29
Maltings Ms, Amer. HP7 77 AP40
Sidcup DA15
off Station Rd 208 EU90
Maltings Pl, SE1 31 P5
SW6 39 M7
Malting Way, Islw. TW7 179 CF83
Malt La, Rad. WD7 99 CG35
Sch Maltman's Grn Sch, Chal.St.P. SL9 off Maltmans La 134 AW55
Maltmans La, Chal.St.P. SL9 134 AW55
Malton Av, Slou. SL1 153 AP72
Malton Ms, SE18
off Malton St 187 ES79
W10 off Malton Rd 14 E8
Malton Rd, W10 14 E8
Malton St, SE18 187 ES79
Maltravers St, WC2 18 D10
Malt St, SE1 44 C2
Malus Cl, Add. KT15 233 BF108
Hemel Hempstead HP2 62 BN19
Malus Dr, Add. KT15 233 BF107
Malva Cl, SW18
off St. Ann's Hill 202 DB85
Malvern Av, E4 123 ED52
Bexleyheath DA7 188 EY80
Harrow HA2 138 BY62
Malvern Cl, SE20
off Derwent Rd 224 DU96
W10 14 G7
Bushey WD23 98 CC44
Hatfield AL10 67 CT17
Mitcham CR4 223 DJ97
Ottershaw KT16 233 BC107
St. Albans AL4 65 CH16
Surbiton KT6 220 CL102
Uxbridge UB10 137 BP61
Malvern Ct, SE14 45 H4
SW7 28 B9
Slough SL3 off Hill Ri 175 BA79
Sutton SM2 off Overton Rd 240 DA108
Malvern Dr, Felt. TW13 198 BX92
Ilford IG3 147 ET63
Woodford Green IG8 124 EJ50
Malvern Gdns, NW2 141 CY61
NW6 15 H1
Harrow HA3 140 CL55
Loughton IG10 107 EM44
Malvern Ms, NW6 15 J3
Malvern Pl, NW6 15 H2
Malvern Rd, E6 166 EL67
E8 10 C7
E11 146 EE61
N8 143 DM55
N17 144 DU55
NW6 15 J2
Enfield EN3 105 DY37
Grays RM17 192 GD77
Hampton TW12 198 CA94
Hayes UB3 177 BS80
Hornchurch RM11 149 FG58
Orpington BR6 246 EV105
Surbiton KT6 220 CL103
Thornton Heath CR7 223 DN98
Malvern Ter, N1 8 E8
N9 122 DT46
Malvern Way, W13
off Templewood 159 CH71
Croxley Green WD3 97 BP43
Hemel Hempstead HP2 62 BM18
Sch Malvern Way Inf & Nurs Sch, Crox.Grn WD3
off Malvern Way 97 BQ43
Malvina Av, Grav. DA12 213 GH89
Malwood Rd, SW12 203 DH86
Malyons, The, Shep. TW17
off Gordon Rd 217 BR100
Malyons Rd, SE13 205 EB85
Swanley BR8 209 FF94
Malyons Ter, SE13 205 EB85
Managers St, E14 34 F3
Manan Cl, Hem.H. HP3 63 BQ22
Manatee Pl, Wall. SM6
off Croydon Rd 223 DK104
Manaton Cl, SE15 44 E10
Manaton Cres, Sthl. UB1 158 CA72
Manbey Gro, E15 13 J4
Manbey Pk Rd, E15 13 J4
Manbey Rd, E15 13 J4
Manbey St, E15 13 J5
Manbre Rd, W6 38 B2
Manbrough Av, E6 25 K3
Sch Manby Lo Inf Sch, Wey. KT13
off Princes Rd 235 BQ105
Manchester Ct, E16 24 B9
Manchester Dr, W10 14 E5
Manchester Gro, E14 34 E10
Manchester Ms, W1 16 G7
Manchester Rd, E14 34 E10
N15 144 DR58
Thornton Heath CR7 224 DQ97
Manchester Sq, W1 16 G8
Manchester St, W1 16 G7
Manchester Way, Dag. RM10 149 FB63
Manchuria Rd, SW11 202 DG86
Manciple St, SE1 31 L5
Mandalay Rd, SW4 203 DJ85
Mandarin St, E14 22 A10
Mandarin Way, Hayes UB4 158 BX72
Mandela Av, Harl. CM20 57 ES13
Mandela Cl, NW10 160 CQ66
Mandela Rd, E16 23 P9
Mandela St, NW1 7 M8
SW9 42 E5
Mandela Way, SE1 31 P8
Mandel Ho, SW18
off Eastfields Av 182 DA84
Mandelyns, Nthch HP4 60 AS16
Coll Mander Portman Woodward 6th Form Tutorial Coll, SW7 28 A9
Mandeville Cl, SE3 47 M5
SW20 221 CY95
Broxbourne EN10 71 DZ20
Guildford GU2 264 AU131
Harlow CM17 74 EW17
Hertford SG13 54 DQ12
Watford WD17 97 BT38
Mandeville Ct, E4 123 DY49
Egham TW20 195 BA91
Mandeville Dr, St.Alb. AL1 65 CD23
Surbiton KT6 219 CK102
Mandeville Ho, SE1 32 B10
Mandeville Ms, SW4
off Clapham Pk Rd 183 DL84
Mandeville Pl, W1 17 H8
Sch Mandeville Prim Sch, E5
off Oswald St 145 DX62
St. Albans AL1
off Mandeville Dr 65 CD23
Mandeville Ri, Welw.G.C. AL8 51 CX07
Mandeville Rd, N14 121 DH47
Enfield EN3 105 DX36
Hertford SG13 54 DQ12
Isleworth TW7 179 CG82
Northolt UB5 158 CA66
Potters Bar EN6 86 DC32
Shepperton TW17 216 BN99
Sch Mandeville Sch, Grnf. UB6
off Horsenden La N 159 CE65
Mandeville St, E5 145 DY62
Mandeville Wk, Hutt. CM13 131 GE44
Mandrake Rd, SW17 202 DF90
Mandrake Way, E15 13 J6
Mandrell Rd, SW2 203 DL85
Manette St, W1 17 P9
Manfield Cl, Slou. SL2 153 AN69
Manford Cl, Chig. IG7 126 EU49
Manford Ct, Chig. IG7
off Manford Way 126 EU50
Manford Cross, Chig. IG7 126 EU50
● Manford Ind Est, Erith DA8 189 FG79
Sch Manford Prim Sch, Chig. IG7
off Manford Way 125 ET50
Manford Way, Chig. IG7 125 ES49
Manfred Rd, SW15 201 CZ85
Manger Rd, N7 8 B4
Mangles Rd, Guil. GU1 264 AX132
Mangold Way, Erith DA18 188 EY76
Mangrove Dr, Hert. SG13 54 DS11
Mangrove La, Hert. SG13 70 DT16
Mangrove Rd, Hert. SG13 54 DS10
Manhattan Av, Wat. WD18 97 BT42
Manhattan Bldg, E3 12 B10
Manhattan Wf, E16 35 N4
Manilla St, E14 34 A4
Manister Rd, SE2 188 EU76
Manitoba Ct, SE16 33 H5
Manitoba Gdns, Grn St Grn BR6
off Superior Dr 245 ET107
Manley Ct, N16 144 DT62
Manley Rd, Hem.H. HP2
off Knightsbridge Way 62 BL19
Manley St, NW1 6 G8
Manly Dixon Dr, Enf. EN3 105 DY37
Mannamead, Epsom KT18 254 CS119
Mannamead Cl, Epsom KT18
off Mannamead 254 CS119
Mann Cl, Croy. CR0
off Scarbrook Rd 224 DQ104
Manneby Prior, N1
off Cumming St 18 D1
Mannicotts, Welw.G.C. AL8 51 CV09
Manningford Cl, EC1 18 G2
Manning Gdns, Croy. CR0 224 DV101
Harrow HA3 139 CK59
Manning Pl, Rich. TW10
off Grove Rd 200 CM86
Manning Rd, E17
off Southcote Rd 145 DY57
Dagenham RM10 168 FA65
Orpington BR5 228 EX99
Manning St, Aveley RM15 170 FQ74
Manningtree Cl, SW19 201 CY88
Manningtree Rd, Ruis. HA4 137 BV63
Manningtree St, E1 20 C8
Mannin Rd, Rom. RM6 148 EV59
Mannock Cl, NW9 140 CR55
Mannock Dr, Loug. IG10 107 EQ40
Mannock Ms, E18 124 EH53
Mannock Rd, N22 143 DP55
Dartford DA1
off Barnwell Rd 190 FM83
Manns Cl, Islw. TW7 199 CF85
Manns Rd, Edg. HA8 118 CN51
Manoel Rd, Twick. TW2 198 CC89
Manor Av, SE4 45 P9
Caterham CR3 258 DS124
Hemel Hempstead HP3 62 BK23
Hornchurch RM11 150 FJ57
Manor Av, Hounslow TW4 178 BX83
Northolt UB5 158 BZ66
Manorbrook, SE3 186 EG84
Manor Chase, Wey. KT13 235 BP106
Jct Manor Circ, Rich. TW9 180 CN83
Manor Cl, E17 off Manor Rd 123 DY54
NW7 off Manor Dr 118 CR50
NW9 140 CP57
SE28 168 EW72
Aveley RM15 170 FQ74
Barnet EN5 101 CY42
Berkhamsted HP4 60 AW19
Crayford DA1 189 FD84
Dagenham RM10 169 FD65
East Horsley KT24 267 BS128
Hatfield AL10 67 CT15
Hertford SG14 54 DR07
Horley RH6 290 DF148
Romford RM1
off Manor Rd 149 FG57
Ruislip HA4 137 BT60
Warlingham CR6 259 DY117
Wilmington DA2 209 FG90
Woking GU22 249 BF116
Worcester Park KT4 220 CS102
Manor Cl S, Aveley RM15
off Manor Cl 170 FQ74
Sch Manor Comm Prim Sch, Swans. DA10
off Keary Rd 212 FZ87
Manor Cotts, Nthwd. HA6 115 BT53
Manor Cotts App, N2 120 DC54
Manor Ct, E10
off Grange Pk Rd 145 EB60
N2 142 DF57
SW2 off St. Matthew's Rd 203 DM85
SW6 39 M7
Enfield EN1 104 DV36
Harefield UB9 114 BJ54
Radlett WD7 99 CF38
Slough SL1
off Richards Way 153 AM74
Twickenham TW2 198 CC89
Wembley HA9 140 CL64
Weybridge KT13 235 BP105
Manor Ct Rd, W7 159 CE73
Manor Cres, Byfleet KT14 234 BM113
Epsom KT19 238 CN112
Guildford GU2 264 AV132
Hornchurch RM11 150 FJ57
Seer Green HP9 111 AR51
Surbiton KT5 220 CN100
Sch Manorcroft Prim Sch, Egh. TW20
off Wesley Dr 195 BA93
Manorcrofts Rd, Egh. TW20 195 BA93
Manordene Cl, T.Ditt. KT7 219 CG102
Manordene Rd, SE28 168 EW72
Manor Dr, N14 121 DH45
N20 120 DE48
NW7 118 CR50
Amersham HP6 77 AP36
Epsom KT19 238 CS107
Esher KT10 219 CF103
Feltham TW13
off Lebanon Av 198 BX92
Horley RH6 290 DF148
New Haw KT15 234 BG110
St. Albans AL2 82 CA27
Sunbury-on-Thames TW16 217 BU96
Surbiton KT5 220 CM100
Wembley HA9 140 CM63
Manor Dr, The, Wor.Pk. KT4 220 CS102
Manor Dr N, N.Mal. KT3 220 CR101
Worcester Park KT4 220 CS102
Manor Est, SE16 32 E9
Manor Fm, Fnghm DA4 230 FM101
Manor Fm Av, Shep. TW17 217 BP100
Manor Fm Cl, Wind. SL4 173 AM83
Worcester Park KT4 220 CS102
Manor Fm Ct, Egh. TW20
off Manor Fm La 195 BA92
Manor Fm Dr, E4 124 EE48
Manor Fm La, Egh. TW20 195 BA92
Manor Fm Rd, Enf. EN1 104 DV35
Thornton Heath CR7 223 DN96
Wembley HA0 159 CK68
Manor Fm Way, Seer Grn HP9
off Orchard Rd 111 AR51
Manorfield Cl, N19
off Junction Rd 143 DJ63
Sch Manorfield Prim & Nurs Sch, Horl. RH6 off Sangers Dr 290 DF148
Sch Manorfield Prim Sch, E14 22 D6
Manor Flds, SW15 201 CX86
Manorfields Cl, Chis. BR7 227 ET97
Manor Gdns, N7 143 DL62
SW20 221 CZ96
W3 180 CN77
W4 off Devonshire Rd 180 CS78
Effingham KT24 268 BX128
Godalming GU7
off Farncombe St 280 AS144
Guildford GU2 264 AV132
Hampton TW12 198 CB94
Richmond TW9 180 CM84
Ruislip HA4 138 BW64
South Croydon CR2 242 DT107
Sunbury-on-Thames TW16 217 BU96
Wooburn Green HP10 132 AE58
Manor Gate, Nthlt. UB5 158 BY66
Manorgate Rd, Kings.T. KT2 220 CN95
Manor Grn Rd, Epsom KT19 238 CP113
Manor Gro, SE15 44 G3
Beckenham BR3 225 EB96
Fifield SL6 172 AD80
Richmond TW9 180 CN84
Manor Hall Av, NW4 119 CW54
Manor Hall Dr, NW4 119 CX54
Manorhall Gdns, E10 145 EA60
Manor Hatch Cl, Harl. CM18 74 EV16
⊖ Manor House 143 DP59
Manor Ho Ct, Epsom KT18 238 CQ113
Shepperton TW17 217 BP101
Manor Ho Dr, NW6 4 D7
Hersham KT12 235 BT107
Northwood HA6 115 BP52
Manor Ho Est, Stan. HA7 117 CH51
Manor Ho Gdns, Abb.L. WD5 81 BR31
Manor Ho La, Bkhm KT23 268 BY126
Datchet SL3 174 AV81
Sch Manor Ho Sch, Bkhm KT23
off Manor Ho La 268 BY127
Manor Ho Way, Islw. TW7 179 CH83
Sch Manor Inf & Nurs Sch, Til. RM18 off Dickens Av 193 GH80
Sch Manor Inf Sch, Bark. IG11
off Sandringham Rd 167 ET65
(Longbridge) Dag. RM9 148 EV63
Sch Manor Jun Sch, Bark. IG11
off Sandringham Rd 167 ET65
Manor La, SE12 206 EE86
SE13 186 EE84
Fawkham Green DA3 231 FW101
Feltham TW13 197 BU89
Gerrards Cross SL9 134 AX59
Harlington UB3 177 BR79
Lower Kingswood KT20 272 DA129
Sevenoaks TN15 231 FW103
Sunbury-on-Thames TW16 217 BU96
Sutton SM1 240 DC106
Manor La Ter, SE13 186 EE84
Manor Leaze, Egh. TW20 195 BB92
Manor Lo, Guil. GU2 264 AV132
Sch Manor Lo Sch, Shenley WD7
off Rectory La 84 CQ30
Sch Manor Mead Sch, Shep. TW17
off Laleham Rd 217 BP99
Manor Ms, NW6 5 K10
SE4 45 P8
Manor Mt, SE23 204 DW88
Sch Manor Oak Prim Sch, Orp. BR5
off Sweeps La 228 EX99
Manor Par, NW10
off Station Rd 161 CT68
Hatfield AL10 67 CT15
MANOR PARK, E12 146 EL63
MANOR PARK, Slou. SL2 153 AQ70
≠ Manor Park 146 EK63
Manor Pk, SE13 185 ED84
Chislehurst BR7 227 ER96
Richmond TW9 180 CM84
Staines-upon-Thames TW18 195 BD90
Manor Pk Cl, W.Wick. BR4 225 EB102
Manor Pk Cres, Edg. HA8 118 CN51
Manor Pk Dr, Har. HA2 138 CB55
Manor Pk Gdns, Edg. HA8 118 CN50
Manor Pk Par, SE13
off Lee High Rd 185 ED84
Sch Manor Pk Prim Sch, Sutt. SM1
off Greyhound Rd 240 DC106
Manor Pk Rd, E12 146 EK63
N2 142 DC55
NW10 161 CT67
Chislehurst BR7 227 EQ95
Sutton SM1 240 DC106
West Wickham BR4 225 EB102
Manor Pl, SE17 43 H1
Bookham KT23 268 CA126
Chislehurst BR7 227 ER95
Feltham TW14 197 BU88
Mitcham CR4 223 DJ97
Staines-upon-Thames TW18 196 BH92
Sutton SM1 240 DB105
Walton-on-Thames KT12 217 BT101
Sch Manor Prim Sch, E15 13 J10
Sch Manor Prim Sch, The, Rom. RM1 off Shaftesbury Rd 149 FF57
Manor Rd, E10 145 EA59
E15 23 J1
E16 23 J4
E17 123 DY54
N16 144 DR61
N17 122 DU53
N22 121 DL51
SE25 224 DU98
SW20 221 CZ96
W13 159 CG73
Ashford TW15 196 BM92
Barking IG11 167 ET65
Barnet EN5 101 CY43
Beckenham BR3 225 EB96
Bexley DA5 209 FB88
Chadwell Heath RM6 148 EX58
Chesham HP5
off Lansdowne Rd 76 AQ29
Chigwell IG7 125 EP50
Dagenham RM10 169 FC65
Dartford DA1 189 FE84
East Molesey KT8 219 CD98
Enfield EN2 104 DR40
Erith DA8 189 FF79
Gravesend DA12 213 GH86
Grays RM17 192 GC79
Guildford GU2 264 AV132
Harlow CM17 58 EW10
Harrow HA1 139 CG58
Hatfield AL10 67 CT15
Hayes UB3 157 BU72
High Beach IG10 106 EH38
Hoddesdon EN11 71 EA16
Lambourne End RM4 126 EW47
London Colney AL2 83 CJ26
Loughton IG10 106 EH44
Mitcham CR4 223 DJ98
Potters Bar EN6 85 CZ31
Reigate RH2 271 CZ132
Richmond TW9 180 CM83
Ripley GU23 249 BF123
Romford RM1 149 FG57
Ruislip HA4 137 BR60
St. Albans AL1 65 CE19
Seer Green HP9 111 AR50
Sidcup DA15 207 ET90
South Merstham RH1 273 DJ129
Sundridge TN14 262 EX124
Sutton SM2 239 CZ108
Swanscombe DA10 211 FX86
Tatsfield TN16 260 EL120
Teddington TW11 199 CH92
Tilbury RM18 193 GG82
Twickenham TW2 198 CC89
Wallington SM6 241 DH105
Waltham Abbey EN9 89 ED33
Walton-on-Thames KT12 217 BT101
Watford WD17 97 BV39
West Thurrock RM20 191 FW79
West Wickham BR4 225 EB103
Windsor SL4 173 AL82
Woking GU21 248 AW116
Woodford Green IG8 125 EM51
Manor Rd N, Esher KT10 219 CF104
Thames Ditton KT7 219 CG103
Wallington SM6 241 DH105
Manor Rd S, Esher KT10 237 CE105
Sch Manor Sch, NW10 4 B9
Manorside, Barn. EN5 101 CY42
Manorside Cl, SE2 188 EW77
Sch Manorside Prim Sch, N3
off Squires La 120 DC53
Manor Sq, Dag. RM8 148 EX61
Manor St, Berk. HP4 60 AX19
Manor Vale, Brent. TW8 179 CJ78
Manor Vw, N3 120 DB54
Manorville Rd, Hem.H. HP3 62 BJ24
Manor Wk, Wey. KT13 235 BP106
Manor Way, E4 123 ED49
NW9 140 CS55
Manor Way, SE3 186 EF84
SE23 204 DW87
SE28 168 EW74
Banstead SM7 256 DF116
Beckenham BR3 225 EA96
Bexley DA5 208 FA88
Bexleyheath DA7 189 FD83
Borehamwood WD6 100 CQ42
Brentwood CM14 130 FU48
Bromley BR2 226 EL100
Chesham HP5 76 AR30
Cheshunt EN8
off Russells Ride 89 DY31
Coleshill HP7 77 AM44
Croxley Green WD3 96 BN42
Egham TW20 195 AZ93
Manorway, Enf. EN1 122 DS45
Manor Way, Grays RM17 192 GB80
Guildford GU2 280 AS137
Harrow HA2 138 CB56
Mitcham CR4 223 DJ97
Oxshott KT22 252 CC115
Petts Wood BR5 227 EQ98
Potters Bar EN6 86 DA30
Purley CR8 241 DL112
Rainham RM13 169 FE70
Ruislip HA4 137 BS59
South Croydon CR2 242 DS107
Southall UB2 178 BX77
Swanscombe DA10 191 FX84
Woking GU22 249 BB121
Manorway, Wdf.Grn. IG8 124 EJ50
Manor Way, Wor.Pk. KT4 220 CS102
Manor Way, The, Wall. SM6 241 DH105
● Manor Way Business Cen, Rain. RM13 off Marsh Way 169 FD71
● Manor Way Business Pk, Swans. DA10 192 FY84
Manor Waye, Uxb. UB8 156 BK67
● Manor Way Ind Est, Grays RM17 192 GC80
Manor Wd Rd, Pur. CR8 241 DL113
Manpreet Ct, E12 147 EM64
Manresa Rd, SW3 40 C1
Mansard Beeches, SW17 202 DG92
Mansard Cl, Horn. RM12 149 FG61
Pinner HA5 138 BX55
Mansards, The, St.Alb. AL1
off Avenue Rd 65 CE19
Manscroft Rd, Hem.H. HP1 62 BH17
Manse Cl, Harling. UB3 177 BR79
Mansel Cl, Guil. GU2 264 AV129
Slough SL2 154 AV71
Mansel Gro, E17 123 EA53
Mansell Cl, Wind. SL4 173 AL82
Mansell Rd, W3 180 CR75
Greenford UB6 158 CB71
Mansell St, E1 32 B1
Mansell Way, Cat. CR3 258 DQ122
Mansel Rd, SW19 201 CY93
Mansergh Cl, SE18 186 EL80
Manse Rd, N16 144 DT62
Manser Rd, Rain. RM13 169 FE69
Manse Way, Swan. BR8 229 FG98
Mansfield, High Wych CM21 58 EU06
Mansfield Av, N15 144 DR56
Barnet EN4 102 DF44
Ruislip HA4 137 BV60
Mansfield Cl, N9 104 DU44
Orpington BR5 228 EX101
Weybridge KT13 235 BP106
Mansfield Dr, Hayes UB4 157 BS70
Merstham RH1 273 DK128
Mansfield Gdns, Hert. SG14 54 DQ07
Hornchurch RM12 150 FK61
Mansfield Hill, E4 123 EB46
Mansfield Ms, W1 17 J7
Mansfield Pl, NW3
off New End 142 DC63
South Croydon CR2 242 DR107
Mansfield Rd, E11 146 EH58
E17 145 DZ56
NW3 6 F2
W3 160 CP70
Chessington KT9 237 CJ106
Ilford IG1 147 EN61
South Croydon CR2 242 DR107
Swanley BR8 209 FE93
Mansfield St, W1 17 J7
Mansford St, E2 20 D1
Manship Rd, Mitch. CR4 202 DG94
Mansion, The, Albury GU5 282 BL139
Berkhamsted HP4 60 AY17
Mansion Cl, SW9 42 F6
Mansion Gdns, NW3 142 DB62
★ Mansion Ho, EC4 19 L9
⊖ Mansion House 19 K10
Mansion Ho Pl, EC4 19 L9
Mansion Ho St, EC2 19 L9
Mansion La, Iver SL0 155 BC74
Mansion La Caravan Site, Iver SL0 155 BC74
Mansions, The, SW5
off Earls Ct Rd 27 L10
Manson Ms, SW7 27 P9
Manson Pl, SW7 28 A9
Manstead Gdns, Rain. RM13 169 FH72
Mansted Gdns, Rom. RM6 148 EW59
Manston Av, Sthl. UB2 178 CA77
Manston Cl, SE20
off Garden Rd 224 DW95
Cheshunt EN8 88 DW30
Manstone Rd, NW2 4 E2
Manston Gro, Kings.T. KT2 199 CK92
Manston Rd, Guil. GU4 265 BA130
Harlow CM20 73 ES15
Manston Way, Horn. RM12 169 FH65
St. Albans AL4 65 CK21
Manthorp Rd, SE18 187 EQ78
Mantilla Rd, SW17 202 DG91
Mantle Rd, SE4 185 DY83
Mantlet Cl, SW16 203 DJ94
Mantle Way, E15 13 J6
Manton Av, W7 179 CF75
Manton Cl, Hayes UB3 157 BS73
Manton Rd, SE2 188 EU77
Enfield EN3 105 EA37
Mantua St, SW11 40 B10
Mantus Cl, E1 21 H4
Mantus Rd, E1 20 G4
Manuka Cl, W7 159 CG74

Manus Way, N20
off Blakeney Cl 120 DC46
Manville Gdns, SW17 203 DH90
Manville Rd, SW17 202 DG89
Manwood Rd, SE4 205 DZ85
Manwood St, E16 37 K3
Manygate La, Shep. TW17 217 BQ101
Manygates, SW12 203 DH89
Maori Rd, Guil. GU1 265 AZ134
Mapesbury Ms, NW4
off Station Rd 141 CU58
Mapesbury Rd, NW2 4 E4
Mapeshill Pl, NW2 4 B5
Mape St, E2 20 E4
Maple Av, E4 123 DZ50
W3 160 CS74
Harrow HA2 138 CB61
St. Albans AL3 64 CC15
Upminster RM14 150 FP62
West Drayton UB7 156 BL73
Maple Cl, N3 120 DA51
N16 144 DU58
SW4 203 DK86
Brentwood CM13
off Cherry Av 131 FZ48
Buckhurst Hill IG9 124 EK48
Bushey WD23 98 BY40
Hampton TW12 198 BZ93
Hatfield AL10 off Elm Dr 67 CU19
Hayes UB4 158 BX69
Hornchurch RM12 149 FH62
Ilford IG6 125 ES50
Mitcham CR4 223 DH95
Petts Wood BR5 227 ER99
Ruislip HA4 137 BV58
Swanley BR8 229 FE96
Theydon Bois CM16
off Loughton La 107 ER35
Whyteleafe CR3 258 DT117
Maple Ct, Eng.Grn TW20
off Ashwood Rd 194 AV93
Erith DA8 189 FF80
New Malden KT3 220 CR97
Stanstead Abbotts SG12 55 ED11
Maplecourt Wk, Wind. SL4
off Common Rd 173 AN78
Maple Cres, Sid. DA15 208 EU86
Slough SL2 154 AV73
Maplecroft Cl, E6 24 G8
Maplecroft La, Lwr Naze. EN9 72 EE21
MAPLE CROSS, Rick. WD3 113 BD49
Sch Maple Cross JMI Sch, Rick.
WD3 off Denham Way 113 BE50
Jct Maple Cross Rbt, Rick.
WD3 113 BE48
Mapledale Av, Croy. CR0 224 DU103
Mapledene, Chis. BR7 207 EQ92
Mapledene Est, E8 10 C6
Mapledene Rd, E8 10 B6
Sch Mapledown Spec Sch, NW2
off Claremont Rd 141 CW59
Maple Dr, Bkhm KT23 268 CB125
South Ockendon RM15 171 FX70
Maplefield, Park St AL2 82 CB29
Maplefield La, Ch.St.G. HP8 94 AV41
Maple Gdns, Edg. HA8 118 CS52
Staines-upon-Thames TW19 196 BL89
Maple Gate, Loug. IG10 107 EN40
Maple Grn, Hem.H. HP1 61 BE18
Maple Gro, NW9 140 CQ59
W5 179 CK76
Bookham KT23 268 CA127
Brentford TW8 179 CH80
Guildford GU1 264 AX132
Southall UB1 158 BZ71
Watford WD17 97 BU39
Welwyn Garden City AL7 51 CZ06
Woking GU22 248 AY121
Maple Gro Business Cen,
Houns. TW4
off Lawrence Rd 178 BW84
Maple Ho, NW3
off Maitland Pk Vil 6 F4
Maplehurst, Lthd. KT22 253 CD123
Maplehurst Cl, Dart. DA2
off Sandringham Dr 209 FE89
Kingston upon Thames
KT1 220 CL98
● Maple Ind Est, Felt. TW13
off Maple Way 197 BV90
Sch Maple Inf Sch, Surb. KT6
off Maple Rd 219 CK99
Maple Leaf Cl, Abb.L. WD5 81 BU32
Biggin Hill TN16
off Main Rd 260 EK116
Mapleleaf Cl, S.Croy. CR2 243 DX111
Maple Leaf Cl, Stans.Abb.
SG12 55 ED12
Maple Leaf Dr, Sid. DA15 207 ET88
Mapleleafe Gdns, Ilf. IG6 147 EP55
Maple Leaf Sq, SE16 33 K5
Maple Lo Cl, Map.Cr. WD3 113 BE49
Maple Ms, NW6 5 L10
SW16 203 DM92
● Maple Pk, Hodd. EN11 71 EC17
Maple Pl, N17 off Park La 122 DU52
W1 17 M5
Banstead SM7 239 CX114
West Drayton UB7 156 BL73
● Maple River Ind Est, Harl.
CM20 58 EV09
Maple Rd, E11 146 EE58
SE20 224 DV95
Ashtead KT21 253 CK119
Dartford DA1 210 FJ88
Gravesend DA12 213 GJ91
Grays RM17 192 GC79
Hayes UB4 158 BW69
Redhill RH1 288 DF138
Ripley GU23 250 BG124
Surbiton KT6 220 CL99
Whyteleafe CR3 258 DT117
Maples, The, Bans. SM7 240 DB114
Claygate KT10 237 CG108
Goffs Oak EN7 88 DS28
Harlow CM19 73 EP19
Ottershaw KT16 233 BB107
St. Albans AL1
off Granville Rd 65 CF20
Sch Maple Sch, St.Alb. AL1
off Hall Pl Gdns 65 CE19
Maplescombe La, Fnghm
DA4 230 FN104
Maples Pl, E1 20 F6
Maple Springs, Wal.Abb. EN9 90 EG33
Maplestead Rd, SW2 203 DM87
Dagenham RM9 168 EV67
Maple St, E2 20 D1
W1 17 L6
Romford RM7 149 FC56
Maplethorpe Rd, Th.Hth. CR7 223 DN98
Mapleton Cl, Brom. BR2 226 EG100
Mapleton Cres, SW18 202 DB86
Enfield EN3 104 DW38
Mapleton Rd, E4 123 EC48
SW18 202 DB86
Edenbridge TN8 277 ET133
Enfield EN1 104 DV40
Westerham TN16 277 ES130
Maple Wk, W10 14 D4
Sutton SM2 240 DB110
Maple Way, Couls. CR5 257 DH121
Feltham TW13 197 BU90
Waltham Abbey EN9 off Breach
Barn Mobile Home Pk 90 EH29
Maplewood Gdns, Beac. HP9 110 AH54
Maplin Cl, N21 103 DM44
Maplin Ho, SE2
off Wolvercote Rd 188 EX75
Maplin Pk, Slou. SL3 175 BC75
Maplin Rd, E16 24 A8
Maplin St, E3 21 N3
Mapperley Dr, Wdf.Grn. IG8
off Forest Dr 124 EE52
Marabou Cl, E12 146 EL64
Maran Way, Erith DA18 188 EX75
Marathon Ho, NW1 16 E6
Marathon Way, SE28 187 ET75
Marbaix Gdns, Islw. TW7 179 CD81
Marban Rd, W9 14 G2
Marbeck Cl, Wind. SL4 173 AK81
★ Marble Arch, W1 16 F10
⊖ Marble Arch 16 F10
Marble Arch Apts, W1
off Harrowby St 16 D8
Marble Cl, W3 160 CP74
Marble Dr, NW2 141 CX60
Marble Hill Cl, Twick. TW1 199 CH87
Marble Hill Gdns, Twick. TW1 199 CH87
★ Marble Hill Ho, Twick.
TW1 199 CJ87
Marble Ho, SE18
off Felspar Cl 187 ET78
Marble Quay, E1 32 C2
Marbles Way, Tad. KT20 255 CX119
Marbrook Ct, SE12 206 EJ90
Marcella Rd, SW9 42 F9
Marcellina Way, Orp. BR6 227 ES104
Marcet Rd, Dart. DA1 210 FJ85
Marchant Cl, NW7 118 CS51
Marchant Rd, E11 145 ED61
Marchant St, SE14 45 L3
Marchbank Rd, W14 39 H2
Marchmant Cl, Horn. RM12 150 FJ62
Marchmont Gdns, Rich. TW10
off Marchmont Rd 200 CM85
Marchmont Grn, Hem.H. HP2
off Paston Rd 62 BK18
Marchmont Rd, Rich. TW10 200 CM85
Wallington SM6 241 DJ108
Marchmont St, WC1 18 A4
March Rd, Twick. TW1 199 CG87
Weybridge KT13 234 BN106
Marchside Cl, Houns. TW5 178 BX81
Marchwood Cl, SE5 43 P5
Marchwood Cres, W5 159 CJ72
Marcia Ct, Slou. SL1 153 AM74
Marcia Rd, SE1 31 P9
Marcilly Rd, SW18 202 DD85
Marco Dr, Pnr. HA5 116 BZ52
Marconi Gdns, Pilg.Hat.
CM15 130 FW43
Marconi Pl, N11 121 DH49
Marconi Rd, E10 145 EA60
Northfleet DA11 212 GD90
Marconi Way, St.Alb. AL4 65 CK20
Southall UB1 158 CB72
Marcon Pl, E8 10 E3
Marco Rd, W6 181 CW76
Marcourt Lawns, W5 160 CL70
Marcus Ct, E15 13 K8
Marcuse Rd, Cat. CR3 258 DR123
Marcus Garvey Ms, SE22
off St. Aidan's Rd 204 DV85
Marcus Garvey Way, SE24 183 DN84
Marcus Rd, Dart. DA1 209 FG87
Marcus St, E15 13 K8
SW18 202 DB86
Marcus Ter, SW18 202 DB86
Mardale Dr, NW9 140 CR57
Mardell Rd, Croy. CR0 225 DX99
Marden Av, Brom. BR2 226 EG100
Marden Cl, Chig. IG7 126 EV47
Marden Cres, Bex. DA5 209 FC85
Croydon CR0 223 DM100
Marden Ho, E8 10 E2
Sch Marden Lo Prim Sch, Cat. CR3
off Croydon Rd 258 DV121
Marden Pk, Wold. CR3 275 DZ125
Marden Rd, N17 144 DS55
Croydon CR0 223 DM100
Romford RM1 149 FE58
Marden Sq, SE16 32 E7
Marder Rd, W13 179 CG75
Mardyke Cl, Rain. RM13 169 FC68
Mardyke Ho, SE17
off Crosslet St 31 M8
Rainham RM13
off Lower Mardyke Av 169 FD68
Mardyke Rd, Harl. CM20 58 EU13
Marechal Niel Av, Sid. DA15 207 ER90
Mareschal Rd, Guil. GU2 280 AW136
Marescroft Rd, Slou. SL2 153 AL70
Maresfield, Croy. CR0 224 DS104
Maresfield Gdns, NW3 5 P3
Mare St, E8 10 F9
Marfleet Cl, Cars. SM5 222 DE103
Marford Rd, Welw.G.C. AL8 50 CS10
Wheathampstead AL4 50 CN07
Margaret Av, E4 105 EB44
St. Albans AL3 65 CD18
Shenfield CM15 131 FZ45
Margaret Bondfield Av, Bark.
IG11 168 EU66
Margaret Bldgs, N16
off Margaret Rd 144 DT60
Margaret Cl, Abb.L. WD5 81 BT32
Epping CM16
off Margaret Rd 92 EU29
Potters Bar EN6 86 DC33
Margaret Cl, Romford RM2
off Margaret Rd 149 FH57
Staines-upon-Thames TW18
off Charles Rd 196 BK93
Waltham Abbey EN9 89 ED33
Margaret Ct, W1 17 L8
Margaret Dr, Horn. RM11 150 FM60
Margaret Gardner Dr, SE9 207 EM89
Margaret Ingram Cl, SW6 38 G3
Margaret Lockwood Cl, Kings.T.
KT1 220 CM98
Margaret McMillan Ho, E16 24 C9
Margaret Rd, N16 144 DT60
Barnet EN4 102 DD43
Bexley DA5 208 EX86
Epping CM16 92 EU29
Guildford GU1 280 AW135
Romford RM2 149 FH57
Sch Margaret Roper Cath Prim Sch,
Pur. CR8 off Russell Hill Rd 241 DN110
Margaret Rutherford Pl, SW12 203 DJ88
Margaret Sq, Uxb. UB8 156 BJ67
Margaret St, W1 17 K8
Margaretta Ter, SW3 40 C2
Margaretting Rd, E12 146 EJ61
Margaret Way, Couls. CR5 257 DP118
Ilford IG4 146 EL58
Sch Margaret Wix Prim Sch, St.Alb.
AL3 off High Oaks 64 CC16
Margate Rd, SW2 203 DL85
Margeholes, Wat. WD19 116 BY47
MARGERY, Tad. KT20 272 DA129
Margery Fry Ct, N7 143 DL62
Margery Gro, Lwr Kgswd
KT20 271 CY129
Margery La, Lwr Kgswd KT20 271 CZ129
Tewin AL6 52 DD05
Margery Pk Rd, E7 13 N6
Margery Rd, Dag. RM8 148 EX62
Margery St, WC1 18 E3
Margery Wd, Welw.G.C. AL7 52 DA06
Margery Wd La, Lwr Kgswd
KT20 271 CZ129
Margherita Pl, Wal.Abb. EN9 90 EF34
Margherita Rd, Wal.Abb. EN9 90 EG34
Margin Dr, SW19 201 CX92
Margravine Gdns, W6 26 D10
Margravine Rd, W6 38 D1
Marham Dr, NW9
off Kenley Av 118 CS53
Marham Gdns, SW18 202 DE88
Morden SM4 222 DC100
Mar Ho, SE7
off Springfield Gro 186 EJ79
Maria Cl, SE1 32 D8
Sch Maria Fidelis Conv Sch,
Lwr Sch, NW1 17 M3
Upr Sch, NW1 17 N2
Mariam Gdns, Horn. RM12 150 FM61
Marian Cl, Hayes UB4 158 BX70
Marian Ct, Sutt. SM1 240 DB106
Marian Lawson Ct, Chig. IG7
off Manford Way 126 EU50
Marian Pl, E2 10 E10
Marian Rd, SW16 223 DJ95
Marian Sq, E2 10 D10
Marian St, E2 10 E10
Sch Marian Vian Prim Sch, Beck.
BR3 off Shirley Cres 225 DY99
Marian Way, NW10 161 CT66
Maria Ter, E1 21 J6
Maria Theresa Cl, N.Mal. KT3 220 CR99
Maricas Av, Har. HA3 117 CD53
Marie Curie, SE5
off Sceaux Gdns 43 P6
Marie Lloyd Gdns, N19 143 DL59
Marie Lloyd Ho, N1 19 L1
Marie Lloyd Wk, E8 10 B5
Marie Manor Way, Dart. DA2 191 FS84
Mariette Way, Wall. SM6 241 DL109
Marigold All, SE1 30 G1
Marigold Cl, Sthl. UB1
off Lancaster Rd 158 BY73
Marigold Ct, Guil. GU1 264 AY131
Marigold Pl, Harl. CM17 58 EV11
Marigold Rd, N17 122 DW52
Marigold St, SE16 32 E5
Marigold Way, Croydon CR0 225 DX102
H Marillac Hosp, Warley
CM13 129 FX51
Marina App, Hayes UB4 158 BY71
Marina Av, N.Mal. KT3 221 CV99
Marina Cl, Brom. BR2 226 EG97
Chertsey KT16 216 BH102
Marina Dr, Dart. DA1 210 FN88
Northfleet DA11 213 GF87
Welling DA16 187 ES82
Marina Gdns, Chsht EN8 88 DW30
Romford RM7 149 FC58
Marina Pl, Hmptn W. KT1 219 CK95
Marina Pt, SW6
off Lensbury Ave 39 P8
Marina Way, Iver SL0 155 BF73
Slough SL1 153 AK73
Teddington TW11
off Fairways 199 CK94
Marine Dr, SE18 37 K9
Barking IG11 168 EV70
Marinefield Rd, SW6 39 M8
● Mariner Business Cen,
Croy. CR0 241 DM106
Mariner Gdns, Rich. TW10 199 CJ90
Mariner Rd, E12
off Dersingham Av 147 EN63
Mariners Cl, Barn. EN4 102 DD43
Mariners Ct, Green. DA9
off High St 191 FV84
Mariners Ms, E14 34 G8
Mariners Wk, Erith DA8
off Cornwallis Cl 189 FF79
Mariner's Way, Grav. DA11 212 GE87
Mariner Way, Hem.H. HP2 62 BN21
Marine St, SE16 32 C6
Marine Twr, SE8 45 N2
Marion Av, Shep. TW17 217 BP99
Marion Cl, Bushey WD23 98 BZ39
Ilford IG6 125 ER52
Marion Cres, Orp. BR5 228 EU99
Marion Gro, Wdf.Grn. IG8 124 EE50
Marion Ms, SE21 204 DR90
Sch Marion Richardson Prim Sch,
E1 21 J9
Marion Rd, NW7 119 CU50
Thornton Heath CR7 224 DQ99
Marion Wk, Hem.H. HP2
off Washington Av 62 BM15
Marischal Rd, SE13 185 ED83
Marisco Cl, Grays RM16 193 GH77
Marish La, Denh. UB9 135 BC56
Sch Marish Prim Sch,
Langley SL3
off Swabey Rd 175 BA76
Marish Wf, Mdgrn SL3 174 AY75
Sch Marist Catholic Prim Sch, The,
W.Byf. KT14
off Old Woking Rd 233 BF113
Maritime Cl, Green. DA9 211 FV85
Maritime Gate, Grav. DA11 212 GE87
Maritime Ho, SE18 37 N8
Maritime Quay, E14 34 B10
Maritime St, E3 21 P5
Marius Pas, SW17
off Marius Rd 202 DG89
Marius Rd, SW17 202 DG89
Marjoram Cl, Guil. GU2 264 AU130
Marjorams Av, Loug. IG10 107 EM40
Marjorie Gro, SW11 182 DF84
Marjorie Ms, E1 21 J9
Sch Marjory Kinnon Sch, Felt.
TW14 off Hatton Rd 197 BS85
Markab Rd, Nthwd. HA6 115 BT50
Mark Av, E4 105 EB44
Mark Cl, Bexh. DA7 188 EY81
Southall UB1
off Longford Av 158 CB74
Mark Dr, Chal.St.P. SL9 112 AX49
Marke Cl, Kes. BR2 244 EL105
Markedge La, Chipstead CR5 256 DE124
Merstham RH1 272 DF126
Markenfield Rd, Guil. GU1 264 AX134
Markeston Grn, Wat. WD19 116 BX49
Market, The, Cars. SM5
off Wrythe La 222 DC102
Sutton SM1 off Rose Hill 222 DC102
Market App, W12 26 A4
Market Ct, W1 17 L8
Market Dr, W4 180 CS80
Market Est, N7 8 A4
Marketfield Rd, Red. RH1 272 DF134
Marketfield Way, Red. RH1 272 DF134
Market Hill, SE18 37 M7
Market Ho, Harl. CM20
off Birdcage Wk 57 ER14
Market La, W12 26 A5
Edgware HA8 118 CQ53
Iver SL0 175 BC75
Slough SL3 175 BC76
Market Link, Rom. RM1 149 FE56
Market Meadow, Orp. BR5 228 EW98
Market Ms, W1 29 J3
Market Oak La, Hem.H. HP3 62 BN24
Market Pl, N2 142 DE55
SE16 32 D8
W1 17 L8
W3 160 CQ74
Abridge RM4 108 EV41
Beaconsfield HP9
off London End 111 AM54
Bexleyheath DA6 188 FA84
Brentford TW8 179 CJ80
Chalfont St. Peter SL9 112 AX53
Dartford DA1
off Market St 210 FL87
Enfield EN2 off The Town 104 DR41
Hatfield AL10
off Kennelwood La 67 CV17
Hertford SG14 off Fore St 54 DR09
Kingston upon Thames KT1 219 CK96
Romford RM1 149 FE57
St. Albans AL3 65 CD20
Tilbury RM18 193 GF82
Market Pl, The, NW11 142 DB56
Market Rd, N7 8 A5
Richmond TW9 180 CN83
Market Row, SW9
off Atlantic Rd 183 DN84
Market Service Rd, The, Sutt. SM1
off Rosehill Av 222 DC102
Market Sq, N9 off Edmonton
Grn Shop Cen 122 DV47
Uxbridge UB8
off The Mall Pavilions 156 BJ66
Market Sq, E14 22 D9
Amersham HP7 off High St 77 AP40
Bromley BR1 226 EG96
Chesham HP5 off High St 76 AP31
Harlow CM20 off East Gate 57 ER14
Staines-upon-Thames TW18
off Clarence St 195 BE91
Waltham Abbey EN9
off Church St 89 EC33
Westerham TN16 277 EQ127
Woking GU21
off Cawsey Way 248 AY117
Market St, E1 20 A6
E6 167 EM68
SE18 37 M8
Dartford DA1 210 FL87
Guildford GU1 280 AX135
Harlow CM17 58 EW11
Hertford SG14 54 DR09
Watford WD18 97 BV42
Windsor SL4 173 AR81
● Market Trading Est,
Sthl. UB2 177 BV77
Market Way, E14 22 D9
Wembley HA0 off Turton Rd 140 CL64
Westerham TN16
off Costell's Meadow 277 ER126
Market Yd Ms, SE1 31 N6
Markfield, Croy. CR0 243 DZ110
Markfield Gdns, E4 123 EB45
Markfield Rd, N15 144 DU56
Caterham CR3 274 DV126
Sch Mark Hall Comm Sch &
Sports Coll, Harl. CM17
off First Av 58 EW12
Mark Hall Moors, Harl. CM20 58 EV12
MARK HALL NORTH, Harl.
CM20 58 EU12
MARK HALL SOUTH, Harl.
CM20 58 EV14
Markham Cl, Borwd. WD6 100 CM41
Markham Pl, SW3 28 E10
Markham Rd, Chsht EN7 88 DQ26
Markham Sq, SW3 28 E10
Markham St, SW3 28 D10
Markhole Cl, Hmptn. TW12 198 BZ94
Markhouse Av, E17 145 DY58
Markhouse Rd, E17 145 DZ57
Markland Ho, W10 14 C10
Mark La, EC3 31 P1
Gravesend DA12 213 GL86
Markmanor Av, E17 145 DY59
Mark Oak La, Lthd. KT22 252 CA122
Mark Rd, N22 121 DP54
Hemel Hempstead HP2 62 BN18
Marksbury Av, Rich. TW9 180 CN83
MARK'S GATE, Rom. RM6 126 EY54
Sch Marks Gate Inf Sch,
Chad.Hth RM6
off Lawn Fm Gro 148 EY55
Sch Marks Gate Jun Sch,
Chad.Hth RM6
off Rose La 148 EY55
Mark Sq, EC2 19 N4
Marks Rd, Rom. RM7 149 FC57
Warlingham CR6 259 DY118
Marks Sq, Nthflt DA11 213 GF91
Mark St, E15 13 J7
EC2 19 N4
Reigate RH2 272 DB133
Markville Gdns, Cat. CR3 274 DU125
Mark Wade Cl, E12 146 EK60
Markway, Sun. TW16 218 BW96
Mark Way, Swan. BR8 229 FG99
Markwell Cl, SE26 204 DV91
Markwell Wd, Harl. CM19 73 EP21
Markyate Rd, Dag. RM8 148 EV64
Marlands Rd, Ilf. IG5 146 EL55
Marlborough, SW3 28 D8
Marlborough Av, E8 10 C9
N14 121 DJ48
Edgware HA8 118 CP48
Ruislip HA4 137 BQ58
Marlborough Cl, N20 120 DF48
SE17 31 H9
SW19 202 DE93
Grays RM16 192 GC75
Hersham KT12 218 BX104
Orpington BR6
off Aylesham Rd 227 ET100
Upminster RM14 151 FS60
Marlborough Ct, W1 17 L9
W8 27 J8
Dorking RH4
off Marlborough Hill 285 CH136
Wallington SM6
off Cranley Gdns 241 DJ108
Marlborough Cres, W4 180 CR76
Harlington UB3 177 BR80
Sevenoaks TN13 278 FE124
Marlborough Dr, Ilf. IG5 146 EL55
Weybridge KT13 217 BQ104
Sch Marlborough First & Mid Sch,
Har. HA1
off Marlborough Hill 139 CE56
Marlborough Gdns, N20 120 DF48
Upminster RM14 151 FR60
Marlborough Gate, St.Alb. AL1 65 CE20
Marlborough Gate Ho, W2 16 A10
Marlborough Gro, SE1 44 C1
Marlborough Hill, NW8 5 P9
Dorking RH4 285 CH136
Harrow HA1 139 CF56
★ Marlborough Ho, SW1 29 M3
Marlborough La, SE7 186 EJ79
Marlborough Ms, SW2
off Acre La 183 DM84
Banstead SM7 256 DA115
Marlborough Par, Uxb. UB10
off Uxbridge Rd 157 BP70
Marlborough Pk Av, Sid.
DA15 208 EU87
Marlborough Pl, NW8 15 N1
Sch Marlborough Prim Sch,
SW3 28 D9
Isleworth TW7
off London Rd 179 CG81
Marlborough Ri, Hem.H. HP2 62 BL17
Marlborough Rd, E4 123 EA51
E7 166 EJ66
E15 13 K1
E18 146 EG55
N9 122 DT46
N19 143 DK61
N22 121 DL52
SE18 37 P6
SW1 29 M3
SW19 202 DE93
W4 180 CQ78
W5 179 CK75
Ashford TW15 196 BK92
Bexleyheath DA7 188 EX83
Bromley BR2 226 EJ98
Dagenham RM8 148 EV63
Dartford DA1 210 FJ86
Dorking RH4 285 CH136
Feltham TW13 198 BX89
Hampton TW12 198 CA93
Isleworth TW7 179 CH81
Pilgrim's Hatch CM15 130 FU44
Richmond TW10 200 CL86
Romford RM7 148 FA56
St. Albans AL1 65 CE20
Slough SL3 174 AX77
South Croydon CR2 242 DQ108
Southall UB2 178 BW76
Sutton SM1 222 DA104
Uxbridge UB10 157 BP70
Watford WD18 97 BV42
Woking GU21 249 BA116
Sch Marlborough Sch, St.Alb. AL1
off Watling St 64 CC23
Sidcup DA15
off Marlborough Pk Av 208 EU87
Marlborough St, SW3 28 C9
Marlborough Yd, N19 143 DK61
Marld, The, Ashtd. KT21 254 CM118
Marle Gdns, Wal.Abb. EN9 89 EC32
Marler Rd, SE23 205 DY88
Marlescroft Way, Loug. IG10 107 EP43
Marley Av, Bexh. DA7 188 EX79
Marley Cl, N15 143 DP56
Addlestone KT15 233 BF107
Greenford UB6 158 CA69
Marley Ct, Brox. EN10 71 DZ23
Marley Ho, E16
off University Way 37 N1
Marley Ri, Dor. RH4 285 CG139
Marley Rd, Welw.G.C. AL7 52 DA11
Marley St, SE16 33 J9
Marley Wk, NW2 4 A3
Marl Fld Cl, Wor.Pk. KT4 221 CU102
Marlin Cl, Berk. HP4 60 AT18
Sunbury-on-Thames TW16 197 BS93
Marlin Copse, Berk. HP4 60 AU20
Marlin End, Berk. HP4 60 AT20
Marlingdene Cl, Hmptn.
TW12 198 CA93
Marlings Cl, Chis. BR7 227 ES98
Whyteleafe CR3 258 DS117
Marlings Pk Av, Chis. BR7 227 ES98
Marling Way, Grav. DA12 213 GL92
Marlin Pk, Felt. TW14 197 BV85
Marlins, The, Nthwd. HA6 115 BT51
Marlins Cl, Chorl. WD3 95 BE40

Marlins Cl, Sutton SM1
off Turnpike La 240 DC106
Marlins Meadow, Wat. WD18 97 BR44
Marlin Sq, Abb.L. WD5 81 BT31
Marlins Turn, Hem.H. HP1 62 BH17
Marloes Cl, Wem. HA0 139 CK63
Marloes Rd, W8 27 L7
Marlow Av, Purf. RM19 190 FN77
Marlow Cl, SE20 224 DV97
Marlow Ct, NW6 4 D6
NW9 141 CT55
Marlow Cres, Twick. TW1 199 CF86
Marlow Dr, Sutt. SM3 221 CX103
Marlowe Cl, Chis. BR7 207 ER93
Ilford IG6 125 EQ53
Marlowe Ct, SE19
off Lymer Av 204 DT92
Marlowe Gdns, SE9 207 EN86
Romford RM3 128 FJ53
Marlowe Path, SE8 46 C2
Marlowe Rd, E17 145 EC56
Marlowes, Hem.H. HP1 62 BK21
Marlowes, The, NW8 6 A9
Dartford DA1 189 FD84
Marlowes Cen, The, Hem.H. HP1 62 BK21
Marlowe Sq, Mitch. CR4 223 DJ98
Marlowe Way, Croy. CR0 223 DL103
Marlow Gdns, Hayes UB3 177 BR76
Marlow Rd, E6 25 J3
SE20 224 DV97
Southall UB2 178 BZ76
Marlow Way, SE16 33 J4
Marlpit Av, Couls. CR5 257 DL117
Marlpit La, Couls. CR5 257 DK116
Marl Rd, SW18 182 DB84
Marlton St, SE10 35 M10
Marlwood Cl, Sid. DA15 207 ES89
Marlyns Cl, Guil. GU4 265 BA130
Marlyns Dr, Guil. GU4 265 BA130
Marlyon Rd, Ilf. IG6 126 EV50
Marmadon Rd, SE18 187 ET77
Marmara Apts, E16
off Western Gateway 35 P1
Marmion App, E4 123 EA49
Marmion Av, E4 123 DZ49
Marmion Cl, E4 123 DZ49
Marmion Ms, SW11
off Taybridge Rd 182 DG83
Marmion Rd, SW11 182 DG84
Marmont Rd, SE15 44 D6
Marmora Rd, SE22 204 DW86
Marmot Rd, Houns. TW4 178 BX83
Marne Av, N11 121 DH49
Welling DA16 188 EU83
Marnell Way, Houns. TW4 178 BX83
Sch Marner Prim Sch, E3 22 D4
Marne St, W10 14 E2
Marney Rd, SW11 182 DG84
Marneys Cl, Epsom KT18 254 CN115
Marnfield Cres, SW2 203 DM88
Marnham Av, NW2 141 CY63
Marnham Cres, Grnf. UB6 158 CB69
Marnham Pl, Add. KT15 234 BJ105
Marnham Ri, Hem.H. HP1 62 BG18
Marnock Rd, SE4 205 DY85
Maroon St, E14 21 L7
Maroons Way, SE6 205 EA92
Marquess Est, N1 9 K4
Marquess Rd, N1 9 L5
Marquis Cl, Wem. HA0 160 CM66
Marquis Rd, N4 143 DM60
N22 121 DM51
NW1 7 P5
Marrabon Cl, Sid. DA15 208 EU88
Marram Ct, Grays RM17
off Medlar Rd 192 GE79
Marrick Cl, SW15 181 CU84
Marrilyne Av, Enf. EN3 105 DZ38
Marriott Cl, Felt. TW14 197 BR86
Marriot Ter, Chorl. WD3 95 BF42
Marriott Lo Cl, Add. KT15 234 BJ105
Marriott Rd, E15 13 J8
N4 143 DM60
N10 120 DF53
Barnet EN5 101 CX41
Dartford DA1 210 FN87
Marriotts, Harl. CM17 58 EW10
Marriotts Cl, NW9 141 CT58
Marriotts Way, Hem.H. HP3 62 BK22
Mar Rd, S.Ock. RM15 171 FW70
Marrods Bottom, Beac. HP9 110 AJ47
Marrowells, Wey. KT13 217 BS104
Marryat Cl, Houns. TW4 178 BZ84
Marryat Pl, SW19 201 CY91
Marryat Rd, SW19 201 CX92
Enfield EN1 104 DV35
Marryat Sq, SW6 38 E6
Marsala Rd, SE13 185 EB84
Marsden Cl, Welw.G.C. AL8 51 CV11
Marsden Gdns, Dart. DA1 190 FM82
Marsden Grn, Welw.G.C. AL8 51 CV10
Marsden Rd, N9 122 DV47
SE15 184 DT83
Welwyn Garden City AL8 51 CV10
Marsden St, NW5 6 G5
Marsden Way, Orp. BR6 245 ET105
Marshall, W2
off Hermitage St 16 A7
Marshall Av, St.Alb. AL3 65 CE17
Marshall Cl, SW18
off Allfarthing La 202 DC86
Harrow HA1 off Bowen Rd 139 CD59
Hounslow TW4 198 BZ85
South Croydon CR2 242 DU113
Marshall Ct, SE20
off Anerley Pk 204 DV94
Marshall Dr, Hayes UB4 157 BT71
Marshall Est, NW7 119 CU49
Marshall Path, SE28
off Attlee Rd 168 EV73
Marshall Pl, New Haw KT15 234 BJ109
Marshall Rd, E10 145 EB62
N17 122 DR53
Marshalls Cl, N11 121 DH49
Epsom KT19 238 CQ113
Marshalls Dr, Rom. RM1 149 FE55
Marshall's Gro, SE18 37 H8
Sch Marshalls Pk Sch, Rom. RM1
off Pettits La 127 FE54
Marshalls Pl, SE16 32 B7
Marshalls Rd, Rom. RM7 149 FD56
Marshall's Rd, Sutt. SM1 240 DB105
Marshall St, NW10 160 CR66
W1 17 M9
Marshals Dr, St.Alb. AL1 65 CG17
Marshalsea Rd, SE1 31 K4
MARSHALSWICK, St.Alb. AL1 65 CG17
Marshalswick La, St.Alb. AL1 65 CH17
Marsham Cl, Chis. BR7 207 EP92
Marsham La, Ger.Cr. SL9 134 AY58
Marsham Lo, Ger.Cr. SL9 134 AY58
Marsham St, SW1 29 P7
Marsham Way, Ger.Cr. SL9 134 AY57
Marsh Av, Epsom KT19 238 CS110
Mitcham CR4 222 DF96
Marshbrook Cl, SE3 186 EK83
Marsh Cl, NW7 119 CT48
Waltham Cross EN8 89 DZ33
Marsh Ct, SW19 222 DC95
Uxb. UB3 off Uxbridge Rd 157 BS71
Marshcroft Dr, Chsht EN8 89 DY30
Marsh Dr, NW9 141 CT58
Marshe Cl, Pot.B. EN6 86 DD32
Marsh Fm Rd, Twick. TW2 199 CF88
Marshfield, Datchet SL3 174 AW81
Sch Marshfields C of E Inf Sch, Ott. KT16 off Fletcher Cl 233 BE107
Marshfield St, E14 34 E6
Marshfoot Interchange, Grays RM16, RM17 192 GE79
Marshfoot Rd, Grays RM16, RM17 192 GE78
Marshgate, Harl. CM20
off School La 57 ES12
Marshgate Cen, Harl. CM19 72 EK15
Marshgate Dr, Hert. SG13 54 DS08
Marshgate La, E15 12 E10
Marshgate Path, SE28
off Tom Cribb Rd 187 EQ76
Sch Marshgate Prim Sch, Rich. TW10 off Queens Rd 180 CM84
Marshgate Trd Est, Tap. SL6 152 AG72
Sch Marsh Grn Prim Sch, Dag. RM10 off South Cl 168 FA67
Marsh Grn Rd, Dag. RM10 168 FA67
Marsh Hill, E9 11 L3
Marsh La, E10 145 EA61
N17 122 DV52
NW7 118 CS49
Addlestone KT15 234 BH105
Dorney SL4 172 AF75
Harlow CM17 58 EY10
Maidenhead SL6 172 AF75
Stanmore HA7 117 CJ50
Stanstead Abbotts SG12 55 ED12
Ware SG12 55 DY07
Marshmoor Cres, N.Mymms AL9 67 CW22
Marshmoor La, N.Mymms AL9 67 CW22
Marsh Rd, Pnr. HA5 138 BY56
Wembley HA0 159 CK68
Marshside Cl, N9 122 DW46
Marsh St, E14 34 C9
Dartford DA1 190 FN84
Marsh St N, Dart. DA1 190 FN82
Marsh Ter, Orp. BR5
off Buttermere Rd 228 EX98
Marsh Vw, Grav. DA12 213 GM88
Marsh Wall, E14 34 A3
Marsh Way, Rain. RM13 169 FD70
Marsland Cl, SE17 43 H1
Marston, SE17 off Deacon Way 31 K8
Epsom KT19 238 CQ111
Marston Av, Chess. KT9 238 CL107
Dagenham RM10 148 FA61
Marston Cl, NW6 5 P6
Chesham HP5 76 AN27
Dagenham RM10 148 FA62
Hemel Hempstead HP3 62 BN21
Marston Ct, Green. DA9 191 FU84
Walton-on-Thames KT12
off St. Johns Dr 218 BW102
Marston Dr, Warl. CR6 259 DY118
Marston Ho, Grays RM17 192 GA79
Marston Rd, Hodd. EN11 71 EB16
Ilford IG5 124 EL53
Teddington TW11 199 CH92
Woking GU21 248 AV117
Marston Way, SE19 203 DP94
Marsworth Av, Pnr. HA5 116 BX53
Marsworth Cl, Hayes UB4 158 BY71
Watford WD18 97 BS44
Marsworth Ho, E2 10 C9
Martaban Rd, N16 144 DS61
Martara Ms, SE17 43 J1
Martello St, E8 10 E6
Martello Ter, E8 10 E6
Martell Rd, SE21 204 DR90
Martel Pl, E8 10 B4
Marten Gate, St.Alb. AL4 65 CG16
Marten Rd, E17 123 EA54
Martens Av, Bexh. DA7 189 FC84
Martens Cl, Bexh. DA7 189 FC84
Martha Ct, E2 10 F10
Martham Cl, SE28 168 EX73
Ilford IG6 125 EP53
Martha Rd, E15 13 K4
Martha's Bldgs, EC1 19 L4
Martha St, E1 20 F9
Marthorne Cres, Har. HA3 117 CD54
Martian Av, Hem.H. HP2 62 BM17
Martina Ter, Chig. IG7
off Manford Way 125 ES50
Martin Bowes Rd, SE9 187 EM83
Martinbridge Trd Est, Enf. EN1 104 DU43
Martin Cl, N9 123 DX46
Hatfield AL10 67 CU20
South Croydon CR2 243 DX111
Uxbridge UB10 156 BL68
Warlingham CR6 258 DV116
Windsor SL4 172 AJ81
Martin Cres, Croy. CR0 223 DN102
Martindale, SW14 200 CQ85
Iver SL0 155 BD70
Martindale Av, E16 23 P10
Orpington BR6 246 EU106
Martindale Cl, Guil. GU4
off Gilliat Dr 265 BD132
Sch Martindale Prim & Nurs Sch, Hem.H. HP1 off Boxted Rd 61 BF19
Martindale Rd, SW12 203 DH87
Hemel Hempstead HP1 61 BF19
Hounslow TW4 178 BY83
Woking GU21 248 AT118
Martin Dene, Bexh. DA6 208 EZ85
Martin Dr, Nthlt. UB5 138 BZ64
Rainham RM13 169 FH70
Stone DA2 210 FQ86
Martineau Cl, Esher KT10 237 CD105
Martineau Dr, Dor. RH4 285 CH138
Twickenham TW1 179 CH84
Martineau Ms, N5 8 G1
Martineau Rd, N5 8 F1
Martineau St, E1 20 G9
Martinfield, Welw.G.C. AL7 51 CZ08
Martinfield Business Pk, Welw.G.C. AL7
off Martinfield 51 CZ08
Martingale Cl, Sun. TW16 217 BU98
Martingales Cl, Rich. TW10 199 CK90
Martin Gdns, Dag. RM8 148 EW63
Martin Gro, Mord. SM4 222 DA97
Martin Ho, SE1 31 K7
Martini Dr, Enf. EN3 105 EA37
Martin Kinggett Gdns, Dag. RM9 168 EY67
Martin La, EC4 19 M10
Sch Martin Prim Sch, N2
off Plane Tree Wk 120 DE54
Martin Ri, Bexh. DA6 208 EZ85
Martin Rd, Aveley RM15 171 FR73
Dagenham RM8 148 EW63
Dartford DA2 210 FJ90
Guildford GU2 264 AU132
Slough SL1 174 AS76
Martins, The, Wem. HA9 140 CM62
Martins Cl, Guil. GU1 265 BC133
Orpington BR5 228 EX97
Radlett WD7 99 CE36
West Wickham BR4 225 ED102
Martins Ct, St.Alb. AL1
off Swallow La 65 CJ23
Martins Dr, Chsht EN8 89 DY28
Hertford SG13 54 DV09
Martinsfield Cl, Chig. IG7 125 ES49
Martins Mt, New Barn. EN5 102 DA42
Martins Pl, SE28
off Martin St 167 ES74
Martin's Plain, Stoke P. SL2 154 AT69
Martins Rd, Brom. BR2 226 EE96
Martins Shaw, Chipstead TN13 278 FC122
Martinstown Cl, Horn. RM11 150 FN58
Martin St, SE28 167 ES74
Martins Wk, N8
off Alexandra Rd 143 DN55
N10 120 DG53
SE28 167 ES74
Borehamwood WD6
off Siskin Cl 100 CN42
Martinsyde, Wok. GU22 249 BC117
Martin Way, SW20 221 CY97
Morden SM4 221 CY97
Woking GU21 248 AU118
Martlands Ind Est, Wok. GU22 248 AU123
Martlesham, Welw.G.C. AL7 52 DE09
Martlesham Cl, Horn. RM12 150 FJ64
Martlesham Wk, NW9
off Kenley Av 118 CS54
Martlet Gro, Nthlt. UB5 158 BX69
Martlett Ct, WC2 18 B9
Martley Dr, Ilf. IG2 147 EP57
Martock Cl, Har. HA3 139 CG56
Martock Gdns, N11 120 DF50
Marton Cl, SE6 205 EA90
Marton Rd, N16 144 DS61
Martyr Cl, St.Alb. AL1
off Creighton Av 65 CD24
Martyr Rd, Guil. GU1 280 AX135
MARTYR'S GREEN, Wok. GU23 251 BR120
Martyrs La, Wok. GU21 233 BB112
Martys Yd, NW3 6 A1
Marunden Grn, Slou. SL2 153 AM69
Marvell Av, Hayes UB4 157 BU71
Marvels Cl, SE12 206 EH89
Marvels La, SE12 206 EH89
Sch Marvels La Prim Sch, SE12
off Riddons Rd 206 EJ91
Marville Rd, SW6 38 G5
Marvin St, E8 10 F4
Marwell, West. TN16 277 EP126
Marwell Cl, Rom. RM1 149 FG57
West Wickham BR4
off Deer Pk Way 226 EF103
Marwood Cl, Kings L. WD4 80 BN29
Welling DA16 188 EV83
Marwood Dr, NW7 119 CX52
Mary Adelaide Cl, SW15 200 CS91
Mary Ann Gdns, SE8 46 A3
Maryatt Av, Har. HA2 138 CB61
Marybank, SE18 37 J8
Mary Cl, Stan. HA7 140 CM56
Mary Datchelor Cl, SE5 43 M6
Maryfield Cl, Bex. DA5 209 FE90
Marygold Wk, Amer. HP6 94 AV39
Mary Grn, NW8 5 M9
Maryhill Cl, Ken. CR8 258 DQ117
Maryland 13 J4
Maryland, Hat. AL10 67 CT19
Maryland Conv, St.Alb. AL3
off Townsend Dr 65 CD18
Maryland Ind Est, E15
off Maryland Rd 13 H3
Maryland Pk, E15 13 K3
Maryland Pt, E15
off The Grove 13 J4
Sch Maryland Prim Sch, E15 13 K2
Maryland Rd, E15 13 H3
N22 121 DM51
Thornton Heath CR7 223 DP95
Maryland Sq, E15 13 K3
Marylands Rd, W9 15 K5
Maryland St, E15 13 H3
Maryland Wk, N1 9 J8
Maryland Way, Sun. TW16 217 BU96
Mary Lawrenson Pl, SE3 47 N5
MARYLEBONE, NW1 16 E8
Marylebone 16 E5
Marylebone 16 E5
Marylebone Flyover, NW1 16 B7
W2 16 B7
Marylebone Gdns, Rich. TW9
off Manor Rd 180 CM84
Marylebone High St, W1 17 H6
Marylebone La, W1 17 J9
Marylebone Ms, W1 17 J7
Marylebone Pas, W1 17 M8
Marylebone Rd, NW1 16 D6
Marylebone St, W1 17 H7
Marylee Way, SE11 30 D10
Mary Macarthur Ho, E2 21 J2
W6 38 E2
Mary Morgan Ct, Slou. SL2
off Douglas Rd 153 AR71
Sch Marymount Int Sch, Kings.T. KT2 off George Rd 200 CQ94
Mary Neuner Rd, N8 143 DM55
Maryon Gro, SE7 37 H9
Maryon Ms, NW3 6 C1
Maryon Rd, SE7 36 G8
SE18 36 G8
Mary Peters Dr, Grnf. UB6 139 CD64
Mary Pl, W11 26 E1
Mary Rd, Guil. GU1 280 AW135
Mary Rose Cl, Chaff.Hun. RM16 191 FW77
Hampton TW12
off Ashley Rd 218 CA95
Mary Rose Mall, E6 25 K7
Maryrose Way, N20 120 DD46
Mary Seacole Cl, E8 10 A8
Mary Seacole Ho, W6
off Invermead Cl 181 CU76
Maryside, Slou. SL3 174 AY75
Mary's Ter, Twick. TW1 199 CG87
Mary St, E16 23 L6
N1 9 K9
Mary Ter, NW1 7 K9
Coll Mary Ward Adult Ed Cen, The, WC1 18 B6
Mary Way, Wat. WD19 116 BW49
Masbro Rd, W14 26 D7
Mascalls Ct, SE7 186 EJ79
Mascalls Gdns, Brwd. CM14 130 FT49
Mascalls La, Brwd. CM14 130 FT49
H Mascalls Pk, Gt Warley CM14 129 FV51
Mascalls Rd, SE7 186 EJ79
Mascoll Path, Slou. SL2 153 AM69
Mascotte Rd, SW15 181 CX84
Mascotts Cl, NW2 141 CV62
Masefield Av, Borwd. WD6 100 CP43
Southall UB1 158 CA73
Stanmore HA7 117 CF50
Masefield Cl, Chesh. HP5 76 AP28
Erith DA8 189 FF81
Romford RM3 128 FJ53
Masefield Ct, Brwd. CM14 130 FW49
Masefield Cres, N14 103 DJ44
Romford RM3 128 FJ53
Masefield Dr, Upmin. RM14 150 FQ59
Masefield Gdns, E6 25 L4
Masefield La, Hayes UB4 157 BV70
Masefield Rd, Dart. DA1 210 FP85
Grays RM16 192 GE75
Hampton TW12
off Wordsworth Rd 198 BZ91
Northfleet DA11 212 GD90
Masefield Vw, Orp. BR6 227 EQ104
Masefield Way, Stai. TW19 196 BM88
Masham Ho, Erith DA18
off Kale Rd 188 EX75
Mashie Rd, W3 160 CS72
Mashiters Hill, Rom. RM1 127 FD53
Mashiters Wk, Rom. RM1 149 FE55
Maskall Cl, SW2 203 DN88
Maskani Wk, SW16
off Bates Cres 203 DJ94
Maskell Rd, SW17 202 DC90
Maskelyne Cl, SW11 40 D6
Maslen Rd, St.Alb. AL4 65 CJ23
Mason Cl, E16 23 N10
SE16 32 D10
SW20 221 CX95
Bexleyheath DA7 189 FB83
Borehamwood WD6 100 CQ40
Hampton TW12 218 BZ95
Waltham Abbey EN9 90 EF34
Mason Ct, Wem. HA9
off The Avenue 140 CN61
Mason Dr, Harold Wd RM3
off Whitmore Av 128 FL54
Masonic Hall Rd, Cher. KT16 215 BF100
Mason Rd, Sutt. SM1
off Manor Pl 240 DB106
Woodford Green IG8 124 EE49
Masons Arms Ms, W1 17 K9
Masons Av, EC2 19 L8
Croydon CR0 224 DQ104
Harrow HA3 139 CF56
Masons Br Rd, Red. RH1 289 DH139
Masons Ct, Slou. SL1 153 AL73
Masons Grn La, W3 160 CN71
Masons Hill, SE18 37 P9
Bromley BR1, BR2 226 EG97
Masons Paddock, Dor. RH4 269 CG134
Masons Pl, EC1 19 H2
Mitcham CR4 222 DF95
Masons Rd, Enf. EN1 104 DW36
Hemel Hempstead HP2 63 BP19
Slough SL1 153 AL73
Mason St, SE17 31 M9
Masons Yd, EC1 19 H2
Mason's Yd, SW1 29 M2
SW19 off High St Wimbledon 201 CX92
Mason Way, Wal.Abb. EN9 90 EF34
Massetts Rd, Horl. RH6 290 DF149
Massey Cl, N11 121 DH50
Massey Ct, E6 166 EJ67
Massie Rd, E8 10 C5
Massingberd Way, SW17 203 DH91
Massinger St, SE17 31 N9
Massingham St, E1 21 J4
Masson Av, Ruis. HA4 158 BW65
Mast, The, E16 37 P1
Master Cl, Oxt. RH8
off Church La 276 EE129
Master Gunner Pl, SE18 186 EL80
Masterman Ho, SE5 43 K4
Masterman Rd, E6 24 G3
Masters Cl, SW16 203 DJ93
Masters Dr, SE16 44 E1
Masters St, E1 21 K6
Masthead Cl, Dart. DA2 190 FQ84
Mast Ho Terrace, E14 34 B9
Riv Masthouse Terrace Pier 34 B10
Mast Leisure Pk, SE16 33 K7
Mastmaker Rd, E14 34 B5
Mast Quay, SE18 37 K6
off Woolwich Ch St 37 K6
Maswell Pk Cres, Houns. TW3 198 CC85
Maswell Pk Rd, Houns. TW3 198 CB85
Matcham Rd, E11 146 EE62
Matching Rd, Hat.Hth CM22 59 FH06
Old Harlow CM17 59 FB11
Ongar CM5 75 FH18
MATCHING TYE, Harl. CM17 59 FF12
Matchless Dr, SE18 187 EN80
Matfield Cl, Brom. BR2 226 EG99
Matfield Rd, Belv. DA17 188 FA79
Matham Gro, SE22 184 DT84
Matham Rd, E.Mol. KT8 219 CD99
Mathecombe Rd, Slou. SL1 173 AM75
Matheson Lang Gdns, SE1
off Baylis Rd 30 E5
Matheson Rd, W14 26 G9
Mathews Av, E6 25 M1
Mathews Pk Av, E15 13 M5
Mathews Yd, Croy. CR0
off Surrey St 224 DQ104
Mathias Cl, Epsom KT18 238 CQ113
Sch Mathilda Marks-Kennedy Prim Sch, NW7
off Hale La 118 CR50
Mathisen Way, Colnbr. SL3 175 BE81
Mathon Ct, Guil. GU1 265 AZ134
Matilda Cl, SE19
off Elizabeth Way 204 DR94
Matilda Gdns, E3 22 A1
Matilda St, N1 8 D9
Matisse Rd, Houns. TW3 178 CB83
Matlock Cl, SE24 184 DQ84
Barnet EN5 101 CX43
Matlock Ct, SE5
off Denmark Hill Est 184 DR84
Matlock Cres, Sutt. SM3 239 CY105
Watford WD19 116 BW48
Matlock Gdns, Horn. RM12 150 FL62
Sutton SM3 239 CY105
Matlock Pl, Sutt. SM3 239 CY105
Matlock Rd, E10 145 EC58
Caterham CR3 258 DS121
Matlock St, E14 21 L8
Matlock Way, N.Mal. KT3 220 CR95
Matrimony Pl, SW8 41 L9
Matson Ct, Wdf.Grn. IG8
off The Bridle Path 124 EE52
Matson Ho, SE16 32 F6
Matthew Arnold Cl, Cob. KT11 235 BU114
Staines-upon-Thames TW18
off Elizabeth Av 196 BJ93
Sch Matthew Arnold Sch, The, Stai. TW18 off Kingston Rd 196 BJ93
Matthew Cl, W10 14 C5
Matthew Ct, Mitch. CR4 223 DK99
Matthew Parker St, SW1 29 P5
Matthews Cl, Rom. RM3
off Oak Rd 128 FM53
Matthews Gdns, New Adgtn CR0 243 ED111
Matthews La, Stai. TW18
off Kingston Rd 196 BG91
Matthews Rd, Grnf. UB6 139 CD64
Matthews St, SW11 40 E8
Reigate RH2 288 DA138
Matthews Yd, WC2 18 A9
Matthias Rd, N16 9 M2
Mattingley Way, SE15 44 A4
Mattison Rd, N4 143 DN58
Mattock La, W5 159 CH74
W13 159 CH74
Maud Cashmore Way, SE18 37 K7
Maud Chadburn Pl, SW4
off Balham Hill 203 DH86
Maude Cres, Wat. WD24 97 BV37
Maude Rd, E17 145 DY57
SE5 43 N7
Beaconsfield HP9 111 AN54
Swanley BR8 209 FG93
Maudesville Cotts, W7 159 CE74
Maude Ter, E17 145 DY56
Maud Gdns, E13 13 M10
Barking IG11 167 ET68
Maudlin's Grn, E1 32 C2
Maud Rd, E10 145 EC62
E13 13 M10
Maudslay Rd, SE9 187 EM83
H Maudsley Hosp, SE5 43 M8
Maudsley Ho, Brent. TW8
off Green Dragon La 180 CL78
Maud St, E16 23 L7
Maud Wilkes Cl, NW5 7 L3
Maughan Way, W3 180 CQ76
Mauleverer Rd, SW2 203 DL85
Maundeby Wk, NW10
off Neasden La 160 CS65
Maunder Cl, Chaff.Hun. RM16 191 FX77
Maunder Rd, W7 159 CF74
Maunds Fm, Harl. CM18 73 ER20
Maunds Hatch, Harl. CM18 73 ER19
Maunsel St, SW1 29 N8
Maurer Ct, SE10 35 M6
Maurice Av, N22 121 DP54
Caterham CR3 258 DR122
Maurice Brown Cl, NW7 119 CX50
Maurice St, W12 161 CV72
Maurice Wk, NW11 142 DC56
Maurier Cl, Nthlt. UB5 158 BW67
Mauritius Rd, SE10 35 K9
Maury Rd, N16 144 DU61
Mauveine Gdns, Houns. TW3 178 CA84
Mavelstone Cl, Brom. BR1 226 EL95
Mavelstone Rd, Brom. BR1 226 EL95
Maverton Rd, E3 12 A9
Mavis Av, Epsom KT19 238 CS106
Mavis Cl, Epsom KT19 238 CS106
Mavis Gro, Horn. RM12 150 FL61
Mavis Wk, E6 24 G7
Mawbey Est, SE1 44 C1
Mawbey Ho, SE1
off Old Kent Rd 44 B1
Mawbey Pl, SE1 44 B1
Mawbey Rd, SE1 44 B1
Ottershaw KT16 233 BD107
Mawbey St, SW8 42 A5
Mawney Cl, Rom. RM7 127 FB54
Sch Mawney Prim Sch, The, Rom. RM7
off Mawney Rd 149 FD57
Mawney Rd, Rom. RM7 149 FC56
Mawson Cl, SW20 221 CY96
Mawson La, W4
off Great W Rd 181 CT79
Maxey Gdns, Dag. RM9 148 EY63
Maxey Rd, SE18 187 EQ77
Dagenham RM9 148 EY63
Maxfield Cl, N20 120 DC45
Maxilla Gdns, W10 14 D8
Maxilla Wk, W10 14 D9
Maximfeldt Rd, Erith DA8 189 FE78
Maxim Rd, N21 103 DN44
Dartford DA1 209 FE85
Erith DA8
off West St 189 FE78
Maxim Twr, Rom. RM1
off Mercury Gdns 149 FE56
Maxted Cl, Hem.H. HP2 63 BQ18
Maxted Pk, Har. HA1 139 CE59
Maxted Rd, SE15 44 B10
Hemel Hempstead HP2 63 BP17

Maxwell Cl, Croy. CR0 223 DL102
Hayes UB3 157 BU73
Mill End WD3 114 BG47
Maxwell Dr, W.Byf. KT14 234 BJ111
Maxwell Gdns, Orp. BR6 227 ET104
Maxwell Ri, Wat. WD19 116 BY45
Maxwell Rd, SW6 39 L5
Ashford TW15 197 BQ93
Beaconsfield HP9 111 AK52
Borehamwood WD6 100 CP41
Northwood HA6 115 BR52
St. Albans AL1 65 CH21
Welling DA16 187 ET83
West Drayton UB7 176 BM77
● **Maxwells W**, Chsht EN8 88 DW31
Maxwelton Av, NW7 118 CR50
Maxwelton Cl, NW7 118 CR50
Maya Angelou Ct, E4
off Bailey Cl 123 EC49
Maya Cl, SE15 44 E8
Mayall Cl, Enf. EN3 105 EA38
Mayall Rd, SE24 203 DP85
Maya Pl, N11 121 DK52
Maya Rd, N2 142 DC56
May Av, Nthflt DA11 213 GF88
Orpington BR5 228 EV99
● **May Av Ind Est**, Nthflt DA11
off May Av 213 GF88
Maybank Av, E18 124 EH54
Hornchurch RM12 149 FH64
Wembley HA0 139 CF64
Maybank Gdns, Pnr. HA5 137 BU57
Maybank Lo, Horn. RM12
off Maybank Av 150 FJ64
Maybank Rd, E18 124 EH53
May Bate Av, Kings.T. KT2 219 CK95
● **Maybells Commercial Est**,
Bark. IG11 168 EX68
Mayberry Pl, Surb. KT5 220 CM101
Maybourne Cl, SE26 204 DV92
Maybourne Ri, Wok. GU22 248 AX124
Maybrick Rd, Horn. RM11 150 FJ58
Maybrook Meadow Est,
Bark. IG11 168 EU66
MAYBURY, Wok. GU22 249 BB117
Maybury Av, Chsht EN8 88 DV28
Dartford DA2 210 FQ88
Maybury Cl, Enf. EN1 104 DV38
Loughton IG10 107 EP42
Petts Wood BR5 227 EP99
Slough SL1 153 AK72
Tadworth KT20
off Ballards Grn 255 CY119
Maybury Gdns, NW10 161 CV65
Maybury Hill, Wok. GU22 249 BB116
Sch **Maybury Inf Sch**,
Wok. GU21
off Walton Rd 249 BA116
Maybury Ms, N6 143 DJ59
Maybury Rd, E13 24 C5
Barking IG11 167 ET68
Woking GU21 249 AZ117
Maybury St, SW17 202 DE92
Maybush Rd, Horn. RM11 150 FL59
Maychurch Cl, Stan. HA7 117 CK52
May Cl, Chess. KT9 238 CM107
St. Albans AL3 65 CD18
Maycock Gro, Nthwd. HA6 115 BT51
May Cotts, Wat. WD18 98 BW43
May Ct, SW19 222 DB95
Grays RM17 *off Medlar Rd* 192 GE79
Maycroft, Pnr. HA5 115 BV54
Maycroft Av, Grays RM17 192 GD78
Maycroft Gdns, Grays RM17 192 GD78
Maycroft Rd, Chsht EN7 88 DS26
Maycross Av, Mord. SM4 221 CZ97
Mayday Gdns, SE3 186 EL82
Mayday Rd, Th.Hth. CR7 223 DP100
H **Mayday Uni Hosp**, Th.Hth.
CR7 223 DP100
Maydew Ho, SE16 32 G8
Maydwell Lo, Borwd. WD6 100 CM40
Mayell Cl, Lthd. KT22 253 CJ123
Mayerne Rd, SE9 206 EK85
Mayer Rd, Wal.Abb. EN9
off Deer Pk Way 105 EB36
Mayesbrook Rd, Bark. IG11 167 ET67
Dagenham RM8 148 EU62
Ilford IG3 148 EU62
Mayes Cl, New Adgtn CR0 243 ED108
Swanley BR8 229 FG98
Warlingham CR6 259 DX118
Mayesford Rd, Rom. RM6 148 EW59
Sch **Mayespark Prim Sch**, Ilf. IG3
off Goodmayes La 148 EU62
Mayes Rd, N22 121 DN54
Mayeswood Rd, SE12 206 EJ90
MAYFAIR, W1 29 J1
Mayfair Av, Bexh. DA7 188 EX81
Ilford IG1 147 EM61
Romford RM6 148 EX58
Twickenham TW2 198 CC87
Worcester Park KT4 221 CU102
Mayfair Cl, Beck. BR3 225 EB95
St. Albans AL4 65 CJ15
Surbiton KT6 220 CL102
Mayfair Gdns, N17 122 DR51
Woodford Green IG8 124 EG52
Mayfair Ms, NW1 6 F7
Mayfair Pl, W1 29 K2
Mayfair Rd, Dart. DA1 210 FK85
Mayfair Ter, N14 121 DK45
Mayfare, Crox.Grn WD3 97 BR43
Mayfield, Bexh. DA7 188 EZ83
Leatherhead KT22 253 CJ121
Waltham Abbey EN9 89 ED34
Welwyn Garden City AL8 51 CW05
Mayfield Av, N12 120 DC49
N14 121 DJ47
W4 180 CS77
W13 179 CH76
Gerrards Cross SL9 134 AX56
Harrow HA3 139 CH57
New Haw KT15 234 BH110
Orpington BR6 227 ET102
Woodford Green IG8 124 EG52
Mayfield Cl, E8 10 A5
SW4 203 DK85
Ashford TW15 197 BP93
Harlow CM17 58 EZ11
Hersham KT12 235 BU105
Mayfield Cl, New Haw KT15 234 BJ110
Redhill RH1 288 DG140
Thames Ditton KT7 219 CH102
Uxbridge UB10 157 BP69
Mayfield Cres, N9 104 DV44
Thornton Heath CR7 223 DM98
Mayfield Dr, Pnr. HA5 138 BZ56
Windsor SL4 173 AN83
Mayfield Gdns, NW4 141 CX58
W7 159 CD72
Brentwood CM14 130 FV46
Hersham KT12 235 BU105
New Haw KT15 234 BH110
Staines-upon-Thames TW18 195 BF93
Mayfield Grn, Bkhm KT23 268 CA126
Mayfield Gro, Rain. RM13 170 FJ69
Sch **Mayfield Inf & Nurs Sch**, Wal.Cr.
EN8 *off Cheshunt Wash* 89 DY27
Mayfield Mans, SW15
off West Hill 201 CX87
Mayfield Pk, West Dr. UB7 176 BJ76
Sch **Mayfield Prim Sch**, W7
off High La 159 CD72
Mayfield Rd, E4 123 EC47
E8 10 A7
E13 23 M5
E17 123 DY54
N8 143 DM58
SW19 221 CZ95
W3 160 CP73
W12 180 CS75
Belvedere DA17 189 FC77
Bromley BR1 226 EL99
Dagenham RM8 148 EW60
Enfield EN3 105 DX40
Gravesend DA11 213 GF87
Hersham KT12 235 BU105
South Croydon CR2 242 DR109
Sutton SM2 240 DD107
Thornton Heath CR7 223 DM98
Weybridge KT13 234 BM106
Wooburn Green HP10 132 AE57
Mayfields, Grays RM16 192 GC75
Swanscombe DA10 211 FX86
Wembley HA9 140 CN61
Sch **Mayfield Sch & Coll**, Dag. RM8
off Pedley Rd 148 EW60
Mayfields Cl, Wem. HA9 140 CN61
Mayflower Av, Hem.H. HP2 62 BK20
Mayflower Cl, SE16 33 K8
Hertingfordbury SG14 53 DL11
Lower Nazeing EN9 72 EE22
Ruislip HA4 137 BQ58
South Ockendon RM15 171 FW70
Mayflower Ct, SE16 32 G5
off St. Marychurch St 32 G5
Harlow CM19 73 EP19
Sch **Mayflower Prim Sch**, E14 22 C9
Mayflower Rd, SW9 42 A10
Chafford Hundred RM16 191 FW78
Park Street AL2 82 CB27
Mayflower St, SE16 32 G5
Mayflower Way, Beac. HP9 132 AG55
Farnham Common SL2 133 AQ64
Mayfly Cl, Eastcote HA5 138 BW59
Orpington BR5 228 EX98
Mayfly Gdns, Nthlt. UB5
off Seasprite Cl 158 BX69
MAYFORD, Wok. GU22 248 AW122
Mayford Cl, SW12 202 DF87
Beckenham BR3 225 DX97
Woking GU22 248 AX122
Mayford Grn, Wok. GU22
off Smarts Heath Rd 248 AX122
Mayford Rd, SW12 202 DF87
May Gdns, Els. WD6 99 CK44
Wembley HA0 159 CJ68
Maygoods Cl, Uxb. UB8 156 BK71
Maygoods Grn, Uxb. UB8 156 BK71
Maygoods La, Uxb. UB8 156 BK71
Maygood St, N1 8 D10
Maygoods Vw, Cowley UB8 156 BJ71
Maygreen Cres, Horn. RM11 149 FG59
Maygrove Rd, NW6 4 G5
Mayhall La, Amer. HP6 77 AP35
Mayhew Cl, E4 123 EA48
Mayhill Rd, SE7 186 EH79
Barnet EN5 101 CY44
Mayhurst Av, Wok. GU22 249 BC116
Mayhurst Cl, Wok. GU22 249 BC116
Mayhurst Cres, Wok. GU22 249 BC116
Maylands Av, Hem.H. HP2 63 BP17
Hornchurch RM12 149 FH63
Maylands Dr, Sid. DA14 208 EX90
Uxbridge UB8 156 BK65
Maylands Rd, Wat. WD19 116 BW49
Maylands Way, Rom. RM3 128 FQ51
Maylins Dr, Saw. CM21 58 EX05
Maynard Cl, N15
off Brunswick Rd 144 DS57
SW6 39 M5
Erith DA8 189 FF80
Maynard Ct, Enf. EN3
off Harston Dr 105 EA38
Waltham Abbey EN9 90 EF34
Maynard Dr, St.Alb. AL1 65 CD23
Maynard Path, E17 145 EC57
Maynard Pl, Cuffley EN6 87 DL29
Maynard Rd, E17 145 EC57
Hemel Hempstead HP2 62 BK21
Maynards, Horn. RM11 150 FL59
Maynards Quay, E1 32 G1
Mayne Av, St.Alb. AL3 64 BZ22
Maynooth Gdns, Cars. SM5 222 DF101
Mayo Cl, Chsht EN8 88 DW28
Mayo Gdns, Hem.H. HP1 62 BH21
Mayola Rd, E5 144 DW63
Mayo Rd, NW10 160 CS65
Croydon CR0 224 DR99
Walton-on-Thames KT12 217 BT101
Mayor's La, Dart. DA2 210 FJ92
Mayow Rd, SE23 205 DX90
SE26 205 DX91
Mayplace Av, Dart. DA1 189 FG84
Mayplace Cl, Bexh. DA7 189 FB83
Mayplace La, SE18 187 EP80
Sch **Mayplace Prim Sch**, Barne. DA7
off Woodside Rd 189 FD84
Mayplace Rd E, Bexh. DA7 189 FB83
Dartford DA1 189 FC83
Mayplace Rd W, Bexh. DA7 188 FA84
MAYPOLE, Orp. BR6 246 EZ106
Maypole Cres, Erith DA8 190 FK79
Ilford IG6 125 ER52
Maypole Dr, Chig. IG7 126 EU48
Sch **Maypole Prim Sch**, Dart. DA2
off Franklin Rd 209 FE90
Maypole Rd, Grav. DA12 213 GM88
Orpington BR6 246 EZ106
Maypole Rd, Taplow SL6 152 AG71
Maypole St, Harl. CM17
off Alba Rd 58 EW14
May Rd, E4 123 EA51
E13 13 P10
Hawley DA2 210 FM91
Twickenham TW2 199 CE88
Mayroyd Av, Surb. KT6 220 CN103
May's Bldgs Ms, SE10 46 F5
Mays Cl, Wey. KT13 234 BM110
Mays Ct, WC2 30 A1
Maysfield Rd, Send GU23 249 BD123
MAY'S GREEN, Cob. KT11 251 BT121
Mays Gro, Send GU23 249 BD124
Mays Hill Rd, Brom. BR2 226 EE96
Mays La, E4 123 ED47
Barnet EN5 101 CY43
Maysoule Rd, SW11 182 DD84
Mays Rd, Tedd. TW11 199 CD92
Mayston Ms, SE10
off Westcombe Hill 47 P1
May St, W14 39 H1
Mayswood Gdns, Dag. RM10 169 FC65
Maythorne Cl, Wat. WD18 97 BS42
Mayton St, N7 143 DM62
Maytree Cl, Edg. HA8 118 CQ48
Guildford GU1 264 AV131
Rainham RM13 169 FE68
Maytree Cres, Wat. WD24 97 BT35
Maytree Gdns, W5 179 CK76
May Tree La, Stan. HA7 117 CF52
Maytrees, Rad. WD7 99 CG37
Maytree Wk, SW2 203 DN89
Mayville Est, N16 9 N2
Sch **Mayville Prim Sch**, E11
off Lincoln St 146 EE62
Mayville Rd, E11 146 EE61
Ilford IG1 147 EP64
May Wk, E13 166 EH68
Maywater Cl, S.Croy. CR2 242 DR111
Maywin Dr, Horn. RM11 150 FM60
Maywood Cl, Beck. BR3 205 EB94
⇌ **Maze Hill** 47 J2
Maze Hill, SE3 47 J3
SE10 47 J2
Mazenod Av, NW6 5 K7
Maze Rd, Rich. TW9 180 CN80
Mead, The, N2 120 DC54
W13 159 CH71
Ashtead KT21 254 CL119
Beaconsfield HP9 111 AL53
Beckenham BR3 225 EC95
Cheshunt EN8 88 DW29
Uxbridge UB10 136 BN61
Wallington SM6 241 DK107
Watford WD19 116 BY48
West Wickham BR4 225 ED102
Mead Av, Red. RH1 288 DG142
Slough SL3 175 BB75
● **Mead Business Cen**, Hert.
SG13 54 DS08
● **Mead Business Pk**, Chesh. HP5
off Berkhampstead Rd 76 AQ30
Mead Cl, NW1 7 H6
Denham UB9 136 BG61
Egham TW20 195 BB93
Grays RM16 192 GB75
Harrow HA3 117 CD53
Loughton IG10 107 EP40
Redhill RH1 272 DG131
Romford RM2 127 FG54
Slough SL3 175 BB75
Swanley BR8 229 FG99
Mead Ct, NW9 140 CQ57
Addlestone KT15 216 BK104
Egham TW20
off Holbrook Meadow 195 BC93
Knaphill GU21 248 AS116
Waltham Abbey EN9 89 EB34
Mead Cres, E4 123 EC49
Bookham KT23 268 CA125
Dartford DA1 *off Beech Rd* 210 FK88
Sutton SM1 240 DE105
Meadcroft Rd, SE11 42 G3
Meade Cl, W4 180 CN79
Meade Ct, Walt.Hill KT20 255 CU124
Mead End, Ashtd. KT21 254 CM116
Meades, The, Wey. KT13 235 BQ107
Meades La, Chesh. HP5 76 AP32
Meadfield, Edg. HA8 118 CP47
Mead Fld, Har. HA2
off Kings Rd 138 BZ62
Meadfield Av, Slou. SL3 175 BA76
Meadfield Grn, Edg. HA8 118 CP47
Meadfield Rd, Slou. SL3 175 BA76
Meadfoot Rd, SW16 203 DJ94
Meadgate Av, Wdf.Grn. IG8 124 EL50
Meadgate Rd, Lwr Naze. EN9 71 ED20
Roydon CM19 71 ED20
Mead Gro, Rom. RM6 148 EX55
Mead Ho La, Hayes UB4 157 BR70
Meadhurst Pk, Sun. TW16 197 BS93
Meadhurst Rd, Cher. KT16 216 BH102
Sch **Mead Inf Sch, The**, Ewell KT19
off Newbury Gdns 239 CT105
Meadlands Dr, Rich. TW10 199 CK89
Sch **Meadlands Prim Sch**, Rich.
TW10 *off Broughton Av* 199 CJ91
Mead La, Cher. KT16 216 BH102
Hertford SG13 54 DR08
● **Mead La Ind Est**, Hert.
SG13 54 DT08
Meadow, The, Chis. BR7 207 EQ93
Hailey SG13 55 DY13
Meadow Av, Croy. CR0 225 DX100
Meadow Bk, N21 103 DM44
Meadowbank, NW3 6 E7
SE3 186 EF83
Meadow Bk, E.Hors. KT24 267 BT128
Guildford GU1
off Stoughton Rd 264 AW132
Meadowbank, Kings L. WD4 80 BN30
Surbiton KT5 220 CM100
Watford WD19 116 BW45
Meadowbank Cl, SW6 38 B5
Isleworth TW7 179 CE81
Meadow Bk Cl, Amer. HP7 77 AS38
Meadowbank Cl, Bov. HP3 79 BB28
Meadowbank Gdns, Houns.
TW5 177 BU82
Meadowbank Rd, NW9 140 CR59
Meadowbanks, Barn. EN5 101 CT43
Meadowbrook, Oxt. RH8 275 EC130
Meadowbrook Cl, Colnbr. SL3 175 BF82
Meadowbrook Rd, Dor. RH4 285 CG135
Meadow Bungalows, Chilw.
GU4 281 BB140
Meadow Cl, E4 123 EB46
E9 11 P3
Meadow Cl, SE6 205 EA92
SW20 221 CW98
Barking IG11 167 ET67
Barnet EN5 101 CZ44
Bexleyheath DA6 208 EZ85
Bricket Wood AL2 82 CA29
Chesham HP5
off Little Hivings 76 AN27
Chislehurst BR7 207 EP92
Enfield EN3 105 DY38
Esher KT10 219 CF104
Godalming GU7 280 AS144
Hersham KT12 236 BZ105
Hertford SG13 54 DT08
Hounslow TW4 198 CA86
London Colney AL2 83 CK27
North Mymms AL9 67 CX24
Northolt UB5 158 CA68
Old Windsor SL4 194 AV86
Purley CR8 241 DK113
Richmond TW10 200 CL88
Ruislip HA4 137 BT58
St. Albans AL4 65 CJ17
Sevenoaks TN13 278 FG123
Sutton SM1
off Aultone Way 222 DC103
Meadowcot La, Colesh. HP7 77 AM44
Meadow Cotts, Beac. HP9 111 AL54
Meadow Ct, Epsom KT18 238 CQ113
Harlow CM18 *off Lodge Hall* 73 ES19
Redhill RH1 273 DJ130
Staines-upon-Thames TW18 195 BE90
Meadowcourt Rd, SE3 186 EF84
Meadowcroft, Brom. BR1 227 EM97
Bushey WD23 98 CB44
Chalfont St. Peter SL9 112 AX54
Meadow Cft, Hat. AL10 67 CT18
Meadowcroft, St.Alb. AL1 65 CG23
Meadowcroft Cl, Horl. RH6 291 DJ151
Sch **Meadowcroft Comm Inf Sch**,
Cher. KT16 *off Little Grn La* 215 BF104
Meadowcroft Rd, N13 121 DN47
Meadowcross, Wal.Abb. EN9 90 EE34
Meadow Dell, Hat. AL10 67 CT18
Meadow Dr, N10 143 DH55
NW4 119 CW54
Amersham HP6 77 AS37
Ripley GU23 249 BF123
Meadowford Cl, SE28 168 EU73
Meadow Gdns, Edg. HA8 118 CP51
Staines-upon-Thames TW18 195 BD92
Meadow Garth, NW10 160 CQ66
Meadow Gate, Ashtd. KT21 254 CL117
Meadowgate Cl, NW7 119 CT50
Sch **Meadowgate Sch**, SE4
off Revelon Rd 185 DY83
Meadow Grn, Welw.G.C. AL8 51 CW09
Sch **Meadow High Sch**, Hlgdn UB8
off Royal La 156 BM71
Meadow Hill,
New Malden KT3 220 CS100
Purley CR8 241 DJ113
Meadowlands, Cob. KT11 235 BU113
Hornchurch RM11 150 FL59
Oxted RH8 276 EG134
West Clandon GU4 266 BH130
Meadowlands Pk, Add. KT15 216 BL104
Meadow La, SE12 206 EH90
Beaconsfield HP9 111 AM53
Eton SL4 173 AQ80
Fetcham KT22 252 CC121
Meadowlea Cl, Harm. UB7 176 BK79
Meadow Ms, SW8 42 C3
Meadow Pl, SW8 42 B4
W4 *off Edensor Rd* 180 CS80
Sch **Meadow Prim Sch**, Epsom
KT17 *off Sparrow Fm Rd* 239 CV105
Meadow Ri, Couls. CR5 241 DK113
Meadow Rd, SW8 42 C4
SW19 202 DC94
Ashford TW15 197 BR92
Ashtead KT21 254 CL117
Barking IG11 167 ET66
Berkhamsted HP4 60 AU17
Borehamwood WD6 100 CP40
Bromley BR2 226 EE95
Bushey WD23 98 CB43
Claygate KT10 237 CE107
Dagenham RM9 168 EZ65
Epping CM16 91 ET29
Feltham TW13 198 BY89
Gravesend DA11 213 GG89
Guildford GU4 265 BA130
Hemel Hempstead HP3 62 BN24
Loughton IG10 106 EL43
Pinner HA5 138 BX57
Romford RM7 149 FC60
Slough SL3 174 AY76
Southall UB1 158 BZ73
Sutton SM1 240 DE106
Virginia Water GU25 214 AS99
Watford WD25 81 BU34
Meadow Row, SE1 31 J7
Meadows, The, Amer. HP7 77 AS39
Guildford GU2 280 AW137
Halstead TN14 246 EZ113
Hemel Hempstead HP1 61 BE19
Orpington BR6 246 EW107
Sawbridgeworth CM21 58 FA05
Warlingham CR6 259 DX117
Watford WD25 98 BX36
Welwyn Garden City AL7 52 DC09
Meadows Cl, E10 145 EA61
Meadows End, Sun. TW16 217 BU95
Meadows Est, SE6
off Chestnut Cl 205 EC92
Meadowside, SE9 186 EJ84
Bookham KT23 252 CA123
Dartford DA1 210 FK88
Horley RH6 *off Stockfield* 291 DH147
Jordans HP9 112 AT52
Walton-on-Thames KT12 218 BW103
Meadow Side, Wat. WD25 81 BV31
Meadowside Rd, Sutt. SM2 239 CY109
Upminster RM14 150 FQ64
Meadows Leigh Cl, Wey.
KT13 217 BQ104
Sch **Meadows Sch, The**, Woob.Grn
HP10 *off School Rd* 132 AE57
Meadow Stile, Croy. CR0
off High St 224 DQ104
Meadowsweet Cl, E16 24 E7
SW20 221 CW98
Meadow Vw, Ch.St.G. HP8 112 AU48
Chertsey KT16 216 BJ102
Harrow HA1 139 CE60
Orpington BR5 228 EW97
Sidcup DA15 208 EV87
Staines-upon-Thames TW19 195 BF85
Meadowview Rd, SE6 205 DZ92
Bexley DA5 208 EY86
Epsom KT19 238 CS109
Meadow Vw Rd, Hayes UB4 157 BQ70
Thornton Heath CR7 223 DP99
Meadow Wk, E18 146 EG56
Dagenham RM9 168 EZ65
Dartford DA2 210 FJ91
Epsom KT17, KT19 238 CS107
Penn HP10 110 AC46
Wallington SM6 223 DH104
Walton on the Hill KT20 255 CV124
Meadow Way, NW9 140 CR57
Addlestone KT15 234 BH105
Bedmond WD5 81 BT27
Bookham KT23 252 CB123
Chessington KT9 238 CL106
Chigwell IG7 125 EQ48
Dartford DA2 210 FQ87
Dorney Reach SL6 172 AF75
Fifield SL6 172 AD81
Hemel Hempstead HP3 61 BF23
Kings Langley WD4 80 BN30
Old Windsor SL4 194 AV86
Orpington BR6 227 EN104
Potters Bar EN6 86 DA34
Reigate RH2 288 DB138
Rickmansworth WD3 114 BJ45
Ruislip HA4 137 BV58
Sawbridgeworth CM21 58 FA06
Tadworth KT20 255 CY118
Upminster RM14 150 FQ62
Wembley HA9 139 CK63
West Horsley KT24 267 BR125
Meadow Way, The, Har. HA3 117 CE53
Meadow Waye, Houns. TW5 178 BY79
Sch **Meadow Wd Sch**, Bushey
WD23 *off Coldharbour La* 98 CC43
● **Mead Pk**, Harl. CM20 57 ET11
Mead Path, SW17 202 DC92
Mead Pl, E9 11 H5
Croydon CR0 223 DP102
Rickmansworth WD3 114 BH46
Mead Plat, NW10 160 CQ65
Sch **Mead Prim Sch**, Harold Hill
RM3 *off Amersham Rd* 128 FM51
Mead Rd, Cat. CR3 258 DT123
Chislehurst BR7 207 EQ93
Dartford DA1 210 FK88
Edgware HA8 118 CN51
Gravesend DA11 213 GH89
Hersham KT12 236 BY105
Richmond TW10 199 CJ90
Shenley WD7 84 CN33
Uxbridge UB8 156 BK65
Sch **Mead Rd Inf Sch**, Chis. BR7
off Mead Rd 207 EQ93
Mead Row, SE1 30 E6
Meads, The, Brick.Wd AL2 82 BZ29
Edgware HA8 118 CR51
Northchurch HP4 60 AS17
Sutton SM3 221 CY104
Upminster RM14 151 FS61
Uxbridge UB8 156 BL70
Coll **Meads Cor**, Purf. RM19 190 FP77
Meadside Cl, Beck. BR3 225 DY95
Meads La, Ilf. IG3 147 ES59
Meads Rd, N22 121 DP54
Enfield EN3 105 DY39
Guildford GU1 265 BA134
Meadsway, Gt Warley CM13 129 FV51
Mead Ter, Wem. HA9
off Meadow Way 139 CK63
MEAD VALE, Red. RH1 288 DD136
Meadvale Rd, W5 159 CH70
Croydon CR0 224 DT101
Meadview Rd, Ware SG12 55 DX07
Mead Wk, Slou. SL3 175 BB75
Meadway, N14 121 DK47
NW11 142 DB58
SW20 221 CW98
Ashford TW15 196 BN91
Barnet EN5 102 DA42
Beckenham BR3 225 EC95
Berkhamsted HP4 60 AY18
Mead Way, Brom. BR2 226 EF100
Bushey WD23 98 BY40
Meadway, Coln.Hth AL4 66 CR23
Mead Way, Couls. CR5 257 DL118
Croydon CR0 225 DY103
Meadway, Eff. KT24 268 BY128
Enfield EN3 104 DW36
Epsom KT19 238 CQ112
Esher KT10 236 CB109
Grays RM17 192 GD77
Mead Way, Guil. GU4 265 BC129
Meadway, Halst. TN14 246 EZ113
Hoddesdon EN11 71 EA19
Ilford IG3 147 ES63
Meadway, Oxshott KT22 237 CD114
Romford RM2 127 FG54
Ruislip HA4 137 BR58
Mead Way, Slou. SL1 153 AK71
Meadway, Stai. TW18 196 BG94
Surbiton KT5 220 CQ102
Twickenham TW2 199 CD88
Warlingham CR6 258 DW115
Welwyn Garden City AL7 51 CZ11
Woodford Green IG8 124 EJ50
Meadway, The, SE3 47 H9
Buckhurst Hill IG9 124 EK46
Cuffley EN6 87 DM28
Horley RH6 291 DJ148
Loughton IG10 107 EM44
Orpington BR6 246 EV106
Sevenoaks TN13 278 FF122
Meadway Cl, NW11 142 DB58
Barnet EN5 102 DA42
Pinner HA5
off Highbanks Rd 116 CB51
Staines-upon-Thames TW18 195 BF94
Meadway Ct, NW11 142 DB58
Meadway Dr, Add. KT15 234 BJ108
Woking GU21 248 AW116
Meadway Gdns, Ruis. HA4 137 BR58
Meadway Gate, NW11 142 DA58
Meadway Pk, Ger.Cr. SL9 134 AX60
Meaford Way, SE20 204 DV94
Meakin Est, SE1 31 N6
Meanley Rd, E12 146 EL63
Meard St, W1 17 N9
Meare Cl, Tad. KT20 255 CW123
Meare Est, Woob.Grn HP10 132 AD55
Mears Cl, E1 *off Settles St* 20 D7
Meath Cl, Orp. BR5 228 EV99
Meath Cres, E2 21 J3
Meath Gdns, Horl. RH6 290 DE146
MEATH GREEN, Horl. RH6 290 DE146
Meath Grn Av, Horl. RH6 290 DF146

Sch Meath Grn Inf Sch, Horl. RH6 off Kiln La 290 DF146
Sch Meath Grn Jun Sch, Horl. RH6 off Greenfields Rd 290 DF146
Meath Grn La, Horl. RH6 288 DE143
Meath Rd, E15 13 L10
Ilford IG1 147 EQ62
Sch Meath Sch, Ott. KT16 off Brox Rd 233 BD108
Meath St, SW11 41 J6
Meautys, St.Alb. AL3 64 BZ22
Sch Mechinah Liyeshiva Zichron Moshe Sch, N16 off Amhurst Pk 144 DR59
Mecklenburgh Pl, WC1 18 C4
Mecklenburgh Sq, WC1 18 C4
Mecklenburgh St, WC1 18 C4
Medburn St, NW1 7 N10
Medbury Rd, Grav. DA12 213 GM88
Medcalf Rd, Enf. EN3 105 DZ37
Medcroft Gdns, SW14 180 CQ84
Medebourne Cl, SE3 47 P10
Mede Cl, Wrays. TW19 194 AX88
Mede Fld, Fetch. KT22 253 CD124
Medesenge Way, N13 121 DP51
Medfield St, SW15 201 CV87
Medhurst Cl, E3 21 M1
Chobham GU24 232 AT109
Medhurst Cres, Grav. DA12 213 GM90
Medhurst Dr, Brom. BR1 205 ED92
Medhurst Gdns, Grav. DA12 213 GM90
Median Rd, E5 10 G2
Medici Cl, Ilf. IG3 off Barley La 148 EU58
★ Medici Galleries, W1 29 L1
Medick Ct, Grays RM17 192 GE79
Medina Av, Esher KT10 219 CE104
Medina Gro, N7 143 DN62
Medina Ho, Erith DA8 off Waterhead Cl 189 FE80
Medina Rd, N7 143 DN62
Grays RM17 192 GD77
Medina Sq, Epsom KT19 238 CN109
Medlake Rd, Egh. TW20 195 BC93
Medland Cl, Wall. SM6 222 DG102
Medland Ho, E14 21 L10
Medlar Cl, Guil. GU1 264 AW132
Northolt UB5 off Parkfield Av 158 BY68
Medlar Ct, Slou. SL2 154 AW74
Medlar Ho, SW16 off Hemlock Cl 223 DK96
Medlar Rd, Grays RM17 192 GD79
Medlar St, SE5 43 K6
Medley Rd, NW6 5 K5
Medman Cl, Uxb. UB8 156 BJ68
Medora Rd, SW2 203 DM87
Romford RM7 149 FD56
Medow Mead, Rad. WD7 83 CF33
Medusa Rd, SE6 205 EB86
Medway Bldgs, E3 21 M1
Medway Cl, Croy. CR0 224 DW100
Ilford IG1 147 EQ64
Watford WD25 82 BW34
Medway Dr, Perivale UB6 159 CF68
Medway Gdns, Wem. HA0 139 CG63
Medway Ms, E3 21 M1
Medway Par, Perivale UB6 159 CF68
Medway Rd, E3 21 M1
Dartford DA1 189 FG83
Hemel Hempstead HP2 62 BM15
Medway St, SW1 29 P7
Medwick Ms, Hem.H. HP2 off Hunters Oak 63 BP15
Medwin St, SW4 183 DM84
Meecham Ct, SW11 40 B8
Meerbrook Rd, SE3 186 EJ83
Meeson Rd, E15 13 L8
Meesons La, Grays RM17 192 FZ77
Meeson St, E5 11 L1
Meeting Fld Path, E9 11 H4
Meeting Ho All, E1 32 F2
Meeting Ho La, SE15 44 E6
Megg La, Chipper. WD4 80 BH29
Mehetabel Rd, E9 10 G4
Meister Cl, Ilf. IG1 147 ER60
Melancholy Wk, Rich. TW10 199 CJ89
Melanda Cl, Chis. BR7 207 EM92
Melanie Cl, Bexh. DA7 188 EY81
Melba Gdns, Til. RM18 193 GG80
Melba Way, SE13 46 D7
Melbourne Av, N13 121 DM51
W13 159 CG74
Pinner HA5 138 CB55
Slough SL1 153 AQ72
Melbourne Cl, Orp. BR6 227 ES101
St. Albans AL3 65 CF16
Uxbridge UB10 136 BN63
Wallington SM6 off Melbourne Rd 241 DJ106
Melbourne Ct, E5 off Daubeney Rd 145 DY63
SE20 204 DU94
Waltham Cross EN8 off Alexandra Way 89 DZ34
Welwyn Garden City AL8 51 CV10
Melbourne Gdns, Rom. RM6 148 EY57
Melbourne Gro, SE22 184 DS84
Melbourne Ho, Hayes UB4 158 BW70
Melbourne Ms, SE6 205 EC87
SW9 42 E7
Melbourne Pl, WC2 18 D10
Melbourne Rd, E6 167 EM67
E10 145 EB59
E17 145 DY56
SW19 222 DA95
Bushey WD23 98 CB44
Ilford IG1 147 EP60
Teddington TW11 199 CJ93
Tilbury RM18 192 GE81
Wallington SM6 241 DH106
Melbourne Sq, SW9 42 E7
Melbourne Ter, SW6 off Moore Pk Rd 39 L5
Melbourne Way, Enf. EN1 104 DT44
Melbourne Yd, SE19 off Westow St 204 DS93
Melbray Ms, SW6 38 G9
Melbreak Ho, SE22 off Pytchley Rd 184 DS83
Melbury Av, Sthl. UB2 178 CB76
Melbury Cl, Cher. KT16 216 BG101
Chislehurst BR7 206 EL93
Claygate KT10 237 CH107
West Byfleet KT14 234 BG114
Melbury Ct, W8 27 H6
Melbury Dr, SE5 43 N5
Melbury Gdns, SW20 221 CV95
South Croydon. CR2 242 DS111
Melbury Rd, W14 26 G6
Melbury Rd, Harrow HA3 140 CM57
Melchester Ho, N19 off Wedmore St 143 DK62
Melcombe Gdns, Har. HA3 140 CM58
Melcombe Ho, SW8 off Dorset Rd 42 C5
Melcombe Pl, NW1 16 E6
Sch Melcombe Prim Sch, W6 38 C2
Melcombe St, NW1 16 F5
Meldex Cl, NW7 119 CW51
Meldon Cl, SW6 39 M7
Meldone Cl, Surb. KT5 220 CP100
Meldrum Cl, Orp. BR5 off Killewarren Way 228 EW100
Oxted RH8 276 EF132
Meldrum Rd, Ilf. IG3 148 EU61
Melfield Gdns, SE6 205 EB91
Melford Av, Bark. IG11 167 ES65
Melford Cl, Chess. KT9 238 CM106
Melford Rd, E6 25 J4
E11 146 EE61
E17 145 DY56
SE22 204 DU87
Ilford IG1 147 ER61
Melfort Av, Th.Hth. CR7 223 DP97
Melfort Rd, Th.Hth. CR7 223 DP97
Melgund Rd, N5 8 F3
Melia Cl, Wat. WD25 98 BW35
Melina Cl, Hayes UB3 157 BR71
Melina Pl, NW8 16 A3
Melina Rd, W12 181 CV75
Melings, The, Hem.H. HP2 63 BP15
Melior Pl, SE1 31 N4
Melior St, SE1 31 M4
Meliot Rd, SE6 205 ED89
Melksham Cl, Rom. RM3 128 FL52
Melksham Dr, Rom. RM3 off Melksham Gdns 128 FM52
Melksham Gdns, Rom. RM3 128 FL52
Melksham Grn, Rom. RM3 off Melksham Gdns 128 FM52
Meller Cl, Croy. CR0 223 DL104
Mellersh Hill Rd, Won. GU5 281 BB144
Mellifont Cl, Cars. SM5 222 DD101
Melling Dr, Enf. EN1 104 DU39
Melling St, SE18 187 ES79
Mellish Cl, Bark. IG11 167 ET67
Mellish Gdns, Wdf.Grn. IG8 124 EG50
● Mellish Ind Est, SE18 36 F6
Mellish St, E14 34 A6
Mellish Way, Horn. RM11 150 FJ57
Mellison Rd, SW17 202 DE92
Melliss Av, Rich. TW9 180 CP81
Mellitus St, W12 161 CT72
Mellor Cl, Walt. KT12 218 BZ101
Mellor Wk, Wind. SL4 173 AR81
Mellow Cl, Bans. SM7 240 DB114
Mellow La E, Hayes UB4 157 BQ69
Sch Mellow La Sch, Hayes End UB4 off Hewens Rd 157 BQ70
Mellow La W, Uxb. UB10 157 BQ69
Mellows Rd, Ilf. IG5 147 EM55
Wallington SM6 241 DK106
Mells Cres, SE9 207 EM91
Mell St, SE10 47 J1
Melody Ct, W4 off Wellesley Rd 180 CN78
Melody La, N5 9 H2
Melody Rd, SW18 202 DC85
Biggin Hill TN16 260 EJ118
Melon Pl, W8 27 L4
Melon Rd, E11 146 EE62
SE15 44 C6
Melrose Av, N22 121 DP53
NW2 4 B2
SW16 223 DM97
SW19 202 DA89
Borehamwood WD6 100 CP43
Dartford DA1 209 FE87
Greenford UB6 158 CB68
Mitcham CR4 203 DH94
Potters Bar EN6 86 DB32
Twickenham TW2 198 CB87
Melrose Cl, SE12 206 EG88
Greenford UB6 158 CB68
Hayes UB4 157 BU71
Melrose Ct, W13 off Williams Rd 159 CG74
Melrose Cres, Orp. BR6 245 ER105
Melrose Dr, Sthl. UB1 158 CA74
Melrose Gdns, W6 26 B6
Edgware HA8 118 CP54
Hersham KT12 236 BW106
New Malden KT3 220 CR97
Melrose Pl, Wat. WD17 97 BT38
Melrose Rd, SW13 181 CT82
SW18 201 CZ86
SW19 222 DA96
W3 off Stanley Rd 180 CQ76
Biggin Hill TN16 260 EJ116
Coulsdon CR5 257 DH115
Pinner HA5 138 BZ56
Weybridge KT13 234 BN106
Sch Melrose Sch, Mitch. CR4 off Church Rd 222 DE97
Melrose Ter, W6 26 B5
Melsa Rd, Mord. SM4 222 DC100
Melsted Rd, Hem.H. HP1 62 BH20
Melstock Av, Upmin. RM14 150 FQ63
Melthorne Dr, Ruis. HA4 138 BW62
Melthorpe Gdns, SE3 186 EL81
Melton Cl, Ruis. HA4 138 BW60
Melton Ct, SW7 28 B9
Sutton SM2 240 DC108
Melton Flds, Epsom KT19 238 CR109
Melton Gdns, Rom. RM1 149 FF59
Melton Pl, Epsom KT19 238 CR109
Melton Rd, S.Merst. RH1 273 DJ130
Melton St, NW1 17 M3
Melville Av, SW20 201 CU94
Greenford UB6 139 CF64
South Croydon CR2 242 DT106
Melville Cl, Uxb. UB10 137 BR62
Melville Ct, W4 off Stonehill Rd 180 CN78
W12 off Goldhawk Rd 181 CV76
Melville Gdns, N13 121 DP50
Melville Pl, N1 9 J7
Melville Rd, E17 145 DZ55
NW10 160 CR66
SW13 181 CU81
Rainham RM13 169 FG70
Romford RM5 127 FB52
Sidcup DA14 208 EW89
Melville Vil Rd, W3 off High St 160 CR74
Melvin Rd, SE20 224 DW95
Melvinshaw, Lthd. KT22 253 CJ121
Melvyn Cl, Goffs Oak EN7 87 DP28
Melwas Ct, N9 off Galahad Rd 122 DU48
Melyn Cl, N7 7 M1
Memel Ct, EC1 19 J5
Memel St, EC1 19 J5
Memess Path, SE18 187 EN79
Memorial Av, E15 23 J2
Memorial Cl, Houns. TW5 178 BZ79
Oxted RH8 275 ED127
Memorial Hts, Ilf. IG2 147 ER58
H Memorial Hosp, SE18 187 EN82
Menai Pl, E3 12 A10
Mendez Way, SW15 201 CU86
Mendip Cl, SE26 204 DW91
Harlington UB3 177 BR80
St. Albans AL4 65 CJ15
Slough SL3 175 BA78
Worcester Park KT4 221 CW102
Mendip Dr, NW2 141 CX61
Mendip Ho, N9 off Edmonton Grn Shop Cen 122 DU47
Mendip Hos, E2 21 H2
Mendip Rd, SW11 182 DC83
Bexleyheath DA7 189 FE81
Bushey WD23 98 CC44
Hornchurch RM11 149 FG59
Ilford IG2 147 ES57
Mendip Way, Hem.H. HP2 62 BL17
Mendlesham, Welw.G.C. AL7 52 DE09
Mendora Rd, SW6 38 F4
Mendoza Cl, Horn. RM11 150 FL57
Menelik Rd, NW2 4 F2
★ Menier Chocolate Factory, SE1 off Southwark St 31 K3
Menlo Gdns, SE19 204 DR94
Menon Dr, N9 122 DV48
Sch Menorah Foundation Sch, Edg. HA8 off Abbots Rd 118 CQ52
Sch Menorah Gram Sch, Edg. HA8 off Abbots Rd 118 CQ52
Sch Menorah Prim Sch, NW11 off Woodstock Av 141 CY59
Menotti St, E2 20 D4
Menthone Pl, Horn. RM11 150 FK59
Mentmore Cl, Har. HA3 139 CJ58
Mentmore Rd, St.Alb. AL1 65 CD22
Mentmore Ter, E8 10 F7
Meon Cl, Tad. KT20 255 CV122
Meon Ct, Islw. TW7 179 CE82
Meon Rd, W3 180 CQ75
Meopham Rd, Mitch. CR4 223 DJ95
Mepham Cres, Har. HA3 116 CC52
Mepham Gdns, Har. HA3 116 CC52
Mepham St, SE1 30 D3
Mera Dr, Bexh. DA7 188 FA84
Merantun Way, SW19 222 DC95
Merbury Cl, SE13 205 EC85
SE28 167 ER74
Merbury Rd, SE28 187 ES75
Mercator Pl, E14 34 B10
Mercator Rd, SE13 185 ED84
Mercer Cl, T.Ditt. KT7 219 CF101
Merceron Hos, E2 off Globe Rd 20 G2
Merceron St, E1 20 E5
Mercer Pl, Pnr. HA5 116 BW54
Mercers, Harl. CM19 73 EN18
Hemel Hempstead HP2 62 BL18
Mercers Cl, SE10 35 L9
Mercers Ms, N19 143 DK62
Mercers Pl, W6 26 B8
Mercers Rd, N19 143 DK62
Mercers Row, St.Alb. AL1 64 CC22
Mercer St, WC2 18 A9
Mercer Wk, Uxb. UB8 off The Mall Pavilions 156 BJ66
Merchant Dr, Hert. SG13 54 DT08
Merchants Cl, SE25 off Clifford Rd 224 DU98
Merchants Ho, SE10 off Collington St 47 H1
Merchants Row, SE10 off Hoskins St 47 H1
Merchant St, E3 21 P3
Sch Merchant Taylors' Sch, Nthwd. HA6 off Sandy Lo La 115 BS46
Merchiston Rd, SE6 205 ED89
Merchland Rd, SE9 207 EQ88
Mercia Gro, SE13 185 EC84
Mercian Way, Slou. SL1 153 AK74
Mercia Wk, Wok. GU21 off Commercial Way 249 AZ117
Mercier Rd, SW15 201 CY85
● Mercury Cen, Felt. TW14 197 BU85
Mercury Gdns, Rom. RM1 149 FE56
Mercury Ho, E3 off Garrison Rd 12 A9
● Mercury Pk, Woob.Grn HP10 132 AE56
Mercury Wk, Hem.H. HP2 62 BM17
Mercury Way, SE14 45 J2
Mercy Ter, SE13 185 EB84
Merebank La, Croy. CR0 241 DM106
Mere Cl, SW15 201 CX87
Orpington BR6 227 EP103
Meredith Av, NW2 4 B2
Meredith Cl, Pnr. HA5 116 BX52
Meredith Ms, SE4 185 DZ84
Meredith Rd, Grays RM16 193 GG77
Meredith St, E13 23 P3
EC1 18 G3
Meredyth Rd, SW13 181 CU82
Mere End, Croy. CR0 225 DX101
Merefield, Saw. CM21 58 EY06
Merefield Gdns, Tad. KT20 255 CX119
Mere Rd, SE2 188 EX75
Shepperton TW17 217 BP100
Slough SL1 174 AT76
Tadworth KT20 255 CV124
Weybridge KT13 217 BR104
Mereside, Orp. BR6 227 EN103
Mereside Pl, Vir.W. GU25 214 AX100
Meretone Cl, SE4 185 DY84
Mereton Mans, SE8 46 B6
Merevale Cres, Mord. SM4 222 DC100
Mereway Rd, Twick. TW2 199 CD88
Merewood Cl, Brom. BR1 227 EN96
Merewood Gdns, Croy. CR0 225 DX101
Merewood Rd, Bexh. DA7 189 FC82
Mereworth Cl, Brom. BR2 226 EF99
Mereworth Dr, SE18 187 EP80
Merganser Gdns, SE28 off Avocet Ms 187 ER76
MERIDEN, Wat. WD25 98 BY35
Meriden Cl, Brom. BR1 206 EK94
Ilford IG6 125 EQ53
Meriden Way, Wat. WD25 98 BY36
Meridia Ct, E15 off Biggerstaff Rd 12 F8
● Meridian Business Pk, Enf. EN3 105 DY44
Waltham Abbey EN9 105 EB35
Meridian Cl, NW7 118 CR49
Meridian Ct, SE16 off East La 32 C4
Meridian Gate, E14 34 E4
Meridian Gro, Horl. RH6 291 DJ147
Meridian Pl, E14 34 D4
Sch Meridian Prim Sch, SE10 47 H1
Meridian Rd, SE7 186 EK80
Meridian Sq, E15 12 G6
● Meridian Trd Est, SE7 36 B8
Meridian Wk, N17 off Commercial Rd 122 DS51
Meridian Way, N9 122 DW50
N18 122 DW51
Enfield EN3 105 DX44
Stanstead Abbotts SG12 55 EB10
Waltham Abbey EN9 105 EB35
Meriel Wk, Green. DA9 off The Avenue 191 FV84
Merifield Rd, SE9 186 EJ84
Merino Cl, E11 146 EJ56
Merino Pl, Sid. DA15 off Blackfen Rd 208 EU86
Merivale Rd, SW15 181 CY84
Harrow HA1 138 CC59
Merland Cl, Tad. KT20 255 CW120
Merland Grn, Tad. KT20 255 CW120
Merland Ri, Epsom KT18 255 CW119
Tadworth KT20 255 CW119
Sch Merland Ri Comm Prim Sch, Epsom KT18 off Merland Ri 255 CW119
Merle Av, Hare. UB9 114 BH54
Merlewood, Sev. TN13 279 FH123
Merlewood Cl, Cat. CR3 258 DR120
Merlewood Dr, Chis. BR7 227 EM95
Merley Ct, NW9 140 CQ60
Merlin Cl, Chaff.Hun. RM16 192 FY76
Croydon CR0 242 DS105
Ilford IG6 126 EW50
Mitcham CR4 222 DE97
Northolt UB5 158 BW69
Romford RM5 127 FD51
Slough SL3 175 BB79
Wallington SM6 241 DM107
Waltham Abbey EN9 90 EG34
Merlin Ct, Brom. BR2 off Durham Av 226 EF98
Woking GU21 off Blackmore Cres 233 BC114
Merlin Cres, Edg. HA8 118 CM53
Merlin Gdns, Brom. BR1 206 EG90
Romford RM5 127 FD51
Merling Cl, Chess. KT9 off Coppard Gdns 237 CK106
Merling Ct, Nthch HP4 60 AS17
Merlin Gro, Beck. BR3 225 DZ98
Ilford IG6 125 EP52
Merlin Ho, Enf. EN3 off Allington Ct 105 DX43
Sch Merlin Prim Sch, Downham BR1 off Ballamore Rd 206 EG90
Merlin Rd, E12 146 EJ61
Romford RM5 127 FD51
Welling DA16 188 EU84
Merlin Rd N, Well. DA16 188 EU84
Merlins Av, Har. HA2 138 BZ62
Sch Merlin Sch, SW15 off Carlton Dr 201 CX85
Merlin St, WC1 18 E3
Merlin Way, Lvsdn WD25 81 BT34
North Weald Bassett CM16 92 FA27
Merlot Ms, St.Alb. AL3 65 CD16
Mermagen Dr, Rain. RM13 169 FH66
Mermaid Cl, Grav. DA11 212 GD87
Mermaid Ct, SE1 31 L4
SE16 33 N3
Mermaid Twr, SE8 45 N3
Mermerus Gdns, Grav. DA12 213 GM91
Merredene St, SW2 203 DM86
Merriam Av, E9 11 P4
Merriam Cl, E4 123 EC50
Merrick Rd, Sthl. UB2 178 BZ75
Merrick Sq, SE1 31 K6
Merridale, SE12 206 EG85
Merridene, N21 103 DP44
Merrielands Cres, Dag. RM9 168 EZ67
Merrifield Ct, Welw.G.C. AL7 51 CX12
Merrilands Rd, Wor.Pk. KT4 221 CW102
Merrilees Rd, Sid. DA15 207 ES88
Merrilyn Cl, Clay. KT10 237 CG107
Merriman Rd, SE3 186 EJ81
Merrington Rd, SW6 39 K2
Merrin Hill, S.Croy. CR2 242 DS111
Merrion Av, Stan. HA7 117 CK50
Merrion Ct, Ruis. HA4 off Pembroke Rd 137 BT60
Merritt Gdns, Chess. KT9 237 CJ107
Merritt Rd, SE4 205 DZ85
Merritt Wk, N.Mymms AL9 67 CV23
Merrivale, N14 103 DK44
Merrivale Av, Ilf. IG4 146 EK56
Merrivale Gdns, Wok. GU21 248 AW117
Merrivale Ms, West Dr. UB7 156 BK74
MERROW, Guil. GU1 265 BB133
● Merrow Business Cen, Guil. GU4 265 BD131
Merrow Chase, Guil. GU1 265 BC134
Sch Merrow C of E Inf Sch, Guil. GU4 off Kingfisher Dr 265 BD132
Merrow Common Rd, Guil. GU4 265 BC131
Merrow Copse, Guil. GU1 265 BB133
Merrow Ct, Guil. GU1 265 BD134
Merrow Cft, Guil. GU1 265 BC133
Merrow Downs, Guil. GU1 281 BD135
Merrow Dr, Hem.H. HP1 61 BE19
● Merrow Ind Est, Guil. GU4 265 BD131
Merrow La, Guil. GU4 265 BC129
Merrow Pl, Guil. GU4 265 BD132
Merrow Rd, Sutt. SM2 239 CX109
Merrows Cl, Nthwd. HA6 off Rickmansworth Rd 115 BQ51
Merrow St, SE17 43 L2
Guildford GU4 265 BD132
Merrow Wk, SE17 31 M10
Merrow Way, Guil. GU1 265 BD133
New Addington CR0 243 EC107
Merrow Wds, Guil. GU1 265 BB132
Merrydown Way, Chis. BR7 226 EL95
Merryfield, SE3 47 M9
Merryfield Gdns, Stan. HA7 117 CJ50
Merryfield Ho, SE9 off Grove Pk Rd 206 EJ90
Merryfields, St.Alb. AL4 off Firwood Av 66 CL20
Uxbridge UB8 156 BK68
Merryfields Way, SE6 205 EB87
MERRY HILL, Bushey WD23 116 CA46
Merryhill Cl, E4 123 EB45
Sch Merry Hill Inf Sch & Nurs, Bushey WD23 off School La 116 CB45
Merry Hill Mt, Bushey WD23 116 CB46
Merry Hill Rd, Bushey WD23 116 CB46
Merryhills Cl, Bigg.H. TN16 260 EK116
Merryhills Ct, N14 103 DJ43
Merryhills Dr, Enf. EN2 103 DK42
Sch Merryhills Prim Sch, Enf. EN2 off Bincote Rd 103 DM41
Merrylands, Cher. KT16 215 BE104
Merrylands Rd, Bkhm KT23 252 BZ123
Merrymeade Chase, Brwd. CM15 130 FX46
Merrymeet, Bans. SM7 240 DF114
Merryweather Cl, Dart. DA1 210 FM86
Merryweather Ct, N.Mal. KT3 off Rodney Cl 220 CS99
Merrywood Gro, Lwr Kgswd KT20 271 CX130
Merrywood Pk, Box H. KT20 270 CP130
Reigate RH2 272 DB132
Mersea Ho, Bark. IG11 167 EP65
Mersey Av, Upmin. RM14 151 FR58
Mersey Pl, Hem.H. HP2 off Colne Way 62 BM15
Mersey Rd, E17 145 DZ55
Mersey Wk, Nthlt. UB5 off Brabazon Rd 158 CA68
Mersham Dr, NW9 140 CN57
Mersham Pl, SE20 224 DV95
Mersham Rd, Th.Hth. CR7 224 DR97
MERSTHAM, Red. RH1 273 DJ128
⇌ Merstham 273 DJ128
Sch Merstham Prim Sch, Merst. RH1 off London Rd S 273 DJ129
Merstham Rd, Red. RH1 273 DN129
Merten Rd, Rom. RM6 148 EY59
Merthyr Ter, SW13 181 CV79
MERTON, SW19 222 DA95
Merton Abbey Mills, SW19 off Watermill Way 222 DC95
Sch Merton Abbey Prim Sch, SW19 off High Path 222 DB95
Coll Merton Adult Ed, SW20 off Whatley Av 221 CY97
Merton Av, W4 181 CT77
Northolt UB5 138 CC64
Uxbridge UB10 157 BP66
Merton Ct, Borwd. WD6 off Bennington Dr 100 CM39
Ilford IG1 off Castleview Gdns 146 EL58
Sch Merton Ct Sch, Sid. DA14 off Knoll Rd 208 EW91
Merton Gdns, Petts Wd BR5 227 EP99
Tadworth KT20 255 CX119
Merton Hall Gdns, SW20 221 CY95
Merton Hall Rd, SW19 221 CY95
Merton High St, SW19 202 DB94
● Merton Ind Pk, SW19 222 DC95
Merton La, N6 142 DF61
Merton Mans, SW20 221 CX96
MERTON PARK, SW19 222 DA96
Tra Merton Park 222 DA95
Merton Pk Par, SW19 off Kingston Rd 221 CZ95
Sch Merton Pk Prim Sch, SW19 off Church La 222 DA96
Merton Pl, Grays RM16 193 GG77
Merton Ri, NW3 6 D7
Merton Rd, E17 145 EC57
SE25 224 DU99
SW18 202 DA85
SW19 202 DB94
Barking IG11 167 ET66
Enfield EN2 104 DR38
Harrow HA2 138 CC60
Ilford IG3 147 ET59
Slough SL1 174 AU76
Watford WD18 97 BV42
Merton Wk, Lthd. KT22 253 CG118
Merton Way, Lthd. KT22 253 CG119
Uxbridge UB10 157 BP68
West Molesey KT8 218 CB98
Merttins Rd, SE15 205 DX85
Meru Cl, NW5 7 H2
Mervan Rd, SW2 183 DN84
Mervyn Av, SE9 207 EQ90
Mervyn Rd, W13 179 CG76
Shepperton TW17 217 BQ101
Merwin Way, Wind. SL4 173 AK83
Meryfield Cl, Borwd. WD6 100 CM40
Sch Meryfield Comm Prim Sch, Borwd. WD6 off Theobald St 100 CM39
Mesne Way, Shore. TN14 247 FF112
Messaline Av, W3 160 CQ72
Messant Cl, Harold Wd RM3 128 FK54
Messent Rd, SE9 206 EJ85
Messeter Pl, SE9 207 EN86
Messina Av, NW6 5 J7
Metcalfe Ct, SE10 35 M6
Metcalf Rd, Ashf. TW15 197 BP92
Metcalf Wk, Felt. TW13 off Cresswell Rd 198 BY91
★ Met Collection, The, SW6 39 J2
Meteor St, SW11 182 DG84
Meteor Way, Wall. SM6 241 DL108
Metford Cres, Enf. EN3 105 EA38
Methley St, SE11 42 F1
★ Methodist Cen Hall, SW1 29 P5
Methuen Cl, Edg. HA8 118 CN52
Methuen Pk, N10 121 DH54
Methuen Rd, Belv. DA17 189 FB77
Bexleyheath DA6 188 EZ84
Edgware HA8 118 CN52
Methven Ct, N9 off The Broadway 122 DU48
Methwold Rd, W10 14 C6
Metro Apts, The, Wok. GU21 off Goldsworth Rd 248 AY117
● Metro Business Cen, SE26 205 DZ92
Metro Cen Hts, SE1 31 J7
● Metro Cen, St.Alb. AL4 65 CF16
● Metro Ind Cen, Islw. TW7 179 CE82
● Metropolitan Cen, The, Grnf. UB6 158 CB67

Metropolitan Cl, E14 22 B7
Metropolitan Ms, Wat. WD18 97 BS42
Coll Metropolitan Pol Cadet Training Cen, Loug. IG10 off Lippitts Hill 106 EF40
Coll Metropolitan Pol Mounted Branch Training Sch, E.Mol. KT8 off Ember La 219 CD100
Metropolitan Sta App, Wat. WD18 97 BT41
Meux Cl, Chsht EN7 88 DU31
Mews, The, N1 9 K8
N8 off Turnpike La 143 DN55
Grays RM17 192 GC77
Guildford GU1 off Walnut Tree Cl 280 AW135
Harlow CM18 off Lodge Hall 73 ES19
Ilford IG4 146 EK57
Romford RM1 off Market Link 149 FE56
Sevenoaks TN13 278 FG123
Twickenham TW1 off Bridge Rd 199 CH86
Mews, Islw. TW7 off Worton Rd 179 CD84
Mews Deck, E1 32 F1
Mews End, Bigg.H. TN16 260 EK118
Mews Pl, Wdf.Grn. IG8 124 EG49
Mews St, E1 32 C2
Mexfield Rd, SW15 201 CZ85
Meyer Grn, Enf. EN1 104 DU38
Meyer Rd, Erith DA8 189 FC79
Meymott St, SE1 30 G3
Meynell Cres, E9 11 J6
Meynell Gdns, E9 11 J6
Meynell Rd, E9 11 J6
Romford RM3 127 FH52
Meyrick Cl, Knap. GU21 248 AS116
Meyrick Rd, NW10 161 CU65
SW11 40 B10
Mezen Cl, Nthwd. HA6 115 BR50
★ MI5 (Security Service) Thames Ho, SW1 30 A8
Miah Ter, E1 32 D3
Miall Wk, SE26 205 DY91
Micawber Av, Uxb. UB8 156 BN70
Micawber St, N1 19 K2
Michael Cliffe Ho, EC1 18 F3
Michael Cres, Horl. RH6 290 DG150
Michael Faraday Ho, SE17 43 M1
Sch Michael Faraday Prim Sch, SE17 43 M2
Michael Gdns, Grav. DA12 213 GL92
Hornchurch RM11 150 FK56
Michael Gaynor Cl, W7 159 CF74
Michael La, Guil. GU2 264 AV129
Michaelmas Cl, SW20 221 CW97
Michael Rd, E11 146 EE60
SE25 224 DS97
SW6 39 M6
Michaels Cl, SE13 186 EE84
Michaels La, Ash TN15 231 FV103
Fawkham Green DA3 231 FV103
Sch Michael Sobell Sinai Sch, Har. HA3 off Shakespeare Dr 140 CN58
Michael Stewart Ho, SW6 off Clem Attlee Ct 39 H3
Sch Michael Tippett Sch, SE24 off Heron Rd 184 DQ84
Micheldever Rd, SE12 206 EE86
Michelham Gdns, Tad. KT20 off Waterfield 255 CW120
Twickenham TW1 199 CF90
Michelsdale Dr, Rich. TW9 off Rosedale Rd 180 CL84
Michels Row, Rich. TW9 off Kew Foot Rd 180 CL84
Michel Wk, SE18 187 EP78
Michigan Av, E12 146 EL63
Michigan Bldg, E14 34 F1
Michigan Cl, Brox. EN10 89 DY26
Michleham Down, N12 119 CZ49
Micholls Av, Ger.Cr. SL9 112 AY49
Micklefield Rd, Hem.H. HP2 63 BQ20
Sch Micklefield Sch, Reig. RH2 off Somers Rd 272 DA133
Micklefield Way, Borwd. WD6 100 CL38
MICKLEHAM, Dor. RH5 269 CJ128
Mickleham Bypass, Mick. RH5 269 CH127
Mickleham Cl, Orp. BR5 227 ET96
Mickleham Downs, Mick. RH5 269 CK127
Mickleham Dr, Lthd. KT22 269 CJ126
Mickleham Gdns, Sutt. SM3 239 CY107
Mickleham Rd, Orp. BR5 227 ET95
Mickleham Way, New Adgtn CR0 243 ED108
Micklem Dr, Hem.H. HP1 61 BF19
Sch Micklem Prim Sch, Hem.H. HP1 off Boxted Rd 62 BG19
Micklethwaite Rd, SW6 39 K3
● Midas Ind Est, Cowley UB8 156 BH68
Midcot Way, Berk. HP4 60 AT17
Midcroft, Ruis. HA4 137 BS60
Slough SL2 153 AP70
Mid Cross La, Chal.St.P. SL9 112 AY50
Middle Boy, Abridge RM4 108 EW41
Middle Cl, Amer. HP6 94 AT37
Coulsdon CR5 257 DN120
Epsom KT17 238 CS112
Middle Cres, Denh. UB9 135 BD59
Middle Dartrey Wk, SW10 off Blantyre St 40 A4
Middle Dene, NW7 118 CR48
Middle Down, Ald. WD25 98 CB36
Middle Dr, Beac. HP9 111 AK50
Middle Fm Cl, Eff. KT24 268 BX127
Middle Fm Pl, Eff. KT24 268 BW127
Middle Fld, NW8 6 A8
Middlefield, Hat. AL10 67 CU17
Horley RH6 291 DJ147
Welwyn Garden City AL7 51 CY13
Middlefield Av, Hodd. EN11 71 EA15
Middlefield Cl, Hodd. EN11 71 EA15
St. Albans AL4 65 CJ17
Middlefielde, W13 159 CH71
Middlefield Gdns, Ilf. IG2 147 EP58
Middlefield Rd, Hodd. EN11 71 EA15
Middlefields, Croy. CR0 243 DY109
Middle Furlong, Bushey WD23 98 CB42
Middle Gorse, Croy. CR0 243 DY112
MIDDLE GREEN, Slou. SL3 154 AY73
Middle Grn, Brock. RH3 286 CP136
Slough SL3 154 AY74
Staines-upon-Thames TW18 196 BK94
Middle Grn Cl, Surb. KT5 off Alpha Rd 220 CM100
Middle Grn Rd, Slou. SL3 174 AX75
Middleham Gdns, N18 122 DU51
Middleham Rd, N18 122 DU51
Middle Hill, Egh. TW20 194 AW91
Hemel Hempstead HP1 61 BE20
Middleknights Hill, Hem.H. HP1 62 BG17
Middle La, N8 143 DL57
Bovingdon HP3 79 BA29
Epsom KT17 238 CS112
Seal TN15 off Church Rd 279 FM121
Teddington TW11 199 CF93
Middle La Ms, N8 off Middle La 143 DL57
Middlemead Cl, Bkhm KT23 268 CA125
Middle Meadow, Ch.St.G. HP8 112 AW48
Middlemead Rd, Bkhm KT23 268 BZ125
Middle Ope, Wat. WD24 97 BV37
Middle Pk Av, SE9 206 EK86
Sch Middle Pk Prim Sch, SE9 off Middle Pk Av 206 EK87
Middle Path, Har. HA2 off Middle Rd 139 CD60
Middle Rd, E13 23 N1
SW16 223 DK96
Berkhamsted HP4 60 AV19
Denham UB9 135 BC59
East Barnet EN4 102 DE44
Harrow HA2 139 CD61
Ingrave CM13 131 GC50
Leatherhead KT22 253 CH121
Waltham Abbey EN9 89 EB32
Middle Row, W10 14 E5
Sch Middle Row Prim Sch, W10 14 E4
Middlesborough Rd, N18 122 DU51
● Middlesex Business Cen, Sthl. UB2 178 BZ75
Middlesex Cl, Sthl. UB1 158 CB70
Middlesex Ct, W4 181 CT78
Addlestone KT15 off Garfield Rd 234 BJ105
Middlesex Ho, Uxb. UB8 off High St 156 BJ66
Middlesex Pas, EC1 19 H7
Middlesex Rd, Mitch. CR4 223 DL99
Middlesex St, E1 19 P7
Uni Middlesex Uni, Cat Hill Campus, Barn. EN4 off Cat Hill 102 DG43
Hendon Campus, NW4 off The Burroughs 141 CV56
New Southgate Campus, N11 off Oakleigh Rd S 120 DG48
Trent Pk Campus, N14 off Bramley Rd 103 DJ40
Middlesex Wf, E5 144 DW61
Middle St, EC1 19 J6
Betchworth RH3 286 CP136
Croydon CR0 off Surrey St 224 DQ103
Lower Nazeing EN9 72 EG23
Shere GU5 282 BN139
Middle Temple, EC4 18 E10
Middle Temple La, EC4 18 E9
Middleton Av, E4 123 DZ49
Greenford UB6 159 CD68
Sidcup DA14 208 EW93
Middleton Cl, E4 123 DZ48
Middleton Dr, SE16 33 K5
Pinner HA5 137 BU55
Middleton Gdns, Ilf. IG2 147 EP58
Middleton Gro, N7 8 A2
Middleton Hall La, Brwd. CM15 130 FY47
Middleton Ms, N7 8 A2
Middleton Pl, W1 17 L7
Middleton Rd, E8 10 B7
NW11 142 DA59
Carshalton SM5 222 DE101
Downside KT11 251 BV119
Epsom KT19 238 CR110
Hayes UB3 157 BR71
Mill End WD3 114 BG46
Morden SM4 222 DC100
Shenfield CM15 130 FY46
Middleton St, E2 20 E2
Middleton Way, SE13 185 ED84
Middle Wk, Burn. SL1 152 AH69
Woking GU21 off Commercial Way 248 AY117
Middleway, NW11 142 DB57
Middle Way, SW16 223 DK96
Erith DA18 188 EY76
Hayes UB4 158 BW70
Watford WD24 97 BV37
Middle Way, The, Har. HA3 117 CF54
Middlewich Ho, Nthlt. UB5 off Taywood Rd 158 BZ69
Middle Yd, SE1 31 M2
Middlings, The, Sev. TN13 278 FF125
Middlings Ri, Sev. TN13 278 FF126
Middlings Wd, Sev. TN13 278 FF125
Coll Mid Essex Adult Comm Coll, Bishops Hill, Hutt. CM13 off Rayleigh Rd 131 GB44
Warley Cen, Warley CM13 off Essex Way 129 FW51
Midfield Av, Bexh. DA7 189 FC83
Swanley BR8 209 FH93
Midfield Par, Bexh. DA7 189 FC83
Sch Midfield Prim Sch, St.P.Cray BR5 off Grovelands Rd 208 EU94
Midfield Way, Orp. BR5 228 EV95
Midford Pl, W1 17 M5
Midgarth Cl, Oxshott KT22 236 CC114
Coll Mid Herts Music Cen, Hat. AL10 off Birchwood Av 67 CV16
Midholm, NW11 142 DB56
Wembley HA9 140 CN60
Midholm Cl, NW11 142 DB56
Midholm Rd, Croy. CR0 225 DY103
MID HOLMWOOD, Dor. RH5 285 CJ142
Mid Holmwood La, Mid Holm. RH5 285 CJ142
Midhope Cl, Wok. GU22 248 AY119
Midhope Gdns, Wok. GU22 off Midhope Rd 248 AY119
Midhope Rd, Wok. GU22 248 AY119
Midhope St, WC1 18 B3
Midhurst Av, N10 142 DG55
Croydon CR0 223 DN101
Midhurst Cl, Horn. RM12 149 FG63
Midhurst Gdns, Uxb. UB10 157 BQ66
Midhurst Hill, Bexh. DA6 208 FA86
Midhurst Rd, W13 179 CG75
Midhurst Way, E5 144 DU63
Midland Cres, NW3 5 N4
Midland Pl, E14 34 F10
Midland Rd, E10 145 EC59
NW1 17 P1
Hemel Hempstead HP2 62 BK20
Midland Ter, NW2 141 CX62
NW10 160 CS70
● Midleton Ind Est, Guil. GU2 264 AV133
Midleton Rd, Guil. GU2 264 AV133
New Malden KT3 220 CQ97
Midlothian Rd, E3 21 N5
Midmoor Rd, SW12 203 DJ88
SW19 221 CX95
Midship Cl, SE16 33 K3
Midship Pt, E14 34 A5
Midstrath Rd, NW10 140 CS63
Mid St, S.Nutfld RH1 273 DM134
Midsummer Av, Houns. TW4 178 BZ84
Midsummer Wk, Wok. GU21 248 AX116
Midway, St.Alb. AL3 64 CB23
Sutton SM3 221 CZ101
Walton-on-Thames KT12 217 BV103
Midway Av, Cher. KT16 216 BG97
Egham TW20 215 BB97
Midway Cl, Stai. TW18 196 BH90
Midwinter Cl, Well. DA16 188 EU83
Midwood Cl, NW2 141 CV62
Miena Way, Ashtd. KT21 253 CK117
Miers Cl, E6 167 EN67
Mighell Av, Ilf. IG4 146 EK57
Mikado Cl, Hare. UB9 114 BK54
Mike Spring Ct, Grav. DA12 213 GK91
Milan Rd, Sthl. UB1 178 BZ75
Milan Wk, Brwd. CM14 130 FV46
Milborne Gro, SW10 39 P1
Milborne St, E9 11 H5
Milborough Cres, SE12 206 EE86
Milbourne La, Esher KT10 236 CC107
Sch Milbourne Lo Jun Sch, Esher KT10 off Milbourne La 236 CC107
Sch Milbourne Lo Sch, Esher KT10 off Arbrook La 237 CD107
Milbrook, Esher KT10 236 CC107
Milburn Dr, West Dr. UB7 156 BL73
Milburn Wk, Epsom KT18 254 CS115
Milby Ct, Borwd. WD6 off Blyth Cl 100 CM39
Milcombe Cl, Wok. GU21 off Inglewood 248 AV118
Milcote St, SE1 30 G5
Mildenhall Rd, E5 144 DW63
Slough SL1 154 AS72
Mildmay Av, N1 9 M4
Mildmay Gro N, N1 9 M3
Mildmay Gro S, N1 9 M3
Mildmay Pk, N1 9 M2
Mildmay Pl, N16 9 P3
Shoreham TN14 247 FF111
Mildmay Rd, N1 9 M2
Ilford IG1 off Albert Rd 147 EP62
Romford RM7 149 FC57
Mildmay St, N1 9 M4
Mildred Av, Borwd. WD6 100 CN42
Hayes UB3 177 BR77
Northolt UB5 138 CB64
Watford WD18 97 BT42
Mildred Cl, Dart. DA1 210 FN86
Mildred Ct, Croy. CR0 224 DU102
Mildred Rd, Erith DA8 189 FE78
Mile Cl, Wal.Abb. EN9 89 EC33
MILE END, E1 21 L3
⊖ Mile End 21 N4
Mile End, The, E17 123 DX53
MILE END GREEN, Dart. DA2 231 FW96
H Mile End Hosp, E1 21 K4
Mile End Pl, E1 21 J4
Mile End Rd, E1 20 F6
E3 20 F6
Mile Ho Cl, St.Alb. AL1 65 CG23
Mile Ho La, St.Alb. AL1 65 CG23
Mile Path, Wok. GU22 248 AV120
Mile Rd, Wall. SM6 222 DG102
Miles Cl, SE28 167 ER74
Harlow CM19 73 EP16
Sch Miles Coverdale Prim Sch, W12 26 A4
Miles Dr, SE28 167 ER74
Miles La, Cob. KT11 236 BY113
Milespit Hill, NW7 119 CV50
Miles Pl, NW1 16 B6
Surbiton KT5 off Villiers Av 220 CM98
Miles Rd, N8 143 DL55
Epsom KT19 238 CR112
Mitcham CR4 222 DE97
Miles St, SW8 42 A3
Milestone Cl, N9 122 DU47
Ripley GU23 250 BG122
Sutton SM2 240 DD107
Milestone Dr, Pur. CR8 241 DM114
Jct Milestone Grn, SW14 180 CQ84
Milestone Rd, SE19 204 DT93
Dartford DA2 210 FP86
Harlow CM17 58 EW13
Miles Way, N20 120 DE47
Milfoil St, W12 161 CU73
Milford Cl, SE2 188 EY79
St. Albans AL4 65 CK16
Milford Gdns, Croy. CR0 225 DX99
Edgware HA8 118 CN52
Wembley HA0 139 CK64
Milford Gro, Sutt. SM1 240 DC105
Milford La, WC2 18 D10
Milford Ms, SW16 203 DM90
Milford Rd, W13 159 CH74
Southall UB1 158 CA73
Milford Twrs, SE6 off Thomas La 205 EB87
Milkhouse Gate, Guil. GU1 off High St 280 AX136
Milking La, Downe BR6 244 EL112
Keston BR2 244 EK111
Milk St, E16 37 N3
EC2 19 K9
Bromley BR1 206 EH93
Milkwell Gdns, Wdf.Grn. IG8 124 EH52
Milkwell Yd, SE5 43 K7
Milkwood Rd, SE24 203 DP85
Milk Yd, E1 32 G1
Mill, The, Hertingfordbury SG14 53 DM10
Millacres, Ware SG12 55 DX06
Millais Av, E12 147 EN64
Millais Cres, Epsom KT19 238 CS106
Millais Gdns, Edg. HA8 118 CN54
Millais Pl, Til. RM18 193 GG80
Millais Rd, E11 145 EC63
Enfield EN1 104 DT43
New Malden KT3 220 CS101
Millais Way, Epsom KT19 238 CQ105
Millan Cl, New Haw KT15 234 BH110
Milland Ct, Borwd. WD6 100 CR39
Millard Cl, N16 9 P2
Millard Rd, SE8 33 N10
Millard Ter, Dag. RM10 off Church Elm La 168 FA65
Mill Av, Uxb. UB8 156 BJ68
Millbank, SW1 30 A7
Hemel Hempstead HP3 62 BK24
Millbank Ct, SW1 30 A8
Pier Millbank Millennium Pier 30 B9
Sch Millbank Prim Sch, SW1 29 P9
● Millbank Twr, SW1 30 A9
Millbank Way, SE12 206 EG85
Mill Bottom, S.Holm. RH5 285 CK144
Millbourne Rd, Felt. TW13 198 BY91
Mill Br, Barn. EN5 101 CZ44
Millbridge, Hert. SG14 54 DQ09
Millbridge Ms, Hert. SG14 off Millbridge 54 DQ09
Mill Br Pl, Uxb. UB8 156 BH68
Millbro, Swan. BR8 209 FG94
Millbrook, Guil. GU1 280 AX136
Weybridge KT13 235 BS105
Millbrook Av, Well. DA16 187 ER84
Millbrook Ct, Ware SG12 55 DX05
Millbrook Gdns, Chad.Hth RM6 148 EZ58
Gidea Park RM2 127 FE54
Millbrook Pl, NW1 off Hampstead Rd 7 L10
Sch Millbrook Prim Sch, Chsht EN8 off Gews Cor 89 DX29
Millbrook Rd, N9 122 DV46
SW9 183 DP83
Bushey WD23 98 BZ39
Mill Brook Rd, St.M.Cray BR5 228 EW98
Millbrook Way, Colnbr. SL3 175 BE82
Mill Cl, Bkhm KT23 252 CA124
Carshalton SM5 222 DG103
Chesham HP5 76 AS34
Hemel Hempstead HP3 80 BN25
Horley RH6 290 DE147
Lemsford AL8 51 CU10
Piccotts End HP1 62 BH16
Ware SG12 55 DX06
West Drayton UB7 176 BK76
Mill Cor, Barn. EN5 101 CZ39
Mill Ct, E10 145 EC62
Harlow CM20 57 ER12
Millcrest Rd, Goffs Oak EN7 87 DP28
Millcroft Ho, SE6 205 EC91
Mill Dr, Ruis. HA4 137 BR59
Millen Ct, Hort.Kir. DA4 230 FP98
MILL END, Rick. WD3 113 BF46
Millender Wk, SE16 33 H9
Millennium Br, EC4 19 J10
SE1 19 J10
● Millennium Business Cen, NW2 141 CV61
Millennium Cl, E16 23 P8
Uxbridge UB8 156 BH68
Millennium Dr, E14 34 G8
Millennium Harbour, E14 33 P4
Millennium Pl, E2 20 F1
Sch Millennium Prim Sch, SE10 35 L7
Millennium Sq, SE1 32 A4
Millennium Way, SE10 35 J4
Millennium Wf, Rick. WD3 off Wharf La 114 BL45
Miller Av, Enf. EN3 105 EA38
Miller Cl, Brom. BR1 206 EG92
Collier Row RM5 126 FA52
Mitcham CR4 222 DF101
Pinner HA5 116 BW54
Miller Pl, Ger.Cr. SL9 134 AX57
Miller Rd, SW19 202 DD93
Croydon CR0 223 DM102
Guildford GU4 265 BC131
Miller's Av, E8 10 A2
Millers Cl, NW7 119 CU49
Chigwell IG7 126 EV47
Chorleywood WD3 95 BE41
Dartford DA1 210 FK87
Staines-upon-Thames TW18 196 BH92
Millers Copse, Epsom KT18 254 CR119
Redhill RH1 289 DP144
Millers Ct, W4 off Chiswick Mall 181 CT78
Hertford SG14 off Parliament Sq 54 DR10
Millersdale, Harl. CM19 73 EP19
Millers Grn Cl, Enf. EN2 103 DP41
Miller's La, Chig. IG7 126 EV46
Millers La, Stans.Abb. SG12 55 EC11
Windsor SL4 194 AT86
Millers Meadow Cl, SE3 206 EF85
Millers Ri, St.Alb. AL1 65 CE21
Miller's Ter, E8 10 A2
Miller St, NW1 7 L10
Millers Way, W6 26 B5
Miller Wk, SE1 30 F3
Millet Rd, Grnf. UB6 158 CB69
Mill Fm Av, Sun. TW16 197 BS94
● Mill Fm Business Pk, Houns. TW4 198 BY87
Mill Fm Cl, Pnr. HA5 116 BW54
Mill Fm Cres, Houns. TW4 198 BY88
Millfield, N4 off Six Acres Est 143 DN61
Berkhamsted HP4 60 AX18
Mill Fld, Harl. CM17 58 EW11
Millfield, Sun. TW16 217 BR95
Welwyn Garden City AL7 52 DC08
Millfield Av, E17 123 DY53
Millfield Cl, Lon.Col. AL2 83 CK26
Millfield Dr, Nthflt DA11 212 GE89
Millfield La, N6 142 DF61
Lower Kingswood KT20 271 CZ125
Millfield Pl, N6 142 DG61
Millfield Rd, Edg. HA8 118 CQ54
Hounslow TW4 198 BY88
Millfields, Chesh. HP5 76 AQ33
Millfields Cl, Orp. BR5 228 EV97
Sch Millfields Comm Sch, E5 off Hilsea St 144 DW63
Millfields Cotts, Orp. BR5 off Millfields Cl 228 EV98
Millfields Est, E5 145 DX62
Millfields Rd, E5 144 DW63
Millfield Wk, Hem.H. HP3 62 BN22
Millford, Wok. GU21 248 AV117
Mill Gdns, SE26 204 DV91
MILL GREEN, Hat. AL9 67 CY15
Mill Grn, Mitch. CR4 222 DG101
● Mill Grn Business Pk, Mitch. CR4 off Mill Grn Rd 222 DG101
Mill Grn La, Hat. AL9 67 CY15
★ Mill Green Mus, Hat. AL9 67 CX15
Mill Grn Rd, Mitch. CR4 222 DF101
Welwyn Garden City AL7 51 CY10
Millgrove St, SW11 40 G8
Millharbour, E14 34 C6
Millhaven Cl, Rom. RM6 148 EV58
Millhedge Cl, Cob. KT11 252 BY116
MILL HILL, NW7 119 CU50
Mill Hill, SW13 181 CU83
Shenfield CM15 130 FY45
⇌ Mill Hill Broadway 118 CS51
Jct Mill Hill Circ, NW7 119 CT50
Sch Mill Hill Co High Sch, NW7 off Worcester Cres 118 CS47
Oakhill Campus, Barn. EN4 off Church Hill Rd 120 DF46
⊖ Mill Hill East 119 CX52
Mill Hill Gro, W3 160 CP74
● Mill Hill Ind Est, NW7 119 CT51
Mill Hill La, Brock. RH3 270 CP134
Mill Hill Rd, SW13 181 CU82
W3 180 CP75
Sch Mill Hill Sch, NW7 off The Ridgeway 119 CV49
Millhoo Ct, Wal.Abb. EN9 90 EF34
Mill Ho Cl, Eyns. DA4 off Mill La 230 FL102
Millhouse La, Bedmond WD5 81 BT27
Mill Ho La, Cher. KT16 215 BB98
Egham TW20 215 BB98
Millhouse Pl, SE27 203 DP91
Millhurst Ms, Harl. CM17 58 EY11
Millicent Rd, E10 145 DZ60
Milligan St, E14 33 P1
Milliners Ct, Loug. IG10 off The Croft 107 EN40
Milliner's Ct, St.Alb. AL1 65 CE20
Milliners Ho, SW18 off Eastfields Av 182 DA84
Milling Rd, Edg. HA8 118 CR52
Millington Cl, Slou. SL1 153 AM74
Millington Rd, Hayes UB3 177 BS76
Mill La, E4 105 EB41
NW6 5 H3
SE18 37 M10
Albury GU5 281 BF139
Amersham HP7 77 AN39
Beaconsfield HP9 111 AL54
Broxbourne EN10 71 DZ21
Byfleet KT14 234 BM113
Carshalton SM5 240 DF105
Chadwell Heath RM6 148 EY58
Chafford Hundred RM16 191 FX77
Chalfont St. Giles HP8 112 AU47
Cheshunt EN8 89 DY28
Chilworth GU4 281 BF139
Croxley Green WD3 97 BQ44
Croydon CR0 223 DM104
Dorking RH4 285 CH135
Downe BR6 245 EN110
Egham TW20 215 BC98
Epsom KT17 239 CT109
Eynsford DA4 230 FL102
Fetcham KT22 253 CG122
Gerrards Cross SL9 135 AZ58
Grays RM20 191 FX78
Guildford GU1 off Quarry St 280 AX136
Harlow CM17 58 EY11
Hookwood RH6 290 DD148
Horton SL3 175 BB83
Kings Langley WD4 80 BN29
Limpsfield Chart RH8 277 EM131
Navestock RM4 109 FH40
Oxted RH8 276 EF132
Ripley GU23 250 BK119
Sevenoaks TN14 279 FJ121
Shoreham TN14 247 FF110
South Merstham RH1 273 DJ131
Taplow SL6 152 AC71
Toot Hill CM5 93 FE29
Westerham TN16 277 EQ127
Windsor SL4 173 AN80
Woodford Green IG8 124 EF50
Mill La Cl, Brox. EN10 71 DZ21
● Mill La Trd Est, Croy. CR0 223 DM104
Millman Ms, WC1 18 C5
Millman Pl, WC1 off Millman St 18 C5
Millman Rd, E16 25 K10
Millman St, WC1 18 C5
Millmark Gro, SE14 45 M9
Millmarsh La, Enf. EN3 105 DY40
Millmead, Byfleet KT14 234 BM112
Guildford GU1, GU2 280 AW136
Mill Mead, Stai. TW18 195 BF91
Mill Mead Rd, N17 144 DV56
Sch Mill Mead Sch, Hert. SG14 off Port Vale 54 DQ09
Millmead Ter, Guil. GU2 280 AW136
Millmead Way, Hert. SG14 53 DP08
Mill Pk Av, Horn. RM12 150 FL61
Mill Pl, E14 21 M9
Chislehurst BR7 off Old Hill 227 EP95
Dartford DA1 189 FG84
Datchet SL3 174 AX82
Kingston upon Thames KT1 220 CM97
Mill Pl Caravan Pk, Datchet SL3 174 AW82
Mill Plat, Islw. TW7 179 CG82
Mill Plat Av, Islw. TW7 179 CG82
Mill Pond Cl, SW8 41 P5
Sevenoaks TN14 279 FK121
Millpond Ct, Add. KT15 234 BL106
Millpond Est, SE16 32 E5
Millpond Pl, Cars. SM5 222 DG104
Mill Pond Rd, Dart. DA1 210 FL86
Mill Race, Stans.Abb. SG12 55 ED11
Mill Ridge, Edg. HA8 118 CM50
Mill Rd, E16 36 B2
SW19 202 DC94
Aveley RM15 170 FQ73
Cobham KT11 252 BW115
Dunton Green TN13 278 FE121
Epsom KT17 239 CT112
Erith DA8 189 FC80
Esher KT10 218 CA103
Hawley DA2 210 FM91
Hertford SG14 54 DR08
Ilford IG1 147 EN62
Northfleet DA11 212 GE87
Purfleet RM19 190 FP79
South Holmwood RH5 285 CJ144

Mill Rd, Tadworth KT20 255 CX123
Twickenham TW2 198 CC89
West Drayton UB7 176 BJ76
Mill Row, N1 9 P9
Mills Cl, Uxb. UB10 156 BN68
Mills Ct, EC2 19 P3
Mills Gro, E14 22 E7
NW4 141 CX55
Mill Shaw, Oxt. RH8 276 EF132
Millshot Dr, Amer. HP7 77 AR40
Millshott Cl, SW6 38 B6
Millside, B.End SL8 132 AC60
Carshalton SM5 222 DF103
Millside Ct, Iver SL0 176 BH75
● **Millside Ind Est**, Dart. DA1 190 FK84
Millside Pl, Islw. TW7 179 CH82
Millsmead Way, Loug. IG10 107 EM40
Millson Cl, N20 120 DD47
Mills Rd, Hersham KT12 236 BW106
Mills Row, W4 180 CR77
Mills Spur, Old Wind. SL4 194 AV87
Millstead Cl, Tad. KT20 255 CV122
Millstone Cl, E15 13 H4
South Darenth DA4 230 FQ96
Millstone Ms, S.Darenth DA4 230 FQ95
Millstream Cl, N13 121 DN50
Hertford SG14 53 DP09
Millstream La, Slou. SL1 153 AL74
Millstream Rd, SE1 32 A5
Millstream Way, Woob.Moor HP10 132 AD55
Mill St, SE1 32 B5
W1 17 K10
Berkhamsted HP4 60 AW19
Colnbrook SL3 175 BD80
Harlow CM17 74 EY17
Hemel Hempstead HP3
off Fourdinier Way 62 BK23
Kingston upon Thames KT1 220 CL97
Redhill RH1 288 DE135
Slough SL2 154 AT74
Westerham TN16 277 ER127
Mills Way, Hutt. CM13 131 GC46
Mills Yd, SW6 39 L10
Millthorne Cl, Crox.Grn WD3 96 BM43
Mill Vale, Brom. BR2 226 EF96
Mill Vw, Park St AL2
off Park St 83 CD27
Mill Vw Cl, Ewell KT17 239 CT108
Millview Cl, Reig. RH2 272 DD132
Mill Vw Gdns, Croy. CR0 225 DX104
MILLWALL, E14 34 C8
Millwall Dock Rd, E14 34 A6
★ **Millwall FC**, SE16 45 H1
Millwards, Hat. AL10 67 CV21
Millway, NW7 118 CS50
Mill Way, Bushey WD23 98 BY40
Feltham TW14 197 BV85
Leatherhead KT22 254 CM124
Mill End WD3 113 BF46
Millway, Reig. RH2 272 DD134
Millway Gdns, Nthlt. UB5 158 BZ65
Millwell Cres, Chig. IG7 125 ER50
Millwood Rd, Houns. TW3 198 CC85
Orpington BR5 228 EW97
Millwood St, W10 14 E7
Millwrights Wk, Hem.H. HP3
off Stephenson Wf 80 BM25
Mill Yd, E1 20 C10
● **Mill Yd Indusrial Est**, Edg. HA8 118 CP53
Milman Cl, Pnr. HA5 138 BX55
Milman Rd, NW6 4 D10
Milman's St, SW10 40 A3
● **Milmead Ind Cen**, N17 122 DV54
Milne Ct, E18
off Churchfields 124 EG53
Milne Feild, Pnr. HA5 116 CA52
Milne Gdns, SE9 206 EL85
Milne Pk E, New Adgtn CR0 243 ED111
Milne Pk W, New Adgtn CR0 243 ED111
Milner App, Cat. CR3 258 DU121
Milner Cl, Cat. CR3 258 DT121
Watford WD25 81 BV34
Milner Ct, Bushey WD23 98 CB44
Milner Dr, Cob. KT11 236 BZ112
Twickenham TW2 199 CD87
Milner Pl, N1 8 F8
Carshalton SM5
off High St 240 DG105
Milner Rd, E15 23 J3
SW19 222 DB95
Burnham SL1 152 AG71
Caterham CR3 258 DU122
Dagenham RM8 148 EW61
Kingston upon Thames KT1 219 CK97
Morden SM4 222 DD99
Thornton Heath CR7 224 DR97
Milner Sq, N1 8 G7
Milner St, SW3 28 E8
Milner Wk, SE9 207 ER89
Milne Way, Hare. UB9 114 BH53
Milnthorpe Rd, W4 180 CR79
Milo Gdns, SE22
off Milo Rd 204 DT86
Milo Rd, SE22 204 DT86
Milroy Av, Nthflt DA11 212 GE89
Milroy Wk, SE1 30 G2
Milson Rd, W14 26 D6
Milstead Ho, E5 10 F2
MILTON, Grav. DA12 213 GK86
Milton Av, E6 166 EK66
N6 143 DJ59
NW9 140 CQ55
NW10 160 CQ67
Badgers Mount TN14 247 FB110
Barnet EN5 101 CZ43
Chalfont St. Peter SL9 134 AX56
Croydon CR0 224 DR101
Gravesend DA12 213 GJ88
Hornchurch RM12 149 FF61
Sutton SM1 222 DD104
Westcott RH4 285 CD137
Milton Cl, N2 142 DC58
SE1 32 A9
Hayes UB4 157 BU72
Horton SL3 175 BA83
Sutton SM1 222 DD104
Milton Ct, EC2 19 L6
Chadwell Heath RM6
off Cross Rd 148 EW59
Hemel Hempstead HP2
off Milton Dene 63 BP15
Uxbridge UB10 137 BP62
Waltham Abbey EN9 89 EC34
Milton Ct La, Dor. RH4 285 CF136
Milton Ct Rd, SE14 45 M3
Milton Cres, Ilf. IG2 147 EQ59
Milton Dene, Hem.H. HP2 63 BP15
Milton Dr, Borwd. WD6 100 CP43
Shepperton TW17 216 BL98
Milton Flds, Ch.St.G. HP8 112 AV48
Milton Gdn Est, N16 9 N1
Milton Gdns, Epsom KT18 238 CS114
Staines-upon-Thames TW19
off Chesterton Dr 196 BM88
Tilbury RM18 193 GH81
Milton Gro, N11 121 DJ50
N16 9 M1
Milton Hall Rd, Grav. DA12 213 GK88
Milton Hill, Ch.St.G. HP8 112 AV48
Milton Lawns, Amer. HP6 77 AR36
● **Milton Pk**, Egh. TW20 195 BA94
Milton Pk, N6 143 DJ59
Milton Pl, N7 8 E2
Gravesend DA12 213 GJ86
Milton Rd, E17 145 EA56
N6 143 DJ59
N15 143 DP56
NW7 119 CU50
NW9 *off West Hendon Bdy* 141 CU59
SE24 203 DP85
SW14 180 CR83
SW19 202 DC93
W3 160 CR74
W7 159 CF73
Addlestone KT15 234 BG107
Belvedere DA17 188 FA77
Caterham CR3 258 DR121
Chesham HP5 76 AP29
Croydon CR0 224 DR102
Dunton Green TN13 278 FE121
Egham TW20 195 AZ92
Gravesend DA12 213 GJ86
Grays RM17 192 GB78
Hampton TW12 198 CA94
Harrow HA3 139 CE56
Mitcham CR4 202 DG94
Romford RM1 149 FG58
Slough SL2 153 AR70
Sutton SM1 222 DA104
Swanscombe DA10 212 FY86
Uxbridge UB10 136 BN63
Wallington SM6 241 DJ107
Walton-on-Thames KT12 218 BX104
Ware SG12 55 DX05
Warley CM14 130 FV49
Welling DA16 187 ET81
● **Milton Rd Business Pk**, Grav. DA12 *off Milton Rd* 213 GJ87
★ **Milton's Cottage**, Ch.St.G. HP8 112 AV48
Milton St, EC2 19 L6
Swanscombe DA10 211 FX86
Waltham Abbey EN9 89 EC34
Watford WD24 97 BV38
Westcott RH4 285 CD137
Milton Way, Fetch. KT22 268 CC125
West Drayton UB7 176 BM77
Milverton Dr, Uxb. UB10 137 BQ63
Milverton Gdns, Ilf. IG3 147 ET61
Milverton Ho, SE23 205 DY90
Milverton Rd, NW6 4 B7
Milverton St, SE11 42 F1
Milverton Way, SE9 207 EN91
Milwards, Harl. CM19 73 EP19
Sch **Milwards Prim Sch & Nurs**, Harl. CM19
off Paringdon Rd 73 EP19
Milward St, E1 20 F7
Milward Wk, SE18
off Spearman St 187 EN79
Mimas Rd, Hem.H. HP2 62 BM17
off Saturn Way
MIMBRIDGE, Wok. GU24 232 AV113
Mimms Hall Rd, Pot.B. EN6 85 CX31
Mimms La, Ridge EN6 84 CQ33
Shenley WD7 84 CN33
Mimosa Cl, Orp. BR6 228 EW103
Pilgrim's Hatch CM15 130 FV43
Romford RM3 128 FJ52
Mimosa Rd, Hayes UB4 158 BW71
Mimosa St, SW6 38 G7
Mimram Rd, Hert. SG14 53 DP10
Mina Av, Slou. SL3 174 AX75
Minard Rd, SE6 206 EE87
Mina Rd, SE17 43 P1
SW19 222 DA95
Minchenden Cres, N14 121 DJ48
Minchen Rd, Harl. CM20 57 ET13
Minchin Cl, Lthd. KT22 253 CG122
Mincing La, EC3 19 N10
Chobham GU24 232 AT108
Minden Rd, SE20 224 DV95
Sutton SM3 221 CZ103
Minehead Rd, SW16 203 DM92
Harrow HA2 138 CA62
Mineral Cl, Barn. EN5 101 CW44
Mineral La, Chesh. HP5 76 AQ32
Mineral St, SE18 187 ES77
Minera Ms, SW1 29 H8
Minerva Cl, SW9 42 F5
Sidcup DA14 207 ES90
Staines-upon-Thames TW19 196 BG85
Minerva Dr, Wat. WD24 97 BS36
Minerva Est, E2 *off Minerva St* 20 E1
Minerva Rd, E4 123 EB52
NW10 160 CQ70
Kingston upon Thames KT1 220 CM96
Minerva St, E2 20 E1
Minerva Way, Beac. HP9 111 AP54
Minet Av, NW10 160 CS68
Minet Dr, Hayes UB3 157 BU74
Minet Gdns, NW10 160 CS68
Hayes UB3 157 BU74
Sch **Minet Inf Sch**, Hayes UB3
off Avondale Dr 157 BV74
Sch **Minet Jun Sch**, Hayes UB3
off Avondale Dr 157 BV74
Minet Rd, SW9 42 G8
Minford Gdns, W14 26 C5
Mingard Wk, N7
off Hornsey Rd 143 DM62
Ming St, E14 22 B10
Minims, The, Hat. AL10 67 CU17
Minister Ct, Frog. AL2 83 CE28
Ministers Gdns, St.Alb. AL2
off Frogmore 83 CE28
★ **Ministry of Defence**, SW1 30 A4
★ **Ministry of Justice**, SW1 29 M6
Ministry Way, SE9 207 EM89
Miniver Pl, EC4
off Garlick Hill 19 K10
Mink Ct, Houns. TW4 178 BW83
Minniecroft Rd, Burn. SL1 152 AH69
Minniedale, Surb. KT5 220 CM99
Minnow St, SE17 31 P9
Minnow Wk, SE17
off Minnow St 31 P9
Minoan Dr, Hem.H. HP3 62 BL24
Minorca Rd, Wey. KT13 234 BN105
Minories, EC3 20 A10
Minshull Pl, Beck. BR3 205 EA94
Minshull St, SW8 41 N7
Minson Rd, E9 11 K8
Minstead Gdns, SW15 201 CT87
Minstead Way, N.Mal. KT3 220 CS100
Minster Av, Sutt. SM1
off Leafield Rd 222 DA103
Minster Cl, Hat. AL10 67 CU20
● **Minster Ct**, EC3 19 N10
Minster Ct, Horn. RM11 150 FN61
Minster Dr, Croy. CR0 242 DS105
Minster Gdns, W.Mol. KT8 218 BZ98
Minsterley Av, Shep. TW17 217 BS98
Minster Pavement, EC3
off Mincing La 19 N10
Minster Rd, NW2 4 F3
Bromley BR1 206 EH94
Minster Wk, N8
off Lightfoot Rd 143 DL56
Minster Way, Horn. RM11 150 FM60
Slough SL3 175 AZ75
Minstrel Cl, Hem.H. HP1 62 BH19
Minstrel Gdns, Surb. KT5 220 CM98
● **Mint Business Pk**, E16 23 P7
Mint Cl, Hlgdn UB10 157 BP69
Mintern Cl, N13 121 DP48
Minterne Av, Sthl. UB2 178 CA77
Minterne Rd, Har. HA3 140 CM57
Minterne Waye, Hayes UB4 158 BW72
Mintern St, N1 9 M10
Minter Rd, Bark. IG11 168 EU70
Mint Gdns, Dor. RH4
off Church St 285 CG136
Mint La, Lwr Kgswd KT20 272 DA129
Minton Ho, SE11
off Walnut Tree Wk 30 E8
Minton La, Harl. CM17 74 EW15
Minton Ms, NW6 5 M4
Minton Ri, Tap. SL6 152 AH72
Mint Rd, Bans. SM7 256 DC116
Wallington SM6 241 DH105
Mint St, SE1 31 J4
Mint Wk, Croy. CR0
off High St 224 DQ104
Knaphill GU21 248 AS117
Warlingham CR6 259 DX118
Mintwater Cl, Ewell KT17 239 CU110
Mirabel Rd, SW6 39 H4
Mirador Cres, Slou. SL2 154 AV73
Miramar Way, Horn. RM12 150 FK64
Miranda Cl, E1 20 G7
Miranda Ct, W3
off Queens Dr 160 CM72
Miranda Rd, N19 143 DJ60
Mirfield St, SE7 36 E8
Miriam Rd, SE18 187 ES78
● **Mirravale Trd Est**, Dag. RM8 148 EZ59
Mirren Cl, Har. HA2 138 BZ63
Mirrie La, Denh. UB9 135 BC57
Mirror Path, SE9
off Lambscroft Av 206 EJ90
Misbourne Av, Chal.St.P. SL9 112 AY50
Misbourne Cl, Chal.St.P. SL9 112 AY50
Misbourne Ct, Slou. SL3
off High St 175 BA77
Misbourne Meadows, Denh. UB9 135 BC60
Misbourne Rd, Uxb. UB10 156 BN67
Misbourne Vale, Chal.St.P. SL9 112 AX50
Miskin Rd, Dart. DA1 210 FJ87
Miskin Way, Grav. DA12 213 GK93
Missden Dr, Hem.H. HP3 63 BQ22
Missenden Cl, Felt. TW14 197 BT88
Missenden Gdns, Burn. SL1 152 AH72
Morden SM4 222 DC100
Missenden Rd, Amer. HP7 77 AL39
Chesham HP5 76 AL32
Mission Gro, E17 145 DY57
Sch **Mission Gro Prim Sch**, E17
off Buxton Rd 145 DZ56
Mission Pl, SE15 44 D6
Mission Sq, Brent. TW8 180 CL79
Mistletoe Cl, Croy. CR0
off Marigold Way 225 DX102
Mistley Gdns, Hkwd RH6 290 DD149
Mistley Rd, Harl. CM20 58 EU13
Mistral, SE5 *off Sceaux Gdns* 43 P6
Misty's Fld, Walt. KT12 218 BW102
Mitali Pas, E1 20 C9
MITCHAM, CR4 222 DG97
Trm **Mitcham** 222 DE98
⇌ **Mitcham Eastfields** 222 DG96
Mitcham Gdn Village, Mitch. CR4 222 DG99
● **Mitcham Ind Est**, Mitch. CR4 222 DG95
⇌ **Mitcham Junction** 222 DG99
Trm **Mitcham Junction** 222 DG99
Mitcham La, SW16 203 DJ93
Mitcham Pk, Mitch. CR4 222 DF98
Mitcham Rd, E6 25 H2
SW17 202 DF92
Croydon CR0 223 DL100
Ilford IG3 147 ET59
Mitchell Av, Nthflt DA11 212 GD89
Sch **Mitchell Brook Prim Sch**, NW10 *off Bridge Rd* 160 CR65
Mitchellbrook Way, NW10 160 CR65
Mitchell Cl, SE2 188 EW77
Abbots Langley WD5 81 BU32
Belvedere DA17 189 FC76
Bovingdon HP3 79 AZ27
Dartford DA1 210 FL89
Rainham RM13 170 FJ68
St. Albans AL1 65 CD24
Slough SL1 173 AN75
Welwyn Garden City AL7 52 DC09
Mitchell Rd, N13 121 DP50
Orpington BR6 245 ET105
Mitchells Cl, Shalf. GU4
off Station Rd 280 AY140
Mitchell's Pl, SE21
off Dulwich Village 204 DS87
Mitchells Row, Shalf. GU4 280 AY141
Mitchell St, EC1 19 J4
Mitchell Wk, E6 24 G7
Amersham HP6 77 AS38
Swanscombe DA10 212 FY87
Mitchell Way, NW10 160 CQ65
Bromley BR1 226 EG95
Mitchison Rd, N1 9 L5
Mitchley Av, Pur. CR8 242 DQ113
Mitchley Av, South Croydon CR2 242 DQ113
Mitchley Gro, S.Croy. CR2 242 DU113
Mitchley Hill, S.Croy. CR2 242 DT113
Mitchley Rd, N17 144 DU55
Mitchley Vw, S.Croy. CR2 242 DU113
Mitford Cl, Chess. KT9
off Merritt Gdns 237 CJ107
Mitford Rd, N19 143 DL61
Mitre, The, E14 21 N10
Mitre Av, E17
off Greenleaf Rd 145 DZ55
● **Mitre Br Ind Est**, W10 161 CV70
Mitre Cl, Brom. BR2
off Beckenham La 226 EF96
Shepperton TW17 217 BR100
Sutton SM2 240 DC108
Mitre Ct, EC2 19 K8
Hertford SG14 54 DR09
Mitre Rd, E15 13 J10
SE1 30 F4
Mitre Sq, EC3 19 P9
Mitre St, EC3 19 P9
Mitre Way, W10 161 CV70
Mitre Wf, NW10 161 CV70
Mixbury Gro, Wey. KT13 235 BR107
Mixnams La, Cher. KT16 216 BG97
Mizen Cl, Cob. KT11 236 BX114
Mizen Way, Cob. KT11 252 BW115
Mizzen Mast Ho, SE18 37 L6
Moat, The, N.Mal. KT3 220 CS95
Toot Hill CM5 93 FF29
Sch **Moatbridge Sch**, SE9
off Eltham Palace Rd 206 EK86
Moat Cl, Bushey WD23 98 CB43
Chipstead TN13 278 FB123
Orpington BR6 245 ET107
Moat Ct, Ashtd. KT21 254 CL117
Moat Cres, N3 142 DB55
Moat Cft, Well. DA16 188 EW83
Moat Dr, E13 24 D1
Harrow HA1 138 CC56
Ruislip HA4 137 BS59
Slough SL2 154 AW71
Moated Fm Dr, Add. KT15 234 BJ108
Moat Fm Rd, Nthlt. UB5 158 BZ65
Moatfield Rd, Bushey WD23 98 CB43
Moat La, Erith DA8 189 FG81
Moat Pl, SW9 42 D10
W3 160 CP72
Denham UB9 136 BH63
Moatside, Enf. EN3 105 DX42
Feltham TW13 198 BW91
Moats La, S.Nutfld RH1 289 DN140
Moatview Ct, Bushey WD23 98 CB43
Moatwood Grn, Welw.G.C. AL7 51 CY10
Moberly Rd, SW4 203 DK87
Moberly Way, Ken. CR8 258 DR120
Jct **Moby Dick**, Rom. RM6 148 EZ56
Mocatta Ms, Red. RH1 273 DJ131
Mockford Ms, Red. RH1 273 DJ131
Modbury Gdns, NW5 6 F5
Modder Pl, SW15 181 CX84
Model Cotts, SW14 180 CQ83
Model Fm Cl, SE9 206 EL90
Modena Ms, Wat. WD18 97 BS42
Modling Ho, E2 21 J1
Moelwyn Hughes Ct, N7 7 P3
Moelyn Ms, Har. HA1 139 CG57
Moffat Ho, SE5
off Comber Gro 43 J5
Moffat Rd, N13 121 DL51
SW17 202 DE91
Thornton Heath CR7 224 DQ96
Moffats Cl, Brook.Pk AL9 86 DA26
Moffats La, Brook.Pk AL9 85 CZ27
MOGADOR, Tad. KT20 271 CY129
Mogador Cotts, Tad. KT20
off Mogador Rd 271 CX128
Mogador Rd, Lwr Kgswd KT20 271 CX128
Mogden La, Islw. TW7 199 CE85
Mohmmad Khan Rd, E11
off Harvey Rd 146 EF60
Moira Cl, N17 122 DS54
Moira Ct, SW17 202 DG89
Moira Rd, SE9 187 EM84
Moir Cl, S.Croy. CR2 242 DU109
Molash Rd, Orp. BR5 228 EX98
Molasses Row, SW11 39 P10
Mole Abbey Gdns, W.Mol. KT8 218 CA97
● **Mole Business Pk**, Lthd. KT22 253 CG121
Mole Ct, Epsom KT19 238 CQ105
Molember Ct, E.Mol. KT8 219 CE99
Molember Rd, E.Mol. KT8 219 CE99
Mole Rd, Fetch. KT22 253 CD121
Hersham KT12 236 BX106
Molescroft, SE9 207 EQ90
Coll **Molesey Adult Learning Cen**, W.Mol. KT8
off Ray Rd 218 CB99
Molesey Av, W.Mol. KT8 218 BZ98
Molesey Cl, Hersham KT12 236 BY105
Molesey Dr, Sutt. SM3 221 CY103
H **Molesey Hosp**, W.Mol. KT8 218 CA99
Molesey Pk Av, W.Mol. KT8 218 CB99
Molesey Pk Cl, E.Mol. KT8 218 CC99
Molesey Pk Rd, E.Mol. KT8 219 CD99
West Molesey KT8 218 CB99
Molesey Rd, Walt. KT12 236 BX106
West Molesey KT8 218 BY99
Molesford Rd, SW6 39 J7
Molesham Cl, W.Mol. KT8 218 CB97
Molesham Way, W.Mol. KT8 218 CB97
Moles Hill, Oxshott KT22 237 CD111
Molesworth, Hodd. EN11 55 EA13
Molesworth Rd, Cob. KT11 235 BU113
Molesworth St, SE13 185 EC83
Mole Valley Pl, Ashtd. KT21 253 CK119
Molewood Rd, Hert. SG14 53 DP08
Mollands La, S.Ock. RM15 171 FW70
Mollison Av, Enf. EN3 105 DY43
Mollison Dr, Wall. SM6 241 DL107
Mollison Ri, Grav. DA12 213 GL92
Mollison Sq, Wall. SM6
off Mollison Dr 241 DL108
Mollison Way, Edg. HA8 118 CN54
Molloy Ct, Wok. GU21
off Courtenay Rd 249 BA116
Molly Huggins Cl, SW12 203 DJ87
Molteno Rd, Wat. WD17 97 BU39
Molyneaux Av, Bov. HP3 79 AZ27
Molyneux Dr, SW17 203 DH91
Molyneux Rd, Gdmg. GU7 280 AT144
Weybridge KT13 234 BN106
Molyneux St, W1 16 D7
Molyns Ms, Slou. SL1
off Nicholas Gdns 153 AL74
Momples Rd, Harl. CM20 58 EV13
Monaco Wks, Kings L. WD4 81 BP30
Monahan Av, Pur. CR8 241 DM112
Monarch Cl, Felt. TW14 197 BS87
Rainham RM13
off Wymark Cl 169 FG68
Tilbury RM18 193 GH82
West Wickham BR4 244 EF105
Monarch Dr, E16 24 E7
Monarch Ms, E17 145 EB57
SW16 203 DN92
Monarch Par, Mitch. CR4
off London Rd 222 DF96
Monarch Pl, Buck.H. IG9 124 EJ47
Monarch Rd, Belv. DA17 188 FA76
Monarchs Ct, NW7
off Grenville Pl 118 CR50
Monarchs Way, Ruis. HA4 137 BR60
Waltham Cross EN8 89 DY34
Monarch Way, Ilf. IG2 147 ER58
Mona Rd, SE15 45 H8
Monastery Gdns, Enf. EN2 104 DR40
Mona St, E16 23 M7
Monaveen Gdns, W.Mol. KT8 218 CA97
Monck St, SW1 29 P7
Monclar Rd, SE5 184 DR84
Moncorvo Cl, SW7 28 C5
Moncrieff Cl, E6 24 G8
Moncrieff Pl, SE15 44 C8
Moncrieff St, SE15 44 D8
Mondial Way, Harling. UB3 177 BQ80
Sch **Monega Prim Sch**, E12
off Monega Rd 166 EK65
Monega Rd, E7 166 EJ65
E12 166 EK65
Money Av, Cat. CR3 258 DR122
MONEYHILL, Rick. WD3 114 BH46
Moneyhill Ct, Rick. WD3
off Dellwood 114 BH46
Moneyhill Par, Rick. WD3
off Uxbridge Rd 114 BH46
Money Hill Rd, Rick. WD3 114 BJ46
Money Hole La, Tewin AL6 52 DE08
Money La, West Dr. UB7 176 BK76
Money Rd, Cat. CR3 258 DR122
Mongers La, Epsom KT17 239 CT110
Monica Cl, Wat. WD24 98 BW40
Monier Rd, E3 12 A7
Monivea Rd, Beck. BR3 205 DZ94
Monkchester Cl, Loug. IG10 107 EN39
Monk Dr, E16 23 N9
MONKEN HADLEY, Barn. EN5 101 CZ39
Sch **Monken Hadley C of E Prim Sch**, Barn. EN4 *off Camlet Way* 102 DA39
Monkey Island La, Bray SL6 172 AE78
Monkfrith Av, N14 103 DH44
Monkfrith Cl, N14 121 DH45
Sch **Monkfrith Prim Sch**, N14
off Knoll Dr 120 DG45
Monkfrith Way, N14 120 DG45
Monkhams, Wal.Abb. EN9 89 EC29
Monkhams Av, Wdf.Grn. IG8 124 EG50
Monkhams Dr, Wdf.Grn. IG8 124 EH49
Monkhams La, Buck.H. IG9 124 EH48
Woodford Green IG8 124 EG50
Monkleigh Rd, Mord. SM4 221 CY97
Monk Pas, E16 23 N10
Monks Av, Barn. EN5 102 DC44
West Molesey KT8 218 BZ99
Monksbury, Harl. CM18 74 EU18
Monks Chase, Ingrave CM13 131 GC50
Monks Cl, SE2 188 EX77
Broxbourne EN10 71 EA20
Enfield EN2 104 DQ40
Harrow HA2 138 CB61
Ruislip HA4 138 BX63
St. Albans AL1 65 CE22
Monks Cres, Add. KT15 234 BH106
Walton-on-Thames KT12 217 BV102
Monksdene Gdns, Sutt. SM1 222 DB104
Monks Dr, W3 160 CN71
Monksfield Way, Slou. SL2 153 AN69
Monksgate, St.Alb. AL1
off Monks Cl 65 CE22
Monks Grn, Fetch. KT22 252 CC121
Monksgrove, Loug. IG10 107 EN43
Monks Horton Way, St.Alb. AL1 65 CH18
Monksmead, Borwd. WD6 100 CQ42
Sch **Monksmead Sch**, Borwd. WD6
off Hillside Av 100 CQ41
MONKS ORCHARD, Croy. CR0 225 DZ101
Monks Orchard, Dart. DA1 210 FJ89
Sch **Monks Orchard Prim Sch**, Croy. CR0
off The Glade 225 DX99
Monks Orchard Rd, Beck. BR3 225 EA102
Monks Pk, Wem. HA9 160 CQ65
Monks Pk Gdns, Wem. HA9 160 CP65
Monks Pl, Cat. CR3
off Tillingdown Hill 258 DV122
Monk's Ridge, N20 119 CV46
Monks Ri, Welw.G.C. AL8 51 CX05
Monks Rd, Bans. SM7 256 DA116
Enfield EN2 104 DQ40
Virginia Water GU25 214 AX98
Windsor SL4 173 AK82
Monk St, SE18 37 M8
Monks Wk, Cher. KT16 215 BE98
Monk's Wk, Reig. RH2 272 DB134
Monks Wk, Sthflt DA13 212 GA93
Monks Way, NW11 141 CZ56
Beckenham BR3 225 EA100
Harmondsworth UB7 176 BL79
Orpington BR5 227 EQ102
Staines-upon-Thames TW18 196 BK94
Monks Well, Green. DA9 191 FV84
Monkswell Ct, N10 120 DG53
Monkswick Rd, Harl. CM20 57 ET13
Monkswood, Welw.G.C. AL8 51 CW05
Monkswood Av, Wal.Abb. EN9 89 ED33
Monkswood Gdns, Borwd. WD6 100 CR43
Ilford IG5 147 EN55
Monkton Ho, E5
off Pembury Rd 10 E2

Monkton Rd, Well. DA16 187 ET82
Monkton St, SE11 30 F8
Monkville Av, NW11 141 CZ56
Monkwell Sq, EC2 19 K7
Monkwood Cl, Rom. RM1 149 FG57
Monmouth Av, E18 146 EH56
Kingston upon Thames KT1 199 CJ94
Monmouth Cl, W4 180 CR76
Mitcham CR4
off Recreation Way 223 DL98
Welling DA16 188 EU84
Monmouth Gro, Brent. TW8
off Sterling Pl 180 CL77
Monmouth Ho, NW5 7 K4
Monmouth Pl, W2 15 K9
Monmouth Rd, E6 25 J3
N9 122 DV47
W2 15 K9
Dagenham RM9 148 EZ64
Hayes UB3 177 BS77
Watford WD17 97 BV41
Monmouth St, WC2 18 A9
Monnery Rd, N19 143 DJ62
Monnow Grn, Aveley RM15
off Monnow Rd 170 FQ73
Monnow Rd, SE1 32 C10
Aveley RM15 170 FQ73
Mono La, Felt. TW13 197 BV89
Monoux Gro, E17 123 EA53
Monro Dr, Guil. GU2 264 AU131
Monroe Cres, Enf. EN1 104 DV39
Monroe Dr, SW14 200 CP85
Monro Gdns, Har. HA3 117 CE52
● Monro Ind Est, Wal.Cr. EN8 89 DY34
Monro Pl, Epsom KT19 238 CN109
Monro Way, E5 144 DU63
Monsal Ct, E5 *off Redwald Rd* 145 DY63
Monsell Ct, N4
off Monsell Rd 143 DP62
Monsell Gdns, Stai. TW18 195 BE92
Monsell Rd, N4 143 DP62
Sch Monson Prim Sch, SE14 45 J4
Monson Rd, NW10 161 CU68
SE14 45 J5
Broxbourne EN10 71 DZ20
Redhill RH1 272 DF130
Mons Wk, Egh. TW20 195 BC92
Mons Way, Brom. BR2 226 EL100
Montacute Rd, SE6 205 DZ87
Bushey Heath WD23 117 CE45
Morden SM4 222 DD100
New Addington CR0 243 EC109
Montagu Cres, N18 122 DV49
Montague Av, SE4 185 DZ84
W7 159 CF74
South Croydon CR2 242 DS112
Montague Cl, SE1 31 L2
Barnet EN5 101 CZ42
Farnham Royal SL2 153 AP68
Walton-on-Thames KT12 217 BU101
Montague Dr, Cat. CR3 258 DQ122
Montague Gdns, W3 160 CN73
Montague Hall Pl, Bushey
WD23 98 CA44
Montague Pl, WC1 17 P6
Montague Rd, E8 10 C3
E11 146 EF61
N8 143 DM57
N15 144 DU56
SW19 202 DB94
W7 159 CF74
W13 159 CH72
Berkhamsted HP4 60 AV19
Croydon CR0 223 DP102
Hounslow TW3 178 CB83
Richmond TW10 200 CL86
Slough SL1 154 AT73
Southall UB2 178 BY77
Uxbridge UB8 156 BK66
Montague Sq, SE15 45 H5
Montague St, EC1 19 J7
WC1 18 A6
Montague Waye, Sthl. UB2 178 BY76
Montagu Gdns, N18 122 DW49
Wallington SM6 241 DJ105
Montagu Mans, W1 16 F6
Montagu Ms N, W1 16 F7
Montagu Ms S, W1 16 F8
Montagu Ms W, W1 16 F8
Montagu Pl, W1 16 E7
Montagu Rd, N9 122 DW49
N18 122 DV50
NW4 141 CU58
Datchet SL3 174 AV81
● Montagu Rd Ind Est, N18 122 DW49
Montagu Row, W1 16 F7
Montagu Sq, W1 16 F7
Montagu St, W1 16 F8
Montaigne Cl, SW1 29 P9
Montalt Rd, Wdf.Grn. IG8 124 EF50
Montana Bldg, SE13
off Deals Gateway 46 C6
Montana Cl, S.Croy. CR2 242 DR110
Montana Gdns, SE26 205 DZ92
Sutton SM1 *off Lind Rd* 240 DC106
Montana Rd, SW17 202 DG91
SW20 221 CW95
Montayne Rd, Chsht EN8 89 DX32
Sch Montbelle Prim Sch, SE9
off Milverton Way 207 EN91
Montbelle Rd, SE9 207 EP90
Montbretia Cl, Orp. BR5 228 EW98
Montcalm Cl, Brom. BR2 226 EG100
Hayes UB4 157 BV69
Montcalm Rd, SE7 186 EK80
Montclare St, E2 20 A3
Monteagle Av, Bark. IG11 167 EQ65
Sch Monteagle Prim Sch, Dag.
RM9 *off Burnham Rd* 168 EV67
Monteagle Way, E5 144 DU62
SE15 44 F10
Montefiore St, SW8 41 K9
Montego Cl, SE24
off Railton Rd 183 DN84
Montem La, Slou. SL1 153 AR74
Sch Montem Prim Sch, N7
off Hornsey Rd 143 DM62
Slough SL1
off Chalvey Gro 173 AP75
Montem Rd, SE23 205 DZ87
New Malden KT3 220 CS98
Montem St, N4
off Thorpedale Rd 143 DM60
Montenotte Rd, N8 143 DJ57
Monterey Cl, NW7
off The Broadway 118 CS50
Bexley DA5 209 FC89
Uxbridge UB10 156 BN66
Montesole Ct, Pnr. HA5 116 BW54
Montevetro, SW11 40 A6
Montfichet Rd, E20 12 E7
Montford Pl, SE11 42 E1
Montford Rd, Sun. TW16 217 BU98
Montfort Gdns, Ilf. IG6 125 EQ51
Montfort Pl, SW19 201 CX88
Montfort Ri, Red. RH1 288 DF142
Montgolfier Wk, Nthlt. UB5
off Wayfarer Rd 158 BY69
Montgomerie Cl, Berk. HP4
off Mortain Dr 60 AU17
Montgomerie Dr, Guil. GU2 264 AU129
Montgomerie Ms, SE23 204 DW87
Montgomery Av, Esher KT10 219 CE104
Hemel Hempstead HP2 62 BN19
Montgomery Cl, Grays RM16 192 GC75
Mitcham CR4 223 DL98
Sidcup DA15 207 ET86
Montgomery Ct, W2
off Harrow Rd 16 A7
W4 *off St. Thomas' Rd* 180 CQ79
Dagenham RM10
off St. Mark's Pl 168 FA65
Montgomery Cres, Rom. RM3 128 FJ50
Montgomery Dr, Chsht EN8 89 DY28
Montgomery Gdns, Sutt.
SM2 240 DD108
Montgomery Pl, Slou. SL2 154 AW72
Montgomery Rd, W4 180 CQ77
Edgware HA8 118 CM51
South Darenth DA4 231 FR95
Woking GU22 248 AY118
Montgomery St, E14 34 D3
Montgomery Way, Ken. CR8 258 DR120
Montholme Rd, SW11 202 DF86
Monthope Rd, E1 20 C7
Montolieu Gdns, SW15 201 CV85
Montpelier Av, W5 159 CJ71
Bexley DA5 208 EX87
Montpelier Cl, Uxb. UB10 156 BN67
Montpelier Ct, Wind. SL4
off St. Leonards Rd 173 AQ82
Montpelier Gdns, E6 24 F2
Romford RM6 148 EW59
Montpelier Gro, NW5 7 M2
Montpelier Ms, SW7 28 D6
Montpelier Pl, E1 20 G9
SW7 28 D6
Sch Montpelier Prim Sch, W5
off Montpelier Rd 159 CK71
Montpelier Ri, NW11 141 CY59
Wembley HA9 139 CK60
Montpelier Rd, N3 120 DC53
SE15 44 F6
W5 159 CK71
Purley CR8 241 DP110
Sutton SM1 240 DC105
Montpelier Row, SE3 47 L9
Twickenham TW1 199 CH87
Montpelier Sq, SW7 28 D5
Montpelier St, SW7 28 D5
Montpelier Ter, SW7 28 D5
Montpelier Vale, SE3 47 L9
Montpelier Wk, SW7 28 D6
Montpelier Way, NW11 141 CY59
Montrave Rd, SE20 204 DW93
Montreal Pl, WC2 18 C10
Montreal Rd, Ilf. IG1 147 EQ59
Sevenoaks TN13 278 FE123
Tilbury RM18 193 GG83
Montrell Rd, SW2 203 DL88
Montrose Av, NW6 4 F10
Datchet SL3 174 AW80
Edgware HA8 118 CQ54
Romford RM2 128 FJ54
Sidcup DA15 208 EU87
Slough SL1 153 AP72
Twickenham TW2 198 CB87
Welling DA16 187 ER83
Montrose Cl, Ashf. TW15 197 BQ93
Welling DA16 187 ET83
Woodford Green IG8 124 EG49
Montrose Ct, SW7 28 B5
Montrose Cres, N12 120 DC51
Wembley HA0 160 CL65
Montrose Gdns, Mitch. CR4 222 DF97
Oxshott KT22 237 CD112
Sutton SM1 222 DB103
Montrose Pl, SW1 29 H5
Montrose Rd, Felt. TW14 197 BR86
Harrow HA3 117 CE54
Montrose Wk, Wey. KT13 217 BP104
Montrose Way, SE23 205 DX88
Datchet SL3 174 AX81
Montrouge Cres, Epsom KT17 255 CW116
Montserrat Av, Wdf.Grn. IG8 123 ED52
Montserrat Cl, SE19 204 DR92
Montserrat Rd, SW15 181 CY84
⊖ Monument 19 M10
★ Monument, The, EC3 19 M10
● Monument Business Cen,
Wok. GU21
off Monument Way E 249 BB115
Monument Gdns, SE13 205 EC85
Monument Grn, Wey. KT13 217 BP104
Monument Hill, Wey. KT13 235 BP105
Monument La, Chal.St.P. SL9 112 AY51
Monument Rd, Wey. KT13 235 BP105
Woking GU21 233 BA114
Monument St, EC3 31 M1
Monument Way, N17 144 DT55
Monument Way E, Wok.
GU21 249 BB115
Monument Way W, Wok.
GU21 249 BA115
Monza St, E1 32 G1
Moodkee St, SE16 32 G6
Moody Rd, SE15 44 A5
Moody St, E1 21 K3
Moon La, Barn. EN5 101 CZ41
Moon St, N1 8 G8
Moorcroft Gdns, Brom. BR2
off Southborough Rd 226 EL99
Moorcroft La, Uxb. UB8 156 BN71
Moorcroft Rd, SW16 203 DL90
Sch Moorcroft Sch, Hlgdn UB8
off Bramble Cl 156 BM72
Moorcroft Way, Pnr. HA5 138 BY57
Moordown, SE18 187 EP81
Moore Av, Grays RM20 192 FY78
Tilbury RM18 193 GH82
Moore Cl, SW14 180 CQ83
Addlestone KT15 234 BH106
Dartford DA2 211 FR89
Mitcham CR4 223 DH96
Slough SL1 173 AP75
Moore Ct, Wem. HA0
off Station Gro 160 CL65
Moore Cres, Dag. RM9 168 EV67
Moorefield Rd, N17 122 DT54
Moore Gro Cres, Egh. TW20 194 AY94
Moorehead Way, SE3 186 EH83
Moore Ho, E14 34 B5
Mooreland Rd, Brom. BR1 206 EF94
Moor End, Maid. SL6 172 AC78
Moorend, Welw.G.C. AL7 52 DA12
Moor End Rd, Hem.H. HP1 62 BJ21
Moore Pk Rd, SW6 39 L5
Moore Rd, SE19 204 DQ93
Berkhamsted HP4 60 AT17
Swanscombe DA10 212 FY86
Moores La, Eton Wick SL4 173 AM77
Moores Pl, Brwd. CM14 130 FX47
Moores Rd, Dor. RH4 285 CH135
Moore St, SW3 28 E8
Moore Wk, E7 13 P2
Moore Way, Sutt. SM2 240 DA109
Moorey Cl, E15 13 L9
Moorfield, Harl. CM18 73 EQ20
South Holmwood RH5 285 CK144
Moorfield Av, W5 159 CK70
● Moorfield Pt, Guil. GU1 264 AY130
Moorfield Rd, Chess. KT9 238 CL106
Denham UB9 136 BG59
Enfield EN3 104 DW39
Guildford GU1 264 AX130
Orpington BR6 228 EU101
Uxbridge UB8 156 BK72
Moorfields, EC2 19 L7
Moorfields Cl, Stai. TW18 215 BE95
H Moorfields Eye Hosp, EC1 19 L3
Moorfields Highwalk, EC2 19 L7
Moor Furlong, Slou. SL1 153 AL74
⇌ Moorgate 19 L7
⊖ Moorgate 19 L7
Moorgate, EC2 19 L8
Moorgate Pl, EC2 19 L8
Moorhall Rd, Hare. UB9 136 BH58
Moor Hall Rd, Harl. CM17 58 EZ11
Moorhayes Dr, Stai. TW18 216 BJ97
Moorhen Cl, Erith DA8 189 FH80
Moorhen Wk, Green. DA9
off Waterstone Way 211 FU86
Moorholme, Wok. GU22
off Oakbank 248 AY119
MOORHOUSE, West. TN16 277 EM127
MOORHOUSE BANK, West.
TN16 277 EM128
Moorhouse Rd, W2 15 J8
Harrow HA3 139 CK55
Oxted RH8 277 EM131
Westerham TN16 277 EM128
Sch Moor Ho Sch, Oxt. RH8
off Mill La 276 EF132
Moorhurst Av, Goffs Oak EN7 87 DN29
Moorings, SE28 168 EV73
Moorings, The, E16
off Prince Regent La 24 C7
Bookham KT23 268 CA125
Windsor SL4
off Straight Rd 194 AW87
Moorings Ho, Brent. TW8
off Tallow Rd 179 CJ80
Moorland Cl, Rom. RM5 127 FB52
Twickenham TW2 198 CA87
Moorland Rd, SW9 183 DP84
Harmondsworth UB7 176 BJ79
Hemel Hempstead HP1 62 BG22
Moorlands, Frog. AL2 83 CD28
Welwyn Garden City AL7 52 DA12
Moorlands, The, Wok. GU22 249 AZ121
Moorlands Av, NW7 119 CV51
Moorlands Est, SW9 183 DN84
Moorlands Reach, Saw. CM21 58 EZ06
Moor La, EC2 19 L7
Chessington KT9 238 CL105
Harmondsworth UB7 176 BJ79
Rickmansworth WD3 114 BM47
Sarratt WD3 95 BE36
Staines-upon-Thames
TW18, TW19 195 BE90
Upminster RM14 151 FS60
Woking GU22 248 AY122
Moor La Crossing, Wat. WD18 115 BQ46
Moormead Dr, Epsom KT19 238 CS106
Moor Mead Rd, Twick. TW1 199 CG86
Moormede Cres, Stai. TW18 195 BF91
Moor Mill La, Coln.St AL2 83 CE29
MOOR PARK, Nthwd. HA6 115 BQ49
★ Moor Park, Rick. WD3 114 BN48
⊖ Moor Park 115 BR48
Moor Pk Est, Nthwd. HA6 115 BQ49
Moor Pk Gdns, Kings.T. KT2 200 CS94
● Moor Pk Ind Cen, Wat.
WD18 115 BQ45
Moor Pk Rd, Nthwd. HA6 115 BR50
Moor Pl, EC2 19 L7
Moor Rd, Chesh. HP5 76 AQ32
Sevenoaks TN14 263 FH120
Moors, The, Welw.G.C. AL7 52 DA08
Moorside, Hem.H. HP3 62 BH23
Welwyn Garden City AL7 52 DA12
Wooburn Green HP10 132 AE55
Moorside Rd, Brom. BR1 206 EE90
Moors La, Orch.L. HP5 78 AV28
Moorsom Way, Couls. CR5 257 DK117
Moorstown Ct, Slou. SL1 174 AS75
Moor St, W1 17 P9
Moors Wk, Welw.G.C. AL7 52 DC09
Moor Twr, Harl. CM18 73 ET16
Moortown Rd, Wat. WD19 116 BW49
Moor Vw, Wat. WD18 115 BU45
Moot Ct, NW9 140 CN57
Moran Cl, Brick.Wd AL2 82 BZ31
Morant Gdns, Rom. RM5 127 FB50
Morant Pl, N22 121 DM53
Morant Rd, Grays RM16 193 GH76
Jct Morants Ct Cross, Dunt.Grn
TN14 263 FB118
Morants Ct Rd, Dunt.Grn
TN13 263 FC118
Morant St, E14 22 B10
Sch Mora Prim Sch, NW2
off Mora Rd 141 CW63
Mora Rd, NW2 141 CW63
Mora St, EC1 19 K3
Morat St, SW9 42 D6
Moravian Pl, SW10 40 B3
Moravian St, E2 20 G1
Moray Av, Hayes UB3 157 BT74
Moray Cl, Edg. HA8
off Pentland Av 118 CP47
Romford RM1 127 FE52
Moray Dr, Slou. SL2 154 AU72
Moray Ms, N7 143 DM61
Moray Rd, N4 143 DM61
Moray Way, Rom. RM1 127 FD52
Morcote Cl, Shalf. GU4 280 AY141
Mordaunt Gdns, Dag. RM9 168 EY66
Mordaunt Rd, NW10 160 CR67
Mordaunt St, SW9 42 C10
MORDEN, SM4 222 DA97
⊖ Morden 222 DB97
Morden Cl, Tad. KT20 255 CX120
Morden Ct, Mord. SM4 222 DB98
Morden Gdns, Grnf. UB6 139 CF64
Mitcham CR4 222 DD98
★ Morden Hall Pk NT, Mord.
SM4 222 DB97
Morden Hall Rd, Mord. SM4 222 DB97
Morden Hill, SE13 46 E8
Morden La, SE13 46 F7
Sch Morden Mt Prim Sch, SE13 46 D8
MORDEN PARK, Mord. SM4 221 CY99
Sch Morden Prim Sch,
Mord. SM4
off London Rd 222 DA99
Tra Morden Road 222 DB96
Morden Rd, SE3 47 N8
SW19 202 DB94
Mitcham CR4 222 DC98
Romford RM6 148 EY59
Morden Rd Ms, SE3 47 N9
⇌ Morden South 222 DA99
Morden St, SE13 46 D7
Morden Way, Sutt. SM3 222 DA101
Morden Wf Rd, SE10 35 J7
Mordon Rd, Ilf. IG3 147 ET59
Mordred Ct, N9
off Galahad Rd 122 DU47
Mordred Rd, SE6 206 EE89
Moreau Wk, Geo.Grn SL3
off Alan Way 154 AY72
Morecambe Cl, E1 21 J6
Hornchurch RM12 149 FH64
Morecambe Gdns, Stan. HA7 117 CK49
Morecambe St, SE17 31 K9
Morecambe Ter, N18 122 DR49
More Circle, Gdmg. GU7 280 AS144
More Cl, E16 23 M8
W14 26 D9
Purley CR8 241 DN111
Morecoombe Cl, Kings.T. KT2 200 CP94
Moree Way, N18 122 DU49
Sch More Ho Sch, SW1 28 F7
Moreland Av, Colnbr. SL3 175 BC80
Grays RM16 192 GC75
Moreland Cl, Colnbr. SL3
off Moreland Av 175 BC80
Moreland Dr, Ger.Cr. SL9 135 AZ59
Sch Moreland Prim Sch, EC1 19 H2
Moreland St, EC1 19 H2
Moreland Way, E4 123 EB48
More La, Esher KT10 218 CB103
Morel Ct, Sev. TN13 279 FH122
Morella Cl, Vir.W. GU25 214 AW98
Morella Rd, SW12 202 DF87
Morell Cl, Barn. EN5 102 DC41
Morello Av, Uxb. UB8 157 BP71
Morello Cl, Swan. BR8 229 FD98
Morello Dr, Slou. SL3 155 AZ74
Morel Ms, Dag. RM8
off Ager Ave 148 EX60
More London Pl, SE1
off Tooley St 31 N3
More London Riverside, SE1
off Tooley St 31 P3
Moremead, Wal.Abb. EN9 89 ED33
Moremead Rd, SE6 205 DZ91
Morena St, SE6 205 EB87
More Rd, Gdmg. GU7 280 AS144
Moresby Av, Surb. KT5 220 CP101
Moresby Rd, E5 144 DV60
Moresby Wk, SW8 41 L9
Moretaine Rd, Ashf. TW15
off Hengrove Cres 196 BK90
MORETON, Ong. CM5 75 FH20
Moreton Av, Islw. TW7 179 CE81
Moreton Cl, E5 144 DW61
N15 144 DR58
NW7 119 CW51
SW1 29 M10
Cheshunt EN7 88 DV27
Swanley BR8 229 FE96
Moreton Gdns, Wdf.Grn. IG8 124 EL50
Moreton Ho, SE16 32 F6
● Moreton Ind Est, Swan.
BR8 229 FG98
Moreton Pl, SW1 29 M10
Moreton Rd, N15 144 DR58
Moreton CM5 75 FG24
South Croydon CR2 242 DR106
Worcester Park KT4 221 CU103
Moreton St, SW1 29 M10
Moreton Ter, SW1 29 M10
Moreton Ter Ms N, SW1 29 M10
Moreton Ter Ms S, SW1 29 M10
Moreton Twr, W3 160 CP74
Moreton Way, Slou. SL1 153 AK74
Morewood Cl, Sev. TN13 278 FF123
● Morewood Cl Ind Pk, Sev.
TN13 *off Morewood Cl* 278 FF123
Morford Cl, Ruis. HA4 137 BV59
Morford Way, Ruis. HA4 137 BV59
Morgan Av, E17 145 ED56
Morgan Cl, Dag. RM10 168 FA66
Northwood HA6 115 BT51
Morgan Ct, N9
off Galahad Rd 122 DU48
SW11
off Battersea High St 40 B7
Morgan Cres, They.B. CM16 107 ER36
Morgan Dr, Green. DA9 211 FS87
Morgan Gdns, Ald. WD25 98 CB38
Morgan Ho, SW1
off Vauxhall Br Rd 29 M9
Morgan Rd, N7 8 E3
W10 14 G6
Bromley BR1 206 EG94
Morgans Cl, Hert. SG13 54 DR11
Sch Morgans JMI Sch, Hert. SG13
off Morgans Rd 54 DR11
Morgans La, SE1 31 N3
Hayes UB3 157 BR71
Morgans Rd, Hert. SG13 54 DR11
Morgan St, E3 21 M3
E16 23 M6
Morgans Wk, Hert. SG13 54 DR12
Morgan Way, Rain. RM13 170 FJ69
Morgan Way, Woodford Green
IG8 124 EL51
Sch Moriah Jewish Day Sch, Pnr.
HA5 *off Cannon La* 138 BY60
Moriarty Cl, Brom. BR1 227 EP98
Moriatry Cl, N7 143 DL63
Morice Rd, Hodd. EN11 71 DZ15
Morie St, SW18 182 DB84
Morieux Rd, E10 145 DZ60
Moring Rd, SW17 202 DG91
Morkyns Wk, SE21 204 DS90
Morland Av, Croy. CR0 224 DS102
Dartford DA1 209 FH85
Morland Cl, NW11 142 DB60
Hampton TW12 198 BZ92
Mitcham CR4 222 DE97
Morland Est, E8 10 D6
Morland Gdns, NW10 160 CR66
Southall UB1 158 CB74
Morland Ms, N1 8 F7
Morland Pl, N15 144 DS56
Morland Rd, E17 145 DX57
SE20 205 DX93
Croydon CR0 224 DS102
Dagenham RM10 168 FA66
Harrow HA3 140 CL57
Ilford IG1 147 EP61
Sutton SM1 240 DC106
Morland Way, Chsht EN8 89 DY28
Morley Av, E4 123 ED52
N18 122 DU49
N22 121 DN54
Morley Cl, Orp. BR6 227 EP103
Slough SL3 175 AZ75
Coll Morley Coll, SE1 30 F6
Morley Cres, Edg. HA8 118 CQ47
Ruislip HA4 138 BW61
Morley Cres E, Stan. HA7 117 CJ54
Morley Cres W, Stan. HA7 117 CJ54
Morley Gro, Harl. CM20 57 EQ13
Morley Hill, Enf. EN2 104 DR38
Morley Rd, E10 145 EC60
E15 13 L10
SE13 185 EC84
Barking IG11 167 ER67
Chislehurst BR7 227 EQ95
Romford RM6 148 EY57
South Croydon CR2 242 DT110
Sutton SM3 221 CZ102
Twickenham TW1 199 CK86
Morley Sq, Grays RM16 193 GG77
Morley St, SE1 30 F6
Morna Rd, SE5 43 K8
Morning La, E9 10 G4
Morning Ri, Loud. WD3 96 BK41
Sch Morningside Prim Sch, E9 11 H4
Morningside Rd, Wor.Pk. KT4 221 CV103
Mornington Av, W14 26 G9
Bromley BR1 226 EJ97
Ilford IG1 147 EN59
Mornington Cl, Bigg.H. TN16 260 EK117
Woodford Green IG8 124 EG49
Mornington Ct, Bex. DA5 209 FC88
⊖ Mornington Crescent 7 L10
Mornington Cres, NW1 7 L10
Hounslow TW5 177 BV81
Mornington Gro, E3 22 A3
Mornington Ms, SE5 43 J6
Mornington Pl, NW1 7 K10
Mornington Rd, E4 123 ED45
E11 146 EF60
SE8 45 P5
Ashford TW15 197 BQ92
Greenford UB6 158 CB71
Loughton IG10 107 EQ41
Radlett WD7 83 CG34
Woodford Green IG8 124 EF49
Morningtons, Harl. CM19 73 EQ19
Mornington St, NW1 7 K10
Mornington Ter, NW1 7 K9
Mornington Wk, Rich. TW10 199 CJ91
Morocco St, SE1 31 N5
Morpeth Av, Borwd. WD6 100 CM38
Morpeth Cl, Hem.H. HP2
off York Way 62 BL21
Morpeth Gro, E9 11 J8
Morpeth Rd, E9 11 H9
Sch Morpeth Sch, E2 21 H3
Annexe, E2 20 G3
Morpeth St, E2 21 J2
Morpeth Ter, SW1 29 L7
Morpeth Wk, N17 *off West Rd* 122 DV52
Morphou Rd, NW7 119 CY51
Morrab Gdns, Ilf. IG3 147 ET62
Morrell Ct, Welw.G.C. AL7 51 CZ08
Morrells Yd, SE11 30 F10
Morrice Cl, Slou. SL3 175 AZ77
Morris Ave, E12 147 EM64
Uxbridge UB10 156 BL65
Morris Cl, Chal.St.P. SL9 113 AZ53
Croydon CR0 225 DY100
Orpington BR6 227 ES104
Morris Ct, E4 123 EB48
E5 *off Mount Pleasant Hill* 144 DW61
Enfield EN3 *off Rigby Pl* 105 EA37
Waltham Abbey EN9 90 EF34
Morris Gdns, SW18 202 DA87
Dartford DA1 210 FN85
Morris Ho, W3
off Swainson Rd 181 CT75
Harlow CM18 73 EQ18
Morrish Rd, SW2 203 DL87
Morrison Av, E4 123 EA51
N17 144 DS55
Morrison Rd, SW9 42 F9
Barking IG11 168 EY68
Hayes UB4 157 BV69
Morrison St, SW11 40 G10
Morris Pl, N4 143 DN61
Morris Rd, E14 22 C6
E15 146 EE63
Dagenham RM8 148 EZ61
Isleworth TW7 179 CF83
Romford RM3 127 FH52
South Nutfield RH1 289 DL136
Morris St, E1 20 F9
Morriston Cl, Wat. WD19 116 BW50
Morris Wk, Dart. DA1
off Birdwood Ave 190 FN82
Morris Way, Lon.Col. AL2 83 CK26
Morse Cl, E13 23 N3
Harefield UB9 114 BJ54
Morshead Mans, W9
off Morshead Rd 15 K3
Morshead Rd, W9 15 K3
Morson Rd, Enf. EN3 105 DY44
Morston Cl, Tad. KT20
off Waterfield 255 CV120
Morston Gdns, SE9 207 EM91

Mortain Dr, Berk. HP4 60 AT17
Morten Cl, SW4 203 DK86
Morten Gdns, Denh. UB9 136 BG59
Mortens Wd, Amer. HP7 77 AR40
Morteyne Rd, N17 122 DR53
Mortham St, E15 13 J9
Mortimer Cl, NW2 141 CZ62
SW16 203 DK89
Bushey WD23 98 CB44
Mortimer Cres, NW6 5 L9
Saint Albans AL3 64 CA22
Worcester Park KT4 220 CR104
Mortimer Dr, Bigg.H. TN16 244 EJ112
Enf. EN1 104 DR43
Mortimer Est, NW6 5 L9
Mortimer Gate, Chsht EN8 89 DZ27
Mortimer Ho, W11 26 D2
off St. Anns Rd
Mortimer Mkt, WC1 17 M5
Mortimer Pl, NW6 5 L9
Mortimer Rd, E6 25 J3
N1 9 P7
NW10 14 A2
W13 159 CJ72
Erith DA8 189 FD79
Mitcham CR4 222 DF95
Orpington BR6 228 EU103
Slough SL3 174 AX76
Mortimer Sq, W11 26 D1
Mortimer St, W1 17 L8
Mortimer Ter, NW5 143 DH63
off Gordon Ho Rd
MORTLAKE, SW14 180 CQ83
⇌ Mortlake 180 CQ83
Mortlake Cl, Croy. CR0 223 DL104
Mortlake Dr, Mitch. CR4 222 DE95
Mortlake High St, SW14 180 CR83
Mortlake Rd, E16 24 B8
Ilford IG1 147 EQ63
Richmond TW9 180 CN80
Mortlake Sta Pas, SW14 180 CQ83
off Sheen La
Mortlake Ter, Rich. TW9 180 CN80
off Kew Rd
Mortlock Cl, SE15 44 E7
Morton, Tad. KT20 255 CX121
Morton Cl, E1 20 G9
Uxbridge UB8 156 BM70
Wallington SM6 241 DM108
Woking GU21 248 AW115
Morton Ct, Nthlt. UB5 138 CC64
Morton Cres, N14 121 DK49
Morton Dr, Slou. SL2 133 AL64
Morton Gdns, Wall. SM6 241 DJ106
Morton Ms, SW5 27 L9
Morton Pl, SE1 30 E7
Morton Rd, E15 13 L7
N1 9 K7
Morden SM4 222 DD99
Woking GU21 248 AW115
Morton Way, N14 121 DJ48
Morvale Cl, Belv. DA17 188 EZ77
Morval Rd, SW2 203 DN85
Morven Cl, Pot.B. EN6 86 DC31
Morven Rd, SW17 202 DF90
Morville Ho, SW18 202 DD86
off Fitzhugh Gro
Morville St, E3 12 A10
Morwell St, WC1 17 P7
Mosbach Gdns, Hutt. CM13 131 GB47
Moscow Pl, W2 15 L10
Moscow Rd, W2 15 L10
Moseley Row, SE10 35 M8
Moselle Av, N22 121 DN54
Moselle Cl, N8 off Miles Rd 143 DL55
Moselle Ho, N17 122 DT52
off William St
Moselle Pl, N17 122 DT52
Moselle Rd, Bigg.H. TN16 260 EL118
Sch Moselle Sch, Main Site, N17 122 DS54
off Adams Rd
Sch Moselle Spec Sch, Upr Sch,
N17 off Downhills Pk Rd 144 DQ55
Moselle St, N17 122 DT52
Mosford Cl, Horl. RH6 290 DF146
Mospey Cres, Epsom KT17 255 CT115
Mosquito Cl, Wall. SM6 241 DL108
Mosquito Way, Hat. AL10 66 CS17
Moss Bk, Grays RM17 192 FZ78
Mossborough Cl, N12 120 DB51
Sch Mossbourne Comm Acad,
E5 10 D2
Mossbury Rd, SW11 182 DE83
Moss Cl, E1 20 D6
N9 122 DU46
Pinner HA5 116 BZ54
Rickmansworth WD3 114 BK47
Moss Ct, Seer Grn HP9 111 AR51
off Orchard Rd
Mossdown Cl, Belv. DA17 188 FA77
Mossendew Cl, Hare. UB9 114 BK53
Mossfield, Cob. KT11 235 BU113
Mossford Ct, Ilf. IG6 147 EP55
Mossford Grn, Ilf. IG6 147 EP55
Sch Mossford Grn Prim Sch,
Barkingside IG6 125 EQ54
off Fairlop Rd
Mossford La, Ilf. IG6 125 EP54
Mossford St, E3 21 N4
Moss Gdns, Felt. TW13 197 BU89
South Croydon CR2 243 DX108
off Warren Av
Moss Grn, Welw.G.C. AL7 51 CY11
Moss Hall Ct, N12 120 DB51
Moss Hall Cres, N12 120 DB51
Moss Hall Gro, N12 120 DB51
Sch Moss Hall Inf Sch, N12 120 DB51
off Moss Hall Gro
Sch Moss Hall Jun Sch, N3 120 DB51
off Nether St
Mossington Gdns, SE16 32 G9
Moss La, Pnr. HA5 138 BZ55
Romford RM1 off Albert Rd 149 FF58
Mosslea Rd, SE20 204 DW94
Bromley BR2 226 EK99
Orpington BR6 227 EQ104
Whyteleafe CR3 258 DT116
Mossop St, SW3 28 D8
Moss Rd, Dag. RM10 168 FA66
South Ockendon RM15 171 FW71
Watford WD25 81 BV34
Moss Side, Brick.Wd AL2 82 BZ30
Mossville Gdns, Mord. SM4 221 CZ97
Moss Way, Beac. HP9 110 AJ51
Lane End DA2 211 FR91
Moston Cl, Hayes UB3 177 BT78
Mostyn Av, Wem. HA9 140 CM64
Mostyn Gdns, NW10 14 C2
Mostyn Gro, E3 21 P1
Mostyn Rd, SW9 42 E7
SW19 221 CZ95
Bushey WD23 98 CC43
Edgware HA8 118 CR52
Mostyn Ter, Red. RH1 288 DG135
Mosul Way, Brom. BR2 226 EL100
Mosyer Dr, Orp. BR5 228 EX103
Motcomb St, SW1 28 F6
Moth Cl, Wall. SM6 241 DL108
Mothers' Sq, E5 10 F1
Motherwell Way, Grays RM20 191 FU78
Motley Av, EC2 19 N4
Motley St, SW8 41 L8
MOTSPUR PARK, N.Mal. KT3 221 CV100
⇌ Motspur Park 221 CV99
Motspur Pk, N.Mal. KT3 221 CT100
MOTTINGHAM, SE9 206 EJ89
⇌ Mottingham 206 EL88
Mottingham Gdns, SE9 206 EK88
Mottingham La, SE9 206 EJ88
SE12 206 EJ88
Sch Mottingham Prim Sch, SE9
off Ravensworth Rd 207 EM90
Mottingham Rd, N9 105 DX44
SE9 206 EL89
Mottisfont Rd, SE2 188 EU76
Motts Hill La, Tad. KT20 255 CU123
Motts La, Dag. RM8 148 EZ61
off Becontree Av
Mott St, E4 105 ED38
High Beach IG10 106 EF39
Mouchotte Cl, Bigg.H. TN16 244 EH112
Moulins Rd, E9 11 H7
Moulsford Ho, N7 7 P3
Moultain Hill, Swan. BR8 229 FG98
Moulton Av, Houns. TW3 178 BY82
Moultrie Way, Upmin. RM14 151 FS59
Mound, The, SE9 207 EN90
Moundfield Rd, N16 144 DU58
Moundsfield Way, Slou. SL1 173 AL75
Mount, The, E5 144 DV61
N20 120 DC47
NW3 off Heath St 142 DC63
W3 160 CP74
Brentwood CM14 130 FW48
Cheshunt EN7 88 DR26
Coulsdon CR5 256 DG115
Esher KT10 236 CA107
Ewell KT17 239 CT110
Fetcham KT22 253 CE123
Guildford GU1, GU2 280 AV137
Lower Kingswood KT20 271 CZ126
New Malden KT3 221 CT97
Potters Bar EN6 86 DB30
Rickmansworth WD3 96 BJ44
Romford RM3 128 FJ48
St. John's GU21 248 AU119
Virginia Water GU25 214 AX100
Warlingham CR6 258 DU119
Wembley HA9 140 CP61
Weybridge KT13 217 BS103
Woking GU21 248 AX118
Worcester Park KT4 239 CV105
Mountacre Cl, SE26 204 DT91
Mount Adon Pk, SE22 204 DU87
Mountague Pl, E14 22 E10
Mountain Ho, SE11 30 C10
H Mount Alvernia Hosp,
Guil. GU1 280 AY136
Mount Angelus Rd, SW15 201 CT87
Mount Ararat Rd, Rich. TW10 200 CL85
Mount Ash Rd, SE26 204 DV90
Mount Av, E4 123 EA48
W5 159 CK71
Brentwood CM13 131 GA44
Chaldon CR3 258 DQ124
Romford RM3 128 FQ51
Southall UB1 158 CA72
Mountbatten Cl, SE18 187 ES79
SE19 204 DS92
St. Albans AL1 65 CH23
Slough SL1 174 AU76
Mountbatten Ct, SE16 33 H3
off Rotherhithe St
Buckhurst Hill IG9 124 EK47
Mountbatten Gdns, Beck. BR3 225 DY98
off Balmoral Av
Mountbatten Ms, SW18 202 DC88
off Inman Rd
Mountbatten Sq, Wind. SL4 173 AQ81
off Ward Royal
Mountbel Rd, Stan. HA7 117 CG53
Sch Mount Carmel RC Prim Sch,
W5 off Little Ealing La 179 CJ77
Sch Mount Carmel RC Tech Coll
for Girls, N19 143 DK60
off Holland Wk
Mount Cl, W5 159 CJ71
Bromley BR1 226 EL95
Carshalton SM5 240 DG109
Cockfosters EN4 102 DG42
Farnham Common SL2 133 AQ63
Fetcham KT22 253 CE123
Hemel Hempstead HP1 61 BF20
Kenley CR8 258 DQ116
Sevenoaks TN13 278 FF123
Woking GU22 248 AV121
Mount Cl, The, Vir.W. GU25 214 AX100
Mountcombe Cl, Surb. KT6 220 CL101
Mount Cor, Felt. TW13 198 BX89
Mount Ct, SW15 181 CY83
off Weimar St
Guildford GU2 280 AW136
off The Mount
West Wickham BR4 226 EE103
Mount Cres, Warley CM14 130 FX49
Mount Culver Av, Sid. DA14 208 EX93
Mount Dr, Bexh. DA6 208 EY85
Harrow HA2 138 BZ57
Park Street AL2 83 CD25
Wembley HA9 140 CQ61
Mount Dr, The, Reig. RH2 272 DC132
Mountearl Gdns, SW16 203 DM90
Mount Echo Av, E4 123 EB47
Mount Echo Dr, E4 123 EB46
MOUNT END, Epp. CM16 92 EZ32
Mount Ephraim La, SW16 203 DK90
Mount Ephraim Rd, SW16 203 DK90
Mount Felix, Walt. KT12 217 BT102
Mountfield Cl, SE6 205 ED87
Mountfield Rd, E6 25 L1
N3 142 DA55
W5 159 CK72
Hemel Hempstead HP2 62 BL20
Mountfield Ter, SE6 205 ED87
off Mountfield Cl
Mountfield Way, Orp. BR5 228 EW98
Mountford Mans, SW11 41 H7
Mountfort Cres, N1 8 E6
Mountfort Ter, N1 8 E7
Mount Gdns, SE26 204 DV90
Mount Grace Rd, Pot.B. EN6 86 DA31
Sch Mount Grace Sch, Pot.B. EN6
off Church Rd 86 DB30
Mount Gro, Edg. HA8 118 CQ48
Mountgrove Rd, N5 143 DP62
Mount Harry Rd, Sev. TN13 278 FG123
MOUNT HERMON, Wok.
GU22 248 AX118
Mount Hermon Cl, Wok. GU22 248 AX118
Mount Hermon Rd, Wok.
GU22 248 AX119
Mount Hill La, Ger.Cr. SL9 134 AV60
Mount Holme, T.Ditt. KT7 219 CH101
Mounthurst Rd, Brom. BR2 226 EF101
Mountington Pk Cl, Har. HA3 139 CK58
Mountjoy Cl, SE2 188 EV75
Mountjoy Ho, EC2 19 K7
off The Barbican
Mount La, Denh. UB9 135 BD61
Mount Lee, Egh. TW20 194 AY92
Mount Ms, Hmptn. TW12 218 CB95
Mount Mills, EC1 19 H3
Mountnessing Bypass, Brwd.
CM15 131 GD41
Jct Mountnessing Rbt, Brwd.
CM15 131 GC41
Mount Nod Rd, SW16 203 DM90
Mount Nugent, Chesh. HP5 76 AN27
Mount Pk, Cars. SM5 240 DG109
Mount Pk Av, Har. HA1 139 CD61
South Croydon CR2 241 DP109
Mount Pk Cres, W5 159 CK72
Mount Pk Rd, W5 159 CK71
Harrow HA1 139 CD62
Pinner HA5 137 BU57
Mount Pl, W3 off High St 160 CP74
Guildford GU2 280 AW136
off The Mount
Mount Pleasant, SE27 204 DQ91
WC1 18 D5
Barnet EN4 102 DE42
Biggin Hill TN16 260 EK117
Effingham KT24 268 BY128
Epsom KT17 239 CT110
Guildford GU2 280 AW136
Harefield UB9 114 BG53
Hertford Heath SG13 54 DW11
Ruislip HA4 138 BW61
St. Albans AL3 64 CB19
Wembley HA0 160 CL67
West Horsley KT24 267 BP129
Weybridge KT13 216 BN104
Mount Pleasant Av, Hutt.
CM13 131 GE44
Mount Pleasant Cl, Hat. AL9 67 CW15
Mount Pleasant Cres, N4 143 DM59
Mount Pleasant Est, Ilf. IG1 147 EQ64
off Ilford La
Mount Pleasant Hill, E5 144 DV61
Mount Pleasant La, E5 144 DV61
Bricket Wood AL2 82 BY30
Hatfield AL9 51 CW14
Sch Mount Pleasant La JMI Sch,
Brick.Wd AL2 82 BY30
off Mount Pleasant La
Mount Pleasant Pl, SE18 187 ER77
Mount Pleasant Rd, E17 123 DY54
N17 122 DS54
NW10 4 B7
SE13 205 EB86
W5 159 CJ70
Caterham CR3 258 DU123
Chigwell IG7 125 ER49
Dartford DA1 210 FM86
New Malden KT3 220 CQ97
Romford RM5 127 FD51
Mount Pleasant Vil, N4 143 DM59
Mount Pleasant Wk, Bex. DA5 209 FC85
Sch Mount Prim Sch, The, N.Mal.
KT3 off Dickerage La 220 CP97
Mount Ri, Red. RH1 288 DD136
Mount Rd, NW2 141 CV62
NW4 141 CU58
SE19 204 DR93
SW19 202 DA89
Barnet EN4 102 DE43
Bexleyheath DA6 208 EX85
Chessington KT9 238 CM106
Chobham GU24 232 AV112
Dagenham RM8 148 EZ60
Dartford DA1 209 FF86
Epping CM16 92 EW32
Feltham TW13 198 BY90
Hayes UB3 177 BT75
Hertford SG14 53 DN10
Ilford IG1 147 EP64
Mitcham CR4 222 DE96
New Malden KT3 220 CR97
Woking GU22 248 AV121
Mount Row, W1 29 J1
Sch Mount Sch, The, NW7
off Milespit Hill 119 CV50
Mountsfield Cl, Stai. TW19 196 BG86
Mountsfield Ct, SE13 205 ED86
Mountside, Felt. TW13 198 BY90
Guildford GU2 280 AV136
Stanmore HA7 117 CF53
Mountsorrel, Hert. SG13 54 DT08
Mounts Pond Rd, SE3 46 G8
Mount Sq, The, NW3 142 DC62
off Heath St
Mounts Rd, Green. DA9 211 FV85
Mount Stewart Av, Har. HA3 139 CK58
Sch Mount Stewart Inf Sch,
Kenton HA3 139 CK59
off Carlisle Gdns
Sch Mount Stewart Jun Sch,
Kenton HA3 139 CK59
off Mount Stewart Av
Mount St, W1 29 H1
Dorking RH4 285 CG136
Mount St Ms, W1 29 J1
Mount Ter, E1 20 E7
Mount Vernon, NW3 142 DC63
H Mount Vernon Hosp, Nthwd.
HA6 115 BP51
Mount Vw, NW7 118 CR48
W5 159 CK70
Enfield EN2 103 DM38
London Colney AL2 84 CL27
Mountview, Nthwd. HA6 115 BT51
Mount Vw, Rick. WD3 114 BH46
Coll Mountview Acad of Thea Arts,
Crouch End, N8 143 DL58
off Crouch Hill
Wood Grn, N22 121 DM54
off Kingfisher Pl
Mountview Cl, NW11 142 DB60
Redhill RH1 288 DE136
Mountview Ct, N8 143 DP56
off Green Las
Mountview Dr, Red. RH1 288 DD136
Mount Vw Rd, E4 123 EC45
N4 143 DL59
NW9 140 CR56
Mountview Rd, Chsht EN7 88 DS26
Claygate KT10 237 CH108
Orpington BR6 228 EU101
Mount Vil, SE27 203 DP90
Mount Way, Cars. SM5 240 DG109
Mountway, Pot.B. EN6 86 DA30
Welwyn Garden City AL7 51 CZ12
Mountway Cl, Welw.G.C. AL7 51 CZ12
Mountwood, W.Mol. KT8 218 CA97
Mountwood Cl, S.Croy. CR2 242 DV110
Jct Movers La, Bark. IG11 167 ES68
Movers La, Bark. IG11 167 ER67
● Mowat Ind Est, Wat. WD24 98 BW38
Mowatt Cl, N19 143 DK60
Mowbray Av, Byfleet KT14 234 BL113
Mowbray Cres, Egh. TW20 195 BA92
Mowbray Gdns, Dor. RH4 269 CH134
Mowbray Rd, NW6 4 E6
SE19 224 DT95
Edgware HA8 118 CN49
Harlow CM20 57 ET13
New Barnet EN5 102 DC42
Richmond TW10 199 CJ90
Mowbrays Cl, Rom. RM5 127 FC53
Mowbrays Rd, Rom. RM5 127 FC54
Mowbrey Gdns, Loug. IG10 107 EQ40
Sch Mowlem Prim Sch, E2 10 G10
Mowlem St, E2 10 F10
● Mowlem Trd Est, N17 122 DW52
Mowll St, SW9 42 E5
Moxey Cl, Bigg.H. TN16 244 EJ113
Moxom Av, Chsht EN8 89 DY30
Moxon Cl, E13 23 M1
Moxon St, W1 16 G7
Barnet EN5 101 CZ41
Moye Cl, E2 10 D10
Moyers Rd, E10 145 EC59
Moylan Rd, W6 38 F3
Moyne Ct, Wok. GU21 248 AT118
off Iveagh Rd
Moyne Pl, NW10 160 CN68
Moynihan Dr, N21 103 DL43
Moys Cl, Croy. CR0 223 DL100
Moyser Rd, SW16 203 DH92
Mozart St, W10 14 G3
Mozart Ter, SW1 29 H9
Muchelney Rd, Mord. SM4 222 DC100
Muckhatch La, Egh. TW20 215 BB97
MUCKINGFORD, S.le H. SS17 193 GM76
Muckingford Rd, Linford SS17 193 GM77
West Tilbury RM18 193 GL77
DLR Mudchute 34 D9
Muddy La, Slou. SL2 154 AS71
● Mudlands Ind Est, Rain.
RM13 169 FE69
Mud La, W5 159 CK71
Mudlarks Boul, SE10 35 M6
off John Harrison Way
Muggeridge Cl, S.Croy. CR2 242 DR106
Muggeridge Rd, Dag. RM10 149 FB63
MUGSWELL, Couls. CR5 272 DB125
Muirdown Av, SW14 180 CQ84
Muir Dr, SW18 202 DE86
Muirfield, W3 160 CS72
Muirfield Cl, SE16 44 F1
Watford WD19 116 BW49
Muirfield Cres, E14 34 C6
Muirfield Grn, Wat. WD19 116 BW49
Muirfield Rd, Wat. WD19 116 BX49
Woking GU21 248 AU118
Muirkirk Rd, SE6 205 EC88
Muir Rd, E5 144 DU62
Muir St, E16 37 J3
Mulberry Av, Stai. TW19 196 BL88
Windsor SL4 174 AT82
● Mulberry Business Cen,
SE16 33 K5
Mulberry Cl, E4 123 EA47
N8 143 DL57
NW3 6 A1
NW4 141 CW55
SE7 186 EK79
SE22 204 DU85
SW3 off Beaufort St 40 B3
SW16 203 DJ91
Amersham HP7 94 AT39
Barnet EN4 102 DD42
Broxbourne EN10 71 DZ24
Feltham TW13 197 BV90
Northolt UB5 158 BY68
off Parkfield Av
Park Street AL2 82 CB28
Romford RM2 149 FH56
Watford WD17 97 BS36
Weybridge KT13 217 BP104
Woking GU21 232 AY114
● Mulberry Ct, Dart. DA1 209 FE85
off Bourne Ind Pk
Mulberry Ct, EC1 19 H3
off Tompion St
N2 off Great N Rd 142 DE55
Barking IG11 167 ET65
Beaconsfield HP9 133 AM55
Guildford GU4 265 BD132
off Gilliat Dr
Surbiton KT6 219 CK101
Mulberry Cres, Brent. TW8 179 CH80
West Drayton UB7 176 BN75
Mulberry Dr, Purf. RM19 190 FM77
Slough SL3 174 AY78
Mulberry Gdns, Harl. CM17 58 EX11
Shenley WD7 84 CL33
Mulberry Gate, Bans. SM7 255 CZ116
Mulberry Grn, Harl. CM17 58 EX11
Mulberry Hill, Shenf. CM15 131 FZ45
Sch Mulberry Ho Sch, The,
NW2 4 F3
Mulberry La, Croy. CR0 224 DT102
Mulberry Mead, Hat. AL10 51 CT14
Mulberry Ms, SE14 45 N6
Wallington SM6 241 DJ107
Mulberry Par, West Dr. UB7 176 BN76
Mulberry Pl, SE9 186 EK84
W6 off Chiswick Mall 181 CU78
Sch Mulberry Prim Sch, N17 122 DU54
off Parkhurst Rd
Mulberry Rd, E8 10 A6
Northfleet DA11 212 GE90
Sch Mulberry Sch for Girls, E1 20 E9
Coll Mulberry Sch for Girls -
St. George's, E1 20 E10
Mulberry St, E1 20 C8
Mulberry Tree Ms, W4 180 CQ75
off Clovelly Rd
Mulberry Trees, Shep. TW17 217 BQ101
Mulberry Wk, SW3 40 B2
Mulberry Way, E18 124 EH54
Belvedere DA17 189 FC75
Ilford IG6 147 EQ56
Mulgrave Rd, NW10 141 CT63
SE18 37 K9
SW6 38 G2
W5 159 CK69
Croydon CR0 224 DR104
Harrow HA1 139 CG61
Sutton SM2 240 DA107
Sch Mulgrave Sch & Early Years Cen,
SE18 37 N7
Mulgrave Way, Knap. GU21 248 AS118
Mulholland Cl, Mitch. CR4 223 DH96
Mulkern Rd, N19 143 DK60
Mullards Cl, Mitch. CR4 222 DF102
Mullein Ct, Grays RM17 192 GD79
Mullens Rd, Egh. TW20 195 BB92
Muller Ho, SE18 37 M10
Muller Rd, SW4 203 DK86
Mullet Gdns, E2 20 D2
Mullins Path, SW14 180 CR83
Mullion Cl, Har. HA3 116 CB53
Mullion Wk, Wat. WD19 116 BX49
off Ormskirk Rd
Mull Wk, N1 9 K5
Mulready St, NW8 16 C5
Mulready Wk, Hem.H. HP3 62 BL24
Multi Way, W3 180 CS75
Multon Rd, SW18 202 DD87
Mulvaney Way, SE1 31 M5
Mumford Mills, SE10 46 C6
Mumford Rd, SE24 203 DP85
Mumfords La, Chal.St.P. SL9 134 AU55
Muncaster Cl, Ashf. TW15 196 BN91
Muncaster Rd, SW11 202 DF85
Ashford TW15 197 BP92
Muncies Ms, SE6 205 EC89
Mundania Rd, SE22 204 DV86
Munday Rd, E16 23 N9
Mundells, Chsht EN7 88 DU27
Welwyn Garden City AL7 51 CZ07
Mundells Ct, Welw.G.C. AL7 51 CZ07
MUNDEN, Wat. WD25 82 CB34
Munden Dr, Wat. WD25 98 BY37
Munden Gro, Wat. WD24 98 BW38
Munden Ho, E3 22 D2
off Bromley High St
Munden St, W14 26 E8
Munden Vw, Wat. WD25 98 BX36
Mundesley Cl, Wat. WD19 116 BW49
Mundesley Spur, Slou. SL1 154 AS72
Mundford Rd, E5 144 DW61
Mundon Gdns, Ilf. IG1 147 ER60
Mund St, W14 39 H1
Mundy Ct, Eton SL4 173 AR80
off Eton Ct
Mundy St, N1 19 N2
Munford Dr, Swans. DA10 212 FY87
Mungo Pk Cl, Bushey Hth
WD23 116 CC47
Mungo Pk Rd, Grav. DA12 213 GK92
Rainham RM13 169 FG65
Mungo Pk Way, Orp. BR5 228 EW101
Munkenbeck, W2 16 A7
off Hermitage St
Munnery Way, Orp. BR6 227 EN104
Munnings Gdns, Islw. TW7 199 CD85
Munro Dr, N11 121 DJ51
Munro Ho, SE1 off Murphy St 30 E5
Munro Ms, W10 14 F6
Munro Ter, SW10 40 A3
Munslow Gdns, Sutt. SM1 240 DD105
Munstead Vw, Art. GU3 280 AV138
Munster Av, Houns. TW4 178 BZ84
Munster Ct, Tedd. TW11 199 CJ93
Munster Gdns, N13 121 DP49
Munster Ms, SW6 38 E4
Munster Rd, SW6 38 E4
Teddington TW11 199 CH93
Munster Sq, NW1 17 K3
Munton Rd, SE17 31 K8
Murchison Av, Bex. DA5 208 EX88
Murchison Rd, E10 145 EC61
Hoddesdon EN11 55 EB14
Murdoch Cl, Stai. TW18 196 BG92
Murdock Cl, E16 23 M8
Murdock St, SE15 44 E3
Murfett Cl, SW19 201 CY89
Murfitt Way, Upmin. RM14 150 FN63
Muriel Av, Wat. WD18 98 BW43
Muriel St, N1 8 D10
Murillo Rd, SE13 185 ED84
Murphy St, SE1 30 E5
Murray Av, Brom. BR1 226 EH96
Hounslow TW3 198 CB85
● Murray Business Cen, Orp.
BR5 228 EV97
Murray Cl, SE28 167 ES74
Murray Ct, W7 179 CE76
Murray Cres, Pnr. HA5 116 BX53
Murray Grn, Wok. GU21 233 BC114
off Bunyard Dr
Murray Gro, N1 19 K1
Murray Ms, NW1 7 N6
Murray Rd, SW19 201 CX93
W5 179 CJ77
Berkhamsted HP4 60 AV18
Northwood HA6 115 BS53
Orpington BR5 228 EV97
Ottershaw KT16 233 BC107
Richmond TW10 199 CH89
Murrays La, Byfleet KT14 234 BK114
Murray Sq, E16 23 P9
Murray St, NW1 7 M6
Murrays Yd, SE18 37 N8
Murray Ter, NW3 off Flask Wk 142 DD63
W5 off Murray Rd 179 CK77
Murrells Wk, Bkhm KT23 252 CA123
Murreys, The, Ashtd. KT21 253 CK118
Mursell Est, SW8 42 C6
Murthering La, Rom. RM4 109 FG43
Murton Ct, St.Alb. AL1 65 CE19
Murtwell Dr, Chig. IG7 125 EQ51
Musard Rd, W6 38 F2
W14 38 F2

Musbury St, E1 20 G8
Muscal, W6 38 E2
Muscatel Pl, SE5 43 P5
Sch Muschamp Prim Sch, Cars.
SM5 off Muschamp Rd 222 DE103
Muschamp Rd, SE15 184 DT83
Carshalton SM5 222 DE103
Muscovy Ho, Erith DA18
off Kale Rd 188 EY75
Muscovy St, EC3 31 P1
Museum La, SW7 28 B7
★ Museum of Childhood at
Bethnal Grn, E2 20 F2
★ Museum of Croydon, Croy.
CR0 224 DQ104
★ Museum of Harlow, Harl.
CM20 58 EV12
★ Museum of Instruments
(Royal Coll of Music), SW7 28 A6
★ Museum of London, EC2 19 J7
★ Museum of London
Docklands, E14 34 B1
★ Museum of Richmond,
Rich. TW9 199 CK85
★ Museum of St. Albans,
St.Alb. AL1 65 CE19
Museum Pas, E2 20 G2
Museum St, WC1 18 A7
Museum Way, W3 180 CN75
Musgrave Cl, Barn. EN4 102 DC39
Cheshunt EN7 off Allwood Rd 88 DT27
Musgrave Cres, SW6 39 K5
Musgrave Rd, Islw. TW7 179 CF81
Musgrove Cl, Ken. CR8 241 DM113
Musgrove Rd, SE14 45 K7
Musjid Rd, SW11 40 B9
Muskalls Cl, Chsht EN7 88 DU27
Musket Cl, E.Barn. EN4
off East Barnet Rd 102 DD43
Muskham Rd, Harl. CM20 58 EU12
Musk Hill, Hem.H. HP1 61 BE21
Musleigh Manor, Ware SG12 55 DZ06
Musley Hill, Ware SG12 55 DY05
Musley La, Ware SG12 55 DY05
Musquash Way, Houns. TW4 178 BW82
Mussenden La, Fawk.Grn DA3 231 FS101
Horton Kirby DA4 230 FQ99
Mustard Mill Rd, Stai. TW18 195 BF91
Muston Rd, E5 144 DV61
Mustow Pl, SW6 39 H8
Muswell Av, N10 121 DH54
MUSWELL HILL, N10 143 DH55
Muswell Hill, N10 143 DH55
Muswell Hill Bdy, N10 143 DH55
Muswell Hill Pl, N10 143 DH56
Sch Muswell Hill Prim Sch, N10
off Muswell Hill 143 DH55
Muswell Hill Rd, N6 142 DG58
N10 142 DG56
Muswell Ms, N10 143 DH55
Muswell Rd, N10 143 DH55
Mutchetts Cl, Wat. WD25 82 BY33
Mutrix Rd, NW6 5 K8
Mutton La, Pot.B. EN6 85 CY31
Mutton Pl, NW1 7 H5
Muybridge Rd, N.Mal. KT3 220 CQ96
Sch Myatt Gdn Prim Sch, SE4 45 P8
Myatt Rd, SW9 42 G6
Myatts Flds S, SW9
off St. Lawrence Way 42 F8
Myatts N, SW9
off Fairbairn Grn 42 F6
Mycenae Rd, SE3 47 N4
Myddelton Av, Enf. EN1 104 DS38
Myddelton Cl, Enf. EN1 104 DT39
Myddelton Gdns, N21 121 DP45
Myddelton Pk, N20 120 DD48
Myddelton Pas, EC1 18 F2
Myddelton Rd, N8 143 DL56
Myddelton Sq, EC1 18 F2
Myddelton St, EC1 18 F3
Myddleton Av, N4 144 DQ61
Myddleton Cl, Stan. HA7 117 CG47
Myddleton Ct, Horn. RM11 149 FF59
Myddleton Ms, N22 121 DL52
Myddleton Path, Chsht EN7 88 DV31
Myddleton Rd, N22 121 DL52
Uxbridge UB8 156 BJ67
Ware SG12 55 DX07
Myers Cl, Shenley WD7 84 CL32
Myers Dr, Slou. SL2 133 AP64
Myers La, SE14 45 J2
Mygrove Cl, Rain. RM13 170 FK68
Mygrove Gdns, Rain. RM13 170 FK68
Mygrove Rd, Rain. RM13 170 FK68
Myles Ct, Goffs Oak EN7 88 DQ29
Mylis Cl, SE26 204 DV91
Mylius Cl, SE14 45 H6
Mylne Cl, W6 181 CU78
Cheshunt EN8 88 DW27
Mylner Ct, Hodd. EN11
off Ditchfield Rd 71 EA15
Mylne St, EC1 18 E1
Mylor Cl, Wok. GU21 232 AY114
Mymms Dr, Brook.Pk AL9 86 DA26
Mynchen Cl, Beac. HP9 111 AK49
Mynchen End, Beac. HP9 111 AK49
Mynchen Rd, Beac. HP9 111 AK50
Mynns Cl, Epsom KT18 238 CP114
Mynterne Ct, SW19
off Swanton Gdns 201 CX88
MYNTHURST, Reig. RH2 287 CV144
Myra St, SE2 188 EU78
Myrdle St, E1 20 D7
Myrke, The, Datchet SL3 174 AT77
Myrna Cl, SW19 202 DE94
Myron Pl, SE13 185 EC83
Myrtle All, SE18 37 M7
Myrtle Av, Felt. TW14 177 BS84
Ruislip HA4 137 BU59
Myrtleberry Cl, E8 10 A5
Myrtle Cl, Colnbr. SL3 175 BE81
East Barnet EN4 120 DF46
Erith DA8 189 FE81
Uxbridge UB8 156 BM71
West Drayton UB7 176 BM76
Myrtle Cres, Slou. SL2 154 AT73
Myrtledene Rd, SE2 188 EU78
Myrtle Gdns, W7 159 CE74
Myrtle Grn, Hem.H. HP1
off Newlands Rd 61 BE19
Myrtle Gro, Aveley RM15 190 FQ75
Enfield EN2 104 DR38
New Malden KT3 220 CQ96
Myrtle Pl, Dart. DA2 211 FR87
Myrtle Rd, E6 166 EL67
E17 145 DY58
N13 122 DQ48
W3 160 CQ74
Croydon CR0 225 EA104
Dartford DA1 210 FK88
Dorking RH4 285 CG135
Hampton Hill TW12 199 CC93
Hounslow TW3 178 CC82
Ilford IG1 147 EP61
Romford RM3 128 FJ51
Sutton SM1 240 DC106
Warley CM14 130 FW49
Myrtleside Cl, Nthwd. HA6 115 BR52
Myrtle Wk, N1 19 N1
Mysore Rd, SW11 182 DF83
Myton Rd, SE21 204 DR90

N

● N17 Studios, N17 122 DT52
N1 Shop Cen, N1 8 F10
Nacovia Ho, SW6
off Townmead Rd 39 P8
Nadine Ct, Wall. SM6
off Woodcote Rd 241 DJ109
Nadine St, SE7 186 EJ78
Nafferton Ri, Loug. IG10 106 EK43
Nagle Cl, E17 123 ED54
Jct Nags Head, N7 143 DM63
Nags Head Cen, N7 143 DM63
Nags Head Cl, Hert. SG13 54 DV08
Nag's Head Ct, EC1 19 J5
Nags Head La, Brwd. CM14 129 FR51
Upminster RM14 128 FQ53
Welling DA16 188 EV83
Nags Head Rd, Enf. EN3 104 DW42
Nailsworth Cres, Merst. RH1 273 DK129
Nailzee Cl, Ger.Cr. SL9 134 AY59
Nairn Ct, Til. RM18
off Dock Rd 193 GF82
Nairne Gro, SE24 204 DR85
Nairn Grn, Wat. WD19 115 BU48
Nairn Rd, Ruis. HA4 158 BW65
Nairn St, E14 22 F7
Nalders Rd, Chesh. HP5 76 AR29
NALDERSWOOD, Reig. RH2 287 CW144
Nallhead Rd, Felt. TW13 198 BW92
Namba Roy Cl, SW16 203 DM91
Namton Dr, Th.Hth. CR7 223 DM98
Nan Clark's La, NW7 119 CT47
Nancy Downs, Wat. WD19 116 BW45
Nankin St, E14 22 B9
Nansen Rd, SW11 182 DG84
Gravesend DA12 213 GK92
Nansen Village, N12 120 DB49
Nant Ct, NW2
off Granville Rd 141 CZ61
Nanterre Ct, Wat. WD17 97 BU40
Nantes Cl, SW18 182 DC84
Nantes Pas, E1 20 A6
Nant Rd, NW2 141 CZ61
Nant St, E2 20 F2
Naoroji St, WC1 18 E3
Nap, The, Kings L. WD4 80 BN29
Napier Av, E14 34 B10
SW6 38 G10
Napier Cl, SE8 45 P4
W14 26 G6
Hornchurch RM11 149 FH60
London Colney AL2 83 CK25
West Drayton UB7 176 BM76
Napier Ct, SE12 206 EH90
SW6 off Ranelagh Gdns 38 G10
Cheshunt EN8
off Flamstead End Rd 88 DV28
Surbiton KT6 219 CK100
Napier Dr, Bushey WD23 98 BY42
Napier Gdns, Guil. GU1 265 BB133
Napier Gro, N1 19 K1
Napier Ho, Rain. RM13 169 FF69
Napier Pl, W14 26 G7
Napier Rd, E6 167 EN67
E11 146 EE63
E15 23 K1
N17 144 DS55
NW10 161 CV69
SE25 224 DV98
W14 26 G7
Ashford TW15 197 BR94
Belvedere DA17 188 EZ77
Bromley BR2 226 EH98
Enfield EN3 105 DX43
Isleworth TW7 179 CG84
London Heathrow Airport
TW6 176 BK81
Northfleet DA11 213 GF88
South Croydon CR2 242 DR108
Wembley HA0 139 CK64
Napier Ter, N1 8 G7
Napier Wk, Ashf. TW15 197 BR94
Napoleon Rd, E5 144 DV62
Twickenham TW1 199 CH87
Napsbury Av, Lon.Col. AL2 83 CJ26
Napsbury La, St.Alb. AL1 65 CG23
Napton Cl, Hayes UB4 158 BY70
Narbonne Av, SW4 203 DJ85
Narboro Ct, Rom. RM1 149 FG58
Narborough Cl, Uxb. UB10 137 BQ61
Narborough St, SW6 39 L9
Narcissus Rd, NW6 5 J3
Narcot La, Ch.St.G. HP8 112 AU48
Chalfont St. Peter SL9 112 AV52
Narcot Rd, Ch.St.G. HP8 112 AU48
Narcot Way, Ch.St.G. HP8 112 AU49
Nare Rd, Aveley RM15 170 FQ73
Naresby Fold, Stan. HA7 117 CJ51
Narford Rd, E5 144 DU62
Narrow Boat Cl, SE28
off Ridge Cl 187 ER75
Narrow La, Warl. CR6 258 DV119
Narrow St, E14 21 L10
Narrow Way, Brom. BR2 226 EL100
Nascot Pl, Wat. WD17 97 BV39
Nascot Rd, Wat. WD17 97 BV40
Nascot St, W12 14 A8
Watford WD17 97 BV40
Sch Nascot Wd Inf & Nurs Sch, Wat.
WD17 off Nascot Wd Rd 97 BU38
Sch Nascot Wd Jun Sch, Wat.
WD17 off Nascot Wd Rd 97 BU38
Nascot Wd Rd, Wat. WD17 97 BT37
Naseberry Ct, E4
off Merriam Cl 123 EC50
Naseby Cl, NW6 6 P6
Isleworth TW7 179 CE81
Naseby Ct, Walt. KT12
off Clements Rd 218 BW103
Naseby Rd, SE19 204 DR93
Dagenham RM10 148 FA62
Ilford IG5 125 EM53
Nash Cl, Els. WD6 100 CM42
North Mymms AL9 67 CX23
Sutton SM1 222 DD104
Coll Nash Coll, Brom. BR2
off Croydon Rd 226 EF104
Nash Cft, Nthflt DA11 212 GE91
Nashdom La, Burn. SL1 152 AG66
Nash Dr, Red. RH1 272 DF132
Nashes Farm La, St.Alb. AL4 66 CL15
Nash Gdns, Red. RH1 272 DF132
Nash Grn, Brom. BR1 206 EG93
Hemel Hempstead HP3 80 BM25
Nash Ho, SW1 41 K1
Nash La, Kes. BR2 244 EG106
Nashleigh Hill, Chesh. HP5 76 AQ29
Sch Nash Mills C of E Prim Sch,
Hem.H. HP3
off Belswains La 80 BM25
Nash Mills La, Hem.H. HP3 80 BM26
Nash Rd, N9 122 DW47
SE4 185 DX84
Romford RM6 148 EX56
Slough SL3 175 AZ77
Nash St, NW1 17 K3
Nash's Yd, Uxb. UB8
off George St 156 BK66
Nash Way, Kenton HA3 139 CH58
Nasmyth St, W6 181 CV76
Nassau Path, SE28
off Disraeli Cl 168 EW74
Nassau Rd, SW13 181 CT81
Nassau St, W1 17 L7
Nassington Rd, NW3 142 DE63
Natalie Cl, Felt. TW14 197 BR87
Natalie Ms, Twick. TW2
off Sixth Cross Rd 199 CD90
Natal Rd, N11 121 DL51
SW16 203 DK93
Ilford IG1 147 EP63
Thornton Heath CR7 224 DR97
Nathan Ct, Upmin. RM14 151 FS60
Nathaniel Cl, E1 20 B7
Nathans Rd, Wem. HA0 139 CJ61
Nathan Way, SE28 187 ES77
★ National Archives, The, Rich.
TW9 180 CP80
★ National Army Mus, SW3 40 F2
H National Blood Service,
Brentwood Transfusion Cen,
Brwd. CM15 131 FZ46
N London Blood Transfusion Cen,
NW9 118 CR54
S Thames Blood Transfusion Cen,
SW17 202 DD92
Coll National Film & Television Sch
Beaconsfield Studios, Beac.
HP9 off Station Rd 111 AL54
★ National Gall, WC2 29 P1
H National Hosp for Neurology &
Neurosurgery, The, WC1 18 B5
★ National Maritime Mus,
SE10 46 G3
★ National Portrait Gall, WC2 29 P1
Coll National Sch of Govt, SW1 29 L9
National Ter, SE16
off Bermondsey Wall E 32 E5
★ National Thea, SE1 30 D2
National Wks, Houns. TW4
off Bath Rd 178 BZ83
Nation Way, E4 123 EC46
★ Natural History Mus, SW7 28 A7
Natwoke Cl, Beac. HP9 111 AK50
Naunton Way, Horn. RM12 150 FK62
Naval Row, E14 22 F10
Naval Wk, Brom. BR1
off High St 226 EG96
Navarino Gro, E8 10 D4
Navarino Rd, E8 10 D4
Navarre Ct, Kings L. WD4
off Primrose Hill 81 BP28
Navarre Gdns, Rom. RM5 127 FB51
Navarre Rd, E6 166 EL68
Navarre St, E2 20 A4
Navenby Wk, E3 22 B4
Navestock Cl, E4
off Mapleton Rd 123 EC48
Navestock Cres, Wdf.Grn. IG8 124 EJ53
Navigation Bldg, Hayes UB3
off Station Rd 177 BT76
Navigation Ct, E16
off Albert Basin Way 167 EQ73
Navigation Dr, Enf. EN3 105 EA38
Navigator Dr, Sthl. UB2 178 CC75
Navy St, SW4 41 N10
Naxos Bldg, E14 34 A5
Nayim Pl, E8 10 E3
Nayland Ct, Rom. RM1
off Market Pl 149 FE56
Naylor Gro, Enf. EN3
off South St 105 DX43
Naylor Rd, N20 120 DC47
SE15 44 E4
Naylor Ter, Colnbr. SL3
off Vicarage Way 175 BC80
Nazareth Gdns, SE15 44 E8
NAZEING, Wal.Abb. EN9 72 EJ22
Nazeingbury Cl, Lwr Naze.
EN9 71 ED22
Nazeingbury Par, Wal.Abb. EN9
off Nazeing Rd 71 ED22
Nazeing Common, Naze. EN9 72 EH24
NAZEING GATE, Wal.Abb. EN9 90 EJ25
Nazeing New Rd, Brox. EN10 71 EA21
Sch Nazeing Prim Sch, Naze. EN9
off Hyde Mead 72 EE23
Nazeing Rd, Lwr Naze. EN9 71 EC22
Nazeing Wk, Rain. RM13
off Ongar Way 169 FF67
Nazrul St, E2 20 A2
● NCR Business Cen, NW10
off Great Cen Way 140 CS64
Neagle Cl, Borwd. WD6
off Balcon Way 100 CQ39
Neal Av, Sthl. UB1 158 BZ70
Neal Cl, Ger.Cr. SL9 135 BB60
Northwood HA6 115 BU53
Neal Ct, Hert. SG14 54 DQ09
Waltham Abbey EN9 90 EF33
Nealden St, SW9 42 C10
Neale Cl, N2 142 DC55
Neal St, WC2 18 A9
Watford WD18 98 BW43
Neal's Yd, WC2 18 A9
Near Acre, NW9 119 CT53
NEASDEN, NW2 140 CS62
⊖ Neasden 140 CS64
Neasden Cl, NW10 140 CS64
Jct Neasden Junct, NW10
off North Circular Rd 140 CS63
Neasden La, NW10 140 CS63
Neasden La N, NW10 140 CR62
Neasham Rd, Dag. RM8 148 EV64
Neatby Ct, Chsht EN8
off Coopers Wk 89 DX28
Neate St, SE5 44 A2
Neath Gdns, Mord. SM4 222 DC100
Neathouse Pl, SW1 29 L8
Neats Acre, Ruis. HA4 137 BR59
Neatscourt Rd, E6 24 F7
Neave Cres, Rom. RM3 128 FJ53
Neb La, Oxt. RH8 275 EC131
Nebraska Bldg, SE13
off Deals Gateway 46 C7
Nebraska St, SE1 31 L5
★ NEC Harlequins RFC, Twick.
TW2 199 CE87
Neckinger, SE16 32 B6
Neckinger Est, SE16 32 B6
Neckinger St, SE1 32 B5
Nectarine Way, SE13 46 D8
Necton Rd, Wheat. AL4 50 CL07
Needham Cl, Wind. SL4 173 AL81
Needham Ct, Enf. EN3
off Manton Rd 105 EA37
Needham Rd, W11 15 J9
Needham Ter, NW2
off Kara Way 141 CX62
Needleman St, SE16 33 J5
Needles Bk, Gdse. RH9 274 DV131
Neela Cl, Uxb. UB10 137 BP63
Neeld Cres, NW4 141 CV57
Wembley HA9 140 CN64
Neeld Par, Wem. HA9
off Harrow Rd 140 CN64
Neil Cl, Ashf. TW15 197 BQ92
Neild Way, Rick. WD3 113 BF45
Neil Wates Cres, SW2 203 DN88
Nelgarde Rd, SE6 205 EA87
Nella Rd, W6 38 C3
Nelldale Rd, SE16 32 G8
Nellgrove Rd, Uxb. UB10 157 BP70
Nell Gwynn Cl, Shenley WD7 84 CL32
Nell Gwynne Av, Shep. TW17 217 BR100
Nell Gwynne Cl, Epsom KT19 238 CN111
Nello James Gdns, SE27 204 DR91
Nelmes Cl, Horn. RM11 150 FM57
Nelmes Cres, Horn. RM11 150 FL57
Sch Nelmes Prim Sch, Horn. RM11
off Wingletye La 150 FM56
Nelmes Rd, Horn. RM11 150 FL59
Nelmes Way, Horn. RM11 150 FL56
Nelson Av, St.Alb. AL1 65 CH23
Nelson Cl, NW6 15 J2
Biggin Hill TN16 260 EL117
Croydon CR0 223 DP102
Feltham TW14 197 BT88
Romford RM7 127 FB53
Slough SL3 174 AX77
Uxbridge UB10 157 BP69
Walton-on-Thames KT12 217 BV102
Warley CM14 130 FX50
Nelson Ct, SE16
off Brunel Rd 33 H3
Gravesend DA12 213 GJ88
Nelson Gdns, E2 20 D2
Guildford GU1 265 BA133
Hounslow TW3 198 CA86
Nelson Gro Rd, SW19 222 DB95
H Nelson Hosp, SW20 221 CZ96
Nelson Ho, Green. DA9 211 FW85
Nelson La, Uxb. UB10 157 BP69
Nelson Mandela Cl, N10 120 DG54
Nelson Mandela Ho, N16
off Cazenove Rd 144 DU61
Nelson Mandela Rd, SE3 186 EJ83
Nelson Pas, EC1 19 K3
Nelson Pl, N1 19 H1
Sidcup DA14
off Sidcup High St 208 EU91
Sch Nelson Prim Sch, E6
off Napier Rd 167 EN68
Whitton TW2 off Nelson Rd 198 CB87
Nelson Rd, E4 123 EB51
E11 146 EG56
N8 143 DM57
N9 122 DV47
N15 144 DS56
SE10 46 F3
SW19 202 DB94
Ashford TW15 196 BL92
Belvedere DA17 188 EZ78
Bromley BR2 226 EJ98
Caterham CR3 258 DR123
Dartford DA1 210 FJ86
Enfield EN3 105 DX44
Harrow HA1 139 CD60
Hounslow TW3, TW4 198 CA86
London Heathrow Airport
TW6 176 BM81
New Malden KT3 220 CR99
Northfleet DA11 213 GF89
Rainham RM13 169 FF68
Sidcup DA14
off Sidcup High St 208 EU91
South Ockendon RM15 171 FW68
Stanmore HA7 117 CJ51
Twickenham TW2 198 CC86
Uxbridge UB10 157 BP69
Windsor SL4 173 AM83
★ Nelson's Column, WC2 30 A2
Nelson Sq, SE1 30 G4
Nelson's Row, SW4 183 DK84
Nelson St, E1 20 E8
E6 167 EM68
E16 23 L10
Hertford SG14 53 DP08
Nelsons Yd, NW1 7 L10
Nelson Ter, N1 19 H1
● Nelson Trd Est, SW19 222 DB95
Nelson Wk, E3 22 D4
SE16 33 M3
Epsom KT19 238 CN109
Nelwyn Av, Horn. RM11 150 FM57
Nemor Ct, Edg. HA8
off Atlas Cres 118 CQ47
Nemoure Rd, W3 160 CQ73
Nene Gdns, Felt. TW13 198 BZ89
Nene Rd, Lon.Hthrw Air. TW6 177 BP81
Nepaul Rd, SW11 40 C9
Nepean St, SW15 201 CU86
Neptune Cl, Rain. RM13 169 FF68
Neptune Ct, Borwd. WD6
off Clarendon Rd 100 CN41
Neptune Dr, Hem.H. HP2 62 BL18
Neptune Ho, E3
off Garrison Rd 12 A9
Neptune Rd, Har. HA1 139 CD58
London Heathrow Airport
TW6 177 BR81
Neptune St, SE16 32 G6
Neptune Wk, Erith DA8 189 FD77
Neptune Way, Slou. SL1
off Hunters Way 173 AL75
Nero Ct, Brent. TW8
off Justin Cl 179 CK80
Nesbit Rd, SE9 186 EK84
Nesbitt Cl, SE3 47 J9
Nesbitts All, Barn. EN5
off Bath Pl 101 CZ41
Nesbitt Sq, SE19
off Coxwell Rd 204 DS94
Coll Nescot, Ewell KT17
off Reigate Rd 239 CU111
Nesham St, E1 32 C2
Ness Rd, Erith DA8 190 FK79
Ness St, SE16 32 C6
Nesta Rd, Wdf.Grn. IG8 124 EE51
Nestles Av, Hayes UB3 177 BT76
Neston Rd, Wat. WD24 98 BW37
Nestor Av, N21 103 DP44
Nethan Dr, Aveley RM15 170 FQ73
Netheravon Rd, W4 181 CT77
W7 159 CF74
Netheravon Rd S, W4 181 CT78
Netherbury Rd, W5 179 CK76
Netherby Gdns, Enf. EN2 103 DL42
Netherby Pk, Wey. KT13 235 BS106
Netherby Rd, SE23 204 DW87
Nether Cl, N3 120 DA52
Nethercote Av, Wok. GU21 248 AT117
Nethercourt Av, N3 120 DA51
Netherfield Ct, Stans.Abb.
SG12 55 ED12
Netherfield Gdns, Bark. IG11 167 ER65
Netherfield La, Stans.Abb.
SG12 56 EE12
Netherfield Rd, N12 120 DB50
SW17 202 DG90
Netherford Rd, SW4 41 M9
Netherhall Gdns, NW3 5 P4
Netherhall Rd, Roydon CM19 72 EF17
Netherhall Way, NW3 5 P3
Netherheys Dr, S.Croy. CR2 241 DP108
Netherlands, The, Couls. CR5 257 DJ119
Netherlands Rd, New Barn.
EN5 102 DD44
Netherleigh Cl, N6 143 DH60
Netherleigh Pk, Red. RH1 289 DL137
Nether Mt, Guil. GU2 280 AV136
Nethern Ct Rd, Wold. CR3 259 EA123
Netherne Dr, Couls. CR5 257 DH121
Netherne La, Couls. CR5 257 DK121
Merstham RH1 257 DJ123
Netherpark Dr, Rom. RM2 127 FF54
Nether St, N3 120 DA53
N12 120 DB50
Netherton Gro, SW10 39 P3
Netherton Rd, N15 144 DR58
Twickenham TW1 199 CG85
Netherway, St.Alb. AL3 64 CA23
Netherwood, N2 120 DD54
Netherwood Pl, W14 26 C6
Netherwood Rd, W14 26 C6
Beaconsfield HP9 111 AK50
Netherwood St, NW6 5 H6
Netley Cl, Goms. GU5 283 BQ138
New Addington CR0 243 EC108
Sutton SM3 239 CX106
Netley Dr, Walt. KT12 218 BZ101
Netley Gdns, Mord. SM4 222 DC101
Sch Netley Prim Sch, NW1 17 L3
Netley Rd, E17 145 DZ57
Brentford TW8 180 CL79
Ilford IG2 147 ER57
London Heathrow Airport
TW6 177 BR81
Morden SM4 222 DC101
Netley St, NW1 17 L3
NETTESWELL, Harl. CM20 57 ET14
Netteswellbury Fm, Harl.
CM18 73 ET16
Netteswell Orchard, Harl.
CM20 57 ER14
Netteswell Rd, Harl. CM20 57 ES12
Netteswell Twr, Harl. CM20 57 ER14
Nettlecombe Cl, Sutt. SM2 240 DB109
Nettlecroft, Hem.H. HP1 62 BH21
Welwyn Garden City AL7 52 DB08
Nettleden Av, Wem. HA9 160 CN65
Nettleden Rd, Hem.H. HP1 61 BB15
Potten End HP4 61 BA16
Nettlefold Pl, SE27 203 DP90
Nettlestead Cl, Beck. BR3 225 DZ95
Nettles Ter, Guil. GU1 264 AX134
Nettleton Rd, SE14 45 K6
London Heathrow Airport
TW6 177 BP81
Uxbridge UB10 136 BM63
Nettlewood Rd, SW16 203 DK94
Neuchatel Rd, SE6 205 DZ89
Nevada Bldg, SE10
off Blackheath Rd 46 C6
Nevada Cl, N.Mal. KT3 220 CQ98
Nevada St, SE10 46 F4
Navarre Ct, Kings L. WD4
off Primrose Hill 81 BP28
Nevell Rd, Grays RM16 193 GH76
Nevern Pl, SW5 27 K9
Nevern Rd, SW5 27 J9
Nevern Sq, SW5 27 K9
Nevil Cl, Nthwd. HA6 115 BQ50
Neville Av, N.Mal. KT3 220 CR95
Neville Cl, E11 146 EF62
NW1 17 P1
NW6 15 H1
SE15 44 C5
W3 off Acton La 180 CQ75
Banstead SM7 240 DB114
Esher KT10 236 BZ107
Hounslow TW3 178 CB82
Potters Bar EN6 85 CZ31
Sidcup DA15 207 ET91
Stoke Poges SL2 154 AT65
Neville Ct, Slou. SL1
off Dropmore Rd 152 AJ69
Uxb. UB3 off Uxbridge Rd 157 BS71
Neville Dr, N2 142 DC58

Neville Gdns, Dag. RM8 **148** EX62
Neville Gill Cl, SW18 **202** DA86
Neville Pl, N22 **121** DM53
Neville Rd, E7 **13** P7
NW6 **15** H1
W5 **159** CK70
Croydon CR0 **224** DR101
Dagenham RM8 **148** EX61
Ilford IG6 **125** EQ53
Kingston upon Thames KT1 **220** CN96
Richmond TW10 **199** CJ90
Nevilles Ct, NW2 **141** CU62
Neville St, SW7 **28** A10
Neville Ter, SW7 **28** A10
Neville Wk, Cars. SM5 **222** DE101
Nevill Gro, Wat. WD24 **97** BV39
Nevill Rd, N16 **144** DS63
Nevill Way, Loug. IG10
off Valley Hill **106** EL44
Nevin Dr, E4 **123** EB46
Nevinson Cl, SW18 **202** DD86
Nevis Cl, E13 **24** B1
Rom. RM1 **127** FE51
Nevis Rd, SW17 **202** DG89
New Acres Rd, SE28 **187** ES75
NEW ADDINGTON, Croy. CR0 **243** ED109
Tra **New Addington** **243** EC110
Newall Ct, W12
off Heathstan Rd **161** CU72
Newall Ho, SE1 **31** K6
Newall Rd, Lon.Hthrw Air.
TW6 **177** BQ81
New Arc, Uxb. UB8
off High St **156** BK67
Newark Cl, Guil. GU4
off Dairyman's Wk **265** BB129
Ripley GU23 **250** BG121
Newark Cotts, Ripley GU23 **250** BG121
Newark Ct, Walt. KT12 **218** BW102
Newark Cres, NW10 **160** CR69
Newark Grn, Borwd. WD6 **100** CR41
Newark Knok, E6 **25** L8
Newark La, Ripley
GU22, GU23 **249** BF118
Newark Rd, S.Croy. CR2 **242** DR107
Newark St, E1 **20** E7
Newark Way, NW4 **141** CU56
New Ash Cl, N2 **142** DD55
New Atlas Wf, E14 **33** P7
New Barn Cl, Wall. SM6 **241** DM107
New Barnes Av, St.Alb. AL1 **65** CG23
NEW BARNET, Barn. EN5 **102** DB42
⇌ **New Barnet** **102** DD43
New Barn La, Cudham TN14 **261** EQ116
Newbarn La, Seer Grn HP9 **112** AS49
New Barn La, West. TN16 **261** EQ118
Whyteleafe CR3 **258** DS117
New Barn Rd, Sthflt DA13 **212** GC90
Swanley BR8 **229** FE95
New Barns Av, Mitch. CR4 **223** DK98
New Barn St, E13 **23** P4
New Barns Way, Chig. IG7 **125** EP48
New Battlebridge La, Red.
RH1 **273** DH130
Sch **New Beacon Sch, The**,
Sev. TN13
off Brittains La **278** FG127
NEW BECKENHAM, Beck.
BR3 **205** DZ93
⇌ **New Beckenham** **205** DZ94
New Bell Yd, EC4 *off Carter La* **19** H9
Newberries Av, Rad. WD7 **99** CJ35
Sch **Newberries Prim Sch**, Rad.
WD7 *off Newberries Av* **99** CJ36
Newberry Cres, Wind. SL4 **173** AK82
New Berry La, Hersham KT12 **236** BX106
Newbery Rd, Erith DA8 **189** FF81
Newbery Way, Slou. SL1 **173** AR75
Newbiggin Path, Wat. WD19 **116** BW49
Newbolt Av, Sutt. SM3 **239** CW106
Newbolt Rd, Stan. HA7 **117** CF51
New Bond St, W1 **17** J9
Newborough Grn, N.Mal. KT3 **220** CR98
New Brent St, NW4 **141** CW57
Newbridge Pt, SE23
off Windrush La **205** DX90
Sch **Newbridge Sch**,
Barley La Campus, Ilf. IG3
off Barley La **148** EV57
Loxford La Campus, Ilf. IG3
off Loxford La **147** ES63
New Br St, EC4 **18** G9
New Broad St, EC2 **19** N7
New Bdy, W5 **159** CJ73
Hampton Hill TW12
off Hampton Rd **199** CD92
Uxb. UB10 *off Uxbridge Rd* **157** BP69
New Bdy Bldgs, W5
off New Bdy **159** CK73
Newburgh Rd, W3 **160** CQ74
Grays RM17 **192** GD78
Newburgh St, W1 **17** L9
New Burlington Ms, W1 **17** L10
New Burlington Pl, W1 **17** L10
New Burlington St, W1 **17** L10
Newburn St, SE11 **42** D1
Newbury Av, Enf. EN3 **105** DZ38
Newbury Cl, Dart. DA2
off Lingfield Av **210** FP87
Northolt UB5 **158** BZ65
Romford RM3 **128** FK51
Newbury Gdns, Epsom KT19 **239** CT105
Romford RM3 **128** FK51
Upminster RM14 **150** FM62
Newbury Ho, N22 **121** DL53
Newbury Ms, NW5 **7** H5
NEWBURY PARK, Ilf. IG2 **147** ER57
⊖ **Newbury Park** **147** ER58
Sch **Newbury Pk Prim Sch**,
Barkingside IG2
off Perrymans Fm Rd **147** ER58
Newbury Rd, E4 **123** EC51
Bromley BR2 **226** EG97
Ilford IG2 **147** ES58
London Heathrow Airport
TW6 **176** BM81
Romford RM3 **128** FK50
Newbury St, EC1 **19** J7
Newbury Wk, Rom. RM3 **128** FK50
Newbury Way, Nthlt. UB5 **158** BY65
New Butt La, SE8 **46** B5
New Butt La N, SE8 **46** B5
Newby Cl, Enf. EN1 **104** DS40
Newby Pl, E14 **22** E10
Newby St, SW8 **41** K10
New Caledonian Wf, SE16 **33** N6
Newcastle Av, Ilf. IG6 **126** EU51
Newcastle Cl, EC4 **18** G8
Newcastle Pl, W2 **16** B7
Newcastle Row, EC1 **18** F4
New Causeway, Reig. RH2 **288** DB137
New Cavendish St, W1 **17** K6
New Change, EC4 **19** J9
New Chapel Rd, Felt. TW13
off High St **197** BV88
New Chapel Sq, Felt. TW13 **197** BV88
New Charles St, EC1 **19** H2
NEW CHARLTON, SE7 **36** C8
New Ch Ct, SE19
off Waldegrave Rd **204** DU94
New Ch Rd, SE5 **43** K4
Newchurch Rd, Slou. SL2 **153** AM71
Sch **New City Prim Sch**, E13 **24** D3
New City Rd, E13 **24** C2
New Clocktower Pl, N7 **8** A4
New Cl, SW19 **222** DC97
Feltham TW13 **198** BY92
New Coll Ct, NW3
off Finchley Rd **5** P5
New Coll Ms, N1 **8** F6
New Coll Par, NW3
off Finchley Rd **6** A5
Newcombe Gdns, SW16 **203** DL91
Hounslow TW4 **178** BZ84
Newcombe Pk, NW7 **118** CS50
Wembley HA0 **160** CM67
Newcombe Ri, West Dr. UB7 **156** BL72
Newcombe St, W8 **27** K2
Newcomen Rd, E11 **146** EF62
SW11 **182** DD83
Newcomen St, SE1 **31** L4
Newcome Path, Shenley WD7
off Newcome Rd **84** CN34
Newcome Rd, Shenley WD7 **84** CN34
New Compton St, WC2 **17** P9
New Concordia Wf, SE1 **32** B4
New Coppice, Wok. GU21 **248** AT119
New Cotts, Wenn. RM13 **170** FJ72
New Ct, EC4 **18** E10
Addlestone KT15 **216** BJ104
Northolt UB5 **138** CB64
Newcourt, Uxb. UB8 **156** BJ71
Newcourt St, NW8 **16** C1
🔒 **New Covent Gdn Flower Mkt**,
SW8 **41** P3
🔒 **New Covent Gdn Mkt**,
SW8 **41** N5
New Crane Pl, E1 **32** G2
Newcroft Cl, Uxb. UB8 **156** BM71
NEW CROSS, SE14 **45** L6
⇌ **New Cross** **45** P5
⊖ **New Cross** **45** P5
Jct **New Cross**, SE14 **45** N5
NEW CROSS GATE, SE14 **45** J6
⇌ **New Cross Gate** **45** L5
⊖ **New Cross Gate** **45** L5
New Cross Rd, SE14 **45** H5
Guildford GU2 **264** AU132
New Cut, Slou. SL1 **152** AG70
Newdales Cl, N9 **122** DU47
Newdene Av, Nthlt. UB5 **158** BX68
Newdigate Grn, Hare. UB9 **114** BK53
Newdigate Rd, Hare. UB9 **114** BJ53
Leigh RH2 **286** CS141
Newdigate Rd E, Hare. UB9 **114** BK53
New Ealing Bdy, W5
off Haven Grn **159** CK73
Newell Ri, Hem.H. HP3 **62** BL23
Newell Rd, Hem.H. HP3 **62** BL23
Newell St, E14 **21** N9
NEW ELTHAM, SE9 **207** EN89
⇌ **New Eltham** **207** EP88
New End, NW3 **142** DC63
Sch **New End Prim Sch**, NW3
off Streatley Pl **142** DC63
New End Sq, NW3 **142** DD63
● **New England Ind Est**, Bark.
IG11 **167** EQ68
New England St, St.Alb. AL3 **64** CC20
Newenham Rd, Bkhm KT23 **268** CA126
Newent Cl, SE15 **43** N4
Carshalton SM5 **222** DF102
H **New Epsom & Ewell Cottage
Hosp**, Epsom KT19 **238** CL111
New Era Est, N1
off Whitmore Rd **9** N9
New Fm Av, Brom. BR2 **226** EG98
New Fm Cl, Stai. TW18 **216** BJ95
New Fm Dr, Abridge RM4 **108** EV41
New Fm La, Nthwd. HA6 **115** BS53
New Ferry App, SE18 **37** L6
New Fetter La, EC4 **18** F8
Newfield Cl, Hmptn. TW12 **218** CA95
Newfield La, Hem.H. HP2 **62** BL20
Sch **Newfield Prim Sch**, NW10
off Longstone Av **161** CT66
Newfield Ri, NW2 **141** CV62
Newfields, Welw.G.C. AL8 **51** CV10
Newfield Way, St.Alb. AL4 **65** CJ22
● **New Ford Business Cen**,
Wal.Cr. EN8 **89** DZ34
Newford Cl, Hem.H. HP2 **63** BP19
New Ford Rd, Wal.Cr. EN8 **89** DZ34
New Forest La, Chig. IG7 **125** EN51
● **New Frontiers Science Pk**,
Harl. CM19 **73** EM16
Newgale Gdns, Edg. HA8 **118** CM53
New Gdn Dr, West Dr. UB7
off Drayton Gdns **176** BL75
Newgate, Croy. CR0 **224** DQ102
Newgate Cl, Felt. TW13 **198** BY89
St. Albans AL4 **65** CK17
NEWGATE STREET, Hert. SG13 **69** DK24
Newgate St, E4 **124** EF48
EC1 **19** H8
Hertford SG13 **69** DK22
Newgatestreet Rd, Goffs Oak
EN7 **87** DP27
Newgate St Village, Hert. SG13 **87** DL25
New Globe Wk, SE1 **31** J2
New Goulston St, E1 **20** A8
New Grn Pl, SE19 **204** DS93
NEW GREENS, St.Alb. AL3 **65** CD16
New Grns Av, St.Alb. AL3 **65** CD15
New Hall Cl, Bov. HP3 **79** BA27
Newhall Ct, Wal.Abb. EN9 **90** EF33
New Hall Dr, Rom. RM3 **128** FL53
Newhall Gdns, Walt. KT12 **218** BW103
Newhall Ho, NW7
off Morphou Rd **119** CY50
Coll **Newham Acad of Music**, E6
off Wakefield St **166** EL67
H **Newham Cen for Mental
Health**, E13 **24** E5
Coll **Newham Coll of Further Ed**,
SE1 **31** P4
East Ham Campus, E6
off High St S **167** EM68
Coll **Newham Coll of Further Ed**,
Little Ilford Cen, E12
off Browning Rd **147** EM64
Stratford Campus, E15 **13** K7
● **Newham Dockside**, E16 **36** G1
Coll **Newham 6th Form Coll**,
Main Site, E13 **24** B4
Stratford Site, E15 **13** H7
Newhams Row, SE1 **31** P5
H **Newham Uni Hosp**, E13 **24** D4
Gateway Surgical Cen, E13 **24** E5
Newham Way, E6 **25** P2
E16 **23** N7
Newhaven Cl, Hayes UB3 **177** BT77
Newhaven Cres, Ashf. TW15 **197** BR92
Newhaven Gdns, SE9 **186** EK84
Newhaven La, E16 **23** M5
Newhaven Rd, SE25 **224** DR99
Newhaven Spur, Slou. SL2 **153** AP70
NEW HAW, Add. KT15 **234** BK108
Sch **New Haw Comm Jun Sch**,
New Haw KT15
off The Avenue **234** BG110
New Haw Rd, Add. KT15 **234** BJ106
New Heston Rd, Houns. TW5 **178** BZ80
New Hope Ct, NW10 **161** CV69
New Horizons, Borwd. WD6 **100** CQ40
● **New Horizons Ct**, Brent.
TW8 **179** CG79
Newhouse Av, Rom. RM6 **148** EX55
Newhouse Cl, N.Mal. KT3 **220** CS101
Newhouse Cres, Wat. WD25 **81** BV32
New Ho La, Grav. DA11 **213** GF90
North Weald Bassett CM16 **75** FC24
Redhill RH1 **289** DK142
New Ho Pk, St.Alb. AL1 **65** CG23
Newhouse Rd, Bov. HP3 **79** BA26
Newhouse Wk, Mord. SM4 **222** DC101
Newick Cl, Bex. DA5 **209** FB86
Newick Rd, E5 **144** DV62
Newing Grn, Brom. BR1 **206** EK94
NEWINGTON, SE1 **31** J8
Newington Barrow Way, N7 **143** DM62
Newington Butts, SE1 **31** H9
SE11 **31** H9
Newington Causeway, SE1 **31** H7
Newington Grn, N1 **9** M2
N16 **9** M2
Sch **Newington Grn Prim Sch**,
N16 **9** M2
Newington Grn Rd, N1 **9** L3
New Inn Bdy, EC2 **19** P4
New Inn La, Guil. GU4 **265** BB130
New Inn Pas, WC2 **18** D9
New Inn Sq, EC2 **19** P4
New Inn St, EC2 **19** P4
New Inn Yd, EC2 **19** P4
New James Ct, SE15
off Nunhead La **184** DV83
New Jersey Ter, SE15
off Nunhead La **184** DV83
New Jubilee Ct, Wdf.Grn. IG8
off Grange Av **124** EG52
New Kent Rd, SE1 **31** J7
St. Albans AL1 **65** CD20
Sch **New King's Prim Sch**, SW6 **39** H8
New Kings Rd, SW6 **38** F9
New King St, SE8 **46** A2
Newland Cl, Pnr. HA5 **116** BY51
St. Albans AL1 **65** CG23
Newland Ct, EC1 **19** L4
off St. Luke's Est
Wembley HA9 **140** CN61
Newland Dr, Enf. EN1 **104** DV39
Newland Gdns, W13 **179** CG75
Hertford SG13 **54** DS09
Sch **Newland Ho Sch**, Twick. TW1
off Waldegrave Pk **199** CF91
Newland Rd, N8 **143** DL55
Newlands, Hat. AL9 **67** CW16
Newlands, The, Wall. SM6 **241** DJ108
Newlands Av, Rad. WD7 **83** CF34
Thames Ditton KT7 **219** CE102
Woking GU22 **249** AZ121
Newlands Cl, Edg. HA8 **118** CL48
Hersham KT12 **236** BY105
Horley RH6 **290** DF146
Hutton CM13 **131** GD45
Southall UB2 **178** BY78
Wembley HA0 **159** CJ65
Newlands Cor, Guil. GU4 **282** BG136
Newlands Ct, SE9 **207** EN86
Caterham CR3 **258** DQ121
Newlands Cres, Guil. GU1 **281** AZ136
Newlands Dr, Colnbr. SL3 **175** BE83
Newlands Pk, SE26 **205** DX92
Bedmond WD5 **81** BT26
Newlands Pl, Barn. EN5 **101** CX43
Newlands Quay, E1 **32** G1
Newlands Rd, SW16 **223** DL96
Hemel Hempstead HP1 **61** BE19
Woodford Green IG8 **124** EF47
Newlands Ter, SW8
off Queenstown Rd **41** J8
Newland St, E16 **37** H3
Newlands Wk, Wat. WD25 **82** BX33
Newlands Way, Chess. KT9 **237** CJ106
Potters Bar EN6 **86** DB30
Newlands Wds, Croy. CR0 **243** DZ109
New La, Sutt.Grn GU4 **248** AY122
Newling Cl, E6 **25** K8
New Lo Dr, Oxt. RH8 **276** EF128
Sch **New Lo Sch**, Dor. RH4
off Chichester Rd **269** CH134
New London St, EC3 **19** P10
● **New Lydenburg Commercial Est**,
SE7 *off New Lydenburg St* **36** D7
New Lydenburg St, SE7 **36** D7
Newlyn Cl, Brick.Wd AL2 **82** BY30
Orpington BR6 **245** ET105
Uxbridge UB8 **156** BN71
Newlyn Gdns, Har. HA2 **138** BZ59
Newlyn Rd, N17 **122** DT53
Barnet EN5 **101** CZ42
Welling DA16 **187** ET82
NEW MALDEN, KT3 **220** CR97
⇌ **New Malden** **220** CS97
Newman Cl, Horn. RM11 **150** FL57
Newman Pas, W1 **17** M7
Newman Rd, E13 **24** A3
E17 **145** DX56
Bromley BR1 **226** EG95
Croydon CR0 **223** DM102
Hayes UB3 **157** BV73
Newmans Cl, Loug. IG10 **107** EP41
Newman's Ct, EC3 **19** M9
Newmans Dr, Hutt. CM13 **131** GC45
NEWMAN'S END, Harl. CM17 **59** FE10
Newmans Gate, Hutt.. CM13 **131** GC45
Newmans La, Loug. IG10 **107** EN41
Surbiton KT6 **219** CK100
Newmans Rd, Nthflt DA11 **213** GF89
Newman's Row, WC2 **18** D7
Newman St, W1 **17** M7
Newmans Way, Barn. EN4 **102** DC39
Newman Yd, W1 **17** M8
Newmarket Av, Nthlt. UB5 **138** CA64
Newmarket Ct, St.Alb. AL3 **64** CC19
Newmarket Grn, SE9
off Middle Pk Av **206** EK87
Newmarket Way, Horn. RM12 **150** FL63
Newmarsh Rd, SE28 **167** ET74
New Mill Rd, Orp. BR5 **228** EW95
Newminster Rd, Mord. SM4 **222** DC100
Sch **New Monument Prim Sch**,
Wok. GU22 *off Alpha Rd* **249** BC115
New Mt St, E15 **13** H8
Newnes Path, SW15
off Putney Pk La **181** CV84
Newnham Av, Ruis. HA4 **138** BW60
Newnham Cl, Loug. IG10 **106** EK44
Northolt UB5 **138** CC64
Slough SL2 **154** AU74
Thornton Heath CR7 **224** DQ96
Newnham Gdns, Nthlt. UB5 **138** CC64
Sch **Newnham Inf & Jun Schs**, Ruis.
HA4 *off Newnham Av* **138** BW60
Newnham Ms, N22 **121** DM53
Newnham Pl, Grays RM16 **193** GG77
Newnham Rd, N22 **121** DM53
Newnhams Cl, Brom. BR1 **227** EM97
Newnham Ter, SE1 **30** E6
Newnham Way, Har. HA3 **140** CL57
Sch **New N Comm Sch**, N1 **9** J8
New N Pl, EC2 **19** N5
New N Rd, N1 **19** M1
Ilford IG6 **125** ER52
Reigate RH2 **287** CZ137
New N St, WC1 **18** C6
Newnton Cl, N4 **144** DR59
New Oak Rd, N2 **120** DC54
New Orleans Wk, N19 **143** DK59
New Oxford St, WC1 **17** P8
New Par, Ashf. TW15
off Church Rd **196** BM91
Chorleywood WD3
off Whitelands Av **95** BC42
Croxley Green WD3
off The Green **96** BM44
New Par Flats, Chorl. WD3
off Whitelands Av **95** BC42
New Pk Av, N13 **122** DQ48
New Pk Cl, Nthlt. UB5 **158** BY65
New Pk Ct, SW2 **203** DL87
New Pk Dr, Hem.H. HP2 **63** BP19
● **New Pk Ind Est**, N18 **122** DW50
New Pk Par, SW2
off New Pk Rd **203** DL87
New Pk Rd, SW2 **203** DK88
Ashford TW15 **197** BQ92
Harefield UB9 **114** BJ53
Newgate Street SG13 **69** DK24
New Peachey La, Uxb. UB8 **156** BK72
Newpiece, Loug. IG10 **107** EP41
New Pl Gdns, Upmin. RM14 **151** FR61
New Pl Sq, SE16 **32** E6
New Plaistow Rd, E15 **13** K8
New Plymouth Ho, Rain.
RM13 **169** FF69
New Pond Par, Ruis. HA4
off West End Rd **137** BU62
Newport Av, E13 **24** B5
E14 **35** H1
Newport Cl, Enf. EN3 **105** DY37
Newport Ct, WC2 **17** P10
Newport Mead, Wat. WD19
off Kilmarnock Rd **116** BX49
Newport Pl, WC2 **17** P10
Newport Rd, E10 **145** EC61
E17 **145** DY56
SW13 **181** CU81
W3 **180** CQ75
Hayes UB4 **157** BR71
London Heathrow Airport
TW6 **176** BN81
Slough SL2 **153** AL70
Newports, Saw. CM21 **58** EW06
Swanley BR8 **229** FD101
Sch **Newport Sch**, E10
off Newport Rd **145** EC61
Newport St, SE11 **30** C9
New Priory Ct, NW6 **5** K7
New Providence Wf, E14 **34** G2
New Provident Pl, Berk. HP4
off Holliday St **60** AX19
Newquay Cres, Har. HA2 **138** BY61
Newquay Gdns, Wat. WD19
off Fulford Gro **115** BV47
Newquay Rd, SE6 **205** EB89
New Quebec St, W1 **16** F9
New Ride, SW7 **28** E4
Jct **New River Arms**, Brox.
EN10 **89** DY25
New River Av, N8 **143** DM55
Stanstead Abbotts SG12 **55** EB11
New River Cl, Hodd. EN11 **71** EB16
New River Ct, N5 **9** L1
Cheshunt EN7 **88** DV31
New River Cres, N13 **121** DP49
New River Head, EC1 **18** F2
● **New River Trd Est**, Chsht
EN8 **89** DX26
New River Wk, N1 **9** J5
New River Way, N4 **144** DR59
New Rd, E1 **20** E7
E4 **123** EB49
N8 **143** DL57
N9 **122** DV47
N17 **122** DT53
N22 **122** DQ53
NW7 **119** CY52
NW7 (Barnet Gate) **119** CT45
SE2 **188** EX77
Albury GU5 **282** BK139
Amersham HP6 **77** AS37
Berkhamsted HP4 **60** AX18
Brentford TW8 **179** CK79
Brentwood CM14 **130** FX47
Broxbourne EN10 **71** DZ19
Chalfont St. Giles HP8 **94** AY41
Chilworth GU4 **281** BB141
Chipperfield WD4 **79** BF30
Church End WD3 **95** BF39
Claygate KT10 **237** CF110
Coleshill HP7 **77** AM42
Croxley Green WD3 **96** BN43
Dagenham RM9, RM10 **168** FA67
Datchet SL3 **174** AX81
New Rd, Dorking RH5 **285** CK137
East Bedfont TW14 **197** BR86
East Clandon GU4 **266** BL131
Elstree WD6 **99** CK44
Epping CM16 **92** FA32
Esher KT10 **218** CC104
Feltham TW14 **197** BV88
Gomshall GU5 **283** BQ139
Gravesend DA11 **213** GH86
Grays RM17 **192** GA79
Grays (Bridge Rd) RM17 **192** GB79
Hanworth TW13 **198** BY92
Harlington UB3 **177** BQ80
Harlow CM17 **58** EX11
Harrow HA1 **139** CF63
Hertford SG14 **54** DQ07
Hextable BR8 **209** FF94
Hounslow TW3 **178** CB84
Ilford IG3 **147** ES61
Kingston upon Thames KT2 **200** CN94
Lambourne End RM4 **108** EX44
Langley SL3 **175** BA76
Leatherhead KT22 **237** CF110
Letchmore Heath WD25 **99** CE39
Limpsfield RH8 **276** EH130
Mitcham CR4 **222** DF102
Northchurch HP4 **60** AS17
Orpington BR6 **228** EU101
Penn HP10 **110** AC47
Radlett WD7 **99** CE36
Rainham RM13 **169** FG69
Richmond TW10 **199** CJ91
Shenley WD7 **84** CN34
Shepperton TW17 **217** BP97
Smallfield RH6 **291** DP148
South Darenth DA4 **230** FQ96
South Mimms EN6 **85** CU33
Staines-upon-Thames TW18 **195** BC92
Stanborough AL8 **51** CU12
Sundridge TN14 **262** EX124
Swanley BR8 **229** FF97
Tadworth KT20 **255** CW123
Uxbridge UB8 **157** BQ70
Ware SG12 **55** DX06
Watford WD17 **98** BW42
Welling DA16 **188** EV82
West Molesey KT8 **218** CA97
Weybridge KT13 **235** BQ106
Wonersh GU5 **281** BB143
New Rd Hill, Downe BR6 **244** EL109
Keston BR2 **244** EL109
New Row, WC2 **18** A10
Sch **New Rush Hall Sch**, Ilf. IG6
off Fencepiece Rd **125** EQ52
Newry Rd, Twick. TW1 **179** CG84
Newsam Av, N15 **144** DR57
Sch **New Sch at W Heath, The**, Sev.
TN13 *off Ashgrove Rd* **279** FH129
★ **New Scotland Yd**, SW1 **29** N6
Newsham Rd, Wok. GU21 **248** AT117
Newsholme Dr, N21 **103** DM43
Newsom Pl, St.Alb. AL1 **65** CE19
NEW SOUTHGATE, N11 **121** DK49
⇌ **New Southgate** **121** DH50
● **New Southgate Ind Est**,
N11 **121** DJ50
🔒 **New Spitalfields Mkt**, E10 **145** EA62
New Spring Gdns Wk, SE11 **42** B1
● **New Sq**, Felt. TW14 **197** BQ88
New Sq, WC2 **18** D8
Slough SL1 **174** AS75
Newstead, Hat. AL10 **67** CT21
Newstead Av, Orp. BR6 **227** ER104
Newstead Cl, N12 **120** DE51
Newstead Ri, Cat. CR3 **274** DV126
Newstead Rd, SE12 **206** EE87
Newstead Wk, Cars. SM5 **222** DC101
Newstead Way, SW19 **201** CX91
Harlow CM20 **57** EQ13
Sch **Newstead Wd Sch for Girls**,
Orp. BR6 *off Avebury Rd* **227** ER104
New St, EC2 **19** P7
Berkhamsted HP4 **60** AX19
Staines-upon-Thames TW18 **196** BG91
Watford WD18 **98** BW42
Westerham TN16 **277** EQ127
New St Hill, Brom. BR1 **206** EH92
New St Sq, EC4 **18** F8
New Swan Yd, Grav. DA12
off Bank St **213** GH86
New Tank Hill Rd, Purf. RM19 **190** FN76
Newteswell Dr, Wal.Abb. EN9 **89** ED32
Newton Abbot Rd, Nthflt
DA11 **213** GF89
Newton Av, N10 **120** DG53
W3 **180** CQ75
Newton Cl, E17 **145** DY58
Harrow HA2 **138** CA61
Hoddesdon EN11 **55** EB13
Slough SL3 **175** AZ75
Newton Ct, Old Wind. SL4 **194** AU86
Newton Cres, Borwd. WD6 **100** CQ42
Newton Dr, Saw. CM21 **58** EX06
Sch **Newton Fm First & Mid Sch**,
S.Har. HA2
off Ravenswood Cres **138** BZ61
Newton Gro, W4 **180** CS77
Newton Ho, Enf. EN3
off Exeter Rd **105** DX41
● **Newton Ind Est**, Rom.
RM6 **148** EX56
Newton La, Old Wind. SL4 **194** AV86
Newton Lo, SE10 **35** M7
Newton Pk Pl, Chis. BR7 **207** EM94
Newton Pl, E14 **34** A8
Sch **Newton Prep Sch**, SW8 **41** K6
Newton Rd, E15 **13** H2
N15 **144** DT57
NW2 **141** CW62
SW19 **201** CY94
W2 **15** K9
Chigwell IG7 **126** EV50
Harrow HA3 **117** CE54
Isleworth TW7 **179** CF82
Purley CR8 **241** DJ112
Tilbury RM18 **193** GG82
Welling DA16 **188** EU83
Wembley HA0 **160** CM66
Newtons Cl, Rain. RM13 **169** FF66
Jct **Newtons Cor**, Rain. RM13 **169** FE66
● **Newtons Ct**, Dart. DA2 **191** FR84

Newtonside Orchard, Wind. SL4 194 AU86
Sch Newtons Prim Sch, Rain. RM13 off Lowen Rd 169 FD68
Newton St, WC2 18 B8
Newtons Yd, SW18 off Wandsworth High St 202 DA85
Newton Wk, Edg. HA8 off Roscoff Cl 118 CQ53
Newton Way, N18 122 DQ50
Newton Wd, Ashtd. KT21 238 CL114
Newton Wd Rd, Ashtd. KT21 254 CM116
NEWTOWN, Chesh. HP5 76 AP30
NEW TOWN, Dart. DA1 210 FN86
Sch Newtown Inf Sch & Nurs, Chesh. HP5 off Berkhampstead Rd 76 AQ29
Newtown Rd, Denh. UB9 156 BH65
Newtown St, SW11 41 J6
New Trinity Rd, N2 142 DD55
New Turnstile, WC1 18 C7
New Union Cl, E14 34 F6
New Union St, EC2 19 L7
H New Victoria Hosp, The, Kings.T. KT2 220 CS95
New Wanstead, E11 146 EF58
New Way La, Thres.B. CM17 75 FB16
New Way Rd, NW9 140 CS56
New Wf Rd, N1 8 B10
New Wickham La, Egh. TW20 195 BA94
New Windsor St, Uxb. UB8 156 BJ67
New Wd, Welw.G.C. AL7 52 DC08
Sch New Woodlands Sch, Brom. BR1 off Shroffold Rd 206 EE91
NEWYEARS GREEN, Uxb. UB9 136 BN59
New Years Grn La, Hare. UB9 136 BL58
New Years La, Knock. TN14 261 ET116
New Zealand Av, Walt. KT12 217 BT102
New Zealand Way, W12 161 CV73
Rainham RM13 169 FF69
Nexus Ct, E11 off Kirkdale Rd 146 EE59
Niagara Av, W5 179 CJ77
Niagara Cl, N1 off Cropley St 9 K10
Cheshunt EN8 89 DX29
Nibthwaite Rd, Har. HA1 139 CE57
● Nice Business Pk, SE15 44 F3
Sch Nicholas Breakspear RC Sch, St.Alb. AL4 off Colney Heath La 66 CL21
Nicholas Cl, Grnf. UB6 158 CB68
St. Albans AL3 65 CD17
South Ockendon RM15 171 FW69
Watford WD24 97 BV37
Nicholas Ct, E13 24 B3
N7 8 C3
Nicholas Gdns, W5 179 CK75
Slough SL1 153 AL74
Woking GU22 249 BE116
Nicholas La, EC4 19 M10
Hertford SG14 off Old Cross 54 DQ09
Nicholas Ms, W4 off Short Rd 180 CS79
Nicholas Pas, EC4 19 M10
Nicholas Rd, E1 21 H4
W11 26 C1
Croydon CR0 241 DL105
Dagenham RM8 148 EZ61
Elstree WD6 100 CM44
Nicholas Way, Hem.H. HP2 62 BM18
Northwood HA6 115 BQ53
Nicholay Rd, N19 143 DK61
Nichol Cl, N14 121 DK46
Nicholes Rd, Houns. TW3 178 CA84
Nichol La, Brom. BR1 206 EG94
Nicholl Rd, Epp. CM16 91 ET31
Nicholls, Wind. SL4 172 AJ83
Nicholls Av, Uxb. UB8 156 BN70
Nicholls Cl, Cat. CR3 258 DQ122
Nicholls Fld, Harl. CM18 74 EV16
Nichollsfield Wk, N7 8 C3
Nicholls Pt, E15 13 P8
Nicholls Twr, Harl. CM18 74 EU16
Nicholl St, E2 10 C9
Nichols Cl, N4 off Osborne Rd 143 DN60
Chessington KT9 off Merritt Gdns 237 CJ107
Nichols Ct, E2 20 A1
Nichols Grn, W5 160 CL71
● Nicholson Ct, Hodd. EN11 71 EB17
Nicholson Rd, Croy. CR0 224 DT102
Nicholson St, SE1 30 G3
Nicholson Wk, Egh. TW20 195 BA92
Nicholson Way, Sev. TN13 279 FK122
Nickelby Cl, SE28 168 EW72
Nickleby Cl, Uxb. UB8 157 BP72
Nickols Wk, SW18 off Jew's Row 182 DB84
Nicola Cl, Har. HA3 117 CD54
South Croydon CR2 242 DQ107
Nicola Ms, Ilf. IG6 125 EP52
Nicolas Wk, Grays RM16 off Godman Rd 193 GH75
Nicol Cl, Chal.St.P. SL9 112 AX53
Twickenham TW1 off Cassilis Rd 199 CH86
Nicol End, Chal.St.P. SL9 112 AW53
Nicoll Pl, NW4 141 CV58
Nicoll Rd, NW10 160 CS67
Nicoll Way, Borwd. WD6 100 CR43
Nicol Rd, Chal.St.P. SL9 112 AW53
Nicolson Dr, Bushey Hth WD23 116 CC46
Nicolson Rd, Orp. BR5 228 EX101
Nicosia Rd, SW18 202 DE87
Nidderdale, Hem.H. HP2 off Wharfedale 62 BM17
Nido Twr, E1 20 A7
Niederwald Rd, SE26 205 DY91
Nield Rd, Hayes UB3 177 BT75
Nigel Cl, Nthlt. UB5 158 BY67
Nigel Fisher Way, Chess. KT9 237 CJ108
Nigel Ms, Ilf. IG1 147 EP63
Nigel Playfair Av, W6 off King St 181 CV77
Nigel Rd, E7 146 EJ64
SE15 44 C10
Nigeria Rd, SE7 186 EJ80
Nightingale Av, E4 124 EE50
Harrow HA1 139 CH59
Upminster RM14 151 FT60
West Horsley KT24 251 BR124
Nightingale Cl, E4 124 EE49
W4 180 CQ79
Abbots Langley WD5 81 BU31
Biggin Hill TN16 260 EJ115
Carshalton SM5 222 DG103
Cobham KT11 236 BX111
Epsom KT19 238 CN112
Northfleet DA11 212 GE91
Pinner HA5 138 BW57
Radlett WD7 99 CF36
Nightingale Ct, E11 off Nightingale La 146 EH57
Hertford SG14 54 DQ09
Slough SL1 off St. Laurence Way 174 AU76
Sutton SM1 off Lind Rd 240 DC106
Woking GU21 off Inkerman Way 248 AT118
Nightingale Cres, Harold Wd RM3 128 FL54
West Horsley KT24 251 BQ124
Nightingale Dr, Epsom KT19 238 CP107
Nightingale Est, E5 144 DU62
Nightingale Gro, SE13 205 ED85
Dartford DA1 190 FN84
Nightingale Hts, SE18 off Nightingale Vale 187 EP79
Nightingale Ho, E1 off Thomas More St 32 C2
W12 off Du Cane Rd 14 A9
Nightingale La, E11 146 EG57
N6 142 DE60
N8 143 DL56
SW4 202 DF87
SW12 202 DF87
Bromley BR1 226 EJ96
Ide Hill TN14 278 FB130
Richmond TW10 200 CL87
St. Albans AL1 65 CJ24
Nightingale Ms, E3 11 L10
E11 146 EG57
SE11 30 F8
Kingston upon Thames KT1 off South La 219 CK97
Nightingale Pk, Farn.Com. SL2 153 AM66
Nightingale Pl, SE18 187 EN79
SW10 39 P2
Rickmansworth WD3 off Nightingale Rd 114 BK45
Sch Nightingale Prim Sch, E5 off Rendlesham Rd 144 DU63
E18 off Ashbourne Av 146 EJ56
N22 off Bounds Grn Rd 121 DM53
SE18 off Bloomfield Rd 187 EP78
Nightingale Rd, E5 144 DV62
N1 9 K5
N9 104 DW44
N22 121 DL53
NW10 161 CT68
W7 159 CF74
Bushey WD23 98 CA43
Carshalton SM5 222 DF104
Chesham HP5 76 AP29
Cheshunt EN7 88 DQ25
East Horsley KT24 267 BT125
Esher KT10 236 BZ106
Guildford GU1 264 AX134
Hampton TW12 198 CA92
Petts Wood BR5 227 EQ100
Rickmansworth WD3 114 BJ46
South Croydon CR2 243 DX111
Walton-on-Thames KT12 217 BV101
West Molesey KT8 218 CB99
Nightingales, Harl. CM17 74 EW17
Waltham Abbey EN9 off Roundhills 90 EE34
Nightingales, The, Stai. TW19 196 BM87
Sch Nightingale Sch, SW17 off Beechcroft Rd 202 DE89
Nightingales Cor, Amer. HP7 off Chalfont Sta Rd 94 AW40
Nightingale Shott, Egh. TW20 195 AZ93
Nightingales La, Ch.St.G. HP8 112 AX46
Nightingale Sq, SW12 202 DG87
Nightingale Vale, SE18 187 EN79
Nightingale Wk, SW4 203 DH86
Windsor SL4 173 AQ83
Nightingale Way, E6 25 H6
Bletchingley RH1 274 DS134
Denham UB9 135 BF59
Swanley BR8 229 FE97
Nile Cl, N16 144 DT62
Nile Dr, N9 122 DW47
Nile Path, SE18 off Jackson St 187 EN79
Nile Rd, E13 24 C1
Nile St, N1 19 K2
Nile Ter, SE15 44 A1
Nimbus Rd, Epsom KT19 238 CR110
Nimegen Way, SE22 204 DS85
Nimmo Dr, Bushey Hth WD23 117 CD45
Nimrod Cl, Nthlt. UB5 158 BX69
St. Albans AL4 65 CJ18
Nimrod Dr, Hat. AL10 66 CR17
Nimrod Pas, N1 9 P5
Nimrod Rd, SW16 203 DH93
Nina Mackay Cl, E15 13 J8
Nina Wk, N20 off Friern Barnet La 120 DC47
Nine Acre La, Hat. AL10 67 CT19
Nine Acres, Slou. SL1 153 AM74
Nine Acres Cl, E12 146 EL64
Hayes UB3 177 BQ76
Nineacres Way, Couls. CR5 257 DL116
Nine Ashes, Hunsdon SG12 off Acorn St 56 EK08
NINE ELMS, SW8 41 M4
Nine Elms Av, Uxb. UB8 156 BK71
Nine Elms Cl, Felt. TW14 197 BT88
Uxbridge UB8 156 BK72
Nine Elms Gro, Grav. DA11 213 GG87
Nine Elms La, SW8 41 M3
Ninefields, Wal.Abb. EN9 90 EF33
Ninehams Cl, Cat. CR3 258 DR120
Ninehams Gdns, Cat. CR3 258 DR120
Ninehams Rd, Cat. CR3 258 DR121
Tatsfield TN16 260 EJ121
Nine Stiles Cl, Denh. UB9 156 BH65
Nineteenth Rd, Mitch. CR4 223 DL98
Ninhams Wd, Orp. BR6 245 EN105
Ninian Rd, Hem.H. HP2 62 BL15
Ninnings Rd, Chal.St.P. SL9 113 AZ52
Ninnings Way, Chal.St.P. SL9 113 AZ52
Ninth Av, Hayes UB3 157 BU73
Nisbet Ho, E9 11 K3
Nisbett Wk, Sid. DA14 off Sidcup High St 208 EU91
Nita Rd, Warley CM14 130 FW50
Nithdale Rd, SE18 187 EP80
Nithsdale Gro, Uxb. UB10 137 BQ62
Niton Cl, Barn. EN5 101 CX44
Niton Rd, Rich. TW9 180 CN83
Niton St, SW6 38 C4
Niven Cl, Borwd. WD6 100 CQ39
Nixey Cl, Slou. SL1 174 AU75
No. 1 St, SE18 37 P7
Noahs Ct Gdns, Hert. SG13 54 DS10
NOAK HILL, Rom. RM4 128 FK47
Noak Hill Rd, Rom. RM3 128 FJ49
Nobel Dr, Harling. UB3 177 BR80
Nobel Rd, N18 122 DW50
Noble Ct, Mitch. CR4 222 DD96
Slough SL2 154 AT74
Noble St, EC2 19 J8
Walton-on-Thames KT12 217 BV104
Nobles Way, Egh. TW20 194 AY93
Noel Coward Ho, SW1 off Vauxhall Br Rd 29 M9
NOEL PARK, N22 121 DN54
Sch Noel Pk Prim Sch, N22 off Gladstone Av 121 DN54
Noel Pk Rd, N22 121 DN54
Noel Rd, E6 24 G5
N1 8 G10
W3 160 CP72
Noel Sq, Dag. RM8 148 EW63
Noel St, W1 17 M9
Noel Ter, SE23 off Dartmouth Rd 204 DW89
Noke Dr, Red. RH1 272 DG133
Noke Fm Barns, Couls. CR5 256 DF122
Noke La, St.Alb. AL2 82 BY26
Nokes, The, Hem.H. HP1 62 BG18
Noke Side, St.Alb. AL2 82 CA27
Noko, W10 14 D2
Nolan Path, Borwd. WD6 100 CM39
Nolan Way, E5 144 DU63
Nolton Pl, Edg. HA8 118 CM53
Nonsuch Cl, Ilf. IG6 125 EP51
Nonsuch Ct Av, Epsom KT17 239 CV110
Sch Nonsuch High Sch for Girls, Cheam SM3 off Ewell Rd 239 CX108
Nonsuch Ho, SW19 off Chapter Way 222 DD95
● Nonsuch Ind Est, Epsom KT17 238 CS111
★ Nonsuch Mansion, Sutt. SM3 239 CW107
Sch Nonsuch Prim Sch, Stoneleigh KT17 off Chadacre Rd 239 CV106
Nonsuch Wk, Sutt. SM2 239 CW110
Nook, The, Stans.Abb. SG12 55 EB11
Noons Cor Rd, Dor. RH5 284 BZ143
Nora Gdns, NW4 141 CX56
NORBITON, Kings.T. KT2 220 CP96
⇌ Norbiton 220 CN95
Norbiton Av, Kings.T. KT1 220 CN96
Norbiton Common Rd, Kings.T. KT1 220 CP97
Norbiton Rd, E14 21 N8
Norbreck Gdns, NW10 off Lytham Gro 160 CM69
Norbreck Par, NW10 off Lytham Gro 160 CM69
Norbroke St, W12 161 CT73
Norburn St, W10 14 E7
NORBURY, SW16 223 DN95
⇌ Norbury 223 DM95
Norbury Av, SW16 223 DM95
Hounslow TW3 199 CD85
Thornton Heath CR7 223 DN96
Watford WD24 98 BW39
Norbury Cl, SW16 223 DN95
Norbury Ct Rd, SW16 223 DL97
Norbury Cres, SW16 223 DM95
Norbury Cross, SW16 223 DL97
Norbury Gdns, Rom. RM6 148 EX57
Norbury Gro, NW7 118 CS48
Norbury Hill, SW16 203 DN94
Sch Norbury Manor Business & Enterprise Coll for Girls, Th.Hth. CR7 off Kensington Av 223 DN95
Sch Norbury Manor Prim Sch, SW16 off Abingdon Rd 223 DL95
Norbury Pk, Mick. RH5 269 CF127
Norbury Ri, SW16 223 DL97
Norbury Rd, E4 123 EA50
Feltham TW13 197 BT90
Reigate RH2 271 CZ134
Thornton Heath CR7 224 DQ96
Sch Norbury Sch, Har. HA1 off Welldon Cres 139 CE57
Norbury Way, Bkhm KT23 268 CC125
Norcombe Gdns, Har. HA3 139 CJ58
Norcombe Ho, N19 off Wedmore St 143 DK62
Norcott Cl, Hayes UB4 158 BW70
Norcott Rd, N16 144 DU61
Norcroft Gdns, SE22 204 DU87
Norcutt Rd, Twick. TW2 199 CE88
Nordenfeldt Rd, Erith DA8 189 FD78
Nordmann Pl, S.Ock. RM15 171 FX70
Norelands Dr, Burn. SL1 152 AJ68
Norfield Rd, Dart. DA2 209 FC91
Norfolk Av, N13 121 DP51
N15 144 DT58
Slough SL1 153 AQ71
South Croydon CR2 242 DU110
Watford WD24 98 BW38
Norfolk Cl, N2 142 DE55
N13 121 DP51
Barnet EN4 102 DG42
Dartford DA1 210 FN86
Horley RH6 290 DF149
Twickenham TW1 off Cassilis Rd 199 CH86
Norfolk Ct, Dor. RH5 285 CK140
Norfolk Cres, W2 16 D8
Sidcup DA15 207 ES87
Norfolk Fm Cl, Wok. GU22 249 BD116
Norfolk Fm Rd, Wok. GU22 249 BD115
Norfolk Gdns, Bexh. DA7 188 EZ81
Borehamwood WD6 100 CR42
Norfolk Ho, SW1 off Regency St 29 P8
Norfolk Ho Rd, SW16 203 DK90
Norfolk La, Mid Holm. RH5 285 CH142
Norfolk Ms, W10 14 F7
Norfolk Pl, W2 16 B8
Chafford Hundred RM16 191 FW78
Norfolk Pl, Welling DA16 188 EU82
Norfolk Rd, E6 167 EM67
E17 123 DX54
NW8 6 B9
NW10 160 CS66
SW19 202 DE94
Barking IG11 167 ES66
Barnet EN5 102 DA41
Claygate KT10 237 CE106
Dagenham RM10 149 FB64
Dorking RH4 285 CG136
Enfield EN3 104 DV44
Feltham TW13 198 BW88
Gravesend DA12 213 GK86
Harrow HA1 138 CB57
Ilford IG3 147 ES60
Rickmansworth WD3 114 BL46
Romford RM7 149 FC58
South Holmwood RH5 285 CJ144
Thornton Heath CR7 224 DQ97
Upminster RM14 150 FN62
Uxbridge UB8 156 BK65
Norfolk Row, SE1 30 C8
Norfolk Sq, W2 16 B9
Norfolk Sq Ms, W2 16 B9
Norfolk St, E7 13 N2
Norfolk Ter, W6 38 E1
Norgrove Pk, Ger.Cr. SL9 134 AY56
Norgrove St, SW12 202 DG87
Norheads La, Bigg.H. TN16 260 EJ116
Warlingham CR6 260 EG119
Norhyrst Av, SE25 224 DT97
NORK, Bans. SM7 255 CY115
Nork Gdns, Bans. SM7 239 CY114
Nork Ri, Bans. SM7 255 CX116
Nork Way, Bans. SM7 255 CY115
Norland Ho, W11 26 D3
Norland Pl, W11 26 F3
Sch Norland Pl Sch, W11 26 E3
Norland Rd, W11 26 D3
Norlands Cres, Chis. BR7 227 EP95
Norlands Gate, Chis. BR7 227 EP95
Norlands La, Egh. TW20 215 BE97
Norland Sq, W11 26 F3
Norley Vale, SW15 201 CU88
Norlington Rd, E10 145 EC60
E11 145 EC60
Sch Norlington Sch, E10 off Norlington Rd 145 ED60
Norman Av, N22 121 DP53
Epsom KT17 239 CT112
Feltham TW13 198 BY89
South Croydon CR2 242 DQ110
Southall UB1 158 BY73
Twickenham TW1 199 CH87
Normanby Cl, SW15 201 CZ85
Normanby Rd, NW10 141 CT63
Norman Cl, Epsom KT18 255 CV119
Orpington BR6 227 EQ104
Romford RM5 127 FB54
St. Albans AL1 65 CE23
Waltham Abbey EN9 89 ED33
Norman Colyer Ct, Epsom KT19 off Hollymoor La 238 CR110
Norman Ct, Ilf. IG2 147 ER59
Potters Bar EN6 86 DC30
Woodford Green IG8 off Monkhams Av 124 EH50
Norman Cres, Brwd. CM13 131 GA48
Hounslow TW5 178 BX81
Pinner HA5 116 BW53
Sch Normand Cft Comm Sch for Early Years & Prim Ed, W14 39 H2
Normand Gdns, W14 off Greyhound Rd 38 F2
Normand Ms, W14 38 F2
Normand Rd, W14 38 G2
Normandy Av, Barn. EN5 101 CZ43
Normandy Cl, SE26 205 DY90
Normandy Ct, Hem.H. HP2 62 BK19
Normandy Dr, Berk. HP4 60 AV17
Hayes UB3 157 BQ72
Normandy Ho, Enf. EN2 off Cedar Rd 104 DQ38
Normandy Pl, W12 off Bourbon La 26 C3
Sch Normandy Prim Sch, Barne. DA7 off Fairford Av 189 FD81
Normandy Rd, SW9 42 E7
St. Albans AL3 65 CD18
Normandy Ter, E16 24 A9
Normandy Wk, Egh. TW20 off Mullens Rd 195 BC92
Normandy Way, Erith DA8 189 FE81
Hoddesdon EN11 71 EC16
Norman Gro, E3 21 M1
Normanhurst, Ashf. TW15 196 BN92
Hutton CM13 131 GC44
Normanhurst Av, Bexh. DA7 188 EX81
Normanhurst Dr, Twick. TW1 off St. Margarets Rd 199 CH85
Normanhurst Rd, SW2 203 DM89
Orpington BR5 228 EV96
Walton-on-Thames KT12 218 BX103
Sch Normanhurst Sch, E4 off Station Rd 123 ED45
Norman Rd, E6 25 K4
E11 145 ED61
N15 144 DT57
SE10 46 D4
SW19 202 DC94
Ashford TW15 197 BR93
Belvedere DA17 189 FB76
Dartford DA1 210 FL88
Hornchurch RM11 149 FG59
Ilford IG1 147 EP64
Sutton SM1 240 DA106
Thornton Heath CR7 223 DP99
Normans, The, Slou. SL2 154 AV72
Normans Cl, NW10 160 CR65
Gravesend DA11 213 GG87
Uxbridge UB8 156 BL71
Normansfield Av, Tedd. TW11 199 CJ94
Normansfield Cl, Bushey WD23 116 CB45
Normanshire Av, E4 123 EC49
Normanshire Dr, E4 123 EA49
Normans Mead, NW10 160 CR65
Norman St, EC1 19 J3
Normanton Av, SW19 202 DA89
Normanton Pk, E4 124 EE48
Normanton Rd, S.Croy. CR2 242 DS107
Normanton St, SE23 205 DX89
Norman Way, N14 121 DL47
W3 160 CP71
Normington Cl, SW16 203 DN92
Norrels Dr, E.Hors. KT24 267 BT126
Norrels Ride, E.Hors. KT24 267 BT125
Norrice Lea, N2 142 DD57
Norris Cl, Epsom KT19 238 CP111
London Colney AL2 83 CH26
Norris Gro, Brox. EN10 71 DY20
Norris La, Hodd. EN11 71 EA16
Norris Ri, Hodd. EN11 71 DZ16
Norris Rd, Hodd. EN11 71 EA17
Staines-upon-Thames TW18 195 BF91
Norris St, SW1 29 N1
Norris Way, Dart. DA1 189 FF83
Norroy Rd, SW15 181 CX84
Norrys Cl, Cockfos. EN4 102 DF43
Norrys Rd, Cockfos. EN4 102 DF42
Norseman Cl, Ilf. IG3 148 EV60
Norseman Way, Grnf. UB6 off Olympic Way 158 CB67
Norstead Pl, SW15 201 CU89
Norsted La, Pr.Bot. BR6 246 EU110
North Access Rd, E17 145 DX58
North Acre, NW9 118 CS53
Banstead SM7 255 CZ116
NORTH ACTON, W3 160 CR70
⊖ North Acton 160 CR70
North Acton Rd, NW10 160 CR69
Northallerton Way, Rom. RM3 128 FK50
Northall Rd, Bexh. DA7 189 FC82
Northampton Av, Slou. SL1 153 AQ72
Northampton Gro, N1 9 L3
Northampton Pk, N1 9 K4
Northampton Rd, EC1 18 F4
Croydon CR0 224 DU103
Enfield EN3 105 DY42
Northampton Row, EC1 18 F3
Northampton Sq, EC1 18 G3
Northampton St, N1 9 J6
Coll North & W Essex Adult Comm Coll, Northbrooks Ho, Harl. CM19 off Northbrooks 73 EQ16
Rivermill Cen, Harl. CM20 off Hodings Rd 57 EQ13
Northanger Rd, SW16 203 DL93
North App, Nthwd. HA6 115 BQ47
Watford WD25 97 BT35
North Arc, Croy. CR0 off North End 224 DQ103
North Audley St, W1 16 G9
North Av, N18 122 DU49
W13 159 CH72
Brentwood CM14 129 FR45
Carshalton SM5 240 DG108
Harrow HA2 138 CB58
Hayes UB3 157 BU73
Richmond TW9 off Sandycombe Rd 180 CN81
Shenley WD7 84 CL32
Southall UB1 158 BZ73
Whiteley Village KT12 235 BS109
NORTHAW, Pot.B. EN6 86 DF30
Northaw Cl, Hem.H. HP2 63 BP15
Sch Northaw C of E Prim Sch, Northaw EN6 off Vineyards Rd 86 DG30
Northaw Pl, Northaw EN6 86 DD30
Northaw Rd E, Cuffley EN6 87 DK31
Northaw Rd W, Northaw EN6 86 DG30
North Bk, NW8 16 B3
Northbank Rd, E17 123 EC54
North Barn, Brox. EN10 71 EA21
NORTH BECKTON, E6 25 H5
Sch North Beckton Prim Sch, E6 25 K6
North Birkbeck Rd, E11 145 ED62
Northborough Rd, SW16 223 DK97
Slough SL2 153 AN70
Northbourne, Brom. BR2 226 EG101
Godalming GU7 280 AT143
Northbourne Ho, E5 off Pembury Rd 10 E2
Northbourne Rd, SW4 183 DK84
North Branch Av, W10 14 B3
Sch North Br Ho Jun Sch, NW3 5 P3
Sch North Br Ho Sen Sch, NW1 7 J9
Northbridge Rd, Berk. HP4 60 AT17
Sch Northbrook C of E Sch, SE13 off Leahurst Rd 205 ED85
Northbrook Dr, Nthwd. HA6 115 BS53
Northbrook Rd, N22 121 DL52
SE13 205 ED85
Barnet EN5 101 CY44
Croydon CR0 224 DR99
Ilford IG1 147 EN61
Northbrooks, Harl. CM19 73 EQ16
Northburgh St, EC1 19 H4
North Burnham Cl, Burn. SL1 off Wyndham Cres 152 AH68
Sch Northbury Inf & Jun Schs, Bark. IG11 off North St 167 EQ65
North Carriage Dr, W2 16 C10
NORTH CHEAM, Sutt. SM3 239 CW105
NORTHCHURCH, Berk. HP4 60 AT17
Northchurch, SE17 31 M10
Northchurch Rd, N1 9 L6
Wembley HA9 160 CM65
Northchurch Ter, N1 9 N7
North Circular Rd, E4 (A406) 123 DZ52
E6 (A406) 167 EP68
E11 (A406) 124 EJ54
E12 (A406) 147 EP64
E17 (A406) 123 DZ52
E18 (A406) 124 EJ54
N3 (A406) 142 DB55
N11 (A406) 120 DD53
N12 (A406) 120 DD53
N13 (A406) 121 DN50
N18 (A406) 122 DS50
NW2 (A406) 140 CS62
NW10 (A406) 160 CP66
NW11 (A406) 141 CY56
W3 (A406) 180 CM75
W4 (A406) 180 CM75
W5 (A406) 180 CM75
Barking (A406) IG11 167 EP68
Ilford (A406) IG1, IG4 146 EL60
Northcliffe Cl, Wor.Pk. KT4 220 CS104
Northcliffe Dr, N20 119 CZ46
North Cl, Barn. EN5 101 CW43
Beaconsfield HP9 132 AH55
Bexleyheath DA6 188 EX84
Chigwell IG7 126 EU50
Dagenham RM10 168 FA67
Feltham TW14 off North Rd 197 BR86
Morden SM4 221 CY98
North Holmwood RH5 285 CJ140
St. Albans AL2 82 CB25
Windsor SL4 173 AM81
North Colonnade, The, E14 34 B2
North Common, Wey. KT13 235 BP105
North Common Rd, W5 160 CL73
Uxbridge UB8 136 BK64
Northcote, Add. KT15 234 BK105

Northcote, Oxshott KT22 236 CC114
Pinner HA5 116 BW54
Northcote Av, W5 160 CL73
Isleworth TW7 199 CG85
Southall UB1 158 BY73
Surbiton KT5 220 CN101
Northcote Cl, W.Hors. KT24 267 BQ125
Northcote Cres, W.Hors. KT24 267 BQ125
Sch Northcote Lo Sch, SW11
off Bolingbroke Gro 202 DF86
Northcote Ms, SW11
off Northcote Rd 182 DE84
Northcote Rd, E17 145 DY56
NW10 160 CS66
SW11 182 DE84
Croydon CR0 224 DR100
Gravesend DA11 213 GF88
New Malden KT3 220 CQ97
Sidcup DA14 207 ES91
Twickenham TW1 199 CG85
West Horsley KT24 267 BQ125
North Cotts, Lon.Col. AL2 83 CG25
Northcott Av, N22 121 DL53
Northcotts, Abb.L. WD5
off Long Elms 81 BR33
Hatfield AL9 67 CW17
North Countess Rd, E17 123 DZ54
Northcourt, Mill End WD3
off Springwell Av 114 BG46
NORTH CRAY, Sid. DA14 208 FA90
North Cray Rd, Bex. DA5 208 EZ90
Sidcup DA14 208 EY93
North Cres, E16 23 H5
N3 119 CZ54
WC1 17 N6
Northcroft, Slou. SL2 153 AP70
Wooburn Green HP10 132 AE56
Northcroft Cl, Eng.Grn TW20 194 AV92
Northcroft Gdns, Eng.Grn
TW20 194 AV92
Northcroft Rd, W13 179 CH75
Englefield Green TW20 194 AV92
Epsom KT19 238 CR108
Northcroft Ter, W13
off Northcroft Rd 179 CH75
Northcroft Vil, Eng.Grn TW20 194 AV92
North Cross Rd, SE22 204 DT85
Ilford IG6 147 EQ56
North Dene, NW7 118 CR48
Northdene, Chig. IG7 125 ER50
North Dene, Houns. TW3 178 CB81
Northdene Gdns, N15 144 DT58
North Down, S.Croy. CR2 242 DS111
Northdown Cl, Ruis. HA4 137 BT62
Northdown Gdns, Ilf. IG2 147 ES57
Northdown La, Guil. GU1 280 AY137
Northdown Rd, Chal.St.P. SL9 112 AY51
Hatfield AL10 67 CU21
Hornchurch RM11 149 FH59
Longfield DA3 231 FX96
Sutton SM2 240 DA110
Welling DA16 188 EV82
Woldingham CR3 259 EA123
● North Downs Business Pk,
Dunt.Grn TN13 263 FC117
North Downs Cres, New Adgtn
CR0 243 EB110
H North Downs Private Hosp,
The, Cat. CR3 274 DT125
North Downs Rd, New Adgtn
CR0 243 EB110
Northdown St, N1 8 B10
North Downs Way, Bet. RH3 271 CU130
Caterham CR3 273 DN126
Dorking RH5 269 CE133
Godstone RH9 275 DY128
Guildford GU3, GU4 280 AT138
Oxted RH8 276 EE126
Redhill RH1 272 DG128
Reigate RH2 272 DD130
Sevenoaks TN13, TN14 263 FD118
Tadworth KT20 271 CX130
Westerham TN16 261 ER121
North Dr, SW16 203 DJ91
Beaconsfield HP9 132 AG55
Beckenham BR3 225 EB98
Hatfield AL9
off Great N Rd 67 CW16
Hounslow TW3 178 CC82
Oaklands AL4 66 CL18
Orpington BR6 245 ES105
Romford RM2 150 FJ55
Ruislip HA4 137 BS59
Slough SL2 154 AS69
Virginia Water GU25 214 AS100
⇌ North Dulwich 204 DR85
⊖ North Ealing 160 CM72
Sch North Ealing Prim Sch, W5
off Pitshanger La 159 CH70
North End, NW3 142 DC61
Buckhurst Hill IG9 124 EJ45
Croydon CR0 224 DQ103
Northend, Hem.H. HP3 63 BP22
North End, Noak Hill RM3 128 FJ47
Northend, Warley CM14 130 FW50
North End Av, NW3 142 DC61
Northend Cl, Flack.Hth HP10 132 AC56
North End Cres, W14 26 G9
North End Ho, W14 26 F9
North End La, Downe BR6 245 EN110
North End Par, W14 26 F9
Sch Northend Prim Sch, Erith DA8
off Peareswood Rd 189 FF81
North End Rd, NW11 142 DA60
SW6 39 H2
W14 26 G10
Northend Rd, Dart. DA1 189 FF80
Erith DA8 189 FF80
North End Rd, Wem. HA9 140 CN62
● Northend Trd Est, Erith
DA8 189 FE81
North End Way, NW3 142 DC61
Northern Av, N9 122 DT47
Northernhay Wk, Mord. SM4 221 CY98
Northern Perimeter Rd,
Lon.Hthrw Air. TW6 177 BQ81
Northern Perimeter Rd W,
Lon.Hthrw Air. TW6 176 BK81
Northern Relief Rd, Bark. IG11 167 EP66
Northern Rd, E13 166 EH67
Slough SL2 153 AR70
Northern Service Rd, Barn.
EN5 101 CY41
Northern Wds, Flack.Hth HP10 132 AC56
Northey Av, Sutt. SM2 239 CZ110
North Eyot Gdns, W6 181 CU78
Northey St, E14 21 M10
● North Feltham Trading Est,
Felt. TW14 197 BV85
Northfield, Hat. AL10
off Longmead 67 CV15
Loughton IG10 106 EK42
Shalford GU4 280 AY142
Northfield Av, W5 179 CH75
W13 179 CH75
Orpington BR5 228 EW100
Pinner HA5 138 BX56
Northfield Cl, Brom. BR1 226 EL95
Hayes UB3 177 BS76
Northfield Ct, Stai. TW18 216 BH95
Northfield Cres, Sutt. SM3 239 CY105
Northfield Fm Ms, Cob. KT11 235 BU113
Northfield Gdns, Dag. RM9
off Northfield Rd 148 EZ63
Watford WD24 98 BW37
Northfield Pk, Hayes UB3 177 BT76
Northfield Path, Dag. RM9 148 EZ62
Northfield Pl, Wey. KT13 235 BP108
Northfield Rd, E6 167 EM66
N16 144 DS59
W13 179 CH75
Barnet EN4 102 DE41
Borehamwood WD6 100 CP39
Cobham KT11 235 BU113
Dagenham RM9 148 EZ63
Enfield EN3 104 DV43
Eton Wick SL4 173 AM77
Hounslow TW5 178 BX79
Staines-upon-Thames TW18 216 BH95
Waltham Cross EN8 89 DY32
⊖ Northfields 179 CH76
Northfields, SW18 182 DA84
Ashtead KT21 254 CL119
Grays RM17 192 GC77
● Northfields Ind Est, Wem.
HA0 160 CN67
Northfields Rd, W3 160 CP71
NORTH FINCHLEY, N12 120 DD50
NORTHFLEET, Grav. DA10 212 GD86
⇌ Northfleet 212 GA86
NORTHFLEET GREEN, Grav.
DA13 212 GC92
Northfleet Grn Rd, Grav.
DA13 212 GC93
● Northfleet Ind Est, Nthflt
DA11 192 GA84
Sch Northfleet Sch for Girls, Grav.
DA11 off Hall Rd 212 GD89
Sch Northfleet Tech Coll, Nthflt
DA11 off Colyer Rd 212 GD88
North Flockton St, SE16 32 C4
North Gdn, E14
off Westferry Circ 33 P2
North Gdns, SW19 202 DD94
North Gate, NW8 16 C1
Harl. CM20 57 EQ14
Northgate, Gat. RH6 290 DF151
Nthwd. HA6 115 BQ52
Northgate Ct, SW9
off Canterbury Cres 183 DN83
Northgate Dr, NW9 140 CS58
● Northgate Ind Pk, Rom.
RM5 126 EZ54
Northgate Path, Borwd. WD6 100 CM38
North Gates, N12 off High Rd 120 DC53
North Glade, The, Bex. DA5 208 EZ87
North Gower St, NW1 17 M3
North Grn, NW9
off Clayton Fld 118 CS52
Slough SL1 154 AS73
⊖ North Greenwich 35 J4
⊖ North Greenwich 35 J4
North Gro, N6 142 DG59
N15 144 DR57
Chertsey KT16 215 BF100
Harlow CM18 74 EU16
Sch North Harringay Prim Sch, N8
off Falkland Rd 143 DN56
NORTH HARROW, Har. HA2 138 CA58
⊖ North Harrow 138 CA57
North Hatton Rd, Lon.Hthrw Air.
TW6 177 BR81
North Hill, N6 142 DF57
Rickmansworth WD3 95 BE40
North Hill Av, N6 142 DF58
North Hill Dr, Rom. RM3 128 FK48
North Hill Grn, Rom. RM3 128 FK49
NORTH HILLINGDON, Uxb.
UB10 157 BQ66
Coll North Hillingdon Adult Ed Cen,
Uxb. UB10 off Long La 137 BP64
NORTH HOLMWOOD, Dor.
RH5 285 CH141
North Ho, Harl. CM18
off Bush Fair 73 ET17
NORTH HYDE, Sthl. UB2 178 BY77
North Hyde Gdns, Hayes UB3 177 BU77
North Hyde La, Houns. TW5 178 BY78
Southall UB2 178 BY78
North Hyde Rd, Hayes UB3 177 BT76
Northiam, N12 120 DA48
Northiam St, E9 10 F9
Northington St, WC1 18 C5
NORTH KENSINGTON, W10 14 D7
North Kent Av, Nthflt DA11 212 GC86
Coll North Kingston Cen, Kings.T.
KT2 off Richmond Rd 200 CL93
Northlands, Pot.B. EN6 86 DD31
Northlands Av, Orp. BR6 245 ES105
Northlands St, SE5 43 J9
North La, Tedd. TW11 199 CF93
North Lo Cl, SW15 201 CX85
● North London Business Pk,
N11 120 DF47
Sch North London Collegiate Sch,
Edg. HA8 off Canons Dr 118 CL50
Sch North London Int Sch, The,
IB Diploma Cen, N11
off Friern Barnet La 120 DF50
Upr Sch, N11
off Friern Barnet Rd 120 DF50
Lwr Sch, N12
off Woodside Av 120 DC48
Lwr Sch, N12
off Woodside Pk Rd 120 DB49
NORTH LOOE, Epsom KT17 239 CW113
North Loop Rd, Uxb. UB8 156 BK69
North Mall, N9 off Edmonton
Grn Shop Cen 122 DV47
North Mead, Red. RH1 272 DF131
Sch Northmead Jun Sch, Guil.
GU2 off Grange Rd 264 AV131
Northmead Rd, Slou. SL2 153 AM70
North Ms, WC1 18 D5
H North Middlesex Uni Hosp,
N18 122 DS50
North Moors, Guil. GU1 264 AY130
NORTH MYMMS, Hat. AL9 85 CU25
North Mymms Pk, N.Mymms
AL9 85 CT25
NORTH OCKENDON, Upmin.
RM14 151 FV64
Northolm, Edg. HA8 118 CR49
Northolme Cl, Grays RM16
off Premier Av 192 GC76
Northolme Gdns, Edg. HA8 118 CN53
Northolme Ri, Orp. BR6 227 ES103
Northolme Rd, N5 144 DQ63
NORTHOLT, UB5 158 BZ66
⊖ Northolt 158 CA66
Northolt, N17 122 DR54
Northolt Av, Ruis. HA4 137 BV64
Northolt Gdns, Grnf. UB6 139 CF64
Sch Northolt High Sch, Nthlt. UB5
off Eastcote La 158 BZ65
⇌ Northolt Park 138 CB63
Northolt Rd, Har. HA2 138 CB63
London Heathrow Airport
TW6 176 BK81
● Northolt Trading Est,
Nthlt. UB5 158 CB66
Northolt Way, Horn. RM12 170 FJ65
● North Orbital Commercial Pk,
St.Alb. AL1 65 CG24
North Orbital Rd, Denh. UB9 135 BF60
Hatfield AL10 51 CV14
Rickmansworth WD3 135 BF55
St. Albans AL1, AL2, AL4 83 CK25
Watford WD25 81 BU34
Northover, Brom. BR1 206 EF90
North Par, Chess. KT9 238 CL106
Edgware HA8
off Mollison Way 118 CN54
Southall UB1 off North Rd 158 CA72
North Pk, SE9 207 EM86
Chalfont St. Peter SL9 134 AY56
Iver SL0 175 BC76
North Pk La, Gdse. RH9 274 DU129
North Pas, SW18 182 DA84
North Perimeter Rd, Uxb. UB8
off Kingston La 156 BL69
North Pl, Guil. GU1 280 AX135
Mitcham CR4 202 DF94
Teddington TW11 199 CF93
Waltham Abbey EN9
off Highbridge St 89 EB33
North Pt, N8 143 DM57
Northpoint, Brom. BR1
off Sherman Rd 226 EG95
Northpoint Cl, Sutt. SM1 222 DC104
Northpoint Ho, N1
off Essex Rd 9 L5
Northpoint Sq, NW1 7 N4
North Pole La, Kes. BR2 244 EF107
North Pole Rd, W10 14 A7
Northport St, N1 9 M9
Sch North Prim Sch, Sthl. UB1
off Meadow Rd 158 BZ73
North Ride, W2 28 C1
Northridge Rd, Grav. DA12 213 GJ90
Northridge Way, Hem.H. HP1 61 BF21
North Riding, Brick.Wd AL2 82 CA30
North Ri, W2
off St. Georges Flds 16 D9
North Rd, N6 142 DG59
N7 7 P4
N9 122 DV46
SE18 187 ES77
SW19 202 DC93
W5 179 CK76
Belvedere DA17 189 FB76
Berkhamsted HP4 60 AV19
Brentford TW8 180 CL79
Brentwood CM14 130 FW46
Bromley BR1 226 EH95
Chadwell Heath RM6 148 EY57
Chesham Bois HP6 77 AQ36
Chorleywood WD3 95 BD43
Dartford DA1 209 FF86
Edgware HA8 118 CP53
Feltham TW14 197 BR86
Guildford GU2 264 AV131
Havering-atte-Bower RM4 127 FE48
Hayes UB3 157 BR71
Hersham KT12 236 BW106
Hertford SG14 54 DQ09
Hoddesdon EN11 71 EA16
Ilford IG3 147 ES61
Purfleet RM19 190 FQ77
Reigate RH2 287 CZ137
Richmond TW9 180 CN83
South Ockendon RM15 171 FW68
Southall UB1 158 CA73
Surbiton KT6 219 CK100
Waltham Cross EN8 89 DY33
West Drayton UB7 176 BM76
West Wickham BR4 225 EB102
Woking GU21 249 BA116
North Rd Av, Brwd. CM14 130 FW46
Hertford SG14 53 DN08
North Rd Gdns, Hert. SG14 53 DP09
Northrop Rd, Lon.Hthrw Air.
TW6 177 BS81
North Row, W1 16 F10
North Several, SE3 47 H8
NORTH SHEEN, Rich. TW9 180 CN82
⇌ North Sheen 180 CN84
Sch Northside Prim Sch, N12
off Albert St 120 DC50
Northside Rd, Brom. BR1
off Mitchell Way 226 EG95
North Side Wandsworth Common,
SW18 202 DC85
Northspur Rd, Sutt. SM1 222 DA104
North Sq, N9 off Edmonton
Grn Shop Cen 122 DV47
North Sq, NW11 142 DA57
North Sta App, S.Nutfld RH1 289 DM136
Northstead Rd, SW2 203 DN89
North St, E13 24 A1
NW4 141 CW57
SW4 41 L10
Barking IG11 167 EP65
Bexleyheath DA7 188 FA84
Bromley BR1 226 EG95
Carshalton SM5 222 DF104
Dartford DA1 210 FK87
Dorking RH4 285 CG136
Egham TW20 195 AZ92
Godalming GU7
off Station Rd 280 AT144
Gravesend DA12
off South St 213 GH87
Guildford GU1 280 AX135
Hornchurch RM11 150 FK59
Isleworth TW7 179 CG83
Leatherhead KT22 253 CG121
North St, Lower Nazeing EN9 72 EE22
Redhill RH1 272 DF133
Romford RM1, RM5 149 FD55
Westcott RH4 284 CC137
North St Pas, E13 166 EH68
North Tenter St, E1 20 B9
North Ter, SW3 28 C7
Windsor SL4
off Windsor Castle 174 AS80
Northumberland All, EC3 19 P9
Northumberland Av, E12 146 EJ60
WC2 30 A2
Enfield EN1 104 DV39
Hornchurch RM11 150 FJ57
Isleworth TW7 179 CF81
Welling DA16 187 ER84
Northumberland Cl, Erith DA8 189 FC80
Stanwell TW19 196 BL86
Northumberland Cres, Felt.
TW14 197 BS86
Northumberland Gdns, N9 122 DT48
Bromley BR1 227 EN98
Isleworth TW7 179 CG80
Mitcham CR4 223 DK99
Northumberland Gro, N17 122 DV52
NORTHUMBERLAND HEATH,
Erith DA8 189 FC80
Sch Northumberland Heath Prim Sch,
Erith DA8 off Byron Dr 189 FB80
⇌ Northumberland Park 122 DV53
Northumberland Pk, N17 122 DT52
Erith DA8 189 FC80
Sch Northumberland Pk Comm Sch,
N17 off Trulock Rd 122 DU52
● Northumberland Pk Ind Est,
N17 off Willoughby La 122 DV52
Northumberland Pl, W2 15 J8
Richmond TW10 199 CK85
Northumberland Rd, E6 25 H8
E17 145 EA59
Northumberland Rd, Har. HA2 138 BZ57
Istead Rise DA13 213 GF94
New Barnet EN5 102 DC44
Northumberland Row, Twick. TW2
off Colne Rd 199 CE88
Northumberland St, WC2 30 A2
Northumberland Way, Erith
DA8 189 FC81
Northumbria St, E14 22 B8
North Verbena Gdns, W6
off St. Peter's Sq 181 CU78
Northview, N7 143 DL62
North Vw, SW19 201 CV92
W5 159 CJ70
Northview, Hem.H. HP1
off Winkwell 61 BD22
North Vw, Ilf. IG6 126 EU52
Pinner HA5 138 BW59
Northview, Swan. BR8 229 FE96
North Vw Av, Til. RM18 193 GG81
Northview Cres, NW10 141 CT63
North Vw Cres, Epsom KT18 255 CV117
North Vw Dr, Wdf.Grn. IG8 124 EK54
Sch Northview Prim Sch, NW10
off Northview Cres 141 CT64
North Vw Rd, N8 143 DK55
Sevenoaks TN14 off Seal Rd 279 FJ121
North Vil, NW1 7 N5
North Wk, W2 27 N1
New Addington CR0 243 EB106
NORTH WATFORD, Wat. WD24 97 BV37
North Way, N9 122 DW47
N11 121 DJ51
NW9 140 CP55
Northway, NW11 142 DB57
Guildford GU2 264 AU132
Morden SM4 221 CY97
North Way, Pnr. HA5 138 BW55
Northway, Rick. WD3 114 BK45
North Way, Uxb. UB10 156 BL66
Northway, Wall. SM6 241 DJ105
Welwyn Garden City AL7
off Nursery Hill 51 CZ06
Northway Circ, NW7 118 CR49
Northway Cres, NW7 118 CR49
Northway Ho, N20 120 DC46
Northway Rd, SE5 184 DQ83
Croydon CR0 224 DT100
Sch Northway Sch, NW7
off The Fairway 118 CR48
Northways Par, NW3
off Finchley Rd 6 A6
North Weald Airfield, N.Wld Bas.
CM16 92 EZ26
NORTH WEALD BASSETT, Epp.
CM16 93 FB27
North Weald Cl, Horn. RM12 169 FH66
Northweald La, Kings.T. KT2 199 CK92
NORTH WEMBLEY, Wem.
HA0 139 CH61
⊖ North Wembley 139 CK62
⊖ North Wembley 139 CK62
North Western Av, Wat.
WD24, WD25 97 BU35
● North Western Commercial Cen,
NW1 off Broadfield La 8 A7
Coll North W Kent Coll,
Dartford Campus, Dart.
DA1 off Oakfield La 210 FJ89
Gravesend Campus, Grav.
DA12 off Dering Way 213 GM88
H North West London Health
Protection Unit, NW9 140 CR55
Sch North W London Jewish
Prim Sch, NW6 4 E6
Northwest Pl, N1 8 F10
North Wf Rd, W2 16 A7
Northwick Av, Har. HA3 139 CG58
Northwick Circle, Har. HA3 139 CJ58
Northwick Cl, NW8 16 A4
Harrow HA1 139 CH60
⊖ Northwick Park 139 CG59
H Northwick Pk Hosp, Har.
HA1 139 CG59
Northwick Pk Rd, Har. HA1 139 CF58
Northwick Rd, Wat. WD19 116 BW49
Wembley HA0
off Glacier Wy 159 CK67
Northwick Ter, NW8 16 A4
Northwick Wk, Har. HA1 139 CF59
Northwold Dr, Pnr. HA5
off Cuckoo Hill 138 BW55
Northwold Est, E5 144 DU61
Sch Northwold Prim Sch, E5
off Northwold Rd 144 DU61
Northwold Rd, E5 144 DT61
N16 144 DT61
NORTHWOOD, HA6 115 BR51
⊖ Northwood 115 BS52
Northwood, Grays RM16 193 GH75
Welwyn Garden City AL7 52 DD09
Northwood Av, Horn. RM12 149 FG63
Purley CR8 241 DN113
Northwood Cl, Chsht EN7 88 DT27
Sch Northwood Coll, Nthwd. HA6
off Maxwell Rd 115 BR52
North Wd Ct, SE25
off Regina Rd 224 DU97
Northwood Dr, Green. DA9
off Stone Castle Dr 211 FU86
Northwood Gdns, N12 120 DD50
Greenford UB6 139 CF64
Ilford IG5 147 EN56
Northwood Hall, N6 143 DJ59
NORTHWOOD HILLS, Nthwd.
HA6 115 BT54
⊖ Northwood Hills 115 BU54
Northwood Ho, SE27 204 DR91
Northwood Pl, Erith DA18 188 EZ76
Sch Northwood Prep Sch, Rick.
WD3 off Sandy Lo Rd 115 BQ47
Sch Northwood Prim Sch, Erith
DA18 off Northwood Pl 188 EZ76
Northwood Rd, N6 143 DH59
SE23 205 DZ88
Carshalton SM5 240 DG107
Harefield UB9 114 BJ53
London Heathrow Airport
TW6 176 BK81
Thornton Heath CR7 223 DP96
Sch Northwood Sch, Nthwd. HA6
off Potter St 115 BU53
Northwood Twr, E17 145 EC56
Northwood Way, SE19
off Roman Ri 204 DR93
Harefield UB9 114 BK53
Northwood HA6 115 BU52
NORTH WOOLWICH, E16 37 H4
North Woolwich Rd, E16 35 M2
Jct North Woolwich Rbt, E16 36 E3
North Worple Way, SW14 180 CR83
Nortoft Rd, Chal.St.P. SL9 113 AZ51
Norton Av, Surb. KT5 220 CP101
Norton Cl, E4 123 EA50
Borehamwood WD6 100 CN39
Enfield EN1 off Brick La 104 DV40
Norton Folgate, E1 19 P6
Norton Gdns, SW16 223 DL96
Norton La, Cob. KT11 251 BT119
Norton Rd, E10 145 DZ60
Dagenham RM10 169 FD65
Uxbridge UB8 156 BK69
Wembley HA0 159 CK65
Norval Rd, Wem. HA0 139 CH61
Norvic Ho, Erith DA8
off Waterhead Cl 189 FF80
Norway Dr, Slou. SL2 154 AV71
Norway Gate, SE16 33 M6
Norway Pl, E14 21 N9
Norway St, SE10 46 D3
Norway Wk, Rain. RM13
off The Glen 170 FJ70
Sch Norwegian Sch in London, The,
SW20 off Arterberry Rd 201 CW94
Norwich Cres, Chad.Hth RM6 148 EV57
Norwich Ho, E14 22 D8
Norwich Ms, Ilf. IG3 148 EU60
Norwich Pl, Bexh. DA6 188 FA84
Norwich Rd, E7 13 N3
Dagenham RM9 168 FA68
Greenford UB6 158 CB67
Northwood HA6 137 BT55
Thornton Heath CR7 224 DQ97
Norwich St, EC4 18 E8
Norwich Wk, Edg. HA8 118 CQ52
Norwich Way, Crox.Grn WD3 97 BP41
NORWOOD, SE19 204 DR93
Norwood Av, Rom. RM7 149 FE59
Wembley HA0 160 CM67
Norwood Cl, NW2 141 CY62
Effingham KT24 268 BY128
Hertford SG14 53 DM08
Southall UB2 178 CA77
Twickenham TW2
off Fourth Cross Rd 199 CD89
Norwood Ct, Amer. HP7 77 AP40
Norwood Cres, Lon.Hthrw Air.
TW6 177 BQ81
Norwood Dr, Har. HA2 138 BZ58
Norwood Fm La, Cob. KT11 235 BU111
Norwood Gdns, Hayes UB4 158 BW70
Southall UB2 178 BZ77
NORWOOD GREEN, Sthl.
UB2 178 CA77
Sch Norwood Grn Inf & Nurs Sch,
Sthl. UB2 off Thorncliffe Rd 178 BZ78
Sch Norwood Grn Jun Sch, Sthl.
UB2 off Thorncliffe Rd 178 BY78
Norwood Grn Rd, Sthl. UB2 178 CA77
Norwood High St, SE27 203 DP90
⇌ Norwood Junction 224 DT98
⊖ Norwood Junction 224 DT98
Norwood La, Iver SL0 155 BD70
NORWOOD NEW TOWN,
SE19 204 DQ93
Norwood Pk Rd, SE27 204 DQ92
Norwood Rd, SE24 203 DP88
SE27 203 DP89
Cheshunt EN8 89 DY30
Effingham KT24 268 BY128
Southall UB2 178 BZ77
Sch Norwood Sch, The, SE19
off Crown Dale 204 DQ92
Norwood Ter, Sthl. UB2
off Tentelow La 178 CB77
Notley End, Eng.Grn TW20 194 AW93
Notley St, SE5 43 L4
Notre Dame Est, SW4 183 DJ84
Sch Notre Dame Prep Sch, Cob.
KT11 off Burwood Pk 235 BT112
Sch Notre Dame RC Prim Sch,
SE18 off Eglinton Rd 187 EP79
Sch Notre Dame Sch, SE1 30 G6
Sch Notre Dame Sen Sch, Cob.
KT11 off Burwood Pk 235 BT111
Notson Rd, SE25 224 DV98
Notting Barn Rd, W10 14 C5
Nottingdale Sq, W11 26 E1
Nottingham Av, E16 24 C7
Nottingham Cl, Wat. WD25 81 BU33

Nottingham Cl, Woking GU21 248 AT118
Nottingham Ct, WC2 18 A9
St. John's GU21
off Nottingham Cl 248 AT118
Nottingham Pl, W1 16 G5
Nottingham Rd, E10 145 EC58
SW17 202 DF88
Heronsgate WD3 113 BC45
Isleworth TW7 179 CF82
South Croydon CR2 242 DQ105
Nottingham St, W1 16 G6
Nottingham Ter, NW1 16 G5
NOTTING HILL, W11 14 F10
Sch Notting Hill & Ealing High Sch, Sen Sch & 6th Form, W13 *off Cleveland Rd* 159 CH71
⊖ Notting Hill Gate 27 J1
Notting Hill Gate, W11 27 J2
Nova, E14 34 A8
Nova Ms, Sutt. SM3 221 CY102
Novar Cl, Orp. BR6 227 ET101
Nova Rd, Croy. CR0 223 DP102
Novar Rd, SE9 207 EQ88
Novello St, SW6 39 J7
Novello Way, Borwd. WD6 100 CR39
Nowell Rd, SW13 181 CU79
Nower, The, Sev. TN14 261 ET119
Nower Cl E, Dor. RH4 285 CF137
Nower Cl W, Dor. RH4 285 CF137
Nower Hill, Pnr. HA5 138 BZ56
Sch Nower Hill High Sch, Pnr. HA5 *off George V Av* 138 CA56
Nower Rd, Dor. RH4 285 CG136
Noyna Rd, SW17 202 DF90
Nubia Way, Brom. BR1 206 EE90
Nuding Cl, SE13 185 EA83
H Nuffield Hosp Brentwood, Brwd. CM15 130 FY46
H Nuffield Hosp N London (Enfield), Enf. EN2 103 DN40
Nuffield Rd, Swan. BR8 209 FG93
H Nuffield Speech & Language Unit, W5 159 CJ71
● Nugent Ind Pk, Orp. BR5 228 EW99
Nugent Rd, N19 143 DL60
SE25 224 DT97
Nugents Ct, Pnr. HA5 116 BY53
Nugent Shop Pk, Orp. BR5 228 EW98
Nugents Pk, Pnr. HA5 116 BY53
Nugent Ter, NW8 15 P1
Numa Ct, Brent. TW8 *off Justin Cl* 179 CK80
Nunappleton Way, Oxt. RH8 276 EG132
Nun Ct, EC2 19 L8
Nuneaton Rd, Dag. RM9 168 EX66
Nuneham Est, SW16 203 DK91
Nunfield, Chipper. WD4 80 BH31
NUNHEAD, SE15 184 DW83
⇌ Nunhead 44 G9
Nunhead Cres, SE15 184 DV83
Nunhead Est, SE15 184 DV84
Nunhead Grn, SE15 44 F10
Nunhead Gro, SE15 184 DV83
Nunhead La, SE15 184 DV83
Nunhead Pas, SE15 *off Peckham Rye* 184 DU83
Nunnery Cl, St.Alb. AL1 65 CD22
Nunnery Stables, St.Alb. AL1 65 CD22
Nunnington Cl, SE9 206 EL90
Nunns Rd, Enf. EN2 104 DQ40
Nunns Way, Grays RM17 192 GD77
Nunsbury Dr, Brox. EN10 89 DY25
Nuns La, St.Alb. AL1 65 CE24
Nuns Wk, Vir.W. GU25 214 AX99
NUPER'S HATCH, Rom. RM4 127 FE45
Nupton Dr, Barn. EN5 101 CW44
Nurse Cl, Edg. HA8 *off Gervase Rd* 118 CQ53
Nurseries Rd, Wheat. AL4 50 CL08
Nursery, The, Erith DA8 189 FF80
Nursery Av, N3 120 DC54
Bexleyheath DA7 188 EZ83
Croydon CR0 225 DX103
Nursery Cl, SE4 45 N9
SW15 181 CX84
Amersham HP7 77 AS39
Croydon CR0 225 DX103
Dartford DA2 210 FQ87
Enfield EN3 105 DX39
Epsom KT17 238 CS110
Feltham TW14 197 BV87
Orpington BR6 227 ET101
Penn HP10 110 AC47
Romford RM6 148 EX58
Sevenoaks TN13 279 FJ122
South Ockendon RM15 171 FW70
Swanley BR8 229 FC96
Walton on the Hill KT20 271 CV125
Watford WD19 115 BV46
Woking GU21 248 AW116
Woodford Green IG8 124 EH50
Woodham KT15 233 BF110
Nursery Ct, N17 *off Nursery St* 122 DT52
Nursery Flds, Saw. CM21 58 EX05
Nursery Gdns, Chilw. GU4 281 BB140
Chislehurst BR7 207 EP93
Enfield EN3 105 DX39
Goffs Oak EN7 88 DR28
Hampton TW12 198 BZ91
Hounslow TW4 198 BZ85
Staines-upon-Thames TW18 196 BH94
Sunbury-on-Thames TW16 217 BT96
Ware SG12 55 DY06
Welwyn Garden City AL7 51 CY06
Nursery Hill, Welw.G.C. AL7 51 CY06
Nursery La, E2 10 A9
E7 13 P4
W10 14 A7
Hookwood RH6 290 DD149
Penn HP10 110 AC47
Slough SL3 154 AW74
Uxbridge UB8 156 BK70
Nurserymans Rd, N11 120 DG47
Nursery Pl, Old Wind. SL4 *off Gregory Dr* 194 AV86
Sevenoaks TN13 278 FD122
Nursery Rd, E9 10 G4
N2 120 DD53
Nursery Rd, N14 121 DJ45
SW9 183 DM84
Broxbourne EN10 89 DY25
Godalming GU7 280 AT144
Hoddesdon EN11 55 EB14
Loughton IG10 106 EJ43
Lower Nazeing EN9 71 ED22
Pinner HA5 138 BW55
Sunbury-on-Thames TW16 217 BS96
Sutton SM1 240 DC105
Taplow SL6 152 AH72
Thornton Heath CR7 224 DR98
Walton on the Hill KT20 271 CU125
Nursery Rd Merton, SW19 222 DB96
Nursery Rd Mitcham, Mitch. CR4 222 DE97
Nursery Rd Wimbledon, SW19 *off Worple Rd* 201 CY94
Nursery Row, SE17 31 L9
Barnet EN5 *off St. Albans Rd* 101 CY41
Nursery St, N17 122 DT52
Nursery Ter, Pott.End HP4 *off The Front* 61 BB16
Nursery Wk, NW4 141 CV55
Romford RM7 149 FD59
Nursery Way, Wrays. TW19 194 AX86
Nursery Waye, Uxb. UB8 156 BK67
Nurstead Rd, Erith DA8 188 FA80
Nutberry Av, Grays RM16 192 GA75
Nutberry Cl, Grays RM16 *off Long La* 192 GA75
Nutbourne St, W10 14 E2
Nutbrook St, SE15 184 DU83
Nutbrowne Rd, Dag. RM9 168 EZ67
Nutcombe La, Dor. RH4 285 CF136
Nutcroft Gro, Fetch. KT22 253 CE121
Nutcroft Rd, SE15 44 E4
NUTFIELD, Red. RH1 273 DM133
⇌ Nutfield 289 DL136
Nutfield, Welw.G.C. AL7 52 DA06
Sch Nutfield Ch C of E Prim Sch, S.Nutfld RH1 *off Mid St* 289 DM135
Nutfield Cl, N18 122 DU51
Carshalton SM5 222 DE104
Nutfield Gdns, Ilf. IG3 147 ET61
Northolt UB5 158 BW68
Nutfield Marsh Rd, Nutfld RH1 273 DJ130
Nutfield Pk, S.Nutfld RH1 289 DN137
Nutfield Rd, E15 145 EC63
NW2 141 CU61
SE22 204 DT85
Coulsdon CR5 256 DG116
Redhill RH1 272 DG134
South Merstham RH1 273 DJ129
Thornton Heath CR7 223 DP98
Nutfield Way, Orp. BR6 227 EN103
Nutford Pl, W1 16 D8
Nut Gro, Welw.G.C. AL8 51 CX06
Nuthatch Cl, Stai. TW19 196 BM88
Nuthatch Gdns, SE28 187 ER75
Reigate RH2 288 DC138
Nuthurst Av, SW2 203 DM89
Nutkins Way, Chesh. HP5 76 AQ29
Nutkin Wk, Uxb. UB8 156 BL66
Nutley Cl, Swan. BR8 229 FF95
Nutley Ct, Reig. RH2 *off Nutley La* 271 CZ134
Nutley La, Reig. RH2 271 CZ133
Nutley Ter, NW3 5 P4
Nutmead Cl, Bex. DA5 209 FC88
Nutmeg Cl, E16 23 K4
Nutmeg La, E14 22 G9
Nuttall St, N1 9 P10
Nutter La, E11 146 EJ58
Nuttfield Cl, Crox.Grn WD3 97 BP44
Nutt Gro, Edg. HA8 117 CK47
Nut Tree Cl, Orp. BR6 228 EX104
Nutt St, SE15 44 B4
Nutty La, Shep. TW17 217 BQ98
Nutwell St, SW17 202 DE92
Nutwood Av, Brock. RH3 286 CQ135
Nutwood Cl, Brock. RH3 286 CQ135
Nutwood Gdns, Chsht EN7 *off Great Stockwood Rd* 88 DS26
Nuxley Rd, Belv. DA17 188 EZ79
Nyall Ct, Gidea Pk RM2 150 FJ56
Nyanza St, SE18 187 ER79
Nye Bevan Est, E5 145 DX62
Nyefield Pk, Walt.Hill KT20 271 CU126
Nye Way, Bov. HP3 79 BA28
Nylands Av, Rich. TW9 180 CN81
Nymans Gdns, SW20 *off Hidcote Gdns* 221 CV97
Nynehead St, SE14 45 L4
Nyon Gro, SE6 205 DZ89
Nyssa Cl, Wdf.Grn. IG8 *off Gwynne Pk Av* 125 EM51
Nyth Cl, Upmin. RM14 151 FR58
Nyton Cl, N19 *off Courtauld Rd* 143 DL60

O

★ O2, The, SE10 35 J3
★ O2 Academy Brixton, SW9 42 E10
O2 Shop Cen, NW3 5 N4
Oakapple Cl, S.Croy. CR2 242 DV114
Oak Apple Ct, SE12 206 EG89
Oak Av, N8 143 DL56
N10 121 DH52
N17 122 DR52
Bricket Wood AL2 82 CA30
Croydon CR0 225 EA103
Egham TW20 195 BC94
Enfield EN2 103 DM38
Hampton TW12 198 BY92
Hounslow TW5 178 BX80
Sevenoaks TN13 279 FH128
Upminster RM14 150 FP62
Uxbridge UB10 137 BP61
West Drayton UB7 176 BN76
Oakbank, Fetch. KT22 252 CC123
Hutton CM13 131 GE43
Oak Bk, New Adgtn CR0 243 EC107
Oakbank, Wok. GU22 248 AY119
Oakbank Av, Walt. KT12 218 BZ101
Oakbank Gro, SE24 184 DQ84
Oakbark Ho, Brent. TW8 *off High St* 179 CJ80
Oakbrook Cl, Brom. BR1 206 EH91
Oakbury Rd, SW6 39 M9
Oak Cl, N14 121 DH45
Box Hill KT20 270 CP130
Oak Cl, Dartford DA1 189 FE84
Godalming GU7 280 AS143
Hemel Hempstead HP3 62 BM24
Oxted RH8 276 EG132
Sutton SM1 222 DC103
Waltham Abbey EN9 89 ED34
Oakcombe Cl, N.Mal. KT3 220 CS95
Oak Cottage Cl, SE6 206 EE88
Oak Ct E, Stan. HA7 *off Valencia Rd* 117 CJ49
Oak Ct W, Stan. HA7 *off Valencia Rd* 117 CJ49
Oak Cres, E16 23 K7
Oakcroft Cl, Pnr. HA5 115 BV54
West Byfleet KT14 233 BF114
Oakcroft Rd, SE13 46 G9
Chessington KT9 238 CM105
West Byfleet KT14 233 BF114
Oakcroft Vil, Chess. KT9 238 CM105
Oakdale, N14 121 DH46
Welwyn Garden City AL8 51 CW05
Oakdale Av, Har. HA3 140 CL57
Northwood HA6 115 BU54
Oakdale Cl, Wat. WD19 116 BW49
Oakdale Gdns, E4 123 EC50
Sch Oakdale Infants' Sch, E18 *off Woodville Rd* 124 EH54
Sch Oakdale Jun Sch, E18 *off Oakdale Rd* 124 EH54
Oakdale La, Crock.H. TN8 277 EP133
Oakdale Rd, E7 166 EH66
E11 145 ED61
E18 124 EH54
N4 144 DQ58
SE15 45 H10
SW16 203 DL92
Epsom KT19 238 CR109
Watford WD19 116 BW48
Weybridge KT13 216 BN104
Oakdale Way, Mitch. CR4 222 DG101
Oakdene, SE15 44 E6
Oak Dene, W13 *off The Dene* 159 CH71
Oakdene, Beac. HP9 111 AL52
Cheshunt EN8 89 DY30
Chobham GU24 232 AT110
Romford RM3 128 FM54
Tadworth KT20 255 CY120
Oakdene Av, Chis. BR7 207 EN92
Erith DA8 189 FC79
Thames Ditton KT7 219 CG102
Oakdene Cl, Bkhm KT23 268 CC127
Brockham RH3 286 CQ136
Hornchurch RM11 149 FH58
Pinner HA5 116 BZ52
Oakdene Ct, Walt. KT12 217 BV104
Oakdene Dr, Surb. KT5 220 CQ101
Oakdene Ms, Sutt. SM3 221 CZ102
Oakdene Par, Cob. KT11 *off Anyards Rd* 235 BV114
Oakdene Pk, N3 119 CZ52
Oakdene Pl, Peasm. GU3 280 AW142
Oakdene Rd, Bkhm KT23 252 BZ124
Brockham RH3 286 CQ136
Cobham KT11 235 BV114
Hemel Hempstead HP3 62 BM24
Hillingdon UB10 157 BP68
Orpington BR5 227 ET99
Peasmarsh GU3 280 AW142
Redhill RH1 272 DE134
Sevenoaks TN13 278 FG122
Watford WD24 97 BV36
Oakdene Way, St.Alb. AL1 65 CJ20
Oakden St, SE11 30 F8
Oak Dr, Berk. HP4 60 AX20
Box Hill KT20 270 CP130
Sawbridgeworth CM21 58 EW07
Oake Ct, SW15 *off Portinscale Rd* 201 CY85
Oaken Coppice, Ashtd. KT21 254 CN119
Oak End, Harl. CM18 73 ET17
Oak End Dr, Iver SL0 155 BC68
Oaken Dr, Clay. KT10 237 CF107
Oak End Way, Ger.Cr. SL9 135 AZ57
Woodham KT15 233 BE112
Oakengate Wd, Tad. KT20 270 CQ131
Oaken Gro, Welw.G.C. AL7 51 CY11
Oakenholt Ho, SE2 *off Hartslock Dr* 188 EX75
Oaken La, Clay. KT10 237 CE106
Oakenshaw Cl, Surb. KT6 220 CL101
Warlingham CR6 258 DW115
Oakes Cl, E6 25 K9
Oakeshott Av, N6 142 DG61
Oakey La, SE1 30 E6
Oak Fm, Borwd. WD6 100 CQ43
Sch Oak Fm Inf & Jun Schs, Hlgdn UB10 *off Windsor Av* 157 BP67
Oakfield, E4 123 EB50
Oak Fld, Chesh. HP5 76 AP30
Oakfield, Mill End WD3 113 BF45
Woking GU21 248 AS116
Oakfield Av, Har. HA3 139 CH55
Slough SL1 153 AP74
Oakfield Cl, Amer. HP6 77 AQ37
New Malden KT3 *off Blakes La* 221 CT99
Potters Bar EN6 85 CZ31
Ruislip HA4 137 BT58
Weybridge KT13 235 BQ105
Sch Oakfield Co Inf & Nurs Sch, Dart. DA1 *off Oakfield La* 210 FL89
Oakfield Ct, N8 143 DL59
NW2 *off Hendon Way* 141 CX59
Borehamwood WD6 100 CP41
Oakfield Dr, Reig. RH2 272 DA132
Sch Oakfield First Sch, Wind. SL4 *off Imperial Rd* 173 AP82
Oakfield Gdns, N18 122 DS49
SE19 204 DS92
Beckenham BR3 225 EA99
Carshalton SM5 222 DE102
Greenford UB6 159 CD70
Oakfield Glade, Wey. KT13 235 BQ105
Sch Oakfield Jun Sch, Dart. DA1 *off Oakfield La* 210 FK89
Fetcham KT22 *off Bell La* 253 CD123
Oakfield La, Bex. DA5 209 FF89
Dartford DA1, DA2 209 FG89
Keston BR2 244 EJ105
Oakfield Lo, Ilf. IG1 *off Albert Rd* 147 EP62
Oakfield Pk Rd, Dart. DA1 210 FK89
Oakfield Pl, Dart. DA1 210 FK89
Sch Oakfield Prep Sch, SE21 *off Thurlow Pk Rd* 204 DR88
Oakfield Rd, E6 166 EL67
E17 123 DY54
N3 120 DB53
Oakfield Rd, N4 143 DN58
N14 121 DL48
SE20 204 DV94
SW19 201 CX90
Ashford TW15 197 BP92
Ashtead KT21 253 CK117
Cobham KT11 235 BV113
Croydon CR0 224 DQ102
Ilford IG1 147 EP61
● Oakfield Rd Ind Est, SE20 *off Oakfield Rd* 204 DV94
Oakfields, Guil. GU3 264 AS132
Sevenoaks TN13 279 FH126
Walton-on-Thames KT12 217 BU102
West Byfleet KT14 234 BH114
Sch Oakfield Sch, Pyrford GU22 *off Coldharbour Rd* 249 BF115
Oakfields Rd, NW11 141 CY58
Oakfield St, SW10 39 N2
Oakford Rd, NW5 7 L1
Oak Gdns, Croy. CR0 225 EA103
Edgware HA8 118 CQ54
Oak Glade, Cooper. CM16 *off Coopersale Common* 92 EX29
Epsom KT19 *off Christ Ch Rd* 238 CN112
Northwood HA6 115 BP53
Oak Glen, Horn. RM11 150 FL55
Oak Gra Rd, W.Clan. GU4 266 BH128
Oak Grn, Abb.L. WD5 81 BS32
Oak Grn Way, Abb.L. WD5 81 BS32
Oak Gro, NW2 141 CY63
Hatfield AL10 67 CT18
Hertford SG13 54 DS11
Ruislip HA4 137 BV59
Sunbury-on-Thames TW16 197 BV94
West Wickham BR4 225 EC103
Oak Gro Rd, SE20 224 DW95
Oakhall Ct, E11 146 EH58
Oak Hall Ct, Sun. TW16 197 BT92
Oakhall Dr, Sun. TW16 197 BT92
Oak Hall Rd, E11 146 EH58
Oakham Cl, SE6 *off Rutland Wk* 205 DZ89
Barnet EN4 102 DF41
Oakham Dr, Brom. BR2 226 EF98
Oakhampton Rd, NW7 119 CX52
Oak Hill, Burpham GU4 265 BC129
Oakhill, Clay. KT10 237 CG107
Oak Hill, Epsom KT18 254 CR116
Surbiton KT6 220 CL101
Woodford Green IG8 123 ED52
Oakhill Av, NW3 5 L1
Pinner HA5 116 BY54
Oakhill Cl, Ashtd. KT21 253 CJ118
Maple Cross WD3 113 BE49
Oak Hill Cl, Wdf.Grn. IG8 123 EC52
Coll Oak Hill Coll, N14 *off Chase Side* 102 DG44
Oakhill Ct, SW19 201 CX94
Oak Hill Cres, Surb. KT6 220 CL101
Woodford Green IG8 123 ED52
Oakhill Dr, Surb. KT6 220 CL101
Oakhill Gdns, Wey. KT13 217 BS103
Oak Hill Gdns, Wdf.Grn. IG8 124 EE53
Oak Hill Gro, Surb. KT6 220 CL100
Oak Hill Pk, NW3 142 DB63
Oak Hill Pk Ms, NW3 142 DC63
Oakhill Path, Surb. KT6 220 CL100
Oakhill Pl, SW15 *off Oakhill Rd* 202 DA85
Sch Oakhill Prim Sch, Wdf.Grn. IG8 *off Alders Av* 124 EE51
Oakhill Rd, SW15 201 CZ85
SW16 223 DL95
Addlestone KT15 233 BF107
Ashtead KT21 253 CJ118
Beckenham BR3 225 EC96
Maple Cross WD3 113 BD49
Orpington BR6 227 ET102
Purfleet RM19 190 FP78
Reigate RH2 288 DB135
Sevenoaks TN13 278 FG124
Oak Hill Rd, Stap.Abb. RM4 127 FD45
Surbiton KT6 220 CL100
Oakhill Rd, Sutt. SM1 222 DB104
Oak Hill Way, NW3 142 DC63
Oak Ho, NW3 *off Maitland Pk Vil* 6 F4
Romford RM7 *off Cottons App* 149 FD57
Oakhouse Rd, Bexh. DA6 208 FA85
Oakhurst, Chobham GU24 232 AS109
Oakhurst Av, Bexh. DA7 188 EY80
East Barnet EN4 120 DE45
Oakhurst Cl, E17 146 EE56
Chislehurst BR7 227 EM95
Ilford IG6 125 EQ53
Teddington TW11 199 CE92
Oakhurst Gdns, E4 124 EF46
E17 146 EE56
Bexleyheath DA7 188 EY80
Oakhurst Gro, SE22 184 DU84
Oakhurst Pl, Wat. WD18 *off Cherrydale* 97 BT42
Oakhurst Ri, Cars. SM5 240 DE110
Oakhurst Rd, Enf. EN3 105 DX36
Epsom KT19 238 CQ107
Sch Oakhyrst Gra Sch, Cat. CR3 *off Stanstead Rd* 274 DR126
Oakington, Welw.G.C. AL7 52 DD08
Oakington Av, Amer. HP6 94 AY39
Harrow HA2 138 CA59
Hayes UB3 177 BR77
Wembley HA9 140 CM62
Oakington Cl, Sun. TW16 218 BW96
Oakington Dr, Sun. TW16 218 BW96
Oakington Manor Dr, Wem. HA9 140 CN64
Sch Oakington Manor Prim Sch, Wem. HA9 *off Oakington Manor Dr* 140 CP64
Oakington Rd, W9 15 K4
Oakington Way, N8 143 DL58
Oakland Gdns, Hutt. CM13 131 GC43
Oakland Pl, Buck.H. IG9 124 EG47
Oakland Rd, E15 13 H1
Oaklands, N21 121 DM47
Berkhamsted HP4 60 AU19
Fetcham KT22 253 CD124
Horley RH6 291 DJ148
Kenley CR8 242 DQ114
Loughton IG10 106 EJ44
Twickenham TW2 198 CC87
Oaklands Av, N9 104 DV44
Brookmans Park AL9 85 CY27
Esher KT10 219 CD102
Isleworth TW7 179 CF79
Romford RM1 149 FE55
Oaklands Av, Sidcup DA15 207 ET87
Thornton Heath CR7 223 DN98
Watford WD19 115 BV46
West Wickham BR4 225 EB104
Oaklands Cl, Bexh. DA6 208 EZ85
Chessington KT9 237 CJ105
Petts Wood BR5 227 ES100
Shalford GU4 280 AY142
Coll Oaklands Coll, Borehamwood Campus, Borwd. WD6 *off Elstree Way* 100 CQ40
Cen for Construction Crafts, St.Alb. AL4 *off Acrewood Way* 66 CN20
St. Albans City Campus, St.Alb. AL1 *off St. Peters Rd* 65 CE20
St. Albans Smallford Campus, St.Alb. AL4 *off Hatfield Rd* 66 CL19
Welwyn Garden City Campus, Welw.G.C. AL8 *off The Campus* 51 CX08
Oaklands Ct, W12 *off Uxbridge Rd* 161 CV74
Addlestone KT15 216 BH104
Watford WD17 97 BU39
Wembley HA0 139 CK64
Oaklands Dr, Harl. CM17 74 EW16
Redhill RH1 289 DH136
South Ockendon RM15 171 FW71
Oaklands Est, SW4 203 DJ86
Oaklands Gdns, Ken. CR8 242 DQ114
Oaklands Gate, Nthwd. HA6 115 BS51
Oaklands Gro, W12 161 CU74
Broxbourne EN10 71 DY24
Oaklands Ho, NW6 *off Belsize Rd* 5 N7
Sch Oaklands Inf Sch, Bigg.H. TN16 *off Norheads La* 260 EJ116
Sch Oaklands Jun Sch, Bigg.H. TN16 *off Oaklands La* 260 EJ116
Oaklands La, Barn. EN5 101 CV42
Biggin Hill TN16 244 EH113
Smallford AL4 66 CL18
Oaklands Ms, NW2 4 C1
Oaklands Pk, Hutt. CM13 131 GB46
Oaklands Pk Av, Ilf. IG1 *off High Rd* 147 ER61
Oaklands Pl, SW4 *off St. Alphonsus Rd* 183 DJ84
Sch Oaklands Prim Sch, W7 *off Oaklands Rd* 179 CF75
Oaklands Rd, N20 119 CZ45
NW2 4 C2
SW14 180 CR83
W7 179 CF75
Bexleyheath DA6 188 EZ84
Bromley BR1 206 EE94
Cheshunt EN7 88 DS26
Dartford DA2 210 FP88
Northfleet DA11 213 GF91
Sch Oaklands Sch, E2 20 E2
Isleworth TW7 *off Woodlands Rd* 179 CD83
Loughton IG10 *off Albion Hill* 106 EK43
Oaklands Way, Tad. KT20 255 CW122
Wallington SM6 241 DK108
Oaklands Wd, Hat. AL10 67 CU18
Oakland Way, Epsom KT19 238 CR107
Oak La, E14 21 N10
N2 120 DD54
N11 121 DK51
Cuffley EN6 87 DM28
Englefield Green TW20 194 AW90
Isleworth TW7 179 CE84
Sevenoaks TN13 278 FG127
Twickenham TW1 199 CG87
Windsor SL4 173 AN81
Woking GU22 *off Beaufort Rd* 249 BC116
Woodford Green IG8 124 EF49
Oaklawn Rd, Lthd. KT22 253 CE118
Oak Leaf Cl, Epsom KT19 238 CQ112
Oakleafe Gdns, Ilf. IG6 147 EP55
Oaklea Pas, Kings.T. KT1 219 CK97
Oakleigh Av, N20 120 DD47
Edgware HA8 118 CP54
Surbiton KT6 220 CN102
Oakleigh Cl, N20 120 DF48
Swanley BR8 229 FE97
Oakleigh Ct, N1 19 L1
Barnet EN4 102 DE44
Edgware HA8 118 CQ54
Oakleigh Cres, N20 120 DE47
Oakleigh Dr, Crox.Grn WD3 97 BQ44
Oakleigh Gdns, N20 120 DC46
Edgware HA8 118 CM50
Orpington BR6 245 ES105
Oakleigh Ms, N20 *off Oakleigh Rd N* 120 DC47
OAKLEIGH PARK, N20 120 DD46
⇌ Oakleigh Park 120 DD45
Oakleigh Pk Av, Chis. BR7 227 EN95
Oakleigh Pk N, N20 120 DD46
Oakleigh Pk S, N20 120 DE47
Oakleigh Ri, Epp. CM16 92 EU32
Oakleigh Rd, Pnr. HA5 116 BZ51
Uxbridge UB10 157 BQ66
Oakleigh Rd N, N20 120 DD47
Oakleigh Rd S, N11 120 DG48
Sch Oakleigh Spec Sch, N20 *off Oakleigh Rd N* 120 DF48
Oakleigh Way, Mitch. CR4 223 DH95
Surbiton KT6 220 CN102
Oakley Av, W5 160 CN73
Barking IG11 167 ET66
Croydon CR0 241 DL105
Oakley Cl, E4 123 EC48
E6 25 H8
W7 159 CE73
Addlestone KT15 234 BK105
Grays RM20 191 FW79
Isleworth TW7 179 CD81
Oakley Ct, Loug. IG10 *off Hillyfields* 107 EN40
Mitcham CR4 222 DG101
Oakley Cres, EC1 19 H1
Slough SL1 154 AS73
Oakley Dell, Guil. GU4 265 BC132
Oakley Dr, SE9 207 ER88
SE13 205 ED86
Bromley BR2 226 EL104
Romford RM3 128 FN50
Oakley Gdns, N8 143 DM57
SW3 40 D2
Banstead SM7 256 DB115
Betchworth RH3 286 CQ140
OAKLEY GREEN, Wind. SL4 172 AH82
Oakley Grn Rd, Oakley Grn SL4 172 AG82

Oakley Ho, SE11
off Hotspur St 30 E9
Oakley Pk, Bex. DA5 208 EW87
Oakley Pl, SE1 44 A1
Oakley Rd, N1 9 L6
SE25 224 DV99
Bromley BR2 226 EL104
Harrow HA1 139 CE58
Warlingham CR6 258 DU118
Oakley Sq, NW1 17 M1
Oakley St, SW3 40 C2
Oakley Wk, W6 38 D2
Oakley Yd, E2 20 B4
Oak Lock Ms, W4 180 CS78
Oak Lo Av, Chig. IG7 125 ER50
Oak Lo Cl, Hersham KT12 236 BW106
Stanmore HA7
off Dennis La 117 CJ50
Oak Lo Dr, Red. RH1 288 DG142
West Wickham BR4 225 EB101
Oak Lo La, West. TN16 277 ER125
Sch Oak Lo Prim Sch, W.Wick. BR4
off Chamberlain Cres 225 EB101
Sch Oak Lo Sch, SW12
off Nightingale La 202 DG87
Sch Oak Lo Spec Sch, N2
off Heath Vw 142 DC56
Oaklodge Way, NW7 119 CT50
Oak Manor Dr, Wem. HA9
off Oakington Manor Dr 140 CM64
Oakmead Av, Brom. BR2 226 EG100
Oakmeade, Pnr. HA5 116 CA51
Oakmead Gdns, Edg. HA8 118 CR49
Oakmead Grn, Epsom KT18 254 CP115
Oakmead Pl, Mitch. CR4 222 DE95
Oakmead Rd, SW12 202 DG88
Croydon CR0 223 DK100
Oakmere Av, Pot.B. EN6 86 DC33
Oakmere Cl, Pot.B. EN6 86 DD31
Oakmere La, Pot.B. EN6 86 DC32
Oakmere Ms, Pot.B. EN6 86 DC32
Sch Oakmere Prim Sch, Pot.B. EN6
off Chace Av 86 DD32
Oakmere Rd, SE2 188 EU79
Oakmont Pl, Orp. BR6 227 ER102
Oakmoor Way, Chig. IG7 125 ES50
Oak Pk, Hunsdon SG12 56 EH06
West Byfleet KT14 233 BE113
Oak Pk Gdns, SW19 201 CX87
Oak Pk Ms, N16 144 DT62
Oak Path, Bushey WD23
off Mortimer Cl 98 CB44
Oak Piece, N.Wld Bas. CM16 93 FC25
Oak Pl, SW18 off East Hill 202 DB85
Oakridge, Brick.Wd AL2 82 BZ29
Oak Ridge, Dor. RH4 285 CH139
Oakridge Av, Rad. WD7 83 CF34
Oakridge Dr, N2 142 DD55
Oakridge La, Ald. WD25 99 CD35
Bromley BR1 205 ED92
Radlett WD7 83 CF33
Oakridge Rd, Brom. BR1 205 ED91
Oak Ri, Buck.H. IG9 124 EK48
Oak Rd, W5 off The Broadway 159 CK73
Caterham CR3 258 DS122
Cobham KT11 252 BX115
Epping CM16 91 ET30
Gravesend DA12 213 GJ90
Grays RM17 192 GC79
Greenhithe DA9 211 FS86
Leatherhead KT22 253 CG118
New Malden KT3 220 CR96
Northumberland Heath
DA8 189 FC80
Orpington BR6 246 EU108
Reigate RH2 272 DB133
Romford RM3 128 FM53
Slade Green DA8 189 FG81
Westerham TN16 277 ER125
Oak Row, SW16 223 DJ96
Oakroyd Av, Pot.B. EN6 85 CZ33
Oakroyd Cl, Pot.B. EN6 85 CZ34
Oaks, The, N12 120 DB49
SE18 187 EQ78
Berkhamsted HP4 60 AU19
Dartford DA2 210 FP86
Dorking RH4 off Oak Ridge 285 CH139
Epsom KT18 239 CT114
Fetcham KT22 252 CC123
Hayes UB4 157 BQ68
Morden SM4 221 CY98
Ruislip HA4 137 BS59
Staines-upon-Thames TW18
off Moormede Cres 195 BF91
Swanley BR8 229 FE96
Tadworth KT20 255 CW123
Watford WD19 116 BW46
West Byfleet KT14 234 BG113
Woodford Green IG8 124 EE51
Oaks Av, SE19 204 DS92
Feltham TW13 198 BY89
Romford RM5 127 FC54
Worcester Park KT4 221 CV104
Oaks Cl, Lthd. KT22 253 CG121
Radlett WD7 99 CF35
Oaksford Av, SE26 204 DV90
Oaks Gro, E4 124 EE47
Oakshade Rd, Brom. BR1 205 ED91
Oxshott KT22 236 CC114
Oakshaw, Oxt. RH8 275 ED127
Oakshaw Rd, SW18 202 DB87
Oakside, Denh. UB9 156 BH65
Oakside Ct, Horl. RH6
off Oakside La 291 DJ147
Ilford IG6 125 ER53
Oakside La, Horl. RH6 291 DJ147
Oaks La, Croy. CR0 224 DW104
Ilford IG2 147 ES57
Mid Holmwood RH5 285 CH143
Sch Oaks Pk High Sch, Ilf. IG2
off Oaks La 147 ES57
Oaks Pavilion Ms, SE19 204 DS91
Oak Sq, Sev. TN13
off High St 279 FJ126
Oaks Retail Pk, The, Harl.
CM20 57 ET12
Oaks Rd, Croy. CR0 242 DV106
Kenley CR8 241 DP114
Reigate RH2 272 DC133
Stanwell TW19 196 BK86
Woking GU21 248 AY117
Oaks Shop Cen, W3
off High St 160 CQ74
Oak Sq, SW9 42 C9
Oaks Sq, The, Epsom KT19
off Waterloo Rd 238 CR113
Oaks Track, Cars. SM5 240 DF111
Wallington SM6 241 DH110
Oak St, Hem.H. HP3 62 BM24
Oak St, Romford RM7 149 FC57
Oak Stubbs La, Dorney R. SL6 172 AF75
Oaks Way, Cars. SM5 240 DF108
Epsom KT18
off Epsom La N 255 CV119
Kenley CR8 242 DQ114
Long Ditton KT6 219 CK103
Ripley GU23 250 BG124
Sch Oakthorpe Prim Sch, N13
off Tile Kiln La 122 DQ50
Oakthorpe Rd, N13 121 DN50
Oaktree Av, N13 121 DP48
Oak Tree Av, Bluewater DA9 211 FT87
Oak Tree Cl, W5 159 CJ72
Abbots Langley WD5 81 BR32
Oaktree Cl, Brwd. CM13
off Hawthorn Av 131 FZ48
Oak Tree Cl, Burpham GU4 265 BB129
Oaktree Cl, Goffs Oak EN7 87 DP28
Oak Tree Cl, Hat. AL10 67 CU17
Hertford Heath SG13 54 DW12
Jacobs Well GU4 264 AW128
Loughton IG10 107 EQ39
Stanmore HA7 117 CJ52
Virginia Water GU25 214 AX101
Oak Tree Ct, Els. WD6 99 CK44
Oak Tree Dell, NW9 140 CQ57
Oak Tree Dr, N20 120 DB46
Englefield Green TW20 194 AW92
Guildford GU1 264 AW130
Slough SL3 175 BB78
Oak Tree Gdns, Brom. BR1 206 EH92
Oaktree Gdns, Ch.Lang. CM17
off Burley Hill 74 EX16
Oak Tree Gdns, Guil. GU1 265 BB131
Oaktree Garth, Welw.G.C. AL7 51 CY10
Oaktree Gro, Ilf. IG1 147 ER64
Oak Tree Rd, NW8 16 B3
Sch Oaktree Sch, N14
off Chase Side 102 DG44
Sch Oaktree Sch, The, St.John's
GU21 off Gorsewood Rd 248 AS119
Oaktree Wk, Cat. CR3 258 DS122
Oak Vw, Wat. WD18 97 BS41
Oakview Cl, Chsht EN7 88 DV28
Watford WD19 98 BW44
Oakview Gdns, N2 142 DD56
Oak Vw Gdns, Slou. SL3 175 AZ77
Oakview Gro, Croy. CR0 225 DY102
Sch Oak Vw Prim & Nurs Sch,
Hat. AL10 off Woods Av 67 CV19
Oakview Rd, SE6 205 EB92
Sch Oak Vw Sch, Loug. IG10
off Whitehills Rd 107 EN42
Oak Village, NW5 7 H2
Oak Wk, Saw. CM21 58 EX07
Wallington SM6
off Helios Rd 222 DG102
Oak Warren, Sev. TN13 278 FG129
Oak Way, N14 121 DH45
Oakway, SW20 221 CW98
Oak Way, W3 160 CS74
Oakway, Amer. HP6 77 AP35
Oak Way, Ashtd. KT21 254 CN116
Oakway, Brom. BR2 225 ED96
Oak Way, Croy. CR0 225 DX100
Feltham TW14 197 BS88
Reigate RH2 288 DD135
Oakway, Wok. GU21 248 AS119
Oakway Cl, Bex. DA5 208 EY86
Oakway Pl, Rad. WD7
off Watling St 83 CG34
Oakways, SE9 207 EP86
Oakwell Dr, Northaw EN6 87 DH32
OAKWOOD, N14 103 DK44
⊖ Oakwood 103 DJ43
Oakwood, Berk. HP4 60 AT20
Guildford GU2 264 AU129
Wallington SM6 241 DH109
Waltham Abbey EN9
off Fairways 90 EE34
Oakwood Av, N14 121 DK45
Beckenham BR3 225 EC96
Borehamwood WD6 100 CP42
Bromley BR2 226 EH97
Epsom KT19 238 CN109
Hutton CM13 131 GE44
Mitcham CR4 222 DD96
Purley CR8 241 DP112
Southall UB1 158 CA73
Oakwood Chase, Horn. RM11 150 FM58
Oakwood Cl, N14 103 DJ44
SE13 205 ED87
Chislehurst BR7 207 EM93
Dartford DA1 210 FP88
East Horsley KT24 267 BS127
Redhill RH1 272 DG134
South Nutfield RH1
off Mid St 289 DM136
Woodford Green IG8
off Green Wk 124 EL51
Oakwood Ct, W14 26 G6
Slough SL1
off Oatlands Dr 154 AS72
Oakwood Cres, N21 103 DL44
Greenford UB6 159 CG65
Oakwood Dr, SE19 204 DR93
Bexleyheath DA7 189 FD84
East Horsley KT24 267 BS127
Edgware HA8 118 CQ51
St. Albans AL4 65 CJ19
Sevenoaks TN13 279 FH123
● Oakwood Est, Harl. CM20 58 EV11
Oakwood Gdns, Ilf. IG3 147 ET61
Orpington BR6 227 EQ103
Sutton SM1 222 DA103
Oakwood Hill, Loug. IG10 107 EM44
● Oakwood Hill Ind Est, Loug.
IG10 107 EP43
Oakwood La, W14 26 G6
Oakwood Ms, Harl. CM17
off Station Rd 58 EW11
Oakwood Pk Rd, N14 121 DK45
Oakwood Pl, Croy. CR0 223 DN100
Sch Oakwood Prim Sch, St.Alb.
AL4 off Oakwood Dr 65 CJ19
Oakwood Ri, Cat. CR3 274 DS125
Oakwood Rd, NW11 142 DB57
SW20 221 CU95
Bricket Wood AL2 82 BY29
Croydon CR0 223 DN100
Horley RH6 290 DG147
Merstham RH1 273 DN129
Orpington BR6 227 EQ103
Pinner HA5 115 BV54
Virginia Water GU25 214 AW99
Woking GU21 248 AS119
Sch Oakwood Sch, Bexh. DA7
off Woodside Rd 189 FD84
Sch Oakwood Sch, Horley RH6
off Balcombe Rd 291 DJ148
Purley CR8
off Godstone Rd 241 DP113
Oakwood Vw, N14 103 DK44
Oakworth Rd, W10 14 B6
Oarsman Pl, E.Mol. KT8 219 CE98
Sch Oasis Acad Coulsdon,
Couls. CR5
off Homefield Rd 257 DP120
Sch Oasis Acad Shirley Pk,
Croy. CR0 off Shirley Rd 224 DV101
Sch Oasis Acad Enfield,
Enf. EN3 off Kinetic Cres 105 DZ37
Sch Oasis Acad Hadley,
Enf. EN3 off Bell La 105 DX38
Oast Ho Cl, Wrays. TW19 194 AY87
Oasthouse Way, Orp. BR5 228 EV98
Oast Rd, Oxt. RH8 276 EF131
Oates Cl, Brom. BR2 225 ED97
Oates Rd, Rom. RM5 127 FB50
Oatfield Ho, N15 144 DS58
Oatfield Rd, Orp. BR6 227 ET102
Tadworth KT20 255 CV120
Oatland Ri, E17 123 DY54
Oatlands, Horl. RH6 291 DH147
Oatlands Av, Wey. KT13 235 BR106
Oatlands Chase, Wey. KT13 217 BS104
Oatlands Cl, Wey. KT13 235 BQ105
Oatlands Dr, Slou. SL1 153 AR72
Weybridge KT13 217 BR104
Oatlands Grn, Wey. KT13 217 BR104
Sch Oatlands Inf Sch,
Wey. KT13
off St. Marys Rd 235 BR105
Oatlands Mere, Wey. KT13 217 BR104
OATLANDS PARK, Wey. KT13 235 BR105
Oatlands Rd, Enf. EN3 104 DW39
Tadworth KT20 255 CY119
Oat La, EC2 19 J8
Oatridge Gdns, Hem.H. HP2 63 BP19
Oban Cl, E13 24 C5
Oban Ct, Slou. SL1
off Montem La 173 AR75
Oban Ho, E14 23 H8
Barking IG11
off Wheelers Cross 167 ER68
Oban Rd, E13 24 D3
SE25 224 DR98
Oban St, E14 23 H8
Obelisk Ride, Egh. TW20 194 AS93
Oberon Cl, Borwd. WD6 100 CQ39
Oberon Ct, Denh. UB9
off Patrons Way E 135 BF58
Oberon Way, Shep. TW17 216 BL97
Oberstein Rd, SW11 182 DD84
Oborne Cl, SE24 203 DP85
O'Brien Ho, E2 21 K2
Observatory Gdns, W8 27 J4
Observatory Ms, E14 34 G9
Observatory Rd, SW14 180 CQ84
Observatory Shop Cen,
Slou. SL1 174 AU75
Observatory Wk, Red. RH1
off Lower Br Rd 272 DF134
Observer Dr, Wat. WD18 97 BS42
Occupation La, SE18 187 EP81
W5 179 CK77
Roydon CM19 72 EH15
Occupation Rd, SE17 31 J10
W13 179 CH75
Watford WD18 97 BV43
Ocean Est, E1 21 K5
Oceanis, E16 off Seagull La 23 N10
Ocean St, E1 21 K6
Ocean Wf, E14 34 A5
Ockenden Cl, Wok. GU22
off Ockenden Rd 249 AZ118
Ockenden Gdns, Wok. GU22
off Ockenden Rd 249 AZ118
Ockenden Rd, Wok. GU22 249 AZ118
⇌ Ockendon 171 FX69
Ockendon Ms, N1 9 L5
Ockendon Rd, N1 9 L5
Upminster RM14 150 FQ64
Sch Ockendon Sch, The,
S.Ock. RM15
off Erriff Dr 171 FU71
OCKHAM, Wok. GU23 250 BN121
Ockham Dr, Grnf. UB6 158 CC66
Orpington BR5 208 EU94
West Horsley KT24 251 BR124
Ockham La, Cob. KT11 251 BT118
Ockham GU23 251 BP120
Jct Ockham Pk, Wok. GU23 250 BL119
Ockham Rd N, Lthd. KT24 251 BQ124
Ockham GU23 250 BN121
Ockham Rd S, E.Hors. KT24 267 BS126
Ockley Ct, Guil. GU4
off Cotts Wd Dr 265 BB129
Sutton SM1 off Oakhill Rd 240 DC105
Ockley Rd, SW16 203 DL90
Croydon CR0 223 DM101
Ockleys Mead, Gdse. RH9 274 DW129
Octagon, The, Ware SG12 55 DX05
Octagon Arc, EC2 19 N7
Octagon Rd, Whiteley Vill.
KT12 235 BS109
Octavia Cl, Mitch. CR4 222 DE99
Octavia Ct, Wat. WD24 98 BW40
Octavia Ms, W9 14 G4
Octavia Rd, Islw. TW7 179 CF82
Octavia St, SW11 40 C7
Octavia Way, SE28
off Booth Cl 168 EV73
Staines-upon-Thames TW18 196 BG93
Octavius St, SE8 46 A4
Odard Rd, W.Mol. KT8
off Down St 218 CA98
Oddesey Rd, Borwd. WD6 100 CP39
Odds Fm Est, Woob.Grn HP10 132 AH59
Odelia Ct, E15
off Biggerstaff Rd 12 F8
Odell Cl, Bark. IG11 167 ET66
Odell Wk, SE13
off Bankside Av 185 EB83
Odencroft Rd, Slou. SL2 153 AN69
Odeon, The, Bark. IG11
off Longbridge Rd 167 ER66
Odeon Par, Grnf. UB6
off Allendale Rd 159 CH65
Sch Odessa Inf Sch, E7 13 N2
Odessa Rd, E7 13 M1
NW10 161 CU68
Odessa St, SE16 33 N5
Odger St, SW11 40 F8
● Odhams Trading Est,
Wat. WD24 98 BW37
Odhams Wk, WC2 18 B9
● Odyssey Business Pk, Ruis.
HA4 137 BV64
Offa Rd, St.Alb. AL3 64 CC20
Offa's Mead, E9 11 M1
Offenbach Ho, E2 21 J1
Offenham Rd, SE9 207 EM91
Offers Ct, Kings.T. KT1
off Winery La 220 CM97
Offerton Rd, SW4 183 DJ83
Offham Slope, N12 119 CZ50
Offley Pl, Islw. TW7 179 CD82
Offley Rd, SW9 42 E4
Offord Cl, N17 122 DU51
Offord Rd, N1 8 C6
Offord St, N1 8 C6
Ogard Rd, Hodd. EN11 71 EC15
Ogilby St, SE18 37 J9
Oglander Rd, SE15 184 DT84
Ogle St, W1 17 L6
Oglethorpe Rd, Dag. RM10 148 EZ62
Ohio Bldg, SE13
off Deals Gateway 46 C7
Ohio Rd, E13 23 M5
Oil Mill La, W6 181 CU78
Okeburn Rd, SW17 202 DG92
Okehampton Cl, N12 120 DD50
Okehampton Cres, Well. DA16 188 EV81
Okehampton Rd, NW10 4 B9
Romford RM3 128 FJ51
Okehampton Sq, Rom. RM3 128 FJ51
Okemore Gdns, Orp. BR5 228 EW98
Olaf St, W11 26 D1
Old Acre, Wok. GU22 234 BG114
Oldacre Ms, SW12
off Balham Gro 203 DH87
★ Old Admiralty Bldg (MoD),
SW1 29 P3
Old Amersham Rd, Ger.Cr.
SL9 135 BB60
Old Av, W.Byf. KT14 233 BE113
Weybridge KT13 235 BR107
Old Av Cl, W.Byf. KT14 233 BE113
Old Bailey, EC4 19 H9
Old Bakery Ms, Albury GU5 282 BH139
Old Barge Ho All, SE1
off Upper Grd 30 F2
Old Barn Cl, Sutt. SM2 239 CY108
Old Barn La, Crox.Grn WD3 96 BM43
Kenley CR8 258 DT116
Old Barn Ms, Crox.Grn WD3
off Old Barn La 96 BM43
Old Barn Rd, Epsom KT18 254 CQ117
Old Barn Way, Bexh. DA7 189 FD83
Old Barrack Yd, SW1 28 G4
Old Barrowfield, E15 13 K9
Old Bath Rd, Colnbr. SL3 175 BE81
Old Beaconsfield Rd, Farn.Com.
SL2 153 AQ65
Old Bell Ct, Hem.H. HP2
off George St 62 BK19
Old Bellgate Pl, E14 34 A7
Oldberry Rd, Edg. HA8 118 CR51
Old Bethnal Grn Rd, E2 20 D2
OLD BEXLEY, Bex. DA5 209 FB87
● Old Bexley Business Pk,
Bex. DA5 209 FB87
Sch Old Bexley C of E Prim Sch,
Bex. DA5 off Hurst Rd 208 EZ88
Old Bexley La, Bex. DA5 209 FD89
Dartford DA1 209 FF88
★ Old Billingsgate, EC3 31 N1
Old Billingsgate Wk, EC3
off Lower Thames St 31 N1
Old Bond St, W1 29 L1
Oldborough Rd, Wem. HA0 139 CJ61
Old Brewers Yd, WC2 18 A9
Old Brewery Ms, NW3 6 A1
Old Br Cl, Nthlt. UB5 158 CA68
Old Br La, Epsom KT17 239 CT112
Old Br St, Hmptn W. KT1 219 CK96
Old Broad St, EC2 19 M9
Old Bromley Rd, Brom. BR1 205 ED92
Old Brompton Rd, SW5 39 K1
SW7 39 K1
Old Bldgs, WC2 18 E8
Old Burlington St, W1 17 L10
Oldbury Cl, Cher. KT16
off Oldbury Rd 215 BE101
Orpington BR5 228 EX98
Oldbury Gro, Beac. HP9 111 AK50
Old Bury Hill, Westc. RH4 285 CE138
Oldbury Pl, W1 17 H6
Oldbury Rd, Cher. KT16 215 BE101
Enfield EN1 104 DU40
Old Canal Ms, SE15 44 B1
Old Carriageway, The, Sev.
TN13 278 FC123
Old Castle St, E1 20 A7
Old Cavendish St, W1 17 J8
Old Change Ct, EC4
off Carter La 19 J9
Old Chapel Rd, Swan. BR8 229 FC101
Old Charlton Rd, Shep. TW17 217 BQ99
● Old Char Wf, Dor. RH4 285 CF135
Old Chelsea Ms, SW3 40 B3
Old Chertsey Rd, Chobham
GU24 232 AV110
Old Chestnut Av, Esher KT10 236 CA107
Old Chorleywood Rd, Rick. WD3
off Chorleywood Rd 96 BK44
Old Ch Cl, Orp. BR6 228 EV102
Oldchurch Gdns, Rom. RM7 149 FD59
Old Ch La, NW9 140 CQ61
Mountnessing CM13 131 GE42
Perivale UB6
off Perivale La 159 CG69
Stanmore HA7 117 CJ52
Old Ch Path, Esher KT10
off High St 236 CB105
Oldchurch Ri, Rom. RM7 149 FE58
Old Ch Rd, E1 21 J9
E4 123 EA49
Oldchurch Rd, Rom. RM7 149 FD59
Old Ch St, SW3 40 B1
Old Claygate La, Clay. KT10 237 CG107
Old Clem Sq, SE18
off Kempt St 187 EN79
Old Coach Rd, Cher. KT16 215 BD99
Old Coach Rd, The, Cole Grn
SG14 52 DF12
Old Coal Yd, SE28
off Pettman Cres 187 ER77
Old Common Rd, Chorl. WD3
off Common Rd 95 BD42
Cobham KT11 235 BU112
Old Compton St, W1 17 N10
Old Cote Dr, Houns. TW5 178 CA79
OLD COULSDON, Couls. CR5 257 DN119
Old Ct, Ashtd. KT21 254 CL119
Old Ct Grn, Pott.End HP4
off Hempstead La 61 BC17
Old Ct Pl, W8 27 L4
Old Ct Rd, Guil. GU2 280 AU135
Old Crabtree La, Hem.H. HP2 62 BL21
Old Cross, Hert. SG14 54 DQ09
Old Cross Wf, Hert. SG14
off Old Cross 54 DQ09
★ Old Curiosity Shop, WC2 18 C8
Old Dairy, The, Wok. GU21
off Goldsworth Rd 248 AX117
Old Dairy Ms, SW4
off Tintern St 183 DL84
SW12 202 DG88
Old Dairy Sq, N21
off Wades Hill 121 DN45
Old Dartford Rd, Fnghm DA4 230 FM100
Old Dean, Bov. HP3 79 BA27
Old Deer Pk Gdns, Rich. TW9 180 CL83
Old Devonshire Rd, SW12 203 DH87
Old Dock App Rd, Grays
RM17 192 GE77
Old Dock Cl, Rich. TW9 180 CN79
Old Dover Rd, SE3 47 P4
Old Dr, The, Welw.G.C. AL8 51 CV10
Olden La, Pur. CR8 241 DN112
Old Esher Cl, Hersham KT12 236 BX106
Old Esher Rd, Hersham KT12 236 BX106
Old Essex Rd, Hodd. EN11 71 EB16
Old Farleigh Rd, S.Croy. CR2 242 DW110
Warlingham CR6 243 DY113
Old Fm Av, N14 121 DJ45
Sidcup DA15 207 ER88
Old Fm Cl, Houns. TW4 178 BZ84
Knotty Green HP9 110 AJ50
Old Fm Gdns, Swan. BR8 229 FF97
Old Farmhouse Dr, Oxshott
KT22 253 CD115
Old Fm Pas, Hmptn. TW12 218 CC95
Old Fm Rd, N2 120 DD53
Guildford GU1 264 AX131
Hampton TW12 198 BZ93
West Drayton UB7 176 BK75
Old Fm Rd E, Sid. DA15 208 EU89
Old Fm Rd W, Sid. DA15 207 ET89
Old Fm Yd, The, Sheering
CM22 59 FC07
Old Ferry Dr, Wrays. TW19 194 AW86
Sch Oldfield Cen, Hmptn. TW12
off Oldfield Rd 218 BZ95
Oldfield Circ, Nthlt. UB5 158 CC65
Old Fld Cl, Amer. HP6 94 AY39
Oldfield Cl, Brom. BR1 227 EM98
Cheshunt EN8 89 DY28
Greenford UB6 139 CE64
Horley RH6
off Oldfield Rd 290 DF150
Stanmore HA7 117 CG50
Oldfield Dr, Chsht EN8 89 DY28
Oldfield Fm Gdns, Grnf. UB6 159 CD67
Oldfield Gdns, Ashtd. KT21 253 CK119
Oldfield Gro, SE16 33 J9
Oldfield La N, Grnf. UB6 159 CE65
Oldfield La S, Grnf. UB6 158 CC70
Oldfield Ms, N6 143 DJ59
Sch Oldfield Prim Sch, Grnf. UB6
off Oldfield La N 159 CD68
Oldfield Rd, N16 144 DS62
NW10 161 CT66
SW19 201 CY93
W3 off Valetta Rd 181 CT75
Bexleyheath DA7 188 EY82
Bromley BR1 227 EM98
Hampton TW12 218 BZ95
Hemel Hempstead HP1 61 BE21
Horley RH6 290 DF150
London Colney AL2 83 CK25
Oldfields Rd, Sutt. SM1 221 CZ104
● Oldfields Trd Est, Sutt.
SM1 222 DA104
Oldfield Wd, Wok. GU22
off Maybury Hill 249 BB117
Old Fishery La, Hem.H. HP1 61 BF22
Old Fish St Hill, EC4 19 J10
Old Fives Ct, Burn. SL1 152 AH69
Old Fleet La, EC4 18 G8
Old Fold Cl, Barn. EN5
off Old Fold La 101 CZ39
Old Fold La, Barn. EN5 101 CZ39
Old Fold Vw, Barn. EN5 101 CW41
OLD FORD, E3 11 N7
Sch Old Ford Prim Sch, E3 11 N10
Old Ford Rd, E2 20 F2
E3 11 K10
Old Forge Cl, Stan. HA7 117 CG49
Watford WD25 81 BU33
Welwyn AL6 51 CZ05
Old Forge Cres, Shep. TW17 217 BP100
Old Forge Ms, W12
off Goodwin Rd 181 CV75
Old Forge Rd, N19 143 DK61
Enfield EN1 104 DT38
Loudwater HP10 110 AC53
Old Forge Way, Sid. DA14 208 EV91
Old Fox Cl, Cat. CR3 257 DP121
Old Fox Footpath,
S.Croy. CR2
off Essenden Rd 242 DS108
Old French Horn La, Hat. AL10 67 CV17
Old Gannon Cl, Nthwd. HA6 115 BQ50
Old Gdn, The, Sev. TN13 278 FD123
Old Gdn Ct, St.Alb. AL3 64 CC20
Old Gloucester St, WC1 18 B6
Old Gro Cl, Chsht EN7 88 DR26
Old Hall Cl, Pnr. HA5 116 BY53
Old Hall Dr, Pnr. HA5 116 BY53
Old Hall Ri, Harl. CM17 74 EY15
Old Hall St, Hert. SG14 54 DR09
Oldham Ter, W3 160 CQ74
OLD HARLOW, Harl. CM17 58 EX11
Old Harpenden Rd, St.Alb. AL3 65 CE17
Old Harrow La, West. TN16 261 EQ119
Old Hatch Manor, Ruis. HA4 137 BT59
OLD HATFIELD, Hat. AL9 67 CX17
Old Heath Rd, Wey. KT13 234 BN107
Old Herns La, Welw.G.C. AL7
off Herns La 52 DC07
Old Hertford Rd, Hat. AL9 67 CW16
Old Highway, Hodd. EN11 55 EB14
Old Hill, Chis. BR7 227 EN95
Orpington BR6 245 ER107

Old Hill, Woking GU22 248 AX120
Oldhill St, N16 144 DU60
Old Homesdale Rd, Brom. BR2 226 EJ98
Old Hosp Cl, SW12 202 DF88
Old Ho Cl, SW19 201 CY92
Epsom KT17 239 CT110
Old Ho Ct, Hem.H. HP2 62 BM20
Oldhouse Cft, Harl. CM20 57 ES13
Old Ho Gdns, Twick. TW1 199 CJ85
Old Ho La, Kings L. WD4 96 BL35
Lower Nazeing EN9 72 EF23
Roydon CM19 72 EK18
Old Ho Rd, Hem.H. HP2 62 BM20
Old Howlett's La, Ruis. HA4 137 BQ58
Old Jamaica Rd, SE16 32 C6
Old James St, SE15 184 DV83
Old Jewry, EC2 19 L9
Old Kenton La, NW9 140 CP57
Old Kent Rd, SE1 31 M7
SE15 44 D2
Old Kiln La, Brock. RH3 286 CQ135
Old Kiln Rd, Penn HP10 110 AC45
Old Kingston Rd, Wor.Pk. KT4 220 CQ104
Old La, Cob. KT11 251 BP117
Oxted RH8 276 EF129
Tatsfield TN16 260 EK121
Old La Gdns, Cob. KT11 251 BT122
Old Leys, Hat. AL10 67 CU22
Old Lib La, Hert. SG14
off Old Cross 54 DQ09
Old Lo Dr, Beac. HP9 111 AL54
Old Lo La, Ken. CR8 257 DN115
Purley CR8 241 DM113
Old Lo Pl, Twick. TW1
off St. Margarets Rd 199 CH86
Old Lo Way, Stan. HA7 117 CG50
Old London Rd, Bad.Mt TN14 246 FA110
East Horsley KT24 267 BU126
Epsom KT18 255 CU118
Hertford SG13 54 DS09
Kingston upon Thames KT2 220 CL96
Knockholt Pound TN14 262 EY115
Mickleham RH5 269 CJ127
St. Albans AL1 65 CD21
Old Long Gro, Beac. HP9 111 AQ51
Old Maidstone Rd, Sid. DA14 208 EZ94
OLD MALDEN, Wor.Pk. KT4 220 CR102
Old Malden La, Wor.Pk. KT4 220 CR103
Old Malt Way, Wok. GU21 248 AX117
Old Manor Dr, Grav. DA12 213 GJ88
Isleworth TW7 198 CC86
Old Manor Gdns, Chilw. GU4 281 BD140
Old Manor Ho Ms, Shep. TW17
off Squires Br Rd 216 BN97
Old Manor La, Chilw. GU4 281 BC140
Old Manor Rd, Sthl. UB2 178 BX77
Old Manor Way, Bexh. DA7 189 FD82
Chislehurst BR7 207 EM92
Old Manor Yd, SW5 27 K10
Old Mkt Sq, E2 20 A2
Old Marsh La, Tap. SL6 172 AF75
Old Marylebone Rd, NW1 16 D7
Old Mead, Chal.St.P. SL9 112 AY51
Old Meadow Cl, Berk. HP4 60 AU21
Old Merrow St, Guil. GU4 265 BC131
Old Ms, Har. HA1
off Hindes Rd 139 CE57
Old Mill Cl, Eyns. DA4 230 FL102
Old Mill Ct, E18 146 EJ55
Old Mill Gdns, Berk. HP4 60 AX19
Old Mill La, Bray SL6 172 AD75
Merstham RH1 273 DH128
Uxbridge UB8 156 BH72
Old Mill Pl, Rom. RM7 149 FD58
Wraysbury TW19 195 BB86
Old Mill Rd, SE18 187 ER79
Denham UB9 136 BG62
Hunton Bridge WD4 81 BQ33
Old Mitre Ct, EC4 18 F9
Old Montague St, E1 20 C7
Old Moor La, Woob.Moor
HP10 132 AE55
Old Nazeing Rd, Brox. EN10 71 EA21
Old Nichol St, E2 20 A4
Old N St, WC1 18 C6
Old Nurseries La, Cob. KT11 235 BV113
Old Nursery Ct, Hedg. SL2 133 AQ61
Old Nursery Pl, Ashf. TW15
off Park Rd 197 BP92
Old Oak, St.Alb. AL1 65 CE23
Old Oak Av, Chipstead CR5 256 DE119
Old Oak Cl, Chess. KT9 238 CM105
Cobham KT11 235 BV113
OLD OAK COMMON, NW10 161 CT71
Old Oak Common La, NW10 160 CS71
W3 160 CS71
Old Oak La, NW10 160 CS69
[Sch] Old Oak Prim Sch, W12
off Mellitus St 161 CT72
Old Oak Rd, W3 161 CT73
Old Oaks, Wal.Abb. EN9 90 EE32
★ Old Operating Thea Mus &
Herb Garret, SE1 31 M3
Old Orchard, Byfleet KT14 234 BM112
Harlow CM18 73 ER17
Park Street AL2 82 CC26
Sunbury-on-Thames TW16 218 BW96
Old Orchard, The, NW3
off Nassington Rd 142 DF63
Iver SL0 155 BF72
Old Orchard Cl, Barn. EN4 102 DD38
Uxbridge UB8 156 BN72
Old Orchard Ms, Berk. HP4 60 AW20
Old Otford Rd, Sev. TN14 263 FH117
Old Palace La, Rich. TW9 199 CJ85
[Sch] Old Palace of John Whitgift
Jun Sch, S.Croy. CR2
off Melville Av 242 DT107
[Sch] Old Palace of John Whitgift
Sen Sch, Croy. CR0
off Old Palace Rd 223 DP104
[Sch] Old Palace Prim Sch, E3 22 D2
Old Palace Rd, Croy. CR0 223 DP104
Guildford GU2 280 AU135
Weybridge KT13 217 BP104
Old Palace Ter, Rich. TW9
off King St 199 CK85
Old Palace Yd, SW1 30 A6
Richmond TW9 199 CJ85
Old Papermill Ct, Woob.Grn HP10
off Glory Mill La 132 AE56
Old Paradise St, SE11 30 C8
Old Pk Av, SW12 202 DG86
Enfield EN2 104 DQ42
Old Parkbury La, Coln.St AL2 83 CF30
Old Pk Gro, Enf. EN2 104 DQ42
Old Pk La, W1 29 H3
Old Pk Ms, Houns. TW5 178 BZ80
Old Pk Ride, Wal.Cr. EN7 88 DT33
Old Pk Ridings, N21 103 DP44
Old Pk Rd, N13 121 DM49
SE2 188 EU78
Enfield EN2 103 DP41
Old Pk Rd S, Enf. EN2 103 DP42
Old Pk Vw, Enf. EN2 103 DN41
Old Parsonage Yd, Hort.Kir.
DA4 230 FQ97
Old Parvis Rd, W.Byf. KT14 234 BK112
Old Pearson St, SE10 46 D4
Old Perry St, Chis. BR7 207 ES94
Northfleet DA11 212 GE89
Old Polhill, Sev. TN14 263 FD115
Old Portsmouth Rd, Gdmg.
GU7 280 AV142
Guildford GU3 280 AV142
Old PO La, SE3 186 EH83
Old Post Office Wk, Surb. KT6
off St. Marys Rd 219 CK100
Old Pottery Cl, Reig. RH2 288 DB136
Old Pound Cl, Islw. TW7 179 CG81
Old Priory, Hare. UB9 137 BP59
Old Pye St, SW1 29 N6
Old Quebec St, W1 16 F9
Old Queen St, SW1 29 P5
Old Rectory Cl, Walt.Hill KT20 255 CU124
Old Rectory Dr, Hat. AL10 67 CV18
Old Rectory Gdns, Edg. HA8 118 CN51
Old Rectory La, Denh. UB9 135 BE59
East Horsley KT24 267 BS126
Old Redding, Har. HA3 116 CC49
Old Redstone Dr, Red. RH1 288 DG135
Old Reigate Rd, Bet. RH3 270 CP134
Dorking RH4 270 CL134
Oldridge Rd, SW12 202 DG87
Old Rd, SE13 186 EE84
Addlestone KT15 233 BF108
Buckland RH3 270 CS134
Dartford DA1 189 FD84
Enfield EN3 104 DW39
Harlow CM17 58 EX11
Old Rd E, Grav. DA12 213 GH88
Old Rd W, Grav. DA11 213 GF88
Old Rope Wk, Sun. TW16
off The Avenue 217 BV97
Old Royal Free Pl, N1
off Old Royal Free Sq 8 F9
Old Royal Free Sq, N1 8 F9
Old Ruislip Rd, Nthlt. UB5 158 BX68
Old St. Mary's, W.Hors. KT24
off Ripley La 267 BP129
Olds App, Wat. WD18 115 BP46
Old Savill's Cotts, Chig. IG7
off The Chase 125 EQ49
Old Sch Cl, SE10 35 K7
SW19 222 DA96
Beckenham BR3 225 DX96
Guildford GU1
off Markenfield Rd 264 AX134
Old Sch Ct, Wrays. TW19 194 AY87
Old Sch Cres, E7 13 N5
Old Sch Ho, Godden Grn
TN15 279 FN124
Old Sch La, E5 145 DX61
Brockham RH3 286 CN138
Old Sch Ms, Stai. TW18 195 BD92
Weybridge KT13 235 BR105
Old Sch Pl, Croy. CR0 241 DN105
Woking GU22 248 AY121
Old Sch Rd, Uxb. UB8 156 BM70
Old Schs La, Epsom KT17 239 CT109
Old Sch Sq, E14 22 A9
Thames Ditton KT7 219 CF100
Olds Cl, Wat. WD18 115 BP46
Old Seacoal La, EC4 18 G8
Old Shire La, Chorl. WD3 95 BB44
Gerrards Cross SL9 113 BA46
Waltham Abbey EN9 106 EG35
Old Slade La, Iver SL0 175 BE76
Old Solesbridge La, Chorl.
WD3 96 BG41
Old Sopwell Gdns, St.Alb. AL1 65 CE22
Old S Cl, Hatch End HA5 116 BX53
Old S Lambeth Rd, SW8 42 B4
🔒 Old Spitalfields Mkt, E1 20 A6
Old Sq, WC2 18 D8
Old Stable Ms, N5 144 DQ62
Old Sta App, Lthd. KT22 253 CG121
Old Sta Pas, Rich. TW9
off Little Grn 179 CK84
Old Sta Rd, Hayes UB3 177 BT76
Loughton IG10 106 EL43
Old Sta Way, SW4
off Voltaire Rd 183 DK83
Wooburn Green HP10 132 AE58
Old Sta Yd, Brom. BR2
off Bourne Way 226 EF102
Oldstead Rd, Brom. BR1 205 ED91
Old Stede Cl, Ashtd. KT21 254 CM117
Old Stockley Rd, West Dr.
UB7 177 BP75
⇌ Old Street 19 L3
⊖ Old Street 19 L3
Old St, E13 24 B1
EC1 19 J4
Old St, The, Fetch. KT22 253 CD123
Old Studio Cl, Croy. CR0 224 DR101
Old Swan Yd, Cars. SM5 240 DF105
Old Thea Ct, SE1
off Porter St 31 K2
Old Thieves La, Hertingfordbury
SG14 off Thieves La 53 DM10
Old Tilburstow Rd, Gdse. RH9 274 DW134
Old Town, SW4 183 DJ83
Croydon CR0 223 DP104
Old Town Cl, Beac. HP9 111 AL54
★ Old Town Hall Arts Cen,
Hem.H. HP1 62 BK19
Old Tram Yd, SE18
off Lakedale Rd 187 ES77
Old Twelve Cl, W7 159 CE70
Old Tye Av, Bigg.H. TN16 260 EL116
Old Uxbridge Rd, W.Hyde WD3 113 BE53
[Sch] Old Vicarage Sch,
Rich. TW10
off Richmond Hill 200 CL86
Old Vicarage Way, Woob.Grn
HP10 132 AE59
Old Wk, The, Otford TN14 263 FH117
Old Watery La, Woob.Grn
HP10 132 AE55
Old Watford Rd, Brick.Wd AL2 82 BY30
Old Watling St, Grav. DA11 213 GG92
Oldway La, Slou. SL1 173 AK75
Old Westhall Cl, Warl. CR6 258 DW119
Old Wf Way, Wey. KT13
off Weybridge Rd 234 BM105
OLD WINDSOR, Wind. SL4 194 AU86
Old Windsor Lock, Old Wind.
SL4 194 AW85
OLD WOKING, Wok. GU22 249 BA121
Old Woking Rd, W.Byf. KT14 233 BF113
Woking GU22 249 BE116
Old Woolwich Rd, SE10 47 H2
Old Yd, The, West. TN16 262 EW124
Old York Rd, SW18 202 DB85
Oleander Cl, Orp. BR6 245 ER106
O'Leary Sq, E1 20 G6
[Sch] Olga Prim Sch, E3 21 M1
Olga St, E3 21 M1
Olinda Rd, N16 144 DT58
Oliphant St, W10 14 D2
Olive Cl, St.Alb. AL1 65 CH21
Olive Gro, N15 144 DQ56
Oliver Av, SE25 224 DT97
● Oliver Business Pk, NW10
off Oliver Rd 160 CQ68
Oliver Cl, W4 180 CP79
Addlestone KT15 234 BG105
Grays RM20 191 FT80
Hemel Hempstead HP3 62 BL24
Hoddesdon EN11 71 EB15
Park Street AL2 83 CD27
Oliver Cres, Fnghm DA4 230 FM101
Oliver Gdns, E6 25 H8
Oliver-Goldsmith Est, SE15 44 D6
[Sch] Oliver Goldsmith Prim Sch,
NW9 off Coniston Gdns 140 CR57
SE5 44 A6
Oliver Gro, SE25 224 DT98
Oliver Ms, SE15 44 C8
Olive Rd, E13 24 D3
NW2 141 CW63
SW19 off Norman Rd 202 DC94
W5 179 CK76
Dartford DA1 210 FK88
Oliver Ri, Hem.H. HP3 62 BL24
Oliver Rd, E10 145 EB61
E17 145 EC57
NW10 160 CQ68
Grays RM20 191 FU80
Hemel Hempstead HP3 62 BL24
New Malden KT3 220 CQ96
Rainham RM13 169 FF67
Shenfield CM15 131 GA43
Sutton SM1 240 DD105
Swanley BR8 229 FD97
Olivers Cl, Pott.End HP4 61 BC16
Olivers Yd, EC1 19 M4
Olive St, Rom. RM7 149 FD57
Olivette St, SW15 181 CX83
Olivia Dr, Slou. SL3 175 AZ78
Olivia Gdns, Hare. UB9 114 BJ53
Olivier Ct, Denh. UB9
off Patrons Way E 135 BF58
Olivier Cres, Dor. RH4
off Stubs Cl 285 CJ138
Ollards Gro, Loug. IG10 106 EK42
Olleberrie La, Sarratt WD3 79 BD32
Ollerton Grn, E3 11 P8
Ollerton Rd, N11 121 DK50
Olley Cl, Wall. SM6 241 DL108
Ollgar Cl, W12 161 CT74
Olliffe St, E14 34 F7
Olmar St, SE1 44 C2
Olney Rd, SE17 43 J2
Olron Cres, Bexh. DA6 208 EX85
Olven Rd, SE18 187 EQ80
Olveston Wk, Cars. SM5 222 DD100
Olwen Ms, Pnr. HA5 116 BX54
Olyffe Av, Well. DA16 188 EU82
Olyffe Dr, Beck. BR3 225 EC95
★ Olympia, W14 26 F7
Olympia Ms, W2 27 M1
Olympia Way, W14 26 F7
[H] Olympic Med Inst, Har.
HA1 139 CH59
Olympic Sq, Wem. HA9 140 CN62
★ Olympic Stadium, E20 12 C7
Olympic Way, Grnf. UB6 158 CB67
Wembley HA9 140 CN63
Olympus Gro, N22 121 DN53
Olympus Sq, E5
off Nolan Way 144 DU62
Oman Av, NW2 141 CW63
O'Meara St, SE1 31 K3
Omega Bldg, SW18
off Smugglers Way 182 DB84
Omega Cl, E14 34 C6
Omega Ct, Rom. RM7 149 FC58
Ware SG12 off Crib St 55 DX06
Omega Maltings, Ware SG12
off Star St 55 DY06
Omega Pl, N1 18 B1
Omega Rd, Wok. GU21 249 BA115
Omega St, SE14 45 P6
Omega Way, Egh. TW20 215 BC95
● Omega Wks, E3 12 B6
Ommaney Rd, SE14 45 L7
Omnibus Ho, N22
off Redvers Rd 121 DN54
Omnibus Way, E17 123 EA54
Ondine Rd, SE15 184 DT84
Onega Gate, SE16 33 L6
O'Neill Path, SE18
off Kempt St 187 EN79
● One New Change, EC4 19 J9
One Pin La, Farn.Com. SL2 133 AQ63
One Tree Cl, SE23 204 DW86
One Tree Hill Rd, Guil. GU4 281 BB135
One Tree La, Beac. HP9 111 AL52
Ongar Cl, Add. KT15 233 BF107
Romford RM6 148 EW57
Ongar Hill, Add. KT15 234 BG107
Ongar Par, Add. KT15
off Ongar Hill 234 BG107
Ongar Pl, Add. KT15 234 BG107
[Sch] Ongar Pl Inf Sch, Add. KT15
off Milton Rd 234 BG107
Ongar Rd, SW6 39 J2
Addlestone KT15 234 BG106
Brentwood CM15 130 FV45
Romford RM4 108 EW40
Ongar Way, Rain. RM13 169 FE67
Onra Rd, E17 145 EA59
Onslow Av, Rich. TW10 200 CL85
Sutton SM2 239 CZ110
Onslow Cl, E4 123 EC47
W10 14 G2
Hatfield AL10 67 CV18
Onslow Cl, Thames Ditton KT7 219 CE102
Woking GU22 249 BA117
Onslow Cres, SW7 28 B9
Chislehurst BR7 227 EP95
Woking GU22 249 BA117
Onslow Dr, Sid. DA14 208 EX89
Onslow Gdns, E18 146 EH55
N10 143 DH57
N21 103 DN43
SW7 28 A9
South Croydon CR2 242 DU112
Thames Ditton KT7 219 CE102
Wallington SM6 241 DJ107
[Sch] Onslow Inf Sch, Ons.Vill.
GU2 off Powell Cl 280 AT136
Onslow Ms, Cher. KT16 216 BG100
Onslow Ms E, SW7 28 A9
Onslow Ms W, SW7 28 A9
Onslow Par, N14
off Osidge La 121 DH46
Onslow Rd, Croy. CR0 223 DM101
Guildford GU1 264 AX134
Hersham KT12 235 BT105
New Malden KT3 221 CU98
Richmond TW10 200 CL85
[Sch] Onslow St. Audrey's Sch, Hat.
AL10 off Old Rectory Dr 67 CV18
Onslow Sq, SW7 28 B8
Onslow St, EC1 18 F5
Guildford GU1 280 AW135
ONSLOW VILLAGE, Guil. GU2 280 AS136
Onslow Way, T.Ditt. KT7 219 CE102
Woking GU22 249 BF115
Ontario Cl, Brox. EN10 89 DY25
Smallfield RH6 291 DN149
Ontario St, SE1 31 H7
Ontario Twr, E14 34 F1
Ontario Way, E14 34 A1
On The Hill, Wat. WD19 116 BY47
Onyx Ms, E15 off Vicarage La 13 K5
Opal Cl, E16 24 F9
Opal Ct, Wexham SL3 154 AW70
Opal Ms, NW6 5 H8
Ilford IG1 147 EP61
Opal St, SE11 30 G9
Opecks Cl, Wexham SL2 154 AV70
Opendale Rd, Burn. SL1 152 AH71
Openshaw Rd, SE2 188 EV77
[Uni] Open Uni in London, The,
NW1 7 K6
Openview, SW18 202 DC88
Ophelia Gdns, NW2
off Hamlet Sq 141 CY62
Ophir Ter, SE15 44 C7
Opossum Way, Houns. TW4 178 BW82
Oppenheim Rd, SE13 46 E8
Oppidans Ms, NW3 6 E7
Oppidans Rd, NW3 6 E7
● Optima Business Pk, Hodd.
EN11 71 EC16
● Optima Pk, Cray. DA1 189 FG83
Opulens Pl, Nthwd. HA6 115 BP52
Oram Pl, Hem.H. HP3 62 BK23
Orange Ct, E1
off Hermitage Wall 32 D3
Orange Ct La, Downe BR6 245 EN109
Orange Gro, E11 145 ED62
Chigwell IG7 125 EQ51
Orange Hill Rd, Edg. HA8 118 CQ52
Orange Pl, SE16 33 H7
Orangery, The, Rich. TW10 199 CJ89
Orangery La, SE9 207 EM85
Orange Sq, SW1 29 H9
Orange St, WC2 29 N1
Orange Tree Hill, Hav.at.Bow.
RM4 127 FD50
Orange Yd, W1 17 P9
Oransay Rd, N1 9 K5
Oransay Wk, N1
off Oransay Rd 9 K5
Oratory La, SW3 28 B10
[Sch] Oratory RC Prim Sch, SW3 28 C10
Orbain Rd, SW6 38 F5
Orbel St, SW11 40 C7
● Orbital 25 Business Pk, Wat.
WD18 115 BR45
Orbital Cres, Wat. WD25 97 BT35
Orbital One, Dart. DA1 210 FP89
Orb St, SE17 31 L9
Orchard, The, N14 103 DH43
N20 120 DB46
N21 104 DR44
NW11 142 DA57
SE3 47 H8
W4 180 CR77
W5 off Montpelier Rd 159 CK71
Banstead SM7 256 DA115
Croxley Green WD3 96 BM43
Dunton Green TN13 263 FE120
Epsom KT17 239 CT108
Ewell KT17
off Tayles Hill Dr 239 CT110
Hertford SG14 54 DQ06
Hounslow TW3 178 CC82
Kings Langley WD4 80 BN29
North Holmwood RH5 285 CJ140
Swanley BR8 229 FD96
Virginia Water GU25 214 AY99
Welwyn Garden City AL8 51 CX07
Weybridge KT13 235 BP105
Woking GU22 248 AY122
Orchard Av, N3 142 DA55
N14 103 DJ44
N20 120 DD47
Ashford TW15 197 BQ93
Belvedere DA17 188 EY79
Berkhamsted HP4 60 AU19
Brentwood CM13 131 FZ48
Croydon CR0 225 DY101
Dartford DA1 209 FH87
Feltham TW14 197 BR85
Gravesend DA11 213 GH92
Hounslow TW5 178 BY80
Mitcham CR4 222 DG102
New Malden KT3 220 CS96
Rainham RM13 170 FJ70
Slough SL1 153 AK71
Southall UB1 158 BY74
Thames Ditton KT7 219 CG102
Watford WD25 81 BV32
Windsor SL4 173 AN81
Woodham KT15 233 BF111
Orchard Bungalow Caravan Site,
Slou. SL2 153 AM66
● Orchard Business Cen, Red.
RH1 289 DH143
Orchard Cl, E4
off Chingford Mt Rd 123 EA49
E11 146 EH56
Orchard Cl, N1 9 K7
NW2 141 CU62
SE23 204 DW86
SW20 221 CW98
W10 14 F6
Ashford TW15 197 BQ93
Banstead SM7 240 DB114
Beaconsfield HP9
off Seeleys Rd 111 AK52
Bexleyheath DA7 188 EY81
Bushey Heath WD23 117 CD46
Chorleywood WD3 95 BD42
Cuffley EN6 87 DL28
Denham UB9 156 BH65
East Horsley KT24 251 BT124
Edgware HA8 118 CL51
Egham TW20 195 BB92
Elstree WD6 100 CM42
Fetcham KT22 253 CD122
Guildford GU1 265 BB134
Hemel Hempstead HP2 62 BM18
Horley RH6 290 DF147
Leatherhead KT22 253 CF119
Little Berkhamsted SG13 69 DJ19
Long Ditton KT6 219 CH101
Northolt UB5 138 CC64
Radlett WD7 99 CE37
Ruislip HA4 137 BQ59
St. Albans AL1 65 CF21
Sheering CM22 59 FC07
South Ockendon RM15 171 FW70
Stanstead Abbotts SG12 55 EC11
Walton-on-Thames KT12 217 BV101
Ware SG12 55 DX05
Watford WD17 97 BT40
Wembley HA0 160 CL67
West Ewell KT19 238 CP107
Woking GU22 249 BB116
Orchard Ct, Bov. HP3 79 BA27
Twickenham TW2 199 CD89
Wallington SM6
off Parkgate Rd 241 DH106
Worcester Park KT4 221 CU102
Orchard Cres, Edg. HA8 118 CQ50
Enfield EN1 104 DT39
Orchard Cft, Harl. CM20 58 EU13
Orchard Dr, SE3 47 H8
Ashtead KT21 253 CK120
Chorleywood WD3 95 BC41
Edgware HA8 118 CM50
Grays RM17 192 GA75
Park Street AL2 82 CB27
Theydon Bois CM16 107 ES36
Uxbridge UB8 156 BK70
Watford WD17 97 BT39
Woking GU21 249 AZ115
Wooburn Green HP10 132 AD59
Orchard End, Cat. CR3 258 DS122
Fetcham KT22 252 CC124
Weybridge KT13 217 BS103
Orchard End Av, Amer. HP7 94 AT39
Orchard Est, Wdf.Grn. IG8 124 EJ52
Orchard Fm Pk, Red. RH1 289 DM143
Orchard Fld Rd, Gdmg. GU7 280 AT144
Orchard Gdns, Chess. KT9 238 CL105
Effingham KT24 268 BY128
Epsom KT18 238 CQ114
Sutton SM1 240 DA106
Waltham Abbey EN9 89 EC34
Orchard Gate, NW9 140 CS56
Esher KT10 219 CD102
Farnham Common SL2 133 AQ64
Greenford UB6 159 CH65
Orchard Grn, Orp. BR6 227 ES103
Orchard Gro, SE20 204 DU94
Chalfont St. Peter SL9 112 AW53
Croydon CR0 225 DY101
Edgware HA8 118 CN53
Harrow HA3 140 CM57
Orpington BR6 227 ET103
Orchard Hill, SE13 46 D8
Carshalton SM5 240 DF106
Dartford DA1 209 FE85
[Coll] Orchard Hill Coll, Wall. SM6
off Woodcote Rd 241 DH107
Orchard Ho, Erith DA8 189 FF81
[Sch] Orchard Inf & Nurs & Jun
Schs, The, Houns. TW4
off Orchard Rd 198 CA85
Orchard La, SW20 221 CV95
Amersham HP6 77 AR38
East Molesey KT8 219 CD100
Pilgrim's Hatch CM15 130 FT43
Woodford Green IG8 124 EJ49
Orchard Lea, Saw. CM21 58 EW06
Orchard Lea Cl, Wok. GU22 249 BE115
ORCHARD LEIGH, Chesh. HP5 78 AV28
Orchard Leigh, Chesh. HP5 78 AU28
Orchardleigh, Lthd. KT22 253 CH122
Orchardleigh Av, Enf. EN3 104 DW40
Orchard Mains, Wok. GU22 248 AW119
Orchard Mead, Hat. AL10
off Days Mead 67 CT18
Orchard Mead Ho, NW11 141 CZ61
Orchardmede, N21 104 DR44
Orchard Ms, N1 9 M7
N6 off Orchard Rd 143 DH59
SW17 off Franche Ct Rd 202 DC90
Seer Green HP9
off Orchard Rd 111 AR51
Orchard Path, Slou. SL3 155 BA72
Orchard Pl, E5 10 F3
E14 23 J10
N17 122 DT52
Cheshunt EN8
off Turners Hill 89 DX30
Keston BR2 244 EJ109
Sundridge TN14 262 EY124
[Sch] Orchard Prim Sch, E9 11 H7
SW2 off Christchurch Rd 203 DM88
Sidcup DA14 off Oxford Rd 208 EV92
[Sch] Orchard Prim Sch, The, Wat.
WD24 off Gammons La 97 BT36
Orchard Ri, Croy. CR0 225 DY102
Kingston upon Thames KT2 220 CQ95
Pinner HA5 137 BT55
Richmond TW10 180 CP84
Orchard Ri E, Sid. DA15 207 ET85
Orchard Ri W, Sid. DA15 207 ES85
Orchard Rd, N6 143 DH59
SE3 47 J8
SE18 187 ER77
Barnet EN5 101 CZ42
Beaconsfield HP9 111 AM54
Belvedere DA17 188 FA77
Brentford TW8 179 CJ79
Bromley BR1 226 EJ95
Burpham GU4 265 BB130
Chalfont St. Giles HP8 112 AW47

Orchard Rd, Chessington KT9 238 CL105
Dagenham RM10 168 FA67
Dorking RH4 285 CH137
Enfield EN3 104 DW43
Farnborough BR6 245 EP106
Feltham TW13 197 BU88
Hampton TW12 198 BZ94
Hayes UB3 157 BT73
Hounslow TW4 198 BZ85
Kingston upon Thames KT1 220 CL96
Mitcham CR4 222 DG102
Northfleet DA11 212 GC89
Old Windsor SL4 194 AV86
Onslow Village GU2 280 AT136
Otford TN14 263 FF116
Pratt's Bottom BR6 246 EW110
Reigate RH2 272 DB134
Richmond TW9 180 CN83
Riverhead TN13 278 FE122
Romford RM7 127 FB53
Seer Green HP9 111 AQ50
Shalford GU4 280 AY140
Shere GU5 282 BN139
Sidcup DA14 207 ES91
Smallfield RH6 291 DP148
South Croydon CR2 242 DV114
South Ockendon RM15 171 FW70
Sunbury-on-Thames TW16
off Hanworth Rd 197 BV94
Sutton SM1 240 DA106
Swanscombe DA10 212 FY85
Twickenham TW1 199 CG85
Welling DA16 188 EV83
Orchards, The, Epp. CM16 92 EU32
Sawbridgeworth CM21 58 EY05
Sch Orchard Sch, The, E.Mol. KT8
off Bridge Rd 219 CD98
Orchards Cl, W.Byf. KT14 234 BG114
Sch Orchards Inf Sch, Reig. RH2
off Alexander Rd 288 DA137
Orchardson Ho, NW8 16 B4
off Orchardson St 16 B4
Orchardson St, NW8 16 A5
Orchard Sq, W14 38 G1
Broxbourne EN10 71 DZ24
Orchards Residential Pk, The,
Slou. SL3 155 AZ74
Orchards Shop Cen, Dart.
DA1 210 FL86
Orchard St, E17 145 DY56
W1 16 G9
Dartford DA1 210 FL86
Hemel Hempstead HP3 62 BK24
St. Albans AL3 64 CC21
Orchard Ter, Enf. EN1 104 DU44
Orchard Vw, Cher. KT16 216 BG100
Uxbridge UB8 156 BK70
Orchard Vil, Sid. DA14 208 EV93
Orchardville, Burn. SL1 152 AH70
Orchard Wk, Kings.T. KT2
off Clifton Rd 220 CN95
Orchard Way, Add. KT15 234 BH106
Ashford TW15 196 BM89
Beckenham BR3 225 DY99
Bovingdon HP3 79 BA28
Chigwell IG7 126 EU48
Croydon CR0 225 DY102
Dartford DA2 210 FK90
Dorking RH4 285 CH137
Enfield EN1 104 DS41
Esher KT10 236 CC107
Goffs Oak EN7 87 DP27
Lower Kingswood KT20 271 CZ126
Mill End WD3 114 BG45
Oxted RH8 276 EG133
Potters Bar EN6 86 DB28
Reigate RH2 288 DB138
Send GU23 265 BC125
Slough SL3 154 AY74
Sutton SM1 240 DD105
Orchard Waye, Uxb. UB8 156 BK68
Sch Orchard Way Prim Sch, Croy.
CR0 *off Orchard Way* 225 DY101
Orchehill Av, Ger.Cr. SL9 134 AX56
Orchehill Ct, Ger.Cr. SL9 134 AY57
Orchehill Ri, Ger.Cr. SL9 134 AY57
Orchestra Cl, Edg. HA8
off Symphony Cl 118 CP52
Orchid Cl, E6 24 G6
SE13 205 ED85
Abridge RM4 108 EV41
Chessington KT9 237 CJ108
Goffs Oak EN7 88 DQ30
Hatfield AL10 51 CT14
Southall UB1 158 BY72
Orchid Ct, Egh. TW20 195 BB91
Romford RM7 149 FE61
Orchid Gdns, Houns. TW3 178 BZ84
Orchid Rd, N14 121 DJ45
Orchid St, W12 161 CU73
Orchis Gro, Bad.Dene RM17 192 FZ78
Orchis Way, Rom. RM3 128 FM51
Orde Hall St, WC1 18 C5
Ordell Rd, E3 21 P1
Ordnance Cl, Felt. TW13 197 BU89
Ordnance Cres, SE10 35 H4
Ordnance Hill, NW8 6 B9
Ordnance Ms, NW8 6 B10
Ordnance Rd, E16 23 L6
SE18 187 EN79
Enfield EN3 105 DX37
Gravesend DA12 213 GJ86
Oregano Cl, West Dr. UB7 156 BL72
Oregano Dr, E14 23 H9
Oregano Way, Guil. GU2 264 AU129
Oregon Av, E12 147 EM63
Oregon Bldg, SE13
off Deals Gateway 46 C6
Oregon Cl, N.Mal. KT3
off Georgia Rd 220 CQ98
Oregon Sq, Orp. BR6 227 ER102
Orestan La, Eff. KT24 267 BV127
Orestes Ms, NW6 5 J2
Oreston Rd, Rain. RM13 170 FK69
Orewell Gdns, Reig. RH2 288 DB136
Orford Ct, SE27 203 DP89
Orford Gdns, Twick. TW1 199 CF89
Orford Rd, E17 145 EA57
E18 146 EH55
SE6 205 EB90
Jct Organ Crossroads, Epsom
KT17 239 CU108
Organ Hall Rd, Borwd. WD6 100 CL39
Organ La, E4 123 EC47
Oriel Cl, Mitch. CR4 223 DK98
Oriel Ct, NW3 5 P1
Oriel Dr, SW13 181 CV79
Oriel Gdns, Ilf. IG5 147 EM55
Oriel Pl, NW3 5 P1
Sch Oriel Prim Sch, Han. TW13
off Hounslow Rd 198 BY90
Oriel Rd, E9 11 K4
Oriel Way, Nthlt. UB5 158 CB66
Oriental Cl, Wok. GU22
off Oriental Rd 249 BA117
Oriental Rd, E16 36 F2
Woking GU22 249 BA117
Oriental St, E14 22 B10
Orient Cl, St.Alb. AL1 65 CE22
● Orient Ind Pk, E10 145 EA61
Orient St, SE11 30 G8
Orient Way, E5 145 DX62
E10 145 DY61
Oriole Cl, Abb.L. WD5 81 BU31
Oriole Way, SE28 168 EV73
● Orion Business Cen, SE14 45 J1
● Orion Cen, The, Croy. CR0 223 DL103
Orion Ho, E1 20 F5
Orion Ms, Mord. SM4
off Woodville Rd 222 DA98
Orion Pt, E14 34 A8
Sch Orion Prim Sch, The, NW9
off Lanacre Av 119 CT54
Orion Rd, N11 121 DH51
Orion Way, Nthwd. HA6 115 BT49
Orissa Rd, SE18 187 ES78
Orkney Ct, Tap. SL6 152 AE66
Orkney St, SW11 40 G8
Orlando Gdns, Epsom KT19 238 CR110
Orlando Rd, SW4 183 DJ83
Orleans Cl, Esher KT10 219 CD103
★ Orleans Ho Gall, Twick.
TW1 199 CH88
Sch Orleans Inf Sch, Twick. TW1
off Hartington Rd 199 CH87
Sch Orleans Pk Sch, Twick. TW1
off Richmond Rd 199 CH87
Orleans Rd, SE19 204 DR93
Twickenham TW1 199 CH87
Orlestone Gdns, Orp. BR6 246 EY106
Orleston Ms, N7 8 F4
Orleston Rd, N7 8 F4
Orley Fm Rd, Har. HA1 139 CE62
Sch Orley Fm Sch, Har.Hill HA1
off South Hill Av 139 CD62
Orlop St, SE10 47 J1
Ormanton Rd, SE26 204 DU91
Orme Ct, W2 27 L1
Orme Ct Ms, W2 27 M1
Orme La, W2 27 L1
Ormeley Rd, SW12 203 DH88
Orme Rd, Kings.T. KT1 220 CP96
Sutton SM1 *off Grove Rd* 240 DB107
Ormerod Gdns, Mitch. CR4 222 DG96
Ormesby Cl, SE28
off Wroxham Rd 168 EX73
Ormesby Dr, Pot.B. EN6 85 CX32
Ormesby Way, Har. HA3 140 CM58
Orme Sq, W2 27 L1
Ormiston Gro, W12 161 CV74
Ormiston Rd, SE10 47 N1
Ormond Av, Hmptn. TW12 218 CB95
Richmond TW10
off Ormond Rd 199 CK85
Ormond Cl, WC1 18 B6
Harold Wood RM3
off Chadwick Dr 128 FK54
Ormond Cres, Hmptn. TW12 218 CB95
Ormond Dr, Hmptn. TW12 198 CB94
Ormonde Av, Epsom KT19 238 CR109
Orpington BR6 227 EQ103
Ormonde Gate, SW3 40 F1
Ormonde Pl, SW1 28 G9
Ormonde Ri, Buck.H. IG9 124 EJ46
Ormonde Rd, SW14 180 CP83
Northwood HA6 115 BR49
Woking GU21 248 AW116
Ormonde Ter, NW8 6 E9
Ormond Ms, WC1 18 B5
Ormond Rd, N19 143 DL60
Richmond TW10 199 CK85
Ormond Yd, SW1 29 M2
Ormsby, Sutt. SM2
off Grange Rd 240 DB108
Ormsby Gdns, Grnf. UB6 158 CC68
Ormsby Pl, N16 144 DT62
Ormsby Pt, SE18 37 P9
Ormsby St, E2 10 A10
Ormside St, SE15 44 G3
Ormside Way, Red. RH1 273 DH130
Ormskirk Rd, Wat. WD19 116 BX49
Ornan Rd, NW3 6 C3
Oronsay, Hem.H. HP3
off Northend 63 BP22
Orpen Wk, N16 144 DS62
Orphanage Rd, Wat.
WD17, WD24 98 BW40
Coll Orpheus Cen, Gdse. RH9
off North Pk La 274 DU130
Orpheus St, SE5 43 L7
ORPINGTON, BR5 & BR6 227 ES102
≠ Orpington 227 ET103
⊖ Orpington 227 ET103
Orpington Bypass, Orp. BR6 228 EV103
Sevenoaks TN14 246 FA109
Coll Orpington Coll, Orp. BR6
off The Walnuts 228 EU102
Orpington Gdns, N18 122 DS48
H Orpington Hosp, Orp. BR6 245 ET105
Orpington Rd, N21 121 DP46
Chislehurst BR7 227 ES97
Orpin Rd, S.Merst. RH1 273 DH130
Orpwood Cl, Hmptn. TW12 198 BZ92
ORSETT HEATH, Grays RM16 193 GG75
Orsett Heath Cres, Grays
RM16 193 GG76
Orsett Rd, Grays RM17 192 GA78
Orsett St, SE11 30 D10
Orsett Ter, W2 15 M8
Woodford Green IG8 124 EJ52
Orsman Rd, N1 9 N9
Orton Cl, St.Alb. AL4 65 CG16
Orton Gro, Enf. EN1 104 DU39
Orton Pl, SW19 202 DB94
Orton St, E1 32 C3
Orville Rd, SW11 40 B8
Orwell Cl, Hayes UB3 157 BS73
Rainham RM13 169 FD71
Windsor SL4 173 AR83
Orwell Ct, N5 9 K1
Orwell Rd, E13 166 EJ68
Osbaldeston Rd, N16 144 DU61
Osberton Rd, SE12 206 EG85
Osbert St, SW1 29 N9
Osborn Cl, E8 10 C8
Osborne Av, Stai. TW19 196 BL88
Osborne Cl, Barn. EN4 102 DF41
Beckenham BR3 225 DY98
Osborne Cl, Feltham TW13 198 BX92
Hornchurch RM11 149 FH58
Osborne Ct, Pot.B. EN6 86 DB29
Windsor SL4
off Osborne Rd 173 AQ82
Osborne Gdns, Pot.B. EN6 86 DB30
Thornton Heath CR7 224 DQ96
Osborne Gro, E17 145 DZ56
N4 143 DN60
Osborne Hts, Warley CM14 130 FV49
Osborne Ms, E17
off Osborne Gro 145 DZ56
Windsor SL4 173 AQ82
Osborne Pl, Sutt. SM1 240 DD106
Osborne Rd, E7 146 EH64
E9 11 P4
E10 145 EB62
N4 143 DM60
N13 121 DN48
NW2 161 CV65
W3 180 CP76
Belvedere DA17 188 EZ78
Broxbourne EN10 71 EA19
Buckhurst Hill IG9 124 EH46
Cheshunt EN8 89 DY27
Dagenham RM9 148 EZ64
Egham TW20 195 AZ93
Enfield EN3 105 DY40
Hornchurch RM11 149 FH58
Hounslow TW3 178 BZ83
Kingston upon Thames KT2 200 CL94
Pilgrim's Hatch CM15 130 FU44
Potters Bar EN6 86 DB30
Redhill RH1 272 DG131
Southall UB1 158 CC72
Thornton Heath CR7 224 DQ96
Uxbridge UB8
off Oxford Rd 156 BJ66
Walton-on-Thames KT12 217 BU102
Watford WD24 98 BW38
Windsor SL4 173 AQ82
Osborne Sq, Dag. RM9 148 EZ63
Osborne St, Slou. SL1 174 AT75
Osborne Ter, SW17
off Church La 202 DG92
Osborne Way, Chess. KT9
off Bridge Rd 238 CM106
Osborn Gdns, NW7 119 CX52
Osborn La, SE23 205 DY87
Osborn St, E1 20 B7
Osborn Ter, SE3 *off Lee Rd* 186 EF84
Osborn Way, Welw.G.C. AL8 51 CX10
Osborn Way Tunnel, Welw.G.C.
AL8 *off Osborn Way* 51 CX09
Osbourne Av, Kings L. WD4 80 BM28
Osbourne Ct, W5 160 CL71
Osbourne Rd, Dart. DA2 210 FP86
Oscar Cl, Pur. CR8 241 DN110
Oscar Faber Pl, N1 9 P7
Oscar St, SE8 46 A8
Oseney Cres, NW5 7 M4
Osgood Av, Orp. BR6 245 ET106
Osgood Gdns, Orp. BR6 245 ET106
OSIDGE, N14 121 DH46
Osidge La, N14 120 DG46
Sch Osidge Prim Sch, N14
off Chase Side 121 DJ46
Osier Cres, N10 120 DF53
Osier La, SE10 35 M7
Osier Ms, W4 181 CT79
Osier Pl, Egh. TW20 195 BC93
Osiers, The, Crox.Grn WD3 97 BQ44
Osiers Rd, SW18 182 DA84
Osier St, E1 21 H5
Osier Way, E10 145 EB62
Banstead SM7 239 CY114
Mitcham CR4 222 DE99
Oslac Rd, SE6 205 EB92
Oslo Ct, NW8 16 C1
Oslo Sq, SE16 33 M6
Osman Cl, N15 *off Pulford Rd* 144 DR58
Sch Osmani Prim Sch, E1 20 D6
Osman Rd, N9 122 DU48
W6 26 B6
Osmington Ho, SW8 42 C5
Osmond Cl, Har. HA2 138 CC61
Osmond Gdns, Wall. SM6 241 DJ106
Osmund St, W12
off Braybrook St 161 CT71
Osnaburgh St, NW1 17 K5
NW1 (north section) 17 K3
Osnaburgh Ter, NW1 17 K4
Osney Ho, SE2
off Hartslock Dr 188 EX75
Osney Wk, Cars. SM5 222 DD100
Osney Way, Grav. DA12 213 GM89
Osprey Cl, E6 24 G7
E11 146 EG56
E17 123 DY52
Bromley BR2 226 EL102
Fetcham KT22 252 CC122
Sutton SM1
off Sandpiper Rd 239 CZ106
Watford WD25 82 BY34
West Drayton UB7 176 BK75
Osprey Ct, Wal.Abb. EN9 90 EG34
Osprey Dr, Epsom KT18 255 CV117
Osprey Gdns, S.Croy. CR2 243 DX110
Osprey Hts, SW11
off Bramlands Cl 182 DE83
Osprey Ms, Enf. EN3 104 DV43
Osprey Rd, Wal.Abb. EN9 90 EG34
Ospringe Cl, SE20 204 DW94
Ospringe Ct, SE9 207 ER86
Ospringe Rd, NW5 7 L1
Osram Ct, W6 26 B7
Osram Rd, Wem. HA9 139 CK62
Osric Path, N1 19 N1
Ossian Ms, N4 143 DM59
Ossian Rd, N4 143 DM59
Jct Ossie Garvin Rbt, Hayes
UB4 158 BW73
Ossington Bldgs, W1 16 G6
Ossington Cl, W2 27 K1
Ossington St, W2 27 K1
Ossory Rd, SE1 44 C1
Ossulston St, NW1 17 N1
Ossulton Pl, N2 142 DC55
Ossulton Way, N2 142 DC56
Ostade Rd, SW2 203 DM87
Ostell Cres, Enf. EN3 105 EA38
Osten Ms, SW7 27 M7
Osterberg Rd, Dart. DA1 190 FM84
OSTERLEY, Islw. TW7 178 CC80
⊖ Osterley 179 CD80
Osterley Av, Islw. TW7 179 CD80
Osterley Cl, Orp. BR5 228 EU95
Osterley Ct, Islw. TW7 179 CD81
Osterley Cres, Islw. TW7 179 CE81
Osterley Gdns, Sthl. UB2 178 CC75
Thornton Heath CR7 224 DQ96
Osterley Ho, E14 22 C8
Osterley La, Islw. TW7 179 CE78
Southall UB2 178 CA78
Osterley Pk, Islw. TW7 179 CD78
★ Osterley Park Ho, Islw.
TW7 178 CC78
Osterley Pk Rd, Sthl. UB2 178 BZ76
Osterley Pk Vw Rd, W7 179 CE75
Osterley Rd, N16 144 DS63
Isleworth TW7 179 CE80
Osterley Views, Sthl. UB2 158 CC74
Oster St, St.Alb. AL3 64 CC19
Oster Ter, E17
off Southcote Rd 145 DX57
Ostlers Dr, Ashf. TW15 197 BQ92
Ostliffe Rd, N13 122 DQ50
Oswald Bldg, SW8 41 J3
Oswald Cl, Fetch. KT22 252 CC122
Oswald Rd, Fetch. KT22 252 CC122
St. Albans AL1 65 CE21
Southall UB1 158 BY74
Oswald's Mead, E9
off Lindisfarne Way 145 DY63
Oswald St, E5 145 DX62
Oswald Ter, NW2
off Temple Rd 141 CW62
Osward, Croy. CR0 243 DZ109
Osward Pl, N9 122 DV47
Osward Rd, SW17 202 DF89
Oswell Ho, E1 32 F2
Oswin St, SE11 31 H8
Oswyth Rd, SE5 43 P8
OTFORD, Sev. TN14 263 FH116
Otford Cl, SE20 224 DW95
Bexley DA5
off Southwold Rd 209 FB86
Bromley BR1 227 EN97
Otford Cres, SE4 205 DZ86
Otford La, Halst. TN14 246 EZ112
Sch Otford Prim Sch, Otford TN14
off High St 263 FH116
Otford Rd, Sev. TN14 263 FH118
Othello Cl, SE11 30 G10
Otho Ct, Brent. TW8 179 CK80
Otis St, E3 22 E2
Otley App, Ilf. IG2 147 EP58
Otley Dr, Ilf. IG2 147 EP57
Otley Rd, E16 24 C8
Otley Ter, E5 145 DX61
Otley Way, Wat. WD19 116 BW48
Otlinge Rd, Orp. BR5 228 EX98
Ottawa Ct, Brox. EN10 89 DY25
Ottawa Gdns, Dag. RM10 169 FD66
Ottawa Rd, Til. RM18 193 GG82
Ottaway St, E5 144 DU62
Ottenden Cl, Orp. BR6
off Southfleet Rd 245 ES105
Otterbourne Rd, E4 123 ED48
Croydon CR0 224 DQ103
Otterburn Gdns, Islw. TW7 179 CG80
Otterburn Ho, SE5 43 J4
Otterburn St, SW17 202 DF93
Otter Cl, E15 12 E9
Ottershaw KT16 233 BB107
Otterden St, SE6 205 EA91
Otterfield Rd, West Dr. UB7 156 BL73
Otter Gdns, Hat. AL10 67 CV19
Ottermead La, Ott. KT16 233 BC107
Otter Meadow, Lthd. KT22 253 CF119
Otter Rd, Grnf. UB6 158 CC70
Otters Cl, Orp. BR5 228 EX98
OTTERSHAW, Cher. KT16 233 BC106
Ottershaw Pk, Ott. KT16 233 BA109
Otterspool La, Wat. WD25 98 BY38
Otterspool Service Rd, Wat.
WD25 98 BZ39
Otterspool Way, Wat. WD25 98 BY37
Otto Cl, SE26 204 DV90
Ottoman Ter, Wat. WD17
off Ebury Rd 98 BW41
Otto St, SE17 42 G3
Ottways Av, Ashtd. KT21 253 CK119
Ottways La, Ashtd. KT21 253 CK120
Otway Gdns, Bushey WD23 117 CE45
Otways Cl, Pot.B. EN6 86 DB32
Oulton Cl, E5
off Mundford Rd 144 DW61
SE28 *off Rollesby Way* 168 EW72
Oulton Cres, Bark. IG11 167 ET65
Potters Bar EN6 85 CX32
Oulton Rd, N15 144 DR57
Oulton Way, Wat. WD19 116 BY49
Oundle Av, Bushey WD23 98 CC44
Sch Our Lady & St. John's RC
Prim Sch, Brent. TW8
off Boston Pk Rd 179 CJ78
Sch Our Lady & St. Joseph RC
Prim Sch, N1 9 N5
Sch Our Lady & St. Philip Neri
Prim Sch, Annexe, SE23
off Mayow Rd 205 DX90
SE26 *off Sydenham Rd* 205 DY91
Sch Our Lady Immaculate Cath
Prim Sch, Surb. KT6
off Ewell Rd 220 CP102
Sch Our Lady of Dolours RC
Prim Sch, W2 15 L6
Sch Our Lady of Grace Inf Sch,
NW2 *off Dollis Hill Av* 141 CW61
Sch Our Lady of Grace Jun Sch,
NW2 *off Dollis Hill La* 141 CV62
Sch Our Lady of Grace RC Prim Sch,
SE7 *off Charlton Rd* 186 EH79
Sch Our Lady of Lourdes Cath
Prim Sch, E11
off Chestnut Dr 146 EG58
SE13 *off Belmont Hill* 185 ED83
Sch Our Lady of Lourdes Prim Sch,
NW10 *off Wesley Rd* 160 CQ67
Sch Our Lady of Lourdes RC
Prim Sch, N11
off The Limes Avenue 121 DJ50
N12 *off Bow La* 120 DC53
Sch Our Lady of Muswell Cath
Prim Sch, N10
off Pages La 142 DG55
Sch Our Lady of Peace Catholic
Inf & Nurs Sch, Slou. SL1
off Derwent Dr 152 AJ71
Sch Our Lady of Peace Catholic
Jun Sch, Slou. SL1
off Derwent Dr 152 AJ71
Sch Our Lady of the Rosary RC
Prim Sch, Sid. DA15
off Holbeach Gdns 207 ES86
Staines-upon-Thames TW18
off Park Av 196 BG93
Sch Our Lady of the Visitation
RC Prim Sch, Grnf. UB6
off Greenford Rd 158 CC70
Sch Our Lady of Victories RC
Prim Sch, SW7 27 P9
SW15 *off Clarendon Dr* 181 CX84
Sch Our Lady Queen of Heaven
RC Prim Sch, SW19
off Victoria Dr 201 CX87
Sch Our Lady's Catholic Prim Sch,
Chesh.B. HP6
off Amersham Rd 77 AP35
Dartford DA1
off King Edward Av 210 FK86
Sch Our Lady's Conv High Sch,
N16 *off Amhurst Pk* 144 DS59
Sch Our Lady's Prim Sch, E14 21 P9
Sch Our Lady's RC Prim Sch,
NW1 7 L8
Welwyn Garden City AL7
off Woodhall La 51 CY11
Ousden Cl, Chsht EN8 89 DY30
Ousden Dr, Chsht EN8 89 DY30
Ouseley Rd, SW12 202 DF88
Old Windsor SL4 194 AW87
Wraysbury TW19 194 AW87
Outdowns, Eff. KT24 267 BV129
Outer Circle, NW1 16 G5
Outfield Rd, Chal.St.P. SL9 112 AX52
Outgate Rd, NW10 161 CT66
Outlook Dr, Ch.St.G. HP8 112 AX48
Outlook Ho, Enf. EN3
off Tysoe Av 105 DZ36
Outram Pl, N1 8 B8
Weybridge KT13 235 BQ106
Outram Rd, E6 166 EL67
N22 121 DK53
Croydon CR0 224 DT102
Outwich St, EC3 19 P8
OUTWOOD, Red. RH1 289 DP143
Outwood La, Chipstead CR5 256 DF118
Kingswood KT20 256 DB122
⊖ Oval 42 E3
Oval, The, E2 10 E10
Banstead SM7 240 DA114
Broxbourne EN10 89 DY25
Godalming GU7 280 AT144
Guildford GU2 280 AU135
Sidcup DA15 208 EU87
Oval Gdns, Grays RM17 192 GC76
Oval Pl, SW8 42 C4
Sch Oval Prim Sch, Croy. CR0
off Cherry Orchard Rd 224 DS102
Oval Rd, NW1 7 J7
Croydon CR0 224 DS102
Oval Rd N, Dag. RM10 169 FB67
Oval Rd S, Dag. RM10 169 FB68
Ovaltine Ct, Kings L. WD4 81 BP29
Ovaltine Dr, Kings L. WD4 81 BP29
Oval Way, SE11 42 D1
Gerrards Cross SL9 134 AY56
Ovanna Ms, N1 9 P5
Ovenden Rd, Sund. TN14 262 EX120
Overbrae, Beck. BR3 205 EA93
Overbrook, W.Hors. KT24 267 BP129
Overbrook Wk, Edg. HA8 118 CN52
Overbury Av, Beck. BR3 225 EB97
Overbury Cres, New Adgtn
CR0 243 EC110
Overbury Rd, N15 144 DR58
Overbury St, E5 145 DX63
Overchess Ridge, Chorl. WD3 95 BF41
Overcliffe, Grav. DA11 213 GG86
Overcliff Rd, SE13 185 EA83
Grays RM17 192 GD77
Overcourt Cl, Sid. DA15 208 EV86
Overdale, Ashtd. KT21 254 CL115
Bletchingley RH1 274 DQ133
Dorking RH5 285 CJ135
Overdale Av, N.Mal. KT3 220 CQ96
Overdale Rd, W5 179 CJ76
Chesham HP5 76 AP28
Overdown Rd, SE6 205 EA91
Overhill, Warl. CR6 258 DW119
Overhill Rd, SE22 204 DU87
Purley CR8 241 DN109
Overhill Way, Beck. BR3 225 ED99
Overlea Rd, E5 144 DU59
Overlord Cl, Brox. EN10 71 DY20
Overlord Ct, Lthd. KT22 253 CD121
Overmead, Sid. DA15 207 ER87
Swanley BR8 229 FE99
Oversley Ho, W2 15 J6
Overstand Cl, Beck. BR3 225 EA99
Overstone Gdns, Croy. CR0 225 DZ101
Overstone Rd, W6 26 A7
Overstrand Ho, Horn. RM12 149 FH61
Overstream, Loud. WD3 96 BH42
Over The Misbourne, Denh.
UB9 135 BC58
Gerrards Cross SL9 135 BA58
Overthorpe Cl, Knap. GU21 248 AS117
Overton Cl, NW10 160 CQ65
Isleworth TW7 179 CF81
Overton Ct, E11 146 EG59
Overton Dr, E11 146 EH59
Romford RM6 148 EW59
Sch Overton Gra Sch, Sutt. SM2
off Stanley Rd 240 DB109
Overton Ho, SW15
off Tangley Gro 201 CT87
Overton Rd, E10 145 DY60
N14 103 DL43
SE2 188 EW76
SW9 42 F9
Sutton SM2 240 DA107
Overton Rd E, SE2 188 EX76
Overtons Yd, Croy. CR0 224 DQ104
Overy St, Dart. DA1 210 FL86
Ovesdon Av, Har. HA2 138 BZ60
Oveton Way, Bkhm KT23 268 CA126
Ovett Cl, SE19 204 DS93
Ovex Cl, E14 34 F5
Ovington Ct, Wok. GU21
off Roundthorn Way 248 AT116
Ovington Gdns, SW3 28 D7
Ovington Ms, SW3 28 D7
Ovington Sq, SW3 28 D7
Ovington St, SW3 28 D7
Owen Cl, SE28 168 EW74
Croydon CR0 224 DR100

Owen Cl, Hayes UB4 157 BV69
Northolt UB5 158 BY65
Romford RM5 127 FB51
Slough SL3 *off Parsons Rd* 175 AZ78
Owen Gdns, Wdf.Grn. IG8 124 EL51
Owenite St, SE2 188 EV77
Owen Pl, Lthd. KT22
off Church Rd 253 CH122
Owen Rd, N13 122 DQ50
Hayes UB4 157 BV69
Owens Ms, E11 *off Short Rd* 146 EE61
Owen's Row, EC1 18 G2
Owen St, EC1 18 G1
Owens Way, SE23 205 DY87
Croxley Green WD3 96 BN43
Owen Wk, SE20
off Sycamore Gro 224 DU95
Owen Waters Ho, Ilf. IG5 125 EM53
Owen Way, NW10 160 CQ65
Owgan Cl, SE5 43 M5
Owl, The, High Beach IG10 106 EF40
Owl Cl, S.Croy. CR2 243 DX110
Owlets Hall Cl, Horn. RM11
off Prospect Rd 150 FM55
Owlsears Cl, Beac. HP9 111 AK51
Ownstead Gdns, S.Croy. CR2 242 DT111
Ownsted Hill, New Adgtn CR0 243 EC110
Oxberry Av, SW6 38 F8
Oxdowne Cl, Stoke D'Ab.
KT11 236 CB114
Oxenden Dr, Hodd. EN11 71 EA18
Oxenden Wd Rd, Orp. BR6 246 EV107
Oxendon St, SW1 29 N1
Oxenford St, SE15 184 DT83
Oxenholme, NW1 17 M1
Oxenpark Av, Wem. HA9 140 CL59
Oxestalls Rd, SE8 33 M10
Oxfield Cl, Berk. HP4 60 AU20
Oxford Av, N14 121 DJ46
SW20 221 CY96
Burnham SL1 152 AG68
Grays RM16 193 GG77
Hayes UB3 177 BT80
Hornchurch RM11 150 FN56
Hounslow TW5 178 CA78
St. Albans AL1 65 CJ21
Slough SL1 153 AM71
⊖ **Oxford Circus** 17 L9
Oxford Circ Av, W1 17 L9
Oxford Cl, N9 122 DV47
Ashford TW15 197 BQ94
Cheshunt EN8 89 DX29
Gravesend DA12 213 GM89
Mitcham CR4 223 DJ97
Northwood HA6 115 BQ49
Romford RM2 149 FG57
Oxford Ct, EC4 19 L10
W3 160 CN72
Feltham TW13
off Oxford Way 198 BX91
Warley CM14 130 FX49
Oxford Cres, N.Mal. KT3 220 CR100
Oxford Dr, SE1 31 N3
Ruislip HA4 138 BW61
Oxford Gdns, N20 120 DD46
N21 122 DQ45
W4 180 CN78
W10 14 F7
Denham UB9 135 BF62
Sch **Oxford Gdns Prim Sch**,
W10 14 C8
Oxford Gate, W6 26 D8
Oxford Ms, Bex. DA5 208 FA88
Oxford Pl, NW10 *off Press Rd* 140 CR62
Hatfield AL10 66 CS16
Oxford Rd, E15 13 H5
N4 143 DN60
N9 122 DV47
NW6 15 K1
SE19 204 DR93
SW15 181 CY84
W5 159 CK73
Beaconsfield HP9 133 AP55
Carshalton SM5 240 DE107
Enfield EN3 104 DV43
Gerrards Cross SL9 135 BA60
Guildford GU1 280 AX136
Harrow HA1 138 CC58
High Wycombe HP10 110 AE54
Holtspur HP9 110 AE54
Ilford IG1 147 EQ63
Redhill RH1 272 DE133
Romford RM3 128 FM51
Sidcup DA14 208 EV92
Teddington TW11 199 CD92
Uxbridge UB8, UB9 156 BJ65
Wallington SM6 241 DJ106
Wealdstone HA3 139 CF55
Windsor SL4 173 AQ81
Woodford Green IG8 124 EJ50
Oxford Rd E, Wind. SL4 173 AQ81
Oxford Rd N, W4 180 CP78
Oxford Rd S, W4 180 CN78
Oxford Sq, W2 16 D9
Oxford St, W1 17 M8
Watford WD18 97 BV43
Oxford Ter, Guil. GU1
off Pewley Hill 280 AX136
Oxford Wk, Sthl. UB1 158 BZ74
Oxford Way, Felt. TW13 198 BX91
● **Oxgate Cen Ind Est, The**,
NW2 141 CV60
Oxgate Gdns, NW2 141 CV62
Oxgate La, NW2 141 CV61
Oxhawth Cres, Brom. BR2 227 EN99
OXHEY, Wat. WD19 98 BW44
Oxhey Av, Wat. WD19 116 BX45
Oxhey Dr, Nthwd. HA6 115 BV50
Watford WD19 116 BW48
Oxhey Dr S, Nthwd. HA6 115 BV50
Oxhey La, Har. HA3 116 CA50
Pinner HA5 116 CA50
Watford WD19 116 BZ47
Oxhey Ridge Cl, Nthwd. HA6 115 BU50
Oxhey Rd, Wat. WD19 98 BW44
Sch **Oxhey Wd Prim Sch**, S.Oxhey
WD19 *off Oxhey Dr* 116 BW48
Ox La, Epsom KT17 239 CU109
Oxleas, E6 25 N8
Oxleas Cl, Well. DA16 187 ER82
OXLEASE, Hat. AL10 67 CV19
Oxlease Dr, Hat. AL10 67 CV19
Oxleay Ct, Har. HA2 138 CA60
Oxleay Rd, Har. HA2 138 CA60
Oxleigh Cl, N.Mal. KT3 220 CS99
Oxley Cl, SE1 32 B10
Romford RM2 128 FJ54
Oxleys, The, Harl. CM17 58 EX11
Oxley Sq, E3 22 D4
Oxleys Rd, NW2 141 CV62
Waltham Abbey EN9 90 EG32
Oxlip Cl, Croy. CR0
off Marigold Way 225 DX102
Oxlow La, Dag. RM9, RM10 148 FA63
Oxonian St, SE22 184 DT84
Oxo Twr Wf, SE1 30 F1
OXSHOTT, Lthd. KT22 237 CD113
≠ **Oxshott** 236 CC113
Oxshott Ri, Cob. KT11 236 BX113
Oxshott Rd, Lthd. KT22 253 CE115
Oxshott Way, Cob. KT11 252 BY115
OXTED, RH8 275 ED129
≠ **Oxted** 276 EE129
Oxted Cl, Mitch. CR4 222 DD97
Oxted Rd, Gdse. RH9 274 DW130
Sch **Oxted Sch**, Oxt. RH8
off Bluehouse La 276 EF128
Oxtoby Way, SW16 223 DK96
Oxygen, E16 23 N10
● **Oyo Business Units Belvedere**,
Belv. DA17
off Crabtree Manorway N 189 FC75
Oyster Catchers Cl, E16 24 A8
Oyster Catcher Ter, Ilf. IG5
off Tiptree Cres 147 EN55
Oysterfields, St.Alb. AL3 64 CB19
Oystergate Wk, EC4
off Swan La 31 L1
Oyster La, Byfleet KT14 234 BK110
Oyster Row, E1 21 H9
Oyster Wf, SW11 40 A8
Ozolins Way, E16 23 N8

P

Pablo Neruda Cl, SE24
off Shakespeare Rd 183 DP84
Paceheath Cl, Rom. RM5 127 FD51
Pace Pl, E1 20 F9
PACHESHAM PARK, Lthd.
KT22 253 CF116
Pachesham Pk, Lthd. KT22 253 CG117
Pacific Cl, Felt. TW14 197 BT88
Swanscombe DA10 212 FY85
Pacific Ms, SW9
off Saltoun Rd 183 DN84
Pacific Rd, E16 23 N8
● **Pacific Wf**, Bark. IG11 167 EP66
Pacific Wf, SE16
off Rotherhithe St 33 J3
Packet Boat La, Uxb. UB8 156 BH72
Packham Cl, Orp. BR6 228 EV104
Packham Ct, Wor.Pk. KT4 221 CW104
off Lavender Av
Packham Rd, Nthflt DA11 213 GF90
Packhorse Cl, St.Alb. AL4 65 CJ17
Packhorse La, Borwd. WD6 100 CS37
Ridge EN6 84 CR31
Packhorse Rd, Ger.Cr. SL9 134 AY58
Sevenoaks TN13 278 FC123
Packington Rd, W3 180 CQ76
Packington Sq, N1 9 J9
Packington St, N1 9 H8
Packmores Rd, SE9 207 ER85
Padbrook, Oxt. RH8 276 EG129
Padbrook Cl, Oxt. RH8 276 EH128
Padbury, SE17 43 N1
Padbury Cl, Felt. TW14 197 BR88
Padbury Ct, E2 20 B3
Padcroft Rd, West Dr. UB7 156 BK74
Paddenswick Rd, W6 181 CU76
Paddick Cl, Hodd. EN11 71 DZ16
PADDINGTON, W2 15 N7
≠ **Paddington** 16 A8
⊖ **Paddington** 16 A8
Sch **Paddington Acad**, W9 15 K5
Paddington Cl, Hayes UB4 158 BX70
Paddington Grn, W2 16 B6
Sch **Paddington Grn Prim Sch**,
W2 16 A5
Paddington St, W1 16 G6
Paddock, The, Brox. EN10 71 EA20
Chalfont St. Peter SL9 112 AY50
Dartford DA2 211 FS89
Datchet SL3 174 AV81
Guildford GU1 265 BD133
Hatfield AL10 67 CU16
Ickenham UB10 137 BP63
Westcott RH4 284 CB137
Westerham TN16 277 EQ126
Paddock Cl, SE3 47 P9
SE26 205 DX91
Farnboro. BR6 *off State Fm Av* 245 EP105
Hunsdon SG12 56 EK06
Northolt UB5 158 CA68
Oxted RH8 276 EF131
South Darenth DA4 230 FQ95
Watford WD19 98 BY44
Worcester Park KT4 220 CS102
Paddock Gdns, SE19
off Westow St 204 DS93
Paddock Mead, Harl. CM18 73 EQ20
Paddock Rd, NW2 141 CU62
Bexleyheath DA6 188 EY84
Ruislip HA4 138 BX62
Paddocks, The, NW7 119 CY51
Bookham KT23
off Leatherhead Rd 268 CB126
Chorleywood WD3 95 BF42
Cockfosters EN4 102 DF41
Hertford Heath SG13 54 DV12
New Haw KT15 234 BH110
Sevenoaks TN13 279 FK124
Stapleford Abbotts RM4 109 FF44
Virginia Water GU25 214 AY100
Welwyn Garden City AL7 52 DB08
Wembley HA9 140 CP61
Weybridge KT13 217 BS104
Sch **Paddock Sch**, SW15
off Priory La 181 CT84
Paddocks Cl, Ashtd. KT21 254 CL118
Cobham KT11 236 BW114
Harrow HA2 138 CB63
Orpington BR5 228 EX103
Paddocks End, Seer Grn HP9
off Orchard Rd 111 AR51
Paddocks Mead, Wok. GU21 248 AS116
Paddocks Retail Pk, Wey.
KT13 234 BL111
Paddocks Rd, Guil. GU4 265 BA130
Paddocks Way, Ashtd. KT21 254 CL118
Chertsey KT16 216 BH102
Paddock Wk, Warl. CR6 258 DV119
Paddock Way, SW15 201 CW87
Ashley Green HP5 78 AT25
Chislehurst BR7 207 ER94
Hemel Hempstead HP1 61 BE20
Oxted RH8 276 EF131
Woking GU21 233 BB114
Padelford La, Stan. HA7 117 CG47
Padfield Ct, Wem. HA9
off Forty Av 140 CM62
Padfield Rd, SE5 43 J10
Padgets, The, Wal.Abb. EN9 89 ED34
Padley Cl, Chess. KT9 238 CM106
Padnall Ct, Rom. RM6
off Padnall Rd 148 EX55
Padnall Rd, Rom. RM6 148 EX56
Padstow Cl, Orp. BR6 245 ET105
Slough SL3 174 AY76
Padstow Rd, Enf. EN2 103 DP40
Padstow Wk, Felt. TW14 197 BT88
Padua Rd, SE20 224 DW95
Pagden St, SW8 41 K6
Pageant Av, NW9 118 CR53
Pageant Cl, Til. RM18 193 GJ81
Pageant Cres, SE16 33 M2
Pageantmaster Ct, EC4 18 G9
Pageant Rd, St.Alb. AL1 65 CD21
Pageant Wk, Croy. CR0 224 DS104
Page Av, Wem. HA9 140 CQ62
Page Cl, Bean DA2 211 FW90
Dagenham RM9 148 EY64
Hampton TW12 198 BY93
Harrow HA3 140 CM58
Page Cres, Croy. CR0 241 DN106
Erith DA8 189 FF80
Page Grn Rd, N15 144 DU57
Page Grn Ter, N15 144 DT57
Page Heath La, Brom. BR1 226 EK97
Page Heath Vil, Brom. BR1 226 EK97
Page Hill, Ware SG12 54 DV05
Pagehurst Rd, Croy. CR0 224 DV101
Page Meadow, NW7 119 CU52
Page Pl, Frog. AL2
off Frogmore 83 CE27
Page Rd, Felt. TW14 197 BR86
Hertford SG13 54 DU9
Pages Cft, Berk. HP4 60 AU17
Pages Hill, N10 120 DG54
Pages La, N10 120 DG54
Romford RM3 128 FP54
Uxbridge UB8 156 BJ65
Page St, NW7 119 CU53
SW1 29 P8
Pages Wk, SE1 31 N8
Pages Yd, W4 *off Church St* 180 CS79
Paget Av, Sutt. SM1 222 DD104
Paget Cl, Hmptn. TW12 199 CD91
Paget Gdns, Chis. BR7 227 EP95
Paget La, Islw. TW7 179 CD83
Paget Pl, Kings.T. KT2 200 CQ93
Thames Ditton KT7
off Brooklands Rd 219 CG102
Paget Ri, SE18 187 EN80
Paget Rd, N16 144 DR60
Ilford IG1 147 EP63
Slough SL3 175 AZ77
Uxbridge UB10 157 BQ70
Paget St, EC1 18 G2
Paget Ter, SE18 187 EN79
Pagette Way, Bad.Dene RM17 192 GA77
Pagitts Gro, Barn. EN4 102 DB39
Paglesfield, Hutt. CM13 131 GC44
Pagnell St, SE14 45 N4
Pagoda Av, Rich. TW9 180 CM83
Pagoda Gdns, SE3 46 G9
Pagoda Gro, SE27 204 DQ89
Pagoda Vista, Rich. TW9 180 CM82
Paignton Cl, Rom. RM3 128 FK53
Paignton Rd, N15 144 DS58
Ruislip HA4 137 BU62
Paines Brook Rd, Rom. RM3
off Paines Brook Way 128 FM51
Paines Brook Way, Rom. RM3 128 FM51
Paines Cl, Pnr. HA5 138 BY55
Painesfield Dr, Cher. KT16 216 BG103
Paines La, Pnr. HA5 116 BY53
Pains Cl, Mitch. CR4 223 DH96
Painshill, Cob. KT11 235 BT113
Pains Hill, Oxt. RH8 276 EJ132
★ **Painshill Park**, Cob. KT11 235 BS114
Painsthorpe Rd, N16
off Oldfield Rd 144 DS62
Painter Ho, E1 *off Sidney St* 20 F8
Painters Ash La, Nthflt DA11 212 GD90
Sch **Painters Ash Prim Sch**, Nthflt
DA11 *off Masefield Rd* 212 GD90
Painters La, Enf. EN3 105 DY35
Painters Ms, SE16
off Macks Rd 32 D8
Painters Rd, Ilf. IG2 147 ET55
Paisley Rd, N22 121 DP53
Carshalton SM5 222 DD102
Paisley Ter, Cars. SM5 222 DD101
Sch **Pakeman Prim Sch**, N7
off Hornsey Rd 143 DM62
Pakeman St, N7 143 DM62
Pakenham Cl, SW12
off Balham Pk Rd 202 DG88
Pakenham St, WC1 18 D3
Pakes Way, They.B. CM16 107 ES37
Palace Av, W8 27 M3
Palace Cl, E9 11 P5
Kings Langley WD4 80 BM30
Slough SL1 153 AM74
Palace Ct, NW3 5 M2
W2 15 L10
Harrow HA3 140 CL58
Palace Ct Gdns, N10 143 DJ55
Palace Dr, Wey. KT13 217 BP104
● **Palace Ex**, Enf. EN2 104 DR42
Palace Gdns, Enf. EN2 104 DR42
Palace Gdns, Buck.H. IG9 124 EK46
Palace Gdns Ms, W8 27 K2
Palace Gdns Ter, W8 27 K2
Palace Gate, W8 27 N5
Palace Gates Rd, N22 121 DK53
Palace Grn, W8 27 M4
Croydon CR0 243 DZ108
Palace Gro, SE19 204 DT94
Bromley BR1 226 EH95
Palace Ms, E17 145 DZ56
SW1 29 H9
SW6 39 H5
● **Palace of Industry**,
Wem. HA9
off Fulton Rd 140 CN63
Palace Par, E17 145 DZ56
Palace Pl, SW1 29 L6
Palace Rd, N8 143 DK57
N11 121 DL52
SE19 204 DT94
SW2 203 DM88
Bromley BR1 226 EH95
East Molesey KT8 219 CD97
Kingston upon Thames KT1 219 CK98
Ruislip HA4 138 BY63
Westerham TN16 261 EN121
Palace Rd Est, SW2 203 DM88
Palace Sq, SE19 204 DT94
Palace St, SW1 29 L6
Palace Vw, SE12 206 EG89
Bromley BR1 226 EG97
Croydon CR0 243 DZ105
Palace Vw Rd, E4 123 EB50
Palace Way, Wey. KT13
off Palace Dr 217 BP104
Woking GU22 249 BB120
Palamos Rd, E10 145 EA60
Palatine Av, N16 9 P1
Palatine Rd, N16 9 P1
Palemead Cl, SW6 38 C6
Palermo Rd, NW10 161 CU68
Palestine Gro, SW19 222 DD95
Palewell Cl, Orp. BR5 228 EV96
Palewell Common Dr, SW14 200 CR85
Palewell Pk, SW14 200 CR85
Paley Gdns, Loug. IG10 107 EP41
Palfrey Cl, St.Alb. AL3 65 CD18
Palfrey Pl, SW8 42 D4
Palgrave Av, Sthl. UB1 158 CA73
Palgrave Gdns, NW1 16 D4
Palgrave Ho, NW3 6 E2
Palgrave Rd, W12 181 CT76
Palissy St, E2 20 A3
Palladian Circ, Green. DA9 191 FW84
Palladino Ho, SW17
off Laurel Cl 202 DE92
Palladio Ct, SW18
off Mapleton Rd 202 DB86
Pallant Way, Orp. BR6 227 EN104
Pallas Rd, Hem.H. HP2 62 BM18
Pallet Way, SE18 186 EL81
Palliser Dr, Rain. RM13 169 FG71
Palliser Rd, W14 26 E10
Chalfont St. Giles HP8 112 AU48
Pallister Ter, SW15
off Roehampton Vale 201 CT90
Pall Mall, SW1 29 M3
Pall Mall E, SW1 29 P2
Palmar Cres, Bexh. DA7 188 FA83
Palmar Rd, Bexh. DA7 188 FA82
Palmarsh Rd, Orp. BR5
off Wotton Grn 228 EX98
Palm Av, Sid. DA14 228 EX93
Palm Cl, E10 145 EB62
Palmeira Rd, Bexh. DA7 188 EX83
Palmer Av, Bushey WD23 98 CB43
Gravesend DA12 213 GK91
Sutton SM3 239 CW105
Palmer Cl, Hert. SG14 54 DQ07
Horley RH6 290 DF145
Hounslow TW5 178 CA81
Northolt UB5 158 BY65
Redhill RH1 288 DG135
West Wickham BR4 225 ED104
Palmer Cres, Kings.T. KT1 220 CL97
Ottershaw KT16 233 BD107
Palmer Dr, Brom. BR1 227 EP98
Palmer Gdns, Barn. EN5 101 CX43
Palmer Ho, SE14
off Lubbock St 45 J5
Palmer Pl, N7 8 E3
Palmer Rd, E13 24 B5
Dagenham RM8 148 EX60
Hertford SG14 54 DR07
Palmers Av, Grays RM17 192 GC78
Coll **Palmer's Coll**,
Grays RM17
off Chadwell Rd 192 GE77
Palmers Dr, Grays RM17 192 GC77
Palmersfield Rd, Bans. SM7 240 DA114
PALMERS GREEN, N13 121 DN48
≠ **Palmers Green** 121 DM49
Sch **Palmers Grn High Sch**,
N21 *off Hoppers Rd* 121 DN47
Palmers Gro, Lwr Naze. EN9 72 EF22
West Molesey KT8 218 CA98
Palmers Hill, Epp. CM16 92 EU29
Palmers La, Enf. EN1, EN3 104 DV39
Palmer's Lo, Guil. GU2
off Old Palace Rd 280 AV135
Palmers Moor La, Iver SL0 156 BG70
Palmers Orchard, Shore. TN14 247 FF111
Palmers Pas, SW14
off Palmers Rd 180 CQ83
Palmers Rd, E2 21 K1
N11 121 DJ50
SW14 180 CQ83
SW16 223 DM96
Borehamwood WD6 100 CP39
Palmerston Av, Slou. SL3 174 AV76
Palmerston Cl, Red. RH1
off Reed Dr 288 DG137
Welwyn Garden City AL8 51 CW09
Woking GU21 233 AZ114
Palmerston Cres, N13 121 DM50
SE18 187 EQ79
Palmerstone Ct, Vir.W. GU25
off Sandhills La 214 AY99
Palmerston Gdns, Grays
RM20 191 FX78
Palmerston Gro, SW19 202 DA94
Palmerston Ho, SW11
off Strasburg Rd 41 H7
W8 27 J3
Palmerston Rd, E7 146 EH64
E17 145 DZ56
N22 121 DM52
NW6 5 J6
SW14 180 CQ84
SW19 202 DA94
W3 180 CQ76
Buckhurst Hill IG9 124 EH47
Carshalton SM5 240 DF105
Croydon CR0 224 DR99
Grays RM20 191 FX78
Harrow HA3 139 CF55
Hounslow TW3 178 CC81
Orpington BR6 245 EQ105
Rainham RM13 170 FJ68
Sutton SM1 *off Vernon Rd* 240 DC106
Twickenham TW2 199 CE86
Palmerston Way, SW8 41 K5
Palmer St, SW1 29 N5
Palmers Way, Chsht EN8 89 DY29
Palm Gro, W5 180 CL76
Guildford GU1 264 AW129
Palm Rd, Rom. RM7 149 FC57
Pamela Av, Hem.H. HP3 62 BM23
Pamela Gdns, Pnr. HA5 137 BV57
Pamela Wk, E8 10 C8
Pampisford Rd, Pur. CR8 241 DN111
South Croydon CR2 241 DP108
Pams Way, Epsom KT19 238 CR106
Pancake La, Hem.H. HP2 63 BR21
Pancras La, EC4 19 K9
Pancras Rd, N1 8 A10
NW1 7 N10
Pancras Way, E3 12 A10
Pancroft, Abridge RM4 108 EV41
Pandian Way, NW1 7 N4
Pandora Rd, NW6 5 J4
Panfield Ms, Ilf. IG2 147 EN58
Panfield Rd, SE2 188 EU76
Pangbourne Av, W10 14 B6
Pangbourne Dr, Stan. HA7 117 CK50
Pangbourne Ho, N7 7 P3
Panhard Pl, Sthl. UB1 158 CB73
Pank Av, Barn. EN5 102 DC43
Pankhurst Av, E16 36 B2
Pankhurst Cl, SE14 45 J5
Isleworth TW7 179 CF83
Pankhurst Ho, W12
off Du Cane Rd 14 A9
Pankhurst Pl, Wat. WD24 98 BW41
Pankhurst Rd, Walt. KT12 218 BW101
Panmuir Rd, SW20 221 CV95
Panmure Cl, N5 9 H1
Panmure Rd, SE26 204 DV90
Pannells Cl, Cher. KT16 215 BF102
Pannells Ct, Guil. GU1 280 AX135
Hounslow TW5 178 BZ79
Panoramic, The, NW3 6 D2
Pan Peninsula Sq, E14
off Millharbour 34 C5
PANSHANGER, Welw.G.C. AL7 52 DB09
Panshanger Dr, Welw.G.C. AL7 52 DB09
Panshanger La, Cole Grn SG14 52 DF10
Sch **Panshanger Prim Sch**, Welw.G.C.
AL7 *off Daniells* 52 DA08
Pansy Gdns, W12 161 CU73
Panters, Swan. BR8 209 FF94
Panther Dr, NW10 140 CR64
Pantile Rd, Wey. KT13 235 BR105
Pantile Row, Slou. SL3 175 BA77
Pantiles, The, NW11 141 CZ56
Bexleyheath DA7 188 EZ80
Bromley BR1 226 EL97
Bushey Heath WD23 117 CD45
Pantiles Cl, N13 121 DP50
Woking GU21 248 AV118
Pantile Wk, Uxb. UB8
off The Mall Pavilions 156 BJ66
Panton Cl, Croy. CR0 223 DP102
Panton St, SW1 29 N1
Panxworth Rd, Hem.H. HP3 62 BL22
Panyer All, EC4 19 J9
Panyers Gdns, Dag. RM10 149 FB62
Papercourt La, Ripley GU23 249 BF122
Paper Ms, Dor. RH4 285 CH135
Papermill Cl, Cars. SM5 240 DG105
Paper Mill La, Dart. DA1
off Lawson Rd 190 FK84
Sch **Papillon Ho Sch**, Tad. KT20
off Pebble Cl 270 CS129
Papillons Wk, SE3 47 N9
Papworth Gdns, N7 8 D3
Papworth Way, SW2 203 DN87
Parade, The, SW11 40 F4
Aveley RM15 190 FQ75
Brentwood CM14
off Kings Rd 130 FW48
Burgh Heath KT20 255 CY119
Carpenders Park WD19 116 BY48
Carshalton SM5
off Beynon Rd 240 DF106
Claygate KT10 237 CE107
Dartford DA1
off Crayford Way 209 FF85
Epsom KT17, KT18 238 CR113
Epsom Common KT18
off Spa Dr 238 CN114
Hampton TW12
off Hampton Rd 199 CD92
Romford RM3 128 FP51
South Oxhey WD19
off Prestwick Rd 116 BX48
Sunbury-on-Thames TW16 197 BT94
Virginia Water GU25 214 AX100
Watford WD17 97 BV41
Windsor SL4 173 AK81
Parade Ms, SE27 203 DP89
Paradise, Hem.H. HP2 62 BK21
Paradise Cl, Chsht EN7 88 DV28
Paradise Pk, E5 145 DX61
Paradise Pas, N7 8 E3
Paradise Path, SE28
off Birchdene Dr 168 EU74
Paradise Pl, SE18 37 H9
Paradise Rd, SW4 42 A8
Richmond TW9 199 CK85
Waltham Abbey EN9 89 EC34
Paradise Row, E2 20 F2
Paradise St, SE16 32 E5
Paradise Wk, SW3 40 E2
Paragon, The, SE3 47 M8
Paragon Cl, E16 23 N8
Paragon Gro, Surb. KT5 220 CM100
Paragon Ms, SE1 31 M8
Paragon Pl, SE3 47 M8
Surbiton KT5
off Berrylands Rd 220 CM100
Paragon Rd, E9 10 F5
● **Paramount Ind Est**,
Wat. WD24 98 BW38
Parbury Ri, Chess. KT9 238 CL107
Parbury Rd, SE23 205 DY86
Parchment Cl, Amer. HP6 77 AS37
Parchmore Rd, Th.Hth. CR7 223 DP96
Parchmore Way, Th.Hth. CR7 223 DP96
Par Cl, Hert. SG13
off Birdie Way 54 DV08
Sch **Pardes Ho Gram Sch**, N3
off Hendon La 119 CZ54
Sch **Pardes Ho Prim Sch**, N3
off Hendon La 119 CZ54
Pardoe Rd, E10 145 EB59
Pardoner St, SE1 31 M6
Pardon St, EC1 19 H4
Pares Cl, Wok. GU21 248 AX116
Parfett St, E1 20 D7

Parfitt Cl, NW3
off North End 142 DC61
Parfour Dr, Ken. CR8 258 DQ116
Parfrey St, W6 38 B2
Parham Dr, Ilf. IG2 147 EP58
Parham Way, N10 121 DJ54
Sch Paringdon Jun Sch, Harl.
CM18 off Paringdon Rd 73 ER19
Paringdon Rd, Harl.
CM18, CM19 73 EP19
Paris Gdn, SE1 30 G2
Sch Parish Ch C of E Junior, Inf &
Nurs Schs, Croy. CR0
off Warrington Rd 223 DP104
Parish Cl, Horn. RM11 149 FH61
Watford WD25 off Crown Ri 82 BX34
Sch Parish C of E Prim Sch, Brom.
BR1 off London La 206 EG94
Parish Gate Dr, Sid. DA15 207 ES86
Parish La, SE20 205 DX93
Farnham Common SL2 133 AP61
Parish Ms, SE20 205 DX94
Parish Wf, SE18 37 H8
Park, The, N6 142 DG58
N11 142 DB60
SE19 204 DS94
SE23 off Park Hill 204 DW88
W5 159 CK74
Bookham KT23 252 CA123
Carshalton SM5 240 DF106
St. Albans AL1 65 CG18
Sidcup DA14 208 EU92
Park App, Well. DA16 188 EV84
Park Av, E6 167 EN67
E15 13 J5
N3 120 DB53
N13 121 DN48
N18 122 DU49
N22 121 DL54
NW2 161 CV65
NW10 160 CM69
NW11 142 DB60
SW14 180 CR84
Barking IG11 167 EQ65
Bromley BR1 206 EF93
Bushey WD23 98 BZ40
Carshalton SM5 240 DG107
Caterham CR3 258 DS124
Chorleywood WD3 96 BG43
Egham TW20 195 BC93
Enfield EN1 104 DS44
Farnborough BR6 227 EM104
Gravesend DA12 213 GJ88
Grays RM20 191 FU79
Harlow CM17 74 EW18
Hounslow TW3 198 CB86
Hutton CM13 131 GC46
Ilford IG1 147 EN61
Mitcham CR4 203 DH94
Northfleet DA11 212 GE88
Orpington BR6 228 EU103
Potters Bar EN6 86 DC34
Radlett WD7 83 CH33
Redhill RH1 288 DF142
Ruislip HA4 137 BR58
St. Albans AL1 65 CG19
Southall UB1 158 CA74
Staines-upon-Thames TW18 195 BF93
Upminster RM14 151 FS59
Watford WD18 97 BU42
West Wickham BR4 225 EC103
Woodford Green IG8 124 EH50
Wraysbury TW19 194 AX85
Park Av E, Epsom KT17 239 CU107
Park Av Ms, Mitch. CR4
off Park Av 203 DH94
Park Av N, N8 143 DK55
NW10 141 CV64
Park Av Rd, N17 122 DV52
Park Av S, N8 143 DK56
Park Av W, Epsom KT17 239 CU107
PARK BARN, Guil. GU2 264 AS133
Park Barn Dr, Guil. GU2 264 AS132
Park Barn E, Guil. GU2 264 AT133
Park Boul, Rom. RM2 127 FF53
Park Cen Bldg, E3
off Fairfield Rd 12 B10
Park Chase, Guil. GU1 264 AY134
Wembley HA9 140 CM63
Park Cliff Rd, Green. DA9 191 FW84
Park Cl, E9 11 H8
NW2 141 CV62
NW10 160 CM69
SW1 28 E5
W4 180 CR78
W14 27 H6
Brookmans Park AL9 85 CZ26
Bushey WD23 98 BX41
Carshalton SM5 240 DF107
Esher KT10 236 BZ107
Fetcham KT22 253 CD124
Hampton TW12 218 CC95
Harrow HA3 117 CE53
Hatfield AL9 67 CW17
Hounslow TW3 198 CC85
Kingston upon Thames KT2 220 CN95
New Haw KT15 234 BH110
North Weald Bassett CM16 92 FA27
Oxted RH8 276 EF128
Rickmansworth WD3 115 BP49
Strood Green RH3 286 CP139
Walton-on-Thames KT12 217 BT103
Windsor SL4 173 AR82
Park Copse, Dor. RH5 285 CK136
Park Cor, Coln.Hth AL4 66 CP23
Windsor SL4 173 AL83
Park Cor Dr, E.Hors. KT24 267 BS128
Park Cor Rd, Sthflt DA13 212 FZ91
Park Ct, SE21 204 DQ90
SE26 204 DV93
SW11 41 J6
Bookham KT23 268 CA125
Hampton Wick KT1 219 CJ95
Harlow CM20 57 ER14
New Malden KT3 220 CR98
Wembley HA9 140 CL64
West Byfleet KT14 234 BG113
Woking GU22 off Park Dr 249 AZ118
Park Cres, N3 120 DB52
W1 17 J5
Elstree WD6 100 CM41
Enfield EN2 104 DR42
Erith DA8 189 FC79
Harrow HA3 117 CE53
Hornchurch RM11 149 FG59
Twickenham TW2 199 CD88
Park Cres Ms E, W1 17 K5
Park Cres Ms W, W1 17 J6
Park Cres Rd, Erith DA8 189 FD79
Park Cft, Edg. HA8 118 CQ53
Parkcroft Rd, SE12 206 EF87
Park Dale, N11 121 DK51
Parkdale Cres, Wor.Pk. KT4 220 CR104
Parkdale Rd, SE18 187 ES78
Park Dr, N21 104 DQ44
NW11 142 DB60
SE7 186 EL79
SW14 180 CR84
W3 180 CN76
Ashtead KT21 254 CN118
Dagenham RM10 149 FC62
Harrow Weald HA3 117 CE51
Hatfield Heath CM22 59 FH05
North Harrow HA2 138 CA59
Potters Bar EN6 86 DA31
Romford RM1 149 FD56
Upminster RM14 150 FQ63
Weybridge KT13 235 BP106
Woking GU22 249 AZ118
Park Dr Cl, SE7 186 EL78
Park E Bldg, E3
off Fairfield Rd 12 B10
Park End, NW3 6 D1
Bromley BR1 226 EF95
Park End Rd, Rom. RM1 149 FE56
Parker Av, Hert. SG14 54 DR07
Tilbury RM18 193 GJ81
Parker Cl, E16 36 G3
Carshalton SM5 240 DF107
Parker Ms, WC2 18 B8
Parke Rd, SW13 181 CU81
Sunbury-on-Thames TW16 217 BU98
Parker Rd, Croy. CR0 242 DQ105
Grays RM17 192 FZ78
Parkers Cl, Ashtd. KT21 254 CL119
Parkers Hill, Ashtd. KT21 254 CL119
Parkers La, Ashtd. KT21 254 CL119
Parkers Row, SE1 32 B5
Parker St, E16 36 G3
WC2 18 B8
Watford WD24 97 BV39
Parkes Rd, Chig. IG7 125 ES50
Park Fm Cl, N2 142 DC55
Pinner HA5 137 BV57
Park Fm Rd, Brom. BR1 226 EK95
Kingston upon Thames KT2 200 CL94
Upminster RM14 150 FM64
Parkfield, Chorl. WD3 95 BF42
Sevenoaks TN15 279 FM123
Parkfield Av, SW14 180 CS84
Amersham HP6 77 AR37
Feltham TW13 197 BU90
Harrow HA2 116 CC54
Hillingdon UB10 157 BP69
Northolt UB5 158 BX68
Parkfield Cl, Edg. HA8 118 CP51
Northolt UB5 158 BY68
Parkfield Cres, Felt. TW13 197 BU90
Harrow HA2 116 CC54
Ruislip HA4 138 BY62
Parkfield Dr, Nthlt. UB5 158 BX68
Parkfield Gdns, Har. HA2 138 CB55
Sch Parkfield Prim Sch, NW4
off Park Rd 141 CV59
Parkfield Rd, NW10 161 CU66
SE14 45 N6
Feltham TW13 197 BU90
Harrow HA2 138 CC62
Ickenham UB10 137 BP61
Northolt UB5 158 BY68
Parkfields, SW15 181 CW84
Croydon CR0 225 DZ102
Oxshott KT22 237 CD111
Roydon CM19 72 EH16
Welwyn Garden City AL8 51 CX09
Parkfields Av, NW9 140 CR60
SW20 221 CV95
Parkfields Cl, Cars. SM5 240 DG105
Parkfields Rd, Kings.T. KT2 200 CM92
Parkfield St, N1 8 F10
Parkfield Vw, Pot.B. EN6 86 DB32
Parkfield Way, Brom. BR2 227 EM100
Park Gdns, NW9 140 CP55
Erith DA8 off Valley Rd 189 FD77
Kingston upon Thames KT2 200 CM92
Park Gate, N2 142 DD55
N21 121 DM45
Parkgate, SE3 186 EF83
Park Gate, W5 159 CK71
Parkgate, Burn. SL1 152 AJ70
Parkgate Av, Barn. EN4 102 DC39
Parkgate Cl, Kings.T. KT2
off Warboys App 200 CP93
Park Gate Ct, Wok. GU22
off Constitution Hill 248 AY118
Parkgate Cres, Barn. EN4 102 DC40
Parkgate Gdns, SW14 200 CR85
Sch Parkgate Inf & Nurs Sch, Wat.
WD24 off Northfield Gdns 98 BW37
Sch Parkgate Jun Sch, Wat. WD24
off Southwold Rd 98 BW37
Parkgate Ms, N6 143 DJ59
Parkgate Rd, SW11 40 C5
Orpington BR6 247 FB105
Reigate RH2 288 DB135
Wallington SM6 240 DG106
Watford WD24 98 BW37
Park Gates, Har. HA2 138 CA63
Park Gra Gdns, Sev. TN13
off Solefields Rd 279 FJ127
Park Grn, Bkhm KT23 252 CA124
Park Gro, E15 13 N8
N11 121 DK52
Bexleyheath DA7 189 FC84
Bromley BR1 226 EH95
Chalfont St. Giles HP8 94 AX41
Edgware HA8 118 CM50
Knotty Green HP9 110 AJ48
Park Gro Rd, E11 146 EE61
Park Hall Rd, N2 142 DE56
SE21 204 DQ90
Reigate RH2 272 DA132
● Park Hall Trd Est, SE21 204 DQ90
Parkham Ct, Brom. BR2 226 EE96
Parkham St, SW11 40 B7
Park Hts, Wok. GU22
off Constitution Hill 248 AY118
Sch Park High Sch, Stan. HA7
off Thistlecroft Gdns 117 CK54
Park Hill, SE23 204 DV89
SW4 203 DK85
W5 159 CK71
Bromley BR1 226 EL98
Carshalton SM5 240 DE107
Harlow CM17 58 EV12
Loughton IG10 106 EK43
Richmond TW10 200 CM86
Park Hill Cl, Cars. SM5 240 DE106
Parkhill Cl, Horn. RM12 150 FJ62
Park Hill Ct, SW17
off Beeches Rd 202 DF90
Sch Parkhill Inf & Jun Schs, Ilf. IG5
off Lord Av 147 EN55
Sch Park Hill Inf Sch, Croy. CR0
off Stanhope Rd 224 DS104
Sch Park Hill Jun Sch, Croy. CR0
off Stanhope Rd 224 DS104
Park Hill Ri, Croy. CR0 224 DS103
Parkhill Rd, E4 123 EC46
NW3 6 F4
Bexley DA5 208 EZ87
Park Hill Rd, Brom. BR2 226 EE96
Croydon CR0 224 DS103
Epsom KT17 239 CT111
Parkhill Rd, Hem.H. HP1 62 BH20
Sidcup DA15 207 ER90
Park Hill Rd, Wall. SM6 241 DH108
Sch Park Hill Sch, Kings.T. KT2
off Queens Rd 200 CN94
Parkhill Wk, NW3 6 F3
Parkholme Rd, E8 10 B4
Park Homes, Lon.Col. AL2
off Peters Av 83 CJ26
Park Horsley, E.Hors. KT24 267 BU129
Parkhouse 67 CT17
Park Ho, N21 121 DM45
Parkhouse Ct, Hat. AL10 66 CS17
Park Ho Dr, Reig. RH2 287 CZ136
Park Ho Gdns, Twick. TW1 199 CJ86
Parkhouse St, SE5 43 M4
Parkhurst, Epsom KT19 238 CQ110
Parkhurst Gdns, Bex. DA5 208 FA87
Parkhurst Gro, Horl. RH6 290 DE147
Parkhurst Ho, W12 14 A9
Parkhurst Rd, E12 147 EN63
E17 145 DY56
N7 8 A1
N11 120 DG49
N17 122 DU54
N22 121 DM52
Bexley DA5 208 FA87
Guildford GU2 264 AU133
Hertford SG14 53 DP08
Horley RH6 290 DE147
Sutton SM1 240 DD105
● Park Ind Est, Frog. AL2 83 CE27
Parkinson Ho, SW1
off Tachbrook St 29 N10
Parkland Av, Rom. RM1 149 FE55
Slough SL3 174 AX77
Upminster RM14 150 FP64
Parkland Cl, Chig. IG7 125 EQ48
Hoddesdon EN11 55 EB14
Sevenoaks TN13 279 FJ129
Parkland Dr, St.Alb. AL3 64 CA21
Parkland Gdns, SW19 201 CX88
Parkland Gro, Ashf. TW15 196 BN91
Parkland Mead, Brom. BR1
off Gardenia Rd 227 EP97
Parkland Rd, N22 121 DM54
Ashford TW15 196 BN91
Woodford Green IG8 124 EG52
Parklands, N6 143 DH59
Addlestone KT15 234 BJ106
Bookham KT23 252 CA123
Chigwell IG7 125 EQ48
Coopersale CM16 92 EX29
Guildford GU2 264 AU130
Hemel Hempstead HP1 61 BF18
North Holmwood RH5 285 CH140
Oxted RH8 276 EE131
Shere GU5 282 BN141
Surbiton KT5 220 CM99
Waltham Abbey EN9 89 ED32
Parklands Cl, SW14 200 CQ85
Barnet EN4 102 DD38
Ilford IG2 147 EQ59
Parklands Ct, Houns. TW5 178 BX82
Parklands Dr, N3 141 CY55
Parklands Gro, Islw. TW7 179 CF81
Sch Parklands Inf Sch, Rom. RM1
off Havering Rd 127 FD54
Sch Parklands Jun Sch, Rom. RM1
off Havering Rd 149 FD55
Parklands Pl, Guil. GU1 265 BB134
Parklands Rd, SW16 203 DH92
Parklands Way, Wor.Pk. KT4 220 CS104
Parkland Wk, N4 143 DM59
N6 143 DK59
N10 143 DH56
Park La, E15 12 G8
N9 122 DT48
N17 122 DU52
W1 29 H3
Ashtead KT21 254 CM118
Aveley RM15 171 FR74
Banstead SM7 256 DD118
Beaconsfield HP9 111 AM54
Broxbourne EN10 71 DY19
Burnham SL1 133 AL64
Carshalton SM5 240 DG105
Chadwell Heath RM6 148 EX58
Cheshunt EN7 88 DU26
Colney Heath AL4 66 CP23
Coulsdon CR5 257 DK121
Cranford TW5 177 BU80
Croydon CR0 224 DR104
Elm Pk RM12 169 FH65
Greenhithe DA9 211 FU86
Guildford GU4 265 BC131
Harefield UB9 114 BG53
Harlow CM20 57 ER13
Harrow HA2 138 CB62
Hayes UB4 157 BS71
Hemel Hempstead HP1, HP2 62 BK21
Hornchurch RM11 149 FG58
Horton SL3 175 BA83
Reigate RH2 287 CY135
Richmond TW9 179 CK84
Seal TN15 279 FN121
Sevenoaks TN13 279 FJ124
Slough SL3 174 AV76
Stanmore HA7 117 CG48
Sutton SM3 239 CY107
Swanley BR8 230 FJ96
Teddington TW11 199 CF93
Wallington SM6 240 DG105
Waltham Cross EN8 89 DX33
Wembley HA9 140 CL64
Wormley EN10 70 DV22
Park La Cl, N17 122 DU52
Park La E, Reig. RH2 288 DA136
Park La Paradise, Chsht EN7 70 DU24
Sch Park La Prim Sch, Wem. HA9
off Park La 140 CL63
PARK LANGLEY, Beck. BR3 225 EC99
Park Lawn, Farn.Royal SL2 153 AQ69
Parklawn Av, Epsom KT18 238 CP113
Horley RH6 290 DF146
Park Lawn Rd, Wey. KT13 235 BQ105
Park Lawns, Wem. HA9 140 CM63
Parklea Cl, NW9 118 CS53
Parkleigh Rd, SW19 222 DB96
Park Ley Rd, Wold. CR3 259 DX120
Parkleys, Rich. TW10 199 CK91
Park Lo Av, West Dr. UB7 176 BM75
Park Mans, SW1
off Knightsbridge 28 E5
SW8 42 B2
Parkmead, SW15 201 CV86
Park Mead, Harl. CM20 57 EP14
Harrow HA2 138 CB62
Parkmead, Loug. IG10 107 EN43
Park Mead, Sid. DA15 208 EV85
Parkmead Cl, Croy. CR0 225 DX100
Parkmead Gdns, NW7 119 CT51
Park Meadow, Hat. AL9 67 CW17
Park Ms, SE10 47 M1
SE24 off Croxted Rd 204 DQ86
Chislehurst BR7 207 EP93
East Molesey KT8 218 CC98
Hatfield AL9 67 CW16
Oxted RH8 276 EF128
Rainham RM13 169 FG65
Parkmore Cl, Wdf.Grn. IG8 124 EG49
Park Nook Gdns, Enf. EN2 104 DR37
Parkpale La, Bet. RH3 286 CN139
Park Par, NW10 161 CT68
Park Piazza, SE13
off Highfield Cl 205 ED86
Park Pl, E14 34 A2
N1 9 M8
SW1 29 L3
W3 180 CN77
W5 159 CK74
Amersham HP6 94 AT38
Gravesend DA12 213 GJ86
Hampton Hill TW12 198 CC93
Park Street AL2 83 CD27
Seer Green HP9 111 AR50
Sevenoaks TN13 278 FD123
Wembley HA9 140 CM63
Woking GU22
off Hill Vw Rd 249 AZ118
Park Pl Vil, W2 15 P6
Sch Park Prim Sch, E15 13 M6
Park Ridings, N8 143 DN55
Park Ri, SE23 205 DY88
Harrow HA3 117 CE53
Leatherhead KT22 253 CH121
Northchurch HP4 60 AS17
Park Ri Cl, Lthd. KT22 253 CH121
Park Ri Rd, SE23 205 DY88
Park Rd, E6 166 EJ67
E10 145 EA60
E12 146 EH60
E15 13 N8
E17 145 DZ57
N2 142 DD55
N8 143 DJ56
N11 121 DK52
N14 121 DK45
N15 143 DP56
N18 122 DT49
NW1 16 C2
NW4 141 CU59
NW8 16 C2
NW9 140 CR59
NW10 160 CS67
SE25 224 DS98
SW19 202 DD93
W4 180 CQ80
W7 159 CF73
Albury GU5 282 BL140
Amersham HP6 94 AT37
Ashford TW15 197 BP92
Ashtead KT21 254 CL118
Banstead SM7 256 DB115
Beckenham BR3 205 DZ94
Brentwood CM14 130 FV46
Bromley BR1 226 EH95
Bushey WD23 98 CA44
Caterham CR3 258 DS123
Chesham HP5 76 AP31
Chislehurst BR7 207 EP93
Dartford DA1 210 FN87
East Molesey KT8 218 CC98
Egham TW20 195 BA91
Enfield EN3 105 DY36
Esher KT10 236 CB105
Feltham TW13 198 BX91
Gravesend DA11 213 GH88
Grays RM17 192 GB78
Guildford GU1 264 AX134
Hackbridge SM6 223 DH103
Hampton Hill TW12 198 CB91
Hampton Wick KT1 219 CJ95
Hayes UB4 157 BS71
Hemel Hempstead HP1 62 BJ22
Hertford SG13 54 DS09
High Barnet EN5 101 CZ42
Hoddesdon EN11 71 EA17
Hounslow TW3 178 CC84
Ilford IG1 147 ER62
Isleworth TW7 179 CH81
Kenley CR8 257 DP115
Kingston upon Thames KT2 200 CM92
New Barnet EN4 102 DE42
New Malden KT3 220 CR98
Northaw EN6 86 DG30
Orpington BR5 228 EW99
Oxted RH8 276 EF128
Radlett WD7 99 CG35
Redhill RH1 272 DF132
Richmond TW10 200 CM86
Rickmansworth WD3 114 BK45
Shepperton TW17 216 BN102
Slough SL2 153 AQ68
Stanwell TW19 196 BH86
Sunbury-on-Thames TW16 197 BV94
Surbiton KT5 220 CM99
Sutton SM3 239 CY107
Swanley BR8 229 FF97
Swanscombe DA10 212 FY86
Teddington TW11 199 CF93
Twickenham TW1 199 CJ86
Uxbridge UB8 156 BL66
Wallington SM6 241 DH106
Waltham Cross EN8 89 DX33
Ware SG12 54 DV05
Warlingham CR6 244 EE114
Watford WD17 97 BU39
Wembley HA0 160 CL65
Woking GU22 249 BA117
Park Rd E, W3 180 CP75
Uxbridge UB10 156 BK68
Park Rd N, W3 180 CP75
W4 180 CR78
Park Row, SE10 46 G2
PARK ROYAL, NW10 160 CN69
⊖ Park Royal 160 CN70
H Park Royal Cen for Mental
Health, NW10 160 CQ68
● Park Royal Metro Cen,
NW10 160 CP70
Park Royal Rd, NW10 160 CQ69
W3 160 CQ69
Sch Park Sch, The, Wok. GU22
off Onslow Cres 249 BA117
Sch Park Sch for Girls, Ilf. IG1
off Park Av 147 EP60
Parkshot, Rich. TW9 180 CL84
Parkside, N3 120 DB53
NW2 141 CU62
NW7 119 CU51
SE3 47 L4
SW19 201 CX91
Buckhurst Hill IG9 124 EH47
Chalfont St. Peter SL9
off Lower Rd 135 AZ56
Park Side, Epp. CM16 92 EV29
Parkside, Grays RM16 192 GE76
Halstead TN14 246 EZ113
Hampton Hill TW12 199 CD92
Matching Tye CM17 59 FE12
New Haw KT15 234 BH110
Potters Bar EN6
off High St 86 DC32
Sidcup DA14 208 EV89
Sutton SM3 239 CY107
Waltham Cross EN8 89 DY34
Watford WD19 98 BW44
Parkside Av, SW19 201 CX92
Bexleyheath DA7 189 FD82
Bromley BR1 226 EL98
Romford RM1 149 FD55
Tilbury RM18 193 GH82
● Parkside Business Est, SE8 45 M2
Parkside Cl, SE20 204 DW94
East Horsley KT24 267 BT125
Sch Parkside Comm Prim Sch,
Borwd. WD6
off Aycliffe Rd 100 CM38
Parkside Ct, Wey. KT13 234 BN105
Parkside Cres, N7 143 DN62
Surbiton KT5 220 CQ100
Parkside Cross, Bexh. DA7 189 FE82
Parkside Dr, Edg. HA8 118 CN48
Watford WD17 97 BS40
Parkside Est, E9 11 H8
Parkside Gdns, SW19 201 CX91
Coulsdon CR5 257 DH117
East Barnet EN4 120 DF46
H Parkside Hosp, SW19 201 CX90
Parkside Ho, Dag. RM10 149 FC62
Parkside Ms, Warl. CR6 259 EA116
H Parkside Oncology Clinic,
SW19 201 CX90
Parkside Pl, E.Hors. KT24 267 BS125
Staines-upon-Thames TW18 196 BG93
Parkside Rd, SW11 40 G7
Belvedere DA17 189 FC77
Hounslow TW3 198 CB85
Northwood HA6 115 BT50
Sch Parkside Sch, Stoke D'Ab.
KT11 off Stoke Rd 252 CA118
Parkside Ter, N18
off Great Cambridge Rd 122 DR49
Orpington BR6
off Willow Wk 227 EP104
Parkside Wk, SE10 35 J7
Slough SL1 174 AU76
Parkside Way, Har. HA2 138 CB56
Park S, SW11 40 G7
Parkspring Ct, Erith DA8
off Erith High St 189 FF79
Park Sq, Esher KT10
off Park Rd 236 CB105
Lambourne End RM4 108 EY44
Park Sq E, NW1 17 J4
Park Sq Ms, NW1 17 J5
Park Sq W, NW1 17 J4
Parkstead Rd, SW15 201 CU85
Park Steps, W2
off St. Georges Flds 16 D10
Parkstone Av, N18 122 DT50
Hornchurch RM11 150 FK58
Parkstone Rd, E17 145 EC55
SE15 44 D9
PARK STREET, St.Alb. AL2 83 CD26
⇌ Park Street 83 CD26
Park St, SE1 31 J2
W1 16 G10
Berkhamsted HP4 60 AV18
Colnbrook SL3 175 BD80
Croydon CR0 224 DQ103
Guildford GU1 280 AW136
Hatfield AL9 67 CW17
St. Albans AL2 83 CD26
Slough SL1 174 AT76
Teddington TW11 199 CE93
Windsor SL4 173 AR81
Sch Park St C of E Prim Sch & Nurs,
Park St AL2 off Branch Rd 83 CD27
Park St La, Park St AL2 82 CB30
Jct Park St Rbt, St.Alb. AL2 64 CC24
Park Ter, Green. DA9 211 FV85
Sundridge TN14
off Main Rd 262 EX124
Worcester Park KT4 221 CU102
Parkthorne Cl, Har. HA2 138 CB58
Parkthorne Dr, Har. HA2 138 CA58
Parkthorne Rd, SW12 203 DK87
Park Twrs, W1 off Brick St 29 J3
Park Vw, N21 121 DM45
W3 160 CQ71
Aveley RM15 171 FR74
Bookham KT23 268 CA125
Caterham CR3 274 DU125
Hatfield AL9 67 CW16
Hoddesdon EN11 71 EA18
Horley RH6
off Brighton Rd 290 DG148
New Malden KT3 221 CT97
Pinner HA5 116 BZ53
Potters Bar EN6 86 DC33
Park Vw, Wem. HA9 140 CP64

Sch **Park Vw Acad**, N15
off Langham Rd 144 DQ56
Parkview Chase, Slou. SL1 153 AL72
Parkview Cl, Cars. SM5 240 DF108
Park Vw Cl, St.Alb. AL1 65 CG21
Parkview Ct, SW18
off Broomhill Rd 202 DA86
Park Vw Ct, E3 *off Devons Rd* 22 B6
Ilf. IG2 147 ES58
Woking GU22 248 AY119
Parkview Cres, Wor.Pk. KT4 221 CW102
Park Vw Cres, N11 121 DH49
Parkview Dr, Mitch. CR4 222 DD96
Park Vw Est, E2 11 H10
N5 144 DQ63
Park Vw Gdns, NW4 141 CW57
Grays RM17 192 GB78
Ilford IG4 147 EM56
Park Vw Ho, SE24
off Hurst St 203 DP86
Parkview Ho, Horn. RM12 149 FH61
Park Vw Ms, SW9 42 D8
Parkview Ms, Rain. RM13 169 FH71
Park Vw Rd, N3 120 DB53
N17 144 DU55
NW10 141 CT63
Parkview Rd, SE9 207 EP88
Park Vw Rd, W5 160 CL71
Berkhamsted HP4 60 AV19
Parkview Rd, Croy. CR0 224 DU102
Park Vw Rd, Lthd. KT22 253 CF120
Pinner HA5 115 BV52
Redhill RH1 288 DG141
Southall UB1 158 CA74
Uxbridge UB8 156 BN72
Welling DA16 188 EW83
Woldingham CR3 259 DY122
Park Vw Rd Est, N17 122 DV54
Parkview Vale, Guil. GU4 265 BC131
Park Village E, NW1 7 J9
Park Village W, NW1 7 J10
Park Vil, Rom. RM6 148 EX58
Parkville Rd, SW6 38 G5
Park Vista, SE10 47 H3
Park Wk, N6 *off North Rd* 142 DG59
SE10 46 G5
SW10 39 P2
Ashtead KT21
off Rectory La 254 CM119
Sch **Park Wk Prim Sch**, SW10 40 A3
Parkway, N14 121 DL47
Park Way, N20 120 DF49
Parkway, NW1 7 J9
Park Way, NW11 141 CY57
Parkway, SW20 221 CX98
Park Way, Bex. DA5 209 FE90
Bookham KT23 252 CA123
Parkway, Dor. RH4 285 CG135
Park Way, Edg. HA8 118 CP53
Enfield EN2 103 DN40
Parkway, Erith DA18 188 EY76
Park Way, Felt. TW14 197 BV87
Parkway, Guil. GU1 264 AY133
Harlow CM19 72 EL15
Park Way, Horl. RH6 290 DG148
Parkway, Ilf. IG3 147 ET62
New Addington CR0 243 EC109
Porters Wood AL3 65 CF16
Rainham RM13
off Upminster Rd S 169 FG70
Park Way, Rick. WD3 114 BJ46
Parkway, Rom. RM2 149 FF55
Park Way, Ruis. HA4 137 BU60
Parkway, Saw. CM21 58 EY06
Park Way, Shenf. CM15 131 FZ46
Parkway, Uxb. UB10 156 BN66
Welwyn Garden City AL8 51 CW11
Park Way, W.Mol. KT8 218 CB97
Parkway, Wey. KT13 235 BR105
Woodford Green IG8 124 EJ50
Parkway, The, Cran. TW4, TW5 177 BV82
Hayes UB3, UB4 158 BW72
Iver SL0 155 BC68
Northolt UB5 158 BX69
Southall UB2 177 BU78
Parkway Cl, Welw.G.C. AL8 51 CW09
Parkway Ct, St.Alb. AL1 65 CH23
Parkway Cres, E15 12 F2
Parkway Gdns, Welw.G.C. AL8 51 CW10
Sch **Parkway Prim Sch**, Erith
DA18 *off Alsike Rd* 188 EY76
● **Parkway Trd Est**, Houns.
TW5 178 BW79
Park W, W2 16 D9
Park W Bldg, E3
off Fairfield Rd 12 B10
Park W Pl, W2 16 D8
Parkwood, N20 120 DF48
Beckenham BR3 225 EA95
Parkwood Av, Esher KT10 218 CC102
Parkwood Cl, Bans. SM7 255 CX115
Broxbourne EN10 71 DZ19
Parkwood Dr, Hem.H. HP1 61 BF20
Parkwood Gro, Sun. TW16 217 BU97
Sch **Parkwood Hall Sch**, Swan.
BR8 *off Beechenlea La* 229 FH97
Parkwood Ms, N6 143 DH58
Sch **Parkwood Prim Sch**, N4
off Queens Dr 143 DP61
Parkwood Rd, SW19 201 CZ92
Banstead SM7 255 CX115
Bexley DA5 208 EZ87
Isleworth TW7 179 CF81
Nutfield RH1 273 DL133
Tatsfield TN16 260 EL121
Parkwood Vw, Bans. SM7 255 CW116
Park Wks Rd, Red. RH1 273 DM133
Sch **Parlaunt Pk Prim Sch**, Langley
SL3 *off Kennett Rd* 175 BB76
Parlaunt Rd, Slou. SL3 175 BA77
Parley Dr, Wok. GU21 248 AW117
Parliament Ct, E1 19 P7
Parliament Hill, NW3 6 D1
Sch **Parliament Hill Sch**, NW5
off Highgate Rd 142 DG63
Parliament La, Burn. SL1 152 AF66
Parliament Ms, SW14
off Thames Bk 180 CQ82
Parliament Sq, SW1 30 A5
Hertford SG14 54 DR09
Parliament St, SW1 30 A5
Parliament Vw Apts, SE1 30 C8
Parma Cres, SW11 182 DF84
● **Parmiter Ind Cen**, E2 10 F10
Sch **Parmiter's Sch**, Wat. WD25
off High Elms La 82 BW31
Parmiter St, E2 10 F10
Parmoor Ct, EC1 19 J4
Parnall Rd, Harl. CM18 73 ER18
Parndon Mill La, Harl. CM20 57 EP12
Parndon Wd Rd, Harl. CM19 73 EQ20
Parnell Cl, W12 181 CV76
Abbots Langley WD5 81 BT30
Chafford Hundred RM16 191 FW78
Edgware HA8 118 CP49
Parnell Gdns, Wey. KT13 234 BN111
Parnell Rd, E3 11 P9
Parnell Way, Har. HA3
off Weston Dr 117 CH53
Parnel Rd, Ware SG12 55 DZ05
Parnham Cl, Brom. BR1
off Stoneleigh Rd 227 EP97
Parnham St, E14 21 M8
Parolles Rd, N19 143 DJ60
Paroma Rd, Belv. DA17 188 FA76
Parr Av, Epsom KT17 239 CV109
Parr Cl, N9 122 DV49
N18 122 DV49
Chafford Hundred RM16 191 FW77
Leatherhead KT22 253 CF120
Parr Ct, N1 9 L10
Feltham TW13 198 BW91
Parr Cres, Hem.H. HP2 63 BP15
Parris Cft, Dor. RH4
off Goodwyns Rd 285 CJ139
Parritt Rd, Red. RH1 273 DH132
Parrock, The, Grav. DA12 213 GJ88
Parrock Av, Grav. DA12 213 GJ88
PARROCK FARM, Grav. DA12 213 GK91
Parrock Rd, Grav. DA12 213 GJ88
Parrock St, Grav. DA12 213 GH87
Parrotts Cl, Crox.Grn WD3 96 BN42
Parrotts Fld, Hodd. EN11 71 EB16
Parr Pl, W4
off Chiswick High Rd 181 CT77
Parr Rd, E6 166 EK67
Stanmore HA7 117 CK53
Parrs Cl, S.Croy. CR2 242 DR109
Parrs Pl, Hmptn. TW12 198 CA94
Parr St, N1 9 L10
Parry Av, E6 25 J9
Parry Cl, Epsom KT17 239 CU108
Parry Dr, Wey. KT13 234 BN110
Parry Grn N, Slou. SL3 175 AZ77
Parry Grn S, Slou. SL3 175 AZ77
Parry Pl, SE18 37 P8
Parry Rd, SE25 224 DS97
W10 14 F2
Parry St, SW8 42 A2
Parsifal Rd, NW6 5 K2
Parsley Gdns, Croy. CR0
off Primrose La 225 DX102
Parsloe Rd, Epp.Grn CM16 73 EN21
Harlow CM19 73 EP20
Parsloes Av, Dag. RM9 148 EX63
Sch **Parsloes Prim Sch**, Dag. RM9
off Spurling Rd 168 EZ65
Parsonage Bk, Eyns. DA4
off Pollyhaugh 230 FL103
Parsonage Cl, Abb.L. WD5 81 BS30
Hayes UB3 157 BT72
Warlingham CR6 259 DY116
Westcott RH4 284 CC138
Parsonage Ct, Loug. IG10 107 EP41
Sch **Parsonage Fm Prim Sch**, Rain.
RM13 *off Farm Rd* 170 FJ69
Parsonage Gdns, Enf. EN2 104 DQ40
Parsonage La, Chesh. HP5
off Blucher St 76 AP31
Enfield EN1, EN2 104 DR40
North Mymms AL9 67 CV23
Sidcup DA14 208 EZ91
Slough SL2 153 AQ68
Sutton at Hone DA4 210 FP93
Westcott RH4 284 CC137
Windsor SL4 173 AN81
Parsonage Leys, Harl. CM20 57 ET14
Parsonage Manorway, Belv.
DA17 188 FA79
Parsonage Rd, Ch.St.G. HP8 112 AV48
Englefield Green TW20 194 AX92
Grays RM20 191 FW79
North Mymms AL9 67 CV23
Rainham RM13 170 FJ69
Rickmansworth WD3 114 BK45
Parsonage Sq, Dor. RH4 285 CG135
Parsonage St, E14 34 F9
Parsons Cl, Horl. RH6 290 DE147
Sutton SM1 222 DB104
Parsons Ct, Borwd. WD6
off Chaucer Gro 100 CN42
Parsons Cres, Edg. HA8 118 CN48
Parsonsfield Cl, Bans. SM7 255 CX115
Parsonsfield Rd, Bans. SM7 255 CX116
PARSONS GREEN, SW6 39 J6
⊖ **Parsons Green** 39 H7
Parsons Grn, SW6 39 J7
Guildford GU1
off Bellfields Rd 264 AX132
Parsons Grn Ct, Guil. GU1
off Bellfields Rd 264 AX132
Parsons Grn La, SW6 39 J6
Parsons Gro, Edg. HA8 118 CN48
Parsons Hill, SE18
off John Wilson St 37 L7
Parsons Ho, SW2
off New Pk Rd 203 DL87
Parson's Ho, W2 16 A5
Parsons La, Dart. DA2 209 FH90
Parson's Mead, Croy. CR0 223 DP102
Parsons Mead, E.Mol. KT8 218 CC97
Parsons Pightle, Couls. CR5 257 DN120
Parsons Rd, E13 24 C1
Slough SL3 175 AZ79
Parson St, NW4 141 CW56
Parsons Wd, Farn.Com. SL2 153 AQ65
Parthenia Rd, SW6 39 K7
Parthia Cl, Tad. KT20 255 CV119
Partingdale La, NW7 119 CX50
Partington Cl, N19 143 DK60
Partridge Cl, E16 24 E7
Barnet EN5 101 CW44
Bushey WD23 116 CB46
Chesham HP5 76 AS28
Stanmore HA7 118 CL49
Partridge Ct, Harl. CM18 73 ER17
Partridge Dr, Orp. BR6 227 EQ104
Partridge Grn, SE9 207 EN90
Partridge Knoll, Pur. CR8 241 DP112
Partridge Mead, Bans. SM7 255 CW116
Partridge Rd, Hmptn. TW12 198 BZ93
Harlow CM18 73 ER17
St. Albans AL3 65 CD16
Sidcup DA14 207 ES90
Partridges, Hem.H. HP3
off Reddings 62 BN22
Partridge Sq, E6 25 H6
Partridge Way, N22 121 DL53
Guildford GU4 265 BD132
Parvills, Wal.Abb. EN9 89 ED32
Parvin St, SW8 41 N6
Parvis Rd, W.Byf. KT14 234 BG113
Pasadena Cl, Hayes UB3 177 BV75
● **Pasadena Trd Est**, Hayes
UB3 177 BU75
Pascal Ms, SE19
off Anerley Hill 204 DU94
Pascal St, SW8 41 P4
Pascoe Rd, SE13 205 ED85
Pasfield, Wal.Abb. EN9 89 ED33
Pasgen Ct, N9
off Galahad Rd 122 DU47
Pasley Cl, SE17 43 J1
Pasquier Rd, E17 145 DY55
Passey Pl, SE9 207 EM86
Passfield Dr, E14 22 D6
Passfield Path, SE28
off Booth Cl 168 EV73
Passfields, SE6 205 EB90
Passing All, EC1 19 H5
Passmore Gdns, N11 121 DK51
PASSMORES, Harl. CM18 73 ER17
Sch **Passmores Sch & Tech Coll**,
Harl. CM18
off Tendring Rd 73 ER17
Passmore St, SW1 28 G9
★ **Passport Office**, SW1 29 K8
Pastens Rd, Oxt. RH8 276 EJ131
Pasteur Cl, NW9 118 CS54
Pasteur Dr, Harold Wd RM3 128 FK54
Pasteur Gdns, N18 121 DP50
Paston Cl, E5
off Caldecott Way 145 DX62
Wallington SM6 223 DJ104
Paston Cres, SE12 206 EH87
Paston Rd, Hem.H. HP2 62 BK18
Pastoral Way, Warley CM14 130 FV50
Pastor St, SE11 31 H8
Pasture Cl, Bushey WD23 116 CC45
Wembley HA0 139 CH62
Pasture Rd, SE6 206 EF88
Dagenham RM9 148 EZ63
Wembley HA0 139 CH61
Pastures, The, N20 119 CZ46
Hatfield AL10 67 CV19
Hemel Hempstead HP1 61 BE19
St. Albans AL2 64 CA24
Watford WD19 116 BW45
Welwyn Garden City AL7 52 DA11
Pastures Mead, Uxb. UB10 156 BN65
Pastures Path, E11 146 EE61
Pasture Vw, St.Alb. AL4 65 CK17
Patch, The, Sev. TN13 278 FE122
Patcham Ct, Sutt. SM2 240 DC109
Patcham Ter, SW8 41 K6
Patch Cl, Uxb. UB10 156 BM67
PATCHETTS GREEN, Wat.
WD25 98 CC39
Patching Way, Hayes UB4 158 BY71
Paternoster Cl, Wal.Abb. EN9 90 EF33
Paternoster Hill, Wal.Abb. EN9 90 EF32
Paternoster La, EC4
off Warwick La 19 H9
Paternoster Row, EC4 19 J9
Noak Hill RM4 128 FJ47
Paternoster Sq, EC4 19 H9
Paterson Ct, EC1
off St. Luke's Est 19 L3
Paterson Rd, Ashf. TW15 196 BK92
Pater St, W8 27 J7
Pates Manor Dr, Felt. TW14 197 BR87
Path, The, SW19 222 DB95
Pathfield Rd, SW16 203 DK93
Pathfields, Shere GU5 282 BN140
Pathway, The, Rad. WD7 99 CF36
Send GU23 265 BF125
Watford WD19
off Anthony Cl 116 BX46
Patience Rd, SW11 40 C9
Patio Cl, SW4 203 DK86
Patmore Est, SW8 41 L6
Patmore La, Hersham KT12 235 BT107
Patmore Link Rd, Hem.H. HP2 63 BQ20
Patmore Rd, Wal.Abb. EN9 90 EE34
Patmore St, SW8 41 M6
Patmore Way, Rom. RM5 127 FB50
Patmos Rd, SW9 42 G5
Paton Cl, E3 22 B2
Paton St, EC1 19 J3
Patricia Cl, Slou. SL1 153 AL73
Patricia Ct, Chis. BR7
off Manor Pk Rd 227 ER95
Welling DA16 188 EV80
Patricia Dr, Horn. RM11 150 FL60
Patricia Gdns, Sutt. SM2 240 DA111
Patrick Connolly Gdns, E3 22 D3
Patrick Gro, Wal.Abb. EN9
off Beaulieu Dr 89 EB33
Patrick Rd, E13 24 D3
Patrington Cl, Uxb. UB8 156 BJ69
Patriot Sq, E2 20 F1
Patrol Pl, SE6 205 EB86
Patrons Way E, Denh. UB9 135 BF58
Patrons Way W, Denh. UB9 135 BF58
Patshull Pl, NW5 7 L5
Patshull Rd, NW5 7 K4
Patten All, Rich. TW10
off The Hermitage 199 CK85
Pattenden Rd, SE6 205 DZ88
Patten Rd, SW18 202 DE87
Patterdale Cl, Brom. BR1 206 EF93
Patterdale Rd, SE15 44 G4
Dartford DA2 211 FR88
Patterson Ct, SE19 204 DT94
Dartford DA1 210 FN85
Wooburn Green HP10
off Glory Mill La 132 AE56
Patterson Rd, SE19 204 DT93
Chesham HP5 76 AP28
Pattina Wk, SE16 33 M3
Pattison Rd, NW2 142 DA62
Pattison Wk, SE18 187 EQ78
Paul Cl, E15 13 J7
Cheshunt EN7
off Gladding Rd 88 DQ25
Paulet Rd, SE5 43 H8
Paulet Way, NW10 160 CS66
Paul Gdns, Croy. CR0 224 DT103
Paulhan Rd, Har. HA3 139 CK56
Paulin Dr, N21 121 DN45
Pauline Cres, Twick. TW2 198 CC88
Pauline Ho, E1 20 D6
Paulinus Cl, Orp. BR5 228 EW96
Paul Julius Cl, E14 34 G1
Paul Robeson Cl, E6 25 M2
Pauls Grn, Wal.Cr. EN8 89 DY33
Pauls Hill, Penn HP10 110 AF48
Pauls La, Hodd. EN11 71 EA17
off Taverners Way
Paul's Nurs Rd, High Beach
IG10 106 EH39
Paul's Pl, Ashtd. KT21 254 CP119
Paul St, E15 13 J8
EC2 19 M5
Paul's Wk, EC4 19 H10
Paultons Sq, SW3 40 B2
Paultons St, SW3 40 B3
Pauntley St, N19 143 DJ60
Paved Ct, Rich. TW9 199 CK85
Paveley Ct, NW7 119 CX52
Paveley Dr, SW11 40 C5
Paveley Ho, N1
off Priory Grn Est 18 C1
Paveley St, NW8 16 D4
Pavement, The, SW4 183 DJ84
W5 *off Popes La* 180 CL76
Isleworth TW7
off South St 179 CG83
Pavement Ms, Rom. RM6
off Clarissa Rd 148 EX59
Pavement Sq, Croy. CR0 224 DU102
Pavet Cl, Dag. RM10 169 FB65
Pavilion End, Knot.Grn HP9 110 AJ50
Pavilion Gdns, Stai. TW18 196 BH94
Pavilion Ho, SE16
off Canada St 33 J5
Pavilion La, SE10
off Ordnance Cres 35 J5
Beck. BR3 205 DZ93
Pavilion Ms, N3
off Windermere Av 120 DA54
Pavilion Par, W12 14 A8
Pavilion Rd, SW1 28 F7
Ilford IG1 147 EM59
Pavilions, Wind. SL4 173 AP81
Pavilions, The, Byfleet KT14 234 BK111
North Weald Bassett CM16 93 FC25
Pavilion Sq, SW17 202 DE90
🔒 **Pavilions Shop Cen**, Wal.Cr.
EN8 89 DX34
Pavilion St, SW1 28 F7
Pavilion Ter, W12 14 A8
East Molesey KT8 219 CF98
Ilford IG2
off Southdown Cres 147 ES57
Pavilion Way, Amer. HP6 94 AW39
Edgware HA8 118 CP52
Ruislip HA4 138 BW61
Pavillion Ms, N4 143 DM61
Pawleyne Ct, SE20 204 DW94
Pawsey Cl, E13 13 P8
Pawson's Rd, Croy. CR0 224 DQ100
Paxford Rd, Wem. HA0 139 CH61
Paxton Av, Slou. SL1 173 AQ76
Paxton Cl, Rich. TW9 180 CM82
Walton-on-Thames KT12 218 BW101
Paxton Ct, SE12 206 EJ90
Borwd. WD6 *off Manor Way* 100 CQ42
Paxton Gdns, Wok. GU21 233 BE112
Paxton Pl, SE27 204 DS91
Sch **Paxton Prim Sch**, SE19
off Woodland Rd 204 DS93
Paxton Rd, N17 122 DT52
SE23 205 DY90
W4 180 CS79
Berkhamsted HP4 60 AX19
Bromley BR1 206 EG94
St. Albans AL1 65 CE21
Paxton Ter, SW1 41 K2
Paycock Rd, Harl. CM19 73 EN17
Payne Cl, Bark. IG11 167 ES66
Paynell Ct, SE3 47 K10
Payne Rd, E3 22 C1
Paynesfield Av, SW14 180 CR83
Paynesfield Rd, Bushey Hth
WD23 117 CF45
Tatsfield TN16 260 EK119
Paynes La, Lwr Naze. EN9 71 EC24
Payne St, SE8 45 P3
Paynes Wk, W6 38 E3
Paynetts Ct, Wey. KT13 235 BR106
Payzes Gdns, Wdf.Grn. IG8
off Chingford La 124 EF50
Peabody Av, SW1 29 J10
Peabody Cl, SE10 46 D6
SW1 41 K2
Croydon CR0 224 DW102
Peabody Cotts, SE24
off Rosendale Rd 204 DQ87
Peabody Ct, Enf. EN3
off Martini Dr 105 EA37
Peabody Dws, WC1 18 A4
Peabody Est, EC1 (Clerkenwell)
off Farringdon La 18 F5
EC1 (St. Luke's) 19 K5
N1 (Islington) 9 J7
N17 122 DS53
SE1 30 F3
SE17 31 L9
SE24 203 DP87
SW1 29 L8
SW3 40 D2
SW6 39 J2
W6 38 B1
W10 14 B6
Peabody Hill, SE21 203 DP88
Peabody Hill Est, SE21 203 DP87
Peabody Sq, SE1 30 G5
Peabody Twr, EC1
off Golden La 19 K5
Peabody Trust, SE1 31 J3
Peabody Trust Camberwell Grn Est,
SE5 43 L6
Peabody Trust Old Pye St Est,
SW1 *off Old Pye St* 29 N7
Peabody Yd, N1 9 J8
Peace Cl, N14 103 DH43
SE25 224 DS98
Cheshunt EN7 88 DU29
Greenford UB6 159 CD67
Peace Dr, Wat. WD17 97 BU41
Peace Gro, Wem. HA9 140 CP62
Peace Prospect, Wat. WD17 97 BU41
Peace Rd, Iver SL0 155 BA67
Slough SL3 155 BA68
Peace St, SE18
off Nightingale Vale 187 EP79
Peach Cft, Nthflt DA11 212 GE90
Peaches Cl, Sutt. SM2 239 CY108
Peachey Cl, Uxb. UB8 156 BK72
Peachey La, Uxb. UB8 156 BK71
Peach Gro, E11 145 ED62
Peach Rd, W10 14 D2
Feltham TW13 197 BU88
Peach Tree Av, West Dr. UB7
off Pear Tree Av 156 BM72
Peachum Rd, SE3 47 M2
Peachwalk Ms, E3 11 K10
Peachy Cl, Edg. HA8
off Manor Pk Cres 118 CN51
Peacock Av, Felt. TW14 197 BR88
Peacock Cl, E4 123 DZ52
NW7 119 CY50
Dagenham RM8 148 EW60
Hornchurch RM11 150 FL56
Peacock Gdns, S.Croy. CR2 243 DY110
● **Peacock Ind Est**, N17 122 DT52
Peacock Pl, N1 *off Laycock St* 8 F5
Peacocks, Harl. CM19 73 EM17
🔒 **Peacocks Cen, The**, Wok.
GU21 248 AY117
Peacocks Cl, Berk. HP4 60 AT16
Peacock St, SE17 31 H9
Gravesend DA12 213 GJ87
Peacock Wk, E16 24 B8
Abbots Langley WD5 81 BU31
Dorking RH4 *off Rose Hill* 285 CG137
Peacock Yd, SE17 31 H9
Peak, The, SE26 204 DW90
Peakes La, Chsht EN7 88 DT27
Peakes Pl, St.Alb. AL1
off Granville Rd 65 CF20
Peakes Way, Chsht EN7 88 DT27
Peaketon Av, Ilf. IG4 146 EK56
Peak Hill, SE26 204 DW91
Peak Hill Av, SE26 204 DW91
Peak Hill Gdns, SE26 204 DW91
Peak Rd, Guil. GU2 264 AU131
Peaks Hill, Pur. CR8 241 DK110
Peaks Hill Ri, Pur. CR8 241 DL110
Pea La, Upmin. RM14 171 FU66
Peal Gdns, W13 159 CG70
Peall Rd, Croy. CR0 223 DM100
Pearce Cl, Mitch. CR4 222 DG96
Pearcefield Av, SE23 204 DW88
Pearce Rd, Chesh. HP5 76 AP29
Pearces Wk, St.Alb. AL1
off Albert St 65 CD21
Pear Cl, NW9 140 CR56
SE14 45 M5
Pearcroft Rd, E11 145 ED61
Pearcy Cl, Harold Hill RM3 128 FL52
Peardon St, SW8 41 K9
Peareswood Gdns, Stan. HA7 117 CK53
Peareswood Rd, Erith DA8 189 FF81
Pearfield Rd, SE23 205 DY90
Pearing Cl, Wor.Pk. KT4 221 CX103
Pearl Cl, E6 25 L8
NW2 141 CX59
Pearl Ct, Wok. GU21
off Langmans Way 248 AS116
Pearl Gdns, Slou. SL1 153 AP74
Pearl Rd, E17 145 EA55
Pearl St, E1 32 F2
Pearmain Cl, Shep. TW17 217 BP99
Pearman St, SE1 30 F6
Pear Pl, SE1 30 E4
Pear Rd, E11 145 ED62
Pearscroft Ct, SW6 39 M7
Pearscroft Rd, SW6 39 L8
Pearse St, SE15 43 P3
Pearson Av, Hert. SG13 54 DQ11
Pearson Cl, SE5 43 K6
Barnet EN5 102 DB42
Hertford SG13
off Pearson Av 54 DQ11
Purley CR8 241 DP111
Pearson Ms, SW4 183 DK83
Pearsons Av, SE14 46 A6
Pearson St, E2 9 P10
Pearson Way, Dart. DA1 210 FM89
Mitcham CR4 222 DG95
Pears Rd, Houns. TW3 178 CC83
PEARTREE, Welw.G.C. AL7 51 CZ09
Peartree Av, SW17 202 DC90
Pear Tree Av, West Dr. UB7 156 BM72
Pear Tree Cl, E2 10 A9
Addlestone KT15
off Pear Tree Rd 234 BG106
Amersham HP7
off Orchard End Av 94 AT39
Bromley BR2 226 EK99
Chessington KT9 238 CN106
Peartree Cl, Erith DA8 189 FD81
Hemel Hempstead HP1 62 BG19
Pear Tree Cl, Mitch. CR4 222 DE96
Seer Green HP9 111 AQ51
Slough SL1 153 AM74
Peartree Cl, S.Croy. CR2 242 DV114
South Ockendon RM15 171 FW68
Pear Tree Cl, Swan. BR8 229 FD96
Peartree Cl, Welw.G.C. AL7 51 CY09
Peartree Ct, E18
off Churchfields 124 EH53
Pear Tree Ct, EC1 18 F5
Peartree Ct, Welw.G.C. AL7 51 CY10
Peartree Fm, Welw.G.C. AL7 51 CY09
Peartree Gdns, Dag. RM8 148 EV63
Romford RM7 127 FB54
Pear Tree Hill, Salf. RH1 288 DG143
Peartree La, E1 33 H1
Welwyn Garden City AL7 51 CY10
Pear Tree Mead, Harl. CM18 74 EU18
Sch **Pear Tree Mead Prim & Nurs
Sch**, Harl. CM18
off Pear Tree Mead 74 EU18
Sch **Peartree Prim Sch**, Welw.G.C.
AL7 *off Peartree La* 51 CY10
Pear Tree Rd, Add. KT15 234 BG106
Ashford TW15 197 BQ92
Peartree Rd, Enf. EN1 104 DS41
Hemel Hempstead HP1 62 BG19
Pear Tree St, EC1 19 H4
Pear Tree Wk, Chsht EN7 88 DR26
Peartree Way, SE10 35 N8
Peary Pl, E2 21 H2
Peascod Pl, Wind. SL4
off Peascod St 173 AR81
Peascod St, Wind. SL4 173 AR81
Peascroft Rd, Hem.H. HP3 62 BN23
Pease Cl, Horn. RM12
off Dowding Way 169 FH66
PEASMARSH, Guil. GU3 280 AW142
Peatfield Cl, Sid. DA15
off Woodside Rd 207 ES90
Peatmore Av, Wok. GU22 250 BG116
Peatmore Cl, Wok. GU22 250 BG116

Pebble Cl, Tad. KT20 270 CS128
PEBBLE COOMBE, Tad. KT20 270 CS128
Pebble Hill, Lthd. KT24 267 BQ133
Pebble Hill Rd, Bet. RH3 270 CS131
Tadworth KT20 270 CS131
Pebble La, Epsom KT18 254 CN121
Leatherhead KT22 270 CL125
Pebble Way, W3 160 CP74
Pebworth Rd, Har. HA1 139 CG61
Peckarmans Wd, SE26 204 DU90
Peckett Sq, N5 9 H1
Peckford Pl, SW9 42 F9
PECKHAM, SE15 44 A8
Peckham Gro, SE15 43 P4
Peckham High St, SE15 44 C7
Peckham Hill St, SE15 44 C4
Peckham Pk Rd, SE15 44 C4
Sch Peckham Pk Sch, SE15 44 D5
Peckham Rd, SE5 43 N7
SE15 43 N7
⇌ Peckham Rye 44 C8
Peckham Rye, SE15 44 D10
SE22 184 DU84
Pecks Hill, Lwr Naze. EN9 72 EE21
Pecks Yd, E1 20 A6
Peckwater St, NW5 7 L3
● Pedham Pl Ind Est, Swan. BR8 229 FG99
Pedlars End, Moreton CM5 75 FH21
Pedlars Wk, N7 8 B4
Pedley Rd, Dag. RM8 148 EW60
Pedley St, E1 20 B5
PEDNORMEAD END, Chesh. HP5 76 AN32
Pednormead End, Chesh. HP5 76 AP32
Pednor Rd, Chesh. HP5 76 AM30
Pedro St, E5 145 DX62
Pedworth Gdns, SE16 32 G9
Peek Cres, SW19 201 CX92
Peeks Brook La, Horl. RH6 291 DM150
Coll Peel Cen (Met Pol Training & Driving Sch), NW9
off Aerodrome Rd 141 CT55
Peel Cl, E4 123 EB47
N9 off Plevna Rd 122 DU48
Windsor SL4 173 AP83
Peel Ct, Slou. SL1 153 AP71
Peel Cres, Hert. SG14 53 DP07
Peel Dr, NW9 141 CT55
Ilford IG5 146 EL55
Peel Gro, E2 20 G1
Peel Pas, W8 27 J3
Peel Pl, Ilf. IG5 124 EL54
Peel Prec, NW6 15 J1
Peel Rd, E18 124 EF53
Orpington BR6 245 EQ106
Wealdstone HA3 139 CF55
Wembley HA9 139 CK62
Peel St, W8 27 J3
Peel Way, Rom. RM3 128 FM54
Uxbridge UB8 156 BL71
Peerage Way, Horn. RM11 150 FL59
● Peerglow Cen, Ware SG12 55 DY07
● Peerglow Est, Enf. EN3 104 DW43
● Peerglow Ind Est, Wat. WD18
off Olds App 115 BP46
Peerless Dr, Hare. UB9 136 BJ57
Peerless St, EC1 19 L3
Pegamoid Rd, N18 122 DW48
Pegasus Cl, N16 9 L1
Pegasus Ct, W3 off Horn La 160 CQ72
Abbots Langley WD5
off Furtherfield 81 BT32
Gravesend DA12 213 GJ90
Harrow HA3 139 CK57
Pegasus Pl, SE11 42 E2
SW6 off Ackmar Rd 39 J7
St. Albans AL3 65 CD18
Pegasus Rd, Croy. CR0 241 DN107
Pegasus Way, N11 121 DH51
Pegelm Gdns, Horn. RM11 150 FM59
Peggotty Way, Uxb. UB8 157 BP72
Pegg Rd, Houns. TW5 178 BX80
Pegley Gdns, SE12 206 EG89
Pegmire La, Ald. WD25 98 CC39
Pegrams Rd, Harl. CM18 73 EQ18
Pegrum Dr, Lon.Col. AL2 83 CH26
Pegs La, Hert. SG13 54 DR11
Pegwell St, SE18 187 ES80
Peket Cl, Stai. TW18 215 BE95
Pekin Cl, E14 22 B9
Pekin St, E14 22 B9
Peldon Ct, Rich. TW9 180 CM84
Peldon Pas, Rich. TW10
off Worple Way 180 CM84
Peldon Rd, Harl. CM19 73 EN17
Pelham Av, Bark. IG11 167 ET67
Pelham Cl, SE5 43 P10
Pelham Ct, Hem.H. HP2 63 BQ20
Welwyn Garden City AL7 52 DC10
Pelham Cres, SW7 28 C9
Pelham Ho, W14 26 G9
Pelham La, Ald. WD25 98 CB36
Pelham Pl, SW7 28 C9
W13 off Ruislip Rd E 159 CF70
Sch Pelham Prim Sch, SW19
off Southey Rd 202 DA94
Bexleyheath DA7
off Pelham Rd 188 FA83
Pelham Rd, E18 146 EH55
N15 144 DT56
N22 121 DN54
SW19 202 DA94
Beckenham BR3 224 DW96
Bexleyheath DA7 188 FA83
Gravesend DA11 213 GF87
Ilford IG1 147 ER61
Pelham Rd S, Grav. DA11 213 GF88
Pelhams, The, Wat. WD25 98 BX35
Pelhams Cl, Esher KT10 236 CA105
Pelham St, SW7 28 B8
Pelhams Wk, Esher KT10 218 CA104
Pelham Ter, Grav. DA11
off Campbell Rd 213 GF87
Pelham Way, Bkhm KT23 268 CB126
Pelican Est, SE15 44 A7
Pelican Ho, SE15
off Peckham Rd 44 A7
Pelican Pas, E1 20 G4
Pelier St, SE17 43 K2
Pelinore Rd, SE6 206 EE89
Pellant Rd, SW6 38 F3
Pellatt Gro, N22 121 DN53
Pellatt Rd, SE22 204 DT85
Wembley HA9 140 CL61
Pellerin Rd, N16 9 P2
Pelling Hill, Old Wind. SL4 194 AV87
Pellings Cl, Brom. BR2 226 EE97
Pelling St, E14 22 A8
Pellipar Cl, N13 121 DN48
Pellipar Gdns, SE18 37 J10
Pellow Cl, Barn. EN5 101 CZ44
Pelly Ct, Epp. CM16 91 ET31
Pelly Rd, E13 13 P10
Pelman Way, Epsom KT19 238 CP110
Pelter St, E2 20 A2
Pelton Av, Sutt. SM2 240 DB110
Pelton Rd, SE10 35 J10
Pembar Av, E17 145 DY55
Pemberley Chase, W.Ewell KT19 238 CP106
Pemberley Cl, W.Ewell KT19 238 CP106
Pember Rd, NW10 14 C3
Pemberton Av, Rom. RM2 149 FH55
Pemberton Cl, St.Alb. AL1 65 CD23
Stai. TW19 196 BL88
Pemberton Gdns, N19 143 DJ62
Romford RM6 148 EY57
Swanley BR8 229 FE97
Pemberton Ho, SE26
off High Level Dr 204 DU91
Pemberton Pl, E8 10 F7
Esher KT10
off Carrick Gate 218 CC104
Pemberton Rd, N4 143 DN57
East Molesey KT8 218 CC98
Slough SL2 153 AL70
Pemberton Row, EC4 18 F8
Pemberton Ter, N19 143 DJ62
Pembrey Way, Horn. RM12 170 FJ65
Pembridge Av, Twick. TW2 198 BZ88
Pembridge Chase, Bov. HP3 79 AZ28
Pembridge Cl, Bov. HP3 79 AZ28
Pembridge Cres, W11 15 J10
Pembridge Gdns, W2 27 J1
Coll Pembridge Hall, W2 27 K1
Sch Pembridge Hall Sch, W2 27 K1
Pembridge La, Brickendon SG13 70 DQ19
Broxbourne EN10 70 DR21
Pembridge Ms, W11 15 J10
Pembridge Pl, SW15 202 DA85
W2 15 K10
Pembridge Rd, W11 27 J1
Bovingdon HP3 79 BA28
Pembridge Sq, W2 27 J1
Pembridge Vil, W2 15 J10
W11 15 J10
Pembroke Av, N1 8 B8
Enfield EN1 104 DV38
Harrow HA3 139 CG55
Hersham KT12 236 BX105
Pinner HA5 138 BX60
Surbiton KT5 220 CP99
Pembroke Cl, SW1 29 H5
Banstead SM7 256 DB117
Broxbourne EN10 71 DY23
Erith DA8 off Pembroke Rd 189 FD77
Hornchurch RM11 150 FM56
Pembroke Cotts, W8
off Pembroke Sq 27 J7
Pembroke Dr, Aveley RM15 190 FP75
Goffs Oak EN7 87 DP29
Pembroke Gdns, W8 27 H8
Dagenham RM10 149 FB62
Woking GU22 249 BA118
Pembroke Gdns Cl, W8 27 H7
Pembroke Ms, E3 21 M2
N10 120 DG53
W8 27 J7
Sevenoaks TN13 279 FH125
Pembroke Pl, W8 27 J7
Edgware HA8 118 CN52
Isleworth TW7
off Thornbury Rd 179 CE82
Sutton at Hone DA4 230 FP95
Pembroke Rd, E6 25 J6
E17 145 EB57
N8 143 DL56
N10 120 DG53
N13 122 DQ48
N15 144 DT57
SE25 224 DS98
W8 27 J8
Bromley BR1 226 EJ96
Erith DA8 189 FC78
Greenford UB6 158 CB70
Ilford IG3 147 ET60
Mitcham CR4 222 DG96
Northwood HA6 115 BQ48
Ruislip HA4 137 BS60
Sevenoaks TN13 279 FH125
Wembley HA9 139 CK62
Woking GU22 249 BA118
Pembroke Sq, W8 27 J7
Pembroke St, N1 8 B7
Pembroke Studios, W8 27 H7
Pembroke Vil, W8 27 J8
Richmond TW9 179 CK84
Pembroke Wk, W8 27 J8
Pembroke Way, Hayes UB3 177 BQ76
Pembury Cl, SW9 42 E7
Pembury Av, Wor.Pk. KT4 221 CU101
Pembury Cl, E5 10 F2
Bromley BR2 226 EF101
Coulsdon CR5 240 DG114
Pembury Ct, Harling. UB3 177 BR79
Pembury Cres, Sid. DA14 208 EY89
Pembury Pl, E5 10 E3
Pembury Rd, E5 10 E3
N17 122 DT54
SE25 224 DU98
Bexleyheath DA7 188 EY80
Pemdevon Rd, Croy. CR0 223 DN101
Pemell Cl, E1 21 H4
Pemerich Cl, Hayes UB3 177 BT78
Pempath Pl, Wem. HA9 139 CK61
Pemsel Ct, Hem.H. HP3
off Crabtree La 62 BL22
Penally Pl, N1 9 M8
Penang St, E1 32 F2
Penard Rd, Sthl. UB2 178 CA76
Penarth St, SE15 44 G2
Penates, Esher KT10 237 CD105
Penberth Rd, SE6 205 EC89
Penbury Rd, Sthl. UB2 178 BZ77
Pencombe Ms, W11 15 H10
Pencraig Way, SE15 44 E3
Pencroft Dr, Dart. DA1
off Shepherds La 210 FJ87
Pendall Cl, Barn. EN4 102 DE42
Penda Rd, Erith DA8 189 FB80
Pendarves Rd, SW20 221 CW95
Penda's Mead, E9 11 M1
Pendell Av, Hayes UB3 177 BT80
Pendell Ct, Bletch. RH1 273 DP131
Pendell Rd, Bletch. RH1 273 DP131
Pendennis Cl, W.Byf. KT14 234 BG114
Pendennis Rd, N17 144 DR55
SW16 203 DL91
Orpington BR6 228 EW103
Sevenoaks TN13 279 FH123
Pendenza, Cob. KT11 252 BY116
Penderel Rd, Houns. TW3 198 CA85
Penderry Ri, SE6 205 ED89
Penderyn Way, N7 143 DK63
Pendle Ct, Uxb. UB10
off Sutton Ct Rd 157 BP67
Pendle Rd, SW16 203 DH93
Pendlestone Rd, E17 145 EB57
Pendleton Cl, Red. RH1 288 DF136
Pendleton Rd, Red. RH1 288 DE136
Reigate RH2 288 DC137
Pendlewood Cl, W5 159 CJ71
Pendolino Way, NW10 160 CN66
Pendragon Rd, Brom. BR1 206 EF90
Sch Pendragon Sch, Downham BR1 off Pendragon Rd 206 EG90
Pendragon Wk, NW9 140 CS58
Pendrell Rd, SE4 45 L9
Pendrell St, SE18 187 ER80
Pendula Dr, Hayes UB4 158 BX70
Pendulum Ms, E8 10 A3
Penerley Rd, SE6 205 EB88
Rainham RM13 169 FH71
Penfields Ho, N7 8 A5
Penfold Cl, Croy. CR0 223 DN104
Penfold La, Bex. DA5 208 EX89
Penfold Pl, NW1 16 B6
Penfold Rd, N9 123 DX46
Penfold St, NW1 16 B5
NW8 16 B5
● Penfold Trading Est, Wat. WD24 98 BW39
Penford Gdns, SE9 186 EK83
Penford St, SE5 42 G8
Pengarth Rd, Bex. DA5 208 EX85
PENGE, SE20 204 DW94
⇌ Penge East 204 DW93
Penge Ho, SW11 40 B10
Penge La, SE20 204 DW94
Pengelly Cl, Chsht EN7 88 DV30
Penge Rd, E13 166 EJ66
SE20 224 DU97
SE25 224 DU97
⇌ Penge West 204 DV93
⊖ Penge West 204 DV93
Penhale Cl, Orp. BR6 246 EU105
Penhall Rd, SE7 36 E8
Penhill Rd, Bex. DA5 208 EW87
Penhurst, Wok. GU21 233 AZ114
Penhurst Pl, SE1 30 D7
Penhurst Rd, Ilf. IG6 125 EP52
Penifather La, Grnf. UB6 159 CD69
Penington Rd, Beac. HP9 132 AH55
Peninsula Apts, W2
off Praed St 16 C7
Peninsula Hts, SE1 30 B10
Peninsular Cl, Felt. TW14 197 BR86
Peninsular Pk Rd, SE7 35 P9
Penistone Rd, SW16 203 DL94
Penistone Wk, Rom. RM3
off Okehampton Rd 128 FJ51
Penketh Dr, Har. HA1 139 CD62
Penlow Rd, Harl. CM18 73 EQ18
Penman Cl, St.Alb. AL2 82 CA27
Penman's Grn, Kings L. WD4 79 BF32
Penmans Hill, Chipper. WD4 79 BF33
Penmon Rd, SE2 188 EU76
PENN, H.Wyc. HP10 110 AE48
Pennack Rd, SE15 44 B3
Pennant Ms, W8 27 L8
Pennant Ter, E17 123 DZ54
Pennard Mans, W12 26 A5
Pennard Rd, W12 26 A4
Pennards, The, Sun. TW16 218 BW96
Penn Av, Chesh. HP5 76 AN30
Penn Bottom, Penn HP10 110 AG47
Penn Cl, Chorl. WD3 95 BD44
Greenford UB6 158 CB68
Harrow HA3 139 CJ56
Uxbridge UB8 156 BK70
Penn Dr, Denh. UB9 135 BF58
Penne Cl, Rad. WD7 83 CF34
Penner Cl, SW19 201 CY89
Penners Gdns, Surb. KT6 220 CL101
Pennethorne Cl, E9 10 G9
Pennethorne Ho, SW11 40 B10
Pennethorne Rd, SE15 44 E5
Penney Cl, Dart. DA1 210 FK87
Penn Gdns, Chis. BR7 227 EP96
Romford RM5 126 FA52
Penn Gaskell La, Chal.St.P. SL9 113 AZ50
Penn Grn, Beac. HP9 111 AK51
Penn Ho, Burn. SL1 152 AJ69
Pennine Dr, NW2 141 CY61
Pennine Ho, N9 off Edmonton Grn Shop Cen 122 DU48
Pennine La, NW2 141 CY61
Pennine Rd, Slou. SL2 153 AN71
Pennine Way, Bexh. DA7 189 FE81
Harlington UB3 177 BR80
Hemel Hempstead HP2 62 BM17
Northfleet DA11 212 GE90
Pennings Av, Guil. GU2 264 AT132
Pennington Cl, SE27
off Hamilton Rd 204 DR91
Romford RM5 126 FA50
Pennington Dr, N21 103 DL43
Weybridge KT13 217 BS104
Pennington Rd, Chal.St.P. SL9 112 AX52
Penningtons, The, Amer. HP6 77 AS37
Pennington St, E1 32 D1
Pennington Way, SE12 206 EH89
Pennis La, Fawk.Grn DA3 231 FX100
Penniston Cl, N17 122 DQ54
Penniwell Cl, Edg. HA8 118 CM49
Penn La, Bex. DA5 208 EX85
Penn Meadow, Stoke P. SL2 154 AT67
Penn Pl, Rick. WD3
off Northway 114 BK45
Penn Rd, N7 8 B2
Beaconsfield HP9 110 AJ48
Chalfont St. Peter SL9 112 AX53
Datchet SL3 174 AX81
Mill End WD3 113 BF46
Park Street AL2 82 CC27
Slough SL2 153 AR70
Watford WD24 97 BV39
Sch Penn Sch, Penn HP10
off Church Rd 110 AD48
Penn St, N1 9 M9
Penn Way, Chorl. WD3 95 BD44
Penny Brookes St, E15 12 G4
Penny Cl, Rain. RM13 169 FH69
Pennycroft, Croy. CR0 243 DY109
Pennyfather La, Enf. EN2 104 DQ40
Pennyfield, Cob. KT11 235 BU113
Pennyfields, E14 22 A10
Warley CM14 130 FW49
Penny La, Shep. TW17 217 BS101
Pennylets Grn, Stoke P. SL2 154 AT66
Pennymead, Harl. CM20 74 EU15
Pennymead Dr, E.Hors. KT24 267 BT127
Pennymead Ri, E.Hors. KT24 267 BT127
Pennymead Twr, Harl. CM20 74 EU15
Penny Ms, SW12 203 DH87
Pennymoor Wk, W9 15 H4
Penny Rd, NW10 160 CP69
Pennyroyal Av, E6 25 L9
Pennys La, High Wych CM21 57 ER05
Penpoll Rd, E8 10 E4
Penpool La, Well. DA16 188 EV83
Penrhyn Av, E17 123 DZ53
Penrhyn Cl, Cat. CR3 258 DR120
Penrhyn Cres, E17 123 EA53
SW14 180 CQ84
Penrhyn Gdns, Kings.T. KT1
off Surbiton Rd 219 CK98
Penrhyn Gro, E17 123 EA53
Penrhyn Rd, Kings.T. KT1 220 CL97
Penrith Cl, SW15 201 CY85
Beckenham BR3 225 EB95
Reigate RH2 272 DE133
Uxbridge UB8 156 BK66
Penrith Cres, Rain. RM13 149 FG64
Penrith Pl, SE27 203 DP89
Penrith Rd, N15 144 DR57
Ilford IG6 125 ET51
New Malden KT3 220 CR98
Romford RM3 128 FN51
Thornton Heath CR7 224 DQ96
Penrith St, SW16 203 DJ93
Penrose Av, Wat. WD19 116 BX47
Penrose Ct, Eng.Grn TW20 194 AW93
Hemel Hempstead HP2 62 BL16
Penrose Dr, Epsom KT19 238 CN111
Penrose Gro, SE17 43 J1
Penrose Ho, SE17 43 J1
Penrose Rd, Fetch. KT22 252 CC122
Penrose St, SE17 43 J1
Penryn St, NW1 7 N10
Penry St, SE1 31 P9
Pensbury Pl, SW8 41 M8
Pensbury St, SW8 41 M8
Penscroft Gdns, Borwd. WD6 100 CR42
Pensford Av, Rich. TW9 180 CN82
Penshurst, Harl. CM17 58 EV12
Penshurst Av, Sid. DA15 208 EU86
Penshurst Cl, Chal.St.P. SL9 112 AX54
Penshurst Gdns, Edg. HA8 118 CP50
Penshurst Grn, Brom. BR2 226 EF99
Penshurst Rd, E9 11 J7
N17 122 DT52
Bexleyheath DA7 188 EZ81
Potters Bar EN6 86 DD31
Thornton Heath CR7 223 DP99
Penshurst Wk, Brom. BR2
off Penshurst Rd 226 EF99
Penshurst Way, Orp. BR5
off Star La 228 EW98
Sutton SM2 240 DA108
Pensilver Cl, Barn. EN4 102 DE42
Pensons La, Ong. CM5 93 FG28
Penstemon Cl, N3 120 DA52
Penstock Footpath, N22 143 DL55
🔒 Pentavia Retail Pk, NW7 119 CT52
Pentelow Gdns, Felt. TW14 197 BU86
Pentire Cl, Horsell GU21 232 AY114
Upminster RM14 151 FS58
Pentire Rd, E17 123 ED53
Pentland, Hem.H. HP2
off Mendip Way 62 BM17
Pentland Av, Edg. HA8 118 CP47
Shepperton TW17 216 BN99
Pentland Cl, N9 122 DW47
NW11 141 CY61
Pentland Gdns, SW18 202 DC86
Pentland Pl, Nthlt. UB5 158 BY67
Pentland Rd, NW6 15 J2
Bushey WD23 98 CC44
Slough SL2 153 AN71
Pentlands Cl, Mitch. CR4 223 DH97
Pentland St, SW18 202 DC86
Pentland Way, Uxb. UB10 137 BQ62
Pentley Cl, Welw.G.C. AL8 51 CX06
Pentley Pk, Welw.G.C. AL8 51 CX06
Pentlow St, SW15 38 B10
Pentlow Way, Buck.H. IG9 124 EL45
Pentney Rd, E4 123 ED46
SW12 203 DJ88
SW19 off Midmoor Rd 221 CY95
Penton Av, Stai. TW18 195 BF94
Penton Dr, Chsht EN8 89 DX29
Penton Gro, N1 18 E1
Penton Hall Dr, Stai. TW18 216 BG95
Penton Hook Rd, Stai. TW18 196 BG94
Penton Ho, SE2 off Hartslock Dr 188 EX75
Penton Pk, Cher. KT16 216 BG97
Penton Pl, SE17 31 H10
Penton Ri, WC1 18 D2
Penton Rd, Stai. TW18 195 BF94
Penton St, N1 8 E10
PENTONVILLE, N1 18 E1
Pentonville Rd, N1 18 C1
Pentreath Av, Guil. GU2 280 AT135
Pentrich Av, Enf. EN1 104 DU38
Pentridge St, SE15 44 A4
Pentstemon Dr, Swans. DA10 212 FY85
Pentyre Av, N18 122 DR50
Penwerris Av, Islw. TW7 178 CC80
Penwith Rd, SW18 202 DB89
Penwith Wk, Wok. GU22 248 AX119
Penwood End, Wok. GU22 248 AV121
Penwood Ho, SW15
off Tunworth Cres 201 CT86
Sch Penwortham Prim Sch, SW16
off Penwortham Rd 203 DH93
Penwortham Rd, SW16 203 DH93
South Croydon CR2 242 DQ110
Penylan Pl, Edg. HA8 118 CN52
Penywern Rd, SW5 27 K10
Penzance Cl, Hare. UB9 114 BK53
Penzance Gdns, Rom. RM3 128 FN51
Penzance Pl, W11 26 E2
Penzance Rd, Rom. RM3 128 FN51
Penzance Spur, Slou. SL2 153 AP70
Penzance St, W11 26 E2
Peony Cl, Pilg.Hat. CM15 130 FV44
Peony Ct, Wdf.Grn. IG8
off The Bridle Path 124 EE52
Peony Gdns, W12 161 CU73
● Peoplebuilding, Hem.H. HP2 63 BP19
Pepler Ms, SE5 44 A2
Pepler Way, Burn. SL1 152 AH69
Peplins Cl, Brook.Pk AL9 85 CY26
Peplins Way, Brook.Pk AL9 85 CY25
Peploe Rd, NW6 4 D10
Peplow Cl, West Dr. UB7 156 BK74
Pepper All, High Beach IG10 106 EG39
Pepper Cl, E6 25 K6
Caterham CR3 274 DS125
Peppercorn Cl, Th.Hth. CR7 224 DR96
Pepper Hill, Gt Amwell SG12 55 DZ10
Northfleet DA11 212 GC90
Pepperhill La, Nthflt DA11 212 GC90
Peppermead Sq, SE13 205 EA85
Peppermint Cl, Croy. CR0 223 DL101
Peppermint Hts, Wem. HA0 159 CK67
Peppermint Pl, E11
off Birch Gro 146 EE62
Pepper St, E14 34 C6
SE1 31 J4
Peppie Cl, N16 144 DS61
Pepys Cl, Ashtd. KT21 254 CN117
Dartford DA1 190 FN84
Northfleet DA11 212 GD90
Slough SL3 175 BB79
Tilbury RM18 193 GJ81
Uxbridge UB10 137 BP63
Pepys Cres, E16 35 P2
Barnet EN5 101 CW43
Pepys Ri, Orp. BR6 227 ET102
Pepys Rd, SE14 45 K7
SW20 221 CW95
Pepys St, EC3 19 P10
Perceval Av, NW3 6 C2
Percheron Cl, Islw. TW7 179 CG83
Percheron Rd, Borwd. WD6 100 CR44
Perch St, E8 10 B1
Percival Cl, Oxshott KT22 236 CB111
Percival Ct, N17 122 DT52
Northolt UB5 138 CA64
★ Percival David Foundation of Chinese Art, WC1
off Gordon Sq 17 P5
Percival Gdns, Rom. RM6 148 EW58
Percival Rd, SW14 180 CQ84
Enfield EN1 104 DT42
Feltham TW13 197 BT89
Hornchurch RM11 150 FJ58
Orpington BR6 227 EP103
Percival St, EC1 18 G4
Percival Way, Epsom KT19 238 CQ105
Percy Av, Ashf. TW15 196 BN92
Percy Bryant Rd, Sun. TW16 197 BS94
Percy Bush Rd, West Dr. UB7 176 BM76
Percy Circ, WC1 18 D2
Percy Gdns, Enf. EN3 105 DX43
Hayes UB4 157 BS69
Isleworth TW7 179 CG82
Worcester Park KT4 220 CR102
Percy Ho, SW16
off Pringle Gdns 203 DJ91
Percy Ms, W1 17 N7
Percy Pas, W1 17 M7
Percy Pl, Datchet SL3 174 AV81
Percy Rd, E11 146 EE59
E16 23 K6
N12 120 DC50
N21 122 DQ45
SE20 225 DX95
SE25 224 DU99
W12 181 CU75
Bexleyheath DA7 188 EY82
Guildford GU2 264 AV132
Hampton TW12 198 CA94
Ilford IG3 148 EU59
Isleworth TW7 179 CG84
Mitcham CR4 222 DG101
Romford RM7 149 FB55
Twickenham TW2 198 CB88
Watford WD18 97 BV42
Percy St, W1 17 N7
Grays RM17 192 GC79
Percy Ter, Brom. BR1 227 EP97
Percy Way, Twick. TW2 198 CC88
Percy Yd, WC1 18 D2
Peregrine Cl, NW10 140 CR64
Watford WD25 82 BY34
Peregrine Ct, SW16 203 DM91
Welling DA16 187 ET81
Peregrine Gdns, Croy. CR0 225 DY103
Peregrine Ho, EC1 19 H2
Peregrine Rd, N17 122 DQ52
Ilford IG6 126 EV50
Sunbury-on-Thames TW16 217 BT96
Waltham Abbey EN9 90 EG34
Peregrine Wk, Horn. RM12
off Heron Flight Av 169 FH65
Peregrine Way, SW19 201 CW94
Perham Rd, W14 38 F1
Perham Way, Lon.Col. AL2 83 CK26
Peridot St, E6 25 H6
Perifield, SE21 204 DQ88
Perimeade Rd, Perivale UB6 159 CJ68
Perimeter Rd E, Lon.Gat.Air. RH6 290 DG154
Perimeter Rd N, Lon.Gat.Air. RH6 290 DF151
Perimeter Rd S, Lon.Gat.Air. RH6 290 DC154
Periton Rd, SE9 186 EK84
PERIVALE, Grnf. UB6 159 CJ67
⊖ Perivale 159 CG68
Perivale, Grnf. UB6 159 CF69
Perivale Gdns, W13 159 CH70
Watford WD25 81 BV34
Perivale Gra, Perivale UB6 159 CG69
Perivale La, Perivale UB6 159 CG69
● Perivale New Business Cen, Perivale UB6 159 CH68
● Perivale Pk, Perivale UB6 159 CG68
Sch Perivale Prim Sch, Perivale UB6 off Federal Rd 159 CJ68
Periwood Cres, Perivale UB6 159 CG67
Perkin Cl, Houns. TW3 178 CB84
Wembley HA0 139 CH64
Perkins Cl, Green. DA9 211 FT85
Perkins Ct, Ashf. TW15 196 BM92
Perkin's Rents, SW1 29 N6
Perkins Rd, Ilf. IG2 147 ER57
Perkins Sq, SE1 31 K2
Perks Cl, SE3 47 J9

Perleybrooke La, Wok. GU21
off Bampton Way 248 AU117
Permain Cl, Shenley WD7 83 CK33
Perpins Rd, SE9 207 ES86
Perram Cl, Brox. EN10 89 DY26
Perran Rd, SW2
off Christchurch Rd 203 DP89
Perran Wk, Brent. TW8 180 CL78
Perren St, NW5 7 J4
Perrers Rd, W6 181 CV77
Perrett Gdns, Hert. SG14 53 DL08
Perrin Cl, Ashf. TW15
off Fordbridge Rd 196 BM92
Perrin Ct, Wok. GU21
off Blackmore Cres 249 BB115
Perrin Rd, Wem. HA0 139 CG63
Perrins Ct, NW3 5 P1
Perrins La, NW3 5 P1
Perrin's Wk, NW3 5 P1
Perrior Rd, Gdmg. GU7 280 AS144
Perriors Cl, Chsht EN7 88 DU27
Perronet Ho, SE1
off Princess St 31 H7
Perrott St, SE18 187 EQ77
Perry Av, W3 160 CR72
Perry Cl, Rain. RM13
off Lowen Rd 169 FD68
Uxbridge UB8 157 BP72
Perry Ct, E14
off Maritime Quay 34 B10
N15 144 DS58
Perrycroft, Wind. SL4 173 AL83
Perryfields Way, Burn. SL1 152 AH70
Perryfield Way, NW9 141 CT58
Richmond TW10 199 CH89
Perry Gdns, N9 122 DS48
Perry Garth, Nthlt. UB5 158 BW67
Perry Gro, Dart. DA1 190 FN84
Perry Hall Cl, Orp. BR6 228 EU101
Sch Perry Hall Prim Sch, Orp. BR6
off Perry Hall Rd 227 ET100
Perry Hall Rd, Orp. BR6 227 ET100
Perry Hill, SE6 205 DZ90
Lower Nazeing EN9 72 EF23
Worplesdon GU3 264 AS128
Perry Ho, SW2 off Tierney Rd 203 DL87
Rainham RM13
off Lowen Rd 169 FD68
Perry How, Wor.Pk. KT4 221 CT102
Perrylands La, Smallfield RH6 291 DM149
Perryman Ho, Bark. IG11 167 EQ67
Perrymans Fm Rd, Ilf. IG2 147 ER58
Perryman Way, Slou. SL2 153 AM69
Perry Mead, Bushey WD23 116 CB45
Enfield EN2 103 DP40
Perrymead St, SW6 39 K7
Sch Perrymount Prim Sch, SE23
off Sunderland Rd 205 DX89
Perryn Rd, SE16 32 E6
W3 160 CR73
Perry Ri, SE23 205 DY90
Perry Rd, Dag. RM9 168 EZ70
Harlow CM18 73 EQ18
Perrysfield Rd, Chsht EN8 89 DY27
Perrys La, Knock.P. TN14 246 EV113
Perrys Pl, W1 17 N8
Perry Spring, Harl. CM17 74 EW17
PERRY STREET, Grav. DA11 212 GE88
Perry St, Chis. BR7 207 ER93
Dartford DA1 189 FE84
Northfleet DA11 212 GE88
Perry St Gdns, Chis. BR7
off Old Perry St 207 ES93
Perrys Way, S.Ock. RM15 171 FW71
Perry Vale, SE23 204 DW89
Perry Way, Aveley RM15 170 FQ73
● Perrywood Business Pk, Red. RH1 289 DH142
Perrywood Ho, E5
off Pembury Rd 10 E2
Persant Rd, SE6 206 EE89
Perseverance Cotts, Ripley GU23 250 BJ121
Perseverance Pl, SW9 42 F5
Richmond TW9
off Shaftesbury Rd 180 CL83
Persfield Cl, Epsom KT17 239 CT110
Pershore Cl, Ilf. IG2 147 EP57
Pershore Gro, Cars. SM5 222 DD100
Perspective Ho, Enf. EN3
off Tysoe Av 105 DY36
Pert Cl, N10 121 DH52
Perth Av, NW9 140 CR59
Hayes UB4 158 BW70
Slough SL1 153 AP72
Perth Cl, SW20
off Huntley Way 221 CU96
Northolt UB5 138 CA64
Perth Rd, E10 145 DY60
E13 24 A1
N4 143 DN60
N22 121 DP53
Barking IG11 167 ER68
Beckenham BR3 225 EC96
Ilford IG2 147 EN58
Perth Ter, Ilf. IG2 147 EQ59
● Perth Trd Est, Slou. SL1 153 AP71
Perwell Av, Har. HA2 138 BZ60
Perwell Ct, Har. HA2 138 BZ60
Pescot Hill, Hem.H. HP1 62 BH18
Sch Petchey Acad, E8 10 B2
Peter Av, NW10 161 CV66
Oxted RH8 275 ED129
Peterboat Cl, SE10 35 K8
Sch Peterborough & St. Margaret's Sch, Stan. HA7
off Common Rd 117 CE48
Peterborough Av, Upmin. RM14 151 FS60
Peterborough Gdns, Ilf. IG1 146 EL59
Peterborough Ms, SW6 39 J8
Sch Peterborough Prim Sch, SW6 39 K9
Peterborough Rd, E10 145 EC57
SW6 39 J8
Carshalton SM5 222 DE100
Guildford GU2 264 AT132
Harrow HA1 139 CE60
Peterborough Vil, SW6 39 L6
Peterchurch Ho, SE15 44 E4
Peter Dwight Dr, Amer. HP6
off Woodside Rd 77 AS38
Petergate, SW11 182 DC84
Peterhead Ms, Slou. SL3 175 BA78
Peter Heathfield Ho, E15
off Wise Rd 12 G8
Peterhill Cl, Chal.St.P. SL9 112 AY50
Sch Peter Hills with St. Mary's & St. Paul's C of E Prim Sch, SE16 33 K2
Peter Ho, E1 off Commercial Rd 20 F8
Peterhouse Gdns, SW6 39 M7
● Peter James Business Cen, Hayes UB3 177 BU75
Peterlee Ct, Hem.H. HP2 62 BM16
● Peterley Business Cen, E2 20 E1
Peter Moore Ct, N9
off Menon Dr 122 DV48
★ Peter Pan Statue, W2 28 A2
Peters Av, Lon.Col. AL2 83 CJ26
Peters Cl, Dag. RM8 148 EX60
Stanmore HA7 117 CK51
Welling DA16 187 ES82
Petersfield, St.Alb. AL3 65 CE16
Petersfield Av, Rom. RM3 128 FL51
Slough SL2 154 AU74
Staines-upon-Thames TW18 196 BJ92
Petersfield Cl, N18 122 DQ50
Romford RM3 128 FN51
Petersfield Cres, Couls. CR5 257 DL115
Petersfield Ri, SW15 201 CV88
Petersfield Rd, W3 180 CQ75
Staines-upon-Thames TW18 196 BJ92
PETERSHAM, Rich. TW10 200 CL88
Petersham Av, Byfleet KT14 234 BL112
Petersham Cl, Byfleet KT14 234 BL112
Richmond TW10 199 CK89
Sutton SM1 240 DA106
Petersham Dr, Orp. BR5 227 ET96
Petersham Gdns, Orp. BR5 227 ET96
Petersham La, SW7 27 N6
Petersham Ms, SW7 27 N7
Petersham Pl, SW7 27 N6
Petersham Rd, Rich. TW10 200 CL86
Peters Hill, EC4 19 J10
Peter's La, EC1 19 H6
Peterslea, Kings L. WD4 81 BP29
Petersmead Cl, Tad. KT20 255 CW123
Peters Path, SE26 204 DV91
Peterstone Rd, SE2 188 EV76
Peterstow Cl, SW19 201 CY89
Peter St, W1 17 M10
Gravesend DA12 213 GH87
Peterswood, Harl. CM18 73 ER19
Peters Wd Hill, Ware SG12 55 DX07
Sch Peterswood Inf Sch & Nurs, Harl. CM18
off Paringdon Rd 73 ER19
Peterwood Way, Croy. CR0 223 DM103
Petham Ct, Swan. BR8 229 FF100
Petherton Rd, N5 9 K3
Petiver Cl, E9 11 H6
Petley Rd, W6 38 B3
Peto Pl, NW1 17 K4
Peto St N, E16 23 L9
Petridge Rd, Red. RH1 288 DF139
Petridgewood Common, Red. RH1 288 DF140
Petrie Cl, NW2 4 F4
★ Petrie Mus of Egyptian Archaeology, WC1
off Malet Pl 17 N5
Petros Gdns, NW3 5 N3
Pettacre Cl, SE28 187 EQ76
Pett Cl, Horn. RM11 149 FH61
Petten Cl, Orp. BR5 228 EX102
Petten Gro, Orp. BR5 228 EW102
Petters Rd, Ashtd. KT21 254 CM116
Petticoat La, E1 19 P7
Petticoat Sq, E1 20 A8
Petticoat Twr, E1 20 A8
Pettits Boul, Rom. RM1 127 FE53
Pettits Cl, Rom. RM1 127 FE54
Pettits La, Rom. RM1 127 FE54
Pettits La N, Rom. RM1 127 FD53
Pettits Pl, Dag. RM10 148 FA64
Pettits Rd, Dag. RM10 148 FA64
Pettiward Cl, SW15 181 CW84
Pettley Gdns, Rom. RM7 149 FD57
Pettman Cres, SE28 187 ER76
Pettsgrove Av, Wem. HA0 139 CJ64
Petts Hill, Nthlt. UB5 138 CB64
Sch Petts Hill Prim Sch, Nthlt. UB5 off Newmarket Av 138 CB64
Petts La, Shep. TW17 216 BN98
Pett St, SE18 36 G8
PETTS WOOD, Orp. BR5 227 ER99
⇌ Petts Wood 227 EQ99
Petts Wd Rd, Petts Wd BR5 227 EQ99
Petty Cross, Slou. SL1 153 AL72
Petty France, SW1 29 M6
Pettys Cl, Chsht EN8 89 DX28
Petty Wales, EC3
off Lower Thames St 31 P1
Petworth Cl, Couls. CR5 257 DJ119
Northolt UB5 158 BZ66
Petworth Ct, Wind. SL4 173 AP81
Petworth Gdns, SW20
off Hidcote Gdns 221 CV97
Uxbridge UB10 157 BQ67
Petworth Ho, SE22
off Pytchley Rd 184 DS83
Petworth Rd, N12 120 DE50
Bexleyheath DA6 208 FA85
Petworth St, SW11 40 D6
Petworth Way, Horn. RM12 149 FF63
Petyt Pl, SW3 40 C3
Petyward, SW3 28 D9
Pevensey Av, N11 121 DK50
Enfield EN1 104 DR40
Pevensey Cl, Islw. TW7 178 CC80
Pevensey Rd, E7 146 EF63
SW17 202 DD91
Feltham TW13 198 BY88
Slough SL2 153 AN71
Pevensey Way, Crox.Grn WD3 97 BP42
Peverel, E6 25 L8
Peverel Ho, Dag. RM10 148 FA61
Peveret Cl, N11 121 DH50
Peveril Dr, Tedd. TW11 199 CD92
Pewley Bk, Guil. GU1 280 AY136
Sch Pewley Down Inf Sch, Guil. GU1 off Semaphore Rd 280 AY136
Pewley Hill, Guil. GU1 280 AX136
Pewley Pt, Guil. GU1 280 AY136
Pewley Way, Guil. GU1 280 AY136
Pewsey Cl, E4 123 EA50
Peyton Pl, SE10 46 E4
Peyton's Cotts, Red. RH1 273 DM132
Pharaoh Cl, Mitch. CR4 222 DF101
Pharaoh's Island, Shep. TW17 216 BM103
Pheasant Cl, E16 23 P8
Berkhamsted HP4 60 AW20
Purley CR8
off Partridge Knoll 241 DP113
Pheasant Ct, Wat. WD25 98 BW35
Pheasant Hill, Ch.St.G. HP8 112 AW47
Pheasant Ri, Chesh. HP5 76 AR33
Pheasants Way, Rick. WD3 114 BH45
Pheasant Wk, Chal.St.P. SL9 112 AV49
Phelips Rd, Harl. CM19 73 EN20
Phelp St, SE17 43 L2
Phelps Way, Hayes UB3 177 BT77
Phene St, SW3 40 D2
Philanthropic Rd, Red. RH1 288 DG135
Philan Way, Rom. RM5 127 FD51
Philbeach Gdns, SW5 27 H10
Phil Brown Pl, SW8 41 K10
Philbye Ms, Slou. SL1 173 AM75
Philchurch Pl, E1 20 D9
Philimore Cl, SE18 187 ES78
Philip Av, Rom. RM7 149 FD60
Swanley BR8 229 FD98
Philip Cl, Pilg.Hat. CM15 130 FV44
Romford RM7 off Philip Av 149 FD60
Philip Dr, Flack.Hth HP10 132 AC56
Philip Gdns, Croy. CR0 225 DZ103
Philip La, N15 144 DR56
Philipot Path, SE9 207 EM86
Philippa Gdns, SE9 206 EK85
Philippa Way, Grays RM16 193 GH77
Philip Rd, Rain. RM13 169 FE69
Staines-upon-Thames TW18 196 BK93
Philips Cl, Cars. SM5 222 DG102
Philip Sidney Ct, Chaff.Hun. RM16 191 FX78
Sch Philip Southcote Sch, Add. KT15 off Addlestone Moor 216 BJ103
Philip St, E13 23 N4
Philip Sydney Rd, Grays RM16 191 FX78
Philip Wk, SE15 44 D10
Phillida Rd, Rom. RM3 128 FN54
Phillimore Ct, Rad. WD7
off Phillimore Pl 99 CE36
Phillimore Gdns, NW10 4 A8
W8 27 J5
Phillimore Gdns Cl, W8 27 J6
Phillimore Pl, W8 27 J5
Radlett WD7 99 CE36
Phillimore Wk, W8 27 J6
Phillipers, Wat. WD25 98 BY35
Phillipp St, N1 9 N9
Phillips Cl, Dart. DA1 209 FH86
Phillips Hatch, Won. GU5 281 BC143
Philpot La, EC3 19 N10
Chobham GU24 232 AV113
Philpot Path, Ilf. IG1
off Richmond Rd 147 EQ62
Philpots Cl, West Dr. UB7 156 BK73
Philpot Sq, SW6
off Peterborough Rd 182 DB83
Philpot St, E1 20 F8
Phineas Pett Rd, SE9 186 EL83
Tra Phipps Bridge 222 DC97
Phipps Br Rd, SW19 222 DC96
Mitcham CR4 222 DC96
Phipps Hatch La, Enf. EN2 104 DQ38
Phipp's Ms, SW1 29 K7
Phipps Rd, Slou. SL1 153 AK71
Phipp St, EC2 19 N4
Phoebe Rd, Hem.H. HP2 62 BM17
Phoebeth Rd, SE4 205 EA85
Phoebe Wk, E16 off Garvary Rd 24 B9
Phoenix Ave, SE10 35 K4
● Phoenix Business Cen, Chesh. HP5 off Higham Rd 76 AP30
Phoenix Cl, E8 10 A8
E17 123 DZ54
W12 161 CV73
Epsom KT19 238 CN112
Northwood HA6 115 BT49
West Wickham BR4 226 EE103
Phoenix Ct, Felt. TW13 197 BS91
Guildford GU1 off High St 280 AX136
New Malden KT3 221 CT97
Northfleet DA11 212 GA85
Phoenix Dr, Kes. BR2 226 EK104
Sch Phoenix High Sch, W12
off The Curve 161 CU73
● Phoenix Ind Est, Har. HA1 139 CF56
● Phoenix Pk, Brent. TW8 179 CK78
Phoenix Pl, WC1 18 D4
Dartford DA1 210 FK87
Phoenix Pt, SE28 168 EW74
Phoenix Rd, NW1 17 N2
SE20 204 DW93
Sch Phoenix Sch, E3 21 P2
Sch Phoenix Sch, The, NW3 5 P5
Phoenix St, WC2 17 P9
● Phoenix Trd Est, Perivale UB6 159 CJ67
Phoenix Way, SW18 off North Side Wandsworth Common 202 DC85
Hounslow TW5 178 BW79
Phoenix Wf, SE10 35 L4
Phoenix Wf Rd, SE1 32 B5
Phoenix Wks, Pnr. HA5
off Cornwall Rd 116 BZ52
Phoenix Yd, WC1 18 D3
★ Photographers' Gall, W1 17 L9
Phygtle, The, Chal.St.P. SL9 112 AY51
Phyllis Av, N.Mal. KT3 221 CV99
★ Physical Energy Statue, W2 27 P3
Physic Pl, SW3 40 E2
Picardy Ho, Enf. EN2
off Cedar Rd 104 DQ38
Picardy Manorway, Belv. DA17 189 FB76
Picardy Rd, Belv. DA17 188 FA78
Picardy St, Belv. DA17 188 FA76
Piccadilly, W1 29 K3
Piccadilly Arc, SW1 29 L2
⊖ Piccadilly Circus 29 M1
Piccadilly Circ, W1 29 N1
Piccadilly Ct, N7 8 C4
Piccadilly Pl, W1 29 M1
Piccards, The, Guil. GU2
off Chestnut Av 280 AW138
PICCOTTS END, Hem.H. HP2 62 BJ16
Piccotts End La, Hem.H. HP2 62 BJ17
Piccotts End Rd, Hem.H. HP1 62 BJ18
Pickard Cl, N14 121 DK46
Pickard St, EC1 19 H2
Pickering Av, E6 25 M1
Pickering Cl, E9 11 J6
Pickering Gdns, N11 120 DG51
Croydon CR0 224 DT100
Pickering Ms, W2 15 M8
Pickering Pl, SW1 29 M3
Guildford GU2 264 AU132
Pickering Rd, Bark. IG11 167 EQ65
Pickering St, N1 9 H8
Pickets Cl, Bushey Hth WD23 117 CD46
Pickets St, SW12 203 DH87
Pickett Cft, Stan. HA7 117 CK53
Picketts, Welw.G.C. AL8 51 CX06
Picketts La, Red. RH1 289 DJ144
Picketts Lock La, N9 122 DW47
Pickford Cl, Bexh. DA7 188 EY82
Pickford Dr, Slou. SL3 155 AZ74
Pickford La, Bexh. DA7 188 EY82
Pickford Rd, Bexh. DA7 188 EY83
St. Albans AL1 65 CH20
Pickfords Gdns, Slou. SL1 153 AR73
Pickfords Wf, N1 19 J1
Pick Hill, Wal.Abb. EN9 90 EF32
Pickhurst Grn, Brom. BR2 226 EF101
Sch Pickhurst Inf Sch, W.Wick. BR4 off Pickhurst La 226 EF100
Sch Pickhurst Jun Sch, W.Wick. BR4 off Pickhurst La 226 EF100
Pickhurst La, Brom. BR2 226 EF102
West Wickham BR4 226 EE100
Pickhurst Mead, Brom. BR2 226 EF101
Pickhurst Pk, Brom. BR2 226 EE99
Pickhurst Ri, W.Wick. BR4 225 EC101
Pickins Piece, Horton SL3 175 BA82
Pickmoss La, Otford TN14 263 FH116
Pickwick Cl, Houns. TW4
off Dorney Way 198 BY85
Pickwick Ct, SE9 206 EL88
Pickwick Gdns, Nthflt DA11 212 GD90
Pickwick Ms, N18 122 DS50
Pickwick Pl, Har. HA1 139 CE59
Pickwick Rd, SE21 204 DR87
Pickwick St, SE1 31 J5
Pickwick Ter, Slou. SL2
off Maple Cres 154 AV73
Pickwick Way, Chis. BR7 207 EQ93
Pickworth Cl, SW8 42 B5
Picquets Way, Bans. SM7 255 CY116
Picton Pl, W1 17 H9
Surbiton KT6 220 CN102
Picton St, SE5 43 L5
Picture Ho, SW16 203 DL89
Pied Bull Yd, N1
off Theberton St 8 G8
Piedmont Rd, SE18 187 ER78
Pield Heath Av, Uxb. UB8 156 BN70
Sch Pield Heath Ho Sch, Uxb. UB8 off Pield Heath Rd 156 BL70
Pield Heath Rd, Uxb. UB8 156 BM71
Piercing Hill, They.B. CM16 107 ER35
Pier Head, E1 32 E3
Pierian Spring, Hem.H. HP1 62 BH18
Pieris Ho, Felt. TW13
off High St 197 BU89
Piermont Grn, SE22 204 DV85
Piermont Pl, Brom. BR1 226 EL96
Piermont Rd, SE22 204 DV85
Pier Par, E16 37 L3
Pierrepoint Arc, N1 8 G10
Pierrepoint Rd, W3 160 CP73
Pierrepoint Row, N1 8 G10
Pier Rd, E16 37 L5
Erith DA8 189 FE79
Feltham TW14 197 BV85
Greenhithe DA9 191 FV84
Northfleet DA11 213 GF86
Pierson Rd, Wind. SL4 173 AK82
Pier St, E14 34 F8
Pier Ter, SW18 off Jew's Row 182 DB84
Pier Wk, Grays RM17 192 GA80
Pier Way, SE28 187 ER76
Pigeonhouse La, Chipstead CR5 272 DC125
Pigeon La, Hmptn. TW12 198 CA91
Piggotts End, Amer. HP7 77 AP40
Piggotts Orchard, Amer. HP7 77 AP40
Piggs Cor, Grays RM17 192 GC76
Piggy La, Chorl. WD3 95 BB44
Pigott St, E14 22 A9
Pike Cl, Brom. BR1 206 EH92
Uxbridge UB10 156 BM67
Pike La, Upmin. RM14 151 FT64
Pike Rd, NW7
off Ellesmere Av 118 CR49
Pikes End, Pnr. HA5 137 BV56
Pikes Hill, Epsom KT17 238 CS113
Pikestone Cl, Hayes UB4
off Berrydale Rd 158 BY70
Pike Way, N.Wld Bas. CM16 92 FA27
Pilgrimage St, SE1 31 L5
Pilgrim Cl, Mord. SM4 222 DB101
Park Street AL2 82 CC27
Pilgrim Hill, SE27 204 DQ91
Orpington BR5 228 EY96
Pilgrims Cl, N13 121 DM49
Northolt UB5 138 CC64
Pilgrim's Hatch CM15 130 FT43
Shere GU5 282 BN139
Watford WD25 off Kytes Dr 82 BX33
Westhumble RH5 269 CG131
Pilgrims Ct, SE3 47 P6
Dartford DA1 210 FN85
PILGRIM'S HATCH, Brwd. CM15 130 FU42
Pilgrim's La, NW3 6 B1
Pilgrims La, Chaldon CR3 273 DM125
North Stifford RM16 171 FW74
Titsey RH8 276 EH125
Westerham TN16 260 EL123
Pilgrims Ms, E14 23 H10
Pilgrims Pl, NW3 6 A1
Reigate RH2 272 DA132
Pilgrims Ri, Barn. EN4 102 DE43
Pilgrim St, EC4 18 G9
Pilgrims Vw, Green. DA9 211 FW86
Pilgrims Way, E6 off High St N 166 EL67
N19 143 DK60
Pilgrims' Way, Albury GU5 282 BL138
Betchworth RH3 271 CY131
Caterham CR3 273 DP126
Pilgrims Way, Chev. TN14 262 EV121
Dartford DA1 210 FN88
Pilgrims' Way, Dor. RH4 269 CE134
Pilgrims' Way, Guil. GU4 280 AX138
Pilgrims' Way, Red. RH1 273 DJ127
Pilgrims Way, Reig. RH2 272 DA131
Shere GU5 282 BN139
South Croydon CR2 242 DT106
Pilgrim's Way, Wem. HA9 140 CP60
Pilgrims' Way, West. TN16 261 EM123
Westhumble RH5 269 CH131
Sch Pilgrims' Way Prim Sch, SE15 44 G3
Pilgrims Way W, Otford TN14 263 FD116
Pilkington Rd, SE15 44 E9
Orpington BR6 227 EQ103
Pilkingtons, Harl. CM17 74 EX15
Pillions La, Hayes UB4 157 BR70
Pilot Busway, SE10 35 K5
Pilot Cl, SE8 45 N2
Pilots Pl, Grav. DA12 213 GJ86
Pilsdon Cl, SW19 201 CX88
Piltdown Rd, Wat. WD19 116 BX49
● Pilton Ind Est, Croy. CR0 223 DP103
Pilton Pl, SE17 31 K10
Pimento Ct, W5 off Olive Rd 179 CK76
PIMLICO, SW1 29 L10
⊖ Pimlico 29 N10
Sch Pimlico Acad, SW1 41 M1
Pimlico Rd, SW1 28 G10
Pimlico Wk, N1 19 N2
Pimms Cl, Guil. GU4 265 BA130
Pimpernel Way, Rom. RM3 128 FK51
Pinceybrook Rd, Harl. CM18 73 EQ19
Pinchbeck Rd, Orp. BR6 245 ET107
Pinchfield, Map.Cr. WD3 113 BE50
Pinchin St, E1 20 D10
Pincott La, W.Hors. KT24 267 BP129
Pincott Pl, SE4 45 K10
Pincott Rd, SW19 202 DC94
Bexleyheath DA6 208 FA85
Pindar Rd, Hodd. EN11 71 EC16
Pindar St, EC2 19 N6
PINDEN, Dart. DA2 231 FW96
Pindock Ms, W9 15 M5
Pineapple Ct, SW1 29 L6
Pineapple Rd, Amer. HP7 94 AT39
Pine Av, E15 13 H2
Gravesend DA12 213 GK88
West Wickham BR4 225 EB102
Pine Cl, E10 145 EA61
N14 121 DJ45
N19 143 DJ61
SE20 224 DW95
Berkhamsted HP4 60 AV19
Cheshunt EN8 89 DX28
Kenley CR8 258 DR117
New Haw KT15 234 BH111
Stanmore HA7 117 CH49
Swanley BR8 229 FF98
Woking GU21 248 AW117
Pine Coombe, Croy. CR0 243 DX105
Pine Ct, Upmin. RM14 150 FN63
Pine Cres, Cars. SM5 240 DD111
Hutton CM13 131 GD43
Pinecrest Gdns, Orp. BR6 245 EP105
Pinecroft, Gidea Pk RM2 150 FJ56
Hemel Hempstead HP3 62 BM24
Hutton CM13 131 GB45
Pinecroft Cres, Barn. EN5 101 CY42
Pine Dean, Bkhm KT23 268 CB125
Pinedene, SE15 44 E6
Pinefield Cl, E14 22 A10
Pine Gdns, Horl. RH6 290 DG149
Ruislip HA4 137 BV60
Surbiton KT5 220 CN100
Pine Glade, Orp. BR6 245 EM105
Pine Gro, N4 143 DL61
N20 119 CZ46
SW19 201 CZ92
Bricket Wood AL2 82 BZ30
Brookmans Park AL9 86 DB25
Bushey WD23 98 BZ40
Weybridge KT13 235 BP106
Pine Gro Ms, Wey. KT13 235 BQ106
Pine Hill, Epsom KT18 254 CR115
Pinehurst, Sev. TN14 279 FL121
Pinehurst Cl, Abb.L. WD5 81 BS32
Kingswood KT20 256 DA122
Pinehurst Gdns, W.Byf. KT14 234 BJ112
Pinehurst Wk, Orp. BR6 227 ES102
Pinelands Cl, SE3 47 M5
Pinel Cl, Vir.W. GU25 214 AY98
Pinemartin Cl, NW2 141 CW62
Pine Ms, NW10 4 C10
Pineneedle La, Sev. TN13 279 FH123
Pine Pl, Bans. SM7 239 CX114
Hayes UB4 157 BT70
Pine Ridge, Cars. SM5 240 DG109
Pineridge Cl, Wey. KT13 235 BS105
Pine Rd, N11 120 DG47
NW2 141 CW63
Woking GU22 248 AW120
Pines, The, N14 103 DJ43
Borehamwood WD6
off Anthony Rd 100 CM40
Coulsdon CR5 257 DH118
Dorking RH4 off South Ter 285 CH137
Hemel Hempstead HP3 61 BF24
Purley CR8 241 DP113
Slough SL3 155 AZ74
Sunbury-on-Thames TW16 217 BU97
Woking GU21 233 AZ114
Woodford Green IG8 124 EG48
Pines Av, Enf. EN1 104 DV36
Pines Cl, Amer. HP6 77 AP36
Northwood HA6 115 BS51
Pines Rd, Brom. BR1 226 EL96
● Pines Trd Est, The, Guil. GU3 264 AS132
Pine St, EC1 18 E4
Pinetree Cl, Chal.St.P. SL9 112 AW52
Pine Tree Cl, Hem.H. HP2 62 BK19
Hounslow TW5 177 BV81
Pinetree Gdns, Hem.H. HP3 62 BL22
Pine Tree Hill, Wok. GU22 249 BD116
Pine Trees Dr, Uxb. UB10 136 BL63
Pine Tree Way, SE13
off Elmira St 185 EB83
Pine Vw Cl, Chilw. GU4 281 BF140
Pine Vw Manor, Epp. CM16 92 EU30
Pine Wk, Bans. SM7 256 DF117
Pinewalk, Bkhm KT23 268 CB125
Pine Wk, Brom. BR1 226 EJ95
Carshalton SM5 240 DD110
Caterham CR3 258 DS122
Cobham KT11 236 BX114
East Horsley KT24 267 BT128
Surbiton KT5 220 CN100
Pine Way, Eng.Grn TW20
off Ashwood Rd 194 AV93
Pine Wd, Sun. TW16 217 BU95
Pinewood, Welw.G.C. AL7 51 CY11
Pinewood Av, New Haw KT15 234 BJ109
Pinner HA5 116 CB51
Rainham RM13 169 FH70
Sevenoaks TN14 279 FK121
Sidcup DA15 207 ES88
Uxbridge UB8 156 BM72
Pinewood Cl, Borwd. WD6 100 CR39
Croydon CR0 225 DY104

Pinewood Cl, Gerrards Cross SL9
off Oxford Rd 134 AY59
Harlow CM17 74 EW16
Iver SL0 155 BC66
Northwood HA6 115 BV50
Orpington BR6 227 ER103
Pinner HA5 116 CB51
St. Albans AL4 65 CJ20
Watford WD17 97 BU39
Woking GU21 233 BA114
Pinewood Dr, Orp. BR6 245 ES106
Potters Bar EN6 85 CZ31
Staines-upon-Thames TW18 196 BG92
Pinewood Gdns, Hem.H. HP1 62 BH20
Pinewood Grn, Iver SL0 155 BC66
Pinewood Gro, W5 159 CJ72
New Haw KT15 234 BH110
Pinewood Ms, Stanw. TW19 196 BK86
Pinewood Pk, New Haw KT15 234 BH111
Pinewood Pl, Dart. DA2 209 FE89
Epsom KT19 238 CR105
Sch **Pinewood Prim Sch**,
Coll.Row RM5
off Thistledene Av 127 FB50
Pinewood Ride, Iver SL0 155 BA68
Slough SL3 155 BA68
Pinewood Rd, SE2 188 EX79
Bromley BR2 226 EG98
Feltham TW13 197 BV90
Havering-atte-Bower RM4 127 FC49
Iver SL0 155 BB67
Virginia Water GU25 214 AU98
Sch **Pinewood Sch**, Ware SG12
off Hoe La 55 DX08
Pinewood Way, Hutt. CM13 131 GD43
Pinfold Rd, SW16 203 DL91
Bushey WD23 98 BZ40
Pinglestone Cl, Harm. UB7 176 BL80
Pinkcoat Cl, Felt. TW13
off Tanglewood Way 197 BV90
Pinkerton Pl, SW16 203 DK91
Pinkham Way, N11 120 DG52
Pink La, Burn. SL1 152 AH68
Pinkneys Ct, Tap. SL6 152 AG72
Pinks Hill, Swan. BR8 229 FE99
Pinkwell Av, Hayes UB3 177 BR77
Pinkwell La, Hayes UB3 177 BQ77
Sch **Pinkwell Prim Sch**, Hayes UB3
off Pinkwell La 177 BQ77
Pinley Gdns, Dag. RM9
off Stamford Rd 168 EV67
Pinnace Ho, E14
off Manchester Rd 34 F6
Pinnacle, The, RM6 148 EY58
Pinnacle, NW9
off Heritage Ave 119 CT54
Pinnacle Hill, Bexh. DA7 189 FB84
Pinnacle Hill N, Bexh. DA7 189 FB83
PINNACLES, Harl. CM19 73 EN15
Pinnacles, Wal.Abb. EN9 90 EE34
Pinnata Cl, Enf. EN2 104 DQ39
Pinnate Pl, Welw.G.C. AL7 51 CY13
Pinn Cl, Uxb. UB8 156 BK72
Pinnell Rd, SE9 186 EK84
PINNER, HA5 138 BY56
⊖ **Pinner** 138 BY56
Pinner Ct, Pnr. HA5 138 CA56
PINNER GREEN, Pnr. HA5 116 BX54
Pinner Grn, Pnr. HA5 116 BW54
Pinner Gro, Pnr. HA5 138 BY56
Pinner Hill, Pnr. HA5 116 BW53
Pinner Hill Rd, Pnr. HA5 116 BW54
Pinner Pk, Pnr. HA5 116 CA53
Pinner Pk Av, Har. HA2 138 CB55
Sch **Pinner Pk First Sch**, Pnr. HA5
off Melbourne Av 138 CB55
Pinner Pk Gdns, Har. HA2 116 CC54
Sch **Pinner Pk Mid Sch**, Pnr. HA5
off Melbourne Av 138 CB55
Pinner Rd, Har. HA1, HA2 138 CB57
Northwood HA6 115 BT53
Pinner HA5 138 BZ56
Watford WD19 98 BX44
Pinner Vw, Har. HA1, HA2 138 CC58
PINNERWOOD PARK, Pnr.
HA5 116 BW52
Sch **Pinner Wd Sch**, Pnr. HA5
off Latimer Gdns 116 BW53
Pinnocks Av, Grav. DA11 213 GH88
Pinn Way, Ruis. HA4 137 BS59
Pinstone Way, Ger.Cr. SL9 135 BB61
Pintail Cl, E6 24 G7
Pintail Rd, Wdf.Grn. IG8 124 EH52
Pintail Way, Hayes UB4 158 BX71
Pinter Ho, SW9 42 B9
Pinto Cl, Borwd. WD6 100 CR44
Pinto Way, SE3 186 EH84
Pioneer Cl, E14 22 C7
Pioneer Pl, Croy. CR0 243 EA109
● **Pioneers Ind Pk**, Croy.
CR0 223 DL102
Pioneer St, SE15 44 C6
Pioneer Way, W12
off Du Cane Rd 161 CV72
Swanley BR8 229 FE97
Watford WD18 97 BT44
Piper Cl, N7 8 C3
Piper Rd, Kings.T. KT1 220 CN97
Pipers Cl, Burn. SL1 152 AJ69
Cobham KT11 252 BX115
PIPERS END, Hert. SG14 53 DJ13
Pipers End, Hert. SG14 53 DJ13
Virginia Water GU25 214 AX97
Piper's Gdns, Croy. CR0 225 DY101
Pipers Grn, NW9 140 CQ57
Pipers Grn La, Edg. HA8 118 CL48
Piper Way, Ilf. IG1 147 ER60
Pipewell Rd, Cars. SM5 222 DE100
Pippbrook, Dor. RH4 285 CH135
Pippbrook Gdns, Dor. RH4
off London Rd 285 CH135
Pippens, Welw.G.C. AL8 51 CY06
Pippin Cl, NW2 141 CV62
Croydon CR0 225 DZ102
Shenley WD7 84 CL33
Pippins, The, Slou. SL3
off Pickford Dr 155 AZ74
Watford WD25 82 BW34
Pippins Cl, West Dr. UB7 176 BK76
Pippins Ct, Ashf. TW15 197 BP93
Sch **Pippins Sch**, Colnbr. SL3
off Raymond Cl 175 BF81
Pippit Ct, Enf. EN3
off Teal Cl 104 DW37
Piquet Rd, SE20 224 DW96
Pirbright Cres, New Adgtn
CR0 243 EC107
Pirbright Rd, SW18 201 CZ88
Pirie Cl, SE5 43 M10
Pirie St, E16 36 B3
Pirrip Cl, Grav. DA12 213 GM89
Pirton Cl, St.Alb. AL4 65 CJ15
Pishiobury Dr, Saw. CM21 58 EW07
Pishiobury Ms, Saw. CM21 58 EX08
Pitcairn Cl, Rom. RM7 148 FA56
Pitcairn Rd, Mitch. CR4 202 DF94
Pitcairn's Path, Har. HA2
off Eastcote Rd 138 CC62
Pitchfont La, Oxt. RH8 260 EF124
Pitchford St, E15 13 H7
PITCH PLACE, Guil. GU3 264 AT129
Pitch Pond Cl, Knot.Grn HP9 110 AH50
Pit Fm Rd, Guil. GU1 265 BA134
Pitfield Cres, SE28 168 EU74
Pitfield Est, N1 19 M2
Pitfield St, N1 19 N3
Pitfield Way, NW10 160 CQ65
Enfield EN3 104 DW39
Pitfold Cl, SE12 206 EG86
Pitfold Rd, SE12 206 EG86
Pitlake, Croy. CR0 223 DP103
Pitman Ho, SE8
off Tanners Hill 46 A6
Pitman St, SE5 43 J4
Pitmaston Ho, SE13 46 E8
Pitmaston Rd, SE13 46 E8
Pitsea Pl, E1 21 K9
Pitsea St, E1 21 K9
Pitsfield, Welw.G.C. AL8 51 CX06
Pitshanger La, W5 159 CH70
★ **Pitshanger Manor Ho & Gall**,
W5 159 CJ74
Pitshanger Pk, W13 159 CH69
Pitson Cl, Add. KT15 234 BK105
Pitstone Cl, St.Alb. AL4
off Highview Gdns 65 CJ15
Pitt Cres, SW19 202 DB91
Pitt Dr, St.Alb. AL4 65 CJ23
Pitteway Wk, Hert. SG14
off Port Vale 54 DQ09
Pitt Ho, SW11
off Maysoule Rd 182 DD84
Pittman Cl, Ingrave CM13 131 GC50
Pittman Gdns, Ilf. IG1 147 EQ64
Pittmans Fld, Harl. CM20 57 ET14
Pitt Pl, Epsom KT17 238 CS114
Pitt Rd, Croy. CR0 224 DQ99
Epsom KT17 238 CS114
Orpington BR6 245 EQ105
Thornton Heath CR7 224 DQ99
Pitt's Head Ms, W1 29 H3
Pittsmead Av, Brom. BR2 226 EG101
Pitts Rd, Slou. SL1 153 AQ74
Pitt St, W8 27 K4
Pittville Gdns, SE25 224 DU97
Pittwood, Shenf. CM15 131 GA46
Pitwood Grn, Tad. KT20 255 CW120
● **Pitwood Pk Ind Est**,
Tad. KT20
off Waterfield 255 CV120
Pix Fm La, Hem.H. HP1 61 BB21
Pixfield Ct, Brom. BR2
off Beckenham La 226 EF96
PIXHAM, Dor. RH4 269 CJ133
● **Pixham End**, Dor. RH4 269 CJ133
Pixham La, Dor. RH4 269 CJ133
Pixholme Gro, Dor. RH4 269 CJ134
Pixies Hill Cres, Hem.H. HP1 61 BF22
Sch **Pixies Hill JMI Sch**, Hem.H.
HP1 *off Hazeldell Rd* 61 BF21
Pixies Hill Rd, Hem.H. HP1 61 BF21
Pixley St, E14 21 P8
Pixton Way, Croy. CR0 243 DY109
Place Fm Av, Orp. BR6 227 ER102
Place Fm Rd, Bletch. RH1 274 DR130
Placehouse La, Couls. CR5 257 DM119
Plackett Way, Slou. SL1 153 AK74
Plain, The, Epp. CM16 92 EV29
Plaines Cl, Slou. SL1 153 AM74
PLAISTOW, E13 23 L2
PLAISTOW, Brom. BR1 206 EF93
⊖ **Plaistow** 13 M10
Plaistow Gro, E15 13 L9
Bromley BR1 206 EH94
H **Plaistow Hosp**, E13 24 C1
Plaistow La, Brom. BR1 206 EG94
Plaistow Pk Rd, E13 166 EH68
Sch **Plaistow Prim Sch**, E13
off Junction Rd 166 EH68
Plaistow Rd, E13 13 L9
E15 13 L9
Plaitford Cl, Rick. WD3 114 BL47
Plane Av, Nthflt DA11 212 GD87
Planes, The, Cher. KT16 216 BJ101
Plane St, SE26 204 DV90
Plane Tree Cres, Felt. TW13 197 BV90
Planetree Path, E17
off Rosebank Vil 145 EA56
Plane Tree Wk, N2 142 DD55
SE19 *off Lunham Rd* 204 DS93
Plantaganet Pl, Wal.Abb. EN9 89 EB33
Plantagenet Cl, Wor.Pk. KT4 238 CR105
Plantagenet Gdns, Rom. RM6 148 EX59
Plantagenet Pl, Rom. RM6 148 EX59
Plantagenet Rd, Barn. EN5 102 DC42
Plantain Gdns, E11
off Hollydown Way 145 ED62
Plantain Pl, SE1 31 L4
Plantation, The, SE3 47 P9
Plantation Cl, SW4
off King's Av 203 DL85
Greenhithe DA9 211 FT86
Plantation Dr, Orp. BR5 228 EX102
Plantation La, EC3
off Rood La 19 N10
Warlingham CR6 259 DY119
Plantation Rd, Amer. HP6 77 AS37
Erith DA8 189 FG81
Swanley BR8 209 FG94
Plantation Wk, Hem.H. HP1 62 BG17
Plantation Way, Amer. HP6 77 AS37
Plantation Wf, SW11 39 P10
Plashet Gdns, Brwd. CM13 131 GA49
Plashet Gro, E6 166 EJ67
Plashet Rd, E13 13 P8
Plashets, The, Sheering CM22 59 FC07
Sch **Plashet Sch**, E6
off Plashet Gro 166 EL66
Plassy Rd, SE6 205 EB87
Platford Grn, Horn. RM11 150 FL56
Platina St, EC2 19 M4
Platinum Ho, Har. HA1
off Lyon Rd 139 CF58
Platinum Ms, N15
off Crowland Rd 144 DT57
Plato Rd, SW2 183 DL84
Platt, The, SW15 38 D10
Amersham HP7 77 AP40
Platt Meadow, Guil. GU4
off Eustace Rd 265 BD131
Platts Av, Wat. WD17 97 BV41
Platt's Eyot, Hmptn. TW12 218 CA96
Platt's La, NW3 142 DA63
Platts Rd, Enf. EN3 104 DW39
Platt St, NW1 7 N10
Plawsfield Rd, Beck. BR3 225 DX95
Plaxtol Cl, Brom. BR1 226 EJ95
Plaxtol Rd, Erith DA8 188 FA80
Plaxton Ct, E11
off Woodhouse Rd 146 EF62
Playfair St, W6 38 B1
Playfield Av, Rom. RM5 127 FC53
Playfield Cres, SE22 204 DT85
Playfield Rd, Edg. HA8 118 CQ54
Playford Rd, N4 143 DM61
Playgreen Way, SE6 205 EA91
Playground Cl, Beck. BR3
off Churchfields Rd 225 DX96
Playhouse Ct, SE1
off Southwark Br Rd 31 J4
Playhouse Sq, Harl. CM20
off College Gate 73 EQ15
Playhouse Yd, EC4 18 G9
● **Plaza Business Cen**, Enf. EN3
off Stockingswater La 105 DZ40
Plaza Par, NW6
off Kilburn High Rd 5 L10
🛍 **Plaza Shop Cen, The**, W1 17 M8
Pleasance, The, SW15 181 CV84
Pleasance Rd, SW15 201 CV85
Orpington BR5 228 EV96
Pleasant Gro, Croy. CR0 225 DZ104
Pleasant Pl, N1 9 H7
Hersham KT12 236 BW107
West Hyde WD3 113 BE52
Pleasant Ri, Hat. AL9 67 CW15
Pleasant Row, NW1 7 K9
Pleasant Vw, Erith DA8 189 FE78
Pleasant Vw Pl, Orp. BR6
off High St 245 EP106
Pleasant Way, Wem. HA0 159 CJ68
Pleasure Pit Rd, Ashtd. KT21 254 CP118
Plender St, NW1 7 L9
Pleshey Rd, N7 7 N1
Plesman Way, Wall. SM6 241 DL109
Plevna Cres, N15 144 DS58
Plevna Rd, N9 122 DU48
Hampton TW12 218 CB95
Plevna St, E14 34 E6
Pleydell Av, SE19 204 DT94
W6 181 CT77
Pleydell Ct, EC4 18 F9
Pleydell Est, EC1
off Radnor St 19 K3
Pleydell St, EC4 18 F9
Plimley Pl, W12 26 C4
Plimsoll Cl, E14 22 C9
Plimsoll Rd, N4 143 DN62
Plomer Av, Hodd. EN11 55 DZ14
Plough Ct, EC3 19 M10
Plough Fm Cl, Ruis. HA4 137 BR58
Plough Hill, Cuffley EN6 87 DL28
● **Plough Ind Est**, Lthd.
KT22 253 CG120
Plough La, SE22 204 DT86
SW17 202 DB92
SW19 202 DB92
Downside KT11 251 BU116
Harefield UB9 114 BJ51
Potten End HP4 61 BB16
Purley CR8 241 DL109
Sarratt WD3 79 BF33
Stoke Poges SL2 154 AV67
Teddington TW11 199 CG92
Wallington SM6 241 DL105
Plough La Cl, Wall. SM6 241 DL106
Ploughlees La, Slou. SL1 154 AS73
Ploughmans Cl, NW1 7 N8
Ploughmans End, Islw. TW7 199 CD85
Welwyn Garden City AL7 52 DC10
Ploughmans Wk, N2
off Long La 120 DC54
Plough Ms, SW11
off Plough Ter 182 DD84
Plough Pl, EC4 18 F8
Plough Ri, Upmin. RM14 151 FS59
Plough Rd, SW11 40 A10
Epsom KT19 238 CR109
Smallfield RH6 291 DP148
Jct **Plough Rbt**, Hem.H. HP1 62 BK22
Plough St, E1 20 C8
Plough Ter, SW11 182 DD84
Plough Way, SE16 33 K8
Plough Yd, EC2 19 P5
Plover Cl, Berk. HP4 60 AW20
Staines-upon-Thames TW18 195 BF90
Plover Ct, Enf. EN3
off Teal Cl 104 DW36
Plover Gdns, Upmin. RM14 151 FT60
Plover Way, SE16 33 L6
Hayes UB4 158 BX72
Plowden Bldgs, EC4
off Middle Temple La 18 E10
Plowman Cl, N18 122 DR50
Plowman Way, Dag. RM8 148 EW60
Ployters Rd, Harl. CM18 73 EQ18
Plumbers Row, E1 20 C7
Plumbridge St, SE10 46 E6
Plum Cl, Felt. TW13 197 BU88
Sch **Plumcroft Prim Sch**, SE18
off Plum La 187 EQ79
Plum Garth, Brent. TW8 179 CK77
Plum La, SE18 187 EP80
Plummer La, Mitch. CR4 222 DF96
Plummer Rd, SW4 203 DK87
Plummers Cft, Dunt.Grn TN13 278 FE121
Plumpton Av, Horn. RM12 150 FL63
Plumpton Cl, Nthlt. UB5 158 CA65
Plumpton Rd, Hodd. EN11 71 EC15
Plumpton Way, Cars. SM5 222 DE104
PLUMSTEAD, SE18 187 ES78
⇌ **Plumstead** 187 ER77
Plumstead Common Rd,
SE18 187 EP79
Plumstead High St, SE18 187 ES77
Sch **Plumstead Manor Sch**, SE18
off Old Mill Rd 187 ER79
Plumstead Rd, SE18 37 P8
Plumtree Cl, Dag. RM10 169 FB65
Wallington SM6 241 DK108
Plumtree Ct, EC4 18 F8
Plumtree Mead, Loug. IG10 107 EN41
Pluto Cl, Slou. SL1 173 AL75
Pluto Ri, Hem.H. HP2 62 BL18
Plymouth Dr, Sev. TN13 279 FJ124
Plymouth Pk, Sev. TN13 279 FJ124
Plymouth Rd, E16 23 N7
Plymouth Rd, Bromley BR1 226 EH95
Chafford Hundred RM16 191 FW77
Slough SL1 153 AL71
Plymouth Wf, E14 34 G8
Plympton Av, NW6 4 G7
Plympton Cl, Belv. DA17
off Halifield Dr 188 EY76
Plympton Pl, NW8 16 C5
Plympton Rd, NW6 4 G7
Plympton St, NW8 16 C5
Plymstock Rd, Well. DA16 188 EW80
Pocket Hill, Sev. TN13 278 FG128
Pocketsdell La, Bov. HP3 78 AX28
Pocklington Cl, NW9 118 CS54
Pocock Av, West Dr. UB7 176 BM76
Pococks La, Eton SL4 174 AS78
Pocock St, SE1 30 G4
Podium, The, E2 21 H2
Podmore Rd, SW18 182 DC84
Poets Chase, Hem.H. HP1
off Laureate Way 62 BH18
Poets Gate, Chsht EN7 88 DR28
Poets Rd, N5 9 L2
Poets Way, Har. HA1
off Blawith Rd 139 CE56
Point, The, Ruislip HA4 137 BU63
Point, The, E17 *off Tower Ms* 145 EA56
Pointalls Cl, N3 120 DC54
Point Cl, SE10 46 F6
Pointer Cl, SE28 168 EX72
Pointers, The, Ashtd. KT21 254 CL120
Sch **Pointer Sch, The**, SE3 47 N5
Pointers Cl, E14 34 C10
Pointers Hill, Westc. RH4 284 CC138
Pointers Rd, Cob. KT11 251 BQ116
Point Hill, SE10 46 F5
Point of Thomas Path, E1 33 H1
Point Pl, Wem. HA9 160 CP66
Point Pleasant, SW18 182 DA84
Point W, SW7 27 M8
Point Wf La, Brent. TW8
off Town Meadow 180 CL80
Poland Ho, E15 12 G8
Poland St, W1 17 M9
● **Polar Pk**, West Dr. UB7 176 BM80
Polayn Garth, Welw.G.C. AL8 51 CW08
Polebrook Rd, SE3 186 EJ83
Pole Cat All, Brom. BR2 226 EF103
Polecroft La, SE6 205 DZ89
Polehamptons, The, Hmptn.
TW12 218 CC95
Polehanger La, Hem.H. HP1 61 BE18
Pole Hill Rd, E4 123 EC45
Hayes UB4 157 BQ69
Uxbridge UB10 157 BQ69
Pole La, Ong. CM5 75 FE17
Polesden Gdns, SW20 221 CV96
★ **Polesden Lacey, Ho & Gdn**,
Dor. RH5 268 CA130
Polesden La, Ripley GU23 249 BF122
Polesden Rd, Bkhm KT23 268 CB129
Polesden Vw, Bkhm KT23 268 CB127
Poles Hill, Chesh. HP5 76 AN29
Sarratt WD3 79 BE33
Polesteeple Hill, Bigg.H. TN16 260 EK117
Polesworth Ho, W2 15 K6
Polesworth Rd, Dag. RM9 168 EX66
Polhill, Halst. TN13, TN14 263 FC115
Polhill Pk, Halst. TN14 263 FD117
Police Sta La, Bushey WD23
off Sparrows Herne 116 CB45
Police Sta Rd, Hersham KT12 236 BW107
★ **Polish Inst & Sikorski Mus**,
SW7 *off Princes Gate* 28 B5
Jct **Polish War Mem**, Ruis.
HA4 157 BV66
Pollard Av, Denh. UB9 135 BF58
Pollard Cl, E16 23 N10
N7 8 D2
Chigwell IG7 126 EU50
Old Windsor SL4 194 AV85
Pollard Hatch, Harl. CM19 73 EP18
Pollard Rd, N20 120 DE47
Morden SM4 222 DD99
Woking GU22 249 BB116
Pollard Row, E2 20 D2
Pollards, Map.Cr. WD3 113 BD50
Pollards Cl, Goffs Oak EN7 88 DQ29
Loughton IG10 106 EJ43
Welwyn Garden City AL7 52 DA09
Pollards Cres, SW16 223 DL97
Pollards Hill E, SW16 223 DM97
Pollards Hill N, SW16 223 DL97
Pollards Hill S, SW16 223 DL97
Pollards Hill W, SW16 223 DL97
Pollards Oak Cres, Oxt. RH8 276 EG132
Pollards Oak Rd, Oxt. RH8 276 EG132
Pollard St, E2 20 D2
Pollards Wd Hill, Oxt. RH8 276 EH130
Pollards Wd Rd, SW16 223 DL96
Oxted RH8 276 EH131
Pollard Wk, Sid. DA14 208 EW93
Pollen St, W1 17 K9
Pollicott Cl, St.Alb. AL4 65 CJ15
Pollitt Dr, NW8 16 A4
★ **Pollock's Toy Mus**, W1 17 M6
Pollyhaugh, Eyns. DA4 230 FL104
Polperro Cl, Orp. BR6
off Cotswold Ri 227 ET100
Polperro Ms, SE11 30 F8
Polsted Rd, SE6 205 DZ87
Polsten Ms, Enf. EN3 105 EA37
Polthorne Est, SE18 187 EQ77
Polthorne Gro, SE18 187 EQ77
Poltimore Rd, Guil. GU2 280 AU136
Polworth Rd, SW16 203 DL92
Polygon, The, SW4
off Old Town 183 DJ84
● **Polygon Business Cen**,
Colnbr. SL3 175 BF82
Polygon Rd, NW1 17 N1
Polytechnic St, SE18 37 M8
Pomell Way, E1 20 B8
Pomeroy Cl, Amer. HP7 77 AR40
Twickenham TW1 179 CH84
Pomeroy Cres, Wat. WD24 97 BV36
Pomeroy St, SE14 45 H5
Pomfret Rd, SE5 43 H10
Pomoja La, N19 143 DK61
Pompadour Cl, Warley CM14
off Queen St 130 FW50
Pond Cl, N12 120 DE51
SE3 47 M9
Ashtead KT21 254 CL117
Harefield UB9 114 BJ54
Hersham KT12 235 BU107
Pond Cottage La, W.Wick.
BR4 225 EA102
Pond Cotts, SE21 204 DS88
Pond Cft, Hat. AL10 67 CT18
Pondcroft, Welw.G.C. AL7 51 CY10
PONDERS END, Enf. EN3 104 DW43
⇌ **Ponders End** 105 DX43
● **Ponders End Ind Est**, Enf.
EN3 105 DZ42
Ponder St, N7 8 C6
Pond Fm Cl, Walt.Hill KT20 255 CU124
Pond Fm Est, E5
off Millfields Rd 144 DW62
Pond Fld, Welw.G.C. AL7 52 DA06
Pondfield Cres, St.Alb. AL4 65 CH16
Pond Fld End, Loug. IG10 124 EJ45
Pondfield Ho, SE27
off Elder Rd 204 DQ92
Pondfield La, Brwd. CM13 131 GA49
Pondfield Rd, Brom. BR2 226 EE102
Dagenham RM10 149 FB64
Godalming GU7 280 AT144
Kenley CR8 257 DP116
Orpington BR6 227 EP104
Pond Grn, Ruis. HA4 137 BS61
Pond Hill Gdns, Sutt. SM3 239 CY107
Pond La, Chal.St.P. SL9 112 AV53
Peaslake GU5 283 BQ144
Pond Lees Cl, Dag. RM10
off Leys Av 169 FD66
Pond Mead, SE21 204 DR86
Pond Meadow, Guil. GU2 264 AS134
Sch **Pond Meadow Sch**,
Guil. GU1
off Larch Av 264 AW131
Pond Pk Rd, Chesh. HP5 76 AP29
Pond Path, Chis. BR7
off Heathfield La 207 EQ93
Pond Piece, Oxshott KT22 236 CB114
Pond Pl, SW3 28 C9
Pond Rd, E15 13 J10
SE3 47 M8
Egham TW20 195 BC93
Hemel Hempstead HP3 80 BN25
Woking GU22 248 AU120
Ponds, The, Wey. KT13
off Ellesmere Rd 235 BS107
Pondside Ave, Wor.Pk. KT4 221 CW102
Pondside Cl, Harling. UB3 177 BR80
Ponds La, Guil. GU5 282 BL142
Pond Sq, N6 *off South Gro* 142 DG60
Pond St, NW3 6 C2
Pond Wk, Upmin. RM14 151 FS61
Pond Way, Tedd. TW11
off Holmesdale Rd 199 CJ93
Pondwicks, Amer. HP7 77 AP39
Pondwicks Cl, St.Alb. AL1 64 CC21
Pondwood Ri, Orp. BR6 227 ES101
Ponler St, E1 20 E9
Ponsard Rd, NW10 161 CV69
Sch **Ponsbourne St. Mary's C of E**
Prim Sch, Hert. SG13
off Newgate St Village 69 DL24
Ponsford St, E9 11 H4
Ponsonby Pl, SW1 29 P10
Ponsonby Rd, SW15 201 CV87
Ponsonby Ter, SW1 29 P10
Pontefract Rd, Brom. BR1 206 EF92
Pontes Ave, Houns. TW3 178 BZ84
Pontoise Cl, Sev. TN13 278 FF122
Ponton Rd, SW8 41 P3
DLR **Pontoon Dock** 36 C3
Pont St, SW1 28 E7
Pont St Ms, SW1 28 E7
Pontypool Pl, SE1 30 G4
Pontypool Wk, Rom. RM3 128 FJ51
Pony Chase, Cob. KT11 236 BZ113
Pool Cl, Beck. BR3 205 EA92
West Molesey KT8 218 BZ99
Pool Ct, SE6 205 EA89
Poole Cl, Ruis. HA4 137 BS61
Poole Ct Rd, Houns. TW4 178 BY82
Poole Ho, SE11
off Lambeth Wk 30 D7
Grays RM16 193 GJ75
Pool End Cl, Shep. TW17 216 BN99
Poole Rd, E9 11 J5
Epsom KT19 238 CR107
Hornchurch RM11 150 FM59
Woking GU21 248 AY117
Pooles Bldgs, EC1 18 E5
Pooles La, SW10 39 N5
Dagenham RM9 168 EY68
Pooles Pk, N4 143 DN61
Sch **Pooles Pk Prim Sch**, N4
off Lennox Rd 143 DM61
Poole St, N1 9 L9
Poole Way, Hayes UB4 157 BR69
Pooley Av, Egh. TW20 195 BB92
Pooley Dr, SW14
off Sheen La 180 CQ83
POOLEY GREEN, Egh. TW20 195 BC92
Pooley Grn Cl, Egh. TW20 195 BC92
Pooley Grn Rd, Egh. TW20 195 BB92
Pooleys La, N.Mymms AL9 67 CV23
Pool Gro, Croy. CR0 243 DY112
Pool La, Slou. SL1 154 AS73
Poolmans Rd, Wind. SL4 173 AK83
Poolmans St, SE16 33 J4
Pool Rd, Har. HA1 139 CD59
West Molesey KT8 218 BZ100
Poolsford Rd, NW9 140 CS56
Poonah St, E1 21 H9
Pootings Rd, Crock.H. TN8 277 ER134
Pope Cl, SW19 202 DD93
Feltham TW14 197 BT88
Pope Ho, SE16 32 E9
Sch **Pope John RC Prim Sch**, W12
off Commonwealth Av 161 CV73
Sch **Pope Paul Cath Prim Sch**,
Pot.B. EN6 *off Baker St* 85 CZ33
Pope Rd, Brom. BR2 226 EK99
Popes Av, Twick. TW2 199 CE89
Popes Cl, Amer. HP6 94 AT37
Colnbrook SL3 175 BB80
Popes Dr, N3 120 DA53
Popes Gro, Croy. CR0 225 DZ104
Twickenham TW1, TW2 199 CF89
Pope's Head All, EC3
off Cornhill 19 M9
Popes La, W5 179 CK76
Oxted RH8 276 EE134
Watford WD24 97 BV37
Popes Rd, SW9 183 DN83

Popes Rd, Abbots Langley WD5 81 BS31
Pope St, SE1 31 P5
Popham Cl, Han. TW13 198 BZ90
Popham Gdns, Rich. TW9
off Lower Richmond Rd 180 CN83
Popham Rd, N1 9 J9
Popham St, N1 9 H8
● Popin Business Cen, Wem. HA9 140 CP64
POPLAR, E14 34 C2
DLR Poplar 34 C1
Poplar Av, Amer. HP7 94 AT39
Gravesend DA12 213 GJ91
Leatherhead KT22 253 CH122
Mitcham CR4 222 DF95
Orpington BR6 227 EP103
Southall UB2 178 CB76
West Drayton UB7 156 BM73
Poplar Bath St, E14 22 D10
● Poplar Business Pk, E14 34 E1
Poplar Cl, E9 11 N2
Chesham HP5 76 AQ28
Colnbrook SL3 175 BE81
Epsom KT17 255 CV115
Pinner HA5 116 BX53
South Ockendon RM15 171 FX70
Poplar Ct, SW19 202 DA92
Poplar Cres, Epsom KT19 238 CQ107
Poplar Dr, Bans. SM7 239 CX114
Hutton CM13 131 GC44
Poplar Fm Cl, Epsom KT19 238 CQ107
Poplar Gdns, N.Mal. KT3 220 CR96
Poplar Gro, N11 120 DG51
W6 26 B5
New Malden KT3 220 CR97
Wembley HA9 140 CQ62
Woking GU22 248 AY119
Poplar High St, E14 22 C10
Poplar Ho, Langley SL3 175 AZ78
Poplar Mt, Belv. DA17 189 FB77
Poplar Pl, SE28 168 EW73
W2 15 L10
Hayes UB3 157 BU73
Sch Poplar Prim Sch, SW19
off Poplar Rd S 222 DA97
Poplar Rd, SE24 184 DQ84
SW19 222 DA96
Ashford TW15 197 BQ92
Denham UB9 136 BJ64
Leatherhead KT22 253 CH122
Shalford GU4 280 AY141
Sutton SM3 221 CZ102
Wooburn Green HP10
off Glory Mill La 132 AE56
Poplar Rd S, SW19 222 DA97
Poplar Row, They.B. CM16 107 ES37
Poplars, Welw.G.C. AL7 52 DB08
Poplars, The, N14 103 DH43
Abridge RM4 off Hoe La 108 EV41
Borehamwood WD6
off Grove Rd 100 CN39
Cheshunt EN7 88 DS26
Gravesend DA12 213 GL87
Hemel Hempstead HP1 62 BH21
Magdalen Laver CM5 75 FB19
St. Albans AL1 65 CH24
Poplars Av, NW10 4 A5
Hatfield AL10 66 CR18
Poplars Cl, Hat. AL10 66 CQ18
Ruislip HA4 137 BS60
Watford WD25 81 BV32
Poplar Shaw, Wal.Abb. EN9 90 EF33
Poplars Rd, E17 145 EB58
Poplar St, Rom. RM7 149 FC56
Poplar Vw, Wem. HA9
off Magnet Rd 139 CK61
Poplar Wk, SE24 184 DQ84
Caterham CR3 258 DS123
Croydon CR0 224 DQ103
Poplar Way, Felt. TW13 197 BU90
Ilford IG6 147 EQ56
Poppins Ct, EC4 18 G9
Poppleton Rd, E11 146 EE58
Poppy Cl, Barn. EN5 102 DC44
Belvedere DA17 189 FB76
Hemel Hempstead HP1 61 BE19
Northolt UB5 158 BZ65
Pilgrim's Hatch CM15 130 FV43
Wallington SM6 222 DG102
★ Poppy Factory Mus, The, Rich. TW10 199 CK86
Poppyfields, Welw.G.C. AL7 52 DC09
Poppy La, Croy. CR0 224 DW101
Poppy Wk, Hat. AL10 67 CT15
Waltham Cross EN7 88 DR28
Porchester Cl, SE5 184 DQ84
Hornchurch RM11 150 FL58
Porchester Gdns, W2 15 L10
Porchester Gdns Ms, W2 15 M9
Porchester Gate, W2
off Bayswater Rd 27 N1
Porchester Mead, Beck. BR3 205 EA93
Porchester Ms, W2 15 M8
Porchester Pl, W2 16 D9
Porchester Rd, W2 15 L8
Kingston upon Thames KT1 220 CP96
Porchester Sq, W2 15 M8
Porchester Sq Ms, W2 15 M8
Porchester Ter, W2 15 N9
Porchester Ter N, W2 15 M8
Porchfield Cl, Grav. DA12 213 GJ89
Sutton SM2 240 DB110
Porch Way, N20 120 DF48
Porcupine Cl, SE9 206 EL89
Porden Rd, SW2 183 DM84
Porlock Av, Har. HA2 138 CC60
Porlock Rd, Enf. EN1 122 DT45
Porlock St, SE1 31 L4
Porridge Pot All, Guil. GU2
off Bury Flds 280 AW136
Porrington Cl, Chis. BR7 227 EM95
Portal Cl, SE27 203 DN90
Ruislip HA4 137 BU63
Uxbridge UB10 156 BL66
Portal Way, W3 160 CR71
Port Av, Green. DA9 211 FV86
Portbury Cl, SE15 44 D7
Port Cres, E13 24 A5
★ Portcullis Ho, SW1
off Bridge St 30 B5
Portcullis Lo Rd, Enf. EN2 104 DR41
Portelet Ct, N1 9 M8
Portelet Rd, E1 21 J3
Porten Rd, W14 26 E7
Porter Cl, Grays RM20 191 FW79
Porter Rd, E6 25 K8
Porters Av, Dag. RM8, RM9 168 EV65
Porters Cl, Brwd. CM14 130 FU46
Portersfield Rd, Enf. EN1 104 DS42
Porters Pk Dr, Shenley WD7 83 CK33
Porter Sq, N19 143 DL60
Porter St, SE1 31 K2
W1 16 F6
Porters Wk, E1 32 F1
Porters Way, N12 120 DE52
West Drayton UB7 176 BM76
Porters Wd, St.Alb. AL3 65 CE16
Porteus Rd, W2 15 P7
Portgate Cl, W9 15 H4
Porthallow Cl, Orp. BR6 245 ET105
Porthcawe Rd, SE26 205 DY91
Port Hill, Hert. SG14 54 DQ09
Orpington BR6 246 EV112
Porthkerry Av, Well. DA16 188 EU84
Portia Way, E3 21 N5
Coll Portico City Learning Cen, E5 10 G1
Portinscale Rd, SW15 201 CY85
Portland Av, N16 144 DT59
Gravesend DA12 213 GH89
New Malden KT3 221 CT101
Sidcup DA15 208 EU86
● Portland Business Cen, Datchet SL3 off Manor Ho La 174 AV81
Portland Cl, Rom. RM6 148 EY57
Slough SL2 153 AK70
Worcester Park KT4 221 CV101
● Portland Commercial Est, Bark. IG11 168 EW68
Portland Ct, SE1
off Falmouth Rd 31 L6
Portland Cres, SE9 206 EL89
Feltham TW13 197 BR91
Greenford UB6 158 CB70
Stanmore HA7 117 CK54
Portland Dr, Chsht EN7 88 DU31
Enfield EN2 104 DS38
Merstham RH1 273 DK129
Portland Gdns, N4 143 DP58
Romford RM6 148 EX57
Portland Gro, SW8 42 C6
Portland Hts, Nthwd. HA6 115 BT49
H Portland Hosp for Women & Children, The, W1 17 K5
Portland Ho, Merst. RH1 273 DJ129
Portland Ms, W1 17 M9
Portland Pk, Ger.Cr. SL9 134 AX58
Portland Pl, W1 17 J5
Epsom KT17 238 CS112
Greenhithe DA9 191 FW84
Hertford Heath SG13 54 DW11
Sch Portland Pl Sch, W1 17 K6
Portland Ri, N4 143 DP60
Portland Ri Est, N4 143 DP60
Portland Rd, N15 144 DT56
SE9 206 EL89
SE25 224 DU98
W11 26 F2
Ashford TW15 196 BL90
Bromley BR1 206 EJ91
Dorking RH4 285 CG135
Gravesend DA12 213 GH88
Hayes UB4 157 BS69
Kingston upon Thames KT1 220 CL97
Mitcham CR4 222 DE96
Southall UB2 178 BZ76
Portland Sq, E1 32 E2
Portland St, SE17 31 L10
St. Albans AL3 64 CC20
Portland Ter, Rich. TW9 179 CK84
Portland Wk, SE17 43 M2
Portley La, Cat. CR3 258 DS121
Portley Wd Rd, Whyt. CR3 258 DT120
Portman Av, SW14 180 CR83
Portman Cl, W1 16 F8
Bexley DA5 209 FE88
Bexleyheath DA7
off Queen Anne's Gate 188 EX83
St. Albans AL4 65 CJ15
Portman Dr, Wdf.Grn. IG8 124 EK54
Portman Gdns, NW9 118 CR54
Uxbridge UB10 156 BN66
Portman Gate, NW1 16 D5
Portman Hall, Har. HA3 117 CD50
Portman Ho, St.Alb. AL3 65 CD17
Portman Ms S, W1 16 G9
Portman Pl, E2 21 H3
Portman Rd, Kings.T. KT1 220 CM96
Portman Sq, W1 16 F8
Portman St, W1 16 G9
Portmeadow Wk, SE2 188 EX75
Portmeers Cl, E17
off Lennox Rd 145 EA58
Portmore Gdns, Rom. RM5 126 FA50
Portmore Pk Rd, Wey. KT13 234 BN105
Portmore Quays, Wey. KT13
off Weybridge Rd 234 BM105
Portmore Way, Wey. KT13 216 BN104
Portnall Dr, Vir.W. GU25 214 AT99
Portnall Ri, Vir.W. GU25 214 AT99
Portnall Rd, W9 14 G4
Virginia Water GU25 214 AT99
Portnalls Cl, Couls. CR5 257 DH116
Portnalls Ri, Couls. CR5 257 DH116
Portnalls Rd, Couls. CR5 257 DH118
Portnoi Cl, Rom. RM1 127 FD54
Portobello Cl, Chesh. HP5 76 AN29
Portobello Ct, W11 15 H9
Portobello Ms, W11 27 J1
Portobello Rd, W10 14 G8
W11 15 H10
Port of Tilbury, Til. RM18 192 GE84
Porton Ct, Surb. KT6 219 CJ100
Portpool La, EC1 18 E6
Portree Cl, N22 121 DM52
Portree St, E14 23 H8
Portsdown, Edg. HA8
off Rectory La 118 CN50
Portsdown Av, NW11 141 CZ58
Portsdown Ms, NW11 141 CZ58
Portsea Ms, W2 16 D9
Portsea Pl, W2 16 D9
Portsea Rd, Til. RM18 193 GJ81
Portslade Rd, SW8 41 L8
Portsmouth Av, T.Ditt. KT7 219 CG101
Portsmouth Cl, Slou. SL1 154 AS73
Portsmouth Ms, E16 36 B2
Portsmouth Rd, SW15 201 CV87
Cobham KT11 235 BU114
Esher KT10 236 CC105
Portsmouth Rd, Guildford GU1, GU3 280 AW138
Kingston upon Thames KT1 219 CJ99
Surbiton KT6 219 CJ99
Thames Ditton KT7 219 CE103
Woking GU23 250 BM119
Portsmouth St, WC2 18 C9
Portsoken St, E1 20 A10
Portswood Pl, SW15
off Danebury Ave 201 CT87
Portugal Gdns, Twick. TW2
off Fulwell Pk Av 198 CC89
Portugal Rd, Wok. GU21 249 AZ116
Portugal St, WC2 18 C9
Port Vale, Hert. SG14 53 DP08
Portway, E15 13 M8
Epsom KT17 239 CU110
Rainham RM13 169 FG67
Portway Cres, Epsom KT17 239 CU109
Portway Gdns, SE18
off Shooters Hill Rd 186 EK81
Sch Portway Prim Sch, E15 13 N9
Postern Grn, Enf. EN2 103 DN40
Postfield, Welw.G.C. AL7 52 DA06
Post Ho La, Bkhm KT23 268 CA125
Post La, Twick. TW2 199 CD88
Post Meadow, Iver SL0 155 BD69
Postmill Cl, Croy. CR0 225 DX104
Post Office App, E7 146 EH64
Post Office Ct, EC3 19 M9
Post Office La, Beac. HP9 111 AK52
George Green SL3 154 AX72
Post Office Rd, Harl. CM20 57 EQ14
Post Office Row, Oxt. RH8 276 EL131
Post Office Wk, Harl. CM20 57 ER14
Post Office Way, SW8 41 N4
Post Rd, Sthl. UB2 178 CB76
Postway Ms, Ilf. IG1
off Clements Rd 147 EP62
Postwood Grn, Hert.Hth SG13 54 DW12
Potash Rd, Ware SG12 55 DY08
Potier St, SE1 31 M7
Potiphar Pl, Warley CM14 130 FV49
Potkiln La, Jordans HP9 133 AQ55
POTTEN END, Berk. HP4 61 BC16
Sch Potten End First Sch, Pott.End HP4 off Church Rd 61 BB17
Potten End Hill, Hem.H. HP1 61 BD16
Potten End HP4 61 BD16
Potter Cl, Mitch. CR4 223 DH96
Potterells, N.Mymms AL9 85 CX25
Potteries, The, Barn. EN5 102 DA43
Ottershaw KT16 233 BE107
Potterne Cl, SW19 201 CX87
POTTERS BAR, EN6 86 DA32
⇌ Potters Bar 86 DA32
H Potters Bar Comm Hosp, Pot.B. EN6 86 DC34
Potters Cl, SE15 43 P4
Croydon CR0 225 DY102
Loughton IG10 106 EL40
Potters Ct, Pot.B. EN6 86 DA32
Potters Cross, Iver SL0 155 BE69
POTTERS CROUCH, St.Alb. AL2 82 BX25
Potters Fld, Harl. CM17 74 EX17
St. Albans AL3 65 CE16
Potters Flds, SE1 31 P3
Potters Gro, N.Mal. KT3 220 CQ98
Potters Hts Cl, Pnr. HA5 115 BV52
Potters La, SW16 203 DK93
Barnet EN5 102 DA42
Borehamwood WD6 100 CQ39
Send GU23 249 BB123
Potters Ms, Els. WD6 99 CK44
Potters Rd, SW6 39 N9
Barnet EN5 102 DB42
POTTER STREET, Harl. CM17 74 EW16
Potter St, Harl. CM17 74 EW16
Northwood HA6 115 BU53
Pinner HA5 115 BV53
Potter St Hill, Pnr. HA5 115 BV51
Sch Potter St Prim Sch, Harl. CM17
off Carters Mead 74 EW17
Potters Way, Reig. RH2 288 DC138
Pottery Cl, SE25 224 DV98
Pottery La, W11 26 E1
Pottery Rd, Bex. DA5 209 FC89
Brentford TW8 180 CL79
Pottery St, SE16 32 E5
Pott St, E2 20 F3
Pouchen End La, Hem.H. HP1 61 BD21
Poulcott, Wrays. TW19 194 AY86
Poulett Gdns, Twick. TW1 199 CG88
Poulett Rd, E6 167 EM68
Poulters Wd, Kes. BR2 244 EK106
Poultney Cl, Shenley WD7 84 CM32
Poulton Av, Sutt. SM1 222 DD104
Poulton Cl, E8 10 E4
Poulton Ct, W3
off Victoria Rd 160 CR71
Poultry, EC2 19 L9
Pound, The, Burn. SL1
off Hogfair La 152 AJ70
Pound Cl, Epsom KT19 238 CR111
Long Ditton KT6 219 CJ102
Lower Nazeing EN9 72 EE23
Orpington BR6 227 ER103
Pound Ct, Ashtd. KT21 254 CM118
Pound Ct Dr, Orp. BR6 227 ER103
Pound Cres, Fetch. KT22 253 CD121
Pound Fm Cl, Esher KT10 219 CD102
Pound Fld, Guil. GU1 264 AX133
Poundfield, Wat. WD25 97 BT35
Poundfield Ct, Wok. GU22
off High St 249 BC121
Poundfield Gdns, Wok. GU22 249 BC120
Poundfield Rd, Loug. IG10 107 EN43
Pound La, NW10 161 CU65
Epsom KT19 238 CR112
Knockholt Pound TN14 262 EX115
Sevenoaks TN13 279 FH124
Shenley WD7 84 CM33
Pound Pk Rd, SE7 36 E9
Pound Pl, SE9 207 EN86
Shalford GU4 281 AZ140
Pound Pl Cl, Shalf. GU4 281 AZ140
Pound Rd, Bans. SM7 255 CZ117
Chertsey KT16 216 BH101
Pound St, Cars. SM5 240 DF106
Poundwell, Welw.G.C. AL7 52 DA10
Pounsley Rd, Dunt.Grn TN13 278 FE121
Pountney Rd, SW11 40 G10
POVEREST, Orp. BR5 227 ET99
Sch Poverest Prim Sch, St.M.Cray BR5 off Tillingbourne Grn 228 EU99
Poverest Rd, Orp. BR5 227 ET99
Povey Cross Rd, Horl. RH6 290 DD150
Powder Mill La, Dart. DA1 210 FL89
Powder Mill La, Twickenham TW2 198 BZ88
Powdermill La, Wal.Abb. EN9 89 EB33
Powdermill Ms, Wal.Abb. EN9
off Powdermill La 89 EB33
Powdermill Way, Wal.Abb. EN9 89 EB32
Powell Av, Dart. DA2 211 FS89
Powell Cl, Chess. KT9
off Coppard Gdns 237 CK106
Edgware HA8 118 CM51
Guildford GU2 280 AT136
Horley RH6 290 DE147
Sch Powell Corderoy Prim Sch, Dor. RH4 off Longfield Rd 285 CF137
Powell Gdns, Dag. RM10 148 FA63
Redhill RH1 273 DH132
Powell Pl, E4 105 EB42
Powell Rd, E5 144 DV62
Buckhurst Hill IG9 124 EJ45
Powells Cl, Dor. RH4
off Goodwyns Rd 285 CJ139
Powell's Wk, W4 180 CS79
Power Cl, Guil. GU1 264 AW133
● Powergate Business Pk, NW10 160 CR69
● Power Ind Est, Erith DA8 189 FG81
Power Rd, W4 180 CN77
Powers Ct, Twick. TW1 199 CK87
Powerscroft Rd, E5 10 G1
Sidcup DA14 208 EW93
Powis Ct, Pot.B. EN6 86 DC34
Powis Gdns, NW11 141 CZ59
W11 15 H8
Powis Ms, W11 15 H8
Powis Pl, WC1 18 B5
Powis Rd, E3 22 D3
Powis Sq, W11 15 H8
Powis St, SE18 37 L7
Powis Ter, W11 15 H8
Powle Ter, Ilf. IG1
off Oaktree Gro 147 ER64
Powlett Pl, NW1 7 H6
Pownall Gdns, Houns. TW3 178 CB84
Pownall Rd, E8 10 B9
Hounslow TW3 178 CB84
Pownsett Ter, Ilf. IG1
off Buttsbury Rd 147 EQ64
Powster Rd, Brom. BR1 206 EH92
Powys Cl, Bexh. DA7 188 EX79
Powys Ct, Borwd. WD6 100 CR41
Powys La, N13 121 DL50
N14 121 DL49
POYLE, Slou. SL3 175 BE81
Poyle La, Burn. SL1 152 AH67
Poyle New Cotts, Colnbr. SL3 175 BF82
Poyle Pk, Colnbr. SL3 175 BE83
Poyle Rd, Colnbr. SL3 175 BE83
Guildford GU1 280 AY136
● Poyle Tech Cen, Slou. SL3 175 BE82
Poyle Ter, Guil. GU1
off Sydenham Rd 280 AX136
Poynder Rd, Til. RM18 193 GH81
Poynders Ct, SW4
off Poynders Rd 203 DJ86
Poynders Gdns, SW4 203 DJ87
Poynders Hill, Hem.H. HP2 63 BQ21
Poynders Rd, SW4 203 DJ86
Poynes Rd, Horl. RH6 290 DE146
Poynings, The, Iver SL0 175 BF77
Poynings Cl, Orp. BR6 228 EV103
Poynings Rd, N19 143 DJ62
Poynings Way, N12 120 DA50
Romford RM3
off Arlington Gdns 128 FL53
Poyntell Cres, Chis. BR7 227 ER95
Poynter Ho, W11 26 D2
Poynter Rd, Enf. EN1 104 DU43
Poynton Rd, N17 122 DU54
Poyntz Rd, SW11 40 E9
Poyser St, E2 20 F1
Prae, The, Wok. GU22 249 BF118
Prae Cl, St.Alb. AL3 64 CB19
Praed Ms, W2 16 B8
Praed St, W2 16 C7
Praetorian Ct, St.Alb. AL1 64 CC23
Sch Prae Wd Prim Sch, St.Alb. AL3 off King Harry La 64 CA22
Pragel St, E13 24 B1
Pragnell Rd, SE12 206 EH89
Prague Pl, SW2 203 DL85
Prah Rd, N4 143 DN61
Prairie Cl, Add. KT15 216 BH104
Prairie Rd, Add. KT15 216 BH104
Prairie St, SW8 41 H9
Pratt Ms, NW1 7 L9
PRATT'S BOTTOM, Orp. BR6 246 EV110
Sch Pratts Bottom Prim Sch, Pr.Bot. BR6 off Hookwood Rd 246 EW111
Pratts La, Hersham KT12
off Molesey Rd 236 BX105
Pratts Pas, Kings.T. KT1
off Clarence St 220 CL96
Pratt St, NW1 7 L9
Pratt Wk, SE11 30 D8
Prayle Gro, NW2 141 CX60
Prebend Gdns, W4 181 CT76
W6 181 CT76
Prebend St, N1 9 J9
Precinct, The, Egh. TW20
off High St 195 BA92
West Molesey KT8
off Victoria Av 218 CB97
Precinct Rd, Hayes UB3 157 BU73
Precincts, The, Burn. SL1 152 AH70
Morden SM4 off Green La 222 DA100
Premier Av, Grays RM16 192 GC75
Premier Cor, W9 14 G1
Premiere Pl, E14 34 A1
● Premier Pk, NW10 160 CP67
Premier Pk Rd, NW10 160 CP68
Premier Pl, Wat. WD18 97 BT43
Sch Prendergast - Hilly Flds Coll, SE4 off Adelaide Av 185 EA84
Sch Prendergast - Ladywell Flds Coll, SE4 off Manwood Rd 205 EA86
Prendergast Rd, SE3 47 K10
Prentice Pl, Harl. CM17 74 EW17
Prentis Rd, SW16 203 DK91
Prentiss Ct, SE7 36 E9
Presburg Rd, N.Mal. KT3 220 CS99
Prescelly Pl, Edg. HA8 118 CM53
Prescot St, E1 20 B10
Prescott Av, Petts Wd BR5 227 EP100
Prescott Cl, SW16 203 DL94
Prescott Grn, Loug. IG10 107 EQ41
Prescott Ho, SE17 43 H3
Prescott Pl, SW4 183 DK83
Prescott Rd, Chsht EN8 89 DY27
Colnbrook SL3 175 BE82
Presdales Ct, Ware SG12
off Presdales Dr 55 DY07
Presdales Dr, Ware SG12 55 DX07
Sch Presdales Sch, Ware SG12
off Hoe La 55 DX08
Presentation Ms, SW2 203 DM89
Preshaw Cres, Mitch. CR4
off Lower Grn W 222 DE97
President Dr, E1 32 E2
President St, EC1 19 J2
Prespa Cl, N9 off Hudson Way 122 DW47
Press Ct, SE1 32 C10
Press Rd, NW10 140 CR62
Uxbridge UB8 156 BK65
Prestage Way, E14 22 F10
Prestbury Ct, Wok. GU21
off Muirfield Rd 248 AU118
Prestbury Cres, Bans. SM7 256 DF116
Prestbury Rd, E7 166 EJ66
Prestbury Sq, SE9 207 EM91
Prested Rd, SW11
off St. John's Hill 182 DE84
Prestige Way, NW4
off Heriot Rd 141 CW57
PRESTON, Wem. HA9 139 CK59
Preston Av, E4 123 ED51
Preston Cl, SE1 31 N8
Twickenham TW2 199 CE90
Preston Ct, Walt. KT12 218 BW102
Jct Preston Cross, Lthd. KT23 268 BZ126
Preston Dr, E11 146 EJ57
Bexleyheath DA7 188 EX81
Epsom KT19 238 CS107
Preston Gdns, NW10
off Church Rd 160 CS65
Enfield EN3 105 DY37
Ilford IG1 146 EL58
Preston Gro, Ashtd. KT21 253 CJ117
Preston Hill, Chesh. HP5 76 AR29
Harrow HA3 140 CM58
Preston La, Tad. KT20 255 CV121
Sch Preston Manor High Sch, Wem. HA9 off Carlton Av E 140 CM61
Sch Preston Pk Prim Sch, Wem. HA9 off College Rd 139 CK60
Preston Pl, NW2 161 CU65
Richmond TW10 200 CL85
⊖ Preston Road 140 CL60
Preston Rd, E11 146 EE58
SE19 203 DP93
SW20 201 CT94
Harrow HA3 140 CL59
Northfleet DA11 212 GE88
Romford RM3 128 FK49
Shepperton TW17 216 BN99
Slough SL2 154 AW73
Wembley HA9 140 CL61
Prestons Rd, E14 34 F4
Bromley BR2 226 EG104
Preston Waye, Har. HA3 140 CL60
Prestwick Cl, Sthl. UB2
off Ringway 178 BY78
Prestwick Rd, Wat. WD19 116 BX50
Prestwood, Slou. SL2 154 AV72
Prestwood Av, Har. HA3 139 CH56
Prestwood Cl, SE18 188 EU80
Harrow HA3 139 CH56
Prestwood Dr, Rom. RM5 127 FC50
Prestwood Gdns, Croy. CR0 224 DQ101
Prestwood St, N1 19 K1
Pretoria Av, E17 145 DY56
Pretoria Cl, N17 122 DT52
Pretoria Cres, E4 123 EC46
Pretoria Ho, Erith DA8
off Waterhead Cl 189 FE80
Pretoria Rd, E4 123 EC46
E11 145 ED60
E16 23 L4
N17 122 DT52
SW16 203 DH93
Chertsey KT16 215 BF102
Ilford IG1 147 EP64
Romford RM7 149 FC56
Watford WD18 97 BU42
Pretoria Rd N, N18 122 DT51
Pretty La, Couls. CR5 257 DJ121
Prevost Rd, N11 120 DG47
Prey Heath, Wok. GU22 248 AV123
Prey Heath Cl, Wok. GU22 248 AW124
Prey Heath Rd, Wok. GU22 248 AV124
Price Cl, NW7 119 CY51
SW17 202 DF90
Price Rd, Croy. CR0 241 DP106
Price's Ct, SW11 40 A10
Prices La, Reig. RH2 288 DA137
Prices Ms, N1 8 D8
Price's St, SE1 31 H3
Price Way, Hmptn. TW12
off Victors Dr 198 BY93
Prichard Ct, N7 8 C3
Prichard Ho, SE11
off Hotspur St 30 E9
Pricklers Hill, Barn. EN5 102 DB44
Prickley Wd, Brom. BR2 226 EF102
Priddy Pl, Red. RH1 273 DJ131
Priddy's Yd, Croy. CR0
off Church St 224 DQ103
Prideaux Pl, W3 160 CR73
WC1 18 D2
Prideaux Rd, SW9 42 B10
Pridham Rd, Th.Hth. CR7 224 DR98
Priest Ct, EC2 19 J8
Priestfield Rd, SE23 205 DY90
Priest Hill, Egh. TW20 194 AW90
Old Windsor SL4 194 AW90
Priestland Gdns, Berk. HP4 60 AY17
Priestlands Cl, Horl. RH6 290 DF147
Priestlands Pk Rd, Sid. DA15 207 ET90
Priestley Cl, N16 144 DT59
Priestley Gdns, Rom. RM6 148 EV58
Priestley Rd, Mitch. CR4 222 DG96
Priestley Way, E17 145 DX55
NW2 141 CU60
Priestly Gdns, Wok. GU22 249 BA120
Priestman Pt, E3 22 C3
Sch Priestmead First & Mid Schs, Kenton HA3
off Hartford Av 139 CH55
Priest Pk Av, Har. HA2 138 CA61
Priests Av, Rom. RM1 127 FD54
Priests Br, SW14 180 CS84
SW15 180 CS84
Priests Fld, Ingrave CM13 131 GC50
Priests La, Brwd. CM15 130 FY47
Priests Paddock, Knot.Grn HP9 110 AJ50
Prima Rd, SW9 42 E4
Primary Rd, Slou. SL1 173 AR76
Primeplace Ms, Th.Hth. CR7 224 DQ96

Prime Zone Ms, N8 143 DL58
Primley La, Sheering CM22 59 FC06
Primrose Av, Enf. EN2 104 DR39
Horley RH6 291 DH150
Romford RM6 148 EV59
Primrose Cl, E3 22 A1
N3 120 DB54
SE6 205 EC92
Harrow HA2 138 BZ62
Hatfield AL10 67 CV19
Hemel Hempstead HP1 61 BE21
Wallington SM6 223 DH102
Primrose Ct, Brwd. CM14
off White Lyons Rd 130 FW48
Primrose Dr, Hert. SG13 54 DV09
West Drayton UB7 176 BK77
Primrose Fld, Harl. CM18 73 ET18
Primrose Gdns, NW3 6 D4
Bushey WD23 116 CB45
Radlett WD7
off Aldenham Rd 99 CG35
Ruislip HA4 138 BW64
Primrose Glen, Horn. RM11 150 FL56
PRIMROSE HILL, NW8 6 E8
Primrose Hill, EC4 18 F9
Brentwood CM14 130 FW48
Kings Langley WD4 81 BP28
Primrose Hill Ct, NW3 6 E7
Sch Primrose Hill Prim Sch, NW1 7 H8
Primrose Hill Rd, NW3 6 E6
Primrose Hill Studios, NW1 6 G8
Primrose La, Ald. WD25 99 CD38
Croydon CR0 225 DX102
Primrose Ms, NW1 6 F7
SE3 186 EH80
W5 *off St. Mary's Rd* 179 CK75
Primrose Path, Chsht EN7 88 DU31
Primrose Pl, Islw. TW7 179 CF82
Primrose Rd, E10 145 EB60
E18 124 EH54
Hersham KT12 236 BW106
Primrose Sq, E9 11 H7
Primrose St, EC2 19 N6
Primrose Wk, SE14 45 M4
Ewell KT17 239 CT108
Primrose Way, Wem. HA0 159 CK68
Primula St, W12 161 CU72
Prince Albert Rd, NW1 16 D1
NW8 16 D1
Prince Albert Sq, Red. RH1 288 DF139
Prince Alberts Wk, Wind. SL4 174 AU81
Prince Arthur Ms, NW3 5 P1
Prince Arthur Rd, NW3 5 P2
Prince Charles Av, S.Darenth DA4 231 FR96
Prince Charles Dr, NW4 141 CW59
Prince Charles Rd, SE3 47 L6
Prince Charles Way, Wall. SM6 223 DH104
Prince Consort Cotts, Wind. SL4 173 AR82
Prince Consort Dr, Chis. BR7 227 ER95
Prince Consort Rd, SW7 27 P6
Princedale Rd, W11 26 F2
Prince Edward Rd, E9 11 P5
Prince Edward St, Berk. HP4 60 AW19
Prince George Av, N14 103 DJ42
Prince George Duke of Kent Ct, Chis. BR7 *off Holbrook La* 207 ER94
Prince George Rd, N16 9 P1
Prince George's Av, SW20 221 CW96
Prince George's Rd, SW19 222 DD95
Prince Henry Rd, SE7 186 EK80
★ Prince Henry's Room, EC4 18 E9
Prince Imperial Rd, SE18 187 EM81
Chislehurst BR7 207 EP94
Prince John Rd, SE9 206 EL85
Princelet St, E1 20 B6
Prince of Orange La, SE10 46 E4
Prince of Wales Cl, NW4 *off Church Ter* 141 CV56
Prince of Wales Dr, SW8 41 K5
SW11 40 E7
Prince of Wales Footpath, Enf. EN3 105 DY38
Prince of Wales Gate, SW7 28 C4
Prince of Wales Pas, NW1 17 L3
Sch Prince of Wales Prim Sch, Enf. EN3 *off Salisbury Rd* 105 DZ37
Prince of Wales Rd, NW5 7 H5
SE3 47 M7
Outwood RH1 289 DN143
Sutton SM1 222 DD103
Prince of Wales Ter, W4 180 CS78
W8 27 M5
Prince Pk, Hem.H. HP1 62 BG21
DLR Prince Regent 24 C10
⊖ Prince Regent 24 D10
Prince Regent La, E13 24 C7
E16 24 C7
Prince Regent Ms, NW1 17 L3
Prince Regent Rd, Houns. TW3 178 CC83
Prince Rd, SE25 224 DS99
Prince Rupert Rd, SE9 187 EM84
Prince's Arc, SW1 29 M2
Princes Av, N3 120 DA53
N10 142 DG55
N13 121 DN50
N22 121 DK53
NW9 140 CP56
W3 180 CN76
Carshalton SM5 240 DF108
Dartford DA2 210 FP88
Enfield EN3 105 DY36
Greenford UB6 158 CB72
Petts Wood BR5 227 ES99
South Croydon CR2 258 DV115
Surbiton KT6 220 CN102
Watford WD18 97 BT43
Woodford Green IG8 124 EH49
Princes Cl, N4 143 DP60
NW9 140 CN56
SW4 *off Old Town* 183 DJ83
Berkhamsted HP4 60 AU17
Edgware HA8 118 CN50
Eton Wick SL4 173 AM78
North Weald Bassett CM16 93 FC25
Sidcup DA14 208 EX90
South Croydon CR2 258 DV115
Teddington TW11 199 CD91
Princes Ct, SE16 33 N7
SW3 *off Brompton Rd* 28 E6
Hemel Hempstead HP3 62 BH23
Wembley HA9 140 CL64
● Princes Ct Business Cen, E1 32 F1
Princes Dr, Har. HA1 139 CE55
Prince's Dr, Oxshott KT22 237 CE112
Princesfield Rd, Wal.Abb. EN9 90 EH33
Coll Prince's Foundation, The, EC2 19 N4
Princes Gdns, SW7 28 B6
W3 160 CN71
W5 159 CJ70
Princes Gate, Harl. CM20 57 ES12
Princes Gate, SW7 28 C5
Princes Gate Ct, SW7 28 B5
Princes Gate Ms, SW7 28 B6
Princes La, N10 143 DH55
Ruislip HA4 137 BS60
Princes Ms, W2 15 L10
Hounslow TW3 178 CA84
Princes Par, Pot.B. EN6 *off High St* 86 DC32
Princes Pk, Rain. RM13 169 FG66
Princes Pk Av, NW11 141 CY58
Hayes UB3 157 BR73
Princes Pk Circle, Hayes UB3 157 BR73
Princes Pk Cl, Hayes UB3 157 BR73
Princes Pk La, Hayes UB3 157 BR73
Princes Pk Par, Hayes UB3 157 BR73
Princes Pl, SW1 29 M2
W11 26 E2
Princes Plain, Brom. BR2 226 EL101
Sch Princes Plain Prim Sch, Brom. BR2 *off Church La* 226 EL101
Princes Ri, SE13 46 F8
Princes Riverside Rd, SE16 33 J2
Princes Rd, N18 122 DW49
SE20 205 DX93
SW14 180 CR83
SW19 202 DA93
W13 *off Broomfield Rd* 159 CH74
Ashford TW15 196 BM92
Bourne End SL8 132 AC60
Buckhurst Hill IG9 124 EJ47
Dartford DA1, DA2 209 FG86
Egham TW20 195 AZ93
Feltham TW13 197 BT89
Gravesend DA12 213 GJ90
Ilford IG6 147 ER56
Kew TW9 180 CM81
Kingston upon Thames KT2 200 CN94
Redhill RH1 288 DF136
Richmond TW10 200 CM85
Romford RM1 149 FG57
Swanley BR8 209 FG93
Teddington TW11 199 CD91
Weybridge KT13 235 BP106
Jct Princes Rd Interchange, Dart. DA1 210 FP88
H Princess Alexandra Hosp, Harl. CM20 57 EP14
Princess Alice Way, SE28 187 ER75
Princess Av, Wem. HA9 140 CL61
Windsor SL4 173 AP83
Princess Cl, SE28 168 EX72
Princess Cres, N4 143 DP61
Princess Diana Dr, St.Alb. AL4 65 CK21
Princesses Wk, Kew TW9 *off Royal Botanic Gdns* 180 CL80
Sch Princess Frederica C of E Prim Sch, NW10 14 A1
Princess Gdns, Wok. GU22 249 BB116
H Princess Grace Hosp, The, W1 16 G5
Princess Gro, Seer Grn HP9 111 AR49
Princess Louise Cl, W2 16 B6
H Princess Margaret Hosp, Wind. SL4 173 AR82
Princess Mary Cl, Guil. GU2 264 AU130
Princess Mary's Rd, Add. KT15 234 BJ105
Sch Princess May Prim Sch, N16 10 A2
Princess May Rd, N16 9 P1
Princess Ms, NW3 6 B4
Kingston upon Thames KT1 220 CM97
Princess Par, Orp. BR6 *off Crofton Rd* 227 EN104
Princess Pk Manor, N11 120 DG50
Princess Prec, Horl. RH6 *off High St* 291 DH148
Princes Sq, W2 15 L10
Princess Rd, NW1 6 G8
NW6 15 J1
Croydon CR0 224 DQ100
Woking GU22 249 BB116
H Princess Royal Uni Hosp, The, Orp. BR6 227 EN104
Princess St, SE1 31 H7
Princes St, EC2 19 L8
N17 122 DS51
W1 17 K9
Bexleyheath DA7 188 EZ84
Gravesend DA11 213 GH86
Richmond TW9 *off Sheen Rd* 200 CL85
Slough SL1 174 AV75
Sutton SM1 240 DD105
Ware SG12 55 DX06
Princess Way, Red. RH1 272 DG133
Princes Ter, E13 166 EH67
Prince St, SE8 45 P2
Watford WD17 98 BW41
Princes Vw, Dart. DA1 210 FN88
Princes Way, SW19 201 CX87
Buckhurst Hill IG9 124 EJ47
Croydon CR0 241 DM106
Hutton CM13 131 GA46
Ruislip HA4 138 BY63
West Wickham BR4 244 EF105
Princes Yd, W11 26 F3
Princethorpe Ho, W2 15 K6
Princethorpe Rd, SE26 205 DX91
Princeton Ct, SW15 *off Felsham Rd* 181 CX83
Princeton St, WC1 18 C6
Principal Cl, N14 121 DJ46
Principal Sq, E9 *off Chelmer Rd* 11 K2
Pringle Gdns, SW16 203 DJ91
Purley CR8 241 DM110
Sch Prins Willem Alexander Sch, Wok. GU22 *off Old Woking Rd* 249 BC117
Printers Av, Wat. WD18 97 BS43
Printers Inn Ct, EC4 18 E8
Printers Ms, E3 11 M9
Printer St, EC4 18 F8
Printers Way, Harl. CM20 58 EU10
Printing Ho La, Hayes UB3 177 BS75
Printing Ho Sq, Guil. GU1 *off Martyr Rd* 280 AX135
Printing Ho Yd, E2 19 P2
Print Village, SE15 44 B9
Priolo Rd, SE7 186 EJ78
Prior Av, Sutt. SM2 240 DE108
Prior Bolton St, N1 9 H5
Prior Chase, Bad.Dene RM17 192 FZ77
Prioress Cres, Green. DA9 191 FW84
Prioress Ho, E3 *off Bromley High St* 22 D2
Prioress Rd, SE27 203 DP90
Prioress St, SE1 31 M7
Prior Gro, Chesh. HP5 76 AQ30
Prior Rd, Ilf. IG1 147 EN62
Priors, The, Ashtd. KT21 253 CK119
Priors Cl, Hert.Hth SG13 54 DV12
Slough SL1 174 AU76
Priors Ct, Wok. GU21 248 AU118
Priors Cft, E17 123 DY54
Woking GU22 249 BA120
Priors Fm La, Nthlt. UB5 158 BZ65
Priors Fld, Nthlt. UB5 *off Arnold Rd* 158 BY65
Priorsford Av, Orp. BR5 228 EU98
Priors Gdns, Ruis. HA4 138 BW64
Priors Mead, Bkhm KT23 268 CC125
Enfield EN1 104 DS39
Priors Pk, Horn. RM12 150 FJ62
Priors Rd, Wind. SL4 173 AK83
Prior St, SE10 46 E5
Priors Wd Rd, Hert.Hth SG13 54 DW12
Sch Prior Weston Prim Sch, EC1 19 K5
Priory, The, SE3 186 EF84
Croydon CR0 *off Epsom Rd* 241 DN105
Godstone RH9 274 DV131
Priory Av, E4 123 DZ48
E17 145 EA57
N8 143 DK56
W4 180 CS77
Harefield UB9 136 BJ56
Harlow CM17 58 EW10
Petts Wood BR5 227 ER100
Sutton SM3 239 CX105
Wembley HA0 139 CF63
Priory Cl, E4 123 DZ48
E18 124 EG53
N3 119 CZ53
N14 103 DH43
N20 119 CZ45
SW19 *off High Path* 222 DB95
Beckenham BR3 225 DY97
Broxbourne EN10 71 DY24
Chislehurst BR7 227 EM95
Dartford DA1 210 FJ85
Denham UB9 136 BG62
Dorking RH4 285 CG138
Hampton TW12 218 BZ95
Harefield UB9 136 BH56
Hayes UB3 157 BV73
Hoddesdon EN11 71 EA18
Horley RH6 290 DF147
Pilgrim's Hatch CM15 130 FU43
Ruislip HA4 137 BT60
Stanmore HA7 117 CF48
Sudbury HA0 139 CF63
Sunbury-on-Thames TW16 *off Staines Rd E* 197 BU94
Walton-on-Thames KT12 217 BU104
Woking GU21 233 BD113
Sch Priory C of E Prim Sch, The, SW19 *off Queens Rd* 202 DB92
Priory Ct, E17 145 DZ55
EC4 *off Carter La* 19 H9
SW8 41 P7
Berkhamsted HP4 60 AW19
Bushey WD23 *off Sparrows Herne* 116 CC46
Epsom KT17 *off Old Schs La* 239 CT109
Guildford GU2 *off Portsmouth Rd* 280 AW137
Harlow CM18 74 EV17
Priory Ct Est, E17 *off Priory Ct* 123 DZ54
Priory Ct Ho, SE6 205 EB88
Priory Cres, SE19 204 DQ94
Sutton SM3 239 CX105
Wembley HA0 139 CG62
Priory Dr, SE2 188 EX78
Reigate RH2 288 DA136
Stanmore HA7 117 CF48
Priory Fld Dr, Edg. HA8 118 CP49
Priory Flds, Eyns. DA4 230 FM103
Watford WD17 97 BT39
Priory Gdns, N6 143 DH58
SE25 224 DT98
SW13 181 CT83
W4 180 CS77
W5 *off Hanger La* 160 CM69
Ashford TW15 197 BR92
Berkhamsted HP4 60 AW19
Dartford DA1 210 FK85
Hampton TW12 198 BZ94
Harefield UB9 136 BJ56
Wembley HA0 139 CG63
Priory Gate, Chsht EN8 89 DZ27
Priory Grn, Stai. TW18 196 BH92
Priory Grn Est, N1 8 C10
Priory Gro, SW8 42 A8
Barnet EN5 102 DA43
Romford RM3 128 FL48
Priory Hts, N1 8 C10
Slough SL1 *off Buckingham Av* 153 AL72
Priory Hill, Dart. DA1 210 FK86
Wembley HA0 139 CG63
H Priory Hosp, The, SW15 181 CT84
H Priory Hosp Hayes Gro, The, Hayes BR2 226 EG103
H Priory Hosp N London, N14 121 DL46
Priory Ho, SE7 *off Springfield Gro* 186 EJ79
Priory La, SW15 200 CS86
Eynsford DA4 230 FM102
Richmond TW9 180 CN80
West Molesey KT8 218 CA98
Priory Ms, SW8 42 A7
Hornchurch RM11 149 FH60
Staines-upon-Thames TW18 196 BH92
Priory Pk, SE3 186 EF83
Priory Pk Rd, NW6 5 H8
Wembley HA0 139 CG63
Priory Path, Rom. RM3 128 FL48
Priory Pl, Dart. DA1 210 FK86
Walton-on-Thames KT12 217 BU104
Priory Post 16 Cen, SE19 *off Hermitage Rd* 204 DR93
Priory Rd, E6 166 EK67
N8 143 DK56
NW6 5 L8
SW19 202 DD94
Priory Rd, W4 180 CR76
Barking IG11 167 ER66
Chalfont St. Peter SL9 134 AX55
Chessington KT9 220 CL104
Croydon CR0 223 DN101
Hampton TW12 198 BZ94
Hounslow TW3 198 CC85
Loughton IG10 106 EL42
Reigate RH2 288 DA136
Richmond TW9 180 CN79
Romford RM3 128 FL48
Slough SL1 152 AJ71
Sutton SM3 239 CX105
Priory Rd N, Dart. DA1 190 FK84
Priory Rd S, Dart. DA1 210 FK85
Sch Priory Sch, SE25 *off Tennison Rd* 224 DT98
Slough SL1 *off Orchard Av* 153 AK71
Sch Priory Sch, The, Bans. SM7 *off Bolters La* 256 DA115
Dorking RH4 *off West Bk* 285 CF137
Orpington BR5 *off Tintagel Rd* 228 EW102
Priory Shop Cen, Dart. DA1 210 FL86
Priory St, E3 22 D2
Hertford SG14 54 DR09
Ware SG12 54 DW06
Priory Ter, NW6 5 L8
Sunbury-on-Thames TW16 *off Staines Rd E* 197 BU94
Priory Vw, Bushey Hth WD23 117 CE45
Priory Wk, SW10 39 P1
Saint Albans AL1 65 CE23
Priory Way, Chal.St.P. SL9 134 AX55
Datchet SL3 174 AV80
Harmondsworth UB7 176 BL79
Harrow HA2 138 CB56
Southall UB2 178 BX76
Priory Wf, Hert. SG14 *off Priory St* 54 DR09
Priscilla Cl, N15 144 DQ57
Pritchard's Rd, E2 10 D9
Pritchett Cl, Enf. EN3 105 EA37
Priter Rd, SE16 32 D7
Private Rd, Enf. EN1 104 DS43
Probert Rd, SW2 203 DN85
Probyn Ho, SW1 *off Page St* 29 P8
Probyn Rd, SW2 203 DP89
Procter Ho, SE1 32 C10
Procter St, WC1 18 C7
Proctor Cl, Mitch. CR4 222 DG95
Proctor Gdns, Bkhm KT23 268 CB125
Proctors Cl, Felt. TW14 197 BU88
Profumo Rd, Hersham KT12 236 BX106
● Progress Business Cen, Slou. SL1 153 AK72
● Progress Business Pk, Croy. CR0 223 DM103
● Progression Cen, The, Hem.H. HP2 62 BN17
Progress Way, N22 121 DN53
Croydon CR0 223 DM103
Enfield EN1 104 DU43
● Prologis Pk Heathrow, West Dr. UB7 177 BP76
Promenade, Edg. HA8 118 CN50
Promenade, The, W4 180 CS81
Promenade App Rd, W4 180 CS80
Promenade de Verdun, Pur. CR8 241 DK111
Promenade Mans, Edg. HA8 *off Hale La* 118 CN50
● Prospect Business Pk, Loug. IG10 107 ER42
Prospect Cl, SE26 204 DV91
Belvedere DA17 188 FA77
Bushey WD23 117 CD45
Hounslow TW3 178 BZ81
Ruislip HA4 138 BX59
Prospect Cotts, SW18 182 DA84
Prospect Cres, Twick. TW2 198 CC86
Prospect Gro, Grav. DA12 213 GK87
Prospect Hill, E17 145 EB56
Prospect Ho, SW19 *off Chapter Way* 222 DD95
Prospect La, Eng.Grn TW20 194 AT92
Prospect Pl, Dart. DA1 210 FK86
Prospect Pl, E1 32 G2
N2 142 DD56
N7 8 B1
N17 122 DS52
NW2 *off Ridge Rd* 141 CZ62
NW3 5 N1
SW20 201 CV94
W4 *off Chiswick High Rd* 180 CR78
Bromley BR2 226 EH97
Epsom KT17 238 CS113
Gravesend DA12 213 GK87
Grays RM17 192 GB79
Romford RM5 127 FC54
Staines-upon-Thames TW18 195 BF92
Prospect Quay, SW18 182 DA84
Prospect Ring, N2 142 DD55
Prospect Rd, NW2 141 CZ62
Barnet EN5 102 DA43
Cheshunt EN8 88 DW29
Hornchurch RM11 150 FM55
Long Ditton KT6 219 CJ100
St. Albans AL1 65 CD22
Sevenoaks TN13 279 FJ123
Woodford Green IG8 124 EJ50
Prospect St, SE16 32 F6
Prospect Vale, SE18 36 G8
Prospect Way, Hutt. CM13 131 GE42
Prospero Rd, N19 143 DJ60
Prossers, Tad. KT20 255 CX121
Protea Cl, E16 23 L4
Prothero Gdns, NW4 141 CV57
Prothero Rd, SW6 38 F4
Prout Gro, NW10 140 CS63
Prout Rd, E5 144 DV62
Provence St, N1 9 J10
Providence Av, Har. HA2 *off Goodwill Dr* 138 CA60
Providence Cl, E9 11 K8
Providence Ct, W1 17 H10
Providence La, Harling. UB3 177 BR80
Providence Pl, N1 8 G8
Epsom KT17 238 CS112
Romford RM5 126 EZ54
Woking GU22 234 BG114
Providence Rd, West Dr. UB7 156 BL74
Providence Row, N1 *off Pentonville Rd* 18 C1
Providence Row Cl, E2 *off Ainsley St* 20 F3
Providence Sq, SE1 *off Jacob St* 32 C4
Providence St, Green. DA9 211 FU85
Providence Yd, E2 20 C2
● Provident Ind Est, Hayes UB3 177 BU75
Provost Est, N1 19 L2
Provost Rd, NW3 6 F6
Provost St, N1 19 L3
Prowse Av, Bushey Hth WD23 116 CC47
Prowse Pl, NW1 7 L6
Prudence La, Orp. BR6 245 EN105
Pruden Cl, N14 121 DJ47
Prudent Pas, EC2 19 K8
Prune Hill, Eng.Grn TW20 194 AX94
Prusom St, E1 32 F3
Pryor Cl, Abb.L. WD5 81 BT32
Pryors, The, NW3 142 DD62
★ P.S. Tattershall Castle, SW1 30 B3
Puck La, Wal.Abb. EN9 89 ED29
Pucknells Cl, Swan. BR8 229 FC95
Puddenhole Cotts, Bet. RH3 270 CN133
Pudding La, EC3 31 M1
Chigwell IG7 125 ET46
Hemel Hempstead HP1 62 BG18
St. Albans AL3 *off Market Pl* 65 CD20
Seal TN15 *off Church St* 279 FN121
DLR Pudding Mill Lane 12 C9
Pudding Mill La, E15 12 D9
Puddingstone Dr, St.Alb. AL4 65 CJ22
Puddle Dock, EC4 19 H10
Puddledock La, Dart. DA2 209 FE92
Westerham TN16 277 ET133
PUDDS CROSS, Hem.H. HP3 78 AX29
Puers Fld, Jordans HP9 112 AS51
Puers La, Jordans HP9 112 AS51
Puffin Cl, Bark. IG11 168 EV69
Beckenham BR3 225 DX99
Puffin Ter, Ilf. IG5 *off Tiptree Cres* 147 EN55
Pulborough Rd, SW18 201 CZ87
Pulborough Way, Houns. TW4 178 BW84
Pulford Rd, N15 144 DR58
Pulham Av, N2 142 DC56
Broxbourne EN10 71 DX21
Pulham Ho, SW8 *off Dorset Rd* 42 C5
Puller Rd, Barn. EN5 101 CY40
Hemel Hempstead HP1 62 BG21
Pulleyns Av, E6 25 H2
Pulleys Cl, Hem.H. HP1 61 BF19
Pulleys La, Hem.H. HP1 61 BF19
Pullfields, Chesh. HP5 76 AN30
Pullman Cl, St.Alb. AL1 *off Ramsbury Rd* 65 CE22
Pullman Ct, SW2 203 DL88
Pullman Gdns, SW15 201 CW86
Pullman Ms, SE12 206 EH90
Pullman Pl, SE9 206 EL85
Pullmans Pl, Stai. TW18 196 BG92
Pulpit Cl, Chesh. HP5 76 AN29
Pulross Rd, SW9 183 DM83
Pulse, The, Colnbr. SL3 175 BE81
Pulse Apts, NW6 5 M3
Pulteney Cl, E3 11 N9
Isleworth TW7 *off Gumley Gdns* 179 CG83
Pulteney Gdns, E18 *off Pulteney Rd* 146 EH55
Pulteney Rd, E18 146 EH55
Pulteney Ter, N1 8 D9
Pulton Pl, SW6 39 J5
Puma Ct, E1 20 A6
Pump All, Brent. TW8 179 CK80
Pump Cl, Nthlt. UB5 *off Union Rd* 158 CA68
Pump Ct, EC4 18 E9
Pumphandle Path, N2 *off Tarling Rd* 120 DC54
Pump Hill, Loug. IG10 107 EM40
Pump Ho Cl, SE16 33 H5
Bromley BR2 226 EF96
★ Pumphouse Ed Mus, Rotherhithe, SE16 33 M2
Pump Ho Ms, E1 20 C10
Pumping Sta Rd, W4 180 CS80
Pumpkin Hill, Burn. SL1 153 AL65
Pump La, SE14 45 H4
Chesham HP5 76 AS32
Epping Green CM16 73 EP24
Hayes UB3 177 BV75
Orpington BR6 247 FB106
Pump Pail N, Croy. CR0 *off Old Town* 224 DQ104
Pump Pail S, Croy. CR0 *off Southbridge Rd* 224 DQ104
Punchard Cres, Enf. EN3 105 EB38
Punch Bowl La, Chesh. HP5 *off Red Lion St* 76 AQ32
Punchbowl La, Dor. RH5 285 CK135
Punch Bowl La, Hem.H. HP2 63 BR17
St. Albans AL3 63 BT16
Pundersons Gdns, E2 20 F2
Punjab La, Sthl. UB1 *off Herbert Rd* 158 BZ74
Purbeck Av, N.Mal. KT3 221 CT100
Purbeck Cl, Merst. RH1 273 DK128
Purbeck Ct, Guil. GU2 264 AS134
Purbeck Dr, NW2 141 CY61
Woking GU21 233 AZ114
Purbeck Ho, SW8 *off Bolney St* 42 C5
Purbeck Rd, Horn. RM11 149 FG60
Purberry Gro, Epsom KT17 239 CT110
Purbrock Av, Wat. WD25 98 BW36
Purbrook Est, SE1 31 P5
Purbrook St, SE1 31 P6
Purcell Cl, Borwd. WD6 99 CK39
Kenley CR8 242 DR114
Purcell Cres, SW6 38 E4
Purcell Ho, Enf. EN1 104 DT38
Purcell Rd, Grnf. UB6 158 CB71
Purcells Av, Edg. HA8 118 CN50
Sch Purcell Sch, The, Bushey WD23 *off Aldenham Rd* 98 CA41
Purcells Cl, Ashtd. KT21 *off Albert Rd* 254 CM118
Purcell St, N1 9 N10
Purchese St, NW1 7 P10
Purdom Rd, Welw.G.C. AL7 51 CY12
Purdy St, E3 22 C4
Purelake Ms, SE13 185 ED83

PURFLEET, RM19 190 FP77
⇌ **Purfleet** 190 FN78
Purfleet Bypass, Purf. RM19 190 FP77
● **Purfleet Ind Pk**, Aveley RM15 190 FM75
Sch **Purfleet Prim Sch**, Purf. RM19 *off Tank Hill Rd* 190 FN77
Purfleet Rd, Aveley RM15 190 FN75
● **Purfleet Thames Terminal**, Purf. RM19 190 FQ80
Purford Grn, Harl. CM18 74 EU16
Sch **Purford Grn Inf Sch**, Harl. CM18 *off Purford Grn* 74 EU17
Sch **Purford Grn Jun Sch**, Harl. CM18 *off Purford Grn* 74 EU17
Purkis Cl, Uxb. UB8 *off Dawley Rd* 157 BQ72
Purkiss Rd, Hert. SG13 54 DQ12
Purland Cl, Dag. RM8 148 EZ60
Purland Rd, SE28 187 ET75
Purleigh Av, Wdf.Grn. IG8 124 EL51
PURLEY, CR8 241 DM111
⇌ **Purley** 241 DP112
Purley Av, NW2 141 CY62
Purley Bury Av, Pur. CR8 242 DQ110
Purley Bury Cl, Pur. CR8 242 DQ111
Purley Cl, Ilf. IG5 125 EN54
Sch **Purley Cross**, Pur. CR8 241 DN111
Purley Downs Rd, Pur. CR8 242 DQ110
South Croydon CR2 242 DR111
Purley Hill, Pur. CR8 241 DP112
Purley Knoll, Pur. CR8 241 DM111
⇌ **Purley Oaks** 242 DQ109
Sch **Purley Oaks Prim Sch**, S.Croy. CR2 *off Bynes Rd* 242 DR108
Purley Oaks Rd, S.Croy. CR2 242 DR109
Purley Par, Pur. CR8 *off High St* 241 DN111
Purley Pk Rd, Pur. CR8 241 DP110
Purley Pl, N1 8 G6
Purley Ri, Pur. CR8 241 DM112
Purley Rd, N9 122 DR48
Purley CR8 241 DN111
South Croydon CR2 242 DR108
Purley Vale, Pur. CR8 241 DP113
H **Purley War Mem Hosp**, Pur. CR8 241 DN111
Purley Way, Croy. CR0 223 DM101
Purley CR8 241 DN108
Purley Way Centre, Croy. CR0 223 DN103
Purley Way Cres, Croy. CR0 *off Purley Way* 223 DM101
Purlieu Way, They.B. CM16 107 ES35
Purlings Rd, Bushey WD23 98 CB43
Purneys Rd, SE9 186 EK84
Purrett Rd, SE18 187 ET78
Pursers Ct, Slou. SL2 154 AS72
Purser's Cross Rd, SW6 39 H6
Pursers La, Peasl. GU5 283 BR142
Pursers Lea, Peasl. GU5 283 BR144
Pursewardens Cl, W13 159 CJ74
Pursley Gdns, Borwd. WD6 100 CN38
Pursley Rd, NW7 119 CV52
Purton Ct, Farn.Royal SL2 153 AQ66
Purton La, Farn.Royal SL2 153 AQ66
Purves Rd, NW10 14 A1
Puteaux Ho, E2 21 J1
PUTNEY, SW15 181 CY84
⇌ **Putney** 181 CY84
⊖ **Putney Bridge** 38 G10
Putney Br, SW6 181 CY83
SW15 181 CY83
Putney Br App, SW6 38 F10
Putney Br Rd, SW15 181 CY84
SW18 181 CY84
Putney Common, SW15 38 A10
Putney Gdns, Chad.Hth RM6 *off Heathfield Pk Dr* 148 EV57
PUTNEY HEATH, SW15 201 CW86
Putney Heath, SW15 201 CW86
Putney Heath La, SW15 201 CX86
Sch **Putney High Sch**, SW15 *off Putney Hill* 201 CX85
Putney High St, SW15 181 CX84
Putney Hill, SW15 201 CX86
Putney Pk Av, SW15 181 CU84
Putney Pk La, SW15 181 CV84
Sch **Putney Pk Sch**, SW15 *off Woodborough Rd* 181 CV84
Putney Pier 38 E10
Putney Rd, Enf. EN3 105 DX36
Coll **Putney Sch of Art & Design**, SW15 *off Oxford Rd* 181 CY84
PUTNEY VALE, SW15 201 CT90
Putney Wf Twr, SW15 181 CY83
Puttenham Cl, Wat. WD19 116 BW48
Putters Cft, Hem.H. HP2 62 BM15
Puttocks Cl, N.Mymms AL9 67 CW23
Puttocks Dr, N.Mymms AL9 67 CW23
Pycroft Way, N9 122 DU49
Pyebush La, Beac. HP9 133 AN56
Pye Cl, Cat. CR3 *off St. Lawrence Way* 258 DR123
Pyecombe Cor, N12 119 CZ49
PYE CORNER, Harl. CM20 57 ER10
Pyenest Rd, Harl. CM19 73 EP18
Pyghtle, The, Denh. UB9 136 BG60
Pylbrook Rd, Sutt. SM1 222 DA104
Pyle Hill, Wok. GU22 248 AX124
Pylon Way, Croy. CR0 223 DL102
Pym Cl, E.Barn. EN4 102 DD43
Pymers Mead, SE21 204 DQ88
Pymmes Brook Dr, Barn. EN4 102 DE42
Pymmes Cl, N13 121 DM50
N17 122 DV53
Pymmes Gdns N, N9 122 DT48
Pymmes Gdns S, N9 122 DT48
Pymmes Grn Rd, N11 121 DH49
Pymmes Rd, N13 121 DL51
Pym Orchard, Brasted TN16 262 EW124
Pym Pl, Grays RM17 192 GA77
Pynchester Cl, Uxb. UB10 136 BN61
Pyne Rd, Surb. KT6 220 CN102
Pynest Grn La, Wal.Abb. EN9 106 EG38
Pynfolds, SE16 32 F5
Pynham Cl, SE2 188 EU76
Pynnacles Cl, Stan. HA7 117 CH50
Pypers Hatch, Harl. CM20 73 ET15
Sch **Pyrcroft Gra Prim Sch**, Cher. KT16 *off Pyrcroft Rd* 215 BE100
Pyrcroft La, Wey. KT13 235 BP106
Pyrcroft Rd, Cher. KT16 215 BF101
PYRFORD, Wok. GU22 249 BE115
Sch **Pyrford C of E Prim Sch**, Pyrford GU22 *off Coldharbour Rd* 250 BG116
Pyrford Common Rd, Wok. GU22 249 BD116
Pyrford Ct, Wok. GU22 249 BE117
PYRFORD GREEN, Wok. GU22 250 BH117
Pyrford Heath, Wok. GU22 249 BF116
Pyrford Lock, Wisley GU23 250 BJ116
Pyrford Rd, W.Byf. KT14 234 BG113
Woking GU22 234 BG114
PYRFORD VILLAGE, Wok. GU22 250 BG118
Pyrford Wds, Wok. GU22 249 BE115
Pyrford Wds Cl, Wok. GU22 249 BF115
Pyrford Wds Rd, Wok. GU22 249 BE115
Sch **Pyrgo Priory Prim Sch**, Harold Hill RM3 *off Dagnam Pk Dr* 128 FN50
Pyrian Cl, Wok. GU22 249 BD117
Pyrland Rd, N5 9 L2
Richmond TW10 200 CM86
Pyrles Grn, Loug. IG10 107 EP39
Pyrles La, Loug. IG10 107 EP40
Pyrmont Gro, SE27 203 DP90
Pyrmont Rd, W4 180 CN79
Pytchley Cres, SE19 204 DQ93
Pytchley Rd, SE22 184 DS83
Pytt Fld, Harl. CM17 74 EV16

Q

● **QED Distribution Pk**, Purf. RM19 191 FR77
Quadrangle, The, SE24 204 DQ85
SW10 39 P6
W2 16 C8
Guildford GU2 *off The Oval* 280 AU135
Horley RH6 291 DH148
Welwyn Garden City AL8 51 CW08
Quadrangle Cl, SE1 31 N8
Quadrangle Ho, E15 13 K5
Quadrangle Ms, Stan. HA7 117 CJ52
Quadrant, The, Epsom KT17 238 CR113
Quadrant, The, SW20 221 CY95
Bexleyheath DA7 188 EX80
Purfleet RM19 190 FQ77
Richmond TW9 180 CL84
Rickmansworth WD3 114 BL45
St. Albans AL4 65 CH17
Sutton SM2 240 DC107
Quadrant Arc, Rom. RM1 149 FE57
Quadrant Arc, W1 29 M1
Quadrant Cl, NW4 *off The Burroughs* 141 CV57
● **Quadrant Ct**, Green. DA9 191 FT84
Quadrant Gro, NW5 6 F3
Quadrant Ho, Sutt. SM2 240 DC107
● **Quadrant Pk**, Welw.G.C. AL7 51 CZ07
Quadrant Rd, Rich. TW9 179 CK84
Thornton Heath CR7 223 DP98
Quadrant Way, Wey. KT13 234 BM105
Quadrivium Pt, Slou. SL1 153 AQ74
Quad Rd, Wem. HA9 139 CK62
● **Quadrum Ind Pk**, Peasm. GU3 280 AV141
Quaggy Wk, SE3 186 EG84
Quail Gdns, S.Croy. CR2 243 DY110
Sch **Quainton Hall Sch**, Har. HA1 *off Hindes Rd* 139 CE57
Quainton St, NW10 140 CR62
Quaker Cl, Sev. TN13 279 FK123
Quaker Ct, E1 20 A5
EC1 19 L4
Quaker La, Sthl. UB2 178 CA76
Waltham Abbey EN9 89 EC34
Quakers Course, NW9 119 CT53
Quakers Hall La, Sev. TN13 279 FJ122
Quakers La, Islw. TW7 179 CG81
Potters Bar EN6 86 DB30
Quaker's Pl, E7 146 EK64
Quaker St, E1 20 A5
Quakers Wk, N21 104 DR44
Quality Ct, WC2 18 E8
Quality St, Merst. RH1 273 DH128
Quantock Cl, Harling. UB3 177 BR80
St. Albans AL4 65 CJ16
Slough SL3 175 BA78
Quantock Dr, Wor.Pk. KT4 221 CW103
Quantock Gdns, NW2 141 CX61
Quantock Ms, SE15 44 C9
Quantock Rd, Bexh. DA7 *off Cumbrian Av* 189 FE82
Quantocks, Hem.H. HP2 62 BM17
Quarles Cl, Rom. RM5 126 FA52
Quarles Pk Rd, Chad.Hth RM6 148 EV58
Quarrendon Fm La, Colesh. HP7 77 AQ42
Quarrendon Rd, Amer. HP7 77 AR40
Quarrendon St, SW6 39 K7
Quarr Rd, Cars. SM5 222 DD100
Quarry, The, Bet. RH3 270 CR132
Quarry Cl, Grav. DA11 213 GF87
Lthd. KT22 253 CK121
Oxted RH8 276 EE130
Quarry Cotts, Sev. TN13 278 FG123
Quarry Gdns, Lthd. KT22 253 CK121
Quarry Hill, Grays RM17 192 GA78
Sevenoaks TN15 279 FK123
Sch **Quarry Hill Inf Sch**, Grays RM17 *off Dell Rd* 192 GB78
Sch **Quarry Hill Jun Sch**, Grays RM17 *off Bradleigh Av* 192 GB78
Quarry Hill Pk, Reig. RH2 272 DC131
Quarry Ms, Purf. RM19 190 FN77
Quarry Pk Rd, Sutt. SM1 239 CZ107
Quarry Ri, Sutt. SM1 239 CZ107
Quarry Rd, SW18 202 DC86
Godstone RH9 274 DW128
Oxted RH8 276 EE130
● **Quarryside Business Pk**, Red. RH1 273 DH130
Quarry Spring, Harl. CM20 74 EU15
Quarry St, Guil. GU1 280 AX136
Quarterdeck, The, E14 34 A5
Quartermaine Av, Wok. GU22 249 AZ122
Quartermass Cl, Hem.H. HP1 *off Quartermass Rd* 62 BG19
Quartermass Rd, Hem.H. HP1 62 BG19
Quaves Rd, Slou. SL3 174 AV76
Quay La, Green. DA9 191 FV84
Quayside Ho, W10 *off Kensal Rd* 14 E4
Quayside Wk, Kings.T. KT1 *off Bishop's Hall* 219 CK96
Quay W, Tedd. TW11 199 CH92
Quebec Av, West. TN16 277 ER126
Quebec Cl, Smallfield RH6 *off Alberta Dr* 291 DN148
★ **Quebec Ho** (Wolfe's Ho), West. TN16 277 ER126
Quebec Ms, W1 16 F9
Quebec Rd, Hayes UB4 158 BW73
Ilford IG1, IG2 147 EP59
Tilbury RM18 193 GG82
Quebec Sq, West. TN16 277 ER126
Quebec Way, SE16 33 K5
Queen Adelaide Rd, SE20 204 DW93
Queen Alexandra's Ct, SW19 201 CZ92
Queen Alexandra's Way, Epsom KT19 238 CN111
Queen Anne Av, N15 *off Suffield Rd* 144 DT57
Bromley BR2 226 EF97
Queen Anne Dr, Clay. KT10 237 CE108
Queen Anne Ms, W1 17 K7
Queen Anne Rd, E9 11 J5
Sch **Queen Anne Royal Free C of E First Sch, The**, Wind. SL4 *off Chaucer Cl* 173 AR83
Queen Anne's Cl, Twick. TW2 199 CD90
Queen Anne's Gdns, W4 180 CS76
Queen Annes Gdns, W5 180 CL75
Enfield EN1 104 DS44
Leatherhead KT22 *off Linden Rd* 253 CH121
Queen Anne's Gdns, Mitch. CR4 222 DF97
Queen Anne's Gate, SW1 29 N5
Bexleyheath DA7 188 EX83
Queen Anne's Gro, W4 180 CS76
Queen Annes Gro, W5 180 CL75
Enfield EN1 122 DR45
Queen Anne's Ms, Lthd. KT22 *off Fairfield Rd* 253 CH121
Queen Annes Pl, Enf. EN1 104 DS44
Queen Annes Rd, Wind. SL4 173 AQ84
Queen Annes Sq, SE1 32 C8
Queen Annes Ter, Lthd. KT22 *off Fairfield Rd* 253 CH121
Queen Anne St, W1 17 J8
Queen Anne's Wk, WC1 *off Queen Sq* 18 B5
Queen Anne Ter, E1 *off Sovereign Cl* 32 F1
Queen Bee Ct, Hat. AL10 66 CR16
Queenborough Gdns, Chis. BR7 207 ER93
Ilford IG2 147 EN56
Queen Caroline Est, W6 38 A1
Queen Caroline St, W6 26 B9
H **Queen Charlotte's & Chelsea Hosp**, W12 161 CU72
Queen Charlotte St, Wind. SL4 *off High St* 173 AR81
Queendale Ct, Wok. GU21 *off Roundthorn Way* 248 AT116
Sch **Queen Eleanor's C of E Jun Sch**, Guil. GU2 *off Queen Eleanor's Rd* 280 AU135
Queen Eleanor's Rd, Guil. GU2 280 AT135
Queen Elizabeth Ct, Brox. EN10 *off Groom Rd* 89 DZ26
Queen Elizabeth Gdns, Mord. SM4 222 DA98
★ **Queen Elizabeth Hall & Purcell Room**, SE1 30 C2
H **Queen Elizabeth Hosp**, SE18 186 EL80
★ **Queen Elizabeth Olympic Pk**, E20 12 C3
Queen Elizabeth Rd, E17 145 DY55
Kingston upon Thames KT2 220 CM95
Queen Elizabeths Cl, N16 144 DR61
Queen Elizabeth's Coll, SE10 46 E4
Queen Elizabeth's Ct, Wal.Abb. EN9 *off Greenwich Way* 105 EC36
Queen Elizabeths Dr, N14 121 DL46
Queen Elizabeth's Dr, New Adgtn CR0 243 ED110
Queen Elizabeth II Br, Dart. DA1 191 FR82
Purfleet RM19 191 FR82
★ **Queen Elizabeth II Conf Cen**, SW1 29 P5
H **Queen Elizabeth II Hosp**, Welw.G.C. AL7 52 DA13
Sch **Queen Elizabeth II Jubilee Sch**, W9 15 H4
Coll **Queen Elizabeth's Foundation**, Training Coll, Lthd. KT22 *off Woodlands Rd* 253 CD117
Queen Elizabeth's Gdns, New Adgtn CR0 243 ED110
Sch **Queen Elizabeth's Girls' Sch**, Barn. EN5 *off High St* 101 CZ42
★ **Queen Elizabeth's Hunting Lo**, E4 124 EF45
Sch **Queen Elizabeth's Sch**, Barn. EN5 *off Queens Rd* 101 CX41
Queen Elizabeth St, SE1 31 P4
Queen Elizabeths Wk, N16 144 DR61
Queen Elizabeth's Wk, Wall. SM6 241 DK105
Queen Elizabeth Wk, SW13 181 CV81
Windsor SL4 174 AS82
Queen Elizabeth Way, Wok. GU22 249 AZ119
Queenhill Rd, S.Croy. CR2 242 DV110
Queenhithe, EC4 19 K10
Queenhythe Cres, Guil. GU4 264 AX128
Queenhythe Rd, Jacobs Well GU4 264 AX128
Queen Margaret's Gro, N1 9 N3
Uni **Queen Mary**, Mile End Campus, E1 21 L4
Uni **Queen Mary - Barts & The London Sch of Med & Dentistry**, EC1 19 H5
Royal London Hosp, E1 20 E7
Queen Mary Av, E18 124 EG53
Mord. SM4 221 CX99
Queen Mary Cl, Rom. RM1 149 FF58
Surbiton KT6 220 CN104
Woking GU22 249 BC116
Queen Mary Ct, Stai. TW19 *off Victory Cl* 196 BL88
Queen Mary Ho, SW15 201 CU86
Queen Mary Rd, SE19 203 DP93
Shepperton TW17 217 BQ96
Queen Mary's Av, Cars. SM5 240 DF108
Queen Marys Av, Wat. WD18 97 BS42
Queen Marys Bldgs, SW1 *off Stillington St* 29 M8
Queen Mary's Ct, Wal.Abb. EN9 *off Greenwich Way* 105 EC35
Queen Marys Dr, New Haw KT15 233 BF110
★ **Queen Mary's Gdns**, NW1 16 G3
H **Queen Mary's Hosp**, NW3 142 DC62
Sidcup DA14 208 EU93
H **Queen Mary's Hosp for Children**, Cars. SM5 222 DC102
H **Queen Mary's Hosp (Roehampton)**, SW15 201 CU86
Queen Mother's Dr, Denh. UB9 135 BF58
Queen of Denmark Ct, SE16 33 N6
Queens Acre, Sutt. SM3 239 CX108
Windsor SL4 173 AR84
Queens All, Epp. CM16 91 ET31
Queens Av, N3 120 DC52
N10 142 DG55
N20 120 DD47
Queen's Av, N21 121 DP46
Queens Av, Byfleet KT14 234 BK112
Feltham TW13 198 BW91
Greenford UB6 158 CB72
Stanmore HA7 139 CJ55
Watford WD18 97 BT42
Woodford Green IG8 124 EH50
Queensberry Ms W, SW7 28 A8
Queensberry Pl, E12 146 EK64
SW7 28 A8
Richmond TW9 *off Friars La* 199 CK85
Queensberry Way, SW7 28 A8
Queensborough Ms, W2 15 N10
Queensborough Pas, W2 15 N10
Queensborough Studios, W2 15 N10
Queensborough Ter, W2 15 M10
Queensbridge Pk, Islw. TW7 199 CE85
Sch **Queensbridge Prim Sch**, E8 10 B7
Queensbridge Rd, E2 10 B8
E8 10 B5
QUEENSBURY, Har. HA3 139 CK55
⊖ **Queensbury** 140 CM55
Queensbury Circle Par, Har. HA3 *off Streatfield Rd* 140 CL55
Stanmore HA7 *off Streatfield Rd* 140 CL55
Queensbury Rd, NW9 140 CR59
Wembley HA0 160 CM68
Queensbury Sta Par, Edg. HA8 140 CM55
Queensbury St, N1 9 K7
Queen's Circ, SW8 41 J5
SW11 41 J5
Queens Cl, Edg. HA8 118 CN50
Old Windsor SL4 194 AU85
Wallington SM6 *off Queens Rd* 241 DH106
Walton on the Hill KT20 255 CU124
★ **Queen's Club, The** (Tennis Cen), W14 38 E1
Queens Club Gdns, W14 38 F2
Sch **Queen's C of E Prim Sch, The**, Kew TW9 *off Cumberland Rd* 180 CN80
Sch **Queen's Coll**, W1 17 J7
Queen's Cotts, Wind. SL4 173 AR84
Queens Ct, SE23 204 DW88
Borwd. WD6 *off Bennington Dr* 100 CM39
Broxbourne EN10 71 DZ24
Hertford SG13 *off Queens Rd* 54 DR10
Richmond TW10 200 CM86
St. Albans AL1 65 CH20
Slough SL1 154 AT73
Waltham Cross EN8 *off Queens Way* 89 DZ34
Queenscourt, Wem. HA9 140 CL63
Queens Ct, Wey. KT13 235 BR106
Woking GU22 *off Hill Vw Rd* 249 AZ118
Queens Ct Ride, Cob. KT11 235 BU113
Queen's Cres, NW5 6 G5
Queens Cres, Rich. TW10 200 CM85
St. Albans AL4 65 CH17
Queenscroft Rd, SE9 206 EK85
Queensdale Cres, W11 26 D2
Queensdale Pl, W11 26 E2
Queensdale Rd, W11 26 D3
Queensdale Wk, W11 26 E3
Queensdown Rd, E5 144 DV63
Queens Dr, E10 145 EA59
N4 143 DP61
W3 160 CM72
W5 160 CM72
Abbots Langley WD5 81 BT32
Guildford GU2 264 AU131
Oxshott KT22 236 CC111
Queen's Dr, Slou. SL3 155 AZ66
Queens Dr, Surb. KT5 220 CN101
Thames Ditton KT7 219 CG101
Waltham Cross EN8 89 EA34
Queens Dr, The, Mill End WD3 113 BF45
Queens Elm Par, SW3 *off Old Ch St* 28 B10
Queen's Elm Sq, SW3 40 B1
Queensferry Wk, N17 *off Jarrow Rd* 144 DV56
★ **Queen's Gall, The**, SW1 29 K5
Queens Gdns, NW4 141 CW57
W2 15 N10
W5 159 CJ71
Dartford DA2 210 FP88
Queen's Gdns, Houns. TW5 178 BY81
Queens Gdns, Rain. RM13 169 FD68
Upminster RM14 151 FT58
Queen's Gate, SW7 27 P5
Queensgate, Cob. KT11 236 BX112
Queen's Gate, Gat. RH6 290 DG152
Queensgate, Wal.Cr. EN8 89 DZ34
Queens Gate, Wat. WD17 *off Lord St* 98 BW41
Queensgate Cen, Harl. CM20 57 ES11
Queensgate Centre, Grays RM17 *off Orsett Rd* 192 GA78
Queen's Gate Gdns, SW7 27 P7
Queens Gate Gdns, SW15 181 CV84
Queensgate Gdns, Chis. BR7 227 ER95
Queensgate Ho, E3 *off Hereford Rd* 21 P1
Queen's Gate Ms, SW7 27 P5
Queensgate Ms, Beck. BR3 *off Queens Rd* 225 DY95
Queensgate Pl, NW6 5 J7
Queen's Gate Pl, SW7 27 P7
Queen's Gate Pl Ms, SW7 27 P7
Sch **Queen's Gate Sch**, SW7 28 A8
Queen's Gate Ter, SW7 27 N6
Queens Gro, NW8 6 A9
Queen's Gro Ms, NW8 6 A9
Queens Gro Rd, E4 123 ED46
Queen's Head Pas, EC4 19 J8
Queen's Head St, N1 9 H9
Queens Head Wk, Brox. EN10 *off High Rd Wormley* 71 DY23
Queens Head Yd, SE1 31 L3
H **Queen's Hosp**, Rom. RM7 149 FE59
Queens Ho, Tedd. TW11 199 CF93
★ **Queen's Ho, The**, SE10 46 G3
★ **Queen's Ice & Bowl**, W2 27 M1
Queenside Ms, Horn. RM12 150 FL61
Queensland Av, N18 122 DQ51
SW19 222 DB95
Queensland Cl, E17 123 DZ54
Queensland Ho, E16 *off Rymill St* 37 L3
Queensland Rd, N7 8 E1
Queens La, N10 143 DH55
Ashford TW15 *off Clarendon Rd* 196 BM91
Sch **Queen's Manor Prim Sch**, SW6 38 C5
Queens Mkt, E13 *off Green St* 166 EJ67
Queensmead, NW8 6 B8
Datchet SL3 174 AV80
Queens Mead, Edg. HA8 118 CM51
Queensmead, Oxshott KT22 236 CC111
Queensmead Av, Epsom KT17 239 CV110
Queensmead Rd, Brom. BR2 226 EF96
Sch **Queensmead Sch**, S.Ruis. HA4 *off Queens Wk* 138 BX63
Queensmere Cl, SW19 201 CX89
Queensmere Rd, SW19 201 CX89
Slough SL1 *off Wellington St* 174 AU75
Queensmere Shop Cen, Slou. SL1 174 AT75
Queens Ms, W2 15 M10
Queensmill Rd, SW6 38 C5
Sch **Queensmill Sch**, SW6 39 K9
Queens Par, N11 120 DF50
W5 160 CM72
Queens Par Cl, N11 *off Colney Hatch La* 120 DF50
⊖ **Queen's Park** 14 F1
⊖ **Queen's Park** 14 F1
Sch **Queens Pk Comm Sch**, NW6 4 C8
Queens Pk Ct, W10 14 D3
Queens Pk Gdns, Felt. TW13 *off Vernon Rd* 197 BU90
Sch **Queen's Pk Prim Sch**, W10 14 F4
★ **Queens Park Rangers FC**, W12 161 CV74
Queens Pk Rd, Cat. CR3 258 DS123
Romford RM3 128 FM53
Queens Pas, Chis. BR7 *off High St* 207 EP93
Queens Pl, Mord. SM4 222 DA98
Watford WD17 98 BW41
Queen's Prom, Kings.T. KT1 219 CK97
Queen Sq, WC1 18 B5
Queen Sq Pl, WC1 18 B5
Queens Reach, E.Mol. KT8 219 CE98
Queens Ride, SW13 181 CU83
SW15 181 CU83
Queen's Ride, Rich. TW10 200 CP88
Queens Ri, Rich. TW10 200 CM86
Queens Rd, E11 145 ED59
E13 166 EH67
Queen's Rd, E17 145 DZ58
Queens Rd, N3 120 DC53
N9 122 DV48
Queen's Rd, N11 121 DL52
Queens Rd, NW4 141 CW57
SE14 44 E6
SE15 44 E6
SW14 180 CR83
SW19 201 CZ93
W5 160 CL72
Barking IG11 167 EQ66
Barnet EN5 101 CX41
Beckenham BR3 225 DY96
Berkhamsted HP4 60 AU18
Brentwood CM14 130 FW48
Bromley BR1 226 EG96
Buckhurst Hill IG9 124 EH47
Chesham HP5 76 AQ30
Chislehurst BR7 207 EP93
Queen's Rd, Croy. CR0 223 DP100
Queens Rd, Datchet SL3 174 AU81
Egham TW20 195 AZ93
Enfield EN1 104 DS42
Queen's Rd, Erith DA8 189 FE79
Queens Rd, Eton Wick SL4 173 AL78
Feltham TW13 197 BV88
Gravesend DA12 213 GJ90
Guildford GU1 264 AX134
Hampton Hill TW12 198 CB91
Hayes UB3 157 BS72
Hersham KT12 235 BV106
Hertford SG13, SG14 54 DR11
Horley RH6 290 DG148
Queen's Rd, Houns. TW3 178 CB83
Queens Rd, Kings.T. KT2 200 CN94
Loughton IG10 106 EL41
Morden SM4 222 DA98
New Malden KT3 221 CT98
North Weald Bassett CM16 93 FB26
Richmond TW10 200 CM85
Queen's Rd, Slou. SL1 154 AT73
Queens Rd, Sthl. UB2 178 BX75
Sutton SM2 240 DA110
Queen's Rd, Tedd. TW11 199 CE93
Thames Ditton KT7 219 CF99
Queens Rd, Twick. TW1 199 CF88
Queen's Rd, Uxb. UB8 156 BJ69
Queens Rd, Wall. SM6 241 DH106
Waltham Cross EN8 89 DY34
Ware SG12 55 DZ05
Watford WD17 98 BW42
Queen's Rd, Well. DA16 188 EV82
Queens Rd, West Dr. UB7 176 BM75
Weybridge KT13 235 BQ105

Queens Rd, Windsor SL4 173 AQ82
⇌ Queens Road Peckham 44 F6
Queens Rd W, E13 13 P10
Queen's Row, SE17 43 L2
Sch Queens' Sch, Bushey WD23
off Aldenham Rd 98 BZ41
Queen's Sq, The, Hem.H. HP2 62 BM20
Queens Ter, E13 166 EH67
Queen's Ter, NW8 6 A10
Queens Ter, Islw. TW7 179 CG84
Queens Ter Cotts, W7
off Boston Rd 179 CE75
Queensthorpe Rd, SE26 205 DX91
★ Queen's Twr, SW7 28 A6
Queenstown Gdns, Rain.
RM13 169 FF69
Queenstown Ms, SW8 41 J7
Queenstown Rd, SW8 41 J3
⇌ Queenstown Road
(Battersea) 41 K6
Queen St, EC4 19 K10
N17 122 DS51
W1 29 J2
Bexleyheath DA7 188 EZ83
Chertsey KT16 216 BG102
Chipperfield WD4 80 BG31
Croydon CR0 242 DQ105
Erith DA8 189 FE79
Gomshall GU5 283 BQ139
Gravesend DA12 213 GH86
Romford RM7 149 FD58
St. Albans AL3 64 CC20
Warley CM14 130 FW50
Queen St Pl, EC4 31 K1
Queensville Rd, SW12 203 DK87
Queens Wk, E4 123 ED46
NW9 140 CQ61
Queen's Wk, SW1 29 L3
Queens Wk, W5 159 CJ70
Ashford TW15 196 BK91
Queen's Wk, Har. HA1 139 CE56
Queens Wk, Ruis. HA4 138 BX62
Queen's Wk, The, SE1 30 C3
⊖ Queensway 27 M1
Queens Way, NW4 141 CW57
Queensway, W2 15 M9
Queens Way, Croy. CR0 241 DM107
Queensway, Enf. EN3 104 DV42
Queens Way, Felt. TW13 198 BW91
Queensway, Hat. AL10 67 CU18
Hemel Hempstead
HP1, HP2 62 BM18
Petts Wood BR5 227 EQ99
Redhill RH1 272 DF133
Queens Way, Shenley WD7 84 CL32
Queensway, Sun. TW16 217 BV96
Queens Way, Wal.Cr. EN8 89 DZ34
Queensway, W.Wick. BR4 226 EE104
Queensway, The, Chal.St.P.
SL9 134 AX55
● Queensway Business Cen,
Enf. EN3 *off Queensway* 104 DW42
Queensway N, Hersham KT12
off Robinsway 236 BW105
Queensway S, Hersham KT12
off Trenchard Cl 236 BW106
Queenswell Av, N20 120 DE49
Sch Queenswell Inf & Nurs Sch,
N20 *off Sweets Way* 120 DD47
Sch Queenswell Jun Sch, N20
off Sweets Way 120 DD47
Queenswood Av, E17 123 EC53
Hampton TW12 198 CB93
Hounslow TW3 178 BZ82
Hutton CM13 131 GD43
Thornton Heath CR7 223 DN99
Wallington SM6 241 DK105
Queenswood Cres, Wat. WD25 81 BU33
Queenswood Gdns, E11 146 EG60
Queenswood Pk, N3 119 CY54
Queen's Wd Rd, N10 143 DH58
Queenswood Rd, SE23 205 DX90
Sidcup DA15 207 ET85
Sch Queenswood Sch, Brook.Pk
AL9 *off Shepherds Way* 86 DD28
Queens Yd, WC1 17 M5
Jct Queen Victoria, Sutt. SM3 239 CW105
Queen Victoria Av, Wem. HA0 159 CK66
★ Queen Victoria Mem, SW1 29 L4
Queen Victoria St, EC4 19 H10
Queen Victoria's Wk, Wind.
SL4 174 AS81
Queen Victoria Ter, E1
off Sovereign Cl 32 F1
Quemerford Rd, N7 8 C2
Quendell Wk, Hem.H. HP2 62 BL20
Quendon Dr, Wal.Abb. EN9 89 ED33
Quennell Cl, Ashtd. KT21
off Parkers La 254 CM119
Quennell Way, Hutt. CM13 131 GC45
Quentin Pl, SE13 186 EE83
Quentin Rd, SE13 186 EE83
Quentins Dr, Berry's Grn
TN16 261 EP116
Quentins Wk, Berry's Grn TN16
off St. Anns Way 261 EP116
Quentin Way, Vir.W. GU25 214 AV98
Quernmore Cl, Brom. BR1 206 EG93
Quernmore Rd, N4 143 DN58
Bromley BR1 206 EG93
Querrin St, SW6 39 N9
● Questor, Dart. DA1 210 FL89
Quex Ms, NW6 5 K8
Quex Rd, NW6 5 K8
Quickbeams, Welw.G.C. AL7 52 DA06
Quickberry Pl, Amer. HP7 77 AR39
Quickley La, Chorl. WD3 95 BB44
Quickley Ri, Chorl. WD3 95 BC44
Quickmoor La, Kings L. WD4 80 BH33
Quick Rd, W4 180 CS78
Quicks Rd, SW19 202 DB94
Quick St, N1 19 H1
Quick St Ms, N1 18 G1
Quickswood, NW3 6 D6
Quickwood Cl, Rick. WD3 96 BG44
Quiet Cl, Add. KT15 234 BG105
Quiet Nook, Brom. BR2
off Croydon Rd 226 EK104
Quill Hall La, Amer. HP6 94 AT37
Quill La, SW15 181 CX84
Quillot, The, Hersham KT12 235 BT106
Quill St, N4 143 DN62
W5 160 CL69
Quilp St, SE1 31 J4
Quilter Gdns, Orp. BR5
off Tintagel Rd 228 EW102
Quilter Rd, Orp. BR5 228 EW102
Quilters Pl, SE9 207 EQ88
Quilter St, E2 20 C2
Quilter St, SE18 187 ET78
Quilting Ct, SE16
off Poolmans St 33 J4
Quinbrookes, Slou. SL2 154 AW72
Quince Ho, SW16
off Hemlock Cl 223 DK96
Felt. TW13 *off High St* 197 BV88
Quince Rd, SE13 46 D8
Quinces Cft, Hem.H. HP1 62 BG18
Quince Tree Cl, S.Ock. RM15 171 FW70
Quincy Rd, Egh. TW20 195 BA92
Quinnell Cl, SE18
off Rippolson Rd 187 ET78
Quinta Dr, Barn. EN5 101 CV43
Quintin Av, SW20 221 CZ95
Quintin Cl, Pnr. HA5
off High Rd 137 BV57
Sch Quintin Kynaston Sch,
NW8 6 A9
Quinton Cl, Beck. BR3 225 EC97
Hounslow TW5 177 BV80
Wallington SM6 241 DH105
Quinton Rd, T.Ditt. KT7 219 CG102
Quinton St, SW18 202 DC89
Quintrell Cl, Wok. GU21 248 AV117
Quixley St, E14 22 G10
Quorn Rd, SE22 184 DS84

R

Raans Rd, Amer. HP6 94 AT38
Rabbit La, Hersham KT12 235 BU108
Rabbit Row, W8 27 K2
Rabbits Rd, E12 146 EL63
South Darenth DA4 231 FR96
Sch Rabbsfarm Prim Sch, Yiew.
UB7 *off Gordon Rd* 156 BL73
Rabbs Mill Ho, Uxb. UB8 156 BJ68
Rabies Heath Rd, Bletch. RH1 274 DS133
Godstone RH9 274 DU134
Rabournmead Dr, Nthlt. UB5 138 BY64
Raby Rd, N.Mal. KT3 220 CR98
Raby St, E14 21 L8
Raccoon Way, Houns. TW4 178 BW82
Racecourse Way, Gat. RH6 290 DF151
Rachel Cl, Ilf. IG6 147 ER55
Rachels Way, Chesh. HP5
off Cresswell Rd 76 AR34
Rackham Cl, Well. DA16 188 EV82
Rackham Ms, SW16 203 DJ93
Racks Ct, Guil. GU1 280 AX136
Racton Rd, SW6 39 J3
Radbourne Av, W5 179 CJ77
Radbourne Cl, E5 145 DX63
Radbourne Ct, Har. HA3 139 CH58
Radbourne Cres, E17 123 ED54
Radbourne Rd, SW12 203 DK88
Radburn Cl, Harl. CM18 74 EU19
Radcliffe Av, NW10 161 CU68
Enfield EN2 104 DQ39
Radcliffe Gdns, Cars. SM5 240 DE108
Radcliffe Ms, Hmptn H. TW12
off Taylor Cl 198 CC92
Radcliffe Path, SW8 41 K9
Radcliffe Rd, N21 121 DP46
SE1 31 P6
Croydon CR0 224 DT103
Harrow HA3 117 CG54
Radcliffe Sq, SW15 201 CX86
Radcliffe Way, Nthlt. UB5 158 BX69
Radcot Av, Slou. SL3 175 BB76
Radcot Pt, SE23 205 DX90
Radcot St, SE11 42 F1
Raddington Rd, W10 14 F7
Radfield Dr, Dart. DA2
off Teynham Rd 210 FQ87
Radfield Way, Sid. DA15 207 ER87
Radford Rd, SE13 205 EC86
Radford Way, Bark. IG11 167 ET69
Radipole Rd, SW6 38 G6
● Radius Pk, Felt. TW14 177 BT84
Radland Rd, E16 23 M9
Rad La, Abin.Ham. RH5 283 BS141
Peaslake GU5 283 BS140
Radlet Av, SE26 204 DV90
RADLETT, WD7 99 CH35
⇌ Radlett 99 CG35
Radlett Cl, E7 13 M4
Radlett La, Shenley WD7 99 CK35
Sch Radlett Lo Sch, Rad. WD7
off Harper La 83 CH31
Radlett Pk Rd, Rad. WD7 83 CG34
Radlett Pl, NW8 6 C8
Sch Radlett Prep Sch, Rad. WD7
off Watling St 99 CJ38
Radlett Rd, Ald. WD25 98 CB39
St. Albans AL2 83 CE28
Watford WD17, WD24 98 BW41
Radley Av, Ilf. IG3 147 ET63
Radley Cl, Felt. TW14 197 BT88
Radley Ct, SE16 33 K4
Radley Gdns, Har. HA3 140 CL56
Radley Ho, SE2
off Wolvercote Rd 188 EX75
Radley Ms, W8 27 K7
Radley Rd, N17 122 DS54
Radley's La, E18 124 EG54
Radleys Mead, Dag. RM10 169 FB65
Radley Sq, E5
off Dudlington Rd 144 DW61
Radlix Rd, E10 145 EA60
Radnor Av, Har. HA1 139 CE57
Welling DA16 208 EV85
Radnor Cl, Chis. BR7 207 ES93
Mitcham CR4 223 DL98
Radnor Cres, SE18 188 EU79
Ilford IG4 147 EM57
Radnor Gdns, Enf. EN1 104 DS39
Twickenham TW1 199 CF89
Radnor Gro, Uxb. UB10 156 BN68
Radnor Ho, SW16 223 DM96
Radnor La, Holm.St.M. RH5 283 BU144
Radnor Ms, W2 16 B9
Radnor Pl, W2 16 C9
Radnor Rd, NW6 4 E9
SE15 44 C4
Harrow HA1 139 CD57
Twickenham TW1 199 CF89
Weybridge KT13 216 BN104
Radnor St, EC1 19 K3
Radnor Ter, W14 26 G8
Radnor Wk, E14 34 B8
SW3 40 D1
Croydon CR0 225 DZ100
Radnor Way, NW10 160 CP70
Radnor Way, Slough SL3 174 AY77
Radolphs, Tad. KT20 255 CX122
Radstock Av, Har. HA3 139 CG55
Radstock Cl, N11 120 DG50
Radstock St, SW11 40 C5
Radstock Way, Merst. RH1 273 DK128
Radstone Ct, Wok. GU22 249 AZ118
Radzan Cl, Dart. DA2 209 FE89
Raebarn Gdns, Barn. EN5 101 CV43
Raeburn Av, Dart. DA1 209 FH85
Surbiton KT5 220 CP100
Raeburn Cl, NW11 142 DC58
Kingston upon Thames KT1 199 CK94
Raeburn Ct, Wok. GU21
off Martin Way 248 AU118
Raeburn Rd, Edg. HA8 118 CN54
Hayes UB4 157 BR68
Sidcup DA15 207 ES86
Raeburn St, SW2 183 DL84
Raeside Cl, Seer Grn HP9 111 AQ51
Raffles Ct, Edg. HA8 118 CM49
Rafford Way, Brom. BR1 226 EH96
★ R.A.F. Northolt, Ruis. HA4 137 BT64
Raft Rd, SW18 *off North Pas* 182 DA84
Ragged Hall La, St.Alb. AL2 64 BZ24
★ Ragged Sch Mus, E3 21 M6
Raggleswood, Chis. BR7 227 EN95
Rag Hill Cl, Tats. TN16 260 EL121
Rag Hill Rd, Tats. TN16 260 EK121
Raglan Av, Wal.Cr. EN8 89 DX34
Raglan Cl, Houns. TW4 198 BZ85
Reigate RH2 272 DC132
Raglan Ct, SE12 206 EG85
South Croydon CR2 241 DP106
Wembley HA9 140 CM63
Raglan Gdns, Wat. WD19 115 BV46
Sch Raglan Inf Sch, Enf. EN1
off Wellington Rd 122 DS45
Sch Raglan Jun Sch, Enf. EN1
off Raglan Rd 122 DS45
Raglan Prec, Cat. CR3 258 DS122
Sch Raglan Prim Sch, Brom. BR2
off Raglan Rd 226 EJ98
Raglan Rd, E17 145 EC57
SE18 37 P10
Belvedere DA17 188 EZ77
Bromley BR2 226 EJ98
Enfield EN1 122 DS45
Knaphill GU21 248 AS118
Reigate RH2 288 DB131
Raglan St, NW5 7 K4
Raglan Ter, Har. HA2 138 CB63
Raglan Way, Nthlt. UB5 158 CC65
Ragley Cl, W3 *off Church Rd* 180 CQ75
Rags La, Chsht EN7 88 DS27
Ragstone Rd, Slou. SL1 173 AR76
Ragwort Ct, SE26 204 DV92
Rahere Ho, EC1 19 J2
Rahn Rd, Epp. CM16 92 EU31
Raider Cl, Rom. RM7 126 FA53
Raikes Hollow, Abin.Ham. RH5 283 BV142
Raikes La, Abin.Ham. RH5 283 BV141
Railey Ms, NW5 7 L2
Railpit La, Warl. CR6 260 EE115
Railshead Rd, Islw. TW7 179 CH84
Railstore, The, Gidea Pk RM2 150 FJ55
Railton Rd, SE24 183 DN84
Guildford GU2 264 AV130
Railway App, N4
off Wightman Rd 143 DN58
SE1 31 M2
Harrow HA1, HA3 139 CF56
Hertford SG14 54 DQ09
Twickenham TW1 199 CG87
Wallington SM6 241 DH107
Railway Arches, W12 26 A5
Railway Av, SE16 33 H4
Railway Children Wk, SE12 206 EG89
Bromley BR1 206 EG89
Railway Cotts, Rad. WD7 99 CH35
Watford WD24 97 BV39
Railway Ms, E3 22 A3
W10 14 F8
Railway Pas, Tedd. TW11
off Victoria Rd 199 CG93
Railway Pl, Belvedere DA17 188 FA76
Gravesend DA12 *off Stone St* 213 GH86
Hertford SG13 54 DS09
Railway Ri, SE22
off Grove Vale 184 DS84
Railway Rd, Grnf. UB6 159 CD66
Tedd. TW11 199 CF91
Waltham Cross EN8 89 DY33
Railway Side, SW13 180 CS83
Railway Sq, Brwd. CM14
off Fairfield Rd 130 FW48
Railway St, N1 18 B1
Hertford SG13, SG14 54 DR09
Northfleet DA11 212 GA85
Romford RM6 148 EW60
Railway Ter, E17 123 EC53
SE13 *off Ladywell Rd* 205 EB85
Kings Langley WD4 80 BN27
Slough SL2 154 AT74
Staines-upon-Thames TW18 195 BD92
Westerham TN16 277 ER125
Rainborough Cl, NW10 160 CQ65
Rainbow Av, E14 34 C10
Rainbow Ct, Wat. WD19
off Oxhey Rd 98 BW44
Woking GU21
off Langmans Way 248 AS116
● Rainbow Ind Est, West Dr.
UB7 156 BK73
● Rainbow Ind Pk, SW20 221 CV96
Rainbow Quay, SE16 33 M7
Rainbow Rd, Chaff.Hun.
RM16 191 FW77
Matching Tye CM17 59 FE12
Rainbow St, SE5 43 N5
Rainer Cl, Chsht EN8 89 DX29
Raines Ct, N16
off Northwold Rd 144 DT61
Sch Raine's Foundation Sch,
Lwr Sch, E2 20 F2
Upr Sch, E2 21 H1
Raine St, E1 32 F2
RAINHAM, RM13 169 FG69
⇌ Rainham 169 FF70
Rainham Cl, SE9 207 ER86
SW11 202 DE86
★ Rainham Hall, Rain. RM13 169 FG70
Rainham Rd, NW10 14 B3
Rainham RM13 169 FE66
Rainham Rd N, Dag. RM10 149 FB61
Rainham Rd S, Dag. RM10 149 FB63
Sch Rainham Village Prim Sch,
Rain. RM13
off Upminster Rd S 169 FG70
Rainhill Way, E3 22 B2
Rainsborough Av, SE8 33 L9
Rainsborough Ct, Hert. SG13
off Lilbourne Dr 54 DU08
Rainsford Cl, Stan. HA7 117 CJ49
Rainsford Rd, NW10 160 CP69
Rainsford St, W2 16 C8
Rainsford Way, Horn. RM12 149 FG60
Rainton Rd, SE7 35 P10
Rainville Rd, W6 38 B3
Raisins Hill, Pnr. HA5 138 BW55
Raith Av, N14 121 DK48
Raleana Rd, E14 34 F2
Raleigh Av, Hayes UB4 157 BV71
Wallington SM6 241 DK105
Raleigh Cl, NW4 141 CW57
Erith DA8 189 FF79
Pinner HA5 138 BX59
Ruislip HA4 137 BT61
Slough SL1 153 AN74
Raleigh Ct, SE19
off Lymer Av 204 DT92
Beckenham BR3 225 EB95
Staines-upon-Thames TW18 196 BG91
Wallington SM6 241 DH107
Raleigh Dr, N20 120 DE48
Claygate KT10 237 CD106
Smallfield RH6 291 DN148
Surbiton KT5 220 CQ102
Raleigh Gdns, SW2
off Brixton Hill 203 DM86
Mitcham CR4 222 DF96
Raleigh Ms, N1
off Queen's Head St 9 H9
Orpington BR6
off Osgood Av 245 ET106
Raleigh Rd, N8 143 DN56
SE20 205 DX94
Enfield EN2 104 DR42
Feltham TW13 197 BT90
Richmond TW9 180 CM83
Southall UB2 178 BY78
Sch Raleigh Sch, The, W.Hors.
KT24 *off Northcote Cres* 267 BQ125
Raleigh St, N1 9 H9
Raleigh Way, N14 121 DK46
Feltham TW13 198 BW92
Rale La, E4 *off Buxton Rd* 123 ED45
Ralliwood Rd, Ashtd. KT21 254 CN119
Ralph Ct, W2 15 M8
Ralph Perring Ct, Beck. BR3 225 EA98
Ralston Ct, Wind. SL4
off Russell St 173 AR81
Ralston St, SW3 40 E1
Ralston Way, Wat. WD19 116 BX47
Rama Cl, SW16 203 DK94
Rama Ct, Har. HA1 139 CE61
Ramac Way, SE7 35 A9
Rama La, SE19 204 DT94
Coll Rambert Sch of Ballet &
Contemporary Dance, Twick.
TW1 *off St. Margarets Rd* 199 CH85
Rambler Cl, SW16 203 DJ91
Taplow SL6 152 AH72
Rambler La, Slou. SL3 174 AW76
Ramblers La, Harl. CM17
off Crossway 58 EX14
Ramblers Way, Welw.G.C. AL7 52 DB10
Rambling Way, Pott.End HP4 61 BC17
Ram Cl, SW17 202 DG92
Ram Gorse, Harl. CM20 57 EP13
Ramilles Cl, SW2 203 DL86
Ramillies Pl, W1 17 L9
Ramillies Rd, NW7 118 CS47
W4 180 CR77
Sidcup DA15 208 EV86
Ramillies St, W1 17 L9
Ramin Ct, Guil. GU1 264 AW131
Ramney Dr, Enf. EN3 105 DY37
Ramornie Cl, Hersham KT12 236 BZ106
Ramparts, The, St.Alb. AL3 64 CB21
Rampart St, E1 20 E9
Ram Pas, Kings.T. KT1
off High St 219 CK96
Rampayne St, SW1 29 N10
Ram Pl, E9 11 H4
Rampton Cl, E4 123 EA48
Ramsay Cl, Brox. EN10 71 DY21
Ramsay Gdns, Rom. RM3 128 FJ53
Ramsay Pl, Har. HA1 139 CE60
Ramsay Rd, E7 146 EE63
W3 180 CQ76
Ramsbury Rd, St.Alb. AL1 65 CE21
Ramscote La, Bell. HP5 76 AN25
Ramscroft Cl, N9 122 DS45
Ramsdale Rd, SW17 202 DG92
RAMSDEN, Orp. BR5 228 EW102
Ramsden Cl, Orp. BR5 228 EW102
Ramsden Dr, Rom. RM5 126 FA52
Ramsden Rd, N11 120 DF50
SW12 202 DG86
Erith DA8 189 FD80
Orpington BR5, BR6 228 EV101
Ramsey Cl, NW9 141 CT58
Brookmans Park AL9 86 DD27
Greenford UB6 139 CD64
Horley RH6 290 DF148
St. Albans AL1 65 CG22
Ramsey Ct, Slou. SL2
off Lower Britwell Rd 153 AK70
Ramsey Ho, SW11
off Maysoule Rd 182 DD84
Ramsey Lo Ct, St.Alb. AL1 65 CE19
Ramsey Pl, Cat. CR3 258 DQ122
Ramsey Rd, Th.Hth. CR7 223 DM100
Ramsey St, E2 20 D4
Ramsey Wk, N1 9 L5
Ramsey Way, N14 121 DJ45
Ramsfort Ho, SE16
off Manor Est 32 E9
Ramsgate Cl, E16 36 A3
Ramsgate St, E8 10 B4
Ramsgill App, Ilf. IG2 147 ET56
Ramsgill Dr, Ilf. IG2 147 ET57
Rams Gro, Rom. RM6 148 EY56
Ramson Ri, Hem.H. HP1 61 BE21
Ram St, SW18 202 DB85
Ramulis Dr, Hayes UB4 158 BX70
Ramus Wd Av, Orp. BR6 245 ES106
Rancliffe Gdns, SE9 186 EL84
Rancliffe Rd, E6 25 H1
Sch Randal Cremer Prim Sch, E2 10 A10
Randal Cres, Reig. RH2 288 DA136
Randall Av, NW2 141 CT62
Randall Cl, SW11 40 C6
Erith DA8 189 FC79
Slough SL3 175 AZ78
Randall Ct, NW7 119 CU52
SW6 *off Dairy Cl* 39 J7
Randall Dr, Horn. RM12 150 FJ63
Randall Pl, SE10 46 E4
Randall Rd, SE11 30 C10
Randall Row, SE11 30 C9
Randalls Cres, Lthd. KT22 253 CG120
Randalls Dr, Hutt. CM13 131 GE44
Randalls Pk Av, Lthd. KT22 253 CG120
Randalls Pk Dr, Lthd. KT22
off Randalls Rd 253 CG121
Randalls Ride, Hem.H. HP2 62 BK18
Randalls Rd, Lthd. KT22 253 CE119
Randall's Wk, Brick.Wd AL2 82 BZ30
Randalls Way, Lthd. KT22 253 CG121
Randell's Rd, N1 8 B8
Randisbourne Gdns, SE6 205 EB90
Randle Rd, Rich. TW10 199 CJ91
Randlesdown Rd, SE6 205 EA91
Randles La, Knock.P. TN14 262 EX115
Randolph App, E16 24 D9
Randolph Av, W9 15 P4
Randolph Cl, Bexh. DA7 189 FC83
Kingston upon Thames KT2 200 CQ92
Knaphill GU21
off Creston Av 248 AS117
Stoke D'Abernon KT11 252 CA115
Randolph Cres, W9 15 N5
Randolph Gdns, NW6 15 L1
Randolph Gro, Rom. RM6
off Donald Dr 148 EW57
● Randolph Ho, Croy. CR0 224 DQ102
Randolph Ms, W9 15 P5
Randolph Rd, E17 145 EB57
W9 15 N5
Bromley BR2 227 EM102
Epsom KT17 239 CT114
Slough SL3 174 AY76
Southall UB1 178 BZ75
Randolph's La, West. TN16 277 EP126
Randolph St, NW1 7 L7
Randon Cl, Har. HA2 116 CB54
Ranelagh Av, SW6 38 G10
SW13 181 CU82
Ranelagh Br, W2
off Gloucester Ter 15 M7
Ranelagh Cl, Edg. HA8 118 CN49
Ranelagh Dr, Edg. HA8 118 CN49
Twickenham TW1 199 CH85
★ Ranelagh Gdns, SW3 40 G1
Ranelagh Gdns, E11 146 EJ57
SW6 38 G10
W4 180 CQ80
W6 181 CT76
Ilford IG1 147 EN60
Northfleet DA11 213 GF87
Ranelagh Gdns Mans, SW6
off Ranelagh Gdns 38 F10
Ranelagh Gro, SW1 29 H10
Ranelagh Ms, W5 179 CK75
Ranelagh Pl, N.Mal. KT3 220 CS99
Sch Ranelagh Prim Sch, E15 13 K10
Ranelagh Rd, E6 167 EN67
E11 146 EE63
E15 13 K9
N17 144 DS55
N22 121 DM53
NW10 161 CT68
SW1 41 M1
W5 179 CK75
Hemel Hempstead HP2 63 BP20
Redhill RH1 272 DE134
Southall UB1 158 BX74
Wembley HA0 139 CK64
Ranfurly Rd, Sutt. SM1 222 DA103
Sch Rangefield Prim Sch, Downham
BR1 *off Glenbow Rd* 206 EE92
Rangefield Rd, Brom. BR1 206 EE92
Rangemoor Rd, N15 144 DT57
Range Rd, Grav. DA12 213 GL87
Rangers Rd, E4 124 EE45
Loughton IG10 124 EE45
Rangers Sq, SE10 46 G6
Ranger Wk, Add. KT15
off Monks Cres 234 BH106
Range Way, Shep. TW17 216 BN101
Rangeworth Pl, Sid. DA15
off Priestlands Pk Rd 207 ET90
Rangoon St, EC3 20 A9
Rankin Cl, NW9 140 CS55
Rankine Ho, SE1 *off Bath Ter* 31 J7
Ranleigh Gdns, Bexh. DA7 188 EZ80
Ranmere St, SW12
off Ormeley Rd 203 DH88
Ranmoor Cl, Har. HA1 139 CD56
Ranmoor Gdns, Har. HA1 139 CD56
Ranmore Av, Croy. CR0 224 DT104
Ranmore Cl, Red. RH1 272 DG131
★ Ranmore Common, Dor.
RH5 268 CB133
Ranmore Common Rd, Westh.
RH5 269 CD133
Ranmore Path, Orp. BR5 228 EU98
Ranmore Rd, Dor. RH4 268 CC134
Sutton SM2 239 CX109
Rannoch Cl, Edg. HA8 118 CP47
Rannoch Rd, W6 38 B2
Rannoch Wk, Hem.H. HP2 62 BK16
Rannock Av, NW9 140 CS59
Ranskill Rd, Borwd. WD6 100 CN39
Ransom Cl, Wat. WD19 116 BW45
● Ransome's Dock Business Cen,
SW11 40 D5
Ransom Rd, SE7 36 D10
Ransom Wk, SE7 36 D9
Ranston Cl, Denh. UB9
off Nightingale Way 135 BF58
Ranston St, NW1 16 C6
Rant Meadow, Hem.H. HP3 62 BN22
Ranulf Cl, Harl. CM17 58 EW09
Ranulf Rd, NW2 141 CZ63
Ranwell Cl, E3 11 N9
Ranwell St, E3 11 N9
Ranworth Av, Hodd. EN11 55 EB13
Ranworth Cl, Erith DA8 189 FE82
Hemel Hempstead HP3
off Panxworth Rd 62 BK22
Ranworth Gdns, Pot.B. EN6 85 CX31
Ranworth Rd, N9 122 DW47
Ranyard Cl, Chess. KT9 220 CM104
Raphael Av, Rom. RM1 149 FF55
Tilbury RM18 193 GG80
Raphael Cl, Kings.T. KT1 219 CK98

Raphael Cl, Shenley WD7 84 CL32
Raphael Dr, Loug. IG10 107 EP40
T.Ditt. KT7 219 CF101
Watford WD24 98 BX40
Sch Raphael Indep Sch, Horn. RM11 off Park La 149 FG59
Raphael Rd, Grav. DA12 213 GK87
Raphael St, SW7 28 E5
Rapier Cl, Purf. RM19 190 FN77
Rasehill Cl, Rick. WD3 96 BJ43
Rashleigh St, SW8 41 K9
Rashleigh Way, Hort.Kir. DA4 230 FQ98
Rasper Rd, N20 120 DC47
Rastell Av, SW2 203 DK89
Ratcliffe Cl, SE12 206 EG87
Uxbridge UB8 156 BK69
Ratcliffe Cross St, E1 21 K9
Ratcliffe La, E14 21 L9
Ratcliffe Orchard, E1 21 K10
Ratcliff Rd, E7 146 EJ64
Rathbone Mkt, E16 23 L7
Rathbone Pl, W1 17 N8
Rathbone St, E16 23 L7
W1 17 M7
Rathcoole Av, N8 143 DM56
Rathcoole Gdns, N8 143 DM57
Sch Rathfern Prim Sch, SE6 off Rathfern Rd 205 DZ88
Rathfern Rd, SE6 205 DZ88
Rathgar Av, W13 159 CH74
Rathgar Cl, N3 119 CZ54
Redhill RH1 288 DG139
Rathgar Rd, SW9 43 H10
Rathlin, Hem.H. HP3 63 BP22
Rathmell Dr, SW4 203 DK86
Rathmore Rd, SE7 36 A10
Gravesend DA11 213 GH87
Rathwell Path, Borwd. WD6 100 CL39
Rats La, High Beach IG10 106 EH38
Rattray Rd, SW2 183 DN84
Ratty's La, Hodd. EN11 71 ED17
Raul Rd, SE15 44 D8
Raveley St, NW5 7 L1
Ravel Gdns, Aveley RM15 170 FQ72
Ravel Rd, Aveley RM15 170 FQ72
Raven Cl, NW9 118 CS54
Rickmansworth WD3 114 BJ45
Raven Ct, E5 off Stellman Cl 144 DU62
Hatfield AL10 67 CU19
Ravencroft, Grays RM16 off Alexandra Cl 193 GH75
Ravendale Rd, Sun. TW16 217 BT96
Ravenet St, SW11 41 J7
Ravenfield, Eng.Grn TW20 194 AW93
Ravenfield Rd, SW17 202 DF90
Welwyn Garden City AL7 51 CZ09
Ravenhill Rd, E13 166 EJ68
Ravenna Rd, SW15 201 CX85
Ravenoak Way, Chig. IG7 125 ES50
Ravenor Pk Rd, Grnf. UB6 158 CB69
Sch Ravenor Prim Sch, Grnf. UB6 off Greenway Gdns 158 CA69
Raven Rd, E18 124 EJ54
Raven Row, E1 20 F6
⇌ Ravensbourne 205 ED94
Ravensbourne Av, Beck. BR3 205 ED94
Bromley BR2 205 ED94
Staines-upon-Thames TW19 196 BL88
● Ravensbourne Business Cen, Kes. BR2 244 EK105
Coll Ravensbourne Coll of Design & Communication, SE10 35 K4
Ravensbourne Cres, Rom. RM3 150 FM55
Ravensbourne Gdns, W13 159 CH71
Ilford IG5 125 EN53
Ravensbourne Pk, SE6 205 EA87
Ravensbourne Pk Cres, SE6 205 DZ87
Ravensbourne Pl, SE13 46 D8
Ravensbourne Rd, SE6 205 DZ87
Bromley BR1 226 EG97
Dartford DA1 189 FG83
Twickenham TW1 199 CJ86
Sch Ravensbourne Sch, Rom. RM3 off Neave Cres 128 FK53
Sch Ravensbourne Sch, The, Brom. BR2 off Hayes La 226 EH98
Ravensbourne Ter, Stanw. TW19 off Ravensbourne Av 196 BM88
Ravensbury Av, Mord. SM4 222 DC99
Ravensbury Ct, Mitch. CR4 off Ravensbury Gro 222 DD98
Ravensbury Gro, Mitch. CR4 222 DD98
Ravensbury La, Mitch. CR4 222 DD98
Ravensbury Path, Mitch. CR4 222 DD98
Ravensbury Rd, SW18 202 DA89
Orpington BR5 227 ET98
Ravensbury Ter, SW18 202 DB89
Ravenscar Rd, Brom. BR1 206 EE91
Surbiton KT6 220 CM103
Ravens Cl, Brom. BR2 226 EF96
Enfield EN1 104 DS40
Redhill RH1 272 DF132
Surbiton KT6 219 CK100
Ravens Ct, Berk. HP4 off Benningfield Gdns 60 AY17
Ravenscourt, Brwd. CM15 130 FX46
Sun. TW16 217 BT95
Ravenscourt Av, W6 181 CU77
Ravenscourt Cl, Horn. RM12 off Ravenscourt Dr 150 FL62
Ruislip HA4 137 BQ59
Ravenscourt Dr, Horn. RM12 150 FL62
Ravenscourt Gdns, W6 181 CU77
Ravenscourt Gro, Horn. RM12 150 FL61
⊖ Ravenscourt Park 181 CU77
Ravenscourt Pk, W6 181 CU76
Ravenscourt Pl, W6 181 CV77
Ravenscourt Rd, W6 181 CV77
Orpington BR5 228 EU97
Ravenscourt Sq, W6 181 CU76
Ravenscraig Rd, N11 121 DH49
Ravenscroft, Brox. EN10 71 DZ20
Watford WD25 82 BY34
Ravenscroft Av, NW11 141 CZ59
Wembley HA9 140 CM60
Ravenscroft Cl, E16 23 N6
Ravenscroft Cres, SE9 207 EM90
Ravenscroft Pk, Barn. EN5 101 CX42
Ravenscroft Pt, E9 11 J5
Sch Ravenscroft Prim Sch, E16 23 P5
Ravenscroft Rd, E16 23 P6
W4 180 CQ77
Beckenham BR3 224 DW96
Weybridge KT13 235 BQ111
Sch Ravenscroft Sch, The, N20 off Barnet La 119 CZ45
Ravenscroft St, E2 20 B1
Ravensdale Av, N12 120 DC49
Ravensdale Gdns, SE19 204 DR94
Hounslow TW4 178 BY83
● Ravensdale Ind Est, N16 144 DU58
Ravensdale Ms, Stai. TW18 off Worple Rd 196 BH93
Ravensdale Rd, N16 144 DT59
Hounslow TW4 178 BY83
Ravensdell, Hem.H. HP1 61 BF19
Ravensdon St, SE11 42 F1
Ravensfield, Slou. SL3 174 AX75
Ravensfield Cl, Dag. RM9 148 EX63
Ravensfield Gdns, Epsom KT19 238 CS106
Ravens Gate Ms, Brom. BR2 off Meadow Rd 226 EE96
Ravenshaw St, NW6 5 H3
Ravenshead Cl, S.Croy. CR2 242 DW111
Ravenshill, Chis. BR7 227 EP95
Ravenshurst Av, NW4 141 CW56
Ravenside Cl, N18 123 DX51
Ravenside Retail Pk, N18 123 DX50
Ravens La, Berk. HP4 60 AX19
Ravenslea Rd, SW12 202 DF87
Ravensleigh Gdns, Brom. BR1 off Pike Cl 206 EH92
Ravensmead, Chal.St.P. SL9 113 AZ50
Ravensmead Rd, Brom. BR2 205 ED94
Ravensmede Way, W4 181 CT77
Ravensmere, Epp. CM16 92 EU31
Ravens Ms, SE12 off Ravens Way 206 EG85
Ravenstone, SE17 43 P1
Sch Ravenstone Prim Sch, SW12 off Ravenstone St 203 DH88
Ravenstone Rd, N8 143 DM55
NW9 off West Hendon Bdy 141 CT58
Ravenstone St, SW12 202 DG88
Ravens Way, SE12 206 EG85
Ravens Wf, Berk. HP4 60 AX19
Ravenswold, Ken. CR8 258 DQ115
Ravenswood, Bex. DA5 208 EY88
Ravenswood Av, Surb. KT6 220 CM103
West Wickham BR4 225 EC102
Ravenswood Cl, Cob. KT11 252 BX115
Romford RM5 127 FB50
Ravenswood Ct, Kings.T. KT2 200 CP93
Woking GU22 249 AZ118
Ravenswood Cres, Har. HA2 138 BZ61
West Wickham BR4 225 EC102
Ravenswood Gdns, Islw. TW7 179 CE81
● Ravenswood Ind Est, E17 off Shernhall St 145 EC56
Ravenswood Pk, Nthwd. HA6 115 BU51
Ravenswood Rd, E17 145 EB56
SW12 203 DH87
Croydon CR0 223 DP104
Sch Ravens Wd Sch, Brom. BR2 off Oakley Rd 226 EK104
Ravensworth Rd, NW10 161 CV69
SE9 207 EM91
Slough SL2 153 AN69
Ravey St, EC2 19 N4
Ravine Gro, SE18 187 ES79
Rav Pinter Cl, N16 144 DS59
Rawdon Dr, Hodd. EN11 71 EA18
Rawlings Cl, Beck. BR3 225 EC99
Orpington BR6 245 ET106
Rawlings Cres, Wem. HA9 140 CP62
Rawlings La, Seer Grn HP9 111 AQ48
Rawlings St, SW3 28 E8
Rawlins Cl, N3 141 CY55
South Croydon CR2 243 DY108
Rawlinson Ho, SE13 off Mercator Rd 185 ED84
Rawlyn Cl, Chaff.Hun. RM16 191 FV78
Rawnsley Av, Mitch. CR4 222 DD99
Rawreth Wk, N1 9 K8
Rawson Ct, SW11 off Strasburg Rd 41 J7
Rawson St, SW11 41 H7
Rawsthorne Cl, E16 37 J3
Rawstone Wk, E13 13 P10
Rawstorne Pl, EC1 18 G2
Rawstorne St, EC1 18 G2
Raybarn Rd, Hem.H. HP1 62 BG18
Rayburn Rd, Horn. RM11 150 FN59
Ray Cl, Chess. KT9 237 CJ107
Raydean Rd, New Barn. EN5 102 DB43
Raydon Rd, Chsht EN8 89 DX32
Raydons Gdns, Dag. RM9 148 EY63
Raydons Rd, Dag. RM9 148 EY64
Raydon St, N19 143 DH61
Rayfield, Epp. CM16 92 EU30
Welwyn Garden City AL8 51 CX06
Rayfield Cl, Brom. BR2 226 EL100
Rayford Av, SE12 206 EF87
Rayford Cl, Dart. DA1 210 FJ85
Ray Gdns, Bark. IG11 168 EU68
Stanmore HA7 117 CH50
Ray Lamb Way, Erith DA8 189 FH79
Raylands Mead, Ger.Cr. SL9 134 AW57
Rayleas Cl, SE18 187 EP81
Rayleigh Av, Tedd. TW11 199 CE93
Rayleigh Cl, N13 122 DR48
Hutton CM13 131 GC44
Rayleigh Ct, Kings.T. KT1 220 CM96
Rayleigh Ri, S.Croy. CR2 242 DS107
Rayleigh Rd, E16 36 B2
N13 122 DQ48
SW19 221 CZ95
Hutton CM13 131 GB44
Woodford Green IG8 124 EJ51
Rayley La, N.Wld Bas. CM16 74 FA24
Sch Ray Lo Prim Sch, Wdf.Grn. IG8 off Snakes La E 124 EK51
Ray Lo Rd, Wdf.Grn. IG8 124 EJ51
Ray Massey Way, E6 off Ron Leighton Way 166 EL67
Raymead, NW4 141 CW56
Raymead Av, Th.Hth. CR7 223 DN99
Raymead Cl, Fetch. KT22 253 CE122
Ray Mead Ct, Maid. SL6 off Boulters La 152 AC70
Raymead Pas, Th.Hth. CR7 off Raymead Av 223 DN99
Ray Mead Rd, Maid. SL6 152 AC72
Raymead Way, Fetch. KT22 253 CE122
Raymer Cl, St.Alb. AL1 65 CE19
Raymere Gdns, SE18 187 ER80
Raymer Wk, Horl. RH6 291 DJ147
Raymond Av, E18 146 EF55
W13 179 CG76
Raymond Bldgs, WC1 18 D6
Raymond Cl, SE26 204 DW92
Abbots Langley WD5 81 BR32
Colnbrook SL3 175 BE81
Raymond Ct, N10 off Pembroke Rd 120 DG52
Potters Bar EN6 off St. Francis Cl 86 DC34
Raymond Cres, Guil. GU2 280 AT135
Raymond Gdns, Chig. IG7 126 EV48
Raymond Rd, E13 166 EJ66
SW19 201 CY93
Beckenham BR3 225 DY98
Ilford IG2 147 ER59
Slough SL3 175 BA76
Raymonds Cl, Welw.G.C. AL7 51 CY11
Raymonds Plain, Welw.G.C. AL7 51 CY11
Raymond Way, Clay. KT10 237 CG107
Raymouth Rd, SE16 32 F8
Rayne Ct, E18 146 EF56
Sch Raynehurst Comm Prim Sch, Grav. DA12 off Cerne Rd 213 GM90
Rayners Av Mobile Home Pk, Loud. HP10 110 AC52
Rayners Cl, Colnbr. SL3 175 BC80
Loudwater HP10 110 AC52
Wembley HA0 139 CK64
Rayners Ct, Grav. DA11 212 GB86
Harrow HA2 138 CA60
Rayners Cres, Nthlt. UB5 157 BV69
Rayners Gdns, Nthlt. UB5 157 BV68
RAYNERS LANE, Har. HA2 138 BZ60
⊖ Rayners Lane 138 BZ59
Rayners La, Har. HA2 138 CB61
Pinner HA5 138 BZ58
Rayners Rd, SW15 201 CY85
Rayner Twrs, E10 145 EA59
Raynes Av, E11 146 EJ59
RAYNES PARK, SW20 221 CV97
⇌ Raynes Park 221 CW96
Sch Raynes Pk High Sch, SW20 off Bushey Rd 221 CV97
Raynham, W2 16 C9
Raynham Av, N18 122 DU51
Sch Raynham Prim Sch, N18 off Raynham Av 122 DU50
Raynham Rd, N18 122 DU50
W6 181 CV77
Raynham St, Hert. SG13 54 DS08
Raynham Ter, N18 122 DU50
Raynor Cl, Sthl. UB1 158 BZ74
Raynor Pl, N1 9 K7
Raynsford Rd, Ware SG12 55 DY06
Raynton Cl, Har. HA2 138 BY60
Hayes UB4 157 BT70
Raynton Dr, Hayes UB4 157 BT70
Raynton Rd, Enf. EN3 105 DX37
Ray Rd, Rom. RM5 127 FB50
West Molesey KT8 218 CB99
Rays Av, N18 122 DW49
Windsor SL4 173 AM80
Rays Hill, Hort.Kir. DA4 230 FQ98
Rays La, Penn HP10 110 AC47
Rays Rd, N18 122 DW49
West Wickham BR4 225 EC101
Ray St, EC1 18 F5
Ray St Br, EC1 18 F5
Ray Wk, N7 off Andover Rd 143 DM61
Raywood Cl, Harling. UB3 177 BQ80
Reach, The, SE28 187 ES75
Reachview Cl, NW1 7 M7
Read Cl, T.Ditt. KT7 219 CG101
Read Ct, Wal.Abb. EN9 90 EG33
Reade Ct, Farn.Com. SL2 off Victoria Rd 153 AQ65
Readens, The, Bans. SM7 256 DF116
Reading Arch Rd, Red. RH1 272 DF134
Reading Cl, SE22 204 DU86
Reading La, E8 10 E5
Reading Rd, Nthlt. UB5 138 CB64
Sutton SM1 240 DC106
Readings, The, Chorl. WD3 95 BF41
Harlow CM18 73 ET18
Reading Way, NW7 119 CX50
Read Rd, Ashtd. KT21 253 CK117
Reads Cl, Ilf. IG1 off Chapel Rd 147 EP62
Reads Rest La, Tad. KT20 255 CZ119
Read Way, Grav. DA12 213 GK92
Reapers Cl, NW1 7 N8
Reapers Way, Islw. TW7 off Hall Rd 199 CD85
Reardon Ct, N21 122 DQ47
Reardon Path, E1 32 F3
Reardon St, E1 32 E2
Reaston St, SE14 45 H4
Sch Reay Prim Sch, SW9 42 D5
Reckitt Rd, W4 180 CS78
Record St, SE15 44 G2
Recovery St, SW17 202 DE92
Recreation Av, Harold Wd RM3 128 FM54
Romford RM7 149 FC57
Recreation Rd, SE26 205 DX91
Bromley BR2 226 EF96
Guildford GU1 264 AW134
Sidcup DA15 off Woodside Rd 207 ES90
Southall UB2 178 BY77
Recreation Way, Mitch. CR4 223 DK97
Rector St, N1 9 J9
Rectory Chase, Lt.Warley CM13 151 FX56
Rectory Cl, E4 123 EA48
N3 119 CZ53
SW20 221 CW97
Ashtead KT21 254 CM119
Byfleet KT14 234 BL113
Dartford DA1 189 FE84
Essendon AL9 68 DF17
Farnham Royal SL2 153 AQ69
Guildford GU4 265 BD132
Hunsdon SG12 56 EK07
Long Ditton KT6 219 CJ102
Shepperton TW17 216 BN97
Sidcup DA14 208 EV91
Stanmore HA7 117 CH51
Windsor SL4 173 AN81
Rectory Cres, E11 146 EJ58
Rectory Fm Rd, Enf. EN2 103 DM38
Rectory Fld, Harl. CM19 73 EP17
Rectory Fld Cres, SE7 186 EJ80
Rectory Gdns, N8 143 DL56
SW4 41 L10
Rectory Gdns, Chalfont St. Giles HP8 112 AV48
Hatfield AL10 67 CV18
Northolt UB5 158 BZ67
Upminster RM14 151 FR61
Rectory Grn, Beck. BR3 225 DZ95
Rectory Gro, SW4 41 L10
Croydon CR0 223 DP103
Hampton TW12 198 BZ91
Rectory Hill, Amer. HP6, HP7 77 AP39
Rectory La, SW17 202 DG93
Ashtead KT21 254 CM118
Banstead SM7 240 DF114
Berkhamsted HP4 60 AW19
Bookham KT23 268 BZ126
Brasted TN16 262 EW123
Buckland RH3 271 CT131
Byfleet KT14 234 BL113
Edgware HA8 118 CN51
Harlow CM19 73 EP17
Kings Langley WD4 80 BN28
Long Ditton KT6 219 CH102
Loughton IG10 107 EN40
Rickmansworth WD3 114 BK46
Sevenoaks TN13 279 FJ126
Shenley WD7 84 CN33
Shere GU5 282 BM139
Sidcup DA14 208 EV91
Stanmore HA7 117 CH50
Wallington SM6 241 DJ105
Westerham TN16 260 EL123
Rectory Meadow, Sthflt DA13 212 GA93
Rectory Orchard, SW19 201 CY91
Rectory Pk, S.Croy. CR2 242 DS113
Rectory Pk Av, Nthlt. UB5 158 BZ69
Rectory Pl, SE18 37 L7
⇌ Rectory Road 144 DT62
Rectory Rd, E12 147 EM64
E17 145 EB55
N16 144 DT62
SW13 181 CU82
W3 160 CP74
Beckenham BR3 225 EA95
Chipstead CR5 272 DD125
Dagenham RM10 168 FA66
Grays RM17 192 GD76
Hayes UB3 157 BU72
Hounslow TW4 177 BV81
Keston BR2 244 EK108
Rickmansworth WD3 114 BK46
Southall UB2 178 BZ76
Sutton SM1 222 DA104
Swanscombe DA10 212 FY87
Taplow SL6 152 AD70
Welwyn Garden City AL8 51 CV06
West Tilbury RM18 193 GK79
Rectory Sq, E1 21 K6
Rectory Way, Amer. HP7 77 AP39
Uxbridge UB10 137 BP62
Rectory Wd, Harl. CM20 57 EQ14
Reculver Ms, N18 122 DU49
Reculver Rd, SE16 33 J10
Red Anchor Cl, SW3 40 C3
Redan Pl, W2 15 L9
Redan St, W14 26 D6
Redan Ter, SE5 43 H8
Redbarn Cl, Pur. CR8 off Whytecliffe Rd N 241 DP111
Red Barracks Rd, SE18 37 K9
Redberry Gro, SE26 204 DW90
Redbourne Av, N3 120 DA53
Redbourne Dr, SE28 168 EX72
Redbourn Rd, Hem.H. HP2 62 BN16
St. Albans AL3 64 CA18
REDBRIDGE, Ilf. IG1 147 EM58
⊖ Redbridge 146 EK58
Coll Redbridge Coll, Rom. RM6 off Little Heath 148 EV57
Coll Redbridge Drama Cen, E18 off Churchfields 124 EG53
● Redbridge Enterprise Cen, Ilf. IG1 147 EQ61
Redbridge Gdns, SE5 43 P5
Redbridge Ho, E16 off University Way 37 N1
Coll Redbridge Inst of Adult Ed, Ilf. IG2 off Gaysham Av 147 EP57
Redbridge La E, Ilf. IG4 146 EK58
Redbridge La W, E11 146 EH58
Coll Redbridge Music Sch, Ilf. IG6 off Fencepiece Rd 125 EQ52
Sch Redbridge Prim Sch, Ilf. IG4 off College Gdns 146 EL57
Redbridge Rbt, Ilf. IG4 146 EJ58
Redburn St, SW3 40 E2
Redbury Cl, Rain. RM13 169 FH70
Redcar Cl, Nthlt. UB5 138 CB64
Redcar Rd, Rom. RM3 128 FM50
Redcar St, SE5 43 J5
Redcastle Cl, E1 20 G10
Red Cedars Rd, Orp. BR6 227 ES101
Redchurch St, E2 20 A4
Redcliffe Cl, SW5 off Old Brompton Rd 39 L1
Redcliffe Ct, E5 off Napoleon Rd 144 DV62
Redcliffe Gdns, SW5 39 M1
SW10 39 M1
W4 180 CP80
Ilford IG1 147 EN60
Redcliffe Ms, SW10 39 M1
Redcliffe Pl, SW10 39 N3
Redcliffe Rd, SW10 39 N1
Sch Redcliffe Sch, SW10 39 N2
Redcliffe Sq, SW10 39 M1
Redcliffe St, SW10 39 M2
Redclose Av, Mord. SM4 222 DA99
Redclyffe Rd, E6 166 EJ67
Redcote Pl, Dor. RH4 269 CK134
Red Cottage Ms, Slou. SL3 174 AW76
Red Ct, Slou. SL1 154 AS74
Redcourt, Wok. GU22 249 BD115
Red Cow, Slou. SL1 174 AT76
Redcroft Rd, Sthl. UB1 158 CC73
Redcross Way, SE1 31 K4
Redden Ct Rd, Rom. RM3 150 FL55
Sch Redden Ct Sch, Harold Wd RM3 off Cotswold Rd 150 FM55
Redding Cl, Dart. DA2 211 FS89
Redding Dr, Amer. HP6 77 AN37
Reddings, Hem.H. HP3 62 BM22
Welwyn Garden City AL8 51 CW08
Reddings, The, NW7 119 CT48
Borehamwood WD6 100 CM41
Reddings Av, Bushey WD23 98 CB43
Reddings Cl, NW7 119 CT49
Sch Reddings Prim & Nurs Sch, The, Hem.H. HP3 off Bennetts End Rd 62 BN22
Reddington Cl, S.Croy. CR2 242 DR109
Reddington Dr, Slou. SL3 174 AY76
Reddington Ho, N1 8 D10
Reddins Rd, SE15 44 C3
Redditch Ct, Hem.H. HP2 62 BM16
Reddons Rd, Beck. BR3 205 DY94
Reddown Rd, Couls. CR5 257 DK118
Reddy Rd, Erith DA8 189 FF79
Rede Ct, Wey. KT13 217 BP104
Redehall Rd, Smallfield RH6 291 DP148
Redenham Ho, SW15 off Tangley Gro 201 CT87
Rede Pl, W2 15 K9
Redesdale Gdns, Islw. TW7 179 CG80
Redesdale St, SW3 40 D2
Redfern Av, Houns. TW4 198 CA87
Redfern Cl, Uxb. UB8 156 BJ67
Redfern Gdns, Rom. RM2 128 FK54
Redfern Rd, NW10 160 CS66
SE6 205 EC87
Redfield La, SW5 27 K8
Redfield Ms, SW5 27 K8
Redford Av, Couls. CR5 241 DH114
Thornton Heath CR7 223 DM98
Wallington SM6 241 DL107
Redford Cl, Felt. TW13 197 BT89
H Redford Lo Psychiatric Hosp, N9 122 DU47
Redford Rd, Wind. SL4 173 AK81
Redford Wk, N1 9 H8
Redford Way, Uxb. UB8 156 BJ66
Redgate Dr, Brom. BR2 226 EH103
Sch Red Gates Sch, Croy. CR0 off Purley Way 241 DN106
Redgate Ter, SW15 201 CY86
Redgrave Cl, Croy. CR0 224 DT100
Redgrave Ct, Denh. UB9 off Patrons Way E 135 BF57
Redgrave Rd, SW15 181 CX83
Redhall Cl, Hat. AL10 67 CT21
Redhall Ct, Cat. CR3 258 DR123
Redhall Dr, Hat. AL10 67 CT22
Redhall End, St.Alb. AL4 off Roestock La 66 CS22
Redhall La, Chan.Cr. WD3 96 BL39
Redheath Cl, Wat. WD25 97 BT35
REDHILL, RH1 272 DG134
⇌ Redhill 272 DG133
⊖ Redhill 272 DG133
Red Hill, Chis. BR7 207 EN92
Denham UB9 135 BD61
Redhill Common, Red. RH1 288 DE135
Redhill Dr, Edg. HA8 118 CQ54
Sch Red Hill Prim Sch, Chis. BR7 off Red Hill 207 EP92
Redhill Rd, Cob. KT11 235 BP113
Red Hills, Hodd. EN11 70 DV19
Redhill St, NW1 17 K2
★ Red Ho, The (William Morris Ho), Bexh. DA6 188 EY84
Red Ho Cl, Knot.Grn HP9 110 AH51
Ware SG12 55 DY07
Red Ho La, Bexh. DA6 188 EX84
Walton-on-Thames KT12 217 BU103
Red Ho Rd, Croy. CR0 223 DK100
Redhouse Rd, Tats. TN16 260 EJ120
Red Ho Sq, N1 9 K5
Redington Gdns, NW3 142 DB63
Redington Rd, NW3 142 DB63
Redland Gdns, W.Mol. KT8 off Dunstable Rd 218 BZ98
Redlands, Couls. CR5 257 DL116
Sch Redlands C of E Prim Sch, The, Dor. RH4 off Goodwyns Rd 285 CH139
Redlands Ct, Brom. BR1 206 EF94
Redlands La, Mid Holm. RH5 285 CG142
Sch Redlands Prim Sch, E1 21 H6
Redlands Rd, Enf. EN3 105 DY39
Sevenoaks TN13 278 FF124
Redlands Way, SW2 203 DM87
Red La, Clay. KT10 237 CG107
Dorking RH5 286 CL142
Oxted RH8 276 EH133
Redleaf Cl, Belv. DA17 188 FA79
Fetcham KT22 253 CE124
Red Leaf Cl, Slou. SL3 off Pickford Dr 155 AZ74
Redleaves Av, Ashf. TW15 197 BP93
Redlees Cl, Islw. TW7 179 CG84
Red Leys, Uxb. UB8 156 BL66
● Red Lion Business Pk, Surb. KT6 220 CM103
Red Lion Cl, SE17 43 K2
Aldenham WD25 off Church La 98 CC37
Orpington BR5 228 EW100
Red Lion Ct, EC4 18 F8
Hatfield AL9 67 CW16
Red Lion Cres, Harl. CM17 74 EW17
Red Lion Dr, Hem.H. HP3 80 BM25
Red Lion Hill, N2 120 DD54
Red Lion La, SE18 187 EN80
Chobham GU24 232 AS109
Harlow CM17 74 EW17
Hemel Hempstead HP3 80 BM26
Sarratt WD3 96 BG35
Red Lion Par, Pnr. HA5 138 BY55
Red Lion Pl, SE18 off Shooters Hill Rd 187 EN81
Red Lion Rd, Chobham GU24 232 AS109
Surbiton KT6 220 CM103
Red Lion Row, SE17 43 K2
Red Lion Sq, SW18 off Wandsworth High St 202 DA85
WC1 18 C7
Red Lion St, WC1 18 C6
Chesham HP5 76 AP32
Richmond TW9 199 CK85
Red Lion Way, Woob.Grn HP10 132 AE57
Red Lion Yd, W1 29 H2
Red Lo Cres, Bex. DA5 209 FD90
Red Lo Gdns, Berk. HP4 60 AU20
Red Lo Rd, Beck. BR3 225 ED100
Bexley DA5 209 FD90
West Wickham BR4 225 EC102
Redman Cl, Nthlt. UB5 158 BW68
Redmans La, Shore. TN14 247 FE107
Redmans Rd, E1 20 G6
Redmead La, E1 32 C3
Redmead Rd, Hayes UB3 177 BS77
Redmore Rd, W6 181 CV77
Red Oak Cl, Croy. CR0 225 EA103
Orpington BR6 227 EP104
Red Oaks Mead, They.B. CM16 107 ER37
Red Path, E9 11 M4
Red Pl, W1 16 G10
Redpoll Way, Erith DA18 188 EX76

Red Post Hill, SE21 204 DR85
SE24 184 DR84
Redricks La, Saw. CM21 57 ES09
Redriffe Rd, E13 13 M9
Redriff Est, SE16 33 M6
Sch Redriff Prim Sch, SE16 33 M4
Redriff Rd, SE16 33 K7
Romford RM7 127 FB54
Red Rd, Borwd. WD6 100 CM41
Warley CM14 130 FV49
Redroofs Cl, Beck. BR3 225 EB95
Jct Red Rover, SW15 181 CT83
Redruth Cl, N22 121 DM52
Redruth Gdns, Clay. KT10 237 CF108
Romford RM3 128 FM50
Redruth Rd, E9 11 H8
Romford RM3 128 FN50
Redruth Wk, Rom. RM3 128 FN50
Redsan Cl, S.Croy. CR2 242 DR108
Red Sq, N16 144 DR62
Redstart Cl, E6 24 G6
SE14 45 L4
New Addington CR0 243 ED110
Redstart Mans, Ilf. IG1
off Mill Rd 147 EN62
Redstone Hill, Red. RH1 272 DG134
Redstone Hollow, Red. RH1 288 DG135
Redstone Manor, Red. RH1 272 DG134
Redstone Pk, Red. RH1 272 DG134
Redstone Rd, Red. RH1 288 DG135
Redston Rd, N8 143 DK56
REDSTREET, Grav. DA13 212 GB93
Red St, Sthflt DA13 212 GA93
Redtiles Gdns, Ken. CR8 257 DP115
Redvers Rd, N22 121 DN54
Warlingham CR6 258 DW118
Redvers St, N1 19 P2
Redwald Rd, E5 11 K1
Redway Dr, Twick. TW2 198 CC87
Red Willow, Harl. CM19 73 EM18
Redwing Cl, S.Croy. CR2 243 DX111
Redwing Ct, W.Byf. KT14 234 BH112
Redwing Gro, Abb.L. WD5 81 BU31
Redwing Ms, SE5 43 J9
Redwing Path, SE28 187 ER75
Redwing Ri, Guil. GU4 265 BD132
Redwing Rd, Wall. SM6 241 DL108
Redwood, Burn. SL1 152 AG68
Egham TW20 215 BE96
Redwood Chase, S.Ock. RM15 171 FW70
Redwood Cl, E3 12 A10
N14 121 DK45
SE16 33 M3
Kenley CR8 242 DQ114
St. Albans AL1 65 CJ20
Sidcup DA15 208 EU87
Uxbridge UB10 157 BP68
Watford WD19 116 BW49
Redwood Ct, NW6 4 E7
Redwood Dr, Hem.H. HP3 62 BL22
Redwood Est, Houns. TW5 177 BV79
Redwood Gdns, E4 105 EB44
Chigwell IG7 126 EU50
Slough SL1
off Godolphin Rd 153 AR73
Redwood Gro, W5 179 CH76
Chilworth GU4 281 BC140
Redwood Ms, SW4 41 K10
Ashford TW15
off Napier Wk 197 BR94
Redwood Mt, Reig. RH2 272 DA131
Redwood Pl, Beac. HP9 111 AK54
Redwood Ri, Borwd. WD6 100 CN37
Redwoods, SW15 201 CU88
Addlestone KT15 234 BG107
Hertford SG14 54 DQ08
Redwoods, The, Wind. SL4 173 AR83
Redwoods Cl, Buck.H. IG9 124 EH47
Redwood Wk, Surb. KT6 219 CK102
Redwood Way, Barn. EN5 101 CX43
Reece Ms, SW7 28 A8
Reed Av, Orp. BR6 227 ES104
Reed Cl, E16 23 N7
SE12 206 EG85
Iver SL0 155 BE72
London Colney AL2 83 CK27
Reed Ct, Green. DA9 191 FW84
Reed Dr, Red. RH1 288 DG137
Reede Gdns, Dag. RM10 149 FB64
Reede Rd, Dag. RM10 168 FA65
Reede Way, Dag. RM10 149 FB64
⇌ Reedham 241 DM113
Reedham Cl, N17 144 DV56
Bricket Wood AL2 82 CA29
Reedham Dr, Pur. CR8 241 DM113
Reedham Pk Av, Pur. CR8 257 DN116
Reedham Rd, Burn. SL1 152 AJ69
Reedham St, SE15 44 C9
Reedholm Vil, N16 144 DR63
Reed Ho, SW19
off Durnsford Rd 202 DB91
Reed Pl, SW4 183 DK84
Shepperton TW17 216 BM102
West Byfleet KT14 233 BE113
Reed Pond Wk, Rom. RM2 127 FF54
Reed Rd, N17 122 DT54
Reeds, The, Welw.G.C. AL7 51 CX10
Reeds Cres, Wat. WD24 98 BW40
Reedsfield Cl, Ashf. TW15
off Reedsfield Rd 197 BP91
Reedsfield Rd, Ashf. TW15 197 BP91
Reeds Pl, NW1 7 L6
Sch Reed's Sch, Cob. KT11
off Sandy La 236 CA112
Reeds Wk, Wat. WD24 98 BW40
Reed Way, Slou. SL1 153 AM73
Reedworth St, SE11 30 F9
Reef Ho, E14 off Manchester Rd 34 F6
Ree La Cotts, Loug. IG10
off Englands La 107 EN39
Reenglass Rd, Stan. HA7 117 CK49
Rees Dr, Stan. HA7 118 CL49
Rees Gdns, Croy. CR0 224 DT100
Reesland Cl, E12 167 EN65
Rees St, N1 9 K9
Reets Fm Cl, NW9 140 CS58
Reeve Rd, Reig. RH2 288 DC138
Reeves Av, NW9 140 CR59
Tr Reeves Corner 223 DP103
Reeves Cor, Croy. CR0
off Roman Way 223 DP103
Reeves Cres, Swan. BR8 229 FD97
Reeves La, Roydon CM19 72 EJ19
Reeves Ms, W1 28 G1
Reeves Rd, E3 22 C4
SE18 187 EP79
Reflection, The, E16 37 N4
Reform Row, N17 122 DT54
Reform St, SW11 40 E8
Regal Cl, E1 20 D6
W5 159 CK71
Regal Ct, N18 122 DT50
Regal Cres, Wall. SM6 223 DH104
Regal Dr, N11 121 DH50
Regalfield Cl, Guil. GU2 264 AU130
Regal Ho, SW6
off Lensbury Av 39 P8
Ilford IG2 off Royal Cres 147 ER58
Regal La, NW1 7 H9
Regal Pl, E3 21 P3
SW6 39 M5
Regal Row, SE15 44 G6
Regal Way, Har. HA3 140 CL58
Watford WD24 98 BW38
Regan Cl, Guil. GU2 264 AV129
Regan Ho, N18 122 DT51
Regan Way, N1 19 N1
Regarder Rd, Chig. IG7 126 EU50
Regarth Av, Rom. RM1 149 FE58
Regatta Ho, Tedd. TW11
off Twickenham Rd 199 CG91
Regency Cl, W5 160 CL72
Chigwell IG7 125 EQ50
Hampton TW12 198 BZ92
Regency Ct, E18 124 EG54
Brentwood CM14 130 FW47
Broxbourne EN10
off Berners Way 71 DZ23
Harlow CM18 74 EU18
Hemel Hempstead HP2
off Alexandra Rd 62 BK20
Sutton SM1
off Brunswick Rd 240 DB105
Regency Cres, NW4 119 CX54
Regency Dr, Ruis. HA4 137 BS60
West Byfleet KT14 233 BF113
Regency Gdns, Horn. RM11 150 FJ59
Walton-on-Thames KT12 218 BW102
Regency Ho, SW6
off The Boulevard 39 P7
Regency Lo, Buck.H. IG9 124 EK47
Regency Ms, NW10 161 CU65
SW9 43 H5
Beckenham BR3 225 EC95
Isleworth TW7
off Queensbridge Pk 199 CE85
Regency Pl, SW1 29 P8
Regency St, NW10 160 CS70
SW1 29 N8
Regency Ter, SW7
off Fulham Rd 28 A10
Regency Wk, Croy. CR0 225 DY100
Richmond TW10
off Grosvenor Rd 200 CL85
Regency Way, Bexh. DA6 188 EX83
Woking GU22 249 BD115
Regeneration Rd, SE16 33 J9
Regent Av, Uxb. UB10 157 BP66
● Regent Business Cen, Hayes UB3
off Pump La 177 BU75
Regent Cl, N12 off Nether St 120 DC50
Grays RM16 192 GC75
Harrow HA3 140 CL58
Hounslow TW4 177 BV81
Kings Langley WD4 80 BN29
New Haw KT15 234 BK109
Redhill RH1 273 DJ129
St. Albans AL4 65 CJ16
Sch Regent Coll, Har. HA2
off Imperial Dr 138 CA59
Regent Ct, Slou. SL1 154 AS72
Welwyn Garden City AL7 51 CY10
Windsor SL4 173 AR81
Regent Cres, Red. RH1 272 DF132
Regent Gdns, Ilf. IG3 148 EU58
Regent Gate, Wal.Cr. EN8 89 DX34
● Regent Pk, Lthd. KT22 253 CG118
Regent Pk, Barn. EN4 102 DB39
Regent Pl, SW19
off Haydons Rd 202 DB92
W1 17 M10
Croydon CR0 off Grant Rd 224 DT102
Regent Rd, SE24 203 DP86
Epping CM16 91 ET30
Surbiton KT5 220 CM99
Regents Av, N13 121 DM50
Regents Br Gdns, SW8 42 B4
Regents Cl, Hayes UB4 157 BS71
Radlett WD7 83 CG34
South Croydon CR2 242 DS107
Whyteleafe CR3 258 DS118
Coll Regent's Coll, NW1 16 G4
Regents Dr, Kes. BR2 244 EK106
Woodford Green IG8 125 EN51
Regents Ms, NW8 5 P10
Horley RH6
off Victoria Rd 290 DG148
REGENT'S PARK, NW1 17 H1
⊖ Regent's Park 17 J5
★ Regent's Park, The, NW1 16 F1
Regent's Pk Est, NW1 17 K3
Regents Pk Rd, N3 141 CZ55
NW1 6 F8
Regents Pk Ter, NW1 7 J8
Regent's Pl, SE3 47 N8
Regents Pl, Loug. IG10 124 EK45
Regent Sq, E3 22 C3
WC1 18 B3
Belvedere DA17 189 FB77
Regents Row, E8 10 C9
Regent St, NW10 14 D3
SW1 29 N1
W1 17 K8
W4 180 CN78
Watford WD24 97 BV38
Regents Wf, N1 8 C10
Regina Cl, Barn. EN5 101 CX41
Sch Regina Coeli Catholic Prim Sch, S.Croy. CR2
off Pampisford Rd 241 DP108
Reginald Ms, Harl. CM17
off Green St 58 EX14
Reginald Rd, E7 13 N6
SE8 46 A5
Northwood HA6 115 BT53
Romford RM3 128 FN53
Reginald Sq, SE8 46 A5
Regina Pt, SE16 33 H6
Regina Rd, N4 143 DM60
SE25 224 DU97
W13 159 CG74
Southall UB2 178 BY77
Regina Ter, W13 159 CG74
Regis Pl, SW2 183 DM84
Regis Rd, NW5 7 J3
Regius Ct, Penn HP10 110 AD47
Regnart Bldgs, NW1 17 M4
Reid Av, Cat. CR3 258 DR121
Reid Cl, Couls. CR5 257 DH116
Hayes UB3 157 BS72
Pinner HA5 137 BU56
Reidhaven Rd, SE18 187 ES77
REIGATE, RH2 272 DA134
⇌ Reigate 272 DA133
Reigate Av, Sutt. SM1 222 DA102
● Reigate Business Ms, Reig. RH2 off Albert Rd N 271 CZ133
Coll Reigate Coll, Reig. RH2
off Castlefield Rd 272 DB134
Sch Reigate Gram Sch, Reig. RH2
off Reigate Rd 272 DC134
Reigate Heath, Reig. RH2 287 CX135
Reigate Hill, Reig. RH2 272 DB130
Reigate Hill Cl, Reig. RH2 272 DA131
Jct Reigate Hill Interchange, Tad. KT20 272 DB129
Sch Reigate Parish Ch Sch, Reig. RH2 off Blackborough Rd 272 DC134
Sch Reigate Priory Sch, Reig. RH2
off Bell St 272 DA134
Reigate Rd, Bet. RH3 270 CS132
Bromley BR1 206 EF90
Dorking RH4 285 CJ135
Epsom KT17, KT18 239 CT110
Hookwood RH6 290 DC146
Ilford IG3 147 ET61
Leatherhead KT22 253 CJ123
Redhill RH1 272 DB134
Reigate RH2 272 DB134
Sidlow RH2 288 DB141
Tadworth KT20 255 CX117
Sch Reigate St. Mary's Prep & Choir Sch, Reig. RH2
off Chart La 272 DB134
Sch Reigate Sch, Reig. RH2
off Pendleton Rd 288 DC137
Reigate Way, Wall. SM6 241 DL106
Reighton Rd, E5 144 DU62
Reindeer Cl, E13 13 P9
Reindorp Cl, Guil. GU2
off Old Ct Rd 280 AU135
Reinickendorf Av, SE9 207 EQ85
Reizel Cl, N16 144 DT60
Relay Rd, W12 26 B1
Relf Rd, SE15 44 D10
Reliance Sq, EC2 19 P4
Relko Ct, Epsom KT19 238 CR110
Relko Gdns, Sutt. SM1 240 DD106
Relton Ms, SW7 28 D6
Rembrandt Cl, E14 34 G7
SW1 28 G9
Rembrandt Ct, Epsom KT19 239 CT107
Rembrandt Dr, Nthflt DA11 212 GD90
Rembrandt Rd, SE13 186 EE84
Edgware HA8 118 CN54
Rembrandt Way, Walt. KT12 217 BV104
Remington Rd, E6 24 G8
N15 144 DR58
Remington St, N1 19 H1
Remnant St, WC2 18 C8
Remus Cl, St.Alb. AL1 65 CD24
Remus Rd, E3 12 A7
Renaissance Ct, Houns. TW3
off Prince Regent Rd 178 CC83
Renaissance Wk, SE10 35 M6
Rendel Ho, Bans. SM7 256 DC118
Rendle Cl, Croy. CR0 224 DT99
Rendlesham Av, Rad. WD7 99 CF37
Rendlesham Cl, Ware SG12 54 DV05
Rendlesham Rd, E5 144 DU63
Enfield EN2 103 DP39
Rendlesham Way, Chorl. WD3 95 BC44
Renforth St, SE16 33 H5
Renfree Way, Shep. TW17 216 BM101
Renfrew Cl, E6 25 L9
Renfrew Ho, E17
off Sherwood Cl 123 DZ54
Renfrew Rd, SE11 30 G8
Hounslow TW4 178 BX82
Kingston upon Thames KT2 200 CP94
Renmans, The, Ashtd. KT21 254 CM116
Renmuir St, SW17 202 DF93
Rennell St, SE13 185 EC83
Rennels Way, Islw. TW7 179 CE82
Renness Rd, E17 145 DY55
Rennets Cl, SE9 207 ES85
Rennets Wd Rd, SE9 207 ER85
Rennie Cl, Ashf. TW15 196 BK90
Rennie Ct, SE1 off Upper Grd 30 G2
Enfield EN3
off Brunswick Rd 105 EA38
Rennie Dr, Dart. DA1
off Marsh St N 190 FN82
Rennie Est, SE16 32 F9
Rennie Ho, SE1 off Bath Ter 31 J7
Rennie St, SE1 30 G2
Rennie Ter, Red. RH1 288 DG135
Rennison Cl, Chsht EN7 88 DT27
Renovation, The, E16 37 N4
Renown Cl, Croy. CR0 223 DP102
Romford RM7 126 FA53
Rensburg Rd, E17 145 DX57
Renshaw Cl, Belv. DA17
off Grove Rd 188 EZ79
Renters Av, NW4 141 CW58
Renton Dr, Orp. BR5 228 EX101
● Renwick Ind Est, Bark. IG11 168 EV67
Renwick Rd, Bark. IG11 168 EV70
Repens Way, Hayes UB4 158 BX70
Rephidim St, SE1 31 N7
Replingham Rd, SW18 201 CZ88
Reporton Rd, SW6 38 F5
Repository Rd, SE18 187 EM79
Repton Av, Hayes UB3 177 BR77
Romford RM2 149 FG55
Wembley HA0 139 CJ63
Repton Cl, Cars. SM5 240 DE106
Repton Ct, Beck. BR3 225 EB95
Ilford IG5 off Repton Gro 125 EM53
Repton Dr, Rom. RM2 149 FG56
Repton Gdns, Rom. RM2 149 FG55
Repton Grn, St.Alb. AL3 65 CD16
Repton Gro, Ilf. IG5 125 EM53
Repton Pl, Amer. HP7 94 AU39
Repton Rd, Har. HA3 140 CM56
Orpington BR6 228 EU104
Repton St, E14 21 M8
Repton Way, Crox.Grn WD3 96 BN43
Repulse Cl, Rom. RM5 126 FA53
Reservoir Cl, Green. DA9 211 FW86
Thornton Heath CR7 224 DR98
Reservoir Rd, N14 103 DJ43
SE4 45 L9
Reservoir Rd, Ruislip HA4 137 BQ57
Resham Cl, Sthl. UB2 178 BW76
Residence, Pnr. HA5
off Marsh Rd 138 BY56
Resolution Wk, SE18 37 J6
Resolution Way, SE8 46 A4
Reson Way, Hem.H. HP1 62 BH21
Restavon Pk, Berry's Grn TN16 261 EP116
Restell Cl, SE3 47 K2
Restmor Way, Wall. SM6 222 DG103
Reston Cl, Borwd. WD6 100 CN38
Reston Path, Borwd. WD6 100 CN38
Reston Pl, SW7 27 N5
Restons Cres, SE9 207 ER86
Restoration Sq, SW11 40 B7
Restormel Cl, Houns. TW3 198 CA85
Retcar Cl, N19
off Dartmouth Pk Hill 143 DH61
Retcar Pl, N19 143 DH61
Retford Cl, Borwd. WD6 100 CN38
Romford RM3 128 FN51
Retford Path, Rom. RM3 128 FN51
Retford Rd, Rom. RM3 128 FM51
Retford St, N1 19 P1
Retingham Way, E4 123 EB47
Retreat, The, NW9 140 CR57
SW14
off South Worple Way 180 CS83
Addlestone KT15 234 BK106
Amersham HP6 94 AY39
Brentwood CM14 130 FV46
Englefield Green TW20 194 AX92
Fifield SL6 172 AD80
Grays RM17 192 GB79
Harrow HA2 138 CA59
Hutton CM13 131 GB44
Kings Langley WD4 81 BQ31
Orpington BR6 246 EV107
Surbiton KT5 220 CM100
Thornton Heath CR7 224 DR98
Worcester Park KT4 221 CV104
Retreat Cl, Har. HA3 139 CJ57
Retreat Pl, E9 11 H5
Retreat Rd, Rich. TW9 199 CK85
Retreat Way, Chig. IG7 126 EV48
Reubens Rd, Hutt. CM13 131 GB44
Reunion Row, E1
off Tobacco Dock 32 F1
Reuters Plaza, E14 34 B3
Reveley Sq, SE16 33 M5
Revell Cl, Fetch. KT22 252 CB122
Revell Dr, Fetch. KT22 252 CB122
Revell Ri, SE18 187 ET79
Revell Rd, Kings.T. KT1 220 CP95
Sutton SM1 239 CZ107
Revelon Rd, SE4 185 DY84
Revel Rd, Woob.Grn HP10 132 AD55
Revels Cl, Hert. SG14 54 DR07
Revels Rd, Hert. SG14 54 DR07
Revelstoke Rd, SW18 201 CZ89
Reventlow Rd, SE9 207 EQ88
Reverdy Rd, SE1 32 C9
Reverend Cl, Har. HA2 138 CB62
Revere Way, Epsom KT19 238 CS109
Revesby Rd, Cars. SM5 222 DD100
Review Lodge, Dag. RM10 169 FA68
Review Rd, NW2 141 CT61
Dagenham RM10 169 FB67
Rewell St, SW6 39 N5
Rewley Rd, Cars. SM5 222 DD100
Rex Av, Ashf. TW15 196 BN93
Rex Cl, Rom. RM5 127 FB52
Rex Pl, W1 29 H1
Reydon Av, E11 146 EJ58
Reynard Cl, SE4 45 M10
Bromley BR1 227 EM97
Reynard Ct, Pur. CR8 241 DN111
Reynard Dr, SE19 204 DT94
Reynard Pl, SE14
off Milton Ct Rd 45 M3
Reynardson Rd, N17 122 DQ52
Reynards Way, Brick.Wd AL2 82 BZ29
Reynard Way, Hert. SG13 54 DU09
Reynolah Gdns, SE7 36 B10
Reynolds Av, E12 147 EN64
Chessington KT9 238 CL108
Redhill RH1 273 DH132
Romford RM6 148 EW59
Reynolds Cl, NW11 142 DB59
SW19 222 DD95
Carshalton SM5 222 DF102
Hemel Hempstead HP1 62 BG19
Reynolds Ct, E11
off Cobbold Rd 146 EF62
Romford RM6 148 EX55
Reynolds Cres, Sand. AL4 65 CH15
Reynolds Dr, Edg. HA8 140 CM55
Reynolds Ho, Enf. EN1
off Ayley Cft 104 DU43
Reynolds Pl, SE3 186 EH80
Richmond TW10
off Cambrian Rd 200 CM86
Reynolds Rd, SE15 204 DW85
W4 180 CQ76
Beaconsfield HP9 110 AJ52
Hayes UB4 158 BW70
New Malden KT3 220 CR101
Reynolds Wk, Chesh. HP5
off Great Hivings 76 AN27
Reynolds Way, Croy. CR0 242 DS105
Rhapsody Cres, Warley CM14 130 FV50
Rheidol Ms, N1 9 J10
Rheidol Ter, N1 9 H10
Rheingold Way, Wall. SM6 241 DL109
Rheola Cl, N17 122 DT53
Rhoda St, E2 20 B4
Rhodes Av, N22 121 DJ53
Sch Rhodes Av Prim Sch, N22
off Rhodes Av 121 DJ53
Rhodes Cl, Egh. TW20 195 BB92
Rhodesia Rd, E11 145 ED61
SW9 42 B9
Rhodes Moorhouse Ct, Mord. SM4 222 DA100
Rhodes St, N7 8 D3
Rhodes Way, Wat. WD24 98 BX40
Rhodeswell Rd, E14 21 M6
Rhododendron Ride, Egh. TW20 194 AT94
Slough SL3 155 AZ69
Rhodrons Av, Chess. KT9 238 CL106
Rhondda Gro, E3 21 M3
Sch Rhyl Prim Sch, NW5 7 H4
Rhyl Rd, Perivale UB6 159 CF68
Rhyl St, NW5 7 H4
Rhymes, The, Hem.H. HP1 62 BH18
Rhys Av, N11 121 DK52
Rialto Rd, Mitch. CR4 222 DG96
Ribble Cl, Wdf.Grn. IG8
off Prospect Rd 124 EJ51
Ribbledale, Lon.Col. AL2 84 CM27
Ribblesdale, Dor. RH4
off Roman Rd 285 CH138
Hemel Hempstead HP2 62 BL17
Ribblesdale Av, N11 120 DG51
Northolt UB5 158 CB65
Ribblesdale Rd, N8 143 DM56
SW16 203 DH93
Dartford DA2 210 FQ88
Ribbon Dance Ms, SE5 43 M7
Ribchester Av, Perivale UB6 159 CF69
Ribston Cl, Brom. BR2 227 EM102
Shenley WD7 83 CK33
Rib Vale, Hert. SG14 54 DR06
Ricardo Path, SE28
off Byron Cl 168 EW74
Ricardo Rd, Old Wind. SL4 194 AV86
Ricardo St, E14 22 C9
Sch Ricards Lo High Sch, SW19
off Lake Rd 201 CZ92
Ricards Rd, SW19 201 CZ92
Ricebridge La, Reig. RH2 287 CV137
Rice Cl, Hem.H. HP2 62 BM19
Rices Cor, Shalf. GU4 281 BA141
Sch Richard Alibon Prim Sch, Dag. RM10 off Alibon Rd 148 FA64
Sch Richard Atkins Prim Sch, SW2
off New Pk Rd 203 DL87
Sch Richard Challoner Sch, N.Mal. KT3 off Manor Dr N 220 CR101
Richard Cl, SE18 37 H9
Sch Richard Cloudesley Sch, EC1 19 J5
Sch Richard Cobden Prim Sch, NW1 7 M10
Richard Fell Ho, E12
off Walton Rd 147 EN63
Richard Foster Cl, E17 145 DZ59
Sch Richard Hale Sch, Hert. SG13
off Hale Rd 54 DR10
Richard Ho Dr, E16 24 F9
Richard Meyjes Rd, Guil. GU2 280 AS135
Richard Robert Res, The, E15
off Salway Pl 13 H5
Richard Ryan Pl, Dag. RM9 168 EY67
Richards Av, Rom. RM7 149 FC57
Richards Cl, Bushey WD23 117 CD45
Harlington UB3 177 BR79
Harrow HA1 139 CG57
Uxbridge UB10 156 BN67
Richards Fld, Epsom KT19 238 CR109
Richardson Cl, E8 10 A8
Greenhithe DA9
off Steele Av 211 FU85
London Colney AL2 84 CL27
Richardson Cres, Chsht EN7 87 DP25
Richardson Gdns, Dag. RM10 169 FB65
Richardson Pl, Coln.Hth AL4 66 CP22
Richardson Rd, E15 13 J10
Richardson's Ms, W1 17 L5
Richards Pl, E17 145 EA55
SW3 28 D8
Richards Rd, Stoke D'Ab. KT11 236 CB114
Richards St, Hat. AL10 66 CR16
Richard Stagg Cl, St.Alb. AL1 65 CJ22
Richard St, E1 20 E9
Richards Way, Slou. SL1 153 AN74
Richbell Cl, Ashtd. KT21 253 CK118
Richbell Pl, WC1 18 C6
Richborne Ter, SW8 42 D4
Richborough Cl, Orp. BR5 228 EX98
Richborough Ho, E5
off Pembury Rd 10 E2
Richborough Rd, NW2 4 D1
Richbourne Ct, W1
off Harrowby St 16 D8
Richens Cl, Houns. TW3 179 CD82
Riches Rd, Ilf. IG1 147 EQ61
Richfield Rd, Bushey WD23 116 CC45
Richford Gate, W6 26 A6
Richford Rd, E15 13 L8
Richford St, W6 26 A5
● Rich Ind Est, SE1 31 P7
RICHINGS PARK, Iver SL0 175 BE76
Richings Pl, Iver SL0 175 BE76
Richings Way, Iver SL0 175 BF76
Richland Av, Couls. CR5 240 DG114
Richlands Av, Epsom KT17 239 CU105
Rich La, SW5 39 L1
Richmer Rd, Erith DA8 189 FG80
★ Rich Mix Cen, The, E1
off Bethnal Grn Rd 20 B4
RICHMOND, TW9 & TW10 200 CL86
⇌ Richmond 180 CL84
Richmond 180 CL84
⊖ Richmond 180 CL84
Richmond 199 CK85
Coll Richmond Adult Comm Coll, Clifden, Twick. TW1
off Clifden Rd 199 CF88
Parkshot, Rich. TW9
off Parkshot 179 CK84
Richmond Av, E4 123 ED50
N1 8 C8
NW10 4 A5
SW20 221 CY95
Brentwood CM14 130 FW46
Feltham TW14 197 BS86
Uxbridge UB10 157 BP65
Richmond Br, Rich. TW9 199 CK86
Twickenham TW1 199 CK86
Richmond Bldgs, W1 17 N9
Jct Richmond Circ, Rich. TW9 180 CL84
Richmond Cl, E17 145 DZ58
Amersham HP6 94 AT38
Biggin Hill TN16 260 EH119
Borehamwood WD6 100 CR43
Cheshunt EN8 88 DW29
Epsom KT18 238 CS114
Fetcham KT22 252 CC124
Richmond Ct, Brox. EN10 71 DZ20
Hatfield AL10
off Cooks Way 67 CV20
Mitcham CR4
off Phipps Br Rd 222 DD97
Potters Bar EN6 86 DC31
Richmond Cres, E4 123 ED50
N1 8 D8
N9 122 DU46

Richmond Cres, Slough SL1 154 AU74
Staines-upon-Thames TW18 195 BF92
Richmond Dr, Grav. DA12 213 GL89
Shepperton TW17 217 BQ100
Watford WD17 97 BS39
Woodford Green IG8 125 EN52
Richmond Gdns, NW4 141 CU57
Harrow HA3 117 CF51
Richmond Grn, Croy. CR0 223 DL104
Richmond Gro, N1 8 G7
Surbiton KT5 off Ewell Rd 220 CM100
Richmond Hill, Rich. TW10 200 CL86
Richmond Hill Ct, Rich. TW10 200 CL86
Sch Richmond Ho, Hmptn. TW12 off Buckingham Rd 198 BZ92
Richmond Ho, NW1 off Park Village E 17 K1
Richmond Ms, W1 17 N9
Teddington TW11 off Church Rd 199 CF92
★ Richmond Park, Rich. TW10 200 CN88
Richmond Pk, Kings.T. KT2 200 CN88
Loughton IG10 off Fallow Flds 124 EK45
Richmond TW10 200 CN88
Richmond Pk Rd, SW14 200 CQ85
Kingston upon Thames KT2 200 CL94
Richmond Pl, SE18 187 EQ77
Richmond Rd, E4 123 ED46
E7 146 EH64
E8 10 A6
E11 145 ED61
N2 120 DC54
N11 121 DL51
N15 144 DS58
SW20 221 CV95
W5 180 CL75
Coulsdon CR5 257 DH115
Croydon CR0 223 DL104
Grays RM17 192 GC79
Ilford IG1 147 EQ62
Isleworth TW7 179 CG83
Kingston upon Thames KT2 199 CK92
New Barnet EN5 102 DB43
Potters Bar EN6 86 DC31
Romford RM1 149 FF58
Staines-upon-Thames TW18 195 BF92
Thornton Heath CR7 223 DP97
Twickenham TW1 199 CJ86
H Richmond Royal Hosp, Rich. TW9 180 CL83
Richmond St, E13 23 P1
Richmond Ter, SW1 30 A4
Uni Richmond Uni - The American Int Uni In London, Kensington Campus, W8 27 M6
Richmond Hill Campus, Rich. TW10 off Queens Rd 200 CL87
Coll Richmond upon Thames Coll, Twick. TW2 off Egerton Rd 199 CE87
Richmond Wk, St.Alb. AL4 65 CK16
Richmond Way, E11 146 EG61
W12 26 D5
W14 26 D6
Croxley Green WD3 97 BQ42
Fetcham KT22 252 CB123
Richmount Gdns, SE3 186 EG83
Rich St, E14 21 P10
Rickard Cl, NW4 141 CV56
SW2 203 DM88
West Drayton UB7 176 BK76
Rickards Cl, Surb. KT6 220 CL102
Ricketts Hill Rd, Tats. TN16 260 EK118
Rickett St, SW6 39 K2
Rickfield Cl, Hat. AL10 67 CU20
Rickman Ct, Add. KT15 off Rickman Cres 216 BH104
Rickman Cres, Add. KT15 216 BH104
Rickman Hill, Couls. CR5 257 DH118
Rickman Hill Rd, Chipstead CR5 257 DH118
Rickmans La, Stoke P. SL2 134 AS64
Rickman St, E1 21 H4
RICKMANSWORTH, WD3 114 BL45
⇌ Rickmansworth 114 BK45
⊖ Rickmansworth 114 BK45
Rickmansworth La, Chal.St.P. SL9 113 AZ50
Rickmansworth Pk, Rick. WD3 114 BK45
Sch Rickmansworth Pk JMI Sch, Rick. WD3 off Park Rd 114 BL45
Sch Rickmansworth PNEU Sch, Rick. WD3 off The Drive 96 BJ44
Rickmansworth Rd, Amer. HP6 77 AQ37
Chorleywood WD3 95 BE41
Harefield UB9 114 BJ53
Northwood HA6 115 BR52
Pinner HA5 115 BV54
Watford WD17, WD18 97 BS42
Sch Rickmansworth Sch, Crox.Grn WD3 off Scots Hill 96 BM44
Rick Roberts Way, E15 12 F9
Ricksons La, W.Hors. KT24 267 BP127
Rickthorne Rd, N19 143 DL61
Rickwood, Horl. RH6 291 DH147
Rickyard Path, SE9 186 EL84
Ridding La, Grnf. UB6 139 CF64
Riddings, The, Cat. CR3 274 DT125
Riddings La, Harl. CM18 73 ET19
⇌ Riddlesdown 242 DR113
Riddlesdown Av, Pur. CR8 242 DQ112
Sch Riddlesdown High Sch, Pur. CR8 off Dunmail Dr 242 DS114
Riddlesdown Rd, Pur. CR8 242 DQ111
Riddons Rd, SE12 206 EJ90
Ride, The, Brent. TW8 179 CH78
Enfield EN3 104 DW41
Ride La, Far.Grn GU5 282 BK144
Rideout St, SE18 37 J9
Rider Cl, Sid. DA15 207 ES86
Riders Way, Gdse. RH9 274 DW131
Ridgdale St, E3 22 B1
RIDGE, Pot.B. EN6 84 CS34
Ridge, The, Barn. EN5 101 CZ43
Bexley DA5 208 EZ87
Coulsdon CR5 241 DL114
Epsom KT18 254 CP117
Fetcham KT22 253 CD124
Orpington BR6 227 ER103
Purley CR8 241 DJ110
Ridge, The, Surbiton KT5 220 CN99
Twickenham TW2 199 CD87
Woking GU22 249 BB117
Woldingham CR3 275 EB126
Ridge Av, N21 122 DQ45
Dartford DA1 209 FF86
Ridgebank, Slou. SL1 153 AM73
Ridgebrook Rd, SE3 186 EJ84
Ridge Cl, NW4 119 CX54
NW9 140 CR56
SE28 187 ER75
Strood Green RH3 286 CP138
Woking GU22 248 AV121
Ridge Crest, Enf. EN2 103 DM39
Ridgecroft Cl, Bex. DA5 209 FC88
Ridgefield, Wat. WD17 97 BS37
Ridgegate Cl, Reig. RH2 272 DD132
RIDGE GREEN, Red. RH1 289 DL137
Ridge Grn, S.Nutfld RH1 289 DL137
Ridge Grn Cl, S.Nutfld RH1 289 DL137
RIDGE HILL, Rad. WD7 84 CQ30
Ridge Hill, NW11 141 CY60
Ridgehurst Av, Wat. WD25 81 BT34
Ridgelands, Fetch. KT22 253 CD124
Ridge La, Wat. WD17 97 BS38
Ridge Langley, S.Croy. CR2 242 DU109
Ridge Lea, Hem.H. HP1 61 BF20
Ridgemead Cl, N14 121 DL47
Ridgemead Rd, Eng.Grn TW20 194 AU90
Ridgemont Gdns, Edg. HA8 118 CQ49
Ridgemont Pl, Horn. RM11 150 FK58
Ridgemount, Guil. GU2 280 AV135
Weybridge KT13 off Oatlands Dr 217 BS103
Ridgemount Av, Couls. CR5 257 DH117
Croydon CR0 225 DX102
Ridgemount Cl, SE20 204 DV94
Ridgemount End, Chal.St.P. SL9 112 AY50
Ridgemount Gdns, Enf. EN2 103 DP40
Ridgemount Way, Red. RH1 288 DD136
Ridge Pk, Pur. CR8 241 DK110
Ridge Rd, N8 143 DM58
N21 122 DQ46
NW2 141 CZ62
Mitcham CR4 203 DH94
Sutton SM3 221 CY102
Ridges, The, Art. GU3 280 AW139
Ridge St, Wat. WD24 97 BV38
Ridge's Yd, Croy. CR0 223 DP104
Ridgeview Cl, Barn. EN5 101 CX44
Ridgeview Lo, Lon.Col. AL2 84 CM28
Ridgeview Rd, N20 120 DB48
Ridge Way, SE19 off Vicars Oak Rd 204 DS93
Ridgeway, SE28 off Pettman Cres 187 ER77
Berkhamsted HP4 60 AT19
Bromley BR2 226 EG103
Ridge Way, Cray. DA1 209 FF86
Ridgeway, Epsom KT19 238 CQ112
Ridge Way, Felt. TW13 198 BY90
Ridgeway, Grays RM17 192 GE77
Horsell GU21 248 AX115
Hutton CM13 131 GB46
Iver SL0 155 BF73
Lane End DA2 211 FS92
Rickmansworth WD3 114 BH45
Virginia Water GU25 214 AY99
Welwyn Garden City AL7 52 DA09
Woodford Green IG8 124 EJ49
Ridgeway, The, E4 123 EB47
N3 120 DB52
N11 120 DF49
N14 121 DL47
NW7 119 CU49
NW9 140 CS56
NW11 141 CZ60
W3 180 CN75
Amersham HP7 77 AR40
Chalfont St. Peter SL9 134 AY55
Croydon CR0 223 DM104
Cuffley EN6 86 DE28
Enfield EN2 103 DN39
Fetcham KT22 253 CD123
Gidea Park RM2 149 FG56
Guildford GU1 281 BA135
Harold Wood RM3 128 FL53
Hertford SG14 53 DM08
Horley RH6 290 DG150
Kenton HA3 139 CJ58
North Harrow HA2 138 CA58
Oxshott KT22 236 CC114
Potters Bar EN6 86 DD34
Radlett WD7 99 CF37
Ruislip HA4 137 BU59
St. Albans AL4 65 CH17
Ridge Way, The, S.Croy. CR2 242 DS110
Ridgeway, The, Stan. HA7 117 CJ51
Walton-on-Thames KT12 217 BT102
Watford WD17 97 BS37
Ridgeway Av, Barn. EN4 102 DF44
Gravesend DA12 213 GH90
Ridgeway Cl, Chesh. HP5 76 AP28
Dorking RH4 285 CG138
Fetcham KT22 253 CE124
Hemel Hempstead HP3 off London Rd 80 BM25
Oxshott KT22 236 CC114
Woking GU21 248 AX116
Ridgeway Ct, Red. RH1 288 DE135
Ridgeway Cres, Orp. BR6 227 ES104
Ridgeway Cres Gdns, Orp. BR6 227 ES103
Ridgeway Dr, Brom. BR1 206 EH91
Dorking RH4 285 CG139
Ridgeway E, Sid. DA15 207 ET85
Ridgeway Gdns, N6 143 DJ59
Ilford IG4 146 EL57
Woking GU21 248 AX115
Sch Ridgeway Prim Sch, S.Croy. CR2 off Southcote Rd 242 DS110
Ridgeway Rd, SW9 183 DP83
Chesham HP5 76 AN28
Dorking RH4 285 CG139
Isleworth TW7 179 CE80
Redhill RH1 272 DE134
Ridgeway Rd N, Islw. TW7 179 CE79
Ridgeways, Harl. CM17 74 EY15
Ridgeway Wk, Nthlt. UB5 off Arnold Rd 158 BY65
Ridgeway W, Sid. DA15 207 ES85
Ridgewell Cl, N1 9 K8
SE26 205 DZ91
Dagenham RM10 169 FB67
Ridgewell Gro, Horn. RM12 off North Weald Cl 169 FH66
Ridgmont Rd, St.Alb. AL1 65 CE21
Ridgmount Gdns, WC1 17 N5
Ridgmount Pl, WC1 17 N6
Ridgmount Rd, SW18 202 DB85
Ridgmount St, WC1 17 N6
Ridgway, SW19 201 CX93
Pyrford GU22 249 BF115
Ridgway, The, Sutt. SM2 240 DD108
Ridgway Gdns, SW19 201 CX93
Ridgway Pl, SW19 201 CY93
Ridgway Rd, Pyrford GU22 249 BF115
Ridgwell Rd, E16 24 D6
Riding, The, NW11 off Golders Grn Rd 141 CZ59
Woking GU21 233 BB114
Riding Ct Rd, Datchet SL3 174 AW80
Riding Hill, S.Croy. CR2 242 DU113
Riding Ho St, W1 17 L7
Riding La, Beac. HP9 110 AF53
Ridings, The, E11 off Malcolm Way 146 EG57
W5 160 CM70
Addlestone KT15 233 BF107
Amersham HP6 77 AR35
Ashtead KT21 253 CK117
Biggin Hill TN16 260 EL117
Chigwell IG7 126 EV49
Cobham KT11 236 CA112
East Horsley KT24 267 BS125
Epsom KT18 254 CS115
Ewell KT17 239 CT109
Hertford SG14 53 DN10
Iver SL0 175 BF77
Kingswood KT20 255 CZ120
Latimer HP5 94 AX36
Reigate RH2 272 DD131
Ripley GU23 250 BG123
Sunbury-on-Thames TW16 217 BU95
Surbiton KT5 220 CN99
Windsor SL4 off River Rd 173 AK80
Ridings Av, N21 103 DP42
Ridings Cl, N6 143 DJ59
Ridings La, Wok. GU23 250 BN123
Ridlands Gro, Oxt. RH8 276 EL130
Ridlands La, Oxt. RH8 276 EK130
Ridlands Ri, Oxt. RH8 276 EL130
Ridler Rd, Enf. EN1 104 DS38
Ridley Av, W13 179 CH76
Ridley Cl, Bark. IG11 167 ET66
Romford RM3 127 FH53
Ridley Rd, E7 146 EJ63
E8 10 A3
NW10 161 CU68
SW19 202 DB94
Bromley BR2 226 EF97
Warlingham CR6 258 DW118
Welling DA16 188 EV81
Ridsdale Rd, SE20 224 DV95
Woking GU21 248 AV117
Riefield Rd, SE9 187 EQ84
Riesco Dr, Croy. CR0 242 DW107
Riffel Rd, NW2 4 A2
Riffhams, Brwd. CM13 131 GB48
Rifle Butts All, Epsom KT18 255 CT115
Rifle Ct, SE11 42 F2
Rifle Pl, W11 off St. Anns Rd 26 D2
Rifle St, E14 22 D7
Riga Ms, E1 off Commercial Rd 20 C8
Rigault Rd, SW6 38 F9
Rigby Cl, Croy. CR0 223 DN104
Rigby Gdns, Grays RM16 193 GH77
Rigby La, Hayes UB3 177 BR75
Rigby Ms, Ilf. IG1 147 EN61
Rigby Pl, Enf. EN3 105 EA37
Rigden St, E14 22 C9
Rigeley Rd, NW10 161 CU69
Rigg App, E10 145 DX60
Rigge Pl, SW4 183 DK84
Riggindale Rd, SW16 203 DK92
Riley Cl, Epsom KT19 238 CP111
Riley Rd, SE1 31 P6
Enfield EN3 104 DW38
Riley St, SW10 40 A4
Rill Ct, Bark. IG11 off Spring Pl 167 EQ68
Rinaldo Rd, SW12 203 DH87
Ring, The, W2 16 C10
Ring Cl, Brom. BR1 206 EH94
Ringcroft St, N7 8 E3
Ringers Rd, Brom. BR1 226 EG97
Ringford Rd, SW18 201 CZ85
Ringlet Cl, E16 24 A7
Ringlewell Cl, Enf. EN1 off Central Av 104 DV40
Ringley Av, Horl. RH6 290 DG148
Ringley Pk Av, Reig. RH2 288 DD135
Ringley Pk Rd, Reig. RH2 272 DC134
Ringmer Av, SW6 38 F7
Ringmer Gdns, N19 143 DL61
Ringmer Ho, SE22 off Pytchley Rd 184 DS83
Ringmer Pl, N21 104 DR43
Ringmer Way, Brom. BR1 227 EM99
Ringmore Dr, Guil. GU4 265 BC131
Ringmore Ri, SE23 204 DV87
Ringmore Rd, Walt. KT12 218 BW104
Ringmore Vw, SE23 off Ringmore Ri 204 DV87
Ring Rd, W12 26 A1
Ring Rd N, Gat. RH6 291 DH152
Ring Rd S, Gat. RH6 291 DH152
Ringshall Rd, Orp. BR5 228 EU97
Ringside Ct, SE28 168 EW74
Ringslade Rd, N22 121 DM54
Ringstead Rd, SE6 205 EB87
Sutton SM1 240 DD105
Ringway, N11 121 DJ51
Southall UB2 178 BY78
Ringway Rd, Park St AL2 82 CB27
Ringwold Cl, Beck. BR3 205 DY94
Ringwood Av, N2 120 DF54
Croydon CR0 223 DL101
Hornchurch RM12 150 FK61
Orpington BR6 246 EW110
Redhill RH1 272 DF131
Ringwood Cl, Pnr. HA5 138 BW55
Ringwood Gdns, E14 34 B8
SW15 201 CU89
Ringwood Rd, E17 145 DZ58
Ringwood Way, N21 121 DP46
Hampton Hill TW12 198 CA91
RIPLEY, Wok. GU23 250 BJ122
Ripley Av, Egh. TW20 194 AY93
Ripley Bypass, Wok. GU23 250 BK122
Ripley Cl, Brom. BR1 227 EM99
New Addington CR0 243 EC107
Slough SL3 174 AY77
Sch Ripley C of E Inf Sch, Ripley GU23 off Georgelands 250 BH121
Sch Ripley Ct Sch, Ripley GU23 off Rose La 250 BJ122
Ripley Gdns, SW14 180 CR83
Sutton SM1 240 DC105
Ripley La, W.Hors. KT24 266 BN125
Woking GU23 250 BL123
Ripley Ms, E11 146 EE58
Ripley Rd, E16 24 C8
Belvedere DA17 188 FA77
East Clandon GU4 266 BJ127
Enfield EN2 104 DQ39
Hampton TW12 198 CA94
Ilford IG3 147 ET61
Send GU23 266 BJ127
★ Ripley's Believe It or Not! W1 29 N1
RIPLEY SPRINGS, Egh. TW20 194 AY93
Ripley Vw, Loug. IG10 107 EP38
Ripley Vil, W5 159 CJ72
Ripley Way, Chsht EN7 88 DV30
Epsom KT19 238 CN111
Hemel Hempstead HP1 61 BE19
Riplington Ct, SW15 201 CU87
Ripon Cl, Guil. GU2 264 AT131
Northolt UB5 138 CA64
Ripon Gdns, Chess. KT9 237 CK106
Ilford IG1 146 EL58
Ripon Rd, N9 122 DV45
N17 144 DR55
SE18 187 EP79
Ripon Way, Borwd. WD6 100 CQ43
St. Albans AL4 65 CK16
Rippersley Rd, Well. DA16 188 EU81
Sch Ripple Inf & Jun Schs, Bark. IG11 off Suffolk Rd 167 ES67
Ripple Rd, Bark. IG11 167 EQ66
Dagenham RM9 168 EV67
● Rippleside Commercial Est, Bark. IG11 168 EW68
Ripplevale Gro, N1 8 D7
Rippolson Rd, SE18 187 ET78
Ripston Rd, Ashf. TW15 197 BR92
Risborough, SE17 off Deacon Way 31 J8
Risborough Dr, Wor.Pk. KT4 221 CU101
Risborough St, SE1 31 H4
Risdens, Harl. CM18 73 EQ19
Risdon St, SE16 33 H5
Rise, The, E11 146 EG57
N13 121 DN49
NW7 119 CT51
NW10 140 CR63
Amersham HP7 77 AQ39
Bexley DA5 208 EW87
Buckhurst Hill IG9 124 EK45
Dartford DA1 189 FF84
East Horsley KT24 267 BS126
Edgware HA8 118 CP50
Elstree WD6 100 CM43
Epsom KT17 239 CT110
Gravesend DA12 213 GL91
Greenford UB6 139 CG64
Greenhithe DA9 211 FU86
Park Street AL2 83 CD25
Sevenoaks TN13 279 FJ129
South Croydon CR2 242 DW109
Tadworth KT20 255 CW121
Uxbridge UB10 156 BM68
Waltham Abbey EN9 off Breach Barn Mobile Home Pk 90 EH30
Risebridge Chase, Rom. RM1 127 FF52
Risebridge Rd, Rom. RM2 127 FF54
Rise Cotts, Ware SG12 off Widford Rd 56 EK05
Risedale Cl, Hem.H. HP3 off Risedale Hill 62 BL23
Risedale Hill, Hem.H. HP3 62 BL23
Risedale Rd, Bexh. DA7 189 FB83
Hemel Hempstead HP3 62 BL23
Riseholme Ho, SE22 off Albrighton Rd 184 DS83
Riseldine Rd, SE23 205 DY86
Rise Pk Boul, Rom. RM1 127 FF53
Sch Rise Pk Inf Sch, Rom. RM1 off Annan Way 127 FD53
Sch Rise Pk Jun Sch, Rom. RM1 off Annan Way 127 FD53
Rise Pk Par, Rom. RM1 127 FE54
Riseway, Brwd. CM15 130 FY48
Rising Hill Cl, Nthwd. HA6 off Ducks Hill Rd 115 BQ51
Risinghill St, N1 8 D10
Risingholme Cl, Bushey WD23 116 CB45
Harrow HA3 117 CE53
Risingholme Rd, Har. HA3 117 CE54
Risings, The, E17 145 ED56
Rising Sun Ct, EC1 19 H7
Risley Av, N17 122 DQ53
Sch Risley Av Prim Sch, N17 off The Roundway 122 DS53
Rita Rd, SW8 42 B3
Ritches Rd, N15 144 DQ57
Ritchie Rd, Croy. CR0 224 DV100
Ritchie St, N1 8 F10
Ritchings Av, E17 145 DY56
Ritcroft Cl, Hem.H. HP3 63 BP21
Ritcroft Dr, Hem.H. HP3 63 BP21
Ritcroft St, Hem.H. HP3 63 BP21
Ritherdon Rd, SW17 202 DG89
Ritson Rd, E8 10 B4
Ritter St, SE18 187 EN79
Ritz Ct, Pot.B. EN6 86 DA31
Ritz Par, W5 off Connell Cres 160 CM70
Rivaz Pl, E9 11 H4
Rivenhall End, Welw.G.C. AL7 52 DC09
Rivenhall Gdns, E18 146 EF56
River App, Edg. HA8 118 CQ53
River Ash Est, Shep. TW17 217 BS101
River Av, N13 121 DP48
Hoddesdon EN11 71 EB16
Thames Ditton KT7 219 CG101
River Bk, N21 122 DQ45
East Molesey KT8 219 CE97
Riverbank, Picc.End HP1 off Piccotts End Rd 62 BJ16
Staines-upon-Thames TW18 195 BF93
River Bk, T.Ditt. KT7 219 CF99
West Molesey KT8 218 BZ97
Riverbank, The, Wind. SL4 173 AP80
Riverbank Rd, Brom. BR1 206 EG90
Riverbank Way, Brent. TW8 179 CJ79
River Barge Cl, E14 34 F5
● River Brent Business Pk, W7 179 CE76
River Cl, E11 146 EJ58
Guildford GU1 264 AW132
Rainham RM13 169 FH71
Ruislip HA4 137 BT58
Southall UB2 178 CC75
Surbiton KT6 off Catherine Rd 219 CK99
Waltham Cross EN8 89 EA34
● River Ct, Wok. GU21 249 BC115
River Ct, SE1 30 G1
Shepperton TW17 217 BQ101
Taplow SL6 152 AC72
Rivercourt Rd, W6 181 CV77
River Crane Wk, Felt. TW13 198 BX88
Hounslow TW4 198 BX88
River Crane Way, Felt. TW13 off Watermill Way 198 BZ89
Riverdale, SE13 off Lewisham High St 185 EC83
Riverdale Cl, Bark. IG11 168 EV70
Riverdale Dr, SW18 off Knaresborough Dr 202 DB88
Woking GU22 249 AZ121
Riverdale Gdns, Twick. TW1 199 CJ86
Riverdale Rd, SE18 187 ET78
Bexley DA5 208 EZ87
Erith DA8 189 FB78
Feltham TW13 198 BY91
Twickenham TW1 199 CJ86
Riverdene, Edg. HA8 118 CQ48
Riverdene Rd, Ilf. IG1 147 EN62
River Dr, Upmin. RM14 150 FQ58
Riverfield Rd, Stai. TW18 195 BF93
River Front, Enf. EN1 104 DR41
River Gdns, Bray SL6 172 AD75
Carshalton SM5 222 DG103
Feltham TW14 197 BV85
● River Gdns Business Cen, Felt. TW14 off River Gdns 177 BV84
Rivergate Cen, The, Bark. IG11 168 EU70
River Gro Pk, Beck. BR3 225 DZ95
RIVERHEAD, Sev. TN13 278 FD122
Riverhead Cl, E17 123 DX54
Riverhead Dr, Sutt. SM2 240 DA110
Sch Riverhead Infants' Sch, Sev. TN13 off Worships Hill 278 FE123
Riverhill, Cob. KT11 251 BV115
Sevenoaks TN15 279 FL130
Worcester Park KT4 220 CR103
Riverhill Ms, Wor.Pk. KT4 220 CR104
Riverholme Dr, Epsom KT19 238 CR109
River Island Cl, Fetch. KT22 253 CD121
River La, Lthd. KT22 253 CD120
Richmond TW10 199 CK88
Sch Riverley Prim Sch, E10 off Park Rd 145 EA60
Rivermead, Byfleet KT14 234 BM113
East Molesey KT8 218 CC97
Kingston upon Thames KT1 219 CK99
Rivermead Cl, Add. KT15 234 BJ108
Teddington TW11 199 CH92
Rivermead Ct, SW6 38 G10
Rivermead Ho, E9 off Kingsmead Way 11 M2
Rivermead Rd, N18 123 DX51
River Meads, Stans.Abb. SG12 55 EC10
Rivermeads Av, Twick. TW2 198 CA90
Rivermill, SW1 41 P1
Harlow CM20 57 EQ13
River Mt, Walt. KT12 217 BT101
Rivermount Gdns, Guil. GU2 280 AW137
Rivernook Cl, Walt. KT12 218 BW99
River Pk, Berk. HP4 60 AU18
Hemel Hempstead HP1 62 BG22
River Pk Av, Stai. TW18 195 BD91
River Pk Gdns, Brom. BR2 205 ED94
River Pk Rd, N22 121 DM54
River Pk Vw, Orp. BR6 228 EV101
River Pl, N1 9 J7
River Reach, Tedd. TW11 199 CJ92
River Rd, Bark. IG11 167 ES68
Brentwood CM14 130 FS49
Buckhurst Hill IG9 124 EL46
Staines-upon-Thames TW18 215 BF95
Taplow SL6 152 AC73
Windsor SL4 172 AJ80
● River Rd Business Pk, Bark. IG11 167 ET69
Riversdale, Nthflt DA11 212 GE89
Sch Riversdale Prim Sch, SW18 off Merton Rd 202 DA88
Riversdale Rd, N5 143 DP62
Romford RM5 127 FB52
Thames Ditton KT7 219 CG99
Riversdell Cl, Cher. KT16 215 BF101
Riversend Rd, Hem.H. HP3 62 BJ23
Riversfield Rd, Enf. EN1 104 DS41
H Rivers Hosp, The, Saw. CM21 58 EW06
Rivers Ho, Brent. TW8 off Chiswick High Rd 180 CN78
Riverside, Hem.H. HP1 62 BJ22
Riverside, NW4 141 CV59
SE7 36 A7
Chertsey KT16 216 BG97
Dorking RH4 269 CK134
Eynsford DA4 230 FK103
Guildford GU1 264 AX132
Hertford SG14 off The Folly 54 DR09
Horley RH6 290 DG150
London Colney AL2 84 CL27
Richmond TW9, TW10 off Water La 199 CK85
Runnymede TW20 195 BA90
Shepperton TW17 217 BS101
Staines-upon-Thames TW18 215 BF95
Stanstead Abbotts SG12 55 EC11
Twickenham TW1 199 CH88
Wraysbury TW19 194 AW87
Riverside, The, E.Mol. KT8 219 CD97
Riverside Av, Brox. EN10 71 EA22
East Molesey KT8 219 CD99
● Riverside Business Cen, SW18 202 DB88
Guildford GU1 264 AW134
Tilbury RM18 193 GH84
Riverside Cl, E5 144 DW60
W7 159 CE70
Kings Langley WD4 81 BP29
Kingston upon Thames KT1 219 CK98
Orpington BR5 228 EW96
Romford RM1 149 FD56
St. Albans AL1 off Riverside Rd 65 CE22
Staines-upon-Thames TW18 215 BF95
Wallington SM6 223 DH104

Riverside Cotts, Woob.Moor HP10 132 AE55
Riverside Ct, E4
off Chelwood Cl 105 EB44
SW8 41 P2
Harlow CM17 58 EW09
St. Albans AL1 65 CE22
Riverside Dr, NW11 141 CY58
W4 180 CS80
Bramley GU5 281 BA144
Esher KT10 236 CA105
Mitcham CR4 222 DE99
Richmond TW10 199 CH89
Rickmansworth WD3 114 BK46
Staines-upon-Thames TW18 195 BE92
● Riverside Est, Lon.Col. AL2 84 CL27
Riverside Gdns, N3 141 CY55
W6 181 CV78
Berkhamsted HP4 60 AU18
Enfield EN2 104 DQ40
Old Woking GU22 249 BB121
Wembley HA0 160 CL68
Riverside Hts, Til. RM18 193 GG82
● Riverside Ind Est, Bark. IG11 168 EU69
Dartford DA1 210 FL85
Riverside Mans, E1 32 G1
Riverside Pk, West Dr. UB7 176 BJ76
Weybridge KT13 234 BL106
Riverside Path, Chsht EN8
off Dewhurst Rd 88 DW29
Riverside Pl, Stanw. TW19 196 BK86
Sch Riverside Prim Sch, SE16 32 D5
Riverside Retail Pk, Sev. TN14 263 FH119
Riverside Rd, E15 22 F1
N15 144 DU58
SW17 202 DB91
Hersham KT12 236 BX105
St. Albans AL1 65 CE21
Sidcup DA14 208 EY90
Staines-upon-Thames TW18 195 BF94
Stanwell TW19 196 BK85
Watford WD19 97 BV44
Sch Riverside Sch, St.P.Cray BR5 off Main Rd 228 EW96
Riverside Twr, SW6 39 P8
Riverside Wk, E14
off Ferry St 46 E1
Bexley DA5 208 EW87
Isleworth TW7 179 CE83
Kingston upon Thames KT1
off High St 219 CK97
Loughton IG10 107 EP44
West Wickham BR4
off The Alders 225 EB102
Windsor SL4 off Farm Yd 173 AR80
Riverside Way, Cowley UB8 156 BH67
Dartford DA1 210 FL85
St. Albans AL2 83 CD32
● Riverside W, Woob.Grn HP10 132 AE55
Riverside Yd, SW17 202 DC91
Riversmead, Hodd. EN11 71 EA18
Riversmeet, Hert. SG14 53 DP10
Riverstone Cl, Har. HA2 139 CD60
Riverstone Ct, Kings.T. KT2
off Queen Elizabeth Rd 220 CM95
Sch Riverston Sch, SE12
off Eltham Rd 206 EG85
River St, EC1 18 E2
Ware SG12 55 DY06
Windsor SL4 173 AR80
River Ter, W6 38 A1
Riverton Cl, W9 15 H3
River Vw, Enf. EN2
off Chase Side 104 DQ41
Grays RM16 193 GG77
Welwyn Garden City AL7 51 CZ05
Sch Riverview C of E Prim Sch & Nurs, W.Ewell KT19
off Riverview Rd 238 CR105
Riverview Gdns, SW13 181 CV79
Cobham KT11 235 BU113
Twickenham TW1 199 CF89
Riverview Gro, W4 180 CP79
River Vw Hts, SE16 32 C4
Sch Riverview Inf Sch, Grav. DA12 off Cimba Wd 213 GL91
Sch Riverview Jun Sch, Grav. DA12 off Cimba Wd 213 GL91
RIVERVIEW PARK, Grav. DA12 213 GK92
Riverview Pk, SE6 205 EA89
Riverview Rd, W4 180 CP80
Epsom KT19 238 CQ105
Greenhithe DA9 211 FU85
River Wk, E4
off Winchester Rd 123 EC52
Denham UB9 136 BJ64
Walton-on-Thames KT12 217 BU100
● Riverwalk Business Pk, Enf. EN3 105 DZ41
Riverwalk Rd, Enf. EN3 105 DZ42
Riverway, N13 121 DN50
River Way, SE10 35 L6
Epsom KT19 238 CR106
Harlow CM20 58 EU10
Loughton IG10 107 EN44
Riverway, Stai. TW18 216 BH95
River Way, Twick. TW2 198 CB89
● Riverway Est, Peasm. GU3 280 AW142
River Wey Navigation, Guil. GU1 264 AX132
Woking GU23 249 BB122
Riverwood La, Chis. BR7 227 ER95
Rivet Ho, SE1 32 B10
Rivett-Drake Cl, Guil. GU2 264 AV130
Rivey Cl, W.Byf. KT14 233 BF114
Rivington Av, Wdf.Grn. IG8 124 EK54
Rivington Ct, NW10 161 CU67
Dagenham RM10
off St. Mark's Pl 169 FB65
Rivington Cres, NW7 119 CT52
Rivington Pl, EC2 19 P3
Rivington St, EC2 19 N3
Rivington Wk, E8 10 D8
Rivulet Rd, N17 122 DQ52
Rixon Cl, Geo.Grn SL3 154 AY72
Rixon Ho, SE18 187 EP79
Rixon St, N7 143 DN62
Rixsen Rd, E12 146 EL64
Sch R.J. Mitchell Prim Sch, The, Horn. RM12
off Tangmere Cres 169 FH65
Roach Rd, E3 12 A6
Road Ho Est, Old Wok. GU22
off High St 249 BA120

Roads Pl, N19 143 DL61
Roakes Av, Add. KT15 216 BH103
Roan St, SE10 46 E3
Roasthill La, Dorney SL4 173 AK79
Robarts Cl, Pnr. HA5 137 BV57
Robb Rd, Stan. HA7 117 CG51
Robbs Cl, Hem.H. HP1 62 BG17
Robe End, Hem.H. HP1 61 BF18
Robert Adam St, W1 16 G8
Roberta St, E2 20 C2
Robert Av, St.Alb. AL1 64 CB24
Sch Robert Blair Prim Sch, N7 8 B5
Sch Robert Browning Prim Sch, SE17 31 L10
Robert Burns Ms, SE24
off Mayall Rd 203 DP85
Sch Robert Clack Sch, Lwr Site, Dag. RM8 off Green La 148 EZ61
Upr Site, Dag. RM8
off Gosfield Rd 148 FA60
Robert Cl, W9 15 P5
Chigwell IG7 125 ET50
Hersham KT12 235 BV106
Potters Bar EN6 85 CY33
Robert Daniels Ct, They.B. CM16 107 ES37
Robert Dashwood Way, SE17 31 J9
Robert Keen Cl, SE15 44 D7
Robert Lowe Cl, SE14 45 K4
Roberton Dr, Brom. BR1 226 EJ95
Robert Owen Ho, SW6 38 D6
Robert Rd, Hedg. SL2 133 AR61
Robertsbridge Rd, Cars. SM5 222 DC102
Roberts Cl, SE9 207 ER88
SE16 33 K5
Barking IG11
off Tanner St 167 EQ65
Cheshunt EN8
off Norwood Rd 89 DY30
Orpington BR5
off Sholden Gdns 228 EW99
Romford RM3 127 FH53
Stanwell TW19 196 BJ86
Sutton SM3 239 CX108
Thornton Heath CR7
off Kitchener Rd 224 DR97
West Drayton UB7 156 BL74
Roberts La, Chal.St.P. SL9 113 BA50
Roberts Ms, SW1 28 G7
Orpington BR6 228 EU102
Robertson Cl, Brox. EN10 89 DY26
Robertson Ct, Wok. GU21 248 AS118
Robertson Rd, E15 12 F8
Berkhamsted HP4 60 AX19
Robertson St, SW8 41 J10
Robert's Pl, EC1 18 F4
Roberts Pl, Dag. RM10 168 FA65
Robert Sq, SE13 185 EC84
Roberts Rd, E17 123 EB53
NW7 119 CY51
Belvedere DA17 188 FA78
Watford WD18
off Tucker St 98 BW43
Robert St, E16 37 N3
NW1 17 K3
SE18 187 ER77
WC2 30 B1
Croydon CR0 off High St 224 DQ104
Robert Sutton Ho, E1
off Tarling St 20 G9
Roberts Way, Eng.Grn TW20 194 AW94
Hatfield AL10 67 CT19
Sch Robertswood Comb Sch, Chal.St.P. SL9
off Denham La 113 AZ52
Roberts Wd Dr, Chal.St.P. SL9 113 AZ50
Robeson St, E3 21 P6
Robeson Way, Borwd. WD6 100 CQ39
Robina Cl, Bexh. DA6 188 EX84
Northwood HA6 115 BT53
Robina Rd, Brox. EN10 89 DZ25
Robin Cl, NW7 118 CS48
Addlestone KT15 234 BK106
Hampton TW12 198 BY92
Romford RM5 127 FD52
Stanstead Abbotts SG12 55 EC12
Robin Ct, E14 off New Union Cl 34 F6
SE16 32 C8
Wallington SM6
off Carew Rd 241 DJ107
Robin Cres, E6 24 F6
Robin Gdns, Red. RH1 272 DG131
Robin Gro, N6 142 DG61
Brentford TW8 179 CJ79
Harrow HA3 140 CM58
Robin Hill, Berk. HP4 60 AW20
Robin Hill Dr, Chis. BR7 206 EL93
Jct Robin Hood, SW15 200 CS90
Robinhood Cl, Mitch. CR4 223 DJ97
Robin Hood Cl, Slou. SL1 153 AL74
Woking GU21 248 AT118
Robin Hood Cres, Knap. GU21 248 AS117
Robin Hood Dr, Bushey WD23 98 BZ39
Harrow HA3 117 CF52
Robin Hood Gdns, E14 22 F10
Robin Hood Grn, Orp. BR5 228 EU99
Sch Robin Hood Infants' Sch, Sutt. SM1 off Robin Hood La 240 DA106
Sch Robin Hood Jun Sch, Sutt. SM1 off Thorncroft Rd 240 DB106
Robin Hood La, E14 22 F10
SW15 200 CS91
Bexleyheath DA6 208 EY85
Hatfield AL10 67 CU17
Robinhood La, Mitch. CR4 223 DJ97
Robin Hood La, Sutt. SM1 240 DA106
Sutton Green GU4 249 AZ124
Robin Hood Meadow, Hem.H. HP2 62 BM15
Sch Robin Hood Prim Sch, SW15
off Bowness Cres 200 CS92
Robin Hood Rd, SW19 201 CV92
Brentwood CM15 130 FV45
Woking GU21 248 AT118
Robin Hood Way, SW15 200 CS91
SW20 200 CS91
Greenford UB6 159 CF65
● Robin Hood Wks, Knap. GU21
off Robin Hood Rd 248 AS117
Robin Ho, NW8
off Newcourt St 16 C1
Robinia Av, Nthflt DA11 212 GD87
Robinia Cl, SE20
off Sycamore Gro 224 DU95
Ilford IG6 125 ES51
Robinia Cres, E10 145 EB61
Robin La, NW4 141 CX55
Robin Mead, Welw.G.C. AL7 52 DA06

Robin Pl, Wat. WD25 81 BV32
Robins, The, Harl. CM17 58 EW09
Robins Cl, Lon.Col. AL2 84 CL27
Uxbridge UB8
off Newcourt 156 BJ71
Robins Ct, SE12 206 EJ90
Robinscroft Ms, SE10 46 D7
Robinsfield, Hem.H. HP1 62 BG20
Sch Robinsfield Inf Sch, NW8 6 C10
Robins Gro, W.Wick. BR4 226 EG104
Robins La, They.B. CM16 107 ES36
Robins Nest Hill, Lt.Berk. SG13 69 DJ19
Robinson Av, Goffs Oak EN7 87 DP28
Robinson Cl, E11 146 EE62
Enfield EN2 104 DQ41
Hornchurch RM12 169 FH66
Woking GU22 249 BC120
Robinson Cres, Bushey Hth WD23 116 CC46
Robinson Ho, W10 14 D9
Robinson Rd, E2 20 G1
SW17 202 DE93
Dagenham RM10 148 FA63
Robinsons Cl, W13 159 CG71
Robinson St, SW3 40 E2
Robinson Way, Nthflt DA11 212 GA85
Robins Orchard, Chal.St.P. SL9 112 AY51
Robins Rd, Hem.H. HP3 62 BN22
Robins Way, Hat. AL10 67 CT21
Robinsway, Hersham KT12 236 BW105
Waltham Abbey EN9
off Roundhills 90 EE34
Robinswood Cl, Beac. HP9 110 AJ50
Robinswood Ms, N5 8 G3
Robin Way, Cuffley EN6 87 DL28
Guildford GU2 264 AV130
Orpington BR5 228 EV97
Staines-upon-Thames TW18 195 BF90
Robin Willis Way, Old Wind. SL4 194 AU86
Robinwood Gro, Uxb. UB8 156 BM70
Robinwood Pl, SW15 200 CR91
Roborough Wk, Horn. RM12 170 FJ65
Robsart St, SW9 42 D8
Robson Av, NW10 161 CU67
Robson Cl, E6 24 G8
Chalfont St. Peter SL9 112 AY50
Enfield EN2 103 DP40
Robson Rd, SE27 203 DP90
Robsons Cl, Chsht EN8 88 DW29
Robyns Cft, Nthflt DA11 212 GE90
Robyns Way, Sev. TN13 278 FF122
Rocastle Rd, SE4 205 DY85
Roch Av, Edg. HA8 118 CM54
Rochdale Rd, E17 145 EA59
SE2 188 EV78
Rochdale Way, SE8 46 A4
Rochelle Cl, SW11 182 DD84
Rochelle St, E2 20 A3
Rochemont Wk, E8 10 B9
Roche Rd, SW16 223 DM95
Sch Roche Sch, The, SW18
off Frogmore 202 DA85
Rochester Av, E13 166 EJ67
Bromley BR1 226 EH96
Feltham TW13 197 BT89
Rochester Cl, SW16 203 DL94
Enfield EN1 104 DS39
Sidcup DA15 208 EV86
Rochester Dr, Bex. DA5 208 EZ86
Pinner HA5 138 BX57
Watford WD25 82 BW34
Rochester Gdns, Cat. CR3 258 DS122
Croydon CR0 224 DS104
Ilford IG1 147 EM59
Rochester Ms, NW1 7 L6
Rochester Pl, NW1 7 M6
Rochester Rd, NW1 7 L5
Carshalton SM5 240 DF105
Dartford DA1 210 FN87
Gravesend DA12 213 GL87
Hornchurch RM12 169 FH66
Northwood HA6 137 BT55
Staines-upon-Thames TW18 195 BD92
Rochester Row, SW1 29 M8
Rochester Sq, NW1 7 M6
Rochester St, SW1 29 N7
Rochester Ter, NW1 7 L5
Rochester Wk, SE1 31 L2
Reigate RH2 off Castle Dr 288 DB139
Rochester Way, SE3 186 EH81
SE9 187 EM83
Croxley Green WD3 97 BP42
Dartford DA1 209 FD87
Rochester Way Relief Rd, SE3 186 EH81
SE9 186 EL84
Roche Wk, Cars. SM5 222 DD100
Rochford Av, Loug. IG10 107 EQ41
Romford RM6 148 EW57
Shenfield CM15 131 GA43
Waltham Abbey EN9 89 ED33
Rochford Cl, E6
off Boleyn Rd 166 EK68
Broxbourne EN10 89 DY26
Hornchurch RM12 169 FH65
Rochford Grn, Loug. IG10 107 EQ41
Rochfords Gdns, Slou. SL2 154 AW74
Rochford St, NW5 6 F2
Rochford Wk, E8 10 D6
Rochford Way, Croy. CR0 223 DL100
Taplow SL6 152 AG73
Rockall Ct, Slou. SL3 175 BB76
Rock Av, SW14
off South Worple Way 180 CR83
Rockbourne Rd, SE23 205 DX88
Rockchase Gdns, Horn. RM11 150 FL58
Sch Rockcliffe Manor Prim Sch, SE18 off Bassant Rd 187 ET79
Rock Cl, Mitch. CR4 222 DD96
Rockdale Gdns, Sev. TN13 279 FH125
Rockdale Rd, Sev. TN13 279 FH125
Rockells Pl, SE22 204 DV86
Rockfield Cl, Oxt. RH8 276 EF131
Rockfield Rd, Oxt. RH8 276 EF129
Rockford Av, Perivale UB6 159 CG68
Rock Gdns, Dag. RM10 149 FB64
Rock Gro Way, SE16 32 D8
Rockhall Rd, NW2 4 C1
Rockhall Way, NW2
off Midland Ter 141 CX62
Rockhampton Cl, SE27 203 DN91
Rockhampton Rd, SE27 203 DN91
South Croydon CR2 242 DS107
Rock Hill, SE26 204 DT91
Orpington BR6 246 FA107
Rockingham Av, Horn. RM11 149 FH58
Rockingham Cl, SW15 181 CT84
Uxbridge UB8 156 BJ67

Rockingham Est, SE1 31 J7
Rockingham Gate, Bushey WD23 98 CC44
Rockingham Par, Uxb. UB8 156 BJ66
Rockingham Pl, Beac. HP9 111 AM54
Rockingham Rd, Uxb. UB8 156 BH67
Rockingham St, SE1 31 J7
Rockland Rd, SW15 181 CY84
Rocklands Dr, Stan. HA7 117 CH54
Rockleigh, Hert. SG14 53 DP09
Rockleigh Ct, Shenf. CM15 131 GA45
Rockley Rd, W14 26 C5
Rockliffe Av, Kings L. WD4 80 BN30
Sch Rockmount Prim Sch, SE19
off Chevening Rd 204 DR93
Rockmount Rd, SE18 187 ET78
SE19 204 DR93
Rockshaw Rd, Merst. RH1 273 DM127
Rocks La, SW13 181 CU81
Rock St, N4 143 DN61
Rockware Av, Grnf. UB6 159 CD67
Rockways, Barn. EN5 101 CT44
Rockwell Gdns, SE19 204 DS92
Rockwell Rd, Dag. RM10 149 FB64
Rockwood Pl, W12 26 B4
Rocky La, Merst. RH1 272 DG129
Reigate RH2 272 DF128
Rocliffe St, N1 19 H1
Rocombe Cres, SE23 204 DW87
Rocque La, SE3 47 M10
Rodborough Rd, NW11 142 DA60
Roden Cl, Harl. CM17 58 EZ11
Roden Ct, N6 143 DK59
Roden Gdns, Croy. CR0 224 DS100
Rodenhurst Rd, SW4 203 DJ86
Roden St, N7 143 DM62
Ilford IG1 147 EN62
Rodeo Cl, Erith DA8 189 FH81
Roderick Rd, NW3 6 F1
Rodgers Cl, Els. WD6 99 CK44
Roding Av, Wdf.Grn. IG8 124 EL51
Roding Ct, Ilf. IG1 147 EN62
Roding Gdns, Loug. IG10 106 EL44
Roding La, Buck.H. IG9 124 EL46
Chigwell IG7 125 EN46
Roding La N, Wdf.Grn. IG8 124 EK54
Roding La S, Ilf. IG4 146 EK56
Woodford Green IG8 146 EK56
Roding Ms, E1 32 D2
Sch Roding Prim Sch, Dag. RM8
off Hewett Rd 148 EX63
Woodford Green IG8
off Roding La N 124 EL52
Roding Rd, E5 11 K1
E6 25 N6
Loughton IG10 106 EL43
Rodings, The, Upmin. RM14 151 FR58
Woodford Green IG8 124 EJ51
Rodings Row, Barn. EN5
off Leecroft Rd 101 CY43
⊖ Roding Valley 124 EK49
Sch Roding Valley High Sch, Loug. IG10 off Alderton Hill 106 EL43
Roding Vw, Buck.H. IG9 124 EK46
Roding Way, Rain. RM13 170 FK68
Rodmarton St, W1 16 F7
Rodmell Cl, Hayes UB4 158 BY70
Rodmell Slope, N12 119 CZ50
Rodmere St, SE10 47 K1
Rodmill La, SW2 203 DL87
Rodney Av, St.Alb. AL1 65 CG22
Rodney Cl, Croy. CR0 223 DP102
New Malden KT3 220 CS99
Pinner HA5 138 BY59
Walton-on-Thames KT12 218 BW102
Rodney Ct, W9 15 P4
Rodney Cres, Hodd. EN11 71 EA15
Rodney Gdns, Pnr. HA5 137 BV57
West Wickham BR4 244 EG105
Rodney Grn, Walt. KT12 218 BW103
Rodney Pl, E17 123 DY54
SE17 31 K8
SW19 222 DC95
Rodney Rd, E11 146 EH56
SE17 31 K8
Mitcham CR4 222 DE96
New Malden KT3 220 CS99
Twickenham TW2 198 CA86
Walton-on-Thames KT12 218 BW103
Rodney St, N1 8 D10
Rodney Way, Colnbr. SL3 175 BE81
Guildford GU1 265 BA133
Romford RM7 126 FA53
Rodona Rd, Wey. KT13 235 BR111
Rodway Rd, SW15 201 CU87
Bromley BR1 226 EH95
Rodwell Cl, Ruis. HA4 138 BW60
Rodwell Ct, Add. KT15
off Garfield Rd 234 BJ105
Rodwell Pl, Edg. HA8 118 CN51
Rodwell Rd, SE22 204 DT86
Roebourne Way, E16 37 L4
Roebuck Cl, Ashtd. KT21 254 CL120
Feltham TW13 197 BV91
Hertford SG13 54 DU09
Reigate RH2 272 DB134
Roebuck Grn, Slou. SL1 153 AL74
Roebuck La, N17 off High Rd 122 DT51
Buckhurst Hill IG9 124 EJ45
Roebuck Rd, Chess. KT9 238 CN106
Ilford IG6 126 EV50
Roedean Av, Enf. EN3 104 DW39
Roedean Cl, Enf. EN3 104 DW39
Orpington BR6 246 EV105
Roedean Cres, SW15 200 CS86
Roedean Dr, Rom. RM1 149 FE56
Roe End, NW9 140 CQ56
Roefields Cl, Felden HP3 62 BG24
ROE GREEN, Hat. AL10 67 CU18
Roe Grn, NW9 140 CQ57
Roe Grn Cl, Hat. AL10 66 CS19
Sch Roe Grn Inf & Jun Schs, NW9
off Princes Av 140 CP56
Roe Grn La, Hat. AL10 67 CT18
ROEHAMPTON, SW15 201 CU85
Roehampton Cl, SW15 181 CU84
Gravesend DA12 213 GL87
Sch Roehampton C of E Prim Sch, SW15 off Roehampton La 201 CV87
Roehampton Dr, Chis. BR7 207 EQ93
Roehampton Gate, SW15 200 CS86
Roehampton High St, SW15 201 CV87
Jct Roehampton La, SW15 201 CV88
Roehampton La, SW15 181 CU84
Uni Roehampton Uni - Digby Stuart Coll, SW15
off Roehampton La 201 CU85
Uni Roehampton Uni - Downshire Ho, SW15
off Roehampton La 201 CU86

Uni Roehampton Uni - Froebel Coll, SW15 off Roehampton La 201 CT86
Halls of Res, SW15
off Minstead Gdns 201 CT87
Uni Roehampton Uni - Southlands Coll, SW15
off Roehampton La 201 CU85
Uni Roehampton Uni - Whitelands Coll, SW15
off Holybourne Av 201 CU87
Roehampton Vale, SW15 200 CS90
Roe Hill Cl, Hat. AL10 67 CT19
Roehyde Way, Hat. AL10 66 CS20
Roe La, NW9 140 CP56
Roesel Pl, Petts Wd BR5 227 EP99
ROESTOCK, St.Alb. AL4 66 CR23
Roestock Gdns, Coln.Hth AL4 66 CS22
Roestock La, Coln.Hth AL4 66 CR23
Roe Way, Wall. SM6 241 DL107
Rofant Rd, Nthwd. HA6 115 BS51
Roffes La, Chaldon CR3 258 DR124
Roffey Cl, Horl. RH6 290 DF148
Purley CR8 257 DP116
Roffey St, E14 34 E5
Roffords, Wok. GU21 248 AV117
Rogate Ho, E5 off Muir Rd 144 DV62
Sch Roger Ascham Prim Sch, E17
off Wigton Rd 123 DZ53
Roger Dowley Ct, E2 10 G10
Rogers Cl, Cat. CR3
off Tillingdown Hill 258 DV122
Cheshunt EN7 88 DR26
Coulsdon CR5 257 DP118
Rogers Ct, Swan. BR8 229 FG98
Rogers Est, E2 off Globe Rd 21 H3
Rogers Gdns, Dag. RM10 148 FA64
Rogers Ho, SW1 off Page St 29 P8
Rogers La, Stoke P. SL2 154 AT67
Warlingham CR6 259 DZ118
Rogers Mead, Gdse. RH9
off Ivy Mill La 274 DV132
Rogers Rd, E16 23 M9
SW17 202 DD91
Dagenham RM10 148 FA64
Grays RM17 192 GC77
Rogers Ruff, Nthwd. HA6 115 BQ53
Roger St, WC1 18 D5
Rogers Wk, N12
off Holden Rd 120 DB48
Rojack Rd, SE23 205 DX88
Rokeby Ct, Wok. GU21 248 AT117
Rokeby Gdns, Wdf.Grn. IG8 124 EG53
Rokeby Pl, SW20 201 CV94
Rokeby Rd, SE4 45 N8
Sch Rokeby Sch, E16 23 M6
Kingston upon Thames KT2
off George Rd 200 CQ94
Rokeby St, E15 13 H8
Roke Cl, Ken. CR8 242 DQ114
Rokefield, Dor. RH4 284 CB136
Roke Lo Rd, Ken. CR8 241 DP113
Sch Roke Prim Sch, Ken. CR8
off Little Roke Rd 242 DQ114
Roke Rd, Ken. CR8 258 DQ115
Roker Pk Av, Uxb. UB10 136 BL63
Rokesby Cl, Well. DA16 187 ER82
Rokesby Pl, Wem. HA0 139 CK64
Rokesby Rd, Slou. SL2 153 AM69
Rokesly Av, N8 143 DL57
Sch Rokesly Inf Sch, N8
off Hermiston Av 143 DL57
Sch Rokesly Jun Sch, N8
off Rokesly Av 143 DL57
Rokewood Ms, Ware SG12 55 DX05
Roland Gdns, SW7 27 P10
Feltham TW13 198 BY90
Roland Ms, E1 21 J6
Roland Rd, E17 145 ED56
Roland St, St.Alb. AL1 65 CG20
Roland Way, SE17 43 M1
SW7 27 P10
Worcester Park KT4 221 CT103
Roles Gro, Rom. RM6 148 EX56
Rolfe Cl, Barn. EN4 102 DE42
Beaconsfield HP9 111 AL54
Rolinsden Way, Kes. BR2 244 EK105
Rollason Way, Brwd. CM14 130 FV48
Rollesby Rd, Chess. KT9 238 CN107
Rollesby Way, SE28 168 EW73
Rolleston Av, Petts Wd BR5 227 EP100
Rolleston Cl, Petts Wd BR5 227 EP101
Rolleston Rd, S.Croy. CR2 242 DR108
Roll Gdns, Ilf. IG2 147 EN57
Rollins St, SE15 45 H2
Rollit Cres, Houns. TW3 198 CA85
Rollit St, N7 8 E2
Rollo Rd, Swan. BR8 209 FF94
Rolls Bldgs, EC4 18 E8
Rolls Cotts, Magd.Lav. CM5
off Hastingwood Rd 75 FB19
Rollscourt Av, SE24 204 DQ85
Rolls Pk Av, E4 123 EA51
Rolls Pk Rd, E4 123 EB50
Jct Rolls Pk Rbt, Chig. IG7 125 ER45
Rolls Pas, EC4 18 E8
Rolls Rd, SE1 32 B10
Rolls Royce Cl, Wall. SM6 241 DL108
Rollswood, Welw.G.C. AL7 51 CY12
Rolt St, SE8 45 L2
Rolvenden Gdns, Brom. BR1 206 EK94
Rolvenden Pl, N17 122 DU52
Romanby Ct, Red. RH1
off Mill St 288 DF135
Roman Cl, W3
off Avenue Gdns 180 CP75
Feltham TW14 198 BW85
Harefield UB9 114 BH53
Rainham RM13 169 FD68
Romanfield Rd, SW2 203 DM87
Roman Gdns, Kings L. WD4 81 BP30
Roman Ho, Rain. RM13
off Roman Cl 169 FD68
Romanhurst Av, Brom. BR2 226 EE98
Romanhurst Gdns, Brom. BR2 226 EE98
● Roman Ind Est, Croy. CR0 224 DS101
Roman Ms, Hodd. EN11
off North Rd 71 EA16
Roman Ri, SE19 204 DR93
Sawbridgeworth CM21 58 EX05

Roman Rd, E2 20 G3
E3 21 L1
E6 24 F5
N10 121 DH52
NW2 141 CW62
W4 180 CS77
Brentwood CM15 131 GC41
Dorking RH4 285 CG138
Ilford IG1 167 EP65
Northfleet DA11 212 GC90
Roman Rd Prim Sch, E6 24 F4
Roman Rbt, Harl. CM20 58 EU11
Romans End, St.Alb. AL3 64 CC22
Roman Sq, SE28 168 EU74
Roman St, Hodd. EN11 71 EA16
Romans Way, Wok. GU22 250 BG115
Roman Vale, Harl. CM17 58 EW10
Roman Vil Rd, Dart. DA2, DA4 210 FQ92
Roman Way, N7 8 D5
SE15 44 G5
Carshalton SM5 240 DF109
Croydon CR0 223 DP103
Dartford DA1 209 FE85
Enfield EN1 104 DT43
Waltham Abbey EN9 105 EB35
● **Roman Way Ind Est**, N1 8 C6
Romany Ct, Hem.H. HP2
off Wood End Cl 63 BQ19
Romany Gdns, E17
off McEntee Av 123 DY53
Sutton SM3 222 DA101
Romany Ri, Orp. BR5 227 EQ102
Roma Read Cl, SW15 201 CV87
Roma Rd, E17 145 DY55
Romberg Rd, SW17 202 DG90
Romborough Gdns, SE13 205 EC85
Romborough Way, SE13 205 EC85
Rom Cres, Rom. RM7 149 FF59
Romeland, Els. WD6 99 CK44
St. Albans AL3 64 CC20
Waltham Abbey EN9 89 EC33
Romeland Hill, St.Alb. AL3 64 CC20
Romero Cl, SW9 42 D10
Romero Sq, SE3 186 EJ84
Romeyn Rd, SW16 203 DM90
ROMFORD, RM1 - RM7 149 FF57
⇌ **Romford** 149 FE58
Romford Rd, E7 13 M4
E12 146 EL63
E15 13 J6
Aveley RM15 170 FQ73
Chigwell IG7 126 EU48
Romford RM5 126 EY52
● **Romford Seedbed Cen**, Rom.
RM7 149 FE59
Romford St, E1 20 D7
Romilly Dr, Wat. WD19 116 BY49
Romilly Rd, N4 143 DP61
Romilly St, W1 17 N10
Rommany Rd, SE27 204 DR91
Romney Chase, Horn. RM11 150 FM58
Romney Cl, N17 122 DV53
NW11 142 DC60
SE14 45 H5
Ashford TW15 197 BQ92
Chessington KT9 238 CL105
Harrow HA2 138 CA59
Romney Dr, Brom. BR1 206 EK94
Harrow HA2 138 CA59
Romney Gdns, Bexh. DA7 188 EZ81
Romney Ho, Enf. EN1
off Ayley Cft 104 DU43
Romney Lock, Wind. SL4 174 AS79
Romney Lock Rd, Wind. SL4 173 AR80
Romney Ms, W1 16 G6
Romney Par, Hayes UB4
off Romney Rd 157 BR68
Romney Rd, SE10 46 F3
Hayes UB4 157 BR68
New Malden KT3 220 CR100
Northfleet DA11 212 GE90
Romney Row, NW2
off Brent Ter 141 CX61
Romney St, SW1 29 P7
Romola Rd, SE24 203 DP88
Romsey Cl, Orp. BR6 245 EP105
Slough SL3 175 AZ76
Romsey Dr, Farn.Com. SL2 133 AR62
Romsey Gdns, Dag. RM9 168 EX67
Romsey Rd, W13 159 CG73
Dagenham RM9 168 EX67
Romside Pl, Rom. RM7
off Brooklands La 149 FD56
Romulus Ct, Brent. TW8
off Justin Cl 179 CK80
Romulus Rd, Grav. DA12 213 GJ86
Rom Valley Way, Rom. RM7 149 FE59
Ronald Av, E15 23 K3
Ronald Cl, Beck. BR3 225 DZ98
Ronald Ct, St.Alb. AL2 82 BY29
Ronald Rd, Beac. HP9 111 AM53
Romford RM3 128 FN53
Ronald Ross Prim Sch,
SW19
off Castlecombe Dr 201 CY87
Ronaldsay Spur, Slou. SL1 154 AS71
Ronalds Rd, N5 8 F3
Bromley BR1 226 EG95
Ronaldstone Rd, Sid. DA15 207 ES86
Ronald St, E1 21 H9
Ronan Way, Denh. UB9 135 BF61
Rona Rd, NW3 6 G1
Ronart St, Wealds. HA3 139 CF55
Rona Wk, N1 9 L5
Rondu Rd, NW2 4 E2
Ronelean Rd, Surb. KT6 220 CM104
Roneo Cor, Horn. RM12 149 FF60
Roneo Link, Horn. RM12 149 FF60
Ronfearn Av, Orp. BR5 228 EX99
Ron Grn Ct, Erith DA8 189 FD79
Ron Leighton Way, E6 166 EL67
Ronneby Cl, Wey. KT13 217 BS104
Ronnie La, E12 147 EN63
Ronsons Way, St.Alb. AL4 65 CF17
Ronson Way, Lthd. KT22 253 CF121
Ron Todd Cl, Dag. RM10 168 FA67
Ronver Rd, SE12 206 EF87
Rood La, EC3 19 N10
Roof of the World Pk Homes Est,
Box H. KT20 270 CP132
Rookby Ct, N21 121 DP47
Rook Cl, Horn. RM12 169 FG66
Wembley HA9 140 CP62
Rookdean, Chipstead TN13 278 FC122
Rookeries Cl, Felt. TW13 197 BV90
Rookery, The, Grays RM20 191 FU79
Rookery Cl, NW9 141 CT57
Fetcham KT22 253 CE124
Rookery Ct, Grays RM20 191 FU79
Rookery Cres, Dag. RM10 169 FB66
Rookery Dr, Chis. BR7 227 EN95
Westcott RH4 284 CA138
Rookery Gdns, Orp. BR5 228 EW99
Rookery Hill, Ashtd. KT21 254 CN118
Outwood RH1 291 DN145
Rookery La, Brom. BR2 226 EK100
Grays RM17 192 GD78
Smallfield RH6 291 DN146
Rookery Mead, Couls. CR5 257 DJ122
Rookery Rd, SW4 183 DJ84
Downe BR6 245 EM110
Staines-upon-Thames TW18 196 BH92
Rookery Vw, Grays RM17 192 GD78
Rookery Way, NW9 141 CT57
Lower Kingswood KT20 271 CZ127
Rookes All, Hert. SG13
off Mangrove Rd 54 DS10
Rookesley Rd, Orp. BR5 228 EX101
Rooke Way, SE10 35 L10
Rookfield Av, N10 143 DJ56
Rookfield Cl, N10 143 DJ56
Rook La, Chaldon CR3 257 DM124
Rookley Cl, Sutt. SM2 240 DB110
Rook Rd, Woob.Grn HP10 132 AD59
Rooks Cl, Welw.G.C. AL8 51 CX10
Rooks Heath Coll,
S.Har. HA2
off Eastcote La 138 CA62
Rooks Hill, Loud. WD3 96 BJ42
Welwyn Garden City AL8 51 CW10
Rooksmead Rd, Sun. TW16 217 BT96
Rooks Nest, Gdse. RH9 275 DY130
Rookstone Rd, SW17 202 DF92
Rook Wk, E6 24 G8
Rookwood Av, Loug. IG10 107 EQ41
New Malden KT3 221 CU98
Wallington SM6 241 DK105
Rookwood Cl, Grays RM17 192 GB77
Merstham RH1 273 DH129
Rookwood Ct, Guil. GU2 280 AW137
Rookwood Gdns, E4 124 EF47
Loughton IG10 107 EQ41
Rookwood Ho, Bark. IG11
off St. Marys 167 ER68
Rookwood Rd, N16 144 DT59
★ **Roosevelt Mem**, W1 17 H10
Roosevelt Way, Dag. RM10 169 FD65
Rootes Dr, W10 14 C5
Roothill La, Bet. RH3 286 CN140
Ropemaker Pl, EC2 19 L6
Ropemaker Rd, SE16 33 L5
Ropemakers Flds, E14 33 N1
Ropemaker St, EC2 19 L6
Roper La, SE1 31 P4
Ropers Av, E4 123 EC50
Ropers Orchard, SW3 40 B3
Roper St, SE9 207 EM86
Ropers Wk, SW2
off Brockwell Pk Gdns 203 DN87
Roper Way, Mitch. CR4 222 DG96
● **Ropery Business Pk**, SE7
off Anchor And Hope La 36 C8
Ropery St, E3 21 N5
Rope St, SE16 33 M7
Rope Wk, Sun. TW16 218 BW97
Ropewalk Gdns, E1 20 D9
Ropewalk Ms, E8 10 C7
Rope Yd Rails, SE18 37 N7
Ropley St, E2 20 C1
Rosa Alba Ms, N5
off Kelross Rd 144 DQ63
Rosa Av, Ashf. TW15 196 BN91
Rosalind Franklin Cl, Guil.
(Surr.Res.Pk) GU2 280 AS135
Rosaline Rd, SW6 38 F5
Rosamond St, SE26 204 DV90
Rosamund Cl, S.Croy. CR2 242 DR105
Rosamun St, Sthl. UB2 178 BY77
Rosary, The, Egh. TW20 215 BD96
Rosary Cl, Houns. TW3 178 BY82
Rosary Ct, Pot.B. EN6 86 DB30
Rosary Gdns, SW7 27 N9
Ashford TW15 197 BP91
Bushey WD23 117 CE45
Rosary RC Prim Sch, NW3 6 C2
Heston TW5 *off The Green* 178 CA79
Rosaville Rd, SW6 38 G5
Roscoe St, EC1 19 K5
Roscoff Cl, Edg. HA8 118 CQ53
Roseacre, Oxt. RH8 276 EG134
Roseacre Cl, W13 159 CH71
Hornchurch RM11 150 FM60
Shepperton TW17 216 BN99
Sutton SM1 222 DC103
Roseacre Gdns, Chilw. GU4 281 BF140
Welwyn Garden City AL7 52 DC09
Roseacre Rd, Well. DA16 188 EV83
Rose All, EC2 *off New St* 19 P7
SE1 31 K2
Rose & Crown Ct, EC2 19 J8
Rose & Crown Yd, SW1 29 M2
Roseary Cl, West Dr. UB7 176 BK77
Rose Av, E18 124 EH54
Gravesend DA12 213 GL88
Mitcham CR4 222 DF95
Morden SM4 222 DC99
Rosebank, SE20 204 DV94
Rose Bk, Brwd. CM14 130 FX48
Rosebank, Epsom KT18 238 CQ114
Waltham Abbey EN9 90 EE33
Rosebank Av, Horn. RM12 150 FJ64
Wembley HA0 139 CF63
Rosebank Cl, N12 120 DE50
Teddington TW11 199 CG93
Rose Bk Cotts, Wok. GU22 248 AY122
Rosebank Gdns, E3 21 M1
Northfleet DA11 212 GE88
Rosebank Gro, E17 145 DZ55
Rosebank Rd, E17 145 EB58
W7 179 CE75
Rosebank Vil, E17 145 EA56
Rosebank Wk, NW1 7 P6
SE18 37 H8
Rosebank Way, W3 160 CR72
Rose Bates Dr, NW9 140 CN56
Roseberry Cl, Upmin. RM14 151 FT58
Roseberry Ct, Wat. WD17
off Grandfield Av 97 BU39
Roseberry Gdns, N4 143 DP58
Roseberry Gdns, Dartford DA1 210 FJ87
Orpington BR6 227 ES104
Upminster RM14 151 FT59
Roseberry Pl, E8 10 A5
Roseberry St, SE16 32 E9
Rosebery Av, E12 166 EL65
EC1 18 E5
N17 122 DU54
Epsom KT17 238 CS114
Harrow HA2 138 BY63
New Malden KT3 221 CT96
Sidcup DA15 207 ES87
Thornton Heath CR7 224 DQ96
Rosebery Cl, Mord. SM4 221 CX100
Rosebery Ct, EC1
off Rosebery Av 18 E4
Northfleet DA11 213 GF88
Rosebery Cres, Wok. GU22 249 AZ121
Rosebery Gdns, N8 143 DL57
W13 159 CG72
Sutton SM1 240 DB105
● **Rosebery Ind Pk**, N17 122 DV54
Rosebery Ms, N10 121 DJ54
SW2 *off Rosebery Rd* 203 DL86
Rosebery Rd, N10 121 DJ54
SW2 203 DL86
Bushey WD23 116 CB45
Epsom KT18 254 CR119
Grays RM17 192 FY79
Hounslow TW3 198 CC85
Kingston upon Thames KT1 220 CP96
Sutton SM1 239 CZ107
Roseberys, Epsom KT18 238 CS114
Rosebery Sch, Epsom KT18
off White Horse Dr 238 CQ114
Rosebery Sq, EC1 18 E5
Kingston upon Thames KT1 220 CN96
Rosebine Av, Twick. TW2 199 CD87
Rosebriar Cl, Wok. GU22 250 BG116
Rosebriars, Cat. CR3 258 DS120
Esher KT10 236 CC106
Rosebriar Wk, Wat. WD24 97 BT36
Rose Bruford Coll,
Sid. DA15
off Burnt Oak La 208 EV88
Rosebury Rd, SW6 39 M9
Rosebury Sq, Wdf.Grn. IG8 125 EN52
Rosebury Vale, Ruis. HA4 137 BT60
Rose Bushes, Epsom KT17 255 CV116
Rose Ct, E1 20 A7
Amersham HP6
off Chestnut La 77 AS37
Pinner HA5 *off Nursery Rd* 138 BW55
Waltham Cross EN7 88 DU27
Rosecourt Rd, Croy. CR0 223 DM100
Rosecrest Ct, N15 *off High Rd* 144 DT55
Rosecroft Av, NW3 142 DA62
Rosecroft Cl, Bigg.H. TN16
off Lotus Rd 261 EM118
Orpington BR5 228 EW100
Rosecroft Dr, Wat. WD17 97 BS36
Rosecroft Gdns, NW2 141 CU62
Twickenham TW2 199 CD88
Rosecroft Rd, Sthl. UB1 158 CA70
Rosecroft Wk, Pnr. HA5 138 BX57
Wembley HA0 139 CK64
Rosedale, Ashtd. KT21 253 CJ118
Caterham CR3 258 DS123
Rose Dale, Orp. BR6 227 EP103
Rosedale, Welw.G.C. AL7 51 CZ05
Rosedale Av, Chsht EN7 88 DT29
Hayes UB3 157 BR71
Rosedale Cl, SE2 188 EV76
W7 *off Boston Rd* 179 CF75
Bricket Wood AL2 82 BY30
Dartford DA2 210 FP87
Stanmore HA7 117 CH51
Rosedale Coll, Hayes UB3
off Wood End Grn Rd 157 BS72
Rosedale Ct, N5 8 G1
Rosedale Dr, Dag. RM9 168 EV67
Rosedale Gdns, Dag. RM9 168 EV66
Rosedale Pl, Croy. CR0 225 DX101
Rosedale Rd, E7 146 EJ64
Dagenham RM9 168 EV66
Epsom KT17 239 CU106
Grays RM17 192 GD78
Richmond TW9 180 CL84
Romford RM1 127 FC54
Rosedale Ter, W6
off Dalling Rd 181 CV76
Rosedale Way, Chsht EN7 88 DU29
Rosedene, NW6 4 D8
Rosedene Av, SW16 203 DM90
Croydon CR0 223 DM101
Greenford UB6 158 CA69
Morden SM4 222 DA99
Rosedene Ct, Dart. DA1
off Shepherds La 210 FJ87
Ruislip HA4 137 BS60
Rosedene End, St.Alb. AL2 82 CA26
Rosedene Gdns, Ilf. IG2 147 EN56
Rosedene Ms, Uxb. UB8 156 BJ69
Rosedene Ter, E10 145 EB61
Rosedew Rd, W6 38 C3
Rose Dr, Chesh. HP5 76 AS32
Rose End, Wor.Pk. KT4 221 CX102
Rosefield, Sev. TN13 278 FG124
Rosefield Cl, Cars. SM5 240 DE106
Rosefield Gdns, E14 22 A10
Ottershaw KT16 233 BD107
Rosefield Rd, Stai. TW18 196 BG91
Roseford Ct, W12 26 C5
Rose Gdn Cl, Edg. HA8 118 CL51
Rose Gdns, W5 179 CK76
Feltham TW13 197 BU89
Southall UB1 158 CA70
Stanwell TW19 196 BK87
Watford WD18 97 BU43
Rosegate Ho, E3 21 P1
Rose Glen, NW9 140 CR56
Romford RM7 149 FE60
Rosehart Ms, W11 15 J9
Rose Hatch Av, Rom. RM6 148 EX55
Roseheath, Hem.H. HP1 61 BE19
Roseheath Rd, Houns. TW4 198 BZ85
ROSE HILL, Dor. RH4 285 CG136
ROSEHILL, Sutt. SM1 222 DB102
Rose Hill, Sutt. SM1 222 DB101
Rose Hill, Burn. SL1 152 AG66
Rosehill, Clay. KT10 237 CG107
Rose Hill, Dor. RH4 285 CH136
Rosehill, Hmptn. TW12 218 CA95
Rose Hill, Sutt. SM1 222 DB103
Rose Hill App, Dor. RH4
off Rose Hill 285 CG136
Rosehill Av, Sutt. SM1 222 DC102
Woking GU21 248 AW116
Rosehill Cl, Hodd. EN11 71 DZ17
Rosehill Ct, Hem.H. HP1
off Green End Rd 62 BG22
Slough SL1 174 AU76
Rosehill Fm Meadow, Bans.
SM7 256 DB115
Rosehill Gdns, Abb.L. WD5 81 BQ32
Greenford UB6 139 CF64
Sutton SM1 222 DB103
Rose Hill Pk W, Sutt. SM1 222 DC102
Rosehill Rd, SW18 202 DC86
Biggin Hill TN16 260 EJ117
Rose Joan Ms, NW6 5 J1
Roseland Cl, N17 122 DR52
Roselands Av, Hodd. EN11 71 DZ15
Roselands Prim Sch, Hodd.
EN11 *off High Wd Rd* 55 DZ14
Rose La, Ripley GU23 250 BJ121
Romford RM6 148 EX55
Rose Lawn, Bushey Hth
WD23 116 CC46
Roseleigh Av, N5 9 H1
Roseleigh Cl, Twick. TW1 199 CK86
Roseley Cotts, Eastwick CM20 57 EP11
Rosemary Av, N3 120 DB54
N9 122 DV46
Enfield EN2 104 DR39
Hounslow TW4 178 BX82
Romford RM1 149 FF55
West Molesey KT8 218 CA97
Rosemary Cl, Croy. CR0 223 DL100
Harlow CM17 58 EW11
Oxted RH8 276 EG133
South Ockendon RM15 171 FW69
Uxbridge UB8 156 BN71
Rosemary Ct, Horl. RH6 290 DE147
Rosemary Cres, Guil. GU2 264 AT130
Rosemary Dr, E14 22 G9
Ilford IG4 146 EK57
London Colney AL2 83 CG26
Rosemary Gdns, SW14
off Rosemary La 180 CQ83
Chessington KT9 238 CL105
Dagenham RM8 148 EZ60
Rosemary La, SW14 180 CQ83
Egham TW20 215 BB97
Horley RH6 291 DH149
Rosemary Rd, SE15 44 B4
SW17 202 DC90
Welling DA16 187 ET81
Rosemary St, N1 9 L8
Rosemead, NW9 141 CT59
Chertsey KT16 216 BH101
Potters Bar EN6 86 DC30
Rosemead Av, Felt. TW13 197 BT89
Mitcham CR4 223 DJ96
Wembley HA9 140 CL64
Rosemead Cl, Red. RH1 288 DD136
Rosemead Gdns, Hutt. CM13 131 GD42
Rosemead Prep Sch, SE21
off Thurlow Pk Rd 204 DQ89
Rosemere Pl, Beck. BR2 226 EE98
Rose Ms, N18 122 DV49
Rosemont Av, N12 120 DC51
Rosemont Rd, NW3 5 N4
W3 160 CP73
New Malden KT3 220 CQ97
Richmond TW10 200 CL86
Wembley HA0 160 CL67
Rosemoor Cl, Welw.G.C. AL7 51 CZ10
Rosemoor St, SW3 28 E9
Rosemount, Harl. CM19 73 EP18
Wallington SM6 241 DJ107
Rosemount Av, W.Byf. KT14 234 BG113
Rosemount Cl, Wdf.Grn. IG8
off Chapelmount Rd 125 EM51
Rosemount Dr, Brom. BR1 227 EM98
Rosemount Pt, SE23
off Dacres Rd 205 DX90
Rosemount Rd, W13 159 CG72
Rosenau Cres, SW11 40 D7
Rosenau Rd, SW11 40 D6
Rosendale Prim Sch, SE21
off Rosendale Rd 204 DQ87
Rosendale Rd, SE21 204 DQ87
SE24 204 DQ87
Roseneath Av, N21 121 DP46
Roseneath Cl, Orp. BR6 246 EW108
Roseneath Pl, SW16
off Curtis Fld Rd 203 DM91
Roseneath Rd, SW11 202 DG86
Roseneath Wk, Enf. EN1 104 DR42
Rosens Wk, Edg. HA8 118 CP48
Rosenthal Rd, SE6 205 EB86
Rosenthorpe Rd, SE15 205 DX85
Rose Pk, Add. KT15 233 BE109
Rose Pk Cl, Hayes UB4 158 BW70
Rosepark Ct, Ilf. IG5 125 EM54
Roserton St, E14 34 E5
Rosery, The, Croy. CR0 225 DX100
Roses, The, Wdf.Grn. IG8 124 EF52
Roses La, Wind. SL4 173 AK82
Rose Sq, SW3 28 B10
Rose St, EC4 19 H8
WC2 18 A10
Northfleet DA11 212 GB86
Rosethorn Cl, SW12 203 DJ87
Rose Tree Ms, Wdf.Grn. IG8
off Chigwell Rd 124 EL51
Rosetree Pl, Hmptn. TW12 218 CA95
Rosetrees, Guil. GU1 281 BA135
Rosetta Arts Centre, E15 23 K3
Rosetta Cl, SW8 42 B5
Rosetta Prim Sch, E16 24 B7
Rosetti Ter, Dag. RM8
off Marlborough Rd 148 EV63
Rose Vale, Hodd. EN11 71 EA17
Rose Valley, Brwd. CM14 130 FW48
Roseveare Rd, SE12 206 EJ91
Rose Vil, Dart. DA1 210 FP87
Roseville Av, Houns. TW3 198 CA85
Roseville Rd, Hayes UB3 177 BU78
Rosevine Rd, SW20 221 CW95
Rose Wk, Pur. CR8 241 DK111
St. Albans AL4 65 CJ18
Slough SL2 153 AP71
Surbiton KT5 220 CP99
West Wickham BR4 225 ED103
Rose Wk, The, Rad. WD7 99 CH37
Rosewall Cl, Wok. GU21
off Muirfield Rd 248 AU118
Rose Way, SE12 206 EG85
Roseway, SE21 204 DR86
Rose Way, Edg. HA8 118 CQ49
Rosewell Cl, SE20 204 DV94
Rosewood, Dart. DA2 209 FE91
Esher KT10 219 CG103
Sutton SM2 240 DC110
Woking GU22 249 BA119
Rosewood Av, Grnf. UB6 139 CG64
Rosewood Av, Hornch. RM12 149 FG64
Rosewood Cl, Sid. DA14 208 EW90
Rosewood Ct, Brom. BR1 226 EJ95
Hemel Hempstead HP1 61 BE19
Kings.T. KT2 200 CN94
Romford RM6 148 EW57
Rosewood Dr, Enf. EN2 103 DN35
Shepperton TW17 216 BM99
Rosewood Gdns, SE13
off Morden Hill 46 E8
Rosewood Gro, Sutt. SM1 222 DC103
Rosewood Sq, W12
off Primula St 161 CU72
Rosewood Ter, SE20
off Laurel Gro 204 DW94
Rosewood Way, Farn.Com.
SL2 133 AQ64
Rosher Cl, E15 12 G7
ROSHERVILLE, Grav. DA11 213 GF85
Rosherville C of E Prim Sch,
Nthflt DA11 *off London Rd* 212 GE86
Rosherville Way, Grav. DA11 212 GE87
Rosh Pinah Jewish Prim Sch,
Edg. HA8 *off Glengall Rd* 118 CP48
Rosie's Way, S.Ock. RM15 171 FX72
Rosina St, E9 11 J3
Roskell Rd, SW15 181 CX83
Rosken Gro, Farn.Royal SL2 153 AP68
Roslin Rd, W3 180 CP76
● **Roslin Sq**, W3 180 CP76
Roslin Way, Brom. BR1 206 EG92
Roslyn Cl, Brox. EN10 71 DY21
Mitcham CR4 222 DD96
Roslyn Ct, Wok. GU21
off St. John's Rd 248 AU118
Roslyn Gdns, Rom. RM2 127 FF54
Roslyn Rd, N15 144 DR57
Rosmead Rd, W11 14 F10
Rosoman Pl, EC1 18 F4
Rosoman St, EC1 18 F3
Ross, E16 *off Seagull La* 23 N10
Rossall Cl, Horn. RM11 149 FG58
Rossall Cres, NW10 160 CM69
Ross Av, Dag. RM8 148 EZ61
Ross Cl, Har. HA3 116 CC52
Hatfield AL10
off Homestead Rd 67 CU15
Hayes UB3 177 BR77
Northolt UB5 139 CD63
Ross Ct, E5 *off Napoleon Rd* 144 DV63
SW15 201 CX87
Ross Cres, Wat. WD25 97 BU35
Rossdale, Sutt. SM1 240 DE106
Rossdale Dr, N9 104 DW44
NW9 140 CQ60
Rossdale Rd, SW15 181 CW84
Rosse Gdns, SE13
off Desvignes Dr 205 ED86
Rosse Ms, SE3 186 EH81
Rossendale Cl, Enf. EN2 103 DP37
Rossendale St, E5 144 DV61
Rossendale Way, NW1 7 M7
Rossetti Gdns, Couls. CR5 257 DM118
Rossetti Ms, NW8 6 B9
Rossetti Rd, SE16 32 E10
Rossgate, Hem.H. HP1
off Galley Hill 62 BG18
Rossgate Prim Sch, Hem.H.
HP1 *off Galley Hill* 62 BG18
Ross Haven Pl, Nthwd. HA6 115 BT53
Rossignol Gdns, Cars. SM5 222 DG103
Rossindel Rd, Houns. TW3 198 CA85
Rossington Av, Borwd. WD6 100 CL38
Rossington Cl, Enf. EN1 104 DV38
Rossington St, E5 144 DU61
Rossiter Cl, SE19 204 DQ94
Slou. SL3 174 AY77
Rossiter Flds, Barn. EN5 101 CY44
Rossiter Gro, SW9 183 DN83
Rossiter Rd, SW12 203 DH88
Rossland Cl, Bexh. DA6 209 FB85
Rosslare Cl, West. TN16 277 ER125
Rosslyn Av, E4 124 EF47
SW13 180 CS83
Dagenham RM8 148 EZ59
East Barnet EN4 102 DE44
Feltham TW14 197 BU86
Romford RM3 128 FM54
Rosslyn Cl, Hayes UB3 157 BR71
Sunbury-on-Thames TW16
off Cadbury Rd 197 BS93
West Wickham BR4 226 EF104
Rosslyn Cres, Har. HA1 139 CF57
Wembley HA9 140 CL63
Rosslyn Gdns, Wem. HA9
off Rosslyn Cres 140 CL62
Rosslyn Hill, NW3 6 B1
Rosslyn Ms, NW3 6 B1
Rosslyn Pk, Wey. KT13 235 BR105
Rosslyn Pk Ms, NW3 6 B2
Rosslyn Rd, E17 145 EC56
Barking IG11 167 ER66
Twickenham TW1 199 CJ86
Watford WD18 97 BV41
Rossmore Cl, Enf. EN3 105 DX42
Rossmore Ct, NW1 16 E4
Rossmore Rd, NW1 16 D5
Ross Par, Wall. SM6 241 DH107
Ross Rd, SE25 224 DR97
Cobham KT11 236 BW113
Dartford DA1 209 FG86
Twickenham TW2 198 CB88
Wallington SM6 241 DJ106
Ross Way, SE9 186 EL83
Northwood HA6 115 BT49
Rossway Dr, Bushey WD23 98 CC43
Rosswood Gdns, Wall. SM6 241 DJ107
Rostella Rd, SW17 202 DD91
Rostrevor Av, N15 144 DT58
Rostrevor Gdns, Hayes UB3 157 BS74
Iver SL0 155 BD68
Southall UB2 178 BY78
Rostrevor Ms, SW6 38 G7
Rostrevor Rd, SW6 38 G6
SW19 202 DA92
Roswell Cl, Chsht EN8 89 DY30
Rotary St, SE1 30 G6
Rothbury Av, Rain. RM13 169 FH71
Rothbury Gdns, Islw. TW7 179 CG80
Rothbury Rd, E9 11 P6
Rothbury Wk, N17 122 DU52
Roth Dr, Hutt. CM13 131 GB47
Rother Cl, Wat. WD25 82 BW34
Rotherfield Prim Sch, N1 9 K8
Rotherfield Rd, Cars. SM5 240 DG105
Enfield EN3 105 DX37
Rotherfield St, N1 9 K7
Rotherham Wk, SE1 30 G3
Rotherhill Av, SW16 203 DK93

ROTHERHITHE, SE16 33 J6
⊖ Rotherhithe 33 H4
Rotherhithe New Rd, SE16 44 D1
Rotherhithe Old Rd, SE16 33 J7
Sch Rotherhithe Prim Sch, SE16 33 J8
Rotherhithe St, SE16 33 H4
Rotherhithe Tunnel, E1 33 J2
Rotherhithe Tunnel App, E14 21 L10
SE16 32 G5
Rothervale, Horl. RH6 290 DF145
Rotherwick Hill, W5 160 CM70
Rotherwick Rd, NW11 142 DA59
Rotherwood Cl, SW20 221 CY95
Rotherwood Rd, SW15 38 C10
Rothery St, N1 8 G8
Rothery Ter, SW9 42 G5
Rothesay Av, SW20 221 CY96
Greenford UB6 159 CD65
Richmond TW10 180 CP84
Rothesay Rd, SE25 224 DR98
Rothes Rd, Dor. RH4 285 CH135
Rothsay Rd, E7 166 EJ66
Rothsay St, SE1 31 N6
Rothsay Wk, E14 34 B8
Rothschild Rd, W4 180 CQ77
Rothschild St, SE27 203 DP91
Roth Wk, N7 off Durham Rd 143 DN61
Rothwell Gdns, Dag. RM9 168 EW67
Rothwell Ho, Houns. TW5 off Biscoe Cl 178 CA79
Rothwell Rd, Dag. RM9 168 EW67
Rothwell St, NW1 6 F8
Rotten Row, SW1 28 G4
SW7 28 C4
Rotterdam Dr, E14 34 F7
Rouel Rd, SE16 32 C7
Rouge La, Grav. DA12 213 GH88
Rougemont Av, Mord. SM4 222 DA100
Roughdown Av, Hem.H. HP3 62 BG23
Roughdown Rd, Hem.H. HP3 62 BH23
Roughdown Vil Rd, Hem.H. HP3 62 BG23
Roughets La, Bletch. RH1 274 DS129
Godstone RH9 274 DS129
Roughlands, Wok. GU22 249 BE115
Rough Rew, Dor. RH4 285 CH139
Roughs, The, Nthwd. HA6 115 BT48
Roughtallys, N.Wld Bas. CM16 92 EZ27
Roughwood Cl, Wat. WD17 97 BS38
Roughwood La, Ch.St.G. HP8 112 AY45
Roundacre, SW19 201 CX89
Roundaway Rd, Ilf. IG5 125 EM54
ROUND BUSH, Wat. WD25 98 CC38
Roundbush La, Ald. WD25 98 CC38
Roundcroft, Chshrt EN7 88 DT26
Roundel Cl, SE4 185 DZ84
Round Gro, Croy. CR0 225 DX101
Roundhay Cl, SE23 205 DX89
Roundheads End, Forty Grn HP9 110 AH51
Roundhedge Way, Enf. EN2 103 DM38
Round Hill, SE26 204 DW89
Roundhill, Wok. GU22 249 BB119
Roundhill Dr, Enf. EN2 103 DM42
Woking GU22 249 BB118
Roundhills, Wal.Abb. EN9 90 EE34
Roundhill Way, Cob. KT11 236 CB111
Guildford GU2 264 AT134
Round Ho Ct, Chshrt EN8 off Hobbs Cl 89 DX29
Roundhouse La, E20 12 E5
Roundings, The, Hert.Hth SG13 54 DV14
Roundlyn Gdns, St.M.Cray BR5 off Lynmouth Ri 228 EV98
Roundmead Av, Loug. IG10 107 EN41
Roundmead Cl, Loug. IG10 107 EN41
Roundmoor Dr, Chshrt EN8 89 DX29
Round Oak Rd, Wey. KT13 234 BM105
Roundtable Rd, Brom. BR1 206 EF90
Roundthorn Way, Wok. GU21 248 AT116
Roundtree Rd, Wem. HA0 139 CH64
Roundway, Bigg.H. TN16 off Norheads La 260 EK116
Egham TW20 195 BC92
Roundway, The, N17 122 DQ53
Claygate KT10 237 CF106
Watford WD18 97 BT44
Roundways, Ruis. HA4 137 BT62
Roundwood, Chis. BR7 227 EP96
Kings Langley WD4 80 BL26
Roundwood Av, Hutt. CM13 131 GA46
Uxbridge UB11 157 BQ74
Roundwood Cl, Ruis. HA4 137 BR59
Roundwood Dr, Welw.G.C. AL8 51 CW07
Roundwood Gro, Hutt. CM13 131 GB45
Roundwood Lake, Hutt. CM13 131 GB46
Roundwood Pk, NW10 161 CU66
Roundwood Rd, NW10 161 CT65
Amersham HP6 77 AS38
Roundwood Vw, Bans. SM7 255 CX115
Roundwood Way, Bans. SM7 255 CX115
Rounton Rd, E3 22 B4
Waltham Abbey EN9 90 EE33
Roupell Rd, SW2 203 DM88
Roupell St, SE1 30 F3
Rousden St, NW1 7 L7
Rousebarn La, Rick. WD3 97 BQ41
Rouse Gdns, SE21 204 DS91
Rous Rd, Buck.H. IG9 124 EL46
Routemaster Cl, E13 24 A2
Routh Ct, Felt. TW14 197 BR88
Routh Rd, SW18 202 DE87
Routh St, E6 25 K7
Rover Av, Ilf. IG6 125 ET51
Rover Ho, N1 off Phillipp St 9 P9
Rowallan Par, Dag. RM8 off Green La 148 EW60
Rowallan Rd, SW6 38 E5
Rowan Av, E4 123 DZ51
Egham TW20 195 BC92
Rowan Cl, SW16 223 DJ95
W5 180 CL75
Ashford TW15 196 BK91
Banstead SM7 255 CX115
Beaconsfield HP9 110 AH54
Bricket Wood AL2 82 CA31
Guildford GU1 264 AV131
Ilford IG1 147 ER64
New Malden KT3 220 CS96
Reigate RH2 288 DC136
St. Albans AL4 66 CL20
Shenley WD7 off Juniper Gdns 84 CL33
Stanmore HA7 117 CF51
Wembley HA0 139 CG62
Rowan Ct, Borwd. WD6 off Theobald St 100 CL39
Rowan Cres, SW16 223 DJ95
Dartford DA1 210 FJ88
Rowan Dr, NW9 141 CU56
Broxbourne EN10 89 DZ25
Rowan Gdns, Croy. CR0 224 DT104
Iver SL0 155 BC68
Rowan Grn, Wey. KT13 235 BR105
Rowan Grn E, Brwd. CM13 131 FZ48
Rowan Grn W, Brwd. CM13 131 FZ49
Rowan Gro, Aveley RM15 170 FQ73
Coulsdon CR5 257 DH121
Rowan Ho, NW3 off Maitland Pk Rd 6 F4
Rowanhurst Dr, Farn.Com. SL2 133 AQ64
Rowan Pl, Amer. HP6 94 AT38
Hayes UB3 157 BT73
Sch Rowan Prep Sch, Rowan Brae, Esher KT10 off Gordon Rd 237 CE108
Rowan Hill, Esher KT10 off Fitzalan Rd 237 CF108
Rowan Rd, SW16 223 DJ96
W6 26 C9
Bexleyheath DA7 188 EY83
Brentford TW8 179 CH80
Swanley BR8 229 FD97
West Drayton UB7 176 BK77
Rowans, Welw.G.C. AL7 52 DA06
Rowans, The, N13 122 DQ48
Aveley RM15 off Purfleet Rd 170 FQ74
Chalfont St. Peter SL9 134 AX55
Hemel Hempstead HP1 62 BG20
Sunbury-on-Thames TW16 197 BT92
Woking GU22 248 AY118
Rowans Cl, Long. DA3 231 FX96
Sch Rowans Prim Sch, Welw.G.C. AL7 off Rowans 52 DA06
Sch Rowans Sch, The, SW20 off Drax Av 201 CU94
Rowans Way, Loug. IG10 107 EM42
Rowan Ter, SE20 off Sycamore Gro 224 DU95
W6 26 C9
Rowantree Cl, N21 122 DR46
Rowantree Rd, N21 122 DR46
Enfield EN2 103 DP40
Rowan Wk, N2 142 DC58
N19 off Bredgar Rd 143 DJ61
W10 14 E4
Barnet EN5 102 DB43
Bromley BR2 227 EM104
Chesham HP5 76 AN30
Hatfield AL10 67 CU21
Hornchurch RM11 150 FK56
Rowan Way, Rom. RM6 148 EW55
Slough SL2 153 AP71
South Ockendon RM15 171 FX70
Rowanwood Av, Sid. DA15 208 EU88
Rowanwood Ms, Enf. EN2 103 DP40
Rowbarns Way, E.Hors. KT24 267 BT130
Rowben Cl, N20 120 DB46
Rowberry Cl, SW6 38 B5
Rowbourne Pl, Cuffley EN6 87 DK28
Rowbury, Gdmg. GU7 280 AU143
Rowcroft, Hem.H. HP1 61 BE21
Rowcross St, SE1 32 A10
Rowdell Rd, Nthlt. UB5 158 CA67
Rowden Pk Gdns, E4 off Rowden Rd 123 EA51
Rowden Rd, E4 123 EA51
Beckenham BR3 225 DY95
Epsom KT19 238 CP105
Rowditch La, SW11 40 G8
Rowdon Av, NW10 161 CV66
Rowdown Cres, New Adgtn CR0 243 ED109
Sch Rowdown Inf Sch, New Adgtn CR0 off Calley Down Cres 243 ED110
Rowdowns Rd, Dag. RM9 168 EZ67
Rowe Gdns, Bark. IG11 167 ET68
Rowe La, E9 10 G2
Rowena Cres, SW11 40 D9
Rowe Wk, Har. HA2 138 CA62
Rowfant Rd, SW17 202 DG88
Rowhedge, Brwd. CM13 131 GA48
Row Hill, Add. KT15 233 BF107
Rowhill Rd, E5 10 F1
Dartford DA2 209 FF93
Swanley BR8 209 FF93
Sch Rowhill Sch, Wilm. DA2 off Stock La 210 FJ91
Rowhurst Av, Add. KT15 234 BH107
Leatherhead KT22 253 CF117
Rowington Cl, W2 15 L6
Rowland Av, Har. HA3 139 CJ55
Rowland Cl, Wind. SL4 173 AK83
Rowland Ct, E16 23 L4
Rowland Cres, Chig. IG7 125 ES49
Rowland Gro, SE26 off Dallas Rd 204 DV90
Rowland Hill Av, N17 122 DQ52
Rowland Hill St, NW3 6 C2
Rowlands Av, Pnr. HA5 116 CA51
Rowlands Cl, N6 142 DG58
NW7 119 CU52
Cheshunt EN8 89 DX30
Rowlands Flds, Chshrt EN8 89 DX29
Rowlands Rd, Dag. RM8 148 EZ61
Rowland Wk, Hav.at.Bow. RM4 127 FE48
Rowland Way, SW19 222 DB95
Ashford TW15 off Littleton Rd 197 BQ94
Rowlatt Cl, Dart. DA2 210 FJ91
Rowlatt Ct, St.Alb. AL1 off Hillside Rd 65 CE19
Rowlatt Dr, St.Alb. AL3 64 CA22
Rowlatt Rd, Dart. DA2 off Whitehead Cl 210 FJ90
Rowley Av, Sid. DA15 208 EV87
Rowley Cl, Pyrford GU22 250 BG116
Watford WD19 off Lower Paddock Rd 98 BY44
Wembley HA0 160 CM66
Rowley Ct, Cat. CR3 258 DQ122
Rowley Gdns, N4 144 DQ59
Cheshunt EN8 89 DX28
ROWLEY GREEN, Barn. EN5 101 CT42
Rowley Grn Rd, Barn. EN5 101 CT43
● Rowley Ind Pk, W3 180 CP76
Rowley La, Barn. EN5 101 CT43
Borehamwood WD6 100 CR39
Wexham SL3 154 AW67
Rowley Mead, Thnwd CM16 92 EW25
Rowley Rd, N15 144 DQ57
Rowleys Rd, Hert. SG13 54 DT08
Rowley Wk, Hem.H. HP2 63 BQ15
Rowley Way, NW8 5 M8
Rowlheys Pl, West Dr. UB7 176 BL76
Rowlls Rd, Kings.T. KT1 220 CM97
Rowmarsh Cl, Nthflt DA11 212 GD91
Rowney Gdns, Dag. RM9 168 EW65
Sawbridgeworth CM21 58 EW07
Rowney Rd, Dag. RM9 168 EV65
Rowney Wd, Saw. CM21 58 EW06
Rowntree Clifford Cl, E13 24 A4
Rowntree Cl, NW6 5 K5
Rowntree Path, SE28 off Booth Cl 168 EV73
Rowntree Rd, Twick. TW2 199 CE88
Rows, The, Harl. CM20 off East Gate 57 ER14
Rowse Cl, E15 12 F8
Rowsley Av, NW4 141 CW55
Rowstock Gdns, N7 7 P3
Rowton Rd, SE18 187 EQ80
ROW TOWN, Add. KT15 233 BF108
Rowtown, Add. KT15 233 BF108
Rowzill Rd, Swan. BR8 209 FF93
Roxborough Av, Har. HA1 139 CD59
Isleworth TW7 179 CF80
Roxborough Hts, Har. HA1 off College Rd 139 CE58
Roxborough Pk, Har. HA1 139 CE59
Roxborough Rd, Har. HA1 139 CD57
Roxbourne Cl, Nthlt. UB5 158 BX65
Sch Roxbourne First & Mid Schs, S.Har. HA2 off Torbay Rd 138 BY61
Roxburgh Av, Upmin. RM14 150 FQ62
Roxburgh Rd, SE27 203 DP92
Roxburn Way, Ruis. HA4 137 BT62
Roxby Pl, SW6 39 K2
ROXETH, Har. HA2 139 CD61
Roxeth Ct, Ashf. TW15 196 BN92
Sch Roxeth First & Mid Sch, Har. HA2 off Brickfields 139 CD61
Roxeth Grn Av, Har. HA2 138 CB62
Roxeth Gro, Har. HA2 138 CB63
Roxeth Hill, Har. HA2 139 CD61
Sch Roxeth Manor First & Mid Schs, S.Har. HA2 off Eastcote La 138 CA62
Roxford Cl, Shep. TW17 217 BS99
Roxley Rd, SE13 205 EB86
Roxton Gdns, Croy. CR0 243 EA106
Roxwell Cl, Slou. SL1 153 AL74
Roxwell Gdns, Hutt. CM13 131 GC43
Roxwell Rd, W12 181 CU75
Barking IG11 168 EU68
● Roxwell Trd Pk, E10 145 DX59
Roxwell Way, Wdf.Grn. IG8 124 EJ52
Roxy Av, Rom. RM6 148 EW59
★ Royal Acad of Arts, W1 29 L1
Coll Royal Acad of Dance, SW11 40 B7
★ Royal Acad of Dramatic Art (R.A.D.A.), WC1 17 P6
Uni Royal Acad of Music, NW1 17 H5
★ Royal Air Force Mus, NW9 119 CU54
DLR Royal Albert 24 G10
Royal Albert Dock, E16 37 J1
★ Royal Albert Hall, SW7 28 A5
Jct Royal Albert Rbt, E16 24 G10
Royal Albert Way, E16 24 F10
Sch Royal Alexandra & Albert Sch, Reig. RH2 off Rocky La 272 DE129
Royal Arc, W1 29 L1
Royal Artillery Barracks, SE18 37 L10
Royal Av, SW3 28 E10
Waltham Cross EN8 89 DY33
Worcester Park KT4 220 CS103
Coll Royal Ballet Sch, The, Upr Sch, WC2 18 B9
Coll Royal Ballet Sch, The, Lwr Sch, Rich. TW10 off Richmond Pk 200 CR88
★ Royal Berkshire Yeomanry Mus (Windsor TA Cen), Wind. SL4 173 AR83
★ Royal Botanic Gdns, Kew, Rich. TW9 180 CL80
H Royal Brompton Hosp, SW3 28 C10
Annexe, SW3 28 B10
Royal Carriage Ms, SE18 off Major Draper Rd 37 P7
Royal Circ, SE27 203 DN90
Royal Cl, N16 144 DS60
SE8 45 N2
SW19 201 CX90
Ilford IG3 148 EU59
Orpington BR6 245 EP105
Uxbridge UB8 156 BM72
Worcester Park KT4 220 CS103
Coll Royal Coll of Anaesthetists, The, WC1 18 C7
Uni Royal Coll of Art, SW7 27 P5
Coll Royal Coll of Art, Sculpture Sch, SW11 40 C5
Coll Royal Coll of Defence Studies, SW1 29 H6
Coll Royal Coll of Music, SW7 28 A6
Coll Royal Coll of Nursing, W1 17 J8
Coll Royal Coll of Obstetricians & Gynaecologists, NW1 16 E4
Coll Royal Coll of Physicians, NW1 17 K4
★ Royal Coll of Surgeons of England, WC2 18 D8
Royal Coll St, NW1 7 L6
Royal Connaught Dr, Bushey WD23 98 BZ42
Royal Ct, EC3 off Royal Ex Bldgs 19 M9
SE16 33 N6
Hemel Hempstead HP3 62 BL23
★ Royal Courts of Justice, WC2 18 D9
Royal Cres, W11 26 D3
Ilford IG2 147 ER58
Ruislip HA4 138 BY63
Royal Cres Ms, W11 26 D3
Sch Royal Docks Comm Sch, The, E16 24 D9
Royal Docks Rd, E6 25 P10
★ Royal Dress Collection (Kensington Palace), W8 27 M3
Royal Dr, N11 120 DG50
Epsom KT18 255 CV118
Royal Duchess Ms, SW12 off Dinsmore Rd 203 DH87
Royal Earlswood Pk, Red. RH1 288 DG138
Royale Leisure Pk, W3 160 CN70
Royal Ex, EC3 19 M9
Royal Ex Av, EC3 19 M9
Royal Ex Bldgs, EC3 19 M9
★ Royal Festival Hall, SE1 30 D3
Uni Royal Free & Uni Coll Med Sch, Royal Free Campus, NW3 6 D2
H Royal Free Hosp, The, NW3 6 D2
Royal Gdns, W7 179 CG76
★ Royal Geographical Society, SW7 28 A5
Sch Royal Gram Sch, Guil. GU1 off High St 280 AY135
Royal Herbert Pavilions, SE18 187 EM81
Royal Hill, SE10 46 E4
Uni Royal Holloway Coll, Egh. TW20 off Egham Hill 194 AX93
Inst for Environmental Research, Vir.W. GU25 off Callow Hill 214 AW96
Kingswood Hall of Res, Egh. TW20 off Coopers Hill La 194 AX91
Royal Horticultural Society Cotts, Wisley GU23 off Wisley La 250 BL116
★ Royal Horticultural Society Gdn Wisley, Wok. GU22 250 BL119
★ Royal Horticultural Society (Lawrence Hall), SW1 29 N7
★ Royal Horticultural Society (Lindley Hall), SW1 29 N8
★ Royal Hosp Chelsea & Mus, SW3 40 G1
H Royal Hosp for Neuro-Disability, SW15 201 CY86
Royal Hosp Rd, SW3 40 E2
Royal Jubilee Ct, Rom. RM2 149 FG55
Sch Royal Kent C of E Prim Sch, The, Oxshott KT22 off Oakshade Rd 236 CC114
Royal La, Uxb. UB8 156 BM69
West Drayton UB7 156 BM72
Sch Royal Liberty Sch, The, Gidea Pk RM2 off Upper Brentwood Rd 150 FJ55
H Royal London Homoeopathic Hosp, WC1 18 B6
H Royal London Hosp, The, St. Clements, E3 21 P3
Whitechapel, E1 20 E7
Whitechapel - Dentistry Cen, E1 20 E7
H Royal Marsden Hosp, The, SW3 28 B10
Sutton SM2 240 DC110
Sch Royal Masonic Sch for Girls, The, Rick. WD3 off Chorleywood Rd 96 BK44
★ Royal Mews, The, SW1 29 K6
Royal Mews, Lon.Col. AL2 83 CK26
Coll Royal Military Sch of Music, Twick. TW2 off Kneller Rd 199 CD86
Royal Mint Ct, EC3 32 B1
Royal Mint Pl, E1 20 B10
Royal Mint St, E1 20 B10
Royal Mt Ct, Twick. TW2 199 CE90
Sch Royal Nat Inst for the Blind Sunshine Ho Sch, Nthwd. HA6 off Dene Rd 115 BR51
H Royal Nat Orthopaedic Hosp, W1 17 K5
Stanmore HA7 117 CJ47
★ Royal National Rose Society - Gdns of the Rose, The, St.Alb. AL2 82 BY26
H Royal National Throat, Nose & Ear Hosp, WC1 18 C2
Royal Naval Pl, SE14 45 N4
⊖ Royal Oak 15 M7
Royal Oak Ct, N1 19 N2
Royal Oak Ms, Tedd. TW11 off High St 199 CG92
Royal Oak Pl, SE22 204 DV86
Royal Oak Rd, E8 10 E4
Bexleyheath DA6 208 EZ85
Woking GU21 248 AW118
Royal Oak Ter, Grav. DA12 off Constitution Hill 213 GJ88
Royal Oak Yd, SE1 31 N5
★ Royal Observatory Greenwich (Flamsteed Ho), SE10 47 H4
Royal Opera Arc, SW1 29 N2
★ Royal Opera Ho, WC2 18 B10
Royal Orchard Cl, SW18 201 CY87
Royal Par, SE3 47 L9
SW6 off Dawes Rd 38 E4
W5 off Western Av 160 CL69
Chislehurst BR7 227 EQ94
Richmond TW9 off Station App 180 CN81
Royal Par Ms, SE3 47 L9
Chislehurst BR7 207 EQ94
Sch Royal Pk Prim Sch, Sid. DA14 off Riverside Rd 208 EY90
Royal Pier Ms, Grav. DA12 off Royal Pier Rd 213 GH86
Royal Pier Rd, Grav. DA12 213 GH86
Royal Pl, SE10 46 F5
Royal Quarter, Kings.T. KT2 220 CL95
Royal Rd, E16 24 E9
SE17 42 G2
Darenth DA2 210 FN92
St. Albans AL1 65 CH20
Sidcup DA14 208 EX90
Teddington TW11 199 CD92
Royal Route, Wem. HA9 140 CM63
Sch Royal Russell Prep Sch, Croy. CR0 off Coombe La 242 DV106
Sch Royal Russell Sen Sch, Croy. CR0 off Coombe La 242 DV107
Sch Royal Sch Hampstead, The, NW3 6 A1
Coll Royal Sch of Needlework, E.Mol. KT8 off Hampton Ct Palace 219 CF98
Royal St, SE1 30 D6
H Royal Surrey Co Hosp, Guil. GU2 264 AS134
Royal Swan Quarter, Lthd. KT22 off Leret Way 253 CH121
Royalty Ms, W1 17 N9
Uni Royal Vet Coll - Boltons Pk Fm, Pot.B. EN6 off Hawkshead Rd 86 DA29
Uni Royal Vet Coll - Camden Campus, Beaumont Animal's Hosp, NW1 7 M9
Royal Coll St, NW1 7 N9
Uni Royal Vet Coll - Hawkshead Campus, N.Mymms AL9 off Hawkshead La 85 CX28
DLR Royal Victoria 23 N10
Royal Victoria Dock, E16 36 A1
● Royal Victoria Patriotic Bldg, SW18 202 DD86
Royal Victoria Pl, E16 36 B2
Royal Victoria Sq, E16 36 A1
Royal Victor Pl, E3 21 K1
Royal Wk, Wall. SM6 off Prince Charles Way 223 DH104
Royce Cl, Brox. EN10 71 DZ21
Royce Gro, Lvsdn WD25 81 BT34
Roycraft Av, Bark. IG11 167 ET68
Roycraft Cl, Bark. IG11 167 ET68
Roycroft Cl, E18 124 EH53
SW2 203 DN88
Roydene Rd, SE18 187 ES79
ROYDON, Harl. CM19 72 EH15
⇌ Roydon 56 EG13
● Roydonbury Ind Est, Harl. CM19 72 EL15
Roydon Cl, SW11 40 F8
Loughton IG10 124 EL45
Roydon Ct, Hersham KT12 235 BU105
ROYDON HAMLET, Harl. CM19 72 EJ19
Roydon Lo Chalet Est, Roydon CM19 56 EJ14
Roydon Marina Village, Roydon CM19 56 EG14
Sch Roydon Prim Sch, Roydon CM19 off Epping Rd 72 EH15
Roydon Rd, Harl. CM19 56 EL14
Stanstead Abbotts SG12 56 EE11
Roydon St, SW11 41 J6
Roy Gdns, Ilf. IG2 147 ES56
Roy Gro, Hmptn. TW12 198 CB93
Royle Bldg, N1 9 J10
Royle Cl, Chal.St.P. SL9 113 AZ52
Romford RM2 149 FH57
Royle Cres, W13 159 CG70
Roy Richmond Way, Epsom KT19 238 CS110
Roy Rd, Nthwd. HA6 115 BT52
Roy Sq, E14 21 M10
Royston Av, E4 123 EA50
Byfleet KT14 234 BL112
Sutton SM1 222 DD104
Wallington SM6 241 DK105
Royston Cl, Hert. SG14 53 DP09
Hounslow TW5 177 BV81
Walton-on-Thames KT12 217 BU102
Royston Ct, SE24 204 DQ86
Richmond TW9 180 CM81
Surbiton KT6 220 CN104
Royston Gdns, Ilf. IG1 146 EK58
Royston Gro, Pnr. HA5 116 BZ51
Royston Par, Ilf. IG1 146 EK58
Royston Pk Rd, Pnr. HA5 116 BZ51
Sch Royston Prim Sch, SE20 off High St 225 DX95
Royston Rd, SE20 225 DX95
Byfleet KT14 234 BL112
Dartford DA1 209 FF86
Richmond TW10 200 CL85
Romford RM3 128 FN52
St. Albans AL1 65 CH21
Roystons, The, Surb. KT5 220 CP99
Royston St, E2 21 H1
Royston Way, Slou. SL1 152 AJ71
Rozel Ct, N1 9 N8
Rozel Rd, SW4 41 L9
Rubastic Rd, Sthl. UB2 178 BW76
Rubeck Cl, Red. RH1 273 DH132
Rubens Pl, SW4 off Dolman St 183 DM84
Rubens Rd, Nthlt. UB5 158 BW68
Rubens St, SE6 205 DZ89
Rubin Pl, Enf. EN3 105 EA37
Ruby Cl, Slou. SL1 173 AN75
Ruby Ms, E17 off Ruby Rd 145 EA55
Ruby Rd, E17 145 EA55
Ruby St, NW10 160 CQ66
SE15 44 E2
Ruby Triangle, SE15 44 E2
Ruby Way, NW9 119 CT53
Ruckholt Cl, E10 145 EB62
Ruckholt Rd, E10 12 B1
Rucklers La, Kings L. WD4 80 BK27
Ruckles Way, Amer. HP7 77 AQ40
Rucklidge Av, NW10 161 CT68
Rudall Cres, NW3 off Willoughby Rd 142 DD63
Ruddington Cl, E5 145 DY63
Ruddlesway, Wind. SL4 173 AK81
Ruddock Cl, Edg. HA8 118 CQ52
Ruddstreet Cl, SE18 37 P9
Ruden Way, Epsom KT17 255 CV116
Rudge Ri, Add. KT15 233 BF106
Rudgwick Keep, Horl. RH6 off Langshott La 291 DJ147
Rudgwick Ter, NW8 6 D9
Rudland Rd, Bexh. DA7 189 FB83
Rudloe Rd, SW12 203 DJ87
Rudolf Pl, SW8 42 B3
Sch Rudolf Steiner Sch - Kings Langley, Kings L. WD4 off Langley Hill 80 BM29
Rudolph Rd, E13 23 M1
NW6 15 K1
Bushey WD23 98 CA44
Rudstone Ho, E3 off Bromley High St 22 C2
Rudsworth Cl, Colnbr. SL3 175 BD80
Rudyard Gro, NW7 118 CQ51
Rue de St. Lawrence, Wal.Abb. EN9 off Quaker La 89 EC34
Ruffets Wd, Grav. DA12 213 GJ93
Ruffetts, The, S.Croy. CR2 242 DV108
Ruffetts Cl, S.Croy. CR2 242 DV108
Ruffetts Way, Tad. KT20 255 CY118
Ruffle Cl, West Dr. UB7 176 BL75
Rufford Cl, Har. HA3 139 CG58
Watford WD17 97 BT37
Rufford St, N1 8 B8
Rufford Twr, W3 160 CP74
● Rufus Business Cen, SW18 202 DB89
Rufus Cl, Ruis. HA4 138 BY62
Rufus St, N1 19 N3
Rugby Av, N9 122 DT46
Greenford UB6 159 CD65
Wembley HA0 139 CH64
Rugby Cl, Har. HA1 139 CE57
★ Rugby Football Union Twickenham, Twick. TW1 199 CE86
Rugby Gdns, Dag. RM9 168 EW65
Rugby La, Sutt. SM2 off Nonsuch Wk 239 CX109

Rugby Rd, NW9 140 CP56
W4 180 CS75
Dagenham RM9 168 EV66
Twickenham TW1 199 CE86
Rugby St, WC1 18 C5
Rugby Way, Crox.Grn WD3 97 BP43
Rugged La, Wal.Abb. EN9 90 EK33
Ruggles-Brise Rd, Ashf. TW15 196 BK92
Rugg St, E14 22 A10
RUISLIP, HA4 137 BS59
⊖ Ruislip 137 BS60
Coll Ruislip Adult Learning Cen, Ruis. HA4
off Sidmouth Dr 137 BU62
Ruislip Cl, Grnf. UB6 158 CB70
RUISLIP COMMON, Ruis. HA4 137 BR57
Ruislip Ct, Ruis. HA4
off Courtfield Gdns 137 BT61
RUISLIP GARDENS, Ruis. HA4 137 BS63
⊖ Ruislip Gardens 137 BU63
Sch Ruislip Gdns Prim Sch, Ruis. HA4 off Stafford Rd 137 BT63
Sch Ruislip High Sch, Ruis. HA4
off Sidmouth Dr 137 BU62
RUISLIP MANOR, Ruis. HA4 137 BU61
⊖ Ruislip Manor 137 BU60
Ruislip Retail Pk, Ruis. HA4 138 BY63
Ruislip Rd, Grnf. UB6 158 CA69
Northolt UB5 158 BX69
Ruislip Rd E, W7 159 CD70
W13 159 CD70
Greenford UB6 159 CD70
Ruislip St, SW17 202 DF91
Rumania Wk, Grav. DA12 213 GM90
Rumballs Cl, Hem.H. HP3 62 BN23
Rumballs Rd, Hem.H. HP3 62 BN23
Rumbold Rd, SW6 39 M5
Hoddesdon EN11 71 EC15
Rum Cl, E1 32 G1
Rumford Ho, SE1 off Bath Ter 31 J6
Rumford Shop Hall, Rom. RM1 off Market Pl 149 FE56
Rumsey Cl, Hmptn. TW12 198 BZ93
Rumsey Ms, N4 143 DP62
Rumsey Rd, SW9 42 D10
Rumsley, Wal.Cr. EN7 88 DU27
Runbury Circle, NW9 140 CR61
Runcie Cl, St.Alb. AL4 65 CG16
Runciman Cl, Orp. BR6 246 EW110
Runcorn Cl, N17 144 DV56
Runcorn Cres, Hem.H. HP2 62 BM16
Runcorn Pl, W11 14 E10
Rundell Cres, NW4 141 CV57
Rundells, Harl. CM18 74 EU19
Rundell Twr, SW8 42 C6
Runes Cl, Mitch. CR4 222 DD98
Runham Rd, Hem.H. HP3 62 BL22
Runnel Ct, Bark. IG11
off Spring Pl 167 EQ68
Runnelfield, Har. HA1 139 CE62
Runnemede Rd, Egh. TW20 195 AZ91
Running Horse Yd, Brent. TW8
off Pottery Rd 180 CL79
Running Waters, Brwd. CM13 131 GA49
Runnymede, SW19 222 DD95
Coll Runnymede Cen, The, Add. KT15 off Chertsey Rd 216 BH103
Runnymede Cl, Twick. TW2 198 CB86
Runnymede Ct, SW15 201 CU88
Croydon CR0 224 DT103
Egham TW20 195 BA91
Runnymede Cres, SW16 223 DK95
Runnymede Gdns, Grnf. UB6 159 CD68
Twickenham TW2 198 CB86
H Runnymede Hosp, Cher. KT16 215 BD104
Runnymede Ho, E9
off Kingsmead Way 11 M1
Runnymede Rd, Twick. TW2 198 CB86
Runrig Hill, Amer. HP6 77 AS35
Runsley, Welw.G.C. AL7 51 CZ06
Runtley Wd La, Sutt.Grn GU4 265 AZ125
Runway, The, Hat. AL10 66 CR16
Ruislip HA4 137 BV64
Runway Cl, NW9
off Great Strand 119 CT54
Rupack St, SE16 32 G5
Rupert Av, Wem. HA9 140 CL64
Rupert Ct, W1 17 N10
West Molesey KT8
off St. Peter's Rd 218 CA98
Rupert Gdns, SW9 42 G9
Rupert Rd, N19
off Holloway Rd 143 DK61
NW6 15 H1
W4 180 CS76
Guildford GU2 280 AV135
Rupert St, W1 17 N10
Rural Cl, Horn. RM11 149 FH60
Rural Vale, Nthflt DA11 212 GE87
Rural Way, SW16 203 DH94
Redhill RH1 272 DG134
Rusbridge Cl, E8 10 C2
Ruscoe Dr, Wok. GU22
off Pembroke Rd 249 BA117
Ruscoe Rd, E16 23 L8
Ruscombe Dr, Park St AL2 82 CB26
Ruscombe Gdns, Datchet SL3 174 AU80
Ruscombe Way, Felt. TW14 197 BT87
Rush, The, SW19
off Kingston Rd 221 CZ95
Rusham Ct, Egh. TW20
off Rusham Pk Av 195 BA93
Rusham Pk Av, Egh. TW20 195 AZ93
Rusham Rd, SW12 202 DF86
Egham TW20 195 AZ93
Rushbridge Cl, Croy. CR0 224 DQ100
Rushbrook Cres, E17 123 DZ53
Rushbrook Rd, SE9 207 EQ89
Rushburn, Woob.Grn HP10 132 AF57
Rush Cl, Stans.Abb. SG12 55 EC11
Rush Common Ms, SW2 203 DM87
Rush Cft, Gdmg. GU7 280 AU143
Rushcroft Rd, E4 123 EA52
SW2 183 DN84
Sch Rush Cft Sch, E4
off Rushcroft Rd 123 EB52
Rushden Cl, SE19 204 DR94
Rushdene, SE2 188 EX76
Rushdene Av, Barn. EN4 120 DE45
Rushdene Cl, Nthlt. UB5 158 BW68
Rushdene Cres, Nthlt. UB5 158 BW68
Rushdene Rd, Brwd. CM15 130 FW45
Pinner HA5 138 BX58
Rushdene Wk, Bigg.H. TN16 260 EK117
Rushden Gdns, NW7 119 CW51
Ilford IG5 147 EN55
Rushdon Cl, Grays RM17 192 GA76
Romford RM1 149 FG57
Rush Dr, Wal.Abb. EN9 105 EC40
Rushen Dr, Hert.Hth SG13 54 DW12
Rushen Wk, Cars. SM5
off Paisley Rd 222 DD102
Rushes Mead, Harl. CM18 73 ES17
Uxbridge UB8
off Frays Waye 156 BJ67
Rushet Rd, Orp. BR5 228 EU96
Rushett Cl, T.Ditt. KT7 219 CH102
Rushett Dr, Dor. RH4 285 CH139
Rushett La, Epsom KT18 237 CJ111
Rushett Rd, T.Ditt. KT7 219 CH101
Rushetts Rd, Reig. RH2 288 DC138
Rushey Cl, N.Mal. KT3 220 CR98
Rushey Grn, SE6 205 EB87
Sch Rushey Grn Prim Sch, SE6
off Culverley Rd 205 EB88
Rushey Hill, Enf. EN2 103 DM42
Rushey Mead, SE4 205 EA85
Rushfield, Pot.B. EN6 85 CX33
Sawbridgeworth CM21 58 EY05
Rushford Rd, SE4 205 DZ86
RUSH GREEN, Rom. RM7 149 FC59
Rush Grn Gdns, Rom. RM7 149 FC60
Sch Rush Grn Inf Sch, Rom. RM7
off Dagenham Rd 149 FD60
Sch Rush Grn Jun Sch, Rom. RM7
off Dagenham Rd 149 FE60
Rush Grn Rd, Rom. RM7 149 FC60
Rushgrove Av, NW9 141 CT57
Rushgrove St, SE18 37 K9
Rush Hill Ms, SW11
off Rush Hill Rd 182 DG83
Rush Hill Rd, SW11 182 DG83
Rushleigh Av, Chsht EN8 89 DX31
Rushley Cl, Kes. BR2 244 EK105
Rushmead, E2 20 E3
Richmond TW10 199 CH90
Rushmead Cl, Croy. CR0 242 DT105
Rushmere Av, Upmin. RM14 150 FQ62
Rushmere Ct, Hem.H. HP3
off Ebberns Rd 62 BL24
Wor.Pk. KT4 off The Avenue 221 CU103
Rushmere Ho, SW15
off Fontley Way 201 CU88
Rushmere La, Orch.L. HP5 78 AU28
Rushmere Pl, SW19 201 CX92
Englefield Green TW20 194 AY92
Rushmon Gdns, Walt. KT12
off Collingwood Pl 217 BV104
Rushmoor Cl, Guil. GU2 264 AT131
Pinner HA5 137 BV56
Rickmansworth WD3 114 BK47
Rushmore Cl, Brom. BR1 226 EL97
Rushmore Cres, E5
off Rushmore Rd 145 DX63
Rushmore Hill, Knock.P. TN14 246 EX112
Orpington BR6 246 EW110
Sch Rushmore Prim Sch, E5
off Elderfield Rd 145 DX63
Rushmore Rd, E5 144 DW63
Rusholme Av, Dag. RM10 148 FA62
Rusholme Gro, SE19 204 DS92
Rusholme Rd, SW15 201 CX86
Rushout Av, Har. HA3 139 CH58
Rushton Av, Wat. WD25 97 BU35
Rushton Gro, Harl. CM17 74 EX15
Rushton St, N1 9 M10
Rushworth Rd, Reig. RH2 272 DA133
Rushworth St, SE1 31 H4
Rushy Meadow La, Cars. SM5 222 DE103
Sch Rushy Meadow Prim Sch, Cars. SM5
off Rushy Meadow La 222 DE104
Ruskin Av, E12 166 EL65
Feltham TW14 197 BT86
Richmond TW9 180 CN80
Upminster RM14 150 FQ59
Waltham Abbey EN9 90 EE34
Welling DA16 188 EU83
Ruskin Cl, NW11 142 DB58
Cheshunt EN7 88 DS26
Ruskin Dr, Orp. BR6 227 ES104
Welling DA16 188 EU83
Worcester Park KT4 221 CV103
Ruskin Gdns, W5 159 CK70
Harrow HA3 140 CM56
Romford RM3 127 FH52
Ruskin Gro, Dart. DA1 210 FN85
Welling DA16 188 EU82
Ruskin Pk Ho, SE5 43 M10
Ruskin Rd, N17 122 DT53
Belvedere DA17 188 FA77
Carshalton SM5 240 DF106
Croydon CR0 223 DP103
Grays RM16 193 GG77
Isleworth TW7 179 CF83
Southall UB1 158 BY73
Staines-upon-Thames TW18 195 BF94
Ruskin Wk, N9 122 DU47
SE24 204 DQ85
Bromley BR2 227 EM100
Ruskin Way, SW19 222 DD95
Rusland Av, Orp. BR6 227 ER104
Rusland Hts, Har. HA1
off Rusland Pk Rd 139 CE56
Rusland Pk Rd, Har. HA1 139 CE56
Rusper Cl, NW2 141 CW62
Stanmore HA7 117 CJ49
Rusper Rd, N22 122 DQ54
Dagenham RM9 168 EW65
Russell Av, N22 121 DP54
St. Albans AL3 65 CD20
Russell Cl, NW10 160 CQ66
SE7 186 EJ80
W4 181 CT79
Amersham HP6 94 AX39
Beckenham BR3 225 EB97
Bexleyheath DA7 188 FA84
Brentwood CM15 130 FV45
Dartford DA1 189 FG83
Northwood HA6 115 BQ50
Ruislip HA4 138 BW61
Walton on the Hill KT20 271 CU125
Woking GU21 248 AW115
Russell Ct, SW1 29 M3
Bricket Wood AL2 82 CA30
Russell Ct, Chesham HP5 76 AR29
Guildford GU1 264 AW131
Leatherhead KT22 253 CH122
Surbiton KT6 220 CL101
Russell Cres, Wat. WD25 97 BT35
Russellcroft Rd, Welw.G.C. AL8 51 CW08
Russell Dr, Stanw. TW19 196 BK86
Russell Gdns, N20 120 DE47
NW11 141 CY58
W14 26 E6
Richmond TW10 199 CJ89
Sipson UB7 176 BN78
Russell Gdns Ms, W14 26 E5
Russell Grn Cl, Pur. CR8 241 DN110
Russell Gro, NW7 118 CS50
SW9 42 F5
Russell Hill, Pur. CR8 241 DM110
Russell Hill Pl, Pur. CR8 241 DN111
Russell Hill Rd, Pur. CR8 241 DN111
Russell Kerr Cl, W4 180 CQ80
Russell La, N20 120 DE47
Watford WD17 97 BR36
Russell Lo, SE1
off Spurgeon St 31 L6
Russell Mead, Har.Wld HA3 117 CF53
Russell Par, NW11
off Golders Grn Rd 141 CY58
Russell Pl, NW3 6 D2
SE16 33 L7
Hemel Hempstead HP3 62 BH23
Sutton at Hone DA4 230 FN95
Sch Russell Prim Sch, The, Rich. TW10 off Petersham Rd 199 CK88
Russell Rd, E4 123 DZ49
E10 145 EB58
E16 23 P8
E17 145 DZ55
N8 143 DK58
N13 121 DM51
N15 144 DS57
N20 120 DE47
NW9 141 CT58
SW19 202 DA94
W14 26 E6
Buckhurst Hill IG9 124 EH46
Enfield EN1 104 DT38
Gravesend DA12 213 GK86
Grays RM17 192 GA77
Mitcham CR4 222 DE97
Northolt UB5 138 CC64
Northwood HA6 115 BQ49
Shepperton TW17 217 BQ101
Tilbury RM18 192 GE81
Tilbury (cul-de-sac) RM18 193 GF82
Twickenham TW2 199 CF86
Walton-on-Thames KT12 217 BU100
Woking GU21 248 AW115
Russells, Tad. KT20 255 CX122
Sch Russell Sch, The, Chorl. WD3
off Brushwood Dr 95 BB42
Russells Cres, Horl. RH6 290 DG149
Russell's Footpath, SW16 203 DL92
⊖ Russell Square 18 A5
Russell Sq, WC1 18 A5
Longfield DA3
off Cavendish Sq 231 FX97
Russells Ride, Chsht EN8 89 DX31
Russell St, WC2 18 B10
Hertford SG14 54 DQ09
Windsor SL4 173 AR81
Russell's Way, S.Ock. RM15 171 FX72
Russell's Wf Flats, W10 14 G4
Russell Wk, Rich. TW10
off Park Hill 200 CM86
Russell Way, Sutt. SM1 240 DA106
Watford WD19 115 BV45
Russell Wilson Ct, Rom. RM3
off Church Rd 128 FN53
Russet Cl, Chsht EN7 88 DS26
Hersham KT12 218 BX104
Horley RH6
off Carlton Tye 291 DJ148
Staines-upon-Thames TW19 195 BF86
Uxbridge UB10 157 BQ70
Russet Cres, N7 8 C2
Russet Dr, Croy. CR0 225 DY102
St. Albans AL4 65 CJ21
Shenley WD7 84 CL32
Sch Russet Ho Sch, Enf. EN1
off Autumn Cl 104 DV39
Russets, The, Chal.St.P. SL9
off Austenwood Cl 112 AX54
Russets Cl, E4
off Larkshall Rd 123 ED49
Russett Cl, Orp. BR6 246 EV106
Russett Ct, Cat. CR3 274 DU125
Russett Hill, Chal.St.P. SL9 134 AY55
Russetts, Horn. RM11 150 FL56
Russetts Cl, Wok. GU21 249 AZ115
Russett Way, Swan. BR8 229 FD96
Russettwood, Welw.G.C. AL7 52 DD10
Russet Way, N.Holm. RH5 285 CK140
Russia Dock Rd, SE16 33 M3
Russia La, E2 10 G10
Russia Row, EC2 19 K9
Russia Wk, SE16 33 K5
Russington Rd, Shep. TW17 217 BR100
Rusthall Av, W4 180 CR77
Rusthall Cl, Croy. CR0 224 DW100
Rustic Av, SW16 203 DH94
Rustic Cl, Upmin. RM14 151 FS60
Rustic Pl, Wem. HA0 139 CK63
Rustic Wk, E16 24 A8
Rustington Wk, Mord. SM4 221 CZ101
Ruston Av, Surb. KT5 220 CP101
Ruston Gdns, N14 off Byre Rd 102 DG44
Ruston Ms, W11 14 E9
Ruston Rd, SE18 36 G7
Ruston St, E3 11 P8
Rust Sq, SE5 43 L4
Rutford Rd, SW16 203 DL92
Ruth Cl, Stan. HA7 140 CM56
Ruthen Cl, Epsom KT18 238 CP114
Rutherford Cl, Borwd. WD6 100 CQ40
Sutton SM2 240 DD107
Uxbridge UB8 156 BM70
Windsor SL4 173 AM81
Sch Rutherford Sch, S.Croy. CR2
off Melville Av 242 DT106
Rutherford St, SW1 29 N8
Rutherford Twr, Sthl. UB1 158 CB72
Rutherford Way, Bushey Hth WD23 117 CD46
Wembley HA9 140 CN63
Rutherglen Rd, SE2 188 EU79
Rutherwick Cl, Horl. RH6 290 DF148
Rutherwick Ri, Couls. CR5 257 DL117
Rutherwyke Cl, Epsom KT17 239 CU107
Rutherwyk Rd, Cher. KT16 215 BE101
Ruthin Cl, NW9 140 CS58
Ruthin Rd, SE3 47 N2
Ruthven Av, Wal.Cr. EN8 89 DX33
Ruthven St, E9 11 J8
Rutland App, Horn. RM11 150 FN57
Rutland Av, Sid. DA15 208 EU87
Slough SL1 153 AR71
Rutland Cl, SW14 180 CP83
SW19 off Rutland Rd 202 DE94
Ashtead KT21 254 CL117
Bexley DA5 208 EX88
Chessington KT9 238 CM107
Dartford DA1 210 FK87
Epsom KT19 238 CR110
Redhill RH1 272 DF133
Rutland Ct, SW7
off Rutland Gdns 28 D5
Chis. BR7 227 EN95
Enfield EN3 104 DW43
Rutland Dr, Horn. RM11 150 FN57
Morden SM4 221 CZ100
Richmond TW10 199 CK88
Rutland Gdns, N4 143 DP58
SW7 28 D5
W13 159 CG71
Croydon CR0 242 DS105
Dagenham RM8 148 EW64
Hemel Hempstead HP2 62 BM19
Rutland Gdns Ms, SW7 28 D5
Rutland Gate, SW7 28 D5
Belvedere DA17 189 FB78
Bromley BR2 226 EF98
Rutland Gate Ms, SW7 28 C5
Rutland Gro, W6 181 CV78
Rutland Ms, NW8 5 M9
Rutland Ms E, SW7 28 C6
Rutland Ms S, SW7 28 C6
Rutland Ms W, SW7
off Ennismore St 28 C6
Rutland Pk, NW2 4 B5
SE6 205 DZ89
Rutland Pk Gdns, NW2
off Rutland Pk 4 B5
Rutland Pk Mans, NW2
off Rutland Pk 4 B5
Rutland Pl, EC1 19 J5
Bushey Heath WD23
off The Rutts 117 CD46
Rutland Rd, E7 166 EK66
E9 11 H8
E11 146 EH57
E17 145 EA58
SW19 202 DE94
Harrow HA1 138 CC58
Hayes UB3 177 BR77
Ilford IG1 147 EP63
Southall UB1 158 CA71
Twickenham TW2 199 CD89
Rutland St, SW7 28 D6
Rutland Wk, SE6 205 DZ89
Rutland Way, Orp. BR5 228 EW100
Rutley Cl, SE17 42 G2
Harold Wood RM3
off Pasteur Dr 128 FK54
Rutlish Rd, SW19 222 DA95
Sch Rutlish Sch, SW20
off Watery La 221 CZ96
Rutson Rd, Byfleet KT14 234 BM114
Rutter Gdns, Mitch. CR4 222 DC98
Rutters Cl, West Dr. UB7 176 BN75
Rutts, The, Bushey Hth WD23 117 CD46
Rutts Ter, SE14 45 J7
Ruvigny Gdns, SW15 38 D10
Ruxbury Rd, Cher. KT16 215 BC100
Ruxley Cl, Epsom KT19 238 CP106
Sidcup DA14 208 EX93
Ruxley Cor, Sid. DA14 208 EY93
Ruxley Cor Ind Est, Sid. DA14 208 EX93
Ruxley Cres, Clay. KT10 237 CH107
Ruxley Gdns, Shep. TW17 217 BQ99
Ruxley La, Epsom KT19 238 CR106
Ruxley Ms, Epsom KT19 238 CP106
Ruxley Ridge, Clay. KT10 237 CG108
Ruxton Cl, Couls. CR5 257 DJ115
Swanley BR8 229 FE97
Ryall Cl, Brick.Wd AL2 82 BY29
Ryalls Ct, N20 120 DF48
Ryan Cl, SE3 186 EJ84
Ruislip HA4 137 BV60
Ryan Dr, Brent. TW8 179 CG79
Ryan Way, Wat. WD24 98 BW39
Ryarsh Cres, Orp. BR6 245 ES105
Rybrook Dr, Walt. KT12 218 BW103
Rycott Path, SE22
off Lordship La 204 DU87
Rycroft, Wind. SL4 173 AM83
Rycroft La, Sev. TN14 278 FE130
Rycroft Way, N17 144 DT55
Ryculff Sq, SE3 47 M8
Rydal Cl, NW4 119 CY53
Purley CR8 242 DR113
Rydal Ct, Wat. WD25
off Grasmere Cl 81 BV32
Rydal Cres, Perivale UB6 159 CH69
Rydal Dr, Bexh. DA7 188 FA81
West Wickham BR4 226 EE103
Rydal Gdns, NW9 140 CS57
SW15 200 CS92
Hounslow TW3 198 CB86
Wembley HA9 139 CJ60
Rydal Rd, SW16 203 DK91
Rydal Way, Egh. TW20 195 BB94
Enfield EN3 104 DW44
Ruislip HA4 138 BW63
RYDE, THE, Hat. AL9 67 CW15
Ryde, The, Hat. AL9 67 CW16
Staines-upon-Thames TW18 216 BH95
Ryde Cl, Ripley GU23 250 BJ121
Ryde Heron, Knap. GU21 248 AS117
RYDENS, Walt. KT12 218 BW103
Rydens Av, Walt. KT12 217 BV103
Rydens Cl, Walt. KT12 218 BW103
Rydens Gro, Hersham KT12 236 BX105
Rydens Pk, Walt. KT12 218 BX103
Rydens Rd, Walt. KT12 218 BX103
Sch Rydens Sch, Hersham KT12
off Hersham Rd 236 BW105
Rydens Way, Wok. GU22 249 BA120
Ryde Pl, Twick. TW1 199 CJ86
Ryder Av, E10 145 EB59
Ryder Cl, Bov. HP3 79 BA28
Bromley BR1 206 EH92
Bushey WD23 98 CB44
Hertford SG13 54 DV08
Ryder Ct, SW1 29 M2
Ryder Dr, SE16 44 E1
Ryder Gdns, Rain. RM13 169 FF65
Ryder Ms, E9 11 H3
Ryders Av, Coln.Hth AL4 66 CS20
Ryder Seed Ms, St.Alb. AL1
off Pageant Rd 65 CD21
Ryders Ter, NW8 5 N10
Ryder St, SW1 29 M2
Ryder Yd, SW1 29 M2
Rydes Av, Guil. GU2 264 AT131
Sch Ryde Sch, The, Hat. AL9
off Pleasant Ri 67 CW15
Rydes Cl, Wok. GU22 249 BC120
RYDESHILL, Guil. GU3 264 AS131
Rydes Hill Cres, Guil. GU2 264 AT130
Sch Rydes Hill Prep Sch, Guil. GU2 off Aldershot Rd 264 AT132
Rydes Hill Rd, Guil. GU2 264 AT132
Ryde Vale Rd, SW12 203 DH89
Rydings, Wind. SL4 173 AM83
Rydon Business Cen, Lthd. KT22 253 CH119
Rydon Ms, SW19 201 CW94
Rydons Cl, SE9 186 EL83
Rydon's La, Couls. CR5 258 DQ120
Rydon St, N1 9 K8
Rydons Way, Red. RH1 288 DG135
Rydon's Wd Cl, Couls. CR5 258 DQ120
Rydston Cl, N7 8 B6
Rye, The, N14 121 DJ45
Ryebridge Cl, Lthd. KT22 253 CG118
Ryebrook Rd, Lthd. KT22 253 CG118
Rye Cl, Bex. DA5 209 FB86
Borwd. WD6 100 CR42
Guildford GU2 264 AS132
Hornchurch RM12 150 FJ64
Ryecotes Mead, SE21 204 DS88
Rye Ct, Slou. SL1
off Alpha St S 174 AU76
Rye Cres, Orp. BR5 228 EW102
Ryecroft, Grav. DA12 213 GL92
Harlow CM19 73 EP15
Hatfield AL10 67 CT20
Ryecroft Av, Ilf. IG5 125 EP54
Twickenham TW2 198 CB87
Ryecroft Cl, Hem.H. HP2
off Poynders Hill 63 BQ21
Ryecroft Ct, St.Alb. AL4 66 CM20
Ryecroft Cres, Barn. EN5 101 CV43
Ryecroft Rd, SE13 205 EC85
SW16 203 DN93
Chesham HP5 76 AN32
Otford TN14 263 FG116
Petts Wood BR5 227 ER100
Ryecroft St, SW6 39 L7
Ryedale, SE22 204 DV86
Ryedale Ct, Sev. TN13
off London Rd 278 FE121
Ryefield Cl, Hodd. EN11 55 EB13
Rye Fld, Ashtd. KT21 253 CK117
Orpington BR5 228 EX102
Ryefield Av, Uxb. UB10 157 BP66
Ryefield Ct, Nthwd. HA6
off Ryefield Cres 115 BU54
Ryefield Cres, Nthwd. HA6 115 BU54
Ryefield Par, Nthwd. HA6
off Ryefield Cres 115 BU54
Ryefield Path, SW15 201 CU88
Sch Ryefield Prim Sch, Hlgdn UB10 off Ryefield Av 157 BQ67
Ryefield Rd, SE19 204 DQ93
Ryegates, SE15 44 F8
RYE HILL, Harl. CM18 73 ES22
Rye Hill Pk, SE15 184 DW84
Rye Hill Rd, Harl. CM18 73 ES22
Thornwood CM16 74 EU23
Rye Ho, NW7 off Peacock Cl 119 CY50
Rye House 71 EC15
Ryeland Cl, West Dr. UB7 156 BL72
Ryelands, Horl. RH6 291 DJ147
Welwyn Garden City AL7 51 CZ12
Ryelands Cl, Cat. CR3 258 DS121
Ryelands Ct, Lthd. KT22 253 CG118
Ryelands Cres, SE12 206 EJ86
Ryelands Pl, Wey. KT13 217 BS104
Sch Ryelands Prim Sch, SE25
off Albert Rd 224 DV99
Rye La, SE15 44 C7
Sevenoaks TN14 263 FG117
Sch Rye Oak Prim Sch, SE15
off Whorlton Rd 184 DV83
RYE PARK, Hodd. EN11 71 EB16
Rye Pk Ind Est, Hodd. EN11
off Salisbury Rd 71 EC15
Rye Pas, SE15 44 D10
Ryepeck Meadow Moorings, Shep. TW17 216 BL101
Rye Rd, SE15 185 DX84
Hoddesdon EN11 71 EB15
Stanstead Abbotts SG12 56 EE13
Rye Wk, SW15 201 CX85
Rye Way, Edg. HA8
off Canons Dr 118 CM51
Ryfold Rd, SW19 202 DA90
Ryhope Rd, N11 121 DH49
Rykens La, Bet. RH3 286 CQ139
Rykhill, Grays RM16 193 GH76
Ryland Cl, Felt. TW13 197 BT91
Rylandes Rd, NW2 141 CU62
South Croydon CR2 242 DV109
Ryland Ho, Croy. CR0 224 DQ104
Ryland Rd, NW5 7 J4
Rylett Cres, W12 181 CT76
Rylett Rd, W12 181 CT75
Rylston Rd, N13 122 DR48
SW6 38 G3
Rymer Rd, Croy. CR0 224 DS101
Rymer St, SE24 203 DP86
Rymill Cl, Bov. HP3 79 BA28
Rymill St, E16 37 L3
Rysbrack St, SW3 28 E6
Rysted La, West. TN16 277 EQ126
Rythe Cl, Chess. KT9
off Nigel Fisher Way 237 CJ108
Claygate KT10 237 CE106
Rythe Ct, T.Ditt. KT7 219 CG101
Rythe Rd, Clay. KT10 237 CD106
Sch Ryvers Comb Sch, Langley SL3 off Trelawney Av 174 AX76
Ryvers Rd, Slou. SL3 175 AZ76

S

★ Saatchi Gall, The, SW3 28 F9
Sabah Ct, Ashf. TW15 196 BN91
Sabbarton St, E16 23 L9
Sabella Ct, E3 21 P1
Sabina Rd, Grays RM16 193 GJ77

Sabine Rd, SW11 40 E10
Sable Cl, Houns. TW4 178 BW83
Sable St, N1 9 H6
Sachfield Dr, Chaff.Hun. RM16 192 FY76
Sach Rd, E5 144 DV61
Sackville Av, Brom. BR2 226 EG102
Sackville Cl, Har. HA2 139 CD62
Sevenoaks TN13 279 FH122
Sackville Ct, Rom. RM3
off Sackville Cres 128 FL53
Sackville Cres, Rom. RM3 128 FL53
Sackville Est, SW16 203 DL90
Sackville Gdns, Ilf. IG1 147 EM60
Sackville Rd, Dart. DA2 210 FK89
Sutton SM2 240 DA108
Sackville St, W1 29 M1
Sacombe Rd, Hem.H. HP1 61 BF18
Sacred Heart Cath Prim Sch, N.Mal. KT3
off Burlington Rd 221 CU98
Sacred Heart Cath Prim Sch & Nurs, Bushey WD23
off Merry Hill Rd 98 BZ44
Sacred Heart High Sch, W6 26 B9
Sacred Heart Language Coll, The, Wealds. HA3 off High St 117 CE54
Sacred Heart of Mary Girls' Sch, Upmin. RM14
off St. Mary's La 150 FP61
Sacred Heart RC Prim Sch, N7 8 D3
N20 off Oakleigh Pk S 120 DE47
SW11 40 D9
SW15 off Roehampton La 201 CU85
Ruislip HA4
off Herlwyn Av 137 BS61
Teddington TW11
off St. Mark's Rd 199 CH94
Ware SG12 off Broadmeads 55 DX06
Sacred Heart RC Sch, SE5 43 J6
Saddington St, Grav. DA12 213 GH87
Saddlebrook Pk, Sun. TW16 197 BS94
Saddlers Cl, Arkley EN5 101 CV43
Borehamwood WD6
off Farriers Way 100 CR44
Pinner HA5 116 CA51
Saddlers Ms, SW8
off Portland Gro 42 B6
Hampton Wick KT1 219 CJ95
Wembley HA0
off The Boltons 139 CF63
Saddler's Pk, Eyns. DA4 230 FK104
Saddlers Path, Borwd. WD6 100 CR43
Saddlers Way, Epsom KT18 254 CR119
Saddlescombe Way, N12 120 DA50
Saddleworth Rd, Rom. RM3 128 FJ51
Saddleworth Sq, Rom. RM3 128 FJ51
Saddle Yd, W1 29 J2
Sadleir Rd, St.Alb. AL1 65 CE22
Sadler Cl, Chshl EN7
off Markham Rd 88 DQ25
Mitcham CR4 222 DF96
Sadler Ho, E3
off Bromley High St 22 D2
Sadlers Cl, Guil. GU4 265 BD133
Sadlers Gate Ms, SW15 38 A10
Sadlers Mead, Harl. CM18 74 EU16
Sadlers Ride, W.Mol. KT8 218 CC96
Sadlers Way, Hert. SG14 53 DN09
Sadler's Wells Thea, EC1 18 G2
Saffer Inst, N7 8 B3
Saffron Av, E14 22 G10
Saffron Cl, NW11 141 CZ57
Croydon CR0 223 DL100
Datchet SL3 174 AV81
Hoddesdon EN11 71 DZ16
Saffron Ct, Felt. TW14
off Staines Rd 197 BQ87
Saffron Grn First Sch, Borwd. WD6 off Nicoll Way 100 CR42
Saffron Hill, EC1 18 F5
Saffron La, Hem.H. HP1 62 BH19
Saffron Platt, Guil. GU2 264 AU130
Saffron Rd, Chaff.Hun. RM16 191 FW77
Romford RM5 127 FC54
Saffron St, EC1 18 F6
Saffron Way, Surb. KT6 219 CK102
Sage Cl, E6 25 J7
Sage Ms, SE22
off Lordship La 204 DT85
Sage St, E1 20 G10
Sage Way, WC1 18 C3
Saigasso Cl, E16 24 E9
Sailacre Ho, SE10
off Calvert Rd 186 EF78
Sail Ct, E14 off Newport Av 23 H10
Sailmakers Ct, SW6 39 N10
Sail St, SE11 30 D8
Sainfoin Rd, SW17 202 DG89
Sainsbury Cen, The, Cher. KT16 off Guildford St 216 BG101
Sainsbury Rd, SE19 204 DS92
St. Adrian's RC Prim Sch & Nurs, St.Alb. AL1
off Watling Vw 64 CC23
St. Agatha's Cath Prim Sch, Kings.T. KT2
off St. Agatha's Dr 200 CM93
St. Agatha's Dr, Kings.T. KT2 200 CM93
St. Agathas Gro, Cars. SM5 222 DF102
St. Agnells Ct, Hem.H. HP2 62 BN16
St. Agnells La, Hem.H. HP2 62 BM15
St. Agnes Cl, E9 10 G9
St. Agnes Pl, SE11 42 G3
St. Agnes RC Prim Sch, E3 22 C2
St. Agnes' RC Prim Sch, NW2
off Thorverton Rd 141 CY62
St. Agnes Well, EC1
off Old St 19 M4
St. Aidan's Cath Prim Sch, Couls. CR5 off Portnalls Rd 257 DJ116
Ilford IG1 off Benton Rd 147 ER60
St. Aidans Ct, W13
off St. Aidans Rd 179 CJ75
Barking IG11
off Choats Rd 168 EV69
St. Aidan's Prim Sch, N4
off Albany Rd 143 DN59
St. Aidan's Rd, SE22 204 DV86
St. Aidans Rd, W13 179 CH75
St. Aidan's Way, Grav. DA12 213 GL90
St. Alban & Stephen RC Inf & Nurs Sch, St.Alb. AL1
off Vanda Cres 65 CF21
St. Alban & Stephen RC Jun Sch, St.Alb. AL1
off Cecil Rd 65 CG20
ST. ALBANS, AL1 - AL4 65 CE20
St. Albans Abbey 65 CD22
St. Albans Av, E6 25 K2
St. Alban's Av, W4 180 CR77
St. Albans Av, Felt. TW13 198 BX92
Upminster RM14 151 FS60
Weybridge KT13 216 BN104
St. Albans Cath, St.Alb. AL3 65 CD20
St. Alban's Catholic Prim Sch, E.Mol. KT8
off Beauchamp Rd 218 CC99
St. Albans Catholic Prim Sch, Harl. CM20 off First Av 57 ET13
St. Alban's Cath Prim Sch, Horn. RM12 off Heron Flight Av 169 FH66
St. Albans City 65 CE20
St. Albans City Hosp, St.Alb. AL3 64 CC18
St. Albans Cl, NW11 142 DA60
Gravesend DA12 213 GK90
Windsor SL4
off St. Alban's St 173 AR81
St. Alban's C of E Prim Sch, EC1 18 E6
St. Albans Ct, EC2 19 K8
St. Albans Cres, N22 121 DN53
St. Alban's Cres, Wdf.Grn. IG8 124 EG52
St. Albans Enterprise Cen, St.Alb. AL3 off Long Spring 65 CF16
St. Albans Gdns, Grav. DA12 213 GK90
St. Alban's Gdns, Tedd. TW11 199 CG92
St. Albans Girls' Sch, St.Alb. AL3 off Sandridgebury La 65 CE16
St. Albans Gro, W8 27 M6
St. Alban's Gro, Cars. SM5 222 DE101
St. Albans High Sch for Girls, St.Alb. AL1
off Townsend Av 65 CE19
St. Albans Hill, Hem.H. HP3 62 BL23
St. Albans La, NW11 142 DA60
Bedmond WD5 81 BT26
St. Albans Music Sch, St.Alb. AL3 off Townsend Dr 65 CD17
St. Albans Organ Mus, St.Alb. AL1 off Camp Rd 65 CH21
St. Alban's Pl, N1 8 G9
St. Albans Retail Pk, St.Alb. AL1 65 CD22
St. Albans Rd, NW5 142 DG62
NW10 160 CS67
Barnet EN5 101 CX39
Coopersale CM16 92 EX29
Dancers Hill EN6 101 CV35
Dartford DA1 210 FM87
Hemel Hempstead HP2, HP3 62 BN21
Ilford IG3 147 ET60
St. Alban's Rd, Kings.T. KT2 200 CL93
St. Albans Rd, Lon.Col. AL2 84 CN28
Reigate RH2 272 DA133
Sandridge AL4 65 CF17
Shenley WD7 84 CN28
South Mimms EN6 85 CV34
St. Alban's Rd, Sutt. SM1 239 CZ105
St. Albans Rd, Wat. WD17, WD24, WD25 97 BV40
St. Alban's Rd, Wdf.Grn. IG8 124 EG52
St. Albans Rd E, Hat. AL10 67 CV17
St. Albans Rd Inf Sch, Dart. DA1 off St. Albans Rd 210 FM86
St. Albans Rd W, Hat. AL10 66 CR18
Roe Green AL10 67 CT17
St. Albans Sch, St.Alb. AL3
off Abbey Gateway 64 CC20
St. Albans St, SW1 29 N1
St. Alban's St, Wind. SL4 173 AR81
St. Albans Ter, W6 38 E2
St. Alban's Vil, NW5
off Highgate Rd 142 DG62
St. Albert the Gt RC Prim Sch, Hem.H. HP3 off Acorn Rd 62 BN21
St. Alfege Pas, SE10 46 E3
St. Alfege Rd, SE7 186 EK79
St. Alfege with St. Peter's C of E Prim Sch, SE10 46 E3
St. Aloysius' Coll, N6
off Hornsey La 143 DJ60
St. Aloysius RC Inf Sch, NW1 17 N2
St. Aloysius RC Jun Sch, NW1 17 M1
St. Alphage Gdns, EC2 19 K7
St. Alphage Highwalk, EC2 19 L7
St. Alphage Wk, Edg. HA8 118 CQ54
St. Alphege Rd, N9 122 DW45
St. Alphonsus Rd, SW4 183 DJ84
St. Amunds Cl, SE6 205 EA91
St. Andrew & St. Francis C of E Prim Sch, NW2
off Belton Rd 161 CU65
St. Andrew Ms, Hert. SG14 54 DQ09
St. Andrew's & St. Mark's C of E Jun Sch, Surb. KT6
off Maple Rd 219 CK99
St. Andrews Av, Horn. RM12 149 FG64
Wembley HA0 139 CG63
Windsor SL4 173 AM82
St. Andrew's Cl, N12 120 DC49
St. Andrews Cl, NW2 141 CV62
SE16 44 F1
SE28 168 EX72
SW19 202 DB93
St. Andrew's Cl, Islw. TW7 179 CD81
St. Andrews Cl, N.Wld Bas. CM16 75 FC24
Old Windsor SL4 194 AU86
St. Andrews Cl, Reig. RH2
off St. Marys Rd 288 DB135
Ruislip HA4 138 BX61
St. Andrew's Cl, Shep. TW17 217 BR98
St. Andrews Cl, Stan. HA7 117 CJ54
Thames Ditton KT7 219 CH102
Woking GU21 248 AW117
St. Andrew's Cl, Wrays. TW19 194 AY87
St. Andrews C of E High Sch, Croy. CR0
off Warrington Rd 241 DP105
St. Andrew's C of E Prim Sch, N1 8 D8
N14 off Chase Rd 121 DK46
N20 off Totteridge Village 119 CZ47
SW9 42 B9
Enfield EN1
off Churchbury La 104 DS40
North Weald Bassett CM16
off School Grn La 93 FC25
Stanstead Abbotts SG12
off Mill Race 55 ED11
Uxbridge UB8
off Nursery Waye 156 BK67
St. Andrew's Ct, SW18 202 DC89
St. Andrews Ct, Colnbr. SL3
off High St 175 BD80
Watford WD17 97 BV39
St. Andrews Cres, Wind. SL4 173 AM82
St. Andrews Dr, Orp. BR5 228 EV100
St. Albans AL1 65 CH23
Stanmore HA7 117 CJ53
St. Andrews Gdns, Cob. KT11 236 BW113
St. Andrew's Gro, N16 144 DR60
St. Andrew's Hill, EC4 19 H10
St. Andrews Meadow, Harl. CM18 73 ET16
St. Andrew's Ms, N16 144 DS60
St. Andrews Ms, SE3 47 N4
SW12 off Emmanuel Rd 203 DK88
St. Andrews Pl, NW1 17 K4
Shenfield CM15 131 FZ47
St. Andrew's Prim Sch, Cob. KT11
off Lockhart Rd 236 BW113
St. Andrew's RC Prim Sch, SW16 off Polworth Rd 203 DL92
St. Andrews Rd, E11 146 EE58
E13 24 A3
E17 123 DX54
N9 122 DW45
NW9 140 CR60
NW10 161 CV65
NW11 141 CZ58
W3 160 CS73
W7 off Churchfield Rd 179 CE75
W14 38 F2
Carshalton SM5 222 DE104
Coulsdon CR5 256 DG116
Croydon CR0
off Lower Coombe St 242 DQ105
Enfield EN1 104 DR41
St. Andrew's Rd, Grav. DA12 213 GJ87
St. Andrews Rd, Hem.H. HP3
off West Valley Rd 62 BJ24
Ilford IG1 147 EM59
Romford RM7 149 FD58
Sidcup DA14 208 EX90
St. Andrew's Rd, Surb. KT6 219 CK100
St. Andrews Rd, Til. RM18 192 GE81
Uxbridge UB10 156 BM66
Watford WD19 116 BX48
St. Andrew's Sch, Lthd. KT22
off Grange Rd 253 CK120
Woking GU21
off Wilson Way 248 AX116
St. Andrews Sq, W11 14 E9
St. Andrew's Sq, Surb. KT6 219 CK100
St. Andrews Twr, Sthl. UB1 158 CC73
St. Andrew St, EC4 18 F7
Hertford SG14 54 DQ09
St. Andrews Wk, Cob. KT11 251 BV115
St. Andrews Way, E3 22 C5
Oxted RH8 276 EL130
Slough SL1 153 AK73
St. Angela's Ursuline Sch, E7
off St. Georges Rd 166 EH65
St. Anna Rd, Barn. EN5
off Sampson Av 101 CX43
St. Annes Av, Stanw. TW19 196 BK87
St. Annes Boul, Red. RH1 273 DH132
St. Anne's Cath High Sch for Girls, Upr Sch, N13
off Oakthorpe Rd 121 DN49
Lwr Sch, Enf. EN2
off London Rd 104 DR42
St. Anne's Catholic Prim Sch, Bans. SM7 off Court Rd 256 DA116
Chertsey KT16
off Free Prae Rd 216 BG102
St. Anne's Cl, N6 142 DG62
St. Annes Cl, Chsht EN7 88 DU28
St. Anne's Cl, Wat. WD19 116 BW49
St. Anne's C of E Prim Sch, SW18 off St. Ann's Hill 202 DB85
St. Anne's Ct, W1 17 N9
St. Anne's Dr, Red. RH1 272 DG133
St. Annes Dr N, Red. RH1 272 DG132
St. Annes Gdns, NW10 160 CM69
St. Anne's Mt, Red. RH1 272 DG133
St. Annes Pk, Brox. EN10 71 EA20
St. Annes Pas, E14 21 N9
St. Anne's Prim Sch, E1 20 C5
St. Anne's RC Prim Sch, SE11 42 C2
St. Annes Ri, Red. RH1 272 DG133
St. Annes Rd, E11 145 ED61
St. Anne's Rd, Hare. UB9 136 BJ55
London Colney AL2 83 CK27
Wembley HA0 139 CK64
St. Anne's Row, E14 21 P9
St. Anne St, E14 21 P9
St. Anne's Way, Red. RH1
off St. Anne's Dr 272 DG133
St. Ann's, Bark. IG11 167 EQ67
St. Anns Cl, Cher. KT16 215 BF100
St. Ann's C of E Prim Sch, N15 off Avenue Rd 144 DR57
St. Ann's Cres, SW18 202 DC86
St. Ann's Gdns, NW5 6 G4
St. Ann's Heath Jun Sch, Vir.W. GU25 off Sandhills La 214 AY99
St. Ann's Hill, SW18 202 DB85
St. Anns Hill Rd, Cher. KT16 215 BC100
St. Ann's Hosp, N15 144 DQ57
St. Ann's La, SW1 29 P6
St. Ann's Pk Rd, SW18 202 DC86
St. Ann's Pas, SW13 180 CS83
St. Anns Rd, N9 122 DT47
St. Ann's Rd, N15 143 DP57
SW13 181 CT82
St. Anns Rd, W11 26 D1
St. Ann's Rd, Bark. IG11
off Axe St 167 EQ67
St. Anns Rd, Cher. KT16 215 BF100
St. Ann's Rd, Har. HA1 139 CE58
St. Ann's Sch, W7
off Springfield Rd 159 CE74
Morden SM4
off Bordesley Rd 222 DB99
St. Ann's Shop Cen, Har. HA1 139 CE58
St. Ann's St, SW1 29 P6
St. Ann's Ter, NW8 6 B10
St. Anns Vil, W11 26 D3
St. Anns Way, Berry's Grn TN16 261 EP116
South Croydon CR2 241 DP107
St. Anselm's Cath Prim Sch, Dart. DA1 off Littlebrook Manor Way 210 FN85
St. Anselm's Pl, W1 17 J9
St. Anselm's RC Prim Sch, SW17 off Tooting Bec Rd 202 DG90
St. Anselm's RC Prim Sch, Harrow HA1 off Roxborough Pk 139 CE59
St. Anselms RC Prim Sch, Sthl. UB2 off Church Av 178 BZ76
St. Anselms Rd, Hayes UB3 177 BT75
St. Anthonys Av, Hem.H. HP3 63 BP22
Woodford Green IG8 124 EJ51
St. Anthony's Cath Prim Sch, SE20 off Genoa Rd 224 DV95
SE22 off Etherow St 204 DU86
Farnham Royal SL2
off Farnham Rd 153 AQ70
Woodford Green IG8
off Mornington Rd 124 EG49
St. Anthonys Cl, E1 32 C2
SW17 off College Gdns 202 DE89
St. Anthonys Ct, Beac. HP9
off Walkwood Ri 132 AJ55
St. Anthony's Hosp, Sutt. SM3 221 CX102
St. Anthony's Prep Sch, NW3 6 A2
St. Anthony's RC Prim Sch, Wat. WD18 off Croxley Vw 97 BS43
St. Anthony's Way, Felt. TW14 177 BT84
St. Antony's RC Prim Sch, E7
off Upton Av 166 EH66
St. Antony's Rd, E7 166 EH66
St. Arvans Cl, Croy. CR0 224 DS104
St. Asaph Rd, SE4 45 J10
St. Aubins Ct, N1
off De Beauvoir Est 9 M8
St. Aubyn's Av, SW19 201 CZ92
St. Aubyns Av, Houns. TW3 198 CA85
St. Aubyns Cl, Orp. BR6 227 ET104
St. Aubyns Gdns, Orp. BR6 227 ET103
St. Aubyn's Rd, SE19 204 DT93
St. Aubyn's Sch, Wdf.Grn. IG8 off Bunces La 124 EF52
St. Audrey Av, Bexh. DA7 188 FA82
St. Audreys Cl, Hat. AL10 67 CV21
St. Audreys Grn, Welw.G.C. AL7 51 CZ10
St. Augustine of Canterbury C of E Prim Sch, Belv. DA17
off St. Augustine's Rd 188 EZ76
St. Augustine Rd, Grays RM16 193 GH77
St. Augustine's Av, W5 160 CL68
St. Augustines Av, Brom. BR2 226 EL99
St. Augustine's Av, S.Croy. CR2 242 DQ107
St. Augustines Av, Wem. HA9 140 CL62
St. Augustine's Cath Prim Sch, Ilf. IG2 off Cranbrook Rd 147 EP57
St. Augustines Cl, Brox. EN10 71 DZ20
St. Augustine's C of E High Sch, NW6 15 K1
St. Augustine's C of E Prim Sch, NW6 5 L10
St. Augustines Ct, SE1 32 E10
St. Augustines Dr, Brox. EN10 71 DZ19
St. Augustine's Path, N5 9 K1
St. Augustine's Priory Sch, W5
off Hillcrest Rd 160 CM71
St. Augustine's RC Prim Sch, SE6 off Dunfield Rd 205 EC92
W6 38 F3
Hoddesdon EN11
off Riversmead 71 EA17
St. Augustines Rd, NW1 7 N6
St. Augustine's Rd, Belv. DA17 188 EZ77
St. Austell Cl, Edg. HA8 118 CM54
St. Austell Rd, SE13 46 F8
St. Awdry's Rd, Bark. IG11 167 ER66
St. Awdry's Wk, Bark. IG11
off Station Par 167 EQ66
St. Barnabas & St. Philip's C of E Prim Sch, W8 27 J7
St. Barnabas Cl, SE22
off East Dulwich Gro 204 DS85
Beckenham BR3 225 EC96
St. Barnabas C of E Prim Sch, SW1 29 H10
St. Barnabas Ct, Har. HA3 116 CC53
St. Barnabas Gdns, W.Mol. KT8 218 CA99
St. Barnabas Ms, SW1
off St. Barnabas St 29 H10
St. Barnabas Rd, E17 145 EA58
Mitcham CR4 202 DG94
Sutton SM1 240 DD106
Woodford Green IG8 124 EH53
St. Barnabas St, SW1 29 H10
St. Barnabas Ter, E9 11 J3
St. Barnabas Vil, SW8 42 B6
St. Bartholomew's Catholic Prim Sch, Swan. BR8
off Sycamore Dr 229 FE97
St. Bartholomews Cl, SE26 204 DW91
St. Bartholomew's C of E Prim Sch, SE26
off The Peak 204 DW91
St. Bartholomews Ct, Guil. GU1 281 AZ135
St. Bartholomew's Hosp, EC1 19 H7
St. Bartholomew's Rd, E6 166 EL67
St. Bartholomew-the-Great Ch, EC1 19 H7
St. Bart's Cl, St.Alb. AL4 65 CK21
St. Bede's Cath Prim Sch, Chad.Hth RM6
off Canon Av 148 EW57
St. Bede's C of E Jun Sch, Send GU23 off Bush La 249 BD124
St. Bede's RC Inf Sch, SW12
off Thornton Rd 203 DK88
St. Bede's Sch, Red. RH1
off Carlton Rd 272 DE131
St. Benedict's Av, Grav. DA12 213 GK89
St. Benedict's Cl, SW17
off Church La 202 DG92
St. Benedict's Sch, Nurs & Jun Sch, W5
off Montpelier Av 159 CJ71
Sen Sch & 6th Form, W5
off Eaton Ri 159 CK71
St. Benet's Cl, SW17
off College Gdns 202 DE89
St. Benet's Gro, Cars. SM5 222 DC101
St. Benet's Pl, EC3 19 M10
St. Benjamins Dr, Pr.Bot. BR6 246 EW109
St. Bernadette Cath Prim Sch, Uxb. UB10 off Long La 157 BP67
St. Bernadette RC Nurs & Prim Sch, Lon.Col. AL2
off Walsingham Way 83 CK27
St. Bernadette's Catholic Prim Sch, Kenton HA3
off Clifton Rd 140 CM56
St. Bernadette's RC Jun Sch, SW12 off Atkins Rd 203 DJ87
St. Bernards, Croy. CR0 224 DS104
St. Bernard's Cl, SE27 204 DR91
St. Bernard's Conv Sch, Slou. SL3 off Langley Rd 174 AW75
St. Bernard's Hosp, Sthl. UB1 179 CD75
St. Bernard's Prep Sch, Slou. SL1 off Hawtrey Cl 174 AV75
St. Bernard's Rd, E6 166 EK67
St. Bernards Rd, St.Alb. AL3 65 CD19
Slough SL3 174 AW76
St. Blaise Av, Brom. BR1 226 EH96
St. Bonaventure's Cath Comp Sch, E7 13 P7
St. Boniface RC Prim Sch, SW17 off Undine St 202 DF92
St. Botolph Rd, Nthflt DA11 212 GC90
St. Botolph Row, EC3 20 A9
St. Botolph's Av, Sev. TN13 278 FG124
St. Botolph's C of E Prim Sch, Nthflt DA11 off Dover Rd 212 GD87
St. Botolph's Rd, Sev. TN13 278 FG124
St. Botolph St, EC3 20 A9
St. Brelades Cl, Dor. RH4 285 CG138
St. Brelades Ct, N1
off Balmes Rd 9 M8
St. Brelades Pl, St.Alb. AL4
off Harvesters 65 CK16
St. Brides Av, EC4 18 G9
Edgware HA8 118 CM53
St. Bride's Ch, EC4 18 G9
St. Brides Cl, Erith DA18
off St. Katherines Rd 188 EX75
St. Bride's Pas, EC4
off Salisbury Ct 18 G9
St. Bride St, EC4 18 G8
St. Catharines Rd, Brox. EN10 71 EA19
St. Catherine of Siena Cath Prim Sch, Wat. WD25
off Horseshoe La 82 BX33
St. Catherines, Wok. GU22 248 AW119
St. Catherine's Bletchingley Village Sch, Bletch. RH1
off Coneybury 274 DS133
St. Catherine's Cath Sch for Girls, Bexh. DA6
off Watling St 189 FB84
St. Catherines Cl, SW17 202 DE89
Chessington KT9 237 CK107
St. Catherine's C of E Prim Sch, Hodd. EN11
off Haslewood Av 71 EA17
Ware SG12 off Park Rd 54 DV05
St. Catherines Ct, Felt. TW13 197 BU88
St. Catherines Cross, Bletch. RH1 274 DS134
St. Catherines Dr, SE14 45 K9
Guildford GU2 280 AV138
St. Catherines Fm Ct, Ruis. HA4 137 BQ58
St. Catherines Hill, Guil. GU2
off Portsmouth Rd 280 AW138
St. Catherine's Ms, SW3 28 E8
St. Catherines Pk, Guil. GU1 281 AZ136
St. Catherine's RC Prim Sch, Barn. EN5 off Vale Dr 102 DA42
West Drayton UB7
off Money La 176 BK75
St. Catherines Rd, E4 123 EA47
Ruislip HA4 137 BR57
St. Catherine's Sch, Sen Sch, Bramley GU5
off Station Rd 281 AZ144
Twickenham TW1
off Cross Deep 199 CG89
St. Cecelia's Pl, SE3 47 N1
St. Cecilia Rd, Grays RM16 193 GH77
St. Cecilia's Cl, Sutt. SM3 221 CY102
St. Cecilia's RC Prim Sch, Sutt. SM3 off London Rd 221 CX103
St. Cecilia's, Wandsworth Sch, SW18 off Sutherland Gro 201 CZ87
St. Chad's Cath Prim Sch, SE25 off Alverston Gdns 224 DS99
St. Chads Cl, Long Dit. KT6 219 CJ101
St. Chad's Dr, Grav. DA12 213 GL90
St. Chad's Gdns, Rom. RM6 148 EY59
St. Chad's Pl, WC1 18 B2
St. Chad's Rd, Rom. RM6 148 EY58
Tilbury RM18 193 GG80
St. Chad's St, WC1 18 B2
St. Charles Borromeo Catholic Prim Sch, Wey. KT13
off Portmore Way 216 BN104
St. Charles Catholic 6th Form Coll, W10 14 D7
St. Charles Ct, Wey. KT13 234 BN106
St. Charles Hosp, W10 14 D6
St. Charles Pl, W10 14 E7
Weybridge KT13 234 BN106
St. Charles RC Prim Sch, W10 14 D6
St. Charles Rd, Brwd. CM14 130 FV46
St. Charles Sq, W10 14 E6
St. Christina's Sch, NW8 6 D10
St. Christopher Rd, Uxb. UB8 156 BK71
St. Christopher's Cl, Islw. TW7 179 CE81
St. Christopher's Dr, Hayes UB3 157 BV73
St. Christophers Gdns, Th.Hth. CR7 223 DN97
St. Christophers Ms, Wall. SM6 241 DJ106
St. Christopher's Pl, W1 17 H8
St. Christopher's Sch, NW3 6 B3
Epsom KT18 off Downs Rd 238 CS114
Wembley HA9
off Wembley Pk Dr 140 CM62
St. Christopher's The Hall Sch, Beck. BR3 off Bromley Rd 225 EC96
St. Clair Cl, Ilf. IG5 125 EM54
Oxted RH8 275 EC130
Reigate RH2 272 DC134
St. Clair Dr, Wor.Pk. KT4 221 CV104
St. Clair Rd, E13 24 B1
St. Clair's Rd, Croy. CR0 224 DS103

● St. Clare Business Pk, Hmptn. TW12 198 CC93
St. Clare St, EC3 20 A9
St. Clement Cl, Uxb. UB8 156 BK72
★ St. Clement Danes Ch, WC2 18 D9
St. Clement Danes C of E Prim Sch, WC2 18 C9
St. Clement Danes Sch, Chorl. WD3 off Chenies Rd 95 BD40
St. Clements & St. James C of E Prim Sch, W11 26 E2
St. Clements Av, Grays RM20 191 FV79
St. Clement's Catholic Prim Sch, Ewell KT17 off Fennells Mead 239 CT109
St. Clement's Cl, Nthflt DA11 off Coldharbour Rd 213 GF90
St. Clement's C of E Jun Sch, Wal.Cr. EN8 off Cheshunt Wash 89 DY27
St. Clements Ct, EC4 off Clements La 19 M10
N7 8 E5
Purfleet RM19 190 FN77
St. Clements Hts, SE26 204 DU90
St. Clement's La, WC2 18 D9
St. Clements Rd, Grays RM20 191 FW80
Greenhithe DA9 191 FW84
St. Clements St, N7 8 E5
St. Clements Way, Grays RM20 191 FT79
Greenhithe DA9 211 FU85
St. Clements Yd, SE22 off Archdale Rd 204 DT85
St. Cloud Rd, SE27 204 DQ91
St. Columba's Cath Boys' Sch, Bexh. DA6 off Halcot Av 209 FB85
St. Columba's Cl, Grav. DA12 213 GL90
St. Columba's Coll, St.Alb. AL3 off King Harry La 64 CC22
St. Crispins Cl, NW3 6 D1
Southall UB1 158 BZ72
St. Crispins Way, Ott. KT16 233 BC109
St. Cross Ct, Hodd. EN11 71 EA19
St. Cross RC Prim Sch, Hodd. EN11 off Upper Marsh La 71 EA19
St. Cross St, EC1 18 F6
St. Cuthbert La, Uxb. UB8 156 BK72
St. Cuthbert Mayne Catholic Jun Sch, Hem.H. HP1 off Clover Way 62 BH19
St. Cuthbert's Catholic Prim Sch, Eng.Grn TW20 off Bagshot Rd 194 AW94
St. Cuthberts Cl, Eng.Grn TW20 194 AX92
St. Cuthberts Gdns, Pnr. HA5 off Westfield Pk 116 BZ52
St. Cuthberts Rd, N13 121 DN51
NW2 4 G4
Hoddesdon EN11 55 EC14
St. Cuthbert with St. Matthias C of E Prim Sch, SW5 27 L10
St. Cyprian's Greek Orthodox Prim Sch, Th.Hth. CR7 off Springfield Rd 224 DQ95
St. Cyprian's St, SW17 202 DF91
St. David Cl, Uxb. UB8 156 BK71
St. Davids, Couls. CR5 257 DM117
St. Davids Cl, SE16 44 F1
Hemel Hempstead HP3 63 BR21
Iver SL0 155 BD67
St. David's Cl, Reig. RH2 272 DC133
St. Davids Cl, Wem. HA9 140 CQ62
St. David's Cl, W.Wick. BR4 225 EB101
St. David's Coll, W.Wick. BR4 off Beckenham Rd 225 EB101
St. Davids Ct, E17 145 EC55
St. David's Cres, Grav. DA12 213 GK91
St. David's Dr, Brox. EN10 71 DZ19
St. Davids Dr, Edg. HA8 118 CM53
St. David's Dr, Eng.Grn TW20 194 AW94
St. Davids Ms, E3 off Morgan St 21 M3
St. Davids Pl, NW4 141 CV59
St. Davids Rd, Swan. BR8 209 FF93
St. David's Sch, Ashf. TW15 off Church Rd 196 BM90
Purley CR8 off Woodcote Valley Rd 241 DM111
St. Davids Sq, E14 34 D10
St. Denis Rd, SE27 204 DR91
St. Denys Cl, Pur. CR8 241 DP110
St. Dionis Rd, SW6 39 H8
St. Dominic's RC Prim Sch, E9 11 L4
NW5 6 F3
St. Dominic's 6th Form Coll, Har.Hill HA1 off Mount Pk Av 139 CE61
St. Donatts Rd, SE14 45 N7
St. Dunstans, Sutt. SM1 off Cheam Rd 239 CZ107
St. Dunstan's All, EC3 off Great Tower St 19 N10
St. Dunstans Av, W3 160 CR73
St. Dunstan's Catholic Prim Sch, Wok. GU22 off Onslow Cres 249 BA117
St. Dunstans Cl, Hayes UB3 177 BT77
St. Dunstan's C of E Prim Sch, Cheam SM3 off Anne Boleyn's Wk 239 CY108
St. Dunstan's Coll, SE6 off Stanstead Rd 205 EA88
St. Dunstan's Ct, EC4 off Fleet St 18 F9
St. Dunstan's Dr, Grav. DA12 213 GL91
St. Dunstans Gdns, W3 160 CR73
St. Dunstan's Hill, EC3 off Great Tower St 31 N1
Sutton SM1 239 CY106
St. Dunstan's La, EC3 31 N1
Beckenham BR3 225 EC100
St. Dunstan's Rd, E7 166 EJ65
St. Dunstans Rd, SE25 224 DT98
W6 38 C1
W7 179 CE75
St. Dunstan's Rd, Felt. TW13 197 BT90
St. Dunstans Rd, Houns. TW4 178 BW82
Hunsdon SG12 56 EK07
St. Ebba's Hosp, Epsom KT19 238 CQ109
St. Edith Cl, Epsom KT18 238 CQ114
St. Edmunds, Berk. HP4 60 AW20
St. Edmunds Av, Ruis. HA4 137 BR58
St. Edmunds Cl, NW8 6 E9
SW17 off College Gdns 202 DE89
Erith DA18 off St. Katherines Rd 188 EX75
St. Edmunds Dr, Stan. HA7 117 CG53
St. Edmund's La, Twick. TW2 198 CB87
St. Edmund's RC Prim Sch, E14 34 B8
N9 off Hertford Rd 122 DV46
Whitton TW2 off Nelson Rd 198 CB87
St. Edmunds Rd, N9 122 DU45
Dartford DA1 190 FM84
Ilford IG1 147 EM58
St. Edmunds Sq, SW13 38 A3
St. Edmunds Ter, NW8 6 D10
St. Edmunds Wk, St.Alb. AL4 65 CJ21
St. Edmunds Way, Harl. CM17 58 EW11
St. Edward's Catholic First Sch, Wind. SL4 off Parsonage La 173 AN81
St. Edwards Cl, NW11 142 DA58
New Addington CR0 243 ED111
St. Edward's C of E Comp Sch, Rom. RM7 off London Rd 148 FA58
St. Edward's C of E Prim Sch, Rom. RM1 off Havering Dr 149 FE56
St. Edward's RC Prim Sch, E13 off Green St 166 EJ67
NW1 16 D5
St. Edward's Royal Free Ecumenical Mid Sch, Wind. SL4 off Parsonage La 173 AN81
St. Edwards Way, Rom. RM1 149 FD57
St. Egberts Way, E4 123 EC46
St. Elizabeth Dr, Epsom KT18 238 CQ114
St. Elizabeth's Catholic Prim Sch, Rich. TW10 off Queens Rd 200 CM86
St. Elizabeth's Prim Sch, E2 11 H10
St. Elmo Cl, Slou. SL2 off St. Elmo Cres 153 AR70
St. Elmo Cres, Slou. SL2 153 AR70
St. Elmo Rd, W12 161 CT74
St. Elmos Rd, SE16 33 L4
St. Elphege's RC Infants' & Jun Schs, Wall. SM6 off Mollison Dr 241 DL107
St. Erkenwald Ms, Bark. IG11 off St. Erkenwald Rd 167 ER67
St. Erkenwald Rd, Bark. IG11 167 ER67
St. Ermin's Hill, SW1 29 N6
St. Ervans Rd, W10 14 F6
St. Ethelbert's Catholic Prim Sch, Slou. SL2 off Wexham Rd 154 AV72
St. Etheldredas Dr, Hat. AL10 67 CW18
St. Eugene de Mazenod RC Prim Sch, NW6 5 K7
St. Faiths Cl, Enf. EN2 104 DQ39
St. Faith's C of E Prim Sch, SW18 off Alma Rd 202 DC85
St. Faith's Rd, SE21 203 DP88
St. Fidelis Cath Prim Sch, Erith DA8 off Bexley Rd 189 FC79
St. Fidelis Rd, Erith DA8 189 FD77
St. Fillans Rd, SE6 205 EC88
St. Francesca Cabrini RC Prim Sch, SE23 off Honor Oak Pk 204 DW86
St. Francis Av, Grav. DA12 213 GL91
St. Francis Cath Prim Sch, SE15 44 D4
Caterham CR3 off Whyteleafe Rd 258 DT121
St. Francis Cl, Petts Wd BR5 227 ES100
Potters Bar EN6 86 DC33
Watford WD19 115 BV46
St. Francis de Sales RC Inf & Jun Schs, N17 off Church Rd 122 DT52
St. Francis of Assisi RC Prim Sch, W11 26 D1
St. Francis Pl, SW12 off Malwood Rd 203 DH86
St. Francis' RC Prim Sch, E15 13 J3
St. Francis Rd, SE22 184 DS84
Denham UB9 135 BF58
Erith DA8 off West St 189 FD77
St. Francis Way, Grays RM16 193 GJ77
Ilford IG1 147 ES63
St. Francis Xavier 6th Form Coll, SW12 off Malwood Rd 203 DH86
St. Frideswides Ms, E14 22 E9
St. Gabriel's Cl, E11 146 EH61
E14 22 C7
St. Gabriel's C of E Prim Sch, SW1 41 L1
St. Gabriels Manor, SE5 off Cormont Rd 42 G6
St. Gabriels Rd, NW2 4 C3
St. George's, SW17 off Cranmer Ter 202 DD92
St. George's, Har. HA1 139 CE58
St. Georges Av, E7 166 EH66
N7 143 DK63
NW9 140 CQ56
St. George's Av, W5 179 CK75
St. Georges Av, Grays RM17 192 GC77
Hornchurch RM11 150 FM59
Southall UB1 158 BZ73
St. George's Av, Wey. KT13 235 BP107
St. George's Bickley C of E Prim Sch, Brom. BR1 off Tylney Rd 226 EK96
St. George's Cath RC Prim Sch, SE1 30 G6
St. George's Cath School, Maida Vale, W9 15 M1
St. George's Cen, Grav. DA11 213 GH86
St. Georges Circ, SE1 30 G6
St. Georges Cl, NW11 141 CZ58
SE28 off Redbourne Dr 168 EX72
St. George's Cl, SW8 41 M6
St. Georges Cl, Horl. RH6 291 DH148
Wembley HA0 139 CG62
St. George's Cl, Wey. KT13 235 BQ106
Windsor SL4 173 AL81
St. George's C of E Inf Sch, Amer. HP7 off White Lion Rd 94 AT39
St. George's C of E Prim Sch, SE5 43 N4
SW8 41 M5
St. George's C of E Sch, Grav. DA11 off Meadow Rd 213 GG89
St. George's Coll, Add. KT15 off Weybridge Rd 216 BK104
Jun Sch, Wey. KT13 off Thames St 217 BP104
St. Georges Ct, E6 25 J4
EC4 18 G8
SW7 27 N6
St. Georges Cres, Grav. DA12 213 GK91
St. George's Cres, Slou. SL1 153 AK73
St. George's Dr, SW1 29 K9
St. Georges Dr, Uxb. UB10 136 BM62
Watford WD19 116 BY48
St. Georges Flds, W2 16 D9
St. Georges Gdns, Epsom KT17 239 CT114
St. George's Gdns, Surb. KT6 220 CP103
St. Georges Gro, SW17 202 DD90
St. George's Hanover Sq Prim Sch, W1 29 H1
ST. GEORGE'S HILL, Wey. KT13 235 BQ110
St. George's Hosp, SW17 202 DD92
Hornchurch RM12 150 FK63
● St. George's Ind Est, N22 121 DP52
● St. Georges Ind Est, Kings.T. KT2 199 CK92
St. Georges La, EC3 off Pudding La 19 M10
St. George's Lo, Wey. KT13 235 BR106
St. Georges Ms, NW1 6 F7
SE1 30 F6
SE8 33 N8
St. Georges Pl, Twick. TW1 off Church St 199 CG88
St. George's RC Prim Sch, Enf. EN2 off Gordon Rd 104 DR40
Harrow HA1 off Sudbury Hill 139 CF62
St. Georges Rd, E7 166 EH65
E10 145 EC62
N9 122 DU48
N13 121 DM48
NW11 141 CZ58
SE1 30 F6
St. George's Rd, SW19 201 CZ93
St. Georges Rd, W4 180 CS75
W7 159 CF74
Addlestone KT15 234 BJ105
St. George's Rd, Beck. BR3 225 EB95
St. Georges Rd, Brom. BR1 227 EM96
Dagenham RM9 148 EY64
Enfield EN1 104 DT38
St. George's Rd, Felt. TW13 198 BX91
St. Georges Rd, Hem.H. HP3 62 BJ24
Ilford IG1 147 EM59
St. George's Rd, Kings.T. KT2 200 CN94
Mitcham CR4 223 DH97
Petts Wood BR5 227 ER100
St. Georges Rd, Red. RH1 289 DK142
Richmond TW9 180 CM83
St. George's Rd, Sev. TN13 279 FH122
Sidcup DA14 208 EX93
St. Georges Rd, Swan. BR8 229 FF98
Twickenham TW1 199 CH85
Wallington SM6 241 DH106
Watford WD24 97 BV38
St. George's Rd, Wey. KT13 235 BR107
St. Georges Rd W, Brom. BR1 226 EL95
St. George's Sch, Wind. SL4 off Windsor Castle 173 AR80
St. Georges Sq, E7 166 EH66
E14 21 L10
SE8 33 N8
St. George's Sq, SW1 29 N10
New Malden KT3 off High St 220 CS97
St. George's Sq Ms, SW1 41 N1
St. Georges Ter, NW1 6 F7
St. George St, W1 17 K9
St. Georges Wk, Croy. CR0 224 DQ104
St. Georges Way, SE15 43 N3
St. George the Martyr C of E Prim Sch, WC1 18 C5
St. George Wf, SW8 42 A1
St. Gerards Cl, SW4 203 DJ85
St. German's Pl, SE3 47 N7
St. Germans Rd, SE23 205 DY88
St. Gilda's RC Jun Sch, N8 off Oakington Way 143 DL59
St. Giles Av, Dag. RM10 169 FB66
South Mimms EN6 85 CV32
Uxbridge UB10 137 BQ63
St. Giles Cl, Dag. RM10 off St. Giles Av 169 FB66
Hounslow TW5 178 BY80
Orpington BR6 245 ER106
St. Giles C of E Inf Sch, Ashtd. KT21 off Dene Rd 254 CM118
St. Giles' C of E Prim Sch, S.Mimms EN6 off Blanche La 85 CU32
St. Giles Ct, WC2 off St. Giles High St 18 A8
St. Giles High St, WC2 17 P8
St. Giles Pas, WC2 17 P9
St. Giles Rd, SE5 43 N5
St. Giles' Sch, S.Croy. CR2 off Pampisford Rd 241 DP107
St. Gilles Ho, E2 21 J1
St. Gothard Rd, SE27 204 DR91
St. Gregory Cl, Ruis. HA4 138 BW63
St. Gregory's Catholic Science Coll, Kenton HA3 off Donnington Rd 139 CK57
St. Gregorys Cres, Grav. DA12 213 GL89
St. Gregory's RC Prim Sch, W5 off Woodfield Rd 159 CK71
St. Helena Rd, SE16 33 J9
St. Helena St, WC1 18 E3
St. Helen's Catholic Inf Sch, E17 off Shernhall St 145 EC57
Brentwood CM14 off Queens Rd 130 FX47
St. Helen's Catholic Jun Sch, Brwd. CM15 off Sawyers Hall La 130 FX45
St. Helen's Catholic Prim Sch, E13 23 N4
St. Helens Cl, Uxb. UB8 156 BK72
St. Helen's Coll, Uxb. UB10 off Parkway 157 BP66
St. Helens Ct, Epp. CM16 off Hemnall St 92 EU30
Rainham RM13 169 FG70
St. Helens Cres, SW16 off St. Helens Rd 223 DM95
St. Helens Gdns, W10 14 C7
St. Helen's Ms, Brwd. CM15 130 FX47
St. Helens Pl, E10 145 DY59
EC3 19 N8
St. Helen's RC Prim Sch, SW9 42 E10
St. Helens Rd, SW16 223 DM95
St. Helen's Rd, W13 off Dane Rd 159 CJ74
St. Helens Rd, Erith DA18 188 EX75
Ilford IG1 147 EM58
St. Helen's Sch, Nthwd. HA6 off Eastbury Rd 115 BS51
ST. HELIER, Cars. SM5 222 DD101
⇌ St. Helier 222 DA100
St. Helier Av, Mord. SM4 222 DC101
St. Helier Hosp, Cars. SM5 222 DC102
St. Helier Rd, Sand. AL4 65 CH15
St. Heliers Av, Houns. TW3 198 CA85
St. Heliers Rd, E10 145 EC58
St. Hildas Av, Ashf. TW15 196 BL92
St. Hildas Cl, NW6 4 D7
SW17 202 DE89
Horley RH6 291 DH148
St. Hilda's Rd, SW13 181 CV79
St. Hilda's Sch, Bushey WD23 off High St 116 CB45
St. Hilda's Way, Grav. DA12 213 GK91
St. Huberts Cl, Ger.Cr. SL9 134 AY60
St. Huberts La, Ger.Cr. SL9 135 AZ61
St. Hughe's Cl, SW17 202 DE89
St. Hughs Rd, SE20 off Ridsdale Rd 224 DV95
St. Ignatious RC Prim Sch, N15 off St. Ann's Rd 144 DT58
St. Ignatius Coll, Enf. EN1 off Turkey St 104 DV37
St. Ignatius RC Prim Sch, Sun. TW16 off Green St 217 BU95
St. Ives Cl, Rom. RM3 128 FM52
St. Ivian Ct, N10 off Colney Hatch La 120 DG54
St. Ivians Dr, Rom. RM2 149 FG55
St. James' & St. Michael's C of E Prim Sch, W2 15 P10
St. James Av, N20 120 DE48
W13 159 CG74
Epsom KT17 239 CT111
Sutton SM1 240 DA106
St. James' Cath High Sch, NW9 off Great Strand 119 CT53
St. James' Cath Prim Sch, Orp. BR5 off Maybury Cl 227 EP99
St. James Cen, Harl. CM20 58 EU11
St. James Cl, N20 120 DE48
NW8 off St. James's Ter 6 E9
SE18 off Congleton Gro 187 EQ78
Barnet EN4 102 DD42
Epsom KT18 238 CS114
New Malden KT3 221 CT99
Ruislip HA4 138 BW61
Woking GU21 248 AU118
St. James' C of E Jun Sch, E7 13 N2
St. James C of E Prim Sch, N10 off Woodside Av 142 DG56
St. James' C of E Prim Sch, SE16 32 C6
Enfield EN3 off Frederick Cres 104 DW40
Harlow CM18 off Paringdon Rd 73 ER19
St. James C of E Prim Sch, Wey. KT13 off Grotto Rd 217 BQ104
St. James Ct, Green. DA9 211 FT86
St. James Dr, Rom. RM3 128 FL51
St. James Gdns, Lt.Hth RM6 148 EV56
Wembley HA0 159 CK66
St. James Gate, NW1 7 P7
St. James Gro, SW11 40 F8
St. James Hatcham C of E Prim Sch, SE14 45 M6
St. James Indep Sch for Sen Boys, Twick. TW1 off Cross Deep 199 CG89
St. James Indep Schs for Jun Boys & Girls & Sen Girls, W14 26 F8
St. James La, Green. DA9 211 FS88
St. James Ms, E14 34 F7
E17 145 DY57
Weybridge KT13 235 BP105
St. James Oaks, Grav. DA11 213 GG87
St. James Pl, Dart. DA1 off Spital St 210 FK86
Slough SL1 off Greenfern Av 152 AJ72
St. James Rd, E15 13 L2
N9 122 DV47
Brentwood CM14 130 FW48
Carshalton SM5 222 DE104
Goffs Oak EN7 88 DQ28
Kingston upon Thames KT1 220 CL96
Mitcham CR4 202 DG94
Purley CR8 241 DP113
Sevenoaks TN13 279 FH122
Surbiton KT6 219 CK100
Sutton SM1 240 DA106
Watford WD18 97 BV43
ST. JAMES'S, SW1 29 N3
St. James's, SE14 45 M6
St. James's & Lucie Clayton Coll, SW5 27 N9
St. James's Av, E2 21 H1
Beckenham BR3 225 DY97
Gravesend DA11 213 GG87
Hampton Hill TW12 198 CC92
St. James's Cath Prim Sch, Twick. TW2 off Stanley Rd 199 CD90
St. James's Cl, SW17 202 DF89
St. James's Cotts, Rich. TW9 off Paradise Rd 200 CL85
St. James's Ct, SW1 29 M6
St. James's Cres, SW9 42 F10
St. James's Dr, SW12 202 DF88
SW17 202 DF88
St. James's Gdns, W11 26 E2
St. James's La, N10 143 DH56
St. James's Mkt, SW1 29 N1
★ St. James's Palace, SW1 29 M4
★ St. James's Park, SW1 29 N4
⊖ St. James's Park 29 N6
St. James's Pk, Croy. CR0 224 DQ101
St. James's Pas, EC3 19 P9
St. James's Pl, SW1 29 L3
Grav. DA11 213 GF86
St. James's Rd, SE1 32 D10
St. James's Rd, SE16 32 D6
Croydon CR0 223 DP101
Gravesend DA11 213 GG86
Hampton Hill TW12 198 CB92
St. James's Sq, SW1 29 M2
St. James's St, E17 145 DY57
SW1 29 L2
Gravesend DA11 213 GG86
St. James's Ter, NW8 6 E10
St. James's Ter Ms, NW8 6 E9
⇌ St. James Street 145 DY57
St. James St, W6 38 A1
St. James's Wk, EC1 18 G4
St. James Ter, SW12 202 DG88
St. James the Gt Cath Prim & Nurs Sch, Th.Hth. CR7 off Windsor Rd 223 DP96
St. James the Gt Cath Prim Sch, SE15 44 B6
St. James Wk, Iver SL0 175 BE75
St. James Way, Sid. DA14 208 EY92
St. Jeromes Gro, Hayes UB3 157 BQ72
St. Joachim's RC Prim Sch, E16 24 C9
St. Joan of Arc Cath Sch, Rick. WD3 off High St 114 BL45
St. Joan of Arc RC Prim Sch, N5 off Northolme Rd 144 DQ63
St. Joans Rd, N9 122 DT46
St. John & St. James C of E Prim Sch, E9 10 G3
N18 off Grove St 122 DT50
St. John Baptist Prim Sch, Downham BR1 off Beachborough Rd 205 EC91
St. John Bosco Sch, SW11 40 C7
St. John Evangelist RC Prim Sch, N1 8 G10
St. John Fisher Cath Prim Sch, Erith DA18 off Kale Rd 188 EY76
Loughton IG10 off Burney Dr 107 EQ40
St. John Fisher RC First & Mid Sch, Pnr. HA5 off Melrose Rd 138 CA56
St. John Fisher RC Prim Sch, SW20 off Grand Dr 221 CX99
Perivale UB6 off Thirlmere Av 159 CJ69
St. Albans AL4 off Hazelmere Rd 65 CJ17
St. John Fisher Rd, Erith DA18 188 EX76
St. John of Jerusalem C of E Prim Sch, E9 11 H7
ST. JOHN'S, SE8 46 A8
ST. JOHN'S, Wok. GU21 248 AV118
⇌ St. John's 46 B8
St. Johns, N.Holm. RH5 285 CH140
St. John's, Red. RH1 288 DE136
St. John's & St. Clement's C of E Prim Sch, SE15 off Adys Rd 184 DU83
St. John's (Angell Town) C of E Prim Sch, SW9 42 F9
St. Johns Av, N11 120 DF50
St. John's Av, NW10 161 CT67
SW15 201 CX85
Epsom KT17 239 CT112
Harlow CM17 58 EW11
St. Johns Av, Lthd. KT22 253 CH121
Warley CM14 130 FX49
St. John's Beaumont Sch, Old Wind. SL4 off Priest Hill 194 AV89
St. John's Catholic Comp Sch, Grav. DA12 off Rochester Rd 213 GK88
St. John's Catholic Prim Sch, Grav. DA12 off Rochester Rd 213 GK87
Mill End WD3 off Berry La 114 BH46
St. John's Ch Rd, E9 10 G3
Wotton RH5 off Coast Hill 284 BZ139
St. Johns Cl, N14 103 DJ44
St. John's Cl, SW6 39 J4
St. Johns Cl, Berry's Grn TN16 off St. Johns Ri 261 EP116
St. John's Cl, Guil. GU2 off St. John's Rd 280 AU135
St. Johns Cl, Hem.H. HP1 off Anchor La 62 BH22
Leatherhead KT22 253 CJ120
St. John's Cl, Pot.B. EN6 86 DC33
St. Johns Cl, Rain. RM13 169 FG66
St. John's Cl, Uxb. UB8 156 BH67
Wembley HA9 140 CL64
St. John's C of E Prim Sch, N11 off Crescent Rd 120 DF49
N20 off Swan La 120 DC47
SE20 off Maple Rd 204 DW94
Buckhurst Hill IG9 off High Rd 124 EH46
Caterham CR3 off Markfield Rd 274 DV125
Croydon CR0 off Spring Pk Rd 225 DX104
Enfield EN2 off Theobalds Pk Rd 103 DP36
Kingston upon Thames KT1 off Portland Rd 220 CL97
Lemsford AL8 off Lemsford Village 51 CT10
Sevenoaks TN13 off Bayham Rd 279 FK123
Welwyn AL6 off Hertford Rd 51 CZ05
St. John's C of E Sch, Epp. CM16 off Tower Rd 91 ES30
St. John's C of E School, Stanmore, Stan. HA7 off Green La 117 CG49
St. John's C of E Walham Grn Prim Sch, SW6 38 F6
St. John's Cotts, SE20 off Maple Rd 204 DW94
St. Johns Cotts, Rich. TW9 off Kew Foot Rd 180 CL83
St. Johns Ct, Buck.H. IG9 124 EH46
St. John's Ct, Egh. TW20 195 BA92
St. Johns Ct, Hert. SG14 off St. John's St 54 DR09
St. John's Ct, Islw. TW7 179 CF82
St. Johns Ct, Nthwd. HA6 off Murray Rd 115 BS52
St. Albans AL1 65 CH19
Westcott RH4 off St. John's Rd 284 CC137

St. John's Ct, Wok. GU21 off St. Johns Hill Rd 248 AU119
St. John's Cres, SW9 42 E10
St. Johns Dr, SW18 202 DB88
Walton-on-Thames KT12 218 BW102
Windsor SL4 173 AM82
St. John's Est, N1 19 M1
SE1 32 A5
St. John's Gdns, W11 26 G1
★ St. John's Gate & Mus of the Order of St. John, EC1 18 G5
St. Johns Gro, N19 143 DJ61
SW13 off Terrace Gdns 181 CT82
Richmond TW9 off Kew Foot Rd 180 CL84
Sch St. John's Highbury Vale C of E Prim Sch, N5 off Conewood St 143 DP62
St. John's Hill, SW11 182 DD84
Coulsdon CR5 257 DN117
Purley CR8 257 DN116
Sevenoaks TN13 279 FJ123
St. John's Hill Gro, SW11 182 DD84
St. Johns Hill Rd, Wok. GU21 248 AU119
★ St. John's Jerusalem, Dart. DA4 210 FP94
St. John's La, EC1 18 G5
Great Amwell SG12 55 EA09
St. Johns Lo, Wok. GU21 248 AU119
St. John's Lye, Wok. GU21 248 AT119
St. John's Ms, W11 15 J9
Woking GU21 248 AU119
St. Johns Par, Sid. DA14 208 EU91
St. Johns Pk, SE3 47 M5
St. Johns Pk Home Est, Enf. EN2 103 DP37
St. John's Pas, SW19 off Ridgway Pl 201 CY93
St. John's Path, EC1 18 G5
St. Johns Pathway, SE23 off Devonshire Rd 204 DW88
St. John's Pl, EC1 18 G5
Sch St. John's Prep Sch, Pot.B. EN6 off The Ridgeway 86 DE34
Sch St. John's Prim Sch, E2 20 G1
W13 off Felix Rd 159 CG73
Knaphill GU21 off Victoria Rd 248 AS118
Redhill RH1 off Pendleton Rd 288 DE136
Sch St. John's RC Prim Sch, SE16 33 L5
Sch St. John's R. C. Sch, Wdf.Grn. IG8 off Turpins La 125 EN50
St. Johns Ri, Berry's Grn TN16 261 EP116
Woking GU21 248 AV119
St. John's Rd, E4 123 EB48
E6 off Ron Leighton Way 166 EL67
St. Johns Rd, E16 23 N8
St. John's Rd, E17 123 EB54
N15 144 DS58
St. Johns Rd, NW11 141 CZ58
St. John's Rd, SE20 204 DW94
SW11 182 DE84
SW19 201 CY94
Barking IG11 167 ES67
Carshalton SM5 222 DE104
St. Johns Rd, Croy. CR0 off Waddon Rd 223 DP104
St. John's Rd, Dart. DA2 210 FQ87
St. Johns Rd, E.Mol. KT8 219 CD98
St. John's Rd, Epp. CM16 91 ET30
St. Johns Rd, Erith DA8 189 FD78
St. John's Rd, Felt. TW13 198 BY91
St. Johns Rd, Grav. DA12 213 GK87
Grays RM16 193 GH78
St. John's Rd, Guil. GU2 280 AT135
Hampton Wick KT1 219 CJ96
Harrow HA1 139 CF58
St. Johns Rd, Hem.H. HP1 62 BG22
Ilford IG2 147 ER59
St. John's Rd, Islw. TW7 179 CE82
St. Johns Rd, Lthd. KT22 253 CJ121
Loughton IG10 107 EM40
New Malden KT3 220 CQ97
St. John's Rd, Petts Wd BR5 227 ER100
Redhill RH1 288 DF136
Richmond TW9 180 CL84
St. Johns Rd, Rom. RM5 127 FC50
St. John's Rd, Sev. TN13 279 FH121
St. Johns Rd, Sid. DA14 208 EV91
Slough SL2 154 AU74
Southall UB2 178 BY76
Sutton SM1 222 DA103
Uxbridge UB8 156 BH67
Watford WD17 97 BV40
St. John's Rd, Well. DA16 188 EV83
Wembley HA9 139 CK63
Westcott RH4 284 CC137
St. Johns Rd, Wind. SL4 173 AN82
St. John's Rd, Wok. GU21 248 AV118
Sch St. John's Sch, Lthd. KT22 off Epsom Rd 253 CH121
Northwood HA6 off Wieland Rd 115 BV51
Coll St. John's Seminary, Won. GU5 off Cranleigh Rd 281 BC144
Sch St. John's Sen Sch, Enf. EN2 off The Ridgeway 102 DG35
St. John's Sq, EC1 18 G5
St. John's St, Gdmg. GU7 280 AT144
Hertford SG14 54 DR09
St. Johns Ter, E7 166 EH65
SE18 187 EQ79
SW15 off Kingston Vale 200 CS90
W10 14 D4
St. John's Ter, Enf. EN2 104 DR37
Redhill RH1 off St. John's Ter Rd 288 DF136
St. John's Ter Rd, Red. RH1 288 DF136
St. John St, EC1 19 H5
Sch St. John's Upr Holloway C of E Prim Sch, N19 off Pemberton Gdns 143 DK61
St. Johns Vale, SE8 46 B8
St. Johns Vil, N19 143 DK61
St. John's Vil, W8 27 M7
St. Johns Wk, Harl. CM17 58 EW11
Sch St. John's Walworth C of E Prim Sch, SE17 31 K9
St. John's Waterside, Wok. GU21 off Copse Rd 248 AT118
St. Johns Way, N19 143 DK60
St. John's Way, Cher. KT16 216 BG102
St. Johns Well Ct, Berk. HP4 60 AV18
St. Johns Well La, Berk. HP4 60 AV18
ST. JOHN'S WOOD, NW8 16 A2
⊖ St. John's Wood 6 A10
St. John's Wd Ct, NW8 16 B3
St. John's Wd High St, NW8 16 B1
St. John's Wd Pk, NW8 6 B9
St. John's Wd Rd, NW8 16 A4
St. John's Wd Ter, NW8 6 C10
Sch St. John the Baptist C of E Jun Sch, Hmptn W. KT1 off Lower Teddington Rd 199 CK94
Sch St. John the Baptist C of E Prim Sch, N1 19 N1
Great Amwell SG12 off Hillside La 55 EA10
Sch St. John the Baptist Sch, Wok. GU22 off Elmbridge La 249 BA119
Sch St. John the Divine C of E Prim Sch, SE5 42 G4
Sch St. John Vianney RC Prim Sch, N15 off Stanley Rd 143 DP56
Sch St. Joseph's Catholic Comb Sch, Chal.St.P. SL9 off Priory Rd 134 AW55
Sch St. Joseph's Catholic High Sch, Slou. SL2 off Shaggy Calf La 154 AU73
Sch St. Joseph's Cath Infants' & Jun Schs, SE5 43 J4
Sch St. Joseph's Cath Inf Sch, E10 off Marsh La 145 EA61
Sch St. Joseph's Cath Jun Sch, E10 off Vicarage Rd 145 EB60
Sch St. Joseph's Cath Prim Sch, Bark. IG11 off Broadway 167 EQ67
Bromley BR1 off Plaistow La 206 EH94
Crayford DA1 off Old Rd 189 FE84
Dagenham RM9 off Connor Rd 148 EZ63
Dorking RH4 off Norfolk Rd 285 CG136
Epsom KT18 off Rosebank 238 CQ114
Guildford GU2 off Aldershot Rd 264 AT132
Harrow HA3 off Dobbin Cl 117 CG54
Hertford SG14 off North Rd 53 DN08
Kingston upon Thames KT1 off Fairfield S 220 CM96
Northfleet DA11 off Springhead Rd 212 GD87
South Oxhey WD19 off Ainsdale Rd 116 BW48
Upminster RM14 off St. Mary's La 150 FP61
Sch St. Joseph's Catholic Prim Sch Redhill, Red. RH1 off Linkfield La 272 DE133
St. Josephs Cl, W10 14 F7
St. Joseph's Cl, Orp. BR6 245 ET105
Sch St. Joseph's Coll, SE19 off Beulah Hill 203 DP93
Sch St. Joseph's Conv Prep Sch, Grav. DA12 off Old Rd E 213 GJ89
Sch St. Joseph's Conv Sch, E11 off Cambridge Pk 146 EG58
St. Josephs Ct, SE2 188 EX79
St. Joseph's Ct, SE7 186 EH79
St. Josephs Dr, Sthl. UB1 158 BY74
St. Josephs Grn, Welw.G.C. AL7 51 CX12
St. Joseph's Gro, NW4 141 CV56
Sch St. Joseph's In The Pk Sch, Hertingfordbury SG14 off St. Mary's La 53 DN11
St. Joseph's Ms, Beac. HP9 111 AM53
Sch St. Joseph's Prim Sch, SE8 46 A4
SW3 28 E9
Sch St. Joseph's RC Inf & Jun Schs, NW4 off Watford Way 141 CV56
Sch St. Joseph's RC Inf Sch, SE19 off Crown Dale 204 DQ93
Wembley HA9 off Waverley Av 140 CM64
Sch St. Joseph's RC Jun Sch, SE19 off Woodend 204 DQ93
Wembley HA9 off Chatsworth Av 140 CM64
Sch St. Joseph's RC Prim Sch, N19 off Highgate Hill 143 DH60
NW10 off Goodson Rd 160 CS66
SE1 31 K4
SE10 35 K10
Bermondsey, SE16 32 C5
Rotherhithe, SE16 33 H7
SW15 off Oakhill Rd 202 DA85
W7 off York Av 159 CE74
W9 15 N3
WC2 18 B8
Waltham Cross EN8 off Royal Av 89 DY32
St. Josephs Rd, N9 122 DV45
St. Joseph's Rd, Wal.Cr. EN8 89 DY33
St. Josephs St, SW8 41 K6
St. Joseph's Vale, SE3 47 H9
Sch St. Joseph the Worker Catholic Prim Sch, Hutt. CM13 off Highview Cres 131 GC44
Sch St. Jude's & St. Paul's C of E Prim Sch, N1 9 N4
St. Judes Cl, Eng.Grn TW20 194 AW92
Sch St. Jude's C of E Prim Sch, SE1 30 G6
SE24 off Regent Rd 203 DP85
Sch St. Jude's C of E Sch, Eng.Grn TW20 off Bagshot Rd 194 AW93
St. Jude's Rd, E2 20 F1
Englefield Green TW20 194 AW90
St. Jude St, N16 9 P3
ST. JULIANS, St.Alb. AL1 65 CD23
St. Julians, Sev. TN15 279 FN128
St. Julian's Cl, SW16 203 DN91
St. Julian's Fm Rd, SE27 203 DN91
St. Julian's Rd, NW6 5 H7
St. Julians Rd, St.Alb. AL1 65 CD22
St. Justin Cl, Orp. BR5 228 EX97
★ St. Katharine Docks, E1 32 B1
Pier St. Katharine's Pier 32 A2
St. Katharines Prec, NW1 7 J10
St. Katharine's Way, E1 32 B2
Sch St. Katherine's Knockholt C of E Prim Sch, Knock. TN14 off Main Rd 262 EV117
St. Katherines Rd, Cat. CR3 274 DU125
Erith DA18 188 EX75
St. Katherine's Row, EC3 off Fenchurch St 19 P9
St. Katherine's Wk, W11 26 D2
St. Katherines Way, Berk. HP4 60 AT16
St. Keverne Rd, SE9 206 EL91
St. Kilda Rd, W13 159 CG74
St. Kilda Rd, Orpington BR6 227 ET102
St. Kilda's Rd, N16 144 DR60
Brentwood CM15 130 FV45
Harrow HA1 139 CE58
St. Kitts Ter, SE19 204 DS92
St. Laurence Cl, NW6 4 D9
Orpington BR5 228 EX97
Uxbridge UB8 156 BJ71
St. Laurence Dr, Brox. EN10 71 DZ23
St. Laurence Way, Slou. SL1 174 AU76
St. Lawrence Cl, Abb.L. WD5 81 BS30
Bovingdon HP3 79 BA27
Edgware HA8 118 CM52
Sch St. Lawrence C of E Jun Sch, E.Mol. KT8 off Church Rd 218 CC98
St. Lawrence Ct, Abb.L. WD5 off St. Lawrence Cl 81 BS30
St. Lawrence Dr, Pnr. HA5 137 BV58
★ St. Lawrence Jewry Ch, EC2 19 K8
Sch St. Lawrence Prim Sch, Eff. KT24 off Lower Rd 268 BX127
Feltham TW13 off Victoria Rd 197 BV88
St. Lawrence Rd, Upmin. RM14 150 FQ61
St. Lawrence St, E14 34 F2
St. Lawrence's Way, Reig. RH2 off Church St 272 DA134
St. Lawrence Ter, W10 14 E6
St. Lawrence Way, SW9 42 F7
Bricket Wood AL2 82 BZ30
Caterham CR3 258 DQ123
St. Leonards Av, E4 123 ED51
Harrow HA3 139 CJ56
Windsor SL4 173 AQ82
St. Leonards Cl, Bushey WD23 98 BY42
Grays RM17 192 FZ79
Hertford SG14 54 DS07
St. Leonard's Cl, Well. DA16 188 EU83
Sch St. Leonard's C of E Prim Sch, SW16 off Mitcham La 203 DK92
St. Leonards Ct, N1 19 M2
St. Leonard's Gdns, Houns. TW5 178 BY80
St. Leonards Gdns, Ilf. IG1 147 EQ64
St. Leonards Hill, Wind. SL4 173 AK84
St. Leonards Ri, Orp. BR6 245 ES105
St. Leonards Rd, E14 22 D7
NW10 160 CR70
St. Leonard's Rd, SW14 180 CP83
St. Leonards Rd, W13 159 CJ73
Amersham HP6 77 AS35
Claygate KT10 237 CF107
Croydon CR0 223 DP104
Epsom KT18 255 CW119
Hertford SG14 54 DR07
Nazeing EN9 90 EE25
St. Leonard's Rd, Surb. KT6 219 CK99
St. Leonards Rd, T.Ditt. KT7 219 CG100
Windsor SL4 173 AQ82
St. Leonards Sq, NW5 7 H5
St. Leonard's Sq, Surb. KT6 219 CK99
St. Leonards St, E3 22 D2
St. Leonard's Ter, SW3 40 E1
St. Leonards Wk, SW16 203 DM94
Iver SL0 175 BF76
St. Leonards Way, Horn. RM11 149 FH61
St. Loo Av, SW3 40 D2
St. Louis Cl, Pot.B. EN6 86 DC33
St. Louis Rd, SE27 204 DQ91
St. Loy's Rd, N17 122 DS54
St. Lucia Dr, E15 13 L8
St. Luke Cl, Uxb. UB8 156 BK72
ST. LUKE'S, EC1 19 K4
St. Luke's Av, SW4 183 DK84
St. Lukes Av, Enf. EN2 104 DR38
St. Luke's Av, Ilf. IG1 147 EP64
Sch St. Luke's Catholic Prim Sch, Harl. CM19 off Pyenest Rd 73 EQ17
St. Luke's Cl, EC1 19 K4
SE25 224 DV100
St. Lukes Cl, Lane End DA2 211 FS92
Swanley BR8 229 FD96
Sch St. Luke's C of E Prim Sch, EC1 19 K3
SE27 off Linton Gro 204 DQ92
W9 14 G2
Kingston upon Thames KT2 off Acre Rd 220 CM95
Sch St. Luke's C of E (VA) Prim Sch, E16 23 M8
St. Lukes Ct, Hat. AL10 67 CV17
St. Luke's Est, EC1 19 L3
H St. Luke's Hosp for the Clergy, W1 17 L5
St. Lukes Ms, W11 15 H8
Sch St. Luke's Prim Sch, E14 34 G9
St. Lukes Rd, W11 15 H7
Old Windsor SL4 194 AU86
Whyteleafe CR3 off Whyteleafe Hill 258 DT118
St. Lukes Sq, E16 23 M9
Guildford GU1 281 AZ135
St. Luke's St, SW3 28 C10
H St. Luke's Woodside Hosp, N10 142 DG56
St. Luke's Yd, W9 14 G1
St. Magnus Ct, Hem.H. HP3 63 BP22
St. Malo Av, N9 122 DW48
Sch St. Margaret Clitherow RC Prim Sch, NW10 off Quainton St 140 CR63
SE28 off Cole Cl 168 EV74
St. Margaret Dr, Epsom KT18 238 CR114
ST. MARGARETS, Twick. TW1 199 CG85
ST. MARGARETS, Ware SG12 55 EB10
St. Margarets, Bark. IG11 167 ER67
Guildford GU1 265 AZ133
St. Margarets Av, N15 143 DP56
N20 120 DC47
Ashford TW15 197 BP92
Berry's Green TN16 off St. Anns Way 261 EP116
Harrow HA2 138 CC62
Sidcup DA15 207 ER90
St. Margaret's Av, Sutt. SM3 221 CY104
St. Margarets Av, Uxb. UB8 156 BN70
St. Margarets Cl, EC2 off Lothbury 19 L8
Berkhamsted HP4 60 AX20
Dartford DA2 211 FR89
Iver SL0 155 BD68
Orpington BR6 246 EV105
Penn HP10 110 AC47
Sch St. Margaret's C of E Prim Sch, SE18 off St. Margaret's Gro 187 EQ78
Barking IG11 off North St 167 EQ66
St. Margaret's Ct, SE1 31 K3
St. Margaret's Cres, SW15 201 CV85
Gravesend DA12 213 GL90
St. Margaret's Dr, Twick. TW1 199 CH85
St. Margarets Gate, Iver SL0 off St. Margarets Cl 155 BD68
St. Margaret's Gro, E11 146 EF62
SE18 187 EQ79
St. Margarets Gro, Twick. TW1 199 CG86
H St. Margaret's Hosp, Epp. CM16 92 EV29
St. Margarets La, W8 27 L7
Sch St. Margaret's Lee C of E Prim Sch, SE13 off Lee Ch St 186 EE84
St. Margarets Pas, SE13 off Church Ter 186 EE83
St. Margarets Path, SE18 187 EQ78
St. Margarets Rd, E12 146 EJ61
St. Margaret's Rd, N17 144 DS55
NW10 14 A1
St. Margarets Rd, SE4 185 DZ84
W7 179 CE75
Coulsdon CR5 257 DH121
Edgware HA8 118 CP50
Isleworth TW7 179 CH84
St. Margaret's Rd, Nthflt DA11 212 GE89
Ruislip HA4 137 BR58
St. Margarets Rd, S.Darenth DA2, DA4 211 FS93
St. Margaret's Rd, Stans.Abb. SG12 55 EA13
St. Margarets Rd, Twick. TW1 179 CH84
Jct St. Margarets Rbt, Twick. TW1 199 CH85
Sch St. Margaret's Sch, NW3 off Kidderpore Gdns 142 DB63
Tadworth KT20 off Tadworth Ct 255 CX121
Sch St. Margaret's Sch Bushey, Bushey WD23 off Merry Hill Rd 116 CA45
Prep Sch, Bushey WD23 off Merry Hill Rd 116 CA46
⇌ St. Margarets (SG12) 55 EC11
St. Margarets Sq, SE4 off Adelaide Av 185 DZ84
St. Margaret's St, SW1 30 A5
St. Margaret's Ter, SE18 187 EQ78
⇌ St. Margarets (TW1) 199 CH86
St. Margarets Way, Hem.H. HP2 63 BR20
St. Margaret Way, Slou. SL1 off Grimsby Rd 173 AM75
St. Marks Av, Nthflt DA11 213 GF87
Sch St. Mark's Catholic Sch, Houns. TW3 off Bath Rd 178 BZ83
St. Marks Cl, SE10 46 E5
SW6 39 J7
W11 14 E9
St. Mark's Cl, Barn. EN5 102 DB41
St. Marks Cl, Coln.Hth AL4 66 CP22
Harrow HA1 139 CH59
Sch St. Mark's C of E Acad, Mitch. CR4 off Acacia Rd 223 DH96
Sch St. Mark's C of E Prim Sch, N19 off Sussex Way 143 DL61
SE11 42 D2
SE25 off Albert Rd 224 DU98
Bromley BR2 off Aylesbury Rd 226 EG97
St. Marks Cres, NW1 7 H8
St. Mark's Gate, E9 11 P7
St. Mark's Gro, SW10 39 M3
St. Mark's Hill, Surb. KT6 220 CL100
H St. Mark's Hosp, Har. HA1 139 CH59
St. Mark's Pl, SW19 off Wimbledon Hill Rd 201 CZ93
St. Marks Pl, W11 14 F9
St. Mark's Pl, Dag. RM10 169 FB65
St. Marks Pl, Wind. SL4 173 AQ82
Sch St. Mark's Prim Sch, W7 off Lower Boston Rd 179 CE75
Mitcham CR4 off St. Marks Rd 222 DF96
St. Marks Ri, E8 10 B3
St. Marks Rd, SE25 off Coventry Rd 224 DU98
St. Mark's Rd, W5 160 CL74
St. Marks Rd, W7 179 CE75
W10 14 D8
W11 14 E9
Bromley BR2 226 EH97
Enfield EN1 104 DT44
St. Mark's Rd, Epsom KT18 255 CW118
St. Marks Rd, Mitch. CR4 222 DF96
St. Mark's Rd, Tedd. TW11 199 CH94
St. Marks Rd, Wind. SL4 173 AQ82
St. Marks Sq, NW1 6 G8
St. Mark St, E1 20 B9
Sch St. Mark's W Essex Catholic Sch, Harl. CM18 off Tripton Rd 73 ES16
St. Martha's Av, Wok. GU22 249 AZ121
Sch St. Martha's Conv Jun Sch, Barn. EN5 off Wood St 101 CY42
Sch St. Martha's Conv Sen Sch, Had.Wd EN4 off Camlet Way 102 DA39
St. Marthas Ct, Chilw. GU4 off Nursery Gdns 281 BB140
St. Martin Cl, Uxb. UB8 156 BK72
★ St. Martin-in-the-Fields Ch, WC2 30 A1
Sch St. Martin-in-the-Fields High Sch for Girls, SW2 off Tulse Hill 203 DP88
Sch St. Martin of Porres RC Prim Sch, N11 off Blake Rd 121 DJ51
St. Martins, Nthwd. HA6 115 BR50
St. Martins App, Ruis. HA4 137 BS59
St. Martins Av, E6 24 E1
Epsom KT18 238 CS114
St. Martins Cl, NW1 7 L8
East Horsley KT24 267 BS129
Enfield EN1 104 DV39
Epsom KT17 239 CT113
Erith DA18 off St. Helens Rd 188 EX75
St. Martin's Cl, Wat. WD19 116 BW49
West Drayton UB7 off St. Martin's Rd 176 BK76
Sch St. Martin's C of E Inf & Jun Schs, Epsom KT18 off Worple Rd 254 CR115
Sch St. Martin's C of E Prim Sch, Pixham La, Dor. RH4 off Pixham La 269 CJ134
Ranmore Rd, Dor. RH4 off Ranmore Rd 285 CG135
St. Martin's Ct, WC2 off St. Martin's La 18 A10
Ashford TW15 196 BJ92
St. Martin's Ctyd, WC2 18 A10
St. Martins Dr, Walt. KT12 218 BW104
St. Martins Est, SW2 203 DN88
St. Martin's La, WC2 18 A10
St. Martins La, Beck. BR3 225 EB99
St. Martin's-le-Grand, EC1 19 J8
St. Martins Meadow, Brasted TN16 262 EW123
St. Martin's Ms, WC2 30 A1
St. Martins Ms, Dor. RH4 off Church St 285 CG136
Pyrford GU22 250 BG116
St. Martin's Pl, WC2 30 A1
St. Martins Rd, N9 122 DV47
St. Martin's Rd, SW9 42 C8
St. Martins Rd, Dart. DA1 210 FM86
Hoddesdon EN11 71 EC17
St. Martin's Rd, West Dr. UB7 176 BJ76
Sch St. Martin's Sch, Hutt. CM13 off Hanging Hill La 131 GC46
Northwood HA6 off Moor Pk Rd 115 BR50
St. Martin's St, WC2 29 P1
St. Martins Ter, N10 off Pages La 120 DG54
St. Martins Wk, Dor. RH4 off High St 285 CH136
St. Martins Way, SW17 202 DC90
Sch St. Mary Abbots C of E Prim Sch, W8 27 L5
St. Mary Abbots Pl, W8 27 H7
St. Mary Abbots Ter, W14 27 H7
Sch St. Mary & All Saints C of E Prim Sch, Beac. HP9 off Maxwell Rd 111 AL52
Sch St. Mary & St. Joseph's Cath Sch, Sid. DA14 off Chislehurst Rd 208 EU92
Sch St. Mary & St. Michael Prim Sch, E1 20 G9
Sch St. Mary & St. Pancras C of E Prim Sch, NW1 17 N1
St. Mary at Hill, EC3 31 N1
★ St. Mary at Hill Ch, EC3 31 N1
St. Mary Av, Wall. SM6 222 DG104
St. Mary Axe, EC3 19 N9
St. Marychurch St, SE16 32 G5
ST. MARY CRAY, Orp. BR5 228 EW99
⇌ St. Mary Cray 228 EU98
Sch St. Mary Cray Prim Sch, St.M.Cray BR5 off High St 228 EW100
St. Mary Graces Ct, E1 20 B10
St. Marylebone Cl, NW10 off Craven Pk 160 CS67
Sch St. Marylebone C of E Sch, W1 17 H6
★ St. Mary-le-Bow Ch, EC2 19 K9
Sch St. Mary Magdalene Acad, N7 8 E4
Sch St. Mary Magdalene C of E Prim Sch, SE15 44 E9
SE18 37 L8
Sch St. Mary Magdalene's Cath Prim Sch, SW14 off Worple St 180 CR83
Sch St. Mary Magdalene's C of E Prim Sch, W2 15 L6
Sch St. Mary Magdalen's Cath Prim Sch, SE4 off Howson Rd 185 DY84
Sch St. Mary Magdalen's RC Jun Sch, NW2 off Linacre Rd 161 CV65
St. Mary Newington Cl, SE17 off Surrey Sq 31 P10
Sch St. Mary of the Angels RC Prim Sch, W2 15 J8
St. Mary Rd, E17 145 EA56
St. Marys, Bark. IG11 167 ER67
Sch St. Mary's & St. John's C.E. Prim Sch, NW4 off Prothero Gdns 141 CV57
Sch St. Mary's & St. Peter's C of E Prim Sch, Tedd. TW11 off Somerset Rd 199 CF92
St. Marys App, E12 147 EM64
St. Marys Av, E11 146 EH58
St. Mary's Av, N3 119 CY54
Bromley BR2 226 EE97
Northwood HA6 115 BS50
St. Marys Av, Shenf. CM15 131 GA43
St. Mary's Av, Stanw. TW19 196 BK87
Teddington TW11 199 CF93
St. Mary's Av Cen, Sthl. UB2 178 CB77
St. Mary's Av N, Sthl. UB2 178 CB77
St. Mary's Av S, Sthl. UB2 178 CB77
Sch St. Mary's Bryanston Sq C of E Prim Sch, W1 16 E6
Sch St. Mary's Cath Inf Sch, Croy. CR0 off Bedford Pk 224 DR102
Sch St. Mary's Cath Jun Sch, E17 off Shernhall St 145 EC55
Croydon CR0 off Sydenham Rd 224 DR102
Sch St. Mary's Cath Prim Sch, E4 off Station Rd 123 ED46
SW19 off Russell Rd 202 DA94
Beckenham BR3 off Westgate Rd 205 EC94
Hornchurch RM12 off Hornchurch Rd 149 FG60
Uxbridge UB8 off Rockingham Cl 156 BJ67
St. Mary's Ch Rd, Hat. AL9 85 CU25
St. Mary's Cl, N17 122 DU53
St. Marys Cl, Chess. KT9 238 CM108
Epsom KT17 239 CU108
St. Mary's Cl, Fetch. KT22 253 CD123
Gravesend DA12 213 GJ89
St. Marys Cl, Grays RM17 off Dock Rd 192 GD79
St. Mary's Cl, Hare. UB9 136 BH55
Loughton IG10 106 EL42
St. Marys Cl, Orp. BR5 228 EV96
St. Mary's Cl, Oxt. RH8 276 EE129
Stanwell TW19 196 BK87
Sunbury-on-Thames TW16 off Green Way 217 BU98
St. Marys Cl, Wat. WD18 off Church St 98 BW42

St. Mary's C of E Comb Sch, Amer. HP7 off School La 77 AP39
St. Mary's C of E First Sch, Nthch HP4 off New Rd 60 AS17
St. Mary's C of E High Sch, NW4 off Downage 141 CW55
St. Mary's C of E Inf Sch, N8 off Church La 143 DM56
St. Mary's C of E Jun Sch, N8 off Rectory Gdns 143 DL56
Oxted RH8 off Silkham Rd 276 EE128
St. Mary's C of E Prim Sch,
E17 off The Drive 145 EB56
N1 9 H8
N3 off Dollis Pk 119 CZ52
NW10 off Garnet Rd 160 CS65
SE13 off Lewisham High St 205 EC85
SW15 off Felsham Rd 181 CX83
Barnet EN4 off Littlegrove 102 DE44
Byfleet KT14 off Hart Rd 234 BL113
Chessington KT9 off Church La 238 CM107
North Mymms AL9 off Dellsome La 67 CV23
Rickmansworth WD3 off Stockers Fm Rd 114 BK48
Shenfield CM15 off Hall La 131 FZ44
Slough SL1 off Yew Tree Rd 174 AU76
Swanley BR8 off St. Marys Rd 229 FE98
Inf Site, Twick. TW1 off Amyand Pk Rd 199 CG87
Jun Site, Twick. TW1 off Richmond Rd 199 CH88
St. Mary's C of E Prim School, Stoke Newington, N16 off Lordship Rd 144 DS61
St. Mary's Coll, Twick. TW1 off Waldegrave Rd 199 CF90
St. Mary's Copse, Wor.Pk. KT4 220 CS103
St. Marys Ct, E6 25 J3
St. Mary's Ct, SE7 186 EK80
W5 off St. Mary's Rd 179 CK75
Beaconsfield HP9 off Malthouse Sq 133 AM55
St. Mary's Cres, NW4 141 CV55
Hayes UB3 157 BT73
St. Marys Cres, Islw. TW7 179 CD80
St. Mary's Cres, Stanw. TW19 196 BK87
St. Marys Dr, Felt. TW14 197 BQ87
St. Mary's Dr, Sev. TN13 278 FE123
St. Marys Est, SE16 off St. Marychurch St 32 G5
St. Mary's Gdns, SE11 30 F8
St. Mary's Gate, W8 27 L7
St. Marys Grn, N2 142 DC55
Biggin Hill TN16 260 EJ118
St. Mary's Gro, N1 9 H5
SW13 181 CV83
W4 180 CP79
St. Marys Gro, Bigg.H. TN16 260 EJ118
St. Mary's Gro, Rich. TW9 180 CM84
St. Mary's Hare Pk Sch, Gidea Pk RM2 off South Dr 150 FJ55
St. Mary's High Sch, Croydon CR0 off Woburn Rd 224 DQ102
St. Mary's Hosp, W2 16 B8
St. Mary's Kilburn C of E Prim Sch, NW6 5 K8
St. Mary's La, Hert. SG14 53 DM11
Upminster RM14 150 FN61
St. Marys Mans, W2 16 A6
St. Mary's Ms, NW6 5 L7
Richmond TW10 off Wiggins La 199 CJ89
St. Mary's Mt, Cat. CR3 258 DT124
St. Marys Path, N1 9 H8
St. Mary's Pl, SE9 off Eltham High St 207 EN86
W5 179 CK75
W8 27 L7
St. Mary's RC Inf Sch, N15 off Hermitage Rd 144 DR58
St. Mary's RC Infants' Sch, Cars. SM5 off West St 240 DF105
St. Mary's RC Jun Sch, N15 off Hermitage Rd 144 DR57
Carshalton SM5 off Shorts Rd 240 DF106
St. Mary's RC Prim Sch, NW6 5 J10
SE9 off Glenure Rd 207 EN85
SW4 off Crescent La 183 DJ84
SW8 41 K6
W4 off Duke Rd 180 CS78
W10 14 E5
W14 26 D7
Enfield EN3 off Durants Rd 105 DX42
Isleworth TW7 off South St 179 CG83
Tilbury RM18 off Calcutta Rd 193 GF82
St. Marys Rd, E10 145 EC62
E13 166 EH68
N8 off High St 143 DL56
N9 122 DW46
St. Mary's Rd, NW10 160 CS67
St. Marys Rd, NW11 141 CY59
St. Mary's Rd, SE15 44 G7
SE25 224 DS97
SW19 (Wimbledon) 201 CY92
W5 179 CK75
Barnet EN4 120 DF45
Bexley DA5 209 FC88
Cheshunt EN8 88 DW29
Denham UB9 135 BF58
St. Marys Rd, E.Mol. KT8 219 CD99
St. Mary's Rd, Grays RM16 193 GH77
Greenhithe DA9 211 FS85
Harefield UB9 136 BH56
Hayes UB3 157 BT73
Hemel Hempstead HP2 62 BK19
St. Marys Rd, Ilf. IG1 147 EQ61
Leatherhead KT22 253 CH122
St. Marys Rd, Long Ditton KT6 219 CJ101
Reigate RH2 288 DB135
St. Mary's Rd, Slou. SL3 154 AY74
South Croydon CR2 242 DR110
St. Marys Rd, Surb. KT6 219 CK100
Swanley BR8 229 FD98
St. Mary's Rd, Wat. WD18 97 BV42
St. Marys Rd, Wey. KT13 235 BR105
St. Mary's Rd, Wok. GU21 248 AW117
Worcester Park KT4 220 CS103
St. Mary's Sch, NW3 6 A3
Gerrards Cross SL9 off Packhorse Rd 134 AY56
St. Marys Sq, W2 16 A6
St. Mary's Sq, W5 off St. Mary's Rd 179 CK75
St. Marys Ter, W2 16 A6
St. Mary's Twr, EC1 off Fortune St 19 K5
St. Mary St, SE18 37 K8
St. Marys Vw, Har. HA3 139 CJ57
St. Mary's Vw, Wat. WD18 98 BW42
St. Mary's Wk, SE11 30 F8
Bletchingley RH1 274 DR133
Hayes UB3 157 BT73
St. Marys Wk, St.Alb. AL4 65 CH16
St. Mary's Way, Chal.St.P. SL9 112 AX54
Chesham HP5 76 AP31
Chigwell IG7 125 EN50
Guildford GU2 264 AS132
St. Matthew Acad, SE3 47 J10
St. Matthew Cl, Uxb. UB8 156 BK72
St. Matthew's Av, Surb. KT6 220 CL102
St. Matthews Cl, Rain. RM13 169 FG66
Watford WD19 98 BX44
St. Matthew's C of E Inf Sch, Cob. KT11 off Downside Rd 251 BV118
St. Matthew's C of E Prim Sch, SW1 29 P6
Enfield EN3 off South St 104 DW43
St. Matthews C of E Prim Sch, Red. RH1 off Linkfield La 272 DF132
St. Matthew's C of E Prim Sch, Surb. KT6 off Langley Rd 220 CL101
St. Matthew's Dr, Brom. BR1 227 EM97
St. Matthews Prim Sch, SW20 off Cottenham Pk Rd 221 CU95
St. Matthew's Prim Sch, Yiew. UB7 off High St 156 BL74
St. Matthew's Rd, SW2 183 DM84
St. Matthews Rd, W5 off The Common 160 CL74
St. Matthew's Rd, Red. RH1 272 DF133
St. Matthew's Row, E2 20 C3
St. Matthew St, SW1 29 N7
St. Matthias Cl, NW9 141 CT57
St. Matthias C of E Prim Sch, E2 20 B4
N16 9 N2
St. Maur Rd, SW6 39 H6
St. Mawes Cl, Crox.Grn WD3 97 BP42
St. Mellion Cl, SE28 168 EX72
St. Merryn Cl, SE18 187 ER80
St. Meryl Sch, Carp.Pk WD19 off The Mead 116 BY48
St. Michael & All Angels C of E Acad, SE5 43 J5
St. Michael & St. Martin RC Prim Sch, Houns. TW4 off Belgrave Rd 178 BZ83
St. Michael at Bowes C of E Jun Sch, N13 off Tottenhall Rd 121 DN51
St. Michael Cath Prim Sch, Ashf. TW15 off Feltham Hill Rd 196 BN92
St. Michael's, Oxt. RH8 276 EG129
St. Michael's All, EC3 19 M9
St. Michaels Av, N9 122 DW45
Hemel Hempstead HP3 63 BP21
St. Michael's Av, Wem. HA9 160 CN65
St. Michael's Camden Town C of E Prim Sch, NW1 7 L8
St. Michael's Catholic Gram Sch, N12 off Nether St 120 DC50
St. Michael's Catholic High Sch, Wat. WD25 off High Elms La 82 BX32
St. Michaels Cl, E16 24 E7
St. Michael's Cl, N3 119 CZ54
St. Michaels Cl, N12 120 DE50
Aveley RM15 170 FQ73
Bromley BR1 226 EL97
Erith DA18 off St. Helens Rd 188 EX75
Harlow CM20 57 ES14
Walton-on-Thames KT12 218 BW103
Worcester Park KT4 221 CT103
St. Michael's C of E First Sch, Mick. RH5 off School La 269 CJ127
N6 off North Rd 142 DG59
N22 off Bounds Grn Rd 121 DM53
SE26 off Champion Rd 205 DY91
SW18 off Granville Rd 201 CZ87
Enfield EN2 off Brigadier Hill 104 DQ39
St. Albans AL3 off St. Michaels St 64 CB20
St. Michael's C of E Prim Sch, Well. DA16 off Wrotham Rd 188 EW81
St. Michael's Ct, Slou. SL2 153 AK70
St. Michaels Cres, Pnr. HA5 138 BY58
St. Michaels Dr, Wat. WD25 81 BV33
St. Michaels Gdns, W10 14 E7
St. Michael's Grn, Beac. HP9 111 AL52
St. Michael's Ms, SW1 28 G9
St. Michael's RC Prim Sch, E6 off Howard Rd 167 EM68
St. Michael's RC Sch, SE16 32 C5
St. Michaels Rd, NW2 141 CW63
St. Michael's Rd, SW9 42 C8
Ashford TW15 196 BN92
St. Michaels Rd, Brox. EN10 71 DZ20
Caterham CR3 258 DR122
Croydon CR0 224 DQ102
Grays RM16 193 GH78
Wallington SM6 241 DJ107
Welling DA16 188 EV83
St. Michael's Rd, Wok. GU21 233 BD114
St. Michaels St, W2 16 B8
St. Albans AL3 64 CB20
St. Michaels Ter, N22 121 DL54
St. Michaels Vw, Hat. AL10 off Homestead Rd 67 CV16
St. Michaels Way, Pot.B. EN6 86 DB30
St. Mildred's Ct, EC2 off Poultry 19 L9
St. Mildreds Rd, SE12 206 EE87
Guildford GU1 265 AZ133
St. Monica's RC Prim Sch, N1 19 N2
N14 off Cannon Rd 121 DL48
St. Monica's Rd, Kgswd KT20 255 CZ121
St. Nazaire Cl, Egh. TW20 off Mullens Rd 195 BC92
St. Neots Cl, Borwd. WD6 100 CN38
St. Neots Rd, Rom. RM3 128 FM52
St. Nicholas Av, Bkhm KT23 268 CB125
Hornchurch RM12 149 FG62
St. Nicholas Cen, Sutt. SM1 off St. Nicholas Way 240 DB106
St. Nicholas Cl, Amer. HP7 94 AV39
Elstree WD6 99 CK44
Uxbridge UB8 156 BK72
St. Nicholas C of E Prim Sch, Els. WD6 off St. Nicholas Cl 99 CK44
Shepperton TW17 off Manor Fm Av 217 BP100
St. Nicholas Cres, Pyrford GU22 250 BG116
St. Nicholas Dr, Sev. TN13 279 FH126
Shepperton TW17 216 BN101
St. Nicholas Glebe, SW17 202 DG93
St. Nicholas Grn, Harl. CM17 58 EW14
St. Nicholas Gro, Ingrave CM13 131 GC50
St. Nicholas Hill, Lthd. KT22 253 CH122
St. Nicholas Ho, Enf. EN2 103 DH35
St. Nicholas Mt, Hem.H. HP1 61 BF20
St. Nicholas Pl, Loug. IG10 107 EN42
St. Nicholas Prep Sch, SW7 28 B5
St. Nicholas Rd, SE18 187 ET78
Sutton SM1 240 DB106
Thames Ditton KT7 219 CF100
St. Nicholas Sch, Harl. CM17 off Hobbs Cross Rd 58 EY12
Merstham RH1 off Taynton Dr 273 DK129
Purley CR8 off Old Lo La 241 DN113
St. Nicholas St, SE8 45 P7
St. Nicholas Way, Sutt. SM1 240 DB105
St. Nicolas' C of E Comb Sch, Tap. SL6 off Rectory Rd 152 AE70
St. Nicolas C of E Inf Sch, Guil. GU2 off Portsmouth Rd 280 AW136
St. Nicolas La, Chis. BR7 226 EL95
St. Ninian's Ct, N20 120 DF48
St. Norbert Grn, SE4 185 DY84
St. Norbert Rd, SE4 185 DY84
St. Normans Way, Epsom KT17 239 CU110
St. Olaf's Rd, SW6 38 F5
St. Olaves Cl, Stai. TW18 195 BF94
St. Olaves Ct, EC2 19 L9
St. Olave's Est, SE1 31 P4
St. Olaves Gdns, SE11 30 E8
St. Olave's Gram Sch, Orp. BR6 off Goddington La 228 EV104
St. Olave's Prep Sch, SE9 off Southwood Rd 207 EP89
St. Olaves Rd, E6 167 EN67
St. Olave's Wk, SW16 223 DJ96
St. Olav's Sq, SE16 32 G6
St. Omer Ridge, Guil. GU1 281 BA135
St. Omer Rd, Guil. GU1 281 BA135
St. Osmund's Cath Prim Sch, SW13 off Church Rd 181 CT81
St. Oswald's Pl, SE11 42 C1
St. Oswald's Rd, SW16 223 DP95
St. Oswulf St, SW1 29 P9
ST. PANCRAS, WC1 18 A3
St. Pancras Commercial Cen, NW1 off Pratt St 7 M8
St. Pancras Hosp, NW1 7 N9
St. Pancras 18 A1
Saint Pancras International 18 A1
St. Pancras Way, NW1 7 M8
St. Patrick's Cath Prim Sch, E17 off Longfield Av 145 DY56
NW5 7 K4
Collier Row RM5 off Lowshoe La 127 FB53
St. Patrick's Ct, Wdf.Grn. IG8 124 EE52
St. Patrick's Gdns, Grav. DA12 213 GK90
St. Patricks Pl, Grays RM16 193 GJ77
St. Patrick's RC Prim Sch, SE18 off Griffin Rd 187 ER77
St. Paul & All Hallows C.E. Inf & Jun Schs, N17 off Park La 122 DU52
St. Paul Cl, Uxb. UB8 156 BK71
St. Paulinus C of E Prim Sch, Cray. DA1 off Iron Mill La 189 FE84
St. Paul's 19 J8
St. Paul's Acad, SE2 off Wickham La 188 EU79
St. Paul's All, EC4 off St. Paul's Chyd 19 H9
St. Paul's Av, NW2 161 CV65
SE16 33 K2
St. Pauls Av, Har. HA3 140 CM57
Slough SL2 154 AT73
St. Paul's Cath, EC4 19 J9
St. Paul's Cath Sch, EC4 19 J9
St. Paul's Catholic Coll, Sun. TW16 off Green St 217 BU95
St. Paul's Cath Prim Sch, T.Ditt. KT7 off Hampton Ct Way 219 CE101
St. Paul's Chyd, EC4 19 H9
St. Paul's Cl, SE7 186 EK78
W5 180 CM75
St. Pauls Cl, Add. KT15 234 BG106
St. Paul's Cl, Ashf. TW15 197 BQ92
St. Pauls Cl, Aveley RM15 170 FQ73
Borehamwood WD6 100 CQ43
St. Paul's Cl, Cars. SM5 222 DE102
St. Pauls Cl, Chess. KT9 237 CK105
Harlington UB3 177 BR78
St. Paul's Cl, Houns. TW3 178 BY82
St. Pauls Cl, Swans. DA10 212 FY87
St. Paul's C of E Comb Sch, Woob.Grn HP10 off Stratford Dr 132 AD59
St. Paul's C of E Jun Sch, Kings.T. KT2 off Princes Rd 200 CN94
St. Paul's C of E Prim Sch, E1 20 D10
N11 off The Avenue 121 DH50
N21 off Ringwood Way 121 DP45
NW3 6 E7
NW7 off The Ridgeway 119 CV49
SE17 43 J1
W6 26 A10
Addlestone KT15 off School La 234 BG105
Brentford TW8 off St. Paul's Rd 179 CK79
St. Pauls C of E Prim Sch, Chess. KT9 off Orchard Rd 238 CL105
St. Paul's C of E Prim Sch, Chipper. WD4 off The Common 80 BG31
Dorking RH4 off St. Pauls Rd W 285 CH137
Hunton Bridge WD4 off Langleybury La 81 BQ34
Swanley BR8 off School La 229 FH95
St. Paul's Ct, W14 26 D9
St. Pauls Ct, Chipper. WD4 off The Common 80 BG31
St. Pauls Ctyd, SE8 off Mary Ann Gdns 46 A3
ST. PAUL'S CRAY, Orp. BR5 228 EU96
St. Paul's Cray C of E Prim Sch, St.P.Cray BR5 off Buttermere Rd 228 EX97
St. Pauls Cray Rd, Chis. BR7 227 ER95
St. Paul's Cres, NW1 7 P6
St. Pauls Dr, E15 12 G3
St. Paul's Girls' Sch, W6 26 C8
St. Paul's Ms, NW1 7 P6
St. Pauls Ms, Dor. RH4 285 CH137
St. Paul's Pl, N1 9 L4
St. Pauls Pl, Aveley RM15 170 FQ73
St. Albans AL1 65 CG20
St. Paul's Prep Sch, SW13 off Lonsdale Rd 181 CU78
St. Paul's RC Prim Sch, N22 off Bradley Rd 121 DM54
Cheshunt EN7 off Park La 88 DV27
St. Pauls Ri, N13 121 DP51
St. Paul's Rd, N1 8 G5
N17 122 DU52
Barking IG11 167 EQ67
Brentford TW8 179 CK79
Erith DA8 189 FC80
St. Pauls Rd, Hem.H. HP2 62 BK19
St. Paul's Rd, Rich. TW9 180 CM83
Staines-upon-Thames TW18 195 BD92
Thornton Heath CR7 224 DQ97
St. Pauls Rd, Wok. GU22 249 BA117
St. Paul's Rd E, Dor. RH4 285 CH137
St. Pauls Rd W, Dor. RH4 285 CG137
St. Paul's Sch, SW13 off Lonsdale Rd 181 CU78
St. Paul's Shrubbery, N1 9 L4
St. Pauls Sq, Brom. BR2 226 EG96
St. Paul's Ter, SE17 43 H2
St. Paul St, N1 9 J9
St. Pauls Wk, Kings.T. KT2 off Alexandra Rd 200 CN94
St. Pauls Way, E3 21 N7
E14 21 N7
St. Paul's Way, N3 120 DB52
St. Pauls Way, Wal.Abb. EN9 off Rochford Av 89 ED33
Watford WD24 98 BW40
St. Paul's Way Comm Sch, E3 22 A6
St. Paul's with St. Luke's Prim Sch, E3 21 P6
St. Paul's with St. Michael's C of E Prim Sch, E8 10 D8
St. Pauls Wd Hill, Orp. BR5 227 ES96
St. Peter & Paul's Cath Prim Sch, Ilf. IG1 off Gordon Rd 147 ER62
St. Peter & St. Paul Cath Prim Sch, St.P.Cray BR5 off St. Pauls Wd Hill 227 ES96
St. Peter & St. Paul C of E Inf Sch, Chaldon CR3 off Rook La 273 DN125
St. Peter & St. Paul RC Prim Sch, Mitch. CR4 off Cricket Grn 222 DF98
St. Peter & St. Paul's RC Prim Sch, EC1 19 H4
St. Peter Chanel Cath Prim Sch, Sid. DA14 off Baugh Rd 208 EW92
St. Peter in Chains RC Inf Sch, N8 off Elm Gro 143 DL58
St. Peter's All, EC3 19 M9
St. Peter's Av, E2 20 D1
E17 146 EE56
St. Peters Av, N18 122 DU49
Berry's Green TN16 261 EP116
St. Petersburgh Ms, W2 15 L10
St. Petersburgh Pl, W2 15 L10
St. Peter's Catholic Comp Sch, Guil. GU1 off Horseshoe La E 265 BC133
St. Peter's Cath Prim Sch, Dag. RM9 off Goresbrook Rd 168 EZ67
Leatherhead KT22 off Grange Rd 253 CJ120
Romford RM1 off Dorset Av 149 FE55
St. Peter's Cl, E2 20 D1
St. Peters Cl, SW17 202 DE89
St. Peter's Cl, Barn. EN5 101 CV43
Burnham SL1 152 AH70
St. Peters Cl, Bushey Hth WD23 117 CD46
Chalfont St. Peter SL9 off Lewis La 112 AY53
Chislehurst BR7 207 ER94
Hatfield AL10 67 CU17
Ilford IG2 147 ES56
Mill End WD3 114 BH46
Old Windsor SL4 off Church Rd 194 AU85
St. Peter's Cl, Ruis. HA4 138 BX61
St. Peters Cl, St.Alb. AL1 65 CD19
Staines-upon-Thames TW18 195 BF93
Swanscombe DA10 212 FZ87
Woking GU22 249 BC120
St. Peter's C of E Comb Sch, Burn. SL1 off Minniecroft Rd 152 AH69
St. Peter's C of E Inf Sch, Tand. RH8 off Tandridge La 275 EA133
St. Peter's C of E Mid Sch, Old Wind. SL4 off Crimp Hill Rd 194 AT86
St. Peter's C of E Prim Sch, SE17 43 L1
W6 off St. Peter's Rd 181 CU77
W9 15 J5
Mill End WD3 off Church La 114 BH46
South Weald CM14 off Wigley Bush La 130 FS47
St. Peters Ct, Chal.St.P. SL9 off High St 112 AY53
St. Peter's Ct, NW4 141 CW57
St. Peters Ct, SE3 off Eltham Rd 206 EF85
SE4 45 P9
West Molesey KT8 218 CA98
St. Peter's Eaton Sq C of E Prim Sch, SW1 29 K7
St. Peter's Gdns, SE27 203 DN90
St. Peter's Gro, W6 181 CU77
St. Peter's Hosp, Cher. KT16 215 BD104
St. Peters La, St.P.Cray BR5 228 EU96
St. Peters Ms, N4 143 DP57
St. Peter's Pl, W9 15 L5
St. Peter's Prim Sch, E1 32 G2
South Croydon CR2 off Normanton Rd 242 DS107
St. Peter's RC Prim Sch, SE18 37 N10
St. Peters Rd, N9 122 DW46
St. Peter's Rd, W6 181 CU78
Croydon CR0 242 DR105
Grays RM16 193 GH77
St. Peters Rd, Kings.T. KT1 220 CN96
St. Albans AL1 65 CE20
Southall UB1 158 CA71
Twickenham TW1 199 CH85
Uxbridge UB8 156 BK71
Warley CM14 off Crescent Rd 130 FV49
St. Peter's Rd, W.Mol. KT8 218 CA98
St. Peters Rd, Wok. GU22 249 BB121
St. Peter's Sch, St.Alb. AL1 off Cottonmill La 65 CE21
St. Peter's Sq, E2 20 D1
W6 181 CU78
St. Peters St, N1 9 H9
St. Albans AL1 65 CD20
St. Peter's St, S.Croy. CR2 242 DR106
St. Peter's St Ms, N1 9 H10
St. Peters Ter, SW6 38 F5
St. Peter's Vil, W6 181 CT77
St. Peter's Way, N1 9 P7
St. Peters Way, W5 159 CK71
St. Peter's Way, Add. KT15 216 BG104
Chertsey KT16 233 BD105
St. Peters Way, Chorl. WD3 95 BB43
Harlington UB3 177 BR78
St. Philip Howard RC Prim Sch, Hat. AL10 off Woods Av 67 CV18
St. Philip's Av, Wor.Pk. KT4 221 CV103
St. Philips Gate, Wor.Pk. KT4 221 CV103
St. Philip Sq, SW8 41 J8
St. Philip's Rd, E8 10 C5
St. Philips Rd, Surb. KT6 219 CK100
St. Philip's Sch, SW7 27 P9
Chessington KT9 off Harrow Cl 237 CK107
St. Philip St, SW8 41 J10
St. Philip's Way, N1 9 K8
St. Philomena's Cath Prim Sch, Orp. BR5 off Chelsfield Rd 228 EW101
St. Philomena's Sch, Cars. SM5 off Pound St 240 DF106
St. Pinnock Av, Stai. TW18 216 BG95
St. Quentin Ho, SW18 off Fitzhugh Gro 202 DD86
St. Quentin Rd, Well. DA16 187 ET83
St. Quintin Av, W10 14 B7
St. Quintin Gdns, W10 14 A7
St. Quintin Rd, E13 24 A1
St. Raphaels Ct, St.Alb. AL1 off Avenue Rd 65 CE19
St. Raphael's RC Prim Sch, Nthlt. UB5 off Hartfield Av 157 BV68
St. Raphael's Way, NW10 140 CQ64
St. Regis Cl, N10 121 DH54
St. Richard's with St. Andrew's C of E Prim Sch, Rich. TW10 off Ashburnham Rd 199 CH90
St. Robert Southwell Cath Prim Sch, NW9 off Slough La 140 CQ58
St. Ronan's Cl, Barn. EN4 102 DD38
St. Ronans Cres, Wdf.Grn. IG8 124 EG52
St. Ronans Vw, Dart. DA1 210 FM87
St. Rose's Catholic Inf Sch, Hem.H. HP1 off Green End Rd 62 BG22
St. Rule St, SW8 41 L8
St. Saviour's & St. Olave's Sch, SE1 31 M7
St. Saviour's C of E Inf Sch, W5 off The Grove 159 CK74
St. Saviour's C of E Prim Sch, E17 off Verulam Av 145 DZ59
SE24 off Herne Hill Rd 184 DQ83
W9 15 M5
St. Saviours Ct, Har. HA1 139 CD57
St. Saviour's Ct, Pur. CR8 off Old Lo La 241 DM113
St. Saviour's Est, SE1 32 A6
St. Saviours Pl, Guil. GU1 off Leas Rd 264 AW134
St. Saviour's Prim Sch, E14 22 C7
St. Saviour's RC Prim Sch, SE13 off Bonfield Rd 185 EC84
St. Saviour's Rd, SW2 203 DM85
St. Saviours Rd, Croy. CR0 224 DQ100
St. Saviours Vw, St.Alb. AL1 off Summerhill Ct 65 CF19
St. Scholastica's RC Prim Sch, E5 off Kenninghall Rd 144 DU62
Saints Cl, SE27 off Wolfington Rd 203 DP91
Saints Dr, E7 146 EK64
St. Silas Pl, NW5 6 G5
St. Silas St Est, NW5 6 G4
St. Simon's Av, SW15 201 CW85
ST. STEPHENS, St.Alb. AL3 64 CC22
St. Stephens Av, E17 145 EC57
W12 181 CV75
W13 159 CH72
St. Stephen's Av, Ashtd. KT21 254 CL116
St. Stephens Av, St.Alb. AL3 64 CB22
St. Stephen's Cath Prim Sch, Well. DA16 off Deepdene Rd 188 EU82
St. Stephens Cl, E17 145 EB57
NW8 6 D9
St. Albans AL3 64 CB23
Southall UB1 158 CA71
St. Stephen's C of E Jun Sch, Twick. TW1 off Winchester Rd 199 CH86
St. Stephen's C of E Prim Sch, SE8 46 B8
SW8 42 C4
W2 15 K7
W12 26 A4
St. Stephens Cres, W2 15 K8
Brentwood CM13 131 GA49
Thornton Heath CR7 223 DN97
St. Stephens Gdn Est, W2 15 J8

St. Stephens Gdns, SW15
off Manfred Rd 201 CZ85
W2 15 K7
Twickenham TW1 199 CJ86
St. Stephens Gro, SE13 46 F10
St. Stephens Hill, St.Alb. AL1 64 CC22
St. Stephens Ms, W2 15 K7
St. Stephen's Par, E7
off Green St 166 EJ66
St. Stephen's Pas, Twick. TW1
off Richmond Rd 199 CJ86
Sch St. Stephen's Prim Sch, E6
off Whitfield Rd 166 EJ66
St. Stephens Rd, E3 11 N10
E6 166 EJ66
St. Stephen's Rd, E17 145 EB57
St. Stephens Rd, W13 159 CH72
St. Stephen's Rd, Barn. EN5 101 CX43
St. Stephens Rd, Enf. EN3 105 DX37
Hounslow TW3 198 CA86
St. Stephen's Rd, West Dr.
UB7 156 BK74
St. Stephens Row, EC4 19 L9
St. Stephens Ter, SW8 42 C5
St. Stephen's Wk, SW7 27 N8
Saints Wk, Grays RM16 193 GJ77
St. Swithin's La, EC4 19 L10
St. Swithun's Rd, SE13 205 ED85
Sch St. Swithun Wells RC Prim Sch,
Hlgdn HA4 off Hunters Hill 138 BX62
Sch St. Teresa Cath Prim Sch, The,
Dag. RM8 off Bowes Rd 148 EW63
Sch St. Teresa's Cath Prim Sch,
Borwd. WD6 off Brook Rd 100 CP40
Sch St. Teresa's Prep Sch, Dor. RH5
off Effingham Hill 268 BX132
Sch St. Teresa's RC First & Mid Sch,
Har.Wld HA3
off Long Elmes 116 CC53
Sch St. Teresa's RC Prim Sch, Mord.
SM4 off Montacute Rd 222 DD100
Sch St. Teresa's Sch, Dor. RH5
off Effingham Hill 268 BX132
St. Teresa Wk, Grays RM16 193 GH76
St. Theresa Ct, Epsom KT18 238 CQ114
St. Theresa's Cl, E9 145 EA63
Sch St. Theresa's RC Prim Sch, N3
off East End Rd 142 DB55
St. Theresa's Rd, Felt. TW14 177 BT84
Sch St. Thomas à Becket RC Prim
Sch, SE2 off Mottisfont Rd 188 EU76
Sch St. Thomas Becket Cath Prim
Sch, SE25 off Becket Cl 224 DU100
Sch St. Thomas' Catholic Prim Sch,
Sev. TN13 off South Pk 279 FH125
St. Thomas Cl, Chilw. GU4 281 BC140
St. Thomas' Cl, Surb. KT6 220 CM102
St. Thomas Cl, Wok. GU21
off St. Mary's Rd 248 AW117
Sch St. Thomas C of E Prim Sch,
W10 14 F5
St. Thomas Ct, Bex. DA5 208 FA87
St. Thomas Dr, E.Clan. GU4
off The Street 266 BL131
Orpington BR5 227 EQ102
St. Thomas' Dr, Pnr. HA5 116 BY53
St. Thomas Gdns, Ilf. IG1 167 EQ65
H St. Thomas' Hosp, SE1 30 C6
Coll St. Thomas' Med Sch & the
Nightingale Sch, SE1 30 C7
Sch St. Thomas More Cath Prim Sch,
Bexh. DA7
off Sheldon Rd 188 EZ82
Sch St. Thomas More RC Prim Sch,
SE9 off Appleton Rd 186 EL83
Berkhamsted HP4
off Greenway 60 AU19
Sch St. Thomas More RC Sch,
N22 off Glendale Av 121 DN52
SE9 off Footscray Rd 207 EN86
Sch St. Thomas More Sch, SW3 28 E9
Sch St. Thomas of Canterbury
Cath Prim Sch, SW6 38 G4
Grays RM17 off Ward Av 192 GB77
Guildford GU1
off Horseshoe La W 265 BB134
Mitcham CR4
off Commonside E 222 DG97
Sch St. Thomas of Canterbury
C of E Inf & Jun Schs, Brwd.
CM15 off Sawyers Hall La 130 FX45
St. Thomas Rd, E16 23 N8
N14 121 DK45
St. Thomas' Rd, W4 180 CQ79
St. Thomas Rd, Belv. DA17 189 FC75
Brentwood CM14 130 FX47
Northfleet DA11
off St. Margaret's Rd 212 GE89
St. Thomas's Av, Grav. DA11 213 GH88
St. Thomas's Cl, Wal.Abb. EN9 90 EH33
St. Thomas's Gdns, NW5 6 G4
St. Thomas's Ms, SW18
off West Hill 202 DA85
Guil. GU1
off St. Catherines Pk 281 AZ136
St. Thomas's Pl, E9 10 G6
St. Thomas's Rd, N4 143 DN61
NW10 160 CS67
St. Thomas's Sq, E9 10 F6
St. Thomas St, SE1 31 L3
St. Thomas's Way, SW6 38 G4
Sch St. Thomas the Apostle Coll,
SE15 44 G8
St. Thomas Wk, Colnbr. SL3 175 BD80
St. Timothy's Ms, Brom. BR1
off Wharton Rd 226 EH95
St. Ursula Gro, Pnr. HA5 138 BX57
St. Ursula Rd, Sthl. UB1 158 CA72
Sch St. Ursula's Cath Inf Sch,
Harold Hill RM3
off Straight Rd 128 FJ51
Sch St. Ursula's Conv Sch,
SE10 46 G5
Sch St. Ursula's Jun Sch, Harold Hill
RM3 off Straight Rd 127 FH51
St. Vincent Cl, SE27 203 DP92
Sch St. Vincent de Paul RC Prim Sch,
SW1 29 L7
St. Vincent Dr, St.Alb. AL1 65 CG23
St. Vincent Rd, Twick. TW2 198 CC86
Walton-on-Thames KT12 217 BV104
St. Vincents Av, Dart. DA1 210 FN85
Sch St. Vincent's Cath Prim Sch,
SE9 off Harting Rd 206 EL91
Dagenham RM8
off Burnside Rd 148 EW61
ST. VINCENT'S HAMLET, Brwd.
CM14 128 FP46
St. Vincents La, NW7 119 CW50
Sch St. Vincent's RC Prim Sch,
NW7 off The Ridgeway 119 CW50
W1 17 H7
W3 off Pierrepoint Rd 160 CP73
St. Vincents Rd, Dart. DA1 210 FN86
St. Vincent St, W1 17 H7
St. Vincents Way, Pot.B. EN6 86 DC33
St. Wilfrids Cl, Barn. EN4 102 DE43
St. Wilfrids Rd, Barn. EN4 102 DD43
Sch St. William of York RC Prim Sch,
SE23 off Brockley Pk 205 DY88
St. Williams Ct, N1
off Gifford St 8 B7
St. Winefride's Av, E12 147 EM64
Sch St. Winefride's RC Prim Sch,
E12 off Church Rd 147 EM64
St. Winifreds, Ken. CR8 258 DQ115
Sch St. Winifred's Catholic Jun Sch,
SE12 off Newstead Rd 206 EF86
Sch St. Winifred's Catholic Nurs &
Inf Sch, SE12
off Effingham Rd 206 EE85
St. Winifreds Cl, Chig. IG7 125 EQ50
St. Winifred's Rd, Bigg.H.
TN16 261 EM118
Teddington TW11 199 CH93
St. Yon Ct, St.Alb. AL4 65 CK20
Sakins Cft, Harl. CM18 73 ET18
Sakura Dr, N22 121 DK53
Saladin Dr, Purf. RM19 190 FN77
Salamanca Pl, SE1 30 C9
Salamanca St, SE1 30 B9
Salamander Cl, Kings.T. KT2 199 CJ92
Salamander Quay, Hare. UB9 114 BG52
Salamons Way, Rain. RM13 169 FE72
Salbrook Rd, Salf. RH1 288 DG142
Salcombe Dr, Mord. SM4 221 CX102
Romford RM6 148 EZ58
Salcombe Gdns, NW7 119 CW51
Salcombe Pk, Loug. IG10 106 EK43
Sch Salcombe Prep Sch, Inf Dept,
N14 off Green Rd 103 DH43
Jun Dept, N14
off Chase Side 121 DH45
Salcombe Rd, E17 145 DZ59
N16 9 P2
Ashford TW15 196 BL91
Salcombe Vil, Rich. TW10
off The Vineyard 200 CL85
Salcombe Way, Hayes UB4 157 BS69
Ruislip HA4 137 BU61
Salcot Cres, New Adgtn CR0 243 EC110
Salcote Rd, Grav. DA12 213 GL92
Salcott Rd, SW11 202 DE85
Croydon CR0 223 DL104
Salehurst Cl, Har. HA3 140 CL57
Salehurst Rd, SE4 205 DZ86
Salem Pl, Croy. CR0 224 DQ104
Northfleet DA11 212 GD87
Salem Rd, W2 15 M10
Salento Cl, N3 120 DA52
Sale Pl, W2 16 C7
Salesian Gdns, Cher. KT16 216 BG102
Sch Salesian Sch, Cher. KT16
off Highfield Rd 216 BG102
Sale St, E2 20 C4
Salford Rd, SW2 203 DK88
SALFORDS, Red. RH1 288 DF142
⇌ Salfords 288 DG142
Sch Salfords Prim Sch, Salf. RH1
off Copsleigh Av 288 DG140
Salfords Way, Red. RH1 288 DG142
Salhouse Cl, SE28
off Rollesby Way 168 EW72
Salisbury Av, N3 141 CZ55
Barking IG11 167 ER66
St. Albans AL1 65 CH19
Slough SL2 153 AQ70
Sutton SM1 239 CZ107
Swanley BR8 229 FG98
Salisbury Cl, SE17 31 L8
Amersham HP7 77 AS39
Potters Bar EN6 86 DC32
Upminster RM14 151 FT61
Worcester Park KT4 221 CT104
Salisbury Ct, EC4 18 G9
Edgware HA8 118 CM49
Salisbury Cres, Chsht EN8 89 DX32
Salisbury Gdns, SW19 201 CY94
Buckhurst Hill IG9 124 EK47
Welwyn Garden City AL7 51 CZ10
Salisbury Hall Dr, Hat. AL10 66 CR16
Salisbury Hall Gdns, E4 123 EA51
Salisbury Ho, E14 22 C8
Salisbury Ms, SW6 38 G5
Bromley BR2 226 EL99
Salisbury Pl, SW9 43 H5
W1 16 E6
West Byfleet KT14 234 BJ111
Sch Salisbury Prim Sch, E12
off Romford Rd 146 EL64
Salisbury Rd, E4 123 EA48
E7 13 N5
E10 145 EC61
E12 146 EK64
E17 145 EC57
N4 143 DP57
N22 121 DP53
SE25 224 DU100
SW19 201 CY94
W13 179 CG75
Banstead SM7 240 DB114
Barnet EN5 101 CY41
Bexley DA5 208 FA88
Bromley BR2 226 EL99
Carshalton SM5 240 DF107
Dagenham RM10 169 FB65
Dartford DA2 210 FQ88
Enfield EN3 105 DZ37
Feltham TW13 198 BW88
Godstone RH9 274 DW131
Gravesend DA11 213 GF88
Grays RM17 192 GC79
Harrow HA1 139 CD57
Hoddesdon EN11 71 EC15
Hounslow TW4 178 BW83
Ilford IG3 147 ES61
London Heathrow Airport
TW6 197 BQ85
New Malden KT3 220 CR97
Pinner HA5 137 BU56
Richmond TW9 180 CL84
Romford RM2 149 FH57
Southall UB2 178 BY77
Uxbridge UB8 156 BH68
Watford WD24 97 BV38
Welwyn Garden City AL7 51 CZ10
Woking GU22 248 AY119
Worcester Park KT4 221 CT104
Sch Salisbury Sch, Lwr Sch, N9
off Turin Rd 122 DW45
Upr Sch, N9
off Nightingale Rd 122 DW45
Salisbury Sq, EC4 18 F9
Hatfield AL9 off Park St 67 CW17
Hertford SG14
off Railway St 54 DR09
Salisbury St, NW8 16 B5
W3 180 CQ75
Salisbury Ter, SE15 45 H10
Salisbury Wk, N19 143 DJ61
Salix Cl, Fetch. KT22 252 CB123
Sunbury-on-Thames TW16
off Oak Gro 197 BV94
Salix Rd, Grays RM17 192 GD79
Salliesfield, Twick. TW2 199 CD86
Sally Murray Cl, E12 147 EN63
Salmen Rd, E13 23 M1
Salmon Cl, Welw.G.C. AL7 52 DA06
Salmond Cl, Stan. HA7 117 CG51
Salmonds Gro, Ingrave CM13 131 GC50
Salmon La, E14 21 L8
Salmon Meadow Footpath,
Hem.H. HP3 62 BK24
Salmon Rd, Belv. DA17 188 FA78
Dartford DA1 190 FM83
Salmons La, Whyt. CR3 258 DU119
Salmons La W, Cat. CR3 258 DS120
Salmons Rd, N9 122 DU46
Chessington KT9 237 CK107
Effingham KT24 267 BV129
Salmon St, E14 21 N9
NW9 140 CP60
Salomons Rd, E13 24 C6
Salop Rd, E17 145 DX58
Saltash Cl, Sutt. SM1 239 CZ105
Saltash Rd, Ilf. IG6 125 ER52
Welling DA16 188 EW81
Salt Box Hill, Bigg.H. TN16 244 EH113
Salt Box Rd, Guil. GU3, GU4 264 AT129
Saltcoats Rd, W4 180 CS75
Saltcote Cl, Dart. DA1 209 FE86
Saltcroft Cl, Wem. HA9 140 CP60
Salter Cl, Har. HA2 138 BZ62
Salterford Rd, SW17 202 DG93
Saltern Ct, Bark. IG11
off Puffin Cl 168 EV69
Salter Rd, SE16 33 J3
Salters Cl, Berk. HP4 60 AT17
Rickmansworth WD3 114 BL46
Salters Gdns, Wat. WD17 97 BU39
Salters Hall Ct, EC4 19 L10
Salters Hill, SE19 204 DR92
Salters Rd, E17 145 ED56
W10 14 C5
Salter St, E14 22 A10
NW10 161 CU69
Salter St Alleyway, NW10
off Hythe Rd 161 CU70
Salterton Rd, N7 143 DL62
Saltford Cl, Erith DA8 189 FE78
Salt Hill Av, Slou. SL1 153 AQ74
Salthill Cl, Uxb. UB8 136 BL64
Salt Hill Dr, Slou. SL1 153 AQ74
Salt Hill Way, Slou. SL1 153 AQ74
Saltings, The, Green. DA9 191 FW84
Saltley Cl, E6 25 H8
Salton Cl, N3
off East End Rd 120 DA54
Saltoun Rd, SW2 183 DN84
Saltram Cl, N15 144 DT56
Saltram Cres, W9 15 H2
Saltwell St, E14 22 B10
Saltwood Cl, Orp. BR6 246 EW105
Saltwood Gro, SE17 43 L1
Sch Salusbury Prim Sch, NW6 4 G9
Salusbury Rd, NW6 14 G1
Salutation Rd, SE10 35 K8
Sch Salvatorian Coll, Wealds.
HA3 off High St 117 CE54
Salvia Gdns, Perivale UB6 159 CG68
Salvin Rd, SW15 181 CX83
Salway Cl, Wdf.Grn. IG8 124 EF52
Salway Pl, E15 13 H5
Salway Rd, E15 13 H5
Salwey Cres, Brox. EN10 71 DZ20
Samantha Cl, E17 145 DZ59
Samantha Ms, Hav.at.Bow.
RM4 127 FE48
Sam Bartram Cl, SE7 36 D10
Sambrook Ho, SE11 30 E9
Sambruck Ms, SE6 205 EB88
Samels Ct, W6
off South Black Lion La 181 CU78
Samford Ho, N1 8 E9
Samford St, NW8 16 B5
Samian Gate, St.Alb. AL3 64 BZ22
Samira Cl, E17
off Colchester Rd 145 DZ58
Samos Rd, SE20 224 DV96
Samphire Ct, Grays RM17
off Salix Rd 192 GE79
Sample Oak La, Chilw. GU4 281 BE140
Sampson Av, Barn. EN5 101 CX43
Sampson Cl, Belv. DA17
off Carrill Way 188 EX76
Sampsons Ct, Shep. TW17
off Linden Way 217 BQ99
Sampsons Grn, Slou. SL2 153 AM69
Sampson St, E1 32 D3
Samson St, E13 24 C1
Samuel Cl, E8 10 B8
SE14 45 J3
SE18 37 H8
Stanmore HA7 117 CG47
Samuel Gray Gdns, Kings.T.
KT2 219 CK95
Samuel Johnson Cl, SW16 203 DM91
Samuel Lewis Trust Dws, N1 8 F5
SW3 28 C9
SW6 39 K4
W14 26 F8
Samuel Lewis Trust Est, SE5
off Warner Rd 43 K7
Samuels Ct, W6 181 CU78
Samuel Sq, St.Alb. AL1
off Pageant Rd 65 CD21
Samuel St, SE15 44 A4
SE18 37 J8
Sancroft Cl, NW2 141 CV62
Sancroft Rd, Har. HA3 117 CF54
Sancroft St, SE11 30 D10
Sanctuary, The, SW1 29 P5
Bexley DA5 208 EX86
Morden SM4 222 DA100
Sanctuary Cl, Dart. DA1 210 FJ86
Harefield UB9 114 BJ52
Sanctuary Ms, E8 10 B5
Sanctuary Rd, Lon.Hthrw Air.
TW6 196 BN86
Sanctuary St, SE1 31 K5
Sandall Cl, W5 160 CL70
Sandall Ho, E3 11 M10
Sandall Rd, NW5 7 M5
W5 160 CL70
Sandalls Spring, Hem.H. HP1 61 BF18
Sandal Rd, N18 122 DU50
New Malden KT3 220 CR99
Sandal St, E15 13 J8
Sandalwood, Guil. GU2 280 AV135
Sandalwood Av, Cher. KT16 215 BD104
Sandalwood Cl, E1 21 L5
Sandalwood Dr, Ruis. HA4 137 BQ59
Sandalwood Rd, Felt. TW13 197 BV90
Sanday Cl, Hem.H. HP3 63 BP22
Sandbach Pl, SE18 187 EQ78
Sandbanks, Felt. TW14 197 BS88
Sandbanks Hill, Bean DA2 211 FV93
Sandbourne Av, SW19 222 DB97
Sandbourne Rd, SE4 45 L8
Sandbrook Cl, NW7 118 CR51
Sandbrook Rd, N16 144 DS62
Sandby Grn, SE9 186 EL83
Sandcliff Rd, Erith DA8 189 FD77
Sandcroft Cl, N13 121 DP51
Sandcross La, Reig. RH2 287 CZ137
Sch Sandcross Sch, Reig. RH2
off Sandcross La 287 CZ137
Sandells Av, Ashf. TW15 197 BQ91
Sandell St, SE1 30 E4
Sandels Way, Beac. HP9 111 AK51
Sandelswood End, Beac. HP9 111 AK50
Sandelswood Gdns, Beac.
HP9 111 AK51
Sandeman Gdns, Ware SG12 55 DY05
Sanderling Way, Green. DA9 211 FU85
Sanders Cl, Hmptn H. TW12 199 CC92
Hemel Hempstead HP3 62 BM24
London Colney AL2 83 CK27
Sanders Ct, Brwd. CM14 130 FW49
Sch Sanders Draper Sch, The,
Horn. RM12
off Suttons La 150 FK63
Sandersfield Gdns, Bans.
SM7 256 DA115
Sandersfield Rd, Bans. SM7 256 DB115
Sanders La, NW7 119 CX52
Sanderson Cl, NW5 7 J1
Sanderson Rd, Uxb. UB8 156 BJ65
Sandersons Av, Bad.Mt TN14 246 FA110
Sanderson Sq, Brom. BR1 227 EN97
Sanders Pl, St.Alb. AL1 65 CG21
Sanders Rd, Hem.H. HP3 62 BM23
SANDERSTEAD, S.Croy. CR2 242 DT111
⇌ Sanderstead 242 DR109
Sanderstead Av, NW2 141 CY61
Sanderstead Cl, SW12 203 DJ87
Sanderstead Ct Av, S.Croy.
CR2 242 DU113
Sanderstead Hill, S.Croy. CR2 242 DS111
Sanderstead Rd, E10 145 DY60
Orpington BR5 228 EV100
South Croydon CR2 242 DR108
Sanders Way, N19
off Sussex Way 143 DK60
Sandes Pl, Lthd. KT22 253 CG118
Sandfield Gdns, Th.Hth. CR7 223 DP97
Sandfield Pas, Th.Hth. CR7 224 DQ97
Sch Sandfield Prim Sch, Guil.
GU1 off York Rd 280 AX135
Sandfield Rd, St.Alb. AL1 65 CG20
Thornton Heath CR7 223 DP97
Sandfields, Send GU23 249 BD124
Sandfield Ter, Guil. GU1 280 AX135
Sandford Av, N22 122 DQ52
Loughton IG10 107 EQ41
Sandford Cl, E6 25 J4
Sandford Ct, N16 144 DS60
Sandford Rd, E6 25 H2
Bexleyheath DA7 188 EY84
Bromley BR2 226 EG98
Sandford St, SW6 39 M5
Sandgate Cl, Rom. RM7 149 FD59
Sandgate Ho, E5 10 F1
W5 159 CJ71
Sandgate La, SW18 202 DE88
Sandgate Rd, Well. DA16 188 EW80
Sandgates, Cher. KT16 215 BE103
Sandgate St, SE15 44 E2
Sandham Pt, SE18 37 P9
Sandhills, Wall. SM6 241 DK105
Sandhills, The, SW10
off Limerston St 39 P2
Sandhills Ct, Vir.W. GU25 214 AY99
Sandhills La, Vir.W. GU25 214 AY99
Sandhills Meadow, Shep.
TW17 217 BQ101
Sandhills Rd, Reig. RH2 288 DA136
Sandhurst Av, Har. HA2 138 CB58
Surbiton KT5 220 CP101
Sandhurst Cl, NW9 140 CN55
South Croydon CR2 242 DS109
Sandhurst Dr, Ilf. IG3 147 ET63
Sch Sandhurst Inf & Jun Schs,
SE6 off Minard Rd 206 EE88
Sandhurst Rd, N9 104 DW44
NW9 140 CN55
SE6 205 ED88
Bexley DA5 208 EX85
Orpington BR6 228 EU104
Sidcup DA15 207 ET90
Tilbury RM18 193 GJ82
Sandhurst Way, S.Croy. CR2 242 DS108
Sandifer Dr, NW2 141 CX62
Sandifield, Hat. AL10 67 CU21
Sandiford Rd, Sutt. SM3 221 CZ103
Sandiland Cres, Brom. BR2 226 EF103
Tra Sandilands 224 DT103
Sandilands, Croy. CR0 224 DU103
Sevenoaks TN13 278 FD122
Sandilands Rd, SW6 39 L7
Sandison St, SE15 44 B10
Sandlands Gro, Walt.Hill KT20 255 CU123
Sandlands Rd, Walt.Hill KT20 255 CU123
Sandland St, WC1 18 D7
Sandlers End, Slou. SL2 153 AP70
Sandlewood Cl, Barn. EN5 101 CT43
Sandling Ri, SE9 207 EN90
Sandlings, The, N22 121 DN54
Sandlings Cl, SE15 44 E9
Sandmartin Way, Wall. SM6 222 DG101
Sandmere Cl, Hem.H. HP2
off St. Albans Rd 62 BN21
Sandmere Rd, SW4 183 DL84
Sandon Cl, Esher KT10 219 CD101
Sandon Rd, Chsht EN8 88 DW30
Sandow Cres, Hayes UB3 177 BT76
Sandown Av, Dag. RM10 169 FC65
Esher KT10 236 CC106
Hornchurch RM12 150 FK61
Sandown Cl, Houns. TW5 177 BU81
Sandown Ct, Sutt. SM2
off Grange Rd 240 DB108
Sandown Dr, Cars. SM5 240 DG109
Sandown Gate, Esher KT10 218 CC104
● Sandown Ind Pk, Esher
KT10 218 CA103
★ Sandown Park Racecourse,
Esher KT10 218 CB104
Sandown Rd, SE25 224 DV99
Coulsdon CR5 256 DG116
Esher KT10 236 CC105
Gravesend DA12 213 GJ93
Slough SL2 153 AM71
Watford WD24 98 BW38
● Sandown Rd Ind Est, Wat.
WD24 98 BW37
Sandown Way, Nthlt. UB5 158 BY65
Sandpiper Cl, E17 123 DX53
SE16 33 N4
Greenhithe DA9 211 FU85
Sandpiper Ct, E14
off Stewart St 34 F6
Sandpiper Dr, Erith DA8 189 FH80
Sandpiper Ho, West Dr. UB7
off Wraysbury Dr 156 BK73
Sandpiper Rd, S.Croy. CR2 243 DX111
Sutton SM1 239 CZ106
Sandpipers, The, Grav. DA12 213 GK89
Sandpiper Way, Orp. BR5 228 EX98
Sandpit Hall Rd, Chobham
GU24 232 AU112
Sandpit La, Brwd.
CM14, CM15 130 FT46
St. Albans AL1, AL4 65 CJ18
Sandpit Pl, SE7 37 H10
Sandpit Rd, Brom. BR1 206 EE92
Dartford DA1 190 FJ84
Redhill RH1 288 DE135
Welwyn Garden City AL7 51 CY11
Sandpits La, Penn HP10 110 AC48
Sandpits Rd, Croy. CR0 243 DX105
Richmond TW10 199 CK89
Sandra Cl, N22 122 DQ53
Hounslow TW3 198 CB85
Sandridgebury La, St.Alb. AL3 65 CE16
Sandridge Cl, Barn. EN4 102 DE37
Harrow HA1 139 CE56
● Sandridge Gate Business Cen,
St.Alb. AL4 65 CF16
● Sandridge Pk, Port.Wd AL3 65 CF15
Sandridge Rd, St.Alb. AL1 65 CE18
Sandridge St, N19 143 DJ61
Sandringham Av, SW20 221 CY95
Harlow CM19 72 EL15
Sandringham Cl, SW19 201 CX88
Enfield EN1 104 DS40
Ilford IG6 147 EQ55
Woking GU22 250 BG116
Sandringham Ct, W9 15 P3
Kingston upon Thames KT2
off Skerne Wk 219 CK95
Slough SL1 153 AK72
Sandringham Cres, Har. HA2 138 CA61
St. Albans AL4 65 CJ15
Sandringham Dr, Ashf. TW15 196 BK91
Dartford DA2 209 FE89
Welling DA16 187 ES82
Sandringham Flats, WC2
off Charing Cross Rd 17 P10
Sandringham Gdns, N8 143 DL58
N12 120 DC51
Hounslow TW5 177 BU81
Ilford IG6 147 EQ55
West Molesey KT8 218 CA98
Sandringham Lo, Hodd. EN11
off Taverners Way 71 EA17
Sandringham Ms, W5
off High St 159 CK73
Hampton TW12 218 BZ95
Sandringham Pk, Cob. KT11 236 BZ112
Sch Sandringham Prim Sch, E7
off Sandringham Rd 146 EJ64
Sandringham Rd, E7 146 EJ64
E8 10 A3
E10 145 ED58
N22 144 DQ55
NW2 161 CV65
NW11 141 CY59
Barking IG11 167 ET65
Bromley BR1 206 EG92
London Heathrow Airport
TW6 196 BL85
Northolt UB5 158 CA66
Pilgrim's Hatch CM15 130 FV43
Potters Bar EN6 86 DB30
Thornton Heath CR7 224 DQ99
Watford WD24 98 BW37
Worcester Park KT4 221 CU104
Sch Sandringham Sch, St.Alb.
AL4 off The Ridgeway 65 CH16
Sandringham Way, Wal.Cr. EN8 89 DX34
Sandrock Pl, Croy. CR0 243 DX105
Sandrock Rd, SE13 46 B10
Westcott RH4 284 CB138
Sandroyd Way, Cob. KT11 236 CA113
SANDS END, SW6 39 N7
Sand's End La, SW6 39 M6
Sands Fm Dr, Burn. SL1 152 AJ70
Sandstone La, E16 24 B10
Sandstone Pl, N19 143 DH61
Sandstone Rd, SE12 206 EH89
Sands Way, Wdf.Grn. IG8 124 EL51
Sandtoft Rd, SE7 186 EH79
Sandway Path, St.M.Cray BR5
off Okemore Gdns 228 EW98
Sandway Rd, Orp. BR5 228 EW98
Sandwell Cres, NW6 5 K4
Sandwich St, WC1 18 A3
Sandwick Cl, NW7 119 CU52
Sandy Bk Rd, Grav. DA12 213 GH88
Sandy Bury, Orp. BR6 227 ER104
Sandy Cl, Hert. SG14 53 DP09
Woking GU22 off Sandy La 249 BC117
Sandycombe Rd, Felt. TW14 197 BU88
Richmond TW9 180 CN83
Sandycoombe Rd, Twick. TW1 199 CJ86
Sandycroft, SE2 188 EU79

Sandy Cft, Epsom KT17 239 CW110
Sandycroft Rd, Amer. HP6 94 AV39
Sandy Dr, Cob. KT11 236 CA111
Feltham TW14 197 BS88
Sandy Gro, Borwd. WD6 100 CM40
Sandy Hill Av, SE18 187 EP78
Sandy Hill Rd, SE18 37 N9
Sandyhill Rd, Ilf. IG1 147 EP63
Sandy Hill Rd, Wall. SM6 241 DJ109
Sandy La, Alb.Hth GU5 282 BJ141
Aveley RM15 170 FM73
Bean DA2 211 FW89
Betchworth RH3 286 CS135
Bletchingley RH1 273 DP132
Bushey WD23 98 CC41
Chadwell St. Mary RM16 193 GH79
Chobham GU24 232 AS109
Cobham KT11 236 CA112
Guildford GU3 280 AU139
Harrow HA3 140 CM58
Kingston upon Thames KT1 199 CG94
Kingswood KT20 256 DA123
Leatherhead KT22 236 CA112
Limpsfield RH8 276 EH127
Mitcham CR4 222 DG95
Northwood HA6 115 BU50
Orpington BR6 228 EU101
Oxted RH8 275 EC129
Pyrford GU22 249 BF117
Reigate RH2 287 CW135
Richmond TW10 199 CJ89
St. Paul's Cray BR5 228 EX95
Send GU23 249 BC123
Sevenoaks TN13 279 FJ123
Shere GU5 282 BN139
Sidcup DA14 208 EX94
South Nutfield RH1 289 DK135
Sutton SM2 239 CY108
Teddington TW11 199 CG94
Virginia Water GU25 214 AY98
Walton-on-Thames KT12 217 BV100
Watford WD25 98 CC41
West Thurrock RM20
off London Rd W Thurrock 191 FV79
Westerham TN16 277 ER125
Woking GU22 249 BC116
Sandy La Caravan Site, Wat. WD25
off Sandy La 98 CC41
Sandy La Est, Rich. TW10 199 CK89
Sandy La N, Wall. SM6 241 DK107
Sandy La S, Wall. SM6 241 DK107
Sandy Lo, Nthwd. HA6 115 BS47
Sandy Lo La, Nthwd. HA6 115 BR47
Sandy Lo Rd, Rick. WD3 115 BP47
Sandy Lo Way, Nthwd. HA6 115 BS50
Sandy Mead, Epsom KT19 238 CN109
Maidenhead SL6 172 AC78
Sandymount Av, Stan. HA7 117 CJ50
Sandy Ridge, Chis. BR7 207 EN93
Sandy Ri, Chal.St.P. SL9 112 AY53
Sandy Rd, NW3 142 DB62
Addlestone KT15 234 BG107
Sandys Ct, Hounslow TW4
off Bath Rd 178 BY82
Sandy's Row, E1 19 P7
Sandy Way, Cob. KT11 236 CA112
Croydon CR0 225 DZ104
Walton-on-Thames KT12 217 BT102
Woking GU22 249 BC117
Sanfoin End, Hem.H. HP2 62 BN18
Sanford La, N16
off Lawrence Bldgs 144 DT61
Sanford St, SE14 45 L3
Sanford Ter, N16 144 DT62
Sanford Wk, N16
off Sanford Ter 144 DT61
SE14 45 L3
Sangam Cl, Sthl. UB2 178 BY76
Sanger Av, Chess. KT9 238 CL106
Sanger Dr, Send GU23 249 BC123
Sangers Dr, Horl. RH6 290 DF148
Sangers Wk, Horl. RH6
off Sangers Dr 290 DF148
Sangley Rd, SE6 205 EB87
SE25 224 DS98
Sangora Rd, SW11 182 DD84
San Ho, E9 11 K5
San Juan Dr, Chaff.Hun.
RM16 191 FW77
San Luis Dr, Chaff.Hun. RM16 191 FW77
San Marcos Dr, Chaff.Hun.
RM16 191 FW77
Sansom Rd, E11 146 EE61
Sansom St, SE5 43 M5
Sans Wk, EC1 18 F4
Santers La, Pot.B. EN6 85 CY33
Santiago Way, Chaff.Hun.
RM16 191 FX78
Santley St, SW4 183 DM84
Santos Rd, SW18 202 DA85
Santway, The, Stan. HA7 117 CE50
Sanway Cl, Byfleet KT14 234 BL114
Sanway Rd, Byfleet KT14 234 BL114
● Sapcote Trd Cen, NW10 141 CT64
Saperton Wk, SE11 30 D8
Sapho Pk, Grav. DA12 213 GM91
Saphora Cl, Orp. BR6 245 ER106
Sappers Cl, Saw. CM21 58 EZ05
Sapperton Ct, EC1 19 J4
Sapphire Cl, E6 25 K8
Dagenham RM8 148 EW60
Sapphire Ct, NW9
off Ruby Way 119 CT53
Sapphire Rd, NW10 160 CQ66
SE8 33 M9
Sappho Ct, Wok. GU21
off Langmans Way 248 AS116
Saracen Cl, Croy. CR0 224 DR100
● Saracen Ind Area, Hem.H.
HP2 63 BP18
Saracens Head, Hem.H. HP2
off Adeyfield Rd 62 BN19
Saracen's Head Yd, EC3 19 P9
★ Saracens RFC, Wat. WD18 97 BV43
Saracen St, E14 22 B9
Sara Ct, Beck. BR3 225 EB95
Sara Cres, Green. DA9 191 FU84
Sch Sarah Bonnell Sch, E15 13 K5
Sarah Ho, SW15 181 CT84
Sara Ho, Erith DA8
off Larner Rd 189 FE80
Sara La Ct, N1 off Stanway St 9 P10
Sara Pk, Grav. DA12 213 GL91
Saratoga Rd, E5 144 DW63
● Sarbir Ind Pk, Harl. CM20 58 EW10
Sardinia St, WC2 18 C9
Sarel Way, Horl. RH6 291 DH146
Sargeant Cl, Uxb. UB8 156 BK69
Sarita Cl, Har. HA3 117 CD54
Sarjant Path, SW19
off Queensmere Rd 201 CX89
Sark Cl, Houns. TW5 178 CA80
Sark Ho, N1 off Clifton Rd 9 K5
Enfield EN3
off Eastfield Rd 105 DX38
Sark Twr, SE28 187 EQ75
Sark Wk, E16 24 B8
Sarnesfield Ho, SE15 44 E3
Sarnesfield Rd, Enf. EN2
off Church St 104 DR41
SARRATT, Rick. WD3 96 BG35
Sarratt Bottom, Sarratt WD3 95 BE36
Sch Sarratt C of E Sch, Sarratt
WD3 off The Green 96 BG36
Sarratt La, Rick. WD3 96 BH40
Sarratt Rd, Rick. WD3 96 BM41
Sarre Av, Horn. RM12 170 FJ65
Sarre Rd, NW2 4 G2
Orpington BR5 228 EW99
Sarsby Dr, Stai. TW19 195 BA89
Sarsen Av, Houns. TW3 178 BZ82
Sarsfeld Rd, SW12 202 DF88
Sarsfield Rd, Perivale UB6 159 CH68
Sartor Rd, SE15 185 DX84
● Sarum Complex, Uxb.
UB8 156 BH68
Sarum Grn, Wey. KT13 217 BS104
Sch Sarum Hall Sch, NW3 6 C6
Sarum Pl, Hem.H. HP2 62 BL16
Sarum Ter, E3 21 N5
Satanita Cl, E16 24 E8
Satchell Mead, NW9 119 CT53
Satchwell Rd, E2 20 C3
Satinwood Ct, Hem.H. HP3 62 BL22
Satis Ct, Epsom KT17 239 CT111
Sattar Ms, N16
off Clissold Rd 144 DR62
Saturn Ho, E3
off Garrison Rd 12 A9
Saturn Way, Hem.H. HP2 62 BM18
Sauls Grn, E11 off Napier Rd 146 EE62
Saunder Cl, Chsht EN8
off Welsummer Way 89 DX27
Saunders Cl, E14 21 P10
Ilford IG1 147 ER60
Northfleet DA11 212 GE89
Saunders Copse, Wok. GU22 248 AV122
Saunders La, Wok. GU22 248 AS122
Saunders Ness Rd, E14 34 F10
Saunders Rd, SE18 187 ET78
Uxbridge UB10 156 BM66
Saunders St, SE11 30 E9
Saunders Way, SE28
off Oriole Way 168 EV73
Dartford DA1 210 FM89
Saunderton Rd, Wem. HA0 139 CH64
Saunton Av, Hayes UB3 177 BT80
Saunton Rd, Horn. RM12 149 FG61
Savage Gdns, E6 25 K9
EC3 19 P10
Savannah Cl, SE15 44 A5
Savay Cl, Denh. UB9 136 BG59
Savay La, Denh. UB9 136 BG58
Savera Cl, Sthl. UB2 178 BW76
Savernake Rd, N9 104 DU44
NW3 6 F1
Savery Dr, Long Dit. KT6 219 CJ101
Savile Cl, N.Mal. KT3 220 CS99
Thames Ditton KT7 219 CF102
Savile Gdns, Croy. CR0 224 DT103
Savile Row, W1 17 L10
Savill Cl, Chsht EN7
off Markham Rd 88 DQ25
Saville Cl, Epsom KT19 238 CP111
Saville Cres, Ashf. TW15 197 BR93
Saville Ho, E16 off Robert St 37 N3
Saville Rd, E16 37 H3
W4 180 CR76
Romford RM6 148 EZ58
Twickenham TW1 199 CF88
Saville Row, Brom. BR2 226 EF102
Enfield EN3 105 DX40
Savill Gdns, SW20
off Bodnant Gdns 221 CU97
Savill Ms, Eng.Grn TW20 194 AX93
Savill Row, Wdf.Grn. IG8 124 EF51
Savona Cl, SW19 201 CY94
Savona Est, SW8 41 L5
Savona St, SW8 41 L5
Savoy Av, Hayes UB3 177 BS78
Savoy Bldgs, WC2 30 C1
Jct Savoy Circ, W3 161 CT73
Savoy Cl, E15 13 J8
Edgware HA8 118 CN50
Harefield UB9 114 BK54
Savoy Ct, Har. HA2
off Station Rd 138 CB57
WC2 30 B1
Savoy Hill, WC2 30 C1
Savoy Ms, SW9 42 A9
St. Albans AL1 64 CB23
Savoy Pl, W12 off Bourbon La 26 C3
WC2 30 B1
Savoy Rd, Dart. DA1 210 FK85
Savoy Row, WC2 18 C10
Savoy Steps, WC2
off Savoy Row 30 C1
Savoy St, WC2 18 C10
Savoy Way, WC2 30 C1
Savoy Wd, Harl. CM19 73 EN20
Sawbill Cl, Hayes UB4 158 BX71
SAWBRIDGEWORTH, CM21 58 EW05
Sawells, Brox. EN10 71 DZ21
Sawkins Cl, SW19 201 CY89
Sawley Rd, W12 161 CU74
Saw Mill Way, N16 144 DU58
Sawmill Yd, E3 11 M9
Sawpit La, E.Clan. GU4 266 BL131
Sawtry Cl, Cars. SM5 222 DD101
Sawtry Way, Borwd. WD6 100 CN38
Sawyer Cl, N9 122 DU47
Sawyers Chase, Abridge RM4 108 EV41
Sawyers Cl, Dag. RM10 169 FC65
Windsor SL4 173 AL80
Sawyers Ct, Wal.Cr. EN8
off Sturlas Way 89 DY33
Sawyers Gro, Brwd. CM15 130 FX46
Coll Sawyers Hall Coll of Science &
Tech, The, Brwd. CM15
off Sawyers Hall La 130 FW45
Sawyers Hall La, Brwd. CM15 130 FW45
Sawyer's Hill, Rich. TW10 200 CP87
Sawyers La, Els. WD6 99 CH40
Potters Bar EN6 85 CX34
Sawyers Lawn, W13 159 CF72
Sawyer St, SE1 31 J4
Sawyers Way, Hem.H. HP2 62 BM20
Saxby Rd, SW2 203 DL87
Saxham Rd, Bark. IG11 167 ES68
Saxley, Horl. RH6
off Ewelands 291 DJ147
Saxlingham Rd, E4 123 ED48
Saxon Av, Felt. TW13 198 BZ89
Saxonbury Av, Sun. TW16 217 BV97
Saxonbury Cl, Mitch. CR4 222 DD97
Saxonbury Gdns, Long Dit.
KT6 219 CJ102
Saxon Cl, E17 145 EA59
Amersham HP6 77 AR38
Brentwood CM13 131 GA48
Northfleet DA11 212 GC90
Otford TN14 263 FF117
Romford RM3 128 FM54
Slough SL3 175 AZ75
Surbiton KT6 219 CK100
Uxbridge UB8 156 BM71
Saxon Ct, Borwd. WD6 100 CL40
Whyteleafe CR3
off Godstone Rd 258 DU119
Saxon Dr, W3 160 CP72
Saxonfield Cl, SW2 203 DM87
Saxon Gdns, Sthl. UB1 158 BY73
Taplow SL6 152 AD70
Saxon Pl, Hort.Kir. DA4 230 FQ99
Sch Saxon Prim Sch,
Shep. TW17
off Briar Rd 216 BN99
Saxon Rd, E3 21 N1
E6 25 J5
N22 121 DP53
SE25 224 DR99
Ashford TW15 197 BR93
Bromley BR1 206 EF94
Hawley DA2 210 FL91
Ilford IG1 167 EP65
Kingston upon Thames KT2 220 CL95
Southall UB1 158 BY74
Walton-on-Thames KT12 218 BX104
Wembley HA9 140 CQ62
Saxons, Tad. KT20 255 CX121
Saxon Shore Way, Grav. DA12 213 GM86
Saxon Ter, SE6
off Neuchatel Rd 205 DZ89
Saxon Wk, Sid. DA14 208 EW93
Saxon Way, N14 103 DK44
Harmondsworth UB7 176 BJ79
Old Windsor SL4 194 AV86
Reigate RH2 271 CZ133
Waltham Abbey EN9 89 EC33
Saxony Par, Hayes UB3 157 BQ71
Saxton Cl, SE13 185 ED83
Saxton Ms, Wat. WD17 97 BU40
Saxville Rd, Orp. BR5 228 EV97
Sayer Cl, Green. DA9 211 FU85
Sayers Cl, Fetch. KT22 252 CC124
Sayers Gdns, Berk. HP4 60 AU16
Sayers Wk, Rich. TW10
off Stafford Pl 200 CM87
Sayesbury La, N18 122 DU50
Sayesbury Rd, Saw. CM21 58 EX05
Sayes Ct, SE8 45 P2
Addlestone KT15 234 BJ106
Sayes Ct Fm Dr, Add. KT15 234 BH106
Sch Sayes Ct Jun Sch, Add. KT15
off Sayes Ct Fm Dr 234 BH106
Sayes Ct Rd, Orp. BR5 228 EU98
Sayes Ct St, SE8 45 P2
Sayes Gdns, Saw. CM21 58 EZ05
Sayward Cl, Chesh. HP5 76 AR29
Scadbury Gdns, Orp. BR5 228 EU96
Scadbury Pk, Chis. BR7 207 ET93
Scads Hill Cl, Orp. BR6 227 ET100
Scafell Rd, Slou. SL2 153 AM71
Scala St, W1 17 M6
Scales Rd, N17 144 DT55
Scammell Way, Wat. WD18 97 BT44
Scampston Ms, W10 14 D8
Scandrett St, E1 32 E3
Scarab Cl, E16 35 L1
Scarba Wk, N1 9 L5
Scarborough Cl, Bigg.H. TN16 260 EJ118
Sutton SM2 239 CZ111
Scarborough Dr, Crox.Grn WD3 97 BP42
Scarborough Rd, E11 145 ED60
N4 143 DN59
N9 122 DW45
London Heathrow Airport TW6
off Southern Perimeter Rd 197 BQ86
Scarborough St, E1 20 B9
Scarborough Way, Slou. SL1 173 AP75
Scarbrook Rd, Croy. CR0 224 DQ104
Sch Scargill Inf & Jun Schs, Rain.
RM13 off Mungo Pk Rd 169 FG65
Scarle Rd, Wem. HA0 159 CK65
Scarlet Cl, St.P.Cray BR5 228 EV98
Scarlet Rd, SE6 206 EE90
Scarlett Cl, Wok. GU21 248 AT118
Scarlette Manor Way, SW2
off Papworth Way 203 DN87
Scarsbrook Rd, SE3 186 EK83
Scarsdale Pl, W8 27 L6
Scarsdale Rd, Har. HA2 138 CC62
Scarsdale Vil, W8 27 K7
Scarth Rd, SW13 181 CT83
Scatterdells La, Chipper. WD4 79 BF30
Scawen Cl, Cars. SM5 240 DG105
Scawen Rd, SE8 45 L1
Scawfell St, E2 20 B1
Scaynes Link, N12 120 DA50
Sceaux Gdns, SE5 43 P6
Sceptre Rd, E2 21 H3
Uni Schiller Int Uni, SE1 30 E3
Schofield Wk, SE3
off Dornberg Cl 186 EH80
Scholars Cl, Barn. EN5 101 CY42
Scholars Ms, Welw.G.C. AL8 51 CX07
Scholars Pl, N16 144 DS62
Scholars Rd, E4 123 EC46
SW12 203 DJ88
Scholars Wk, Chal.St.P. SL9 112 AY51
Guildford GU2 280 AV135
Hatfield AL10 67 CU21
Langley SL3 175 BA75
Scholars Way, Amer. HP6 94 AT38
Dagenham RM9 148 EU63
Romford RM2 149 FG57
Scholefield Rd, N19 143 DK60
Schomberg Ho, SW1
off Page St 29 P8
Schonfeld Sq, N16 144 DR61
Schoolbank Rd, SE10 35 L8
Schoolbell Ms, E3 21 M1
School Cl, Chesh. HP5 76 AP28
Essendon AL9
off School La 68 DF17
Guildford GU1 264 AX132
School Cres, Cray. DA1 189 FF84
Schoolfield Rd, Grays RM20 191 FU79
School Gdns, Pott.End HP4 61 BB17
Schoolgate Dr, Mord. SM4 222 DB99
School Grn La, N.Wld Bas.
CM16 93 FC25
School Hill, Merst. RH1 273 DJ128
Schoolhouse Gdns, Loug.
IG10 107 EP42
Schoolhouse La, E1 21 J10
School Ho La, Tedd. TW11 199 CH94
Schoolhouse Yd, SE18
off Bloomfield Rd 187 EP78
School La, Add. KT15 234 BG105
Amersham Old Town HP7 77 AM39
Bean DA2 211 FW90
Bricket Wood AL2 82 CA31
Bushey WD23 116 CB45
Caterham CR3 274 DT126
Chalfont St. Giles HP8 112 AV47
Chalfont St. Peter SL9 112 AX54
Chigwell IG7 125 ET49
East Clandon GU4 266 BL131
Egham TW20 195 BA92
Essendon AL9 68 DE17
Fetcham KT22 253 CD122
Harlow CM20 57 ES12
Hatfield AL10 67 CV17
Horton Kirby DA4 230 FQ98
Kingston upon Thames KT1
off School Rd 219 CJ95
Longfield DA3 231 FT100
Magdalen Laver CM5 75 FD17
Mickleham RH5 269 CJ127
Ockham GU23 251 BP122
Pinner HA5 138 BY56
Seal TN15 279 FM121
Seer Green HP9 111 AR51
Shepperton TW17 217 BP100
Slough SL2 154 AT73
Stoke Poges SL2 154 AV67
Surbiton KT6 220 CN102
Swanley BR8 229 FH95
Tewin AL6 52 DE06
Walton on the Hill KT20
off Chequers La 271 CU125
Welling DA16 188 EV83
West Horsley KT24 267 BP129
Westcott RH4 285 CD137
School Mead, Abb.L. WD5 81 BS32
School Meadow, Guil. GU2 264 AS132
Coll School of Economic Science,
W1 17 H8
Coll School of Horticulture, Rich.
TW9 off Kew Grn 180 CM80
Uni School of Oriental & African
Studies, Russell Sq Campus,
WC1 17 P5
Vernon Sq Campus, WC1 18 D2
Uni School of Pharmacy, WC1 18 B4
Sch School of the Islamic
Republic of Iran, The,
NW6 15 J1
School Pas, Kings.T. KT1 220 CM96
Southall UB1 158 BZ74
School Rd, E12 off Sixth Av 147 EM63
NW10 160 CR70
Ashford TW15 197 BP93
Chislehurst BR7 227 EQ95
Dagenham RM10 168 FA67
East Molesey KT8 219 CD98
Hampton Hill TW12 198 CC93
Harmondsworth UB7 176 BK79
Hounslow TW3 178 CC83
Kingston upon Thames KT1 219 CJ95
Ongar CM5 93 FG32
Penn HP10 110 AC47
Potters Bar EN6 86 DC30
Wooburn Green HP10 132 AE57
School Rd Av, Hmptn H. TW12 198 CC93
School Row, Hem.H. HP1 61 BF21
School Sq, SE10
off Greenroof Way 35 M7
School Wk, Horl. RH6
off Thornton Cl 290 DE148
Slough SL2
off Grasmere Av 154 AV73
Sunbury-on-Thames TW16 217 BT98
School Way, N12 120 DC49
Schoolway, N12
(Woodhouse Rd) 120 DD51
School Way, Dag. RM8 148 EW62
Schooner Cl, E14 34 G7
SE16 33 J4
Barking IG11 168 EV69
Schooner Ct, Dart. DA2 190 FQ84
Schrier, Bark. IG11
off Ripple Rd 167 EQ66
Schroder Ct, Eng.Grn TW20 194 AV92
Schubert Rd, SW15 201 CZ85
Elstree WD6 99 CK44
★ Science Mus, SW7 28 B7
Scilla Ct, Grays RM17 192 GD79
Scillonian Rd, Guil. GU2 280 AU135
Jct Scilly Isles, Esher KT10 219 CE103
● Scimitar Pk, Harl. CM19 56 EL14
Sclater St, E1 20 A4
Scoble Pl, N16 10 B1
Scoles Cres, SW2 203 DN88
★ Scoop at More London, SE1
off Tooley St 31 P3
Scope Way, Kings.T. KT1 220 CL98
Scoresby St, SE1 30 G3
Scorton Av, Perivale UB6 159 CG68
Scotch Common, W13 159 CG71
Scoter Cl, Wdf.Grn. IG8 124 EH52
Scot Gro, Pnr. HA5 116 BX52
Scotia Rd, SW2 203 DN87
Scotland Br Rd, New Haw
KT15 234 BG111
Scotland Grn, N17 122 DT54
Scotland Grn Rd, Enf. EN3 105 DX43
Scotland Grn Rd N, Enf. EN3 105 DX42
Scotland Pl, SW1 30 A2
Scotland Rd, Buck.H. IG9 124 EJ46
Scotlands Dr, Farn.Com. SL2 153 AP65
Scotney Cl, Crox.Grn WD3 97 BP42
Orpington BR6 245 EN105
Scotney Wk, Horn. RM12
off Bonington Rd 150 FK64
Scotscraig, Rad. WD7 99 CF35
Scotsdale Cl, Petts Wd BR5 227 ES98
Scotsdale Cl, Sutton SM3 239 CY108
Scotsdale Rd, SE12 206 EH85
Scotshall La, Warl. CR6 243 EC114
Scots Hill, Crox.Grn WD3 96 BM44
Scots Hill Cl, Crox.Grn WD3 96 BM44
Scotsmill La, Crox.Grn WD3 96 BM44
Scotswood Cl, Beac. HP9 111 AK50
Scotswood St, EC1 18 F4
Scotswood Wk, N17 122 DU52
Scott Av, SW15 201 CY86
Stanstead Abbotts SG12 55 EB11
Scott Cl, SW16 223 DM95
Epsom KT19 238 CQ106
Farnham Common SL2 133 AQ64
Guildford GU2 264 AU132
Saint Albans AL3 64 CA22
West Drayton UB7 176 BM77
Scott Ct, SW8
off Silverthorne Rd 41 K9
W3 off Petersfield Rd 180 CR75
Scott Cres, Erith DA8
off Cloudesley Rd 189 FF81
Harrow HA2 138 CB60
Scott Ellis Gdns, NW8 16 A3
Scottes La, Dag. RM8
off Valence Av 148 EX60
Scott Fm Cl, T.Ditt. KT7 219 CH102
Scott Gdns, Houns. TW5 178 BX80
Scott Ho, E13 13 P10
N18 122 DU50
Scott Lidgett Cres, SE16 32 C5
Scott Rd, Edg. HA8 118 CP54
Gravesend DA12 213 GK92
Grays RM16 193 GG77
Scott Russell Pl, E14 34 C10
Scotts Av, Brom. BR2 225 ED96
Sunbury-on-Thames TW16 197 BS94
Scotts Cl, Horn. RM12
off Rye Cl 150 FJ64
Staines-upon-Thames TW19 196 BK88
Ware SG12 55 DX07
Scotts Dr, Hmptn. TW12 198 CB94
Scotts Fm Rd, Epsom KT19 238 CQ107
Scotts La, Brom. BR2 225 ED97
Walton-on-Thames KT12 236 BX105
Sch Scotts Pk Prim Sch, Brom.
BR1 off Orchard Rd 226 EJ95
Scotts Pas, SE18
off Spray St 37 P8
Sch Scotts Prim Sch,
Horn. RM12
off Bonington Rd 150 FJ64
Scotts Rd, E10 145 EC60
W12 181 CV75
Bromley BR1 206 EG94
Southall UB2 178 BW76
Ware SG12 55 DX07
Scott St, E1 20 E5
Scotts Vw, Welw.G.C. AL8 51 CW10
Scotts Way, Sev. TN13 278 FE122
Sunbury-on-Thames TW16 197 BS93
Scottswood Cl, Bushey WD23
off Scottswood Rd 98 BY40
Scottswood Rd, Bushey WD23 98 BY40
Scott Trimmer Way, Houns.
TW3 178 BY82
Scottwell Dr, NW9 141 CT57
Sch Scott Wilkie Prim Sch, E16 24 E8
Scoulding Rd, E16 23 M8
Scouler St, E14 34 G1
Scout App, NW10 140 CS63
Scout La, SW4 off Old Town 183 DJ83
Scout Way, NW7 118 CR49
Scovell Cres, SE1 31 J5
Scovell Rd, SE1 31 J5
Scratchers La, Fawk.Grn DA3 231 FR103
Scrattons Ter, Bark. IG11 168 EX67
Scriveners Cl, Hem.H. HP2 62 BL20
Scriven St, E8 10 B8
Scrooby St, SE6 205 EB86
Scrubbitts Pk Rd, Rad. WD7 99 CG35
Scrubbitts Sq, Rad. WD7 99 CG35
Scrubs La, NW10 161 CU69
W10 161 CU69
Scrutton Cl, SW12 203 DK87
Scrutton St, EC2 19 N5
Scudamore La, NW9 140 CQ55
Scudders Hill, Fawk.Grn DA3 231 FV100
Scutari Rd, SE22 204 DW85
Scylla Cres, Lon.Hthrw Air.
TW6 197 BP87
Scylla Pl, St.John's GU21
off Church Rd 248 AU119
Scylla Rd, SE15 44 D10
London Heathrow Airport
TW6 197 BP86
Seaborough Rd, Grays RM16 193 GJ76
Seabright St, E2 20 E3
Seabrook Ct, Pot.B. EN6 86 DA32
Seabrook Dr, W.Wick. BR4 226 EE103
Seabrooke Ri, Grays RM17 192 GB79
Seabrook Gdns, Rom. RM7 148 FA59
Seabrook Rd, Dag. RM8 148 EX62
Kings Langley WD4 81 BR27
Seaburn Cl, Rain. RM13 169 FE68
Seacole Cl, W3 160 CR71
Seacon Twr, E14 33 P5
Seacourt Rd, SE2 188 EX75
Slough SL3 175 BB77
Seacroft Gdns, Wat. WD19 116 BX48
Seafield Rd, N11 121 DK49
Seaford Cl, Ruis. HA4 137 BR61
Seaford Rd, E17 145 EB55
N15 144 DR57
W13 159 CH74
Enfield EN1 104 DS42
London Heathrow Airport
TW6 196 BK85
Seaford St, WC1 18 B3
Seaforth Av, N.Mal. KT3 221 CV99
Seaforth Cl, Rom. RM1 127 FE52
Seaforth Cres, N5 9 J2
Seaforth Dr, Wal.Cr. EN8 89 DX34
Seaforth Gdns, N21 121 DM45
Epsom KT19 239 CT105
Woodford Green IG8 124 EJ50
Seaforth Pl, SW1
off Buckingham Gate 29 M6
Seagrave Cl, E1 21 J7
Seagrave Rd, SW6 39 K2
Beaconsfield HP9 110 AJ51
Seagry Rd, E11 146 EG58
Seagull Cl, Bark. IG11 168 EU69
Seagull La, E16 23 P10
SEAL, Sev. TN15 279 FN121
Sealand Rd, Lon.Hthrw Air.
TW6 196 BN86
Sealand Wk, Nthlt. UB5
off Wayfarer Rd 158 BY69

Seal Dr, Seal TN15 279 FM121
Seale Hill, Reig. RH2 288 DA136
Seal Hollow Rd, Sev. TN13, TN15 279 FJ124
Seally Rd, Grays RM17 192 GA78
Seal Rd, Sev. TN14, TN15 279 FJ121
Seal St, E8 10 B1
Seaman Cl, Park St AL2 83 CD25
Searches La, Bedmond WD5 81 BV28
Searchwood Rd, Warl. CR6 258 DV118
Searle Pl, N4 143 DM60
Searles Cl, SW11 40 D5
Searles Dr, E6 25 N7
Searles Rd, SE1 31 M8
Sears St, SE5 43 L4
Seasalter Ct, Beck. BR3
off Kingsworth Cl 225 DY99
Seasons Cl, W7 159 CE74
Seasprite Cl, Nthlt. UB5 158 BX69
Seaton Av, Ilf. IG3 147 ES64
Seaton Cl, E13 23 P5
SE11 30 F10
SW15 201 CV88
Twickenham TW2 199 CD86
Seaton Dr, Ashf. TW15 196 BL89
Seaton Gdns, Ruis. HA4 137 BU62
Sch Seaton Ho Sch, Sutt. SM2
off Banstead Rd S 240 DD110
Seaton Pt, E5 144 DU63
Seaton Rd, Dart. DA1 209 FG87
Hayes UB3 177 BR77
Hemel Hempstead HP3 62 BK23
London Colney AL2 83 CK26
Mitcham CR4 222 DE96
Twickenham TW2 198 CC86
Welling DA16 188 EW80
Wembley HA0 160 CL68
Seaton Sq, NW7
off Tavistock Av 119 CX52
Seaton St, N18 122 DU50
Seawall Ct, Bark. IG11
off Dock Rd 167 EQ68
Sebastian Av, Shenf. CM15 131 GA44
Sebastian Ct, Bark. IG11
off Meadow Rd 167 ET66
Sebastian St, EC1 19 H3
Sebastopol Rd, N9 122 DU49
Sebbon St, N1 9 H7
Sebergham Gro, NW7 119 CU52
Sebert Rd, E7 146 EH64
Sebright Pas, E2 20 D1
Sch Sebright Prim Sch, E2 10 C10
Sebright Rd, Barn. EN5 101 CX40
Hemel Hempstead HP1 62 BG21
Secker Cres, Har. HA3 116 CC53
Secker St, SE1 30 E3
Second Av, E12 146 EL63
E13 23 N2
E17 145 EA57
N18 122 DW49
NW4 141 CX56
SW14 180 CS83
W3 161 CT74
W10 14 F4
Dagenham RM10 169 FB67
Enfield EN1 104 DT43
Grays RM20 191 FU79
Harlow CM18 73 ES15
Hayes UB3 157 BT74
Romford RM6 148 EW57
Waltham Abbey EN9 off Breach Barn Mobile Home Pk 90 EH30
Walton-on-Thames KT12 217 BV100
Watford WD25 98 BX35
Wembley HA9 139 CK61
Second Cl, W.Mol. KT8 218 CC98
Second Cres, Slou. SL1 153 AQ71
Second Cross Rd, Twick. TW2 199 CE89
Second Way, Wem. HA9 140 CP63
Sedan Way, SE17 31 N10
Sedcombe Cl, Sid. DA14 208 EV91
Sedcote Rd, Enf. EN3 104 DW43
Sedding St, SW1 28 G8
Seddon Highwalk, EC2
off The Barbican 19 J6
Seddon Ho, EC2
off The Barbican 19 J6
Seddon Rd, Mord. SM4 222 DD99
Seddon St, WC1 18 D3
Sedgebrook Rd, SE3 186 EK82
Sedgecombe Av, Har. HA3 139 CJ57
Sedge Ct, Grays RM17 192 GE80
Sedgefield Cl, Rom. RM3 128 FM49
Sedgefield Cres, Rom. RM3 128 FM49
Sedgeford Rd, W12 161 CT74
Sedge Grn, Lwr Naze. EN9 72 EE20
Roydon CM19 72 EE20
Sedgehill Rd, SE6 205 EA91
Sch Sedgehill Sch, SE6
off Sedgehill Rd 205 EB92
Sedgemere Av, N2 142 DC55
Sedgemere Rd, SE2 188 EW76
Sedgemoor Dr, Dag. RM10 148 FA63
Sedge Rd, N17 122 DW52
Sedgeway, SE6 206 EF88
Sedgewood Cl, Brom. BR2 226 EF101
Sedgmoor Pl, SE5 43 P5
Sedgwick Av, Uxb. UB10 157 BP66
Sedgwick Rd, E10 145 EC61
Sedgwick St, E9 11 J3
Sedleigh Rd, SW18 201 CZ86
Sedlescombe Rd, SW6 39 H3
Sedley, Sthflt DA13 212 GA93
Sedley Cl, Enf. EN1 104 DV38
Sedley Gro, Hare. UB9 136 BJ56
Sedley Pl, W1 17 J9
Sedley Ri, Loug. IG10 107 EM40
Sch Sedley's C of E Prim Sch, Sthflt DA13 off Church St 212 GA92
Sedum Cl, NW9 140 CP57
Seeley Dr, SE21 204 DS91
Seeleys, Harl. CM17 58 EW12
Seeleys Cl, Beac. HP9 110 AJ51
Seeleys La, Beac. HP9
off Seeleys Wk 111 AK52
Seeleys Rd, Beac. HP9 110 AJ50
Seeleys Wk, Beac. HP9 110 AJ52
Seelig Av, NW9 141 CU59
Seely Rd, SW17 202 DG93
SEER GREEN, Beac. HP9 111 AR52
⇌ Seer Green & Jordans 111 AR52
Sch Seer Grn C of E Comb Sch, Seer Grn HP9 off School La 111 AQ51
Seer Grn La, Jordans HP9 112 AS52
Seer Mead, Seer Grn HP9 111 AR52
Seething La, EC3 31 P1
Seething Wells La, Surb. KT6 219 CJ100
Sefton Av, NW7 118 CR50
Harrow HA3 117 CD53
Sefton Cl, Petts Wd BR5 227 ET98
St. Albans AL1
off Blenheim Rd 65 CF19
Stoke Poges SL2 154 AT66
Sefton Ct, Welw.G.C. AL8 51 CV11
Sefton Paddock, Stoke P. SL2 154 AU66
● Sefton Pk, Stoke P. SL2 154 AU66
Sefton Rd, Croy. CR0 224 DU102
Epsom KT19 238 CR110
Petts Wood BR5 227 ET98
Sefton St, SW15 38 B9
Sefton Way, Uxb. UB8 156 BJ72
Segal Cl, SE23 205 DY87
Segrave Cl, Wey. KT13 234 BN108
Sekforde St, EC1 18 G5
Sekhon Ter, Felt. TW13 198 CA90
Selah Dr, Swan. BR8 229 FC95
Selan Gdns, Hayes UB4 157 BV71
Selbie Av, NW10 141 CT64
Selborne Av, E12
off Walton Rd 147 EN63
Bexley DA5 208 EY88
Selborne Gdns, NW4 141 CU56
Perivale UB6 159 CG67
Sch Selborne Prim Sch, Perivale UB6 off Conway Cres 159 CF68
Selborne Rd, E17 145 DZ57
N14 121 DL48
N22 121 DM53
SE5 43 L8
Croydon CR0 224 DS104
Ilford IG1 147 EN61
New Malden KT3 220 CS96
Sidcup DA14 208 EV91
Selborne Wk, E17
off The Mall Walthamstow 145 DZ56
Selbourne Av, E17 145 DZ56
New Haw KT15 234 BH110
Surbiton KT6 220 CM103
Selbourne Cl, New Haw KT15 234 BH109
Selbourne Rd, Guil. GU4 265 BA131
Selbourne Sq, Gdse. RH9 274 DW130
Selby Av, St.Alb. AL3 65 CD20
Selby Chase, Ruis. HA4 137 BV61
Selby Cl, E6 24 G7
Chessington KT9 238 CL108
Chislehurst BR7 207 EN93
Selby Gdns, Sthl. UB1 158 CA70
Selby Grn, Cars. SM5 222 DE101
Selby Rd, E11 146 EE62
E13 24 B6
N17 122 DS51
SE20 224 DU96
W5 159 CH70
Ashford TW15 197 BQ93
Carshalton SM5 222 DE101
Selby Sq, W10 14 F2
Selby St, E1 20 D5
Selby Wk, Wok. GU21
off Wyndham Rd 248 AV118
Selcroft Rd, Pur. CR8 241 DP112
Selden Hill, Hem.H. HP2 62 BK21
Selden Rd, SE15 45 H9
Selden Wk, N7 off Durham Rd 143 DM61
Seldon Ho, SW8 41 L5
Sele Mill, Hert. SG14 53 DP09
Sele Rd, Hert. SG14 53 DP09
Sch Sele Sch, The, Hert. SG14
off Welwyn Rd 53 DM09
★ Selfridges, W1 16 G9
SELHURST, SE25 224 DS100
⇌ Selhurst 224 DS99
Selhurst Cl, SW19 201 CX88
Woking GU21 249 AZ115
Selhurst New Rd, SE25 224 DS100
Selhurst Pl, SE25 224 DS100
Selhurst Rd, N9 122 DR48
SE25 224 DS99
Selinas La, Dag. RM8 148 EY59
Selkirk Dr, Erith DA8 189 FE81
Selkirk Rd, SW17 202 DE91
Twickenham TW2 198 CC89
Sell Cl, Chsht EN7
off Gladding Rd 88 DQ26
Sellers Cl, Borwd. WD6 100 CQ39
Sellers Hall Cl, N3 120 DA52
Sch Sellincourt Prim Sch, SW17
off Sellincourt Rd 202 DE93
Sellincourt Rd, SW17 202 DE92
Sellindge Cl, Beck. BR3 205 DZ94
Sellons Av, NW10 161 CT67
Sells Cl, Guil. GU1 281 AZ136
Sells Rd, Ware SG12 55 DZ05
Sellwood Dr, Barn. EN5 101 CX43
Sellwood St, SW2
off Brockwell Pk Row 203 DN87
SELSDON, S.Croy. CR2 242 DW110
Selsdon Av, S.Croy. CR2 242 DR107
Selsdon Cl, Rom. RM5 127 FC53
Surbiton KT6 220 CL99
Selsdon Cres, S.Croy. CR2 242 DW109
Sch Selsdon High Sch, S.Croy. CR2 off Farnborough Av 243 DX108
Selsdon Pk Rd, S.Croy. CR2 243 DX109
Sch Selsdon Prim Sch, S.Croy. CR2 off Addington Rd 242 DW109
Selsdon Rd, E11 146 EG59
E13 166 EJ67
NW2 141 CT61
SE27 203 DP90
New Haw KT15 234 BG111
South Croydon CR2 242 DR106
● Selsdon Rd Ind Est, S.Croy. CR2 off Selsdon Rd 242 DR108
Selsdon Way, E14 34 D7
Selsea Pl, N16 9 P2
Selsey Cres, Well. DA16 188 EX81
Selsey St, E14 22 A7
Selvage La, NW7 118 CR50
Selway Cl, Pnr. HA5 137 BV56
Selway Ho, SW8
off South Lambeth Rd 42 B6
Selwood Cl, Stanw. TW19 196 BJ86
Selwood Gdns, Stanw. TW19 196 BJ86
Selwood Pl, SW7 28 A10
Selwood Rd, Brwd. CM14 130 FT48
Chessington KT9 237 CK105
Croydon CR0 224 DV103
Sutton SM3 221 CZ102
Woking GU22 249 BB120
Selwood Ter, SW7 28 A10
Selworthy Cl, E11 146 EG57
Selworthy Ho, SW11 40 B6
Selworthy Rd, SE6 205 DZ90
Selwyn Av, E4 123 EC51
Hatfield AL10 66 CR19
Ilford IG3 147 ES58
Richmond TW9 180 CL83
Selwyn Cl, Houns. TW4 178 BY84
Selwyn Cl, Windsor SL4 173 AL82
Selwyn Ct, SE3 47 L10
Edgware HA8 118 CP52
Selwyn Cres, Hat. AL10 66 CS18
Welling DA16 188 EV84
Selwyn Dr, Hat. AL10 66 CR18
Selwyn Pl, Orp. BR5 228 EV97
Sch Selwyn Prim Sch, E4
off Selwyn Av 123 EC51
E13 13 P8
Selwyn Rd, E3 21 N1
E13 166 EH67
NW10 160 CR66
New Malden KT3 220 CR99
Tilbury RM18 off Dock Rd 193 GF82
Semaphore Rd, Guil. GU1 280 AY136
Semley Gate, E9
off Osborne Rd 11 P4
Semley Pl, SW1 29 H9
SW16 off Semley Rd 223 DM96
Semley Rd, SW16 223 DL96
Semper Cl, Knap. GU21 248 AS117
Semper Rd, Grays RM16 193 GJ75
Sempill Rd, Hem.H. HP3 62 BL23
Senate St, SE15 45 H9
Senator Wk, SE28
off Garrick Dr 187 ER76
SEND, Wok. GU23 249 BC124
Sendall Ct, SW11 182 DD83
Send Barns La, Send GU23 249 BD124
Send Cl, Send GU23 249 BC123
Sch Send C of E First Sch, Send GU23
off Send Barns La 249 BE124
SENDGROVE, Wok. GU23 265 BC126
Send Hill, Send GU23 265 BC125
SEND MARSH, Wok. GU23 249 BF124
Send Marsh Grn, Send M. GU23
off Send Marsh Rd 249 BF123
Send Marsh Rd, Wok. GU23 249 BF123
Send Par Cl, Send GU23
off Send Rd 249 BC123
Send Rd, Send GU23 249 BB122
Seneca Rd, Th.Hth. CR7 224 DQ98
Senga Rd, Wall. SM6 222 DG102
Senhouse Rd, Sutt. SM3 221 CX104
Senior St, W2 15 L6
Senlac Rd, SE12 206 EH88
Sennen Rd, Enf. EN1 122 DT45
Sennen Wk, SE9 206 EL90
Senrab St, E1 21 J8
Sentamu Cl, SE24 203 DP88
Sentinel Ct, Nthlt. UB5 158 BY70
Sentinel Pt, SW8
off St. George Wf 42 A2
Sentinel Sq, NW4 141 CW56
Sentis Ct, Nthwd. HA6
off Carew Rd 115 BT51
September Way, Stan. HA7 117 CH51
Sequoia Cl, Bushey Hth WD23
off Giant Tree Hill 117 CD46
Sequoia Gdns, Orp. BR6 227 ET101
Sequoia Pk, Pnr. HA5 116 CB51
Serbin Cl, E10 145 EC59
Serenaders Rd, SW9 42 F9
Seren Park Gdns, SE3 47 K2
Sergeants Grn La, Wal.Abb. EN9 90 EJ33
Sergeants Pl, Cat. CR3 258 DQ122
Sergehill La, Bedmond WD5 81 BT27
Serjeants Inn, EC4 18 F9
Serle St, WC2 18 D8
Sermed Ct, Slou. SL2 154 AW74
Sermon Dr, Swan. BR8 229 FC97
Sermon La, EC4 19 J9
★ Serpentine, The, W2 28 C3
Serpentine Ct, Sev. TN13 279 FK122
★ Serpentine Gall, W2 28 B3
Serpentine Grn, Merst. RH1
off Malmstone Av 273 DK129
Serpentine Rd, W2 28 E3
Sevenoaks TN13 279 FJ123
Service Rd, The, Pot.B. EN6 86 DA32
Serviden Dr, Brom. BR1 226 EK95
Sch Servite RC Prim Sch, SW10 39 N2
Setchell Rd, SE1 32 A8
Setchell Way, SE1 32 A8
Seth St, SE16 33 H5
Seton Gdns, Dag. RM9 168 EW66
Settle Pt, E13 23 N1
Settle Rd, E13 13 N10
Romford RM3 128 FN49
Settlers Ct, E14
off Newport Av 23 H10
Settles St, E1 20 D7
Settrington Rd, SW6 39 L9
Seven Acres, Cars. SM5 222 DE103
Northwood HA6 115 BU51
Swanley BR8 229 FD100
Seven Arches App, Wey. KT13 234 BM108
Seven Arches Rd, Brwd. CM14 130 FX48
Seven Hills Cl, Walt. KT12 235 BS109
Seven Hills Rd, Cob. KT11 235 BS111
Iver SL0 155 BC65
Walton-on-Thames KT12 235 BS109
Seven Hills Rd S, Cob. KT11 235 BS113
SEVEN KINGS, Ilf. IG3 147 ES59
⇌ Seven Kings 147 ES60
Sch Seven Kings High Sch, Ilf. IG2 off Ley St 147 ER59
Seven Kings Rd, Ilf. IG3 147 ET61
Seven Kings Way, Kings.T. KT2 220 CL95
Sch Seven Mills Prim Sch, E14 34 B5
SEVENOAKS, TN13 - TN15 279 FJ125
⇌ Sevenoaks 278 FG124
Sevenoaks 279 FJ125
Coll Sevenoaks Adult Ed Cen, Sev. TN13 off Bradbourne Rd 279 FH122
● Sevenoaks Business Cen, Sev. TN14 279 FH121
Sevenoaks Bypass, Sev. TN14 278 FC123
Sevenoaks Cl, Bexh. DA7 189 FC84
Romford RM3 128 FJ49
Sutton SM2 240 DA110
SEVENOAKS COMMON, Sev. TN13 279 FH129
Sevenoaks Ct, Nthwd. HA6 115 BQ52
H Sevenoaks Hosp, Sev. TN13 279 FJ121
Sevenoaks Ho, SE25 224 DU97
★ Sevenoaks Mus, Sev. TN13 279 FJ125
Sch Sevenoaks Prep Sch, Godden Grn TN15
off Fawke Common Rd 279 FN126
Sch Sevenoaks Prim Sch, Sev. TN13
off Bradbourne Pk Rd 279 FH122
Sevenoaks Rd, SE4 205 DY86
Orpington BR6 245 ET106
Otford TN14 263 FH116
Pratt's Bottom BR6 245 ET108
Sch Sevenoaks Sch, Sev. TN13
off High St 279 FJ126
Sevenoaks Way, Orp. BR5 208 EW94
Sidcup DA14 208 EW94
Sevens Cl, Berk. HP4 60 AX19
Sevenseas Rd, Lon.Hthrw Air. TW6 197 BQ86
Seven Sisters, N15 144 DT57
⇌ Seven Sisters 144 DS57
⊖ Seven Sisters 144 DS57
Sch Seven Sisters Prim Sch, N15
off South Gro 144 DR57
Seven Sisters Rd, N4 143 DM62
N7 143 DM62
N15 144 DQ59
Seven Stars Cor, W12
off Goldhawk Rd 181 CU76
Seven Stars Yd, E1 20 B6
Seventh Av, E12 147 EM63
Hayes UB3 157 BU74
Severalls Av, Chesh. HP5 76 AQ30
Severnake Cl, E14 34 B8
Severn Av, W10 14 F2
Romford RM2 149 FH55
Severn Cres, Slou. SL3 175 BB78
Severn Dr, Enf. EN1 104 DU38
Esher KT10 219 CG103
Upminster RM14 151 FR58
Walton-on-Thames KT12 218 BX103
Severnmead, Hem.H. HP2 62 BL17
Severn Rd, Aveley RM15 170 FQ72
Severns Fld, Epp. CM16 92 EU29
Severnvale, Lon.Col. AL2
off Thamesdale 84 CM27
Severn Way, NW10 141 CT64
Watford WD25 82 BW34
Severus Rd, SW11 182 DE84
Seville Ms, N1 9 N7
Seville St, SW1 28 F5
Sevington Rd, NW4 141 CV58
Sevington St, W9 15 L5
Seward Rd, W7 179 CG75
Beckenham BR3 225 DX96
SEWARDSTONE, E4 105 EC39
SEWARDSTONEBURY, E4 106 EE42
Sewardstone Cl, E4 105 EC39
Sewardstone Gdns, E4 105 EB43
Sewardstone Grn, E4 106 EE42
Sewardstone Rd, E2 11 H10
E4 123 EB45
Waltham Abbey EN9 105 EC38
Jct Sewardstone Rbt, Wal.Abb. EN9 105 ED35
Sewardstone St, Wal.Abb. EN9 89 EC34
Seward St, EC1 19 H4
Sewdley St, E5 145 DX62
Sewell Cl, Chaff.Hun. RM16 191 FW78
St. Albans AL4 66 CL20
Sewell Harris Cl, Harl. CM20 57 ET14
Sewell Rd, SE2 188 EU76
Sewells, Welw.G.C. AL8 51 CY05
Sewell St, E13 23 P2
Sextant Av, E14 34 G8
Sexton Cl, Chsht EN7
off Shambrook Rd 88 DQ25
Rainham RM13
off Blake Cl 169 FF67
Sexton Ct, E14 off Newport Av 23 H10
Sexton Rd, Til. RM18 193 GF81
Seymer Rd, Rom. RM1 149 FD55
Seymore Ms, SE14
off New Cross Rd 45 N5
Seymour Av, N17 122 DU54
Caterham CR3 258 DQ123
Epsom KT17 239 CV109
Morden SM4 221 CX101
Seymour Chase, Epp. CM16
off Boleyn Row 92 EV29
Seymour Cl, E.Mol. KT8 218 CC99
Loughton IG10 106 EL44
Pinner HA5 116 BZ53
Seymour Ct, E4 124 EF47
N10 120 DG54
N16 off Cazenove Rd 144 DU60
Seymour Cres, Hem.H. HP2 62 BL20
Seymour Dr, Brom. BR2 227 EM102
Seymour Gdns, SE4 45 L10
Feltham TW13 198 BW91
Ilford IG1 147 EM60
Ruislip HA4 138 BX60
Surbiton KT5 220 CM99
Twickenham TW1 199 CH87
Seymour Ms, W1 16 G8
Ewell KT17 239 CU110
Sawbridgeworth CM21 58 EY08
Seymour Pl, SE25 224 DV98
W1 16 E7
Hornchurch RM11 150 FK59
Seymour Rd, E4 123 EB46
E6 166 EK68
E10 145 DZ60
N3 120 DB52
N8 143 DN57
N9 122 DV47
SW18 201 CZ87
SW19 201 CX89
W4 180 CQ77
Carshalton SM5 240 DG106
Chalfont St. Giles HP8 112 AW49
East Molesey KT8 218 CC99
Hampton Hill TW12 198 CC92
Kingston upon Thames KT1 219 CK95
Mitcham CR4 222 DG101
Northchurch HP4 60 AS17
Northfleet DA11 213 GF88
St. Albans AL3 65 CE17
Slough SL1 173 AR75
Tilbury RM18 193 GF81
Seymours, Harl. CM19 73 EM18
Seymours, The, Loug. IG10 107 EN39
Seymour St, SE18 187 EQ76
W1 16 E9
W2 16 E9
Seymour Ter, SE20 224 DV95
Seymour Vil, SE20 224 DV95
Seymour Wk, SW10 39 N2
Swanscombe DA10 212 FY87
Seymour Way, Sun. TW16 197 BS93
Seyssel St, E14 34 F8
Shaa Rd, W3 160 CR73
Shacklands Rd, Sev. TN14 247 FB111
Shackleford Rd, Wok. GU22 249 BA121
Shacklegate La, Tedd. TW11 199 CE91
Shackleton Cl, SE23
off Featherstone Av 204 DV89
Shackleton Ct, E14
off Maritime Quay 34 B10
W12 181 CV75
Shackleton Rd, Slou. SL1 154 AT73
Southall UB1 158 BZ73
Shackleton Wk, Guil. GU2
off Humbolt Cl 264 AT134
Shackleton Way, Abb.L. WD5
off Lysander Way 81 BU32
Welwyn Garden City AL7 52 DD09
SHACKLEWELL, N16 10 A1
Shacklewell Grn, E8 10 B1
Shacklewell La, E8 10 A2
N16 10 A2
Sch Shacklewell Prim Sch, E8 10 A1
Shacklewell Rd, N16 10 B1
Shacklewell Row, E8 10 B1
Shacklewell St, E2 20 B4
Shadbolt Av, E4 123 DY50
Shadbolt Cl, Wor.Pk. KT4 221 CT103
Shad Thames, SE1 32 A3
SHADWELL, E1 32 G1
⊖ Shadwell 20 F10
DLR Shadwell 20 F10
Shadwell Ct, Nthlt. UB5
off Shadwell Dr 158 BZ68
Shadwell Dr, Nthlt. UB5 158 BZ69
Shadwell Gdns Est, E1 20 G10
Shadwell Pierhead, E1 33 H1
Shadwell Pl, E1 20 G10
Shady Bush Cl, Bushey WD23 116 CC45
Shady La, Wat. WD17 97 BV40
Shaef Way, Tedd. TW11 199 CG94
Shafter Rd, Dag. RM10 169 FC65
Shaftesbury, Loug. IG10 106 EK41
Shaftesbury Av, W1 17 N10
WC2 17 N10
Enfield EN3 105 DX40
Feltham TW14 197 BU86
Kenton HA3 139 CK58
New Barnet EN5 102 DC42
South Harrow HA2 138 CB60
Southall UB2 178 CA77
Shaftesbury Circle, S.Har. HA2
off Shaftesbury Av 138 CC60
Shaftesbury Ct, N1 19 L1
SE1 off Alderney Ms 31 L6
Shaftesbury Cres, Stai. TW18 196 BK94
Shaftesbury Gdns, NW10 160 CS70
Sch Shaftesbury High Sch, Har.Wld HA3 off Headstone La 116 CB53
Shaftesbury La, Dart. DA1 190 FP84
Shaftesbury Ms, SW4 203 DJ85
W8 27 K7
Sch Shaftesbury Pk Prim Sch, SW11 40 G9
Shaftesbury Pl, W14 27 H9
Shaftesbury Pt, E13 23 P1
Sch Shaftesbury Prim Sch, E7
off Shaftesbury Rd 166 EJ66
Shaftesbury Quay, Hert. SG14
off Railway St 54 DR09
Shaftesbury Rd, E4 123 ED46
E7 166 EJ66
E10 145 EA60
E17 145 EB58
N18 122 DS51
N19 143 DL60
Beckenham BR3 225 DZ96
Carshalton SM5 222 DD101
Epping CM16 91 ET29
Richmond TW9 180 CL83
Romford RM1 149 FF58
Watford WD17 98 BW41
Woking GU22 249 BA117
Shaftesburys, The, Bark. IG11 167 EQ67
Shaftesbury St, N1 19 K1
Shaftesbury Way, Kings L. WD4 81 BQ28
Twickenham TW2 199 CD90
Shaftesbury Waye, Hayes UB4 157 BV71
Shafto Ms, SW1 28 E7
Shafton Rd, E9 11 K8
Shaggy Calf La, Slou. SL2 154 AU73
Shakespeare Av, N11 121 DJ50
NW10 160 CR67
Feltham TW14 197 BU86
Hayes UB4 157 BV70
Tilbury RM18 193 GH82
Shakespeare Cres, E12 167 EM65
Shakespeare Dr, Borwd. WD6 100 CN42
Har. HA3 140 CM58
Shakespeare Gdns, N2 142 DF56
● Shakespeare Ind Est, Wat. WD24 97 BU38
Shakespeare Rd, E17 123 DX54
N3 off Popes Dr 120 DA53
NW7 119 CT49
NW10 160 CR67
SE24 203 DP85
W3 160 CQ74
W7 159 CF73
Addlestone KT15 234 BK105
Bexleyheath DA7 188 EY81
Dartford DA1 190 FN84
Romford RM1 149 FF58
★ Shakespeare's Globe Thea, SE1 31 J1
Shakespeare Sq, Ilf. IG6 125 EQ51
Shakespeare St, Wat. WD24 97 BV38
Shakespeare Twr, EC2 19 K6
Shakespeare Way, Felt. TW13 198 BW91
Shakspeare Ms, N16
off Shakspeare Wk 144 DS63
Shakspeare Wk, N16 9 N1
Shalbourne Sq, E9 11 N4
Shalcomb St, SW10 39 P3
Shalcross Dr, Chsht EN8 89 DZ30
Shalden Ho, SW15
off Tunworth Cres 201 CT86
Shaldon Dr, Mord. SM4 221 CY99
Ruislip HA4 138 BW62
Shaldon Rd, Edg. HA8 118 CM53
Shaldon Way, Walt. KT12 218 BW104
Shale Ct, E15 off Romford Rd 13 L5
Shale Grn, Merst. RH1
off Bletchingley Rd 273 DK129
Shalfleet Dr, W10 14 C10
SHALFORD, Guil. GU4 280 AX141
⇌ Shalford 280 AY140

Shalford Cl, Orp. BR6 245 EQ105
Sch Shalford Inf Sch, Guil. GU4 off Station Row 280 AY140
Shalford Rd, Guil. GU1, GU4 280 AX137
Shalimar Gdns, W3 160 CQ73
Shalimar Rd, W3 160 CQ73
Shallcross Cres, Hat. AL10 67 CU21
Shallons Rd, SE9 207 EP91
Shalstone Rd, SW14 180 CP83
Shalston Vil, Surb. KT6 220 CM100
Shambles, The, Sev. TN13 off London Rd 279 FJ125
Shambrook Rd, Chsht EN7 87 DP25
Shamrock Cl, Fetch. KT22 253 CD121
Shamrock Ho, SE26 off Talisman Sq 204 DU91
Shamrock Rd, Croy. CR0 223 DM100
Gravesend DA12 213 GL87
Shamrock St, SW4 41 N10
Shamrock Way, N14 121 DH46
Shandon Rd, SW4 203 DJ86
Shand St, SE1 31 N4
Shandy St, E1 21 K5
Shanklin Cl, Chsht EN7 88 DT29
Shanklin Gdns, Wat. WD19 116 BW49
Shanklin Ho, E17 off Sherwood Cl 123 DZ54
Shanklin Rd, N8 143 DK57
N15 144 DU56
Shannon Cl, NW2 141 CX62
Southall UB2 178 BX78
● Shannon Commercial Cen, N.Mal. KT3 off Beverley Way 221 CU98
Jct Shannon Cor, N.Mal. KT3 221 CU98
Shannon Cor Retail Pk, N.Mal. KT3 221 CU98
Shannon Gro, SW9 183 DM84
Shannon Pl, NW8 6 D10
Shannon Way, Aveley RM15 170 FQ73
Beckenham BR3 205 EB93
Shantock Hall La, Bov. HP3 78 AY29
Shantock La, Bov. HP3 78 AX30
Shap Cres, Cars. SM5 222 DF102
Shapland Way, N13 121 DM50
Sch Shapla Prim Sch, E1 20 C10
Shapwick Cl, N11 120 DF50
Shard, The, SE1 31 M3
Shardcroft Av, SE24 203 DP85
Shardeloes Rd, SE4 45 N9
SE14 45 N8
Sharland Cl, Th.Hth. CR7 off Dunheved Rd N 223 DN100
Sharland Rd, Grav. DA12 213 GJ89
Sharman Ct, Sid. DA14 208 EU91
Sharman Row, Slou. SL3 175 AZ78
Sharnbrooke Cl, Well. DA16 188 EW83
Sharnbrook Ho, W14 39 J2
Sharney Av, Slou. SL3 175 BB76
Sharon Cl, Bkhm KT23 252 CA124
Epsom KT19 238 CQ113
Long Ditton KT6 219 CJ102
Sharon Gdns, E9 10 G8
Sharon Rd, W4 180 CR78
Enfield EN3 105 DY40
Sharpcroft, Hem.H. HP2 62 BK18
Sharpe Cl, W7 off Templeman Rd 159 CF71
Sharpecroft, Harl. CM19 73 EQ15
Sharpes La, Hem.H. HP1 61 BB21
Sharpleshall St, NW1 6 F7
Sharpness Cl, Hayes UB4 158 BY71
Sharps La, Ruis. HA4 137 BR60
Sharp Way, Dart. DA1 190 FM83
Sharratt St, SE15 45 H2
Sharsted St, SE17 42 G1
Sharvel La, Nthlt. UB5 157 BU67
Shavers Pl, SW1 29 N1
Shaw Av, Bark. IG11 168 EY68
Shawbridge, Harl. CM19 73 EQ18
Shawbrooke Rd, SE9 206 EJ85
Shawbury Cl, NW9 118 CS54
Shawbury Rd, SE22 204 DT85
Shaw Cl, SE28 168 EV74
Bushey Heath WD23 117 CE47
Cheshunt EN8 88 DW28
Epsom KT17 239 CT111
Hornchurch RM11 149 FH60
Ottershaw KT16 233 BC107
South Croydon CR2 242 DT112
Shaw Ct, SW11 182 DD83
Morden SM4 222 DC101
Windsor SL4 194 AU85
Shaw Cres, E14 21 M7
Hutton CM13 131 GD43
South Croydon CR2 242 DT112
Tilbury RM18 193 GH81
Shaw Dr, Walt. KT12 218 BW101
Shawfield Ct, West Dr. UB7 176 BL76
Shawfield Pk, Brom. BR1 226 EK96
Shawfield St, SW3 40 D1
Shawford Ct, SW15 201 CU87
Shawford Rd, Epsom KT19 238 CR107
Shaw Gdns, Bark. IG11 168 EY68
Slough SL3 175 AZ78
Shaw Gro, Couls. CR5 258 DQ120
Shaw Ho, E16 off Claremont St 37 M3
N17 off Queen St 122 DS51
Banstead SM7 256 DC118
Sch Shawley Comm Prim Sch, Epsom KT18 off Shawley Way 255 CW118
Shawley Cres, Epsom KT18 255 CW118
Shawley Way, Epsom KT18 255 CV118
Shaw Path, Brom. BR1 off Shroffold Rd 206 EF90
Sch Shaw Prim Sch, S.Ock. RM15 off Avon Grn 171 FV72
Shaw Rd, SE22 184 DS84
Bromley BR1 206 EF90
Enfield EN3 105 DX39
Tatsfield TN16 260 EJ120
Shaws, The, Welw.G.C. AL7 52 DC10
Shaws Cotts, SE23 205 DY90
Shaw Sq, E17 123 DY53
Shaw Way, Wall. SM6 241 DL108
Shaxton Cres, New Adgtn CR0 243 EC109
Sheares Hoppit, Hunsdon SG12 56 EK05
Shearing Dr, Cars. SM5 off Stavordale Rd 222 DC101
Shearling Way, N7 8 B4
Shearman Rd, SE3 186 EF84
Jct Shears, The, Sun. TW16 197 BS94
Shears Cl, Dart. DA1 210 FJ89
Shears Ct, Sun. TW16 off Staines Rd W 197 BS94
Sch Shears Grn Inf Sch, Nthflt DA11 off Packham Rd 213 GF90
Sch Shears Grn Jun Sch, Nthflt DA11 off White Av 213 GF90
Shearsmith Ho, E1 20 D10
Shearwater Cl, Bark. IG11 168 EU69
Shearwater Rd, Sutt. SM1 239 CZ106
Shearwater Way, Hayes UB4 158 BX72
Shearwood Cres, Dart. DA1 189 FF83
Sheath La, Oxshott KT22 236 CB113
Sheaveshill Av, NW9 140 CS56
Sheba Pl, E1 20 B5
Sheehy Way, Slou. SL2 154 AV73
Sheen Common, SW14 200 CP85
Sheen Common Dr, Rich. TW10 180 CN84
Sheen Ct, Rich. TW10 180 CN84
Sheen Ct Rd, Rich. TW10 180 CN84
Sheendale Rd, Rich. TW9 180 CM84
Sheenewood, SE26 204 DV92
Sheen Gate Gdns, SW14 180 CQ84
Sheen Gate Mans Pas, SW14 off East Sheen Av 180 CR84
Sheen Gro, N1 8 E8
Sheen La, SW14 180 CQ83
Sch Sheen Mt Prim Sch, SW14 off West Temple Sheen 200 CP85
Sheen Pk, Rich. TW9 180 CM84
Sheen Rd, Orp. BR5 227 ET98
Richmond TW9, TW10 200 CL85
Sheen Way, Wall. SM6 241 DM106
Sheen Wd, SW14 200 CQ85
Sheepbarn La, Warl. CR6 244 EF112
Sheepcot Dr, Wat. WD25 82 BW34
Sheepcote, Welw.G.C. AL7 52 DA12
Sheepcote Cl, Beac. HP9 110 AJ51
Hounslow TW5 177 BU80
Sheepcote Gdns, Denh. UB9 136 BG58
Sheepcote La, SW11 40 E9
Burnham SL1 132 AF62
Orpington BR5 228 EZ99
Swanley BR8 228 EZ98
Wheathampstead AL4 50 CL07
Wooburn Green HP10 132 AG61
Sheepcote Rd, Eton Wick SL4 173 AN78
Harrow HA1 139 CF58
Hemel Hempstead HP2 62 BM20
Windsor SL4 173 AL82
Sheepcotes Rd, Rom. RM6 148 EX56
Sheepcot La, Wat. WD25 81 BV34
Sheepfold La, Amer. HP7 77 AR39
Sheepfold Rd, Guil. GU2 264 AT131
Sheephouse Grn, Wotton RH5 284 BZ140
Sheephouse La, Dor. RH5 284 BZ139
Sheephouse Rd, Hem.H. HP3 62 BM22
Sheephouse Way, N.Mal. KT3 220 CS101
Sheeplands Av, Guil. GU1 265 BC132
Sheep La, E8 10 E9
Sheep Wk, Epsom KT18 254 CR122
Reigate RH2 271 CY131
Shepperton TW17 216 BM101
Sheep Wk, The, Wok. GU22 249 BE118
Sheepwalk La, E.Hors. KT24 267 BT134
Sheep Wk Ms, SW19 201 CX93
Sheer Cft, Chesh. HP5 76 AM29
SHEERING, B.Stort. CM22 59 FC07
Sch Sheering C of E Prim Sch, Sheering CM22 off The Street 59 FD06
Sheering Dr, Harl. CM17 58 EX12
Sheering Hall Dr, Harl. CM17 58 FA08
Sheering Lwr Rd, Harl. CM17 58 EZ09
Sawbridgeworth CM21 58 FA06
Sheering Mill La, Saw. CM21 58 EZ05
Sheering Rd, Harl. CM17 58 EY11
Hatfield Heath CM22 59 FF05
Sheerness Ms, E16 37 P4
SHEERWATER, Wok. GU21 233 BC113
Sheerwater Av, Wdhm KT15 233 BE112
Sheerwater Rd, E16 24 E6
West Byfleet KT14 233 BE112
Woking GU21 233 BE112
Woodham KT15 233 BE112
Sheethanger La, Felden HP3 62 BG24
Sheet St, Wind. SL4 173 AR82
Sheffield Dr, Rom. RM3 128 FN50
Sheffield Gdns, Rom. RM3 128 FN50
Sheffield Rd, Lon.Hthrw Air. TW6 off Shrewsbury Rd 197 BQ86
Slough SL1 153 AQ72
Sheffield Sq, E3 21 P2
Sheffield St, WC2 18 C9
Sheffield Ter, W8 27 J3
Shefton Ri, Nthwd. HA6 115 BU52
Sheila Cl, Rom. RM5 127 FB52
Sheila Rd, Rom. RM5 127 FB52
Sheilings, The, Horn. RM11 150 FM57
Shelbourne Cl, Pnr. HA5 138 BZ55
Shelbourne Pl, Beck. BR3 205 DZ94
Shelbourne Rd, N17 122 DV54
Shelburne Dr, Houns. TW4 off Hanworth Rd 198 CA86
Shelburne Rd, N7 143 DM63
Shelbury Cl, Sid. DA14 208 EU90
Shelbury Rd, SE22 204 DV85
Sheldon Av, N6 142 DE59
Ilford IG5 125 EP54
Sheldon Cl, SE12 206 EH85
SE20 224 DV95
Cheshunt EN7 88 DS26
Harlow CM17 74 EY15
Reigate RH2 288 DB135
Sheldon Ct, SW8 off Thorncroft St 42 A5
Guildford GU1 off Lower Edgeborough Rd 281 AZ135
Sheldon Pl, E2 20 D1
Sheldon Rd, N18 122 DS49
NW2 4 D1
Bexleyheath DA7 188 EZ81
Dagenham RM9 168 EY66
Sheldon Sq, W2 15 P7
Sheldon St, Croy. CR0 224 DQ104
Sheldrake Cl, E16 37 J3
Sheldrake Pl, W8 27 J4
Sheldrick Cl, SW19 222 DD96
Shelduck Cl, E15 13 M2
Sheldwich Ter, Brom. BR2 226 EL100
Shelford, Kings.T. KT1 off Burritt Rd 220 CN96
Shelford Pl, N16 144 DR62
Shelford Ri, SE19 204 DT94
Shelford Rd, Barn. EN5 101 CW44
Shelgate Rd, SW11 202 DE85
Shellbank La, Dart. DA2 211 FU93
★ Shell Cen, SE1 30 D3
Shell Cl, Brom. BR2 226 EL100
Shellduck Cl, NW9 off Swan Dr 118 CS54
Shelley Av, E12 166 EL65
Greenford UB6 159 CD69
Hornchurch RM12 149 FF61
Shelley Cl, SE15 44 F8
Banstead SM7 255 CX115
Borehamwood WD6 100 CN42
Coulsdon CR5 257 DM117
Edgware HA8 118 CN49
Greenford UB6 159 CD69
Hayes UB4 157 BU71
Northwood HA6 115 BT50
Orpington BR6 227 ES104
Slough SL3 175 AZ78
Wooburn Moor HP10 off Falcons Cft 132 AE55
Shelley Ct, N4 143 DM60
Waltham Abbey EN9 off Bramley Shaw 90 EF33
Shelley Cres, Houns. TW5 178 BX82
Southall UB1 158 BZ72
Shelley Dr, Well. DA16 187 ES81
Shelley Gdns, Wem. HA0 139 CJ61
Shelley Gro, Loug. IG10 107 EM42
Shelley Ho, SW1 41 M2
Shelley La, Hare. UB9 114 BG53
Shelley Pl, Til. RM18 193 GH81
Shelley Rd, NW10 160 CR67
Chesham HP5 76 AP29
Hutton CM13 131 GD45
Shelleys La, Knock. TN14 261 ET116
Shelley Way, SW19 202 DD93
Shellfield Cl, Stai. TW19 196 BG85
Shellgrove Est, N16 9 P2
Shellness Rd, E5 10 F2
Shell Rd, SE13 185 EB83
Shellwood Dr, N.Holm. RH5 285 CJ140
Shellwood Rd, SW11 40 E9
Leigh RH2 286 CQ141
Shelmerdine Cl, E3 22 A6
Shelson Av, Felt. TW13 197 BT90
Shelton Av, Warl. CR6 258 DW117
Shelton Cl, Guil. GU2 264 AU129
Warlingham CR6 258 DW117
Shelton Rd, SW19 222 DA95
Shelton St, WC2 18 A9
Shelvers Grn, Tad. KT20 255 CW121
Shelvers Hill, Tad. KT20 off Ashurst Rd 255 CV121
Shelvers Spur, Tad. KT20 255 CW121
Shelvers Way, Tad. KT20 255 CW121
Shenden Cl, Sev. TN13 279 FJ128
Shenden Way, Sev. TN13 279 FJ128
Shendish Edge, Hem.H. HP3 off London Rd 80 BM25
Sch Shene Sch, SW14 off Park Av 180 CS84
SHENFIELD, Brwd. CM15 131 GA45
⇌ Shenfield 131 GA45
Shenfield Cl, Couls. CR5 off Woodfield Cl 257 DJ119
Shenfield Common, Brwd. CM15 130 FY48
Shenfield Cres, Brwd. CM15 130 FY47
Shenfield Gdns, Hutt. CM13 131 GB44
Shenfield Grn, Shenf. CM15 131 GA45
Sch Shenfield High Sch, Shenf. CM15 off Alexander La 131 GA43
Shenfield Ho, SE18 off Shooters Hill Rd 186 EK80
Shenfield Pl, Shenf. CM15 130 FY45
Shenfield Rd, Brwd. CM15 130 FX46
Woodford Green IG8 124 EH52
Shenfield St, N1 19 P1
SHENLEY, Rad. WD7 84 CN33
Shenley Av, Ruis. HA4 137 BT61
Shenleybury, Shenley WD7 84 CL30
Shenleybury Cotts, Shenley WD7 84 CL31
Shenley Cl, S.Croy. CR2 242 DT110
Shenley Hill, Rad. WD7 99 CG35
Shenley La, Lon.Col. AL2 83 CJ27
Sch Shenley Prim Sch, Shenley WD7 off London Rd 84 CM34
Shenley Rd, SE5 43 P7
Borehamwood WD6 100 CN42
Dartford DA1 210 FN86
Hounslow TW5 178 BY81
Radlett WD7 83 CH34
Shenstone Cl, Dart. DA1 189 FD84
Shenstone Dr, Burn. SL1 153 AK70
Shenstone Gdns, Rom. RM3 128 FJ53
Shenstone Hill, Berk. HP4 60 AX18
Sch Shenstone Sch, Cray. DA1 off Old Rd 189 FD84
Shepcot Ho, N14 103 DJ44
Shepherd Cl, Abb.L. WD5 81 BT30
Hanworth TW13 198 BY91
Shepherdess Pl, N1 19 K2
Shepherdess Wk, N1 9 K10
Shepherd Ho, E16 37 N1
Shepherd Mkt, W1 29 J2
Sch Shepherd Prim Sch, Mill End WD3 off Shepherds La 114 BG46
SHEPHERD'S BUSH, W12 26 B2
⇌ Shepherd's Bush 26 D4
Shepherd's Bush 26 D4
⊖ Shepherd's Bush 26 C4
Shepherds Bush Grn, W12 26 B4
⊖ Shepherd's Bush Market 26 A3
Shepherds Bush Mkt, W12 26 A5
Shepherds Bush Pl, W12 26 C4
Shepherds Bush Rd, W6 26 B9
Shepherds Cl, N6 143 DH58
W1 off Lees Pl 16 G10
Beaconsfield HP9 111 AM54
Cowley UB8 156 BJ70
Leatherhead KT22 254 CL124
Orpington BR6 off Stapleton Rd 227 ET104
Romford RM6 148 EX57
Shepperton TW17 217 BP100
Stanmore HA7 117 CG50
Shepherds Ct, W12 26 C4
Hertford SG14 54 DQ06
Shepherds Farm, Rickmansworth WD3 114 BG46
Shepherds Grn, Chis. BR7 207 ER94
Hemel Hempstead HP1 61 BE21
Shepherds Hill, N6 143 DH58
Guildford GU2 264 AU132
Shepherds Hill, Merstham RH1 273 DJ126
Romford RM3 128 FN54
Shepherds Ho, N7 off York Way 8 A5
Shepherds La, E9 11 J3
SE28 167 ES74
Beaconsfield HP9 111 AM54
Shepherd's La, Brwd. CM14 130 FS45
Shepherds La, Dart. DA1 209 FG88
Guildford GU2 264 AT131
Rickmansworth WD3 113 BF45
Shepherds Path, Nthlt. UB5 off Cowings Mead 158 BY65
Shepherd's Pl, W1 16 G10
Shepherds Rd, Wat. WD18 97 BT41
Shepherd St, W1 29 J3
Northfleet DA11 212 GD87
Shepherds Wk, NW2 141 CU61
NW3 6 A2
Bushey Heath WD23 117 CD47
Shepherds' Wk, Epsom KT18 254 CP121
Shepherds Way, Brook.Pk AL9 86 DC27
Chesham HP5 76 AR33
Rickmansworth WD3 114 BH45
Shalford GU4 280 AY138
South Croydon CR2 243 DX108
Shepiston La, Hayes UB3 177 BR77
West Drayton UB7 177 BQ77
Shepley Cl, Cars. SM5 222 DG104
Shepley Ms, Enf. EN3 105 EA37
Sheppard Cl, Enf. EN1 104 DV38
Kingston upon Thames KT1 off Beaufort Rd 220 CL98
Sheppard Dr, SE16 32 E10
Sheppards, Harl. CM19 off Heighams 73 EM18
Sheppards Cl, St.Alb. AL3 65 CE17
Sheppard St, E16 23 M4
SHEPPERTON, TW17 216 BN101
⇌ Shepperton 217 BQ99
● Shepperton Business Pk, Shep. TW17 217 BQ99
Shepperton Cl, Borwd. WD6 100 CR39
Shepperton Ct, Shep. TW17 217 BP100
Shepperton Ct Dr, Shep. TW17 217 BP99
Shepperton Rd, N1 9 K8
Petts Wood BR5 227 EQ100
Staines-upon-Thames TW18 216 BJ97
Shepperton Studios, Shep. TW17 216 BM97
Sheppey Cl, Erith DA8 189 FH80
Sheppey Gdns, Dag. RM9 off Sheppey Rd 168 EW66
Sheppey Rd, Dag. RM9 168 EV66
Sheppeys La, Bedmond WD5 81 BS28
Sheppy Pl, Grav. DA12 213 GH87
Shepton Hos, E2 off Welwyn St 21 H2
Sherard Ct, N7 off Manor Gdns 143 DL62
Sherard Rd, SE9 206 EL85
Sherards Orchard, Harl. CM19 73 EP17
● Sheraton Business Cen, Perivale UB6 159 CH68
Sheraton Cl, Els. WD6 100 CM43
Sheraton Dr, Epsom KT19 238 CQ113
Sheraton Ms, Wat. WD18 97 BS42
Sheraton St, W1 17 N9
Sherborne Av, Enf. EN3 104 DW40
Southall UB2 178 CA77
Sherborne Cl, Colnbr. SL3 175 BE81
Epsom KT18 255 CW117
Hayes UB4 158 BW72
Sherborne Ct, Guil. GU2 off The Mount 280 AW136
Sherborne Cres, Cars. SM5 222 DE101
Sherborne Gdns, NW9 140 CN55
W13 159 CH72
Romford RM5 126 FA50
Sherborne Ho, SW8 off Bolney St 42 C5
Sherborne La, EC4 19 L10
Sherborne Pl, Nthwd. HA6 115 BR51
Sherborne Rd, Chess. KT9 238 CL106
Feltham TW14 197 BR87
Orpington BR5 227 ET98
Sutton SM3 222 DA103
Sherborne St, N1 9 L8
Sherborne Wk, Lthd. KT22 off Windfield 253 CJ121
Sherborne Way, Crox.Grn WD3 97 BP42
Sherboro Rd, N15 144 DT58
Sherbourne, Albury GU5 282 BK139
Sherbourne Cl, Hem.H. HP2 62 BL21
Sherbourne Cotts, Albury GU5 282 BL138
Watford WD18 off Lammas Rd 98 BW43
Sherbourne Dr, Wind. SL4 173 AM84
Sherbourne Gdns, Shep. TW17 217 BS101
Sherbourne Pl, Stan. HA7 117 CG51
Sherbourne Wk, Farn.Com. SL2 133 AQ63
Sherbrooke Cl, Bexh. DA6 188 FA84
Sherbrooke Rd, SW6 38 F5
Sherbrooke Way, Wor.Pk. KT4 221 CV101
Sherbrook Gdns, N21 121 DP45
SHERE, Guil. GU5 282 BN139
Shere Av, Sutt. SM2 239 CW110
Shere Cl, Chess. KT9 237 CK106
North Holmwood RH5 285 CJ140
Sch Shere C of E Inf Sch, Shere GU5 off Gomshall La 282 BN139
Sheredan Rd, E4 123 ED50
Sheredes Dr, Hodd. EN11 71 DZ19
Sch Sheredes Prim Sch, Hodd. EN11 off Benford Rd 71 DZ19
Sch Sheredes Sch, Hodd. EN11 off Cock La 71 DZ18
Shere La, Shere GU5 282 BN139
★ Shere Mus, Guil. GU5 282 BN139
Shere Rd, Guil. GU4, GU5 282 BL138
Ilford IG2 147 EN57
West Horsley KT24 267 BP130
Sherfield Av, Rick. WD3 114 BK47
Sherfield Cl, N.Mal. KT3 220 CP98
Sherfield Gdns, SW15 201 CT86
Sherfield Ms, Hayes UB3 157 BS72
Sherfield Rd, Grays RM17 192 GB79
Sheridan Cl, Hem.H. HP1 62 BH21
Romford RM3 127 FH52
Swanley BR8 off Willow Av 229 FF97
Uxbridge UB10 off Alpha Rd 157 BQ70
Sheridan Ct, Houns. TW4 off Vickers Way 198 BY85
Sheridan Ct, Northolt UB5 138 CB64
Sheridan Cres, Chis. BR7 227 EP96
Sheridan Dr, Reig. RH2 272 DB132
Sheridan Gdns, Har. HA3 139 CK58
Sheridan Hts, E1 off Spencer Way 20 F9
Sheridan Ho, Lthd. KT22 off Highbury Dr 253 CG121
Sheridan Ms, E11 off Woodbine Pl 146 EH58
Sheridan Pl, SW13 181 CT82
Bromley BR1 226 EK96
Hampton TW12 218 CB95
Sheridan Rd, E7 146 EF62
E12 146 EL64
SW19 221 CZ95
Belvedere DA17 188 FA77
Bexleyheath DA7 188 EY83
Richmond TW10 199 CJ90
Watford WD19 116 BX45
Sheridans Rd, Bkhm KT23 268 CC126
Sheridan Ter, Nthlt. UB5 138 CB64
Sheridan Wk, NW11 142 DA58
Broxbourne EN10 71 DY20
Carshalton SM5 off Carshalton Pk Rd 240 DF106
Sheridan Way, Beck. BR3 off Turners Meadow Way 225 DZ95
Sheriff Way, Wat. WD25 81 BU33
Sch Sheringdale Prim Sch, SW18 off Standen Rd 201 CZ88
Sheringham Av, E12 147 EM63
N14 103 DK43
Feltham TW13 197 BU90
Romford RM7 149 FC58
Twickenham TW2 198 BZ88
Sheringham Ct, Hayes UB3 177 BT75
Sheringham Dr, Bark. IG11 147 ET64
Sch Sheringham Jun Sch, E12 off Sheringham Av 147 EM63
Sheringham Rd, N7 8 D4
SE20 224 DV97
Sheringham Twr, Sthl. UB1 158 CB73
Sherington Av, Pnr. HA5 116 CA52
Sch Sherington Prim Sch, SE7 off Sherington Rd 186 EH79
Sherington Rd, SE7 186 EH79
Sherland Rd, Twick. TW1 199 CF88
Sherlies Av, Orp. BR6 227 ES103
★ Sherlock Holmes Mus, NW1 16 F5
Sherlock Ms, W1 16 G6
Shermanbury Cl, Erith DA8 189 FF80
Sherman Gdns, Chad.Hth RM6 148 EW58
Sherman Rd, Brom. BR1 226 EG95
Slough SL1 154 AS71
Shernbroke Rd, Wal.Abb. EN9 90 EF34
Shernhall St, E17 145 EC57
Sherpa Rd, Hem.H. HP2 62 BN19
Sherrard Rd, E7 166 EJ65
E12 166 EK65
Sherrards, Welw.G.C. AL8 51 CV06
Sherrards Mansion, Welw.G.C. AL8 off Sherrards 51 CV06
Sherrards Ms, Welw.G.C. AL8 off Sherrards 51 CV06
SHERRARDSPARK, Welw.G.C. AL8 51 CV07
Sherrardspark Rd, Welw.G.C. AL8 51 CW07
Sherrards Way, Barn. EN5 102 DA43
Sherrick Grn Rd, NW10 141 CV64
Sherriff Cl, Esher KT10 218 CB103
Sherriff Rd, NW6 5 K5
Sherringham Av, N17 122 DU54
Sherrin Rd, E10 145 EA63
Sherrock Gdns, NW4 141 CU56
Sherry Ms, Bark. IG11 167 ER66
Sherwin Rd, SE14 45 J7
Sherwood Av, E18 146 EH55
SW16 203 DK94
Greenford UB6 159 CE65
Hayes UB4 157 BV70
Potters Bar EN6 85 CY32
Ruislip HA4 137 BS58
St. Albans AL4 65 CH17
Sherwood Cl, E17 123 DZ54
SW13 off Lower Common S 181 CV83
W13 159 CH74
Bexley DA5 208 EW86
Fetcham KT22 252 CC122
Slough SL3 174 AY76
Sherwood Ct, Colnbr. SL3 off High St 175 BD80
Watford WD25 off High Rd 81 BU34
Sherwood Cres, Reig. RH2 288 DB138
Sherwood Gdns, E14 34 B8
SE16 44 D1
Barking IG11 167 ER66
Sherwood Ho, Harl. CM18 off Bush Fair 73 ET17
Sherwood Pk Av, Sid. DA15 208 EU87
Sch Sherwood Pk Prim Sch, Sid. DA15 off Sherwood Pk Av 208 EV86
Sherwood Pk Rd, Mitch. CR4 223 DJ98
Sutton SM1 240 DA106
Sch Sherwood Pk Sch, Wall. SM6 off Streeters La 223 DK104
Sherwood Pl, Hem.H. HP2 off Turnpike Grn 62 BM16
Sherwood Rd, NW4 141 CW55
SW19 201 CZ94
Coulsdon CR5 257 DJ116
Croydon CR0 224 DV101
Hampton Hill TW12 198 CC92
Harrow HA2 138 CC61
Ilford IG6 147 ER56
Knaphill GU21 248 AS117
Welling DA16 187 ES82
Sch Sherwood Sch, The, Mitch. CR4 off Abbotts Rd 223 DJ98
Sherwoods Rd, Wat. WD19 116 BY45
Sherwood St, N20 120 DD48
W1 17 M10
Sherwood Ter, N20 120 DD48
Sherwood Way, W.Wick. BR4 225 EB103
Shetland Cl, Borwd. WD6 100 CR44
Guildford GU4 off Weybrook Dr 265 BB129
Shetland Rd, E3 21 N1
Shevon Way, Brwd. CM14 130 FT49
Shewens Rd, Wey. KT13 235 BR105
Shey Copse, Wok. GU22 249 BC117
Shield Dr, Brent. TW8 179 CG79
Shieldhall St, SE2 188 EW77
Shield Rd, Ashf. TW15 197 BQ91
Shifford Path, SE23 205 DX90
Shilburn Way, Wok. GU21 248 AU118

Shillibeer Pl, W1 16 D6
Shillibeer Wk, Chig. IG7 125 ET48
Shillingford Cl, NW7 119 CX52
Shillingford St, N1 9 H7
Shillitoe Av, Pot.B. EN6 85 CX32
Shimmings, The, Guil. GU1 265 BA133
Shinecroft, Otford TN14 263 FG116
Shinfield St, W12 14 A9
Shingle Ct, Wal.Abb. EN9 90 EG33
Shinglewell Rd, Erith DA8 188 FA80
Shinners Cl, SE25 224 DU99
Ship All, W4 *off Thames Rd* 180 CN79
Ship & Half Moon Pas, SE18 37 N6
Ship & Mermaid Row, SE1 31 M4
Shipfield Cl, Tats. TN16 260 EJ121
Ship Hill, H.Wyc. HP10 133 AL60
Tatsfield TN16 260 EJ121
Shipka Rd, SW12 203 DH88
Ship La, SW14 180 CQ82
Aveley RM15 191 FR75
Mountnessing CM13 131 GF41
Purfleet RM19 191 FS76
Sutton at Hone DA4 230 FK95
Swanley BR8 230 FK95
Ship La Caravan Site, Aveley RM15 191 FR76
SHIPLEY BRIDGE, Horl. RH6 291 DM153
Shipman Rd, E16 24 B9
SE23 205 DX89
Ship St, SE8 46 A6
Ship Tavern Pas, EC3 19 N10
Shipton Cl, Dag. RM8 148 EX62
Shipton St, E2 20 B2
Shipwright Rd, SE16 33 L5
Shipwright Yd, SE1 31 N3
Ship Yd, E14 34 C10
Weybridge KT13 *off High St* 235 BP105
Shirburn Cl, SE23 *off Tyson Rd* 204 DW87
Shirbutt St, E14 22 C10
Shirebrook Rd, SE3 186 EK82
Shire Cl, Brox. EN10 *off Groom Rd* 89 DZ26
Shire Ct, Epsom KT17 239 CT108
Erith DA18 *off St. John Fisher Rd* 188 EX76
Shirehall Cl, NW4 141 CX58
Shirehall Gdns, NW4 141 CX58
Shirehall La, NW4 141 CX58
Shirehall Pk, NW4 141 CX58
Shirehall Rd, Dart. DA2 210 FK92
Shire Horse Way, Islw. TW7 179 CF83
Shire La, Chal.St.P. SL9 113 BD54
Chorleywood WD3 95 BB43
Denham UB9 135 BE55
Keston BR2 245 EM108
Orpington BR6 245 ER107
Shiremeade, Els. WD6 100 CM43
Shire Ms, Whitton TW2 198 CC86
● Shire Pk, Welw.G.C. AL7 51 CY07
Shire Pl, SW18 202 DB87
Redhill RH1 288 DF136
Shires, The, Ham TW10 200 CL91
Watford WD25 81 BV31
Shires Cl, Ashtd. KT21 253 CK118
Shires Ho, Byfleet KT14 234 BL113
Shirland Ms, W9 15 H3
Shirland Rd, W9 15 J3
SHIRLEY, Croy. CR0 225 DX104
Shirley Av, Bex. DA5 208 EX87
Cheam SM2 239 CZ109
Coulsdon CR5 257 DP119
Croydon CR0 224 DW102
Redhill RH1 288 DF139
Sutton SM1 240 DE105
Windsor SL4 173 AM81
Shirley Ch Rd, Croy. CR0 225 DX104
Shirley Cl, E17 *off Addison Rd* 145 EB57
Broxbourne EN10 71 DZ24
Cheshunt EN8 88 DW29
Dartford DA1 190 FJ84
Hounslow TW3 198 CC85
Shirley Ct, Croy. CR0 225 DX104
Shirley Cres, Beck. BR3 225 DY98
Shirley Dr, Houns. TW3 198 CC85
Shirley Gdns, W7 159 CF74
Barking IG11 167 ES65
Hornchurch RM12 150 FJ61
Shirley Gro, N9 122 DW45
SW11 182 DG83
Shirley Hts, Wall. SM6 241 DJ109
[Sch] Shirley High Sch, Croy. CR0 *off Shirley Ch Rd* 225 DX104
Shirley Hills Rd, Croy. CR0 243 DX106
Shirley Ho Dr, SE7 186 EJ80
[H] Shirley Oaks Hosp, Croy. CR0 224 DW101
Shirley Oaks Rd, Croy. CR0 225 DX102
Shirley Pk Rd, Croy. CR0 224 DV102
Shirley Rd, E15 13 K6
W4 180 CR75
Abbots Langley WD5 81 BT32
Croydon CR0 224 DV101
Enfield EN2 104 DQ41
St. Albans AL1 65 CF21
Sidcup DA15 207 ES90
Wallington SM6 241 DJ109
Shirley St, E16 23 L8
Shirley Way, Croy. CR0 225 DY104
Shirlock Rd, NW3 6 F1
Shirwell Cl, NW7 119 CX52
Shobden Rd, N17 122 DR53
Shobroke Cl, NW2 141 CW62
Shoebury Rd, E6 167 EM66
Shoe La, EC4 18 F8
Harlow CM17 74 EZ16
Sholden Gdns, Orp. BR5 228 EW99
Sholto Rd, Lon.Hthrw Air. TW6 196 BM85
Shona Ho, E13 24 C6
Shonks Mill Rd, Nave. RM4 109 FG37
Shooters Av, Har. HA3 139 CJ56
Shooters Dr, Lwr Naze. EN9 72 EE22
SHOOTER'S HILL, SE18 187 EQ81
Shooters Hill, SE18 187 EN81
Welling DA16 187 EN81
[Coll] Shooters Hill Post 16 Campus, SE18 *off Red Lion La* 187 EN81
Shooters Hill Rd, SE3 47 M6
SE10 46 F7
SE18 186 EH80
Shooters Rd, Enf. EN2 103 DP39
Shootersway, Berk. HP4 60 AU20
Shootersway La, Berk. HP4 60 AT20
Shootersway Pk, Berk. HP4 60 AT20
Shoot Up Hill, NW2 4 E3
Shophouse La, Albury GU5 282 BK144
Shoplands, Welw.G.C. AL8 51 CX05
Shord Hill, Ken. CR8 258 DR116
Shore, The, Nthflt DA11 212 GD85
Rosherville DA11 213 GF86
Shore Cl, Felt. TW14 197 BU87
Hampton TW12 *off Stewart Cl* 198 BY92
Shorediche Cl, Uxb. UB10 136 BM62
SHOREDITCH, E1 20 A5
⊖ Shoreditch High Street 19 P5
Shoreditch High St, E1 19 P5
Shoreditch Ho, N1 19 M3
Shore Gro, Felt. TW13 198 CA89
SHOREHAM, Sev. TN14 247 FG111
⇌ Shoreham 247 FG111
Shoreham Cl, SW18 *off Ram St* 202 DB85
Bexley DA5 208 EX88
Croydon CR0 224 DW100
Shoreham La, Halst. TN14 246 EZ112
Orpington BR6 246 FA107
Sevenoaks TN13 278 FF122
Shoreham Pl, Shore. TN14 247 FG112
Shoreham Ri, Slou. SL2 *off Lower Britwell Rd* 153 AK70
Shoreham Rd, Orp. BR5 228 EV95
Sevenoaks TN14 247 FH111
Shoreham Rd E, Lon.Hthrw Air. TW6 196 BL85
Shoreham Rd W, Lon.Hthrw Air. TW6 196 BL85
[Sch] Shoreham Village Sch, Shore. TN14 *off Church St* 247 FF111
Shoreham Way, Brom. BR2 226 EG100
Shore Pl, E9 10 G7
Shore Pt, Buck.H. IG9 124 EH47
Shore Rd, E9 10 G7
Shores Rd, Wok. GU21 232 AY114
Shore Way, SW9 42 F8
Shorncliffe Rd, SE1 32 A10
Shorndean St, SE6 205 EC88
Shorne Cl, Orp. BR5 228 EX98
Sidcup DA15 208 EV86
Shornefield Cl, Brom. BR1 227 EN97
Shornells Way, SE2 *off Willrose Cres* 188 EW78
Shorrolds Rd, SW6 39 H4
Shortacres, Red. RH1 273 DM133
Shortcroft Rd, Epsom KT17 239 CT108
Shortcrofts Rd, Dag. RM9 168 EZ65
Shorter Av, Shenf. CM15 131 FZ44
Shorter St, E1 20 A10
Shortfern, Slou. SL2 154 AW72
Shortgate, N12 119 CZ49
Short Hedges, Houns. TW3, TW5 178 CB81
Short Hill, Har. HA1 *off High St* 139 CE60
SHORTLANDS, Brom. BR1 226 EE97
⇌ Shortlands 226 EE96
Shortlands, W6 26 C9
Harlington UB3 177 BR79
Shortlands Cl, N18 122 DR48
Belvedere DA17 188 EZ76
Shortlands Gdns, Brom. BR2 226 EE96
Shortlands Grn, Welw.G.C. AL7 51 CZ10
Shortlands Gro, Brom. BR2 225 ED97
Shortlands Rd, E10 145 EB59
Bromley BR2 225 ED97
Kingston upon Thames KT2 200 CM94
Short La, Brick.Wd AL2 82 BZ30
Oxted RH8 276 EH132
Staines-upon-Thames TW19 196 BM88
Shortmead Dr, Chsht EN8 89 DY31
Short Path, SE18 *off Long Wk* 187 EP79
Short Rd, E11 146 EE61
W4 180 CS79
London Heathrow Airport TW6 196 BL86
Shorts Cft, NW9 140 CP56
Shorts Gdns, WC2 18 A9
Shorts Rd, Cars. SM5 240 DE105
Short St, NW4 *off New Brent St* 141 CW56
SE1 30 F4
Short Wall, E15 22 F2
Shortway, N12 120 DE51
Short Way, SE9 186 EL83
Shortway, Amer. HP6 77 AR37
Chesham HP5 76 AP29
Short Way, Twick. TW2 198 CC87
Shortwood Av, Stai. TW18 196 BH90
Shortwood Common, Stai. TW18 196 BH91
[Sch] Shortwood Inf Sch, Stai. TW18 *off Stanwell New Rd* 196 BH90
Shotfield, Wall. SM6 241 DH107
Shothanger Way, Bov. HP3 79 BC26
Shott Cl, Sutt. SM1 *off Turnpike La* 240 DC106
Shottendane Rd, SW6 39 J6
Shottery Cl, SE9 206 EL90
Shottfield Av, SW14 180 CS84
Shoulder of Mutton All, E14 21 M10
Shouldham St, W1 16 D7
Showers Way, Hayes UB3 157 BU74
Shrapnel Cl, SE18 186 EL80
Shrapnel Rd, SE9 187 EM83
SHREDING GREEN, Iver SL0 155 BB72
Shrewsbury Av, SW14 180 CQ84
Harrow HA3 140 CL56
Shrewsbury Cl, Surb. KT6 220 CL103
Shrewsbury Ct, EC1 *off Whitecross St* 19 K5
[Sch] Shrewsbury Ho Sch, Surb. KT6 *off Ditton Rd* 220 CL103
Shrewsbury La, SE18 187 EP81
Shrewsbury Ms, W2 15 J7
Shrewsbury Rd, E7 146 EK64
N11 121 DJ51
NW10 *off Shakespeare Rd* 160 CR67
W2 15 J8
Beckenham BR3 225 DY97
Carshalton SM5 222 DE100
London Heathrow Airport TW6 197 BQ86
Redhill RH1 272 DE134
Shrewsbury St, W10 14 B5
Shrewsbury Wk, Islw. TW7 *off South St* 179 CG83
Shrewton Rd, SW17 202 DF94
Shrimpton Cl, Beac. HP9 111 AK49
Shrimpton Rd, Beac. HP9 111 AK49
Shroffold Rd, Brom. BR1 206 EE91
Shropshire Cl, Mitch. CR4 223 DL98
Shropshire Ho, N18 122 DV50
Shropshire Pl, WC1 17 M5
Shropshire Rd, N22 121 DM52
Shroton St, NW1 16 C6
Shrubberies, The, E18 124 EG54
Chigwell IG7 125 EQ50
Shrubbery, The, E11 146 EH57
Hemel Hempstead HP1 61 BE19
Upminster RM14 150 FQ62
Shrubbery Cl, N1 9 K9
Shrubbery Gdns, N21 121 DP45
Shrubbery Rd, N9 122 DU48
SW16 203 DL91
Gravesend DA12 213 GH88
South Darenth DA4 231 FR95
Southall UB1 158 BZ74
Shrubhill Rd, Hem.H. HP1 61 BF21
Shrubland Gro, Wor.Pk. KT4 221 CW104
Shrubland Rd, E8 10 B8
E10 145 EA59
E17 145 EA57
Banstead SM7 255 CZ116
Shrublands, Brook.Pk AL9 86 DB26
Shrublands, The, Pot.B. EN6 85 CY33
Shrublands Av, Berk. HP4 60 AU19
Croydon CR0 243 EA105
Shrublands Cl, N20 120 DD46
SE26 204 DW90
Chigwell IG7 125 EQ51
Shrublands Rd, Berk. HP4 60 AU18
Shrubsall Cl, SE9 206 EL88
Shrubs Rd, Rick. WD3 114 BM51
Shuna Wk, N1 *off St. Paul's Rd* 9 L4
Shurland Av, Barn. EN4 102 DD44
Shurland Gdns, SE15 44 B4
Shurlock Av, Swan. BR8 229 FD96
Shurlock Dr, Orp. BR6 245 EQ105
Shuters Sq, W14 38 G1
Shuttle Cl, Sid. DA15 207 ET87
Shuttlemead, Bex. DA5 208 EZ87
Shuttle Rd, Dart. DA1 189 FG83
Shuttle St, E1 20 C5
Shuttleworth Rd, SW11 40 B8
Siamese Ms, N3 120 DA53
Siani Ms, N8 143 DP56
Sibella Rd, SW4 41 N9
Sibford Ct, Mitch. CR4 *off Lower Grn W* 222 DF97
Sibley Cl, Bexh. DA6 208 EY85
Bromley BR1 226 EL99
Sibley Ct, Uxb. UB8 157 BQ71
Sibley Gro, E12 166 EL66
Sibneys Grn, Harl. CM18 73 ES19
Sibthorpe Rd, SE12 206 EH86
North Mymms AL9 67 CX24
Sibthorp Rd, Mitch. CR4 *off Holborn Way* 222 DF96
Sibton Rd, Cars. SM5 222 DE101
Sicilian Av, WC1 18 B7
Sicklefield Cl, Chsht EN7 88 DT26
Sidbury St, SW6 38 E6
SIDCUP, DA14 & DA15 207 ET91
⇌ Sidcup 208 EU89
[Coll] Sidcup Arts & Adult Ed Cen, Sid. DA14 *off Alma Rd* 208 EV90
Sidcup Bypass, Chis. BR7 207 ES91
Orpington BR5 208 EX94
Sidcup DA14 207 ES91
Sidcup High St, Sid. DA14 208 EU91
Sidcup Hill, Sid. DA14 208 EV91
Sidcup Hill Gdns, Sid. DA14 *off Sidcup Hill* 208 EW92
Sidcup Pl, Sid. DA14 208 EU92
Sidcup Rd, SE9 206 EK87
SE12 206 EH85
● Sidcup Tech Cen, Sid. DA14 208 EX92
Siddeley Dr, Houns. TW4 178 BY83
Siddeley Rd, E17 *off Fulbourne Rd* 123 EC54
Siddons La, NW1 16 F5
Siddons Rd, N17 122 DU53
SE23 205 DY89
Croydon CR0 223 DN104
Side Rd, E17 145 DZ57
Denham UB9 135 BD59
Sideways La, Hkwd RH6 290 DD149
Sidewood Rd, SE9 207 ER88
Sidford Cl, Hem.H. HP1 61 BF20
Sidford Ho, SE1 *off Briant Est* 30 D7
Sidford Pl, SE1 30 D7
Sidi Ct, N15 143 DP55
Sidings, The, E11 145 EC60
Dunton Green TN13 263 FE120
Hatfield AL10 66 CS19
Loughton IG10 106 EL44
Staines-upon-Thames TW18 196 BH91
Sidings Apts, The, E16 37 M4
Sidings Ct, Hert. SG14 54 DQ09
Sidings Ms, N7 143 DN62
Siding Way, Lon.Col. AL2 83 CH26
SIDLOW, Reig. RH2 288 DB141
Sidmouth Av, Islw. TW7 179 CE82
Sidmouth Cl, Wat. WD19 115 BV47
Sidmouth Dr, Ruis. HA4 137 BU62
Sidmouth Par, NW2 *off Sidmouth Rd* 4 A7
Sidmouth Rd, E10 145 EC62
NW2 4 B6
Orpington BR5 228 EV99
Welling DA16 188 EW80
Sidmouth St, WC1 18 B3
Sidney Av, N13 121 DM50
Sidney Cl, Uxb. UB8 156 BJ66
Sidney Ct, Wal.Cr. EN8 *off Queens Way* 89 DZ34
Sidney Elson Way, E6 25 L1
Sidney Gdns, Brent. TW8 179 CJ79
Sidney Gro, EC1 18 G1
Sidney Rd, E7 146 EG62
N22 121 DM52
SE25 224 DU99
SW9 42 C9
Beckenham BR3 225 DY96
Harrow HA2 138 CC55
Staines-upon-Thames TW18 196 BG91
Theydon Bois CM16 107 ER36
Twickenham TW1 199 CG86
Walton-on-Thames KT12 217 BU101
Windsor SL4 172 AJ83
Sidney Sq, E1 20 G7
Sidney St, E1 20 G8
Sidney Webb Ho, SE1 31 M6
Sidworth St, E8 10 F7
Siebert Rd, SE3 47 P3
Siege Ho, E1 *off Sidney St* 20 F8
Siemens Rd, SE18 36 F7
Sienna Cl, Chess. KT9 237 CK107
Sigdon Pas, E8 10 D3
Sigdon Rd, E8 10 D3
Sigers, The, Pnr. HA5 137 BV58
Signal Bldg, Hayes UB3 *off Station Rd* 177 BT76
Signal Ho, Har. HA1 *off Lyon Rd* 139 CF58
Signmakers Yd, NW1 7 K9
Sigrist Sq, Kings.T. KT2 220 CL95
Silbury Av, Mitch. CR4 222 DE95
Silbury Ho, SE26 *off Sydenham Hill Est* 204 DU90
Silbury St, N1 19 L2
[Sch] Silchester Manor Sch, Tap. SL6 *off Bath Rd* 152 AD72
Silchester Rd, W10 14 D9
Silecroft Rd, Bexh. DA7 188 FA81
[Jct] Silent Pool Junct, Guil. GU5 282 BK138
Silesia Bldgs, E8 10 F6
Silex St, SE1 31 H5
Silk Br Retail Pk, NW9 141 CT58
Silk Cl, SE12 206 EG85
Silkfield Rd, NW9 140 CS57
Silkham Rd, Oxt. RH8 275 ED127
Silkin Ms, SE15 44 D5
Silk Ms, SE11 *off Kennington Rd* 42 F1
Silk Mill Ct, Wat. WD19 *off Silk Mill Rd* 115 BV45
Silk Mill Rd, Wat. WD19 115 BV45
Silk Mills Cl, Sev. TN14 279 FJ121
Silk Mills Pas, SE13 46 D8
Silk Mills Path, SE13 46 D9
Silk Mills Sq, E9 11 P4
Silkmore La, W.Hors. KT24 266 BN125
Silkstream Rd, Edg. HA8 118 CQ53
Silk St, EC2 19 K6
Silo Cl, Gdmg. GU7 280 AT143
Silo Dr, Gdmg. GU7 280 AT143
Silo Rd, Gdmg. GU7 280 AT143
Silsden Cres, Ch.St.G. HP8 *off London Rd* 112 AX48
Silsoe Ho, NW1 *off Park Village E* 17 K1
Silsoe Rd, N22 121 DM54
Silverbeck Way, Stanw.M. TW19 196 BG85
Silver Birch Av, E4 123 DZ51
North Weald Bassett CM16 92 EY27
Silver Birch Cl, N11 120 DG51
SE6 205 DZ90
SE28 168 EU74
Dartford DA2 209 FE91
Uxbridge UB10 136 BL63
Woodham KT15 233 BE112
Silver Birch Ct, Chsht EN8 89 DX31
Silver Birches, Hutt. CM13 131 GA46
Silver Birch Gdns, E6 25 J5
Silver Birch Ms, Ilf. IG6 *off Fencepiece Rd* 125 EQ51
Upminster RM14 151 FS60
Silverbirch Wk, NW3 6 F5
Silvercliffe Gdns, Barn. EN4 102 DE42
Silver Cl, SE14 45 L4
Harrow HA3 117 CD52
Kingswood KT20 255 CY124
● Silver Ct, Welw.G.C. AL7 52 DA08
Silver Cres, W4 180 CP77
Silverdale, NW1 17 L2
SE26 204 DW91
Enfield EN2 103 DL42
Silverdale Av, Ilf. IG3 147 ES57
Oxshott KT22 236 CC114
Walton-on-Thames KT12 217 BT104
Silverdale Cl, W7 159 CE74
Brockham RH3 286 CP138
Northolt UB5 138 BZ64
Sutton SM1 239 CZ105
Silverdale Ct, Stai. TW18 *off Leacroft* 196 BH92
Silverdale Dr, SE9 206 EL89
Hornchurch RM12 149 FH64
Sunbury-on-Thames TW16 217 BV96
Silverdale Gdns, Hayes UB3 177 BU75
● Silverdale Ind Est, Hayes UB3 *off Silverdale Rd* 177 BU75
Silverdale Rd, E4 123 ED51
Bexleyheath DA7 189 FB82
Bushey WD23 98 BY43
Hayes UB3 177 BU75
Petts Wood BR5 227 EQ98
St. Paul's Cray BR5 228 EU97
Silver Dell, Wat. WD24 97 BT35
Silverfield, Brox. EN10 71 DZ22
Silvergate, Epsom KT19 238 CQ106
● Silverglade Business Pk, Chess. KT9 237 CJ112
Silverhall St, Islw. TW7 179 CG83
Silver Hill, Ch.St.G. HP8 112 AV47
Well End WD6 100 CQ36
Silverholme Cl, Har. HA3 139 CK59
Silver Jubilee Way, Houns. TW4 177 BV82
Silverlands Cl, Ott. KT16 215 BD104
Silverland St, E16 37 K3
Silver La, Pur. CR8 241 DK112
West Wickham BR4 225 ED103
Silverlea Gdns, Horl. RH6 291 DJ149
Silverleigh Rd, Th.Hth. CR7 223 DM98
Silverlocke Rd, Grays RM17 192 GD79
Silvermead, E18 *off Churchfields* 124 EG53
Silvermere Av, Rom. RM5 127 FB51
Silvermere Dr, N18 123 DX51
Silvermere Rd, SE6 205 EB86
Silver Pl, W1 17 M10
Watford WD18 *off Metropolitan Ms* 97 BS42
Silver Rd, SE13 185 EB83
W12 26 C1
Gravesend DA12 213 GL89
Silversmiths Way, Wok. GU21 248 AW118
Silver Spring Cl, Erith DA8 189 FB79
Silverstead La, West. TN16 261 ER121
Silverstone Cl, Red. RH1 *off Goodwood Rd* 272 DF132
Silverston Way, Stan. HA7 117 CJ51
⇌ Silver Street 122 DT50
Silver St, N18 122 DS49
Abridge RM4 108 EV41
Enfield EN1 104 DR41
Goffs Oak EN7 88 DR30
Waltham Abbey EN9 89 EC33
Silverthorn Dr, Hem.H. HP3 63 BP24
Silverthorne Rd, SW8 41 J8
Silverthorn Gdns, E4 123 EA47
Silverton Rd, W6 38 C3
SILVERTOWN, E16 36 C4
Silvertown Way, E16 23 K8
Silver Tree Cl, Walt. KT12 217 BU104
Silvertree La, Grnf. UB6 159 CD69
Silver Trees, Brick.Wd AL2 82 BZ30
Silver Wk, SE16 33 N3
Silver Way, Hlgdn UB10 157 BP68
Romford RM7 149 FB55
● Silverwing Ind Est, Croy. CR0 241 DM106
Silverwood Cl, Beck. BR3 205 EA94
Croydon CR0 243 DZ109
Northwood HA6 115 BQ53
Silverwood Cotts, Shere GU5 282 BL138
Silvester Rd, SE22 204 DT85
Silvesters, Harl. CM19 73 EM17
Silvester St, SE1 31 K5
Silvocea Way, E14 23 H9
Silwood Est, SE16 *off Concorde Way* 33 J9
Silwood St, SE16 33 H9
Sime Cl, Guil. GU3 264 AT130
Simla Ho, SE1 31 M5
Simmil Rd, Clay. KT10 237 CE106
Simmonds Ri, Hem.H. HP3 62 BK22
Simmons Cl, N20 120 DE46
Chessington KT9 237 CJ107
Slough SL3 *off Common Rd* 175 BA77
Simmons Ct, Guil. GU1 264 AW130
Simmons Dr, Dag. RM8 148 EY62
Simmons Gate, Esher KT10 236 CC106
Simmons La, E4 123 ED47
Simmons Pl, Stai. TW18 *off Chertsey La* 195 BE92
Simmons Rd, SE18 37 N10
Simmons Way, N20 120 DE47
Simms Cl, Cars. SM5 222 DE103
Simms Gdns, N2 120 DC54
Simms Rd, SE1 32 C9
Simnel Rd, SE12 206 EH87
[Sch] Simon Balle Sch, Hert. SG13 *off Mangrove Rd* 54 DS10
Simon Cl, W11 15 H10
Simon Ct, N11 *off Ringway* 121 DJ51
Simon Dean, Bov. HP3 79 BA27
Simonds Rd, E10 145 EA61
Simone Cl, Brom. BR1 226 EK95
Simone Dr, Ken. CR8 258 DQ116
[Sch] Simon Marks Jewish Prim Sch, N16 *off Cazenove Rd* 144 DT61
Simons Cl, Ott. KT16 233 BC107
Simons Wk, E15 13 H3
Englefield Green TW20 194 AW94
Simplemarsh Ct, Add. KT15 *off Simplemarsh Rd* 234 BH105
Simplemarsh Rd, Add. KT15 234 BG105
Simplicity La, Harl. CM17 58 EX14
Simpson Cl, N21 *off Macleod Rd* 103 DL43
Croy. CR0 224 DQ99
Simpson Dr, W3 160 CR72
Simpson Rd, Houns. TW4 198 BZ86
Rainham RM13 169 FF65
Richmond TW10 199 CJ91
Simpsons Rd, E14 34 D1
Bromley BR2 226 EG97
Simpson St, SW11 40 C8
Simpsons Way, Slou. SL1 154 AS74
Simpson Way, Long Dit. KT6 219 CJ100
Simrose Ct, SW18 *off Wandsworth High St* 202 DA85
Sims Cl, Rom. RM1 149 FF56
Sims Wk, SE3 186 EF84
Sinclair Ct, Beck. BR3 205 EA94
Sinclair Dr, Sutt. SM2 240 DB109
Sinclair Gdns, W14 26 D5
Sinclair Gro, NW11 141 CX58
Sinclair Pl, SE4 205 EA86
Sinclair Rd, E4 123 DZ50
W14 26 D5
Windsor SL4 173 AQ83
Sinclair Way, Lane End DA2 211 FR91
Sinclare Cl, Enf. EN1 104 DT39
Sincots Rd, Red. RH1 *off Lower Br Rd* 272 DF134
Sinderby Cl, Borwd. WD6 100 CL39
Singapore Rd, W13 159 CG74
Singer St, EC2 19 M3
[Sch] Singlegate Prim Sch, SW19 *off South Gdns* 202 DD94
Singles Cross La, Knock.P. TN14 246 EW114
SINGLE STREET, West. TN16 261 EN115
Single St, Berry's Grn TN16 261 EP115
Singleton Cl, SW17 202 DF94
Croydon CR0 *off St. Saviours Rd* 224 DQ101
Hornchurch RM12 *off Carfax Rd* 149 FF63
Singleton Rd, Dag. RM9 148 EZ64
Singleton Scarp, N12 120 DA50
SINGLEWELL, Grav. DA12 213 GK93
[Sch] Singlewell Prim Sch, Grav. DA12 *off Mackenzie Way* 213 GK93
Singlewell Rd, Grav. DA11 213 GH89
Singret Pl, Cowley UB8 156 BJ70
Sinnott Rd, E17 123 DX53
[Sch] Sion-Manning RC Girls' Sch, W10 14 E7
Sion Rd, Twick. TW1 199 CH88
SIPSON, West Dr. UB7 176 BN79
Sipson Cl, Sipson UB7 176 BN79
Sipson La, Harling. UB3 176 BN79
Sipson UB7 176 BN79
Sipson Rd, West Dr. UB7 176 BN78
Sipson Way, Sipson UB7 176 BN80
Sir Alexander Cl, W3 161 CT74
Sir Alexander Rd, W3 161 CT74
Sir Cyril Black Way, SW19 202 DA94
Sirdar Rd, N22 143 DP55
W11 26 D1
Mitcham CR4 *off Grenfell Rd* 202 DG93
Sirdar Strand, Grav. DA12 213 GM92
[Sch] Sir Francis Drake Prim Sch, SE8 45 L1
Sir Francis Way, Brwd. CM14 130 FV47
[Sch] Sir Frederic Osborn Sch, Welw.G.C. AL7 *off Herns La* 52 DB08

Coll Sir George Monoux Coll, E17
off Chingford Rd 123 EB54
Sir Giles Gilbert Scott Bldg, The, SW15 201 CY86
Sir Henry Peek's Dr, Slou. SL2 153 AN65
Sirinham Pt, SW8 42 C3
Sirius Rd, Nthwd. HA6 115 BU50
Sch Sir James Barrie Prim Sch, SW8 41 M7
Sir James Black Ho, SE5
off Coldharbour La 43 L8
Sch Sir John Cass's Foundation & Redcoat Sch, E1 21 K7
Sch Sir John Cass's Foundation C of E Prim Sch, EC3 20 A9
Sch Sir John Heron Prim Sch, E12
off School Rd 147 EM63
Sir John Kirk Cl, SE5 43 J4
Sch Sir John Lillie Prim Sch, SW6 38 F3
Sir John Lyon Ho, EC4
off Gardners La 19 J10
Sir John Newsom Way, Welw.G.C. AL7 51 CY12
★ Sir John Soane's Mus, WC2
off Lincoln's Inn Flds 18 C8
Sir Martin Bowles Ho, SE18
off Calderwood St 37 M8
Sir Robert Ms, Slou. SL3
off Cheviot Rd 175 BA78
Sir Steve Redgrave Br, E16 37 N1
Sch Sir Thomas Abney Sch, N16
off Fairholt Rd 144 DR60
Sir Thomas More Est, SW3 40 B3
Sch Sir William Burrough Prim Sch, E14 21 M8
Sch Sir William Perkin's Sch, Cher. KT16 off Guildford Rd 215 BF102
Sise La, EC4 19 L9
Siskin Cl, Borwd. WD6 100 CN42
Bushey WD23 98 BY42
Sisley Rd, Bark. IG11 167 ES67
Sispara Gdns, SW18 201 CZ86
Sissinghurst Cl, Brom. BR1 206 EE92
Sissinghurst Rd, Croy. CR0 224 DU101
Sissulu Ct, E6 166 EJ67
Sister Mabel's Way, SE15 44 C4
Sisters Av, SW11 182 DF84
Sistova Rd, SW12 203 DH88
Sisulu Pl, SW9 183 DN83
Sittingbourne Av, Enf. EN1 104 DR44
Sitwell Gro, Stan. HA7 117 CF50
Siverst Cl, Nthlt. UB5 158 CB65
Sivill Ho, E2 20 B2
Siviter Way, Dag. RM10 169 FB66
Siward Rd, N17 122 DR53
SW17 202 DC90
Bromley BR2 226 EH97
Six Acres, Hem.H. HP3 62 BN23
Six Acres Est, N4 143 DN61
Six Bells La, Sev. TN13 279 FJ126
● Six Bridges Trd Est, SE1 44 D1
Sixpenny Ct, Bark. IG11 167 EQ65
Sixth Av, E12 147 EM63
W10 14 E3
Hayes UB3 157 BT74
Watford WD25 98 BX35
Sixth Cross Rd, Twick. TW2 198 CC90
Skardu Rd, NW2 4 E2
Skarnings Ct, Wal.Abb. EN9 90 EG33
Skeena Hill, SW18 201 CY87
Skeet Hill La, Orp. BR5, BR6 228 EY103
Skeffington Rd, E6 166 EL67
Skeffington St, SE18 187 EQ76
Skelbrook St, SW18 202 DB89
Skelgill Rd, SW15 181 CZ84
Skelley Rd, E15 13 L7
Skelton Cl, E8 10 B5
Beaconsfield HP9 132 AG55
Skelton Rd, E7 13 P5
Skeltons La, E10 145 EB59
Skelwith Rd, W6 38 B3
Skenfrith Ho, SE15 44 E3
Skerne Rd, Kings.T. KT2 219 CK95
Skerne Wk, Kings.T. KT2 219 CK95
Sketchley Gdns, SE16 33 J10
Sketty Rd, Enf. EN1 104 DS41
Skibbs La, Orp. BR5, BR6 228 EZ103
Skid Hill La, Warl. CR6 244 EF113
Skidmore Way, Rick. WD3 114 BL46
Skiers St, E15 13 J9
Skiffington Cl, SW2 203 DN88
Skillet Hill, Wal.Abb. EN9 106 EH35
Skimpans Cl, N.Mymms AL9 67 CX24
Skinner Ct, E2 10 F10
Skinner Pl, SW1 28 G9
★ Skinners' Hall, EC4
off Dowgate Hill 19 L10
Skinners La, EC4 19 K10
Ashtead KT21 253 CK118
Hounslow TW5 178 CB81
Skinner St, EC1 18 F3
Skinney La, Hort.Kir. DA4 230 FQ97
Skip La, Hare. UB9 136 BL60
Skippers Cl, Green. DA9 211 FV85
Skipsea Ho, SW18 202 DD86
Skipsey Av, E6 25 K3
Skipton Cl, N11 120 DG51
Skipton Dr, Hayes UB3 177 BQ76
Skipton Way, Horl. RH6 291 DH145
Skipworth Rd, E9 11 H8
Skomer Wk, N1 off Ashby Gro 9 K6
● Sky Business Pk, Egh. TW20
off Eversley Way 215 BC96
Skydmore Path, Slou. SL2
off Umberville Way 153 AM69
Skylark Av, Green. DA9 211 FU86
Skylark Rd, Denh. UB9 135 BC60
Skylines Village, E14 34 E5
Sky Peals Rd, Wdf.Grn. IG8 123 ED53
Skyport Dr, Harm. UB7 176 BK80
Sch Skyswood Prim Sch, St.Alb. AL4 off Chandlers Rd 65 CJ16
Skys Wd Rd, St.Alb. AL4 65 CH16
Skyvan Cl, Lon.Hthrw Air. TW6 197 BQ85
● Skyway 14, Colnbr. SL3 175 BF83
Slacksbury Hatch, Harl. CM19
off Helions Rd 73 EP15
Slade, The, SE18 187 ES79
Sladebrook Rd, SE3 186 EK83
Slade Ct, Ott. KT16 233 BD107
Radlett WD7 99 CG35
Sladedale Rd, SE18 187 ES78
Slade End, They.B. CM16 107 ES36
Slade Gdns, Erith DA8 189 FF81
⇌ Slade Green 189 FG81
Sch Slade Grn Inf Sch, Erith DA8
off Slade Grn Rd 189 FG80
Sch Slade Grn Jun Sch, Erith DA8
off Slade Grn Rd 189 FG80
Slade Grn Rd, Erith DA8 189 FG80
Slade Ho, Houns. TW4 198 BZ86
Slade Oak La, Denh. UB9 135 BD59
Gerrards Cross SL9 135 BB55
Slade Rd, Ott. KT16 233 BD107
Slades Cl, Enf. EN2 103 DN41
Slades Dr, Chis. BR7 207 EQ90
Slades Gdns, Enf. EN2 103 DN40
Slades Hill, Enf. EN2 103 DN41
Slades Ri, Enf. EN2 103 DN41
Slade Twr, E10 145 EA61
Slade Wk, SE17 43 H3
Slade Way, Mitch. CR4 222 DG95
Slagrove Pl, SE13 205 EA85
Slaidburn St, SW10 39 P3
Slaithwaite Rd, SE13 185 EC84
Slaney Pl, N7 8 E2
Slaney Rd, Rom. RM1 149 FE57
Slapleys, Wok. GU22 248 AX120
Slater Cl, SE18 37 M9
Slattery Rd, Felt. TW13 198 BW88
Sleaford Grn, Wat. WD19 116 BX48
Sleaford Ho, E3 22 B5
Sleaford St, SW8 41 L4
Sleapcross Gdns, Smallford AL4 66 CP21
SLEAPSHYDE, St.Alb. AL4 66 CP21
Sleapshyde La, Smallford AL4 66 CP21
Sleddale, Hem.H. HP2 62 BL17
Sledmere Ct, Felt. TW14
off Kilross Rd 197 BS88
Sleepers Fm Rd, Grays RM16 193 GH75
Sleets End, Hem.H. HP1 62 BH18
Slewins Cl, Horn. RM11 150 FJ57
Slewins La, Horn. RM11 150 FJ57
Slievemore Cl, SW4
off Voltaire Rd 183 DK83
Slimmons Dr, St.Alb. AL4 65 CG16
Slines Oak Rd, Warl. CR6 259 EA119
Woldingham CR3 259 EA123
Slingsby Pl, WC2 18 A10
Slip, The, West. TN16 277 EQ126
Slipe La, Brox. EN10 71 DZ24
Slippers Hill, Hem.H. HP2 62 BK19
Slippers Pl, SE16 32 F6
Slippers Pl Est, SE16 32 F7
Slipshatch Rd, Reig. RH2 287 CX138
Slipshoe St, Reig. RH2
off West St 272 DA134
Sloane Av, SW3 28 D9
Sloane Ct E, SW3 28 G10
Sloane Ct W, SW3 28 G10
Sloane Gdns, SW1 28 G9
Orpington BR6 227 EQ104
H Sloane Hosp, The, Beck. BR3 225 ED95
Sloane Ms, N8 143 DL57
⊖ Sloane Square 28 G9
Sloane Sq, SW1 28 G9
Sloane St, SW1 28 F6
Sloane Ter, SW1 28 F8
Sloane Wk, Croy. CR0 225 DZ100
Slocan Way, Welw.G.C. AL7 51 CZ06
Slocock Hill, Wok. GU21 248 AW117
Slocum Cl, SE28 168 EW73
SLOUGH, SL1 - SL3 154 AS74
⇌ Slough 154 AT74
Sch Slough & Eton C of E Sch, Slou. SL1 off Ragstone Rd 173 AR76
● Slough Business Pk, Slou. SL1 153 AQ73
Sch Slough Gram Sch, Slou. SL3
off Lascelles Rd 174 AV76
● Slough Interchange, Slou. SL2 154 AU74
Sch Slough Islamic Sch, Slou. SL2 off Wexham Rd 154 AV73
Slough La, NW9 140 CQ58
Buckland RH3 271 CU133
Epping CM16 75 FD24
Headley KT18 270 CQ125
★ Slough Mus, Slou. SL1 174 AU75
Slough Retail Pk, Slou. SL1 153 AP74
Slough Rd, Datchet SL3 174 AU78
Eton SL4 173 AR78
Iver SL0 155 BE68
● Slough Trd Est, Slou. SL1 153 AN72
Slowmans Cl, Park St AL2 82 CC28
Slyfield Ct, Guil. GU1
off Slyfield Grn 264 AY131
Slyfield Grn, Guil. GU1 264 AX130
● Slyfield Ind Est, Guil. GU1 264 AY130
Sly St, E1 20 E9
Smaldon Cl, West Dr. UB7
off Walnut Av 176 BN76
Small Acre, Hem.H. HP1 61 BF20
Smallberry Av, Islw. TW7 179 CF82
Sch Smallberry Grn Prim Sch, Islw. TW7 off Turnpike Way 179 CG81
Smallbrook Ms, W2 16 A9
Smallcroft, Welw.G.C. AL7 52 DB08
Smalley Cl, N16 144 DT62
Smalley Rd Est, N16
off Smalley Cl 144 DT61
SMALLFIELD, Horl. RH6 291 DP149
Smallfield Rd, Horl. RH6 291 DH148
SMALLFORD, St.Alb. AL4 66 CP19
Smallford La, Smallford AL4 66 CP21
Small Grains, Fawk.Grn DA3 231 FV104
Smallholdings Rd, Epsom KT17 239 CW114
Smallmead, Horl. RH6 291 DH148
Small's Hill Rd, Leigh RH2 287 CU141
Smallwood Cl, Wheat. AL4 50 CL08
Sch Smallwood Prim Sch, SW17
off Smallwood Rd 202 DD91
Smallwood Rd, SW17 202 DD91
Smardale Rd, SW18
off Alma Rd 202 DC85
Smarden Cl, Belv. DA17
off Essenden Rd 188 FA78
Smarden Gro, SE9 207 EM91
Smart Cl, Rom. RM3 127 FH53
Smarts Grn, Chsht EN7 88 DT27
Smarts Heath La, Wok. GU22 248 AU123
Smarts Heath Rd, Wok. GU22 248 AT123
Smarts La, Loug. IG10 106 EK42
Smarts Pl, N18 122 DU50
Smart's Pl, WC2 18 B8
Smarts Rd, Grav. DA12 213 GH89
Smart St, E2 21 J2
Smead Way, SE13 185 EB83
Smeaton Cl, Chess. KT9 237 CK107
Waltham Abbey EN9 90 EE32
Smeaton Ct, SE1 31 J7
Smeaton Dr, Wok. GU22 249 BB120
Smeaton Rd, SW18 202 DA87
Enfield EN3 105 EA37
Woodford Green IG8 125 EM50
Smeaton St, E1 32 E2
Smedley St, SW4 41 P8
SW8 41 P8
Smeed Rd, E3 12 A7
Smiles Pl, SE13 46 E8
Woking GU22 249 BB116
Smitham Bottom La, Pur. CR8 241 DJ111
Smitham Downs Rd, Pur. CR8 241 DK113
Sch Smitham Prim Sch, Couls. CR5 off Portnalls Rd 257 DJ116
Smithbarn Cl, Horl. RH6 291 DH147
Smith Cl, SE16 33 J3
Smithers, The, Brock. RH3 286 CP136
Smithfield, Hem.H. HP2 62 BK18
Smithfield St, EC1 18 G7
Smithies Rd, SE2 188 EV77
Smith Rd, Reig. RH2 287 CZ137
Smith's Ct, W1 17 M10
Smiths Ct, Thnwd CM16 92 EW25
Smiths Cres, Smallford AL4 66 CP21
Smiths Fm Est, Nthlt. UB5 158 CA68
Smiths La, Chsht EN7 88 DR26
Crockham Hill TN8 277 EQ133
Windsor SL4 173 AL82
Smithson Rd, N17 122 DR53
Smiths Pt, E13 13 N9
Smith Sq, SW1 30 A7
Smith St, SW3 28 E10
Surbiton KT5 220 CM100
Watford WD18 98 BW42
Smiths Yd, SW18
off Summerley St 202 DC89
Smith's Yd, Croy. CR0
off St. Georges Wk 224 DQ104
Smith Ter, SW3 40 E1
Smithwood Cl, SW19 201 CY88
Smithy Cl, Lwr Kgswd KT20 271 CZ126
Smithy La, Lwr Kgswd KT20 271 CZ127
Smithy St, E1 20 G6
Sch Smithy St Prim Sch, E1 21 H6
Smock Wk, Croy. CR0 224 DQ100
Smokehouse Yd, EC1 19 H6
Smoke La, Reig. RH2 288 DB136
SMOKY HOLE, Guil. GU5 283 BR144
Smoothfield Ct, Houns. TW3
off Hibernia Rd 178 CA84
Smugglers Wk, Green. DA9 211 FV85
Smugglers Way, SW18 182 DB84
● Smug Oak Grn Business Cen, Brick.Wd AL2 82 CA29
Smug Oak La, St.Alb. AL2 82 CB30
Smyrks Rd, SE17 43 P1
Smyrna Rd, NW6 5 J7
Smythe Cl, N9 122 DU48
Smythe Rd, Sutt.H. DA4 230 FN95
Smythe St, E14 22 D10
Snag La, Cudham TN14 245 ES109
Snakeley Cl, Loud. HP10 110 AC54
Snakes La, Barn. EN4 103 DH41
Snakes La E, Wdf.Grn. IG8 124 EJ51
Snakes La W, Wdf.Grn. IG8 124 EG51
Snakey La, Felt. TW13 197 BU91
Snape Spur, Slou. SL1 154 AS72
SNARESBROOK, E11 146 EE57
⊖ Snaresbrook 146 EG57
Sch Snaresbrook Coll, E18
off Woodford Rd 146 EG55
Snaresbrook Dr, Stan. HA7 117 CK49
Sch Snaresbrook Prim Sch, E18
off Meadow Wk 146 EG56
Snaresbrook Rd, E11 146 EE56
Snarsgate St, W10 14 A7
Snatts Hill, Oxt. RH8 276 EF129
Sneath Av, NW11 141 CZ59
Snelling Av, Nthflt DA11 212 GE89
Snellings Rd, Hersham KT12 236 BW106
Snells La, Amer. HP7 94 AV39
Snells Pk, N18 122 DT51
Snells Wd Ct, Amer. HP7 94 AW40
Sneyd Rd, NW2 4 A2
Sniggs La, Penn HP10
off Beacon Hill 110 AD50
Snipe Cl, Erith DA8 189 FH80
Snodland Cl, Downe BR6
off Mill La 245 EN110
Snowberry Cl, E15 13 H1
Barnet EN5 101 CZ41
Snowbury Rd, SW6 39 M9
Snowden Av, Hlgdn UB10 157 BP68
Snowden Cl, Wind. SL4 173 AK84
Snowden Hill, Nthflt DA11 212 GA85
Snowden St, EC2 19 N5
off Finsbury Mkt
Snowdon Cres, Hayes UB3 177 BQ76
Snowdon Dr, NW9 140 CS58
Snowdon Rd, Lon.Hthrw Air. TW6
off Southern Perimeter Rd 197 BQ85
Snowdown Cl, SE20 225 DX95
Snowdrop Cl, Hmptn. TW12
off Gresham Rd 198 CA93
Snowdrop Path, Rom. RM3 128 FK52
Snowerhill Rd, Bet. RH3 286 CS136
Snow Hill, EC1 18 G7
Snowhill Cotts, Chesh. HP5 60 AT24
Snow Hill Ct, EC1 19 H8
Snowman Ho, NW6 5 L8
Snowsfields, SE1 31 M4
Sch Snowsfields Prim Sch, SE1 31 N4
Snowshill Rd, E12 146 EL64
Snowy Fielder Waye, Islw. TW7 179 CH82
Soames Pl, Barn. EN4 102 DB40
Soames St, SE15 184 DT83
Soames Wk, N.Mal. KT3 220 CS95
Soane Cl, W5 179 CK75
Soap Ho La, Brent. TW8
off Ferry La 180 CL79
Socket La, Brom. BR2 226 EH100
SOCKETT'S HEATH, Grays RM16 192 GD76
Soham Rd, Enf. EN3 105 DZ37
SOHO, W1 17 N10
Soho Cres, Woob.Grn HP10 132 AD59
● Soho Mills Ind Est, Woob.Grn HP10 132 AD59
Sch Soho Parish Sch, W1 17 N10
Soho Sq, W1 17 N8
Soho St, W1 17 N8
Sojourner Truth Cl, E8 10 F5
Solander Gdns, E1 20 G10
Solar Way, Enf. EN3 105 DZ36
Soldene Ct, N7 8 C4
Solebay St, E1 21 L5
Solecote, Bkhm KT23 268 CA125
Sole Fm Av, Bkhm KT23 268 BZ125
Sole Fm Cl, Bkhm KT23 252 BZ124
Sole Fm Rd, Bkhm KT23 268 BZ125
Sch Solefield Sch, Sev. TN13
off Solefields Rd 279 FJ126
Solefields Rd, Sev. TN13 279 FH128
Solent Ri, E13 23 N3
Solent Rd, NW6 5 J3
Soleoak Dr, Sev. TN13 279 FH127
Solesbridge Cl, Chorl. WD3 95 BF41
Solesbridge La, Rick. WD3 96 BG40
Soley Ms, WC1 18 E2
Solna Av, SW15 201 CW85
Solna Rd, N21 122 DR46
Solomon Av, N9 122 DU49
Solomons Ct, N12 off High Rd 120 DC52
Solomons Hill, Rick. WD3
off Northway 114 BK45
Solomon's Pas, SE15 184 DV84
Solom's Ct Rd, Bans. SM7 256 DD117
Solon New Rd, SW4 183 DL84
Solon Rd, SW2 183 DL84
Solway, Hem.H. HP2 62 BM18
Solway Cl, E8 10 B5
Hounslow TW4 178 BY83
Solway Rd, N22 121 DP53
SE22 184 DU84
Somaford Gro, Barn. EN4 102 DD44
Somali Rd, NW2 4 G1
Somborne Ho, SW15
off Fontley Way 201 CU87
Somerby Cl, Brox. EN10 71 EA21
Somerby Rd, Bark. IG11 167 ER66
Somercoates Cl, Barn. EN4 102 DE41
Somerden Rd, Orp. BR5 228 EX101
Somerfield Cl, Tad. KT20 255 CY119
Somerfield Rd, N4 143 DP61
Somerfield St, SE16 33 J10
Somerford Cl, Eastcote HA5 137 BU56
Somerford Gro, N16 10 A1
N17 122 DU52
Somerford Gro Est, N16 10 A1
Somerford Pl, Beac. HP9 111 AK52
Somerford St, E1 20 E5
Somerford Way, SE16 33 L5
Somerhill Av, Sid. DA15 208 EV87
Somerhill Rd, Well. DA16 188 EV82
Someries Rd, Hem.H. HP1 61 BF18
Somerleyton Pas, SW9 183 DP84
Somerleyton Rd, SW9 183 DN84
Somersby Gdns, Ilf. IG4 147 EM57
Somers Cl, NW1 7 N10
Reigate RH2 272 DA133
Somers Cres, W2 16 C9
Somerset Av, SW20 221 CV96
Chessington KT9 237 CK105
Welling DA16 207 ET85
Somerset Cl, N17 122 DR54
Epsom KT19 238 CS109
Hersham KT12
off Queens Rd 235 BV106
New Malden KT3 220 CS100
Sutt. SM3 221 CW104
Woodford Green IG8 124 EG53
Somerset Est, SW11 40 B6
Somerset Gdns, N6 142 DG59
N17 122 DS52
SE13 46 C9
SW16 223 DM97
Hornchurch RM11 150 FN60
Teddington TW11 199 CE92
Wem. HA0 139 CJ64
Somerset Hall, N17 122 DS52
★ Somerset Ho, WC2 18 C10
Somerset Ho, SW19 201 CX90
Somerset Rd, E17 145 EA57
N17 144 DT55
N18 122 DT50
NW4 141 CW56
SW19 201 CY91
W4 180 CR76
W13 159 CH74
Brentford TW8 179 CJ79
Dartford DA1 209 FH86
Enfield EN3 105 EA38
Harrow HA1 138 CC58
Kingston upon Thames KT1 220 CM96
New Barnet EN5 102 DB43
Orpington BR6 228 EU101
Redhill RH1 288 DD136
Southall UB1 158 BZ71
Teddington TW11 199 CE92
Somerset Sq, W14 26 F5
Somerset Way, Iver SL0 175 BF75
Somerset Waye, Houns. TW5 178 BY79
Somersham, Welw.G.C. AL7 52 DD09
Somersham Rd, Bexh. DA7 188 EY82
Sch Somers Heath Prim Sch, S.Ock. RM15
off Foyle Dr 171 FU73
Somers Ms, W2 16 C9
Somers Pl, SW2 203 DM87
Reigate RH2 272 DA133
Somers Rd, E17 145 DZ56
SW2 203 DM86
North Mymms AL9 67 CW24
Reigate RH2 271 CZ133
Somers Sq, N.Mymms AL9 67 CW23
SOMERS TOWN, NW1 17 P2
Somers Way, Bushey WD23 116 CC45
Somerswey, Shalf. GU4 280 AY142
Somerton Av, Rich. TW9 180 CP83
Somerton Cl, Pur. CR8 257 DN115
Somerton Rd, NW2 141 CY62
SE15 184 DV84
Somertons Cl, Guil. GU2 264 AU131
Somertrees Av, SE12 206 EH89
Somervell Rd, Har. HA2 138 BZ64
Somerville Av, SW13 181 CV79
Somerville Cl, SW9 42 D8
Somerville Rd, SE20 205 DX94
Cobham KT11 236 CA114
Dartford DA1 210 FM86
Eton SL4 173 AQ78
Romford RM6 148 EW58
Sommer's Ct, Ware SG12
off Crane Mead 55 DY07
Sommerville Ct, Borwd. WD6
off Alconbury Cl 100 CM39
Sonderburg Rd, N7 143 DM61
Sondes Fm, Dor. RH4 285 CF136
Sondes Pl Dr, Dor. RH4 285 CF136
Sondes St, SE17 43 L2
Songhurst Cl, Croy. CR0 223 DM100
Sonia Cl, Wat. WD19 116 BW45
Sonia Ct, Har. HA1 139 CF58
Sonia Gdns, N12 120 DC49
NW10 141 CT63
Hounslow TW5 178 CA80
Sonic Ct, Guil. GU1 264 AW133
Sonnets, The, Hem.H. HP1 62 BH19
Sonnet Wk, Bigg.H. TN16
off Kings Rd 260 EH118
Sonning Gdns, Hmptn. TW12 198 BY93
Sonning Rd, SE25 224 DU100
Soothouse Spring, St.Alb. AL3 65 CF16
Soper Cl, E4 123 DZ50
SE23 205 DX88
Soper Dr, Cat. CR3 258 DR123
Soper Ms, Enf. EN3
off Harston Dr 105 EA38
Soper Sq, Harl. CM17
off Square St 58 EW14
Sopers Rd, Cuffley EN6 87 DM29
Sophia Cl, N7 8 C4
Sophia Rd, E10 145 EB60
E16 24 A8
Sophia Sq, SE16 33 L1
Sophie Gdns, Slou. SL3 174 AX75
Soprano Ct, E15
off Plaistow Rd 13 L9
Sopwell La, St.Alb. AL1 65 CD21
Sopwith Av, Chess. KT9 238 CL106
Sopwith Cl, Bigg.H. TN16 260 EK116
Kingston upon Thames KT2 200 CM92
Sopwith Dr, W.Byf. KT14 234 BL111
Weybridge KT13 234 BL111
Sopwith Rd, Houns. TW5 178 BW80
Sopwith Way, SW8 41 J4
Kingston upon Thames KT2 220 CL95
Sorbie Cl, Wey. KT13 235 BR107
Sorbus Rd, Brox. EN10 89 DZ25
Sorrel Bk, Croy. CR0 243 DY110
Sorrel Cl, SE28 168 EU74
Sorrel Ct, Grays RM17
off Salix Rd 192 GD79
Sorrel Gdns, E6 24 G6
Sorrel La, E14 23 H9
Sorrell Cl, SE14 45 L4
SW9 42 F8
Sorrel Wk, Rom. RM1 149 FF55
Sorrel Way, Nthflt DA11 212 GE91
Sorrento Rd, Sutt. SM1 222 DB104
Sospel Ct, Farn.Royal SL2 153 AQ68
Sotheby Rd, N5 143 DP62
Sotheran Cl, E8 10 D8
Sotheron Rd, SW6 39 M5
Watford WD17 98 BW40
Soudan Rd, SW11 40 E7
Souldern Rd, W14 26 D7
Souldern St, Wat. WD18 97 BU43
Sounds Lo, Swan. BR8 229 FC100
South Access Rd, E17 145 DY59
Southacre Way, Pnr. HA5 116 BW53
SOUTH ACTON, W3 180 CN76
⊖ South Acton 180 CQ76
South Acton Est, W3 180 CP75
South Africa Rd, W12 161 CV74
South Albert Rd, Reig. RH2 271 CZ133
SOUTHALL, UB1 & UB2 158 BX74
⇌ Southall 178 BZ75
Coll Southall & W London Coll, Sthl. UB1 off Beaconsfield Rd 158 BY74
Southall Cl, Ware SG12 55 DX05
● Southall Enterprise Centre, Sthl. UB2 off Bridge Rd 178 CA75
Southall La, Houns. TW5 177 BV79
Southall UB2 177 BV79
Southall Pl, SE1 31 L5
Southall Way, Brwd. CM14 130 FT49
Southam Ms, Crox.Grn. WD3 97 BP44
Southampton Bldgs, WC2 18 E8
Southampton Gdns, Mitch. CR4 223 DL99
Southampton Ms, E16 36 A2
Southampton Pl, WC1 18 B7
Southampton Rd, NW5 6 F3
Southampton Rd E, Lon.Hthrw Air. TW6 196 BN86
Southampton Rd W, Lon.Hthrw Air. TW6 196 BL86
Southampton Row, WC1 18 B6
Southampton St, WC2 18 B10
Southampton Way, SE5 43 M4
Southam St, W10 14 F5
South App, Nthwd. HA6 115 BR48
South Audley St, W1 29 H1
South Av, E4 123 EB45
Carshalton SM5 240 DG108
Egham TW20 195 BC93
Richmond TW9
off Sandycombe Rd 180 CN82
Southall UB1 158 BZ73
Whiteley Village KT12 235 BS110
South Av Gdns, Sthl. UB1 158 BZ73
South Bk, Chis. BR7 207 EQ90
Southbank, Hext. BR8 209 FF94
South Bk, Surb. KT6 220 CL100
Southbank, T.Ditt. KT7 219 CH101
South Bk, West. TN16 277 ER126
● Southbank Business Cen, SW8 41 P3
Sch Southbank Int Sch - Hampstead Campus, NW3 5 P4
Sch Southbank Int Sch - Kensington Campus, W11 27 J1
Sch Southbank Int Sch - Westminster Campus, Conway St, W1 17 L5
Portland Pl, W1 17 J6
South Bk Rd, Berk. HP4 60 AT17
South Bk Ter, Surb. KT6 220 CL100
SOUTH BEDDINGTON, Wall. SM6 241 DK107
⇌ South Bermondsey 32 G10
South Birkbeck Rd, E11 145 ED62
South Black Lion La, W6 181 CU78
South Bolton Gdns, SW5 27 M10
Sch South Bookham Sch, Bkhm KT23 off Oakdene Cl 268 CC127
South Border, The, Pur. CR8 241 DK111
SOUTHBOROUGH, Brom. BR2 227 EM100
Southborough Cl, Surb. KT6 219 CK102
Southborough La, Brom. BR2 226 EL99
Sch Southborough Prim Sch, Brom. BR2 off Southborough La 227 EN99
Southborough Rd, E9 11 J8
Bromley BR1 226 EL97
Surbiton KT6 220 CL102

Sch Southborough Sch, Surb. KT6 off Hook Rd 220 CL104
Southbourne, Brom. BR2 226 EG101
Southbourne Av, NW9 118 CQ54
Southbourne Cl, Pnr. HA5 138 BY59
Southbourne Cres, NW4 141 CY56
Southbourne Gdns, SE12 206 EH85
Ilford IG1 147 EQ64
Ruislip HA4 137 BV60
Southbridge Pl, Croy. CR0 242 DQ105
Southbridge Rd, Croy. CR0 242 DQ105
Southbridge Way, Sthl. UB2 178 BY75
Southbrook, Saw. CM21 58 EY06
Southbrook Dr, Chsht EN8 89 DX28
Southbrook Ms, SE12 206 EF86
Southbrook Rd, SE12 206 EF86
SW16 223 DL95
≠ Southbury 104 DV42
Southbury Av, Enf. EN1 104 DU43
Southbury Cl, Horn. RM12 150 FK64
Sch Southbury Prim Sch, Enf. EN3 off Swansea Rd 104 DW42
Southbury Rd, Enf. EN1, EN3 104 DR41
Coll South Camden City Learning Cen, NW1 7 N10
Sch South Camden Comm Sch, NW1 7 N10
South Carriage Dr, SW1 28 E4
SW7 28 B5
SOUTH CHINGFORD, E4 123 DZ50
Southchurch Rd, E6 25 J1
South Circular Rd, SE6 (A205) 205 ED87
SE9 (A205) 187 EM83
SE12 (A205) 206 EH86
SE18 (A205) 187 EN79
SE21 (A205) 204 DS88
SE22 (A205) 204 DV88
SE23 (A205) 205 DZ88
SW2 (A205) 203 DN88
SW4 (A205) 202 DG85
SW11 (A3) 202 DE85
SW12 (A205) 203 DN88
SW14 (A205) 180 CS84
SW15 (A205) 181 CW84
SW18 (A3) 202 DE85
W4 (A205) 180 CN78
Brentford (A205) TW8 180 CN78
Richmond (A205) TW9 180 CP82
South City Ct, SE15 43 P4
Southcliffe Dr, Chal.St.P. SL9 112 AY50
South Cl, N6 143 DH58
Barnet EN5 101 CZ41
Bexleyheath DA6 188 EX84
Dagenham RM10 168 FA67
Morden SM4 222 DA100
Pinner HA5 138 BZ59
St. Albans AL2 82 CB25
Slough SL1 off St. George's Cres 153 AK73
Twickenham TW2 198 CA90
West Drayton UB7 176 BM76
Woking GU21 248 AW116
South Cl Grn, Merst. RH1 273 DH129
South Colonnade, The, E14 34 B2
Southcombe St, W14 26 E8
South Common Rd, Uxb. UB8 156 BL65
Southcote, Wok. GU21 248 AX115
Southcote Av, Felt. TW13 197 BT89
Surbiton KT5 220 CP101
Southcote Ri, Ruis. HA4 137 BR59
Southcote Rd, E17 145 DX57
N19 143 DJ63
SE25 224 DV100
South Croydon CR2 242 DS110
South Merstham RH1 273 DJ129
South Cottage Dr, Chorl. WD3 95 BF43
South Cottage Gdns, Chorl. WD3 95 BF43
Southcott Ms, NW8 16 C1
Southcott Rd, Tedd. TW11 219 CJ95
South Countess Rd, E17 145 DZ55
South Cres, E16 22 G5
WC1 17 N7
South Cft, Eng.Grn TW20 194 AV92
Southcroft, Slou. SL2 153 AP70
Southcroft Av, Well. DA16 187 ES83
West Wickham BR4 225 EC103
Southcroft Rd, SW16 202 DG93
SW17 202 DG93
Orpington BR6 227 ES104
South Cross Rd, Ilf. IG6 147 EQ57
South Croxted Rd, SE21 204 DR90
SOUTH CROYDON, CR2 242 DQ107
≠ South Croydon 242 DR106
Southdale, Chig. IG7 125 ER51
SOUTH DARENTH, Dart. DA4 231 FR95
Southdean Gdns, SW19 201 CZ89
South Dene, NW7 118 CR48
Southdene, Halst. TN14 246 EY113
Southdown Av, W7 179 CG76
Southdown Ct, Hat. AL10 67 CV21
Southdown Cres, Har. HA2 138 CB60
Ilford IG2 147 ES57
Southdown Dr, SW20 201 CX94
Southdown Rd, SW20 221 CX95
Carshalton SM5 240 DG109
Hatfield AL10 67 CU21
Hersham KT12 236 BY105
Hornchurch RM11 149 FH59
Woldingham CR3 259 DZ122
Southdowns, S.Darenth DA4 231 FR96
South Dr, Bans. SM7 240 DE113
Beaconsfield HP9 132 AH55
Coulsdon CR5 257 DK115
Cuffley EN6 87 DL30
Dorking RH5 285 CJ136
Orpington BR6 245 ES106
Romford RM2 150 FJ55
Ruislip HA4 137 BS60
St. Albans AL4 65 CK20
Sutton SM2 239 CY110
Virginia Water GU25 214 AU102
Warley CM14 130 FX49
⊖ South Ealing 179 CJ76
South Ealing Rd, W5 179 CK75
South Eastern Av, N9 122 DT48
South Eaton Pl, SW1 29 H8
South Eden Pk Rd, Beck. BR3 225 EB100
South Edwardes Sq, W8 27 H7
SOUTHEND, SE6 205 EB91
South End, W8 27 M6
Bookham KT23 268 CB126
Croydon CR0 242 DQ105
Southend Arterial Rd, Brwd. CM13 151 FV57
Hornchurch RM11 128 FK54
Romford RM2, RM3 128 FK54
Upminster RM14 151 FR57
South End Cl, NW3 6 D1
Southend Cl, SE9 207 EP86
Southend Cres, SE9 207 EN86
South End Grn, NW3 6 D1
Southend La, SE6 205 DZ91
SE26 205 DZ91
Waltham Abbey EN9 90 EH34
Southend Rd, E4 123 DY50
E6 167 EM66
E17 123 EB53
E18 124 EG53
South End Rd, NW3 6 C1
Southend Rd, Beck. BR3 205 EA94
Grays RM17 192 GC77
South End Rd, Horn. RM12 169 FH65
Rainham RM13 169 FG67
Southend Rd, Wdf.Grn. IG8 124 EJ54
South End Row, W8 27 M6
Southerland Cl, Wey. KT13 235 BQ105
Southern Av, SE25 224 DT97
Feltham TW14 197 BU88
Redhill RH1 288 DG141
Southern Dr, Loug. IG10 107 EM44
Southerngate Way, SE14 45 L4
Southern Gro, E3 21 N4
Southernhay, Loug. IG10 106 EK43
Southern Lo, Harl. CM19 73 EQ18
Southern Perimeter Rd, Lon.Hthrw Air. TW6 197 BR85
Southern Pl, Har. HA1 139 CF63
Swanley BR8 229 FD98
Southern Rd, E13 24 B1
N2 142 DF56
Sch Southern Rd Prim Sch, E13 off Southern Rd 166 EH68
Southern Row, W10 14 E5
Southerns La, Chipstead CR5 272 DC125
Southern St, N1 8 C10
Southern Way, SE10 35 M8
Harlow CM17, CM18 73 EN18
Romford RM7 148 FA58
Southernwood Cl, Hem.H. HP2 62 BN19
Southerton Rd, W6 26 A7
Southerton Way, Shenley WD7 84 CL33
South Esk Rd, E7 166 EJ65
Southey Ms, E16 35 P2
Southey Rd, N15 144 DS57
SW9 42 E6
SW19 202 DA94
Southey St, SE20 205 DX94
Southey Wk, Til. RM18 193 GH81
Southfield, Barn. EN5 101 CX44
Welwyn Garden City AL7 51 CX11
Southfield Av, Wat. WD24 98 BW38
Southfield Cl, Dorney SL4 172 AJ76
Uxbridge UB8 156 BN69
Southfield Cotts, W7 off Oaklands Rd 179 CF75
Southfield Gdns, Burn. SL1 152 AH71
Twickenham TW1 199 CF91
Southfield Pk, Har. HA2 138 CB56
Sch Southfield Pk Prim Sch, Epsom KT19 off Long Grv Rd 238 CQ111
Southfield Pl, Wey. KT13 235 BP108
Sch Southfield Prim Sch, W4 off Southfield Rd 180 CS75
Southfield Rd, N17 off The Avenue 122 DS54
W4 180 CS76
Chislehurst BR7 227 ET97
Enfield EN3 104 DV44
Hoddesdon EN11 71 EA15
Waltham Cross EN8 89 DY32
SOUTHFIELDS, SW18 202 DA88
⊖ Southfields 201 CZ88
Southfields, NW4 141 CU55
East Molesey KT8 219 CE100
Swanley BR8 209 FE94
Southfields Av, Ashf. TW15 197 BP93
Sch Southfield Sch, Hat. AL10 off Travellers La 67 CV21
Sch Southfields Comm Coll, SW18 off Merton Rd 202 DA88
Southfields Ct, SW19 201 CY88
Sutton SM1 off Sutton Common Rd 222 DA103
Southfields Grn, Grav. DA11 213 GH92
Southfields Ms, SW18 off Southfields Rd 202 DA86
Southfields Pas, SW18 202 DA86
Southfields Rd, SW18 202 DA86
Woldingham CR3 259 EB123
Southfield Way, St.Alb. AL4 65 CK18
SOUTHFLEET, Grav. DA13 212 GB93
Southfleet Rd, Bean DA2 211 FW91
Northfleet DA11 213 GF89
Orpington BR6 227 ES104
Swanscombe DA10 212 FZ87
South Gdns, SW19 202 DD94
Wembley HA9 off The Avenue 140 CM61
SOUTHGATE, N14 121 DJ47
⊖ Southgate 121 DJ46
South Gate, Harl. CM20 73 ER15
Southgate, Purf. RM19 190 FQ77
Southgate Av, Felt. TW13 197 BR91
Southgate Circ, N14 off The Bourne 121 DK46
Southgate Gro, N1 9 M7
Southgate Rd, N1 9 M8
Potters Bar EN6 86 DC33
Sch Southgate Sch, Cockfos. EN4 off Sussex Way 103 DH43
South Gipsy Rd, Well. DA16 188 EX83
South Glade, The, Bex. DA5 208 EZ88
South Grn, NW9 off Clayton Fld 118 CS53
Slough SL1 153 AS73
≠ South Greenford 159 CE69
South Gro, E17 145 DZ57
N6 142 DG60
N15 144 DR57
Chertsey KT16 215 BF100
South Gro Ho, N6 142 DG60
Sch South Gro Prim Sch, E17 off Ringwood Rd 145 DZ58
SOUTH HACKNEY, E9 10 F7
South Hall Cl, Fnghm DA4 230 FM101
South Hall Dr, Rain. RM13 169 FH71
SOUTH HAMPSTEAD, NW6 5 M6
⊖ South Hampstead 5 P7
Sch South Hampstead High Sch, NW3 5 P5
Jun Dept, NW3 5 P4
SOUTH HAREFIELD, Uxb. UB9 136 BJ56
Sch South Harringay Inf Sch, N4 off Pemberton Rd 143 DP57
Sch South Harringay Jun Sch, N4 off Mattison Rd 143 DP57
SOUTH HARROW, Har. HA2 138 CB62
⊖ South Harrow 138 CC62
SOUTH HATFIELD, Hat. AL10 67 CU20
South Hill, Chis. BR7 207 EM93
Guildford GU1 280 AX136
South Hill Av, Har. HA1, HA2 138 CC62
South Hill Gro, Har. HA1 139 CE63
South Hill Pk, NW3 6 C1
South Hill Pk Gdns, NW3 142 DE63
Sch South Hill Prim Sch, Hem.H. HP1 off Heath La 62 BJ21
South Hill Rd, Brom. BR2 226 EE97
Gravesend DA12 213 GH88
Hemel Hempstead HP1 62 BJ20
Southholme Cl, SE19 224 DS95
SOUTH HOLMWOOD, Dor. RH5 285 CJ144
SOUTH HORNCHURCH, Rain. RM13 169 FE67
South Huxley, N18 122 DR50
Southill La, Pnr. HA5 137 BU56
Southill Rd, Chis. BR7 206 EL94
Southill St, E14 22 D8
South Island Pl, SW9 42 D5
SOUTH KENSINGTON, SW7 27 N9
⊖ South Kensington 28 B8
South Kensington Sta Arc, SW7 off Pelham St 28 B8
South Kent Av, Nthflt DA11 212 GC86
⊖ South Kenton 139 CJ60
⊖ South Kenton 139 CJ60
SOUTH LAMBETH, SW8 42 B6
South Lambeth Est, SW8 off Dorset Rd 42 C5
South Lambeth Pl, SW8 42 B2
South Lambeth Rd, SW8 42 B3
Southland Rd, SE18 187 ET80
Southlands Av, Horl. RH6 290 DF147
Orpington BR6 245 ER105
Southlands Cl, Couls. CR5 257 DM117
Southlands Dr, SW19 201 CX89
Southlands Gro, Brom. BR1 226 EL97
Southlands La, Tand. RH8 275 EB134
Southlands Rd, Brom. BR1, BR2 226 EJ99
Denham UB9 135 BF63
Iver SL0 135 BF64
Southland Way, Houns. TW3 199 CD85
South La, Kings.T. KT1 219 CK97
New Malden KT3 220 CR98
South La W, N.Mal. KT3 220 CR98
South Lawns Apts, Wat. WD25 off Holbrook Gdns 98 CB36
SOUTHLEA, Slou. SL3 174 AV82
Southlea Rd, Datchet SL3 174 AV81
Windsor SL4 174 AU84
South Ley, Welw.G.C. AL7 51 CY12
South Ley Ct, Welw.G.C. AL7 off South Ley 51 CY12
South Lo, NW8 16 A2
SW7 off Knightsbridge 28 D5
South Lo Av, Mitch. CR4 223 DL98
South Lo Cres, Enf. EN2 103 DK42
South Lo Dr, N14 103 DL43
South Lo Rd, Walt. KT12 235 BU109
★ South London Art Gall, SE5 43 P6
South Loop Rd, Uxb. UB8 156 BK70
Southly Cl, Sutt. SM1 222 DA104
(shop) South Mall, N9 off Edmonton Grn Shop Cen 122 DU48
South Mead, NW9 119 CT53
Epsom KT19 238 CS108
Redhill RH1 272 DF131
Southmead Cres, Chsht EN8 89 DY30
Southmead Gdns, Tedd. TW11 199 CG93
South Meadow La, Eton SL4 173 AQ80
South Meadows, Wem. HA9 140 CL64
Sch Southmead Prim Sch, SW19 off Princes Way 201 CY88
Southmead Rd, SW19 201 CY88
Southmere Dr, SE2 188 EX75
SOUTH MERSTHAM, Red. RH1 273 DJ130
≠ South Merton 221 CZ97
SOUTH MIMMS, Pot.B. EN6 85 CT32
South Molton La, W1 17 J9
South Molton Rd, E16 23 P8
South Molton St, W1 17 J9
Southmont Rd, Esher KT10 219 CE103
Southmoor Way, E9 11 P4
South Mundells, Welw.G.C. AL7 51 CZ08
SOUTH NORWOOD, SE25 224 DT97
Coll South Norwood CETS Cen, SE25 off Sandown Rd 224 DV99
South Norwood Hill, SE25 224 DS96
Sch South Norwood Prim Sch, SE25 off Crowther Rd 224 DU98
SOUTH NUTFIELD, Red. RH1 289 DL136
South Oak Rd, SW16 203 DM91
SOUTH OCKENDON, RM15 171 FW70
Southold Ri, SE9 207 EM90
Southolm St, SW11 41 J7
South Ordnance Rd, Enf. EN3 105 EA37
Southover, N12 120 DA49
Bromley BR1 206 EG92
SOUTH OXHEY, Wat. WD19 116 BW48
South Par, SW3 28 B10
W4 180 CR77
Edgware HA8 off Mollison Way 118 CN54
SOUTH PARK, Reig. RH2 287 CZ138
South Pk, SW6 39 K9
Gerrards Cross SL9 135 AZ57
Sevenoaks TN13 279 FH125
South Pk Av, Chorl. WD3 95 BF43
South Pk Cres, SE6 206 EF88
Gerrards Cross SL9 134 AY56
Ilford IG1 147 ER62
South Pk Dr, Bark. IG11 147 ES63
Gerrards Cross SL9 134 AY56
Ilford IG3 147 ES63
South Pk Gdns, Berk. HP4 60 AV18
South Pk Gro, N.Mal. KT3 220 CQ98
South Pk Hill Rd, S.Croy. CR2 242 DR106
South Pk Ms, SW6 39 L10
Sch South Pk Prim Sch, Seven Kings IG3 off Water La 147 ES62
South Pk Rd, SW19 202 DA93
Ilford IG1 147 ER62
South Pk Ter, Ilf. IG1 147 ER62
South Pk Vw, Ger.Cr. SL9 135 AZ56
South Pk Way, Ruis. HA4 158 BW65
South Path, Wind. SL4 173 AQ81
South Penge Pk Est, SE20 224 DV96
South Perimeter Rd, Uxb. UB8 off Kingston La 156 BL69
South Pier Rd, Gat. RH6 291 DH152
South Pl, EC2 19 M6
Enfield EN3 104 DW43
Harlow CM20 58 EU12
Surbiton KT5 220 CM101
Waltham Abbey EN9 off Sun St 89 EC33
South Pl Ms, EC2 19 M7
South Pt, Sutt. SM1 240 DC107
Southport Rd, SE18 187 ER77
DLR South Quay 34 D5
● South Quay Plaza, E14 34 C4
South Quay Sq, E14 34 C4
South Ridge, Wey. KT13 235 BP110
Southridge Pl, SW20 201 CX94
South Riding, Brick.Wd AL2 82 CA30
South Ri, Cars. SM5 240 DE109
Sch South Ri Prim Sch, SE18 off Brewery Rd 187 ER78
South Ri Way, SE18 187 ER78
South Rd, N9 122 DU46
SE23 205 DX89
SW19 202 DC93
W5 179 CK77
Amersham HP6 77 AQ36
Chadwell Heath RM6 148 EY58
Chorleywood WD3 95 BC43
Edgware HA8 118 CP53
Englefield Green TW20 194 AW93
Erith DA8 189 FF79
Feltham TW13 198 BX92
Guildford GU2 264 AV132
Hampton TW12 198 BY93
Harlow CM20 58 EU12
Little Heath RM6 148 EW57
Reigate RH2 288 DB135
St. George's Hill KT13 235 BP109
South Ockendon RM15 171 FW72
Southall UB1 178 BZ75
Twickenham TW2 199 CD90
West Drayton UB7 176 BM76
Weybridge KT13 235 BQ106
Woking GU21 232 AX114
South Row, SE3 47 M8
SOUTH RUISLIP, Ruis. HA4 138 BW63
≠ South Ruislip 138 BW63
⊖ South Ruislip 138 BW63
Southsea Av, Wat. WD18 97 BU42
Southsea Rd, Kings.T. KT1 220 CL98
South Sea St, SE16 33 N6
South Side, W6 181 CT76
Southside, Chal.St.P. SL9 134 AX55
South Side, Cher. KT16 216 BG97
Southside Common, SW19 201 CW93
(shop) Southside Shop Cen, SW18 202 DB86
Southspring, Sid. DA15 207 ER87
South Sq, NW11 142 DB58
WC1 18 E7
Southstand Apts, N5 off Avenell Rd 143 DP63
South Sta App, S.Nutfld RH1 289 DL136
SOUTH STIFFORD, Grays RM20 191 FW78
SOUTH STREET, West. TN16 261 EM119
South St, W1 29 H2
Brentwood CM14 130 FW47
Bromley BR1 226 EG96
Dorking RH4 285 CG137
Enfield EN3 105 DX43
Epsom KT18 238 CR113
Gravesend DA12 213 GH87
Hertford SG14 54 DR09
Isleworth TW7 179 CG83
Rainham RM13 169 FC68
Romford RM1 149 FF58
Staines-upon-Thames TW18 195 BF92
Stanstead Abbotts SG12 55 EC11
South Tenter St, E1 20 B10
South Ter, SW7 28 C8
Dorking RH4 285 CH137
Surbiton KT6 220 CL100
Coll South Thames Coll, Mord. SM4 off London Rd 222 DA99
Roehampton Cen, SW15 off Roehampton La 201 CU86
Tooting Cen, SW17 off Tooting High St 202 DE92
Wandsworth Cen, SW18 off Wandsworth High St 202 DB85
SOUTH TOTTENHAM, N15 144 DS57
⊖ South Tottenham 144 DT57
South Vale, SE19 204 DS93
Harrow HA1 139 CE63
Southvale Rd, SE3 47 K9
South Vw, Brom. BR1 226 EH96
Epsom KT19 238 CN110
Southview Av, NW10 141 CT64
South Vw Av, Til. RM18 193 GG81
Southview Cl, SW17 202 DG92
South Vw Cl, Bex. DA5 208 EZ86
Southview Cl, Chsht EN7 88 DS26
Swanley BR8 229 FF98
South Vw Ct, Wok. GU22 off Constitution Hill 248 AY118
Southview Cres, Ilf. IG2 147 EP58
South Vw Dr, E18 146 EH55
Upminster RM14 150 FN62
Southview Gdns, Wall. SM6 241 DJ108
South Vw Rd, N8 143 DK55
Ashtead KT21 253 CK119
Southview Rd, Brom. BR1 205 ED91
South Vw Rd, Dart. DA2 210 FK90
Gerrards Cross SL9 134 AX56
Grays RM20 191 FW79
Loughton IG10 107 EM44
Pinner HA5 115 BV51
Southview Rd, Warl. CR6 258 DU119
Woldingham CR3 259 EB124
Southviews, S.Croy. CR2 243 DX109
South Vil, NW1 7 P5
Southville, SW8 41 P6
Southville Cl, Epsom KT19 238 CR109
Feltham TW14 197 BS88
Southville Cres, Felt. TW14 197 BS88
Sch Southville Inf & Nurs & Jun Schs, Felt. TW14 off Bedfont La 197 BT88
Southville Rd, Felt. TW14 197 BS88
Thames Ditton KT7 219 CG101
South Wk, Hayes UB3 off Middleton Rd 157 BR71
Reigate RH2 off Chartway 272 DB134
West Wickham BR4 226 EE104
SOUTHWARK, SE1 31 H3
⊖ Southwark 30 G3
Coll Southwark Adult Ed, Nunhead Cen, SE15 off Whorlton Rd 184 DV83
Thomas Calton Cen, SE15 44 C9
Southwark Br, EC4 31 K2
SE1 31 K2
Southwark Br Rd, SE1 31 H6
★ Southwark Cath, SE1 31 L2
Coll Southwark Coll, Bermondsey Cen, SE16 32 E6
Camberwell Cen, SE5 43 N5
Waterloo Cen, SE1 30 G4
Southwark Pk, SE16 32 F7
Southwark Pk Est, SE16 32 F8
Sch Southwark Pk Prim Sch, SE16 32 F7
Southwark Pk Rd, SE16 32 B8
Southwark Pl, Brom. BR1 227 EM97
Southwark St, SE1 31 H2
Southwater Cl, E14 21 N8
Beckenham BR3 205 EB94
South Way, N9 122 DW47
N11 off Ringway 121 DJ51
Southway, N20 120 DA47
NW11 142 DB58
SW20 221 CW98
South Way, Abb.L. WD5 81 BT33
Beaconsfield HP9 132 AG55
Southway, Cars. SM5 240 DD110
South Way, Croy. CR0 225 DY104
Southway, Guil. GU2 264 AT134
South Way, Har. HA2 138 CA56
Southway, Hat. AL10 67 CU22
South Way, Hayes BR2 226 EG101
Purfleet RM19 191 FS76
Southway, Wall. SM6 241 DJ105
South Way, Wem. HA9 140 CN64
Southway Cl, W12 181 CV75
Southway Ct, Guil. GU2 264 AS134
SOUTH WEALD, Brwd. CM14 130 FS47
South Weald Dr, Wal.Abb. EN9 89 ED33
South Weald Rd, Brwd. CM14 130 FU48
Southwell Av, Nthlt. UB5 158 CA65
Southwell Cl, Chaff.Hun. RM16 191 FW78
Southwell Gdns, SW7 27 N8
Southwell Gro Rd, E11 146 EE61
Southwell Rd, SE5 43 J10
Croydon CR0 223 DN100
Kenton HA3 139 CK58
South Western Rd, Twick. TW1 199 CG86
Southwest Rd, E11 145 ED60
South Wf Rd, W2 16 A8
Southwick Ms, W2 16 B8
Southwick Pl, W2 16 C9
Southwick St, W2 16 C8
SOUTH WIMBLEDON, SW19 202 DB94
⊖ South Wimbledon 202 DB94
Southwold Dr, Bark. IG11 148 EU64
Sch Southwold Prim Sch, E5 off Detmold Rd 144 DW61
Southwold Rd, E5 144 DV61
Bexley DA5 209 FB86
Watford WD24 98 BW38
Southwold Spur, Slou. SL3 175 BC75
Southwood Av, N6 143 DH59
Coulsdon CR5 257 DJ115
Kingston upon Thames KT2 220 CQ95
Ottershaw KT16 233 BC108
Southwood Cl, Brom. BR1 227 EM98
Worcester Park KT4 221 CX102
Southwood Dr, Surb. KT5 220 CQ101
SOUTH WOODFORD, E18 124 EF54
⊖ South Woodford 124 EG54
Southwood Gdns, Esher KT10 219 CG104
Ilford IG2 147 EP56
Southwood La, N6 142 DG59
Southwood Lawn Rd, N6 142 DG59
Southwood Pk, N6 142 DG59
Sch Southwood Prim Sch, Dag. RM9 off Keppel Rd 148 EY63
Southwood Rd, SE9 207 EP89
SE28 168 EV74
Southwood Smith St, N1 8 G9
South Worple Av, SW14 180 CS83
South Worple Way, SW14 180 CR83
Soval Ct, Nthwd. HA6 115 BR52
● Sovereign Business Cen, Enf. EN3 105 DZ40
Sovereign Cl, E1 32 F1
W5 159 CJ71
Purley CR8 241 DM110
Ruislip HA4 137 BS60
Sovereign Ct, Harl. CM19 off Rosemount 73 EP18
West Molesey KT8 218 BZ98
Sovereign Cres, SE16 33 L1
Sovereign Gro, Wem. HA0 139 CK62
Sovereign Hts, Slou. SL3 175 BA79
Sovereign Ms, E2 10 A10
Barnet EN4 102 DF41
Sovereign Pk, NW10 160 CP70
St. Albans AL4 65 CK21
Sovereign Pl, Har. HA1 139 CF57
Sovereign Rd, Bark. IG11 168 EW69
Sowerby Cl, SE9 206 EL85
Sowrey Av, Rain. RM13 169 FF65
Soyer Ct, Wok. GU21 off Raglan Rd 248 AS118
Space Waye, Felt. TW14 197 BV85
Spackmans Way, Slou. SL1 173 AQ76
Spa Cl, SE25 224 DS95
Spa Dr, Epsom KT18 238 CN114
Spafield St, EC1 18 E4
Spa Grn Est, EC1 18 F2
Spa Hill, SE19 224 DR95
Spalding Cl, Edg. HA8 118 CS52
Spalding Rd, NW4 141 CW58
SW17 203 DH92
Spalt Cl, Hutt. CM13 131 GB47
Spanby Rd, E3 22 B5
Spaniards Cl, NW11 142 DD60
Spaniards End, NW3 142 DC60
Spaniards Rd, NW3 142 DC61
Spanish Pl, W1 17 H8
Spanish Rd, SW18 202 DC85
Spareleaze Hill, Loug. IG10 107 EM43
Sparepenny La, Dart. DA4 230 FL102
Sparkbridge Rd, Har. HA1 139 CE56
Sparkes Cl, Brom. BR2 226 EH98
Sparke Ter, E16 23 L8
Sparkford Gdns, N11 120 DG50
Sparkford Ho, SW11 40 B6
Sparks Cl, W3 160 CR72

Sparks Cl, Dagenham RM8 148 EX61
Hampton TW12
off Victors Dr 198 BY93
Spa Rd, SE16 32 A7
Sparrow Cl, Hmptn. TW12 198 BY93
Sparrow Dr, Orp. BR5 227 EQ102
Sparrow Fm Dr, Felt. TW14 198 BX87
Sch Sparrow Fm Inf & Nurs Sch, Felt. TW14 *off Denham Rd* 198 BW87
Sch Sparrow Fm Jun Sch, Felt. TW14 *off Sparrow Fm Dr* 198 BW87
Sparrow Fm Rd, Epsom KT17 239 CU105
Sparrow Grn, Dag. RM10 149 FB62
Sparrows Herne, Bushey WD23 116 CB45
Sparrows La, SE9 207 EQ87
Sparrows Mead, Red. RH1 272 DG131
Sparrows Way, Bushey WD23 116 CC45
Sparrowswick Ride, St.Alb. AL3 64 CC15
Sparrow Wk, Wat. WD25
off Gullet Wd Rd 97 BU35
Sparsholt Rd, N19 143 DL60
Barking IG11 167 ES67
Spartan Cl, Wall. SM6 241 DL108
Sparta St, SE10 46 D7
Sch Spa Sch, SE1 32 C9
★ Speaker's Cor, W2 16 F10
Speaker's Ct, Croy. CR0
off St. James's Rd 224 DR102
Spearman St, SE18 187 EN79
Spear Ms, SW5 27 K9
Spearpoint Gdns, Ilf. IG2 147 ET56
Spears Rd, N19 143 DL60
Speart La, Houns. TW5 178 BY80
Spectacle Wks, E13 24 C2
Spectrum Ho, Enf. EN3
off Tysoe Av 105 DY36
Spectrum Pl, SE17 43 L2
Spedan Cl, NW3 142 DB62
Speechly Ms, E8 10 B2
Speedbird Way, Harm. UB7 176 BH80
Speedgate Hill, Fawk.Grn DA3 231 FU103
Speed Highwalk, EC2
off Silk St 19 K6
Speed Ho, EC2
off The Barbican 19 L6
● Speedway Ind Est, Hayes UB3 177 BR75
Speedwell Cl, Guil. GU4 265 BB131
Hemel Hempstead HP1
off Campion Rd 61 BE21
Speedwell Ct, Grays RM17 192 GE80
Speedwell St, SE8 46 A5
Speedy Pl, WC1 18 A3
Speer Rd, T.Ditt. KT7 219 CF99
Speirs Cl, N.Mal. KT3 221 CT100
Spekehill, SE9 207 EM90
Speke Rd, Th.Hth. CR7 224 DR96
Speldhurst Cl, Brom. BR2 226 EF99
Speldhurst Rd, E9 11 J7
W4 180 CR76
Spellbrook Wk, N1 9 K8
Spelman St, E1 20 C6
Spelthorne Gro, Sun. TW16 197 BT94
Sch Spelthorne Inf & Nurs Sch, Ashf. TW15
off Chertsey Rd 197 BS93
Sch Spelthorne Jun Sch, Ashf. TW15
off Feltham Hill Rd 197 BR93
Spelthorne La, Ashf. TW15 217 BQ95
Spence Av, Byfleet KT14 234 BL114
Spence Cl, SE16 33 N5
Spencer Av, N13 121 DM51
Cheshunt EN7 88 DS26
Hayes UB4 157 BU71
Spencer Cl, N3 119 CZ54
NW10 160 CM69
Epsom KT18 254 CS119
Orpington BR6 227 ES103
Uxbridge UB8 156 BJ69
Woking GU21 233 BC113
Woodford Green IG8 124 EJ50
Spencer Ctyd, N3
off Regents Pk Rd 119 CZ54
Spencer Dr, N2 142 DC58
Spencer Gdns, SE9 207 EM85
SW14 200 CQ85
Englefield Green TW20 194 AX92
Spencer Gate, St.Alb. AL1 65 CE18
Spencer Hill, SW19 201 CY93
Spencer Hill Rd, SW19 201 CY94
★ Spencer Ho, SW1 29 L3
Spencer Ms, SW8 42 C7
W6 38 E2
Spencer Pk, SW18 202 DD85
Spencer Pas, E2 10 E10
Spencer Pl, N1 8 G6
Croydon CR0 224 DR101
Spencer Ri, NW5 143 DH63
Spencer Rd, E6 166 EK67
E17 123 EC54
N8 143 DM57
N11 121 DH49
N17 122 DU53
SW18 182 DD84
SW20 221 CV95
W3 160 CQ74
W4 180 CQ80
Beddington Corner CR4 222 DG101
Bromley BR1 206 EE94
Caterham CR3 258 DR121
Cobham KT11 251 BV115
East Molesey KT8 218 CC99
Harrow HA3 117 CE54
Ilford IG3 147 ET60
Isleworth TW7 179 CD81
Mitcham CR4 222 DG97
Rainham RM13 169 FD69
Slough SL3 175 AZ76
South Croydon CR2 242 DS106
Twickenham TW2 199 CE90
Wembley HA0 139 CJ61
Spencers Cft, Harl. CM18 74 EV17
Spencer St, EC1 18 G3
Gravesend DA11 213 GG87
Hertford SG13 54 DS08
St. Albans AL3 65 CD20
Southall UB2 178 BX75
Spencer Wk, NW3 5 P1
SW15 181 CX84
Rickmansworth WD3 96 BJ43
Tilbury RM18 193 GG82
Spencer Way, E1 20 F9
Hemel Hempstead HP1 62 BG17
Redhill RH1 288 DG139
Spencer Yd, SE3 47 L9
Spenser Av, Wey. KT13 234 BN108
Spenser Cres, Upmin. RM14 150 FQ59
Spenser Gro, N16 9 N1
Spenser Ms, SE21 204 DR88
Spenser Rd, SE24 203 DN85
Spenser St, SW1 29 M6
Spensley Wk, N16 144 DR62
Speranza St, SE18 187 ET78
Sperling Rd, N17 122 DS54
Spert St, E14 21 L10
Speyhawk Pl, Pot.B. EN6 86 DB30
Speyside, N14 103 DJ44
Spey St, E14 22 E7
Spey Way, Rom. RM1 127 FE52
Spezia Rd, NW10 161 CU68
Sphere, The, E16 23 L9
● Sphere Ind Est, St.Alb. AL1 65 CG20
Spice Ct, NW9 *off Ruby Way* 119 CT53
Spice Quay Hts, SE1 32 B3
Spicer Cl, SW9 43 H8
Walton-on-Thames KT12 218 BW100
Spicersfield, Chshf EN7 88 DU27
Spicers Fld, Oxshott KT22 237 CD113
Spicers La, Harl. CM17
off Wayre St 58 EW11
Spicer St, St.Alb. AL3 64 CC20
Spice's Yd, Croy. CR0 242 DQ105
Spielman Rd, Dart. DA1 190 FM84
Spiers Way, Horl. RH6 291 DH150
Spigurnell Rd, N17 122 DR53
Spikes Br Moorings, Hayes UB4 158 BY73
Spikes Br Rd, Sthl. UB1 158 BY72
Spilsby Rd, Rom. RM3 128 FK52
Spindle Cl, SE18 37 H7
Spindles, Til. RM18 193 GG80
Spindlewood Gdns, Croy. CR0 242 DS105
Spindlewoods, Tad. KT20 255 CV122
Spindrift Av, E14 34 C8
Spinel Cl, SE18 187 ET78
Spingate Cl, Horn. RM12 150 FK64
Spinnaker Cl, Bark. IG11 168 EV69
Spinnells Rd, Har. HA2 138 BZ60
Spinners Wk, Wind. SL4 173 AQ81
Spinney, Slou. SL1 153 AP74
Spinney, The, N21 121 DN45
SW16 203 DK90
Aldenham WD25 99 CD38
Barnet EN5 102 DB40
Beaconsfield HP9 133 AK55
Berkhamsted HP4 60 AT20
Bookham KT23 252 CB124
Broxbourne EN10 71 DZ19
Chesham HP5 76 AR29
Epsom KT18 255 CV119
Gerrards Cross SL9 134 AX60
Guildford GU2
off Southway 264 AU133
Headley KT18 270 CQ126
Hertford SG13 54 DT09
Horley RH6 290 DG146
Hutton CM13 131 GC44
Loughton IG10 107 EP42
Oxshott KT22 236 CC112
Potters Bar EN6 86 DD31
Purley CR8 241 DP111
Send GU23 266 BJ127
Sidcup DA14 208 EY92
Stanmore HA7 118 CL49
Sunbury-on-Thames TW16 217 BU95
Sutton SM3 239 CW105
Swanley BR8 229 FE96
Watford WD17 97 BU39
Welwyn Garden City AL7 51 CY10
Wembley HA0 139 CG62
Spinney Cl, Beck. BR3 225 EB98
Cobham KT11 236 CA111
New Malden KT3 220 CS99
Rainham RM13 169 FE68
West Drayton UB7 156 BL73
Worcester Park KT4 221 CT104
Spinneycroft, Oxshott KT22 253 CD115
Spinney Dr, Felt. TW14 197 BQ87
Spinney Gdns, SE19 204 DT92
Dagenham RM9 148 EY64
Spinney Hill, Add. KT15 233 BE106
Sch Spinney Inf Sch, Harl. CM20
off Cooks Spinney 58 EU14
Sch Spinney Jun Sch, Harl. CM20
off Cooks Spinney 58 EU14
Spinney Oak, Brom. BR1 226 EL96
Ottershaw KT16 233 BD107
Spinneys, The, Brom. BR1 227 EM96
Spinneys Dr, St.Alb. AL3 64 CB22
Spinney St, Hert. SG13 54 DU09
Spinney Way, Cudham TN14 245 ER111
Spinning Wk, The, Shere GU5 282 BN139
Spinning Wheel Mead, Harl. CM18 74 EU18
H Spire Bushey Hosp, Bushey WD23 117 CF46
Spire Cl, Grav. DA12 213 GH88
H Spire Gatwick Pk Hosp, Horl. RH6 290 DE149
● Spire Grn Cen, Harl. CM19 72 EL16
H Spire Hartswood Hosp, Warley CM13 129 FV51
Spire Ho, W2 15 P10
Spire Pl, Warl. CR6 259 DY118
H Spire Roding Hosp, Ilf. IG4 146 EK55
Spires, The, Dart. DA1 210 FK89
🔒 Spires Shop Cen, The, Barn. EN5 101 CY41
Spirit Quay, E1 32 D2
SPITALBROOK, Hodd. EN11 71 EA19
★ Spitalfields City Fm, E1 20 C5
Spital Heath, Dor. RH4 285 CJ135
Spital La, Brwd. CM14 130 FT48
Spital Sq, E1 19 P6
Spital St, E1 20 C6
Dartford DA1 210 FK86
Spital Yd, E1 19 P6
● Spitfire Business Pk, Croy. CR0 241 DN107
Spitfire Cl, Slou. SL3 175 BA77
● Spitfire Est, Houns. TW5 178 BW78
Spitfire Rd, Wall. SM6 241 DL108
Spitfire Way, Houns. TW5 178 BW78
Splendour Wk, SE16
off Verney Rd 44 G1
Spode Ho, SE11
off Lambeth Wk 30 E7
Spode Wk, NW6 5 M3
Spondon Rd, N15 144 DU56
Spook Hill, N.Holm. RH5 285 CH141
Spoonbill Way, Hayes UB4
off Cygnet Way 158 BX71
Spooners Dr, Park St AL2 82 CC27
Spooners Ms, W3
off Churchfield Rd 160 CR74
Spooner Wk, Wall. SM6 241 DK106
Sporle Ct, SW11 182 DD83
Sportsbank St, SE6 205 EC87
Sportsman Ms, E2 10 C9
Spotted Dog Path, E7 13 P5
Spottiswood Ct, Croy. CR0
off Pawson's Rd 224 DQ100
Spottons Gro, N17 122 DQ53
Spout Hill, Croy. CR0 243 EA106
Spout La, Crock.H. TN8 277 EQ134
Staines-upon-Thames TW19 196 BG85
Spout La N, Stai. TW19 176 BH84
Spratt Hall Rd, E11 146 EG58
Spratts All, Ott. KT16 233 BE107
Spratts La, Ott. KT16 233 BE107
Spray La, Twick. TW2 199 CE86
Spray St, SE18 37 P8
🔒 Spread Eagle Wk Shop Cen, Epsom KT19 *off High St* 238 CR113
Spreighton Rd, W.Mol. KT8 218 CB98
Spriggs Oak, Epp. CM16
off Palmers Hill 92 EU29
Sprimont Pl, SW3 28 E10
Springall St, SE15 44 F5
Springate Fld, Slou. SL3 174 AY75
Spring Av, Egh. TW20 194 AY93
Springbank, N21 103 DM44
Springbank Av, Horn. RM12 150 FJ64
Springbank Rd, SE13 205 ED86
Springbank Wk, NW1 7 P6
Springbottom La, Bletch. RH1 273 DN127
Springbourne Ct, Beck. BR3 225 EC95
Spring Br Ms, W5
off Spring Br Rd 159 CK73
Spring Br Rd, W5 159 CK73
Spring Cl, Barn. EN5 101 CX43
Borehamwood WD6 100 CN39
Dagenham RM8 148 EX60
Godalming GU7 280 AS143
Harefield UB9 114 BK53
Latimer HP5 94 AX36
Springclose La, Sutt. SM3 239 CY107
Springcopse Rd, Reig. RH2 288 DC135
Spring Cotts, Surb. KT6 219 CK99
Spring Ct, Guil. GU2
off Dayspring 264 AV130
Sidcup DA15
off Station Rd 208 EU90
Spring Ct Rd, Enf. EN2 103 DN38
Springcroft Av, N2 142 DF56
Spring Cfts, Bushey WD23 98 CA43
Springdale Ms, N16 9 L1
Springdale Rd, N16 9 L1
Spring Dr, Maid. SL6 152 AE65
Pinner HA5 137 BU58
Springett Ho, SW2
off St. Matthew's Rd 203 DN85
Spring Fm Cl, Rain. RM13 170 FK69
Springfield, E5 144 DV60
Bushey Heath WD23 117 CD46
Epping CM16 91 ET32
Oxted RH8 275 ED130
Springfield Av, N10 143 DJ55
SW20 221 CZ97
Hampton TW12 198 CB93
Hutton CM13 131 GE45
Swanley BR8 229 FF98
Springfield Cl, N12 120 DB50
Chesham HP5 76 AQ33
Croxley Green WD3 97 BP43
Knaphill GU21 248 AS118
Potters Bar EN6 86 DD31
Stanmore HA7 117 CG48
Windsor SL4 173 AP82
Sch Springfield Comm Prim Sch, N16 *off Castlewood Rd* 144 DU58
Springfield Ct, Wall. SM6
off Springfield Rd 241 DH106
Springfield Dr, Ilf. IG2 147 EQ58
Leatherhead KT22 253 CE119
Springfield Gdns, E5 144 DV60
NW9 140 CR57
Bromley BR1 227 EM98
Ruislip HA4 137 BV60
Upminster RM14 150 FP62
West Wickham BR4 225 EB103
Woodford Green IG8 124 EJ52
Springfield Gro, SE7 186 EJ79
Sunbury-on-Thames TW16 217 BT95
Springfield Gro Est, SE7 186 EJ79
Springfield La, NW6 5 L9
Weybridge KT13 235 BP105
Springfield Meadows, Wey. KT13 235 BP105
Springfield Mt, NW9 140 CS57
Springfield Par Ms, N13
off Hazelwood La 121 DN49
Springfield Pl, Ger.Cr. SL9 134 AY57
New Malden KT3 220 CQ98
Sch Springfield Prim Sch, Sun. TW16
off Nursery Rd 217 BT96
Springfield Ri, SE26 204 DV90
Springfield Rd, E4 124 EE46
E6 167 EM66
E15 23 K2
E17 145 DZ58
N11 121 DH50
N15 144 DU56
NW8 5 N9
SE26 204 DV92
SW19 201 CZ92
W7 159 CE74
Ashford TW15 196 BM92
Berkhamsted HP4 60 AT16
Bexleyheath DA7 189 FB83
Bromley BR1 227 EM98
Chesham HP5 76 AQ33
Cheshunt EN8 89 DY32
Epsom KT17 239 CW110
Grays RM16 192 GD75
Guildford GU1 280 AY135
Harrow HA1 139 CE58
Hayes UB4 158 BW74
Hemel Hempstead HP2 62 BM19
Kingston upon Thames KT1 220 CL97
St. Albans AL1 65 CG21
Slough SL3 175 BB80
Smallford AL4 66 CP20
Springfield Rd, Teddington TW11 199 CG92
Thornton Heath CR7 224 DQ95
Twickenham TW2 198 CA88
Wallington SM6 241 DH106
Watford WD25
off Haines Way 81 BV33
Welling DA16 188 EV83
Westcott RH4 284 CB137
Windsor SL4 173 AP82
● Springfield Rd Business Cen, Hayes UB4 158 BW74
Springfields, Amer. HP6 77 AQ37
Broxbourne EN10 71 DZ19
Waltham Abbey EN9 90 EE34
Welwyn Garden City AL8 51 CV11
Springfields Cl, Cher. KT16 216 BH102
H Springfield Uni Hosp, SW17 202 DE89
Springfield Wk, NW6 5 L9
Orpington BR6
off Place Fm Av 227 ER102
Spring Gdns, N5 9 J3
SW1 29 P2
Biggin Hill TN16 260 EJ118
Dorking RH4 285 CG136
Hornchurch RM12 149 FH63
Orpington BR6 246 EV107
Romford RM7 149 FC57
Wallington SM6 241 DJ106
Watford WD25 98 BW35
West Molesey KT8 218 CC99
Wooburn Green HP10 132 AE55
Woodford Green IG8 124 EJ52
● Spring Gdns Business Pk, Rom. RM7 149 FC57
Spring Glen, Hat. AL10 67 CT19
SPRING GROVE, Islw. TW7 179 CF81
Spring Gro, SE19 *off Alma Pl* 204 DT94
W4 180 CN78
Fetcham KT22 252 CB123
Godalming GU7 280 AS143
Gravesend DA12 213 GH88
Hampton TW12
off Plevna Rd 218 CB95
Loughton IG10 106 EK44
Mitcham CR4 222 DG95
Spring Gro Cres, Houns. TW3 178 CC81
Sch Spring Gro Prim Sch, Islw. TW7 *off Star Rd* 179 CD82
Spring Gro Rd, Houns. TW3 178 CB81
Isleworth TW7 178 CB81
Richmond TW10 200 CM85
Springhall La, Saw. CM21 58 EY06
Sch Springhallow Sch, W13
off Compton Cl 159 CG72
Springhall Rd, Saw. CM21 58 EY05
Springhaven Cl, Guil. GU1 265 BA134
● Springhead Enterprise Pk, Nthflt DA11 212 GC88
Springhead Parkway, Nthflt. DA11 212 GC89
Springhead Rd, Erith DA8 189 FF79
Northfleet DA11 212 GC87
Spring Hill, E5 144 DU59
SE26 204 DW91
Springhill Cl, SE5 184 DR83
Spring Hills, Harl. CM20 57 EN14
Springholm Cl, Bigg.H. TN16 260 EJ118
Springhurst Cl, Croy. CR0 243 DZ105
Spring Lake, Stan. HA7 117 CH49
Spring La, E5 144 DV60
N10 142 DG55
SE25 224 DV100
Farnham Royal SL2 153 AP66
Hemel Hempstead HP1 61 BF18
Oxted RH8 275 ED131
Slough SL1 153 AM74
Springle La, Hailey SG13 55 DZ12
Sch Springmead JMI Sch, Welw.G.C. AL7 *off Hilly Flds* 52 DC08
Spring Ms, W1 16 F6
Epsom KT17
off Old Schs La 239 CT109
Richmond TW9
off Rosedale Rd 180 CL84
Spring Pk Av, Croy. CR0 225 DX103
Spring Pk Dr, N4 144 DQ60
Springpark Dr, Beck. BR3 225 EC97
Sch Spring Pk Prim Sch, Croy. CR0 *off Bridle Rd* 225 EA104
Spring Pk Rd, Croy. CR0 225 DX103
Spring Pas, SW15 38 C10
Spring Path, NW3 6 A3
Spring Pl, N3
off Windermere Av 120 DA54
NW5 7 J3
Barking IG11 167 EQ68
Springpond Rd, Dag. RM9 148 EY64
Springrice Rd, SE13 205 EC86
Spring Ri, Egh. TW20 194 AY93
Spring Rd, Felt. TW13 197 BT90
Springs, The, Brox. EN10 89 DY25
Hertford SG13 54 DT08
Springshaw Cl, Sev. TN13 278 FD123
Spring Shaw Rd, Orp. BR5 228 EU95
Springside Ct, Guil. GU1 264 AW133
Spring St, W2 16 A9
Epsom KT17 239 CT109
Spring Ter, Rich. TW9 200 CL85
Spring Tide Cl, SE15 44 D6
Spring Vale, Bexh. DA7 189 FB84
Greenhithe DA9 211 FW86
Springvale Av, Brent. TW8 179 CK78
Springvale Cl, Bkhm KT23 268 CB126
Spring Vale Cl, Swan. BR8 229 FF95
Springvale Est, W14 26 D7
Spring Vale N, Dart. DA1 210 FK87
🔒 Springvale Retail Pk, Orp. BR5 228 EW97
Spring Vale S, Dart. DA1 210 FK87
Springvale Ter, W14 26 D7
Springvale Way, Orp. BR5 228 EW97
● Spring Valley Enterprise Cen, Port.Wd AL3 65 CE16
Spring Vw Rd, Ware SG12 54 DW07
Spring Vil Rd, Edg. HA8 118 CN52
Spring Wk, E1 20 D6
Broxbourne EN10 70 DW22
Horley RH6
off Court Lo Rd 290 DF148
Springwater Cl, SE18 187 EN81
Springway, Har. HA1 139 CD59
Spring Way, Hem.H. HP2 63 BP18
Springwell Av, NW10 161 CT67
Mill End WD3 114 BG47
Springwell Cl, SW16
off Etherstone Rd 203 DN91
Springwell Ct, Houns. TW4 178 BX82
Stanstead Abbotts SG12 55 EC11
Springwell Hill, Hare. UB9 114 BH51
Sch Springwell Inf & Nurs Sch, Heston TW5 *off Speart La* 178 BY80
Sch Springwell Jun Sch, Heston TW5 *off Vicarage Fm Rd* 178 BY80
Springwell La, Hare. UB9 114 BG49
Rickmansworth WD3 114 BG49
Springwell Rd, SW16 203 DN91
Hounslow TW4, TW5 178 BX81
Springwood, Chsht EN7 88 DU26
Springwood Cl, E3 22 A1
Harefield UB9 114 BK53
Springwood Cres, Edg. HA8 118 CP47
Springwood Pl, Wey. KT13 235 BP108
Spring Wds, Vir.W. GU25 214 AV98
Springwood Wk, St.Alb. AL4 65 CK17
Springwood Way, Rom. RM1 149 FG57
Sprowston Ms, E7 13 N4
Sprowston Rd, E7 13 P3
Spruce Cl, Red. RH1 272 DF133
Spruce Ct, W5 180 CL76
Sprucedale Cl, Swan. BR8 229 FE96
Sprucedale Gdns, Croy. CR0 243 DX105
Wallington SM6 241 DK109
Spruce Hill, Harl. CM18 73 ES20
Spruce Hills Rd, E17 123 EC54
Spruce Pk, Brom. BR2
off Cumberland Rd 226 EF98
Spruce Rd, Bigg.H. TN16 260 EK116
Spruce Way, Park St AL2 82 CB27
Sprules Rd, SE4 45 L9
Spur, The, Chsht EN8
off Welsummer Way 89 DX28
Slough SL1 153 AK71
Walton-on-Thames KT12 218 BW103
Spur Cl, Abb.L. WD5 81 BR33
Abridge RM4 108 EV41
Spurfield, W.Mol. KT8 218 CB97
Spurgate, Hutt. CM13 131 GA47
Spurgeon Av, SE19 224 DR95
Spurgeon Cl, Grays RM17 192 GC79
Spurgeon Rd, SE19 224 DR95
Coll Spurgeon's Coll, SE25
off South Norwood Hill 224 DS96
Spurgeon St, SE1 31 L7
Spurling Rd, SE22 184 DT84
Dagenham RM9 168 EZ65
Spurrell Av, Bex. DA5 209 FD91
Spur Rd, N15 *off Philip La* 144 DR56
SE1 30 E4
SW1 29 L5
Barking IG11 167 EQ68
Edgware HA8 118 CL49
Feltham TW14 197 BV85
Isleworth TW7 179 CH80
Orpington BR6 228 EU103
Spur Rd Est, Edg. HA8
off Green La 118 CM49
Spurstowe Rd, E8 10 E3
Spurstowe Ter, E8 10 E3
Squadrons App, Horn. RM12 170 FJ65
Square, The, E10 145 EC62
W6 38 B1
Broxbourne EN10 71 DY23
Carshalton SM5 240 DG106
Caterham CR3
off Godstone Rd 258 DU124
Guildford GU2 280 AT136
Hemel Hempstead HP1
off Marlowes 62 BK20
Ilford IG1 147 EN59
Loug. IG10 107 EP42
Potten End HP4 61 BB16
Richmond TW9 199 CK85
Sawbridgeworth CM21 58 EY05
Sevenoaks TN13
off Amherst Hill 278 FE122
Shere GU5 282 BN139
Swanley BR8 229 FD97
Tatsfield TN16 260 EJ120
Uxbridge UB11 157 BR74
Watford WD24 97 BV37
West Drayton UB7 176 BH81
Weybridge KT13 235 BQ105
Wisley GU23 250 BL116
Woodford Green IG8 124 EG50
● Square One, Sthl. UB2 178 BW77
Square Rigger Row, SW11
off York Pl 182 DC83
Square St, Harl. CM17 58 EW14
Squarey St, SW17 202 DC90
Squerryes, The, Cat. CR3 258 DS121
★ Squerryes Ct & Gdns, West. TN16 277 EQ128
Squerryes Mede, West. TN16 277 EQ127
Squire Gdns, NW8 16 A3
Squires, The, Rom. RM7 149 FC58
Squires Br Rd, Shep. TW17 216 BM98
Squires Ct, SW19 202 DA91
Chertsey KT16
off Springfields Cl 216 BH102
Squires Fld, Swan. BR8 229 FF95
Squires La, N3 120 DB54
Squires Mt, NW3
off East Heath Rd 142 DD62
Squires Rd, Shep. TW17 216 BM98
Squire's Wk, Ashf. TW15 197 BR94
Squires Way, Dart. DA2 209 FD91
Squires Wd Dr, Chis. BR7 206 EL94
Squirrel Chase, Hem.H. HP1 61 BE19
Squirrel Cl, Houns. TW4 178 BW82
Squirrel Keep, W.Byf. KT14 234 BH112
Squirrel Ms, W13 159 CG73
Squirrels, The, SE13 185 ED83
Bushey WD23 99 CD44
Hertford SG13 54 DU09
Pinner HA5 138 BZ55
Welwyn Garden City AL7 52 DC10
Squirrels Chase, Orsett RM16
off Hornsby La 193 GG75
Squirrels Cl, N12 120 DC49
Orpington BR6 227 ES102
Uxbridge UB10 156 BN66
Squirrels Grn, Bkhm KT23 252 CA123
Worcester Park KT4 221 CT102
Squirrels Heath Av, Rom. RM2 149 FH55
Sch Squirrels Heath Inf & Jun Schs, Rom. RM2
off Salisbury Rd 149 FH57
Squirrels Heath La, Horn. RM11 150 FJ56
Romford RM2 150 FJ56
Squirrels Heath Rd, Rom. RM3 150 FL55
Squirrels La, Buck.H. IG9 124 EK48
● Squirrels Trd Est, Hayes UB3 177 BU76
Squirrels Way, Epsom KT18 254 CR115

Squirrel Wd, W.Byf. KT14 234 BH112
Squirries St, E2 20 D2
Stable Cl, Epsom KT18 254 CS119
Kingston upon Thames KT2 200 CM93
Northolt UB5 158 CA68
Stable La, Seer Grn HP9 111 AQ51
Stable Ms, NW5 7 J4
Twickenham TW1 199 CF88
Stables, The, Ald. WD25 98 CB36
Buckhurst Hill IG9 124 EJ45
Cobham KT11 236 BZ114
Guildford GU1
off Old Fm Rd 264 AX131
Stables End, Orp. BR6 227 EQ104
Stables Ms, SE27 204 DQ92
Stables Way, SE11 30 E10
Stable Wk, N1
off Wharfdale Rd 163 DL68
N2 off Old Fm Rd 120 DD53
Stable Way, W10 14 B9
Stable Yd, SW1 29 L4
SW9 42 D9
SW15 38 B10
Stable Yd Rd, SW1 29 L3
Staburn Ct, Edg. HA8 118 CQ54
Stacey Av, N18 122 DW49
Stacey Cl, E10 145 ED57
Gravesend DA12 213 GL92
Stacey St, N7 143 DN62
WC2 17 P9
Stackfield, Harl. CM20 58 EU12
Stackhouse St, SW3 28 E6
Stacklands, Welw.G.C. AL8 51 CV11
Stack Rd, Hort.Kir. DA4 231 FR97
Stacy Path, SE5 43 N5
Staddon Cl, Beck. BR3 225 DY98
● Stadium Business Cen, Wem. HA9 140 CP62
Stadium Retail Pk, Wem. HA9 140 CN62
Stadium Rd, NW2 141 CV59
SE18 186 EL80
Stadium Rd E, NW2 141 CW59
Stadium St, SW10 39 P5
Stadium Way, Dart. DA1 209 FE85
Harlow CM19 57 EM14
Wembley HA9 140 CM63
Staffa Rd, E10 145 DY60
Stafford Av, Horn. RM11 150 FK55
Slough SL2 153 AQ70
Stafford Cl, E17 145 DZ58
N14 103 DJ43
NW6 15 J3
Caterham CR3 258 DT123
Chafford Hundred RM16 191 FW77
Cheshunt EN8 88 DY29
Greenhithe DA9 211 FT85
Sutton SM3 239 CY107
Taplow SL6 152 AH72
Stafford Ct, SW8
off Allen Edwards Dr 42 A5
W8 27 J6
Stafford Cripps Ho, E2 21 H3
SW6 off Clem Attlee Ct 39 H3
● Stafford Cross Business Pk, Croy. CR0 241 DM106
Stafford Dr, Brox. EN10 71 EA20
Stafford Gdns, Croy. CR0 241 DM106
● Stafford Ind Est, Horn. RM11 150 FK55
Stafford Pl, SW1 29 L6
Richmond TW10 200 CM87
Stafford Ri, Cat. CR3 258 DU122
Stafford Rd, E3 21 N1
E7 166 EJ66
NW6 15 J2
Caterham CR3 258 DT122
Croydon CR0 241 DN105
Harrow HA3 116 CC52
New Malden KT3 220 CQ97
Ruislip HA4 137 BT63
Sidcup DA14 207 ES91
Wallington SM6 241 DJ107
Staffords, Harl. CM17 58 EY11
Staffordshire St, SE15 44 D6
Staffords Pl, Horl. RH6 291 DH150
Stafford Sq, Wey. KT13
off Rosslyn Pk 235 BR105
Stafford St, W1 29 L2
Stafford Ter, W8 27 J6
Stafford Way, Sev. TN13 279 FJ127
Staff St, EC1 19 M3
Stagbury Av, Chipstead CR5 256 DE118
Stagbury Cl, Chipstead CR5 256 DE119
Stag Cl, Edg. HA8 118 CP54
Staggart Grn, Chig. IG7 125 ET51
Stagg Hill, Barn. EN4 102 DD35
Potters Bar EN6 102 DD35
Stag Grn Av, Hat. AL9 67 CW16
STAG HILL, Guil. GU2 280 AU135
Stag Hill, Guil. GU2 280 AU135
Jct Stag La, SW15 201 CT89
Stag La, NW9 140 CQ55
SW15 201 CT89
Berkhamsted HP4 60 AU18
Buckhurst Hill IG9 124 EH47
Chorleywood WD3 95 BC44
Edgware HA8 118 CP54
Sch Stag La First & Mid Schs, Edg. HA8 off Collier Dr 118 CN54
Stag Leys, Ashtd. KT21 254 CL120
Stag Leys Cl, Bans. SM7 256 DD115
Stag Ride, SW19 201 CT90
Stagshaw Ho, SE22
off Pytchley Rd 184 DS83
Stags Way, Islw. TW7 179 CF79
Stainash Cres, Stai. TW18 196 BH92
Stainash Par, Stai. TW18
off Kingston Rd 196 BH92
Stainbank Rd, Mitch. CR4 223 DH97
Stainby Cl, West Dr. UB7 176 BL76
Stainby Rd, N15 144 DT56
Stainer Rd, Borwd. WD6 99 CK39
Stainer St, SE1 31 M3
⇌ Staines 196 BG92
⊖ Staines 195 BF92
Staines Av, Sutt. SM3 221 CX103
Staines Br, Stai. TW18 195 BE92
Staines Bypass, Ashf. TW15 196 BH91
Staines-upon-Thames TW18, TW19 196 BH91
Staines Grn, Hert. SG14 53 DK11
Staines La, Cher. KT16 215 BF99
Staines La Cl, Cher. KT16 215 BF100
Sch Staines Prep Sch, Stai. TW18
off Gresham Rd 196 BG92
Staines Rd, Cher. KT16 215 BF97
Feltham TW14 197 BR87
Staines Rd, Hounslow TW3, TW4 178 CB83
Ilford IG1 147 EQ63
Staines-upon-Thames TW18 216 BH95
Twickenham TW2 198 CA90
Wraysbury TW19 194 AY87
Staines Rd E, Sun. TW16 197 BU94
Staines Rd W, Ashf. TW15 197 BP93
Sunbury-on-Thames TW16 197 BP93
STAINES-UPON-THAMES, TW18 & TW19 196 BG91
Staines Wk, Sid. DA14
off Evry Rd 208 EW93
Stainford Cl, Ashf. TW15 197 BR92
Stainforth Rd, E17 145 EA56
Ilford IG2 147 ER59
Staining La, EC2 19 K8
Stainmore Cl, Chis. BR7 227 ER95
Stainsbury St, E2 21 H1
Stainsby Rd, E14 22 A8
Stains Cl, Chsht EN8 89 DY28
Stainton Rd, SE6 205 ED86
Enfield EN3 104 DW39
Stainton Wk, Wok. GU21
off Inglewood 248 AW118
Stairfoot La, Chipstead TN13 278 FC122
Staithes Way, Tad. KT20 255 CV120
Stakescorner Rd, Littleton GU3 280 AU142
Stalbridge St, NW1 16 D6
Stalham St, SE16 32 F7
Stalham Way, Ilf. IG6 125 EP53
Stalisfield Pl, Downe BR6
off Mill La 245 EN110
Stambourne Way, SE19 204 DS94
West Wickham BR4 225 EC104
⊖ Stamford Brook 181 CT77
Stamford Brook Av, W6 181 CT76
Stamford Brook Gdns, W6
off Stamford Brook Rd 181 CT76
Stamford Brook Rd, W6 181 CT76
Stamford Cl, N15 144 DU56
NW3 off Hampstead Sq 142 DC62
Harrow HA3 117 CE52
Potters Bar EN6 86 DD32
Southall UB1 158 CA73
Stamford Cotts, SW10 39 M4
Stamford Ct, W6 181 CU77
Edgware HA8 118 CM49
Stamford Dr, Brom. BR2 226 EF98
Stamford Gdns, Dag. RM9 168 EW66
Stamford Grn, Epsom KT18 238 CP113
Sch Stamford Grn Prim Sch, Epsom KT19 off Christ Ch Mt 238 CP112
Stamford Grn Rd, Epsom KT18 238 CP113
Stamford Gro E, N16 144 DU60
Stamford Gro W, N16 144 DU60
STAMFORD HILL, N16 144 DS60
⇌ Stamford Hill 144 DS59
Stamford Hill, N16 144 DT61
Stamford Hill Est, N16 144 DT60
Sch Stamford Hill Prim Sch, N15
off Berkeley Rd 144 DR58
Stamford Rd, E6 166 EL67
N1 9 P6
N15 144 DU57
Dagenham RM9 168 EV67
Walton-on-Thames KT12
off Kenilworth Dr 218 BX104
Watford WD17 97 BV40
Stamford St, SE1 30 E3
Stamp Pl, E2 20 A2
Stanard Cl, N16 144 DS59
STANBOROUGH, Welw.G.C. AL8 51 CT12
Stanborough Av, Borwd. WD6 100 CN37
Stanborough Cl, Borwd. WD6 100 CN38
Hampton TW12 198 BZ93
Welwyn Garden City AL8 51 CW10
Stanborough Grn, Welw.G.C. AL8 51 CW11
Stanborough Ms, Welw.G.C. AL8 51 CX11
Stanborough Pk, Wat. WD25 97 BV35
Stanborough Pas, E8 10 A4
Sch Stanborough Prim Sch, Wat. WD25 off Appletree Wk 98 BW35
Stanborough Rd, Houns. TW3 179 CD83
Welwyn Garden City AL8 51 CV12
Sch Stanborough Sch, Wat. WD25
off Stanborough Pk 97 BV35
Welwyn Garden City AL8
off Lemsford La 51 CV11
Stanbridge Pl, N21 121 DP47
Stanbridge Rd, SW15 181 CW83
Stanbrook Rd, SE2 188 EV75
Gravesend DA11 213 GF88
Sch Stanburn First & Mid Schs, Stan. HA7 off Abercorn Rd 117 CJ52
Stanbury Av, Wat. WD17 97 BS37
Stanbury Rd, SE15 44 F7
Stancroft, NW9 140 CS56
Standale Gro, Ruis. HA4 137 BQ57
● Standard Ind Est, E16 37 J4
Standard Pl, EC2 19 P3
Standard Rd, NW10 160 CQ70
Belvedere DA17 188 FA78
Bexleyheath DA6 188 EY84
Downe BR6 245 EN110
Enfield EN3 105 DY38
Hounslow TW4 178 BY83
Standen Av, Horn. RM12 150 FK62
Standen Rd, SW18 201 CZ87
Standfield, Abb.L. WD5 81 BS31
Standfield Gdns, Dag. RM10
off Standfield Rd 168 FA65
Standfield Rd, Dag. RM10 148 FA64
Standingford, Harl. CM19 73 EP20
Standish Ho, SE3
off Elford Cl 186 EJ84
Standish Rd, W6 181 CU77
Standlake Pt, SE23 205 DX90
Standring Ri, Hem.H. HP3 62 BH23
Stane Cl, SW19 202 DB94
Stane Gro, SW9 42 A9
Stane St, Lthd. KT22 270 CL126
Mickleham RH5 269 CK127
Stane Way, SE18 186 EK80
Epsom KT17 239 CU110
Stanfield Ho, NW8
off Frampton St 16 B4
Stanfield Rd, E3 21 M1
Stanfields Ct, Harl. CM20
off Broadfield 57 ES14
Stanford Cl, Hmptn. TW12 198 BZ93
Romford RM7 149 FB58
Ruislip HA4 137 BQ58
Woodford Green IG8 124 EL50
Stanford Ct, SW6 39 M7
Waltham Abbey EN9 90 EG33
Stanford Gdns, Aveley RM15 171 FR74
Stanford Ms, E8 10 C3
Stanford Pl, SE17 31 N9
Sch Stanford Prim Sch, SW16
off Chilmark Rd 223 DK95
Stanford Rd, N11 120 DF50
SW16 223 DK96
W8 27 M6
Grays RM16 192 GD76
Stanford St, SW1 29 N9
Stanford Way, SW16 223 DK96
Stangate, SE1 30 C6
Stangate Cres, Borwd. WD6 100 CS43
Stangate Gdns, Stan. HA7 117 CH49
Stanger Rd, SE25 224 DU98
Stanham Pl, Dart. DA1
off Crayford Way 189 FG84
Stanham Rd, Dart. DA1 210 FJ85
Stanhope Av, N3 141 CZ55
Bromley BR2 226 EF102
Harrow HA3 117 CD53
Stanhope Cl, SE16 33 K4
Stanhope Gdns, N4 143 DP58
N6 143 DH58
NW7 119 CT50
SW7 27 P8
Dagenham RM8 148 EZ62
Ilford IG1 147 EM60
Stanhope Gate, W1 29 H2
Stanhope Gro, Beck. BR3 225 DZ99
Stanhope Heath, Stanw. TW19 196 BJ86
Stanhope Ms E, SW7 27 P8
Stanhope Ms S, SW7 27 P9
Stanhope Ms W, SW7 27 P8
Stanhope Par, NW1
off Stanhope St 17 L2
Stanhope Pk Rd, Grnf. UB6 158 CC70
Stanhope Pl, W2 16 E9
Sch Stanhope Prim Sch, Grnf. UB6 off Mansell Rd 158 CC70
Stanhope Rd, E17 145 EB57
N6 143 DJ58
N12 120 DC50
Barnet EN5 101 CW44
Bexleyheath DA7 188 EY82
Carshalton SM5 240 DG108
Croydon CR0 224 DS104
Dagenham RM8 148 EZ61
Greenford UB6 158 CC71
Rainham RM13 169 FG68
St. Albans AL1 65 CF21
Sidcup DA15 208 EU91
Slough SL1 153 AK72
Swanscombe DA10 212 FZ85
Waltham Cross EN8 89 DY33
Stanhope Row, W1 29 J3
Stanhopes, Oxt. RH8 276 EH128
Stanhope St, NW1 17 L3
Stanhope Ter, W2 16 B10
Stanhope Way, Sev. TN13 278 FD122
Stanwell TW19 196 BJ86
Stanier Cl, W14 39 H1
Stanier Ri, Berk. HP4 60 AT16
Staniland Dr, Wey. KT13 234 BM111
Stanlake Ms, W12 26 A3
Stanlake Rd, W12 161 CV74
Stanlake Vil, W12 26 A3
Stanley Av, Bark. IG11 167 ET68
Beckenham BR3 225 EC96
Chesham HP5 76 AP31
Dagenham RM8 148 EZ60
Greenford UB6 158 CC67
New Malden KT3 221 CU99
Romford RM2 149 FG56
St. Albans AL2 82 CA25
Wembley HA0 160 CL66
Stanley Cl, SE9 207 EQ88
SW8 42 C3
Coulsdon CR5 257 DM117
Greenhithe DA9 211 FS85
Hornchurch RM12
off Stanley Rd 150 FJ61
Romford RM2 149 FG56
Uxbridge UB8 156 BK67
Wembley HA0 160 CL66
Stanley Cotts, Slou. SL2 154 AT74
Stanley Ct, Cars. SM5
off Stanley Pk Rd 240 DG108
Stanley Cres, W11 14 G10
Gravesend DA12 213 GK92
Stanleycroft Cl, Islw. TW7 179 CE81
Stanley Dr, Hat. AL10 67 CV20
Stanley Gdns, NW2 4 B3
W3 160 CS74
W11 14 G10
Borehamwood WD6 100 CL39
Hersham KT12 236 BW107
Mitcham CR4
off Ashbourne Rd 202 DG93
South Croydon CR2 242 DU112
Wallington SM6 241 DJ107
Stanley Gdns Ms, W11 15 H10
Stanley Gdns Rd, Tedd. TW11 199 CE92
Stanley Grn E, Slou. SL3 175 AZ77
Stanley Grn W, Slou. SL3 175 AZ77
Stanley Gro, SW8 41 H9
Croydon CR0 223 DN100
Stanley Hill, Amer. HP7 77 AR40
Stanley Hill Av, Amer. HP7 77 AR39
Sch Stanley Inf & Nurs Sch, Tedd. TW11 off Strathmore Rd 199 CE91
Sch Stanley Jun Sch, Tedd. TW11
off Stanley Rd 199 CE91
Stanley Pk Dr, Wem. HA0 160 CM66
Sch Stanley Pk High Sch, Cars. SM5 off Stanley Pk Rd 240 DG107
Sch Stanley Pk Infants' Sch, Cars. SM5 off Stanley Pk Rd 240 DF108
Sch Stanley Pk Jun Sch, Cars. SM5 off Stanley Pk Rd 240 DF108
Stanley Pk Rd, Cars. SM5 240 DF108
Wallington SM6 241 DH107
Stanley Rd, E4 123 ED46
E10 145 EB58
E12 146 EL64
E18 124 EF53
N2 142 DD55
N9 122 DT46
N10 121 DH52
N11 121 DK51
N15 143 DP56
NW9 off West Hendon Bdy 141 CU59
SW14 180 CP84
SW19 202 DA94
W3 180 CQ76
Ashford TW15 196 BL92
Stanley Rd, Bromley BR2 226 EH98
Carshalton SM5 240 DG108
Croydon CR0 223 DN101
Enfield EN1 104 DS41
Grays RM17 192 GB78
Harrow HA2 138 CC61
Hertford SG13 54 DS09
Hornchurch RM12 150 FJ61
Hounslow TW3 178 CC84
Ilford IG1 147 ER61
Mitcham CR4 202 DG94
Morden SM4 222 DA98
Northfleet DA11 212 GE88
Northwood HA6 115 BU53
Orpington BR6 228 EU102
Sidcup DA14 208 EU90
Southall UB1 158 BY73
Sutton SM2 240 DB107
Swanscombe DA10 212 FZ86
Teddington TW11 199 CE91
Twickenham TW2 199 CD90
Watford WD17 98 BW41
Wembley HA9 160 CM65
Woking GU21 249 AZ116
Stanley Rd N, Rain. RM13 169 FE67
Stanley Rd S, Rain. RM13 169 FF68
Stanley Sq, Cars. SM5 240 DF109
Stanley St, SE8 45 P5
Caterham CR3 258 DQ121
Stanley Ter, N19 143 DL61
Stanley Way, Orp. BR5 228 EV99
Stanliff Ho, E14 34 B6
Stanmer St, SW11 40 D7
STANMORE, HA7 117 CG50
⊖ Stanmore 117 CK50
Stanmore Chase, St.Alb. AL4 65 CK21
Coll Stanmore Coll, Stan. HA7
off Elm Pk 117 CJ51
Stanmore Gdns, Rich. TW9 180 CM83
Sutton SM1 222 DC104
Stanmore Hall, Stan. HA7 117 CH48
Stanmore Hill, Stan. HA7 117 CG48
Stanmore Rd, E11 146 EF60
N15 143 DP56
Belvedere DA17 189 FC77
Richmond TW9 180 CM83
Watford WD24 97 BV39
Stanmore St, N1 8 C8
Stanmore Ter, Beck. BR3 225 EA96
Stanmore Twrs, Stan. HA7
off Church Rd 117 CJ50
Stanmore Way, Loug. IG10 107 EN39
Stanmount Rd, St.Alb. AL2 82 CA25
Stannard Ho, SW19
off Plough La 202 DC91
Stannard Ms, E8 10 C4
Stannard Rd, E8 10 C4
Stannary St, SE11 42 F2
Stannet Way, Wall. SM6 241 DJ105
Stannington Path, Borwd. WD6 100 CN39
Stansbury Sq, W10 14 F2
Stansfeld Rd, E6 24 F7
E16 24 F7
Stansfield Ho, SE1 32 B9
Stansfield Rd, SW9 183 DM83
Hounslow TW4 177 BV82
Stansgate Rd, Dag. RM10 148 FA61
STANSTEAD ABBOTTS, Ware SG12 55 ED11
Stanstead Bury, Stans.Abb. SG12 56 EF12
Stanstead Cl, Brom. BR2 226 EF99
Caterham CR3 258 DS124
Stanstead Dr, Hodd. EN11 71 EB15
Stanstead Gro, SE6
off Stanstead Rd 205 DZ88
Stanstead Manor, Sutt. SM1 240 DA107
Stanstead Rd, E11 146 EH57
SE6 205 DX88
SE23 205 DX88
Caterham CR3 274 DR125
Hertford SG13 54 DT08
Hoddesdon EN11 71 EB16
Hunsdon SG12 56 EG09
London Heathrow Airport TW6 196 BM86
Stanstead Abbotts SG12 56 EH12
Ware SG12 54 DW09
Stansted Cl, Horn. RM12 169 FH65
Stansted Cres, Bex. DA5 208 EX88
Stanswood Gdns, SE5 43 P5
● Stanta Business Cen, St.Alb. AL3 off Soothouse Spring 65 CF16
Stanthorpe Cl, SW16 203 DL92
Stanthorpe Rd, SW16 203 DL92
Stanton Av, Tedd. TW11 199 CE93
Stanton Cl, Epsom KT19 238 CP106
Orpington BR5 228 EW101
St. Albans AL4 65 CK16
Worcester Park KT4 221 CX102
Stanton Ct, Dag. RM10
off St. Mark's Pl 168 FA65
Stanton Ho, SE16 33 N4
Stanton Rd, SE26
off Stanton Way 205 DZ91
SW13 181 CT82
SW20 221 CX96
Croydon CR0 224 DQ101
Stantons, Harl. CM20 73 EN15
Stanton Sq, SE26
off Stanton Way 205 DZ91
Stantons Wf, Bramley GU5 281 BA144
Stanton Way, SE26 205 DZ91
Slough SL3 174 AY77
Stants Vw, Hert. SG13
off Rowleys Rd 54 DT08
Stanway Cl, Chig. IG7 125 ES50
Stanway Ct, N1 19 P1
Stanway Gdns, W3 160 CN74
Edgware HA8 118 CQ50
Stanway Rd, Wal.Abb. EN9 90 EG33
Stanway St, N1 9 P10
STANWELL, Stai. TW19 196 BL87
Stanwell Cl, Stanw. TW19 196 BK86
Sch Stanwell Flds C of E Prim Sch, Stanw. TW19
off Clare Rd 196 BL87
Stanwell Gdns, Stanw. TW19 196 BK86
STANWELL MOOR, Stai. TW19 196 BG85
Stanwell Moor Rd, Stai. TW19 196 BH85
Stanwell New Rd, Stai. TW18 196 BH90
Stanwell Rd, Ashf. TW15 196 BL89
Feltham TW14 197 BQ87
Horton SL3 175 BA83
Stanwick Rd, W14 26 G9
Stanworth St, SE1 32 A5
Stanwyck Dr, Chig. IG7 125 EQ50
Stanwyck Gdns, Rom. RM3 127 FH50
Stapenhill Rd, Wem. HA0 139 CH62
Staple Cl, Bex. DA5 209 FD90
Staplefield Cl, SW2 203 DL88
Pinner HA5 116 BY52
Stapleford, Welw.G.C. AL7 52 DD09
STAPLEFORD ABBOTTS, Rom. RM4 109 FC43
Sch Stapleford Abbotts Prim Sch, Stap.Abb. RM4
off Stapleford Rd 109 FB43
★ Stapleford Aerodrome, Rom. RM4 108 EZ40
Stapleford Av, Ilf. IG2 147 ES57
Stapleford Cl, E4 123 EC48
SW19 201 CY87
Kingston upon Thames KT1 220 CN97
Stapleford Ct, Sev. TN13 278 FF123
Stapleford Gdns, Rom. RM5 126 FA51
Stapleford Rd, Rom. RM4 109 FB42
Wembley HA0 159 CK66
STAPLEFORD TAWNEY, Rom. RM4 109 FC37
Stapleford Way, Bark. IG11 168 EV69
Staple Hill Rd, Chob.Com. GU24 232 AS105
Staplehurst Ct, Reig. RH2 288 DC138
Staplehurst Rd, SE13 206 EE85
Carshalton SM5 240 DE108
Reigate RH2 288 DC138
Staple Inn, WC1 18 E7
Staple Inn Bldgs, WC1 18 E7
Staple La, Shere GU5 266 BK132
Staples, The, Swan. BR8 229 FH95
Staples Cl, SE16 33 L2
Jct Staples Cor, NW2 141 CV60
● Staples Cor Retail Pk, NW2
off Geron Way 141 CV61
Staples Rd, Loug. IG10 106 EL41
Sch Staples Rd Inf Sch, Loug. IG10 off Staples Rd 106 EL41
Sch Staples Rd Jun Sch, Loug. IG10 off Staples Rd 106 EL41
Staple St, SE1 31 M5
Stapleton Cl, Pot.B. EN6 86 DD31
Stapleton Cres, Rain. RM13 169 FG65
Stapleton Gdns, Croy. CR0 241 DN106
Stapleton Hall Rd, N4 143 DM59
Stapleton Rd, SW17 202 DG90
Bexleyheath DA7 188 EZ80
Borehamwood WD6 100 CN38
Orpington BR6 227 ET104
Staple Tye Shop Cen, Harl. CM18 73 EQ18
Staple Tye Shop Ms, Harl. CM18 off Perry Rd 73 EQ18
Stapley Rd, Belv. DA17 188 FA78
St. Albans AL3 65 CD19
Stapylton Rd, Barn. EN5 101 CY41
Star All, EC3 19 P10
Star & Garter Hill, Rich. TW10 200 CL88
Starboard Av, Green. DA9 211 FV86
Starboard Way, E14 34 B6
Starbuck Cl, SE9 207 EN87
● Star Business Cen, Rain. RM13 off Marsh Way 169 FD71
Starch Ho La, Ilf. IG6 125 ER54
Star Cl, Enf. EN3 104 DW44
Starcross St, NW1 17 M3
Star Est, Grays RM16 193 GH78
Starfield Rd, W12 181 CU75
Star Hill, Dart. DA1 209 FE85
Woking GU22 248 AW119
Star Hill Rd, Dunt.Grn TN14 262 EZ116
Star Holme Ct, Ware SG12 55 DY06
Sch Starhurst Sch, Dor. RH5
off Chart La S 285 CJ138
Starkey Cl, Chsht EN7
off Shambrook Rd 88 DQ25
Sch Starks Fld Prim Sch, N9
off Church St 122 DS47
Star La, E16 23 J5
Coulsdon CR5 256 DG122
Epping CM16 92 EU30
Orpington BR5 228 EW98
DLR Star Lane 23 J5
Starlight Way, Lon.Hthrw Air. TW6 197 BQ85
St. Albans AL4 65 CJ22
Starling Cl, Buck.H. IG9 124 EG46
Croydon CR0 225 DY100
Pinner HA5 138 BW55
Starling La, Cuffley EN6 87 DM28
Starling Pl, Wat. WD25 82 BW32
Starlings, The, Oxshott KT22 236 CC113
Starling Wk, Hmptn. TW12
off Oak Av 198 BY92
Starmans Cl, Dag. RM9 168 EY67
Star Path, Nthlt. UB5
off Brabazon Rd 158 CA68
Star Pl, E1 32 B1
Sch Star Prim Sch, E16 23 K5
Star Rd, W14 38 G2
Isleworth TW7 179 CD82
Uxbridge UB10 157 BQ70
Starrock La, Chipstead CR5 256 DF120
Starrock Rd, Couls. CR5 257 DH119
Star St, E16 23 M6
W2 16 B8
Ware SG12 55 DY06
Starts Cl, Orp. BR6 227 EN104
Starts Hill Av, Farnboro. BR6 245 EP106
Starts Hill Rd, Orp. BR6 227 EN104
Starveall Cl, West Dr. UB7 176 BM76
Star Wf, NW1 7 M8
Starwood Cl, W.Byf. KT14 234 BJ111
Star Yd, WC2 18 E7
State Fm Av, Orp. BR6 245 EP105
Staten Bldg, E3
off Fairfield Rd 12 B10
Staten Gdns, Twick. TW1 199 CF88
Statham Ct, N7 143 DL62
Statham Gro, N16
off Green Las 144 DR63
N18 122 DS50
Station App, E4 (Chingford)
off Station Rd 124 EE45
E4 (Highams Pk)
off The Avenue 123 ED51
E7 off Woodgrange Rd 146 EH63
E11 (Snaresbrook)
off High St 146 EG57

Station App, N11
off Friern Barnet Rd 121 DH50
N12 (Woodside Pk) 120 DB49
N16 (Stoke Newington)
off Stamford Hill 144 DT61
NW10 off Station Rd 161 CT69
SE1 30 D3
SE3 off Kidbrooke Pk Rd 186 EH83
SE9 (Mottingham) 207 EM88
SE26 (Lwr Sydenham)
off Worsley Br Rd 205 DZ92
SE26 (Sydenham)
off Sydenham Rd 204 DW91
SW6 38 F10
SW16 203 DK92
SW20 221 CW96
W7 159 CE74
Amersham HP6 77 AQ38
Ashford TW15 196 BM91
Barnehurst DA7 189 FC82
Beckenham BR3
off Rectory Rd 225 EA95
Belmont SM2
off Brighton Rd 240 DB110
Berkhamsted HP4
off Brownlow Rd 60 AW18
Bexley DA5
off Bexley High St 208 FA87
Bexleyheath DA7
off Avenue Rd 188 EY82
Bromley BR1 off High St 226 EG97
Buckhurst Hill IG9
off Cherry Tree Ri 124 EK49
Carpenders Park WD19
off Prestwick Rd 116 BX48
Cheam SM2 239 CY108
Chelsfield BR6 246 EV106
Cheshunt EN8 89 DZ30
Chipstead CR5 256 DF118
Chislehurst BR7 227 EN95
Chorleywood WD3 95 BD42
Coulsdon CR5 257 DK116
Croy. CR0 off George St 224 DR103
Crayford DA1 209 FF86
Dartford DA1 210 FL86
Debden IG10 107 EQ42
Denham UB9 off Middle Rd 135 BD59
Dorking RH4 269 CJ134
Dunton Green TN13 263 FE120
East Horsley KT24 267 BS126
Elmstead Woods BR7 206 EL93
Epping CM16 92 EU31
Epsom KT19 238 CR113
Ewell East KT17 239 CV110
Ewell West KT19
off Chessington Rd 239 CT109
Gerrards Cross SL9 134 AY57
Gomshall GU5 283 BR139
Grays RM17 192 GA79
Greenford UB6 159 CD66
Guildford GU1 280 AY135
Hampton TW12
off Milton Rd 218 CA95
Harlow (Harl. Mill) CM20 58 EW10
Harlow (Harl. Town) CM20 57 EQ12
Harrow HA1 139 CE59
Hatch End HA5
off Uxbridge Rd 116 CA52
Hayes BR2 226 EG102
Hayes UB3 off Station Rd 177 BT75
Hemel Hempstead HP3 62 BG23
High Barnet EN5
off Barnet Hill 102 DA42
Hinchley Wood KT10 219 CF104
Horley RH6 291 DH148
Kenley CR8 off Hayes La 242 DQ114
Kingston upon Thames KT1 220 CN95
Leatherhead KT22 253 CG121
Little Chalfont HP7
off Chalfont Sta Rd 94 AX39
Loughton IG10 106 EL43
New Barnet EN5 102 DC42
Northwood HA6 115 BS52
Orpington BR6 227 ET103
Oxshott KT22 236 CC113
Oxted RH8 276 EE128
Pinner HA5 138 BY55
Purley CR8 241 DN111
Radlett WD7
off Shenley Hill 99 CG35
Richmond TW9 180 CN81
Ruislip HA4 137 BS60
St. Mary Cray BR5 228 EV98
Shalford GU4
off Horsham Rd 280 AY140
Shepperton TW17 217 BQ100
South Croydon CR2
off Sanderstead Rd 242 DR109
South Ruislip HA4 137 BV64
Staines-upon-Thames TW18 196 BG92
Stoneleigh KT19 239 CU106
Sunbury-on-Thames TW16 217 BU95
Swanley BR8 229 FE98
Tadworth KT20 255 CW122
Theydon Bois CM16 107 ES36
Upminster RM14 150 FQ61
Virginia Water GU25 214 AX98
Waltham Cross EN8 89 DY34
Wembley HA0 159 CH65
West Byfleet KT14 234 BG112
West Drayton UB7 156 BL74
West Wickham BR4 225 EC102
Weybridge KT13 234 BN107
Whyteleafe CR3 258 DU117
Woking GU22 249 AZ117
Woodford Green IG8
off The Broadway 124 EH51
Worcester Park KT4 221 CU102
Station App E, Earls. RH1
off Earlsbrook Rd 288 DF136
Station App N, Sid. DA15 208 EU89
Station App Path, SE9
off Glenlea Rd 207 EM85
Station App Rd, W4 180 CQ80
Coulsdon CR5 257 DK115
Gatwick RH6
off London Rd 291 DH151
Station App W, Earls. RH1
off Earlswood Rd 288 DF136
Station Av, SW9 43 H10
Caterham CR3 258 DU124
Station Av, Epsom KT19 238 CS109
Kew TW9
off Station App 180 CN81
New Malden KT3 220 CS97
Walton-on-Thames KT12 235 BU105
Station Cl, N3 120 DA53
N12 (Woodside Pk) 120 DB49
Brookmans Park AL9 85 CY26
Hampton TW12 218 CB95
Potters Bar EN6 85 CZ31
Station Ct, SW6 39 N7
Station Cres, N15 144 DR56
SE3 47 N1
Ashford TW15 196 BK90
Wembley HA0 159 CH65
Stationers Hall Ct, EC4
off Ludgate Hill 19 H9
Stationers Pl, Hem.H. HP3 80 BL25
● Station Est, E18
off George La 124 EH54
Station Est, Beck. BR3
off Elmers End Rd 225 DX98
Station Est Rd, Felt. TW14 197 BV88
Station Footpath, Kings L.
WD4 81 BP31
Station Forecourt, Rick. WD3
off Rectory Rd 114 BK45
Station Gar Ms, SW16
off Estreham Rd 203 DK93
Station Gdns, W4 180 CQ80
Station Gro, Wem. HA0 160 CL65
Station Hill, Brom. BR2 226 EG103
They.B. CM16
off Abridge Rd 107 ET37
Station Ho Ms, N9 122 DU49
Station La, E20 12 E5
Hornchurch RM12 150 FK62
Station Ms Ter, SE3
off Halstow Rd 47 N1
Station Par, E11 146 EG57
N14 off High St 121 DK46
NW2 4 B4
SW12 off Balham High Rd 202 DG88
W3 160 CN72
W5 off Uxbridge Rd 160 CM74
Ashford TW15
off Woodthorpe Rd 196 BM91
Barking IG11 167 EQ66
Barnet EN4
off Cockfosters Rd 102 DG42
Beaconsfield HP9 111 AK52
Denham UB9 136 BG59
East Horsley KT24
off Ockham Rd S 267 BS126
Edgware HA8 118 CL52
Feltham TW14 197 BV87
Har. HA3 117 CG54
Hornchurch RM12
off Rosewood Av 149 FH63
Nthlt. HA2 138 CB63
Nthlt. UB5 off Dorchester Rd 138 CB63
Richmond TW9 180 CN81
Rom. RM1 off South St 149 FE58
Sevenoaks TN13
off London Rd 278 FG124
Virginia Water GU25 214 AX98
Station Pas, E18
off Cowslip Rd 124 EH54
SE15 44 G6
Station Path, E8 10 F4
Staines-upon-Thames TW18 195 BF91
Station Pl, N4
off Seven Sisters Rd 143 DN61
Godalming GU7
off Summers Rd 280 AT144
Station Ri, SE27
off Norwood Rd 203 DP89
Station Rd, E4 (Chingford) 123 ED46
E7 146 EG63
E12 146 EK63
E17 145 DY58
N3 120 DA53
N11 121 DH50
N17 144 DU55
N19 143 DJ62
N21 121 DP46
N22 121 DM54
NW4 141 CU58
NW7 118 CS50
NW10 161 CT68
SE13 46 E10
SE20 204 DW93
SE25 (Norwood Junct.) 224 DT98
SW13 181 CU83
SW19 222 DC95
W5 160 CM72
W7 (Hanwell) 159 CE74
Addlestone KT15 234 BJ105
Amersham HP6, HP7 77 AQ38
Ashford TW15 196 BM91
Barkingside IG6 147 ER55
Beaconsfield HP9 111 AK52
Belmont SM2 240 DA110
Belvedere DA17 188 FA76
Berkhamsted HP4 60 AW18
Betchworth RH3 270 CS131
Bexleyheath DA7 188 EY83
Borehamwood WD6 100 CN42
Bramley GU5 281 AZ144
Brasted TN16 262 EV123
Brentford TW8 179 CJ79
Bricket Wood AL2 82 CA31
Bromley BR1 226 EG95
Broxbourne EN10 71 DZ20
Carshalton SM5 240 DF105
Chadwell Heath RM6 148 EX59
Chertsey KT16 215 BF102
Chesham HP5 76 AP31
Chessington KT9 238 CL106
Chigwell IG7 125 EP48
Chobham GU24 232 AT111
Cippenham SL1 153 AL72
Claygate KT10 237 CD106
Crayford DA1 209 FF86
Croydon CR0 224 DQ102
Cuffley EN6 87 DM29
Dorking RH4 285 CG135
Dunton Green TN13 263 FE120
Edgware HA8 118 CN51
Egham TW20 195 BA92
Epping CM16 91 ET31
Esher KT10 219 CD103
Eynsford DA4 230 FK104
Farncombe GU7 280 AT144
Gerrards Cross SL9 134 AY57
Gidea Park RM2 149 FH56
Gomshall GU5 283 BQ139
Greenhithe DA9 191 FU84
Halstead TN14 246 EZ111
Station Rd, Hampton TW12 218 CA95
Hampton Wick KT1 219 CJ95
Harlow CM17 58 EW11
Harold Wood RM3 128 FM53
Harrow HA1 139 CF58
Hayes UB3 177 BS77
Hemel Hempstead HP1 62 BH22
Horley RH6 291 DH148
Hounslow TW3 178 CB84
Ilford IG1 147 EP62
Kenley CR8 242 DQ114
Kings Langley WD4 81 BP29
Kingston upon Thames KT2 220 CN95
Langley SL3 175 BA76
Leatherhead KT22 253 CG121
Letty Green SG14 52 DG12
Loudwater HP10 110 AC53
Loughton IG10 106 EL42
Merstham RH1 273 DJ128
Motspur Park KT3 221 CV99
New Barnet EN5 102 DB43
North Harrow HA2 138 CB57
North Mymms AL9 85 CX25
North Weald Bassett CM16 93 FB27
Northfleet DA11 212 GB86
Orpington BR6 227 ET103
Otford TN14 263 FH116
Radlett WD7 99 CG35
Redhill RH1 272 DG133
Rickmansworth WD3 114 BK45
St. Paul's Cray BR5 228 EW98
Shalford GU4 280 AY140
Shepperton TW17 217 BQ99
Shoreham TN14 247 FG111
Shortlands BR2 226 EE96
Sidcup DA15 208 EU91
Smallford AL4 66 CP19
South Darenth DA4 230 FP96
Southfleet DA13 212 GA91
Stanstead Abbotts SG12 55 EA11
Stoke D'Abernon KT11 252 BY117
Sunbury-on-Thames TW16 197 BU94
Swanley BR8 229 FE98
Taplow SL6 152 AF72
Teddington TW11 199 CF92
Thames Ditton KT7 219 CF101
Twickenham TW1 199 CF88
Upminster RM14 150 FQ61
Uxbridge UB8 156 BJ70
Waltham Abbey EN9 89 EA34
Waltham Cross EN8 89 EA34
Ware SG12 55 DX06
Watford WD17 97 BV40
West Byfleet KT14 234 BG112
West Drayton UB7 156 BK74
West Wickham BR4 225 EC102
Whyteleafe CR3 258 DT118
Woldingham CR3 259 DZ123
Wraysbury TW19 195 AZ86
Station Rd E, Oxt. RH8 276 EE128
Station Rd N, Belv. DA17 189 FB76
Egham TW20 195 BA92
Merstham RH1 273 DJ128
Station Rd S, Merst. RH1 273 DJ128
Station Rd W, Oxt. RH8 276 EE129
Station Row, Shalf. GU4 280 AY140
Station Sq, Petts Wd BR5 227 EQ99
Station St, E15 12 G6
E16 37 N3
Station Ter, NW10 14 C1
SE5 43 K6
Dorking RH4
off Chalkpit La 285 CG135
Park Street AL2
off Park St 83 CD26
Station Vw, Grnf. UB6 159 CD67
Guildford GU1 280 AW135
Station Way, SE15
off Blenheim Gro 44 C8
Cheam SM3 239 CY107
Claygate KT10 237 CE107
Epsom KT19 238 CR113
Roding Valley IG9 124 EJ49
St. Albans AL1 65 CF20
Station Yd, Denh. UB9 136 BG59
Smallford AL4 66 CP20
Twickenham TW1 199 CG87
Staunton Rd, Kings.T. KT2 200 CL93
Slough SL2 153 AR71
Staunton St, SE8 45 P2
★ Stave Hill Ecological Pk,
SE16 33 L4
Staveley Cl, E9 11 H2
N7 8 B1
SE15 44 F6
Staveley Gdns, W4 180 CR81
Staveley Rd, W4 180 CR80
Ashford TW15 197 BR93
Staveley Way, Knap. GU21 248 AS117
Staverton Rd, NW2 4 A6
Hornchurch RM11 150 FK58
Stave Yd Rd, SE16 33 L3
Stavordale Rd, N5 143 DP63
Carshalton SM5 222 DC101
Stayne End, Vir.W. GU25 214 AU98
Stayner's Rd, E1 21 J4
Stayton Rd, Sutt. SM1 222 DA104
Steadfast Rd, Kings.T. KT1 219 CK95
Stead St, SE17 31 L9
Steam Fm La, Felt. TW14 177 BT84
Stean St, E8 10 A8
Stebbing Ho, W11 26 D2
Stebbing Way, Bark. IG11 168 EU68
Stebondale St, E14 34 F10
Sch Stebon Prim Sch, E14 22 A7
Stedham Pl, WC1 18 A8
Stedman Cl, Bex. DA5 209 FE90
Uxbridge UB10 136 BN62
Steed Cl, Horn. RM11 149 FH61
Steedman St, SE17 31 J9
Steeds Rd, N10 120 DF53
Steeds Way, Loug. IG10 106 EL41
Steele Av, Green. DA9 211 FT85
Steele Rd, E11 146 EE63
N17 144 DS55
NW10 160 CQ68
W4 180 CQ76
Isleworth TW7 179 CG84
Steeles Ms N, NW3 6 E5
Steeles Ms S, NW3 6 F5
Steeles Rd, NW3 6 E5
Steele Wk, Erith DA8 189 FB79
Steel's La, E1 21 H9
Steels La, Oxshott KT22 236 CB114
Steelyard Pas, EC4 31 L1
Steen Way, SE22
off East Dulwich Gro 204 DS85
Steep Cl, Orp. BR6 245 ET107
Steep Hill, SW16 203 DK90
Steep Hill, Croydon CR0 242 DS105
Steeplands, Bushey WD23 116 CB45
Steeple Cl, SW6 38 F9
SW19 201 CY92
Steeple Ct, E1
off Coventry Rd 20 F4
Egham TW20
off The Chantries 195 BA92
Steeple Gdns, Add. KT15
off Weatherall Cl 234 BH106
Steeple Hts Dr, Bigg.H. TN16 260 EK117
Steeplestone Cl, N18 122 DQ50
Steeple Wk, N1 9 K8
Steerforth St, SW18 202 DB89
Steering Cl, N9 122 DW46
Steers Mead, Mitch. CR4 222 DF95
Steers Way, SE16 33 M5
Stella Cl, Uxb. UB8 157 BP71
Stellar Ho, N17 122 DT51
Stella Rd, SW17 202 DF93
Stelling Rd, Erith DA8 189 FD80
Stellman Cl, E5 144 DU62
Stembridge Rd, SE20 224 DV96
Sten Cl, Enf. EN3 105 EA37
Stents La, Cob. KT11 252 BZ120
Stepbridge Path, Wok. GU21
off Goldsworth Rd 248 AX117
Stepgates, Cher. KT16 216 BH101
Stepgates Cl, Cher. KT16 216 BH101
Sch Stepgates Comm Sch, Cher.
KT16 off Stepgates 216 BH101
Stephan Cl, E8 10 D8
Stephen Av, Rain. RM13 169 FG65
Stephen Cl, Egh. TW20 195 BC93
Orpington BR6 227 ET104
Stephendale Rd, SW6 39 M8
Sch Stephen Hawking Sch, E14 21 M9
Stephen Ms, W1 17 N7
Stephen Pl, SW4 41 L10
Stephen Rd, Bexh. DA7 189 FC83
Stephens Cl, Rom. RM3 128 FJ50
Stephenson Av, Til. RM18 193 GG81
Stephenson Cl, E3 22 C3
Hoddesdon EN11 71 ED17
Welling DA16 188 EU82
Stephenson Ct, Ware SG12 55 DY07
Stephenson Dr, Wind. SL4 173 AP80
Stephenson Ho, SE1
off Bath Ter 31 J6
Stephenson Rd, E17 145 DY57
W7 159 CF72
Twickenham TW2 198 CA87
Stephenson St, E16 23 J5
NW10 160 CS69
Stephenson Way, NW1 17 M4
Watford WD24 98 BX41
Stephenson Wf, Hem.H. HP3 80 BL25
Stephen's Rd, E15 13 K9
Stephen St, W1 17 N7
Stephyns Chambers, Hem.H.
HP1 off Waterhouse St 62 BJ21
STEPNEY, E1 21 J7
Stepney Causeway, E1 21 K9
Stepney City, E1 off Jubilee St 20 G7
Stepney Cl, Mitch. CR4 222 DG95
⊖ Stepney Green 21 J5
Stepney Grn, E1 21 H6
Sch Stepney Greencoat C of E
Prim Sch, E14 21 N8
Sch Stepney Grn Sch, E1 21 K7
Stepney High St, E1 21 K7
Stepney Way, E1 20 E7
Sterling Av, Edg. HA8 118 CM49
Waltham Cross EN8 89 DX34
Sterling Cl, NW10 161 CU66
Sterling Gdns, SE14 45 L3
● Sterling Ind Est, Dag.
RM10 149 FB63
Sterling Pl, W5 180 CL77
Weybridge KT13 235 BS105
Sterling Rd, Enf. EN2 104 DR39
Sterling St, SW7 28 D6
Sterling Way, N18 122 DR50
★ Sternberg Cen, N3 120 DB54
Stern Cl, Bark. IG11 168 EW68
Sterndale Rd, W14 26 C7
Dartford DA1 210 FM87
Sterne St, W12 26 C4
Sternhall La, SE15 44 D10
Sternhold Av, SW2 203 DK89
Sterry Cres, Dag. RM10
off Alibon Rd 148 FA64
Sterry Dr, Epsom KT19 238 CS105
Thames Ditton KT7 219 CE100
Sterry Gdns, Dag. RM10 168 FA65
Sterry Rd, Bark. IG11 167 ET67
Dagenham RM10 148 FA63
Sterry St, SE1 31 L5
Steucers La, SE23 205 DY87
Steve Biko La, SE6 205 EA91
Steve Biko Rd, N7 143 DN62
Steve Biko Way, Houns. TW3 178 CA83
Stevedale Rd, Well. DA16 188 EW82
Stevedore St, E1 32 E2
Stevenage Cres, Borwd. WD6 100 CL39
Stevenage Ri, Hem.H. HP2 62 BM16
Stevenage Rd, E6 167 EN65
SW6 38 C5
Stevens Av, E9 11 H4
Stevens Cl, Beck. BR3 205 EA93
Bexley DA5 209 FD91
Epsom KT17 238 CS113
Hampton TW12 198 BY93
Steven's Cl, Lane End DA2 211 FS92
Stevens Cl, Pnr. HA5 138 BW57
Potters Bar EN6 85 CX33
Stevens Grn, Bushey Hth
WD23 116 CC46
Stevens La, Clay. KT10 237 CG108
Stevenson Cl, Barn. EN5 102 DD44
Erith DA8 189 FH80
Stevenson Cres, SE16 32 D10
Stevenson Rd, Hedg. SL2 133 AR61
Stevens Pl, Pur. CR8 241 DP113
Stevens Rd, Dag. RM8 148 EV62
Stevens St, SE1 31 P6
Steven's Wk, Croy. CR0 243 DY111
Stevens Way, Amer. HP7 77 AP40
Chigwell IG7 125 ES49
Steventon Rd, W12 161 CT73
Steward Cl, Chsht EN8 89 DY30
STEWARDS, Harl. CM18 73 ER19
Stewards Cl, Epp. CM16 92 EU33
Stewards Grn La, Epp. CM16 92 EV32
Stewards Grn Rd, Epp. CM16 92 EU33
Stewards Holte Wk, N11
off Coppies Gro 121 DH49
Sch Stewards Sch, Harl. CM18
off Parnall Rd 73 ER19
Steward St, E1 19 P7
🛍 Stewards Wk, Rom. RM1
off Western Rd 149 FE57
Stewart, Tad. KT20 255 CX121
Stewart Av, Shep. TW17 216 BN98
Slough SL1 154 AT71
Upminster RM14 150 FP62
Stewart Cl, NW9 140 CQ58
Abbots Langley WD5 81 BT32
Chislehurst BR7 207 EP92
Fifield SL6 172 AD81
Hampton TW12 198 BY92
Woking GU21 248 AT117
Stewart Ct, Denh. UB9
off Patrons Way West 135 BF58
Sch Stewart Fleming Prim Sch,
SE20 off Witham Rd 224 DW97
Sch Stewart Headlam Prim Sch,
E1 20 E4
Stewart Pl, Ware SG12 55 DX06
Stewart Rainbird Ho, E12 147 EN64
Stewart Rd, E15 12 F1
Stewartsby Cl, N18 122 DQ50
Stewart's Dr, Farn.Com. SL2 133 AP64
Stewart's Gro, SW3 28 B10
Stewart's Rd, SW8 41 L5
Stewart St, E14 34 F5
Stew La, EC4 19 J10
Steyne Rd, W3 160 CQ74
Steyning Cl, Ken. CR8 257 DP116
Steyning Gro, SE9 207 EM91
Steyning Way, N12 120 DA50
Steyning Way, Houns. TW4 178 BW84
Steynton Av, Bex. DA5 208 EX89
Stickland Rd, Belv. DA17 188 FA77
Stickleton Cl, Grnf. UB6 158 CB69
Stifford Hill, N.Stfd RM16 171 FX74
South Ockendon RM15 171 FW73
Sch Stifford Prim Sch, Grays
RM17 off Parker Rd 192 FY78
Stifford Rd, S.Ock. RM15 171 FR74
Stile Cft, Harl. CM18 74 EU17
Stilecroft Gdns, Wem. HA0 139 CH62
Stile Hall Gdns, W4 180 CN78
Stile Hall Mans, W4
off Wellesley Rd 180 CN78
Stile Hall Par, W4
off Chiswick High Rd 180 CN78
Stile Meadow, Beac. HP9 111 AL52
Stile Path, Sun. TW16 217 BU98
Stile Rd, Slou. SL3 174 AX76
Stiles Cl, Brom. BR2 227 EM100
Erith DA8
off Riverdale Rd 189 FB78
Stillingfleet Rd, SW13 181 CU79
Stillington St, SW1 29 M8
Sch Stillness Inf & Jun Schs,
SE23 off Brockley Ri 205 DY86
Stillness Rd, SE23 205 DY86
Stilton Path, Borwd. WD6 100 CN38
Stilwell Dr, Uxb. UB8 156 BM70
Jct Stilwell Rbt, Uxb. UB8 157 BP72
Stipularis Dr, Hayes UB4 158 BX70
Stirling Av, Pnr. HA5 138 BY59
Wallington SM6 241 DL108
Stirling Cl, SW16 223 DJ95
Banstead SM7 255 CZ117
Rainham RM13 169 FH69
Sidcup DA14 207 ES91
Uxbridge UB8
off Ferndale Cres 156 BJ69
Windsor SL4 173 AK82
Jct Stirling Cor, Barn. EN5 100 CR44
Borehamwood WD6 100 CR44
Stirling Dr, Cat. CR3 258 DQ121
Orpington BR6 246 EV106
Stirling Gro, Houns. TW3 178 CC82
● Stirling Ind Cen, Borwd.
WD6 100 CR43
🛍 Stirling Retail Pk, Borwd.
WD6 100 CR44
Stirling Rd, E13 24 A1
E17 145 DY55
N17 122 DU53
N22 121 DP53
SW9 42 A9
W3 180 CP76
Harrow HA3 139 CF55
Hayes UB3 157 BV73
London Heathrow Airport
TW6 196 BM86
Slough SL1 153 AP72
Twickenham TW2 198 CA87
Stirling Rd Path, E17 145 DY55
Stirling Wk, N.Mal. KT3 220 CQ99
Surbiton KT5 220 CP100
Stirling Way, Abb.L. WD5 81 BU32
Borehamwood WD6 100 CR44
Croydon CR0 223 DL101
Welwyn Garden City AL7 52 DE09
Stites Hill Rd, Couls. CR5 257 DP120
Stiven Cres, Har. HA2 138 BZ62
Sch St John's Inf & Nurs Sch,
Rad. WD7 off Gills Hill La 99 CF36
Sch St. Mary's Farnham Royal
C of E Prim Sch, Farn.Royal
SL2 off Church Rd 153 AQ69
Stoat Cl, Hert. SG13 54 DU09
Stoats Nest Rd, Couls. CR5 241 DL114
Stoats Nest Village, Couls.
CR5 257 DL115
Stockbreach Cl, Hat. AL10 67 CU17
Stockbreach Rd, Hat. AL10 67 CU17
Stockbury Rd, Croy. CR0 224 DW100
Stockdale Rd, Dag. RM8 148 EZ61
Stockdales Rd, Eton Wick SL4 173 AM77
Stockdove Way, Perivale UB6 159 CF69
Stocker Gdns, Dag. RM9 168 EW66
Stockers Fm Rd, Rick. WD3 114 BK48
Stockers La, Wok. GU22 249 AZ120
★ Stock Exchange, EC4 19 H8
Stockfield, Horl. RH6 291 DH147
Stockfield Av, Hodd. EN11 71 EA15
Stockfield Rd, SW16 203 DM90
Claygate KT10 237 CE106
Stockford Av, NW7 119 CX52
Stockham's Cl, S.Croy. CR2 242 DR111
Stock Hill, Bigg.H. TN16 260 EK116
Stockholm Ho, E1 20 E10
Stockholm Rd, SE16 45 H1
Stockholm Way, E1 32 C2
Stockhurst Cl, SW15 38 B9
Stocking La, Bayford SG13 69 DN18
Stockings La, Lt.Berk. SG13 69 DK18
Stockingswater La, Enf. EN3 105 DY41
Stockland Rd, Rom. RM7 149 FD58
Stock La, Dart. DA2 210 FJ91
Stockleigh Hall, NW8
off Prince Albert Rd 6 E10

Stockley Acad, Yiew. UB7
off Apple Tree Av 156 BM72
Stockley Cl, West Dr. UB7 177 BP75
Stockley Fm Rd, West Dr. UB7
off Stockley Rd 177 BP76
● Stockley Pk, Uxb. UB11 157 BP74
Stockley Pk Rbt, Uxb.
UB11 156 BN74
Stockley Rd, Uxb. UB8 157 BP73
West Drayton UB7 177 BP77
Stock Orchard Cres, N7 8 C2
Stock Orchard St, N7 8 C3
Stockport Rd, SW16 223 DK95
Heronsgate WD3 113 BC45
Stocksbridge Cl, Chsht EN7 88 DS26
Stocks Cl, Horl. RH6 291 DH149
Stocksfield Rd, E17 145 EC55
Stocks Meadow, Hem.H. HP2 62 BN19
Stocks Pl, E14 21 P10
Hillingdon UB10 156 BN67
Stock St, E13 23 N1
Stockton Cl, New Barn. EN5 102 DC42
Stockton Gdns, N17 122 DQ52
NW7 118 CR48
Stockton Ho, E2
off Ellsworth St 20 E2
Stockton Rd, N17 122 DQ52
N18 122 DU51
Reigate RH2 288 DA137
STOCKWELL, SW9 42 E9
Stockwell 42 B8
Stockwell Av, SW9 183 DM83
Stockwell Cl, Brom. BR1 226 EH96
Cheshunt EN7 88 DU28
Edgware HA8 118 CQ54
Stockwell Gdns, SW9 42 C7
Stockwell Gdns Est, SW9 42 B8
Stockwell Grn, SW9 42 C9
Stockwell La, SW9 42 D9
Cheshunt EN7 88 DU28
Stockwell Ms, SW9
off Stockwell Rd 42 C9
Stockwell Pk Cres, SW9 42 D8
Stockwell Pk Est, SW9 42 D9
Stockwell Pk Rd, SW9 42 C7
Stockwell Pk Sch, SW9 42 C7
Stockwell Pk Wk, SW9 42 D10
Stockwell Prim Sch, SW9 42 D10
Stockwell Rd, SW9 42 C8
Stockwells, Tap. SL6 152 AD70
Stockwell St, SE10 46 F3
Stockwell Ter, SW9 42 C7
Stocton Cl, Guil. GU1 264 AW133
Stocton Rd, Guil. GU1 264 AW133
Stodart Rd, SE20 224 DW95
Stofield Gdns, SE9
off Aldersgrove Av 206 EK90
Stoford Cl, SW19 201 CY87
Stoke Av, Ilf. IG6 126 EU51
Stoke Cl, Stoke D'Ab. KT11 252 BZ116
Stoke Common Rd, Fulmer
SL3 134 AU63
Stoke Ct Dr, Stoke P. SL2 154 AS67
STOKE D'ABERNON, Cob.
KT11 252 BZ116
Stoke Flds, Guil. GU1
off Stoke Rd 264 AX134
Stoke Gdns, Slou. SL1 154 AS74
STOKE GREEN, Slou. SL2 154 AU70
Stoke Grn, Stoke P. SL2 154 AU70
Stoke Gro, Guil. GU1
off Stoke Rd 264 AX134
Stoke Hosp, Guil. GU1
off Stoke Rd 264 AX134
Stoke Ms, Guil. GU1
off Stoke Rd 280 AX135
Stoke Mill Cl, Guil. GU1
off Mangles Rd 264 AX132
Stokenchurch St, SW6 39 L7
STOKE NEWINGTON, N16 144 DS61
Stoke Newington 144 DT61
Stoke Newington Ch St, N16 144 DR62
Stoke Newington Common,
N16 144 DT62
Stoke Newington High St,
N16 144 DT62
Stoke Newington Rd, N16 10 A2
Stoke Newington Sch, N16
off Clissold Rd 144 DR62
Stoke Pk Av, Farn.Royal SL2 153 AQ69
Stoke Pl, NW10 161 CT69
STOKE POGES, Slou. SL2 154 AT66
Stoke Poges La, Slou.
SL1, SL2 154 AS72
Stoke Poges Sch, The, Stoke P.
SL2 off Rogers La 154 AT66
Stoke Rd, Cob. KT11 252 BW115
Guildford GU1 264 AX133
Kingston upon Thames KT2 200 CQ94
Rainham RM13 170 FK68
Slough SL2 154 AT71
Walton-on-Thames KT12 218 BW104
Stokers Cl, Gat. RH6 290 DE151
Stokesay, Slou. SL2 154 AT73
Stokesby Rd, Chess. KT9 238 CM107
Stokesheath Rd, Oxshott
KT22 236 CC111
Stokesley Ri, Woob.Grn HP10 132 AE55
Stokesley St, W12 161 CT72
Stokes Ridings, Tad. KT20 255 CX123
Stokes Rd, E6 24 G5
Croydon CR0 225 DX100
Stoke Wd, Stoke P. SL2 134 AT63
Stoll Cl, NW2 141 CW62
Stompond La, Walt. KT12 217 BU103
Stomp Rd, Burn. SL1 152 AJ71
Stoms Path, SE6
off Maroons Way 205 EA92
Stonard Rd, N13 121 DN48
Dagenham RM8 148 EV64
Stonards Hill, Epp. CM16 92 EW31
Loughton IG10 107 EM44
Stondon Pk, SE23 205 DY87
Stondon Wk, E6 166 EK68
STONE, Green. DA9 211 FT85
Stonebank, Welw.G.C. AL8
off Stonehills 51 CX08
Stonebanks, Walt. KT12 217 BU101
STONEBRIDGE, NW10 160 CP67
STONEBRIDGE, Dor. RH5 286 CL139
Stonebridge Common, E8 10 A7
Stonebridge Fld, Eton SL4 173 AP78
Stonebridge Flds, Shalf. GU4 280 AX141
Stonebridge Ms, SE19 204 DR94
Stonebridge Park 160 CN66
Stonebridge Park 160 CN66
Stonebridge Pk, NW10 160 CR66
Stonebridge Prim Sch, The,
NW10 off Shakespeare Av 160 CQ67
Stonebridge Rd, N15 144 DS57
Northfleet DA11 212 GA85
Stonebridge Shop Cen, NW10
off Shakespeare Rd 160 CR67
Stonebridge Way, Wem. HA9 160 CP65
Stonebridge Wf, Shalf. GU4 280 AX141
Stone Bldgs, WC2 18 D7
Stone Castle Dr, Green. DA9 211 FU86
Stonechat Ms, Green. DA9 211 FU86
Stonechat Sq, E6 25 H6
Stone Cl, SW4 41 M9
Dagenham RM8 148 EZ61
West Drayton UB7 156 BM74
Stonecot Cl, Sutt. SM3 221 CY102
Stonecot Hill, Sutt. SM3 221 CY102
Stonecourt Cl, Horl. RH6 291 DJ148
Stone Cres, Felt. TW14 197 BT87
Stonecroft Av, Iver SL0 155 BE72
Stonecroft Cl, Barn. EN5 101 CV42
Stonecroft Rd, Erith DA8 189 FC80
Stonecroft Way, Croy. CR0 223 DL101
Stonecrop Cl, NW9 140 CR55
Stonecrop Rd, Guil. GU4 265 BC132
Stone Cross, Harl. CM20
off Post Office Rd 57 ER14
Stonecross, St.Alb. AL1 65 CE19
Stonecross Cl, St.Alb. AL1 65 CE19
Stone Crossing 211 FS85
Stonecross Rd, Hat. AL10 67 CV16
Stonecutter St, EC4 18 G8
Stonefield, N4 143 DM61
Stonefield Cl, Bexh. DA7 188 FA83
Ruislip HA4 138 BY64
Stonefield St, N1 8 F8
Stonefield Way, SE7
off Greenbay Rd 186 EK80
Ruislip HA4 138 BY63
Stonegate Cl, Orp. BR5
off Main Rd 228 EW97
Stonegrove, Edg. HA8 118 CL49
Stonegrove Est, Edg. HA8
off Lacey Dr 118 CM49
Stonegrove Gdns, Edg. HA8 118 CM50
Stonehall Av, Ilf. IG1 146 EL58
● Stonehall Business Pk,
Match.Grn CM17 59 FH10
Stone Hall Gdns, W8 27 L7
Stone Hall Pl, W8 27 L7
Stone Hall Rd, N21 121 DM45
Stoneham Rd, N11 121 DJ51
STONEHILL, Cher. KT16 232 AY107
● Stonehill Business Pk, N18
off Silvermere Dr 123 DX51
Stonehill Cl, SW14 200 CR85
Bookham KT23 268 CA125
Stonehill Cres, Ott. KT16 232 AY107
Stonehill Grn, Dart. DA2 209 FC94
Stonehill Rd, SW14 200 CQ85
W4 180 CN78
Chobham GU24 232 AW108
Ottershaw KT16 233 BA105
Stonehills, Welw.G.C. AL8 51 CX09
Stonehills Ct, SE21 204 DS90
Stonehill Wds Pk, Sid. DA14 209 FB93
Stonehorse Rd, Enf. EN3 104 DW43
Stonehouse Cor, Purf.
RM19 191 FR79
Stone Ho Ct, EC3 19 N8
Stone Ho Gdns, Cat. CR3 274 DS125
Stonehouse La, Halst. TN14 246 EX109
Purfleet RM19 191 FS78
Stonehouse Rd, Halst. TN14 246 EW110
Stoneings La, Knock. TN14 261 ET118
Stone Lake Retail Pk, SE7 36 B9
Stone Lake Rbt, SE7 36 C9
Stonelea Rd, Hem.H. HP3 62 BM23
STONELEIGH, Epsom KT17 239 CU106
Stoneleigh 239 CU106
Stoneleigh Av, Enf. EN1 104 DV39
Worcester Park KT4 239 CU105
Stoneleigh Bdy, Epsom KT17 239 CU106
Stoneleigh Cl, Wal.Cr. EN8 89 DX33
Stoneleigh Cres, Epsom KT19 239 CT106
Stoneleigh Dr, Hodd. EN11 55 EB14
Stoneleigh Ms, E3 21 M1
Stoneleigh Pk, Wey. KT13 235 BQ106
Stoneleigh Pk Av, Croy. CR0 225 DX100
Stoneleigh Pk Rd, Epsom
KT19 239 CT107
Stoneleigh Pl, W11 26 D1
Stoneleigh Rd, N17 144 DT55
Bromley BR1 227 EP97
Carshalton SM5 222 DE101
Ilford IG5 146 EL55
Oxted RH8 276 EL130
Stoneleigh St, W11 14 D10
Stoneleigh Ter, N19 143 DH61
Stoneley Cres, Green. DA9 191 FW84
Stonells Rd, SW11
off Chatham Rd 202 DF85
Stonemasons Cl, N15 144 DR56
Stoneness Rd, Grays RM20 191 FV79
Stonenest St, N4 143 DM60
Stone Pk Av, Beck. BR3 225 EA98
Stone Pl, Wor.Pk. KT4 221 CU103
Stone Pl Rd, Green. DA9 211 FS85
Stone Rd, Brom. BR2 226 EF99
Stone St. Mary's C of E
Prim Sch, Stone DA9
off Hayes Rd 211 FS87
Stones All, Wat. WD18 97 BV42
Stones Cross Rd, Swan. BR8 229 FC99
Stones End St, SE1 31 J5
Stones La, Westc. RH4 284 CC137
Stones Rd, Epsom KT17 238 CS112
Stone St, Grav. DA11 213 GH86
Stoneswood Rd, Oxt. RH8 276 EH130
Stonewall, E6 25 M7
Stonewood, Bean DA2 211 FW90
Stonewood Rd, Erith DA8 189 FE78
Stoney All, SE18 187 EN82
Stoneyard La, E14 34 C1
Stoney Br Dr, Wal.Abb. EN9 90 EG34
Stoney Brook, Guil. GU2 264 AS133
Stoney Cl, Nthch HP4 60 AT17
Stoney Cft, Couls. CR5 257 DJ122
Stoneycroft, Hem.H. HP1 62 BG20
Welwyn Garden City AL7 52 DA08
Stoneycroft Cl, SE12 206 EF87
Stoneycroft Rd, Wdf.Grn. IG8 124 EL51
Stoneydeep, Tedd. TW11
off Twickenham Rd 199 CG91
Stoneydown, E17 145 DY56
Stoneydown Av, E17 145 DY56
Stoneydown Pk Prim Sch,
E17 off Pretoria Av 145 DY56
Stoneyfield, Ger.Cr. SL9 134 AW60
Stoneyfield Rd, Couls. CR5 257 DM117
Stoneyfields Gdns, Edg. HA8 118 CQ49
Stoneyfields La, Edg. HA8 118 CQ50
Stoney Gro, Chesh. HP5 76 AR30
Stoneylands Ct, Egh. TW20 195 AZ92
Stoneylands Rd, Egh. TW20 195 AZ92
Stoney La, E1 19 P8
SE19 off Church Rd 204 DT93
Bovingdon HP3 79 BB27
Chipperfield WD4 79 BE30
East Burnham SL2 153 AN67
Hemel Hempstead HP1 61 BB23
Stoney Meade, Slou. SL1
off Weekes Dr 153 AP74
Stoney St, SE1 31 L2
Stonhouse St, SW4 183 DK83
Stonny Cft, Ashtd. KT21 254 CM117
Stonor Rd, W14 26 G9
Stonycroft Cl, Enf. EN3
off Brimsdown Av 105 DY40
Stony Dean Sch, Amer. HP7
off Orchard End Av 94 AT39
Stony La, Amer. HP6 94 AY38
Stony Path, Loug. IG10 107 EM40
Stonyrock La, Dor. RH5 268 BY131
Stonyshotts, Wal.Abb. EN9 90 EE34
Stony Wd, Harl. CM18 73 ES16
Stoop Ct, W.Byf. KT14 234 BH112
Stopes St, SE15 44 B5
Stopford Rd, E13 13 P8
SE17 43 H1
Store Rd, E16 37 L4
Storers Quay, E14 34 G9
Store St, E15 13 H3
WC1 17 N7
Storey Cl, Uxb. UB10 136 BQ61
Storey Ct, NW8
off St. John's Wd Rd 16 A3
Storey Rd, E17 145 DZ56
N6 142 DF58
Storey's Gate, SW1 29 P5
Storey St, E16 37 M3
Hemel Hempstead HP3 62 BK24
Stories Ms, SE5 43 N9
Stories Rd, SE5 43 N10
Stork Rd, E7 13 M5
Storksmead Rd, Edg. HA8 118 CS52
Storks Rd, SE16 32 D7
Stormont Ho Sch, E5 10 E1
Stormont Rd, N6 142 DF59
SW11 182 DG83
Stormont Sch, Pot.B. EN6
off The Causeway 86 DD31
Stormont Way, Chess. KT9 237 CJ106
Stormount Dr, Hayes UB3 177 BQ75
Stornaway Rd, Slou. SL3 175 BC77
Stornaway Strand, Grav.
DA12 213 GM91
Stornoway, Hem.H. HP3 63 BP22
Storr Gdns, Hutt. CM13 131 GD43
Storrington Rd, Croy. CR0 224 DT102
Stortford Rd, Hodd. EN11 71 EB16
Stort Mill, Harl. CM20 58 EV09
Stort Twr, Harl. CM20 57 ET13
Story St, N1 8 C7
Stothard Pl, E1
off Spital Yd 19 P6
Stothard St, E1 20 G4
Stott Cl, SW18 202 DD86
STOUGHTON, Guil. GU2 264 AV131
Stoughton Av, Sutt. SM3 239 CX106
Stoughton Cl, SE11 30 D9
SW15 off Bessborough Rd 201 CU88
Stoughton Inf Sch, Guil.
GU2 off Stoughton Rd 264 AV131
Stoughton Rd, Guil.
GU1, GU2 264 AU131
Stour Av, Sthl. UB2 178 CA76
Stourcliffe St, W1 16 E9
Stour Cl, Kes. BR2 244 EJ105
Slough SL1 173 AP76
Stourhead Cl, SW19 201 CX87
Stourhead Gdns, SW20 221 CU97
Stourhead Ho, SW1
off Tachbrook St 29 N10
Stour Rd, E3 12 A7
Dagenham RM10 148 FA61
Dartford DA1 189 FG83
Grays RM16 193 GG78
Stourton Av, Felt. TW13 198 BZ91
Stour Way, Upmin. RM14 151 FS58
Stovell Rd, Wind. SL4 173 AP80
Stow, The, Harl. CM20 57 ET13
Stowage, SE8 46 B3
Stow Cres, E17 123 DY52
Stowe Ct, Dart. DA2 210 FQ87
Stowe Cres, Ruis. HA4 137 BP58
Stowe Gdns, N9 122 DT46
Stowell Av, New Adgtn CR0 243 ED110
Stowe Pl, N15 144 DS55
Stowe Rd, W12 181 CV75
Orpington BR6 246 EV105
Slough SL1 153 AL73
Stowford Coll, Sutt. SM2
off Brighton Rd 240 DC108
Stowting Rd, Orp. BR6 245 ES105
Stox Mead, Har. HA3 117 CD53
Stracey Rd, E7 13 P1
NW10 160 CR67
Strachan Pl, SW19 201 CW93
Stradbroke Dr, Chig. IG7 125 EN51
Stradbroke Gro, Buck.H. IG9 124 EK46
Ilford IG5 146 EL55
Stradbroke Pk, Chig. IG7 125 EP51
Stradbroke Rd, N5 9 K1
Stradbrook Cl, Har. HA2
off Stiven Cres 138 BZ62
Stradella Rd, SE24 204 DQ86
Strafford Av, Ilf. IG5 125 EN54
Strafford Cl, Pot.B. EN6 86 DA32
Strafford Gate, Pot.B. EN6 86 DA32
Strafford Rd, W3 180 CQ75
Barnet EN5 101 CY41
Hounslow TW3 178 BZ83
Twickenham TW1 199 CG87
Strafford St, E14 34 A4
Strahan Rd, E3 21 M2
Straight, The, Sthl. UB1 178 BX75
Straight Bit, Flack.Hth HP10 132 AC55
Straight Rd, Old Wind. SL4 194 AU85
Romford RM3 128 FJ52
Straightsmouth, SE10 46 E4
Strait Rd, E6 25 K10
Straker's Rd, SE15 184 DV84
STRAND, WC2 18 A10
Strand, WC2 30 A1
Strand Cl, Epsom KT18 254 CR119
Strand Ct, SE18
off Strandfield Cl 187 ES78
Strand Dr, Rich. TW9 180 CP80
Strandfield Cl, SE18 187 ES78
Strand Ho, SE28
off Merbury Cl 167 ER74
Strand La, WC2 18 D10
Strand on the Grn, W4 180 CN79
Strand on the Grn Br,
Rich. TW9 180 CP80
Strand-on-the-Grn Inf &
Nurs & Jun Schs, W4
off Thames Rd 180 CN79
Strand Pl, N18 122 DR49
Strand Sch App, W4
off Thames Rd 180 CN79
Strangeways, Wat. WD17 97 BS36
Strangways Ter, W14 26 G6
Stranraer Gdns, Slou. SL1 154 AS74
Stranraer Rd, Lon.Hthrw Air.
TW6 196 BL86
Stranraer Way, N1 8 B7
Strasburg Rd, SW11 41 H7
Stratfield Dr, Brox. EN10 71 DY19
Stratfield Pk Cl, N21 121 DP45
Stratfield Rd, Borwd. WD6 100 CN41
Slough SL1 174 AU75
STRATFORD, E15 12 F4
Stratford 12 G6
Stratford Av, W8 27 K7
Uxbridge UB10 156 BM68
Stratford Cen, The, E15 13 H6
Stratford Cl, Bark. IG11 168 EU66
Dagenham RM10 169 FC66
Slough SL2 153 AK70
Stratford Ct, N.Mal. KT3 220 CR98
Stratford Dr, Woob.Grn HP10 132 AD59
Stratford Gro, SW15 181 CX84
Stratford Ho Av, Brom. BR1 226 EL97
● Stratford Hub, E15 12 C10
Stratford High Street 12 G7
Stratford International 12 D5
● Stratford Office Village, The,
E15 13 J6
Stratford Pl, W1 17 J9
Stratford Regional 12 F6
Stratford Regional 12 F6
Stratford Regional 12 F6
Stratford Rd, E13 13 M9
NW4 141 CX56
W8 27 K8
Hayes UB4 157 BV70
London Heathrow Airport
TW6 197 BP86
Southall UB2 178 BY77
Thornton Heath CR7 223 DN98
Watford WD17 97 BU40
Stratford Sch, E7 13 P6
Stratford Vil, NW1 7 M6
Stratford Way, Brick.Wd AL2 82 BZ29
Hemel Hempstead HP3 62 BH23
Watford WD17 97 BT40
Stratford Workshops, E15
off Burford Rd 13 H8
Strathan Cl, SW18 201 CY86
Strathaven Rd, SE12 206 EH86
Strathblaine Rd, SW11 182 DD84
Strathbrook Rd, SW16 203 DM94
Strathcona Av, Bkhm KT23 268 BY128
Strathcona Cl, Flack.Hth HP10 132 AC56
Strathcona Rd, Wem. HA9 139 CK61
Strathcona Way, Flack.Hth
HP10 132 AC56
Strathdale, SW16 203 DM92
Strathdon Dr, SW17 202 DD90
Strathearn Av, Hayes UB3 177 BT80
Twickenham TW2 198 CB88
Strathearn Pl, W2 16 B10
Strathearn Rd, SW19 202 DA92
Sutton SM1 240 DA106
Stratheden Par, SE3
off Stratheden Rd 47 P5
Stratheden Rd, SE3 47 N6
Strathfield Gdns, Bark. IG11 167 ER65
Strathleven Rd, SW2 203 DL85
Strathmore Cl, Cat. CR3 258 DS121
Strathmore Gdns, N3 120 DB53
W8 27 K2
Edgware HA8 118 CP54
Hornchurch RM12 149 FF60
Strathmore Rd, SW19 202 DA90
Croydon CR0 224 DQ101
Teddington TW11 199 CE91
Strathmore Sch, Rich. TW10
off Meadlands Dr 199 CK89
Strathnairn St, SE1 32 D9
Strathray Gdns, NW3 6 C5
Strath Ter, SW11 182 DE84
Strathville Rd, SW18 202 DB89
Strathyre Av, SW16 223 DN97
Stratton Av, Enf. EN2 104 DR37
Wallington SM6 241 DK109
Stratton Chase Dr, Ch.St.G.
HP8 112 AU47
Stratton Cl, SW19 222 DA96
Bexleyheath DA7 188 EY83
Edgware HA8 118 CM52
Hounslow TW3 178 BZ81
Walton-on-Thames KT12
off St. Johns Dr 218 BW102
Stratton Ct, Surb. KT6
off Adelaide Rd 220 CL99
Strattondale St, E14 34 E6
Stratton Dr, Bark. IG11 147 ET64
Stratton Gdns, Sthl. UB1 158 BZ72
Stratton Rd, SW19 222 DA96
Beaconsfield HP9 110 AH53
Bexleyheath DA7 188 EY83
Romford RM3 128 FN50
Sunbury-on-Thames TW16 217 BT96
Stratton St, W1 29 K2
Stratton Ter, West. TN16
off High St 277 EQ127
Stratton Wk, Rom. RM3 128 FN50
Strauss Rd, W4 180 CR75
Strawberry Cres, Lon.Col. AL2 83 CH26
Strawberry Fld, Hat. AL10 67 CU21
Strawberry Flds, Farnboro.
BR6 245 EP106
Swanley BR8 229 FE95
Ware SG12 54 DV05
STRAWBERRY HILL, Twick.
TW1 199 CE90
Strawberry Hill 199 CE90
Strawberry Hill, Twick. TW1 199 CF90
Strawberry Hill Cl, Twick. TW1 199 CF90
Strawberry Hill Rd, Twick.
TW1 199 CF90
Strawberry La, Cars. SM5 222 DF104
Strawberry Vale, N2 120 DD53
Twickenham TW1 199 CG90
Straw Cl, Cat. CR3 258 DQ123
Strawfields, Welw.G.C. AL7 52 DB08
Strawmead, Hat. AL10 67 CV16
Strawson Ct, Horl. RH6 290 DF147
Strayfield Rd, Enf. EN2 103 DP37
Streakes Fld Rd, NW2 141 CU61
Stream Cl, Byfleet KT14 234 BK112
Streamdale, SE2 188 EU79
Stream La, Edg. HA8 118 CP50
Streamline Ms, SE22 204 DU88
Streamside, Slou. SL1
off Richards Way 153 AM74
Streamside Cl, N9 122 DT46
Bromley BR2 226 EG98
Streamway, Belv. DA17 188 FA79
Streatfeild Av, E6 167 EM67
Streatfield Rd, Har. HA3 139 CK55
STREATHAM, SW16 203 DL91
Streatham 203 DL92
Streatham & Clapham High
Sch, Jun Dept, SW2
off Wavertree Rd 203 DM88
SW16 off Abbotswood Rd 203 DK90
Streatham Cl, SW16 203 DL89
Streatham Common 203 DK94
Streatham Common N, SW16 203 DL92
Streatham Common S, SW16 203 DL93
Streatham Ct, SW16 203 DL90
Streatham High Rd, SW16 203 DL92
STREATHAM HILL, SW2 203 DM87
Streatham Hill 203 DL89
Streatham Hill, SW2 203 DL89
STREATHAM PARK, SW16 203 DJ91
Streatham Pl, SW2 203 DL87
Streatham Rd, SW16 222 DG95
Mitcham CR4 222 DG95
Streatham St, WC1 17 P8
STREATHAM VALE, SW16 203 DK94
Streatham Vale, SW16 203 DJ94
Streatham Wells Prim Sch,
SW2 off Palace Rd 203 DN89
Streathbourne Rd, SW17 202 DG89
Streatley Pl, NW3
off New End 142 DC63
Streatley Rd, NW6 4 G7
Street, The, Albury GU5 282 BH139
Ashtead KT21 254 CL119
Betchworth RH3 286 CS135
Chipperfield WD4 80 BG31
East Clandon GU4 266 BK131
Effingham KT24 268 BX127
Fetcham KT22 253 CD122
Horton Kirby DA4 230 FP98
Shalford GU4 280 AY139
Sheering CM22 59 FC07
West Clandon GU4 266 BH131
West Horsley KT24 267 BP129
Wonersh GU5 281 BA144
Streeters La, Wall. SM6 223 DK104
Streetfield Ms, SE3 47 P10
Streimer Rd, E15 12 F10
Strelley Way, W3 160 CS73
Stretton Mans, SE8 46 B1
Stretton Pl, Amer. HP6 94 AT38
Stretton Rd, Croy. CR0 224 DS101
Richmond TW10 199 CJ89
Stretton Way, Borwd. WD6 100 CL38
Strickland Av, Dart. DA1 190 FL83
Strickland Row, SW18 202 DD87
Strickland St, SE8 46 B7
Strickland Way, Orp. BR6 245 ET105
Stride Rd, E13 23 M1
Strides Ct, Ott. KT16
off Brox Rd 233 BC107
Strimon Cl, N9 122 DW47
Stringers Av, Jacobs Well
GU4 264 AX128
Stringer's Common, Guil.
GU1, GU4 264 AV129
Stringhams Copse, Ripley
GU23 249 BF124
Stripling Way, Wat. WD18 97 BU44
Strode Cl, N10 120 DG52
Strode Rd, E7 146 EG63
N17 122 DS54
NW10 161 CU65
SW6 38 D4
Strodes Coll, Egh. TW20
off High St 195 AZ92
Strodes Coll La, Egh. TW20 195 AZ92
Strodes Cres, Stai. TW18 196 BJ92
Strode St, Egh. TW20 195 BA91
Stroma Cl, Hem.H. HP3 63 BQ22
Stroma Ct, Slou. SL1
off Lincoln Way 153 AK73
Strone Rd, E7 166 EJ65
E12 166 EK65
Strone Way, Hayes UB4 158 BY70
Strongbow Cres, SE9 207 EM85
Strongbow Rd, SE9 207 EM85
Strongbridge Cl, Har. HA2 138 CA60
Stronsa Rd, W12 181 CT75
Stronsay Cl, Hem.H. HP3
off Northend 63 BQ22
Strood Av, Rom. RM7 149 FD60
STROOD GREEN, Bet. RH3 286 CP138
Stroud Cl, Wind. SL4 173 AK83
Stroud Cres, SW15 201 CU90
STROUDE, Vir.W. GU25 215 AZ96
Stroude Rd, Egh. TW20 195 BA93
Virginia Water GU25 214 AY98
Stroudes Cl, Wor.Pk. KT4 220 CS101
Stroud Fld, Nthlt. UB5 158 BY65
Stroud Gate, Har. HA2 138 CB63
STROUD GREEN, N4 143 DM58
Stroud Grn Gdns, Croy. CR0 224 DW101
Stroud Grn Prim Sch, N4
off Woodstock Rd 143 DN60
Stroud Grn Rd, N4 143 DM60
Stroud Grn Way, Croy. CR0 224 DV101
Stroudley Wk, E3 22 C2
Stroud Rd, SE25 224 DU100
SW19 202 DA90
Strouds Cl, Chad.Hth RM6 148 EV57
Stroudwater Pk, Wey. KT13 235 BP107
Stroud Way, Ashf. TW15
off Courtfield Rd 197 BP93
● Stroud Wd Business Cen,
Frog. AL2 off Frogmore 83 CE27
Strouts Pl, E2 20 A4
Struan Gdns, Wok. GU21 248 AY115
Strutton Grd, SW1 29 N6
Struttons Av, Nthflt DA11 213 GF89

Strype St, E1 20 A7
Stuart Av, NW9 141 CU59
W5 160 CM74
Bromley BR2 226 EG102
Harrow HA2 138 BZ62
Walton-on-Thames KT12 217 BV102
Stuart Cl, Pilg.Hat. CM15 130 FV43
Swanley BR8 209 FF94
Uxbridge UB10 156 BN65
Windsor SL4 173 AM82
Stuart Ct, Els. WD6
off High St 99 CK44
Stuart Cres, N22 121 DM53
Croydon CR0 225 DZ104
Hayes UB3 157 BQ72
Reigate RH2 288 DA137
Stuart Evans Cl, Well. DA16 188 EW83
Stuart Gro, Tedd. TW11 199 CE92
Stuart Mantle Way,
Erith DA8 189 FD80
Stuart Pl, Mitch. CR4 222 DF95
Stuart Rd, NW6 15 J3
SE15 184 DW84
SW19 202 DA90
W3 160 CQ74
Barking IG11 167 ET66
East Barnet EN4 120 DE45
Gravesend DA11 213 GG86
Grays RM17 192 GB78
Harrow HA3 117 CF54
Reigate RH2 288 DA137
Richmond TW10 199 CH89
Thornton Heath CR7 224 DQ98
Warlingham CR6 258 DV120
Welling DA16 188 EV81
Stuarts Cl, Hem.H. HP3
off Marriotts Way 62 BK22
Stuart Twr, W9 15 P3
Stuart Way, Chsht EN7 88 DV31
Staines-upon-Thames TW18 196 BH93
Virginia Water GU25 214 AU97
Windsor SL4 173 AL82
Stubbers La, Upmin. RM14 171 FR65
Stubbins Hall La, Wal.Abb.
EN9 89 EB28
Stubbs Cl, NW9 140 CQ57
Stubbs Dr, SE16 32 E10
Stubbs End Cl, Amer. HP6 77 AS36
Stubbs Hill, Knock.P. TN14 246 EW113
Stubbs La, Lwr Kgswd KT20 271 CZ128
Stubbs Ms, Dag. RM8 148 EV63
Stubbs Pt, E13 24 A5
Stubbs Way, SW19
off Ruskin Way 222 DD95
Stubbs Wd, Amer. HP6 77 AS36
Stubs Cl, Dor. RH4 285 CJ138
Stubs Hill, Dor. RH4 285 CJ139
Stucley Pl, NW1 7 K7
Stucley Rd, Houns. TW5 178 CC80
Studdridge St, SW6 39 K9
Studd St, N1 8 G8
Stud Grn, Wat. WD25 81 BV32
Studholme Ct, NW3 5 K1
Studholme St, SE15 44 E5
Studio Ms, NW4
off Glebe Cres 141 CW56
Studio Pl, SW1 28 F5
Studios, The, Bushey WD23 98 CA44
Studios Rd, Shep. TW17 216 BM97
Studio Way, Borwd. WD6 100 CQ40
Studland, SE17 31 L10
Studland Cl, Sid. DA15 207 ET90
Studland Ho, E14 21 L8
Studland Rd, SE26 205 DX92
W7 159 CD72
Byfleet KT14 234 BM113
Kingston upon Thames KT2 200 CL93
Studland St, W6 181 CV77
Studley Av, E4 123 ED52
Studley Cl, E5 11 L3
Studley Ct, E14
off Jamestown Way 35 H1
Sidcup DA14 208 EV92
Studley Dr, Ilf. IG4 146 EK58
Studley Est, SW4 42 A7
Studley Gra Rd, W7 179 CE75
Studley Rd, E7 166 EH65
SW4 42 A7
Dagenham RM9 168 EX66
Sch Study Prep Sch, The,
Spencer Ho, SW19
off Peek Cres 201 CX92
Wilberforce Ho, SW19
off Camp Rd 201 CW92
Sch Study Sch, The,
N.Mal. KT3
off Thetford Rd 220 CS99
Stukeley Rd, E7 166 EH66
Stukeley St, WC1 18 B8
WC2 18 B8
Stump Rd, Epp. CM16 92 EW27
Stumps Hill La, Beck. BR3 205 EA93
Stumps La, Whyt. CR3 258 DS117
Stumpwell La, Penn HP10 110 AD48
Sturdy Rd, SE15 44 E9
Sturge Av, E17 123 EB54
Sturgeon Rd, SE17 43 J1
Sturges Fld, Chis. BR7 207 ER93
Sturgess Av, NW4 141 CV59
Sturge St, SE1 31 J4
Sturla Cl, Hert. SG14 53 DP08
Sturlas Way, Wal.Cr. EN8 89 DX33
Sturmer Cl, St.Alb. AL4 65 CJ21
Sturmer Way, N7 8 C2
Sturminster Cl, Hayes UB4 158 BW72
Sturrock Cl, N15 144 DR56
Sturry St, E14 22 C9
Sturt Ct, Guil. GU4 265 BB132
Sturts La, Walt.Hill KT20 271 CT127
Sturt St, N1 19 K1
Stutfield St, E1 20 D9
Stychens Cl, Bletch. RH1 274 DQ133
Stychens La, Bletch. RH1 274 DQ132
Stylecroft Rd, Ch.St.G. HP8 112 AX47
Styles End, Bkhm KT23 268 CB127
Styles Gdns, SW9 43 H10
Styles Way, Beck. BR3 225 EC98
Stylus Ho, E1
off Devonport St 21 H9
Styventon Pl, Cher. KT16 215 BF101
Subrosa Dr, Merst. RH1 273 DH130

● Subrosa Pk, Merst. RH1 273 DH130
Succombs Hill, Warl. CR6 258 DV120
Whyteleafe CR3 258 DV120
Succombs Pl, Warl. CR6 258 DV120
Sch Sudbourne Prim Sch, SW2
off Hayter Rd 203 DM85
Sudbourne Rd, SW2 203 DL85
Sudbrooke Rd, SW12 202 DF86
Sudbrook Gdns, Rich. TW10 199 CK90
Sudbrook La, Rich. TW10 200 CL88
SUDBURY, Wem. HA0 139 CG64
Sudbury, E6 25 M8
⇌ Sudbury & Harrow Road 139 CH64
Sudbury Av, Wem. HA0 139 CK62
Sudbury Ct, SW8
off Allen Edwards Dr 42 A6
Sudbury Ct Dr, Har. HA1 139 CF62
Sudbury Ct Rd, Har. HA1 139 CF62
Sudbury Cres, Brom. BR1 206 EG93
Wembley HA0 139 CH64
Sudbury Cft, Wem. HA0 139 CF63
Sudbury Gdns, Croy. CR0 242 DS105
Sudbury Hts Av, Grnf. UB6 139 CF64
⊖ Sudbury Hill 139 CE63
Sudbury Hill, Har. HA1 139 CE61
Sudbury Hill Cl, Wem. HA0 139 CF63
⇌ Sudbury Hill Harrow 139 CE63
Sudbury Ho, SW18
off Wandsworth High St 202 DB85
Sch Sudbury Prim Sch, Wem.
HA0 off Watford Rd 139 CH63
Sudbury Rd, Bark. IG11 147 ET64
⊖ Sudbury Town 159 CH65
Sudeley St, N1 19 H1
Sudicamps Ct, Wal.Abb. EN9 90 EG33
Sudlow Rd, SW18 182 DA84
Sudrey St, SE1 31 J5
Suez Av, Grnf. UB6 159 CF68
Suez Rd, Enf. EN3 105 DY42
Suffield Cl, S.Croy. CR2 243 DX112
Suffield Rd, E4 123 EB48
N15 144 DT57
SE20 224 DW96
Suffolk Cl, Borwd. WD6 100 CR43
Horley RH6 290 DG149
London Colney AL2 83 CJ25
Slough SL1 153 AL72
Suffolk Ct, E10 145 EA59
Ilford IG3 147 ES58
Suffolk Dr, Guil. GU4 265 BB129
Suffolk La, EC4 19 L10
Suffolk Pk Rd, E17 145 DY56
Suffolk Pl, SW1 29 P2
Suffolk Rd, E13 23 M3
N15 144 DR58
NW10 160 CS66
SE25 224 DT98
SW13 181 CT80
Barking IG11 167 ER66
Dagenham RM10 149 FC64
Dartford DA1 210 FL86
Enfield EN3 104 DV43
Gravesend DA12 213 GK86
Harrow HA2 138 BZ58
Ilford IG3 147 ES58
Potters Bar EN6 85 CY32
Sidcup DA14 208 EW93
Worcester Park KT4 221 CT103
Sch Suffolks Prim Sch, Enf. EN1
off Brick La 104 DV40
Suffolk St, E7 13 N2
SW1 29 P2
Suffolk Way, Horn. RM11 150 FN56
Sevenoaks TN13 279 FJ125
Sugar Bakers Ct, EC3
off Creechurch La 19 P9
Sugar Ho La, E15 12 E10
Sugar La, Berk. HP4 61 AZ22
Hemel Hempstead HP1 61 BB22
Sugar Loaf Wk, E2 20 G2
Sugar Quay Wk, EC3 31 P1
Sugden Rd, SW11 182 DG83
Thames Ditton KT7 219 CH102
Sugden Way, Bark. IG11 167 ET68
Sulgrave Gdns, W6 26 B5
Sulgrave Rd, W6 26 B5
Sulina Rd, SW2 203 DL87
Sulivan Ct, SW6 39 J9
● Sulivan Enterprise Cen, SW6
off Sulivan Rd 182 DA83
Sch Sulivan Prim Sch, SW6 39 J9
Sulivan Rd, SW6 182 DA83
Sulkin Ho, E2
off Knottisford St 21 J2
Sullivan Av, E16 24 E6
Sullivan Cl, SW11 40 C10
Dartford DA1 209 FH86
Hayes UB4 158 BW71
Sullivan Cres, Hare. UB9 114 BK54
Sullivan Ho, SW1
off Churchill Gdns 41 K1
Sullivan Rd, SE11 30 F8
Tilbury RM18 193 GG81
Sullivans Reach, Walt. KT12 217 BT101
Sullivan Way, Els. WD6 99 CJ44
Sultan Rd, E11 146 EH56
Sultan St, SE5 43 J4
Beckenham BR3 225 DX96
Sultan Ter, N22
off Vincent Rd 121 DN54
Sumatra Rd, NW6 5 K4
Sumburgh Rd, SW12 202 DG86
Sumburgh Way, Slou. SL1 154 AS71
Summer Av, E.Mol. KT8 219 CE99
Summer Cl, Byfleet KT14 234 BM114
Summer Ct, Hem.H. HP2
off Townsend 62 BK18
Summercourt Rd, E1 21 H8
Summer Crossing, T.Ditt. KT7 219 CE98
Summerdale, Welw.G.C. AL8 51 CX05
Summerene Cl, SW16 203 DJ94
Summerfield, Ashtd. KT21 253 CK119
Hatfield AL10 67 CU21
Summerfield Av, NW6 4 F10
Summerfield Cl, Add. KT15
off Spinney Hill 233 BF106
London Colney AL2 83 CJ26
Summerfield La, Long Dit.
KT6 219 CK103
Summerfield Pl, Ott. KT16
off Crawshaw Rd 233 BD107
Summerfield Rd, W5 159 CH70
Loughton IG10 106 EK44
Watford WD25 97 BU35
Summerfields Av, N12 120 DE51
Summerfield St, SE12 206 EF87
Summer Gdns, E.Mol. KT8 219 CE99
Summer Gro, Els. WD6 99 CK44
West Wickham BR4 226 EE103

Summerhayes Cl, Wok. GU21 232 AY114
Summerhays, Cob. KT11 236 BX113
Summer Hill, Chis. BR7 227 EN96
Elstree WD6 100 CN43
Summerhill Cl, Orp. BR6 227 ES104
Summerhill Ct, St.Alb. AL1 65 CF19
Summerhill Gro, Enf. EN1 104 DS44
Summerhill Rd, N15 144 DR56
Dartford DA1 210 FK87
Summer Hill Vil, Chis. BR7 227 EN95
Summerhill Way, Mitch. CR4 222 DG95
Summerhouse Av, Houns.
TW5 178 BY81
Summerhouse Dr, Bex. DA5 209 FD91
Dartford DA2 209 FD91
Summerhouse La, Ald. WD25 98 CC40
Harefield UB9 114 BG52
Harmondsworth UB7 176 BK79
Summerhouse Rd, N16 144 DS61
Summerhouse Way, Abb.L.
WD5 81 BT30
Summerland Gdns, N10 143 DH55
Summerlands Av, W3 160 CQ73
Summerlands Rd, St.Alb. AL4 65 CJ16
Summerlay Cl, Kgswd KT20 255 CY120
Summerlea, Slou. SL1 153 AP74
Summerleas Cl, Hem.H. HP2 62 BL20
Summerlee Av, N2 142 DF56
Summerlee Gdns, N2 142 DF56
Summerley St, SW18 202 DB89
Summerly Av, Reig. RH2
off Burnham Dr 272 DA133
Summer Pl, Chal.St.P. SL9 112 AY52
Wat. WD18 off Tolpits La 97 BT44
Summer Rd, E.Mol. KT8 219 CE99
Thames Ditton KT7 219 CF99
Summersbury Dr, Shalf. GU4 280 AY142
Summersbury Hall, Shalf. GU4
off Summersbury Dr 280 AY142
Summersby Rd, N6 143 DH58
Summers Cl, Sutt. SM2
off Overton Rd 240 DA108
Wembley HA9 140 CP60
Weybridge KT13 234 BN111
Sch Summerside Prim Sch, N12
off Crossway 120 DD51
Summerskill Cl, SE15
off Manaton Cl 44 E10
Summerskille Cl, N9 122 DV47
Summers La, N12 120 DD52
Summers Rd, Burn. SL1 152 AJ69
Godalming GU7 280 AT144
Summers Row, N12 120 DE51
Summers St, EC1 18 E5
SUMMERSTOWN, SW17 202 DB90
Summerstown, SW17 202 DC90
Summerswood Cl, Ken. CR8
off Longwood Rd 258 DR116
Summerswood La, Borwd.
WD6 84 CS34
Sch Summerswood Prim Sch,
Borwd. WD6
off Furzehill Rd 100 CP42
Summerton Way, SE28 168 EX72
Summer Trees, Sun. TW16
off The Avenue 217 BV95
Summerville Gdns, Sutt. SM1 239 CZ107
Summerwood Rd, Islw. TW7 199 CF85
Summit, The, Loug. IG10 107 EM39
Summit Av, NW9 140 CR57
Summit Cl, N14 121 DJ47
NW9 140 CR56
Edgware HA8 118 CN52
Summit Ct, NW2 4 F4
Summit Dr, Wdf.Grn. IG8 124 EK54
Summit Est, N16 144 DU59
Summit Pl, Wey. KT13 234 BN108
Summit Rd, E17 145 EB56
Northolt UB5 158 CA66
Potters Bar EN6 85 CY30
Summit Way, N14 121 DH47
SE19 204 DS94
Sumner Av, SE15 44 B6
Sumner Cl, Fetch. KT22 253 CD124
Orpington BR6 245 EQ105
Sumner Ct, SW8
off Darsley Dr 42 A6
Sumner Gdns, Croy. CR0 223 DN102
Sumner Pl, SW7 28 B9
Addlestone KT15 234 BG106
Sumner Pl Ms, SW7 28 B9
Sumner Rd, SE15 44 B3
Croydon CR0 223 DN102
Harrow HA1 138 CC59
Sumner Rd S, Croy. CR0 223 DN102
SUMNERS, Harl. CM19 73 EN19
Sumners Fm Cl, Harl. CM19 73 EN20
Sumner St, SE1 31 H2
Sumpter Cl, NW3 5 P5
Sumpter Yd, St.Alb. AL1 65 CD20
Sun All, Rich. TW9
off Kew Rd 180 CL84
Sunbeam Cres, W10 14 B5
Sunbeam Rd, NW10 160 CQ70
SUNBURY, Sun. TW16 217 BV97
⇌ Sunbury 217 BT95
Coll Sunbury Adult Learning Cen,
Sun. TW16
off The Avenue 217 BV95
Sunbury Av, NW7 118 CR50
SW14 180 CR84
Sunbury Cl, Walt. KT12 217 BU100
Sunbury Ct, Sun. TW16 218 BX96
Sunbury Ct Island, Sun. TW16 218 BX97
Sunbury Ct Ms, Sun. TW16
off Lower Hampton Rd 218 BX97
Sunbury Ct Rd, Sun. TW16 218 BW96
Sunbury Cres, Felt. TW13
off Ryland Cl 197 BT91
Jct Sunbury Cross, Sun.
TW16 197 BT94
Sunbury Cross Cen, Sun.
TW16 197 BT94
Sunbury Gdns, NW7 118 CR50
Sunbury La, SW11 40 B6
Walton-on-Thames KT12 217 BU100
Sunbury Lock Ait, Walt. KT12 217 BV98
Sch Sunbury Manor Sch, Sun.
TW16 off Nursery Rd 217 BT95
Sunbury Rd, Eton SL4 173 AR79
Feltham TW13 197 BT90
Sutton SM3 221 CX104
Sunbury St, SE18 37 K7
Sunbury Way, Han. TW13 198 BW92
● Sunbury Workshops, E2
off Swanfield St 20 A3
Sun Ct, EC3 19 M9
Erith DA8 189 FF82
Suncroft Pl, SE26 204 DW90

Sundale Av, S.Croy. CR2 242 DW110
Sunderland Av, St.Alb. AL1 65 CG18
Sunderland Ct, SE22 204 DU87
Sunderland Gro, Lvsdn WD25 81 BT34
Sunderland Mt, SE23 205 DX89
Sunderland Rd, SE23 205 DX88
W5 179 CK76
Sunderland Ter, W2 15 L8
Sunderland Way, E12 146 EK61
Sundew Av, W12 161 CU73
Sundew Cl, W12 161 CU73
Sundew Ct, Grays RM17
off Salix Rd 192 GD79
Sundew Rd, Hem.H. HP1 61 BE21
Sundial Av, SE25 224 DT97
Sundon Cres, Vir.W. GU25 214 AV99
Sundorne Rd, SE7 186 EH78
Sundown Av, S.Croy. CR2 242 DT111
Sundown Rd, Ashf. TW15 197 BQ92
Sundra Wk, E1 21 J5
SUNDRIDGE, Brom. BR1 206 EJ93
SUNDRIDGE, Sev. TN14 262 EZ124
Sundridge Av, Brom. BR1 226 EK95
Chislehurst BR7 206 EK94
Welling DA16 187 ER82
Sundridge Cl, Dart. DA1 210 FN86
Sundridge Hill, Sev. TN14 262 EW118
Sundridge Ho, Brom. BR1
off Burnt Ash La 206 EH92
Sundridge La, Sev. TN14 262 EV117
⇌ Sundridge Park 206 EH94
Sundridge Pl, Croy. CR0
off Inglis Rd 224 DU102
Sundridge Rd, Croy. CR0 224 DT101
Dunton Green TN14 262 FA120
Woking GU22 249 BA119
Sunfields Pl, SE3 186 EH80
Sunflower Way, Rom. RM3 128 FK53
Sun Hill, Fawk.Grn DA3 231 FU104
Woking GU22 248 AU121
Jct Sun-In-The-Sands, SE3 186 EH80
Sunken Rd, Croy. CR0 242 DW106
Sunkist Way, Wall. SM6 241 DL109
Sunland Av, Bexh. DA6 188 EY84
Sun La, SE3 186 EH80
Gravesend DA12 213 GJ89
Sunleigh Rd, Wem. HA0 160 CL67
Sunley Gdns, Perivale UB6 159 CG67
Sunlight Cl, SW19 202 DC93
Sunlight Sq, E2 20 F3
Sunmead Cl, Fetch. KT22 253 CF122
Sunmead Rd, Hem.H. HP2 62 BK18
Sunbury-on-Thames TW16 217 BU97
Sunna Gdns, Sun. TW16 217 BV96
Sunningdale, N14 121 DK50
Sunningdale Av, W3 160 CS73
Barking IG11 167 ER67
Feltham TW13 198 BY89
Rainham RM13 169 FH70
Ruislip HA4 138 BW60
Sunningdale Cl, E6 25 J2
SE16 44 E1
SE28 168 EY72
Stanmore HA7 117 CG52
Surbiton KT6
off Culsac Rd 220 CL103
Sunningdale Gdns, NW9 140 CQ57
W8 27 K7
Sunningdale Ms, Welw.G.C.
AL7 51 CY05
Sunningdale Rd, Brom. BR1 226 EL98
Rainham RM13 169 FG66
Sutton SM1 239 CZ105
Sunningfields Cres, NW4 119 CV54
Sunningfields Rd, NW4 119 CV54
Sunning Hill, Nthflt DA11 212 GE89
Sunninghill Ct, W3
off Bollo Br Rd 180 CQ75
Sunninghill Rd, SE13 46 C9
Sunnings La, Upmin. RM14 170 FQ65
Sunningvale Av, Bigg.H. TN16 260 EJ115
Sunningvale Cl, Bigg.H. TN16 260 EK116
Sunny Bk, SE25 224 DU97
Sunnybank, Epsom KT18 254 CQ116
Sunny Bk, Warl. CR6 259 DY117
Sch Sunny Bk Prim Sch, Pot.B.
EN6 off Field Vw Rd 86 DA34
Sunnybank Rd, Pot.B. EN6 86 DA33
Sunnybank Vil, Red. RH1 274 DT132
Sunny Cres, NW10 160 CQ66
Sunny Cft, Harl. CM18 73 ET18
Sunnycroft Gdns, Upmin.
RM14 151 FT59
Sunnycroft Rd, SE25 224 DU97
Hounslow TW3 178 CB82
Southall UB1 158 CA71
Sunnydale, Orp. BR6 227 EN103
Sunnydale Gdns, NW7 118 CR51
Sunnydale Rd, SE12 206 EH85
Sunnydell, St.Alb. AL2 82 CB26
Sunnydene Av, E4 123 ED50
Ruislip HA4 137 BU60
Sunnydene Cl, Rom. RM3 128 FM52
Sunnydene Gdns, Wem. HA0 159 CJ65
Sunnydene Rd, Pur. CR8 241 DP113
Sunnydene St, SE26 205 DY91
Sch Sunnydown Sch, Cat. CR3
off Whyteleafe Rd 258 DT121
Sunnyfield, NW7 119 CT49
Hatfield AL9 67 CX15
Sunnyfield Rd, Chis. BR7 228 EU97
Sch Sunnyfields Prim Sch, NW4
off Hatchcroft 141 CV55
Sunny Gdns Par, NW4
off Great N Way 119 CW54
Sunny Gdns Rd, NW4 119 CV54
Sunny Hill, NW4 141 CV55
Sunnyhill Cl, E5 145 DY63
Sch Sunnyhill Prim Sch, SW16
off Sunnyhill Rd 203 DM91
Sunnyhill Rd, SW16 203 DL91
Hemel Hempstead HP1 62 BH20
West Hyde WD3 113 BD51
Sunnyhurst Cl, Sutt. SM1 222 DA104
Sunnymead Av, Mitch. CR4 223 DJ97
Sunnymead Rd, NW9 140 CR59
SW15 201 CV85
SUNNYMEADS, Stai. TW19 174 AY84
⇌ Sunnymeads 174 AY83
Sunnymede, Chig. IG7 126 EV48
Sunnymede Av, Cars. SM5 240 DD111
Chesham HP5 76 AS28
Epsom KT19 238 CS109
Sunnymede Dr, Ilf. IG6 147 EP56
Sunny Ms, Rom. RM5 127 FC52
Sunny Nook Gdns, S.Croy.
CR2 242 DR107
Sunny Pl, NW4
off Sunny Gdns Rd 141 CW56

Sunny Ri, Chaldon CR3 258 DR124
Sunny Rd, The, Enf. EN3 105 DX39
Sunnyside, NW2 141 CZ62
SW19 201 CY93
Lower Nazeing EN9 72 EF22
Walton-on-Thames KT12 218 BW99
Sunnyside Cotts, Chesh. HP5 78 AU26
Sunnyside Dr, E4 123 EC45
Sunnyside Gdns, Upmin.
RM14 150 FQ61
Sunnyside Pas, SW19 201 CY93
Sunnyside Pl, SW19
off Sunnyside 201 CY93
Sunnyside Rd, E10 145 EA60
N19 143 DK59
W5 159 CK74
Chesham HP5 76 AP30
Epping CM16 91 ET32
Ilford IG1 147 EQ62
Teddington TW11 199 CD91
Sunnyside Rd E, N9 122 DU48
Sunnyside Rd N, N9 122 DT48
Sunnyside Rd S, N9 122 DT48
Sunnyside Ter, NW9
off Edgware Rd 140 CR55
Sunny Vw, NW9 140 CR56
Sunny Way, N12 120 DE52
Sun Pas, SE16 32 C6
Windsor SL4
off Bachelors Acre 173 AR81
Sunray Av, SE24 184 DR84
Bromley BR2 226 EL100
Hutton CM13 131 GE44
Surbiton KT5 220 CP103
West Drayton UB7 176 BK75
Sunrise Av, Horn. RM12 150 FJ62
Sunrise Cl, Felt. TW13
off Exeter Rd 198 BZ90
Sunrise Cres, Hem.H. HP3 62 BL23
Sun Rd, W14 38 G1
Swanscombe DA10 212 FZ86
Sunset Av, E4 123 EB46
Woodford Green IG8 124 EF49
Sunset Ct, Erith DA8 189 FH80
Sunset Ct, Wdf.Grn. IG8
off Navestock Cres 124 EJ52
Sunset Dr, Hav.at.Bow. RM4 127 FH50
Sunset Gdns, SE25 224 DT96
Sunset Ms, Rom. RM5 127 FC51
Sunset Rd, SE5 184 DQ84
SE28 188 EU75
Sunset Vw, Barn. EN5 101 CY40
Sunshine Way, Mitch. CR4 222 DF96
Sun Sq, Hem.H. HP1
off High St 62 BK19
Sunstone Gro, Merst. RH1 273 DL129
Sun St, EC2 19 N7
Sawbridgeworth CM21 58 EZ06
Waltham Abbey EN9 89 EC33
Sun Wk, E1 32 C1
Sunwell Cl, SE15 44 E7
Superior Dr, Grn St Grn BR6 245 ET107
SURBITON, KT5 & KT6 220 CM101
⇌ Surbiton 219 CK100
Surbiton Ct, Surb. KT6 219 CJ100
Surbiton Cres, Kings.T. KT1 220 CL98
Surbiton Hall Cl, Kings.T. KT1 220 CL98
Sch Surbiton High Sch, Kings.T.
KT1 off Surbiton Cres 220 CL98
Surbiton Hill Pk, Surb. KT5 220 CN99
Surbiton Hill Rd, Surb. KT6 220 CL98
H Surbiton Hosp, Surb. KT6 220 CL100
Sch Surbiton Jun Girls' Sch,
Kings.T. KT1
off Surbiton Rd 220 CL98
Surbiton Par, Surb. KT6
off St. Mark's Hill 220 CL100
Surbiton Plaza, Surb. KT6
off St. Marys Rd 219 CK100
Sch Surbiton Prep Sch, Surb.
KT6 off Avenue Elmers 220 CL99
Surbiton Rd, Kings.T. KT1 220 CL98
Surlingham Cl, SE28 168 EX73
Surly Hall Wk, Wind. SL4 173 AM81
Surma Cl, E1 20 E5
Surman Cres, Hutt. CM13 131 GC45
Surmans Cl, Dag. RM9 168 EW67
Surrendale Pl, W9 15 K5
Surrey Av, Slou. SL2 153 AQ71
Surrey Canal Rd, SE14 45 H2
SE15 45 H2
Surrey Cl, N3 141 CY55
Surrey Cres, W4 180 CN78
★ Surrey Docks Fm, SE16 33 N5
Surrey Dr, Horn. RM11 150 FN56
Surrey Gdns, N4 144 DQ58
Effingham Junction KT24 251 BT123
Surrey Gro, SE17 43 N1
Sutton SM1 222 DD104
Surrey Hills Av, Box H. KT20 270 CQ130
● Surrey Hills Business Pk,
Wotton RH5 284 BZ139
Surrey Hills Pk, Box H. KT20 270 CP130
Coll Surrey Inst of Art & Design,
The, Epsom KT18
off Ashley Rd 238 CS114
Surrey La, SW11 40 C7
Surrey La Est, SW11 40 C6
Surrey Ms, SE27
off Hamilton Rd 204 DS91
Surrey Mt, SE23 204 DV88
⊖ Surrey Quays 33 J8
Surrey Quays Rd, SE16 33 H6
Surrey Quays Shop Cen,
SE16 33 J7
Surrey Rd, SE15 205 DX85
Barking IG11 167 ES67
Dagenham RM10 149 FB64
Harrow HA1 138 CC57
West Wickham BR4 225 EB102
Surrey Row, SE1 30 G4
Surrey Sq, SE17 31 N10
Sch Surrey Sq Inf & Jun Schs,
SE17 31 N10
Surrey St, E13 24 B3
WC2 18 D10
Croydon CR0 224 DQ104
Surrey Ter, SE17 31 P9
Surrey Twrs, Add. KT15
off Garfield Rd 234 BJ106
Surrey Water Rd, SE16 33 K3
Surridge Cl, Rain. RM13 170 FJ69
Surridge Gdns, SE19
off Hancock Rd 204 DR93
Surr St, N7 8 B3
Sury Basin, Kings.T. KT2 220 CL95
Susan Cl, Rom. RM7 149 FC55
Susan Constant Ct, E14
off Newport Av 23 H10

Susan Lawrence Ho, E12
off Walton Rd 147 EN63
Susannah St, E14 22 D9
Susan Rd, SE3 186 EH82
Susan Wd, Chis. BR7 227 EN95
Sussex Av, Islw. TW7 179 CE83
Romford RM3 128 FM52
Sussex Border Path, Horl. RH6 290 DF150
Sussex Cl, N19 143 DL61
Chalfont St. Giles HP8 112 AV47
Hoddesdon EN11
off Roman St 71 EA16
Ilford IG4 147 EM58
New Malden KT3 220 CS98
Reigate RH2 288 DD135
Slough SL1 174 AV75
Twickenham TW1
off Westmorland Cl 199 CH86
Sussex Ct, Add. KT15
off Garfield Rd 234 BJ106
Sussex Cres, Nthlt. UB5 158 CA65
Sussex Gdns, N4 144 DQ57
N6 142 DF57
W2 16 A10
Chessington KT9 237 CK107
Sussex Ho Sch, SW1 28 E8
Sussex Keep, Slou. SL1
off Sussex Cl 174 AV75
Sussex Ms, SE6
off Ravensbourne Pk 205 EA87
Sussex Ms E, W2 16 B9
Sussex Ms W, W2 16 B10
Sussex Pl, NW1 16 E3
W2 16 B9
W6 26 A10
Erith DA8 189 FB80
New Malden KT3 220 CS98
Slough SL1 174 AV75
Sussex Ring, N12 120 DA50
Sussex Rd, E6 167 EN67
Carshalton SM5 240 DF107
Dartford DA1 210 FN87
Erith DA8 189 FB80
Harrow HA1 138 CC57
Mitcham CR4
off Lincoln Rd 223 DL99
New Malden KT3 220 CS98
Orpington BR5 228 EW100
Sidcup DA14 208 EV92
South Croydon CR2 242 DR107
Southall UB2 178 BX76
Uxbridge UB10 137 BQ63
Warley CM14 130 FV49
Watford WD24 97 BU38
West Wickham BR4 225 EB102
Sussex Sq, W2 16 B10
Sussex St, E13 24 B3
SW1 41 K1
Sussex Way, N7 143 DL61
N19 143 DL60
Cockfosters EN4 102 DG43
Sutcliffe Cl, NW11 142 DB57
Bushey WD23 98 CC42
Sutcliffe Ho, Hayes UB3 157 BU72
Sutcliffe Rd, SE18 187 ES79
Welling DA16 188 EW82
Sutherland Av, W9 15 N3
W13 159 CH72
Biggin Hill TN16 260 EK117
Cuffley EN6 87 DK28
Hayes UB3 177 BU77
Jacobs Well GU4 264 AX128
Petts Wood BR5 227 ET100
Sunbury-on-Thames TW16 217 BT96
Welling DA16 187 ES84
Sutherland Cl, Barn. EN5 101 CY42
Greenhithe DA9 211 FT85
Sutherland Ct, NW9 140 CP57
Welwyn Garden City AL7 51 CZ08
Sutherland Dr, SW19 222 DD95
Burpham GU4 265 AZ131
Sutherland Gdns, SW14 180 CS83
Sunbury-on-Thames TW16
off Sutherland Av 217 BT96
Worcester Park KT4 221 CV102
Sutherland Gro, SW18 201 CY86
Teddington TW11 199 CE92
Sutherland Pl, W2 15 J8
Sutherland Rd, E17 123 DX54
N9 122 DU46
N17 122 DU52
W4 180 CS79
W13 159 CG72
Belvedere DA17 188 FA76
Croydon CR0 223 DN101
Enfield EN3 105 DX43
Southall UB1 158 BZ72
Sutherland Rd Path, E17 145 DX55
Sutherland Row, SW1 29 K10
Sutherland Sq, SE17 43 J1
Sutherland St, SW1 29 J10
Sutherland Wk, SE17 43 K1
Sutherland Way, Cuffley EN6 87 DK28
Sutlej Rd, SE7 186 EJ80
Sutterton St, N7 8 C5
SUTTON, SM1 - SM3 240 DB107
Sutton 240 DC107
SUTTON ABINGER, Dor. RH5 283 BU143
SUTTON AT HONE, Dart. DA4 230 FN95
Sutton at Hone C of E Prim Sch,
Sutt.H. DA4 off Church Rd 210 FN94
Sutton Av, Slou. SL3 174 AW75
Woking GU21 248 AS119
Sutton Cl, Beck. BR3 225 EB95
Broxbourne EN10 71 DY19
Loughton IG10 124 EL45
Pinner HA5 137 BU57
Sutton Coll of Learning for
Adults, Sutton Cen, Sutt.
SM1 off St. Nicholas Way 240 DB106
Sutton W Cen, Sutt. SM1
off Robin Hood La 240 DA106
Sutton Common 222 DB103
Sutton Common Rd, Sutt.
SM1, SM3 221 CZ101
Sutton Ct, W4 180 CQ79
Sutton SM2 240 DC107
Ware SG12 off Crane Mead 55 DY07
Sutton Ct Rd, E13 24 C3
W4 180 CQ80
Sutton SM1 240 DC107
Uxbridge UB10 157 BP67
Sutton Cres, Barn. EN5 101 CX43
Sutton Dene, Houns. TW3 178 CB81
Sutton Est, SW3 28 D10
W10 14 A6
Sutton Est, The, N1 8 G6
Sutton Gdns, Bark. IG11
off Sutton Rd 167 ES68
Sutton Gdns, Croydon CR0 224 DT99
Merstham RH1 273 DK129
Sutton Gram Sch for Boys,
Sutt. SM1 off Manor La 240 DC106
SUTTON GREEN, Guil. GU4 265 AZ125
Sutton Grn, Bark. IG11
off Sutton Rd 167 ES67
Sutton Grn Rd, Sutt.Grn GU4 264 AY126
Sutton Gro, Sutt. SM1 240 DD105
Sutton Hall Rd, Houns. TW5 178 CA80
Sutton Hts, Sutt. SM2 240 DD108
Sutton High Sch, Sutt. SM1
off Cheam Rd 240 DB107
Sutton Hill, Guil. GU4 265 BC129
Sutton Hosp, Sutt. SM2 240 DB110
★ Sutton Ho, E9 10 G3
Sutton Ho, Hem.H. HP2 62 BL16
Sutton La, EC1 19 H5
Abinger Common RH5 283 BV143
Banstead SM7 256 DB115
Hounslow TW3 178 BZ83
Slough SL3 175 BC78
Sutton SM2 240 DB111
Sutton La N, W4 180 CQ78
Sutton La S, W4 180 CQ79
Sutton Par, NW4
off Church Rd 141 CW56
Sutton Pk, Sutt.Grn GU4 265 AZ127
Sutton Pk Rd, Sutt. SM1 240 DB107
Sutton Path, Borwd. WD6 100 CN40
★ Sutton Pl, Guil. GU4 265 BA127
Sutton Pl, E9 10 G3
Abinger Hammer RH5 283 BT143
Dartford DA4 210 FN92
Slough SL3 175 BB79
Sutton Rd, E13 23 M4
E17 123 DX53
N10 120 DG54
Barking IG11 167 ES68
Hounslow TW5 178 CA81
St. Albans AL1 65 CH21
Watford WD17 98 BW41
Sutton Row, W1 17 P8
Suttons Av, Horn. RM12 150 FJ62
● Suttons Business Pk,
Rain. RM13 169 FD69
Suttons Gdns, Horn. RM12 150 FK62
Suttons La, Horn. RM12 150 FK64
Suttons Prim Sch, Horn.
RM12 off Suttons La 150 FK63
Sutton Sq, E9 10 G3
Hounslow TW5 178 BZ81
Sutton St, E1 20 G10
Sutton's Way, EC1 19 K5
Sutton Wk, SE1 30 D3
Sutton Way, W10 14 A5
Hounslow TW5 178 BZ81
Swabey Rd, Slou. SL3 175 BA77
Swaby Rd, SW18 202 DC88
Swaffham Way, N22 121 DP52
Swaffield Prim Sch, SW18
off St. Ann's Hill 202 DC86
Swaffield Rd, SW18 202 DB87
Sevenoaks TN13 279 FJ122
Swain Cl, SW16 203 DH93
Swain Rd, Th.Hth. CR7 224 DQ99
Swains Cl, West Dr. UB7 176 BL75
Swains La, N6 142 DG62
Swainson Rd, W3 181 CT75
Swains Rd, SW17 202 DF94
Swain St, NW8 16 C4
Swaisland Dr, Cray. DA1 209 FF85
Swaisland Rd, Dart. DA1 209 FH85
Swakeleys Dr, Uxb. UB10 136 BM63
Swakeleys Rd, Ickhm UB10 136 BM62
Swakeleys Rbt, Uxb. UB9 136 BL63
Swakeleys Sch, Hlgdn UB10
off Clifton Gdns 157 BP68
Swale Cl, Aveley RM15 170 FQ72
Swaledale Cl, N11
off Ribblesdale Av 120 DG51
Swaledale Rd, Dart. DA2 210 FQ88
Swale Rd, Dart. DA1 189 FG83
Swaley's Way, S.Ock. RM15 171 FX72
Swallands Rd, SE6 205 EA90
Swallow Cl, SE14 45 H7
Bushey WD23 116 CC46
Chafford Hundred RM16 191 FW77
Erith DA8 189 FE81
Greenhithe DA9 211 FT85
Rickmansworth WD3 114 BJ45
Staines-upon-Thames TW18 195 BF91
Swallow Ct, W13
off Gurnell Gro 159 CF70
Hert. SG14 54 DQ09
Swallowdale, Iver SL0 155 BD69
South Croydon CR2 243 DX109
Swallowdale La, Hem.H. HP2 63 BP17
Swallow Dell Prim Sch,
Welw.G.C. AL7
off Blackthorn Rd 52 DA10
Swallow Dr, NW10
off Kingfisher Way 160 CR65
Northolt UB5 158 CA68
Swallow End, Welw.G.C. AL7 51 CZ09
Swallowfield, NW1
off Munster Sq 17 K3
Englefield Green TW20
off Heronfield 194 AV93
Swallowfield Rd, SE7 186 EH78
Swallow Flds, Iver SL0 155 BD70
Swallowfields, Nthflt DA11 212 GE90
Welwyn Garden City AL7 51 CZ09
Swallowfield Way, Hayes UB3 177 BR75
Swallow Gdns, SW16 203 DK92
Hatfield AL10 67 CU20
Swallow Ho, NW8
off Allitsen Rd 6 C10
Swallow La, Mid Holm. RH5 285 CH142
St. Albans AL1 65 CH23
Swallow Pas, W1
off Swallow Pl 17 K9
Swallow Pl, W1 17 K9
Swallows, Harl. CM17 58 EW11
Swallows, The, Welw.G.C. AL7 51 CZ05
Swallows Oak, Abb.L. WD5 81 BT31
Swallow St, E6 25 H7
W1 29 M1
Iver SL0 155 BD69
Swallowtail Cl, Orp. BR5 228 EX98
Swallowtail Wk, Berk. HP4
off Springfield Rd 60 AT16
Swallow Wk, Horn. RM12
off Heron Flight Av 169 FH65
Swaminarayan Sch, The,
NW10 off Brentfield Rd 160 CR65
Swanage Ho, SW8 42 C5
Swanage Rd, E4 123 EC52
SW18 202 DC86
Swanage Waye, Hayes UB4 158 BW72
Swan All, Wat. WD18
off Lower High St 98 BW43
Swan & Pike Rd, Enf. EN3 105 EA38
Swan App, E6 24 G7
Swan Av, Upmin. RM14 151 FT60
Swanbourne, SE17 31 J9
Swanbourne Dr, Horn. RM12 150 FJ64
Swanbridge Rd, Bexh. DA7 188 FA81
● Swan Business Pk, Dart.
DA1 190 FJ84
● Swan Cen, The, SW17
off Rosemary Rd 202 DC90
Swan Cl, E17 123 DY53
Chesham HP5 76 AP27
Croydon CR0 224 DS101
Feltham TW13 198 BY91
Orpington BR5 228 EU97
Rickmansworth WD3
off Parsonage Rd 114 BK45
Swan Ct, SW3 40 D1
Guildford GU1 264 AX132
Hemel Hempstead HP1
off Waterhouse St 62 BJ21
Swandon Way, SW18 202 DB85
Swan Dr, NW9 118 CS54
Swanfield Rd, Wal.Cr. EN8 89 DY33
Swanfield St, E2 20 A3
Swanhill, Welw.G.C. AL7 52 DA06
Swan Junct, The, W.Wick.
BR4 225 EC103
Swanland Rd, N.Mymms AL9 85 CV28
South Mimms EN6 85 CV33
Swan La, EC4 31 L1
N20 120 DC48
Dartford DA1 209 FF87
Guildford GU1 280 AX135
Loughton IG10 124 EJ45
Swanlea Sch, E1 20 E6
SWANLEY, BR8 229 FE98
Swanley 229 FD98
Swanley Adult Ed Cen, Swan.
BR8 off St. Marys Rd 229 FE97
Swanley Bar La, Pot.B. EN6 86 DB28
Swanley Bypass, Sid. DA14 229 FC97
Swanley BR8 229 FC97
Swanley Cen, Swan. BR8 229 FE97
Swanley Cres, Pot.B. EN6 86 DB29
Swanley La, Swan. BR8 229 FF97
Swanley Rd, Well. DA16 188 EW81
Swanley Sch, Swan. BR8
off St. Marys Rd 229 FE97
SWANLEY VILLAGE, Swan.
BR8 230 FJ95
Swanley Village Rd, Swan.
BR8 229 FH95
Swan Mead, SE1 31 N7
Hemel Hempstead HP3 80 BM25
Swan Ms, SW6
off Purser's Cross Rd 39 J6
Romford RM7 149 FB56
Swan Mill Gdns, Dor. RH4 269 CJ134
Swanns Meadow, Bkhm
KT23 268 CA126
Swan Pas, E1
off Cartwright St 32 B1
Swan Path, E10 off Jesse Rd 145 EC60
Kingston upon Thames KT1
off Villiers Rd 220 CM97
Swan Pl, SW13 181 CT82
Swan Rd, SE16 33 H4
SE18 36 F7
Feltham TW13 198 BY92
Iver SL0 155 BF72
Southall UB1 158 CB72
West Drayton UB7 176 BK75
Swans Cl, St.Alb. AL4 66 CL21
SWANSCOMBE, DA10 212 FZ86
Swanscombe 212 FZ85
● Swanscombe Business Cen,
Swans. DA10 212 FY85
Swanscombe Ho, W11
off St. Anns Rd 26 D2
Swanscombe Rd, W4 180 CS78
W11 26 D3
Swanscombe St, Swans.
DA10 212 FY87
Swansea Cl, Coll.Row RM5 127 FD52
Swansea Ct, E16 37 P3
Swansea Rd, Enf. EN3 104 DW42
London Heathrow Airport TW6
off Shrewsbury Rd 197 BR86
Swanshope, Loug. IG10 107 EP40
Swansland Gdns, E17
off McEntee Av 123 DY53
Swans Rd, Wal.Cr. EN8 89 DX34
Swanston Path, Wat. WD19 116 BW48
Swan St, SE1 31 K6
Isleworth TW7 179 CH83
Swan Ter, Wind. SL4
off Mill La 173 AN80
Swanton Gdns, SW19 201 CX88
Swanton Rd, Erith DA8 189 FB80
Swan Valley Comm Sch, Swans.
DA10 off Southfleet Rd 212 FZ87
Swan Wk, Rom. RM1
off Market Pl 149 FE57
Swan Wk, SW3 40 E2
Shepperton TW17 217 BS101
Swan Way, Enf. EN3 105 DX40
● Swan Wf Business Cen,
Uxb. UB8 off Waterloo Rd 156 BJ68
Swanwick Cl, SW15 201 CT87
Swanworth La, Mick. RH5 269 CH128
Swan Yd, N1 8 G5
Sward Rd, Orp. BR5 228 EU100
Swaton Rd, E3 22 B5
Swaylands Rd, Belv. DA17 188 FA79
Swaynesland Rd, Eden. TN8 277 EM134
Swaynes La, Guil. GU1 265 BE134
Swaythling Cl, N18 122 DV49
Swaythling Ho, SW15
off Tunworth Cres 201 CT86
Swedenborg Gdns, E1 20 D10
Sweden Gate, SE16 33 L7
Swedish Sch, The, SW13
off Lonsdale Rd 181 CT79
Sweeney Cres, SE1 32 B5
Sweeps Ditch Cl, Stai. TW18 216 BG95
Sweeps La, Egh. TW20 195 AZ92
Orpington BR5 228 EX99
Sweet Briar, Welw.G.C. AL7 52 DA11
Sweetbriar Cl, Hem.H. HP1 62 BG17
Sweet Briar Grn, N9 122 DT48
Sweet Briar Gro, N9 122 DT48
Sweet Briar La, Epsom KT18 238 CR114
Sweet Briar Wk, N18 122 DT49
Sweetcroft La, Uxb. UB10 156 BN66
Sweet La, Peasl. GU5 283 BR143
Sweetmans Av, Pnr. HA5 138 BX55
Sweets Way, N20 120 DD47
Swetenham Wk, SE18
off Raglan Rd 187 EQ78
Swete St, E13 23 P1
Sweyne Rd, Swans. DA10 212 FY86
Sweyn Pl, SE3 47 P9
Sweyns, Harl. CM17 74 EW17
Swievelands Rd, Bigg.H.
TN16 260 EH119
Swift Cl, E17 123 DY52
SE28 168 EV73
Harrow HA2 138 CB61
Hayes UB3 157 BT72
Slough SL1 153 AM73
Stanstead Abbotts SG12 55 EC12
Upminster RM14 151 FS60
Swiftfields, Welw.G.C. AL7 51 CZ08
Swift Rd, Felt. TW13 198 BY90
Southall UB2 178 BZ76
Swiftsden Way, Brom. BR1 206 EE93
Swift St, SW6 38 F6
Swiftsure Rd, Chaff.Hun.
RM16 191 FW77
SWILLET, THE, Rick. WD3 95 BB44
Swinbrook Rd, W10 14 F6
Swinburne Ct, SE5
off Basingdon Way 184 DR84
Swinburne Cres, Croy. CR0 224 DW100
Swinburne Gdns, Til. RM18 193 GH82
Swinburne Rd, SW15 181 CU84
Swinderby Rd, Wem. HA0 160 CL65
Swindon Cl, Ilf. IG3
off Salisbury Rd 147 ES61
Romford RM3 128 FM50
Swindon Gdns, Rom. RM3 128 FM50
Swindon La, Rom. RM3 128 FM50
Swindon Rd, Lon.Hthrw Air.
TW6 197 BQ85
Swindon St, W12 161 CV74
Swinfield Cl, Felt. TW13 198 BY91
Swinford Gdns, SW9 42 G10
Swingate La, SE18 187 ES79
Swing Gate First & Nurs Sch,
Berk. HP4
off Swing Gate La 60 AX20
Swing Gate La, Berk. HP4 60 AX22
Swinnerton St, E9 11 L3
Swinton Cl, Wem. HA9 140 CP60
Swinton Pl, WC1 18 C2
Swinton St, WC1 18 C2
Swires Shaw, Kes. BR2 244 EK105
Swiss Av, Wat. WD18 97 BS42
Swiss Cl, Wat. WD18 97 BS41
Swiss Cottage 6 A6
Swiss Cottage Sch, NW8 6 B7
Swiss Ct, W1 29 P1
Swiss Ter, NW6 6 A6
Switch Ho, E14 23 H10
Swithland Gdns, SE9 207 EN91
Sword Cl, Brox. EN10 71 DX20
Swyncombe Av, W5 179 CH77
Swynford Gdns, NW4 141 CU56
Sybil Elgar Sch, W5
off Florence Rd 160 CL73
Southall UB2
off Havelock Rd 178 BZ76
Sybil Ms, N4 143 DP58
Sybil Phoenix Cl, SE8 33 K10
Sybourn Infants' Sch, E17
off Sybourn St 145 DZ59
Sybourn Jun Sch, E17
off Sybourn St 145 DZ59
Sybourn St, E17 145 DZ59
Sycamore App, Crox.Grn WD3 97 BQ43
Sycamore Av, E3 11 N8
W5 179 CK76
Hatfield AL10 67 CU19
Hayes UB3 157 BS73
Sidcup DA15 207 ET86
Upminster RM14 150 FN62
Sycamore Cl, E16 23 J5
N9 122 DU49
SE9 206 EL89
W3 off Bromyard Av 160 CS74
Amersham HP6 77 AR37
Barnet EN4 102 DD44
Bushey WD23 98 BY40
Carshalton SM5 240 DF105
Chalfont St. Giles HP8 112 AU48
Cheshunt EN7 88 DT27
Edgware HA8 off Ash Cl 118 CQ49
Feltham TW13 197 BU90
Fetcham KT22 253 CE123
Gravesend DA12 213 GK87
Loughton IG10 107 EP40
Northolt UB5 158 BY67
South Croydon CR2 242 DS106
Tilbury RM18 193 GG81
Watford WD25 97 BV35
West Drayton UB7 156 BM73
Sycamore Ct, Surb. KT6
off Penners Gdns 220 CL101
Sycamore Dene, Chesh. HP5 76 AR28
Sycamore Dr, Brwd. CM14
off Copperfield Gdns 130 FW46
Park Street AL2 83 CD27
Swanley BR8 229 FE97
Sycamore Fld, Harl. CM19 73 EN19
Sycamore Gdns, W6 181 CV75
Mitcham CR4 222 DD96
Sycamore Gro, NW9 140 CQ59
SE6 205 EC86
SE20 204 DU94
New Malden KT3 220 CR97
Romford RM2 127 FG54
Sycamore Hill, N11 120 DG51
Sycamore Ho, NW3
off Maitland Pk Vil 6 F4
Warlingham CR6
off East Parkside 259 EB115
Sycamore Ms, SW4 183 DJ83
Sycamore Path, E17
off Poplars Rd 145 EB58
Sycamore Pl, Brom. BR1 227 EN97
Sycamore Ri, Bans. SM7 239 CX114
Berkhamsted HP4 60 AX20
Chalfont St. Giles HP8 112 AU48
Sycamore Rd, SW19 201 CW93
Amersham HP6 77 AR37
Chalfont St. Giles HP8 112 AU48
Croxley Green WD3 97 BQ43
Dartford DA1 210 FK88
Guildford GU1 264 AX134
Sycamores, The, Aveley RM15
off Dacre Av 171 FR74
Bookham KT23 252 CC124
Hemel Hempstead HP3 61 BF23
Radlett WD7 83 CH34
Sycamore St, EC1 19 J5
Sycamore Wk, W10 14 E4
Englefield Green TW20 194 AV93
George Green SL3 154 AY72
Ilford IG6 off Civic Way 147 EQ56
Reigate RH2 288 DC137
Sycamore Way, S.Ock. RM15 171 FX70
Teddington TW11 199 CJ93
Thornton Heath CR7 223 DN99
SYDENHAM, SE26 204 DW92
Sydenham 204 DW91
Sydenham 204 DW91
Sydenham Av, N21
off Fleming Dr 103 DM43
SE26 204 DV92
Sydenham Cl, Rom. RM1 149 FF56
Sydenham Gdns, Slou. SL1 173 AQ76
Sydenham High Sch, SE26
off Westwood Hill 204 DV92
Jun Dept, SE26
off Westwood Hill 204 DV91
Sydenham Hill 204 DT90
Sydenham Hill, SE23 204 DV88
SE26 204 DU90
Sydenham Hill Est, SE26 204 DU90
Sydenham Pk, SE26 204 DW90
Sydenham Pk Rd, SE26 204 DW90
Sydenham Pl, SE27
off Lansdowne Hill 203 DP90
Sydenham Ri, SE23 204 DV89
Sydenham Rd, SE26 204 DW91
Croydon CR0 224 DR101
Guildford GU1 280 AX136
Sydenham Sch, SE26
off Dartmouth Rd 204 DV90
Sydmons Ct, SE23 204 DW87
Sydner Ms, N16 144 DT63
Sydner Rd, N16 144 DT63
Sydney Av, Pur. CR8 241 DM112
Sydney Chapman Way, Barn.
EN5 101 CZ40
Sydney Cl, SW3 28 B9
Sydney Cres, Ashf. TW15 197 BP93
Sydney Gro, NW4 141 CW57
Slough SL1 153 AQ72
Sydney Ms, SW3 28 B9
Sydney Pl, SW7 28 B9
Guildford GU1 281 AZ135
Sydney Rd, E11
off Mansfield Rd 146 EH58
N8 143 DN56
N10 120 DG53
SE2 188 EW76
SW20 221 CX96
W13 159 CG74
Bexleyheath DA6 188 EX84
Enfield EN2 104 DR42
Feltham TW14 197 BU88
Guildford GU1 281 AZ135
Ilford IG6 125 EQ54
Richmond TW9 180 CL84
Sidcup DA14 207 ES91
Sutton SM1 240 DA105
Teddington TW11 199 CF92
Tilbury RM18 193 GG82
Watford WD18 97 BS43
Woodford Green IG8 124 EG49
Sydney Russell Comp Sch,
Dag. RM9 off Parsloes Av 148 EX64
Sydney St, SW3 28 C10
Syke Cluan, Iver SL0 175 BE75
Syke Ings, Iver SL0 175 BE76
Sykes Dr, Stai. TW18 196 BH92
Sykes Rd, Slou. SL1 153 AP72
Sylvana Cl, Uxb. UB10 156 BM67
Sylvan Av, N3 120 DA54
N22 121 DM52
NW7 119 CT51
Hornchurch RM11 150 FL58
Romford RM6 148 EZ58
Sylvan Cl, Chaff.Hun. RM16 192 FY77
Hemel Hempstead HP3 62 BN21
Oxted RH8 276 EH129
South Croydon CR2 242 DV110
Woking GU22 249 BB117
Sylvan Ct, N12 120 DB49
Sylvandale, Welw.G.C. AL7 52 DC10
Sylvan Est, SE19 224 DT95
Sylvan Gdns, Surb. KT6 219 CK101
Sylvan Gro, NW2 4 D1
SE15 44 F4
Sylvan Hill, SE19 224 DS95
Sylvan Ms, Green. DA9
off Watermans Way 191 FV84
Sylvan Rd, E7 13 P4
E11 146 EG57
E17 145 EA57
SE19 224 DT95
Ilford IG1 147 EQ61
Sylvan Wk, Brom. BR1 227 EM97
Sylvan Way, Chig. IG7 126 EV48
Dagenham RM8 148 EV62
Redhill RH1 288 DG135
Welwyn Garden City AL7 52 DC10
West Wickham BR4 244 EE105
Sylverdale Rd, Croy. CR0 223 DP104
Purley CR8 241 DP113
Sylvester Av, Chis. BR7 207 EM93
Sylvester Gdns, Ilf. IG6 126 EV50
Sylvester Path, E8 10 F4
Sylvester Rd, E8 10 F4
E17 145 DZ59
N2 120 DC54
Wembley HA0 139 CJ64
Sylvestres, Rvrhd TN13 278 FD121
Sylvestrus Cl, Kings.T. KT1 220 CN95
Sylvia Av, Hutt. CM13 131 GC47
Pinner HA5 116 BZ51
Sylvia Ct, Wem. HA9
off Harrow Rd 160 CP66
Sylvia Gdns, Wem. HA9 160 CP66
Sylvia Young Thea Sch,
NW1 16 D5
Symes Ms, NW1 7 L10
Symington Ho, SE1 31 K2
Symington Ms, E9 11 K2
Symister Ms, N1 19 N3
Symonds Ct, Chsht EN8 89 DX28
Symonds Hyde, Hat. AL10 50 CP13
Symons Cl, SE15 44 G9
Symons St, SW3 28 F9

Symphony Cl, Edg. HA8 118 CP52
Symphony Ms, W10 14 F2
Syon Gate Way, Brent. TW8 179 CG80
★ **Syon Ho & Pk**, Brent. TW8 179 CJ81
⇌ **Syon Lane** 179 CG80
Syon La, Islw. TW7 179 CH80
Syon Pk Gdns, Islw. TW7 179 CF80
Sch **Syon Pk Sch**, Islw. TW7 *off Twickenham Rd* 179 CH81
Syon Vista, Rich. TW9 179 CK81
Syracuse Av, Rain. RM13 170 FL69
Uni **Syracuse Uni - London Program**, WC1 18 B6
Syringa Ct, Grays RM17 192 GD80
Sythwood, Wok. GU21 248 AV117
Sch **Sythwood Prim Sch**, Horsell GU21 *off Sythwood* 248 AV116

T

Tabard Cen, SE1 *off Prioress St* 31 M7
Tabard Gdns Est, SE1 31 M5
Tabard St, SE1 31 L5
Tabarin Way, Epsom KT17 255 CW116
Tabernacle Av, E13 23 N5
Tabernacle St, EC2 19 M5
Tableer Av, SW4 203 DJ85
Tabley Rd, N7 143 DL63
Tabor Gdns, Sutt. SM3 239 CZ107
Tabor Gro, SW19 201 CY94
Tabor Rd, W6 181 CV76
Tabors Ct, Shenf. CM15 *off Shenfield Rd* 131 FZ45
Tabrums Way, Upmin. RM14 151 FS59
Tachbrook Est, SW1 41 P1
Tachbrook Ms, SW1 29 L8
Tachbrook Rd, Felt. TW14 197 BT87
Southall UB2 178 BX77
Uxbridge UB8 156 BJ68
Tachbrook St, SW1 29 M9
Tack Ms, SE4 46 A10
Tadema Ho, NW8 16 B5
Tadema Rd, SW10 39 P4
Tadlows Cl, Upmin. RM14 150 FP64
Tadmor Cl, Sun. TW16 217 BT98
Tadmor St, W12 26 C3
Tadorne Rd, Tad. KT20 255 CW121
TADWORTH, KT20 255 CV121
⇌ **Tadworth** 255 CW122
Tadworth Av, N.Mal. KT3 221 CT99
Tadworth Cl, Tad. KT20 255 CX122
Tadworth Par, Horn. RM12 *off Maylands Av* 149 FH63
Sch **Tadworth Prim Sch**, Tad. KT20 *off Tadworth St* 255 CX122
Tadworth Rd, NW2 141 CU61
Tadworth St, Tad. KT20 255 CW123
Taeping St, E14 34 C8
Taffy's How, Mitch. CR4 222 DE97
Taft Way, E3 22 D2
Tagalie Pl, Shenley WD7 84 CL32
Tagg's Island, Hmptn. TW12 219 CD96
Tailworth St, E1 20 C7
Tait Ct, SW8 *off Darsley Dr* 41 P6
Tait Rd, Croy. CR0 224 DS101
● **Tait Rd Ind Est**, Croy. CR0 224 DS101
Tait St, E1 20 E9
Takeley Cl, Rom. RM5 127 FD54
Waltham Abbey EN9 89 ED33
Takhar Ms, SW11 40 D9
Talacre Rd, NW5 7 H4
Jct **Talbot, The**, N.Wld Bas. CM16 75 FD24
Talbot Av, N2 142 DD55
Slough SL3 175 AZ76
Watford WD19 116 BY45
Talbot Cl, N15 144 DT56
Mitcham CR4 223 DJ98
Reigate RH2 288 DB135
Talbot Ct, EC3 19 M10
Hemel Hempstead HP3 *off Forest Av* 62 BK22
Talbot Cres, NW4 141 CU57
Talbot Gdns, Ilf. IG3 148 EU61
Talbot Ho, E14 22 C8
N7 *off Harvist Est* 143 DN62
Talbot Pl, SE3 47 J8
Datchet SL3 174 AW81
Talbot Rd, E6 167 EN68
E7 146 EG63
N6 142 DG58
N15 144 DT56
N22 121 DJ54
SE22 184 DS84
W2 15 K8
W11 15 H8
W13 159 CG73
Ashford TW15 196 BK92
Carshalton SM5 240 DG106
Dagenham RM9 168 EZ65
Harrow HA3 117 CF54
Hatfield AL10 67 CU15
Isleworth TW7 179 CG84
Rickmansworth WD3 114 BL46
Southall UB2 178 BY77
Thornton Heath CR7 224 DR98
Twickenham TW2 199 CE88
Wembley HA0 139 CK64
Talbot Sq, W2 16 B9
Talbot St, Hert. SG13 54 DS09
Talbot Wk, NW10 *off Garnet Rd* 160 CS65
W11 14 E9
Talbot Yd, SE1 31 L3
Talbrook, Brwd. CM14 130 FT48
Talehangers Cl, Bexh. DA6 188 EX84
Taleworth Cl, Ashtd. KT21 253 CK120
Taleworth Pk, Ashtd. KT21 253 CK120
Taleworth Rd, Ashtd. KT21 253 CK119
Talfourd Pl, SE15 44 A7
Talfourd Rd, SE15 44 A7
Talfourd Way, Red. RH1 288 DF137
Talgarth Rd, W6 26 B10
W14 26 D10
Talgarth Wk, NW9 140 CS57
Talia Ho, E14 *off New Union Cl* 34 F6
Talisman Cl, Ilf. IG3 148 EV60
Talisman Sq, SE26 204 DU91
Talisman Way, Epsom KT17 255 CW116
Wembley HA9 140 CM62
Tallack Cl, Har. HA3 117 CE52
Tallack Rd, E10 145 DZ60
Tall Elms Cl, Brom. BR2 226 EF99
Tallents Cl, Sutt.H. DA4 210 FP94
Tallis Cl, E16 24 A9
Tallis Ct, Gidea Pk RM2 150 FJ55
Tallis Gro, SE7 186 EH79
Tallis St, EC4 18 F10
Tallis Vw, NW10 160 CR65
Tallis Way, Borwd. WD6 99 CK39
Warley CM14 130 FV50
Tall Oaks, Amer. HP6 77 AR37
Tallon Rd, Hutt. CM13 131 GE43
Tallow Cl, Dag. RM9 168 EX65
Tallow Rd, Brent. TW8 179 CJ79
Tall Trees, SW16 223 DM97
Colnbrook SL3 175 BE81
Tall Trees Cl, Horn. RM11 150 FK58
Jct **Tally Ho Cor**, N12 120 DC50
Tally Rd, Oxt. RH8 276 EL131
Talma Gdns, Twick. TW2 199 CE86
Talmage Cl, SE23 *off Tyson Rd* 204 DW87
Talman Gro, Stan. HA7 117 CK51
Talma Rd, SW2 183 DN84
Sch **Talmud Torah Machzikei Hadass Sch**, E5 *off Clapton Common* 144 DU59
Talus Cl, Purf. RM19 *off Brimfield Rd* 191 FR77
Talwin St, E3 22 D3
Tamar Cl, E3 11 P9
Upminster RM14 151 FS58
Tamar Dr, Aveley RM15 170 FQ72
Tamar Grn, Hem.H. HP2 62 BM15
Tamarind Cl, Guil. GU2 264 AU129
Tamarind Yd, E1 32 D2
Tamarisk Cl, St.Alb. AL3 *off New Grns Av* 65 CD16
South Ockendon RM15 171 FW70
Tamarisk Rd, S.Ock. RM15 171 FW69
Tamarisk Sq, W12 161 CT73
Tamarisk Way, Slou. SL1 173 AN75
Tamarix Cres, Lon.Col. AL2 83 CG26
Tamar Sq, Wdf.Grn. IG8 124 EH51
Tamar St, SE7 36 G8
Tamar Way, N17 *off Park Vw Rd* 144 DU55
Slough SL3 175 BB78
Tamblin Way, Hat. AL10 66 CS17
Tamerton Sq, Wok. GU22 248 AY119
Tamesis Gdns, Wor.Pk. KT4 220 CS102
Tamesis Strand, Grav. DA12 213 GL92
Tamian Way, Houns. TW4 178 BW84
Tamworth Av, Wdf.Grn. IG8 124 EE51
Tamworth La, Mitch. CR4 223 DH96
Tamworth Pk, Mitch. CR4 223 DH98
Tamworth Pl, Croy. CR0 224 DQ103
Tamworth Rd, Croy. CR0 223 DP103
Hertford SG13 54 DS08
Tamworth St, SW6 39 J2
Tancred Rd, N4 143 DP58
Tandem Cen, SW19 222 DD95
Tandem Way, SW19 222 DD95
TANDRIDGE, Oxt. RH8 275 EA133
Tandridge Cl, Cat. CR3 258 DU122
Tandridge Dr, Orp. BR6 227 ER102
Tandridge Gdns, S.Croy. CR2 242 DT113
Tandridge Hill La, Gdse. RH9 275 DZ128
Tandridge La, Tand. RH8 275 EA131
Tandridge Pl, Orp. BR6 227 ER102
Tandridge Rd, Warl. CR6 259 DX119
Tanfield Av, NW2 141 CT63
Tanfield Cl, Chsht EN7 88 DU27
Tanfield Rd, Croy. CR0 242 DQ105
Tangent Link, Harold Hill RM3 128 FK53
Tangent Rd, Rom. RM3 *off Ashton Rd* 128 FK53
Tangier La, Eton SL4 173 AR79
Tangier Rd, Guil. GU1 281 BA135
Richmond TW10 180 CP83
Tangier Way, Tad. KT20 255 CY117
Tangier Wd, Tad. KT20 255 CY118
Tangleberry Cl, Brom. BR1 226 EL98
Tangle Tree Cl, N3 120 DB54
Tanglewood Cl, Croy. CR0 224 DW104
Longcross KT16 214 AV104
Stanmore HA7 117 CE47
Uxbridge UB10 156 BN69
Woking GU22 249 BD116
Tanglewood Way, Felt. TW13 197 BV90
Tangley Gro, SW15 201 CT87
Tangley La, Guil. GU3 264 AT130
Tangley Pk Rd, Hmptn. TW12 198 BZ93
Tanglyn Av, Shep. TW17 217 BP99
Tangmere Cres, Horn. RM12 169 FH65
Tangmere Gdns, Nthlt. UB5 158 BW68
Tangmere Gro, Kings.T. KT2 199 CK92
Tangmere Way, NW9 118 CS54
Tanhouse Rd, Oxt. RH8 275 ED132
Tanhurst Wk, SE2 *off Alsike Rd* 188 EX76
Tankerton Rd, Surb. KT6 220 CM103
Tankerton St, WC1 18 B3
Tankerton Ter, Croy. CR0 *off Mitcham Rd* 223 DM101
Tankerville Rd, SW16 203 DK93
Tank Hill Rd, Purf. RM19 190 FN78
Tank La, Purf. RM19 190 FN77
Tankridge Rd, NW2 141 CV61
Tanner Pt, E13 13 N9
Tanners Cl, St.Alb. AL3 64 CC19
Walton-on-Thames KT12 217 BV100
Tanners Cl, Brock. RH3 286 CQ138
Tanners Cres, Hert. SG13 54 DQ11
Tanners Dean, Lthd. KT22 253 CJ122
Tanners End La, N18 122 DS49
Tannersfield, Shalf. GU4 280 AY142
Tanners Hill, SE8 45 P7
Abbots Langley WD5 81 BT31
Tanners La, Ilf. IG6 147 EQ55
Tanners Meadow, Brock. RH3 286 CP138
Tanners Ms, SE8 45 P7
Tanner St, SE1 31 P5
Barking IG11 167 EQ65
Tanners Way, Hunsdon SG12 56 EJ06
Tanners Wd Cl, Abb.L. WD5 *off Tanners Wd La* 81 BS32
Sch **Tanners Wd JMI Sch**, Abb.L. WD5 *off Hazelwood La* 81 BS32
Tanners Wd La, Abb.L. WD5 81 BS32
Tanners Yd, E2 20 E1
Tannery, The, Red. RH1 272 DE134
Tannery Cl, Beck. BR3 225 DX99
Tannery Cl, Dagenham RM10 149 FB62
Tannery La, Bramley GU5 280 AY144
Send GU23 249 BF122
Tannington Ter, N5 143 DN62
Tannsfeld Rd, SE26 205 DX92
Tannsfield Dr, Hem.H. HP2 62 BM18
Tannsmore Cl, Hem.H. HP2 62 BM18
Tansley Cl, N7 7 P2
Tanswell Est, SE1 30 E5
Tanswell St, SE1 30 E5
Tansy Cl, E6 25 M9
Guildford GU4 265 BC132
Romford RM3 128 FL51
Tansycroft, Welw.G.C. AL7 52 DB08
Tantallon Rd, SW12 202 DG88
Tant Av, E16 23 L8
Tantony Gro, Rom. RM6 148 EX55
Tanworth Cl, Nthwd. HA6 115 BQ51
Tanworth Gdns, Pnr. HA5 115 BV54
Tanyard Ho, Brent. TW8 *off London Rd* 179 CJ80
Tanyard La, Bex. DA5 208 FA88
Tanyard Way, Horl. RH6 291 DH146
Tanys Dell, Harl. CM20 58 EU12
Sch **Tany's Dell Comm Prim Sch**, Harl. CM20 *off Mowbray Rd* 58 EU12
Tanza Rd, NW3 142 DF63
Tapestry Cl, Sutt. SM2 240 DB108
TAPLOW, Maid. SL6 152 AE70
⇌ **Taplow** 152 AF72
Taplow, NW3 6 B7
SE17 31 M10
Taplow Common Rd, Burn. SL1 152 AG67
Taplow Rd, N13 122 DQ49
Taplow SL6 152 AG71
Taplow St, N1 19 K1
Tapners Rd, Bet. RH3 287 CT139
Leigh RH2 287 CT139
Tappesfield Rd, SE15 44 G10
Tapp St, E1 20 E4
Tapster St, Barn. EN5 101 CZ42
Tara Ms, N8 143 DK58
Taransay, Hem.H. HP3 63 BP22
Taransay Wk, N1 9 L4
Tarbay La, Oakley Grn SL4 172 AH82
Tarbert Ms, N15 144 DS57
Tarbert Rd, SE22 204 DS85
Tarbert Wk, E1 20 G10
Target Cl, Felt. TW14 197 BS86
Jct **Target Rbt**, Nthlt. UB5 *off Western Av* 158 BZ67
Tarham Cl, Horl. RH6 290 DE146
Tariff Cres, SE8 33 N8
Tariff Rd, N17 122 DU51
Tarleton Gdns, SE23 204 DV88
Tarling Cl, Sid. DA14 208 EV90
Tarling Rd, E16 23 M9
N2 120 DC54
Tarling St, E1 20 G9
Tarling St Est, E1 20 G9
Tarnbank, Enf. EN2 103 DL43
Tarn St, SE1 31 J7
Tarnwood Pk, SE9 207 EM88
Tarnworth Rd, Rom. RM3 128 FN50
Tarpan Way, Brox. EN10 89 DZ26
Tarquin Ho, SE26 204 DU91
Tarragon Cl, SE14 45 L4
Tarragon Dr, Guil. GU2 264 AU129
Tarragon Gro, SE26 205 DX93
Tarrant Pl, W1 16 E7
Tarrington Cl, SW16 203 DK90
Tartar Rd, Cob. KT11 236 BW113
Tarver Rd, SE17 43 H1
Tarves Way, SE10 46 D4
Taryn Gro, Brom. BR1 227 EM97
Tash Pl, N11 121 DH50
Sch **TASIS, The American Sch in England**, Thorpe TW20 *off Coldharbour La* 215 BC97
Tasker Cl, Harling. UB3 177 BQ80
Tasker Ho, Bark. IG11 *off Dovehouse Mead* 167 ER68
Tasker Rd, NW3 6 E3
Grays RM16 193 GH76
Tasman Ct, E14 *off Westferry Rd* 34 C9
Sunbury-on-Thames TW16 197 BS94
Tasmania Ho, Til. RM18 *off Hobart Rd* 193 GG81
Tasmania Ter, N18 122 DQ51
Tasman Rd, SW9 183 DL83
Tasman Wk, E16 24 E9
Tasso Rd, W6 38 E2
Tatam Rd, NW10 160 CQ66
Tatchbury Ho, SW15 *off Tunworth Cres* 201 CT86
Tate & Lyle Jetty, E16 36 G5
★ **Tate Britain**, SW1 30 A9
Tate Cl, Lthd. KT22 253 CJ123
Tate Gdns, Bushey WD23 117 CE45
★ **Tate Modern**, SE1 31 H2
Tate Rd, E16 37 J3
Chalfont St. Peter SL9 113 AZ50
Sutton SM1 240 DA106
Tatham Pl, NW8 6 B10
TATLING END, Ger.Cr. SL9 135 BB61
Tatnell Rd, SE23 205 DY86
TATSFIELD, West. TN16 260 EL120
Tatsfield App Rd, Tats. TN16 260 EH123
Tatsfield Av, Lwr Naze. EN9 71 ED23
Tatsfield La, Tats. TN16 261 EM121
TATTENHAM CORNER, Epsom KT18 255 CV118
⇌ **Tattenham Corner** 255 CV118
Tattenham Cor Rd, Epsom KT18 255 CT117
Tattenham Cres, Epsom KT18 255 CU118
Tattenham Gro, Epsom KT18 255 CV118
Tattenham Way, Tad. KT20 255 CX118
Tattersall Cl, SE9 206 EL85
Tattle Hill, Hert. SG14 53 DL05
Tatton Cl, Cars. SM5 222 DG102
Tatton Cres, N16 144 DT59
Tatton St, Harl. CM17 58 EW14
Tatum St, SE17 31 M9
Tauber Cl, Els. WD6 100 CM42
Tauheed Cl, N4 144 DQ61
Taunton Av, SW20 221 CV96
Caterham CR3 258 DT123
Hounslow TW3 178 CC82
Taunton Cl, Bexh. DA7 189 FD82
Ilford IG6 125 ET51
Sutton SM3 222 DA102
Taunton Dr, N2 120 DC54
Enfield EN2 103 DN41
Taunton La, Couls. CR5 257 DN119
Taunton Ms, NW1 16 E5
Taunton Pl, NW1 16 E4
Taunton Rd, SE12 206 EE85
Greenford UB6 158 CB67
Northfleet DA11 212 GA85
Romford RM3 128 FJ49
Taunton Vale, Grav. DA12 213 GK90
Taunton Way, Stan. HA7 140 CL55
Tavern Cl, Cars. SM5 222 DE101
Taverners, Hem.H. HP2 62 BL18
Taverners Cl, W11 26 E3
Taverner Sq, N5 9 J1
Taverners Way, E4 124 EE46
Hoddesdon EN11 71 EA17
Tavern La, SW9 42 F8
Tavern Quay, SE16 *off Sweden Gate* 33 L8
Tavistock Av, E17 145 DY55
NW7 119 CX52
Perivale UB6 159 CG68
St. Albans AL1 64 CC23
Tavistock Cl, N16 9 P3
Potters Bar EN6 86 DD31
Romford RM3 128 FK53
St. Albans AL1 65 CD24
Staines-upon-Thames TW18 196 BK94
Tavistock Ct, WC2 *off Tavistock St* 18 B10
Tavistock Cres, W11 15 H7
Mitcham CR4 223 DL98
Tavistock Gdns, Ilf. IG3 147 ES63
Tavistock Gate, Croy. CR0 224 DR102
Tavistock Gro, Croy. CR0 224 DR101
Tavistock Ms, E18 *off Tavistock Pl* 146 EG56
N19 *off Tavistock Terr* 143 DL62
Tavistock Pl, E18 146 EG56
N14 103 DH44
WC1 17 P4
Tavistock Rd, E7 146 EF63
E15 13 L5
E18 146 EG55
N4 144 DR58
NW10 161 CT68
W11 14 G8
Bromley BR2 226 EF98
Carshalton SM5 222 DD102
Croydon CR0 224 DR102
Edgware HA8 118 CN53
Uxbridge UB10 137 BQ64
Watford WD24 98 BX39
Welling DA16 188 EW81
West Drayton UB7 156 BK74
Tavistock Sq, WC1 17 P4
Tavistock St, WC2 18 B10
Tavistock Ter, N19 143 DK62
Tavistock Twr, SE16 33 L7
Tavistock Wk, Cars. SM5 *off Tavistock Rd* 222 DD102
Taviton St, WC1 17 N4
Tavy Cl, SE11 30 F10
Tawney Common, They.Mt CM16 92 FA32
Tawney La, Ong. CM5 93 FC32
Stapleford Tawney RM4 109 FD35
Tawney Rd, SE28 168 EV73
Tawneys Rd, Harl. CM18 73 ES16
Tawny Av, Upmin. RM14 150 FP64
Tawny Cl, W13 159 CH74
Feltham TW13 *off Chervil Cl* 197 BU90
Tawny Way, SE16 33 K8
Tayben Av, Twick. TW2 199 CE86
Taybridge Rd, SW11 182 DG83
Tayburn Cl, E14 22 E8
Tayfield Cl, Uxb. UB10 137 BQ62
Tayler Cotts, Ridge EN6 *off Crossoaks La* 85 CT34
Tayles Hill, Epsom KT17 *off Tayles Hill Dr* 239 CT110
Tayles Hill Dr, Epsom KT17 239 CT110
Taylifers, Harl. CM19 73 EN20
Taylor Av, Rich. TW9 180 CP82
Taylor Cl, N17 122 DU52
SE8 45 N2
Epsom KT19 238 CN111
Hampton Hill TW12 198 CC92
Harefield UB9 *off High St* 114 BJ53
Hounslow TW3 178 CC81
Orpington BR6 245 ET105
Romford RM5 126 FA52
St. Albans AL4 65 CG16
Taylor Pl, E3 *off Payne Rd* 22 C1
Taylor Rd, Ashtd. KT21 253 CK117
Mitcham CR4 202 DE94
Wallington SM6 241 DH106
Taylor Row, Dart. DA2 210 FJ90
Noak Hill RM3 *off Cummings Hall La* 128 FJ47
Taylors Av, Hodd. EN11 71 EA18
Taylors Bldgs, SE18 37 P8
Taylors Cl, Sid. DA14 207 ET91
Taylors Ct, Felt. TW13 197 BU89
Taylors Grn, W3 160 CS72
Taylors La, NW10 160 CS66
SE26 204 DV91
Barnet EN5 101 CZ39
Taylors Rd, Chesh. HP5 76 AR29
Taymount Ri, SE23 204 DW89
Taynton Dr, Merst. RH1 273 DK129
Tayport Cl, N1 8 B7
Tayside Dr, Edg. HA8 118 CP48
Tay Way, Rom. RM1 127 FF53
Taywood Rd, Nthlt. UB5 158 BZ69
Teak Cl, SE16 33 M3
Teal Av, Orp. BR5 228 EX98
Tealby Ct, N7 8 C4
Teal Cl, E16 24 E7
Enfield EN3 104 DW37
South Croydon CR2 243 DX111
Teal Ct, Wall. SM6 *off Carew Rd* 241 DJ107
Teal Dr, Nthwd. HA6 115 BQ52
Teale St, E2 10 D10
Tealing Dr, Epsom KT19 238 CR105
Teal Pl, Sutt. SM1 *off Sandpiper Rd* 239 CZ106
Teal St, SE10 35 M6
Teal Way, Hem.H. HP3 80 BM25
● **Teardrop Cen**, Swan. BR8 229 FH99
Teasel Cl, Croy. CR0 225 DX102
Teasel Cres, SE28 167 ES74
Teasel Way, E15 23 K2
Teazle Meade, Thnwd CM16 92 EV25
Teazle Wd Hill, Lthd. KT22 253 CE117
Teazlewood Pk, Lthd. KT22 253 CG117
Tebworth Rd, N17 122 DT52
● **Technology Pk, The**, NW9 140 CR55
Teck Cl, Islw. TW7 179 CG82
Tedder Cl, Chess. KT9 237 CJ107
Ruislip HA4 *off West End Rd* 137 BV64
Tedder Cl, Uxbridge UB10 156 BM66
Tedder Rd, Hem.H. HP2 62 BN19
South Croydon CR2 242 DW108
TEDDINGTON, TW11 199 CG93
⇌ **Teddington** 199 CG93
Teddington Cl, Epsom KT19 238 CR110
Teddington Lock, Tedd. TW11 199 CG91
H **Teddington Mem Hosp**, Tedd. TW11 199 CE93
Teddington Pk, Tedd. TW11 199 CF92
Teddington Pk Rd, Tedd. TW11 199 CF91
Sch **Teddington Sch**, Tedd. TW11 *off Broom Rd* 199 CJ93
Tedworth Gdns, SW3 40 E1
Tedworth Sq, SW3 40 E1
Tee, The, W3 160 CS72
Tees Av, Perivale UB6 159 CE68
Tees Cl, Upmin. RM14 151 FR59
Teesdale, Hem.H. HP2 62 BL17
Teesdale Av, Islw. TW7 179 CG81
Teesdale Cl, E2 20 D1
Teesdale Gdns, SE25 224 DS96
Isleworth TW7 179 CG81
Teesdale Rd, E11 146 EF58
Dartford DA2 210 FQ88
Slough SL2 153 AM71
Teesdale St, E2 20 E1
Teesdale Yd, E2 10 D10
Tees Dr, Rom. RM3 128 FK48
Tee Side, Hert. SG13 54 DV08
Teeswater Ct, Erith DA18 *off Middle Way* 188 EX76
Teevan Cl, Croy. CR0 224 DU101
Teevan Rd, Croy. CR0 224 DU101
Tegan Cl, Sutt. SM2 240 DA108
Teggs La, Wok. GU22 249 BF116
Teign Ms, SE9 206 EL89
Teignmouth Cl, SW4 183 DK84
Edgware HA8 118 CM54
Teignmouth Gdns, Perivale UB6 159 CF68
Teignmouth Par, Perivale UB6 *off Teignmouth Gdns* 159 CH68
Teignmouth Rd, NW2 4 C3
Welling DA16 188 EW82
Sch **Teikyo Sch UK Teikyo Women's Coll London**, Stoke P. SL2 *off Framewood Rd* 154 AX66
Telcote Way, Ruis. HA4 *off Woodlands Av* 138 BW59
★ **Telecom Twr**, W1 17 L6
Telegraph Hill, NW3 142 DB62
Telegraph La, Clay. KT10 237 CF107
Telegraph Ms, Ilf. IG3 148 EU60
Telegraph Path, Chis. BR7 207 EP92
Telegraph Pl, E14 34 C8
Telegraph Rd, SW15 201 CV87
Telegraph St, EC2 19 L8
Telegraph Track, Cars. SM5 240 DG110
Telemann Sq, SE3 186 EH83
Telephone Pl, SW6 39 H2
Telfer Cl, W3 *off Church Rd* 180 CQ75
Sch **Telferscot Prim Sch**, SW12 *off Telferscot Rd* 203 DK88
Telferscot Rd, SW12 203 DK88
Telford Av, SW2 203 DL88
Telford Cl, E17 145 DY59
SE19 *off St. Aubyn's Rd* 204 DT93
Watford WD25 98 BX35
Telford Ct, Guil. GU1 265 AZ134
St. Albans AL1 65 CE21
Telford Dr, Slou. SL1 173 AN75
Walton-on-Thames KT12 218 BW101
Telford Ho, SE1 31 J7
Telford Rd, N11 121 DJ51
NW9 *off West Hendon Bdy* 141 CU58
SE9 207 ER89
W10 14 E6
London Colney AL2 83 CJ27
Southall UB1 158 CB73
Twickenham TW2 198 CA87
Telfords Yd, E1 32 D1
Telford Ter, SW1 41 L2
Telford Way, W3 160 CS71
Hayes UB4 158 BY71
Telham Rd, E6 25 L1
Tell Gro, SE22 184 DT84
Tellisford, Esher KT10 236 CB105
Tellson Av, SE18 186 EL81
Telscombe Cl, Orp. BR6 227 ES103
Telston La, Otford TN14 263 FF117
Temair Ho, SE10 *off Tarves Way* 46 D4
Temeraire Pl, Brent. TW8 180 CM78
Temeraire St, SE16 33 H5
Temperance St, St.Alb. AL3 64 CC20
Temperley Rd, SW12 202 DG87
Tempest Av, Pot.B. EN6 86 DC32
Tempest Mead, N.Wld Bas. CM16 93 FB27
Tempest Rd, Egh. TW20 195 BC93
Tempest Way, Rain. RM13 169 FG65
Templar Ct, NW8 *off St. John's Wd Rd* 16 A3
Templar Dr, SE28 168 EX72
Gravesend DA11 213 GG92
Templar Ho, NW2 4 G4
Harrow HA2 *off Northolt Rd* 139 CD61
Rainham RM13 *off Chantry Way* 169 FD68
Templar Pl, Hmptn. TW12 198 CA94
Templars Av, NW11 141 CZ58
Templars Ct, Dart. DA1 210 FN85
Templars Cres, N3 120 DA54
Templars Dr, Har. HA3 117 CD51
Templars Ho, E16 *off University Way* 37 P1
Templar St, SE5 43 H7
⊖ **Temple** 18 D10
★ **Temple, The**, EC4 18 E10
Temple Av, EC4 18 F10
N20 120 DD45
Croydon CR0 225 DZ103
Dagenham RM8 148 FA60
Temple Bk, Harl. CM20 58 EV09
★ **Temple Bar**, EC4 19 H9
★ **Temple Bar Mem**, EC4 18 E9
Temple Bar Rd, Wok. GU21 248 AT119
Temple Cl, E11 146 EE59
N3 119 CZ54
SE28 187 EQ76
Cheshunt EN7 88 DU31
Epsom KT19 238 CR112
Watford WD17 97 BT40
Templecombe Ms, Wok. GU22 *off Dorchester Ct* 249 BA116
Templecombe Rd, E9 10 G8
Templecombe Way, Mord. SM4 221 CY99

Temple Ct, E1 off Rectory Sq 21 J6
SW8 off Thorncroft St 42 A5
Hertford SG14 54 DR06
Potters Bar EN6 85 CY31
Templecroft, Ashf. TW15 197 BR93
Templedene Av, Stai. TW18 196 BH94
Temple Dws, E2 off Temple Yd 20 E1
Templefield Cl, Add. KT15 234 BH107
● Temple Flds, Harl. CM20 58 EU11
Temple Flds, Hert. SG14 54 DR06
Temple Fortune Hill, NW11 142 DA57
Temple Fortune La, NW11 142 DA58
Temple Fortune Mans, NW11
off Finchley Rd 141 CZ57
Temple Fortune Par, NW11
off Finchley Rd 141 CZ57
Temple Gdns, N21
off Barrowell Grn 121 DP47
NW11 141 CZ58
Dagenham RM8 148 EX62
Rickmansworth WD3 115 BP49
Staines-upon-Thames TW18 215 BF95
Temple Gro, NW11 142 DA58
Enfield EN2 103 DP41
Temple Hill, Dart. DA1 210 FM86
Sch Temple Hill Comm Prim & Nurs Sch, Dart. DA1
off St. Edmunds Rd 210 FN85
Temple Hill Sq, Dart. DA1 210 FM85
Templehof Av, NW2 141 CW59
Temple La, EC4 18 F9
Templeman Cl, Pur. CR8
off Croftleigh Av 257 DP116
Templeman Rd, W7 159 CF71
Temple Mead, Hem.H. HP2 62 BK18
Roydon CM19 72 EH15
Templemead Cl, W3 160 CS72
Temple Mead Cl, Stan. HA7 117 CH51
Templemead Ho, E9
off Kingsmead Way 11 M1
Templemere, Wey. KT13 217 BR104
Temple Mills La, E20 12 E1
★ Temple of Mithras, EC4
off Queen Victoria St 19 L9
Templepan La, Chan.Cr. WD3 96 BL37
Temple Pk, Uxb. UB8 156 BN69
Temple Pl, WC2 18 D10
Templer Av, Grays RM16 193 GG77
Temple Rd, E6 166 EL67
N8 143 DM56
NW2 141 CW63
W4 180 CQ76
W5 179 CK76
Biggin Hill TN16 260 EK117
Croydon CR0 242 DR105
Epsom KT19 238 CR112
Hounslow TW3 178 CB84
Richmond TW9 180 CM83
Windsor SL4 173 AQ82
Temple Sheen, SW14 200 CQ85
Temple Sheen Rd, SW14 180 CP84
Temple St, E2 20 E1
Templeton Av, E4 123 EA49
Templeton Cl, N16 9 P2
SE19 224 DR95
Templeton Ct, NW7
off Kingsbridge Dr 119 CX52
Borwd. WD6 off Eaton Way 100 CM39
Templeton Pl, SW5 27 K9
Templeton Rd, N15 144 DR58
Temple Vw, St.Alb. AL3 64 CC18
Temple Way, Farn.Com. SL2 133 AQ64
Sutton SM1 222 DD104
Temple W Ms, SE11 30 G7
Templewood, W13 159 CH71
Welwyn Garden City AL8 51 CX06
Templewood Av, NW3 142 DB62
Temple Wd Dr, Red. RH1 272 DF131
Templewood Gdns, NW3 142 DB62
Templewood Gate, Farn.Com.
SL2 133 AQ64
Templewood La, Slou. SL2 134 AS63
Templewood Pk, Slou. SL2 134 AT63
Templewood Pt, NW2 141 CZ61
Sch Templewood Prim Sch,
Welw.G.C. AL8
off Pentley Pk 51 CX07
Temple Yd, E2 20 E1
Tempsford, Welw.G.C. AL7 52 DD09
Tempsford Av, Borwd. WD6 100 CR42
Tempsford Cl, Enf. EN2
off Gladbeck Way 104 DQ41
Tempus, Har. HA2 138 CC61
Tempus Ct, E18 124 EG53
Temsford Cl, Har. HA2 116 CC54
Ten Acre, Wok. GU21
off Chirton Wk 248 AU118
Ten Acre La, Egh. TW20 215 BC96
Ten Acres, Fetch. KT22 253 CD124
Ten Acres Cl, Fetch. KT22 253 CD124
Tenbury Cl, E7
off Romford Rd 146 EK64
Tenbury Ct, SW2 203 DK88
Tenby Av, Har. HA3 117 CH54
Tenby Cl, N15 144 DT56
Romford RM6 148 EY58
Tenby Gdns, Nthlt. UB5 158 CA65
Tenby Rd, E17 145 DY57
Edgware HA8 118 CM53
Enfield EN3 104 DW41
Romford RM6 148 EY58
Welling DA16 188 EX81
Tenchleys La, Oxt. RH8 276 EK131
Tench St, E1 32 E3
Tenda Rd, SE16 32 E9
Tendring Ms, Harl. CM18 73 ES16
Tendring Rd, Harl. CM18 73 EQ17
Tendring Way, Rom. RM6 148 EW57
Tenham Av, SW2 203 DK88
Tenison Ct, W1 17 L10
Tenison Way, SE1 30 E3
Tennand Cl, Chsht EN7 88 DT26
Tenniel Cl, W2 15 N9
Guildford GU2 264 AV132
Tennis Ct La, E.Mol. KT8
off Hampton Ct Way 219 CE97
Tennison Av, Borwd. WD6 100 CP43
Tennison Cl, Couls. CR5 257 DP120
Tennison Rd, SE25 224 DT98
Tennis St, SE1 31 L4
Tenniswood Rd, Enf. EN1 104 DT39
Tennyson Av, E11 146 EG59
E12 166 EL66
NW9 140 CQ55
Grays RM17 192 GB76
New Malden KT3 221 CV99
Twickenham TW1 199 CF88
Waltham Abbey EN9 90 EE34
Tennyson Cl, Enf. EN3 105 DX43
Tennyson Cl, Feltham TW14 197 BT86
Welling DA16 187 ES81
Tennyson Rd, E10 145 EB61
E15 13 J6
E17 145 DZ58
NW6 4 G8
NW7 119 CU50
SE20 205 DX94
SW19 202 DC93
W7 159 CF73
Addlestone KT15 234 BL105
Ashford TW15 196 BL92
Dartford DA1 210 FN85
Hounslow TW3 178 CC82
Hutton CM13 131 GC45
Romford RM3 128 FJ52
St. Albans AL2 82 CA26
Tennyson St, SW8 41 J9
Tennyson Wk, Nthflt DA11 212 GD90
Tilbury RM18 193 GH82
Tennyson Way, Horn. RM12 149 FF61
Slough SL2 153 AL70
Tensing Av, Nthflt DA11 212 GE90
Tensing Rd, Sthl. UB2 178 CA76
Tentelow La, Sthl. UB2 178 CA78
Tenterden Cl, NW4 141 CX55
SE9 207 EM91
Tenterden Dr, NW4 141 CX55
Tenterden Gdns, NW4 141 CX55
Croydon CR0 224 DU101
Tenterden Gro, NW4 141 CW56
Tenterden Rd, N17 122 DT52
Croydon CR0 224 DU101
Dagenham RM8 148 EZ61
Tenterden St, W1 17 K9
Tenter Grd, E1 20 A7
Tenter Pas, E1 20 B9
Tent Peg La, Orp. BR5 227 EQ99
Tent St, E1 20 E4
Tenzing Rd, Hem.H. HP2 62 BN20
Tequila Wf, E14
off Commercial Rd 21 M9
Terborch Way, SE22
off East Dulwich Gro 204 DS85
Tercel Path, Chig. IG7 126 EV49
Teredo St, SE16 33 K7
Terence Cl, Grav. DA12 213 GM88
Terence Ct, Belv. DA17
off Nuxley Rd 188 EZ79
Teresa Gdns, Wal.Cr. EN8 88 DW34
Teresa Ms, E17 145 EA56
Teresa Wk, N10
off Connaught Gdns 143 DH57
Terling Cl, E11 146 EF62
Terling Rd, Dag. RM8 148 FA61
Terlings, The, Brwd. CM14 130 FU48
Terling Wk, N1 9 J8
Jct Terminal Four Rbt,
Lon.Hthrw Air. TW6 197 BQ86
Terminus Pl, SW1 29 K7
Terminus St, Harl. CM20 57 ER14
Tern Gdns, Upmin. RM14 151 FS60
Tern Way, Brwd. CM14 130 FS49
Terrace, The, E4
off Chingdale Rd 124 EE48
N3 off Hendon La 119 CZ54
NW6 5 J8
SW13 180 CS82
Addlestone KT15 234 BL106
Bray SL6 172 AC76
Dorking RH5 285 CJ137
Gravesend DA12 213 GH86
Sevenoaks TN13 278 FD122
Woodford Green IG8
off Broadmead Rd 124 EG51
Terrace Apts, N5
off Drayton Pk 8 F2
Terrace Gdns, SW13 181 CT82
Watford WD17 97 BV40
Terrace La, Rich. TW10 200 CL86
Terrace Rd, E9 11 H6
E13 13 P9
Walton-on-Thames KT12 217 BU101
Terraces, The, Dart. DA2 210 FQ87
Terrace St, Grav. DA12 213 GH86
Terrace Wk, Dag. RM9 148 EY64
Terrapin Rd, SW17 203 DH90
Terretts Pl, N1 8 G7
Terrick Rd, N22 121 DL53
Terrick St, W12 161 CV72
Terrilands, Pnr. HA5 138 BZ55
Terront Rd, N15 144 DQ57
Tersha St, Rich. TW9 180 CM84
Tessa Sanderson Pl, SW8 41 K10
Tessa Sanderson Way, Grnf.
UB6 off Lilian Board Way 139 CD64
Testard Rd, Guil. GU2 280 AW136
Testers Cl, Oxt. RH8 276 EH132
Testerton Wk, W11 14 D10
Testwood Rd, Wind. SL4 173 AK81
Tetbury Pl, N1 8 G9
Tetcott Rd, SW10 39 N4
Tetherdown, N10 142 DG55
Coll Tetherdown Adult Ed Cen,
N10 off Tetherdown 142 DG55
Sch Tetherdown Prim Sch, N10
off Grand Av 142 DG56
Tethys Rd, Hem.H. HP2 62 BM17
Tetty Way, Brom. BR2 226 EG96
Teversham La, SW8 42 B6
Teviot Av, Aveley RM15 170 FQ72
Teviot Cl, Guil. GU2 264 AU131
Welling DA16 188 EV81
Teviot St, E14 22 E6
TEWIN, Welw. AL6 52 DE05
Tewin Cl, St.Alb. AL4 65 CJ16
Tewin Ct, Welw.G.C. AL7 51 CZ08
Sch Tewin Cowper C of E Prim Sch,
Tewin AL6
off Cannons Meadow 52 DE05
Tewin Mill Ho, Tewin AL6 52 DE07
Tewin Rd, Hem.H. HP2 63 BQ20
Welwyn Garden City AL7 51 CZ09
Tewin Water, Welw. AL6 52 DB05
Tewkesbury Av, SE23 204 DV88
Pinner HA5 138 BY57
Tewkesbury Cl, N15
off Pulford Rd 144 DR58
Barnet EN4
off Approach Rd 102 DD42
Byfleet KT14 234 BK111
Loughton IG10 106 EL44
Tewkesbury Gdns, NW9 140 CP55
Tewkesbury Rd, N15 144 DR58
W13 159 CG73
Carshalton SM5 222 DD102
Tewkesbury Ter, N11 121 DJ51
Tewson Rd, SE18 187 ES78
Teynham Av, Enf. EN1 104 DR44
Teynham Grn, Brom. BR2 226 EG99
Teynham Rd, Dart. DA2 210 FQ87
Teynton Ter, N17 122 DQ53
Thackeray Av, N17 122 DU54
Tilbury RM18 193 GH81
Thackeray Cl, SW19 201 CX94
Isleworth TW7 179 CG82
Uxbridge UB8 157 BP72
Thackeray Dr, Rom. RM6 148 EU59
Thackeray Rd, E6 166 EK68
SW8 41 J9
Thackeray St, W8 27 M5
Thackrah Cl, N2 off Tarling Rd 120 DC54
Thakeham Cl, SE26 204 DV92
Thalia Cl, SE10 47 H2
Thalmassing Cl, Hutt. CM13 131 GB47
Thame Rd, SE16 33 K4
Thames Av, SW10 39 P6
Chertsey KT16 216 BG97
Dagenham RM9 169 FB70
Hemel Hempstead HP2 62 BM15
Perivale UB6 159 CF68
Windsor SL4 173 AR80
Wor.Pk. 221 CW102
Thames Bk, SW14 180 CQ82
Thamesbank Pl, SE28 168 EW72
★ Thames Barrier Information &
Learning Cen, SE18 36 E6
Coll Thames Christian Coll,
SW11 40 B10
Thames Circle, E14 34 B8
Thames Cl, Cher. KT16 216 BH101
Hampton TW12 218 CB96
Rainham RM13 169 FH72
Thames Ct, W.Mol. KT8 218 CB96
Thames Cres, W4 180 CS80
Thamesdale, Lon.Col. AL2 84 CM27
THAMES DITTON, KT7 219 CF100
⇌ Thames Ditton 219 CF101
Sch Thames Ditton Inf Sch, T.Ditt.
KT7 off Speer Rd 219 CF100
Thames Ditton Island, T.Ditt.
KT7 219 CG99
Sch Thames Ditton Jun Sch, T.Ditt.
KT7 off Mercer Cl 219 CF101
Thames Dr, Grays RM16 193 GG78
Ruislip HA4 137 BQ58
Thames Edge Ct, Stai. TW18
off Clarence St 195 BE91
● Thames Europort, Dart.
DA2 191 FS84
Thames Eyot, Twick. TW1 199 CG88
Thamesfield Ct, Shep. TW17 217 BQ101
Thames Gate, Dart. DA1 210 FN85
Thamesgate Cl, Rich. TW10 199 CH91
Thamesgate Shop Cen,
Grav. DA11 off New Rd 213 GH86
Thames Gateway, Dag. RM9 168 EZ68
Rainham RM13 169 FG72
South Ockendon RM15 190 FP75
Coll Thames Gateway Coll,
CEME Campus, Rain.
RM13 off Marsh Way 169 FD70
● Thames Gateway Pk, Dag.
RM9 168 EZ69
Thameshill Av, Rom. RM5 127 FC54
Thameside, Cher. KT16 216 BJ101
Staines-upon-Thames TW18 216 BH97
Teddington TW11 199 CK94
● Thameside Cen, Brent.
TW8 180 CM79
● Thameside Ind Est, E16 36 F4
Sch Thameside Inf Sch, Grays
RM17 off Manor Rd 192 GC79
Sch Thameside Jun Sch, Grays
RM17 off Manor Rd 192 GC79
Thameside Wk, SE28 167 ET72
Thames Link, SE16 33 J3
THAMESMEAD, SE28 167 ET73
Thames Mead, Walt. KT12 217 BU101
Windsor SL4 173 AL81
Coll Thamesmead Cen, Erith DA18
off Yarnton Way 188 EY75
THAMESMEAD NORTH, SE28 168 EX72
Thames Meadow, Shep.
TW17 217 BR102
West Molesey KT8 218 CA96
Sch Thamesmead Sch, Shep.
TW17 off Manygate La 217 BQ100
Thamesmead Spine Rd, Belv.
DA17 189 FB75
THAMESMEAD WEST, SE18 187 EP76
Thamesmere Dr, SE28 168 EU73
Thames Pl, SW15 181 CX83
Thames Pt, SW6 39 P7
Thamespoint, Tedd. TW11 199 CK94
Thames Quay, SW10 39 P7
Thames Rd, E16 36 E3
W4 180 CN79
Barking IG11 167 ET69
Dartford DA1 189 FG82
Grays RM17 192 GB80
Slough SL3 175 BA77
Thames Side, Kings.T. KT1 219 CK95
Windsor SL4 173 AR80
Thames St, SE10 46 D2
Greenhithe DA9 191 FT84
Hampton TW12 218 CB95
Kingston upon Thames KT1 219 CK96
Staines-upon-Thames TW18 195 BE91
Sunbury-on-Thames TW16 217 BV98
Walton-on-Thames KT12 217 BT101
Weybridge KT13 217 BP103
Windsor SL4 173 AR81
Thames Tunnel Mills, SE16
off Rotherhithe St 32 G4
Thamesvale Cl, Houns. TW3 178 CA83
H Thames Valley Nuffield Hosp,
Wexham SL2 154 AW67
H Thames Valley Nuffield Hosp,
The, Wexham Pk Hall,
Wexham SL3 154 AV68
Thames Vw, Grays RM16 193 GG78
Ilford IG1 off Axon Pl 147 EQ61
Sch Thames Vw Inf Sch, Bark.
IG11 off Bastable Av 168 EU68
Sch Thames Vw Jun Sch, Bark.
IG11 off Bastable Av 167 ET68
Sch Thamesview Sch, Grav. DA12
off Thong La 213 GM90
Thames Village, W4 180 CQ81
Thames Way, Grav. DA11 212 GB86
Thames Wf, E16 35 L2
Thamley, Purf. RM19 190 FN77
Thanescroft Gdns, Croy. CR0 224 DS104
Thanet Dr, Kes. BR2
off Phoenix Dr 226 EK104
Thanet Pl, Croy. CR0 242 DQ105
Thanet Rd, Bex. DA5 208 FA87
Thanet Rd, Erith DA8 189 FE80
Thanet St, WC1 18 A3
Thane Vil, N7 143 DM62
Thane Wks, N7 143 DM62
Thanington Ct, SE9 207 ES86
Thanstead Copse, Loud. HP10 110 AC53
Thanstead Ct, Loud. HP10 110 AC53
Thant Cl, E10 145 EB62
Tharp Rd, Wall. SM6 241 DK106
Thatcham Gdns, N20 120 DC45
Thatcher Cl, West Dr. UB7
off Classon Cl 176 BL75
Thatcher Ct, Dart. DA1
off Heath St 210 FK87
Thatchers Cl, Horl. RH6
off Wheatfield Way 291 DH146
Loughton IG10 107 EQ40
Thatchers Cft, Hem.H. HP2 62 BL16
Thatchers Way, Islw. TW7 199 CD85
Thatches Gro, Rom. RM6 148 EY56
Thavies Inn, EC1 18 F8
Thaxted Ct, N1 19 L1
SE16 off Abbeyfield Rd 32 G8
Thaxted Grn, Hutt. CM13 131 GC43
Thaxted Ho, Dag. RM10 169 FB66
Thaxted Pl, SW20 201 CX94
Thaxted Rd, SE9 207 EQ89
Buckhurst Hill IG9 124 EL45
Thaxted Wk, Rain. RM13
off Ongar Way 169 FF67
Thaxted Way, Wal.Abb. EN9 89 ED33
Thaxton Rd, W14 39 H2
Thayers Fm Rd, Beck. BR3 225 DY95
Thayer St, W1 17 H7
Thaynesfield, Pot.B. EN6 86 DD31
★ Theatre Royal, WC2 18 B9
Theatre Sq, E15 13 H5
Theatre St, SW11 40 F10
Theberton St, N1 8 F8
Theed St, SE1 30 E3
Thele Av, Stans.Abb. SG12 55 ED11
Theleway Cl, Hodd. EN11 55 EB14
Thellusson Way, Rick. WD3 113 BF45
Thelma Cl, Grav. DA12 213 GM92
Thelma Gdns, SE3 186 EK81
Feltham TW13 198 BY90
Thelma Gro, Tedd. TW11 199 CG93
Theobald Cres, Har. HA3 116 CB53
Theobald Rd, E17 145 DZ59
Croydon CR0 223 DP103
Theobalds Av, N12 120 DC49
Grays RM17 192 GC78
Theobalds Cl, Cuffley EN6 87 DM30
Theobalds Ct, N4
off Queens Dr 144 DQ62
⇌ Theobalds Grove 89 DX32
Theobalds La, Chsht EN7, EN8 88 DV32
Theobalds Pk Rd, Enf. EN2 103 DP35
Theobald's Rd, WC1 18 C6
Theobalds Rd, Cuffley EN6 87 DL30
Theobald St, SE1 31 L7
Borehamwood WD6 100 CM40
Radlett WD7 99 CH36
Theodora Way, Pnr. HA5 137 BT55
Theodore Rd, SE13 205 EC86
Thepps Cl, S.Nutfld RH1 289 DM137
Tra Therapia Lane 223 DL101
Therapia La, Croy. CR0 223 DL100
Therapia Rd, SE22 204 DW86
Theresa Rd, W6 181 CU77
Theresas Wk, S.Croy. CR2
off St. Mary's Rd 242 DR110
Therfield Ct, N4
off Brownswood Rd 144 DQ61
Therfield Rd, St.Alb. AL3 65 CD16
Sch Therfield Sch, Lthd. KT22
off Dilston Rd 253 CG119
Thermopylae Gate, E14 34 D9
Theseus Wk, N1 19 H1
Thesiger Rd, SE20 205 DX94
Thessaly Ho, SW8 41 L5
Thessaly Rd, SW8 41 L5
Thetford Cl, N13 121 DP52
Thetford Gdns, Dag. RM9 168 EX66
Thetford Rd, Ashf. TW15 196 BL91
Dagenham RM9 168 EX67
New Malden KT3 220 CR100
Thetis Ter, Rich. TW9
off Kew Grn 180 CN79
Theven St, E1 off Globe Rd 21 H4
THEYDON BOIS, Epp. CM16 107 ET36
⊖ Theydon Bois 107 ET36
Sch Theydon Bois Prim Sch, They.B.
CM16 off Orchard Dr 107 ES36
Theydon Bower, Epp. CM16 92 EU31
Theydon Ct, Wal.Abb. EN9 90 EG33
Theydon Gdns, Rain. RM13 169 FE66
THEYDON GARNON, Epp.
CM16 108 EW35
Theydon Gate, They.B. CM16
off Coppice Row 107 ES36
Theydon Gro, Epp. CM16 92 EU30
Woodford Green IG8 124 EJ51
THEYDON MOUNT, Epp.
CM16 92 FA34
Theydon Pk Rd, They.B. CM16 107 ES39
Theydon Pl, Epp. CM16 91 ET31
Theydon Rd, E5 144 DW61
Epping CM16 91 ER34
Theydon St, E17 145 DZ59
Thicket, The, West Dr. UB7 156 BL72
Thicket Cres, Sutt. SM1 240 DC105
Thicket Gro, SE20
off Anerley Rd 204 DU94
Dagenham RM9 168 EW65
Thicket Rd, SE20 204 DU94
Sutton SM1 240 DC105
Thicketts, Sev. TN13 279 FJ123
Thickthorne La, Stai. TW18 196 BJ94
Thieves La, Hert. SG14 53 DM10
Ware SG12 54 DW08
Third Av, E12 146 EL63
E13 23 P2
E17 145 EA57
W3 161 CT74
W10 14 F4
Dagenham RM10 169 FB67
Enfield EN1 104 DT43
Grays RM20 191 FU79
Harlow CM18, CM19 73 EM16
Hayes UB3 157 BT74
Romford RM6 148 EW57
Waltham Abbey EN9 off Breach
Barn Mobile Home Pk 90 EH30
Watford WD25 98 BX35
Wembley HA9 139 CK61
Third Cl, W.Mol. KT8 218 CB98
Third Cres, Slou. SL1 153 AQ71
Third Cross Rd, Twick. TW2 199 CD89
Third Way, Wem. HA9 140 CP63
Thirkleby Cl, Slou. SL1 153 AQ74
Thirleby Rd, NW7 119 CY50
SW1 29 M7
Edgware HA8 118 CR53
Thirlmere Av, Perivale UB6 159 CJ69
Slough SL1 152 AJ71
Thirlmere Cl, Egh. TW20 195 BB94
Thirlmere Dr, St.Alb. AL1 65 CH22
Thirlmere Gdns, Nthwd. HA6 115 BQ51
Wembley HA9 139 CJ60
Thirlmere Ho, Islw. TW7
off Summerwood Rd 199 CF85
Thirlmere Ri, Brom. BR1 206 EF93
Thirlmere Rd, N10 121 DH53
SW16 203 DK91
Bexleyheath DA7 189 FC82
Thirlstane, St.Alb. AL1 65 CE19
Thirsk Cl, Nthlt. UB5 158 CA65
Thirsk Rd, SE25 224 DR98
SW11 182 DG83
Borehamwood WD6 100 CN37
Mitcham CR4 202 DG94
Thirston Path, Borwd. WD6 100 CN40
Thirza Rd, Dart. DA1 210 FM86
Thistlebrook, SE2 188 EW76
● Thistlebrook Ind Est, SE2 188 EW75
Thistle Cl, Hem.H. HP1 61 BE21
Thistlecroft, Hem.H. HP1 62 BH21
Thistlecroft Gdns, Stan. HA7 117 CK53
Thistlecroft Rd, Hersham
KT12 236 BW105
Thistledene, T.Ditt. KT7 219 CF100
West Byfleet KT14 233 BF113
Thistledene Av, Har. HA2 138 BY62
Romford RM5 127 FB50
Thistledown, Grav. DA12 213 GK93
Thistle Dr, Hat. AL10 67 CT15
Thistlefield Cl, Bex. DA5 208 EX88
Thistle Gro, SW10 27 P10
Welwyn Garden City AL7 52 DC12
Thistlemead, Chis. BR7 227 EP96
Thistle Mead, Loug. IG10 107 EN41
Thistle Rd, Grav. DA12 213 GL87
Thistles, The, Hem.H. HP1 62 BH19
Leatherhead KT22 253 CJ122
Thistlewaite Rd, E5 144 DV62
Thistlewood Cl, N7 143 DM61
Thistlewood Cres, New Adgtn
CR0 243 ED112
Thistleworth Cl, Islw. TW7 179 CD80
Thistley Cl, N12 120 DE51
Coulsdon CR5 257 DK122
Thistley Ct, SE8
off Glaisher St 46 C2
Thomas a'Beckett Cl, Wem.
HA0 139 CF63
Sch Thomas Arnold Prim Sch, Dag.
RM9 off Rowdowns Rd 168 EZ66
Thomas Av, Cat. CR3 258 DQ121
Thomas Baines Rd, SW11 182 DD83
Sch Thomas Buxton Inf & Jun Schs,
E1 20 D5
Thomas Cl, Brwd. CM15 130 FY48
Sch Thomas Coram Mid Sch, The,
Berk. HP4 off Swing Gate La 60 AX21
Thomas Cribb Ms, E6 25 K8
Thomas Darby Ct, W11 14 E9
Thomas Dean Rd, SE26 205 DZ91
Thomas Dinwiddy Rd, SE12 206 EH89
Thomas Doyle St, SE1 30 G6
Thomas Dr, Rom. RM2 150 FJ56
Grav. DA12 213 GK89
Sch Thomas Fairchild Comm Sch,
N1 9 K10
Sch Thomas Gamuel Prim Sch,
E17 off Colchester Rd 145 EA58
Sch Thomas Harding Jun Sch,
Chesh. HP5 off Fullers Hill 76 AP32
Thomas Hardy Ho, N22 121 DM52
Thomas Hollywood Ho, E2 20 G1
Thomas Jacomb Pl, E17 145 DZ56
Sch Thomas Jones Prim Sch,
W11 14 E9
Sch Thomas Knyvett Coll, Ashf.
TW15 off Stanwell Rd 196 BL90
Thomas La, SE6 205 EA87
Thomas More Bldg, The, Ruis.
HA4 137 BS60
Sch Thomas More Cath Sch,
Pur. CR8
off Russell Hill Rd 241 DN110
Thomas More Ho, EC2
off The Barbican 19 J7
Thomas More Sq, E1
off Thomas More St 32 C1
Thomas More St, E1 32 C1
Thomas More Way, N2 142 DC55
Thomas N Ter, E16
off Barking Rd 23 L7
Thomas Pl, W8 27 L7
Thomas Rd, E14 21 P8
Crayford DA1 189 FG82
Wooburn Green HP10 132 AD59
● Thomas Rd Ind Est, E14 22 A7
Thomas Rochford Way, Chsht
EN8 89 DZ27
Thomas Sims Ct, Horn. RM12 149 FH64
Sch Thomas's School, Battersea,
SW11 40 B7
Sch Thomas's School, Clapham,
SW11 off Broomwood Rd 202 DF86
Sch Thomas's School, Fulham,
SW6 39 L10
Sch Thomas's School, Kensington,
Lwr Sch, W8 27 N6
Prep Sch, W8 27 M6
Thomas St, SE18 37 M8
Sch Thomas Tallis Sch, SE3
off Kidbrooke Pk Rd 186 EH83
Thomas Wall Cl, Sutt. SM1
off Clarence Rd 240 DB106
Sch Thomas Willingale Sch,
Loug. IG10
off The Broadway 107 EQ41
Thompkins La, Farn.Royal
SL2 153 AM66
Thompson Av, Rich. TW9 180 CN83
Thompson Cl, Ilf. IG1
off High Rd 147 EQ61
Slough SL3 175 BA77

Thompson Cl, Sutton SM3
off Barrington Rd 222 DA102
Thompson Ho, W3
off Larden Rd 180 CS75
Thompson Rd, SE22 204 DT86
Dagenham RM9 148 EZ62
Hounslow TW3 178 CB84
Thompsons Av, SE5 43 J4
Thompsons Cl, Chsht EN7 88 DT29
Thompson's La, High Beach IG10 106 EF39
Thompson Way, Rick. WD3 114 BG45
Thomson Cres, Croy. CR0 223 DN102
Thomson Rd, Har. HA3 139 CE55
Thong La, Grav. DA12 213 GM90
Thorburn Sq, SE1 32 C9
Thorburn Way, SW19 222 DC95
Thoresby St, N1 19 K2
Thorkhill Gdns, T.Ditt. KT7 219 CG102
Thorkhill Rd, T.Ditt. KT7 219 CH101
Thorley Cl, W.Byf. KT14 234 BG114
Thorley Gdns, Wok. GU22 234 BG114
Thornaby Gdns, N18 122 DU51
Thornaby Pl, Woob.Grn HP10 132 AE55
Thornash Cl, Wok. GU21 248 AW115
Thornash Rd, Wok. GU21 248 AW115
Thornash Way, Wok. GU21 248 AW115
Thorn Av, Bushey Hth WD23 116 CC46
Thorn Bk, Guil. GU2 280 AU136
Thornbank Cl, Stai. TW19 196 BG85
Thornberry Way, Guil. GU1 265 AZ130
Thornbridge Rd, Iver SL0 155 BC67
Thornbrook, Thnwd CM16 92 EX25
Thornbury Av, Islw. TW7 179 CD80
Thornbury Cl, N16 9 P2
NW7 off Kingsbridge Dr 119 CX52
Hoddesdon EN11 55 EB13
Thornbury Gdns, Borwd. WD6 100 CQ42
Thornbury Rd, SW2 203 DL86
Isleworth TW7 179 CD81
Thornbury Sq, N6 143 DJ60
Thornby Rd, E5 144 DW62
Thorncliffe Rd, SW2 203 DL86
Southall UB2 178 BZ78
Thorn Cl, Brom. BR2 227 EN100
Northolt UB5 158 BZ69
Thorncombe Rd, SE22 204 DS85
Thorncroft, Eng.Grn TW20 194 AW94
Hemel Hempstead HP3 63 BP22
Hornchurch RM11 149 FH58
Thorncroft Cl, Couls. CR5
off Waddington Av 257 DN119
Thorncroft Dr, Lthd. KT22 253 CH123
Thorncroft Rd, Sutt. SM1 240 DB105
Thorncroft St, SW8 42 A5
Thorndales, Warley CM14 130 FX49
Thorndean St, SW18 202 DC89
Thorndene Av, N11 120 DG46
Thorndike, Slou. SL2 153 AN71
Thorndike Av, Nthlt. UB5 158 BX67
Thorndike Cl, SW10 39 N4
Thorndike Ho, SW1
off Vauxhall Br Rd 29 N10
Thorndike Rd, N1 9 K5
Thorndike St, SW1 29 N9
Thorndon Cl, Orp. BR5 227 ET96
Thorndon Ct, Gt Warley CM13 129 FW51
Thorndon Gdns, Epsom KT19 238 CS105
Thorndon Gate, Ingrave CM13 131 GC50
Thorndon Rd, Orp. BR5 227 ET96
Thorn Dr, Geo.Grn SL3 154 AY72
Thorndyke Ct, Pnr. HA5
off Westfield Pk 116 BZ52
Thorne Cl, E11 146 EE63
E16 23 N8
Ashford TW15 197 BQ94
Claygate KT10 237 CG108
Erith DA8 189 FC79
Hemel Hempstead HP1 62 BH22
Thorneloe Gdns, Croy. CR0 241 DN106
Thorne Pas, SW13 180 CS82
Thorne Rd, SW8 42 A5
Thornes Cl, Beck. BR3 225 EC97
Thorne St, E16 23 M8
SW13 180 CS83
Thornet Wd Rd, Brom. BR1 227 EN97
THORNEY, Iver SL0 176 BH76
Thorney Cres, SW11 40 B5
Thorneycroft Cl, Walt. KT12 218 BW100
Thorneycroft Dr, Enf. EN3 105 EA38
Thorney Hedge Rd, W4 180 CP77
Thorney La N, Iver SL0 155 BF74
Thorney La S, Iver SL0 175 BF75
Thorney Mill Rd, Iver SL0 176 BG76
West Drayton UB7 176 BG76
Thorney St, SW1 30 A8
Thornfield Av, NW7 119 CY53
Thornfield Rd, W12 181 CV75
Banstead SM7 256 DA117
Thornford Rd, SE13 205 EC85
Thorngate Rd, W9 15 K4
Thorngrove Rd, E13 166 EH67
Thornham Gro, E15 12 G3
Thornham St, SE10 46 D3
Thornhaugh Ms, WC1 17 P5
Thornhaugh St, WC1 17 P6
Thornhill, N.Wld Bas. CM16 93 FC26
Thornhill Av, SE18 187 ES80
Surbiton KT6 220 CL103
Thornhill Br Wf, N1 8 C9
Thornhill Cl, Amer. HP7 77 AP40
Thornhill Cres, N1 8 C7
Thornhill Gdns, E10 145 EB61
Barking IG11 167 ES66
Thornhill Gro, N1 8 D7
Sch Thornhill Prim Sch, N1 8 E7
Thornhill Rd, E10 145 EB61
N1 8 E6
Croydon CR0 224 DQ101
Northwood HA6 115 BQ49
Surbiton KT6 220 CL103
Uxbridge UB10 136 BM63
Thornhill Sq, N1 8 D7
Thornhill Way, Shep. TW17 216 BN99
Thorn La, Rain. RM13 170 FK68
Thornlaw Rd, SE27 203 DN91
Thornleas Pl, E.Hors. KT24
off Station App 267 BS126
Thornley Cl, N17 122 DU52
Thornley Dr, Har. HA2 138 CB61
Thornley Pl, SE10 47 J1
Thornridge, Brwd. CM14 130 FV45
Thornsbeach Rd, SE6 205 EC88
Thornsett Pl, SE20 224 DV96
Thornsett Rd, SE20 224 DV96
SW18 202 DB89
Thornside, Edg. HA8 118 CN51
Thorns Meadow, Brasted TN16 262 EW123
Thorn Ter, SE15
off Nunhead Gro 184 DW83
Thornton Av, SW2 203 DK88
W4 180 CS77
Croydon CR0 223 DM100
West Drayton UB7 176 BM76
Thornton Cl, Guil. GU2 264 AU130
Horley RH6 290 DE148
West Drayton UB7 176 BM76
Thornton Ct, SW20 221 CX99
Thornton Cres, Couls. CR5 257 DN119
Thornton Dene, Beck. BR3 225 EA96
Thornton Gdns, SW12 203 DK88
Thornton Gro, Pnr. HA5 116 CA51
THORNTON HEATH, CR7 223 DP98
⇌ Thornton Heath 224 DQ98
Thornton Heath 223 DN99
Jct Thornton Heath Pond, Th.Hth. CR7 223 DN99
Thornton Hill, SW19 201 CY94
Thornton Ho, SE17 31 M9
Thornton Pl, W1 16 F6
Horley RH6 290 DE148
Thornton Rd, E11 145 ED61
N18 122 DW48
SW12 203 DK87
SW14 180 CR83
SW19 201 CX93
Barnet EN5 101 CY41
Belvedere DA17 189 FB77
Bromley BR1 206 EG92
Carshalton SM5 222 DD102
Croydon CR0 223 DM101
Ilford IG1 147 EP63
Potters Bar EN6 86 DC30
Thornton Heath CR7 223 DM101
Thornton Rd E, SW19
off Thornton Rd 201 CX93
● Thornton Rd Ind Est, Croy. CR0 223 DL100
Thornton Row, Th.Hth. CR7
off London Rd 223 DN99
Thorntons Fm Av, Rom. RM7 149 FD60
Thornton Side, Red. RH1 273 DH131
Thornton St, SW9 42 E8
Hertford SG14 54 DR09
St. Albans AL3 64 CC19
Thornton Wk, Horl. RH6
off Thornton Pl 290 DE148
Thornton Way, NW11 142 DB57
Sch Thorntree Prim Sch, SE7 36 F10
Thorntree Rd, SE7 186 EK78
Thornville Gro, Mitch. CR4 222 DC96
Thornville St, SE8 46 A7
THORNWOOD, Epp. CM16 92 EW25
Thornwood Cl, E18 124 EH54
Thornwood Gdns, W8 27 J4
Thornwood Rd, SE13 206 EE85
Epping CM16 92 EV29
Thorogood Gdns, E15 13 K3
Thorogood Way, Rain. RM13 169 FE67
Thorold Cl, S.Croy. CR2 243 DX110
Thorold Rd, N22 121 DL52
Ilford IG1 147 EP61
Thoroughfare, The, Walt.Hill KT20 271 CU125
Thorparch Rd, SW8 41 P6
THORPE, Egh. TW20 215 BC97
Thorpebank Rd, W12 161 CU74
Thorpe Bypass, Egh. TW20 215 BB96
Thorpe Cl, W10 14 F8
New Addington CR0 243 EC111
Orpington BR6 227 ES103
Sch Thorpe C of E Inf Sch, Thorpe TW20 off The Bence 215 BB97
H Thorpe Coombe Hosp, E17 145 EC55
Thorpe Cres, E17 123 DZ54
Watford WD19 116 BW45
Thorpedale Gdns, Ilf. IG2, IG6 147 EN56
Thorpedale Rd, N4 143 DL60
Thorpefield Cl, St.Alb. AL4 65 CK17
THORPE GREEN, Egh. TW20 215 BA98
Sch Thorpe Hall Prim Sch, E17
off Hale End Rd 123 EC53
Thorpe Hall Rd, E17 123 EC53
Sch Thorpe Ho Sch, Ger.Cr. SL9
off Oval Way 134 AY56
● Thorpe Ind Est, Egh. TW20 215 BC96
THORPE LEA, Egh. TW20 195 BB93
Sch Thorpe Lea Prim Sch, Egh. TW20 off Huntingfield Way 195 BD93
Thorpe Lea Rd, Egh. TW20 195 BB93
Thorpe Lo, Horn. RM11 150 FK59
★ Thorpe Park, Cher. KT16 215 BE98
Thorpe Rd, E6 167 EM67
E7 146 EF63
E17 123 EC54
N15 144 DS58
Barking IG11 167 ER66
Chertsey KT16 215 BD99
Kingston upon Thames KT2 200 CL94
St. Albans AL1 65 CD21
Staines-upon-Thames TW18 195 BD93
Thorpes Cl, Guil. GU2 264 AU131
Thorpeside Cl, Stai. TW18 215 BE96
Thorpe Wk, Grnf. UB6 159 CE68
Thorpewood Av, SE26 204 DV89
Thorpland Av, Uxb. UB10 137 BQ62
Thorsden Cl, Wok. GU22 248 AY118
Thorsden Ct, Wok. GU22
off Guildford Rd 248 AY118
Thorsden Way, SE19
off Oaks Av 204 DS92
Thorverton Rd, NW2 141 CY62
Thoydon Rd, E3 21 L1
Thrale Rd, SW16 203 DJ92
Thrale St, SE1 31 K3
Thrasher Cl, E8 10 A8
Thrawl St, E1 20 B7
Threadneedle St, EC2 19 M9
Three Arches Pk, Red. RH1 288 DF138
Three Arch Rd, Red. RH1 288 DF138
Three Barrels Wk, EC4 31 K1
Three Bridges Path, Kings.T. KT1
off Portland Rd 220 CL97
Sch Three Bridges Prim Sch, Sthl. UB2 off Melbury Av 178 CB76
Three Cherry Trees La, Hem.H. HP2 63 BP16
Three Cl La, Berk. HP4 60 AW20
Three Colts Cor, E2 20 C4
Three Colts La, E2 20 E4
Three Colt St, E14 21 P9
Three Cors, Bexh. DA7 189 FB82
Hemel Hempstead HP3 62 BN22
Three Cranes Wk, EC4
off Bell Wf La 31 K1
Three Cups Yd, WC1 18 D7
Three Forests Way, Broad.Com. EN9 72 EL21
Chigwell IG7 126 EW48
Epping CM16 73 EM23
Harlow CM19 72 EH18
Loughton IG10
off The Clay Rd 106 EK38
Mark Hall North CM20 58 EU10
Romford RM4 126 EW48
Waltham Abbey EN9 106 EK36
Ware SG12 56 EL12
Three Gates, Guil. GU1 265 BC132
Three Gates Rd, Fawk.Grn DA3 231 FU102
Three Horseshoes Rd, Harl. CM19 73 EP17
Three Households, Ch.St.G. HP8 112 AT49
Three Kings Rd, Mitch. CR4 222 DG97
Three Kings Yd, W1 17 J10
Three Meadows Ms, Har. HA3 117 CF53
Three Mill La, E3 22 E2
Three Oak La, SE1 32 A4
Three Oaks Cl, Uxb. UB10 136 BM62
Three Pears Rd, Guil. GU1 265 BE134
Three Quays Wk, EC3 31 P1
Three Valleys Way, Bushey WD23 98 BX43
THRESHERS BUSH, Harl. CM17 75 FB16
Threshers Bush, Harl. CM17 58 FA14
Threshers Pl, W11 14 E10
Thriffwood, SE26 204 DW90
Thrift, The, Bean DA2 211 FW90
Thrift Fm La, Borwd. WD6 100 CP40
Thriftfield, Hem.H. HP2 62 BK18
Thrift Grn, Brwd. CM13
off Knight's Way 131 GA48
Thrift La, Cudham TN14 261 ER117
Ware SG12 55 DZ08
Thrifts Mead, They.B. CM16 107 ES37
Thrift Vale, Guil. GU4 265 BD131
Thrigby Rd, Chess. KT9 238 CM107
Throckmorton Rd, E16 24 B9
Throgmorton Av, EC2 19 M8
Throgmorton St, EC2 19 M8
Throstle Pl, Wat. WD25 82 BW32
Thrower Pl, Dor. RH5 285 CJ138
Throwley Cl, SE2 188 EW76
Throwley Rd, Sutt. SM1 240 DB106
Throwley Way, Sutt. SM1 240 DB105
Thrums, The, Wat. WD24 97 BV37
Thrupp Cl, Mitch. CR4 223 DH96
Thrupps Av, Hersham KT12 236 BX106
Thrupps La, Hersham KT12 236 BX106
Thrush Av, Hat. AL10 67 CU20
Thrush Grn, Har. HA2 138 CA56
Rickmansworth WD3 114 BJ45
Thrush La, Cuffley EN6 87 DL28
Thrush St, SE17 31 J10
Thumbswood, Welw.G.C. AL7 52 DA12
Thumpers, Hem.H. HP2 62 BL18
Thundercourt, Ware SG12 55 DX05
Thunderer Rd, Dag. RM9 168 EY70
Thundridge Cl, Welw.G.C. AL7
off Amwell Common 52 DB10
Thurbarn Rd, SE6 205 EB92
Thurgood Rd, Hodd. EN11 71 EA15
Thurland Ho, SE16
off Manor Est 32 E9
Thurland Rd, SE16 32 C6
Thurlby Cl, Har. HA1
off Gayton Rd 139 CG58
Woodford Green IG8 125 EM50
Thurlby Rd, SE27 203 DN91
Wembley HA0 159 CK65
Thurleigh Av, SW12 202 DG86
Thurleigh Rd, SW12 202 DG86
Thurleston Av, Mord. SM4 221 CY99
Thurlestone Av, N12 120 DF51
Ilford IG3 147 ET63
Thurlestone Cl, Shep. TW17 217 BQ100
Thurlestone Rd, SE27 203 DN90
Thurloe Cl, SW7 28 C8
Thurloe Gdns, Rom. RM1 149 FF58
Thurloe Pl, SW7 28 B8
Thurloe Pl Ms, SW7 28 B8
Thurloe Sq, SW7 28 C8
Thurloe St, SW7 28 B8
Thurloe Wk, Grays RM17 192 GA76
Thurlow Cl, E4
off Higham Sta Av 123 EB51
Thurlow Gdns, Ilf. IG6 125 ER51
Wembley HA0 139 CK64
Thurlow Hill, SE21 204 DQ88
Thurlow Pk Rd, SE21 203 DP88
Thurlow Rd, NW3 6 A2
W7 179 CG75
Thurlow St, SE17 31 M10
Thurlow Ter, NW5 6 G3
Thurlstone Rd, Ruis. HA4 137 BU62
Thurlton Ct, Wok. GU21
off Chobham Rd 248 AY116
Thurnby Ct, Twick. TW2 199 CE90
Thurnham Way, Tad. KT20 255 CW120
Coll Thurrock Adult Comm Coll - Grays Adult Ed Cen, Grays RM17
off Richmond Rd 192 GB78
Coll Thurrock & Basildon Coll, Woodview Campus, Grays RM16 off Woodview 193 GF77
● Thurrock Commercial Centre, S.Ock. RM15 190 FM75
Thurrock Pk Way, Til. RM18 192 GD80
● Thurrock Trade Pk, Grays RM20 191 FU80
Thursby Rd, Wok. GU21 248 AU118
Thursland Rd, Sid. DA14 208 EY92
Thursley Cres, New Adgtn CR0 243 ED108
Thursley Gdns, SW19 201 CX89
Thursley Rd, SE9 207 EM90
Thurso Cl, Rom. RM3 128 FP51
Thurso Ho, NW6 15 L1
Thurso St, SW17 202 DD91
Thurstan Rd, SW20 201 CV94
Thurstans, Harl. CM19 73 EP20
Thurston Rd, SE13 46 D9
Slough SL1 154 AS72
Southall UB1 158 BZ72
● Thurston Rd Ind Est, SE13 46 C10
Thurtle Rd, E2 10 B9
Thwaite Cl, Erith DA8 189 FC79
Thyer Cl, Orp. BR6
off Isabella Dr 245 EQ105
Thyme Cl, SE3 186 EJ83
Thyme Ct, Guil. GU4
off Mallow Cres 265 BB131
Thyra Gro, N12 120 DB51
Tibbatts Rd, E3 22 C4
Tibbenham Pl, SE6 205 EA89
Tibbenham Wk, E13 23 M1
Tibberton Sq, N1 9 J7
Tibbets Cl, SW19 201 CX88
Jct Tibbet's Cor, SW15 201 CX87
Tibbet's Cor Underpass, SW15
off West Hill 201 CX87
Tibbet's Ride, SW15 201 CX87
Tibbles Cl, Wat. WD25 98 BY35
Tibbs Hill Rd, Abb.L. WD5 81 BT30
Tiber Cl, E3 12 A9
Tiber Gdns, N1 8 B9
Tiberius Sq, St.Alb. AL3 64 CA22
Ticehurst Cl, Orp. BR5 208 EU94
Ticehurst Rd, SE23 205 DY89
Tichborne, Map.Cr. WD3 113 BD50
Tichmarsh, Epsom KT19 238 CQ110
Tickenhall Dr, Harl. CM17 74 EX15
Tickford Cl, SE2
off Ampleforth Rd 188 EW75
Tidal Basin Rd, E16 35 M1
Tide Cl, Mitch. CR4 222 DG95
Tideham Ho, SE28
off Merbury Cl 167 ER74
Sch Tidemill Academy, SE8 46 B4
Tidemill Way, SE8 46 B4
Tidenham Gdns, Croy. CR0 224 DS104
Tideslea Path, SE28 167 ER74
Tideslea Twr, SE28 187 ER75
Tideswell Rd, SW15 201 CW85
Croydon CR0 225 EA104
Tideway Cl, Rich. TW10 199 CH91
● Tideway Ind Est, SW8 41 M3
Tideway Wk, SW8 41 L3
Tidey St, E3 22 B6
Tidford Rd, Well. DA16 187 ET82
Tidlock Ho, SE28 187 ER75
Tidworth Ho, SE22
off Albrighton Rd 184 DS83
Tidworth Rd, E3 22 A4
Tidy's La, Epp. CM16 92 EV29
Tiepigs La, Brom. BR2 226 EE103
West Wickham BR4 226 EE103
Tierney Rd, SW2 203 DL88
Sch Tiffin Girl's Sch, The, Kings.T. KT2 off Richmond Rd 200 CL93
Sch Tiffin Sch for Boys, Kings.T. KT2 off Queen Elizabeth Rd 220 CM96
Tiger Moth Way, Hat. AL10 66 CR17
Tiger Way, E5 144 DV63
Tigris Cl, N9 122 DW47
Tilbrook Rd, SE3 186 EJ83
Tilburstow Hill Rd, Gdse. RH9 274 DW132
TILBURY, RM18 193 GG81
Tilbury Cl, SE15 44 B4
Orpington BR5 228 EV96
Pinner HA5 116 BZ52
Coll Tilbury Energy & Environment Cen, Til. RM18 off Fort Rd 193 GK83
★ Tilbury Fort, Til. RM18 193 GJ84
Sch Tilbury Manor Jun Sch, Til. RM18 off Dickens Av 193 GH80
Tilbury Mead, Harl. CM18 74 EU17
Tilbury Rd, E6 25 J1
E10 145 EC59
⇌ Tilbury Town 192 GE82
Tilbury Wk, Slou. SL3 175 BB76
Tildesley Rd, SW15 201 CW86
Tilecroft, Welw.G.C. AL8 51 CX06
Tile Fm Rd, Orp. BR6 227 ER104
Tilegate Rd, Harl. CM18 73 ET17
Ongar CM5 75 FC19
Tilehouse Cl, Borwd. WD6 100 CM41
Sch Tilehouse Comb Sch, Denh. UB9
off Nightingale Way 135 BF58
Tilehouse La, Denh. UB9 135 BE58
Gerrards Cross SL9 113 BE53
West Hyde WD3 113 BE53
Tilehouse Rd, Guil. GU4 280 AY138
Tilehouse Way, Denh. UB9 135 BF59
Tilehurst La, Dor. RH5 286 CL137
Tilehurst Pt, SE2
off Yarnton Way 188 EW75
Tilehurst Rd, SW18 202 DD88
Sutton SM3 239 CY106
Tilekiln Cl, Chsht EN7 88 DS29
Tile Kiln Cl, Hem.H. HP3 63 BP21
Tile Kiln Cres, Hem.H. HP3 63 BP21
Tile Kiln La, N6 143 DJ60
N13 122 DQ50
Bexley DA5 209 FC89
Harefield UB9 137 BP59
Hemel Hempstead HP3 62 BN21
Tilers Cl, S.Merst. RH1 273 DJ131
Tiler's Wk, Reig. RH2 288 DC138
Tiler's Way, Reig. RH2 288 DC138
Tile Yd, E14 21 P9
Tileyard Rd, N7 8 A6
Tilford Av, New Adgtn CR0 243 EC109
Tilford Gdns, SW19 201 CX89
Tilgate Common, Bletch. RH1 274 DQ133
Tilia Cl, Sutt. SM1 239 CZ106
Tilia Rd, E5 10 F1
Tilia Wk, SW9 183 DP84
Tillage Cl, St.Alb. AL4 65 CK22
Till Av, Fnghm DA4 230 FM102
Tiller Rd, E14 34 A6
Tillett Cl, NW10 160 CQ65
Tillett Sq, SE16 33 M5
Tillett Way, E2 20 C2
Tilley La, Headley KT18 254 CQ123
Tilley Rd, Felt. TW13 197 BU88
Tillingbourne Gdns, N3 141 CZ55
Tillingbourne Grn, Orp. BR5 228 EU98
Sch Tillingbourne Jun Sch, Chilw. GU4 off New Rd 281 BB141
Tillingbourne Rd, Shalf. GU4 280 AY140
Tillingbourne Way, N3
off Tillingbourne Gdns 141 CZ56
Tillingdown Hill, Cat. CR3 258 DU122
Tillingdown La, Cat. CR3 258 DV124
Tillingham Ct, Wal.Abb. EN9 90 EG33
Tillingham Way, N12 120 DA49
Tilling Rd, NW2 141 CW60
Tillings Cl, SE5 43 K7
Tilling Way, Wem. HA9 139 CK61
Tillman St, E1 20 F9
Tilloch St, N1 8 C7
Tillotson Ct, SW8
off Wandsworth Rd 42 A5
Tillotson Rd, N9 122 DT47
Harrow HA3 116 CB52
Ilford IG1 147 EN59
Tillwicks Rd, Harl. CM18 74 EU17
Tilly's La, Stai. TW18 195 BF91
Tilmans Mead, Fnghm DA4 230 FM101
Tilney Cl, Lthd. KT22
off Randalls Cres 253 CG120
Tilney Ct, EC1 19 K4
Tilney Dr, Buck.H. IG9 124 EG47
Tilney Gdns, N1 9 M5
Tilney Rd, Dag. RM9 168 EZ65
Southall UB2 178 BW77
Tilney St, W1 29 H2
Tilson Cl, SE5 43 N4
Tilson Gdns, SW2 203 DL87
Tilson Ho, SW2 203 DL87
Tilson Rd, N17 122 DU53
Tilston Cl, E11
off Matcham Rd 146 EF62
Tilstone Av, Eton Wick SL4 173 AL78
Tilstone Cl, Eton Wick SL4 173 AL78
Tilsworth Rd, Beac. HP9 132 AJ55
Tilsworth Wk, St.Alb. AL4
off Larkswood Ri 65 CJ15
Tilt Cl, Cob. KT11 252 BY116
Tilthams Cor Rd, Gdmg. GU7 280 AV143
Tilthams Grn, Gdmg. GU7 280 AV143
Tiltman Pl, N7 143 DM62
Tilt Meadow, Cob. KT11 252 BY116
Tilton St, SW6 38 F3
Tilt Rd, Cob. KT11 252 BW115
Tiltwood, The, W3 160 CQ73
Tilt Yd App, SE9 207 EM86
Timber Cl, Bkhm KT23 268 CC126
Chislehurst BR7 227 EN96
Woking GU22 233 BF114
Timber Ct, Grays RM17
off Columbia Wf Rd 192 GA79
Timbercroft, Epsom KT19 238 CS105
Welwyn Garden City AL7 51 CZ06
Timbercroft La, SE18 187 ES79
Sch Timbercroft Prim Sch, SE18
off Timbercroft La 187 ES80
Timberdene, NW4 119 CX54
Timberdene Av, Ilf. IG6 125 EP53
Timberham Fm Rd, Gat. RH6 290 DD151
Timberham Way, Horl. RH6 290 DE152
Timberhill, Ashtd. KT21 254 CL119
Timber Hill Cl, Ott. KT16 233 BC108
Timber Hill Rd, Cat. CR3 258 DU124
Timberidge, Loud. WD3 96 BJ42
Timberland Cl, SE15 44 C5
Timberland Rd, E1
off Hainton Cl 20 F9
Timber La, Cat. CR3
off Timber Hill Rd 258 DU124
Timberling Gdns, S.Croy. CR2
off St. Mary's Rd 242 DR110
Timber Mill Way, SW4 41 N10
Timber Orchard, Waterf. SG14 53 DN05
Timber Pond Rd, SE16 33 K3
Timberslip Dr, Wall. SM6 241 DK109
Timber St, EC1 19 J4
Timbertop Rd, Bigg.H. TN16 260 EJ118
Timber Wf, E2 10 A9
Timberwharf Rd, N16 144 DU58
Timberwood, Slou. SL2 133 AR62
Timbrell Pl, SE16 33 N3
Time Sq, E8 10 A3
Times Sq, Sutt. SM1 240 DB106
Times Sq, E1 20 C9
Times Sq Shop Cen, Sutt. SM1 off High St 240 DB106
Timms Cl, Brom. BR1 227 EM98
Timothy Cl, SW4 off Elms Rd 203 DJ85
Bexleyheath DA6 208 EY85
Timothy Ho, Erith DA18
off Kale Rd 188 EY75
Timperley Gdns, Red. RH1 272 DE132
Timplings Row, Hem.H. HP1 62 BH18
Timsbury Wk, SW15 201 CU88
Timsway, Stai. TW18 195 BF92
Tindale Cl, S.Croy. CR2 242 DR111
Tindall Cl, Rom. RM3 128 FM54
Tindall Ms, Horn. RM12 150 FJ62
Tindal St, SW9 42 G6
Tinderbox All, SW14 180 CR83
Tine Rd, Chig. IG7 125 ES50
Tingeys Top La, Enf. EN2 103 DN36
Tinkers La, Roydon CM19 72 EJ20
Windsor SL4 173 AK82
Tinniswood Cl, N5
off Drayton Pk 8 E2
Tinsey Cl, Egh. TW20 195 BB92
Tinsley Cl, SE25 224 DV97
Tinsley Est, Wat. WD18 97 BS42
Tinsley Rd, E1 21 H6
Tintagel Cl, Epsom KT17 239 CT114
Hemel Hempstead HP2 62 BK15
Tintagel Cres, SE22 184 DT84
Tintagel Dr, Stan. HA7 117 CK49
Tintagel Gdns, SE22
off Oxonian St 184 DT84
Tintagel Rd, Orp. BR5 228 EW103
Tintagel Way, Wok. GU22 249 BA116
Tintells La, W.Hors. KT24 267 BP128
Tintern Av, NW9 140 CP55
Tintern Cl, SW15 201 CY85
SW19 202 DC94
Slough SL1 173 AQ76
Tintern Ct, W13
off Green Man La 159 CG73
Tintern Gdns, N14 121 DL45
Tintern Path, NW9
off Ruthin Cl 140 CS58
Tintern Rd, N22 122 DQ53
Carshalton SM5 222 DD102
Tintern St, SW4 183 DL84
Tintern Way, Har. HA2 138 CB60
Tinto Rd, E16 23 P5
Tinwell Ms, Borwd. WD6 100 CQ43
Tinworth St, SE11 30 B10
Tippendell La, St.Alb. AL2 82 CB26
Tippetts Cl, Enf. EN2 104 DQ39
Tipthorpe Rd, SW11 40 G10
Tipton Cotts, Add. KT15
off Oliver Cl 234 BH105
Tipton Dr, Croy. CR0 242 DS105
Tiptree Cl, E4
off Mapleton Rd 123 EC48
Hornchurch RM11 150 FN60
Tiptree Cres, Ilf. IG5 147 EN55
Tiptree Dr, Enf. EN2 104 DR42
Tiptree Est, Ilf. IG5 147 EN55
Tiptree Rd, Ruis. HA4 137 BV63
Tiree Cl, Hem.H. HP3 63 BP22

Tirlement Rd, S.Croy. CR2 242 DQ108
Tirrell Rd, Croy. CR0 224 DQ100
Tisbury Ct, W1 *off Rupert St* 17 N10
Tisbury Rd, SW16 223 DL96
Tisdall Pl, SE17 31 M9
Tissington Ct, SE16
off Rotherhithe New Rd 33 J9
Titan Rd, Grays RM17 192 GA78
Hemel Hempstead HP2 62 BM17
Titchborne Row, W2 16 D9
Titchfield Rd, NW8 6 D9
Carshalton SM5 222 DD102
Enfield EN3 105 DY37
Titchfield Wk, Cars. SM5
off Titchfield Rd 222 DD101
Titchwell Rd, SW18 202 DD87
Tite Hill, Egh. TW20 194 AX92
Tite St, SW3 40 E1
Tithe Barn Cl, Kings.T. KT2 220 CM95
St. Albans AL1 64 CC23
Tithe Barn Ct, Abb.L. WD5 81 BT29
Tithe Barn Dr, Maid. SL6 172 AE78
Tithebarns La, Send GU23 266 BG126
Tithe Barn Way, Nthlt. UB5 157 BV68
Tithe Cl, NW7 119 CU53
Hayes UB4 157 BT71
Maidenhead SL6 172 AC78
Virginia Water GU25 214 AX100
Walton-on-Thames KT12 217 BV100
Tithe Ct, Slou. SL3 175 BA77
Tithe Fm Av, Har. HA2 138 CA62
Tithe Fm Cl, Har. HA2 138 CA62
Tithelands, Harl. CM19 73 EM18
Tithe La, Wrays. TW19 195 BA86
Tithe Meadows, Vir.W. GU25 214 AW100
Tithepit Shaw La, Warl. CR6 258 DV115
Tithe Wk, NW7 119 CU53
Titian Av, Bushey Hth WD23 117 CE45
Titley Cl, E4 123 EA50
Titmus Cl, Uxb. UB8 157 BQ72
Titmuss Av, SE28 168 EV73
Titmuss St, W12
off Goldhawk Rd 181 CW75
TITSEY, Oxt. RH8 276 EH125
Titsey Hill, Titsey RH8 260 EF123
Titsey Rd, Oxt. RH8 276 EH125
Tiverton Av, Ilf. IG5 147 EN55
Tiverton Cl, Croy. CR0
off Exeter Rd 224 DT101
Tiverton Dr, SE9 207 EQ88
Tiverton Gro, Rom. RM3 128 FN50
Tiverton Ho, Enf. EN3 105 DX41
Sch Tiverton Prim Sch, N15
off Pulford Rd 144 DR58
Tiverton Rd, N15 144 DR58
N18 122 DS50
NW10 4 C9
Edgware HA8 118 CM54
Hounslow TW3 178 CC82
Potters Bar EN6 86 DD31
Ruislip HA4 137 BU62
Thornton Heath CR7
off Willett Rd 223 DN99
Wembley HA0 160 CL68
Tiverton St, SE1 31 J7
Tiverton Way, NW7 119 CX52
Chessington KT9 237 CJ106
Tivoli Ct, SE16 33 N4
Tivoli Gdns, SE18 36 G8
Tivoli Ms, Grav. DA12 213 GH88
Tivoli Rd, N8 143 DK57
SE27 204 DQ92
Hounslow TW4 178 BY84
Toad La, Houns. TW4 178 BZ84
Tobacco Dock, E1 32 E1
Tobacco Quay, E1 32 E1
Tobago St, E14 34 A4
Tobermory Cl, Slou. SL3 174 AY77
Tobin Cl, NW3 6 D6
Epsom KT19 238 CP111
Toby La, E1 21 L5
Toby Way, Surb. KT5 220 CP103
Tockley Rd, Burn. SL1 152 AH68
Todd Brook, Harl. CM19 73 EP16
Todd Cl, Rain. RM13 170 FK70
Todds Cl, Horl. RH6 290 DE146
Todds Wk, N7
off Andover Rd 143 DM61
Todhunter Ter, Barn. EN5
off Prospect Rd 102 DA42
Toft Av, Grays RM17 192 GD77
Tokenhouse Yd, EC2 19 L8
Token Yd, SW15 181 CY84
TOKYNGTON, Wem. HA9 160 CP65
Tokyngton Av, Wem. HA9 160 CN65
Toland Sq, SW15 201 CU85
Tolcarne Dr, Pnr. HA5 137 BV55
Toldene Ct, Couls. CR5 257 DM120
Toley Av, Wem. HA9 140 CL59
Tolhurst Dr, W10 14 F2
Toll Bar Ct, Sutt. SM2 240 DB109
Tollbridge Cl, W10 14 F4
Tolldene Cl, Knap. GU21
off Robin Hood Rd 248 AS117
Tollers La, Couls. CR5 257 DM119
Tollesbury Gdns, Ilf. IG6 147 ER55
Tollet St, E1 21 J4
Tollgate, Guil. GU1 265 BD133
Tollgate Av, Red. RH1 288 DF139
Tollgate Cl, Chorl. WD3 95 BF41
Tollgate Dr, SE21 204 DS89
Hayes UB4 158 BX73
Tollgate Gdns, NW6 5 L10
Tollgate Ho, NW6 5 K10
Sch Tollgate Prim Sch, E13 24 D4
Tollgate Rd, E6 24 E7
E16 24 C6
Colney Heath AL4 66 CS24
Dartford DA2 211 FR87
Dorking RH4 285 CH139
North Mymms AL9 85 CU25
Waltham Cross EN8 105 DX35
Tollhouse La, Wall. SM6 241 DJ109
Tollhouse Way, N19 143 DJ61
Tollington Pk, N4 143 DM61
Tollington Pl, N4 143 DM61
Tollington Rd, N7 143 DM63
Tollington Way, N7 143 DL62
Tollpit End, Hem.H. HP1 62 BG17
Tolmers Av, Cuffley EN6 87 DL28
Tolmers Gdns, Cuffley EN6 87 DL29
Tolmers Ms, Newgate St
SG13 87 DL25
Tolmers Pk, Newgate St SG13 87 DL25
Tolmers Rd, Cuffley EN6 87 DL27
Tolmers Sq, NW1 17 M4
Tolpaide Ho, SE11 30 E9
Tolpits Cl, Wat. WD18 97 BT43
Tolpits La, Wat. WD18 97 BT44
Tolpuddle Av, E13
off Rochester Av 166 EJ67
Tolpuddle St, N1 8 E10
Tolsford Rd, E5 10 F2
Tolson Rd, Islw. TW7 179 CG83
Tolvaddon, Wok. GU21
off Cardingham 248 AU117
Tolverne Rd, SW20 221 CW95
TOLWORTH, Surb. KT6 220 CN103
⇌ Tolworth 220 CP103
Tolworth Bdy, Surb. KT6 220 CP103
Tolworth Cl, Surb. KT6 220 CP102
Tolworth Gdns, Rom. RM6 148 EX57
Sch Tolworth Girls' Sch & Cen for
Cont Ed, Surb. KT6
off Fullers Way N 220 CM104
H Tolworth Hosp, Surb. KT6 220 CN103
Sch Tolworth Infants' Sch, Surb.
KT6 *off School La* 220 CM102
Jct Tolworth Junct, Surb. KT5 220 CP103
Sch Tolworth Jun Sch, Surb.
KT6 *off Douglas Rd* 220 CM102
Tolworth Pk Rd, Surb. KT6 220 CM103
Tolworth Ri N, Surb. KT5
off Elmbridge Av 220 CQ101
Tolworth Ri S, Surb. KT5
off Warren Dr S 220 CQ102
Tolworth Rd, Surb. KT6 220 CL103
Tolworth Twr, Surb. KT6 220 CP103
Tomahawk Gdns, Nthlt. UB5
off Javelin Way 158 BX69
Tom Coombs Cl, SE9 186 EL84
Tom Cribb Rd, SE28 187 EQ76
Tom Gros Cl, E15 13 H3
Tom Hood Cl, E15 13 H3
Sch Tom Hood Sch, E11
off Terling Cl 146 EF62
Tom Jenkinson Rd, E16 35 P2
Tomkins Cl, Borwd. WD6
off Tallis Way 100 CL39
Tomkyns La, Upmin. RM14 151 FR56
Tomlin Cl, Epsom KT19 238 CR111
Tomlin Rd, Slou. SL2 153 AL70
Tomlins Gro, E3 22 B2
Tomlinson Cl, E2 20 B3
W4 180 CP78
Tomlins Orchard, Bark. IG11 167 EQ67
Tomlins Ter, E14 21 M8
Tomlins Wk, N7
off Briset Way 143 DM61
Tomlyns Cl, Hutt. CM13 131 GE44
Tom Mann Cl, Bark. IG11 167 ES67
Tom Nolan Cl, E15 23 K1
● Tomo Ind Est, Uxb. UB8 156 BJ72
Tompion Ho, EC1
off Percival St 19 H4
Tompion St, EC1 18 G3
Toms Cft, Hem.H. HP2 62 BL21
Tomsfield, Hat. AL10 66 CS19
Toms Hill, Kings L. WD4 96 BL36
Rickmansworth WD3 96 BL36
Toms La, Bedmond WD5 81 BR28
Kings Langley WD4 81 BP29
Tom Smith Cl, SE10 47 J2
Tomswood Ct, Ilf. IG6 125 EQ53
Tomswood Hill, Ilf. IG6 125 EP52
Tomswood Rd, Chig. IG7 125 EN51
Tom Thumbs Arch, E3
off Malmesbury Rd 22 A1
Tom Williams Ho, SW6
off Clem Attlee Ct 38 G3
Tonbridge Cl, Bans. SM7 240 DF114
Tonbridge Cres, Har. HA3 140 CL56
Tonbridge Ho, SE25 224 DU97
Tonbridge Rd, Harold Hill RM3 128 FK52
Sevenoaks TN13 279 FJ127
West Molesey KT8 218 BY98
Tonbridge St, WC1 18 A2
Tonbridge Wk, WC1
off Bidborough St 18 A2
Tonfield Rd, Sutt. SM3 221 CZ102
Tonge Cl, Beck. BR3 225 EA99
Tonsley Hill, SW18 202 DB85
Tonsley Pl, SW18 202 DB85
Tonsley Rd, SW18 202 DB85
Tonsley St, SW18 202 DB85
Tonstall Rd, Epsom KT19 238 CR110
Mitcham CR4 222 DG96
Tony Cannell Ms, E3 21 N3
Tooke Cl, Pnr. HA5 116 BY53
Tookey Cl, Har. HA3 140 CM59
Took's Ct, EC4 18 E8
Tooley St, SE1 31 M2
Northfleet DA11 212 GD87
Toorack Rd, Har. HA3 117 CD54
TOOT HILL, Ong. CM5 93 FF30
Toot Hill Rd, Ong. CM5 93 FF29
⇌ Tooting 202 DG93
⊖ Tooting Bec 202 DF90
Jct Tooting Bec, SW17 202 DF90
Tooting Bec Gdns, SW16 203 DK91
Tooting Bec Rd, SW16 202 DG90
SW17 202 DG90
⊖ Tooting Broadway 202 DE92
Jct Tooting Bdy, SW17 202 DE91
TOOTING GRAVENEY, SW17 202 DE93
Tooting Gro, SW17 202 DE92
Tooting High St, SW17 202 DE93
Tooting Mkt, SW17
off Tooting High St 202 DF91
Tootswood Rd, Brom. BR2 226 EE99
Tooveys Mill Cl, Kings L. WD4 80 BN28
Topaz Cl, Slou. SL1
off Pearl Gdns 153 AP74
Topaz Ct, E11
off High Rd Leytonstone 146 EE60
Topaz Ho, E15 *off Romford Rd* 13 L5
Topaz Wk, NW2 *off Marble Dr* 141 CX59
Topcliffe Dr, Orp. BR6 245 ER105
Top Dartford Rd, Dart. DA2 209 FF94
Swanley BR8 209 FF94
Top Fm Cl, Beac. HP9 110 AG54
Topham Sq, N17 122 DQ53
Topham St, EC1 18 E4
Top Ho Ri, E4
off Parkhill Rd 123 EC45
Topiary, The, Ashtd. KT21 254 CL120
Topiary Sq, Rich. TW9 180 CM83
Topland Rd, Chal.St.P. SL9 112 AX52
Toplands Av, Aveley RM15 170 FP74
Topley St, SE9 186 EK84
Topmast Pt, E14 34 A5
Top Pk, Beck. BR3 226 EE99
Gerrards Cross SL9 134 AW58
Topping La, Uxb. UB8 156 BK69
Topp Wk, NW2 141 CW61
Topsfield Cl, N8 143 DK57
Topsfield Par, N8
off Tottenham La 143 DL57
Topsfield Rd, N8 143 DL57
Topsham Rd, SW17 202 DF90
Torbay Rd, NW6 4 G7
Harrow HA2 138 BY61
Torbay St, NW1 7 K7
Torbitt Way, Ilf. IG2 147 ET57
Torbridge Cl, Edg. HA8 118 CL52
Torbrook Cl, Bex. DA5 208 EY86
Torcross Dr, SE23 204 DW89
Torcross Rd, Ruis. HA4 137 BV62
Tor Gdns, W8 27 J4
Tor Gro, SE28 167 ES74
Torin Ct, Eng.Grn TW20 194 AW92
Torland Dr, Oxshott KT22 237 CD114
Tor La, Wey. KT13 235 BQ111
Tormead Cl, Sutt. SM1 240 DA107
Tormead Rd, Guil. GU1 265 AZ134
Sch Tormead Sch, Jun Sch, Guil.
GU1 *off Cranley Rd* 265 AZ134
Sen Sch, Guil. GU1
off Cranley Rd 265 AZ134
Tormount Rd, SE18 187 ES79
Tornay Ho, N1
off Priory Grn Est 8 C10
Toronto Av, E12 147 EM63
Toronto Dr, Smallfield RH6 291 DN148
Toronto Rd, Ilf. IG1 147 EP60
Tilbury RM18 193 GG82
Torquay Gdns, Ilf. IG4 146 EK56
Torquay Spur, Slou. SL2 153 AP70
Torquay St, W2 15 L7
Torrance Cl, SE7 186 EK79
Hornchurch RM11 149 FH60
Torrens Cl, Guil. GU2 264 AU131
Torrens Rd, E15 13 L4
SW2 203 DM85
Torrens Sq, E15 13 K4
Torrens St, EC1 18 F1
Torrens Wk, Grav. DA12 213 GL92
Torres Sq, E14
off Maritime Quay 34 B10
Torre Wk, Cars. SM5 222 DE102
Torrey Dr, SW9 42 F8
Torriano Av, NW5 7 N3
Torriano Cotts, NW5 7 M3
Sch Torriano Inf Sch, NW5 7 N4
Sch Torriano Jun Sch, NW5 7 N3
Torriano Ms, NW5 7 M2
Torridge Gdns, SE15 184 DW84
Torridge Rd, Slou. SL3 175 BB79
Thornton Heath CR7 223 DP99
Torridge Wk, Hem.H. HP2
off The Dee 62 BM15
Torridon Cl, Wok. GU21 248 AV117
Torridon Ho, NW6 15 L1
Sch Torridon Inf Sch, SE6
off Torridon Rd 205 ED89
Sch Torridon Jun Sch, SE6
off Hazelbank Rd 205 ED89
Torridon Rd, SE6 205 ED88
SE13 205 ED87
Torrington Av, N12 120 DD50
Torrington Cl, N12 120 DD49
Claygate KT10 237 CE107
Torrington Dr, Har. HA2 138 CB63
Loughton IG10 107 EQ42
Potters Bar EN6 86 DD32
Torrington Gdns, N11 121 DJ51
Loughton IG10 107 EQ42
Perivale UB6 159 CJ67
Torrington Gro, N12 120 DE50
Torrington Pk, N12 120 DC50
Torrington Pl, E1 32 D2
WC1 17 M6
Torrington Rd, E18 146 EG55
Berkhamsted HP4 60 AV19
Claygate KT10 237 CE107
Dagenham RM8 148 EZ60
Perivale UB6 159 CJ67
Ruislip HA4 137 BT62
Torrington Sq, WC1 17 P5
Croydon CR0
off Tavistock Gro 224 DR101
Torrington Way, Mord. SM4 222 DA100
Tor Rd, Well. DA16 188 EW81
Torr Rd, SE20 205 DX94
Tortoiseshell Way, Berk. HP4 60 AT17
Torver Rd, Har. HA1 139 CE56
Torver Way, Orp. BR6 227 ER104
Torwood Cl, Berk. HP4 60 AT19
Torwood La, Whyt. CR3 258 DT120
Torwood Rd, SW15 201 CU85
Torworth Rd, Borwd. WD6 100 CM39
Tothill Ho, SW1 *off Page St* 29 P8
Tothill St, SW1 29 N5
Totnes Rd, Well. DA16 188 EV80
Totnes Wk, N2 142 DD56
Tottan Ter, E1 21 K8
Sch Tottenhall Inf Sch, N13
off Tottenhall Rd 121 DN51
Tottenhall Rd, N13 121 DN51
TOTTENHAM, N17 122 DS53
⊖ Tottenham Court Road 17 N8
Tottenham Ct Rd, W1 17 M5
Tottenham Grn E, N15 144 DT56
TOTTENHAM HALE, N17 144 DV55
⇌ Tottenham Hale 144 DV55
⊖ Tottenham Hale 144 DV55
Jct Tottenham Hale, N17 144 DT56
Tottenham Hale Retail Pk,
N15 144 DU56
★ Tottenham Hotspur FC,
N17 122 DT52
Tottenham La, N8 143 DL57
Tottenham Ms, W1 17 M6
Tottenham Rd, N1 9 N5
Tottenham St, W1 17 M7
Totterdown St, SW17 202 DF91
TOTTERIDGE, N20 119 CY46
⊖ Totteridge & Whetstone 120 DB47
Totteridge Common, N20 119 CU47
Totteridge Grn, N20 120 DA47
Totteridge Ho, SW11 40 B9
Totteridge La, N20 120 DA47
Totteridge Rd, Enf. EN3 105 DX37
Totteridge Village, N20 119 CY46
Totternhoe Cl, Har. HA3 139 CJ57
Totton Rd, Th.Hth. CR7 223 DN97
Toucan Cl, NW10 160 CN69
Toulmin Dr, St.Alb. AL3 64 CC16
Toulmin St, SE1 31 J5
Toulon St, SE5 43 J4
Tournay Rd, SW6 39 H4
Tours Pas, SW11 182 DD84
Toussaint Wk, SE16 32 D6
Tovey Av, Hodd. EN11 71 EA15
Tovey Cl, Lon.Col. AL2 83 CK26
Lower Nazeing EN9 72 EE23
Tovil Cl, SE20 224 DU96
Tovy Ho, SE1 44 C1
Towcester Rd, E3 22 D5
Tower, The, Couls. CR5 257 DK122
● Tower 42, EC2 19 N8
Tower Br, E1 32 A3
SE1 32 A3
Tower Br App, E1 32 A2
★ Tower Br Exhib, SE1 32 A3
Tower Br Ms, Har. HA1
off Greenford Rd 139 CF63
Tower Br Piazza, SE1 32 A3
Sch Tower Br Prim Sch, SE1 32 A4
Tower Br Rd, SE1 31 N7
Tower Br Wf, E1 32 C3
Tower Bldgs, E1
off Brewhouse La 32 F3
Tower Cen, Hodd. EN11 71 EA17
Tower Cl, NW3 6 B2
SE20 204 DV94
Berkhamsted HP4 60 AU20
Flackwell Heath HP10 132 AC56
Gravesend DA12 213 GL92
Hertford Heath SG13 54 DW13
Horley RH6 290 DF148
Ilford IG6 125 EP51
North Weald Bassett CM16 75 FD24
Orpington BR6 227 ET103
Woking GU21 248 AX117
Tower Ct, WC2 18 A9
Brentwood CM14 130 FV47
Egham TW20
off The Chantries 195 BA92
Tower Cft, Eyns. DA4 230 FL103
Tower Gdns, Clay. KT10 237 CG108
Tower Gdns Rd, N17 122 DQ53
Towergate Cl, Uxb. UB8 136 BL64
DLR Tower Gateway 20 B10
Tower Gro, Wey. KT13 217 BS103
Coll Tower Hamlets Coll,
Arbour Sq Cen, E1 21 J8
Bethnal Grn Cen, E2 20 C3
East India Dock Rd, E14 22 D9
Poplar Cen, E14 34 C1
Tower Hamlets Rd, E7 13 M1
E17 145 EA55
Tower Hts, Hodd. EN11
off Amwell St 71 EA17
TOWER HILL, Dor. RH4 285 CH138
⊖ Tower Hill 19 P10
Tower Hill, EC3 32 A1
Brentwood CM14 130 FW47
Chipperfield WD4 79 BE29
Dorking RH4 285 CH138
Gomshall GU5 283 BQ140
Tower Hill La, Goms. GU5 283 BQ140
Sandridge AL4 50 CM10
Tower Hill Ri, Goms. GU5 283 BQ140
Tower Hill Rd, Dor. RH4 285 CH138
Tower Hill Ter, EC3
off Byward St 31 P1
Tower Ho, Slou. SL1 174 AS75
Uxb. UB8 *off High St* 156 BJ66
Sch Tower Ho Sch, SW14
off Sheen La 180 CQ84
Tower La, Wem. HA9
off Main Dr 139 CK62
Tower Ms, E17 145 EA56
★ Tower Millennium Pier,
EC3 31 P2
Tower Mill Rd, SE15 43 N3
★ Tower of London, EC3 32 A1
Tower Pk Rd, Cray. DA1 209 FF85
Tower Pl, Warl. CR6 259 EA115
● Tower Pl E, EC3 31 P1
● Tower Pl W, EC3 31 P1
Tower Pt, Enf. EN2 104 DR42
Tower Retail Pk, Cray.
DA1 209 FF85
Tower Ri, Rich. TW9
off Jocelyn Rd 180 CL83
Tower Rd, NW10 161 CU66
Belvedere DA17 189 FC77
Bexleyheath DA7 189 FB84
Coleshill HP7 77 AN43
Dartford DA1 210 FJ86
Epping CM16 91 ES30
Orpington BR6 227 ET103
Tadworth KT20 255 CW123
Twickenham TW1 199 CF90
Ware SG12 55 DY05
Tower Royal, EC4 19 K10
Towers, The, Ken. CR8 258 DQ115
Towers Av, Hlgdn UB10 157 BQ69
● Towers Business Pk, Wem.
HA9 *off Carey Way* 140 CQ63
Sch Towers Inf Sch, Horn. RM11
off Osborne Rd 150 FJ59
Sch Towers Jun Sch, Horn. RM11
off Windsor Rd 150 FJ59
Towers Pl, Rich. TW9 200 CL85
Towers Rd, Grays RM17 192 GC78
Hemel Hempstead HP2 62 BL19
Pinner HA5 116 BY53
Southall UB1 158 CA70
Tower St, WC2 17 P9
Hertford SG14 54 DQ07
Towers Wk, Wey. KT13 235 BP107
Towers Wd, S.Darenth DA4 231 FR95
Tower Ter, N22 *off Mayes Rd* 121 DM54
SE4 *off Foxberry Rd* 185 DY84
Tower Vw, Bushey Hth WD23 117 CE45
Croydon CR0 225 DX101
Towfield Rd, Felt. TW13 198 BZ89
Towing Path, Guil. GU1 280 AW138
Towing Path Wk, N1 8 A10
Town, The, Enf. EN2 104 DR41
Town Br Ct, Chesh. HP5
off Watermeadow 76 AP32
Town Cen, Hat. AL10 67 CU17
Towncourt Cres, Petts Wd
BR5 227 EQ99
Towncourt La, Petts Wd BR5 227 ER100
Town Ct Path, N4 144 DQ60
Town End, Cat. CR3 258 DS122
Town End Cl, Cat. CR3 258 DS122
Towney Mead, Nthlt. UB5 158 BZ68
Towney Mead Ct, Nthlt. UB5
off Towney Mead 158 BZ68
Sch Town Fm Prim Sch, Stanw.
TW19 *off St. Mary's Cres* 196 BK87
Town Fm Way, Stanw. TW19
off Town La 196 BK87
Townfield, Chesh. HP5 76 AP32
Rickmansworth WD3 114 BJ45
Townfield Cor, Grav. DA12 213 GJ88
Townfield Ct, Dor. RH4
off Horsham Rd 285 CG137
Town Fld La, Ch.St.G. HP8 112 AW48
Townfield Rd, Dor. RH4 285 CG137
Townfield Rd, Hayes UB3 157 BT74
Townfields, Hat. AL10 67 CU17
Townfield Sq, Hayes UB3 157 BT74
Town Fld Way, Islw. TW7 179 CG82
Towngate, Cob. KT11 252 BY115
Town Hall App, N16 9 M1
Town Hall App Rd, N15 144 DT56
Town Hall Av, W4 180 CR78
Town Hall Rd, SW11 182 DF83
Townholm Cres, W7 179 CF76
Town La, Stanw. TW19 196 BK86
Wooburn Green HP10 132 AD59
Townley Ct, E15 13 L5
Sch Townley Gram Sch for Girls,
Bexh. DA6 *off Townley Rd* 208 EZ85
Townley Rd, SE22 204 DS85
Bexleyheath DA6 208 EZ85
Townley St, SE17 31 L10
Townmead Rd, Bletch. RH1 274 DR133
● Townmead Business Cen,
SW6 39 N10
Town Meadow, Brent. TW8 179 CK79
Townmead Rd, SW6 39 N9
Richmond TW9 180 CP82
Waltham Abbey EN9 89 EC34
Town Mill Ms, Hert. SG14
off Millbridge 54 DQ09
Town Path, Egh. TW20 195 BA92
Town Pier, Grav. DA11
off West St 213 GH86
Town Quay, Bark. IG11 167 EP67
Town Rd, N9 122 DV47
TOWNSEND, St.Alb. AL3 65 CD17
Townsend, Hem.H. HP2 62 BK18
Townsend Av, N14 121 DK49
St. Albans AL1 65 CE19
Sch Townsend C of E Sch, St.Alb.
AL3 *off Sparrowswick Ride* 64 CC15
Townsend Dr, St.Alb. AL3 65 CD18
● Townsend Ind Est, NW10 160 CQ68
Townsend La, NW9 140 CR59
Woking GU22
off St. Peters Rd 249 BB121
Townsend Ms, SW18
off Waynflete St 202 DC89
Sch Townsend Prim Sch, SE17 31 N8
Townsend Rd, N15 144 DT57
Ashford TW15 196 BL92
Chesham HP5 76 AP30
Southall UB1 158 BY74
Townsend St, SE17 31 M9
Townsend Way, Nthwd. HA6 115 BT52
Townsend Yd, N6 143 DH60
Townshend Cl, Sid. DA14 208 EV93
Townshend Est, NW8 6 C10
Townshend Rd, NW8 6 C9
Chislehurst BR7 207 EP92
Richmond TW9 180 CM84
Townshend Ter, Hert. SG13 54 DS09
Townshend Ter, Rich. TW9 180 CM84
Townshott Cl, Bkhm KT23 268 CA125
Townslow La, Wisley GU23 250 BK116
Townson Av, Nthlt. UB5 157 BU69
Townson Way, Nthlt. UB5
off Townson Av 157 BU68
Town Sq, Bark. IG11
off Clockhouse Av 167 EQ67
Erith DA8 *off Pier Rd* 189 FE79
Woking GU21
off Church St E 249 AZ117
Town Sq Cres, Bluewater DA9 211 FT87
Town Tree Rd, Ashf. TW15 196 BN92
Towpath, Shep. TW17 216 BM103
Towpath Rd, N18 123 DX51
Towpath Wk, E9 11 N2
Towpath Way, Croy. CR0 224 DT100
Towton Rd, SE27 204 DQ89
Toynbec Cl, Chis. BR7
off Beechwood Ri 207 EP91
Toynbee Rd, SW20 221 CY95
Toynbee St, E1 20 A7
Toyne Way, N6 142 DF58
Tozer Wk, Wind. SL4 173 AK83
Tracery, The, Bans. SM7 256 DB115
Tracey Av, NW2 4 A2
Tracious Cl, Wok. GU21
off Sythwood 248 AV116
Tracious La, Wok. GU21 248 AV116
Tracy Av, Slou. SL3 175 AZ78
Tracy Ct, Stan. HA7 117 CJ52
Tracyes Rd, Harl. CM18 74 EV17
● Trade City, Wey. KT13 234 BL110
● Trade City Bus Pk,
Uxb. UB8 156 BJ68
Trade Cl, N13 121 DN49
Trader Rd, E6 25 N9
Tradescant Rd, SW8 42 B5
Trading Est Rd, NW10 160 CQ70
Trafalgar Av, N17 122 DS51
SE15 44 B1
Broxbourne EN10 71 DZ21
Worcester Park KT4 221 CX102
● Trafalgar Business Cen, Bark.
IG11 167 ET70
Trafalgar Cl, SE16 33 L8
Trafalgar Ct, E1 33 H1
Cobham KT11 235 BU113
Trafalgar Dr, Walt. KT12 217 BV104
Trafalgar Gdns, E1 21 K6
W8 27 L6
Trafalgar Gro, SE10 47 H2
Sch Trafalgar Inf Sch, Twick. TW2
off Elmsleigh Rd 199 CD89
Sch Trafalgar Jun Sch, Twick. TW2
off Elmsleigh Rd 199 CD89
Trafalgar Ms, E9 11 N4
Trafalgar Pl, E11 146 EG56
N18 122 DU50
Trafalgar Rd, SE10 47 H2
SW19 202 DB94
Dartford DA1 210 FL89
Gravesend DA11 213 GG87
Rainham RM13 169 FF68
Twickenham TW2 199 CD89
Trafalgar Sq, SW1 29 P2
WC2 29 P2
Trafalgar St, SE17 31 L10
Trafalgar Ter, Har. HA1
off Nelson Rd 139 CE60
● Trafalgar Trd Est, Enf. EN3 105 DY42
Trafalgar Way, E14 34 E2

Trafalgar Way, Croydon CR0 223 DM103
Trafalgar Way Retail Pk, Croy. CR0 223 DM103
Trafford Cl, Ilf. IG6 125 ET51
Shenley WD7 84 CL32
Trafford Rd, Th.Hth. CR7 223 DM99
Trafford Way, Beck. BR3 205 EA93
Trahorn Cl, E1 20 E5
Tralee Ct, SE16 32 E10
Tram Cl, SE24 off Hinton Rd 183 DP83
Tramsheds Ind Est, Croy. CR0 223 DK101
Tramway Av, E15 13 J6
N9 122 DV45
Tramway Cl, SE20 224 DW95
Tramway Ho, Erith DA8
off Stonewood Rd 189 FE78
Tramway Path, Mitch. CR4 222 DF99
Tranby Pl, E9 11 K3
Tranley Ms, NW3 6 D2
Tranmere Rd, N9 122 DT45
SW18 202 DC89
Twickenham TW2 198 CB87
Tranquil Dale, Buckland RH3 271 CT132
Tranquil Pas, SE3 47 L9
Tranquil Ri, Erith DA8
off West St 189 FE78
Tranquil Vale, SE3 47 K9
Transept St, NW1 16 C7
Transmere Cl, Petts Wd BR5 227 EQ100
Transmere Rd, Petts Wd BR5 227 EQ100
Transom Cl, SE16 33 M8
Transom Sq, E14 34 C9
Transport Av, Brent. TW8 179 CG78
Tranton Rd, SE16 32 D6
Trappes Ho, SE16
off Manor Est 32 E9
Trapps La, Chesh. HP5 76 AR32
Traps Hill, Loug. IG10 107 EM41
Traps La, N.Mal. KT3 220 CS95
Trapstyle Rd, Ware SG12 54 DU05
Trasher Mead, Dor. RH4 285 CJ139
Travellers Cl, N.Mymms AL9 67 CW23
Travellers La, Hat. AL10 67 CU19
North Mymms AL9 67 CW22
Travellers Way, Houns. TW4 178 BW82
Travers Cl, E17 123 DX53
Travers Rd, N7 143 DN62
Travic Rd, Slou. SL2 153 AM69
Travis Ct, Farn.Royal SL2 153 AP69
Treachers Cl, Chesh. HP5 76 AP31
Treacle Mine Rbt, Grays RM16 192 FZ75
Treacy Cl, Bushey Hth WD23 116 CC47
Treadgold St, W11 14 D10
Treadway St, E2 20 E1
Treadwell Rd, Epsom KT18 254 CS115
Treasury Cl, Wall. SM6 241 DK106
Treaty Cen, Houns. TW3 178 CB83
Treaty St, N1 8 C9
Trebble Rd, Swans. DA10 212 FY86
Trebeck St, W1 29 J2
Trebellan Dr, Hem.H. HP2 62 BM19
Trebovir Rd, SW5 27 K10
Treby St, E3 21 N5
Trecastle Way, N7 7 P1
Tredegar Ms, E3 21 N2
Tredegar Rd, E3 21 N1
N11 121 DK52
Dartford DA2 209 FG89
Tredegar Sq, E3 21 N2
Tredegar Ter, E3 21 N2
Trederwen Rd, E8 10 D8
Tredown Rd, SE26 204 DW92
Tredwell Cl, SW2
off Hillside Rd 203 DM89
Bromley BR2 226 EL98
Tredwell Rd, SE27 203 DP91
Treebourne Rd, Bigg.H. TN16 260 EJ117
Treeby Ct, Enf. EN3
off George Lovell Dr 105 EA37
Treebys Av, Jacobs Well GU4 264 AX128
Tree Cl, Rich. TW10 199 CK88
Treehouse Sch, N10
off Woodside Av 142 DG56
Treelands, N.Holm. RH5 285 CJ139
Treemount Ct, Epsom KT17 238 CS113
Treen Av, SW13 181 CT83
Tree Rd, E16 24 C8
Treeside Cl, West Dr. UB7 176 BK77
Tree Tops, Brwd. CM15 130 FW46
Treetops, Grav. DA12 213 GH92
Whyteleafe CR3 258 DU118
Treetops Cl, SE2 188 EY78
Northwood HA6 115 BR50
Treetops Vw, Loug. IG10 124 EK45
Treeview Cl, SE19 224 DS95
Treewall Gdns, Brom. BR1 206 EH91
Tree Way, Reig. RH2 272 DB131
Trefgarne Rd, Dag. RM10 148 FA61
Trefil Wk, N7 143 DL63
Trefoil Ho, Erith DA18
off Kale Rd 188 EY75
Trefoil Rd, SW18 202 DC85
Trefusis Wk, Wat. WD17 97 BS39
Tregaron Av, N8 143 DL58
Tregaron Gdns, N.Mal. KT3 220 CS98
Tregarthen Pl, Lthd. KT22 253 CJ121
Tregarth Pl, Wok. GU21 248 AT117
Tregarvon Rd, SW11 182 DG84
Tregelles Rd, Hodd. EN11 55 EA14
Tregenna Av, Har. HA2 138 BZ63
Tregenna Cl, N14 103 DJ43
Tregenna Ct, Har. HA2 138 CA63
Tregony Rd, Orp. BR6 245 ET105
Trego Rd, E9 11 P6
Tregothnan Rd, SW9 42 A10
Tregunter Rd, SW10 39 N2
Trehaven Par, Reig. RH2
off Hornbeam Rd 288 DB137
Trehearn Rd, Ilf. IG6 125 ER52
Treherne Ct, SW9 42 F6
SW17 202 DG91
Trehern Rd, SW14 180 CR83
Trehurst St, E5 11 L2
Trelawn Cl, Ott. KT16 233 BC108
Trelawney Av, Slou. SL3 174 AX76
Trelawney Cl, E17
off Orford Rd 145 EB56
Trelawney Est, E9 10 G5
Trelawney Gro, Wey. KT13 234 BN107
Trelawney Rd, Ilf. IG6 125 ER52
Trelawn Rd, E10 145 EC62
SW2 203 DN85
Trellick Twr, W10 14 G5
Trellis Sq, E3 21 P2
Treloar Gdns, SE19
off Hancock Rd 204 DR93
Tremadoc Rd, SW4 183 DK84
Tremaine Cl, SE4 46 A9
Tremaine Gro, Hem.H. HP2 62 BL16
Tremaine Rd, SE20 224 DV96
Trematon Pl, Tedd. TW11 199 CJ94
Tremlett Gro, N19 143 DJ62
Tremlett Ms, N19 143 DJ62
Tremolo Grn, Dag. RM8 148 EY60
Trenance, Wok. GU21
off Cardingham 248 AU117
Trenance Gdns, Ilf. IG3 148 EU62
Trenchard Av, Ruis. HA4 137 BV63
Trenchard Cl, NW9
off Fulbeck Dr 118 CS53
Hersham KT12 236 BW106
Stanmore HA7 117 CG51
Trenchard Ct, Mord. SM4
off Green La 222 DA100
Trenchard St, SE10 47 H1
Trenches La, Slou. SL3 155 BA73
Trenchold St, SW8 42 A3
Trenear Cl, Orp. BR6 246 EU105
Trenham Dr, Warl. CR6 258 DW116
Trenholme Cl, SE20 204 DV94
Trenholme Ct, Cat. CR3 258 DU122
Trenholme Rd, SE20 204 DV94
Trenholme Ter, SE20 204 DV94
Trenmar Gdns, NW10 161 CV69
Trent Av, W5 179 CJ76
Upminster RM14 151 FR58
Trentbridge Cl, Ilf. IG6 125 ET51
Trent Cl, Shenley WD7
off Edgbaston Dr 84 CL32
Trent C of E Prim Sch, Cockfos. EN4 off Church Way 102 DF42
Trent Gdns, N14 103 DH44
Trentham Ct, W3
off Victoria Rd 160 CR71
Trentham Cres, Wok. GU22 249 BA121
Trentham Dr, Orp. BR5 228 EU98
Trentham Rd, Red. RH1 288 DF136
Trentham St, SW18 202 DA88
Trent Park Country Pk, Barn. EN4 102 DG40
Trent Rd, SW2 203 DM85
Buckhurst Hill IG9 124 EH46
Slough SL3 175 BB79
Trent Way, Hayes UB4 157 BS69
Worcester Park KT4 221 CW104
Trentwood Side, Enf. EN2 103 DM41
Treport St, SW18 202 DB87
Tresco Cl, Brom. BR1 206 EE93
Trescoe Gdns, Har. HA2 138 BY59
Romford RM5 127 FC50
Tresco Gdns, Ilf. IG3 148 EU61
Tresco Rd, SE15 184 DV84
Berkhamsted HP4 60 AT19
Tresham Cres, NW8 16 C4
Tresham Rd, Bark. IG11 167 ET66
Tresham Wk, E9 11 H2
Tresilian Av, N21 103 DM43
Tresilian Sq, Hem.H. HP2 62 BM15
Tresillian Way, Wok. GU21 248 AU116
Tressell Cl, N1 9 H7
Tressillian Cres, SE4 46 A10
Tressillian Rd, SE4 185 DZ84
Tresta Wk, Wok. GU21 248 AU115
Trestis Cl, Hayes UB4
off Jollys La 158 BY71
Treston Ct, Stai. TW18 195 BF92
Treswell Rd, Dag. RM9 168 EY67
Tretawn Gdns, NW7 118 CS49
Tretawn Pk, NW7 118 CS49
Trevalga Way, Hem.H. HP2 62 BL16
Trevanion Rd, W14 26 F10
Treve Av, Har. HA1 138 CC59
Trevellance Way, Wat. WD25 82 BW33
Trevelyan Av, E12 147 EM63
Trevelyan Cl, Dart. DA1 190 FM84
Trevelyan Ct, Wind. SL4 173 AP82
Trevelyan Cres, Har. HA3 139 CK59
Trevelyan Gdns, NW10 4 A9
Trevelyan Ho, E2
off Morpeth St 21 J3
Trevelyan Mid Sch, Wind. SL4 off Wood Cl 173 AQ84
Trevelyan Rd, E15 13 K1
SW17 202 DE92
Trevelyan Way, Berk. HP4 60 AV17
Trevera Ct, Wal.Cr. EN8
off Eleanor Rd 89 DY33
Trevereux Hill, Oxt. RH8 277 EM131
Treveris St, SE1 30 G3
Treverton St, W10 14 D5
Treves Cl, N21 103 DM43
Treville St, SW15 201 CV87
Treviso Rd, SE23
off Farren Rd 205 DY89
Trevithick Cl, Felt. TW14 197 BT88
Trevithick Dr, Dart. DA1 190 FM84
Trevithick Ho, SE16 32 F9
Trevithick St, SE8 46 A2
Trevone Gdns, Pnr. HA5 138 BY58
Trevor Cl, Brom. BR2 226 EF101
East Barnet EN4 102 DD43
Harrow HA3 off Kenton La 117 CF52
Isleworth TW7 199 CF85
Northolt UB5 158 BW68
Trevor Cres, Ruis. HA4 137 BT63
Trevor Gdns, Edg. HA8 118 CR53
Northolt UB5 158 BW68
Ruislip HA4
off Clyfford Rd 137 BU63
Trevor Pl, SW7 28 D5
Trevor Rd, SW19 201 CY94
Edgware HA8 118 CR53
Hayes UB3 177 BS75
Woodford Green IG8 124 EG52
Trevor Sq, SW7 28 E5
Trevor St, SW7 28 D5
Trevor Wk, SW7 off Trevor Sq 28 E5
Trevose Av, W.Byf. KT14 233 BF114
Trevose Rd, E17 123 ED53
Trevose Way, Wat. WD19 116 BW48
Trewarden Av, Iver SL0 155 BD68
Trewenna Dr, Chess. KT9 237 CK106
Potters Bar EN6 86 DD32
Trewince Rd, SW20 221 CW95
Trewint St, SW18 202 DC89
Trewsbury Ho, SE2
off Hartslock Dr 188 EX75
Trewsbury Rd, SE26 205 DX92
Triandra Way, Hayes UB4 158 BX71
Triangle, The, EC1 19 H4
N13 off Green Las 121 DM49
Barking IG11
off Tanner St 167 EQ65
Kingston upon Thames KT1
off Kenley Rd 220 CQ96
Woking GU21 248 AW118
Triangle Business Cen, NW10
off Enterprise Way 161 CU69
Triangle Ct, E16 24 E6
Triangle Est, SE11 42 E1
Triangle Ms, West Dr. UB7 156 BM74
Triangle Pas, Barn. EN4
off Station App 102 DC42
Triangle Pl, SW4 183 DK84
Triangle Rd, E8 10 E8
Triangle Wks, N9
off Centre Way 122 DW47
Tricorn Ho, SE28
off Miles Dr 167 ER74
Trident Cen, Wat. WD24 98 BW39
Trident Gdns, Nthlt. UB5
off Jetstar Way 158 BX69
Trident Ho, SE28
off Merbury Rd 167 ER74
Trident Ind Est, Colnbr. SL3 175 BE83
Hoddesdon EN11 71 EC17
Trident Rd, Wat. WD25 81 BT34
Trident St, SE16 33 K8
Trident Way, Sthl. UB2 177 BV76
Trigg's Cl, Wok. GU22 248 AX119
Trigg's La, Wok. GU21, GU22 248 AW118
Trig La, EC4 19 J10
Trigo Ct, Epsom KT19
off Blakeney Cl 238 CR111
Trigon Rd, SW8 42 D4
Trilby Rd, SE23 205 DX89
Trimmer Wk, Brent. TW8 180 CL79
Trim St, SE14 45 N3
Trinder Gdns, N19 143 DL60
Trinder Ms, Tedd. TW11 199 CG92
Trinder Rd, N19 143 DL60
Barnet EN5 101 CW43
Trindles Rd, S.Nutfld RH1 289 DM136
Tring Av, W5 160 CM74
Southall UB1 158 BZ72
Wembley HA9 160 CN65
Tring Cl, Ilf. IG2 147 EQ58
Romford RM3 128 FM49
Tring Gdns, Rom. RM3 128 FL49
Tring Grn, Rom. RM3 128 FM49
Tringham Cl, Ott. KT16 233 BC107
Tring Wk, Rom. RM3 128 FL49
Trinidad Gdns, Dag. RM10 169 FD66
Trinidad St, E14
off Limehouse Causeway 21 P10
Trinity Av, N2 142 DD55
Enfield EN1 104 DT44
Trinity Buoy Wf, E14 35 L1
Trinity Business Pk, E4
off Trinity Way 123 DZ51
Trinity Cath High Sch, Lwr Sch, Wdf.Grn. IG8
off Sydney Rd 124 EG49
Upr Sch, Wdf.Grn. IG8
off Mornington Rd 124 EG49
Trinity Ch Pas, SW13 181 CV79
Trinity Ch Rd, SW13 181 CV79
Trinity Ch Sq, SE1 31 K6
Trinity Chyd, Guil. GU1
off High St 280 AX135
Trinity Cl, E8 10 B4
E11 146 EE61
NW3 6 A1
SE13 185 ED84
SW4 off The Pavement 183 DJ84
Bromley BR2 226 EL102
Hounslow TW4 178 BY84
Northwood HA6 115 BS51
South Croydon CR2 242 DS109
Stanwell TW19 196 BJ86
Trinity Coll of Music, SE10 46 F2
Trinity Cotts, Rich. TW9
off Trinity Rd 180 CM83
Trinity Ct, N1 9 N8
N18 122 DT51
NW2 4 A1
SE7 36 E9
Rick. WD3 114 BL47
Trinity Cres, SW17 202 DF89
Trinity Dr, Uxb. UB8 157 BQ72
Trinity Gdns, E16 23 M6
SW9 183 DM84
Dartford DA1
off Summerhill Rd 210 FK86
Trinity Gate, Guil. GU1
off Epsom Rd 280 AY135
Trinity Gro, SE10 46 E6
Hertford SG14 54 DQ07
Trinity Hall Cl, Wat. WD24 98 BW41
Trinity Ho, EC3 19 P10
Trinity Ho, SE1 off Bath Ter 31 K6
Trinity La, Wal.Cr. EN8 89 DY32
Trinity Ms, SE20 224 DV95
W10 14 D8
Hemel Hempstead HP2 63 BR21
Trinity Path, SE26 204 DW90
Trinity Pl, EC3 32 A1
Bexleyheath DA6 188 EZ84
Windsor SL4 173 AQ82
Trinity Ri, SW2 203 DN88
Trinity Rd, N2 142 DD55
N22 121 DL53
SW17 202 DF89
SW18 202 DD85
SW19 202 DA93
Gravesend DA12 213 GJ87
Hertford Heath SG13 54 DW12
Ilford IG6 147 EQ55
Richmond TW9 180 CM83
Southall UB1 158 BY74
Ware SG12 55 DY05
Trinity St. Mary's C of E Prim Sch, SW12
off Balham Pk Rd 202 DG88
Trinity St. Stephen C of E First Sch, Wind. SL4
off Vansittart Rd 173 AP81
Trinity Sch, SE13 206 EF85
Belvedere DA17 off Erith Rd 189 FC77
Dagenham RM10
off Heathway 148 FA63
Trinity Sch of John Whitgift, Croy. CR0 off Shirley Rd 224 DW103
Trinity Sq, EC3 31 P1
Trinity St, E16 23 N7
SE1 31 K5
Trinity St, Enfield EN2 104 DQ40
Trinity Wk, NW3 5 P5
Hemel Hempstead HP2 63 BR21
Hertford Heath SG13 54 DW12
Trinity Way, E4 123 DZ51
W3 160 CS73
Trio Pl, SE1 31 K5
Tripps Hill, Ch.St.G. HP8 112 AU48
Tripps Hill Cl, Ch.St.G. HP8 112 AU48
Tripton Rd, Harl. CM18 73 ES16
Tristan Ct, Wem. HA0
off King George Cres 139 CK64
Tristan Sq, SE3 186 EE83
Tristram Cl, E17 145 ED55
Tristram Dr, N9 122 DU48
Tristram Rd, Brom. BR1 206 EF91
Triton Sq, NW1 17 L4
Triton Way, Hem.H. HP2 62 BM18
Tritton Av, Croy. CR0 241 DL105
Tritton Rd, SE21 204 DR90
Trittons, Tad. KT20 255 CW121
Triumph Cl, Chaff.Hun. RM16 191 FW77
Harlington UB3 177 BQ80
Triumph Ho, Bark. IG11 168 EU69
Triumph Rd, E6 25 K8
Triumph Trd Est, N17 122 DU51
Trivett Cl, Green. DA9 211 FU85
Trocette Mansion, SE1
off Bermondsey St 31 P6
Trodd's La, Guil. GU1 281 BF135
Trojan Way, Croy. CR0 223 DM104
Trolling Down Hill, Dart. DA2 210 FP89
Troon Cl, SE16 32 F10
SE28 off Fairway Dr 168 EX72
Troon St, E1 21 L8
Troopers Dr, Rom. RM3 128 FK49
Trosley Av, Grav. DA11 213 GH89
Trosley Rd, Belv. DA17 188 FA79
Trossachs Rd, SE22 204 DS85
Trothy Rd, SE1 32 D8
Trotsworth Av, Vir.W. GU25 214 AX98
Trotsworth Ct, Vir.W. GU25 214 AX98
Trotters Bottom, Barn. EN5 101 CU37
Trotters Gap, Stans.Abb. SG12 55 ED11
Trotters La, Mimbr. GU24 232 AV112
Trotters Rd, Harl. CM18 74 EU17
Trotter Way, Epsom KT19 238 CN112
Trott Rd, N10 120 DF52
Trotts La, West. TN16 277 EQ127
Trott St, SW11 40 C7
Trotwood, Chig. IG7 125 ER51
Trotwood Cl, Shenf. CM15
off Middleton Rd 130 FY46
Troughton Rd, SE7 36 A10
Troutbeck Cl, Slou. SL2 154 AU73
Troutbeck Rd, SE14 45 L6
Trout La, West Dr. UB7 156 BJ73
Trout Ri, Loud. WD3 96 BH41
Trout Rd, West Dr. UB7 156 BK74
Troutstream Way, Loud. WD3 96 BK42
Trouvere Pk, Hem.H. HP1 62 BH18
Trouville Rd, SW4 203 DJ86
Trowbridge Est, E9 11 N4
Trowbridge Rd, E9 11 P5
Romford RM3 128 FK51
Trowers Way, Red. RH1 273 DH131
Trowley Ri, Abb.L. WD5 81 BS31
Trowlock Av, Tedd. TW11 199 CJ93
Trowlock Island, Tedd. TW11 199 CK92
Trowlock Way, Tedd. TW11 199 CK93
Troy Cl, Tad. KT20 255 CV120
Troy Ct, SE18 37 P9
W8 27 J6
Troy Rd, SE19 204 DR93
Troy Town, SE15 44 D10
Trubshaw Rd, Sthl. UB2
off Havelock Rd 178 CB76
Trueman Cl, Edg. HA8 118 CQ52
Trueman Rd, Ken. CR8 258 DR120
Truesdale Dr, Hare. UB9 136 BJ56
Truesdale Rd, E6 25 K9
Trulock Ct, N17 122 DU52
Trulock Rd, N17 122 DU52
Truman's Rd, N16 9 P2
Truman Wk, E3 22 D4
Trumpers Way, W7 179 CE76
Trumper Way, Slou. SL1 153 AM74
Uxbridge UB8 156 BJ67
Trumpets Hill Rd, Reig. RH2 287 CU135
Trumpington Dr, St.Alb. AL1 65 CD23
Trumpington Rd, E7 146 EF63
Trumps Grn Av, Vir.W. GU25 214 AX100
Trumps Grn Cl, Vir.W. GU25
off Trumpsgreen Rd 214 AY99
Trumps Grn Inf Sch, Vir.W. GU25 off Crown Rd 214 AX100
Trumpsgreen Rd, Vir.W. GU25 214 AX100
Trumps Mill La, Vir.W. GU25 215 AZ100
Trump St, EC2 19 K9
Trundlers Way, Bushey Hth WD23 117 CE46
Trundle St, SE1 31 J4
Trundleys Rd, SE8 33 K10
Trundleys Ter, SE8 33 K9
Trunks All, Swan. BR8 229 FB96
Trunley Heath Rd, Bramley GU5 280 AW144
Truro Gdns, Ilf. IG1 146 EL59
Truro Rd, E17 145 DZ56
N22 121 DL52
Gravesend DA12 213 GK90
Truro St, NW5 6 G5
Truro Wk, Rom. RM3 128 FJ51
Truro Way, Hayes UB4 157 BS69
Truslove Rd, SE27 203 DN92
Trussley Rd, W6 26 A7
Trustees Cl, Denh. UB9
off Patrons Way West 135 BF58
Trustees Way, Denh. UB9 135 BF57
Trustons Gdns, Horn. RM11 149 FG59
Trust Rd, Wal.Cr. EN8 89 DY34
Trust Wk, SE21
off Peabody Hill 203 DP88
Tryfan Cl, Ilf. IG4 146 EK57
Tryon Cres, E9 10 G8
Tryon St, SW3 28 E10
Trys Hill, Lyne KT16 215 AZ103
Trystings Cl, Clay. KT10 237 CG107
Tuam Rd, SE18 187 ER79
Tubbenden Cl, Orp. BR6 227 ES103
Tubbenden Dr, Orp. BR6 245 ER105
Tubbenden Inf Sch, Orp. BR6 off Sandy Bury 227 ER104
Tubbenden Jun Sch, Orp. BR6 off Sandy Bury 227 ER104
Tubbenden La, Orp. BR6 227 ES104
Tubbenden La S, Orp. BR6 245 ER106
Tubbs Cft, Welw.G.C. AL7 52 DB10
Tubbs Rd, NW10 161 CT68
Tubs Hill Par, Sev. TN13 278 FG124
Tubwell Rd, Stoke P. SL2 154 AV67
Tucker Rd, Ott. KT16 233 BD107
Tucker St, Wat. WD18 98 BW43
Tuckey Gro, Ripley GU23 249 BF124
Tuck Rd, Rain. RM13 169 FG65
Tudor Av, Chsht EN7 88 DU31
Hampton TW12 198 CA93
Romford RM2 149 FG55
Watford WD24 98 BX38
Worcester Park KT4 221 CV104
Tudor Circle, Gdmg. GU7 280 AS144
Tudor Cl, N6 143 DJ59
NW3 6 C3
NW7 119 CU51
NW9 140 CQ61
SW2 203 DM86
Ashford TW15 196 BL91
Banstead SM7 255 CY115
Bookham KT23 252 CA124
Cheshunt EN7 88 DV31
Chessington KT9 238 CL106
Chigwell IG7 125 EN49
Chislehurst BR7 227 EM95
Cobham KT11 236 BZ113
Coulsdon CR5 257 DN118
Dartford DA1 209 FH86
Epsom KT17 239 CT110
Hatfield AL10 66 CS21
Hunsdon SG12 56 EK07
Northfleet DA11 212 GE88
Pinner HA5 137 BU57
Shenfield CM15 131 FZ44
Smallfield RH6 291 DP148
South Croydon CR2 258 DV115
Sutton SM3 239 CX106
Wallington SM6 241 DJ108
Woking GU22 249 BA117
Woodford Green IG8 124 EH50
Tudor Ct, E17 145 DY59
Borehamwood WD6 100 CL40
Crockenhill BR8 229 FC101
Egham TW20
off The Chantries 195 BA92
Feltham TW13 198 BW91
Tudor Ct N, Wem. HA9 140 CN64
Tudor Ct Prim Sch, Chaff.Hun. RM16 off Bark Burr Rd 192 FZ75
Tudor Ct S, Wem. HA9 140 CN64
Tudor Cres, Enf. EN2 103 DP39
Ilford IG6 125 EP51
Tudor Dr, Kings.T. KT2 200 CL92
Morden SM4 221 CX100
Romford RM2 149 FG56
Walton-on-Thames KT12 218 BX102
Watford WD24 98 BX38
Wooburn Green HP10 132 AD55
Tudor Enterprise Pk, Har. HA3
off Tudor Rd 139 CD55
Tudor Est, NW10 160 CP68
Tudor Gdns, NW9 140 CQ61
SW13 off Treen Av 180 CS83
W3 160 CN72
Harrow HA3 off Tudor Rd 117 CD54
Romford RM2 149 FG56
Slough SL1 152 AJ72
Twickenham TW1 199 CF88
Upminster RM14 150 FQ61
West Wickham BR4 225 EC104
Tudor Gro, E9 10 G7
N20 120 DE48
Tudor Ho, Surb. KT6
off Lenelby Rd 220 CN102
Tudor La, Old Wind. SL4 194 AW87
Tudor Manor Gdns, Wat. WD25 82 BX32
Tudor Ms, Rom. RM1
off Eastern Rd 149 FF57
Tudor Par, Rick. WD3
off Berry La 114 BG45
Tudor Pk, Amer. HP6 77 AR37
Tudor Pl, Mitch. CR4 202 DE94
Tudor Prim Sch, N3
off Queens Rd 120 DC53
Hemel Hempstead HP3
off Redwood Dr 62 BL22
Southall UB1 off Tudor Rd 158 BY73
Tudor Ri, Brox. EN10 71 DY21
Tudor Rd, E4 123 EB51
E6 166 EJ67
E9 10 F8
N9 122 DV45
SE19 204 DT94
SE25 224 DV99
Ashford TW15 197 BR93
Barking IG11 167 ET67
Barnet EN5 102 DA41
Beckenham BR3 225 EB97
Godalming GU7 280 AS144
Hampton TW12 198 CA94
Harrow HA3 117 CD54
Hayes UB3 157 BR72
Hazlemere HP15 110 AC45
Hounslow TW3 179 CD84
Kingston upon Thames KT2 200 CN94
Pinner HA5 116 BW54
St. Albans AL3 65 CE16
Southall UB1 158 BY73
Wheathampstead AL4 50 CL07
Tudors, The, Reig. RH2 272 DC131
Tudor Sq, Hayes UB3 157 BR71
Tudor St, EC4 18 F10
Tudor Wk, Bex. DA5 208 EY86
Leatherhead KT22 253 CF120
Watford WD24 98 BX37
Weybridge KT13
off West Palace Gdns 217 BP104
Tudor Wks, Hayes UB4
off Beaconsfield Rd 158 BW74
Tudor Way, N14 121 DK46
W3 180 CN75
Hertford SG14 53 DN09
Petts Wood BR5 227 ER100
Rickmansworth WD3 114 BG46
Uxbridge UB10 156 BN65
Waltham Abbey EN9 89 ED33
Windsor SL4 173 AL81
Tudor Well Cl, Stan. HA7 117 CH50
Tudway Rd, SE3 186 EH83
Tuffnell Ct, Chsht EN8
off Coopers Wk 89 DX28
Tufnail Rd, Dart. DA1 210 FM86
TUFNELL PARK, N7 143 DK63
Tufnell Park 143 DJ63
Tufnell Pk Prim Sch, N7 7 P1
Tufnell Pk Rd, N7 143 DJ63
N19 143 DJ63
Tufter Rd, Chig. IG7 125 ET50
Tufton Gdns, W.Mol. KT8 218 CB96
Tufton Rd, E4 123 EA49

Tufton St, SW1 29 P6
Tugboat St, SE28 187 ES75
Tugela Rd, Croy. CR0 224 DR100
Tugela St, SE6 205 DZ89
Tugmutton Cl, Orp. BR6 245 EP105
Tugswood Cl, Couls. CR5 257 DK121
Tuilerie St, E2 10 C10
Tuition Cen, The, NW4
off Lodge Rd 141 CW56
Tuke Sch, SE15 44 E7
Tulip Cl, E6 25 J7
Croydon CR0 225 DX102
Hampton TW12
off Partridge Rd 198 BZ93
Pilgrim's Hatch CM15
off Poppy Cl 130 FV43
Romford RM3 128 FJ51
Southall UB2 *off Chevy Rd* 178 CC75
Tulip Ct, Pnr. HA5 138 BW55
Tulip Gdns, Ilf. IG1 167 EP65
Tulip Tree Ct, Sutt. SM2
off The Crescent 240 DA111
Tulip Way, West Dr. UB7 176 BK77
Tull St, Mitch. CR4 222 DF101
Tulse Cl, Beck. BR3 225 EC97
TULSE HILL, SE21 204 DQ88
Tulse Hill 203 DP89
Tulse Hill, SW2 203 DP88
Tulse Hill, SW2 203 DN86
Tulse Hill Est, SW2 203 DN86
Tulsemere Rd, SE27 204 DQ89
Tulyar Cl, Tad. KT20 255 CV120
Tumber St, Headley KT18 270 CQ125
Tumbler Rd, Harl. CM18 74 EU17
Tumblewood Rd, Bans. SM7 255 CY116
Tumbling Bay, Walt. KT12 217 BU100
Tummons Gdns, SE25 224 DS96
Tump Ho, SE28 167 ES74
Tuncombe Rd, N18 122 DS49
Tunfield Rd, Hodd. EN11 55 EB14
Tunis Rd, W12 161 CV74
Tunley Grn, E14
off Burdett Rd 21 P7
Tunley Rd, NW10 160 CS67
SW17 202 DG88
Tunmarsh La, E13 24 B2
Tunmers End, Chal.St.P. SL9 112 AW53
Tunnan Leys, E6 25 M8
Tunnel Av, SE10 35 H4
Tunnel Av Trd Est, SE10 35 H5
Tunnel Gdns, N11 121 DJ52
Tunnel Rd, SE16 32 G4
Reigate RH2 *off Church St* 272 DA134
Tunnel Wd Cl, Wat. WD17 97 BT37
Tunnel Wd Rd, Wat. WD17 97 BT37
Tunnmeade, Harl. CM20 58 EU14
Tunsgate, Guil. GU1 280 AX136
Tunsgate Sq, Guil. GU1
off High St 280 AX136
Tuns La, Slou. SL1 173 AQ76
Tunstall Av, Ilf. IG6 126 EU51
Tunstall Cl, Orp. BR6 245 ES105
Tunstall Rd, SW9 183 DM84
Croydon CR0 224 DS102
Tunstall Wk, Brent. TW8 180 CL79
Tunstock Way, Belv. DA17 188 EY76
Tunworth Cl, NW9 140 CQ58
Tunworth Cres, SW15 201 CT86
Tun Yd, SW8 41 K10
Tupelo Rd, E10 145 EB61
Tuppy St, SE28 187 EQ76
Tupwood Ct, Cat. CR3 274 DU125
Tupwood La, Cat. CR3 274 DU125
Tupwood Scrubbs Rd, Cat.
CR3 274 DU128
Turenne Cl, SW18 182 DC84
Turfhouse La, Chobham
GU24 232 AS109
Turin Rd, N9 122 DW45
Turin St, E2 20 C3
Turkey Oak Cl, SE19 224 DS95
Turkey Street 104 DW37
Turkey St, Enf. EN1, EN3 104 DV37
Turks Cl, Uxb. UB8 156 BN69
Turks Head Yd, Eton SL4
off High St 173 AR80
Turk's Head Yd, EC1 18 G6
Turks Row, SW3 28 F10
Turle Rd, N4 143 DM60
SW16 223 DL96
Turlewray Cl, N4 143 DM60
Turley Cl, E15 13 K9
Turmore Dale, Welw.G.C. AL8 51 CW10
Turnagain La, EC4 18 G8
Dartford DA2 209 FG90
Turnage Rd, Dag. RM8 148 EY60
Turnberry Cl, NW4 119 CX54
SE16 44 F1
Turnberry Ct, Wat. WD19 116 BW48
Turnberry Dr, Brick.Wd AL2 82 BY30
Turnberry Quay, E14 34 D6
Turnberry Way, Orp. BR6 227 ER102
Turnbull Cl, Green. DA9 211 FS87
Turnbury Cl, SE28 168 EX72
Turnchapel Ms, SW4
off Cedars Rd 183 DH83
Turner Av, N15 144 DS56
Bigg. H. TN16 244 EJ112
Mitcham CR4 222 DF95
Twickenham TW2 198 CC90
Turner Cl, NW11 142 DB58
SW9 43 H6
Guildford GU4 265 AZ131
Hayes UB4 157 BQ68
Wembley HA0 139 CK64
Turner Ct, N15
off St. Ann's Rd 144 DR57
Dartford DA1 210 FJ85
Turner Cres, Croy. CR0 224 DQ100
Turner Dr, NW11 142 DB58
Turner Ho, E14 *off Cassilis Rd* 34 B5
Turner Ms, Sutt. SM2 240 DB108
Turner Pl, SW11 202 DE85
Turner Rd, E17 145 EC55
Bean DA2 211 FV90
Bushey WD23 98 CC42
Edgware HA8 140 CM55
Hornchurch RM12 149 FF61
New Malden KT3 220 CR101
Slough SL3 174 AW75
Turners Cl, N20 120 DF48
Staines-upon-Thames TW18 196 BH92
Turners Ct, Abridge RM4 108 EV41
Turners Gdns, Sev. TN13 279 FJ128
Turners Hill, Chsht EN8 89 DX30
Hemel Hempstead HP2 62 BL21
Turners La, Hersham KT12 235 BV107
Turners Meadow Way, Beck.
BR3 225 DZ95
Turners Rd, E3 21 N7
Turner St, E1 20 E7
E16 23 L9
Turners Wk, Chesh. HP5 76 AQ30
Turners Way, Croy. CR0 223 DN103
Turners Wd, NW11 142 DC60
Turners Wd Dr, Ch.St.G. HP8 112 AX48
Turneville Rd, W14 38 G2
Turney Prim & Sec Spec Sch,
SE21 *off Turney Rd* 204 DQ87
Turney Rd, SE21 204 DR87
Turneys Orchard, Chorl. WD3 95 BD43
TURNFORD, Brox. EN10 89 DZ26
Turnford, Brox. EN10 89 DY25
Turnford Sch, Chsht EN8
off Mill La 89 DY28
Turnford Vil, Turnf. EN10 89 DZ26
Turnham Cl, Guil. GU2 280 AW138
Turnham Green 180 CS77
Turnham Grn Ter, W4 180 CS77
Turnham Grn Ter Ms, W4 180 CS77
Turnham Prim Sch, SE4
off Turnham Rd 185 DY84
Turnham Rd, SE4 205 DY85
Turnmill St, EC1 18 F5
Turnoak Av, Wok. GU22 248 AY120
Turnoak La, Wok. GU22 248 AY120
Turnoak Pk, Wind. SL4 173 AL84
Turnors, Harl. CM20 73 EQ15
Turnpike Cl, SE8 45 P4
Turnpike Dr, Orp. BR6 246 EW109
Turnpike Grn, Hem.H. HP2 62 BL16
Turnpike Ho, EC1 19 H3
Turnpike Lane 143 DN55
Turnpike Lane 143 DP55
Turnpike La, N8 143 DM56
Sutton SM1 240 DC106
Uxbridge UB10 156 BL69
West Tilbury RM18 193 GK78
Turnpike Link, Croy. CR0 224 DS103
Turnpike Ms, N8 143 DN56
Turnpike Way, Islw. TW7 179 CG81
Turnpin La, SE10 46 F3
Turnstone Cl, E13 23 N3
NW9 *off Kestrel Cl* 118 CS54
Ickenham UB10 137 BP64
South Croydon CR2 243 DY110
Turnstones, The, Grav. DA12 213 GK89
Watford WD25 98 BY36
Turp Av, Grays RM16 192 GC75
Turpentine La, SW1 29 K10
Turpin Av, Rom. RM5 126 FA52
Turpin Cl, Enf. EN3 105 EA37
Turpington Cl, Brom. BR2 226 EL100
Turpington La, Brom. BR2 226 EL101
Turpin Ho, SW11 41 J6
Turpin La, Erith DA8 189 FG80
Turpin Rd, Felt. TW14 197 BT86
off Staines Rd
Turpins Cl, Hert. SG14 53 DM09
Turpins La, Wdf.Grn. IG8 125 EM50
Turpin Way, N19 143 DK61
Wallington SM6 241 DH108
Turquand St, SE17 31 K9
Turret Gro, SW4 41 L10
Turton Rd, Wem. HA0 140 CL64
Turton Way, Slou. SL1 173 AR76
Turville Ct, Bkhm KT23
off Proctor Gdns 268 CB125
Turville St, E2 20 A4
Tuscan Ho, E2 21 H2
Tuscan Rd, SE18 187 ER78
Tuscany Ho, E17
off Sherwood Cl 123 DZ54
Ilf. IG3 148 EU58
Tuskar St, SE10 47 J1
Tussauds Cl, Crox.Grn WD3 96 BN43
Tustin Est, SE15 44 G3
Tuttlebee La, Buck.H. IG9 124 EG47
Tuxford Cl, Borwd. WD6 100 CL38
Twankhams All, Epp. CM16
off Hemnall St 92 EU30
Tweed Cl, Berk. HP4 60 AV18
Tweeddale Gro, Uxb. UB10 137 BQ62
Tweeddale Prim Sch, Cars.
SM5 *off Tweeddale Rd* 222 DD101
Tweeddale Rd, Cars. SM5 222 DD102
Tweed Glen, Rom. RM1 127 FD52
Tweed Grn, Rom. RM1 127 FD52
Tweed Ho, E14 22 E5
Tweed La, Strood Grn RH3 286 CP139
Tweedmouth Rd, E13 24 A1
Tweed Rd, Slou. SL3 175 BA79
Tweed Way, Rom. RM1 127 FD52
Tweedy Cl, Enf. EN1 104 DT43
Tweedy Rd, Brom. BR1 226 EF95
Tweenways, Chesh. HP5 76 AR30
Tweezer's All, WC2 18 E10
Twelve Acre Cl, Bkhm KT23 252 BZ124
Twelve Acre Ho, E12
off Grantham Rd 147 EN62
Twelve Acres, Welw.G.C. AL7 51 CY11
Twelvetrees Business Pk,
E3 22 G5
Twelvetrees Cres, E3 22 E4
Twentyman Cl, Wdf.Grn. IG8 124 EG50
TWICKENHAM, TW1 & TW2 199 CG89
Twickenham 199 CF87
Twickenham Br, Rich. TW9 199 CJ85
Twickenham TW1 199 CJ85
Twickenham Cl, Croy. CR0 223 DM104
Twickenham Gdns, Grnf. UB6 139 CG64
Harrow HA3 117 CE52
Twickenham Prep Sch, Hmptn.
TW12 *off High St* 218 CC95
Twickenham Rd, E11 145 ED61
Feltham TW13 198 BZ90
Isleworth TW7 179 CG83
Richmond TW9 179 CJ84
Teddington TW11 199 CG92
Twickenham Trd Est, Twick.
TW1 199 CF86
Twig Folly Cl, E2 21 K1
Twigg Cl, Erith DA8 189 FE80
Twilley St, SW18 202 DB87
Twinches La, Slou. SL1 153 AP74
Twine Cl, Bark. IG11
off Thames Rd 168 EV69
Twine Ct, E1 20 G10
Twineham Grn, N12 120 DA49
Twine Ter, E3 *off Ropery St* 21 N5
Twining Av, Twick. TW2 198 CC90
Twinn Rd, NW7 119 CY51
Twinoaks, Cob. KT11 236 CA113
Twin Tumps Way, SE28 168 EU73
Twisden Rd, NW5 143 DH63
Twisleton Ct, Dart. DA1
off Priory Hill 210 FK86
Twitchells La, Jordans HP9 112 AT51
TWITTON, Sev. TN14 263 FF116
Twitten Gro, Brom. BR1 227 EM97
Twitton La, Otford TN14 263 FD115
Twitton Meadows, Otford TN14 263 FE116
Two Acres, Welw.G.C. AL7 51 CZ11
Two Beeches, Hem.H. HP2 62 BM15
Two Dells La, Chesh. HP5 60 AT24
Two Mile Dr, Slou. SL1 153 AK74
Two River's Ct, Felt. TW14 197 BR86
Two Rivers Retail Pk, Stai.
TW18 195 BE91
Two Waters Prim Sch, Hem.H.
HP3 *off High Ridge Cl* 80 BK25
Two Waters Rd, Hem.H. HP3 62 BJ22
Two Waters Way, Hem.H. HP3 62 BJ24
Twybridge Way, NW10 160 CQ66
Twycross Ms, SE10 35 K9
Twyford Abbey Rd, NW10 160 CM69
Twyford Av, N2 142 DF55
W3 160 CN73
Twyford C of E High Sch, W3
off Twyford Cres 160 CP74
Twyford Cres, W3 160 CN74
Twyford Ho, N15 144 DS58
Twyford Pl, WC2 18 C8
Twyford Rd, Cars. SM5 222 DD102
Harrow HA2 138 CB60
Ilford IG1 147 EQ64
St. Albans AL4 65 CJ16
Twyford St, N1 8 C8
Twyner Cl, Horl. RH6 291 DK147
Twynersh Av, Cher. KT16 215 BF100
Twysdens Ter, N.Mymms AL9
off Dellsome La 67 CW24
Tyas Rd, E16 23 L5
Tybenham Rd, SW19 222 DA97
Tyberry Rd, Enf. EN3 104 DV41
Tyburn La, Har. HA1 139 CE59
Tyburns, The, Hutt. CM13 131 GC47
Tyburn Way, W1 16 F10
Tycehurst Hill, Loug. IG10 107 EM42
Tychbourne Dr, Guil. GU4 265 BC131
Tydcombe Rd, Warl. CR6 258 DW119
TYE GREEN, Harl. CM18 73 ES17
Tye Grn Village, Harl. CM18 73 ES18
Tye La, Headley KT18 270 CR127
Orpington BR6 245 EQ106
Tadworth KT20 270 CS128
Tyers Est, SE1 31 N4
Tyers Gate, SE1 31 N4
Tyers St, SE11 30 C10
Tyers Ter, SE11 42 C1
Tyeshurst Cl, SE2 188 EY78
Tyfield Cl, Chsht EN8 88 DW30
Tykeswater La, Els. WD6 99 CJ39
Tylecroft Rd, SW16 223 DL96
Tyle Grn, Horn. RM11 150 FL56
Tylehost, Guil. GU2 264 AU130
Tylehurst Dr, Red. RH1 288 DF135
Tylehurst Gdns, Ilf. IG1 147 EQ64
Tyle Pl, Old Wind. SL4 194 AU85
Tyler Cl, E2 10 A10
Erith DA8 189 FB80
Tyler Gdns, Add. KT15 234 BJ105
Tyler Gro, Dart. DA1
off Spielman Rd 190 FM84
Tyler Rd, Sthl. UB2
off McNair Rd 178 CB76
TYLERS CAUSEWAY, Hert.
SG13 69 DK22
Tylers Causeway, Newgate St
SG13 69 DH23
Tylers Cl, Gdse. RH9 274 DV130
Kings Langley WD4 80 BL28
Loughton IG10 124 EL45
Tyler's Ct, W1 17 N9
Tylers Cres, Horn. RM12 150 FJ64
Tylersfield, Abb.L. WD5 81 BT31
Tylers Gate, Har. HA3 140 CL58
Tylers Grn First Sch, Penn
HP10 *off School Rd* 110 AD47
Tylers Grn Rd, Swan. BR8 229 FC100
Tylers Hill Rd, Chesh. HP5 78 AT30
Tylers Path, Cars. SM5
off Rochester Rd 240 DF105
Tylers Rd, Roydon CM19 72 EJ19
Tyler St, SE10 47 K1
Tylers Way, Wat. WD25 99 CD42
Tyler Wk, Slou. SL3
off Gilbert Way 175 AZ78
Tyler Way, Brwd. CM14 130 FV46
Tylney Av, SE19 204 DT92
Tylney Cl, Chig. IG7 125 ET49
Tylney Cft, Harl. CM19 73 EP17
Tylney Rd, E7 146 EJ63
Bromley BR1 226 EK96
Tylsworth Cl, Amer. HP6 77 AR38
Tymperley Ct, SW19
off Windlesham Gro 201 CY88
Tynan Cl, Felt. TW14 197 BU88
Tyndale Ct, E14 34 C10
Tyndale La, N1 8 G6
Tyndale Ms, Slou. SL1 173 AP75
Tyndale Ter, N1 8 G6
Tyndall Rd, E10 145 EC61
Welling DA16 187 ET83
Tyne Cl, Upmin. RM14 151 FR58
Tynedale, Lon.Col. AL2
off Thamesdale 84 CM27
Tynedale Cl, Dart. DA2 211 FR88
Tynedale Rd, Strood Grn RH3 286 CP138
Tyne Gdns, Aveley RM15 170 FQ73
Tyneham Cl, SW11 41 H10
Tyneham Rd, SW11 41 H9
Tynemouth Cl, E6 25 N9
Tynemouth Dr, Enf. EN1 104 DU38
Tynemouth Rd, N15 144 DT56
SE18 187 ET78
Mitcham CR4 202 DG94
Tynemouth St, SW6 39 N8
Tyne St, E1
off Old Castle St 20 B8
Tynley Gro, Jacobs Well GU4 264 AX128
Tynsdale Rd, NW10 160 CS66
Tynwald Ho, SE26
off Sydenham Hill Est 204 DU90
Type St, E2 21 J1
Typhoon Way, Wall. SM6 241 DL108
Typleden Cl, Hem.H. HP2 62 BK18
Tyrawley Rd, SW6 39 L6
Tyre La, NW9 140 CS56
Tyrell Cl, Har. HA1 139 CE63
Tyrell Ct, Cars. SM5 240 DF105
Tyrell Gdns, Wind. SL4 173 AM83
Tyrell Ri, Warley CM14 130 FW50
Tyrells Cl, Upmin. RM14 150 FN61
Tyrells Pl, Guil. GU1 281 AZ135
Tyrols Rd, SE23
off Wastdale Rd 205 DX88
Tyrone Rd, E6 25 K1
Tyron Way, Sid. DA14 207 ES91
Tyrrell Av, Well. DA16 208 EU85
Tyrrell Rd, SE22 184 DU84
Tyrrells Hall Cl, Grays RM17 192 GD79
Tyrrell Sq, Mitch. CR4 222 DE95
TYRRELL'S WOOD, Lthd. KT22 254 CM123
Tyrrel Way, NW9 141 CT59
Tyrwhitt Ct, Guil. GU2
off Henderson Av 264 AV130
Tyrwhitt Rd, SE4 185 EA83
Tysea Cl, Harl. CM18 73 ET18
Tysea Hill, Stap.Abb. RM4 127 FF45
Tysea Rd, Harl. CM18 73 ET18
Tysoe Av, Enf. EN3 105 DZ36
Tysoe St, EC1 18 E3
Tyson Rd, SE23 204 DW87
Tyssen Comm Prim Sch,
N16 *off Oldhill St* 144 DU60
Tyssen Pas, E8 10 A4
Tyssen Pl, S.Ock. RM15 171 FW69
Tyssen Rd, N16 144 DT62
Tyssen St, E8 10 B4
N1 9 P10
Tythebarn Cl, Guil. GU4
off Dairyman's Wk 265 BB129
Tytherton Rd, N19 143 DK62
TYTTENHANGER, St.Alb. AL4 65 CK23
Tyttenhanger Grn, Tytten. AL4 65 CK23

U

Uamvar St, E14 22 D6
Uckfield Gro, Mitch. CR4 222 DG95
Uckfield Rd, Enf. EN3 105 DX37
Udall Gdns, Rom. RM5 126 FA51
Udall St, SW1 29 M9
Udney Pk Rd, Tedd. TW11 199 CG92
Uffington Rd, NW10 161 CU67
SE27 203 DN91
Ufford Cl, Har. HA3 116 CB52
Ufford Rd, Har. HA3 116 CB52
Ufford St, SE1 30 F4
Ufton Gro, N1 9 M6
Ufton Rd, N1 9 M7
Uhura Sq, N16 144 DS62
Ujima Ct, N19 *off Hornsey Ri* 143 DL60
SW16 203 DL91
Ullathorne Rd, SW16 203 DJ91
Ulleswater Rd, N14 121 DL49
Ullin St, E14 22 E7
Ullswater Business Pk,
Couls. CR5 257 DL116
Ullswater Cl, SW15 200 CR91
Bromley BR1 206 EE93
Hayes UB4 157 BS68
Slough SL1
off Buttermere Av 152 AJ71
Ullswater Ct, Har. HA2 138 CA59
Ullswater Cres, SW15 200 CR91
Coulsdon CR5 257 DL116
Ullswater Rd, SE27 203 DP89
SW13 181 CU80
Hemel Hempstead HP3 63 BQ22
Ullswater Way, Horn. RM12 149 FG64
Ulstan Cl, Wold. CR3 259 EA123
Ulster Gdns, N13 122 DQ49
Ulster Pl, NW1 17 J5
Ulster Ter, NW1 17 J5
Ulundi Rd, SE3 47 K3
Ulva Rd, SW15 201 CX85
Ulverscroft Rd, SE22 204 DT85
Ulverston, Purf. RM19 190 FQ78
Ulverston Cl, St.Alb. AL1 65 CF20
Ulverstone Rd, SE27 203 DP89
Ulverston Rd, E17 123 ED54
Ulwin Av, Byfleet KT14 234 BL113
Ulysses Rd, NW6 5 H2
Umberstones, Vir.W. GU25 214 AX100
Umberston St, E1 20 E8
Umberville Way, Slou. SL2 153 AM70
Umbria St, SW15 201 CU86
Umbriel Pl, E13 23 P1
Umfreville Rd, N4 143 DP58
Underacres Cl, Hem.H. HP2 62 BN19
Undercliff Rd, SE13 46 B10
UNDERHILL, Barn. EN5 102 DA43
Underhill, Barn. EN5 102 DA43
Underhill Inf Sch, Barn. EN5
off Mays La 101 CY43
Underhill Jun Sch, Barn. EN5
off Mays La 101 CY43
Underhill Pk Rd, Reig. RH2 272 DA131
Underhill Pas, NW1 7 K8
Underhill Rd, SE22 204 DV86
Underhill St, NW1 7 K9
Underne Av, N14 121 DH47
UNDERRIVER, Sev. TN15 279 FN130
Underriver Ho Rd, Undrvr
TN15 279 FP130
Undershaft, EC3 19 N9
Undershaw Rd, Brom. BR1 206 EE90
Underwood, New Adgtn CR0 243 EC106
Underwood, The, SE9 207 EM89
Underwood Rd, E1 20 C5
E4 123 EB50
Caterham CR3 274 DS126
Woodford Green IG8 124 EK52
Underwood Row, N1 19 K2
Underwood St, N1 19 K2
Undine Rd, E14 34 D8
Undine St, SW17 202 DF92
Uneeda Dr, Grnf. UB6 159 CD67
Unicorn Pas, SE1
off Tooley St 31 P3
Unicorn Prim Sch,
Beck. BR3
off Creswell Dr 225 EB99
Unicorn Sch, Rich. TW9
off Kew Rd 180 CM81
Unicorn Wk, Green. DA9 211 FT85
Union Business Pk, Uxb.
UB8 156 BH66
Union Cl, E11 145 ED63
Union Cotts, E15 13 K6
Union Ct, EC2 19 N8
Richmond TW9 *off Eton St* 200 CL85
Union Dr, E1 21 M4
Union Grn, Hem.H. HP2
off Church St 62 BK19
Union Gro, SW8 41 N9
Union Jack Club, SE1 30 E4
Union La, Islw. TW7 179 CG81
Union Pk, SE10 47 L1
Uxbridge UB8 156 BJ72
Union Rd, N11 121 DK51
SW4 41 N8
SW8 41 N8
Bromley BR2 226 EK99
Croydon CR0 224 DQ101
Northolt UB5 158 CA68
Romford RM7 149 FD58
Wembley HA0 160 CL65
Union Sq, N1 9 J9
Union St, SE1 31 H3
Barnet EN5 101 CY42
Kingston upon Thames KT1 219 CK96
Union Wk, E2 19 P2
Union Wf, N1 19 J1
West Drayton UB7
off Bentinck Rd 156 BL74
Unity Cl, NW10 161 CU65
SE19 *off Crown Dale* 204 DQ92
New Addington CR0 243 EB109
Unity Ct, SE1 *off Mawbey Pl* 32 B10
Unity Rd, Enf. EN3 104 DW37
Unity Ter, Har. HA2
off Scott Cres 138 CB60
Unity Trd Est, Wdf.Grn.
IG8 146 EK55
Unity Way, SE18 36 E6
Unity Wf, SE1 32 B4
University Cl, NW7 119 CT52
Bushey WD23 98 CA42
University Coll Hosp, NW1 17 M4
Elizabeth Garrett Anderson
Wing, NW1 17 M4
Hosp for Tropical Diseases,
WC1 17 M5
Obstetric Hosp, WC1 17 M5
Private Wing, WC1 17 M5
University Coll London,
WC1 17 N4
Arthur Stanley Ho, W1 17 M6
Eastman Dental Inst, WC1 18 C3
Inst of Ophthalmology, EC1 19 L3
Ludwig Inst for Cancer
Research, W1 17 M6
Prankerd Ho, NW1 17 M4
Ramsay Hall, W1 17 L5
Slade Research Cen, WC1 17 P5
Inst of Neurology, WC1 18 B5
The Warburg Inst, WC1 17 P5
Windeyer Bldg, W1 17 M6
Wolfson Ho, NW1 17 M3
Wolfson Inst for Biomedical
Research, WC1 17 M5
University Coll Sch,
Jun Branch, NW3
off Holly Hill 142 DC63
Sen Sch, NW3 5 N2
University Gdns, Bex. DA5 208 EZ87
University Hosp Lewisham,
SE13 205 EB85
University of Cumbria,
Tower Hamlets E3 21 N5
University of E London - London Docklands Campus,
E16 25 M10
University of E London - Stratford Campus,
Arthur Edwards Bldg, E15 13 K4
Cen for Clinical Ed, E15 13 K5
Duncan Ho, E15 12 G8
Sch of Ed, E15 13 K4
Student Services Cen, E15 13 K4
Uni Ho, E15 13 K5
University of Greenwich - Avery Hill Campus, Mansion
Site, SE9 *off Bexley Rd* 207 EQ86
Southwood Site, SE9
off Avery Hill Rd 207 EQ87
University of Greenwich - Maritime Greenwich Campus,
Cooper Bldg, SE10 46 G2
Old Royal Naval Coll, SE10 46 G2
University of Hertfordshire,
Bayfordbury Fld Sta &
Observatory, Hert. SG13
off Lower Hatfield Rd 53 DN14
College La Campus, Hat.
AL10 *off College La* 67 CT20
de Havilland Campus, Hat.
AL10 *off Mosquito Way* 66 CR18
University of London,
Canterbury Hall, WC1 18 A3
Commonwealth Hall, WC1 18 A3
Hughes Parry Hall, WC1 18 A3
International Hall, WC1 18 B5
Senate Ho, WC1 17 P6
Stewart Ho, WC1 17 P6
Union, WC1 17 N5
University of Surrey,
Frances Harrison Ho,
Guil. GU2 *off Gill Av* 280 AS135
HPRU, Guil. GU2
off Gill Av 280 AS135
Post Grad Med Sch, Guil.
GU2 *off Gill Av* 280 AS135
Sch of Acting, Guil. GU2
off Gill Av 264 AU134
Stag Hill Campus, Guil. GU2
off Alresford Rd 264 AV134
Wealden Ho, Guil. GU2
off Gill Av 280 AS135
University of the Arts, W1 17 J9
University of West London,
Brentford Site TW8
off Boston Manor Rd 179 CJ78
Ealing Site W5
off St. Mary's Rd 159 CK74
Vestry Hall W5
off Ranelagh Rd 179 CK75
University of Westminster - Cavendish Campus, W1 17 L6
University of Westminster - Harrow Campus,
Har. HA1
off Watford Rd 139 CG59
University of Westminster - Marylebone Campus, NW1 16 G6
University of Westminster - Regent Campus, W1 17 K8
Great Portland St, W1 17 K6
Little Titchfield St, W1 17 L7
Riding Ho St, W1 17 L7

University Pl, Erith DA8
off Belmont Rd 189 FC80
University Rd, SW19 202 DD93
University St, WC1 17 M5
University Way, E16 37 M1
Dartford DA1 190 FP84
Unstead La, Bramley GU5 280 AW144
Unstead Wd, Peasm. GU3 280 AW142
Unwin Av, Felt. TW14 197 BR85
Unwin Cl, SE15 44 C3
Unwin Rd, SW7 28 B6
Isleworth TW7 179 CE83
Upbrook Ms, W2 15 P9
Upcerne Rd, SW10 39 P5
Upchurch Cl, SE20 204 DV94
Up Cor, Ch.St.G. HP8 112 AW47
Up Cor Cl, Ch.St.G. HP8 112 AV47
Upcroft, Wind. SL4 173 AP83
Upcroft Av, Edg. HA8 118 CQ50
Updale Cl, Pot.B. EN6 85 CY33
Updale Rd, Sid. DA14 207 ET91
Upfield, Croy. CR0 224 DV103
Horley RH6 290 DG149
Upfield Cl, Horl. RH6 290 DG150
Upfield Rd, W7 159 CF71
Upfolds Grn, Guil. GU4 265 BC130
Upgrove Manor Way, SW2
off Trinity Ri 203 DN87
Sch Uphall Prim Sch, Ilf. IG1
off Uphall Rd 147 EP64
Uphall Rd, Ilf. IG1 147 EP64
Upham Pk Rd, W4 180 CS77
Uphavering Ho, Horn. RM12 149 FH61
Uphill Dr, NW7 118 CS50
NW9 140 CQ57
Uphill Gro, NW7 118 CS49
Uphill Rd, NW7 118 CS49
Upland Av, Chesh. HP5 76 AP28
Upland Ct Rd, Rom. RM3 128 FM54
Upland Dr, Brook.Pk AL9 86 DB25
Epsom KT18 255 CW118
Upland Ms, SE22 204 DU85
Sch Upland Prim Sch, Bexh.
DA7 off Church Rd 188 EZ83
Upland Rd, E13 23 M4
SE22 204 DU85
Bexleyheath DA7 188 EZ83
Caterham CR3 259 EB120
Epping CM16 91 ET25
South Croydon CR2 242 DR106
Sutton SM2 240 DD108
Uplands, Ashtd. KT21 253 CK120
Beckenham BR3 225 EA96
Croxley Green WD3 96 BM44
Ware SG12 55 DZ05
Welwyn Garden City AL8 51 CW05
Uplands, The, Brick.Wd AL2 82 BY30
Gerrards Cross SL9 134 AY60
Loughton IG10 107 EM41
Ruislip HA4 137 BU60
Uplands Av, E17
off Blackhorse La 123 DX54
● Uplands Business Pk, E17 123 DX54
Uplands Cl, SE18 187 EP78
SW14 off Monroe Dr 200 CP85
Gerrards Cross SL9 134 AY60
Sevenoaks TN13 278 FF123
Uplands Dr, Oxshott KT22 237 CD113
Uplands End, Wdf.Grn. IG8 124 EL52
Uplands Pk Rd, Enf. EN2 103 DN41
Uplands Rd, N8 143 DM57
East Barnet EN4 120 DG46
Kenley CR8 258 DQ116
Orpington BR6 228 EV102
Romford RM6 148 EX55
Warley CM14 130 FY50
Woodford Green IG8 124 EL52
Uplands Way, N21 103 DN43
Sevenoaks TN13 278 FF123
Upland Way, Epsom KT18 255 CW118
UPMINSTER, RM14 150 FQ62
⇌ Upminster 150 FQ61
⊖ Upminster 150 FQ61
⊖ Upminster Bridge 150 FN61
Sch Upminster Inf Sch, Upmin.
RM14 off St. Mary's La 150 FQ62
Sch Upminster Jun Sch, Upmin.
RM14 off St. Mary's La 150 FQ62
Upminster Rd, Horn.
RM11, RM12 150 FM61
Upminster RM14 150 FM61
Upminster Rd N, Rain. RM13 170 FJ69
Upminster Rd S, Rain. RM13 169 FG70
★ Upminster Tithe Barn Mus of
Nostalgia, Upmin. RM14 150 FQ59
● Upminster Trd Pk, Upmin.
RM14 151 FX59
⊖ Upney 167 ET66
Upney Cl, Horn. RM12
off Tylers Cres 150 FK64
Upney La, Bark. IG11 167 ES65
Upnor Way, SE17 31 P10
Uppark Dr, Ilf. IG2 147 EQ58
Upper Abbey Rd, Belv. DA17 188 EZ77
Upper Addison Gdns, W14 26 E4
Upper Ashlyns Rd, Berk. HP4 60 AV20
Upper Bk St, E14 34 C3
Upper Bardsey Wk, N1
off Bardsey Wk 9 K4
Upper Barn, Hem.H. HP3 62 BM23
Upper Belgrave St, SW1 29 H6
Upper Belmont Rd, Chesh.
HP5 76 AP28
Upper Berenger Wk, SW10
off Blantyre St 40 A4
Upper Berkeley St, W1 16 E9
Upper Beulah Hill, SE19 224 DS95
Upper Blantyre Wk, SW10
off Blantyre St 40 A4
Upper Bourne End La, Hem.H.
HP1 79 BA25
Upper Bray Rd, Bray SL6 172 AC77
Upper Brentwood Rd, Rom.
RM2 150 FJ56
Upper Br Rd, Red. RH1 272 DE134
Upper Brighton Rd, Surb. KT6 219 CK100
Upper Brockley Rd, SE4 45 P8
Upper Brook St, W1 28 G1
Upper Butts, Brent. TW8 179 CJ79
Upper Caldy Wk, N1
off Clifton Rd 164 DQ65
Upper Camelford Wk, W11
off St. Marks Rd 161 CY72
Upper Cavendish Av, N3 142 DA55
Upper Cheyne Row, SW3 40 C3
Upper Ch Hill, Green. DA9 211 FS85
Upper Clabdens, Ware SG12 55 DZ05
UPPER CLAPTON, E5 144 DV60
Upper Clapton Rd, E5 144 DV60
Upper Clarendon Wk, W11
off Clarendon Wk 161 CY72
Upper Cornsland, Brwd.
CM14 130 FX48
Upper Ct Rd, Epsom KT19 238 CQ111
Woldingham CR3 259 EA123
Upper Culver Rd, St.Alb. AL1 65 CE18
Upper Dagnall St, St.Alb. AL3 65 CD20
Upper Dartrey Wk, SW10
off Blantyre St 40 A4
Upper Dengie Wk, N1
off Popham Rd 164 DQ67
Upper Dr, Beac. HP9 111 AK50
Biggin Hill TN16 260 EJ118
Upper Dunnymans, Bans. SM7
off Basing Rd 239 CZ114
Upper Edgeborough Rd, Guil.
GU1 281 AZ135
UPPER EDMONTON, N18 122 DU51
UPPER ELMERS END, Beck.
BR3 225 DZ100
Upper Elmers End Rd, Beck.
BR3 225 DY98
Upper Fairfield Rd, Lthd.
KT22 253 CH121
Upper Fm Rd, W.Mol. KT8 218 BZ98
Upperfield Rd, Welw.G.C. AL7 51 CZ11
Upper Forecourt, Gat. RH6 291 DH152
Upper Fosters, NW4
off New Brent St 141 CW57
UPPER GATTON, Reig. RH2 272 DC127
Upper George St, Chesh. HP5
off Frances St 76 AQ30
Upper Gladstone Rd, Chesh.
HP5 76 AQ30
Upper Grn E, Mitch. CR4 222 DF97
Upper Grn Rd, Tewin AL6 52 DE05
Upper Grn W, Mitch. CR4
off London Rd 222 DF97
Upper Grosvenor St, W1 28 G1
Upper Grotto Rd, Twick. TW1 199 CF89
Upper Grd, SE1 30 E2
Upper Gro, SE25 224 DS98
Upper Gro Rd, Belv. DA17 188 EZ79
🛍 Upper Guild Hall,
Bluewater DA9
off Bluewater Shop Cen 211 FT87
Upper Guildown Rd, Guil.
GU2 280 AV137
Upper Gulland Wk, N1
off Nightingale Rd 9 K5
UPPER HALLIFORD, Shep.
TW17 217 BS97
⇌ Upper Halliford 217 BS96
Upper Halliford Bypass, Shep.
TW17 217 BS99
Upper Halliford Grn, Shep.
TW17 217 BS98
Upper Halliford Rd, Shep.
TW17 217 BS96
Upper Hall Pk, Berk. HP4 60 AX20
Upper Hampstead Wk, NW3
off New End 142 DC63
Upper Ham Rd, Kings.T. KT2 199 CK91
Richmond TW10 199 CK91
Upper Handa Wk, N1
off Handa Wk 9 K4
Upper Harestone, Cat. CR3 274 DU127
Upper Hawkwell Wk, N1
off Popham Rd 164 DQ67
Upper Heath Rd, St.Alb. AL1 65 CF18
Upper High St, Epsom KT17 238 CS113
Upper Highway, Abb.L. WD5 81 BR33
Kings Langley WD4 81 BQ32
Upper Hill Ri, Rick. WD3 96 BH44
Upper Hitch, Wat. WD19 116 BY46
UPPER HOLLOWAY, N19 143 DJ62
⊖ Upper Holloway 143 DK61
Upper Holly Hill Rd, Belv.
DA17 189 FB78
Upper Hook, Harl. CM18 73 ET17
Upper James St, W1 17 M10
Upper John St, W1 17 M10
Upper Lattimore Rd, St.Alb.
AL1 65 CE20
Upper Lees Rd, Slou. SL2 153 AP69
Upper Lismore Wk, N1
off Mull Wk 9 K5
Upper Lo Way, Couls. CR5
off Netherne Dr 257 DK122
Upper Mall, W6 181 CU78
Upper Manor Rd, Gdmg. GU7 280 AS144
Upper Marlborough Rd, St.Alb.
AL1 65 CE20
Upper Marsh, SE1 30 D6
Upper Marsh La, Hodd. EN11 71 EA18
Upper Meadow, Chesh. HP5
off Stanley Av 76 AP30
Gerrards Cross SL9 134 AW60
Upper Mealines, Harl. CM18 74 EU18
Upper Montagu St, W1 16 E6
Upper Mulgrave Rd, Sutt.
SM2 239 CY108
Upper N St, E14 22 B10
UPPER NORWOOD, SE19 204 DR94
Upper Paddock Rd, Wat. WD19 98 BY44
Upper Palace Rd, E.Mol. KT8 218 CC97
Upper Pk, Harl. CM20 57 EP14
Loughton IG10 106 EK42
Upper Pk Rd, N11 121 DH50
NW3 6 E4
Belvedere DA17 189 FB77
Bromley BR1 226 EH95
Kingston upon Thames KT2 200 CN93
Upper Phillimore Gdns, W8 27 J5
Upper Pillory Down, Cars.
SM5 240 DG113
Upper Pines, Bans. SM7 256 DF117
Upper Rainham Rd, Horn.
RM12 149 FF63
Upper Ramsey Wk, N1
off Ramsey Wk 9 L5
Upper Rawreth Wk, N1
off Popham Rd 164 DQ67
Upper Richmond Rd, SW15 181 CY84
Upper Richmond Rd W, SW14 180 CP84
Richmond TW10 180 CN84
Upper Riding, Beac. HP9 110 AG54
Upper Rd, E13 23 N2
Denham UB9 135 BD59
Wallington SM6 241 DK106
🛍 Upper Rose Gall,
Bluewater DA9
off Bluewater Shop Cen 211 FU87
Upper Rose Hill, Dor. RH4 285 CH137
Upper Ryle, Brwd. CM14 130 FV45
Upper St. Martin's La, WC2 18 A10
Upper Sales, Hem.H. HP1 61 BF21
Upper Sawley Wd, Bans. SM7 239 CZ114
Upper Selsdon Rd, S.Croy.
CR2 242 DT108
Upper Sheridan Rd, Belv. DA17
off Coleman Rd 188 FA77
Upper Shirley Rd, Croy. CR0 224 DW103
Upper Shot, Welw.G.C. AL7 52 DA08
Upper Shott, Chsht EN7 88 DT26
Upper Sq, Islw. TW7 179 CG83
Upper Sta Rd, Rad. WD7 99 CG35
Upper Stoneyfield, Harl. CM19 73 EP15
Upper St, N1 8 F10
Shere GU5 282 BM138
Upper Sunbury Rd, Hmptn.
TW12 218 BY95
Upper Sutton La, Houns. TW5 178 CA80
Upper Swaines, Epp. CM16 91 ET30
UPPER SYDENHAM, SE26 204 DU91
Upper Tachbrook St, SW1 29 L8
Upper Tail, Wat. WD19 116 BY48
Upper Talbot Wk, W11
off Talbot Wk 161 CY72
Upper Teddington Rd, Kings.T.
KT1 219 CJ95
Upper Ter, NW3 142 DC62
Upper Thames St, EC4 19 H10
🛍 Upper Thames Wk,
Bluewater DA9
off Bluewater Shop Cen 211 FT88
Upper Tollington Pk, N4 143 DN60
Upperton Rd, Guil. GU2 280 AW136
Sidcup DA14 207 ET92
Upperton Rd E, E13 24 D2
Upperton Rd W, E13 24 C3
UPPER TOOTING, SW17 202 DE90
Upper Tooting Pk, SW17 202 DF89
Upper Tooting Rd, SW17 202 DF91
Upper Town Rd, Grnf. UB6 158 CB70
Upper Tulse Hill, SW2 203 DM87
Upper Vernon Rd, Sutt. SM1 240 DD106
Upper Wk, Vir.W. GU25 214 AY98
UPPER WALTHAMSTOW, E17 145 EB56
Upper Walthamstow Rd, E17 145 ED56
⇌ Upper Warlingham 258 DU118
Upper W St, Reig. RH2 271 CZ134
Upper Whistler Wk, SW10
off Blantyre St 39 P4
Upper Wickham La, Well.
DA16 188 EV80
Upper Wimpole St, W1 17 J6
Upper Woburn Pl, WC1 17 P3
Upper Woodcote Village, Pur.
CR8 241 DK112
Uppingham Av, Stan. HA7 117 CH53
Upsdell Av, N13 121 DN51
UPSHIRE, Wal.Abb. EN9 90 EJ32
Upshirebury Grn, Wal.Abb. EN9
off Horseshoe Hill 90 EK33
Sch Upshire Prim Foundation Sch,
Wal.Abb. EN9
off Upshire Rd 90 EH33
Upshire Rd, Wal.Abb. EN9 90 EF32
Upshot La, Wok. GU22 249 BF117
Upstall St, SE5 43 H7
UPTON, E7 166 EH66
UPTON, Slou. SL1 174 AU76
Upton, Wok. GU21 248 AV117
Upton Av, E7 13 P6
St. Albans AL3 65 CD19
Upton Cl, NW2 141 CY62
Bexley DA5 208 EZ86
Park Street AL2 83 CD25
Slough SL1 174 AT76
Upton Ct, SE20 off Blean Gro 204 DW94
Upton Ct Rd, Slou. SL3 174 AU76
Sch Upton Cross Prim Sch, E13
off Churston Av 166 EH67
Upton Dene, Sutt. SM2 240 DB108
Upton Gdns, Har. HA3 139 CH57
H Upton Hosp, Slou. SL1 174 AT76
Sch Upton Ho Sch, Wind. SL4
off St. Leonards Rd 173 AQ82
Upton La, E7 13 P8
Upton Lo Cl, Bushey WD23 116 CC45
UPTON PARK, E6 166 EJ67
UPTON PARK, Slou. SL1 174 AT76
⊖ Upton Park 166 EH67
Upton Pk, Slou. SL1 174 AT76
Upton Pk Rd, E7 166 EH66
Sch Upton Prim Sch, Bexh. DA6
off Upton Rd 208 EZ85
Upton Rd, N18 122 DU50
SE18 187 EQ79
Bexley DA5 208 EZ86
Bexleyheath DA6 188 EY84
Hounslow TW3 178 CA83
Slough SL1 174 AU76
Thornton Heath CR7 224 DR96
Watford WD18 97 BV42
Upton Rd S, Bex. DA5 208 EZ86
Upway, N12 120 DE52
Chalfont St. Peter SL9 113 AZ53
Upwood Rd, SE12 206 EF86
SW16 223 DL95
Uranus Rd, Hem.H. HP2 62 BM18
Urban Av, Horn. RM12 150 FJ62
Urban Ms, N4 143 DP59
Coll Urdang Acad, The, EC1 18 F3
Urlwin St, SE5 43 J3
Urlwin Wk, SW9 42 F7
Urmston Dr, SW19 201 CY88
Ursula Ms, N4 143 DP60
Ursula St, SW11 40 C7
Sch Ursuline Conv Prep Sch,
SW20 off The Downs 201 CX94
Sch Ursuline High Sch, SW20
off Crescent Rd 221 CX95
Urswick Gdns, Dag. RM9 168 EY66
Urswick Rd, E9 10 G2
Dagenham RM9 168 EX66
Sch Urswick Sch, The, E9 10 G5
Usborne Ms, SW8 42 C4
Usher Rd, E3 11 P10
Usherwood Cl, Box H. KT20 270 CP131
Usk Rd, SW11 182 DC84
Aveley RM15 170 FQ72
Usk St, E2 21 J2
Utah Bldg, SE13
off Deals Gateway 46 C6
Utopia Village, NW1 6 G8
Uvedale Cl, New Adgtn CR0
off Uvedale Cres 243 ED111
Uvedale Cres, New Adgtn
CR0 243 ED111
Uvedale Rd, Dag. RM10 148 FA62
Enfield EN2 104 DR43
Oxted RH8 276 EF129
Uverdale Rd, SW10 39 P5
UXBRIDGE, UB8 - UB11 156 BK66
⊖ Uxbridge 156 BK66
● Uxbridge Business Pk, Uxb.
UB8 136 BJ64
Coll Uxbridge Coll, Hayes Comm
Campus, Hayes UB3
off Coldharbour La 157 BU73
Uxbridge Campus, Uxb. UB8
off Park Rd 156 BL65
Sch Uxbridge High Sch, Uxb.
UB8 off The Greenway 156 BK68
UXBRIDGE MOOR, Iver SL0 156 BG67
UXBRIDGE MOOR, Uxb. UB8 156 BG67
Uxbridge Rd, W3 160 CL73
W5 159 CJ73
W5 (Ealing Com.) 160 CL73
W7 159 CE74
W12 26 B4
W13 159 CH74
Feltham TW13 198 BW89
Hampton TW12 198 CA91
Harrow HA3 116 CC52
Hayes UB4 158 BW73
Iver SL0 154 AY71
Kingston upon Thames KT1 219 CK98
Pinner HA5 116 CB52
Rickmansworth WD3 113 BF47
Slough SL1, SL2, SL3 174 AU75
Southall UB1 158 CA74
Stanmore HA7 117 CF51
Uxbridge UB10 156 BN69
Uxbridge St, W8 27 J2
Uxendon Cres, Wem. HA9 140 CL60
Uxendon Hill, Wem. HA9 140 CM60
Sch Uxendon Manor Prim Sch,
Kenton HA3 off Vista Way 140 CL57

V

Vache La, Ch.St.G. HP8 112 AW47
Vache Ms, Ch.St.G. HP8 112 AX46
Vaillant Rd, Wey. KT13 235 BQ105
Valance Av, E4 124 EF46
Valan Leas, Brom. BR2 226 EE97
Vale, The, N10 120 DG53
N14 121 DK45
NW11 141 CX62
SW3 40 A2
W3 160 CR74
Brentwood CM14 130 FW46
Chalfont St. Peter SL9 112 AX53
Coulsdon CR5 241 DK114
Croydon CR0 225 DX103
Feltham TW14 197 BV86
Hounslow TW5 178 BY79
Ruislip HA4 138 BW63
Sunbury-on-Thames TW16 197 BU93
Woodford Green IG8 124 EG52
Vale Av, Borwd. WD6 100 CP43
Vale Border, Croy. CR0 243 DX111
Vale Cl, N2 142 DF55
W9 15 N3
Chalfont St. Peter SL9 112 AX53
Epsom KT18 254 CS119
Orpington BR6 245 EN105
Pilgrim's Hatch CM15 130 FT43
Weybridge KT13 217 BR104
Woking GU21 248 AY116
Vale Cotts, SW15 200 CS90
Vale Ct, W3 off The Vale 161 CT74
W9 15 N3
Weybridge KT13 217 BR104
Vale Cres, SW15 200 CS90
Vale Cft, Clay. KT10 237 CE109
Pinner HA5 138 BY57
Vale Dr, Barn. EN5 101 CZ42
Vale End, SE22
off Grove Vale 184 DS84
Vale Fm Rd, Wok. GU21 248 AX117
Vale Gro, N4 144 DQ59
W3 off The Vale 160 CR74
Slough SL1 174 AS76
● Vale Ind Est, Wat. WD18 115 BP46
● Vale Ind Pk, SW16 223 DJ95
Vale La, W3 160 CN71
Valence Av, Dag. RM8 148 EX62
Valence Circ, Dag. RM8 148 EX62
Valence Dr, Chsht EN7 88 DU28
★ Valence Ho Mus, Dag.
RM8 148 EX62
Sch Valence Inf & Jun Schs, Dag.
RM8 off Bonham Rd 148 EX61
Valence Rd, Erith DA8 189 FD80
Sch Valence Sch, West. TN16
off Westerham Rd 277 ET126
Valence Wd Rd, Dag. RM8 148 EX62
Valencia Rd, Stan. HA7 117 CJ49
Valency Cl, Nthwd. HA6 115 BT49
Valentia Pl, SW9
off Brixton Sta Rd 183 DN84
Valentine Av, Bex. DA5 208 EY89
Valentine Ct, SE23 205 DX89
Valentine Ho, E3
off Garrison Rd 11 P9
Valentine Pl, SE1 30 G4
Valentine Rd, E9 11 J5
Harrow HA2 138 CC62
Valentine Row, SE1 30 G5
Sch Valentines High Sch, Ilf. IG2
off Cranbrook Rd 147 EN58
Valentines Rd, Ilf. IG1 147 EP60
Valentines Way, Rom. RM7 149 FE61
Valentine Way, Ch.St.G. HP8 112 AX48
Valentyne Cl, New Adgtn CR0 244 EE111
Vale of Health, NW3 142 DD62
Vale Par, SW15
off Kingston Vale 200 CS90
Sch Vale Prim Sch, The, Epsom
KT18 off Beaconsfield Rd 254 CS119
Valerian Wk, N11
off Nurserymans Rd 120 DG47
Valerian Way, E15 23 K3
Valerie Cl, St.Alb. AL1 65 CH20
Valerie Ct, Bushey WD23 116 CC45
Sutton SM2 off Stanley Rd 240 DB108
Vale Ri, NW11 141 CZ60
Chesham HP5 76 AQ28
Vale Rd, E7 166 EH65
N4 144 DQ59
Vale Rd, Bromley BR1 227 EN96
Bushey WD23 98 BY43
Chesham HP5 76 AQ27
Claygate KT10 237 CE109
Dartford DA1 209 FH88
Epsom KT19 239 CT105
Mitcham CR4 223 DK97
Northfleet DA11 212 GD87
Sutton SM1 240 DB105
Weybridge KT13 217 BR104
Windsor SL4 173 AM80
Worcester Park KT4 239 CT105
Vale Rd N, Surb. KT6 220 CL103
Vale Rd S, Surb. KT6 220 CL103
Vale Row, N5
off Gillespie Rd 143 DP62
Vale Royal, N7 8 A7
Valery Pl, Hmptn. TW12 198 CA94
Sch Vale Sch, The, SW7 27 N7
Valeside, Hert. SG14 53 DN10
Vale St, SE27 204 DR90
Valeswood Rd, Brom. BR1 206 EF92
Vale Ter, N4 144 DQ58
Valetta Gro, E13 13 N10
Valetta Rd, W3 180 CS75
Valette St, E9 10 F4
Valiant Cl, Nthlt. UB5
off Ruislip Rd 158 BX69
Romford RM7 126 FA54
Valiant Ho, SE7 36 D10
Valiant Path, NW9 118 CS53
Valiant Way, E6 25 J7
Vallance Rd, E1 20 D3
E2 20 D3
N22 121 DJ54
Vallentin Rd, E17 145 EC56
Valley, The, Guil. GU2
off Portsmouth Rd 280 AW138
Valley Av, N12 120 DD49
Valley Cl, Dart. DA1 209 FF86
Hertford SG13 54 DR10
Loughton IG10 107 EM44
Pinner HA5 115 BV54
Waltham Abbey EN9 89 EC32
Ware SG12 54 DV05
Valley Ct, Cat. CR3
off Beechwood Gdns 258 DU122
Kenley CR8 off Hayes La 242 DQ114
Valley Dr, NW9 140 CN58
Gravesend DA12 213 GK91
Sevenoaks TN13 279 FH125
Valleyfield Rd, SW16 203 DM92
Valley Flds Cres, Enf. EN2 103 DN40
Valley Gdns, SW19 202 DD94
Greenhithe DA9 211 FV86
Wembley HA0 160 CM66
★ Valley Gdns, The, Egh.
TW20 214 AS96
Valley Grn, The, Welw.G.C. AL8 51 CW08
Valley Gro, SE7 36 D10
Valley Hill, Loug. IG10 124 EL45
● Valley Ind Pk, Kings L. WD4 81 BP28
● Valleylink Est, Enf. EN3
off Meridian Way 105 DY44
Valley Ms, Twick. TW1
off Cross Deep 199 CG89
● Valley Pt Ind Est, Croy.
CR0 223 DL101
Sch Valley Prim Sch, Brom. BR2
off Beckenham La 226 EF96
Valley Ri, Wat. WD25 81 BV33
Valley Rd, SW16 203 DM91
Belvedere DA17 189 FB77
Bromley BR2 226 EE96
Dartford DA1 209 FF86
Erith DA8 189 FD77
Fawkham Green DA3 231 FV102
Kenley CR8 258 DR115
Northchurch HP4 60 AT17
Orpington BR5 228 EV95
Rickmansworth WD3 96 BG43
St. Albans AL3 65 CE15
Uxbridge UB10 156 BL68
Welwyn Garden City AL8 51 CV10
Valley Side, E4 123 EA47
Valleyside, Hem.H. HP1 61 BF20
Valley Side Par, E4
off Valley Side 123 EA47
Valley Vw, Barn. EN5 101 CY44
Biggin Hill TN16 260 EJ118
Chesham HP5 76 AN29
Goffs Oak EN7 88 DQ28
Greenhithe DA9 211 FV86
Valley Vw Gdns, Ken. CR8 258 DS115
Valley Wk, Crox.Grn WD3 97 BQ43
Croydon CR0 224 DW103
Valley Way, Ger.Cr. SL9 134 AW58
Valliere Rd, NW10 161 CV69
Valliers Wd Rd, Sid. DA15 207 ER88
Vallis Way, W13 159 CG71
Chessington KT9 237 CK105
Valmar Rd, SE5 43 K7
● Valmar Trd Est, SE5 43 K7
Val McKenzie Av, N7
off Parkside Cres 143 DN62
Valnay St, SW17 202 DF92
Valognes Av, E17 123 DY53
Valonia Gdns, SW18 201 CZ86
Vambery Rd, SE18 187 EQ79
Vanbrough Cres, Nthlt. UB5 158 BW67
Vanbrugh Cl, E16 24 E7
Vanbrugh Dr, Walt. KT12 218 BW101
Vanbrugh Flds, SE3 47 L3
Vanbrugh Hill, SE3 47 L2
SE10 47 K1
Vanbrugh Pk, SE3 47 L5
Vanbrugh Pk Rd, SE3 47 M4
Vanbrugh Pk Rd W, SE3 47 L4
Vanbrugh Rd, W4 180 CR76
Vanbrugh Ter, SE3 47 M6
Vanburgh Cl, Orp. BR6 227 ES102
Vancouver Cl, Epsom KT19 238 CQ111
Orpington BR6 246 EU105
Vancouver Ct, Smallfield RH6 291 DN148
Vancouver Rd, SE23 205 DY89
Broxbourne EN10 89 DY25
Edgware HA8 118 CP53
Hayes UB4 157 BV70
Richmond TW10 199 CJ91
Vanda Cres, St.Alb. AL1 65 CF21
Vanderbilt Rd, SW18 202 DB88
Vanderville Gdns, N2 120 DC54
Vandome Cl, E16 24 A9
Vandon Pas, SW1 29 M6
Vandon St, SW1 29 M6
Van Dyck Av, N.Mal. KT3 220 CR101
Vandyke Cl, SW15 201 CX87
Redhill RH1 272 DF131
Vandyke Cross, SE9 206 EL85

Vandy St, EC2 19 N5
Vane Cl, NW3 6 A1
Harrow HA3 140 CM58
Vanessa Cl, Belv. DA17 188 FA78
Vanessa Wk, Grav. DA12 213 GM92
Vanessa Way, Bex. DA5 209 FD90
Vane St, SW1 29 M8
Van Gogh Cl, Islw. TW7
off Twickenham Rd 179 CG83
Vanguard Cl, E16 23 P7
Croydon CR0 223 DP102
Romford RM7 127 FB54
Vanguard Ho, E8 10 F6
Vanguard St, SE8 46 A6
Vanguard Way, Cat. CR3 259 EB121
Wallington SM6 241 DL108
Warlingham CR6 259 EB121
Vanneck Sq, SW15 201 CU85
Vanner Pt, E9 11 J5
Vanners Par, Byfleet KT14
off Brewery La 234 BL113
Vanoc Gdns, Brom. BR1 206 EG91
Vanquish Cl, Twick. TW2 198 CA87
Vanquisher Wk, Grav. DA12 213 GM90
● **Vansittart Est**, Wind. SL4 173 AQ81
Vansittart Rd, E7 13 M1
Windsor SL4 173 AP80
Vansittart St, SE14 45 M4
Vanston Pl, SW6 39 J4
Vantage Bldg, Hayes UB3
off Station Rd 177 BT75
● **Vantage Business Pk**,
Enfield EN3 105 DY44
Vantage Ms, E14 34 F3
Northwood HA6 115 BR51
Vantage Pl, W8 27 K7
Feltham TW14 197 BU86
Vantage Pt, S.Croy. CR2 242 DR109
Vantage Rd, Slou. SL1 153 AP74
Vantorts Cl, Saw. CM21 58 EY05
Vantorts Rd, Saw. CM21 58 EY06
Vant Rd, SW17 202 DF92
Varcoe Gdns, Hayes UB3 157 BR72
Varcoe Rd, SE16 44 F1
Vardens Rd, SW11 182 DD84
Varden St, E1 20 E8
Vardon Cl, W3 160 CR72
Varley Dr, Twick. TW1 179 CH84
Varley Par, NW9 140 CS56
Varley Rd, E16 24 B8
Varley Way, Mitch. CR4 222 DD96
Varna Rd, SW6 38 F4
Hampton TW12 218 CB95
Varndell St, NW1 17 L2
Varney Cl, Chsht EN7 88 DU27
Hemel Hempstead HP1 61 BF20
Varney Rd, Hem.H. HP1 61 BF20
Varnishers Yd, N1 18 B1
Varsity Dr, Twick. TW1 199 CE85
Varsity Row, SW14 180 CQ82
Vartry Rd, N15 144 DR58
Vassall Rd, SW9 42 E5
Vauban Est, SE16 32 B7
Vauban St, SE16 32 B7
Vaughan Av, NW4 141 CU57
W6 181 CT77
Hornchurch RM12 150 FK63
Vaughan Cl, Dart, DA1 210 FK87
Hampton TW12
off Oak Av 198 BY93
Vaughan Ct, Guil. GU2
off Railton Rd 264 AV130
Sch **Vaughan First & Mid Sch**,
Har. HA1
off Vaughan Rd 138 CC58
Vaughan Gdns, Eton Wick SL4 173 AM77
off Moores La
Ilford IG1 147 EM59
Vaughan Rd, E15 13 L5
SE5 43 J9
Harrow HA1 138 CC59
Thames Ditton KT7 219 CH101
Welling DA16 187 ET82
Vaughan St, SE16 33 N5
Vaughan Way, E1 32 C1
Dorking RH4 285 CG136
Slough SL2 153 AL70
Vaughan Williams Cl, SE8 46 A5
Vaughan Williams Way, Warley
CM14 129 FU51
Vaux Cres, Hersham KT12 235 BV107
VAUXHALL, SE11 42 B1
⇌ **Vauxhall** 42 B2
⊖ **Vauxhall** 42 B2
Vauxhall Br, SE1 42 A1
SW1 42 A1
Vauxhall Br Rd, SW1 29 M8
Vauxhall Cl, Nthflt DA11 213 GF87
Vauxhall Gdns, S.Croy. CR2 242 DQ107
Vauxhall Gdns Est, SE11 42 C1
Vauxhall Gro, SW8 42 C2
Vauxhall Pl, Dart. DA1 210 FL87
Sch **Vauxhall Prim Sch**, SE11 30 D10
Vauxhall Rd, Hem.H. HP2 62 BN20
Vauxhall St, SE11 30 D10
Vauxhall Wk, SE11 30 C10
Vawdrey Cl, E1 20 G5
Veals Mead, Mitch. CR4 222 DE95
Vectis Gdns, SW17
off Vectis Rd 203 DH93
Vectis Rd, SW17 203 DH93
Veda Rd, SE13 185 EA84
Vega Cres, Nthwd. HA6 115 BT50
Vegal Cres, Eng.Grn TW20 194 AW92
Vega Rd, Bushey WD23 116 CC45
Veitch Cl, Felt. TW14 197 BT88
Veldene Way, Har. HA2 138 BZ62
Velde Way, SE22
off East Dulwich Gro 204 DS85
Velizy Av, Harl. CM20 73 ER15
Vellacott Cl, Purf. RM19 191 FR79
Vellacott Ho, W12 161 CV72
Velletri Ho, E2 21 J1
Vellum Dr, Cars. SM5 222 DG104
Venables Cl, Dag. RM10 149 FB63
Venables St, NW8 16 B5
Vencourt Pl, W6 181 CU78
Venetian Rd, SE5 43 K9
Venetia Rd, N4 143 DP58
W5 179 CK75
Venette Cl, Rain. RM13 169 FH71
Venice Av, Wat. WD18 97 BS42
Venice Wk, W2 15 P6
Venner Cl, Red. RH1 272 DG133
Venner Rd, SE26 204 DW93
Venners Cl, Bexh. DA7 189 FE82
Venn St, SW4 183 DJ84
Ventnor Av, Stan. HA7 117 CH53
Ventnor Dr, N20 120 DB48
Ventnor Gdns, Bark. IG11 167 ES65
Ventnor Rd, SE14 45 K5
Sutton SM2 240 DB108
Venton Cl, Wok. GU21 248 AV117
● **Ventura Pk**, Coln.St AL2 83 CF29
Venture Cl, Bex. DA5 208 EY87
Venture Ct, Grav. DA12 213 GK86
Venue St, E14 22 E6
Venus Cl, Slou. SL2 153 AM70
Venus Hill, Bov. HP3 79 BA31
Venus Ho, E3 *off Garrison Rd* 12 A9
E14 *off Crews St* 34 A8
Venus Ms, Mitch. CR4 222 DE97
Venus Rd, SE18 37 J7
Veny Cres, Horn. RM12 150 FK64
Vera Av, N21 103 DN43
Vera Ct, Wat. WD19 116 BX45
Vera Lynn Cl, E7 13 P1
Vera Rd, SW6 38 F7
Verbena Cl, E16 23 L4
South Ockendon RM15 171 FW72
West Drayton UB7
off Magnolia St 176 BK78
Verbena Gdns, W6 181 CU78
Verdant La, SE6 206 EE88
Verdayne Av, Croy. CR0 225 DX102
Verdayne Gdns, Warl. CR6 258 DW116
Verderers Rd, Chig. IG7 126 EU50
Verdi Cres, W10 14 F1
Verdun Rd, SE18 188 EU79
SW13 181 CU79
Verdure Cl, Wat. WD25 82 BY32
Vereker Dr, Sun. TW16 217 BU97
Vereker Rd, W14 38 F1
Vere Rd, Loug. IG10 107 EQ42
Vere St, W1 17 J9
Veridion Way, Erith DA18 188 EZ75
Verity Cl, W11 14 E9
Veritys, Hat. AL10 67 CU18
Vermeer Gdns, SE15
off Elland Rd 184 DW84
Vermont Cl, Enf. EN2 103 DP42
Vermont Rd, SE19 204 DR93
SW18 202 DB86
Slough SL2 153 AM70
Sutton SM1 222 DB104
Verney Cl, Berk. HP4 60 AT18
Verney Gdns, Dag. RM9 148 EY63
Verney Rd, SE16 44 D2
Dagenham RM9 148 EY64
Slough SL3 175 BA77
Verney St, NW10 140 CR62
Verney Way, SE16 44 E1
Vernham Rd, SE18 187 EQ79
Vernon Av, E12 147 EM63
SW20 221 CX96
Enfield EN3 105 DY36
Woodford Green IG8 124 EH52
Vernon Cl, Epsom KT19 238 CQ107
Orpington BR5 228 EV97
Ottershaw KT16 233 BD107
St. Albans AL1 65 CE21
Staines-upon-Thames TW19 196 BL88
Vernon Ct, Stan. HA7
off Vernon Dr 117 CH53
Vernon Cres, Barn. EN4 102 DG44
Brentwood CM13 131 GA48
Vernon Dr, Cat. CR3 258 DQ122
Harefield UB9 114 BJ53
Stanmore HA7 117 CG53
Sch **Vernon Ho Sch**, NW10
off Drury Way 140 CR64
Vernon Ms, E17 *off Vernon Rd* 145 DZ56
W14 26 F9
Vernon Pl, WC1 18 B7
Vernon Ri, WC1 18 D2
Greenford UB6 139 CD64
Vernon Rd, E3 11 P10
E11 146 EE60
E15 13 K6
E17 145 DZ57
N8 143 DN55
SW14 180 CR83
Bushey WD23 98 BY43
Feltham TW13 197 BT89
Ilford IG3 147 ET60
Romford RM5 127 FC50
Sutton SM1 240 DC106
Swanscombe DA10 212 FZ86
Vernon Sq, WC1 18 D2
Vernon St, W14 26 E9
Vernon Wk, Tad. KT20 255 CX120
Vernon Way, Guil. GU2 264 AT133
Vernon Yd, W11 14 G10
Vern Pl, Tats. TN16
off Paynesfield Rd 260 EJ121
Veroan Rd, Bexh. DA7 188 EY82
Verona Cl, Uxb. UB8 156 BJ72
Verona Ct, W4
off Chiswick La 180 CS78
Verona Dr, Surb. KT6 220 CL103
Verona Gdns, Grav. DA12 213 GL91
Verona Ho, Erith DA8
off Waterhead Cl 189 FF80
Verona Rd, E7 13 P6
Veronica Cl, Rom. RM3 128 FJ52
Veronica Gdns, SW16 223 DJ95
Veronica Rd, SW17 203 DH90
Veronique Gdns, Ilf. IG6 147 EP57
Verralls, Wok. GU22 249 BB117
Verran Rd, SW12 203 DH87
Ver Rd, St.Alb. AL3 64 CC20
Versailles Rd, SE20 204 DU94
Verulam Av, E17 145 DZ58
Purley CR8 241 DJ112
Verulam Bldgs, WC1 18 D6
Verulam Cl, Welw.G.C. AL7 51 CZ09
Verulam Ct, NW9 141 CU59
Verulam Ho, W6
off Hammersmith Gro 26 A5
● **Verulam Ind Est**, St.Alb.
AL1 65 CF22
★ **Verulamium Mus & Pk**, St.Alb.
AL3 64 CB20
Verulam Pas, Wat. WD17 97 BV40
Verulam Rd, Grnf. UB6 158 CA70
St. Albans AL3 64 CB19
Sch **Verulam Sch**, St.Alb. AL1
off Brampton Rd 65 CG19
Verulam St, WC1 18 E6
Verwood Dr, Barn. EN4 102 DF41
Verwood Lo, E14
off Manchester Rd 34 F8
Verwood Rd, Har. HA2 116 CC54
Veryan, Wok. GU21 248 AU117
Veryan Cl, Orp. BR5 228 EW98
Vesage Ct, EC1 18 F7
Vesey Path, E14 22 D9
Vespan Rd, W12 181 CU75
Vesta Av, St.Alb. AL1 64 CC23
Vesta Ct, SE1 *off Morocco St* 31 N5
Vesta Ho, E3 *off Garrison Rd* 12 A9
Vesta Rd, SE4 45 L9
Hemel Hempstead HP2
off Saturn Way 62 BM18
Vestris Rd, SE23 205 DX89
Vestry Ms, SE5 43 N7
Vestry Rd, E17 145 EB56
SE5 43 N7
Vestry St, N1 19 L2
Vevers Rd, Reig. RH2 288 DB137
Vevey St, SE6 205 DZ89
Vexil Cl, Purf. RM19 191 FR77
Veysey Cl, Hem.H. HP1
off Halwick Cl 62 BH22
Veysey Gdns, Dag. RM10 148 FA62
Viaduct Pl, E2 20 E3
Viaduct Rd, Ware SG12 55 DY06
Viaduct St, E2 20 E3
Viaduct Way, Welw.G.C. AL7 51 CZ06
Vian Av, Enf. EN3 105 DY35
Vian St, SE13 46 D10
Vibart Gdns, SW2 203 DM87
Vibart Wk, N1 8 B8
Vibia Cl, Stanw. TW19 196 BK87
Vicarage Av, SE3 47 P5
Egham TW20 195 BB93
Vicarage Causeway, Hert.Hth
SG13 54 DV11
Vicarage Cl, Bkhm KT23 268 CA125
Brentwood CM14 130 FS49
Erith DA8 189 FC79
Hemel Hempstead HP1 62 BJ22
Kingswood KT20 255 CY124
Northaw EN6 86 DF30
Northolt UB5 158 BZ66
Potters Bar EN6 85 CY32
Ruislip HA4 137 BR59
St. Albans AL1 64 CC23
Seer Green HP9 111 AQ52
Worcester Park KT4 220 CS102
Vicarage Ct, W8 27 L4
off Vicarage Gate
Egham TW20 195 BB93
Feltham TW14 197 BQ87
Vicarage Cres, SW11 40 A7
Egham TW20 195 BB92
Vicarage Dr, SW14 200 CR85
Barking IG11 167 EQ66
Beckenham BR3 225 EA95
Bray SL6 172 AC75
Northfleet DA11 212 GC86
Vicarage Fm Rd, Houns.
TW3, TW5 178 BY82
Vicarage Flds, Walt. KT12 218 BW100
🔒 **Vicarage Fld Shop Cen**, Bark.
IG11 167 EQ66
Vicarage Gdns, SW14 200 CQ85
off Vicarage Rd
W8 27 K3
Mitcham CR4 222 DE97
Potten End HP4 61 BB16
Vicarage Gate, W8 27 L4
Guildford GU2 280 AU136
Vicarage Gate Ms, Tad. KT20 255 CY124
Vicarage Gro, SE5 43 M6
Vicarage Hill, West. TN16 277 ER126
Vicarage La, E6 25 K2
E15 13 K8
Bovingdon HP3 79 BB26
Chigwell IG7 125 EQ47
Dunton Green TN13
off London Rd 263 FD119
Epsom KT17 239 CU109
Horley RH6 290 DF147
Ilford IG1 147 ER60
Kings Langley WD4 80 BM29
Laleham TW18 216 BH97
Leatherhead KT22 253 CH122
North Weald Bassett CM16 74 FA24
Send GU23 265 BC126
Wraysbury TW19 194 AY88
Vicarage Par, N15
off West Grn Rd 144 DQ56
Vicarage Pk, SE18 187 EQ78
Vicarage Path, N8 143 DL59
Vicarage Pl, Slou. SL1 174 AU76
Sch **Vicarage Prim Sch**, E6 25 K2
Vicarage Rd, E10 145 EB60
E15 13 L6
N17 122 DU52
NW4 141 CU58
SE18 187 EQ78
SW14 200 CQ85
Bexley DA5 209 FB88
Coopersale CM16 92 EW29
Croydon CR0 223 DN104
Dagenham RM10 169 FB65
Egham TW20 195 BB93
Hampton Wick KT1 219 CJ95
Hornchurch RM12 149 FG60
Kingston upon Thames KT1 219 CK96
Potten End HP4 61 BA16
Staines-upon-Thames TW18 195 BE91
Sunbury-on-Thames TW16 197 BT92
Sutton SM1 240 DB105
Teddington TW11 199 CG92
Twickenham TW2 199 CE89
Ware SG12 55 DY06
Watford WD18 97 BU44
Whitton TW2 198 CC86
Woking GU22 249 AZ121
Woodford Green IG8 124 EL52
Vicarage Sq, Grays RM17 192 GA79
Vicarage Wk, SW11 40 A7
Reigate RH2 *off Chartway* 272 DB134
Vicarage Way, NW10 140 CR62
Colnbrook SL3 175 BC80
Gerrards Cross SL9 135 AZ58
Harrow HA2 138 CA59
Vicarage Wd, Harl. CM20 58 EU14
Vicars Br Cl, Wem. HA0 160 CL68
Vicars Cl, E9 10 G9
E15 13 N8
Enfield EN1 104 DS40
Sch **Vicar's Grn Prim Sch**, Wem.
HA0 *off Lily Gdns* 159 CJ68
Vicars Hill, SE13 185 EB84
Vicars Moor La, N21 121 DN45
Vicars Oak Rd, SE19 204 DS93
Vicars Rd, NW5 6 G2
Vicars Wk, Dag. RM8 148 EV62
Viceroy Cl, N2 142 DE55
Viceroy Ct, NW8 6 D10
Croy. CR0 *off Dingwall Rd* 224 DR102
Viceroy Par, N2 *off High Rd* 142 DE56
Viceroy Rd, SW8 42 A6
Vickers Cl, Wall. SM6 241 DM108
Vickers Dr N, Wey. KT13 234 BL110
Vickers Dr S, Wey. KT13 234 BL111
Vickers Rd, Erith DA8 189 FD78
Vickers Way, Houns. TW4 198 BY85
Vickery's Wf, E14 22 A8
Victor App, Horn. RM12
off Abbs Cross Gdns 150 FK60
Victor Cl, Horn. RM12 150 FK60
Victor Ct, Horn. RM12 150 FK60
Rainham RM13
off Askwith Rd 169 FD68
Victor Gdns, Horn. RM12 150 FK60
Victor Gro, Wem. HA0 160 CL66
⇌ **Victoria** 29 K8
⊖ **Victoria** 29 K8
★ **Victoria & Albert Mus**, SW7 28 B7
Victoria Arc, SW1
off Terminus Pl 29 K7
Victoria Av, E6 166 EK67
EC2 19 P7
N3 119 CZ53
Barnet EN4 102 DD42
Gravesend DA12
off Sheppy Pl 213 GH87
Grays RM16 192 GC75
Hounslow TW3 198 BZ85
Romford RM5 127 FB51
South Croydon CR2 242 DQ110
Surbiton KT6 219 CK101
Uxbridge UB10 157 BP66
Wallington SM6 222 DG104
Wembley HA9 160 CP65
West Molesey KT8 218 CA97
🚌 **Victoria Bus Sta** 29 K7
H **Victoria Cen**, Rom. RM1 149 FF56
Victoria Cl, SE22
off Underhill Rd 204 DU85
Barnet EN4 102 DD42
Cheshunt EN8 89 DX30
Grays RM16 192 GC75
Hayes UB3 157 BR72
Horley RH6 290 DG148
Rickmansworth WD3
off Nightingale Rd 114 BK45
West Molesey KT8
off Victoria Av 218 CA97
Weybridge KT13 217 BR104
🚌 **Victoria Coach Sta** 29 J9
Sch **Victoria C of E First Sch**, Berk.
HP4 *off Prince Edward St* 60 AW19
Victoria Cotts, Rich. TW9 180 CM81
Victoria Ct, Red. RH1 288 DG137
Wembley HA9 160 CN65
Victoria Cres, N15 144 DS57
SE19 204 DS93
SW19 201 CZ94
Iver SL0 156 BG73
Victoria Dock Rd, E16 24 B10
Victoria Dr, SW19 201 CX87
Slough SL1, SL2 153 AL65
South Darenth DA4 231 FR96
Victoria Embk, EC4 30 C1
SW1 30 B4
WC2 30 C1
★ **Victoria Embankment Gdns**,
WC2 30 B1
Victoria Gdns, W11 27 J2
Biggin Hill TN16 260 EJ115
Hounslow TW5 178 BY81
Victoria Gate, Harl. CM17 74 EW15
Victoria Gro, N12 120 DC50
W8 27 N6
Victoria Gro Ms, W2 27 K1
Victoria Hill Rd, Swan. BR8 229 FF95
Victoria Ho, SW8
off South Lambeth Rd 42 B4
Romford RM2 150 FJ56
● **Victoria Ind Est**, NW10 160 CS69
W3 160 CR71
● **Victoria Ind Pk**, Dart. DA1 210 FL85
Sch **Victoria Jun Sch**, Felt. TW13
off Victoria Rd 197 BV88
Victoria La, Barn. EN5 101 CZ42
Harlington UB3 177 BQ78
Victoria Mans, SW8
off South Lambeth Rd 42 B4
Victoria Ms, E8 10 C4
NW6 5 J8
SW4 *off Victoria Ri* 183 DH84
SW18 202 DC88
Bayfordbury SG13 53 DN14
Englefield Green TW20 194 AW93
Victoria Mills Studios, E15 12 G8
Victorian Gro, N16 144 DS62
Victorian Hts, SW8
off Thackeray Rd 41 K9
Victorian Rd, N16 144 DS62
★ **Victoria Park**, E9 11 L8
● **Victoria Pk Ind Cen**, E9 11 P6
Victoria Pk Rd, E9 10 F9
Victoria Pk Sq, E2 20 G2
Victoria Pas, NW8 16 A4
Watford WD18 97 BV42
🔒 **Victoria Pl**, SW1 29 K8
Victoria Pl, Epsom KT17 238 CS112
Richmond TW9 199 CK85
Victoria Pt, E13 13 N10
🔒 **Victoria Retail Pk**, Ruis.
HA4 138 BX64
Victoria Ri, SW4 183 DH83
Victoria Rd, E4 124 EE46
E11 146 EE63
E13 23 N1
E17 123 EC54
E18 124 EH54
N4 143 DM59
N9 122 DT49
N15 144 DU56
N18 122 DT49
N22 121 DJ53
NW4 141 CW56
NW6 5 H9
NW7 119 CT50
NW10 160 CR71
SW14 180 CR83
W3 160 CR71
W5 159 CH71
W8 27 N7
Addlestone KT15 234 BK105
Barking IG11 167 EP65
Barnet EN4 102 DD42
Berkhamsted HP4 60 AW20
Bexleyheath DA6 188 FA84
Bromley BR2 226 EK99
Buckhurst Hill IG9 124 EK47
Bushey WD23 116 CB46
Chesham HP5 76 AQ31
Chislehurst BR7 207 EN92
Coulsdon CR5 257 DK115
Victoria Rd, Dagenham RM10 149 FB64
Dartford DA1 210 FK85
Erith DA8 189 FE79
Eton Wick SL4 173 AM78
Farnham Common SL2 153 AQ65
Feltham TW13 197 BV88
Guildford GU1 264 AY134
Horley RH6 290 DG148
Kingston upon Thames KT1 220 CM96
Mitcham CR4 202 DE94
Northfleet DA11 213 GF88
Redhill RH1 288 DG135
Romford RM1 149 FE58
Ruislip HA4 138 BW64
Sevenoaks TN13 279 FH125
Sidcup DA15 207 ET90
Slough SL2 154 AV74
Southall UB2 178 BZ76
Staines-upon-Thames TW18 195 BE90
Surbiton KT6 219 CK100
Sutton SM1 240 DD106
Teddington TW11 199 CG93
Twickenham TW1 199 CH87
Uxbridge UB8 156 BJ66
Waltham Abbey EN9 89 EC34
Warley CM14 130 FW49
Watford WD24 97 BV38
Weybridge KT13 217 BR104
Woking GU22 248 AY117
Victoria Scott Ct, Dart. DA1 189 FE83
● **Victoria Sq**, St.Alb. AL1 65 CF21
Victoria Sq, SW1 29 K6
Victoria Steps, Brent. TW8
off Kew Br Rd 180 CM79
Victoria St, E15 13 J6
SW1 29 L7
Belvedere DA17 188 EZ78
Englefield Green TW20 194 AW93
St. Albans AL1 65 CD20
Slough SL1 174 AT75
Windsor SL4 173 AQ81
Victoria's Way, S.Ock. RM15 171 FW72
Victoria Ter, N4 143 DN60
NW10 *off Old Oak La* 160 CS70
Dorking RH4 *off South St* 285 CG136
Harrow HA1 139 CE60
Victoria Vil, Rich. TW9 180 CM83
Victoria Way, SE7 36 A10
Ruislip HA4 138 BX64
Weybridge KT13 217 BR104
Woking GU21 248 AY117
Victoria Wf, E14 33 M1
Victoria Yd, E1 20 D9
Victor Rd, NW10 161 CV69
SE20 205 DX94
Harrow HA2 138 CC55
Teddington TW11 199 CE91
Windsor SL4 173 AQ83
Victors Cres, Hutt. CM13 131 GB47
Victors Dr, Hmptn. TW12 198 BY93
Sch **Victor Seymour Infants' Sch**,
Cars. SM5
off Denmark Rd 240 DF105
Victor Smith Ct, Brick.Wd AL2 82 CA31
Victors Way, Barn. EN5 101 CZ41
Victor Vil, N9 122 DR48
Victor Wk, NW9 118 CS54
Hornchurch RM12
off Abbs Cross Gdns 150 FK60
Victor Way, Coln.St AL2 83 CF31
Victory Av, Mord. SM4 222 DC99
● **Victory Business Cen**, Islw.
TW7 179 CF83
Victory Cl, Chaff.Hun. RM16 191 FW77
Staines-upon-Thames TW19 196 BL88
Victory Ms, Sthl. UB2 178 BY76
Victory Pk Rd, Add. KT15 234 BJ105
Victory Pl, E14 21 M10
SE17 31 L8
SE19 *off Westow St* 204 DS93
Sch **Victory Prim Sch**, SE17 31 K8
Victory Rd, E11 146 EH56
SW19 202 DC94
Berkhamsted HP4
off Gossoms End 60 AU18
Chertsey KT16 216 BG102
Rainham RM13 169 FG68
Victory Rd Ms, SW19
off Victory Rd 202 DC94
Victory Wk, SE8 46 A6
Victory Way, SE16 33 M5
Dartford DA2 190 FQ84
Hounslow TW5 178 BW78
Romford RM7 127 FB54
Vidler Cl, Chess. KT9
off Merritt Gdns 237 CJ107
Vienna Cl, Ilf. IG5 146 EK55
View, The, SE2 188 EY78
View Cl, N6 142 DF59
Biggin Hill TN16 260 EJ116
Chigwell IG7 125 ER50
Harrow HA1 139 CD56
View Cres, N8 143 DK57
Viewfield Cl, Har. HA3 140 CL59
Viewfield Rd, SW18 201 CZ86
Bexley DA5 208 EW88
Viewland Rd, SE18 187 ET78
Viewlands Av, West. TN16 261 ES120
View Rd, N6 142 DF59
Potters Bar EN6 86 DC32
Viga Rd, N21 103 DN44
Vigerons Way, Grays RM16 193 GH77
Viggory La, Wok. GU21 248 AW115
Vigilant Cl, SE26 204 DU91
Vigilant Way, Grav. DA12 213 GL92
Vignoles Rd, Rom. RM7 148 FA59
Vigors Cft, Hat. AL10 67 CT19
Vigo St, W1 29 L1
Viking Cl, E3 21 M1
Viking Ct, SW6 39 K2
Viking Gdns, E6 24 G5
Viking Pl, E10 145 DZ60
Sch **Viking Prim Sch**, Nthlt. UB5
off Radcliffe Way 158 BX69
Viking Rd, Nthflt DA11 212 GC90
Southall UB1 158 BY73
Viking Way, Erith DA8 189 FC76
Pilgrim's Hatch CM15 130 FV45
Rainham RM13 169 FG70
Villa Ct, Dart. DA1
off Greenbanks 210 FL89

Villacourt Rd, SE18 188 EU80
Village, The, Bluewater DA9 211 FT87
Slough SL1 174 AT75
Village, The, SE7 186 EJ79
Village Arc, E4
off Station Rd 123 ED46
Village Cl, E4 123 EC50
NW3 6 B3
Hoddesdon EN11 71 ED15
Weybridge KT13 217 BR104
Village Ct, E17 off Eden Rd 145 EB57
Village Gdns, Epsom KT17 239 CT110
Village Grn Av, Bigg.H. TN16 260 EL117
Village Grn Rd, Dart. DA1 189 FG84
Village Grn Way, Bigg.H. TN16
off Main Rd 260 EL117
Village Hts, Wdf.Grn. IG8 124 EF50
Village Infants' Sch, Dag. RM10 off Ford Rd 168 FA66
Village La, Hedg. SL2 133 AR60
Village Ms, NW9 140 CR61
Village Pk Cl, Enf. EN1 104 DS44
Village Rd, N3 119 CY53
Coleshill HP7 77 AM44
Denham UB9 135 BF61
Dorney SL4 172 AH76
Egham TW20 215 BC97
Enfield EN1 104 DS44
Village Row, Sutt. SM2 240 DA108
Village Sq, The, Couls. CR5
off Netherne Dr 257 DK122
Village Way, NW10 140 CR63
SE21 204 DR86
Amersham HP7 94 AX40
Ashford TW15 196 BM91
Beckenham BR3 225 EA96
Ilford IG6 147 EQ55
Pinner HA5 138 BY59
South Croydon CR2 242 DU113
Village Way E, Har. HA2 138 BZ59
Villa Rd, SW9 42 E10
Villas Rd, SE18 187 EQ77
Villa St, SE17 43 M1
Villiers, The, Wey. KT13 235 BR107
Villiers Av, Surb. KT5 220 CM99
Twickenham TW2 198 BZ88
Villiers Cl, E10 145 EA61
Surbiton KT5 220 CM98
Villiers Ct, N20
off Buckingham Av 120 DC45
Villiers Cres, St.Alb. AL4 65 CK17
Villiers Gro, Sutt. SM2 239 CX109
Villiers High Sch, Sthl. UB1
off Boyd Av 158 BZ74
Villiers Path, Surb. KT5 220 CL99
Villiers Rd, NW2 161 CU65
Beckenham BR3 225 DX96
Isleworth TW7 179 CE82
Kingston upon Thames KT1 220 CM97
Slough SL2 153 AR71
Southall UB1 158 BZ74
Watford WD19 98 BY44
Villiers St, WC2 30 A1
Hertford SG13 54 DS09
Villier St, Uxb. UB8 156 BK68
Vimy Cl, Houns. TW4 198 BZ85
Vincam Cl, Twick. TW2 198 CA87
Vince Ct, N1 off Charles Sq 19 M3
Vincent Av, Cars. SM5 240 DD111
Croydon CR0 243 DY111
Surbiton KT5 220 CP102
Vincent Cl, SE16 33 L5
Barnet EN5 102 DA41
Bromley BR2 226 EH98
Chertsey KT16 215 BE101
Cheshunt EN8 89 DY28
Esher KT10 218 CB104
Fetcham KT22 252 CB123
Ilford IG6 125 EQ51
Sidcup DA15 207 ES88
Sipson UB7 176 BN79
Vincent Dr, Dor. RH4 285 CG137
Shepperton TW17 217 BS97
Uxbridge UB10 156 BM67
Vincent Gdns, NW2 141 CT62
Vincent Grn, Couls. CR5 256 DF120
Vincentia Quay, SW11 39 P9
Vincent La, Dor. RH4 285 CG136
Vincent Ms, E3 off Menai Pl 12 A10
Vincent Rd, E4 123 ED51
N15 144 DQ56
N22 121 DN54
SE18 37 N8
W3 180 CQ76
Chertsey KT16 215 BE101
Coulsdon CR5 257 DJ116
Croydon CR0 224 DS101
Dagenham RM9 168 EY66
Dorking RH4 285 CG136
Hounslow TW4 178 BX82
Isleworth TW7 179 CD81
Kingston upon Thames KT1 220 CN97
Rainham RM13 170 FJ70
Stoke D'Abernon KT11 252 BY116
Wembley HA0 160 CM66
Vincent Row, Hmptn H. TW12 198 CC93
Vincents Cl, Chipstead CR5 256 DF120
Vincents Dr, Dor. RH4
off Nower Rd 285 CG137
Vincents Path, Nthlt. UB5
off Arnold Rd 158 BY65
Vincent Sq, N22 121 DN54
SW1 29 M8
Biggin Hill TN16 244 EJ113
Vincent St, E16 23 M7
SW1 29 N8
Vincents Wk, Dor. RH4
off Arundel Rd 285 CG136
Vincent Ter, N1 8 G10
Vincent Wks, Dor. RH4 285 CG136
Vincenzo Cl, N.Mymms AL9 67 CW23
Vince St, EC1 19 M3
Vine, The, Sev. TN13 279 FH124
Vine Av, Sev. TN13 279 FH124
Vine Cl, E5
off Rendlesham Rd 144 DU63
Staines-upon-Thames TW19 196 BG85
Surbiton KT5 220 CM100
Sutton SM1 222 DC104
Welwyn Garden City AL8 51 CY07
West Drayton UB7 176 BN77
Vine Ct, E1 20 D7
Harrow HA3 140 CL58
Vine Ct Rd, Sev. TN13 279 FJ124
Vinegar All, E17 145 EB56
Vine Gdns, Ilf. IG1 147 EQ64
Vinegar St, E1 32 E2
Vinegar Yd, SE1 31 N4
Vine Gate, Farn.Com. SL2 153 AQ65
Vine Gro, Harl. CM20 57 ER10
Uxbridge UB10 156 BN66
Vine Hill, EC1 18 E5
Vine La, SE1 31 P3
Uxbridge UB10 156 BM67
Vine Pl, W5
off St. Mark's Rd 160 CL74
Hounslow TW3 178 CB84
Viner Cl, Walt. KT12 218 BW100
Vineries, The, N14 103 DJ44
SE6 205 EA88
Enfield EN1 104 DS41
Vineries Bk, NW7 119 CV50
Vineries Cl, Dag. RM9 168 FA65
Sipson UB7 176 BN79
Vine Rd, E15 13 L6
SW13 181 CT83
East Molesey KT8 218 CC98
Orpington BR6 245 ET107
Stoke Poges SL2 154 AT65
Vines Av, N3 120 DB53
Vine Sq, W14 39 H1
Vine St, EC3 20 A10
W1 29 M1
Romford RM7 149 FC57
Uxbridge UB8 156 BK67
Vine St Br, EC1 18 F5
Vine Way, Brwd. CM14 130 FW46
Vine Yd, SE1 31 K4
Vineyard, The, Hert. SG14 54 DR07
Richmond TW10 200 CL85
Ware SG12 55 EA05
Welwyn Garden City AL8 51 CX07
Vineyard Av, NW7 119 CY52
Vineyard Cl, SE6 205 EA88
Kingston upon Thames KT1 220 CM97
Vineyard Gro, N3 120 DB53
Vineyard Hill, Northaw EN6 86 DG29
Vineyard Hill Rd, SW19 202 DA91
Vineyard Pas, Rich. TW9
off Paradise Rd 200 CL85
Vineyard Path, SW14 180 CR83
Vineyard Prim Sch, The, Rich. TW10
off Friars Stile Rd 200 CL86
Vineyard Rd, Felt. TW13 197 BU90
Vineyard Row, Hmptn W. KT1 219 CJ95
Vineyards Rd, Northaw EN6 86 DF30
Vineyard Wk, EC1 18 E4
Viney Bk, Croy. CR0 243 DZ109
Viney Rd, SE13 185 EB83
Vining St, SW9 183 DN84
Vinlake Av, Uxb. UB10 136 BM62
Vinopolis, SE1 31 K2
Vinson Cl, Orp. BR6 228 EU102
Vintage Ms, E4
off Cherrydown Ave 123 EA49
Vintners Ct, EC4 19 K10
Vintners Pl, EC4
off Vintners Ct 19 K10
Vintry Ms, E17
off Cleveland Pk Cres 145 EA56
Viola Av, SE2 188 EV77
Feltham TW14 198 BW86
Staines-upon-Thames TW19 196 BK88
Viola Cl, S.Ock. RM15 171 FW69
Viola Sq, W12 161 CT73
Violet Av, Enf. EN2 104 DR38
Uxbridge UB8 156 BM71
Violet Cl, E16 23 K5
SE8 45 N2
Sutton SM3 221 CY102
Wallington SM6 222 DG102
Violet Gdns, Croy. CR0 241 DP106
Violet Hill, NW8 15 N1
Violet La, Croy. CR0 241 DP106
Violet Rd, E3 22 C5
E17 145 EA58
E18 124 EH54
Violet St, E2 20 F4
Violet Way, Loud. WD3 96 BJ42
Virgil Dr, Brox. EN10 71 DZ23
Virgil Pl, W1 16 E7
Virgil St, SE1 30 D6
Virginia Av, Vir.W. GU25 214 AW99
Virginia Beeches, Vir.W. GU25 214 AW97
Virginia Cl, Ashtd. KT21
off Skinners La 253 CK118
Bromley BR2 225 ED97
New Malden KT3
off Willow Rd 220 CQ98
Romford RM5 127 FC52
Staines-upon-Thames TW18
off Blacksmiths La 216 BJ97
Weybridge KT13 235 BQ107
Virginia Dr, Vir.W. GU25 214 AW99
Virginia Gdns, Ilf. IG6 125 EQ54
Virginia Pl, Cob. KT11 235 BU114
Virginia Prim Sch, E2 20 A3
Virginia Rd, E2 20 A3
Thornton Heath CR7 223 DP95
Virginia St, E1 32 D1
Virginia Wk, SW2 203 DM86
Gravesend DA12 213 GK93
VIRGINIA WATER, GU25 214 AX99
Virginia Water 214 AY99
Virgo Fidelis Conv Sen Sch, SE19 off Central Hill 204 DR93
Virgo Fidelis Prep Sch, SE19
off Central Hill 204 DR93
Viridian Apts, SW8 41 L5
Visage Apts, NW3 6 B7
Viscount Cl, N11 121 DH50
Viscount Dr, E6 25 J6
Viscount Gdns, W.Byf. KT14 234 BL112
Viscount Gro, Nthlt. UB5 158 BX69
Viscount Rd, Stanw. TW19 196 BK88
Viscount St, EC1 19 J5
Viscount Way, Lon.Hthrw Air. TW6 177 BS84
Vista, The, E4 123 ED45
SE9 206 EK86
Sidcup DA14 207 ET92
Vista Av, Enf. EN3 105 DX40
Vista Bldg, The, SE18 37 M8
Vista Dr, Ilf. IG4 146 EK57
Vista Ho, SW19
off Chapter Way 222 DD95
Vista Office Cen, TW4 178 BW83
Vista Way, Har. HA3 140 CL58
Vitae, W6 off Goldhawk Rd 181 CU76
Vita et Pax Sch, N14
off Priory Cl 103 DH43
Vittoria Prim Sch, N1 8 E10
Viveash Cl, Hayes UB3 177 BT76
Vivian Av, NW4 141 CV57
Wembley HA9 140 CN64
Vivian Cl, Wat. WD19 115 BU46
Vivian Comma Cl, N4 143 DP62
Vivian Ct, W9 5 L10
Vivian Gdns, Wat. WD19 115 BU46
Vivian Gdns, Wembley HA9 140 CN64
Vivian Rd, E3 11 L10
Vivian Sq, SE15 44 E10
Vivian Way, N2 142 DD57
Vivien Cl, Chess. KT9 238 CL108
Vivien Ct, N9 off Galahad Rd 122 DU47
Vivienne Cl, Twick. TW1 199 CJ86
Vixen Ct, Hat. AL10 67 CV16
Vixen Dr, Hert. SG13 54 DU09
Voce Rd, SE18 187 ER80
Voewood Cl, N.Mal. KT3 221 CT100
Vogan Cl, Reig. RH2 288 DB137
Vogans Mill, SE1 32 B4
Volta Cl, N9 off Hudson Way 122 DW48
Voltaire Bldgs, SW18 202 DB88
Voltaire Rd, SW4 183 DK83
Voltaire Way, Hayes UB3 157 BS73
Volt Av, NW10 160 CR69
Volta Way, Croy. CR0 223 DM102
Voluntary Pl, E11 146 EG58
Vorley Rd, N19 143 DJ61
Voss Ct, SW16 203 DL93
Voss St, E2 20 D3
Voyager Business Est, SE16
off Spa Rd 32 C6
Voyagers Cl, SE28 168 EW72
Voysey Cl, N3 141 CY55
Vulcan Cl, E6 25 M9
Vulcan Gate, Enf. EN2 103 DN40
Vulcan Rd, SE4 45 N8
Vulcan Sq, E14 34 B9
Vulcan Ter, SE4 45 N8
Vulcan Way, N7 8 D4
New Addington CR0 244 EE110
Wallington SM6 241 DL109
Vyne, The, Bexh. DA7 189 FB83
Vyner Rd, W3 160 CR73
Vyners Sch, Ickhm UB10
off Warren Rd 136 BM63
Vyner St, E2 10 F10
Vyners Way, Uxb. UB10 136 BN64
Vyse Cl, Barn. EN5 101 CW42

W

Wacketts, Chsht EN7 88 DU27
Wadbrook St, Kings.T. KT1 219 CK96
Wadding St, SE17 31 L9
Waddington Av, Couls. CR5 257 DN120
Waddington Cl, Couls. CR5 257 DP119
Enfield EN1 104 DS42
Waddington Rd, E15 13 H3
St. Albans AL3 65 CD20
Waddington St, E15 13 H4
Waddington Way, SE19 204 DQ94
WADDON, Croy. CR0 223 DN103
Waddon 241 DN105
Waddon Cl, Croy. CR0 223 DN104
Waddon Ct Rd, Croy. CR0 241 DN105
Waddon Marsh 223 DN103
Waddon Marsh Way, Croy. CR0 223 DM102
Waddon New Rd, Croy. CR0 223 DP104
Waddon Pk Av, Croy. CR0 241 DN105
Waddon Rd, Croy. CR0 223 DN104
Waddon Way, Croy. CR0 241 DP107
Wade, The, Welw.G.C. AL7 51 CZ12
Wade Av, Orp. BR5 228 EX101
Wade Dr, Slou. SL1 153 AN74
Wades, The, Hat. AL10 67 CU21
Wades Gro, N21 121 DN45
Wades Hill, N21 103 DN44
Wades La, Tedd. TW11
off High St 199 CG92
Wadesmill Rd, Chap.End SG12 54 DQ06
Hertford SG14 54 DQ06
Wadeson St, E2 10 F10
Wades Pl, E14 22 C10
Wadeville Av, Rom. RM6 148 EZ59
Wadeville Cl, Belv. DA17 188 FA79
Wadham Av, E17 123 EB52
Wadham Cl, Shep. TW17 217 BQ101
Wadham Gdns, NW3 6 C8
Greenford UB6 159 CD65
Wadham Rd, E17 123 EB53
SW15 181 CY84
Abbots Langley WD5 81 BT31
Wadhurst Cl, SE20 224 DV96
Wadhurst Rd, SW8 41 L6
W4 180 CR76
Wadley Cl, Hem.H. HP2
off White Hart Dr 62 BM21
Wadley Rd, E11 146 EE59
Wadsworth Business Cen, Grnf. UB6 159 CJ68
Wadsworth Cl, Enf. EN3 105 DX43
Perivale UB6 159 CJ68
Wadsworth Rd, Perivale UB6 159 CH68
Wager St, E3 21 N5
Waggon Cl, Guil. GU2 264 AS133
Waggoners Rbt, Houns. TW5 177 BV81
Waggon Ms, N14
off Chase Side 121 DJ46
Waggon Rd, Barn. EN4 102 DC37
Waghorn Rd, E13 166 EJ67
Harrow HA3 139 CK55
Waghorn St, SE15 44 C10
Wagner St, SE15 44 G4
Wagon Rd, Barn. EN4 102 DB36
Wagon Way, Loud. WD3 96 BJ41
Wagstaff Gdns, Dag. RM9 168 EW66
Wagtail Cl, NW9 118 CS54
Enfield EN1 104 DV39
Wagtail Gdns, S.Croy. CR2 243 DY110
Wagtail Wk, Beck. BR3 225 EC99
Wagtail Way, Orp. BR5 228 EX98
Waid Cl, Dart. DA1 210 FM86
Waight Cl, Hat. AL10 66 CS16
Waights Ct, Kings.T. KT2 220 CL95
Wain Cl, Pot.B. EN6 86 DB29
Wainfleet Av, Rom. RM5 127 FC54
Wainford Cl, SW19
off Windlesham Gro 201 CX88
Wainwright Av, Hutt. CM13 131 GD44
Wainwright Gro, Islw. TW7 179 CD84
Waite Davies Rd, SE12 206 EF87
Waite St, SE15 44 A2
Waithman St, EC4 18 G9
Wake Arms, Epp. CM16 107 EM36
Wake Cl, Guil. GU2 264 AV129
Wakefield Cl, Byfleet KT14 234 BL112
Wakefield Cres, Stoke P. SL2 154 AT66
Wakefield Gdns, SE19 204 DS94
Ilford IG1 146 EL58
Wakefield Ms, WC1 18 B3
Wakefield Rd, N11 121 DK50
N15 144 DT57
Greenhithe DA9 211 FW85
Richmond TW10 199 CK85
Wakefield St, E6 166 EK67
N18 122 DU50
Wakefield St, WC1 18 B4
Wakefields Wk, Chsht EN8 89 DY31
Wakeford Cl, SW4 203 DJ85
Bexley DA5 208 EX87
Wakehams Hill, Pnr. HA5 138 BZ55
Wakeham St, N1 9 L5
Wakehurst Path, Wok. GU21 233 BC114
Wakehurst Rd, SW11 202 DE85
Wakeling La, Wem. HA0 139 CH62
Wakeling Rd, W7 159 CF71
Wakeling St, E14 21 L9
Wakelin Rd, E15 13 J10
Wakely Cl, Bigg.H. TN16 260 EJ118
Wakeman Rd, NW10 14 C2
Wakemans Hill Av, NW9 140 CR57
Wakerfield Cl, Horn. RM11 150 FM57
Wakering Rd, Bark. IG11 167 EQ66
Wakerley Cl, E6 25 J9
Wake Rd, High Beach IG10 106 EJ38
Wakley St, EC1 18 G2
Walberswick St, SW8 42 B5
Walbrook, EC4 19 L10
Walbrook Ho, N9 122 DW47
Walbrook Wf, EC4
off Bell Wf La 31 K1
Walburgh St, E1 20 E9
Walburton Rd, Pur. CR8 241 DJ113
Walcorde Av, SE17 31 K9
Walcot Ho, SE22
off Albrighton Rd 184 DS83
Walcot Rd, Enf. EN3 105 DZ40
Walcot Sq, SE11 30 F8
Walcott St, SW1 29 M8
Waldair Ct, E16 37 N4
Waldair Wf, E16 37 N4
Waldeck Gro, SE27 203 DP90
Waldeck Rd, N15 143 DP56
SW14
off Lower Richmond Rd 180 CQ83
W4 180 CN79
W13 159 CH72
Dartford DA1 210 FM86
Waldeck Ter, SW14
off Lower Richmond Rd 180 CQ83
Waldegrave Av, Tedd. TW11
off Waldegrave Rd 199 CF92
Waldegrave Ct, Upmin. RM14 150 FP60
Waldegrave Gdns, Twick. TW1 199 CF89
Upminster RM14 150 FP60
Waldegrave Pk, Twick. TW1 199 CF91
Waldegrave Rd, N8 143 DN55
SE19 204 DT94
W5 160 CM72
Bromley BR1 226 EL98
Dagenham RM8 148 EW61
Teddington TW11 199 CF91
Twickenham TW1 199 CF91
Waldegrave Sch for Girls, Twick. TW2 off Fifth Cross Rd 199 CD90
Waldegrove, Croy. CR0 224 DT104
Waldemar Av, SW6 38 F7
W13 159 CJ74
Waldemar Rd, SW19 202 DA92
Walden Av, N13 122 DQ49
Chislehurst BR7 207 EM91
Rainham RM13 169 FD68
Waldenbury Pl, Beac. HP9 132 AG55
Walden Cl, Belv. DA17 188 EZ78
Walden Ct, SW8
off Wandsworth Rd 41 P6
Walden Gdns, Th.Hth. CR7 223 DM97
Waldenhurst Rd, Orp. BR5 228 EX101
Walden Par, Chis. BR7
off Walden Rd 207 EM93
Walden Pl, Welw.G.C. AL8 51 CX07
Walden Rd, N17 122 DR53
Chislehurst BR7 207 EM93
Hornchurch RM11 150 FK58
Welwyn Garden City AL8 51 CX07
Waldens Cl, Orp. BR5 228 EX101
Waldenshaw Rd, SE23 204 DW88
Waldens Pk Rd, Wok. GU21 248 AW116
Waldens Rd, Orp. BR5 228 EY101
Woking GU21 248 AX117
Walden St, E1 20 E8
Walden Way, NW7 119 CX51
Hornchurch RM11 150 FK58
Ilford IG6 125 ES52
Waldo Cl, SW4 203 DJ85
Waldo Pl, Mitch. CR4 202 DE94
Waldorf Cl, S.Croy. CR2 241 DP109
Waldorf Sch of S W London, The, SW16 off Abbotswood Rd 203 DJ89
Waldo Rd, NW10 161 CU69
Bromley BR1 226 EK97
Waldram Cres, SE23 204 DW88
Waldram Pk Rd, SE23 205 DX88
Waldram Pl, SE23
off Waldram Cres 204 DW88
Waldrist Way, Erith DA18 188 EZ75
Waldron Gdns, Brom. BR2 225 ED97
Waldronhyrst, S.Croy. CR2 241 DP105
Waldron Ms, SW3 40 B2
Waldron Rd, SW18 202 DC90
Harrow HA1, HA2 139 CE60
Waldrons, The, Croy. CR0 241 DP105
Oxted RH8 276 EF131
Waldrons Path, S.Croy. CR2 242 DQ105
Waldrons Yd, Har. HA2
off Northolt Rd 139 CD61
Waldstock Rd, SE28 168 EU73
Waleran Cl, Stan. HA7 117 CF51
Walerand Rd, SE13 46 F9
Waleran Flats, SE1 31 N8
Wales Av, Cars. SM5 240 DF106
Wales Cl, SE15 44 E4
Wales Fm Rd, W3 160 CR71
Waleton Acres, Wall. SM6 241 DJ107
Waley St, E1 21 K6
Walfield Av, N20 120 DB45
Walford Rd, N16 144 DS63
North Holmwood RH5 285 CH140
Uxbridge UB8 156 BJ68
Walfords Cl, Harl. CM17 58 EW12
Walfrey Gdns, Dag. RM9 168 EY66
WALHAM GREEN, SW6 39 L5
Walham Grn Ct, SW6 39 L5
Walham Gro, SW6 39 J4
Walham Ri, SW19 201 CY93
Walham Yd, SW6 39 J4
Walk, The, Eton Wick SL4 173 AN78
Hertford SG14
off Chelmsford Rd 53 DN10
Hornchurch RM11 150 FM61
Potters Bar EN6 86 DA32
Sunbury-on-Thames TW16 197 BT94
Tandridge RH8 275 EA133
Walkden Rd, Chis. BR7 207 EN92
Walker Cl, N11 121 DJ49
SE18 187 EQ77
W7 159 CE74
Dartford DA1 189 FF83
Feltham TW14 197 BT87
Hampton TW12
off Fearnley Cres 198 BZ93
Walker Cl, New Addington CR0 243 EC108
Walker Cres, Slou. SL3 175 AZ78
Walker Gro, Hat. AL10 66 CR17
Walker Ms, SW2 off Effra Rd 203 DN85
Walker Prim Sch, N14
off Waterfall Rd 121 DK47
Walkers Ct, E8 10 C4
W1 17 N10
Walkerscroft Mead, SE21 204 DQ88
Walkers Pl, SW15
off Felsham Rd 181 CY84
Walkfield Dr, Epsom KT18 255 CV117
Walkley Rd, Dart. DA1 209 FH85
Walks, The, N2 142 DD55
Walkwood End, Beac. HP9 110 AJ54
Walkwood Ri, Beac. HP9 132 AJ55
Walkynscroft, SE15 44 F8
Wallace Cl, SE28
off Haldane Rd 168 EX73
Shepperton TW17 217 BR98
Uxbridge UB10 156 BL68
Wallace Collection, W1 16 G8
Wallace Ct, Enf. EN3
off Eden Cl 105 EA37
Wallace Cres, Cars. SM5 240 DF106
Wallace Flds, Epsom KT17 239 CT112
Wallace Flds Inf Sch, Ewell KT17 off Wallace Flds 239 CU113
Wallace Flds Jun Sch, Ewell KT17 off Dorling Dr 239 CU112
Wallace Gdns, Swans. DA10 212 FY86
Wallace Rd, N1 9 K4
Grays RM17 192 GA76
Wallace Sq, Couls. CR5
off Cayton Rd 257 DK122
Wallace Wk, Add. KT15 234 BJ105
Wallace Way, N19
off Giesbach Rd 143 DK61
Romford RM1 127 FD53
Wallasey Cres, Uxb. UB10 136 BN61
Wallbrook Business Cen, Houns. TW4 off Green La 177 BV83
Wallbutton Rd, SE4 45 L9
Wallcote Av, NW2 141 CX60
Walled Gdn, The, Bet. RH3 286 CR135
Tadworth KT20 255 CX122
Walled Gdn Cl, Beck. BR3 225 EB98
Wall End Rd, E6 167 EM66
Wallenger Av, Rom. RM2 149 FH55
Waller Dr, Nthwd. HA6 115 BU54
Waller La, Cat. CR3 258 DT123
Waller Rd, SE14 45 J7
Beaconsfield HP9 111 AM53
Wallers Cl, Dag. RM9 168 EY67
Woodford Green IG8 125 EM51
Waller's Hoppet, Loug. IG10 106 EL40
Wallers Way, Hodd. EN11 55 EB14
Waller Way, SE10 46 D4
Wallfield All, Hert. SG13 54 DQ10
Wallflower St, W12 161 CT73
Wallgrave Rd, SW5 27 L8
Wall Hall Dr, Ald. WD25 98 CB36
Wall Hall Fm Cotts, Ald. WD25
off Pelham La 98 CB36
Wall Hall Mansion, Ald. WD25 98 CB36
Wallhouse Rd, Erith DA8 189 FH80
Wallingford Av, W10 14 C7
Wallingford Rd, Uxb. UB8 156 BH68
Wallingford Wk, St.Alb. AL1 65 CD23
WALLINGTON, SM6 241 DJ106
Wallington 241 DH107
Wallington Cl, Ruis. HA4 137 BQ58
Wallington Cor, Wall. SM6
off Manor Rd N 241 DH105
Wallington Co Gram Sch, Wall. SM6 off Croydon Rd 241 DH105
Wallington Grn, Wall. SM6
off Croydon Rd 241 DH105
Wallington High Sch for Girls, Wall. SM6 off Woodcote Rd 241 DH109
Wallington Rd, Chesh. HP5 76 AP30
Ilford IG3 147 ET59
Wallington Sq, Wall. SM6
off Woodcote Rd 241 DH107
Wallis All, SE1 31 K4
Wallis Cl, SW11 182 DD83
Dartford DA2 209 FF90
Hornchurch RM11 149 FH60
Wallis Ct, Slou. SL1 174 AU75
Wallis Ho, Brent. TW8 180 CL78
Wallis Ms, N8 off Courcy Rd 143 DN55
Fetcham KT22 253 CG122
Wallis Pk, Nthflt DA11 212 GB85
Wallis Rd, E9 11 P5
Lon.Hthrw Air. TW6
off Western Perimeter Rd 176 BH82
Southall UB1 158 CB72
Wallis's Cotts, SW2 203 DL87
Wallman Pl, N22
off Bounds Grn Rd 121 DM53
Wallorton Gdns, SW14 180 CR84
Wallside, EC2
off The Barbican 19 K7
Wall St, N1 9 M5
Wallwood Rd, E11 145 ED60
Wallwood St, E14 21 P7
Walmar Cl, Barn. EN4 102 DD39
Walmer Cl, E4 123 EB47
Farnborough BR6
off Tubbenden La S 245 ER105
Romford RM7 127 FB54
Walmer Gdns, W13 179 CG75
Walmer Ho, N9 122 DT45
Walmer Pl, W1 16 E6
Walmer Rd, W10 14 B9
W11 14 E10
Walmer St, W1 16 E6
Walmer Ter, SE18 187 EQ77
Walmgate Rd, Perivale UB6 159 CH67
Walmington Fold, N12 120 DA51
Walm La, NW2 4 B5
Walmsley Ho, SW16
off Colson Way 203 DJ91
Walney Wk, N1 9 K4
Walnut Av, West Dr. UB7 176 BN76
Walnut Cl, SE8 45 P3
Carshalton SM5 240 DF106
Epsom KT18 255 CT115
Eynsford DA4 230 FK104
Hayes UB3 157 BS73
Ilford IG6 147 EQ56
Park Street AL2 82 CB27
Walnut Ct, W5 180 CL75
Welwyn Garden City AL7 51 CY12
Walnut Dr, Kgswd KT20 255 CY123
Walnut Gdns, E15 13 H2
Walnut Grn, Bushey WD23 98 BZ40
Walnut Gro, Bans. SM7 239 CX114
Enfield EN1 104 DR43
Harlow CM20 57 EP14
Hemel Hempstead HP2 62 BK20
Hornchurch RM12 150 FK60
Welwyn Garden City AL7 51 CY12
Wooburn Green HP10 132 AE57

Walnut Ms, Sutt. SM2 240 DC108
Wooburn Green HP10 132 AE57
Walnut Rd, E10 145 EA61
Walnuts, The, Orp. BR6
off High St 228 EU102
Walnut Shop Cen, Orp. BR6 228 EU102
Walnuts Rd, Orp. BR6 228 EU102
Walnut Tree Av, Dart. DA1 210 FL89
Mitcham CR4
off De'Arn Gdns 222 DE97
Walnut Tree Cl, SW13 181 CT81
Banstead SM7 239 CY112
Cheshunt EN8 89 DX31
Chislehurst BR7 227 EQ95
Guildford GU1 264 AW134
Hoddesdon EN11 71 EA17
Uxbridge UB10 136 BL63
Westerham TN16 277 ER126
Walnut Tree Cotts, SW19
off Church Rd 201 CY92
Walnut Tree Gdns, Gdmg. GU7 280 AS144
Walnut Tree La, Byfleet KT14 234 BK112
Walnut Tree Pk, Guil. GU1 264 AW134
Walnut Tree Pl, Send GU23 249 BD123
Walnut Tree Rd, SE10 47 K1
Brentford TW8 180 CL79
Dagenham RM8 148 EX61
Erith DA8 189 FE78
Hounslow TW5 178 BZ79
Shepperton TW17 217 BQ96
Walnut Tree Wk, SE11 30 E8
Ware SG12 55 DX09
Walnut Tree Wk Prim Sch, SE11 30 E8
Walnut Way, Buck.H. IG9 124 EK48
Ruislip HA4 158 BW65
Swanley BR8 229 FD96
Walpole Av, Chipstead CR5 256 DF118
Richmond TW9 180 CM82
Walpole Cl, W13 179 CJ75
Grays RM17
off Palmers Dr 192 GC77
Pinner HA5 116 CA51
Walpole Cres, Tedd. TW11 199 CF92
Walpole Gdns, W4 180 CQ78
Twickenham TW2 199 CE89
Walpole Ho, SE1
off Westminster Br Rd 30 E5
Walpole Ms, NW8 6 A9
SW19 off Walpole Rd 202 DD93
Walpole Pk, W5 159 CJ74
Weybridge KT13 234 BN108
Walpole Pl, SE18 37 N9
Teddington TW11 199 CF92
Walpole Rd, E6 166 EJ66
E17 145 DY56
E18 124 EF53
N17 (Downhills Way) 144 DQ55
N17 (Lordship La) 122 DQ54
SW19 202 DD93
Bromley BR2 226 EK99
Croydon CR0 224 DR103
Old Windsor SL4 194 AV87
Slough SL1 153 AK72
Surbiton KT6 220 CL101
Teddington TW11 199 CF92
Twickenham TW2 199 CE89
Walpole St, SW3 28 E10
Walrond Av, Wem. HA9 140 CL64
Walrus Rd, Lon.Hthrw Air. TW6
off Western Perimeter Rd 176 BH83
Walsham Cl, N16
off Clarke Path 144 DU60
SE28 168 EX73
Walsham Rd, SE14 45 J8
Feltham TW14 197 BV87
Walsh Cres, New Adgtn CR0 244 EE112
Walshford Way, Borwd. WD6 100 CN38
Walsingham Cl, Hat. AL10 67 CT17
Walsingham Gdns, Epsom KT19 238 CS105
Walsingham Pk, Chis. BR7 227 ER96
Walsingham Pl, SW4 off Clapham Common W Side 182 DF84
SW11 202 DG86
Walsingham Rd, E5 144 DU62
W13 159 CG74
Enfield EN2 104 DR42
Mitcham CR4 222 DF99
New Addington CR0 243 EC110
Orpington BR5 228 EV95
Walsingham Wk, Belv. DA17 188 FA79
Walsingham Way, Lon.Col. AL2 83 CJ27
Walter Rodney Cl, E6
off Stevenage Rd 167 EM65
Walters Cl, SE17 31 K9
Cheshunt EN7 87 DP25
Hayes UB3 177 BT75
Walters Ho, SE17 42 G3
Walters Mead, Ashtd. KT21 254 CL117
Walters Rd, SE25 224 DS98
Enfield EN3 104 DW43
Walter St, E2 21 J3
Kingston upon Thames KT2
off Sopwith Way 220 CL95
Walters Way, SE23 205 DX86
Walters Yd, Brom. BR1 226 EG96
Walter Ter, E1 21 K8
Walterton Rd, W9 15 H5
Walter Wk, Edg. HA8 118 CQ51
WALTHAM ABBEY, EN9 106 EF35
★ Waltham Abbey (ruins), Wal.Abb. EN9 89 EC33
Waltham Av, NW9 140 CN58
Guildford GU2 264 AV131
Hayes UB3 177 BQ76
Waltham Cl, Dart. DA1 209 FG86
Hutton CM13 off Bannister Dr 131 GC44
Orpington BR5 228 EX102
WALTHAM CROSS, EN7 & EN8 89 DZ33
⇌ Waltham Cross 89 DY34
Waltham Cross 89 DY34
Waltham Dr, Edg. HA8 118 CN54
Waltham Forest Coll, E17
off Forest Rd 145 EB55
Waltham Gdns, Enf. EN3 104 DW36
Waltham Gate, Wal.Cr. EN8 89 DZ26
Waltham Holy Cross Inf Sch, Wal.Abb. EN9
off Quendon Dr 89 ED33
Waltham Holy Cross Jun Sch, Wal.Abb. EN9
off Quendon Dr 89 ED33
Waltham Pk Way, E17 123 EA53
Waltham Rd, Cars. SM5 222 DD101
Caterham CR3 258 DV122
Nazeing Gate EN9 90 EF26
Southall UB2 178 BY76
Woodford Green IG8 124 EL51
WALTHAMSTOW, E17 123 EB54
Walthamstow Acad, E17
off Billet Rd 123 DZ53
Walthamstow Adult Ed Cen, E17 off Greenleaf Rd 145 DZ55
Walthamstow Av, E4 123 DZ52
● Walthamstow Business Cen, E17 123 EC54
⇌ Walthamstow Central 145 EA56
⊖ Walthamstow Central 145 EA56
Walthamstow Central 145 EA56
Walthamstow Hall Sch, Jun Sch, Sev. TN13
off Bradbourne Pk Rd 279 FH122
Sen Sch, Sev. TN13
off Holly Bush La 279 FJ123
Walthamstow Queens Road 145 DZ57
Walthamstow Sch for Girls, E17 off Church Hill 145 EB56
Waltham Way, E4 123 DZ49
Waltheof Av, N17 122 DR53
Waltheof Gdns, N17 122 DR53
Walton Av, Har. HA2 138 BZ64
New Malden KT3 221 CT98
Sutton SM3 221 CZ104
Wembley HA9 140 CP62
Walton Br, Shep. TW17 217 BS101
Walton-on-Thames KT12 217 BS101
Walton Br Rd, Shep. TW17 217 BS101
Walton Cl, E5 off Orient Way 145 DX62
NW2 141 CV61
SW8 42 B4
Harrow HA1 139 CD56
Walton Comm Hosp, Walt. KT12 217 BV103
Walton Ct, Wok. GU21 249 BA116
Walton Cres, Har. HA2 138 BZ63
Walton Dr, NW10 160 CR65
Harrow HA1 139 CD56
Walton Gdns, W3 160 CP71
Feltham TW13 197 BT91
Hutton CM13 131 GC43
Waltham Abbey EN9 89 EB33
Wembley HA9 140 CL61
Walton Grn, New Adgtn CR0 243 EC108
Walton La, Farn.Royal SL2 153 AL69
Shepperton TW17 217 BR101
Walton-on-Thames KT12 217 BQ102
Weybridge KT13 217 BP103
Walton Leigh Sch, Walt. KT12 off Queens Rd 235 BT105
Walton Oak Sch, Walt. KT12
off Ambleside Av 218 BW102
WALTON-ON-THAMES, KT12 217 BT103
⇌ Walton-on-Thames 235 BU105
WALTON ON THE HILL, Tad. KT20 271 CT125
Walton-on-the-Hill Prim Sch, Walt.Hill KT20
off Walton St 255 CV124
Walton Pk, Walt. KT12 218 BX103
Walton Pk La, Walt. KT12 218 BX103
Walton Pl, SW3 28 E6
Walton Rd, E12 147 EN63
E13 166 EJ68
N15 144 DT56
Bushey WD23 98 BX42
East Molesey KT8 218 CA98
Epsom Downs KT18 255 CT118
Harrow HA1 139 CD56
Headley KT18 254 CQ121
Hoddesdon EN11 71 EB15
Romford RM5 126 EZ52
Sidcup DA14 208 EW89
Walton-on-Thames KT12 218 BW99
Ware SG12 55 DX07
West Molesey KT8 218 BY99
Woking GU21 249 AZ116
Walton St, SW3 28 D8
Enfield EN2 104 DR39
St. Albans AL1 65 CF19
Walton on the Hill KT20 255 CU124
Walton Ter, Borwd. WD6
off Watford Rd 99 CK44
Wok. GU21 249 BB115
Walton Way, W3 160 CP71
Mitcham CR4 223 DJ98
Walt Whitman Cl, SE24
off Shakespeare Rd 183 DP84
Walverns Cl, Wat. WD19 98 BW44
WALWORTH, SE17 31 J10
Walworth Acad, SE1 43 P1
★ Walworth Garden Fm - Horticultural Training Cen, SE17 43 H1
Walworth Pl, SE17 43 K1
Walworth Rd, SE1 31 J8
SE17 31 J8
Walwyn Av, Brom. BR1 226 EK97
Wambrook Cl, Hutt. CM13 131 GC46
Wanborough Dr, SW15 201 CV88
Wanderer Dr, Bark. IG11 168 EV69
Wander Wf, Kings L. WD4 81 BP30
Wandle Bk, SW19 202 DD93
Croydon CR0 223 DL104
Wandle Ct, Epsom KT19 238 CQ105
Wandle Ct Gdns, Croy. CR0 223 DL104
Wandle Park 223 DN103
Wandle Rd, SW17 202 DE89
Beddington CR0 223 DL104
Croydon CR0 224 DQ104
Morden SM4 222 DC98
Wallington SM6 223 DH103
Wandle Side, Croy. CR0 223 DM104
Wallington SM6 223 DH104
● Wandle Tech Pk, Mitch. CR4 222 DF101
● Wandle Trd Est, Mitch. CR4
off Budge La 222 DF101
Wandle Valley Sch, Cars. SM5 off Welbeck Rd 222 DE101
Wandle Way, SW18 202 DB88
Mitcham CR4 222 DF99
Wandon Rd, SW6 39 M5
WANDSWORTH, SW18 201 CZ85
Wandsworth Br, SW6 182 DB83
SW18 182 DB83
Wandsworth Br Rd, SW6 39 L6
⇌ Wandsworth Common 202 DF88
Wandsworth Common, SW12 202 DE86
Wandsworth Common W Side, SW18 202 DC85
Wandsworth High St, SW18 202 DA85
★ Wandsworth Mus, SW18 202 DA85
Wandsworth Plain, SW18 202 DB85
Wandsworth Riverside Quarter Pier 182 DA84
⇌ Wandsworth Road 41 M9
Wandsworth Rd, SW8 42 A2
⇌ Wandsworth Town 182 DB84
Wandsworth Town, SW18 202 DA85
Wangey Rd, Rom. RM6 148 EX59
Wanless Rd, SE24 184 DQ83
Wanley Rd, SE5 184 DR84
Wanlip Rd, E13 24 A4
Wanmer Ct, Reig. RH2
off Birkheads Rd 272 DA133
Wannions Cl, Chesh. HP5 78 AU30
Wannock Gdns, Ilf. IG6 125 EP52
Wansbeck Rd, E3 11 P6
E9 11 P6
Wansbury Way, Swan. BR8 229 FG99
Wansdown Pl, SW6 39 L4
Wansey St, SE17 31 K9
Wansford Cl, Brwd. CM14 130 FT48
Wansford Grn, Wok. GU21 248 AT117
Wansford Pk, Borwd. WD6 100 CS42
Wansford Rd, Wdf.Grn. IG8 124 EJ53
WANSTEAD, E11 146 EH59
⊖ Wanstead 146 EH58
Wanstead Ch Prim Sch, E11
off Church Path 146 EG57
Wanstead Cl, Brom. BR1 226 EJ96
Wanstead High Sch, E11
off Redbridge La W 146 EJ58
Wanstead La, Ilf. IG1 146 EK58
Wanstead Park 146 EH63
Wanstead Pk, E11 146 EK59
Wanstead Pk Av, E12 146 EK61
Wanstead Pk Rd, Ilf. IG1 147 EM60
Wanstead Pl, E11 146 EG58
Wanstead Rd, Brom. BR1 226 EJ96
Wansunt Rd, Bex. DA5 209 FC88
Wantage Rd, SE12 206 EF85
Wantz La, Rain. RM13 169 FH70
Wantz Rd, Dag. RM10 149 FB63
Waplings, The, Tad. KT20 255 CV124
WAPPING, E1 32 D2
Wapping 32 G3
Wapping Dock St, E1 32 F3
Wapping High St, E1 32 C3
Wapping La, E1 32 F1
Wapping Wall, E1 32 G2
Wapseys La, Hedg. SL2 134 AS58
Wapshott Rd, Stai. TW18 195 BE93
Warbank Cl, New Adgtn CR0 244 EE111
Warbank Cres, New Adgtn CR0 244 EE110
Warbank La, Kings.T. KT2 201 CT94
Warbeck Rd, W12 161 CV74
Warberry Rd, N22 121 DM54
Warblers Grn, Cob. KT11 236 BZ114
Warboys App, Kings.T. KT2 200 CP93
Warboys Cres, E4 123 EC50
Warboys Rd, Kings.T. KT2 200 CP93
Warburton Cl, N1 9 N4
Harrow HA3 117 CD51
Warburton Ho, E8
off Warburton Rd 10 E8
Warburton Rd, E8 10 E8
Twickenham TW2 198 CB88
Warburton St, E8 10 E8
Warburton Ter, E17 123 EB54
War Coppice Rd, Cat. CR3 274 DR127
Wardalls Gro, SE14 45 H4
Ward Av, Grays RM17 192 GA77
Ward Cl, Chsht EN7 88 DU27
Erith DA8 189 FD79
Iver SL0 155 BF72
South Croydon CR2 242 DS106
Ware SG12 54 DW05
Wardell Cl, NW7 118 CS52
Wardell Fld, NW9 118 CS53
Warden Av, Har. HA2 138 BZ60
Romford RM5 127 FC50
Warden Rd, NW5 7 H4
Wardens Fld Cl, Grn St Grn BR6 245 ES107
Wardens Gro, SE1 31 J3
Ward Gdns, Harold Wd RM3
off Whitmore Av 128 FL54
Slough SL1 153 AL73
Ward Hatch, Harl. CM20 58 EU12
Ward La, Warl. CR6 258 DW116
Wardle St, E9 11 J3
Wardley St, SW18 202 DB87
Wardo Av, SW6 38 E7
Wardour Ms, W1 17 M9
Wardour St, W1 17 N10
Ward Pl, Amer. HP7 77 AP40
Ward Pt, SE11 30 E9
Ward Rd, E15 12 G8
N19 143 DJ62
Wardrobe Pl, EC4
off St. Andrew's Hill 19 H9
Wardrobe Ter, EC4 19 H9
Ward Royal, Wind. SL4 173 AQ81
Wards Dr, Sarratt WD3 95 BF36
Wards La, Els. WD6 99 CG40
Ward's Pl, Egh. TW20 195 BC93
Wards Rd, Ilf. IG2 147 ER59
Ward St, Guil. GU1
off Martyr Rd 280 AX135
Wards Wf App, E16 36 E4
WARE, SG12 55 DX06
⇌ Ware 55 DY07
Wareham Cl, Houns. TW3 178 CB84
Wareham Ho, SW8 42 C4
Warehams La, Hert. SG14 54 DQ10
Warehouse W, E16 24 A10
Waremead Rd, Ilf. IG2 147 EP57
★ Ware Mus, Ware SG12 55 DX06
Warenford Way, Borwd. WD6 100 CN39
Warenne Hts, Red. RH1 288 DD136
Warenne Rd, Fetch. KT22 252 CC122
WARE PARK, Ware SG12 54 DT06
Ware Pk Rd, Hert. SG14 54 DR07
Ware Pt Dr, SE28 187 ER75
Ware Rd, Chad.Spr. SG12 54 DU08
Hailey SG13 55 EA12
Hertford SG13, SG14 54 DS09
Hoddesdon EN11 55 EA14
Widford SG12 55 EC05
Warescot Cl, Brwd. CM15 130 FV45
Warescot Rd, Brwd. CM15 130 FV45
Wareside Cl, Welw.G.C. AL7 52 DB10
Warfield Rd, NW10 14 C3
Feltham TW14 197 BS87
Hampton TW12 218 CB95
Warfield Yd, NW10 14 C3
Wargrave Av, N15 144 DT58
Wargrave Rd, Har. HA2 138 CC62
Warham Rd, N4 143 DN57
Harrow HA3 117 CF54
Otford TN14 263 FH116
South Croydon CR2 241 DP106
Warham St, SE5 43 H4
Waring Cl, Orp. BR6 245 ET107
Waring Dr, Orp. BR6 245 ET107
Waring Rd, Sid. DA14 208 EW93
Waring St, SE27 204 DQ91
Warkworth Gdns, Islw. TW7 179 CG80
Warkworth Rd, N17 122 DR52
Warland Rd, SE18 187 ER80
WARLEY, Brwd. CM14 130 FW50
Warley Av, Dag. RM8 148 EZ59
Hayes UB4 157 BU71
Warley Cl, E10 145 DZ60
Warley Gap, Lt.Warley CM13 129 FV52
Warley Hill, Brwd. CM13, CM14 129 FV51
● Warley Hill Business Pk, Gt Warley CM13 off The Dr 129 FW51
Warley Mt, Warley CM14 130 FW49
Warley Prim Sch, Warley CM14 off Chindits La 130 FW50
Warley Rd, N9 122 DW47
Great Warley CM13 129 FT54
Hayes UB4 157 BU72
Ilford IG5 125 EN53
Upminster RM14 128 FQ54
Woodford Green IG8 124 EH52
Warley St, E2 21 J2
Great Warley CM13 151 FW58
Upminster RM14 151 FW58
Warley St Flyover, Brwd. CM13 151 FX57
Warley Wds Cres, Brwd. CM14
off Crescent Rd 130 FV49
WARLINGHAM, CR6 259 DX118
Warlingham Pk Sch, Warl. CR6
off Chelsham Common 259 EA116
Warlingham Rd, Th.Hth. CR7 223 DP98
Warlingham Sch, Warl. CR6
off Tithepit Shaw La 258 DV116
Warlock Rd, W9 15 J4
Warlow Cl, Enf. EN3 105 EA37
Warlters Cl, N7
off Warlters Rd 143 DL63
Warlters Rd, N7 143 DL63
Warltersville Rd, N19 143 DL59
Warltersville Way, Horl. RH6 291 DJ150
Warmark Rd, Hem.H. HP1 61 BE18
Warmington Cl, E5
off Denton Way 145 DX62
Warmington Rd, SE24 204 DQ86
Warmington St, E13 23 P4
Warminster Gdns, SE25 224 DU96
Warminster Rd, SE25 224 DT96
Warminster Sq, SE25 224 DU96
Warminster Way, Mitch. CR4 223 DH95
Warmwell Av, NW9 118 CS53
Warndon St, SE16 33 H9
Warneford Ct, NW9
off Annesley Ave 140 CR55
Warneford Pl, Wat. WD19 98 BY44
Warneford Rd, Har. HA3 139 CK55
Lon.Hthrw Air. TW6 176 BH82
Warneford St, E9 10 F8
Warne Pl, Sid. DA15
off Shorne Cl 208 EV86
Warner Av, Sutt. SM3 221 CY103
Warner Cl, E15 13 K3
NW9 141 CT59
Barnet EN4 102 DE37
Hampton TW12
off Tangley Pk Rd 198 BZ92
Harlington UB3 177 BR80
Slough SL1 153 AL74
Warner Ho, SE13 46 D8
Warner Par, Hayes UB3 177 BR80
Warner Pl, E2 20 D1
Warner Rd, E17 145 DY56
N8 143 DK56
SE5 43 J7
Bromley BR1 206 EF94
Ware SG12 54 DW07
Warners Av, Hodd. EN11 71 DZ19
Warners Cl, Wdf.Grn. IG8 124 EG50
WARNERS END, Hem.H. HP1 61 BE19
Warners End Rd, Hem.H. HP1 62 BG20
Warners La, Albury GU5 282 BL141
Kingston upon Thames KT2 199 CK91
Warners Path, Wdf.Grn. IG8 124 EG50
Warner St, EC1 18 E5
Warner Ter, E14 22 B7
Warner Yd, EC1 18 E5
Warnford Ho, SW15
off Tunworth Cres 200 CS86
● Warnford Ind Est, Hayes UB3 177 BS75
Warnford Rd, Orp. BR6 245 ET106
Warnham Ct Rd, Cars. SM5 240 DF108
Warnham Rd, N12 120 DE50
Warple Ms, W3
off Warple Way 180 CS75
Warple Way, W3 160 CS74
Warren, The, E12 146 EL63
Ashtead KT21 254 CL119
Carshalton SM5 240 DD109
Chalfont St. Peter SL9 113 AZ52
Chesham HP5 76 AL28
East Horsley KT24 267 BT130
Gravesend DA12 213 GK91
Hayes UB4 157 BU72
Hounslow TW5 178 BZ80
Kings Langley WD4 80 BM29
Kingswood KT20 255 CY123
Oxshott KT22 236 CC112
Park Street AL2
off How Wd 82 CC28
Radlett WD7 83 CG33
Worcester Park KT4 238 CR105
Warren Av, E10 145 EC62
Bromley BR1 206 EE94
Orpington BR6 245 ET106
Richmond TW10 180 CP84
South Croydon CR2 243 DX108
Sutton SM2 239 CZ110
Warren Cl, N9 123 DX45
SE21 204 DQ87
Bexleyheath DA6 208 FA85
Esher KT10 236 CB105
Hatfield AL10 67 CV15
Hayes UB4 158 BW71
Slough SL3 174 AY76
Wembley HA9 139 CK61
Warren Comp Sch, The, Chad.Hth RM6
off Whalebone La N 148 EZ57
Warren Ct, N17
off High Cross Rd 144 DU55
SE7 186 EJ78
Ashtead KT21
off Ashfield Cl 254 CL119
Chigwell IG7 125 ER49
Sevenoaks TN13 279 FJ125
Weybridge KT13 234 BN106
Warren Cres, N9 122 DT45
Warren Cutting, Kings.T. KT2 200 CR94
Warren Dale, Welw.G.C. AL8 51 CX06
Warren Dell Prim Sch, S.Oxhey WD19 off Gosforth La 116 BW48
Warrender Prim Sch, Ruis. HA4 off Old Hatch Manor 137 BT59
Warrender Rd, N19 143 DJ62
Chesham HP5 76 AS29
Warrender Way, Ruis. HA4 137 BU59
Warren Dr, Grnf. UB6 158 CB70
Hornchurch RM12 149 FG62
Kingswood KT20 255 CZ122
Orpington BR6 246 EV106
Ruislip HA4 138 BX59
Warren Dr, The, E11 146 EJ59
Warren Dr N, Surb. KT5 220 CP102
Warren Dr S, Surb. KT5 220 CQ102
Warreners La, Wey. KT13 235 BR109
Warren Fm Home Pk, Wok. GU22 250 BH119
Warren Fld, Epp. CM16 92 EU32
Iver SL0 155 BC68
Warrenfield Cl, Chsht EN7 88 DU31
Warren Flds, Stan. HA7
off Valencia Rd 117 CJ49
Warren Footpath, Twick. TW1 199 CK87
Warren Gdns, E15 12 G3
Orpington BR6 246 EU106
Warrengate La, S.Mimms EN6 85 CW31
Warrengate Rd, N.Mymms AL9 85 CW28
Warren Grn, Hat. AL10 67 CV15
Warren Gro, Borwd. WD6 100 CR42
Warren Hastings Ct, Grav. DA11
off Pier Rd 213 GF86
Warren Hts, Chaf.Hun. RM16 192 FY77
Loughton IG10 106 EJ43
Warren Hill, Epsom KT18 254 CR116
Loughton IG10 106 EJ44
Warren Ho, E3 22 C2
W14 27 H8
Warrenhyrst, Guil. GU1
off Warren Rd 281 BA135
Warren Jun Sch, Chad.Hth RM6 off Gordon Rd 148 EZ57
Warren La, SE18 37 N7
Albury GU5 282 BJ139
Grays RM16 191 FX77
Oxshott KT22 236 CC111
Oxted RH8 276 EF134
Stanmore HA7 117 CF48
Woking GU22 250 BH118
Warren La Gate, SE18 37 N7
Warren Lo, Kgswd KT20 255 CY124
Warren Mead, Bans. SM7 255 CW115
Warren Mead Inf Sch, Bans. SM7 off Partridge Mead 255 CX115
Warren Mead Jun Sch, Nork SM7 off Roundwood Way 255 CX115
Warren Ms, W1 17 L5
Warrenne Rd, Brock. RH3 286 CP136
Warrenne Way, Reig. RH2 272 DA134
Warren Pk, Box H. KT20 270 CQ131
Kingston upon Thames KT2 200 CQ93
Warlingham CR6 259 DX118
Warren Pk Rd, Hert. SG14 54 DQ08
Sutton SM1 240 DD107
Warren Pond Rd, E4 124 EF46
Warren Prim Sch, Chaff.Hun. RM16 off Gilbert Rd 191 FW76
Warren Ri, N.Mal. KT3 220 CR95
Warren Rd, E4 123 EC47
E10 145 EC62
E11 146 EJ60
NW2 141 CT61
SW19 202 DE93
Ashford TW15 197 BS94
Banstead SM7 239 CW114
Bexleyheath DA6 208 FA85
Bromley BR2 226 EG103
Bushey Heath WD23 116 CC46
Croydon CR0 224 DS102
Dartford DA1 210 FK90
Godalming GU7 280 AS144
Guildford GU1 281 AZ135
Ilford IG6 147 ER57
Kingston upon Thames KT2 200 CQ93
New Haw KT15 234 BG110
Orpington BR6 245 ET106
Purley CR8 241 DP111
Reigate RH2 272 DB133
St. Albans AL1 64 CC24
Sidcup DA14 208 EW90
Southfleet DA13 212 GB92
Twickenham TW2 198 CC86
Uxbridge UB10 136 BL63
Warren Rd Prim Sch, Orp. BR6 off Warren Rd 245 ET106
Warrens Shawe La, Edg. HA8 118 CP46
⊖ Warren Street 17 M4
Warren St, W1 17 K5
Warren Ter, Grays RM16
off Arterial Rd W Thurrock 191 FX75
Hertford SG14 54 DR07
Romford RM6 148 EX56
Warren Wk, SE7 186 EJ79
Warren Way, Edg. HA8 118 CP54
Weybridge KT13 235 BQ106
Warren Wd Cl, Brom. BR2 226 EF103
Warren Wd Ms, Hat. AL9 68 DD22
Warriner Av, Horn. RM12 150 FK61
Warriner Dr, N9 122 DU48
Warriner Gdns, SW11 40 F7
Warrington Av, Slou. SL1 153 AQ72
Warrington Cres, W9 15 N5
Warrington Gdns, W9 15 N5
Hornchurch RM11 150 FJ58
Warrington Rd, Croy. CR0 223 DP104
Dagenham RM8 148 EX61
Harrow HA1 139 CE57
Richmond TW10 199 CK85
Warrington Spur, Old Wind. SL4 194 AV87
Warrington Sq, Dag. RM8 148 EX61
Warrior Av, Grav. DA12 213 GJ91
Warrior Cl, SE28 167 ER74
Warrior Sq, E12 147 EN63
Warsaw Cl, Ruis. HA4
off Glebe Av 157 BV65
Warsdale Dr, NW9
off Mardale Dr 140 CR57
Warspite Rd, SE18 36 G6
Warton Rd, E15 12 E8
Warwall, E6 25 N8
⊖ Warwick Avenue 15 N5
Warwick Av, W2 15 N5
W9 15 N5
Cuffley EN6 87 DK27
Edgware HA8 118 CP48
Egham TW20 215 BC95
Harrow HA2 138 BZ63
Slough SL2 153 AQ70
Staines-upon-Thames TW18 196 BJ93
Warwick Bldg, SW8 41 J4
Warwick Chambers, W8
off Pater St 27 J6
Warwick Cl, Barn. EN4 102 DD43
Bexley DA5 208 EZ87
Bushey Heath WD23
off Magnaville Rd 117 CE45
Cuffley EN6 87 DK27
Hampton TW12 198 CC94
Hertford SG13 54 DQ11

Warwick Cl, Hornchurch RM11 150 FM56
Orpington BR6 228 EU104
South Holmwood RH5 285 CH144
Warwick Ct, SE15 44 D9
WC1 18 D7
Chorleywood WD3 95 BF41
Surbiton KT6 220 CL103
Warwick Cres, W2 15 N6
Hayes UB4 157 BT70
Warwick Deeping, Ott. KT16 233 BC106
Warwick Dene, W5 160 CL74
Warwick Dr, SW15 181 CV83
Cheshunt EN8 89 DX28
Warwick Est, W2 15 L7
Warwick Gdns, N4 144 DQ57
W14 27 H7
Ashtead KT21 253 CJ117
Barnet EN5 101 CZ38
Ilford IG1 147 EP60
Romford RM2 150 FJ55
Thames Ditton KT7 219 CF99
Thornton Heath CR7
off London Rd 223 DN97
Warwick Gro, E5 144 DV60
Surbiton KT5 220 CM101
Warwick Ho St, SW1 29 P2
Warwick La, EC4 19 H9
Rainham RM13 170 FM68
Upminster RM14 170 FP68
Woking GU21 248 AU119
Warwick Ms, Crox.Grn WD3 96 BN44
Warwick Pas, EC4 19 H8
Warwick Pl, W5
off Warwick Rd 179 CK75
W9 15 N6
Northfleet DA11 212 GB85
Uxbridge UB8 156 BJ66
Warwick Pl N, SW1 29 L9
🔒 Warwick Quad Shop Mall, Red. RH1 off London Rd 272 DG133
Warwick Rd, E4 123 EA50
E11 146 EH57
E12 146 EL64
E15 13 M5
E17 123 DZ53
N11 121 DK51
N18 122 DS49
SE20 224 DV97
SW5 26 G8
W5 179 CK75
W14 26 G8
Ashford TW15 196 BL92
Barnet EN5 102 DB42
Beaconsfield HP9 111 AK52
Borehamwood WD6 100 CR41
Coulsdon CR5 241 DJ114
Enfield EN3 105 DZ37
Hounslow TW4 177 BV83
Kingston upon Thames KT1 219 CJ95
New Malden KT3 220 CQ97
Rainham RM13 170 FJ70
Redhill RH1 272 DF133
St. Albans AL1 65 CF18
Sidcup DA14 208 EV92
Southall UB2 178 BZ76
Sutton SM1 240 DC105
Thames Ditton KT7 219 CF99
Thornton Heath CR7 223 DN97
Twickenham TW2 199 CE88
Welling DA16 188 EW83
West Drayton UB7 176 BL75
Warwick Row, SW1 29 K6
Warwicks Bench, Guil. GU1 280 AX136
Warwicks Bench La, Guil. GU1 280 AY137
Warwicks Bench Rd, Guil. GU1 280 AY137
Sch Warwick Sch, The, Red. RH1 off Noke Dr 272 DG133
Warwickshire Path, SE8 45 P4
Warwick Sq, EC4 19 H8
SW1 29 L10
Warwick Sq Ms, SW1 29 L9
Warwick St, W1 17 M10
Warwick Ter, SE18 187 ER79
Warwick Way, SW1 29 L9
Croxley Green WD3 97 BQ42
Dartford DA1 210 FL89
WARWICK WOLD, Red. RH1 273 DN129
Warwick Wold Rd, Red. RH1 273 DN128
Warwick Yd, EC1 19 K5
Wash, The, Hert. SG14 54 DR09
Wash Hill, Woob.Grn HP10 132 AE60
Wash Hill Lea, Woob.Grn HP10 132 AD59
Washington Av, E12 146 EL63
Hemel Hempstead HP2 62 BM15
Washington Bldg, SE13 off Deals Gateway 46 C6
Washington Cl, E3 22 D2
Reigate RH2 272 DA131
Washington Dr, Slou. SL1 153 AK73
Windsor SL4 173 AL83
Washington Rd, E6 off St. Stephens Rd 166 EJ66
E18 124 EF54
SW13 181 CU80
Kingston upon Thames KT1 220 CN96
Lon.Hthrw Air. TW6 off Wayfarer Rd 176 BH82
Worcester Park KT4 221 CV103
Washington Row, Amer. HP7 off London Rd W 77 AQ40
Wash La, S.Mimms EN6 85 CV33
Washneys Rd, Orp. BR6 246 EV113
Washpond La, Warl. CR6 259 EC118
Wash Rd, Hutt. CM13 131 GD44
Wasp Grn La, Outwood RH1 289 DP143
Wasp Rd, Lon.Hthrw Air. TW6 off Wayfarer Rd 176 BH82
Wastdale Rd, SE23 205 DX88
Watchfield Ct, W4 180 CQ78
Watchgate, Lane End DA2 211 FR91
Watchlytes, Welw.G.C. AL7 52 DC09
Sch Watchlytes Sch, Welw.G.C. AL7 off Watchlytes 52 DC09
Watchmead, Welw.G.C. AL7 52 DA09
Watcombe Cotts, Rich. TW9 180 CN79
Watcombe Pl, SE25 off Albert Rd 224 DV98
Watcombe Rd, SE25 224 DV99
Waterbank Rd, SE6 205 EC91
Waterbeach, Welw.G.C. AL7 52 DD08
Waterbeach Cl, Slou. SL1 153 AR72
Waterbeach Rd, Dag. RM9 168 EW65
Slough SL1 153 AR72
Waterbourne Way, Ken. CR8 242 DR114
Water Brook La, NW4 141 CW57
Watercress Pl, N1 9 P7
Watercress Rd, Chsht EN7 88 DR26
Watercress Way, Wok. GU21 248 AV117
Watercroft Rd, Halst. TN14 246 EZ110
Sch Waterdale, Wat. WD25 82 BX30
Waterdale, Hert. SG13 54 DQ11
Waterdale Rd, SE2 188 EU79
Waterdales, Nthflt DA11 212 GD88
Waterdell Pl, Rick. WD3 off Uxbridge Rd 114 BG47
Waterden Cl, Guil. GU1 281 AZ135
Waterden Rd, E20 12 B4
Guildford GU1 280 AY135
WATER END, Hat. AL9 85 CV26
Water End Cl, Borwd. WD6 100 CM40
Waterend La, Ayot St.P. AL6 50 CQ07
Wheathampstead AL4 50 CQ07
Water End Rd, Pott.End HP4 61 BB17
Waterer Gdns, Tad. KT20 255 CX118
Waterer Ri, Wall. SM6 241 DK107
Waterfall Cl, N14 121 DJ48
Hoddesdon EN11 71 DZ16
Virginia Water GU25 214 AU97
Waterfall Cotts, SW19 202 DD93
Waterfall Rd, N11 121 DH49
N14 121 DJ48
SW19 202 DD93
Waterfall Ter, SW17 202 DE93
Waterfield, Herons. WD3 113 BC45
Tadworth KT20 255 CV119
Welwyn Garden City AL7 52 DB08
Waterfield Cl, SE28 168 EV74
Belvedere DA17 188 FA76
Waterfield Dr, Warl. CR6 258 DW119
Waterfield Gdns, SE25 224 DR98
Waterfield Grn, Tad. KT20 255 CW120
Waterfields, Lthd. KT22 253 CH119
Watford WD17 98 BX42
🔒 Waterfields Retail Pk, Wat. WD17 98 BX42
Waterfields Way, Wat. WD17 98 BX42
WATERFORD, Hert. SG14 53 DM05
Waterford Cl, Cob. KT11 236 BY111
Waterford Common, Waterf. SG14 53 DP05
Waterford Grn, Welw.G.C. AL7 52 DB09
Waterford Rd, SW6 39 M6
Waterford Way, NW10 141 CV64
Waterfront, The, Els. WD6 99 CH44
Hertford SG14 54 DR09
Waterfront Ms, N1 off Arlington Av 9 K10
● Waterfront Studios Business Cen, E16 35 N2
🔒 Water Gdns, Harl. CM20 73 ER15
Water Gdns, Stan. HA7 117 CH51
Water Gdns, The, W2 16 D8
Watergardens, The, Kings.T. KT2 200 CQ93
Water Gdns Sq, SE16 33 J5
Watergate, EC4 18 G10
Watergate, The, Wat. WD19 116 BX47
Sch Watergate Sch, SE6 off Lushington Rd 205 EB92
Watergate St, SE8 46 A3
Watergate Wk, WC2 30 B2
● Waterglade Ind Pk, Grays RM20 191 FT78
Waterglades, Knot.Grn HP9 110 AJ49
Waterhall Av, E4 124 EE49
Waterhall Cl, E17 123 DX53
Waterhead Cl, Erith DA8 189 FE80
Waterhouse Cl, E16 24 E6
NW3 6 B2
W6 26 D10
Waterhouse La, Bletch. RH1 274 DT132
Kenley CR8 258 DQ119
Kingswood KT20 255 CY121
Waterhouse Moor, Harl. CM18 73 ES16
Waterhouse Sq, EC1 18 E7
Waterhouse St, Hem.H. HP1 62 BJ20
Wateridge Cl, E14 34 A7
Wateringbury Cl, Orp. BR5 228 EV97
Water La, E15 13 K4
EC3 31 N1
N9 122 DV46
NW1 7 K7
SE14 45 H4
Abinger Hammer RH5 283 BV143
Albury GU5 282 BH137
Berkhamsted HP4 60 AW19
Bookham KT23 268 BY125
Bovingdon HP3 79 BA29
Chesham HP5 76 AP32
Cobham KT11 252 BY115
Hertford SG14 54 DQ10
Ilford IG3 147 ES62
Kings Langley WD4 81 BP29
Kingston upon Thames KT1 219 CK95
Purfleet RM19 190 FN77
Redhill RH1 273 DP130
Richmond TW9 199 CK85
Roydon CM19 72 EL19
Shoreham TN14 247 FF112
Sidcup DA14 208 EZ89
Titsey RH8 276 EG126
Twickenham TW1 off The Embankment 199 CG88
Watford WD17 98 BW42
Westerham TN16 277 ER127
Sch Water La Prim Sch, Harl. CM19 off Broadley Rd 73 EN19
Water Lily Cl, Sthl. UB2 off Navigator Dr 178 CC75
⇌ Waterloo 30 E4
⊖ Waterloo 30 E4
Waterloo Br, SE1 30 C1
WC2 30 C1
Waterloo Cl, E9 11 H2
Feltham TW14 197 BT88
⇌ Waterloo East 30 E3
Waterloo Est, E2 10 G10
Waterloo Gdns, E2 10 G10
N1 8 G7
Romford RM7 149 FD58
Waterloo Pas, NW6 5 H7
Waterloo Pl, SW1 29 N2
Kew TW9 off Kew Grn 180 CN79
Richmond TW9 off The Quadrant 180 CL84
Waterloo Rd, E6 166 EJ66
E7 13 M2
E10 145 EA59
NW2 141 CU60
SE1 30 E4
Brentwood CM14 130 FW46
Epsom KT19 238 CR112
Ilford IG6 125 EQ54
Romford RM7 149 FE57
Sutton SM1 240 DD106
Uxbridge UB8 156 BJ67
Waterloo St, Grav. DA12 213 GJ87
Waterloo Ter, N1 8 G7
Waterlow Ct, NW11 off Heath Cl 142 DB59
Waterlow Rd, N19 143 DJ60
Reigate RH2 288 DC135
Waterman Cl, Wat. WD19 97 BV44
Waterman Ct, Slou. SL1 153 AL74
Watermans, Rom. RM1 149 FF57
● Watermans, The, Stai. TW18 195 BE91
★ Watermans Art Cen, Brent. TW8 180 CL79
Waterman's Cl, Kings.T. KT2 off Woodside Rd 200 CL94
Waterman St, SW15 181 CX83
Waterman's Wk, EC4 off Allhallows La 31 L1
Watermans Wk, SE16 33 L6
Watermans Way, Green. DA9 191 FV84
North Weald Bassett CM16 92 FA27
Waterman Way, E1 32 E2
Watermark Way, Hert. SG13 54 DT09
Water Mead, Chipstead CR5 256 DF117
Watermead, Felt. TW14 197 BS88
Tadworth KT20 255 CV121
Woking GU21 248 AT116
Watermead Ho, E9 off Kingsmead Way 11 M2
Watermead La, Cars. SM5 off Middleton Rd 222 DF101
Watermeadow, Chesh. HP5 76 AP32
Watermeadow Cl, Erith DA8 189 FH80
Watermeadow La, SW6 39 N9
Water Meadows, Frog. AL2 off Frogmore 83 CE28
Watermead Rd, SE6 205 EC91
Watermead Way, N17 144 DV55
Watermen's Sq, SE20 204 DW94
Water Ms, SE15 184 DW84
● Watermill Business Cen, Enf. EN3 105 DZ40
Watermill Cl, Rich. TW10 199 CJ90
Watermill La, N18 122 DS50
Hertford SG14 54 DR06
Watermill La N, Hert. SG14 54 DQ06
Watermill Way, SW19 222 DC95
Feltham TW13 198 BZ89
Water Mill Way, S.Darenth DA4 230 FP96
Watermint Cl, Orp. BR5 off Wagtail Way 228 EX98
Watermint Quay, N16 144 DU59
Waterperry La, Chobham GU24 232 AT110
Water Rd, Wem. HA0 160 CM67
Water Row, Ware SG12 55 DX06
Waters Dr, Rick. WD3 114 BL46
Staines-upon-Thames TW18 195 BF90
Watersedge, Epsom KT19 238 CQ105
Waters Edge Ct, Erith DA8 off Erith High St 189 FF78
Watersfield Way, Edg. HA8 117 CK52
Waters Gdns, Dag. RM10 148 FA64
WATERSIDE, Chesh. HP5 76 AR32
Waterside, Beck. BR3 225 EA95
Berkhamsted HP4 off Holliday St 60 AX19
Chesham HP5 76 AQ32
Dartford DA1 209 FE85
Gravesend DA11 212 GE86
Horley RH6 290 DG146
Water Side, Kings L. WD4 80 BN29
Waterside, Lon.Col. AL2 84 CL27
Radlett WD7 83 CH34
Uxbridge UB8 156 BJ71
Welwyn Garden City AL7 52 DA07
Wooburn Green HP10 132 AE56
Waterside Av, Beck. BR3 off Brockwell Av 225 EB99
● Waterside Business Cen, Islw. TW7 off Railshead Rd 179 CH84
Waterside Cl, E3 11 N8
SE16 32 D5
SE28 167 ET74
Barking IG11 148 EU63
Harold Wood RM3 128 FN52
Northolt UB5 158 BZ69
Surbiton KT6 off Culsac Rd 220 CL103
Sch Waterside Comb Sch, Chesh. HP5 off Blackhorse Av 76 AR33
Waterside Ct, SE13 off Weardale Rd 185 ED84
Kings Langley WD4 off Water Side 81 BP29
Waterside Dr, Langley SL3 175 AZ75
Walton-on-Thames KT12 217 BU99
Waterside Ms, Guil. GU1 264 AW132
Harefield UB9 114 BG51
Waterside Path, SW18 off Smugglers Way 182 DB84
Waterside Pl, NW1 7 H8
Sawbridgeworth CM21 58 FA05
Waterside Pt, SW11 40 D4
Waterside Rd, Guil. GU1 264 AX131
Southall UB2 178 CA76
Sch Waterside Sch, SE18 off Robert St 187 ER78
Waterside Twr, SW6 39 P8
● Waterside Trd Cen, W7 179 CE76
Waterside Way, SW17 202 DC91
Woking GU21 off Winnington Way 248 AV118
Waterslade, Red. RH1 272 DE134
Watersmeet, Harl. CM19 73 EP19
Watersmeet Cl, Guil. GU4 off Cotts Wd Dr 265 BA129
Watersmeet Way, SE28 168 EW72
Waterson Rd, Grays RM16 193 GH77
Waterson St, E2 19 P2
Waters Pl, SW15 38 B9
Watersplash Cl, Kings.T. KT1 220 CL97
Watersplash Ct, Lon.Col. AL2 off Thamesdale 84 CM27
Watersplash La, Hayes UB3 177 BU77
Hounslow TW5 177 BV78
Watersplash Rd, Shep. TW17 216 BN98
Waters Rd, SE6 206 EE90
Kingston upon Thames KT1 220 CP96
Waters Sq, Kings.T. KT1 220 CP97
Waterstone Way, Green. DA9 211 FU86
Water St, WC2 18 D10
Waterton, Swan. BR8 229 FD98
Waterton Av, Grav. DA12 213 GL87
Water Twr Cl, Uxb. UB8 136 BL64
Water Twr Hill, Croy. CR0 242 DR105
Water Twr Pl, N1 8 F9
Water Twr Rd, Gt Warley CM14 130 FW50
Water Vw, Horl. RH6 off Carlton Tye 291 DJ148
Waterview Cl, Bexh. DA6 208 EX85
Waterview Ho, E14 21 M7
Waterway Av, SE13 185 EB83
● Waterway Business Pk, Hayes UB3 177 BR75
Waterway Rd, Lthd. KT22 253 CG122
● Waterways Business Cen, Enf. EN3 105 EA38
Jct Waterworks Cor, E18 124 EE54
Waterworks Cotts, Brox. EN10 71 DY22
Waterworks La, E5 145 DX61
Waterworks Rd, SW2 203 DL86
Waterworks Yd, Croy. CR0 off Surrey St 224 DQ104
Watery La, SW20 221 CZ96
Broxbourne EN10 89 DY25
Flamstead AL3 83 CK28
Hatfield AL10 66 CS19
Lyne KT16 215 BD101
Northolt UB5 158 BW68
Sidcup DA14 208 EV93
Wooburn Green HP10 110 AE54
Wates Way, Brwd. CM15 130 FX46
Mitcham CR4 222 DF100
● Wates Way Ind Est, Mitch. CR4 222 DF100
Wateville Rd, N17 122 DQ53
WATFORD, WD17 - WD19; WD24 & WD25 97 BT41
⊖ Watford 97 BT41
🔒 Watford Arches Retail Pk, Wat. WD17 98 BX43
● Watford Business Pk, Wat. WD18 97 BS44
Watford Bypass, Borwd. WD6 117 CG45
Watford Cl, SW11 40 D6
Guildford GU1 265 AZ134
Watford Fld Rd, Wat. WD18 98 BW43
★ Watford FC, Wat. WD18 97 BV43
H Watford Gen Hosp, Wat. WD18 97 BV43
Sch Watford Gram Sch for Boys, Wat. WD18 off Rickmansworth Rd 97 BT42
Sch Watford Gram Sch for Girls, Wat. WD18 off Lady's Cl 98 BW43
WATFORD HEATH, Wat. WD19 116 BY46
Watford Heath, Wat. WD19 116 BX45
⊖ Watford High Street 98 BW42
Watford Ho La, Wat. WD17 off Clarendon Rd 97 BV41
⇌ Watford Junction 98 BW40
⊖ Watford Junction 98 BW40
● Watford Metro Cen, Wat. WD18 115 BQ45
★ Watford Mus, Wat. WD17 98 BW42
⇌ Watford North 98 BW37
Watford Rd, E16 23 P7
Croxley Green WD3 97 BQ43
Elstree WD6 99 CJ44
Harrow HA1 139 CG61
Kings Langley WD4 81 BP32
Northwood HA6 115 BT52
Radlett WD7 99 CE36
St. Albans AL1, AL2 82 CA27
Wembley HA0 139 CG61
Watford Way, NW4 141 CU56
NW7 119 CT51
Wathen Rd, Dor. RH4 285 CH135
Watkin Ms, Enf. EN3 105 EA37
Watkin Rd, Wem. HA9 140 CP62
Watkins Cl, Nthwd. HA6 off Chestnut Av 115 BT53
Watkinson Rd, N7 8 C4
Watkins Ri, Pot.B. EN6 off The Walk 86 DB32
Watkins Way, Dag. RM8 148 EY60
Watling Av, Edg. HA8 118 CR52
Watling Cl, Hem.H. HP2 62 BL17
Watling Ct, EC4 19 K9
Borehamwood WD6 99 CK44
Watling Fm Cl, Stan. HA7 117 CJ46
Watling Gdns, NW2 4 F5
Watling Knoll, Rad. WD7 83 CF33
Watlings Cl, Croy. CR0 225 DY100
Watling St, EC4 19 J9
SE15 43 P3
Bexleyheath DA6 189 FB84
Dartford DA1, DA2 210 FP87
Elstree WD6 99 CJ40
Gravesend DA11, DA12, DA13 213 GL94
Radlett WD7 83 CF32
St. Albans AL1, AL2 82 CC25
Watling St Caravan Site (Travellers), Park St AL2 82 CC25
Watlington Gro, SE26 205 DY92
Watlington Rd, Harl. CM17 58 EX11
Watling Vw, St.Alb. AL1 64 CC24
Sch Watling Vw Sch, St.Alb. AL1 off Watling Vw 65 CD24
Watney Cl, Pur. CR8 241 DM113
Watney Cotts, SW14 off Lower Richmond Rd 180 CQ83
Watney Mkt, E1 20 F9
Watney Rd, SW14 180 CQ83
Watneys Rd, Mitch. CR4 223 DK99
Watney St, E1 20 F9
Watson Av, E6 167 EN66
St. Albans AL3 65 CF17
Sutton SM3 221 CY103
Watson Cl, N16 9 M2
SW19 202 DE93
Grays RM20 191 FU81
Watson Gdns, Harold Wd. RM3 128 FK54
Watson Ho, Har. HA1 139 CF57
Watson Pl, SE25 224 DT99
Watson Rd, Westc. RH4 284 CC137
Watsons Ms, W1 16 D7
Watsons Rd, N22 121 DM53
Watson's St, SE8 46 A5
Watson St, E13 166 EH68
Watsons Wk, St.Alb. AL1 65 CE21
Sch Wattenden Prim Sch, The, Pur. CR8 off Old Lo La 257 DP116
Wattendon Rd, Ken. CR8 257 DP116
Wattisfield Rd, E5 144 DW62
Wattleton Rd, Beac. HP9 111 AK54
Watton Rd, Ware SG12 54 DW05
Watts Cl, N15 144 DS57
Tadworth KT20 255 CX122
Watts Cres, Purf. RM19 190 FQ77
Watts Down Cl, E13 13 N9
Watts Fm Par, Chobham GU24 off Barnmead 232 AT110
Watts Gro, E3 22 C6
Watts La, Chis. BR7 227 EP95
Tadworth KT20 255 CX122
Teddington TW11 199 CG92
Watts Lea, Horsell GU21 248 AU115
Watts Mead, Tad. KT20 255 CX122
Watts Rd, T.Ditt. KT7 219 CG101
Watts St, E1 32 F2
SE15 44 B6
Watts Way, SW7 28 B6
Wat Tyler Rd, SE3 46 F8
SE10 46 F8
Wauthier Cl, N13 121 DP50
Wavell Cl, Chsht EN8 89 DY27
Wavell Dr, Sid. DA15 207 ES86
Wavell Gdns, Slou. SL2 153 AM69
Wavell Rd, Beac. HP9 111 AP54
Wavel Ms, N8 143 DK56
NW6 5 L7
Wavel Pl, SE26 off Sydenham Hill 204 DT91
Wavendene Av, Egh. TW20 195 BB94
Wavendon Av, W4 180 CR78
Waveney, Hem.H. HP2 62 BM15
Waveney Av, SE15 184 DV84
Waveney Cl, E1 32 D2
Waverley Av, E4 123 DZ49
E17 145 ED55
Kenley CR8 258 DS116
Surbiton KT5 220 CP100
Sutton SM1 222 DB103
Twickenham TW2 198 BZ88
Wembley HA9 140 CM64
Waverley Cl, E18 124 EJ53
Bromley BR2 226 EK99
Hayes UB3 177 BR77
West Molesey KT8 218 CA99
Waverley Ct, Wok. GU22 248 AY118
Waverley Cres, SE18 187 ER78
Romford RM3 128 FJ52
Waverley Dr, Cher. KT16 215 BD104
Virginia Water GU25 214 AU97
Waverley Gdns, E6 25 H7
NW10 160 CM69
Barking IG11 167 ES68
Grays RM16 192 GA75
Ilford IG6 125 EQ54
Northwood HA6 115 BU53
Waverley Gro, N3 141 CX55
● Waverley Ind Pk, Har. HA1 139 CD55
Waverley Pl, N4 143 DP60
NW8 6 A10
Leatherhead KT22 off Church Rd 253 CH122
Waverley Rd, E17 145 EC55
E18 124 EJ53
N8 143 DK58
N17 122 DV52
SE18 187 EQ78
SE25 224 DV98
Enfield EN2 103 DP42
Epsom KT17 239 CV106
Harrow HA2 138 BZ60
Oxshott KT22 236 CB114
Rainham RM13 169 FH69
St. Albans AL3 65 CD18
Slough SL1 153 AQ71
Southall UB1 158 CA73
Stoke D'Abernon KT11 236 CB114
Weybridge KT13 234 BN106
Sch Waverley Sch, Enf. EN3 off The Ride 104 DW42
Waverley Vil, N17 122 DT54
Waverley Wk, W2 15 K6
Waverley Way, Cars. SM5 240 DE107
Waverton Ho, E3 11 P8
Waverton Rd, SW18 202 DC87
Waverton St, W1 29 H2
Wavertree Ct, SW2 off Streatham Hill 203 DL88
Wavertree Rd, E18 124 EG54
SW2 203 DL88
Waxham, NW3 6 F2
Waxlow Cres, Sthl. UB1 158 CA72
Waxlow Rd, NW10 160 CQ68
Waxlow Way, Nthlt. UB5 158 BZ70
Waxwell Cl, Pnr. HA5 116 BX54
Waxwell La, Pnr. HA5 116 BX54
Way, The, Reig. RH2 272 DD133
Waybourne Gro, Ruis. HA4 137 BQ58
Waycross Rd, Upmin. RM14 151 FS58
Waye Av, Houns. TW5 177 BU81
Wayfarer Rd, Lon.Hthrw Air. TW6 176 BH82
Nthlt. UB5 158 BX70
Wayfarers Pk, Berk. HP4 60 AT19
Wayfaring Grn, Bad.Dene RM17 off Curling La 192 FZ78
Wayfield Link, SE9 207 ER86
Wayford St, SW11 40 D9
Wayland Av, E8 10 D3
Wayland Ho, SW9 42 E8
Waylands, Hayes UB3 157 BR71
Swanley BR8 229 FF98
Wraysbury TW19 194 AY86
Waylands Cl, Knock.P. TN14 262 EY115
Waylands Mead, Beck. BR3 225 EB95
Wayleave, The, SE28 168 EV73
Waylen Gdns, Dart. DA1 190 FM82
Waylett Ho, SE11 42 E1
Waylett Pl, SE27 203 DP90
Wembley HA0 139 CK63
Wayman Ct, E8 10 E5
Wayne Cl, Orp. BR6 227 ET104
Wayneflete Pl, Esher KT10 off More La 218 CB104
Wayneflete Twr Av, Esher KT10 218 CA104
Waynflete Av, Croy. CR0 223 DP104
Waynflete Sq, W10 14 C10
Waynflete St, SW18 202 DC89
Wayre, The, Harl. CM17 58 EW11
Wayre St, Harl. CM17 58 EW11
Wayside, NW11 141 CY60
SW14 200 CQ85
Chipperfield WD4 80 BH30
New Addington CR0 243 EB107
Potters Bar EN6 86 DD33
Shenley WD7 83 CK33
Wayside, The, Hem.H. HP3 63 BQ21
Wayside Av, Bushey WD23 99 CD44
Hornchurch RM12 150 FK61
Wayside Cl, N14 103 DJ44
Romford RM1 149 FF55
● Wayside Commercial Est, Bark. IG11 168 EU67
Wayside Ct, Twick. TW1 199 CJ86
Wembley HA9 140 CN62
Woking GU21 off Langmans Way 248 AS116
Wayside Gdns, SE9 off Wayside Gro 207 EM91
Dagenham RM10 148 FA64
Gerrards Cross SL9 134 AX59
Wayside Gro, SE9 207 EM91
Wayside Ms, Ilf. IG2 off Gaysham Av 147 EN57
Wayville Rd, Dart. DA1 210 FP87
Way Volante, Grav. DA12 213 GL91
Weald, The, Chis. BR7 207 EM93
Weald Br Rd, N.Wld Bas. CM16 75 FD24
Weald Cl, SE16 32 E10
Brentwood CM14 130 FU48
Bromley BR2 226 EL103
Istead Rise DA13 212 GE94
Shalford GU4 off Station Rd 280 AY140
★ Weald Country Pk, Brwd. CM14 130 FS45

Sch **Weald First & Mid Schs**, Har. HA3
off Robin Hood Dr 117 CF52
● **Weald Hall Fm Commercial Cen**, Hast. CM17 92 EZ25
Weald Hall La, Thnwd CM16 92 EW25
Weald La, Har. HA3 117 CD54
Wealdon Ct, Guil. GU2
off Chapelhouse Cl 264 AS134
Weald Pk Way, S.Wld CM14 130 FS48
Weald Ri, Har. HA3 117 CF52
Weald Rd, Brwd. CM14 129 FR46
Sevenoaks TN13 279 FH129
Uxbridge UB10 156 BN68
Weald Sq, E5 144 DU61
WEALDSTONE, Har. HA3 139 CF55
Wealdstone Rd, Sutt. SM3 221 CZ103
Wealdway, Cat. CR3 274 DS128
Wealdway, Grav. DA13 213 GH93
Weald Way, Hayes UB4 157 BS69
Reigate RH2 288 DC138
Romford RM7 149 FB58
Wealdwood Gdns, Pnr. HA5
off Highbanks Rd 116 CB51
Weale Rd, E4 123 ED48
Weall Cl, Pur. CR8 241 DM113
Weall Grn, Wat. WD25 81 BV32
Weardale Av, Dart. DA2 210 FQ89
Weardale Gdns, Enf. EN2 104 DR39
Weardale Rd, SE13 185 EB84
Wear Pl, E2 20 E3
Wearside Rd, SE13 185 EB84
Weasdale Ct, Wok. GU21
off Roundthorn Way 248 AT116
Weatherall Cl, Add. KT15 234 BH106
Weatherbury Ho, N19
off Wedmore St 143 DK62
Weatherhill Cl, Horl. RH6 291 DM148
Weatherhill Common, Smallfield RH6 291 DM147
Weatherhill Rd, Smallfield RH6 291 DM148
Weatherley Cl, E3 21 P6
Weaver Cl, E6 25 N10
Croydon CR0 242 DT105
Weavers Almshouses, E11
off New Wanstead 146 EG58
Weavers Cl, Grav. DA11 213 GG88
Isleworth TW7 179 CE84
Weavers La, SE1 31 P3
Sevenoaks TN14 279 FJ121
Weavers Orchard, Sthflt DA13 212 GA93
Weavers Ter, SW6 39 K3
Weaver St, E1 20 C5
Weavers Way, NW1 7 N8
Weaver Wk, SE27 203 DP91
Webb Cl, W10 14 A5
Chesham HP5 76 AP30
Slough SL3 174 AX77
Webber Cl, Els. WD6
off Rodgers Cl 99 CK44
Erith DA8 189 FH80
Webber Row, SE1 30 F5
Webber St, SE1 30 F4
Webb Est, E5 144 DU59
Webb Gdns, E13 23 P4
Webb Ho, SW8 41 P5
Webb Pl, NW10 161 CT69
Webb Rd, SE3 47 M2
Webb's All, Sev. TN13, TN15 279 FJ125
Webbscroft Rd, Dag. RM10 149 FB63
Webbs Rd, SW11 202 DF85
Hayes UB4 157 BV69
Webb St, SE1 31 N7
Webheath Est, NW6 5 H6
Webley Ct, Enf. EN3
off Sten Cl 105 EA37
Webster Cl, Horn. RM12 150 FK62
Oxshott KT22 236 CB114
Waltham Abbey EN9 90 EG33
Webster Gdns, W5 159 CK74
Webster Rd, E11 145 EC62
SE16 32 D7
Websters Cl, Wok. GU22 248 AU120
Wedderburn Rd, NW3 6 A3
Barking IG11 167 ER67
Wedgewood Cl, Epp. CM16 92 EU30
Northwood HA6 115 BQ52
Wedgewood Dr, Harl. CM17 74 EX16
Wedgwood Ho, SE11 30 E7
Wedgewood Ms, W1 17 P9
Wedgwood Pl, Cob. KT11 235 BU114
Wedgwoods, Tats. TN16
off Redhouse Rd 260 EJ121
Wedgwood Wk, NW6
off Dresden Cl 5 M3
Wedgwood Way, SE19 204 DQ94
Wedhey, Harl. CM19 73 EQ15
Wedlake Cl, Horn. RM11 150 FL60
Wedlake St, W10 14 F4
Wedmore Av, Ilf. IG5 125 EN53
Wedmore Gdns, N19 143 DK61
Wedmore Ms, N19 143 DK62
Wedmore Rd, Grnf. UB6 159 CD69
Wedmore St, N19 143 DK62
Wednesbury Gdns, Rom. RM3 128 FM52
Wednesbury Grn, Rom. RM3
off Wednesbury Gdns 128 FM52
Wednesbury Rd, Rom. RM3 128 FM52
Weech Rd, NW6 5 J1
Weedington Rd, NW5 6 G2
Weedon Cl, Chal.St.P. SL9 112 AV53
Weedon La, Amer. HP6 77 AN36
Weekes Dr, Slou. SL1 153 AP74
Weekley Sq, SW11
off Thomas Baines Rd 182 DD83
Weigall Rd, SE12 186 EG84
Weighhouse St, W1 17 H9
Weighton Rd, SE20 224 DV96
Harrow HA3 117 CD53
Weihurst Gdns, Sutt. SM1 240 DD106
Weimar St, SW15 181 CY83
Weind, The, They.B. CM16 107 ES36
Weirdale Av, N20 120 DF47
Weir Est, SW12 203 DJ87
Weir Hall Av, N18 122 DR51
Weir Hall Gdns, N18 122 DR50
Weir Hall Rd, N17 122 DR50
N18 122 DR50
Weir Pl, Stai. TW18 215 BE95
Weir Rd, SW12 203 DJ87
SW19 202 DB90
Bexley DA5 209 FB87
Chertsey KT16 216 BH101
Walton-on-Thames KT12 217 BU100
Weirside Gdns, West Dr. UB7 156 BK74
Weir's Pas, NW1 17 P2
Weiss Rd, SW15 181 CX83
Welbeck Av, Brom. BR1 206 EG91
Hayes UB4 157 BV70
Sidcup DA15 208 EU88
Welbeck Cl, N12 120 DD50
Borehamwood WD6 100 CN41
Epsom KT17 239 CU108
Welbeck Cl, New Malden KT3 221 CT99
Welbeck Rd, E6 24 E2
Barnet EN4 102 DD44
Carshalton SM5 222 DE102
Harrow HA2 138 CB60
Sutton SM1 222 DD103
Welbeck St, W1 17 J8
Welbeck Wk, Cars. SM5
off Welbeck Rd 222 DE102
Welbeck Way, W1 17 J8
Sch **Welbourne Prim Sch**, N17
off High Cross Rd 144 DU55
Welby St, SE5 43 H7
Welch Ho, Enf. EN3
off Beaconsfield Rd 105 DX37
Welch Pl, Pnr. HA5 116 BW53
Welclose St, St.Alb. AL3 64 CC20
Welcomes Rd, Ken. CR8 258 DQ115
Welcote Dr, Nthwd. HA6 115 BR51
Welden, Slou. SL2 154 AW72
Welders La, Chal.St.P. SL9 112 AT52
Jordans HP9 112 AT52
Weldon Cl, Ruis. HA4 157 BV65
Weldon Dr, W.Mol. KT8 218 BZ98
Weldon Way, Merst. RH1 273 DK129
Weld Pl, N11 121 DH50
Welfare Rd, E15 13 K6
Welford Cl, E5
off Denton Way 145 DX62
Welford Ho, Nthlt. UB5
off Waxlow Way 158 BZ70
Welford Pl, SW19 201 CY91
Welham Cl, Borwd. WD6 100 CN39
N.Mymms AL9 67 CW24
Welham Ct, N.Mymms AL9
off Dixons Hill Rd 67 CW24
WELHAM GREEN, Hat. AL9 67 CV23
⇌ **Welham Green** 67 CX23
Welham Manor, N.Mymms AL9 67 CW24
Welham Rd, SW16 202 DG92
SW17 202 DG92
Welhouse Rd, Cars. SM5 222 DE102
Welkin Grn, Hem.H. HP2
off Wood End Cl 63 BQ19
Wellacre Rd, Har. HA3 139 CH58
Wellan Cl, Sid. DA15 208 EV85
Welland Cl, Slou. SL3 175 BA79
Welland Gdns, Perivale UB6 159 CF68
Welland Ms, E1 32 D2
Welland Rd, Lon.Hthrw Air. TW6 off Wayfarer Rd 176 BH82
Wellands, Hat. AL10 67 CU16
Wellands Cl, Brom. BR1 227 EM96
Welland St, SE10 46 E2
Well App, Barn. EN5 101 CW43
Wellbank, Tap. SL6
off Rectory Rd 152 AE70
Wellbrook Rd, Orp. BR6 245 EN105
Wellbury Ter, Hem.H. HP2 63 BQ20
Wellby Cl, N9 122 DU46
Well Cl, SW16 203 DM91
Ruislip HA4
off Parkfield Cres 138 BY62
Woking GU21 248 AW117
Wellclose Sq, E1 20 D10
Wellclose St, E1 32 D1
Wellcome Av, Dart. DA1 190 FM84
Coll **Wellcome Trust**, NW1 17 N4
Well Cottage Cl, E11 146 EJ59
Well Ct, EC4 19 K9
SW16 203 DM91
Wellcroft, Hem.H. HP1
off Gadebridge Rd 62 BH19
Wellcroft Cl, Welw.G.C. AL7 52 DA11
Wellcroft Rd, Slou. SL1 153 AP74
Welwyn Garden City AL7 52 DA11
Welldon Cres, Har. HA1 139 CE58
Sch **Welldon Pk First Sch**, S.Har. HA2 off Kingsley Rd 138 CC63
Sch **Welldon Pk Mid Sch**, S.Har. HA2 off Wyvenhoe Rd 138 CC63
WELL END, Borwd. WD6 100 CR38
Well End Rd, Borwd. WD6 100 CQ37
Weller Cl, Amer. HP6 77 AS37
Weller Ms, Brom. BR2 226 EH98
Enfield EN2 103 DN39
Weller Pl, Downe BR6 245 EN111
Weller Rd, Amer. HP6 77 AS37
Wellers Cl, West. TN16 277 EQ127
Wellers Ct, Shere GU5 282 BN139
Wellers Gro, Chsht EN7 88 DU28
Weller St, SE1 31 J4
Wellesford Cl, Bans. SM7 255 CZ117
Wellesley, Harl. CM19 73 EN20
Wellesley Av, W6 181 CV76
Iver SL0 175 BF76
Northwood HA6 115 BT50
Wellesley Cl, SE7
off Wellington Gdns 186 EJ78
Wellesley Ct, W9 15 N2
Sutton SM3
off Stonecot Hill 221 CY102
Wellesley Ct Rd, Croy. CR0 224 DR103
Wellesley Cres, Pot.B. EN6 85 CY33
Twickenham TW2 199 CE89
Wellesley Gro, Croy. CR0 224 DR103
Wellesley Pk Ms, Enf. EN2 103 DP40
Wellesley Pas, Croy. CR0
off Wellesley Rd 224 DQ103
Wellesley Path, Slou. SL1
off Wellesley Rd 174 AU75
Wellesley Pl, NW1 17 N3
Tra **Wellesley Road** 224 DQ103
Wellesley Rd, E11 146 EG57
E17 145 EA58
N22 121 DN54
NW5 6 G3
W4 180 CN78
Brentwood CM14 130 FW46
Croydon CR0 224 DQ102
Harrow HA1 139 CE57
Ilford IG1 147 EP61
Slough SL1 174 AU75
Sutton SM2 240 DC107
Twickenham TW2 199 CD90
Wellesley St, E1 21 J7
Wellesley Ter, N1 19 K2
Welley Av, Wrays. TW19 174 AY84
Welley Rd, Horton SL3 174 AY84
Wraysbury TW19 194 AX85
Well Fm Rd, Cat. CR3 258 DU119
Wellfield Av, N10 143 DH55
Wellfield Cl, Hat. AL10 67 CU17
Wellfield Gdns, Cars. SM5 240 DE109
Wellfield Rd, SW16 203 DL91
Hatfield AL10 67 CU16
Wellfields, Loug. IG10 107 EN41
Wellfield Wk, SW16 203 DM92
Wellfit St, SE24
off Hinton Rd 183 DP83
Wellgarth, Grnf. UB6 159 CH65
Welwyn Garden City AL7 51 CY10
Wellgarth Rd, NW11 142 DB60
Well Gro, N20 120 DC45
Well Hall Par, SE9
off Well Hall Rd 187 EM84
Well Hall Rd, SE9 187 EM83
Jct **Well Hall Rbt**, SE9 186 EL83
WELL HILL, Orp. BR6 247 FB107
Well Hill, Orp. BR6 247 FB107
Well Hill La, Orp. BR6 247 FB108
Well Hill Rd, Sev. TN14 247 FC107
Wellhouse La, Barn. EN5 101 CW42
Betchworth RH3 286 CQ138
Wellhouse Rd, Beck. BR3 225 DZ98
Wellhurst Cl, Orp. BR6 245 ET108
WELLING, DA16 188 EU83
⇌ **Welling** 188 EU82
Welling High St, Well. DA16 188 EV83
Sch **Welling Sch**, Well. DA16
off Elsa Rd 188 EV81
Wellings Ho, Hayes UB3 157 BV74
★ **Wellington Arch**, W1 29 H4
Wellington Av, E4 123 EA47
N9 122 DV48
N15 144 DT58
Hounslow TW3 198 CA85
Pinner HA5 116 BZ53
Sidcup DA15 208 EU86
Virginia Water GU25 214 AV99
Worcester Park KT4 221 CW104
Wellington Bldgs, SW1 41 H1
Wellington Cl, SE14 45 J7
W11 15 J9
Dagenham RM10 169 FC66
Walton-on-Thames KT12 217 BT102
Watford WD19 116 BZ48
Wellington Cotts, E.Hors. KT24 267 BS129
Wellington Ct, NW8 16 A1
Ashford TW15
off Wellington Rd 196 BL92
Staines-upon-Thames TW19 off Clare Rd 196 BL87
Surb. KT6 off Glenbuck Rd 220 CL100
Wellington Cres, N.Mal. KT3 220 CQ97
Wellington Dr, Dag. RM10 169 FC66
Purley CR8 241 DM110
Welwyn Garden City AL7 52 DC09
Wellington Gdns, SE7 186 EJ79
Twickenham TW2 199 CD91
Wellington Gro, SE10 46 G5
Wellington Hill, High Beach IG10 106 EG37
H **Wellington Hosp**, NW8 16 B1
Wellington Ho, Gidea Pk RM2
off Kidman Cl 150 FJ55
Wellingtonia Av, Hav.at.Bow. RM4 127 FE48
Wellington Ms, SE7 186 EJ79
SE22 184 DU84
SW16 off Woodbourne Av 203 DK90
★ **Wellington Mus**, W1 28 G4
Wellington Par, Sid. DA15 208 EU85
● **Wellington Pk Est**, NW2 141 CU61
Wellington Pas, E11 146 EG57
Wellington Pl, N2 142 DE57
NW8 16 B2
Broxbourne EN10 70 DW23
Cobham KT11 236 BZ112
Warley CM14 130 FW50
Sch **Wellington Prim Sch**, E3 22 A3
E4 off Wellington Av 123 EB47
Hounslow TW3
off Sutton La 178 BZ82
Wellington Rd, E6 167 EM68
E7 13 M1
E10 145 DY60
E11 146 EG57
E17 145 DY55
NW8 6 A10
NW10 14 D3
SW19 202 DA89
W5 179 CJ76
Ashford TW15 196 BL92
Belvedere DA17 188 EZ78
Bexley DA5 208 EX86
Bromley BR2 226 EJ98
Caterham CR3 258 DQ122
Croydon CR0 223 DP101
Dartford DA1 210 FJ86
Enfield EN1 104 DS42
Feltham TW14 197 BS85
Hampton TW12 199 CD91
Harrow HA3 139 CE55
London Colney AL2 83 CK26
North Weald Bassett CM16 92 FA27
Orpington BR5 228 EV100
Pinner HA5 116 BZ53
St. Albans AL1 65 CH21
Tilbury RM18 193 GG83
Twickenham TW2 199 CD91
Uxbridge UB8 156 BJ67
Watford WD17 97 BV40
Wellington Rd N, Houns. TW4 178 BZ83
Wellington Rd S, Houns. TW4 178 BZ84
Wellington Row, E2 20 B2
Wellington Sq, N1 8 C8
SW3 28 E10
Wellington St, SE18 37 L9
WC2 18 B10
Gravesend DA12 213 GJ87
Hertford SG14 53 DP08
Slough SL1 174 AT75
Wellington Ter, E1 32 E2
W2 off Notting Hill Gate 27 L1
Harrow HA1 off West St 139 CD60
Knaphill GU21
off Victoria Rd 248 AS118
Wellington Way, E3 22 A3
Horley RH6 290 DF146
Weybridge KT13 234 BN110
Welling Way, SE9 187 ER83
Welling DA16 187 ER83
Well La, SW14 200 CQ85
Harlow CM19 57 EN14
Pilgrim's Hatch CM15 130 FT41
Woking GU21 248 AW117
Wellmeade Dr, Sev. TN13 279 FH127
Wellmeadow Rd, SE6 206 EE87
SE13 206 EE86
W7 179 CG77
Wellow Wk, Cars. SM5 222 DD102
Well Pas, NW3 142 DD62
Well Path, Wok. GU21
off Well La 248 AW117
Well Rd, NW3 142 DD62
Barnet EN5 101 CW43
Northaw EN6 86 DE28
Well Row, Bayford SG13 69 DM17
Wells, The, N14 121 DK45
Wells Cl, Chsht EN7
off Bloomfield Rd 88 DQ25
Leatherhead KT23 252 CB124
Northolt UB5
off Yeading La 158 BW69
St. Albans AL3
off Artisan Cres 64 CC19
Wells Cl, South Croydon CR2 242 DS106
Windsor SL4 173 AN81
Wells Ct, Rom. RM1
off Regarth Av 149 FE58
Wells Dr, NW9 140 CR60
Wellsfield, Bushey WD23 98 BY43
Wells Gdns, Dag. RM10 149 FB64
Ilford IG1 146 EL59
Rainham RM13 169 FF65
Wells Ho Rd, NW10 160 CS71
Wellside Cl, Barn. EN5 101 CW42
Wellside Gdns, SW14
off Well La 200 CQ85
Wells Ms, W1 17 M7
Wellsmoor Gdns, Brom. BR1 227 EN97
Wells Pk Rd, SE26 204 DU90
Sch **Wells Pk Sch & Training Cen**, Chig. IG7
off Lambourne Rd 125 ET49
Wells Path, Hayes UB4 157 BS69
Wells Pl, SW18 202 DC87
Merstham RH1 273 DH130
Westerham TN16 277 EQ127
Sch **Wells Prim Sch**, Wdf.Grn. IG8 off Barclay Oval 124 EG49
Wellspring Cres, Wem. HA9 140 CP62
Wellspring Ms, SE26 204 DV91
Wells Ri, NW8 6 E9
Wells Rd, W12 26 A5
Bromley BR1 227 EM96
Epsom KT18 238 CN114
Guildford GU4 265 BC131
Wells Sq, WC1 18 C3
Wells St, W1 17 L7
Wellstead Av, N9 122 DW45
Wellstead Rd, E6 25 L1
Wells Ter, N4 143 DN61
Wellstones, Wat. WD17 97 BV41
Wellstones Yd, Wat. WD17
off Wellstones 97 BV41
Well St, E9 10 F7
E15 13 J4
Wells Way, SE5 43 M2
SW7 28 A6
Wellswood Cl, Hem.H. HP2 63 BP19
Wells Yd S, N7 8 E2
Well Wk, NW3 142 DD63
Well Way, Epsom KT18 254 CN115
Wellwood Cl, Couls. CR5
off The Vale 241 DL114
Wellwood Rd, Ilf. IG3 148 EU60
Welmar Ms, SW4 183 DK84
Welsford St, SE1 32 C10
Welsh Cl, E13 23 N3
Welshpool Ho, E8 10 D8
Welshpool St, E8 10 D8
Sch **Welsh Sch, The**, NW10
off Shakespeare Av 160 CQ67
Welshside Wk, NW9
off Fryent Gro 140 CS58
Welstead Way, W4 181 CT77
Welsummer Way, Chsht EN8 89 DX27
● **Weltech Business Cen**, Welw.G.C. AL7 52 DA09
Weltje Rd, W6 181 CU78
Welton Rd, SE18 187 ES80
Welwyn Av, Felt. TW14 197 BT86
Welwyn Ct, Hem.H. HP2 62 BM16
WELWYN GARDEN CITY, AL7 & AL8 51 CX09
⇌ **Welwyn Garden City** 51 CY09
Welwyn Garden City 51 CX08
Welwyn Rd, Hert. SG14 52 DG08
Welwyn St, E2 21 H2
Welwyn Way, Hayes UB4 157 BS70
WEMBLEY, HA0 & HA9 140 CL64
★ **Wembley Arena**, Wem. HA9 140 CN63
⇌ **Wembley Central** 140 CL64
⊖ **Wembley Central** 140 CL64
⊖ **Wembley Central** 140 CL64
● **Wembley Commercial Cen**, Wem. HA9 139 CK61
Sch **Wembley High Tech Coll**, Wem. HA0 off East La 139 CJ62
Wembley Hill Rd, Wem. HA9 140 CM64
WEMBLEY PARK, Wem. HA9 140 CM61
⊖ **Wembley Park** 140 CN62
● **Wembley Pk Business Cen**, Wem. HA9 140 CP62
Wembley Pk Dr, Wem. HA9 140 CM62
Wembley Pt, Wem. HA9 160 CP66
Sch **Wembley Prim Sch**, Wem. HA9 off East La 140 CL62
Wembley Rd, Hmptn. TW12 198 CA94
★ **Wembley Stadium**, Wem. HA9 140 CN63
⇌ **Wembley Stadium** 140 CM64
Wembley Way, Wem. HA9 160 CP65
Wemborough Rd, Stan. HA7 117 CJ52
Wembury Ms, N6
off Wembury Rd 143 DH59
Wembury Rd, N6 143 DH59
Wemyss Rd, SE3 47 L9
Wend, The, Couls. CR5 241 DK114
Croydon CR0 243 DZ111
Wendela Cl, Wok. GU22 249 AZ118
Wendela Ct, Har. HA1 139 CE62
Sch **Wendell Pk Prim Sch**, W12
off Cobbold Rd 181 CT75
Wendell Rd, W12 181 CT75
Wendle Ct, SW8 42 A3
Wendle Sq, SW11 40 D6
Wendley Dr, New Haw KT15 233 BF110
Wendling, NW5 6 F2
Wendling Rd, Sutt. SM1 222 DD102
Wendon St, E3 11 P8
Wendover, SE17 31 N10
Wendover Cl, Hayes UB4 158 BX70
St. Albans AL4
off Highview Gdns 65 CJ15
Wendover Ct, W3 160 CP70
Wendover Dr, N.Mal. KT3 221 CT100
Wendover Gdns, Brwd. CM13 131 GB47
Wendover Pl, Stai. TW18 195 BD92
Wendover Rd, NW10 161 CT68
SE9 186 EK83
Bromley BR2 226 EH97
Burnham SL1 152 AH71
Staines-upon-Thames TW18 195 BC92
Wendover Way, Bushey WD23 98 CC44
Hornchurch RM12 150 FJ64
Orpington BR6
off Glendower Cres 228 EU100
Welling DA16 208 EU85
Wendron Cl, Wok. GU21 248 AU118
Wendy Cl, Enf. EN1 104 DT44
Wendy Cres, Guil. GU2 264 AU132
Wendy Way, Wem. HA0 160 CL67
Wengeo La, Ware SG12 54 DV05
Wenham Gdns, Hutt. CM13
off Bannister Dr 131 GC44
Wenham Ho, SW8
off Ascalon St 41 L5
Wenham Pl, Hat. AL10 67 CU17
Wenlack Cl, Denh. UB9 136 BG62
Wenlock Ct, N1 19 M1
Wenlock Edge, Dor. RH4 285 CJ138
Wenlock Gdns, NW4 141 CU56
Wenlock Rd, N1 9 J10
Edgware HA8 118 CP52
Wenlock St, N1 19 K1
WENNINGTON, Rain. RM13 170 FK73
Wennington Rd, E3 21 K1
Rainham RM13 169 FG70
Wensley Av, Wdf.Grn. IG8 124 EF52
Wensley Cl, N11 120 DG51
SE9 207 EM86
Romford RM5 126 FA50
Wensleydale, Hem.H. HP2 62 BM17
Wensleydale Av, Ilf. IG5 124 EL54
Wensleydale Gdns, Hmptn. TW12 198 CB94
Wensleydale Pas, Hmptn. TW12 218 CA95
Wensleydale Rd, Hmptn. TW12 198 CA93
Wensley Rd, N18 122 DV51
Wensum Way, Rick. WD3 114 BK46
● **Wenta Business Cen**, Watford WD24 98 BX37
Wentbridge Path, Borwd. WD6 100 CN38
Wentland Cl, SE6 205 ED89
Wentland Rd, SE6 205 ED89
WENTWORTH, Vir.W. GU25 214 AS100
Wentworth Av, N3 120 DA52
Elstree WD6 100 CM43
Slough SL2 153 AN68
Wentworth Av Shop Par, Slou. SL2
off Wentworth Av 153 AN69
Wentworth Cl, N3 120 DB52
SE28 168 EX72
Ashford TW15
off Reedsfield Rd 197 BP91
Gravesend DA11 213 GG92
Hayes BR2 off Hillside La 226 EG103
Long Ditton KT6 219 CK103
Morden SM4 222 DA101
Orpington BR6 245 ES106
Potters Bar EN6 86 DA31
Ripley GU23 250 BH121
Watford WD17 97 BT38
Wentworth Cotts, Brox. EN10 71 DY22
Wentworth Ct, Surb. KT6
off Culsac Rd 220 CL103
Wentworth Cres, SE15 44 D5
Hayes UB3 177 BR76
Wentworth Dene, Wey. KT13 235 BP106
Wentworth Dr, Dart. DA1 209 FG86
Lon.Hthrw Air. TW6
off Widgeon Rd 176 BH83
Pinner HA5 137 BU57
Virginia Water GU25 214 AT98
Watford WD19 116 BX50
Wentworth Gdns, N13 121 DP49
★ **Wentworth Golf Course**, Vir.W. GU25 214 AT100
Wentworth Hill, Wem. HA9 140 CM60
● **Wentworth Ind Ct**, Slou. SL2 off Goodwin Rd 153 AN69
Wentworth Ms, E3 21 M4
W3 160 CS72
Wentworth Pk, N3 120 DA52
Wentworth Pl, Grays RM16 192 GD76
Stanmore HA7
off Greenacres Dr 117 CH51
Sch **Wentworth Prim Sch**, Dart. DA1
off Wentworth Dr 209 FG87
Wentworth Rd, E12 146 EK63
NW11 141 CZ58
Barnet EN5 101 CX41
Croydon CR0 223 DN101
Hertford SG13 54 DQ12
Southall UB2 178 BW77
Wentworth St, E1 20 A8
Wentworth Way, Pnr. HA5 138 BX56
Rainham RM13 169 FH69
South Croydon CR2 242 DU114
Wenvoe Av, Bexh. DA7 189 FB82
Wepham Cl, Hayes UB4 158 BX71
Wernbrook St, SE18 187 EQ79
Werndee Rd, SE25 224 DU98
Werneth Hall Rd, Ilf. IG5 147 EM55
Werrington St, NW1 17 M1
Werter Rd, SW15 181 CY84
Wescott Way, Uxb. UB8 156 BJ68
Wesleyan Pl, NW5 7 J1
Wesley Apts, SW8
off Wandsworth Rd 41 P6
Wesley Av, E16 35 P2
NW10 160 CR69
Hertford SG13 off Hale Rd 54 DR10
Hounslow TW3 178 BY82
Wesley Cl, N7 143 DM61
SE17 31 H9
Goffs Oak EN7 88 DQ28
Harrow HA2 138 CC61
Horley RH6 290 DG146
Orpington BR5 228 EW97
Reigate RH2 287 CZ135
Wesley Ct, SW19 202 DB94
Wesley Dr, Egh. TW20 195 BA93
Wesley Hill, Chesh. HP5 76 AP30
Wesley Rd, E10 145 EC59
NW10 160 CQ67
Hayes UB3 157 BU73
★ **Wesley's Ho**, EC1 19 L5
Wesley Sq, W11 14 E9
Wesley St, W1 17 H7
Wessels, Tad. KT20 255 CX121
Wessex Av, SW19 222 DA96
Wessex Cl, Ilf. IG3 147 ES58
Kingston upon Thames KT1 220 CP95
Thames Ditton KT7 219 CF103
Wessex Ct, Wem. HA9 140 CM61
Wessex Dr, Erith DA8 189 FE81
Pinner HA5 116 BY52
Wessex Gdns, NW11 141 CY60
Sch **Wessex Gdns Prim Sch**, NW11 off Wessex Gdns 141 CY60
Wessex Ho, SE1 32 B10
Wessex La, Grnf. UB6 159 CD68
Wessex St, E2 21 H3
Wessex Wk, Dart. DA2
off Sandringham Dr 209 FE89
Wessex Way, NW11 141 CY59
Wessonmead, SE5
off Camberwell Rd 43 K5
● **West 12 Shop Cen**, W12 26 C4
Westacott, Hayes UB4 157 BS71

Westacott Cl, N19 143 DK60
West Acres, Amer. HP7 77 AR40
Westacres, Esher KT10 236 BZ108
WEST ACTON, W3 160 CN72
⊖ West Acton 160 CN72
Sch West Acton Prim Sch, W3 off Noel Rd 160 CP72
Westall Cl, Hert. SG13 54 DQ10
Westall Ms, Hert. SG13 off West St 54 DQ10
Westall Rd, Loug. IG10 107 EP41
Westanley Av, Amer. HP7 77 AR39
West App, Petts Wd BR5 227 EQ99
West Arbour St, E1 21 H8
Sch West Ashtead Prim Sch, Ashtd. KT21 off Taleworth Rd 254 CL120
West Av, E17 145 EB56
N3 120 DA51
NW4 141 CX57
Hayes UB3 157 BT73
Penn HP10 110 AC46
Pinner HA5 138 BZ58
Redhill RH1 288 DG140
St. Albans AL2 82 CB25
Southall UB1 158 BZ73
Wallington SM6 241 DL106
Whiteley Village KT12 235 BS109
West Av Rd, E17 145 EA56
West Bk, N16 144 DS59
Barking IG11 off Highbridge Rd 167 EP67
Dorking RH4 285 CF137
Enfield EN2 104 DQ40
Westbank Rd, Hmptn H. TW12 198 CC93
WEST BARNES, N.Mal. KT3 221 CU99
West Barnes La, SW20 221 CV96
New Malden KT3 221 CV97
Westbeech Rd, N22 143 DN55
Westbere Dr, Stan. HA7 117 CK49
Westbere Rd, NW2 4 G2
Westbourne Av, W3 160 CR72
Sutton SM3 221 CY103
Westbourne Br, W2 15 N7
Westbourne Cl, Hayes UB4 157 BV70
Westbourne Cres, W2 16 A10
Westbourne Cres Ms, W2 16 A10
Westbourne Dr, SE23 205 DX89
Brentwood CM14 130 FT49
Westbourne Gdns, W2 15 L8
WESTBOURNE GREEN, W2 15 J7
Westbourne Gro, W2 15 K9
W11 15 H10
Westbourne Gro Ms, W11 15 J9
Westbourne Gro Ter, W2 15 L8
Westbourne Ho, Houns. TW5 178 CA79
Westbourne Ms, St.Alb. AL1 off London Rd 65 CD20
⊖ Westbourne Park 15 H6
Westbourne Pk Ms, W2 15 L8
Westbourne Pk Pas, W2 15 K7
Westbourne Pk Rd, W2 15 K7
W11 14 F9
Westbourne Pk Vil, W2 15 K7
Westbourne Pl, N9 122 DV48
Sch Westbourne Prim Sch, Sutt. SM1 off Anton Cres 222 DA104
Westbourne Rd, N7 8 E5
SE26 205 DX93
Bexleyheath DA7 188 EY80
Croydon CR0 224 DT100
Feltham TW13 197 BT90
Staines-upon-Thames TW18 196 BH94
Uxbridge UB8 157 BP70
Westbourne St, W2 16 A10
Westbourne Ter, SE23 off Westbourne Dr 205 DX89
W2 15 P8
Westbourne Ter Ms, W2 15 N8
Westbourne Ter Rd, W2 15 N7
West Br Cl, W12 off Percy Rd 161 CU74
Sch Westbridge Prim Sch, SW11 40 C6
Westbridge Rd, SW11 40 B7
WEST BROMPTON, SW10 39 L2
⇌ West Brompton 39 K1
⊖ West Brompton 39 K1
⊖ West Brompton 39 K1
Westbrook, Maid. SL6 172 AE78
Westbrook Av, Hmptn. TW12 198 BZ94
Westbrook Cl, Barn. EN4 102 DD41
Westbrook Cres, Cockfos. EN4 102 DD41
Westbrook Dr, Orp. BR5 228 EW102
Westbrooke Cres, Well. DA16 188 EW83
Westbrooke Rd, Sid. DA15 207 ER89
Welling DA16 188 EV83
Sch Westbrooke Sch, Well. DA16 off South Gipsy Rd 188 EX83
Sch Westbrook Hay Prep Sch, Hem.H. HP1 off London Rd 61 BD24
Westbrook Rd, SE3 186 EH81
Hounslow TW5 178 BZ80
Staines-upon-Thames TW18 off South St 195 BF92
Thornton Heath CR7 224 DR95
Westbrook Sq, Barn. EN4 off Westbrook Cres 102 DD41
West Burrowfield, Welw.G.C. AL7 51 CX11
Westbury, Chsht EN8 off Turners Hill 89 DX30
Westbury Av, N22 143 DP55
Claygate KT10 237 CF107
Southall UB1 158 CA70
Wembley HA0 160 CL66
Westbury Cl, Ruis. HA4 137 BU59
Shepperton TW17 off Burchetts Way 217 BP100
Whyteleafe CR3 off Station App 258 DU118
Westbury Dr, Brwd. CM14 130 FV47
Westbury Gro, N12 120 DA51
Sch Westbury Ho Sch, N.Mal. KT3 off Westbury Rd 220 CR99
Westbury La, Buck.H. IG9 124 EJ47
Westbury Lo Cl, Pnr. HA5 138 BX55
Westbury Par, SW12 off Balham Hill 203 DH86
Westbury Pl, Brent. TW8 179 CK79
Westbury Ri, Harl. CM17 74 EX16
Westbury Rd, E7 146 EH64
E17 145 EA56
N11 121 DL51
N12 120 DA51
SE20 225 DX95
W5 160 CL72
Westbury Rd, Barking IG11 167 ER67
Beckenham BR3 225 DY97
Brentwood CM14 130 FW47
Bromley BR1 226 EK95
Buckhurst Hill IG9 124 EJ47
Croydon CR0 224 DR100
Feltham TW13 198 BX88
Ilford IG1 147 EM61
New Malden KT3 220 CR98
Northwood HA6 115 BS49
Watford WD18 97 BV43
Wembley HA0 160 CL66
Westbury St, SW8 41 L9
Westbury Ter, E7 166 EH65
Upminster RM14 151 FS61
Westerham TN16 277 EQ127
Westbush Cl, Hodd. EN11 55 DZ14
WEST BYFLEET, KT14 234 BH113
⇌ West Byfleet 234 BG112
Sch West Byfleet Comm Inf Sch, W.Byf. KT14 off Camphill Rd 234 BH112
Sch West Byfleet Jun Sch, W.Byf. KT14 off Camphill Rd 234 BH112
Westcar La, Hersham KT12 235 BV107
West Carriage Dr, W2 28 B3
West Cen St, WC1 18 A8
West Cen Av, W10 off Harrow Rd 161 CV69
West Chantry, Har. HA3 off Chantry Rd 116 CB53
Westchester Dr, NW4 141 CX55
WEST CLANDON, Guil. GU4 266 BH129
Westcliffe Apts, W2 16 B7
West Cl, N9 122 DT48
Ashford TW15 196 BL91
Barnet EN5 101 CV43
Cockfosters EN4 102 DG42
Greenford UB6 158 CC68
Hampton TW12 off Oak Av 198 BY93
Hoddesdon EN11 71 EA16
Rainham RM13 169 FH70
Wembley HA9 140 CM60
Westcombe Av, Croy. CR0 223 DL100
Westcombe Ct, SE3 47 L4
Westcombe Dr, Barn. EN5 102 DA43
Westcombe Hill, SE3 47 P2
SE10 47 N1
Westcombe Lo Dr, Hayes UB4 157 BR71
⇌ Westcombe Park 47 P1
Westcombe Pk Rd, SE3 47 K3
West Common, Ger.Cr. SL9 134 AX57
West Common Cl, Ger.Cr. SL9 134 AY57
West Common Rd, Brom. BR2 226 EG103
Keston BR2 244 EH105
Uxbridge UB8 136 BK64
Westcoombe Av, SW20 221 CT95
Westcote Ri, Ruis. HA4 137 BQ59
Westcote Rd, SW16 203 DJ92
Epsom KT19 238 CP111
WESTCOTT, Dor. RH4 284 CC138
Westcott, Welw.G.C. AL7 52 DD08
West Cotts, NW6 5 K3
Westcott Av, Nthflt DA11 213 GG90
Westcott Cl, N15 144 DT58
Bromley BR1 226 EL99
New Addington CR0 off Castle Hill Av 243 EB109
Sch Westcott C of E First Sch, Westc. RH4 off School La 285 CD137
Westcott Common, Westc. RH4 284 CB138
Westcott Cres, W7 159 CE72
Westcott Ho, E14 22 B10
Westcott Keep, Horl. RH6 off Langshott La 291 DJ147
Westcott Rd, SE17 42 G2
Dorking RH4 285 CE137
Westcott St, Westc. RH4 284 CB137
Westcott Way, Sutt. SM2 239 CW110
WESTCOURT, Grav. DA12 213 GL89
West Ct, SE18 off Prince Imperial Rd 187 EM81
Hounslow TW5 178 CC80
Westcourt, Sun. TW16 217 BV96
West Ct, Wem. HA0 139 CJ61
Coll Westcourt Cen, The, Grav. DA12 off Jubilee Cres 213 GL89
Sch Westcourt Prim Sch, Grav. DA12 off Silver Rd 213 GL89
West Cres, Wind. SL4 173 AM81
West Cres Rd, Grav. DA12 213 GH86
Westcroft, Slou. SL2 153 AP70
Westcroft Cl, NW2 4 F2
Enfield EN3 104 DW38
Westcroft Ct, Brox. EN10 71 EA19
Westcroft Gdns, Mord. SM4 221 CZ97
Westcroft Rd, Cars. SM5 240 DG105
Wallington SM6 240 DG105
Westcroft Sq, W6 181 CU77
Westcroft Way, NW2 141 CY63
West Cromwell Rd, SW5 27 J9
W14 26 G10
● West Cross Cen, Brent. TW8 179 CG79
West Cross Route, W10 14 C10
W11 14 C10
West Cross Way, Brent. TW8 179 CH79
⇌ West Croydon 224 DQ102
⊖ West Croydon 224 DQ102
Tram West Croydon 224 DQ102
⊖ West Croydon 224 DQ102
Westdale Pas, SE18 187 EP79
Westdale Rd, SE18 187 EP79
Westdean Av, SE12 206 EH88
Westdean Cl, SW18 202 DB85
Westdene, Hersham KT12 235 BV105
West Dene, Sutt. SM3 off Park La 239 CY107
West Dene Dr, Rom. RM3 128 FK50
Sch West Dene Sch, Pur. CR8 off Brighton Rd 241 DM114
Westdene Way, Wey. KT13 217 BS104
West Down, Bkhm KT23 268 CB127
Westdown Rd, E15 145 EC63
SE6 205 EA87
WEST DRAYTON, UB7 176 BK76
⇌ West Drayton 156 BL74
West Drayton Pk Av, West Dr. UB7 176 BL76
Sch West Drayton Prim Sch, West Dr. UB7 off Kingston La 176 BL75
West Drayton Rd, Hayes End UB8 157 BP71
West Dr, SW16 203 DJ91
Carshalton SM5 240 DD110
Cheam SM2 239 CX109
Harrow HA3 117 CD51
Tadworth KT20 255 CX118
Virginia Water GU25 214 AT101
Watford WD25 97 BV36
West Dr Gdns, Har. HA3 117 CD51
WEST DULWICH, SE21 204 DR90
⇌ West Dulwich 204 DR88
⇌ West Ealing 159 CH73
West Eaton Pl, SW1 28 G8
West Eaton Pl Ms, SW1 28 G8
Wested La, Swan. BR8 229 FG101
West Ella Rd, NW10 160 CS66
WEST END, Esher KT10 236 BZ107
WEST END, Hat. AL9 68 DC18
West End Av, E10 145 EC57
Pinner HA5 138 BX56
West End Cl, NW10 160 CQ66
West End Ct, Pnr. HA5 138 BX56
Stoke Poges SL2 154 AT67
West End Gdns, Esher KT10 236 BZ106
Northolt UB5 158 BW68
West End La, NW6 5 K9
Barnet EN5 101 CX42
Esher KT10 236 BZ107
Essendon AL9 68 DC18
Harlington UB3 177 BQ80
Pinner HA5 138 BX55
Stoke Poges SL2 154 AS67
West End Rd, Brox. EN10 70 DS23
Northolt UB5 158 BW66
Ruislip HA4 137 BV64
Southall UB1 158 BY74
Westerdale, Hem.H. HP2 62 BL17
Westerdale Rd, SE10 47 N1
Westerfield Rd, N15 144 DT57
Westerfolds Cl, Wok. GU22 249 BC116
Westergate Rd, SE2 188 EY79
WESTERHAM, TN16 277 EQ126
Westerham Av, N9 122 DR48
Westerham Cl, Add. KT15 234 BJ107
Sutton SM2 240 DA110
Westerham Dr, Sid. DA15 208 EV86
Westerham Hill, West. TN16 261 EN121
Westerham Rd, E10 145 EB58
Keston BR2 244 EK107
Oxted RH8 276 EF129
Sevenoaks TN13 278 FC123
Westerham TN16 277 EM128
● Westerham Trade Cen, West. TN16 off The Flyer's Way 277 ER126
Westerley Cres, SE26 205 DZ92
Westerley Ware, Rich. TW9 off Kew Grn 180 CN79
Westermain, New Haw KT15 234 BJ110
Western Av, NW11 141 CX58
W3 160 CR71
W5 160 CM69
Brentwood CM14 130 FW46
Chertsey KT16 216 BG97
Dagenham RM10 169 FC65
Denham UB9 136 BJ63
Egham TW20 215 BB97
Epping CM16 91 ET32
Greenford UB6 159 CF69
Ickenham UB10 157 BP65
Northolt UB5 158 BZ67
Romford RM2 128 FJ54
Ruislip HA4 157 BP65
● Western Av Business Pk, W3 off Mansfield Rd 160 CP70
Western Av Underpass, W5 off Western Av 160 CM69
Western Beach Apts, E16 35 N2
Western Cl, Cher. KT16 off Western Av 216 BG97
Western Ct, N3 off Huntly Dr 120 DA51
Western Cross Cl, Green. DA9 off Johnsons Way 211 FW86
Western Dr, Shep. TW17 217 BR100
Wooburn Green HP10 132 AE58
H Western Eye Hosp, NW1 16 E6
Western Gdns, W5 160 CN73
Brentwood CM14 130 FW47
Western Gateway, E16 35 N1
Sch Western Ho Prim Sch, Slou. SL1 off Richards Way 153 AL74
Shop Western Int Mkt, Sthl. UB2 177 BV77
Western La, SW12 202 DG87
Western Ms, W9 15 H5
Western Par, New Barn. EN5 off Great N Rd 102 DA43
Reigate RH2 off Prices La 288 DB137
Western Pathway, Horn. RM12 170 FJ65
Western Perimeter Rd, Lon.Hthrw Air. TW6 176 BH83
Western Pl, SE16 33 H4
Western Rd, E13 166 EJ67
E17 145 EC57
N2 142 DF56
N22 121 DM54
NW10 160 CQ70
SW9 183 DN83
SW19 222 DD95
W5 159 CK73
Brentwood CM14 130 FW47
Epping CM16 91 ET32
Lower Nazeing EN9 72 EE22
Mitcham CR4 222 DD95
Romford RM1 149 FE57
Southall UB2 178 BX76
Sutton SM1 240 DA106
Western Ter, W6 off Chiswick Mall 181 CU78
● Western Trd Est, NW10 160 CQ70
Western Vw, Hayes UB3 177 BT75
Westernville Gdns, Ilf. IG2 147 EQ59
Western Way, SE28 187 ER76
Barnet EN5 102 DA44
WEST EWELL, Epsom KT19 238 CS108
Sch West Ewell Inf Sch, W.Ewell KT19 off Ruxley La 238 CR106
West Fm Av, Ashtd. KT21 253 CJ118
West Fm Cl, Ashtd. KT21 253 CJ119
West Fm Dr, Ashtd. KT21 253 CK119
DLR Westferry 22 A10
Westferry Circ, E14 34 A2
Westferry Rd, E14 33 P2
WESTFIELD, Wok. GU22 249 AZ122
Westfield, Abin.Ham. RH5 283 BS143
Ashtead KT21 254 CM118
Harlow CM18 73 ES16
Hatfield AL9 68 DA23
Loughton IG10 106 EJ43
Reigate RH2 272 DB131
Sevenoaks TN13 279 FJ122
Welwyn Garden City AL7 52 DA08
Westfield Ave, E20 12 E5
South Croydon CR2 242 DR113
Watford WD24 98 BW37
Woking GU22 248 AY121
Westfield Cl, NW9 140 CQ55
SW10 39 N5
Enfield EN3 105 DY41
Gravesend DA12 213 GJ93
Sutton SM1 239 CZ105
Waltham Cross EN8 89 DZ31
Westfield Common, Wok. GU22 248 AY122
Sch Westfield Comm Prim Sch, Hodd. EN11 off Westfield Rd 71 DZ16
Sch Westfield Comm Tech Coll, Wat. WD18 off Tolpits La 97 BT44
Westfield Ct, St.Alb. AL4 65 CK17
Westfield Dr, Bkhm KT23 252 CA122
Harrow HA3 139 CK57
Sch Westfield First Sch, Berk. HP4 off Durrants La 60 AT18
Westfield Gdns, Dor. RH4 off Westcott Rd 285 CG136
Harrow HA3 139 CK56
Romford RM6 148 EW58
Westfield Gro, Wok. GU22 248 AY120
Westfield La, Geo.Grn SL3 154 AX73
Harrow HA3 139 CK57
Shop Westfield London, W12 26 C3
Westfield Par, New Haw KT15 234 BK110
Westfield Pk, Pnr. HA5 116 BZ52
Westfield Pk Dr, Wdf.Grn. IG8 124 EL51
Sch Westfield Prim Sch, Wok. GU22 off Bonsey La 248 AY121
Westfield Rd, NW7 118 CR48
W13 159 CG74
Beaconsfield HP9 110 AJ54
Beckenham BR3 225 DZ96
Berkhamsted HP4 60 AS17
Bexleyheath DA7 189 FC82
Croydon CR0 223 DP103
Dagenham RM9 148 EY63
Guildford GU1 264 AY130
Hertford SG14 53 DP07
Hoddesdon EN11 71 DZ16
Mitcham CR4 222 DF96
Slough SL2 153 AP70
Surbiton KT6 219 CK99
Sutton SM1 239 CZ105
Walton-on-Thames KT12 218 BY101
Woking GU22 248 AX122
Westfields, SW13 181 CT83
St. Albans AL3 64 CA22
Westfields Av, SW13 180 CS83
Westfields Rd, W3 160 CP71
Shop Westfield Stratford City, E15 12 E5
Westfield St, SE18 36 E7
Westfield Wk, Wal.Cr. EN8 89 DZ31
Westfield Way, E1 21 L3
W12 26 C2
Ruislip HA4 137 BS62
Woking GU22 248 AY122
⊖ West Finchley 120 DB51
West Gdn Pl, W2 16 D9
West Gdns, E1 32 F1
SW17 202 DE93
Epsom KT17 238 CS110
Westgate, E16 23 P10
West Gate, W5 160 CL69
Harlow CM20 73 EQ15
Westgate Cl, Epsom KT18 off Chalk La 254 CR115
Westgate Ct, SW9 off Canterbury Cres 183 DN83
Waltham Cross EN8 off Holmesdale 105 DX35
Westgate Cres, Slou. SL1 153 AM73
● Westgate Est, Felt. TW14 196 BN88
Westgate Houe, Islw. TW7 off London Rd 179 CD82
Sch Westgate Prim Sch, Dart. DA1 off Summerhill Rd 210 FK87
Shop Westgate Retail Pk, Slou. SL1 153 AN73
Westgate Rd, SE25 224 DV98
Beckenham BR3 225 EB96
Dartford DA1 210 FK86
Sch Westgate Sch, Slou. SL1 off Cippenham La 153 AN74
Westgate St, E8 10 E8
Westgate Ter, SW10 39 M1
Westglade Ct, Har. HA3 139 CK57
West Gorse, Croy. CR0 243 DY112
WEST GREEN, N15 144 DQ55
West Grn Pl, Grnf. UB6 off Uneeda Dr 159 CD67
Sch West Grn Prim Sch, N15 off Woodlands Pk Rd 144 DQ56
West Grn Rd, N15 143 DP56
West Gro, SE10 46 F6
Hersham KT12 235 BV105
Woodford Green IG8 124 EJ51
Westgrove La, SE10 46 F6
Sch West Gro Prim Sch, N14 off Chase Rd 121 DK45
West Halkin St, SW1 28 G6
West Hallowes, SE9 206 EK88
Westhall Pk, Warl. CR6 258 DW119
West Hall Rd, Rich. TW9 180 CP81
Westhall Rd, Warl. CR6 258 DV119
WEST HAM, E15 13 M7
⇌ West Ham 23 K2
⊖ West Ham 23 K2
DLR West Ham 23 J2
Sch West Ham Ch Prim Sch, E15 13 L8
West Ham La, E15 13 J7
West Ham Pk, E7 13 N6
WEST HAMPSTEAD, NW6 5 L3
⊖ West Hampstead 5 K5
⊖ West Hampstead 5 L5
West Hampstead Ms, NW6 5 L5
⇌ West Hampstead (Thameslink) 5 K4
★ West Ham United FC, E13 166 EJ68
West Harding St, EC4 18 F8
West Harold, Swan. BR8 229 FD97
WEST HARROW, Har. HA1 138 CC59
⊖ West Harrow 138 CC58
Sch West Hatch High Sch, Chig. IG7 off High Rd 125 EM50
West Hatch Manor, Ruis. HA4 137 BT60
Westhay Gdns, SW14 200 CP85
WEST HEATH, SE2 188 EX79
West Heath, Oxt. RH8 276 EG130
West Heath Av, NW11 142 DA60
West Heath Cl, NW3 142 DA62
Dartford DA1 off West Heath Rd 209 FF86
West Heath Dr, NW11 142 DA60
West Heath Gdns, NW3 142 DA61
West Heath La, Sev. TN13 279 FH128
West Heath Rd, NW3 142 DA61
SE2 188 EW79
Dartford DA1 209 FF86
WEST HENDON, NW9 140 CS59
West Hendon Bdy, NW9 141 CT58
● West Herts Business Cen, Borwd. WD6 off Brook Rd 100 CP41
Coll West Herts Coll, Dacorum Campus, Hem.H. HP1 off Marlowes 62 BJ19
Watford Campus, Wat. WD17 off Hempstead Rd 97 BU41
West Hill, SW15 201 CX87
SW18 202 DA85
West Hill, Dartford DA1 210 FK86
Downe BR6 245 EM112
Epsom KT19 238 CQ113
Harrow HA2 139 CE61
Oxted RH8 275 ED130
South Croydon CR2 242 DS110
Wembley HA9 140 CM60
West Hill Av, Epsom KT19 238 CQ112
West Hill Bk, Oxt. RH8 275 ED130
Westhill Cl, Grav. DA12 off Leith Pk Rd 213 GH88
West Hill Ct, N6 142 DG62
West Hill Dr, Dart. DA1 210 FJ86
West Hill Pk, N6 142 DF61
Sch West Hill Prim Sch, SW18 off Merton Rd 202 DA85
Dartford DA1 off Dartford Rd 210 FJ86
Westhill Ri, Dart. DA1 210 FK86
West Hill Rd, SW18 202 DA86
Westhill Rd, Hodd. EN11 71 DZ16
West Hill Rd, Wok. GU22 248 AX119
Sch West Hill Sch, Lthd. KT22 off Kingston Rd 253 CG118
West Hill Way, N20 120 DB46
Westholm, NW11 142 DB56
West Holme, Erith DA8 189 FC81
Westholme, Orp. BR6 227 ES101
Westholme Gdns, Ruis. HA4 137 BU60
Westhorne Av, SE9 206 EJ86
SE12 206 EG87
Westhorpe Gdns, NW4 141 CW55
Westhorpe Rd, SW15 181 CW83
WEST HORSLEY, Lthd. KT24 267 BP127
West Ho Cl, SW19 201 CY88
WESTHUMBLE, Dor. RH5 269 CG131
Westhumble St, Westh. RH5 269 CH131
Westhurst Dr, Chis. BR7 207 EP92
WEST HYDE, Rick. WD3 113 BE52
West Hyde La, Chal.St.P. SL9 113 AZ52
West India Av, E14 34 A2
West India Dock Rd, E14 21 P9
DLR West India Quay 34 C1
⊖ West Kensington 26 G10
West Kensington Ct, W14 26 G10
West Kent Av, Nthflt DA11 212 GC86
● West Kent Cold Storage, Dunt.Grn TN14 263 FF120
WEST KILBURN, W9 14 G2
Westlake Cl, N13 121 DN48
Hayes UB4 158 BY70
Westlake Rd, Wem. HA9 139 CK61
Westland Av, Horn. RM11 150 FL60
Westland Cl, Lvsdn WD25 81 BT34
Stanwell TW19 196 BL86
Westland Dr, Brom. BR2 226 EF103
Brookmans Park AL9 85 CY27
Westland Ho, E16 off Rymill St 37 L3
Westland Pl, N1 19 L2
Westland Rd, Wat. WD17 97 BV40
Westlands Av, Slou. SL1 152 AJ72
Westlands Cl, Hayes UB3 177 BU77
Slough SL1 off Westlands Av 152 AJ72
Westlands Ct, Epsom KT18 254 CQ115
Westlands Ter, SW12 off Gaskarth Rd 203 DJ86
Westlands Way, Oxt. RH8 275 ED127
West La, SE16 32 E5
Abinger Hammer RH5 284 BX139
West Lawn Apts, Wat. WD25 off Broadfield Way 98 CB36
Westlea Av, Wat. WD25 98 BY37
Westlea Cl, Brox. EN10 71 DZ24
Westlea Rd, W7 179 CG76
Broxbourne EN10 71 DZ23
Westleas, Horl. RH6 290 DE146
Sch West Lea Sch, N9 off Haselbury Rd 122 DS48
Westlees Cl, N.Holm. RH5 285 CJ139
Westleigh Av, SW15 201 CV85
Coulsdon CR5 256 DG116
Westleigh Dr, Brom. BR1 226 EL95
Westleigh Gdns, Edg. HA8 118 CN53
● Westlinks, Wem. HA0 off Alperton La 159 CK68
Westlinton Cl, NW7 119 CY51
West Lo Av, W3 160 CN74
Sch West Lo Prim Sch, Pnr. HA5 off West End La 138 BX56
Sch West Lo Sch, Sid. DA15 off Station Rd 208 EU90
Sch West London Acad, Nthlt. UB5 off Compton Cres 158 BY67
Coll West London Coll, W1 17 H9
Westlyn Cl, Rain. RM13 170 FJ69
Westly Wd, Welw.G.C. AL7 52 DA08
Westmacott Dr, Felt. TW14 197 BT88
West Mall, N9 off Plevna Rd 122 DU48
W8 27 K2
West Malling Way, Horn. RM12 150 FJ64
Westmark Pt, SW15 off Norley Vale 201 CV88
Westmead, SW15 201 CV86
West Mead, Epsom KT19 238 CS107
Ruislip HA4 138 BW63
Welwyn Garden City AL7 52 DB12
Westmead, Wind. SL4 173 AP83
Woking GU21 248 AV117
Westmead Cor, Cars. SM5 off Colston Av 240 DE105
Westmead Dr, Red. RH1 288 DG142
Westmeade Cl, Chsht EN7 88 DV29
Westmead Rd, Sutt. SM1 240 DD105
West Meads, Guil. GU2 280 AT135
Horley RH6 291 DJ148
Westmede, Chig. IG7 125 EQ51
Westmere Dr, NW7 118 CR48
West Mersea Cl, E16 36 A3
West Ms, N17 122 DV51
SW1 29 K9
H West Middlesex Uni Hosp, Islw. TW7 179 CG82
West Mill, Grav. DA11 213 GF86
WESTMINSTER, SW1 29 L6
⊖ Westminster 30 B5
★ Westminster Abbey, SW1 30 A6
Sch Westminster Abbey Choir Sch, SW1 29 P6
★ Westminster Abbey Mus, SW1 30 A6
Sch Westminster Acad, W2 15 K6
Coll Westminster Adult Ed Service, Amberley Rd Cen, W9 15 L5
Ebury Br Cen, SW1 29 J10
Frith St Cen, W1 17 P9
Westminster Av, Th.Hth. CR7 223 DP96
Westminster Br, SE1 30 B5
SW1 30 B5
Westminster Br Rd, SE1 30 D5
● Westminster Business Sq, SE11 off Durham St 42 C1
★ Westminster Cath, SW1 29 L7

Westminster Cath Choir Sch, SW1 29 M7
Westminster Cath RC Prim Sch, SW1 29 P10
★ Westminster City Hall, SW1 29 M6
Westminster City Sch, SW1 29 M6
Westminster Cl, Felt. TW14 197 BU88
Ilford IG6 125 ER54
Teddington TW11 199 CG92
Westminster Ct, St.Alb. AL1 64 CC22
Waltham Cross EN8 off Eleanor Way 89 DZ33
Westminster Dr, N13 121 DL50
Westminster Gdns, E4 124 EE46
SW1 30 A8
Barking IG11 167 ES68
Ilford IG6 125 EQ54
Westminster Kingsway Coll, Castle La Cen, SW1 29 M6
Kings Cross Cen, WC1 18 C3
Peter St Cen, W1 17 N10
Regent's Pk Cen, NW1 17 L4
Vincent Sq Cen, SW1 29 N8
Westminster Millennium Pier 30 B4
Westminster Palace Gdns, SW1 off Artillery Row 29 N7
Westminster Rd, N9 122 DV46
W7 159 CE74
Sutton SM1 222 DD103
Westminster Sch, SW1 30 A6
Westminster Under Sch, SW1 29 N9
Westmoat Cl, Beck. BR3 205 EC94
WEST MOLESEY, KT8 218 BZ99
Westmont Rd, Esher KT10 219 CE103
Westmoor Gdns, Enf. EN3 105 DX40
Westmoor Rd, Enf. EN3 105 DX40
Westmoor St, SE7 36 D7
Westmore Grn, Tats. TN16 260 EJ121
Westmoreland Av, Horn. RM11 150 FJ57
Welling DA16 187 ES83
Westmoreland Dr, Sutt. SM2 240 DB109
● Westmoreland Pl, Brom. BR1 226 EG97
Westmoreland Pl, SW1 41 K1
W5 159 CK71
Westmoreland Rd, NW9 140 CN56
SE17 43 K2
SW13 181 CT81
Bromley BR1, BR2 226 EE99
Westmoreland St, W1 17 H7
Westmoreland Ter, SE20 204 DV94
SW1 41 K1
Westmoreland Wk, SE17 43 M2
Westmore Rd, Tats. TN16 260 EJ121
Westmorland Cl, E12 146 EK61
Epsom KT19 238 CS110
Twickenham TW1 199 CH86
Westmorland Rd, E17 145 EA58
Harrow HA1 138 CB57
Westmorland Sq, Mitch. CR4 off Westmorland Way 223 DL99
Westmorland Way, Mitch. CR4 223 DK98
West Mt, Guil. GU2 off The Mount 280 AW136
Westmount Apts, Wat. WD18 off Linden Av 97 BT42
Westmount Av, Amer. HP7 77 AQ39
Westmount Rd, SE9 187 EM82
WEST NORWOOD, SE27 204 DQ90
⇌ West Norwood 203 DP90
West Oak, Beck. BR3 225 ED95
Westoe Rd, N9 122 DV47
Weston Av, Add. KT15 234 BG105
Grays RM20 191 FT77
Thames Ditton KT7 219 CE101
West Molesey KT8 218 BY97
Weston Cl, Couls. CR5 257 DM120
Godalming GU7 280 AS144
Hutton CM13 131 GC45
Potters Bar EN6 85 CZ32
Weston Ct, N4 off Queens Dr 144 DQ62
N20 off Farnham Cl 120 DC45
Weston Dr, Cat. CR3 258 DQ122
Stanmore HA7 117 CH53
West One Shop Cen, W1 17 H9
Weston Flds, Albury GU5 282 BJ139
Weston Gdns, Islw. TW7 179 CD81
Woking GU22 249 BE116
WESTON GREEN, T.Ditt. KT7 219 CF102
Weston Grn, Dag. RM9 148 EZ63
Thames Ditton KT7 219 CE102
Weston Grn Rd, Esher KT10 219 CD102
Thames Ditton KT7 219 CE102
Weston Gro, Brom. BR1 226 EF95
Weston Lea, W.Hors. KT24 267 BR125
Weston Pk, N8 143 DL58
Kingston upon Thames KT1 off Clarence St 220 CL96
Thames Ditton KT7 219 CE102
Weston Pk Cl, T.Ditt. KT7 219 CE102
Weston Pk Prim Sch, N8 off Denton Rd 143 DM57
Weston Ri, WC1 18 D1
Weston Rd, W4 180 CQ76
Bromley BR1 206 EF94
Dagenham RM9 148 EY63
Enfield EN2 104 DR39
Epsom KT17 238 CS111
Guildford GU2 264 AV133
Slough SL1 153 AM71
Thames Ditton KT7 219 CE102
Weston St, SE1 31 M5
Weston Wk, E8 10 F7
Weston Way, Wok. GU22 249 BE116
Weston Yd, Albury GU5 282 BJ139
Westover Cl, Sutt. SM2 240 DB109
Westover Hill, NW3 142 DA61
Westover Rd, SW18 202 DC86
Westow Hill, SE19 204 DS93
Westow St, SE19 204 DS93
West Palace Gdns, Wey. KT13 217 BP104
West Pk, SE9 206 EL89
West Pk Av, Rich. TW9 180 CN81
West Pk Cl, Houns. TW5 178 BZ79
Romford RM6 148 EX57
West Pk Hill, Brwd. CM14 130 FU48
West Pk Hosp, Epsom KT19 238 CM112
West Pk Rd, Epsom KT19 238 CM112
Richmond TW9 180 CN81
Southall UB2 158 CC74
West Parkside, SE10 35 M7
Warlingham CR6 259 EA115
West Pier, E1 32 E3
● West Pl, Harl. CM20 58 EU12
West Pl, SW19 201 CW92
West Pt, SE1 32 C10
Slough SL1 153 AK74
Westpoint Apts, N8 off Turnpike La 143 DM56
West Pt Cl, Houns. TW4 178 BZ83
● Westpoint Trd Est, W3 160 CP71
Westpole Av, Cockfos. EN4 102 DG42
Westport Rd, E13 24 A5
Westport St, E1 21 K8
West Poultry Av, EC1 18 G7
West Quarters, W12 161 CU72
West Quay Dr, Hayes UB4 158 BY71
West Ramp, Lon.Hthrw Air. TW6 176 BN81
Westray, Hem.H. HP3 63 BQ22
Westridge Cl, Chesh. HP5 76 AM30
Hemel Hempstead HP1 61 BF20
West Ridge Gdns, Grnf. UB6 158 CC68
West Riding, Brick.Wd AL2 82 BZ30
West Rd, E15 13 M9
N17 122 DV51
SW3 40 F1
SW4 203 DK85
W5 160 CL71
Barnet EN4 120 DG46
Berkhamsted HP4 60 AU18
Chadwell Heath RM6 148 EX58
Chessington KT9 237 CJ112
Feltham TW14 197 BR86
Guildford GU1 280 AY135
Harlow CM20 58 EU11
Kingston upon Thames KT2 220 CQ95
Reigate RH2 288 DB135
Rush Green RM7 149 FD59
South Ockendon RM15 171 FV69
West Drayton UB7 176 BM76
Weybridge KT13 235 BP109
Westrow, SW15 201 CW85
West Row, W10 14 E4
Westrow Dr, Bark. IG11 167 ET65
Westrow Gdns, Ilf. IG3 147 ET61
⇌ West Ruislip 137 BQ61
⊖ West Ruislip 137 BQ61
West Shaw, Long. DA3 231 FX96
West Sheen Vale, Rich. TW9 180 CM84
Westside, NW4 119 CV54
West Side, Turnf. EN10 89 DY25
Westside Apts, Ilf. IG1 off Roden St 147 EN62
● West Side Business Cen, Harl. CM19 72 EL16
West Side Common, SW19 201 CW92
West Silvertown 35 P3
West Smithfield, EC1 18 G7
West Spur Rd, Uxb. UB8 156 BK69
West Sq, SE11 30 G7
Harlow CM20 57 EQ14
Iver SL0 off High St 155 BF72
Weststand Apts, N5 off Avenell Rd 143 DP62
West St, E2 20 F1
E11 146 EE62
E17 145 EB57
WC2 17 P9
Bexleyheath DA7 188 EZ84
Brentford TW8 179 CJ79
Bromley BR1 226 EG95
Carshalton SM5 222 DF104
Croydon CR0 242 DQ105
Dorking RH4 285 CG136
Epsom KT18 238 CR113
Erith DA8 189 FD77
Ewell KT17 238 CS110
Gravesend DA11 213 GG86
Grays RM17 192 GA79
Harrow HA1 139 CD60
Hertford SG13 54 DQ10
Reigate RH2 271 CY133
Sutton SM1 240 DB106
Ware SG12 55 DX06
Watford WD17 97 BV40
Woking GU21 off Church St E 249 AZ117
West St La, Cars. SM5 240 DF105
⇌ West Sutton 240 DA105
West Temple Sheen, SW14 180 CP84
West Tenter St, E1 20 B9
West Thames Coll, Islw. TW7 off London Rd 179 CE81
Feltham Skills Cen, Felt. TW13 off Boundaries Rd 198 BX88
● West Thamesmead Business Pk, SE28 187 ET76
West Thornton Prim Sch, Croy. CR0 off Rosecourt Rd 223 DM100
WEST THURROCK, Grays RM20 191 FU78
West Thurrock Prim Sch, W.Thur. RM20 off The Rookery 191 FU79
West Thurrock Way, Grays RM20 191 FT77
WEST TILBURY, Til. RM18 193 GL79
West Twrs, Pnr. HA5 138 BX58
West Twyford Prim Sch, NW10 off Twyford Abbey Rd 160 CN68
Westvale Ms, W3 160 CS74
West Valley Rd, Hem.H. HP3 80 BJ25
West Vw, NW4 141 CW56
Ashtead KT21 253 CJ119
Chesham HP5 76 AR29
Feltham TW14 197 BQ87
Hatfield AL10 67 CU16
Loughton IG10 107 EM41
West Vw Av, Whyt. CR3 off Station Rd 258 DT118
Westview Cl, NW10 141 CT64
W7 159 CE72
W10 14 B8
Rainham RM13 170 FJ69
Redhill RH1 288 DE136
West Vw Ct, Els. WD6 off High St 99 CK44
Westview Cres, N9 122 DS45
Westview Dr, Wdf.Grn. IG8 124 EK54
West Vw Gdns, Els. WD6 off High St 99 CK44
Westview Ri, Hem.H. HP2 62 BK19
West Vw Rd, Crock. BR8 229 FD100
Dartford DA1 210 FM86
St. Albans AL3 65 CD19
Swanley BR8 229 FG98
Westview Rd, Warl. CR6 258 DV119
Westville Rd, W12 181 CU75
Thames Ditton KT7 219 CG102
West Wk, W5 160 CL71
East Barnet EN4 120 DG45
Harlow CM20 57 EQ14
Hayes UB3 157 BU74
West Walkway, The, Sutt. SM1 off Cheam Rd 240 DB106
Westward Ho, Guil. GU1 265 AZ132
Westward Prep Sch, Walt. KT12 off Hersham Rd 217 BV103
Westward Rd, E4 123 DZ50
Westward Way, Har. HA3 140 CL58
West Warwick Pl, SW1 29 L9
WEST WATFORD, Wat. WD18 97 BU42
Westway, Rom. RM1 off South St 149 FE57
West Way, N18 122 DR49
NW10 140 CR62
Westway, SW20 221 CV97
W2 15 J6
W9 15 J6
W10 14 F8
W12 161 CU73
West Way, Beac. HP9 110 AF54
Brentwood CM14 130 FU48
Carshalton SM5 240 DD110
Westway, Cat. CR3 258 DR122
West Way, Croy. CR0 225 DY103
Edgware HA8 118 CP51
Westway, Gat. RH6 291 DH152
Guildford GU2 264 AT132
West Way, Houns. TW5 178 BZ81
Petts Wood BR5 227 ER99
Pinner HA5 138 BX56
Rickmansworth WD3 114 BH46
Ruislip HA4 137 BT60
Shepperton TW17 217 BR100
West Wickham BR4 225 ED100
Westway Cl, SW20 221 CV97
West Way Gdns, Croy. CR0 225 DX103
Westway Gdns, Red. RH1 272 DG131
Westways, Epsom KT19 239 CT105
Westerham TN16 277 EQ126
Westway Shop Pk, Grnf. UB6 159 CE67
Westwell Cl, Orp. BR5 228 EX102
Westwell Rd, SW16 203 DL93
Westwell Rd App, SW16 off Westwell Rd 203 DL93
Westwick Cl, Hem.H. HP2 63 BR21
Westwick Gdns, W14 26 C5
Hounslow TW4 177 BV82
WEST WICKHAM, BR4 225 EC103
⇌ West Wickham 225 EC101
Westwick Pl, Wat. WD25 82 BW34
Westwick Row, Hem.H. HP2 63 BR20
West Wimbledon Prim Sch, SW20 off Bodnant Gdns 221 CV97
Westwood Av, SE19 224 DQ95
Brentwood CM14 130 FU49
Harrow HA2 138 CB63
Woodham KT15 233 BF112
Westwood Cl, Amer. HP6 94 AX39
Bromley BR1 226 EK97
Esher KT10 218 CC104
Potters Bar EN6 86 DA30
Ruislip HA4 137 BP58
Westwood Ct, Guil. GU2 off Hillcrest Rd 264 AT133
Westwood Dr, Amer. HP6 94 AX39
Westwood Gdns, SW13 181 CT83
Westwood Hill, SE26 204 DU92
Westwood La, Sid. DA15 208 EU85
Welling DA16 187 ET83
Westwood Language Coll for Girls, SE19 off Spurgeon Rd 204 DR94
Westwood Pk, SE23 204 DV87
● Westwood Pk Trd Est, W3 160 CN71
Westwood Pl, SE26 204 DU91
Westwood Rd, E16 36 A3
SW13 181 CT83
Coulsdon CR5 257 DK118
Ilford IG3 147 ET60
Southfleet DA13 212 FY93
West Woodside, Bex. DA5 208 EY87
Westwood Way, Sev. TN13 278 FF122
West Yoke, Ash TN15 231 FX103
Wetheral Dr, Stan. HA7 117 CH53
Wetherall Ms, St.Alb. AL1 off Watsons Wk 65 CE21
Wetherby Cl, Nthlt. UB5 158 CB65
Wetherby Gdns, SW5 27 N9
Wetherby Ms, SW5 27 L10
Wetherby Pl, SW7 27 N9
Wetherby Pre-Prep Sch, W2 27 K1
Wetherby Rd, Borwd. WD6 100 CL39
Enfield EN2 104 DQ39
Wetherby Way, Chess. KT9 238 CL108
Wetherden St, E17 145 DZ59
Wethered Dr, Burn. SL1 152 AH71
Wetherell Rd, E9 11 K8
Wetherill Rd, N10 120 DG53
Wetherly Cl, Harl. CM17 58 EZ11
Wettern Cl, S.Croy. CR2 off Purley Oaks Rd 242 DS110
Wetton Pl, Egh. TW20 195 AZ92
Wexfenne Gdns, Wok. GU22 250 BH116
Wexford Rd, SW12 202 DF87
Wexham Ct Prim Sch, Wexham SL3 off Church La 154 AW71
Wexham Lo, Wexham SL2 154 AV71
Wexham Pk Hosp, Slou. SL2 154 AW70
Wexham Pk La, Wexham SL3 154 AW70
Wexham Pl, Wexham SL2 154 AX65
Wexham Rd, Slou. SL1, SL2 154 AV71
Wexham Sch, Slou. SL2 off Norway Dr 154 AW71
● Wexham Springs, Wexham SL2 154 AW66
WEXHAM STREET, Slou. SL3 154 AW67
Wexham St, Slou. SL2, SL3 154 AW67
Wexham Wds, Wexham SL3 154 AW71
Wey Av, Cher. KT16 216 BG97
Weybank, Wisley GU23 250 BL116
Wey Barton, Byfleet KT14 234 BM113
Weybourne Pl, S.Croy. CR2 242 DR110
Weybourne St, SW18 202 DC89
WEYBRIDGE, KT13 234 BN105
⇌ Weybridge 234 BN107
● Weybridge Business Pk, Add. KT15 234 BL105
Weybridge Ct, SE16 44 D1
Weybridge Hosp, Wey. KT13 234 BN105
Weybridge Pk, Wey. KT13 234 BN106
Weybridge Pt, SW11 40 F8
Weybridge Rd, Add. KT15 216 BK104
Thornton Heath CR7 223 DN98
Weybridge KT13 216 BL104
Weybrook Dr, Guil. GU4 265 BB129
Wey Cl, W.Byf. KT14 off Broadoaks Cres 234 BH113
Wey Ct, Epsom KT19 238 CQ105
New Haw KT15 234 BK109
Weydown Cl, SW19 201 CY88
Guildford GU2 264 AU129
Weydown La, Guil. GU2 off Cumberland Av 264 AU129
Weyfield Prim Sch, Guil. GU1 off School Cl 264 AX131
Weyhill Rd, E1 20 D8
Wey Ho, Nthlt. UB5 off Taywood Rd 158 BZ69
Wey Ho Sch, Bramley GU5 off Horsham Rd 280 AY143
Weylands Cl, Walt. KT12 218 BZ102
Weylands Pk, Wey. KT13 235 BR107
Wey La, Chesh. HP5 76 AP32
Weylea Av, Guil. GU4 265 BA131
Weylond Rd, Dag. RM8 148 EZ62
Wey Manor Rd, New Haw KT15 234 BK109
Weyman Rd, SE3 186 EJ81
Weymead Cl, Cher. KT16 216 BJ102
Wey Meadows, Wey. KT13 234 BL106
Weymede, Byfleet KT14 234 BM112
Weymouth Av, NW7 118 CS50
W5 179 CJ76
Weymouth Cl, E6 25 N9
Weymouth Ct, Sutt. SM2 240 DA108
Weymouth Dr, Chaff.Hun. RM16 191 FX78
Weymouth Ho, SW8 42 C5
Weymouth Ms, W1 17 J6
Weymouth Rd, Hayes UB4 157 BS69
Weymouth St, W1 17 H7
Hemel Hempstead HP3 62 BK24
Weymouth Ter, E2 10 B10
Weymouth Wk, Stan. HA7 117 CG51
Wey Retail Pk, Byfleet KT14 234 BL112
Wey Rd, Wey. KT13 216 BM104
Weyside Cl, Byfleet KT14 234 BM112
Weyside Gdns, Guil. GU1 264 AV132
Weyside Rd, Guil. GU1 264 AV132
Weystone Rd, Wey. KT13 off Weybridge Rd 234 BM105
Weyver Ct, St.Alb. AL1 off Avenue Rd 65 CE19
● Weyvern Pk, Peasm. GU3 off Old Portsmouth Rd 280 AV142
Weyview Cl, Guil. GU1 264 AW132
Wey Vw Ct, Guil. GU1 off Walnut Tree Cl 280 AW135
Whadcote St, N4 143 DN61
Whaddon Ho, SE22 off Albrighton Rd 184 DS83
Whalebone Av, Rom. RM6 148 EZ58
Whalebone Ct, EC2 19 L8
Whalebone Gro, Rom. RM6 148 EZ58
Whalebone La, E15 13 J7
Whalebone La N, Rom. RM6 148 EY57
Whalebone La S, Dag. RM8 148 EZ59
Romford RM6 148 EZ59
Whales Yd, E15 13 J7
Whaley Rd, Pot.B. EN6 86 DC33
Wharfdale Cl, N11 120 DG51
Wharfdale Ct, E5 off Pedro St 145 DX63
Wharfdale Rd, N1 8 B10
Wharfedale, Hem.H. HP2 62 BL17
Wharfedale Gdns, Th.Hth. CR7 223 DM98
Wharfedale Rd, Dart. DA2 210 FQ88
Wharfedale St, SW10 39 L1
Wharf Ho, Erith DA8 off West St 189 FE78
Wharf La, E14 21 N9
Rickmansworth WD3 114 BL46
Ripley GU23 250 BJ118
Send GU23 249 BC123
Twickenham TW1 199 CG88
Wharf Pl, E2 10 D9
Wharf Rd, N1 9 J10
N1 (King's Cross) 8 A10
Brentwood CM14 130 FW48
Broxbourne EN10 71 DZ23
Enfield EN3 105 DY44
Gravesend DA12 213 GL86
Grays RM17 192 FZ79
Guildford GU1 264 AW134
Hemel Hempstead HP1 62 BH22
Wraysbury TW19 194 AW87
Wharf Rd S, Grays RM17 192 FZ79
Wharfside Cl, Erith DA8 189 FF78
Wharfside Rd, E16 23 J7
Wharf St, E16 23 J7
Wharf Way, Hunt.Br WD4 81 BQ33
Wharley Hook, Harl. CM18 73 ET18
Wharncliffe Dr, Sthl. UB1 159 CD74
Wharncliffe Gdns, SE25 224 DS96
Wharncliffe Rd, SE25 224 DS96
Wharton Cl, NW10 160 CS65
Wharton Cotts, WC1 off Wharton St 18 D3
Wharton Rd, Brom. BR1 226 EH95
Wharton St, WC1 18 D3
Whateley Cl, Guil. GU2 264 AV129
Whateley Rd, SE20 205 DX94
SE22 204 DT85
Whatley Av, SW20 221 CY97
Whatman Rd, SE23 205 DX87
Whatmore Cl, Stai. TW19 196 BG86
Wheatash Rd, Add. KT15 216 BH103
Wheatbarn, Welw.G.C. AL7 52 DB08
Wheatbutts, The, Eton Wick SL4 173 AM77
Wheat Cl, Sand. AL4 65 CG16
Wheatcroft, Chsht EN7 88 DV28
Wheatcroft Ct, Sutt. SM1 off Cleeve Way 222 DB102
Wheatcroft Sch, Hert. SG13 off Stanstead Rd 54 DU08
Wheatfield, Hat. AL10 off Stonecross Rd 67 CV17
Hemel Hempstead HP2 62 BK18
Wheatfields, E6 25 N8
Enfield EN3 105 DY40
Harlow CM17 58 EW09
Wheatfields Inf & Nurs Sch, St.Alb. AL4 off Downes Rd 65 CH16
Wheatfields Jun Sch, St.Alb. AL4 off Downes Rd 65 CH16
Wheatfield Way, Horl. RH6 291 DH147
Kingston upon Thames KT1 220 CL96
WHEATHAMPSTEAD, St.Alb. AL4 50 CL06
Wheathill Rd, SE20 224 DV97
Wheat Knoll, Ken. CR8 258 DQ116
Wheatland Ho, SE22 off Albrighton Rd 184 DS83
Wheatlands, Houns. TW5 178 CA79
Wheatlands Rd, SW17 off Stapleton Rd 202 DG90
Slough SL3 174 AV76
Wheatley Cl, NW4 119 CU54
Greenhithe DA9 off Steele Av 211 FU85
Hornchurch RM11 150 FK58
Sawbridgeworth CM21 58 EW06
Welwyn Garden City AL7 52 DA11
Wheatley Cres, Hayes UB3 157 BU73
Wheatley Dr, Wat. WD25 82 BW34
Wheatley Gdns, N9 122 DS47
Wheatley Ho, SW15 off Tangley Gro 201 CU87
Wheatley Rd, Islw. TW7 179 CF83
Welwyn Garden City AL7 51 CZ10
Wheatleys, St.Alb. AL4 65 CJ18
Wheatleys Eyot, Sun. TW16 217 BU99
Wheatley St, W1 17 H7
Wheatley Ter Rd, Erith DA8 189 FF79
Wheatley Way, Chal.St.P. SL9 112 AY51
Wheat Sheaf Cl, E14 34 C8
Wheatsheaf Cl, Nthlt. UB5 138 BY64
Ottershaw KT16 233 BD107
Woking GU21 248 AY116
Wheatsheaf Hill, Halst. TN14 246 EZ109
Wheatsheaf La, SW6 38 B4
SW8 42 B4
Staines-upon-Thames TW18 195 BF94
Wheatsheaf Rd, Hunsdon SG12 56 EK06
Romford RM1 149 FF58
Wheatsheaf Ter, SW6 39 H5
Wheatstone Cl, Mitch. CR4 222 DE95
Slough SL3 174 AU76
Wheatstone Rd, W10 14 F6
Erith DA8 189 FD78
Wheeler Av, Oxt. RH8 275 ED129
Penn HP10 110 AC47
Wheeler Cl, Wdf.Grn. IG8 off Chigwell Rd 125 EM50
Wheeler Gdns, N1 8 B8
Wheeler Pl, Brom. BR2 226 EH98
Wheelers, Epp. CM16 91 ET29
Wheelers Cl, Lwr Naze. EN9 72 EE22
Wheelers Cross, Bark. IG11 167 ER68
Wheelers Dr, Ruis. HA4 off Wallington Cl 137 BQ58
Wheelers Fm Gdns, N.Wld Bas. CM16 93 FB26
Wheelers La, Brock. RH3 286 CP136
Epsom KT18 238 CP113
Hemel Hempstead HP3 62 BL22
Smallfield RH6 291 DN149
Wheelers Orchard, Chal.St.P. SL9 112 AY51
Wheel Fm Dr, Dag. RM10 149 FC62
Wheelock Cl, Erith DA8 189 FB80
Wheelwright Cl, Bushey WD23 off Ashfield Av 98 CB44
Wheelwright St, N7 8 C6
Whelan Way, Wall. SM6 223 DK104
Wheler St, E1 20 A5
Whellock Rd, W4 180 CS76
WHELPLEY HILL, Chesh. HP5 78 AX26
Whelpley Hill Pk, Whel.Hill HP5 78 AX26
Whenman Av, Bex. DA5 209 FC89
Whernside Cl, SE28 168 EW73
Wherwell Rd, Guil. GU2 280 AW136
WHETSTONE, N20 120 DB47
Whetstone Cl, N20 120 DD47
Whetstone Pk, WC2 18 C8
Whetstone Rd, SE3 186 EJ82
Whewell Rd, N19 143 DL61
Whichcote Gdns, Chesh. HP5 76 AR33
Whichcote St, SE1 30 E3
Whichert Cl, Knot.Grn HP9 110 AJ49
Whidborne Cl, SE8 46 B9
Whidborne St, WC1 18 B3
Whielden Cl, Amer. HP7 77 AP40
Whielden Gate, Winch.Hill HP7 77 AL43
Whielden Grn, Amer. HP7 77 AP40
Whielden Hts, Amer. HP7 77 AN41
Whielden La, Amer. HP7 77 AL43
Whielden St, Amer. HP7 77 AN41
Whieldon Gra, Ch.Lang. CM17 74 EY16
Whiffins Orchard, Cooper. CM16 92 EX29
Whimbrel Cl, SE28 168 EW73
South Croydon CR2 242 DR111
Whimbrel Way, Hayes UB4 158 BX72
Whinchat Rd, SE28 187 ER76
Whinfell Cl, SW16 203 DK92
Whinfell Way, Grav. DA12 213 GM91
Whinneys Rd, Loud. HP10 110 AC52
Whinyates Rd, SE9 186 EL83
Whipley Cl, Guil. GU4 off Weybrook Dr 265 BB129
Whippendell Cl, Orp. BR5 228 EV95
Whippendell Hill, Kings L. WD4 80 BJ30
Whippendell Rd, Wat. WD18 97 BU43
Whippendell Way, Orp. BR5 228 EV95
Whipps Cross, E17 145 ED57
Whipps Cross Rd, E11 145 ED57
Whipps Cross University Hospital, E11 145 ED58
Whiskin St, EC1 18 G3
Whisperwood, Loud. WD3 96 BH41
Whisperwood Cl, Har. HA3 117 CE52
Whistler Gdns, Edg. HA8 118 CM54
Whistler Ms, SE15 44 B5
Dagenham RM8 off Fitzstephen Rd 148 EV64
Whistlers Av, SW11 40 B5
Whistlers Ct, Wold. CR3 275 ED125
Whistler St, N5 8 G2
Whistler Twr, SW10 39 P4
Whistler Wk, SW10 off Blantyre St 39 P4
Whiston Rd, E2 10 A10
Whitacre Ms, SE11 42 F1
Whitakers Way, Loug. IG10 107 EM39
Whitbread Cl, N17 122 DU53
Whitbread Rd, SE4 185 DY84
Whitburn Rd, SE13 185 EB84
Whitby Av, NW10 160 CP69
Whitby Cl, Bigg.H. TN16 260 EH119
Greenhithe DA9 211 FU85
Whitby Ct, N7 8 B1
Whitby Gdns, NW9 140 CN55
Sutton SM1 222 DD103
Whitby Rd, SE18 37 J8
Harrow HA2 138 CC62
Ruislip HA4 137 BV62
Slough SL1 153 AQ73
Sutton SM1 222 DD103
Whitby St, E1 20 A4
Whitcher Cl, SE14 45 L3
Whitcher Pl, NW1 7 L5
Whitchurch Av, Edg. HA8 118 CM52
Whitchurch Cl, Edg. HA8 118 CM51
Whitchurch First & Mid Schs, Stan. HA7 off Wemborough Rd 117 CK52
Whitchurch Gdns, Edg. HA8 118 CM51
Whitchurch La, Edg. HA8 117 CK52
Whitchurch Rd, W11 14 D10
Romford RM3 128 FK49
Whitcomb Ct, WC2 off Whitcomb St 29 P1
Whitcomb St, WC2 29 P1
Whitcome Ms, Rich. TW9 180 CP81
Whiteadder Way, E14 34 D8
Whitear Wk, E15 13 H4
White Av, Nthflt DA11 213 GF90
Whitebarn La, Dag. RM10 168 FA67
Whitebeam Av, Brom. BR2 227 EN100
Whitebeam Cl, SW9 42 D5

Whitebeam Cl, Shenley WD7
off Mulberry Gdns 84 CM33
Waltham Cross EN7 88 DS26
Whitebeam Dr, Reig. RH2 288 DB137
South Ockendon RM15 171 FW69
Whitebeam Ho, NW3
off Maitland Pk Rd 6 F4
Whitebeams, Hat. AL10 67 CU21
White Beams, Park St AL2 82 CC28
White Beam Way, Tad. KT20 255 CU121
White Bear Pl, NW3
off New End Sq 142 DD63
Whiteberry Rd, Dor. RH5 284 CB143
White Br Av, Mitch. CR4 222 DD98
Whitebridge Cl, Felt. TW14 197 BT86
Sch White Br Comm Inf Sch, The, Loug. IG10
off Greensted Rd 125 EM45
Sch White Br Jun Sch, The, Loug. IG10 off Greensted Rd 125 EM45
Whitebroom Rd, Hem.H. HP1 61 BE18
WHITE BUSHES, Red. RH1 289 DH139
White Butts Rd, Ruis. HA4 138 BX62
WHITECHAPEL, E1 20 C9
⊖ Whitechapel 20 E6
⊖ Whitechapel 20 E6
★ Whitechapel Art Gall, E1 20 B8
Whitechapel High St, E1 20 B8
Whitechapel Rd, E1 20 C8
White Ch La, E1 20 C8
White Ch Pas, E1 20 C8
⊖ White City 26 B1
⊖ White City 26 B2
White City Cl, W12 26 A1
White City Est, W12 161 CV73
White City Rd, W12 14 A10
White Cl, Slou. SL1 153 AR74
White Conduit St, N1 8 F10
Whitecote Rd, Sthl. UB1 158 CB72
White Craig Cl, Pnr. HA5 116 CA50
Whitecroft, Horl. RH6
off Woodhayes 291 DH147
St. Albans AL1 65 CH23
Swanley BR8 229 FE96
Whitecroft Cl, Beck. BR3 225 ED98
Whitecroft Way, Beck. BR3 225 EC99
Whitecross Pl, EC2 19 M6
Whitecross St, EC1 19 K4
★ White Cube, N1
off Hoxton Sq 19 N3
★ White Cube, SW1 29 M2
White Down Rd, Dor. RH5 284 BW135
Whitefield Av, NW2 141 CW59
Purley CR8 257 DN116
Whitefield Cl, SW15 201 CY86
Orpington BR5 228 EW97
Sch Whitefield Sch, NW2
off Claremont Rd 141 CX59
Sch Whitefield Schs & Cen, E17
off Macdonald Rd 123 ED54
Whitefields Rd, Chsht EN8 88 DW28
Whitefoot La, Brom. BR1 205 EC91
Whitefoot Ter, Brom. BR1 206 EE90
Whiteford Rd, Slou. SL2 154 AS71
White Friars, Sev. TN13 278 FG127
Whitefriars Av, Har. HA3 117 CE54
Whitefriars Dr, Har. HA3 117 CD54
Sch Whitefriars First & Mid Sch, Wealds. HA3
off Whitefriars Av 117 CE54
● Whitefriars Ind Est, Harrow HA3 117 CD54
Whitefriars St, EC4 18 F9
White Gdns, Dag. RM10 168 FA65
Whitegate Gdns, Har. HA3 117 CF52
White Gates, Horn. RM12 150 FJ61
Whitegates, Whyt. CR3
off Court Bushes Rd 258 DU119
Woking GU22 off Loop Rd 249 AZ120
Whitegates Cl, Crox.Grn WD3 96 BN42
Whitegate Way, Tad. KT20 255 CV120
Whitehall, SW1 30 A2
White Hall, Abridge RM4
off Market Pl 108 EV41
Whitehall Cl, Borwd. WD6 100 CN42
Chigwell IG7 126 EU48
Lower Nazeing EN9 72 EE22
Uxbridge UB8 156 BJ67
Whitehall Ct, SW1 30 A3
Whitehall Cres, Chess. KT9 237 CK106
Whitehall Fm La, Vir.W. GU25 214 AY96
Whitehall Gdns, E4 124 EE46
SW1 30 A3
W3 160 CN74
W4 180 CP79
Sch Whitehall Inf Sch, Uxb. UB8 off Cowley Rd 156 BJ67
Sch Whitehall Jun Sch, Uxb. UB8 off Cowley Rd 156 BJ68
Whitehall La, Buck.H. IG9 124 EG47
Egham TW20 195 AZ94
Erith DA8 189 FF82
Grays RM17 192 GC78
South Park RH2 287 CZ138
Wraysbury TW19 195 BA86
Whitehall Pk, N19 143 DJ60
Whitehall Pk Rd, W4 180 CP79
Whitehall Pl, E7 13 P2
SW1 30 A3
Wallington SM6
off Bernard Rd 241 DH105
Sch Whitehall Prim Sch, E4
off Normanton Pk 124 EE47
Whitehall Rd, E4 124 EE47
W7 179 CG75
Bromley BR2 226 EK99
Grays RM17 192 GC77
Harrow HA1 139 CE59
Thornton Heath CR7 223 DN99
Uxbridge UB8 156 BK67
Woodford Green IG8 124 EE47
Jct Whitehall Rbt, Harl. CM19 73 EM16
Whitehall St, N17 122 DT52
Whitehands Cl, Hodd. EN11 71 DZ17
White Hart Av, SE18 187 ET76
SE28 187 ET76
White Hart Cl, Ch.St.G. HP8 112 AU48
Sevenoaks TN13 279 FJ128
White Hart Ct, EC2 19 N7
Ripley GU23 250 BJ121
White Hart Dr, Hem.H. HP2 62 BM21
⇌ White Hart Lane 122 DT52
White Hart La, N17 122 DR52
N22 121 DN53
NW10 off Church Rd 161 CT65
SW13 180 CS83
Romford RM7 126 FA53
White Hart Meadow, Beac. HP9 111 AL54
White Hart Meadows, Ripley GU23 250 BJ121
White Hart Rd, SE18 187 ES77
Hemel Hempstead HP2 62 BN21
Orpington BR6 228 EU101
Slough SL1 173 AR76
Jct White Hart Rbt, Nthlt. UB5 158 BX68
White Hart Row, Cher. KT16
off Heriot Rd 216 BG101
White Hart Slip, Brom. BR1
off Market Sq 226 EG96
White Hart St, EC4 19 H8
SE11 30 F10
White Hart Wd, Sev. TN13 279 FJ129
White Hart Yd, SE1 31 L3
Gravesend DA11
off High St 213 GH86
Whitehaven, Slou. SL1 154 AT73
Whitehaven Cl, Brom. BR2 226 EG98
Goffs Oak EN7 88 DS28
Whitehaven St, NW8 16 C5
Whitehead Cl, N18 122 DR50
SW18 202 DC87
Dartford DA2 210 FJ90
Whitehead's Gro, SW3 28 D10
Whiteheart Av, Uxb. UB8 157 BQ71
Whiteheath Av, Ruis. HA4 137 BQ59
Sch Whiteheath Inf Sch, Ruis. HA4 off Ladygate La 137 BP58
Sch Whiteheath Jun Sch, Ruis. HA4 off Whiteheath Av 137 BP58
White Hedge Dr, St.Alb. AL3 64 CC19
White Heron Ms, Tedd. TW11 199 CF93
White Hill, Beac. HP9 132 AG55
Whitehill, Berk. HP4 60 AX18
White Hill, Chesh. HP5 76 AQ31
Chipstead CR5 256 DC124
Hemel Hempstead HP1 61 BF21
Northwood HA6 114 BN51
Rickmansworth WD3 114 BN51
South Croydon CR2
off St. Mary's Rd 242 DR109
Whitehill, Welw. AL6 51 CU05
Whitehill Cl, Berk. HP4
off Whitehill 60 AX18
White Hill Cl, Chesh. HP5 76 AQ30
Whitehill Ct, Berk. HP4
off Whitehill 60 AX18
Sch Whitehill Infants' & Nurs Sch, Grav. DA12 off Sun La 213 GJ90
Sch Whitehill Jun Sch, Grav. DA12 off Sun La 213 GJ90
White Hill La, Bletch. RH1 274 DR127
Whitehill La, Grav. DA12 213 GK90
Ockham GU23 251 BQ123
Whitehill Par, Grav. DA12 213 GJ90
Whitehill Pl, Vir.W. GU25 214 AY99
White Hill Rd, Berk. HP4 60 AV21
Chesham HP5 78 AX26
Whitehill Rd, Dart. DA1 209 FG85
Gravesend DA12 213 GJ89
Longfield DA3 231 FX96
Southfleet DA13 231 FX96
Whitehills Rd, Loug. IG10 107 EN41
White Horse All, EC1 18 G6
White Horse Dr, Epsom KT18 238 CQ114
White Horse Hill, Chis. BR7 207 EN91
White Horse La, E1 21 J5
Whitehorse La, SE25 224 DR98
White Horse La, Lon.Col. AL2 84 CL25
Ripley GU23 250 BJ121
Sch Whitehorse Manor Inf & Jun Schs, Th.Hth. CR7
off Whitehorse Rd 224 DR98
White Horse Ms, SE1 30 F6
White Horse Rd, E1 21 L9
E6 25 K2
Whitehorse Rd, Croy. CR0 224 DR100
Thornton Heath CR7 224 DR100
White Horse Rd, Wind. SL4 173 AK83
White Horse St, W1 29 J3
White Horse Yd, EC2 19 L8
Whitehouse Apts, SE1
off Belvedere Rd 30 D3
Whitehouse Av, Borwd. WD6 100 CP41
White Ho Cl, Chal.St.P. SL9 112 AY52
Whitehouse Cl, Woob.Grn HP10 110 AE54
White House Ct, Amer. HP6 77 AQ37
White Ho Dr, Guil. GU1 265 BB134
Stanmore HA7 117 CJ49
Whitehouse La, Bedmond WD5 81 BV26
White Ho La, Enf. EN2
off Brigadier Hill 104 DQ39
Jacobs Well GU4 264 AX129
Sevenoaks TN14 278 FF130
Whitehouse La, Woob.Grn HP10 110 AE54
White Ho Rd, Sev. TN14 278 FF130
Whitehouse Way, N14 121 DH47
Iver SL0 155 BD69
Slough SL3 174 AW76
Whitehurst Dr, N18 123 DX51
White Kennett St, E1 19 P8
White Knights Rd, Wey. KT13 235 BQ108
White Knobs Way, Cat. CR3 274 DU125
Whitelands Av, Chorl. WD3 95 BC42
Whitelands Cres, SW18 201 CY87
Whitelands Ho, SW3 28 E10
Whitelands Way, Rom. RM3 128 FK54
White La, Guil. GU4, GU5 281 BC136
Oxted RH8 260 EH123
Warlingham CR6 260 EH123
Whiteleaf Rd, Hem.H. HP3 62 BJ23
Whiteledges, W13 159 CJ72
Whitelegg Rd, E13 23 M1
Whiteley, Wind. SL4 173 AL80
Whiteley Rd, SE19 204 DR92
🔒 Whiteleys Shop Cen, W2 15 L9
Whiteleys Way, Han. TW13 198 CA90
WHITELEY VILLAGE, Walt. KT12 235 BS110
White Lion Cl, Amer. HP7 94 AU39
White Lion Ct, EC3 19 N9
White Lion Gate, Cob. KT11 235 BU114
White Lion Hill, EC4 19 H10
White Lion Hos, Hat. AL10
off Robin Hood La 67 CU17
White Lion Rd, Amer. HP7 94 AT38
White Lion Sq, Hat. AL10
off Robin Hood La 67 CV17
White Lion St, N1 18 E1
Hemel Hempstead HP3 62 BK24
🔒 White Lion Wk, Guil. GU1
off High St 280 AX136
White Lo, SE19 203 DP94
White Lo Cl, N2 142 DD58
Isleworth TW7 179 CG82
Sevenoaks TN13 279 FH123
Sutton SM2 240 DC108
White Lo Gdns, Red. RH1 288 DG142
White Lyon Ct, EC2 19 J6
White Lyons Rd, Brwd. CM14 130 FW47
Whitemore Rd, Guil. GU1 264 AX130
White Oak Dr, Beck. BR3 225 EC96
White Oak Gdns, Sid. DA15 207 ET87
Sch White Oak Prim Sch, Swan. BR8 off Hilda May Av 229 FE96
Whiteoaks, Bans. SM7 240 DB113
Whiteoaks La, Grnf. UB6 159 CD68
● White Oak Sq, Swan. BR8 229 FE97
White Orchards, N20 119 CZ45
Stanmore HA7 117 CG50
Whitepit La, H.Wyc. HP10 132 AE57
Jct White Post Cor, Rain. RM13 170 FL68
White Post Fld, Saw. CM21 58 EX05
White Post Hill, Fnghm DA4 230 FN101
Whitepost Hill, Red. RH1 272 DE134
White Post La, E9 11 P6
SE13 185 EA83
White Post St, SE15 45 H4
White Rd, E15 13 K6
Betchworth RH3 270 CN133
Box Hill KT20 270 CN133
White Rose La, Wok. GU22 249 AZ117
Whites Av, Ilf. IG2 147 ES58
Whites Cl, Green. DA9 211 FW86
Whites Grds, SE1 31 P5
Whites Grds Est, SE1
off Whites Grds 31 P4
White Shack La, Chan.Cr. WD3 96 BM37
Whites La, Datchet SL3 174 AV79
Whites Meadow, Brom. BR1
off Blackbrook La 227 EN98
White's Row, E1 20 A7
White's Sq, SW4
off Nelson's Row 183 DK84
White Star Cl, Gdmg. GU7 280 AT144
Whitestile Rd, Brent. TW8 179 CJ78
Whitestone La, NW3 142 DC62
Whitestone Wk, NW3
off North End Way 142 DC62
Hemel Hempstead HP1
off Fennycroft Rd 62 BG17
Whitestone Way, Croy. CR0 223 DN104
White St, Sthl. UB1 178 BX75
White Stubbs Fm, Brox. EN10 70 DU21
White Stubbs La, Bayford SG13 69 DK21
Broxbourne EN10 69 DP21
White Swan Ms, W4
off Bennett St 180 CS79
Whitethorn, Welw.G.C. AL7 52 DB10
Whitethorn Av, Couls. CR5 256 DG115
West Drayton UB7 156 BL73
Whitethorn Gdns, Croy. CR0 224 DV103
Enfield EN2 104 DR43
Hornchurch RM11 150 FJ58
Whitethorn Pl, West Dr. UB7 156 BM74
Whitethorn St, E3 22 B5
White Twr Way, E1 21 L6
Whitewaits, Harl. CM20 57 ES14
White Way, Bkhm KT23 268 CB126
Whiteways Ct, Stai. TW18
off Pavilion Gdns 196 BH94
Whitewebbs La, Enf. EN2 104 DS35
Whitewebbs Pk, Enf. EN2 104 DQ35
Whitewebbs Rd, Enf. EN2 103 DP35
Whitewebbs Way, Orp. BR5 227 ET95
Whitewood Cotts, Tats. TN16 260 EJ120
Whitewood Rd, Berk. HP4 60 AU19
Whitfield Cl, Guil. GU2 264 AU131
Whitfield Cres, Dart. DA2 210 FQ87
Whitfield Pl, W1 17 L5
Whitfield Rd, E6 166 EJ66
SE3 47 H7
Bexleyheath DA7 188 EZ80
Whitfield St, W1 17 N7
Whitfield Way, Mill End WD3 113 BF46
Whitford Gdns, Mitch. CR4 222 DF97
Whitgift Av, S.Croy. CR2 241 DP106
🔒 Whitgift Cen, Croy. CR0 224 DQ103
Whitgift Ho, SW11
off Randall Cl 40 C6
Sch Whitgift Sch, S.Croy. CR2
off Haling Pk Rd 242 DQ106
Whitgift St, SE11 30 C8
Croydon CR0 224 DQ104
Whit Hern Ct, Chsht EN8 88 DW30
Whiting Av, Bark. IG11 167 EP66
Whitings, Ilf. IG2 147 ER57
Sch Whitings Hill Prim Sch, Barn. EN5 off Whitings Rd 101 CW43
Whitings Rd, Barn. EN5 101 CW43
Whitings Way, E6 25 L6
Whitland Rd, Cars. SM5 222 DD102
Whitlars Dr, Kings L. WD4 80 BM28
Whitley Cl, Abb.L. WD5 81 BU32
Stanwell TW19 196 BL86
Whitley Ho, SW1 41 M1
Whitley Rd, N17 122 DS54
Hoddesdon EN11 71 EB15
Whitlock Dr, SW19 201 CY87
Whitman Rd, E3 21 M4
Whitmead Cl, S.Croy. CR2 242 DS107
Whitmoor Common, Worp. GU3 264 AV127
Whitmoor La, Guil. GU4 264 AX126
Whitmore Av, Harold Wd RM3 128 FL54
Whitmore Cl, N11 121 DH50
Whitmore Est, N1 9 P9
Whitmore Gdns, NW10 4 A10
Sch Whitmore High Sch, Har. HA2 off Porlock Av 138 CC60
Sch Whitmore Prim Sch, N1 9 M9
Whitmore Rd, N1 9 N9
Beckenham BR3 225 DZ97
Harrow HA1 138 CC59
Whitmores Cl, Epsom KT18 254 CQ115
Whitmore's Wd, Hem.H. HP2 63 BP19
Whitmore Way, Horl. RH6 290 DE147
Whitnell Way, SW15 201 CX85
Whitney Av, Ilf. IG4 146 EK56
Whitney Ho, SE22
off Albrighton Rd 184 DS83
Whitney Rd, E10 145 EB59
Whitney Wk, Sid. DA14 208 EY93
Whitstable Cl, Beck. BR3 225 DZ95
Ruislip HA4 137 BS61
Whitstable Ho, W10 14 D9
Whitstable Pl, Croy. CR0 242 DQ105
Whitstone La, Beck. BR3 225 EB99
Whittaker Av, Rich. TW9
off Hill St 199 CK85
Whittaker Rd, E6 166 EJ66
Slough SL2 153 AK70
Sutton SM3 221 CZ104
Whittaker St, SW1 28 G9
Whittaker Way, SE1 32 D9
Whitta Rd, E12 146 EK63
Whittell Gdns, SE26 204 DW90
Whittenham Cl, Slou. SL2 154 AU74
Whittets Ait, Wey. KT13
off Jessamy Rd 216 BN103
Sch Whittingham Comm Prim Sch, E17
off Higham Hill Rd 123 DY53
Whittingstall Rd, SW6 39 H7
Hoddesdon EN11 71 EB15
Whittington Av, EC3 19 N9
Hayes UB4 157 BT71
Whittington Ct, N2 142 DF57
H Whittington Hosp, N19 143 DJ61
Whittington Ms, N12 120 DC49
Whittington Rd, N22 121 DL52
Hutton CM13 131 GC44
Whittington Way, Pnr. HA5 138 BY57
Whittlebury Cl, Cars. SM5 240 DF108
Whittle Cl, E17 145 DY58
Leavesden WD25 81 BT34
Southall UB1 158 CB72
Whittle Parkway, Slou. SL1 153 AK72
Whittle Rd, Houns. TW5 178 BW80
Lon.Hthrw Air. TW6
off Western Perimeter Rd 176 BH83
Southall UB2 off Post Rd 178 CB75
Whittlesea Cl, Har. HA3 116 CC52
Whittlesea Path, Har. HA3 116 CC53
Whittlesea Rd, Har. HA3 116 CC53
Whittlesey St, SE1 30 E3
WHITTON, Twick. TW2 198 CB87
⇌ Whitton 198 CC87
Whitton Av E, Grnf. UB6 139 CE64
Whitton Av W, Grnf. UB6 138 CC64
Northolt UB5 138 CC64
Whitton Cl, Grnf. UB6 159 CH65
Whitton Dene, Houns. TW3 198 CB85
Isleworth TW7 199 CD85
Whitton Dr, Grnf. UB6 159 CG65
Whitton Manor Rd, Islw. TW7 198 CC85
Whitton Rd, Houns. TW3 178 CB84
Twickenham TW1, TW2 199 CF86
Jct Whitton Rd Rbt, Twick. TW1 199 CF86
Sch Whitton Sch, Whitton TW2
off Percy Rd 198 CB89
Whitton Wk, E3 22 A2
Whitton Waye, Houns. TW3 198 CA86
Whitwell Rd, E13 23 N3
Watford WD25 98 BX35
Whitworth Cres, Enf. EN3 105 EA37
Whitworth Ho, SE1 31 K7
Whitworth Rd, SE18 187 EN80
SE25 224 DS97
Whitworth St, SE10 35 K10
Whopshott Av, Wok. GU21 248 AW116
Whopshott Cl, Wok. GU21 248 AW116
Whopshott Dr, Wok. GU21 248 AW116
Whorlton Rd, SE15 184 DV83
Whybridge Cl, Rain. RM13 169 FE67
Sch Whybridge Inf Sch, Rain. RM13 off Ford La 169 FG67
Sch Whybridge Jun Sch, Rain. RM13 off Blacksmiths La 169 FF67
Whybrow Gdns, Berk. HP4 60 AY17
Whychcote Pt, NW2
off Claremont Rd 141 CW59
Whymark Av, N22 143 DN55
Whytebeam Vw, Whyt. CR3 258 DT118
Whytecliffe Rd N, Pur. CR8 241 DP111
Whytecliffe Rd S, Pur. CR8 241 DN111
Whytecroft, Houns. TW5 178 BX80
WHYTELEAFE, Cat. CR3 258 DS118
⇌ Whyteleafe 258 DT117
● Whyteleafe Business Village, Whyt. CR3
off Whyteleafe Hill 258 DT117
Whyteleafe Hill, Whyt. CR3 258 DT118
Whyteleafe Rd, Cat. CR3 258 DS120
Sch Whyteleafe Sch, Whyt. CR3
off Whyteleafe Hill 258 DT118
⇌ Whyteleafe South 258 DU119
Whyte Ms, Sutt. SM3 239 CY108
Whyteville Rd, E7 166 EH65
Wichling Cl, Orp. BR5 228 EX102
Wick, The, Hert. SG14 53 DP06
Wickenden Rd, Sev. TN13 279 FJ122
Wicken's Meadow, Dunt.Grn TN14 263 FF119
Wickersley Rd, SW11 41 H9
Wickers Oake, SE19 204 DT91
Wicker St, E1 20 E9
Wicket, The, Croy. CR0 243 EA106
Wicket Rd, Perivale UB6 159 CG69
Wickets, The, Ashf. TW15 196 BL91
Wickets End, Shenley WD7 84 CL33
Wickets Way, Ilf. IG6 125 ET51
Wickford Cl, Rom. RM3
off Wickford Dr 128 FM50
Wickford Dr, Rom. RM3 128 FM50
Wickford St, E1 20 G4
Wickford Way, E17 145 DX56
Wickham Av, Croy. CR0 225 DY103
Sutton SM3 239 CW106
Wickham Chase, W.Wick. BR4 225 ED101
Wickham Cl, E1 21 H7
Enfield EN3 104 DV41
Harefield UB9 114 BK53
Horley RH6 290 DF147
New Malden KT3 221 CT99
Sch Wickham Common Prim Sch, W.Wick. BR4
off Gates Grn Rd 244 EG105
Wickham Ct, St.Alb. AL1 65 CH18
Wickham Ct Rd, W.Wick. BR4 225 EC103
Sch Wickham Ct Sch, W.Wick. BR4 off Layhams Rd 244 EE105
Wickham Cres, W.Wick. BR4 225 EC103
Wickham Fld, Otford TN14 263 FF116
Wickham Gdns, SE4 185 DZ83
Wickham La, SE2 188 EU78
Egham TW20 195 BA94
Welling DA16 188 EU78
Wickham Ms, SE4 45 P9
Wickham Rd, E4 123 EC52
SE4 45 P9
Beckenham BR3 225 EB96
Croydon CR0 225 DX103
Grays RM16 193 GJ75
Harrow HA3 117 CD54
Wickham St, SE11 30 C10
Welling DA16 187 ES82
Wickhams Wf, Ware SG12
off Crane Mead 55 DY06
Wickham Way, Beck. BR3 225 EC98
Wicklands Rd, Hunsdon SG12 56 EK07
Wick La, E3 12 A10
Englefield Green TW20 194 AT92
Wickliffe Av, N3 119 CY54
Wickliffe Gdns, Wem. HA9 140 CP61
Wicklow St, WC1 18 C2
Wick Rd, E9 11 J5
Englefield Green TW20 194 AV94
Teddington TW11 199 CH94
Wicks Cl, SE9 206 EK91
Wicksteed Cl, Bex. DA5 209 FD90
Wicksteed Ho, SE1 31 K7
Brentford TW8
off Green Dragon La 180 CM78
Wick Way, St.Alb. AL1 65 CH17
Wickway Ct, SE15 44 A3
Wickwood St, SE5 43 H9
Widbury Gdns, Ware SG12 55 DZ06
Widbury Hill, Ware SG12 55 DZ06
Wid Cl, Hutt. CM13 131 GD43
Widdecombe Av, Har. HA2 138 BY61
Widdenham Rd, N7 8 C1
Widdin St, E15 13 H7
Widecombe Cl, Rom. RM3 128 FK53
Widecombe Gdns, Ilf. IG4 146 EL56
Widecombe Rd, SE9 206 EL90
Widecombe Way, N2 142 DD57
Widecroft Rd, Iver SL0 155 BE72
Widegate St, E1 19 P7
Widenham Cl, Pnr. HA5 138 BW57
Widewater Pl, Hare. UB9 136 BH57
Wide Way, Mitch. CR4 223 DK97
Widewing Cl, Tedd. TW11 199 CH94
Widford Rd, Hunsdon SG12 56 EK05
Welwyn Garden City AL7 52 DB09
Widgeon Cl, E16 24 A8
Widgeon Rd, Erith DA8 189 FH80
Lon.Hthrw Air. TW6 176 BH82
Widgeon Way, Wat. WD25 98 BY36
Widley Rd, W9 15 K3
Widmoor, Woob.Grn HP10 132 AE60
WIDMORE, Brom. BR1 226 EH97
Widmore Dr, Hem.H. HP2 62 BN18
WIDMORE GREEN, Brom. BR1 226 EJ95
Widmore Lo Rd, Brom. BR1 226 EK96
Widmore Rd, Brom. BR1 226 EG96
Uxbridge UB8 157 BP70
Widvale Rd, Mtnsg CM15 131 GC41
Widworthy Hayes, Hutt. CM13 131 GB46
Wieland Rd, Nthwd. HA6 115 BU52
Wigan Ho, E5 144 DV60
Wigeon Path, SE28 187 ER76
Wigeon Way, Hayes UB4 158 BX72
Wiggenhall Rd, Wat. WD18 97 BV43
Wiggenhall Rd Goods Yd, Wat. WD18 97 BV44
Wiggie La, Red. RH1 272 DG132
Wiggins La, Rich. TW10 199 CJ89
Wiggins Mead, NW9 119 CT52
Wigginton Av, Wem. HA9 160 CP65
Wightman Rd, N4 143 DN57
N8 143 DN56
Wighton Ms, Islw. TW7 179 CE82
Wigley Bush La, S.Wld CM14 130 FS47
Wigley Rd, Felt. TW13 198 BX88
Wigmore Ct, W13
off Singapore Rd 159 CG74
Wigmore Pl, W1 17 J8
Wigmore Rd, Cars. SM5 222 DD103
Wigmores N, Welw.G.C. AL8 51 CX08
Wigmores S, Welw.G.C. AL8 51 CX09
Wigmore St, W1 16 G9
Wigmore Wk, Cars. SM5 222 DD103
Wigram Rd, E11 146 EJ58
Wigram Sq, E17 123 EC54
Wigston Cl, N18 122 DS50
Wigston Rd, E13 24 A4
Wigton Gdns, Stan. HA7 118 CL53
Wigton Pl, SE11 42 F1
Wigton Rd, E17 123 DZ53
Romford RM3 128 FL49
Wigton Way, Rom. RM3 128 FL49
Wilberforce Ct, Edg. HA8 118 CM49
Keston BR2 244 EK107
Wilberforce Ms, SW4 183 DK84
Sch Wilberforce Prim Sch, W10 14 F2
Wilberforce Rd, N4 143 DP61
NW9 141 CU58
Wilberforce Wk, E15 13 K3
Wilberforce Way, SW19 201 CX93
Gravesend DA12 213 GK92
Wilbraham Pl, SW1 28 F8
Wilbur Rd, Lon.Hthrw Air. TW6 off Wayfarer Rd 176 BH82
Wilbury Av, Sutt. SM2 239 CZ110
Sch Wilbury Prim Sch, N18
off Wilbury Way 122 DR50
Wilbury Rd, Wok. GU21 248 AX117
Wilbury Way, N18 122 DR50
Wilby Ms, W11 27 H2
Wilcon Way, Wat. WD25 82 BX34
Wilcot Av, Wat. WD19 116 BY45
Wilcot Cl, Wat. WD19
off Wilcot Av 116 BY45
Wilcox Cl, SW8 42 B4
Borehamwood WD6 100 CQ39
Wilcox Gdns, Shep. TW17 216 BM97
Wilcox Pl, SW1 29 M7
Wilcox Rd, SW8 42 A4
Sutton SM1 240 DB105
Teddington TW11 199 CD91
Wildacres, Nthwd. HA6 115 BT49
West Byfleet KT14 234 BJ111
Wildbank Ct, Wok. GU22
off White Rose La 249 AZ118
Wildberry Cl, W7 179 CG77
Wildcat Rd, Lon.Hthrw Air. TW6 off Widgeon Rd 176 BH83
Wild Ct, WC2 18 C8
Wildcroft Dr, N.Holm. RH5 285 CK139
Wildcroft Gdns, Edg. HA8 117 CK51
Wildcroft Rd, SW15 201 CW87
Wilde Cl, E8 10 C8
Tilbury RM18
off Coleridge Rd 193 GJ82
Wilde Pl, N13 121 DP51
SW18 202 DD87
Wilder Cl, Ruis. HA4 137 BV60
Wilderness, The, Berk. HP4 60 AW19
East Molesey KT8 218 CC99
Hampton Hill TW12
off Park Rd 198 CB91
WILDERNESSE, Sev. TN15 279 FL122
Wildernesse Av, Sev. TN15 279 FL122
Wildernesse Mt, Sev. TN13 279 FK122
Wilderness Ms, SW4 183 DH84
Wilderness Rd, Chis. BR7 207 EP94
Guildford GU2 280 AT135
Oxted RH8 276 EE130
Wilde Rd, Erith DA8 189 FB80
Wilders Cl, Wok. GU21 248 AW118
Wilderton Rd, N16 144 DS59
Wildfell Rd, SE6 205 EB87
Wild Goose Dr, SE14 45 H7
Wild Grn N, Slou. SL3
off Verney Rd 175 BA77
Wild Grn S, Slou. SL3 175 BA77
Wild Hatch, NW11 142 DA58
WILDHILL, Hat. AL9 68 DD21
Wild Hill, Hat. AL9 68 DC21
Wildhill Rd, Hat. AL9 67 CY23
Wild Oaks Cl, Nthwd. HA6 115 BT51
Wild's Rents, SE1 31 N6
Wild St, WC2 18 B9
Wildwood, Nthwd. HA6 115 BR51
Wildwood Av, Brick.Wd AL2 82 BZ30

Wildwood Cl, SE12 206 EF87
East Horsley KT24 267 BT125
Woking GU22 249 BF115
Wildwood Ct, Ken. CR8 258 DR115
Wildwood Gro, NW3
off North End Way 142 DC60
Wildwood Ri, NW11 142 DC60
Wildwood Rd, NW11 142 DC59
Wildwood Ter, NW3 142 DC60
Wilford Cl, Enf. EN2 104 DR41
Northwood HA6 115 BR52
Wilford Rd, Slou. SL3 174 AY77
Wilfred Av, Rain. RM13 169 FG71
Wilfred Owen Cl, SW19 202 DC93
Wilfred St, SW1 29 L6
Gravesend DA12 213 GH86
Woking GU21 248 AX117
Wilfred Turney Est, W6
off Hammersmith Gro 181 CW75
Wilfrid Gdns, W3 160 CQ71
Wilhelmina Av, Couls. CR5 257 DJ119
Wilkes Rd, Brent. TW8 180 CL79
Hutton CM13 131 GD43
Wilkes St, E1 20 B6
Wilkins Cl, Hayes UB3 177 BT78
Mitcham CR4 222 DE95
WILKIN'S GREEN, Hat. AL10 66 CQ19
Wilkins Grn La, Hat. AL10 66 CQ19
Smallford AL4 66 CP20
Wilkins Gro, Welw.G.C. AL8 51 CX10
Wilkins Ho, SW1
off Churchill Gdns 41 L2
Wilkinson Cl, Chsht EN7 88 DQ26
Dartford DA1 190 FM84
Uxbridge UB10 157 BP67
Wilkinson Gdns, SE25 224 DS95
Wilkinson Rd, E16 24 D8
Wilkinson St, SW8 42 C5
Wilkinson Way, W4 180 CR75
Hemel Hempstead HP3 62 BM24
Wilkin St, NW5 7 J4
Wilkin St Ms, NW5 7 J4
Wilkins Way, Brasted TN16 262 EV124
Wilks Av, Dart. DA1 210 FM89
Wilks Gdns, Croy. CR0 225 DY102
Wilks Pl, N1 19 P1
Willan Rd, N17 122 DR54
Willan Wall, E16 23 L10
Willard St, SW8 41 J10
Willats Cl, Cher. KT16 215 BF100
Willcocks Cl, Chess. KT9 220 CL104
Willcott Rd, W3 160 CP74
Will Crooks Gdns, SE9 186 EJ84
Willen Fld Rd, NW10 160 CQ68
Willenhall Av, New Barn. EN5 102 DC44
Willenhall Dr, Hayes UB3 157 BS73
Willenhall Rd, SE18 187 EP78
Willersley Av, Orp. BR6 227 ER104
Sidcup DA15 207 ET88
Willersley Cl, Sid. DA15 207 ET88
WILLESDEN, NW10 161 CT65
WILLESDEN GREEN, NW10 161 CV66
⊖ Willesden Green 4 B4
Willesden Junction 161 CT69
⊖ Willesden Junction 161 CT69
Willesden La, NW2 4 B5
NW6 4 F7
Willes Rd, NW5 7 K4
Willett Cl, Nthlt. UB5
off Broomcroft Av 158 BW69
Petts Wood BR5 227 ES100
Willett Ho, E13
off Queens Rd W 166 EG68
Willett Pl, Th.Hth. CR7
off Willett Rd 223 DN99
Willett Rd, Th.Hth. CR7 223 DN99
Willetts La, Denh. UB9 135 BF63
Willetts Ms, Hodd. EN11 71 EA16
Willett Way, Petts Wd BR5 227 ER99
Willey Broom La, Chaldon
CR3 273 DN125
Willey Fm La, Chaldon CR3 274 DQ126
Willey La, Chaldon CR3 274 DR125
William Ash Cl, Dag. RM9 168 EV65
William Atkinson Ho, N17
off Beaufoy Rd 122 DS52
William Barefoot Dr, SE9 207 EN91
Sch William Bellamy Inf Sch, Dag.
RM10 off Frizlands La 148 FA61
Sch William Bellamy Jun Sch, Dag.
RM10 off Frizlands La 148 FA61
William Bonney Est, SW4 183 DK84
Coll William Booth Coll, SE5 43 M9
William Booth Rd, SE20 224 DU95
Sch William Byrd Prim Sch,
Harling. UB3
off Victoria La 177 BR79
William Carey Way, Har. HA1 139 CE59
Sch William C. Harvey Sch, N17
off Adams Rd 122 DR54
William Cl, N2 120 DD54
SE13 46 F9
SW6 38 F4
Romford RM5 127 FC53
Southall UB2
off Windmill Av 178 CC75
William Cory Prom, Erith DA8 189 FE78
William Ct, Hem.H. HP3
off King Edward St 62 BK24
William Covell Cl, Enf. EN2 103 DM38
Sch William Davies Prim Sch,
E7 off Stafford Rd 166 EK65
Sch William Davis Prim Sch, E2 20 C4
William Dr, Stan. HA7 117 CG51
William Dunbar Ho, NW6 14 G1
William Dyce Ms, SW16
off Babington Rd 203 DK91
William Ellis Cl, Old Wind. SL4 194 AU85
Sch William Ellis Sch, NW5
off Highgate Rd 142 DG62
William Ellis Way, SE16 32 D7
William Evans Rd, Epsom
KT19 238 CN111
William Evelyn Ct, Wotton
RH5 284 BZ139
Sch William Ford C of E Jun Sch,
Dag. RM10 off Ford Rd 168 FA66
William Foster La, Well. DA16 188 EU82
William IV St, WC2 30 A1
William Gdns, SW15 201 CV85
Smallfield RH6 291 DN148
William Guy Gdns, E3 22 D3
William Harvey Ho, SW19
off Whitlock Dr 201 CY88
William Henry Wk, SW8 41 N3
Sch William Hogarth Sch, The,
W4 off Duke Rd 180 CS78
William Hunter Way, Brwd.
CM14 130 FW47
William Margrie Cl, SE15 44 D8
Sch William Martin C of E Inf &
Nurs Sch, Harl. CM18
off Tawneys Rd 73 ES17
Sch William Martin C of E Jun Sch,
Harl. CM18 off Tawneys Rd 73 ET17
William Ms, SW1 28 F5
William Morley Cl, E6 166 EK67
William Morris Cl, E17 145 DZ55
★ William Morris Gall, E17
off Lloyd Pk 145 EA55
Sch William Morris Prim Sch, Mitch.
CR4 off Recreation Way 223 DK97
Sch William Morris Sch, E17
off Folly La 123 DY53
Coll William Morris 6th Form,
W6 38 C1
William Morris Way, SW6 39 N10
William Moulder Ct, Chesh.
HP5 76 AP28
William Nash Ct, Orp. BR5
off Brantwood Way 228 EW97
Sch William Patten Prim Sch, N16
off Stoke Newington Ch St 144 DT61
Sch William Penn Sch, The, Slou.
SL2 off Penn Rd 153 AR70
William Perkin Ct, Grnf. UB6
off Greenford Rd 159 CE65
William Petty Way, Orp. BR5 228 EW102
William Pl, E3 11 N10
William Rainbird Ho, N17
off Beaufoy Rd 122 DT52
William Rd, NW1 17 L3
SW19 201 CY94
Caterham CR3 258 DR122
Guildford GU1 264 AW134
Sutton SM1 240 DC106
William Rushbrooke Ho, SE16
off Eveline Lowe Est 32 C8
William Russell Ct, Wok.
GU21 248 AS118
Williams Av, E17 123 DZ53
William Saville Ho, NW6 15 H1
Williams Bldgs, E2 20 G4
Williams Cl, N8
off Coolhurst Rd 143 DK58
Addlestone KT15
off Monks Cres 234 BH106
Williams Dr, Houns. TW3 178 CA84
Williams Gro, N22 121 DN53
Long Ditton KT6 219 CJ101
William's La, SW14 180 CQ83
Williams La, Mord. SM4 222 DC99
Williamson Cl, SE10 35 L10
Williamson Rd, N4 143 DP58
Williamson St, N7 8 B1
Williamson Way, Rick. WD3 114 BG46
William Sq, SE16 33 M1
Williams Rd, W13 159 CG73
Southall UB2 178 BY77
Williams Ter, Croy. CR0 241 DN107
William St, E10 145 EB58
N17 122 DT52
SW1 28 F5
Barking IG11 167 EQ66
Berkhamsted HP4 60 AX19
Bushey WD23 98 BX41
Carshalton SM5 222 DE104
Gravesend DA12 213 GH87
Grays RM17 192 GB79
Slough SL1 154 AT74
Windsor SL4 173 AR81
Williams Wk, Guil. GU2
off Grange Rd 264 AV130
Williams Way, Dart. DA2 209 FD89
Radlett WD7 99 CJ35
William Swayne Pl, Guil. GU1
off Station App 280 AY135
Sch William Torbitt Prim Sch, Ilf.
IG2 off Eastern Av 147 ET57
Sch William Tyndale Prim Sch,
N1 9 H6
Willifield Way, NW11 141 CZ56
Willingale Cl, Hutt. CM13
off Fairview Av 131 GE44
Loughton IG10
off Willingale Rd 107 EQ40
Woodford Green IG8 124 EJ51
Willingale Rd, Loug. IG10 107 EQ41
Willingdon Rd, N22 121 DP54
Willinghall Cl, Wal.Abb. EN9 89 ED32
Willingham Cl, NW5 7 M3
Willingham Ter, NW5 7 M3
Willingham Way, Kings.T. KT1 220 CN97
Willington Ct, E5
off Mandeville St 145 DY62
Willington Rd, SW9 183 DL83
Sch Willington Sch, SW19
off Worcester Rd 201 CZ92
Willis Av, Sutt. SM2 240 DE107
Willis Cl, Epsom KT18 238 CP113
Willis Ho, E12 off Grantham Rd 147 EN62
Willis Rd, E15 13 L10
Croydon CR0 224 DQ101
Erith DA8 189 FC77
Willis St, E14 22 D9
Willmore End, SW19 222 DB95
Willoners, Slou. SL2 153 AN70
Willoughby Av, Croy. CR0 241 DM105
Willoughby Cl, Brox. EN10 71 DY21
Willoughby Ct, Lon.Col. AL2 83 CK26
Willoughby Dr, Rain. RM13 169 FE66
Willoughby Gro, N17 122 DV52
Willoughby Ho, EC2
off The Barbican 19 L7
Willoughby La, N17 122 DV52
Willoughby Ms, SW4
off Wixs La 183 DH84
Willoughby Pk Rd, N17 122 DV52
Willoughby Pas, E14 34 A2
Willoughby Rd, N8 143 DN55
NW3 6 A1
Kingston upon Thames KT2 220 CM95
Slough SL3 175 BA76
Twickenham TW1 199 CK86
Willoughbys, The, SW14
off Upper Richmond Rd W 180 CS83
Willoughby St, WC1 18 A7
Willoughby Way, SE7 36 A8
Willow Av, SW13 181 CT82
Denham UB9 136 BJ64
Sidcup DA15 208 EU86
Swanley BR8 229 FF97
West Drayton UB7 156 BM73
Willow Bk, SW6 38 F10
Richmond TW10 199 CH90
Woking GU22 248 AY122
Willowbank Gdns, Tad. KT20 255 CV122
Willowbank Pl, Pur. CR8
off Kingsdown Av 241 DP109
Willowbay Cl, Barn. EN5 101 CX44
Willow Brean, Horl. RH6 290 DE147
Willow Br Rd, N1 9 J5
Willowbrook, Eton SL4 173 AR77
Willowbrook Est, SE15
off Shurland Gdns 44 B4
Sch Willow Brook Prim Sch, E10
off Church Rd 145 EA60
Sch Willowbrook Prim Sch,
Hutt. CM13
off Brookfield Cl 131 GD44
Willowbrook Rd, SE15 44 B3
Southall UB2 178 CA76
Staines-upon-Thames TW19 196 BL89
● Willow Cen, Mitch. CR4 222 DF99
Willow Chase, Chesh. HP5 76 AP30
Willow Cl, SE6
off Verdant La 206 EF88
Bexley DA5 208 EZ86
Brentford TW8 179 CJ79
Bromley BR2 227 EM99
Buckhurst Hill IG9 124 EK48
Chalfont St. Peter SL9 112 AY54
Chertsey KT16 215 BE103
Cheshunt EN7 88 DS26
Colnbrook SL3 175 BC80
Erith DA8 off Willow Rd 189 FG81
Flackwell Heath HP10 132 AC57
Hornchurch RM12 149 FH62
Hutton CM13 131 GB44
Orpington BR5 228 EV101
Thornton Heath CR7 223 DP100
Woodham KT15 233 BF111
Willow Cor, Bayford SG13 69 DM18
Willow Cotts, Mitch. CR4 223 DJ97
Richmond TW9 off Kew Grn 180 CN79
Willow Ct, EC2 19 N4
Edgware HA8 118 CL49
Hemel Hempstead HP3 62 BL24
Horley RH6 291 DH145
Sawbridgeworth CM21 58 EX06
Willowcourt Av, Har. HA3 139 CH57
Willow Cres, St.Alb. AL1 65 CJ20
Willow Cres E, Denh. UB9 136 BJ64
Willow Cres W, Denh. UB9 136 BJ64
Willowdene, N6 off View Rd 142 DF59
Willow Dene, Bushey Hth
WD23 117 CE45
Willowdene, Chsht EN8 89 DY27
Pilgrim's Hatch CM15 130 FT43
Willow Dene, Pnr. HA5 116 BX54
Willowdene Cl, Twick. TW2 198 CC87
Willowdene Ct, Warley CM14 130 FW49
Sch Willow Dene Sch, SE18
off Swingate La 187 ES81
Willow Dr, Barn. EN5 101 CY42
Ripley GU23 250 BG124
Willow Edge, Kings L. WD4 80 BN29
Willow End, N20 120 DA47
Northwood HA6 115 BU51
Surbiton KT6 220 CL102
Willow Fm La, SW15
off Queens Ride 181 CV83
Willowfield, Harl. CM18 73 ER17
Sch Willowfield Sch, E17
off Clifton Av 145 DX55
Willowfields Cl, SE18 187 ES78
Willow Gdns, Houns. TW3 178 CA81
Ruislip HA4 137 BT61
Willow Glade, Reig. RH2
off Hornbeam Rd 288 DB137
Willow Grn, NW9
off Clayton Fld 118 CS53
Borehamwood WD6 100 CR43
North Holmwood RH5 285 CH140
Willow Gro, E13 13 N10
Chislehurst BR7 207 EN93
Ruislip HA4 137 BT61
Willowhayne Dr, Walt. KT12 217 BV101
Willowhayne Gdns, Wor.Pk.
KT4 221 CW104
Willowherb Wk, Rom. RM3
off Clematis Cl 128 FJ52
Willow Ho, NW3
off Maitland Pk Vil 6 F4
Warlingham CR6
off East Parkside 259 EB115
Willow La, SE18 37 K8
Amersham HP7 94 AT41
Guildford GU1
off Boxgrove Rd 265 BA133
Mitcham CR4 222 DF99
Watford WD18 97 BU43
● Willow La Ind Est, Mitch.
CR4 222 DF99
Willow Lo, Rom. RM7
off Cottons App 149 FD57
Willowmead, Chig. IG7 126 EU48
Willow Mead, Dor. RH4 285 CG135
Willowmead, Hert. SG14 53 DN10
Willow Mead, Saw. CM21 58 EY06
Willowmead, Stai. TW18 216 BH95
Willowmead Cl, W5 159 CK71
Woking GU21 248 AU116
Willowmere, Esher KT10 236 CC105
Willow Mt, Croy. CR0
off Langton Way 224 DS104
Willow Pk, Otford TN14 263 FF117
Stoke Poges SL2 154 AU66
Willow Path, Wal.Abb. EN9 90 EE34
Willow Pl, SW1 29 M8
Eton SL4 173 AQ78
Hastingwood CM17 74 EZ19
Willow Rd, NW3 142 DD63
W5 180 CL75
Colnbrook SL3 175 BE82
Dartford DA1 210 FJ88
Enfield EN1 104 DS41
Erith DA8 189 FG81
Godalming GU7 280 AT143
New Malden KT3 220 CQ98
Redhill RH1 288 DC137
Romford RM6 148 EY58
Wallington SM6 241 DH108
Willows, The, Amer. HP6 77 AP35
Buckhurst Hill IG9 124 EK48
Byfleet KT14 234 BL113
Claygate KT10 237 CE107
Grays RM17 192 GE79
Guildford GU4
off Collier Way 265 BD132
Mill End WD3
off Uxbridge Rd 114 BG47
St. Albans AL1 65 CH24
Watford WD19
off Brookside Rd 115 BV45
Weybridge KT13 216 BN104
Windsor SL4 173 AK80
Willows Av, Mord. SM4 222 DB99
Willows Cl, Pnr. HA5 116 BW54
Willowside, Lon.Col. AL2 84 CL27
Willows Path, Epsom KT18 238 CP114
Windsor SL4 172 AJ81
Willows Riverside Pk, Wind.
SL4 172 AJ80
Sch Willows Sch, The, Hayes
UB4 off Stipularis Dr 158 BX70
Willow St, E4 123 ED45
EC2 19 N4
Romford RM7 149 FC56
Willow Tree Cl, E3 11 M9
SW18 off Cargill Rd 202 DB88
Abridge RM4 108 EV41
Hayes UB4 158 BW70
Northolt UB5 158 BY65
Uxbridge UB10 137 BQ62
Willow Tree La, Hayes UB4 158 BW70
Willowtree Marina, Hayes
UB4 158 BY72
Willow Tree Pl, Chal.St.P. SL9 112 AV54
Sch Willow Tree Prim Sch, Nthlt.
UB5 off Arnold Rd 158 BY65
Jct Willow Tree Rbt, Hayes
UB4 158 BX71
Willow Tree Wk, Brom. BR1 226 EH95
Willowtree Way, Th.Hth. CR7
off Kensington Av 223 DN95
Willow Vale, W12 161 CU74
Chislehurst BR7 207 EP93
Fetcham KT22 252 CB123
Willow Vw, SW19 222 DD95
Ware SG12 55 DY07
Willow Wk, E17 145 DZ57
N2 120 DD54
N15 143 DP56
N21 103 DM44
SE1 31 P8
Box Hill KT20 off Oak Dr 270 CQ130
Chertsey KT16 216 BG101
Dartford DA1 210 FJ85
Englefield Green TW20 194 AW92
Orpington BR6 227 EP104
Redhill RH1 off Ash Dr 289 DH136
Shere GU5 282 BN139
Sutton SM3 221 CZ104
Upminster RM14 151 FS60
Willow Way, N3 120 DB52
SE26 204 DV90
W11 26 D1
Box Hill KT20 off Oak Dr 270 CP130
Epsom KT19 238 CR107
Godstone RH9 274 DV132
Guildford GU1 264 AV130
Hatfield AL10 67 CT21
Hemel Hempstead HP1 62 BH18
Potters Bar EN6 86 DB33
Radlett WD7 99 CE36
Romford RM3 128 FP51
St. Albans AL2 82 CA27
Sunbury-on-Thames TW16 217 BU98
Twickenham TW2 198 CB89
Wembley HA0 139 CG62
West Byfleet KT14 234 BJ111
Woking GU22 248 AX121
Willow Wd Cl, Burn. SL1 152 AH68
Willow Wd Cres, SE25 224 DS100
Willrose Cres, SE2 188 EW78
Wills Cres, Houns. TW3 198 CB86
Wills Gro, NW7 119 CU50
Willson Rd, Eng.Grn TW20 194 AV92
Wilman Gro, E8 10 D6
Wilmar Cl, Hayes UB4 157 BR70
Uxbridge UB8 156 BK66
Wilmar Gdns, W.Wick. BR4 225 EB102
Wilmcote Ho, W2 15 K6
Wilmer Cl, Kings.T. KT2 200 CM92
Wilmer Cres, Kings.T. KT2 200 CM92
Wilmer Gdns, N1 9 N9
Wilmerhatch La, Epsom KT18 254 CP118
Wilmer Ho, E3 11 M10
Wilmer Lea Cl, E15 12 G7
Wilmer Pl, N16 144 DT61
Wilmer Way, N14 121 DK50
WILMINGTON, Dart. DA2 210 FK91
Wilmington Av, W4 180 CR80
Orpington BR6 228 EW103
Wilmington Cl, Wat. WD17 97 BV41
Wilmington Ct Rd, Dart. DA2 209 FG90
Sch Wilmington Enterprise Coll,
Wilm. DA2 off Common La 209 FH90
Wilmington Gdns, Bark. IG11 167 ER65
Sch Wilmington Gram Sch for Boys,
Wilm. DA2 off Common La 209 FH90
Sch Wilmington Prim Sch, Wilm.
DA2 off Common La 209 FH90
Wilmington Sq, WC1 18 E3
Wilmington St, WC1 18 E3
Wilmot Cl, N2 120 DC54
SE15 44 C5
Wilmot Grn, Gt Warley CM13 129 FW51
Wilmot Pl, NW1 7 L6
W7 159 CE74
Wilmot Rd, E10 145 EB61
N17 144 DR55
Burnham SL1 152 AH69
Carshalton SM5 240 DF106
Dartford DA1 209 FG85
Purley CR8 241 DN112
Wilmots Cl, Reig. RH2 272 DC133
Wilmot St, E2 20 E4
Wilmot Way, Bans. SM7 240 DA114
Wilmount St, SE18 37 N9
Wilna Rd, SW18 202 DC87
Wilsham St, W11 26 D2
Wilshaw Cl, NW4 141 CU55
Wilshaw St, SE14 46 A6
Wilshere Av, St.Alb. AL1 64 CC23
Wilsman Rd, S.Ock. RM15 171 FW68
Wilsmere Dr, Har.Wld HA3 117 CE52
Northolt UB5 138 BY64
Wilson Av, Mitch. CR4 202 DE94
Wilson Cl, S.Croy. CR2
off Bartlett St 242 DR106
Wembley HA9 140 CM59
Wilson Dr, Ott. KT16 233 BB106
Wembley HA9 140 CM59
Wilson Gdns, Har. HA1 138 CC59
Wilson Gro, SE16 32 E5
Wilson Ho, SE7
off Springfield Gro 186 EJ79
Wilson La, Dart. DA4 231 FT96
Wilson Rd, E6 24 E2
SE5 43 N7
Chessington KT9 238 CM107
Ilford IG1 147 EM59
Wilsons, Tad. KT20 255 CX121
Wilsons Cor, Brwd. CM15 130 FX47
Wilsons Pl, E14 21 N9
Wilsons Rd, W6 26 D10
Sch Wilson's Sch, Wall. SM6
off Mollison Dr 241 DL107
Wilson St, E17 145 EC57
EC2 19 M6
N21 121 DN45
Wilson Way, Wok. GU21 248 AX116
Wilstone Cl, Hayes UB4 158 BY70
Wilstone Dr, St.Alb. AL4 65 CJ15
Wilthorne Gdns, Dag. RM10
off Acre Rd 169 FB66
Wilton Av, W4 180 CS78
Wilton Cl, Harm. UB7 176 BK79
Wilton Cres, SW1 28 G5
SW19 221 CZ95
Beaconsfield HP9 111 AL52
Hertford SG13 54 DQ12
Windsor SL4 173 AK84
Wilton Dr, Rom. RM5 127 FC52
Wilton Est, E8 10 D5
Wilton Gdns, Walt. KT12 218 BX102
West Molesey KT8 218 CA97
Wilton Gro, SW19 201 CZ94
New Malden KT3 221 CT100
Wilton Ho, SE22
off Albrighton Rd 184 DS83
Wilton La, Jordans HP9 111 AR52
Wilton Ms, SW1 29 H6
Wilton Par, Felt. TW13
off High St 197 BV88
Wilton Pk, Beac. HP9 111 AP53
Wilton Pk Ct, SE18
off Prince Imperial Rd 187 EN81
Wilton Pl, SW1 28 G5
New Haw KT15 234 BK109
Wilton Rd, N10 120 DG54
SE2 188 EW76
SW1 29 K7
SW19 202 DE94
Beaconsfield HP9 111 AL51
Cockfosters EN4 102 DF42
Hounslow TW4 178 BX83
Ilford IG1 147 EP63
Redhill RH1 288 DF135
Wilton Row, SW1 28 G5
Wilton Sq, N1 9 L8
Wilton St, SW1 29 J6
Wilton Ter, SW1 28 G6
Wilton Vil, N1 9 L9
Wilton Way, E8 10 C5
Hertford SG13 54 DQ11
Wiltshire Av, Horn. RM11 150 FM56
Slough SL2 153 AQ70
Wiltshire Cl, NW7 119 CT50
SW3 28 E8
Dartford DA2 211 FR87
Wiltshire Gdns, N4 144 DQ58
Twickenham TW2 198 CC88
Wiltshire La, Pnr. HA5 137 BT55
Wiltshire Rd, SW9 183 DN83
Orpington BR6 228 EU101
Thornton Heath CR7 223 DN97
Wiltshire Row, N1 9 L9
Wilverley Cres, N.Mal. KT3 220 CS100
Wimbart Rd, SW2 203 DM87
WIMBLEDON, SW19 201 CY93
⇌ Wimbledon 201 CZ93
⊖ Wimbledon 201 CZ93
Tram Wimbledon 201 CZ93
★ Wimbledon (All England Tenn &
Croquet Club), SW19 201 CY91
Wimbledon Br, SW19 201 CZ93
⇌ Wimbledon Chase 221 CY96
Sch Wimbledon Chase Prim Sch,
SW19 off Merton Hall Rd 221 CY95
Sch Wimbledon Coll, SW19
off Edge Hill 201 CX94
★ Wimbledon Common,
SW19 201 CT91
Sch Wimbledon Common Prep Sch,
SW19 off Ridgway 201 CX94
Sch Wimbledon High Sch, SW19
off Mansel Rd 201 CZ93
Wimbledon Hill Rd, SW19 201 CY93
WIMBLEDON PARK, SW19 201 CZ90
⊖ Wimbledon Park 202 DA90
Wimbledon Pk, SW19 201 CZ89
Wimbledon Pk Est, SW19 201 CY88
Sch Wimbledon Pk Prim Sch,
SW19 off Havana Rd 202 DB89
Wimbledon Pk Rd, SW18 201 CZ87
SW19 201 CZ88
Wimbledon Pk Side, SW19 201 CX89
Wimbledon Rd, SW17 202 DC91
Coll Wimbledon Sch of Art, SW19
off Merton Hall Rd 221 CY95
Terry Bruen Bldg, SW19
off Palmerston Rd 202 DA94
● Wimbledon Stadium Business
Cen, SW17 202 DB90
★ Wimbledon Windmill Mus,
SW19 201 CV89
Wimbolt St, E2 20 C2
Wimborne Av, Chis. BR7 227 ET98
Hayes UB4 157 BV72
Orpington BR5 227 ET98
Redhill RH1 288 DF139
Southall UB2 178 CA77
Wimborne Cl, SE12 206 EF85
Buckhurst Hill IG9 124 EH47
Epsom KT17 238 CS113
Sawbridgeworth CM21 58 EX05
Worcester Park KT4 221 CW102
Wimborne Dr, NW9 140 CN55
Pinner HA5 138 BX59
Wimborne Gdns, W13 159 CH72
Wimborne Gro, Wat. WD17 97 BS37
Wimborne Ho, SW8 42 D5
Wimborne Rd, N9 122 DU47
N17 122 DS54
Wimborne Way, Beck. BR3 225 DX97
Wimbourne Ct, N1 9 L10
Wimbourne St, N1 9 L10
Wimpole Cl, Brom. BR2 226 EJ98
Kingston upon Thames KT1 220 CM96
Wimpole Ms, W1 17 J6
Wimpole Rd, West Dr. UB7 156 BK74
Wimpole St, W1 17 J8
Wimshurst Cl, Croy. CR0 223 DL102
Winans Wk, SW9 42 E9
Wincanton Cres, Nthlt. UB5 138 CA64
Wincanton Gdns, Ilf. IG6 147 EP55
Wincanton Rd, SW18 201 CZ87
Romford RM3 128 FK48
Winchcombe Rd, Cars. SM5 222 DD101
Winchcomb Gdns, SE9 186 EK83
Winchdells, Hem.H. HP3 62 BN23
Winchelsea Av, Bexh. DA7 188 EZ80
Winchelsea Cl, SW15 201 CX85
Winchelsea Rd, E7 146 EG62
N17 144 DS55
NW10 160 CR67
Winchelsey Ri, S.Croy. CR2 242 DT107
Winchendon Rd, SW6 38 G5
Teddington TW11 199 CD91
Winchester Av, NW6 4 F8
NW9 140 CN55
Hounslow TW5 178 BZ79
Upminster RM14 151 FT60
Winchester Cl, E6 25 J9
SE17 31 H9
Amersham HP7 77 AS39
Bromley BR2 226 EF97
Colnbrook SL3 175 BE81
Enfield EN1 104 DS43
Esher KT10 236 CA105
Kingston upon Thames KT2 200 CP94
Waltham Abbey EN9
off Highbridge St 89 EB33
Winchester Ct, E17
off Billet Rd 123 DY53

Winchester Cres, Grav. DA12 213 GK90
Winchester Dr, Pnr. HA5 138 BX57
Winchester Gro, Sev. TN13 279 FH123
Winchester Ho, SE18
off Shooters Hill Rd 186 EK80
Winchester Ms, NW3 6 B6
Worcester Park KT4 221 CX103
Winchester Pk, Brom. BR2 226 EF97
Winchester Pl, E8 10 A3
N6 143 DH60
Winchester Rd, E4 123 EC52
N6 143 DH60
N9 122 DU46
NW3 6 B6
Bexleyheath DA7 188 EX82
Bromley BR2 226 EF97
Feltham TW13 198 BZ90
Harrow HA3 140 CL56
Hayes UB3 177 BS80
Ilford IG1 147 ER62
Northwood HA6 137 BT55
Orpington BR6 246 EW105
Twickenham TW1 199 CH86
Walton-on-Thames KT12 217 BU102
Winchester Sq, SE1 31 L2
Winchester St, SW1 29 K10
W3 160 CQ74
Winchester Wk, SE1 31 L2
Winchester Way, Crox.Grn WD3 97 BP43
Winchet Wk, Croy. CR0 224 DW100
Winchfield Cl, Har. HA3 139 CJ58
Winchfield Ho, SW15
off Highcliffe Dr 201 CT86
Winchfield Rd, SE26 205 DY92
Winchfield Way, Rick. WD3 114 BJ45
Winchilsea Cres, W.Mol. KT8 218 CC96
WINCHMORE HILL, N21 121 DM45
WINCHMORE HILL, Amer. HP7 110 AJ45
⇌ Winchmore Hill 121 DN46
Winchmore Hill Rd, N14 121 DK46
N21 121 DK46
Sch Winchmore Sch, N21
off Laburnum Gro 122 DQ47
Winchstone Cl, Shep. TW17 216 BM98
Winckley Cl, Har. HA3 140 CM57
Wincott St, SE11 30 F8
Wincrofts Dr, SE9 187 ER84
Windall Cl, SE19 224 DU95
Windborough Rd, Cars. SM5 240 DG108
Windermere Av, N3 142 DA55
NW6 4 F9
SW19 222 DB97
Harrow HA3 139 CJ59
Hornchurch RM12 149 FG64
Purfleet RM19 190 FQ78
Ruislip HA4 138 BW59
St. Albans AL1 65 CH22
Wembley HA9 139 CJ59
Windermere Cl, Chorl. WD3 95 BC43
Dartford DA1 209 FH88
Egham TW20 195 BB94
Feltham TW14 197 BT88
Hemel Hempstead HP3 63 BQ21
Orpington BR6 227 EP104
Staines-upon-Thames TW19 196 BK89
Windermere Ct, SW13 181 CT79
Kenley CR8 257 DP115
Wembley HA9
off Windermere Av 139 CJ59
Windermere Gdns, Ilf. IG4 146 EL57
Windermere Gro, Wem. HA9
off Windermere Av 139 CJ60
Windermere Ho, Islw. TW7
off Summerwood Rd 199 CF85
Windermere Pt, SE15 44 G5
Sch Windermere Prim Sch, St.Alb. AL1 off Windermere Av 65 CH22
Windermere Rd, N10 121 DH53
N19 143 DJ61
SW15 200 CS91
SW16 223 DJ95
W5 179 CJ76
Bexleyheath DA7 189 FC82
Coulsdon CR5 257 DL115
Croydon CR0 224 DT102
Southall UB1 158 BZ71
West Wickham BR4 226 EE103
Windermere Way, Reig. RH2 272 DD133
Slough SL1 152 AJ71
West Drayton UB7 156 BL74
Winders Rd, SW11 40 C8
Windfield, Lthd. KT22 253 CH121
Windfield Cl, SE26 205 DX91
Windgates, Guil. GU4
off Tychbourne Dr 265 BC131
Windham Av, New Adgtn CR0 243 ED110
Windham Rd, Rich. TW9 180 CM83
Wind Hill, Magd.Lav. CM5 75 FF20
Windhill, Welw.G.C. AL7 52 DA08
Windhover Way, Grav. DA12 213 GL91
Windings, The, S.Croy. CR2 242 DT111
Winding Shot, Hem.H. HP1 62 BG19
Winding Way, Dag. RM8 148 EW62
Harrow HA1 139 CE63
Windlass Pl, SE8 33 M9
Windlesham Gro, SW19 201 CX88
Windley Cl, SE23 204 DW89
Windmill All, W4
off Windmill Rd 180 CS77
Windmill Av, Epsom KT17 239 CT111
St. Albans AL4 65 CJ16
Southall UB2 178 CC75
Windmill Br Ho, Croy. CR0 224 DR102
● Windmill Business Village, Sun. TW16 off Brooklands Cl 217 BS95
Windmill Centre, Sthl. UB2 158 CC74
Windmill Cl, SE1 32 D8
SE13 46 F8
Caterham CR3 258 DQ121
Epsom KT17 239 CT112
Horley RH6 291 DH148
Long Ditton KT6 219 CH102
Sunbury-on-Thames TW16 197 BS94
Upminster RM14 150 FN61
Waltham Abbey EN9 90 EE34
Windsor SL4 173 AP82
Windmill Ct, NW2 4 F4
Ruis. HA4 off West Way 137 BT60
Windmill Dr, NW2 141 CY62
SW4 203 DH85
Croxley Green WD3 96 BM44
Keston BR2 244 EJ105
Leatherhead KT22 253 CJ123
Reigate RH2 272 DD132
Windmill End, Epsom KT17 239 CT112
Windmill Fld, Ware SG12 55 DX07
Windmill Flds, Harl. CM17 58 EZ11
Windmill Gdns, Enf. EN2 103 DN41
Windmill Grn, Shep. TW17 217 BS101
Windmill Gro, Croy. CR0 224 DQ101
WINDMILL HILL, Grav. DA11 213 GG88
Windmill Hill, NW3 142 DC62
Chipperfield WD4 79 BF32
Coleshill HP7 111 AM45
Enfield EN2 103 DP41
Ruislip HA4 137 BT59
Windmill Ho, E14 34 A8
Windmill La, E15 13 H4
Barnet EN5 101 CT44
Bushey Heath WD23 117 CE46
Cheshunt EN8 89 DX30
Epsom KT17 239 CT112
Greenford UB6 158 CC71
Isleworth TW7 179 CE77
Long Ditton KT6 219 CH100
Southall UB2 178 CC76
Windmill Ms, W4 180 CS77
Windmill Pas, W4 180 CS77
Windmill Ri, Kings.T. KT2 200 CP94
Windmill Rd, N18 122 DR49
SW18 202 DD86
SW19 201 CV88
W4 180 CS77
W5 179 CJ77
Brentford TW8 179 CK78
Chalfont St. Peter SL9 112 AX52
Croydon CR0 224 DQ101
Fulmer SL3 134 AX64
Hampton Hill TW12 198 CB92
Hemel Hempstead HP2 62 BL21
Mitcham CR4 223 DJ99
Sevenoaks TN13 279 FH130
Slough SL1 153 AR74
Sunbury-on-Thames TW16 217 BS95
Windmill Rd W, Sun. TW16 217 BS96
Windmill Row, SE11 42 E1
Windmill Shott, Egh. TW20
off Rusham Rd 195 AZ93
Windmill St, W1 17 N7
Bushey Heath WD23 117 CE46
Gravesend DA12 213 GH86
Windmill Wk, SE1 30 F3
Windmill Way, Reig. RH2 272 DD132
Ruislip HA4 137 BT60
Windmill Wd, Amer. HP6 77 AN37
Windmore Av, Pot.B. EN6 85 CW31
Windmore Cl, Wem. HA0 139 CG64
Windover Av, NW9 140 CR56
Windridge Cl, St.Alb. AL3 64 CA22
Windrose Cl, SE16 33 J4
Windrush, N.Mal. KT3 220 CP98
Windrush Av, Slou. SL3 175 BB76
Windrush Cl, N17 122 DS53
SW11 off Maysoule Rd 182 DD84
W4 180 CQ81
Uxbridge UB10 136 BM63
Windrushes, Cat. CR3 274 DU125
Windrush La, SE23 205 DX90
Sch Windrush Prim Sch, SE28
off Bentham Rd 168 EV74
Windrush Rd, NW10 160 CR67
Windrush Sq, SW2
off Rushcroft Rd 183 DN84
Winds End Cl, Hem.H. HP2 62 BN18
Windsock Cl, SE16 33 N8
Windsock Way,
Lon.Hthrw Air. TW6
off Western Perimeter Rd 176 BH82
WINDSOR, SL4 174 AS82
⇌ Windsor & Eton Central 173 AR81
Windsor & Eton Relief Rd, Wind. SL4 173 AP80
⇌ Windsor & Eton Riverside 173 AR80
Windsor Av, E17 123 DY54
SW19 222 DC95
Edgware HA8 118 CP49
Grays RM16 192 GB75
New Malden KT3 220 CQ99
Sutton SM3 221 CY104
Uxbridge UB10 157 BP67
West Molesey KT8 218 CA97
Sch Windsor Boys' Sch, The, Wind. SL4 off Maidenhead Rd 173 AP81
★ Windsor Castle, Wind. SL4 174 AS80
● Windsor Cen, The, SE27 204 DQ91
Windsor Cl, N3 119 CY54
SE27 204 DQ91
Borehamwood WD6 100 CN39
Bovingdon HP3 79 BA28
Brentford TW8 179 CH79
Cheshunt EN7 88 DU30
Chislehurst BR7 207 EP92
Guildford GU2 280 AT136
Harrow HA2 138 CA62
Hemel Hempstead HP2 62 BL22
Lon.Hthrw Air. TW6
off Western Perimeter Rd 176 BH83
Northwood HA6 115 BU54
Windsor Ct, N14 121 DJ45
Borehamwood. WD6
off Rutherford Cl 100 CQ40
Pnr. HA5 off Westbury Lo Cl 138 BX55
Sunbury-on-Thames TW16 197 BU94
Windsor Ct Rd, Chobham GU24 232 AS109
Windsor Cres, Har. HA2 138 CA63
Loudwater HP10 110 AC53
Wembley HA9 140 CP62
Windsor Dr, Ashf. TW15 196 BK91
Barnet EN4 102 DF44
Dartford DA1 209 FG86
Hertford SG14 53 DM09
Orpington BR6 246 EU107
Windsor End, Beac. HP9 133 AM55
Windsor Gdns, W9 15 J6
Croydon CR0
off Richmond Rd 223 DL104
Hayes UB3 177 BR76
Sch Windsor Girls' Sch, Wind. SL4 off Imperial Rd 173 AN83
★ Windsor Great Pk, Ascot SL5, Egh. TW20 & Wind. SL4 194 AS93
Windsor Gt Pk, Ascot SL5 194 AS93
Egham TW20 194 AS93
Windsor Gro, SE27 204 DQ91
Windsor Hill, Woob.Grn HP10 132 AF58
Windsor Ho, N1 9 J10
Bushey WD23
off Royal Connaught Dr 98 BZ42
Windsor La, Burn. SL1 152 AJ70
Wooburn Green HP10 132 AE58
Windsor Ms, SE6 205 EC88
SE23 205 DY88
Windsor Pk Rd, Hayes UB3 177 BT80
Windsor Pl, SW1 29 M7
Chertsey KT16
off Windsor St 216 BG100
Harlow CM20 58 EU11
★ Windsor Racecourse (Royal), Wind. SL4 173 AM79
Windsor Rd, E4
off Chivers Rd 123 EB49
E7 146 EH64
E10 145 EB61
E11 146 EG60
N3 119 CY54
N7 143 DL62
N13 121 DN48
N17 122 DU54
NW2 161 CV65
W5 160 CL73
Barnet EN5 101 CX44
Beaconsfield HP9 133 AN57
Bexleyheath DA6 188 EY84
Chesham HP5 76 AP28
Chobham GU24 232 AS109
Dagenham RM8 148 EY62
Datchet SL3 174 AT80
Enfield EN3 105 DX36
Englefield Green TW20 195 AZ90
Eton SL4 173 AR79
Gerrards Cross SL9 134 AW60
Gravesend DA12 213 GH90
Harrow HA3 117 CD53
Hornchurch RM11 150 FJ59
Hounslow TW4 177 BV82
Ilford IG1 147 EP63
Kingston upon Thames KT2 200 CL94
Old Windsor SL4 194 AX88
Pilgrim's Hatch CM15 130 FV44
Richmond TW9 180 CM82
Slough SL1 174 AS76
Southall UB2 178 BZ76
Stoke Poges SL2 154 AU63
Sunbury-on-Thames TW16 197 BU93
Teddington TW11 199 CD92
Thornton Heath CR7 223 DP96
Water Oakley SL4 172 AF79
Watford WD24 98 BW38
Worcester Park KT4 221 CU103
Wraysbury TW19 194 AY86
Windsors, The, Buck.H. IG9 124 EL47
Windsor St, N1 9 H8
Chertsey KT16 216 BG100
Uxbridge UB8 156 BJ66
Windsor Ter, N1 19 K2
Windsor Wk, SE5 43 M9
Walton-on-Thames KT12
off King George Av 218 BX102
Weybridge KT13 235 BP106
Windsor Way, W14 26 D8
Rickmansworth WD3 114 BG46
Woking GU22 249 BC116
Windsor Wf, E9 11 P3
Windsor Wd, Wal.Abb. EN9
off Monkswood Av 90 EE33
Windspoint Dr, SE15 44 E3
Winds Ridge, Send GU23 265 BC125
Windus Rd, N16 144 DT60
Windus Wk, N16 144 DT60
Windward Cl, Enf. EN3
off Bullsmoor La 105 DX35
Windycroft Cl, Pur. CR8 241 DK113
Windy Hill, Hutt. CM13 131 GC46
Windy Ridge, Brom. BR1 226 EL95
Windy Ridge Cl, SW19 201 CX92
Wine Cl, E1 32 G1
Wine Office Ct, EC4 18 F8
Winern Glebe, Byfleet KT14 234 BK113
Winery La, Kings.T. KT1 220 CM97
Winey Cl, Chess. KT9
off Nigel Fisher Way 237 CJ108
Winfield Mobile Home Pk, Wat. WD25 98 CB39
Winford Dr, Brox. EN10 71 DZ22
Winford Ho, E3 11 P7
Winford Par, Sthl. UB1
off Telford Rd 158 CB72
Winforton St, SE10 46 E6
Winfrith Rd, SW18 202 DC87
Wingate Cres, Croy. CR0 223 DK100
Wingate Rd, W6 181 CV76
Ilford IG1 147 EP64
Sidcup DA14 208 EW92
Wingate Sq, SW4
off Old Town 183 DJ84
Wingate Way, St.Alb. AL1 65 CG21
Wing Cl, N.Wld Bas. CM16 92 FA27
Wingfield, Bad.Dene RM17 192 FZ78
Wingfield Bk, Nthflt DA11 212 GC89
Wingfield Cl, Brwd. CM13
off Pondfield La 131 GA48
New Haw KT15 234 BH110
Wingfield Ct, E14
off Newport Av 34 G1
Banstead SM7 256 DA115
Wingfield Gdns, Upmin. RM14 151 FT58
Wingfield Ho, NW6
off Tollgate Gdns 5 L10
Wingfield Ms, SE15 44 C10
Sch Wingfield Prim Sch, SE3
off Moorehead Way 186 EH83
Wingfield Rd, E15 13 J1
E17 145 EB57
Gravesend DA12 213 GH87
Kingston upon Thames KT2 200 CN93
Wingfield St, SE15 44 C10
Wingfield Way, Ruis. HA4 157 BV65
Wingford Rd, SW2 203 DL86
Wingletye La, Horn. RM11 150 FM60
Wingmore Rd, SE24 184 DQ83
Wingrave Cres, Brwd. CM14 130 FS49
Wingrave Rd, W6 38 B3
Wingrove Dr, Purf. RM19 190 FP78
Wingrove Rd, SE6 206 EE89
Wings Cl, Sutt. SM1 240 DA105
Wings Rd, Lon.Hthrw Air. TW6
off Wayfarer Rd 176 BH83
Wing Way, Brwd. CM14
off Geary Dr 130 FW46
Winifred Av, Horn. RM12 150 FK63
Winifred Cl, Barn. EN5 101 CT44
Winifred Gro, SW11 182 DF84
Winifred Pl, N12 off High Rd 120 DC50
Winifred Rd, SW19 222 DA95
Coulsdon CR5 256 DG116
Dagenham RM8 148 EY61
Dartford DA1 209 FH85
Erith DA8 189 FE78
Hampton Hill TW12 198 CA91
Hemel Hempstead HP3 62 BK24
Winifred St, E16 37 K3
Winifred Ter, E13 23 N1
Enfield EN1 122 DT45
Winkers Cl, Chal.St.P. SL9 113 AZ53
Winkers La, Chal.St.P. SL9 113 AZ53
Winkfield Rd, E13 24 A1
N22 121 DN53
Winkley St, E2 20 E1
Winkwell, Hem.H. HP2 61 BD22
Winkworth Pl, Bans. SM7
off Bolters La 239 CZ114
Winkworth Rd, Bans. SM7 239 CZ114
Winlaton Rd, Brom. BR1 205 ED91
Winmill Rd, Dag. RM8 148 EZ62
Winnards, Wok. GU21
off Abercorn Way 248 AV118
Winn Common Rd, SE18 187 ES79
Winnett St, W1 17 N10
Winningales Ct, Ilf. IG5
off Vienna Cl 146 EL55
Winnings Wk, Nthlt. UB5
off Arnold Rd 158 BY65
Winnington Cl, N2 142 DD58
Winnington Rd, N2 142 DD59
Enfield EN3 104 DW38
Winnington Way, Wok. GU21 248 AV118
Winnipeg Dr, Grn St Grn BR6 245 ET107
Winnipeg Way, Brox. EN10 89 DY25
Winnock Rd, West Dr. UB7 156 BK74
Winn Rd, SE12 206 EG88
Winns Av, E17 145 DY55
Winns Ms, N15 144 DS56
Sch Winns Prim Sch, E17
off Fleeming Rd 123 DZ54
Winns Ter, E17 123 EA54
Winsbeach, E17 145 ED55
Winscombe Cres, W5 159 CK70
Winscombe St, N19 143 DH61
Winscombe Way, Stan. HA7 117 CG50
Winsford Rd, SE6 205 DZ90
Winsford Ter, N18 122 DR50
Winsham Gro, SW11 202 DG85
Winslade Rd, SW2 203 DL85
Winslade Way, SE6
off Rushey Grn 205 EB87
Winsland Ms, W2 16 A8
Winsland St, W2 16 A8
Winsley St, W1 17 L8
Winslow, SE17 43 N1
Winslow Cl, NW10
off Neasden La N 140 CS62
Pinner HA5 137 BV58
Winslow Gro, E4 124 EE47
Winslow Rd, W6 38 B2
Winslow Way, Felt. TW13 198 BX90
Walton-on-Thames KT12 218 BW104
Sch Winsor Prim Sch, E6 25 L9
Winsor Ter, E6 25 L7
Winstanley Cl, Cob. KT11 235 BV114
Winstanley Est, SW11 40 B10
Winstanley Rd, SW11 182 DD83
Winstanley Wk, Cob. KT11
off Winstanley Cl 235 BV114
Winstead Gdns, Dag. RM10 149 FC64
Winston Av, NW9 140 CS59
Sch Winston Churchill Sch, The, St.John's GU21
off Hermitage Rd 248 AT118
Winston Churchill Way, Chsht EN8 88 DW33
Winston Cl, Green. DA9 211 FT86
Harrow HA3 117 CF51
Romford RM7 149 FB56
Winston Ct, Har. HA3 116 CB52
Winston Dr, Bigg.H. TN16
off Polesteeple Hill 260 EK117
Stoke D'Abernon KT11 252 BY116
Winstone Cl, Amer. HP6 76 AP34
Winston Gdns, Berk. HP4 60 AT19
Winston Rd, N16 9 M2
Winston Wk, W4
off Beaconsfield Rd 180 CR76
Winston Way, Ilf. IG1 147 EP62
Old Woking GU22 249 BB120
Potters Bar EN6 86 DA34
Sch Winston Way Prim Sch, Ilf. IG1 off Winston Way 147 EQ61
Winstre Rd, Borwd. WD6 100 CN39
Winter Av, E6 166 EL67
Winterborne Av, Orp. BR6 227 ER104
Winterbourne Gro, Wey. KT13 235 BQ107
Sch Winterbourne Inf & Nurs Sch, Th.Hth. CR7
off Winterbourne Rd 223 DN98
Sch Winterbourne Jun Boys' Sch, Th.Hth. CR7
off Winterbourne Rd 223 DN98
Sch Winterbourne Jun Girls' Sch, Th.Hth. CR7
off Winterbourne Rd 223 DN98
Winterbourne Ms, Oxt. RH8
off Brook Hill 275 EC130
Winterbourne Rd, SE6 205 DZ88
Dagenham RM8 148 EW61
Thornton Heath CR7 223 DN98
Winter Box Wk, Rich. TW10 180 CM84
Winterbrook Rd, SE24 204 DQ86
Winterburn Cl, N11 120 DG51
Winterdown Gdns, Esher KT10 236 BZ107
Winterdown Rd, Esher KT10 236 BZ107
Winterfold Cl, SW19 201 CY89
Wintergarden, Bluewater DA9 off Bluewater Parkway 211 FU87
Winter Gdn Cres, Bluewater DA9 211 FU87
Winter Gdn Ho, WC2
off Macklin St 18 B8
Wintergreen Cl, E6 24 G7
Winterhill Way, Guil. GU4 265 BB130
Winters Cft, Grav. DA12 213 GK93
Winterscroft Rd, Hodd. EN11 71 DZ16
Wintersells Rd, Byfleet KT14 234 BK110
Winters Rd, T.Ditt. KT7 219 CH101
Winterstoke Gdns, NW7 119 CU50
Winterstoke Rd, SE6 205 DZ88
Winters Way, Wal.Abb. EN9 90 EG33
Winterton Ho, E1 20 F9
Winterton Pl, SW10 39 P2
Winterwell Rd, SW2 203 DL85
Winthorpe Gdns, Borwd. WD6 100 CM39
Winthorpe Rd, SW15 181 CY84
Winthrop St, E1 20 E6
Winthrop Wk, Wem. HA9
off Everard Way 140 CL62
Winton App, Crox.Grn WD3 97 BQ43
Winton Av, N11 121 DJ52
Winton Cl, N9 123 DX45
Winton Cres, Crox.Grn WD3 97 BP43
Winton Dr, Chsht EN8 89 DY29
Croxley Green WD3 97 BP44
Winton Gdns, Edg. HA8 118 CM52
Sch Winton Prim Sch, N1 18 C1
Winton Rd, Orp. BR6 245 EP105
Ware SG12 55 DZ06
Winton Way, SW16 203 DN92
Wintoun Path, Slou. SL2 153 AL70
Winvale, Slou. SL1 174 AS76
Winwood, Slou. SL2 154 AW72
Wireless Rd, Bigg.H. TN16 260 EK115
Wirrall Ho, SE26
off Sydenham Hill Est 204 DU90
Wirral Wd Cl, Chis. BR7 207 EN93
Wirra Way, Lon.Hthrw Air. TW6 off Wayfarer Rd 176 BH82
Wisbeach Rd, Croy. CR0 224 DR99
Wisborough Rd, S.Croy. CR2 242 DT109
Wisdom Dr, Hert. SG13 54 DS09
Wisdons Cl, Dag. RM10 149 FB60
Wise La, NW7 119 CV51
West Drayton UB7 176 BK77
Wiseman Ct, SE19 204 DS92
Wiseman Rd, E10 145 EA61
Wisemans Gdns, Saw. CM21 58 EW06
Wise Rd, E15 12 F9
Wise's La, Hat. AL9 85 CW27
Wiseton Rd, SW17 202 DE88
Wishart Rd, SE3 186 EK81
Wishaw Wk, N13
off Elvendon Rd 121 DL51
Wishbone Way, Wok. GU21 248 AT116
Wishford Ct, Ashtd. KT21
off The Marld 254 CM118
Sch Wishmore Cross Sch, Chobham GU24 off Alpha Rd 232 AT110
WISLEY, Wok. GU23 250 BL116
Wisley Common, Wok. GU23 250 BN117
Wisley Ct, S.Croy. CR2
off Sanderstead Rd 242 DR110
Jct Wisley Interchange, Cob. KT11 251 BQ116
Wisley La, Wisley GU23 250 BL116
Wisley Rd, SW11 202 DG85
Orpington BR5 208 EU94
Wissants, Harl. CM19 73 EP19
Wistaria Cl, Orp. BR6 227 EP103
Pilgrim's Hatch CM15 130 FW43
Wistaria Dr, Lon.Col. AL2 83 CH26
Wisteria Apts, E9
off Chatham Pl 10 G4
Wisteria Cl, NW7 119 CT51
Ilford IG1 147 EP64
Wisteria Gdns, Swan. BR8 229 FD96
Wisteria Rd, SE13 185 ED84
Wistlea Cres, Coln.Hth AL4 66 CP22
Witanhurst La, N6 142 DG60
Witan St, E2 20 F3
Witches La, Sev. TN13 278 FD122
Witchford, Welw.G.C. AL7 52 DD09
Witcombe Pt, SE15 44 E7
Witham Cl, Loug. IG10 106 EL44
Witham Rd, SE20 224 DW97
W13 159 CG74
Dagenham RM10 148 FA64
Isleworth TW7 179 CD81
Romford RM2 149 FH57
Withens Cl, Orp. BR5 228 EW98
Witherby Cl, Croy. CR0 242 DS106
Wither Dale, Horl. RH6 290 DE147
Witheridge La, Knot.Grn HP9 110 AF48
Penn HP10 110 AF48
Witherings, The, Horn. RM11 150 FL57
Witherington Rd, N5 8 F3
Withers Cl, Chess. KT9
off Coppard Gdns 237 CJ107
Withers Mead, NW9 119 CT53
Witherston Way, SE9 207 EN89
Withey Brook, Hkwd RH6 290 DD150
Withey Cl, Wind. SL4 173 AL81
Witheygate Av, Stai. TW18 196 BH93
Withey Meadows, Hkwd RH6 290 DD150
Withies, The, Knap. GU21 248 AS117
Leatherhead KT22 253 CH120
Withybed Cor, Walt.Hill KT20 255 CV123
Withycombe Rd, SW19 201 CX87
Withycroft, Geo.Grn SL3 154 AY72
Withy La, Ruis. HA4 137 BQ57
Withy Mead, E4 123 ED48
Withy Pl, Park St AL2 82 CC28
Witley Cres, New Adgtn CR0 243 EC107
Witley Gdns, Sthl. UB2 178 BZ77
● Witley Ind Est, Sthl. UB2
off Witley Gdns 178 BZ77
Witley Pt, SW15
off Wanborough Dr 201 CV88
Witley Rd, N19 143 DJ61
Witney Cl, Pnr. HA5 116 BZ51
Uxbridge UB10 136 BM63
Witney Path, SE23 205 DX90
Wittenham Way, E4 123 ED48
Wittering Cl, Kings.T. KT2 199 CK92
Wittering Wk, Horn. RM12 170 FJ65
Wittersham Rd, Brom. BR1 206 EF92
Wivenhoe Cl, SE15 44 E10
Wivenhoe Ct, Houns. TW3 178 BZ84
Wivenhoe Rd, Bark. IG11 168 EU68
Wiverton Rd, SE26 204 DW93
Wix Hill, W.Hors. KT24 267 BP130
Wix Hill Cl, W.Hors. KT24 267 BP131
Sch Wix Prim Sch, SW4
off Wixs La 183 DH83
Wix Rd, Dag. RM9 168 EX67
Wixs La, SW4 183 DH84
Woburn Av, Horn. RM12 149 FG63
Purley CR8 off High St 241 DN111
Theydon Bois CM16 107 ES37
Woburn Cl, SE28
off Summerton Way 168 EX72
SW19 202 DC93
Bushey WD23 98 CC43
Woburn Ct, SE16
off Masters Dr 44 F1
Woburn Hill, Add. KT15 216 BJ103
Woburn Pk, Add. KT15 216 BK103
Woburn Pl, WC1 17 P4
Woburn Rd, Cars. SM5 222 DE102
Croydon CR0 224 DQ102
Woburn Sq, WC1 17 P5
Woburn Wk, WC1 17 P3
Wodeham Gdns, E1 20 D6
Wodehouse Av, SE5 44 A6
Wodehouse Rd, Dart. DA1 190 FN84
Wodeland Av, Guil. GU2 280 AV136
Woffington Cl, Kings.T. KT1 219 CJ95
Wokindon Rd, Grays RM16 193 GH76
WOKING, GU22 - GU24 249 AZ117
⇌ Woking 249 AZ117
Sch Woking Adult Learning Cen, Wok. GU22 off Bonsey La 248 AX121
● Woking Business Pk, Wok. GU21 249 BB115
Woking Cl, SW15 181 CT84
Sch Woking Coll, Wok. GU22
off Rydens Way 249 BA120
H Woking Comm Hosp, Wok. GU22 249 AZ118
Sch Woking High Sch, Horsell GU21 off Morton Rd 248 AX115
H Woking Nuffield Hosp, The, Wok. GU21 232 AY114
Woking Rd, Guil. GU1, GU4 264 AX130
Wold, The, Wold. CR3 259 EA122
Woldham Pl, Brom. BR2 226 EJ98
Woldham Rd, Brom. BR2 226 EJ98
WOLDINGHAM, Cat. CR3 259 EB122
⇌ Woldingham 259 DX122
WOLDINGHAM GARDEN VILLAGE, Cat. CR3 259 DY121
Woldingham Rd, Wold. CR3 258 DV120
Sch Woldingham Sch, Wold. CR3 off Marden Pk 275 DY125
Wolds Dr, Orp. BR6 245 EN105

Wolfe Cl, Brom. BR2 226 EG100
Hayes UB4 157 BV69
Wolfe Cres, SE7 186 EK78
SE16 33 J5
Wolferton Rd, E12 147 EM63
Wolffe Gdns, E15 13 L5
Sch Wolf Flds Prim Sch, Sthl. UB2 off Norwood Rd 178 BZ77
Wolffram Cl, SE13 206 EE85
Wolfington Rd, SE27 203 DP91
Wolf La, Wind. SL4 173 AK83
Wolfs Hill, Oxt. RH8 276 EG131
Sch Wolfson Hillel Prim Sch, N14 off Chase Rd 103 DK44
H Wolfson Neurorehabilitation Cen, SW20 201 CV94
Wolf's Row, Oxt. RH8 276 EH130
Wolfs Wd, Oxt. RH8 276 EG132
Wolftencroft Cl, SW11 40 B10
Wollaston Cl, SE1 31 J8
Wolmer Cl, Edg. HA8 118 CP49
Wolmer Gdns, Edg. HA8 118 CN48
Wolseley Av, SW19 202 DA89
Wolseley Gdns, W4 180 CP79
Wolseley Rd, E7 166 EH66
N8 143 DK58
N22 121 DM53
W4 180 CQ77
Harrow HA3 139 CE55
Mitcham CR4 222 DG101
Romford RM7 149 FD59
Wolseley St, SE1 32 B5
Wolsey Av, E6 25 L3
E17 145 DZ55
Cheshunt EN7 88 DT29
Thames Ditton KT7 219 CF99
● Wolsey Business Pk, Wat. WD18 115 BR45
Wolsey Cl, SW20 201 CV94
Hounslow TW3 178 CC84
Kingston upon Thames KT2 220 CP95
Southall UB2 178 CC76
Worcester Park KT4 239 CU105
Wolsey Cres, Green. DA9 off The Ri 211 FU86
Morden SM4 221 CY101
New Addington CR0 243 EC109
Wolsey Dr, Kings.T. KT2 200 CL92
Walton-on-Thames KT12 218 BX102
Wolsey Gdns, Ilf. IG6 125 EQ51
Wolsey Gro, Edg. HA8 118 CR52
Esher KT10 236 CB105
Sch Wolsey Inf Sch, Croy. CR0 off King Henry's Dr 243 EC108
Sch Wolsey Jun Sch, New Adgtn CR0 off King Henry's Dr 243 EC108
Wolsey Ms, NW5 7 L4
Orpington BR6 245 ET106
Wolsey Pl Shop Cen, Wok. GU21 off Commercial Way 249 AZ117
Wolsey Rd, N1 9 M3
Ashford TW15 196 BL91
East Molesey KT8 219 CD98
Enfield EN1 104 DV40
Esher KT10 236 CB105
Hampton Hill TW12 198 CB93
Hemel Hempstead HP2 62 BK21
Northwood HA6 115 BQ47
Sunbury-on-Thames TW16 197 BT94
Wolsey St, E1 20 G7
Wolsey Wk, Wok. GU21 248 AY117
Wolsey Way, Chess. KT9 238 CN106
Wolsley Cl, Dart. DA1 209 FE85
Wolstan Cl, Denh. UB9 136 BG62
Wolstonbury, N12 120 DA50
Wolvens La, Dor. RH4, RH5 284 CA140
Wolvercote Rd, SE2 188 EX75
Wolverley St, E2 20 E3
Wolverton, SE17 31 M10
Wolverton Av, Kings.T. KT2 220 CN95
Wolverton Cl, Horl. RH6 290 DF150
Wolverton Gdns, W5 160 CM73
W6 26 C8
Horley RH6 290 DF149
Wolverton Rd, Stan. HA7 117 CH51
Wolverton Way, N14 103 DJ43
Wolves La, N13 121 DN52
N22 121 DN52
Wombwell Gdns, Nthflt DA11 212 GE89
WOMBWELL PARK, Grav. DA11 212 GD89
Womersley Rd, N8 143 DM58
WONERSH, Guil. GU5 281 BB144
Wonersh Common, Won. GU5 281 BB141
Wonersh Common Rd, Won. GU5 281 BB142
Wonersh Way, Sutt. SM2 239 CX109
Wonford Cl, Kings.T. KT2 220 CS95
Walton on the Hill KT20 271 CU126
Wonham La, Bet. RH3 286 CS135
Wonham Way, Guil. GU5 283 BR139
Wonnacott Pl, Enf. EN3 105 DX36
Wontford Rd, Pur. CR8 257 DN115
Wontner Cl, N1 9 J7
Wontner Rd, SW17 202 DF89
WOOBURN, H.Wyc. HP10 132 AD58
Wooburn Cl, Uxb. UB8 off Aldenham Dr 157 BP70
Wooburn Common, Woob.Grn HP10 132 AH59
Wooburn Common Rd, Slou. SL1 132 AH61
Wooburn Green HP10 132 AH61
Wooburn Gra, Woob.Grn HP10 132 AD60
WOOBURN GREEN, H.Wyc. HP10 132 AF56
Wooburn Grn La, Beac. HP9 132 AG56
● Wooburn Ind Pk, Woob.Grn HP10 132 AD59
Wooburn Manor Pk, Woob.Grn HP10 132 AE58
Wooburn Mead, Woob.Grn HP10 132 AE57
Wooburn Ms, Woob.Grn HP10 132 AE58
Wooburn Town, Woob.Grn HP10 132 AD59
Woodall Cl, E14 22 D10
Chessington KT9 237 CK108
Woodall Rd, Enf. EN3 105 DX44
Wood Av, Purf. RM19 190 FQ77
Woodbank, Rick. WD3 96 BJ44
Woodbank Av, Ger.Cr. SL9 134 AX58
Woodbank Dr, Ch.St.G. HP8 112 AX48
Woodbank Rd, Brom. BR1 206 EF90
Woodbastwick Rd, SE26 205 DX92
Woodberry Av, N21 121 DN47
Harrow HA2 138 CB56
Woodberry Cl, NW7 119 CX52
Sunbury-on-Thames TW16 197 BU93
Woodberry Cres, N10 143 DH55
Woodberry Down, N4 144 DQ59
Epping CM16 92 EU29
Sch Woodberry Down Comm Prim Sch, N4 off Woodberry Gro 144 DQ59
Woodberry Down Est, N4 144 DQ59
Woodberry Gdns, N12 120 DC51
Woodberry Gro, N4 144 DQ59
N12 120 DC51
Bexley DA5 209 FD90
Woodberry Way, E4 123 EC46
N12 120 DC51
Woodbine Cl, Harl. CM19 73 EQ17
Twickenham TW2 199 CD89
Waltham Abbey EN9 106 EJ35
Woodbine Gro, SE20 204 DV94
Enfield EN2 104 DR38
Woodbine La, Wor.Pk. KT4 221 CV104
Woodbine Pl, E11 146 EG58
Woodbine Rd, Sid. DA15 207 ES88
Woodbines Av, Kings.T. KT1 219 CK97
Woodbine Ter, E9 11 H4
Woodborough Rd, SW15 181 CV84
Woodbourne Av, SW16 203 DK90
Woodbourne Cl, SW16 off Woodbourne Av 203 DL90
Woodbourne Dr, Clay. KT10 237 CF107
Woodbourne Gdns, Wall. SM6 241 DH108
Woodbridge Av, Lthd. KT22 253 CG118
● Woodbridge Business Pk, Guil. GU1 264 AW133
Woodbridge Cl, N7 143 DM61
NW2 141 CU62
Romford RM3 128 FK49
Woodbridge Ct, Wdf.Grn. IG8 124 EL52
Woodbridge Gro, Lthd. KT22 253 CG118
Sch Woodbridge High Sch & Language Coll, Wdf.Grn. IG8 off St. Barnabas Rd 124 EH52
WOODBRIDGE HILL, Guil. GU2 264 AU132
Woodbridge Hill, Guil. GU2 264 AV133
Woodbridge Hill Gdns, Guil. GU2 264 AU133
Woodbridge La, Rom. RM3 128 FK48
Woodbridge Meadows, Guil. GU1 264 AW133
Woodbridge Rd, Bark. IG11 147 ET64
Guildford GU1 264 AW133
Woodbridge St, EC1 18 G4
Woodbrook Gdns, Wal.Abb. EN9 90 EE33
Woodbrook Rd, SE2 188 EU79
Woodburn Cl, NW4 141 CX57
Woodbury Cl, E11 146 EH56
Biggin Hill TN16 261 EM118
Bourne End SL8 132 AC59
Croydon CR0 224 DT103
Woodbury Dr, Sutt. SM2 240 DC110
Woodbury Gdns, SE12 206 EH90
Woodbury Hill, Loug. IG10 106 EL41
Woodbury Hollow, Loug. IG10 106 EL40
Woodbury Pk Rd, W13 159 CH70
Woodbury Rd, E17 145 EB56
Biggin Hill TN16 261 EM118
Woodbury St, SW17 202 DE92
Woodchester Pk, Knot.Grn HP9 110 AJ50
Woodchester Sq, W2 15 L6
Woodchurch Cl, Sid. DA14 207 ER90
Woodchurch Dr, Brom. BR1 206 EK94
Woodchurch Rd, NW6 5 K7
Wood Cl, E2 20 C4
NW9 140 CR59
Bexley DA5 209 FE90
Harrow HA1 139 CD59
Hatfield AL10 67 CV18
Redhill RH1 288 DG143
Windsor SL4 173 AQ84
Woodclyffe Dr, Chis. BR7 227 EN96
Woodcock Ct, Har. HA3 140 CL59
Woodcock Dell Av, Har. HA3 139 CK59
Woodcock Hill, Berk. HP4 60 AS18
Harrow HA3 139 CK59
Rickmansworth WD3 114 BL50
Sandridge AL4 66 CN15
● Woodcock Hill Ind Est, Rick. WD3 114 BL49
Woodcocks, E16 24 D7
Woodcombe Cres, SE23 204 DW88
Wood Common, Hat. AL10 67 CV15
WOODCOTE, Epsom KT18 254 CQ116
WOODCOTE, Pur. CR8 241 DK111
Woodcote, Guil. GU2 280 AV138
Horley RH6 291 DH147
Woodcote Av, NW7 119 CW51
Hornchurch RM12 149 FG63
Thornton Heath CR7 223 DP98
Wallington SM6 241 DH108
Woodcote Cl, Chsht EN8 88 DW30
Enfield EN3 104 DW44
Epsom KT18 238 CR114
Kingston upon Thames KT2 200 CM92
Woodcote Dr, Orp. BR6 227 ER102
Purley CR8 241 DK110
Woodcote End, Epsom KT18 254 CR115
Woodcote Grn, Wall. SM6 241 DJ109
Woodcote Grn Rd, Epsom KT18 254 CQ116
Woodcote Gro, Couls. CR5 241 DH112
Woodcote Gro Rd, Couls. CR5 257 DK115
Sch Woodcote High Sch, Couls. CR5 off Meadow Ri 241 DK113
Woodcote Hurst, Epsom KT18 254 CQ116
Woodcote La, Pur. CR8 241 DK111
Woodcote Lawns, Chesh. HP5 off Little Hivings 76 AN27
Woodcote Ms, Loug. IG10 124 EK45
Wallington SM6 241 DH107
WOODCOTE PARK, Couls. CR5 241 DH113
Woodcote Pk, Epsom KT18 254 CQ117
Woodcote Pk Av, Pur. CR8 241 DJ112
Woodcote Pk Rd, Epsom KT18 254 CQ116
Woodcote Pl, SE27 203 DP92
Sch Woodcote Prim Sch, Couls. CR5 off Dunsfold Ri 241 DK114
Woodcote Rd, E11 146 EG59
Epsom KT18 238 CR114
Purley CR8 241 DJ109
Wallington SM6 241 DH107
Woodcote Side, Epsom KT18 254 CP115
Woodcote Valley Rd, Pur. CR8 241 DK113
Woodcott Ho, SW15 off Ellisfield Dr 201 CU87
Wood Ct, W12 off Heathstan Rd 161 CU72
Edg. HA8 off South Rd 118 CP53
Wood Cres, Hem.H. HP3 62 BK21
Woodcrest Rd, Pur. CR8 241 DL113
Woodcrest Wk, Reig. RH2 272 DE132
Woodcroft, N21 121 DM46
SE9 207 EM90
Greenford UB6 159 CG65
Harlow CM18 73 EQ17
Woodcroft Av, NW7 118 CS52
Woodgate Cres, Stanmore HA7 117 CF53
Stanstead Abbotts SG12 55 ED11
Woodcroft Cres, Uxb. UB10 157 BP67
Woodcroft Ms, SE8 33 L9
Sch Woodcroft Prim Sch, Edg. HA8 off Goldbeaters Gro 118 CS52
Woodcroft Rd, Chesh. HP5 76 AR28
Thornton Heath CR7 223 DP99
Sch Woodcroft Sch, Loug. IG10 off Whitakers Way 107 EM39
Woodcutter Pl, St.Alb. AL2 82 CC27
Woodcutters Av, Grays RM16 192 GC75
Woodcutters Cl, Horn. RM11 150 FK56
Wood Dr, Chis. BR7 206 EL93
Sevenoaks TN13 278 FF126
Woodedge Cl, E4 124 EF46
Jct Wooden Br, Guil. GU2 264 AU133
Woodend, SE19 204 DQ93
Esher KT10 218 CC103
Wood End, Hayes UB3 157 BS72
Woodend, Lthd. KT22 269 CJ125
Wood End, Park St AL2 82 CC28
Woodend, Sutt. SM1 222 DC103
Wood End, Swan. BR8 229 FC98
Woodend, The, Wall. SM6 241 DH109
Wood End Av, Har. HA2 138 CB63
Wood End Cl, Farn.Com. SL2 133 AR62
Hemel Hempstead HP2 63 BQ19
Northolt UB5 139 CD64
Woodend Cl, Wok. GU21 248 AU119
Woodend Gdns, Enf. EN2 103 DL42
Wood End Gdns, Nthlt. UB5 138 CC64
Wood End Grn Rd, Hayes UB3 157 BR71
Sch Wood End Inf Sch, Nthlt. UB5 off Whitton Av W 139 CD64
Sch Wood End Jun Sch, Grnf. UB6 off Vernon Ri 139 CD64
Wood End La, Nthlt. UB5 158 CB65
Woodend Pk, Cob. KT11 252 BX115
Sch Wood End Pk Comm Sch, Hayes UB3 off Judge Heath La 157 BQ73
Woodend Rd, E17 123 EC54
Wood End Rd, Har. HA1 139 CD63
Wood End Way, Nthlt. UB5 138 CC64
Wooder Gdns, E7 13 N1
Wooderson Cl, SE25 224 DS98
Woodfall Av, Barn. EN5 101 CZ43
Woodfall Dr, Dart. DA1 189 FE84
Woodfall Rd, N4 143 DN60
Woodfall St, SW3 40 E1
Wood Fm Rd, Hem.H. HP2 62 BL20
Woodfarrs, SE5 184 DR84
Wood Fld, NW3 6 E3
Woodfield, Ashtd. KT21 253 CK117
Woodfield Av, NW9 140 CS56
SW16 203 DK90
W5 159 CJ70
Carshalton SM5 240 DG107
Gravesend DA11 213 GH88
Northwood HA6 115 BS49
Wembley HA0 139 CJ62
Woodfield Cl, SE19 204 DQ94
Ashtead KT21 253 CK117
Coulsdon CR5 257 DJ119
Enfield EN1 104 DS42
Redhill RH1 272 DE133
Woodfield Cres, W5 159 CJ70
Woodfield Dr, E.Barn. EN4 120 DG46
Hemel Hempstead HP3 63 BR22
Romford RM2 149 FG56
Woodfield Gdns, Hem. H. HP3 63 BQ22
New Malden KT3 221 CT99
Woodfield Gro, SW16 203 DK90
Woodfield Hill, Couls. CR5 257 DH119
Woodfield La, SW16 203 DK90
Ashtead KT21 254 CL116
Hatfield AL9 68 DD23
Hertford SG13 68 DD23
Woodfield Pk, Amer. HP6 77 AN37
Woodfield Pl, W9 15 H5
Woodfield Ri, Bushey WD23 117 CD45
Woodfield Rd, W5 159 CJ70
W9 15 H6
Ashtead KT21 253 CK117
Hounslow TW4 177 BV82
Radlett WD7 99 CG36
Thames Ditton KT7 219 CF103
Welwyn Garden City AL7 51 CZ09
Woodfields, Sev. TN13 278 FD122
Woodfields, The, S.Croy. CR2 242 DT111
Sch Woodfield Sch, NW9 off Glenwood Av 140 CS60
Hemel Hempstead HP3 off Malmes Cft 63 BQ22
Merstham RH1 off Sunstone Gro 273 DL129
Woodfield Ter, Hare. UB9 114 BH54
Thornwood CM16 92 EW25
Woodfield Way, N11 121 DK52
Hornchurch RM12 150 FK60
Redhill RH1 272 DE132
St. Albans AL4 65 CJ17
Woodfines, The, Horn. RM11 150 FK58
WOODFORD, Wdf.Grn. IG8 124 EH51
⊖ Woodford 124 EH51
Woodford Av, Ilf. IG2, IG4 147 EM57
Woodford Green IG8 146 EK55
WOODFORD BRIDGE, Wdf.Grn. IG8 125 EM52
Woodford Br Rd, Ilf. IG4 146 EK55
Sch Woodford Co High Sch for Girls, Wdf.Grn. IG8 off High Rd Woodford Grn 124 EF51
Woodford Ct, W12 26 C4
Waltham Abbey EN9 90 EG33
Woodford Cres, Pnr. HA5 115 BV54
WOODFORD GREEN, IG8 124 EF49
Sch Woodford Grn Prep Sch, Wdf.Grn. IG8 off Glengall Rd 124 EG51
Sch Woodford Grn Prim Sch, Wdf.Grn. IG8 off Sunset Av 124 EG50
Woodford New Rd, E17 146 EE56
E18 124 EE53
Woodford Green IG8 124 EE53
Woodford Pl, Wem. HA9 140 CL60
Woodford Rd, E7 146 EH63
E18 146 EG56
Watford WD17 97 BV40
● Woodford Trd Est, Wdf.Grn. IG8 124 EJ54
Woodford Way, Slou. SL2 153 AN69
WOODFORD WELLS, Wdf.Grn. IG8 124 EH49
Woodgate, Wat. WD25 81 BV33
Woodgate Av, Chess. KT9 237 CK106
Northaw EN6 87 DH33
Woodgate Cl, Cob. KT11 235 BV113
Woodgate Ct, Horn. RM11 150 FK55
Woodgate Cres, Nthwd. HA6 115 BU51
Woodgate Dr, SW16 203 DK94
Woodgate Ms, Wat. WD17 97 BU39
Woodgavil, Bans. SM7 255 CZ116
Woodger Cl, Guil. GU4 265 BC132
Woodger Ct, Croy. CR0 off Lion Rd 224 DQ99
Woodger Rd, W12 26 B5
Woodgers Gro, Swan. BR8 229 FF96
Woodget Cl, E6 24 G8
Woodgrange Av, N12 120 DD51
W5 160 CN74
Enfield EN1 104 DU44
Harrow HA3 139 CJ57
Woodgrange Cl, Har. HA3 139 CK57
Woodgrange Gdns, Enf. EN1 104 DU44
Sch Woodgrange Inf Sch, E7 off Sebert Rd 146 EH63
⊖ Woodgrange Park 146 EK64
Woodgrange Rd, E7 13 P2
Woodgrange Ter, Enf. EN1 104 DU44
WOOD GREEN, N22 121 DL53
⊖ Wood Green 121 DM54
Woodgreen Rd, Wal.Abb. EN9 106 EJ35
Wood Grn Way, Chsht EN8 89 DY31
WOODHALL, Welw.G.C. AL7 51 CY11
Woodhall, NW1 17 L3
Woodhall Av, SE21 204 DT90
Pinner HA5 116 BY54
Woodhall Cl, Hert. SG14 54 DQ07
Uxbridge UB8 136 BK64
Woodhall Ct, Welw.G.C. AL7 51 CY10
Woodhall Cres, Horn. RM11 150 FM59
Woodhall Dr, SE21 204 DT90
Pinner HA5 116 BX53
Woodhall Gate, Pnr. HA5 116 BX52
Woodhall Ho, SW18 off Fitzhugh Gro 202 DD86
Woodhall La, Hem.H. HP2 62 BL19
Shenley WD7 100 CL35
Watford WD19 116 BX49
Welwyn Garden City AL7 51 CY10
Woodhall Par, Welw.G.C. AL7 51 CZ11
Sch Woodhall Prim Sch, S.Oxhey WD19 off Woodhall La 116 BY49
Woodhall Rd, Pnr. HA5 116 BX52
WOODHAM, Add. KT15 233 BF111
Woodham Ct, E18 146 EF56
Woodham Gate, Wok. GU21 233 BC113
Woodham La, Add. KT15 234 BG110
Woking GU21 233 BB114
Woodham Lock, W.Byf. KT14 233 BF112
Woodham Pk Rd, Wdhm KT15 233 BF109
Woodham Pk Way, Wdhm KT15 233 BF111
Woodham Ri, Wok. GU21 233 AZ114
Woodham Rd, SE6 205 EC90
Woking GU21 248 AY115
Woodham Way, Stans.Abb. SG12 55 EC11
Woodham Waye, Wok. GU21 233 BB113
WOODHATCH, Reig. RH2 288 DC137
Woodhatch Cl, E6 24 G7
Woodhatch Rd, Red. RH1 288 DB137
Reigate RH2 288 DB137
Woodhatch Spinney, Couls. CR5 257 DL116
Woodhaven Gdns, Ilf. IG6 off Brandville Gdns 147 EQ56
Woodhaw, Egh. TW20 195 BB91
Woodhayes, Horl. RH6 291 DH147
Woodhayes Rd, SW19 201 CW94
Woodhead Dr, Orp. BR6 off Sherlies Av 227 ES103
Woodheyes Rd, NW10 140 CR64
Woodhill, SE18 37 H8
Harlow CM18 73 ES18
Send GU23 265 BD125
Woodhill Av, Ger.Cr. SL9 135 BA58
Woodhill Ct, Send GU23 265 BD125
Woodhill Cres, Har. HA3 139 CK58
Sch Woodhill Prim Sch, SE18 37 H9
Wood Ho, SW17 off Laurel Cl 202 DE92
Woodhouse Av, Perivale UB6 159 CF68
Woodhouse Cl, SE22 184 DU84
Hayes UB3 177 BS76
Perivale UB6 159 CF68
Coll Woodhouse Coll, N12 off Woodhouse Rd 120 DD51
Woodhouse Eaves, Nthwd. HA6 115 BU50
Woodhouse Gro, E12 166 EL65
Wood Ho La, Brox. EN10 70 DT21
Woodhouse La, Holm.St.M. RH5 283 BU143
Woodhouse Rd, E11 146 EF62
N12 120 DD51
Woodhurst Av, Petts Wd BR5 227 EQ100
Watford WD25 98 BX35
Woodhurst Dr, Denh. UB9 135 BF57
Woodhurst La, Oxt. RH8 276 EE130
Woodhurst Pk, Oxt. RH8 276 EE130
Woodhurst Rd, SE2 188 EU78
W3 160 CQ73
Woodhyrst Gdns, Ken. CR8 257 DP115
Woodin Cl, Dart, DA1 210 FK86
Wooding Gro, Harl. CM19 73 EP15
Woodington Cl, SE9 207 EN86
Woodknoll Dr, Chis. BR7 227 EM95
Woodland App, Grnf. UB6 159 CG65
Woodland Av, Hem.H. HP1 62 BH21
Hutton CM13 131 GC43
Slough SL1 153 AR73
Windsor SL4 173 AM84
Woodland Chase, Crox.Grn WD3 115 BP45
Woodland Cl, NW9 140 CQ58
SE19 204 DS93
Epsom KT19 238 CS107
Hemel Hempstead HP1 62 BH21
Hutton CM13 131 GC43
Ickenham UB10 137 BP61
Weybridge KT13 235 BR105
Woodford Green IG8 124 EH48
Woodland Ct, Oxt. RH8 275 ED128
Woodland Cres, SE10 47 J2
SE16 33 J5
Wood Land, E.Hors. KT24 267 BT127
St. Albans AL4 65 CJ18
Watford WD17 87 BT39
Woodland Gdns, N10 143 DH57
Isleworth TW7 179 CE82
South Croydon CR2 242 DW111
Woodland Glade, Farn.Com. SL2 133 AR62
Woodland Gra, Iver SL0 175 BE76
Woodland Gro, SE10 47 J1
Epping CM16 92 EU31
Weybridge KT13 235 BR105
Woodland Hts, SE3 47 K2
Woodland Hill, SE19 204 DS93
Woodland La, Chorl. WD3 95 BD41
Woodland Ms, SW16 203 DL90
Woodland Mt, Hert. SG13 54 DT09
Woodland Pl, Chorl. WD3 95 BF42
Woodland Pl, Hemel Hempstead HP1 62 BH21
Woodland Ri, N10 143 DH56
Greenford UB6 159 CG65
Oxted RH8 276 EE130
Sevenoaks TN15 279 FL123
Welwyn Garden City AL8 51 CW07
Woodland Rd, E4 123 EC46
N11 121 DH50
SE19 204 DS92
Hertford Heath SG13 54 DV12
Loughton IG10 106 EL41
Maple Cross WD3 113 BD50
Thornton Heath CR7 223 DN98
WOODLANDS, Islw. TW7 179 CE82
Woodlands, NW11 141 CY58
SW20 221 CW98
Brookmans Park AL9 86 DB26
Epping CM16 92 EU31
Gerrards Cross SL9 135 AZ57
Harrow HA2 138 CA56
Horley RH6 291 DJ147
Park Street AL2 82 CC27
Radlett WD7 83 CG34
Send Marsh GU23 off Clandon Rd 265 BF125
Woking GU22 off Constitution Hill 248 AY118
Woodlands, The, N14 121 DH46
SE13 205 ED87
SE19 204 DQ94
Amersham HP6 77 AQ35
Beckenham BR3 225 EC95
Esher KT10 218 CC103
Guildford GU1 265 BC133
Isleworth TW7 179 CF82
Orpington BR6 246 EV107
Smallfield RH6 291 DP148
Wallington SM6 241 DH109
Woodlands Av, E11 146 EH60
N3 120 DC52
W3 160 CP74
Berkhamsted HP4 60 AW20
Hornchurch RM11 150 FK57
New Malden KT3 220 CQ95
Redhill RH1 288 DF135
Romford RM6 148 EY58
Ruislip HA4 138 BW60
Sidcup DA15 207 ES88
West Byfleet KT14 233 BF113
Worcester Park KT4 221 CT103
Woodlands Cl, NW11 141 CY57
Borehamwood WD6 100 CP42
Bromley BR1 227 EM96
Claygate KT10 237 CF108
East Horsley KT24 267 BT127
Gerrards Cross SL9 135 BA58
Grays RM16 192 GE76
Guildford GU1 264 AY130
Hoddesdon EN11 71 EA18
Ottershaw KT16 233 BB110
Swanley BR8 229 FF97
Woodlands Copse, Ashtd. KT21 253 CK116
Woodlands Ct, Wok. GU22 off Constitution Hill 248 AY119
Woodlands Dr, Beac. HP9 110 AJ51
Hoddesdon EN11 71 EA19
Kings Langley WD4 81 BQ28
Stanmore HA7 117 CF51
Sunbury-on-Thames TW16 218 BW96
Sch Woodlands First & Mid Sch, Edg. HA8 off Bransgrove Rd 118 CM53
Woodlands Gdns, Epsom KT18 255 CW117
Woodlands Glade, Beac. HP9 110 AJ51
Woodlands Gro, Couls. CR5 256 DG117
Isleworth TW7 179 CE82
Woodlands Hill, Beac. HP9 133 AL58
Sch Woodlands Inf Sch, Ilf. IG1 off Loxford La 147 ER64
Sch Woodlands Jun Sch, Ilf. IG1 off Loxford La 147 ER64
Woodlands La, Stoke D'Ab. KT11 252 CA117
Woodlands Par, Ashf. TW15 197 BQ93
Woodlands Pk, Add. KT15 233 BF106
Bexley DA5 209 FC91
Box Hill KT20 270 CP131
Guildford GU1 265 BB132
Woking GU21 off Blackmore Cres 233 BC114
Woodlands Pk Rd, N15 143 DP57
SE10 47 J2
Woodlands Pl, Cat. CR3 274 DU126
Sch Woodlands Prim Sch, Borwd. WD6 off Alban Cres 100 CN39
Woodlands Ri, Swan. BR8 229 FF96
Woodlands Rd, E11 146 EE61
E17 145 EC55
N9 122 DW46
SW13 181 CT83
Bexleyheath DA7 188 EY83
Bookham KT23 268 BY128
Bromley BR1 226 EL96
Bushey WD23 98 BY43
Enfield EN2 104 DR39
Epsom KT18 254 CN115
Guildford GU1 264 AX130
Harold Wood RM3 128 FN53
Harrow HA1 139 CF57
Hemel Hempstead HP3 80 BN27
Hertford SG13 54 DT09
Ilford IG1 147 EQ62
Isleworth TW7 179 CE82
Leatherhead KT22 253 CD117
Orpington BR6 246 EU107
Redhill RH1 288 DF135
Romford RM1 149 FF55
Southall UB1 158 BX74
Surbiton KT6 219 CK101
Virginia Water GU25 214 AW98
West Byfleet KT14 233 BF114
Woodlands Rd E, Vir.W. GU25 214 AW98
Woodlands Rd W, Vir.W. GU25 214 AW97
Sch Woodlands Sch, Gt Warley CM13 off Warley St 151 FX56
Leatherhead KT22 off Fortyfoot Rd 253 CJ122
Woodlands St, SE13 205 ED87
Woodland St, E8 10 B4
Woodlands Vw, Bad.Mt TN14 246 FA110
Dorking RH5 285 CH142
Woodlands Way, SW15 201 CZ85
Ashtead KT21 254 CN116
Box Hill KT20 270 CQ130
Woodland Ter, SE7 36 G9

Woodland Vw, Chesh. HP5 76 AR32
Godalming GU7 280 AS142
Woodland Wk, NW3 6 D2
SE10 47 K1
Bromley BR1 206 EE91
Epsom KT19 238 CN107
Woodland Way, N21 121 DN47
NW7 118 CS51
SE2 188 EX77
Bedmond WD5 81 BT27
Caterham CR3 274 DS128
Croydon CR0 225 DY102
Goffs Oak EN7 87 DP28
Greenhithe DA9 191 FU84
Kingswood KT20 255 CY122
Mitcham CR4 202 DG94
Morden SM4 221 CZ98
Petts Wood BR5 227 EQ98
Purley CR8 241 DN113
Surbiton KT5 220 CP103
Theydon Bois CM16 107 ER35
West Wickham BR4 243 EB105
Weybridge KT13 235 BR106
Woodford Green IG8 124 EH48
⊖ **Wood Lane** 26 B1
Wood La, N6 143 DH58
NW9 140 CS59
W12 14 B10
Caterham CR3 258 DR124
Dagenham RM8, RM9, RM10 148 EW63
Hedgerley SL2 134 AS61
Hemel Hempstead HP2 62 BK21
Hornchurch RM12 149 FG64
Isleworth TW7 179 CF80
Iver SL0 155 BC71
Lane End DA2 211 FR91
Ruislip HA4 137 BR60
Slough SL1 173 AM76
Stanmore HA7 117 CG48
Tadworth KT20 255 CZ116
Ware SG12 55 EA05
Weybridge KT13 235 BQ109
Woodford Green IG8 124 EF50
Wood La Cl, Iver SL0 155 BB69
Wood La End, Hem.H. HP2 62 BN19
Sch **Woodlane High Sch**, W12 *off Du Cane Rd* 161 CV72
Woodlawn Cl, SW15 201 CZ85
Woodlawn Cres, Twick. TW2 198 CB89
Woodlawn Dr, Felt. TW13 198 BX89
Woodlawn Gro, Wok. GU21 249 AZ115
Woodlawn Rd, SW6 38 C4
Woodlea, St.Alb. AL2 *off Hammers Gate* 82 CA25
Woodlea Dr, Brom. BR2 226 EE99
Woodlea Gro, Nthwd. HA6 115 BQ51
Sch **Woodlea Prim Sch**, Wold. CR3 *off Long Hill* 259 EA122
Woodlea Rd, N16 144 DS62
Woodlee Cl, Vir.W. GU25 214 AW96
Woodleigh, E18 *off Churchfields* 124 EG53
Woodleigh Av, N12 120 DE51
Woodleigh Gdns, SW16 203 DL90
Woodley Cl, SW17 *off Arnold Rd* 202 DF94
Woodley Hill, Chesh. HP5 76 AR34
Woodley La, Cars. SM5 222 DD104
Woodley Rd, Orp. BR6 228 EW103
Ware SG12 55 DZ05
Wood Lo Gdns, Brom. BR1 206 EL94
Wood Lo La, W.Wick. BR4 225 EC104
Woodmancote Gdns, W.Byf. KT14 234 BG113
Woodman La, E4 106 EE43
Woodman Ms, Rich. TW9 180 CP81
Woodman Path, Ilf. IG6 125 ES51
Woodman Rd, Couls. CR5 257 DJ115
Hemel Hempstead HP3 62 BL22
Warley CM14 130 FW50
Woodmans Gro, NW10 141 CT64
Woodmans Ms, W12 161 CV71
WOODMANSTERNE, Bans. SM7 256 DD115
⇌ **Woodmansterne** 257 DH116
Woodmansterne La, Bans. SM7 256 DB115
Carshalton SM5 240 DF112
Wallington SM6 241 DH111
Sch **Woodmansterne Prim Sch**, SW16 *off Stockport Rd* 223 DK95
Banstead SM7 *off Carshalton Rd* 240 DF114
Woodmansterne Rd, SW16 223 DK95
Carshalton SM5 240 DE109
Coulsdon CR5 257 DJ115
Woodmansterne St, Bans. SM7 256 DE115
Woodman St, E16 37 M3
Wood Martyn Ct, Orp. BR6 *off Augustus La* 228 EU103
Wood Meads, Epp. CM16 92 EU29
Woodmere, SE9 207 EM88
Woodmere Av, Croy. CR0 225 DX101
Watford WD24 98 BX38
Woodmere Cl, SW11 *off Lavender Hill* 182 DG83
Croydon CR0 225 DX101
Woodmere Gdns, Croy. CR0 225 DX101
Woodmere Way, Beck. BR3 225 ED99
Woodmill Ms, Hodd. EN11 *off Whittingstall Rd* 71 EB15
Woodmill Rd, E5 144 DW61
Woodmount, Swan. BR8 229 FC101
Woodnook Rd, SW16 203 DH92
Woodpecker Cl, N9 104 DV44
Bushey WD23 116 CC46
Cobham KT11 236 BY112
Harrow HA3 117 CF53
Hatfield AL10 67 CT21
Woodpecker Dr, Green. DA9 211 FU86
Woodpecker Ms, SE13 *off Mercator Rd* 185 ED84
Woodpecker Mt, Croy. CR0 243 DY109
Woodpecker Rd, SE14 45 L3
SE28 168 EW73
Woodpecker Way, Wok. GU22 248 AX123
Woodplace Cl, Couls. CR5 257 DJ119
Woodplace La, Couls. CR5 257 DJ118
Wood Pond Cl, Seer Grn HP9 111 AQ51
Woodquest Av, SE24 204 DQ85
Woodredon Cl, Roydon CM19 *off Epping Rd* 72 EH16
Woodredon Fm La, Wal.Abb. EN9 106 EK35
Wood Retreat, SE18 187 ER80
Woodridden Hill, Wal.Abb. EN9 106 EK35
Wood Ride, Barn. EN4 102 DD39
Petts Wood BR5 227 ER98
Woodridge Cl, Enf. EN2 103 DN39
Sch **Woodridge Prim Sch**, N12 *off Southover* 120 DA48
Woodridge Way, Nthwd. HA6 115 BS51
Wood Riding, Wok. GU22 *off Pyrford Wds* 249 BF115
Woodridings Av, Pnr. HA5 116 BZ53
Woodridings Cl, Pnr. HA5 116 BY52
Woodriffe Rd, E11 145 ED59
Wood Ri, Guil. GU3 264 AS132
Pinner HA5 137 BU57
Wood Rd, NW10 160 CQ66
Biggin Hill TN16 260 EJ118
Godalming GU7 280 AT144
Shepperton TW17 216 BN98
Woodrow, SE18 37 J9
Woodrow Av, Hayes UB4 157 BT71
Woodrow Cl, Perivale UB6 159 CH66
Woodrow Ct, N17 122 DV52
Woodroyd Av, Horl. RH6 290 DF149
Woodroyd Gdns, Horl. RH6 290 DF150
Woodruff Av, Guil. GU1 265 BA131
Woodrush Cl, SE14 45 L4
Woodrush Way, Rom. RM6 148 EX56
Woods, The, Nthwd. HA6 115 BU50
Radlett WD7 83 CH34
Uxbridge UB10 137 BP63
Woods Av, Hat. AL10 67 CV18
Wood's Bldgs, E1 20 E6
Woods Dr, Slou. SL2 133 AM64
Woodseer St, E1 20 B6
Woodsford, SE17 43 L1
Woodsford Sq, W14 26 F5
Woodshire Rd, Dag. RM10 149 FB62
Woodshore Cl, Vir.W. GU25 214 AV100
Woodshots Meadow, Wat. WD18 97 BR43
WOODSIDE, SE25 224 DU100
WOODSIDE, Hat. AL9 67 CZ21
WOODSIDE, Wat. WD25 81 BT33
Trm **Woodside** 224 DV100
Woodside, NW11 142 DA57
SW19 201 CZ93
Buckhurst Hill IG9 124 EJ47
Cheshunt EN7 88 DU31
Elstree WD6 100 CM42
Fetcham KT22 252 CB122
Flackwell Heath HP10 132 AC57
Hertford Heath SG13 54 DW12
Lower Kingswood KT20 271 CZ128
Orpington BR6 246 EU106
Thornwood CM16 92 EX27
Walton-on-Thames KT12 *off Ashley Rd* 217 BU102
Watford WD24 97 BU36
West Horsley KT24 267 BQ126
Woodside Av, N6 142 DF57
N10 142 DF57
N12 120 DC49
SE25 224 DV100
Amersham HP6 77 AR36
Beaconsfield HP9 110 AJ52
Chislehurst BR7 207 EQ92
Esher KT10 219 CE101
Flackwell Heath HP10 132 AC57
Hersham KT12 235 BV105
Wembley HA0 160 CL67
Woodside Cl, Amer. HP6 77 AR37
Beaconsfield HP9 110 AJ52
Bexleyheath DA7 189 FD84
Caterham CR3 258 DS124
Chalfont St. Peter SL9 112 AY54
Hutton CM13 131 GD43
Rainham RM13 170 FJ70
Ruislip HA4 137 BR58
Stanmore HA7 117 CH50
Surbiton KT5 220 CQ101
Wembley HA0 160 CL67
● **Woodside Commercial Est**, Thnwd CM16 92 EX26
Woodside Ct, N12 120 DB49
Woodside Ct Rd, Croy. CR0 224 DU101
Woodside Cres, Sid. DA15 207 ES90
Smallfield RH6 291 DN148
Woodside Dr, Dart. DA2 209 FE91
Woodside End, Wem. HA0 160 CL67
Woodside Gdns, E4 123 EB50
N17 122 DS54
Woodside Gra Rd, N12 120 DB49
Woodside Grn, SE25 224 DV100
Hatfield AL9 68 DA21
Woodside Gro, N12 120 DC48
Sch **Woodside High Sch**, N22 *off White Hart La* 121 DP52
Woodside Hill, Chal.St.P. SL9 112 AY54
Sch **Woodside Junior, Inf & Nurs Schs**, Croy. CR0 *off Morland Rd* 224 DU101
Sch **Woodside Jun Sch**, Amer. HP6 *off Mitchell Wk* 77 AS38
Woodside La, N12 120 DB48
Bexley DA5 208 EX86
Hatfield AL9 67 CZ21
Woodside Ms, SE22 204 DT86
⊖ **Woodside Park** 120 DB49
Woodside Pk, SE25 224 DU99
Woodside Pk Av, E17 145 ED56
Woodside Pk Rd, N12 120 DB49
Woodside Pl, Hat. AL9 67 CZ21
Wembley HA0 160 CL67
Sch **Woodside Prim Sch**, Chsht EN7 *off Jones Rd* 87 DP29
Grays RM16 *off Grangewood Av* 193 GF76
Woodside Rd, E13 24 C4
N22 121 DM52
SE25 224 DV100
Abbots Langley WD5 81 BV31
Amersham HP6 77 AR37
Beaconsfield HP9 110 AJ52
Bexleyheath DA7 189 FD84
Bricket Wood AL2 82 BZ30
Bromley BR1 226 EL99
Cobham KT11 236 CA113
Guildford GU2 264 AT133
Kingston upon Thames KT2 200 CL94
New Malden KT3 220 CR96
Northwood HA6 115 BT52
Purley CR8 241 DK113
Sevenoaks TN13 278 FG123
Sidcup DA15 207 ES90
Sundridge TN14 262 EX124
Sutton SM1 222 DC104
Watford WD25 81 BV31
Woodford Green IG8 124 EG49
Sch **Woodside Sch**, Belv. DA17 *off Halt Robin Rd* 189 FB77
Sch **Woodside Sch, The**, E17 *off Wood St* 145 EC55
Woodside Way, Croy. CR0 224 DV100
Mitcham CR4 223 DH95
Woodside Way, Penn HP10 110 AC46
Redhill RH1 288 DG135
Salfords RH1 288 DG140
Virginia Water GU25 214 AV97
Woods Ms, W1 16 F10
Woodsome Lo, Wey. KT13 235 BQ107
Woodsome Rd, NW5 142 DG62
Woods Pl, SE1 31 P7
Woodspring Rd, SW19 201 CY89
Woods Rd, SE15 44 E7
Woodstead Gro, Edg. HA8 118 CL51
Woodstock, W.Clan. GU4 266 BH128
Jct **Woodstock, The**, Sutt. SM3 221 CY101
Woodstock Av, NW11 141 CY59
W13 179 CG76
Isleworth TW7 199 CG85
Romford RM3 128 FP50
Slough SL3 174 AX77
Southall UB1 158 BZ69
Sutton SM3 221 CZ101
Woodstock Cl, Bex. DA5 208 EZ88
Hertford Heath SG13 *off Hogsdell La* 54 DV11
Stanmore HA7 118 CL54
Woking GU21 248 AY116
Woodstock Ct, SE12 206 EG86
Woodstock Cres, N9 104 DV44
Woodstock Dr, Uxb. UB10 136 BL63
Woodstock Gdns, Beck. BR3 225 EB95
Hayes UB4 157 BT71
Ilford IG3 148 EU61
Woodstock Gro, W12 26 D4
Coll **Woodstock Ho**, Long Dit. KT6 *off Woodstock La N* 219 CJ103
Woodstock La N, Long Dit. KT6 219 CJ103
Woodstock La S, Chess. KT9 237 CJ105
Claygate KT10 237 CH106
Woodstock Ms, W1 17 H7
Woodstock Ri, Sutt. SM3 221 CZ101
Woodstock Rd, E7 166 EJ66
E17 123 ED54
N4 143 DN60
NW11 141 CZ59
W4 180 CS76
Broxbourne EN10 71 DY19
Bushey Heath WD23 117 CF45
Carshalton SM5 240 DG106
Coulsdon CR5 *off Chipstead Valley Rd* 257 DH116
Croydon CR0 224 DR104
Wembley HA0 160 CM66
Woodstock Rd N, St.Alb. AL1 65 CH18
Woodstock Rd S, St.Alb. AL1 65 CH20
Woodstock St, W1 17 J9
Woodstock Ter, E14 22 D10
Woodstock Way, Mitch. CR4 223 DH96
Woodstone Av, Epsom KT17 239 CU106
⇌ **Wood Street** 145 EC56
Jct **Wood St**, E17 123 EC54
Wood St, E17 145 EC55
EC2 19 K9
W4 180 CS78
Barnet EN5 101 CW42
Grays RM17 192 GC79
Kingston upon Thames KT1 219 CK95
Merstham RH1 273 DJ129
Mitcham CR4 222 DG101
Swanley BR8 230 FJ96
Woodsway, Oxshott KT22 237 CE114
Woodsyre, SE26 204 DT91
Woodthorpe Rd, SW15 181 CV84
Ashford TW15 196 BL91
Woodtree Cl, NW4 119 CW54
Wood Vale, N10 143 DJ57
SE23 204 DV88
Hatfield AL10 67 CV18
Woodvale Av, SE25 224 DT97
Wood Vale Est, SE23 204 DW86
Woodvale Est, SE27 204 DQ92
Woodvale Pk, St.Alb. AL1 65 CH20
Woodvale Wk, SE27 204 DQ92
Woodvale Way, NW11 141 CX62
Woodview, Chess. KT9 237 CJ111
Wood Vw, Cuffley EN6 87 DL27
Woodview, Grays RM16, RM17 192 GE76
Wood Vw, Hem.H. HP1 62 BH18
Woodview Av, E4 123 EC49
Woodview Cl, N4 143 DP59
SW15 200 CR91
Ashtead KT21 254 CN116
Orpington BR6 227 EQ103
South Croydon CR2 242 DV114
Wood View Ms, Rom. RM1 127 FD53
Woodview Rd, Swan. BR8 229 FC96
Woodville, SE3 186 EH81
Woodville Cl, SE12 206 EG85
Teddington TW11 199 CG91
Woodville Ct, Wat. WD17 97 BU40
Woodville Gdns, NW11 141 CX59
W5 160 CL72
Ilford IG6 147 EP55
Ruislip HA4 137 BQ59
Woodville Gro, Well. DA16 188 EU83
Woodville Pl, Grav. DA12 213 GH87
Hertford SG14 53 DP07
Woodville Rd, E11 146 EF60
E17 145 DY56
E18 124 EH54
N16 9 N3
NW6 5 H10
NW11 141 CX59
W5 159 CK72
Barnet EN5 102 DB41
Morden SM4 222 DA98
Richmond TW10 199 CH90
Thornton Heath CR7 224 DQ98
Woodville St, SE18 37 H9
Woodvill Rd, Lthd. KT22 253 CH120
Wood Wk, Chorl. WD3 95 BE40
Woodward Av, NW4 141 CU57
Woodward Cl, Clay. KT10 237 CF107
Grays RM17 192 GB77
Woodwarde Rd, SE22 204 DS86
Woodward Gdns, Dag. RM9 *off Woodward Rd* 168 EW66
Stanmore HA7 117 CF52
Woodward Hts, Grays RM17 192 GB77
Woodward Rd, Dag. RM9 168 EV66
Woodwards, Harl. CM19 73 EQ17
Woodward Ter, Green. DA9 211 FS86
Woodway, Beac. HP9 110 AF54
Brentwood CM13, CM15 131 GA46
Guildford GU1 265 BB133
Wood Way, Orp. BR6 227 EN103
Woodway Cres, Har. HA1 139 CG58
Woodwaye, Wat. WD19 116 BW45
Woodwell St, SW18 *off Huguenot Pl* 202 DC85
Wood Wf, SE10 46 D2
Wood Wf Apts, SE10 *off Horseferry Pl* 46 E2
Woodwicks, Map.Cr. WD3 113 BD50
Woodyard, The, Epp. CM16 92 EW28
Woodyard Cl, NW5 7 H3
Woodyard La, SE21 204 DS87
Woodyates Rd, SE12 206 EG86
Woodyers Cl, Won. GU5 281 BB144
Woolacombe Rd, SE3 186 EJ81
Woolacombe Way, Hayes UB3 177 BS77
Woolborough La, Outwood RH1 289 DM143
Woolbrook Rd, Dart. DA1 209 FE86
Wooldridge Cl, Felt. TW14 197 BQ88
Wooler St, SE17 43 L1
Woolf Cl, SE28 168 EV74
Woolf Ms, WC1 17 P4
Woolf Wk, Til. RM18 *off Brennan Rd* 193 GJ82
Woolhampton Way, Chig. IG7 126 EV48
Woolhams, Cat. CR3 274 DT126
Woollam Cres, St.Alb. AL3 64 CC16
Woollard St, Wal.Abb. EN9 89 EC34
Woollaston Rd, N4 143 DP58
WOOLLENSBROOK, Hodd. EN11 71 DX15
Woollens Gro, Hodd. EN11 71 DZ16
Woollett Cl, Cray. DA1 189 FG84
Woolmans Cl, Brox. EN10 71 DZ22
Woolmead Av, NW9 141 CU59
Woolmer Cl, Borwd. WD6 100 CN38
Woolmerdine Ct, Bushey WD23 98 BX41
Woolmer Dr, Hem.H. HP2 63 BQ20
Woolmer Gdns, N18 122 DU51
Woolmer Rd, N18 122 DU50
Woolmers La, Letty Grn SG14 53 DH13
Woolmers Pk, Hert. SG13, SG14 53 DH14
Woolmers Pk Ms, Letty Grn SG14 53 DH14
Sch **Woolmore Prim Sch**, E14 22 F10
Woolmore St, E14 22 E10
Woolneigh St, SW6 39 L10
Woolpack Ho, Enf. EN3 105 DX37
Woolridge Way, E9 11 H6
Wool Rd, SW20 201 CV93
Woolstaplers Way, SE16 32 C8
Woolston Cl, E17 *off Riverhead Cl* 123 DX54
Woolstone Rd, SE23 205 DY89
WOOLWICH, SE18 37 M6
⇌ **Woolwich Arsenal** 37 P8
DLR **Woolwich Arsenal** 37 P8
RB **Woolwich Arsenal Pier** 37 P6
Woolwich Ch St, SE18 36 G7
★ **Woolwich Common**, SE18 187 EM80
Woolwich Common, SE18 187 EN79
Woolwich Ct, Enf. EN3 *off Hodson Pl* 105 EA38
⇌ **Woolwich Dockyard** 37 J8
● **Woolwich Dockyard Ind Est**, SE18 37 H7
Woolwich Ferry Pier, E16 37 K5
Woolwich Foot Tunnel, E16 37 L5
SE18 37 L5
Woolwich Garrison, SE18 186 EL79
Woolwich High St, SE18 37 K7
Woolwich Manor Way, E6 25 K5
E16 37 N3
Woolwich Mkt, SE18 37 N8
Woolwich New Rd, SE18 187 EN78
Sch **Woolwich Poly Sch**, SE28 *off Hutchins Rd* 168 EU74
Woolwich Rd, SE2 188 EX79
SE7 36 D9
SE10 35 L10
Belvedere DA17 188 EX79
Bexleyheath DA6, DA7 188 FA84
● **Woolwich Trade Pk**, SE28 187 ER76
Wooster Gdns, E14 22 G8
Wooster Ms, Har. HA2 *off Fairfield Dr* 138 CC55
Wooster Pl, SE1 31 M8
Wooster Rd, Beac. HP9 110 AJ51
Wootton Cl, Epsom KT18 255 CT115
Hornchurch RM11 150 FK57
Wootton Dr, Hem.H. HP2 62 BM15
Wooburn Green HP10 132 AE55
Wootton Gro, N3 120 DA53
Wootton St, SE1 30 F4
Worbeck Rd, SE20 224 DV96
Worcester Av, N17 122 DU52
Upminster RM14 151 FT61
Worcester Cl, NW2 *off Newfield Ri* 141 CV62
SE20 224 DU95
Croydon CR0 225 DZ103
Greenhithe DA9 191 FV84
Istead Rise DA13 213 GF94
Mitcham CR4 222 DG96
Worcester Ct, Walt. KT12 218 BW103
Worcester Cres, NW7 118 CS48
Woodford Green IG8 124 EH50
Worcester Dr, W4 180 CS75
Ashford TW15 197 BP93
Worcester Gdns, SW11 *off Grandison Rd* 202 DF85
Greenford UB6 158 CC65
Ilford IG1 146 EL59
Slough SL1 173 AR75
Worcester Park KT4 220 CS104
Worcester Ho, SE11 *off Kennington Rd* 30 E7
Worcester Ms, NW6 5 M4
WORCESTER PARK, KT4 221 CT103
⇌ **Worcester Park** 221 CU102
Worcester Pk Rd, Wor.Pk. KT4 220 CQ104
Worcester Rd, E12 147 EM63
E17 123 DX54
SW19 201 CZ92
Cowley UB8 156 BJ71
Guildford GU2 264 AT132
Hatfield AL10 67 CT17
Reigate RH2 271 CZ133
Sutton SM2 240 DB107
Worcesters Av, Enf. EN1 104 DU38
Sch **Worcesters Prim Sch**, Enf. EN1 *off Goat La* 104 DT38
Wordsworth Av, E12 166 EL66
E18 146 EF55
Greenford UB6 159 CD68
Kenley CR8 *off Valley Rd* 258 DR115
Wordsworth Cl, Rom. RM3 128 FJ53
Saint Albans AL3 64 CB22
Tilbury RM18 193 GJ82
Wordsworth Dr, Sutt. SM3 239 CW105
Wordsworth Gdns, Borwd. WD6 100 CN43
Wordsworth Mead, Red. RH1 272 DG132
Wordsworth Pl, NW5 6 F3
Wordsworth Rd, N16 9 P2
SE1 32 A9
SE20 205 DX94
Addlestone KT15 234 BK105
Hampton TW12 198 BZ91
Slough SL2 153 AK70
Wallington SM6 241 DJ107
Wordsworth Rd, Welling DA16 187 ES81
Wordsworth Wk, NW11 141 CZ56
Wordsworth Way, Dart. DA1 190 FN84
West Drayton UB7 176 BL77
Worfield St, SW11 40 D5
Worgan St, SE11 30 C10
SE16 33 K7
Workers Rd, Harl. CM17 75 FB16
Ongar CM5 75 FD17
Coll **Working Men's Coll, The**, NW1 7 M10
Worland Rd, E15 13 K6
World Cargo Cen, Gat. RH6 290 DD152
WORLD'S END, Enf. EN2 103 DN41
World's End, Cob. KT11 235 BU114
Worlds End La, N21 103 DM43
Enfield EN2 103 DM43
Orpington BR6 245 ET107
World's End Pas, SW10 40 A4
World's End Pl, SW10 *off King's Rd* 39 P4
Worley Pl, Seer Grn HP9 111 AR50
Worley Rd, St.Alb. AL3 64 CC19
Worleys Dr, Orp. BR6 245 ER105
Worlidge St, W6 26 A10
Worlingham Rd, SE22 184 DT84
Sch **Wormholt Pk Prim Sch**, W12 *off Bryony Rd* 161 CU73
Wormholt Rd, W12 161 CU73
WORMLEY, Brox. EN10 71 DY24
Wormleybury, Brox. EN10 70 DW23
Wormley Ct, Wal.Abb. EN9 90 EG33
Wormley Lo Cl, Brox. EN10 71 DZ23
Sch **Wormley Prim Sch**, Brox. EN10 *off St. Laurence Dr* 71 DY23
WORMLEY WEST END, Brox. EN10 70 DS22
Wormwood St, EC2 19 N8
Wormyngford Ct, Wal.Abb. EN9 *off Ninefields* 90 EG33
Wornington Rd, W10 14 E5
Woronzow Rd, NW8 6 B9
Worple, The, Wrays. TW19 195 AZ86
Worple Av, SW19 201 CX94
Isleworth TW7 199 CG85
Staines-upon-Thames TW18 196 BH93
Worple Cl, Har. HA2 138 BZ60
Sch **Worple Prim Sch**, Islw. TW7 *off Queens Ter* 179 CG84
Worple Rd, SW19 201 CY94
SW20 221 CW96
Epsom KT18 238 CS114
Isleworth TW7 179 CG84
Leatherhead KT22 253 CH123
Staines-upon-Thames TW18 196 BH94
Worple Rd Ms, SW19 201 CZ93
⇌ **Worplesdon** 248 AV124
Worplesdon Rd, Guil. GU2, GU3 264 AT129
Worple St, SW14 180 CR83
Worple Way, Har. HA2 138 BZ60
Richmond TW10 200 CL85
Worrall La, Uxb. UB10 156 BL65
Worrin Cl, Shenf. CM15 131 FZ46
Worrin Pl, Shenf. CM15 131 FZ46
Worrin Rd, Shenf. CM15 131 FZ47
Worsfold Cl, Send GU23 249 BB123
Worships Hill, Sev. TN13 278 FE123
Worship St, EC2 19 M5
Worslade Rd, SW17 202 DD91
Sch **Worsley Br Jun Sch**, Beck. BR3 *off Brackley Rd* 205 EA94
Worsley Br Rd, SE26 205 DZ91
Beckenham BR3 205 DZ92
Worsley Gra, Chis. BR7 207 EQ93
Worsley Gro, E5 144 DU63
Worsley Rd, E11 146 EE63
Worsopp Dr, SW4 203 DJ85
Worsted Grn, Merst. RH1 273 DJ129
Worth Cl, Orp. BR6 245 ES105
Worthfield Cl, Epsom KT19 238 CR108
Worth Gro, SE17 43 L1
Worthies, The, Amer. HP7 77 AP40
Worthing Cl, E15 13 J9
Grays RM17 192 FY79
Worthing Rd, Houns. TW5 178 BZ79
Worthington Cl, Mitch. CR4 223 DH97
Worthington Rd, Surb. KT6 220 CM102
Worthy Down Ct, SE18 *off Prince Imperial Rd* 187 EN81
Wortley Rd, E6 166 EK66
Croydon CR0 223 DN101
Worton Gdns, Islw. TW7 179 CD82
● **Worton Hall Est**, Islw. TW7 179 CE84
Worton Rd, Islw. TW7 179 CE83
Worton Way, Houns. TW3 179 CD82
Isleworth TW7 178 CC81
WOTTON, Dor. RH5 284 BZ139
Wotton Dr, Dor. RH5 284 BZ139
Wotton Grn, Orp. BR5 228 EX98
Wotton Rd, NW2 141 CW63
SE8 45 P3
Wotton Way, Sutt. SM2 239 CW110
Wouldham Rd, E16 23 L8
Grays RM20 192 FY79
Wrabness Way, Stai. TW18 216 BH95
Wragby Rd, E11 146 EE62
Wrampling Pl, N9 122 DU46
Wrangley Ct, Wal.Abb. EN9 90 EG33
Wrangthorn Wk, Croy. CR0 *off Fernleigh Cl* 241 DN105
Wray Av, Ilf. IG5 147 EN55
Wray Cl, Horn. RM11 150 FJ59
Wray Common, Reig. RH2 272 DD132
Sch **Wray Common Prim Sch**, Reig. RH2 *off Kendal Cl* 272 DD133
Wray Common Rd, Reig. RH2 272 DC133
Wray Cres, N4 143 DL61
Wrayfield Av, Reig. RH2 272 DC133
Wrayfield Rd, Sutt. SM3 221 CX104
Wraylands Dr, Reig. RH2 272 DD132
Wray La, Reig. RH2 272 DC130
Wraymead Pl, Reig. RH2 *off Wray Pk Rd* 272 DB133
Wray Mill Pk, Reig. RH2 272 DD132
Wray Pk Rd, Reig. RH2 272 DB133
Wray Rd, Sutt. SM2 239 CZ109
WRAYSBURY, Stai. TW19 195 AZ86
⇌ **Wraysbury** 195 BA86
Wraysbury Cl, Houns. TW4 198 BY85
Wraysbury Dr, West Dr. UB7 156 BK73
Wraysbury Gdns, Stai. TW18 195 BE91
Sch **Wraysbury Prim Sch**, Wrays. TW19 *off Welley Rd* 194 AY86
Wraysbury Rd, Stai. TW18, TW19 195 BC90
Wrays Way, Hayes UB4 157 BS70
Wrekin Rd, SE18 187 EQ80
Sch **Wren Acad**, N12 *off Hilton Av* 120 DD50
Wren Av, NW2 4 B2
Southall UB2 178 BZ77
Wren Cl, E16 23 M8
N9 *off Chaffinch Cl* 123 DX46
Lon.Hthrw Air. TW6 *off Widgeon Rd* 176 BH83

Wren Cl, Orpington BR5 228 EX97
South Croydon CR2 243 DX109
Wren Ct, Slou. SL3 175 BA76
Warlingham CR6 258 DW117
Wren Cres, Add. KT15 234 BK106
Bushey WD23 116 CC46
Wren Dr, Wal.Abb. EN9 90 EG34
West Drayton UB7 176 BK76
Wren Gdns, Dag. RM9 148 EX64
Hornchurch RM12 149 FF60
Wren Landing, E14 34 B2
Wren La, Ruis HA4 137 BV58
Wren Ms, SE13
off Lee High Rd 186 EE84
Wren Path, SE28 187 ER76
Wren Pl, Brwd. CM14 130 FX48
Wren Rd, SE5 43 L7
Dagenham RM9 148 EX64
Sidcup DA14 208 EW91
Wrens, The, Harl. CM19 73 EP15
Wrens Av, Ashf. TW15 197 BQ92
Wrens Cft, Nthflt DA11 212 GE91
Wrensfield, Hem.H. HP1 62 BG21
Wrens Hill, Oxshott KT22 252 CC115
Wren St, WC1 18 D4
Wren Ter, Ilf. IG5
off Tiptree Cres 147 EN55
Wrentham Av, NW10 4 C10
Wrenthorpe Rd, Brom. BR1 206 EE91
Wren Wk, Til. RM18 193 GH80
Wren Wd, Welw.G.C. AL7 52 DA08
Wrenwood Way, Pnr. HA5 137 BV56
Wrestlers Cl, Hat. AL10 67 CW15
Wrestlers Ct, EC3
off Camomile St 19 N8
Wrexham Rd, E3 22 B1
Romford RM3 128 FK48
Wricklemarsh Rd, SE3 186 EH81
Wrigglesworth St, SE14 45 J4
Wright, Wind. SL4 172 AJ83
Wright Cl, Swans. DA10 211 FX86
Wright Gdns, Shep. TW17
off Laleham Rd 216 BN99
Wright Rd, N1 9 P4
Hounslow TW5 178 BW80
Wrights All, SW19 201 CW93
Wrightsbridge Rd, S.Wld
CM14 128 FN46
Wrights Cl, SE13 185 ED84
Dagenham RM10 149 FB62
Wrights Ct, Harl. CM17
off Potter St 74 EW17
Wrights Grn, SW4
off Nelson's Row 183 DK84
Wrights La, W8 27 L6
Wrights Pl, NW10
off Mitchell Way 160 CQ65
Wright Sq, Wind. SL4
off Wright 173 AK83
Wrights Rd, E3 11 N10
SE25 224 DS97
Wrights Row, Wall. SM6 241 DH105
Wrights Wk, SW14 180 CR83
Wright Way, Wind. SL4
off Wright 172 AJ83
Wrigley Cl, E4 123 ED50
Wriotsley Way, Add. KT15
off Coombelands La 234 BG107
Writtle Wk, Rain. RM13 169 FF67
● **Wrotham Business Pk**,
Barn. EN5 101 CZ37
★ **Wrotham Pk**, Barn. EN5 101 CZ36
Wrotham Rd, NW1 7 M7
W13 *off Mattock La* 159 CJ74
Barnet EN5 101 CY40
Gravesend DA11, DA13 213 GG88
Welling DA16 188 EW81
Sch Wrotham Rd Prim Sch,
Grav. DA11
off Wrotham Rd 213 GH87
Wroths Path, Loug. IG10 107 EM39
Wrottesley Rd, NW10 161 CU68
SE18 187 EQ79
Wroughton Rd, SW11 202 DF86
Wroughton Ter, NW4 141 CW56
Wroxall Rd, Dag. RM9 168 EW65
Sch Wroxham, The,
Pot.B. EN6
off Wroxham Gdns 85 CX31
Wroxham Av, Hem.H. HP3 62 BK22
Wroxham Gdns, N11 121 DJ52
Enfield EN2 103 DN35
Potters Bar EN6 85 CX31
Wroxham Rd, SE28 168 EX73
Wroxham Way, Ilf. IG6 125 EP53
Wroxton Rd, SE15 44 F9
WRYTHE, THE, Cars. SM5 222 DF103
Wrythe Grn, Cars. SM5
off Wrythe Grn Rd 222 DF104
Wrythe Grn Rd, Cars. SM5 222 DF104
Wrythe La, Cars. SM5 222 DC102
Wulfstan St, W12 161 CT72
Wulstan Pk, Pot.B. EN6
off Tempest Av 86 DD32
Wyatt Cl, SE16 33 N5
Bushey Heath WD23 117 CE45
Feltham TW13 198 BW88
Hayes UB4 157 BU71
Wyatt Dr, SW13 181 CW80
Wyatt Pk Rd, SW2 203 DL89
Wyatt Pt, SE28 *off Erebus Dr* 187 EQ75
Wyatt Rd, E7 13 P5
N5 144 DQ62
Dartford DA1 189 FF83
Staines-upon-Thames TW18 196 BG92
Windsor SL4 173 AK83
Wyatts Cl, Chorl. WD3 96 BG41
Wyatts Covert, Denh. UB9 135 BF56
Wyatts La, E17 145 EC55
Wyatts Rd, Chorl. WD3 95 BF42
Wybert St, NW1 17 K4
Sch Wyborne Prim Sch, SE9
off Footscray Rd 207 EP88
Wyborne Way, NW10 160 CQ66
Wyburn Av, Barn. EN5 101 CZ41
Wyche Gro, S.Croy. CR2 242 DQ108
Wych Elm, Harl. CM20 57 EQ14
Wych Elm Cl, Horn. RM11 150 FN59
Kingston upon Thames KT2 200 CM94
Wych Elm Pas, Kings.T. KT2
off Acre Rd 200 CM94
Wych Elm Ri, Guil. GU1 280 AY137
Wych Elm Rd, Horn. RM11 150 FN58
Wych Elms, Park St AL2 82 CB28
Wycherley Cl, SE3 47 L4
Wycherley Cres, New Barn.
EN5 102 DB44
Wychford Dr, Saw. CM21 58 EW06
Wych Hill, Wok. GU22 248 AW119
Wych Hill La, Wok. GU22 248 AY119
Wych Hill Pk, Wok. GU22 248 AX119
Wych Hill Ri, Wok. GU22 248 AW119
Wych Hill Way, Wok. GU22 248 AX120
Wychwood Av, Edg. HA8 117 CK51
Thornton Heath CR7 224 DQ97
Wychwood Cl, Edg. HA8 117 CK51
Sunbury-on-Thames TW16 197 BU93
Wychwood End, N6 143 DJ59
Wychwood Gdns, Ilf. IG5 147 EM56
Wychwood Way, SE19
off Roman Ri 204 DR93
Northwood HA6 115 BT52
Wyclif Ct, EC1 *off Wyclif St* 18 G3
Wycliffe Cl, Chsht EN8 89 DX28
Welling DA16 187 ET81
Wycliffe Ct, Abb.L. WD5 81 BS32
Wycliffe Rd, SW11 41 H9
SW19 202 DB93
Wycliffe Row, Nthflt DA11 213 GF88
Wyclif St, EC1 18 G3
Wycombe End, Beac. HP9 133 AK55
Wycombe Gdns, NW11 142 DA61
Wycombe La, Woob.Grn
HP10 132 AE56
Wycombe Pl, SW18 202 DC86
St. Albans AL4 65 CH17
Wycombe Rd, N17 122 DU53
Ilford IG2 147 EM57
Wembley HA0 160 CN67
Wycombe Sq, W8 27 J3
Wycombe Way, St.Alb. AL4 65 CJ17
Wyddial Grn, Welw.G.C. AL7
off Widford Rd 52 DB09
Wydehurst Rd, Croy. CR0 224 DU101
Wydell Cl, Mord. SM4 221 CW100
Wydeville Manor Rd, SE12 206 EH91
Wye, The, Hem.H. HP2 62 BN15
Wyecliffe Gdns, S.Merst. RH1 273 DJ130
Wye Cl, Ashf. TW15 197 BP91
Orpington BR6 227 ET101
Ruislip HA4 137 BQ58
Wyedale, Lon.Col. AL2 84 CM27
Wyemead Cres, E4 124 EE47
Wye Rd, Grav. DA12 213 GK89
Wooburn Green HP10 132 AD55
Wye St, SW11 40 B9
Wyeth's Ms, Epsom KT17 239 CT113
Wyeths Rd, Epsom KT17 239 CT113
Wyevale Cl, Pnr. HA5 137 BU55
Wyfields, Ilf. IG5
off Ravensbourne Gdns 125 EP53
Wyfold Ho, SE2
off Wolvercote Rd 188 EX75
Wyfold Rd, SW6 38 E6
Wyhill Wk, Dag. RM10 169 FC65
Wyke Cl, Islw. TW7 179 CF79
Wykeham Av, Dag. RM9 168 EW65
Hornchurch RM11 150 FK58
Wykeham Cl, Grav. DA12 213 GL93
Sipson UB7 176 BN78
Wykeham Grn, Dag. RM9 168 EW65
Wykeham Hill, Wem. HA9 140 CM60
Sch Wykeham Prim Sch, NW10
off Aboyne Rd 140 CS62
Hornchurch RM12
off Rainsford Way 149 FG60
Wykeham Ri, N20 119 CY46
Wykeham Rd, NW4 141 CW57
Guildford GU1 265 BD133
Harrow HA3 139 CH56
Wykeridge Cl, Chesh. HP5 76 AP27
Wyke Rd, E3 12 A7
SW20 221 CW96
Wylands Rd, Slou. SL3 175 BA77
Wylchin Cl, Pnr. HA5 137 BT56
Wyldes Cl, NW11 142 DC60
Wyldfield Gdns, N9 122 DT47
Wyld Way, Wem. HA9 160 CP65
Wyldwood Cl, Harl. CM17 58 EW09
Wyleu St, SE23 205 DY87
Wylie Rd, Sthl. UB2 178 CA76
Wyllen Cl, E1 20 G5
★ **Wyllyotts Cen & Potters
Bar Mus**, Pot.B. EN6 85 CZ32
Wyllyotts Cl, Pot.B. EN6 85 CZ32
Wyllyotts La, Pot.B. EN6 85 CZ32
Wyllyotts Pl, Pot.B. EN6 85 CZ32
Wylo Dr, Barn. EN5 101 CU44
Wymark Cl, Rain. RM13 169 FF68
Wymering Rd, W9 15 K3
Wymers Cl, Burn. SL1 152 AH68
Wymers Wd Rd, Burn. SL1 152 AG67
Wymond St, SW15 38 B10
Wynan Rd, E14 34 C10
Wynash Gdns, Cars. SM5 240 DE106
Wynaud Ct, N22 121 DM51
Wyncham Av, Sid. DA15 207 ES88
Wynches Fm Dr, St.Alb. AL4 65 CK19
Wynchgate, N14 121 DK46
N21 121 DL46
Harrow HA3 117 CE52
Wynchlands Cres, St.Alb. AL4 65 CK20
Wyncote Way, S.Croy. CR2 243 DX109
Wyncroft Cl, Brom. BR1 227 EM97
Wyndale Av, NW9 140 CN58
Wyndcliff Rd, SE7 186 EH79
Wyndcroft Cl, Enf. EN2 103 DP41
Wyndham Av, Cob. KT11 235 BU113
Wyndham Cl, Orp. BR6 227 EQ102
Sutton SM2 240 DA108
Wyndham Cres, N19 143 DJ62
Burnham SL1 152 AH69
Hounslow TW4 198 CA86
Wyndham Est, SE5 43 J4
Wyndham Ms, W1 16 E7
Wyndham Pl, W1 16 E7
Wyndham Rd, E6 166 EK66
SE5 43 H5
W13 179 CH76
Barnet EN4 120 DF46
Kingston upon Thames KT2 200 CM94
Woking GU21 248 AV118
Wyndhams End, Welw.G.C.
AL7 51 CZ13
Wyndham St, W1 16 E6
Wyndham Yd, W1 16 E7
Wyndhurst Cl, S.Croy. CR2 241 DP108
Wyneham Rd, SE24 204 DR85
Wynell Rd, SE23 205 DX90
Wynford Gro, Orp. BR5 228 EV97
Wynford Pl, Belv. DA17 188 FA79
Wynford Rd, N1 8 C10
Wynford Way, SE9 207 EM90
Wyngrave Pl, Knot.Grn HP9 110 AJ50
Wynlie Gdns, Pnr. HA5 115 BV54
Wynn Br Cl, Wdf.Grn. IG8
off Chigwell Rd 124 EJ53
Wynndale Rd, E18 124 EH53
Wynne Rd, SW9 42 E9
Wynns Av, Sid. DA15 208 EU85
Wynnstay Gdns, W8 27 K6
Wynnstow Pk, Oxt. RH8 276 EF131
Wynnswick Rd, Seer Grn HP9 111 AQ50
Wynter St, SW11 182 DC84
Wynton Gdns, SE25 224 DT99
Wynton Gro, Walt. KT12 217 BU104
Wynton Pl, W3 160 CP72
Wynyard Cl, Sarratt WD3 96 BG36
Wynyard Ter, SE11 30 D10
Wynyatt St, EC1 18 G3
Wyre Gro, Edg. HA8 118 CP48
Hayes UB3 177 BU77
Wyresdale Cres, Perivale UB6 159 CF69
Wysemead, Horl. RH6 291 DJ147
Wyteleaf Cl, Ruis. HA4 137 BQ58
Wythburn Pl, W1 16 E9
Wythenshawe Rd, Dag. RM10 148 FA62
Wythens Wk, SE9 207 EP86
Wythes Cl, Brom. BR1 227 EM96
Wythes Rd, E16 36 G3
Wythfield Rd, SE9 207 EM86
Wyton, Welw.G.C. AL7 52 DD09
Wyvenhoe Rd, Har. HA2 138 CC62
Wyvern Cl, Dart. DA1 210 FJ87
Orpington BR6 228 EV104
● **Wyvern Est**, N.Mal. KT3 221 CU98
Wyvern Gro, Hayes UB3 177 BP80
Wyvern Pl, Add. KT15
off Green La 234 BH105
Wyvern Rd, Pur. CR8 241 DP110
Wyvern Way, Uxb. UB8 156 BJ67
Wyvil Est, SW8 42 A4
Sch Wyvil Prim Sch, SW8 42 B4
Wyvil Rd, SW8 42 A3
Wyvis St, E14 22 D6

X

● **X2 Hatton Cross Centre**,
Hounslow TW6
off Eastern Perimeter Rd 177 BT84

Y

Yabsley St, E14 34 F2
Yaffle Rd, Wey. KT13 235 BQ110
Yalding Gro, Orp. BR5 228 EX98
Yalding Rd, SE16 32 C7
Yale Cl, Houns. TW4 198 BZ85
Yale Way, Horn. RM12 149 FG63
Yarborough Rd, SW19 222 DD95
Yarbridge Cl, Sutt. SM2 240 DB110
Yardley Cl, E4 105 EB43
Reigate RH2 272 DB132
Yardley Ct, Sutt. SM3
off Hemingford Rd 239 CW105
Yardley La, E4 105 EB43
Sch Yardley Prim Sch, E4
off Hawkwood Cres 105 EC43
Yardley St, WC1 18 E3
Yard Mead, Egh. TW20 195 BA90
Yarm Cl, Lthd. KT22 253 CJ123
Yarm Ct Rd, Lthd. KT22 253 CJ123
Yarmouth Cres, N17 144 DV57
Yarmouth Pl, W1 29 J3
Yarmouth Rd, Slou. SL1 153 AQ73
Watford WD24 98 BW38
Yarm Way, Lthd. KT22 253 CJ123
Yarnfield Sq, SE15 44 D7
Yarnton Way, SE2 188 EX75
Erith DA18 188 EZ76
Yarrow Cres, E6 24 G6
Yarrowfield, Wok. GU22 248 AX123
Yarrowside, Amer. HP7 94 AV41
Yateley St, SE18 36 F7
Yates Ct, NW2 4 D5
Yates Ho, E2 *off Roberta St* 20 D2
Yattendon Rd, Horl. RH6 291 DH148
Sch Yattendon Sch, Horl. RH6
off Oakwood Rd 290 DG147
Sch Yavneh Coll, Borwd. WD6
off Hillside Av 100 CQ42
YEADING, Hayes UB4 157 BV69
Yeading Av, Har. HA2 138 BY61
Yeading Fork, Hayes UB4 158 BW71
Yeading Gdns, Hayes UB4 157 BV71
Sch Yeading Inf Sch,
Hayes UB4
off Carlyon Rd 158 BW71
Sch Yeading Jun Sch,
Hayes UB4
off Carlyon Rd 158 BW71
Yeading La, Hayes UB4 157 BV72
Northolt UB5 158 BW69
Yeames Cl, W13 159 CG72
Yearling Cl, Gt Amwell SG12 55 DZ08
Yeate St, N1 9 L7
Yeatman Rd, N6 142 DF58
Yeats Cl, NW10 160 CS65
W7 159 CF73
Redhill RH1 288 DC137
Yeats Ct, N15
off Tynemouth Rd 144 DT56
N18 *off Baxter Rd* 122 DV49
Ye Cor, Wat. WD19 98 BY44
Yeend Cl, W.Mol. KT8 218 CA98
Sch Yehudi Menuhin Sch,
Stoke D'Ab. KT11
off Cobham Rd 252 CA119
**Sch Yeishiva Gedolah
Lubavitch Sch**, N2
off Kingsley Way 142 DC57
Yeldham Rd, W6 38 C1
Yellow Hammer Ct, NW9
off Eagle Dr 118 CS54
Yellowpine Way, Chig. IG7 126 EV49
Yellow Stock Ms, N.Ock.
RM14 151 FU64
Yelverton Cl, Rom. RM3 128 FK53
Yelverton Rd, SW11 40 B9
Ye Meads, Tap. SL6 152 AE73
Yenston Cl, Mord. SM4 222 DA100
Yeoman Cl, E6 25 N10
SE27 203 DP90
Yeoman Dr, Stai. TW19 196 BL88
Yeoman Rd, Nthlt. UB5 158 BY66
Yeomanry Cl, Epsom KT17 239 CT112
Yeomans Acre, Ruis. HA4 137 BU58
Yeomans Ct, Hert. SG13 54 DS09
Yeomans Cft, Bkhm KT23
off Vicarage Cl 268 CA125
Yeomans Keep, Chorl. WD3 95 BF41
Yeomans Meadow, Sev. TN13 278 FG126
Yeoman's Ms, Islw. TW7
off Queensbridge Pk 199 CE85
Yeoman's Row, SW3 28 D7
Yeoman St, SE8 33 L8
Yeomans Way, Enf. EN3 104 DW40
Yeomans Yd, E1 20 B10
Yeoman Way, Red. RH1 289 DH139
Yeomen Way, Ilf. IG6 125 EQ51
Yeo St, E3 22 C6
Yeoveney Cl, Stai. TW19 195 BD89
Yeovil Cl, Orp. BR6 227 ES103
Yeovil Rd, Slou. SL1 153 AL72
Yeovilton Pl, Kings.T. KT2 199 CJ92
Sch Yerbury Prim Sch, N19
off Foxham Rd 143 DK62
Yerbury Rd, N19 143 DK62
Sch Yesodey Hatorah Sch,
N16 *off Amhurst Pk* 144 DT59
**Sch Yesodey Hatorah Sec Sch
for Girls**, N16
off Egerton Rd 144 DT59
Yester Dr, Chis. BR7 206 EL94
Yester Pk, Chis. BR7 207 EM94
Yester Rd, Chis. BR7 207 EM94
Yevele Way, Horn. RM11 150 FL59
Yew Av, West Dr. UB7 156 BL73
Yewbank Cl, Ken. CR8 258 DR115
Yew Cl, Buck.H. IG9 124 EK47
Cheshunt EN7 88 DS27
Yewdale Cl, Brom. BR1 206 EE93
Yewdells Cl, Buckland RH3 271 CU133
Yewfield Rd, NW10 161 CT66
Yew Gro, NW2 4 D1
Welwyn Garden City AL7 52 DC10
Yewlands, Hodd. EN11 71 EA18
Sawbridgeworth CM21 58 EY06
Yewlands Cl, Bans. SM7 256 DC115
Yewlands Dr, Hodd. EN11 71 EA18
Yew Pl, Wey. KT13 217 BT104
Yews, The, Ashf. TW15
off Reedsfield Rd 197 BP91
Gravesend DA12 213 GK88
Yews Av, Enf. EN1 104 DV36
Yew Tree Bottom Rd, Epsom
KT17, KT18 255 CV116
Yew Tree Cl, N21 121 DN45
Yewtree Cl, N22 121 DJ53
Yew Tree Cl, SE13
off Bankside Av 185 EC83
Beaconsfield HP9 111 AM54
Chipstead CR5 256 DF119
Yewtree Cl, Har. HA2 138 CB56
Yew Tree Cl, Horl. RH6 290 DF147
Hutton CM13 131 GB44
Ley Hill HP5 78 AU30
Sevenoaks TN13 278 FD123
Welling DA16 188 EU81
Worcester Park KT4 220 CS102
Yew Tree Ct, Els. WD6
off Barnet La 99 CK44
Hemel Hempstead HP1 62 BG22
Yew Tree Dr, Bov. HP3 79 BB28
Caterham CR3 274 DT125
Guildford GU1 264 AW130
Yewtree End, Park St AL2 82 CB27
Yew Tree Gdns, Chad.Hth RM6 148 EY57
Epsom KT18 254 CP115
Romford RM7 149 FD57
Yew Tree La, Reig. RH2 272 DB131
Yew Tree Lo, SW16 203 DJ91
Yew Tree Ms, West. TN16 277 ER127
Yew Tree Rd, W12 161 CT73
Beckenham BR3 225 DZ97
Dorking RH4 269 CG134
Slough SL1 174 AU76
Uxbridge UB10 156 BM67
Yew Trees, Egh. TW20 215 BC97
Shepperton TW17
off Laleham Rd 216 BM98
Yew Tree Wk, Eff. KT24 268 BX127
Hounslow TW4 198 BZ85
Maidenhead SL6 132 AD63
Purley CR8 242 DQ110
Yew Tree Way, Croy. CR0 243 DY110
Yew Wk, Har. HA1 139 CE60
Hoddesdon EN11 71 EA18
YIEWSLEY, West Dr. UB7 156 BL74
Yoakley Rd, N16 144 DS61
Yoga Way, Wor.Pk. KT4 221 CU103
Yoke Cl, N7 8 B4
Yolande Gdns, SE9 206 EL85
Yonge Pk, N4 143 DN62
York Av, SW14 200 CQ85
W7 159 CE74
Hayes UB3 157 BQ71
Sidcup DA15 207 ES89
Slough SL1 153 AQ72
Stanmore HA7 117 CH53
Windsor SL4 173 AP82
York Br, NW1 16 G4
York Bldgs, WC2 30 B1
York Cl, E6 25 J9
W7 *off York Av* 159 CE74
Amersham HP7 94 AT39
Byfleet KT14 234 BL112
Kings Langley WD4 80 BN29
Morden SM4 222 DB98
Shenfield CM15 131 FZ45
York Cres, Borwd. WD6 100 CR40
Loughton IG10 106 EL41
Yorke Gdns, Reig. RH2 272 DA133
Yorke Gate, Cat. CR3 258 DR122
Sch Yorke Mead Prim Sch, Crox.Grn
WD3 *off Dulwich Way* 96 BN43
Yorke Rd, Crox.Grn WD3 96 BN44
Reigate RH2 271 CZ133
Yorkes, Harl. CM18 73 ET17
York Gdns, Walt. KT12 218 BX103
York Gate, N14 121 DL45
NW1 16 G5
York Gro, SE15 44 G7
York Hill, SE27 203 DP90
Loughton IG10 106 EL41
York Hill Est, SE27 203 DP90
York Ho, Bushey WD23
off Royal Connaught Dr 98 CA42
● **York Ho**, Wem. HA9 140 CN63
York Ho Pl, W8 27 L4
Sch York Ho Sch, Rick. WD3
off Sarratt Rd 96 BM40
Yorkland Av, Well. DA16 187 ET83
York Ms, NW5 7 K3
Ilford IG1 147 EN62
York Par, Brent. TW8 179 CK78
York Pl, SW11 182 DD83
WC2 30 B1
Dagenham RM10 169 FC65
Ilford IG1 *off York Rd* 147 EN61
York Ri, NW5 143 DH62
Orpington BR6 227 ES102
York Rd, E4 123 EA50
E7 13 N5
E10 145 EC62
E17 145 DX57
N11 121 DK51
N18 122 DV51
N21 122 DR45
SE1 30 D4
SW11 182 DC84
SW18 182 DC84
SW19 202 DC93
W3 160 CQ72
W5 179 CJ76
Biggin Hill TN16 260 EH119
Brentford TW8 179 CK78
Byfleet KT14 234 BK112
Croydon CR0 223 DN101
Dartford DA1 210 FM87
Gravesend DA12 213 GJ90
Guildford GU1 280 AX135
Hounslow TW3 178 CB83
Ilford IG1 147 EN62
Kingston upon Thames KT2 200 CM94
New Barnet EN5 102 DD43
North Weald Bassett CM16 92 FA27
Northfleet DA11 212 GD87
Northwood HA6 115 BU54
Rainham RM13 169 FD66
Richmond TW10
off Albert Rd 200 CM85
St. Albans AL1 65 CF19
Shenfield CM15 131 FZ45
South Croydon CR2 243 DX110
Sutton SM2 240 DA107
Teddington TW11 199 CE91
Uxbridge UB8 156 BK66
Waltham Cross EN8 89 DY34
Watford WD18 98 BW43
Weybridge KT13 235 BQ105
Windsor SL4 173 AP82
Woking GU22 248 AY118
**Sch York Rd Jun Sch & Language
Unit**, Dart. DA1 *off York Rd* 210 FM87
Yorkshire Cl, N16 144 DS62
Yorkshire Gdns, N18 122 DV50
Jct Yorkshire Grey, SE9 206 EK85
Yorkshire Grey Pl, NW3 5 P1
Yorkshire Grey Yd, WC1 18 C7
Yorkshire Rd, E14 21 L9
Mitcham CR4 223 DL99
York Sq, E14 21 L9
York St, W1 16 F6
Mitcham CR4 222 DG101
Twickenham TW1 199 CG88
York Ter, Enf. EN2 104 DQ38
Erith DA8 189 FC81
York Ter E, NW1 17 H5
York Ter W, NW1 16 G5
Yorkton St, E2 20 C1
York Way, N1 7 P4
N7 8 B9
N20 120 DF48
Borehamwood WD6 100 CR40
Chessington KT9 238 CL108
Feltham TW13 198 BZ90
Hemel Hempstead HP2 62 BL21
Watford WD25 98 BX36
York Way Ct, N1 8 B9
York Way Est, N7
off York Way 8 A5
Youngfield Rd, Hem.H. HP1 61 BF19
Youngmans Cl, Enf. EN2 104 DQ39
Young Rd, E16 24 C7
Young's Bldgs, EC1 19 K4
Youngs Ct, SW11 41 H7
Youngs Ri, Welw.G.C. AL8 51 CV09
Youngs Rd, Ilf. IG2 147 ER57
Young St, W8 27 L5
Fetcham KT22 269 CE125
Youngstroat La, Wok. GU21,
GU24 232 AY110
Yoxley App, Ilf. IG2 147 EQ58
Yoxley Dr, Ilf. IG2 147 EQ58
Yukon Rd, SW12 203 DH87
Broxbourne EN10 89 DY25
Yule Cl, Brick.Wd AL2 82 BZ30
Yunus Khan Cl, E17 145 EA57
Yvon Ho, SW11 40 G7

Z

Zambezie Dr, N9 122 DW48
Zampa Rd, SE16 44 G1
Zander Ct, E2 20 D1
Zangwill Rd, SE3 186 EK81
Zealand Av, Harm. UB7 176 BK80
Zealand Rd, E3 11 L10
Zelah Rd, Orp. BR5 228 EV101
Zennor Rd, SW12 203 DJ88
● **Zennor Rd Ind Est**, SW12
off Zennor Rd 203 DJ88
Zenoria St, SE22 184 DT84
Zermatt Rd, Th.Hth. CR7 224 DQ98
Zetex Apts, Rom. RM1
off Mercury Gdns 149 FF56
Zetland St, E14 22 D7
Zig Zag, The, Mick. RH5 269 CK130
Zig Zag Rd, Box H. KT20 269 CK132
Kenley CR8 258 DQ116
Zion Ho, E1 20 G8
Zion Pl, Grav. DA12 213 GH87
Thornton Heath CR7 224 DR98
Zion Rd, Th.Hth. CR7 224 DR98
Zion St, Seal TN15
off Church Rd 279 FM121
● **ZK Pk**, Croy. CR0 223 DM104
Zoar St, SE1 31 J2
● **Zodiac Business Pk**, Cowley
UB8 156 BK72
Zodiac Ct, Croy. CR0
off London Rd 223 DP102
Zoffany St, N19 143 DK61
★ **ZSL London Zoo**, NW1 6 G10
Zulu Ms, SW11 40 D9

HERTFORDSHIRE
AYLESBURY VALE
TRING
DACORUM
BERKHAMSTED
HEMEL HEMPSTEAD
HARPENDEN
WHEATHAMPSTEAD
ST. ALBANS
ST. ALBANS
LONDON COLNEY
WELWYN
WELWYN GARDEN CITY
WELWYN
HATFIELD
ESSENDON
HATFIELD
A1(M)
POTTERS BAR
CUFFLE
WENDOVER
PRINCES RISBOROUGH
GREAT MISSENDEN
CHESHAM
BUCKINGHAMSHIRE
CHILTERN
AMERSHAM
LITTLE CHALFONT
CHALFONT ST. GILES
TYLERS GREEN
WYCOMBE
HIGH WYCOMBE
M40
LOUDWATER
BEACONSFIELD
WOOBURN
MARLOW
GERRARDS CROSS
SOUTH BUCKS
STOKE POGES
BURNHAM
DENHAM
16/1A
M1
21/6A
21A
M25
ABBOTS LANGLEY
WATFORD
WATFORD
BUSHEY
THREE RIVERS
RICKMANSWORTH
HERTSMERE
BOREHAMWOOD
NEW BARNET
BARNET
EAST BARNET
SOUTHGATE
BARNET
23/1
EDGWARE
STANMORE
HARROW
PINNER
HARROW
FINCHLEY
HENDON
HAREFIELD
NORTHWOOD
RUISLIP
HILLINGDON
UXBRIDGE
GREAT
WEMBLEY
BRENT
HAMPSTEAD
CAMDEN
WILLESDEN
NORTHOLT
HENLEY-ON-THAMES
MAIDENHEAD
A404(M)
SLOUGH
SLOUGH
LANGLEY
IVER
EALING
EALING
HAYES
SOUTHALL
ACTON
PADDINGTON
WESTMINSTER
MARYLE
KENSINGTON & CHELSEA
HAMMERSMITH & FULHAM
WEST DRAYTON
M4
15/4B
8/9
WINDSOR & MAIDENHEAD
ETON
WINDSOR
DATCHET
London Heathrow
4A
HAMMERSMITH
KEW
BATTERSEA
TWYFORD
WOKINGHAM
OLD WINDSOR
WRAYSBURY
HOUNSLOW
HOUNSLOW
RICHMOND
RICHMOND UPON THAMES
TWICKENHAM
WANDSWORTH
WANDSWORTH
BRIXTON
WINKFIELD
FELTHAM
ASHFORD
STAINES-UPON-THAMES
SPELTHORNE
EGHAM
STREATHAM
A329(M)
BRACKNELL
WOKINGHAM
BRACKNELL FOREST
ASCOT
VIRGINIA WATER
TEDDINGTON
KINGSTON UPON THAMES
WIMBLEDON
MERTON
MERTON
MORDEN
MITCHAM
M3
12/2
CHERTSEY
SURBITON
KINGSTON UPON THAMES
WALTON-ON-THAMES
LON
RUNNYMEDE
OTTERSHAW
WEYBRIDGE
ESHER
SUTTON
SUTTON
BAGSHOT
SURREY HEATH
CHOBHAM
ELMBRIDGE
EWELL
EPSOM & EWELL
EPSOM
SANDHURST
CAMBERLEY
BYFLEET
OXSHOTT
STOKE D'ABERNON
HART
FRIMLEY
WOKING
WOKING
ASHTEAD
BANSTEAD
COULS
RIPLEY
FETCHAM
LEATHERHEAD
TADWORTH
FARNBOROUGH
FLEET
MYTCHETT
REIGATE & BANSTEAD
HAMPSHIRE
RUSHMOOR
GREAT BOOKHAM
EAST HORSLEY
ALDERSHOT
NORMANDY
EAST CLANDON
GUILDFORD
GUILDFORD
MOLE VALLEY
REDHILL
REIGATE
BROCKHAM
TONGHAM
DORKING
WESTCOTT
GOMSHALL
FARNHAM
COMPTON
SHALFORD
LEIGH
SALFORDS
SURREY
SHACKLEFORD
HOLMBURY ST MARY
EAST HANTS
ELSTEAD
GODALMING
BEARE GREEN
HORLEY
MILFORD
WAVERLEY
WITLEY
CHARLWOOD
London Gatwick
CRAWLEY
WEST
EA
HA

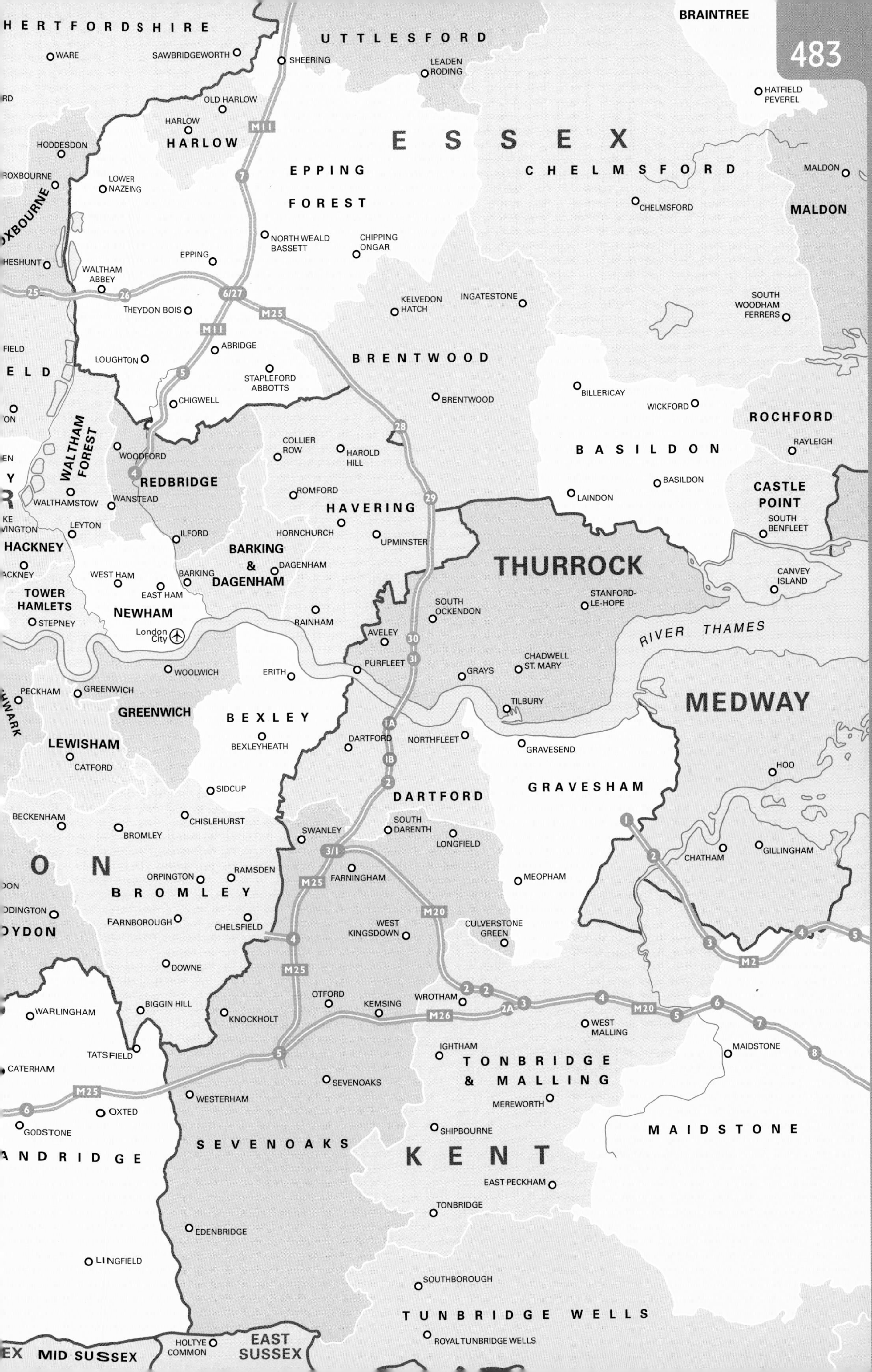

HERTFORDSHIRE
WARE
SAWBRIDGEWORTH
SHEERING
UTTLESFORD
BRAINTREE
LEADEN RODING
HATFIELD PEVEREL
OLD HARLOW
HARLOW
HARLOW
M11
ESSEX
HODDESDON
ROXBOURNE
LOWER NAZEING
EPPING
FOREST
CHELMSFORD
MALDON
CHELMSFORD
MALDON
NORTH WEALD BASSETT
CHIPPING ONGAR
EPPING
HESHUNT
WALTHAM ABBEY
25
26
6/27
THEYDON BOIS
M25
KELVEDON HATCH
INGATESTONE
SOUTH WOODHAM FERRERS
FIELD
ABRIDGE
LOUGHTON
STAPLEFORD ABBOTTS
BRENTWOOD
CHIGWELL
BRENTWOOD
BILLERICAY
WICKFORD
ROCHFORD
WALTHAM FOREST
WOODFORD
COLLIER ROW
HAROLD HILL
BASILDON
RAYLEIGH
REDBRIDGE
ROMFORD
BASILDON
LAINDON
CASTLE POINT
WALTHAMSTOW
WANSTEAD
HAVERING
SOUTH BENFLEET
LEYTON
ILFORD
HORNCHURCH
UPMINSTER
HACKNEY
BARKING & DAGENHAM
DAGENHAM
THURROCK
CANVEY ISLAND
WEST HAM
BARKING
EAST HAM
STANFORD-LE-HOPE
TOWER HAMLETS
NEWHAM
SOUTH OCKENDON
STEPNEY
London City
RAINHAM
RIVER THAMES
AVELEY
30
31
PURFLEET
CHADWELL ST. MARY
WOOLWICH
ERITH
GRAYS
PECKHAM
GREENWICH
TILBURY
MEDWAY
GREENWICH
BEXLEY
1A
LEWISHAM
BEXLEYHEATH
DARTFORD
NORTHFLEET
GRAVESEND
CATFORD
1B
HOO
SIDCUP
DARTFORD
GRAVESHAM
BECKENHAM
CHISLEHURST
BROMLEY
SWANLEY
SOUTH DARENTH
LONGFIELD
CHATHAM
GILLINGHAM
3/1
ORPINGTON
RAMSDEN
FARNINGHAM
MEOPHAM
M25
BROMLEY
FARNBOROUGH
CHELSFIELD
M20
WEST KINGSDOWN
CULVERSTONE GREEN
DOWNE
M25
M2
OTFORD
KEMSING
WROTHAM
BIGGIN HILL
WARLINGHAM
KNOCKHOLT
M26
2A
WEST MALLING
M20
TATSFIELD
IGHTHAM
MAIDSTONE
CATERHAM
TONBRIDGE & MALLING
SEVENOAKS
M25
WESTERHAM
MEREWORTH
OXTED
GODSTONE
SHIPBOURNE
MAIDSTONE
SEVENOAKS
KENT
EAST PECKHAM
TONBRIDGE
EDENBRIDGE
LINGFIELD
SOUTHBOROUGH
TUNBRIDGE WELLS
ROYAL TUNBRIDGE WELLS
HOLTYE COMMON
EAST SUSSEX
MID SUSSEX